AMERICAN WRITERS

AMERICAN WRITERS

JAY PARINI
Editor

SUPPLEMENT XXVIII

CHARLES SCRIBNER'S SONS
A part of Gale, a Cengage Company

GALE
A Cengage Company

Farmington Hills, Mich • San Francisco • New York • Waterville, Maine
Meriden, Conn • Mason, Ohio • Chicago

American Writers Supplement XXVIII

Editor in Chief: Jay Parini

Project Editor: Jennifer Stock

Permissions: Carissa Poweleit

Composition and Electronic Capture: Gary Oudersluys

Manufacturing: Rita Wimberley

For product information and technology assistance, contact us at **Gale Customer Support, 1-800-877-4253.** For permission to use material from this text or product, submit all requests online at **www.cengage.com/permissions** Further permissions questions can be emailed to **permissionrequest@cengage.com**

While every effort has been made to ensure the reliability of the information presented in this publication, Gale, a Cengage Company, does not guarantee the accuracy of the data contained herein. Gale accepts no payment for listing; and inclusion in the publication of any organization, agency, institution, publication, service, or individual does not imply endorsement of the editors or publisher. Errors brought to the attention of the publisher and verified to the satisfaction of the publisher will be corrected in future editions.

EDITORIAL DATA PRIVACY POLICY. Does this publication contain information about you as an individual? If so, for more information about our editorial data privacy policies, please see our Privacy Statement at www.gale.cengage.com

LIBRARY OF CONGRESS CATALOGING-IN-PUBLICATION DATA

American writers: a collection of literary biographies / Leonard Unger, editor in chief.
    p. cm.
    The 4-vol. main set consists of 97 of the pamphlets originally published as the University of Minnesota pamphlets on American writers; some have been rev. and updated. The supplements cover writers not included in the original series.
    Supplement 2, has editor in chief, A. Walton Litz; Retrospective suppl. 1, c. 1998, was edited by A. Walton Litz & Molly Weigel; Suppl. 5–26 have as editor-in-chief, Jay Parini.
    Includes bibliographies and index.
    Contents: v. 1. Henry Adams to T.S. Eliot — v. 2. Ralph Waldo Emerson to Carson McCullers — v. 3. Archibald MacLeish to George Santayana — v. 4. Isaac Bashevis Singer to Richard Wright — Supplement\[s\]: 1, pt. 1. Jane Addams to Sidney Lanier. 1, pt. 2. Vachel Lindsay to Elinor Wylie. 2, pt. 1. W.H. Auden to O. Henry. 2, pt. 2. Robinson Jeffers to Yvor Winters. — 4, pt. 1. Maya Angelou to Linda Hogan. 4, pt. 2. Susan Howe to Gore Vidal — Suppl. 5. Russell Banks to Charles Wright — Suppl. 6. Don DeLillo to W. D. Snodgrass — Suppl. 7. Julia Alvarez to Tobias Wolff — Suppl. 8. T.C. Boyle to August Wilson. — Suppl. 11 Toni Cade Bambara to Richard Yates.
    ISBN 978-0-684-32512-5
    1. American literature—History and criticism. 2. American literature—Bio-bibliography. 3. Authors, American—Biography. I. Unger, Leonard. II. Litz, A. Walton. III. Weigel, Molly. IV. Parini, Jay. V. University of Minnesota pamphlets on American writers.

PS129 .A55
810'.9
\[B\]   73-001759

ISBN-13: 978-0-684-32517-0

This title is also available as an e-book.
ISBN-13: 978-0-684-32518-7
Contact your Gale, a Cengage Company sales representative for ordering information.

Charles Scribner's Sons, an imprint of Gale, a Cengage Company
27500 Drake Rd.
Farmington Hills, MI 48331-3535

Printed in Mexico
1 2 3 4 5 6 7 21 20 19 18 17

Acknowledgments

The editors wish to thank the copyright holders of the excerpted criticism included in this volume and the permissions managers of many book and magazine publishing companies for assisting us in securing reproduction rights. Following is a list of the copyright holders who have granted us permission to reproduce material in this volume of *American Writers*. Every effort has been made to trace copyright, but if omissions have been made, please let us know.

COPYRIGHTED EXCERPTS IN *AMERICAN WRITERS*, SUPPLEMENT 28, WERE REPRODUCED FROM THE FOLLOWING SOURCES:

BIALOSKY, JILL. "Cover Blurb", Carnegie Mellon University Press, 2002. Courtesy of Carnegie Mellon University Press.

BOTTOMS, DAVID. "Husks", Copper Canyon Press, 2011. Courtesy of Copper Canyon Press. / "In Jimmy's Grill", Copper Canyon Press, 1995. Courtesy of Copper Canyon Press. / "Crawling Out at Parties", Copper Canyon Press, 1995. Courtesy of Copper Canyon Press. / "The Catfish", Copper Canyon Press, 1995. Courtesy of Copper Canyon Press. / "Rubbing the Faces of Angels", Copper Canyon Press, 1995. Courtesy of Copper Canyon Press. / "Wakulla: Chasing the Gator's Eye", Copper Canyon Press, 1995. Courtesy of Copper Canyon Press. / "Sign for My Father, Who Stressed the Bunt", Copper Canyon Press, 1995. Courtesy of Copper Canyon Press. / "In the Ice Pasture", Copper Canyon Press, 1995. Courtesy of Copper Canyon Press. / "Barriers", Copper Canyon Press, 1995. Courtesy of Copper Canyon Press. / "Shooting Rats at the Bibb County Dump", Copper Canyon Press, 1995. Copyright © 1995 Copper Canyon Press. / "Dedication", Copper Canyon Press, 1995. Courtesy of Copper Canyon Press. / "Stumptown Attends the Picture Show", Copper Canyon Press, 1995. Copyright © 1995 Copper Canyon Press. / "Oglethorpe's Dream", University of Georgia Press, 2001. Courtesy of University of Georgia Press. / "Dedication", Copper Canyon Press, 2004. Courtesy of Copper Canyon Press. / "Easter Shoes Epistle", Copper Canyon Press, 2004. Courtesy of Copper Canyon Press. / "Under the Vulture-Tree", Copper Canyon Press, 1995. Copyright © 1995 Copper Canyon Press. / "Three-Quarter Moon and Moment of Grace", Copper Canyon Press, 2004. Courtesy of Copper Canyon Press. / "First Woods", Copper Canyon Press, 2011. Courtesy of Copper Canyon Press. / "Violets", Copper Canyon Press, 2011. Courtesy of Copper Canyon Press. / "Country Store and Moment of Grace", Copper Canyon Press, 1999. Copyright © 1999 Copper Canyon Press. / "Night Strategies", Copper Canyon Press, 1995. Copyright © 1995 Copper Canyon Press. / "Walking a Battlefield: A Love Story", Copper Canyon Press, 2011. Courtesy of Copper Canyon Press. / "Shooting Rats In the Afterlife", Copper Canyon Press, 2004.

ACKNOWLEDGEMENTS

Copyright © 2004 Copper Canyon Press. / "Campfire In a Light Rain", Copper Canyon Press, 2011. Copyright © 2011 Copper Canyon Press. / "My Daughter Works the Heavy Bag", Copper Canyon Press, 2011. Copyright © 2011 Copper Canyon Press. / "Otherworld, Underworld, Prayer Porch", Cortland Review, 2015. Copyright © 2015 Cortland Review.

BYRAYN, LOUSE. Louise Bryant, "Forward", Thomas Seltzer, Inc., 1923. Courtesy of Thomas Seltzer, Inc / Ron Charles, "It's Banned Books Week Again. Can We Stop Yelling At Each Other About It?", Washington Post, 2015. Courtesy of The Washington Post. / Ron Charles, "'Another Brooklyn' Remind Us of a Brooklyn Far From the Tony Borough of Today", Washington Post, August 12, 2016. Courtesy of Washington Post. / Karen Coats, "Review of Tupac and D Foster", University of Illinois, January 2008. Courtesy of University of Illinois. / Janice M. Del Negro, "Review of The Other Side", University of Illinois, February 2001. Courtesy of University of Illinois.

ECK, DIANA. "Preface", Columbia University Press, 1999. Courtesy of Columbia University Press. / "Preface", Anima Poetry Press, 1981. Courtesy of Anima Press. / "Heart", Beacon Press, 1993. Courtesy of Beacon Press.

FOLSOM, MICHAEL BREWSTER. "The Book of Poverty", The Nation, February 28, 1966. Courtesy of The Nation.

GLIICK, LOUISE. "Foreward", Yale University Press, 2005. Courtesy of Yale University Press.

GOLD, MICHAEL. "Three Whose Hatred Killed Them", International Publishers Co., 1972. Courtesy of International Publishers Co. / "A Strange Funeral in Braddock", International Publishers Co., 1929. Courtesy of International Publishers Co.

GRIEST, STEPHANIE ELIZONDO. "Prologue", Villard Books / Random House, Inc., 2004. Courtesy of Villard Books / Random House, Inc.

KELLOGG, CAROLYN. "Jacqueline Woodson Named the New Young People's Poet Laureate", Los Angeles Times, 2015. Courtesy of Los Angeles Times.

KIRKUS MEDIA. "Review of Maizon at Blue Hill", Kirkus Media, 1992. Courtesy of Kirkus Media.

LEA, SYDNEY. "Father's Game", University of Illinois Press, 1980. Courtesy of University of Illinois Press. / "To Our Son", University of Illinois Press, 1980. Courtesy of University of Illinois Press. / "Recalling the Horseman Billy Farrell From An Airplane In Vermont", University of Illinois Press, 1980. Courtesy of University of Illinois Press. / "Searching The Drowned Man: The Third Day", University of Illinois Press, 1980. Courtesy of University of Illinois Press. / "The President of Flowers", University of Illinois Press, 1980. Courtesy of University of Illinois Press. / "Making Sense", University of Georgia Press, 1987. Courtesy of University of Georgia Press. / "Horn", University of Georgia Press, 1987. Courtesy of University of Georgia Press. / "The Art Of The Son", University of Georgia Press, 1987. Courtesy of University of Georgia Press. / "At the Flyfisher's Shack", Lea Sydney, 1990. Courtesy of Lea Sydney. / "Manifest", Lea Sydney, 1990. Courtesy of Lea Sydney. / "The 1950s", Four Way Books, 2011. Copyright © 2011 Four Way Books. / "Prefatory Poem", Lea Sydney, 1990. Copyright © 1990 Lea Sydney. / "Title Poem", Red Hen Press, 1992. Courtesy of Red Hen Press. / "Two Chets", Lea Sydney, 1990. Copyright © 1990 Lea Sydney. / "Title Poem", University of Illinois Press, 1996. Courtesy of University of Illinois Press. / "Reasons to Hate Poetry", University of Illinois Press, 2000. Courtesy of University of Illinois Press. / "Well, Everything", University of Illinois Press, 2000. Courtesy of University of Illinois Press. / "Girls In Their Upstairs Windows", University of Illinois Press, 2000. Courtesy of University of Illinois Press. / "Phases - In Praise of Zoloft", University of Illinois Press, 2000. Courtesy of University of Illinois Press. / "Sun Rising", Lea

ACKNOWLEDGEMENTS

Sydney, 1990. Copyright © 1990 Lea Sydney. / "Getting Involved", Sarabande Books, 2005. Courtesy of Sarabande Books. / "The Jetty", Sarabande Books, 2005. Courtesy of Sarabande Books. / "Over Brongo", Lea Sydney, 1990. Copyright © 1990 Lea Sydney. / "Man Walked Out", Sarabande Books, 2005. Courtesy of Sarabande Books. / "Unknown", Sarabande Books, 2005. Courtesy of Sarabande Books. / "V.Predator", Sarabande Books, 2005. Courtesy of Sarabande Books. / "Unknown", Sarabande Books, 2005. Courtesy of Sarabande Books. / "vii: Dry Drunk: The Rowing", Sarabande Books, 2005. Courtesy of Sarabande Books. / "ix. Talent From Birth", Sarabande Books, 2005. Courtesy of Sarabande Books. / "Title Poem", Sarabande Books, 2005. Courtesy of Sarabande Books. / "House of Women", Four Way Books, 2013. Courtesy of Four Way Books. / "Road Agent", Red Hen Press, 1992. Copyright © 1992 Red Hen Press / "1959", Sarabande Books, 2005. Copyright © 2005 Sarabande Books. / "Was Blind But Now", Sarabande Books, 2005. Copyright © 2005 Sarabande Books. / "666: Father of Lies", Sarabande Books, 2005. Copyright © 2005 Sarabande Books. / "x. Noon for Good", Sarabande Books, 2005. Copyright © 2005 Sarabande Books. / "Wonder: Red Beans and Ricely", Sarabande Books, 2005. Copyright © 2005 Sarabande Books. / "Lenora's Kitchen", Lea Sydney, 1987. Copyright © 1987 Lea Sydney. / "Waiting for the Armistice", Lea Sydney, 1987. Copyright © 1987 Lea Sydney. / "Annual Report", Lea Sydney, 1987. Copyright © 1987 Lea Sydney. / "Young Man Leaving Home", University of Illinois Press, 1980. Copyright © 1980 University of Illinois Press. / "Dirge For My Brother: Dawn to Dawn", University of Illinois Press, 1982. Copyright © 1982 University of Illinois Press. / "The Feud", University of Illinois Press, 1982. Copyright © 1982 University of Illinois Press.

MANN, THOMAS. "Preface", Farrar, Straus & Giroux, 1965. Courtesy of Farrar, Straus & Giroux.

NAFISI, AZAR. "Letter to Michael Folsom", University of Michigan, July 28, 1979. Courtesy of University of Michigan.

PATCHETT, ANN. "Cover Blurb", Carnegie Mellon University Press, 2006. Courtesy of Carnegie Mellon University Press.

PAYLOR, DIANE R. "Bold Type", Ms Magazine, November / December 1994. Courtesy of Ms Magazine.

ROCHMAN, HAZEL. "Review of Show Way", American Library Association, 2005. Courtesy of American Library Association. / "Review of Each Kindess", American Library Association, 2012. Courtesy of American Library Association. / "Booklist Interview", American Library Association, 2005. Courtesy of American Library Association.

SCHNEIDER, DEAN. "Interview", American Library Association, 2008. Courtesy of American Library Association.

SCOTT, WHITNEY. "Review of Autobiography of A Family", American Library Association, 1994. Courtesy of American Library Association.

SIKEN, RICHARD. "War of The Foxes", Copper Canyon Press, 2015. Copyright © 2015 Copper Canyon Press. / "Boot Theory", Yale University Press, 2005. Courtesy of Yale University Press. / "Little Beast", Yale University Press, 2005. Courtesy of Yale University Press. / "The Torn-Up Road", Yale University Press, 2005. Courtesy of Yale University Press. / "Unfinished Duet", Yale University Press, 2005. Courtesy of Yale University Press. / "Scheherarzade", Yale University Press, 2005. Courtesy of Yale University Press. / "Snow and Dirty Rain", Yale University Press, 2005. Courtesy of Yale University Press. / "Landscape With Black Coats In Snow", Copper Canyon Press, 2015. Courtesy of Copper Canyon Press. / "The Stag and The Quiver", Copper Canyon

ACKNOWLEDGEMENTS

Press, 2015. Courtesy of Copper Canyon Press. / Logic", Copper Canyon Press, 2015. Courtesy of Copper Canyon Press.

SUTTON, ROGER. "Review of Melanin Sun", University of Illinois, July / August 1995. Courtesy of University of Illinois.

WAKOSKI, DIANE. "The Green of Oxygen", Anhinga Press, 2010. Copyright © 2010 Anhinga Press. / "Amber Disks", Anhinga Press, 2010. Copyright © 2010 Anhinga Press. / "The Bowl of Gardenias", Anhinga Press, 2010. Copyright © 2010 Anhinga Press. / "Spending the New Year with the Man from Receiving at Sears", Diane Wakoski, 1980. Copyright © 1980 Diane Wakoski. / "Breakfast", Diane Wakoski, 1982. Copyright © 1982 Diane Wakoski. / "Making a Sacher Torte", Diane Wakoski, 1982. Copyright © 1982 Diane Wakoski. / "Joyce Carol Oates Plays the Saturn Piano", Diane Wakoski, 1988. Copyright © 1988 Diane Wakoski. / "Frontmatter Bio", Black Sparrow Press, 1973. Courtesy of Black Sparrow Press. / "Cover Declaration", Simon & Schuster, 1971. Courtesy of Simon & Schuster. / "The Greed for Control Over Death & Life", Black Sparrow Press, 1984. Courtesy of Black Sparrow Press. / "The Archeology of Movies & Books", Black Sparrow Press, 1995. Courtesy of Black Sparrow Press.

WIND, LEE. "Blog Interview", LeeWind.org, December 11, 2009. Courtesy of LeeWind.org.

WOODSON, JACQUELINE. "The Selfish Giant", Penguin Books, 2016. Courtesy of Penguin Books. / "A Girl Named Jack", Penguin Books, 2016. Courtesy of Penguin Books. / "Each World" Penguin Books, 2016. Courtesy of Penguin Books. / "Parents Poem", Penguin Books, 2017. Courtesy of Penguin Books. / Excerpt from …", Penguin Books, 2001. Courtesy of Penguin Books. / "Back Cover", Penguin Books, 2004. Courtesy of Penguin Books. / "Excerpt from …", Penguin Books, 2012. Courtesy of Penguin Books. / "Response To Winning Margaret A. Edwards Award", American Library Association, 2006. Courtesy of American Library Association. / "Quotes From Author's Website", Woodson Jacqueline, various. Courtesy of Jacqueline Woodson. / "The Pain Of The Watermelon Joke", New York Times, 2014. Courtesy of The New York Times Company. / "Lift Every Voice", Poetry Foundation, Courtesy of Poetry Foundation.

List of Subjects

Introduction	*xi*	LUDWIG LEWISOHN	145
		Jack Fischel	
List of Contributors	*xiii*		
		SOLOMON NORTHUP	163
HARRIETTE SIMPSON ARNOW	1	*Sarah Peters*	
Phoebe Jackson			
		OLIVE HIGGINS PROUTY	177
DAVID BOTTOMS	21	*Elaine Roth*	
Christopher Buck			
		RICHARD SIKEN	195
LOUISE BRYANT	37	*Ryan L. Winet*	
Judith Barlow			
		DANA SPIOTTA	205
DIANA L. ECK	49	*Elizabeth Freudenthal*	
Susan Butterworth			
		RUTH McENERY STUART	225
MICHAEL GOLD	65	*Joan Wylie Hall*	
Patrick Chura			
		EDWIN WAY TEALE	243
DIANE GOODMAN	85	*Dan Brayton*	
Ashley Cowger			
		DIANE WAKOSKI	259
STEPHANIE ELIZONDO GRIEST	97	*Nancy Bunge*	
Kristin Winet			
		JACQUELINE WOODSON	277
GRACE KING	111	*Amy Alessio*	
Windy Petrie			
		Cumulative Index	291
SYDNEY LEA	129		
David Gullette			

Introduction

In *America and Americans*, John Steinbeck underscored the importance of literature for understanding the United States as a whole, its history and intellectual texture: "In considering the American past, how poor we would be in information without *Huckleberry Fin, An American Tragedy, Winesburg, Ohio, Main Street, The Great Gatsby,* and *As I Lay Dying.*" These classic works define the American character, but so do thousands of other works: poems and stories, travelogues, plays, personal essays. As this volume of critical essays will suggest, American literature is a vast terrain, and it's the essence of this country.

In this twentieth-eighth supplement of *American Writers*, we assemble a rich sequence of writers from a wide variety of genres; they are mostly well-known authors who make a genuine and indelible contribution to the definition of the American character, and yet none has yet been a focus in this series. Readers who want to dig into their lives and writing should find these essays useful for biographical and historical context, close readings of texts, and supplementary material chosen to enhance the reading of these authors and their work.

This series itself has its origins in a series of critical and biographical monographs that appeared between 1959 and 1972. The *Minnesota Pamphlets on American Writers* achieved fame in their time; they were incisively written and informative, treating ninety-seven American writers in a format and style that attracted a devoted following of readers. The series proved invaluable to a generation of students and teachers who could depend on these reliable and interesting critiques of major figures. The idea of reprinting these essays occurred to Charles

Scribner, Jr. (1921–1995). The series appeared in four volumes entitled *American Writers: A Collection of Literary Biographies* (1974).

Since then, our yearly supplements have discussed hundreds of well-known and lesser known writers: poets, novelists, essayists, playwrights, screenwriters, and memoirists, even a handful of literary critics. The idea has been consistent and reaches back to the earliest models: to provide detailed essays that address students and the general reader. These essays often rise to a high level of craft and vision, but they are meant to introduce notable American writers and give a view of their developing career, with some historical context for making sense of their writing. Each essay examines the writer in the context of his or her time and place.

This supplement takes up a range of writers from the past and present. Some of them, such as novelists Louise Bryant, Michael Gold, Grace King, Ludwig Lewisohn, Olive Higgins Prouty, and Ruth McEnery Stuart, were born in the nineteenth century, as was memoirist Solomon Northup and travel writer and naturalist Edwin Way Teale. The rest of the authors included in this collection were born in the twentieth century, writing fiction (Harriet Simpson Arnow, Diane Goodman, Dana Spiotta), poetry (David Bottoms, Sydney Lea, Richard Siken, and Diane Wakoski), memoirs (Stephanie Elizaondo Griest), books for children (Jacqueline Woodson), or theology (Diana L. Eck). In fact, a number of these authors managed to cross genres quite easily, writing in multiple forms. While each of these writers has been written about in journals and newspapers, none has received the kind of sustained critical attention

INTRODUCTION

he or she deserves, and we hope to provide a beginning here, as their work deserves reading and, indeed, rereading.

The definition of an American character seems never to end, and it will never easily be pinned down; writers from a wide range of backgrounds, working in very different genres, contribute to its texture and definition. This supplement offers what strikes me as an arresting collection of portraits of influential literary figures, most of whom have not been given their due. Their voices and visions are worth taking seriously, and in these essays we hope to move in that direction.

—Jay Parini

List of Contributors

Amy Alessio. Amy Alessio is an award-winning teen librarian with a black belt in karate. She served on the YALSA Board of Directors and has written several books on library programming. Her passions for books as well as vintage foods and crafts are shared through presentations around the United States. JACQUELINE WOODSON

Judith Barlow. Judith Barlow is Professor Emerita of English and Women's Studies at the University at Albany, SUNY. Her books include *Final Acts: The Creation of Three Late O'Neill; Plays by American Women, 1900–1930; Plays by American Women, 1930–1960; Women Writers of the Provincetown Players: A Collection of Short Works;* and *Howe in an Hour.* She has been a visiting professor at Nankai University in China and Sofia University in Bulgaria. LOUISE BRYANT

Dan Brayton. Dan Brayton is Associate Professor in the Department of English and American Literatures and the Program in Environmental Studies at Middlebury College. He has also taught for the Williams-Mystic Program in Maritime Studies, and for Sea Education Association in Woods Hole, Massachusetts. His publications have appeared in such journals and magazines as *ELH, PMLA, Forum for Modern Language Studies,* and *WoodenBoat.* His book, *Shakespeare's Ocean: An Ecocritical Exploration,* published in 2012 by the University of Virginia Press, won the Northeast Modern Language Association Book Prize. EDWIN WAY TEALE

Christopher Buck. Christopher Buck, independent scholar and Pittsburgh attorney, publishes broadly in American studies, Native American studies, African American studies, religious studies, Islamic studies, and Baha'i studies. Author of: *God and Apple Pie* (2015), *Religious Myths and Visions of America* (2009), *Alain Locke: Faith and Philosophy* (2005), *Paradise and Paradigm* (1999), *Symbol and Secret* (1995/2004), and *Religious Celebrations* (co-author, 2011), with book chapters in *'Abdu'l-Bahá's Journey West* (2013), *The Blackwell Companion to the Qur'an* (2006/2015), *The Islamic World* (2008), *American Writers* (2004/2010/2015), and *British Writers* (2014). DAVID BOTTOMS

Nancy Bunge. A professor at Michigan State University, Nancy Bunge has also held senior Fulbright lectureships at the University of Vienna, the Free University of Brussels, the University of Ghent, and the University of Siegen. She was a visiting scholar at Harvard Divinity School. Her essays have appeared in places like *Poets & Writers Magazine, The Writers Chronicle,* and *The Chronicle of Higher Education;* her most recent book is *The Midwestern Novel: Literary Populism from Huckleberry Finn to the Present.* DIANE WAKOSKI

Susan Butterworth. Susan Butterworth is a recent Master of Divinity graduate of Episcopal Divinity School in Cambridge, Massachusetts, where her area of special competency includes Global, Ecumenical, and Interfaith Studies. She has been a professor of English composition and literature at Salem State University. She is currently working as a chaplain at Massachusetts Institute of Technology, where she leads a Sunday evening ecumenical, contemplative Taizé prayer service. She writes for the Episcopal Digital Nnetwork and is working on a book

LIST OF CONTRIBUTORS

about the anti-apartheid work of the Anglican dean of Johannesburg Cathedral, Gonville ffrench-Beytagh. DIANA L. ECK

Patrick Chura. Patrick Chura is a professor at the University of Akron, where he teaches courses in nineteenth and twentieth century American literature and culture studies. He is the author of two books and has published articles on a variety of literary-historical topics. His second book, *Thoreau the Land Surveyor,* won the College English Association of Ohio's Dasher Award for outstanding literary scholarship. His new edition of Ernest Poole's *The Harbor* was recently published in the Penguin Classics series. MICHAEL GOLD

Ashley Cowger. Ashley Cowger is the author of the short story collection *Peter Never Came,* which was awarded the Autumn House Press Fiction Prize. Her short fiction, articles, and book reviews have appeared in several journals and anthologies. She holds an M.F.A. from the University of Alaska Fairbanks, and she teaches English at Penn State Harrisburg. DIANE GOODMAN

Jack Fischel. Jack Fischel is Emeritus Professor of History at Millersville University and Visiting Professor of the Humanities at Messiah College. He is the author/editor of a number of books on the Holocaust as well as on Jewish-American history and popular culture. He is also a frequent contributor the *American Writers* series. LUDWIG LEWISOHN

Elizabeth Freudenthal. Elizabeth Freudenthal received a doctorate in English from University of California, Santa Barbara, where she conducted interdisciplinary research on the medicalization of personality in contemporary fiction and culture. She has published essays in *New Literary History, Postmodern Culture,* and *Moving On: Essays on the Aftermath of Leaving Academia.* Her current research interests include fiction by contemporary women writers and intersections of disability, trauma, and poverty in health care policy. DANA SPIOTTA

David Gullette. David Gullette is Professor Emeritus of English at Simmons College, Boston. He was one of the first editors of the esteemed literary quarterly, *Ploughshares,* and has published poetry, translations and two books about revolutionary Nicaraguan poetry plus a novel set in Nicaragua. He is Literary Director of the Poets' Theatre in Cambridge; his adaptation for the stage of Seamus Heaney's rendering of *Beowulf* was presented by the Poets' Theatre in December 2015. SYDNEY LEA

Joan Wylie Hall. Joan Wylie Hall is a senior lecturer in English at the University of Mississippi. She is the author of *Shirley Jackson: A Study of the Short Fiction* and editor of *Conversations with Audre Lorde* and *Conversations with Natasha Trethewey.* Her essays on Trethewey, Ann Patchett, and Janisse Ray appeared in previous volumes of the *American Writers Supplement.* RUTH McENERY STUART

Phoebe Jackson. Phoebe Jackson is a professor of English at William Paterson University, where she teaches courses in American literature. Her research interests include twentieth- and twenty-first century American women writers with a focus on the intersectionality of race, class, and gender and composition studies. HARRIETTE SIMPSON ARNOW

Sarah Peters. Sarah Peters, Ph.D., is an Assistant Professor of English at East Central University in Ada, Oklahoma, where she teaches literature, humanities, and writing. Her publications include scholarship on the works of Eudora Welty, Anne Sexton, and Hannah Webster Foster. SOLOMON NORTHUP

Windy Petrie. Windy Counsell Petrie, Ph.D., is Professor and Chair of English at Azusa Pacific University. Her areas of specialization include literary autobiography, transatlantic authorship and readership in the long nineteenth, and late nineteenth and early twentieth century female Künstlerroman. She has published essays and reviews in *a/b: Autobiography Studies, Christianity and Literature, Literatura, American Writ-*

xiv

ers and American Writers Retrospective, and in the collections *American Writers in Europe* (Palgrave Macmillan) and *Postmodernism and Beyond* (Cambridge Scholars Press). Her book manuscript, *Professions of Authorship: American Women's Literary Autobiography in the 1930s,* is nearing completion. GRACE KING

Elaine Roth. Elaine Roth is Professor of Film Studies at Indiana University South Bend, where she is Associate Chair of the English department. Co-editor of the collection *Motherhood Misconceived* (2009, SUNY Press), her work has appeared in *Genders, Quarterly Review of Film and Literature,* and *Feminist Media Studies.* She teaches Film Genres and History of the Motion Picture, among other courses, and is currently working on a project on early women screenwriters. OLIVE HIGGINS PROUTY

Kristin Winet. Kristin Winet is Assistant Professor of English at Rollins College in Winter Park, Florida, where she also directs the First-Year and Academic Writing Program. She holds a Ph.D. in Rhetoric and Composition and an M.F.A. in Creative Writing from the University of Arizona and is an award-winning travel writer and photographer. Her research combines the fields of rhetoric, feminism, and tourism and examines how feminist rhetoric can positively impact digital travel writing. Her work has been published or is forthcoming in *Kairos: Rhetoric, Technology, and Pedagogy* and *English Journal,* as well as in the edited collections *Feminist Challenges or Feminist Rhetorics?: Locations, Scholarship, Discourse* and *Food, Feminism, and Rhetorics.* STEPHANIE ELIZONDO GRIEST

Ryan L. Winet. Ryan L. Winet teaches English at Rollins College and serves as an editor for *The Offending Adam,* an online poetry journal. RICHARD SIKEN

HARRIETTE SIMPSON ARNOW

(1908—1986)

Phoebe Jackson

DISCOURAGED FROM WRITING at a young age by her mother, Harriette Simpson Arnow went on to write five works of fiction, a historical novel, a memoir, and two social histories. Her unwillingness to conform to parental guidance or other people's expectations demonstrates a feature that many of her characters possess as well. Arnow is perhaps best known for her 1954 novel *The Dollmaker*, a runner-up for the National Book Award in 1955 that was made into a movie starring Jane Fonda in 1984. Early in her career Arnow focused her literary production on fiction set in Appalachia, beginning with the trilogy *Mountain Path* (1936), *Hunter's Horn* (1949), and *The Dollmaker*. For students of Appalachian literature, Arnow figures prominently as an author who depicted rural Kentucky in the 1930s, peopled by farmers who were trying to make do in an area that was increasingly losing its population to cities. Arnow's novels give readers a glimpse of life in Appalachia without resorting to stereotypes more typical of earlier regional literature. Her novels continue to resonate with readers for their strong female characters, who navigate the socially prescribed challenges of life in rural and urban America.

BIOGRAPHY

Arnow was born Harriette Louisa Simpson in Wayne County, Kentucky, on July 7, 1908. Arnow's parents were Mollie Jane Denney and Elias Thomas Simpson, both of whom at one time were schoolteachers. Once they had children, six in total, both parents gave up teaching. Mollie Jane stayed home to take care of Arnow and her siblings, and at various times the children were homeschooled. Elias Simpson worked at a number of different jobs including work as a bookkeeper, a boilermaker, and a tool dresser.

In her 1977 memoir, *Old Burnside*, Arnow talks about the family's move from rural Bronston, Kentucky, where her father was a teacher, to Burnside, Kentucky, where her father got a job as a bookkeeper in 1913. At the same time, her mother ran a boardinghouse to make extra money. Though she does not remember the move itself, it was nonetheless a significant one for her. In her memoir, Arnow vividly evokes a sense of place in the Cumberland River basin, where as a child she was intrigued by everything the town of Burnside had to offer but especially all of the action involved with the logging industry on the Cumberland River. Because Arnow's mother did not think highly of lower Burnside, the family eventually moved farther up the river to Tyree's Corner.

Arnow recalls how storytelling was an important part of her family's life. Her grandmother would tell stories about Indian attacks, the American Revolution, and the War of 1812. However, she was most impressed with her father's storytelling, claiming "he was the best storyteller of all" (*Old Burnside*, p. 63). Later in her life, Arnow would write a historical novel about the American Revolution, *The Kentucky Trace* (1974), clearly influenced by the storytelling of her youth. At an early age, Arnow was already an inquisitive student, eager to learn about life around her.

Her early education consisted of going to school until 1918, when she was homeschooled because of the influenza pandemic that year. In 1918 the family moved to Torrent, Kentucky,

where her father got a job in an oil field. According to Sandra Ballard, the move to Torrent gave Arnow the background information with which to write her first short story, "Marigolds and Mules," published in 1934. While her family was in Torrent, her mother decided to send her to St. Helen's Academy, which Arnow attended for only a year because of her displeasure with the school. The next year she was sent to Stanton Academy. Because there was no more work for her father in the oil field, the family returned to Burnside, and Arnow graduated from Burnside High School 1924.

In an address she gave in 1985 to the Appalachian Writers Association, Arnow explained her initial foray into the publishing world while still in junior high school. Arnow surreptitiously wrote her first story and sent it to a children's magazine, *Child Life*. Though this initial attempt resulted in a letter of rejection, the editors of the magazine thought the story worthy enough that they encouraged her to send another piece. Even so, her mother disapproved of her writing. To her mother's way of thinking, Arnow would be better off pursuing a career in teaching rather than spending her time "scribbling." But as Arnow comments, "I continued to want to scribble" ("Help and Hindrances," p. 285).

After high school Arnow attended Berea College for two years before embarking on her first teaching assignment in rural Pulaski County, Kentucky, in 1926. Teaching in a one-room school in rural Kentucky would prove instrumental in the writing of her first novel, *Mountain Path*, published in 1936. Her tenure teaching at this rural school lasted only a year; she then moved on to continue her education at the University of Louisville. After finishing college in 1930, Arnow resumed teaching until ill health and stress brought an end to that work. In 1934 Arnow moved to Cincinnati to begin her life as a writer, remaining there until 1939. In an interview with Danny L. Miller, Arnow talks about the reading she did during this period, which included novelists such as Leo Tolstoy, Fyodor Dostoyevsky, Sigrid Undset, Èmile Zola, Gustave Flaubert, and, especially, Thomas Hardy.

In 1935, during her time in Cincinnati, two of her short stories were published: "A Mess of Pork" by the magazine *New Talent* and "Marigolds and Mules" by the literary magazine *Kosmos: Dynamic Stories of Today*. Her short story "The Washerwoman's Day" was published the next year by the *Southern Review*, which was edited by Cleanth Brooks and Robert Penn Warren. It is also during this time that Arnow wrote two novels. The first, *Mountain Path*, was published by Covici-Friede (1936), but the second, *Between the Flowers*, could not find a publisher and would only be released posthumously by Michigan State University Press in 1999.

During these Great Depression years, Arnow worked at the Federal Writers Project (FWP), where she met her future husband, Harold Arnow, a newspaper writer who was also employed by the FWP. They were married in March 1939. From that time until 1945, Arnow and her husband tried their hand at subsistence farming in Kentucky. Their lack of success at this endeavor finally led them, with their daughter, Marcella (b. 1941), to move to Detroit, where Harold got a job as a reporter for the *Detroit Times*. In Detroit they had a second child, Thomas, who was born in 1946. Two of her short stories were also published during this time: "The Two Hunters" (July 1942) in *Esquire* and "The Hunter" (November 1944) in the *Atlantic Monthly*.

In 1949 Arnow's novel *Hunter's Horn* was published by Macmillan. A best seller, it received acclaim in the *New York Times Book Review*, where it was selected as one of the top ten novels published that year. The critics at *Saturday Review* went a step further in their admiration, naming it the best book written in 1949. A year later *Hunter's Horn* garnered one more accolade, when it was one of three novels nominated for a Pulitzer Prize for Fiction in 1950.

That year the Arnows purchased rural acreage, which included a farm, outside of Ann Arbor, where they would spend the rest of their lives. The year 1954 would see the publication of her most acclaimed novel, *The Dollmaker*. The novel was a best seller as well as a runner-up for the

HARRIETTE SIMPSON ARNOW

1955 National Book Award. Like *Hunter's Horn*, *The Dollmaker* was voted the best work of fiction for 1954 by *Saturday Review*. In 1984 the novel would be made into a TV movie for ABC, produced by and starring Jane Fonda, who headed up the entire project. According to a *New York Times* article of that year, Jane Fonda had read *The Dollmaker* in 1971 and was so impressed with the story that she was determined to see it made into a movie.

For Arnow's next book projects, she turned to writing two social histories: *Seedtime on the Cumberland* (1960) and *Flowering of the Cumberland* (1963). According to Sandra Ballard, Arnow had been researching life on the Cumberland River basin for about twenty years and had so much material after completing the first volume that she was able to write and publish a second. These books focus on life in the Cumberland River basin during the late eighteenth century.

After the publication of these two social histories, Arnow returned to writing fiction, and in 1970 her novel *The Weedkiller's Daughter* was published by Knopf. It was less well received by critics and remained out of print until it was reissued by Michigan State University Press in 2012. In 1997 Arnow's memoir, *Old Burnside*, was published. It is a vivid historical description of the Cumberland River and its environs combined with an outline of Arnow's childhood until she went off to Berea College. The memoir is a look back at the land and at her life and how they were intertwined at an early age.

In 1974 Arnow's historical novel, *The Kentucky Trace: A Novel of the American Revolution*, was published by Knopf. According to Martha Billips, this book was better received by some critics, though it sold poorly. At the time of Arnow's death, she was at work on a longer novel tentatively titled "Belle." This work remains unpublished. Arnow died in March 22, 1986. Beginning with the reprint of *Hunter's Horn* in 1997, Michigan State University Press has reissued all of Arnow's works, including the two social histories. The only exceptions are *The Dollmaker*, which has been in continuous print with trade presses since its publication, and *Old Burnside*, which was published by the University Press of Kentucky. In addition to its publication of *Between the Flowers*, Michigan State University Press has published a posthumous collection of Arnow's short stories, *The Collected Short Stories of Harriette Simpson Arnow* (2005), edited by Sandra L. Ballard and Haeja K. Chung.

APPALACHIAN NOVELS

Arnow's first novel, *Mountain Path*, was published in 1936. In an introduction Arnow wrote for the 1964 University Press of Kentucky edition, she sketches out what life was like in the hill communities of Kentucky. Arnow had already published her two nonfiction social histories of the Cumberland region, and her introduction makes explicit the changes that took place there during the 1920s and 1930s. According to her account, people had to move away from these communities because of "worn-out soil and other depleted natural resources" (p. viii) as well as the demise of the timber industry. Change in the hill communities is a topic Arnow explores in all three Appalachian novels (*Mountain Path*, *Hunter's Horn*, and *The Dollmaker*).

Important to *Mountain Path*, in particular, is Arnow's short discussion in her introduction about the economic reasons farmers turned to running stills to make money. Hill people could feed their families through farming, but it was difficult to make any money from it. In order to get cash, farmers turned to selling corn alcohol to "put shoes on the children, pay the taxes, and buy a trinket for the baby" (p. ix). While the stills clearly remained an economic necessity to people in the hill communities during the period she writes about, the vagaries of history eventually worked to change people's attitudes toward them. It was the appearance of larger distillers, taxes, Prohibition, and eventually public sentiment that coalesced to work against the local distiller in the hill communities.

Mountain Path might have been a different book had her editor not interfered with the writing of it. In his book *Harriette Arnow*, written in 1974, William Eckley discusses the relationship that Arnow had with her publisher, Harold Strauss

of Covici-Friede. Having read a short story of hers in the magazine *New Talent*, Strauss asked her to send anything else she was working on. At his encouragement, she sent him the manuscript for *Mountain Path*. While he thought highly of her manuscript, Strauss had some editorial changes to suggest and went as far as to urge her to rewrite the book. According to Glenda Hobbs, in his correspondence with Arnow, Strauss recommended that she include a feud in the narrative, which at the time was a stock characteristic for fiction about the region. From his perspective, inclusion of a feud would help to ensure that the book would sell well. Though no prior manuscript of the book exists, Hobbs thinks Arnow most likely took his advice.

While the sympathetic depiction of rural poverty combined with a stereotypical narration of feuds might have been a selling point for the book in the 1930s, much of the critical focus since the novel's reissue in 1985 has been on the depiction of women in the novel. Though critics are right to highlight the novel's female characters, specifically Louisa and Corie, two of the main characters, what remains patently important to Arnow is the economic circumstances of the schoolteacher Louisa and of the people who populate the hill community where she has come to teach. In her article "Fact and Fancy in *Mountain Path*," Joan R. Griffin rightly argues that the making of moonshine, along with the feuds that are its by-product, ultimately affect the characters and their futures. In a sense, there are two parallel stories in Arnow's novel: the need for Louisa to make money in order to return to college and the need for the people in the hill communities to make money for their own survival. Unfortunately, one has a future (Louisa) while the other's future is overdetermined by its circumstances, as the families in the hill communities will continue to feud in part because of a real lack of economic resources.

Many critics see *Mountain Path* as a quasi-autobiographical narrative, which lends the book an air of authenticity. Martha Billips explains that it was economic necessity that compelled Arnow herself to get a teaching position for one year in 1926 in a rural valley in Pulaski County.

Though Arnow did not like the comparison made between her and her fictional character, many critics who have studied her life and work maintain that Arnow's experiences as a teacher in a one-room school clearly informed her depiction of Louisa's experiences.

In the novel, Louisa has left her hometown of Lexington, Kentucky, to teach in rural Cavecreek, teaching being one of the few ways available to her to earn the money to finish her college studies back home. Much like the people she will eventually encounter in Cavecreek, Louisa is realistic about what she needs to do to survive even before she gets there. Though she is not exactly sure what to expect moving to a rural county, she does realize what is at stake and acts accordingly: "She would keep her mouth shut and teach the earth was flat with four corners if necessary. She had to keep the job. She had to have the fifty-six dollars a month, and save thirty-five from each pay day in order to go back to school to chemistry and mathematics and people of her own kind" (p. 12). This quote suggests that she already expects to see a difference between herself and the people of the hill community and that she initially is disparaging of "their kind." Nonetheless, Louisa displays a distinct determination to succeed at her new quest. Realizing that the trip to get to rural Cavecreek will require riding a mule, she even lies that she has done so before, unwilling to advertise her difference. From the outset, it is clear that the stakes are high for Louisa, and that she is capable of meeting the challenges that will confront her. She is eager to return to college, she needs the money to do so, and she will do what it takes to succeed.

Though initially disparaging of those who live in a rural county, Louisa finds that her own education begins when she becomes a boarder with the Lee Buck Cal family and starts to teach. From Lee Buck Cal's wife, Corie, and from the schoolchildren, specifically Rie, Louisa learns how to navigate life in the hill community. The basic plot of the novel concerns Louisa and her experiences learning to live in a rural county and learning to teach in a one-room classroom that lacks any of the teaching materials one would

expect. Two subplots run parallel to Louisa's story. First, the reader is introduced to Chris Bledsoe, who, Louisa finds out even before she arrives in Cavecreek, is a murderer. Quite quickly, in order to advance the romantic plot, Louisa realizes there is more to Chris than meets the eye, and she falls in love with him. But like the other people in Cavecreek, Chris is caught up in the vicissitudes of the moonshine business. He finds himself hiding out in Cavecreek, though he is from Tennessee, because he has killed another man, Sol Joe Coager, in retaliation for the death of his brother. Louisa learns from Chris that his brother was shot trying to bury a jug of whiskey.

According to the novel, at this time a person could get a fifty-dollar reward for turning in a person's still. This law is the basis for the second subplot, the feud between the Cals and the Barnetts. Their feud began because in order to make some money, one of the Barnetts turned Lee Buck in to the authorities for his still. In retaliation, Lee Buck gets revenge by killing one of the Barnetts, and at the same time, a member of the Cal family gets shot. Thus, the dividing lines are drawn in the valley. Arnow reminds the reader that the tragedy stretches beyond the deaths of immediate family members: the feuding also results in the breaking apart of former family members (Corie and her sister) and friends. The threads of the novel revolve around these two narrative lines and eventually come together at the end of the novel, when Chris is shot in Lee Buck's cave, where they make moonshine.

As these two subplots suggest, the illegal making of moonshine to earn money keeps people like Chris, the Cals, and the Barnetts trapped in a never-ending spiral of violence. But Louisa comes to see another side of making moonshine and its importance to everyone in the hill community, cognizant that the violence will remain a part of their lives. After getting to know Chris better, she comes to realize that "it was not wrong to make good whiskey, and no law could make it wrong. Always they had made it; the Bledsoes, and the Andersons, and the Calhouns. She saw that they would continue to make it. Nothing could stop them" (p. 123). Arnow's

introduction to the 1964 edition, in effect, allows the reader to understand the economic dynamics of making moonshine, thereby elevating the novel from one about a stereotypical feud to one that underscores the economic significance of stills in rural Kentucky. As the novel ably demonstrates, the lack of opportunity for rural people to make money any other way creates significant challenges for them.

Many critics have rightly observed Arnow's sympathetic portrayal of rural women from the Cumberland region, beginning with *Mountain Path*. Especially significant to Louisa's growth while she lives in Cavecreek is her interaction with Corie Cals. Throughout her stay with the Cals family, Louisa observes how Corie handles living under the shadow of the feud between the families and with the dangerous business of making moonshine. Though Corie lives her daily life with these troubles, Louisa notes that she nonetheless has a lot of gratitude: "Without being a pessimist Corie expected the worst of all possible combinations in all things, and as a result was eternally grateful for some little thing" (p. 215). Moreover, rather than dwelling on her troubles, according to Louisa, "she only laid them away in a corner of her mind where they were not easily stumbled upon" (p. 141). It is this type of life lesson Louisa learns from Corie, something that cannot be read in a college text or gleaned from a teacher's lecture, heretofore the main sources of her learning.

The focus of much of the novel is the conflict that Louisa experiences over her plan to leave Cavecreek for the broader world beyond. For her, the decision becomes whether to make a life in this place, where she has learned so much about life, or to return to Lexington to continue her studies. While her time in rural Kentucky has been a life-changing and meaningful one, she also never quite forgets the reason she came to Cavecreek in the first place or the feeling that she was meant to do more in life. In one particular scene, Louisa proves herself cunningly adept at making up a story in order to chase away two men who are looking for Chris Bledsoe. Even so, Louisa realizes that this life cannot be hers: "This is not my life. I am preparing for my real life.

Someday I shall live and be a success" (p. 205). Though she frequently wavers in her thoughts about whether to leave or stay, she also knows that the life for women living in the valley is a difficult one. Unlike her, girls like Rie, Corie's daughter, will undoubtedly be married quite young and have children without proper medical care. Then there are the many women buried in the graveyard, who, "it seemed, often died in their thirties and forties" (p. 237). Ultimately she acknowledges that "she was not fitted for a life here in the hills" (p. 287). As Barbara Baer notes, Louisa never really has to make the decision, because when Chris dies, the decision is made for her.

In the end, there is a big difference in opportunities for people living in the hill communities and those, like Louisa, who have other options. Arnow's novel sympathetically narrates the difficult lives of the people of this period who stayed on in places like the fictional Cavecreek. Without industry or good farming land, they were limited in what they were able to do to make a living. Corn alcohol was just one way they were able to survive. However, in the years after the 1920s, there would be an emptying out of the hill communities as people migrated to the cities in the North. *Mountain Path*, like her other Appalachian novels, documents a way of life that Arnow wants her readers to remember did exist at one time.

Arnow's second novel, *Hunter's Horn*, published in 1949 by Macmillan, was well received and remained on the *New York Times* best-seller list for five weeks. The theme and the characters of the novel first appeared in a short story, "The Hunter," published in the *Atlantic Monthly* in 1949. In the novel, the short story becomes chapter 4. The general arc of the story and the novel involves Nunn Ballew and his determination to hunt down a fox whom the hill community calls King Devil. The fox has posed a nuisance to the community by stealing chickens, killing sheep, and even leading hound dogs to their deaths. For those reasons, residents are eager to see King Devil dead by whatever means. For Nunn, the fox becomes a personal obsession. In chapter 4, Nunn has the opportunity to shoot the fox, but much to the chagrin of the other hunters present, he refuses. The novel revolves around Nunn's insistence on getting King Devil in what he considers the only honorable way: capturing the fox through hunting with foxhounds.

The distinguishing feature of *Hunter's Horn* is the fleshing out of the individual characters. In *Mountain Path*, the reader gets to know the characters, but they are overall less defined. In *Hunter's Horn*, the depiction of the characters is more nuanced, Nunn in particular. Nunn shares characteristics of other male characters found in Arnow's novels, like Chris Bledsoe in *Mountain Path*, Marsh Gregory in *Between the Flowers*, and William David Leslie Collins in *Kentucky Trace*. Like these other men, Nunn is to some degree an outsider. In Nunn's case, after spending a number of years working in the coal mines, he has returned to Little Smokey Creek, where he was brought up, to buy land and farm. As a character, Nunn seems to be a composite of two of Arnow's earlier characters, Marsh Gregory and Delphine Costello from her previously unpublished book, *Between the Flowers*. Like Marsh Gregory, Nunn finds a certain amount of pleasure working the land and shows an interest in learning about how to improve his soil from the women agents at the Agriculture Adjustment Administration, a government bureau that was created in the 1930s to help equalize profits for farmers by paying them not to grow certain crops, thereby creating scarcity to improve prices. Nunn also shares a family history similar to that of Delphine Costello. Nunn's father, like Delphine's, died when he was young, and his mother, a schoolteacher, left Little Smokey Creek to move to Missouri, leaving Nunn to be raised by his Aunt Marthie and his uncle, Preacher John. Nunn remarks that his mother, again like Delphine's, "could not sit and accept life like a dead tree in a snowstorm; she had gone out and gathered it with her own two hands, even if in gathering it she had to leave her widow's weeds and her baby" (p. 141). This characteristic of not settling in life is a frequent theme in Arnow's fiction. It will also come to define in part both of Nunn's children—his daughter, Suse, and his son, Lee Roy.

The difference that marks Nunn's character is his obsession with hunting King Devil. Nunn goes back and forth in the novel between accusing King Devil of ruining his life and readily accepting responsibility for the adverse effects his obsession has created for his family. His ability to see both sides of his behavior makes him a complex and interesting character, one with whom a reader can sympathize while at the same time recognizing his personal deficiencies. In her discussion of the novel, Janet Holtman argues that Nunn's obsession can be attributed to one factor: his need to see himself as different from the rest of the hill community. His obsession, in effect, defines and differentiates him.

When Nunn has the opportunity to shoot King Devil but does not, the other farmers are clearly bewildered by his inexplicable behavior. To their mind, King Devil needs to die or they will keep losing livestock. For Nunn, King Devil is not just a fox but an object lesson laden with moral value. He represents something larger than life. In response to the farmers' outrage, Nunn makes a grandiose proclamation befitting a moral quest: "I hope th good Lord God in heaven sends me to brile in hell through eternity without end if I ever stop chasen that fox till I git him . . . I'll chase him till I'm crippled an blind an bald . . ." (p. 41). His proclamation suggests his need to be committed to something bigger than himself, something that distinguishes him as a person. Regardless of what others think, his obsession elevates him above the quotidian. Nunn has, for all intents and purposes, done the unthinkable by tying his future to King Devil.

Though he is aware that others laugh "because he was fool enough to waste his life and starve his family for a fox that could never be caught" (p. 80), Nunn is resolute. He realizes that "the damned fox had put a wall between him and the rest of the world; other men did what they pleased; he chased a fox because he had to" (p. 80). His obsession is his defining feature among his peers, but at the same time it also gives meaning to his life.

To the surprise of this family and of the community, Nunn does the inconceivable by selling much of his family livestock in order to buy two pedigreed foxhound pups to help trap King Devil. Doing so means that his family will suffer the consequences of not having a cow for milk and pigs for meat. But the death of his beloved foxhound Zing in pursuit of King Devil gives Nunn an even stronger motivation to capture the fox. Nunn rationalizes his decision to purchase the foxhound pups by appealing to his own self virtue: "I made my brags that I'd raise me up a pair a pups, fine pups that ud git King Devil. . . . I couldn't go back on my word, could I? White trash does that" (p. 83). It is significant that Nunn uses the term "white trash" to distinguish himself. The term is a class signification denoting poverty, but in Nunn's sense of the word, it also denotes a way of acting. People who are "white trash" do not act honorably; they make boasts that have no substance to them. But Nunn's words are different. He stands behind their meaning.

In using the words "white trash," Nunn also wants his family to see that his actions distinguish him and his family from other people in the community. The pups themselves have what Marxist theorists term a "sign value" because they impart a type of social status on Nunn and his family. As Nunn notes, "nobody between the Big South Fork and the Cumberland had ever heard of a pedigree" (p. 79). For his daughter, Suse, the fact that these dogs are pedigreed enables her to have bragging rights with her classmate whose uncle has a pedigreed bull. The day after the arrival of the foxhound pups, the children in the family cannot wait to run off after breakfast to tell everyone that they are the owners of two pedigreed pups, thus elevating their own status in the community.

Nunn can acknowledge the hardships that will accrue for his family as a result of buying the foxhound pups, and for this he feels guilty. He is wholly cognizant that "the money that had gone for the pups, their feed, and their medicine by rights belonged to Milly and the children" (p. 141). This ability to give voice to his own limitations also makes him a compelling character, one who struggles with his own inner demons. His actions, however, are also quite telling of what life is like for women living in the hill communities. Milly did not want to sell their

pregnant cow because they would need the milk. But Milly's practical reasons get overruled by Nunn's obsession with King Devil. Milly's voice in effect is silenced.

The problems faced by the women of Little Smokey Creek are a prominent part of the novel. For Milly, it is the practical considerations in life that are important: that her children are healthy and that "she wasn't in the family way" (p. 89) are as much as she can hope for. Unlike Nunn, who has high hopes for his daughter to become a schoolteacher like his mother, Milly is much more conscious of what can happen to young women who live in the hill communities. She thus worries about her daughter's future. To Milly's way of thinking, "It would be better never to have a girl child; they saw nothing but pain and trouble and work, and so many went wrong, or else married some good-for-nothing little feist when they were too little to know that kisses come easier than victuals and that a houseful of youngens comes easiest of all" (p. 48). While Suse does evince a more defiant attitude than any of the women in the novel except Sue Annie, the midwife, unfortunately circumstances conspire against her, and she becomes pregnant.

One of the most compelling chapters in the book, chapter 30, displays the immense strength of character that hill women like Sue Annie and Milly possess. Ironically, this chapter was excised from *Hunter's Horn* at the behest of the Fiction Book Club in 1949 for its edition of the novel. According to Sandra Ballard, the editors considered the graphic scene too unpleasant for its readers. In the chapter, Sue Annie saves a young boy suffering from gastrointestinal worms by using a number of homeopathic remedies to force the worms up his throat and removing them. The chapter ably demonstrates Sue Annie's fortitude and skill in doctoring rural children to keep them from dying, a common phenomenon in the hill communities, which lacked proper medical care. In Arnow's next novel, *The Dollmaker*, Gertie demonstrates the same fortitude when she must cut a hole in her son's throat to help him breathe. Though many of these women were trapped by their gender and their poverty, Arnow's fiction pays homage to their ability to do the unthinkable in order to save lives.

In the end, Nunn's two foxhounds, Vinie and Sam, do get King Devil, who in an ironic twist of events turns out to be a pregnant vixen and not a fox. Having accomplished his goal of killing King Devil, Nunn, in an interesting turn of events, accepts his position back in the community. His first action is to sell the foxhounds, thus eliminating his difference and putting him on equal par with others in his community. Having failed his daughter in pursuit of King Devil, Nunn seeks to make amends by buying Suse a dress with the money he has made from the sale of the dogs. But his purchase is bittersweet when he learns that his daughter is pregnant. For Milly, the sale adds more tragedy to the news of her daughter because the foxhounds represented a sign value for her: "Th hounds was th onliest real fine things we've ever had" (p. 371). From Milly's perspective, she has lost her daughter, who will now be forced into a dismal situation living with her in-laws and taking care of someone else's children. Much to Milly's surprise, because she had thought Nunn different from the others, Nunn does not allow his daughter to remain in his house even though he knows what that means for her. The ending of the novel seems to foreclose any possibility that difference can make a foothold in the hill community.

Published in 1954 by Macmillan, *The Dollmaker* is Arnow's most renowned and accomplished novel. The final book in her trilogy on Appalachia, *The Dollmaker* charts the migration of the Nevels family, who move from Kentucky north to Detroit to work in the factories during World War II. The migration northward represents the possibility of economic improvement for the family, but it also means assimilating to a wholly new cultural environment. Arnow's novel examines this transformation of the Nevels family from rural tenant farmers in Kentucky to working-class urban denizens in Detroit.

Though the novel begins in Kentucky, much of the action of the story takes place after the family has moved to Detroit. *The Dollmaker* is a record of the myriad problems the family mem-

bers face in trying to fit into a place where they are clearly outsiders. Much like the "Okies" who migrated westward from the Great Plains during the Dust Bowl era, the Nevelses are labeled "hillbillies" on their arrival in Detroit. Though Arnow focuses on the problems that the family endures in the city, she is not given to portraying rural Kentucky in a sentimental light by comparison. She makes it clear that Kentucky before the family's move has undergone considerable change. Men have left the area in order to sign up for the military or, like Clovis Nevels, have moved to the North to get jobs in factories during World War II. Change in the Cumberland is writ large even if the hill people still do subsistence farming and still, if need be, use farm animals for transportation. From the secret nuclear research at the laboratory in Oak Ridge, Tennessee, to the signs tacked on trees urging hill people to come north to work in Willow Run, the 1940s were bringing tremendous change to the region.

Gertie, the main character of the novel, is Arnow's most singular female character. Wedded to her life in rural Kentucky, she demonstrates a command of self-sufficient living skills all but lost to modern 1940s America. The opening chapter of the novel illustrates Gertie's abilities when her son's life is at stake. Riding a mule to try to get her son to a doctor, Gertie hails down a passing car carrying an army officer and his driver. The two watch in disbelief as she cuts her son's throat to give him a tracheotomy in their car, thereby saving his life. Though one would expect that the army officer would see much worse in the war, Gertie proves herself the stronger and more capable one as he faints dead away at the sight of her impromptu surgery. Thus the opening chapter sets the stage, establishing the strength of Gertie's character.

During the period when her husband, Clovis, first goes alone to Detroit to work in a factory, Gertie ably works their tenant farm in Kentucky with the help of her son. Unbeknownst to her husband, she has also been saving money through her own work of selling eggs and molasses to buy a nearby farm so that they no longer have to be beholden as tenant farmers. Her farming skills

secure her purchase of her Uncle John's farm. As he freely admits, "Many's th time, Gertie, I've wished you could ha been one a my own. You're mighty nigh as good a hand at farmen as I am, an if I don't watch out you'll git th better a me in this trade" (p. 106). Unlike the other women who are left behind in their rural community while their husbands seek employment in the city, Gertie by herself has been able to maintain the farm. She thus differentiates herself from the other women in the community, who want to abandon the rural life to move to the city. Gertie would prefer to remain on the farm.

In her rural community, Gertie is an anomaly. Her estrangement will continue in her new community after she agrees to move to Detroit to join her husband. In Arnow's refusal to privilege the rural over the urban and vice versa, the reader learns that Detroit exists on a continuum with rural Kentucky. As with her life in the hill community, Gertie, as a woman, finds herself not quite fitting in with the mores of her new environment in Detroit. This time, however, it is two of her own children out of the five she had who are eager to see their mother change and adapt to life in the city. Gertie's two middle children, Clytie and Enoch, feel ashamed of the way that their mother talks and encourage her to rid herself of expressions that identify her as a "hillbilly." Gertie therefore must rethink her ways of parenting and of interacting with others to satisfy the demands of her children, who see her as a liability at times. Her children challenge her to embrace the way things are done in Detroit in her working-class community, implying that her rural practices have no place in this new urban setting.

But not all members of her family have been able to adapt to Detroit. Reuben, the eldest son, is still wedded to his life back in Kentucky, where he farmed alongside his mother. Though Gertie tries to encourage him to change in order to get along, he refuses to adjust to his new life: "I ain't maken myself over fer Detroit" (p. 316). Likewise, her youngest daughter, Cassie, has a difficult time adjusting. In Kentucky, Cassie had her imaginary friend Callie Lou to talk to. But in Detroit, her desire to stay inside and play with

her make-believe friend seems out of place. Going outside to play, Cassie becomes an easy target for the other children, who make fun of her talking to an imaginary friend. With both children, Gertie feels torn between the belief that they should be allowed to be themselves, to be individuals, and her awareness that they need to adapt to their new environment. In their decided difference, Reuben and Cassie suffer the consequences of their inability to adapt to the social and cultural practices of Detroit. For Reuben, it means abandoning his family as he runs away to Kentucky to live with his grandmother. Sadly, the consequences for Cassie are even graver. In one of the most heart-wrenching scenes in any literary text, Cassie, who has been playing with Callie Lou in the railroad yard, has her legs severed when she does not hear an oncoming "backward-moving switch engine" (p. 406).

Besides adapting to life in the ironically named Merry Hill, a housing project in Detroit, Gertie finds herself confronted with new challenges that will increasingly become a part of modern urban living. In an interesting twist, Gertie finds that Clovis' purchase of a refrigerator has suddenly made her a minor celebrity in the neighborhood. The refrigerator, aptly named the "Icy Heart," represents the height of modernization in the 1940s. One neighbor, Mrs. Daly, admiringly looks at the refrigerator, exclaiming, "A refrigerator—such a big one an so fine. . . . An ina war when stuff's so hard to git" (p. 277). For the other female neighbors, it is an object of desire, one "every American woman dreams of" (p. 279). Her husband, Clovis, is proud that he is able to buy his wife this appliance. The refrigerator for him signals their rise in socioeconomic terms, leaving behind their "hillbilly" roots.

However, for Gertie, who is not captivated by the commodification of household appliances, the "Icy Heart" represents capitalism's grip on poor people. The family's participation in consumerism sinks them further and further into debt. It is an economic system that makes money off their physical labor in wartime factories and keeps them tied to monthly payments on appliances like the refrigerator and their house. While the Neveleses assumed they were going to improve their economic situation by migrating north, Arnow's novel painfully documents how the working poor from regions like Appalachia often fared worse than they could have imagined.

Besides participation in a new type of consumerism, Gertie's relationship to work undergoes dramatic change, one that neither she nor the reader could foresee. In Kentucky, Gertie could exist on a somewhat equal footing with men because she worked on the farm. Her physical labor was essential in maintaining the economic viability of the whole family. However, in Detroit, her labor as a housewife holds little if any economic value, except for her ability to save money on buying cheaper food, which her family resents. Even the cottage industry of making carved crosses affords her little remuneration in a neighborhood where few residents have any money to buy such things. Even though women of the time were able to work in wartime factories, Clovis discourages Gertie from pursuing such avenues of employment by explaining to her that she is physically unsuited for such labor. The largeness of her body, which was an asset on the farm, becomes a liability in the city. According to Clovis, "[Gertie] was too big for the factory machinery, [which was] set up for little slim women," and because "she was so given to wool gathering she might get a hand or her head smashed the first day" (p. 249). Though she contributed financially to the well-being of her family in Kentucky, she finds herself economically dependent on her husband in Detroit.

The economic picture is further complicated for women during this time period by the contingent nature of their wartime employment. Though some of Gertie's female neighbors work in the factories and have even suffered injuries on the job, everyone knows that by the end of the war these jobs will be gone. They will be given to men who are returning from the war. In that respect, Arnow's book anticipates the criticism that emerged from the feminist movement in the 1960s that decried the cultural more that women remain at home. Arnow seems keenly aware that job opportunities for women would no longer exist after the war and that women would once

again be dependent upon their husbands economically.

By the end of the novel, Clovis no longer has a job either, and Gertie learns that economic insecurity will remain a factor in her life. In an ironic twist, Gertie resorts to her whittling, a skill she has learned on the farm, to help with her family's financial needs. To get the material to whittle the dolls to sell, Gertie decides to cut up the block of cherrywood she brought with her from Kentucky. Out of this block of wood, she has been slowly carving an image of Christ, the whittling representing her last connection to her life in Kentucky. She is characteristically sanguine about her decision, realizing that necessity trumps sentimental and artistic factors. Ultimately Arnow's novel argues that the migration north to Detroit belies the dream that rural people from the hill communities in Kentucky would be able to achieve a better life.

While her novel offers an explicit critique of modern urban America, Arnow refuses to sentimentalize life back in rural Appalachia. Gertie's older son, Reuben, had returned to Kentucky to live with his grandmother because he could not "adapt" to life in Detroit. His return, however, has not improved his economic chances. Since his grandfather will eventually sell his farm, the only jobs available are those in the coal mines or as a factory hand—choices that Gertie dismisses as untenable for a person like Reuben, who wanted to farm. Reviewing Reuben's options, Gertie concludes, "There weren't any answers" (p. 564). The same could be said for the rest of the Nevels family who remained in Detroit.

LATER WORKS

Among Arnow's later works are two novels, *The Weedkiller's Daughter* and *The Kentucky Trace: A Novel of the American Revolution*. These two books mark a clear departure from her earlier works, where the focus was primarily a commentary on Appalachia. In the case of *The Weedkiller's Daughter*, Arnow moves her setting to the suburbs of Detroit for an examination of urban America in the 1960s, depicting a society that is polarized by a cold war mentality. With her last work of fiction, *The Kentucky Trace: A Novel of the American Revolution*, Arnow expands her narrative range to write a historical novel. Though Arnow's book is in part a social history of the American Revolution, it is also paints a rather bleak picture of a society where people feel disenfranchised, humane values have little value, and ecological destruction is the rule. Read together, both of these latter books offer an interesting social commentary of contemporary culture in the 1960s and 1970s.

Addressing the suburban setting of *The Weedkiller's Daughter*, Arnow explained to Barbara Baer that she did not want to be seen as a regionalist writer but instead wanted to write about "Middle America" (p. 60). As such, this novel seems very much of its day, enabling Arnow to examine the contemporary culture of the 1960s.

Sandra Ballard reports that the book had respectable sales, but reviewers did not respond positively to *The Weedkiller's Daughter*. Interestingly, when interviewed later in her life, Arnow told Haeja Chung that she had expected the novel to do better than *The Dollmaker*. Unlike her other works, none of which ever went out of print, *The Weedkiller's Daughter* had a less-than-successful publishing history. It was published originally in 1970 and reprinted in 1974. Thereafter the novel remained out of print until it was reissued by Michigan State University Press in 2012.

Critics who have written about Arnow's work all concede that *The Weedkiller's Daughter* does not quite live up to the expectations of her earlier trilogy. The main character, Susie, unlike the protagonists in her former novels, is a difficult one to embrace, and the other characters in the novel seem more like types rather than fleshed-out individuals. Fifteen-year-old Susie Schnitzer does, however, share the streak of individualism seen not only in Arnow herself but in many of her female characters, including Louisa of *Mountain Path*, Suse in *Hunter's Horn*, Delphina in *Between the Flowers*, and Gertie in *The Dollmaker*.

The Weedkiller's Daughter takes place in the 1960s, when much of society, according to Arnow, is polarized. In Arnow's depiction the divid-

ing lines are drawn between two types of people: those who conform to the dictates of contemporary society and those who prefer to take an alternate path. Susie admires the nonconformists. They include her grandmother, who was deported back to Canada because of her supposed "communist" leanings, as well as the parents of some of her friends: Robert's mother, who is a doctor volunteering in Vietnam; Iggy's father, who is an artist; and Katy's father, who has gotten fired from his post at a university and refuses to testify against others. Last but not least is the elderly Mrs. Nevels, making an appearance from *The Dollmaker*.

These minor characters are set against the novel's antagonists, Susie's parents, whom she calls Bismarck (her father) and the Popsicle Queen (her mother). Susie's parents and others of similar ilk represent the other side of the political spectrum in their over-the-top conservative attitudes about society. Mr. Schnitzer, a product of the cold war mentality, perceives danger all around him. Like many suburbanites of the 1960s anxious about a nuclear war, he has built his own bomb shelter and surrounds his home both inside and out with excessive security systems. People like Mr. Schnitzer are equally worried about their neighbors, fearful that they will attempt to get into their bomb shelter when a nuclear explosion occurs. His is a walled-in fortress that Susie refers to as "The House of Usher," with all of its obvious gothic overtones. Their suburb reflects the socially stratified society taking form in the 1960s: new money people (like Susie's family), who live in executive homes made possible by denuding the area of all fauna and flora, in a development ironically named Eden Hills; old money people who live in "The Village"; and people lower down the socioeconomic ladder, who are buying their first homes in the vicinity of the shopping center. To make way for these new developments, Arnow narrates a harrowing scene where the ducks and their habitat are literally burned alive to clear land. Arnow does not hold back on critiquing the damage that can be done when land development trumps wildlife habitat.

In the midst of this divisive and stratified society, Susie attempts to navigate the perceived treacherous waters as a teenager in a world where she feels alienated from family, peers, and school. The novel is therefore the coming-of-age-story of a teenage girl whose parents, in her opinion, care more about their son, Brandon, than their daughter, who has been scarred psychologically by her overly controlling parents. Susie's goal is to try to convince a school social worker that she is "normal" when in point of fact she feels utterly alienated from most people around her.

Nevertheless, in the arc of the narrative Susie is able to succeed on many levels with people who support her, like Mrs. Nevels and a small group of friends. A pivotal scene in the book occurs when she is invited to go out on a boat with Robert and two other friends. Susie quickly realizes that they are in trouble going out in turbulent weather, which the helmsman Robert, who knows little about navigating a boat, refuses to acknowledge. In this situation, Susie, along with her friend Ben, assume control over the boat, thereby saving it from capsizing. This scene demonstrates to Susie and to the others that she is wholly capable of taking control of her life.

In the last chapter of the book, Susie returns to the "social worker" therapist who is using a group of students at her school for his own research in order to become a psychologist. In this last session with the social worker, she ends up switching roles. In her first session with him, Susie felt terrified about the outcome of his evaluation. At this pivotal moment, Susie takes charge and physically assaults the social worker to uncover the tape recorder that he has hidden on his person, thereby gaining the upper hand. When she leaves his office, he concedes that she is "one of the most normal, healthy-minded American teen-agers I have ever met" (p. 345). Her refusal to go along with his initial assessment leads her to the realization that "she was a normal, normal, a normal American girl, loving the right things, hating the right things (p. 346). For the first time in the novel, Susie seems secure within herself.

By the end of the novel, the reader and Susie learn that all is not what it has appeared to be.

Characters whom Susie thought were abiding by the rules of their parents turn out to be doing something entirely different. Like Susie, her friends Robert and Mary Lou prove their ability to resist parental strictures. Robert secretly dates a woman his father disapproves of, and he will in all likelihood run away with her on his boat. Susie also discovers that Mary Lou disagrees with her parents' racism and anticommunist ideas. While Arnow's novel depicts a seemingly rigid, bifurcated society between conformists and nonconformists, all three teenagers suggest that there are emergent fissures of resistance and that they perhaps will be individual thinkers rather than perpetuate the social and cultural values of their parents. In that sense, Arnow's book seems hopeful about the changes taking place in the 1960s.

In the historical novel *The Kentucky Trace: A Novel of the American Revolution*, readers are introduced to the main character, William David Leslie Collins, known as Leslie, in the opening scene. In the wilderness, a British officer and young lieutenant, who are starving, come upon Leslie's campsite. He has been working as a surveyor, and rather than take them prisoner in rebel territory, he "paroles" them and allows them to ride with him. Though as a rebel he is supposed to kill them, Leslie finds he cannot: "There were some who'd call him traitor to the cause; but then maybe he'd feel a traitor to mankind if in the woods he'd killed two men only because they'd worn the uniform of the enemy" (p. 4). Soon thereafter, however, the three of the them are captured by horse thieves who operate under a different code of ethics.

This scene gives the reader a snapshot of Leslie's character. Like Gertie in *The Dollmaker* or Susie in *The Weedkiller's Daughter*, Leslie is a person who cannot play by societal rules. To his credit, he is honor bound to hold certain humane values, one of which is that the so-called enemy, the Loyalists, are deserving of decent treatment regardless of whose side they are on. But Leslie's values, we soon learn, are out of synch with the society around him, including the horse thieves, whose primary goal is opportunistic theft rather than participation in the war and who intend to hang all three men. He is also at odds with the "overmountain" rebels who capture the horse thieves but who question Leslie's loyalty to the revolutionary cause. A person with real values, Leslie refuses to play along with the overmountain men and does not tell them that he has been a spy for Francis Marion's militia and that he fought in the famous Battle of Camden. Both ventures would have proven that Leslie was on the right side. Instead, Leslie literally and figuratively is trapped by the forces of society. Not willing to participate in what he sees as a corrupt system, Leslie evades his certain death by throwing himself over a bluff to escape.

After he escapes the overmountain men, Leslie continues his journey back to his homestead and his so-called family. Once there, he finds that his wife and her child are missing. At this time, the reader learns the truth about his marriage to his wife, Sadie. Having gotten drunk at a tavern, Leslie was tricked by the tavern keeper into marrying his daughter. Returning from a surveying trip, Leslie finds his wife has had "their" child much earlier than expected, leading him to realize that the child could not have been his. Though he has done the honorable thing by marrying Sadie, he finds himself trapped in a marriage founded on deception.

While the war itself is not the main thrust of the novel, it is an important theme. In Arnow's book *Old Burnside: A Memoir of a Southern Girlhood*, she talks about how war was a frequent topic of conversation for the family. Because her family had been in America for generations, her "Grandma Denney had hair-raising tales of Indian attacks on long-gone ancestors" (p. 62). There were also stories about ancestors who lived through the American Revolution, the War of 1812, and the Civil War. Arnow even recalls how her parents talked about World War I and about her mother's obsession with reading the daily newspaper to find out about the war. In her own time, according to Martha Billips, Arnow "despaired of the escalation of the conflict in Vietnam" ("Harriette Simpson Arnow," p. 331). No doubt the Vietnam War was on her mind when a minor character in *The Kentucky Trace*, John Saufley, remarks, "Right now the East don't want

the West, and the North is a different world from the South. And they've got Spain on their doorstep. But supposen they do clean out Spain, kill every Indian, plow up every acre a ground from the Atlantic to the Pacific? They'll still have their wars" (p. 48). As part of the next generation of her family to be living through yet another war, Arnow critically suggests that the United States will seemingly always be actively participating in wars.

Arnow's book is also a commentary on the ecological destruction that has taken place, a theme that she examined in *The Weedkiller's Daughter*. In *The Kentucky Trace*, Arnow narrates another type of environmental destruction, the devastation of wildlife. Leslie feels a kindred spirit with nature: "trees had always been kind to him; kinder than men" (p. 25). During his journey, Leslie bears witness to the diminishing numbers of bears, buffalo, and wolves. The problem that plagues the natural environment is the incursion of men driven by greed. In spying a beaver dam, Leslie opines, "He hadn't been close to a beaver dam in years; with every man in Christendom wanting a beaver hat, and hunters eager to supply the skins, the beaver hadn't lasted long" (p. 75). Arnow's book offers a striking commentary of what can happen to wildlife and the environment when commercialism is the paramount driver of an economy.

The rest of the novel concerns itself with a ragtag group of people that Leslie encounters while trying to follow a group of neighbors, including, he thinks, his wife and child, who have left the area because of Indian activity. The reader later learns that Sadie and the child have died from a lingering fever, freeing Leslie to pursue his own life. By the end of the novel, Leslie has turned this ragtag group—including a Native American, two slaves, and an abandoned baby—into his own community.

The group Leslie has assembled is made up of outsiders very much like himself, who have been disenfranchised from society. But they are far from a company of equals: members of the group become both figuratively and literally Leslie's property. The Native American man, to whom Leslie gives the name Little Brother Leap-

ing Fish, does not have a tribe and does not speak English. Leslie buys the slave Rachel from her mistress, the "yellow-haired woman." The novel's presumption is that she will have a much better life being owned by Leslie than by the yellow-haired woman. The other slave, Jethro, was given to Leslie by his parents when he turned twenty-one. Lastly, there is the child that Leslie "adopts" and also names after himself, William David. The novel seems to privilege whiteness and patriarchy as the determining factors in a society.

In the novel, Leslie has seemingly made his way through a corrupt world where there is no end to war, where environmental devastation to wildlife is the rule, and where people have no values. He has also created a new community out of people unwelcome in the dominant culture. One would hope that such an ending suggests an optimistic vision of the possibilities for society, but Arnow is also realistic about the havoc that humankind can wreak as Leslie reflects, "The world was a fine place—except for the people in it, including himself" (p. 161).

POSTHUMOUS PUBLICATIONS

Though her second book, *Between the Flowers*, was written in the 1930s, it was not published until 1999, when it was picked up by Michigan State University Press. Martha Billips, in "The Writer and the Land," details how Arnow and her editor Harold Strauss spent three years trying to get her second novel published, with no success. According to the correspondence between the two, editorial staffers who knew little about farm life raised questions about Arnow's depiction of farming. Unable to secure a publisher for the novel, Strauss wrote Arnow, in a letter dated September 15, 1939, that her relative unfamiliarity with the reading public, as well as the impending war, would hinder her chances of finding a publisher.

Between the Flowers interrogates the question that was much on Arnow's mind as a young woman: whether to remain in the hill country of Appalachia or move to the city. In her first novel, *Mountain Path*, Arnow's heroine, Louisa, chooses the same path that Arnow did in real life, when

she left the rural school in Pulaski County to resume her studies at the University of Louisville.

In *Between the Flowers*, Arnow reexamines rural living from a different perspective. To explore this topic, Arnow sets up a three-way dynamic among characters that suggests the possible options available in rural Kentucky. Delphine Costello is a hill country woman who dreams of leaving the rural county to move to the city; Marsh Gregory, her eventual husband, has moved around as an oilman but decides to buy a farm; and finally, Sam Fairchild has left the farming community to go to college to learn about farming but then never returns. Through these three characters, Arnow's text attempts to parse the different ways of thinking about life in a rural community.

The novel primarily narrates the story of Marsh Gregory and Delphine Costello. Arnow immediately sets up the tension between the two that will characterize their entire marriage. The reader learns early on that Delph is someone who does not want to remain in the hill country for the rest of her life. But though Delph is eager to move away from the Little South Fork Country, her present circumstances of living with her uncle and aunt keep her from actualizing that desire. At the beginning of the novel, Delph finds herself struggling with her uncle to let her move into town so that she can attend high school. But her uncle has conservative ideas about letting girls leave the farm and thinks poorly of those who decide to move away to the city. He had to watch all his own siblings desert farm life, leaving him behind to take of his parents and the farm. Clearly resentful that they left, he seems bound and determined to keep Delph on the farm as unacknowledged retribution. Delph's life is thus circumscribed by her conservative uncle and aunt, whose ideas about what young farming women should be doing does not include moving away to get an education.

For Delph, Arnow crafts a family lineage that helps explain why she sees things differently. From her relatives, Delph has inherited the desire to see and live in other places and not stay in the Little South Fork Country. Her ancestor Azariah, who settled in the hill country in the eighteenth century, only stayed around for a while before abandoning his family to move west. Likewise, after Delph's father died, her mother remarried and quickly moved to Oregon. When she tried to take her daughter with her, Delph's uncle had the law intervene on his behalf to ensure that Delph remained behind with him. This passion to move away, the text suggests, is something in Delph's blood, an inherited feature. It is a desire that haunts her entire life. In a conversation with Dorie, whose children have all gone away, Delph admits: "I can't live my days in this back hill country wonderin'" (p. 29). In many ways, her statement will prove to be prescient.

Falling in love with and marrying Marsh, an oilman who has seen some of the world, represents one way to escape her life in the Little South Fork Country. Initially, when Marsh and Delph run off to get married without her uncle's approval, they talk about moving to South America. But as the novel progresses, any such talk of leaving the hill country becomes nonexistent as Marsh decides to try his hand at farming. Isolated and doing the grueling work needed to keep a farm running, Delph finds herself becoming the person she never wanted to be, a farmer's wife. At the same time, with her help, Marsh eventually becomes what he wants to be, a successful farmer. Though her dream of moving away to a city is never realized, the dream never dissipates. Arnow's novel is striking in that she does not take sides with either Marsh, who loves working the land, or with Delph, who is so desperate to leave. Instead, the reader can feel sympathy for both characters, who are clearly ill-suited for each other.

For his part, Marsh represents a different type of farmer than those who have always lived and farmed in rural Kentucky. He is the farmer that the character Dorie Dodson Fairchild had hoped her son, Sam, would be. Though Dorie's alcoholic husband died, she stayed on the farm and worked hard to make it a success. As a result, she was able to send her children off to college, and she had high hopes for Sam, whose interest in fertilizers led him to study chemistry. But Sam does not return to the country. As she explains to Marsh, "He's high up in research in one of th'

biggest munitions plants in th' country—spendin' all his days searchin' out th' cheapest ways to kill th' most men in th' least time. An' he could be workin' out ways to build up th' land" (p. 149). Arnow is clearly critical of those men like Sam who did not return to help the farming community but instead capitalize on their talents to make money for destructive means.

Marsh, meanwhile, is educating himself through government bulletins on advanced farming techniques. Neighbors are skeptical at first of Marsh's new methods. When Mrs. Crouch, the postmistress, sees one of the bulletins Marsh receives, she says: "Here's somethin', but it's nothin' but gover'ment foolishness—some bulletin from Washington tellin' a man how to farm like as if they knowed in Washington" (p. 12). But Dorie, cognizant of Marsh's inherent qualities, understands what is needed in rural Kentucky to keep it alive: "It needs good heads more'n strong backs" (p. 28). Marsh effectively combines both the curiosity to learn about farming and the willingness to work. He represents the possibility of the new type of farmer willing to educate himself about successful farming methods like diversified farming. Ultimately he is successful in his endeavors because he has used his head.

Arnow's novel also describes the insurmountable problems the Great Depression brought to rural Kentucky, when the logging industry completely dried up. Speaking about her children's desire to leave, Dorie readily admits, "Who that's young an' strong an' smart like mine wants to spend their days on a river bottom farm by a dyin' lumber town? Burdine's dead. They've got th' coal an' th' oil an' timber out a these hills, th' money's gone . . . the land's washed out, an' what's to hold th' children?" (p. 27). Because of these economic problems, many of the men out of necessity are leaving to go north to find jobs. In her trips to sell melons, Delph observes the men waiting at bus depots and train stations to make their way out of town: "Usually they were longlimbed hill men with suitcases gripped awkwardly in great-knuckled, sunburned hands, come up from the back hill counties to take the train to some one of the short-houred, easy-jobbed, New Jerusalems of the north" (pp. 183–

184). Arnow's novel lays bare the discouraging reality for those people who hope their lives will be better if they move to the North, a reality she will eloquently describe in *The Dollmaker*.

One of the key moments in the novel occurs when Sam Fairchild, Dorie's son, returns to Burdine for a visit, giving Delph a last opportunity to change her life. Though Sam only makes an appearance at the end of the novel, he is talked about at different times throughout the text. Delph is especially interested in him. As a teenager, she collected articles about people who had left, which she then put into a scrapbook. She was effectively living vicariously through the travels of others who did not remain in rural Kentucky. Sam, in her eyes, "had gone the farthest and seen the most" (p. 56). His return to Burdine then represents a critical moment for her.

At the same time that Sam returns, Marsh has come down with typhoid fever, contracted from drinking water out of a creek. As Marsh lies in bed for days wavering between life and death, Delph, through the encouragement of Dorie, ends up rekindling her friendship with Sam, and it is clear that they are kindred spirits. Like Marsh in Delph's earlier years, Sam represents the opportunity to recapture the dream of moving away and living a life she has always wanted. Sam, she observes, "could drive away the ugliness and the pain, and she would find herself young again and strong, able to dream and plan, and see [her son] Burr-Head grow into the man she wished him to be—someone hungry for the taste of the world, like Sam" (p. 375).

But much like Louisa's situation in *Mountain Path*, suddenly the decision of whether to stay or leave is made for her. Had Marsh died, one presumes Delph would have left with Sam. However, Marsh does not die, and when Delph hears that he will live, she faints straightaway, knowing that she will not be able to leave Marsh and Burr-Head. She also comes to realize that Burr-Head will never have the same hunger she has to be part of the greater world, but will be a farmer like Marsh someday. Rather than leave with Sam, Delph decides to remain behind.

The last scene in the book horrifically depicts how Delph is trapped by farm life. While Sam, as a man, has freedom of movement, Delph, as a farmer's wife, seemingly has no options other than to carry on as she has done. After watching Sam leave, Delph climbs onto a fencepost, where she sees her neighbor, Sadie, approaching. For Delph, Sadie represents all she dislikes about being a farmer's wife, the constant toil with no future to look forward to. Overwhelmed by the sight of her, Delph imagines Sadie's eyes saying "Always and always I will live with you, Delph, be over you and watch and hold you to the ways of a farmer's wife" (p. 419). Moments later, Delph, in despair about her future, spontaneously hops into the field on the other side of the fence. Within minutes, Solomon, the bull, is bearing down on her; Sadie screams and runs toward her. At that moment, both the reader and Delph know that her situation is hopeless and her death imminent.

Between the Flowers, though unpublished during Arnow's lifetime, is an important work. Arnow expands upon the social issues that interest her, like the displacement of farmers and the economic travails of rural Kentucky. Though she was criticized by readers of her manuscript for what they saw as her lack of knowledge about farming in Appalachia, her novel shines an important historical light on a part of rural America that got little literary attention in the 1930s. For that reason, she remains an important writer for Appalachian literature.

MEMOIR

In 1977 Arnow's memoir, *Old Burnside: A Memoir of a Southern Girlhood*, was published by the University Press of Kentucky. According to Barbara L. Baer, Arnow wrote the book as a historical account of her onetime hometown of Burnside, Kentucky, for its bicentennial. In the prologue, Arnow recounts that in 1953 she and her family drove from Michigan to Burnside for a visit. During her absence of a number of years, Burnside itself had been moved to higher ground to make way for Lake Cumberland, a huge manmade lake. On her arrival in the Cumberland River basin, Arnow describes the bewilderment of being completely lost in an area she no longer recognized. Her memoir represents an attempt to recapture the existence of Burnside through weaving together the history of the town along with her own experience of it.

In the first few chapters of the book, Arnow gives the reader a historical overview of the Cumberland River basin beginning with the Cherokee, who thought of the river as their hunting grounds. These chapters also record the social history of the Cumberland River during the nineteenth century, where the reader learns about the daily lives of people who lived there, like girls and boys who were bound to families. Using county records and other historical materials, Arnow describes in detail the importance of the river in terms of the history of the region, including such events like the Civil War, and of its economic importance for commerce and the traffic of goods. Until the arrival of the railroad in the 1880s, the Cumberland River functioned as a significant connection between Burnside and the outside world.

Arnow next turns to narrating her personal history with the town when she and her family first moved to Burnside in March 1913. In her earliest years, Arnow already demonstrated an interest and curiosity about Burnside and the Cumberland River rather than in the domestic affairs of her family and house. While her mother did not think that highly of Burnside, Arnow, as a child, liked nothing more than to run errands that would take her into town, where she was an astute observer of all of the buildings, people, and activities taking place on her walk.

In the autumn of 1913, Arnow and her family move from lower Burnside to Tyree's Knob, where she had an opportunity to spend more time in the woods. Though the book is filled with autobiographical details about her life and the daily life of her family, it is the Cumberland River itself that dominates the memoir. She recounts in one instance how her persistent queries and interest in log booms and boom hands enabled her one spring to prevail upon her father to take her and her sister to see the logs coming down the river. In 1918 the family moved to Tor-

rent, Kentucky, where her father had gotten a job in an oil field, remaining there until 1921, when oil dropped in price and the oil field was no longer producing. No doubt this experience with the oil field helped her to create the character Marsh Gregory in *Between the Flowers*. The family returned to Burnside in the summer of 1921, where Arnow finished her schooling. At age sixteen Arnow left for Berea College, leaving Burnside permanently. That she wrote this book toward the end of her career reinforces the importance of Appalachia to her career as a writer and as a person.

CONCLUSION

Taken together, Harriette Arnow's works bespeak a writer who was actively engaged with the issues of her time, issues that still resonate for readers. The novels of her Appalachian series challenged old stereotypes about people who lived in the hill communities, too often thought of as people with questionable values who were constantly feuding. Instead, her novels direct the reader's attention to important issues about the use of farmland and the economic necessity for people to leave rural areas to make a living. Ahead of her time, Arnow also thought and wrote about women's issues, depicting the struggles women encountered as farmer's wives living and surviving in Appalachia. For these reasons, Arnow continues to be a defining voice in Appalachian studies. With her later works, Arnow remained critically engaged with social and environmental issues, casting a light on land use, environmental destruction, and devastation to wildlife. Her novels demonstrate her forward thinking about issues that are still of concern.

Selected Bibliography

WORKS OF HARRIETTE SIMPSON ARNOW

NOVELS AND SHORT STORIES
Mountain Path. New York: Covici-Friede, 1936. Reprint, University Press of Kentucky, 1964.

Hunter's Horn. New York: Macmillan, 1949. Reprint, East Lansing: Michigan State University Press, 1997.

The Dollmaker. New York: Macmillan, 1954. Reprint, New York; Perennial, 2003.

The Weedkiller's Daughter. New York: Knopf, 1970. Reprint, East Lansing: Michigan State University Press, 2012.

The Kentucky Trace: A Novel of the American Revolution. New York: Knopf, 1974. Reprint, East Lansing: Michigan State University Press, 2012.

Between the Flowers. East Lansing: Michigan State University Press, 1999.

The Collected Short Stories of Harriette Simpson Arnow. Edited by Sandra L. Ballard and Haeja K. Chung. East Lansing: Michigan State University Press, 2005.

NONFICTION
Seedtime on the Cumberland. New York: Macmillan, 1960. Reprint, East Lansing: Michigan State University Press, 2013.

Flowering of the Cumberland. New York: Macmillan, 1963. Reprint, East Lansing: Michigan State University Press, 2013.

Old Burnside: A Memoir of a Southern Girlhood. Lexington: University Press of Kentucky, 1977.

"Help and Hindrances in Writing: A Lecture." Transcribed by Sandra L. Ballard. In *Harriette Simpson Arnow: Critical Essays on Her Work*. Edited by Haeja K. Chung. East Lansing: Michigan State University Press 1995. Pp. 281–291.

PAPERS
Arnow's papers are held in Special Collections at the King Library, University of Kentucky, Lexington.

CRITICAL AND BIOGRAPHICAL STUDIES

Baer, Barbara L. "Harriette Arnow's Chronicles of Destruction." In *Harriette Simpson Arnow: Critical Essays on Her Work*. Edited by Haeja K. Chung. East Lansing: Michigan State University Press 1995. Pp. 53–62.

Ballard, Sandra L. "Harriette Simpson Arnow's Life as a Writer." In *Harriette Simpson Arnow: Critical Essays on Her Work*. Edited by Haeja K. Chung. East Lansing: Michigan State University Press 1995. Pp. 15–31.

Billips, Martha. "The Writer and the Land: Harriette Simpson Arnow and the Genesis of Her Novel 'Between the Flowers.'" *Appalachian Journal* 32, no. 4:468–482 (summer 2005.)

———. ldquo;Harriette Simpson Arnow: A Writer's Life." In *Kentucky Women: Their Lives and Times*. Edited by Melissa A. McEuen and Thomas H. Appleton, Jr. Athens:

HARRIETTE SIMPSON
ARNOW

University of Georgia Press, 2015. Pp. 312–336.

Eckley, William. *Harriette Arnow*. New York: Twayne, 1974.

Farber, Stephen. "'It's as Far from What I Am as Anything I'll Ever Play.'" *New York Times*, May 13, 1984. http://www.nytimes.com/1984/05/13/arts/it-s-as-far-from-what-i-am-as-anything-i-ll-ever-play.html?pagewanted=all

Griffin, Joan R. "Fact and Fancy in *Mountain Path*." In *Harriette Simpson Arnow: Critical Essays on Her Work*. Edited by Haeja K. Chung. East Lansing: Michigan State University Press 1995. Pp.117–127.

Hobbs, Glenda. "Starting Out in the Thirties: Harriette Arnow's Literary Genesis." In *Literature at the Barricades: The American Writer in the 1930s*. Edited by Ralph Bogardus and Fred Hobson. Tuscaloosa: University of Alabama Press, 1982. Pp. 144–161.

Holtman, Janet. "Countering 'What God Thought and the Neighbors Said': Alternative Gender Possibility and Becoming-Animal in Harriette Arnow's *Hunter's Horn*."

Journal of Appalachian Studies 21, no. 1:21–32 (spring 2015).

INTERVIEWS

Chung, Haeja K. "Fictional Characters Come to Life: An Interview." In *Harriette Simpson Arnow: Critical Essays on Her Work*. Edited by Haeja K. Chung. East Lansing: Michigan State University Press 1995. Pp. 263–280.

Miller, Danny. "A MELUS Interview: Harriette Arnow." *Multi-Ethnic Literature of the United States* 9, no. 2:83–97 (summer 1982).

FILM BASED ON THE WORK OF HARRIETTE SIMPSON ARNOW

The Dollmaker. Teleplay by Susan Cooper and Hume Cronyn. Directed by Daniel Petrie. Aired on ABC, May 13, 1984.

DAVID BOTTOMS

(1949—)

Christopher Buck

ACCLAIMED AS POET laureate of Georgia for more than a decade (2000–2012), David Bottoms is a narrative poet whose work reads like creative nonfiction in poetic form. His attention to physical detail creates vivid scenes into which the reader can enter, and vicariously experience, in order to gain metaphysical insight into life—and death. Like the song "Georgia on My Mind" (most familiar as the Ray Charles version), Bottoms has Georgia on his mind, specifically Macon, Georgia. This locale provides canvas and palette for the paintings he creates. Vitalizing his vignettes with local color to register a universal, even archetypal point, Bottoms is even more "down home" in his narrative accounts of close family, sundry friends, local characters, and native flora and fauna as part and parcel of the (mostly) Georgia landscape.

The poems that Bottoms creates are not still-life portraits. Kinetic, not static, his poems are moving scenes—action without much dialogue—that often stir the emotions. His poetry can also be analogized to short video clips, with narration, that operate somewhat in a documentary style, yet are clearly neither journalistic nor otherwise objective. This poetry is intensely personal; each subject is treated subjectively. The author clearly has his audience in mind, but does not speak directly to the intended readers. He is neither a metaphysical poet nor a social poet: in his work scenes are reenacted with scarcely a word of commentary. The poet lets the reader muse on what the Muse has inspired the poet to write. In this sense, the poems have no clear message yet are full of meaning.

LIFE

Born September 11, 1949, in Canton, Georgia, David Bottoms was raised in "the Bible Belt," where "sometimes it felt like we lived right on the hardest part of the buckle" (*The Onion's Dark Core* [*ODC*], p. 63). David Harold Bottoms, Jr., was the only child of David Harold Bottoms, Sr., a funeral director, and Louise Ashe Bottoms, a registered nurse. There was nothing in Canton to predispose Bottoms to higher cultural aspirations. During his childhood, Canton was a small town some fifty miles north of Atlanta. At that time, Canton was a bulwark against change, insulated from significant cultural, racial, and religious diversity. Bottoms describes Canton as "a very small town in which everything of any cultural or historical value was, over the years, systematically bulldozed for the quick bucks of burger joints and car washes" (*ODC*, p. 45). In his childhood years in the late 1950s, Bottoms received his religious education at the Canton First Baptist Church (Southern Baptist), where his mother served as superintendent of the Primary Department of the Sunday School (*ODC*, p. 144). Thus, during his most impressionable years, he had quite a religious upbringing. The indelible imprint of religion on Bottoms' psyche and soul is evident throughout his poetry.

After graduating from Cherokee High School in 1967, Bottoms studied at Mercer University in Macon, where he earned his degree in English in 1971. For a year, Bottoms worked as a guitar salesman. He married Margaret Lynn Bensel, who taught art at an elementary school, on February 5, 1972. He then enrolled in a graduate program in English at West Georgia College (now University of West Georgia), where he earned his master's degree in 1973. From 1974 to 1978, Bottoms taught high school English in Douglasville, Georgia. He also worked part-time in the Georgia Poetry Society's Poets in the Schools program.

In 1979 Bottoms got his first big break as an aspiring poet. His first full-length book, *Shooting Rats at the Bibb County Dump* (1980), won the Walt Whitman Award of the American Academy of American Poets. The judge was none other than Robert Penn Warren—U.S. poet laureate in 1986–1987 and the only author awarded the Pulitzer Prize for both poetry and fiction—who named Bottoms as the winner from more than thirteen hundred submissions that year. This prestigious award brought Bottoms national acclaim.

Later that year, Bottoms accepted a graduate fellowship at Florida State University. There he earned his Ph.D. in American poetry and creative writing in 1982. Shortly after, Bottoms began teaching at Georgia State University in Atlanta, where he served as professor of creative writing. Together with Pam Durban, Bottoms founded and edited the GSU literary magazine, *Five Points*.

In 1986 Bottoms was offered a visiting appointment at the University of Montana as Richard Hugo Poet in Residence. Divorce followed a year later. At the University of Montana, Bottoms met and fell in love with Kelly Jean Beard, a law student. In 1989 they married and he moved to Billings, Montana. While she practiced law, he finished his second novel. In 1990 they moved to Atlanta, and in 1991 their daughter, Rachel, was born. Returning to GSU, Bottoms served as associate dean of fine arts and was named the John B. and Elena Diaz-Verson Amos Distinguished Chair in English Letters.

Bottoms has received a number of prestigious awards for his poetry. These include the 1984 and 1987 Book of the Year in Poetry from the Dixie Council of Authors and Journalists, for *In a U-Haul North of Damascus* (1983)and *Under the Vulture-Tree* (1987), the Levinson Prize from *Poetry* magazine (1985); a Georgia Council for the Arts individual artist grant (1988); the Award in Literature from the American Academy and Institute of Arts and Letters (1988); a National Endowment for the Arts Fellowship (1988); the Ingram Merrill Foundation Award (1988); a Guggenheim Foundation Fellowship (1999); Georgia Author of the Year Award for *Vagrant*

Grace (1999); the post of Georgia Poet Laureate (2000–2012); the Frederick Bock Prize of *Poetry* magazine (2002); an honorary doctor of letters degree from Mercer University (2005); *Irish America* magazine's Stars of the South honor (2006); and *Shenandoah*'s James Boatwright III Prize for Poetry (2007), judged by Eavan Boland. Further honors include election in 2009 to the Georgia Writer's Hall of Fame, sponsored by University of Georgia Libraries; the 2011 Governor's Award in Humanities, sponsored by the governor of Georgia and Georgia Humanities Council; Florida State University's Alumni Award for Distinguished Writers (2012); and inclusion in *Best American Poetry 2016*, selected by Edward Hirsch.

PHILOSOPHY OF POETRY: THE ONION'S DARK CORE

Many poets are reluctant to "betray" their work by commenting on, much less interpreting, their poems. David Bottoms is a notable exception. *The Onion's Dark Core: A Little Book of Poetry Talk* (2010) is a small volume of both new and previously published essays and interviews. This modest work has added value as a primer on poetry—not as a systematic treatise, but as a record of an accomplished poet's reflections on the art and craft of poetry. As such, *The Onion's Dark Core* is filled with insights of use to other poets, especially aspiring poets.

With a somewhat mystical orientation, David Bottoms approaches poetry with a sense of mystery, "a hazy intuition of a reality other than the physical" (p. 42). He believes that "good poems" should "define the mystery for us"—not "solve" the mystery of life ("which is impossible") but rather to "teach us the right questions to ask" (p. 93).

Poets can be "storytellers who are yearners after meaning," and the greatest writers are those who "touch their readers at the deepest emotional and psychological levels" (p. 31). In a sense, such writers approach their subject matter with "a religious sensibility," in "probing the profound questions of the human predicament" (p. 33). Poetry, at its finest, can evoke "epiphanies" of

"deep insight" (p. 31). "Art," for Bottoms, is a "quest for truth" (p. 37).

Bottoms also sheds light on some of the dynamics of his own poetry. "Often," Bottoms explains, "my poems will turn near the end and try to make a figurative leap there," because doing so "seems to give the poem a final punch, a final burst of energy" (p. 86). Indeed, he is a master of this poetic technique, which serves as a signature—practically a trademark—of his literary style.

Bottoms quotes, with approval, Ed Hirsch, who says that poetry is "a mode of thinking that moves beyond the literal" (p. 17). Bottoms understands this to mean that poetry is a process in which "we actually began to think in a different way, to open doors out of the physical landscape into an internal and spiritual landscape of more meaningful meanings and more truthful truths" (p. 17). A narrative poet himself, Bottoms distinguishes himself from those poets who pursue poetic narrative "at the expense of metaphor," which many poets "have identified, quite correctly, as the fundamental element of poetry" (p. 17). One may then ask how a narrative can move beyond the literal into the figurative. Bottoms characterizes metaphor as a "gift" that "makes the world fresh" and "teaches us to see the world from different angles" in such a way that it "connects all things" (p. 19). It's not that every poetic "story" has to have a "moral." Yet, for a poem to be worth its artistic salt, an element of meaning should be present. The poem is not mere entertainment but a vehicle for reflection. The Muse, in other words, wants us to muse.

"All of my poems depend heavily on narrative," writes Bottoms (*Armored Hearts* [*AH*], p. 84). If the narrative itself serves as a canvas for setting the scene and enacting the drama, that "narrative surface" is a platform whereby the poet can "make the language leap into another level of meaning" (p. 84), thereby transcending the literal to read something figurative, symbolic, even archetypal. In his work, Bottoms "leans toward compression, the illustrated moment" (*ODC*, p. 128). Many of Bottoms' poems achieve a flash of implicit insight, especially at the end,

in which the climax is a mystical, even transcendent, moment of self-realization, rather than a plot twist or dramatic high point. Each poem abounds in detail, with signature autobiographical authenticity, where the poet is often as much an actor as he is an observer. That attention to detail registers some psychological insight at a higher level of meaning; the general derives from the specific.

With this background in mind, a brief description and analysis of David Bottoms' first three books of poetry follows. (His 1978 *Jamming with the Band at the VFW* was a mere chapbook of ten poems.) Since the poems in these three volumes were reprinted in the first three sections of his four-part collection *Armored Hearts* (1995), the pagination of this reprise publication will be used throughout.

SHOOTING RATS AT THE BIBB COUNTY DUMP

Bottoms launched his career as a distinguished American poet with his first full collection, *Shooting Rats at the Bibb County Dump* (1980). He tells us in *The Onion's Dark Core* that several poems in this collection were influenced by an idea discussed by Carl Sagan in his 1977 book *Dragons of Eden*, the notion of a "triune brain." In this theory, the human brain evolved as three distinct brains, one after the other. The first is the "reptile brain," located at the top of the spine, said to regulate "eating, sex, and ritual" (*ODC*, p. 100). Above that is the "mammal brain," governing emotion. At the top, the "neo-cortex" allows for abstract thought, which (mostly but not wholly) "differentiates us from other creatures" (p. 100). Indeed, one of the poems he included in his 1980 collection was "The Copperhead" (a distinctly reptilian title), which had just been published in the *Atlantic* (p. 125). Bottoms' favorite reptilian creatures include "snakes, turtles, alligators, rats, vultures" (p. 137).

Many of Bottoms' early poems are anchored in Macon landscapes and culture, and in *Shooting Rats* this is evidenced by titles such as "Below Freezing on Pinelog Mountain," "Writing on Napkins at the Sunshine Club," and

"Watching Gators at Ray Boone's Reptile Farm." Ironically, the book was originally titled "All Systems Break Down" (*ODC*, p. 124), a change that shows a preference for the local (and therefore "real") over the abstract. Because the subject matter, evidently autobiographical, attends so closely to native detail, Bottoms' poems have a ring of authenticity that scarcely requires any "suspension of disbelief" whatsoever—which, by the way, is one way in which David Bottoms' work may be distinguished from that of James Dickey, whose influence Bottoms otherwise acknowledges (*ODC*, pp. 82–83; 166–167; and passim). These poems are not tall tales. They are told matter-of-factly, often with brief, retrospective reflection at the very end.

The title poem deserves special attention. "Shooting Rats at the Bibb County Dump" comes from experience that Bottoms had as a freshman at Mercer University, which, at that time, was a small, private (Southern Baptist affiliated) liberal arts college in Macon, Georgia, with a student population of around fifteen hundred. There, young David pledged a fraternity, Phi Delta Theta. The frat boys were mostly "party guys" not unlike those depicted in the John Belushi movie *Animal House* (*ODC*, p. 68). One of the "more bizarre" of the "fraternity shenanigans" took place at the local Bibb County dump, where a sort of fraternity "ritual" or even "folk art" developed (*ODC*, p. 69), that of shooting rats. Here, predominantly reptilian brains (the rats) met their match in the adolescent brains (the frat boys), who would be the death of the former for the amusement of the latter.

The way it would happen was typically as follows: on Friday and Saturday nights, after the guys had taken their dates back to the women's dorm at Wesleyan College, the frat boys, in two or three cars, would take their .22 rifles (or pistols), along with their beer or whiskey, and drive out to the county dump. There, they would pull their cars into a line facing the garbage mounds, cut the engines, and squat in front of their bumpers and wait. Absolute silence would follow. Then, a scratching sound would emerge from the mounds of garbage. Soon, rats would be swarming. Someone would flash on the headlights, revealing dozens of "little red eyes frozen in the light" (*ODC*, p. 70). Shooting would follow for a minute or two. In the poem, this scene is described tersely and compactly. The poem ends on a dark note of profound, revelatory irony (at least for an adolescent):

It's the light they believe kills.
We drink and load again, let them crawl
for all they're worth into the darkness we're headed
    for.

(AH, p. 5)

This poem, in which the dump becomes a graveyard for the rats, follows the collection's first two poems, "Wrestling Angels" and "Smoking in an Open Grave," which take place in a human graveyard. Death continues to haunt the fourth selection, "The Drunk Hunter," as well as the sixth piece, "Cockfight in a Loxahatchee Grove." While death is a natural fact of life, in these poems, death is precipitated by violence.

A particularly poignant poem is "Stumptown Attends the Picture Show," which, as the poet indicates right after the title, is *on the first attempt at desegregation in Canton, Georgia*" (*AH*, p. 14):

Word has come and Martha the ticket girl
stands behind the candy counter
eating popcorn and smoking Salems.
Beside her the projectionist,
having canned the Vivien Leigh
and come downstairs to watch the real show,
leans folding chairs against the theater doors,
guards his glass counter
like saloon keepers in his Westerns
guard the mirrors hung above their bars.

Outside, good old boys line the sidewalk,
string chain between parking meters
in front of the Canton Theater,
dig in like Rebs in a Kennesaw trench.
From the street, policeman and sheriff's deputies
address their threats to proper names,
try to maintain any stability.
Someone has already radioed the State Boys.

Through the glass door Martha watches
the moon slide over Jones Mercantile.
In front of Landers' Drugstore

a streetlight flickers like a magic lantern,
but Martha cannot follow the plot,
neither can the projectionist.
Only one thing is certain:
elements from different worlds are converging,
spinning toward confrontation,
and the State Boys are winding down some county
    road,
moving in a cloud of dust towards the theater
    marquee.

This poem never attracted the attention and critical acclaim that it rightly deserves. It is a masterpiece of understatement, an almost casual look at profound social change in progress, to which the ticket girl and projectionist are oblivious ("but Martha cannot follow the plot, / neither can the projectionist"). In an almost documentary fashion, "Stumptown Attends the Picture Show" is a showpiece exemplifying the prevailing social "reptile brain" among many white Americans in the Deep South, so steeped as it was in racial prejudice. It is almost a perfect poem as a snapshot of that time and place, where Canton, Georgia, represents America at large. The actual event took place on Monday, August 11, 1964, as four young African American men attempted to integrate the Canton Theater on Main Street.

"Stumptown" is the nickname for an African American section of Canton, where David Bottoms grew up. We are never shown the attempted desegregation of the local movie theater (presumably by unnamed African Americans from Stumptown), but only the prelude (which could well have been the result of a wild rumor). The siege mentality is strikingly depicted, and the poem's ending—"Only one thing is certain: / elements from different worlds are converging, / spinning toward confrontation"—is as close as Bottoms ever comes to outright social commentary.

According to the *Atlanta Constitution*'s story on this event on the following day (August 12, 1964, p. 40), this attempt at desegregation triggered a race riot, as a crowd gathered on Main Street at night. Apparently, a group of African Americans was also present: "There were unconfirmed reports that rocks were thrown at a carload of Negroes passing through the City." On Monday night, four African American men transgressed

the racial divide, where the bright line became the red line, the crossing of which could not be tolerated. Whether or not the "carload of Negroes" were the same four African Americans coming back to the theater for a repeat desegregation attempt is unclear. Although short of these details, the story reports: "The Negroes were peppered with eggs and tomatoes from a crowd of about 700 white persons as they came out of the theater on Main Street." The article further reports: "Chief Orr said the car they used was overturned, apparently by persons resenting the desegregation move." A curfew was imposed at 8 p.m. on Tuesday night, in which Chief Orr commented: "You can't even buy a cup of coffee in this town tonight."

Asking high school and university students to read and discuss "Stumptown Attends the Picture Show" would be an ideal approach in an American studies context to bring to life this historic desegregation attempt, one of many to follow. We do not know if the poet actually witnessed this event. Either way, this poem shows that David Bottoms is capable of writing effective poetry on social issues, although most of his work is made up of reminiscences about boyhood, youth, and family, and scenes in nature while fishing in lakes and rivers.

Several scenes take place in local bars. "In Jimmy's Grill," the waitress, with "eyes painted like we used to paint ours before ball games," sidles over to the jukebox, where "the blue neon of a Budweiser sign / sparkles off the three rings in her ear." The poem ends with a sidelong adolescent glance at the pool room in the back of the bar, "where a beer gut rolls like a melon on the green pool table" (*AH*, p. 17). And the poet explicitly applies the "triune brain" theory in "Crawling Out at Parties" (which, when first published in the May 1978 issue of *Poetry* magazine, bore the dedication, "For Carl Sagan"). The poem opens: "My old reptile loves the Scotch, / the way it drugs the cells that keep him caged / in the ancient swamps of the brain" (*AH*, p. 22).

For all the reptilian violence met with throughout this collection, "The Catfish" offers a respite of compassion and true humanity. The

poet spots a fisherman at the St. Simons Bridge, breaking down his rod and getting ready to leave. Before doing so, the fishermen tosses a catfish "too small to keep" onto the pavement. The catfish struggles to fight off death, and "suck[s] hard, straining to gill air." The poet grabs a beach towel from the backseat of his car and walks to the curb "where the catfish swimming on the sidewalk / [lies] like a document on evolution." The poet picks the catfish up in the towel and watches "the quiver of its precrawling, / [feels] whiskers groping in the darkness of the alien light / then [throws] it high above the concrete railing / back to the current of our breathable past" (*AH*, p. 23). Consistent with theory, the poet speaks of "the animal inside us" (*AH*, p. 24). The final poem, "Rubbing the Faces of Angels," also takes place in a graveyard, where the poet comments: "Yes, after all this time / we are coming to judge death less critically" (*AH*, p. 27). Death is a major theme throughout Bottoms' work, by his own admission and by way of commentary on poetry itself: "all poems are really about death" (*ODC*, p. 140).

IN A U-HAUL NORTH OF DAMASCUS

Bottoms' second book, *In a U-Haul North of Damascus* (1983), departs from the stark, reptilian emphasis of *Shooting Rats*. In this collection of poems, the poet adds a sacred dimension in such poems as "Recording the Spirit Voices," "Sermon of the Fallen," and "Light of the Sacred Harp," the latter set in an abandoned church, where a group of young men light a fire by burning hymnals in the trash can and get drunk, although the scene only pretends at (or portends toward) transcendence. Yet, as seen in "Wakulla: Chasing the Gator's Eye," the primal reptilian creature in the human psyche is ever present, even if submerged and repressed, as reflected in the spotlight that shines on the alligator's eye, whereby "you can see in its deep red shining / the reptile that moves beneath you" (*AH*, p. 55). All but two of the poems from this collection are reprinted in *Armored Hearts*.

One poem, "Under the Boathouse," evokes "The Lifeguard," by James Dickey, whose influ-

ence Bottoms has acknowledged in general. Based on critical acclaim, however, arguably the most notable poem is "Sign for My Father, Who Stressed the Bunt" (*AH*, p. 39). Reminiscing as a young boy, the poet opens the scene "On the rough diamond"—a pasture that the poet's father marked out on "the hand-cut field below the dog lot and barn." There, father and son "rehearsed the strict technique / of bunting." Watching his father demonstrate, the boy envied his father's skill as he placed the baseball with precise dexterity: "You could drop it like a seed / down either base line. I admired your style." That much the son concedes. Yet he could not give up his preference for hitting homers throughout his "three leagues of organized ball." Although his dad "stressed the same technique" throughout all those years, the son never learned, or was unwilling to do so: "That whole tiresome pitch / about basics never changing, / and I never learned what you were laying down." It is only years later that the son acknowledges the value of the skill that his dad was trying to convey: "Like a hand brushed across the bill of a cap, / let this be the sign / I'm getting a grip on the sacrifice."

Bunting is a "sacrifice" technique in baseball. A skill used in offense, the bunter often will not make it to first base before he is tagged out. By sacrificing his position—especially when the bases are loaded—the player can allow his teammates at the other three bases to score runs if the sacrifice succeeds. It's all about being a team player, which is its own form of heroism. Bottoms notes that his father would "still have preached the necessity of the bunt, the necessity of sacrificing for the good of the team" (*ODC*, p. 72). The poet, as young boy, never understood or appreciated the purpose, much less the skill of bunting until years later: "Finally, I came to understand that this whole routine had, perhaps, very little to do with baseball. . . . And baseball was simply his way of communicating" (*ODC*, p. 72).

The poem ends with a wordplay on the word "sacrifice." In *The Onion's Dark Core*, the poet gives us an insight into how this poem came about, especially in his composition technique: "The seed of the poem was the play on the word

'sacrifice,' and as was fairly typical for me at the time, the first line that came became the last line of the poem" (p. 72). Although "sacrifice" is a proper term to describe the technique of bunting, here it stands for the role of fathering. Literary critics can hazard deeper meanings, such as intergenerational conflict on the metaphorical baseball diamond of competitive life, et cetera—all of which does not detract one iota from the poet's memorable (perhaps immortal) tribute to his father, who represents, ideally, all good fathers. In this respect, "Sign for My Father, Who Stressed the Bunt" is a perfect poem. It compares favorably with Robert Hayden's celebrated poem about his stepfather, "Those Winter Sundays."

Bottoms sums up what the poem is ultimately about when he says that "the poem is not so much about learning to bunt as it is about the sacrifice the father has made for the son" (*ODC*, p. 85). The story about the father teaching the boy to bunt is the "narrative surface," which depends on wordplay (following a series of puns), "that allows the figurative possibility to reveal itself." As a professor of English and creative writing, Bottoms teaches his students that figuration triggers the "Deep Hidden Meaning" (*ODC*, p. 85), in which the poem conveys some deep meaning as to the purpose of life.

UNDER THE VULTURE-TREE

Like bookends, the first and last poems of *Under the Vulture-Tree* (1987) are "In the Ice Pasture" and "The Desk." If there is a thematic progression or evolution among the twenty-six poems in between, it may be seen in the transition from the last lines of "In the Ice Pasture" ("of two beasts becoming one, / or one beast being born") to the subject matter of "The Desk," for which this collection of poetry is perhaps best known. This transition, if indeed it is one, advances from the predominant attention given to animals and nature (a recurrent metaphor of the "animal nature" within each human being) to a gradual shift in focus on that which makes us more truly human. "The Desk" (*AH*, pp. 108–109), ranks as one of David Bottoms' finest poems. In this true-to-life narrative, the poet breaks into the class-

room of his dad's old high school. In so doing, of course, the poet breaks the law. His object is to retrieve his father's desk as a keepsake.

Another outstanding piece is "Under the Vulture-Tree," reproduced in full, as follows:

We have all seen them circling pastures,
have looked up from the mouth of a barn, a pine
  clearing,
the fences of our own backyards, and have stood
amazed by the one slow wing beat, the endless
  dihedral drift.
But I had never seen so many so close, hundreds,
every limb of the dead oak feathered black,

and I cut the engine, let the river grab the jon boat
and pull it toward the tree.
The black leaves shined, the pink fruit blossomed
red, ugly as a human heart.
Then, as I passed under their dream, I saw for the
  first time
its soft countenance, the raw fleshy jowls
wrinkled and generous, like the faces of the very old
who have grown to empathize with everything.

And I drifted away from them, slow, on the pull of
  the river,
reluctant, looking back at their roost,
calling them what I'd never called them, what they
  are,
those dwarfed transfiguring angels,
who flock to the side of the poisoned fox, the mud
  turtle
crushed on the shoulder of the road,
who pray over the leaf-graves of the anonymous lost,
with mercy enough to consume us all and give us
  wings.

(*AH*, p. 94)

The vulture is typically looked upon with some cultural loathing and disdain. Vultures are seen as ugly, repugnant, and menacing harbingers of death or impending death. People have little appreciation for the part that vultures play in the wider ecological scheme of things. Vultures prey on carrion, exampled by the poet's mention of "the poisoned fox" and "the mud turtle crushed on the shoulder of the road." Here, the physical figuratively represents the metaphysical, as these vultures are transformed into "those dwarfed, transfiguring angels," which really is "what they are." In the last line, vultures are said to "give us

wings." It would be easy to understand vultures as a metaphor for death. If so, then this poem is a meditation on the positive side of death.

Readers do not know if the poet has faith in life after death, or even if the poet has given much thought to the question as to whether consciousness and memory can live on after death. In this sense, those on whom the vulture of Death preys literally disappear. They vanish from sight, except insofar as they are taken up into the vultures themselves. While this is a novel and fresh appreciation of vultures, the metaphysical meditation on death, while not cynical, is also not hopeful. The reader may expect that the poet will continue his spiritual search. Such an expectation is partly fulfilled in David Bottoms' later work.

ARMORED HEARTS

This volume, as previous stated, republished the poems in Bottoms' first three books. It also contains twenty-seven previously uncollected poems that appeared in various literary journals. Some of the poems are set not in Georgia but in Montana, where he lived and taught for several years.

Several of the titles are suggestively religious in nature, such as "American Mystic," "Last Supper in Montana," "The Pentecostal," "Free Grace at Rose Hill," and "Zion Hill." In Montana the poet's father-in-law is portrayed as a committed Christian, rather strict and unyielding. But beyond the religious names of certain places in Montana, the poet does not have much else to say on the deeper questions of life. In such matters, Bottoms is reticent here, even guarded. This is not the time to indulge in such speculation. The poet's subject matter is down-to-earth, and much more immediate. In this sense, "Armored Hearts" lives up to its name. However, in "Barriers" (p. 123), the poet, in an instinctive premonition, comments: "I am not a father, but I think about the love of fathers." Having later become a father, Bottoms' poems about his daughter, Rachel, such as "A Daughter's Fever," are among his finest work.

VAGRANT GRACE

Vagrant Grace (1999) opens with three epigraphs on the subject of grace. In this way, the author announces a unifying theme. It remains for the reader to see how successfully that theme has been developed, as well as what insights may be gained thereby. The title is a far cry from that soul-stirring Christian hymn "Amazing Grace."

Divided into five parts, *Vagrant Grace* contains twenty-seven poems that are generally longer than in those in previous collections. Religious themes are apparent in several of the titles, such as "A Morning from the Gospel of John" and "My Uncle Sowing Beatitudes," but in a departure from previous collections, *Vagrant Grace* has no title poem. That said, one poem in particular has "grace" in the title: "Country Store and Moment of Grace." This is an uncharacteristically lengthy poem, spanning nineteen pages. This narrative of desultory, impressionistic vignettes culminates in a litany of "Amens" that read like a call-and-response funeral oration, with a single, redemptive message:

What's left in these last moments but memory?
And what is memory
but the mirror image of hope?
So Amen also to hope
and to these blurred receding thoughts of the evening.

(p. 55)

The word "afterlife" is mentioned, in passing, throughout a number of poems across his body of work, yet with scarcely any commentary. For all his talk of "soul," the afterlife remains distant, elusive, and uncertain. And for all his talk of "grace," redemption is not in evidence, save for the eventual coming to terms with the inevitability of death. The lost souls are hardly ever found. The spiritual landscape, not to mention the social reality, is bleak. That said, where there is family, there is hope. Bottoms' work, as wistful and perhaps cynical as it may be, is strong on family values. It practically sacralizes the roles of fatherhood and, to a lesser extent, motherhood. This collection of poetry, after all, is "for my mother and father, and for Kelly and Rachel," the poet's wife and daughter. With this dedication, these personae make their appearances throughout.

DAVID BOTTOMS

One poem stands out in this collection as unpretentiously sermonic as the poet experiences a moment of self-realization about the importance, and sacredness, of fatherhood in particular and respect for life and humanity in general. "Night Strategies" (pp. 27–28) is a poignant narrative that borders on social commentary. While gently tending to his baby daughter, the poet hears a radio news report about a sixteen-year-old Muslim girl in war-torn Sarajevo. She was raped by three soldiers, presumably in full view of "her mother, who clawed all night at the tiles / of their mosque." Moved to empathy by this disturbing report from abroad, the poet concludes:

> I lathered the cloth with our wafer of soap
> and dabbed at my daughter's stomach and thighs,
> knowing the only answer I have
> is this nervous
> exaggeration of tenderness,
> and that every ministry of my hand, clumsy
> and apologetic, asks her
> to practice such a radical faith.

The contrast between the depraved violence in far-off Sarajevo brings home the importance and responsibility of fatherhood, and of the sacredness of life itself. The poet's daughter, Rachel, appears by name in "A Family Parade," "Our Presbyterian Christmas," and "My Daughter at the Gymnastics Party."

Perhaps his most openly religious poem is "A Morning from the Gospel of John" (p. 75), which appears to be a homiletic meditation on John 21:1–11, the story of the miraculous catching of fish as directed by the resurrected Jesus. This, perhaps, presages the theme, or least the title, of his next collection, *Waltzing Through the Endtime* (2004).

In his review of *Vagrant Grace*, David Baker usefully compares—and contrasts—James Dickey and David Bottoms, noting a subtle development in the latter's work. Bottoms' prior work "depicted a fierce natural world, dangerously beautiful with its swamps and wild poisonous growth," where his poems "attend with vigilance to the perilous, often merciless operations of nature." Yet the natural world in *Vagrant Grace* is "considerably more suburban, its wild past recessive, even repressed," in which the poet has

"evolved into a family man and homeowner, a civilized citizen-neighbor whose home is no longer rough country," who "hunts now for meaning rather than survival, . . . shifting subtly from narration to meditation." As a result, Bottoms has "deepened his portrayal of the South beyond alligators and county fairs to a place of genuine spiritual anxiety" (Baker, pp. 152–154).

That spiritual quest explores inner nature—of self and family, of death and memory, of void and legacy. One senses that this shift is as transitional as it is ongoing. The poet's attention gravitates—or levitates—from lake to sky, from cold-blooded reptiles, amphibians, and fish to warm-blooded birds, mammals, and humans, with angels waiting in the wings. There are more birds in these poems. The birds were always part of the flora and fauna of the Georgian landscape. But the poet's gaze is not so earthbound as it turns heavenward as well as inward.

The poetry of David Bottoms represents a spiritual odyssey. This quest for meaning and purpose in life begins, in his early work, with encounters with various reptilian predators and omnivorous vermin, in natural settings brought to life by vivid descriptions in the active tense. Yet, from time to time, the poet reminisces about childhood and youth, especially about time spent with his father and grandparents, in reveries that convey not only wistfulness but a sense of loss, both past and pending. The specter of inevitable death gives pause for thought and occasion for doubt.

OGLETHORPE'S DREAM

Oglethorpe's Dream: A Picture of Georgia, with photographs by Diane Kirkland, was published in 2001 by the University of Georgia Press. This book was commissioned by the State of Georgia in partnership with the Georgia Department of Industry, Trade and Tourism, the Georgia Humanities Council, and the University of Georgia Press. Presumably this was Bottoms' first major project in his public role as Georgia's poet laureate. *Oglethorpe's Dream* is a long poem, shy of epic length, written to accompany photos of various Georgia scenes, at the request of then

governor Roy E. Barnes. The excerpt that follows offers a taste of the many flavors that may be savored in this work that collectively represents the state of Georgia:

On Saturdays in Vidalia the veterans gathered at the
  hardware store.

Occasionally, there was pretense of something
  purchased—
a box of nails, some finishing screws, a tape
  measure—
but mostly the men talking.

Do you remember from your childhood the old men
  gathered?
Do you recall the dust on the bubblegum machine,
your father rocked back
in a straight-backed chair?

An old man in a straw fedora is telling a story you've
  heard before.
This several men listening
have heard it before.

The story has a fish in it,
and a leaking boat. At the bottom of the lake lies a
  deep truth.

What was that truth? Where has it gone?

The rhetorical question "Do you remember from your childhood the old men gathered?" is a welcome shift in perspective, as well as a direct outreach from the poet to his intended audience, the citizens of Georgia, one and all. This is the poet laureate at work in his role as a public poet. Even if his description is retrieved from the archives of the poet's personal memory, it is transformed into something interpersonal, intersubjective, even universal. The last line of this excerpt gives pause for thought: "What was that truth? Where has it gone?" This interrogation of the purpose of such small talk and tall tales raises the greater issue of "truth"—not as factual truth, but as truth relates to the purpose of life itself. This poetic twist adds another dimension—deeper than the fishing lake itself—to an otherwise mundane, commonplace occurrence, turning it into an occasion for reflection. It is not the poet's job to answer the question but to raise it. An

intimation, even an implication, of the answer might certainly fall within the poet's artistic license. But leaving it to the reader to discover whatever the "truth" may be allows the reader to do so by way of a kind of self-realization. This is the poet laureate at his finest, applying his skills at subtlety and restraint to get his readers to pause and reflect.

WALTZING THROUGH THE ENDTIME

Waltzing Through the Endtime (2004) is a collection of fifteen poems in three sections, spanning fifty-nine pages. The dark dance begins with "Easter Shoes Epistle" (pp. 3–6)—a skillful meditation on shoes, such as "an old work boot," "stray shoe in the street," "old shoe," "penny loafers, sans pennies," "Spanish boots, high-topped, waxed to a crow's eye," "my mother's hospital shoes," and "my father's wingtips."

Bottoms experiments with a new style, adapted, perhaps, to his inner focus on the "salvation or loss of the soul," as presaged by his epigraph by Flannery O'Connor. Indeed, Bottoms acknowledges what he describes as a "spiritual shift," defining it more specifically as "a significant shift toward a Christian outlook." In so doing, the poet engages in "a spiritual quest that frames itself in Christian mythology" (*ODC*, pp. 163–164). Nods to "faith" appear throughout, sometimes explicitly so. Yet this faith does not always have certitude: though surrounded by the devout, the author is saddled with doubt.

"Shooting Rats in the Afterlife" (*Waltzing Through the Endtime* [*WTE*], pp. 20–23) echoes the title (and title poem) of *Shooting Rats at the Bibb County Dump*. He again recalls his college days in 1971, concluding that the legacy of memory functions as a kind of afterlife:

as though through memory we create our own afterlives—
which can't be the entire breadth of it all,
but in some way a homeland,
a landscape out of which we might ramble into the
  afterlives, yes,
the memories, of one another. . . .

(p. 20)

This is as close as the poet gets to faith in an afterlife, real or imagined, defined as part of "our psychic terrain" where landscapes of the past "are, perhaps, the only things we take with us" (p. 20). It is not clear whether the "memory" of which the poet speaks is a personal reminiscence or legacy honored by others, or both.

Curiously, in the middle of the poem, the poet indulges in some religious reflection:

Yes, the Word,
   though I don't recall Christ teaching much about
   animals.
Still, calling his children sheep,
some animals he must have loved.
But rodents? Who knows?

(p. 22)

This bit of humor has a serious side, as the poem ends with this meditation on the afterlife: "In Paradise, say the Southern Baptists, every crown is jeweled, every jewel a good deed remembered, / a kindness rewarded." After which the poet concludes, wistfully: "Leroy Lawson leaning into that truck, then salvo of headlights / blinding against garbage / hundreds of startled rubies" (p. 23)—referring, of course, to the redness reflecting back from the headlights shining on the rats' eyes as they stare back at the glare that invades their sanctuary of darkness.

In this small cluster of poems, the "endtime" refers to personal death, not to the end of history by way of apocalypse. Religious imagery, both implicit and explicit, abounds. Compared to his previous work, this is an added dimension of life experience that dwells as much in the past as in the present, with less looking forward to the future. "Afterlife," as a response to the impending "endtime," although religiously nuanced, is defined as jewels of precious memory, practically to the exclusion of any belief in otherworldly immortality.

In some ways this experiment with longer poems creates a fuller vicarious reading experience by expanding the narrative. The poetic description is still rich with imagery, condensed for effect, and skillfully sustained. These poems, moreover, offer deeper insights into the poet's psyche and perspective. In this respect, the author

takes us into his confidence, with all of the vulnerability that such exposure risks. That said, these poems, as a whole, are not likely to be held in such high critical esteem as his other work. Bottoms himself has said, in one or more interviews, that he will probably not return to this longer poetic form. This being the case, *Vagrant Grace* is clearly a transitional work, in what may be described as a process of subtle metamorphosis.

In saying something, should the poet have something to say? He can quote scripture, such as Matthew 24:29: "and the moon will not give its light, and the stars / will fall from the sky" ("Vigilance," *WTE*, p. 57). But this is an incidental reference to the "endtime," a proof text that proves nothing. Although Bottoms is a professed Christian, his poetry never reaches certitude. The poet honestly does not know the answers, yet is still pondering the existential questions of life. His proofs are drawn from personal experience, from real life. This creates a sense of ongoing search, inviting the reader to follow along.

WE ALMOST DISAPPEAR

Published in 2011, this sixty-five-page collection (dedicated to Bottoms' wife Kelly and his daughter, Rachel) is slender in length yet expansive in reflections on life and loss and on how familiarity discloses intimate details—often ugly, even repulsive—yet without breeding contempt. Here we see the poet as storyteller, who is neither mythmaker nor moralist.

Each of the five numbered sections in *We Almost Disappear* begins with one or two short epigraphs that set the tone and, to a certain extent, the reader's expectations. Forty-six poems are presented in this collection, beginning with "First Woods" (p. 5), which recaptures a boyhood experience in a "caravan of trucks" heading to a pine forest on his uncle's land. Hunting dogs are then let loose to pursue the unidentified prey "in the black woods" that the boy "never [sees]," yet clearly is "dragging those frantic voices" into the chase. Here the young poet is given a first intimation of death. "Violets" (p. 6) offers the boy's firsthand view of his grandmother watering her

plants, with tender care, as "she [spits] tobacco juice into her flower boxes," and whose wrinkled mouth is "blackened around the edges like a wilting leaf." "Husks" anticipates the grandmother's imminent end of life, as she slaps cornhusks against a post, all the while not knowing "what's withering inside her," with the last line noticing "those last green scraps blooming in her hand." Similar subject matter follows, with "My Grandpa Builds an Airplane," "After the Stroke," and "We Take My Grandpa Fishing," ending with "The Undertaker's Words." The portraits of family members are loving, but unflinching in unglamorous detail.

This volume marks a notable shift from Bottoms' earlier fascination with animals (especially reptiles), and with the wilderness generally, to a primary focus on close family members. Section 2 begins with "Montana Wedding Day," with the rest of the section primarily reflecting on family. Section 4 is notable for its focus on the poet's father, even though it doesn't bear a formal dedication.

Poignantly, in "Campfire in a Light Rain" (pp. 60–62), night falls, and the "charred logs sizzle in the rain." One gets the sense that the campfire is dampened by the drizzle, and could easily be extinguished. Thereupon the poet, in a pensive moment, poses this rhetorical question:

Whatever happened to the promise of wisdom?

The gray beard came, the cracked teeth,
the vanishing hair, the trembling hand,
but what became
of Solomon's crown?

The poet has spent much of his life "searching for purity" yet "never grasping the nature of ashes." The campfire, for all its ashes, does not quite disappear. But Bottoms, perhaps without explicitly realizing it, may have discovered an example of purity earlier in the collection. Clearly the strongest poem (certainly the most optimistic and affirmative) in the book is "My Daughter Works the Heavy Bag" (p. 23):

A bow to the instructor,
then fighting stance, and the only girl in karate class
    faces the heavy bag.

Small for fifth grade—willowlike, says her mother—
sweaty hair tangled like blown willow branches.

The boys try to ignore her. They fidget against the
    wall, smirk,
practice their routine of huff and feint.
Circle, barks the instructor,
jab, circle, kick, and the black bag wobbles on its
    chain.

Again and again, the bony jewels of her fist
jab out in glistening precision,
her flawless legs remember arabesque and glissade.
Kick, jab, kick, and the bag coughs rhythmically
    from its gut.

The boys fidget and wait—
then a whisper somewhere, a laugh, a jeer.

She circles the bag—jab, jab, jab—flushed, jaw set,
    huffing
with her punches, huffing with her kicks, circles
to her left and glares.
But only at the bag—alone, in herself—
to her own time, in her own rhythm, honing her
    blocks
and feints, her solitary dance,
having mastered already the first move of self-
    defense.

This poem is remarkable for its evocative use of sound ("the bag coughs rhythmically from its gut") with "huffing" throughout, amid "a whisper somewhere, a laugh, a jeer." It's a coming-of-age narrative in the finest sense, in which the daughter (in real life, Rachel) answers the boys' unsportsmanlike jeer when she "circles to her left and glares." Undeterred, and singularly determined, the daughter, in admirable independence and by strength of character, hones her skills, "having mastered already the first move of self-defense," which, perhaps, is learning not to be intimidated, and not to swerve from her discipline in the course of shaping her own destiny.

The title *We Almost Disappear* comes from the last line in the poem "Walking a Battlefield: A Love Story" (p. 30), which begins: "Fog most always suggests the otherworldly." This is immediately followed with a touching line: "where one hand takes another as we almost disappear." This poem, written in honor of the poet's wife,

Kelly, looks to the future (at least what remains of it) as no longer a solo journey or an individual quest. For it is "we" (as a couple) who are coursing through life together. The spiritual journey is shared, even if the vaunted promise of wisdom as the fruit of experience late in life remains as elusive as ever.

There is, moreover, a sense of redemption in the title *We Almost Disappear*. The key redemptive word is "almost" (suggesting the associated phrase, "but not quite"). In other words, we do not face total oblivion. Something remains of our respective individual legacies, even if in just a few memories. This is the poet's personal, rather than Christian, spiritual meditation in progress.

LEGACY

The subject matter of David Bottoms' past work has remained largely consistent, so one can only surmise that his future work is likely to be much the same in nature, although more mature as time goes on. As the poet grows with his art, and as awareness of his work continues to broaden and solidify his position as one of the leading U.S. poets, a progression from poet laureate of Georgia to poet laureate of the United States would be a natural one.

Despite the understated perfection of a political poem like "Stumptown Attends the Picture Show," there are indications that Bottoms will continue to steer clear of social commentary. "Pure art has no moral responsibility or agenda," he says (*ODC*, p. 142), though this may be a disclaimer against art as propaganda. Moreover, it may be a distinction without a real difference: "I like to think of poetry, and all art, as the act of getting back in touch with the soul" (*ODC*, p. 142). Here Bottoms has a clear sense of individual salvation, although he is reticent about social salvation.

One aspect of memory that is notably absent from Bottoms' work is that of profound regret and torment over experiences in war, crime, or, in another context of violence, domestic disputes. Any notion of psychic "hell" is repressed. The author, after all, does not carry the same type of

personal baggage as the acclaimed poet Richard Hugo, for example, whose work Bottoms knows well. By contrast, Bottoms indulges throughout his work in the recreational adventures of hunting and fishing and the refuge of solitude, which offers opportunities for contemplation and reflection on the past. It is as though the poet is evolving through the evolutionary sequence of the reptilian, mammalian, and ultimately distinctively human aspects of the "triune brain," wherein both the animal nature and the soul reside in uncanny tension. The poet cannot be faulted for lack of a social agenda or utopian ideals. That is not his artistic vocation. Still, the reader gets a sense of an ongoing spiritual quest.

In this quest the author's Christian perspective is not parochial. Although there are references to Southern Baptists and Presbyterians, with occasional nods to Methodists, in many ways the author's Christian identity appears to be more cultural than theological; indeed, in his work one gets more of a sense of natural law, as it were, than any denominational doctrine. But that may be changing over time. The Christian experience, including the Bible as scripture, adds a dimension to life's experience and purpose. By necessity, spiritual experience is best described by way of references and allusions to the "myth" of Christian tradition, which provides a rich set of images and vocabulary that complement portrayals of nature, with its reptilian instincts and mammalian imperatives.

When *The Onion's Dark Core* and the body of Bottoms' poetry are read together, the experience is rewarding and enriching. Bottoms exemplifies the finest in the art and craft of poetry. His poetic skill is consummate. As for where he may go from here, in 2015 the *Cortland Review* published "Otherworld, Underworld, Prayer Porch," the title poem of his next collection, scheduled for publication by Copper Canyon Press in 2018. It runs as follows:

Maybe I'll rise from the dead.

Or live as a shadow. Or maybe I'll never leave you.
  At Emeritus
an old man plowing the hallway

with a three-wheeled walker
stopped me and grinned, My goal is to live for-
    ever—so far, so good.

Maybe we never get enough birdsong,
or watery soup
and over-steamed veggies. Still, from the prayer
    porch
eternity sometimes looks like a raw deal.

Eternal leaf blower and weed whacker?

(A few days before he died my old man asked about
    the yard.)
Mostly blue jays at the feeder this morning, rude

and rowdy, and a few cardinals dripping off the trees
like the bloody tears of Christ.

Maybe we only rise again to the good things—
    honeysuckle,
robins, mockingbirds, doves,
fireflies toward evening, and along the back fence

the steady harping of tree frogs.
On the prayer porch, among the icons, such fancy
    thoughts.

If this title is any indication, this forthcoming volume may well complete the evolutionary trajectory of the "triune" progression. "Otherworld" hints at a world of transcendence, whereas "Underworld" suggests a psychic netherworld, with "Prayer Porch" possibly underscoring a spiritual aspiration to that empathy and compassion of which the reptile brain is fully deprived. Bottoms' work is always natural, never supernatural, yet, all the while, the metaphorical becomes increasingly metaphysical, but only in the most tentative, exploratory ways. The poet is at one with nature, at home in suburbia and with family, yet he flows and ebbs, to and from the deeper recesses of the self as he meditates, but scarcely speculates on what may (or may not) lay ahead, way ahead.

The poem opens with "Maybe I'll rise from the dead," and closes with "fancy thoughts." In between, the poet imagines not so much how his life will continue on, but how life itself goes on. Doubt verges on cynicism: "Still, from the prayer porch / eternity sometimes looks like a raw deal." The candor is exquisite. No solace for the soul

here. For the time being, the "otherworld" remains this world. The poet is too physical to be metaphysical, at least in this point in time. But where these "fancy thoughts" might lead is an open question.

In an interview with William Walsh in 2006, Bottoms elaborated on the poet's quest for the meaning of life. He observed that "all serious writers" are "seekers after the big answers." Although we will "never know those big answers," nevertheless "what the writer yearns for" is "a sense of consequence in the world." One of his essays is titled "Articulating the Spirit: Poetry, Community, and the Metaphysical Shortwave" (*ODC*, p. 7–26). In this and in other interviews, Bottoms casts the role of the poet as a kind of "diviner," but not quite a soothsayer. The poet is somehow receptive to what the world is trying to teach us. His or her sensitivity is attuned to the subtleties of life that can only be expressed as rare insights. But those insights are not sermonic. They cannot be "preached." Although discursive words can be heard, or read, they may fall on deaf ears unless, through the artifice of the narrative (in this case, autobiographical accounts), an experience is re-created. If the artifice works, the measure of the poet's success will be that the reader discovers, through a process of self-realization, the hidden "message" the poet is trying to convey. In a sense, the poet is speaking on behalf of the natural order of things, of life itself. This is the core of Bottoms' spiritual quest and experiential odyssey, shared by his readers as they grow and mature along with him.

Selected Bibliography

WORKS OF DAVID BOTTOMS

POETRY
Jamming with the Band at the VFW. Austell, Ga.: Burnt Hickory Press, 1978. (Limited edition chapbook of ten poems.)
Shooting Rats at the Bibb County Dump. New York: William Morrow, 1980.
In a U-Haul North of Damascus. New York: William Morrow, 1983.

DAVID BOTTOMS

Under the Vulture-Tree. New York: William Morrow, 1987.

Armored Hearts: Selected and New Poems. Port Townsend, Wash.: Copper Canyon Press, 1995.

Vagrant Grace. Port Townsend, Wash.: Copper Canyon Press, 1999.

Oglethorpe's Dream: A Picture of Georgia. Photographs by Diane Kirkland. Athens: University of Georgia Press, 2001.

Waltzing Through the Endtime. Port Townsend, Wash.: Copper Canyon Press, 2004.

We Almost Disappear. Port Townsend, Wash.: Copper Canyon Press, 2011.

"Otherworld, Underworld, Prayer Porch." *Cortland Review* 69 (November 2015). http://www.cortlandreview.com/issue/69/bottoms.php

Otherworld, Underworld, Prayer Porch. Port Townsend, Wash.: Copper Canyon Press, Forthcoming

NOVELS

Easter Weekend. Boston: Houghton Mifflin, 1990. Reprint, London: Constable, 1991; Baton Rouge: Louisiana State University Press, 1998.

Any Cold Jordan. Atlanta: Peachtree, 1987. Reprint, New York: Washington Square Press, 1988.

ARTICLES AND ESSAYS

"Note on the Structure of James Seay's 'It All Comes Together Outside the Restroom in Hogansville.'" *Notes on Contemporary Literature* 7, no. 4:6–7 (September 1977).

"Country Music and Poetry." *Poetry Pilot*, June 1980, pp. 2–3.

"On Narrative in Poetry." *Chattahoochee Review* 4, no. 2:75–83 (winter 1984).

"A Cosmic and Ancient Mystery." *Atlanta Weekly*, December 30, 1984, pp. 10–11.

"The Messy Humanity of Randall Jarrell: His Poetry in the Eighties." *South Carolina Review* 17, no. 1:82–95 (fall 1984).

"Norman Blake: A Modern Old-Time Musician." *Atlanta Weekly*, September 22, 1985, p. 30.

"Poet Reaches Out with Only Gifts He Can Offer." *Atlanta Journal-Constitution*, December 25, 1986, p. A19.

"A Sense of Place." In *Georgia on My Mind.* Helena, Mont.: Falcon Press, 1990. (Introductory essay to book of photographs.)

"An Infinite Variation." *Oxford Review* (Atlanta) 6, no. 8:2 (October 1991).

"Literature and the Inevitable." *Atlanta Journal-Constitution*, July 31, 1996, p. A15. (Writers in the South Series, Olympic Special.)

"James Dickey: The Champ of American Poetry." *Atlanta Journal-Constitution*, January 25, 1997. Editorial page.

"James Dickey on the Bank of Lake Katherine." In *Dictionary of Literary Biography Yearbook*, 1997. Edited by Matthew J. Bruccoli and George Garrett. Detroit: Gale, 1998.

"Turn Your Radio On: The Powers of Influence." *Southern Quarterly* 37, nos. 3–4:85–92 (spring–summer 1999). (Paper delivered at "The Poetry of David Bottoms" session, South Central Modern Language Association convention, 1997.)

"Waiting on the Words." *Metropolitan* 4, no. 1:15–16 (fall 1999).

"The Power of Symbols." *Atlanta Journal-Constitution*, February 4, 2001, p. C1.

Articulating the Spirit: Poetry, Community, and the Metaphysical Shortwave. Atlanta: Georgia Humanities Council, 2002. (Georgia Humanities Lecture.)

"Thirst and the Writer's Sense of Consequence." *Kennesaw Review* (spring 2003). Reprinted in *The Best of the Web 2008.* Edited by Steve Almond and Nathan Leslie. Westland, Mich.: Dzanc Books, 2008.

The Onion's Dark Core: A Little Book of Poetry Talk. Winston-Salem, N.C.: Press 53, 2010.

"The Poetry Bridge." In *My Town: Writers on American Cities.* Washington, D.C.: U.S. Department of State, Bureau of International Information Programs, 2010. Pp. 7–11. http://photos.state.gov/libraries/amgov/30145/publications-english/mytown_001.pdf

"Forbidden Water: A Thought on the Nature of Poetry." *CEA Critic* 75, no. 3:191–200 (November 2013). (Keynote address, College English Association National Conference.)

ANTHOLOGY

The Morrow Anthology of Younger American Poets. With Dave Smith. New York: Quill, William Morrow, 1985.

PAPERS

David Bottoms Papers, c. 1970–1992. Stuart A. Rose Manuscript, Archives, and Rare Book Library, Emory University, Atlanta.

CRITICAL AND BIOGRAPHICAL STUDIES

Baker, David. "Story's Stories." *Kenyon Review* 24, no. 2:150–154 (spring 2002). (Review of *Vagrant Grace*).

Chappell, Fred. "David Bottoms and the Evolution of the GOB Aesthetic." *Sewanee Review* 117, no. 4:592–610 (fall 2009).

Ellis, Steven R. "Poetry—Armored Hearts: Selected and New Poems by David Bottoms." *Library Journal* 120, no. 12:84 (July 1995).

Gentry, Bruce. "Introduction: David Bottoms." *Southern Quarterly* 37, no. 3:65 (spring 1999).

DAVID BOTTOMS

Suarez, Ernest. "A Deceptive Simplicity: The Poetry of David Bottoms." *Southern Quarterly* 37, no. 3:73 (spring 1999).

Walsh, William J., ed. *David Bottoms: Critical Essays and Interviews*. Jefferson, N.C., and London: McFarland, 2010.

REVIEWS

Conarroe, Joel. Review of *In a U-Haul North of Damascus*. *Washington Post*, August 7, 1983, p. BW4.

Lieberman, Laurence. "David Bottoms's Grueling Miracle: Faith in Middle Age." *Southern Review* 46, no. 4:567–583 (autumn 2010). (Review of *Waltzing Through the Endtime*.)

INTERVIEWS

"A Conversation with David Bottoms." *Rattle: A Magazine of Poetry* 39:64–86 (spring 2013). http://www.rattle.com/a-conversation-with-david-bottoms/

Fraser, Gregory. "An Instrument of Investigation: An Interview with David Bottoms." *Birmingham Poetry Review* 39 (spring 2012). (Excerpt available from https://www.uab.edu/cas/englishpublications/birmingham-poetry-review/bpr-back-issues/bpr-39-2012/interview-with-david-bottoms.)

Friman, Alice, and Bruce Gentry. "Fishing from the Poetry Boat: A Conversation with David Bottoms." *Southern Quarterly* 37, no. 3–4:93–95 (spring–summer 1999).

"An Interview with David Bottoms." *Habersham Review* 4, no. 2:128–145 (autumn 1995).

"The Poetry Receiver: An Interview with David Bottoms." *Atlanta Review* 1, no. 1:20–28 (July 1994).

Rider, Eddie Lee. "An Interview with David Bottoms." *Chattahoochee Review* 12, no. 1:79–89 (fall 1991).

Suarez, Ernest. "David Bottoms." In his *Southbound: Interviews with Southern Poets*. Columbia and London: University of Missouri Press, 1999. Pp. 85–103.

Walsh, William J. "David Bottoms." In *Speak So I Shall Know Thee: Interviews with Southern Writers*. Jefferson, N.C., and London: McFarland 1991.

———. "David Bottoms: Logic of the Original Dream." *Five Points* 10, nos. 1–2 (fall–spring 2006). Republished online as "An Interview with David Bottoms," *Poetry Daily*, 2006. http://poems.com/special_features/prose/essay_bottoms.php

LOUISE BRYANT

(1885—1936)

Judith E. Barlow

LOUISE BRYANT WAS a pioneering journalist primarily known for covering the Russian Revolution. She wrote two books and dozens of dispatches filed from the front lines, occasionally dodging bullets and bombs as she followed her stories. *Six Red Months in Russia* (1918) and *Mirrors of Moscow* (1923) gave Americans a firsthand look at the complicated events that changed Russia from a czarist state to a Bolshevik stronghold. Even though she participated for less than a year, Bryant was also an important member of the groundbreaking Provincetown Players, which produced her short play *The Game* (1916). She dabbled in poetry, fiction, illustration, and sculpture, but her lasting contribution is her nonfiction prose.

EARLY YEARS

Louise Bryant was born Anna Louisa Mohan in San Francisco on December 5, 1885, to Hugh J. and Anna Louisa Mohan. (Some sources give her middle name as "Louise," but she was likely christened after her mother, Louisa. To confuse matters further, the elder Mohan sometimes also called herself "Louise.") Bryant had both an older sister and an older brother. As a child Louise was told—and continued to believe—that her birth father was dead. He was in fact a reasonably successful journalist though not a particularly reliable family man. Her parents divorced when Louise was three and her mother subsequently married Sheridan Daniel Bryant, a worker for the Southern Pacific Railroad. Louise spent several of her early years on her grandfather's combination horse ranch and mine, but she returned to the family home when she was twelve. Along with her two siblings and two half-brothers, she was given Bryant's last name, and she was among the earliest feminists to refuse to change her name

when she married. She once complained that the French postal service refused to deliver her mail unless the sender used her husband's surname.

Bryant grew up in Reno and various small towns in Nevada. She attended Nevada State University (today the University of Nevada, Reno) and graduated from the University of Oregon in 1909, having taken a few short breaks to try her hand at teaching. After marrying Paul Trullinger, a dentist, on November 13 of that year, she continued contributing sketches and occasional articles to a weekly local tabloid, the *Spectator*. Although Trullinger seems to have been an understanding and generous man who allowed Bryant her own studio, she was growing bored with her marriage and with Portland. When she met the Harvard-educated journalist and activist John Silas (Jack) Reed in 1915, the attraction was instantaneous: shortly after Reed returned to his home in New York City, Bryant followed him. After being granted a divorce from Trullinger, Bryant married Reed on November 9, 1916.

PROVINCETOWN PLAYERS

Like many bohemians at the time, Bryant and Reed joined the Provincetown Players, one of the numerous "little theaters" that were challenging Broadway's hegemony. Political radicalism and artistic innovation went hand in hand: when silk workers in Paterson, New Jersey, called a strike in 1913, New York artists and intellectuals joined with them to stage a fund-raising pageant. Both the Moscow Art Theatre and Dublin's Abbey Theatre toured the United States early in the century, helping spawn the hundreds of acting companies that quickly sprang up across the country.

The vast majority of these troupes produced dramas by modern European and British playwrights, but the Provincetown Players, which began as an informal group of friends on Cape Cod in the summer of 1915, was dedicated to supporting work by American dramatists and involving them in the productions. When they moved to New York City, they dubbed their venue the Playwright's Theatre, and the first of the group's "resolutions" was "to encourage the writing of American plays of real artistic, literary and dramatic—as opposed to Broadway—merit" (qtd. in Barlow, p. 2).

The Provincetown Players saw themselves as radicals who opposed the status quo of their conservative hometowns and dedicated themselves to supporting artistic innovation, questioning the capitalist system, reevaluating relations between women and men, and challenging traditional sexual mores. Bryant was not part of the casual collective that performed plays on a Provincetown wharf in the summer of 1915. She and Reed joined the group the following summer and became members of the executive committee that fall. Reed contributed three plays to the company: a comedy titled *The Eternal Quadrangle*; *Freedom*, about a farcical prison break; and the highly political *The Peace That Passeth Understanding*, which theater historian Robert Károly Sarlós calls "a savage attack on the shapers of the Versailles treaty . . . the most topical piece ever staged by the players" (p. 98). Like most of the members, Reed was also occasionally roped into acting.

In her unpublished memoir, Bryant claims that "I was not only a director, I was secretary, I acted, I put on plays, and I simply lived in the theatre or on the beach" (p. 8). As Cheryl Black suggests in *The Women of Provincetown*, Bryant was using "director" loosely to mean a leader of the group, and she was not the Provincetown's official secretary (p. 36). But Bryant probably did help stage her own play, *The Game* (1916), even though she is not credited in the program. She was also involved in most other aspects of Provincetown work, including acting in Reed's farce *The Eternal Quadrangle* and Eugene O'Neill's *Thirst*. She was apparently a slightly better performer than Reed, who was wont to forget his lines.

Bryant wrote *The Game*, her only produced play, before she joined the company; the typescript in the Library of Congress was copyrighted on August 25, 1915. Edna Kenton, the group's first historian, records in *The Provincetown Players and the Playwrights' Theatre, 1915–1922*, that the Players were "hopelessly divided on the scant merits" of both *The Game* and Wilbur Daniel Steele's comedy *Not Smart* (p. 20). She acknowledges, however, that such controversy was to be expected because "voting was public; making up bills was always a test of sporting blood and friendship" (p. 20). These two works, along with Eugene O'Neill's *Bound East for Cardiff* (his first staged play), premiered in Provincetown in late July 1916. Despite the Players' worries and some negative reviews, audiences apparently liked *The Game*, for it reappeared on a special bill in September, a program that raised eighty dollars for the Players' move to New York City. Two months later the group opened its Greenwich Village theater with *Bound East for Cardiff*, Floyd Dell's *King Arthur's Socks*, and *The Game*.

The Provincetown members were supposed to participate in all aspects of the productions. The performance of *The Game* may well be one of the Provincetown's most successful collaborative efforts, largely due to the set and costumes designed by the artists Marguerite and William Zorach. The program notes describe the drama as "an attempt to synthesize decoration, costume, speech and action into one mood." In his autobiography, *Art Is My Life*, William Zorach recalls:

> Louise said we could do whatever we wished with her play and even asked me to act in it. We were delighted with the opportunity to put on a play and ruthlessly turned an English morality play into a sort of Egyptian pantomime. The backdrop was a decorative and abstract pattern of the sea, trees, the moon, and the moon path in the water designed by Marguerite. . . . It made a hit.
>
> (pp. 45–46)

The Provincetown historian Robert K. Sarlós, writing in *Jig Cook and the Provincetown Players*, describes Marguerite Zorach's backdrop: "the

setting sun [is] . . . framed in a diamond and surrounded by triangular hills. The sun's reflection lies heavily across the sinuous lines of waves from horizon to the bottom of the drop. Ten trees, symmetrically arranged on either side of the sun, resemble ancient columns, their foliage like so many fans" (pp. 24–25). Photographs indicate that the costumes were simple tunics. If the gestures shown in existing photographs reflect those actually used in performance, body movements were heavily stylized to resemble Egyptian friezes.

In emphasizing his and his wife's contributions to the production, Zorach understandably downplays the value of Bryant's script. When the text was published in *The Provincetown Plays: First Series*, theaters interested in performing the work were admonished to "send for photographs and directions." But the Zorachs were taking many of their cues from Bryant. In the 1915 script of *The Game*, for example, stage directions describe the character of Life as wearing "a flowing white robe without ornaments of any kind," Death wears simple black garments, and the Girl "wears a dancer's costume." The play is set on a cliff "overlooking the sea," either at sunset, with the light gradually fading, or at "midnight with bright moonlight to illumine the scene and lend an air of mystery" (p. 2). A nonrealistic, "poetic" staging was evidently integral to Bryant's original conception of the work.

The Game is a symbolic contest between Death and Life, with Youth and Girl as the prizes. He is a writer and she a dancer; both are suicidal because they have failed to find true love. When Youth discovers that Girl has interpreted his poetry in dance, and she finds him a sympathetic admirer of herself and her art, the two decide they have found their soul mates. It is interesting that Bryant envisions Life as female and Death as male, thus identifying the creative force as feminine. Both Youth and Girl are considered "geniuses"; Youth is no more capable of creating without a loved one to appreciate him than Girl is. Instead of the traditional notion that love is central to a woman's life and peripheral to a man's, Bryant gives us young people of both sexes made miserable by an absence of romance.

Whether or not she was acting at the behest of her colleagues, Bryant made a number of revisions to her original script when she prepared it for the Provincetown production. The role of Death was significantly augmented with additional lines, perhaps to better balance the forces of Life and Death. At the same time, several themes that were prominent in the original— themes dear to the heart of most Players—were toned down. While the conflict between art and commerce is evident in both versions, the anticapitalist strain is stronger in the 1915 script. Writing soon after the Ludlow Massacre of April 1914, Bryant may have been worried about a libel suit when she cut Death's boast that John D. Rockefeller "is one of my best friends on earth, he certainly sends me a great many souls from the mines in Colorado" (p. 5). Another line that disappeared during revision was Death's admonition to Youth that his writing will "stir up a social revolution" (p. 12), something many of the Players hoped to do with their work. Finally, several comments about war and the death of soldiers were eliminated. While the Provincetown version ends with Life's lament for the soldiers—"They are the flower of youth—there are dreamers among them"—the original typescript has a more explicit curtain line: "I *must* find a way to stop wars—perhaps Youth will help me" (p. 15).

In February 1917, shortly before the United States entered World War I, Reed and Bryant left the Provincetown Players to pursue their journalism careers. Louise Bryant did, nevertheless, continue her affair with the Provincetown's most famous playwright, Eugene O'Neill. Both Bryant and Reed, despite their obvious devotion to each other, engaged in extramarital relationships. The longest-running and most serious of these was Bryant's liaison with O'Neill, which began before her marriage to Reed and continued afterward. Many biographers speculate that O'Neill married his second wife, Agnes Boulton, because of her resemblance to Louise Bryant. Mary V. Dearborn, author of one of the best Bryant biographies, is among those who believe that several O'Neill characters, notably Nina Leeds in *Strange Interlude*, were modeled on Bryant (p. 55).

Louise and Jack gave domesticity a try, renting a house in Croton-on-Hudson, north of New York City. During this period, Reed was hospitalized at Johns Hopkins for removal of a kidney that had troubled him for many years. Louise continued to see O'Neill during Reed's absence, although much of the time she herself was ill with a serious gynecological infection. The movie *Reds* (1981) shows an abandoned Jack Reed recuperating at their Croton home with no one for company except the puppy he had bought Louise for Christmas. In fact, Louise was there caring for her husband with a trained nurse.

REVOLUTIONARY RUSSIA

Louise sailed for Europe in June 1917, a perilous trip because the United States had recently entered World War I and German U-boats were a threat. She returned to New York a month later, but on August 17 Bryant and Reed started their long and tortuous journey to Russia. She carried credentials from the Bell Syndicate, which particularly wanted her to report from a woman's perspective. According to Dearborn, Bryant "was also appointed as correspondent for the *Metropolitan* . . . and for *Seven Arts* and *Every Week* (which would both go out of business very soon)" (p. 75). Barbara Gelb, who chronicled the lives of the couple in *So Short a Time*, notes that Bryant and Reed jointly published an article in the October 1917 issue of the radical magazine *Masses* that asserted, "The uninteresting war begins to be interesting to liberals" (p. 114). This would soon prove to be an understatement as Bryant and Reed found themselves in the capital of Petrograd the night of November 7–8, when Soviet insurrectionists captured the Winter Palace, toppling Russia's Provisional Government and bringing Vladimir Lenin's Bolsheviks to power.

Louise Bryant sent a large number of dispatches from Russia. Dearborn notes that Louise sold thirty-two stories to the *Philadelphia Ledger*, which in turn syndicated them to the Hearst chain's *New York American* and to more than one hundred newspapers across the United States and Canada; they were eventually translated into five languages (p. 102).

The most important of Bryant's writings are collected in two volumes, *Six Red Months in Russia* (1918), and *Mirrors of Moscow* (1923). (Bryant actually spent about four months in Russia gathering material for the first volume; nearly two months were taken up with travel in the days before commercial aviation.) Reed's major reports were gathered in *Ten Days That Shook the World*, which was published in 1919.

Bryant's reporting style is personal, as the subtitle to *Six Red Months in Russia* suggests: "An Observer's Account of Russia Before and During the Proletarian Dictatorship." Dearborn calls her "a dedicated advocate journalist" (p. 93). In the introduction to *Six Red Months in Russia*, Bryant claims to be "a messenger who lays his notes before you, attempting to give you a picture of what I saw and what you would have seen if you been with me" (p. xix). Her approach in some ways foreshadows the New Journalism championed by Truman Capote, Hunter S. Thompson, and Joan Didion in the 1960s and 1970s. Bryant's prose is lucid, graceful, and direct, well suited to the newspaper readers she was addressing.

She took her assignment seriously, but she clearly also had some fun when she wasn't trying to sort out the various competing factions. On one occasion she took Somerset Maugham and the American consul to the "Thieves Market" in Petrograd, which sold everything from pilfered Bokhara carpets to Chinese porcelain. Though at first shocked by the provenance of the goods, the consul purchased "a pipe owned by Peter the Great, and Maugham picked up two marvellous bead purses" (p. 120).

Virtually every reviewer of Bryant's books commented on her pro-Bolshevik leanings, but most noted that this did not undermine the accuracy of her reportage. Although Bryant was a shrewd observer of people and events, her great love for Russia included a romantic view of what the revolution might produce. At one point in *Mirrors of Moscow*, she asserts that "the Communists are undoubtedly the knights errant of the twentieth century and their slogan of 'internationalism' is but a revival of that old, old banner of 'Brotherhood'" (p. 194). At the conclu-

sion of *Six Red Months in Russia*, she muses, "I wanted to go back and offer my life for the revolution" (p. 235).

Closely based on the original news stories, *Six Red Months in Russia* comprises twenty-three short chapters. Bryant begins with the claim that "We have here in America an all too obvious and objectionable prejudice against Russia" (p. xix). She adds that "Socialism is here, whether we like it or not—just as woman suffrage is here—and it spreads with the years" (p. xx). Bryant attended many official meetings of the Democratic Congress as well as endless discussions of the long-planned Constituent Assembly, which was abolished a mere thirteen hours after it was finally convened. She also interviewed just about every significant person involved in the conflict. Although Bryant emphasizes that *"all the important political parties in Russia are Socialist parties—except the Cadets,"* she acknowledges that the number of different factions was bewildering (p. 29). At one point she even provides a chart attempting to explain the differing attitudes of the Cadets, the Mensheviks, and the Bolsheviks. She is clearly, as she asserts, playing the role of "layman speaking to laymen" (p. 29).

According to Dearborn, Bryant joined the College Equal Suffrage League in 1912; seven years later she was arrested while participating in a suffragist rally at which an effigy of President Woodrow Wilson was burned. Bryant was what today would be called a liberal feminist. She did not believe that women were inferior or superior to men, insisting that "I can never see any spiritual difference between men and women inside or outside of politics. They act and react very much alike" (pp. 127–128). The Bell Syndicate's mandate that she pay particular attention to Russian women fit her interests perfectly. Bryant was delighted that "twenty-three regularly elected women-delegates" (p. 42) attended the Democratic Congress, and added, "I am enough of a feminist to be pleased with the fact that the Cronstadt Soviet has been headed by a middle-aged woman [Madame Stahl] for more than half a year" (p. 122).

Bryant believed that the Bolsheviks offered gender equality, a hope that history has unfortu-

nately not borne out. In a July 1918 *Pearson's Magazine* article headlined "The Russian Gay-Girl and the War," she even makes the unsupported claim that there is less prostitution in revolutionary Russia than elsewhere in the world because women there are treated as comrades, an argument she would return to in *Mirrors of Moscow*. Bryant is more convincing when discussing individuals in *Six Red Months in Russia*. One of the women who fascinated her was Katherine Breshkovsky, whom she describes in breathless prose as

> a Jeanne d'Arc who led the masses to freedom by education instead of bayonets; hunted, imprisoned, tortured, almost half a century exiled in the darkness of Siberia, brought back under the flaming banners of revolution, honoured as no other woman of modern times has been honoured, misunderstanding and misunderstood, deposed again, broken.
>
> (p. 73)

She predicted that Breshkovsky would go down in history as "'Babushka,' the Grandmother of the Revolution" (p. 73).

Bryant was so taken with Breshkovsky that she wrote a short drama about her. Apparently never printed or performed, a copy of this script is housed in the Library of Congress. Titled "The End of the Candle: A Play of the Russian Revolution" (1918), this "little dream of what might have been if the Provisional Government had remained in power and the German advance had still taken place," as stated on the title page, is set in the Winter Palace as the invading German army approaches. *The End of the Candle* is a blend of political fantasy, propaganda, and melodrama that focuses on Breshkovsky and Aleksandr Kerensky, the comparatively moderate Russian revolutionary who headed the Provisional Government before the Bolshevik takeover. The drama reveals the folly in Babushka's faith that "America has always been kind to the revolution. America may yet save Russia" (p. 8). The United States, in this play, is responsible for Kerensky's imminent downfall. The work does not indicate this, but Breshkovsky, like many others, was forced to flee Russia when Kerensky was replaced.

Several chapters in *Six Red Months in Russia* are devoted to other women, including Countess

Panina and Alexandra Kollontay, both of whom served as minister of welfare after the Revolution. Where Bryant's account of Panina is often humorous and dismissive—she quotes a young woman who observes that "Panina really does like poor people—she thinks they are *almost* as good as other people" (p. 88)—she greatly admired Kollontay. As minister, Kollontay lowered the salaries of social workers so more money was available for the poor, aided mothers and orphans, and obtained funds for millions of maimed soldiers by raising the taxes on luxuries like playing cards. In *Mirrors of Moscow*, Bryant notes that Kollontay even had the courage to openly disagree with Lenin. She was, Bryant observes, the only woman in the Russian cabinet—which speaks well for her but not for Russia's vaunted sexual equality.

Maria Spiridonova appears in both *Six Months in Red Russia* and *Mirrors of Moscow*. Bryant is adept at providing brief but vivid descriptions of those she interviewed. In *Six Red Months in Russia*, for example, she writes that Spiridonova "looks as if she came from New England" because of "her puritanical plain black clothes with the chaste little white collars" (p. 123). At age nineteen, Spiridonova had killed the governor of Tambov, a savage man known for encouraging his troops to brutalize peasants, especially women. After being beaten and tortured almost to death, Spiridonova was exiled to Siberia, where she spent some eleven years. Bryant considered her a great hero: "I have not met a woman her equal in any country" (p. 126). Spiridonova did not remain a hero in her own country, however: she was executed in September 1941, along with many others, by order of Joseph Stalin.

As would be expected, Bryant interviewed both Lenin and Leon Trotsky, calling them "symbols representing a new order" (p. 99). (In her first book, she spells the name "Lenine" but later adopts the more common "Lenin.") She admires Lenin for his intelligence but admits that he lacks Kerensky's warmth and charm; "It is not easy to write fairly of Lenine, I confess that. . . . Lenine is sheer intellect—he is absorbed, cold, unattractive, impatient at interruption" (p. 101).

She dismisses the claim that Lenin is pro-German (though the Bolsheviks later were forced into a treaty with their German enemies) and insists that his real wish is to form a relationship with the United States. In her view, she writes in *Mirrors of Moscow*, Lenin became "a great reformer" not because he himself was suffering but because he could not stand to see others "hungry and outcast" (p. 3). To Bryant, Lenin possesses "all the qualities of a 'chief,' including the absolute indifference which is so necessary to such a part" (*Six Red Months*, p. 102)—a chilling remark meant to be a compliment. She also concludes in *Mirrors of Moscow* that Lenin's success was greatly enhanced by the women around him— "his mother, his wife, his sister and his lifelong friend and, in late years, chief secretary, Fotiva" (pp. 5–6).

Although much briefer, Bryant's treatment of Trotsky in *Six Red Months in Russia* also at times approaches hagiography. For her, Trotsky is the man of action while Lenin is the thinker. She considers the slightly built Trotsky "much more human" (p. 104) than the intellectual Lenin, "a brilliant and fiery orator" (p. 108). *Mirrors of Moscow* includes high praise for his wife, Madame Trotsky, who succeeded in protecting many of Russia's art treasures at a time when revolutionaries wanted them destroyed as symbols of the czarist regime.

RADICAL STRUGGLE BACK HOME

Bryant arrived back in the United States in February 1918; Reed would not return until the end of April. She began putting together *Six Red Months in Russia*, which was published late that year by George H. Doran, with illustrations by Oscar Césare, known by the single name Césare. The reviews were mixed but generally positive. Although nowhere in the book does Bryant claim to speak Russian, a critic for *The Nation*, complained that the chapters "appear to have been written in haste, as is indicated by numerous errors. Moreover, while they convey the impression that the author knows Russian, her use of that language does not confirm the impression. Notwithstanding all these shortcom-

ings, the collection is interesting, and it contains a wealth of information about the Soviet government and the various political parties in Russia" (November 18, 1918, p. 591). The reviewer concludes that "Miss Bryant's impressions of Russia, gathered in the midst of the turmoil of the Revolution, should aid to a proper understanding of the Bolshevist movement" (November 16, 1918, p. 591). *The Dial* reviewer took a more consistently positive stance. While noting that "the author is honestly and frankly a pleader for the Bolsheviki. . . . This partisanship, fortunately does not mitigate her reporter's gift for accurate observation, and her book is exceedingly valuable as a straight record of fact" (November 30, 1918, p. 504).

Bryant proved a very popular speaker on the subject of the Russian Revolution. She traveled around the United States talking about her experiences in Russia and her hopes for the country's future. Her biographer Virginia Gardner says that at one point Bryant addressed an audience of four thousand. Yet the muckraker Upton Sinclair, who observed a "wildly enthusiastic" crowd at a speech she gave in Los Angeles, complained that neither of the city's major newspapers bothered to cover the event.

During this period fears of bolshevism taking root on American soil were coalescing into the first Red Scare with the creation of the Overman Committee, a special Senate subcommittee that investigated German and Communist influence in the United States; it was, in essence, a forerunner of the infamous House Un-American Activities Committee. A parade of witnesses testified to the repression and savagery of Russian bolshevism. Bryant demanded—and was granted—a hearing before the committee to offer counterevidence based on what she had seen firsthand, but the hostile lawmakers spent much of the time probing her about her own religious and political beliefs and marriage history. Dearborn reports that when Lee Slater Overman said "we are going to treat you fairly and treat you as a lady," Bryant replied: "I do not want to be treated as a lady, but I want to be treated as a human being" (p. 125). She did manage, with great difficulty, to testify about what she had seen in Russia.

Reed was more inclined toward political activism than Bryant was, and during his 1918–1919 sojourn in the United States he helped establish the Communist Labor Party of America (CLP). He also lectured widely and completed *Ten Days That Shook the* World. Reed was repeatedly arrested for inciting riots and sedition, but he was able to slip away to Russia in the fall of 1919. In February 1920 he attempted to return to the United States bringing funds for the CLP, even though an indictment for criminal anarchy awaited him, but he was arrested and imprisoned in Finland, then ruled by the conservative Whites. Reed managed to smuggle out a message to Louise, who received it in August. The anarchist Emma Goldman reports that Bryant "disguised [herself] as a sailor and, like Reed, soon left New York with forged seaman's papers" (p. 851). Louise joined her husband in Russia in mid-September, but their reunion was short-lived. His always fragile health further undermined by his time in prison, Reed died of typhus in Moscow on October 17, 1920, with Bryant by his side. After a hero's funeral, Reed was interred at the Kremlin Wall Necropolis. Reed's *Ten Days That Shook the World* remains the most famous contemporary book about the Russian Revolution.

EASTERN TRAVELS AND MIRRORS OF MOSCOW

Louise stayed on in Russia, and on October 14, 1920, an interview she conducted with Lenin appeared on the front page of the *Washington Times* with the headline "Russia Europe's Only Solvent Nation, Says Lenin, Soviet Chief." She traveled to eastern regions of the Soviet Union including Bukhara and Turkestan—places few Westerners, especially Western women, would have dared to venture. In fact, most of her journeys were similarly dangerous: there was fighting within and between the nations she visited. Food and housing were often difficult to find, and Bryant, like the majority of Russians, sometimes subsisted on bread soup, although her diet was generally better than most. At times she was followed by spies who tracked her every movement, and during at least one period—in a scenario repre-

sentative of a bad farce—there were spies following her spies.

During her travels throughout the East, Louise met a number of political leaders who were striving for power in this war-torn region. She records in *Mirrors of Moscow*, for example, that she became friends with Enver Pasha, one of the "Young Turks" who held power over the Ottoman Empire from 1913 to 1918. The chapter on him in this volume is one of the longest, and although she praises him for being "extremely liberal in his opinions about women," she also notes that he once told a young actress "that she would be better off in a harem" (p. 154), not exactly the views of a feminist. Bryant was perceptive in observing Enver Pasha's "very obvious opportunism, and the cruelty and lack of conscience which a fatalistic belief inspires" (p. 149). He would later be one of the main perpetrators of the Armenian genocide.

In the foreword to *Mirrors of Moscow*, Bryant explains, "I have tried to show the leaders of the revolution as they really are, as I know them in their homes, where the red glare does not penetrate and they live as other men" (p. xi). She hopes, far too optimistically, that "in the end the peasants will rule Russia" (p. xiii). Ironically, she considers the Russian leaders "frank," while "in the western democracies, politics is the art of seeming frank while not being so" (p. xiii). (History has proven her half-right in this assertion.) *Mirrors of Moscow* is an interesting but less absorbing book than *Six Red Months in Russia*, partly because several chapters are devoted to functionaries like Christian Rakovsky and Abraham Krasnichakov, who would never have the historical impact of a Lenin or Trotsky. She dismisses Leo Kaminev (Kamenev), a member of the All-Russian Central Executive Committee of Soviets, as a genial but mediocre man, and correctly predicts Alexei Ivanovich Rykov to be "the logical successor to Lenin" (p. 39) even though "I do not think he will go down in history as a great figure" because he will always be seen in Lenin's shadow (p. 41).

One of the most compelling pieces in *Mirrors of Moscow* is devoted to the women soldiers ominously called "the Death Battalion." Despite

their name, they seem to have done little killing, but Bryant was impressed by the fact that women were allowed to take combat positions in the Russian military. This chapter also demonstrates her ability to lighten her somber story with a little wit. She recalls one young soldier who, having no superior officers to salute, kept saluting Bryant. A disconcerted Bryant had to beg her to stop.

Bryant insists that in general Russians "hate to kill," although she fails to indicate whether this makes them different from any other people. The actual Bolshevik takeover was a relatively bloodless affair, but violence both preceded and followed it. She herself witnesses the deaths of "two little street boys" caught in the crossfire between warring factions. In *Six Red Months in Russia* she recalls: "One whimpered pitifully when he was shot, the other died instantly, dropping at our feet an inanimate bundle of rags, his pinched little face covered with his own blood" (p. 181). She knew firsthand that war and revolution entail bloodshed, despite her attempts to downplay the ferocity of this upheaval.

More disturbing, in a different way, is Bryant's account of executions taking place in Russia. She relates that Fedore "Dzerzhinsky [has] an unusually classical background for a Chief Executioner" (p. 45) and praises him for seeing that "prisoners were quickly and humanely disposed of" (p. 49). She defends Lenin by saying he believed in the death penalty "only for those who attempted forcibly to overthrow the government" (pp. 47–48), although the examples she provides do not support this claim. Dzerzhinsky and his colleague, Jacob Peters, Bryant insists, are "as much victims of the revolution" as those they put to death (p. 48). Perhaps realizing how harsh her analysis sounds, she cites the electric chair in New York's Sing Sing prison, insisting that she is not supporting executions in either Russia or the United States. Even less convincing is her comparison of the Cheka, the Soviet state security organization, to America's private detective agencies.

Bryant seemed to believe that a Bolshevik state would allow freedoms previously denied to most Russians, but her examples sometimes belie

these claims. Surprisingly for a journalist, Bryant comes perilously close to excusing Soviet silencing of the press. In *Six Red Months in Russia*, she admits that several newspapers had been closed down but counters that "while the Soviets declared a temporary suppression of the press, they never at any time tried to interfere with public speaking or with theatrical performances which ridiculed them or the revolution" (p. 175). Konstantin Stanislavsky's famous Moscow Art Theatre (a favorite of Lenin's) and the ballet continued to thrive, but writers did not fare as well. She also asserts that the only danger to the church in Russia comes from internal corruption. "The church itself will go on because the peasants are religious," she optimistically asserts (*Mirrors*, p. 172).

This is one of several places where Bryant falls into the trap of making somewhat questionable generalizations about the "peasants," meaning the rural poor. She romanticizes the "peasants" who "already hold the balance of power and . . . move towards control with the crushing surety of a glacier" (*Mirrors*, p. 89). At the same time, she claims rather condescendingly that "peasant women are naturally slow-moving and stolidly honest" (p. 113). Bryant may admire what she considers the peasant spirit, but she spent most of her time in Russia observing city dwellers and interviewing the movers and shakers of the Revolution, only a few of whom came from the peasant class.

The first *Mirrors of Moscow* stories appeared on June 4, 1922, in the Hearst press; the volume itself was published the following year. Like the reviews of her first book, the reaction to *Mirrors of Moscow* was largely positive. The *New York Times* had a lukewarm response but devoted a full page to the slim volume, complete with illustrations. The review is titled "Machiavellian Muzhiks of Moscow." Striking a condescending note, the critic argues that "in lieu of delving into the depths which have swallowed up so many other writers of Russia, Miss Bryant has been content to write about it in a casual, feminine, chatty way" (March 11, 1923, p. 3). He concedes, however, that "Miss Bryant manages to give a picture of present-day Russia which certainly has

meritorious points about it" (March 11, 1923, p. 3). Katharine Sergeant Angell, writing for the *Nation*, dubs the book "very useful" (May 9, 1923, p. 548), a word echoed in Arthur Ruhl's remarks in the *Literary Review*, although he considers it too early to evaluate the "shifting" scene in Russia (March 31, 1923, p. 565). A commentator in the *Washington Times* calls it "a notable contribution to the interpretation of present day Russia" (November 19, 1922, p. 8). Perhaps the most perplexing evaluation came from the *Bookman* critic, who complains, "One would be willing to take a Bible oath that every word in [the chapters] is rigidly truthful; for this very reason, they are not as interesting as they might be" (June 1923, p. 464). (He apparently prefers journalists who invent tales rather than report events.) A more positive response appeared in the *Greensboro* (N.C.) *Daily News*, which notes, "Louise Bryant's book will cause the reader at least, to pause and reconsider and herein is its great value. The style is attractive; the movement never lags, and one can get much pleasure from reading it, even one who disagrees entirely with its conclusions" (April 22, 1923, p. 10).

Louise Bryant continued her reporting, obtaining interviews with the Italian war hero Gabriele D'Annunzio and the deposed King Constantine I of Greece. She was also the first American to interview Benito Mussolini shortly after he came to power in 1922. She not only spoke with him but did extensive background research, even tracking down his wife at a small village market. Bryant recognized the power and ambition of the man, who was still an enigma to most of the world, but deplored his conservative attitudes toward women. According to Dearborn, Bryant recounted in a newspaper article that,when the soon-to-be dictator insisted that women do not belong in politics, she "wonder[ed] about those auxiliary legions of women Fascisti. They must annoy Mussolini greatly" (p. 210).

THIRD MARRIAGE AND FINAL YEARS

Despite what she had achieved, in just a few years Bryant's life spiraled out of control. On

LOUISE BRYANT

December 10, 1923, she married William C. Bullitt in Paris. He was a wealthy diplomat and great admirer of John Reed. A few months later, on February 4, 1924, their daughter, Anne, was born. The family lived happily for a short time, although Bill was a complicated individual who, through his wealth and family connections, managed to be taken on as Sigmund Freud's patient. They lived well, mostly in Europe, until Bryant's behavior took a strange turn and she began drinking steadily. She had developed, doctors eventually concluded, an extremely rare disorder called Dercum's disease, or adiposis dolorosa. This disease, more common in women than men, causes painful fatty tissue growths under the skin. The condition is often accompanied by confusion and depression; heavy drinking is one consequence. The disfiguring disease was especially devastating to Bryant, who had always been admired for her beauty.

Bullitt stood by Louise for a while, sending her for treatments that had little effect; even today there is no cure for Dercum's disease. His sympathy, however, seems short-lived. Embarrassed by her behavior—he came from an upperclass Main Line Philadelphia family and traveled in exclusive circles—he divorced her (possibly without her knowledge) in 1930 and took custody of Anne, who was allowed only very limited contact with her mother. One of his complaints against Bryant at the divorce hearing was that she had had a lesbian relationship with the sculptor Gwen Le Gallienne.

During her last years, Louise gave strong support to the Jamaican-born writer Claude McKay, with whom she had become close friends. The two corresponded regularly, and McKay dedicated his first novel, *Home to Harlem* (1928), to Bryant. A voluminous collection of Bryant's writings, many unpublished, are housed at the Yale and Harvard libraries. She spent much of the 1920s attempting to write a book about Reed that would also have been an autobiography; nearly fifty heavily marked typescript pages, apparently part of this work, are titled "Christmas in Petrograd 1917." Gardner adds that Bryant was still writing plays as late as 1926. And somehow, despite her physical and emotional dis-

abilities, in her last years Bryant learned how to fly an airplane.

Bullitt was providing her with some kind of financial support, but it must have been limited: at the end she was living alone in a cheap French hotel. Largely abandoned by her friends and family, Bryant died of a cerebral hemorrhage after collapsing on the steps of that hotel on January 6, 1936, and was buried in Paris. She was fifty years old.

Louise Bryant is probably best known through the 1981 American film *Reds*, an epic drama that tells part of Bryant and Reed's story. Starring Diane Keaton as Bryant, Warren Beatty as Reed, and Jack Nicholson as Eugene O'Neill, the film aspires to be partly a docudrama, with interpolations by several elderly commentators who lived through the period. Beatty, Keaton, and Nicholson were nominated for Academy Awards in acting categories, but the only member of the cast who won was Maureen Stapleton, who played Bryant's erstwhile friend Emma Goldman. Warren Beatty took home the Best Director prize. Not surprisingly, the film focuses on Reed. In the second half of the movie, Bryant's main role is to undertake a harrowing journey to get to his bedside before he dies. She is presented as heroic, though whether she actually skied across the frozen tundra is questionable.

Reds is an action film as well as an attempt at political history, and the movie features dramatic scenes of roaring mobs, camels galloping on the Russian steppes, and Reed igniting immense crowds with his rhetoric. At one point he is seen running for safety when a band of armed horsemen attack the train he's riding. Most of Bryant's writing involved her observations of the common people in the streets and her one-on-one interviews with the prime players in the Revolution—none of which make for exciting screen exploits.

At the time of her death, tributes to Louise Bryant appeared around the world. Gardner reports that the *New Masses* characterized her as an "indomitable fighter for women's rights" and "one of the first-class journalists of her time" (p. 299). Like all too many women, unfortunately, Bryant became best known for the male company

she kept. Although the headline of her obituary in the *New York Times* identifies her as a journalist (and mistakenly gives her age as forty-one), most of the six-paragraph text concerns her marriages to John Reed and William Bullitt: nearly a quarter of the obituary is devoted to a description of her anguish at Reed's funeral sixteen years earlier. She is also characterized as "a communist leader," a description that fits Reed far better than Bryant (p. 19). The *New York Herald Tribune* devoted even more column inches to her, citing Bryant as "an unusually competent journalist [who] sought to dispel many foolish legends concerning the Soviet [Union] that has gained widespread credence in the United States." Still, the obituary makes much of her appearance ("Once a glamorous and exciting figure"), and the headline proclaims in large letters: "Louise Bryant Dead; Widow of John Reed" (p. 16).

In many cases, Bryant was also done no favors by her "friends." Some blamed her for her drinking and losing her looks, others questioned her commitment to the revolution. In the second volume of her autobiography, *Living My Life*, Emma Goldman accused Bryant of "lack of depth" (p. 850). Goldman claimed to have been Bryant's main support—literal and moral—at John Reed's funeral, but she never forgave Bryant for her negative writings about Russian anarchists.

What would Louise Bryant have done had she not succumbed to a devastating disease? She and John Reed were a remarkable couple, encouraging each other and reading each other's work, but Bryant continued important writing even after his death. It's hard to imagine her settling into the sedate life of devoted mother and diplomatic spouse, but the socialist Eden of which she dreamed—with equality for men and women, rich and poor—was already showing ominous rifts. Her preliminary work on Reed's biography, which would have included much about Bryant's life as well, remained unrealized. What Bryant achieved, however, is extraordinary. A highly respected and widely read international correspondent who risked her life to bring the story of the Russian Revolution to a skeptical American populace, Louise Bryant gave readers an inside view of one of the most important events of the twentieth century. The repercussions of that event are still being felt today.

Selected Bibliography

WORKS OF LOUISE BRYANT

JOURNALISM

"The Poets' Revolution." *Masses*, July 1916, p. 29.

"The Russian Gay-Girl and the War." *Pearson's Magazine* 39, no. 3:138–139 (July 1918). Reprinted in *Goodwin's Weekly*, August 3, 1918, p. 11.

Six Red Months in Russia: An Observer's Account of Russia Before and During the Proletarian Dictatorship. New York: George H. Doran, 1918. Reprinted with a preface by Mary V. Dearborn. Portland, Ore.: Powell's Press, 2002.

Mirrors of Moscow. New York: Thomas Seltzer, 1923. Reprint, Westport, Conn.: Hyperion Press, 1973.

PLAYS

The Game. In *The Provincetown Plays: First Series.* New York: Frank Shay, 1916. Pp. 28–42. Reprinted in *Women Writers of the Provincetown Players: A Collection of Short Works.* Edited by Judith E. Barlow. Albany, N.Y.: State University of New York Press, 2009. Pp. 53–64. Earlier typescript, 1915. Manuscript Division, Library of Congress.

"The End of the Candle: A Play of the Russian Revolution." 1918. Typescript, Manuscript Division, Library of Congress.

AUTOBIOGRAPHY

"Christmas in Petrograd, 1917." Typescript, Granville Hicks Papers, Special Collections, Syracuse University Library, Syracuse, N.Y.

PAPERS

Louise Bryant Papers, MS 1840. Yale University Library Manuscripts and Archives, Beinecke Library, New Haven, Conn. http://drs.library.yale.edu/HLTransformer/ HLTransServlet?stylename=yul.ead2002.xhtml. xsl&pid=mssa:ms.1840&query=street%20family&clear-stylesheet-cache=yes&hlon=yes&big=&adv=&filter=&hit PageStart=701&sortFields=&view=tp#titlepage

William C. Bullitt Papers, MS 112. Yale University Library Manuscripts and Archives, Beinecke Library, New Haven,

LOUISE BRYANT

Conn. http://drs.library.yale.edu/HLTransformer/
HLTransServlet?stylename=yul.ead2002.xhtml.
xsl&pid=mssa:ms.0112&query=bullitt&clear-stylesheet-
cache=yes&hlon=yes&big=&adv=&filter=&hitPageStart=
1&sortFields=&view=tp#titlepage

John Reed Papers, Houghton Library, Harvard University,
Cambridge, Mass. http://oasis.lib.harvard.edu/oasis/
deliver/~hou00070

CRITICAL AND BIOGRAPHICAL STUDIES

Barlow, Judith E. "Introduction" and "Introduction to *The Game*." In *Women Writers of the Provincetown Players: A Collection of Short Works*. Albany, N.Y.: State University of New York Press, 2009. Pp. 1–23, 47–52.

Black, Cheryl. *The Women of Provincetown 1915–1922*. Tuscaloosa: University of Alabama Press, 2002.

Dearborn, Mary V. *Queen of Bohemia: The Life of Louise Bryant*. Boston: Houghton Mifflin, 1996.

Gardner, Virginia. *"Friend and Lover": The Life of Louise Bryant*. New York: Horizon Press, 1982.

Gelb, Arthur, and Barbara Gelb. *O'Neill*. Enl. ed., New York: Harper & Row, 1973.

Gelb, Barbara. *So Short a Time: A Biography of John Reed and Louise Bryant*. New York: Norton, 1973. Reprint, New York: Berkley, 1981.

Goldman, Emma. *Living My Life*. Vol. 2. New York: Knopf, 1931. Reprint, New York: Da Capo Press, 1970.

Kenton, Edna. *The Provincetown Players and the Playwrights' Theatre, 1915–1922*. Edited by Travis Bogard and Jackson R. Bryer. Jefferson, N.C.: McFarland, 2004.

"Louise Bryant, 41 [*sic*], Journalist, Dead." *New York Times*, January 10, 1936, p. 19.

"Louise Bryant Dead; Widow of John Reed." *New York Herald Tribune*, January 19, 1936, p. 16.

Reed, John. *Ten Days That Shook the World*. New York, Boni & Liveright, 1919.

Sarlós, Robert Károly. *Jig Cook and the Provincetown Players: Theatre in Ferment*. Amherst: University of Massachusetts Press, 1982.

Sinclair, Upton. "Strangling the News." *New Justice* 1:1–3 (May 1, 1919). Reprinted in *Butte Daily Bulletin*, May 19, 1919, p. 5.

Zorach, William. *Art Is My Life*. Cleveland: World, 1967.

FILMS BASED ON THE LIFE OF LOUISE BRYANT

Reds. Screenplay by Warren Beatty and Trevor Griffiths. Directed by Warren Beatty. Paramount, 1981.

DIANA L. ECK

(1945—)

Susan Butterworth

DIANA L. ECK is a skillful nonfiction writer who weaves together threads of scholarship, field research, and writing as a participant-observer to create works that incorporate Eastern and Western points of view, a travel writer's sense of place, a spiritual journey, and a persuasive call to action. Beginning as a scholar of comparative religion, she became a pioneer of interfaith dialogue. Her study of the Indian city of Banaras (now Varanasi) and her sense of the holiness and faith found in Hindu religion and culture led her to the conviction that God is present in the hearts of the faithful of more than one religion, not only in her own Christian faith. Eck developed this conviction through her interfaith dialogue work with the World Council of Churches (WCC) based in Geneva, Switzerland; the Pluralism Project at Harvard University; her teaching in the Faculty of Arts and Sciences at Harvard University and Harvard Divinity School; her books; and hundreds of journal articles and conference presentations.

Eck describes herself as a student, scholar, and teacher of the comparative study of religion. Her academic specialization is Hindu tradition and the multiple religious traditions of India, where she has lived and worked. She teaches Indian studies, comparative religion, and religious pluralism to undergraduates and graduates at Harvard University, and she is involved in the Harvard-Epworth United Church in Cambridge, Massachusetts. Eck holds polycentricity—the interconnectedness and interdependence of many truths—as a model and an ideal. She has documented her intellectual and spiritual journey in a body of work that forms an organic and fluid whole, from her earliest scholarly work on the multiplicity of Hindu sacred thought in *Banaras: City of Light* (1982) through her reflections on theology in *Encountering God: A Spiritual Journey from Bozeman to Banaras* (1993) and her work on religious pluralism in the United States in *A New Religious America: How a "Christian Country" Has Become the World's Most Religiously Diverse Nation* (2001) to her return to the religious geography of India in *India: A Sacred Geography* (2012).

A METHODIST IN MONTANA

Diana L. Eck was born on July 5, 1945, in Tacoma, Washington, to Hugo and Dorothy Eck, both descended from Swedish immigrants to the Midwest. In 1946 the Ecks moved to Bozeman, Montana, where Hugo, an architect, joined the faculty of Montana State University. There the Ecks were active in the Methodist Church, which spurred Dorothy's involvement with the League of Women Voters and then Democratic politics, eventually becoming one of only four women in the Montana State Senate and a formidable liberal voice in that chamber for the next twenty years. Growing up in Bozeman, situated in the Gallatin Valley in the Rocky Mountains, Diana describes riding horses along the banks of the river in a fertile, farming valley. She was active in the Montana Methodist Youth Fellowship and spent her teenage summers at Methodist church camps, bonding and praying with her fellow campers. At summer work camps, the youth built a church on the Blackfeet Indian Reservation in northwest Montana and a silo on a farm in Mexico. In her spiritual memoir *Encountering God*, she writes, "The most durable product of these teenage summers, at least for me, was a sturdy faith in God, a very portable sense of what constitutes the church, and a commitment to the work of the church in the world" (p. 5).

By the time she was twenty, Eck had gone "back East" to Smith College in Northampton, Massachusetts, which she entered in the fall of 1963, and farther east to India, to Banaras Hindu University on the banks of the Ganges River. She writes in *Encountering God*, "Today these two places, Bozeman and Banaras, both convey the spiritual meaning of the word *home* to me. And these two rivers, the Gallatin and the Ganges, both flow with living waters I would call holy. Worlds apart, they carry currents of life and meaning whose confluence is in me, deep in my own spiritual life" (pp. 1–2).

ENCOUNTERING INDIA

In *Encountering God*, Eck describes her first encounter with India and Hindus. At Smith College, she writes, she was aimed toward the study of Latin America. During her sophomore year, an announcement for the University of Wisconsin's College Year in India captured her attention. She took a summer course in Hindi and left for Banaras in September 1965. Banaras is a teeming, congested city on the banks of the River Ganges in northern India. There she was immediately impressed by what she calls the "religiousness" of the city. Eck writes:

> We had not been there more than a day or two when we rose before dawn and took rickshaws to the riverfront to see the sights for which Banāras is so famous. Thousands of Hindus were there at Dasashwamedh Ghat, bobbing in the water, standing waist deep their hands folded in prayer, chanting to a crescendo of bells as the sun rose over the river. . . . For two miles along the ghats, Hindus bathed in the Ganges and worshiped as the sun broke the horizon. The city pulsed with the life of faith as vibrant as any I had known, and as different.
>
> (p. 7)

Her junior year abroad at Banaras Hindu University was her first encounter with people of faith who were not from her own tradition. She realized that the qualities which she valued in her Christian faith, and in Christian people—a faith centered in love, justice, and human dignity practiced by energetic, committed, visionary people—were to be found in the non-Christian people of strong faith and spiritual presence that she was meeting while doing fieldwork in Banaras. Eck writes, "These people, unbeknownst to them, pushed me into a life of work and inquiry, spiritual and intellectual. I became a student of comparative religion and focused my work on Hinduism and the traditions of India" (p. 9).

Understanding the city of Banaras and its meaning for Hindus was her first great intellectual challenge and the beginning of a life of scholarship devoted to interfaith dialogue and religious pluralism. Eck received her B.A. in religion from Smith College in 1967, and an M.A. in South Asian studies and modern Indian history from the School of Oriental and African Studies, University of London, in 1968. She returned to India in 1972 for further study of Hindi, and spent a year of research in Banaras in 1973–1974, where she received a postgraduate diploma in ancient Indian history and culture from Banaras Hindu University.

In 1976 she received her Ph.D. from Harvard University in the comparative study of religion. Eck wrote her doctoral dissertation on the city of Banaras, a study of what the city, the Ganges, and the gods mean to Hindus. She writes in *Encountering God*, "I first chose to do academic work on the meaning of the city of Banaras because it was widely held to be the most important of the religious centers of India. Hindus call it Kashi, the luminous City of Light" (p. 58). After receiving her doctorate, she became an instructor in Hindu religion at Harvard University, where she would become professor of comparative religion and Indian studies in 1984. Eck returned to Banaras for further research in 1978, while developing her doctoral thesis on Banaras into the book *Banaras: City of Light*.

BANARAS: CITY OF LIGHT

Banaras: City of Light (1982) was published by Alfred Knopf as a 350-page book illustrated with 59 photographs and 7 maps. Many of the photos were taken by Eck. The volume is a significant work of scholarship. Eck writes in the preface:

DIANA L. ECK

My work is based on two primary sources: a voluminous literature of Sanskrit texts which describe and praise Banāras, and the city itself, with its patterns of temples, its seasons of pilgrimage, and its priestly and lay interpreters. It is a study of "text and context," or perhaps more accurately, of classical Sanskrit texts and the "text" of the city, brought together so that we may see this city and understand its sacred structure and meaning as it has been seen and understood by Hindus.

(pp. xiii–xiv)

Two of the Sanskrit texts that deal primarily with Banaras—the *Kashi Khanda* and the *Kashi Rahsya*—had not been previously translated or studied by Western scholars. Eck studied diverse genres: *mahatmya* (praise literature), mythological literature, ritual literature, and geographical description. In addition, she worked in the field, exploring the sacred geography of the city, its temples and ruins, lanes, and pilgrimage routes. She consulted the Brahmins of Banaras, "the knowledgeable keepers of the tradition and those who act as interpreters of myth and *mahatmya*" (p. xv), teachers, priests, and storytellers. She watched the cycles of pilgrimage, following ordinary people to their destinations.

While *Banaras* might be read as an example of the sacred travel genre, Eck's purpose goes far deeper. *Banaras* is a scholarly work. It is also a work that crosses cultures. Eck seeks to reveal a complex Hindu city to the Western eye. She writes:

It is our purpose here to try to see the city Hindus see. We will explore the Sanskrit texts that praise this city. We will hear the popular Hindi tales and listen to the voices of priests and pilgrims. We will walk the ancient streets of Banaras, visit its temples, ponder its ruins, and learn of its gods. And all the while we will attempt to see, in and through the facts we have gathered, a vision of the city Hindus have seen.

(pp. 7–8)

The heart of the city is the Ganges River, its ghats (stairs leading to the river) where pilgrims bathe in the sacred water, its many temples, and the cremation pyres that Hindus believe bring the dead closer to liberation from the earthly round of life and death. The life of the city vibrates with the ancient ritual tradition of Hinduism. In her study, Eck approaches the city from a variety of perspectives: the religious imagination of the Hindu pilgrim, the historical perspective from ancient times through the Muslim centuries to the modern period, the geographical perspective of a city of many shrines and temples dedicated to the gods Shiva, Vishnu, and Krishna and the great goddess Devi. She includes detailed descriptions of temples and shrines with associated stories of the many gods and goddesses represented, as she explores the river Ganges and the great ghats—the site of the salvation of the dead and the purification of the living. She follows the seasons and festivals around the calendar, describes life in Banaras in the context of Hindu culture and theology, and ends her journey at the great cremation grounds of the City of Death and Liberation.

It is especially holy to die in Banaras. Eck writes, "No other city on earth is as famous for death as is Banaras. . . . At the center of the city along the riverfront is Manikarnika, the sanctuary of death, with its ceaselessly smoking cremation pyres" (p. 324). She continues, "For death in Kāshī is death transformed . . . Death in Kashi is Liberation . . . Death, which elsewhere is feared, here is welcomed as a long-expected guest" (p. 325). Eck concludes, "Kashi draws into powerful focus the greatest symbols of Hindu culture—its gods, especially the Great Lord, Shiva; its sacred geography, especially the Heavenly River, Ganga; and its vision of transcendence, *moksha*" (p. 344).

The focus of the volume is solidly on Banaras, but the depth of information opens a window onto broader Hindu traditions, stories, and culture. Always, Eck seeks to enlighten the Western reader about the Hindu way of thinking of the Divine as both one and many-faceted. "Kashi [the City of Light] is the paradigm of the sacred place. . . . The various temples, wells, pools, parks, and streams of the city symbolically embody the whole of India" (pp. 283–284). Thus the book is a comprehensive study of Hindu culture and theology as well as a specific sacred city.

Banaras presents a detailed geography of the city's sacred precincts, the seasons and times of worship, the multiple meanings of the city for

51

the Hindu, the images of Shiva and places of devotion to the many deities of Kashi, the City of Light. Deeply sourced with appendices, notes, illustrations, and extensive bibliography, it is an introduction to India's religious life and to Eck's original concept of sacred geography.

DARŚAN: SEEING THE DIVINE IMAGE OF INDIA

After her work on Banaras, Eck began a study of the sacred rivers, Hindu temples, and wayside shrines that link India into a network of pilgrimage places. *Darśan: Seeing the Divine Image in India*, was first published in 1981, and a second, revised and enlarged edition came out in 1985. In contrast to the substantial volume on Banaras, *Darśan* is a slim volume, an essay of under one hundred pages. Eck's emphasis is on the multiplicity of visual images in the Hindu tradition. The text is an essay on seeing; the book is the first fruit of her decades-long project of mapping India's holy sites and pilgrimage routes.

She writes in *Encountering God*:

> In the course of my research on the sacred geography of Banaras, I began to glimpse in my peripheral vision some indications that Banaras was not *the* sacred city of the Hindus, at least in the way I had imagined Banaras ought to be unique; such is the stake that academics often invest in the importance of their own subject. Yet I became increasingly aware, and with some irritation I must admit, that almost nothing of the praises of this sacred place really was unique.
>
> (p. 58)

Indeed there are other Cities of Light, other sacred rivers, other pilgrimage sites. Thus Eck deepens her study of oneness versus manyness, a Western monotheistic conception versus a Hindu conception of the sacred, and continues to develop her point of view, seeing India as a Hindu sees it. Eck writes in her preface to *Darśan*:

> This is an essay about the power and importance of "seeing" in the Hindu religious tradition . . . This is also an essay about the divine image in the Hindu tradition. . . . In exploring the nature of the divine image, we will not limit ourselves to the images of

the gods as such, but we will consider the ways in which the Hindu temple and the Hindu place of pilgrimage have become "divine images" as well.

(p. 1)

The Western experience is simply not comparable, Eck comments. The Hindu doesn't say "I am going to worship" but rather "I am going for *darśan*," to see and be seen in the presence of the deity. She observes that "contact between devotee and deity is exchanged through the eyes" (pp. 3, 7).

Eck hypothesizes that to begin to know the Hindu tradition, the teacher and student of culture must not only study the scriptural tradition but also attend to the visual tradition of art, image, and landscape. Thus the small volume is rich with black-and-white photos of temples, religious images, pilgrims, and pilgrimage sites, many taken by Eck. An explicit purpose of the volume is to present visual images of India through the medium of film and photography as a means of employing the senses in the process of learning about culture. She calls this a "hermeneutic of the visible," applying it not only to classical images of religion but also to "ordinary images of people's traditions, rites, and daily activities" (p. 14).

Further, seeing is not passive but rather a cognitive process that includes mind, eye, and experience. Seeing unfamiliar images of Hindu life raises questions that are the starting point for learning: "To understand India, we need to raise our eyes from the book to the image, but we also need some means of interpreting and comprehending the images we see" (p. 18). The Western observer must consider the assumptions behind the words "idolatry" and "monotheism" to realize the Hindu's comfort with multiplicity. "At virtually every level of life and thought, India is polycentric and pluralistic" (p. 24).

Eck focuses on the nature of the Hindu image as a real embodiment of the deity, charged with the presence of the god. The Hindu ritual of worship expresses a relational love. The god is honored by acts of humility and also by acts of affection, such as bathing, adorning, and touching the image. Festivals offer a further opportunity for darshan, seeing and being seen by

the deities. She goes on to explore the temple as religious image and the role of the worshipper's journey, the pilgrimage, an important part of India's religious life. She states, "The entire land of India is, to the eyes of Hindu pilgrims, a sacred geography" (p. 65).

Eck brings the reader back to Banaras, where there is a great density of images and where the "whole of the sacred world is gathered together into one place" (p. 74). It is "the destination at the end of the pilgrim road. It brings to an end not only the circuit of pilgrimage in India, but the long soul's pilgrimage through life after life" (p. 75). For the Hindu, in Eck's interpretation, the pilgrimage place itself is an image of the divine.

WORLD COUNCIL OF CHURCHES

In 1976 Eck became one of the twenty-five members of the World Council of Churches' Working Group on Dialogue with People of Living Faiths, which carries out the work of the WCC in interreligious relations. She remained a member of this group until 1991, becoming its moderator in 1984.

In 1977, while a lecturer on Hindu religion at Harvard, Eck was invited by the WCC to a theological consultation on interfaith dialogue in Chiang Mai, Thailand, beginning her formal commitment to ecumenical and interfaith work and her authorship of the first of dozens of moderator's reports and working papers. "Multitraditional Faith: A Personal View of Christians in Dialogue with People of Other Religious Traditions" was published in the *Bulletin of the Center for the Study of World Religions* in 1978, foreshadowing her work in *Encountering God*.

In *Encountering God*, Eck positions her commitment to the ecumenical church and the work of the WCC in the language of Pentecost, "the experience of the worldwide Christian community of many languages, races, and cultures" (p. 131). She writes:

I have felt what I would call Pentecostal energy in the experience of "church" that is most ecumenical—the great assemblies of the World Council of

Churches (WCC), like those in Vancouver in 1983 and in Canberra in 1991. . . . The ecumenical movement became a new Pentecostal movement, gathering from a hundred countries, speaking dozens of languages, and miraculously experiencing the uniting energy of the Holy Spirit.

(p. 131)

She uses spirit language when she extends the Christian ecumenical movement to the interfaith movement: "For those of us who are Christians, we understand it to be the Holy Spirit that drives us beyond the comforts and certainties of what we know to the very boundaries where Christians and Hindus and Muslims meet" (p. 134). On interfaith dialogue, she quotes the final report of one of the large sections of the WCC assembly in Canberra: "The Holy Spirit is at work in ways that pass human understanding: the freedom of the Spirit may challenge and surprise us as we enter into dialogue with people of other faiths" (p. 135).

In January of 1990, she writes, the WCC called a theological consultation in Baar, Switzerland, "to address the theological confusion among Christians about what it means to speak of God's presence among people of other faiths" (p. 188). With others, she forged a statement declaring that because God, the creator of all, is present in the plurality of religions, it is "inconceivable to us that God's saving activity could be confined to any one continent, cultural type, or group of peoples" (p. 188). This inclusive statement is a recasting of Christian language, yet it is an important departure for dialogue: "For if Christians acknowledge—as do those of us who forged this language at Baar—not only the 'seeking' but the 'finding' of God by people of other faiths, then the encounter with the Hindu or Muslim is truly an opportunity to deepen our knowledge and understanding of the one we call God" (p. 188). Eck's experience of world religions was an influence on this open-hearted statement of policy. Her work with the WCC, and the many published reports that resulted, also exemplify her collaborative leadership style and reflect her conviction that the world and its faiths are interdependent.

Eck notes that interreligious dialogue was not on the agenda of the churches until the second

half of the twentieth century. Not until the 1960s and 1970s did the conversation about "other faiths" shift from mission to interfaith dialogue and conversation about global concerns. Joining the WCC's Office on Interreligious Relations in its early days, Eck had the means, opportunity, and scholarly platform to engage in "building relations with people of other faiths . . . [,] addressing the fears and hesitancies of the member churches . . . [and] enabling Christians to think afresh about the theological implications of their relations with neighbors of other faiths" (*Encountering God*, p. 214).

ENCOUNTERING GOD

In *Encountering God: A Spiritual Journey from Bozeman to Banaras* (1993), written from the perspective of an explorer of religious pluralism, Eck turns from explaining India from the Hindu point of view to considering India's religious traditions from the viewpoint of a Christian in a world of many faiths. The book is a spiritual memoir and personal theology, informed by her work in India and her work with the WCC. She writes in the preface, "It is a book about how my encounters with people of other faiths have challenged, changed, and deepened my own faith" (p. xvii).

She clarifies her research question: "As a scholar and professor of religion, this kind of intellectual work is no small challenge—to glimpse the world of meaning in which people of another faith live their lives and die their deaths. But it is another question—equally important but very different—which I am pursuing here: What does all this mean to me, as a Christian?" (p. 10).

How does the reformulation of self-understanding develop in interfaith relations? Eck writes:

> To recognize this plurality of religious claims [to universal truth] as a profoundly important fact of our world does not constitute a betrayal of one's own faith. It is simply a fact among the many facts that emerge from the historical and comparative study of religion. . . . How does the understanding of others, which is the aim of the scholar of

comparative religion, reshape our self-understanding?

(p. 14)

Encountering God addresses theological questions, but it is not about theoretical theology. Eck describes it as "a theology with people in it" (p. 16). She writes:

> Theological questions are not merely theoretical; they are the life and death questions of real people attempting to live with intellectual and personal honesty in a world too complex for simplistic answers. Here I have tried to write for ordinary people who do not think of themselves as theologians, but who struggle with real questions of faith in the world in which we live.

(p. 15)

In *Encountering God*, Eck makes personal some of the ideas that were presented from a third-person point of view in *Banaras: City of Light* and *Darśan*. She also expands her thoughts about the nature of the divine image and polytheistic imagination presented in the *Darśan* essay. It is possible that Eck's openness to religious pluralism flows from her grasp of the diversity of deities in the Hindu tradition. She writes in *Darśan*, referring to the unlimited power of each of a variety of gods: "To celebrate one deity, one sacred place, one temple, does not mean there is no room for the celebration of another" (p. 26).

Eck weaves her view of religious pluralism into her story of learning about the Hindu religion. As she writes about the Hindu concept of the existence of many gods at the same time as there is truly only one god, she notes that the challenge is to hold multiple points of view simultaneously. The Hindu worshipper is accustomed to this challenge. She likens the challenge of religious pluralism to that capacity to hold multiple points of view. One does not relinquish one point of view for another. She explains, "Plurality is not given up in favor of oneness, nor oneness in favor of plurality. Both viewpoints are held—and are understood to be held—simultaneously" (*Encountering God*, p. 63).

Eck articulates some of the concepts that are fundamental to the religious pluralism movement of which she is a spokesperson and pioneer. One

of these concepts is the difference between pluralism and diversity. She explains:

> Diversity, of course, is not pluralism. Diversity is simply a fact, but what will we make of that fact, individually and as a culture? . . . Might [diversity] lead to a genuine pluralism, a positive and interactive interpretation of plurality? These are critical questions for the future, as people decide whether they value a sense of identity that isolates and sets them apart from one another or whether they value a broader identity that brings them into real relationship with one another.
>
> (*Encountering God*, p. 43)

Pluralism includes both a clearer and an expanded understanding of one's own concept of God.

The heart of *Encountering God* is a strong statement of personal, Christian belief, coupled with a simultaneous statement of respect for other faiths and commitment to religious pluralism:

> I do not believe that our faith in Christ can lead us any longer along the road of intolerance and exclusivism. That road runs contrary to the spirit of Jesus of Nazareth. Faith in Christ means that I live my life, and will surely die my death, in terms of my commitment to Christ. It does not mean that no other experience of God's presence and mercy could possibly be true. . . .
>
> (p. 96)

In the chapters "The Names of God," "The Faces of God," "The Breath of God," and "Attention to God," Eck presents Hindu concepts of God to the layperson in terms that convey the inexplicable nature of God to both Hindus and Christians. She connects some Hindu concepts to some Christian concepts, for example *mahatmya*, language of praise, with doxology in psalms and hymnody. She connects concepts; she does not equate them. She emphasizes the complexity of understanding God and points out that many Hindu concepts have no parallels in Christian thought and vice versa. She uses Hindu God-language to explore and enlarge Christian theology. No human being, Hindu or Christian, has enough language or imagination to comprehend the mystery of God. She writes, "The exaltation of one's chosen deity lies not in the condemnation of other images of the divine, but in the multiplication of meaning through the appreciative recognition of others, a kind of mutual inclusivism" (pp. 75–76).

Travel in India deepened her Christian faith as she learned to see what Hindus see. Eck grounds her theological insights in the concrete dimension of travel writing. In the chapter titled "The Faces of God," Eck discusses the Christian concept of incarnation. Eck weaves Hindu and Christian theology in a tapestry of relationship. She articulates the difference between honoring an image of God and the Christian worship of Jesus:

> When I stand in a Hindu sanctuary during the *arati*, when the oil lamps are raised toward the deity, I feel drawn into an attitude of worship. It is not the worship of idols, but the honoring of God through focused attention to the consecrated image in which God is graciously present. . . . This form of worship, called *puja*, has an integrity and beauty all its own, and it must surely be one of the many ways in which God truly enjoys a relationship with men and women. But as Christians, even in those churches where incense and images abound, we don't do *puja* to Jesus. We do not worship Jesus in quite that way and we do not because of the mystery of his humanity.
>
> (p. 85)

After clarifying her point about the difference between Hindu and Christian worship, Eck argues elegantly, in the first person and as a Christian, against an exclusivist view of Christ. As a Christian, she firmly centers her faith in the incarnation of Jesus: "As a Christian, I confess that Jesus enables me to see something of God that I do not know in any other way: God truly grounded in the soil of human life and death" (p. 90). Yet, she affirms that God is present to all of humanity, including the non-Christian faithful: "Christians should not be fearful or suspicious, therefore, of discovering the presence of God, which we know in Christ, in the religious lives of people of other faiths" (p. 92). Christ's love is inclusive of all people: "Whole-hearted commitment to Christ's way is worthy of the faith to which Christians are called; the denigration or demonization of our neighbors is not" (p. 95).

In "The Breath of God," Eck addresses the Holy Spirit, weaving together personal history, travel in India, her work with the WCC, Hindu and Christian theology, practice, and popular culture. She speaks of the Holy Spirit in inclusive,

ecumenical Christian language, and illuminates the divine energy, Shakti, of the Hindu tradition. A study of Shakti, she writes, has steered her toward a larger understanding of the Holy Spirit.

"Attention to God" opens with a lovely meditation on what it means to pay attention, to stay awake, keep watch, referring to Zen Buddhist teaching, personal experience, and the Christian gospel. The chapter examines Buddhist, Christian, and Hindu contemplative traditions and spiritual practice or discipline.

THE CHALLENGE OF RELIGIOUS PLURALISM

In *Encountering God*, Eck asserts, "Among the urgent tasks of theology today is to confront seriously the challenge of religious pluralism" (p. 49). In the chapter titled "Is Our God Listening?" she discusses in some detail the three concepts of exclusivism, inclusivism, and pluralism. These three responses to religious diversity provide an intellectual framework for practical interfaith work on the ground.

Exclusivism. Our way of thinking about God is correct and excludes all others. Inclusivism. We see God fully, others less clearly. Our way of thinking about God includes other, less adequate, views. Pluralism. God transcends comprehension. Each religion understands God only partially.

Pluralism for the Christian is a response to the infinite greatness of God: "Religiously, the move to pluralism begins for Christians the moment we imagine that the one we call God is greater than our knowledge or understanding of God. . . . Humility or simple honesty before God requires that we not limit God to the God we know or to the particular language and image through which we know God" (p. 186).

Religious pluralism requires commitment:

> The pluralist . . . stands in a particular community and is willing to be committed to the struggles of that community. . . . Pluralists recognize that others also have communities and commitments. They are unafraid to encounter one another and realize that they must all live with each other's particularities. . . . The theological task, and the task of a pluralist society, is to create the space and the means

for the encounter of commitments, not to neutralize all commitment.

(p. 195)

Pluralism is based on interreligious dialogue: "We do not enter into dialogue to produce an agreement, but to produce real relationship, even friendship, which is premised upon mutual understanding, not upon agreement" (p. 197).

Eck makes an important point about the diversity within Christian thinking, and by extension the diversity within other religious groups. She writes, "Intra-religious tension is today as powerful as inter-religious tension. Very often the religious conflicts that flare up have less to do with what one believes than with how one believes what one believes" (p. 169). She exhibits the influence of her study of the Hindu worldview, when she writes, "The idea that the human apprehension of truth is multi-sided, a view developed so extensively in the traditions originating in India, is quite alien to the monotheistic consciousness of the West" (p. 173). Thus the monotheistic traditions, with their emphasis on one God, one way, and one truth have much to learn from India and Eck's work. Pluralists work to understand others on their own terms, as Eck has done in *Banāras* and *Darśan*.

A CALL TO ACTION: THE NEED FOR INTER-RELIGIOUS DIALOGUE IN AN INTERDEPENDENT WORLD

In *Encountering God*, written in the last decade of the twentieth century, Eck is aware of living in an interdependent world. She writes, "Interdependence describes not only the inextricable relatedness of nations and economies, but also that of peoples, religious traditions, and cultures" (p. 202). She points out that the ecumenical movement is a response to this interdependence when she considers the phrase "global ,"—or in Christian terms, "the household of God." At the WCC, "the ecumenical movement found this term expressive of the worldwide reach of the church, a worldwide household" (p. 203). Clearly, she urges, the meaning of the word "we" must expand beyond culture, religion, or clan.

The chapter continues the tone of spiritual memoir as she writes about Mahatma Gandhi

and her experience in twentieth-century Delhi after her time in Banaras, "the most old-fashioned of Hindu cities" (p. 204). In Delhi, Eck meets intellectuals, activists, and feminists who work with women's cooperatives and grassroots movements for social justice, people who characterize themselves as Gandhians. Gandhi is a model for expanding the meaning of "we." The communities he created were expansively inclusive. Further, "Gandhi refused to demonize his opponent as a person, even when he was in profound disagreement with everything the opponent stood for. For him, only in the give and take of relationship would it be possible to construct a world which both could affirm" (p. 210).

Eck asserts that our lives and religious traditions have grown interrelated. "In my own case," she writes, "there is no doubt that by writing an interpretive study of the city of Banaras I have participated as a Christian, in a small way, in the history of the Hindu tradition. It is also true that my Hindu friends and teachers have participated in the history of the Christian tradition through their influence on me and my thinking" (p. 212). Further, interreligious dialogue "is at the very heart of a workable society" (p. 218). American and worldwide religious interdependence demands that we tackle "the basic ignorance, the fear, and the misunderstanding that separate us from one another" (p. 218).

Drawing on personal experience, the work of the WCC, Mahatma Gandhi, the Jewish philosopher Abraham Joshua Heschel, and Martin Luther King, Jr., Eck issues a call for interreligious dialogue, for knowing our neighbors, for genuine relationship and engagement with people of all faiths. *Encountering God* ends with a plea for a household of world religions, a community of communities, where acknowledgment of diversity walks with commitment to a specific faith. Eck's final words describe an imaginative vision of the river of life that includes images from the Book of Revelation of the Christian scripture. Surely, she writes, the river of heaven includes the Ganges in India and the Gallatin in Montana.

Encountering God: A Spiritual Journey from Bozeman to Banaras has become a classic in the genre of spiritual memoir and in the field of religious pluralism. Eck won the University of Louisville Grawemeyer Award in Religion in 1995 and the Melcher Award of the Unitarian Universalist Association in 1994 for *Encountering God*.

THE PLURALISM PROJECT

By 1990 the influx of American students of Asian heritage in her classes on religion at Harvard sent Eck on a new curve in the path of her research. She writes in *A New Religious America* (2001):

> When I first met these new students—Muslims from Providence, Hindus from Baltimore, Sikhs from Chicago, Jains from New Jersey—they signaled to me the emergence in America of a new cultural and religious reality about which I knew next to nothing. At that point I had not been to an American mosque. I had never visited a Sikh community in my own country and I could imagine a Hindu summer camp only by analogy with my Methodist camp experience. I felt the very ground under my feet as a teacher and scholar begin to shift. My researcher's eye began to refocus—from Banaras to Detroit, from Delhi to Boston.
>
> (pp. 17–18)

Beginning with a research seminar at Harvard called World Religions in New England, she and her students began to explore multireligious America. Visiting mosques, temples, gurdwaras, and shrines around Boston and New England, a new landscape of religious America emerged and a new conversation began.

In 1991 Eck founded and became the director of the Pluralism Project, a research project studying the changing religious landscape of the United States and the implications of religious pluralism for American public life. Student interns spread out across the country, seeking to map the new religious diversity of the United States, particularly the increasing presence of Hindu, Buddhist, and Muslim communities.

Eck urges a study of the dynamic changes that are occurring as America and religious diversity interact. "How will Christians and Jews, long dominant in America, respond to this new diversity?" (*A New Religious America*, p. 23).

"What does this new religious diversity mean for American electoral politics, for the continuing interpretation of church-state issues by the Supreme Court? What does it mean for American public education . . . for colleges and universities with an increasingly multireligious student body?" (p. 22).

The Pluralism Project has produced an educational multimedia CD-ROM, *On Common Ground: World Religions in America* (New York: Columbia University Press, 1997). Its ongoing work on religious pluralism in a multireligious society, case studies, and research reports have been compiled in the award-winning Pluralism Project website (http://www.pluralism.org). In 1998 President Bill Clinton and the National Endowment for the Humanities awarded Eck the National Humanities Medal for the work of the Pluralism Project in the investigation of America's religious diversity.

The Pluralism Project celebrated its twenty-fifth anniversary in 2016. Its student interns have gone on to become chaplains, professional researchers, oral historians, and spokespeople for the growing interfaith movement in America.

A NEW RELIGIOUS AMERICA

Eck ended *Encountering God* by calling for an expanded vision of "we" to include the entire household of world religions. *A New Religious America: How a "Christian Country" Has Become the World's Most Religiously Diverse Nation* (2001) opens with the news that the United States has become the most religiously diverse nation on earth. That expanded vision of "we" must take place in our own backyard, not on the other side of the world. Eck writes:

> "We the people of the United States" now form the most profusely religious nation on earth. But many, if not most, Christian, Jewish, or secular Americans have never visited a mosque or a Hindu or Buddhist temple. Many Americans are not so sure what Sikhs or Muslims believe, let alone Jains and Zoroastrians. Similarly, Muslim or Hindu Americans may have sketchy and stereotypical views of Christians and Jews.
>
> (p. 5)

A New Religious America is an exploration of the ways American society has been transformed by its new religious diversity. In *Banāras* and *Darśan*, Eck writes about religious diversity in India. In *Encountering God*, she writes about the challenge of religious pluralism in theological and methodological terms. In *A New Religious America*, she turns to the work on the ground in her own neighborhood. She writes, "Our first challenge in America today is simply to open our eyes . . . to discover America anew, and to explore the many ways in which the new immigration has changed the religious landscape of our cities and town our neighborhoods and schools" (p. 2). Commitment to the principle of religious freedom demands that "we will all need to know more than we do about one another and listen for the new ways in which new Americans articulate the 'we' and contribute to the sound and spirit of America" (p. 6).

In the chapter titled "From Many, One," Eck presents a history and commentary on the origins of religious freedom in the United States. From the narrative of a Christian America to religious diversity in the public square, the dilemma of religious pluralism, especially since the Immigration Act of 1965 eliminated the exclusion of Asians from immigration, has met American attitudes toward difference: exclusion, assimilation, and pluralism. To address the misinformation, misunderstanding, and isolation among diverse religious groups, she urges "an instructive first step toward a new religious America: simply to begin to know one another" (p. 32). The first step toward knowing one another is an integral part of the American ethos of freedom of religion, the "freedom to exercise religious hospitality" (p. 39)

In the chapters on American Hindus, American Buddhists, and American Muslims, Eck takes the reader along on her travels around the country in displays of descriptive writing designed to create images of the multiplicity of religious experience in America. Much of the material is surprising to the reader. The sights she describes are exotic; yet they are hidden in plain sight in strip malls, warehouses, and in beautiful, large new temple construction in affluent suburbs. Eck

roams the country visiting mosques and Islamic centers, attending the consecration of a temple here or a holiday celebration there, weaving history with stories of community building and distinctively American manifestations of traditional practices. Emphasis is on the multiplicity of experience, the internal diversity of each tradition.

Eck refers to interviews conducted by herself and the student researchers of the Pluralism Project as they search out and find expressions of the new religious America. She travels from the interfaith groundbreaking of a new Islamic Center in Sharon, Massachusetts, to the consecration of the Sri Lakshmi Temple in suburban Boston, a visit to the Vedanta Society of New York, and the celebration of the King's Birthday at the Wat Thai in North Hollywood, California. She writes:

> I had to go looking for these places, as did all of our Pluralism Project researchers. The new religious America did not simply present itself in a coherent group photo. Rather we made it a point to search out its various expressions. So I often wondered as I drove America's highways from temple to mosque to gurdwara just how many people had any idea that this is all here and what they would think if they did.
>
> (pp. 294–295)

In the chapter titled "Afraid of Ourselves," she addresses the climate of suspicion, American xenophobia, and the challenges of welcoming newcomers of every religion. Response to visible difference and change is too often fear. Stereotypes and deep ignorance of other religious traditions have led to vandalism and hate crimes. These are expressions of "a view of a normative Christian America that many still hold, despite our constitutional commitment to religious freedom and despite the facts of our multireligious society" (p. 309).

The final chapter of *A New Religious America* is titled "Bridge-Building: A New Multireligious America." Eck writes, "Many stories of vandalism and violence, like the ones we told in the last chapter, have a sequel: the story of new beginnings and new bridges of understanding and cooperation built across the lines of religious difference" (p. 340). The book ends on a note of hope, with stories of neighbors cooperating and

supporting each other in projects such as Peace Terrace in Fremont, California, where a Methodist church and an Islamic society built a new church and a new mosque side by side. She asserts that it is the task of the religious pluralist to bring these stories of cooperation to the attention of the public.

Narratives of her travels in the new religious America continue with journeys to observe interfaith dialogue around the United States. A surprising example is at America's largest shopping mall, the Mall of America in Minneapolis, Minnesota, which has an interfaith council of its own. The Mall Area Religious Council (MARC), she writes, "wants to capitalize on the magnetic power of the mall. It says it hopes to provide a spiritual presence in the mall, to embody the values of understanding, community, dignity, respect, and peace, and to provide opportunities for interfaith dialogue, study, and conversation between people of differing cultures and traditions" (p. 374).

In this book Eck was prophetic about the new interfaith and multifaith environment in America. "America's religious diversity is here to stay," she asserts. "The very principles on which America was founded will be tested for their strength and vision in the new religious America" (p. 383). Those principles are "the twin principles of religious freedom and nonestablishment [of a state religion]," which, Eck proclaims, "provide the guidelines for something far more valuable than a Christian or Judeo-Christian nation. They provide the guidelines for a multireligious nation, the likes of which the world has rarely seen. The presence of new neighbors of other faiths in America has made crystal clear both the strength of these twin principles and the need to reaffirm them again and again" (p. 384).

Eck challenges her reader to imagine a new, multireligious nation. The image of America now includes mosques and temples and new immigrants. She concludes, "Whether the vibrant new religious diversity that is now part and parcel of the United States will, in the years ahead, bring us together or tear us apart depends greatly on whether we are able to imagine our national community anew" (p. 385).

DIANA L. ECK

THE VOICES OF WOMEN

In *Encountering God*, Eck writes about hearing the voices of interfaith dialogue in her work and travels:

> For me this task is doubly complex because I hear not only the voices of Hindu or Buddhist friends and teachers as I write, but also the voices of women within my own tradition who have never been given much narrative space. . . . Our voices have been suppressed in the texts and in the leadership of most of the world's religious traditions.
>
> (p. 17)

Eck has done her part in her scholarly work not only to listen to the voices of the women who are reshaping religious traditions but to make them heard. *Speaking of Faith: Global Perspectives on Women, Religion, and Social Change*, her third book, edited with Devaki Jain, was published in New Delhi in 1985. Such scholarly papers as "Women and Anger: The Power of Prophecy and Revolution," "Liberty, Equality, 'Fraternity'—Women in the Light of Changing Religious Consciousness," and "Religious Revolution in Our Time: A Woman's Perspective," published in the winter 1989 bulletin of the International Council of Christians and Jews, have brought women's voices to the conference table. She has aired women's voices in her work with the World Council of Churches as well, in such papers as her moderator's report for the WCC, "Working Group on Dialogue:"Women and Interfaith Dialogue—The Experience of the Toronto Consultation" (published in *Current Dialogue* 16 [August 1989]).

Eck has also made the voices of women heard in her lived experience. She and her partner, Dorothy A. Austin, an Episcopal priest, met as graduate students at Harvard in 1976. In the fall of 1998, Eck and Austin became the first same-sex couple to be masters of Lowell House, one of the twelve undergraduate residences at Harvard. In 1999 Eck and Austin became foster parents to four refugee ethnic Albanian teenagers from Kosovo, who lived with them in the master's residence at Lowell House. Amidst the international diversity of a Harvard residence, becoming housemasters gave them "the opportunity to help create a pluralist community in a living context" (*New Religious America*, p. 16). Eck and Austin were married in Harvard's Memorial Church, where Austin was associate minister, on July 4, 2004, weeks after same-sex marriage became legal in Massachusetts.

Diana Eck received the Melcher Lifetime Achievement Award from the Unitarian Universalist Association in 2003. In 2006 she served as president of the American Academy of Religion.

INDIA: A SACRED GEOGRAPHY

Diana Eck is an intrepid traveler, not an armchair scholar. Her early work in Banaras forged a new path in religious studies, a path of extensive fieldwork on the ground. In *India: A Sacred Geography* (2012), she writes:

> The long train trips, the midnight crowds on station platforms and in waiting rooms, the bumpy bus trips standing up, the terrifying road trips up and down mountainsides stitched with hairpin turns, and the blessed time on foot, on the trail—this was my life in India for more than a decade of research on this project.
>
> (p. 457)

Her research in India for this book, begun in the 1980s, she explains, was interrupted by life, illness, and death, and the decision to turn to the more theological *Encountering God*, as well as the politics of Hindu nationalism, a "confrontational Hindu extremism that steamed on through the 1990s" (*India*, p. 459). The global movements of history, the immigration to the United States of so many South Asians, the launch of the Pluralism Project, the CD-ROM *On Common Ground: World Religions in America*, and her book *A New Religious America* also intervened with work on *India: A Sacred Geography*. Eck returned frequently to India through all these years. This volume is a magnum opus, the culmination of decades of research and travel and experience. "During these subsequent years," she writes, "I have traveled many thousands of miles on the pilgrim tracks of this wider sacred geography, trying to understand from the ground up the ways in which India has been composed through the centuries as a sacred landscape" (p. 4).

She has journeyed a long way since she wrote her thesis on Banaras in the 1970s. Her early studies focused on unique pilgrimage sites. She embraces the interconnectedness of India's sacred sites. She began with the study of Banaras from the Hindu point of view, then pondered the meaning of the Hindu worldview for herself as a Christian, then moved to a consideration of the interconnectedness of all the world's religions, especially in America, and in her 2012 book brings all of her experience to bear in a masterwork on the interconnectedness of the landscape of pilgrimage in India.

India's sacred landscape does not emphasize uniqueness: for example, the place where Lord Shiva's light (or *linga*) first pierced the earth is said to be in Banaras. But it is also said to be in at least twelve other places of pilgrimage. To the Hindu worldview, there is no contradiction in such duplication. The sacred is too vast to be constrained by geography. As she describes networks of sacred cities and rivers, Eck emphasizes the multiplicity of India:

> The pilgrim's India is a vividly imagined landscape that has been created not by homing in on the singular importance of one place, but by the linking, duplication, and multiplication of places so as to constitute an entire world. The critical rule of thumb is this: Those things that are deeply important are to be widely repeated. The repetition of places . . . constitutes a vivid symbolic landscape characterized not by exclusivity and uniqueness, but by polycentricity, pluralism, and duplication.
>
> (p. 5)

Eck links the great rivers, mountains, and places of India to the myths of gods and heroes in an intricately related landscape of stories and pilgrimage sites. Each place and each story is part of a complex and cumulative landscape that endows the whole with layers of meaning and connection. She links past and present as well:

> For at least two thousand years, pilgrimage to the *tirthas* [spiritual crossing places] has been one of the most widespread of the many streams of religious practice that have come to be called "Hindu." The modern world has not seen the waning of pilgrimage traditions but has made transportation more readily available for a burgeoning pilgrim traffic.
>
> (p. 10)

What is India? Eck asks, as she maps a widely diverse society, sometimes shattered by conflict, with an underlying "practical everyday pluralism" (p. 44) that makes it function. She theorizes that it is the network of pilgrimage, not the modern notion of a nation-state, that unites and defines India:

> Many of India's great places of pilgrimage have a transregional magnetism, and the circulation of pilgrims to these *tirthas* creates a broader arc of experience for people all over India. . . . In the far north on the trail to Kedarnath or on the beach of Rameshvara in the south, pilgrims will find themselves in multilingual crowds with fellow pilgrims from many parts of India.
>
> (p. 15)

Eck enters the realm of spiritual travel writing when she speaks of a sacred geography. The methodology of mapping goes beyond an exploration of place as she explains, "The imagined landscape bears imprints of meaning: the self-manifest eruptions of the gods, the footprints of the heroes, the divine origins of the rivers, the body of the Goddess. In this mental map, geography is overlaid with layer upon layer of story and connected in a storied landscape" (p. 17).

In *India: A Sacred Geography*, Eck develops the gracious concept of "myth on earth." She posits: "The extent to which mythology and topography overlap or diverge in the shaping of an imagined landscape is a critically important question for students of religion, culture, and politics today" (p. 40).

As in *Banaras*, Eck's approach is to explain India from a distinctly Indian idiom, the India of myths and stories, rather than a Western geopolitical understanding of the great peninsula. The book is packed with information. Page after page, in great detail, she links traditional stories, Hindu scripture, places, gods and goddesses, her own pilgrimage, and the pilgrimage of India's people to the whole of interconnected India, emphasizing the significance of pilgrimage and its economic, social, and cultural implications.

Eck connects some of India's twenty-first century tensions as part of the narrative of sacred geography. She confronts the rise of new strains of Hindu nationalism since the 1990s, the tensions between Hindu and Muslim that have

erupted at contested temple sites. The "narrative of temple looting and destruction, followed by rebuilding and resistance, followed by looting and destruction once again" (p. 222) goes back at least a thousand years. Today it is represented by polarization and sporadic violence leading, for example, to a security gateway of metal detectors at the great Shiva temple of Somnath. But from the pilgrim's standpoint, she points out, the pilgrimage circuit that incorporates Somnath "is not all infused with the narrative of destruction and resurrection that informs Hindu nationalist discourse" (p. 226).

She devotes several pages to the politicization of the disputed temple site at Ayodhya, where a mosque was destroyed amid bloody mayhem on December 6, 1992. "As we conclude our study of the landscape of Hindu India, with its many networks of tīrthas, we recognize just how volatile and powerful the links to sacred places can be and how readily they can be deployed in a context far removed from the practices and patterns of pilgrimage that have been in place for centuries" (p. 436).

The final chapter is titled "A Pilgrim's India Today." The flow of pilgrimage traffic in India continues to grow exponentially. Eck makes the distinction between tourism, seeing the sights, and pilgrimage, beholding a sacred image or sacred place. "How does all this pilgrimage traffic relate to the concerns for the environment?" she asks (p. 444). She confronts the pollution of India's sacred rivers as a dissonant discourse among religious leaders, environmental activists, and political activists. For the faithful, by definition a sacred river cannot be impure. Is it human and industrial waste that pollutes the rivers or is it the spiritual and political corruption of the age? How can these discourses be bridged? These questions and connections are what make *India: A Sacred Geography* far more than a guide to the connections between mythology and place, the network of sacred sites of gods and heroes, but a commentary on the complex culture and geopolitics of India.

MAPPING RELIGIOUS GEOGRAPHY

How has Eck been able to catalog and analyze such a sheer volume of detail, from her work on Banaras early in her academic career to her comprehensive survey of India's sacred geography thirty years later? She writes in *India: A Sacred Geography*, "I gradually learned to inspect the trees and view the forest at the same time" (p. 447).

In India, landscape is composed by the footsteps of pilgrims. Eck comments, "The landscape interlaced with their footsteps is part and parcel of the cumulative knowledge passed on as culture. It is cultural knowledge embedded in the day-to-day life of society. And culture, of course, is always in the making, always being composed once again, in a new context, with each new journey" (p. 451). Culture is always in the making in the new religious America as well. It seems natural and inevitable that Eck would set about mapping religious sites in America, even while she continued her long labor of mapping the religious sites of India.

In his review of *Banaras* in 1984, Paul Younger, professor of religion at McMaster University, labeled Eck's academic field "religious geography," an original field that she created. Philip Dare of Lexington Theological Seminary, reviewing *Encountering God* in 1994, found the book unlike any other he had read in its message to Christians to abandon tribalism and embrace pluralism, while Bardwell Smith, writing in *Anglican Theological Review*, calls her perspective "rare" and "original." Ten years later, Randall Balmer, reviewing *A New Religious America*, described Eck's work as "tireless." Indeed, Eck is energetic in her personal style and in traveling thousands of miles in her dedication to mapping religious diversity on the ground in India and America.

Eck writes in *India: A Sacred Geography*, "As we think about the significance of this pilgrim's landscape, there is an important theological perspective that emerges" (p. 451). She continues, "The particularity of the sacred, the differentiation of the multitude of places in which sacred presence is apprehended, and yet the affirmation of the everywhere of the sacred—this is the particular genius of the theology given expression in the landscape of India" (p. 453).

Religious pluralism is about the differentiation of a multitude of religious expression and the "affirmation of the everywhere of the sacred."

India's multireligious culture is far more ancient than America's, and certainly it is not without its tensions. But if in America we could grasp the simultaneity of here and everywhere, one and many, if this might become part of the cultural knowledge embedded in day-to-day life, we might be closer to imagining a new, multireligious America.

Eck's extensive work of mapping in India is a major contribution to scholarship in the field of Indian studies. Her work of mapping in America is a major contribution to scholarship in the study of the new religious America. Her work on religious pluralism connects the multiplicity in Indian culture with the new religious reality in America. Her work as a pioneer of interfaith dialogue is perhaps her greatest achievement.

In her later works, from *Encountering God* to *India: A Sacred Geography*, Eck is both researcher and prophetic activist, concluding each book with a call to action. In each case, the material is considered from viewpoints of past, present, and future as well as multiple religious viewpoints. Her ability to hold many viewpoints at the same time is a lesson from her early work in India, applied to a lifetime of scholarship. Her tirelessness and energy as a traveler and researcher and her articulate voice for religious pluralism provide an intellectual framework for practical interfaith work on the ground in the twenty-first century.

Selected Bibliography

WORKS OF DIANA L. ECK

Darśan: Seeing the Divine Image in India. Chambersburg, Pa.: Anima Books, 1981; 2nd ed., rev. and enl., 1985.

Banaras: City of Light. New York: Knopf, 1982.

Speaking of Faith: Global Perspectives on Women, Religion, and Social Change. Edited with Devaki Jain. New Delhi: Kali for Women, 1985. Reprint, Philadelphia: New Society, 1987.

Encountering God: A Spiritual Journey from Bozeman to Banaras. Boston: Beacon Press, 1993. Rev. 10th anniversary ed., with a new introduction by the author, Boston: Beacon Press, 2003.

A New Religious America: How a "Christian Country" Has Become the World's Most Religiously Diverse Nation. San Francisco: HarperSanFrancisco, 2001.

India: A Sacred Geography. New York: Harmony Books, 2012.

REVIEWS

Balmer, Randall Herbert. Review of *A New Religious America. Theology Today* 60, no. 2:248–249 (July 2003).

Dare, Philip N. Review of *Encountering God. Lexington Theological Quarterly* 29, no. 4:267–269 (winter 1994).

Haberman, David L. *Review of India: A Sacred Geography. Journal of the American Academy of Religion* 81, no. 1:278–281 (March 2014).

Prothero, Stephen R. "On Common Ground: World Religions in America." *Church History* 68, no. 3:742–732 (September 1999).

Smith, Bardwell L. "Encountering God: A Spiritual Journey from Bozeman to Banaras." *Anglican Theological Review* 77, no. 2:259–261 (Spring 1995).

Younger, Paul. "*Banaras: City of Light.*" *Journal of the American Academy of Religion* 52, no. 2:407–408 (June 1984).

INTERVIEWS

Pitney, Nico. "Her Modern Family: Four Moms, Four Refugee Kids, and Plenty More: Some Life Lessons from Harvard Professor Diana Eck." *Huffington Post*, August 27, 2016. http://www.huffingtonpost.com/entry/diana-eck-interview_us_57bf669de4b04193420e6e65#comments

MICHAEL GOLD

(1893—1967)

Patrick Chura

As NOVELIST, ESSAYIST, dramatist, poet, journalist, and editor, Michael Gold was the leading advocate of leftist, "proletarian" literature in the United States between the world wars. His acclaimed autobiographical novel of 1930, *Jews Without Money*, is a vivid and historically important account of early-twentieth-century Jewish immigrant life in the tenements of Manhattan's Lower East Side. *Jews Without Money* earned admiring reviews and reached a wide audience, going through eleven printings in 1930 alone. In that year, Sinclair Lewis mentioned the novel in his Nobel Prize acceptance speech, crediting Gold with revealing "the new frontier of the Jewish East Side."

During the 1930s Michael Gold became a national figure—the most famous Communist writer in America—as editor of the radical journal *New Masses* and columnist for the American Communist Party's *Daily Worker*. In a decade when many American artists explored working-class life and took Marxist-influenced positions, Gold was the acknowledged dean of proletarian writers, with a roster of professional allies that included Ernest Hemingway, Theodore Dreiser, Eugene O'Neill, Langston Hughes, Dorothy Day, and Upton Sinclair. Ironically Gold's notoriety as literary spokesman and aggressive crusader for working-class culture embroiled him in Depression-era public controversies that added to his celebrity but inhibited his productivity as a writer, making him "as much an accomplished character as an accomplished author" (Folsom, "The Education of Mike Gold," p. 222).

While the context of the "red decade" elevated Michael Gold, a second historical factor—the end of the Great Depression and the onset of World War II—had the opposite effect,

marginalizing him as a cultural figure and further destabilizing his writing career. After the Moscow Trials of 1936–1938 and the German-Soviet Non-Aggression Pact of 1939, many leftist writers and critics began to repudiate their Communist ties, and Gold became by default a "critical hatchet man," the unofficial gatekeeper of the American Communist Party's rigid artistic standards. This role forced him to denounce all but a narrow range of modernist literary works and put him at odds with scores of writers who had once been his friends. Its consequences were apparent in *The Hollow Men*, a collection of *Daily Worker* columns Gold expanded for publication in 1941. Intended to admonish artists who had renounced the Party in the wake of the Hitler-Stalin pact, the inflammatory book in effect damaged Gold, permanently ending many of his relationships with major literary figures of his generation.

When the anti-Left persecutions of McCarthyism took hold of the United States in 1950, Gold was living in France. But he returned to the United States in time to face the worst of the McCarthy hysteria. With the Communist Party under relentless attack, his newspaper work evaporated. Living on the brink of poverty, he took on menial jobs to support his family. An unsuccessful national speaking tour in 1954 made it clear that he had lost his audience and all but a few adherents, though he was now followed closely by the FBI. Through the 1950s Gold kept up correspondence with fellow dissidents Pete Seeger, W. E. B. Dubois, and the longtime radical Elizabeth Gurley Flynn, but the movement he had once led was in disarray and he was clearly outstripped by the disasters of a reactionary time. Though Michael Gold had been "among the cultural luminaries of his generation" (Wald, p. 55), by midcentury he was an outcast, his life's

work, and his politics, generally disregarded or disparaged.

This was the situation in 1966, when Michael Brewster Folsom, then a graduate student at the University of California, Berkeley, initiated a new and still significant conversation about Gold's importance to American literary history. Folsom, reviewing for the *Nation* a mistake-plagued reprint edition of Gold's only novel, declared that "no literary achievement of the 1930s has suffered more from the obscurity and calumny which a frightened generation has heaped on that decade than Michael Gold's *Jews Without Money*" (Folsom, "The Book of Poverty," p. 242). Folsom alleged that the novel had not been forgotten but "erased," and for a single, telling reason: its author remained a Communist (and a public figure) long after that ceased to be fashionable. Bolstering this claim was the edition Folsom was reviewing, which, like a previous reprint in the McCarthy period, had omitted the novel's final paragraphs, the passage that describes the main character's conversion to socialism and constitutes the book's central argument. In Folsom's view, the textual corruption produced the direct opposite of Gold's intention, and did so in a way that symbolized the participation of the literary establishment in "the expurgation of radical opinion from American political life" (p. 242). The remedy Folsom proposed was not only to restore Gold's text and recognize the novel as a powerful work of art but to canonize it: "*Jews Without Money* belongs in an undergraduate course in 20th-century American literature, for it is a work of literary art with an imagination and style of its own" (p. 244).

Until Folsom died in 1990, he did more than anyone else to counteract and repair Mike Gold's elimination from twentieth-century literary history, publishing a Gold anthology along with increasingly detailed critical articles. He also did substantial work on a full-scale biography, becoming Gold's personal friend and recording long interviews with him in the 1960s. That biography was never completed. In 1979 John Pyros self-published a short critical biography, brave in its promotion of Gold, that is far from definitive but remains a valuable resource.

Though there has been a resurgence of academic interest in *Jews Without Money* since the end of the Cold War, with more than thirty journal articles and book chapters published on various aspects of the novel since 1990, other phases of Gold's career await in-depth treatment, and one can still find signs that old animosities linger. Alfred Kazin's 1996 introduction to the 1996 Carrol & Graf edition of *Jews Without Money* insulted the author, calling Gold "a monumentally injured soul but clearly not very bright" (p. 4). In this Kazin echoed Paul Berman's 1983 account of Gold's life in the *Village Voice*, which felt it necessary to remind readers in its first paragraph that Gold "was no genius" (p. 39). In the first decades of the twenty-first century the leading Gold scholar was Alan Wald, who had high regard for Gold's accomplishments. Wald published an authoritative critical-biographical chapter, "Inventing Mike Gold," in his 2002 study, *Exiles from a Future Time*. The fact that as of 2017 no definitive biography of Gold had yet been published justifies Wald's claim that his influence and reputation had yet to be fully assessed.

EARLY LIFE AND RADICALISM

Gold was born Itzok Isaac Granich in New York on April 12, 1893, the first surviving child of Eastern European Jewish immigrants. As a young man he used the Americanized first names Irving and Irwin, then in his late twenties, as a response to persecutions of American leftists by the U.S. Department of Justice, he adopted the name Michael Gold, the protective pseudonym he kept for the rest of his life. Gold's father, Chaim (Americanized to Charles) Granich, immigrated to the United States from Iaşi, Romania, in 1885. He was an erratic breadwinner but a charismatic storyteller, a lover of Yiddish theater and classic drama who inculcated literary values in his sons. Gold's mother, Gittel (Kate) Schwartz, came to the United States from Budapest, Hungary, in 1886. The couple met and married in New York. Their first child, a girl, was born in the late 1880s but died of natural causes several years before Mike was born. Gold's two younger brothers,

George and Emmanuel (Manny), were born in 1895 and 1898.

For a time in Gold's childhood, Charles Granich ran a small storefront business making and selling suspender fasteners. When that failed, an unknown illness damaged his health, keeping him from other laboring jobs and eventually making him bedridden. Growing up in the slums, Gold, a talented student, was forced to quit school at age twelve to help support his family, working at a gas mantle factory and later at a series of menial jobs. In his teenage years Gold was traumatized by his father's physical decline and increasingly depressive, sometimes suicidal states. The death of Charles Granich when Gold was only eighteen was a devastating shock that stayed with him for the rest of his life.

At age twenty-one Gold became involved in the labor movement when, after being laid off as a factory worker and shipping clerk, he wandered into a protest rally in New York's Union Square, heard passionate anticapitalist speeches, and witnessed an authoritarian crackdown on the right to free assembly. The crowd was attacked by police, and Gold was beaten with other demonstrators as he attempted to help an injured woman. For years Gold had been writing autobiographical poetry and sketches without an intended audience, but soon after this event he bought his first copy of the radical journal *Masses* and began submitting politically charged poetry to editors Floyd Dell and Max Eastman, literary mentors who boosted Gold's confidence and encouraged his work on the sketches and anecdotes about slum life that would later appear in *Jews Without Money*.

There is still some uncertainty about whose oratory inspired Gold's conversion to socialism on that pivotal day in 1914. In interviews Gold gave in the 1930s, he claimed that the Union Square speaker was Elizabeth Gurley Flynn, the fiery Communist-feminist "rebel girl" who had risen to prominence in strikes led by the Industrial Workers of the World (IWW). But separate studies by Folsom and Wald give credence to Gold's original claim that the speaker was Emma Goldman, whose anarchist views later become anathema to the Depression-era Communist Party. In

either case, the speaker's words may not have been the most crucial factor in Gold's political awakening. Recalling the incident in 1932, Gold stated, "I have always been grateful to that cop and that club. For one thing, he introduced me to literature and the revolution" ("Why I Am a Communist," p. 203).

Gold's first published poem, "Three Whose Hatred Killed Them," appeared in the *Masses* in August 1914 and marked the beginning of the author's long association with the journal, first as Irwin Granich and later as Mike Gold. The poem espouses violence in the cause of radical labor by extolling three anarchists accidentally killed in a New York tenement by a bomb they had made themselves for use against enemies of the working class. The "iron hatred" of the anarchists had "burst too soon," the poet acknowledges, but Gold cautions his comrades to "Judge them not harshly." In reminding his audience that "They hated, but it was the enemy of man they hated," Gold refers to the probable intended target of the bomb, John D. Rockefeller, who had used hired militia to crush a strike in his Colorado coal mines by setting fire to strikers' tents, killing thirteen women and children, in the horrific Ludlow Massacre of April 20, 1914. The poem documents a tragic setback to the revolutionary cause, but like much of Gold's later verse, it eventually finds hope, treating the accidental deaths of the "Undisciplined warriors" in New York as a precursor to renewed ardor. For the remainder of his long career, Gold's enduring optimism about a worker-led future conformed neatly to Communist Party artistic standards but displeased critics who saw his revolutionary prophecies as unconvincing and formulaic.

Gold's multiple pursuits in New York and Boston during his early twenties managed to combine radical politics with conventionally ambitious self-improvement. Seeking the economic security he had never known while growing up, Gold enrolled in night-school classes, worked as a cub reporter for the New York *Globe*, and turned these experiences into a year of study at New York University's journalism school. He also took on stringer assignments for several New York suburban newspapers and briefly managed

a printing plant (Wald, p. 49). These exploits won Gold permission to attend Harvard University as a "special," or provisional, student in 1914. While at Harvard he took a course from renowned drama professor George Pierce Baker and probably became acquainted with Eugene O'Neill, who was also studying with Baker at that time (Brogna, p. 19). Gold also wrote a daily newspaper column for the *Boston Journal*, "A Freshman at Harvard," in which he shared lively observations from the perspective of an unsophisticated outsider.

The Harvard adventure ended abruptly after just one semester when Gold suffered a severe nervous breakdown. Overwork, inadequate food, a romantic setback, and a probable delayed reaction to his father's death were immediate factors, but the crash almost certainly had to do as well with Gold's attempt to move in unfamiliar territory where cultural and class background were concerned. A short story published in the *New Masses* more than a decade later, "Love on a Garbage Dump," seems to be an intense and complex reaction to the failure of Gold's remarkable attempt at elite education. The story opens with a fictional rejection of Harvard that Folsom interprets as a self-defining moment: "Certain enemies have spread the slander that I once attended Harvard college. This is a lie. I worked on the garbage dump in Boston, city of Harvard. But that's all ("Love," p. 177).

Critics from the Depression era to the Cold War cited this passage to charge Gold with an anti-intellectualism that made it easier to disparage his work and outlook. What it actually expressed was its author's status as a rebellious outsider who harbored legitimate hostility toward an American educational system that destroyed rather than nurtured the creative intellect of those in the laboring class: "Well balanced intellectuals among the workers become revolutionists. The others become freaks and madmen" ("Love," p. 176).

After leaving Cambridge, Gold moved to Boston, roomed in an anarchist boardinghouse, dressed as a pauper, joined the IWW, and became newly active in strikes, labor reform, and the liberalization of birth control. While sending regular contributions to the Socialist *New York Call*, Gold convinced his wealthy friend Van Kleek Allison to found and coedit the *Flame*, a short-lived anarchist "journal of revolution," whose purpose, as stated in its August 1916 masthead, was "to burn against oppression and authority love everywhere." In early 1917 Theodore Dreiser, seeking material for a play about life in the tenements, asked Gold to show him the life and conditions of the Lower East Side. Gold obliged by escorting the famous author to Chrystie Street and showing him the apartment he still shared with his mother.

During this period Gold had accepted an assignment from the anarchist newspaper *Blast* to report on a strike at the Plymouth cordage factory, where he met Bartolomeo Vanzetti and produced his first journalism about the labor movement. Upton Sinclair later wrote sympathetically about Gold in this period. In his 1928 novel *Boston*, a detailed account of the infamous " Sacco and Vanzetti case," Sinclair imagines the young reporter as "a Jewish lad out of the slums of New York" who came to Plymouth as both a witness and participant, attending radical meetings with a "band of rebels" who were determined to fight on the side of the strikers (p. 77). A decade later Gold was arrested along with John Dos Passos, Katherine Anne Porter, and other literary activists during protest demonstrations for Nicola Sacco and Bartolomeo Vanzetti when the case culminated in the execution of the two anarchists.

PROVINCETOWN PLAYWRIGHT

Sinclair's description of Gold in the same chapter of *Boston* as a "proletarian playwright, a very scarce article" (p. 79), refers accurately to a contiguous and underappreciated phase of his versatile career. In 1916–1917 Gold not only began drafting the sketches that would later become *Jews Without Money*, he found further creative outlet as a member of the Provincetown Players, eventually contributing three one-act plays that were produced alongside works by major modernist playwrights including Eugene O'Neill and Susan Glaspell at the Players' theater in Greenwich Village. The Players staged Gold's *Ivan's Homecoming* alongside O'Neill's *The*

Sniper in February 1917, and in December of the same year Gold's *Down the Airshaft* was presented on a bill with works by Glaspell and Floyd Dell.

No copies have been found of these early plays, but late in his life Gold remembered *Ivan's Homecoming* as an antiwar drama in which the ghost of a Russian peasant killed in battle returns to beg that his death be "avenged on the heads of the war makers" (Roessel, p. 236). In *Down the Airshaft*, Gold drew from his Lower East Side childhood to tell the story of Sammy Cohen, a boy inwardly torn by a need to earn money for his destitute family and a longing for beauty in the form of flute music heard in a tenement airshaft (Roessel, p. 237). O'Neill, who enthusiastically supported Gold's dramatic writing through the 1920s, praised *Down the Airshaft* for its sensitive, genuine portrayal of slum conditions.

A third Provincetown play, *Money*, was performed on a bill with works by Edna Ferber and Djuna Barnes in January 1920 and was published nine years later in *One-Act Plays*, an anthology of short drama intended for use in secondary schools. The simple plot involves a group of immigrant Jewish men living in a crowded, "gloomy East Side cellar" (p. 205) that resembles the basement shop on Chrystie Street where Gold's family struggled to survive during his childhood. Moisha, a cobbler, has lost his savings of $112, a sum he had intended to use to bring his wife and children from Poland. Tormented by this life-and-death calamity, Moisha is unable to sleep for several nights. His obsessive searching awakens the other boarders and turns inevitably to interrogation when he concludes that the savings must have been stolen and that one of his roommates is guilty. Finally, Yonkel, a peddler, cannot endure the pressure; he confesses to the crime and apologizes. The stunned workers are left to consider and debate differences between rich and poor, the Old World and the New, and how the "disease of money" (p. 227) corrupts even fellow Jews with essentially kind hearts. A key moment comes when a policeman appears, summoned by the loud argument, and Moisha chooses not to report Yonkel's crime. The eldest of the boarders, Abram, offers the double-edged excuse that the men had not been

fighting but only talking about money. The policeman departs, greatly amused at the confirmation of the anti-Jewish stereotype. As the play closes, Mendel, the youngest character, tells of a speaker he had once heard, a man standing on an East Side street corner "saying that one day there would be no money, no rich and poor, only everyone working together like brothers and sisters" (p. 229).

It is interesting that this play, which was written in 1920 but did not see publication until 1929, rehearses an ending that has become closely identified with Gold's life, art, and politics. The East Side street-corner speaker vaguely resembles the revolutionary speaker that had electrified Gold in 1914 and is strikingly similar to the speaker described in 1930 in the final chapter of *Jews Without Money*, a work that was soon to receive national attention and make Gold a major cultural figure of the Depression era. With slight reworking, *Money* could be inserted seamlessly into the series of ghetto sketches that make up Gold's loosely plotted autobiographical novel. The correspondence between the early play and the famous novel underscores the long gestation of Gold's only major book and its roots in experiences that were fictionally refined over a long period but found a receptive audience after the stock market crash of October 1929. Thomas R. Cook, one of the editors who had found and selected *Money* for its 1929 publication, wrote prophetically of Gold's one-act as a "typically American" play that "succeeded in throwing light on one of our most complex sociological problems" (*Money*, p. xvi).

David Roessel's research into Gold's affiliation with the Provincetown Players focuses on aesthetic similarities and differences between Gold and O'Neill. Roessel argues that while both playwrights participated in a broad movement to dramatize class-based realities, O'Neill disagreed with Gold's overtly political emphasis and consistently advised his friend to eschew propaganda in favor of simple realism, which in O'Neill's view was more politically effective. O'Neill nevertheless believed that if Gold could break away from the financial necessities of magazine editing and journalism, he would be a major dramatist. In 1925 he wrote to the producer Kenneth McGowan, urging him to offer the Com-

munist playwright a contract and adding, "This Gold, as I've told you before, has the stuff!" (qtd. in Roessel, p. 243). In hindsight, Gold's association with the Provincetown experimental theater was natural; the Provincetown group actively sought worker-artists who could authentically express the lives of the downtrodden and bring class war to the stage.

Deeper consideration of the Gold-O'Neill artistic friendship offers evidence that it also had much to do with the life experience they shared as the sons of theater-loving immigrant fathers and that Gold may have influenced O'Neill, prompting him to explore the possibilities of ethnic theater. Along with his knowledge of ghetto life, Gold brought to the Provincetown Players a sampling of methods he had learned as a boy from attending (and sometimes acting in) the Lower Manhattan Yiddish theater, a drama milieu that was viewed by many critics as artistically superior to Broadway. Like the turn-of-the-century Yiddish drama that Gold knew, O'Neill's early plays experimented with a wide range of styles. As in works by Mike Gold and many Yiddish dramatists, O'Neill's characters often came from social classes that had not previously appeared on stage. Gold's sustained interest in writing plays about marginalized groups—not only Jews but African Americans, Irish, and Mexican peons—parallels O'Neill's strong interest in black American life and working-class reality during the same period. O'Neill's sense of belonging to a victimized minority, the Irish, was undoubtedly an important factor that mirrored Gold's sense of otherness as an American Jew. If, as Nahma Sandrow maintains, O'Neill was the modernist playwright whose work had "most in common" (p. 201) with New York Yiddish drama, it may have been because Gold served as a conduit for influence and cross-ethnic collaboration.

MEXICO AND THE LIBERATOR

With American entry into World War I, Gold moved to Mexico to avoid the draft. While living there for more than a year (early 1918 to 1920), he learned fluent Spanish and immersed himself in a peasant culture involved in its own form of class conflict. He labored in the fields alongside Mexican peons near Tampico but also did translation work for newspapers and canvased the streets of Mexico City to raise funds to publish a Spanish-language version of the Soviet constitution (Wald, p. 51).

A short story based this experience, "Two Mexicos," dissects the contradictory political views of the country's elite landowning classes and draws analogies between the rural Mexican laborers and those equally exploited in the ghettos of urban America. The contrast between brothers, Don Felipe and the younger Enrique, is the contrast between feudalism and an egalitarian future. The elder brother, who abuses the landless peons, seeing them as subhuman and enforcing submission through violence, is the incarnation of "brutal, primitive aristocracy" (p. 54). He rapes and lynches, but claims to value pride and personal valor while bemoaning the Mexican Revolution that has afforded a minimum of rights to the "slaves" on his ranch. Enrique is a Marxist revolutionary who treats the peasant workers "almost as equals" and has plans to transfer his land to them. While the story's diction emphasizes obvious parallels between systemic worker exploitation in Mexico and that in the United States, the story does not resolve the conflict between good and evil simplistically. The warring brothers stand "facing each other in the vast, silent moonlight," but the only outcome is implied in the narrator's expectation that there will be "no peace till the younger [brother] shall have forever slain the elder" (p. 61).

Published in the *Liberator* in 1920, this story was later turned into a full-length drama, "Fiesta," which saw production with the newly commercialized Provincetown Players in 1929 and drew praise from *New York Times* critic Brooks Atkinson, who called Gold "a genuine playwright." The reviewer for the *New Republic*, Stark Young, similarly extolled the author's "genuine poetic feeling for types, fresh feeling, contrasts of personality, [and] raw color" (qtd. in Pyros, p. 73). As Wald notes, Gold's sojourn in Mexico was productive, resulting in "a full-length play, a short story, an unfinished novel, and a life-long love of Mexican songs, the spirit of the

Mexican Revolution, and the Spanish language" (p. 51).

Before leaving Mexico, Gold received news of the Palmer Raids, widespread arrests and detentions of radicals and anarchists by the U.S. Department of Justice. This alarming anti-Left atrocity prompted him to change his name permanently, an act that resonated in both actual and symbolic terms. The new pseudonym—Michael Gold—was taken from a person known to him, a Jewish friend of his father who had been a corporal in the Civil War, fighting for the North against the Southern slavocracy. To the extent that the name figuratively united the nineteenth-century war against chattel slavery with the twentieth-century struggle against wage slavery, it points to one of Gold's long-standing passions. If there is one aspect of Gold's career as both editor and writer that deserves renewed attention, it is his lifelong effort to espouse and in some ways embody the aims of disparate races and ethnicities by suggesting shared links between the liberation histories of African Americans and working-class Jewish Americans.

In 1921 Gold was elected to the editorial board of the *Liberator*, the successor journal to the suppressed *Masses* and the namesake of William Lloyd Garrison's famed antislavery newspaper of the antebellum era. In this role, Gold encouraged and published works from the "mass poets" of the working classes to counter what he termed the "ego-poets" of the bourgeoisie. In the February 1921 issue, he published the seminal essay "Towards Proletarian Art," an impassioned manifesto in which he broke with the liberal-individualist aesthetic theory of mentors Dell and Eastman. Citing Walt Whitman as "the heroic spiritual grandfather" (*Mike Gold: A Literary Anthology*, p. 67) of proletarian culture, Gold called for heightened social consciousness in literature and asserted that "a mighty national art cannot arise save out of the soil of the masses" (p. 70). The new art, Gold implied, would express the experience of the poor and without exception be created either by the poor themselves or by artists who had lived sympathetically among them. The American currency of the term "proletarian literature" dates from the publication of this article, which Folsom describes as "a major document in radical literary theory" (p. 62).

In January 1922 Gold became coeditor of the *Liberator* with the black poet Claude McKay, and although their collaboration would last only six months, they published poetry and prose that would help initiate the Harlem Renaissance. While the declarations about working-class literature Gold published in the *Liberator* had immediate impact, it has taken far longer for critics to recognize the significance of what Gold and McKay accomplished through this unusual cross-racial collaboration. Harold Cruse's 1967 study *Crisis of the Negro Intellectual*, for example, alleged that Gold's proletarian and McKay's New Negro writing operated antagonistically at the *Liberator* and accused Gold of being "not sympathetic to McKay's literary work" (p. 49). Cruse depicted the coeditorial relationship as adversarial and saw Gold as an enemy of the black aesthetic who forced the Jamaican-born McKay to prioritize laboring-class cultural standards in opposition to the race-centered artistic criteria of the nascent Harlem Renaissance.

While it seems true that Gold and McKay were in some ways "temperamentally incompatible" (Wald, p. 51), the actual products of their collaboration, according to the research of William Maxwell, bespeak a fruitful concord of goals and priorities. Maxwell's 1996 revisionist consideration of the Gold-McKay relationship, "The Proletarian as New Negro: Mike Gold's Harlem Renaissance," argued that the Jewish Communist and New Negro artist did not represent warring aesthetics but instead reinforced each other in important ways. Both Gold and McKay, for example, saw themselves as proletarian writers and agreed that racism was a threat to the aspirations of all workers.

As Maxwell further pointed out, much of the McKay poetry that later became central to the Harlem Renaissance was published in the *Liberator*, and the issues McKay and Gold edited together featured essays, poetry, and art by both black and white contributors on racial oppression and black culture in the United States and the Caribbean. Under their control, the magazine

showed that the core values of proletarian literature and the Harlem Renaissance were not mutually exclusive but in cooperative alignment. That a Marxist journal with an almost completely white staff was also "one of the small number of magazines in and around which the Harlem Renaissance took shape" (Maxwell, p. 100) is significant. In a general sense, this knowledge challenges the still widely held assumption that proletarian and "New Negro" writing were wholly discreet schools.

Acknowledging Mike Gold's sympathetic responsiveness to black experience also helps to explain a number of his later artistic choices. Gold's 1924 biography of the abolitionist John Brown, for example, has been viewed as a tacit commemoration of his joint editorship with McKay, a book that "situates their collaboration within an old American tradition of interracial revolutionary brotherhood" (Maxwell, p. 100). The first project Gold tackled after McKay left the *Liberator, The Life of John Brown* is a fascinating specimen of radical literature, offering fresh ways of thinking about interracial links and commonalities among historical protest movements. Portraying Brown as "a common man to the end" (*Life*, p. 3), a worker-hero and comrade to both white and black proletarians, Gold implicitly offers himself as an inheritor of the abolitionist's militant spirit.

Throughout the 1920s Gold referred to Brown as his favorite American hero and returned to his story more than a decade later by working with Michael Blankfort to transform *The Life of John Brown* into agitprop drama. *Battle Hymn*, produced during the Federal Theatre Project's initial New York season of 1936, blended socialist realism with elements of expressivist theatricality to relate the abolitionist past to the revolutionary present. One fascinating ensemble scene occurs at the home of the New York abolitionist Gerrit Smith just before the Harpers Ferry raid. Brown reveals his daring plan to Ralph Waldo Emerson, William Lloyd Garrison, Frank Sanborn, and Henry Thoreau, who ends the discussion by remarking that Brown "acts on a higher law than governments" and lives "in a world with God" (*Battle Hymn*, p. 84).

In Morgan Himelstein's critical analysis, *Battle Hymn* clearly indicated that the freeing of Negro slaves by revolutionary violence was a necessary prelude to the emancipation of the white wage slaves of the North. Gold and Blankfort "thus implied that the agitational activity of John Brown was a predecessor of the current work of the Communist Party and that the Civil War was a forerunner of the coming proletarian revolution" (*Drama Was a Weapon*, p. 94). While the sweeping predictions the play made at the height of the Depression went unrealized, Gold's take on Brown was nevertheless prescient. Assessing the antislavery militant as "almost our greatest American" (*Life*, p. 3) was then a decidedly minority view, but it is becoming the consensus among historians.

The 1920s were a productive period for Gold's fiction writing as well. In 1924 the Little Red Library, a pamphlet series underwritten by the Communist Party, published *The Damned Agitator and Other Stories*, a book of short prose that blended autobiographical elements with class-based formulas Gold learned from the *Masses* editors and later refined through exposure to Soviet criticism on a trip to the Soviet Union in 1924–1925. The title story, originally published in the *New York Call* in March 1917 but updated for reprint, is an impressionistic psychological sketch of an immigrant labor leader. The setting replicates details from a labor action in the New England textile industry and thus from the pre–World War I period of labor agitation that culminated in a 1911 textile workers' strike led by notorious IWW leader "Big" Bill Haywood in Lawrence, Massachusetts. But while the Lawrence strike ended successfully, the strike led by Gold's Kurelovitch, "a tall, tragic, rough-hewn Pole" (p. 4), seems likely to fail.

The complexity of Gold's psychological portrait of the "damned agitator" matches the untenable set of problems he faces. The story opens when the strike is seven weeks old, scabs are on the way, and the leader's sense is that the action "might soon be a bitter ash in the mouths of the men" (p. 3). As the "woeful conditions" accumulate, it is not surprising that Kurelovitch is under constant threat from police gunmen or

that he is accused of "pocketing half the strike funds," as Haywood and other labor leaders often were. But Kurelovitch's deeper predicament is that "his own side" includes an embittered, overburdened wife and fellow workers who have lost hope. The story follows the strike leader through a long day of anguish, ending in a state of exhaustion and alcohol-induced oblivion that will only be repeated: "Never . . . would he be permitted to know sweetness or rest" (p. 16).

An expanded, Russian-language version of the *Damned Agitator* collection was published in 1925. The pessimistic stories were generally disliked by Russian critics, but the pamphlet managed to reach an audience several times larger than its American readership. Haywood himself, forcibly exiled and living Moscow at the time, wrote the introduction for this edition. Among Gold's fictional subjects and protagonists— harassed strike leaders, imprisoned Wobblies, and starving coal miners—Haywood surely discerned echoes of his own experience.

A final reworking of "The Damned Agitator," in which Gold changed the nationality of the disgruntled strikers from Russian to French Canadian and softened some elements of the brutal and grotesque, appeared in a collection of short fiction and poetry Gold published in 1929 under the title *120 Million*. Gold's second book of short fiction and poetry showed the author's gradual development as reflected in an aesthetic shift from simple, stark realism to a modernist outlook that was influenced by his Soviet Union visit, during which Gold became interested in futurism and enraptured by the innovations of the Russian directors Vladimir Mayakovsky and Vsevolod Meyerhold.

In addition to "Two Mexicos," an important prose work in this collection is "The American Famine," a slightly fictionalized version of an article Gold write for the *Liberator* in 1921 after spending several days wandering among New York's half-million homeless and unemployed. Impersonating a starving worker, Gold visits the "missions" where charity workers "preach humility to the poor" (p. 62), talks with the men in breadlines, and sleeps in Bowery flophouses. Accounts of persons and conditions in the Bowery YMCA, the reading rooms of public libraries, Union Square, Bryant Park, and the employment bureau in Grand Central Terminal both catalog and interpret the misery of suffering thousands while recording the "unconscious wisdom of the proletariat" (p. 69). The narrative concludes with a comparison between Russian famine, which can be endured because it is temporary rather than systemic or endemic, and American famine, which will continue because for the poor under capitalism there is "no plan . . . no vision" (p. 71). Another story, "Faster, America, Faster," paints American decadence as "a private freight train rushing to Hollywood; violent, profligate, licentious and cruel," blindly advancing toward catastrophe and arrogantly "wasting life" (p. 140). V. F. Calverton's review of *120 Million* in the *Nation* found Gold's fiction crude and violent, but "challenging in its very crudity" (qtd. in Pyros, p. 20).

Appended to the twelve short stories in *120 Million* is a section of "Proletarian Chants and Recitations" along with Gold's assertions that such communal theatrical experiments respond to the "needs of American workers" and are "a valuable weapon for propaganda and solidarity" (p. 170). There are chants about the brutal interrogation of a labor leader, the suicide of a pregnant teenage factory girl, the birthday of a long-suffering agitator who would rather die than desert the labor movement, and a recitation excerpted verbatim from the prison letters of Bartolomeo Vanzetti. The book's title is taken from the final chant. It refers to the numerical U.S. population, the millions who are figuratively cataloged by a proletarian poet on a cross-country journey, a people who worship a "Money God" and make war on each other, "whose heart is a Ford car, / Whose brain is a cheap Hollywood Movie, . . . / Whose victims die of hunger" (pp. 191–192).

120 Million also reprints one of Gold's best poems from the early 1920s, "The Strange Funeral at Braddock," which focuses on three reactions to the horrific death of Jan Clepak, an immigrant worker who had fallen into a vat of molten steel. One observer at the funeral chooses self-destructive despair, another pledges never to

let her children work in a mill, and a third, Clepak's widow, responds imaginatively, vowing to transform the death into revolutionary action: "I'll make myself hard as steel, harder, / I'll come some day and make bullets out of Jan's body / and shoot them into a tyrant's heart." The journalist Art Shields called this elegiac piece "the most tragically beautiful poem that has come out of the United States class struggle" (p. 126). Throughout his career, critics tended to characterize Gold's poetry primarily as overly political and formulaic, little more than a tool for welding the masses into solidarity. More recent critics including Wald, however, have expressed strong interest in Gold's verse, noting that he drew perceptively from Walt Whitman and prefigured the early Beat poets, making him an important nexus between nineteenth- and twentieth-century aesthetic movements.

In 1927, working with John Howard Lawson and Jon Dos Passos, Gold secured financial support from the wealthy financier and art patron Otto Kahn to establish the New Playwrights Theatre. Seizing the chance to bring the theories of Mayakovsky and Meyerhold to New York, Gold immediately composed the full-length play *Hoboken Blues*, an exuberantly constructivist version of Harlem life subtitled *The Black Rip Van Winkle: A Modern Negro Fantasia on an Old American Theme*. The play's black main character, Sam Pickens, a child of the Great Migration who came north when his brother was lynched, finds himself unemployed in Harlem and leaves to seek work in Hoboken, where he achieves success and eventually becomes "president" of the city. He returns twenty-five years later to discover that it had all been a dream, that there "ain't no Hoboken," and sums up the racial and class-based determiners of reality: "folks, why can't there be a place for de poor men, black and white. . . . Where no one is hungry, where no one is lynched, where dere's no money or bosses, and men are brudders?" (p. 626).

As it is written, Gold's play was strikingly groundbreaking in its use of surreal characters, futuristic visual style, expressivist staging, and incorporation of modern jazz-dance into what Gold called "simultaneous planes of action" (p.

548). Moreover, Gold's directive that "No White men appear in this play" and that "where white men are indicated, they are played by Negroes in white caricature masks" (p. 549) surpassed many of the risks taken by Gold's theater contemporaries, even in comparison to the innovations of his friend Eugene O'Neill. According to Maxwell, the play attempted nothing less than "to slip the bonds of whiteness and take part in, not merely comment on, the Harlem Renaissance" (p. 106).

As *Hoboken Blues* was produced, however, it conveyed the opposite of Gold's radical intentions. A portent of trouble came when Gold visited the actor-singer Paul Robeson and personally entreated him to play the main character Pickens. Robeson refused, ostensibly because he saw the play as overly pessimistic (Wald, p. 53). When Gold could not assemble an all-black cast, the production went forward with white actors speaking black dialect, a concession that burdened the play with connotations of a minstrel show despite its enlightened thinking and respectful treatment of black culture. Even in his last years Gold became agitated when discussing the missed opportunity represented by *Hoboken Blues*, believing with good reason that the play deserved better treatment.

In fact, most of the handful of plays produced by the New Playwrights Theatre from 1927 to its demise in 1929 met similarly confused receptions. Among the interesting productions were Lawson's *Loudspeaker*, Upton Sinclair's *Jailbirds* and Dos Passos' *Airways, Inc.*, all of which closed after disappointingly short runs and generally negative reviews. Gold nevertheless believed that the company had succeeded in advancing the cause of a new theater that was radical both artistically and politically. Lawson agreed and unselfishly gave Gold the full credit for conceiving the venture, recalling the New Playwrights Theater as "an enormously significant experiment, the first workers' theatre in the English language in the United States" (p. 12).

NEW MASSES *AND* JEWS WITHOUT MONEY

When the *Liberator* became the de facto official organ of the Communist Party of America in the

mid-1920s and narrowed its political and artistic content accordingly, Gold helped found the *New Masses*, becoming editor in chief in 1928. This position offered an influential platform for statements that inspired a generation of leftists but also enmeshed Gold in a series of highly public disagreements.

The unabashed vehemence of Gold's ideas about proletarian culture fueled a long, at times bitter, debate with his former mentor Floyd Dell. While working under Dell at the *Liberator*, Gold spoke, dressed, and acted in ways that heightened contrasts between Dell's middle-class appearance and background. Years later Joseph Freeman, in his memoir *An American Testament*, described this method of working-class posturing:

> He affected dirty shirts, a big, black, uncleaned Stetson with the brim of a sombrero; smoked stinking, twisted, Italian three-cent cigars, and spat frequently and vigorously on the floor—whether that floor was covered by an expensive carpet in a rich aesthete's studio or was the bare wooden floor of the small office where Gold's desk was littered with disorderly papers. These "proletarian" props were as much a costume as the bohemian's sideburns and opera cape.
>
> (p. 257)

In articles for both the *Liberator* and the *New Masses* in the 1920s, Gold proposed direct contact with workers as an essential ingredient of a new art that would express their lives and struggles.

Dell, however, did not believe that transforming one's self into a worker was desirable or possible; he developed a profound distaste for proletarian "impersonation" and a defensible argument against it. His antipathy was made public in a *Liberator* editorial of June 1922 that took issue with Gold's dressing like a worker, associating with workers, trying to live like a worker and talk like a worker. Though Gold, as Dell claimed, "really cherishes the romantic delusion that he belongs to the working class," he was actually "a literary man, an intellectual" and a member of the "salaried middle class" (p. 25) whose identification with workers was transparent and shallow. Dell glibly dissected the psychology behind Gold's class-based charade: "Comrade Mike," he explained, "is for some obscure

reason ashamed of not being a workingman . . . so he is in awe of the workingman when he meets him and says extravagant things in praise of him" (p. 25).

Dell later acknowledged that he had often mocked the simulation of proletarian identity by radical intellectuals. But his offense against Gold's aesthetic was not without ultimate political consequences, especially as the Sacco and Vanzetti case gained currency and began to reinvigorate the proletarian leanings of radicals and even moderate liberals in 1926–1927.

An important document from this period of internecine conflict is Gold's 1927 *New Masses* article "John Reed and the Real Thing." In this essay Gold describes Reed—the Harvard graduate who rallied striking silk workers in Paterson, New Jersey, by teaching them college fight songs and staging a workers' pageant in Madison Square Garden before going off to Russia to fight for and (and ultimately die for) the ideals of the revolution—in hagiographic terms that explain why the Communist Party later founded "John Reed Club" chapters to support leftist art. Reed was exceptional, Gold claimed, because he helped mitigate the worker's prejudice against middle-class intervention in labor-class life. Through his sincere amalgamation with laborers at Paterson and elsewhere, Reed had identified himself completely with the working class: "there was no gap between John Reed and the workers any longer" (p. 154). Implicitly disparaging Dell, Gold argued that Reed's greatness could never be understood by the "pale rootless intellectuals . . .who lead wasted, futile lives in their meek offices" (p. 152).

The decade of contention between Gold and Dell did not end as benignly as it might have, with Dell's laconic resignation from the list of contributing editors to the *New Masses* in May 1929. Instead, in characteristic fashion, Gold felt the need to aggressively ostracize his onetime mentor in the July number of the journal with an essay that Dell's biographer has called "an unrestricted exercise in character assassination" (Clayton, p. 253). The committed Communist asserted that Dell "had none of the contacts with workingmen and strikes and battles that John

Reed made." He was therefore "at no time . . . a real revolutionist" but instead represented a "Greenwich Village playboy" who had tellingly refused to agitate for Sacco and Vanzetti ("Floyd Dell Resigns," p. 10).

Of course Gold knew that the problem was more complex, originating in a polarizing dialectic between bohemian art and revolutionary action, between individualistic and collective consciousness, between Dell's persona as solipsistic artist and the model of a self-abnegating servant to society all class-conscious radicals tried to embody. But the timing of Dell's casting out was auspicious; the imminent stock market crash and the decade-long Depression that followed would dictate a reunification of the literary Left around a newly empowered version of Gold's ideal.

Two essays from 1930 exemplify Gold's theories and the intense debates they incited. First, "Wilder: Prophet of the Genteel Christ," an excoriating *New Republic* review of several novels by Thornton Wilder, scandalized readers and touched off a nationwide "Gold-Wilder controversy" that played out for several years. Gold's economic interpretation of literature saw Wilder as "the poet of the genteel bourgeoisie," whose "irritating and pretentious" novels lacked contemporary relevance because within them "nobody works in a Ford plant, and nobody starves looking for work" (*Literary Anthology*, pp. 201–202). The *New Republic* editor Edmund Wilson, who had commissioned the review, gave Gold credit for exposing "the insipidity and pointlessness of most literary criticism" and for making it "very plain that the economic crisis [the Great Depression] was to be accompanied by a literary one" (*Literary Anthology*, p. 197).

A second telling article, Gold's September 1930 *New Masses* editorial column (later given the title "Proletarian Realism"), enumerated the essential elements of a "new form" of literary expression: "Proletarian realism deals with the *real conflicts* of men and women who work for a living. It has nothing to do with the sickly mental states of the idle Bohemians, their subtleties, their sentimentalities, their fine-spun affairs." Writers of this genre, Gold insisted, must be workers or

must "have the courage of proletarian experience" (*Literary Anthology*, pp. 206, 207).

Gold's authority for making these declarations was based on his recent publication of a successful work of imaginative literature that he believed met his stated criteria. *Jews Without Money*, Gold's only novel and by consensus his best work of fiction, was described by Alfred Kazin as "a great piercing cry of lament and outrage" (p. 2) over the struggles of the poor. The novel is a loosely narrated series of sketches from the author's childhood featuring a young Mikey Gold, a self-announced "truthful book of poverty" (p. 71) that spares no detail in cataloging slum misery while identifying its cause in the capitalist system: "America is so rich and fat," Gold writes, "because it has eaten the tragedy of millions of immigrants" (p. 112). Aside from its central emphasis on the class war, the work is a perceptive critique of urban America, theorizing racism, sexism, and the costs of assimilation for Jewish immigrants struggling with cultural identity in the United States.

The tone and technique of the novel, which Gold originally titled "Poverty Is a Trap," are illustrated in its raw yet lyrical descriptions of slum life, its graphic violence, and the economically determined insights that follow from both. In one representative passage, Gold describes working-class Jewish mothers who "stopped in the shade of the elevated trains, to suckle their babies with big sweaty breasts" (p. 57) and a Bowery bum in "moldy, wrinkled clothes," whose "rusty yellow face was covered with sores . . . like a corpse in the first week of decomposition" (p. 58). The tenement neighborhoods are for Gold a "world of violence and stone" (p. 53) where prostitutes proliferate and "the rose of syphilis bloomed by night and by day" (p. 15), where immigrant girls are gang-raped and a pedophile who assaults a young boy is "kicked, punched and beat with shovels" (p. 60). Later, the victimized boy is decapitated when he falls under a horsecar, his severed head hanging from the bloody axle. On the cruel streets of the Lower East Side, even stray kittens are abused: "We tortured them, they tortured us. It was poverty," Gold explains (p. 64). The agony culminates when the narrator's

six-year-old sister, Esther, is run over by an express truck while gathering stove wood in a snowstorm, prompting the outraged cry of "shame on America! In Russia we could not live for the pogroms, but here our children are killed!" (p. 284).

The ghetto's pervasive death and misery compel profound sentiments and radical questioning. Gold wonders, "Is there any gangster who is as cruel and heartless as the present legal State?" (p. 128). His heroic, overworked mother declares America "a good land, but not for the poor" (p. 159). A kind grocery store owner who gives away bread to starving children laments that "kindness is a form of suicide in a world based on the law of competition" (p. 243). Undergoing the "shame and humiliation" of a fruitless job hunt late in the novel, Gold's narrator concludes, "There can be no freedom in the world while men must beg for jobs" (p. 305). For its starkly naturalistic presentation of characters caught in a web of capitalistic forces, *Jews Without Money* has been compared to Upton Sinclair's 1906 muckraking classic, *The Jungle*.

Appropriately, the only light in the book's dark, brutalizing world is the potential for radical change. The novel ends, and the life of teenaged Mikey Gold is given purpose, when he hears and responds to a speech from "a man on an East Side soap-box" about a world movement to abolish poverty: "O workers' Revolution, you brought hope to me, a lonely suicidal boy. You are the true Messiah. . . . Oh Revolution, that forced me to think, to struggle and to live. O great Beginning!"

In the decade following the 1929 stock market crash, Gold was a controversial national figure as best-selling novelist, committed Communist, and vocal advocate of the literary genre he labeled "proletarian realism." In this decade he also met and married Elisabeth Boussus, eleven years younger than Gold and a French teacher at Rutgers University. After a civil wedding in 1936 the couple had their first son, Nicholas, later that year, followed by a second boy, Carl, in 1940. Wald considers it likely that two factors—Gold's consuming public role as a combative editor-activist and his increasing devo-

tion to family life—cooperated in the abrupt decline of his output as a fiction writer after the success of *Jews Without Money*.

By 1950 *Jews Without Money* had seen twenty-five printings and been translated into sixteen languages. In Germany, as Gold noted in his preface to the 1935 edition, the translated novel was used as a form of propaganda against Nazi anti-Semitism. Gold was proud to have helped counteract Fascist hatred in Germany, but he reminded readers in the same preface that the United States had its demagogues as well. The malicious claims some politicians made to out-of-work Americans that capitalism was Jewish, and that an attack on the Jews would restore prosperity, Gold noted, were comparable to Hitler's venom.

The dual focus of *Jews Without Money* on generic poverty and on the Jewish immigrant experience has kept it relevant long past the decade of the Great Depression. That relevance has not had the effect of making the novel widely read in either secondary schools or universities, and disagreements persist about the novel's artistic merit. In an afterword to the 1965 Avon Books reissue of *Jews Without Money*, Michael Harrington somewhat coldly assessed the novel as "a moment in the American literary tradition, a social documentation of the miserable, hopeful poverty of the immigrant, and a work of modest, but unquestionable aesthetic value" (p. 234). At the other extreme, Robert Forsythe called the novel "an American Classic, not only the best book ever written about the New York slums but a literary achievement of high distinction" (p. 9). Folsom diagnosed a possible factor in the book's absence from school reading lists, observing that as a "truthful book of poverty," *Jews Without Money* inhabited "a genus for which there is no accounting in the phylogeny of polite letters" (Folsom, *The Book of Poverty*, p. 244).

In response to Folsom, the leftist scholar Barbara Foley offered what seems a useful classification of *Jews Without Money*, viewing the book as a paradigm of "proletarian fictional autobiography" that shares key traits with Agnes Smedley's compelling and increasingly popular 1929 novel *Daughter of Earth*. Foley notes that

both texts draw to a significant degree upon the model of the bildungsroman, or novel of education, and that they therefore constitute "a hybrid form, poised between bourgeois and revolutionary discursive traditions" (p. 284). A crucial variation from the norms of the genre is that the learning experiences recorded by Gold and Smedley lead their poverty-stricken alter egos not toward a place in the social order but toward radicalism and revolution, underscoring how the proletarian novel differs in political content from the knowledge gained by the hero of the classic bildungsroman.

Gold's book also has much in common with another Jewish-American chronicle of the Lower East Side, Abraham Cahan's *The Rise of David Levinsky* (1917), a work often viewed as the quintessential immigrant novel for its representation of a Jewish tailor who becomes a millionaire. Gold obviously reused some characters and elements of Cahan's plot, but he gave them new meaning by associating them with stark economic decline. Gold's character Herman, for example, achieves early business success as a salesman of suspender fasteners, but when that livelihood is stolen from him he descends into ever deeper poverty and ends his career as pushcart peddler, the very job with which the greenest of Jewish immigrants usually began life in the New World. The failure prompts Herman's avowal that leaving Romania for New York had been his life's greatest mistake. In essence, *Jews Without Money* reverses the trajectory of the archetypal American narrative of upward mobility, recasting the national myth as a family tragedy in which compassion is denied full expression by capitalist material conditions.

In 1988 Richard Tuerk made a major contribution to Gold studies by pointing out that *Jews Without Money* is more sophisticated and carefully written than critics have recognized. Studying the novel manuscript and comparing the published and unpublished draft versions of its chapters, Tuerk concluded that it is much more than a series of episodic, factual sketches with a tacked-on radical ending and that it was in fact the end product of much revision. Tuerk showed where Gold changed biographical facts to suit his purposes—creating the tragic character of Mikey's sister, Esther, and reworking the experiences of other East Side Jews in the poignant scene where his father fails to sell bananas from a pushcart. These and other imaginative reworkings, along with Gold's conscious attention to prose style, contribute to the overall effect of the book and especially to its ending, which Tuerk does not find discontinuous with the preceding narrative. The novel's combination of episodic elements and a cumulative plot, along with its use of complex, gradually converging strands of imagery, show that Gold was a skilled and capable literary craftsman, and that "*Jews Without Money* is not a series of roughhewn memoirs but a carefully worked, unified piece of art" (p. 77).

From 1933 to 1966 Gold wrote a regular column for the Communist *Daily Worker* titled "Change the World!" Sixty-six of the best early articles were collected and published as an eponymous book in 1937. These pieces, sometimes predictably responsive to current events but often bizarrely digressive or fantastic, have been called "a storehouse of literary riches" by Gold's first editor (Sillen, pp. 15–16), and they remain largely unexplored. It is ironic that, though some *Change the World!* columns from the 1950s can be difficult to find, scholars now have access to a large trove of them in Gold's extensive FBI file, assembled by various agents during and after the McCarthy era and now held in the Gold-Folsom papers at the University of Michigan.

In 1959 Gold published what he considered a "sequel" to *Jews Without Money*. Almost thirty years after that novel's publication the now sixty-six-year-old writer again recalled his youth in a series of columns that ran from April to October in the San Francisco *People's World*. As several critics have noted, the new material was clever, sure-handed, and full of life and humanity; it meshed seamlessly with the style of the earlier novel and showed that Gold still possessed the skills that made him famous.

STATURE

When Folsom collected and published Gold's *People's World* columns in 1972 as chapters

under the title "A Jewish Childhood in the New York Slums," he saw them as a reminder of Gold's real genius, the artless, sincere humanity Gold drew on "before he got tangled in the life of literature and politics" (*Literary Anthology*, p. 292). As such, these sequel chapters—among the last pieces of imaginative literature Gold attempted—also remind us of what his devotion to the Party had cost him. The fact that Gold published little of consequence in the line of imaginative literature after 1930 was inarguably due in part to the sacrifice of his literary talent on behalf of the proletarian struggle. A consideration of Gold's struggles after the 1930s to remain an artist and to support his family while being vilified as a political outcast—or, in Folsom's term, "the pariah of American letters" (*Literary Anthology*, p. 7)—makes one wonder whether, by aspiring to be simultaneously a loyal Communist and a respected writer in a reactionary and philistine country, Gold had attempted the impossible. Gold's comment in 1932, "I want socialism so much that I accept this fierce, crude struggle as my fate in time" ("Communist," p. 214), indicates that he may have wondered about this himself.

Unlike most of the literary leftists of his generation, Michael Gold did not eventually disavow his radicalism, though his refusal to soft-pedal his artistic or political opinions earned him enemies in the cultural establishment. Perhaps more brazenly (or naively as some would have it), Gold never gave up the cause of what he termed "world socialism," instead retaining throughout his life the hope, expressed in the epiphanic ending of *Jews Without Money*, that a worker's messiah would come. What Mike Gold explained about his spirit and temperament at the advent of his fame was as true in the author's final days as in 1921: "The tenement is in my blood. When I think it is the tenement thinking. When I hope it is the tenement hoping. I am not an individual; I am all that the tenement group poured into me during those early years of my spiritual travail" ("Proletarian," p. 65).

By the mid-1960s Gold's eyesight had deteriorated from the effects of diabetes. Nearly blind, he continued to write for the *People's World* and

the Jewish Communist *Freiheit*, dictating articles to his wife, Liz, and using a tape recorder to work on his never-completed autobiography. His last column for the *Daily Worker* was published July 31, 1966. On May 14, 1967, he died of complications following a stroke at the Kaiser Foundation Hospital in Terra Linda, near San Francisco. He was seventy-three.

Four weeks later a memorial service was held in New York. The list of those who came to pay respects represented surprisingly varied strands of American life. Along with the populist poet and "voice of America" Carl Sandburg, whose presence confirmed that Gold still touched some in the dominant culture, there was Gold's associate at the Playwright's Theater, the famously blacklisted John Howard Lawson, one of the Hollywood Ten. Lawson not only spoke but published a tribute, "The Stature of Michael Gold," in that month's *Political Affairs*, calling his subject "a writer of courage, wisdom and—perhaps his greatest quality—stubborn integrity" (p. 11).

Gold's lifelong friend Dorothy Day, the most notorious of all Catholic radicals, also attended. In the June 1967 *Catholic Worker*, she eulogized Gold as "a gentle and loving spirit" (p. 8). The folksinger and social activist Pete Seeger, who had been reading Gold's work since the 1930s and would soon become the embodiment of Vietnam War protest, came to celebrate the man he had often called his hero. The Uruguayan American woodcut master Antonio Frasconi was present too; he would have credited Gold as an inspiration for his visual art, which relentlessly addressed racism, poverty, violence, and social injustice. Frasconi shared with Gold a love of Henry David Thoreau and Walt Whitman, and, like Gold, he wrathfully called attention to the "ugly things in life" in a quest for truthful art. At the time of the memorial Frasconi was exhibiting a set of woodcuts condemning the impact of the deadly U.S. war machine on the impoverished people of Vietnam (Parkhurst, p. 247). One of Frasconi's definitions of art—"the direct expression of a man who is angry about something" (Hentoff, p. 13)—describes as well the creative motivations of Gold.

The twin claims made by Lawson at the time of his friend's death—that there were many readers of literary and scholarly publications who had "never heard of" the once-famous Communist and that Gold had "suffered brutal misjudgments and cold neglect from the cultural establishment" (p. 11)—were accurate. But reclamation work goes on, and one early twenty-first-century testimony to Gold's impact from a perhaps unanticipated source offers perspectives at once deeply interesting and historically revealing.

READING MIKE GOLD IN TEHRAN

In her best-selling 2003 memoir, *Reading Lolita in Tehran*, the Iranian-American author Azar Nafisi wrote about Gold with insight and a curious mixture of sympathy and disdain. Nafisi, who holds a Ph.D. in literature from the University of Oklahoma, completed her doctoral dissertation on "The Literary Wars of Mike Gold" in 1979, just before she returned to Iran and witnessed the start of the Iranian revolution.

Reading Lolita in Tehran describes a meeting Nafisi had with the head of the English Department at the University of Tehran before her first semester teaching a course in Western literature. Asked about her dissertation, Nafisi explained that she had initially envisioned "a comparative study of the literature of the twenties and thirties, the proletarians and non-proletarians" (*Reading Lolita*, p. 87). It was obvious that the best person to represent the twenties was F. Scott Fitzgerald, but identifying a writer who would serve as Fitzgerald's "counterpoint" was difficult until she came across "the real proletarians, whose spirit was best captured by Mike Gold" (p. 87). In the end Nafisi left Fitzgerald out of her dissertation and wrote solely about Gold, analyzing why the proletarian writer's cultural view "took over" in the thirties and forced out writers like Fitzgerald. Nafisi, who in her student days protested the Vietnam War and embraced leftism, accounted for Gold's appeal on a personal level: "I was a revolutionary myself. I wanted to understand the passion that drove the likes of Mike Gold" (p. 88).

A month before this meeting took place, in July 1979, Nafisi had sent a copy of her dissertation to Michael Folsom, thanking him for his advice on the project and asking for his comments. With the manuscript she enclosed a personal note that affirmed her deep commitment to the Communist writer: "I feel close to Gold because of his passion for his people," she wrote, "because I think he never once forgot them or their vision. . . . I love Gold" ("Letter"). Not surprisingly, when the fall academic term began weeks later in Tehran, Nafisi did something Folsom had been calling for since 1959; she took the bold step of incorporating Gold into her survey of twentieth-century fiction, teaching his stories alongside those of Fitzgerald and Hemingway and affording Gold the stature of a major writer.

But at some point between 1979 and the publication of *Reading Lolita in Tehran*, Nafisi's thinking underwent a fundamental change, transforming her love for Gold into contempt. The author doesn't say how Gold was received in the Iranian university classroom (though she remarks that her copy of *Jews Without Money* caused consternation during a search of her belongings at the Tehran airport). Instead, in the memoir published more than two decades later, one purpose of which is to expose the corruption and tyranny of the Islamic Republic of Iran, she equates Gold's communism with the fundamentalism of Ayatollah Khomeini. After witnessing the brutal imposition of state authority in her homeland, "now, in retrospect," Nafisi decides, "the revolution Gold desired was a Marxist one and ours was Islamic, but they had a great deal in common, in that they were both ideological and totalitarian" (p. 109). To prove her point, Nafisi quotes out of context a few sentences from Gold's essay "Towards Proletarian Art," referring to the passage disparagingly. She then delivers a decisive stroke: "Such sentences could have come out of any newspaper in Iran" (p. 109).

The stunning transformation of Nafisi's literary standards from one decade and context to another replicates the arc of Michael Gold's career, exposing the contradictions behind his marginalization as a literary figure. Nafisi's unstable appraisal of proletarian art has several implications for Gold's present and future

standing. First, it serves as a general reminder of the politics of canon formation as they operate now and always. Second, the text's thinly disguised warning that neglect of our "great writers" in favor of Gold could produce a form of totalitarianism in the United States analogous to what Nafisi finds in Iran reflects the reactionary processes by which Michael Gold was erased from cultural memory. A final, contemporary object lesson to be derived from *Reading Lolita in Tehran* involves the recognition that the extremism Nafisi criticizes in Iran resembles twenty-first-century examples of U.S. political intolerance more than many are willing to recognize. The text, after all, articulates Nafisi's passionate argument to Iranian students in 1979—but actually to well over a million American readers in 2003—that Mike Gold is still unworthy of acceptance by the literary establishment, and still dangerous.

In a period of corporate control, wealth disparity, and the apparent mainstreaming of protofascism, Michael Gold should be more than ever of interest to a cultural establishment whose attention to his work has been insufficient. But whether the voice we privilege in *Reading Lolita in Tehran* is that of the twenty-nine-year-old Ph.D. in literature who loved Gold, or the middle-aged famous author who likened his ideals to tyranny and brutality, Nafisi's text suggests reasons to read and reconsider the literary pariah, globally and at home. Meanwhile, the paradox Nafisi explained to her colleagues in Tehran, a statement that came from the Nafisi who loved Gold, is still true and bears repeating: "You may not believe it, but he was a big shot in his day" (p. 107).

Selected Bibliography

WORKS OF MICHAEL GOLD

FICTION AND POETRY

"Three Whose Hatred Killed Them." *Masses*, August 1914. Reprinted in *Mike Gold: A Literary Anthology*. Edited by Michael Folsom. New York: International Publishers, 1972. P. 22.

"Two Mexicos." *Liberator*, May 1920. Reprinted in *Mike Gold: A Literary Anthology*. Edited by Michael Folsom. New York: International Publishers, 1972. Pp. 49–61.

The Damned Agitator and Other Stories. Chicago: Daily Worker Publishing, 1924.

"The Strange Funeral in Braddock." *Liberator*, June 1924. Reprinted in *Mike Gold: A Literary Anthology*. Edited by Michael Folsom. New York: International Publishers, 1972. Pp. 126–128.

"Love on a Garbage Dump." *New Masses*, December 1928. Reprinted in *Mike Gold: A Literary Anthology*. Edited by Michael Folsom. New York: International Publishers, 1972. Pp. 177–185.

120 Million. London: Modern Books, 1929.

Jews Without Money. New York: H. Liveright, 1930. 2nd ed., New York: Carroll & Graf, 1996.

NONFICTION

"Towards Proletarian Art." *Liberator*, February 1921. Reprinted in *Mike Gold: A Literary Anthology*. Edited by Michael Folsom. New York: International, 1972. Pp. 62–70.

Life of John Brown. Girard, Kans.: Haldeman-Julius, 1924. Reprint, New York: Roving Eye Press, 1960.

"John Reed and the Real Thing." *New Masses*, November 1927. Reprinted in *Mike Gold: A Literary Anthology*. Edited by Michael Folsom. New York: International Publishers, 1972. Pp. 152–156.

"Floyd Dell Resigns." *New Masses*, July 1929, pp. 10–11.

"Proletarian Realism." *New Masses*, September 1930. Reprinted in *Mike Gold: A Literary Anthology*. Edited by Michael Folsom. New York: International Publishers, 1972. Pp. 203–208.

"Wilder, Prophet of the Genteel Christ." *New Republic*, October 22, 1930. Reprinted in *Mike Gold: A Literary Anthology*. Edited by Michael Folsom. New York: International Publishers, 1972. Pp. 197–202.

"Why I Am a Communist." *New Masses*, September 1932. Reprinted in *Mike Gold: A Literary Anthology*. Edited by Michael Folsom. New York: International Publishers, 1972. Pp. 209–214.

Change the World! New York: International Publishers, 1937.

The Hollow Men. New York: International Publishers, 1941.

"A Jewish Childhood in the New York Slums." Individual essays first published in *People's World*, April–October, 1959. Reprinted in *Mike Gold: A Literary Anthology*. Edited by Michael Folsom. New York: International Publishers, 1972. Pp. 292–319.

Flame masthead. N.d. Gold-Folsom Papers, University of Michigan.

PUBLISHED PLAYS

Hoboken Blues: The Black Rip Van Winkle; A Modern Negro Fantasia on an Old American Theme. In *The American Caravan: A Yearbook of American Literature*. Edited by Van Wyck Brooks, Alfred Kreymborg, Lewis Mumford, and Paul Rosenfeld. New York: Literary Guild of America, 1927. Pp. 548–626.

Money. 1929. Reprinted in *One-Act Plays*. Edited by Barrett H. Clark and Thomas R. Cook. Boston and New York: D. C. Heath, 1929.

Battle Hymn: A Play in Three Acts, Prologues, and an Epilogue. With Michael Blankfort. New York: Samuel French, 1936.

ANTHOLOGIES

The Mike Gold Reader. New York: International Publishers, 1954.

Mike Gold: A Literary Anthology. Edited by Michael Folsom. New York: International Publishers, 1972.

PAPERS

Mike Gold and Mike Folsom Papers, 1901–1990 (bulk 1930–1967). Joseph A. Labadie Collection, Special Collections Library, University of Michigan, Ann Arbor.

CRITICAL AND BIOGRAPHICAL STUDIES

Aaron, Daniel. *Writers on the Left: Episodes in American Literary Communism*. New York: Avon Books, 1961.

Berman, Paul. "East Side Story: Mike Gold, the Communists, and the Jews." *Village Voice*, March 1983, pp. 39–53.

Brogna, John J. *Michael Gold: Critic and Playwright*. PhD diss., University of Georgia, Athens, Georgia, 1982.

Chura, Patrick. *Vital Contact: Downclassing Journeys in American Literature from Herman Melville to Richard Wright*. New York: Routledge, 2005.

Clayton, Douglas. *Floyd Dell: The Life and Times of an American Rebel*. Chicago: I. R. Dee, 1994.

Cruse, Harold. *The Crisis of the Negro Intellectual*. New York: William Morrow, 1967.

Day, Dorothy. "Mike Gold." *Catholic Worker*, June 1967, p. 8.

Dell, Floyd. "Explanations and Apologies." *Liberator*, June 1922, pp. 25–26.

Foley, Barbara. *Radical Representations: Politics and Form in U.S. Proletarian Fiction, 1929–1941*. Durham, N.C.: Duke University Press, 1993.

Folsom, Michael, "The Book of Poverty." *Nation*, February 28, 1966, pp. 242–245.

———. "The Education of Mike Gold." In *Proletarian Writers of the Thirties*. Edited by David Madden. Carbondale: Southern Illinois University Press, 1968. Pp. 221–251.

Forsythe, Robert. Foreword to *Change the World!* New York: International Publishers, 1936.

Freeman, Joseph. *An American Testament*. New York: Farrar & Rinehart, 1936.

Harrington, Michael. Afterword to *Jews Without Money*. New York: Avon Books, 1965.

Himelstein, Morgan Yale. *Drama Was a Weapon: The Left-Wing Theatre in New York, 1929–1941*. New Brunswick, N.J.: Rutgers University Press, 1963.

Kazin, Alfred. Introduction to *Jews Without Money*. New York: Carroll & Graf, 1996.

Lawson, John Howard. "The Stature of Mike Gold." *Political Affairs* 46, no. 6:11–14 (June 1967).

Lewis, Sinclair. "The American Fear of Literature." Nobel lecture, December 12, 1930. http://www.nobelprize.org/nobel_prizes/literature/laureates/1930/lewis-lecture.html

Madden, David, ed. *Proletarian Writers of the Thirties*. Carbondale: Southern Illinois University Press, 1968.

Maxwell, William J. "The Proletarian as New Negro: Mike Gold's Harlem Renaissance." In *Radical Revisions: Rereading 1930s Culture*. Edited by Bill V. Mullen and Sherry Linkon. Urbana: University of Illinois Press, 1996. Pp. 91–119.

Pyros, John. *Mike Gold: Dean of American Proletarian Writers*. New York: Dramatika Press, 1979.

Roessel, David. "'What Made You Leave the Movement?': O'Neill, Mike Gold, and the Radicalism of the Provincetown Players." In *Eugene O'Neill and His Early Contemporaries: Bohemians, Radicals, Progressives, and the Avant Garde*. Edited by Eileen J. Hermann and Robert M. Dowling. Jefferson, N.C.: McFarland, 2011. Pp. 234–249.

Shields, Art. "Mike Gold, Our Joy and Pride." *Political Affairs* 51, no. 7:126–128 (July 1972).

Sillen, Samuel. Introduction to *The Mike Gold Reader*. International Publishers, 1954.

Sinclair, Upton. *Boston: A Novel*. New York: A. & C. Boni, 1928.

Tuerk, Richard. "*Jews Without Money* as a Work of Art." *Studies in American Jewish Literature* 7, no. 1:67–79 (spring 1988).

Wald, Alan. *Exiles from a Future Time: The Forging of the Mid-Twentieth-Century Literary Left*. Chapel Hill: University of North Carolina Press, 2002.

OTHER SOURCES

Hentoff, Nat. Introduction to *Frasconi Against the Grain: The Woodcuts of Antonio Frasconi*. New York: Macmillan, 1972.

Liberator archive, 1918–1924. Marxist Internet Archive. https://www.marxists.org/history/usa/culture/pubs/liberator/

Nafisi, Azar. Letter to Michael Folsom, July 28, 1979. Gold-

Folsom Papers, University of Michigan, Ann Arbor.

———. *Reading Lolita in Tehran: A Memoir in Books*. New York: Random House, 2003.

New Masses archive, 1926–1923. Marxist Internet Archive. https://www.marxists.org/history/usa/pubs/new-masses/

Parkhurst, Charles. "An Appreciation." In *Frasconi Against the Grain: The Woodcuts of Antonio Frasconi*. New York: Macmillan, 1972.

Rowe, John Carlos. *The Cultural Politics of the New American Studies* Ann Arbor, Mich.: MPublishing, University of Michigan Library, 2012.

Sandrow, Nahma. *Vagabond Stars: A World History of Yiddish Theater*. Syracuse, N.Y.: Syracuse University Press, 1996.

DIANE GOODMAN

(1956—)

Ashley Cowger

STUDIES PUBLISHED BETWEEN 2011 and 2015 uncovered the average American's misperceptions of the income divide in the United States. In spite of outcries against the "1 percent" and movements like Occupy Wall Street, the results of a survey of more than five thousand people living in America showed that the average American grossly underestimated the significance of the American wealth gap. The actual numbers indicated that the wealthiest 20 percent of Americans retained upward of 84 percent of the country's wealth after the recession of 2008–2009, while the bottom 40 percent possessed only 0.3 percent (Fitz). As politicians, filmmakers, and other media figures desperately tried to draw public attention to this imbalance and its accompanying problems, many contemporary fiction writers were also turning their attention to these concerns, since literature has always been a prime venue for social investigation and commentary. One such author is the short-story writer Diane Goodman, whose work has largely flown under the radar of many readers. Goodman's fiction gives voice to the contemporary working-class American woman, turning a much-needed spotlight on the class divide in America. In a blurb on the back cover of *The Plated Heart* (2006), Ann Patchett says that Goodman's stories, which give "a beautiful and deeply felt voice to women who we so rarely see: the ones who serve us," are an accurate representation of "what it means to work in America"; Jill Bialosky, in a blurb on the back cover of *The Genius of Hunger* (2002), says that Goodman's stories provide a glimpse into "unexpectedly dark corners of the secret lives of women, their joys and hungers, sadnesses and lost expectations"; and *Kirkus*'s prepublication review of *The Genius of Hunger* in 2001 describes Goodman's work as "portraits of women battling for understanding in the face of an indifferent world."

Indeed, Goodman's fiction is a necessary and sobering reminder of the stark divide between classes in America, and the distinct effect that divide has on women. Goodman's stories depict characters in a variety of roles, from cashier to chef to displaced housewife, and her stories mine the depths of each character to reveal the messy, complicated nature of working-class life in contemporary America. In a personal interview with Ashley Cowger (2016), Goodman herself put it this way:

> I have something to say, and the only way that I want to say it is through characters and situations that I invent. I want to say it indirectly. I want exploration towards some kind of revelation. I want to think deeply about these issues, want to realize them through how the characters will respond, want to find the way to use language to say things beautifully—even ugly things, even difficult things.

LIFE

Diane Beth Goodman was born in 1956 in Cleveland, Ohio. She had a blue-collar upbringing and was an avid reader from an early age. Although she is known today primarily as a fiction writer, Goodman began her writing career as a poet. She started writing poetry at a young age, but, like the attempts of many young poets, her early poems were marked by adolescent angst. It wasn't until college that Goodman came to identify as a poet. Goodman studied biology at Denison University, where she elected to take various creative writing and literature courses. Studying literature and writing in an academic setting helped Goodman understand the artistry of poetry. According to Goodman, in college she

came to understand "the difference between writing poems in a journal when you're depressed and writing poetry" (Cowger interview).

After earning her bachelor of arts degree, Goodman earned a master of fine arts in creative writing at Antioch University and, later, a second master's degree in English from the University of Delaware. It is her time at Delaware that seems to have had the most profound influence on Goodman as a writer because there she was able to study under her favorite poet, W. D. Snodgrass. In fact, it was because of Snodgrass that Goodman went to the University of Delaware. Goodman discovered Snodgrass during her senior year in college and was deeply affected by his work. She wrote him a letter, telling him she wanted to study with him. Much to her delight, Snodgrass called her and invited her to apply to the University of Delaware. Her application was initially rejected, but Goodman flew from Cleveland to Delaware to talk to someone in the graduate department and was able to "talk her way in" to the program (Cowger interview). She promptly quit her job, sold her car, and moved to Delaware.

In Delaware, Goodman introduced herself to Snodgrass but couldn't afford to take his poetry writing class. He invited her to sit in on the class for free, though he discouraged her from participating as it would not have been fair to the students who had paid to take the course. She eventually received funding and studied with Snodgrass for the rest of her time in Delaware. She finished the program in 1982, and because she wanted to teach at the college level, in 1984 she began working toward her Ph.D. She earned her Ph.D. in English at Case Western Reserve University, where she wrote her dissertation on Snodgrass' 1959 collection *Heart's Needle*. To aid Goodman' study of the cycle of poems, Snodgrass granted her access to a draft of *Heart's Needle* as she worked on her dissertation. After earning her Ph.D., Goodman took a one-year teaching position at Allegheny College in Meadville, Pennsylvania. She earned tenure at Allegheny and stayed for ten years, after which she decided to take what she intended to be a one-year leave of absence. She wanted to be by the

water, so she moved to Miami to work at a private prep school. After spending a year in Miami, she decided not to return to Allegheny, and she continued teaching at the prep school for five years, while teaching part-time at the University of Miami.

With her blue-collar background, Goodman became jaded working with the affluent children at a private school and needed a break from teaching, but the only thing she felt competent to do for a living besides teaching was cooking. She began working as a private chef for the family of one of the children she had been working with in her previous position. She found that she had an easier time working for the rich in a service position than as a teacher. During this time she also started a catering company called Diane Cooks, which she ran for ten years in South Beach, Florida. Goodman eventually returned to academia: she joined the faculty of Grand Canyon University in Phoenix, Arizona, in 2012 and became an associate professor three years later. But it is her time working as a chef near and for the wealthy in Florida that instigated her career as a fiction writer and continues to inform her fiction. Many of her stories were born of her experiences in Florida. It is as though her fiction is a necessary means of making sense of the inequities of the world around her, and her stories, in turn, help expose Goodman's readers to these injustices.

Goodman's first short story was a direct result of an interaction she had with a stranger in a Florida grocery store. She didn't know what to make of the incident, and she found herself compelled to write a story about it. That story became "Spirit," the final story in her first fiction collection, *The Genius of Hunger* (2002). In "Spirit," we meet a first-person narrator whose name is never revealed and whose past, in many ways, lines up with Goodman's. The narrator is a high school teacher who recently relocated to Florida, leaving behind a university job and a failing relationship in Pennsylvania. Her interaction with a strange woman at a grocery store uncovers memories of the life the narrator left behind and her uncertainty about the new life she's embarking upon.

"Spirit" set Goodman off on a journey to examine her experiences in Florida through fiction. Having left behind a tenured professorship at Allegheny, her new life seems to have mirrored that of the narrator in "Spirit" in many ways—a life less stable in some ways, and lonelier, but at the same time far more liberating. Almost all of Goodman's stories to date take place in or around Miami, and while not all of her characters are as recognizably pulled from reality as the narrator in "Spirit," her characters reflect the range of people she met and observed during that period of her life. At the forefront of Goodman's consciousness was the disparity between her new life, cooking for and serving the wealthy, and her old life as a tenured professor. Her stories often provide a very direct comparison between people of different social classes, and her own experiences in and out of the so-called ivory tower have clearly played a role in her ability to recognize so acutely the differences and similarities between these groups.

FROM POETRY TO PROSE

Her early experiences writing and studying poetry surely helped shape Goodman as a short-fiction writer. Many of Goodman's poems included a narrative element, so it was a logical step to move from poetry to storytelling. Like any good literary fiction writer, Goodman's prose contains a level of lyricism and attention to detail found in poetry. In addition to consonance, which she uses to great effect in her fiction, Goodman has a poet's instinct for the sound and emotional resonance of language. The imagery of her prose functions both on the literal and symbolic level, and her word choices are careful and exact.

In her first-person stories, the voices of Goodman's narrators successfully express not only their personalities but also their inner turmoil and needs—in some cases needs they do not even know they have. Many of her characters, though, have a poet's sensibility and mine the contexts of their lives for depth and meaning the way a poet seeks significance from every image. In fact, some of Goodman's characters are literal poets, while others use cooking as their form of

poetry—an art, a skilled craft, that engages the senses fully and serves as a valuable outlet for creativity.

THEMES AND BODY OF WORK

One of the most significant qualities that distinguishes Goodman's fiction from the work of many other authors is the ubiquity of certain themes. Readers of Goodman's work come to recognize certain topics that pop up again and again in different stories, always examined from new and interesting angles. Three recurring themes in particular—food, class, and women—appear in Goodman's fiction most certainly as a result of the substantial role they have played in Goodman's life.

The epigraph to one of Goodman's stories, "Phyllis," is the following quote by M. F. K. Fisher: "sharing food with another human being is an intimate act that should not be indulged in lightly" (*The Genius of Hunger*, p. 83). The intimacy of food—food preparation, food sharing, shopping for and selling food ingredients—is one of the most prominent themes embraced by Goodman's fiction. She believes cooking is an act of love and nurturing, and her fiction often depicts cooking and consuming food as a way of expressing deeper needs. According to Goodman, food has a dual nature in contemporary American culture. We are a food-oriented society, obsessed with foodie culture, celebrity chefs, and television cooking shows; at the same time, however, dieting and healthful eating is a top concern among many Americans. We want to have our elaborately decorated buttercream cake and eat it too—to indulge recklessly, yet to maintain slim, healthy physiques. These opposing desires, born of a basic human need—all living beings must eat to survive—turn an essential, natural practice into something far more complicated and conflicting than it needs to be.

Goodman's personal relationship to food—having worked as a professional chef and even briefly owning her own restaurant—uniquely positions her to comment on and through food in her fiction. In her stories, food signifies social status, as characters often use their food tastes to

signal sophistication. Food links the working-class sellers, preparers, and servers of food to their affluent customers and clients. In addition, the food in her stories often serves as a physical stand-in for the emotional need for love and connection. Just as an anorexic deprives herself of food, Goodman's characters often have trouble navigating social interactions and developing meaningful relationships.

Social status and class is another almost ubiquitous theme in Goodman's work. The majority of Goodman's characters are members of the working class, and many of them find themselves working for or living near the very rich in and around Miami. This juxtaposition of lifestyles and opportunities allows the reader to compare the lives of the working and upper classes. Ultimately all of Goodman's characters are human, with all of the moral and emotional complexity being human entails, but many of her main characters exemplify what it is to be treated as a nameless, expendable servant.

Just as it is impossible to discuss Goodman's fiction without considering the themes of food and class, it is equally necessary to note the frequency of female characters in her stories. Like most female authors, Goodman writes from her perspective as a woman. This certainly doesn't mean that all of Goodman's main characters are female—though most of them are—or that Goodman's work appeals only to a female readership. Goodman writes male characters as expertly as she writes females, but her female characters have backgrounds and personalities shaped distinctly by their roles and identities as women. Alongside many universal matters, Goodman's work deals with motherhood, anorexia, and rape—topics that chiefly affect women. Likewise, the state of being "a woman" affects all women, much the same way everyone is affected by his or her particular ethnicity, culture, or social rank.

All of these themes inform a body of work that to date includes one chapbook of poetry and three short-story collections. As of this writing, she is working on a fourth short-story collection. Her poetry chapbook, *Constellations*, was published in 1993 by Heatherstone Press and is now out of print. Her first short-story collection, *The Genius of Hunger*, was published by Carnegie Mellon University Press in 2002. Her second book, *The Plated Heart*, was also published by Carnegie Mellon and was released in 2006. Her much-anticipated third book, *Party Girls*, was published by Autumn House Press in 2011 and was listed as a notable collection by the Story Prize.

THE GENIUS OF HUNGER

Most of the story titles in *The Genius of Hunger* bear the names of significant female characters. In addition to Goodman's common themes of food, class, and women, the stories in *The Genius of Hunger* incorporate characters working in or shopping at grocery stores. The grocery stores function as a symbolic thread that connects the stories and allows them to comment on and inform each other. Various types of grocery stores are depicted, from major chains to small family-owned businesses to trendy and expensive health food stores. Goodman uses these disparate settings to illustrate a range of very different people from very different social classes and backgrounds. These grocery stores (and, likewise, food) remind us of commonalities among all these characters, no matter the difference in bank account or social rank: we are all, ultimately, made of no stronger stuff than soft flesh and fragile bones; we all need food to survive.

The collection opens with a story that addresses a question commonly raised in Goodman's work: what is it like to be a working woman living amid the very rich? In "Joan," an overweight, middle-aged woman, fraught with self-doubt and angry at the unfairness of her social status, throws her back out in a posh health food store called Wild Oates. When a handsome, spoiled teenaged boy first knocks her over, then comes to her rescue, Goodman reminds the reader not just of the growing epidemic of selfishness and insensitivity but also of those essential glimmers of humanity shared by the rich and poor alike—our insecurities, our uncertainty about right versus wrong, our shame when we've done horrible things that can't be undone.

DIANE GOODMAN

The second story in the collection, "Lily Brown," features an unreliable first-person narrator: a disabled woman seeking a sense of purpose in her life. The narrator, whose name we never learn, goes by many pseudonyms, among them, Lily Brown. Although on the surface she seems satisfied with the way her life has turned out, her quest to resolve other people's problems leads her to a strange, misguided new career while leading the reader to a deeper understanding of her anger and frustration at the unfairness of her situation. The reality that her new career is unlikely to ever generate income seems almost beside the point to the narrator.

One of Goodman's rare stories with a male protagonist, "Dani," introduces the reader to Brian, a produce clerk who finds himself infatuated with one of his customers, in spite of being practically engaged to another woman. When the customers in the store begin finding dangerous objects embedded in the produce—shards of green glass, razor blades, nails—Brian obsessively worries about Dani. What if Dani purchases some of the tampered-with produce? What if Dani is hurt? What if Dani decides to shop elsewhere? So preoccupied is he with his fledgling love affair, he misses the signs of who has been intentionally planting the objects in the produce.

The title character in "Phyllis" is pouring all of her energy into party preparations when the story opens, and as the story unfolds, a surprising truth about the party is revealed. Although "Phyllis" is thematically similar to Goodman's other stories, it is stylistically distinct. The third-person narrator's voice is far more conspicuous than in many of Goodman's other stories. Rather than a third-person narrator who fades into the background, the narrator is almost a character herself. In addition, unlike many of Goodman's other protagonists, Phyllis is not a working-class woman on the fringe of high society but instead a housewife married to a millionaire. Phyllis met her husband when she was working as a flight attendant, and her change in social status works as an interesting lens through which to compare the life of the working-class woman to the life of leisure well-situated women like Phyllis are able to lead. Phyllis, for example, shops for and prepares all the food for the party herself, yet she hires a staff headed by her live-in maid to serve the food, make the drinks, and clean up. As we learn more about Phyllis and her life, it becomes clear that, working class or wealthy, in the end there is no difference. The ravages of aging and mortality await us all.

In "Shiva," Goodman examines the theme of food through the perspective of an anorexic waitress who intentionally seeks out and surrounds herself with food in spite of her eating disorder. Marcie is no typical anorexic, though. She is unaware of her disorder, and her self-imposed starvation stems not from vanity but from the self-loathing instilled in her from childhood abuse. When the wafting smell of the delicious Indian dishes she serves her customers reminds her of her hunger, she takes a moment to refresh herself at the statue of Shiva at the front of the restaurant.

> My first day on the job here, Mr. Saha took me to this statue and explained Shiva, the Hindu deity who represents destruction. Shiva works miracles when you understand that you have to concentrate and be remorseful. So when I think I am going to faint if I don't stick my hand into a steaming bowl of curry and push the food into my mouth, I go and stand in front of Shiva. I close my eyes and I repent; I understand that my pain is my penance.
>
> (*The Genius of Hunger*, p. 107)

To Marcie, the aching of her empty stomach is a fitting punishment, though she may not know for what. Just as, when she was young, her mother would beat her for infractions she often didn't understand, Marcie accepts the pain, apparently believing she deserves all this and more.

The next two stories in the collection, "Rosie" and "Valene," are linked. In "Rosie," we meet Roz, Charlene, and JoAnne, three women who work in the flower department at a Miami Winn-Dixie. Cemented together by their own past heartaches, Roz, Charlene, and JoAnne have developed a bond so close that they are collectively referred to as "Rosie" by the store manager. The story revolves around the women's dislike of a new bakery employee, the flirtatious and voluptuous Mindi, who reminds Roz and

JoAnne of the women who broke up their marriages and who seems to be at risk of disturbing Charlene's budding romance with the stock boy Jack. Woven into the present story of the three women grappling with their prejudice against Mindi are the stories of the days Roz and Charlene returned home to find their husbands with Valene and Lynette, respectively.

In "Valene," JoAnne goes out alone one night and meets a pregnant young woman who is drinking at a bar. The woman turns out to be Valene, the same woman who broke up her friend Roz's marriage. Surprised to find herself face-to-face with a woman she has never met but has long despised, JoAnne is forced to confront her own preconceptions as well as her own behavior of late. JoAnne has taken up with her married creative writing professor, and it is only now, confronted with the reality of Valene before her, that she realizes she may not be so different from women like Valene, Lynette, and even Mindi, after all.

"Alta" is another of Goodman's infrequent stories depicting the perspective of an affluent woman. Born into privilege and living off a large inheritance, Claire has returned to the United States after spending eight years in Haiti, bringing her son and stepdaughter with her. The decision to return to the States was inspired equally by her desire to raise her children in the safe environment she had grown up in and by her anger at her cheating husband, Georges. Like Roz and JoAnne from the previous two stories, Claire returned home from work one day to find her husband in bed with another woman, but unlike Roz and JoAnne, Claire did not sue for divorce. She moved away, taking his children, by his request, but their marriage is still legally binding.

Like the title character from "Phyllis," Claire presents a useful lens through which to compare the lifestyles of the working and upper classes. Though Phyllis married into wealth, Claire was born into it. However, Claire's prolonged period living in Haiti introduced her to an entirely different—and, for her, much more meaningful—way of living. She began to work as a reporter, and she found herself, for the first time ever, with a purpose. Instead of lazing around a large house and reading, she exposed herself to the great injustices around her and wrote about them to expose them to the world. Her love of this new life battles with her wish to keep her children safe, to give them the fortune and comfort she knew as a child. Though her frustration at Georges' teenage daughter, Eva—whom she has legally adopted but seems to see as a stand-in for her philandering, gadabout husband—is clouding her ability to love both children equally, she struggles to be a good mother all the same. When she decides to send Eva home to Haiti, she is forced to confront her own feelings about both her husband and her children and to weigh the consequences of her treatment of this child, whose only chance of a stable childhood lies with Claire.

One of Goodman's favorites of her own stories is "Gina," a first-person narrative about a Costco cashier who has an altercation with a couple of customers. When a man cuts in front of another customer in Gina's line, she finds herself more irritated with the woman he cut in front of, whose jewelry and overall appearance connote a level of wealth Gina and the man will never experience firsthand, than she is with the man himself. It occurs to Gina that the man may have a gun, but the wealthy woman seems almost sure of it, and is so panicky about setting the man off that she chooses to let him get away with his behavior rather than confront him. Gina does confront him, but mainly she is angry at the woman, whose prejudice about the man's (and, therefore, vicariously, Gina's) social status is revealed through her fear. Goodman is partial to "Gina" because writing it allowed her to vent some of her personal frustrations by releasing them into the main character, who deals with her own frustrations much less commendably. According to Goodman, "Gina" illuminates an anger that is very personal but also global: anger about how the class people are born into affects the way they are treated. In the end, even though Gina behaves terribly, she becomes a hero to herself. Goodman particularly enjoys performing this story at readings because she can embody Gina as she reads the story aloud.

DIANE GOODMAN

"Spirit" perhaps comes closer to Goodman's own experience than any of her other stories. Here a woman at a grocery store witnesses an aging woman who speaks only Spanish attempting to buy crab legs and pork feet, for which she cannot pay. After the cashier's repeated attempts to make the woman understand that her credit card is not working, the cashier and the man behind the narrator grow increasingly irritated at the woman. The narrator, a close stand-in for Goodman herself, pays for the woman's groceries to diffuse the situation.

THE PLATED HEART

Goodman's second short-story collection, *The Plated Heart*, continues to explore the themes of food and class through the lens of a mostly female cast of characters in Florida. Whereas most of the story titles in *The Genius of Hunger* are characters' names, most of the titles in *The Plated Heart* are the characters' occupations. In two cases, the main characters' names are not even revealed to the reader. It is as though these people's jobs are their identities. Indeed, many of the characters in these stories, most of whom prepare or serve food as their profession, are essentially nameless to their employers and clients.

In the first story of the collection, "The Manager," a nameless personal chef develops a crush on the store manager at the grocery store where she shops for the ingredients needed to prepare her boss's meals. Like "Dani" from *The Genius of Hunger*, but in reverse, we watch her anguish as she overanalyzes every interaction she has with the man at the grocery store. Her trivial exchanges with a man she does not know seem to be her only meaningful contact with another human being, and the namelessness of the character in the story mimics her lack of identity and significance in the world around her. On the surface, she appreciates her anonymity because she does not know how to interact or engage with other people. She likes her job in part because, to her boss, she is little more than hired help, faceless and replaceable. The narrator tells us:

That was the beauty of her boss and her boss's family—they were not interested in nor curious about her. They did not want to get to know her beyond the service she provided. She slipped into their house quietly, put the groceries away, prepared and packaged meals their servants would later serve them, and left when she was done. . . . sometimes she wondered if her boss would recognize her if she ran into her on the street.

(The Plated Heart, pp. 16–17)

Though the main character embraces her loneliness, it is clear that she desperately needs some form of human connection, and it is for this reason that she has fabricated a fantasy relationship with a man who hardly knows she exists.

"The Caterer" takes us inside a prosperous household and allows us to watch, through the eyes of a nameless caterer-narrator, as a family dinner party degenerates into a full-fledged feud. Unlike most of Goodman's first-person narrators, the narrator in "The Caterer" tells the reader little about herself. She makes no mention of her own background and personality beyond past incidents she has voyeuristically witnessed on the job. She seems to live vicariously through her wealthy clients, whose behavior both fascinates and appalls her. Though she recounts other cases of dinner parties gone awry, this one leaves her dumbstruck, unsure how to handle the fact that she and the other caterers are audience to an episode that is none of their business but unable to look away.

At the dinner party, Marv, a handsome and irritable uncle, is intent on stirring up trouble. Though the full story behind the impetus of his resentment toward the other members of his family is never revealed, it's clear that he has been cut out of the family fortune. The purpose of the dinner party is to provide a platform for Marv's niece to announce her pregnancy, yet Marv interminably steers the conversation in directions the other members of the family find uncomfortable. Unwilling to let his bitterness rest even in light of his niece's good news, Marv grows increasingly hostile as the meal progresses, and the evening culminates with Marv pouring an entire pitcher of water over his own girlfriend's head. Before leaving, Laura, Marv's girlfriend, thanks the narrator for the "superb food. And service. Really. This couldn't have been easy for

you guys. Thanks." "She worked for a caterer for a long time," Marv says, as though this is the only logical explanation for why Laura would acknowledge the caterer and what the family just put her through (p. 72).

Belle, the narrator in "The Tavern," is reminiscent of the nameless narrator from "Lily Brown." After Belle falls from a ladder at work and becomes permanently disabled, her life all but falls apart. Her husband, who is mysteriously missing the day of her accident, eventually leaves her, and Belle now lives a life of routine, living off social security and disability, and dining regularly at the Tavern, a bar and restaurant owned by recently widowed Wade. Belle sees the strange circumstances of Wade's wife's death as an opportunity to create meaning out of the otherwise meaningless. She begins to behave like a character from *Law & Order*—reruns of which she watches almost every night—and tries to solve what she sees as the mystery of Wade's wife's death. While it is obvious to the reader that Wade wants none of her sleuthing—his only wish is to put the incident behind him and move on—Belle needs this chance to have a purpose, to help ease another person's suffering, where her own suffering was left to rot and harden.

In "The Butcher," food plays an even more central role than in many of Goodman's other stories. Janine suffers from crippling anxiety and has difficulty completing the basic errands needed to care for her dying great-aunt Tia. Though Tia is incapable of digesting most food, she requests that Janine make her elaborate meals, so that she might at least smell and sometimes lick them before eating the soft puddings and cream of wheat her body is able to process. Though past trauma has arrested Janine's emotional and social development, she has made an effort to learn to cook to make Tia's final days as happy as possible.

Her willingness to acquiesce to Tia's requests leads her to the grocery store at 2:00 a.m. Janine is uncomfortable driving Tia's large van, and since the crowded streets and grocery store spur her anxiety, Tia suggests that Janine run her errands at night instead, when streets and store alike will be nearly empty. At the store she develops a relationship with the butcher, who

helps her select meats and plan meals, and he eventually even writes down recipes for dishes he assures Janine her great aunt will be able to digest. Though the butcher's behavior raises alarms for the reader, Janine is too naive and socially inept to recognize the danger of her increasingly close relationship with this man. Janine, whose father abandoned her when she was sixteen, sees the butcher as a paternal figure, though his interest in her is clearly carnal. Tia's love of the new delicacies the butcher is teaching Janine to cook causes Janine to let her guard down in a rare instance in which anxiety would actually serve her well.

"The Vendor" introduces the reader to Salim, the mute owner of a food truck who parks at construction sites and prides himself on his relationship with the construction workers. Salim, who lost the ability to speak at age four, when he was caught inside a burning building, makes up for his lack of ability to speak by listening closely to people and paying attention to every detail around him. He knows his customers well, far better than they know him. They have no idea that he knows so much about them—their names, their wives' names, their addresses, and sometimes their bleak and painful histories. Although Salim believes that the construction workers who buy his food remember him from one job to the next, it's clear that he is as faceless and nameless to these blue-collar workers as they likely are to the building owners who employ them. He is a silent friend and confidant, one they will never even know they had.

In "The Customer," Ellen, a personal chef, takes on a new client in her apartment complex, who hires her to cater an upcoming Fourth of July party. Mrs. Fierstein requests picnic food—chicken and pie, traditional home-style cooking—and Ellen is all too happy to accommodate her. She herself longs for the less extravagant meals her mother and grandmother used to cook at the farm where she grew up. Though it was her own choice to move to Florida to attend culinary school and gain an impressive income as a personal chef, she misses the farm and her family terribly. When planning the menu for the party, she eschews her fancy culinary education and instead prepares recipes passed down from her mother and grandmother. Out of habit,

though, she adds elegant garnishes to the down-home food—cherry tomatoes cut into ornamental roses, lemon zest atop the fried chicken, and flowers and confetti sprinkled about the silver tray. Before presenting the tray to the customer to test, Ellen prides herself on the stylish appearance of the food.

Ellen is surprised to discover that Mrs. Fierstein is not only not satisfied with Ellen's chic take on picnic food, she accuses Ellen of purchasing the food from a restaurant and trying to peddle it as homemade. This is not, it turns out, Mrs. Fierstein's idea of picnic food. It is not, Ellen realizes, her own family's idea of picnic food either. The garnish and show of extravagance, which Ellen had thought would dress up the food a bit, "make it look like it deserves to be paid for," ruining the essence of what the food was meant to be.

The final story in the collection, "The Cook," returns us to the familiar grocery store setting. Darlene, another personal chef, has developed a crush on the man who works at the fish counter, whose name she doesn't even know. In spite of his anonymity, Darlene feels as though she knows him—they chat when she shops for fish at his counter, and they share conspiratorial jokes about Darlene's clients. When, on a whim, Darlene invites him to dinner to sample her bouillabaisse, she finds herself frantically trying to finish her shopping so she can complete her day's work and get home to begin preparing for her date. In the checkout line, Darlene realizes something is amiss—the disgruntled man in line behind her seems to be a former lover of the checkout girl, and it's clear the checkout girl wants nothing to do with him. Darlene, who suddenly realizes how little she knows about the man she herself has invited into her home for dinner, finds herself caught in the middle of a potential incident and has no idea what to do or how to help.

PARTY GIRLS

Goodman's third collection of fiction, *Party Girls*, is similar in theme and style to Goodman's first two books and at the same time signals what may be considered a departure. The most obvious change emerges in the stories' titles, which do not follow any noticeable theme or format. Likewise, while the first collection revolves around grocery stores and the second explores characters through their occupations, the stories in *Party Girls* are less easy to pin down in terms of consistent thematic approach. While many of the stories relate in some form or another to parties, not every story contains a party. These shifts may indicate that Goodman is relaxing her thematic inclinations and may be opening the door to stories that will differ dramatically from her earlier work.

Party Girls is arguably a darker set of stories, which pose questions about the human condition that have no satisfactory answer. Many of the characters are dealing with loneliness and their own passing youth, themes that appear in the first two collections but that are more central in this third book. Whereas the theme of social class and social displacement play a significant part in all three of Goodman's books, the pervasive sense of loneliness and helplessness in *Party Girls* seems to stem less from class issues and more from the inability to connect meaningfully with other human beings shared by almost all of the collection's main characters. The title, *Party Girls*, then, is ironic. While parties are certainly a recurring theme in this collection, and some of the women are referred to explicitly as "party girls," in actuality most of these characters are the sort of people who feel out of place at parties, who must force themselves to socialize and often regret the outcomes after they do.

Party Girls immediately begins to explore that darker outlook through "Beloved Child," a story about a chef who finds herself figuratively adopted into a group of friends who consider themselves family but with whom the narrator does not feel a true connection. While Aiko, whose name is Japanese for "beloved child," and Gil, the narrator's boyfriend, commiserate over a shared grief—their fathers, who were both ministers, died years ago—the narrator has closed herself off from her own feelings after having lived through her mother's suicide when she was just fifteen. Though she says she prefers to leave the past in the past, it seems she has not fully dealt with the void her mother's death left behind.

The narrator's quiet, internal sorrow juxtaposed with the drama of Aiko and Gil's perpetual mourning deepens the wedge between the narrator and these characters. They feel she does not understand their pain, and they're right. She does not understand why they must relive this sadness in such an external way. Her sadness is far too deep to rise to the surface and float upon the shallows.

"Abracadabra" involves another chef who has trouble connecting with those around her. This chef realizes the depths of her loneliness only after she develops a relationship with a new employee. The signs that this new employee is not to be trusted are obvious to the reader, but the chef's judgment is clouded by her need to feel tethered to another human being. As she allows him to take more control over her restaurant, she begins to realize what she has been missing for so many years as she has focused solely on her career. However, it's unclear whether the lesson she takes away from the experience is that human connection is essential or, instead, that she should never have let her guard down and let someone in.

The next story, "Candy Land," conveys a similar sense of isolation, although it presents not a chef who has been swindled but a bank manager who has been forced into early retirement. Both characters have, knowingly or not, resigned themselves to loneliness after being left by men in their pasts, and the events of their respective stories force them to confront the consequences of this disengagement. Like the narrator in "Abracadabra," Candace discovers perhaps too late that she has allowed herself to become disconnected from the world around her. In Candace's case, the lesson comes in the form of an elaborate Saint Patrick's Day party. Candace has poured her heart and soul into preparing and cooking for the event, but only her former boss and his wife bother to attend. Candace's response to her lack of social significance is far more aggressive than is the narrator's in "Abracadabra." Whereas the chef in "Abracadabra" seems to have trouble formulating her next step after the events of her story, Candace is emboldened by the events of hers.

"Dancing" is the one exception to the irony of the collection's title: Lucy is in fact a party girl, or at least she was long ago in her youth. She loves going out to her small town's most popular restaurant, and she loves dancing. She does not love her boyfriend, Hank, or at least she understands that he does not love her and she equates this understanding with acceptance. She accepts that Hank does not like to dance, until she discovers that he has gone out dancing without her and spent the evening dancing with a much younger woman. It's no surprise to the reader that Hank would be so nonchalant about his relationship with Lucy, but Lucy is both surprised and enraged. Although she is certainly angry at Hank—and irrationally angry at the young, beautiful woman who has caught Hank's eye—she is perhaps angriest at herself for engaging in a relationship with such a shallow, emotionally unavailable man.

"The Hungry Girl" is arguably one of the more enigmatic of Goodman's stories. In it, we meet a personal chef who has a vendetta against aging Chef Yves, who she believes attempted to rape a student in his food safety class last summer. After being virtually ignored by Chef Yves in the course last summer, Veronica has dieted and studied the behavior of attractive women in hopes of catching the chef's attention this summer and humiliating him for his behavior last year. It is not solely to defend the victim, though, that Veronica has spent an entire year starving herself in preparation for this revenge. In fact, the victim, Charlotte was as oblivious to Veronica as Chef Yves was, and both of them made Veronica feel small and insignificant. She seems to detest the two equally, but it is from Chef Yves she longs to gain her retribution. Her plan, as elaborate as the planning has been, culminates in little more than embarrassing him over dinner, yet Veronica is satisfied with this outcome. Chef Yves insists that he did not rape Charlotte, and Charlotte herself dropped the charges, so it is never fully clear what really happened in the hotel room that night. But Veronica is sated by the knowledge that she was able to become the sort of woman to whom a man like Chef Yves might pay attention.

"Saving Julie" and "Saving Herself" are Goodman's second set of linked stories (the first, "Rosie" and "Valene," having appeared in *The Genius of Hunger*). "Saving Julie" brings together two very different women whose names are similar—Denise, the protagonist, and Doreen, the oblivious vacationer who has propped herself against the outside of Denise's apartment door to engage in an obnoxious cell phone conversation. Doreen complains into her phone about a party whose host, Julie, has no idea Doreen is attending only begrudgingly. Denise grows increasingly infuriated with the stranger, whose attitude about the party seems to affect Denise on a personal level. The next day, in "Saving Herself," Doreen is perched outside Denise's door again. This time, Denise tries to shoo Doreen away by forcefully unlocking the deadbolt and rattling the doorknob, but to no avail. When Doreen paces down the hallway a bit, Denise, on the pretense of taking out the garbage, steps out of her apartment to get a look at this complete stranger who has fueled such a fierce fire within her. Doreen, as it turns out, is nothing like what Denise had imagined— she's much older, as a start—and when Denise becomes so consumed by her rage that she begins to cry in the hallway, Doreen steps forward to comfort her. Doreen, as it turns out, is human, in the end, just like Julie, just like Denise.

Sloane from "The Secret World of Women" is perhaps the least like a party girl of all the women in this collection. Not only is Sloane demonstrably not a girl—her graying hair is one of the first details the reader is given about her— but she also hates parties and has to force herself to attend the one her friend, Abbey, is giving. At the party she meets Billy, who reminds her of Bruce Springsteen and awakens in her a long-dormant interest in romantic relationships. Sloane spends the evening analyzing Billy's interactions with her and convinces herself that he is as interested in her as she is in him. She e-mails him as soon as she returns home, believing that she is on the cusp of a grand romance. It is not until the next morning, when she sees him again, sober and in the light of day, that she realizes their budding passion had been all in her head.

The last story in the collection, "The Other Mothers," gives the reader a final glimpse of the themes of social anxiety and self-doubt by casting them in the light of a housewife, Mallory, who finds herself living on a private island in Florida, surrounded by the very wealthy and beautiful, most of whom speak English as a second (or third or fourth) language. She tells us:

> Since we arrived a month ago, I have tried different ways of making friends but I always get it wrong. It's hard. Sometimes I can't talk at all because everyone is speaking a language I don't understand. . . . Other times, I talk too much, I talk without thinking and I hear words coming out of my own mouth that I don't remember ever being in my head.
>
> *(Party Girls*, p. 111)

This language barrier is the perfect metaphor for the feeling of otherness in which Mallory finds herself drowning. She both figuratively and literally cannot understand the people around her, and they cannot understand her.

This inability to connect plunges Mallory into a deep depression, and her method of coping with her emotional distress is self-harming. When her husband, Roger, suggests she hold a Midwestern-style barbecue to try to get to know the other mothers at the prep school her children attend, Mallory is temporarily comforted. She believes that if she can introduce these women to her lifestyle—the food she eats, the type of party she throws and attends—they will understand her and she will, at last, feel at peace. From the moment the party begins, though, her belief that she does not belong returns with a vengeance. The other mothers will not eat the fatty bratwurst and potato salad she has prepared, many of them having eaten before arriving late at the party, and one even electing to bring her own lightly dressed salad. They have brought, instead, bottles of wine and expensive cake to share. Accustomed to hired help, they let their garbage rest wherever it falls, and Mallory is mistaken for a maid when she attempts to clean up the scattered cups and napkins while the party is still in full swing.

Mallory's emotional distress reaches its peak when she watches Roger mingling easily with the guests. He hardly acknowledges Mallory,

which she takes as a great affront since he is the only person in attendance she can talk to in any meaningful way, and he doesn't even seem to notice when she piles a plate with her greasy cookout comfort food and carries it to the bedroom to eat alone in bed. However, it is not on Roger but on her own children that she takes out the brunt of her dissatisfaction.

CONCLUSION

Like all great literature, Goodman's work will continue to resonate for years to come. Her exploration of class, gender roles, and human connection and disconnection will continue to be relevant even as society changes. Though her stories continue to explore many of the same themes, the complexity of characters and situations in her newer stories cast a much darker light than those in her first two books. It's as though the naive and often desperate hopes of the characters in her early stories have been tracked to their inevitable conclusions: broken hearts, unfulfilled desires, futures that fail to supersede the past. Time will only tell where her next short story collection will lead her, but no doubt she will continue to study ugly, difficult things through beautifully poetic prose and fully realized characters.

Selected Bibliography

WORKS OF DIANE GOODMAN

SHORT-STORY COLLECTIONS

The Genius of Hunger. Pittsburgh, Pa.: Carnegie Mellon University Press, 2002.

The Plated Heart. Pittsburgh, Pa.: Carnegie Mellon University Press, 2006.

Party Girls. Pittsburgh, Pa.: Autumn House Press, 2011.

OTHER WORKS

Constellations. Whately, Mass.: Heatherstone Press, 1993. (Poetry chapbook.)

"Beloved." In *Keeping the Wolves at Bay: Stories by Emerging American Writers.* Edited by Sharon Dilworth. Pittsburgh, Pa.: Autumn House Press, 2010.

"Food for Thought." The Story Prize Blogspot, 2011. http://thestoryprize.blogspot.com/2011/12/diane-goodman-food-for-thought.html

"What I Know." In *Best Food Writing 2013.* Edited by Holly Hughes. Philadelphia: Da Capo Press, 2013.

"The Endless Present." *EatingWell*, July–August 2014.

REVIEWS

Review of *The Genius of Hunger. Kirkus Reviews* 69, no. 24:1704 (December 15, 2001). https://www.kirkusreviews.com/book-reviews/diane-goodman/the-genius-of-hunger/

Ubinas, Helen. "The Poetic Tales of Everyday Women." *Hartford Courant*, March 17, 2002. http://articles.courant.com/2002-03-17/entertainment/0203170625_1_odd-tale-everyday-women-hunger (Review of *The Genius of Hunger*.)

INTERVIEWS

Bannon, Jennifer. "Diane Goodman: The Party Girl Serves Up Short Fiction Delicacies." *Alimentum*, 2011. http://www.alimentumjournal.com/party-girls-interview

Cowger, Ashley. Personal, unpublished interview with Diane Goodman. June 21, 2016.

"Diane Goodman, Ph.D." *Letters, Numbers, Minds & Voices.* Grand Canyon University, n.d. http://blogs.gcu.edu/college-of-humanities-and-social-sciences/diane-goodman-phd/

OTHER SOURCES

Fitz, Nicholas. "Economic Inequality: It's Far Worse Than You Think." *Scientific American*, March 31, 2015. http://www.scientificamerican.com/article/economic-inequality-it-s-far-worse-than-you-think/

"Outstanding and Notable 2011 Collections." *TSP* (The Story Prize), n.d. http://thestoryprize.blogspot.com/2012/02/outstanding-and-notable-2011.html

STEPHANIE ELIZONDO GRIEST

(1974—)

Kristin Winet

STEPHANIE ELIZONDO GRIEST likes to tell the story of her great-great-uncle Jake, an intrepid wanderer who saw all of the United States with his legs hanging off the edge of a freight train. This story is usually followed by stories of her father, who drummed his way around the world with the United States Navy Band, and then of her cousins, a pair of freedom-loving cowboys who chased cattle all across the deserts of South Texas. According to Griest, what these men in her family have in common is that their stories represent the wanderlust that is encoded into her DNA and that actively—and persistently— "pumps through [her] veins" (*100 Places*, p. xiii). Straddling the line between reportage and memoir, a line she declares is arbitrary, Griest's work echoes this lifelong desire to satisfy the wanderlust she was born with, to better understand the complexities of post-Communist countries and places going through immense social change, and to bring to light the magnificent and the ordinary in a complex, globalized world.

Griest's joyful sense of humor and colloquial yet academically curious style resonate in the books that have established this Chicana feminist at the forefront of literary travel journalism. In addition to her three travel books, published between 2004 and 2010, her journalism, which has appeared in such diverse magazines and literary journals as *The Believer, Florida Review, Poets & Writers, Texas Observer*, and *Latina Magazine*, showcases the dexterity of her work and her ability to cross the genres of memoir, reportage, and literary journalism almost seamlessly. With a wide audience and a political agenda focused almost exclusively on exploring feminist issues, advocating for free speech, and investigating the way democracy enhances (and sometimes stifles) lives across the world, she shines most when she is able to weave together her own adventurous travel tales with the lives and experiences of the people she meets and befriends along the way.

In her first book, *Around the Bloc: My Life in Moscow, Beijing, and Havana* (2004), she openly admits her fear of remaining either unknown or stuck for life in her hometown of Corpus Christi, Texas, citing a terrifying dream in which she wakes up at twenty-five "roaming Mary Carroll High's halls in [her] letterman jacket and getting plastered in the Taco Bell parking lot for fun" (p. xi). In *Mexican Enough: My Life Between the Borderlines* (2008), she admits that even after she spent her twenties on four different continents, she still couldn't sit still: the day she turned thirty, she knew it was time to (again) quit her day job, cram everything she owned into storage, and ravage her savings account (p. 4). In her guidebook, *100 Places Every Woman Should Go* (2007), she reaffirms this reality by reminding her readers that although she has explored two dozen countries and all but four U.S. states, she still aches for more (p. xiii).

Though her work often seeks to give voice to the voiceless and explore the wider world of social justice issues through her journalism, she is never personally removed from the people and places she writes about; in fact, she is an integral part—and voice—of the stories she tells, wrestling with her own wanderlust and her desire to rival the stories of her male ancestors. This is the context from which Griest enters the wider world of travel journalism, and why she starts many of her travel narratives by addressing this wander-

STEPHANIE ELIZONDO GRIEST

lust. She has always felt a need to legitimize and explain the gnawing: she is both an unencumbered female wanderer (most of her belongings fit into her backpack) and an observant feminist journalist, falling in love, time and time again, with places around the globe that people had least expected her to love. This gives her work a certain immediacy and credibility, simultaneously legitimizing her penchant for social activism and the reasons she is committed to telling her own stories and giving voice to the voiceless. Her journalism actively reflects this. Her part-memoir, part-reportage blend of travel writing places her directly in the center while observing the issues of revolution, empire, and colonialism as they unfold around her and directly inform her life experience—and stoke her fire for adventure, for a life story she believes to be worth telling.

Griest's work is also an important contribution to the world of travel journalism because she offers a welcome voice to the otherwise male-dominated field she desperately desired to enter. In many ways, her books differ from much mainstream travel journalism—and that of her male predecessors in particular—simply because she is fueled by a lifelong desire to fully understand how she fits in with the intrepid men of her past and to figure out how, as a biracial woman with Mexican roots who grew up calling herself white, she fits into the wider global tapestry of individuals whose lives are marked by migration, exile, and belonging. This tension—how to appreciate her home roots more thoroughly while also stroking her wanderlust—both fueled Griest's original desire to become a travel journalist and now serves as a counternarrative to the many travel tales of women of privilege divorcing themselves from their material possessions and personal commitments in exchange for travel. For this reason, her subject position as a biracial woman of mixed heritage continues to resonate with the many women travelers who face similar dilemmas between staying home and traveling abroad—and provides welcome alternatives to more traditional narratives. Therefore, as a much-needed voice in the field of women's travel journalism, Griest offers us a compelling perspective.

Stephanie Elizondo Griest was born on June 6, 1974, in Corpus Christi, Texas, a place that has become a touchstone in her books as the place from which she constantly escapes and returns. All her life, having barely left the confines of this Texas city on the Gulf of Mexico, Griest grew up wondering if she, too, could participate in—and even rival—the stories of the males in the family. Having grown up in a place that she claims held nothing more for her than strip centers, shopping malls, and a relatively uneventful high school life, she knew that she needed to find the kind of life that suburban America could not satisfy. When the time came to make important life decisions upon graduation, she realized that if she didn't seek an alternative reality for herself, she would likely, for instance, end up buying all of her jewelry from a booth at the mall rather than from its country of origin (*Around the Bloc*, p. xi). In other words, she was terrified that she would never be able to rival the stories her male ancestors could tell around the dinner table and at family holidays. As she writes in the preface to *The Best Women's Travel Writing 2010*, she would never be able to start a conversation like "that time in Burkina Faso" or that time "in Marrakech . . ." (p. xv). This thread—rationalizing and legitimizing her travels—permeates all of Griest's travel books, emphasizing her need to make her presence known and to stand as tall as her traveling ancestors.

This dream started to materialize for her during her senior year in high school, when she applied for and was chosen to attend a prestigious journalism conference in Washington, D.C., that featured a keynote address by a top CNN correspondent who had covered both the fall of the Berlin Wall and the recent collapse of the Soviet Union. Having considered the idea of becoming a journalist for most of her young life, she decided she had to go to the conference, so she raised some money, talked her mother out of her frequent flyer miles, and boarded a plane for the first time in her life. Listening to the keynote speaker, she realized the trajectory of her life didn't have to begin and end in South Texas; she could become an international journalist. Griest

remembers that during the talk, the speaker "vividly described how Lithuanians had flung their bodies in front of Russian tanks to shield their television tower, how Estonians had impaled their Soviet passports upon stakes and set them ablaze in protest, how millions spilled into the street and demanded social change" (*Around the Bloc*, p. xii). As she later put it in an interview with Kristin Winet in 2012, "His stories of Revolution marveled me," because "the only thing that people would take to the streets and shake their fists about in South Texas was football." After his rousing talk, she ran up to the microphone and asked him how she could be just like him. Learn Russian, he said, and then moved on to the next question. Griest took his advice, enrolling in Russian at the University of Texas at Austin in the fall and spending the next four years intimately learning the language's unusual conjugations, inflections, and idiomatic phrases. In 1996, during her junior year, she made her first visit to Russia when she spent a semester at the Moscow Linguistics Institute, experiencing life firsthand in post-Soviet Russia instead of reading about it in a textbook.

Her college years prepared her in unexpected ways for life in the twelve Communist countries she would explore between 1996 and 2000. During her last three years of college Griest lived and worked in a commune-style housing cooperative, a "crunchy granola version of a socialist workers' commune" called Royal (*Around the Bloc*, p. 15). There, she lived with sixteen other vegetarians, growing her own herbs, brewing her own beer, and composting her own waste. Each week, everyone was expected to contribute at least five hours of their time to household chores, including cooking, cleaning, and even "changing the water in the tofu bucket" in order to keep the house and community running smoothly (p. 15). This experience, lovingly called their utopian "cooperativism," felt like paradise to her until a group of Russian exchange students came to live with them and told the Americans that their "utopia" reminded them of a Soviet *komunalnaya kvartira*, communal-style housing in which dozens of family members were stuffed into two-bedroom apartments. When the relationship between the Americans and the Russians became estranged, with the Americans complaining that the Russians wouldn't do their share and the Russians scoffing at the Americans for acting like "commies" (p. 16), Griest realized that the meanings of truth, democracy, and justice—concepts that "had surrounded [her] since birth" (p. 17)—were ideologies she needed to better understand. Overall, Griest believes that those early experiences should have prepared her well for life under communism, but instead, it often left her with more questions than answers. She graduated Phi Beta Kappa in 1997 with dual degrees in journalism and post-Soviet studies and, after the trip in her junior year to Russia, a certificate in advanced Russian from the Moscow Linguistics Institute.

During this first trip to Russia in 1996, she took "notes, mad notes, every single day, even though [she] had no idea what to do with them" (Winet interview). After graduation, she left for China, where she edited and taught writing and news reporting at the *China Daily* in Beijing as a Henry Luce Scholar. This fellowship, which sends fifteen to eighteen young Americans to Asia each year to work on a scholarly project of their choice, gave her the opportunity to get a behind-the-scenes look at censorship and propaganda in the Chinese press. As she tells it, "once again, [she] took mad notes" and returned to the United States with "a fierce set of stories," realizing that she needed to write a book (Winet interview). It would take a while, but the notes she took in both Russia and China found their way into *Around the Bloc* (2004).

Meanwhile, back in the United States, she worked as a freelance writer. She was a political reporter for the Austin bureau of the Associated Press, where she covered such topics as George W. Bush's work as governor of Texas and his campaign for the U.S. presidency. She also served as a Reston Fellow at the *New York Times*, wrote for the *Washington Post*, and freelanced for the *Seattle Post-Intelligencer*. The topics she covered were as broad as they were incisive: from male belly dancers to religious cults (a story that had landed her a spot on the coveted *USA Today* collegiate All-Academic First Team in 1996) to Seattle's 1990s grunge scene, her work is grounded in a passion for understanding the diverse peoples of the world—and the passions

and desire for belonging that drive them—as she, too, seeks to understand her own bicultural, biracial life as a Chicana woman. In 2000 Griest participated in a project called the Odyssey, a forty-five-thousand-mile historical documentation journey she undertook with eight young social justice activists who wanted to explore the people and events in Howard Zinn's *A People's History of the United States* (1980) and rewrite it for K–12 students. During this yearlong journey, Griest and her cohort documented the lives and stories of the people who aren't typically featured in history textbooks, giving voice to the slaves, migrant workers, and indigenous peoples who also played a large role in shaping U.S. history. They filed their dispatches online and encouraged young people to follow them as they visited historic places of interest throughout the nation. Of all her adventures, Griest claims that her work with the Odyssey was "hands-down the greatest adventure" of her life (Winet interview).

For a few years after this, she lived in Brooklyn, New York, in a tiny apartment crammed with multiple roommates and living off a nonprofit salary. After the publication of *Around the Bloc* in the spring of 2004 and a relatively exhausting book tour, she turned thirty and realized that she had been living backward, not forward—and that she needed to move on to the next thing. She came up with a new book idea, to live and study Spanish in Mexico, and although she hadn't been able to find a grant to fund her yet, she left for Mexico on New Year's Eve 2004. One week later, to her astonishment, she opened her e-mail to find that she had been awarded Princeton University's Hodder Fellowship for 2005–2006, which would enable her to stay in Mexico for eight months and then to write her book, which became her second travel memoir, *Mexican Enough* (2008).

After she returned to the United States and completed her Princeton fellowship in the summer of 2006, Griest decided to adopt a completely itinerant lifestyle, moving out of her apartment, putting what she had left into storage, hitting the road, and sleeping in artist colonies, on college campuses, in friends' spare bedrooms, and with family. She became, as she writes in a 2009 *Poets & Writers* article, "Confessions of an Author Nomad," a "colony whore"—that is, an artist who applies to dozens of residencies for the maximum amount of time every year and then lines them up, year after year, so that she can continue to travel and write what she wants. Though some people called her homeless during this time, she preferred the term "nomadic," believing that she could live the rest of her life applying for residencies, grants, and fellowships (p. 105). During these itinerant years, in addition to publishing *Mexican Enough*, she wrote a guidebook for women, *100 Places Every Woman Should Go* (2007), and traveled to more than thirty-five cities promoting it. She remembers these years both fondly and with a dose of wry skepticism, particularly in the areas of romantic life, healthy eating, and the odd habits that develop when a person is alone all the time. Before she began her nomadic lifestyle, she was a staunch vegetarian who cooked her own meals and composted; after becoming itinerant, she memorized every hot dog stand and fast food restaurant in the nation's airports. Once a belly dancer whose daily yoga practice kept her in impeccable shape, now she could barely contort herself into a lotus position. She suffered wrist and back injuries and digestive issues ("Confessions," pp. 105–106). Sometimes she would be so exhausted that she wouldn't be able to write unless she was staying at an art colony. In other words, as she rationalizes this lifestyle, "half of you must be a highly organized hustler who nabs great gigs and airfares. The other half must be a universe-loving hippie who believes that whatever happens is beautiful" ("Confessions," p. 107). These tensions eventually led her to ask herself how much longer she could—or would want to—live this way, and she ultimately decided that since she had always been a writer but felt she knew nothing of the craft, she would quit the nomadic lifestyle she had worked so hard to cultivate and go back to school for her master's degree.

In 2012 Griest completed her M.F.A. in nonfiction at the University of Iowa's esteemed creative writing program, an experience she claims helped her discover that although she loved the life of book tours, traveling, and being partially nomadic, she loved teaching as well. She worked as a visiting professor of creative

writing at St. Lawrence University in upstate New York for one year and then took a position as assistant professor and Margaret R. Shuping Fellow of creative nonfiction at the University of North Carolina at Chapel Hill in 2013. As of 2017 Griest had four travel books to her name (*All the Agents and Saints: Dispatches from the U.S. Borderlands* was released in July 2017) and she had edited a collection of women's travel stories. In addition to this, she has written hundreds of articles for magazines and websites, contributed to a number of travel anthologies and collections, and worked on many additional campaigns and literacy efforts. Along the way, Griest's work has also given her the chance to get involved in social activism work. As a testament to her commitment to freedom of the press, she cofounded the Youth Free Expression Movement, a nonprofit anticensorship organization for teen writers, and also serves as a senior fellow at the World Policy Institute and a board member of the National Coalition Against Censorship (NCAC), an alliance of fifty nonprofit organizations working to educate the public about the consequences of censorship and how to protect the freedom of speech.

For a young woman who grew up worrying that she would never be able to leave the confines of her hometown in South Texas, the fact that she has explored over thirty countries and nearly every U.S. state and now teaches creative writing to hopeful journalists and memoirists stands as a testament to both her commitment to follow in her great-great-uncle's footsteps and her determination to find and make known her own voice. It also shows her dedication to rescuing travel memoir from the hands of the privileged and placing it directly into the hands of all the women, people of color, and minorities who believe a life of travel is not accessible to them.

AROUND THE BLOC: MY LIFE IN MOSCOW, BEIJING, AND HAVANA

Griest's first major book, *Around the Bloc: My Life in Moscow, Beijing, and Havana*, published in 2004, marked her entrance into the world of journalistic memoir and represents the better part of her twenties, a decade she characterizes as one consumed with what she refers to collectively as "the Bloc"—not just the former Eastern Bloc of the Soviet Union and its satellites but present-day Communist countries like China and Cuba as well. Throughout the book, she questions the meaning of democracy and seeks to understand what she grew up thinking of as the "Evil Empire," as well as understanding the role of her generation in shaping the future of the post-Communist (and continuing Communist) world. As a memoir, the book reads like personal diary entries, with each chapter broken into a theme that is loosely chronological; as a piece of reportage, it reads like an intimate immersion piece dedicated to exploring the lives of ordinary people in the aftermath of the fall of the Berlin Wall in 1989 and the Soviet Union in 1991. As both personal journey and historical document, the power in Griest's first book is in its naiveté and its determination; the narrator is simultaneously idealistic, wide-eyed, and passionate, intent on finding excitement and purpose in her travels to parts of the world no one in her family ever expected her to venture.

In the first section, "Moscow," readers are introduced to Griest's backstory on growing up in Texas as she lives out her semester abroad in post-Soviet Russia. Taking place in 1996, her story documents life in Russia as it was transitioning into a democratic republic, emphasizing the impending changes to the nation's fabric and the personal and professional opportunities and limitations faced by its citizens. Her writerly ethos, both as *inostranka* ("foreign girl") and young, hopeful political journalist, shines through as she takes her readers through the experiences she had during her time in Moscow. She opens the book by recounting her dormitory life, for which nothing could have prepared her. In order to demonstrate the deplorable living conditions with which she was suddenly faced, she describes the chronic lightbulb shortage, the wrath of insects, the flooding bathtub, and the burned-out burners on the stove; then she shares stories of cockroaches, washing clothes in a bucket, and sleeping on a flat mattress and pillow "the width of a pantyliner" (*Around the Bloc*, p. 10). After this first shocking experience, she takes readers to the Moscow Linguistics Institute, the school

where she takes advanced Russian classes; she volunteers for a short time at a *priyat*, a temporary children's home, and learns how to properly drink vodka (one bottle per person per party, and all shots should be chased by either pickles or sausages). She recounts her love interests, focusing a whole chapter on a dashing twenty-something male named Andrei who reveals that he was imprisoned after refusing to expose himself to radiation, and she ends her stay in Moscow with a visit to Vladimir Lenin's mausoleum in Red Square.

Befittingly, the journey of this twenty-one-year-old revolutionary from Texas is equal parts coming-of-age story and eyewitness testimony to a period of immense and difficult social change. Throughout the book, revolution and its aftermath are never far from Griest's mind, particularly as they relate to inflation, delayed wages, unemployment, public services and health care, dating, and corruption. In nearly every chapter, she explores the cultural and social tensions that face young Russians as they learn to navigate their new world, focusing on such realities as the apathy many Russians feel toward revolting, the lack of interest in fighting for their rights, and the general pervasiveness of anti-Americanism. In one scene, she waits in line at the Moscow Linguistics Institute for her stipend—300,000 rubles, or about $60—and realizes that she, as a light-skinned American foreigner, is given more than even the highly educated professors at the institute (p. 22). At the same time, she becomes frustrated when she finds that none of the young people at her school want to assemble, noticing that although they gained the right to protest in 1991, "students at MLI celebrated that freedom's reverse—the right not to gather" (p. 25). She also remembers how, on International Women's Day, instead of gathering to defend the rights of women, everyone gathered to try the new McChicken sandwich at the new McDonald's near Red Square. She comes to understand that transitioning to democracy is a lengthy and complicated process, and she is also acutely aware that her Russian friends face painful realities that she, as an outsider, can never really quite understand. Part of her journey is coming to realize that these differences exist regardless of how much students

come together and rally for their rights—and that her privilege as an American who is simply passing through Russia as an exchange student is part of her own growth process.

She writes passionately about the anti-American sentiments directed at her, citing a few stories that emphasize how difficult it can be for a young Chicana woman to travel alone in Russia. In one chapter, she takes readers into the home of a friend where a fellow student named Misha insults her culture and music, claiming that he would never set foot on American soil. In another, she shares the story of trying to buy a ticket at the Moscow Metro to visit her friend Elena, a frustrating experience in which she gets sent to three different counters before realizing that the women selling the tickets are playing a trick on her. Then, seeking help, she knocks on the door of the attendant box down by the train, where she is greeted by an angry old woman yelling "Get out of Russia!" as she stands there helplessly (p. 59). Griest's mission in sharing these stories is not to make her readers feel sorry for her; rather, she wants to portray the very real suspicions that many Russians felt toward Americans in the mid-1990s, a time when relations between the two nations were not much more positive than they had been in the Soviet era. Not surprisingly, she counters these unfortunate situations with plenty of stories of the generosity and warm-spirited nature of many Russians she meets and befriends, always careful to try to present the full picture.

Much of the book focuses on the differences between young, idealistic Americans and young, apathetic Russians—a contrast she notices almost immediately and returns to as a theme throughout the section. Fashion is one indicator of the divide: at the Moscow Linguistics Institute, one of the first things she notices is that the Russian students are "a primped and preened bunch: Their hair was combed, their shoes were polished, their clothes were neatly pressed"; the girls wore lots of makeup and the boys lots of aftershave (p. 17). In her typically wry way, she compares this stylish look with her own laid-back Texas mannerisms and dress, reminding readers that she had honed the art of "rolling out of bed," going

out without makeup, and wearing Levis. Throughout the book, she continues to marvel at the physical differences in femininity and dress that she witnesses, even going so far as to theorize about it, citing the work of sociologists like Francine du Plessix Gray and suggesting that women's primping sessions "generates from centuries of political terror, when citizens learned as a survival technique to quickly size up strangers and determine whether or not they were trustable" (p. 86). She feels like a frumpy, androgynous "pauper" in "mud brown corduroys, bulky sweaters, and hiking boots" until she reaches the *banya* (Russian bathhouse) in chapter 7 and sees Russian women of all shapes and sizes with their inhibitions down (p. 87). Reconciling the differences between these cultural norms of dress and fashion, she leaves Russia with a newfound appreciation for style but also recognizes her roots as a vegetarian Chicana feminist.

The second part of *Around the Bloc* takes place in China, where Griest stays for a year following her time in Moscow. After realizing that she'd "missed out on something by arriving [in Russia] five years after communism's collapse," she decides that she needs to "go where the Revolution prospered and Former Times was the present" to more fully comprehend what life is like under Communist rule (p. 169). During her time there, Griest worked at the *China Daily*, the national newspaper she calls "the English mouthpiece" of the Communist Party, in order to more fully understand the role of censorship and ethics in the media. Unlike the first and third sections of the book, however, Griest feels most out of place in China, a country that continues to elude her. From the first moment to the last, she is confronted by her sense of *laowai*, or foreigner status, wherever she goes and whatever she does. Not only does she have trouble making friends with Chinese women and finding dates (she is even asked by her employer to avoid befriending her Chinese colleagues because it is "too risky") but she continually makes cultural faux pas, has to give up her vegetarian convictions, and struggles to understand some of China's most important cultural norms, such as *mianxi*, or the idea of saving face (p. 221). Though she never

says so directly, Griest struggles with adjusting to life under Communist rule and recognizes the difficulties contemporary men and women living in China face on a day-to-day basis.

Griest begins her tale by emphasizing the olfactory and culinary differences in China, a trope that she uses throughout her stay to demonstrate just how foreign she feels in her new home. Her first "whiff" of Beijing is startling: an unsettling combination of cigarettes, sweat, and soy sauce (p. 173). She can't even see more than a few meters, describing the city's infamous smog as a "billowy greyness" that "hung so heavily" in the sky it made it difficult for her to breathe (p. 175). On her first day, she and some colleagues visit an upscale restaurant for lunch, an experience that leaves her grappling with her strong commitment to vegetarianism, as she is faced with the difficult predicament of eating such delicacies as duck, pork belly, chicken fingers, and fish. She uses the moment, though, to shrug off her convictions and devote her time in China to discovery, asking, "Can't morals be shoved aside for a little culture now and then?" (p. 182). From there, she falls in love with Chinese cuisine, sharing experiences of riding her bicycle through the open-air markets, eating street food, and shopping for fruits and vegetables.

Of course, Griest's reason for being in China is to learn from and report on the state of the media, particularly at the *China Daily*. The entire experience is strange to her, as the business is run as a *danwei*, or an institution that is fully responsible for the lives and careers of its employees: it provides employee housing, sets salaries, pays medical and dental care, approves marriages and divorces, oversees the birth of everyone's one child, holds passports, monitors all travel, allots such goods as toilet paper, shampoo, and soap, and sets contracts that are incredibly difficult to break (pp. 190–191). Griest is amazed by this, especially when she begins hearing how dissatisfied her coworkers are with these restrictions and lack of opportunities. Her coworker Liu, for instance, complains that she hates the shampoo they choose for her; another coworker tells her the story of an unhappy wife who flung herself out of the fourteenth-story

window of the *danwei's* building on her husband's birthday. Griest is uncertain about the stories the paper publishes as well, citing many examples of egregious errors used to make China look better in comparison with places like Tibet and Taiwan; similarly, she discovers that the list of off-limits topics has grown increasingly large, including anything that might make China look less than perfect, and that the Xinhua news agency even provides proper adjectives and phrases to ensure consistency across media outlets (p. 199). As in Russia, Griest is frustrated by the lack of interest in rebellion, never really understanding why no one protests more forcefully and why so many of her coworkers shrug and say that "sometimes you have to sacrifice your principles to be flexible—and [they] think that's ok" (p. 203).

Part of the power of this part of Griest's journey is in her struggle to understand China's complex history and the role of Mao Zedong in shaping the lives and opportunities of the people she meets. As a tourist, she visits a number of important historical sites, such Mao's mausoleum, Tiananmen Square, and even the Natural History Museum, where she encounters human cadavers floating in glass cases. This struggle to understand is intimately tied to the Chinese media's relationship with the truth and culminates in Griest's investigation into the real history of Tiananmen Square. At first she struggles to understand how the media in China could restrict its peoples' access to knowledge and news, wondering how such mind-numbing reports (often hyperbolic at best) about the state's agricultural, social, economic, and industrial achievements could be satisfactory to readers. However, after diving into the archives at the *danwei* library and finding a three-month gap in the *China Daily* archives and a suspicious article published by the *International Herald Tribune* that cites only the government as a source of information, she realizes that the government controls the media and that no original reporting was used. She writes that although some Chinese journalists did try to report on the demonstrations and share what really happened that day, the Chinese people she meets have moved on, claiming that they are powerless to change their situation and therefore

"just focus on the things that affect [them] directly. Like housing and health care, and having a good life" (p. 244). At the end of this section, Griest wonders who has suffered most under Stalin's and Mao's grand experiments, coming to the conclusion at her last banquet meal that the only way to bring about change in China is "through quiet influence," not through grand demonstrations or upending existing social norms (p. 291).

After her stay in China, Griest writes that instead of returning home immediately, she spent time traveling aimlessly through Mongolia, Uzbekistan, Kyrgyzstan, Russia, and Turkey. During that fateful trip, Griest experienced a number of unfortunate events, including the collapse of Russia's currency and getting robbed in Istanbul; these experiences prompted her to abandon Europe for a while and instead seek a different path. She returned home to Corpus Christi, but soon went to Colombia to reunite with her ex-boyfriend, Mario, the "full-blooded, soccer-playing, coffee-picking, sign-of-the-crossing Latino who dominated [her] heart," who had visited her in China and who she had pined for ever since (p. 302). However, the relationship quickly went sour and Griest ended up back in Corpus Christi, "at the washed-up age of twenty-five" and without a plan (p. 303). Along with her friend Machi, she decides to sneak into Cuba illegally through Mexico to see how Cuba is faring as a Communist country at the turn of the millennium, concealing her American identity by claiming she is a Canadian graduate student from a small town near Toronto. During her short but exceptionally positive time in Havana, Griest marches with a group of mothers demanding Elián González's safe return to Cuba, almost gets to see Fidel Castro speak, learns to dance the rumba, interviews students at the University of Havana, and meets Cuba's premier hip-hop musician.

Most of this short section of the book (only fifty-four pages) is devoted to Griest's exploration of the political situation in Cuba at the turn of the twenty-first century, meaning that a great deal is devoted to the controversy in 2000 over Elián González and the lengthy debate over

STEPHANIE ELIZONDO GRIEST

whether or not the young child who made it to Miami should be sent back to his homeland, Cuba. Early in her stay, she hears of a political demonstration rallying for the return of Elián and quickly joins, hoping to finally see—after four years and eleven present and former Communist nations—"some in-the-streets action!" (p. 312). What she discovers, however, is not a solemn political march but something more like a parade, with women and mothers waving flags, playing Celia Cruz songs, and cheering. Her attempts to meet Fidel Castro are thwarted when he opts not to show up at a follow-up rally to the demonstration. Though she had thought that this might be her chance to "see a Communist leader who wasn't bloated behind a pane of glass," Griest is at first disappointed by these setbacks but then comes to realize that life in Cuba is more than just political demonstrations and Communist rallies (p. 314).

Griest reclaims much of her identity in Cuba, owing to the fact that she is suddenly seen as a desirable woman and is in a culture where she doesn't feel so undeniably foreign. In one chapter, she tells the story of how she overcame getting dumped by Mario—twice—by learning to revel in and enjoy the attention she gets from "every male on the block" (p. 321). As she writes, "there's just something about an island full of gorgeous men calling you *linda* that makes you start to believe it" (p. 322). This outward acceptance leads to a more reflective self-acceptance, as Griest comes to the realization that she can be both independent and sexually desirable. At the end of another chapter in which she tries to rumba with a handsome young Cuban named Harold, she realizes that Russians bond over vodka, Chinese over dinner, and Cubans through appreciation for the body and dance. Griest returns home to the United States a confident traveler who, after compromising her convictions, questioning her commitment to feminism, and thinking critically about her claim to her Mexican heritage, no longer sees herself as the "militant-vegetarian-Chicana-feminist" she left thinking she was (p. 365). Instead, she returns with a stronger-than-ever belief in social activism, realizing that demonstrations and protests are not

necessarily as romantic as she once believed they were and that she wants to devote herself to learning Spanish and reclaiming her Chicana identity.

100 PLACES EVERY WOMAN SHOULD GO

Griest's second book, *100 Places Every Woman Should Go*, is a distinct departure from *Around the Bloc* in the sense that it is not really a journalistic memoir; though there are moments when Griest's voice shines through, it is more a guidebook for women about places important to women than a collection of Griest's personal stories. The book was commissioned by Travelers' Tales Press in 2009 to inspire conversations about travel destinations centered around places where women made history, where women sought (and seek) enlightenment or beautification, where women can have adventures, and where women can indulge themselves. Though the places chosen do skew toward the Americas and Europe, leaving out some potentially worthwhile additions, the book fills an important niche in the ever-evolving travel market, and speaks specifically to the kinds of places where "being a woman is affirmed and confirmed; where you will be energized and impassioned" (p. xiv). Griest is also careful to anticipate counterarguments about women's safety, letting her readers know before they even begin reading the first chapter that only places where men are "at least somewhat respectful to foreign women" were chosen for final inclusion in the book.

The book reads like a reimagining of the traditional form of the guidebook, with each chapter meditating on a place that speaks to women. Structurally and thematically, the book works more as a feminist manifesto than a traditional guidebook, undermining the form by supplying all the expected trimmings: lists of entries categorized by theme, with each entry including an introduction, a little bit of historical background, a highlight, and recommended reading. In the first section, for instance, readers are taken to places where powerful women made history, spending a few pages on such important figures as Sappho in Lesbos, Greece; Joan of Arc

in Rouen, France; and seventeenth-century witches in Salem, Massachusetts. In each short chapter, Griest offers relevant and insightful commentary on why each place matters to women and how they can most enjoy their time there. In the Salem chapter, for instance, she suggests that women start their tour at the Salem Witch Museum, walks them through how they might spend their day, and then advises them to travel there in October, when the city hosts two important events: the Haunted Happenings exhibit, a month-long festival that includes a lively children's parade; and the Annual Psychic Fair and Witchcraft Expo, in which women can take aura photography, get astrological guidance, or receive a psychic reading from an expert.

Other sections are just as entertaining. Section 2, "Places of Adventure," covers such diverse places as Antarctica and surfing sites most amenable to women surfers. Section 3, "Places of Purification and Beautification," offers readers a glimpse into the Russian *banya*, Brazilian bikini waxes, and the best destinations for holistic spa treatments. Further sections include famous chocolate sites, best ice cream parlors, and the sexiest lingerie shops. Even though the book presupposes that all women would wish to go on these excursions, Griest nonetheless fills a gap in the available resources for women travelers, ending her tour around the world with a brief meditation on why all women should travel to the homes of their ancestors, writing that no place is "as meaningful as our own motherlands" (p. 309). She suggests that women do this so that they can "leave with the satisfaction that [they] witnessed the same sunset as [their] ancestors, and that [their] boots collected the same dust" (p. 311).

MEXICAN ENOUGH: MY LIFE BETWEEN THE BORDERLINES

Published in 2008, *Mexican Enough: My Life Between the Borderlands* is Griest's second travel memoir and begins as a meditation upon the author's status as a multiethnic travel writer. Though Griest spent her twenties traveling and documenting life in Communist and former Communist countries, she describes herself at thirty as experiencing a professional crisis: having devoted nearly a decade to one book and "living backward," she is eager to begin afresh by living in the present (p. 2). Moreover, growing up in South Texas as the daughter of an Anglo father and a Mexican American mother, she also feels an identity crisis, especially because she can speak Russian fluently but speaks only rudimentary Spanish. The contours of *Mexican Enough* are therefore personal and also global: while Griest seeks to better understand her Mexican heritage, she also desires to understand the broader cultural implications of her own family's journey—and the journey of millions of other Mexican Americans—from Mexico to the United States.

Although Griest travels to many different parts of Mexico in *Mexican Enough*, the first half of the book focuses on her personal journey. After a brief stay in La Zona Rosa ("the Pink Zone"), the heart of Mexico City's gay community, Griest travels to Querétaro, a city 135 miles northwest of the city, to begin her journey. Though she initially plans on staying for a year, she returns to the United States after four months, but sets off for a short trip to Mexico again a few months later, this time with her mother. The pair travel to Cruillas to learn more about their family history from distant relatives who decided to stay rather than migrate to Texas. Then, for purposes that could be described as more journalistic than personal, she travels to the Mexican state of Chiapas, located in the extreme southeast and bordering Guatemala. Chiapas is also the site of the 1994 Zapatista uprising, an armed revolt against the Mexican military and state that sought to secure greater land rights and resources for indigenous peoples, especially Mayas. In Chiapas, Griest learns about the struggles of indigenous Mayas who continue to endure threats, intimidation, and squalid conditions by pro-government forces and business interests. On her fourth excursion, Griest travels to the Mexican state of Oaxaca, just west of Chiapas in southern Mexico. Oaxaca is Mexico's second-poorest state, and Griest continues to meet and work closely with representatives of indigenous peoples in this area. Because the book is so closely connected to

these very different regions of Mexico, each section—Querétaro, Cruillas, Chiapas, and Oaxaca—highlights a particular aspect of Griest's interior—and exterior—journey to better understand her own connection to Mexico.

In the first part of the book, Griest shares her experiences traveling to Querétaro. After arriving in Mexico City, Griest befriends several gay men in the Pink Zone, a former gallery district that has become a place where gay and lesbian Mexican citizens can express their sexuality in comparative safety. Griest also learns in the Pink Zone about *ni modo*, an expression that is often translated into English as "it can't be helped" or "there is nothing to be done" (p. 10). Griest associates this attitude with the many centuries of challenges that have faced people living in Mexico. Early on, Griest recognizes that *ni modo* is used both for situations of frustration (such as lost bags at the airport) and also moments of serendipity, and it is this phrase that she adopts most forcefully as she learns to adjust to life in Mexico.

In Querétaro, Griest learns more about the daily activities, rituals, and attitudes of the gay men that she travels with—and how their actions and rituals represent larger cultural realities. Griest is especially surprised by the frequent cleanings her roommates give their apartment, even when the appliances and floors are already clean. One of her roommates, a former art student named Fabian, opines to Griest that Mexicans are familiar with chaos beyond their control: political chaos, economic chaos, even the chaos of natural disasters, so they like to strictly maintain the cleanliness of their own homes as a measure of control in their lives (p. 26). Fabian also tells Griest about the cultural attitude of *flojera*, or a general laziness that he and others believe afflicts Mexicans. *Flojera* is generally regarded by Griest and Fabian as a positive attribute—a capacity to relax and enjoy moments that Griest, who had been living in New York City, finds desirable but impossible to achieve—but being too laid back can be a barrier to seizing opportunities or making the most out of challenges. Fabian says, "This is the part of our culture that keeps us down, our flojera. I sometimes wonder how we would be if

the Spanish didn't conquer us. They were really flojo. Maybe we would be harder workers if the French had come instead. Or the British. Or even the Portuguese" (p. 30). Fabian, for instance, has not practiced painting in a number of years, claiming that even though he graduated several years ago, he created so much art in college that "he needed to rest" (p. 30). Griest adds the following commentary: "This idea will resurface in conversations throughout my travels in Mexico. Nearly every societal ill, from corruption to gender discrimination to racism, is said to have sprung forth from the moment Spanish explorer Hernan Cortes set foot on this land in 1519 and started Conquesting" (p. 30).

This first section foreshadows the turn toward the journalistic that Griest takes later on in the book. In her third month in Querétaro, Griest becomes fascinated by *luchadores*, or Mexican professional wrestlers, learning that the masks they wear into the ring recall the tradition of Aztec and Maya warriors, who would wear masks of jaguars and other animals in order to "channel their energy" before battle (p. 44). A *luchador* who has his mask ripped off before an audience is therefore not only being exposed but also losing some of his mystical powers. Later that month, Griest encounters art installations protesting the thousands of victims of rape and murder that have gripped northern Mexico, especially in Ciudad Juárez. She meets the artists responsible for these installations, who struggle just to receive permits for their work. When the local government decides, several days early, to take down the installations, Griest is fascinated when the artists tell her that they will go public with their struggles, thus foreshadowing the complex relationships with the press and the government that protesters must negotiate to try to achieve meaningful change in Mexico.

The final leg of Griest's first trip to Mexico culminates with a road trip to Guadalajara and Aguascalientes. The trip proves to be more difficult than Griest and her companions expect, and this tension boils over into direct conflict between Griest and Fabian. Following a long day of interviewing individuals who have lost family members to the very dangerous trip to the United

States (which most locals call "El Norte," or "The North"), Fabian complains that Griest is too cold, too dispassionate, in her role as an interviewing journalist. Griest grows uncomfortably aware that he sees her as an American journalist collecting stories for her own benefit, not unlike the way she has used her Mexican bloodline on college admissions forms just because America "rewards such absurdity" (p. 92). She decides that she must engage more thoughtfully on her second trip.

The next section of the book chronicles the trip she takes with her mother, in which Griest explores the story of how her mother's side of the family came to the United States. The story is intimately connected to the history of ranching in Texas. Griest recalls how she originally learned the story of Richard King, a former riverboat captain who purchased one hundred head of cattle from a small pueblo in northern Mexico called Cruillas and invited the entire village to travel with him to work on his new ranch in Texas. According to legend, the villagers accepted King's offer and left town, thus ending the story of Cruillas and beginning the story of the King Ranch, a spread that, at 825,000 acres, would be larger than twenty-five United Nations members if it were its own sovereign nation (p. 98).

Though at first Griest wonders if Cruillas is just a legend and no longer exists, she comes across an atlas of Mexico that features a small town called Cruillas in the state of Tamaulipas, just south of Texas and the King Ranch. Intrigued by this discovery, Griest travels to the King Ranch in order to visit distant relatives who may be able to help her discover the ultimate fate of Cruillas. There she learns that her own family did not come up to South Texas in 1854, the year of King's legendary offer, but rather some twenty years later. Griest surmises that Cruillas must not have disappeared, but rather endured for at least another generation. Determined to discover her origins, Griest conscripts her mother as a traveling companion so that the two might trace the beginnings of their family and, perhaps, discover a town that everyone in their family thought had disappeared in the nineteenth century.

With some perseverance, the two discover the village of Cruillas. Griest interviews a scholar from the nearby city of Victoria about the discrepancies between what she learned about Richard King and his relations with northern Mexico. The scholar explains that the perception of King could not be more different: in Texas, King is revered as one of the founding fathers of the ranching industry; in Mexico, he is regarded as a scoundrel and a thug who would often pay his Mexican workers to steal horses and cattle from Mexican ranches. Griest's rediscovery of Cruillas is also, in some respects, a rediscovery of the fraught nature of history—and of her own relationship to Mexico.

In July 2005 Griest returns to Mexico City to see her mother off at the airport. While staying in the city, Griest attends the gay pride festival in the Pink Zone and learns that Octavio Acuña, an activist for the gay community in Querétaro, has been killed. While investigating Acuña's death, Griest comes across a headline that declares "Zapatistas Declare Red Alert" (p. 138). Intrigued, she travels to Chiapas to learn more about the Zapatista movement, which represents an armed struggle by the indigenous people of the state against the Mexican government and business interests. The Zapatistas are perhaps best known for their 1994 uprising, when they occupied San Cristóbal de las Casas on the same day that the North American Free Trade Agreement (NAFTA) went into effect. NAFTA and other trade agreements were generally seen by Zapatistas and their sympathizers as bankrupting the traditional, agricultural way of life for indigenous people, who could no longer afford to compete with large-scale agricultural operations in the United States and elsewhere. Another famous figure from the Zapatista uprising was Subcomandante Marcos, a spokesperson for the group who often appeared in public with a ski mask.

Much of this section is focused on the local people's relationship with Subcomandante Marcos. Griest immediately notices, for instance, that many of the local vendors sell dolls with ski masks. The tradition apparently began in the 1990s, when foreign journalists suggested that some of the doll makers and weavers in the community add masks to boost sales (pp. 145–146). Additionally, many of the cinemas in San Cris-

tóbal screen documentaries and films sympathetic to the Zapatistas. Griest meets a group of Maya women who are engaged in preserving and publishing collected songs in Tzotzil, their native language. Griest also meets Ambar Past, a woman originally from the United States who settled in Chiapas and began learning traditional weaving and songs from the Maya women. As she learned Tzotzil, Ambar realized that many of the women were reciting poetry and began an effort to record, transcribe, and publish these works (p. 151).

Griest then travels with a woman named Rebeca to Acteal, one of the communities that has witnessed massacres for its part in mobilizing the indigenous population against the Mexican government. In 1997 an estimated seventy paramilitary soldiers attacked the villagers gathered at Mass, killing forty-five as local police and military units avoided the area (p. 161). The story of the massacre helps to explain why so many indigenous villagers joined the Zapatista movement, as they remained vulnerable to paramilitary elements and in desperate economic straights following the passage of NAFTA. Following this harrowing trip to Acteal, Griest then goes to Oventic and Polhó, autonomous townships operating under the protection of the Zapatistas. In Oventic, Griest meets several international activists seeking to help the indigenous populations achieve greater political and economic sovereignty. One of these activists is a man named Robert, a musician who, much like Ambar, is trying to record and publish folk music created by Zapatistas. As the examples of Ambar and Robert indicate, the fight for greater autonomy by indigenous people is political as well as cultural: without their language, traditions, and songs, many of these populations will forget their origins. This cultural amnesia has been a consistent theme in Griest's many interviews with families who have welcomed back migrants from the United States; these migrants often bring back strange manners of dress and behavior more consistent with Los Angeles than the pueblos of Mexico. Cultural amnesia is also, of course, a profound fear that motivated Griest's own journeys to Mexico.

After her experiences with the Zapatistas, Griest realizes that, as a journalist, she desperately wants to learn more about indigenous struggles in other parts of Mexico. This interest takes her to Oaxaca, one of the poorest states in Mexico and the ancestral land of Zapotecs, the Mixtecs, and Triquis. Here Griest documents the phenomenon of workers' strikes that are a common part of Mexican urban life. These strikes often take place in the plazas, or *zocalos*, in town centers. One of the most common in Oaxaca is teachers' strikes, in which thousands of teachers descend upon the capital (also named Oaxaca) in order to demand higher wages. Locals explain to Griest that strikes occur so frequently because of the recalcitrance of politicians and government managers in Mexico: because average working people cannot rely on local representatives or bureaucrats to effect meaningful change, they must instead strike until the powers that be agree to a small increase in pay. During her stay in Oaxaca, Griest becomes increasingly enmeshed in the story of *Noticias*, the largest circulation newspaper in Oaxaca (p. 191). When Griest visits the offices of *Noticias*, she is shocked to learn that the site has been occupied by striking workers who turn out to be hired goons masquerading as employees: their presence in the office is meant to disrupt the paper's circulation, though this tactic has not proven successful (p. 192). Griest meets with Governor Ulises Ruiz and asks questions about the strikers at the offices of *Noticias*; unfortunately, she finds him reticent to provide any helpful additions to the story beyond denying all the charges that have been levied against him (pp. 202–203). The story of *Noticias* serves as another example of the struggle that activists and the free press face when it comes to achieving their goals.

During the remainder of her stay in Oaxaca—which also serves as the ending to her yearlong, four-part journey to Mexico—Griest works closely with advocates for the many indigenous groups living in the Mexican state. In fact, as she writes, she is struck by the fact that she has met so many *mestizos* who have fully dedicated their lives to improving the lives of and defending the indigenous peoples of Mexico. She lists them fondly: Rebeca, Rafael, and Marta in Chiapas;

Juan, Javier, and women like Rosa and Maríia in Oaxaca. One of the most important conversations she will have about the complicated relationships between geography, identity, and belonging occurs with Maríia , one of the female activists working with Tepeyac, a local human rights organization. During one conversation with Griest, Maríia explains that she is not indigenous because "she does not feel that way"; she doesn't dress "that way," she doesn't "practice their tradition," and she doesn't "speak that language" (p. 222). Instead, she sees herself as fully *mestiza*, because the traditions of her Zapotec ancestors stopped with her grandmother. At the end of their conversation, another activist lays a hand upon Griest's shoulder, bringing her into the tapestry of stories of mixed-race individuals with Mexican heritage: "The important thing is that you realize what you have lost. . . . Now it is only a matter of fighting to regain it" (p. 223). Griest, who prefers to identify herself as biracial in the first chapter of the book, realizes from her experiences that this liminal state of being both American and Mexican, white and brown, is both a challenge and an opportunity: " *poco*," (little by lilttle), she writes, embracing her great-grandmother's language, "we are coming into our own as a people" (p. 286). By embracing the inclusive pronoun to refer to Latinas in the United States, Griest ends her book feeling that she can finally reclaim the term she has used to describe herself since college: a Chicana feminist, with all its rights and responsibilities.

Selected Bibliography

WORKS OF STEPHANIE ELIZONDO GRIEST

NONFICTION

Around the Bloc: My Life in Moscow, Beijing, and Havana. New York: Villard, 2004. New York: Random House, 2007.

100 Places Every Woman Should Go. Palo Alto, Calif.: Travelers' Tales, 2007.

Mexican Enough: My Life Between the Borderlines. New York: Atria Books; New York: Washington Square Press, 2008.

"Confessions of an Author Nomad: Promoting Your Books at All Costs." *Poets & Writers* 37, no. 6:105–108 (November–December 2009).

All the Agents & Saints: Dispatches from the U.S. Borderlands. Chapel Hill: University of North Carolina Press, 2017.

EDITED COLLECTIONS

The Best Women's Travel Writing 2010: True Stories from Around the World. Palo Alto, Calif.: Solas House, 2010.

CRITICAL AND BIOGRAPHICAL STUDIES

Mendoza, Sylvia. "Being 'Mexican Enough': Stephanie Elizondo Griest's Journey to Acceptance." *Hispanic Outlook in Higher Education*, August 2009, pp. 18–20.

REVIEWS

Espinoza, Alex. "Her Heritage Trail." *Los Angeles Times*, August 10, 2008. http://articles.latimes.com/2008/aug/10/entertainment/ca-stephanie-griest10 (Review of *Mexican Enough My Life Between the Borderlines*.)

Fishel, Elizabeth. "Nonfiction Review: *Mexican Enough*." *SF Gate*, August 5. 2008. http://www.sfgate.com/books/article/Nonfiction-review-Mexican-Enough-3202058.php

Hopkins, Alison. "Griest, Stephanie Elizondo. *Around the Bloc: My Life in Moscow, Beijing, and Havana*." *Library Journal* 129, no. 4:96 (2004).

INTERVIEWS

"Interview with Stephanie Elizondo Griest." *Duende*, fall 2014. http://www.duendeliterary.org/griest-interview

Winet, Kristin. "A Conversation with Stephanie Elizondo Griest." Travel Writing 2.0, November 6, 2012. http://travelwriting2.com/a-conversation-with-stephanie-elizondo-griest/

GRACE KING

(1852—1932)

Windy Petrie

IN HER 1932 autobiography, *Memories of a Southern Woman of Letters*, Grace King vividly recalled the day—some seventy years earlier—when she had decided to be a writer. She was ten years old, and she was walking along the levee on her family's country plantation in New Iberia, Louisiana, where they had gone into hiding from the ravages of the Civil War. She noticed the sun shining "like a conflagration behind the cypress forest on the opposite bank." Then she looked down at the "black-looking water of the bayou [which] flowed in a swift current between" (p. 48). Incipient in this imagery of boundaries and hidden depths were the major elements of her career. As a child of war, a Southern loyalist, a feminist literary and social critic, and a popular historian, King would spend her life trying to reconcile the Southern past with the American present, the surface of New Orleans society with its depths, and nineteenth-century ideologies of gender and race with the lived realities of women and people of color. Her readers, in her time and ours, would need to carefully sort through pages upon pages of veiled hints and apparent contradictions to piece together her narrative patterns and explicate her ironic ambiguities. The resolutions and reconciliations she sought from her wartime exile until her death were so elusive, so layered, and so complex that she chased them for forty years through five genres.

EARLY LIFE

Most of her biographies agree that Grace Elizabeth King was born on November 29, 1852 (though some sources give 1851), the eldest girl and third child of William Woodson King, a respected and successful lawyer with familial and educational roots in Kentucky, Alabama, and Virginia, and Sarah Ann Miller King, of New Orleans, Louisiana. The family of eight lived and grew in comfortable, rambunctious prosperity in an elegant neighborhood in the Garden District of the city until the occupation of New Orleans by the federal government during the Civil War forced the family to flee the city and go into hiding miles away on their bayou plantation, L'Embarrass.

W. W. King's position as a successful attorney brought him to the attention of the federal occupation forces, and he would not sign the oath of allegiance to the federal government that was required for him to remain in his home and at his job. The trauma and uncertainty of that flight from the city when she was only ten years old made for one of King's most powerful and telling memories, and the one with which she begins her autobiography. Her father fled the city alone in spring 1862, leaving his wife to face the officers who came to their home to interrogate her, having privately instructed her to bring the family to their country plantation to reunite with him. Sarah King found this easier said than done, but she managed to combine wheedling, commanding, charming, calling in favors, or just blustering through the obstacles in her way as she transported herself, her six children, her mother, and several slaves to L'Embarrass. The children, huddled under blankets in a cart, heard their mother ordering a ferryman to take them across the river in what was left of his half-burned boat and watched her demand hospitality from unwilling strangers based on her social status as a Southern lady. After some close calls, they managed to get to the plantation, having assisted in smuggling medical supplies to Confederate soldiers along the way. They would remain there for nearly four years, facing other uncertainties as battles and troops came closer, children and

slaves fell ill, and medical help and domestic supplies ran short.

The family's years in exile were full of making various adjustments to an isolated rural lifestyle in a potential war zone, where none of them could go to work, school, or social events. However, this time also bore fruit that would be crucial to Grace King's character and career. W. W. King educated his daughters alongside his sons at home in a course of serious reading and academic subjects. Robert Bush, King's biographer, asserts that these years of homeschooling resulted in a "genuine love of learning" for the King girls in particular (*Grace King*, p. 35). The last formal portrait of King as an artist, done six years before her death, reflects this scholarly, domestic circle more than sixty years after the exile: she sits in the foreground, upright and facing the viewer and holding a book in one hand, while her sisters, Nan and Nina, read among piles and piles of books in the background, making the portrait into a triangle with Grace at the apex. By then it was publicly known her sisters sometimes did research to aid Grace's writing.

Sarah King, whom the family all called "Mimi," ensured that her daughters learned proper feminine deportment, music, and French at a Catholic Creole boarding school, Institut St. Louis, when they returned to New Orleans sometime between December 1865 and summer 1866. It was the same school Mrs. King had attended in her youth, even though the Kings were not Catholics of Creole extraction but rather Protestants descended from Huguenots from Alsace. The girls attended as day pupils, as the family now had much less money and a far less fashionable address in a rented house in a working-class Gascoigne neighborhood near the Union barracks.

After graduating from the Institut at age sixteen, Grace chose to pursue further study in foreign languages and in English literature. She remained an avid reader throughout her life. Not only was her father an avid and scholarly reader and her uncle, T. D. Miller, well known in the city for his literary receptions, but King's enthusiasm for books and languages was also likely underscored by the dear family friend and Louisiana historian Charles Gayarré, who would allow her access to his collection of historical materials as her career developed. In addition to history and literary classics, King kept up a reading list that included all the newest fiction and social theory. She read Herbert Spencer, the popular social Darwinist, in the 1870s. She devoured the works of Leo Tolstoy and Fyodor Dostoevsky in the 1880s, studied the biography of George Eliot, and would later follow the careers of Henry James and Edith Wharton with interest.

King had become engaged at age nineteen to a young man named Garrett Walker, who would eventually succeed in the railroad business, but "Mimi" felt he had not enough money and insisted the couple wait two years before getting married. She then used those two years to persuade her daughter to break the engagement, while making Walker feel unwelcome in the King family in every way. We know that King saved all of his love letters—now housed in the Louisiana State University library archives—and never entered into a romantic relationship with a man again, to her mother's great dismay.

W. W. King died in 1881, when Grace was almost thirty. She held vigils up to twenty-four hours long at his bedside in his last days. Not only his scholarliness but his pride and dignity would remain as standards she would bear for herself for the rest of her life. She had taken the initiative to seek a career as a teacher the year before, not wanting to be confined in her home as a dependent. As an unmarried daughter, growing older and resenting her brothers' assumption of authority over her as much as they may have resented having to contribute to the upkeep of their three unmarried sisters, King found constant tension in her household, quarreling with her mother, brothers, and sisters about domestic roles and responsibilities. After particularly significant disagreements with her mother when she was rebuked for being disagreeable to her brothers, she would ride the New Orleans streetcars for hours, unable to return home but having nowhere else to go. It is no wonder that she was looking for some emotional and financial independence in her early thirties.

GRACE KING

There weren't many Southern female role models for King as she sought to find a scholarly career for herself. When she began to write, there was only one Southern woman writer she really respected, Mary Noailles Murfree, who, like many Victorian women, wrote under a male pseudonym (in her case, Charles Eggbert Craddock). Unsatisfied with both the dearth of models and the inaccuracy of the portrayal of women in literature, King began her writing career by criticizing other authors. Ironically, two opportunities came about through the hands of Northern visitors to New Orleans for the 1884–1885 World's Industrial and Cotton Centennial Exposition. King used the word "Yankee" as a pejorative term for Northerners all her life, and disliked the aggressive, businesslike ethos with which she associated them. One can either interpret her cultivation of powerful—and thus valuable to her—Northerners as a "Yankeeish" thing to do, or admire her clever networking, which helped her begin her career without a single rejection letter. The editor Charles Dudley Warner was perhaps the most powerful impetus for King's literary success, and King once wrote to her sister that her time at a party had been wasted until she got Warner into a real conversation. However, it is important to remember that while King definitely cultivated the acquaintance of the literary figures who visited for the exposition, many Northern editors had purposely traveled to the South to find new Southern authors after the Civil War. In this case, King and Warner both found something they were looking for—he found a new Southern author, and she found someone to promote and guide her work.

FIRST PUBLICATIONS

King's first publishing opportunity came in 1885, when she read a paper titled "Heroines of Novels" to a local meeting of like-minded intellectuals brought together by the Northern feminist Julia Ward Howe during her time presiding over the women's division at the centennial. King's breadth of reading and interest in languages allowed her to analyze and comment upon four national literatures—American, British, French, and German—in terms of their portrayal of women. In the essay, she finds French novels to be the best for their realism, and female novelists to be more accurate in their portrayal of their own gender than male authors, bringing Charles Dickens, William Makepeace Thackeray, and Henry James under her critical scrutiny. Her work was so well received that it was published in the *Times-Democrat* on Sunday, May 31, 1885. In print, it exhibits a boldness, definitiveness, and self-assurance that often characterized her public persona throughout her life, although she expressed how fearful and timid she felt about the experience in her private writings. Interestingly enough, some of her last work would be literary and social criticism as well, written with the same self-assuredness as she had shown in her first effort.

The most significant publishing opportunity that arose from the connections King made during the Cotton Centennial started with King's outspoken verbal critique of George Washington Cable, whose literary fame she resented because she felt he made New Orleans society look bad. Upon her expressing her disdain for Cable's pandering to Northern audiences, Richard Watson Gilder, the powerful editor of the *Century Magazine*, a leading literary journal, challenged King to write something better than Cable's work and set the record straight. Although Gilder did not end up publishing the story that resulted, titled "Monsieur Motte," King then sent it to Warner, and he shopped it around New England journals until he landed it in the *New Princeton Review* in late 1885.

The story, first published anonymously, got enough good notices that King quickly decided to reveal her authorship. After she did so, she must have been even more pleased when a local critic wrote, "Miss King shows real power, and after a time some really great work may be expected of her" (qtd. in Kirby, p. 32). The tale was intended to show the love and affection between white women and their black former slaves in a way that did honor to each, although King's view of honoring Marcélite, a former slave who made herself into a highly successful

professional hairdresser, was severely limited by the racist ideologies of her time and place. However, most critics acknowledge that Marcé-lite is the true hero of the tale, the one who "embodies the ideal that King . . . embodies herself as narrator. Marcélite is strong, intelligent, independent, and self-supporting, fully capable of love . . ., yet able to show her anger in astonish-ingly assertive ways" (Jones, *Tomorrow Is Another Day*, p. 104). While critics generally agree on this interpretation, they interpret Marcélite's vocal self-loathing of her dark skin in almost opposite ways, debating whether King is questioning the construction of race and gender or simply underscoring and revealing her own inbred sense of white superiority.

When King received the check for "Monsieur Motte" and went out to spend it, she wrote to her sister Nina that it was "the first really well satis-fied moment of my life" (qtd. in Bush, "Grace King," p. 285). The *Review* wanted more install-ments to deepen the characters and develop the setting and plot, so King ended up turning the story into a novel in four installments, including one that showed plantation life to Northern read-ers and a happily-ever-after wedding in the end, wherein Marcélite walks Marie Modeste down the aisle and gives her away, taking the place of Marie's parents. After all, it was Marcélite who, pretending to be an emissary for Marie's fictional rich uncle, had supported and nurtured her all her life. King later reflected on how raw that first experience writing fiction was, how real the characters and the emotions, and how that type of intensity rarely comes again: "A first novel," she confided in a letter to a friend, "is a first revelation of one's self . . . one can write a first novel only once. Never again will you be so much possessed by your characters" (qtd. in Jones, *Tomorrow*, p. 97). Most writers' first at-tempts don't end up in print, so perhaps there is something to this. Certainly *Monsieur Motte* (1888) is among the most compelling, complex, and confounding texts in King's oeuvre.

Although she first published the story anony-mously, nearly as soon as "Monsieur Motte" was well received, King took public ownership of her work and even allowed her photo to be published

for advertising purposes, an unusual step for a Southern lady. However, her advertising paid off, and in 1887 King was included in a prestigious list of Southern writers and then invited by Warner to visit his home in Hartford, Connecticut. Her stay there confirmed her ambitions and introduced her to some of the most powerful and important American literary figures of that time, from Mark Twain—the pen name of Samuel Langhorne Clemens—to Sarah Orne Jewett, Mary Wilkins Freeman, Ruth McEnery Stuart, and even the redoubtable William Dean Howells. King became an especial admirer of Twain's intellect. She believed he had a place among the greats in American literature before the rest of the literary world did and he believed in her tal-ent, not only encouraging her in their cor-respondence but introducing her to other influen-tial literary figures. King was such a regular guest in Clemens' family circle, both in the United States and in Italy when she traveled there five years later, that Clemens' daughters considered her an honorary sibling. But it was Clemens' wife, Olivia, to whom Grace became especially close, and with whom she corresponded for years. Livvy, as Olivia was called by those who knew her well, was close enough to King to tease her about her stern, rigid pride, and jokingly referred to it as her "Matterhorn" in their correspondence (Bush, *Grace King*, p. 91).

The question of King's aloof demeanor confounded not only her friends but her critics as well. In this case, one might consider it a form of self-defense. It must have been difficult for a loyal Southerner to see the wealth of the Gilded Age in New England when Southern families like hers had been so reduced in their circum-stances, to hear the triumphant speeches of abolitionists and be questioned about the wide-spread sexual abuse of slaves without withdraw-ing into a scornful and silent reserve. Reminding her of how far she was from home, King could see Harriet Beecher Stowe walking in the garden across from her room at the Warners'. King believed Stowe's major work, *Uncle Tom's Cabin* (1852), to be an inaccurate and unfair attack on the South, and seeing Stowe every day made

King want to represent the South with dignity and pride.

Michael Kreyling reads King's notorious pride as an indication that King considered herself a "cultural prophet convinced of the superiority and redemptive merit of the lost society" of the antebellum South (p. 117). Most critics agree with this assessment: Mary Ann Wilson acknowledges that King "set herself this grand task of preservation" of the Southern past (p. 137) and argues that her histories go back to colonial times because she wants to set the record straight. While Lori Robison refers to King's regionalism as a "cultural elegy" (p. 55), she also contends that King can also be read as an auto-ethnographer of the Reconstruction, writing the experience of a white privileged Southerner in a time when those of her class were essentially a colonized people, occupied by federal forces (p. 57) and largely defined by outside voices. This feeling must have been intense enough in the South among Southerners, but to be the lone Southerner among Northerners must have felt lonely indeed. When a fellow dinner guest of the Clemens' went on an extended tirade about how the ravaged South had gotten what it deserved, King maintained a frigid silence. She would only voice her objections in the pages of her work.

As the 1880s ended, King published a new story, "Earthlings," which only Twain seems to have appreciated, but the 1890s brought a good deal more excitement and success along with them. First, King took a long trip to Europe with her sister Nan from fall 1891 to December 1892, which allowed her to meet, interact, and network with a number of influential English and French intellectual and literary figures. While in England, she was invited to lecture at Newnham College, which she did "for the sake of the South" (Bush, *Grace King*, p. 116). In France, she made the acquaintance of Marie Thérèse Blanc, who had studied with the French female novelist George Sand and wrote under the pseudonym Thérèse Bentzon. King would admire Madame Blanc to the end of her life and praise her rapturously in her autobiography as a role model for literary women. Attending Madame Blanc's Parisian literary salon regularly, King was given a chance to

edit some letters George Sand had written to one of her lovers, and she queried her American editor, Warner, about the possibility. He informed her very clearly that American publications would have no place for such work, and the project was given up.

BALCONY STORIES

Despite this disappointment, her first European trip was a major turning point in King's life and career. As a result, Warner invited her to write the introductions to eight French authors for an encyclopedia he was working on. Additionally, when she returned to New Orleans, the experience and authority she had gained through the trip allowed her to host her own literary salon, which she of course wished to model after Madame Blanc's. The years 1892 and 1893 would also see King through the writing (partly in Europe and partly back in the United States), editing, and publishing of a collection titled *Balcony Stories*, comprising stories that first were released in the *Century Magazine*.

Balcony Stories would be issued in book form a total of three times, not only by Century in 1893 but by Graham in 1914 and with new stories in 1925 by Macmillan. The volume is still available in reprint today and is notable for its project of "raising an oral tradition to the level of Literature" (Bush, *Grace King*, p. 144), as the stories themselves are framed by the New Orleans tradition of ladies sitting on their balconies whispering and gossiping to each other in the evenings when their husbands are out and their children are asleep nearby. When these stories are compared to the King family lore, it is clear that many of them are probably revised and reimagined stories that King was told by her mother and grandmother when she was very young.

In her autobiography King explains, "The *Balcony Stories* had been gathering in my mind until I felt I must put them on paper to get relief from them. They wrote themselves" (p. 99). The reviews for the collection tend to emphasize its disjointedness, its ephemeral quality, and either praise or blame what the critics viewed as a lack

of coherence. The stories were characterized as "sketches" or "hints" rather than stories, and King was labeled an "impressionist," which could have been a compliment or a critique depending on who said it. *Balcony Stories* is now considered one of the three definitive collections of Louisiana local color, along with George Washington Cable's *Old Creole Days* (1879) and Kate Chopin's *Bayou Folk* (1894).

Several of the more famous *Balcony Stories* feature African American main characters, including "A Crippled Hope," from the original 1893 edition, and "Joe," which was written for the 1925 edition. The former focuses on a character called "Little Mammy," a valuable healer whose desire for her own family is thwarted by her disability. Because she is so tenderhearted and indefatigable in her care for children and the ill, she is kept working in a warehouse for slaves who are being sold, essentially to get them into better condition and thus bring higher profit. While Little Mammy cannot have a family of her own, she would like to serve in a family, and while many tired-faced, kind-looking ladies would like to hire or purchase her, she is too valuable to the slave dealer and he will not part with her. Therein lies her tragedy: her gift cripples her opportunities more than her injured back and legs do. While Little Mammy is valorized in the story, the narrator makes distressingly racist commentary about how negligent slave mothers are, making Little Mammy's excellent standard of maternal care the exception among her community rather than the rule.

Of the two, "Joe," written decades later, is the more complex story about race, identity, and family. As a valet to a profligate, self-indulgent master, Joe lives—albeit in the role of a servant—a life that participates in the pleasures and luxuries of New Orleans. Joe is smart and his manners are on par with the New Orleans elite: he's also a talented orator and actor, well known for his reenactments of scenes and speeches he has memorized from Shakespearean plays he has attended with his master. But when his master, Mr. Middleton, dies, Joe seems adrift and depressed; the formerly energetic man is now lazy and sluggish. Realizing that the family is in

dire need of money but that Mrs. Middleton will not insist he do other work for her, he rejects her offer to free him and instead asks to be hired out. He then gets the man who hired him to purchase him. Once that purchase is completed, Joe runs away to Canada. The story emphasizes that Joe feels a personal loyalty to the Middleton family, not running away from them and even waiting until they have been paid for him before he disappears. At the story's end, he writes Mrs. Middleton to say "he had not run away from her or the children, or the affection he bore them. He was still their Joe as he had always been" (p. 294).

Loyalty was a deeply admirable value to King—she plays on the same note in "Monsieur Motte" and it was a guiding principle in her own life. She wrote several stories, such as "Bayou L'Ombre," wherein loyal slaves are clearly depicted as superior to disloyal ones and are treated accordingly, in accordance with her theory that it was true, personal, affection that bound slaves and masters together. Michelle Birnbaum notes that in stories such as these King fits into a pattern many postbellum authors utilized to extend antebellum structures of paternalistic slaveholding households into continual labor—after the war, compulsion was translated into affection and duty into desire (p. 19). But surely there is a deeper irony in "Joe," for Joe the slave is clearly more loyal *and* more financially responsible to the family than his white master was. Mr. Middleton left his wife and children vulnerable to poverty; Joe restores them to safe financial ground. As the story ends, Mr. Middleton has died of a lifetime of overindulgence; Joe has survived and is starting a new life to suit his own tastes.

In 1893 King also published a textbook called *A History of Louisiana* with a professor from Tulane. The textbook would be used in the public schools for decades. King supplemented her textbook writing with contracts for other historical works: *Jean Baptiste Le Moyne, Sieur de Bienville* (1892); *New Orleans: The Place and the People* (1895); and *De Soto and His Men in the Land of Florida* (1898). Much of this last volume was made possible by King's access to Charles

Gayarré's extensive library of original copies of narratives written by Spanish and French explorers. This exclusive knowledge and research made her truly expert on the subject, and she would also start lecturing at Chautauqua institutes in Louisiana in 1895. By 1887 she was listed alongside big names like Cable, Joel Chandler Harris, and Lafcadio Hearn in a *Harper's Monthly* article titled "The Recent Movement in Southern Literature." To be mentioned in *Harper's* so early in her career was, King later noted, "equivalent to the presentation of a debutante at court" (qtd. in Kirby, p. 121). She also began to earn the "growing appreciation" of W. D. Howells (Bush, *Grace King*, p. 113), who would later compare her work publicly to that of Nathaniel Hawthorne in its ethos and the French masters in its technique.

During the time in which King was establishing her own new identity as a literary success, her life at home was growing increasingly difficult because of her brother Will's alcoholism. Not only did this cause great emotional pain to the entire family, but it also created financial strain, as his drinking prevented him from supporting his wife and children. Grace and her unmarried siblings ended up having to shoulder Will's financial responsibilities. This situation resulted in significant internal conflict in the home Grace shared with her mother and her unmarried siblings, as Mimi King enabled Will's drinking in what Grace considered an outrageous fashion. In her journal, which had been an outlet for her more honest feelings and darker fears for decades, she recorded her fear that her mother's enabling of Will "would drain us of our last cent. She would crush the life out of us" by taking his part and putting his needs before everyone else's"(qtd. in Bush, *Grace King*, p. 199). When, on New Year's Day 1901, Will died in a locked room with the gas on, the family was divided over whether the death was an accident or suicide, but the grief was shared by them all.

The stress of Will's alcoholism and grief over his death made King conclude that "Will has made me old" (qtd. in Bush, *Grace King*, p. 213). The facts bear out this dramatic-sounding claim: her hair had turned from red-brown to completely white in only two years, and she was now regularly taken for her own sister's mother when they were seen together. Her growing professional success must have provided a necessary counterbalance to the painful burdensome grief in her personal life, which would continue to mount as she lost two more family members one after another. Sadly, both King's mother and her closest brother, Branch, died within a few years of Will.

Having suffered three deaths in her family within four years, King and her sisters decided they had to get away from New Orleans to recover from grief and find new energy and interest in life. The rent they were to receive for the home they had finally been able to buy in New Orleans would finance a two-year stay in Europe this time, if they were careful. Financial caution was indeed required, as King had taken over the guardianship of Will's ten-year-old son, and they had to provide the tuition and room and board for his education in an English boarding school while they traveled. Then an English nerve specialist sent Nina to a sanatorium for a lengthy stay, which resulted in more bills, but left Grace and Nan to travel the Continent together as they had on their first trip. They remained there from 1906 to 1908.

THE PLEASANT WAYS OF ST. MÉDARD

While she was away in Europe, King was again able to turn her energy to a sustained work of fiction. She wrote much of *The Pleasant Ways of St. Médard*, a book she had been trying to write since 1899, in a little village outside of Oxford. It would still not be published for ten more years (in 1916), and then almost by accident when it was reviewed in manuscript by an English critic who thought it had already been published in America. The book is a semiautobiographical account of the King family's first year of struggle when they moved back to New Orleans during Reconstruction. The name St. Médard may be based on the St. Bernard neighborhood on the outskirts of New Orleans (Bush, *Grace King*, p. 250).

The Pleasant Ways of St. Médard is not a pleasant read. It focuses on the frustrations, fears, privations, humiliations, and betrayals suffered by King's parents, whom she calls the Talbots in the book, during Reconstruction. The combined strain of their various physical and psychic suffering nearly results in the death of Mr. Talbot, but he survives and is restored to dignity by finding work that will sustain the family for years: legally sorting out the succession of the ill-gotten wartime gains of one of their neighbors who has died. With her signature irony, King reveals how the greed and corruption of one man unintentionally results in the restoration of another man of integrity. Even more ironic, the Talbots' salvation comes through their former errand boy, who had taken possession of Mr. Talbot's law office and library when Mr. Talbot fled the city and is now—somehow, without a license—a practicing lawyer in the chaotic world of New Orleans during the Reconstruction.

The novel, in fact, is propelled by its ironies, starting with the title itself. Related from the perspective of the children of the Talbot family, one gets the strong impression that their world has been turned upside down. In her introduction, King connects the fiction that will follow to the history of Southern children during and after the war. "Do you remember," she says, when your "Papa" was "the one truth, the one right?" (p. 4). Well, the Papas of the South "came back unlike any Papas that respectable children had ever seen before" (p. 5). Early in the book, one of the Talbot children, in her childish, cruel ignorance of their postbellum situation, tells her Papa he should be ashamed to appear in public in his shabby clothes. This same unsettling sense that everything is backwards now afflicts every character in every chapter of the volume. Mrs. Talbot cannot accept that "the lame boy who used to brush your shoes . . . is practicing law in your office" (p. 19). Although the boy will be the one to save them with his cleverness and industry, all Mrs. Talbot can see are the boy's physical imperfection and former-servant status. We later find out that Mrs. Talbot's own favorite former servant, the children's old governess, has not been inspired to heroic loyalty but instead has

stolen the clothes and household goods Mrs. Talbot left in her care, used them to make herself a prosperous new life, and pretends she doesn't even know Mrs. Talbot when they meet in a shop. Of the two parents, Mr. Talbot has clearly been more successful at inspiring the loyalty King views as a reflection on one's honor than Mrs. Talbot has. Yet the mother's deep anger at and doubts about the father's judgment receive a lot of page space in the novel, while the father's thoughts generally remain unexpressed, although the narrator does speculate about them sometimes, noting he "might well have wondered how [Mrs. Talbot's] idle and futile prejudice could survive" the Civil War (p. 117). Indeed, whether the reader is intended to sympathize with Mr. or Mrs. Talbot in the numerous differences of opinion they have about their new life is quite confusing—perhaps as confusing for the reader as it must have been for the King children themselves.

Readers and critics have long been baffled about how to read and respond to the shifting, often contradictory tones in King's fiction. Robert Bush compares King's irony to Mark Twain's or Ellen Glasgow's (*Grace King*, p. 19). Zita Dresner, in *New Perspectives on Women and Comedy* (1992), claims irony dominates and undercuts the sentimental tone in some of King's scenes. Noting that "Monsieur Motte" can be read as either racist or not, patrician or not, and patriarchal or not, Dresner delineates how such ambivalence "forces the reader to draw their own conclusions" (p. 172). Whether the often dogmatic King *intended* to leave the reader so free seems a tenuous proposition at best, but Dresner proposes that, throughout her fiction, King is representing two related ideologies at once in her ambivalence: first, that Southern life can be particularly cruel to women and people of color, and second, that "a Southern lady must always forgive and accept the selfishness of men" (p. 179).

Because of its painful instabilities, *The Pleasant Ways of St. Médard* was rejected multiple times in ten years by George Brett at Macmillan, the very publisher who had commissioned it. King would never compromise what she felt to be the reality of Reconstruction to make the book

more salable. She proudly rejected the advice to throw in a lovely heroine with a happily-ever-after love story to sweeten the plot, and scornfully recounted her decision to do so in her autobiography. Brett and Macmillan eventually found the book they had been looking for in Margaret Mitchell's *Gone with the Wind*, which paid off in big profits and big publicity for everyone involved, while *The Pleasant Ways of St. Médard* was finally published by Henry Holt and Company, although the novel's unstable narrative and tone made it a mixed bag for reviewers. Alfred Harcourt had politely previewed this in his acceptance letter for the book: "At first I didn't see the pattern," he wrote, "but I found its grateful unfolding very delightful; and thank heaven for the sense of humor that holds the balance all through" (qtd. in Kirby, p. 75). Edward Garnett praised the work's "exquisite shades of feeling, delicate in vibrating sadness" (qtd. in Kirby, p. 75). Yet another reviewer said her work should be more "widely known," but while praising her ability to sketch character, called her "contemptuous of . . . the reader's suspense, and cumulative interest" (qtd. in Kirby, p. 75).

The seemingly fruitless years while she revised *Pleasant Ways* made King question whether she had lost her creative energies permanently. In 1912 she suffered a nervous breakdown, which led to another recuperative trip to Europe with Nan in 1913. She began this trip, as she recounts it, carrying another distressing family burden. Her last surviving brother, Fred, who had become a successful judge, accompanied them on the initial part of the voyage. But far from providing the convenience and assistance he should have, he simply embarrassed his sisters by his drunken antics. This raised again the harbinger of what King viewed as a masculine weakness for whiskey, and may have made her fear that they were in for the same suffering they had endured before Will died. They were grateful when Fred disembarked and left them the only representatives of the King family name on the voyage.

This European trip, like the others, had its beneficent effect and maintained her celebrity status. She was pleased to receive an honorary

doctorate from Tulane University in 1915, and again turned her focus to more historical topics, writing *Creole Families of New Orleans* (1921), which was received (as many books of the 1920s were) as a monument to a disappearing subculture, much as Wharton's 1920 work *The Age of Innocence*, or Willa Cather's *Death Comes for the Archbishop* (1927) would be. King's public opinions on Creole culture seemed to shift with time. Joan DeJean considers King a "critical observer of the politics of creoleness" (p. 111). Earlier in her life, King had been somewhat critical of the pleasure-focused Creole lifestyle, describing Creoles as people who care more about food, wine, card games, parties, and pretty girls than about abstractions like honor and courage. These early judgments may be influenced by her strong Presbyterian upbringing, but in the later book she ties the culture most strongly to its French roots, perhaps more influenced by her three long stays in France. In fact, King's biographer David Kirby argues that in her popular histories King characterizes New Orleans as a Creole city rather than an American one, precisely because it cares more for pleasure than profit (p. 90). It is true that King's letters and journals repeatedly reveal her lingering disgust with what she saw as the "Yankee" focus on industry and profit becoming the broader definition of "American." It was the one bone of contention she had always had with Mark Twain, his beloved Hartford, and the famous Gilded Age.

With her creative energies ebbing, King turned to historical research to revive her career, and her next book was a novel based in and springing out of some of the extensive research her other books had warranted. Called *La Dame de Sainte Hermine* (1926), it tells the story of two women in early colonial New Orleans, an aristocrat and a commoner: how they got there, what became of them, what women of all classes and backgrounds have in common, and perhaps imparts a little of King's own hopes and values for future female destinies. It may also be a slight revision of standard histories of the French women shipped in to early Louisiana, who were generally thought to be little better than tutes, but whom King claims were of solid middle-class

stock and morality. Reviews of the novel credit it for its research but question its quality as fiction. The *New York World* complimented King's "careful research," while the *New York Times* found a "complete absence of narrative skill" in the book (qtd. in Kirby, p. 79).

King also saw her first play produced in 1926, examining familiar questions of female lives and destinies but through comedy rather than sentiment and in a contemporary context. *A Splendid Offer* is a romantic comedy examining three generations of women, wherein the grandmother is flummoxed by the younger generation's refusal to marry according to her principles and traditions, and the younger women engage in successful campaigns to control their own lives. Where the ironies lie in this drama is an intriguing question. Does the grandmother figure perhaps represent Mimi King and her controlling, prideful ideology, which had prevented three of her daughters from marrying? Does it represent any nostalgic reflection on King's part about the engagement she allowed her mother to talk her out of? In her mid-seventies by then, was King wondering if things might have turned out differently, or perhaps trying to understand and forgive her mother now that time had healed some of the wounds of their battles with each other?

Whatever spurred her to write the play, King continued to bring to light the hidden history of women in the South with her next project, *Mount Vernon on the Potomac: History of the Mount Vernon Ladies' Association of the Union*, which Macmillan published in 1929. The book reveals the details of the all-female effort to preserve the home of George Washington, and the spirit, perseverance, and labor it took to accomplish that task. Like her first work, "Monsieur Motte," it was intended as a tribute to the forgotten "ladies" of the Old South and their overlooked accomplishments.

SINS OF THE FATHERS

King often observed, in her fiction and nonfiction, that the real losers in war—any war—were the women and children, sagely observing, "There are no fortunes of war for women and children—it is all misfortune" (*St. Médard*, p. 45). However, a number of her works specifically focus on how the sins of the antebellum fathers and the delusions of the postbellum mothers fall heavily on their children, always confusing their minds, often mutilating their lives. *The Pleasant Ways of St. Médard* reveals this more in terms of its confused narrative distance and mixed senses of sympathy and scorn from the narrator herself, who, one must recall, was constructed by King out of her childhood memories of the family's return to New Orleans. But a number of her stories drive this same point home. Among them, "Bonne Maman" (1886) and "Madrilène" (1890) are perhaps the most notable. As she is about to die, "Bonne Maman" ("good mother" in French), raising a grandchild during the Reconstruction era, finally realizes that her prideful self-delusions, all based on her pre–Civil War identity, will leave the girl—Claire Blanche, or "pure white"—isolated and without resources. Claire, more realistic than her grandmother, has been secretly taking in sewing from her black neighbors to keep from starving, but one wonders what may become of her when her grandmother is gone. She is bored and worn from being confined with her grandmother and can't help being attracted to the outside world, particularly the music of the brothel next door, which makes her feel alive.

As the story "Madrilène" opens, we believe the young title character to be a quadroon servant in a notorious New Orleans house of ill repute. We follow her through her daily tasks and enter her world of thought. But the real story occurs, as in much of King's short fiction, at the very end, when we discover, through a series of serendipitous accidents, that the girl is white. Apparently, the proprietress of the house has kept her as a sort of personal slave because Madrilène's father had died there, wreaking a twisted revenge on a hypocritical, prejudiced society through persecuting the girl.

"The Little Convent Girl" (1893) is perhaps the most notorious, and most perplexing, of King's stories. In it, a teenager takes her first trip outside of her convent school to meet her mother, whom she has never known, because her father

has died. The story consists mostly of meticulous detail about how perfectly proper and pure the convent girl is, how her quiet, rigid self-control makes her stand out on the steamboat on which she travels, and how her strict purity changes and challenges the hardened bargemen. But the story ends abruptly when the girl jumps in the river and drowns. The reader is left to believe it is likely a suicide because the mother whom she has recently met is "colored" and the girl simply cannot live with that knowledge of herself. Still, after reading pages of heavy-handed white-black imagery, wherein the white of the girl's garments are constantly glimpsed underneath the black exterior of her convent school uniform, one has to wonder if King is commenting upon the social construction of whiteness and blackness and questioning the toxic effects of the extreme qualities assigned to each. Anne Goodwyn Jones asserts that "the convent girl's black mother represents her hidden self. . . . Bold and confident, where her daughter is terrified, speaking where her daughter is silent, the black woman shows what the girl could have become" (*Tomorrow*, p. 123). However, it's terribly difficult to reconcile these interpretative possibilities with King's other stories and her overt assumptions about race.

In stories like these, King blurs the lines of race and questions what racial identity actually consists of. Is race determined by ethnic roots, by what one believes about those roots, or by what others believe about race? The story, like much of King's fiction, provides no answer to this question but is unflinchingly clear that Madrilène's father, like Claire's grandmother, has left her in an untenable position on the borderline between white and black, which was a particularly sexually vulnerable position in a city known for its "quadroon balls," wherein white men would select and bid for the favors of beautiful mixed-race mistresses. King loathed the "unwholesome notoriety" the city and the quadroons received from these balls, and wrote about them in *New Orleans: The Place and the People*. The book denounces the "unscrupulous and pitiless" quadroon women who then passed their octoroon daughters as white and married them into the up-

per classes. New Orleans as a city was notorious for its elaborate codes of racial intermixing, inventing and using not just terms like "quadroon" and "octoroon" but also local categories such as "griffe," "quinteroon," and "black drop." King characterizes this racial mixing as being a threat to "family purity, domestic peace, and household dignity, the most insidious and deadly foes a community ever possessed" (p. 348). To counterbalance this portrait of her city, King devotes an entire chapter of the book to the story of three quadroon women who founded a convent, the Sisters of the Holy Family in New Orleans. Declaring that "race, time, and circumstance" conspired to lead to sexual corruption for quadroon women, King praises the quadroon nuns thus: "In their renunciation, they at least, of their race, found the road to social equality. No white woman could do more" (p. 350). To withdraw from the sexualized commerce of their city was, in King's eyes, their only road to dignity.

King's fiction often focuses intently on the injustice to women of all colors, when they are viewed and treated merely objects of beauty and sexual objectification. On this point, at least, most critics agree that King blurs some of the racial lines of her time: Helen Taylor calls King's fiction "skeptical" of gender and racial lines (*Gender, Race, and Religion*, p. 28), while Anna Shannon Elfenbein notes that in their common struggles, King's complex female characters "transcend sexual and racial stereotypes" (p. 74). For instance, the white girls in multiple short stories are as clearly being marketed at their debutante parties as the quadroons at their own balls. The narrator in *St. Médard* says as much when the neglected daughters of the vulgar bootlegger next door are made into attractive young ladies by a society matron, Madame Doucelet. Now without any other means of support, she is hired to "teach them how to dress . . . showing them . . . their own capital of beauty and how it could be profitably increased" (p. 219). King's deep suspicion of the beauty industry, the marriage market, and marriage itself comes through quite clearly from her first book to her last.

Closely reading the fiction as a whole, Elfenbein also finds that King examines the costly constraints of whiteness as much as the conscribed destinies of women of color, particularly in her descriptions of the trappings of Southern femininity, like the spotless white satin boots into which Marie Modeste's feet are painfully forced in "Monsieur Motte"—like Scarlett O'Hara's corsets, they were too tight for the girls to put them on without assistance. The boots, and other trappings that King's female characters generally cannot wait to remove and toss in a heap on their beds like so much lacy, satin refuse, symbolize the double position of Southern femininity: outwardly pampered and inwardly imprisoned.

Kirby's biography of King takes a psychoanalytic perspective on King's life to drive home his theory that King's work—fiction and nonfiction—is often about women who transcend the boundaries of nineteenth-century femininity and become (what she called) a female "man of action" to compensate for the weak or absent men in their lives (p. 24). He argues that this is essentially how King viewed herself and is the touchstone by which all her work can be interpreted. While there is certainly some evidence to support Kirby's essential premise, most subsequent critics have pointed out that this is an oversimplification of the multiple feminine and sometimes feminist discourses in King's oeuvre. Taylor's feminist analysis focuses instead on the "repressive, reactionary influence of the genteel literary tradition" in contrast to the "liberalizing and liberating effect which the lives, works, and friendships of other woman writers were to have on her own" ("The Case of Grace King," p. 687). Noting the disparate tones King used in her letters to male and female correspondents, Taylor labels the differences as "self-deprecatory and flirtatious" with men and "honest" and "ambitio[us]" with women (p. 688). Clara Juncker further theorizes that King's "insistent, monotonous emphasis on female marginality claims for the muted, invisible women of the South a space of their own" (p. 38). This space, Juncker argues, forces the women to create their own systems of language and understanding, which only other women can read: "Through repetition and exag-

geration of insignificance, King invents a linguistic and economic female domain and, in doing so, redefined the his/story of the region" (p. 38). An example is the language of "The Tignon," a very early (1891) article King wrote on the traditional headscarf of black women in her community, in which she describes what the way each women wore it would communicate to other women. The 1894 story "An Interlude" allows white women speak the language of the bonnet instead of the tignon and to express themselves through the music they are expected to play as ladies. Michelle Birnbaum notes that in stories such as "The Drama of an Evening" all the hairdressers and ladies' maids watch the girls whose beauty their labor has manufactured for balls and dances with a "knowingness" that goes beyond that of the dancers themselves (p. 52). King's ability to write so many stories through the eyes of marginalized women raises the question of whether King possibly viewed "knowingness" as one of the compensations for subjugation that people of color and women shared in the nineteenth-century South. This would connect the watchful eyes of the black workers with those of the white mothers that open the *Balcony Stories*. Not only are women of all colors united by knowingness and confinement, but Anne Goodwyn Jones's examination of mothering as a cross-racial symbolic trope throughout King's work weaves all these arguments and observations together.

Most critics agree that King, like many a nineteenth-century female author, "wrote of her own frustrations, feelings of violation and helplessness, and resentment of patriarchal attitudes and regimes women had endured in the south by analogy with the oppression of other groups—notably slaves and then freedmen" (Helen Taylor, qtd. in Elfenbein, p. 115). To this list one could add working-class women of all ethnicities: in *The Pleasant Ways of St. Médard*, a lot of time is spent on Mimi, the private tutor hired for the Talbot children. Mimi's hard work supports her profligate father, a notorious spendthrift who is largely responsible for his daughter's difficult position but who does nothing at all to remedy or even recognize it. Noting that King's

female characters of all possible positions on the color line rise up singularly or in groups and develop their own survival skills or female communities to compensate for and respond to the failure or absence of men, Elfenbein concludes that "the achievement of King's fiction exceeded her conscious grasp of social issues" (p. 75).

One last way in which King's work can be considered feminist is in its continual emphasis on female community. Women rescue other women, turn to other women for strength and understanding, protect and nurture other women repeatedly when the men who were supposed to do so have vanished and failed. From King's first work to her last, women rescue and sustain other women. In her first story, Marcélite pays for Marie Modeste's schooling when she is left destitute by her father. In mid-career, King wrote "A Delicate Affair" (1893), in which two middle-aged women who were once rivals for a young man reunite with one another and completely ignore the man who brought them together. And in her last novel, *La Dame de Sainte Hermine*, it is Madame Catherine, a hardy Louisianan, who picks up Marie Alorge when she faints upon landing in New Orleans and carries her away to nurse her back to health while the men who witness Marie's illness do nothing.

King's views on gender roles were colored by her Southern upbringing as well. As a Southerner, she considered the terms "man" and "woman" to be inadequate and expressed with pride that were it not for the South the terms "lady" and "gentleman" would no longer exist. The ideology of the Southern lady was powerful in King's thinking, and she always overtly considered it a compliment. However, this ideology caused some serious problems in the pragmatic question of surviving in a postbellum world. As Marie Fletcher notes, a Southern lady "was the very epitome of the nobility of helplessness" (p. 50). Jones also notes that it was a prominent Southern myth that "Ladies didn't labor" ("Women Writers," p. 277). But does this inactivity come off as noble *anywhere* in King's oeuvre? In *The Pleasant Ways of St. Médard*, Mrs. Talbot, a character loosely based on King's mother, has to labor to keep her family fed and

clothed while in exile on the plantation. However, when she returns to town she discovers that "the end of the war does not mean the end of her physical toil, for slavery, which had formerly kept women from domestic drudgery, is no more" (Jones, "Tomorrow," p. 54). Mrs. Talbot tries to cling to her training as a Southern lady in Reconstruction New Orleans, but the ideology betrays her again and again. She looks and feels helpless and useless compared to the family's new landlord, a Gascon woman who chides her for being unable to make soup when her own child is burning with a feverish thirst (p. 24). At the same time, the New Orleans shopkeepers in the novel question whether Mrs. Talbot is still a lady when she asks the price of things before she buys them; to them, a "lady" is a preferred customer who always buys the best of everything and would never think of asking, "How much?" *The Pleasant Ways of St. Médard* reflects upon the difference between a lady and a woman in its narrative: ladies are known for their "easy, careless, extravagance, their utter indifference to their money and the trouble they gave [but] . . . to be hardworking, saving . . . that was being a woman" (p. 95). In fact, idleness, thoughtlessness, and ignorance seem to distinguish a "lady" from a mere "woman" in the novel, which hardly seems complimentary.

The novel as a whole showcases the industry and success of working women—as do many of King's short stories—which is perhaps a reflection of one of the effects of the Reconstruction: a new appreciation of work. In fact, the Southern historian Henry Grady, in an 1886 speech called "The New South," proudly declared, "We have fallen in love with work" (qtd. in Robison, p. 57). The shifts in workload and the perception of labor had their impact on the (re)definition of the Southern lady in the latter half of the nineteenth century. Fletcher argues that Grace King, along with Ellen Glasgow, is part of a shift that occurred between the 1860s and the turn of the century from the traditional Southern lady to the "lady of worth" or "lady of merit" (p. 51), thus preserving the Southern distinction between lady and woman but jettisoning decorative helplessness as an admirable quality. Fletcher argues that

"Mrs. Talbot's portrait at once inspires admiration for her efforts to be a lady and explains why the meaning of that word" must change (p. 55).

Another of King's *Balcony Stories*, "The Old Lady's Restoration," might offer some insight into this question as well. In it, a formerly wealthy Southern lady has descended into nearly abject poverty after the war. Then when her family fortune is miraculously restored, the friends who had dropped her come to visit, expecting her to indulge them in the luxury of carriage rides and opera boxes. However, the old lady has moved on, has redefined through hard experience what is "necessary" and what is "luxurious" and will not leave her new working-class community. The society "ladies" who visit her do not understand; they declare her insane and suggest she should be interred in a sanatorium.

It is crucial to note that King referred to herself as a "woman" and not a "lady" in the title of her autobiography. Perhaps King considered herself akin to the old lady in the story: perhaps she had seen too much and worked too hard for luxuries to claim the title of "lady" either. (One must note that King used the money from her first story to buy "nice white cotton toweling," which parallels the old lady's first purchase with her newfound wealth almost word for word.) Or perhaps King's frustrations with her mother's enabling of her brothers while insisting on her daughter's pursuit of a rich suitor ultimately made King decide she would rather be a successful professional woman than a lady, more akin to the robust, efficient Gascon market gardeners or the wealthy colored hairdressers in her stories.

LEGACY

In her last decade, King reigned as the grande dame of New Orleans letters, and her Friday salons drew established and aspiring authors alike. She was regularly featured in American literature textbooks and studies of that decade, including Fred Lewis Pattee's *History of American Literature Since 1870* (1915) and *The Development of the American Short Story* (1923). In July 1923 the *Louisiana Historical Quarterly* devoted itself to printing tributes to King by seven different authors. In 1924 she founded Le Petit Salon exclusively for intellectual women to convene.

King's final work is her autobiography, *Memories of a Southern Woman of Letters* (1932). As a sustained work of art, it generally comes in for more criticism than it does compliments. The book shows the strain of a house divided against itself, to be sure. As Katherine Capshaw Smith observes, King "regales her readers with charming anecdotes of the South's aristocratic heritage while she strains to suppress and minimize ugly moments of regional, economic, and racial tension" (p. 133). Familial tension must also be added to the list of gaping silences in the text. Nearly the first third of the book is taken up by her family stories of war and Reconstruction, including not just the harrowing account of their original flight from New Orleans but an episode wherein Union soldiers fired upon her twelve-year-old brother Fred as he fled into the woods on their plantation. In the rest of the book, King spends a great deal of time describing in detail her three trips to Europe, which only account for about five years of her adult life. King's final work was also historical, but it was her own history this time. Although pieces of it had certainly been woven into everything else she had written, this was the first time she overtly used a first-person perspective. *Memories of a Southern Woman of Letters* was published very shortly after her death, although she did not intend for it to be posthumous, as her fellow Southern woman writer Ellen Glasgow had intended for her 1954 autobiography, *The Woman Within*. Unlike Glasgow's autobiography, King's focuses on her public persona, employing her "Matterhorn" pride, Southern loyalty, and indomitable spirit to the purpose. She leaves out the facts of her life that would complicate or undercut the public image she had crafted so carefully, including her eventual reconciliation with George Washington Cable, the fight with Charles Gayarré that dissolved their friendship, her lifelong trouble with Nina, and all the private opinions of events and people we find in her letters and her journals.

Actually, these narrative gaps and evasions are entirely typical of American women's literary autobiography at the time; moreover, as an overtly *literary* autobiography, King's text simply highlights what she considered to be her most crucial formative experiences as the "woman of letters" the work's title asserts her to be. Like Edith Wharton in her 1933 autobiography, King emphasizes her connection to influential male authors of her time; like Gertrude Atherton in her 1931 autobiography, she traces her family roots to Europe to gain authority over American literary and cultural judgments. Her disdain for American provincialism sets her apart from other Southern women mentioned in the text. Calling on a friend upon her return from her second trip to Europe, King remarks, "Did we talk about Europe and what I had seen and done over there? Not at all. We talked about New Orleans—its news, political, social, and religious. That was what interested her more than anything Europe held" (*Memories*, p. 325). She expresses her indignation at the lack of intellectual interest in the South in general, where her books were not popular, she explains, because books in general were not popular. As she acerbically commented elsewhere, "Books are of no account in the South, I am sorry to say. The Macmillans do not count upon New Orleans at all in the sale of my books" (qtd. in DeJean, p. 111). It also galled her that New Orleans promptly forgot its most prominent—before her—Louisiana historian Charles Gayarré, noting his death "created hardly a ripple of interest in the city in which he had lived and which he had loved" (*Memories*, p. 186). Perhaps she worried that if Gayarré's passing only made a "ripple" in the current of New Orleans' consciousness, her death might go completely unnoticed.

Grace King suffered the stroke that would ultimately end her life during the process of correcting the proofs for her autobiography. To the end, she had lived with her two sisters, Nan and Nina, and their recollections of King's last days reveal the private side of the prideful, dignified King girls, the side that was able to laugh at life and at themselves. The image Nina King recalled of the three King girls as elderly women, the last survivors of their generation, sitting on the floor together, embracing and laughing at their collective physical vulnerability when Nan and Nina were unable to lift Grace back into bed after a fall (Bush, *Grace King*, p. 306), provides some shading to the formality, fatefulness, and frustration that pervades much of her published work. King died on January 14, 1932. Bush notes in his biography that her funeral was as lavish, well attended, and widely publicized as that of a major, well-loved politician might have been. However satisfied she might have been could she have known this, it might have pleased her even more to know that descendants of her proud family continue to live in the New Orleans house her work had helped purchase generations before.

Selected Bibliography

WORKS OF GRACE KING

NOVELS AND SHORT-STORY COLLECTIONS
Monsieur Motte. New York: Armstrong, 1888.
Tales of a Time and Place. New York: Harper, 1892.
Balcony Stories. New York: Century, 1893; Author's ed., New Orleans: L. Graham, 1914. New ed., New York: Macmillan, 1925 (contains two new stories). Reprint, San Bernardino, Calif.: N.p., 2016.
The Pleasant Ways of St. Médard. New York: Holt, 1916. Reprint, Miami: Hardpress, 2016.
La Dame de Sainte Hermine. New York: Macmillan, 1926.

SHORT STORIES AND ARTICLES
"Monsieur Motte." *New Princeton Review* 1:91–133 (January 1886).
"Bonne Maman." *Harper's New Monthly Magazine* 73:293–307 (July 1886).
"Earthlings." *Lippincott's Monthly Magazine* 42:601–679 (November 1888).
"The Self-Made Man: An Impression." *Harper's Bazaar* 23, no. 14:258–259 (April 1890).
"Lagniappe." *Chautauquan* 12:78–79 (October 1890).
"Madrilène; or, The Festival of the Dead." *Harper's New Monthly Magazine* 81:869–886 (November 1890).
"One Woman's Story." *Harper's Bazaar* 24:218–219 (March 1891).

"The Tignon." *Chautauquan* 12:656–657 (February 1891).

"The Chevalier Alain de Triton." *Chautauquan* 13:409–464 (July 1891).

"The Little Convent Girl." *Century Magazine* 46, no. 4:547–551 (August 1893).

"A Delicate Affair." *Century Magazine* 46:884–889 (October 1893).

"An Affair of the Heart." *Harper's New Monthly Magazine* 88:796–799 (April 1894).

"At Chenière Caminada." *Harper's New Monthly Magazine* 88:871–874 (May 1894).

"The Evening Party." *Harper's New Monthly Magazine* 89:192–196 (July 1894).

"An Interlude." *Harper's New Monthly Magazine,* 89:918–920 (November 1894).

"A Domestic Interior." *Harper's New Monthly Magazine* 90:407–411 (February 1895).

"The Higher Life of New Orleans." *Outlook* 53:754–760 (April 1896).

"A Quarrel with God." *Outlook* 55:687–694 (March 6, 1897).

"Fort Louis of Mobile: A Commemoration." *Outlook* 70:433–436 (February 1902).

"On the Prairie." *Appleton's Booklover's Magazine* 7:324–326 (March 1906).

"The Clodhopper." *McClure's Magazine* 28:487–491 (March 1907).

"The Lower Mississippi Valley–Old Louisiana." *Country Life in America* 23:33–37, 66, 68 (November 1912).

"The Centenary of the Battle of New Orleans." *Outlook* 109:178–181 (January 1915).

"The Preservation of Louisiana History." *North Carolina Historical Review* 5, no. 4:363–371 (October 1928).

NONFICTION

Jean Baptiste Le Moyne, Sieur de Bienville. New York: Dodd, Mead, 1892.

A History of Louisiana. With John R. Ficklen. New Orleans: Graham, 1893.

New Orleans: The Place and the People. New York: Macmillan, 1895.

De Soto and His Men in the Land of Florida. New York: Macmillan, 1898.

Creole Families of New Orleans. New York: Macmillan, 1921.

Mount Vernon on the Potomac: History of the Mount Vernon Ladies' Association of the Union. New York: Macmillan, 1929.

JOURNAL AND MEMOIRS

Memories of a Southern Woman of Letters. New York: Macmillan, 1932. Gretna, La.: Pelican, 2007.

To Find My Own Peace: Grace King in Her Journals, 1886–1910. Edited by Melissa Walker Heidari. Athens: University of Georgia Press, 2004.

PAPERS

Grace Elizabeth King Papers, 1781–1933, #1111, Southern Historical Collection, Wilson Library, University of North Carolina at Chapel Hill.

Grace King Papers, 1906–1920, LaRC/Manuscripts Collection 564, Howard-Tilton Memorial Library, Tulane University.

CRITICAL AND BIOGRAPHICAL STUDIES

Allured, Janet, and Judith F. Gentry, eds. *Louisiana Women: Their Lives and Times.* Athens: University of Georgia Press, 2009.

Barreca, Regina, ed. *New Perspectives on Women and Comedy.* Philadelphia: Gordon and Breach, 1992.

Birnbaum, Michele. *Race, Work, and Desire in American Literature.* Cambridge, U.K., and New York: Cambridge University Press, 2003.

Brown, Dorothy H., and Barbara C. Ewell, eds. *Louisiana Women Writers: New Essays and a Comprehensive Bibliography.* Baton Rouge: Louisiana State University Press, 1992.

Bush, Robert. "Grace King and Mark Twain." *American Literature* 44, no. 1:31–51 (March 1972).

———. "Grace King: The Emergence of a Southern Intellectual Woman." *Southern Review* 13, no. 1:272–288 (winter 1977).

———. *Grace King: A Southern Destiny.* Baton Rouge and London: Louisiana State University Press, 1983.

Castille, Philip, and William Osborne, eds. *Southern Literature in Transition: Heritage and Promise.* Memphis, Tenn.: Memphis State University Press, 1983.

DeJean, Joan. "Critical Creolization: Grace King and Writing on French in the American South." In *Southern Literature and Literary Theory.* Edited by Jefferson Humphries. Athens: University of Georgia Press, 1990. Pp. 109–126.

Dresner, Zita Z. "Irony and Ambiguity in Grace King's 'Monsieur Motte.'" In *New Perspectives on Women and Comedy.* Edited by Regina Barreca. Philadelphia: Gordon and Breach, 1992.

Elfenbein, Anna Shannon. *Women on the Color Line: Evolving Stereotypes and the Writings of George Washington Cable, Grace King, Kate Chopin.* Charlottesville: University Press of Virginia, 1989.

Fletcher, Marie. "Grace Elizabeth King: Her Delineation of the Southern Heroine." *Louisiana Studies* 5, no. 1:50–60 (spring 1966).

Humphries, Jefferson, ed. *Southern Literature and Literary Theory.* Athens: University of Georgia Press, 1990.

Inness, Sherrie A., and Royer, Diana. eds. *Breaking Boundaries: New Perspectives on Women's Regional Writing.* Iowa City: University of Iowa Press, 1997.

Jones, Anne Goodwyn. *Tomorrow Is Another Day: The Woman Writer in the South, 1859–1936.* Baton Rouge and London: Louisiana State University Press, 1981.

———. "Women Writers and the Myths of Southern Womanhood." In *The History of Southern Women's Literature.* Edited by Carolyn Perry and Mary Louise Weaks. Baton Rouge: Louisiana State University Press, 2002. Pp. 275–289.

Juncker, Clara. "Grace King: Woman-as-Artist." *Southern Literary Journal* 20, no. 1:37–44 (fall 1987).

———. "Grace King: Feminist, Southern Style." *Southern Quarterly* 26, no. 3:15–30 (winter 1988).

Keely, Karon A. "Marriage Plots and National Reunion: The Trope of Romantic Reconciliation in Postbellum Literature." *Mississippi Quarterly* 51:621–646 (fall 1998).

Kirby, David. *Grace King.* Boston: Twayne, 1980.

Kreyling, Michael. *Inventing Southern Literature.* Jackson: University Press of Mississippi, 1998.

McSherry, Frank Jr., Charles G. Waugh, and Martin Greenberg, eds. *Civil War Women: The Civil War Seen Through Women's Eyes in Stories by Louisa May Alcott, Kate Chopin, Eudora Welty, and Other Great Woman Writers.* New York: Simon & Schuster, 1990.

Perry, Carolyn, and Mary Louise Weaks, eds. *The History of Southern Women's Literature.* Baton Rouge: Louisiana State University Press, 2002.

Piacentino, Edward J. "The Enigma of Black Identity in Grace King's 'Joe.'" *Southern Literary Journal* 19, no. 1:56–67 (fall 1986).

Robison, Lori. "'Why, Why Do We Not Write Our Side?': Gender and Self-Representation in Grace King''s Balcony Stories. In *Breaking Boundaries: New Perspectives on Women's Regional Writing.* Edited by Sherrie A. Inness and Diana Royer. Iowa City: University of Iowa Press, 1997.

Smith, Katharine Capshaw. "Conflicting Visions of the South in Grace King's Memories of a Southern Woman of Letters." *Southern Quarterly* 36, no. 3:133–145 (spring 1988).

Taylor, Helen. "The Case of Grace King." *Southern Review* 18, no. 4:685–702 (autumn 1982).

———. *Gender, Race, and Region in the Writings of Grace King, Ruth McEnery Stuart, and Kate Chopin.* Baton Rouge: Louisiana State University Press, 1989.

Vaughan, Bess. "A Bio-Bibliography of Grace Elizabeth King." *Louisiana Historical Quarterly,* 17, no. 4:751–770 (October 1934).

Wilson, Mary Ann. "Grace King: New Orleans Literary Historian." In *Louisiana Women: Their Lives and Times.* Edited by Janet Allured and Judy Gentry. Athens: University Press of Georgia, 2009. Pp. 137–154.

SYDNEY LEA

(1942—)

David Gullette

SYDNEY LEA IS what critics call a strong poet: plain-speaking, emotionally wide-ranging, with a recognizable "voice," rooted in one geographic location (northern New England), and growing stronger as he and his writing add years. At his best when directly connected to the natural world and the changing seasons, he is a hunter and fisherman, a lover of dogs and small-town life up North, devoted to his family and friends (both the living and the dead), and recognized by the state of Vermont as its poet laureate. This essay will sample his prodigiously productive career as a poet (eleven books of poetry since 1980) and as the author of a novel and a book of short prose pieces that feel like poems.

The key to understanding his writing is to read slowly and carefully, and follow the way his mind lays out a path for the reader to follow. If the reader pays close attention to what's going on in his poems and listens to the music of the lines, the rewards are memorable.

Sydney L. W. Lea, Jr., was born on December 22, 1942, in Chestnut Hill, a suburb of Philadelphia, to Jane Jordan and Sydney L. W. Lea, a businessman. He was the eldest of five children, and from kindergarten through high school he attended Chestnut Hill Academy. In a biographical sketch he provided for this essay, he said that the people who had the greatest impact on him were "one superb French teacher and one superb music teacher." He was an athlete and musician, but, he writes, "had someone predicted that poetry would be my vocation, I'd have been skeptical, to say the least."

Throughout the year he spent as much time as possible (including some years working all summer) at the farm of a bachelor uncle in Montgomery County, Pennsylvania, where, he says, "I kindled my passion for the outdoors,

which has abided ever since." Later, consecutive summers spent at a family camp on an island in West Grand Lake, Maine, intensified this deep connection to the backwoods.

At age seventeen he went to Yale, studying arts and letters, and luckily found himself in a writing course called "Daily Themes," so that sitting down every day to write became a lifelong habit. Outside of class he wrote a lot of prose fiction but never thought he would become a writer.

After earning his B.A. degree from Yale in 1964, he considered going to graduate school but felt he needed "time away from being a student," so he returned to Chestnut Hill Academy, where he taught French and English for a year. In 1965 he began the Ph.D. program in American studies at Yale, completed the preliminary M.A. in 1968, and then switched to the Ph.D. track in comparative literature, where he began a doctoral dissertation on (mostly German) supernatural fiction. But since Yale was a hothouse of literary theory in those days and "theory and I have never gotten along very well," the dissertation remained unfinished when he accepted a job at Dartmouth College.

Dartmouth students wanted a creative writing course, but the English Department saw it as "not a real course." Nonetheless, Lea taught creative writing, purportedly to give him time to finish his dissertation (which in due course he did, receiving his Ph.D. in 1972). But in fact, he says, "I fell in love with my students' awkwardness, their efforts to record experiences that were difficult to get at, and I suddenly felt my own college-era itch to write return—but I turned to poetry rather than fiction." The reasons for this turn to poetry are important to anyone who wants

to understand not just the meaning but also the verbal texture of Lea's poems.

In that remote corner of Maine near the New Brunswick border where he had spent so many summers, he had grown close to the men and women who lived there "prior to the age of power tools (the men were loggers, one and all) and electricity." Mostly uneducated, some even illiterate, these folks were great storytellers. So when Lea "elected to write with a purpose," he tells us:

> [T]heirs were the voices I wanted to get onto the page. I heard them every day in my mind, and do to this day. But I knew I lacked the genius to write in dialect without sounding condescending, which was scarcely how I felt. I concocted the notion that if I wrote stories like theirs in *poetry*, I might capture the rhythms and cadences of their language *without having to imitate it*. This is why in my earlier books I was tagged a narrative poet, and it is true even today that narrative values have a prominent place in my poetic work.

But he was still teaching at Dartmouth, and Dartmouth was blunt: poetry is not scholarship. If he wanted tenure, he should turn parts of his dissertation into articles and publish them in learned journals. He tried to comply, but when he reopened the dissertation, he felt "literal nausea. I decided to go on writing poetry and let fate decide the rest."

He didn't get tenure at Dartmouth, but was hired by Middlebury College, "which had some tradition of writer-professor." During the 1970s he also cofounded, with Jay Parini, the esteemed *New England Review* and began to place poems in prestigious magazines, including the *New Yorker* and *Atlantic Monthly*. He published his first collection, *Searching the Drowned Man*, in 1980. In his academic career, he went on to teach at Yale, Wesleyan, and Vermont Colleges, as well as Franklin College in Switzerland and the Eotvos Lorand University in Budapest. In 1999 he returned to Dartmouth and from 2003 taught in the liberal studies M.A. program until his retirement in 2011. He was appointed that year as poet laureate of Vermont, a position he would hold until 2015.

Over the course of his career, Lea has earned numerous honors, including Rockefeller, Ful-bright, and Guggenheim Fellowships and the 1998 Poets' Prize for his collection *To the Bone*. He has two children, Creston and Erika, from his marriage to Carola Bradford, which ended in divorce; and three children, Jordan, Catherine, and Sydney, from his marriage in 1983 to attorney Robin Barone, who teaches at Vermont Law School. They live in Newbury, Vermont, not far from the Connecticut River.

COLLECTIONS OF THE 1980s

Lea's first published collection, *Searching the Drowned Man* (1980), introduces readers to some of the themes and strategies that he will deploy in the coming years. Here we find multiple perspectives on parents and children. In "Young Man Leaving Home," this archetypal scene begins with his elders' "unaccustomed benedictions" (p. 8) over the last breakfast, and the family assembly as he boards the train and leaves toward

> The Future,
> that unimaginable lode of riches,
>
> this hero, composed of a dozen young rebels
> out of thin novels, groaning with luggage.
>
> (p. 9)

In "Father's Game" we learn that the poet's dad was able to "whistle in" (p. 11) various types of dogs simply by varying the music of his lips—a charming conceit until (as so often in Lea's poetry) he catches us off guard, in this case with an earlier instance of the "siren whistle" early on D-Day. The father's friend, John Whitney, turned his head to hear it "just before / the bullet jolted in / behind his ear near Dieppe" (p. 12). So memories of violence and beauty are shockingly fused in an image carried over from the distant past.

Other parents and children inhabit this first book: the poet himself worries about his own child in "To Our Son," when the youngster comes home from school shattered by the news that his friend, "the nicest girl in class," has died, and the father's first instinct is to rid the house of the "pretty poisons" (p. 21) the Poison Control Center brochure has warned them not to keep in

plain sight. And in "For My Son Creston at the Solstice," the poet recalls camping with his son, and then spending much of the night, as Creston slept, sitting sentry-like before the tent flap, "warding off vague phantoms" (p. 51).

This book is also packed with tributes to old friends, some dead. They linger in the poet's mind and form a part of the self he has made, like Billy Farrell, whose face he can't quite remember, but whose words ring in his ears years later: "Damn the wind! Enough to shake owls from the trees!" (p. 55). Or Alex Lewis, who declared: "Son, I am the President of Flowers" (p. 23). Or in the title poem of the collection, "Searching the Drowned Man: The Third Day," the words of the search boss, Bill White: "I don't like the idea of what we're going to find" (p. 1). Summing up such early experiences, the poet says: "I strained to store these signals up" (p. 2). Deciphering "signs" and "signals" will become a constant theme in Lea's work.

Searching the Drowned Man is not an apprentice effort. Lea's voice is already bold and self-assured and original, despite an occasional echo of Wallace Stevens, Robert Frost, or other influences. And the desire to tell stories and bring alive the landscape of northern New England and the minds, bodies, and words of the people who lived, and live, there becomes the basso continuo of his unfolding career.

Two years later came *The Floating Candles* (1982), which begins with "Dirge for My Brother: Dawn to Dawn," focusing on the life—and death by aneurysm—of his younger brother, whom he calls "Moonman." The older brother always counseled, "Recognize Your Limits" (p. 1), while the younger's "cycle shrieked / far out ahead of me. . . . Your wild eyes rocketed over my preachments of calm" (p. 2). We learn that when Moonman's "great bombed bubble" (p. 1) burst, he lingered for almost four days before he died. The poet's grief tries its best to cling to the formality of a dirge:

Here lies
no mighty chief or leader as the world will measure
such a thing, and yet I feel the republic
stumble, crack.

(p. 3)

The mourners all look away, the poet himself among them: "I, whose words should blast like twenty-one cannons" (p. 3).

The centerpiece of *The Floating Candles* is "The Feud," an ambitious narrative poem in the form of a dramatic monologue. For the full experience of Lea's early experiments with subject matter, voice, and descriptive precision, this is the place to begin. The narrator of the poem is not the poet himself but instead a representative New Englander, whose life gets entangled in a downward spiraling back-and-forth with a backwoods family, the Walkers. They have killed a small deer and end up leaving "their deer guts cooking in the sun" (p. 32) across the road from the narrator's property, where the stench leads the narrator to retaliate by raking the fetid innards into a bag and strewing them in the Walkers' dooryard, along with a signed note:

"Since I'm not eating any deer meat,
I'd just as quick your guts rot somewhere else
as by my house."

(p. 33)

Despite his overheated mind, our narrator declares he doesn't

[. . .]believe in taking up with feuds.
I usually let the Good Lord have His vengeance.

Nothing any good has ever grown
out of revenge.

(p. 33)

This is a lesson he first learned as a schoolboy, when "I slapped up Lemmie Watson, because he broke / the little mill I built down on the brook" (p. 33) and was punished for it with a week of afternoons indoors. But this old lesson fades, and "something else took over" (p. 33). Note the almost Sophoclean simplicity of those ominous words.

Despite telling himself to "Let it go," the tit-for-tat continues: the Walkers stave in his mailbox; he takes in one of their stray dogs, feeds it, hands it over to the pound, but keeps the collar, which he flings into their yard. Ordinarily, he would never mix with people like them with their lowlife ways, but, he says, "It seemed as if / their

style of working things reached up and grabbed me" (p. 36). Four months pass and then they slash all four tires on his new pickup truck.

So our man sees an apple in the store, with a hole in it, and he gets a notion: "Maybe fate is notions / that you might have left alone, but took instead" (p. 38). He buys the apple and some rat poison pellets, stuffs the pellets in the hole, and stores the apple for a week in a shed. Despite repeating over and over to himself, "Nothing good will ever grow from feuds," he tells us the apple "sat inside my mind" (p. 38). But then a full moon rises, and in the middle of the night he seeks out the apple, "as if it was / another person who was going down / inside the shed" (p. 39). He makes his way to the Walkers' place and tosses the apple into the pen of their gigantic hog, which after a while begins to "blow and hoot just like a bear" (p. 41).

A day or two later he gets sick from his nighttime outing, goes to the clinic, and, returning home, sees a "copper-orange" (p. 43) sky and black smoke: it's his own home burning, his son trapped inside; he runs to get the ax, which is frozen in a puddle, "and every step I took / was like a step you take in dreams" (p. 44). He wants to break the upstairs window so the boy can jump out. He throws the ax, misses, and scares the boy back in: "That was the last I saw him. / Like a woman sighing, that old house huffed once and fell" (p. 44). When he tries to figure out how all this happened, our narrator decides that "The part of life you think / you've got done living lies in wait like Satan" (p. 45).

"The Feud" is more than a disturbing short story in verse. It is a carefully crafted meditation on how we stumble into bringing about our own fates, delivered in an American idiom stripped of ornament—sober, direct, unvarnished. The rhythmic, slowly accumulating sense of doom is like something from an old tragedy, but as Lea tells the tale it's happening to people like us, just a town or two over.

No Sign (1987) may seem familiar. Readers of the first two volumes are accustomed by now to retrospective eulogies, but in much of this book there is an insistent calling on the dead, a retrieval of their presence, as well as various meticulous reenactments of their deaths, as when the young wife in "Leonora's Kitchen" (husband and boys away in town) collapses in the yard on the way to gather eggs, "the white hens walking idly near her, / stepping now and then across her ankles" (p. 49). As for the kitchen she has just left, "it seems to do nothing / but replicate the kitchen in any house / of the country working poor" (p. 49). And as for the poet, he has suspended time: her body hasn't been discovered yet, "so the fact that she was pretty and decent, / cannot mean anything yet, / if in fact it will ever mean anything" (p. 50). He invites us to be transfixed along with him in this imagining of a death, in a room not illuminated

[. . .]by anything

like that aura said to rise off the spirit rising.
Yet somehow, still, it is radiant,
and moves us, though unmoving

(p. 50)

The horrified paralysis in the contemplation of tragic endings crops up in other poems early in this volume, and feels related to historical moments. "Waiting for the Armistice," ostensibly set in March 1945, finishes with the image of women in a refugee camp, where both clothes and lives have been yanked away, and the envoi "but there's no safe place to hide" is followed by an unexpected epigraph: "AFTER THE PHALANGIST MASSACRES IN BEIRUT" (p. 33), killings that took place in September 1982. In "Making Sense," we learn that "the word is *Trouble*, / trouble, trouble!" (p. 39). And in "Horn," we are invited to contemplate not catastrophe

but protracted
unease for which
the diagram is there
from the start, and on which
we gradually heap
our meanings[. . .]

(p. 59)

The 1980s was a difficult decade for many, but for Sydney Lea it seems to have darkened his vision.

His "protracted unease" rides shotgun in this volume, alongside intense anxiety about children

(lost, run over by trucks, carelessly careening toward death, committing stupid sins that will haunt them for years). And about violence, toward animals, from people and via machines. And all this haunted by a range of vulnerable or ominous birds: a chicken fed a treble fishing hook by naughty boys ("How to Leave Nothing"), or "drifts of dead tanagers / strewn on the lawn like so many careless dollars" ("The Art of the Son," p. 29), or "nighthawks slicing the last few / ephemerids from air" ("Making Sense," p. 38).

And yet *No Sign* upends our expectations and resets the mood toward the end with a triumphant love poem and tribute to his wife, "Annual Report." How to pull this off in the ironic atmosphere of much twenty-first-century poetic discourse? His way is to be blunt and adult and lyrical and celebratory all at once. The poet marks the twelve-month anniversary of their son's "late birth," who was "encased; released; prostrate; now he uprears / himself on this rich festival of earth" (p. 92). He recalls his own shriek at the child's birth, and then his wife and their daughter of seven with "bug-veils drooping down" (p. 92) from their canvas hats as they broke ground for zinnias and marigolds. Even the death of the old family retriever, Jess, with his "toothless maw" (p. 93), is accepted and memorialized by an apple tree planted on his grave.

All the same, "Who," the poet asks, "can ignore the huff of tragedy / in the first fall gust?" (p. 93). He recalls his firstborn son who, when almost thirteen, would turn "somber / as earth when leaden clouds" would heave overhead. And thinking of that son's dark mood, he exclaims: "How I recall myself in such a season!" (p. 94).

And so it is his wife who brings forth these children, and who with them will militate against his gloom:

How do you do it? Life-love, teach me how.
"Is that," you whisper, pointing to the stairs
down which my sleepyhead daughter treads,
"an emblem of futility and doom?"

(p. 95)

So his rhetorical question to himself (and her) becomes "Why not be content, / why not affirm by will what is?" (p. 96). The poem ends in May,

in "a fête of resurrection" with the beloved wife and mother praised as "creator, creature, riddle, lover, maid" (p. 97). And with this gesture Lea transforms the tenor of this previously harrowing book—as Yeats would say, "gaiety transfiguring all that dread."

A couple of years later, perhaps unsurprisingly for a writer so drawn to narrative, Lea published his only novel, *A Place in Mind* (1989). The narrator is Brant Healey, Ph.D., who, after completing his graduate studies in modern languages, takes a one-year job at "a southern women's college, whose classrooms smelled of expensive perfume, saddle soap, tack leather. Can there be such places on earth any more?" (p. 10). While there, Healey has a passionate affair with Anna Graves, wife of a senior colleague; it ends in bitter disappointment that haunts him on and off for the rest of his (unmarried) life. But heterosexual love is not the emotional focus of the book, which centers instead on his forty-plus-year friendship with Louis McLean, a hunting and fishing guide in the North Country (probably Maine), where Healey owns a cabin on the McLean River. While officially a resident of Boston, Healey is drawn magnetically back to McLean (place and man) and considers himself sane and whole only when hunting or fishing or simply hanging out with Louis: "No women, some whiskey, and a great deal of water" (p. 24). *A Place in Mind* is an unusual novel. The plotting is dutiful, but the dialogue is terse and convincing, and what arrests the reader's mind most are powerful lyrical passages about the immersion of these two men in the natural world over four decades. That they are men from different social classes, that Healey employs McLean throughout the year and throughout the years, is never forgotten, but it becomes less and less important, and the strong male bonding in the world of woods and rapids and lakes, of guns, rods, and axes in a pre-electrical part of America, is what gives this book its steady power. Here's an example:

Fighting the wind, I squatted on the granite, imagined myself in a youthful crouch to dress my fish or fowl, while Louis dressed his next to me: a partridge crop full of haws like scarlet jewels; the

coral roe of a hen salmon; the haloed spots on a brown trout's flank; glint of a knife blade rinsed in the spangled shallows at our feet; feel of the meat—clean, weighty, dripping in our hands.

(p. 93)

If in a skeptical corner of your mind you may have wondered if the poet and professor from Dartmouth and Yale and Middlebury might have been embellishing the sincerity of his friendships with backwoods working folks, this novel is a corrective. It also gives Lea's own repeated sorties in his poems into woods and fields and out on rivers and lakes, alone or with local friends, the authenticity that comes from an unquenchable desire for and intense identification with a place and its critters and its people, in this case north of North of Boston.

COLLECTIONS OF THE 1990s

Prayer for the Little City (1990) draws its title from the prefatory poem's evocation of a cluster of ice-fisher shacks that form a loose community on a frozen lake. The poet is drawn to the scene not by any wonder or mystery, but mainly by

[. . .]the care with which   all night men linger,

as if in prayer   for a novel fish,   or a novel way by which to address   some thing they're feeling.

(p. x)

The attentive reader will notice how the lines are broken into two-beat units, which is not the only structural or rhetorical novelty Lea is playing with in the earlier poems of this collection. Among other things, he draws us into cogitations with religious echoes, something pretty rare in what we have read so far, as rare as the formality and programmatic feel of the poems' formatting. The second poem or titled section, for instance, "Six Sundays Toward a Seventh," consists of seven named and numbered units covering the period of Lent in 1988 and is dedicated to the Reverend Malcolm Grobe. As the story of these seven Sundays unfolds, the poet mainly dissolves himself in the community of worshippers, "I" taking a back seat (or back pew) to "we." We see

and hear the others, learn their names, and each section ends with a free-floating reference to certain passages in the Bible (from which certain italicized fragments in the poem itself have apparently been drawn). What feels mostly missing from this poem is the poet grappling with his individual issues (the one exception being the fourth section, titled "Locked though we were in our own sick, aching flesh," which begins by reenacting the poet and his wife up all night with a sick, sleepless child). So we are left wondering how much this biblical substructure and this communal experience of religious intensity during Lent tell us about the long arc we have been following of the poet's coming to self-knowledge.

A hint comes in the next poem, "Two Chets," in which the poet recounts how one day he found himself driving down Route 22 "simply following Chet / toward the river" (p. 19). Suddenly coming toward him in the opposite lane came a Chevy S-10 driven by someone strangely familiar:

It was Chet, Chet waved,
and when I looked back
to where I was going,
that other Chet ahead of me was gone

without a trace.

(p. 21)

Was this a supernatural moment, a divinely arranged dream? Did he merely imagine it all? Earlier in the poem, after asserting that "Life is stranger / than our inventions" (p. 19), the poet had declared, "I didn't think to be scared of lyrical faith, / to be glad I didn't have it / nor, quite, its absence" (p. 20). But then comes the scene of the two Chets, one coming toward him, one going from him and disappearing, and the poem ends with the baffled poet turning to the reader:

Let me ask you, Stranger:

what are those flashes
when something happens and unhappens
all at once, and you see life,
its starts, its odd reverses?

(p. 20)

134

This is not a rhetorical question. But we're left to share the poet's befuddlement, which is more awkward than intriguing.

The poems that follow mostly relax into Lea's earlier style. "At the Flyfisher's Shack" allows him to imagine an old man whose expertise had been tying flies for trout fishing. He sees "in mind" the head dipping down to the fly currently being tied, with a liquid "bauble" gathering at the tip of the old man's nose: "He couldn't wipe it off, in concentration / rapt, in study, building something fine" (p. 22). This admiration for a fellow craftsman is clear, including the idea that even a rejected fly—rejected because the simulacrum of a specific insect a trout might want was less than perfect—might be exactly what the moment requires: "'Boy,' he'd often tell me, 'there are days / a bungled pattern's what they prefer'" (p. 23). Allowing for departures from rigid patterning is seen as liberating, and fruitful.

This idea is partly echoed in "Manifest" (where every one of eighteen lines begins with "In . . ."), with the evocation of "In illogical woodpeckers' laughter / in their swooping flight, / that suggests assertion crossed by doubt" (p. 38). The tension encapsulated in just those last four words is one key to Lea's finest thinking in poetry.

And as though to dispel the reader's doubts about his experimental formatting, Lea pulls another surprise ending, as he did in *No Sign*. Two of his strongest poems are part of the windup of *Prayer for the Little City*.

"Sun, Rising" entirely fills two pages with text, right up to the margins. There are seventeen three-line stanzas, each beginning with a two-beat phrase, then a gap, then a more-or-less iambic pentameter jamming the right margin. And yet the poem does not feel clotted or ostentatiously overburdened. It's the poet's reflection on his father in the form of a conversation with the long-dead man, who years ago in a moment of pique at his adolescent son ("I'd grown too big for you to handle") had blurted out *You're wearing me* " (p. 58)—a curious expression, probably at that instant meaning "you're wearing me down." The father dies, the years pass, the poet in later life finds himself alone up in the moun-

tains in the snow, even though it's May: "I rebuke myself for wandering up in the dark" (p. 58). But there he is, and realizes "that I make myself the stuff I'm fleeing I'm fleeing" (p. 58). His mind crowded with memories of his father, he suddenly discovers a sky-blue feather "propped in a pure white drift. I drop to a knee. I'm wearing you," he says, "this feather in my hat, and whatever else may be" (p. 59). That rereading of the old phrase, that refitting of worn-out language to a new reality, is an impressive move, an instance of serious wit.

One other strong poem near the end of this volume, "Over Brogno," takes place in northern Italy, near Bellagio on Lake Como (where the poet had been invited to write in peace for a spell). The epigraph is from Rainer Maria Rilke, about how if "the perilous archangel came down, / our thunderous heartbeats would kill us" (p. 60). Then the poem itself: having spent ten or twenty minutes in a lakeside church, the poet mildly rebukes himself for his "bourgeois / reverie and rote prayers / for the absent ones, / wife, children, friends" (p. 60). In the piazza a young woman passes him, but her womanhood has "weighted" him, so his sudden impulse is to climb the snowy mountain behind him, following "the ancient mule paths" (p. 61). On his way up he asks directions of a farmer, whose reply has a Dantean lilt: "At every fork, choose a way that climbs, / if you must" (p. 62). He is glad no one on the mountain has asked him where he's going or why, "for only a troubled abstraction / could have been my answer" (p. 63). On the summit at last, he sees an old tower and a sign with skull and crossbones (*Pericolo di morte!* [Danger!]) and far below, the buildings of the little town of Brogno. But for the narrator up there above everything, there is a moment of vision: he thinks beyond

to our time's angelic throngs:
What deadly secrets? What secret soarings?
What particles abroad?
What specters of light that is more than light?

(p. 63)

He wonders about the radio waves whipping past him, even as he feels his own "Clamorous heartbeat, its clap / within like thunder. Without,

the Angel" (p. 64). His heart must either burst, or draw him down "to cottage and shack, / to human traffic, / where souls move close to ground" (p. 64), where his own beloved people live and die. It is a remarkable moment there at the edge of the Italian Alps, and we recall many earlier poems where the poet wandered up to New England mountaintops, perhaps similarly in search of intensity of vision, of signs revealed, of mysteries acknowledged if not always solved.

The cover of *The Blainville Testament* (1992) announces "Narrative Poems by Sydney Lea." This is a misnomer. With the exception of a reprint of the masterful poem "The Feud," which first appeared in *The Floating Candles* and was discussed above, these poems have narrative elements—character, setting, and suggestions of a plotline or story arc—but none is as whole and rounded-out a story as "The Feud." The closest candidate might be the title poem, "The Blainville Testament," which sketches out an incident in which a younger man, Mark, and a well-known older citizen, Billy Fields, have accepted the unenviable job of burying old Elsie Cammon's cow that "choked to death / on a backwoods apple" (p. 14). Mark used an old tractor to dig a large hole to be the cow's grave, but dropped his brand-new watch into the hole. "Mark jumped down to fetch it. The ground gave way / and half a ton of beef fell in upon him" (p. 15). Despite subsequent town gossip that seventy-nine-year-old Billy murdered Mark on purpose by shoving an eight-hundred-pound cow down on him, the narrator, a local lawyer, scoffs at this, and—now that Billy's dead—breaks the rule of attorney-client secrecy to give Billy's version: Billy set off to seek help, and after a long time ended up at Elsie Cammon's house. They exchanged pleasantries, chatted a long time, Billy seemingly in no hurry, until finally he told her "that Mark was lying out beneath her cow" (p. 22). Elsie, who died soon after, finally told him, "Billy, you ain't magic" (p. 23), as though to say nothing he might try to do could change anything that simply happened. The "testament" or confession that Billy gave the narrator-lawyer, and that the lawyer in turn has just given secondhand to us— "outsider, native, woman, man or child" (p. 23)—

neither condemns nor exonerates Billy. The narrator concludes: "I'll lie here with my story, cool, a while / A little time, while the moon plays on The Bald Man, / I'll hold to it, and you can judge the rest" (p. 23).

The contrast to "The Feud" is obvious: that long narrative poem is driven forward by the narrator's uneasy and growing sense of foreboding, as he steps deeper and deeper into the seductions of the feud with the Walkers, and the drama of the poem comes from our horrified understanding of a man who has only too late become conscious step-by-step of how his own decisions have shaped his fate. But Billy's longer-than-appropriate visit with Elsie while Mark lies crushed under the cow seems mildly comic, and Billy's sense of guilt is almost nonexistent. The poem ends with the narrator simply walking away from judgment, or rather, handing it off to his reader.

The other poems are similar: a slight *donnée*, some visual clarity, but no building of a real narrative arc. "In the Alley" is about a high school production of Oedipus (our speaker plays the title role) recalled years later from a busy square in Florence, where the narrator sees a blind man waiting to cross the street, and while he tries to compose in his mind (in Italian) an offer of help crossing, the blind man walks away and disappears (p. 33). In "Road Agent" the narrator, whose job it is to level the washboard irregularities of backcountry dirt roads with his grader or to plow snow, recalls seeing last week

[. . .]poor young Mrs. Grayson.
She had this flimsy little dress on.
You'd judge she was out for a summer stroll.

Her husband's diplomas would fill a trunk.
(Half-bare, she was, in a foot of snow!
I pretended a wing was loose on the plow.)
He's one of those jacket-and-necktie drunks.

(p. 45)

Now there's a story we'd like to hear, but that's all we get. But of course Lea is aware of this short-circuiting of certain tales. For example, Brian Brodeur, in his blog *How a Poem Happens*, reproduces Lea's poem "Fathomless," then asks Lea a series of questions about it, including,

"Is this a narrative poem?" Lea replies: "It does tell a story, so maybe yes. But that's not the whole enchilada; I think of myself as a poet who, no matter what he addresses, will have an interest if not necessarily in plot, then in other narrative values: character, setting, what have you."

Lea's next volume was *To the Bone: New and Selected Poems* (1996). For a first-time reader of Sydney Lea's poetry, this is a good place to sample the opening sixteen years of his work, which, in addition to some new poems, features Lea's own selections from *Searching the Drowned Man, The Floating Candles, No Sign, Prayer for the Little City*, and *The Blainville Testament*.

The collection draws its name from the first of the new poems, "To the Bone," a deliriously energetic riff on an accident that sent a chainsaw flying into the poet's left leg above the knee. We learn that, doing a favor cutting firewood for a woman whose husband has left her with the kids but no money, the poet's "blade did not plunge through / bone nor artery nor ligament nor center of inscrutable nerves nor tendon" (p. 3) and that, thanks to the quick thinking of the emergency room nurse, Susan Kennedy (to whom the poem is dedicated), who splinted and bound the leg, the muscle did not roll up "like a windowshade" (p. 3).

"Riff" is a fitting description of this poem not only because Lea is a serious jazz aficionado, but because as he whirls us through the immediate aftermath of the accident, including the use of a self-operated morphine pump which both dulls the pain and brings on a storm of fantasies and memory blasts, we feel simultaneously as though we are riding a whirlwind and in the hands of a master of control (think Charles Mingus, think Charlie "Bird" Parker). The lines are (pardon the bad taste) chopped into unpunctuated fragments, and yet they are nicely clustered in stanzas of six lines.

The medical realities are crisp and interesting, but the poem takes off with his immersion in the effects of the morphine, which he thanks "less for killing pain than freeing me to think without muscle" (p. 5). Among the phantoms who make an appearance as he lies semi-stoned in the

hospital bed is Earl Bonness, an old friend from Washington County, Maine, now dead, but fully present in the poet's mind, garrulously rattling on about logging and loggers. Also floating into the morphine-loosened consciousness of the poet is a series of images—of a Pakistani music student being stomped to death by thugs, then other dead people from his past, including his mother. The poem ends first with his admission that he cannot "retrieve for instance / brother or father nor that by mere will I could mend my mother" (p. 14) but also with his insistence on imagining "the wound sealing itself such that I'd refer to me / as a being entire" (p. 14) and the strong possibility "that this ceaseless current bearing every desire / we name it life would come out all right / it would be all right it would be all right / whatever it might be" (p. 14). This is heady, exhilarating poetry.

COLLECTIONS OF THE 2000s

The new century began for Sydney Lea with *Pursuit of a Wound* (2000), which quickly sets up an intermittent drumbeat of defeated lives: a rabid raccoon the poet must shoot ("Yoked Together"); Jimmy, who is hurtled out the back window of his mother's "beat, Bondo-patched Ford" ("Reasons to Hate Poetry"); old Mack, realizing he will die ("November"); Freddy, the "Village Fool," mowed down by a car ("The Drift"); Breck, who hanged himself ("Poor Fool Blues"); Bill McCrae, with cancer "down in his bones" ("Well, Everything"); Dawna, drowning ("Local Story: Reading the Signs"); Lesley, felled by a grand mal seizure ("It Has Orange Teeth"); Pancho the cat, dying ("Fin de Siècle"); an old flame, Angie, dead ("Girls in Their Upstairs Windows"); and Chick the roadhouse owner, dead ("Authority").

These are not weak poems—some are muscular, inventive, and move the reader right along. But there is a sense of thematic repetitiveness. Of course our ever-alert poet is aware this is happening. In "Girls in Their Upstairs Windows" we see his two youngest daughters racing past him toward the pond, "while their father scribbles a poem, / One that—despite the evident bless-

ings—leans / On other dreams that fell all over him" (p. 49). He is leading a fortunate, even privileged life, but can't shake the shadow of the blighted lives of others, whose destinies he feels he must chronicle.

This unresolved bifurcation makes *Pursuit of a Wound* one of the least autobiographical collections of poems so far. But, as with earlier volumes that surprise us with a sudden reversal of gloom, this book ends with a long unstoppered flow of night thoughts, an extended jazz-like blast, "Phases—in praise of Zoloft." He tells us that before starting this wonderful drug, unable to sleep past 3 a.m., he would often wake to "feel quotidian annoyance segue / straight to terror" (p. 69) But now, thanks to costly Zoloft—"Oh God, it does cost" (p. 71)—he returns to an earlier, freer self as father, husband, brother, child, lover, without always being stricken by the thought of "how temporarily one lingers alive" (p. 70). To be able to sidestep a "deeper despond" (p. 72) does not entirely free him from guilt, because he's still aware "there exist too many distresses that have gone too long unaddressed, / not that I am the one to address any—not any!—but that all must / be studied" (p. 72).

The unrestrained outburst that this poem—a sort of allegro companion piece to "To the Bone"—shows us (despite its on-off use of subtle rhymes) a Sydney Lea linked more to Walt Whitman and the Beats than to Robert Frost and William Wordsworth. His mind roams freely (although not quite disconnectedly) from his dead father to "Buddha Monk's 'Misterioso'" (p. 73) to "my first trophy trout" (p. 73) to his first panic attack at Yale to the fact that his aged Ford truck managed to pull him all the way home last night before the alternator died, allowing him to kiss his sleeping children and wife, before taking a cigar to the lawn to watch the full moon climb up over Mt. Moosilauke. He now feels that whether "by drug or God or both . . . it all might at last in fact come round—this my life. / And I vowed to wander, in proper wonder, a valley of the shadow of death" (p. 75).

Ghost Pain (2005) is an impressive and deeply satisfying collection, tightly woven, surefooted. Poem after poem reaches out to us, no two alike, inventiveness—even a polished wildness—at the heart of the enterprise in 2005.

In "1959" the poet, age sixteen, in St. Jean de Luz, buys a pastis for an old World War I veteran (who calls it *La Guerre de quatorze*), and the old fellow picks up his instrument "some crude banjo-y thing" and sings "Badly and long" (p. 7) about the war. The young American is transfixed, with the afternoon light on the Low Pyrenees and a "mollusky stench" coming off the strand, and wishes the people around him could keep quiet "not because the music was good / but because it was long and awful / and it was his and was theirs and was soulful" (p. 8). He doesn't want the moment to end:

If it could just be this light forever.
If every eye could be wet but mine
And that of someone's daughter, which kept shooting
   at me,
though I couldn't determine whether to flirt or rebuke
   me.

To make a soul—I could *tell*—would be so easy.

(p. 8)

The fusion of mildly ironic distance and sympathetic identification with the youngster, along with the detailed rendering of the scene and of those 1959 emotions, recollected in the tranquillity of later life, contribute to the grace of this poem.

Interlarded throughout this collection are Lea's own translations of some almost surreal but not quite Dada prose sketches by Henri Michaux, written with a deadpan mask of realism but based on absurd, dreamlike données. In "Getting Involved" the narrator finds himself bored in the French port of Honfleur and so imports some camels. Tourists are appalled at the smell and blame the inhabitants for being filthy. "The stench soon reached the harbor, where it was mistaken for rotten shrimp" (p. 11). "Soon enough the folks at Honfleur started squinting all the time, showing that suspicious expression so peculiar to camel-drivers as they check to see if anything's missing, if the caravan can keep going" (p. 11). On the fourth day the narrator departs: "Too bad I had to leave like that, and yet I strongly doubt that calm soon returned to that puny town of

shrimp and mussel fishers" (p. 11). In "The Jetty," the narrator has been confined to his room in Honfleur for a month by doctor's orders, but still hasn't seen the sea. So he builds a jetty from his room right out to the edge of the sea, and sits on the end of it, legs dangling above the water. Off to his right he notices another man sitting exactly as he is, who says he wants to bring back everything he's pitched into the sea over the years. Using pulleys, he drags up all sorts of stuff, including "captains from other times, each grandly dressed out in uniform; nailed chests full of precious things; women so lusciously dressed they might not have been dressed at all" (p. 20). The narrator helps the other man stack up huge piles of things dredged up from the deep, but "nothing finally seemed to strike him as satisfactory. No, something had been lost; something he pined to recover had faded for good" (p. 20). So he starts to throw everything back, but the "last thing he shoved from the pier dragged him in with it" (p. 20). As for our narrator: "trembling with fever, I wondered how I'd ever get back to my room" (p. 20).

It's not clear why Lea is inserting these Henri Michaux pieces into a book of his own poems. One guess is that there's something liberating for Lea about paying homage to spurts of comedic irrationality, and about evoking a dream world in which the past rears its lost head and takes on human/ghostlike form, like it or not. To use an analogy from the world of music, it's as if Lea has invited Michaux to sit in and add his wild riffs to the already unbuttoned music of the house band.

Other notable poems in the first third of *Ghost Pain* include "Was Blind but Now," which begins with a story told by an old man whose grandfather owned the property where the Lea family now lives. He asks the poet if he has ever looked *down* on snow. As a boy the storyteller had looked down "into the oxbow where the gray Connecticut River goes, / from a place we thought we'd named The Lookout, but which, as it turns out, / was always so named because that's just what you'd name it" (p. 24). The storyteller's grandpa had failed at several agricultural projects and then one day hanged himself in a barn. ("He didn't tell me that, the courtly old man: it was

known was all.") As a boy, the storyteller was sent off, during a late storm, "to find a cow and her calf and drive them home—drive them home / if calf there were, and if it were living, and the cow living too. I could see / I just had a bad feeling, he told me" (p. 24). The boy never found hide nor hair of either. But, suggests the poet, "it wasn't because / of the cattle, the feeling, and he may later have wondered if it hadn't somehow to do / with what his grandparent was meaning to do (if he yet was meaning to do it / and knew it)" (p. 24).

"Some believe in ghosts, they do, the old man said. He said / it stayed with him all his life, which he thought was mostly a good enough life, / but there'd come a mood, that bad feeling" (p. 24). As he speaks the poet feels the boy sent out into the storm must have "had an unease before he ever set out, or stood to watch / the snow from above it as the fat white flakes kept sifting into the throat" of the Dell (as the poet's family call it when they're down there below) but which he admits to us is "a mighty gulch, so deep it's black all year" (p. 25). The poet tries to make sense of the story, particularly the other man being haunted by that "bad feeling": Maybe it was "Something about those flakes falling in and you couldn't see them after // Maybe it was something as simple as not being so high and mighty / as a young fellow thought after all, with the big round world out there before him" (p. 25).

So the other's story ends, and the two men look each other right in the eye, so that the poet "felt a charge, / a shock of some kind, though I couldn't have said whether scary or bracing or both" (p. 25). But suddenly the poem becomes an exercise in epistemology and whether truth can really be shared. The poet tells us, "I wasn't young, so I knew what he was talking about. No. / I didn't know. I mean to be honest, to speak as plainly as he did." One thing he does know for certain is that "I'd never before felt there what he felt there, never" (p. 25). He continues to interrogate himself: "And so, can I say from that moment / I never again gazed down from The Lookout in snow or calm or rain / the same? I don't know . . . // I'm trying to be as truthful, as unsentimental as I can. / I've tried right along to adorn not a thing, no more than he would do" (p.

25). So he ends, or tries to end, the poem we've been reading:

This isn't a sad account
I don't think but a true one I think. There's something
  of an example for me

His memory is   For me his memory is   His memory
  for me

(p. 26)

That's it; the poem is over. He cannot, or will not continue by using any rhetorical moves that would feel hollow. The implication is that silence would be more truthful about the limits of his empathy. The reader will recall that, in the discussion of "The Blainville Testament" earlier in the essay, the ending of the poem was mildly disappointing in that the narrator walks away from judgment, simply leaving it up to his reader. But in the case of the ending of "Was Blind but Now," we see the poet's epistemological-rhetorical crisis becoming the real subject of the poem, and his refusal to tie up the poem with a neat and tidy ending is consonant with his entire complex (failed) attempt to arrive at a just, unadorned interpretation of the old man's untidy story.

The centerpiece of *Ghost Pain* is a ten-part cycle called "A Man Walked Out," which takes us along on "the man's" nightmare journey through alcohol addiction, hospitalization, an attempt at detox and recovery in a group setting, wrestling with inner demons, and backsliding, to a slow, uncertain return to sanity and relative normalcy. But that's just the topical outline. It's the section-by-section texture of this harrowing of hell—the variety and vivacity—that gives the sequence its deeper power.

In the beginning there's a lot of fighting and drinking and hallucinating, including a dream about ducklings in which

From under waterlogged stump or stone
the longtail hawkjaw turtles
would rise to seize a leg or wing and pull the little
  ones under
one today   another

Tomorrow et cetera.

(p. 36)

That terror of being sucked under runs throughout the early sections of the poem. In "iii. 666: Father of lies," the man "walked out again into was-it-dream" and runs into the devil himself:

no cape no horn no swinging tail.
Fastfood franchise manager, maybe—
frogflesh middle, lividity, polyester shirt,

petty authority's manner:
smirk upon smirk.

(p. 37)

He and Satan wrangle, but next thing he knows, "Grown children, two, conveyed him to hospital lockdown" (p. 37). Meanwhile, the devil tosses psychojargon at him: *"paranoia, depression, anxiety, guilt,"* but when the man looks carefully, "The devil's eyes, unsouled and blue / like his own, were his own" (p. 38). Still, the man insists to himself: "Wherever mercy lay, he *would* be free" (p. 39).

At one point in the midst of this despondency, realizing that with both parents dead he is an orphan and he himself now sixty, he sees two kestrels fly past, "so close their wings seemed almost to jingle" (p. 41), and suddenly, "A change seemed bound to come: not his mother risen, / intact, not his father, his heart and innards quick, // but something. The passing of birds. More scent than sound" (p. 42). But there's no easy resolution. In "v. Predator" the man rehearses all the women he has had, including those of friends "whose women he blighted with semen" (p. 43). When an inner voice asks who he thinks he is, he answers: *I am my world's most vicious lover . . . / I can sicken the whole round planet with my seed"* (p. 44). This section ends with an Inferno vision of those he has betrayed: "half-seen faces, women, fathers, husbands— / specters all, wasting away in his mind— / line up on this new horizon to glare at him" (p. 45).

Rehab begins in regular meetings with a group of other addicts. During the meditation periods, the man sees in his mind his first wife, as well as the "fine, pretty, and patient woman he was married to now, and the five children he had fathered" (p. 48). But visualizing those wives and children (this section is entirely in prose) "made him speak more softly, even when he

wanted to sound bold, confident. The husk of his voice made it seem as though someone else were saying his words for him, like a man possessed" (p. 48). For this man, progress is slow. In "vi. Road rage" he has to struggle, to *concentrate* to keep from stopping and violently confronting a driver of a Ford 350 who is tailgating him. The eighth section, "viii. Dry drunk: the rowing," finds the man staggering out onto the porch in a dream, or maybe from a dream. There's the devil again, offering him a vodka toddy from "a beaker shaped like an owl" (p. 56) after which he "tottered away, grim mystery, / To tell his wife kids doctor cops colleagues even dogs / He hadn't drunk a drop he was fine he was steady / Leave him the fuck alone already. // In sleep he prayed he was asleep" (p. 56). Next thing, he is rowing toward some undefined island, hearing behind him "Devil's cackle abiding," and "he gasps, each pull less than half of what it has been, / His wives and sons and daughters catching on the bottom" (p. 58).

The turning point in this slow stumbling haunted ascent out of the depths comes in "ix. Talent from birth," when the man, driving home at night, hears a Doc Watson rag on the car radio and feels pure envy at the exercise of such a carefully honed craft: "What must it be like to do what you liked / with surfeit of gift? Beethoven. Blake" (p. 60). Suddenly he feels, for the first time since boyhood, "unold, though he was incredibly sixty, / and commonsense showed he was pushing / his limits of creativity" (p. 60). (Hardly true in the case of Sydney Lea.) But here, now, "the man felt forgiven / for each unpardonable word and deed, / even the worst, which he couldn't name," and declares to himself that he "could use what talent he could. / Not all he'd wanted but all he'd need" (p. 61).

This cycle ends with "x. Noon for good" with the man walking out at midday on a Sunday in October, Vermont's best month. He walks northward: "There at least to his thinking / the earth seemed less used up" (p. 62). Looking back on what he has been through, he muses: "For him it wasn't a thing achieved, / recovery, but process, losing, recouping. / He killed his devil hourly" (p. 63). Then, as so often in Lea, a bird appears

to bestow a culmination, in this case a juvenile fish hawk, an osprey. The bird dives down to catch a fish in its claws, drops it, then turns and tries again, successfully: "The hawk had dived and missed, recovered, dived again. / All easy parable was gross" (p. 65). And yet there the bird goes, carrying its trophy toward the hills "with assurèd wings." To the man it seems

[. . .]a miracle, or poem,
a grand ongoing one he smelt as much as felt
and touched as much as heard—a bird retreating
and in retreating moving
the man thus quietly home.

(p. 65)

There are other fine poems in the final third of this volume. "Ghost Pain" takes place in church. Brian has just brought Joan in in a wheelchair: "We wish them all the cheer that humans can, / inquire how the leg is, / now that it's gone. // Is there ghost pain?" (p. 69). The community of the church is clearly more important for Lea as he gets older, for it is "one more safe tiny place amid the great unsafe" (p. 71). And in the charming "Wonder: Red Beans and Ricely" the poet recalls how he and a cousin once took their dates to "the Famous Sunnybrook Ballroom in East Jesus, PA" (p. 78) to listen to Louis Armstrong. Hearing the music, he tells us,

I suddenly dreamed I could see through the tent's canvas top
clear up to stars that stopped their fool blinking and planets that stood
stock-still over cows and great-eyed deer in the moonlight,
and ducks ablaze on their ponds because everything in God's world
understood this was nothing like anything they'd known before.

(p. 78)

Still throbbing with excitement (and some rum), he pledges to get the great man's autograph. Behind the stage he finds a large truck with a set of steps, goes up, knocks on the door. Satchmo sits at a desk in an undershirt and suspenders, sucks down a shot of Johnny Walker, and then writes on a piece of paper: *Red Beans and Ricely Yours at Sunny Brook Ballroom. Pops*" (p.

79). Over the years the piece of paper is lost, as are the "lovely, silken girls, Sally and Barbara" (p. 80), and his cousin, who, because of his drinking, "crossed the foulest river" (p. 80). Nothing is left the poet but "a handful of notes from a horn which are there forever" (p. 80). *Ghost Pain* is a rich and varied book, packed with such pleasures.

Young of the Year (2011) shows us Lea in full control of his craft and contains one of his most memorable poems, "The 1950s." With its cool, third-person narrative voice, this poem has the feel of a short story based on an episode someone else has told the author about. Its structure is also orderly and a bit formal—ten five-line stanzas. The narrative voice tells us about a 1950s high school hockey team's regular practice sessions and a girl who keeps turning up to watch them (and then to offer the boys certain favors, one at a time). The boys themselves are full of braggadocio, boasting after practice about "what they'd make her do, or had" (p. 10). But who is she, and why does she keep turning up? "Some of them must have known her actual name, / so there's no excusing what the young punks called her: / among themselves, the girl was always *Rink Rat*" (p. 10). She doesn't go to their school, so where *does* she go to school? "Nobody cared, or wondered how her family— / if she had a family, that is—could set her free / to hang around with boys at play, and after" (p. 10). The place of assignation is "up a squat little hill that was more or less out of sight. / Not exactly a bower, but atmosphere wasn't the issue / in the dead of winter, when it all had to be quick fun" (p. 10). It is in the fifth stanza, exactly halfway through the poem, that the omniscient narrator pauses, leaves the 1950s frame, and muses:

Much later, driving past some stark cold scene
that sketchily resembles that meeting place,
one of the boys, who may now be a father to
 daughters,
shivers, thinking back on a blurry figure
with bottle-thick glasses lopsided on her face—

her savagely birth-marked face.

(p. 10)

So the team uses her, and cruelly jokes about her, and then in the locker room the talk returns to hockey: "they praised their own teamwork, deception, brotherhood, speed. / In short they swapped the mindless swaggerer's claims / that men have always shared" (p. 11). Then comes the sudden twist, with the poet addressing us directly, elegantly slipping in the poem's only rhyme:

I'm saying *they*,
you'll understand, as I try to skate over shame
it seems to have taken me all these years to name.

(p. 11)

This is confessional poetry in a deeply moral sense, arguably more biting than the verse that grew out of Robert Lowell and his followers, with the possible exception of the brutal honesty of John Berryman.

One last indispensable poem in this collection is "Birds, Farrago." Most of the sections are named after birds, but in this case feels like an *apologia pro vita sua*, putting the poet's entire life into perspective.

Two other collections round out Lea's poetic output as of 2017. *I Was Thinking of Beauty* (2013) has many good poems about childhood, such as "House of Women," where the three-year-old subject, who has been living exclusively with female relatives (all the men are abroad in the Theater of War), is appalled to see a stranger in khaki stride into the house "as if he owned it," pick Mother up and swing her round and round. The child's "days of stardom are over" (p. 6). *No Doubt the Nameless* (2016) is more troubled with thoughts of the passage of time and the shadow of death. "Easy to Love," about his doomed friend, the singer Sean Malley, is a perfect tribute.

CONCLUSION

Perhaps the best way to end an overview of the poetic work of Sydney Lea is to recommend a curious book he published in 2015, *What's the Story: Reflections on a Life Grown Long* (2015), a collection of prose sketches, each the length and density of a long poem. This prose sings.

Even working through stronger episodes of gloom in later life, especially the deaths of friends, what cheers the author are moments of unforeseeable intensity that he was half-convinced were no longer possible for him. When he sees a bald eagle sailing overhead he registers its obvious grace, but his mind feels "crossed by instinctual letdown: there, I thought, goes one more wonder that in older age is a good deal less wondrous than once" (p. 130). But as though to rebuke this self-pity, the sky gives him "that other bird, up higher, which suddenly dwarfed the bald one." It's an extremely rare golden eagle. He's stunned by this visitation: "Did some mysterious higher power feel I'd done some good?" (p. 131). He reviews his possibly insufficient mourning for those he has loved, wondering why he has been spared in "this late welter of crushing disappearances" (p. 131). The privileged moment passes, "And yet to watch the golden eagle's lordly drifting out of sight was unaccountably to hope that in my own small life I'd shown a kindness or two to people. How else, again, to explain this odd compensation?" (p. 131). He has been blessed. So have we, to have been allowed to follow his long, eventful, lyrically chronicled journey through the years.

Selected Bibliography

WORKS OF SYDNEY LEA

POETRY COLLECTIONS
Searching the Drowned Man. Urbana: University of Illinois Press, 1980.
The Floating Candles. Urbana: University of Illinois Press, 1982.
No Sign. Athens: University of Georgia Press, 1987.
Prayer for the 1990. New York: Scribner's, 1989.
The Blainville Testament. Brownsville, Ore.: Story Line Press, 1992.
To the Bone: New and Selected Poems. Urbana: University of Illinois Press, 1996.
Pursuit of a Wound. Urbana: University of Illinois Press, 2000.
Ghost Pain. Louisville, Ky.: Sarabande Books, 2005.
Young of the Year. New York: Four Way Books, 2011.
I Was Thinking of Beauty. New York: Four Way Books, 2013.
No Doubt the Nameless. New York: Four Way Books, 2016.

NOVEL
A Place in Mind. New York: Scribner's, 1989.

NONFICTION
Hunting the Whole Way Home. Hanover, N.H., and London: University Press of New England, 1994.
A Little Wildness: Some Notes on Rambling. Ashland, Ore.: Story Line Press, 2006.
A Hundred Himalayas: Essays on Life and Literature. Ann Arbor: University of Michigan Press, 2012.
A North Country Life: Tales of Woodsmen, Waters, and Wildlife. New York: Skyhorse, 2013.
What's the Story? Reflections on a Life Grown Long. Brattleboro, Vt.: Green Writers Press, 2015.

BIOGRAPHICAL SOURCES

Author's website. www.sydneylea.net
Lea, Sydney. Unpublished biographical sketch provided to David Gullette for the purpose of writing this essay.

INTERVIEWS

Brodeur, Brian. "Sydney Lea." How a Poem Happens: Contemporary Poets Discuss the Making of Poems, February 16, 2011. http:/howapoemhappens.blogspot.com/2011/02/sydney-lea.html

LUDWIG LEWISOHN

(1882—1955)

Jack Fischel

WHEN WE THINK of important American Jewish novelists, such as Saul Bellow, Philip Roth, Bernard Malamud, Cynthia Ozick, Herman Wouk, and Chaim Potok, among others, almost forgotten is the name of Ludwig Lewisohn, who, in the 1920s and early 1930s, was among the most influential Jewish writers in American fiction. He was the author of forty books, including three autobiographies, fifteen novels, works of criticism, and polemics that warned of the corroding effect of assimilation on American Jewish life. Given his belief that art was autobiography, many of Lewisohn's works of fiction are concerned with marital discord based on the tribulations of his own married life, the most autobiographical of which is *The Case of Mr. Crump* (1926). The novel was well received by critics and is considered his masterpiece. Thomas Mann, an influence on Lewisohn, noted that the novel was his effort to liberalize attitudes toward love and marriage.

Writing during the 1930s, when anti-Semitism was widespread in America, and the Nazis were commencing their war against the Jews in Germany, Lewisohn concluded that the rise of Adolf Hitler marked the failure of the Enlightenment, whose ideas influenced the French Revolution with its promise of liberty, equality, and fraternity for all of mankind. He noted that the emancipation of the Jews in France required Jews to subordinate their cultural and religious identity for the promise of equal citizenship. For many Jews in America, argued Lewisohn, the path to acceptance required that they turn their back on their Jewish heritage. Forced to choose between assimilation and their Jewish peoplehood, many Jews chose the former at the cost of the latter. Lewisohn viewed Jews as a nationality, not unlike the Irish, Italians, and others who constituted the American melting pot, but with a difference: Jews lacked an ancestral homeland. Thus Lewisohn became a fervent advocate for a Jewish homeland in Palestine at a time when most American Jews were indifferent to the Zionist movement. Without a Jewish homeland, argued Lewisohn, Jews were doomed to lose the uniqueness of their peoplehood. Like Louis Brandeis, Lewisohn believed that support for a Jewish home in Palestine was compatible with being a patriotic American. Thus his books *The American Jew* (1950), *Israel* (1925), and *What Is This Jewish Heritage?* (1954) were written to remind Jews of their rich heritage, which was threatened by ignorance of their past and, through assimilation, adopting the "religion of Americanism"—that is, the values and mores of a Christian society. His criticism was also directed toward those secular Jews who exchanged their heritage for the false utopian promises of Marxism as it evolved under Joseph Stalin in the Soviet Union.

Influenced by Sigmund Freud, much of Lewisohn's criticism was directed by what he viewed as the repressive influence of Calvinist Christianity (referred to by Lewisohn as "Puritanism") on American life and literature. In his criticism of Puritanism, Lewisohn was not alone. Colleagues such as H. L. Mencken and Theodore Dreiser, among others, also railed against sexually repressive Puritanism and the "formalism" that it spawned. Lewisohn's criticism of Puritanism is best found in *Expression in America* (1932), where he wrote, in regard to the criticism of *Sister Carrie* (1900) by Theodore Dreiser and Dreiser's other novels of realistic fiction:

The Calvinists will not acknowledge and cultivate what they hold to be a life of sin. It must be

LUDWIG LEWISOHN

repressed; it must denied out of existence. . . . It offends, according to the loathsome Pauline saying; it must be plucked out. . . . Hence Dreiser's frank and sharp and profoundly serious dealing with sex as a primordial and pervasive and creative force was from the start and still is an epoch-making act of vicarious liberation. . . . It is the Calvinists who cheapen sex and degrade it, not Dreiser. . . . Dreiser's serious treatment of man's generative instinct remains his great creative act as an American.

(pp. 479–481)

Lewisohn understood the rise of Communism and Nazism as the triumph of the neopaganism that entered into early Christianity at the time Europe was Christianized by Constantine in the fourth century. It was Pauline Christianity, he argued, that altered the Judaism that Jesus practiced and subsequently incorporated a number of pagan beliefs into the new religion, including its hatred of Judaism. Jesus, argued Lewisohn, was not only a Jew but preached a Judaism that was passed down from the Torah to the Prophets down to the Pharisees. For Lewisohn, Christianity, as it evolved over the centuries, was conflicted between its pagan beliefs and the teachings of Jesus, wherein anti-*Judentum* subsequently trumped the teachings of love and peace and manifested itself in the demonization of the Jew. In post-Enlightenment Europe, anti-*Judentum* transformed itself into modern anti-Semitism. For Lewisohn, the Holocaust was the culmination of centuries of hatred toward the Jews, wherein under the Nazis, Jesus was transformed into an Aryan Messiah sent to destroy the Jews. But the pagan element in Christianity was not alone responsible for the murder of European Jewry. Added to the mix was the emergence of the pseudoscience of Social Darwinism, racial hygiene laws, and xenophobic nationalism, which joined Christian anti-*Judentum* with a "science"-based secular anti-Semitism. Jews, however, ignored the new threat to their existence, wagering their future on assimilation. A recurrent theme in Lewisohn's writing is the failure of Jews—including those in the United States—to fully comprehend both the old and new currents of Jew-hatred that refused to accept them as equals.

In his biography of Lewisohn, Seymour Lainoff states that Lewisohn anticipated the tragedy of European Jewry when he noted that many of the Austrian and German prewar writers and intellectuals were almost oblivious to their Jewish heritage. Thus in placing their future in the assimilative process, they were ill prepared for the rise of Hitler. For Lewisohn, the Holocaust proved that the process of assimilation was bankrupt. Germany, wrote Lewisohn, "is the classical land of assimilation: it is the classical land of anti-Semitism" (qtd. in Lainoff, p. 109). In his book *Israel*, Lewisohn states that the failure of assimilation in Germany "could provide a parable to American Jews . . . It was an inescapable part of the modern historic process. But the experiment has failed. It is not necessary that several American generations be sacrificed to foreknown humiliation and predictable disasters" (*Israel*, pp. 79–80). It is not surprising, therefore, that a number of Lewisohn's novels, most notably *The Island Within* (1928; originally published in 1927 as *The Defeated*), deal with the failure of assimilation.

In addition to his work as a novelist and writer of nonfiction about Jewish life, Lewisohn was a major critic whose controversial *Expression in America* was a critical history of American literature and culture. His career also included his work as a translator, working into English the texts of German writers and dramatists such as Gerhard Hauptmann and Jacob Wassermann, among others.

EARLY LIFE AND CAREER

Much of Lewisohn's childhood is told, with some literary license, in the first of his three autobiographies, *Up Stream* (1922). He was born in Berlin on May 30, 1882, to Jacques and Minna Eloesser Lewisohn, who considered themselves German first and Jews afterward. Lewisohn writes, "Although they spoke unexceptional High German they used many Hebrew expressions. . . . But they had assimilated, in a deep sense, Aryan ways of thought and feelings. Their books, their music, their political interests were all German" (*Up Stream*, p. 17). Christmas, for young Ludwig, was more familiar than the Jewish holidays, although, because of his grandmother, he visited her synagogue on the Jewish High Holy days.

LUDWIG LEWISOHN

After his father failed in business, the family immigrated to the United States in 1890 and settled in a village in South Carolina. Two years later, they moved to Charleston. An only child, Ludwig was especially close to his mother and, following his parents' example, assimilated to his new environment. Eschewing any contact with the Jewish community in Charleston, Ludwig gravitated to the Methodist Church where, he writes, he had

> entered into a new faith and sprit of the place. . . . I accepted the Gospel story and the obvious implications of Pauline Christianity without question and felt . . . a spirit and a faith not wholly unlike that of the primitive Church. . . . I accepted Jesus as my personal Savior . . . [and] at the age of ten my emotional assimilation into the social group of which I was a physical member was complete. I would not have touched any alcoholic drink; I would have shrunk in horror from a divorced person. . . .
>
> (*Up Stream*, pp. 50–51)

At age fifteen, Lewisohn saw himself as an American, a southerner, and a Christian. A brilliant student, Lewisohn, after graduation from college, went to Columbia University as a graduate student with the hope of becoming a professor of English literature. His stay at Columbia, however, became a turning point in his life. After receiving his second master's degree in 1903 he was not selected, despite high grades, for a scholarship or fellowship. More significantly, he would discover that he could not get a teaching position because he was a Jew. In response to a letter Lewisohn sent to the secretary of the English Department to discuss the possibility of a teaching appointment, he received the following reply:

> A recent experience has shown me how terribly hard it is for a man of Jewish birth to get a good position. I had always suspected it a matter worth considering, but I had not known how wide-spread and strong it was. While we shall be glad to do anything we can for you, therefore, I cannot help feeling that the chances are going to be greatly against you.
>
> (qtd. in *Up Stream*, p. 122)

The letter, which was Lewisohn's introduction to anti-Semitism, practically destroyed his self-esteem. Despite urging from friendly faculty, Lewisohn felt too discouraged pursue his doctorate. But for Lewisohn, it also made him realize "for the first time in my life my heart turned with grief and remorse to the thoughts of my brethren in exile all over the world" (p. 123).

The letter was not Lewisohn's only encounter with anti-Semitism. Applying for a position at Princeton for which he had excellent qualifications in addition to strong recommendations from faculty at Columbia, he was denied the position after a letter of recommendation "touched on the fact of [his] race" (p. 147). Lewisohn wrote:

> Some years later a university in the farther West needed a professor of German. The attention of the Dean there was called to my work and reputation as a scholar and teacher. He wrote me a tentative letter. I answered but never heard again. Later he confided to a friend of mine that he had sounded the trustees. It would have been useless to propose the name of a Jew. . . . All the men who had refused me at the various universities were Anglo-Americans, pillars of the democracy, proclaimers of its mission to set the bond free and equalize life's opportunities for mankind. . . . Their reactions register accurately the spirit of the nativist oligarchy which rules us. . . .
>
> (p. 147)

These negative experiences planted the seeds that would subsequently lead him to conclude that as patriotic and assimilated as Jews thought themselves to be in the American "melting pot," they would always be "in but not of" America.

In his two-volume biography of Lewisohn, Ralph Melnick notes that following his disappointment at Columbia, Lewisohn was "now determined to wage war upon a world that had so willfully denied him the opportunity to become who he truly was." (vol. 1, p. 66). This included his return to his once-rejected Jewish heritage. Early in his sophomore year in college, Lewisohn discovered the Jewish author Israel Zangwill, whose view of the world and religion seemed to mirror Lewisohn's changing feelings toward Christianity. Lewisohn came to believe that Jesus was not the Christ but a suffering Jew, and personalized his identification with the image of Jesus who, like himself, had been martyred by a Gentile society. Melnick asks: "Might Ludwig

not have already felt, as he undoubtedly did after reading Zangwill, that those who excluded him from their society would also have excluded Jesus in the name of that image of a Christ that barred Ludwig and others from their company of believers?" (vol. 1, p. 67).

Throughout Lewisohn's career, earning a livelihood was always a challenge. Soon after leaving Columbia he thought he could earn a living through writing, but it did not provide a sufficient income, and subsequently he was forced to take a position as a reader at the Doubleday publishing company. According to Lainoff, "he regarded his work there as drudgery and his fellow employees as 'slaves in soul.' For two years, he engaged in this apparently degrading work and in free-lance writing" (p. 8). Describing himself at this point in his life, Lewisohn saw himself as "beaten, broken, breadless . . . a scholar and forbidden to teach, an artist and forbidden to write" (*Up Stream*, p. 145).

Lewisohn's life reached a turning point in 1906, when he married Mary Arnold Crocker Childs, a non-Jewish divorced woman who was twenty years his senior. The mother of four grown children, and a grandmother, she was also a minor poet and playwright who assumed the pen name Bosworth Crocker. The marriage from its beginning was an unhappy one and made more intolerable when she refused to divorce him. She would become the model for Anne Crump in Lewisohn's novel *The Case of Mr. Crump*, the chronicle of his own tortured marital experience. Nostalgic for Charleston (referred to as Queenshaven in his novels, as well as in *Up Stream*), concerned about his elderly parents, finding New York a lonely place, and driven by unfilled sexual needs, he met Mary and shortly thereafter married her. As Melnick informs us, years into the marriage, it turned into an "unending horror" (vol. 1, p. 118), particularly after their separation, when she began an unremitting number of libel suits over alleged unflattering characterizations of her in a number of Lewisohn's publications, including his masterpiece *Crump*, initially published in France. (Unaware that Ludwig had wed someone he did not love, his parents were pleased that he had finally settled down.) Refus-

ing to grant him a divorce (divorce in New York State was possible only if the marriage partners were willing to enter into collusion to establish adultery as grounds, which Mary refused to do), in 1922 a frustrated Ludwig entered into a relationship with Thelma Spear. She was twenty years his junior, part Jewish, something of a poet, and a promising singer. The relationship would last sixteen years, and she would become the mother of James, Lewisohn's only child, in 1933.

Despite the acrimony of his first marriage, Lewisohn published his first novel, *The Broken Snare*, in 1908. Lainoff writes that the novel was "filled with marital discard wherein he (Julian, the main character) saw marriage as a necessary convention"; he argues that "if *The Broken Snare* is an example of 'naturalistic' writing . . . it lacks the greater integrity of the really" naturalistic *Sister Carrie*" (p. 28).

Although committed to the life of the mind, Lewisohn continued to be disappointed by his failure to find a teaching position. So, resigning himself that as a Jew he would not attain a position in a university to teach English literature, he sought one in German literature, an area of study in which he was quite expert. In 1910, after being rejected by a number of universities, he was offered a job at the University of Wisconsin. Early on, however, he found the faculty and its students intellectually bankrupt. Frustrated, he left Wisconsin in 1911 for an instructorship at Ohio University, where he resigned in 1917, on the eve of America's participation in World War I. Lewisohn's resignation was due to the hostility directed at him by the administration because of his seemingly pro-German and pacifist position. During his tenure at both state universities, Lewisohn also became disillusioned with regard to the curriculum and the purpose of state educational institutions in general. Writing in *Up Stream*, Lewisohn complains:

> Our students, then, came to the university not to find truth, but to be engineers or farmers, doctors or teachers. . . . If the aim of education is merely to gain rough, useful tools for striving in the world of matter, and to gain them rapidly—the system works. . . . But when their job leaves these men free they are but little different from people who have not gone to college. They go to foolish plays,

read silly magazines and fight for every poisonous fallacy in politics, religion and conduct.

(pp. 160–161)

Elsewhere in the book, Lewisohn notes that universities erect "charming buildings for the school of veterinary medicine, handsome and commodious ones for agriculture and engineering," but "the ancient arts and studies of man that give vision and wisdom are squeezed in somehow. The students see all that and it falls in with the notions they already have of what is useful and what is not. They tolerate the required Freshman English because of a dim something connected with business letters and advertising 'dope.' Their spoken English remains, as a matter of fact, hopelessly corrupt" (p. 166). At odds with the university administration over the war, he resigned and returned to New York City to pursue his writing career and his work as a translator of German writers and dramatists.

THE BODY OF HIS WORK: SELECTED WRITINGS

Over time Lewisohn's literary and financial prospects improved. In 1919 he was appointed to the drama desk at the *Nation*, where he reviewed productions by the Provincetown Players and the Theater Guild. In 1922 a collection of Lewisohn's reviews were published in *The Drama and the Stage*. Work for the *Nation* also gave Lewisohn a venue for his critical attack on Puritanism and the "genteel tradition."

During the same year, *Up Stream* was published to critical acclaim. As Lewisohn's professional and financial career improved, his open relationship with Thelma Spear was exploited by the Hearst press. Fearful of libel action by Mary and the threat of legal prosecution, Lewisohn resigned his position at the *Nation* and went off to Europe with Thelma. Before leaving for Europe, Lewisohn published his second novel, *Don Juan* (1923), which, among other themes, attacked the difficulties of securing a divorce in New York State. Although he and Thelma traveled throughout Europe and Palestine, it was in France that they spent much of their time. It was also in France that his novel *The Case of Mr. Crump* was privately published in 1926 with a preface by Thomas Mann. In praise of *Crump*, Mann wrote that the novel was "more and less than a novel; it is life, it is concrete and undreamed reality and its artistic silence seems in more than one passage desperately like a cry" (*Crump*, p. vii). Mann continued, "We have here, then, a novelistic document of life, of the *inferno* of a marriage. . . . One must grant him that his power to stir and entertain us is great. His book stands in the very forefront of modern epic narrative" (p. viii). Despite accolades from Mann, the novel was banned by the U.S. Postal Service after its publication in France and appeared in the United States only in 1947.

Lewisohn's next two novels turned to the question of Jewish assimilation in American life. The first, *Roman Summer* (1927), tells about John Austin, a Unitarian and journalist turned poet who meets a beautiful young woman, Esther Azancot, a Jew and Zionist, who believes in her peoplehood. Having fallen in love, Austin hopes to marry Esther and bring her back to his home in the American Midwest, shorn of her Jewish past so that she can assimilate into the American melting pot. But Lewisohn has Esther respond to his overtures scornfully, telling Austin, "The Jews you have known have probably all pretended to be Americans with just a different religion" (*Roman Summer*, p. 120). Late in the novel she tells Austin:

> Because these liberal religious gestures are superficial and misleading . . . you would not have had your little shudder if I had said I was French or if I had said I was Lutheran or even Catholic. It had nothing to do with either a passport or place of birth or creed. It arose from a matter of race and of historical character. I knew that you wanted to know about what you call the real me. That is Jewish. Your little shudder proves it.

(p. 122)

This otherwise mediocre novel prepared the reader for *The Island Within* (1928; first published in London under the title *The Defeated*). Allen Guttmann argues that the novel is "the most eloquent statement of Lewisohn's conviction that the American dream was an illusion and that survival was possible only in Palestine" (p. 103). Short of leaving the American diaspora for Palestine, Lewisohn urged American Jews to

LUDWIG LEWISOHN

rediscover their past. Lewisohn had immersed himself in the religious literature of Judaism. He became versed not only in Old Testament scripture (though the terms "Bible" and "Old Testament" are commonly used by non-Jews to describe Judaism's scriptures, the appropriate term is Tanakh, which is derived as an acronym from the Hebrew letters of its three components, Torah, Nevi'im, and Ketuvim) but also in the Talmud and Jewish mysticism. In a series of books, *Israel* (1925), *The American Jew* (1950), and *What Is This Jewish Heritage?* (1954), Lewisohn outlined the distinction between American Jews who assimilated without recourse to their tradition and those who embraced their Jewish past. He feared that assimilation which turned its back on its Jewish heritage would lead to the extinction of the Jewish people and their contribution to humankind through its emphasis on justice and morality. (Ironically, during the Holocaust, the Nazis made no distinction between assimilated Jews, who eschewed their Jewish peoplehood, and Jews proud of their heritage. The Nazis deported all Jews to the gas chambers.)

An admirer of the Hasidim, whom he encountered in his trip to Europe, Lewisohn lauded them because as diaspora Jews they refused to compromise their religious heritage. Although not an observant Jew in its religious sense, Lewisohn called for Jewish organizations to foster Jewish education in the United States. He also argued that since other religious denominations, such as Catholics, had protected their religious and cultural beliefs with the establishment of private universities—such as Georgetown, Notre Dame, and others—there was no reason why American Jews should not do the same. (Yeshiva University had already been founded in 1886 as a Modern Orthodox institution with the emphasis on Torah study.) In 1948 Brandeis University would be founded as a nonsectarian institution under Jewish auspices.

Short of making Aliyah (a Hebrew term meaning "to go up") to Palestine, Lewisohn called for cultural pluralism to prevail in the United States, wherein Jews could retain their own institutions and character as a people accepting of their own heritage. The Jewish histo-

rian Solomon Grayzel, who sought to understand how Lewisohn viewed the problem of assimilation, wrote:

> Lewisohn initially saw the situation in terms of thwarted ambition—the burning desire to participate in the growth of America hurling itself mainly against the . . . prejudices of his non-Jewish neighbors—later he began to see that greater than the Christian prejudice was the tragedy of the American Jew turning away from his own heritage.
> (qtd. in Lainoff, p. 107)

In addition to *The Island Within*, Lewisohn's novels about the failure of assimilation, intermarriage, anti-Semitism, and Gentile society's unwillingness to accept Jews as equals include *The Last Days of Shylock* (1931), *This People* (1933), *Trumpet of Jubilee* (1937), and *Renegade* (1942). Lewisohn was also a strong supporter of a Jewish state. In the decade of the 1930s, Lewisohn, who had befriended Chaim Weizmann, the future first president of Israel, and other Zionist notables, urged American Jews to become Zionists. In *The Answer: The Jew and the World; Past, Present, and Future* (1939), Lewisohn wrote of the Zionist connection to American democracy. "The only Jew who can be loyal to the spirit of America," he asserted, "is the Zionist. For he who desires freedom for himself will fight for his brother men. Slave and tyrant are psychologically and practically interchangeable terms. Jews cannot be tyrants and dare not be slaves" (*The Answer*, p. 24). At the time *The Answer* was published, the most vociferous opponent of Zionism in the United States was the American Council of Judaism. The organization, in denouncing Zionism, defined Judaism as one religion among other religions in the United States, thus negating the uniqueness of the Jewish heritage. Lewisohn responded that while members of the American Council of Judaism were slaves "in body and in soul, imprisoned in the cold and empty hell of a self-created *Galuth* (exile)," survival in America was possible only if Jews maintained a sense of peoplehood as well as observing the Mosaic laws (*The Answer*, p. 47).

Melnick's biography cites a number of books and people that influenced Lewisohn. The list includes the Hebrew Bible, the Talmud, the writ-

ings of Johann Wolfgang von Goethe, and Freud. In addition, Lewisohn added his admiration for Martin Buber, who, he lamented, "was so little known in America, [but was] perhaps the greatest religious philosopher of our time for all men." He went on to add, "disobedience to God and His Torah is the source of human ills" (qtd. in Melnick, vol. 2, p. 328).

Summarizing Lewisohn's journey from Christianity in his early Charleston years to his strong affirmation of his Jewish identity, Melnick notes that he at first believed that Zionism was a way of validating his identity as a Jew without having to participate in the larger aspect of Jewish culture. This slowly gave way

> through study and exposure to traditional Jewish ritual practices he found meaningful both spiritually and as a way if identifying with his people. Slowly supplanting the Zionist activism of his first years as a self-affirming Jew, he would give greater effort to worrying about the viability of a *Diaspora* community in America. . . . [Despite] remaining a strident proponent of Zionism as a program of cultural identity . . . he was now becoming more concerned with the perpetuation of Judaism as a redemptive truth, seeing in ritual the beauty and values that were needed if there was to be a Jewish future anywhere.
>
> (p. 329)

Lewisohn finally divorced Mary in 1937, just as his relationship with Thelma Spear had deteriorated to the point of a breakup. It is unclear whether Thelma and Ludwig were ever married; Melnick states that Thelma turned down Ludwig's proposal of marriage. In 1940 Lewisohn married Edna Manley, who, on Ludwig's insistence, converted to Judaism. Edna was strongly supportive of Lewisohn's efforts to win custody of his son, James, from Thelma, and the whole tragic story is described in his poorly received third autobiography, *Haven* (1940), cowritten with Edna. From the book, it would appear that Lewisohn had attained a tranquil and happy marriage with Edna. But this was not to be. In 1940, after divorcing Edna, he married Louise Wolk.

Normally the biography of the married life of an author receives scant attention. But in the case of Lewisohn, this is not the situation because much of his fiction about love and marriage is autobiographical. Lainoff notes that "his novels are realistic . . . and sometimes 'naturalistic,' a term he used to indicate nondoctrinaire but bold confrontation with unpleasant truth" (p. 26). According to Lainoff, Lewisohn's first novel, *The Broken Snare*, was written to escape menial writing tasks, but the story also draws on the early days of his marriage to Mary. Fifteen years later, he published his second novel, *Don Juan* (1923), which he wrote in just twenty-nine days. The novel describes the life of an unhappily married man in love with a young woman. At the time the novel was written, the married Lewisohn was already involved with Thelma Spear, who, he wrote in *Mid-Channel*, was a woman "who believed in me, poured life into me and the frozen currents of my spirit melted" (p. 70). With regard to *Don Juan*, Lewisohn, in the midst of his affair with Thelma, writes, "The story dealt with the conflict in which I was involved. That conflict absorbed me wholly; I could think of nothing else. I stripped it, however, and placed it among rather uncomplicated higher middle-class Americans. The characters are nearly all as freely invented as such things are possible" (*Mid-Channel*, p. 71).

The Case of Mr. Crump was possibly Lewisohn's best "naturalistic" novel, and although its story reminds the reader of *Don Juan*, it is much more biographical. The story of the deterioration of a marriage that escalates into a homicide is among the best of the genre. The novel was published in a limited edition of five hundred copies in France in 1926 to great success. Lainoff raises the question that "it is difficult explain this sudden eruption of the exceptional after mediocrity. Could writing on European ground have proven liberating? From a distance, perhaps, the author could face the truths of his own life more openly. Whatever the reason, *Mr. Crump* is Lewisohn's best 'naturalistic' novel, one of the distinctive novels written by an American in the 1920s" (p. 31).

Crump was followed by *Roman Summer* (1927) and *Stephen Escott* (1930). Both novels—except for Lewisohn's introduction of Zionism in *Roman Summer*—pale in comparison with the "naturalism" of *Crump*. Nevertheless, both works

of fiction deal with the problems of marriage, as well as anti-Semitism as a subtheme in *Stephen Escott*. Echoing what obviously was the reason for his marriage to Mary, Lewisohn has Stephen admit, "I married the first nice girl that would have me because of my hunger for sex and the satisfaction of my starved sexual self-esteem couldn't wait any longer" (*Stephen Escott*, p. 212). Both novels were followed by *The Golden Vase* (1931), a short novel, and *An Altar in the Fields* (1934). The former novel was written following Lewisohn's success with *Up Stream*, *Crump*, and *The Island Within*, and it marks the decline of Lewisohn's literary reputation among the critics. The publication of his second autobiography, *Mid-Channel*, did not restore the esteem in which he had long been held. *An Altar in the Fields*, Lewisohn's belated answer to the Jazz Age, deals chiefly with the theme of sexual repression. The novel made little impression on the critics, who described it as a poor book with lifeless characters, not one of Lewisohn's best. Lewisohn's last three novels dealing with marriage and love did not add to his reputation. According to Lainoff, *For Ever Wilt Thou Love* (1939), *Anniversary* (1946), and *In a Summer Season* (1955) "had nothing new to add to what he had already said, and his issues did not seem relevant in periods of drastic social and economic change" (p. 44).

Lewisohn's novels about love and marriage alone do not warrant him consideration as an American Jewish writer, but his novels about his people's history, anti-Semitism, and the failure of assimilation certainly place him among the more important Jewish writers of the twentieth century. His fiction with Jewish content includes *The Island Within* (1928), *The Last Days of Shylock* (1931), *This People* (1933), *Trumpet of Jubilee* (1937), and *Renegade* (1942). Together the novels share a common theme, the self-destruction of the Jewish people because of the loss of their religious identity. As Lainoff notes, Lewisohn argues that "the process of assimilation turns back on itself, breeds internal division, and culminates in despair, sometimes even in suicide" (p. 47).

The Island Within may be the most persuasive argument for Lewisohn's conviction that the American dream was an illusion and that Jewish survival was possible only in Palestine. In this, his best-known novel, Lewisohn concentrates on an American Jew, Arthur Levy, who cannot help noticing the subtle barriers that exist in America for people of Jewish origin. Among other things, the novel is an attack on all forms of anti-Semitism, and it has obvious autobiographical elements. Like Lewisohn, Arthur's father is a Jew who had lived in Germany before he went to America. In the novel Lewisohn develops fully his views on the value and significance of Jewishness, including issues of Jewish self-hatred and the incompatibility of intermarriage for a man like Arthur Levy, who marries a sexually repressed Gentile who feels threatened by her husband's belated sense of Jewish identity. Arthur divorces his wife, Elizabeth, thus also separating himself from the false security of assimilation. Shown a document by the Hasidic Reb Moshe, which details the atrocities of the Crusaders against the Jews in medieval Speyer, Worms, and Mainz in 1096, an event that Christians have overlooked in their praise of the efforts of the Church to free the Holy Land from Islam, Arthur concludes that anti-Semitism is endemic throughout Christianity and decides to cast his lot with the Jewish people. Toward the novel's conclusion, Arthur's father urges him to build up again the House of Israel that his generation had tried to tear down. As for Elizabeth, she magnanimously promises to give their son a Jewish education. Encouraged by Reb Moshe, Arthur sets out to do charitable work among Jews living in the Balkans.

The novel includes a coda wherein Lewisohn sharply makes his argument against an assimilation that ignores the Jewish past. Two Gentile friends of Arthur meet and are confounded by Arthur's decision to leave his comfortable practice for the Balkans in order to help his fellow Jews:

> That doesn't sound like old Arthur. Thoroughly decent chap. I'd want the facts from him. . . . As to casting in his lot with his own people—I don't know but what I like that; it's natural and thoroughly honorable to him. If all Jews did it, I for one would respect them all the more. I don't think that Jews who try not to be Jews do themselves any good in

the eyes of intelligent people. There is something wrong with a man who betrays his own kind.

(p. 349)

Lewisohn's novel is passionate in its sensitivity to prejudice and a warning to his fellow Jews that assimilation without pride in one's heritage can only lead to disaster. Of all Lewisohn's novels, *The Island Within* was the only one to be chosen by the Modern Library as one of the world's best books.

The Last Days of Shylock, unlike Lewisohn's previous fiction, which dealt with the contemporary Jewish issues, draws on Shakespeare's *Merchant of Venice* and imaginatively describes Shylock's life after his forced conversion to Christianity, as well as the fate of his converted daughter, Jessica. The novel is a damning account of Christian anti-Judaism wherein Lewisohn is unsparing in his indictment of Christian avarice and intolerance. Following Shylock's conversion, Gratiano becomes Shylock's Christian godfather. The following excerpt reveals the flavor of the novel wherein Lewisohn, through Shylock, reveals his contempt for the manner in which Jews were treated in Venice during the Renaissance. Shylock sarcastically says to Gratiano:

> Then surely Christian charity will thee to pray for me . . . and I will have the prayers of at least one good Christian. . . . Seeing that thou art to be my godfather my poor soul will be thy particular care. The wine of his jest had been turned into vinegar. Shylock's eyes were stern; they were the eyes of a judge in some court of eternity The Holy martyrs of Ancona had wronged themselves and all Israel by giving their bodies to the fire rather than mouth a few empty words at the command of these brutes who held the sword of the world in their hands. What did the Christian want? He wanted the Jews gold; he wanted to glut his cruelty with the sight of the Jews suffering. The demand that the Jew turn Christian. . . . Shylock inhaled the morning air. He would do calmly as he was bidden. There was none who had power over his soul.

(p. 95)

The novel was well received in the Jewish community. Lainoff cites a letter to Lewisohn from Rabbi Louis Finkelstein, chancellor of the Jewish Theological Seminary, who wrote, "the

book is, to my mind, the finest defense of the medieval Jew against the calumnies usually heaped against him" (p. 55). A letter from Rabbi Stephen S. Wise, dated February 9, 1931, reads, "Dear Lewisohn, you have done a great book. It will live in Jewish history" (qtd. in Lainoff, pp. 55–56). Not all the critics, however, felt the same way about the novel. For example, Granville Hicks, a non-Jew, wrote in the *Nation* that the author did not resolve the problem of Shakespeare's vengeful Shylock with his own more sympathetic picture (qtd. in Lainoff, p. 56). Despite the criticism, the novel was a Book-of-the Month club selection. In the novel's conclusion, Shylock returns to his Judaism, and his apostate daughter Jessica renounces her conversion to Christianity. Together with her children, she returns to Judaism and to her father's house.

This People, consisting of five different novellas, is a portrait of Jews caught up in their denial as Jews, a theme that continued Lewisohn's argument that assimilation can only lead to tragedy for Jews forgetful of their heritage. Written at a time when the Nazis were on the verge of seizing power in Germany, Lewisohn tells of German Jews whose faith in assimilation was betrayed by Hitler's emergence as dictator in Germany:

> For very long the Germans had been accustomed to seeing only those Jews who had been Germanized for generations. . . . In occupied Poland there was fierce hunger . . . and the Jews of the land . . . desirous of saving their wives and children, drifted westward and on all the streets of all the cities of Germany began to appear the Jews of the East, wearing their own costume, speaking their own speech, openly practising the rites of their faith. And these Jews who, precisely like the German nationalists, knew profoundly that they were members of a folk, of a people, nor desired to be ought else and were therefore bent on saving *their* remnant despite the war madness of the heathen—it was these Jews who infuriated the Germans. And not only the Germans. They also infuriated the German Jews, most of whom had sold out their souls and hearts and tradition and history and self-esteem for the grudging tolerance granted to successful mimicry and who were now afraid of being confused and confounded with this alien folk come out of Poland and Ukraine.

(pp. 118–119)

In the story titled "Bolshevik," Lewisohn writes about Jan Zorn, a dedicated Bolshevik filled with Jewish self-hatred, who arrives in Germany from Poland to further the Communist agenda. Lewisohn writes of the emptiness of Zorn, a deracinated Jew for whom there is little in life that matters other than the revolution. He is stabbed to death by a group of young Nazis because he is a Communist and a Jew. In his dying moments, Lewisohn writes, "his blood ran in a little stream toward the gutter. They had stricken him in the back. Upon his unhurt face was an expression of relaxation, almost of ecstasy" (p. 128). In death Zorn at last finds release from his hatred of self. The story combines Lewisohn's antipathy to Jews who exchange their Judaism for Marxism and his hatred of Nazism.

In "Writ of Divorcement," Lewisohn tells of Bob, the son of a Conservative rabbi, who meets Myrtle, the daughter of a wealthy assimilated Jewish businessman. They fall in love, but following their decision to marry, problems arise about the wedding. The story, as told by Bob, informs us that in the first few days after their engagement, serious disagreement about the marriage ceremony took place between them. She was not interested in the tradition of a Jewish wedding—the wedding canopy, the broken glass, and so on. Myrtle tells Bob, "I'll feel funny, if I'm dragged through that hocus-pocus" (pp. 153–154), visualizing the fashionable Gentiles among her Vassar friends who will be attending her wedding. Reluctantly agreeing to a traditional wedding, Myrtle, on the day of the wedding, tells Bob, "'I just don't like the idea of all those . . .' she paused, and Bob understood that she meant to say 'Jews' gawping at me" (p. 157). Myrtle goes through with the Jewish wedding, but it is the beginning of the end. Her hostility toward Jews and Judaism becomes a source of anger that leads to the dissolution of their marriage. Bob concludes (echoing Lewisohn's belief) that throughout her life, Myrtle had fled from her Jewishness and sought to melt into the alien majority. At Vassar she comported herself in conformity to a supposed Nordic ideal, thus embodying the phenomenon of Jewish self-hatred, a not uncommon phenomenon among assimilationist Jews in America.

"The Romantic" tells of a baron of Jewish descent whose father converted to Catholicism. The Baron is given the promise of safe conduct if he returns from exile to his native Carpathia. But he is imprisoned and subsequently executed by the dictatorship because he is a Jew. His lawyer, also of Jewish ancestry, explains that the dictatorship "hates whom they can—the defenseless." But, says the Baron, "I have felt so deeply as one of them." His attorney responds, "But you have not been one of them, only a lover and a friend to them" (p. 219). When asked by the Baron why he stays, the attorney responds, "This is my place. I can help both Carpathians and Jews who suffer." Of course, Carpathia is meant to invoke Nazi Germany, where even the most assimilated of German Jews were targeted for extermination.

The other stories are "The Saint" and "By the Waters of Babylon" (a retelling of the Purim story). Both follow the trajectory of Lewisohn's themes of the failure of assimilation, Jewish survival, and the importance of a Jewish state for Jews worldwide.

Lewisohn's most ambitious and pessimistic novel, *Trumpet of Jubilee* (1937), was written on the eve of World War II. An apocalyptic work of fiction, it chronicles the trials and tribulations of Germany's Jews, the destructive excesses of Stalin's Soviet Union, and the failure of Christians to confront the Nazis in their treatment of the Jews. In one passage, Lewisohn's protagonist Peter Lang speaks to an assimilated German Jew about the responsibility of Christians worldwide to respond to the Nazi treatment of the Jews:

> What ought to have happened is this: thousands and thousands of Christians should have come to Germany and lived with persecuted Jews and the persecuted liberals and pacifists and Christians. Wherever the Nazis turned and whatever they did they should have been met with the intolerable rebuke of Christians from all over the world. Wherever they attacked a Jew they should have found a Christian by his side to offer to share his suffering. The trouble is . . . that the Christianity of most Christians is as dead or dormant in their hearts as your Judaism is in yours. It's an unredeemed world and it's literally going to the devil.
>
> (p. 95)

In a discussion as to whether religion can still be effective in this age of chaos, Lang responds,

"look at National Socialism! Look at orthodox Communism! There you have religions—evil religions. Religions with angels and devils and saviors. . . . It is still as true as ever that you can drive out the devil only by the help of God" (p. 95).

Drawing on a Jewish tradition which states that the world is redeemed by the presence of thirty-six righteous men, Lewisohn includes three such men who are witnesses to a world on the brink of destruction: Peter Lang, a non-Jew, and two Jews, Jehuda Brenner and Andrew Saracen. All three are Lewisohn's voice as they promote moral and religious solutions to the troubles on the eve of World War II. The novel concludes at the end of the Day of Atonement, when the ram's horn, the Trumpet of Jubilee, is sounded, and observant Jews look forward to a better year and the coming of the Messiah will bring world peace. Lainoff notes that Lewisohn's "vision of things to come: the death camps . . . the fall of France, the confrontation of the Russians and the Nazis . . ., have proven to be more true than false" (pp. 58–59).

Published in 1942 to critical praise, *Renegade* tells of Joshua Vidal, a young Jew who leaves the Jewish community of Avignon for Paris to pursue and participate in the world of enlightened ideas, seeking to absorb the teachings of Voltaire and Jean-Jacques Rousseau. He falls in love with Marguerite, a married *comtesse*, and despite their religious differences, Joshua is obsessed with her. Soon, with the help of an apostate Jew, Joshua follows Marguerite to her family estate and seizes the opportunity to "pass" as a young Christian nobleman. In the process Joshua himself becomes a renegade Jew. But at the novel's conclusion Joshua marries Marguerite, now a widow, who then converts to Judaism, and they emigrate to the West Indies, where they become models of piety.

What makes the novel more than a pedestrian work of fiction is Lewisohn's ability to work into the story line his understanding of how the Jews of France react to the possibility of acceptance into French society. Central to this discussion is the German Jewish philosopher and champion of assimilation Moses Mendelssohn (most of whose children, including Abraham, father of the composer Felix Mendelssohn, would convert to Christianity). Lewisohn describes a conversation between a Jewish traveler who has returned from Berlin and a rabbi who is concerned with Mendelssohn's reform ideas. After acknowledging that Mendelssohn is a well-meaning man whom God has given great gifts, the rabbi adds:

> He has been esteemed by great and good men. But they have esteemed him despite the fact that he is a Jew and for his accomplishments which they expected not of a Jew. None esteemed him because he is a Jew. He has caused Jews to be esteemed not in so far as they are Jews but in the hope that they may cease to be such.
>
> (p. 257)

The rabbi concludes that if Jews follow Mendelssohn's path, they will be induced to apostasy and "Israel will crumble away as flint crumbles under the blows of an iron hammer."

Elsewhere, Lewisohn captures the antagonism of both "enlightened" Jews and a Polish visitor from Warsaw in regard to the Hasidim: The visitor says that the goal must be to "fight and restrain, if need be by force, the goings-on of this rabble that calls itself Chasidim. . . . How can we contribute to the perfectibility of the poor backward Jews of Poland, if the masses of them yield to new superstitions and to wild and stupid sectarianism? How, Monsieur, would an account of what is happening here impress . . . Voltaire or the . . . great Lessing?" (p. 268). The encounter concludes with the "enlightened" Jew stating that "we can make progress only by perfecting ourselves" (p. 268). Thus *The Renegade*, in the guise of a romance novel, is also a work of fiction filled with ideas that dovetail with Lewisohn's argument that the siren call of assimilation threatens the ultimate survival of the Jewish people.

THE AUTOBIOGRAPHIES

One of Lewisohn's finest literary works is *Up Stream*, wherein he writes of his life in Queenshaven (Charleston, South Carolina), his warm relations with his mother, strained relations with his father and as an assimilated Jew bereft of any

association with his Jewish peoplehood, his attendance in both church and Sunday schools, and his belief that he was fully accepted in the Charleston community.

Lewisohn, who was a brilliant student with an affinity for German literature and culture, describes how this passion would create problems for him on the eve of World War I, when everything German was removed from the curriculum of many schools, and he was suspected of German sympathies once the country went to war. His autobiography reveals much of what we know about Lewisohn's early life to World War I, including his intellectually life-turning experience at Columbia University. The memoir provides a chilling picture of anti-Semitism in academia, which led Lewisohn, who began life as a believer in assimilation and in Christianity, to condemn assimilation and return to his Jewish heritage:

> The doctrine of assimilation, if driven home by public pressure . . . will create a race of unconscious spiritual helots. We shall become utterly barbarous and desolate. . . . Beware of becoming merely another dweller on an endless Main Street; we must melt naturally and gradually into a richer life, a broader liberty, a more radiant artistic and intellectual culture. . . .
>
> (p. 240)

Whereas *Up Stream* was highly praised by the critics, this cannot be said about *Mid-Channel*, the second of his autobiographies. Lainoff, for example, criticizes the memoir for being disjointed, "beginning with a fulminating defense of his personal affairs and concluding with an attack upon Pauline Christianity. . . . The chronology of events is lost: the reader has trouble reconstructing the decade under discussion. Parts are often interesting and sometimes valuable, but no sense of the whole comes through" (p. 15).

Despite Lainoff's criticism, the memoir is always interesting and perceptive. For example, writing about his marriage and inability to get a divorce in New York State, he writes, "It is several years since I have been in New York and the chances of my returning there are slight. My country and its Christian laws have no regard for love or virtue or the creative mind but give their support to legalized malignity and moral foulness" (p. 17). When it came to divorce, Lewisohn questioned why, as a Jew, he was bound by a Christian law, disguised as a secular one. Elsewhere, commenting on his visiting Rome, he writes of the magnificence of the Sistine Chapel, the Botticelli in Venice, and so on. But discussing other expressions of Christianity, he writes:

> I was touched by the catacombs despite the ominous swastika scratched into these mouldy walls. . . . The martyred and fugitive Church has the sweetness and persuasiveness of all that opposes the spirit to the powers of earth. The militant and triumphant Church, an empire with prisons and engines of war, is even amid the grandeur of St. Peter's a thing that evokes in me both horror and disdain—horror at its long cruelties toward those whom it still calls "perfidious Jews," though not, to be sure, toward them alone.
>
> (p. 110)

Much of Lewisohn's third autobiography, *Haven*, written with his wife, Edna Manley, deals with Ludwig's acrimonious relationship with Thelma over custody of James. The memoir also deals with Lewisohn's loss of popularity as witnessed by declining sales for his novels as well as bad critical reviews for his most recent works. For example, Lewisohn writes that he was hurt that close friends, such as Dorothy Thompson and Sholem Asch, did not acknowledge the merits of *Trumpet of Jubilee*, a novel he considered among his best work. Lewisohn, when learning that *The Island Within* was due to appear in the Modern Library series, wrote, "it is far from being my favorite among my novels and hence . . . I grudge it its extreme and lasting popularity, almost as though that popularity were at the expense of my better and mature book" (pp. 100–101). Elsewhere in *Haven*, Lewisohn bemoans the fact that "had I continued at proper intervals to write feebler and feebler imitations of *The Island Within*, I would have money in the bank and be a respectable American writer. Also I would be dead as an artist and old as a man" (p. 114).

Although other parts of the memoir deal with his impressions of writers—"Thomas Mann and Andre Gide, the two living writers to whom I

feel myself most closely allied" (p. 100)—the work does not lack substance. Written when the Nazis were embarking on their crusade to conquer Europe and beyond, Lewisohn provided an analysis of how cultured Germany fell under the spell of Hitler:

Modern German civilization was most profoundly and disproportionately . . . influenced by the works and ways, the word and song and thought of [a] handful of Jews. And the better half of the split [or schizophrenic] German soul experienced that influence as a thing harmonious with its deep and authentic nature. But the evil, dark, pagan half rebelled. The German rebellion against the Jew is a rebellion against the better part of the German soul. It is self-abasement and self-laceration and self-immolation. From that fact arises the brutal horror of the Nazi roar: "Evil, be thou my good!"

(pp. 80–81)

WORKS OF NONFICTION

Lewisohn's remarks in *Haven* analyzing the "German soul" was of course not the first time he strayed from writing fiction to take up books concerning the future of the Jewish people. His themes—anti-Semitism in American life, the failure of assimilation, the necessity of Jews to reconnect to their Jewish heritage, a critique of Pauline Christianity, prediction of the coming Holocaust, intense commitment to Zionism as manifested in his support for a Jewish state in Palestine, and his vigorous support for Israel after its founding in 1948—can all be found as early as *Up Stream* but more significantly in polemics written about the place of Jews in a world that truly did not welcome them as equal citizens. These books include *Israel* (1925), *The Permanent Horizon: A New Search for Old Truths* (1934), *The Answer* (1939), *The American Jew: Character and Destiny* (1950), and *What Is This Jewish Heritage?* (1954). Lewisohn was a staunch advocate for a pluralistic America wherein Jews could retain their institutions and religious beliefs and unapologetically assimilate in their non-Jewish environment. Solomon Grayzel summarized many of the themes in Lewisohn's nonfiction books when he wrote:

Lewisohn initially saw the situation in terms of thwarted ambition—the American Jew's burning desire to participate in the growth of America hurling itself vainly against the suspicions and prejudices of his non-Jewish neighbors—later he began to see that greater than the tragedy of Christian prejudice was the tragedy of the American Jew turning away from his own heritage.

(qtd. in Lainoff, p. 107)

CRITICISM

During his heyday in the 1920s and early 1930s, Lewisohn was among the most respected literary critics. Alfred Kazin, in his chapter "Liberals and New Humanists" in *On Native Grounds* (1956), wrote the following about Lewisohn:

No critic in America save Paul Elmer More had gone so studiously to the whole history of criticism for guidance. No critic had ever insisted so strenuously on the need of precise study of the basic facts underlying art as a spiritual vocation. Abstractly, indeed, Lewisohn was the most admirable of critics: a naturalist of great imaginative perception and with a salutary insistence on form; a scholar of great sensibility and seemingly the very type of the discerning and generous critical intelligence.

(p. 207)

Before coming to the *Nation* as a theater critic, Lewisohn was a pioneer contributor to the post–World War I literary renaissance, where he adapted modern European literature to American criticism. According to Kazin, "his greatest service at the time was his masterly editorship and partial translation of the Hauptmann plays" (p. 206). (Gerhart Hauptmann [1862–1946], was a German dramatist and novelist. He is counted among the most important promoters of literary naturalism and received the Nobel Prize in Literature in 1912.)

It was characteristic of Lewisohn, writes Kazin, "that his valuable early anthology *A Modern Book of Criticism* (1919) included more of his own criticism than that of any of the other twenty-four French, German, English, and American critics represented. Yet it was entirely in keeping with the progress of American criticism at the time that Lewisohn should have been

among the first to present such an anthology" (p. 275).

Steeped in both American and European literature, Lewisohn's criticism was influenced by Freud and a hatred of Puritanism. Indeed, much of his criticism in *Expression in America* (1932) was based on his reading of the history of American literature through the prism of sex. Writing of Henry David Thoreau, Lewisohn cites a journal passage where Thoreau writes of sex, "I would preserve purity in act and thought, as I would cherish the memory of my mother. A companion can possess no worse quality than vulgarity. If I find that he is not habitually reverent of the fact of sex, I, even I, will not associate with him" (p. 138).

Kazin noted that, in writing on both Thoreau and Ralph Waldo Emerson, Lewisohn asserted, "That they were chilled under-sexed valetudinarians, deprived of helpful and sympathetic social and intellectual atmosphere, renders their achievement only the more remarkable" (p. 279). Kazin and other critics who had praised Lewisohn before *Expression in America* now were disparaging of his reading of American literature, wherein it was argued he was guided by his own prejudices and subjectivity. The result, stated Kazin, was that Lewisohn "carried his postwar discovery of sex . . . to the point of self-ridicule. . . . Few critics in America have ever, indeed, had so moving an ideal of the critic's function or kept to it so stubbornly" (p. 273).

Perhaps Lewisohn's most acclaimed work of criticism was *Cities and Men* (1927), wherein he used his mastery of European as well as American literature to display his scholarly erudition. Lainoff notes, "Regrettably, *Cities and Men . . .*, like *Crump*, is overlooked today. The book is devoid of the flawed Freudianism critics have rightly objected to in *Expression in America. . . .* The book represents a balanced critical Humanism Lewisohn could not always sustain" (p. 127).

LAST YEARS

Lewisohn's last years witnessed his happy marriage to Louise Wolk, whom he married in 1944,

and his appointment as Brandeis' first full professor. When Brandeis was founded in 1948, it was not strictly a "Jewish" college although under Jewish auspices. Applications to Brandeis did not ask for the race, religion, or ancestry of its applicant; in short, the university was a nonsectarian institution that welcomed students on the basis of their ability rather than their race or religion.

Upon his appointment to the faculty, Lewisohn was named professor of comparative literature and in 1955 the university librarian. At Brandeis, Lewisohn became a controversial figure. When Brandeis' president, Abram Leon Sachar, stated that the university was not just another little school but a symbol of what the Jewish people wanted to contribute to the intellectual world, Lewisohn responded that Sachar's objectives were too limited. Lewisohn—who, over the decades, had sought the creation of a Jewish-oriented university, where the Jewish heritage in all its forms would be central to its mission—was disappointed by the direction that Brandeis was taking. Equally disturbing to Lewisohn was Brandeis' decision to earmark a number of its scholarships specifically for Protestant students, which he saw, according to Melnick, "as a manifestation of the university's failure to establish an unapologetic self-affirming identity" (vol. 2, p. 386). Lewisohn denied that he advocated a discriminatory admission policy, stating, "We must accept worthy students irrespective of descent or faith. But that is different from going out into the very streets with bribes, as though we were otherwise not *valid*." As Melnick sums up Lewisohn's position, "Why, he protested, must the American Jewish community always hesitate to be itself uncompromisingly? Why could it not admit to its youth's needs for some place in which they could develop unimpeded by perceptions of obligatory conformity?" (vol. 2, p. 387). Lewisohn went on to accuse Brandeis for not being Jewish enough.

Overall, however, Ludwig's days at Brandeis were fulfilling, despite his ongoing disagreements with Sachar. Lewisohn was a popular teacher and active in Hillel, the Jewish student organization on campus. In fact, *What Is This Jewish Heri-*

tage? was published by Schocken as a Hillel Book—to his last days, Lewisohn was passionate in seeing to it that young Jewish students at Brandeis would become familiar with their history and culture.

On vacation in Miami Beach, Florida, Lewisohn suffered a heart attack and died on December 31, 1955. He was seventy-three years old.

CONCLUSION

Ludwig Lewisohn is an almost forgotten figure on the American literary landscape. Over time his star dimmed despite a body of work that spans novels, poems, literary translations, works of criticism, and a series of books addressing diaspora Jewry, wherein he condemned assimilation at the expense of eschewing Jewish tradition and culture, promoted Zionism, and chronicled his journey from Christianity back to Judaism, the religion of his birth.

It can be argued that, of the Jewish writers who have urged a return of their people to their roots, few have been more passionate and persuasive than Lewisohn. An intellectual who did not suffer fools lightly, Lewisohn contested Jewish Marxists, self-hating Jews, and those who believed that Judaism was a fossil of medieval Europe. If a theme existed in his Jewish fiction it was that Jewish self-destruction was inevitable if assimilation loosened the ties of American Jews to their religion and culture. At first, Lewisohn believed that historic Christian prejudice toward Jews hindered their full integration into American life. Subsequently he concluded that the danger was from within, located in the desire of Jews to assimilate into Christian America by turning their backs on their heritage.

What explains Lewisohn's loss of reputation as an important literary figure and what place does he hold in the history of American literature? The decline in his reputation was in part owing to the negative public response that attended his marital entanglements with his first wife and his sixteen-year affair with Thelma Spear, which ended in a highly publicized court case wherein she claimed to be his legal second wife—a claim rejected by the state's attorney of Maryland. The Hearst press also exploited the litigation over the custody of their son, James. It may be that Lewisohn's creativity as a writer was demeaned in the public mind by the scandal of his personal life.

Literary trends were another factor. The high point of Lewisohn's popularity came in the 1920s and early 1930s. *Crump*, *The Island Within*, and *Up Stream* were among his most critically successful publications. But by the end of the 1930s, his fiction had lost its appeal and a number of critics argued that his early novels, such as *Crump*, were successful works based on his personal life, but his themes of love and marriage now lacked interest with the public.

A third factor may be that Lewisohn wrote books promoting Zionism when most American Jews (before Hitler) were unsupportive of a Jewish homeland in Palestine. His criticism of assimilated Jews who turned their back to their heritage did not resonate with many Jewish intellectuals, including those who, in times of world depression, were lured to the siren call of Stalinism.

American Jewish fiction of the twenty-first century, however, is characterized by its unabashed writing about Jewish life in America—warts and all—and is thus more in accord with Lewisohn's summons for American Jews to embrace their Jewish heritage than with the assimilatory message of Mary Antin's *The Promised Land* (1912). Lewisohn's pioneering of Zionism was vindicated when, after the Holocaust and the subsequent establishment of the State of Israel, pride in their heritage and culture was restored for many American Jews.

Lewisohn's writings would still be worth reading if only because his literary contributions shed light on the fight against the restrictive formalism of American culture. More than this, however, his writings on Jewish life illuminate a period of American history when anti-Semitism was rampant and Jews sought acceptance through assimilating into the majority culture at the expense of turning their back to their heritage.

Selected Bibliography

WORKS OF LUDWIG LEWISOHN

AUTOBIOGRAPHY

Up Stream: An American Chronicle. New York: Boni & Liveright, 1922.

Mid-Channel: An American Chronicle. New York and London: Harper, 1929.

Haven. With Edna Manley Lewisohn. New York: Dial Press, 1940.

FICTION

The Broken Snare: New York: B. W. Dodge, 1908.

Don Juan. New York: Boni & Liveright, 1923.

The Case of Mr. Crump. Paris: Edward W. Titus, 1926. Reprint, New York: Macmillan, 1947.

Roman Summer. New York and London: Harper, 1927.

The Defeated. London: Butterworth, 1927. Reprinted as *The Island Within*, New York: Harper, 1928.

Stephen Escott. New York and London: Harper, 1930.

The Golden Vase. New York and London: Harper, 1931.

The Last Days of Shylock. New York and London: Harper, 1931.

This People. New York and London: Harper, 1933. (Novellas.)

An Altar in the Fields. New York and London: Harper, 1934.

Trumpet of Jubilee. New York and London: Harper, 1937.

For Ever Wilt Thou Love. New York: Dial Press, 1939.

Renegade. New York: Dial Press, 1942.

Breathe upon These. Indianapolis: Bobbs-Merrill, 1944.

Anniversary. New York: Farrar, Straus, 1946.

In a Summer Season. New York: Farrar, Straus, 1955.

CRITICISM

The Spirit of Modern German Literature: Lectures Delivered Before the University of Wisconsin. New York: B. W. Huebsch, 1916.

A Modern Book of Criticism. New York: Boni & Liveright, 1919.

The Drama and the Stage. New York: Harcourt, Brace, 1922.

The Creative Life. New York: Boni & Liveright, 1924.

Cities and Men. New York and London: Harper, 1927.

Expression in America. New York and London: Harper, 1932. Reprinted as *The Story of American Literature*, New York: Random House, 1939.

CRITICAL ESSAYS

"In the Seventh Heaven." *Magazine* 4:23–28 (October 1900).

"A Study of Matthew Arnold." *Sewanee Review* 10, no. 2:143–159 (April 1902).

"German-American Poetry." *Sewanee Review* 12, no. 2:223–230 (April 1904).

"The Modern Novel." *Sewanee Review* 17, no. 4:458–474 (October 1909).

"Thomas Mann." *English Journal* 22, no. 7:527–535 (September 1933).

"The New Meaning of Revolution." *North American Review* 238, no. 3:210–218 (September 1934).

WRITINGS ON JEWISH HISTORY AND CULTURE

Israel. New York: Boni & Liveright, 1925.

The Permanent Horizon: A New Search for Old Truths. New York: Harper, 1934.

The Answer: The Jew and the World; Past, Present, and Future. New York: Liveright, 1939.

The American Jew: Character and Destiny. New York: Farrar, Straus, 1950.

What Is This Jewish Heritage? New York: B'nai B'rith Hillel Foundations, 1954. Rev. ed., Schocken, 1954.

TRANSLATIONS

Dramatic Works. By Gerhart Hauptmann. 7 vols. New York: R. W. Huebsch, 1913.

The World's Illusion. By Jacob Wasserman. New York: Harcourt, Brace and Howe, 1920.

Wedlock. By Jacob Wasserman. New York: Boni & Liveright, 1926.

The Eternal Road: A Drama in Four Parts. By Franz Werfel. New York: Viking, 1936.

Thirty-One Poems. By Rainer Maria Rilke. New York: B. Ackerman, 1936.

For the Sake of Heaven. By Martin Buber. Philadelphia: Jewish Publication Society of America, 1945.

In My Father's Pastures. By Soma Morgenstern. Philadelphia: Jewish Publication Society of America, 1947.

Unambo: A Novel of the War in Israel. By Max Brod. New York: Farrar, Straus and Young, 1952.

The Marked One and Twelve Other Stories. By Jacob Picard. Philadelphia: Jewish Publication Society of America, 1956.

EDITED ANTHOLOGIES AND COLLECTIONS

Creative America: An Anthology. New York and London: Harper and Bros., 1933.

Rebirth: A Book of Modern Jewish Thought. New York and London: Harper, 1935.

Jewish Short Stories. New York: Behrman House, 1945.

Among the Nations: Three Tales and a Play About Jews. New York: Farrar, Straus, 1948.

Goethe: The Story of a Man; Being the Life of Johann Wolfgang Goethe as Told in His Own Words and the

Words of His Contemporaries. 2 vols. New York: Farrar, Straus, 1949.

Theodor Herzl: A Portrait for This Age. New York and Cleveland: World, 1955.

PAPERS

The two primary repositories for Lewisohn's papers are the American Jewish Archives at Hebrew Union College, Cincinnati, Ohio, and the Special Collections Department of Goldfarb Library, Brandeis University, Waltham, Massachusetts.

CRITICAL AND BIOGRAPHICAL STUDIES

Bates, Ernest Sutherland. "Lewisohn into Crump." *American Mercury* 31:441–450 (April 1934).

Bragman, Louis J. "The Case of Ludwig Lewisohn." *American Journal of Psychiatry* 11:319–331 (September 1931).

Chyet, Stanley F. "Ludwig Lewisohn in Charleston (1892–1903)." *Publications of the American Jewish Historical Society* 50:296–322 (March 1965).

Edman, Irwin. Review of *The Island Within. Menorah Journal* 14:508–511 (1928).

Fiedler, Leslie A. "The Jew in the American Novel." In *Collected Essays of Leslie Fiedler*, vol. 2. New York: Stein & Day, 1971.

Gillis, Adolph. *Ludwig Lewisohn: The Artist and His Message.* New York: Duffield and Green, 1933.

Guttmann, Allen. The *Jewish Writer in America: Assimilation and the Crisis of Identity.* New York: Oxford University Press, 1971.

Hindus, Maurice. "Ludwig Lewisohn: From Assimilation to Zionism." *Jewish Frontier* 31:20–30 (February 1964).

Kazin, Alfred. *On Native Grounds: An Interpretation of Modern American Prose Literature.* Garden City, N.Y.: Doubleday, 1956.

Lainoff, Seymour. *Ludwig Lewisohn.* Boston: Twayne, 1982.

Lewisohn, James Elias. "My Father, Ludwig Lewisohn." *Midstream* 12:48–52 (November 1966).

Melnick, Ralph. *The Life and Work of Ludwig Lewisohn.* 2 vols. Detroit: Wayne University Press, 1998.

Mencken, H. L. Review of "The Case of Mr. Crump." *American Mercury* 10:379–380 (March 1927).

Ribalow, Harold U. "Ludwig Lewisohn's" *The Island Within.*" *Jewish Heritage* 5:44–48 (fall 1963).

Singer, David F. "Ludwig Lewisohn: A Paradigm of American-Jewish Return." *Judaism* 14:319–329 (1965).

SOLOMON NORTHUP

(1807—c. 1863)

Sarah Peters

A FREE MAN to the age of thirty-three, Solomon Northup was drugged, kidnapped, and sold into slavery in Washington, D.C., in 1841. He was transported to Louisiana, where he lived in captivity and forced servitude for eleven years, eight months, and twenty-six days. His rescue was publicized in a nationally circulated newspaper story, and his subsequent book, *Twelve Years a Slave*, became a best seller. Although out of print for several decades, it was reintroduced in the mid-twentieth century and in 2013 became a best seller again after an acclaimed film adaptation brought it back into the national spotlight. Northup's story offers unique insight into the daily lives of slaves in the nineteenth-century United States, and as a work of literature both exemplifies and challenges conventions of the slave-narrative genre.

LIFE

Solomon Northup was the son of a freed man, Mintus Northup, and his wife, who was likely named Susanna (Fiske et al., p. 20). Mintus, like many slaves, carried the name of his master, Captain Henry Northup, a loyalist during the American Revolution who chose to remain in New York after the war. On Henry's death in 1789, Mintus was emancipated and later became a successful independent farmer. Connections between the two Northup families continued into the next generation, leading to the lifelong friendship of Solomon Northup and Henry B. Northup, the man who ultimately confirmed Solomon's true identity and removed him from his twelve-year captivity. Solomon was born to free parents in New York in 1808, according to Solomon's own account of his life, but sworn testimonies, letters, and newspaper reports suggest that he was more likely born on July 10, 1807 (Fiske et al., pp. 24, 175). By this time the state of New York had begun a gradual emancipation of slaves, beginning with a 1799 law that defined children of enslaved mothers as free but required them to work as indentured servants for a period of time. All slaves in New York were emancipated in 1827.

Solomon Northup and his elder brother, Joseph, were taught to read and write and probably attended school, "an education," as Northup describes in his book, "surpassing that ordinarily bestowed upon children of our condition" (p. 19). Although he lived in a free state, Northup did contend with other forms of formal and informal racism, and his access to public education was a benefit that many African American children did not receive. Literacy was both an advantage and a danger during Northup's captivity; writing provided him limited opportunities to reach out beyond the plantations, but slaves who were known to read and write were viewed with suspicion and drew negative attention from slave owners and overseers. In addition to formal schooling, Northup gained valuable experience working on his family's farm. Northup's father owned enough land to permit him to vote in a state that required black men to own property valued at a minimum of $250 to qualify for suffrage. By adulthood, Northup had gained knowledge in agricultural operations and management—manual and intellectual skills that helped him support his own family after leaving his father's home.

Northup married Anne Hampton on Christmas Day in 1828, according to a legal statement given by Anne and included as an appendix in *Twelve Years a Slave*, a year later than the date stated in the narrative portion of the book. Anne was a free black woman who worked as a

domestic servant at times, as well as a kitchen manager in restaurants and hotels. While they spoke of their marriage as happy and affectionate, they endured temporary separations for Solomon's work. Because he did not own a farm as his father did, Northup sought work as a laborer in a variety of occupations, including maintenance of the Champlain Canal. In 1829 Northup started his own business as a contractor rafting timber from mills to market. He also worked as a professional woodcutter during the winter when waterways were frozen. In 1830 the Northups leased farmland in Kingsbury, New York, and worked there for four years. Through Anne's kitchen work and Solomon's music—he was hired to play the violin at parties throughout the winter—the Northups developed connections in the nearby community of Sandy Hill that would later assist in Solomon's recovery. The couple had three children: Margaret, Alonzo, and Elizabeth.

The family moved to the resort town of Saratoga Springs in 1834, seeking a life that promised more advancement and independence than they could achieve on a leased farm. While living there, they benefited from seasonal work in the tourism industry, Anne working in hotel kitchens and Solomon working as a driver and a musician. He would also regularly leave to work in the lumber industry.

KIDNAPPING AND CAPTIVITY

In March 1841, while Anne was away working in Sandy Hill, Northup was approached by Merrill Brown and Abram Hamilton, two circus performers who offered him a job playing violin for their shows in New York City. After a few performances, they persuaded him to travel with them to Washington, D.C., for additional shows, and they suggested that Northup take the precaution of procuring free papers since they would be moving south. Their apparent concern for his welfare, combined with other gestures including payment beyond what was promised, encouraged Northup's trust in his new colleagues, and he acknowledges in his book that he never suspected that he was in danger. One night, however, the two men drugged Northup, and he woke up the next morning chained in Williams' Slave Pen in Washington.

When Northup protested his enslavement, James H. Birch, a prominent slave dealer, beat him severely and threatened to murder him if he should mention his status as a free man again. Northup and others who were held in the slave pen were transferred to the ship *Orleans*. Aboard this ship, the first of many attempts to free himself were thwarted. Northup managed to get a letter sent to Henry Northup in New York, but his friend could not secure support for a rescue mission. When they arrived at their destination in New Orleans, Solomon Northup's name was changed to Platt, his new identity forced upon him through violence and threats.

In New Orleans, Northup was sold to his first master, William Ford, whom Northup describes as a "kind, noble, candid, Christian man" (p. 90). Northup distinguished himself as a skilled and innovative worker in Ford's lumber mill, drawing on his knowledge and experience to improve the mill's transport system. His troubles increased, however, when Ford encountered financial difficulties and sold Northup to the cruel John Tibeats. When Tibeats attempted to beat him, Northup turned on him and overpowered him, beating the slave driver instead. In retaliation, Tibeats returned with more men, who tied up Northup, preparing to hang him. He was saved by the intervention of Ford's overseer, Chapin, who stopped the lynching but left Northup bound and immobile in the sun for the rest of the day. (The documentary research of biographers David Fiske, Clifford W. Brown, and Rachel Seligman identifies Tibeats' real name as Tibaut and Chapin's real name as Chafin.)

After this incident Northup was hired out to Peter Tanner, Ford's brother-in-law. On his return to Tibeats, Northup again physically defended himself, almost killing Tibeats, and in fear of being murdered ran away back to Ford. Again he was returned to Tibeats, who hired him out clearing trees in the Big Cane Break. When that job was finished, Northup was sold to Edwin Epps to work on his cotton plantation, under even worse conditions than his volatile time with Tibeats. Under Epps, slaves were subjected to frequent

beatings, and as Northup's skills as a worker and manager became apparent, he was eventually forced into the role of driver and compelled to whip his fellow slaves, increasing his torment and trauma.

RESCUE AND TRIALS

The first known attempt to rescue Northup from slavery came after the letter written to Henry Northup in 1841. New York law allowed the state to appoint agents to rescue New York citizens who had been kidnapped into slavery, and Henry visited the governor to seek assistance. Solomon reports that this initial effort stalled because not enough information was available to locate him in Louisiana; while this was certainly the case, Governor William H. Seward was also actively engaged in a political struggle with the state of Virginia over Seward's refusal to extradite African Americans in New York who were wanted for assisting runaway slaves. This conflict may have deterred Seward from taking the aggressive action of sending a state-appointed agent into the South to free an enslaved man. Henry lacked the resources and authority to pursue a rescue without state support, so he waited for more communication from Solomon.

More than ten years later, Solomon met Samuel Bass, a Canadian carpenter who had been hired to work on Epps's new house. As a skilled carpenter himself, Northup worked alongside Bass and learned that he was an abolitionist who, unlike slaveholders, saw black men and women as human beings. Although Northup's previous attempts to reach out to his friends in New York had failed, and his confidants had betrayed him, Northup took the tremendous personal risk of telling his story to Bass, who agreed to write letters to men who could testify to Northup's identity and take action to free him. One letter, addressed to storekeepers William Perry and Cephas Parker of Saratoga Springs, reached its destination and was forwarded to Anne Northup, who went directly to Henry Northup for help.

Henry Northup gathered evidence in the form of affidavits and petitions that would allow him to prove Solomon Northup's identity as a free citizen of New York and that he was currently being held in slavery. Henry presented these documents to Washington Hunt, by then New York's governor. Hunt appointed Henry as the state's agent in the mission to free Solomon Northup. Henry added to his collection of documents letters of introduction to several Louisianans who might assist him, including attorney John P. Waddill, who accepted the case.

Once Henry made it to Louisiana, it was difficult to locate Solomon. One reason is that the letter that Bass sent included little identifying information about Solomon, his location, or his employer. *Twelve Years a Slave* makes clear throughout the book that Solomon's history as a free man endangered his life. Within days of his kidnapping, he was beaten severely for claiming he was free and for using his real name. His adoption of the name Platt, forced on him by slave traffickers, was necessary for his own survival, so everyone except Bass knew him only as Platt. If Bass's letter had been intercepted and Solomon identified as the sender, Solomon would likely have paid dearly for it. The necessity of secrecy consequently hindered the rescue effort. Henry Northup and Waddill made plans to travel throughout the area to search for Solomon among thousands of slaves, but that plan was cut short when, through interviews in Marksville where the letter was posted, they learned of Bass, whom they deduced to be the author of the letter. With Bass's testimony and the documents they possessed, the men began legal proceedings to take custody of Solomon in the name of the state of New York. They found him on January 3, 1853, and held a tearful reunion at the plantation.

A hearing the next day finalized Solomon's restoration to freedom. From there, Solomon and Henry went to New Orleans, then to Washington, D.C., collecting evidence against Birch, the slave trader. This attention to the paper trail helped the two men gather documentation of the illegal transactions and Birch's role in them. By the time legal proceedings began against Birch on January 18, the story of the rescue had spread and attracted great public interest.

At trial, Birch called two other slave traders, Benjamin O. Shekell and Benjamin A. Thorn, who testified that Northup had consented to the sale himself and had identified himself to Birch

as a native of Georgia hoping to return south. Despite the strong evidence against Birch, and Birch's inability to produce a bill of sale or any records at all corroborating the three slaver traders' alternative account, he was acquitted. Solomon Northup, because he was black, was not permitted to testify against Birch. Birch then sued Solomon for conspiracy to defraud him, and Solomon was arrested. Birch dropped the charge under pressure from Henry Northup, perhaps in fear that Solomon might be permitted to testify in his own defense and expose Birch's perjury. Solomon was finally reunited with his family in New York on January 21, 1853.

After the publication of *Twelve Years a Slave*, a reader recognized descriptions of the kidnappers and identified them as Alexander Merrill and Joseph Russell. In 1854 Merrill and Russell were arrested and indicted for kidnapping Northup with the intent to sell him into slavery. Because the proceedings were held in New York, this time Solomon Northup was able to testify, along with several witnesses who saw him with Merrill and Russell. A battle over jurisdiction led to the case being sent through multiple courts of appeal, with no verdict having been rendered in the original trial. The case was dismissed on the grounds of procedural error, and the two men were held in jail for a total of seven months. Although the case was eligible to be brought to trial again, the new district attorney did not prosecute the kidnappers.

After 1857 little is known of Northup's life. His activities were a mystery to his contemporaries, not just present-day historians. Some speculated that he had gone to England, that he had been killed by his kidnappers, and even that he had been taken into slavery again. Scholars, including biographer David Fiske, have found evidence to suggest that he may have been actively engaged in the Underground Railroad, assisting fugitive slaves in secret and at great personal risk and cost. He was certainly well connected to antislavery activists through his much publicized participation in abolitionist meetings and rallies. His date and place of death and his place of burial are unknown.

TWELVE YEARS A SLAVE

Soon after Northup's rescue, a long front-page story ran in the *New York Times* (then called the *New York Daily Times*) on January 20, 1853, and many other newspapers picked up the story and printed accounts of his ordeal (replicating the spelling error in the *Times* story that identified its subject as Solomon Northrup). Within two weeks Northup began touring the state to speak at abolitionist events alongside Frederick Douglass and other prominent figures in the antislavery campaign, which was by that time at its height. Northup soon began working with author David Wilson, who served as editor for Northup's book-length memoir of his period of enslavement, a project that was in print within five months.

Twelve Years a Slave was published on July 15, 1853, and by January 1855, twenty-seven thousand copies had sold, making it a best seller at the time. The book was widely reviewed, with most reviewers positively noting the factual and impartial relaying of events that offered a true account of the conditions of slavery. One advertisement for Northup's book quoted a review by Douglass, by then internationally famous for his own remarkable slave narrative; Douglass emphasized the unique perspective offered by Northup, who had been a man first, then reduced to chattel. Promoting his book and the abolitionist cause, Northup traveled throughout New England speaking about his experiences. He produced two plays, in 1854 and 1855, which dramatized his story. Northup played himself, a decision not terribly surprising for a longtime musical performer. Another theatrical adaptation, not produced by Northup, ran in 1855 as well.

The print book went through several editions and changed publishers multiple times, up to an 1890 reissue by the International Book Company of New York. After that it remained out of print until the historians Sue Eakin and Joseph Logsdon coedited an annotated edition in 1968. While it was out of print, its prevalence in private collections and occasional mentions in newspapers kept its memory alive. The prominence of the civil rights movement and the emergence of black studies programs in colleges and universities in the 1960s drew popular and academic attention

to Eakin and Logsdon's edition. Within a year, Northup's story was reprinted in the historian Gilbert Osofsky's book *Puttin' on Ole Massa: The Slave Narratives of Henry Bibb, William Wells Brown, and Solomon Northup*. Since then it has been adapted for young readers by Michael Knight in 1971, Sue Eakin in 1998, and Judith and Dennis Fradin in 2012. A television movie titled *Solomon Northup's Odyssey* aired on PBS in 1984. The most famous adaptation of Northup's memoir is Steve McQueen's 2013 film *12 Years a Slave*, which won the Academy Award for Best Picture, the Golden Globe for Best Motion Picture–Drama, and the British Academy of Film and Television Arts (BAFTA) award for Best Film. McQueen is the first black filmmaker to win the Best Picture Oscar.

CONNECTIONS TO UNCLE TOM'S CABIN

The *Sandy Hill Herald* reported on March 8, 1853, that a local man was working on a book about Northup, and the paper joked that it might be called "Uncle Sol." The reference is to Harriet Beecher Stowe's popular novel *Uncle Tom's Cabin*, which began serial publication in June 1851 and was published in book form in March 1852, ten months before Northup's story ran in the *New York Times*. Within a year, Stowe's novel sold three hundred thousand copies in the United States and 1.5 million copies in Britain, an unprecedented best seller in its time. Stowe, a white abolitionist woman born and raised in Connecticut, is said to have been motivated by the passage of the Fugitive Slave Act, which implicated Northerners in maintaining the Southern slavery system.

Stowe's novel is a fictional story of a slave who is sold down the Mississippi into Louisiana. It offers dramatic details of the daily trials of slaves working on plantations as well as those fighting to escape and to save their families. When the novel was published, many celebrated her success in making readers feel the emotional consequences of slavery, emphasizing the humanity of slaves, and garnering support for the abolitionist movement. Proponents of slavery, however, criticized her work as sensationalist,

sentimental propaganda that exaggerated the abuses of slavery. They contended that slavery was a benevolent and paternal institution in which slaves were well treated, clothed, and fed by their masters, protected by a system that sheltered them from the harsh realities they would face if they tried to survive on their own. In her own defense, Stowe wrote the book *A Key to Uncle Tom's Cabin*, published in 1853, that discussed her sources and supporting evidence for the representation of slave life that appears in her novel.

As two books about the lives of slaves in the Deep South, *Uncle Tom's Cabin* and *Twelve Years a Slave* have much in common. They share a common political context, both employed in service of the abolitionist cause to engage the sympathies and incite the outrage of the American public in the years leading up to the Civil War. Both texts address the hardships of work in the fields, the terror at being sold to a cruel master, and the agony of children torn from their mothers, among other horrible truths. Both drew impressive popular attention and were dramatized into theatrical productions shortly after publication, expanding their reach to new audiences. In addition to similarities in content, purpose, and medium, these authors make explicit references to each other.

In *A Key to Uncle Tom's Cabin*, Stowe cites the *New York Times* story of Northup's captivity as evidence that her novel was realistic and based on reliable accounts of slaves' experiences; the similarity was so clear and the novel so fresh in readers' minds that the newspaper named Stowe and her protagonist Tom in the story. Stowe could not have used Northup's story as a source text for *Uncle Tom's Cabin*, but as many contemporary reviewers of *Twelve Years a Slave* noted, the verifiability of Northup's nonfiction account supported Stowe's representations. Stowe herself called it a "singular coincidence that this man was carried to a plantation in the Red River country, that same region where the scene of Tom's captivity was laid; and his account of this plantation, his mode of life there, and some incidents which he describes, form a striking parallel to that history" (*A Key to Uncle Tom's*

Cabin, p. 342). For Northup's part, he dedicated his own book to Stowe. Quoting an excerpt from Stowe's book, Northup added the inscription "To Harriet Beecher Stowe: Whose name, throughout the world, is identified with the Great Reform: This narrative, affording another *Key to Uncle Tom's Cabin*, is respectfully dedicated" (*Twelve Years a Slave*, p. v). The mutual appreciation these authors expressed in print emphasizes the importance of both books to keeping the abolitionist mission in the public consciousness.

A significant theme shared by the books is the use of Christianity within the rhetorics of slavery and abolition. Stowe's novel employs Christian imagery and presents an ethic of love and compassion to resist a common argument that slavery was ordained by God and supported in scripture. Like the fictional Uncle Tom, Northup identifies himself as a Christian, and he cries out to "the Almighty Father of us all—the freeman and the slave" to help him endure his bondage (*Twelve Years a Slave*, p. 77). Northup further demonstrates his faith and his religious education as he integrates references to scripture throughout his narrative. Describing the maternal grief of Eliza, whose children have been sold away from her, Northup describes her dream of freedom as "her cloud by day, her pillar of fire by night," evoking a common image that relates the trials of the African American people to those of the Israelites wandering the desert. He follows this image with a verse from the Old Testament book of Lamentations 1:2: "she weepeth sore in the night, and tears are on her cheeks: all her friends have dealt treacherously with her: they have become her enemies" (p. 88). In addition to the slaves' prayers and devotions, Northup, like Stowe, presents opposing uses of scripture by slave owners, all claiming to be good Christian men while holding human beings in bondage. Ford, the kind master, reads the Bible to his slaves and allows them to keep Bibles of their own, although most did not have the literacy skills to read them without assistance, which Northup himself provided. Ford speaks of the Creator's loving kindness and of rewards promised in the afterlife, encouraging his slaves to treat one another with kindness (p. 97). Tanner,

on the other hand, reads aloud from verses that warn of punishment for a servant who disobeys his master, emphasizing the threat of being "beaten with many *stripes*" (p. 128). Scripture becomes not a comfort but a threat, and Christianity is used to oppress and control slaves. The tension between the use of Christianity in both proslavery and antislavery arguments throughout the nineteenth century is integrated into both books, calling out the hypocrisy of Christian slave owners even as they suggest the potential for their redemption.

It is worth noting here that Northup did not identify himself with Uncle Tom, whose stalwart faith persists to the end as he prays for forgiveness of those who beat him to death. As Northup tells his story of serving as a "driver" forced to whip other slaves, he states, "If Epps was present, I dared not show any lenity, not having the Christian fortitude of a certain well-known Uncle Tom sufficiently to brave his wrath, by refusing to perform the office. In that way, only, I escaped the immediate martyrdom he suffered, and withal, saved my companions much suffering, as it proved in the end" (p. 226). Although he does not criticize Stowe's protagonist, Northup calls upon his image to offer a contrast between the fictional Tom and the impossible bind in which the actual slave is caught. While one might admire the strength and sacrifice of a man who refuses to use the whip against others, the morality of that choice is distorted by the condition of slavery. Northup's choice is not free. If he refuses, he will be beaten and possibly killed. His story dies with him, as the only witnesses are slave owners and other slaves, many of whom have been denied the right to literacy and have no means of communicating beyond the plantation. The fictional Tom's fate can be given meaning by the virtuous white character who learns of his murder and then frees his own slaves, the newly converted white characters who are moved by Tom's unbreakable faith and forgiveness, and the actual white woman who writes the book that speaks to the consciences of her readers. The enslaved Solomon Northup possesses none of those privileges. His alternative is to obey orders and wield the whip, and he real-

izes that while he occupies that position he may spare his fellow slaves a harsher beating at the hands of unsympathetic overseers, or Epps himself. Northup further develops his skills so that he can "handle the whip with marvelous dexterity and precision, throwing the lash within a hair's breadth of the back, the ear, the nose, without, however, touching either of them" (p. 226). The small degree of privilege granted to Northup as the driver allows him to subvert the power of the master just enough to keep himself alive and temporarily protect others.

TWO AMERICAN GENRES

Along with its relevance to the literary context of "works of fiction, professing to portray [slavery's] features in their more pleasing as well as more repugnant aspects" (p. 17), *Twelve Years a Slave* exemplifies two distinctively American genres of nonfiction writing: the slave narrative (or slave's narrative, as some critics prefer) and the captivity narrative. In his influential essay "'I Was Born': Slave Narratives, Their Status as Autobiography and as Literature," James Olney notes the astounding similarities among slave narratives and offers a general outline that many slave narratives follow. Solomon Northup's book contains the standard front matter that Olney lists: a portrait and signature of the author, a preface written by a white editor averring the authenticity of the narrative, and an epigraph by William Cowper, who wrote a number of antislavery poems. As for the narrative itself, Northup's story aligns largely with the outline: a cruel master, an upstanding slave who refuses to be whipped (in this case, Northup himself), a Christian slaveholder, details of a slave's daily life, a slave auction in which children are taken from their mother, failed escape attempts, successful escape, a new last name, comments on the institution of slavery, and an appendix of documentary evidence. The similarities are attributed to the interventions of editors, like David Wilson, who imposed literary structures on the stories told to them by former slaves with the political aim of appealing to white, middle-class readers of nineteenth-century sentimental fiction. Abolition-

ists, who often fell short of believing in true racial equality, relied on appeals to emotions, evoked especially by scenes of violence and familial separation. Speakers at abolitionist meetings, which were often precursors to published narratives, were chosen based on a series of questions to determine whether their experiences would effectively engage white audiences. This screening process might also have contributed to the production of formulaic slave narratives with a narrow view of audience and purpose.

As a genre understood as primarily rhetorical—as abolitionist propaganda—the nature of the narratives changed with the Civil War and the emancipation of Southern slaves. These dramatic changes in the political landscape might also explain the reduced demand for Solomon Northup's public appearances. Scholars recognize the continuing importance of slave narratives, however, both as invaluable historical accounts of the institution of slavery from the perspective of the enslaved and as enduring influences on the development of African American literary traditions.

Many of the conventions of the slave narrative serve to affirm the authenticity of the story as a true, unembellished relation of a sequence of events, in large part to counter the proslavery claims that abuses were exaggerated and slavery was benevolent. Northup's narrative demonstrates that concern, with its editor's preface promising that many of Northup's statements have been "corroborated by abundant evidence" and that other facts have been told without variation by the narrator to the editor, who is satisfied with their veracity (*Twelve Years a Slave*, p. xv). The narrative adds to that assurance frequent references to real places, real people, and official documents, some of which are included as appendices at the end of the book. Acknowledging again the popularity of fictional accounts of slavery, Northup assures the reader in the third paragraph that he intends to tell the truth without decoration:

> I can speak of Slavery only so far as it came under my own observation—only so as I have known and experienced it in my own person. My object is, to give a candid and truthful statement of facts: to

repeat the story of my life, without exaggeration, leaving it for others to determine, whether even the pages of fiction present a picture of more cruel wrong or a severer bondage.

(p. 18)

The necessity of asserting the absolute truth of a slave narrative set it apart from other kinds of autobiography. Memoir as a literary genre works to find patterns that illuminate significance, the autobiographer working as an active shaper of memory and meaning. Reflection and interpretation are central to the art, which establishes unity among disparate episodes. Former slaves as writers and as orators were praised for speaking plainly, not only without embellishment but also without interpretation. Their narratives are primarily episodic, communicating a limited and consistent meaning: they first establish themselves as human, then present the evils of the institution, and finally assure their audience that they intend to assimilate and accept their appropriate role in society, their antiestablishment motives limited to ending slavery.

Northup, however, occupies a unique position within this tradition. He was born a free man, endowed with the privileges of citizenship (limited as they were by racist policies), and he bore witness to slavery as an outsider who retained a kind of emotional distance because he did not consider himself a slave. His struggle to retain his identity among strangers and his final redemption align *Twelve Years a Slave* with another significant American genre, the captivity narrative.

The American captivity narrative gained popularity with the 1682 publication of *The Sovereignty and Goodness of God*, Mary Rowlandson's account of being kidnapped and held captive by Native Americans. Seventeenth-century captivity narratives reflected on the experiences of its authors or subjects through the lens of Puritan theology, understanding the trials as a confrontation with the devil meant to test the faith of the captive, who is ultimately restored to the Christian community. The end of the eighteenth century saw a revival in the popularity of these stories as Americans understood themselves as a people held captive by the tyrannical British crown. Like slave narratives, captivity narratives tend to follow a pattern. An innocent person is thrust suddenly into an alien culture and forced to exist within that culture for an extended period of time. To survive, the captive must balance the need to assimilate into the captor's culture with the need to protect her own identity. The captive adopts the ways of her captors, sometimes identifying as a member of the alien culture, but retains awareness of her old ways and her religion. The trials catalyze a spiritual awakening and development in the captor, who is then redeemed by the grace of God and returned to her original community. Such a narrative emphasizes religious faith as well as personal fortitude, constructing an American ethic of self-reliance, perseverance, and resilience.

Slave narratives and captivity narratives both rely on eyewitness accounts of traumatic experience, and their patterns intersect. However, the captivity narrative, identified primarily with white people kidnapped by "savages," legitimizes the reflective process of meaning-making associated with the genre of autobiography. Whereas slave narratives commonly begin with a slave's uncertain date of birth and parentage, emphasizing the human experiences and self-knowledge denied them from birth, Northup's book begins with details of his heritage that traces paternal lines. The emphasis on his father's identity is a sharp contrast to other slaves' stories; by law, slavery was a condition transmitted through maternal lines, protecting the status of white slave owners who raped enslaved women and fathered their children. Not only does Northup establish his birth to a free father and mother, but he also expresses deep love for his wife and children:

From the time of my marriage to this day the love I have borne my wife has been sincere and unabated; and only those who have felt the glowing tenderness a father cherishes for his offspring, can appreciate my affection for the beloved children which have since been born to us. This much I deem appropriate and necessary to say, in order that those who read these pages, may comprehend the poignancy of those sufferings I have been doomed to bear.

(*Twelve Years a Slave*, p. 22)

Personal and intimate connections to family were regularly denied to slaves, who were rarely

permitted to live with a spouse and were separated from their children by long working hours or permanently torn apart by the sale of a child or parent to another plantation. The first chapter of Northup's book emphasizes a full range of human experience offered to a free man: parental love, childhood education, marriage and children, pursuit of economic independence, success through hard work and intelligence. He wholly embraces an American work ethic, along with a love of liberty that he assures his readers exists among the slaves he happens to meet.

After he is kidnapped, Northup observes slaves and slaveholders as a person encountering a strange and foreign culture. Lying sick in the hospital after acquiring smallpox aboard the Orleans, Northup fears dying "in the midst of strangers" (p. 83). He learns from watching others how to behave in order to protect himself, and he makes decisions about the extent of his assimilation based on careful deliberation. He outlines the options he considers and weighs the potential consequences of each, explaining his choice to "lock the secret" of this identity "closely in [his] heart" and to trust in "Providence and my own shrewdness for deliverance" (pp. 91–92). He is not resigned to slavery but rather strategically employs survival skills to endure his kidnapping until he can return home. Unlike other former slaves, Northup exists at the outset as a speaking subject whose unique experience situates him in a position to analyze, interpret, and construct meaning out of his own memory as he traces his story from independence to captivity to redemption. In this redemption, Northup assures readers that he is "chastened and subdued in spirit by [his] sufferings" and that he intends to live a virtuous life to the end of his days (p. 321). This promise to return to right living with renewed conviction ends many American captivity narratives, as they find useful lessons in their trials and, by the grace of God, are fortified through their endurance.

DETAILS OF SLAVE LIFE

Both slave narratives and captivity narratives feature details of the daily lives and activities of people that would be unfamiliar to many intended readers. Northup's details of his life as a slave have contributed much to the knowledge of the inner workings of antebellum plantations and the intimate lives of slaves. His life on the plantation of Edwin Epps at Bayou Boeuf was his longest residence and hardest labor, and Northup gives extensive details not only of the labor of picking cotton, and the punishments generously doled out to those whose baskets came up short, but also of the daily activities of "cabin life." As Northup reports, cabins were small log buildings with no floors or windows, and slaves slept on planks with pieces of wood for pillows. Eating utensils were limited, and most slaves cut their weekly rations of bacon with the ax they used to chop wood. Slaves were provided blankets, but any other "luxury or convenience"—including dishes or furniture—had to be obtained independently (p. 194). In these explanations, Northup includes an uncommonly detailed account of a slave's economic activity, specifically the custom of "Sunday money." During a time of slow work caused by a caterpillar infestation in the cotton fields, Northup is hired out to a neighboring sugar plantation. While his master, Epps, has the right to all of his wages, he and other slaves are allowed to keep what they earn for work on Sundays. This Sunday work is not optional, and it prevents slaves from observing the Sabbath, but the wages from this labor offer opportunities for slaves to afford a small amount of personal property that they might use to cook and eat their meals and even, Northup says, for the women to purchase "gaudy ribbons, wherewithal to deck their hair in the merry season of the holidays" (p. 196). Because he also receives compensation for playing the violin at parties—those held off of Epps's plantation, that is—he is able to accumulate comparatively large savings. These details give useful facts to readers seeking to understand plantation life, but they also serve to distinguish Northup as exceptional among slaves. He is violently stripped of his name, his family, and his freedom; the will to survive is dependent in part on his ability to maintain a sense of personal identity. He takes pride in his skill as a musician and a craftsman. He innovates lumber

transportation for Ford and impresses Epps by making a curved ax handle, which Epps has never seen. Emphasizing his intelligence and ingenuity both supports Northup's sense of individuality and the injustice at such a man being held in bondage.

Another aspect of plantation life that is rarely told in other sources is the description of the Christmas celebration. At Epps's plantation, slaves are given three days off for Christmas, a time to celebrate in "a little restricted liberty" (p. 213). Hundreds of slaves from neighboring plantations gather for one Christmas supper, and for once during the year, they eat meat, vegetables, and bread, not their measly ration of unsalted bacon and corn meal. After a meal filled with laughter, Northup plays the violin for a joyful dance. Northup reflects in the midst of this story on the comfort found in music for his companions, and for himself specifically, in his violin. Marriages were made during the holiday party, but such unions were not respected as valid by the owners of the slaves. A marriage would be beneficial to the owner of a female slave, as it would contribute to increasing his number of workers or, as it suited him, provide children who could be sold off for profit. However, if slaves lived on separate plantations, their time together would be left to the whim of each master to allow them to travel. The little freedom granted the slaves during these times of celebration was merely a pretense. Relationships formed at Christmas were easily severed by masters. The celebration itself served to inflate the master's reputation as a "generous" man, and the supper and dance were treated as spectacles for the entertainment of the many white people who gathered to watch the scene.

TREATMENT OF WOMEN

While some of the children born to enslaved women were conceived in the unions formed among slaves, many more were the offspring of their own masters. In the institution of slavery, women were subjected to abuses that male slaves had less reason to fear. Northup's book gives attention to two such characters: Eliza, whom he encounters at Williams Slave Pen, and Patsey, a fellow slave at Epps's plantation.

Eliza tells Northup her story of living a comfortable life treated well by a master who promised to free her and her children if she would live with him in a house he built for them. While she trusted her master's word and relates being treated well, her sexual servitude was coerced by her condition as a slave. She had no option for refusing her master's advances, but she had hopes in the promise of liberty for herself and her son and daughter, the latter born of her relationship with her master. A family dispute, however, led to Eliza and her children being sold and her vision of liberty destroyed. Northup relates a scene common in slave narratives—the heartbreaking separation of a mother from her children at the point of sale. The power of Eliza's agony is intensified by contrast to the happy life Northup describes in his first chapter, before he is shockingly ripped from his own devoted wife and beloved children. When Eliza herself is sold, her tremendous grief inspires Eliza's purchaser to offer to buy her daughter, Emily, as well. The response by the slave trader Theophilus Freeman indicates the fate that awaits the child: "There were heaps and piles of money to be made of her, he said, when she was a few years older. There were men enough in New-Orleans who would give five thousand dollars for such an extra, handsome, fancy piece as Emily would be, rather than not get her" (p. 87). Eliza dies in despair never knowing what happened to her children.

Patsey is an exceptional person, admired for her strength, skill, and joyful spirit. She also, as Northup observes, "wept oftener, and suffered more, than any of her companions" (p. 189). Like Eliza, Patsey attracts the lustful attention of her master and, as a result, the jealousy of her mistress. She is whipped frequently, and she asks Northup repeatedly to kill her so that her misery will be ended. Northup encourages her to avoid Epps at one point, which results in Epps threatening Northup with a knife. The desire to help his fellow slave is not enough; when Patsey is accused of having an affair with a neighboring planter, Northup himself is forced to whip her.

He cannot in this instance practice the deception of a near miss that he uses as a driver in the field—Patsey is brutally tortured and her back is split open by the blows delivered first by Northup and, when he refuses to move any more, by Epps until he is fully exhausted and Patsey no longer moves under his whip. Patsey survives this whipping but is forever changed. Both Eliza and Patsey long for freedom, and Northup comments on their stories as evidence to refute common arguments that slaves are incapable of understanding the injustice of their condition.

MORAL REFLECTIONS ON SLAVERY

Many authors of slave narratives were restricted in their moral commentary and reflection on the institution of slavery by interference of the white editors who were instrumental in getting an audience to a speaking engagement or getting a text to press. Frederick Douglass was asked by his mentors, William Lloyd Garrison and John A. Collins, to tell the truth plainly and to leave interpretation to them. When introducing Douglass at events, they would emphasize his body over his mind, asking him to show the scars on his back to corroborate the story he told. Harriot Jacobs, author of *Incidents in the Life of a Slave Girl* (1861), in a "Preface by the Author" (signed "Linda Brent" to protect her identity as a fugitive), includes assurance that her words are "strictly true" and have not been exaggerated; indeed, she says, she has withheld some details of the most horrible abuses out of kindness to the reader who might be overwhelmed by the full reality of her experience (p. 5). Her preface expresses reluctance to tell her story, which is easier left unspoken, and a fear that her limited education has made her "incompetent to such an undertaking" (p. 6). Despite these constraints, both Douglass and Jacobs address the moral degradation inherent in slavery.

Douglass describes a kind mistress who speaks gently, looks him in the eye, and begins to teach him to read. She has not been raised a slaveholder and only married into that lifestyle. Douglass observes the dehumanization of this woman by her connection to the evil institution, by which she receives an education in "irresponsible power" (p. 32):

> Slavery proved as injurious to her as it did to me. When I went there, she was a pious, warm, and tender-hearted woman. There was no sorrow or suffering for which she had not a tear. She had bread for the hungry, clothes for the naked, and comfort for every mourner that came within her reach. Slavery soon proved its ability to divest her of these heavenly qualities. Under its influence, the tender heart became stone, and the lamblike disposition gave way to one of tiger-like fierceness.
>
> (p. 37)

Douglass portrays the slave owner as a monster created by the depravity of slavery itself, which strips both slaves and masters of their humanity. A distorted moral code is pushed upon this woman, who must contort her conscience to align with a worldview that holds slavery to be benevolent and necessary.

Jacobs explains to her intended audience of white female readers that slavery not only corrupts the slave owner but removes the possibility of moral actions from the enslaved: "But, O, ye happy women, whose purity has been sheltered from childhood, who have been free to choose the objects of your affection, whose homes are protected by law, do not judge the poor desolate slave girl too severely!" (p. 83). Telling the story of how, at age fifteen, she deliberately attracted the attention of a white man, she reminds the reader that she would have liked to keep herself "pure" but that she feared that she would be forced into a sexual relationship with her master. Entering into a sexual relationship with a man of similar status to her master, she hoped, would protect her from rape and from the retaliation of her jealous mistress because the master would respect another white man's claim to Jacobs' body above her own refusal (p. 84). Within the system of slavery, the slave has no freedom to make moral choices. Sexual relationships, even if they appear to be consensual, are shaped by denial of an individual's rights to her own body. Although she has been taught right from wrong, she tells the reader, slavery is a powerful demon that holds her in its grasp. The fight to survive overwhelms all other moral concerns.

The narratives of Douglass, Jacobs, and Northup demonstrate how chattel slavery corrupts all it touches. Northup comments on the moral bind of slavery, but his imagery is less stark, a mark of the narrative's balanced and reliable testimony according to Wilson. In his editor's preface, Wilson describes Northup's "fortune" at being owned by multiple masters, "men of humanity as well as of cruelty" (p. xv). Northup's life of freedom, choice, and independence for so many years contributes to a broader perspective from which to judge the conduct of his masters and to render faithfully "a correct picture of Slavery, in all its lights and shadows" (p. xvi). Northup himself promises to "repeat the story of my life, without exaggeration" and to leave the judgment and interpretation of his story to others (p. 18). He reiterates this commitment to objectivity at the end of the book, announcing, "I have no comments to make upon the subject of Slavery. Those who read this book may form their own opinions of 'the peculiar institution'" (p. 321). These announcements belie a complex sense of morality woven throughout the story, in which assumptions about slaves are challenged, cruel slave owners are demonized, and the sins of kind masters are gently revealed.

Northup's family relationship to slavery is complicated. Although Northup was born a free man, his father was born a slave to the family of Henry, the man who would eventually be instrumental in rescuing Solomon from slavery. The shared surname of the two Northup families indicated a strange familial connection through ownership of humans. It is tempting to interpret the emancipation of Mintus Northup as an act of kindness, but that generosity is only enacted on the death of his owner, who presumably benefited from the servitude of Mintus to his last day. Mintus communicated his own feelings to his young children: "although at all times cherishing the warmest emotions of kindness, and even of affection towards the family, in whose house he had been a bondsman, he nevertheless comprehended the system of Slavery, and dwelt with sorrow on the degradation of his race" (p. 20). While Southern slave owners had a personal stake in defending themselves against accusations of cruelty, Northerners in free states—who held their own racist beliefs and also benefited from consumption of goods produced by Southern slave labor—were apt to minimize the injustice of the institution. Stories of affection and loyalty between masters and slaves were popular, and as Northup notes in his book, Northerners were unlikely to witness the mistreatment of a slave firsthand. Slavery in the city was much different from plantation slavery. Those bondsmen whom Northup met "were always dressed well and well provided for, leading an apparently easy life, with but few of its ordinary troubles to perplex them" (p. 25). Here Northup presents a common perception of the well-treated slave who benefits from the care of his owner and lives a relatively carefree and comfortable life. He does not deny this condition but rather assures the reader that despite the lack of physical abuse, each person longs for freedom. The desire for liberty is not born out of the avoidance of pain but rather a deep desire to live as fully human.

Northup's insistence that enslaved people understand and desire liberty subverts the narrative of benevolent slavery prevalent in arguments against abolition, and his description of kind masters, rather than showing the "light" side of slavery as Wilson's preface suggests, contributes further to this subversion. Northup has an abundance of praise for his first master, William Ford, the epitome of the kind slave owner. Ford speaks compassionately to his slaves and appreciates their work. His upbringing, rather than his character, is blamed for the moral blind spot he has toward slavery. In his book, Northup excuses Ford for this flaw and suggests that had he revealed his true identity as a free man, Ford might have assisted him instead of beating him or selling him off quickly as others might do. Ford's slaves hold affection for him and work even harder in hopes of pleasing their master and hearing his words of approval. Considering Northup's book as a work of persuasion on behalf of the abolitionist cause, the rhetorical appeal of such a generous approach is clear. Readers who have social or ancestral connections to slave owners would undoubtedly know examples of good and kind people who nonetheless "never doubted

the moral right of one man holding another in subjection" (*Twelve Years a Slave*, p. 90). It would be difficult for these people to look on their friends and relatives as evildoers, and so the stories of cruel and violent slave drivers might seem irrelevant to what was perceived as the larger, more morally upright, population of slaveholders. Northup's complex approach allows for both the cruel and the humane, arguing that both are inherently immoral while withholding personal condemnation of individuals.

Although Northup speaks so highly of Ford's kindness, his placement under the authority of Tibeats undermines any kindness Ford has displayed and subtly implicates the "kind" master in the behavior of the cruel. Ford's limited moral vision allows him to consider the treatment of Northup and others in economic terms. While Ford prospers, he can treat people well and shelter them from the "remoter depths of Slavery" (p. 91). But when he becomes "embarrassed in his pecuniary affairs," his human property is merely an asset to be exploited; he sells eighteen slaves. Northup, as a consequence of Ford's financial troubles, is sold to Tibeats, who is known to employ physical abuse. When Northup refuses to be whipped and attacks Tibeats, Chapin, an overseer who looks after Ford's interests (Ford holds a mortgage on Northup and loses it if Northup dies), looks after Northup (then called Platt) and prevents Tibeats and his cronies from killing him in retaliation.

While this act saves Northup's life, Chapin's kindness—and Ford's by extension—is undermined by the events that follow. Northup spends the rest of the day tied up and standing in the blazing sun. He cannot move his limbs because they are so tightly bound, and the rope with which Tibeats would have hanged him remains around his neck. Concerned that Tibeats might return, Chapin stands watch, intent on defending Northup's life "at whatever hazard." This puzzling distortion of care and protection is inexplicable to Northup as he reflects on it years later:

Why he did not relieve me—why he suffered me to remain in agony the whole weary day, I never knew. It was not for want of sympathy, I am certain. Perhaps he wished Ford to see the rope about my neck, and the brutal manner in which I had been bound; perhaps his interference with another's property in which he had no legal interest might have been a trespass, which would have subjected him to penalty of the law.

(pp. 119–120)

Northup describes his long, torturous day with no freedom to move or rest, with no food, and with no water but a small cup that a fellow slave, Rachel, takes personal risk to bring him. On the arrival of Ford, who cuts him free, Northup thanks God for his kind master. This horrible scene denies all possibility that the protected and supported slave of a benevolent master lives a happier life than a free black man. It is Northup's protector who submits him to agony for hours, weighing the property rights of another white man over the pain of the human before him. With this scene, Northup convicts not only the slaveholder but also the "benevolent and well-disposed men" in the Northern states who argue that African Americans are safer and more content within the best manifestations of slavery than in the struggles inherent in a free life. In Northup's meditations, slavery corrupts goodness and makes evil seem virtuous, destroying the morality of good white men as it crushes the bodies of black men and women. The reader has insight into the moral struggle that Northup himself faces as he tries to understand and communicate his experiences through his personal sense of justice. The moral reasoning he employs demonstrates an adeptness at navigating racial politics, to remain in the favor of white men while also asserting his own subjectivity. Northup's experience as a free businessman, respected by both black and white people, may have enhanced his ability to survive his imprisonment and also contributed to his ability to escape—had he demonized all white people he might never have trusted Bass to communicate on his behalf.

Fascinating to nineteenth- and twenty-first-century readers alike, *Twelve Years a Slave* is an engaging account of a man's trials and survival, embodying an American ethic of fortitude and perseverance. In its time it served as a compelling rhetorical appeal to those who might use their privilege to end the evil institution of slavery. In our time it offers both historical

evidence to enhance our understanding of a volatile period of U.S. history as well as a literary text that transcends genre. Scholars now recognize the significance of antebellum slave narratives in the history of American literature and African American literature, and Solomon Northup's work occupies an important position in that history.

Selected Bibliography

WORKS OF SOLOMON NORTHUP

Twelve Years a Slave: Narrative of Solomon Northup, a Citizen of New-York, Kidnapped in Washington City in 1841, and Rescued in 1853, from a Cotton Plantation near the Red River, in Louisiana. Auburn, N.Y.: Derby & Miller; Buffalo, N.Y.: Derby, Orton, and Mulligan; London: Sampson Low, Son, 1853. http://docsouth.unc.edu/fpn/northup/northup.html

CRITICAL AND BIOGRAPHICAL STUDIES

Davis, Charles T., and Henry Louis Gates, Jr., eds. *The Slave's Narrative.* Oxford and New York: Oxford University Press, 1985.

Drake, Kimberly. "On the Slave Narrative." In *Critical Insights: The Slave Narrative.* Edited by Kimberly Drake. Ipswich, Mass.: Salem Press, 2014. Pp. xvi–xxxi.

Finkenbine, Roy E. "'Who Will . . . Pay for Their Sufferings?': New York Abolitionists and the Failed Campaign to Compensate Solomon Northup." *New York History* 95, no. 4:637–646 (fall 2014).

Fiske, David, Clifford W. Brown, and Rachel Seligman. *Solomon Northup: The Complete Story of the Author of "Twelve Years a Slave.*" Westport, Conn.: Praegar, 2013.

Green, Tara T. "Black Masculinity and Black Women's Bodies: Representations of Black Bodies in *Twelve Years a Slave.*" *Palimpsest: A Journal on Women, Gender, and the Black International* 4, no. 1:1–23 (2015).

Jones, Ginger. "Solomon Northup: Twelve Years a Slave, Forever a Witness." In *Critical Insights: The Slave Narrative.* Edited by Kimberly Drake. Ipswich, Mass.: Salem Press, 2014. Pp. 31–42.

Olney, James. "'I Was Born': Slave Narratives, Their Status as Autobiography and as Literature." In *The Slave's Narrative.* Edited by Charles T. Davis and Henry Louis Gates, Jr. Oxford: Oxford University Press, 1985. Pp. 148–175.

Sanson, Jerry Purvis. "More Than *Twelve Years A Slave:* The Enduring Legacy of Solomon Northup." *Southern Studies* 22, no. 1:1–15 (2015).

Stauffer, John. "12 Years Between Life and Death." *American Literary History* 26, no. 2:317–325 (summer 2014).

Worley, Sam. "Solomon Northup and the Sly Philosophy of the Slave Pen." *Callaloo* 20, no. 1:243–259 (winter 1997).

OTHER SOURCES

Douglass, Frederick. *Narrative of the Life of Frederick Douglass, an American Slave.* Boston: Anti-Slavery Office, 1845. http://docsouth.unc.edu/neh/douglass/douglass.html

Jacobs, Harriet Ann. *Incidents in the Life of a Slave Girl, Written by Herself.* Edited by L. Maria Child. Boston: Published for the author, 1861. http://docsouth.unc.edu/fpn/jacobs/jacobs.html

Stowe, Harriet Beecher. *Uncle Tom's Cabin; or, Life Among the Lowly.* Boston: John P. Jewett, 1852. http://utc.iath.virginia.edu/uncletom/uthp.html

————. *A Key to Uncle Tom's Cabin.* Boston: John P. Jewett, 1854. http://utc.iath.virginia.edu/uncletom/key/kyhp.html

FILMS BASED ON THE WORK OF SOLOMON NORTHUP

Solomon Northup's Odyssey. Teleplay by Lou Potter and Samm-Art Williams. Directed by Gordon Parks. *American Playhouse,* PBS, 1984.

12 Years a Slave. Screenplay by John Ridley. Directed by Steve McQueen. Regency Enterprises, 2013.

OLIVE HIGGINS PROUTY

(1882—1974)

Elaine Roth

A MOTHER STANDS in the rain peering through the window of a mansion to witness her own daughter's wedding. A woman recovers from a mental breakdown at a beautiful institute in the mountains. A man lights two cigarettes in his mouth and passes one to his female companion. These are some of the moments and subjects for which Olive Higgins Prouty is known: motherhood, mental health, and repressed love affairs. With these images and others, she made a permanent impression on the U.S. imagination in the first part of the twentieth century.

Over a career that spanned almost forty years, Prouty wrote ten novels, two of which were adapted into well-known films, *Stella Dallas* (1925 and 1937) and *Now, Voyager* (1942). She also penned a memoir and a collection of poetry. Prouty created a world of debutante balls, bridge games, and WASPs with nicknames. But she populated that elite world with conflicted characters who break engagements to be married, seeking meaningful work instead, and who shy away from forced social events, preferring the peace of the outdoors. Deeply invested in the narratives of families, more so than romance, Prouty also valued the newly emerging field of psychiatry, championing it as a useful resource.

BIOGRAPHY

Olive Higgins Prouty was born in Worcester, Massachusetts, on January 10, 1882. Her father, Milton Prince Higgins, was president of the Norton Emery Wheel Company, one of Worcester's largest employers, and a trustee of Worcester Polytechnic Institute. Her mother, Katharine Chapin Higgins, was an early advocate for and eventual president of what is now the Parent Teacher Association (PTA). Thus Olive,

along with her two brothers and a sister, grew up in a prominent, well-to-do family with two professionally successful parents in a predominantly blue-collar city. After being anointed class poet at her high school and graduating from Smith College with a bachelor's degree in literature in 1904, she married Lewis Prouty in 1907 and went on to take a writing class at Radcliffe, where she began the short stories that became her first novel, *Bobbie, General Manager* (1913).

The Proutys moved to Brookline, Massachusetts, and by the time she published her first book, the couple had two children, Richard and Jane. Two more daughters, Anne and Olivia, died within a year of their births. After Olivia's death, Prouty completed *Stella Dallas* (1923), but later suffered some form of psychological collapse. Her recovery took place at the Austen Riggs Foundation in Stockbridge, Massachusetts, which was the model for the institutions depicted in her novels *Conflict* (1927) and *Now, Voyager* (1941). Prouty's last novel was *Fabia* in 1951, followed by a memoir, *Pencil Shavings*, in 1961. Her comfortable material circumstances allowed her to contribute generously to various philanthropic endeavors, one of which, an endowment at Smith College for a scholarship for promising young writers, was won by Sylvia Plath, to whom Prouty was particularly dedicated during Plath's own early breakdowns.

BOBBIE, GENERAL MANAGER

Prouty's first novel was published in 1913, when she was thirty-one years old and the mother of two small children. An episodic narrative, probably because it began as a series of stories, *Bobbie, General Manager* often reads like the journal

of a teenager. Told from the perspective of an adolescent girl, Lucy Vars (Bobby is a nickname), the novel features characters who initially play significant roles, like her older brothers, but later recede, while minor characters, like her sister, grow in importance. The effect feels very much like the lived chronicle of an actual family.

Narrated in the first person, the novel begins with Lucy running a motherless household of five siblings, with two older brothers, Tom and Alec, two younger twin brothers, and a little sister, Ruth. By the fourth chapter, a family friend and local doctor, Will Maynard, suggests that Lucy should be sent to boarding school. This triggers an intense social phobia on Lucy's part, a theme which recurs throughout Prouty's work. Returning home after the death of her father, Lucy finds that her role as the "general manager" of the household is to be supplanted by her brother Alec's new wife. The second act of the novel follows Lucy's attempt to live as an unmarried woman in what was formally her own home. There are intimations that the difficulty of this situation will resolve itself into marriage with Dr. Maynard. However, Lucy rejects his proposal, much to her family's dismay. In the third act of the novel, the couple reunites, quickly marries, and sets up house in a college town. The final narrative challenges involve visits from her brother's wife, as well as concern about her sister Ruth, who is engaged to a wealthy man, Breckenridge Sewell, or "Breck," whose mother disapproves of the marriage. Toward the end of the novel, Lucy conspires with the fiancé's mother to disrupt the engagement. In response, Ruth moves to New York and becomes a suffragette. In the final chapter, a happy ending is created when Ruth becomes engaged to a different suitor, Robert Jennings, and Lucy finally conceives a child.

THE FIFTH WHEEL

Prouty's second novel, published in 1916, takes the unusual approach of returning to the characters from her first novel and telling the second half of the story from the perspective of a different character, Lucy's sister Ruth, who played only a minor role in *Bobbie, General Manager*. *The Fifth Wheel* diverges from the first novel's happy ending when Ruth breaks her engagement with her second beau, Robert (Bob) Jennings, and decides instead to return to work for the suffrage movement. Ruth's commitment to this cause has alienated her from Bob, who insists that Ruth not read shocking novels. While Ruth initially complies and in fact burns one novel under dispute, she ultimately chafes under his more conservative view of gender relations. (Very subtly, it is also suggested that Bob's affections may be complicated by his close relationship with his mother, with whom he lives.)

While Ruth appeared to be a superficial social climber in *Bobbie*, in *The Fifth Wheel* her perspective characterizes her time as a debutante as a brief preamble to her real life. She had dallied for many years with the wealthy Breck Sewall, who asked her to marry him but wanted to keep the engagement secret because he suffered qualms about introducing Ruth to his established family. In addition, it turned out that Breck was hiding a secret: he was already married.

Having rejected two proposals, Ruth moves to New York City, where she encounters severe financial difficulties. In a useful coincidence, she eventually finds gainful employment working as a secretary for none other than Breck's mother, who earlier opposed their union. Despite their awkward history, the two women recognize each other's skills, and work together successfully for several years.

The novel resolves when Ruth moves back home to care for her brother Oliver's children. She becomes enchanted by her nieces and nephews and is suddenly concerned that she has missed her own opportunity for a family. The novel's ending quickly delivers two life-changing pieces of news: Ruth has reunited with Bob (whose mother has died), and Mrs. Sewall has died and left Ruth a substantial amount in her will. Like *Bobbie, General Manager*, the novel ends with hopefulness for Ruth's happiness.

This decision to revisit the same story in a different novel is reflected by innovations in the novel's perspective: while mostly delivered from

Ruth's first-person point of view, there are occasional chapters from Lucy's point of view, as well as one in the third person. In chapter 13, titled "Lucy Takes Up the Narrative," Lucy returns as narrator for six chapters, until chapter 19, "Ruth Resumes Her Own Story." Lucy also narrates the novel's last three chapters. While the promise of visiting the same material from the perspective of another character is an interesting approach, in the end, the shifting perspectives may make it hard for readers to feel close to Ruth.

THE STAR IN THE WINDOW

Prouty's third novel, *The Star in the Window* (1918), leaves the Vars family behind. Only two of Prouty's novels tell stories she had no desire to return to; this is one (the other is *Conflict*). All of her other novels follow either the Vars family or the Vale family. (She hoped to develop *Stella Dallas* further but was prevented from pursuing that project by an unauthorized radio serial.)

In this novel, as in the later novel *Now, Voyager*, a young woman, Reba, is tyrannized by an imposing female figure—in this case, Aunt Augusta, who holds sway over the household. Reba's father is unduly influenced by Aunt Augusta, and Reba's mother is a tyrannical invalid (a recurring figure in Prouty's work) confined to a wheelchair. Their domestic monotony is disrupted by a visit from a far-flung cousin, Patience Patterson, a single woman who loves to travel and who encourages Reba to break free of her family bonds. Representing freedom and license, Cousin Pattie is one of the only female characters in Prouty's oeuvre who is both overweight and portrayed positively. Unrepressed in all arenas, verbally as well as physically, Cousin Pattie informs Reba that there is money from her grandfather waiting for her in a safe deposit box.

The determination that has allowed Reba to endure her oppressive family life now allows her to extricate herself from it, and she moves to a rooming house in Boston run by the Women's New England Alliance. There she blossoms, enjoying classes such as gym and domestic science and going to organized dances, where she meets an uneducated sailor missing several fingers.

The next two acts of the novel, uncharacteristically for Prouty, follow the strange romance of Reba and Nathaniel, who is perhaps even more socially awkward than she. He narrates his rough upbringing. They attend movies together. Nathaniel is about to return to sea when Reba's brief spate of intellectual growth and pleasure is disrupted by Aunt Augusta, who announces that she can no longer care for Reba's mother and Reba must return home. Reba, devastated by this prospect, seizes upon the possibility of quickly and secretly marrying Nathaniel as a form of sanctioned escape. They stage a fast wedding and part ways. While tending to her cantankerous mother, she envisions her marriage as a hidden avenue to freedom.

But when Aunt Augusta resumes caring for Reba's mother, releasing her to return to Boston, Reba begins to view her marriage as a restriction. She wonders if it can perhaps remain a secret forever and she can carry on working for the Women's Alliance. After meeting Dr. Chadwick Booth, she falls in love with him before finding out that he is married. When this is revealed to her, she joins him for dinner to confront him, but finds his cavalier attitude toward marriage so appalling that she leaves in the middle of their meal and walks a great distance to town, contracting typhoid fever along the way. Recovering back at home, she grows to appreciate the care of her Aunt Augusta. She also decides that perhaps her marriage doesn't need to be a secret after all.

Meanwhile, unbeknownst to Reba, Nathan has been bettering himself in order to be a worthy mate. Taken under the wing of the minister who married them in Boston, Nathan flourishes in San Francisco, all the while pretending to Reba to be traveling the seas. But when war is declared, Nathan enlists. In her memoir, Prouty describes being preoccupied by the war while writing this novel, which only becomes apparent toward its end. In the final chapter, Nathan and Reba reunite and enjoy a few weeks together before Nathan is deployed, whereupon the family decides to enact the title of the novel and put a star in the window for him.

OLIVE HIGGINS PROUTY

GOOD SPORTS

Prouty's *Good Sports*, a collection of nine short stories, came out in 1919, after she had published three novels but before the publication of her fourth, *Stella Dallas*. Moving between female to male protagonists, shifting from third-person to first-person perspectives, the stories depart from Prouty's novels in several ways, including the fact that they are more explicitly pedantic. There are lessons to be learned in *Good Sports*. A father learns to recognize the professional ambitions of his daughter in "Catalogues" (the daughter is rewarded for this recognition with college catalogs). Meanwhile, hearty athletes learn to recognize the forbearance of the chronically ill in "Pluck." The scenario for "Pluck" is familiar: a man and a woman on an outdoor expedition find themselves alone together in an impromptu shelter (as happens also in *Now, Voyager* and *Home Port*). However, "Pluck" also features admiration for an invalid, whereas Prouty otherwise tends to portray invalids as tyrannical whiners. This uncharacteristic appreciation is echoed in "Broken Ribs," which follows a young man's capitulation in marrying his fiancée after she survives a terrible car accident, although he had planned to break the engagement moments before the crash. As a result, the otherwise wayward young man learns the importance of caring for others, particularly those less able. As in "Pluck," the female invalid is painted in glowing terms, a portrait Prouty never includes in her novels.

In "Why," a young single woman who feels like an outsider in her own community finds her place during World War I in France, only to be killed by shrapnel. Prouty resolves a similar story differently in "Unwanted Lucretia," in which a young single woman who feels like an outsider in her own community is rescued by virtue of her pluck and entertaining writing skills by the romantic interest of a wealthy bachelor. Family members and acquaintances who previously took Lucretia for granted learn a lesson and belatedly acknowledge her value once she has married. The most pedantic story is "Strategy," in which a mother deeply committed to celebrating holidays overhears her adult children bemoaning her

investment in gathering the family for these occasions. The mother promptly retires from such endeavors, but falls into poor health (self-induced, according to the logic of the story), while her family actually misses the festive rituals. Lesson learned, the family gratefully gathers to celebrate Christmas in the final scene. In "From Mars," a recovering veteran finds solace with a woman who has similarly served on the European front of World War I.

The two oddest stories are both told in the first person. In one, "Fifteen Dollars' Worth," Prouty adopts a working-class (as well as male) perspective, complete with dialect, to follow a travelling salesman's trips to a young spinster who enjoys entertaining U.S. troops during World War I. In the final story of the collection, "War Bride," a young single woman distracts herself from loneliness by imaging the life of the French soldier for whom she knits slippers. Written almost in verse, like a poem or a song, the story ends with the French soldier's death.

Taken as a whole, this collection allows Prouty the freedom to adopt a wider range of voices and perspectives than she explores in her novels, which typically follow privileged upper-class lives. In addition, Prouty indulges more freely in judgment in these stories, as opposed to her novels, which often explore multiple perspectives, even on controversial issues like fidelity, and rarely reproach her characters or foreground pedantry.

STELLA DALLAS

Prouty's fourth novel is the work for which she is most remembered. Published in 1923, *Stella Dallas* had phenomenal narrative traction throughout the middle of the twentieth century. The story began as a serial, and Prouty was paid $8,000 for eight installments. These segments became a novel that was quickly adapted into a play, with a script Prouty contributed to but did not care for in its final version. The novel was also adapted for the cinema three times, but again, Prouty approved of neither of the versions made during her lifetime. Finally, the novel was also turned into a radio soap opera that ran for

eighteen years. This adaptation proved the most problematic, in that it was carried out initially without Prouty's permission or even knowledge. Prouty had herself hoped to write a sequel, a desire that seems particularly earnest coming from an author who wrote her first two novels about one family and went on to write five novels about another family. Unfortunately, other writers got to extend Stella Dallas' story before Prouty could. Furthermore, because Prouty was not associated with the radio production in any way, she never received appropriate royalties despite its longevity and success. Years after the radio serial began, she was finally paid $19,500 as the result of an extended legal battle, including an instance in which she herself was served papers.

Stella Dallas follows the life of the eponymous Stella. Born working class, she eschews the humble origins of her family and strives instead for social mobility and beauty. Fairly well educated, she serves as an entertaining diversion for Stephen Dallas, whom she meets shortly after graduating from high school while he is working at the metaphorically named Cataract Mill. Unlike Stella, who is from Cataract, Stephen has fled there in the wake of his father's suicide, convinced his professional and personal ambitions have been dashed. As a result of his abandonment, Helen, the young woman he had been wooing, marries a man thirty-three years older than herself. Stella and Stephen marry after a short four-month courtship and quickly have their daughter, Laurel. As Stephen proves himself at the factory and pursues his ambitions as a lawyer, his professional and personal ambitions return. He finds Stella's pleasure in flirtation and her inability to identify class distinctions depressing. Eventually reunited with Helen, whose older husband has died, he lives separately from Stella and Laurel, spending time with Laurel for a month in the summer (a scenario Prouty revisits in a father-daughter camping team in her later novel *Home Port*).

Narrated from the perspectives of Stella, Laurel, Stephen, and Helen, the novel paints a complicated portrait of Stella as intermittently entertaining and vivacious but also artificial and limited. (Prouty further judges Stella for gaining weight, unlike Helen, who retains her girlish figure even after having four children.) Stella aspires to social recognition for her daughter but inexplicably cannot grasp the role she herself must play for that scenario to work, a role that would necessitate subtlety and marginalization. Instead, Stella continues to enjoy male attention, although the novel reassures us that she is essentially innocent and does not engage in or even imagine any actually disreputable behavior.

Stella is a fascinating character because she contains inherent contradictions; it is no wonder this figure could be developed for eighteen years in a radio serial. She is so excessive that every resident of the summer hotels she and Laurel frequent notices and mocks her, yet she remains sufficiently attuned to nuance that she outfits Laurel in appropriate and tasteful clothing. The disconnect is inexplicable, although it fundamentally turns on Stella's own pride and self-satisfaction. Ultimately, as many feminist film critics later noted, Stella refuses to be relegated to the margins of her own narrative. Prouty objected to the stage version of *Stella Dallas* because she thought the character of Stella was too exaggerated, serving up a working-class caricature for laughs. In contrast, Prouty created a complicated character, occasionally sympathetic and internally at odds.

Stella Dallas begins when Laurel is thirteen, old enough to recognize the rift between her separated parents and canny enough to notice that she and Stella, with whom she primarily resides, are being rebuffed by the elite members of the upper middle class that Stella would like to woo. The very first chapter of the book stages the eventual parting between mother and daughter that is the novel's central preoccupation and the image for which the film adaptations are remembered. The novel ultimately ends with Stella's belated recognition that her daughter can only achieve the social acceptance Stella desires for her if Stella absents herself. She considers suicide, but instead decides to convince her daughter to live with her father and his new wife. Laurel, however, refuses out of loyalty to her mother. So Stella performs a series of acts of disaffection in order to drive Laurel into her

father's arms. Stella stays away when she knows Laurel will be home; misses appointments with Laurel; and finally, and most dramatically, takes up with a man for whom she has no affection, Alfred Munn, whom she knows both Laurel and Stephen loathe for his lack of taste. Stella's performance of desire and lack of maternal affection works, and Laurel moves to live with her father and Helen, who are able to afford a coming-out party that launches Laurel into an established social register. Stella, meanwhile, married to an alcoholic she does not love, refusing to accept the support that Stephen continues to send, lurks outside Stephen and Helen's home, hoping for a glimpse of Laurel's success.

Painted as a model of tact, Helen unceasingly praises Stella's taste to Laurel and refuses to allow her husband to demonize his former wife, all while recognizing the failures of taste that will prohibit Stella and thereby Laurel from achieving social acceptance. When Stella proposes that Laurel live with Helen and Stephen, Helen alone understands the emotional toll this wreaks upon Stella. Their alliance represents not only a cross-class connection but also a daughter's fantasy of multiple mothers entirely dedicated to her well-being.

In 1923, when *Stella Dallas* was published, the motion picture industry was still in its infancy and films were still silent. During the 1920s, 30 percent of screenwriters and directors were women, and perhaps more importantly, the cinema was conceived of as a female diversion; the viewing audience was presumed female and films were designed correspondingly. Prouty wholeheartedly absorbed the power of this new medium in her novel. Early in the second chapter, while Laurel is visiting her father at Helen's house, Laurel has the following revelation when she walks in upon an assembled group as her father gazes adoringly at Helen: "It was like a scene at the 'movies' . . . only it was real! . . . She looked at her father. Suddenly the room faded, disappeared, and a close-up of his face dawned on the screen before her, as it were. . . . Laurel had seen too many close-ups of faces not to recognize that look!" (p. 42). The extent to which cinematic conventions, including camera distance, inform Laurel's understanding of family, affection, and desire is notable. Later in the novel, recognizing that Stella has become a virtual stalker of Laurel from afar, Helen insists on leaving the blinds open so that Stella can gaze upon her daughter from the street. Interestingly, Stella's and Helen's actions further reinforce the emphasis on spectatorship found throughout the novel, and in particular a female audience viewing a female object.

Audiences were quickly able to enjoy the novel as spectators themselves when it was adapted to film in an early silent version of *Stella Dallas* (1925) just two years after its publication. This film, which is not the most famous of the three adaptations, focuses more on Stephen's story than does the novel. Written by Frances Marion, one of the best-known women screenwriters of the era, the film begins by establishing Stephen's wealth and his budding relationship to Helen, which is thwarted by his father's suicide. Stella is introduced only after Helen, and then as a member of an impoverished family. In a scene taken from the novel, she attempts to camouflage her family's poverty by growing attractive flowering vines around the home. While the novel proposes this scene as a passing interest of Stella's, and consistent with her investment in aesthetics, the silent film's intertitles characterize this act as a devious plot to entrap Stephen in particular. After they marry, Stella refuses to follow Stephen to New York, unlike the novel, in which Stephen chooses to leave Stella and Laurel behind. Repeatedly, the film works to vilify Stella and valorize Stephen. In addition, Stella's grammar indicates that she is uneducated, a quick method to indicate her class status, but one that Prouty disliked on both stage and screen, since she felt it was untrue to Stella's character.

The second *Stella Dallas* film (1937), directed by King Vidor, is the adaptation for which the novel is famous, largely based on the strength of Barbara Stanwyck's performance as Stella. Stella is portrayed as working class and, again, specifically intent on wooing Stephen Dallas, having followed his activities in the newspaper; she devises elaborate schemes in order to interact with him. In contrast, in the novel, while Stella does attend college classes solely to meet upwardly mobile men instead of men who work

in the factory, she lays no plot for Stephen in particular.

This film includes a significant departure from both the novel and the other film adaptations, when, years after their separation, Stella amends her ensemble in order to appeal to Stephen. Stephen drops by unexpectedly on Christmas Eve, hoping to spend time with Laurel. In response, Stella dashes into her bedroom and trims the ruffles off a dress, returning to join him with an understated appearance that she understands is in keeping with his preferences. Despite Stella's success in anticipating Stephen's (and thereby his social class's) dictates for women's clothing, their time together is ruined when Ed Munn shows up drunk, disrupting the possibility of a family reunion. Most tellingly, however, this recognition and responsiveness to Stephen's taste flies in the face of the rest of the narrative, as Stella goes on to inadvertently make a spectacle of herself, humiliating Laurel.

After Stella once again refuses to join Stephen in New York, she relies upon Ed Munn for entertainment, which further alienates her from Stephen and Laurel. The film features several famously poignant scenes that are classics of the melodrama genre. One is a failed birthday party for Laurel, with a table laid out with places for partygoers who never arrive; over the course of the scene, mother and daughter's anticipation and excitement turn to disappointment as they belatedly recognize they are being shunned.

Over and above the powerful emotion of that scene, the image for which *Stella Dallas* is most remembered is a strength-in-pathos moment at the very end of the film, which also appears in the silent 1925 version. In the novel, Helen and Stephen stage a coming-out ball for Laurel at their home. In the film, they host Laurel's wedding to an upper-class man, before which Helen carefully pulls up the blinds, knowing that Stella will not want to miss viewing her daughter at this significant event. Meanwhile, Stella stands outside in a crowd in the rain, disrupted in her voyeurism by a policeman forcing her to move along. Lacking all of the sartorial frippery that caused her such unwelcome visibility in the past, suddenly rendered virtually as a homeless woman, Stella stalks off into the darkness, both crying and triumphant in the ascendance of her daughter. This scene of mixed emotions was central to an extended discussion among feminist film scholars almost fifty years later.

The extent to which Stella herself is complicit in her own abjection was taken up in a celebrated debate in the mid-1980s in *Cinema Journal*, a top film studies journal, by feminist film critics such as Linda Williams, E. Ann Kaplan, and Christine Gledhill. Kaplan decried the self-abasing ends to which Stella must descend in order to launch her daughter, while Williams argued that the film revealed the contradictions inherent for women under patriarchy, rather than reveling in them. As rich as this debate was, several aspects of the novel and film were neglected. For one, focusing on maternal masochism overlooks that the novel operates not only as a mother's manual but also a daughter's fantasy, in which the mother never seeks an adult life outside of caring for her child and never actually desires a partner. In the novel, all such desires are false, staged only in order to accomplish more for her daughter. And in fact, not just one but two mothers are utterly devoted to this daughter. The crucial role of Helen and her relationship with Stella was underappreciated until a 2015 article by Kristi Branham, "'Two Mothers United': Interclass Female Friendship in *Stella Dallas*," brought this important connection to light. As Branham's title suggests, Helen and Stella forge an important and unusual cross-class alliance, joining forces to serve the child. While it might be tempting for a resistant reader to judge thin Helen for maintaining the principles of conventional femininity while Stella struggles with weight and rules that she cannot discern, Stella and Helen nonetheless unite in their dedication to Laurel, as well as their recognition of each other as devoted mothers.

A later remake, titled *Stella* (1990), had a hard time conveying the rigid social hierarchy of the original text, despite an energetic performance by Bette Midler as Stella. In this version, Stella, who works in a bar, refuses to marry Stephen when she becomes pregnant, implying to him that she will have an abortion. Instead, she delights in her daughter, but recognizes, as her

daughter becomes an adolescent, that she will face rougher circumstances in her neighborhood than in the social milieu of Stephen and his new wife. The film ends with the famous scene of maternal renunciation, this time outside her daughter's wedding in Manhattan's Central Park, at Tavern on the Green.

CONFLICT

Conflict and *The Star in the Window* are the only two Prouty novels that are not part of a series created by Prouty or others (as in the case of *Stella Dallas*). *Conflict* (1927) is a curious novel, essentially a tragedy, charting the downhill course of both Sheilah Miller and her husband, Felix Nawn. In this work, Prouty allows herself to fully explore an unhappy marriage; she further mentions in her memoir that the adolescent episode in the novel was an autobiographical one. It is no wonder she never chose to return to this narrative.

The novel opens with the characters as teenagers. Felix pursues Sheilah, and although she has no affection for him, a combination of pity and circumstance renders her unable to rebuff his advances, despite the fact that more popular, fun, and attractive boys, such as Roger Dallinger, also extend invitations to her. Sheilah dislikes everything about Felix, from his clothes to his looks to his name, which she considers not sufficiently "American." Nonetheless, she withstands his overtures, although they take a mental toll on her, and she suffers a breakdown. Her sympathetic parents take her to Europe to relieve the strain. Her mother is concerned but overbearing—and also, damningly for Prouty, overweight—while her father is kind but passive. The unhealthy dynamic with Felix continues upon her return to the States, even into college, where he fails out because he dedicates too much time creating an unattractive gift for her. When Felix enlists in the military for World War I, Sheilah agrees to marry him, both because he looks so pathetic in uniform and because she's convinced that he's going to die in the war.

But Felix doesn't die. Instead he returns and marries Sheilah and they have four children, three of whom survive and all of whom Sheilah is convinced resemble Felix in looks and temperament. Felix is unsuccessful at work and the family struggles. When Sheilah, on the verge of another nervous breakdown, runs into an old acquaintance, Cicely Morgan, she tells her: "*This is what life has done to me, Cicely.*" Cicely, who has not married, due to an unrequited lifelong crush on Roger Dallinger, springs into action, finding summer camps for Sheilah's three children, a new wardrobe for Sheilah, and a place for Sheilah at Avidon's, a recuperative institution in the mountains that resembles Cascade, the sanitarium that plays a large role in *Now, Voyager* (and which in turn resembles the Austen Riggs Foundation, where Prouty herself had recently spent time). Coincidentally, Roger Dallinger is also a patient at Avidon's, and he and Sheilah begin one of Prouty's many compromised love affairs.

When Sheilah returns home, she and Roger maintain a correspondence through letters, which Felix eventually discovers. Meanwhile, Felix has resorted to fraud at work, continuing his practice of cheating in high school. Rather than resenting her affair, Felix realizes that he has trapped Sheilah in an unhappy marriage. Unable to imagine resolving his problems in any other way, Felix commits suicide by throwing himself in front of a train. The novel ends with the promise of Sheilah and Roger uniting in the future.

The unremitting descent of the novel serves as a caveat against cross-class marriage, like the one that Fabia Vale considers throughout the five novels dedicated to the Vale family with which Prouty follows *Conflict*. While there is a gesture toward a happy ending, it comes at such a high cost (Felix's very life) that it is hard to appreciate. Ultimately the novel feels like a revisiting of an adolescent impasse or, again, a warning against unpropitious unions.

WHITE FAWN

With *White Fawn* (1931) Prouty launched an exploration of the Vale family of Boston, a subject that was to generate five novels and a well-received film adaptation, *Now, Voyager*. Readers familiar with later installments of the

Vale saga will take special notice of the minor characters in this first installment who later receive novels of their own. There's Charlotte, the maiden aunt, delivering an important piece of advice to a love-struck niece. (She'll reappear later when she stars in *Now, Voyager*.) There's Lisa, another model mother in the vein of Helen from *Stella Dallas*, enduring a marriage to an older man but in love with a man her own age. (Will her current husband die in time for her to have a second family with the man she actually loves? Again, we have to wait for *Now, Voyager*, the third installment, to find out.) This series also allows Prouty to revisit issues she had raised before but not fully developed, such as: is it possible for couples to overcome significant class differences? In *Conflict* and *Stella Dallas*, the answer is no. In *White Fawn*, Prouty considers resolving that question differently.

White Fawn follows the debutante Elizabeth Fabian Vale, known as Fabia. The novel opens with Fabia struggling with the pressures of the social circuit, more comfortablein a nature than at a soiree, walking her dog before the coming-out dance her family is holding for her later that day. While Fabia's story generates the primary narrative of *White Fawn*, her mother Lisa's story provides a significant subplot. Fabia has insisted on this ill-timed walk because she is reeling from having witnessed her beloved mother in an embrace with one of her father's associates. However, Fabia's attentions are startled from this dramatic revelation when her dog is mortally wounded in a hit-and-run accident. Grief-stricken, Fabia must nonetheless host the party shortly afterward, while simultaneously trying to tend to her dying dog in the basement. An unknown, handsome young doctor appears at the house to help minister to her and the dog, but then disappears just as mysteriously. Meanwhile, Fabia, obsessed with enacting justice for her dog, remembers the license plate of the car and searches for the driver. Who of course turns out to be none other than the handsome young doctor, Dan Regan, who had been unable to stop at the time because he was racing to surgery. Guilt-stricken, he later returned from the hospital to discover the dog's fate. Along the way, Fabia

meets his working-class Irish parents. As she and Dan begin a relationship, both her family and his medical associates recommend against their union. Lisa warns Fabia their social circle will never accept her or her children, while Dr. Warburton, the doctor Dan works for, tells Dan not to marry a rich woman because she will resent his commitment to his profession in the face of her wealth. In addition, Dr. Warburton states that while Dan himself might be able to rise in social class, he could only do so by cutting off his salt-of-the-earth family, who have already been introduced as sympathetic characters and whom Dan refuses to abandon.

Meanwhile, Lisa nurses what she believes is a secret love for her husband's business associate, Barry Firth, not knowing that Fabia has witnessed their embrace. Accordingly, Lisa does not understand why her adolescent daughter is suddenly behaving strangely toward her. Lisa wants to believe that her affair is legitimate because she doesn't love her husband, because Barry doesn't love his wife, and because neither of them are prepared to act on their desires. Instead, they primarily admire each other from afar. When Barry's wife becomes ill and may die, Lisa reaches a crisis in her relationship with him, fearing that if he were not unhappily married, he could break off with her and pursue a more satisfying relationship with an unmarried woman. She encourages her husband to transfer Barry to Chicago, then sinks into a depression. This crisis coincides with her steadfast advice to Fabia to seek a more appropriate marital partner than Dan.

Fabia and Dan accordingly break their engagement, but are both miserable. Fabia ultimately devises a plan whereby they navigate their class differences by escaping to the West Coast, where their disparate status will be less visible. The novel ends with the promise of reconciliation between the two. Meanwhile, Barry's wife has in fact died, but Lisa remains in her marriage, hoping that Barry will be able to move on even though she is still in love with him. This first novel of five focused on the Vale family opens many story lines and does not fully

resolve any of them, although Fabia and Dan receive a happy ending of sorts.

LISA VALE

The title of Prouty's second novel in the five-part series on the Vale family seems to promise an investigation of Lisa's story, last seen resolutely married to Rupert while in love with Barry, but instead *Lisa Vale*, published years later in 1938, resumes right where *White Fawn* left off, with Fabia and Dan's story. Like *The Fifth Wheel*, this novel takes up shortly after its predecessor and complicates what looked like a happy ending. Fabia and Dan are once again alienated from each other, a result of Dan's commitment to his job and family, Fabia's jealousy, and their different perspectives, a difference the novel suggests is based on class values. Meanwhile, Lisa continues to struggle with her hidden love for Barry Firth, worries about Fabia's affection for Dan, particularly since she seems so miserable, and, later in the novel, is threatened with blackmail by an acquaintance of her oldest son, Rupert, Jr., who goes by "Windy."

When one of Windy's cousins impregnates a working-class girl, the girl and her family attempt to frame Windy and ask for a large sum of money, in yet another example of the perils of social classes mixing. The Vales are hit with this blackmail effort just as Rupert, Lisa's husband, has lost the family fortune in an ill-advised business venture. In addition, Windy has come down with a malady that Lisa at first appreciates, since it removes him from public scrutiny for a while, but then fears he will die from, and which eventually is diagnosed as infantile paralysis, or polio. He loses mobility in one arm and leg, but by the end of novel he is nevertheless cavorting in the pool with a large group of friends.

Rupert's (and his sister Charlotte's) mother, Mrs. Vale, is introduced as a serious antagonist in this novel when she threatens to sell the family home in which Rupert, Lisa, and their entire family reside unless Fabia breaks her engagement with Dan Regan. In contrast, Barry Firth emerges as a savior figure, finagling a way for Lisa and her family to continue residing in the home. The only casualty in this dynamic is Rupert, who, upon hearing of Barry's successful machinations to save their family home, has a heart episode from which he does not fully recover. At the end of the novel, he sits as an invalid, watching his newly recovered son swim in the pool.

It is a bittersweet resolution to the central narrative conflict of the novel, the suppressed love affair between Lisa and Barry. Readers hoping for Rupert's demise—he is painted in exclusively unflattering terms—will be disappointed by his resilience at the end of the novel.

NOW, VOYAGER

Prouty's second-most-famous novel (after *Stella Dallas*), *Now, Voyager* (1941), follows the dramatic transformation of Charlotte Vale from dumpy maiden aunt into glamorous mistress and benevolent overseer of not only her lover's daughter but also a children's wing of Cascade, a restorative clinic. Thanks to psychiatry and the devotion of Jeremiah Dorrance (who goes by J.D.), her unhappily married love interest, Charlotte rallies against her tyrannical mother and develops a satisfying life of her own. By then an established author, Prouty was promised $50,000 by Warner Bros. studios for screen rights to the novel if it sold fifty thousand copies in the six months after it was published, and $40,000 if it didn't (it didn't, and she received $40,000).

In the two novels about the Vale family that precede *Now, Voyager* (*White Fawn* and *Lisa Vale*), Charlotte has appeared as a near-wraith, whispering warnings to Fabia to pursue her love for Dan Regan regardless of class differences rather than relegate her desires to her family's imperatives, which, as it turns out, was Charlotte's story up to that point. Opening with a line from a Walt Whitman poem, one which we later learn has been given to Charlotte by Dr. Jaquith, her psychiatrist, the novel begins with Charlotte in recovery from a nervous breakdown after a long stint at Cascade, on a cruise that another acquaintance, Renée Beauchamp, intended to take but had to cancel at the last minute. Outfitted in Lisa's clothes and Fabia's

OLIVE HIGGINS PROUTY

shoes, Charlotte is initially misrecognized as Renée; unwilling to return to her true identity, she employs a series of aliases throughout the novel (as does Murray Vale later in *Home Port*). She and her new beau decide upon Camille as a nickname, which he later references by sending her camellias after the cruise. Meanwhile, her love interest also has several names: while he goes by J.D. with friends, he is also called Jerry.

Charlotte's transformation is first physical, as Prouty notes approvingly that she has lost thirty pounds during her time at Cascade. As a result, she now fits into Lisa's dresses and is thrust into new visibility on the cruise as an attractive single woman with a great wardrobe. She looks nothing like earlier photos, and people who met her as recently as two years ago cannot recognize her. However, like many a Prouty protagonist, she struggles psychologically to maintain confidence. Prouty describes Charlotte's difficulties navigating social situations, her newfound pleasure at being received warmly, and the social awkwardness she experiences after years of serving as her elderly mother's domestic companion.

Charlotte's mother is the chief antagonist of the novel, having served as a major antagonist to Fabia in the previous novel, *Lisa Vale*, and according to the logic of the novel, she is the primary reason for Charlotte's nervous breakdown. A fading matriarch, Mrs. Vale dominates Charlotte, unwittingly relegating her to the margins of society. Given Mrs. Vale's inability to read social conventions, she resembles Stella Dallas to some degree, though with more wealth. Alternately ambitious for Charlotte but also undermining her by dictating her clothing choices and overseeing her appearance, Mrs. Vale is a formidable force. Unlike Aunt Augusta from *The Star in the Window*, a similarly tyrannical presence, she never relents. However, similarly to Mrs. Sewall from *The Fifth Wheel*, in perhaps her only benevolent action she wills large sums of money to the women in her family when she dies, with the bulk going to Charlotte. (This inheritance allows Charlotte to endow the children's wing at Cascade.) Appreciated chiefly for her impressive legacy, Mrs. Vale is the most powerful of the bad mothers in Prouty's novels,

wielding a cruel tongue and demanding complete subservience from her daughter. Charlotte's careful, polite negotiation away from her mother's grasp is one of the primary pleasures of the novel. Meanwhile, her mother suffers a fall after an argument with Charlotte and is tended to by none other than Dan Regan, for whom she develops a strong affection and to whom she leaves a generous amount in her will.

Another narrative thread of the novel is Charlotte's love story, which is compromised from beginning to end. Chapter 5 includes a flashback to an earlier cruise that Charlotte took with her mother, during which she became enamored of Leslie Trotter, an officer on the ship. Because he was beneath the Vales in social class, Charlotte's mother opposed the union and successfully undermined it. However, Charlotte mourns the breakup of her only true relationship until she meets J.D. on another cruise. ("Why, it was just as if life were repeating an old pattern! She must see to it it didn't repeat the whole pattern!" [p. 34]). Despite the fact that J.D. is married, after he describes his unhappy circumstances they kiss several times. Prouty goes to great lengths to redeem these moments, much like the kiss between Lisa Vale and Barry Firth in *White Fawn*. While Charlotte does not initiate them and attempts to prevent them from happening again, she does respond to J.D.'s warmth. Nonetheless, the two resolve to never meet again.

Charlotte returns home and begins a relationship with Elliot Livingston, a local widow with two young boys. They become engaged and Charlotte enjoys his attentions, but like Ruth in *The Fifth Wheel*, she worries about Elliot's conservatism; he is shocked, for instance, by some of the novels she reads. (Meanwhile, Charlotte herself wonders why she isn't more embarrassed by the subject material in John Steinbeck's work.) Regardless, Charlotte has relegated herself to a marriage of friendship when J.D. unexpectedly reappears at a Boston party, reminding Charlotte of the nature of true passion. Failing to generate that together, Charlotte and Elliot eventually decide to break their engagement, Elliot saddened that he has not been able to win over Charlotte's affections. Charlotte's

187

mother, extremely disappointed by this revelation, suffers a stroke and then dies. (Given the negative portrayal of Mrs. Vale, the chief strike against Elliot might be the fact that Mrs. Vale approves of him wholeheartedly.)

Along the way, *Now, Voyager* addresses Lisa Vale's earlier predicament: Rupert has died and Lisa is now happily married and pregrant with Barry Firth's son, her fifth child. The novel ends with Tina, J.D.'s youngest daughter, ensconced in Charlotte's home; Charlotte takes her up after the two meet at Cascade. Although she has promised Dr. Jaquith that her relationship with J.D. will not continue, she and J.D. share the rewards of raising a child together, a pleasure that Isobel, his wife, one of Prouty's many demonized mothers, relinquishes readily. Overseeing the new children's wing at Cascade, and happily engaged in Tina's life, complete with multiple dogs, Charlotte rebuffs J.D.'s attempt to rekindle their romance with a famous line, which also provides the film adaptation's ending: "Don't let's ask for the moon! We have the stars!" (p. 263).

The film version of *Now, Voyager* (1942), released just a year after the novel, was the adaptation of which Prouty most approved, perhaps because she helped work on the screenplay. She particularly appreciated Claude Rains's portrayal of Dr. Jaquith (and he does seem to be enjoying himself). The film begins in chapter 8 of the novel, a flashback to Charlotte's original breakdown, triggered by the teasing of June, Lisa's daughter. (While both novel and film work to redeem June, her cruel behavior toward her aunt does undermine Lisa's canonization as an otherwise exemplary mother).

As a visual medium, the film spends more time reveling in Charlotte's makeover, conducted with aplomb by Bette Davis (who also convincingly plays a teenaged Charlotte falling in love with Leslie Trotter). The film anticipates the entrance of Bette Davis as Charlotte, overweight, with heavy eyebrows. But after a breakdown and a stay at Cascade, Charlotte makes a second appearance, this time fully recognizable as Bette Davis, with upswept hair, plucked eyebrows, and a thin figure. In fact, both of Prouty's film adaptations, *Stella Dallas* and *Now, Voyager*, involved

fat suits for the actresses, reinforcing her intense investment in female thinness, an edict mirrored by Hollywood; in contrast to Bette Davis slimming down, Barbara Stanwyck must grow increasingly heavy over the course of *Stella Dallas*.

The film also foregrounds Charlotte's love affair with J.D., here called Jerry, played by Paul Henreid (probably best known for his role as Ingrid Bergman's husband in *Casablanca*, and whose German accent is never explained). Unlike the novel, and despite the prohibitions of the Production Code, the film implies that their relationship has been consummated. A scene in which Jerry joins Charlotte on the balcony outside her hotel room the night before she leaves to return to the United States is followed by a scene in which Jerry gives Charlotte camellias. The juxtaposition of the two shots, omitting as it does an intervening scene from the novel, in which Charlotte rebuffs Jerry and returns to her room alone and locks the door, suggests that the flowers represent a carnal as well as romantic connection.

The film delivers many of the pleasures of the "woman's film," from extensive attention to Charlotte's wardrobe to a fantastically devoted partner, as well as foregrounding the contradictory messages surrounding midcentury femininity. For example, the primary reason Charlotte agrees to marry Elliot is to have a family of her own, even though most of the actual mothers in the film, including Mrs. Vale and Jerry's wife, are portrayed negatively.

HOME PORT

Like *Now, Voyager*, *Home Port* (1947) opens with an epigraph from a Walt Whitman poem, this time "O Captain, My Captain." This is the only Prouty novel narrated almost exclusively from a male point of view, that of Murray Vale, Lisa Vale's second son and her youngest child with Rupert.

The novel begins with an exciting and protracted action sequence: our young adult narrator washes up on shore, unable to recall the events that brought him there. He camps, hikes, and sleeps in the woods, slowly remembering a

boat wreck during a storm at the boys' summer camp where he is a counselor. He and another young camp counselor capsized, and Murray was unable, despite his best efforts, to save the other boy, who drowned. When Murray eventually emerges from the woods, ashamed and afraid that he was responsible for the boy's death or will be met with this charge, he flees, spending much of the middle portion of the book on the lam. As in *Now, Voyager*, the protagonist uses a series of aliases: Tom Brown, Tom Jones, Eliot Jones, Joe Jones. In addition, his nickname has long been "Bug," thanks to his interest in naturalism.

After a physical and psychological collapse, like many a Prouty protagonist, he eventually finds a job working as a guide in a hunting camp in Maine, where he begins to thrive after a long history of playing second fiddle to his more dashing older brother, Windy (Rupert, Jr.). Emerging from that shadow, as well as from the ignominy of having survived the boat wreck, Murray begins to enjoy himself in Maine, particularly after the arrival of Nora and her father, Sam. Like Stella Dallas, Nora is being raised by divorced parents. She and her mother live itinerantly in hotels, while her father seems to be modeled on Stella's boyfriend Alfred Munn—alcoholic and crass, if more benevolent than Munn. Murray, using the pseudonym Joe, and Nora enjoy hiking and fishing together, as well as indulging in what they call psychotherapy sessions.

Toward the end of the novel, this outdoorsy idyll is disrupted when members of his own family, including his mother, Lisa, coincidentally show up at the camp. Nora confesses the subterfuge to Lisa, as well as their plans to marry. In the end, Murray, who continues to conceal his identity from all but his mother and Nora, joins the navy after he and Nora have a son, Murray Victory Jones.

While *Home Port*'s plot maintains an energetic drive, perhaps as a result of the male protagonist—unlike his sister, Fabia, Murray does more than wait for the phone to ring—there are also odd moments. For one, there is an unconvincing attempt to introduce a detective plot, with evidence from the original shipwreck tracked

through the novel by an amateur sleuth. Prouty surely means for the damage on Murray's watch to reveal that he did in fact attempt to rescue his companion, but this connection is never clearly established to the reader.

In addition, the ending of the novel is disconcertingly inconclusive. Murray ceases to narrate, and the third-person perspective shifts to Nora and Lisa. Neither have heard from Murray, who is at sea involved in World War II maneuvers, and both are worried about him. The novel ends without resolving that concern. Although Prouty's next—and final—novel, *Fabia*, takes up the same family narrative and thus could resolve this dilemma, *Fabia* is set before *Home Port*, with the result that the question of whether or not Murray survives the war is never answered.

FABIA

Prouty's last novel, published in 1951, begins with another epigraph of poetry, this time by Alice Meynell, a British poet and suffragist. Beginning ten years earlier, in 1941, *Fabia* uses World War II as a dramatic backdrop. The novel returns to Fabia, Lisa's oldest daughter; in an introduction, Prouty claims that readers have long asked for an update on Fabia's status.

While *White Fawn* ends with Fabia's reconciliation with Dan Regan, and *Lisa Vale* follows their tumultuous engagement and final break, *Fabia* opens with our protagonist trapped in a chaste but long-term love affair with an older married doctor, who physically resembles Dan Regan. Oliver Baird is in one of the bad marriages that abound in Prouty novels; his jealous hypochondriac wife, Irma, resembles Isobel from *Now, Voyager*, who is married to J.D., Charlotte's love interest, and Emma from *Lisa Vale*, who is married to Barry Firth, Lisa's love interest. On top of those unflattering characteristics, Irma has a "chunky body which she had let get too fat" (p. 114), truly a moral failure in Prouty's universe. By contrast, Lisa is Prouty's only female perspective on being trapped in an unhappy marriage.

Oliver has two teenage daughters and is twenty-five years older than Fabia. He feels he cannot leave his family, although this affair has

gone on for seven years when the novel begins. They justify their relationship because it has not been consummated and is thus "innocent," although they meet regularly and have developed an elaborate set of signals for each other: ringing phones and lights left on (they can see each other's respective abodes). Together they fantasize that they have a son, named Oliver, after his father. The novel begins with Fabia's point of view as she waits for Oliver to call and is disappointed when he doesn't. This scenario resembles the many hours Fabia spent in earlier novels hoping that Dan would call. The plot gets going when Lisa discovers Fabia's affair. Then, Renée Beauchamp, a minor character in several of the novels, volunteers that she squandered her youthful love life on an older married man who retired rather than marrying Renée after his wife died. (This story is echoed several times; apparently Miss Fogg, one of Rupert Vale's secretaries, similarly fostered an unrequited affection for him for years.) It is also revealed that this is Oliver's second love affair with a nurse; before marrying Irma, he was almost engaged to a nurse whom he loved but who was beneath him in social class. Unbeknownst to him, his sister interfered in the engagement and discouraged the nurse from pursuing her brother with the unintended result that the nurse committed suicide. Oliver now carries that guilt as well. (Prouty helpfully uses psychiatry to explain Oliver's dilemma: "His mother was responsible" [p. 126].)

Once again, the novel employs multiple perspectives; we hear from Fabia, waiting for the phone to ring; Oliver, wracked with guilt over his responsibilities not only to his family but to Fabia; and Lisa, torn by her daughter's unhappiness and uncertain how to proceed. All the characters accidentally meet at a party at Renée Beauchamp's. Both Oliver and his wife have been invited; Lisa has decided to attend in order to meet Oliver; and Fabia spontaneously crashes the party, having impulsively dropped by Renée's apartment. Oliver's wife, Irma, is so disturbed by this encounter that she and her husband quarrel when they get home. To reconcile with her, Oliver joins her in bed, which rarely happens. When Irma becomes pregnant, Fabia finally

breaks up with Oliver. To add insult to injury, she is blackmailed by her landlady for having an affair.

Once the affair has been discovered, Oliver insists on speaking to Lisa in order to explain himself; the two try to organize an end to the relationship. Lisa encourages Oliver to feign an interest in someone else, while Dr. Jacquith, or "Jake" (Charlotte's therapist from *Now, Voyager*, who seemingly tends to everyone in the novel), suggests that the affair be flushed out into the light of day, believing it cannot withstand visibility. Renée secretly hopes that Irma will die, thus freeing Oliver, although she acknowledges that this would be a fairy-tale solution.

Prouty resists fairy-tale possibilities, instead dragging her characters through bad behavior, however well intentioned, and years of regret. Oliver allows himself to consummate the relationship with Fabia. Fabia is thus doubly betrayed when she learns that Irma has become pregnant. (It is of great moral significance to Oliver, who is never given the opportunity to explain to Fabia that his encounter with Irma occurred before his encounter with Fabia.) The final crushing blow for Fabia is that Irma and Oliver's child is named Oliver, the fictional name that she and Oliver had given their imagined child for years.

Fabia seeks a position as a military nurse after the attack on Pearl Harbor and is stationed in Europe, where she encounters Dan Regan at a dance in a grand hall, in a scene reminiscent of their first meeting. Although Fabia tells Dan about her affair, including its consummation, he continues to pursue her and proposes again. The novel ends with Renée's revelation to Fabia that Oliver deliberately tried to break Fabia's heart by naming his child Oliver in order to end their relationship, knowing that no amount of persuasion would suffice. This piece of information helps Fabia recognize the depths of Oliver's love and, according to the logic of the novel, move on to a relationship with Dan Regan. After mooning for Oliver throughout their seven years together, Fabia quickly switches to swooning with regret for not having spent those years with Dan instead.

The novel stages several ethical dilemmas that continue to have weight decades later, includ-

ing whether older men should date younger women, and whether extramarital relationships of the heart are inherently wrong. Prouty answers the second question differently in different novels: for Barry and Lisa, no; for Oliver and Fabia, yes.

PENCIL SHAVINGS

Like many of her novels, Prouty's memoir, *Pencil Shavings* (1961), begins with an epigraph from a poem, this time by Robert Frost. The work goes on to reflect and echo many of the themes of her novels, from generational accounts of a large family to Prouty's investment in material objects and redecoration; much of the final part of the memoir is taken up with renovations of family homes. Prouty presents herself as a difficult child, one made unhappy by the unattractive front of her substantial family home. While her novels sympathetically portray the sufferings of adolescents and their social anxieties, in her memoir Prouty judiciously switches stances and acknowledges the challenges she must have posed to her parents as such an emotional child. As is her style throughout her novels, Prouty maintains an ability to reflect upon an issue from multiple perspectives. But whereas Prouty's novels abound with terrible, controlling mothers (Charlotte Vale's mother), terrible, infirm mothers (Barry's and J.D.'s wives), or saintly mothers (Helen Morrison Dallas; Lisa Vale), with Stella Dallas as a blend of both, her own mother is presented as complicated and nuanced. Sympathetic to her difficult daughter, Prouty's mother led a professional life of national significance, helping establish the PTA, first in Massachusetts and then nationwide.

Prouty's memoirs share her preoccupation with family; it takes her 90 pages of a 230-page memoir to graduate from high school, while pages 200 on are dedicated to her later life interests of dogs and rehabbing houses. The novels that made her famous and brought her wealth play a fairly minor role.

Writing of the mental breaks she suffered as an adolescent and again after the death of her youngest daughter, she describes her experiences with typical New England calm. But unlike *Now, Voyager*'s clear contention that Charlotte's mother has caused her mental distress, Prouty's difficulties have less obvious sources; she portrays her parents as indulgent and kind, and notes that her second breakdown occurred almost two years after the loss of her daughter. Late in life, her stalwart husband, long suspicious of mental illness, himself declined into a state of anxiety from which he never recovered.

CONCLUSION

Olive Higgins Prouty's strengths as a writer are many. Her most significant literary innovation may be her receptiveness to psychiatry. If such therapy is available primarily to the very wealthy, she nonetheless delivers narratives sympathetic to the fragility of the human mind as well as its capacity for recovery. Her straightforward accounts of the aid therapists bring her characters have a contemporary ring, anticipating the widespread recognition of this field almost a century after her early novels were written.

In addition, she clearly relishes approaching narratives from a range of vantages, so that the superficial social butterfly in *Bobbie, General Manager* returns in *The Fifth Wheel* as a thoughtful young woman, trained into the social milieu but hoping to participate in something larger and more significant, like the national suffrage movement. This expansive perspective prevents Prouty's novels from descending into morality tales or cheap sentimental narratives. Instead, they reflect the complexity of characters who grow and develop.

Correspondingly, her accounts of families resemble actual families, with strong emotional heights and breaks, followed by quiet reconciliations that seem to be accomplished more by the passage of time than any explicit resolution. Again, Prouty resists using characters as types—the bad brother, the sad spinster—but instead describes them differently in different moments across the swath of a lifetime. If, as a result, the characters feel unstable, they also feel familiar.

Consistent with Prouty's willingness to create unstable characters, another of her unique

narrative strengths is the instability of her narratives and plotlines. More than half of her novels feature broken engagements, two of which disrupt the previous happy endings of earlier novels. She restlessly resists closure and traditional endings, which surely helped her to return to the same material.

Despite these thematic and formal innovations, Prouty remains firmly associated with the category of middlebrow fiction, beneath true literature but above pulp fiction. There are several reasons for this. One is that Prouty's investment in the domestic realm and her largely female protagonists align her with sentimental fiction, very much the province of the middlebrow, with its female characters and presumed female reading audience. In addition, Prouty's preoccupations are steadfastly quotidian. She values material objects and domestic questions, rarely connecting them to larger social issues. While women's suffrage plays an important part in her first two novels, and many characters struggle toward meaningful lives, the subject, for instance, of women's work, which she raises repeatedly in her own memoir, is never central to her novels, largely because her characters are insulated by their elite social class. Finally, her novels include little interiority. Notwithstanding the internal musings that fiction allows, Prouty's work generally features dialogue and action. Occasionally, the hand of the author is felt too clearly. Minor characters emerge to play a specific role and then recede abruptly (we leave a learning-disabled boy, Danny, lost in the woods in *Home Port*, never to be referred to again, while a new maid in *Lisa Vale* steps forward to deliver some significant advice, only to disappear completely afterward). There are also minor lapses: it is unclear whether Lisa's time line adds up, for instance. After having four children with Rupert and raising them to adulthood, then nursing him through his convalescence, she apparently still has time to have a second family with Barry after Rupert dies (so that Fabia has a much younger brother, Christopher) and still appear younger than Oliver, Fabia's older paramour.

Despite her relegation to the middlebrow category, and regardless of her occasional (and largely inconsequential) lapses, Prouty produced a rich, complicated, forward-thinking body of work. Her novels seized the popular imagination and continue to provide lasting images that characterize the twentieth century. Sylvia Plath, who benefited from the scholarship that Prouty endowed at Smith College, as well as Prouty's support during one of her breakdowns, was inaccurate in her cruel parody of Prouty's writing in *The Bell Jar*, in which Plath thinly disguises Prouty as Philomena Guinea. "'How could Donald marry her when he learned of the child Elsie, hidden away with Mrs. Rollmop on the secluded country farm? Griselda demanded of her bleak, moonlit pillow.' These books earned Philomena Guinea, who later told me she had been very stupid at college, millions and millions of dollars" (p. 41). Plath indicts Prouty on several levels: for lurid prose, for commercial success, and for academic failure. To begin with the latter charge, it is easy to imagine Prouty, who disliked the limelight and resolutely avoided all publicity for her work, demurring about her college career. More significantly, there are no melodramatic plots in Prouty's work, beyond some contrived coincidences. There are no hidden children, no women longing to marry. Instead, young women are wary of the proposals that come their way, delaying as long as possible and frequently breaking engagements. While all three film versions of *Stella Dallas* end with the marriage of Laurel Dallas, the original novel ends simply with her coming-out party. Prouty would never stage the marriage of a teenager; by contrast, she suggests that marrying young was a mistake for Lisa Vale. Finally, Prouty never received millions for her work, although she was well remunerated and would have been able to support herself as a writer had she needed to, which was true of many midcentury women authors.

It is worth noting that, like her novels, Prouty's charitable giving continued beyond her lifetime. In addition to the scholarship she endowed at Smith College, she provided funding for the Children's Hospital in Boston, in particular a children's garden; created the Olive Higgins Prouty Library Fund, which supports the Worcester Polytechnic Institute's collection in the

Humanities; and gave generously to the Unitarian Church. These projects and more all help inform Prouty's legacy.

Primarily, however, she is remembered as an author. Without drama and without excess, Prouty delivered a steady stream of nuanced, complex, ambivalent characters who continue to inform the contemporary imagination of the twenty-first century. Even those who have never seen the films or read the novel know the character of Stella Dallas, whose aspirations for upward mobility dovetail with the classic American dream. With characters like Stella and others, Prouty helped expand the landscape of twentieth-century U.S. narratives, creating space for the desires of restless, unruly women.

Selected Bibliography

WORKS OF OLIVE HIGGINS PROUTY

NOVELS
Bobbie, General Manager. New York: Frederick A. Stokes, 1913. London: Forgotten Books, 2015.

The Fifth Wheel. New York: Frederick A. Stokes, 1916.

The Star in the Window. New York: Frederick A. Stokes, 1918.

Stella Dallas. Boston: Houghton Mifflin, 1923.

Conflict. Boston: Houghton Mifflin, 1927.

White Fawn. Boston: Houghton Mifflin, 1931.

Lisa Vale. Boston: Houghton Mifflin, 1938. Reprint, New Delhi: Isha Books, 2013. (Page references are to the 2013 edition.)

Now, Voyager. Boston: Houghton Mifflin, 1941. Reprint, New York: Feminist Press at the City University of New York, 2004. (Page references are to the 2004 edition.)

Home Port. Boston: Houghton Mifflin, 1947.

Fabia. Boston: Houghton Mifflin, 1951. New York: Dell, 1951. (Page references are to the Dell edition.)

SHORT STORY COLLECTIONS AND POETRY
Good Sports. New York: Frederick A. Stokes, 1919.

Off the Deep End. N.p., 1945.

Between the Barnacles and Bayberries: and Other Poems. Worcester, Mass.: Friends of the Goddard Library, Clark University, 1997. (Published posthumously after material was released by her children.)

MEMOIR
Pencil Shavings: Memoirs. Cambridge, Mass.: Riverside Press, 1961.

PAPERS
Olive Higgins Prouty Papers. Clark University Archive, Clark University, Worcester, Massachusetts.

CRITICAL AND BIOGRAPHICAL STUDIES

Baric, Neda Rose. "Of Mothers and Mentors: Sylvia Plath and Olive Higgins Prouty." Master's thesis, University of California at Los Angeles, 1991.

Basinger, Jeanine. *A Woman's View: How Hollywood Spoke to Women, 1930–1960.* Hanover, N.H.: Wesleyan University Press, 1993.

Branham, Kristi. "'Two Mothers United': Interclass Female Friendship in *Stella Dallas.*" *Journal of American Studies* 49, no. 1:125–142 (February 2015).

Cavell, Stanley. "Ugly Duckling, Funny Butterfly: Bette Davis and *Now, Voyager.*" *Critical Inquiry* 16, no. 2:213–247 (winter 1990).

———. "Stella's Taste: Reading *Stella Dallas.*" In *Contesting Tears: The Hollywood Melodrama of the Unknown Woman.* Chicago: University of Chicago Press, 1996. Pp. 197–222.

Chandler, Karen M. "Agency and Stella Dallas: Audience, Melodramatic Directives, and Social Determinism in 1920s America." *Arizona Quarterly: A Journal of American Literature, Culture, and Theory* 51, no. 4:27–44 (winter 1995).

Christensen, Inger. "From Heroine to Harlequin: The Representation of Stella Dallas in Novel and Film." *Livstegn: Journal of the Norwegian Association for Semiotic Studies* 3:40–52 (January 1987).

Connolly, Thomas F. "How Now, Voyager? 'Proper' Bostonians on Film." *Popular Culture Review* 21, no. 1:51–60 (winter 2010).

Doane, Mary Ann. "The 'Woman's Film': Possession and Address." In *Home Is Where the Heart Is: Studies in Melodrama and the Woman's Film.* Edited by Christine Gledhill. London: British Film Institute, 1987. Pp. 283–298.

Elsaesser, Thomas. "Tales of Sound and Fury: Observations on the Family Melodrama." In *Home Is Where the Heart Is: Studies in Melodrama and the Woman's Film.* Edited by Christine Gledhill. London: British Film Institute, 1987. Pp. 43–69.

Gallagher, Tag. "Tag Gallagher Responds to Tania Modleski's 'Time and Desire in the Woman's Film' and Linda Williams's 'Something Else Besides a Mother': *Stella Dallas* and the Maternal Melodrama." *Cinema Journal* 25, no. 2:65–66 (winter 1986).

Glancy, Mark. "What Would Bette Davis Do?' British Reactions to Bette Davis in the 1940s: A Case Study of *Now,*

Voyager." *Screen* 49, no. 1:77–85 (spring 2008).

Gledhill, Christine. "Christine Gledhill on *Stella Dallas* and Feminist Film Theory." *Cinema Journal* 25, no. 4:44–48 (summer 1986).

———. "The Melodramatic Field: An Investigation." In *Home Is Where the Heart Is: Studies in Melodrama and the Woman's Film*. Edited by Christine Gledhill. London: British Film Institute, 1987. Pp. 5–39.

Holdstein, Deborah H. "*Dark Victory; Now, Voyager; The Great Lie*: Women's Pictures and the Perfect Moment." *Jump Cut: A Review of Contemporary Media* 32:22–24 (April 1987).

Hughes, Lynn Gordon. "Olive Higgins Prouty." Dictionary of Unitarian & Universalist Biography, August 25, 2000. http://uudb.org/articles/olivehigginsprouty.html

Jacobs, Lea. "*Now, Voyager*: Some Problems of Enunciation and Sexual Difference." *Camera Obscura* 7:89–104 (spring 1981).

Kaplan, E. Ann. "The Case of the Missing Mother: Material Issues in Vidor's *Stella Dallas*" *Heresies* 16:81–85 (1983).

———. "Ann Kaplan Replies to Linda Williams's 'Something Else Besides a Mother': *Stella Dallas* and the Maternal Melodrama." *Cinema Journal* 24, no. 2:40–43 (winter 1985).

———. "Mothering, Feminism, and Representation: The Maternal in Melodrama and the Woman's Film 1910–40." In *Home Is Where the Heart Is: Studies in Melodrama and the Woman's Film*. Edited by Christine Gledhill. London: British Film Institute, 1987. Pp. 113–137.

Keller, Alexandra. "From Stella Dallas to Lila Lipscomb: Reading Real Motherhood Through Reel Motherhood." *West Virginia University Philological Papers* 52:1–16 (fall 2005).

LaPlace, Maria. "Producing and Consuming the Woman's Film: Discursive Struggle in *Now, Voyager*." In *Home Is Where the Heart Is: Studies in Melodrama and the Woman's Film*. Edited by Christine Gledhill. London: British Film Institute, 1987. Pp. 138–166.

"Olive Higgins Prouty." A City of Words: The Worcester Writers Project. Worcester Polytechnic Institute, 2003. http://users.wpi.edu/~cityofwords/prouty.html

Parchesky, Jennifer. "Adapting *Stella Dallas*: Class Boundaries, Consumerism, and Hierarchies of Taste." *Legacy: A Journal of American Women Writers* 23, no. 2:178–199 (2006).

Petro, Patrice, and Carol Flinn. "Patrice Petro and Carol Flinn on Feminist Film Theory." *Cinema Journal* 25, no. 1:50–52 (Autumn 1985).

Plath, Sylvia. *The Bell Jar*. 1971. Reprint, New York: Harper Collins, First Perennial Classics edition, 1999.

Shingler, Martin. "Bette Davis Made over in Wartime: The Feminisation of an Androgynous Star in *Now, Voyager* (1942)." *Film History: An International Journal* 20, no. 3:269–280 (2008).

Siomopoulos, Anna. "'I Didn't Know Anyone Could Be So Unselfish': Liberal Empathy, the Welfare State, and King Vidor's *Stella Dallas*." *Cinema Journal* 38, no. 4:3–23 (summer 1999).

Thornton, Edie. "Teaching Style: The Pedagogy of 'Good Taste' in Olive Higgins Prouty's Early Magazine Fiction, 1909–1912." *Studies in Popular Culture* 19, no. 1:79–85 (October 1996).

———. "Fashion, Visibility, and Class Mobility in *Stella Dallas*." *American Literary History* 11, no. 3:426–447 (fall 1999

Wells, Lynn, and Winston Weathers. "Staging Nontraditional Fiction: *Now, Voyager* as a Case History." *Literature in Performance: A Journal of Literary and Performing Art* 3, no. 2:45–54 (April 1983).

Whelehan, Imelda. "'Don't Let's Ask for the Moon!': Reading and Viewing the Woman's Film." In *The Cambridge Companion to Literature on Screen*. Edited by Deborah Cartmell and Imelda Whelehan. Cambridge, U.K.: Cambridge University Press, 2007. Pp. 138–153.

Williams, Linda. "'Something Else Besides a Mother': *Stella Dallas* and the Maternal Melodrama." *Cinema Journal* 24, no. 1:2–27 (autumn 1984).

FILMS, PLAYS, AND RADIO PLAYS BASED ON THE WORKS OF OLIVE HIGGINS PROUTY

ADAPTATIONS OF *STELLA DALLAS*

Stella Dallas. Play. Adaptation by Gertrude Purcell and Harry Wagstaff Gribble. Directed by Priestly Morrison. Produced by Selwyns, New Haven, Conn., 1924.

Stella Dallas. Screenplay by Frances Marion. Directed by Henry King. Samuel Goldwyn, 1925.

Stella Dallas. Screenplay by Sarah Y. Mason and Victor Heerman. Directed by King Vidor. Samuel Goldwyn, 1937.

Stella Dallas. Radio series. Written and produced by Frank and Anne Hummert. NBC Radio, 1937–1955.

Stella. Screenplay by Robert Getchell. Directed by John Erman. Samuel Goldwyn and Touchstone Pictures, 1990.

ADAPTATIONS OF *NOW, VOYAGER*

Now, Voyager. Screenplay by Casey Robinson. Directed by Irving Rapper. Warner Bros., 1942.

Now, Voyager. Radio drama. Produced by Cecil B. De Mille. Lux Radio Theater, 1943.

Now, Voyager. Television drama. Adapted by Stanley H. Silverman. Directed by James P. Yarbrough. Lux Video Theater, NBC, 1956.

RICHARD SIKEN

(1967—)

Ryan L. Winet

RICHARD SIKEN IS a contemporary American poet, editor, and painter. He is perhaps best known for his first collection of poetry, *Crush* (2005), which was published as the winner of the 2004 Yale Younger Poets Prize. Siken's second collection of poetry, *War of the Foxes*, was published as a Lannan Literary Selection by Copper Canyon Press in 2015.

Born in 1967 in New York City, Siken earned his M.F.A. degree at the University of Arizona. Making his home in Tucson, he has pursued his poetry career while working as a social worker, mainly with disabled adults. He is also a co-founder and editor of a small literary press, Spork Press. His poetry has been recognized with two Lannan Residency Fellowships, two grants from the Arizona Commission on the Arts, and a National Endowment for the Arts Literature Fellowship. His collection *Crush* earned a Lambda Literary Award, Thom Gunn Award, and Pushcart Prize and was a finalist for both the Walt Whitman and National Book Critics Circle Awards.

Beyond his many literary accomplishments, though, Siken remains reticent about sharing details of his biography. In an interview with Legacy Russell in *BOMB*, Siken explains that the reader "gets the page" and Siken keeps the rest. When pressed, Siken reveals that when some of his poems had begun to be published, friends and acquaintances wanted him to discuss his poetry while at work, shopping, or making a stop at the bank—it is these frequent inquiries that have motivated Siken to do his best to keep his life outside of writing to himself. On more than one occasion, he has stressed that readers do not need to know anything about him in order to arrive at an understanding of his work.

THEMES AND WORLDVIEW

Siken is best-known for the raw but masterful portrayals of sex, conflict, and heartbreak that appear in his two poetry collections. Though *Crush* and *War of the Foxes* present very different aesthetics and topics, Siken has argued that these two projects emerged from a common interest in a world that he believes is defined by violence. In an interview with *Tin House*'s Peter Mishler, Siken argues that "everything in the world is actively trying to kill everything else in the world, on every level, and always has." Siken's response to a universal order red in tooth and claw is to study its various "abrasions" through poetry.

Though Siken is a decorated poet, he has turned to other media during his career. Following the publication of *Crush* in 2004, a time when Siken claims he had "nothing left to say," he returned to painting as a means of activating different creative paths. Initially these efforts proved frustrating; however, over time, Siken began to appreciate the fundamentally different ways that painters and poets represent the world. "I realized the hand could say what the voice could not," Siken told Mishler. "That helped inform the new work." Siken's choice of language here is telling: his poetry often gives voices to other characters, animals, and even inanimate objects. That a hand may "say" something different from a "voice" is to acknowledge the fundamentally different approaches to representation that attend different media; however, Siken's observation also opens up the possibility that different artistic approaches may themselves be incorporated into poetry. One of Siken's most consistent techniques in his poetic work is polyvocalism, or the inclusion of several voices into one poem. Unlike the traditional lyric, which is often associated with

the evocations of one speaker, Siken's poems often feature interruptions, interludes, and asides from other speakers. Marked by italics rather than quotes, these additional voices are both technique and philosophy in Siken's writing. Polyvocalism creates additional turns in the narrative of a particular poem and foregrounds the very abrasions that Siken believes is the focus of any proper study of the world.

In interviews, Siken has also discussed the complex relationships between his sexual identity, artistic practices, and his observations about being a gay man in contemporary American culture. One of the lengthier published discussions can be found in an interview with the *Gay & Lesbian Review*. In this interview, Siken was invited, along with fellow poets Jason Schneiderman and Aaron Smith, to a virtual panel slated to discuss everything from whether or not a "gay aesthetic" exists to the state of explicit sexual imagery in modern poetry. When asked about where poetry written by gay authors might be headed, Siken connects his own vanguard practices as a poet with the vulnerable but nevertheless unique role that many gay men and women experience in the United States. For Siken, specificity marks an important stage of poetic maturation. Observing that children begin writing poetry "full of oak trees and lakes" despite their environment, Siken argues that the discovery of a literary space that might accommodate "mac & cheese, thrift stores, their thoughts and feelings" inspires novelty within poetic practice and, by extension, opens up a safe space for gay men and women who do not fit tidily into the "dominate heterosexual template" (p. 28).

Siken also characterizes the role of a gay man as especially liminal, caught between a template of two primary genders in the United States. Not quite a masculine man and not quite a feminine woman, the "feminine male" stereotype had once relegated the gay man to the status of mere pervert; however, more recently, Siken claims to feel more like a rabbi, "drenched in the human experience" (p. 29). Rather like the figure of Tiresias, the blind prophet who had spent life as both a man and a woman, the gay poet may belong nowhere but nevertheless hear everyone.

Despite this alienation, Siken remains hopeful about the role that art plays in the construction and reconstruction of the self and the productions of new templates that may more adequately represent queer experience.

Siken's artistic career has therefore been a study in the abrasions emerging from the incomplete visions of the world that attend any individual perspective. His first book, *Crush*, is a kind of twenty-first-century bildungsroman, a coming-of-age story for a narrator who seeks out passionate encounters and heartbreak as a means of knowing others and himself. Epiphany only occurs after sex or a breakup have taken place: knowledge requires abrasion, it requires heartbreak. Siken's second book, *War of the Foxes*, combines several genres, including the fairy tale, ekphrasis (poetry about painting), and the fable, in order to meditate upon the various ways that tools and language often enable conflict and trauma.

CRUSH

Siken came to national attention when he won the 2004 Yale Series of Younger Poets competition for the manuscript that would become *Crush*. The oldest annual poetry competition in the United States, the Yale Younger Poets Series publishes a first book-length project of a poet under the age of forty, as determined by a literary judge. Though the series by definition highlights the accomplishments of relatively unknown poets, Kate Orazem lists a handful of poetic luminaries whose careers were launched by winning the prize: Muriel Rukeyser, Adrienne Rich, W. S. Merwin, John Ashbery, James Tate, Jack Gilbert, and Robert Hass. The competition is defined as much by its winners as the judges who decide upon the winners. Because there is only one person who makes the final decision on a manuscript, every judge exerts considerable influence upon the style, aesthetics, and priorities of the winners over a period of time. This authority has been, at times, marked by controversy: famously, W. H. Auden (who judged from 1947 to 1959) and W. S. Merwin (1998–2003) opted not to choose winners every year. The judges

over a period of time have also been connected, rightly or wrongly, with the fate of the poetry within the wider world of publishing as a whole: as the poet and critic Peter Davison has noted, the competition itself provided a template for a number of other prestigious prizes that emerged in the 1960s and 1970s as esteem for the award grew.

Crush was submitted during a period of relative calm for the award. This calm was owed, in part, to the proactive oversight of Louise Glück, a decorated American poet and poet laureate of the United States in 2003–2004. The poet and critic Meghan O'Rourke has praised Glück's tenure (she judged the prize from 2003 to 2010) as reviving the prestige of the prize because of her "active editing": whereas earlier judges had balked at reading manuscripts, O'Rourke reports that Glück had read approximately one hundred manuscripts per year for the prize, often encouraging authors to edit and resubmit their manuscripts. *Crush* was one of these manuscripts. According to O'Rourke, Glück and Siken worked closely together between the manuscript's time of selection and publication to reduce the length of the text and rearrange poems. Even as Glück was instrumental to the version of the book that readers encounter, it is also important to know that her editing did not fundamentally change Siken's style or his original vision for the work as a whole.

Though he remains adamant that any poetic work should stand on its own merits rather than a poet's autobiography, Siken acknowledged in a discussion with Nell Casey that the 1991 death of a boyfriend helped to inform the urgency of *Crush*. Love and lust, conquest and abandonment, desire and yearning, wonder and ennui— there are so many pins in the poet's mapping of desperate affections. Siken evokes these states through repetition, line alignments, surprising line breaks, and polyvocalism, or the incorporation of several voices into a single poem. As discussed earlier, polyvocalism marks one of Siken's signature techniques to incorporate multiple perspectives into a single poem, transforming the lyric into a forum of contradicting ideas and conversations. In her foreword to

Crush, Glück connects the considerable emotional range of the collection to Siken's characteristic long lines and irregular alignments: "In the world of *Crush*, panic is a synonym for being: in its delays, in its swerving and rushing syntax, its frantic lists and questions, it fends off time and loss" (p. vii). Each of these observations mark an important element in Siken's various poetic techniques, and in the paragraphs that follow, these formal features will be connected to the many evocations of panic and trauma that lend *Crush* its signature effects.

Though *Crush* is a work that is often autobiographical, Siken has been very careful to distance himself from the character of the poet in the collection. The literary fame afforded to Siken through his first collection also came with significant consequences: in the months and years following publication, Siken would often hear from readers that his work had depressed them despite its accomplished style. To this complaint Siken responds by insisting that the poet is different from the poetry that he makes: "They didn't see the thing," he explained to Mishler, referring to the book he had written. "They only saw me."

FORMAL CHARACTERISTICS AND THEMES IN CRUSH

In *Crush*, Siken often manipulates the pacing of a poem through repetition. These repetitions might appear in the form of a cliché, such as the refrain of "A man walks into a bar . . ." that recurs throughout the poem "Boot Theory." Repetition also sometimes takes the form of mantras and phrasing, at once registering and comforting the speaker through the trauma he has experienced. In "Straw House, Straw Dog," for instance, the number four, dreams, television sets, and Coke appear again and again in different permutations. Siken's lists and questions often carry elements of repetition. Thus the poem "Saying Your Names" derives its propulsive energy from varying the different names Siken must associate with a beloved.

One of the more characteristic features in *Crush* is not only the "swerving and rushing

syntax" that Glück identifies but also the way the poetic lines are arranged on the page. Most of Siken's poems do not adhere to the left alignment traditional to poetry and prose; rather, his language leaps and then retreats back and forth across the page, dramatizing the emotional swings of the speaker as he negotiates his panic. This freer alignment does have some precedent in the poetic tradition, most notably in the tradition of pattern poetry. (More recently, pattern poetry has been called "concrete poetry," or literary texts that derive their meaning from typographic rather than solely lexical or syntactic arrangements.) George Herbert's "Easter Wings" and "Altar" are two famous examples of this kind of poetic form: in the former, the seventeenth-century poet arranges the lines to resemble a pair of wings; in the latter, he creates the appearance of an altar through the lines of his poetry. In *Crush*, Siken does not seek out to create an identifiable shape from the poetic lines; rather, the poet freely arranges the lines across the page, presenting readers with a text that is uneven, meandering, and unpredictable. Though these decisions are typographic in nature, the lines evoke rather than signify; in other words, Siken demonstrates a keen interest in treating the left alignment that has dominated Western printing in the same way poets have treated line and stanza breaks over time, as a tool to be manipulated for stylistic effect. In addition to poetry of free alignment, Siken does include a handful of stichic poems—that is, poems without stanza breaks in the style of epic and long poetry—and one prose poem, "You Are Jeff."

In addition to free alignment, Siken also makes use of enjambment, or using breaks to divide a sentence across several lines. In the last stanza of the sixth section of "Little Beast," for instance, Siken enjambs a sentence that begins with a declaration of amorous interest and then concludes that sentence with evocations of masochism and substance abuse: "But damn if there isn't anything sexier / than a slender boy with a handgun, / a fast car, a bottle of pills." This technique not only serves to offer readers a counterpoint to the traditional, straight, masculine gaze of beauty one finds in American literature,

but it also suggests the escapades (good and bad) that have left the speaker, ultimately, at a point where his own self-destruction is impossible and he is left with nothing but totems of failed relationships as simultaneous trophies and wounds. "I couldn't get the boy to kill me," the poet concludes, "but I wore his jacket for the longest time" (p. 7).

Siken's sentences also vary considerably in length. A common tactic for the poet in the first section is to begin a poem with terse, grammatically unconnected observations. "Little Beast" begins: "An all-night barbeque. A dance on the courthouse lawn" (p. 5). Because these two sentences lack a verb or any connective grammar, the reader must infer the relationship. Both of these scenes evoke moments early in a relationship, amorous revelries in the early hours of the morning, but we are left with a building sense of dread: what fate will befall the lovers? Can such a thing last? In "The Torn-up Road," Siken follows the opening warning, "There is no way to make this interesting," with another incomplete sentence: "A pause, a road, the taste of gravel in the mouth" (p. 9). The poet declares a lack of interesting material only to provide us with details—especially the implied violence connected to the taste of gravel—as a means of at once refusing surprise but also making a larger claim about the trajectory of his relationships: failure and its corollary, violence, will happen again and again.

Another innovation is Siken's use of polyvocalism within a poem. Rather than rely upon only the voice of the poet, Siken will occasionally bestow voice upon an imagined addressee, animals, or even inanimate objects. These additional speakers are marked by italics. The poem "Unfinished Duet," as the name implies, incorporates two speakers whose aims are often at cross-purposes: "His hands keep turning into birds and / flying away from him. *Him being you.* / Yes. *Do you love yourself?* I don't have to / answer that" (p. 26). The second voice, rather than producing harmony, creates a kind of banter that forces the poet to acknowledge discomforts and silences that would otherwise go unrepresented in a lyrical poem.

In addition to these formal characteristics, *Crush* returns frequently to motifs of storytelling and narrative undercutting. In the first section of the collection, the speaker expresses profound fear—even hysteria—that any romantic connection will be destined to follow the same destructive pattern. This fear appears throughout the first seven poems in different examples of storytelling and writing. The first poem in *Crush*, "Scheherazade," takes its title from the character in *The Arabian Nights* who must, as a matter of survival, entertain her captor with a story every night as a means of deferring her demise. This poem dazzles with an array of images suggestive of a delirious whimsy and concluding with an injunction to the beloved: "Tell me we'll never get used to it" (p. 3). Death and ennui are here conflated as the same fearful conclusion for the narrator. The poet also uses stories as a means of distancing himself from the trauma associated with heartbreak and loss, though these efforts often prove unsuccessful. The final poem of the section, "Litany in Which Certain Things Are Crossed Out," portrays a poet who tries out different roles: princess, dragon, writer. Such role-playing amounts to much of the same in "Litany" as with other stories that Siken tells: the poet's efforts at artifice, at imagining himself as anything other than dragon, the monster awakened after love is experienced by the princess, ultimately fail. The poet is the writer is the dragon, and this monstrous character is the producer of the book.

In the second section of *Crush*, the poet shifts to juxtaposing vignettes that portray slightly different versions of a scene. As noted earlier, "Boot Theory" unfolds with the cliché "A man walks into a bar . . ." as its refrain. In the first vignette, the man asks the reader to take his wife, a request the reader obliges. After consummation, the reader is left "a broken man / on an ugly bedspread, staring at the water stains on the ceiling" (p. 20). At this moment, Siken informs the reader that the tenant upstairs removes one boot and, with anticipation, explains that what we're waiting for is the indication of a second shoe; instead, we hear the thudding of a second, third, and fourth shoe. This impossibility is later resolved as a metaphor for the persistence of sad-

ness, which a man (the same who has been walking into a bar over and over) may throw out only to be "left with his hands." "Boot Theory" provides a model for understanding the second section of *Crush*. The poems in this section almost universally employ repetition and slight narrative variation as a formal practice; they ultimately reveal the inescapable facts of suffering and sadness in the narrator. "A Primer for the Small Weird Loves" is a rare instance of the poet offering a glimpse into a childhood filled with terror and bullying because of his sexuality: a scene of drowning elides into scenes of sexual misadventure and even abuse; eventually, the poet will reverse roles, becoming the very character who requires forgiveness from another initiate into the world of desire.

The third section of *Crush* introduces a lyrical sequence with a reappearing beloved/adversary named Henry. The motifs of filmmaking and storytelling appear frequently in the section's first five poems, as do images of freeways and hotels. Such imagery evokes the fleeting nature of the poet's romantic attachments. The image of a bullet first appears in "Planet of Love" and continues as a symbol of stubborn attachment, an object that simultaneously marks a terrible wound but also a connection to an earlier event. Throughout the section, Siken returns to the techniques of refrain and the hypothetical; however, he increasingly employs in the poems the polyvocal technique that first appeared in the second section.

The poet also occasionally uses the language of philosophers and logicians to ambivalent effect. "It's love or it isn't," the poem declares in "The Dislocated Room" (p. 47), oversimplifying a complex range of emotions as a means of protecting himself from a possible affirmative, if qualified, answer. The third section of *Crush* also contains the only poem with true prose blocks in the entire collection ("You Are Jeff") as well as another long stichic poem, "Snow and Dirty Rain." In formal terms, the pseudo-logic of the poet in "The Dislocated Room" and the prose experiments in "You Are Jeff" foreshadow the prose poetry of Siken's 2015 collection, *War of the Foxes*.

Like many poems of the previous section, "Planet of Love" develops according to refrain and repetition: the speaker urges us to imagine different scenarios in which the second-person addressee shifts from being a star in a film to being another character who holds a gun. "Wishbone" seems to pick up exactly where "Planet of Love" left us, in which two voices discuss whether or not the poem's speaker saved a life. Another poem in this section, "The Dislocated Room," employs two voices and introduces readers to a continuing theme in the final section— the speaker's desire to discover a place safe from the consequences of desire. Freeways, road trips, hotels, and restaurants serve as correspondences for the poet's own feelings about the fleeting nature of romantic attachments, and yet, for all of these passing trials and the immense suffering of the poet, *Crush* ends on a note of determination rather than defeat. "Snow and Dirty Rain," much like "Unfinished Duet" in the second section, continues to develop Siken's emerging polyvocality. Though the poem provides a series of troubling images in its closing lines—the poet singing as Rome burns, an urgent plea for another beloved "to mash your lips against me"—Siken concludes with certainty. "We are all going forward," he avers. "None of us are going back" (p. 62). Such sentiments recall the motifs of uninteresting stories that repeat the same conclusions; however, there is also a sense that the speaker will make it through his suffering with experience—however painful—as a form of knowledge. He has learned to negotiate his way through the world, accepting that abrasion and understanding are two aspects of the same experience.

WAR OF THE FOXES

War of the Foxes (2015) marks a significant departure from Siken's first collection in both content and form. The book takes as its principal subjects the problems associated with representation, war, and violence. The collection also draws from the tradition of ekphrasis, or literature about other works of art. Siken, as an accomplished painter, photographer, and filmmaker, well understands the differences in representing subjects visually and poetically.

A decade separates the publication of Siken's critically acclaimed debut collection from *War of the Foxes*. The expectations for a second collection had been very high, as a sophomore effort following a Yale Younger Poets Prize can sometimes be difficult. The critic William Fargason has noted the considerable stylistic and thematic differences between Siken's first and second collections. "*War of the Foxes* is not *Crush*, Part II, nor should it be," Fargason argues. "Siken's newest collection is both familiar and unfamiliar to those who, like myself, fell in love with the power of *Crush*." The critic and psychologist Donna Spruijt-Metz adapts earlier praise to explain the collection: "If *Crush* was about panic, then *War of the Foxes* is about transformation. By transformation, I mean the transformation that takes place when boundaries are blurred and membranes are breached."

These blurred boundaries and breached membranes often involve genre. In addition to ekphrasis, *War of the Foxes* appropriates genres and styles as diverse as the fairy tale, children's stories, the rhetoric of proofs and theorems, and fables. Importantly, these genres and styles are not sequestered to individual poems but erupt unexpectedly. Spruijt-Metz associates the figure of the poet in *War of the Foxes* with the Trickster, a character who establishes certain rules only to undermine them. This language is echoed in the poem "Landscape with Black Coats in Snow," which features a poet haunted by his own efforts to imagine the thoughts and trajectories of other characters that he has made into enemies. At one moment, the poet acknowledges that "to hide somewhere is not surrender, / it is trickery," suggesting that for all of the different voices and genres the poet employs, he is never able to fully write himself out (or paint himself out, as the case may sometimes be) of his own landscape (p. 39). Art may present us with a door that promises an escape, but the door is always a fiction, a convenience of our thinking and emotions.

Unlike *Crush*, *War of the Foxes* is not divided into sections. However, the poems can be divided broadly into types: ekphrastic poems; philosophi-

RICHARD SIKEN

cal poems, such as "Logic," "Three Proofs," "Lovesong of the Square Root of Negative One," and "Glue"; and poems that deliberately play upon children's story titles, such as "War of the Foxes," "The Stag and the Quiver," and "The Worm King's Lullaby." The following discussion will elaborate the different formal characteristics and themes that these different poetic types play in the collection as a whole.

FORMAL CHARACTERISTICS AND THEMES IN WAR OF THE FOXES

A genre associated with magical elements and instruction, the fairy tale provides Siken with narratives and characters in *War of the Foxes* that enable quick leaps between innocence and experience, childhood and adulthood; moreover, the fairy tale, which often anthropomorphizes objects and animals, allows Siken to give voice and subjectivity to creatures and objects that would otherwise remain unspeaking elements in his poems. Take, for instance, "The Stag and the Quiver," which portrays not only two stags caught in a moment of rivalry, but also the hunter and his child. In the second section of the poem, the hunter practices shooting arrows on the trees outside his cabin. "The trees imagine they are deer. The deer imagine they are safe," the poet observes, ascribing attributes of the human to deer and tree alike. However, the poet is quick to add that "The arrows: they have no imagination" (p. 36). By depriving the arrows alone of imagination, the poet reminds us of their use as tools put to use with thinking creatures—creatures with immense capacities for violence but also, in the figure of the hunter's son, of compassion.

The enchanted, if troubled, world that Siken portrays in *War of the Foxes* is all the more counterintuitive because of the many poems that meditate upon different tools. Students of American literature have likely come across the famous section in Henry David Thoreau's essay "Civil Disobedience" that associates unthinking citizens with inanimate objects. "They are the standing army, and the militia, jailers, constables, posse comitatus," Thoreau argues, and in blindly following orders, "they put themselves on a level with wood and earth and stones" (p. 229). By juxtaposing the enchanted alongside the mechanical, the human and the inhuman, Siken brings attention to the ways that representation and, importantly, our use of words justify violent activities. Our failure to imagine different ways of using and making tools will result in more death and suffering. In this vein, Siken worries about the inhumanity of the very tools that we use to conduct war and build civilization. In the poem "Logic," Siken marshals a repeating, declaratory grammar in an effort to locate various items within appropriate categories. "A clock is a machine," the poet observes. "A gear is a tool" (p. 29). Though these efforts begin simply enough, the poet soon discovers uncomfortable slips in the categories where certain words belong. Eventually the poet anthropomorphizes the hammer and the nail, identifying in the moments before the collision of both tools "the dream of / the about-to-be-hit," which the poet acknowledges to be a "bad dream" that nevertheless promises comfort in the end to anxiety, a death in the form of "sleep inside the wood forever" (p. 29). Ostensible examples of the thoughtless and machinelike, the hammer and the nail become characters within a drama about the ends to which people put their tools and machines to use.

The repetitive, declaratory sentences of "Logic" recall the pseudologic of poems like "Boot Theory" and "The Dislocated Room" in *Crush.* In these three cases, the poet directs us to the dilemmas created by impossibilities, Hobson's choices, and false equivocations. In "Glue," which appears toward the end of *War of the Foxes*, the poet experiments with various attempts to remove himself as an active agent in his own thinking. This strategy results again and again in failure. By the end of the poem, the reader understands that the very categories employed in making sense of the world are like bodies, which may be turned over only to discover the spectacle of rot and decay beneath.

In addition to personification, many of the titles in *War of the Foxes* recall the long tradition of ekphrasis, which the fifth edition of the *Dictionary of Literary Terms and Literary Theory*

defines as the "intense pictorial description of an object," with a narrower definition as the "description of art-objects" (p. 228). Siken himself has expressed some ambiguity regarding this act. In his interview with Mishler, Siken explained the attractions and repulsion associated with his notion of ekphrastic writing: "It seemed cheap, seemed like cheating. Much in the way epigraphs are often cheap and easy: at their best, which is infrequently, they show a continuation of the tradition and dialogue of poetry. But most often they are an attempt to bootstrap a poem into importance by name-dropping or by co-opting someone else's thinking." Siken, of course, ultimately overcame these doubts by focusing upon his creative endeavors: by writing about his own experiences painting following the publication of *Crush*, Siken found himself able to address another mode of representation through literature.

Though the most famous examples of ekphrasis concern art objects and paintings, Siken prefers to title his poems after details in paintings that may or may not exist. John Hollander has characterized such poems as "notional" ekphrasis, and Siken's motivation for this shift in attention seems to be humanitarian: rather than emphasize famous paintings or their main subjects, Siken's eye is drawn to moments of frenzy, violence, and suffering that so often make up the tapestry of famous works of art. This attention is immediately grasped in a selection of titles from *War of the Foxes*: "Landscape with a Blur of Conquerors," "Detail of a Hayfield," and "Self-Portrait Against Red Wallpaper." Though the titles of the paintings remain known only to the poet, Siken foregrounds the macabre and mundane aspects of these paintings that so often goes unnoticed in casual trips to the museum, an effort to humanize the often inhuman conditions that fictional scenes portray.

Other poems in the collection, such as the eponymous "War of the Foxes" and "Logic," deal explicitly with war and violence. The first section of "War of the Foxes" was published in the 2008 anthology *State of the Union: 50 Political Poems*, edited by Joshua Beckman and Matthew Zapruder, and the long poem's inclusion in such a collection suggests that Siken's thematic interests were shifting away from the romantic toward the political in the aftermath of the Great Recession. In many of the poems of this collection, Siken uses refrain as a means of registering trauma and also—perhaps—the means through which trauma might finally be processed by the poet. Refrain appears as a central technique in "War of the Foxes," with the poet insisting he tell stories about war before finally concluding with a story about love (pp. 17–19).

Siken also employs several novel techniques not witnessed in *Crush*. One of these techniques is the explicit use of dialogue, typically as banter between characters. This dialogue is delivered by other people, animals, and inanimate objects. Such dialogue enables Siken to vary a particular theme already introduced in a previous poem or section. In "War of the Foxes," for instance, the poet declares: "You cannot have an opponent if you keep saying yes." Later in the section, the poet features two sets of dialogue:

Let me tell you a story about war. A man says to another man, *Can I tell you something?* The other man says, *No.* A man says to another man, *There is something I have to tell you. No*, says the other man. *No, you don't.*

Bird 1: Now we are getting somewhere.
Bird 2: Yes, yes we are.

(p. 17)

Gone is the uneven lineation, the wild variations of line length; instead, Siken prefers geometric and scripted layouts. If *Crush* had deliberately alternated the alignment as a means of registering the speaker's panic, then *War of the Foxes* keeps its material directly in front of the reader, coolly but mercifully dissecting the implications of stories involving war and conflict. In "War of the Foxes" and other poems of the collection, then, the poet's (and painter's) capacity to make and also analyze encourage our renewed attention to the ways that undermining representation in its various guises might promote a more honest, even humane, relationship to a world dominated by abrasions and conflict.

With the publication of his second volume of poetry, Richard Siken has solidified his place as

a vanguard poet with diverse sensibilities and interests. Though he will likely never be accused of being a prolific publisher of his own work, Siken has nevertheless managed to produce two influential and critically acclaimed volumes of poetry, and his readers will wait eagerly for a third volume, even if such a project takes another decade to accomplish.

Selected Bibliography

WORKS OF RICHARD SIKEN

Crush. New Haven, Conn.: Yale University Press, 2005.

War of the Foxes. Port Townsend, Wash.: Copper Canyon Press, 2015.

REVIEWS

Fargason, William. "Review: *War of the Foxes.*" *Southeast Review*, June 2015. http://southeastreview.org/review-war-of-the-foxes/

Spruijt-Metz, Donna. "*War of the Foxes* by Richard Siken." The Rumpus, March 6, 2016. http://therumpus.net/2015/03/war-of-the-foxes-by-richard-siken/

INTERVIEWS

Casey, Nell. "Nerve-Wracked Love: A Profile of Richard Siken." Poetry Foundation, February 27, 2006. https://www.poetryfoundation.org/features/articles/detail/68487

Mishler, Peter. "The Doubting of Self: An Interview with Richard Siken." *Tin House*, December 3, 2014. http://www.tinhouse.com/blog/37462/the-doubling-of-self-an-interview-with-richard-siken.html

Russell, Legacy. "Fight Club: Richard Siken." *BOMB*, October 11, 2011. http://bombmagazine.org/article/6136/fight-club-richard-siken

Schneiderman, Jason, Richard Siken, and Aaron Smith. "Young Poets on the State of the Craft." *Gay & Lesbian Review* 12, no. 5:28–30 (2005).

OTHER SOURCES

Beckman, Joshua, and Matthew Zapruder, eds. *State of the Union: 50 Political Poems.* Minneapolis: Wave Books, 2008.

Cuddon, J. A., and M. A. R. Habib. *A Dictionary of Literary Terms and Literary Theory.* 5th ed. Malden, Mass.: Wiley-Blackwell, 2013.

Davison, Peter. "Discovering Young Poets: How Some of the Best-Known Poets of This Century Got That Way." *Atlantic*, June 1998. http://www.theatlantic.com/magazine/archive/1998/06/discovering-young-poets/377136/

Heffernan, James A. W. *Museum of Words: The Poetics of Ekphrasis from Homer to Ashbery.* Chicago: University of Chicago Press, 1995.

Hollander, John. *The Gazer's Spirit: Poems Speaking to Silent Works of Art.* Chicago: University of Chicago Press, 1995.

Orazem, Kate. "The Rhyme and Reason Behind the Yale Series of Younger Poets." *Yale Herald*, November 10, 2010. http://yaleherald.com/homepage-lead-image/cover-stories/the-rhyme-and-reason-behind-the-yale-series-of-younger-poets/

O'Rourke, Meghan. "On Louise Glück and the Yale Series of Younger Poets." *Kenyon Review*, fall 2008. http://www.kenyonreview.org/kr-online-issue/2008-fall/selections/on-louise-gluck-and-the-yale-series-of-younger-poets/

Thoreau, Henry David. *Walden, Civil Disobedience, and Other Writings.* 3rd ed. Edited by William Rossi. New York: Norton, 2008.

DANA SPIOTTA

(1966—)

Elizabeth Freudenthal

ONE OF THE most exciting American novelists working today, Dana Spiotta writes fiction about thoughtful loners stuck in the machinery of history. Her characters try to build meaningful identities and relationships outside of a mainstream culture of unjust war, exploitative multinational corporations, and corrosive popular media. They try to build a sense of themselves from pop culture ephemera, from relationships with siblings and parents, and from attempts at morality. To tell these stories, Spiotta has developed a version of historical fiction rooted in fidelity to research, to lived experience of the time, and to the critical theories that have dominated the academy since she went to college. Her books are not the postmodern historiographic metafiction theorized by Linda Hutcheon, books that use historical settings to question our ability to know or understand either the past or the present. Nor are they conventional historical fictions of transparent representation of a distinct past. Instead, they are highly researched portrayals of characters shaped by their particular historical moments, whose struggles mirror the present-day experience of the same problems. In Spiotta's work, identities are both fragmented by the forces of history and also grounded in material and affective experiences of bodies in relationship to other bodies.

Critics understand Spiotta's novels in the literary-critical context of novels that emerged after canonical postmodernism. Adam Kelly formulates this generation of "post-postmodernists" as post–baby boom authors, born in the 1960s and 1970s, who went to college or university during the ascendance of critical theory as the dominant mode of humanities scholarship. They read the canonical postmodernists, hold professional positions in M.F.A. programs, and can reshape that knowledge into fiction and teaching that bring ethics, emotion, and character depth into the fragmented world that postmodernism broke. Spiotta, born in 1966, is indeed conversant with the postmodern frame of identities subsumed and fractured by the media, technological, economic, and political systems that shape us. But, like other feminist theorists and writers, she also focuses on the lived, embodied experience of occupying a postmodern, fragmented identity in a world of total domination by social structures. Spiotta articulates in an interview with Liza Johnson this relationship to literature as one that denies the always false but perceived division between "systems novels," which focus on the social-economic-political-media structures that generate individual life, and emotional, character-driven novels:

> No good novels are divisible in that way. There are lots of authentic, moving characters in so-called systems novels, just as there are certainly deep structural ideas in some character-driven novels. I do want to write about social/cultural/historical context, and some people aren't interested in that. I think that's a more interesting way of looking at that division. I'm interested in relationships, in character, but within a specific social context.

In this interview, Spiotta does not mention the perceived gender dynamics of this split: Big systems novels are associated with men writers and are given awards. Character-driven novels of emotion and relationships are associated with women writers and are more likely to be dismissed as unimportant. Spiotta's work, which locates subjective experience in both systems and relationships, has been moderately lauded by the literary world but not given the kind of praise afforded peers such as Jonathan Franzen, whose work also explicitly attempts to synthesize

character and systems concerns with arguably far less artistic success than Spiotta.

Spiotta also joins colleagues including Rachel Kushner and Siri Hustvedt in a deep engagement with other fine arts on their own terms, rather than as metafictional strategies to question the nature of meaning and representation, as was common in much postmodern fiction. Spiotta's characters are intensely, emotionally immersed in music and film. Spiotta has commented in interviews about her own experience with music fandom as formative and generative. And her childhood immersion in Hollywood film culture and industry through her father, a film executive, informs her depictions of the film industry as a dominant force in popular culture for better and worse. Spiotta's attention to the cultural forces that constitute subjectivity draws her to communication technologies as well. Internet writing genres populate her narratives, and her last book develops 1970s phone-system hacking as a proxy for the Internet experience and its associated social forms. Her characters attempt to creatively subvert the structures of domination—they protest the Vietnam war, create an extended fantasy music career, film war criminals with empathy—but they turn to media technologies to do so, technologies that are owned by the same corporations complicit in the domination characters seek to upend.

At least one critic, Michael Szalay, foregrounds the complex class critique in Spiotta's work, which explores the artist's uneasy relationship to corporate ownership of artistic products. Spiotta's work is in part about "selling out," about compromising one's aesthetic or moral values in a market-driven society such that characters can be torn between a morality of aesthetics and one of social relations. In the interview with Johnson, she comments on the novel's capacity to address such moral complexity:

> There are few places in our culture where anything is allowed to be complicated or complex. Most human things are full of conflict and ambivalence, not ease and simplicity. The world has grown increasingly fundamentalist, and the parameters of discussion have become narrowed. People, when they're fearful, are vulnerable to certainty in rhetoric. The novel tries to counter that tendency, I think.

In Spiotta's work, the novel and other arts are compromised tools for resistance, but resistance to degraded discourse remains necessary. As in the work of her friend and mentor Don DeLillo, subjectivity is so completely permeated by corporate media culture that it cannot stand stably on its own. Because subjects are compromised by the capitalist influences shaping consciousness, their ethical actions of resistance are also compromised. But as a feminist concerned with women's lives, Spiotta's characters derive meaning and ethics from embodied experiences of relationships, including sexual desire and motherhood. This feminist investment in subject's habitation in bodies is the key way that Spiotta's work finds ethics in the fragmented subjectivity the postmodern theorists left us.

LIFE

Dana Spiotta's parents, Robert and Emmeline, met each other as college thespians, playing the romantic leads in classmate Francis Ford Coppola's production of *A Streetcar Named Desire*. After college, her father, a son of Italian immigrants, worked his way up through Mobil Oil to an executive position. Dana, born in 1966 in New Jersey, was one of three siblings, along with an older sister and younger brother. The family moved eight times for Robert's job; these frequent moves facilitated Dana's early comforting and stabilizing investments in movies, books, and records. In an interview with Susan Burton, she describes this period as one of discovering the ways that a person can develop an intensely emotional relationship with cultural objects that cannot be dismissed as mere fandom. "It was finding something worthy of your attention . . . and then devoting attention to it until it yielded things that could never be discovered by casual engagement." This experience has reverberated throughout her fiction, in which the metafiction of postmodernism transcends self-reference into deep engagement with alternate art forms on their own terms: Mina's and Meadow's lives shaped by film references in her first and fourth novels,

Nik Worth's fantasy career as a rock star in *Stone Arabia* (2011), and teenager Jason's dependence on the Beach Boys for emotional stability and identification in *Eat the Document* (2006). Media texts serve not only as substitutes for family in Spiotta's work, but also as sources of identification as powerful as race, class, gender, or other forces of history.

When she was thirteen, Spiotta's father left the oil business and moved the family to Los Angeles to work as president of Zoetrope, the film studio founded by his fellow Hofstra alumnus Francis Ford Coppola. Spiotta describes in interviews the deep psychic shift engendered by the family's move to the city from suburban life. Her novels all take place at least in part in Los Angeles, where she spent her adolescence absorbing history, culture, politics, and city life. Perhaps some experience of being a teenager with a high-powered Hollywood mogul father made its way into *Lightning Field* (2001) and *Innocents and Others* (2016), both novels featuring young women in that situation. The family was well off enough for Dana to attend a private school, Crossroads, in Santa Monica—an inspiration for the private school where the two young filmmakers of *Innocents and Others* meet. She worked on the set of *Rumble Fish*, a 1983 Coppola/Zoetrope film that won some critical acclaim, and learned firsthand about the process of making films. She began attending Columbia University but dropped out during her sophomore year as her home life entered a period of dramatic upheaval. Robert Spiotta left Zoetrope to start his own film company, and he lost everything, including the family home. Around then, he and Emmeline divorced. Dana Spiotta went from a life of privilege to having nothing. Supporting herself, she made her way to Seattle, worked in a record store, and attended Evergreen State College. She read widely and deeply. She has said that her encounters with James Joyce's *Dubliners* and *Ulysses* made her want to be a writer by helping her think about the formal possibilities of fiction (Benz). Her entrée into the literary world came through a cold call to an avant-garde literary journal, the *Quarterly*. The editor, writer, and mentor Gordon Lish hired

Spiotta and a friend of hers based on this phone call, and the two young women moved together to New York to work as managing editors of the journal. Spiotta studied with the enormously influential Lish, who introduced her to Don DeLillo. While Lish has said in interviews that her writing did not impress him, her short stories impressed DeLillo. He introduced her to his agent, and the two authors remain friends.

Spiotta supported herself waitressing while she wrote *Lightning Field*, which was published when she was thirty-five. Named a *New York Times* Notable Book of 2001, it was published shortly after the September 11 terrorist attacks on New York City. After this happened, Spiotta quickly married her boyfriend, Clement Cole, a musician and artist, and moved upstate to Cherry Valley, near Cooperstown. Cherry Valley was the locale of several alternative Christian communities in the nineteenth century. "The history of alternative culture in America, you don't hear about it," she told Dinitia Smith of Cooperstown. "It is one of the most profound parts of American history." She taps this rich vein of underground U.S. history primarily in *Eat the Document*, whose protagonist journeys through the country's radical intentional communities throughout the 1970s. By the time Spiotta was writing *Eat the Document*, she and Coleman owned a restaurant in Cherry Valley, the Rose & Kettle, where Coleman was chef and she waited tables. Her writing constituted the kind of secret life that her protagonist would occupy. In between working in the restaurant and caring for her young daughter, Agnes, Spiotta wrote upstairs about a woman-chef with a child, living off the grid with a false identity. With that novel, published in 2006, she was nominated for a National Book Award and won a Rosenthal Foundation Award from the American Academy of Arts and Letters as well as a 2009 Rome Prize from the American Academy in Rome. The novel's success spurred Spiotta's appointment to the writing faculty at Syracuse University, where she moved in 2009. *Stone Arabia*, written mostly in Syracuse, was a National Book Critics Circle Award finalist when it came out in 2011. Spiotta published *Innocents and Others* in 2016. Divorced before this last

book was published, she lives in Syracuse with her daughter and the writer Jonathan Dee.

LIGHTNING FIELD

Spiotta's first book is about wealthy white women wrestling with what is ostensibly typical Los Angeles anomie. The novel emerged in 2001, when film was the primary media register and just before the Internet would dominate cultural production. *Lightning Field* feels like a first novel, inflected with other voices, influenced by other styles, satirizing L.A. characters so steeped in media culture that they cannot seem to build a subjectivity independent of it. In addition, it lays out what will emerge as dominant themes of Spiotta's work: sibling relationships, cultures of media technologies, mental illness, and the nature of contemporary women's identity. The protagonist Mina, who narrates some sections of the novel, is married to David, a screenwriter. She is having "assignations" with her husband's best friend, Max, as well as with a visiting investment banker named Scott, and working for her friend Lorene's elite concept restaurants. Her father was a Hollywood director and is retired in Ojai with a younger partner. Her older brother Michael, suffering from an unnamed illness that may be schizophrenia, lives in a psychiatric hospital. When the novel begins, Mina has not seen Michael in years. She has stopped driving and walks all over Los Angeles, but she is no postmodern flaneur. Unlike Leopold Bloom, *Ulysses'* paradigmatic flaneur, Mina does not meander all around her city. Rather, her wanderings are fixed to single repeated destinations: her home, her lover Max's house, her lover Scott's hotel room, and Lorene's restaurants. Along these routes, she steps into high-end boutiques; her shopping compulsion is almost as unshakable as her sexual compulsions, and she pursues both with a self-conscious understanding that these acquisitive trappings of femininity are inadequate. She frets that she is nothing but "a collection of references" (p. 73) and understands herself and her relationships through film dialogue. The novel takes place at a crisis point: her affairs have become unsustainable, and her brother has left the

hospital. She buys increasingly expensive glamour gear that goes unused. As the structures propping up Mina's life begin to dissolve, the narrative also circulates from Mina to Lorene to Lisa, Lorene's housekeeper.

Lorene and Lisa also struggle to define themselves against norms of femininity, even as they appear to embrace them. Lorene seems to serve as a symbol of femininity itself. She is white, wealthy, beautiful, and concerned almost exclusively with other people's pleasure. While Mina's nonwork time is spent with lovers, Lorene's is spent with various therapeutic professionals who substitute for genuine human connection. She has made a career out of surfaces, first as a life-stylist for men—literally mining masculinity for a surface-level allure comparable to the feminine one she's crafted for herself—then as a developer of high-end concept restaurants. Lorene's body itself is a project—highly controlled, disciplined, plucked, buffed, and augmented. She calls Mina "doll" while turning herself into a doll. And her femininity is explicitly white: "Michael said there is nothing more beautiful than white, white skin because it is so unforgiving, so bruisable, and the person inside seems only barely covered. To me her cheek looks cool and poreless, not at all trembly and translucent. But she may have been different then. Or maybe he could see through skin" (p. 63). Michael perceives Lorene's whiteness as fragility and vulnerability, while Mina perceives the opposite, white skin as invulnerable. While Mina has eroticized Lorene throughout their friendship, including at their first meeting when Mina was fourteen, these different perceptions of her femininity suggest that both femininity and whiteness are generated by another's gaze. Elsewhere in the narrative, Lorene reflects that her augmented breasts look bigger because of her white skin. Femininity is white, and the white woman is an object of others' perceptions and projections.

While Lorene is in part a spoof of L.A.'s culture of wealth, Lisa serves as a sympathetic satire of the white working-class mother: she suffers an aggressive, alcoholic, absentee husband, cleans houses for hourly pay, and has "let herself

go" in a permanent uniform of sweatpants after eating her feelings for the past five years. While Mina's and Lorene's anxieties revolve around their futile bulwarking against the dissolution of their sense of selfhood, Lisa is consumed by stories of missing and tortured children, a particularly maternal form of anxiety (one that prefigures Denise's comparable fixations in *Stone Arabia*). She is so worried about the vulnerability of her children that she overcooks all their tightly budgeted food to kill germs, rendering it inedible. Her mode of motherhood is uniquely born of American culture: unshakeable anxiety about the vulnerability of children converging with both frugality—each grocery shopping trip a tussle with her husband over dollar bills—and the wastefulness endemic to U.S. consumption culture. The food she can barely afford goes in the trash, and her kids eat saltines with jam in front of the TV.

Together, the women of *Lightning Field* literally embody powerful conceptions of contemporary femininity: Lorene is highly controlled, borderline anorexic, virtually sexless, and sheathed in luxury clothing. In "Reading the Slender Body," Susan Bordo identifies the body as a site of the central contradiction of late-capitalist culture: conflicting demands that we exercise restrained self-control during the workday and that we indulge in releasing, expansive consumption during leisure hours. Bulimia is Bordo's paradigmatic example of the body's enactment of this paradox (*Unbearable Weight*, p. 201). Mina and Lisa each embody Bordo's binge capitalism: Mina binges on luxury purchases, food, and, most dominantly, sexual experiences. Lisa binges literally on food, and her overwhelming maternal anxiety is another kind of millennial U.S. excess. Lorene's almost cartoonishly self-controlled, surgically altered body occupies the purgative end of the consumption culture contradiction, even as she produces satirically excessive consumption at her popular restaurants. These women's bodies are fueling late capitalism.

However, through the mentally ill character linking all three women's stories, Spiotta joins a stable of writers, most prominently David Foster

Wallace, that use ill, disabled, or traumatized bodies to work through one basic challenge of post-structuralist theory: if subjectivity is fragmented and socially constructed, how does a person feel like a self, with reliable sources of pleasure and pain? One resolution to this conflict between theory and practice is to focus on embodiment, which itself follows contemporary culture's investment in medical models of personality. A subject, no matter how incoherent, is housed in a body. Even though bodies are themselves shaped by social norms, they also experience impulses, desires, frailties, and impairments ranging (in this book) from anorexia to depression to schizophrenia. Furthermore, Michael's mental illness buttresses Mina's identity with substantive experience. Underneath Mina's and Lorene's postmodern stories of fragmented, media-constructed identity lies a story conceived in the older mode of psychological realism, of two women heartbroken by their brother's and boyfriend's mental illness. The narrative twins Mina and Michael; Mina's identity was fused to her brother's until his illness, which Mina experienced as "a mechanical difference" splitting them and flinging Mina into an identity crisis that is arguably the source of her depression, compulsive infidelity, and experience of herself as nothing but a hollow postmodern subject, "a collection of references." The embodied fact of mental illness serves as a conventional, linear narrative foil to the postmodern excesses of Mina and Lorene. Useful here is Kelly's framework of post–baby boom writers beginning with critical theory in their undergraduate years: Spiotta knowingly writes a stable, linear psychological narrative back into the subjectivity that postmodern Los Angeles had shattered.

The tension between postmodern and realist identity manifests in the novel's narrative structure as well. While Mina's L.A. narrative is circular, mirroring her walks between points on her own map, the Michael-Mina story follows a linear narrative climax by revealing that Michael's mental break was the central loss in Mina's life. The road trip begun on page 1 ends at their mother's house on page 208, where family history clarifies, explicates, and eases Mina's

distress. Her mother reassures Mina that Michael would have developed his illness no matter how she behaved—whether or not she visited him in the hospital, how soon she may have noticed symptoms, or how deeply she loved him. If he would have been sick no matter what, then, Mina wonders why his illness ruptured her sense of self, perhaps permanently:

> How come Mina was just like him through all those years? How come they were so close they didn't even have to whisper to each other, they just knew? How come one day it was this way with Mina and Michael, and the next day it was not? One day the mirror was there, the next day splintered into a thousand pieces? Because that's how it seemed to her, that sudden—like a thing shattering. And she couldn't do anything to change it.
>
> (p. 211)

Mina's fantasy of complete merged bonding with Michael reads in part like a textbook example of psychoanalytic literary theory. According to post-Freudian psychoanalytic theory, infants are merged in union with their mothers. The father breaks that bond by initiating both separate, individuated subjectivity as well as a permanent absence (separation from the mother) structuring that subjectivity. Later, Jacques Lacan built onto Freudian theory a "mirror stage" of human development, when a child learns that she is an individual by relying on external objects—mirrors—reflecting her self-ness back at her. However, Spiotta's text inverts these theories of self-formation in ways suggesting both postmodern self-referential play as well as traditional psychological models of the subject. Mina's mirror, her pre-Oedipal bonding object, is not a parent but an older brother. Instead of learning from her mirror/brother that she is an individual, Mina experiences herself as a merged unit. When he becomes ill, her mirror shatters. She loses her external referent to herself, which results in a profound loss. This is the loss she is chasing throughout the novel—a chase foregrounded by a road trip to her mother's house that frames the narrative.

But while Michael's illness provides a semi-stable referent of Mina's and Lorene's subjectivity and a source of conventional psychological realism, it is also a symbol of L.A.'s self-satirizing culture of commercialized wellness and consumer capitalist binging and purging. Schizophrenia, Michael's likely illness, can be reductively understood as a difficulty navigating the differences between reality and hallucination: a quality endemic to most popular depictions of the town that Hollywood built. As Mina ambles around Los Angeles, her third-person limited narrative reflects on the self-help industry. The narrative identifies as "schizophrenic" these businesses built on the optimism of believing everything can be diagnosed and cured. "It was the schizophrenics, or schizoforensics, of this utopia/dystopia place—things deeply, pathologically wrong, but instantly and infinitely remediable" (p. 16). Los Angeles in this telling is terminally and multiply divided: split in mind, split in its public spaces, and split up ontologically as a good, bad, and nowhere place. The city is located dually—prefiguring Mina's twinning with Michael—as both structural illness and perpetual cure. As Mina ambulates this split urban space, she avoids contemplating the loss of her brother and the existential fear springing from that loss: the fear that she and Michael are still twinned and that she is also ill. She circumambulates this fear as she identifies her environs as schizophrenic; as she continually pockets postcards from Michael without reading them; as the narrative proceeds along a traditional linear climax with information their mother reveals about Michael's illness. Los Angeles is an ill place, suffused with Mina's fear of her own instability and illness. Mina must drive across the country to get better. *Lightning Field* aligns individuals and the places they live to blur the boundaries between inside and out, private and public—the boundaries between our minds and everything our minds experience.

Through this use of illness to both fracture an individual and ground her in a concrete material experience, *Lightning Field* constructs a dialectic between what could be called a postmodern subjectivity of fragmentation and an opposing subjectivity of embodied experience. This dialectic works differently from the layers of mediation and reference that construct Los Angeles and its denizens. Mina's post-Michael

life is one of disconnection and deep technological mediation of the most intimate experiences. For example, early in the novel, in an inversion of Alfred Hitchcock's classic film *Rear Window* (1954), itself the object of Laura Mulvey's classic critical essay on "the male gaze," which constructs desire through mediation and the objectification of women, Mina feels desire for her husband only while watching him at his computer through the front office window of their home. Her observation of him riffs on Hollywood convention so deeply that it seems to rely on shallow postmodern conventions of self-consciousness:

> Mina watched him, examining his profile at twenty paces. Mina watched him, half-shadowed, through a window, half-lit with the amazing dusk light, even, or especially, L.A. movie-fake dusk light that could be thrown by a switch in a soundstage. A fading soft pink light that made her long for soundtrack swells. . . .
>
> (p. 9)

While the whole passage is knowingly metatextual about film manufacturing romantic feeling, this ostensible metatext about the constructedness of romance masks that her feeling for her husband may, in fact, be manufactured. Postmodern subjectivity may still be a means of identifying true feelings. The novel's alternate subjectivity is rooted in connection, embodied experience, and love, but these experiences are not free of the post-structuralist models of subjectivity. For example, Mina's relationship with her brother is the most meaningful in the book: "Then, before all the hospitals, there was the warmth of unbroken companionship. A person so close you hardly needed to speak. The combustible energies and combat closeness of children growing up together, moved around, variously parented. Interior logics developed. Secret reference points. An unquestioned and uncontrived siege bonding" (p. 81). This depiction of a prelapsarian childhood unity broken by sickness is undercut not only by the reference to Michael's illness. "Siege bonding" and the "variously parented" children pull in both the emotional experience of divorce as well as the tie to the generational experience of divorce in the 1970s and 1980s. This reference to divorce links the novel to the social-historical

trends shaping the specific cohort of post–baby boom writers, trends that may enable a distinct generational thematic and formal identity. Many memories of Michael are undercut by questions drawn directly from post-structuralist theory about the loss at the heart of identity and the fallibility of memory. However, they are also shot through with love. Similarly, the depiction of Lorene visiting Michael in the hospital is the most poignant of the novel, framing her plastic surgery, anorexia, and other modes of bodily control as anxious responses to the loss of her only romantic relationship. The housekeeper Lisa's deep anxiety is framed as specifically maternal, focused on news stories of missing and abused children. All three of these characters seem ostensibly to be shaped by their cultures in the mode of postmodernism—fragmented, constructed by technologies and histories, and hollow mouthpieces of cultural ephemera. However, all three also have affective experiences rooted in bodily experiences of sex, love, childbirth, and abuse.

Spiotta's focus on women's embodied experiences begins but does not fully accomplish synthesizing the dialectic of subjectivity formulated in this book. Trappings of postmodern culture—references to film, in particular—enable genuine family connections for Mina. Film is a language that Mina shares with her father and her brother, a language that enfolds her in an affective connection to her community and culture (p. 73). The narrative's statement that her identity feels "like a collection of references" has this context of close familial relationships. This section of narrative plays with the dialectic of subjectivity: on the one hand, Mina feels as if her identity is only and exclusively a collection of the movies she had seen, in the order she had seen them. "They became nearly equally weighted, her memories of her actual life and her memories of the movies she had seen. Was there finally that much difference?" (p. 73). Her confusion between reality and fantasy, between an "actual life" and a life as spectator, parallels a shallow conception of Michael's illness as an inability to tell the difference between reality and fantasy or hallucination. This ontological uncertainty paradoxically strengthens her connection

to her brother and reinforces that an identity as "a collection of references" is as real as any other way of being. By taking affect and embodied experience seriously, *Lightning Field* refreshes postmodern epistemology to enable a way to live with the fragmentation of contemporary life.

EAT THE DOCUMENT

Spiotta's second novel expands on *Lightning Field*'s investigation of the nature of contemporary subjectivity by tracing the journey of a woman through a series of false identities. This novel focuses on a handful of radical activists of two different periods, the 1970s and the 1990s. In particular, it narrates the story of Mary Whittaker, a former radical who fled her life when a Vietnam War protest action inadvertently killed someone. Inspired by the story of Katherine Ann Power, a former Weather Underground member who turned herself in to the FBI in 1993 after years of living under a false identity, the novel traces Mary's transition to becoming Caroline Sherman and then Louise Barrot as she crosses the United States in time as well as space in search of stability and safety. The story alternates with that of Mary's former lover, Bobby Desoto, who now goes by the name Nash Davis, as well as of her Beatles-obsessed son, Jason. Nash's friends, Henry and Miranda, round out the ensemble, all as foils to Mary's story.

A National Book Award finalist when it was published in 2006, *Eat the Document* joined a cluster of novels published during the Iraq War years that reimagine the revolutionary underground of 1970s United States. Historical fiction is always about the time in which it's written as well as the time it represents; these novels sought to better understand the Vietnam War protest movements to better understand the possibilities of resistance to the Iraq War. *Eat the Document* explicitly compares baby boom and generation X protest movements, putting characters loosely affiliated with the antiglobalism protesters from the 1990s Pacific Northwest in dialogue with former hippies. However, the novel is far more invested in the convoluted depredations of late capitalism than it is in the Vietnam War that triggers Mary

and Bobby's initial revolutionary actions. The novel's satirical multinational corporation, Allegecom, has tendrils that creep into almost all aspects of the novel's plot. "Allegecom—the massive corporate entity that contained everything from pharmaceuticals (through its offshoot Pherotek) to genetically modifying seeds with coordinated, matching pesticides (through its biotech arm, Versagro)—was taking an unprecedented foray into developing and running an entire community" (p. 157). This community will be located in the part of the country where Mary and a friend sheltered in a radical feminist commune. Pherotek's pharmaceuticals kill Nash's friend Henry. And a young anticorporate hacker ends up taking a job in marketing for the new Allegecom community, Alphadelphia. The novel's investments in the dominance of late capital, as represented by this conglomerate, come to overwhelm the initial 1970s plot and strongly encourages a reading of Bobby and Mary's actions in the novel's contemporary context, not only of the 1990s but also of the Iraq War. With this novel, Spiotta deepens her work exploring the ways that multilinear histories shapes several generations of individuals.

The novel also pushes further Spiotta's first novel's preoccupations with the ways that women construct selves out of available prefabricated narratives, including those shaped by their historical moments. Much of the novel's affective force is drawn from Mary's attempt to build a new self without one's organic constituent parts: family, memories, a birth name, a hometown. Spiotta spins out the opposition in *Lightning Field* between fragmentary subjectivity and that based on coherent, if fabricated, narrative. Mina argues that the latter is the only way to take possession of one's life. In this book, Mary's attempts to become Caroline and, later, Louise fail because so much of our sense of self depends on the ability to cohere our experiences into a viable story. Mary cannot develop a coherent narration of herself once she abandons her activist life, her birth name, and her origins. Early in her experience as Caroline, the narrative articulates this confusion between her birth and adopted selves. "She realized or guessed that one day she would

get to the point where she wouldn't even know what was true and what she had made up. So she wouldn't be lying any longer, even though some of it wasn't true. Someday time would turn the lies into history" (p. 97). This blurring between truth and fabrication also recalls characters in *Lightning Field* whose media- and technology-constructed identities would not be separable into categories of "truth" and "representation." Caroline assumes, falsely, that if she tells the new story about herself it will be absorbed into truth. The passage then leaps from the individual to the broader scale of group experience. Time turns experiences into history: a publicly acknowledged and shared set of assumed facts about the past. However, in the 1970s, popular American consciousness first encountered the likelihood that state powers turn lies into history all the time, and that this alchemy causes genuine suffering. Lies turned into history through Mary's whole life, but, like President Richard Nixon's lies, Mary's couldn't cohere. Her life is bound to the life of her country on a scale greater than that of schizophrenic Los Angeles in Spiotta's first book.

Despite the clear presence of structures of domination in both the 1970s and the 1990s, the novel does not depict protest action as unequivocally right, an ambivalence primarily demonstrated by SAFE. Just as the name of DeSoto and Mary's radical collective has an ever-changing set of phrases behind the ironic acronym, the moral status of the group remains in flux. Both Mary and Nash grow increasingly skeptical of their earlier conviction about the necessity of countering state violence with terrorist violence. The moral clarity required to plant the bomb remains tenuous even during the act, and fails to resolve into permanence afterward. And the equivalent 1990s movements, represented by the antiglobalization protesters loitering around Nash and Henry's bookstore, are as bogged down by meta-discussions of methods and rhetoric as SAFE was. Reflecting on SAFE and Bobby's love of acronyms while visiting a consciousness-raising group, Mary starts to make a connection between the semiotics of revolution and its politics:

She believed failure of language belied deeper failings in the counterculture. The names just became more and more divorced from their meanings. What was the point of using a name in that way? Shouldn't a name remind you of who you are, or are trying to be? Did they really want a name to be part of a secret, exclusive language—a club that intended to exclude, that deliberately obscured things for outsiders? Was the need to be exclusive sort of reactionary, oppressive and even patriarchal? Caroline knew she was onto something, she was learning how things get away from people. How gradually they, what? Become the very thing they long to escape.

(pp. 101–102)

While the passage takes place in the 1970s, it glances at political concerns that surfaced in the 1990s and are still present: the difficulty of balancing group identity and collective impact; the problems inherent in using language to represent political action; and the difficulty of maintaining a truly democratic governing structure. Mary is thinking through these issues at an all-women group, determining that the exclusionary framework of second-wave feminism threatened to replicate oppressive patriarchal structures. Mary's suspicion resolves into fact, as later third-wave feminists critiqued the second-wavers' tendency to silence women identifying as racial and sexual minorities. The passage also recalls post-1990s investments in subcultural identifications such as Jason's with the Beach Boys, or the revolutionary playing cards displayed for sale to a browsing Miranda Diaz and her boyfriend Josh Marshall. Mary wants a name—a cultural product, a text—to clearly and transparently represent the intentions and potentials of her political group. But group identification itself necessitates exclusion. People are in the group or not. If the group is convened to effect political change, its implicit exclusionary tactics are counterproductive.

At its heart, *Eat the Document* explores whether or not ethical action is possible, given these strictures on movement groups. Kelly argues in his 2012 analysis of *Eat the Document* that the novel explores the deficits implicit in two commonly held positions, which he articulates as the intentions problem and the means-ends problem. Mary explains her actions as

justifiable by her intentions—to end the racist, immoral Vietnam War. But her intentions cannot justify the effect of her actions, the unplanned and unwanted death of the housekeeper. And because intentions are impossible to evaluate without retrospective knowledge of their effects, then the means of an action comes to replace the ends of it. The trappings of action—the drugs, clothes, music, and language—come to substitute culturally for the action itself. Spiotta depicts the commodification of protest movements and puts her young 1990s characters in dialogue about the ethics of using revolution as a fashion without resolving the dialogue neatly. Miranda believes that commodifying the trappings of revolution is part of the dead end of late capital that violates the spirit of revolutionary action. Josh argues that the commodification of all counterculture is an inevitable endpoint of the counterculture itself, that capitalism is a perfect, all-encompassing system that neutralizes all resistance to it. While Miranda is significantly more sympathetic than Josh, Mary seems to echo him, pointing out that tendency of revolutionaries to become what they fight against is an intractable problem with U.S. political movements. In this frame, there are only intentions and means, because just as Allegecom hires its hacker, Josh, capitalism will cannibalize any "end" of a protest action. Kelly argues that Nash's later interest in performative politics can resolve the means-ends problem by uniting both. If a protest action is beautiful, it can accomplish its intent. Kelly's argument finds a viable contemporary politics in the novel. Jenny Turner's essay in the *London Review of Books*, however, points out the political commitments Spiotta chooses not to make, including a curious, anachronistic elision of reference to the Black Panthers, whose culture and politics are represented only via a Funkadelic record that turns up in both Mary's underground journey and her son's later musical life. While the Panthers were a driving force in 1970s revolutionary politics, and while the anti-globalization movements of the 1990s fore-grounded race in their critique of U.S. imperialism, race is oddly absent from *Eat the Document*. Miranda Diaz' name indicates an ethnic identity, but her character does not explicitly address a particular Latina background. Similarly, the book avoids race by giving the housekeeper bomb victim a typically white name. Turner generously and plausibly proposes that Spiotta felt that the story of revolutionaries of color was not hers to tell. By contrast, Susan Choi's *American Woman* (2001), even more explicitly based on the story of Patty Hearst and the Symbionese Liberation Army, puts race at the foreground of the story of these revolutionary movements.

However, by focusing on women's subjectivities, the novel expands the possibilities of resistance. Aliki Varvogli argues that, through the figure of the radical mother, *Eat the Document* offers up a potentially liberatory subjectivity that is shaped by social norms but grounded in empathy, care, and love. A radical challenges dominant norms; a mother is engaged with values that matter; a radical mother can be contradictory in occupying both positions and thus can move past dead-end positions. Once Jason is born, Mary does not turn herself in because she cannot leave her baby alone:

> The baby anchored her, finally, in her world. When she gave birth to Jason, she finally found something she believed time would not ever betray or dwindle. The feeling she had for her son was sentimental, it was frightening, it was unimpeachable. It was self-negating and beyond love. It was an ungentle feeling, this baby love.
>
> (pp. 231–232)

Adolescent Jason is one of the reasons she eventually turns herself in, to be able to be honest with him about who she is.

This passage refuses the sentimentality of clichéd, normative maternal emotions. Instead, it conjures a relationship both destructive and indestructible. Impervious to time, "ungentle," and "frightening," the bodily experience of childbirth nonetheless reinforces Mary's relationship to social life and buttresses her sense of self. Before Jason, she is despairingly lonely primarily because she is unknowable, unrecognized, unfamiliar to people around her. The overwhelming affective message of *Eat the Document* is that without other people knowing our stories, we cannot exist. However, by keeping her birth identity secret from Jason, she compromises the

coherence she believed parenthood would confer upon her. Subjectivity is fragmentary, as the postmodernists taught, but in this book, humans have bodily, "animal" needs for relationships grounded in something like a true story about ourselves—a stable name, a linear narrative of personal history, a set of motives. Those motives do not need to be understandable, though; before she turns herself in, Mary says that no one will understand why she planted that bomb, and it does not matter that no one will understand (p. 282).

This insight about subjectivity enables a more nuanced understanding of the novel's pessimistic depictions of political action. Her act of subversion costs Mary her life—her lover, her family, and her sense of self. She begins to recover from this loss only when she reneges on her underground life, confesses to her son, and chooses to participate in the nation's punitive system of justice. Revolutionary and subversive countercultures themselves are depicted as restrictive, exclusionary, sexist, and ineffectual. The novel affords both Mary and Miranda extensive scenes in which they struggle between their heterosexual desires and their need to develop and express their own thoughts within mixed-gender political groups. When they are in relationships with comrades, their participation in groups must always be balanced by their role as girlfriend. There are additional compromises required by subversive action. SAFE begins as a documentary filmmaking collective. The group eventually begins to believe that film is too impotent to have a chance to stop the war machine. This decision is facilitated by a film Bobby makes of a candid gonzo interview with Louis Feiser, the inventor of napalm. SAFE members believe that the film presents Feiser with too much sympathy. They perceive Bobby's desire to understand Feiser's motives as counterproductive to their goal of destroying the war profiteers Feiser represents (p. 227). Mary and Bobby alternate in their belief in the necessity of direct, violent action, their relationship generating its own ethical momentum that pulls them both along to violence. Bobby's nuanced, empathetic film spurs SAFE's decision to plant the bomb that kills the housekeeper. Later, as Nash, Bobby's attempt to synthesize

aesthetic sophistication and political action is largely ineffectual. Miranda deduces that for Nash, planning the action is equivalent to action itself. None of these actions stop or slow the imperialist trajectory of the United States in either the 1970s or the 1990s.

This leaves open the novel's basic question: When U.S. imperialism in Vietnam morphs directly into Allegecom, what kind of radical politics can effectively counter it? *Eat the Document*'s possibilities fall short. Direct action costs too much for too little return. Aesthetics provide sophistication and nuance, but no social change. Allegecom appears to coopt all subversive action, from developing drugs that cause cancer to building a planned, marketing-driven community on the ground previously occupied by a radical feminist commune. Josh Marshall is the mouthpiece for a cynical stance of accepting the dominance of Allegecom and late capital. Even the title of the novel is weighted by ethical anxiety—it's the title of a 1960s documentary about Bob Dylan moving from acoustic to electric guitar and suffering accusations of "selling out." However, the novel's feminist orientation toward bodily knowledge undercuts Josh's position that all resistance is coopted. The ethics of the novel ultimately rest on that family dyad of Mary and Jason, on embodied knowledge, on subjectivity that is shaped by relationships with other people. Jason's rejection of bodily pleasure and, by extension, of Miranda's desires, broadcast his lack of participation in the novel's ethics of interdependent subjectivity grounded in embodied knowledge. By contrast, Nash's friend Henry experiences radical empathy facilitated by an Allegecom drug, Nepenthex, for the combat-related post-traumatic stress disorder he develops a few years after dodging the Vietnam-era draft. The drug has given him nightmares of war scenes and, in a flight of magical realism, firsthand memories of Bobby's experience bombing the profiteer's home. Later, Nepenthex has also given Henry cancer. Henry's living other people's nightmares is facilitated and then punished by Allegecom, but it nonetheless provides a pathway through the complex ethics of intersubjectivity and empathy that the novel rests on. Henry's

nightmare flashbacks to a Vietnam he never experienced suggest that the detritus of popular culture, including an endless cycling of images of the Vietnam War era, its soldiers and its protesters, have colonized our very selves. Our memories are indistinguishable from the film, TV, and music flooding us. If our subjectivities depend on coherent narratives about our lives, as Mina states and Mary's experience shows, then there is nothing stopping media entities from packaging those stories for us. Postmodern fiction has been asking if and how subjects can exist independently from the media, technological, historical, economic, and political forces shaping them. *Eat the Document* presents Henry, Mary, and Jason to show that caring relationships with friends and family can potentially subvert the machinations of capital and shape an ethics of embodiment.

STONE ARABIA

Spiotta's third novel ostensibly departs from the freighted political concerns of *Eat the Document* to tell a more domestic story. As in *Lightning Field*, this novel is about a sibling pair. Nik Kranis, under the moniker Nik Worth, has fabricated a lifelong music career in a collection of media he calls the "Chronicles." His sister, Denise, pays Nik's bills while taking care of their cognitively declining mother, her own college-age daughter, Ada, and an occasional lover. She also suffers from her own memory problems, as well as a self-described neurotic obsession with Web pages about tragic events. The plot is set in motion by Ada's decision to make a documentary about her uncle Nik, disrupting everyone's fragile routines. The novel begins and ends with Nik's disappearance, which instigates Denise's attempt to record their life together in a book she calls the "Counterchronicles." These three competing stories of Nik establish a commitment to postmodern epistemological concerns and a more focused exploration of the possibilities and compromises required to craft a coherent narrative of selfhood. While *Eat the Document*'s politics turned personal and local, *Stone Arabia*'s domestic story quickly turns political, with the

same investments in the ways that individual lives are shaped by history, the same questions about subjectivity, and the same ethical concerns as her first two novels. In many ways more complex than those for being more domestic, *Stone Arabia* asks how a contemporary subject can make an ethical life in a world that, to paraphrase Nash Davis, tattoos Viacom on our asses.

Stone Arabia branches out formally in a way that will be repeated in *Innocents and Others*, both of which contain multiple kinds of texts written by multiple characters to remind readers of the inadequacy of representation of a single, masterful authorial voice. The novel begins with a letter from Denise to Ada written by Nik, using a sly spoof of a writerly voice his sister may use. The novel also contains clippings from Nik's "Chronicles," Denise's "Counterchronicles," transcripts of Ada's documentary interviews, and conventional third-person narrative about Denise's life. As with many postmodernist formal innovations, the effect of this multitextual polyphony is to deny the reader the comfort of a conventional linear narrative with a single authorial voice about a single character. The reader puts together information the way that Internet-media consumers do, by compiling multiple sources of data, evaluating the epistemological value of each, and cobbling together something like a factual narrative to the extent stable factuality is possible. With a disappearing trickster at the center of a story told by his heartbroken sister, this novel makes clear that narratives are not to be trusted. Moreover, Spiotta doubles down on the unreliability of memory, a clever dig at the memoir craze contemporaneous with the 2011 publication of *Stone Arabia*. Denise opens her memoir with a meditation on her difficulty remembering her past:

> Can I even do it? Can I be accurate at all? I have discovered how much memory can dissolve under pressure. The more I try to hold on to my ability to remember, the more it seems to escape my grasp. I find this terrifying. . . . I have been studying various techniques and even tricks, and I should employ them. Memory, it seems, clings to things. Named things. Spaces. Senses.
>
> (p. 32)

While her sense of self will weaken without stable memories, she turns toward materiality to recover stability. Spaces a body might occupy, sights, sounds, smells, and tastes it might sense, and things it may touch will buttress a person's sense of self by attaching like a barnacle to particular memories. As with her previous work, Spiotta's third novel sets out an ethics of embodiment as an alternative to the effects of fragmented contemporary subjectivity.

In its exploration of contemporary ethics, Stone Arabia also revises the terms of canonical postmodernism's variation of the public square as pure spectacle. A conventional "public square" is a shared civic space of citizen engagement and collective action. The digital public sphere in Spiotta's work is a space for collective anxiety experienced in isolation, which atomizes each individual and degrades the experience of tragedy. Denise calls her experience of Internet-mediated tragedy "Breaking Events"—events that shatter the boundary between herself and society. One of her breaking events is the death of a minor celebrity, Garret Wayne, which recalls the death in 1998 of the comedian Phil Hartman. Denise describes in her memoir her interaction with the digital spectacle: "I was alone and yet right there among thousands of people. We were all together in our puerile, lurid nostalgia, yet we were sitting all alone. It was no comfort, really, it just made it worse. By the next week—at the latest—this would be all quiet and abandoned. A relic site" (p. 115). The group experience of the media event is not affirming or even neutral. Rather than providing a network of social relations that provide solace, the collective Internet experience reinforces the basic loneliness of each individual and replaces grief with shame. Later in the passage, Denise equates the Internet-mediated experience of a celebrity's death with the destruction of her own sense of self:

> We all long to escape our own subjectivity. That's what art can do. . . . But what the televised bombardment of violent events did to me was completely different. I didn't overcome my subjectivity; rather, my person got stretched to include the whole world, stretched to a breaking point. I became pervious, bruised and annihilated. That's what it feels like, this debilitating emotional engagement—annihilation, not affirmation.

(p. 116)

Denise does not feel an Internet-facilitated expansion of self enabled by the ability to reach anyone anywhere in the world at a finger click, sharing the same event with a community of strangers made close by common experience. Instead, she feels that expansion of possibility as destructive. Her language suggests a body is pinned to the bits of information traveling through the World Wide Web, "stretched to a breaking point." Her investment in the digital public sphere annihilates her sense of self.

Denise's third breaking event is an explicit revision of canonical postmodernism's take on the public sphere. The story of an Amish girl who disappeared from the town of Stone Arabia, this breaking event compels Denise to seek out Stone Arabia after Nik disappears. Once there, she recognizes the family's barn from television—a barn that was inspired by "the most photographed barn in the world," from the 1985 novel White Noise, by Spiotta's friend and mentor Don DeLillo. The physical occupation of space of DeLillo's barn is obliterated by its status as a media object. No one sees this barn; people only see photographs of the barn—even people in front of the barn, taking its picture. The barn is subsumed by the phenomenon of the proliferation of images of it. DeLillo's barn serves as a paragon of Jean Baudrillard's postmodern theory of simulation—that representations of the real have come to replace the real itself, so that we now experience only the circulation of representations rather than contact with the things represented. The barn in Stone Arabia, meanwhile, interprets this phenomenon through the feminist lens of emotion and relationships. Rather than experiencing a location and event whose existence is only and exclusively mediated, Denise meets and speaks with the girl's parents. The site is a place where people live, and where loss is processed without technological mediation. As she walks through their property, she reflects on her research about the Amish relationship to technology as one of caution and deliberate decision making. "They don't blindly grab at what-

ever is new. They consider such things with deep skepticism. It wasn't hard to see how much better that might work for someone" (p. 220). In Stone Arabia, family relationships are largely mediated by narrative technologies of film, music, and reams of writing. These circulating representations of Nik literally replace his physical presence. And while valorizing the Amish's stance on technological mediation, the book does not romanticize either the Amish or their skepticism. Denise's talk with the girl's mother brings no solace to either of them. The girl and Nik both remain lost. Denise's first encounter with the story of this family is through news reports that use stock photos and Hollywood film footage of generic Amish life. The barn Denise recognizes from TV is not the barn in front of her at Stone Arabia. The media machine contaminates even the lives conducted outside its sphere. Spiotta's barn is a conflicted site that partially recuperates affect in an oppressively mediated society.

Spiotta's characters struggle with the understanding that their experiences and memories are constructed by corporate entities. Following Nash Davis' wry comment about trying to understand what it feels like not to have Viacom tattooed on our asses, Michael Szalay outlines the connections between the corporate trajectories of Viacom and CBS and Denise and Nik's lives. Nik Worth's "Chronicles" begin the same day as Warner Communications launches MTV. And Denise and Nik split when Viacom splits into Viacom and CBS. CBS owns Simon & Schuster, which owns Scribner, Spiotta's publisher. Tracing these shifting corporate networks, Szalay analyzes the novel as Spiotta's rejection of the trend of literary authors selling their work to premium cable networks. Instead, he argues, Spiotta is honest about Viacom being tattooed on her ass. She writes characters that channel punk's now-defunct refusal into a full rejection of the market. Nik is a brand manager of his fantasy career, with a comprehensive set of false documents including record reviews, interviews, documentaries, CDs, music videos, and posters. Nik Worth has removed himself from economic circulation and created a full simulation of fame without any

possibility of "selling out." He is a hero in a market-driven society. And Nik's alternative career is another way that Spiotta revises the terms of postmodernism: while his career is a perfect simulation of an actual public music career, Stone Arabia makes clear that Nik's simulated career is not ontologically equivalent to a real one. Primarily, he is broke. Denise pays all his bills. So while his CDs are as beautiful as anything published by a record label, major or indie, and while he may be considered a hero for his ultimate refusal of the market-based consumption society, he has not earned anything for his refusal but oblivion.

This is Spiotta's second book about siblings with an overly functional sister and a dependent, ill, absent brother—an unusual theme in literary fiction, which generally focuses on women in the context of heterosexual romance. Spiotta's fiction articulates nuances of women's self-formation through other kinds of family roles. Mina's disappearing brother engenders a profound threat to her identity, a portrait of the absences at the heart of becoming a subject. However, Denise starts writing only after Nik disappears. She requires a loss to rebuild her life through narrative. Denise's writing reinforces the feminist ethic of embodied, empathetic knowledge that is one of Spiotta's major themes. All her novels are enlivened by the restorative power of intimate relationships, from Mina's (briefly glimpsed) with her mother to Mary's with her son, Jason. Denise Kranis finds similar solace and selfhood in serving as her mother's caretaker with an unexpectedly close level of physical intimacy:

> It made sense—we retreated from the mind. The body remained. We lost the memories, and so the past collapsed and disappeared. We were back to the intimacy of our two bodies. And I realized the intimacy was never gone, not completely. It hummed just below our surfaces, held down by our array of vanities and privacies. It felt very simple, and very comforting, that our bodies get returned to each other in the end.
>
> (p. 187)

Soon after, she reflects that memories of her absentee father are also locked in her body. "Inside, beyond my recall of events and dates and talk, there was this hot-wired memory of his

body. I know now how much all of us live in these body places. Your experiences, the hard-felt ones, don't fade. They are written forever in your flesh, your nerves, your fingertips" (p. 189). Both of these passages serve to reinforce the idea that there are aspects of one's experience of self that, while socially constructed, nonetheless exist in a body that has relationships with other bodies. The anxiety about the fallibility of memory that opens Denise's memoir recedes to this belief that the aspects of memory that generate a person's sense of self will be part of one's physical being—flesh, nerves, fingertips. The mother/infant dyad persists and morphs as both age. Reliance on these bodily traces of memory may be the only way to withstand the onslaught of a digital media culture that stretches one's boundaries so thin that they break, to be flooded by the spectacle of never-ending global tragedy.

INNOCENTS AND OTHERS

In Spiotta's fourth book, she returns to material she explored in *Lightning Field*: women trying to be friends and become autonomous subjects in a Los Angeles film culture that does its best to turn women into objects. But this 2016 book distills these themes into a concentrated exploration of the kinds of power women are able to have in a contemporary society for which feminism is a brand. Meadow Mori and Carrie Wexler meet in a private arts school in Los Angeles. Both become filmmakers, but they choose divergent artistic priorities. Meadow is drawn to difficult documentary work—as if Bobby Desoto's SAFE left a legacy for her to push forward. Carrie builds a career in feminist mainstream comedy, putting women at the centers of her stories. Both achieve success, and they remain friends, but the book explores the complexities inherent in both artistic achievement and friendship for women at the millennium. Their stories alternate and briefly cross that of Jelly, a woman with visual impairments who lives in Syracuse and uses phone lines to build intimate and false relationships with powerful Hollywood men. The book builds toward a fourth story to foreground the moral

stakes at issue throughout: a woman in prison for killing her child.

As with Spiotta's other books, *Innocents and Others* dismisses the boundary between fact and fiction, basing characters on real-life oddballs from recent history. Jelly is inspired by a woman calling herself Miranda Grosvenor. In the 1980s, "Miranda" cold-called Hollywood actors, screenwriters, pop stars, composers, and directors and drew them into relationships of passion and intensity, conducted entirely over the phone. Actually a Baton Rouge social worker named Whitney Walton, she fooled famous men into thinking she was a more conventionally beautiful and cultured woman. She did not, however, fake her high-powered social network: a wide circle of major and minor celebrities had phone relationships with her of varying intensities and honesty. Similarly, Jelly's boyfriend, Oz, a blind man with perfect pitch, is based on a figure from the early days of "phone phreaking." Joe Engressia, Jr., calling himself "Joybubbles," was a blind man with perfect pitch who could whistle tones into a phone that would click the automatic switchboard and connect him to distant operators. Thinking he was also an operator, they would connect him long distance for free. Oz has ostensibly similar qualities and introduces Jelly to the world of phone phreaking, a world where people with disabilities and without conventional social standing could hack into the phone system, call long distance for free, and create an international community of people with shared interests. Spiotta's parallels to the contemporary Internet culture of hacking, catfishing, and virtual community are obvious. Less obvious is how deeply invested Spiotta is in taking seriously the sonic world of the visually impaired, as well as the specific technical aspects of production in both the telephone system and film. Her deep attention to these technical details makes clear that she takes these media seriously both as a distinct set of formal, technical, and experiential features and as metaphors for the material underpinnings of cultural phenomena.

The first book since *Lightning Field* that depicts women in positions of cultural power, *Innocents and Others* explores the different ways

that this power takes form. In the earlier book, Lorene builds a lucrative business on understanding men's desires more intimately than they do themselves. In this book, Jelly and Meadow also transform normative feminine traits into tools for social and professional standing—they both draw their own power from cultivating intensive methods of listening, primarily to men. Jelly, overweight, nearly blind, and skilled in phone-based sales, feels compelled to develop relationships with men over the phone. She wants to be "singular. Not even 'a friend.' She wanted a category of her own construction. Something they never knew existed" (pp. 45–46). By creating a new type of relationship, entirely driven by her, something between friendship and romance, she authors a new mode of intersubjectivity. In developing this new mode of social power, she creates a particular way of fulfilling her calling that she calls "body listening"—closing her eyes, leaning back, and "surrendering," as if to a work of art:

> Jelly had a different purpose in listening to anything or anyone. It had something to do with submission, and it had something to do with sympathy. She would lie back and cut off all distraction. The phone was built for this. It had no visual component, no tactile component, no person with hopeful or embarrassed face to read, no scent wafting, no acid collection in the mouth. Just vibrations, long and short waves, and to clutch at them with your own thoughts was just wrong. A distinct resistance to potential. A lack of love, really. Because what is love, if not listening, as uninflected—as uncontained—as possible.

(p. 47)

Jelly's disabilities, vulnerabilities, and beliefs are all evident in this dense passage. Earlier in this section, the narrative explains how Jelly's loss of sight has made common scents almost unbearable to her, as she hides from flowering trees to protect herself. Her hypervigilant senses can be soothed by closing her eyes and focusing on the sound of the phone. The phone also eliminates the difficulties of negotiating a social world of able-bodied people, as Jelly's visual impairments are accompanied by social anxieties that are aggravated by the necessity to find other people's emotional lives visibly legible on their faces. This passage, following her thoughts, also calls

back to her only nonvirtual romantic relationship, with Oz, who showed her how to manipulate the inner workings of the telephone networks using whistles and other tones. To these tones, Jelly attributes a quality of love that is almost chilling in its self-abnegation: that love is purely selfless listening, with no dialogue, not even the listener's thoughts to cloud the experience. This pure passivity inverts feminine traits into means of power over men. Her lover's voice is equivalent to the tones of the hacked telephone system here in a symbiosis recalling Donna Haraway's 1984 "Cyborg Manifesto," an essay about the ethically compromised wartime origins of our beneficial technologies. Haraway writes that we are all cyborgs. Haraway's cyborg is compromised by its origins in nuclear bombs, but Jelly's soulful vulnerability belies her frigid manipulations of the men on the other side of her line.

This frigidity toward her marks puts Jelly on an ethically equal footing with Meadow Mori, the crafty documentary filmmaker whose aesthetic whims subsume her subjects' lives. Jelly may seem more sympathetic than Meadow: Jelly is overweight, disabled, without in-person relationships, and close to broke, while Meadow is thin, professionally successful, and more publicly manipulative. But they use the same tools—goading men into talking about themselves—to achieve their goals. They both privilege their own needs over their partners'. And they are both profoundly lonely. These parallel stories raise the urgency of their meeting, when Meadow woos Jelly into participating in the film and then drops her after manipulating a strained, filmed reunion between her and her virtual ex-lover Jack. Meadow responds to this human tragedy with being disappointed in her documentary technique. She remains ignorant of the emotional havoc she wreaks upon Jelly and Jack. Meadow's next film, about the Argentine soldiers who killed dissidents and raised their children, is perceived—like Bobby Desoto's in *Eat the Document*—as too sympathetic toward self-evidently bad people. Through Meadow's character, Spiotta articulates focused moral quandaries, not only about art-making but also about whether or not it is possible for anyone to be a good person and

whether anyone can be forgiven. Meadow experiences a moral and professional crisis, precipitated by an "aborted" attempt to make a film about Sarah Mills, in prison for starting a fire that killed her boyfriend and toddler daughter; Mills does not start the fire, but she chooses to leave her daughter in the burning apartment building to save the girl from replicating Sarah's life of addiction, violence, sex work, and poverty. The novel aligns Sarah and Meadow as it aligns Meadow and Jelly, putting all their actions—catfishing men, subjugating human lives to an aesthetic vision, and letting a child die in a fire—on the same moral plane. Love and art are matters of life and death.

Her fundamentally generous approach to the myriad ways humans compromise themselves is another way that Spiotta's work revises the postmodern canon and joins fellow good-hearted writers such as David Foster Wallace and Lydia Millet in seeking absolution from the cruelties we inflict on each other and our planet. Spiotta, however, is even more generous than Wallace. For example, both writers create set pieces about the consolations of bad television. In Wallace's *Infinite Jest*, a character dies in front of the television, too fixated on the show *M*A*S*H* to feed himself. In *Innocents and Others*, Carrie writes her own bildungsroman of watching endless, terrible TV as the only child of a divorced, working mother. "But instead of making my taste hackish, I think it made me hunger all the more for something different. It made me imagine what might be good or even better" (p. 207). In Wallace, the pleasures of mass media are fatal. In Spiotta, they are generative. And they are morally sounder than the pleasures of Meadow's difficult work. While Carrie seeks to entertain women like her, Meadow's orientation is fundamentally selfish and inward: she seeks to obliterate and re-form herself. Even in her own moment of transcendence, imagining a film that can show a person "a glimpse of the sublime," she hopes that "everything would change in the doing. Change her vision, and change her, again" (p. 270). None of the women like themselves in this book. But Meadow's realization that her creativity is a manifestation of her own desire to self-

destruct is paired with Sarah's daily ritual of prayer to her daughter. Sarah's prayer is also accompanied by hallucinatory visions of the sublime caused by a neurological phenomenon: When the mind lacks visual stimulation, it invents fantastic images in a multisensory spectacle of automatic neurological self-soothing. "These visions took her through the limits of who she was and what she had done, and for this she felt gratitude, and with this, at last, consolation" (p. 275). By finding a way for Sarah to live with herself, the novel transitively absolves Jelly and Meadow. Through Sarah, Spiotta finds a way for people to forgive themselves.

CONCLUSION

Spiotta's historical fiction conjures the way it feels to walk down Hollywood Boulevard in 1982, or to sit in a weed-fogged political meeting in 1971. She knows what was on the L.A. billboards; she knows what rugs her characters sit on and what they see on the wall through smoky haze. She has discussed in interviews her detailed research methods that focus on the minutiae of lived, quotidian experiences of the period. She watches news footage, reads contemporary newspapers, purchases and uses everyday items like telephones and coffeemakers from the times she represents. She wants to capture how people talked—for example, that people used "women's liberation" instead of "feminism" in the 1960s and 1970s (Johnson interview). She tries to re-create the time period with utmost accuracy through these details, partly in recognition of the fact that plenty of her readers were alive at those times and remember them. But she is also exceptionally invested in the way bodies experience the world. She has described how she fetishizes sound because she uses hearing aids, for example, which displace and rearrange the organic sounds most of us are accustomed to. Her novels brim with technical details about everyday objects and sensory experiences of the times they represent. But for all this dedication to a faithful representation of the time periods her characters occupy, her books remain concerned with the present. Nik's decision to turn

down a record contract in the 1970s mirrors the struggles of current artists with the market's influence on their work—including, as Szalay suggests, Spiotta herself. Furthermore, she compromises historical fidelity by eliding black and other minority experiences from the historical moments she represents. This elision renders inaccurate her depiction of Vietnam War–era radicalism, punk movements, feminist collectives, and other underground histories of the United States.

Her depictions of class are analogously incomplete; her novels decry the power of corporate capitalism to reshape our inner lives, but they do not depict fully the experience of being on the losing end of capital. Lisa, the housekeeper in *Lightning Field*, seems to be fat as a proxy for being poor. While she and Lorene both edge toward satire, Lorene has a poignant, humanizing backstory with Michael while Lisa's cartoonish maternal anxiety fails to do the same for her. Beyond Lisa, Spiotta's characters occupy that ambiguous class status of broke but not poor; they are middle class in experience and expectation no matter the state of their bank accounts. An author does not need to depict the most vulnerable people to critique the worst traits of consumer capitalist society. However, a depiction of working-class identity richer than "overweight and worried" would round out Spiotta's critique. Similarly, Spiotta's depth of respect for the experience of disability is undercut by the way she uses fat bodies as symbols. Jelly's and Oz's visual impairments, as well as Michael's and Nik's mental illnesses, are depicted with nuance and empathy. But representations of Jelly's, Lisa's, and Carrie's body sizes follow the same tired socially constructed narratives: these women eat their feelings and then regret it. In addition, their body sizes serve as foils to wealthier, more successful women. Lisa is fat and poor while Lorene is thin and wealthy. Carrie is fat and middlebrow while Meadow is thin and aesthetically pure. Jelly is fat and lonely while Meadow is thin, has lovers, and manipulates Jelly's life for her own artistic gain. Spiotta's feminism is clear in her focus on women's experiences of patriarchal society. But it is compromised when

she cannot depict a larger-sized woman whose body size is irrelevant to her narrative role.

While Spiotta remains underrepresented in scholarship, various strands of contemporary academic work contextualize her role in the generation of post–baby boomers sharing the awards short lists with her. Kelly references her work in his 2016 analysis of "New Sincerity" in contemporary fiction. With this term, Kelly theorizes the trend of contemporary writers refuting the modernist and postmodernist valorization of craft and instead creating relationships with readers based on trust and faith. This "sincerity" is "new" because these writerly/readerly relationships also acknowledge the post-structuralist deconstruction of representation and authorial voice, as well as the potential corruption of their work by the market. Kelly joins a wide set of critics concerned with the affective and relational features of "post-postmodern" literature and culture; Sianne Ngai's *Ugly Feelings* (2005) and Lee Konstantinou's *Cool Characters: Irony and American Fiction* (2016) are just two examples of book-length works taking emotions as their critical object. There is broad critical consensus that affect is key to understanding and theorizing the newer generation of fiction. With her use of relationships and emotions to revise the terms of postmodernism, Spiotta should be central to these generational assessments of contemporary fiction.

The political stakes of foregrounding affect in novels written by and about women remain high. Spiotta's characters, mostly women, experience ethical crises, depression, loneliness, and body shame. Still, these characters are cooler than you. They hang in Los Angeles clubs listening to punk morph into glam rock. They dance with a drunk Dennis Wilson in a bar in Santa Monica. They build extravagant restaurants that actually turn a profit. They found revolutionary political movements, honing their ideological purity to destroy the military-industrial complex. They hack Ma Bell. They seduce film and pop stars. They join radical feminist communes and teach kids with disabilities. They wear sleek jeans and record avant-garde albums. They make films about war criminals in Argentina and the United States. These characters allow the reader to touch history without nostalgia blinding them to

history's abuses. Spiotta's work is sexy without exploitation, aspirational without elitism, intelligent without obfuscation. Her novels help us understand both our recent past and our contemporary moment. The future for Spiotta's readers looks bright.

Selected Bibliography

WORKS OF DANA SPIOTTA

Lightning Field. New York: Scribner, 2001.

Eat the Document. New York: Scribner, 2006.

Stone Arabia. New York: Scribner, 2011.

Innocents and Others. New York: Scribner, 2016.

CRITICAL AND BIOGRAPHICAL STUDIES

Kelly, Adam. "Beginning with Postmodernism." *Twentieth Century Literature* 57:391–422 (2011).

———. "'Who Is Responsible?' Revisiting the Radical Years in Dana Spiotta's *Eat the Document*." In *Forever Young: The Changing Images of America*. Edited by Philip Coleman and Stephen Matterson. Heidelberg: EAAS, 2012. Pp. 219–230.

———. "The New Sincerity." In *Postmodern/Postwar—and After: Rethinking American Literature*. Edited by Jason Gladstone, Andrew Hoberek, and Daniel Worden. Iowa City: University of Iowa Press, 2016. Pp. 197–208.

Masterson, John. "'It's Not Dark Yet, but It's Getting There': Listening for the End Times in the Contemporary American Novel." *Studia Neophilologica* 88:68–80 (January 2016).

Szalay, Michael. "The Incorporation Artist." *Los Angeles Review of Books*, July 10, 2012. https://lareviewofbooks. org/article/the-incorporation-artist

Varvogli, Aliki. "Radical Motherhood: Narcissism and Empathy in Russell Banks's *The Darling* and Dana Spiotta's *Eat the Document*." *Journal of American Studies* 44, no. 4:657–673 (2010).

INTERVIEWS

Benz, Chanelle. "Interview: Dana Spiotta." Cosmonauts Avenue. http://www.cosmonautsavenue.com/interview-with-dana-spiotta

Burton, Susan. "The Quietly Subversive Fictions of Dana Spiotta." *New York Times Magazine*, February 21, 2016. http://www.nytimes.com/2016/02/21/magazine/the-quietly-subversive-fictions-of-dana-spiotta.html

Johnson, Liza. "Dana Spiotta [author]." *Believer*, fall 2015. http://www.believermag.com/exclusives/?read=interview_spiotta

O'Grady, Megan. "Dana Spiotta's Brilliant New Novel, *Innocents and Others*, Follows the Paths of Two Filmmaking Friends." *Vogue*, February 27, 2016. http://www.vogue.com/13407337/dana-spiotta-innocents-and-others

Smith, Dinitia. "A Radical on the Run as a Novelist's Muse." *New York Times*, February 8, 2006. http://www.nytimes.com/2006/02/08/books/08spio.html

Turner, Jenny. "Whoosh." *London Review of Books*, June 7, 2007, pp. 25–26. http://www.lrb.co.uk/v29/n11/jenny-turner/whoosh

OTHER SOURCES

Bordo, Susan. *Unbearable Weight: Feminism, Western Culture, and the Body*. Berkeley: University of California Press, 2003.

Burn, Stephen. *Jonathan Franzen at the End of Postmodernism*. New York: Continuum, 2008.

Burrough, Bryan. "The Miranda Obsession." *Vanity Fair*, December 15, 1999. http://www.vanityfair.com/culture/1999/12/miranda-catfish-movie-199912

Konstantinou, Lee. *Cool Characters: Irony and Postmodern Fiction*. Cambridge, Mass.: Harvard University Press, 2016.

Lapsley, Phil. *Exploding the Phone: The Untold Story of Teenagers Who Hacked Ma Bell*. New York: Grove Press, 2013.

Martin, Douglas. "Joybubbles, 58, Peter Pan of Phone Hackers, Dies." *New York Times*, August 20, 2007. http://www.nytimes.com/2007/08/20/us/20engressia.html

Ngai, Sianne. *Ugly Feelings*. Cambridge, Mass.: Harvard University Press, 2005.

RUTH McENERY STUART

(1849—1917)

Joan Wylie Hall

RESPONDING TO THE national demand for regionalist fiction after the Civil War, Ruth McEnery Stuart became one of the most popular American women writers of the late nineteenth century. A fragile scrapbook at Tulane University in New Orleans is filled with enthusiastic responses to her twenty books and the readings she gave from Boston to San Francisco. Whether her subject was the loyalty of former slaves on the planation, middle-aged romance, or an Arkansas farmer's pride in his son's childhood escapades, reviewers praised Stuart for the combination of humor and pathos that characterized much local color writing, including the New England tales by Mary Wilkins Freeman and the Louisiana bayou stories of Kate Chopin. In her unpublished letters, Stuart refers to Freeman, Chopin, Mark Twain, and other friends and acquaintances whose literary reputations have outlasted her own.

In 1894 new Southern regionalist books by Stuart (*Carlotta's Intended and Other Tales*) and Chopin (*Bayou Folk*) were both well received. Chopin's "As You Like It" column for the 1897 St. Louis *Criterion* singles out Stuart's title story, "Carlotta's Intended," describing her fellow Louisianan as a "celebrity" who was "recognized throughout the length and breadth of these United States" (p. 712). According to Chopin, Stuart's "deliciously humorous and pathetic" stories are marked by the "wholesome, human note sounding through and through them" (p. 711). Two years later, when many readers were recoiling from the sexual frankness of Chopin's bold new novel, *The Awakening*, they could turn in relief to Stuart's latest book, *Holly and Pizen, and Other Stories*, where "Comedy and Tragedy walked hand and hand," as Stuart says of two characters in her closing black dialect tale, "Picayune: A Child Story" (*Holly and Pizen*, p.

196). Stuart's full-length photograph on the cover of the December 16, 1899 *Harper's Bazar* (as the name was spelled then) marked her selection as "American Authoress of the Hour." With the shift in American tastes by the start of World War I, however, pathos was rejected as sentimentality, humor acquired a sharper edge, and the moderns supplanted the Victorians. Belatedly, Stuart attempted to adapt to these cultural changes, creating a sassy New York narrator and a twentieth-century setting for *The Cocoon: A Rest-Cure Comedy* (1915). Yet her final book was *Plantation Songs and Other Verse* (1916), with E. W. Kemble's cover sketch of a banjo-strumming black man.

When Stuart died in 1917, lengthy obituaries in the *New York Times* and the *New Orleans Times-Picayune* praised her facility with various dialects of American speech and her empathy for humble characters. In more recent decades, scholars have identified Stuart's linguistic skill with racist, xenophobic, and classist attitudes in her portrayals of African Americans, immigrants, and rural Caucasians. Critics have responded more positively to Stuart's treatment of women. Although traditional courtship and marriage plots are prominent in her fiction, the death of her husband after four years of marriage helps to explain the presence of several widows and spinsters. Moreover, Stuart's personal alliances with career women, club women, and the woman's suffrage movement are consistent with her several stories about independent females, especially white women. Reminiscent of Freeman's Louisa Ellis in "A New England Nun," some of Stuart's most memorable characters are content with singleness.

Stuart established her fame with black dialect humor, which constitutes over half of her pub-

lished writing. In addition to several story collections, her works about African Americans include two short novels and two books of verse. Although the male characters, in particular, suffer from the sort of stereotyping that was common in the era's minstrel shows, white Southern authors thought Stuart was an exceptional storyteller. Joel Chandler Harris, author of the Uncle Remus stories, credited her with unusual insight into African American life when he told her: "You have got nearer the heart of the negro than any of us" (qtd. in Stevens, p. 5146). The novelist George Washington Cable, who was virtually exiled from the South for his progressive racial views, nevertheless exchanged witty letters in black dialect with Stuart when she was planning a party for Cable in her New York apartment.

Stuart's dialect fiction is not limited to tales about mammies, laundrywomen, and black "uncles." New Orleans, where she grew up, had distinctive neighborhoods of Germans, Irish, Italians, and Creoles, and Stuart was celebrated for her ethnic characterizations and her fidelity in reproducing language features of each group. For these stories, too, sentimental humor was her typical mode. Although more recent criticism has stressed elements of racism and imperialism in such comic regional writing, earlier critical responses emphasized the role of local color fiction in reuniting North and South during the Reconstruction years. Stuart herself claimed she was a folklorist whose works preserved cultures that were drastically changing.

By the mid-1890s, Stuart branched out from the "folk" of plantations and urban enclaves to depict small-town life—primarily Caucasian life—in Simpkinsville, a fictitious Arkansas village. Many Simpkinsville stories portray Stuart's most popular characters, Deuteronomy Jones and Sonny, the spoiled but lovable child of Jones's middle age. *Sonny* (1896) went into so many printings that she published the sequel *Sonny's Father* in 1910. In contrast, *The Cocoon* and a few of Stuart's other late stories mark a striking departure from her quarter-century of local color writing, raising matters of interest to the "New Woman," from clothing fashions to divorce and eugenics. The metamorphosis from the comic philosophizing in Stuart's first published work, "Uncle Mingo's 'Speculatioms' [sic]," to Blessy Heminway's very modern speculations in *The Cocoon*, sums up Stuart's unusual place in the history of American women's fiction.

BIOGRAPHY

Ruth McEnery Stuart was born Mary Routh McEnery on May 21, probably in 1849, in Marksville, Avoyelles Parish, Louisiana. The loss of many public documents during the Civil War complicates the verification of dates for her early life, and different years between 1848 and 1860 have been cited for her birth. Stuart's gravestone in Metairie Cemetery, New Orleans, lists only the date of death, along with the names of her parents, her husband, and her only son, Stirling McEnery Stuart. The first of eight children of James and Mary Routh (Stirling) McEnery, Stuart was known by her middle name, the spelling of which she changed to Ruth by the time she began publishing in New York magazines in 1888. Her earliest years were spent on the family plantation in Marksville, where her father once served as town mayor, but around 1852 he joined the Custom House staff in New Orleans.

Stuart's Scottish grandfather, Sir John Stirling, dropped his title after immigrating from Dundee. In an essay for *Youth's Companion* in 1900, Stuart mentions Stirling's purchase of the ten-year-old slave Fanny "as nurse for my mother at her birth" ("I Remember," pt. 1, p. 348). In middle age, Fanny cooked for the McEnerys, and her stories and superstitions fascinated Stuart. Although Stuart was an adolescent during the federal occupation of New Orleans, the Civil War is rarely the subject of her fiction. An exception is the story "St. Idyl's Light" (1898), about an orphan girl who dies trying to rescue a local artillery unit from attack by Farragut's fleet on April 23, 1862. Two of Stuart's cousins, John and Samuel McEnery, became governors of Louisiana in the postbellum era. John was quickly removed from office after the disputed election of 1872, but Samuel served from 1881 to 1888 and was later a U.S. senator for several years.

RUTH McENERY STUART

In New Orleans, Stuart's childhood experiences were less circumscribed than they would have been on the family's plantation. Even before the Emancipation Proclamation of 1863 liberated Southern slaves, a large free-black community added to the ethnic diversity of New Orleans. Creole, Irish, Italian, and German communities were likewise later incorporated into Stuart's fiction. Educated in private and public schools, Stuart published unsigned pieces in the city's newspapers while teaching kindergarten at the Locquet-LeRoy Institute for girls. After a visit with her Arkansas relatives in 1879, she taught in Columbus, Arkansas, for four months, then married Alfred Oden Stuart, a plantation owner and merchant from nearby Washington, on August 6. Washington had served as Arkansas' Confederate capital during the Civil War, and A. O. Stuart, who was in his forties during the war, raised food on his plantations to supply rebel forces.

Three times a widower, the fifty-eight-year-old Stuart had eleven children, some of them very young at the time of his marriage to Ruth. Stirling McEnery Stuart, born November 26, 1880, was the only child of this fourth marriage. Ruth Stuart was known as a gracious hostess in Washington, which later served as the model for her Simpkinsville stories. The first work that can definitely be ascribed to Stuart is her parody of Edgar Allan Poe's "The Raven," which she delivered to the Dear Old Town Club, a reading group she founded. Stuart's piece has little in common with the dialect fiction she would begin to publish in 1888, but it does anticipate the comic verses of writers like Carolyn Wells, whom Stuart met after she moved to New York.

After her husband died from a stroke in 1883, Stuart moved back to New Orleans with Stirling and probably resumed teaching. Her youngest stepchildren made homes with their older siblings in Arkansas. Stuart was active in literary circles, where she met such female journalists, editors, and authors as Elizabeth Bisland, Dorothy Dix, Katherine Nobles, and Eliza Jane Poitevent Nicholson. The first two women's clubs in New Orleans were founded in 1884 by Bisland and by the poet and fiction writer Mollie Moore Davis. As a friend of Davis—the wife of *Picayune* edi-

tor Thomas E. Davis—Stuart frequented a salon whose guests included George Washington Cable, Grace King, and other New Orleans writers. Many visitors to the city also came to Davis' Friday afternoons, among them the poet Eugene Field, Robert Louis Stevenson of *Treasure Island* fame, and the *Harper's* editor Charles Dudley Warner.

According to the scholar Ethel C. Simpson, Stuart's encounter with Warner at a North Carolina summer resort in 1887 "marked the real beginning" of her career as a writer (Introduction to *Simpkinsville and Vicinity*, p. 4). Back in New Orleans, Stuart sent him two dialect stories, asking for criticism. Warner accepted "The Lamentations of Jeremiah Johnson" for *Harper's* and recommended "Uncle Mingo's 'Speculatioms [sic]'" to the *New Princeton Review*, which in February 1888 became the first magazine to publish Ruth McEnery Stuart. By 1891 Stuart had moved to New York; she was one of several Southern women who established literary professions and permanent residence in the city. While newcomers typically wrote book reviews, Stuart's reputation for black dialect fiction preceded her. A position as substitute editor for Margaret Sangster at *Harper's Bazar* may have been her original reason for relocating. Stuart served similar brief terms on other journals, and she soon was determined to make her living as a full-time writer.

In 1893 her first collection, *A Golden Wedding and Other Tales*, appeared to favorable reviews. Comprised chiefly of humorous and sentimental black dialect stories, the book contained some important new subject matter. "Camelia Riccardo," a tale about the belle of the French Market, is the first of Stuart's comic pieces on European immigrants and their descendants in New Orleans. Small-town spinsters, a familiar character type in her subsequent fiction, are the protagonists of "The Woman's Exchange of Simpkinsville." The volume concludes with two dialect poems, Stuart's earliest examples of a form that helped to make her famous. She also presented highly successful readings, assuming the speech patterns and personalities of her characters, from black laundresses to aristocratic

white gentlemen. Gena McKinley compares such performances to minstrel shows, arguing that "the fact that she was not in blackface, even though she was acting out the myths of the minstrelsy, whitewashed the racism of the performances and highlighted instead the audience's identification with Stuart herself" (p. 107). Yet, listeners were amused by Stuart's black stereotypes, and her very presence on Northern stages dramatized the conciliatory function that regionalist literature served for decades after the Civil War. A four-month national reading tour by Twain and Cable in 1884–1885 was an even more graphic display of the country's reunification since the men complemented each other so strikingly in temperament, oratorical style, and regional identity.

Like Stuart, some of her closest friends in New York were cultural transplants. During the winter of 1895–1896, she invited Sarah Barnwell Elliott, whom she had met in New Orleans, to share an apartment on East 27th Street. A Tennessee local colorist and daughter of a founder of the University of the South, Elliott had four books to her credit, including the popular novel *Jerry* (1891). Stuart had recently published a second collection, *Carlotta's Intended and Other Tales* (1894), as well as her first novel, *The Story of Babette: A Little Creole Girl* (1894), which she dedicated to the girls of New Orleans. Stuart and Elliott were active in a literary group that included the *Harper*'s editors Sangster and Warner; Cable, who by then had alienated many Southerners with his critical portrayals of white Creole society; Edmund Clarence Stedman, a critic and anthologist; Elizabeth Bacon Custer, the lecturer and widow of General George Armstrong Custer; and Frank Stockton, the *St. Nicholas* editor best remembered for his story "The Lady or the Tiger?" (1882). As a member of the inner circle at *Harper's Bazar*, Stuart was known as a "*Harper's* pet" of the "*Harper's* set." She joined the Barnard, Wednesday Afternoon, and Cosmopolitan clubs; in 1904, she became a member of the Lyceum Club, a woman's organization in London that extended membership to select American writers and artists.

Neighbors of Stuart and Elliott included the pioneer textile designer and interior decorator Candace Wheeler, a business partner of Louis Comfort Tiffany in Associated Artists. The firm decorated Twain's home in Hartford, Connecticut, and they used Celtic knots, dragon designs, and other suggestions of knighthood for the Veterans' Room and Library at the new Park Avenue Armory. This imposing building was headquarters for the elite Seventh Regiment of the New York National Guard, in which Stuart's son Stirling enlisted as a young man. When Stuart became her New York neighbor, Wheeler had recently served as "color director" of the Women's Building at the 1893 World's Columbian Exposition in Chicago, where she organized the display of women's work in the applied arts.

Through Wheeler, Stuart joined artists and writers at the rustic Onteora colony of summer homes in the Catskills. The community became a favorite vacation spot for Stuart, her son, and her sister Sarah McEnery, who moved from New Orleans to live with the Stuarts around 1896. Among the residents and frequent visitors at Onteora were Twain, Stockton, the critic Laurence Hutton, the nature writer John Burroughs (whom Stuart mentions affectionately in her Sonny stories), and several women authors and editors, including Mary Mapes Dodge of *St. Nicholas*, the playwright Marguerite Merington, Jeannette Leonard Gilder of the *Critic* and *Putnam's Monthly*, and Sarah Chauncey Woolsey, who wrote the popular "Katy" series for girls. In her memoir *Yesterdays*, Wheeler describes an elaborate costume party at Onteora, with a "picturesque gipsy-clad tribe" gathered around a large caldron while "Ruth McEnery Stuart, that famous cook of things literary as well as sublunary," presided over "a heaven-smelling stew made after Walter Scott's recipe" (p. 295).

Wheeler's cover story on Stuart for *Harper's Bazar* in 1899 also gives a personal view of the author in the Catskills, emphasizing Stuart's congeniality, her culinary skills, and her knowledge of woodcraft, especially mycology, or the science of mushrooms. The second half of the 1890s had been a fruitful period for Stuart, including a three-week reading tour of Chicago in 1895. Other tours before the end of the decade took her to Boston, Atlanta, Virginia, and

Colorado. *Sonny*, her most popular book, was published in 1896; the collection depicts the doting paternity of the Simpkinsville farmer Deuteronomy Jones in monologues that recall the antebellum genre of Southwest humor. The same year saw the appearance of *Gobolinks; or, Shadow Pictures for Young and Old*, Stuart's collaboration with her friend Albert Bigelow Paine, a novelist and editor who later wrote Twain's biography. A growth in leisure time for middle- and upper-class Americans at the end of the century created a market for such books of easy entertainments as Stuart's series of inkblots. Stuart and Paine preface their whimsical verses with directions for a game of Gobolinks in which readers could make and interpret their own creations from ink and paper. The standard English verses, the rhymes, and the playful tone of *Gobolinks* all recall Stuart's early "Raven" parody.

By the end of 1897, Stuart had completed a short play, *The Snow-Cap Sisters: A Farce*, and the two story collections *In Simpkinsville: Character Tales* and *Solomon Crow's Christmas Pockets and Other Tales*. Two more books followed within the next two years: *Moriah's Mourning and Other Half-Hour Sketches* (1898) and *Holly and Pizen, and Other Stories* (1899). Impressed by Stuart's Southern manners, the journalist Stanhope Sams reported that the "quaint old furniture" she brought from New Orleans gave her New York drawing room "something of the environment of that aristocratic life which was known in the ante-bellum South" (p. 201), but he also observed that "the amount of work she accomplishes would break down a strong man" (p. 204). Sams believed that the "very modern and utilitarian big roll-top desk and type-writer" in Stuart's study showed how completely "she has become part of a great, bustling modern city" (pp. 203, 201). He adds that, without the "tremendous assistance of that prosaic machine, the type-writer," she could never have written so much (p. 204).

In "The Author's Reading in Simpkinsville" (1900), Stuart draws on her own experience when the talkative Deuteronomy Jones relates his "face to face" encounter with an elegantly dressed "genuwine book-factory, femi-nine gender" writer who visits Simpkinsville to read from her books (p. 614). The Arkansas farmer is puzzled that the speaker appears to be "purty tired" after her program, "although she ain't done a stroke o' work since she come" (p. 616). Prone to colds, shingles, and nervous exhaustion, Stuart sometimes needed a more thorough rest than even the Onteora colony provided. She found relief on several trips to the Jackson Sanatorium, a health resort in Dansville, New York; she was recuperating there in March 1905 when her son Stirling suffered a serious fall from the roof of their Long Island home. He had forgotten his key and tried to break into the house with a friend from the Seventh Regiment after a late dinner at the Park Avenue Armory.

In addition to her heavy schedule of readings and social events, Stuart had published three short novels and a collection of short stories in the first five years of the new century, and doctors feared she was too fragile to survive the shock of her son's accident. Stuart had often confided her concerns and hopes for Stirling in letters to her Boston friends, the physicians Augusta and Emily Pope. For at least three years after Stirling's death on Good Friday of 1905, Stuart wrote to the twin sisters on black-bordered mourning stationery. Friends too of Mary Wilkins Freeman, the Popes were crucial members of Stuart's network of supportive women, welcoming her to their Back Bay house on her reading trips to Boston.

Although Stuart cut back drastically on social activities in the months after Stirling's death, later that year she attended the celebration of Mark Twain's seventieth birthday at Delmonico's restaurant, along with many of America's literary stars. Stuart was seated at the head table with Twain and his friend Joseph Twichell, the Standard Oil millionaire Henry Rogers, the poet Bliss Carmen, the *Harper's* editor Henry Mills Alden, the novelist Kate Douglas Wiggin Riggs, and Mary Wilkins Freeman. The following February, Stuart returned with a personal nurse to the Dansville health resort, which was nationally known for its baths and other rest cure treatments. Stuart was disappointed that she seemed to lack

the stamina for writing, and on the Fourth of July she somewhat reluctantly sailed with friends to Europe. She traveled through Scandinavia and the British Isles until December, but the long journey had no immediate impact on the subjects of her work. In the summer of 1911, Stuart again went to Europe; that year, she published a detailed essay, "Browsing About the Ibsen Country," in *Harper's Bazar*. Stuart's interest in folklore and culture is evident in her descriptions of Norwegian dress, Swedish dances, and an exhibit of a decaying Viking ship. She compares impoverished young women of noble Scandinavian ancestry to the "pallid well-bred wom[e]n of the old regime" who took jobs in New Orleans shops after the Civil War (p. 313). Revealing a close knowledge of Henrik Ibsen's plays, Stuart singles out *Peer Gynt* as her favorite. She dismisses the heroine of *A Doll's House* as "the whimsical Nora" and relates a "toothsome bit of gossip" on Ibsen's defense of his unconventional character (p. 312).

After a lapse of about four years following Stirling's death, Stuart's books again appeared regularly. She had resumed her public readings by the spring of 1908, when she hosted her New York friend Candace Wheeler on a visit to New Orleans during Mardi Gras season. The next year, she fulfilled a promise to her friend Libbie Custer by writing an episode about Washington Irving for a four-day program celebrating the history of Westchester County, New York. Between 1909 and 1916, Stuart published seven volumes, including short-story collections, longer fiction, poetry, and a decorated gift book edition of *The Unlived Life of Little Mary Ellen* (1910), one of her longest and most popular Simpkinsville stories. Like her earlier books, most of these later volumes gathered fiction and poetry that she had published in *Century*, *Harper's*, *St. Nicholas*, and other major periodicals.

In 1913 Stuart collected several of her black dialect verses in *Daddy Do-Funny's Wisdom Jingles*, and the *New York Times* printed her "Value of Folklore in Literature," a defense of dialect fiction. Her tone is more mellow in a 1914 *Bookman* essay, "American Backgrounds for Fiction: VI—Arkansas, Louisiana and the Gulf Country," but here too she emphasizes literature's ability to record cultures that are rapidly changing, singling out Grace King in her discussion of New Orleans authors. The next year, Stuart and King sat together on the platform at Tulane University, where they were awarded honorary degrees for their contributions to Southern arts and letters. To hold the parchment diploma, Stuart received a jeweled box from a recently formed literary club, the Ruth McEnery Stuart Clan. Still active in twenty-first-century New Orleans, the elite club was organized in the winter of 1913–1914 by Stuart's friend the attorney Judith Hyman Douglas. Favors for the Clan luncheon were copies of Stuart's new book, *The Cocoon: A Rest-Cure Comedy*. In contrast, at a large banquet hosted in her honor by the Newcomb College Alumnae Association, Stuart recited one of her black dialect poems. Along with nostalgic dialect poetry, her final volume, *Plantation Songs and Other Verse*, includes material that is more modern in both subject matter and voice, especially "Disarmament," "Brotherhood," "Ye Merry Peacemakers," and other poems reflecting Stuart's opposition to World War I.

Stuart died in New York from pneumonia on May 9, 1917, one month after the United States entered the war. After Stirling's death in 1905, she had added a codicil to her will, naming her sister Sarah as her main beneficiary. Stuart originally planned to leave her rolltop desk and typewriter to her son, perhaps symbolically willing him to follow a writing career. Stuart sold at least one of Stirling's story manuscripts, "The Match," to a news syndicate for posthumous publication, and Sarah made similar efforts to give her sister a lasting literary reputation. Part of Stuart's legacy to Sarah was a sheaf of pages covered with her signature; now held by the Historic New Orleans Collection, these autographs were to be pasted into new copies of her books to increase their value.

Herself an occasional author of poetry and essays, Sarah McEnery tried to find a second life for Stuart's dialect fiction on stage. Stuart had published a few verses as lyrics for sheet music during her lifetime, and a few more of her dialect poems appeared posthumously in this popular

form between 1918 and 1923. By the late 1920s, most of Stuart's books were out of print, and a theatrical success could have revived her fading literary reputation. Sarah McEnery's final effort to ensure lasting recognition for her sister was a series of interviews with Mary Frances Fletcher for a 1935 master's thesis on Stuart at the University of Virginia. Twenty years later, Fletcher completed a doctoral degree for Louisiana State University with an expanded manuscript. Fletcher concluded that Stuart, "more than many of her contemporaries, suffered from the reaction against the sentimental era in the years following World War I" (p. v).

A GOLDEN WEDDING *AND DIALECT WRITING*

Stuart's first book introduced the dialects, ethnic groups, settings, and themes that characterize her body of local color writing. On the cover of *A Golden Wedding and Other Tales* (1893), stylized cotton bolls announce that her subject is the South; on the book spine, beribboned bells emphasize the romance theme of the title. Stuart's focus on African American characters is evident in the frontispiece, "The Cake-Walk" by A. B. Frost, who illustrated many of Harris' Uncle Remus stories. While African American rituals and celebrations were sometimes staged to entertain white audiences, African Americans are the only spectators in Frost's ballroom and in "Jessekiah Brown's Courtship," the related story in the *Golden Wedding* volume. The stout couple in Frost's promenade is recognizable as Jessekiah— "the fattest man as well as the oldest bachelor of his color on the plantation" (*A Golden Wedding*, p. 189)—and his dreaded dance partner, "Fat Ann." Stuart's story and Frost's illustration recall a similar comic emphasis on white characters' bodies in Augustus Baldwin Longstreet's "The Dance," one of the most frenetic Southwest humor tales in his *Georgia Scenes* (1835).

The immersion of the Caucasian reader in an African American world was a fairly novel experience in the late 1880s, when Stuart began to publish magazine fiction. In his biographical essay for the *Library of Southern Literature*, Alexander Stephens (presented as Stevens by

mistake of his publisher) asserted that, "although not the first to treat the negro in fiction, Mrs. Stuart has perhaps been the first to show him in his home life independently of his relations with the white man" (p. 5146). In fact, interracial relationships are depicted—often nostalgically—in much of Stuart's fiction, but the title story of *A Golden Wedding* supports Stephens' observation. Sharing a Christmas chicken dinner in their New Orleans tenement, the elderly black neighbors of "A Golden Wedding" discover that they were once husband and wife, married miles away on a distant Christmas.

Slaves on adjoining Louisiana plantations before the war, Cicely and Aleck are separated for decades after Aleck's master, unhappy with their marriage, moves his household to Georgia and later sells Aleck to the Thompson plantation. Cicely, along with their son, Joe, also becomes another man's property when she is sold by the Morgans to the Garretts. Changes in geography, physical appearances, and surnames cause the same complications in "A Golden Wedding" as they do five years later in the African American author Charles Chesnutt's story "The Wife of His Youth" (1898). In Stuart's tale Aleck explains, "quick's de wah was over an' Freedom loosen me, I come clair back ter de coas'—I wucked my way down—a-huntin' fur Cicely; but 'twarn't no use. Her marster done had been kilt in de army, an' look like ev'ything was gone ter rack 'n' ruin" (p. 17).

Eventually, both spouses are drawn from their plantations to New Orleans, a magnet for former slaves. There, Stuart's Christmas setting underscores the wonder of their reunion. Adding to the joy, Cecily and Aleck find their lost son, Joe, at a church gathering for their golden wedding festivities. Now a fifty-year-old minister, Joe had escaped slavery to join the Union Army. And, as testament to his liberty, he changed the family name Smith (from Aleck's early Louisiana owner) to Lincoln. Affirming their marriage, Aleck Thompson and Cecily Garrett reclaim their early surname; Joe is willing to be a Smith for his parents' sake, but he prefers to keep "a name what stood fur freedom" (p. 38). As he tells his father: "I 'ain't nuver spect ter see yer no mo',

an' you 'ain't had no name what yer mought say was borned ter yer nohow" (p. 38). Brother Lincoln's several children include not only "Aberham, to match in wid de Lincoln," but "Phil Sheridam an' Gineral Grant" (p. 40) as well.

Early in 1900, seven years after the *Golden Wedding* volume was published, Stuart traveled to Hampton Normal and Agricultural Institute, a historically black institution in Virginia, to help students present a dramatic version of the title story as a fundraiser for African American education. In February a touring group from the school performed the dramatization in Brooklyn's Memorial Hall to support Hampton's endowment. The program included dialect readings by Stuart and plantation songs by the students.

"A Golden Wedding" is a romance, not a critique of slavery. Yet by relating so precisely the tragic circumstances of the young couple's separation, this keynote story of Stuart's first book acknowledges a master's potential for destroying the lives of his slaves. The *Golden Wedding* collection portrays this same potential more comically in "Christmas Gifts," set some years before the Civil War. In contrast to the meager Christmas dinner in a tenement in the previous story, Stuart introduces a prosperous plantation: "It is a rich Christmas of the olden time" (p. 130). Although the master of Sucrier plantation is "easy-going" and "happy," a reference to his "lax business habits" foreshadows the crisis he casually provokes for Lucindy and Dave, a newlywed slave couple. The distant crisis of the Civil War is implicit in the ominous remark that "old Colonel Slack had grown wealthy simply because he lived on the shore where the tide always came in—the same shore where since '61 the waters move ever to the sea, and those who waited where he stood are stranded" (pp. 130–131).

But the narrator does not suggest any connection between the war and the plantation's large slave population. Instead, "Christmas Gifts" portrays a humorous misunderstanding when Colonel Slack sends the cheerful Lucindy and the pony Lady Gay to the adjoining plantation with a letter bestowing them both on his married daughter Louise. Louise describes the young slave and the pony as "my two best Christmas gifts," but she is "almost frightened" by Lucindy's alarm at hearing about her new home: "The happy-hearted child of a moment ago was transformed into a desperate, grief-stricken woman" (p. 142). Slaves are often portrayed as childlike in Stuart's sentimental fiction, but in his failure to tell Lucindy she would be transferred to another plantation, Colonel Slack is portrayed as both childlike and harmful: "A tender-souled, good old man was he, yet thoughtless, withal, as a growing boy" (p. 132). Lucindy's grief at her separation from Dave turns to rage as she rampages through the kitchen, destroying all of her Christmas presents from the Slacks. She wounds her ears by yanking out the earrings, bares her feet in kicking the shoes into the fire, and tears her skirt trying to remove the new hoop frame. By exaggerating Lucindy's passion to excess, Stuart turns the scene into a burlesque, with slave children rolling on the floor and kitchen workers raucously discussing Lucindy's marriage to a cross-eyed husband.

Meanwhile, the oblivious Dave arrives with a message from the colonel; to his shock, he learns he is Louise's Christmas gift, and he has no idea what has become of Lucindy. Neither spouse knows that the colonel's letter is a "deed of conveyance of 'two adult negroes, by name Lucinda and David.' Then followed descriptions of each, which it was unnecessary to read" (p. 146). Quickly grasping the situation, Louise can tell from the legal document that her father never intended to separate the couple, yet she acts confused when Dave cries and stutters in distress at the apparent loss of his wife. With callous playfulness, Louise protests: "From the way you all are acting to-day, I begin to be afraid of myself. Don't you want to belong to me?" (p. 147). She decides not to enlighten the distraught couple at once because "the situation, which was plain now, had grown so interesting that Louise could not resist the temptation to bring the unconscious actors in the little drama together, that she might witness the happy catastrophe" (p. 147). Calling Lucindy from the kitchen, Louise is startled—not only by the slave's fierce eyes but also by her bloody ears and fingernails, her

torn clothes, and her taut veins: "The girl's appearance was indeed tragic" (p. 148). In a narrative by Harriet Jacobs or Harriet Beecher Stowe, a cruel master or overseer would be the likely reason for such signs of injury, but Colonel Slack is merely "the clumsiest old blunderer" (p. 153), as he admits when he appears at Louise's front door. The alarm Lucindy provoked in Louise vanishes with the colonel's explanation for the comedy of errors.

Colonel Slack says he kept the couple's transfer to Louise's plantation a secret because "saying good-bye will cast a sort of shadow over things" on Christmas, and "Dave and Lucindy are immensely popular among the darkies" (p. 153). With the euphemism "saying good-bye," Colonel Slack describes their uprooting from home and then patronizes them as "darkies." Apologizing to the young couple, he gives them each a five-dollar bill "to pay for spoiling your Christmas" (p. 153). Similarly, in Twain's *Adventures of Huckleberry Finn*, Tom Sawyer pays the slave Jim forty dollars for being a good sport during Tom's dangerous game, a rescue effort that is unnecessary since Miss Watson has already freed Jim in her will. Stuart's slaves are reunited but still enslaved at the end of "Christmas Gifts." Nevertheless, in Stuart's happy ending, they are proud of their new status on Louise's plantation.

That night at the Sucrier festival, Lucindy is dressed in a cast-off gown from her new mistress when she boasts that she is "a house-gal now!" and won't wear "common ornamints, same as you fiel'-han's" (p. 154). She does not explain that she ruined her own prized ornaments in the depths of despair. Describing Stuart's black dialect novel *Napoleon Jackson* (1902), Dorothy H. Brown says that, through the words of a washerwoman, "Stuart frankly states the inadequate payment which has been the lot of Rose Ann and her family" (p. 31). Likewise, in "Christmas Gifts," Colonel Slack's five-dollar bills are inadequate compensation for the reality that Lucindy and Dave are disposable property. Beginning with the title, this fact is repeated in the story's several references to slaves as the belongings of the master and the mistress. Even after slavery was abolished, the phrase "Christ-

mas gifts," spoken by a black child or adult, would elicit a coin or small present from a friendly white person. Stuart places the hopeful recipients Lucindy and Dave in the position of themselves becoming Christmas gifts from the blundering hands of Colonel Slack.

The *Golden Wedding* story "'Blink'" indicates the shattering effect of the Civil War on another plantation master, Colonel Bruce: "Since the beginning of the war Colonel Bruce's history had been the oft-told tale of loss and disaster" (p. 160). Bruce has endured the deaths of his soldier sons and a young daughter, but he is finally overcome by his wife's death and the loss of the family plantation. The old colonel grows wholly dependent on his daughter Evelyn and her aging mammy, a female pattern that also occurs in Stuart's *Story of Babette* (1894) and *The River's Children* (1904). Much as Aleck and Cicely move to New Orleans for a new start in "A Golden Wedding," Evelyn finds a home in the city for the old woman, the colonel, and "Blink," a newly hatched chick smuggled from the plantation by Mammy. "Look like he knowed he warn't righteously in de morgans, an' 'e crave ter clair out an' trabble" (p. 167), says the nursemaid, who—despite emancipation—is reluctant to leave the homeplace.

Mammy's dialect turns the tragedy of the mortgage into the comic mispronunciation "morgans," and her grammar is weak; nevertheless, she becomes a vital literary consultant, reacting frankly to Evelyn's inflated language in the stories the young woman writes and reads aloud. Although Evelyn's fine sewing, decorative fans, and Easter eggs add to the income from Mammy's washing, the young mistress is an aspiring author. She considers her "picturesque surroundings an open book," and, much like Stuart, she gathers regional scenes and voices for her fiction: "Impressions of the quaint old French and Spanish city, with its motley population, were carefully jotted down in her note-book" (p. 171). Under "the unconscious satire" of Mammy's criticism (p. 173), however, Evelyn takes her work in a new direction. Discovering the value of simplicity and realism, she incorporates herself, Mammy, and Blink into a touching account that expresses

"all the wrench of parting with old associations." In response, Mammy "tumble[s] over on the floor, laughing and crying alternately" (p. 174). With her powerful blend of humor and pathos, Evelyn wins first place in a contest sponsored by a New York magazine. When Mammy wonders if the $500 award might buy back the Bruce plantation, Evelyn replies: "We don't want it back, mammy. . . . and if we can write one good story, you know we can write more. It will be only a beginning" (pp. 182–183). As Evelyn implies, and as Peter Schmidt remarks in a 2002 article, "Evelyn's new professional writerly voice, of course, is inextricably intertwined with Mammy's" (p. 82).

Although black dialect is conspicuous in nine of the eleven *Golden Wedding* stories, Stuart's New Orleans characters speak with Italian and French inflections in "Camelia Riccardo," a French Market comedy of cross-dressing and mistaken identity. The final story, "The Woman's Exchange of Simpkinsville," reflects the idiom of rural Arkansas, an area to which Stuart would often return in later volumes. Some critics call these characters hillbillies. In social status, however, postbellum Simpkinsville has less in common with isolated mountaineers than with the New England towns of Freeman and Jewett. The impoverished Simpkins family owned slaves and extensive lands before the Civil War, when Sarey Mirandy and Sophia Falena were "blooming country maidens both" (p. 311). For years afterward, the aging twins have "worn their inherited frugality itself threadbare" (p. 311) until a double crisis comes with the failure of the Little Rock bank and the death of their bachelor brother. Magazine articles about the national growth of woman's exchanges inspire the sisters to open a cooperative business, selling fancywork and baked goods in their home.

After a hopeful rush of activity, they realize the sellers greatly outnumber the buyers of wax fruits, colorful baby stockings, and rows of cakes with names like "Confederate layer" and "General Lee." By narrowing the inventory to breadstuffs, Sarey Mirandy and Sophia Falena can earn a modest income, which they supplement by renting rooms to occasional town visitors. Although

they are embarrassed to charge for a service they would rather give freely, this practical move changes Stuart's story of postbellum survival into a tale of North-South reconciliation. In contrast to the typical romance plot of national union, "The Woman's Exchange of Simpkinsville" offers a different sort of emotional exchange, one based on intense appreciation for the achievement of the twins' dead brother Sonny. When representatives from the Smithsonian Institution stop at the house in search of overnight lodging, they are astonished to discover the rare collection of stuffed birds and the meticulous journals kept by the late naturalist Stephen Decatur Simpkins.

Like some of Charles Chesnutt's *Conjure Woman* stories, Stuart's tale admits that regional harmony brings economic benefits for both North and South. The twins are reluctant to exchange Sonny's life's work for money: "No, sir. They's some things that money don't tech. We wouldn't sell them birds, not ef we got ten cents a head for 'em—an' that's mo' 'n most of 'em 'd be wuth, even if they was baked in a pie 'n' the crust an' gravy throwed in" (pp. 340–341). The sisters worry that their reference to Sonny's old Confederate uniform might have antagonized the strangers; but the men from Washington, D.C., are moved to tears, and they apologize for any hint of Northern aggression on their part: "Your brother's property is yours. No power on earth can take it from you. The war and confiscation are no more" (p. 353). The little delegation tells the sisters that the U.S. government will pay at least ten thousand dollars for the collection while honoring Sonny's memory in the National Museum. His ornithological treatises will enrich public libraries, and his portrait will hang in the Smithsonian. Sophia Falena and Sarey Mirandy weep joyfully at the prospect.

Three years later, Sonny's hundreds of birds have been installed at the Smithsonian; but the Simpkinsville exchange remains open. Affirming that money is not the only benefit of women's employment, Stuart concludes: "A comfortable income gave its machinery just the lubrication it needed for smooth and happy working according to the pleasure of its proprietors" (p. 355). Helen Taylor suggests that "Stuart's lighthearted comic

story suggests various feminist themes consistent with her own and her contemporaries' ideas about women's work, changed social roles, and relations after the war" (p. 123).

The popularity of her first book encouraged Stuart to produce black dialect for magazines and story collections for the rest of her career. Praising this "laureate of the forlorn" in June 1893, the *Critic*'s reviewer emphasizes Stuart's ability to "translate the South into language intelligible over the world" and asserts that the "web of humor and pathos" in her *Golden Wedding* stories is "rarely found in the dialect writing of the day" (p. 377). Like *A Golden Wedding*, some of her subsequent volumes featured a black dialect story in the title, including *Moriah's Mourning and Other Half-Hour Sketches* (1898), *The Second Wooing of Salina Sue and Other Stories* (1905), and *Aunt Amity's Silver Wedding and Other Stories* (1909). Between 1902 and 1904, Stuart published three black dialect novellas: *Napoleon Jackson: The Gentleman of the Plush Rocker*, with its laundress heroine; *George Washington Jones: A Christmas Gift That Went A-Begging*, a sentimental story about an African American orphan; and *The River's Children: An Idyl of the Mississippi*, the tale of a faithful old slave couple who raise the child of their lost master. At the same time, Caucasian characters assumed larger roles in most of Stuart's story collections, notably in the final gathering: *The Haunted Photograph, Whence and Whither, A Case in Diplomacy, The Afterglow* (1911). Perhaps "The Woman's Exchange of Simpkinsville" was a factor in this shift. Separate editions of the popular story were issued as small gift volumes, and Stuart returned many times to Simpkinsville and its outlying farms.

SIMPKINSVILLE FICTION

Both published in 1896, Sarah Orne Jewett's *The Country of the Pointed Firs* and Stuart's *Sonny* are early examples of a short-story cycle or group of loosely connected narratives. Like Jewett's tales of Dunnet Landing, Maine, each of Deuteronomy Jones's seven Simpkinsville monologues can stand alone. Taken together, Stuart's episodes

comprise a coming-of-age narrative, tracing the growth of a beloved only child from a Christmas baby to a young husband and a father himself. More subtly, the stories form a bildungsroman about the unconventional education that shapes an Arkansas farm boy into a naturalist and an author. The middle-aged father Deuteronomy Jones speaks a rural white dialect that recalls the dialogue of the Simpkins twins. In contrast to "The Woman's Exchange of Simpkinsville," however, there is no interplay between standard English and Arkansas patois in the Sonny stories. In his uninterrupted voice, Deuteronomy Jones relates stages of his son's boyhood and adolescence to the family doctor, Jones's good friend.

Beginning with the 1898 edition of *Sonny*, Stuart added the subtitle *A Christmas Guest*, emphasizing just how much Sonny is treasured from the start. Hours after Sonny's arrival, Deuteronomy Jones gives the farm stock an extra measure of food and unchains the dog because "I'd like everything on the place to know *he's* come, an' to feel the difference" (p. 12). Standing in a moonlit yard "full of glory" (p. 11), the exhilarated father says if he could "giggle an' sigh both at once-t, seem like I'd be relieved" (pp. 15–16). Characteristically, Stuart maintains the balance of humor and pathos in describing the crises and triumphs of Sonny's early life: his frightening tantrums as a toddler; his parents' extreme action when he refuses vaccination; his delayed christening at age six, when he selects his own name, "Deuteronomy Jones senior" (after his father, but with a lowercase "senior"); his irregular education, including his nature studies; and his courtship and marriage. Before he is twelve, the precocious Sonny has read *Robinson Crusoe* so often that, according to his father, the book "shows mo' wear 'n tear 'n what my Testament does, I 'm [*sic* spacing] ashamed to say" (p. 71). He wins his high school diploma through unorthodox means in part because the boy has the best library in the county, "'cep'n', of co'se, the doctor's 'n' the preacher's" (p. 82). Afterward, Sonny travels north to visit the real-life naturalist John Burroughs, then studies in New York for three winters. By the time he marries his teen-aged love and becomes a lecturer at the local

academy, Simpkinsville proudly celebrates Sonny "ez a author o' printed books" (p. 121).

Ties with *Sonny: A Christmas Guest* are stressed in the long subtitle of Stuart's 1910 sequel, *Sonny's Father: In which the father, now become grandfather, a kindly observer of life and a genial philosopher, in his desultory talks with the family doctor, carries along the story of Sonny.* Kathryn B. McKee calls attention to the several topical references in this second Deuteronomy Jones chronicle, suggesting that "the superficially benign demeanor of a drawling backwoods narrator mingles with his humorous, understated pronouncements about political and cultural issues to lure the reader into classing his controversial reflections as harmless, uninformed comments by a harmless, uninformed citizen of Simpkinsville, Arkansas" ("Writing in a Different Direction," p. 194). This social commentary is especially conspicuous in the monologue titled "The Women," Jones's positive account of the suffrage meeting he attended with more than forty Simpkinsville women. "The motters on all their banners is thess ez good for our sons ez for our daughters, an' we'll all do mighty well ef we try to live up to 'em," he assures the curious doctor (*Sonny's Father*, p. 96).

While Sonny travels to New York in the earlier volume, Deuteronomy Jones makes a trip north in *Sonny's Father*, and, again, he reports to the doctor on an unusual gathering: the 1909 Manhattan production of Richard Strauss's opera *Salome*, with Mary Garden in her title role. Jones judges that "She shore is supple in the hinges, Mary Garden is, an' she must 'a' had consider'ble drillin' to be able to fling them veils exact, every time" (p. 196). Bemused by the startling performance, he adds that the women in the audience were "all mo' or less stripped" too, and they were "not only respectable an' wealthy, but high class" (p. 196). Deuteronomy Jones is more excited by his discovery that the Waldorf bookstand sells Sonny's nature studies.

Sonny's Father was published five years after the death of Stuart's son, a loss that resonates in the poignant last chapter with the death of Deuteronomy Jones's precocious grandchild. Stirling Stuart's funeral service was held on Easter; the delicate little Doc—named for the Joneses' kind physician—is buried on Easter Sunday. Convinced that "every shadder is shaped in light" (p. 240), the grandfather cherishes the short life of the boy whose "little feet never seemed fully on the earth" (p. 237). Other Simpkinsville characters lose loved ones to death, abandonment, and miscommunication in Stuart's short-story collection *In Simpkinsville: Character Tales* (1897). Humor lightens the pathos in five accounts of widows, widowers, spinsters, and bachelors in midlife. But sorrow is almost relentless in the volume's most interesting narratives, "The Unlived Life of Little Mary Ellen" and "An Arkansas Prophet." Through the rambling reminiscences of old men, Stuart tells two stories of young women deceived in love.

The title character's bizarre state of mind makes "The Unlived Life of Little Mary Ellen" the most grotesque of Stuart's Simpkinsville tales. Chatting with the town's two elderly physicians, Pastor Binney says he has never had "as sad an experience as I did at little Mary Ellen Williams's weddin'—the terrible, terrible weddin' thet never came off" (*In Simpkinsville*, p. 103). The aftermath is even worse because Mary Ellen takes the surname of the fiancé who deserted her, and for four years she is inseparable from a beautiful wax doll that she calls little Mary Ellen. When a dog destroys the doll, the town tries to comfort the bereft Mary Ellen at the "saddest funeral gathering in all the annals of Simpkinsville" (p. 128). With Mary Ellen's collapse and death at the emotional service, the "unlived life" of Stuart's title describes both the woman and her surrogate child.

Born Jeremy but nicknamed Old Proph', the title character of "An Arkansas Prophet" is rare among Simpkinsville's African Americans for his pivotal role. Daniel McMonigle, a longtime Simpkinsville resident, discounts the black man as "a sort o' queer, half-luney, no-'count darky—never done nothin' sence freedom but what he had a mind to, jest livin' on Meredith right along" (p. 13). Yet, three years after Mr. Meredith's beautiful daughter runs off with a stranger from St. Louis, Old Proph' restores order to the whole community. Known for his fortune-telling skills

at the annual New Year's Eve party, Proph' had reluctantly predicted the girl's disappearance; McMonigle tells a newcomer that "sence the day May Meredith dropped out o' Simpkinsville the sky ain't never shone the same" (p. 12). The elderly townsman claims that Proph' isn't even part of the girl's story, "noways in partic'lar. It's only thet sence she could walk an' hold the ol' man's hand he doted on her, an' she was jest ez wropped up in him" (p. 14). It is Proph', however, who maintains hope when many in Simpkinsville assume May Meredith must be dead. After a three-year search that takes him far from home, Old Proph' finds the young woman and brings her to the community's annual gathering, with May's two-year-old child in his arms. When the clock strikes the new year, the noise is "mingled with the sound of joy and of weeping" in "a scene ever to be held dear in the annals of Simpkinsville" (p. 39).

Like Stuart's black dialect fiction, the Simpkinsville annals constitute a large share of her work. Even though the last chapters of *Sonny's Father* are set in the early twentieth century, Stuart continued to publish poetry and fiction that preserved speech patterns and scenes of an older South. Between 1910 and 1913, *Century Magazine* printed many of her comic plantation rhymes for children, which she collected in 1913 in *Daddy Do-Funny's Wisdom Jingles*, illustrated on each page by her friend G. H. Clements. E. W. Kemble's caricatures of a mammy, a preacher, and field workers accompany the first section of Stuart's *Plantation Songs and Other Verse* (1916). In some of the "Other Verse," however, and especially in her final novel, *The Cocoon: A Rest-Cure Comedy* (1915), Stuart exchanges black and white dialects of the South for more cosmopolitan voices.

THE COCOON: A REST-CURE COMEDY *AND A NEW ERA*

Stuart's final short-story collection, *The Haunted Photograph* (1911), reprises many of her familiar character types and dialects, but the closing story, "The Afterglow," reflects a late turn in her work. With its New York artist narrator, "The After-

glow" is closer to Henry James's fiction of art and introspection than it is to Southern local color writing. Stuart's upper-class speaker, Mary Randolph, makes a deprecating reference to "the new woman—or the new way—or new interpretations of the old way" (*The Haunted Photograph*, p. 157); yet, when she is jilted in love, she takes up her work. Determined to make a great painting, she now laments the time lost in middle-aged romance: "How long I have been playing!" (p. 170).

"Jemima of the Seventh Floor" (1909), an uncollected story from the same period, presents a similar narrator, another mature New Yorker with a sense of style. The woman periodically visits Seafair Sanitarium in Virginia, but she admits: "I was in no wise ill, and had come, as many others, to escape from the manifold tyrannies of Gotham's social demands, to be rubbed and smoothed for a while" ("Jemima," p. 98). Intrigued by one of the chambermaids, the patient describes Jemima as "gaunt" and gray-haired at forty-five, decades after she came to Seafair "from the poor hill-country 'up-State'" as "a raw, faded girl of fifteen" (p. 95). When the maid says she would love to own a diamond ring like the narrator's, the affluent woman is puzzled by such an ambition, but she compares the maid's dreaming expression to that of the French artist "Bastien-Lepage's Joan of Arc" (p. 98). Much as Stuart romanticizes the humble characters in her dialect fiction, the New Yorker dwells upon the humor and the pathos in Jemima's hard life. At the same time, this story serves as a transition to the 1915 novel *The Cocoon: A Rest Cure Comedy*—the closest Stuart came to writing the novel on women's issues that she had planned to undertake sometime after 1910.

Like "The Afterglow" and "Jemima of the Seventh Floor," *The Cocoon* departs from Stuart's earlier writing in several ways, notably its standard English prose, its epistolary format, and its many other resemblances to Charlotte Perkins Gilman's feminist classic, "The Yellow Wallpaper" (1892). Helen Taylor points out striking parallels between Gilman's story and Stuart's novel, but she is disappointed that *The Cocoon* "lapses quickly into Stuart's characteristic comic

sentimental narrative mode" (p. 131). However, feminist considerations do not vanish as completely as Taylor claims. Much more thoroughly than the narrator of "Jemima of the Seventh Floor," the novel's young protagonist, Blessy Heminway, introduces the serious issue of women's nervous diseases and the inevitable treatment of these diseases by male practitioners. At the start of her five-week residence at Seafair, Blessy feels like a "glib little fool" after her initial meeting with Dr. Jacques: "Evidently he thinks me frivolous just because I play around a tragic situation" (*Cocoon*, p. 8). A likely model for Blessy's physician is Dr. Weir Mitchell, who popularized the rest cure in the 1870s and died in 1914, the year before Stuart's book was published. Although Stuart took the rest cure several times, Dr. Mitchell was not her physician, but she did engage him as a consulting neurologist in 1905 after her son's fatal fall. Blessy's comment on Dr. Jacques suggests the awe in which Dr. Mitchell's patients held the medical legend: "Haloes always silence me, somehow, and, too, there is a note of finality in all he says" (*Cocoon*, p. 7).

Dr. Mitchell's rest cure was not limited to women, and patients at the Virginia institution in *The Cocoon* include some notable men: a gallant Canadian, a journalist who is recovering from typhoid fever, and a mysterious giant with "long ringlety hair" whom Blessy calls "the Brigand" (p. 11). Yet, Stuart's women characters display more anxiety than the men, mirroring the period's tendency to identify nervous afflictions with the female sex. After gathering loads of jonquils beneath the moon, the previous resident of Blessy's room wandered in her nightgown through the lobby full of smoking men. A somnambulistic "Amazon" from Montana arrives in such a troubled state that she mistakes the Brigand for her fiancé and follows him down hallways for days.

Blessy refers to the source of her own "nerve tire" (p. 7) in a breathless list of daily stresses: "Servants! Bills! Mistakes in bills! The telephone! Wrong wash sent home! Right wash not sent out! Telephone! Soft ice-cream! Subsided soufflé! Wrong entrée sent in from caterers, doubling

home course—guests already arriving, too late to change! Telephone!" (p. 63). Enumerating additional pressures of her domestic and social life in New York, she describes her resulting breakdown: "Tears! Coaxing! Temporary control—then hysteria—Angelic Husband assumes all blame and calls himself a brute! Reconciliation and gr-r-r-r-eat happiness followed by 'nerve disturbance'—and then this place!" (p. 63). Like many of her fellow patients, Blessy spends hours on the roof at Seafair, wrapped in a comforter that transforms her into the cocoon of Stuart's title: "the poor worm going into oblivion to get its wings" (p. 1), as she writes in her first letter home to her lawyer husband, Jack. But she resists many strictures of the cure. She writes long letters to Jack, despite contrary advice, and the food is "so offensively inoffensive" that Blessy drives to town to buy horseradish and Tabasco sauce to sprinkle "promiscuously over these blameless viands" (p. 18). The "patting, rolling and putting to sleep in a specially temperated room" remind her of "Pat-a-cake, pat-a-cake, baker's man" (p. 19), and she is even more sarcastic in her account of the electrical "paraphernalia" in the treatment room: "no end of whizzing, whirring, jostling contraptions at once" (p. 22).

When she describes one of the most popular machines—a "flesh-reducing horse, a wooden beast with the head of a nightmare" (p. 23)— Blessy ridicules not only the less restful sanatorium equipment but women's fashions as well: "In the old days our grandmothers were hourglasses; now we are lead pencils, and I wonder what our daughters will be, or even ourselves next. This navigating in one trouser-leg can't last forever" (p. 23). Familiar with haute couture, Blessy recognizes another resident's elegant dresses by Paquin and Doeuillet. Such allusions to popular culture are extensive in *The Cocoon*, from vaudeville, chorus girls, and Ellen Terry's stage performances to alimony, Reno divorces, and the New York press. Stuart's topicality extends to Blessy's several mentions of sulphites and bromides, Gelett Burgess' comic designations for modern personality types in *Are You a Bromide? or, The Sulphitic Theory* (1906). In contrast, the "musical southern voices" of the

chambermaids are "elemental," and Blessy views Seafair as "a godsend to these people. They come from the turpentine country, most of them, and strongly suggest the Craddock types" (pp. 20–21).

The allusion to Charles Egbert Craddock—the pen name of local colorist Mary Noailles Murfree—indicates the distance between Stuart's own earlier regional types and the New York cosmopolites in her late fiction. Stuart's awareness of changing literary tastes is also evident in her unpublished book manuscript, "Chosen Few," the story of a young widow who leaves Creole New Orleans to edit the women's news for a western newspaper. In July 1914 Stuart published "Sitting Blind by the Sea" in Harriet Monroe's *Poetry*, a journal associated with modernist authors like Ezra Pound and Wallace Stevens; the poem is reprinted in Stuart's final poetry collection, *Plantation Songs*, which also contains references to battle trenches, zeppelins, and the czar—World War I contexts that clash with the volume's nostalgic dialect verses. Although Stuart remains best known for her dialect literature, the mélange of genres in this last book reflects her transitional place in American literary history. The attention to contemporary issues in her late works is consistent with Stuart's public support of woman's suffrage, children's welfare, the Red Cross, African American education, settlement houses, and world peace.

Selected Bibliography

WORKS OF RUTH McENERY STUART

SHORT STORIES AND STORY COLLECTIONS

A Golden Wedding and Other Tales. Illustrated. New York: Harper, 1893. Reprint, Freeport, N.Y.: Books for Libraries, 1972.

Carlotta's Intended and Other Tales. Illustrated. New York: Harper, 1894. Reprint, Freeport, N.Y.: Books for Libraries, 1970.

Sonny. New York: Century, 1896.

In Simpkinsville: Character Tales. With illustrations by Smedley, Carleton, and McNair. New York: Harper, 1897. Reprint, Freeport, N.Y.: Books for Libraries, 1969.

Solomon Crow's Christmas Pockets and Other Tales. Illustrated. New York: Harper, 1897. Reprint, Freeport, N.Y.: Books for Libraries, 1969.

Moriah's Mourning and Other Half-Hour Sketches. Illustrated. New York: Harper, 1898. Reprint, Freeport, N.Y.: Books for Libraries, 1969.

Holly and Pizen, and Other Stories. Illustrated. New York: Century, 1899. Reprint, Freeport, N.Y.: Books for Libraries, 1969.

The Woman's Exchange of Simpkinsville. Little Books by Famous Writers. New York: Harper, 1899. (A gift book edition of the story from Stuart's *Golden Wedding and Other Tales*.)

The Second Wooing of Salina Sue and Other Stories. With illustrations by [E. W.] Kemble and [A. B.] Frost. New York: Harper, 1905. Reprint, New York: Garrett, 1969.

The Woman's Exchange of Simpkinsville. Illustrated. New York: Harper, 1907. (A second gift book edition of the story, reprinted from Stuart's *Golden Wedding and Other Tales*, known as the forget-me-not edition because of the floral cover decorations.)

Aunt Amity's Silver Wedding and Other Stories. Illustrated. New York: Century, 1909. Reprint, Freeport, N.Y.: Books for Libraries, 1970.

Carlotta's Intended. New York: Harper, 1909. (Reprinted as a gift book from its appearance in Stuart's *Carlotta's Intended and Other Tales*.)

Sonny's Father: In which the father, now become grandfather, a kindly observer of life and a genial philosopher, in his desultory talks with the family doctor, carries along the story of Sonny. Illustrated. New York: Century, 1910.

The Unlived Life of Little Mary Ellen. With decorations by Ruth Sypherd Clements. Indianapolis, Ind.: Bobbs-Merrill, 1910. (Reprinted as a gift book from its appearance in Stuart's *In Simpkinsville*.)

The Haunted Photograph, Whence and Whither, A Case in Diplomacy, The Afterglow. Illustrated by William L. Jacobs, Peter Newell, Ethel Pennewill Brown, and Wilson C. Dexter. New York: Century, 1911. Reprint, Freeport, N.Y.: Books for Libraries, 1970.

Simpkinsville and Vicinity: Arkansas Stories of Ruth McEnery Stuart. Edited by Ethel C. Simpson. Fayetteville: University of Arkansas Press, 1983. (Includes an introduction by the editor.)

Uncle 'Riah's Christmas Eve. With illustrations by Jerry Buckley. New York: Starkey & Henricks, 1999. (A Christmas gift edition of the uncollected story for clients of Starkey & Henricks and Allied Reproductions.)

NOVELS AND NOVELLAS

The Story of Babette: A Little Creole Girl. With illustrations by Alice Barber Stephens. New York: Harper, 1894.

Napoleon Jackson: The Gentleman of the Plush Rocker.

With pictures by Edward Potthast. New York: Century, 1902. Reprint, Freeport, N.Y.: Books for Libraries, 1972.

George Washington Jones: A Christmas Gift That Went A-Begging. With pictures by Edward Potthast. Philadelphia: H. Altemus, 1903. Reprint, Freeport, N.Y.: Books for Libraries, 1972.

The River's Children: An Idyl of the Mississippi. With pictures by Harry C. Edwards. New York: Century, 1904.

The Cocoon: A Rest-Cure Comedy. New York: Hearst's International Library, 1915.

POETRY AND OTHER BOOKS

Gobolinks; or, Shadow Pictures for Young and Old. With Albert Bigelow Paine. New York: Century, 1896.

The Snow-Cap Sisters: A Farce. New York: Harper, 1897.

Daddy Do-Funny's Wisdom Jingles. With illustrations by G. H. Clements. New York: Century, 1913.

Plantation Songs and Other Verse. With illustrations by E. W. Kemble. New York: D. Appleton, 1916.

UNCOLLECTED SHORT STORIES

"A Funny Little School." *St. Nicholas* 25, no. 1:40–46 (November 1897).

"An Old Time Christmas Gift." *St. Nicholas* 25, no. 2:94–103 (December 1897).

"The Author's Reading in Simpkinsville: A Monologue." *Century Magazine,* August 1900, pp. 612–619.

"The Broken Story." In *A House-Party: An Account of the Stories Told at a Gathering of Famous American Authors.* Boston: Small, Maynard, 1901. Pp. 236–286. (Anthology of stories by various writers, with an introduction by Paul Leicester Ford.)

"Jemima of the Seventh Floor." *Harper's Monthly Magazine,* December 1909, pp. 95–105. (Set in the fictitious Seafair Sanitarium, later the setting for Stuart's *The Cocoon.*)

"The Luck of Batture Baptiste." *Century Magazine,* May 1914, pp. 63–74.

ESSAYS

"I Remember." *Youth's Companion,* July 12, 1900, p. 348; July 26, 1900, p. 368.

"Browsing About the Ibsen Country." *Harper's Bazar,* July 1911, pp. 312–313, 338.

"Value of Folklore in Literature: Ruth McEnery Stuart Tells Some of Her Experiences and Writes in Defense of Dialect in Fiction." *New York Times Review of Books,* October 12, 1913, pp. 544–545.

"American Backgrounds for Fiction: VI—Arkansas, Louisiana, and the Gulf Country." *Bookman,* August 1914, pp. 620–630.

PAPERS

The Ruth McEnery Stuart Papers at the Williams Research Center of the Historic New Orleans Collection contains about two hundred items, including contracts, sheet music, manuscripts, correspondence, and clippings.

The Tulane University Howard-Tilton Library, New Orleans, holds two boxes of manuscripts, letters, early reviews, and Stuart's honorary doctor of letters diploma in the Ruth McEnery Stuart Papers.

The University of Virginia Clifton Waller Barrett Library of American Literature holds twenty-four items (primarily letters to the *Ladies' Home Journal* editor Edward Bok) in the Papers of Ruth McEnery Stuart, 1896–1908.

CRITICAL AND BIOGRAPHICAL STUDIES

Brady, Patricia. "Literary Ladies of New Orleans in the Gilded Age." *Louisiana History: Journal of the Louisiana Historical Association* 33, no. 2:147–156 (spring 1992). (Treats several features of New Orleans that contributed to the success of Stuart and many other female authors and journalists.)

Brown, Dorothy. "Ruth McEnery Stuart: A Reassessment." *Xavier Review* 7, no. 2:23–36 (1987).

Chopin, Kate. "As You Like It." In *The Complete Works of Kate Chopin.* Edited by Per Seyersted. Baton Rouge: Louisiana State University Press, 1969. Pp. 706–720. (Originally published in 1897, the third of the six "As You Like It" essays describes Chopin's meeting with Stuart.)

DeMenil, Alexander Nicolas. "Ruth McEnery Stuart." In *The Literature of the Louisiana Territory.* St. Louis: St. Louis News Company, 1904. Pp. 286–291. (Biographical sketch, followed by two of Stuart's black dialect stories, "Lady: A Monologue of the Cow-Pen" and "An Easter Symbol," both from *Moriah's Mourning.*)

Ewell, Barbara C. "Changing Places: Women, the Old South; or, What Happens When Local Color Becomes Regionalism." *American Studies* (Heidelberg, Germany) 42, no. 2:159–179 (1997). (Race, gender, place, and other cultural contexts for Stuart, Grace King, Kate Chopin, and other writers associated with the Old South.)

———. "Ruth McEnery Stuart (1848 [*sic*]–1917)." *KnowLA Encyclopedia of Louisiana.* Edited by David Johnson. Louisiana Endowment for the Humanities, March 30, 2011. http://www.knowla.org/entry/521/

Fletcher, Mary Frances. "Ruth McEnery Stuart: A Biographical and Critical Study." Ph.D. diss., Louisiana State University, 1955.

Hall, Joan Wylie. "*Legacy* Profile: Ruth McEnery Stuart (1849–1917)." *Legacy* 10, no. 1:47–56 (1993).

———. "'White mamma . . . black mammy': Replacing the Absent Mother in the Fiction of Ruth McEnery Stuart." In *Southern Mothers: Fact and Fictions in Southern Women's Writing.* Edited by Nagueyalti Warren and Sally Wolff. Baton Rouge: Louisiana State University Press, 1999. Pp. 64–80.

———. "Living 'Amid Romance': Ethnic Cultures in Ruth

McEnery Stuart's New Orleans Stories." In *Songs of the Reconstructing South: Building Literary Louisiana, 1865–1945*. Edited by Suzanne Disheroon-Green and Lisa Abney. Westport, Conn.: Greenwood Press, 2002. Pp. 65–74.

Harkins, E. F. and C. H. L. Johnson. "Ruth McEnery Stuart." In *Little Pilgrimages Among the Women Who Have Written Famous Books*. Boston: L. C. Page, 1902. Pp. 255–265.

Johanningsmeier, Charles. "Ruth McEnery Stuart (1849–1917)." In *Nineteenth-Century American Women Writers: A Bio-Bibliographical Sourcebook*. Edited by Denise D. Knight. Westport, Conn.: Greenwood, 1997. Pp. 414–419.

McKee, Kathryn B. "Writing in a Different Direction: Women Authors and the Tradition of Southwestern Humor, 1875–1910." Ph.D. diss., University of North Carolina at Chapel Hill, 1996. (Discusses, in addition to Stuart, the local color writers Katharine Sherwood Bonner McDowell [Sherwood Bonner], Idora McClellan Moore [Betsy Hamilton], and Mary Noailles Murfree [Charles Egbert Craddock].)

———. "Ruth McEnery Stuart." In *Dictionary of Literary Biography*. Vol. 202, *Nineteenth-Century American Fiction Writers*. Edited by Kent P. Ljungquist. Detroit: Gale, 1999. Pp. 242–250.

McKinley, Gena. "'The Delightful Accent of the South Land': Ruth McEnery Stuart's Dialect Fiction." *Studies in American Fiction* 26, no. 1:97–114 (spring 1998).

Martin, Francis Jr. "To Ignore Is to Deny: E. W. Kemble's Racial Caricature as Popular Art." *Journal of Popular Culture* 40, no. 4:655–682 (2007). (Describes the appeal of Kemble's illustrations for fiction by Stuart, George Washington Cable, Harriet Beecher Stowe, and others, despite the frequent racism of his drawings.)

Reynolds, Claire E. "'Featherbed Resistance' and 'A Dozen Proofs of Women's Superiority.'" *CEA Critic* 67, no. 2:43–61 (2005).

———. "'No time for repinings': Ruth McEnery Stuart Reconstructs the South." *ATQ* 22, no. 4:539–557 (2008).

Rollins, Hyder E. "The Negro in the Southern Short Story." *Sewanee Review Quarterly* 24, no. 1:42–60 (1916). (Discusses Stuart, Sherwood Bonner, Joel Chandler Harris, Paul Laurence Dunbar, and several others.)

Sams, Stanhope. "Ruth McEnery Stuart in New York." In *Women Authors of Our Day in Their Homes: Personal Descriptions and Interviews*. Edited by Francis Whiting Halsey. New York: James Pott, 1903. Pp. 199–208.

Schmidt, Peter. "Command Performances: Black Storytellers in Stuart's 'Blink' and Chesnutt's 'Dumb Witness.'" *Southern Literary Journal* 35, no. 1:70–96 (fall 2002).

Simpson, Ethel C. "Ruth McEnery Stuart: The Innocent Grotesque." *Louisiana Literature: A Review of Literature and Humanities* 4, no. 1:57–65 (spring 1987).

Sneller, Judy E. "'Sambo' and 'The Southern Lady': Humor and the (Re)Construction of Identity in the Local Color Fiction of Ruth McEnery Stuart." In *Gender, Race, and Identity*. Edited by Craig Barrow et al. Chattanooga, Tenn.: Southern Humanities Press, 1993. Pp. 237–245.

———. "Bad Boys/Black Misfits: Ruth McEnery Stuart's Humor and 'The Negro Question.'" In *Images of the Child*. Edited by Harry Eiss. Bowling Green, Ohio: Bowling Green State University Popular Press, 1994. Pp. 215–228.

———. "'Ole Maids' and 'Wily Widders': The Humor of Ruth McEnery Stuart." In *New Directions in American Humor*. Edited by David E. E. Sloane. Tuscaloosa: University of Alabama Press, 1998. Pp. 118–128.

Stevens [Stephens], Edwin Lewis. "Ruth McEnery Stuart." In *Library of Southern Literature*. Vol. 11. Edited by Edwin Anderson Alderman and Joel Chandler Harris. Atlanta: Martin & Hoyt, 1909. Pp. 5145–5162.

Taylor, Helen. *Gender, Race, and Region in the Writings of Grace King, Ruth McEnery Stuart, and Kate Chopin*. Baton Rouge: Louisiana State University Press, 1989.

Tutwiler, Julia R. "The Southern Woman in New York." *Bookman*, February 1904, pp. 624–634.

Wheeler, Candace. "American Authoresses of the Hour: Ruth McEnery Stuart." *Harper's Bazar*, December 16, 1899, pp. 1083–1084.

———. *Yesterdays in a Busy Life*. New York: Harper, 1918. (Memoir by Stuart's friend and neighbor, including a chapter on the Onteora summer community in the Catskills.)

REVIEWS

Cooper, Frederic Taber. Review of *The Cocoon. Bookman*, June 1915, pp. 424–425.

Review of *A Golden Wedding. Critic*, June 10, 1893, pp. 377–378.

"Ruth McEnery Stuart's *Daddy Do-Funny's Wisdom Jingles*—A Holiday Throw-Off." *Brooklyn Daily Eagle*, December 13, 1913, p. 8.

White, N. I. Review of *Plantation Songs. Sewanee Review* 25, no. 2:245–248 (April 1917).

EDWIN WAY TEALE

(1899—1980)

Dan Brayton

EDWIN WAY TEALE was a prominent twentieth-century American science writer, photographer, and naturalist, the author of numerous books on topics ranging from insect predation to observing the changing of the seasons. Born in the Midwestern city of Joliet, Illinois, he spent the majority of his adult life in New York and Connecticut. First smitten with the outdoors at his grandparents' home in Indiana, he became famous for a book about spring arriving on the East Coast. An exuberant lover of the outdoors and the workings of nature, he spent thirteen years working at an office in New York City. A lifelong naturalist and accomplished entomologist, he never took a science course in college, instead choosing to major in English. Now seen as an important voice in a literary genealogy that includes Henry David Thoreau, Aldo Leopold, and Rachel Carson, Teale made many of his most notable treks by automobile with his wife, Nellie.

Teale became a household name for his 1951 nonfiction classic *North with the Spring*, which traces the arrival of spring up the East Coat of the United States in chapters that capture attentive observation of natural phenomena in superb descriptive prose. As the author and his wife follow the advancing season, they note the changes unfolding before them, reflecting on ecological processes and anthropogenic effects. Three more books in the same vein round out the *American Seasons* tetralogy for which Teale is best known today. In 1966 Teale won a Pulitzer Prize for General Nonfiction for his book *Wandering Through Winter*, which concluded his *American Seasons* tetralogy. For the remainder of his life, Teale wrote about nature, cementing his reputation as one of this country's foremost naturalist-writers. By the time of his death, he had published 30 books, 250 articles, and 20,000 photographs.

One of his contemporaries, Roger Tory Peterson, author of highly popular bird guides, compared Teale to the great nature writers Thoreau and John Muir.

Edwin and Nellie Teale should not be confused with John and Mildred Teal, the husband-and-wife team of scientist-writers whose classic study *Life and Death of the Salt Marsh* (1969) established the ecological significance of salt marshes. There is no familial relation between the Teales and the Teals.

EARLY LIFE

Edwin Alfred Teale was born on June 2, 1899, in Joliet, Illinois, an industrial city forty miles southwest of Chicago, to Clara Louise Way and Oliver Cromwell Teale. Oliver Teale had immigrated from England as a youth and worked as a railway mechanic. Clara Way was a schoolteacher. They raised their only son, Edwin, in a strict Quaker household. A hub of heavy industry, Joliet was an unlikely hometown for a budding naturalist. Railways, a limestone quarry, and the U.S. Steel Corporation's Joliet Works were the largest employers in the region. Immigrant workers in the mills breathed toxic fumes, while coal-fired locomotives belched particulate-laden coal smoke into the air. Yet natural beauty could still be found in Joliet at Hickory Creek, a tributary of the Des Plaines River that runs through town. On its shores Teale wandered and played as a child, sometimes for solace from the bullies he encountered at school and from his rather rigid parents.

From an early age Teale cultivated a love of the outdoors and a keen eye for plant, animal, and especially insect life. His maternal grandparents, Edwin Franklin and Jemima George Way,

lived at Lone Oak Farm in northern Indiana, not far from the southern coast of Lake Michigan, where Edwin's mother, Clara, was raised. Here her son returned to visit each summer for his first fifteen years. At Lone Oak, Edwin stayed outdoors most of the time, barefoot and carefree, with permission to wander where he wished in a landscape where the human footprint was light and wildlife abundant. At age twelve he adopted his mother's maiden name in preference to the middle name he was given, in the belief that the latter would be more appropriate for an aspiring writer.

In middle age Teale wrote a memoir, *Dune Boy: The Early Years of a Naturalist* (1943), about his life and adventures at Lone Oak with his Gramp, a Civil War veteran, and his Gram, a simple soul who loved to read aloud. Unlike Edwin's home neighborhood near the railroad tracks on Washington Street in downtown Joliet, the northern Indiana countryside and his grandparents' easygoing ways afforded the budding naturalist the time and space to roam, observe, imagine, and wonder, developing his faculties for observation and his appreciation for the web of life. The young Teale and his friend Verne Bradfield wandered the dune country near the shore of Lake Michigan like a latter-day Tom Sawyer and Huckleberry Finn.

These early experiences in the countryside formed the basis for Teale's first written work, "Tales of Lone Oak," which he began writing when he was only nine years old. The aspiring young writer misspelled the word "tales" as "tails," an understandable and apropos mistake. The tales in this collection derived from the lists of observations kept by the young author to chronicle his daily adventures, including encounters with snakes, birds, insects, and other marvels of nature. Like his later writings, the "Tales" evince a sense of wonder rooted in place and sustained attention to movement (human and animal) and the passage of time, yet writing wasn't the only pastime for the young lad from Joliet. Like so many young naturalists, Teale collected objects—snake skins, stones, arrowheads, wasps' nests, a cow skeleton—for his amateur

natural history museum, which he kept in a shed on his grandparents' property.

At about the same time that he made up his mind to become a writer, Teale also became interested in photography. When he was just eleven, he saw an advertisement for a box camera in the Sears, Roebuck catalog, and decided he must have one. He earned the money to buy the device, along with film and developing material, by picking strawberries for his grandfather. In all he picked twenty thousand of them, enough for the $3.75 he needed for the camera and its accoutrements. When the much-anticipated instrument finally arrived the young naturalist took his first photograph of an easygoing cottontail. Later in life he would dedicate *The Boys' Book of Photography* (1939) to the same animal. Thus began the second artistic calling in which Teale would achieve great success later in life, and one that would remain intimately tied to his writing for the rest of his life. Teale's writing style is a visual one, attentively focused on the specificities that, taken together, create a larger composition. Like photography, his best writing is the verbal equivalent of the landscape photographs of Teale's celebrated contemporary Ansel Adams. Both men would capture the beauties of the twentieth-century American landscape for an appreciative public.

The young Teale's interests and pursuits were not merely of an empirical bent, however, and in high school he became known as an orator, eventually capturing the Indiana state debating championship. After his graduation in 1918, he entered the Student Army Training Corps at the University of Illinois in preparation for service in World War I, intending to become a pilot, but the war ended the same year. He then matriculated at Earlham College, a Quaker institution in Richmond, Indiana, where his uncle, David M. Edwards, was president. In college Teale dedicated himself to studying English literature and courting Nellie Imogene Donovan, a fellow English major who would become his wife and the constant companion of his travels. Nellie was an English major from Colorado who had happy memories of her early summers spent in rural Michigan, not far from the dune country of Lone

Oak Farm. Through the next six decades, their relationship would survive illness, unemployment, tragedy, and fame.

After graduating in 1922 from Earlham, Teale took a job teaching English and public speaking at Friends University in Wichita, Kansas, where he also coached the debate club and helped run a student peace organization. He and Nellie were married on August, 1, 1923, after which they drove to Wichita together in their Model T Ford, inaugurating what would become a lifelong passion for road trips together. Eventually the two would drive more than 75,000 miles on their travels, reading aloud and editing Teale's manuscript drafts. In 1923–1924 Edwin and Nellie were colleagues on the faculty at Friends, both of them members of the English Department. He taught at Friends for two years, she for one.

Even at this transitional time in his life Teale was drawn to exploring backwoods and byways. Not long before his wedding, Teale embarked on a small-boat journey down the Ohio River from Louisville, Kentucky, to Cairo, Illinois, where the river joins the Mississippi, intending to go all the way to New Orleans. His friend Bob Ketchum joined him for the first two days, after which Teale found companionship in reading the works of Thoreau, an adventure he later recounted in *The Lost Woods: Adventures of a Naturalist* (1945). Teale never made it to New Orleans, but he found a kindred spirit and lifelong literary idol in Thoreau.

NEW YORK, COLUMBIA, AND POPULAR SCIENCE

The Teales moved to New York City in 1924 so Edwin could pursue a career as a writer in close proximity to the major literary magazines and publishing houses. There he enrolled in the master's degree program at Columbia University and, after some difficulties finding work and publishing, he became an editorial assistant for Frank Crane, a Presbyterian minister and syndicated columnist whose "Four-Minute Essays" and "Everyday Wisdom" provided readers with pithy, inspirational reflections on general topics ranging from self-motivation to the stages of life and the

vicissitudes of aging. Teale provided Crane with material even before arriving in New York and continued to do so during his first four years in New York.

On September 8, 1925, Nellie gave birth to a son. They named him David Allen Teale, and he would be their only child. Edwin completed his studies, earning a master of arts degree from Columbia in 1926 while also continuing his work for Crane. This era in their lives would not last long. During the years 1927–1928 Teale's father, Oliver, died after a sudden illness, Nellie endured a case of acute appendicitis, little David developed an abscessed ear that threatened to cause hearing loss, and, amid all this calamity, Crane himself died, putting Edwin suddenly out of work. Forced to seek employment to support his family of three, he searched for a position at magazines throughout New York. Eventually he was hired as a staff writer for *Popular Science*, where he worked for the next thirteen years, writing articles on nature, technology, crime (particularly car theft), photography, and a host of other topics.

During the Roaring Twenties, many Americans shared a new optimism about the potential for science to transform everyday life, fostering dreams of flight, space travel, and ever-improving technologies. Teale was no exception in this regard, sharing with many of his contemporaries an abiding interest in flight, particularly in gliders. Much like his fellow Midwesterners the Wright brothers (Wilbur was born in Indiana), he tinkered with aircraft as a young man, at one point even going so far as to build his own glider, the *Dragonette*, which his father and grandfather helped him to launch for its one brief flight (it was soon wrecked in a storm). Later, in New York, Teale continued to be interested in aircraft, particularly gliders, publishing articles on the subject in *Popular Science* throughout the 1920s. In 1930 this interest culminated in *The Book of Gliders*, Teale's first book, which was published with an introduction by the well-known gliding aficionado William Hawley Bowlus. The first of several practical guidebooks that Teale would write, this one combined historical information on the development of gliding with descriptions

of noteworthy gliders and practical considerations for would-be pilots, including how to obtain a pilot's license. It was a far cry from his subsequent books, which would focus almost exclusively (with several exceptions) on what the eco-philosopher David Abram called the "more-than-human-world."

THE WORLD OF INSECTS

Teale nurtured a lifelong love for insects through many years and writings in a variety of places, from his boyhood in Illinois and Indiana to his home in suburban Baldwin, Long Island, during the *Popular Science* years. His interest in insects never waned on his many trips with Nellie throughout the United States or at their final home in the Connecticut countryside. But it was the landscape of Baldwin, where an old orchard next to a swamp offered a wild insectarium, combined with the work of the great French entomologist Jean Henri Fabre, that provided the detailed field observations on which he drew for his series of books on the topic. Teale bought the "insect rights" to this little patch of living landscape from the landlord, paying ten dollars a year to cultivate it with plants attractive to the abundant insects that lived there. At this site Teale developed a novel way of photographing his subjects by putting them in an icebox, thereby immobilizing them, and then posing the chilled bugs before they thawed. In this way he was able to get close-ups of species that otherwise would not have stayed put for the camera. He was soon exhibiting his photos at various venues around New York.

Beginning in 1937 and ending in 1962, Teale published a total of eight books on insects. The first of these was *Grassroot Jungles: A Book of Insects*, which received widespread acclaim, immediately establishing its author as a major voice on the subject and a skilled photographer as well. A photo essay containing 130 illustrations of various insects at all stages of life, this book introduces readers to the fundamentals of entomology with vivid descriptions of the anatomy, physiology, and life cycles of bugs, colorful anecdotes from the history of entomology, and detailed explanations of insect migrations, reproduction, and predation. The opening lines of the book are an invitation to wonder at the natural world. "At our very feet," Teale writes, "often unnoticed in the rush of daily events, is the wonder world of insects. Among the tangled weeds of the roadside or in the grassroot jungles of your own back yard, you encounter strange and incredible forms of life. Observing their activity is like making a Gulliver's journey to another world" (*Grassroot Jungles*, p. 1). Here the use of the second person situates the reader (possibly a child or a young adult) as an initiate being inducted into the mysteries of nature. Beneath our feet and before our very eyes, Teale insists, lies an overlooked world teeming with life. *Grassroot Jungles* is science writing at its best, gracefully harmonizing empirical observations with personal anecdotes and complex explanations in elegantly descriptive prose.

Grassroot Jungles was an immediate hit. Shortly after its publication Teale's photograph of a praying mantis graced the *New York Times Book Review*'s front page, consolidating the book's success and the reputation of its author. Critics expressed equal admiration for Teale's scientific knowledge and artistic presentation in both media, prose and image. Spurred by Teale's growing fame and capitalizing on the second photograph in the book, of the author in the field, with magnifying glass in hand, Robert E. Martin published an article describing Teale as an "insect explorer" along with Teale's photographs of insects ranging from a polyphemus moth to a monarch butterfly, an ant, and a black widow spider, among other celebrity species, spurring public interest in their habits and habitats.

As a staff writer for a popular magazine, Teale knew to capitalize on his own success. The following year, 1939, he came out with *The Boys' Book of Insects*, and in 1940 he published *The Golden Throng: A Book About Bees*, which also included a mix of photos and text, to glowing praise. The success of these early books afforded the Teales a new level of financial independence, and in 1941, less than two months before the United States entered World War II, Teale was able to resign from his staff job at *Popular*

Science. Thereafter he worked as a freelance writer and photographer while continuing to contribute articles to a variety of popular magazines, including *Nature, Better Homes and Gardens, Audubon, New York Times Magazine*, and *Natural History*. Having already established his reputation as a science writer, a string of literary and photographic successes brought him growing acclaim. In 1942 a British edition of *The Golden Throng* came out, and the author was invited to lecture at the Explorers' Club about his entomological adventures. Although he continued writing articles, from this point forward he would focus primarily on publishing full-length books.

After his early successes writing about insects, Teale's perspective on the natural world broadened, as did his literary horizons. In 1942 he published both *Byways to Adventure: A Guide to Nature Hobbies* and *Near Horizons: The Story of an Insect Garden*, which won the 1943 John Burroughs Medal for distinguished natural history writing. *Near Horizons* is at once a treatise on entomology and a work of place-writing in the manner of Gilbert White, whose 1789 book *The Natural History and Antiquities of Selborne* is considered by many to be the first great work of modern nature writing (White has been called the first ecologist). In *Near Horizons*, Teale focuses on a small patch of territory and its abundant insect life. The terrain is lovingly described:

> South of Hempstead and east of Valley Stream, a Long Island hillside slants away from a gray, weather-beaten barn to the borders of a swamp where acres of cattails become a tumbling green sea on a windy day. Slim cedars line the southern edge of the slope and a slow, brown stream cuts its winding track among the sweet-flags and cattails of the lowland. Apple trees, so ancient that one first bore fruit when Abraham Lincoln was President, lift their twisted branches above the grass tangles of the hillside.
>
> (p. 1)

This is more than mere science writing; the lush, poetic prose, with its attentiveness to the beauty and particularities of place, evokes the classic works of American nature writing. These qualities foreshadow Teale's later work, in which the landscape takes center stage.

In 1943 *Dune Boy: The Early Years of a Naturalist* was published, with the U.S. Army issuing a special military edition of 100,000 copies. Teale was now a celebrity. Next came *The Lost Woods: Adventures of a Naturalist* (1945) and *Days Without Time* (1948), which also bore the subtitle *Adventures of a Naturalist*. The titles of Teale's books up to this point reveal his two main interests, insect life and narratives about his own experiences in the field, which nature writers since John Burroughs have called "rambles." Indeed, the majority of Teale's books, and all of his most successful ones, derived from his rambles, on foot or by automobile. But only after he quit working for *Popular Science* did his writing shift from exposition to narrative, mixing scientific descriptions with personal reflections. He was becoming not just a science writer but a nature writer.

Even as Teale's writings diversified, his work on insects continued unabated. In 1949 he published a tribute to Fabre, *The Insect World of J. Henri Fabre*, followed by three more books on entomology: *Insect Friends* (1955), for children; *The Bees* (1961), also for children; and *The Strange Lives of Familiar Insects* (1962). These books, particularly the final one, would later inspire the young Annie Dillard, author of *Pilgrim at Tinker Creek* (1974), *For the Time Being* (1999), and other spiritual meditations on nature and the environment, for their powerful images and descriptions. Yet these books belong to the category of science writing, not nature writing, for they eschew, for the most part, the kind of personal, meditative reflections on the relationship between the human and the nonhuman that characterizes the latter. The relatively narrow lens through which the author chose to focus on the natural world, however, would soon change.

TRAVELS WITH NELLIE: THE AMERICAN SEASONS

The 1940s marked a major transition in Teale's writing, a shift from mostly expository science to a more narrative style marked by an expansion of scope from the minutiae of insect ethology to the broader themes of seasonal change, migration

patterns, and the ecological rhythms affecting all life in the temperate zone. Both *The Lost Woods* and *Days Without Time* were written in a strong first-person voice, and this was a period in his life when Teale read widely in the nature writing tradition. Indeed, he brought out several edited volumes on the subject, including *Green Treasury: A Journey Through the World's Great Nature Writing* (1952), *The Wilderness World of John Muir* (1954), and *The Thoughts of Thoreau* (1962). In 1946 Teale edited a new edition of Thoreau's *Walden; or, Life in the Woods*, penning a new introduction.

During this highly productive era of his professional life, Teale began planning a larger, more ambitious project unlike any he had yet undertaken, which would take him, with Nellie and David accompanying him, on the road again. But just as Teale was expanding his scope and finding his voice as a naturalist in the tradition of Thoreau and Muir, a devastating tragedy befell the family that would affect everything Teale wrote thereafter.

On March 16, 1945, David Teale, nineteen years old and a private first class in the U.S. Army's 346th Infantry Regiment of the 87th Infantry Division, went missing on night patrol at the Moselle River near Koblenz, Germany. World War II was entering its final phase, the Allies making major gains on both fronts and both sides sustaining heavy losses. David had volunteered for a reconnaissance mission with a special battalion called Tiger Patrol. Twelve patrolmen crossed the Moselle on rubber rafts at night. They were met with enemy machine-gun and sniper fire, and only four out of the twelve soldiers who volunteered for the mission survived. David was not among them. For six agonizing months, the Teales only knew their son was missing and likely dead; the details of his death only emerged after the war ended, when his stricken father drove to Massachusetts to interview one of David's surviving comrades on Tiger Patrol. There he learned the details of how David had died just two months before Germany's surrender.

Edwin and Nellie had been planning an ambitious road trip with David, who was himself an eager and knowledgeable naturalist, that would take the three of them up the East Coast, following the arrival of spring as it made its way north. At a conference of scientists in 1940, Teale had learned that spring moves northward at a rate of approximately fifteen miles per day, and this tidbit germinated into a full-fledged plan for a book about the dynamics of seasonal change. The family plotted and planned the journey, nurturing their plans for several years. After David's disappearance and the long-delayed news of his death, the Teales chose to carry out their plans without their son, yet to do so in his honor. In 1947 the grieving parents drove their black Buick to Key West and began chasing the northward movement of spring up the Florida peninsula.

As the days lengthened and warmed, the couple meandered the highways and byways of Florida, following the season's progress, the signs of change, and their own inclinations from one natural site to the next. At one point they got sidetracked all the way to Louisiana, then crisscrossed the Appalachian ridge and the Atlantic coastal plain, seeking out places of particular ecological significance and bio-abundance. Wetlands and coastal islands feature prominently in the narrative, as the two make their way from the Everglades to Lake Okeechobee, Cedar Key, coastal Louisiana, the Okefenokee Swamp, coastal islands in the Carolinas, the Great Dismal Swamp, the Great Smoky Mountains, the Shenandoah Valley, New Jersey's Pine Barrens, Long Island, Cape Cod, and the mountains of northern New England. Everywhere they made observations about birds, insects, unusual plants (such as the Venus flytrap, endemic to coastal North Carolina), as well as interviewing residents with a special attachment to each place.

Toward the end of their northward journey, the Teales crisscrossed much of inland northern New England, traversing the White Mountains of New Hampshire and the Green Mountains of Vermont in their search for wilderness and crossing briefly into the Adirondacks of New York State as well as touching upon the state of Maine. At journey's end they arrived at Mount Washington, near the Maine–New Hampshire border. The record of this journey was published in 1951 with

the title *North with the Spring: A Naturalist's Record of a 17,000 Mile Journey with the North American Spring*, "Dedicated to David, who traveled with us in our hearts." The following three books would be dedicated to him as well.

North with the Spring marked a departure from Teale's previous writings. More encompassing in scope and framed on a grander scale, the narrative allowed room for colorful characters, digressions, side trips, observations, and philosophical reflections. Part travelogue and part natural history essay, the narrative lens zooms outward from the microcosmos of insect life to the macrocosmos of seasonal change, species migrations, and reflections on the human presence in spaces that had long been wild. Unlike his earlier works, the new book was neither practical nor sensational but meditative and lyrical. From the first page Teale acknowledges the influence of Thoreau in the descriptive prose that echoes Walden as well as by naming his forebear explicitly:

> Bare trees imprinted the black lace of their twigs on a gray and somber sky. Dingy with soot, snowdrifts had melted into slush and were freezing again. Behind us, as we drove south, city pallor was increasing. Tempers were growing short in the dead air of underventilated offices. That quiet desperation, which Thoreau says characterizes the mass of men, was taking on new intensity. February, at once the shortest and the longest month of the twelve, had outstayed its welcome. The year seemed stuck on the ridge of winter.
>
> (*North with the Spring*, p. 1)

Here and throughout the book, Teale's beautifully descriptive prose mixes travel writing with precise observations about natural phenomena and philosophical meditations on the spiritual condition of humanity. The narrative then moves from highways and byways to flyways and watersheds, chasing the reemergence of photosynthesis with the growing light of spring. A deep yet subtle melancholia, mixed with calm, runs through the narrative as the Teales strive to reconnect with the deep pulse of life that surrounds them and the civilization whose margins they explore together. Throughout the book there is an abiding sense of loss, mourning, and healing, as if the Teales' love for their son were being transmuted into an attachment to the landscape and all the little lives that populate it, from moths to flowers to eels and even people.

Their roadway rambles struck a deep chord for the Teales, and in 1952 they embarked on another lengthy road trip, chasing a different season. The sequel to their vernal ramble up the coast was an autumnal transcontinental one, east to west, that followed the fall across the land. This trip would be a much longer one than their first, beginning at Monomoy Island, a low-lying spit of sand off the eastern elbow of Cape Cod, Massachusetts, and ending at the rocky bluffs of Point Reyes, in Marin County, California. The record of this coast-to-coast road saga, published in 1956, bore the title *Autumn Across America: A Naturalist's Record of a 20,000-Mile Journey Through the North American Autumn*. Within its pages, as in the other installments of *The American Seasons*, the author's photographs enhance the narrative, providing a visual counterpoint to the descriptive prose. Like his early photos of insects, the book illustrations in the tetralogy tend to focus on a single species, such as a deer, a chipmunk, or a daisy, but here and there we encounter landscape photos, and a few of the author himself, taken by Nellie, standing at various sites of interest.

Teale was now writing at the peak of his powers, his stylistic mastery present on every page of the books that make up the *American Seasons* in a voice attuned to the myriad possibilities for metaphor and metatextual reflection inherent in the attentive, sometimes emotive description of natural phenomena and its effect upon the viewer, or rambler. Thus, in his acknowledgments, Teale writes, "Those who travel over the leaves of this book, I trust, will find there something of the enjoyment we knew as well as what we learned during the days of our autumn journey." Like the gold, red, and orange of autumn leaves, the pages of a book, the author suggests, can delight and instruct. *Autumn Across America* would be another artistic and commercial success.

In 1953 Teale published *Circle of the Seasons: The Journal of a Naturalist's Year*, a book which in some ways harkened back to his earlier

autobiographical writings, *Dune Boy*, *The Lost Woods*, and *Days Without Time*. Once again the book's subtitle identifies the author as a naturalist, a term that suggests Teale's deliberate effort to situate his own work within a broader literary tradition, the one he first encountered when he first read Thoreau while floating down the Ohio River. This set of midcareer books fits more readily within the tradition of American nature writing than Teale's early books on insects, and the self-reflexive gestures to the author-naturalist suggest that the shift was quite deliberate. It is, thus, worth recalling that Teale was also publishing anthologies on nature writing at the time.

The authors who belong to the pantheon of nature writing have tended to focus on a relatively small patch of territory, such as Thoreau's Walden Pond, the Sierras of John Muir, the desert of Mary Austin, the Catskills of John Burroughs, the beach of Henry Beston. So too with Teale's early books on insects, derived as they were from his study of a single, relatively small patch of territory on Long Island. Like these literary forebears, Teale describes the natural phenomena he observed around him, arguably with a great deal more scientific knowledge than his predecessors. Yet whereas Thoreau and Muir attend constantly to the spiritual and aesthetic power of the regions they describe, in Teale's work this acknowledgment of the religious, cultural, and personal impact of the natural world only becomes prominent after his focus shifts from insects to the seasons. In contrast to his earliest works, Teale's *American Seasons* books cover vast amounts of territory, emphasizing the continental scale of the forces that determine seasonal shifts and soaring outward to reflections on the aesthetic and spiritual dimensions of the natural world.

The *American Seasons* constitute a sustained love song to the North American landscape and biosphere, and singing its first two verses—the first two books of the series—he was not yet done making music. So in 1957 the Teales set out on another transcontinental drive, this time beginning near Franconia Notch near the point where they ended the journey recounted in *North with the Spring*, in the White Mountains of New

Hampshire, and headed westward. As summer spread its warmth across the North American continent they made their way across Appalachia, the Midwest, and the Great Plains to the Rockies, finishing their trip at summer's end on top of Pike's Peak, Colorado, looking east as the sun setting behind them turns the mountain into "a titanic, 2½-mile-high sundial," casting its shadow a hundred miles across the plains to the horizon. This book, the third in the series, was published in 1960 with the title *Journey into Summer: A Naturalist's Record of a 19,000-Mile Journey Through the North American Summer*. "With," of course, "Photographs by the Author."

The cycle was not yet complete. Winter remained to explore. The Teales' fourth and final trans-American road trip, completing the cycle of the seasons, began in the far southwest at Silver Strand, the west side of San Diego Bay, and took them east-northeast toward New England once more, concluding in 1962 just north of Caribou, Maine. The culmination of their *American Seasons* tetralogy, and for many readers its crowning achievement, *Wandering Through Winter: A Naturalist's Record of a 20,000-Mile Journey Through the North American Winter* was published in 1965 and quickly became a great success, spurring sales of the previous three books in the series and garnering the author considerable praise. This was a prolific period for Teale. Between their final American road trip and the publication of *Wandering Through Winter*, he came out with another edited volume, *Audubon's Wildlife* (1964).

Readers and critics immediately acknowledged the *American Seasons* tetralogy as Teale's masterpiece. In his front-page review of *Wandering Through Winter* for the *New York Times Book Review*, Teale's friend Roger Tory Peterson described the tetralogy as "the major work of his life." Teale's literary reputation reached its zenith the following year, when he was awarded the Pulitzer Prize for General Nonfiction; he was the first naturalist to receive that honor. (The Pulitzer is awarded for books published in the previous year.) Teale's career was at its zenith, his books, articles, and photographs having found a vast and appreciative audience.

Teale's literary legacy and reputation lie primarily on the success of his *American Seasons* tetralogy. Written in the aftermath of immense personal and global tragedy, the four books of the cycle achieve an emotional and tonal depth surpassing Teale's earlier works, harkening to writings of Ralph Waldo Emerson, Henry David Thoreau, John Muir, Mary Austin, and Henry Beston. Teale's focus on ecology, seasonality, natural cycles, the human desire to be outdoors, and reconciliation with perpetual change reflects a desire for therapeutic experience and healing insight. Undeniably these works evince a striving for wholeness beyond mourning, a desire for reconciliation not just with time and mortality but also with facts and forces that shape the natural world. The tone of calm clarity mixed with insight and delight at nature's variation gives the writing unusual depth and resonance, evoking these literary predecessors at their best.

FINAL YEARS AND LAST WRITINGS

After many years of living on suburban Long Island, which was fast being engulfed by the urban juggernaut of New York City, the Teales decided to seek more space and opportunity to commune with nature. They began looking for a house in the New England countryside. In 1959 they bought an old farmhouse on ten acres in Hampton, Connecticut, in the northeastern part of the state, a backwater region that was still quite rural. With a pond, two streams, woods, meadows, and an 1800 Cape Cod–style farmhouse, this was the kind of home they longed for. They named the property Trail Wood. Reminiscent, in some ways, of Lone Oak Farm, Trail Wood became a refuge for the Teales and a place where Edwin could draw inspiration from the natural habitat. He built a small writer's cottage a few hundred feet from the house for this purpose, with a clear view of woods, a meadow, and a waterfall frequented by birds and wildlife of all kinds. At Trail Wood the couple would spend their final two decades hiking, observing natural phenomena, writing, and receiving visitors, honors, and awards. Later they bought fifty-nine acres adjoining the property.

Even then the Teales did not choose to lead an entirely sedentary life, traveling to the United Kingdom for one last road trip and book project, this time traversing a small but fabled island in the northeast Atlantic. Setting out from Land's End, Cornwall, in southwestern England, the Teales traveled north and east through the English countryside. For the most part they avoided cities, seeking places of biotic abundance. Eventually the couple reached the northern tip of Scotland at John O'Groats, Caithness, 876 miles from their point of departure. In 1970 the record of this journey was published in book form as *Springtime in Britain: An 11,000 Mile Journey Through the Natural History of Britain from Land's End to John O'Groats*. As the title indicates, this is a book along the lines of the *American Seasons* series, part travelogue, part natural history ramble, yet in a landscape very different from the earlier ones.

Upon returning to their home in rural Connecticut, the Teales settled into a more rooted lifestyle. In 1974 Teale published *A Naturalist Buys an Old Farm*, in which he recounts the tale of moving to Trail Wood and occupying the land with his beloved Nellie. As the two aging roadtrippers settle into their ten-acre property, with its menagerie of wild creatures, they become intimate with its spaces, patterns, and rhythms. By this point in his life, Edwin had transitioned fully from science writer to nature writer. His final book, *A Walk Through the Year* (1978), chronicles the details and dynamics of the changing seasons over the course of a complete year at Trail Wood. A palpable yearning for wholeness and completion runs through the text, with echoes here and there of Thoreau's *Walden* and Teale's earlier work *Circle of the Seasons*.

Teale celebrated his eightieth birthday by paddling a canoe with the naturalist and author Ann Zwinger on the Sudbury River in eastern Massachusetts, where Thoreau and his brother, John, had paddled more than a century before, on a voyage recounted in Thoreau's *A Week on the Concord and Merrimack Rivers* (1849). This episode is recounted in *A Conscious Stillness: Two Naturalists on Thoreau's Rivers* (1982), written with Zwinger. In the last year of his life, Ed-

win fought prostate cancer. Knowing that he was dying, Edwin and Nellie decided to bequeath Trail Wood to the Connecticut Audubon Society, which today counts the property, along with some adjoining land, the jewel in its crown. Edwin Way Teale died on October 18, 1980.

Nellie Imogen Teale stayed on at Trail Wood until her death in 1993 at age ninety-two, surviving her husband by thirteen years. In her last decade, she graciously received visitors drawn to the Audubon mission and to Trail Wood and shared stories with them of her life and travels with her late husband. Today the Edwin Way Teale Wildlife Sanctuary is a 186-acre property that maintains the Teales' house and trails that remain open all year, as well as hosting a week-long writer-in-residence program (since 2012) in honor of the author who bequeathed the land to future naturalists and writers.

HONORS AND AWARDS

Among American nature writers, Teale is a neglected figure, at least compared to his fame in the 1960s and 1970s. Yet in his lifetime, he received many honors, in addition to being famous. After being awarded the John Burroughs Medal for distinguished nature writing in 1943, he was made president of the New York Entomological Society (1944–1949). Two years after winning the Pulitzer in 1956, he was elected president of the Thoreau Society (1958). From 1949 to 1953, he was a member of the Brooklyn Entomological Society, which became the New York Entomological Society, and in 1955 he cowrote a segment for the CBS television show *Omnibus* (also aired on radio), hosted by Alistair Cooke.

Teale was awarded honorary degrees by two institutions of learning in his home state, Indiana University and Earlham College, his alma mater, as well as receiving an Indiana Author's Day award. The Massachusetts Horticultural Society honored Teale with its Ecology Award in 1975, and in the same year the New England Wildflower Society bestowed on him its Conservation Medal. He was elected a fellow of the American Association for the Advancement of Science and the New York Academy of Sciences, and he was named an associate of the Royal Photographic Society. The Connecticut Audubon Society dedicated the Trail Wood property as the Edwin Way Teale Nature Trail in 1981, and in 2009 the Indiana Historical Society and the Musette Lewry Trust dedicated a state historical marker to Teale at the site of Lone Oak Farm.

A literary career cannot be measured in honors and awards, yet Teale's prominence, and the respect of his peers, readers, and such a diversity of institutions offers some indication of his standing as a writer during his lifetime and afterward. Other indications of the admiration Teale's work engendered among his readers are subtler, including the many editions issued of his most popular books and even the loyalty of his publishers. Teale's decades-long relationship with Dodd, Mead, and Company, publishers of the majority of his books, is one indicator, among many others, of the author's success. In 1960 Teale's publisher, Edward H. Dodd, came out with a book titled *Of Nature, Time, and Teale: A Biographical Sketch of Edwin Way Teale*, published, of course, by Dodd, Mead. Along with contemporaries such as Dodd and Peterson, Teale would also have a major influence on subsequent environmental writers.

CONTEXTS

Teale's work spans the middle decades of the twentieth century, his best work, arguably, appearing in the decade and a half between 1951 and 1965. It is the *American Seasons* series, from that era, that will stand as his magnum opus. None of Teale's work was written in a vacuum—no literature ever has been—or with a blind eye to developing trends in science and literature. It is instructive, therefore, to situate Teale's oeuvre in context, for by doing so we can tease out the dimensions that make it a singular achievement as well as those features that connect it to its own era.

The postwar period in the United States saw the emergence of the environmental movement on a national and an international scale. The looming threat of nuclear apocalypse motivated

intellectuals and artists to reconsider the value of the natural world in an era when wartime technology provided human beings with the tools to wreak global havoc on human civilization and the biosphere alike. A grassroots environmental movement, shaped by writers motivated by looming catastrophe and a rapidly growing global population, emerged in the 1950s and early 1960s. By the 1950s wartime technologies, such as radar, nuclear power and weapons, and biocides were having alarming effects on nature and wildlife. Teale warned the public about DDT as early as 1945, well over a decade before Rachel Carson's groundbreaking *Silent Spring* (1962) was published, and understood the ways in which industrialization can destroy and transform natural populations and ecosystems.

As the human population along with its consumption and waste all boomed, many Americans sought a simpler life by moving to rural areas. Back-to-the-landers such as Helen and Scott Nearing, whose books on *The Good Life* (beginning with the 1970 volume that bears that title), strove to reconnect with nature's rhythms by homesteading. Others were drawn to conservation as they watched their favorite landscapes being bulldozed as the postwar development boom intensified. Many naturalists and conservationists in this period were inspired by the writings of dissident writers of the past, such as Thoreau, and of the present, such as Edward Abbey. The tradition spawned by the natural history essay, exemplified by the writings of Thoreau, Muir, Burroughs, Austin, Beston, and Teale, acquired a new currency.

The countercultural movements of the 1950s, 1960s, and 1970s created a forum for new voices to be heard and old voices to be reconsidered, not all of them concerned with the simple life. By the late 1950s, when Thoreau was enjoying a renaissance, Rachel Carson's trilogy of the sea, *Under the Sea Wind* (1941), *The Sea Around Us* (1951), and *The Edge of the Sea* (1955), hit the best-seller lists. Within a few years, *Silent Spring*, her painstakingly researched and searingly lucid study of chemical pesticides, would spawn a congressional investigation and take the environmental movement mainstream. Her subsequent

advocacy for environmental issues would become, by the early 1960s, a matter of national and international significance. Along with such like-minded authors as Beston, Abbey, Wallace Stegner, Peter Matthiessen, and Ann Zwinger, Teale played a prominent role in the development of new environmental sensibility.

Yet, for all their dedication to the natural world, the Teales were not homesteaders or priests of the countercultural movement. The gasoline bill for their road trips alone would have financed a hippie commune for a long time. Instead they should be seen as figures in the mainstreaming of the environmental movement, bridging the booming prewar public interest in science with the postwar turn to environmental issues. In this regard it is fascinating to consider the Teales' use of the highway system in the two decades between 1947 and 1965, as they were the beneficiaries, in a sense, of the kind of massive postwar development that also threatened the environment at a hitherto-unprecedented scale.

The national system of highways known as the Eisenhower Interstate System was initially funded by the Federal Aid Highway Act passed in 1956, part of a massive postwar expansion in infrastructural development that also caused immense environmental degradation. In January 1961 President Dwight D. Eisenhower warned of the dangers of the military-industrial complex, but just a year earlier he had vetoed a bill seeking to amend the weak Federal Water Pollution Control Act, which would not be overhauled until the Clean Water Act of 1972. The condition of waterways, such as the Mississippi and the Ohio, which Teale had explored two decades before, lay behind the impetus to pass early environmental legislation. Teale's career thus bridged the momentous mid-twentieth-century developments that led to widespread concern about environmental degradation: world war and its technological juggernaut, the expansion of the military-industrial complex, and the paving of the American landscape.

Subsequent environmental legislation was largely successful, particularly in the 1960s and 1970s. Although he eschewed the kind of advo-

cacy that made Carson famous, Teale can be seen as an important voice in the creation of a national environmental sensibility that led the way to landmark environmental legislation. Just as Henry Beston's book *The Outermost House* was instrumental in motivating the John F. Kennedy administration to create the Cape Cod National Seashore, so too did Teale's writings sway public opinion in favor of environmentalism, paving the way for such landmark laws as the Wilderness Act of 1964. In 1957 Teale had penned an article, published in *Audubon*, arguing for a National Wilderness Preservation System.

These examples highlight his engagement with the pressing environmental issues of his day, yet Teale did not call himself an environmentalist, preferring the term conservationist. "Fundamentally," he wrote, "it is those who have compassion for all life who will best safeguard the life of man." This passage, from *Wandering Through Winter*, is worth quoting at length.

> Those who become aroused only when man is endangered become aroused too late. We cannot make the world uninhabitable for other forms of life and have it inhabitable for ourselves. It is the conservationist who is concerned with the welfare of all the land and life of the country who, in the end, will do most to preserve the world as a fit place for human existence as well.
>
> (p. 162)

When Teale wrote these words a new urgency marked the American public's concern about environmental issues. The threat of nuclear catastrophe and the evident damage of pollution of all kinds raised the possibility that humanity might destroy all life on earth, either in one fell swoop or bit by bit. Then as now those who call themselves conservationists, as opposed to environmentalists or activists, tend to hold back from the kind of environmental advocacy later made popular by the likes of Rachel Carson; nevertheless, Teale anticipated the birth of the Deep Ecology movement when he made a case for a Wildlife Bill of Rights. Those who argue that Teale was not primarily an environmental author, or not truly a nature writer, or for one reason or another not a proper environmentalist (arguments have been made on all three heads),

fail to situate him in historical context or haven't read deeply enough in his oeuvre.

Teale's call for land conservation and land stewardship was a calm one, bespeaking a peaceable temperament (recall that he was raised a Quaker). His temperate voice can too easily be labeled staid or conservative, particularly in the context of the times. For the literary context in which Teale worked was one of upheaval. The tastes and sensibilities of writers in the postwar era were transforming at a rapid pace, along with the interests of the reading public. The Beat Generation of the 1950s took to the road at the same moment as the Teales, traversing the nation on the new roads that were being laid down everywhere, albeit with different goals and results. One could hardly imagine two more antithetical writers than Teale and Jack Kerouac, except, perhaps, Teale and Allen Ginsberg. Kerouac's experimental, confessional novel *On the Road* was completed in 1951 (but not published until 1957), the same year as *North with the Spring*. While it would be difficult to imagine two more different sensibilities, both authors became famous in the fifties for their masterful road trip sagas.

The similarities do not end there. In both books geography features prominently, in *On the Road* as the backdrop for self-discovery, in *North with the Spring* as the stage for natural processes to unfold. In both books the narrator offers observations and philosophical reflections about the cosmos from the vantage point of an itinerant spiritual seeker. In both books the relationships between souls in transit heighten the significance of episodes and observations. Yet whereas Kerouac is interested in heightened spiritual experience and the companionship of kindred spirits, Teale's focus remains squarely on the intricate complexities of nature's workings. We would do well to acknowledge the two books' similarities, as well as their differences, for the two writers derived vastly different artistic insights from their respective travels, yet both converted their experiences into spiritually powerful narratives.

Teale was certainly no beatnik. His writings evince a desire for continuity, not radical change. As contributions to the tradition of American

natural history writing, the *American Seasons* books are paeans to nature's immutable rhythms. In this he had much more in common with his fellow naturalists than he did with avant-gardists. Teale's book reviews of works by Roger Tory Peterson, Sigurd F. Olson, and Edward Abbey attest to his wish to find a place for modern natural history writers in a literary genealogy of naturalists who sought peace and the opportunity for reflection in nature's rhythms. So too do his articles on Gilbert White, John Muir, W. H. Hudson, and John Burroughs, all written during the era of Teale's life when his work can be characterized, however loosely, as nature writing (a characterization some have rejected). It should come as no surprise, then, that so many of Teale's books contain the words "naturalist" or "nature" in the title or subtitle, like a refrain, particularly after he went freelance in 1942. Perhaps it is significant that one of his final books, *A Naturalist Buys an Old Farm*, finally honored the label enough to put it into the title itself.

INFLUENCES AND LEGACY

Few American road-trip narratives were penned before the Teales drove south to Key West and embarked on the trip that generated the *American Seasons* tetralogy. Many have been penned since. The French philosopher Simone de Beauvoir's *America Day by Day* (1948), about her four-month trip across the United States in 1947, may have influenced the Teales' initial plans (recall, however, that the idea initially came to Edwin in 1940). Woodie Guthrie's "This Land Is Your Land," written in 1940 and first recorded in 1944 (it was published in 1945), may have been an influence. One of Teale's primary literary accomplishments was to help foster the growing environmental awareness and support for land conservation among his readers, who ranged throughout North America and the English-speaking world. Certainly the kind of affective relationship to the North American landscape depicted in coast-to-coast imagery connects Guthrie's song and Teale's books, the first of which even starts off at "the Gulf Stream waters." No reader can ignore the powerful affection for American landscapes evident in the books that make up *The American Seasons*, an emotional attachment that redirects nationalist sentiment from the abstraction of the nation itself to the physical realities of its biosphere.

Whatever the sources and inspirations that gave rise to Teale's *American Seasons* project, it is certain that subsequent books about driving across America owe the Teales a debt. For Teale's best-known books are not just about the seasons, nor are they simply natural history musings. They also offered readers a meticulously observed, scientifically informed, and carefully penned introduction to the American landscape, or, more precisely, to various American landscapes, as well as to people they met along the way who cared deeply about those landscapes. Whereas previous nature writers confined their observations about nature history to relatively small regions, Teale experimented with scope and scale, beginning with a magnifying glass in *Grassroot Jungles* and zooming out to a continental perspective in *The American Seasons*. Perhaps it is this multiscalar trajectory of Teale's career that has led some critics and scholars to claim that Teale was not so much a nature writer as a science writer. Perhaps, too, Teale's use of photographic and automotive technology represents a challenge to those environmentalists and ecocritics who prefer their idols to go on foot. Yet it is undeniable that Teale was a nature writer, and one of this country's finest.

One writer who acknowledged Teale's influence was Annie Dillard (born Meta Anne Doak), who won the Pulitzer Prize in 1975 for her first book, *Pilgrim at Tinker Creek*. A lifelong amateur naturalist herself, as well as a Thoreau devotee and innovative prose stylist, Dillard openly acknowledged the impact of Teale's work on the development of her own imagination. Growing up in western Pennsylvania, she pored over Teale's photos of insects and marveled at his descriptions of the behavior and life cycles of the praying mantis and polyphemus moth. In her own work, Dillard frequently gestures to the wonders and horrors of insect life, and often when she does so the reader sometimes feels as if he or she

were being treated to a brilliant refraction of Teale's early work.

Numerous other readers, writers, and scholars have found Teale's work inspiring, and continue to do so. If many scholars of literature and the environment, or ecocritics, tend to overlook Teale in favor of his more famous contemporaries, Rachel Carson and Aldo Leopold, others hold Teale in high esteem. Among them is the professor John R. Harris, who has taught nature and environmental writing at Franklin Pierce University in Rindge, New Hampshire, since 1994. In 2012 Harris set out to follow the vernal road trip recounted in *North with the Spring*, retracing the Teales' footsteps of sixty-five years earlier and visiting the places celebrated by Teale. The result was Harris' 2016 book *Returning North with the Spring*. Part travelogue, part narrative criticism, this thoughtful study moves gracefully between first-person anecdotes, biographical research on the Teales, and sketches of the twenty-first century inhabitants of the places Teale celebrated.

Harris followed the Teales' northward journey with an eye to the ecological changes that had transpired since then. From his journey Harris gleaned surprising insights, such as the following:

> We take it for granted that we live in a diminished world, that the bounty our grandparents knew has passed forever from the face of the earth. In fact, many places along the east coast, even places as seemingly settled as Cape Cod, have grown wilder since the author of *North with the Spring* described them. I know because I have stood in these places, following the footsteps of Edwin Way Teale, the most famous American naturalist in the decades between Aldo Leopold and Rachel Carson.
>
> (p. 2)

As Harris notes, substantial parts of the eastern United States have undergone a process of rewilding, particularly those areas that the Teales successfully sought to conserve. As instrumental as they were in creating a groundswell of conservationist sentiment, the Teales, could they come back and see some of these wild places, would be hard pressed to recognize them. They would also very likely be horrified at the proliferation of roads, traffic, population, and pollution in many of the other landscapes they explored. Writing at a time when the human degradation of the biophysical environment was accelerating, Edwin Way Teale inspired countless Americans to honor, preserve, and where possible to conserve the landscapes and wildlife of home. In an era when conservation and environmentalism have become politicized as never before, the reading public would do well to rediscover and reread his works.

Selected Bibliography

WORKS OF EDWIN WAY TEALE

BOOKS

The Book of Gliders. New York: Dutton, 1930.

Grassroot Jungles: A Book of Insects. New York: Dodd, Mead, 1937.

The Golden Throng: A Book About Bees. New York: Dodd, Mead, 1940.

Byways to Adventure: A Guide to Nature Hobbies. New York: Dodd, Mead, 1942.

Near Horizons: The Story of an Insect Garden. New York: Dodd, Mead, 1942.

Dune Boy: The Early Years of a Naturalist. New York: Dodd, Mead, 1943. Lone Oak edition, with three new chapters, 1957. Reprint, New York: Bantam and Bloomington: Indiana University Press, 1986.

The Lost Woods: Adventures of a Naturalist. New York: Dodd, Mead, 1945.

Days Without Time: Adventures of a Naturalist. New York: Dodd, Mead, 1948.

North with the Spring: A Naturalist's Record of a 17,000 Mile Journey with the North-American Spring. New York: Dodd, Mead, 1951. Reprint, New York: St. Martin's Press, 1990.

Circle of the Seasons: The Journal of a Naturalist's Year. New York: Dodd, Mead, 1953, 1987.

Autumn Across America: A Naturalist's Record of a 20,000-Mile Journey Through the North American Autumn. New York: Dodd, Mead, 1956. Reprint, New York: St. Martin's Press, 1990.

Journey into Summer: A Naturalist's Record of a 19,000-Mile Journey Through the North American Summer. New York: Dodd, Mead, 1960. Reprint, New York: St. Martin's Press, 1990.

The Strange Lives of Familiar Insects. New York: Dodd, Mead, 1962.

Wandering Through Winter: A Naturalist's Record of a 20,000-Mile Journey Through the North American Winter. New York: Dodd, Mead, 1965. Repint, New York: St. Martin's Press, 1990.

Springtime in Britain: An 11,000 Mile Journey Through the Natural History of Britain from Land's End to John O'Groats. New York: Dodd, Mead 1970.

Photographs of American Nature. New York: Dodd, Mead, 1972.

A Naturalist Buys an Old Farm. New York: Dodd, Mead, 1974. Reprint, 1987.

A Walk Through the Year. New York: Dodd, Mead, 1978. Reprint, 1987.

A Conscious Stillness: Two Naturalists on Thoreau's Rivers. With Ann Zwinger. New York: Harper & Row, 1982. Amherst: University of Massachusetts Press, 1983.

CHILDREN'S BOOKS

The Boys' Book of Insects: Interesting Facts About the Lives and Habits of the Common Insects Together with Simple Instructions for Collecting, Rearing, and Studying Them. New York: Dutton, 1939. Rev. ed., *The Junior Book of Insects*, New York: Dutton, 1953; 2nd rev. ed., 1972.

The Boys' Book of Photography. New York: Dutton, 1939.

Insect Friends. New York: Dodd, Mead, 1955.

The Bees. New York: Columbia Record Club, 1961. New ed., Chicago: Childrens Press, 1967.

ANTHOLOGIES

Adventures in Nature: Selections from the Outdoor Writings of Edwin Way Teale. New York: Dodd, Mead, 1959.

The American Seasons. New York: Dodd, Mead, 1976.

EDITED VOLUMES

Walden; or, Life in the Woods, by Henry David Thoreau. New York: Dodd, Mead, 1946.

The Insect World of J. Henri Fabre. Translated by Alexander Teixeira de Mattos. New York: Dodd, Mead, 1949. Rev. ed., Greenwich, Conn.: Fawcett, 1956; Boston: Beacon Press, 1991.

Green Treasury: A Journey Through the World's Great Nature Writing New York: Dodd, Mead, 1952.

The Wilderness World of John Muir. Boston: Houghton Mifflin, 1954.

The Thoughts of Thoreau. New York: Dodd, Mead, 1962. Reprint, 1987.

Audubon's Wildlife; With Selections from the Writings of John James Audubon. New York: Viking, 1964.

BOOK REVIEWS

"Naturalists' Grand Tour." *New York Times Book Review,* October 16, 1955, p. 14. (Review of *Wild America,* by Roger Tory Peterson and James Fisher.)

"This Was—and Is—the North at Its Best." *New York Times Book Review,* April 9, 1961, p. 4. (Review of *The Lonely Land,* by Sigurd F. Olson.)

"Making the Wild Scene." *New York Times Book Review,* January 28, 1968, p. 7. (Review of *Desert Solitaire,* by Edward Abbey.)

ARTICLES

"Dinosaur of the Insect World: The Praying Mantis, Tyrant and Destroyer." *Travel* 64:22–25, 47 (February 1935).

"Gilbert White." *Audubon* 47 (January 1945).

"DDT: The Insect-Killer That Can Be Either Boon or Menace." *Nature* 38:121–124, 162 (March 1945).

With R. Gordon Wasson. "W. H. Hudson's Lost Years." *Saturday Review of Literature* 30, no. 15:15–17 (April 12, 1947).

"Fabre: The Explorer Who Stayed Home." *Coronet* 29: 40–44 (February 1951).

"John Burroughs: Disciple of Nature." *Coronet* 31:90–94 (March 1952).

"Land Forever Wild." *Audubon* 59:108 (May–June, 1957).

"Henry Thoreau and the Realms of Time." *Thoreau Society Bulletin* 64:1–2 (summer 1958).

PAPERS

Edwin Way Teale Papers, Archives & Special Collections at the Thomas J. Dodd Research Center, University of Connecticut, Storrs.

CRITICAL AND BIOGRAPHICAL STUDIES

Dodd, Edward H., Jr. *Of Nature, Time, and Teale: A Biographical Sketch of Edwin Way Teale.* New York: Dodd, Mead, 1960.

Gannett, Lewis. "Lots of June in January." *Herald Tribune Book Week,* October 17, 1965, p. 14. (Review of *Wandering Through Winter.*)

Graham, Frank, Jr. "The Last Naturalist." *Audubon* 83:8, 10 (January 1981).

Harding, Walter. "Edwin Way Teale, 1899–1980." *Thoreau Society Bulletin* 154:6 (winter 1981).

Harris, John R. *Returning North with the Spring.* Gainesville: University Press of Florida, 2016.

Kieran, John. "About Edwin Way Teale." *Audubon* 54:150–154, 190 (May–June 1952).

Peterson, Roger Tory. Review of *Autumn Across America.* *Natural History* 65:452 (November 1956).

———. "Time of Rest, Rebirth, and Hope." *New York Times Book Review,* October 24, 1965, p. 1. (Review of *Wandering Through Winter.*)

Tag, Stan. "Edwin Way Teale." In *American Nature Writers*

II. Edited by John Elder. New York: Scribners, 1996.

Tunley, Roul. "His Backyard Was a Passage to Fame." *Audubon* 71:114 (November 1969).

Weeks, Edward. "The Peripatetic Reviewer: The Four Seasons." *Atlantic* 216:134 (December 1965). (Review of *Wandering Through Winter*.)

Weiss, Jill. "Edwin Way Teale: Traveler in Little Realms." Indiana Historical Bureau: Blogging Hoosier History, April 11, 2016. https://blog.history.in.gov/?p=414

White, E. B. "A Camera in the Concord Woods." *New Yorker*, December 28, 1946, pp. 64–65. (Review of Teale's 1946 edition of *Walden*.)

DIANE WAKOSKI

(1937—)

Nancy Bunge

THE POET DIANE Wakoski was born August 3, 1937, in Whittier, California, to John Joseph and Marie (Mengel) Wakoski. She had one sibling, a younger sister. Her father's job as a petty officer in the U.S. Navy took him away from home frequently and he divorced her mother when Wakoski was thirteen. Her mother supported the three of them by working as a bookkeeper and taking in laundry. They lived in a small house that locked with a skeleton key for sale in any dime store. But this seemingly meager life provided Wakoski with bountiful material for her poetry. Their tiny home sat next to an orange grove, which fascinated Wakoski from a young age. There were also flowers that attracted so many butterflies that if the young Diane stood very still, she could catch them. Her mother bought a piano and paid for Wakoski's lessons, laying the foundation for Wakoski's lifelong love of music. On Saturdays her mother would take Diane and her sister to the public library, where Diane would stock up on books, preferably fairy stories about beautiful lives. Then they would eat out in a café and go to a movie. One can see the imprint of all these events on Wakoski's poetry: the orange grove and flowers made her forever a California girl who offers lush descriptions of nature; the reverence for music she acquired from those piano lessons inspired her to produce musical poetry; the library books provided not only literary models but rich material for Wakoski's imagination; and after turning her back for a time on the Hollywood productions she enjoyed as a child, in more recent decades film has played an important role in Wakoski's poetry. And her father's absence left Wakoski with a yearning for male attention and love that dominated much of her life and her poetry until her happy marriage to the photographer Robert Turney in 1982.

UNIVERSITY OF CALIFORNIA AT BERKELEY

Her outstanding performance in school took her to the University of California at Berkeley, then free to all California residents who won admission. But before she left for Berkeley she spent time in the Florence Crittenden Home for Unwed Mothers, where she gave birth to a child. In the days before birth control pills or legal abortion, pregnancy out of wedlock could ruin a girl's life, since schools sometimes expelled these young women. Given Wakoski's intimate knowledge of the problems one would encounter raising a child as a single mother, she thought it best to give up the child, allowing him to be adopted by someone who, unlike her, could provide him a comfortable life. Even though she believed she did as well as she could by her child, she still felt guilty about her pregnancy and, as a result, during her first year at Berkeley she spent much of her time crying over her supposedly shameful behavior. She also began to discover that she was a poet.

She submitted poetry anonymously to the *Occident*, a literary magazine she also worked for, so she heard her colleagues make fun of her work. She responded by vowing to learn how to write poetry that no one could ever ridicule again. She also accepted that she could never become a professional pianist after hearing others practicing in the music building; she gave up the piano forever, but continued to make music with her poetry. She had a number of excellent teachers at Berkeley. From Josephine Miles, Wakoski learned not only about writing poetry but also about living one's life as fully as possible no matter what one's handicap: arthritis so decimated Miles's body that she could not type or walk, but she could write wonderful poetry; she also became the first woman to achieve tenure in the English

Department at Berkeley and was named a University Professor there. From the poet Thom Gunn, Wakoski learned the important role craft plays in writing poetry that expresses emotions without becoming sentimental. Praise from Tom Parkinson meant a great deal because of his penchant for giving young poets tough criticism, but at the same time, Wakoski learned to see disinterested self-appraisal as essential to improving as a poet; later, after becoming a teacher herself, she felt she had a responsibility not to praise bad work in the classroom and to bring the same demanding standards to her own work. She began to recognize the possibilities for free verse after seeing the power of Gertrude' Stein's language in the *Autobiography of Alice B. Toklas*. While at Berkeley she also fell in love with the poetry of Federico García Lorca, William Butler Yeats, and Wallace Stevens, as well as the surrealism she discovered in French poetry. Her senior thesis, arguing that Wallace Stevens was the first American surrealist, brought these two passions together. Surrealism also came in handy since Wakoski had no desire to write directly about her life. Since birth control pills still had not been invented and abortion continued to be illegal, Wakoski had another child, whom she once again gave up for adoption because she still lacked the resources to provide the child with a good life. Wakoski wanted to write about her children, but her shame made that impossible. She learned that William Wordsworth, like herself, had an illegitimate child, and searched for evidence of this event in his poetry, finding none. Then she realized that she could write about her pregnancies by disguising events but remaining true to their emotional impact.

Wakoski's embarrassment over her children born out of wedlock became transmuted into the shame of committing incest with an invented brother named David in her first published poem, "Justice Is Reason Enough" (1958). This was her first attempt at creating a mythology that both distanced her poems from her literal experiences and expressed their meaning in a way that would allow others to identify with her insights and feelings. So the biographical statement in her books—"The poems in her published books give all the important information about her life" (*Dancing on the Grave of a Son of a Bitch*, p. 139)—means that her poetry is emotionally and philosophically accurate rather than factually true. When babysitting at Berkeley, Wakoski also wandered into a kitchen containing the remnants of a meal that seemed more interesting than the ham sandwiches on white bread she relished when dining out with her mother and sister on Saturday nights. So Wakoski's sojourn at Berkeley from 1956 to 1960 provided her not only with an intense commitment to writing good poetry and a rich sense of how to do it without violating her own privacy, but also an interest in producing intriguing food.

NEW YORK CITY

Wakoski moved to New York City in 1960 with the composer La Monte Young, whom she had met at Berkeley, and felt instantly at home, especially in Greenwich Village. She immediately read the *Village Voice*, and there she learned of the Tenth Street Coffee House, where people could give open readings. This became her social life, since, during those years in New York City, she usually had jobs that required her to work six days a week, leaving her little free time for other activities. Every week this gave her and the other poets a chance to perform before people who took poetry seriously and who shared the praise for presenting the best work read that week with everyone in the group. On her first New Year's Eve in New York, Wakoski attended a party thrown by Le Roi Jones (Amiri Baraka) who included her work in an anthology titled *Four Young Lady Poets* (1962). There, George Stanley's ridicule made her uncomfortable, so when Diane di Prima offered her a pill, she took it—although Wakoski never used drugs before or after this event. Howard Ant invited her to another party, where she met Jerome and Diane Rothenberg, who continue to be important figures in her life, partly because of Rothenberg's enthusiasm for the deep image in poetry. Wakoski suspects that whatever Di Prima gave her helps explain her uncharacteristically outgoing behavior at this felicitous get-together. Rothen-

berg and Robert Kelly, another influence on Wakoski's literary career, had founded Hawk's Well Press, devoted to publishing deep-image poetry. This press published Wakoski's first book, *Coins and Coffins* (1962).

Wakoski and Young split. Subsequently she lived with the sculptor Robert Morris, lived with Tony Weinberger, and married and divorced twice. Her literary life proceeded much more happily. In 1966 Doubleday accepted her second collection, *Discrepancies and Apparitions*, for publication. By the time she left New York City in the mid-1970s, she had published more than thirty books of poetry, including small chapbooks, and had given up the tedious jobs that ate up her time, such as teaching junior high or working in a bookstore. She now made her living traveling around the country giving sixty to eighty poetry readings and workshops a year, primarily at colleges and universities. This confirmed and helped develop Wakoski's commitment to poetry's oral dimension, as well as her ability to present her work powerfully; it also exposed her to other poets and to fresh experiences and events that kept Wakoski and her work alive and engaged. The Guggenheim Fellowship she won in 1972 helped her materially while encouraging her to believe that her work mattered. After teaching as a poet in residence at the California Institute of Technology, University of Virginia, Willamette University, University of California at Irvine, Macalester College, Lake Forest College, Whitman College, and the University of Wisconsin–Madison, Wakoski settled at Michigan State University in 1976, eventually becoming a University Distinguished Professor there.

SURREALISM

Wakoski announces in the introduction to *Trilogy*, a 1974 collection of the first three books she published with small presses, that she has no interest in progressing as a poet insofar as the notion suggests that her work follows one trajectory. Instead, she says, "I would like it if the reader could see in each book a preponderance of the use of one technique or kind of structure for the poems" (*Trilogy*, p. xiv). She does admit that she consistently attempts to uncover the metaphysical dimensions of common objects, to use gorgeous language, to allow an image to shape her poems and to construct what she calls a "personal mythology." But her aversion to following one path helps explain why, when in 1987 *Writer's Digest* asked a group of authors to identify a breakthrough moment, everyone else mentioned one, while Wakoski listed five. This flexibility, along with the overwhelming amount of work she has published, make it difficult to give an accurate overview of her writing. But it seems best to focus on the development of her own "personal mythology" with the understanding that even though she does see it as central to her writing, this approach does not offer a complete rendition of her body of work.

As Wakoski points out, the creation of this mythology begins with the poem "Justice Is Reason Enough," which she first published when she was a student at Berkeley and then included in her first collection, *Coins in Coffins*. In this initial collection, and in this poem, one can see the impact of Wakoski's interest in surrealism, dreams, and the deep image. The work's indefiniteness seems confirmed by Wakoski herself in the different analyses of "Justice Is Reason Enough" she has offered. In her pamphlet *Creating a Personal Mythology* (1975), she says that the poem kills off her brother, just as she has killed off the part of her that could have allowed her to function in the world with confidence after she behaved in a way that society considered taboo. In the introduction to her 2013 collection *Bay of Angels*, she explains that "the missing father in my psyche, early on morphed into a lost boy" (p. xiv). It seems doubtful that most readers would find either reading obvious. But all readers would be struck by the poem's vivid imagery and seductive narrative, perhaps in part because of the poem's elusive meaning. Wakoski in fact argues that readers like poems to have secrets that require effort on their part to discover; a poem's lack of clarity draws them in, coaxing them to own the poem and attempt to discover an order in it.

DIANE WAKOSKI

According to Wakoski, her next collection, *Discrepancies and Apparitions* (1966), includes a number of poems that use bizarre surrealistic images to make ordinary events seem more interesting. In this book, as in *Coins and Coffins*, a number of poems deal with death, including "Apparitions Are Not Singular Occurrences," which Wakoski includes on the list of her best poems in her book *Toward a New Poetry* (1980). There the poem's narrator describes herself riding naked on a zebra wearing only diamonds and being observed by a bird linked to Death. Wakoski explains in a 1988 essay titled "Camera Obscura" that the question of why we need to die has always fascinated her. In *Discrepancies and Apparitions*, she also includes characters from her personal mythology probably too specifically linked to her history for most readers to understand. One is Jennifer Snow, based on a self-possessed young woman Wakoski knew and envied at Berkeley. The other is Daniel, who represents a young man who won a poetry prize the year after Wakoski did, but still while she was attending Berkeley and presumably could have won the award. That these specific references would escape most readers seems to validate Wakoski's claim in an interview with Jody Hoy that younger poets resist allowing readers to share their emotional lives.

Wakoski has explained that *The George Washington Poems* (1967), her next book, focuses on presenting the harsh, unemotional male world, often in a comic way. But the poem in this collection that Wakoski includes on her list of her best poems, "The Father of My Country," explicitly links George Washington and men to Wakoski's longing for her own father when she was young. When Claire Healey points out in an interview with Wakoski that she has become personal in that poem, Wakoski explains that the poem in fact describes how culture impacts us all. She makes a valid point, but so does Healey: the poem clearly comes more directly out of Wakoski's life than the other work in these first three books. This may explain its poignancy. The poem still includes beautiful images, but its accessibility helps make them extremely moving. Wakoski maintains that the poems in this collec-

tion relate to dreams, but that she did not rely on actual dreams for them; instead she consciously created dream images to use. This gave her more control over the process, she claims, making her more like Jennifer Snow. This comment underlines the self-awareness and psychological evolution central to Wakoski's superb work. In his review of *The George Washington Poems*, Norman Martien seems to agree, arguing that Wakoski's voice has become more defined and assertive here than in her earlier collections.

FINDING A VOICE AND EXPANDING IT

Wakoski's next collection, *Inside the Blood Factory* (1968), again includes "The Father of My Country," and her poems continue to weave together accessible information about her life and ideas along with captivating, sometimes bizarre images. The meaning and the imagery in these poems nourish each other. For instance, "Slicing Oranges for Jeremiah" begins with a vivid description of the oranges his mother slices for Jeremiah to devour greedily. Then the narrator backs away to talk about the mother's difficult relationship with her husband and the reality that she keeps both him and their son alive, something they both resent. Then it moves into a discussion of this woman's strength, which becomes expanded into a discussion of all women. In the final stanza, Wakoski returns to the images of oranges, recalling the orange trees she loved as a child so intensely that she may have an orange tree in her throat, waiting for someone to slice its fruit as beautifully as this woman does for her child. "Blue Monday" has a similar movement, beginning with exotic images of blue balls, blue silk, blue teeth, and blue flowers associated with an unnamed woman. Then the poem's narrator makes it clear that she hates Monday because it begins a week during which she will miss an unnamed lover, following this explanation with a barrage of blue images that now have acquired a significance that not only clarifies them but deepens their impact. Thus Wakoski invites the reader into her perspective more generously than she did in her earlier collections, but without in any way diminishing her poems' complexity or her images' power. The poems Wakoski identifies

as working best in this volume—"The Father of My Country," "Ringless," "Blue Monday," "Ice Eagle," "A Sestina from the Home Gardener," and "Slicing Oranges for Jeremiah"—all achieve a synthesis of hinted meaning and vibrant images that create a rich emotional and intellectual experience for the reader.

Wakoski had a sense that *Inside the Blood Factory* included particularly strong poems and that she had found a powerful poetic voice, but rather than rejoicing, she found it frightening because she wanted to spend her career extending herself, not repeating herself. After she delivered the book to Doubleday, but before it appeared, John Martin wrote her explaining that he was starting Black Sparrow Press and asking if she had work for him to consider, suggesting that perhaps she might like to do something too experimental for a conventional press. To liberate herself from the successful approach she just discovered, she wanted to do something didactic. She wrote *Greed, Parts One and Two* (1968), and sent it off to John Martin. who accepted and published it immediately. It differs strikingly from her earlier work.

Wakoski had a plan for *Greed*. Each poem would have one image of a creature that would be a metaphor for what she was discussing. So these poems lack the extravagant, sometimes even bizarre imagery of her earlier work. And the meaning is clear. Part 1 talks about polygamy and betrayal while part 2 discusses lack of integrity in poets, including herself. She pronounces political poetry dishonest because it allows its writers to enjoy more popularity than they would if their work reflected their deepest emotions and thoughts. But she admits that while she advocates for integrity to protect her image, she also likes money and approval. She talks about a childhood memory of finding the silverware at a classmate's party incredibly beautiful and wanting the same opulence for herself, but she disguises her materialism by not seeking luxury in the world; instead she pursues it with extravagant poetic language.

After reviewers confirmed Wakoski's suspicion that *Inside the Blood Factory* offered a particularly excellent collection of poems, instead

of capitalizing on this success by publishing poems using the same technique, she wrote several more entries for *Greed* and one poetry collection, *The Magellanic Clouds* (1970), full of experimentation. Black Sparrow published all this work. In *Greed, Parts 3 and 4* (1969), Wakoski debates with herself. Part 3 exonerates those who own their greed and who move beyond it or use it to make something valuable to others. Part 4 talks about those who enter the world unwanted, intruders, who never feel that they belong. Such people try to create a sense of safety with achievements and possessions. This greed is pointless because the more one fights against the sense of not belonging, the sharper one's awareness of it. Eventually one sees anyone who acquires the money or acceptance one desires as an intruder. Wakoski admits it seems odd to condemn greed that serves only as a hedge against despair. But she answers this by pointing out that when we become too dependent on what we possess, we lose ourselves. Greed diminishes us. She asks if there is an answer to this and concludes it rests in a loving relationship with a man. *The Magellanic Clouds* reads like a long experiment. After reprinting *Greed, Parts One and Two*, it includes some long narrative poems, which Wakoski says she discovered in the late sixties suit her writing best, along with short poems and stories in prose.

Next, she published *Greed, Parts 5–7* (1971), which presents Wakoski's ruthless self-examination. Part 5 talks about giving up her children so that both she and they could have fuller lives, freeing all of them from the syndrome of people producing children so that their offspring can redeem their lives. Then she accuses herself of falsely ennobling her choice, which resulted from the fathers of her children not wanting to marry her. In part 6, which she writes in prose, she talks of jealousy eating her alive and taking her far away from the generosity she wishes guided her life. Instead, she finds herself torn up by anger at poets who win more prizes than she does, or at women whom the men in her life find attractive, or at people who enjoy an economically comfortable life because they have inherited money. She makes an analogy

between suffering from this envy and getting torn apart by sharks: she does not enjoy it. In part 7 she seems to understand the source of this rage. Her mother told her that "pride goeth before a fall," suggesting that honesty and humility would bring rewards. So her anger derives from the realization that her mother gave her bad advice: when her modesty goes unrewarded, Wakoski attempts to comfort herself with self-righteousness. Wakoski argues that pride in fact gives one the self-confidence to transcend the need for external validations of worth. Although lacking the loveliness of Wakoski's poetry, the self-examination taking place in these *Greed* entries plays an important role in the literature Wakoski produces, for besides allowing her to explore new ways of writing, it also provides a place for self-evaluation. Wakoski firmly believes that good poetry rests on ruthless self-examination. As she told Nancy Bunge in an interview in 1985:

> The only writers that interest me are the ones who are original and I think their originality almost always comes out of an organically honest expression of [their] involvement in the world, so I am most interested in writers who are honest creators of their own myth. Even if you're not going to become [a] great writer, you'll become a better writer if you become a very, very honest perceiver of the world and I don't see any way for doing that unless you're a very mean and honest perceiver of yourself.

(p. 88)

The declaration on the cover of *The Motorcycle Betrayal Poems* (1971), dedicating the book "to all those men who betrayed me at one time or another, in hopes they will fall off their motorcycles and break their necks," seems to violate the insight and wisdom Wakoski renders in the last *Greed* entry about rage's destructiveness. But, in fact, the works in this new book talk of longing and sadness more than anger. The first poem, "I Have Had to Learn to Live with My Face," says that she enjoys anger only because it infuses her with pride, however briefly, and concludes that she would rather forgive her betrayers because the problem is her face. But in the poem itself she explains that her goal is to make a good life from the material given to her, and she believes she has achieved that. Those who find her unattractive don't understand how she looked as a child. She believes many people reach the same conclusion about themselves when they look at old photographs. This opening poem reflects a slight shift in the perspective Wakoski presents in her earlier poetry. Although she yearns for love and feels cheated by the men who have left her, she strives to build a life for herself rather than focusing on her partners, and she suspects her own insights may help others.

This also seems to be the central theme of the book's final poem, "The Pink Dress." She will not wear the pink dress left for her because it reminds her of abuse at the hands of her lover and that she can become docile and compliant with such men, disowning her strength and her responsibility to live as fully as possible. In an essay, Wakoski makes it clear that she believes this poem applies to all women: "To me, the idea that women are symbolized by pink has always been hateful. Perhaps because pink is a pastel color, an off shade, a dilution of the primary and powerful color red. . . . The pink dress becomes that dilution of person that a woman is to man in our culture" ("Color Is a Poet's Tool," p. 29). The dress also represents the way men see women as objects.

Another poem in the book is "Thanking My Mother for Piano Lessons," which explains that playing music allows her to imagine a more beautiful life for herself. "My Hell's Angel" describes the joy of simply meeting a kind, vibrant man. In "Letter Number Three" she writes that she believes a lot of women of her time have felt the same despair as she; presumably, they also have the ability to draw on the resources she does in her optimistic poems. Despite the angry proclamation on its cover, in *The Motorcycle Betrayal Poems* Wakoski seems to try to find her way toward the peace she values in her *Greed* entries.

This collection resembles the *Greed* poems in their clarity. Some of the poems have surrealistic, dreamlike qualities, but with most, like "The Pink Dress" or "Thanking My Mother for Piano Lessons," the significance of their images becomes completely clear once the reader has followed the poem's argument. Wakoski's poetry

DIANE WAKOSKI

still discloses a secret, but it generally makes it more easily understood. In this collection Wakoski also includes poems that are letters, another device that provides readers with more intimate access to her meaning.

One aspect of these poems could remain elusive, however, to those unfamiliar with Wakoski's other work. She mentions a number of characters from her developing personal mythology without enough context to make their significance completely clear: the inspiring Beethoven, the King of Spain (her ideal lover), and George Washington, a symbol of patriarchy. These poems do present the Motorcycle Betrayer with brutal clarity.

The Motorcycle Betrayal Poems came out as the women's movement took off. Given Wakoski's predilection for poems about men who betrayed her and her emphasis on the importance of the individual developing his or her own life, one can see why the women's movement attempted to adopt her as well as why interviewers persistently ask her questions about gender and critics often approach her work in terms of gender. Perhaps Wakoski could have ridden this train to a broader readership and more money, but she persistently refused. She sees the process of writing poetry as inherently valuable, but only if the poet can follow where the work leads him or her. Writing poetry for some political purpose immediately undercuts this. Moreover, ideological stances invariably have a simplicity incompatible with good poetry. This does not mean she denies the problems that women often have in American culture, but it does mean she has not, does not, and will not make discussing these her central goal as a poet because it would require her to produce work so shaped by ideology that writing poetry would not only lose its appeal for her, but she would also probably produce stagnant poems. Wakoski has spent her career evading rather than resting in truisms.

Black Sparrow published her next three books, all of them full of new approaches and ideas. The poetry collection *Smudging* (1972) opens with a poem that weaves together images of oranges, smudge pots, and Mexican workers Wakoski recalls from her childhood. The conclu-

sion makes it clear why writing political poetry would violate the complexity of Wakoski's awareness. As it ends, she uses the poem's images to allude to her terror of relationships with men, the warmth and comfort she finds in them, and the potentialities she has yet to develop. The rest of the book collects a variety of poems, including much shorter poems than those Wakoski usually writes, and a short piece of prose called "The Poem."

Next she returned to *Greed*, writing parts 8–11 (1973). In part 8 she argues that poetry provides a way to write about how living through suffering enhances one's life and character. Part 9 continues this theme with a poem in which Wakoski makes it clear people err when they confuse her with Sylvia Plath. Wakoski sees in Plath's suicide an unwillingness to accept the reality of her life that repels her. She declares herself made of stronger material and explains that dealing with problems enhances oneself and one's life rather than making it unbearable. She repeats over and over in this poem that she will never kill herself. She writes nothing substantial for part 10, explaining that she tried in various ways to begin producing something like William Carlos Williams' prose poem *Patterson* (1946), but could not find an approach that worked to her satisfaction. But she leaves part 10 there, explaining that she may come back and write it someday. In part 11, she announces that she will focus on animals because she's tired of people. Nonetheless, she provides a summary of all the men in her personal mythology at this point: the King of Spain, her ideal lover with his gold tooth; the Motorcycle Betrayer; George Washington; Beethoven; and the Homosexual Blue Moon Cowboy. Then she tells a story about two osprey sisters that finally seems to suggest that living well depends on the cooperation of the moon, or the imagination. And, indeed, repeatedly in her poems, Wakoski's imagination has provided her with options that lift her out of traps she feels limit her.

Her next book, *Dancing on the Grave of a Son of a Bitch* (1973), shows Wakoski's imagination at serious work by including one experiment after another. It opens with a collection of poems

about astronomy. Then it moves on to a section of chants, appropriately dedicated to Jerome Rothenberg, followed by a series of poems that involve the Buddha, and finishes with stories in prose. The last one, "The Fable of the Fragile Butterfly," concludes with a numbered list of endings, underlining the open-ended nature not only of the story but of the entire book.

MOVING BEYOND THE PAST

In the preface to her next poetry collection, *Virtuoso Literature for Two and Four Hands* (1975), Wakoski says that here she is trying to "explore the images of fantasy and my past." The view of her history that emerges suggests that she can leave it behind and establish a good life on her own. In "Driving Gloves" she realizes that her mother, like herself, liked to wear driving gloves. She plays with the notion that she has unconsciously imitated her mother, but concludes that she just wears them because she likes them. People shape their own lives. In the poem "On Seeing Two Goldfinches Fly Out of an Alder Tree, the Way You Are Swiftly Flying out of My Life," she regrets the departure of a lover, but concludes that people, like birds, naturally feel compelled to leave situations, including their pasts. "Alone, Like a Window Washer at the 50th Story," plays off the image of a window washer, with Wakoski confessing that she has always looked for company, but, in fact, she enjoys clearing off the debris and helping the light shine through by herself. This activity makes her proud.

The next collection, *Waiting for the King of Spain* (1976), has an even more optimistic tone. Many playful poems talk about her ideal lover, the King of Spain, and recommend self-acceptance. In "Ode to a Lebanese Crock of Olives," she confesses that although she is a California girl, she is neither thin nor tan, and that unlike some women, she has no jewels. But she does have the richness of Lebanese olives. *"To the Thin and Elegant Woman Who Resides Inside of Alix Nelson,"* she urges Alix Nelson to stop aspiring to thinness and accept the beauty of her plump body made that way by delicious American food. Wakoski objects that a critic who

once complained of her thinness has never seen her, and moreover, like Alix, she has a body that reveals the abundance of the American environment. They both need to forgive people who want them to get thin and accept their distinctive opulence.

Some playfulness survives in the introduction to *The Man Who Shook Hands* (1978), but it may be a defense. Wakoski repeatedly tries to begin telling the story of the man who shook her hand after they spent the night together: she's embarrassed in part because she takes this event so seriously, but at bottom it troubles her because it suggests that they saw each other totally differently. How can one connect with others in a world where perceptions of each other are so askew? Part of her reluctance may stem from the reality that she talks directly about herself and her life rather than disguising it with fantasy. And sad poems creep into this collection. "Hitchhikers," although a splendid poem that uses vivid fall imagery to talk about how driving past hitchhikers makes Wakoski profoundly uncomfortable because they need her to reach their destinations, ends in sadness. She lists a series of rationalizations for her choice, but she concludes that the hitchhikers would not want to travel with her. After affirming that she does not have to repeat the sadness of her mother's life in "The Photos," as she glimpses her face in the rearview mirror while changing lanes and realizes that it looks like her mother's, she seems to decide that she is doomed to repeat her mother's life. But positive poems also occur in this collection. When a kind student hugs her, it helps restore her faith in people's goodness. She also begins alluding to a new character in her personal mythology, the Man in Receiving at Sears, Robert Turney, the photographer with whom she has enjoyed a happy marriage since 1982. So although in some poems Wakoski falls back into the sadness and even fatalism that contradicts her repeated earlier declarations that people shape their own lives, in others she moves toward a better future.

Fortunately, *Cap of Darkness* (1980) carries forward the positive dimension of *The Man Who Shook Hands*. The first part reviews once again most of the male characters in her mythology,

with emphasis on the adoring and helpful King of Spain. Then the collection arrives at a good relationship with a real man, Robert Turney, in "Spending the New Year with the Man from Receiving at Sears." That poem opens by saying that her relationship with Robert helps her move past the damage left by her childhood:

> We have dismissed,
> like a doorbell being rung by someone who
> has forgotten his key to the building,
> my childhood.
>
> (Cap of Darkness, p. 31)

This book includes a remarkably large collection of positive poems. In "Aging," for instance, she writes not about loss, but about enjoying the light on a winter morning. Multiple poems discuss flowers. Those about her childhood recall the bees landing on her braids or her capturing butterflies. And she compassionately describes her mother's misguided admiration for their milkman in "My Mother's Milkman."

The next collection, *The Magician's Feastletters*, appeared in 1982, the year she married Robert Turney. She had taught at Michigan State University since 1975, and even though she confesses that she sometimes feels as though she lives in an Edward Hopper painting when she travels the streets of East Lansing, the book indicates she has made peace with living in a small Midwestern city. One thing she loves about East Lansing is the four seasons, and she organizes this collection by the seasons. It begins with the fall, when the school year begins and Michigan is at its most dramatic. The first poem, "Breakfast," talks of her savoring a simple meal while observing the swamp behind her apartment. It concludes that even life's smallest events become powerful when one has the wisdom to completely engage them. People need to find the energy to do this because, as the poem explains, our life consists of moments:

> Everything
> we will ever have
> is present
> in each day's life. There is no more.
>
> (The Magician's Feastletters, p. 13)

"Coprinus Comatus: Evening Mushrooms, Morning Ink" indicates that Robert's presence also helps since he leads her to the mushrooms she celebrates in that poem. The poems in this volume also delight in magic shows, gardenias, students, frogs, thunderstorms, and winter. Here, she recalls her youth with pleasure as she remembers the Halloween she dressed as a pirate and got levitated in a magic show. She describes two eccentric Aunt Pearls who fascinated her and the wonderful Saturdays she enjoyed with her mother and sister. She even feels grateful to an ex-husband for leaving her instead of staying with her and sitting in a chair with his back to her for fifty years like his grandparents. As she bakes in "Making a Sacher Torte," she wonders how having her piano teacher for a mother would have changed her life, but then realizes that the woman who gave her piano lessons, along with many others, mothered her, no matter what their official relationships to her. At poem's end, as she takes a successful Sacher torte from the oven, Wakoski seems pleased with how everything has worked out for her:

> experience and memory are my real roots,
> tangled, complicated, all the freeways I have traveled
> to reach this moment when I lift the firm almond
>   torte
> out of the oven.
>
> (The Magician's Feastletters, p. 46)

In the book that follows, *The Rings of Saturn* (1986), she even writes of taking pride in her contentment. The final poem, "Joyce Carol Oates Plays the Saturn Piano," shows the narrator completely transcending the envy that an early *Greed* entry saw as a sign of weakness. Wakoski admits that she promised herself that if she won a Pulitzer Prize by the time she was forty, she could return to playing the piano. She discovers that Joyce Carol Oates, who has enjoyed spectacular success as a novelist, takes piano lessons, and the poem's narrator wishes her all the best even though Oates quickly achieved the fame, fortune, and solid marriage that Wakoski either had to seek at length or still lacks. Wakoski does not resent this because the process of writing poetry has allowed her entry into worlds wonder-

ful beyond describing: "I hear a music / beyond what anyone can play" (*Rings of Saturn*, p. 121). In this poem, she lets go of the sense of inadequacy that persistently has plagued her because she has discovered that she enjoys and learns so much from writing poetry that the external results matter little.

Along with this emotional resolution of her insecurities, she includes a short poem titled "What Happened?" in which she writes about three of her mentors, Walt Whitman, Wallace Stevens, and Ed Dorn, who all began with a slightly false language and moved into a more natural, expansive way of writing. She concludes the poem by saying that this pattern is hopeful. One could see a similar pattern in Wakoski's work in that her early, surrealistic poems, although interesting in their way, lack the clarity, smoothness, and openness of the easy language in her later work. Understanding her first poems often feels like trying to interpret someone else's dream, and even Wakoski herself interprets these works differently at separate times. Her later poems still have startling images and broad themes, but readers can much more easily enter them. And Wakoski writes more directly out of her life in her later work, mostly leaving aside the characters from her personal mythology. The Man from Receiving at Sears, for instance, has become Robert, or "we." So there seems to be a harmony between the way Wakoski's poems resolve central emotional issues that have surfaced from the start of her work and the direct, open way it expresses them. The surrealistic imagery does not go away; it just has become comprehensible, even when it doesn't make clear intellectual sense. The last image in "Joyce Carol Oates Plays the Saturn Piano" offers a terrific example:

The ring on your long-married, sweetheart, wonderful prize-winning
finger will, perhaps, for a moment
glow, . . .
as a piano always does
when someone with inspired hands throws it into
orbit.

(p. 122)

PAUSING TO SUMMARIZE: THE COLLECTED GREED AND EMERALD ICE

In the mid-1980s, Wakoski began pulling her work together. In 1984 she published *The Collected Greed, Parts 1–13*. In 1988 she published *Emerald Ice: Selected Poems, 1962–1987*, which won the next year's William Carlos Williams Prize from the Poetry Society of America. Part 12 of *Greed* reviews her philosophy and work in that most of the characters from her personal mythology appear, wearing flower masks, in a masque written by George Washington. This entry, written in prose, has a dreamlike quality. Before the masque begins, George Washington asks the character Diane what she has searched for all these years. She identifies the perfect mate and a sense of completion and admits that she has found these things, but she worries that after her difficult childhood and adolescence, she has collapsed into bourgeois comfort. Then she finds herself saying that she will begin a journey reciting "the words almost as if I had been drugged and they were a script I was reading from brainwashed memory" (*The Collected Greed*, p. 153), suggesting that her unconscious pulls her forward. The masque "The Moon Loses Her Shoes" then takes place with the characters from Wakoski's personal mythology playing roles. The devil, played by Wakoski's gay ex-husband, the character M in her personal mythology, steals the magical shoes that make Diane radiant. But she gets them back. When the performance ends, Diane wonders what it says about her new journey and guesses "the masque seemed to imply that my journey is a daily renewal, a daily movement of self though the universe to fulfill an expectation" (p. 179). She muses about harmonizing body and mind, masculine and feminine, Apollonian and Dionysian, solitude and connection, persistent themes in Wakoski's work.

Charles Bukowski, whose work Diane describes as "a constant illustration of rebirth from the death of the deadly bourgeois world" (*The Collected Greed*, p. 191), serves as a master of ceremonies for the bestowal of literary awards named after American wildflowers and given to recent American poets, with Bukowski's irreverence persistently undermining the awards'

seriousness. After this ends, Diane feels as though she has experienced a summation of her past, but still has no understanding of her future journey. George assures her that in five years they may have another masque and awards ceremony, but Diane will be too immersed in her new project to join them. Still, she can count on their support: "The King of Spain and I will always be watching over you. I wish you new countries, with many seasons. One foot in front of another. One foot in front of the other" (p. 217). Diane leaves the ceremony in a car driven by a dog, a Dalmatian that stops the car and, after taking off his clothes and boots, runs away. In the car's trunk, Diane finds a stack of letters. She can find no map, so she once again advocates living in the moment: "I decided not to think of anything, but to concentrate on the movement of the car through this desert landscape; its beauty had always seemed to belong to my life" (p. 219). She finds herself driving west, where her life began.

All these events anticipate Wakoski's next poetry collection, *Medea the Sorceress*, which includes both letters and poems, has a map of Wakoski's life in the front, begins in the west, and deals with the poet's life directly; it even begins with a poem titled "The Orange," a poem about driving toward a new life. In *The Collected Greed*, part 12 ends with a poem about Las Vegas. Las Vegas returns as the subject of *The Emerald City of Las Vegas* (1995), the third of a four-book series (titled *The Archaeology of Movies and Books*), of which *Medea the Sorceress* (1991) is the first volume.

Part 13 of *Greed* returns to poetry and concludes by begging Robert Turney, the person at the center of Wakoski's contented life, to control the drinking and smoking that threaten to diminish his abilities as a photographer. Not incidentally, his death would devastate Wakoski. She ends by praying that Robert be "shaded from /false light" (*The Collected Greed*, p. 248) and dedicates the book to him. This plea apparently worked: she has only good things to say about life with Robert in the books that follow. Moreover, his reliability earns him the name Steel Man.

ENLARGING HER STORY: THE ARCHEOLOGY OF BOOKS AND MOVIES

Wakoski's interest in the story of Medea began in junior high when an English teacher taught Robinson Jeffers' version of the myth. At the time, Wakoski identified with Medea even though it made little logical sense. Later, when she put her children up for adoption, she saw using the myth as a way to tell her story without exposing herself. The title poem at the center of *Medea the Sorceress* makes explicit the links between this myth and her history. She tells of how she awaited the birth of her first child at a home for unwed mothers and received letters from the boy responsible for her pregnancy talking about going out with other girls. She decided that, like Medea, she would have to kill him and go off in her chariot to a new life. So she went to Berkeley and eventually made a good life for herself. She explains that she tells this tale to encourage all the other women who have trusted unreliable men: her experiences show that they can build good futures.

Besides talking directly about her life, Wakoski uses other devices in this book to invite readers into her experience. She alternates letters to her former students, Jonathan Carroll and Craig Cotter, with drafts of poems she included with the letters. Both the letters and the drafts allow readers intimate looks at her thinking and writing processes. She got the idea for the book when she visited Carroll, a writer who lives in Vienna: she liked the way he went to a café every day with his dog and wrote. Back home, sitting at her dining room table and enjoying the light coming through the windows, she realized that she could create a café by bringing her typewriter down to this table. So, she writes from a café and addresses the letters to Craig and Jonathan in other cafés. Wakoski considers poems letters anyway, but she hopes that printing actual letters, besides inviting readers into her thinking, will lend some of the engagement that writing and reading letters brings to her poetry. The sunlight in her dining room also plays a role in the book, which comes back again and again to the image of light. Wakoski repeatedly calls herself "Your lady of light."

DIANE WAKOSKI

The poems and the letters move in an associative way. For instance, after writing to Craig that she doesn't like the night, the poem "Morning Star" talks of sleeping late so she can totally evade the dark. These connections between the letters and poems make the book a lucid presentation of Wakoski's consciousness, but the book broadens out from Wakoski's personal history to consider the situation of women in society and their relationships with men. Sometimes, usually in the poems, she introduces a mythological figure: besides Medea, she tends to favor Persephone or Orpheus. For instance, in a poem about a woman Wakoski suspects is enduring abuse at the hands of her husband, Wakoski compares the woman's situation to that of Persephone and Wakoski herself, enlarging the poem's implications. Making the book even bigger in meaning, Wakoski weaves in quotations about quantum physics underlining the existence, even in science, of multiple realities. Wakoski points out that imagination also creates multiple universes. She writes to Craig:

The idea that many worlds exist simultaneously explains to me how I can be living my middle-aged, middle class life in Michigan while simultaneously meeting you my Rosenkavalier at the Rose Diner in Los Angeles and my friend Jonathan at the Ritter Café in Vienna, and also be at the Mailbag Café that I, the Postmistress, own in Las Vegas, or be meeting all of you at the Café Eau de Vie in Michigan. I can still be the young girl, the teenager who identified with Medea, and simultaneously, the sorceress who escaped and who is now beyond all that.

(*Medea the Sorceress*, p. 27)

To further complicate things, she also discusses movies, particularly ones about adolescence, and Mario Puzo's remarks about Las Vegas. The book generally moves toward the happy ending that Wakoski has found for herself, but it does so in a spiraling, indirect way.

So while *Medea the Sorceress* allows readers access to Diane Wakoski's story, the use of letters, imagery, mythology, and external materials makes her tale very large, complicated, and relatable—even universal. The next three volumes of *The Archeology of Books and Movies* follow the

same format, integrating Wakoski's prose reminiscences and reflections with her poetry, her letters to Jonathan Carroll and Craig Cotter, and quotations explaining quantum physics. The second volume, *Jason the Sailor* (1993), focuses more on men than *Medea* did and includes quotations from Camille Paglia. The letters take up a little less of this volume, which also includes more poems presented consecutively rather than after a letter. Hence it distances itself a bit more from the reader. Wakoski explains that the inspiration for volume 3, *the Emerald City of Las Vegas*, is that as an American, she sees the City of Light not as Paris but Las Vegas (Bunge 2016). This volume still includes letters and quotations about quantum physics, but it also has lengthy quotations from *The Wizard of Oz* and brief excerpts from books about gambling. Unlike the first two books, this volume has separate chapters, with poems arranged under images like "Witches" and "Emerald Light." Like volume 2, it doesn't have that many letters and has longer sequences of poems, and although it continues exploring Wakoski's personal experiences, it also comments on American culture. Wakoski explains that she sees the fourth volume, *Argonaut Rose* (1998), as affirming the connection between her work and the courtier tradition defined by the thirteenth-century *The Romance of the Rose*—hence the word "rose" in the title. But the book has a giant amaryllis on its cover, signaling that this flower, which Wakoski loves, replaces the rose (Bunge 2016). The book seems shaped to some extent by lengthy quotations from "Appollonius Rhodius," part of *Argonautica*, the third-century B.C.E. poem about Jason and the Argonauts. Like volume 3 it has chapter titles, some consisting of images, like "Using Ordinary Waves," and others suggesting a chronological sequence: "And Here They Found Circe." Among many other topics, the poems indicate that Wakoski remains angry because her quest to use her imagination to create great art has been frustrated by the reality that the Orpheus myth still supposedly does not apply to women. But, again, the integration of all this material makes this poetry collection about much more than Diane Wakoski's life. In this

series, Wakoski's personal story becomes the foundation of a mythological narrative with broad implications.

RESTING IN HAPPINESS

In 2000 Diane Wakoski published *The Butcher's Apron: New and Selected Poems*, which also included "Greed, Part 14." This book offers another summation, this time of her poems about eating and drinking. She organizes it by locations, basically following the trajectory of her life set out in the map for her series *The Archeology of Movies and Books*: "California," "Desert and Mountains," "Manhattan," and, finally, "On the Banks of l'Eau de Vie," located in the Village of East Lansing or the world of imagination. The vast majority of these poems are happy; as she points out in the introduction, only a handful of them deal with unpleasantness. Wakoski likes this book because it memorializes the time and energy she devoted to cooking. She believes this activity offered an important physical balance to all her intellectual and imaginative activity and that it nourished her writing by immersing her in the material world. It also seems to have brought her enormous joy. She has had to stop throwing dinner parties because of her health and would like to find another physical activity to balance out her poetic life (Bunge 2016).

The poem that constitutes "Greed, Part 14" begins by recalling a dinner party where someone reprimands Wakoski, accusing her of not paying attention. That night, she dreams of the Motorcycle Betrayer and wonders why he still haunts her. She feels as though others frequently censure her unfairly because she tells the truth, especially about poetry. She sees herself as protecting good work, but she comes to realize that she insults others while doing it. She reprimands herself for being surprised that others react negatively to her criticism. She decides to stop issuing judgments and, instead of trying to protect poetry, put her energy into enjoying the moment. This brings her another kind of gold that she has no need to protect because she cannot lose it.

This honest self-evaluation continues in her next book, *The Diamond Dog* (2010), which col-

lects poems focusing on the image of the Diamond Dog that first appeared in "The Father of My Country" in *The George Washington Poems*. It tells of a dream: in the ash heap left from burning trash behind her childhood home, she digs up a diamond dog, who immediately runs after her departing father. She originally saw the Diamond Dog as underlining how her father's leaving the family devastated her, but now she sees the Diamond Dog as leading her rather than following her father. This makes sense, since Wakoski's poetic career has depended largely upon her articulating her sense of abandonment by her father. And, as she explains in "'Black Ships Drawn Up on a White Beach," her father's absence allowed her to embroider romantic fantasies about him. She underlines this theme in "The Silver " by offering an image of herself not as a child victimized by her father's abandonment but as a princess with a picture of her heroic father in a silver locket. And, indeed, Wakoski sees all her poetry as not only creating a fantasy for her but also laying the foundation for the good life she eventually found. In "Amber Disks" she acknowledges that her father and the Motorcycle Betrayer treated her more generously than her earlier poetry indicated. When her father invited her to spend time with his new family, she acted superior; when he showed up in his navy uniform to visit her at Berkeley, she turned her back on him. And the Motorcycle Betrayer wrote her a letter after their breakup which she never bothered to answer. She also wonders why her friend who lost his boat and then his partner does not talk of betrayals but instead enjoys his life. Another friend points out that he does not hover over the past but allows the present to engage him. Wakoski realizes that curiosity pulls him into the future and frees him from past regrets:

Each breath is new,
orbital. Glittery, glittery, all
the stars in the cosmos, but I focus on only
a dream I had when I was six years old.

(*The Diamond Dog*, p. 29)

In "Blue Ice Wolf," she relates the Diamond Dog to the image of an Icy Wolf she believed she saw looking after her as she recovered in the hospital

from a burst appendix. At this poem's conclusion, she realizes that her father, the Diamond Dog, the Blue Ice Wolf, and the King of Spain have come back for her and will care for her.

These realizations heal Wakoski's relationships with other family members. She feels close to the younger sister she disliked as a child in "The Bowl of Gardenias." She sleeps in a room at her sister's house, heavy with the scent of gardenias, and feels bound to her again through white flowers. She reminds her sister that one struggles to accept that spring flowers will return, but they always do. And she urges her sister to remember, when she hears of Diane's death,

that comets and blossoms
almost always surprise us

when, from sky or earth,
their white cascades invincibly
reappear.

(*The Diamond Dog*, p. 69)

Wakoski feels more kindly toward her mother as well. While earlier she complained of looking like her mother, in "The Green of Oxygen" she suggests that she has inherited from her mother the quiet appreciation of beauty that has nurtured Wakoski all her life:

the green
of oxygen and my own voice,

a spiraling galaxy

(*The Diamond Dog*, p. 83)

When Wakoski dreams of a bottle of Shalimar, her mother's favorite perfume, she hugs it more passionately than she ever could her mother.

Beautiful images and gorgeous language saturate *The Diamond Dog*, like the rest of Wakoski's work, but the collection's compassionate stance distinguishes it from her earlier work and the language seems to ascend with Wakoski's self-awareness. These poems have an astonishing spiritual richness.

After producing a book focusing on one image, preceded by a interconnected series of four books, Diane Wakoski does something both old and new in *Bay of Angels* (2013). She explains in

her introduction that when she contemplated why Alan Tate's name surfaced several times in a dream, she concluded that it alluded to the importance of the New Critics' stance that each poem must stand alone. This book collects various poems under three topics with weak connections to each other: movies and TV, Wakoski's California past, and her relationship with Matthew Dickman, a.k.a. Shadow Boy, a new character in her personal mythology. Like some of her early books, this seems to be a series of experiments with some connections to her most recent work. *The Archeology of Books and Movies* also dealt with film, and a few of these poems reflect the more forgiving stance manifested in *The Diamond Dog*. In "Dancing with My Father" she understands her mother's point of view; in "Cognac in France" she forgives the Motorcycle Betrayer and wishes him well; in "Marilyn Gives Me a White Fleshed Peach" she is grateful for her sister's kindness after their differences and acknowledges that she owes her silver hair to her mother; and in "'The Spiral Staircase': Apples vs. Oranges" she argues that growing up next to an orange grove saved her. So the past no longer torments her but consoles her.

Her relationship with Dickman also seems simultaneously old and new. They have bonded over her first published poem, "Justice Is Reason Enough," where Wakoski's fictional twin brother kills himself. Dickman has a twin and has also lost a brother, so her poem has particular resonance for him. In the poems related to Dickman, Wakoski also returns to her early writing style, full of playfulness and surreal images. But her relationship to Dickman seems to be that of a mentor, a function she has found herself playing as she ages. She began teaching to support her poetry habit, but as the years passed and the poetry community shrank, Wakoski has relied heavily on former students for the simple reason that no one else in her environment cares about poetry as passionately as they do, and in East Lansing, she has little access to other groups of poets. She has created her own community out of former students who still meet at her house to discuss their work and hers. In this context, she

can talk honestly about poetry and be understood, even appreciated.

Taking poetry seriously has allowed Diane Wakoski to produce a remarkable variety of striking work, full of gorgeous imagery, and the self-examination and honesty to which she pledged herself at the start of her career have led her to write ever more complex and compassionate work that emerges from and reflects her constant development not only as a poet but as a person. Her comment in a letter to Jonathan Carroll that she feels proud of what she has made of her life seems totally appropriate: "One of the reasons I don't regret my life or any of its failures is that I feel that I have recreated myself in a way that is quite worthy of merit, and it gives me a sense of what is possible in this world" (*Medea the Sorceress*, p. 123). Her poetry also helps give her readers an enlarged sense of their possibilities through images and music that enhance the impact of what she says and invite the faith that magic persists.

Selected Bibliography

WORKS OF DIANE WAKOSKI

POETRY

Coins and Coffins. New York: Hawk's Well Press, 1962.

Discrepancies and Apparitions. Garden City, N.Y.: Doubleday, 1966.

The George Washington Poems. New York: Riverrun Press, 1967.

Inside the Blood Factory. Garden City, N.Y.: Doubleday, 1968.

The Magellanic Clouds. Los Angeles: Black Sparrow Press, 1970.

The Motorcycle Betrayal Poems. New York: Simon & Schuster, 1971.

Smudging. Los Angeles: Black Sparrow Press, 1972.

Dancing on the Grave of a Son of a Bitch. Los Angeles: Black Sparrow Press, 1973.

Trilogy: Coins and Coffins, Discrepancies and Apparitions, The George Washington Poems. Garden City, N.Y.: Doubleday, 1974.

Virtuoso Literature for Two and Four Hands. Garden City,

N.Y.: Doubleday, 1975.

Waiting for the King of Spain. Santa Barbara, Calif.: Black Sparrow Press, 1976.

The Man Who Shook Hands. Garden City, N.Y.: Doubleday, 1978.

Cap of Darkness. Santa Barbara, Calif.: Black Sparrow Press, 1980.

Toward a New Poetry. Ann Arbor: University of Michigan Press, 1980.

The Magician's Feastletters. Santa Barbara, Calif.: Black Sparrow Press, 1982.

The Rings of Saturn. Santa Barbara, Calif.: Black Sparrow Press, 1986.

Emerald Ice: Selected Poems, 1962–1987. Santa Rosa, Calif.: Black Sparrow Press, 1988.

The Butcher's Apron: New and Selected Poems, Including "Greed: Part 14." Santa Rosa, Calif.: Black Sparrow Press, 2000.

The Diamond Dog. Tallahassee, Fla.: Anhinga Press, 2010.

Bay of Angels. Tallahassee, Fla.: Anhinga Press, 2013.

COMBINED POETRY AND PROSE

The Collected Greed, Parts 1–13. Santa Barbara, Calif.: Black Sparrow Press, 1984.

Medea the Sorceress. Santa Rosa, Calif.: Black Sparrow Press, 1991. (*Archeology of Movies and Books* series.)

Jason the Sailor. Santa Rosa, Calif.: Black Sparrow Press, 1993. (*Archeology of Movies and Books* series.)

The Emerald City of Las Vegas. Santa Rosa, Calif.: Black Sparrow Press, 1995. (*Archeology of Movies and Books* series.)

Argonaut Rose. Santa Rosa, Calif.: Black Sparrow Press, 1998. (*Archeology of Movies and Books* series.)

CRITICISM AND MEMOIR

Creating a Personal Mythology. Los Angeles: Black Sparrow Press, 1975.

Toward a New Poetry. Ann Arbor: University of Michigan Press, 1980.

"Eye & Ear: A Manifesto." *Ohio Review* 38:14–19 (1987).

"Camera Obscura: A Meditation." In *Unveilings* by Lynn Stern. New York: Hudson Hills, 1988. Pp. 61–62.

"The Birth of the San Francisco Renaissance: Something Now Called the Whitman Tradition." *Literary Review* 32:36–41 (fall 1988).

"The New Conservatism in American Poetry." *New Letters* 56:17–38 (1989).

"Whitman? No, Wordsworth: The Song of Myself." In *The Romantics and Us: Essays on Literature and Culture*. Edited by Gene W. Ruoff. New Brunswick, N.J.: Rutgers University Press, 1990. Pp. 15–35.

"Color Is a Poet's Tool." In *Poets' Perspectives: Reading,*

Writing, and Teaching Poetry. Edited by Charles R. Duke and Sally A. Jacobson. Portsmouth, N.H.: Boynton/Cook, 1992. Pp. 24–30.

"Introduction to *The Writer's Digest* Guide to Graduate Writing Programs." *Writer's Digest* 72:34–37 (August 1992).

"Supercharging Forward." With Jane Yolen, Richard Patterson, John Jakes, et al. *Writer's Digest* 77, no. 3:31 (March 1997).

"How My Green Silk Dreams Led to the Concept of Personal Mythology." In *Night Errands: How Poets Use Dreams.* Edited by Roderick Townley. Pittsburgh, Pa.: University of Pittsburgh Press, 1998. Pp. 186–193.

"Remembering the New York 1960s Coffee House World of Poetry." In *Light Years: An Anthology of Sociological Happenings (Multimedia in the East Village, 1960–1966).* Edited by Carol Bergé. New York: Spuyten Duyvil, 2010. Pp. 581–600.

PAPERS

Diane Wakoski Papers, MSS 304. Special Collections, MSU Libraries, Michigan State University, East Lansing.

BIBLIOGRAPHY

Newton, Robert. *Diane Wakoski: A Descriptive Bibliography.* Jefferson, N.C.: McFarland, 1987.

CRITICAL AND BIOGRAPHICAL STUDIES

Allred, Joanne. "Diane Wakoski." In *Updating the Literary West.* Fort Worth: Western Literature Association/Texas Christian University Press, 1997. Pp. 367–378.

Bowers, Susan R. "Diane Wakoski." In *Contemporary American Women Poets: An A-to-Z Guide.* Edited by Catherine Cucinella. Westport, Conn.: Greenwood Press, 2002. Pp. 380–384.

Brown, David M. "Wakoski's 'The Fear of Fat Children.'" *Explicator* 48, no. 4:292 (summer 1990).

Daniel, Rosemary. "Young Poet Stuns with Brilliant Imagery." *Atlanta Constitution,* March 23, 1969, p. 12D.

Ferrier, Carole. "Sexual Politics in Diane Wakoski's Poetry." *Hecate* 1, no. 2:84–89 (1975).

Gannon, Catherine. "Diane Wakoski and the Language of Self." *San Jose Studies* 6, no. 2:84–98 (1979).

Harris, Mark. "Diane Wakoski." In *Dictionary of Literary Biography: American Poets Since World War II.* Vol. 5. Edited by Donald Greiner. Detroit: Gale, 1980. Pp. 355–356.

Kirby, David. "The Diamond Dog." *Christian Science Monitor,* April 17, 2010. http://www.csmonitor.com/Books/Book-Reviews/2010/0417/The-Diamond-Dog

Lauter, Estela. "Diane Wakoski: Disentangling the Woman from the Moon." In *Women as Mythmakers: Poetry and Visual Art by Twentieth-Century Women.* Bloomington, Ind.: 1984. Pp. 98–113.

———."Diane Wakoski." In *Contemporary Poets.* Edited by Thomas Riggs. Detroit: St. James Press, 2001. Pp. 1237–1238.

Martin, Taffy Wynne. "Diane Wakoski's Personal Mythology: Dionysian Music, Created Presence." *Boundary 2* 10, no. 3:155–172 (spring 1982).

Ostriker, Alicia. "In Mind: The Divided Self and Women's Poetry." *Midwest Quarterly* 24, no. 4: 351–356 (June 1, 1983).

———. "'What Are Patterns For?'": Anger and Polarization in Women's Poetry."*Feminist Studies* 10, no. 3:485–503 (fall 1984).

Wagner, Linda W. "Wakoski's Poems: Moving Beyond Confession." In *Still the Frame Holds: Essays on Women Poets and Writers.* Edited by Sheila Roberts. San Bernardino, Calif.: Borgo Press, 1993. Pp. 47–58.

Wirtz, Jason. "Poets on Pedagogy." In *Creative Writing: Teaching Theory and Practice* 2, no. 2:59–86 (December 2010).

REVIEWS

Funsten, Kenneth. "More than Naïve Confessions." *Los Angeles Times,* November 4, 1984, p. J4. (Review of *The Collected Greed.*)

Martien, Norman. "*The George Washington Poems* by Diane Wakoski." *Partisan Review* 38, no. 1:122 (1971).

Zweig, Paul. "Into the Hive of Her Anger." *New York Times Book Review,* December 12, 1971, p. 5. (Review of *The Motorcycle Betrayal Poems.*)

INTERVIEWS

"A Colloquy with Diane Wakoski." *Gypsy Scholar: A Graduate Forum for Literary Criticism* 6:61–73 (1979).

Bartlett, Lee. *Talking Poetry: Conversations in the Workshop with Contemporary Poets.* Albuquerque: University of New Mexico Press, 1987. Pp. 234–254.

Bunge, Nancy. "Good Writing Isn't About Easy Things." In *Master Class: Lessons from Leading Writers.* Iowa City: University of Iowa Press, 2005. Pp. 88–94. (Edited version of "Diane Wakoski" in Bunge's *Finding the Words: Conversations with Writers Who Teach.* Athens, Ohio: Swallow/Ohio Press, 1985).

———. "I Wouldn't Be a True Intellectual If I Weren't Always Combating the World as I See It." *Kalliope* 27, no. 1:36–44 (2005).

———. Personal, unpublished interview with Diane Wakoski, July 6, 2016.

Eisenlohr, Kurt. "Diane Wakoski: A Conversation." *Another Chicago Magazine* 28:182–198 (1994).

DIANE WAKOSKI

Fox, Alan. "Diane Wakoski." In *Rattle Conversations: Interviews with Contemporary American Poets*. Edited by Alan Fox. Los Angeles: Red Hen Press, 2008. Pp. 269–285.

Gillespie, Deborah. "An Interview with Diane Wakoski." *South Carolina Review* 38, no. 1:14–19 (fall 2005).

Healey, Claire. "An Interview with Diane Wakoski." *Contemporary Literature* 18, no.1:1–19 (winter 1977).

Hoy, Jody. "Diane Wakoski." In *The Power to Dream: Interviews with Women in the Creative Arts*. New York: Global City Press, 1995. Pp. 98–119.

Jacobsen, Sally. "Diane Wakoski on the Whitman Tradition in Beat and Later Poetry: An Interview." *Journal of Kentucky Studies* 17:64–75 (2000).

Packard, William. "Diane Wakoski." In *The Poet's Craft: Interviews from the "New York Quarterly."* New York: Paragon House, 1987. Pp. 201–217.

Petroski, Catherine. "Diane Wakoski." *Chelsea* 32:39–45 (August 1973).

Smith, Larry. "A Conversation with Diane Wakoski." *Chicago Review* 29, no. 1:115–125 (summer 1977).

Wirtz, Jason. "It's Musical and It's Beautiful: An Interview with Diane Wakoski." *Writing on the Edge* 19, no. 2:41–52 (spring 2009).

JACQUELINE WOODSON

(1964—)

Amy Alessio

BRINGING TOUGH ISSUES to vibrant, memorable characters through lyrical, poignant writing, Jacqueline Woodson helps young readers and adults discover the value of self-identity. The author of over thirty books, Woodson specializes in young adult fiction and poetry but has also published nonfiction, books for middle grade readers, picture books, and titles for adults. Her works have amassed major literary awards including the National Book Award, the Margaret A. Edwards Award, Newbery Honor Book designations, Coretta Scott King Awards, and more. Diversity and self-acceptance tie together the works of this prolific author through the eyes of characters who feel they are on the outside. Characters represent people not often represented in middle grade or young adult fiction, and through their words and stories she offers points of view that broaden readers' perspectives on important realities in their own worlds. Woodson smashes stereotypes in her work when tragedy, love, and family come together in evocative, emotional situations to show the resilience and intelligence of young people. In response to winning the Edwards Award in 2006, Woodson said, "I feel compelled to write against stereotypes; hoping people will see that some issues know no color, class, sexuality."

Woodson's frank yet humorous voice is distilled into verbal images through her poetry. In her National Book Award–winning *Brown Girl Dreaming* (2014), she writes poems about her childhood. In the poem "The Selfish Giant," Woodson writes of her discovery of the power of words: "And I know now / Words are my Tingalayo. Words are my brilliance" (p. 248).

For more than twenty-five years, Woodson's books, essays, and short stories have delighted and touched readers, and as a teacher of writing to young people and adults, she has inspired other award-winning authors, such as An Na, to find their voices. But it is her own writing that allows her teaching to reach ever further. Short stories and essays encourage young writers to find their own poetry and stories. Despite writing about struggle, suicide, abuse, and other painful issues, Woodson offers characters and their readers a sense of hopefulness. Healing emerges from these situations amid family and friendship.

BIOGRAPHY

Jacqueline Amanda Woodson was born on February 12, 1964, in Columbus, Ohio, to Jack and Mary Ann Woodson. In *Brown Girl Dreaming*, she gives hints of the marriage troubles of her parents in the poem describing how she was named. Her father wanted to name her "Jack," but as Woodson tells the story, her mother named her "Jacqueline, just in case / I grew up and wanted something a little bit longer and further away from Jack" (p. 7).

Her brother, Hope, was three years older and her sister, Odella, two. Odella was named after her uncle Odell, who was killed in a car accident just before she was born. Jack and Mary Ann separated, and Mary Ann took the children to her parents in Greenville, South Carolina. It was there that Jacqueline was raised until her mother took the children to Brooklyn when Jacqueline was four. She and her siblings still spent a lot of time in South Carolina, dividing their time between Brooklyn and the South. Her half-brother, Roman, was born when she was three. In an interview with Jennifer M. Brown for *Publishers Weekly*, Woodson recounted how the experiences of the two cultures left an impact on her and her writing:

I feel so grateful to have had both worlds. . . . The South was so lush and so slow-moving and so much about community. The city was thriving and fast-moving and electric. Brooklyn was so much more diverse: on the block where I grew up, there were German people, people from the Dominican Republic, people from Puerto Rico, African-Americans from the South, Caribbean-Americans, Asians.

The family practiced as Jehovah's Witnesses. Living in two such different places, plus the sense of belonging to a religious minority, fed young Jacqueline's sense of being an outsider. Those feelings would emerge many times in her work. While no longer a practicing Witness, Woodson explained in a *New York Times* interview that she retains the feelings of good and community from those days:

> I still consider myself a Christian. It's hard to grow up with such a foundational system and just let it go. I deeply believe in many Christian values: love people; do the right thing; know that there's good in everyone, that God's looking out for all of us. Being a Witness was too closed an experience. That's what I walked away from, not the things I believe.

Situations among her family also reappear later in her work. *Visiting Day*, her 2002 picture book, follows a little girl who visits her father one special day a month. That the visit is to a prison is not mentioned; the focus instead is on family love and preparations for the reunion each month. Woodson explains on her website: "Once a month when I was a little girl, I would go upstate and visit my favorite uncle. I remember those days well and wanted to write about them. This book isn't completely autobiographical but there is a lot of me in it."

In a 1995 *Horn Book* essay, Woodson said that her awakening as a writer was a direct outgrowth of her political awakening as a child in the early 1970s. During the 1972 presidential election, everyone in her neighborhood had supported George McGovern over Richard Nixon because McGovern represented the best chance to further the dream of Martin Luther King, Jr. When Nixon was forced to resign the presidency two years later, ten-year-old Jacqueline thought that meant that McGovern would take his place, and was devastated to learn that wasn't how the

U.S. Constitution worked. "The word *democracy* no longer existed for me," she wrote. Deeply affected by "the bitterness of Vietnam, the scandal of Watergate, poverty, inadequate housing and education," she turned inward, channeling her feelings into writing ("A Sign of Having Been Here," p. 711).

As she describes on her website, she wrote on many surfaces, as thoughts came to her, including graffiti:

> I wrote on everything and everywhere. I remember my uncle catching me writing my name in graffiti on the side of a building. (It was not pretty for me when my mother found out.) I wrote on paper bags and my shoes and denim binders. I chalked stories across sidewalks and penciled tiny tales in notebook margins. I loved and still love watching words flower into sentences and sentences blossom into stories.

After a fifth-grade teacher praised a poem she had written on Martin Luther King, Jr., her confidence and skills grew. She was asked to edit a school magazine. Her mother encouraged reading and trips to the library, and Woodson had a growing desire to write the stories of her family, friends, and people in her neighborhood. She was not finding those stories in the books from the library.

While being encouraged to write, she was not encouraged to pursue a career as a writer. After she earned a B.A. degree in English from Adelphi University in 1985, she worked as a drama therapist for runaways and homeless children in New York City. When her writing career began to take off, she earned fellowships at the MacDowell Colony in Peterborough, New Hampshire, and the Fine Arts Work Center in Provincetown, Massachusetts. She also taught in the writing programs at Goddard, Eugene Lang, and Vermont Colleges, and at the National Book Foundation's Summer Writing Camp. In 2016 she received an honorary doctorate of humane letters from Adelphi, her alma mater. She now lives in the Park Slope section of Brooklyn with her partner, Dr. Juliet Widoff, and their two children, daughter Toshi and son Jackson-Leroi.

Woodson wrote her first children's book after taking a course on children's writing. An editor

JACQUELINE WOODSON

liked it but then retired, and it languished for a while until the editor Wendy Lamb published it in 1990. It was *Last Summer with Maizon*, which turned into a trilogy. She credits Virginia Hamilton and Judy Blume as memorable influences on her reading, along with "The Selfish Giant" by Oscar Wilde and "The Little Match Girl" by Hans Christian Anderson. When she found stories that she loved as a child she would read and reread them until she had them memorized. She loved the poetry of Nikki Giovanni and Langston Hughes and was inspired to write poetry from the magic of their words and styles.

AWARD-WINNING WRITING

Woodson is one of the most lauded authors for young people living today. While winning awards is important in an author's career, it is her ability to connect with readers, to make her literary writing accessible, that has kept her at the forefront of her craft. In a 2009 interview for the *The Brown Bookshelf*, she admits that awards can be intimidating. "A part of me still can't believe I got a Lifetime Achievement Award. A part of me thinks, 'Goodness, should I stop while I'm ahead?' I don't know. The recognition can sometimes be scary—with it can come an expectation."

Woodson was named the Poetry Foundation's Young People's Poet Laureate in 2015. The two-year position sent her on travels to teach children about great poetry and how to write it. In a podcast for *Publishers Weekly* with Rose Fox and Mark Rotella, she outlined some of her goals for the position. "I try to work with underserved kids, especially in rural areas, kids who have never met an author or poet. I show them the accessibility of poetry and their own ability to write and speak poetry."

Woodson has won most of the major literary awards. In addition to the Edwards Award for the impact of her works, her middle grade and young adult titles have earned four citations as Newbery Honor Books and four Coretta Scott King Awards and Honor Book designations. *Brown Girl Dreaming* won the 2014 National Book Award for Young Adult Fiction, and her 2016 novel

Another Brooklyn was a finalist in the 2016 National Book Award's adult category that year. *Coming On Home Soon*, her 2004 picture book with E. B. Lewis, was selected as a Caldecott Honor Book for his illustrations depicting the World War II era. She writes on her website:

> I am still surprised when I walk into a bookstore and see my name on a book or when the phone rings and someone on the other end is telling me I've just won an award. Sometimes, when I'm sitting at my desk for long hours and nothing's coming to me, I remember my fifth grade teacher, the way her eyes lit up when she said "This is really good."

While praised by many organizations, Woodson also encounters some censorship and racism. After Woodson won the National Book Award for *Brown Girl Dreaming*, the author and ceremony host Daniel Handler made a racist remark at the awards ceremony after her acceptance speech about how she is allergic to watermelon. He also mentioned that he had never won a Coretta Scott King Award. Handler subsequently apologized, then matched donations to the advocacy organization We Need Diverse Books.

Woodson was all too familiar with the stereotypes about African Americans eating watermelon. In her *New York Times* response to the incident, she recounted seeing picture books at the library when she was younger. "In a book I found at the library, a camp song about a watermelon vine was illustrated with caricatures of sleepy-looking black people sitting by trees, grinning and eating watermelon." She felt that the allergy she developed to the fruit was perhaps in response to those "hideous" depictions which associated people who looked like her with jokes and a lowly status. She reviewed how she dreamed of being a writer from fifth grade and what it meant to be standing on the podium to accept this prestigious award:

> In a few short words, the audience and I were asked to take a step back from everything I've ever written, a step back from the power and meaning of the National Book Award, lest we forget, lest I forget, where I came from. By making light of that deep and troubled history, he showed that he believed we were at a point where we could laugh about it all. His historical context, unlike my own, came from a place of ignorance.

Her work also incites some painful responses in book challenges for the subject matter. Mindful of the objections raised about some of her books, Woodson is careful not to include many swear words, trying to keep the conversation about the issues she depicts. In 2015 Woodson won the Langston Hughes Medal from the City College of New York, which honors poets and authors who inspire social change. She has also won Lambda Literary Awards for her depictions of LGBTQIA characters. In her interview with Ron Charles of the *Washington Post* for Banned Books Week, she explained why it's so important to keep discussing challenging topics instead of hiding them away:

> I definitely can understand parents having objections. As a mom, as someone who wants to protect my children in any way that I can, I can kind of get inside the heads of people who are saying, "This is not okay," only because they're fearful. That's where I can begin to have the conversation. I think people are willing to talk about anything if you come to it with kindness. But there are all these conversations that I fear are not being had, and as a result, we get banned and challenged.

In an interview with Carole Boston Weatherford for *Reading Rockets*, she stressed that diverse books are especially important in parts of the country that do not have as much diversity:

> The more people know about other people, the less doubt there will be. I think that we have to constantly publish books that talk about that. . . . I think there is a need of getting more books out into the world and people realizing that this book about this gay white boy from California is very valid in my classroom because I don't want my kids to grow up to beat up this boy. That kind of stuff is so important.

Woodson contributed a story, "July Saturday," to the 1999 anthology *Places I Never Meant to Be*. The author Judy Blume put together the anthology featuring writers whose works were challenged, and proceeds went to the National Coalition Against Censorship. In the *Washington Post* interview, Woodson described how she was surprised to hear that her stories have been banned. She discovered that her works had been challenged in schools and libraries for depictions of drug use, sexuality, and even for having interracial relationships.

In "July Saturday," the narrator and her friend watch as a house burns in their neighborhood. They see their friend Clay Williams, his mother, and a baby forced to leave their home with only a can of quarters. They spot a teenage girl hanging around watching as the family members are helped by the neighborhood women. When the narrator's mother takes in the family, she watches as the father of the burned-out family comes home, only to leave with the teenage girl who has been hanging around the neighborhood all day. Woodson shows that the teen set the fire so that she and the father would be free to go away and live together. The fire allows the father to escape the marriage and domestic problems, leaving his family to struggle.

In her notes on censorship included after the story, Woodson describes the many ways books can be challenged or withheld from readers, ways that people may not even realize exist. She questions whether it is because of funding or because of censorship that books are sometimes not added to library collections, and wonders about the decisions that are being made about her work that she never hears. She writes that although she expected some prejudice, it is hardest for her to accept this kind of silent hatred. She turns to her writing to help her come to terms with this conundrum. "Like the censorship, like racism and homophobia and all the other hatreds in the world, the writing, too, will always be here— giving me a better sense of the world around me, helping me to grow and understand" (p. 82).

WRITING FOR YOUNG ADULTS

Woodson pulls no punches in writing emotional stories for young adults. She shows the powerful pain and joy they experience in their everyday lives and how the prejudices of the larger world affects them. She changes the style and format of the words to match the emotions. When the Young Adult Library Services Association (YALSA) gave Woodson the Margaret A. Edwards achievement award, it specified five books for their impact on young adults: *I Hadn't Meant to Tell You This* and its sequel, *Lena*; *From the Notebooks of Melanin Sun*; *Miracle's Boys*; and *If You Come Softly*.

JACQUELINE WOODSON

I Hadn't Meant to Tell You This (1994) and *Lena* (1999) reveal the effect of sexual abuse in a home. Chauncey, Ohio, is a town with a long history of class and racial divides. Marie's African American friends look down on what they call "poor white trash." Marie's mother left the family when she was ten, and sends her postcards from all over the world. Her father tells her, "Neither one's right, Marie. None of it's right. Just how the world is. White people hate us, and we go on hating them right back" (p. 28). Marie becomes best friends with Lena, who is poor and white, and her other friends tell her she is being "an Uncle Tom." Lena confides in Marie that her father is molesting her and that she is afraid for her little sister. Marie asks her how it makes her feel. "'Like I'm the dirtiest, ugliest thing in the world,' Lena said, wiping her cheeks with the back of her hand. . . . 'You would know by how sick you felt every time he touched you'" (p. 36). Layered over the story of abuse are the racial misconceptions the girls must face. Marie's father does not like his daughter mixing with Lena because she is white and poor, though his life after his wife left him is challenging at best. Lena's biggest problems have nothing to do with race or her class.

The follow-up story, *Lena*, published in 1999, tells what happens next to thirteen-year-old Lena and her eight-year-old sister Dion after they run away from their father. Woodson wrote the story in response to the many letters she received from people wondering what happened to the girls. They disguise themselves as boys and travel to Kentucky, hoping to find some relatives of their deceased mother. They hitchhike and encounter frightening situations, but the life with their father was worse, so they tackle each day. A senior citizen, Ms. Lily, gives them a ride and tries to look out for them. When Lena calls her friend Marie to tell her they are OK, she learns that Marie's father wants to take in the runaways. He has overcome the prejudice he displayed in the first book. *Lena* did not receive critical praise, but it provided hope and closure to young adult readers.

From the Notebooks of Melanin Sun (1995), a Coretta Scott King Honor Book, was Woodson's first book written from a male point of view. Thirteen-year-old Melanin has a terrific relationship with his single mother until she brings home her new girlfriend, a white woman. With her complex, evolving characters, Woodson explores boundaries and love in a book covering subjects not often seen in young adult books. Discussing the book on her website, Woodson writes, "I wanted to say that it's important to love who you want as long as you're happy." In his review of the book, Roger Sutton wrote, "This is one of the most unpreachy—and in the person of EC, unapologetic—accounts we've had of gay parents; it's also a rare YA novel in its belief that parents deserve lives of their own."

Her novel *If You Come Softly* was published in 1998, years before many of the news stories and protests of police shootings of African American people and the spread of the Black Lives Matter movement. The sweet love story of basketball star Jeremiah and quiet Ellie resonates through its message of racism. Jeremiah attends the elite Manhattan prep school Percy Academy on scholarship, and doesn't get along with the other few students of color. He loves going home to Brooklyn, to his author mother and his best friend, Carlton, but he knows this school is a chance at a basketball career for him. Ellie's parents claim they aren't racist, as do her friends, but she understands somehow that she can't be in public often with Jeremiah. She is appalled at comments they get when they are together, but this is mainly the story of the joy experienced by two fifteen-year-olds in love. At the end of the story, Jeremiah is excitedly running and dribbling his ball in Central Park after Ellie gave him her Jewish star necklace, when he is gunned down by police. The end shows Ellie at eighteen, looking at the plaque dedicating the Percy gym to Jeremiah.

In the sequel *Behind You* (2004), Woodson shows in short episodes how the people who surrounded Jeremiah are coping in the months after his death. As she mentioned in an interview with Jessica Ray Patton, grief is handled in small episodes because of its pain. "I think vignettes are about an urgency. For the characters in *Behind You*, the urgency was to try to heal and move on.

JACQUELINE WOODSON

I thought it should be told in really short moments because that's what you're living when you're grieving."

Readers are drawn into Ellie's very slow healing after Jeremiah's death. They see his mother barely surviving. They see how his grandmother can see him as a spirit who is trying to comfort those he left behind. His best friend comes out as gay to Ellie, and readers see the anger of the one remaining black basketball player at Percy Academy, Kennedy, as he lives among comments comparing him to Jeremiah and in fear that something will happen to him too. Interestingly, in *Behind You* it is revealed that there was a huge public outcry over Jeremiah's death and that the two police officers who killed him end up in jail. Characters comment on how rare it is to have that result, in what is a painful foreshadowing of real-world events to come. Woodson explains on her website that it was actually her reaction to the tragic events of September 11, 2001, that spurred her to write *Behind You*: "I was faced with trying to figure out how we move on when we lose people so suddenly. I started thinking about it all and this book began." Both *Behind You* and *If You Come Softly* were YALSA Best Fiction for Young Adults selections.

Three brothers struggle with their grief in the Coretta Scott King Award–winning *Miracle's Boys* (2000). Twelve-year-old Lafayette sees that his brother Charlie is much different since he returned from a stint in the Rahway juvenile facility for robbing a store. His brother Ty'ree works full time at twenty-two to support them and keep them together now that both parents have passed away. Ty'ree had a scholarship to MIT, but his mother died of diabetic shock the day after his high school graduation. Lafayette was the only one home that day, and he wishes he could have done something to save her. Charlie, now referred to as Newcharlie by Lafayette, is hard and angry and blames himself for their mother's death. Ty'ree blames himself for the death of his father, who died of hypothermia after saving a woman and her dog from water. Charlie is reaching a crisis point, and the three brothers must come together to try and heal to move forward. In the

end, *Miracle's Boys* pulls together family, grief, gangs, and resilience to offer hope. "Charlie and Ty'ree went back and forth talking about life and art and things that cost lots of money. I listened to them, feeling good and safe and free," says Lafayette (p. 130). In 2005 Woodson helped script a television miniseries based on *Miracle's Boys*, directed by Spike Lee, LeVar Burton, and other notable directors. Dr. Dre was among the actors in the series.

Hush (2002) garnered many citations on notable lists in addition to a National Book Award nomination. This novel asks readers to imagine what would happen if they were in a witness protection program and had to start their lives over. Toswiah and her older sister Cameron have to turn into Evie and Anna after their father, a police officer in Denver, breaks the so-called blue wall of silence and testifies against two of his white colleagues for their murder of an African American teen. The family gets threats on the phone, and bullets come through the window. So one day they put their belongings into plastic bags and leave their grandmother and Denver to become strangers in an unfamiliar city. Eventually Toswiah, who narrates the story, joins the track team at school and begins to adapt to the situation. But her parents, especially her father, struggle to find their identity in this new life:

All this time I'd been thinking about all the stuff we'd lost—our friends, Grandma, our names, some stupid old clothes. But my father—he'd lost everything. Everything he'd ever known. The morning the lieutenant pinned that medal to his chest, Daddy had looked over at us and grinned. Grinned like the world was complete. Like he had found perfection.

(p. 178)

The question of identity, heard clearly in many other Woodson works as characters struggle with sexual or racial identity and prejudice, is more subtle here. In *Hush*, Toswiah's mother becomes a devout Jehovah's Witness and talks of God's plan for the family. She had to leave her identity but finds a new one. Her father cannot find one, and he tries to commit suicide before realizing he has a lot to live for. This book works especially well for young adults, since the entire period of adolescence is about discovering identity.

People can lose their identity too when they are addicted to drugs. *Beneath a Meth Moon: An Elegy* (2012) is Woodson's portrayal of a hard-hit family of Hurricane Katrina survivors. Teenage Laurel lost her mother and her grandmother to the hurricane, which nearly wiped out the small town of Pass Christian, Mississippi. She and her little brother and her father try to make a new life in Galilee, Iowa, and Laurel finds a best friend and cheerleading. But she also finds T-Boom, who introduces her to meth, then keeps her on it. She writes on every scrap of paper she can find, even when the desire for the drug overpowers everything else. She tries a few times to get off the drug before a friend from the streets gets her to the hospital one night when her heart nearly stops. *Beneath a Meth Moon* was a YALSA selection for Best Book for Young Adults.

EVOKING TIME AND MEMORY: WRITING FOR ADULTS

A writer who is talented in both prose and poetry has the skills to wield words in a variety of styles. Woodson uses different techniques to great effect in her writing. NPR's Terry Gross talked with Woodson about the differences of writing for young adults versus adults. Rather than focus on adult content, though those choices are deliberate, Woodson discussed the intricacies of language that reach people in different stages of life:

> If I have some SAT-type word in there that's going to give me pause when I'm reading it out loud, then it's not going to make it into the narrative. . . . I think that's the same when I'm writing for young people. But . . . I play with language differently when I'm writing for adults. I can adjust the sentences differently. I can move through time. I can play with white space. And that's the way I do things differently—not so much in terms of the words I use.

Discussing *Another Brooklyn* (2016), a finalist for the National Book Award, Woodson told Tess Malone, "I know I can do this and know I can do it a way people will like, but I wanted to push my own boundaries and try something new. I wanted to write more with time, memory. I can go to more haunted places in an adult novel."

Another Brooklyn looks at the lives of four friends who grew up in Brooklyn in the 1970s. August tells the story, remembering the girls' strong friendship and the dangers they faced both in their neighborhood and in 1970s society at large. After August's uncle's death in Vietnam was followed by her mother's death, she, her father, and her brother moved to Brooklyn. August sees how tragedy affects other people in her neighborhood and how many, but not all, survive stronger. Fond memories overlay tragic ones as August reflects on scenes that helped form who she is.

Reviewing the book for the *New York Times*, Tayari Jones found that the success of the novel was in the power of those memories. "Woodson brings the reader so close to her young characters that you can smell the bubble gum on their breath and feel their lips as they brush against your ear. This is both the triumph and challenge of this powerfully insightful novel. 'This is memory,' we are reminded."

Woodson uses form to evoke emotion in her works, such as she did with the short scenes in alternating points of view in *Behind You*. Ron Charles' review in the *Washington Post* found power in *Another Brooklyn*'s evocative style:

> Although less formally experimental than "Brown Girl Dreaming," "Another Brooklyn" still presents its own distinctive structure: Every paragraph is set off by blank lines, which emphasizes the poetic style of Woodson's prose. That structure also effectively slows the narrative down and contributes to its dream-like tone. Time is fluid in this story, as August recalls events that impressed her—and events that she repressed, reaching back to moments in Tennessee and forward to relationships later in life.

Woodson first wrote for adults in 1995 with her look at the effects of the Vietnam War on an African American family, *Autobiography of a Family Photo*. In 1994 Woodson told Diane R. Paylor, "You'd see the neighborhood changing and everyone coming back and being addicted to heroin or having lost their minds or their arms or legs. . . . But nobody was talking about it." In *Autobiography* the nameless narrator begins her story in fifth grade. Her gay brother wears high heels the night before he leaves for Vietnam. He comes home in a casket. One of her remaining

brothers has blue eyes while another is half-white, both appearing to prove her mother's infidelity. The father's anger increases over the twelve-year period of the book until he hits her mother and leaves the family. The narrator wants to escape some of the sadness about the loss of family members to find a new identity in the future. In her review for *Booklist*, Whitney Scott assessed the conclusion and value of the work:

> Woodson brings the narrator to her mid-teens, poised on the brink of an awakening, struggling to come to terms with her sexuality, and literally screaming to leave her earlier life behind, "where we're the pitiful ones." This faux memoir, told with painful clarity and fervor, deserves its share of general readers as well as those who home in on women's and African American literature.

POETRY: MEMOIR AND POWERFUL, SPARE LANGUAGE

As Young People's Poet Laureate, Woodson had an opportunity in 2015 and 2016 to work on projects designed to introduce children to classic poetry and to write their own. Her poetry titles *Brown Girl Dreaming* and *Locomotion* are among the most honored of her works. She has also written notable picture books in verse.

In the podcast with Fox and Rotella for *Publishers Weekly*, Woodson discussed why the poet laureate position was so important to her: "In many areas, kids have never met an author or poet. I enjoy talking to young people about the gospel of poetry. . . . A lot of us grow up thinking poetry is not for us. Langston Hughes, Angelou, Giovanni, Frost. Poetry was a language I could speak too." She realizes that, for young people, "Because of hip hop, spoken word is a form, they recognize it."

Robert Polito, president of the Poetry Foundation, praised Woodson as "an elegant, daring, and restlessly innovative writer. So many writers settle on a style and a repertoire of gestures and subjects, but Woodson, like her characters, is always in motion and always discovering something fresh" (qtd. in Kellogg).

The Poetry Foundation website has links to Woodson's favorite poems and videos of young poets being honored. It has also published some of the many poetry readings and festivals she attended throughout her term. In her essay on children's poetry titled "Lift Every Voice," she discusses how she was afraid of poetry as a child. She didn't understand it, but then she came across some that made her read and reread, and language and phrases began to stick in her mind. She said that this is how writing poetry starts, with reading and rereading. Describing her goals for the position, she wrote, "James Weldon Johnson (1871–1938) wrote the lyrics/poem for what became The Black National lmdash;'Lift Every Voice and Sing.' This is what I'm hoping to do—to lift every young voice in this country."

Brown Girl Dreaming, Woodson's 2014 memoir of her childhood growing up in South Carolina and Brooklyn, is written completely in verse. It garnered more than thirty awards and "best" lists in addition to the National Book Award, including the NAACP Image Award and the Coretta Scott King Award. Remarkably for a book of verse, it was also a *New York Times* best seller for more than twenty weeks. It exemplified the strengths of Woodson's contributions to literature in many ways. It showed her creativity and willingness to experiment with form. It made high-quality, literary poetry accessible and enjoyable in a nonfiction format, rarely seen in youth literature. Poems cover her joy at spending summers with her grandparents, fun with her friends when she returns, love for her family. Interspersed are stories about how her grandfather is getting older and weaker, how her brother Roman got lead poisoning from the paint on the walls of their apartment, how she struggled in school and things came more easily to her sister Odella. The book ends with memories of her grandfather's funeral, words about how she started observing and writing, and her conclusion that all these scenes helped her become who she is.

> When there are many worlds, love can wrap itself
> around you, say, *Don't cry.* Say, *You are as good as*
>   *anyone.*
> Say, *Keep remembering me.* And you know, even as
>   the
> world explodes
> around you—that you are loved . . .
>
> (p. 319)

The logo for the Coretta Scott King awards features a child reading, and words "Peace," "Non-Violent Social Change," and "Brotherhood." *Locomotion* (2003), which was a Coretta Scott King Honor Book in 2004, embodies those ideas through the story of eleven-year-old Lonnie Motion, who loses his parents in a fire and learns how to express his grief through the poetry he is made to write in class. He discovers a talent for it, and writes more. He writes about his new foster mom, about the group home where he had to live, about how his sister's foster mother doesn't approve of him, and about how he will read the Bible and attend church because it allows him to spend more time with his sister. He writes memories of his parents, each poem invoking the palpable grief that Woodson instills in the spare lines:

> The stupid fire couldn't take all of them.
> Nothing could do that.
> Nothing.
>
> (p. 19)

In their analysis "Using Jacqueline Woodson's *Locomotion* with Middle School Students," Mary Napoli and Emily Rose Ritholz describe how the power of Lonnie's words and his discussion of form help readers connect with him as well as find their own poems to tell:

> Through her considerable talents, Woodson has crafted a rich and authentic voice through Lonnie. His words not only express his feelings, but offer opportunities for readers to connect to his life, his story, his heart, and his soul while leaving room to make personal connections. Throughout the novel, Lonnie finds his poetic voice and explains the line breaks and poetry forms that he employs.
>
> (p. 36)

The authors explore several examples of poetry written by their students on themes expressed by Lonnie. Woodson, by having Lonnie write poetry in school and trying to write different forms, brilliantly layered a powerful story with lessons for tweens to find their own unique poetic power.

Woodson followed up Lonnie's story with *Peace, Locomotion* (2009), which is written in prose because he had a teacher who forced him to write that way. Lonnie writes letters to his sister Lili, offering hope that it is possible to find peace after tragic events. It is another lesson in writing crafted within an enjoyable story.

In an interview with Lee Wind for the Society of Children's Book Writers and Illustrators, Woodson was asked about whether or not she had planned to write it in the form of letters. She replied,

> Nope. What I DID know is that it WASN'T going to be poetry. The novel in verse [*Locomotion*] was because Lonnie was just discovering his writer's voice in school. In *Peace, Locomotion*, his "voice" has been silenced by a lame teacher so it wouldn't make sense to have it written in poems. The whole "show don't tell" rule.

Using different styles or mediums to evoke feelings is an important Woodson technique. Wielding language is as important a part of her skill set as layering themes of inclusiveness and equality over an engaging plot.

POETRY AND ILLUSTRATION: PICTURE BOOKS

For younger readers, Woodson has collaborated on picture books with several award-winning illustrators. These illustrated stories and poems offer visions of happy scenes, historical scenes, and family moments, such as the aforementioned *Visiting Day*, illustrated by James Ransome, where the family goes to visit a father without spelling out that the father is in prison.

Some of the titles are written in poetry. *The Other Side* (2001), illustrated by E. B. Lewis, shows a fence with two neighbor girls, one white and one African American, who are not allowed to cross the fence and play with each other. Both of their mothers have told them not to cross it; in their small town, no one crosses any fences to be friends. Clover's friends at first don't like Clover sitting on the fence with Annie.

> Once, when we were jumping rope,
> She asked if she could play.
> And my friend Sandra said no
> Without even asking the rest of us.
>
> (p. 5)

By the end of the book, however, they are all playing together. In an interview with *Booklist*'s Hazel Rochman, Woodson discussed her goals

for *The Other Side*: "I was trying to show young girls as activists, how simple gestures can change the world, and how powerful friendship and dialogue can be. I wanted to say, 'Question. Always question.'"

In picture books and in her poetry collections especially, Woodson paints with pictures. While the girls play together near the fence and sit together on it, they agree at the end to hope for friendlier relations among all people in the future. As in many of her books, Woodson offers hope but no easy answers. In a review of *The Other Side* for the *Bulletin of the Center for Children's Books*, the children's literature professor Janice Del Negro agrees: "This is an emotionally intricate tale presented simply and intimately, and the open-ended conclusion unselfconsciously encourages discussion, examination, and inquiry. Unlike authors of other picture books dealing with racism and prejudice, Woodson doesn't over explain or stack the emotional deck." *The Other Side* was recognized as a School Library Journal Best Book, Booklist Editor's Choice, and one of the New York Public Library's 100 Titles for Reading and Sharing, among other notable lists.

Coming On Home Soon, her 2004 historical picture book, was a Caldecott Honor title for E. B. Lewis' beautiful paintings. In the story, Ada Ruth's mother leaves her and Grandma to take a job in Chicago cleaning trains during the war. Woodson's poetry evokes the rhythm of a worried Grandma trying to comfort a girl missing her mama: "*Keep writing to her*, Grandma says / So I do" (p. 6).

In her interview with Rochman, Woodson explained her desire to write about the history of African American women, and her own family's personal history:

> Black women have been everywhere—building the railroads, cleaning the kitchens, starting revolutions, writing poetry, leading voter registration drives and leading slaves to freedom. We've been there and done that. I want the people who have come before me to be part of the stories that I'm telling, because if it weren't for them, I wouldn't be telling stories.

Grandma marvels that even a "colored woman" can get a job with the railroad. Woodson again layers the story of hard work and loneliness for family with a message about equality. The message and social setting are then provided with a light hand, adding to the tapestry of the book without overwhelming Ada Ruth's story.

Strong women, characters who do what needs to be done, appear in several Woodson books. In her interview with Dean Schneider for *Book Links*, Woodson talked about what she wants from those characters: "I think it's both that I'm inspired by the women who came before me and that I want women represented on the page in a way that's respectful, complicated, and loving. And yes, when I re-read a character on the page who is amazing, I have to go, 'Yes!'"

While the 2005 title *Show Way*, illustrated by Hudson Talbott, is a picture book, the subject matter makes it a title for grade school children. It is about the Underground Railroad and quilts that may have had clues to help guide slaves on their journey. Telling the story of Woodson's own family, it begins with an ancestor sold away from her parents as a child who learned to make Show Way quilts with messages, and how that bravery continued down seven generations of daughters to Woodson's own daughter. Among many notable lists and other awards, *Show Way* was a Newbery Honor Book. In her review of the title for *Booklist*, Rochman wrote, "A Show Way is a quilt with secret meanings, and the image works as both history and haunting metaphor in this exquisite picture book."

In her interview with Weatherford, Woodson said that *Show Way* began with her grandmother trying to tell her about the women who came before her in the family tree, especially Soonie, whose own grandmother was a slave who helped with the Underground Railroad. Woodson traveled to the South and talked with other relatives, piecing together documentation for a family history reaching back into the slavery era, when slaves were not allowed to learn to read or write. She was able to document many people, relationships, and events, but when it came to Soonie's mother, for instance, "history went and lost her name," said Woodson. "I thought as I was writing *Show Way* that I'd make up a name for her, and then I thought no, I think this needs to be written down that we did lose some of our history on this journey."

Identity is preserved in the messages from

Show Way as each generation of women learns to stand tall and do what needs to be done to keep families going. Woodson's own identity spurred her interest in that story, but it traces the unwritten story of many families and constitutes an important part of U.S. history.

The 2012 title *Each Kindness*, illustrated by E. B. Lewis, is another good example of how the picture book medium offers Woodson a palette for her poetic, powerful words. It shows two girls, Maya, who wants to be friends, and Chloe, who ignores her. One day Maya does not come back to school, and Chloe is left with the memory of her own unkindness. Chloe's teacher asks her to drop a pebble in water to see the ripples and think about something kind she has done. She can't think of anything, and she wishes she had a chance to be friendly to Maya. Woodson's free verse inspires feelings and thoughts to ripple from the words like the pebbles in the water of the teacher's analogy for kindness:

The next day, Maya's seat was empty.
In class that morning, we were talking about kindness.

"Kindness" is the word pulled out on its own line, though Maya's seat sits in a line as well. *Each Kindness* landed on numerous state notable lists and won awards that included the Charlotte Zolotow Award, Coretta Scott King Honor Book designation, and Jane Addams Peace Association Children's Book Award. While the text does not openly discuss race, the names of the children and the illustrations show possible racial reasons for the students' separation. Rochman's review for *Booklist* finds racial undertones as well as the strength in telling this story from Chloe's point of view:

Chloe's teacher spells out lessons of kindness, but the story is most powerful in the scenes of malicious bullying in the multiracial classroom and in the school yard. It is rare to tell a story of cruelty from the bully's viewpoint, and both the words and pictures powerfully evoke Chloe's shame and sorrow over the kindness she has not shown, as she looks at the empty seat next to her in the classroom, and then, alone and troubled, throws a stone in the water and watches the ripples move out and away.

MIDDLE GRADE WORKS: MEMOIR AND MEMORABLE, SPARE PROSE

Woodson's first novels were for middle grade readers. Published in 1990, *Last Summer with Maizon* is the story of Margaret and Maizon, two best friends. When they are eleven, Margaret's father dies of a heart attack and Maizon is sent to a boarding school. Throughout the books that became a trilogy, Maizon is unhappy at the school, where she is one of only five African Americans, and she longs to return home to her friend. Woodson published the sequel *Maizon at Blue Hill* in 1992 and, a year later, *Between Madison and Palmetto*, which tells the story of the girls back together in their neighborhood for eighth grade. These books are among the few in her body of work that Woodson feels have any autobiographical elements. Reviews of *Maizon at Blue Hill* were more favorable than those for *Last Summer with Maizon*, which many critics found too short or underdeveloped. Of *Maizon at Blue Hill*, the *Kirkus* reviewer wrote, "Confronted by their ultimatum and stung by the insensitivity of some of the whites, Maizon decides to be friends with no one; and though she eventually responds to her nice roommate and has real liking for some fine teachers, loneliness is the overriding factor in her decision to 'find a place where smart black girls from Brooklyn could feel like they belonged.'" Though these books were written early in her career, Woodson's main themes—the feeling of otherness and the enduring bonds of family and friendship—are already apparent, and their appeal will carry through later works such as *Another Brooklyn*.

Feathers, a Newbery Honor Book published in 2007, follows Frannie, who is trying to find the hope her teacher discusses as the class studies the Emily Dickinson poem "Hope is the thing with feathers." Frannie's mother is depressed after a miscarriage. Frannie frequently acts as translator for her brother Sean, who is deaf, and she is painfully aware of how people often treat him as if he is "different." Sean is hurt by girls who communicate with him through his signing sister: they say it is too bad that someone as good-looking as he is can't talk like they do.

In her interview with Weatherford, Woodson relates that her book was the first for youth to

have a deaf African American character. But she was not thinking about that while writing it. She was trying to present a character who wanted to be a part of a culture that did not always see him as part of that culture. Woodson, in writing Sean, wanted to show his yearning to belong:

> I think it's something we don't think about a lot. I think we think of deafness as other. We think of it as something that is not a culture but, too often, people think of it as a handicap. Deaf should be a capital D just like African-American culture.

> I wanted to put on the page a kid who had his culture, who had the deaf community and his world and a supportive family that wasn't saying be like us, but saying you're a gift to us, and we wanna move into your world.

She wanted *Feathers* to be about hope for all the characters. As always, this hope does not come with simple answers, but a sense of peace still comes with the ending:

> Ms. Johnson says each day holds its own memory— its own moments that we can write about later. She says we should always look for the moments and some of them might be perfect, filled with light and hope and laughter. Moments that stay with us forever and ever. Amen.
>
> (*Feathers*, p. 117)

After Tupac and D Foster (2008), another Newbery Honor title, follows three young girls in the 1990s. D has come into the lives of Neeka and the narrator, who are best friends. They hang and obsess about the hip-hop artist Tupac Shakur, fretting when he is first shot. They don't know much about D except that her mama is largely absent and that she has spent time in foster care. When she comes to say goodbye to them, they learn that D Foster is really Desiree Johnson. "I came on this street and y'all became my friends. That's the D puzzle. I talked about roaming and y'all listened. I sat down and ate with your mamas and it felt like I was finally belonging somewhere. Us three's the puzzle. It's just a three-piece puzzle" (p. 128). In a review for the *Bulletin of the Center of Children's Books*, Karen Coats highlights how the narrator's identity as a friend of D is more important than the missing pieces of D's life: "The narrator's thoughts on D's place in her life—part best friend, part enigma—offer an insightful reminder of the way

we find bits of ourselves in others, and the way our identities are a tapestry of the people and places we love, even if we don't entirely understand them." Identity, friendship, and family reach middle grade readers through Woodson's lyrical poetry and prose.

ANTHOLOGIES

Woodson has contributed stories and poems to more than twenty anthologies, largely for young adults. Themes of the anthologies range from poetry forms to sexual identity and more. For instance, she collaborated on a story called "The Rialto" with Chris Lynch for the anthology *The Color of Absence* in 2001, edited by James Howe, featuring stories on loss.

In *How Beautiful the Ordinary: Twelve Stories of Identity* (2009), edited by Michael Cart, Woodson wrote a nine-page story about transgender Trev, whose father and brother cannot understand who he is. He finds comfort in learning about another relative who had some things in common with him. As with her poetry and picture books, her form invokes feelings. Trev's story is short but memorable and impactful both for readers like him and for those who need to understand people like him. Stories have offered a prolific author such as herself a chance to branch out to reach many new readers on their journeys for self-identity.

IMPACT

Woodson shows no sign of slowing down and continues to find new ways to connect with readers and students, to help them find the importance of their own voices. In her interview Paylor found that Woodson wants to be judged as a writer, not with caveats about who she is as a person: "I have these qualifiers: Jacqueline Woodson, African American, lesbian writer. No one ever says 'Hemingway, a misogynist, anti-Semitic, white, male writer.' How come I can't just be a writer?"

After the painful reminder of African American stereotypes was delivered to her in front of a crowd after she won the National Book Award

for *Brown Girl Dreaming*, Woodson's *New York Times* response emphasized why her work and her writing of diverse voices, of identity and love and hope, is so important:

This mission is what's been passed down to me—to write stories that have been historically absent in this country's body of literature, to create mirrors for the people who so rarely see themselves inside contemporary fiction, and windows for those who think we are no more than the stereotypes they're so afraid of. To give young people—and all people—a sense of this country's brilliant and brutal history, so that no one ever thinks they can walk onto a stage one evening and laugh at another's too often painful past.

Selected Bibliography

WORKS OF JACQUELINE WOODSON

NOVELS

Last Summer with Maizon. New York: Delacorte, 1990.

Maizon at Blue Hill. New York: Delacorte, 1992.

Between Madison and Palmetto. New York: Delacorte, 1993.

I Hadn't Meant to Tell You This. New York: Delacorte, 1994.

Autobiography of a Family Photo. New York: Dutton, 1995.

From the Notebooks of Melanin Sun. New York: Scholastic, 1995.

If You Come Softly. New York: Putnam, 1998.

Lena. New York: Delacorte, 1999.

Miracle's Boys. New York: Putnam, 2000.

Hush. New York: Putnam, 2002.

Behind You. New York: Putnam, 2004.

Feathers. New York: Putnam, 2007.

After Tupac and D Foster. New York: Putnam, 2008.

Peace, Locomotion. New York: Putnam, 2009.

Beneath a Meth Moon: An Elegy. New York: Nancy Paulsen, 2012.

Another Brooklyn: A Novel. New York: Amistad, 2016.

PICTURE BOOKS

The Other Side. Illustrated by E. B. Lewis. New York: Putnam, 2001.

Visiting Day. Illustrated by James Ransome. New York: Scholastic, 2002.

Coming On Home Soon. Illustrated by E. B. Lewis. New York: Putnam, 2004.

Show Way. Illustrated by Hudson Talbott. New York: Putnam, 2005.

Each Kindness. Illustrated by E. B. Lewis. New York: Nancy Paulsen, 2012.

POETRY

Locomotion. New York: Putnam, 2003.

Brown Girl Dreaming. New York: Nancy Paulsen, 2014.

SHORT STORIES

"July Saturday." In *Places I Never Meant to Be: Original Stories by Censored Writers*. Edited by Judy Blume. New York: Simon & Schuster for Young Readers, 1999.

"The Rialto." With Chris Lynch. In *The Color of Absence: 12 Stories About Loss and Hope*. Edited by James Howe. New York: Atheneum for Young Readers, 2001.

"Trev." In *How Beautiful the Ordinary: Twelve Stories of Identity*. Edited by Michael Cart. E-book, HarperCollins, 2009.

ESSAYS

"A Sign of Having Been Here." *Horn Book* 71, no. 3:711 (November–December 1995).

"The Pain of the Watermelon Joke." *New York Times*, November 28, 2014. http://www.nytimes.com/2014/11/29/opinion/the-pain-of-the-watermelon-joke.html

"Lift Every Voice." Poetry Foundation, October 7, 2015. https://www.poetryfoundation.org/resources/children/articles/detail/70271

PAPERS

Jacqueline Woodson Papers, 1989–2002. Archives and Special Collections, Elmer L. Anderson Library, University of Minnesota, Minneapolis.

Jacqueline Woodson Collection, 2001–2003. Special Collections Department, Tampa Library, University of South Florida, Tampa.

CRITICAL AND BIOGRAPHICAL STUDIES

Arnold, Mary. "2006 Margaret A. Edwards Award Winner Jacqueline Woodson." Young Adult Library Services Association (YALSA), November 15, 2011. http://www.ala.org/yalsa/booklistsawards/bookawards/margaretaedwards/maeprevious/06

"Jacqueline Woodson." *The Brown Bookshelf* (blog), February 25, 2009. https://thebrownbookshelf.com/2009/02/22/jacqueline-woodson/

"Jacqueline Woodson (1964–)." In *Something About the Author*. Vol. 189. Edited by Lisa Kumar. Gale, 2009. Pp. 200–209.

Kellogg, Carolyn. "Jacqueline Woodson Named the New Young People's Poet Laureate." *Los Angeles Times*, June 3, 2015. http://www.latimes.com/books/jacketcopy/la-et-jc-jacqueline-woodson-young-peoples-poet-laureate-20150603-story.html

Napoli, Mary, and Emily Rose Ritzholz. "Using Jacqueline

JACQUELINE WOODSON

Woodson's *Locomotion* with Middle School Readers." *Voices from the Middle* 16, no. 3:31–39 (March 2009).

Patton, Jessica Rae. "Jacqueline Woodson: Poetry In Motion." *Teaching K-8 Magazine*, April 2006, pp. 46–48. https://www.essentiallearningproducts.com/jacqueline-woodson-poetry-motion-jessica-rae-patton

"Woodson, Jacqueline (1964–), An Introduction to." *Children's Literature Review*. Vol. 49. Edited by Deborah J. Morad. Detroit: Gale, 1999.

REVIEWS

Charles, Ron. "'Another Brooklyn' Reminds Us of a Brooklyn Far from the Tony Borough of Today." *Washington Post*, August 12, 2016. https://www.washingtonpost.com/entertainment/books/another-brooklyn-by-jacqueline-woodson/2016/08/12/b5272b18-6092-11e6-9d2f-b1a3564181a1_story.html

Coats, Karen. Review of *After Tupac and D Foster. Bulletin of the Center for Children's Books* 61, no. 5:230 (January 2008).

Del Negro, Janice M. Review of *The Other Side. Bulletin of the Center for Children's Books* 54, no. 6:211–212 (February 2001). https://www.ideals.illinois.edu/bitstream/handle/2142/14353/bulletincenterchv00054i00006_opt.pdf?sequence=2

Jones, Tayari. "Jacqueline Woodson's Adult Novel Captures 1970s Brooklyn." *New York Times*, August 18, 2016. http://www.nytimes.com/2016/08/21/books/review/jacqueline-woodson-another-brooklyn.html

Maizon at Blue Hill. Kirkus Reviews, October 1, 1992. https://www.kirkusreviews.com/book-reviews/jacqueline-woodson/maizon-at-blue-hill/

Rochman, Hazel. Review of *Show Way. Booklist*, September 15, 2005, p. 63.

———. Review of *Each Kindness. Booklist*, August 1, 2012, p. 66.

Scott, Whitney. "Autobiography of a Family." *Booklist*, December 15, 1994, p. 736.

Sutton, Roger. Review of *From the Notebooks of Melanin Sun. Bulletin of the Center for Children's Books* 48, no. 11:401 (July–August 1995). https://www.ideals.illinois.edu/bitstream/handle/2142/12875/bulletincenterchv00048i00011_opt.pdf?sequence=2

INTERVIEWS

Brown, Jennifer M. "From Outsider to Insider." *Publishers Weekly*, February 11, 2002. http://www.publishersweekly.com/pw/print/20020211/40294-from-outsider-to-insider.html

Charles, Ron. "It's Banned Books Week Again. Can We Stop Yelling at Each Other About It?" *Washington Post*, September 27, 2015. https://www.washingtonpost.com/entertainment/books/its-banned-books-week-again-can-we-stop-yelling-at-each-other-about-it/2015/09/27/d7860518-6399-11e5-9757-e49273f05f65_story.html

Fox, Rose, and Mark Rotella. "PW Radio 194: Jacqueline Woodson and YA Authors as Advocates." *Publishers Weekly Radio*, October 7, 2016. http://www.publishersweekly.com/pw/podcasts/index.html?podcast=641&channel=8

Gross, Terry. "Jacqueline Woodson on Growing Up, Coming Out, and Saying Hi to Strangers." *Fresh Air*, June 19, 2015. http://www.npr.org/2015/06/19/415747871/jacqueline-woodson-on-growing-up-coming-out-and-saying-hi-to-strangers

Galanes, Philip. "Table for Three: Jimmy Carter and Jacqueline Woodson on Race, Religion, and Rights." *New York Times*, July 24, 2015. http://www.nytimes.com/2015/07/26/fashion/jimmy-carter-and-jacqueline-woodson-on-race-religion-and-rights.html?_r=1

Malone, Tess. "10 Questions for Author Jacqueline Woodson." *Atlanta Magazine*, August 31, 2016. http://www.atlantamagazine.com/news-culture-articles/10-questions-author-jacqueline-woodson/

Paylor, Diane R. "Bold Type: Jacqueline Woodson's Girl Stories." *Ms.*, November–December 1994, p. 77.

Rochman, Hazel. "The *Booklist Interview*: Jacqueline Woodson." *Booklist*, February 1, 2005, p. 968.

Schneider, Dean. "Talking with Jacqueline Woodson." *Book Links*, May 2008. http://www.ala.org/emiert/sites/ala.org.emiert/files/content/cskbookawards/docs/booklinks-200805-JW.pdf

Weatherford, Carole Boston. "Transcript from an Interview with Jacqueline Woodson." *Reading Rockets*, n.d. http://www.readingrockets.org/books/interviews/woodson/transcript

Wind, Lee. "Jacqueline Woodson: An Exclusive SCBWI Team Blog Pre-Conference Interview!" *I'm Here. I'm Queer. What the Hell Do I Read? Society of Children's Book Writers and Illustrators Team Blog*, December 11, 2009. http://www.leewind.org/2009/12/jacqueline-woodson-exclusive-scbwi-team.html

OTHER SOURCES

Author website. www.jacquelinewoodson.com

TELEVISION AND MINISERIES BASED ON THE WORK OF JACQUELINE WOODSON

Miracle's Boys. Six episodes. Adaptations by Kevin Arkadie, Stephen Langford, Dawn Urbont, and Jacqueline Woodson. Episodes directed by Spike Lee, Neema Barnette, LeVar Burton, Ernest R. Dickerson, and Bill Duke. The N, 2005.

Cumulative Index

All references include volume numbers in boldface roman numerals followed by page numbers within that volume. Subjects of articles are indicated by boldface type.

A

"A" (Zukofsky), **Supp. III Part 2:** 611, 612, 614, 617, 619, 620, 621, 622, 623, 624, 626, 627, 628, 629, 630, 631; **Supp. IV Part 1:** 154; **Supp. XVI:** 287, *287*

Aal, Katharyn Machan, **Supp. IV Part 1:** 332; **Supp. XXIII:** 54

Aaron, Daniel, **IV:** 429; **Supp. I Part 2:** 647, 650

Aaron's Rod (Lawrence), **Supp. I Part 1:** 255

Abacus (Karr), **Supp. XI:** 240–242, 248, 254

Abádi-Nagy, Zoltán, **Supp. IV Part 1:** 280, 289, 291

"Abandoned Farmhouse" (Kooser), **Supp. XIX:** 117, 119

"Abandoned House, The" (L. Michaels), **Supp. XVI:** 214

"Abandoned Newborn, The" (Olds), **Supp. X:** 207

"Abandoned Stone Schoolhouse in the Nebraska Sandhills, An" (Kooser), **Supp. XIX:** 124–125

"Abba Jacob" (Nelson), **Supp. XVIII:** 177

"Abbé François Picquet"(Kenny), **Supp. XXIII:** 153

Abbey, Edward, **Supp. VIII:** 42; **Supp. X:** 24, 29, 30, 31, 36; **Supp. XIII:** 1–18; **Supp. XIV:** 179; **Supp. XXV:** 208; **Supp. XXVI:** 31, 37; **Supp. XXVIII:** 253, 255

Abbey's Road (Abbey), **Supp. XIII:** 12

Abbott, Carl, **Supp. XVIII:** 142

Abbott, Clifford F., **Supp. XXVI:** 89

Abbott, Edith, **Supp. I Part 1:** 5

Abbott, Jack Henry, **Retro. Supp. II:** 210

Abbott, Jacob, **Supp. I Part 1:** 38, 39

Abbott, Lyman, **III:** 293

Abbott, Sean, **Retro. Supp. II:** 213

ABC of Color, An: Selections from Over a Half Century of Writings (Du Bois), **Supp. II Part 1:** 186

ABC of Reading (Pound), **III:** 468, 474–475

"Abdication, An" (Merrill), **Supp. III Part 1:** 326

'Abdu'l-Bahá, **Supp. XX: 117, 122**

Abel, Lionel, **Supp. XIII:** 98

Abel, Sam, **Supp. XIII:** 199

Abelard, Peter, **I:** 14, 22

Abeles, Sigmund, **Supp. VIII:** 272

Abeng (Cliff), **Supp. XXII:** 66, 69–71

Abercrombie, Joe, **Supp. XXV:** 74

Abercrombie, Lascelles, **III:** 471; **Retro. Supp. I:** 127, 128

Abernathy, Milton, **Supp. III Part 2:** 616

Abernon, Edgar Vincent, Viscount d', **Supp. XVI:** 191

Aberration of Starlight (Sorrentino), **Supp. XXI:** 234–235

Abhau, Anna. *See* Mencken, Mrs. August (Anna Abhau)

"Abide with Me" (Hoffman), **Supp. XVIII:** 86

Abide with Me (Strout), **Supp. XXIII:** 273, 275, **278–280,** 285

"Ability" (Emerson), **II:** 6

Abingdon, Alexander, **Supp. XVI:** 99

Abish, Walter, **Supp. V:** 44

"Abishag" (Glück), **Supp. V:** 82

"Abnegation, The" (Bronk), **Supp. XXI:** 32

Abney, Lisa, **Supp. XXII:** 9

Abood, Maureen, **Supp. XXII:** 90

"Abortion, The" (Sexton), **Supp. II Part 2:** 682

"Abortions" (Dixon), **Supp. XII:** 153

"About C. D. Wright" (Colburn), **Supp. XV:** 341

"About Effie" (Findley), **Supp. XX: 50**

"About Hospitality" (Jewett), **Retro. Supp. II:** 131

"About Kathryn" (Dubus), **Supp. VII:** 91

"About Language" (Wrigley), **Supp. XVIII:** 300–301

"About Looking Alone at a Place: Arles" (M. F. K. Fisher), **Supp. XVII:** 89, 91

About the House (Auden), **Supp. II Part 1:** 24

About These Stories: Fiction for Fiction Writers and Readers (Huddle, ed.), **Supp. XXVI:** 160

About Town: "The New Yorker" and the World It Made (Yagoda), **Supp. VIII:** 151

"About Zhivago and His Poems"(O'Hara), **Supp. XXIII:** 214

"Above Pate Valley" (Snyder), **Supp. VIII:** 293

Above the River (Wright), **Supp. III Part 2:** 589, 606

Above the Waterfall (Rash), **Supp. XXVII:** 221, 225, 226–227, 228

"Abracadabra"(Goodman), **Supp. XXVIII:** 94

"Abraham" (Schwartz), **Supp. II Part 2:** 663

Abraham, Nelson Algren. *See* Algren, Nelson

Abraham, Pearl, **Supp. XVII:** 49; **Supp. XX: 177; Supp. XXIV: 1–15**

"Abraham Davenport" (Whittier), **Supp. I Part 2:** 699

"Abraham Lincoln" (Emerson), **II:** 13

Abraham Lincoln: The Prairie Years (Sandburg), **III:** 580, 587–589, 590

Abraham Lincoln: The Prairie Years and the War Years (Sandburg), **III:** 588, 590

Abraham Lincoln: The War Years (Sandburg), **III:** 588, 589–590; **Supp. XVII:** 105

"Abraham Lincoln Walks at Midnight" (Lindsay), **Supp. I Part 2:** 390–391

Abram, David, **Supp. XXVIII:** 246

"Abram Morrison" (Whittier), **Supp. I Part 2:** 699

Abramovich, Alex, **Supp. X:** 302, 309

Abrams, David, **Supp. XXII:** 61

Abrams, M. H., **Supp. XVI:** 19; **Supp. XXIII:** 42

Abridgment of Universal Geography, An: Together with Sketches of History (Rowson), **Supp. XV:** 243

"Absalom" (Rukeyser), **Supp. VI:** 278–279

Absalom, Absalom! (Faulkner), **II:** 64, 65–67, 72, 223; **IV:** 207; **Retro. Supp. I:** 75, 81, 82, 84, 85, 86, 87, 88, 89, 90, 92, 382; **Retro. Supp. III:** 74, 80, 83–84; **Supp. V:** 261; **Supp. X:** 51; **Supp. XIV:** 12–13; **Supp. XXVI:** 8, 12

"Absence"(J. Schoolcraft), **Supp. XXIII:** 228, 231

"Absence of Mercy" (Stone), **Supp. V:** 295

"Absentee, The" (Levertov), **Supp. III Part 1:** 284

Absentee Ownership (Veblen), **Supp. I Part 2:** 642

"Absent-Minded Bartender" (X. J. Kennedy), **Supp. XV:** 159

"Absent Thee from Felicity Awhile" (Wylie), **Supp. I Part 2:** 727, 729

Absolutely True Diary of a Part-Time Indian, The (Alexie), **Supp. XXVI:** 108

"Absolution" (Fitzgerald), **Retro. Supp. I:** 108

"Absolution" (Sobin), **Supp. XVI:** 289

"Abuelita's Ache" (Mora), **Supp. XIII:** 218

Abysmal Brute, The (London), **II:** 467

Abyssinia and the Imperialists (C. L. R. James), **Supp. XXI:** 166

Abyss of Human Illusion, The (Sorrentino), **Supp. XXI:** 225, 227, 237–238

"Academic Story, An" (Simpson), **Supp. IX:** 279–280

"Academic Zoo, The: Theory—in Practice" (Epstein), **Supp. XIV:** 107–108, 109

"A Capella" (Wrigley), **Supp. XVIII:** 300

"Accident" (Minot), **Supp. VI:** 208–209

"Accident" (Munro), **Supp. XXVII:** 188

"Accident, The" (Southern), **Supp. XI:** 295

"Accident, The" (Strand), **Supp. IV Part 2:** 624

Accident/A Day's News (Wolf), **Supp. IV Part 1:** 310

Accidental Tourist, The (Tyler), **Supp. IV Part 2:** 657, 668–669; **Supp. V:** 227

Accordion Crimes (Proulx), **Supp. VII:** 259–261

"Accountability" (Dunbar), **Supp. II Part 1:** 197, 204

"Account of the Method of Drawing Birds" (Audubon), **Supp. XVI:** 12

"Accusation, The" (Wright), **Supp. III Part 2:** 595

"Accusation of the Inward Man, The" (Taylor), **IV:** 156

"Accusing Message from Dead Father" (Karr), **Supp. XI:** 244

Ace, Goodman, **Supp. IV Part 2:** 574

Ache of Appetite, The (Hadas), **Supp. XXIII:** 120–121

Achievement in American Poetry (Bogan), **Supp. III Part 1:** 63–64

Acker, Kathy, **Supp. XII:**1–20; **Supp. XXI:** 236

Ackerley, J. R., **Supp. XX: 237**

Ackerman, Diane, **Supp. XIII:** 154

"Acknowledgment" (Lanier), **Supp. I Part 1:** 364

"Acknowledgment, Adaptation, and Shakespeare in Ron Rash's *Serena*" (Morrow), **Supp. XXVII:** 216

Ackroyd, Peter, **Supp. V:** 233; **Supp. XVII:** 180

"Acquaintance in the Heavens, An" (Dillard), **Supp. VI:** 34

"Acquainted with the Night" (Frost), **II:** 155; **Retro. Supp. I:** 137; **Retro. Supp. III:** 102; **Supp. XXI:** 26

Across Spoon River (Masters), **Supp. I Part 2:** 455, 457, 459, 460, 466, 474–475, 476

Across the Layers: Poems Old and New (Goldbarth), **Supp. XII:** 181, **187–189**

Across the River and into the Trees (Hemingway), **I:** 491; **II:** 255–256, 261; **Retro. Supp. I:** 172, **184–185**; **Supp. XIX:** 248

"Acteon" (Stallings), **Supp. XXV:** 231–232

"Actfive" (MacLeish), **III:** 18–19, 22

Actfive and Other Poems (MacLeish), **III:** 3, 17–19, 21

Action (Shepard), **Supp. III Part 2:** 446

Active Anthology (Pound, ed.), **Supp. III Part 2:** 617; **Supp. XXVI:** 224

Active Service (Crane), **I:** 409

"Act of Creation and Its Artifact, The" (Sorrentino), **Supp. XXI:** 229, 235

Act of Love (film), **Supp. XXVI:** 136

Act of Love, An (Wolfert), **Supp. XXI:** 270, **275–277**

Act of Love, An: A Completely Retold Version of the Novel (Wolfert), **Supp. XXI:** 276

Acton, Patricia Nassif, **Supp. X:** 233

Actors and Sin (film), **Supp. XXVII:** 94

"Actor's Blood" (Hecht), **Supp. XXVII:** 94

Actor's Nightmare, The (Durang), **Supp. XXIV:** 116, 119

Acts and Monuments of These Latter and Perilous Days (Fox), **Supp. XXII:** 36

Acts of Faith (Caputo), **Supp. XIX: 29–30**

"Acts of the Apostles, The" (Bronk), **Supp. XXI:** 28

Actual, The (Bellow), **Retro. Supp. II:** 33

"Actual Experience, Preferred Narratives" (Julier), **Supp. IV Part 1:** 211

Acuff, Roy, **Supp. V:** 335

Ada (Nabokov), **Retro. Supp. I:** 265, 266, 270, 276–277, 278, 279

"Ada" (Stein), **IV:** 43

"Adagia" (Stevens), **IV:** 78, 80, 88, 92

"Adagio" (Hull), **Supp. XXI:** 136–137

"Adam" (Hecht), **Supp. X:** 62

"Adam" (W. C. Williams), **Retro. Supp. I:** 422, 423

"Adam and Eve" (Eugene), **Supp. X:** 204

"Adam and Eve" (Shapiro), **Supp. II Part 2:** 708, 712

"Adamantine Practice of Poetry, The" (Wright), **Supp. XV:** 341–342, 343–344

Adam Bede (G. Eliot), **II:** 181

Adamé, Leonard, **Supp. XIII:** 316

Adam & Eve & the City (W. C. Williams), **Retro. Supp. I:** 423

Adamic, Louis, **Supp. XXIII:** 166

"Adamic Purity as Double Agent" (Whalen-Bridge), **Retro. Supp. II:** 211–212

"Adam Robinson Acquires Grandparents and a Little Sister" (P. E. Jones), **Supp. XXII:** 151

"Adams" (Saunders), **Supp. XIX:** 232

Adams, Althea. *See* Thurber, Mrs. James (Althea Adams)

Adams, Annie. *See* Fields, Annie Adams

Adams, Brooks, **Supp. I Part 2:** 484

Adams, Charles, **Supp. I Part 2:** 644

Adams, Charles Francis, **I:** 1, 4; **Supp. I Part 2:** 484

Adams, Franklin P., **Supp. I Part 2:** 653; **Supp. IX:** 190; **Supp. XV:** 294, 297

Adams, Henry, **I:** 1–24, 111, 243, 258; **II:** 278, 542; **III:** 396, 504; **IV:** 191, 349; **Retro. Supp. I:** 53, 59; **Retro. Supp. II:** 207; **Supp. I Part 1:** 299–300, 301, 314; **Supp. I Part 1:** 417, 492, 543, 644; **Supp. II Part 1:** 93–94, 105; **Supp. III Part 2:** 613; **Supp. IV Part 1:** 31, 208; **Supp. XXIV:** 224

Adams, Mrs. Henry (Marian Hooper), **I:** 1, 5, 10, 17–18

Adams, Henry B., **Supp. I Part 1:** 369

Adams, James Truslow, **Supp. I Part 2:** 481, 484, 486

Adams, J. Donald, **IV:** 438

Adams, John, **I:** 1; **II:** 103, 301; **III:** 17, 473; **Supp. I Part 2:** 483, 506, 507, 509, 510, 511, 517, 518, 520, 524

Adams, John Luther, **Supp. XII:** 209

Adams, John Quincy, **I:** 1, 3, 16–17; **Supp. I Part 2:** 685, 686

Adams, Léonie, **Supp. I Part 2:** 707; **Supp. IX:** 229; **Supp. V:** 79; **Supp. XVII:** 75

Adams, Luella, **Supp. I Part 2:** 652

Adams, Noah, **Supp. XVII:** 218

Adams, Phineas, **Supp. XXV:** 37

Adams, Phoebe, **Supp. IV Part 1:** 203; **Supp. VIII:** 124

Adams, Samuel, **Supp. I Part 2:** 516, 525

Adams, Tim, **Supp. XXVII:** 269

Adams, Timothy Dow, **Supp. XVI:** 67, 69

Ada; or Ardor (Nabokov), **III:** 247

Adaptation (film), **Supp. XXV:** 160

"Ad Castitatem" (Bogan), **Supp. III Part 1:** 50

Adcock, Betty, **Supp. XVIII:** 181–182, 182

Addams, Jane, **Supp. I Part 1:** 1–26; **Supp. XI:** 200, 202

Addams, John Huy, **Supp. I Part 1:** 2

"Add Blue to Make White Whiter" (Vaz), **Supp. XXVI:** 263

"Addendum" (Wright), **Supp. V:** 339

Addiego, John, **Supp. XII:** 182

Adding Machine, The (Rice), **I:** 479

Adding Machine, The: Selected Essays (Burroughs), **Supp. III Part 1:** 93, 97

"Adding to the Unhappiness: Those Poems You Are Writing" (Gallagher), **Supp. XXIV:** 172

Addison, Joseph, **I:** 8, 105, 106–107, 108, 114, 131, 300, 304; **III:** 430

"Address Delivered at Lenox, An" (Channing), **Supp. XXIV:** 79–80

"Addressed to a Political Shrimp, or, Fly upon the Wheel" (Freneau), **Supp. II Part 1:** 267

"Address to My Soul" (Wylie), **Supp. I Part 2:** 729

"Address to the Deist, An" (Wheatley), **Supp. XX: 287**

"Address to the Devil" (Jarman), **Supp. XVII:** 114

Address to the Government of the United States on the Cession of Louisiana to the French, An (Brown), **Supp. I Part 1:** 146

"Address to the Scholars of New England" (Ransom), **III:** 491

"Address with Exclamation Points, A" (Simic), **Supp. VIII:** 283

"Adieu to Norman, Bon Jour to Joan and Jean-Paul"(O'Hara), **Supp. XXIII:** 219

Adisa, Opal Palmer, **Supp. XXII:** 66, 74, 78

"Adjutant Bird, The" (Banks), **Supp. V:** 5

Adkins, Nelson F., **II:** 20

Adler, Alfred, **I:** 248

Adler, Betty, **III:** 103

Adler, George J., **III:** 81

Adler, Renata, **Supp. X:** 171

Adler, Stella, **Retro. Supp. III:** 171

Admiral of the Ocean Sea: A Life of Christopher Columbus (Morison), **Supp. I Part 2:** 486–488

"Admirals" (Chabon), **Supp. XI:** 72

"Admonition, An" (Brodsky), **Supp. VIII:** 33

"Adolescence" (Bidart), **Supp. XV:** 32

"Adolescence" (Dove), **Supp. IV Part 1:** 245

"Adolescence" (Olds), **Supp. X:** 211

"Adolescence II" (Dove), **Supp. IV Part 1:** 242, 244–245

Adolescent's Christmas, An: 1944 (C. Bly), **Supp. XVI:** 31–32

"Adolf Eichmann" (Carruth), **Supp. XVI:** 47

"Adonais" (Shelley), **II:** 516, 540

Adonai: The Pilgrim of Eternity (Lippard), **Supp. XXIII:** 180, 189, 190

Adorno, Theodor, **Supp. I Part 2:** 645, 650; **Supp. IV Part 1:** 301

"Adrienne Rich: The Poetics of Change" (Gelpi), **Supp. I Part 2:** 554

Adrift in Macao (Durang), **Supp. XXIV:** 125

"Adultery" (Banks), **Supp. V:** 15

"Adultery" (Dubus), **Supp. VII:** 85

Adultery and Other Choices (Dubus), **Supp. VII:** 83–85

Adulthood Rites (O. Butler), **Supp. XIII:** 63, 64–65

Adult Life of Toulouse Lautrec by Henri Toulouse Lautrec, The (Acker), **Supp. XII:** 5, 6, 8–9

Adventure (London), **II:** 466

Adventures in Ancient Egypt (Goldbarth), **Supp. XII:** 191

Adventures in Value (Cummings), **I:** 430

"Adventures of a Book Reviewer" (Cowley), **Supp. II Part 1:** 137, 142

Adventures of a Novelist (Atherton), **Supp. XXIV:** 17–18, 19–20, 21

Adventures of Augie March, The (Bellow), **I:** 144, 147, 149, 150, 151, 152–153, 154, 155, 157, 158–159, 164; **Retro. Supp. II:** 19, 20, 22–23, 24, 30; **Supp. VIII:** 234, 236–237; **Supp. XXIV:** 220

Adventures of a Young Man (Dos Passos), **I:** 488, 489, 492

Adventures of Captain Bonneville (Irving), **II:** 312

Adventures of Harry Franco, The: A Tale of the Great Panic (Briggs), **Supp. XVIII:** 1, 2, 5–8

Adventures of Harry Richmond, The (Meredith), **Supp. XX: 234**

Adventures of Huckleberry Finn, The (Twain), **I:** 307, 506; **II:** 26, 72, 262, 266–268, 290, 418, 430; **III:** 101, 112–113, 357, 554, 558, 577; **IV:** 198, 201–204, 207; **Retro. Supp. I:** 188; **Retro. Supp. II:** 121; **Retro. Supp. III:** 88, 256, 258, 263, 264–265; **Supp.**

I Part 1: 247; **Supp. IV Part 1:** 247, 257; **Supp. IV Part 2:** 502; **Supp. V:** 131; **Supp. VIII:** 198; **Supp. X:** 230; **Supp. XII:** 16; **Supp. XVI:** 222; **Supp. XX: 171; Supp. XXII:** 81; **Supp. XXVII:** 104; **Supp. XXVIII:** 233

Adventures of Jimmy (Broughton), **Supp. XV:** 146

Adventures of Roderick Random, The (Smollett), **I:** 134

Adventures of the Letter I (Simpson), **Supp. IX:** 266, 273–274

Adventures of Tom Sawyer, The (Twain), **II:** 26; **III:** 223, 572, 577; **IV:** 199–200, 203, 204; **Retro. Supp. III:** 255, 258, 262–264; **Supp. I Part 2:** 456, 470; **Supp. XVI:** 66

Adventures While Preaching the Gospel of Beauty (Lindsay), **Supp. I Part 2:** 374, 376, 381, 382–384, 389, 399

Adventures with Ed (Loeffler), **Supp. XIII:** 1

Advertisements for Myself (Mailer), **III:** 27, 35–38, 41–42, 45, 46; **Retro. Supp. II:** 196, 199, 200, 202, 203, 212; **Supp. IV Part 1:** 90, 284; **Supp. XIV:** 157; **Supp. XXIV:** 281

"Advertisements for Myself on the Way Out" (Mailer), **III:** 37

Advice (Bodenheim), **Supp. XXV:** 22

"Advice to a Prophet" (Wilbur), **Supp. III Part 2:** 555–557

Advice to a Prophet and Other Poems (Wilbur), **Supp. III Part 2:** 554–558

"Advice to a Raven in Russia" (Barlow), **Supp. II Part 1:** 65, 74, 80, 83

"Advice to Players" (Bidart), **Supp. XV:** 35

Advice to the Lovelorn (film), **Retro. Supp. II:** 328

Advice to the Privileged Orders, Part I (Barlow), **Supp. II Part 1:** 80

Aegerter, Lindsay Pentolfe, **Supp. XXII:** 69

"Aeneas and Dido" (Brodsky), **Supp. VIII:** 24–25

"Aeneas at Washington" (Tate), **IV:** 129

Aeneid (Virgil), **I:** 396; **II:** 542; **III:** 124; **Supp. XV:** 23; **Supp. XXIV:** 162–163

Aeneus Tacticus, **I:** 136

Aerial View (Barabtarlo), **Retro. Supp. I:** 278

"Aeria the Evanescent" (Sobin), **Supp. XVI:** 292

Aeschylus, **I:** 274, 433; **III:** 398; **IV:** 358, 368, 370; **Retro. Supp. I:** 65; **Supp. I Part 2:** 458, 494

Aesop, **I:** 387; **II:** 154, 169, 302; **III:** 587

Aesthetic (Croce), **III:** 610

"Aesthetics" (Mumford), **Supp. II Part 2:** 476

"Aesthetics of Silence, The" (Sontag), **Supp. III Part 2:** 459

"Aesthetics of the Shah" (Olds), **Supp. X:** 205

"Affair at Coulter's Notch, The" (Bierce), **I:** 202

Affaire de viol, Une (C. Himes). *See Case of Rape, A* (C. Himes)

"Affair of Outposts, An" (Bierce), **I:** 202

Affliction (Banks), **Supp. V:** 15, 16

Affluent Society, The (Galbraith), **Supp. I Part 2:** 648

Afghanistan Picture Show, An: or, How I Saved the World (Vollmann), **Supp. XVII:** 226, 228–229, 233

"Aficionados, The" (Carver), **Supp. III Part 1:** 137

"Afloat" (Beattie), **Supp. V:** 29

Afloat and Ashore (Cooper), **I:** 351, 355

"Afoot" (P. N. Warren as Kilina), **Supp. XX: 261–262**

Africa, Its Geography, People, and Products (Du Bois), **Supp. II Part 1:** 179

Africa, Its Place in Modern History (Du Bois), **Supp. II Part 1:** 179

"Africa, to My Mother" (D. Diop), **Supp. IV Part 1:** 16

Africana (H. L. Gates, ed.), **Supp. XX: 99**

African American Century, The : How Black Americans Have Shaped Our Country (H. L. Gates), **Supp. XX: 102**

African American Lives (television production), **Supp. XX: 99**

African American Lives 2 (television production), **Supp. XX: 99**

African American National Biography (H. L. Gates, ed.), **Supp. XX: 99**

African American Writers (Smith, ed.), **Supp. XIII:** 115, 127

"African Book" (Hemingway), **II:** 259

"African Chief, The" (Bryant), **Supp. I Part 1:** 168

"African Fragment" (Brooks), **Supp. III Part 1:** 85

African Queen, The (film), **Supp. XI:** 17

"African Roots of War, The" (Du Bois), **Supp. II Part 1:** 174

African Silences (Matthiessen), **Supp. V:** 203

African Treasury, An (Hughes, ed.), **Supp. I Part 1:** 344

"Afrika Revolution" (Baraka), **Supp. II Part 1:** 53

"AFRO-AMERICAN LYRIC" (Baraka), **Supp. II Part 1:** 59

After (Bukiet), **Supp. XVII:** 43, 44–45

After (Hirshfield), **Supp. XXIII:** 133–135, 139

"After a Greek Proverb" (Stallings), **Supp. XXV:** 225

After All: Last Poems (Matthews), **Supp. IX:** 155, 167–169

After and Before the Lightning (Ortiz), **Supp. IV Part 2:** 513

"After a Nightmare" (Davison), **Supp. XXVI:** 69

"After a Party" (Salinas), **Supp. XIII:** 327

"After Apple-Picking" (Frost), **Retro. Supp. I:** 126, 128; **Retro. Supp. III:** 97–98

"After Arguing against the Contention That Art Must Come from Discontent" (Stafford), **Supp. XI:** 327

After Confession: Poetry as Autobiography (Harris), **Supp. XIV:** 269

After Confession: Poetry as Autobiography (K. Sontag and D. Graham), **Supp. XV:** 104

"After Cowboy Chicken Came to Town" (Jin), **Supp. XVIII:** 97–98

"After Disappointment" (Jarman), **Supp. XVII:** 118–119

After Disillusion: Poems (Wolf), **Supp. XXII:** 275

"After Edward Hopper: Somebody in a Bar" (Ferry), **Supp. XXIV:** 162

After Experience (Snodgrass), **Supp. VI:** 314–316, 317

Afterglow, The (Stuart), **Supp. XXVIII:** 235

"Afterglow, The"(Stuart), **Supp. XXVIII:** 237

"After great pain, a formal feeling comes" (Dickinson), **Retro. Supp. I:** 37

"After Hearing a Waltz by Bartók" (A. Lowell), **II:** 522

After Henry (Didion), **Supp. IV Part 1:** 195, 196, 199, 207, 208, 211

"After Henry" (Didion), **Supp. IV Part 1:** 211

"After Holbein" (Wharton), **IV:** 325; **Retro. Supp. I:** 382

After House, The (Rinehart), **Supp. XXV:** 193

After Ikkyu and Other Poems (Harrison), **Supp. VIII:** 42

"After-Image" (Bierds), **Supp. XVII:** 31–32

"After-Image" (Caldwell), **I:** 309

After-Images: Autobiographical Sketches (Snodgrass), **Supp. VI:** 314, **319–323,** 324, 326–327

After I's (Zukofsky), **Supp. III Part 2:** 628, 629

Afterlife (Monette), **Supp. X:** 153

Afterlife (Updike), **Retro. Supp. I:** 322

Afterlife, The (Levis), **Supp. XI:** 259, **260–264**

"After Magritte" (McClatchy), **Supp. XII:** 264

"After Making Love" (Dunn), **Supp. XI:** 153

Aftermath (Longfellow), **II:** 490

"Aftermath" (Longfellow), **II:** 498

After New Formalism (A. Finch, ed.), **Supp. XVII:** 74

"Afternoon" (Ellison), **Supp. II Part 1:** 238

"Afternoon at MacDowell" (Kenyon), **Supp. VII:** 159

"Afternoon Miracle, An" (O. Henry), **Supp. II Part 1:** 390

Afternoon of a Faun (Hearon), **Supp. VIII: 63–64**

Afternoon of an Author: A Selection of Uncollected Stories and Essays (Fitzgerald), **II:** 94

"Afternoon of a Playwright" (Thurber), **Supp. I Part 2:** 620

Afternoon of the Unreal (Salinas), **Supp. XIII:** 311, **316–318**

"Afternoon with the Old Man, An" (Dubus), **Supp. VII:** 84

"After Parting" (Teasdale), **Supp. XXVII:** 283

"After Punishment Was Done with Me" (Olds), **Supp. X:** 213

"After Reading *Barely and Widely,*" (Zukofsky), **Supp. III Part 2:** 625, 631

"After Reading 'In the Clearing' for the Author, Robert Frost" (Corso), **Supp. XII:** 130

"After Reading *Mickey in the Night Kitchen* for the Third Time before Bed" (Dove), **Supp. IV Part 1:** 249

"After Reading the Greek Poet"(Kenny), **Supp. XXIII:** 150

"After Reading Tu Fu, I Go Outside to the Dwarf Orchard" (Wright), **Supp. V:** 343

"After Reading Wang Wei, I Go Outside to the Full Moon" (Wright), **Supp. V:** 343

Aftershocks (Stallings), **Supp. XXV:** 222

"Aftershocks" (Stallings), **Supp. XXV:** 222, 231

After Shocks, Near Escapes (Dobyns), **Supp. XIII: 80–82**

"After Song, An" (W. C. Williams), **Retro. Supp. I:** 413

After Strange Gods (T. S. Eliot), **I:** 588

After Such Knowledge: Memory, History, and the Legacy of the Holocaust (E. Hoffman), **Supp. XVI:** 152–153, **158–161**

"After the Alphabets" (Merwin), **Supp. III Part 1:** 356

"After the Argument" (Dunn), **Supp. XI:** 149

"After the Baptism" (C. Bly), **Supp. XVI:** 40

"After the Burial" (J. R. Lowell), **Supp. I Part 2:** 409

"After the Curfew" (Holmes), **Supp. I Part 1:** 308

"After the Death of John Brown" (Thoreau), **IV:** 185

"After the Denim" (Carver), **Supp. III Part 1:** 144

"After the Dentist" (Swenson), **Supp. IV Part 2:** 645

After the Fall (A. Miller), **III:** 148, 149, 156, 161, 162, 163–165, 166; **Retro. Supp. III:** 170–172, 175–176

"After the Fire" (Merrill), **Supp. III Part 1:** 328

"After the Flood" (Sanders), **Supp. XVI:** 274–275

After the Fox (film), **Supp. IV Part 2:** 575

After the Genteel Tradition (Cowley), **Supp. II Part 1:** 143

"After the Heart's Interrogation" (Komunyakaa), **Supp. XIII:** 120

After the Lost Generation: A Critical Study of the Writers of Two Wars (Aldridge), **Supp. IV Part 2:** 680; **Supp. XIX:** 250

"After the Night Office—Gethsemani Abbey" (Merton), **Supp. VIII:** 195–196

After the Others (Weigl), **Supp. XIX:** 282, 283–284

"After the Persian" (Bogan), **Supp. III Part 1:** 64

After the Plague (Boyle), **Supp. XX: 20**

"After the Plague" (Boyle), **Supp. XX: 20**

"After the Pleasure Party" (Melville), **III:** 93

"After the Rain" (Halliday), **Supp. XIX:** 91

"After the Resolution" (Dunn), **Supp. XI:** 151

After the Stroke (Sarton), **Supp. VIII:** 264

"After the Stroke"(Bottoms), **Supp. XXVIII:** 32

"After the Surprising Conversions" (R. Lowell), **I:** 544, 545; **II:** 550; **Retro. Supp. II:** 187

"After 37 Years My Mother Apologizes for My Childhood" (Olds), **Supp. X:** 208

After This (McDermott), **Supp. XVIII:** 155, **166–167**

Afterthoughts (L. P. Smith), **Supp. XIV:** 339, 345

"Afterthoughts on the Rosenbergs" (Fiedler), **Supp. XIII:** 99

After Tupac and D Foster (Woodson), **Supp. XXVIII:** 288

"After Twenty Years" (Rich), **Supp. I Part 2:** 559–560

"Afterwake, The" (Rich), **Supp. I Part 2:** 553

"Afterward" (Wharton), **Retro. Supp. I:** 372

"Afterword"(Hadas), **Supp. XXIII:** 113

"After Working Long" (Kenyon), **Supp. VII:** 170

"After Yitzl" (Goldbarth), **Supp. XII:** 186

"After You, My Dear Alphonse" (Jackson), **Supp. IX:** 119

"After Your Death" (Trethewey), **Supp. XXI:** 255

"After Your Nap" (B. Kelly), **Supp. XVII:** 124

"Again" (Dixon), **Supp. XII:** 157

"Again, Kapowsin" (Hugo), **Supp. VI:** 141

"Again Just Now" (Budbill), **Supp. XIX:** 11

"Against" (Goldbarth), **Supp. XII:** 193

"Against Decoration" (Karr), **Supp. XI:** 248

"Against Epiphanies" (C. Baxter), **Supp. XVII:** 20

Against Interpretation (Sontag), **Supp. III Part 2:** 451, 455; **Supp. XIV:** 15

"Against Interpretation" (Sontag), **Supp. III Part 2:** 456–458, 463

"Against Modernity" (Ozick), **Supp. V:** 272

"Against Nature" (Karr), **Supp. XI:** 243

Against Nature (Updike), **Retro. Supp. I:** 323

Against Our Vanishing: Winter Conversations with Allen Grossman on the Theory and Practice of Poetry (Halliday), **Supp. XIX: 82–84,** 88

"Against Realism" (Halliday), **Supp. XIX:** 93

Against the Cold (Bynner), **Supp. XV:** 51

"Against the Crusades" (Stern), **Supp. IX:** 300

Against the Current: As I Remember F. Scott Fitzgerald (Kroll Ring), **Supp. IX:** 63

Agamben, Giorgio, **Supp. XVI:** 289

Agapida, Fray Antonio (pseudonym). *See* Irving, Washington

"Agassiz" (J. R. Lowell), **Supp. I Part 2:** 414, 416

Agassiz, Louis, **II:** 343; **Supp. I Part 1:** 312; **Supp. IX:** 180

ge cassant, L' (Char; Sobin, trans.), *Supp. XVI:* 282

"Aged Wino's Counsel to a Young Man on the Brink of Marriage, The" (X. J. Kennedy), **Supp. XV:** 156

Agee, Emma, **I:** 26

Agee, James, **I:** 25–47, 293; **IV:** 215; **Supp. IX:** 109; **Supp. XIV:** 92; **Supp. XV:** 143

"Agency Without Mastery: Chronic Pain and Posthuman Life Writing" (Gilmore), **Supp. XXVI:** 53

"Agent, The" (Wilbur), **Supp. III Part 2:** 557–561

Age of Anxiety, The (Auden), **Supp. II Part 1:** 2, 19, 21

"Age of Conformity, The" (Howe), **Supp. VI:** 117

Age of Grief, The: A Novella and Stories (Smiley), **Supp. VI:** 292, **299–301**

Age of Innocence, The (film, Scorsese), **Retro. Supp. III:** 290

Age of Innocence, The (Wharton), **IV:** 320–322, 327–328; **Retro. Supp. I:** 372, 374, **380–381; Retro. Supp. III:** 287; **Supp. IV Part 1:** 23; **Supp. XXVIII:** 119

Age of Longing, The (Koestler), **I:** 258

Age of Reason, The (Paine), **Supp. I Part 2:** 503, 515–517, 520

"Age of Strolling, The" (Stern), **Supp. IX:** 297

"Ages, The" (Bryant), **Supp. I Part 1:** 152, 155, 166, 167

"Ages of the Women, The" (Gibran), **Supp. XX:** 115

"Aggrandizement, The" (Bronk), **Supp. XXI:** 32

"Aging" (Jarrell), **II:** 388

Aging and Gender in Literature (George), **Supp. IV Part 2:** 450

"Aging"(Wakoski), **Supp. XXVIII:** 267

"Agio Neró" (Mora), **Supp. XIII:** 224

"Agitato ma non Troppo" (Ransom), **III:** 493

"Agnes of Iowa" (Moore), **Supp. X:** 165, 178

Agnes of Sorrento (Stowe), **Supp. I Part 2:** 592, 595–596

Agnon, S. Y., **Supp. V:** 266; **Supp. XXV:** 267

Agony & the Agony, The (Silver), **Supp. XXIV:** 265, **274–275**

"Agosta the Winged Man and Rasha the Black Dove" (Dove), **Supp. IV Part 1:** 246–247

Agrarian Justice (Paine), **Supp. I Part 2:** 517–518

"Agricultural Show, The" (McKay), **Supp. X:** 139

Agrippa: A Book of the Dead (W. Gibson), **Supp. XVI:** 125

Agua de dos ríos/Water from Two Rivers (Espaillat), **Supp. XXI:** 104, 112–113

Agua Fresca: An Anthology of Raza Poetry (Rodríguez, ed.), **Supp. IV Part 2:** 540

Agua Santa/Holy Water (Mora), **Supp. XIII:** 222–225

Agüero Sisters, The (García), **Supp. XI:** 185–190

Aguiar, Marian, **Supp. XXII:** 68

Aguiar, Sarah Appleton, **Supp. XIII:** 30

Aguilar, Carmen, **Supp. XXIII:** 200

Ah, Wilderness! (O'Neill), **III:** 400–401; **Supp. IV Part 2:** 587

Ah, Wilderness!: The Frontier in American Literature (Humphrey), **Supp. IX:** 104

Ahearn, Barry, **Retro. Supp. I:** 415

Ahearn, Frederick L., Jr., **Supp. XI:** 184

Ahearn, Kerry, **Supp. IV Part 2:** 604

Ahmed Arabi Pasha, **I:** 453

Ahnebrink, Lars, **III:** 328

Ahrens, Sylvia, **Supp. XX:** 162

Ah Sin (Harte), **Supp. II Part 1:** 354–355

"Ah! Sun-flower" (Blake), **III:** 19

Ai, **Supp. XXVI:** 66

Aida (rock musical), **Supp. XXI:** 148

Aidoo, Ama Ato, **Supp. XXII:** 68

AIDS and Its Metaphors (Sontag), **Supp. III Part 2:** 452, 466–468

Aids to Reflection (Coleridge), **II:** 10

Aiieeeee! An Anthology of Asian-American Writers (The Combined Asian Resources Project), **Supp. X:** 292

Aiken, Conrad, **I:** 48–70, 190, 211, 243; **II:** 55, 530, 542; **III:** 458, 460; **Retro. Supp. I:** 55, 56, 57, 58, 60, 62; **Supp. X:** 50, 115; **Supp. XV:** 144, 297, 298, 302, 306, 309; **Supp. XVII:** 135; **Supp. XXIV:** 36; **Supp. XXV:** 19; **Supp. XXVI:** 225

"Aimless Love" (Collins), **Supp. XXI:** 61

"Aim Was Song, The" (Frost), **Retro. Supp. I:** 133

Ainger, Arthur Campbell, **Supp. XX:** 230

Ainsworth, Linda, **Supp. IV Part 1:** 274

Ainsworth, William, **III:** 423

Air-Conditioned Nightmare, The (H. Miller), **III:** 186

Airing Dirty Laundry (Reed), **Supp. X:** 241

"Air Is Full of Little Holes, The" (Brockmeier), **Supp. XXII:** 60

"Airmail from Mother" (Kooser), **Supp. XIX:** 120

"Air Plant, The" (Crane), **I:** 401

Air Raid: A Verse Play for Radio (MacLeish), **III:** 21

"Airs above the Ground" (Sarton), **Supp. VIII:** 261

Air Tight: A Novel of Red Russia. See We the Living (Rand)

Air Up There, The (film, Glaser), **Supp. XVII:** 9

"Airwaves" (Mason), **Supp. VIII:** 146

Airways, Inc. (Dos Passos), **I:** 482; **Supp. XXVIII:** 74

A Is for Anne: Mistress Hutchinson Disturbs the Commonwealth (Schott), **Supp. XXIII:** 240, **246–247**

"A is for Dining Alone" (M. F. K. Fisher), **Supp. XVII:** 86

Aitken, Robert, **Supp. I Part 2:** 504

"Aix-les-Bains" (Twain), **Retro. Supp. III:** 267

Aizenberg, Susan, **Supp. XXI:** 131

Akhmadulina, Bella, **Supp. III Part 1:** 268

Akhmatova, Anna, **Supp. III Part 1:** 268, 269; **Supp. VIII:** 20, 21, 25, 27, 30; **Supp. XXI:** 132

Akhmatova Translations, The (Kenyon), **Supp. VII:** 160

"Akhnilo" (Salter), **Supp. IX:** 260

Akins, Zoë, **Supp. XVI:** 187; **Supp. XXVII:** 285

Aksenev, Vasily P., **Retro. Supp. I:** 278

"Al Aaraaf" (Poe), **III:** 426–427

Al Aaraaf, Tamerlane, and Minor Poems (Poe), **III:** 410

"Alabama Jones" (Mosher), **Supp. XXII:** 204, 211

"Alain Locke and Cultural Pluralism" (Kallen), **Supp. XIV:** 197

"Alain Locke: Bahá'í Philosopher" (Buck), **Supp. XIV:** 199

Alain Locke: Faith and Philosophy (Buck), **Supp. XIV:** 200

"Al Araaf" (Poe), **Retro. Supp. III:** 231

Al Araaf, Tamerlane, and Minor Poems (Poe), **Retro. Supp. III:** 224, 231

Alarçon, **Supp. XVII:** 74

Alarcón, Justo, **Supp. IV Part 2:** 538, 539, 540

Alarcón, Norma, **Supp. XXIII:** 194, 204–205

À la Recherche du Temps Perdu (Proust), **IV:** 428

"Alarm" (X. J. Kennedy), **Supp. XV:** 163

"Alastor" (Shelley), **Supp. I Part 2:** 728

"Alatus" (Wilbur), **Supp. III Part 2:** 563

Alaya (Hirshfield), **Supp. XXIII:** 131

"Alba" (Creeley), **Supp. IV Part 1:** 150

Alba, Richard D., **Supp. XX:** 43

Albee, Edward, **I:** 71–96, 113; **II:** 558, 591; **III:** 281, 387; **IV:** 4, 230; **Retro. Supp. II:** 104; **Supp. VIII:** 331; **Supp. XIII:** 196, 197; **Supp. XXIV:** 113, 263, 270

Albers, Joseph, **Supp. IV Part 2:** 621

Alberti, Rafael, **Supp. XV:** 75

Albright, Margery, **Supp. I Part 2:** 613

"Album, The" (Morris), **III:** 220

Album, The (Rinehart), **Supp. XXV:** 197, 200

Alcestiad, The (Wilder), **IV:** 357, 374

"Alchemist, The" (Bogan), **Supp. III Part 1:** 50

"Alchemist in the City, The" (Hopkins), **Supp. IV Part 2:** 639

Alchymist's Journal, The (Connell), **Supp. XIV:** 80

"Alcmena" (Winters), **Supp. II Part 2:** 801

Alcott, Abba. *See* Alcott, Mrs. Amos Bronson (Abigail May)

Alcott, Amos Bronson, **II:** 7, 225; **IV:** 172, 173, 184; **Retro. Supp. I:** 217; **Supp. I Part 1:** 28, 29–32, 35, 39, 41, 45; **Supp. II Part 1:** 290; **Supp. XVI:** 84, 89; **Supp. XXV:** 250

Alcott, Mrs. Amos Bronson (Abigail May), **IV:** 184; **Supp. I Part 1:** 29, 30, 31, 32, 35

Alcott, Anna. *See* Pratt, Anna

Alcott, Louisa May, **IV:** 172; **Supp. I Part 1: 28–46; Supp. IX:** 128; **Supp. XV:** 338; **Supp. XVI:** 84

Alcott, May, **Supp. I Part 1:** 41

Alcuin: A Dialogue (Brown), **Supp. I Part 1:** 126–127, 133

Alden, Hortense. *See* Farrell, Mrs. James T. (Hortense Alden)

Alden, John, **I:** 471; **II:** 502–503

"Alder Fork, The" (Leopold), **Supp. XIV:** 186

Aldington, Perdita, **Supp. I Part 1:** 258

Aldington, Richard, **II:** 517; **III:** 458, 459, 465, 472; **Retro. Supp. I:** 63, 127; **Supp. I Part 1:** 257–262, 270

Aldington, Mrs. Richard. *See* Doolittle, Hilda

Aldo Leopold: His Life and Work (Meine), **Supp. XIV:** 179

"Aldo Leopold's Intellectual Heritage" (Nash), **Supp. XIV:** 191–192

Aldon, Raymond, **Supp. XV:** 297

Aldrich, Thomas Bailey, **II:** 400; **Supp. II Part 1:** 192; **Supp. XIV:** 45; **Supp. XVIII:** 4

Aldrich, Tom, **Supp. I Part 2:** 415

Aldridge, John W., **Supp. I Part 1:** 196; **Supp. IV Part 1:** 286; **Supp. IV Part 2:** 680, 681; **Supp. VIII:** 189; **Supp. XI:** 228; **Supp. XIX:** 250

Aleck Maury Sportsman (Gordon), **II:** 197, 200, 203–204

Alegría, Claribel, **Supp. IV Part 1:** 208

Aleichem, Sholem, **Supp. XXIII:** 4, 7

Aleichem, Sholom, **IV:** 3, 10; **Supp. IV Part 2:** 585

"Alert Lovers, Hidden Sides, and Ice Travelers: Notes on Poetic Form and Energy" (Dunn), **Supp. XI:** 153

"Ale&sacaron; Debeljak" (Simic), **Supp. VIII:** 279

"Alex" (Oliver), **Supp. VII:** 232

Alexander, Doris, **Supp. XVII:** 99

Alexander, Elizabeth, **Supp. XVIII:** 171, 185, 186; **Supp. XXI:** 246, 257

Alexander, George, **II:** 331

Alexander, Michael, **Retro. Supp. I:** 293

Alexander, Paul, **Supp. XXV:** 84

Alexander, Will, **Supp. XXVII:** 163

"Alexander Crummell Dead" (Dunbar), **Supp. II Part 1:** 207, 208–209

Alexander's Bridge (Cather), **I:** 313, 314, 316–317, 326; **Retro. Supp. I:** 1, 6, 7, 8; **Retro. Supp. III:** 22

Alexander the Great, **IV:** 322

"Alexandra" (Cather), **Retro. Supp. I:** 7, 9, 17

Alexandrov, V. E., **Retro. Supp. I:** 270

Alexie, Sherman, **Retro. Supp. III:** 313; **Supp. XVIII:** 58; **Supp. XXVI:** 103, 108

Alger, Horatio, **Supp. XXVII:** 84

Algic Researches (H. Schoolcraft), **Supp. XXIII:** 227

Algonquin Round Table, **Supp. IX:** 190, 191, 197

Algren, Nelson, **I:** 211; **Supp. IX: 1–18; Supp. V:** 4; **Supp. XII:** 126; **Supp. XIII:** 173; **Supp. XIV:** 3; **Supp. XVII:** 161; **Supp. XXI:** 264; **Supp. XXIII:** 165; **Supp. XXV:** 185; **Supp. XXVII:** 87, 134

Alhambra, The (Irving), **II:** 310–311

Ali, Agha Shahid, **Supp. XVII:** 74

Ali, Ayaan Hirsi, **Supp. XXIV:** 15

Alias Grace (Atwood), **Supp. XIII:** 20, **31–32**

Alice (film; Allen), **Supp. XV:** 2, 11

"Alice Doane's Appeal" (Hawthorne), **II:** 227

"Alice Drops Her Cigarette on the Floor … " (Findley), **Supp. XX: 50–51**

"Alice in the Looking Glass" (Stallings), **Supp. XXV:** 234

Alice in Wonderland (Carroll), **Supp. I Part 2:** 622

Alice Ordered Me to Be Made (Notley), **Supp. XXII:** 224, 227, 228

"Alice Ordered Me to Be Made" (Notley), **Supp. XXII:** 227

Alice's Adventures in Wonderland (Carroll), **Supp. XVI:** 261

"Alicia and I Talking on Edna's Steps" (Cisneros), **Supp. VII:** 64

"Alicia Who Sees Mice" (Cisneros), **Supp. VII:** 60

Alien 3 (screenplay, W. Gibson), **Supp. XVI:** 120, 124

"Ali in Havana" (Talese), **Supp. XVII:** 207, 208

Alison, Archibald, **Supp. I Part 1:** 151, 159

Alison's House (Glaspell), **Supp. III Part 1:** 182, 188, 189

Alive (screenplay, Shanley), **Supp. XIV:** 316

Alive and Writing: Interviews with American Authors of the 1980s (McCaffery and Gregory), **Supp. X:** 260

"Alki Beach" (Hugo), **Supp. VI:** 135

Alla Breve Loving (Wright), **Supp. XV:** 339, 340

"Alla Breve Loving" (Wright), **Supp. XV:** 340

"All Apologies" (Biss), **Supp. XXVI:** 56

"All Around the Town" (Benét), **Supp. XI:** 48, 58

"All Around the Town" (Taggard), **Supp. XXVI:** 144

All at Sea (Lardner), **II:** 427

All Aunt Hagar's Children (E. P. Jones), **Supp. XXII:** 140, 143, **150–153**

"All Aunt Hagar's Children" (E. P. Jones), **Supp. XXII:** 151

"All Boy" (Rawlings), **Supp. X:** 222

Allegiances (Stafford), **Supp. XI: 322– 323,** 329

"Allegory of the Cave" (Dunn), **Supp. XI:** 150

"Allegory Unlimited" (Cassill), **Supp. XIX:** 266

Allegro, Johnny (film, Tetzloff), **Supp. XVII:** 62

"Allegro, L' " (Milton), **Supp. XIV:** 8

Allen, Brooke, **Supp. VIII:** 153

Allen, Bruce, **Supp. XXII:** 205, 212; **Supp. XXIII:** 106, 300

Allen, Claudia, **Supp. XXIII:** 79

Allen, Dick, **Supp. IX:** 279

Allen, Donald, **Supp. VIII:** 291; **Supp. XIII:** 112; **Supp. XXIII:** 215, 220; **Supp. XXVI:** 223; **Supp. XXVII:** 25

Allen, Frank, **Supp. XI:** 126; **Supp. XII:** 186; **Supp. XXVI:** 150

Allen, Fred, **Supp. XXV:** 255

Allen, Frederick Lewis, **Supp. I Part 2:** 655

Allen, Gay Wilson, **IV:** 352; **Supp. I Part 2:** 418

Allen, Ivan, **Supp. XXII:** 245

Allen, Paula Gunn. *See* Gunn Allen, Paula

Allen, Robert Moore, **Supp. XX: 164**

Allen, Walter, **I:** 505; **III:** 352; **Supp. IV Part 2:** 685; **Supp. IX:** 231

Allen, Woody, **Supp. I Part 2:** 607, 623; **Supp. IV Part 1:** 205; **Supp. X:** 164; **Supp. XI:** 307; **Supp. XV: 1–18; Supp. XVII:** 48

"*Aller et Retour*" (Barnes), *Supp. III Part 1:* 36

Aller Retour New York (H. Miller), **III:** 178, 182, 183

Allerton, Isaac, **Supp. XXII:** 44

Allessandrini, Goffredo, **Supp. IV Part 2:** 520

Alleys of Eden, The (R. O. Butler), **Supp. XII:** 62, **62–64,** 68

All God's Children Need Traveling Shoes (Angelou), **Supp. IV Part 1:** 2, 9–10, 12–13, 17

All God's Chillun Got Wings (O'Neill), **III:** 387, 391, 393–394

All Gone (Dixon), **Supp. XII:** 148, 149

"All Hallows" (Glück), **Supp. V:** 82

"All I Can Remember" (Jackson), **Supp. IX:** 115

"Alligators, The" (Updike), **IV:** 219

Allingham, John Till, **Supp. XV:** 243

All in the Family (Boyce), **Supp. XXI:** 8

"ALL IN THE STREET" (Baraka), **Supp. II Part 1:** 53

"All in Time" (Stone), **Supp. XXVII:** 251

Allison, Dorothy, **Supp. XVIII:** 195

"All I Want" (Tapahonso), **Supp. IV Part 2:** 508

"All Little Colored Children Should Play the Harmonica" (Patchett), **Supp. XII:** 309

"All Mountains" (Doolittle), **Supp. I Part 1:** 271

All My Friends Are Going to Be Strangers (McMurtry), **Supp. V:** 224, 228, 229

All My Pretty Ones (Sexton), **Supp. II Part 2:** 678, 679–683

"All My Pretty Ones" (Sexton), **Supp. II Part 2:** 681–682
"All My Sad Captains" (Jewett), **Retro. Supp. II:** 134
All My Sons (A. Miller), **III:** 148, 149, 150, 151–153, 154, 155, 156, 158, 159, 160, 164, 166; **Retro. Supp. III:** 165, 167, 168
All New People (Lamott), **Supp. XX:** 135–136
"All Night, All Night" (Schwartz), **Supp. II Part 2:** 665
All Night Long (Caldwell), **I:** 297
"All-Night Melodies" (Nelson), **Supp. XVIII:** 185
All-Night Visitors (Major), **Supp. XXII:** 173–174
"All of Us" (Major), **Supp. XXII:** 185
All of Us: The Collected Poems (Carver), **Supp. XXIV:** 167
All of What We Loved (Bronk), **Supp. XXI:** 32
"All Our Lost Children: Trauma and Testimony in the Performance of Childhood" (Pace), **Supp. XI:** 245
All Our Yesterdays (Parker), **Supp. XIX:** 187–188
"All Out" (Hecht), **Supp. X:** 72
All Over (Albee), **I:** 91–94
"Allowance" (Minot), **Supp. VI:** 206, 207–208
"Alloy" (Rukeyser), **Supp. VI:** 279
"All Parrots Speak" (Bowles), **Supp. IV Part 1:** 89
Allport, Gordon, **II:** 363–364
All Quiet on the Western Front (Remarque), **Supp. IV Part 1:** 380, 381
"ALL REACTION IS DOOMED-!-!-!" (Baraka), **Supp. II Part 1:** 59
"All Revelation" (Frost), **II:** 160–162
"All Riptides Roar with Sand from Opposing Shores" (Vaz), **Supp. XXVI:** 264–265
Allsburg, Christ Van, **Supp. XXV:** 83, 87
"All Shall Love Me and Despair"(Thompson), **Supp. XXIII:** 295
All Shot Up (C. Himes), **Supp. XVI:** 143, 144
"All Souls" (Gioia), **Supp. XV:** 117
"All Souls" (Wharton), **IV:** 315–316; **Retro. Supp. I:** 382
"All Souls' Night" (Yeats), **Supp. X:** 69
All Souls' Rising (Bell), **Supp. X:** 12, 13–16, 17
"All-Star Literary Vaudeville" (Wilson), **IV:** 434–435
Allston, Washington, **II:** 298
All Stories Are True (Wideman), **Supp. X:** 320
"All That Is" (Wilbur), **Supp. III Part 2:** 563
All That Was Possible (Sturgis), **Supp. XX:** 227, 232, 235–237
All the Agents and Saints: Dispatches from the U.S. Borderlands (Griest), **Supp. XXVIII:** 101
"All the Bearded Irises of Life: Confessions of a Homospiritual" (Walker),

Supp. III Part 2: 527
"All the Beautiful Are Blameless" (Wright), **Supp. III Part 2:** 597
ALL: The Collected Poems, 1956–1964 (Zukofsky), **Supp. III Part 2:** 630
ALL: The Collected Short Poems, 1923–1958 (Zukofsky), **Supp. III Part 2:** 629
All the Conspirators (Isherwood), **Supp. XIV:** 156, 159, 160
All the Dark and Beautiful Warriors (Hansberry), **Supp. IV Part 1:** 360, 374
All the Days and Nights: The Collected Stories (Maxwell), **Supp. VIII:** 151, 158, 169
"All the Dead Dears" (Plath), **Retro. Supp. II:** 246; **Supp. I Part 2:** 537
"All the Dead"(P. Benedict), **Supp. XXIII:** 37
"All the Dead Pilots" (Faulkner), **Retro. Supp. III:** 82
All the Good People I've Left Behind (Oates), **Supp. II Part 2:** 510, 522, 523
"All the Hippos Were Boiled in Their Tanks" (Burroughs and Kerouac), **Supp. III Part 1:** 94
All the King's Men (Warren), **I:** 489; **IV:** 243, 248–249, 252; **Supp. V:** 261; **Supp. VIII:** 126; **Supp. X:** 1; **Supp. XVIII:** 77, 79; **Supp. XXIV:** 226
All the Little Live Things (Stegner), **Supp. IV Part 2:** 599, 604, 605, 606, 609–610, 611, 613
All the Pretty Horses (film), **Supp. VIII:** 175
All the Pretty Horses (McCarthy), **Supp. VIII:** 175, 182–183, 188
All the Sad Young Men (Fitzgerald), **II:** 94; **Retro. Supp. I:** 108
"All the Time in the World" (Dubus), **Supp. VII:** 91
"All the Way to Flagstaff, Arizona" (Bausch), **Supp. VII:** 47, 49
"All This and More" (Karr), **Supp. XI:** 243
All Thy Conquests (Hayes), **Supp. XXVI:** 134,135–136
All Tomorrow's Parties (W. Gibson), **Supp. XVI:** 119, 121, 123, 124, 130
"All Too Real" (Vendler), **Supp. V:** 189
All Trivia: Triva, More Trivia, Afterthoughts, Last Words (L. P. Smith), **Supp. XIV:** 339
All-True Travels and Adventures of Lidie Newton (Smiley), **Supp. VI:** 292, 305–307
All We Need of Hell (Crews), **Supp. XI:** 114
Almack, Edward, **Supp. IV Part 2:** 435
al-Maghut, Muhammad, **Supp. XIII:** 278
"Almanac" (Swenson), **Supp. IV Part 2:** 641
Almanac of the Dead (Silko), **Supp. IV Part 2:** 558–559, 560, 561, 570–571
Alma: or, The Dead Women (Notley), **Supp. XXII:** 223, 224, 231, 236
Almon, Bert, **Supp. IX:** 93
"Almost" (Untermeyer), **Supp. XV:** 304

Almost Learning to Live in This World (Schott), **Supp. XXIII:** 247–248
Almost Revolution, The (Priaulx and Ungar), **Supp. XI:** 228
Alnilam (Dickey), **Supp. IV Part 1:** 176, 186, 188–189
"Alone" (Caputo), **Supp. XIX:** 29
"Alone" (Levine), **Supp. V:** 184, 185, 186
"Alone" (Pickering), **Supp. XXI:** 204
"Alone" (Poe), **Retro. Supp. II:** 266
"Alone" (Singer), **IV:** 15
"Alone" (Winters), **Supp. II Part 2:** 786, 811
"Alone, Like a Window Washer at the 50th Story"(Wakoski), **Supp. XXVIII:** 266
"Alone and Lonely" (Budbill), **Supp. XIX:** 10
Aloneness (Brooks), **Supp. III Part 1:** 85, 86
Alone with America (Corso), **Supp. XII:** 131
Alone with America (Howard), **Supp. IX:** 326
"Along America's Edges" (Sobin), **Supp. XVI:** 288
"Along the Color Line" (Du Bois), **Supp. II Part 1:** 173
Along the Illinois (Masters), **Supp. I Part 2:** 472
*Alouette, L' (Anouilh), **Supp. I Part 1:** 286–288
"Alphabet" (Nye), **Supp. XIII:** 283
Alphabet, An (Doty), **Supp. XI:** 120
Alphabet for Gourmets, An (M. F. K. Fisher), **Supp. XVII:** 86, 87, 92
Alphabet of Grace, The (Buechner), **Supp. XII:** 52
"Alphabet of My Dead, An" (Pinsky), **Supp. VI:** 235, 250
"Alphabet of Subjects, An" (Zukofsky), **Supp. III Part 2:** 624
"Alpine Christ, The" (Jeffers), **Supp. II Part 2:** 415, 419
Alpine Christ and Other Poems, The (Jeffers), **Supp. II Part 2:** 419
"Alpine Idyll, An" (Hemingway), **II:** 249; **Retro. Supp. I:** 176
Al Que Quiere! (W. C. Williams), **Retro. Supp. I:** 414, 416, 417, 428
Alraune (Ewers; Endore, trans.), **Supp. XVII:** 54
Alsop, Joseph, **II:** 579
"Alta"(Goodman), **Supp. XXVIII:** 90
"Altar, The" (Herbert), **Supp. IV Part 2:** 646
"Altar, The" (MacLeish), **III:** 4
"Altar Boy" (Fante), **Supp. XI:** 160, 164
"Altar"(Herbert), **Supp. XXVIII:** 198
Altar in the Fields, An (Lewisohn), **Supp. XXVIII:** 152
"Altar of the Dead, The" (James), **Retro. Supp. I:** 229
"Altars in the Street, The" (Levertov), **Supp. III Part 1:** 280
Alter, Robert, **Supp. XII:** 167
Altgeld, John Peter, **Supp. I Part 2:** 382, 455
Althea (Masters), **Supp. I Part 2:** 455, 459

Altick, Richard, **Supp. I Part 2:** 423

Altieri, Charles, **Supp. VIII:** 297, 303; **Supp. XXIII:** 220

Altman, Robert, **Supp. IX:** 143; **Supp. XXIV:** 166, 172

"Alto" (C. Frost), **Supp. XV:** 101

"Altra Ego" (Brodsky), **Supp. VIII:** 31–32

Altruists, The (Silver), **Supp. XXIV: 273**

A Lume Spento (Pound), **Retro. Supp. I:** 283, 285

"Aluminum House" (F. Barthelme), **Supp. XI:** 26

Alvares, Mosseh, **Supp. V:** 11

Alvarez, A., **Supp. I Part 2:** 526, 527; **Supp. II Part 1:** 99; **Supp. IX:** 248

Alvarez, Joseph A., **Supp. XXII:** 13–14

Alvarez, Julia, **Supp. VII: 1–21; Supp. XI:** 177; **Supp. XVII:** 71, 112; **Supp. XXIV:** 86, 89

"Always a Rose" (L.-Y. Lee), **Supp. XV:** 215, 216

"Always in Good Humor" (Adams), **Supp. XV:** 294

Always Outnumbered, Always Outgunned (Mosley), **Supp. XIII:** 242

"Always the Stories" (Ortiz), **Supp. IV Part 2:** 499, 500, 502, 504, 512

Always the Young Strangers (Sandburg), **III:** 577–578, 579

Always Young and Fair (Richter), **Supp. XVIII: 215–216**

Amadeus (Shaffer), **Supp. XIV:** 330

"Amahl and the Night Visitors: A Guide to the Tenor of Love" (Moore), **Supp. X:** 167

"Am and Am Not" (Olds), **Supp. X:** 212

"Amanita, The" (Francis), **Supp. IX:** 81

Amaranth (Robinson), **III:** 509, 510, 512, 513, 522, 523

"Amateur Iconography: Resurrection" (Stallings), **Supp. XXV:** 233

"Amateurs, The" (Swados), **Supp. XIX:** 256

Amazing Adele, The (Barillet and Grédy; Loos, trans.), **Supp. XVI:** 194

Amazing Adventures of Kavalier and Clay, The (Chabon), **Supp. XI:** 68, 76, **77–80; Supp. XXII:** 49

Amazing Adventures of Leticia Carberry (Rinehart), **Supp. XXV:** 194

Amazing Adventures of the Escapist, The (Chabon, ed.), **Supp. XIX:** 174

Amazing Interlude, The (Rinehart), **Supp. XXV:** 194

Amazing Science Fiction Stories, **Supp. XVI:** 121

Amazons: An Intimate Memoir by the First Woman to Play in the National Hockey League (DeLillo), **Supp. VI:** 2

Ambassador Morgenthau's Story (Morgenthau), **Supp. XXIII:** 21, 22

Ambassador of Peace, An (Abernon), **Supp. XVI:** 191

Ambassadors, The (H. James), **II:** 320, 333–334, 600; **III:** 517; **IV:** 322; **Retro. Supp. I:** 215, 218, 219, 220, 221, **232–233**

Ambassador's Son, The (Hickam), **Supp. XXVII:** 111

Ambelain, Robert, **Supp. I Part 1:** 260, 273, 274

"Amber" (Gansworth), **Supp. XXVI:** 114

"Amber Disks"(Wakoski), **Supp. XXVIII:** 271

"Ambition Bird, The" (Sexton), **Supp. II Part 2:** 693

Ambition: The Secret Passion (Epstein), **Supp. XIV:** 113–114

"Ambitious Guest, The" (Hawthorne), **Retro. Supp. III:** 113

Ambler, Eric, **III:** 57

Ambrose Holt and Family (Glaspell), **Supp. III Part 1:** 175, 181, 184, 187, 188

"Ambrose Seyffert" (Masters), **Supp. I Part 2:** 464

"Ambuscade" (Faulkner), **Retro. Supp. III:** 85

"Ambush" (Komunyakaa), **Supp. XIII:** 122

Amen Corner, The (Baldwin), **Retro. Supp. II:** 5, 7; **Supp. I Part 1:** 48, 51, 54, 55, 56

America (Benét), **Supp. XI:** 46, 47, 51

"America" (Ginsberg), **Supp. II Part 1:** 58–59, 317

"America" (song), **IV:** 410

"America, America!" (poem) (Schwartz), **Supp. II Part 2:** 665

"America, Commerce, and Freedom" (Rowson and Reinagle), **Supp. XV:** 240

"America, Home of the Red Man" (Zitkala-Ša), **Supp. XXV:** 281

"America, Seen Through Photographs, Darkly" (Sontag), **Supp. III Part 2:** 464

"America! America!" (story) (Schwartz), **Supp. II Part 2:** 640, 658–659, 660

America and Americans (Steinbeck), **IV:** 52

"America and the Vidal Chronicles" (Pease), **Supp. IV Part 2:** 687

America as a Civilization (Lerner), **III:** 60

America Behind the Color Line (H. L. Gates), **Supp. XX: 102, 105**

America Beyond the Color Line (television program), **Supp. XX: 99**

America Day by Day (de Beauvoir), **Supp. XXVIII:** 255

America Hispana: A Portrait and a Prospect (W. Frank), **Supp. XX: 76**

"America Independent" (Freneau), **Supp. II Part 1:** 261

America Is Worth Saving (Dreiser), **Retro. Supp. II:** 96

American, The (James), **I:** 226; **II:** 326–327, 328, 331, 334; **IV:** 318; **Retro. Supp. I:** 220, **221,** 228, 376, 381

Americana (DeLillo), **Supp. VI:** 2, **3,** 5, 6, 8, 13, 14

American Adam, The (R. W. B. Lewis), **II:** 457–458; **Supp. XIII:** 93

American Almanac (Leeds), **II:** 110

American Anthem (Doctorow and Suares), **Supp. IV Part 1:** 234

"American Apocalypse" (Gunn Allen), **Supp. IV Part 1:** 325

American Aristocracy (film), **Supp. XVI:** 185–186

"American Backgrounds for Fiction: VI—Arkansas, Louisiana and the Gulf Country"(Stuart), **Supp. XXVIII:** 230

American Blood, (Nichols), **Supp. XIII:** 268

American Blues (T. Williams), **IV:** 381, 383

American Buffalo (Mamet), **Supp. XIV:** 239, 241, 242, 244–245, 246, 254, 255

American Caravan: A Yearbook of American Literature (Mumford, ed.), **Supp. II Part 2:** 482

American Cause, The (MacLeish), **III:** 3

American Childhood, An (Dillard), **Supp. VI:** 19–21, 23, 24, 25, 26, 30, 31

"American Childhood in the Dominican Republic, An" (Alvarez), **Supp. VII:** 2, 5

American Child Supreme, An: The Education of a Liberation Ecologist (Nichols), **Supp. XIII:** 256, 257, 258, 264, 265, 266, 267, 268, 269

American Civilization (C. L. R. James), **Supp. XXI:** 169

American Claimant, The (Twain), **IV:** 194, 198–199

American Clock, The (A. Miller), **Retro. Supp. III:** 165–166

American Crisis I (Paine), **Supp. I Part 2:** 508

American Crisis II (Paine), **Supp. I Part 2:** 508

American Crisis XIII (Paine), **Supp. I Part 2:** 509

"American Critic, The" (J. Spingarn), **I:** 266

American Culture, Canons, and the Case of Elizabeth Stoddard (Smith and Weinauer), **Supp. XV:** 270

American Daughter, An (Wasserstein), **Supp. XV: 330–332,** 333

American Democrat, The (Cooper), **I:** 343, 346, 347, 353

American Desert (Everett), **Supp. XVIII: 62–63**

American Diary (Webb), **Supp. I Part 1:** 5

American Drama since World War II (Weales), **IV:** 385

American Dream, An (Mailer), **III:** 27, 33–34, 35, 39, 41, 43, 44; **Retro. Supp. II:** 203, **204–205**

American Dream, The (Albee), **I:** 74–76, 77, 89, 94; **Supp. XXIV:** 113

"American Dreams" (Simpson), **Supp. IX:** 274

American Earth (Caldwell), **I:** 290, 308

"American Emperors" (Poirier), **Supp. IV Part 2:** 690

American English (Marckwardt), **Supp. XXIV:** 255

American Exodus, An (Lange and Taylor), **I:** 293

American Experience, The (Parkes), **Supp. I Part 2:** 617–618

American Express (Corso), **Supp. XII:** 129

"American Express" (Salter), **Supp. IX:** 260–261

"American Famine, The"(Gold), **Supp. XXVIII:** 73

"American Fear of Literature, The" (Lewis), **II:** 451

American Female Patriotism (S. Warner as Wetherell), **Supp. XVIII: 260–261,** 262**,** 263

American Fictions (Hardwick), **Supp. X:** 171

American Fictions, 1940–1980 (Karl), **Supp. IV Part 1:** 384; **Supp. XXI:** 234

"American Financier, The" (Dreiser), **II:** 428

American Folkways (book series), **I:** 290

American Guerilla in the Philippines (Wolfert), **Supp. XXI:** 267

"American Heart of Darkness: The Moral Vision of Five Novels of the Vietnam War" (Palm), **Supp. XXII:** 103

"American Heritage" (Gansworth), **Supp. XXVI:** 114

American Heroine: The Life and Legend of Jane Addams (A. F. Davis), **Supp. I Part 1:** 1

American Historical Novel, The (Leisy), **Supp. II Part 1:** 125

"American Horse" (Erdrich), **Supp. IV Part 1:** 333

American Humor: A Study of the National Character (Rourke), **IV:** 339, 352; **Supp. XIX:** 147

American Hunger (Wright), **Supp. IV Part 1:** 11

"American Husband, The" (Atherton), **Supp. XXIV:** 24

American Indian Anthology, An (Tvedten, ed.), **Supp. IV Part 2:** 505

American Indian Stories (Zitkala-Ša), **Supp. XXV:** 272–273, 282–283, 284–285

"American Indian Women: At the Center of Indigenous Resistance in Contemporary North America" (Jaimes and Halsey), **Supp. IV Part 1:** 331

"American in England, An" (Wylie), **Supp. I Part 2:** 707

Americanize the First American (Zitkala-Ša), **Supp. XXV:** 283

American Jew, The: Character and Destiny (Lewisohn), **Supp. XXVIII:** 145, 150, 157

American Jitters, The: A Year of the Slump (Wilson), **IV:** 427, 428

American Journal (Hayden), **Supp. II Part 1:** 367

American Journey: The Times of Robert F. Kennedy (Plimpton, ed.), **Supp. XVI:** 245

"American Land Ethic, An" (Momaday), **Supp. IV Part 2:** 488

American Landscape, The, **Supp. I Part 1:** 157

American Language, The (Mencken), **II:** 289, 430; **III:** 100, 104, 105, 108, 111, 119–120

American Language, The: Supplement One (Mencken), **III:** 111

American Language, The: Supplement Two (Mencken), **III:** 111

"American Letter" (MacLeish), **III:** 13

"American Liberty" (Freneau), **Supp. II Part 1:** 257

"American Life in Poetry" (column, Kooser), **Supp. XIX:** 116, 127

American Linden (Zapruder), **Supp. XXVI:** 54

American Literary History (Harrison), **Supp. VIII:** 37

American Literature, 1607–1885 (Richardson), **Retro. Supp. III:** 261

"American Literature and the American Language" (T. S. Eliot), **Retro. Supp. III:** 255

American Mercury, **Supp. XI:** 163, 164

American Milk (Stone), **Supp. XXVII:** 257

American Mind, The (Commager), **Supp. I Part 2:** 650

American Moderns: Bohemian New York and the Creation of a New Century (Stansell), **Supp. XVII:** 106

American Moderns: From Rebellion to Conformity (Geismar), **Supp. IX:** 15; **Supp. XI:** 223

"American Mystic"(Bottoms), **Supp. XXVIII:** 28

"American Names" (Benét), **Supp. XI:** 47

American Nature Writers (Elder, ed.), **Supp. IX:** 25

American Nature Writers (Winter), **Supp. X:** 104

American Negro, The (W. H. Thomas), **Supp. II Part 1:** 168

American Notebooks, The (Hawthorne), **II:** 226

American Novel Since World War II, The (Klein, ed.), **Supp. XI:** 233

Americano, The (film), **Supp. XVI:** 185

"American Original, An: Learning from a Literary Master" (Wilkinson), **Supp. VIII:** 164, 165, 168

American Ornithology (Wilson), **Supp. XVI:** 4, 6

American Pastoral (P. Roth), **Retro. Supp. II:** 279, 289, **292–293;** **Supp. XI:** 68

American Pictures: A Personal Journey Through the American Underclass (Holdt), **Supp. XXVI:** 26

American Places (Porter, Stegner and Stegner), **Supp. IV Part 2:** 599

"American Poet" (Shapiro), **Supp. II Part 2:** 701

"American Poetry" (Simpson), **Supp. IX:** 272

American Poetry, 1922: A Miscellany (Untermeyer, ed.), **Supp. XV:** 306

"American Poetry and American Life" (Pinsky), **Supp. VI:** 239–240

American Poetry from the Beginning to Whitman (Untermeyer, ed.), **Supp. XV:** 310

American Poetry since 1900 (Untermeyer, ed.), **Supp. XV:** 306

American Poetry since 1945: A Critical Survey (Stepanchev), **Supp. XI:** 312

American Poetry since 1960 (Mesic), **Supp. IV Part 1:** 175

American Poets since World War II Dictionary of Literary Biography (Gwynn, ed.), **Supp. XV:** 343

American Popular Song (Wilder), **Supp. XXVII:** 42

American Primer, An (Boorstin), **I:** 253

American Primer, An (Whitman), **IV:** 348

"American Primitive" (W. J. Smith), **Supp. XIII:** 333

American Primitive: Poems (Oliver), **Supp. VII:** 234–237, 238

American Procession, An: The Major American Writers from 1830–1930—the Crucial Century (Kazin), **Supp. VIII: 105–106,** 108

"American Prose Writers" articles (Briggs), **Supp. XVIII:** 11

American Psycho (Ellis), **Supp. XXVII:** 67, 71–74, 75, 76

American Psycho (film), **Supp. XXVII:** 68, 79

American Psycho 2 (film), **Supp. XXVII:** 68

American Psycho: The Musical, **Supp. XXVII:** 68

American Radio Company, The (radio show, Keillor), **Supp. XVI:** 176–177

"American Realist Playwrights, The" (McCarthy), **II:** 562

American Register, or General Repository of History, Politics, and Science, The (Brown, ed.), **Supp. I Part 1:** 146

American Renaissance (Matthiessen), **I:** 259–260; **III:** 310; **Supp. XIII:** 93

"American Rendezvous, An" (Beauvoir), **Supp. IX:** 4

American Scene, The (James), **II:** 336; **III:** 460; **Retro. Supp. I:** 232, 235

American Scenes (Kozlenko, ed.), **IV:** 378

"American Scholar, The" (Emerson), **I:** 239; **II:** 8, 12–13; **Retro. Supp. I:** 62, 74–75, 149, 298; **Retro. Supp. II:** 155; **Supp. I Part 2:** 420; **Supp. IX:** 227, 271; **Supp. XIV:** 104

"American Scholar, The" (Pickering), **Supp. XXI:** 196

American Seasons (Teale), **Supp. XXVIII:** 243, 249, 250–252, 255

Americans in England; or, Lessons for Daughters (Rowson), **Supp. XV:** 240

"American Soldier, The" (Freneau), **Supp. II Part 1:** 269

American Songbag, The (Sandburg), **III:** 583

"American Student in Paris, An" (Farrell), **II:** 45

"American Sublime, The" (Stevens), **IV:** 74

American Taliban (Abraham), **Supp. XXIV:** 2, **12–14**

"American Tar, The; or, The Press Gang Defeated" (Rowson and Taylor), **Supp. XV:** 238

"American Temperament, The" (Locke), **Supp. XIV:** 211

American Testament, An (Freeman), **Supp. XXVIII:** 75

American Tragedy, An (Dreiser), **I:** 497, 498, 499, 501, 502, 503, 511–515, 517, 518, 519; **III:** 251; **IV:** 35, 484; **Retro. Supp. II:** 93, 95, **104–108; Supp. XVII:** 155

"American Triptych" (Kenyon), **Supp. VII:** 165

"American Use for German Ideals" (Bourne), **I:** 228

American Village, The (Freneau), **Supp. II Part 1:** 256, 257

"American Village, The" (Freneau), **Supp. II Part 1:** 256

American Wives and English Husbands (Atherton), **Supp. XXIV:** 18, 22

American Woman (Choi), **Supp. XXVIII:** 214

America's Coming-of-Age (Brooks), **I:** 228, 230, 240, 245, 258; **IV:** 427

America's Humor: From Poor Richard to Doonesbury (Blair and Hill), **Retro. Supp. II:** 286

"America's Indian Problem" (Zitkala-Ša), **Supp. XXV:** 282

"America's Part in World Peace" (Locke), **Supp. XIV:** 208

America's Rome (Vance), **Supp. IV Part 2:** 684

America: The Story of a Free People (Commager and Nevins), **I:** 253

America Was Promises (MacLeish), **III:** 16, 17

"Amerika" (Snyder), **Supp. VIII:** 301

Ames, Christopher, **Supp. XVIII:** 242–243

Ames, Fisher, **Supp. I Part 2:** 486

Ames, Lois, **Supp. I Part 2:** 541, 547

Ames, William, **IV:** 158

Ames Stewart, Beatrice, **Supp. IX:** 200

Amichai, Yehuda, **Supp. XI:** 267

Amick, Steve, **Supp. XXII:** 205, 216

Amidon, Stephen, **Supp. XI:** 333

Amiel, Henri F., **I:** 241, 243, 250

Amis, Kingsley, **IV:** 430; **Supp. IV Part 2:** 688; **Supp. VIII:** 167; **Supp. XIII:** 93; **Supp. XV:** 117

Amis, Martin, **Retro. Supp. I:** 278

"Amish, The"(Thompson), **Supp. XXIII:** 295–296

"Amity Hills" (Skloot), **Supp. XX: 204**

Ammons, A. R., **Supp. III Part 2:** 541; **Supp. IX:** 41, 42, 46; **Supp. VII: 23–38; Supp. XII:** 121; **Supp. XIX:** 83; **Supp. XV:** 115; **Supp. XVII:** 242; **Supp. XXVI:** 67

Ammons, Elizabeth, **Retro. Supp. I:** 364, 369; **Retro. Supp. II:** 140

Amnesia Moon (Lethem), **Supp. XVIII:** 136, **138–139**

"Among Children" (Levine), **Supp. V:** 192

Among Friends (M. F. K. Fisher), **Supp. XVII:** 89, 90–91, 92

Among My Books (J. R. Lowell), **Supp. I Part 2:** 407

"Among School Children" (Yeats), **III:** 249; **Supp. IX:** 52; **Supp. XIV:** 8

Among the Believers (Rash), **Supp. XXVII:** 218–220, 221

"Among the Hills" (Whittier), **Supp. I Part 2:** 703

Among the Isles of Shoals (Thaxter), **Supp. XIII:** 152

"Among Those Present" (Benét), **Supp. XI:** 53

"Amoral Moralist" (White), **Supp. I Part 2:** 648

Amory, Cleveland, **Supp. I Part 1:** 316

Amory, Fred, **Supp. III Part 1:** 2

Amos (biblical book), **II:** 166

Amos and Andy (television program), **Supp. XX: 103**

Amplitude (Gallagher), **Supp. XXIV:** 166, 170

Amran, David, **Supp. XIV:** 150

"Am Strand von Tanger" (Salter), **Supp. IX:** 257

"AMTRAK" (Baraka), **Supp. II Part 1:** 60

"Amulet, The" (Antin), **Supp. XX: 10**

"Amulets" (Hull), **Supp. XXI:** 139

Amy and Isabelle (film), **Supp. XXIII:** 275–276

Amy and Isabelle (Strout), **Supp. X:** 86; **Supp. XXIII:** 273, 274–275, **276–278,** 285

"Amy Lowell of Brookline, Mass." (Scott), **II:** 512

Amy Lowell: Portrait of the Poet in Her Time (Gregory), **II:** 512

"Amy Wentworth" (Whittier), **Supp. I Part 2:** 694, 696

Anabase (Perse), **III:** 12

"Anabasis (I)" (Merwin), **Supp. III Part 1:** 342, 346

"Anabasis (II)" (Merwin), **Supp. III Part 1:** 342, 346

Anagrams: A Novel (Moore), **Supp. X:** 163, 164, 167, **169–171,** 172

Analects (Confucius), **Supp. IV Part 1:** 14

Analects, The (Pound, trans.), **III:** 472

Analogy (J. Butler), **II:** 8

"Analysis of a Theme" (Stevens), **IV:** 81

Anarchiad, The, A Poem on the Restoration of Chaos and Substantial Night, in Twenty Four Books (Barlow), **Supp. II Part 1:** 70

Anarchist Woman, An (Hapgood), **Supp. XVII:** 102–103; **Supp. XXI:** 5

Anatomy Lesson, and Other Stories, The (Connell), **Supp. XIV:** 84, 87, 89

"Anatomy Lesson, The" (Connell), **Supp. XIV:** 84, 86, 87

Anatomy Lesson, The (P. Roth), **Retro. Supp. II:** 286, 290; **Supp. III Part 2:** 422–423, 425

"Anatomy Lesson of Dr. Nicholaas Tulp, Amsterdam, 1632, The" (Bierds), **Supp. XVII:** 27–28

Anatomy of Criticism (Frye), **Supp. XIII:** 19; **Supp. XIV:** 15

Anatomy of Melancholy (Burton), **III:** 78; **Supp. XVII:** 229

Anatomy of Nonsense, The (Winters), **Supp. II Part 2:** 811, 812

Anaya, Rudolfo A., **Supp. IV Part 2:** 502; **Supp. XIII:** 213, 220; **Supp. XIX:** 97

"Ancestor" (A. Finch), **Supp. XVII:** 72

Ancestors (Atherton), **Supp. XXIV:** 23, 25

Ancestors (Maxwell), **Supp. VIII:** 152, 168

"Ancestors, The" (Tate), **IV:** 128

Ancestral Voice: Conversations with N. Scott Momaday (Woodard), **Supp. IV Part 2:** 484, 485, 486, 489, 493

"Anchorage" (Harjo), **Supp. XII:** 220–221

Ancient Child, The: A Novel (Momaday), **Supp. IV Part 2:** 488, 489–491, 492, 493

"Ancient Dog Grave, Unearthed During Construction of the Athens Metro, An" (Stallings), **Supp. XXV:** 232

"Ancient Egypt/Fannie Goldbarth" (Goldbarth), **Supp. XII:** 191–192

Ancient Evenings (Mailer), **Retro. Supp. II:** 206, 210, 213

Ancient Law, The (Glasgow), **II:** 179–180, 192

Ancient Musics (Goldbarth), **Supp. XII:** 191–192

"Ancient Semitic Rituals for the Dead" (Goldbarth), **Supp. XII:** 191–192

Ancient Track, The (Lovecraft), **Supp. XXV:** 120

"Ancient World, The" (Doty), **Supp. XI:** 122

& (And) (Cummings), **I:** 429, 431, 432, 437, 445, 446, 448

Andersen, Hans Christian, **I:** 441; **Supp. I Part 2:** 622

Andersen, Hendrik Christian, **Supp. XX: 232**

Anderson, Charles R., **Supp. I Part 1:** 356, 360, 368, 371, 372

Anderson, Frances, **I:** 231

Anderson, Guy, **Supp. X:** 264, 265

Anderson, Henry J., **Supp. I Part 1:** 156

Anderson, Irwin M., **I:** 98–99

Anderson, Mrs. Irwin M., **I:** 98–99

Anderson, Jon, **Supp. V:** 338

Anderson, Judith, **III:** 399

Anderson, Karl, **I:** 99, 103

Anderson, Lorraine, **Supp. XVIII:** 189

Anderson, Margaret, **I:** 103; **III:** 171, 471; **Supp. XXV:** 18; **Supp. XXVII:** 86

Anderson, Marian, **Supp. XXII:** 283

Anderson, Mary Jane. See Lanier, Mrs. Robert Sampson (Mary Jane Anderson)

Anderson, Maxwell, **III:** 159

Anderson, Quentin, **Retro. Supp. I:** 392

Anderson, Robert, **Supp. I Part 1:** 277; **Supp. V:** 108

Anderson, Sally, **Supp. XIII:** 95

Anderson, Sherwood, **I: 97–120,** 211, 374, 375, 384, 405, 423, 445, 480, 487, 495, 506, 518; **II:** 27, 38, 44, 55, 56, 68, 250–251, 263, 271, 289, 451, 456–457; **III:** 220, 224, 382–383, 453, 483, 545, 576, 579; **IV:** 27, 40, 46, 190, 207, 433, 451, 482; **Retro. Supp.**

I: 79, 80, 177; **Retro. Supp. III:** 45, 76; **Supp. I Part 2:** 378, 430, 459, 472, 613; **Supp. IV Part 2:** 502; **Supp. IX:** 14, 309; **Supp. V:** 12, 250; **Supp. VIII:** 39, 152; **Supp. XI:** 159, 164; **Supp. XII:** 343; **Supp. XV:** 298; **Supp. XVI:** 17, 20; **Supp. XVII:** 105; **Supp. XX: 69, 75; Supp. XXIII:** 68, 162, 164; **Supp. XXIV:** 136; **Supp. XXV:** 18; **Supp. XXVII:** 83, 86

Anderson, Mrs. Sherwood (Tennessee Mitchell), I: 100; **Supp. I Part 2:** 459, 460

Anderson, T. J., **Supp. XIII:** 132

Anderson, Wendy, **Supp. XXI:** 255

Anderssen, A., III: 252

"And Hickman Arrives" (Ellison), **Retro. Supp. II:** 118, 126; **Supp. II Part 1:** 248

And in the Hanging Gardens (Aiken), I: 63

"And It Came to Pass" (Wright), **Supp. XV:** 348

And I Worked at the Writer's Trade (Cowley), **Supp. II Part 1:** 137, 139, 141, 143, 147, 148

"...And Ladies of the Club" (J. W. Miller), **Supp. XX:** 161

And Live Apart (Peacock), **Supp. XIX: 196–197**

Andorra (Cameron), **Supp. XII:** 79, 81, **88–91**

"—and Other Poets" (column; Untermeyer), **Supp. XV:** 294

"—and Other Poets" (Untermeyer), *Supp. XV:* 297

"Andoumboulou Brush" (Mackey), **Supp. XXVII:** 156

Andracki, Thaddeus, **Supp. XXVI:** 108

Andral, Gabriel, **Supp. I Part 1:** 302

Andre, Michael, **Supp. XII:** 117–118, 129, 132, 133–134

"Andrea Is Changing Her Name" (Brockmeier), **Supp. XXII:** 61

Andre's Mother (McNally), **Supp. XIII:** 206

Andress, Ursula, **Supp. XI:** 307

"Andrew Jackson" (Masters), **Supp. I Part 2:** 472

Andrews, Bruce, **Supp. IV Part 2:** 426

Andrews, Peter, **Supp. XX:** 87

Andrews, Raymond, **Supp. XXVI: 1–16**

Andrews, Roy Chapman, **Supp. X:** 172

Andrews, Tom, **Supp. XI:** 317

Andrews, Wayne, IV: 310

Andrews, William L., **Supp. IV Part 1:** 13; **Supp. XIX:** 72; **Supp. XX: 105**

Andrews, William P., **Supp. XXV:** 250

Andreyev, Leonid Nikolaevich, I: 53; II: 425

Andria (Terence), IV: 363

"Androgynous Kiss" (Gallagher), **Supp. XXIV:** 170

"Andromache" (Dubus), **Supp. VII:** 84

"And Summer Will Not Come Again" (Plath), **Retro. Supp. II:** 242

"And That Night Clifford Died" (Levine), **Supp. V:** 195

And the Band Played On (Shilts), **Supp. X:** 145

"And the Moon Be Still as Bright" (Bradbury), **Supp. IV Part 1:** 106

"And the Sea Shall Give up Its Dead" (Wilder), IV: 358

And Things That Go Bump in the Night (McNally), **Supp. XIII: 196–197,** 205, 208

And to Think That I Saw It on Mulberry Street (Geisel), **Supp. XVI:** 100, 101, 104

"And *Ut Pictura Poesis* Is Her Name" (Ashbery), **Supp. III Part 1:** 19

And We Are Millions (Ryan), **Supp. XVIII:** 225

"And Winter" (Boyle), **Supp. XXIV:** 63

"Andy Warhol: Andy Do It" (Brainard), **Supp. XXVII:** 25

"Anecdote and Storyteller" (Howe), **Supp. VI:** 127

"Anecdote of the Jar" (Stevens), IV: 83–84

"Anemone" (Rukeyser), **Supp. VI:** 281, 285

"Angel, The" (Buck), **Supp. II Part 1:** 127

"Angel and Unicorn and Butterfly" (Everwine), **Supp. XV:** 76

Angela's Ashes (McCourt), **Supp. XII: 271–279,** 283, 285; **Supp. XXII:** 94

"Angel at the Grave, The" (Wharton), IV: 310; **Retro. Supp. I:** 365

"Angel Butcher" (Levine), **Supp. V:** 181

Angel City (Shepard), **Supp. III Part 2:** 432, 445

Angelica (Holding), **Supp. XXII: 120–121**

"Angel Is My Watermark!, The" (H. Miller), III: 180

Angell, Carol, **Supp. I Part 2:** 655

Angell, Katharine Sergeant. *See* White, Katharine

Angell, Roger, **Supp. I Part 2:** 655; **Supp. V:** 22; **Supp. VIII:** 139

Angel Landing (Hoffman), **Supp. X: 82–83**

"Angel Levine" (Malamud), **Supp. I Part 2:** 431, 432, 433–434, 437

Angel of Bethesda, The (Mather), **Supp. II Part 2:** 464

"Angel of the Bridge, The" (Cheever), **Supp. I Part 1:** 186–187

"Angel of the Odd, The" (Poe), III: 425

Angelo Herndon Jones (Hughes), **Retro. Supp. I:** 203

"Angel on the Porch, An" (Wolfe), IV: 451

Angelou, Maya, **Supp. IV Part 1: 1–19;** **Supp. XI:** 20, 245; **Supp. XIII:** 185; **Supp. XVI:** 259; **Supp. XXI:** 172

"Angel Poem, The" (Stern), **Supp. IX:** 292

Angels and Earthly Creatures (Wylie), **Supp. I Part 2:** 709, 713, 724–730

Angels Flight (Connelly), **Supp. XXI:** 72, **72–73,** 75, 80

"Angels for Djuna Barnes" (Boyle), **Supp. XXIV:** 63

Angels in America: A Gay Fantasia on National Themes (Kushner), **Supp.**

IX: 131, 134, **141–146; Supp. XXIV:** 272

"Angels of the Love Affair" (Sexton), **Supp. II Part 2:** 692

Angels over Broadway (screenplay, Hecht), **Supp. XXVII:** 93

"Angel's Trumpet, The"(P. Benedict), **Supp. XXIII:** 48

"Angel Surrounded by Paysans" (Stevens), IV: 93

Angel That Troubled the Waters, The (Wilder), IV: 356, 357–358

"Anger" (Creeley), **Supp. IV Part 1:** 150–152

Anger (Sarton), **Supp. VIII: 256**

"Anger against Children" (R. Bly), **Supp. IV Part 1:** 73

Angle of Ascent (Hayden), **Supp. II Part 1:** 363, 367, 370

"Angle of Geese" (Momaday), **Supp. IV Part 2:** 485

Angle of Geese and Other Poems (Momaday), **Supp. IV Part 2:** 487, 491

Angle of Repose (Stegner), **Supp. IV Part 2:** 599, 605, 606, 610–611

"*Angle of Repose* and the Writings of Mary Hallock Foote: A Source Study" (Williams-Walsh), **Supp. IV Part 2:** 611

"Anglo-Mongrels and the Rose" (Loy), **Supp. XXII:** 156, 159, 166–167

Anglo-Saxon Century, The (Dos Passos), I: 474–475, 483

Angoff, Charles, III: 107

"Angola Question Mark" (Hughes), **Supp. I Part 1:** 344

Angry Hills, The (Uris), **Supp. XX: 246, 250**

Angry Wife, The (Sedges), **Supp. II Part 1:** 125

"Angry Women Are Building: Issues and Struggles Facing American Indian Women Today" (Gunn Allen), **Supp. IV Part 1:** 324

"Animal, Vegetable, and Mineral" (Bogan), **Supp. III Part 1:** 66

"Animal Acts" (Simic), **Supp. VIII:** 278

Animal and Vegetable Physiology Considered with Reference to Natural Theology (Roget), **Supp. I Part 1:** 312

"Animal Bodies: Corporeality, Class, and Subject Formation in *The Wide, Wide World*" (Mason), **Supp. XVIII:** 263

Animal Dreams (Kingsolver), **Supp. VII:** 199, 204–207

Animal Magnetism (Prose), **Supp. XVI:** 251, 260

"Animals, The" (Merwin), **Supp. III Part 1:** 348

"Animals Are Passing from Our Lives" (Levine), **Supp. V:** 181, 182

Animals in That Country, The (Atwood), **Supp. XIII:** 20, 33

Animals of the Soul: Sacred Animals of the Oglala Sioux (Brown), **Supp. IV Part 2:** 487

"Animals You Eat, The" (X. J. Kennedy), **Supp. XV:** 169

"Animula" (Eliot), **Retro. Supp. I:** 64

Anita Loos Rediscovered (M. A. Loos), **Supp. XVI:** 196

Ankor Wat (Ginsberg), **Supp. II Part 1:** 323

Ann, Leslee, **Supp. XXIV:** 264

"Annabelle" (Komunyakaa), **Supp. XIII:** 117

"Annabel Lee" (Poe), **Retro. Supp. I:** 273; **Retro. Supp. II:** 266; **Retro. Supp. III:** 232

Anna Christie (O'Neill), **III:** 386, 389, 390; **Supp. XXII:** 24

"Anna Grasa" (Weigl), **Supp. XIX:** 278

"Anna in Mourning" (Weigl), **Supp. XIX:** 288

Anna Karenina (Tolstoy), **I:** 10; **II:** 290; **Retro. Supp. I:** 225; **Supp. V:** 323

"Anna Karenina" (Trilling), Supp. III Part 2: 508

Annan, Gabriele, **Retro. Supp. III:** 290

Annan, Noel, **Supp. XX:** 240

"Anna's Grace" (Weigl), **Supp. XIX:** 282–283

"Anna Who Was Mad" (Sexton), **Supp. II Part 2:** 692

"Ann Burlak" (Rukeyser), **Supp. VI:** 280

"Anne" (Oliver), **Supp. VII:** 232

"Anne" (R. H. Davis), **Supp. XVI:** 91, 92

"Anne at the Symphony" (Shields), **Supp. VII:** 310

"Anne Bradstreet's Poetic Voices" (Requa), **Supp. I Part 1:** 107

Anne Bradstreet: The Worldly Puritan (Stanford), **Retro. Supp. III:** 1

Anne of Geierstein: or, The Maiden of the Mist (Scott), **Supp. XX: 234**

Anne Sexton: The Artist and Her Critics (McClatchy), **Supp. XII:** 253

"Ann from the Street" (Dixon), **Supp. XII:** 146–147

"Ann Garner" (Agee), **I:** 27

"Anniad, The" (Brooks), **Supp. III Part 1:** 77, 78

Annie (musical), **Supp. IV Part 2:** 577

Annie Allen (Brooks), **Supp. III Part 1:** 76–79

Annie Dillard Reader, The (Dillard), **Supp. VI:** 23

Annie Hall (film; Allen), **Supp. IV Part 1:** 205; **Supp. XV:** 1, 2, 4, 5, **6–7,** 14

Annie John (Kincaid), **Supp. VII:** 184–186, 193

Annie Kilburn, a Novel (Howells), **II:** 275, 286, 287

"Annihilation" (X. J. Kennedy), **Supp. XV:** 168

"Annihilation of Matter, The" (Bronk), **Supp. XXI:** 30

Anniversary (Lewisohn), **Supp. XXVIII:** 152

Anniversary (Shields), **Supp. VII:** 320, 322, 323, 324

"Anniversary Poem" (Oppen), **Supp. XXVI:** 237

"Annual Report"(Lea), **Supp. XXVIII:** 133

"Annunciation" (Nelson), **Supp. XVIII:** 174

"Annunciation, The" (Le Sueur), **Supp. V:** 130

Ann Vickers (Lewis), **II:** 453

"A No-Account Creole, A" (Chopin), **Retro. Supp. II:** 64

"Anodyne" (Komunyakaa), **Supp. XIII:** 130

"Another" (Bradstreet), **Retro. Supp. III:** 12–13

Another America/Otra America (Kingsolver), **Supp. VII:** 207–209

"Another Animal" (Swenson), **Supp. IV Part 2:** 639

Another Animal: Poems (Swenson), **Supp. IV Part 2:** 639–641, 649

Another Antigone (Gurney), **Supp. V:** 97, 98, 100, 101, 102, 105

"Another August" (Merrill), **Supp. III Part 1:** 326

"Another Beer" (Matthews), **Supp. IX:** 158

Another Brooklyn (Woodson), **Supp. XXVIII:** 279, 283, 287

Another Country (Baldwin), **Retro. Supp. II:** 9–11, 14; **Supp. I Part 1:** 51, 52, 56–58, 63, 67, 337; **Supp. II Part 1:** 40; **Supp. VIII:** 349

"Another Language" (Jong), **Supp. V:** 131

Another Mother Tongue: Gay Words, Gay Worlds (Grahn), **Supp. IV Part 1:** 330

"Another Night in the Ruins" (Kinnell), **Supp. III Part 1:** 239, 251

"Another Night with Snow" (W. V. Davis), **Supp. XXI:** 90, 91

"Another Old Woman" (W. C. Williams), **Retro. Supp. I:** 423

Another Part of the Forest (Hellman), **Supp. I Part 1:** 282–283, 297

Another Republic: 17 European and South American Writers (Strand, trans.), **Supp. IV Part 2:** 630

Another Roadside Attraction (Robbins), **Supp. X:** 259, 261, 262, 263, 264, 265–266, **267–269,** 274, 275, 277, 284

Another Side of Bob Dylan (album, Dylan), **Supp. XVIII:** 25

"Another Spring Uncovered" (Swenson), **Supp. IV Part 2:** 644

Another Thin Man (film), **Supp. IV Part 1:** 355

Another Time (Auden), **Supp. II Part 1:** 15

Another Turn of the Crank (Berry), **Supp. X:** 25, 35

"Another upon the Same" (Taylor), **IV:** 161

"Another Voice" (Wilbur), **Supp. III Part 2:** 557

"Another Wife" (Anderson), **I:** 114

"Another Winter Night" (Budbill), **Supp. XIX:** 10

Another Woman (film; Allen), **Supp. XV:** 11

Another You (Beattie), **Supp. V:** 29, 31, 33–34

Anouilh, Jean, **Supp. I Part 1:** 286–288, 297

Ansa, Tina McElroy, **Supp. XVIII:** 195

Ansay, A. Manette, **Supp. XXV:** 142

"Anselm" (Berrigan), **Supp. XXIV:** 43

Ansen, Alan, **Supp. XXIII:** 112, 122, 123

Ansky, S., **IV:** 6

Ansky, Shloime, **Supp. IX:** 131, 138

"Answer, The" (Jeffers), **Supp. III Part 2:** 423

Answer, The: The Jew and the World; Past, Present, and Future (Lewisohn), **Supp. XXVIII:** 150, 157

Answered Prayers: The Unfinished Novel (Capote), **Supp. III Part 1:** 113, 125, 131–132; **Supp. XVI:** 245

"Answering the Deer: Genocide and Continuance in the Poetry of American Indian Women" (Gunn Allen), **Supp. IV Part 1:** 322, 325

Answering Voice, The: One Hundred Love Lyrics by Women (Teasdale, ed.), **Supp. XXVII:** 283, 286, 289

"Answer of Minerva, The: Pacifism and Resistance in Simone Weil" (Merton), **Supp. VIII:** 204

Antaeus (Wolfe), **IV:** 461

"Ante-Bellum Sermon, An" (Dunbar), **Supp. II Part 1:** 203–204

Antheil, George, **III:** 471, 472; **IV:** 404

"Anthem" (Cohen), **Supp. XXVII:** 52, 63

Anthem (Rand), **Supp. IV Part 2:** 523

Anthology of Holocaust Literature (Glatstein, Knox, and Margoshes, eds.), **Supp. X:** 70

Anthology of Modern American Poetry (Nelson, ed.), **Supp. XXII:** 271

Anthology of Twentieth-Century Brazilian Poetry, An (Bishop and Brasil, eds.), **Retro. Supp. II:** 50; **Supp. I Part 1:** 94

Anthon, Kate, **I:** 452

Anthony, Adelina, **Supp. XXIII:** 197

Anthony, Andrew, **Supp. XVI:** 235, 245, 246

Anthony, Saint, **III:** 395

Anthony, Susan B., **Supp. XI:** 200

"Anthropologist as Hero, The" (Sontag), **Supp. III Part 2:** 451

"Anthropology of Water, The" (Carson), **Supp. XII: 102–103**

Anthropos: The Future of Art (Cummings), **I:** 430

Antichrist (Nietzsche), **III:** 176

"Antietam" (Rash), **Supp. XXVII:** 221

"Anti-Father" (Dove), **Supp. IV Part 1:** 246

"Anti-Feminist Woman, The" (Rich), **Supp. I Part 2:** 550

Antigone (Sophocles), **Supp. I Part 1:** 284; **Supp. X:** 249

"Anti-Memoir"(Dybek), **Supp. XXIII:** 78

Antin, David, **Supp. VIII:** 292; **Supp. XII:** 2, 8

Antin, Mary, **Supp. IX:** 227; **Supp. XVI:** 148, 149; **Supp. XX: 1–16; Supp. XXVIII:** 159

Anti-Oedipus: Capitalism and Schizophrenia (Deleuze and Guattari), **Supp. XII:** 4

Antiphon, The (Barnes), **Supp. III Part 1:** 43–44

"Antiquities" (Mather), **Supp. II Part 2:** 452

"Antiquity of Freedom, The" (Bryant), **Supp. I Part 1:** 168

"Antislavery Tocsin, An" (Douglass), **Supp. III Part 1:** 171

Antoine, Andre, **III:** 387

Antonioni, Michelangelo, **Supp. IV Part 1:** 46, 47, 48

Antony and Cleopatra (Shakespeare), **I:** 285

"Antony on Behalf of the Play" (Burke), **I:** 284

"An trentiesme de mon Eage, L'" (MacLeish), **III:** 9

Antrim, Donald, **Supp. XX:** 90

"Ants" (R. Bly), **Supp. IV Part 1:** 71

Anxiety of Influence, The (Bloom), **Supp. XIII:** 46

"Any City" (Untermeyer), **Supp. XV:** 296

"Any Object" (Swenson), **Supp. IV Part 2:** 640

Any Old Way You Choose It (Christgau), **Supp. XXVII:** 33, 35, 37, 39, 40, 44

Anyplace but Here (Bontemps and Conroy), **Supp. XXII:** 11

"Any Porch" (Parker), **Supp. IX:** 194

Anything Else (film; Allen), **Supp. XV:** 2, 11

Anywhere but Here (Simpson), **Supp. XXVII:** 234–237

"Anywhere Out of This World" (Baudelaire), **II:** 552

Any Woman Can't (Wasserstein), **Supp. XV:** 322

Any Woman's Blues (Jong), **Supp. V:** 115, 123, 126

Anzaldúa, Gloria, **Supp. IV Part 1:** 330; **Supp. XIII:** 223; **Supp. XXIII:** 193, 194, 205

"Apache Tears" (Cliff), **Supp. XXII:** 76

"Aphorisms on Futurism" (Loy), **Supp. XXII:** 159

"Aphorisms on Society" (Stevens), **Retro. Supp. I:** 303

"Apiary IX" (C. Frost), **Supp. XV:** 106

"Apisculptures" (Bierds), **Supp. XVII:** 29

"Apocalypse: What Disaster Reveals" (Díaz), **Supp. XXIV:** 94–95

Apollinaire, Guillaume, **I:** 432; **II:** 529; **III:** 196; **IV:** 80; **Retro. Supp. II:** 326; **Supp. XV:** 182; **Supp. XXIII:** 208

"Apollo Takes Charge of His Muses" (Stallings), **Supp. XXV:** 229

Apologies to the Iroquois (Wilson), **IV:** 429

"Apology" (C. Frost), **Supp. XV:** 103

"Apology, An" (Malamud), **Supp. I Part 2:** 435, 437

"Apology for Bad Dreams" (Jeffers), **Supp. II Part 2:** 427, 438; **Supp. XVII:** 112

"Apology for Crudity, An" (Anderson), **I:** 109

Apology for Poetry (Sidney), **Supp. II Part 1:** 105

Apostle, The (Asch), **Supp. XXIII:** 2, 4, 9, **13–14**

"Apostle of the Tules, An" (Harte), **Supp. II Part 1:** 356

"Apostrophe to a Dead Friend" (Kumin), **Supp. IV Part 2:** 442, 451, 452

"Apostrophe to a Pram Rider" (White), **Supp. I Part 2:** 678

"Apostrophe to Man (on reflecting that the world is ready to go to war again)" (Millay), **III:** 127

"Apostrophe to Vincentine, The" (Stevens), **IV:** 90

"Apotheosis" (Kingsolver), **Supp. VII:** 208

"Apotheosis of Martin Luther King, The" (Hardwick), **Supp. III Part 1:** 203–204

Appalachee Red (Andrews), **Supp. XXVI:** 5–6, 7, 14

Appalachia (Wright), **Supp. V:** 333, 345

Appalachia Inside Out (Miller, Higgs, and Manning, eds.), **Supp. XX:** 166

"Appalachian Book of the Dead III" (Wright), **Supp. V:** 345

"Appalachian Education: A Critique and Suggestions for Reform" (J. W. Miller), **Supp. XX:** 165

"Appalachian Literature: At Home in This World" (J. W. Miller), **Supp. XX:** 165

"Appalachian Values/American Values" (J. W. Miller), **Supp. XX:** 165

Appaloosa (Parker), **Supp. XIX:** 187

"Apparitions Are Not Singular Occurrences" (Wakoski), **Supp. XXVIII:** 262

"Appeal to H. G. Wells" (Sturgis), **Supp. XX:** 233, 240

"Appeal to Progressives, An" (Wilson), **IV:** 429

Appeal to Reason (Paine), **I:** 490

Appeal to the World, An (Du Bois), **Supp. II Part 1:** 184

Appearance and Reality (Bradley), **I:** 572

Appel, Richard, **Supp. XXVII:** 233

"Appendix to 'The Anniad' " (Brooks), **Supp. III Part 1:** 77

"Applause, Applause" (Thompson), **Supp. XXIII:** 289, 291, 301

Apple, Max, **Supp. VIII:** 14; **Supp. XVII:** 1–11, 49–50

Apple, Sam, **Supp. XVII:** 8

"Apple, The" (Kinnell), **Supp. III Part 1:** 250

Applebaum, Anne, **Supp. XVI:** 153

Applebome, Peter, **Supp. XXI:** 38

Applegarth, Mabel, **II:** 465, 478

"Apple-Maggot Fly, The" (Major), **Supp. XXII:** 182

"Apple of Discord, The" (Humphrey), **Supp. IX:** 109

"Apple Peeler" (Francis), **Supp. IX:** 82

"Apple Rind" (C. Frost), **Supp. XV:** 102

"Apples" (Brockmeier), **Supp. XXII:** 51, 53

"Apples, The" (Di Piero), **Supp. XIX:** 46

Appleseed, Johnny (pseudonym). *See* Chapman, John (Johnny Appleseed)

Apple That Astonished Paris, The (Collins), **Supp. XXI:** 53, 57

Appleton, Nathan, **II:** 488

Appleton, Thomas Gold, **Supp. I Part 1:** 306; **Supp. I Part 2:** 415

"Apple Tree, The" (McCarriston), **Supp. XIV:** 263, 268

"Applicant, The" (Plath), **Retro. Supp. II:** 252; **Supp. I Part 2:** 535, 544, 545

"Application, The" (Neugeboren), **Supp. XVI:** 219, 220, 225

"Applications of the Doctrine" (Hass), **Supp. VI:** 100–101

Appointment, The (film), **Supp. IX:** 253

Appointment in Samarra (O'Hara), **III:** 361, 363–364, 365–367, 371, 374, 375, 383

Appreciation of Sarah Orne Jewett (Cary), **Retro. Supp. II:** 132

"Apprentice, The" (Dybek), **Supp. XXIII:** 71

"Approaches, The" (Merwin), **Supp. III Part 1:** 350

"Approaching Artaud" (Sontag), **Supp. III Part 2:** 470–471

"Approaching Prayer" (Dickey), **Supp. IV Part 1:** 175

"Approaching the Mohawk Village: Jogues' Journal" (Kenny), **Supp. XXIII:** 152

Approach to Literature, An: A Collection of Prose and Verse with Analyses and Discussions (Brooks, Warren, and Purser), **Su pp. XIV:**4

"Approach to Thebes, The" (Kunitz), **Supp. III Part 1:** 265–267

Approach to Vedanta, An (Isherwood), **Supp. XIV:** 157, 163, 164

"Appropriation of Cultures, The" (Everett), **Supp. XVIII:** 66

Approximately Paradise (Skloot), **Supp. XX:** 196, 202, **203–204**

"Après-midi d'un faune, L'" (Mallarmé), **III:** 8

"April" (Bierds), **Supp. XVII:** 29

"April" (W. C. Williams), **Retro. Supp. I:** 422

"April" (Winters), **Supp. II Part 2:** 788

April, Steve. *See* Lacy, Ed

April Galleons (Ashbery), **Supp. III Part 1:** 26

"April Galleons" (Ashbery), **Supp. III Part 1:** 26

April Hopes (Howells), **II:** 285, 289

"April Lovers" (Ransom), **III:** 489–490

"April Saturday 1960" (Huddle), **Supp. XXVI:** 150

"April Showers" (Wharton), **Retro. Supp. I:** 361

"April Today Main Street" (Olson), **Supp. II Part 2:** 581

April Twilights (Cather), **I:** 313; **Retro. Supp. I:** 5; **Retro. Supp. III:** 20

"Apt Pupil" (King), **Supp. V:** 152

Arabian Nights, **I:** 204; **II:** 8; **Supp. I Part 2:** 584, 599; **Supp. IV Part 1:** 1

"Arabic Coffee" (Nye), **Supp. XIII:** 276

"Araby" (Joyce), **Supp. VIII:** 15

Aragon, Louis, **I:** 429; **III:** 471; **Retro. Supp. II:** 85, 321

Arana-Ward, Marie, **Supp. VIII:** 84

Ararat (Glück), **Supp. V:** 79, 86–87

Aratani, Mariko, **Supp. XXIII:** 136

"Arbiter, The" (Toole), **Supp. XXVI:** 243

Arbre du voyageur, L' (W. J. Smith; Haussmann, trans.), *Supp. XIII:* 347

Arbus, Diane, **Supp. XII:** 188

Arbuthnott, John (pseudonym). *See* Henry, O.

"Arc, The" (Bidart), **Supp. XV:** 25–26, 27

Archaeologist of Morning (Olson), **Supp. II Part 2:** 557

Archaeology of Books and Movies, The (Wakoski), **Supp. XXVIII:** 269, 270–271, 272

Archaeology of the Circle: New and Selected Poems (Weigl), **Supp. XIX:** 282

"Archaic Maker, The" (Merwin), **Supp. III Part 1:** 357

Archaic Smile (Stallings), **Supp. XXV:** 221, 222, 223, 224, 228–231, 233

"Archaic Torso of Apollo" (Rilke), **Supp. XV:** 148

"Archaischer Torso Apollos" (Rilke), **Supp. XVII:** 244

"Archbishop, The" (Gioia), **Supp. XV:** 126, 127

Archer (television show), **Supp. IV Part 2:** 474

Archer, William, **IV:** 131; **Retro. Supp. I:** 228

Archer at Large (Macdonald), **Supp. IV Part 2:** 473

Archer in Hollywood (Macdonald), **Supp. IV Part 2:** 474

"Archetype and Signature: The Relationship of Poet and Poem" (Fiedler), **Supp. XIII:** 101

"Archibald Higbie" (Masters), **Supp. I Part 2:** 461

"Architect, The" (Bourne), **I:** 223

Architect, The (Briggs and Ranlett), **Supp. XVIII:** 3

Architect, The (Levin), **Supp. XXVII:** 133

Archuleta, Elizabeth, **Supp. XXVI:** 106

Arctic Dreams (Lopez), **Supp. V:** 211

Arctic Refuge: A Circle of Testimony (Haines), **Supp. XII:** 205

"Arcturus" (Connell), **Supp. XIV:** 88

À rebours (Huysmans), **Supp. XX:** 239

Arendt, Hannah, **II:** 544; **Retro. Supp. I:** 87; **Retro. Supp. II:** 28, 117; **Supp. I Part 2:** 570; **Supp. IV Part 1:** 386; **Supp. VIII:** 98, 99, 100, 243; **Supp. XII:** 166–167

Arensberg, Louise, **Supp. XXII:** 162

Arensberg, Walter, **IV:** 408; **Retro. Supp. I:** 416; **Supp. XXII:** 162

Aren't You Happy for Me? (Bausch), **Supp. VII:** 42, 51, 54

Areopagitica (Milton), **Supp. I Part 2:** 422

"Are You a Doctor?" (Carver), **Supp. III Part 1:** 139–141

"Are You Mr. William Stafford?" (Stafford), **Supp. XI:** 317

Are You My Mother? A Comic Drama (Bechdel), **Supp. XXV:** 1, 2, 9–14

"Are You Okay?" (video, Ellis), **Supp. XXVII:** 80

Argall: The True Story of Pocahontas and Captain John Smith (Vollmann), **Supp. XVII:** 225, 226, 231, 232, 233

Argonaut Rose (Wakoski), **Supp. XXVIII:** 270

"Argonauts of 49, California's Golden Age" (Harte), **Supp. II Part 1:** 353, 355

"Arguantando" (Díaz), **Supp. XXIV:** 88–89

"Arguments of Everlasting" (B. Kelly), **Supp. XVII:** 129

"Arguments with the Gestapo Continued: II" (Wright), **Supp. XV:** 344

"Arguments with the Gestapo Continued: Literary Resistance" (Wright), **Supp. XV:** 344

Ari (musical, Uris), **Supp. XX: 247**

Aria da Capo (Millay), **III:** 137–138

"Ariadne and the Rest" (Stallings), **Supp. XXV:** 223, 229

Ariadne's Thread: A Collection of Contemporary Women's Journals (Lifshin, ed.), **Supp. XVI:** 37–38

"Arias, 1971" (Hull), **Supp. XXI:** 135

Ariel (Plath), **Retro. Supp. II: 250–255; Supp. I Part 2:** 526, 539, 541; **Supp. V:** 79; **Supp. XXI:** 58; **Supp. XXII:** 93; **Supp. XXVII:** 296

"Ariel" (Plath), **Supp. I Part 2:** 542, 546

"Ariel Poems" (Eliot), **I:** 579

Ariosto, Ludovico, **Supp. XV:** 175

"Ariosto: Critical Notice of His Life and Genius" (Hunt), **Supp. XV:** 175

Arise, Arise (Zukofsky), **Supp. III Part 2:** 619, 629

Aristides. *See* Epstein, Joseph

"Aristocracy" (Emerson), **II:** 6

Aristocracy and Justice (More), **I:** 223

Aristocrat, The (Richter), **Supp. XVIII:** 220

Aristophanes, **I:** 436; **II:** 577; **Supp. I Part 2:** 406

Aristotle, **I:** 58, 265, 280, 527; **II:** 9, 12, 198, 536; **III:** 20, 115, 145, 157, 362, 422, 423; **IV:** 10, 18, 74–75, 89; **Supp. I Part 1:** 104, 296; **Supp. I Part 2:** 423; **Supp. IV Part 1:** 391; **Supp. IV Part 2:** 526, 530; **Supp. X:** 78; **Supp. XI:** 249; **Supp. XII:** 106; **Supp. XIV:** 242–243

Aristotle Contemplating the Bust of Homer (Rembrandt), **Supp. IV Part 1:** 390, 391

"Arkansas Prophet, An"(Stuart), **Supp. XXVIII:** 236–237

"Arkansas Traveller" (Wright), **Supp. V:** 334

"Arkham" (Howard), **Supp. XXVII:** 118

Arlen, Harold, **Supp. XXII:** 6

"Arm, The" (X. J. Kennedy), **Supp. XV:** 169

"Armadillo, The" (Bishop), **Supp. I Part 1:** 93

Armadillo in the Grass (Hearon), **Supp. VIII: 58–59**

"Armageddon" (Ransom), **III:** 489, 492

Armageddon (Uris), **Supp. XX: 243, 247, 248, 252–253**

Armah, Aiy Kwei, **Supp. IV Part 1:** 373

Armenian Golgotha: A Memoir of the Armenian Genocide, 1915– 1918 (Grigoris Balakian; trans. Peter Balakian and Sevag), **Supp. XXIII:** 28, **29–32**

Armies of the Night, The (Mailer), **III:** 39–40, 41, 42, 44, 45, 46; **Retro. Supp. II:** 205, 206–207, 208; **Supp. IV Part 1:** 207; **Supp. XIV:** 49, 162

"Arm in Arm" (Simpson), **Supp. IX:** 267–268

Arminius, Jacobus, **I:** 557

Armitage, Shelley, **Supp. IV Part 2:** 439

Arm of Flesh, The (Salter), **Supp. IX:** 251

"Armor" (Dickey), **Supp. IV Part 1:** 179

Armored Attack (film), **Supp. I Part 1:** 281

Armored Hearts (Bottoms), **Supp. XXVIII:** 23, 26, 28

"Armored Hearts"(Bottoms), **Supp. XXVIII:** 28

Arms, George W., **Supp. I Part 2:** 416–417

Armstrong, George, **Supp. I Part 2:** 386

Armstrong, Louis, **Retro. Supp. II:** 114

"'Arm the Paper Arm': Kenneth Koch's Postmodern Comedy" (Chinitz), **Supp. XV:** 180, 185

"Army" (Corso), **Supp. XII:** 117, 127

Army Brat (W. J. Smith), **Supp. XIII:** 331, 347

"Army Recruiting Methods" (Bodenheim), **Supp. XXV:** 19

Arna Bontemps Langston Hughes: Letters 1925–1967 (Nichols), **Retro. Supp. I:** 194

"Arna Bontemps Talks About the Renaissance" (Collins), **Supp. XXII:** 7

Arner, Robert D., **Retro. Supp. II:** 62

"Arnie" (Budbill), **Supp. XIX:** 6

Arnold, Edwin T., **Supp. VIII:** 189

Arnold, George W., **Supp. I Part 2:** 411

Arnold, Marilyn, **Supp. IV Part 1:** 220

Arnold, Matthew, **I:** 222, 228, 275; **II:** 20, 110, 338, 541; **III:** 604; **IV:** 349; **Retro. Supp. I:** 56, 325; **Retro. Supp. III:** 261; **Supp. I Part 2:** 416, 417, 419, 529, 552, 602; **Supp. IX:** 298; **Supp. XIV:** 11, 335; **Supp. XIX:** 41; **Supp. XXI:** 90

Arnold, Thurman, **Supp. I Part 2:** 645

Arnow, Harriette Simpson, **Supp. XXVIII: 1–19**

Aronson, Steven M. L., **Supp. V:** 4

Around about America (Caldwell), **I:** 290

Around the Bloc: My Life in Moscow, Beijing, and Havana (Griest), **Supp. XXVIII:** 97, 99, 100, 101–105

"Arrangement in Black and White" (Parker), **Supp. IX:** 198

Arregoces, Christina, **Supp. XXVI:** 148, 158

"Arrival at Santos" (Bishop), **Retro. Supp. II:** 46; **Supp. IX:** 45–46

"Arrival of the Bee Box, The" (Plath), **Retro. Supp. II:** 255

Arrivistes, The: Poem 1940–1949 (Simpson), **Supp. IX:** 265, **267–268**

Arrogance (J. Scott), **Supp. XVII: 186–188,** 189, 191, 192, 194
"Arrow" (Dove), **Supp. IV Part 1:** 250
"Arrowhead Hunting" (Stallings), **Supp. XXV:** 232
Arrow mystery series (Myers), **Supp. XXVII:** 212
Arrowsmith (Lewis), **I:** 362; **II:** 445–446, 449
"Arsenal at Springfield, The" (Longfellow), **Retro. Supp. II:** 168
"Arson at Midnight" (Nelson), **Supp. XVIII:** 186
"Arson Plus" (Hammett), **Supp. IV Part 1:** 343; **Supp. XXI:** 68
"Ars Poetica" (Dove), **Supp. IV Part 1:** 250
"Ars Poetica" (Dunn), **Supp. XI:** 154
"Ars Poetica" (MacLeish), **III:** 9–10
"Ars Poetica" (X. J. Kennedy), **Supp. XV:** 154
"Ars Poetica: A Found Poem" (Kumin), **Supp. IV Part 2:** 455
"Ars Poetica; or, Who Lives in the Ivory Tower" (McGrath), **Supp. X:** 117
"Ars Poetica: Some Recent Criticism" (Wright), **Supp. III Part 2:** 603
"Art" (Emerson), **II:** 13
Art (Reza), **Supp. XXI:** 148
"Art and Architecture of the Double Ending, The"(Painter), **Supp. XXIII:** 295
"Art and Neurosis" (Trilling), **Supp. III Part 2:** 502
Art and Technics (Mumford), **Supp. II Part 2:** 483
Art & Ardor: Essays (Ozick), **Supp. V:** 258, 272
Art as Experience (Dewey), **I:** 266
Art by Subtraction (Reid), **IV:** 41
Art Chronicles 1954–1966 (O'Hara), **Supp. XXIII:** 220
Art de toucher le clavecin, L' (Couperin), *III:* 464
"Artemis" (Davison), **Supp. XXVI:** 69
Artemis to Actaeon and Other Verse (Wharton), **Retro. Supp. I:** 372; **Retro. Supp. III:** 283
Arte of English Poesie (Puttenham), **Supp. I Part 1:** 113
"Art"(Hadas), **Supp. XXIII:** 115–116
"Art History" (Cliff), **Supp. XXII:** 75–76
Arthur, Anthony, **Supp. IV Part 2:** 606
Arthur Mervyn; or, Memoirs of the Year 1793 (Brown), **Supp. I Part 1:** 137–140, 144
"Article of Faith" (Sobin), **Supp. XVI:** 291
Articles of Light & Elation (Sobin), **Supp. XVI:** 291
"Articulating the Spirit: Poetry, Community, and the Metaphysical Shortwave"(Bottoms), **Supp. XXVIII:** 34
Articulation of Sound Forms in Time (Howe), **Supp. IV Part 2:** 419, 431–433
"Artifical Nigger, The" (O'Connor), **Retro. Supp. III:** 213, 218–219
"Artificer" (X. J. Kennedy), **Supp. XV:** 160

"Artificial Nigger, The" (O'Connor), **III:** 343, 351, 356, 358; **Retro. Supp. II:** 229, 232
Art Is My Life (Zorach), **Supp. XXVIII:** 38
Artist, The: A Drama without Words (Mencken), **III:** 104
Artist as Revolutionary, The (Buhle), **Supp. XXI:** 172
"Artist of the Beautiful, The" (Hawthorne), **Retro. Supp. I:** 149; **Retro. Supp. III:** 115
Artistry of Grief (Torsney), **Retro. Supp. I:** 224
Artists and Concubines (Silver), **Supp. XXIV:** 265
"Artists' and Models' Ball, The" (Brooks), **Supp. III Part 1:** 72
Art of Detective Fiction, The (Swales), **Supp. XIX:** 183
"Art of Disappearing, The" (Nye), **Supp. XIII:** 287
Art of Drowning, The (Collins), **Supp. XXI:** 54, 60, 64
Art of Eating, The (M. F. K. Fisher), **Supp. XVII:** 87, 90, 91
Art of Fiction, The (Gardner), **Supp. VI:** 73
"Art of Fiction, The" (H. James), **Retro. Supp. I:** 226; **Retro. Supp. II:** 223
Art of Hunger, The (Auster), **Supp. XII:** 22
"Art of Keeping Your Mouth Shut, The" (Heller), **Supp. IV Part 1:** 383
"Art of Literature and Commonsense, The" (Nabokov), **Retro. Supp. I:** 271
Art of Living and Other Stories, The (Gardner), **Supp. VI:** 72
Art of Love, The (Koch), **Supp. XV:** 182
"Art of Love, The" (Koch), **Supp. XV:** 182
Art of Poetry, The (Koch), **Supp. XV:** 175–176, 178, 188
"Art of Poetry, The" (Koch), **Supp. XV:** 182
"Art of Poetry, The" (McClatchy), **Supp. XII:** 262
Art of Political Murder, The (Goldman), **Supp. XXV:** 49, 57–59
"Art of Romare Bearden, The" (Ellison), **Retro. Supp. II:** 123
"Art of Storytelling, The" (Simpson), **Supp. IX:** 277
Art of Sylvia Plath, The (Newman), **Supp. I Part 2:** 527
Art of the Moving Picture, The (Lindsay), **Supp. I Part 2:** 376, 391–392, 394; **Supp. XVI:** 185
Art of the Novel (H. James), **Retro. Supp. I:** 227
"Art of Theodore Dreiser, The" (Bourne), **I:** 235
Art of the Personal Essay, The (Lopate, comp.), **Supp. XIII:** 280–281; **Supp. XVI:** 266
Art of the Self, The: Essays a Propos "Steps" (Kosinski), **Supp. VII:** 222
Art of the Wasted Day, The (Hampl), **Supp. XXII:** 85

Arts and Sciences (Goldbarth), **Supp. XII: 184–186**
Arts and Sciences: A Seventies Seduction (Mallon), **Supp. XIX:** 132, 135
"Art's Bread and Butter" (Benét), **Retro. Supp. I:** 108
Artsybashev, Mikhail, **Supp. XXIII:** 1
Arvin, Newton, **I:** 259; **II:** 508; **Retro. Supp. I:** 19, 137
Asali, Muna, **Supp. XIII:** 121, 126
"As a Little Child" (Taggard), **Supp. XXII:** 272
"As a Young Man" (Hayes), **Supp. XXVI:** 134–135
Asbury, Herbert, **Supp. IV Part 1:** 353
"Ascent, The" (Rash), **Supp. XXVII:** 228–229
Ascent of F6, The (Auden), **Supp. II Part 1:** 11, 13
Ascent to Truth, The (Merton), **Supp. VIII:** 208
Asch, Nathan, **Supp. XV:** 133, 134; **Supp. XXIII: 4; Supp. XXVI: 17–29**
Asch, Sholem, **IV:** 1, 9, 11, 14; **Retro. Supp. II:** 299; **Supp. XXIII: 1–18; Supp. XXVI:** 18; **Supp. XXVIII:** 156
Ascherson, Neal, **Supp. III:** 167
Ascher-Walsh, Rebecca, **Supp. XIX:** 54
"As Close as Breathing" (Jarman), **Supp. XVII:** 120
As David Danced (Bronk), **Supp. XXI:** 24
"As David Danced" (Bronk), **Supp. XXI:** 26
As Does New Hampshire and Other Poems (Sarton), **Supp. VIII:** 259
"As Evening Lays Dying" (Salinas), **Supp. XIII:** 319
"As Flowers Are" (Kunitz), **Supp. III Part 1:** 265
"Ash" (Sobin), **Supp. XVI:** 284–285
Ash, Nathan, **Supp. XXII:** 277
Ashbery, John, **Retro. Supp. I:** 313; **Supp. I Part 1:** 96; **Supp. III Part 1: 1–29; Supp. III Part 2:** 541; **Supp. IV Part 2:** 620; **Supp. IX:** 52; **Supp. VIII:** 272; **Supp. XI:** 139; **Supp. XIII:** 85; **Supp. XIX:** 40, 83; **Supp. XV:** 176, 177, 178, 188, 250; **Supp. XXI:** 227; **Supp. XXIII:** 207, 209, 210, 211, 215, 217, 220; **Supp. XXIV:** 33, 37, 44; **Supp. XXVI:** 70; **Supp. XXVIII:** 196
"Ashes" (Lamott), **Supp. XX: 141**
"Ashes" (Levine), **Supp. V:** 188
"Ashes of the Beacon" (Bierce), **I:** 209
Ashes: Poems Old and New (Levine), **Supp. V:** 178, 188–189
Ashford, Margaret Mary (Daisy), **II:** 426
Ashman, Angela, **Supp. XXIV:** 200
"Ash Wednesday" (Garrett), **Supp. VII:** 109–110
"Ash Wednesday" (Merton), **Supp. VIII:** 199
Ash Wednesday (T. S. Eliot), **I:** 570, 574–575, 578–579, 580, 582, 584, 585; **Retro. Supp. I:** 64; **Retro. Supp. III:** 58, 65

"Ash Wednesday" (T. S. Eliot), **Supp. IV Part 2:** 436

Asian American Authors (Hsu and Palubinskas, eds.), **Supp. X:** 292

Asian American Heritage: An Anthology of Prose and Poetry (Wand), **Supp. X:** 292

Asian Figures (Mervin), **Supp. III Part 1:** 341

Asian Journal of Thomas Merton, The (Merton), **Supp. VIII:** 196, 206, 208

"Asian Peace Offers Rejected without Publication" (R. Bly), **Supp. IV Part 1:** 61

"Asides on the Oboe" (Stevens), **Retro. Supp. I:** 305

"As I Ebb'd with the Ocean of Life" (Whitman), **IV:** 342, 345–346; **Retro. Supp. I:** 404, 405

As I Lay Dying (Faulkner), **II:** 60–61, 69, 73, 74; **IV:** 100; **Retro. Supp. I:** 75, 82, 84, 85, 86, 88, 89, 91, 92; **Retro. Supp. III:** 80–81, 84; **Supp. IV Part 1:** 47; **Supp. IX:** 99, 103, 251; **Supp. VIII:** 37, 178; **Supp. XIV:** 24

"*As I Lay Dying* and *The Waste Land*: Some Relationships" (Dickerson), **Retro. Supp. III:** 81

"As I Lay with My Head in Your Lap, Camerado" (Whitman), **IV:** 347

Asimov, Isaac, **Supp. IV Part 1:** 116; **Supp. XVI:** 122

Asinof, Eliot, **II:** 424

As I Remember It (PBS documentary), **Supp. XVIII:** 277

Asirvatham, Sandy, **Supp. XVI:** 249

"As Is the Daughter, So Is Her Mother" (Patchett), **Supp. XII:** 310

"As It Was in the Beginning" (Benét), **Supp. XI:** 56

"As I Walked Out One Evening" (Auden), **Supp. II Part 1:** 13; **Supp. XV:** 126; **Supp. XX:** 138

"As I Went Down by Havre de Grace" (Wylie), **Supp. I Part 2:** 723

Ask a Policeman (Hinojosa), **Supp. XIX:** 110–111

"Ask Me" (Stafford), **Supp. XI:** 326–327

Ask Me Tomorrow (Cozzens), **I:** 365–367, 379

Ask the Dust (Fante), **Supp. XI:** 159, 160, 166, **167–169**, 172, 173, 174

"Ask the Optimist!" (Saunders), **Supp. XIX:** 235

Ask Your Mama (Hughes), **Supp. I Part 1:** 339, 341–342

Ask Your Mama: 12 Moods for Jazz (Hughes), **Retro. Supp. I:** 210, 211

As Little Children (R. P. Smith), **Supp. XIV:** 333

"As One Put Drunk into the Packet Boat" (Ashbery), **Supp. III Part 1:** 18

"Asparagus" (Nelson), **Supp. XVIII:** 178

"Aspects of Robinson" (Kees), **Supp. XV:** 134

Aspects of the Novel (Forster), **Retro. Supp. I:** 232; **Supp. VIII:** 155; **Supp. XXI:** 233

"Aspen and the Stream, The" (Wilbur), **Supp. III Part 2:** 555, 556

Aspern Papers, The (James), **Supp. V:** 101, 102

"Aspern Papers, The" (James), **Retro. Supp. I:** 219, 227, 228

Asphalt Georgics (Carruth), **Supp. XVI:** 54

Asphalt Jungle (film, Huston), **Supp. XIII:** 174

"Asphodel" (Welty), **IV:** 265, 271

"Asphodel, That Greeny Flower" (W. C. Williams), **Retro. Supp. I:** 429

"Aspic and Buttermilk" (Olds), **Supp. X:** 213

Asquith, Herbert Henry, **Retro. Supp. I:** 59

"Ass" (Cisneros), **Supp. VII:** 67

Assante, Armand, **Supp. VIII:** 74

Assassin, The: A Play in Three Acts (Shaw), **Supp. XIX:** 248

Assassins, The (Oates), **Supp. II Part 2:** 512, 517–519

"Assault" (Millay), **III:** 130–131

"Assemblage of Husbands and Wives, An" (Lewis), **II:** 455–456

"Assembloir" (Monson), **Supp. XXIV:** 237

Assembly (O'Hara), **III:** 361

As She Climbed Across the Table (Lethem), **Supp. XVIII: 140–141,** 148

Assignment, Wildlife (LaBastille), **Supp. X:** 99, 104

"Assimiliation in Recent American Jewish Autobiographies" (Krupnick), **Supp. XVI:** 153

Assistant, The (Malamud), **Supp. I Part 2:** 427, 428, 429, 431, 435, 441–445, 451; **Supp. XVI:** 220

Assommoir, L' (Zola), **II:** 291; **III:** 318

Assorted Prose (Updike), **IV:** 215–216, 218; **Retro. Supp. I:** 317, 319, 327

Astaire, Adele, **Supp. XVI:** 187

"As the Mist Leaves No Scar" (Cohen), **Supp. XXVII:** 56

As They Were (M. F. K. Fisher), **Supp. XVII:** 88

As They Were (M. F. K. Fisher), **Supp. XVII:** 89, 91

Astor, Mary, **Supp. IV Part 1:** 356; **Supp. XII:** 173

Astoria, or, Anecdotes of an Enterprise beyond the Rocky Mountains (Irving), **II:** 312

"Astounding News by Electric Express via Norfolk! The Atlantic Crossed in Three Days Signal Triumph of Mr. Monck's Flying-Machine . . ." (Poe), **III:** 413, 420

Astraea (Holmes), **III:** 82

Astro, Richard, **Supp. I Part 2:** 429, 445

"Astrological Fricassee" (H. Miller), **III:** 187

"Astronomer's Wife" (Boyle), **Supp. XXIV:** 58

Astrophil and Stella (Sidney), **Supp. XIV:** 128

Asturias, Miguel Ángel, **Supp. XXIV:** 89

"As Weary Pilgrim" (Bradstreet), **Retro. Supp. III:** 14; **Supp. I Part 1:** 103, 109, 122

As We Know (Ashbery), **Supp. III Part 1:** 9, 21–25

"As We Know" (Ashbery), **Supp. III Part 1:** 21–22

Aswell, Edward C., **IV:** 458, 459, 461

"Asylum, The" (Carruth), **Supp. XVI:** 48–49

"As You Like It" (Chopin), **Supp. I Part 1:** 217; **Supp. XXVIII:** 225

As You Like It (Shakespeare), **Supp. I Part 1:** 308

"At a Bar" (Ferry), **Supp. XXIV:** 162

"At a Bar in Charlotte Amalie" (Updike), **IV:** 214

"At a Lecture" (Brodsky), **Supp. VIII:** 33

"At a Low Bar" (Ferry), **Supp. XXIV:** 149

"At a March against the Vietnam War" (R. Bly), **Supp. IV Part 1:** 61

"At a Reading" (McClatchy), **Supp. XII:** 256–257

"Atavism of John Tom Little Bear, The" (O. Henry), **Supp. II Part 1:** 410

"At Chênière Caminada" (Chopin), **Supp. I Part 1:** 220

"At Chinese Checkers" (Berryman), **I:** 182

Atchity, Kenneth John, **Supp. XI:** 227

"At Death's Window" (Lamott), **Supp. XX: 144**

At Eighty-Two (Sarton), **Supp. VIII:** 264

Atet A.D. (Mackey), **Supp. XXVII:** 158–159

"At Every Gas Station There Are Mechanics" (Dunn), **Supp. XI:** 144

At Fault (Chopin), **Retro. Supp. II:** 57, 60, **62–63**; **Supp. I Part 1:** 207, 209–211, 220

"At Fifty" (Bronk), **Supp. XXI:** 31

At Heaven's Gate (Warren), **IV:** 243, 247–248, 251

Atheism Refuted: in a Discourse to Prove the Existence of God (Paine), **Supp. I Part 2:** 517

"Athénaïse" (Chopin), **Retro. Supp. II:** 66, 67; **Supp. I Part 1:** 219–220

At Her Majesty's Request: An African Princess in Victorian England (Myers), **Supp. XXVII:** 209

Atherton, Gertrude, **I:** 199, 207–208; **Supp. XXIV: 17–32; Supp. XXVI:** 276; **Supp. XXVIII:** 125

Athey, Jean L., **Supp. XI:** 184

At Home: Essays, 1982–1988 (Vidal), **Supp. IV Part 2:** 682, 687, 688

"At Home With" (column; Leland), **Supp. XV:** 69

"At Kino Viejo, Mexico" (Ríos), **Supp. IV Part 2:** 541

Atkinson, Brooks, **IV:** 288; **Supp. IV Part 2:** 683; **Supp. XIX:** 244; **Supp. XXVII:** 90; **Supp. XXVIII:** 70

Atlanta (film, July), **Supp. XXIV:** 201, 209–210

Atlantis (Doty), **Supp. XI:** 121, **126–129**

"Atlantis" (Doty), **Supp. XI:** 127–128

"Atlantis" (H. Crane), **Retro. Supp. III:** 48

Atlas, James, **Supp. V:** 233; **Supp. XV:** 25; **Supp. XXIV:** 172

Atlas, The (Vollmann), **Supp. XVII:** 226, 227

"Atlas of the Difficult World, An" (Rich), **Retro. Supp. III:** 251

Atlas of the Difficult World, An: Poems 1988–1991 (Rich), **Retro. Supp. III:** 250

Atlas Shrugged (Rand), **Supp. IV Part 2:** 517, 521, 523, 524–526, 528, 531

At Liberty (T. Williams), **IV:** 378

"At Melville's Tomb" (H. Crane), **I:** 393; **Retro. Supp. II:** 76, 78, 80, 82

"At Mother Teresa's" (Nye), **Supp. XIII:** 276

"At Nightfall" (Kooser), **Supp. XIX:** 122–123

At Night the Salmon Move (Carver), **Supp. III Part 1:** 142

At Night the States (Notley), **Supp. XXII:** 224, 231–232

"At night the states" (Notley), **Supp. XXII:** 232

"At North Farm" (Ashbery), **Supp. III Part 1:** 1–2

At Paradise Gate (Smiley), **Supp. VI:** 292, **293–294**

"At Paso Rojo" (Bowles), **Supp. IV Part 1:** 87

At Play in the Fields of the Lord (Matthiessen), **Supp. V:** 199, 202, 204–206, 212

"At Play in the Paradise of Bombs" (Sanders), **Supp. XVI:** 272–273, 274, 277

"At Pleasure By" (Pinsky), **Supp. VI:** 245

"A-Train / Ziggurat / Elegy"(Balakian), **Supp. XXIII:** 32

At Risk (Hoffman), **Supp. X:** 87

"At Sea" (Hemingway), **II:** 258

"At Shaft 11" (Dunbar), **Supp. II Part 1:** 212

"At Sixty" (Davison), **Supp. XXVI:** 77

"At Slim's River" (Haines), **Supp. XII:** 208–209

"At St. Croix" (Dubus), **Supp. VII:** 83, 87

At Sundown (Whittier), **Supp. I Part 2:** 704

"At Sunset" (Simic), **Supp. VIII:** 282

At Swim-Two-Birds (O'Brien), **Supp. XXV:** 65

Attaway, William, **Supp. XXI:** 264

Attebery, Brian, **Supp. IV Part 1:** 101

Attendant, The (Bronk), **Supp. XXI:** 24

"Attendant, The" (Bronk), **Supp. XXI:** 26

"Attention"(Hadas), **Supp. XXIII:** 121

"At That Time, or The History of a Joke" (Paley), **Supp. VI:** 229–230

"At the Alhambra"(P. Benedict), **Supp. XXIII:** 40

At the Back of the North Wind (Macdonald), **Supp. XIII:** 75

"At the Birth of an Age" (Jeffers), **Supp. II Part 2:** 432

"At the Bomb Testing Site" (Stafford), **Supp. XI:** 317–318, 321, 323

At the Bottom of the River (Kincaid), **Supp. VII:** 182–184, 185

"At the 'Cadian Ball" (Chopin), **Retro. Supp. II:** 64, 65, 68

"At the Cancer Clinic" (Kooser), **Supp. XIX:** 127

"At the Chelton-Pulver Game" (Auchincloss), **Supp. IV Part 1:** 27

"At the Drugstore" (Taylor), **Supp. V:** 323

At the Edge of the Body (Jong), **Supp. V:** 115, 130

"At the End of the Curse, a Blessing" (Verducci), **Supp. XXII:** 209

At the End of the Open Road (Simpson), **Supp. IX:** 265, 269, **271–273,** 277

At the End of This Summer: Poems 1948–1954, **Supp. XII:** 211

"At the End of War" (Eberhart), **I:** 522–523

"At the Executed Murderer's Grave" (Wright), **Supp. III Part 2:** 595, 597

"At the Fishhouses" (Bishop), **Retro. Supp. II:** 45; **Supp. I Part 1:** 90, 92

"At the Flyfisher's Shack"(Lea), **Supp. XXVIII:** 135

At the Gates of the Animal Kingdom (Hempel), **Supp. XXI:** 115, **122–124**

"At the Grave of My Guardian Angel: St. Louis Cemetery, New Orleans" (Levis), **Supp. XI:** 268–269

"At the Gym" (Doty), **Supp. XI:** 135

"At the Indian Store" (McCarriston), **Supp. XIV:** 271

"At the Lake" (Oliver), **Supp. VII:** 244

"At the Landing" (Welty), **IV:** 265–266; **Retro. Supp. I:** 348

"At the Last" (Bynner), **Supp. XV:** 44

"At the Last Rites for Two Hot Rodders" (X. J. Kennedy), **Supp. XV:** 166

At the Mountains of Madness (Lovecraft), **Retro. Supp. III:** 235–236; **Supp. XXII:** 58; **Supp. XXV:** 109, 111, 114

"At the Owl Club, North Gulfport, Mississippi, 1950" (Trethewey), **Supp. XXI:** 249

At the Owl Woman Saloon (Gallagher), **Supp. XXIV:** 166, 172, 173, 174, 175–177

"At the Premiere" (Keillor), **Supp. XVI:** 167

At the Rendezvous of Victory (C. L. R. James), **Supp. XXI:** 172

At the Root of Stars (Barnes), **Supp. III Part 1:** 34

At the Sign of the Sphinx (Wells), **Supp. XXVI:** 274

"At the Site of Last Night's Fire" (Davison), **Supp. XXVI:** 69

"At the Slackening of the Tide" (Wright), **Supp. III Part 2:** 597

"At the Street Corner" (Ferry), **Supp. XXIV:** 162

"At the Tomb of Walt Whitman" (Kunitz), **Supp. III Part 1:** 262

"At the Tourist Centre in Boston" (Atwood), **Supp. XIII:** 33

"At the Town Dump" (Kenyon), **Supp. VII:** 167

"At the Worcester Museum" (Pinsky), **Supp. VI:** 251

"At the Zoo in Spain" (Major), **Supp. XXII:** 182

"Atticus Finch and the Mad Dog: Harper Lee's *To Kill a Mockingbird*" (Jones), **Supp. VIII:** 128

"Atticus Finch—Right and Wrong" (Freedman), **Supp. VIII:** 127–128

"Attic Which Is Desire, The" (W. C. Williams), **Retro. Supp. I:** 422

"At Tikal" (Bronk), **Supp. XXI:** **28–29**

"At Times in Flight: A Parable" (H. Roth), **Supp. IX:** 234

Attitudes toward History (Burke), **I:** 274

Atwan, Robert, **Supp. XVI:** 273, 277

At Weddings and Wakes (McDermott), **Supp. XVIII:** 155, **160–162,** 166

"At White River" (Haines), **Supp. XII:** 208–209

Atwood, Margaret, **Retro. Supp. III:** 253; **Supp. IV Part 1:** 252; **Supp. V:** 119; **Supp. XI:** 317; **Supp. XIII: 19–39,** 291, 306; **Supp. XXI:** 39, 42

"Atwood's Gorgon Touch" (Davey), **Supp. XIII:** 33

"Aubade" (McCarriston), **Supp. XIV:** 271

"Aubade: November" (McCarriston), **Supp. XIV:** 261–262

"Aubade of an Early Homo Sapiens" (C. Frost), **Supp. XV:** 97–98

"Aubade: Opal and Silver" (Doty), **Supp. XI:** 129

"Au Bal Musette" (Van Vechten), **Supp. II Part 2:** 735

Auchincloss, Hugh D., **Supp. IV Part 2:** 679

Auchincloss, Louis, **I:** 375; **III:** 66; **Retro. Supp. I:** 370, 373; **Supp. IV Part 1: 21–38**

"Auction" (Simic), **Supp. VIII:** 278

"Auction, The" (Crane), **I:** 411

"Auction Model 1934" (Z. Fitzgerald), **Supp. IX:** 61

Auden, W. H., **I:** 71, 381, 539; **II:** 367, 368, 371, 376, 586; **III:** 17, 134, 269, 271, 292, 476–477, 504, 527, 530, 542, 615; **IV:** 136, 138, 240, 430; **Retro. Supp. I:** 430; **Retro. Supp. II:** 183, 242, 244, 323; **Retro. Supp. III:** 241, 242; **Supp. I Part 1:** 270; **Supp. I Part 2:** 552, 610; **Supp. II Part 1: 1–28;** **Supp. III Part 1:** 2, 3, 14, 26, 60, 61, 64, 341; **Supp. III Part 2:** 591, 595; **Supp. IV Part 1:** 79, 84, 136, 225, 302, 313; **Supp. IV Part 2:** 440, 465; **Supp. IX:** 94, 287, 288; **Supp. V:** 337; **Supp. VIII:** 19, 21, 22, 23, 30, 32, 155, 190; **Supp. X:** 35, 57, 59, 115–116, 117, 118–119; **Supp. XI:** 243, 244; **Supp. XII:** 253, 264–265, 266, 269–270; **Supp. XIV:** 156, 158, 160, 162, 163; **Supp. XIX:** 147, 151; **Supp. XV:** 74, 117–118, 139, 144, 186; **Supp. XX: 138;** **Supp. XXI:** 60, 98; **Supp. XXIII:** 117, 207; **Supp. XXVIII:** 196

"Auden's OED" (McClatchy), **Supp. XII:** 264–265

"Audition" (Alvarez), **Supp. VII:** 10

Audubon, John James, **III:** 210; **IV:** 265; **Supp. IX:** 171; **Supp. XVI: 1–14**

Audubon, John Woodhouse, **Supp. XVI:** 10

Audubon, Maria Rebecca, **Supp. XVI:** 11

Audubon, Victor Gifford, **Supp. XVI:** 10

Audubon and His Journals (M. Audubon, ed.), **Supp. XVI:** 11, 12

Audubon Reader, The: The Best Writings of John James Audubon (Sanders, ed.), **Supp. XVI:** 269

Audubon's Wildlife (Teale, ed.), **Supp. XXVIII:** 249

Auer, Jane. *See* Bowles, Jane

Auerbach, Eric, **III:** 453

Auerbach, Nina, **Supp. I Part 1:** 40

"August" (Oliver), **Supp. VII:** 235

"August" (Rich), **Supp. I Part 2:** 564

August, Timothy K., **Supp. XXVI:** 210, 211

"August 1968" (Auden), **Supp. II Part 1:** 25

"August 2026: There Will Come Soft Rains" (Bradbury), **Supp. XXVII:** 295

"August Darks, The" (Clampitt), **Supp. IX:** 43, **50–51,** 52

Augustine, Saint, **I:** 279, 290; **II:** 537; **III:** 259, 270, 292, 300; **IV:** 69, 126; **Retro. Supp. I:** 247; **Supp. VIII:** 203; **Supp. XI:** 245; **Supp. XIII:** 89; **Supp. XXI:** 83; **Supp. XXII:** 92–93

August Snow (Price), **Supp. VI:** 264

August Wilson: The Ground on Which I Stand (television documentary), **Retro. Supp. III:** 313, 319

"Au Jardin" (Pound), **III:** 465–466

Aunt Amity's Silver Wedding and Other Stories (Stuart), **Supp. XXVIII:** 235

Aunt Carmen's Book of Practical Saints (Mora), **Supp. XIII: 227–229**

"Aunt Cynthy Dallett" (Jewett), **II:** 393

"Aunt Gladys" (Karr), **Supp. XI:** 241

"Aunt Granny Lith" (Offutt), **Supp. XIX:** 165, 166

"Aunties, The" (Lamott), **Supp. XX: 141**

"Aunt Imogen" (Robinson), **III:** 521

"Aunt Jemima of the Ocean Waves" (Hayden), **Supp. II Part 1:** 368, 379

"Aunt Jennifer's Tigers" (Rich), **Retro. Supp. III:** 242–243; **Supp. XV:** 252

Aunt Jo's Scrapbooks (Alcott), **Supp. I Part 1:** 43

"Aunt Mary" (Oliver), **Supp. VII:** 232

"Aunt Mary" (Stowe), **Supp. I Part 2:** 587

"Aunt Moon's Young Man" (Hogan), **Supp. IV Part 1:** 400

"Aunt Rectita's Good Friday" (X. J. Kennedy), **Supp. XV:** 166

"Aunt Sarah" (R. Lowell), **II:** 554

"Aunt Sue's Stories" (Hughes), **Retro. Supp. I:** 197, 199

"Aunt Violet's Canadian Honeymoon/ 1932" (Shields), **Supp. VII:** 311

"Aunt Violet's Things" (Shields), **Supp. VII:** 311–312

"Aurelia: Moon Jellies" (Mora), **Supp. XIII:** 224

"Aurelio" (Di Piero), **Supp. XIX:** 38

Au revoir les enfants (film, Malle), **Supp. XXIII:** 122

Aurora 7 (Mallon), **Supp. XIX:** 132, **135–136**

Aurora Dawn (Wouk), **Supp. XXV:** 255, 258

Aurora Leigh (E. Browning), **Retro. Supp. I:** 33; **Supp. XI:** 197

Aurora Means Dawn (Sanders), **Supp. XVI:** 268

Auroras of Autumn, The (Stevens), **Retro. Supp. I:** 297, 300, **309–312**

"Auroras of Autumn, The" (Stevens), **Retro. Supp. I:** 311, 312; **Supp. III Part 1:** 12

Auschwitz: the Nazis and the "Final Solution" (television documentary), **Supp. XVII:** 40

Auslander, Joseph, **Supp. XIV:** 120

"Auspex" (Frost), **Retro. Supp. I:** 122

"Auspex" (J. R. Lowell), **Supp. I Part 2:** 424

Austen, Jane, **I:** 130, 339, 375, 378; **II:** 272, 278, 287, 568–569, 577; **IV:** 8; **Retro. Supp. I:** 354; **Supp. I Part 1:** 267; **Supp. I Part 2:** 656, 715; **Supp. IV Part 1:** 300; **Supp. IX:** 128; **Supp. VIII:** 125, 167; **Supp. XII:** 310; **Supp. XV:** 338; **Supp. XX: 108; Supp. XXII:** 206; **Supp. XXVI:** 130; **Supp. XXVII:** 187

Austenfeld, Thomas, **Supp. XXIV:** 64

Auster, Paul, **Supp. XII: 21–39; Supp. XIV:** 292; **Supp. XXI:** 20; **Supp. XXVII:** 26

Austerities (Simic), **Supp. VIII: 276–278,** 283

"Austerities" (Simic), **Supp. VIII:** 277

"Austerity Measures" (Stallings), **Supp. XXV:** 221

"Austerity Measures: A Letter from Greece" (Stallings), **Supp. XXV:** 221, 224, 225

Austin, Mary Hunter, **Retro. Supp. I:** 7; **Supp. IV Part 2:** 503; **Supp. X:** 29; **Supp. XIII:** 154; **Supp. XXVI:** 31; **Supp. XXVIII:** 251, 253

"Authentic Unconscious, The" (Trilling), **Supp. III Part 2:** 512

Author and Agent: Eudora Welty and Diarmuid Russell (Kreyling), **Retro. Supp. I:** 342, 345, 347, 349–350

"Author at Sixty, The" (Wilson), **IV:** 426

"Authority"(Lea), **Supp. XXVIII:** 137

"Author of 'Beltraffio,' The" (James), **Retro. Supp. I:** 227

"Author's Explanation, The" (Larsen), **Supp. XVIII:** 131

"Author's House" (Fitzgerald), **Retro. Supp. I:** 98

"Author's Reading in Simpkinsville, The"(Stuart), **Supp. XXVIII:** 229

"Author's Reflections, An: Willie Loman, Walter Younger, and He Who Must Live" (Hansberry), **Supp. IV Part 1:** 370

"Author to Her Book, The" (Bradstreet), **Retro. Supp. III:** 4, 8; **Supp. I Part 1:** 119; **Supp. V:** 117–118; **Supp. XV:** 125–126

"Autism Poem #20: The Knot Garden"(Crooker), **Supp. XXIII:** 56–57

"Autobiographical Note" (H. Miller), **III:** 174–175

"Autobiographical Notes" (Baldwin), **Supp. I Part 1:** 54

"Autobiographical Notes" (Holmes), **Supp. I Part 1:** 301

"Autobiographic Chapter, An" (Bourne), **I:** 236

Autobiography (Franklin), **II:** 102, 103, 108, 121–122, 302

Autobiography (James), **I:** 462

"Autobiography" (MacLeish), **III:** 20

Autobiography (Van Buren), **III:** 473

Autobiography (W. C. Williams), **Supp. I Part 1:** 254

Autobiography (Zukofsky), **Supp. III Part 2:** 627

Autobiography by Jesus of Nazareth (Pettis), **Supp. XXIII:** 189

"Autobiography"(Dybek), **Supp. XXIII:** 78

"Autobiography in the Shape of a Book Review" (Bynner), **Supp. XV:** 40

"Autobiography of a Confluence, The" (Gunn Allen), **Supp. IV Part 1:** 321

Autobiography of a Family Photo (Woodson), **Supp. XXVIII:** 283–284

Autobiography of Alice B. Toklas, The (Stein), **IV:** 26, 30, 35, 43; **Supp. IV Part 1:** 11, 81; **Supp. XXVIII:** 260

Autobiography of an Ex-Colored Man, The (J. W. Johnson), **Supp. II Part 1:** 33, 194; **Supp. XVIII:** 127; **Supp. XXII:** 7

Autobiography of a Schizophrenic Girl (Renée), **Supp. XVI:** 64, 66

Autobiography of a Thief, The (Hapgood), **Supp. XVII:** 96, 101–102

Autobiography of Benjamin Franklin (Franklin), **Supp. IV Part 1:** 5

Autobiography of LeRoi Jones, The (Baraka), **Retro. Supp. I:** 411

Autobiography of Malcolm X (Little), **Supp. I Part 1:** 66; **Supp. X:** 27; **Supp. XIII:** 264; **Supp. XXII:** 95

Autobiography of Mark Twain, The (Twain), **IV:** 209

Autobiography of My Dead Brother (Myers), **Supp. XXVII:** 204–205

Autobiography of My Mother, The (Kincaid), **Supp. VII:** 182, 188–190, 191, 192, 193

Autobiography of Red: A Novel in Verse (Carson), **Supp. XII:** 97, **106–110**

Autobiography of Upton Sinclair, The (Sinclair), **Supp. V:** 276, 282

Autobiography of W. E. B. Du Bois, The (Du Bois), **Supp. II Part 1:** 159, 186

Autobiography of William Carlos Williams, The (W. C. Williams), **Retro. Supp. I:** 51, 428

Autocrat of the Breakfast-Table, The (Holmes), **Supp. I Part 1:** 306–307

"Autographic Disclosures and Genealogies of Desire in Alison Bechdel's *Fun*

Home" (Watson), **Supp. XXV:** 8

"Automatic Gate, The" (Southern), **Supp. XI:** 294

"Automotive Passacaglia" (H. Miller), **III:** 186

"Autopsy Room, The" (Carver), **Supp. III Part 1:** 137

"Auto Wreck" (Shapiro), **Supp. II Part 2:** 706

"Autre Temps" (Wharton), **IV:** 320, 324

"Autumn" (Berrigan), **Supp. XXIV:** 37

"Autumn, Mist" (Hull), **Supp. XXI:** 133

Autumn Across America (Teale), **Supp. XXVIII:** 249

"Autumn Afternoon" (Farrell), **II:** 45

"Autumnal" (Eberhart), **I:** 540–541

"Autumn Begins in Martins Ferry, Ohio" (Wright), **Supp. III Part 2:** 599

"Autumn Courtship, An" (Caldwell), **I:** 309

"Autumn Equinox" (Skloot), **Supp. XX:** 202

Autumn Garden, The (Hellman), **Supp. I Part 1:** 285–286, 290

"Autumn Garden, The: Mechanics and Dialectics" (Felheim), **Supp. I Part 1:** 297

"Autumn Holiday, An" (Jewett), **II:** 391; **Retro. Supp. II:** 140–141

"Autumn Musings" (Harte), **Supp. II Part 1:** 336

"Autumn of the Revolutionary, The"(Goldman), **Supp. XXV:** 54–55

"Autumn's Day" (Rilke; Berrigan, trans.), **Supp. XXIV:** 37

Autumn Spring (Pickering), **Supp. XXI:** 204–205, 206

"Autumn Within" (Longfellow), **II:** 499

"Autumn Woods" (Bryant), **Supp. I Part 1:** 164

Autum of the Patriarch, The (García Márquez), **Supp. XXIV:** 89

"Au Vieux Jardin" (Aldington), **Supp. I Part 1:** 257

"Aux Imagistes" (W. C. Williams), **Supp. I Part 1:** 266

Available World, The (Monson), **Supp. XXIV:** 230, **239–240**, 241

Avakian, Aram, **Supp. XI:** 294, 295, 309

Avalanche (Boyle), **Supp. XXIV:** 62

Avalanche, The (Atherton), **Supp. XXIV:** 24–25

"Ave Atque Vale" (Bynner), *Supp. XV:* 49

Avedon, Richard, **Supp. I Part 1:** 58; **Supp. V:** 194; **Supp. X:** 15

Aveling, Edward, **Supp. XVI:** 85

"Avenue" (Pinsky), **Supp. VI:** 248

Avenue Bearing the Initial of Christ into the New World: Poems 1946–1964 (Kinnell), **Supp. III Part 1:** 235, 239–241

"Avenue of the Americas" (Simic), **Supp. VIII:** 278

"Average Torture" (Karr), **Supp. XI:** 243

Avery, George C., **Supp. XX: 84**

Avery, John, **Supp. I Part 1:** 153

"Avey" (Toomer), **Supp. IX:** 317

Avi, **Supp. XXVII:** 212

Avon's Harvest (Robinson), **III:** 510

Awake and Sing! (Odets), **Supp. II Part 2:** 530, 531, 536–538, 550; **Supp. IV Part 2:** 587

"Awake at Midnight"(Schott), **Supp. XXIII:** 246

Awake in Spain (O'Hara), **Supp. XXIII:** 216

Awakening, The (Chopin), **Retro. Supp. I:** 10; **Retro. Supp. II:** 57, 59, 60, 67, **68–71**, 73; **Supp. I Part 1:** 200, 201, 202, 211, 220–225; **Supp. V:** 304; **Supp. VIII:** 198; **Supp. XII:** 170; **Supp. XXVIII:** 225

Awakening Land, The (Richter), **Supp. XVIII:** 207, 215

Away from Her (film), **Supp. XXVII:** 193

"Awful German Language, The" (Twain), **Retro. Supp. III:** 268

Awful Rowing Toward God, The (Sexton), **Supp. II Part 2:** 694–696

Awiakta, Marilou, **Supp. IV Part 1:** 319, 335

Awkward Age, The (James), **II:** 332; **Retro. Supp. I:** 229, **230–231**

Axe Handles (Snyder), **Supp. VIII: 303–305**

Axel's Castle: A Study in the Imaginative Literature of 1870 to 1930 (Wilson), **I:** 185; **II:** 577; **IV:** 428, 431, 438, 439, 443; **Supp. VIII:** 101

"Ax-Helve, The" (Frost), **Retro. Supp. I:** 133

Azikewe, Nnamdi, **Supp. IV Part 1:** 361

"Aztec Angel" (Salinas), **Supp. XIII:** 314

Aztec Treasure House, The: New and Selected Essays (Connell), **Supp. XIV:** 80, 97

B

"Bab, the Sub-Deb" (Rinehart), **Supp. XXV:** 195

Babbitt (Lewis), **II:** 442, 443–445, 446, 447, 449; **III:** 63–64, 394; **IV:** 326

Babbitt, Irving, **I:** 247; **II:** 456; **III:** 315, 461, 613; **IV:** 439; **Retro. Supp. I:** 55; **Supp. I Part 2:** 423

Babcock, Elisha, **Supp. II Part 1:** 69

Babel, Isaac, **IV:** 1; **Supp. IX:** 260; **Supp. XII:** 308–309; **Supp. XVII:** 41; **Supp. XXIII:** 68

Babel, Isaak, **Supp. XIV:** 83, 84

Babel to Byzantium (Dickey), **Supp. IV Part 1:** 177, 185

Baber, Asa, **Supp. XXIII:** 52

Baber, Bob Henry, **Supp. XXIII:** 39

Babeuf, François, **Supp. I Part 2:** 518

"Babies, The" (Strand), **Supp. IV Part 2:** 625

Babouk (Endore), **Supp. XVII:** 56–57, 61, **64**

Baby, Come on Inside (Wagoner), **Supp. IX: 335**

"Baby, The" (Barthelme), **Supp. IV Part 1:** 49

Baby Doll (T. Williams), **IV:** 383, 386, 387, 389, 395

"Baby Face" (Sandburg), **III:** 584

"Babylon Revisited" (Fitzgerald), **II:** 95; **Retro. Supp. I:** 109

"Baby or the Botticelli, The" (Gass), **Supp. VI:** 92

"Baby Pictures of Famous Dictators" (Simic), **Supp. VIII:** 276

"Baby's Breath" (Bambara), **Supp. XI:** 15, 16

"Babysitter, The" (Coover), **Supp. V:** 43–44

Baby Sweet's (Andrews), **Supp. XXVI:** 7–9, 12, 14

"Baby Villon" (Levine), **Supp. V:** 182

Baby with the Bathwater (Durang), **Supp. XXIV: 121–122**

Bacall, Lauren, **Supp. IV Part 1:** 130

"Baccalaureate" (MacLeish), **III:** 4

Bacchae, The (Euripides), **Supp. VIII:** 182

Bach, Caleb, **Supp. XXV:** 53

Bach, Johann Sebastian, **Supp. I Part 1:** 363; **Supp. III Part 2:** 611, 612, 619

Bachardy, Don, **Supp. XIV:** 166, 170, 172, 173

Bache, Richard, **Supp. I Part 2:** 504

Bachelard, Gaston, **Supp. XIII:** 225; **Supp. XVI:** 292

"Bachelor Girl, The" (Boyce), **Supp. XXI:** 3

Bachelor Girls (Wasserstein), **Supp. XV: 327–328**, 332

Bachman, John, **Supp. XVI:** 10, 11

Bachmann, Ingeborg, **Supp. IV Part 1:** 310; **Supp. VIII:** 272

Bachofen, J. J., **Supp. I Part 2:** 560, 567

Back Bog Beast Bait (Shepard), **Supp. III Part 2:** 437, 438

Backbone (C. Bly), **Supp. XVI: 34–36**, 37, 40, 41

Back Country, The (Snyder), **Supp. VIII: 296–299**

"Back from the Argentine" (Leopold), **Supp. XIV:** 186

"Background with Revolutionaries" (MacLeish), **III:** 14–15

"Back in the Saddle Again" (Swados), **Supp. XIX:** 259

Back in the World (Wolff), **Supp. VII:** 344, 345

"Back in Tulsa Again" (Brainard), **Supp. XXVII:** 25

Backis, Charles, **Supp. XXI:** 195

"Backlash Blues, The" (Hughes), **Supp. I Part 1:** 343

"Backlash of Kindness, A" (Nye), **Supp. XIII:** 285, 286

"Backslider, The" (R. Fisher), **Supp. XIX:** 70, 71

"Back Street Guy" (Halliday), **Supp. XIX:** 88

Back to China (Fiedler), **Supp. XIII: 102–103**

Back to Methuselah (Shaw), **IV:** 64

"Backwacking: A Plea to the Senator" (Ellison), **Retro. Supp. II:** 126; **Supp. II Part 1:** 248

Backward Glance, A (Wharton), **Retro. Supp. I:** 360, 363, 366, 378, 380, 382; **Retro. Supp. III:** 276; **Supp. XX:** 229; **Supp. XXVI:** 271

"Backward Glance o'er Travel'd Roads, A" (Whitman), **IV:** 348

Bacon, Francis, **II:** 1, 8, 11, 15–16, 111; **III:** 284; **Retro. Supp. I:** 247; **Supp. I Part 1:** 310; **Supp. I Part 2:** 388; **Supp. IX:** 104; **Supp. XIV:** 22, 210

Bacon, Helen, **Supp. X:** 57

Bacon, Katie, **Supp. XXII:** 207; **Supp. XXIII:** 275

Bacon, Leonard, **II:** 530; **Supp. XXII:** 273

Bacon, Roger, **IV:** 69

"Bacterial War, The" (Nemerov), **III:** 272

Bad and the Beautiful, The (film), **Supp. XVIII:** 250

Bad Boy: A Memoir (Myers), **Supp. XXVII:** 209, 210

Bad Boy Brawly Brown (Mosley), **Supp. XIII:** 237, 239, 240–241

Bad Boys (Cisneros), **Supp. VII:** 58

"Bad Company" (Gallagher), **Supp. XXIV:** 174, 176

"Bad Dream" (Taylor), **Supp. V:** 320

Badè, William Frederic, **Supp. IX:** 178

"Badeye" (Rash), **Supp. XXVII:** 216–217

"Bad Fisherman, The" (Wagoner), **Supp. IX:** 328

Bad for Each Other (film), **Supp. XIII:** 174

"Badger" (Clare), **II:** 387

Badger, A. G., **Supp. I Part 1:** 356

"Badger and the Bear, The" (Zitkala-Ša), **Supp. XXV:** 275

Bad Government and Silly Literature (C. Bly), **Supp. XVI:** 37, 38, 40

Badlands (film; Malick), **Supp. XV:** 351

"Bad Lay" (McCarriston), **Supp. XIV:** 267

Badley, Linda, **Supp. V:** 148

Bad Man, A (Elkin), **Supp. VI:** 47

Bad Man Ballad (Sanders), **Supp. XVI:** 268

Bad Man Blues: A Portable George Garrett (Garrett), **Supp. VII:** 111

"Bad Music, The" (Jarrell), **II:** 369

"Bad People" (Halliday), **Supp. XIX:** 90, 91

"Bad Summer on K2, A" (Krakauer and Child), **Supp. XVIII:** 107, 108

"Bad Woman, A" (Fante), **Supp. XI:** 165

Baeck, Leo, **Supp. V:** 260

Baecker, Diann L., **Supp. VIII:** 128

Baer, Barbara L., **Supp. XXVIII:** 6, 11, 17

Baer, William, **Supp. XIII:** 112, 118, 129; **Supp. XXIII:** 124

Baez, Joan, **Supp. IV Part 1:** 200; **Supp. VIII:** 200, 202; **Supp. XVIII:** 24, 25–26, 27

Bag of Bones (King), **Supp. V:** 139, 148, 151

"Bagpipe Music" (MacNeice), **Supp. X:** 117

"Bahá'í Faith: Only Church in World That Does Not Discriminate" (Locke), **Supp. XIV:** 200

Bahá'u'lláh, **Supp. XX:** 117, 121, 122

"Bahá'u'lláh in the Garden of Ridwan" (Hayden), **Supp. II Part 1:** 370, 378

Bahr, David, **Supp. XV:** 66

Bahr, Thomas, **Supp. XXII:** 206, 214

"Bailbondsman, The" (Elkin), **Supp. VI:** 49, **50,** 58

Bailey, Gamaliel, **Supp. I Part 2:** 587, 590

Bailey, Peter, **Supp. XVI:** 69

Bailey, William, **Supp. IV Part 2:** 631, 634

Bailey's Café (Naylor), **Supp. VIII:** 226–228

Bailyn, Bernard, **Supp. I Part 2:** 484, 506

Bair, Deirdre, **Supp. X:** 181, 186, 187, 188, 192, 194, 195, 196, 197

Baird, Linnett, **Supp. XII:** 299

Baird, Peggy, **I:** 385, 401

Baiting the Void (Schott), **Supp. XXIII:** 247–248

Bakan, David, **I:** 59

Baker, Carlos, **II:** 259

Baker, Chet, **Supp. XXI:** 131

Baker, David, **Supp. IX:** 298; **Supp. XI:** 121, 142, 153; **Supp. XII:** 175, 191–192; **Supp. XIX:** 115; **Supp. XXVIII:** 29

Baker, George Pierce, **III:** 387; **IV:** 453, 455; **Supp. XXVIII:** 68

Baker, Gladys, **Supp. XIV:** 121

Baker, Houston, **Supp. XXII:** 6

Baker, Houston A., Jr., **Retro. Supp. II:** 121; **Retro. Supp. III:** 184; **Supp. IV Part 1:** 365; **Supp. X:** 324

Baker, Jeff, **Supp. XXIV:** 166, 178

Baker, Katherine, **Supp. XX:** 69

Baker, Kevin, **Supp. XIV:** 96

Baker, Mabel, **Supp. XVIII:** 259, 263, 266–267, 269

Baker, Nicholson, **Supp. XIII:** 41–57

Baker, Robert, **Supp. XVI:** 288, 290

Bakerman, Jane S., **Supp. IV Part 2:** 468

Bakhtin, Mikhail, **Retro. Supp. II:** 273; **Retro. Supp. III:** 138; **Supp. IV Part 1:** 301; **Supp. X:** 120, 239; **Supp. XXII:** 259

Bakst, Léon, **Supp. IX:** 66

Bakunin, Mikhail Aleksandrovich, **IV:** 429

Balaban, John, **Supp. XIX:** 281

Balakian, Anna, **Supp. XXIII:** 20

Balakian, Diran, **Supp. XXIII:** 28

Balakian, Grigoris, **Supp. XXIII:** 28, 29–32

Balakian, Jan, **Supp. XV:** 327

Balakian, Nona, **Supp. XXIII:** 20

Balakian, Peter, **Supp. XXIII:** 19–34

"Balance" (Bierds), **Supp. XVII:** 31

"Balance" (Nelson), **Supp. XVIII:** 174–175

Balbo, Ned, **Supp. XIX:** 161; **Supp. XVII:** 120

Balbuena, Bernado de, **Supp. V:** 11

Balch, Emily Greene, **Supp. I Part 1:** 25

Balcony, The (Genet), **I:** 84

Balcony Stories (King), **Supp. XXVIII:** 115–116, 122, 124

Bald Soprano, The (Ionesco), **I:** 74

Baldwin, David, **Supp. I Part 1:** 47, 48, 49, 50, 51, 54, 65, 66

Baldwin, James, **Retro. Supp. II:** 1–17; **Retro. Supp. III:** 194; **Supp. I Part 1:** 47–71, 337, 341; **Supp. II Part 1:** 40; **Supp. III Part 1:** 125; **Supp. IV Part 1:** 1, 10, 11, 163, 369; **Supp. V:** 201; **Supp. VIII:** 88, 198, 235, 349; **Supp. X:** 136, 324; **Supp. XI:** 288, 294; **Supp. XIII:** 46, 111, 181, 186, 294; **Supp. XIV:** 54, 71, 73, 306; **Supp. XVI:** 135, 141, 143; **Supp. XVIII:** 25; **Supp. XX:** 147; **Supp. XXI:** 245; **Supp. XXIV:** 185; **Supp. XXVII:** 201

Baldwin, Joseph G., **Retro. Supp. III:** 259

Baldwin, Kara, **Supp. XXVII:** 216

Baldwin, Samuel, **Supp. I Part 1:** 48

Bales, Jack, **Supp. XXVII:** 100, 106

Balint, Benjamin, **Supp. XXVII:** 134

Balitas, Vincent D., **Supp. XVI:** 222; **Supp. XXVI:** 149

Balkian, Nona, **Supp. XI:** 230

Balkun, Mary McAleer, **Supp. XX:** 281

Ball, Gordon, **Supp. XIV:** 148

Ball, John, **Supp. XV:** 202

"Ballad: Between the Box Cars" (Warren), **IV:** 245

"Ballade" (MacLeish), **III:** 4

"Ballade at Thirty-Five" (Parker), **Supp. IX:** 192

"Ballade for the Duke of Orléans" (Wilbur), **Supp. III Part 2:** 556

"Ballade of Broken Flutes, The" (Robinson), **III:** 505

"Ballade of Meaty Inversions" (White), **Supp. I Part 2:** 676

"Ballad of a Thin Man" (song, Dylan), **Supp. XVIII:** 30, 31

"Ballad of Aunt Geneva, The" (Nelson), **Supp. XVIII:** 175

"Ballad of Billie Potts, The" (Warren), **IV:** 241–242, 243, 253

"Ballad of Carmilhan, The" (Longfellow), **II:** 505

"ballad of chocolate Mabbie, the" (Brooks), **Supp. IV Part 1:** 15

"Ballad of Dead Ladies, The" (Villon), **Retro. Supp. I:** 286

Ballad of Dingus Magee, The (Markson), **Supp. XVII:** 139, 141

"Ballad of East and West, The" (Kipling), **Supp. IX:** 246; **Supp. XX:** 23

"Ballad of Jesse Neighbours, The" (Humphrey), **Supp. IX:** 100

"Ballad of Jesus of Nazareth, A" (Masters), **Supp. I Part 2:** 459

"Ballad of John Cable and Three Gentlemen" (Merwin), **Supp. III Part 1:** 342

"Ballad of Larry and Club" (Jarman), **Supp. XVII:** 115

"Ballad of Nat Turner, The" (Hayden), **Supp. II Part 1:** 378

"Ballad of Pearl May Lee, The" (Brooks), **Supp. III Part 1:** 74, 75

"Ballad of Plastic Fred, The" (Gansworth), **Supp. XXVI:** 104

Ballad of Remembrance, A (Hayden), **Supp. II Part 1:** 367

"Ballad of Remembrance, A" (Hayden), **Supp. II Part 1:** 368, 372, 373

"Ballad of Ruby, The" (Sarton), **Supp. VIII:** 259–260

"Ballad of San Isidro, The" (Espaillat), **Supp. XXI:** 108
"Ballad of Sue Ellen Westerfield, The" (Hayden), **Supp. II Part 1:** 364
Ballad of the Brown Girl, The (Cullen), **Supp. IV Part 1:** 167, 168, 169–170, 173
"Ballad of the Brown Girl, The" (Cullen), **Supp. IV Part 1:** 168
"Ballad of the Children of the Czar, The" (Schwartz), **Supp. II Part 2:** 649
"Ballad of the Girl Whose Name Is Mud" (Hughes), **Retro. Supp. I:** 205
"Ballad of the Goodly Fere", **III:** 458
"Ballad of the Harp-Weaver" (Millay), **III:** 135
"Ballad of the Sad Cafe, The" (McCullers), **II:** 586, 587, 588, 592, 595, 596–600, 604, 605, 606
"Ballad of the Sixties" (Sarton), **Supp. VIII:** 259
"Ballad of Trees and the Master, A" (Lanier), **Supp. I Part 1:** 370
"Ballad of Typical Lovers" (Taggard), **Supp. XXII:** 277
"Ballad of William Sycamore, The" (Benét), **Supp. XI:** 44, 47
Ballads and Other Poems (Longfellow), **II:** 489; **III:** 412, 422; **Retro. Supp. II:** 157, 168
Ballads for Sale (A. Lowell), **II:** 527
"Ballads of Lenin" (Hughes), **Supp. I Part 1:** 331
Ballantyne, Sheila, **Supp. V:** 70
Ballard, J. G., **Supp. XVI:** 123, 124; **Supp. XVIII:** 136
Ballard, Josephine. *See* McMurtry, Josephine
Ballard, Sandra, **Supp. XXVIII:** 2, 3, 8, 11
"Ballena" (Mora), **Supp. XIII:** 224
"Ballet in Numbers for Mary Ellen, A" (Karr), **Supp. XI:** 241
"Ballet of a Buffoon, The" (Sexton), **Supp. II Part 2:** 693
"Ballet of Central Park, The" (Boyle), **Supp. XXIV:** 59
"Ballet of the Fifth Year, The" (Schwartz), **Supp. II Part 2:** 650
Ball Four (Bouton), **Supp. XX: 274**
"Ball Game, The" (Creeley), **Supp. IV Part 1:** 140
Ballistics (Collins), **Supp. XXI:** 57, 65
"Ballistics" (Collins), **Supp. XXI:** 65
"Balloon Hoax, The" (Poe), **III:** 413, 420; **Retro. Supp. III:** 226, 230–231
Balloonists, The (Biss), **Supp. XXVI:** 45, 48–50
Balmer, Randall, **Supp. XXVIII:** 62
"Balm of Recognition, The: Rectifying Wrongs through Generations" (E. Hoffman, lecture), **Supp. XVI:** 155
Balo (Toomer), **Supp. III Part 2:** 484
Balsan, Consuelo, **IV:** 313–314
Balthus, **Supp. IV Part 2:** 623
Balthus Poems, The (Dobyns), **Supp. XIII:** 87
Baltimore, Lord, **I:** 132
Balzac, Honoré de, **I:** 103, 123, 339, 376, 474, 485, 499, 509, 518; **II:** 307, 322,

324, 328, 336, 337; **III:** 61, 174, 184, 320, 382; **IV:** 192; **Retro. Supp. I:** 91, 217, 218, 235; **Retro. Supp. II:** 93; **Supp. I Part 2:** 647; **Supp. XVI:** 72
Bambara, Toni Cade, **Retro. Supp. III:** 184, 194; **Supp. XI: 1–23**
Bam opgrunt (At the abyss) (Asch), **Supp. XXIII:** 6
Banana Book, The (Brainard), **Supp. XXVII:** 20, 27–28
Banana Bottom (McKay), **Supp. X:** 132, **139–140**
Bananas (film; Allen), **Supp. XV:** 3, 4
Banaras: City of Light (Eck), **Supp. XXVIII:** 49, 50–52, 54, 58
Bancal, Jean, **Supp. I Part 2:** 514
Bancroft, George, **I:** 544; **Supp. I Part 2:** 479; **Supp. XXII:** 33
Band, Millen, **Supp. XVIII:** 238
Bandaged Nude, The (Ryan as Finnegan), **Supp. XVIII:** 233, **235–236**
"Bandages" (Davison), **Supp. XXVI:** 72
Bandbox (Mallon), **Supp. XIX:** 132, 143
Band of Angels (Warren), **IV:** 245, 254–255
Bandung Files (television series), **Supp. XXI:** 170
Bang the Drum Slowly (Harris), **II:** 424–425
Banjo: A Story without a Plot (McKay), **Supp. X:** 132, **138–139**
"Banjo Song, A" (Dunbar), **Supp. II Part 1:** 197
Bank Director's Son, The: A Real and Intensely Interesting Revelation of City Life (Lippard), **Supp. XXIII:** 184
Bankhead, Tallulah, **IV:** 357; **Supp. IV Part 2:** 574
"Banking Potatoes" (Komunyakaa), **Supp. XIII:** 126
"Bank of England Restriction, The" (Adams), **I:** 4
Banks, Carolyn, **Supp. XXVI:** 9
Banks, Joanne Trautmann, **Supp. XIII:** 297
Banks, Russell, **Supp. IX:** 153; **Supp. V: 1–19,** 227; **Supp. X:** 85; **Supp. XI:** 178; **Supp. XII:** 295, 309, 343; **Supp. XX: 90; Supp. XXIV:** 97
"Banned Poem" (Nye), **Supp. XIII:** 282
Bannon, Barbara, **Supp. XI:** 228
"Banyan" (Swenson), **Supp. IV Part 2:** 651, 652
"Baptism" (Olsen). *See* "O Yes" (Olsen)
"Baptism" (Trethewey), **Supp. XXI:** 246
Baptism, The (Baraka), **Supp. II Part 1:** 40, 41–42, 43
Baptism of Desire (Erdrich), **Supp. IV Part 1:** 259
Barabtarlo, Gennady, **Retro. Supp. I:** 278
Baraka, Imamu Amiri (LeRoi Jones), **Retro. Supp. I:** 411; **Retro. Supp. II:** 280; **Retro. Supp. III:** 316, 317; **Supp. I Part 1:** 63; **Supp. II Part 1: 29–63,** 247, 250; **Supp. III Part 1:** 83; **Supp. IV Part 1:** 169, 244, 369; **Supp. VIII:** 295, 329, 330, 332; **Supp. X:** 324, 328; **Supp. XIII:** 94; **Supp. XIV:** 125, 144; **Supp. XXI:** 172, 227,

228; **Supp. XXIII:** 215; **Supp. XXIV:** 34, 183; **Supp. XXVII:** 18, 22, 160, 161, 166; **Supp. XXVIII:** 260
"Bar at the Andover Inn, The" (Matthews), **Supp. IX:** 168
"Barbados" (Marshall), **Supp. XI:** 281
"Barbara Frietchie" (Whittier), **Supp. I Part 2:** 695–696
Barbarella (film), **Supp. XI:** 293, **307–308**
"Barbarian Status of Women, The" (Veblen), **Supp. I Part 2:** 636–637
Barbarous Coast, The (Macdonald), **Supp. IV Part 2:** 472, 474
Barbary Shore (Mailer), **III:** 27, 28, 30–31, 33, 35, 36, 40, 44; **Retro. Supp. II: 199–200,** 207; **Supp. XIV:** 162
Barber, Charles, **Supp. XXIII:** 125
Barber, David, **Supp. IV Part 2:** 550; **Supp. XII:** 188–189
Barber, Rowland, **Supp. IV Part 2:** 581
Barber, Samuel, **Supp. IV Part 1:** 84
"Barber's Unhappiness, The" (Saunders), **Supp. XIX:** 229
"Barclay of Ury" (Whittier), **Supp. I Part 2:** 693
Barcott, Bruce, **Supp. XVII:** 32
Bard of Savagery, The: Thorstein Veblen and Modern Social Theory (Diggins), **Supp. I Part 2:** 650
"Barefoot Boy, The" (Whittier), **Supp. I Part 2:** 691, 699–700
Barefoot in the Park (Simon), **Supp. IV Part 2:** 575, 578–579, 586, 590
Bare Hills, The (Winters), **Supp. II Part 2:** 786, 788
"Bare Hills, The" (Winters), **Supp. II Part 2:** 790
Barely and Widely (Zukofsky), **Supp. III Part 2:** 627, 628, 635
Barenblat, Rachel, **Supp. XIII:** 274
Barfield, Owen, **III:** 274, 279
"Bargain Lost, The" (Poe), **III:** 411
Barillas, William, **Supp. XIV:** 177
Barillet, Pierre, **Supp. XVI:** 194
Barker, Arthur, **Supp. XIII:** 167
Barker, Clive, **Supp. V:** 142
Barker, Wendy, **Supp. XXVII:** 261, 263
Barking Dog (Budbill), **Supp. XIX:** 1, 5
"Barking Man" (Bell), **Supp. X:** 9
Barking Man and Other Stories (Bell), **Supp. X: 9**
Barksdale, Richard, **Retro. Supp. I:** 202, 205; **Supp. I Part 1:** 341, 346
Barlow, Joel, **Supp. I Part 1:** 124; **Supp. I Part 2:** 511, 515, 521; **Supp. II Part 1: 65–86,** 268
Barlow, Judith, **Supp. XXI:** 6
Barlow, R. H., **Supp. XXV:** 122
Barlow, Ruth Baldwin (Mrs. Joel Barlow), **Supp. II Part 1:** 69
"B.A.R. Man, The" (Yates), **Supp. XI:** 341
Barnaby Rudge (Dickens), **III:** 421
Barnacle Soup and Other Stories of the West of Ireland (Gallagher and Gray), **Supp. XXIV:** 166, 172, 178
Barnard, Frederick, **Supp. I Part 2:** 684
Barnard, Rita, **Retro. Supp. II:** 324
Barn Blind (Smiley), **Supp. VI: 292–293**

"Barn Burning" (Faulkner), **II:** 72, 73; **Retro. Supp. III:** 85; **Supp. IV Part 2:** 682; **Supp. XX:** 174

Barnes, Djuna, **Supp. III Part 1: 31–46; Supp. IV Part 1:** 79, 80; **Supp. XVI:** 282; **Supp. XXII:** 165, 167; **Supp. XXVIII:** 69

Barnes, Kate, **Supp. XXVI:** 36

Barnes, Kim, **Supp. XVIII:** 293

Barnet, Andrea, **Supp. XXII:** 159, 164

Barnett, Claudia, **Supp. XV:** 323, 330, 334

Barnett, Samuel, **Supp. I Part 1:** 2

Barn Fever (Davison), **Supp. XXVI:** 66, 75–76, 77

"Barn Fever" (Davison), **Supp. XXVI:** 75, 77

"Barn-Fox, The" (Rash), **Supp. XXVII:** 222

Barnhardt, Wilton, **Supp. XXII:** 266; **Supp. XXVII: 1–15**

"Barn Owl" (Kooser), **Supp. XIX:** 123

Barnstone, Tony, **Supp. XIII:** 115, 126

Barnstone, Willis, **Supp. I Part 2:** 458

Barnum, P. T., **Supp. I Part 2:** 703

Baro, Gene, **Supp. XXVII:** 253

Baroja, Pío, **I:** 478

Baron, Zach, **Supp. XVIII:** 150

"Baroque Comment" (Bogan), **Supp. III Part 1:** 56, 58

"Baroque Sunburst, A" (Clampitt), **Supp. IX:** 49

"Baroque Wall-Fountain in the Villa Sciarra, A" (Wilbur), **Supp. III Part 2:** 553

Barr, Robert, **I:** 409, 424

Barracks Thief, The (Wolff), **Supp. VII:** 344–345

"Barred Owl" (Offutt), **Supp. XIX:** 170

Barren Ground (Glasgow), **II:** 174, 175, 178, 179, 184–185, 186, 187, 188, 189, 191, 192, 193, 194; **Supp. X:** 228

Barrés, Auguste M., **I:** 228

Barresi, Dorothy, **Supp. XV:** 100, 102

Barrett, Amy, **Supp. XVIII:** 136

Barrett, E. B., **Supp. XV:** 309

Barrett, Elizabeth, **Supp. IV Part 2:** 430

Barrett, George, **Supp. IX:** 250

Barrett, Ralph, **Supp. I Part 2:** 462

Barrie, J. M., **Supp. XX: 234**

"Barrie Cooke Painting" (Gallagher), **Supp. XXIV:** 171

Barrier, Rober G., **Supp. XXI:** 48–49

Barrier of a Common Language: An American Looks at Contemporary British Poetry (Gioia), **Supp. XV:** 112, **116–117**

"Barriers"(Bottoms), **Supp. XXVIII:** 28

"Barroco: An Essay" (Sobin), **Supp. XVI:** 291

Barron, Jonathan, **Supp. IX:** 299

Barrow, John, **II:** 18

Barrus, Clara, **I:** 220

"Barry" (Biss), **Supp. XXVI:** 47

Barry, Iris, **Supp. XIII:** 170

Barry, Philip, **Retro. Supp. I:** 104; **Supp. IV Part 1:** 83; **Supp. V:** 95

Barstow, Elizabeth Drew. *See* Stoddard, Elizabeth

Bart, Lily, **Retro. Supp. III:** 290

Bartas, Seigneur du, **IV:** 157

"Barter" (Teasdale), **Supp. XXVII:** 290, 291

Barth, John, **I: 121–143; Supp. I Part 1:** 100; **Supp. III Part 1:** 217; **Supp. IV Part 1:** 48, 379; **Supp. IX:** 208; **Supp. V:** 39, 40; **Supp. X:** 263, 301, 302, 307; **Supp. XI:** 309; **Supp. XII:** 29, 289, 316; **Supp. XIII:** 41, 101, 104; **Supp. XVII:** 183; **Supp. XVIII:** 136, 140, 141; **Supp. XX:** 21; **Supp. XXII:** 259, 261; **Supp. XXIII:** 42; **Supp. XXVII:** 183

Barth, Karl, **III:** 40, 258, 291, 303, 309; **IV:** 225; **Retro. Supp. I:** 325, 326, 327

Barth, Robert C., **Supp. XV:** 169

Barthé, Richmond, **Retro. Supp. II:** 115

Barthelme, Donald, **Supp. IV Part 1: 39–58**, 227; **Supp. V:** 2, 39, 44; **Supp. VIII:** 75, 138; **Supp. X:** 263; **Supp. XI:** 25; **Supp. XII:** 29; **Supp. XIII:** 41, 46; **Supp. XIX:** 235; **Supp. XVI:** 206; **Supp. XXVII:** 183

Barthelme, Frederick, **Supp. XI: 25–41; Supp. XXI:** 38

Barthelme, Peter, **Supp. XI:** 25

Barthelme, Steven, **Supp. XI:** 25, 27, 37

Barthes, Roland, **Supp. IV Part 1:** 39, 119, 126; **Supp. XIII:** 83; **Supp. XVI:** 285, 294; **Supp. XVII:** 244

Bartholomew and the Oobleck (Geisel), **Supp. XVI:** 104

"Bar Time" (B. Collins), **Supp. XVII:** 245

"Bartleby, the Scrivener; A Story of Wall-Street" (Melville), **III:** 88–89; **Retro. Supp. I:** 255; **Retro. Supp. III:** 147, 149, 159

Bartleby in Manhattan and Other Essays (Hardwick), **Supp. III Part 1:** 204, 210

"Bartleby the Scrivener" (Melville), **Supp. XVIII:** 4

Bartlet, Phebe, **I:** 562

Bartlett, Lee, **Supp. VIII:** 291

Bartlett, Mary Dougherty, **Supp. IV Part 1:** 335

Bartlett, William Irving, **Supp. XXV:** 250–251

Barton, Bruce, **III:** 14; **Retro. Supp. I:** 179

Barton, Priscilla. *See* Morison, Mrs. Samuel Eliot (Priscilla Barton)

Barton, Ralph, **Supp. XVI:** 195

Barton, Rev. William E., **Retro. Supp. I:** 179

Bartov, Omer, **Supp. XVI:** 153–154

Bartram, John, **Supp. I Part 1:** 244

Bartram, William, **II:** 313; **Supp. IX:** 171; **Supp. X:** 223

Barzun, Jacques, **Supp. XIV:** 54

"Basement" (Bambara), **Supp. XI:** 5

Basement Tapes, The (album, Dylan), **Supp. XVIII:** 27, 30, 32

"Base of All Metaphysics, The" (Whitman), **IV:** 348

"Base Stealer, The" (Francis), **Supp. IX:** 82

Bashevis, Isaac. *See* Singer, Isaac Bashevis

Bashir, Antonious, **Supp. XX: 116, 120**

Basil Stories, The (Fitzgerald), **Retro. Supp. I:** 109

Basin and Range (McPhee), **Supp. III Part 1:** 309

"Basin of Eggs, A" (Swenson), **Supp. IV Part 2:** 645

"Basket" (Huddle), **Supp. XXVI:** 150

"Basket, The" (A. Lowell), **II:** 522

"Basketball and Beefeaters" (McPhee), **Supp. III Part 1:** 296

"Basketball and Poetry: The Two Richies" (Dunn), **Supp. XI:** 140

"Basketball Player" (L. Michaels), **Supp. XVI:** 209

"Basket of Trips"(Strout), **Supp. XXIII:** 283, 285

Baskin, Leonard, **Supp. X:** 58, 71; **Supp. XV:** 348

Bass, George, **Supp. XXII:** 6

Bass, Rick, **Supp. XIV:** 227; **Supp. XVI: 15–29; Supp. XXI:** 40, 45; **Supp. XXVI:** 31, 187

Bassard, Katherine Clay, **Supp. XXII:** 148

Bass Cathedral (Mackey), **Supp. XXVII:** 159

Basso, Hamilton, **Retro. Supp. I:** 80

Bastard, The (Caldwell), **I:** 291, 292, 308

"Bastille Day" (Lamott), **Supp. XX: 143**

"Bat, The" (Kenyon), **Supp. VII:** 168

Bat, The (Rinehart and Hopwood), **Supp. XXV:** 195, 200

Bataille, Georges, **Supp. VIII:** 4; **Supp. XII:** 1

"Batard" (London), **II:** 468–469

Batchelor, John Calvin, **Supp. XIX:** 142

Bate, Walter Jackson, **II:** 531; **Supp. XXVI:** 63

"Bateau ivre, Le" (Rimbaud; Berrigan, trans.), **Supp. XXIV:** 40

Bates, Arlo, **Retro. Supp. I:** 35

Bates, Blanche, **Supp. XVI:** 182

Bates, Kathy, **Supp. XIII:** 207

Bates, Lee, **Retro. Supp. II:** 46

Bates, Milton J., **Supp. XII:** 62

Bates, Sylvia Chatfield, **II:** 586

Bateson, Gregory, **Supp. XV:** 146

"Bath, The" (Carver), **Supp. III Part 1:** 144, 145

"Bath, The" (Snyder), **Supp. VIII:** 302

Bathwater Wine (Coleman), **Supp. XI:** 83, 90, **91**

Battaglia, J. F., **Supp. XXVII:** 256, 258, 263

"Batter my heart, three person'd God" (Donne), **Supp. I Part 2:** 726; **Supp. XVII:** 119

"Battle, The" (Simpson), **Supp. IX:** 268–269

Battle Cry (film), **Supp. XX: 246**

Battle Cry (Uris), **Supp. XX: 243, 246, 248–250, 255, 256**

Battlefield Where the Moon Says I Love You, The (Stanford), **Supp. XV:** 345

Battle for the Solomons (Wolfert), **Supp. XXI:** 267

Battle-Ground, The (Glasgow), **II:** 175, 176, 177, 178, 193

Battle Hymn (Gold and Blankfort), **Supp. XXVIII:** 72

"Battle Hymn of the Republic" (Sandburg), **III:** 585

"Battle Hymn of the Republic, The" (Howe), **III:** 505

"Battle Hymn of the Republic, The" (Updike), **Retro. Supp. I:** 324

Battle of Angels (T. Williams), **IV:** 380, 381, 383, 385, 386, 387

"Battle of Aspen, The" (Thompson), **Supp. XXIV:** 286–287

"Battle of Lovell's Pond, The" (Longfellow), **II:** 493

Battle of the Atlantic, The (Morison), **Supp. I Part 2:** 490

"Battle of the Baltic, The" (Campbell), **Supp. I Part 1:** 309

"Battle of the Bunker, The" (Snodgrass), **Supp. VI:** 319–320

"***Battle of the Century!!!, The***" (Goldbarth), **Supp. XII:** 193

Battle of the Little Big Horn, The (Sandoz), **Supp. XXIII:** 146

Battle-Pieces and Aspects of the War (Melville), **II:** 538–539; **III:** 92; **IV:** 350; **Retro. Supp. I:** 257

Battle-Piecs and Aspects of the War (Melville), **Retro. Supp. III:** 161

"Battler, The" (Hemingway), **II:** 248; **Retro. Supp. I:** 175

"Battle That Ended the Century, The" (Lovecraft and Barlow), **Supp. XXV:** 122

Baubles (Wells), **Supp. XXVI:** 275

"Baubles after Bombs" (Peacock), **Supp. XIX:** 200

"Baudelaire" (Schwartz), **Supp. II Part 2:** 663

Baudelaire, Charles, **I:** 58, 63, 384, 389, 420, 569; **II:** 543, 544–545, 552; **III:** 137, 141–142, 143, 409, 417, 418, 421, 428, 448, 466, 474; **IV:** 74, 79, 80, 87, 211, 286; **Retro. Supp. I:** 56, 90; **Retro. Supp. II:** 261, 262, 322, 326; **Retro. Supp. III:** 57, 60, 236; **Supp. I Part 1:** 271; **Supp. III Part 1:** 4, 6, 105; **Supp. XIII:** 77, 284; **Supp. XV:** 165; **Supp. XXI:** 228; **Supp. XXIV:** 152; **Supp. XXVI:** 39

Baudrillard, Jean, **Supp. IV Part 1:** 45

Bauer, Dale, **Retro. Supp. I:** 381

Bauer, Douglas, **Supp. XII:** 290

Baum, L. Frank, **Supp. I Part 2:** 621; **Supp. IV Part 1:** 101, 113; **Supp. XII:** 42

Baumann, Walter, **III:** 478

Bausch, Richard, **Supp. VII:** 39–56; **Supp. XVII:** 21; **Supp. XXVI:** 13

Bawer, Bruce, **Supp. IX:** 135; **Supp. VIII:** 153; **Supp. X:** 187

Baxter, Charles, **Supp. XII:** 22; **Supp. XIV:** 89, 92; **Supp. XVII:** 13–24; **Supp. XXIII:** 289

Baxter, John, **Supp. XI:** 302

Baxter, Richard, **III:** 199; **IV:** 151, 153; **Supp. I Part 2:** 683

"Baxter's Procrustes" (Chesnutt), **Supp. XIV:** 76

"Bay City Blues" (Chandler), **Supp. IV Part 1:** 129

Baylies, William, **Supp. I Part 1:** 153

Baym, Nina, **Supp. IV Part 2:** 463; **Supp. X:** 229; **Supp. XVI:** 92; **Supp. XVIII:** 258, 259; **Supp. XXIV:** 28

Bay of Angels (Wakoski), **Supp. XXVIII:** 261, 272

"Bayou" (Di Piero), **Supp. XIX:** 37

Bayou Folk (Chopin), **Retro. Supp. II:** 64–65, 73; **Supp. I Part 1:** 200, 216, 218; **Supp. XXVIII:** 116, 225

"Bayou L'Ombre"(King), **Supp. XXVIII:** 116

Baziotes, William, **Supp. XV:** 144

"B.C." (Taggard), **Supp. XXII:** 278

Beach, Anna Hampstead, **Supp. XVII:** 75

Beach, Joseph Warren, **I:** 309, 500; **II:** 27; **III:** 319

Beach, Sylvia, **IV:** 404; **Retro. Supp. I:** 109, 422; **Supp. XXII:** 165

"Beaches in Winter" (Kriegel), **Supp. XXIV:** 220, 225

"Beach Women, The" (Pinsky), **Supp. VI:** 241

"Beaded Pear, The" (Simpson), **Supp. IX:** 276

Beagle, Peter, **Supp. X:** 24

Beam, Jeffrey, **Supp. XII:** 98

Beaman, E. O., **Supp. IV Part 2:** 604

Bean, Michael, **Supp. V:** 203

Bean, Robert Bennett, **Supp. II Part 1:** 170

Bean Eaters, The (Brooks), **Supp. III Part 1:** 79–81

Be Angry at the Sun (Jeffers), **Supp. II Part 2:** 434

Bean Spasms (Berrigan, Padgett, and Brainard), **Supp. XXIV:** 41–42

"Beanstalk Country, The" (T. Williams), **IV:** 383

Bean Trees, The (Kingsolver), **Supp. VII:** 197, 199–201, 202, 207, 209

"Bear" (Hogan), **Supp. IV Part 1:** 412

Bear, The (Faulkner), **Supp. VIII:** 184

"Bear, The" (Faulkner), **II:** 71–72, 73, 228; **IV:** 203; **Supp. IV Part 2:** 434; **Supp. IX:** 95; **Supp. X:** 30; **Supp. XIV:** 32; **Supp. XXI:** 37

"Bear, The" (Kinnell), **Supp. III Part 1:** 244

"Bear, The" (Momaday), **Supp. IV Part 2:** 480, 487

Bear and His Daughter: Stories (Stone), **Supp. V:** 295, 308

"Bear Came Over the Mountain, The" (Munro), **Supp. XXVII:** 193

Beard, Charles, **I:** 214; **IV:** 429; **Supp. I Part 2:** 481, 490, 492, 632, 640, 643, 647

Beard, Dan, **Retro. Supp. III:** 266

Beard, James, **I:** 341; **Supp. XVII:** 89, 90

Beard, Mary, **Supp. I Part 2:** 481

"Bearded Oaks" (Warren), **IV:** 240

Bearden, Romare, **Retro. Supp. I:** 209; **Retro. Supp. III:** 318–319; **Supp.**

VIII: 337, 342; **Supp. XXI:** 249

"Beard of Bees, A" (X. J. Kennedy), **Supp. XV:** 171

Beardon, Romare, **Supp. XV:** 144

"Beards, The" (Lethem), **Supp. XVIII:** 148

Beardsley, Aubrey, **II:** 56; **IV:** 77

"Bearings" (Rash), **Supp. XXVII:** 218

Beaser, Robert, **Supp. XV:** 259

"Beast" (Swenson), **Supp. IV Part 2:** 639

"Beast & Burden, The: Seven Improvisations" (Komunyakaa), **Supp. XIII:** 120, 121

Beast God Forgot to Invent, The (Harrison), **Supp. VIII:** 37, 46, 51–52

Beast in Me, The (Thurber), **Supp. I Part 2:** 615

"Beast in the Jungle, The" (H. James), **I:** 570; **II:** 335; **Retro. Supp. I:** 235; **Supp. V:** 103–104; **Supp. XXVI:** 141

Beast in View (Rukeyser), **Supp. VI:** 272, 273, 279, 280

Beasts of Bethlehem, The (X. J. Kennedy), **Supp. XV:** 163

"Beat! Beat! Drums!" (Whitman), **III:** 585

Beat Down to Your Soul: What Was the Beat Generation? (Charters, ed.), **Supp. XIV:** 152

"Beatific Effigies" (Bronk), **Supp. XXI:** 31

Beaton, Cecil, **Supp. XVI:** 191

"Beatrice Palmato" (Wharton), **Retro. Supp. I:** 379; **Retro. Supp. III:** 287–288

Beats, The (Krim, ed.), **Supp. XV:** 338

Beattie, Ann, **Supp. V:** 21–37; **Supp. X:** 26; **Supp. XII:** 80, 139, 294; **Supp. XXI:** 118; **Supp. XXIII:** 289; **Supp. XXVII:** 269

Beattie, L. Elisabeth, **Supp. XX: 164, 165**

Beatty, General Sam, **I:** 193

Beaty, Jerome, **Supp. IV Part 1:** 331

"Beau Monde of Mrs. Bridge, The" (Connell), **Supp. XIV:** 88, 89

Beaumont, Francis, **Supp. I Part 2:** 422

"Beauties of Santa Cruz, The" (Freneau), **Supp. II Part 1:** 260

Beautiful and Damned, The (Fitzgerald), **II:** 88, 89–91, 93, 263; **Retro. Supp. I: 103–105,** 105, 106, 110; **Supp. IX:** 56, 57

Beautiful Changes, The (Wilbur), **Supp. III Part 2:** 544–550

"Beautiful Changes, The" (Wilbur), **Supp. III Part 2:** 549, 550

Beautiful Child (Silver), **Supp. XXIV: 273–274**

"Beautiful Child, A" (Capote), **Supp. III Part 1:** 113, 125

"Beautiful & Cruel" (Cisneros), **Supp. VII:** 63, 67

"Beautiful Gestures, The" (Huddle), **Supp. XXVI:** 154

Beautiful Losers (Cohen), **Supp. XXVII:** 51, 54, 57–58, 59

"Beautiful Wall, Machu Picchu, The" (Bronk), **Supp. XXI:** 31, 32

"Beautiful Woman Who Sings, The" (Gunn Allen), **Supp. IV Part 1:** 326

"Beauty" (Emerson), **II:** 2, 5
"Beauty" (Sanders), **Supp. XVI:** 277
"Beauty" (Wylie), **Supp. I Part 2:** 710
"Beauty and the Beast" (Dove), **Supp. IV Part 1:** 245
"Beauty and the Beast" (fairy tale), **IV:** 266; **Supp. X:** 88
"Beauty and the Shoe Sluts" (Karr), **Supp. XI:** 250
Beauty of the Husband, The: A Fictional Essay in Twenty-Nine Tangos (Carson), **Supp. XII:** 113–114
Beauty Queen, The (P. N. Warren), **Supp. XX:** 268–269
Beauty's Punishment (Rice), **Supp. VII:** 301
Beauty's Release: The Continued Erotic Adventures of Sleeping Beauty (Rice), **Supp. VII:** 301
Beauvoir, Simone de, **IV:** 477; **Retro. Supp. III:** 243; **Supp. I Part 1:** 51; **Supp. III Part 1:** 200–201, 208; **Supp. IV Part 1:** 360; **Supp. IX:** 4; **Supp. XXVIII:** 255
Beaver Men: Spearheads of Empire (Sandoz), **Supp. XXIV:** 244, 246–247
"Be Careful" (Zach; Everwine, trans.), **Supp. XV:** 86
Be Careful How You Live (Lacy), **Supp. XV:** 203–204
"Because I could not stop for Death—" (Dickinson), **Retro. Supp. I:** 38–40, 41, 43, 44
"Because It Happened" (Goldbarth), **Supp. XII:** 192
"Because of Libraries We Can Say These Things" (Nye), **Supp. XIII:** 283
"Because of the Waters of the Flood" (Helprin), **Supp. XXV:** 85
"Because the Body Is a Flower"(Crooker), **Supp. XXIII:** 55
"Because You Mentioned the Spiritual Life" (Dunn), **Supp. XI:** 154
Bech: A Book (Updike), **IV:** 214; **Retro. Supp. I:** 329, 335
Bechdel, Alison, **Supp. XXV:** 1–15
Beck, Dave, **I:** 493
Beck, Ervin, **Supp. XXIII:** 94, 95
Beck, Jack, **Supp. IV Part 2:** 560
Beck, Nicholas, **Supp. XVIII:** 252
Beck, Stefan, **Supp. XXII:** 268
Becker, Carl, **Supp. I Part 2:** 492, 493
Becker, Paula. *See* Modersohn, Mrs. Otto (Paula Becker)
Beckett, Samuel, **I:** 71, 91, 142, 298, 461; **III:** 387; **IV:** 95; **Retro. Supp. I:** 206; **Supp. IV Part 1:** 297, 368–369; **Supp. IV Part 2:** 424; **Supp. V:** 23, 53; **Supp. XI:** 104; **Supp. XII:** 21, 150–151; **Supp. XIII:** 74; **Supp. XIV:** 239; **Supp. XVII:** 185; **Supp. XX:** 17; **Supp. XXI:** 18; **Supp. XXII:** 263
Beckett, Tom, **Supp. IV Part 2:** 419
Beckford, William, **I:** 204
Beckman, Joshua, **Supp. XXVIII:** 202
Beckonings (Brooks), **Supp. III Part 1:** 85
"Becky" (Toomer), **Supp. III Part 2:** 481, 483; **Supp. IX:** 312

Becky and Her Friends (Hinojosa), **Supp. XIX:** 108–109
Becoming a Man: Half a Life Story (Monette), **Supp. X:** 146, 147, 149, 151, 152, **155–157**
"Becoming a Meadow" (Doty), **Supp. XI:** 124–125
"Becoming and Breaking: Poet and Poem" (Ríos), **Supp. IV Part 2:** 539
Becoming Canonical in American Poetry (Morris), **Retro. Supp. I:** 40
Becoming Light: New and Selected Poems (Jong), **Supp. V:** 115
Bécquer, Gustavo Adolfo, **Supp. XIII:** 312
"Bed, The" (Dixon), **Supp. XII:** 154
Beddoes, Thomas Lovell, **III:** 469; **Retro. Supp. I:** 285
Bedichek, Roy, **Supp. V:** 225
Bedient, Calvin, **Supp. IX:** 298; **Supp. XII:** 98
"Bed in the Sky, The" (Snyder), **Supp. VIII:** 300
Bednarik, Joseph, **Supp. VIII:** 39
Bedouin Hornbook (Mackey), **Supp. XXVII:** 157–158
"Bedrock" (Proulx), **Supp. VII:** 253
"Bed Time" (Davison), **Supp. XXVI:** 72
"Bee, The" (Lanier), **Supp. I Part 1:** 364
"Beech" (Frost), **Retro. Supp. III:** 104
Beecher, Catharine, **Supp. I Part 2:** 581, 582–583, 584, 586, 588, 589, 591, 599; **Supp. X:** 103; **Supp. XI:** 193
Beecher, Charles, **Supp. I Part 2:** 588, 589
Beecher, Edward, **Supp. I Part 2:** 581, 582, 583, 584, 588, 591
Beecher, Harriet. *See* Stowe, Harriet Beecher
Beecher, Henry Ward, **II:** 275; **Supp. I Part 2:** 581; **Supp. XI:** 193; **Supp. XVIII:** 4
Beecher, Lyman, **Supp. I Part 2:** 580–581, 582, 583, 587, 588, 599; **Supp. XI:** 193
Beecher, Mrs. Lyman (Roxanna Foote), **Supp. I Part 2:** 580–581, 582, 588, 599
Beeching, Jack, **Supp. X:** 114, 117, 118, 123, 125, 126
"Beehive" (Toomer), **Supp. IX:** 317
"Bee Hunt, The" (Irving), **II:** 313
"Beekeeper's Daughter, The" (Plath), **Retro. Supp. II:** 246–247
"Bee Meeting, The" (Plath), **Retro. Supp. II:** 254–255
Bee Poems (Plath), **Retro. Supp. II:** 254–255
Beer, John, **Supp. XVII:** 239
Beer, Thomas, **I:** 405
Beerbohm, Max, **III:** 472; **IV:** 436; **Supp. I Part 2:** 714
"Beer Bottle" (Kooser), **Supp. XIX:** 117
"Beer in the Sergeant Major's Hat, or The Sun Also Sneezes" (Chandler), **Supp. IV Part 1:** 121
Beers, Henry A., **Supp. XX:** 68
Bees, The (Teale), **Supp. XXVIII:** 247
"Bees Bees Bees" (J. Scott), **Supp. XVII:** 188, 190

Beethoven, Ludwig van, **II:** 536; **III:** 118; **IV:** 274, 358; **Supp. I Part 1:** 363; **Supp. VIII:** 103
Beet Queen, The (Erdrich), **Supp. IV Part 1:** 259, 260, 264–265, 266, 273, 274, 275
Befo' de War: Echoes in Negro Dialect (Gordon), **Supp. II Part 1:** 201
"Before" (Goldbarth), **Supp. XII:** 175
"Before" (Snyder), **Supp. VIII:** 301
Before Adam (London), **II:** 466
Before Breakfast (O'Neill), **Supp. XXII:** 22
Before Disaster (Winters), **Supp. II Part 2:** 786, 800
"Before Disaster" (Winters), **Supp. II Part 2:** 801, 815
"Before I Knocked" (D. Thomas), **III:** 534
Beforelife, The (F. Wright), **Supp. XVII:** 240, 245–246
"Before March" (MacLeish), **III:** 15
Before My Life Began (Neugeboren), **Supp. XVI:** 224–225
"Before the Altar" (A. Lowell), **II:** 516
"Before the Birth of One of Her Children" (Bradstreet), **Retro. Supp. III:** 2; **Supp. I Part 1:** 118
Before the Gringo Came (Atherton), **Supp. XXIV:** 22
"Before the Sky Darkens" (Dunn), **Supp. XI:** 155
"Begat" (Sexton), **Supp. II Part 2:** 693
Beget, Philippe, **Supp. XXIII:** 74
"Beggar Maid, The" (Munro), **Supp. XXVII:** 187
Beggar Maid, The: Stories of Flo and Rose (Munro). *See Who Do You Think You Are?* (Munro)
Beggarman, Thief (Shaw), **Supp. XIX:** 251–252
Beggar on Horseback (Kaufman and Connelly), **III:** 394
"Beggar Said So, The" (Singer), **IV:** 12
Beggars in the House of Plenty (Shanley), **Supp. XIV:** 316, **327–328**
Beggar's Opera, The (Gay), **Supp. I Part 2:** 523
Begiebing, Robert, **Retro. Supp. II:** 210
Begin Again (Paley), **Supp. VI:** 221
Beginners (Carver), **Supp. XXIV:** 177
"Beginning and the End, The" (Jeffers), **Supp. II Part 2:** 420–421, 424
"Beginning of Decadence, The" (Jeffers), **Supp. II Part 2:** 420
"Beginning of Enthusiasm, The" (Salinas), **Supp. XIII:** 327–328
Beginning of Wisdom, The (Benét), **I:** 358; **Supp. XI:** 44
"Beginnings of Sorrow, The"(P. Benedict), **Supp. XXIII:** 48
Be Glad You're Neurotic (Bisch), **Supp. I Part 2:** 608
"Begotten of the Spleen" (Simic), **Supp. VIII:** 277
"Behaving Like a Jew" (Stern), **Supp. IX:** 290–291, 294
"Behavior" (Emerson), **II:** 2, 4
Behavior of Titans, The (Merton), **Supp. VIII:** 201

Behind a Mask (Alcott), **Supp. I Part 1:** 36–37, 43–44
"Behind a Wall" (A. Lowell), **II:** 516
Behind the Movie Camera (radio show), **Supp. XV:** 147
Behind You (Woodson), **Supp. XXVIII:** 281–282, 283
"Behold the Key" (Malamud), **Supp. I Part 2:** 437
Behrendt, Stephen, **Supp. X:** 204
Behrman, S. N., **Supp. V:** 95
Beichman, Arnold, **Supp. XXV:** 254, 258, 264
Beidler, Peter G., **Supp. IV Part 2:** 557
Beidler, Philip D., **Supp. XII:** 69
Beige Dolorosa (Harrison), **Supp. VIII:** 40, 51
Beiles, Sinclair, **Supp. XII:** 129
Beiliss, Mendel, **Supp. I Part 2:** 427, 446, 447, 448
"Being a Constellation" (A. Finch), **Supp. XVII:** 72
"Being a Lutheran Boy-God in Minnesota" (R. Bly), **Supp. IV Part 1:** 59, 67
Being and Race (C. Johnson), **Supp. VI:** 193, 199
Being and Time (Heidegger), **Supp. VIII:** 9
Being Busted (Fiedler), **Supp. XIII:** 95, 102, 104
Being Geniuses Together: 1920–1930 (Boyle), **Supp. XXIV:** 63, 64
Being John Malkovich (Kaufman), **Supp. XV:** 16
Being Perfect (Quindlen), **Supp. XVII:** 167, 179
Being There (Kosinski), **Supp. VII:** 215, 216, 222–223
Beiswanger, George, **Retro. Supp. II:** 220
Beka Lamb (Edgell), **Supp. XXIII:** 83, 85, **86–88,** 93–94, 95
Belasco, David, **Supp. XVI:** 182; **Supp. XXI:** 151
Bel Canto (Patchett), **Supp. XII:** 307, 310, **320–322**
Belchamber (Sturgis), **Supp. XX:** **227, 233, 238–240**
"Beleaguered City, The" (Longfellow), **II:** 498
Belfry of Bruges, The, and Other Poems (Longfellow), **II:** 489; **Retro. Supp. II:** 157, 168
"Belief" (Levine), **Supp. V:** 186, 190
"Belief in the Self Abandoned, The" (Bronk), **Supp. XXI:** 30
"Beliefs of Writers, The" (Doctorow), **Supp. IV Part 1:** 235–236
Believeniks! (Lethem and Sorrentino), **Supp. XVIII:** 148–149
Believers (C. Baxter), **Supp. XVII:** 20–21, 22
"Believers" (C. Baxter), **Supp. XVII:** 21
"Believers, The/Los Creyentes" (Kingsolver), **Supp. VII:** 208
Belinda (Rice), **Supp. VII:** 301–302
"Belinda's Petition" (Dove), **Supp. IV Part 1:** 245
"Belita" (Ríos), **Supp. IV Part 2:** 541

Belitt, Ben, **Supp. XII:** 260
Bell, Archibald, **Supp. XX:** **284, 285**
Bell, Bernard, **Supp. XXII:** 182
Bell, Clive, **IV:** 87
Bell, Daniel, **Supp. I Part 2:** 648
Bell, George Kennedy Allen, **Retro. Supp. I:** 65
Bell, Madison Smartt, **Supp. X:** **1–20;** **Supp. XIX:** 58–59, 60–61; **Supp. XVII:** 236; **Supp. XXI:** 48; **Supp. XXIII:** 43
Bell, Marvin, **Supp. IX:** 152; **Supp. V:** 337, 339; **Supp. XI:** 316; **Supp. XXIV:** 165
Bell, Michael, **Retro. Supp. II:** 139
Bell, Pearl K., **Supp. XI:** 233; **Supp. XXV:** 253; **Supp. XXVII:** 134
Bell, Quentin, **Supp. I Part 2:** 636
Bell, Whitfield J., Jr., **II:** 123
Bellafante, Gina, **Supp. VIII:** 85
Bellamy, Edward, **II:** 276; **Supp. I Part 2:** 641; **Supp. XI:** 200, 203
Bellarosa Connection, The (Bellow), **Retro. Supp. II:** 31, 32
"Belle Dollinger" (Masters), **Supp. I Part 2:** 463
Belleforest, François de, **IV:** 370
"Belle Zoraïde, La" (Chopin), **Supp. I Part 1:** 215–216
Bell in the Fog and Other Stories, The (Atherton), **Supp. XXIV:** 23
Bell Jar, The (Plath), **Retro. Supp. II:** 242, **249–250;** **Supp. I Part 2:** 526, 527, 529, 531–536, 539, 540, 541, 542, 544; **Supp. XXVIII:** 192
Belloc, Hilary, **III:** 176; **IV:** 432
"Bellocq" (Trethewey), **Supp. XXI:** 253
Bellocq, E. J., **Supp. XXI:** 246, 251
Bellocq's Ophelia (Trethewey), **Supp. XXI:** 243, 246, **251–254**
"Bellocq's Ophelia" (Trethewey), **Supp. XXI:** 254
Bellow, Saul, **I:** 113, 138–139, **144–166,** 375, 517; **II:** 579; **III:** 40; **IV:** 3, 19, 217, 340; **Retro. Supp. II: 19–36,** 118, 279, 307, 324; **Supp. II Part 2:** 428, 451; **Supp. I Part 1:** 109; **Supp. IV Part 1:** 30; **Supp. IX:** 212, 227; **Supp. V:** 258; **Supp. VIII:** 98, 176, 234, 236–237, 245; **Supp. XI:** 64, 233; **Supp. XII:** 159, 165, 170, 310; **Supp. XIII:** 106; **Supp. XIX:** 157, 158, 261; **Supp. XV:** 143; **Supp. XVI:** 208; **Supp. XVIII:** 90; **Supp. XX: 244; Supp. XXII:** 268; **Supp. XXIII:** 166; **Supp. XXV:** 79; **Supp. XXVII:** 95
Bellows, George, **Supp. XV:** 295
"Bells, The" (Poe), **III:** 593; **Retro. Supp. II:** 266; **Supp. I Part 2:** 388
"Bells, The" (Sexton), **Supp. II Part 2:** 673
"Bells for John Whiteside's Daughter" (Ransom), **III:** 490
"Bells of Lynn, The" (Longfellow), **II:** 498
"Bells of San Blas, The" (Longfellow), **II:** 490–491, 493, 498
"Bell-Tower, The" (Melville), **III:** 91; **Retro. Supp. III:** 159

"Belly, The" (Dobyns), **Supp. XIII:** 87
'Bel of Prairie Eden (Lippard), **Supp. XXIII:** 178, 186
"Belonging" (Pickering), **Supp. XXI:** 202
"Belonging Kind, The" (W. Gibson and J. Shirley), **Supp. XVI:** 123
Beloved (film, Demme), **Retro. Supp. III:** 185
Beloved (Morrison), **Retro. Supp. III:** 184, 191–192, 193, 194–195, 197; **Supp. III Part 1:** 364, 372–379; **Supp. IV Part 1:** 13–14; **Supp. V:** 259; **Supp. VIII:** 343; **Supp. XIII:** 60; **Supp. XXII:** 78, 109; **Supp. XXIV:** 186
Beloved, The (Gibran), **Supp. XX:** **125**
"Beloved, The" (Halliday), **Supp. XIX:** 92
"Beloved Child"(Goodman), **Supp. XXVIII:** 93–94
Beloved Lady: A History of Jane Addams' Ideas on Reform and Peace (Farrell), **Supp. I Part 1:** 24
Beloved Stranger, The (Bynner), **Supp. XV:** 44, 50
"Below Freezing on Pinelog Mountain"(Bottoms), **Supp. XXVIII:** 23
Bemorse, John, **Supp. XX:** 62
Benchley, Robert, **I:** 48, 482; **II:** 435; **III:** 53; **Supp. IX:** 190, 195, 204
Benda, W. T., **Retro. Supp. I:** 13
"Benda Illustrations to *My Ántonia*, The: Cather's 'Silent' Supplement to Jim Burden's Narrative" (Schwind), **Retro. Supp. III:** 36–37
Bender, Aimee, **Supp. XXII:** 49
Bending of a Twig, The (Coke), **Supp. XX:** 235
Bend Sinister (Nabokov), **III:** 253–254; **Retro. Supp. I:** 265, 266, 270
Beneath a Meth Moon: An Elegy (Woodson), **Supp. XXVIII:** 283
"Beneath the Sidewalk" (Dunn), **Supp. XI:** 145
"Beneath the Smooth Skin of America" (Sanders), **Supp. XVI:** 275
Benedict, Elizabeth, **Supp. XVIII:** 289
Benedict, Laura, **Supp. XXIII:** 35, 36, 49
Benedict, Pinckney, **Supp. XXIII:** **35–50**
Benedict, Ruth, **Supp. IX:** 229
Benefactor, The (Sontag), **Supp. III Part 2:** 451, 455, 468, 469
"Benefit Performance" (Malamud), **Supp. I Part 2:** 431
Benét, Laura, **Supp. XI:** 44
Benét, Rosemary, **Supp. XI:** 44, 51; **Supp. XXV:** 201
Benét, Stephen Vincent, **I:** 358; **II:** 177; **III:** 22; **IV:** 129; **Supp. XI: 43–61**
Benét, William Rose, **II:** 530; **Retro. Supp. I:** 108; **Supp. I Part 2:** 709; **Supp. XI:** 43, 44; **Supp. XIV:** 119, 122, 129
Ben Franklin's Wit and Wisdom (Franklin), **II:** 111
Ben-Gurion, David, **Supp. XX:** 243
Ben-Hur (film), **Supp. IV Part 2:** 683

Benigna Machiavelli (Gilman), **Supp. XI:** 201, 208

Benitez, R. Michael, **Retro. Supp. II:** 264

"Benito Cereno" (Melville), **III:** 91; **Retro. Supp. I:** 255; **Retro. Supp. II:** 188; **Retro. Supp. III:** 147, 149, 159–160, 162; **Supp. XVII:** 185

Benito Cereno (R. Lowell), **II:** 546; **Retro. Supp. II:** 181

Benito's Dream Bottle (Nye), **Supp. XIII:** 278

"Bênitou's Slave, The" (Chopin), **Retro. Supp. II:** 64

Benjamin, Walter, **Supp. IX:** 133; **Supp. XVI:** 290, 291; **Supp. XXIII:** 28, 29, 30, 31

Benjamin Franklin (Van Doren), **Supp. I Part 2:** 486

"Benjamin Pantier" (Masters), **Supp. I Part 2:** 461

Bennet, Mildred, **Retro. Supp. III:** 18

Bennett, Anne Virginia, **II:** 184

Bennett, Arnold, **I:** 103; **II:** 337; **Supp. XVI:** 190

Bennett, Elizabeth, **Supp. VIII:** 58

Bennett, Patrick, **Supp. V:** 225

Bennett, Paula, **Retro. Supp. I:** 29, 33, 42; **Supp. XX:** 286

Bennett, Reginald, **Supp. XXII:** 218

Bennett, William, **Supp. VIII:** 245

Benson, A. C., **Supp. XX:** 238

Benson, Arthur, **Supp. XX:** 233

Benson, E. F., **Supp. XX:** 229

Benson, Heidi, **Supp. XVIII:** 136

Benson, Jackson J., **Supp. IV Part 2:** 613

Benson, Martin, **Supp. XVIII:** 38

Benstock, Shari, **Retro. Supp. I:** 361, 368, 371, 382; **Retro. Supp. III:** 283; **Supp. XX:** 240

Bentham, Jeremy, **I:** 279; **Supp. I Part 2:** 635

Bentley, Anna, **Supp. XXI:** 5

Bentley, Arthur, **Supp. XXI:** 4, 5

Bentley, Eric R., **IV:** 396

Bentley, Nelson, **Supp. IX:** 324

Bentley, Richard, **III:** 79, 86; **Retro. Supp. III:** 157

Benton, Robert, **Supp. IV Part 1:** 236

"Bent Tones" (Wright), **Supp. XV:** 346

Benveniste, Emile, **Supp. XVI:** 292

Benzel, Jan, **Supp. XVI:** 112

Beowulf, **Supp. II Part 1:** 6; **Supp. XVII:** 70, 73

Beran, Carol, **Supp. XIII:** 25

Bercaw-Edwards, Mary, **Retro. Supp. III:** 152

"Berck-Plage" (Plath), **Retro. Supp. II:** 253–254

Bercovitch, Sacvan, **Retro. Supp. I:** 408; **Retro. Supp. II:** 325, 330; **Supp. I Part 1:** 99; **Supp. I Part 2:** 659

Berdyaev, Nikolai, **I:** 494; **III:** 292

"Bereaved Apartments" (Kingsolver), **Supp. VII:** 203

"Bereavement in their death to feel" (Dickinson), **Retro. Supp. I:** 43, 44

"Berenice" (Poe), **III:** 415, 416, 425; **Retro. Supp. II:** 270; **Retro. Supp. III:** 227

Bérénice (Racine), **II:** 573

Berenson, Bernard, **Retro. Supp. I:** 381; **Retro. Supp. III:** 275; **Supp. IV Part 1:** 314; **Supp. XIV:** 335, 336, 337; **Supp. XVII:** 99; **Supp. XXI:** 5

Berenson, Mary Smith, **Supp. XXI:** 4, 5, 6

Berg, James, **Supp. XIV:** 157, 159

Berg, Stephen, **Supp. IV Part 1:** 60

Berger, Alan, **Supp. XVII:** 39

Berger, Charles, **Retro. Supp. I:** 311

Berger, John, **Supp. XVI:** 284; **Supp. XXIII:** 167, 168–169; **Supp. XXIV:** 94

Berger, Roger, **Supp. XIII:** 237

Berger, Thomas, **III:** 258; **Supp. XII:** 171

Berghash, Rachel, **Supp. XXIV:** 172

Bergman, Ingmar, **I:** 291; **Supp. XV:** 7, 8, 12

Bergson, Henri, **I:** 224; **II:** 163, 165, 166, 359; **III:** 8, 9, 488, 619; **IV:** 86, 122, 466, 467; **Retro. Supp. I:** 55, 57, 80; **Retro. Supp. III:** 57; **Supp. IV Part 1:** 42; **Supp. XXII:** 158

Berkeley, Anthony, **Supp. IV Part 1:** 341

Berkeley, George, **II:** 10, 349, 357, 480, 554

Berkman, Alexander, **Supp. XXIII:** 161; **Supp. XXV:** 19

Berkman, Leonard, **Supp. XV:** 321

Berkow, Ira, **Supp. XXVII:** 139

Berkowitz, Gerald, **Supp. IV Part 2:** 590

Berkson, Bill, **Supp. XXIII:** 217, 218; **Supp. XXVII:** 22, 23

Berlin, Isaiah, **Supp. XXII:** 258

Berlin Alexanderplatz (Döblin), **Supp. XV:** 137

Berlin Stories (Isherwood), **Supp. IV Part 1:** 82; **Supp. XIV:** 155, 156, 161, 162, 164, 165

Berlioz, Hector, **Supp. XV:** 33

Berlyne, Daniel E., **Supp. I Part 2:** 672

Berman, Alexander, **Supp. XVII:** 103

Berman, Carolyn Vellenga, **Supp. XXII:** 147

Berman, Paul, **Supp. XXVIII:** 66

Bernard Clare (Farrell), **II:** 38, 39

Bernardin, Susan, **Supp. XXVI:** 111

Bernard of Clairvaux, Saint, **I:** 22; **II:** 538

Bernays, Thekla, **Retro. Supp. II:** 65

Berne, Suzanne, **Supp. XII:** 320

Berne, Victoria (pseudonym). *See* Fisher, M. F. K.

Berneis, Peter, **IV:** 383

Bernhard, Brendan, **Supp. XIV:** 163

Bernhard, Thomas, **Supp. XX:** 91

Bernhardt, Sarah, **I:** 484; **Retro. Supp. I:** 377

Bernice (Glaspell), **Supp. III Part 1:** 179

"Bernice Bobs Her Hair" (Fitzgerald), **II:** 88; **Retro. Supp. I:** 103

Bernstein, Aline, **IV:** 455, 456

Bernstein, Andrea, **Supp. IX:** 146

Bernstein, Carl, **Supp. XXIV:** 293

Bernstein, Charles, **Supp. IV Part 2:** 421, 426; **Supp. XXIV:** 40, 41, 45–46

Bernstein, Elizabeth, **Supp. XII:** 318

Bernstein, Leonard, **I:** 28; **Supp. I Part 1:** 288, 289; **Supp. IV Part 1:** 83, 84

Bernstein, Melvin, **Supp. XIV:** 41, 46

Bernstein, Michael André, **Retro. Supp. I:** 427

Bernstein, Richard, **Supp. IX:** 253, 262; **Supp. XII:** 113; **Supp. XIV:** 33; **Supp. XXII:** 261

Berrett, Jesse, **Supp. XIII:** 241, 242

Berrigan, Ted, **Supp. XIV:** 150; **Supp. XXII:** 224, 225, 228, 231; **Supp. XXIII:** 218, 221; **Supp. XXIV:** 33–47; **Supp. XXVII:** 18, 22, 24

Berroa y Canelo, Quiterio, **Supp. XXI:** 104

"Berry" (Hughes), **Supp. I Part 1:** 329, 330

Berry, Eleanor, **Supp. XXIII:** 246

Berry, Faith, **Retro. Supp. I:** 194, 201

Berry, Walter, **IV:** 313–314, 326; **Retro. Supp. III:** 275, 279

Berry, Wendell, **Supp. VIII:** 304; **Supp. X:** 21–39; **Supp. XII:** 202; **Supp. XIII:** 1–2; **Supp. XIV:** 179; **Supp. XVI:** 39, 56; **Supp. XVIII:** 192; **Supp. XXI:** 90

"Berry Feast, A" (Snyder), **Supp. VIII:** 289, 297

Berryman, John, **I:** 167–189, 405, 441–442, 521; **II:** 554; **III:** 273; **IV:** 138, 430; **Retro. Supp. I:** 430; **Retro. Supp. II:** 175, 178; **Retro. Supp. III:** 14, 243; **Supp. I Part 2:** 546; **Supp. II Part 1:** 109; **Supp. III Part 2:** 541, 561, 595, 596, 603; **Supp. IV Part 2:** 620, 639; **Supp. IX:** 152; **Supp. V:** 179–180, 337; **Supp. XI:** 240; **Supp. XV:** 93; **Supp. XVII:** 111; **Supp. XXII:** 83; **Supp. XXVIII:** 142

Berryman, Mrs. John, **I:** 168–169

Berryman's Sonnets (Berryman), **I:** 168, 175–178

"Berry Territory" (Snyder), **Supp. VIII:** 304

Berthoff, Warner, **Supp. I Part 1:** 133

Berthoff, Werner, **Supp. XXVI:** 23

Bertolucci, Bernardo, **Supp. IV Part 1:** 94

"Bertrand Hume" (Masters), **Supp. I Part 2:** 463–464

Besco, Glenn, **Supp. XXIII:** 125

"Be Serious" (Stone), **Supp. XXVII:** 263

Bessie, Alvah C., **Supp. XXVI:** 28

"Best, the Most, The" (Carruth), **Supp. XVI:** 59

Best American Essays 1987, The (G. Talese and R. Atwan, eds.), **Supp. XVI:** 273

Best American Essays 1988, The (Dillard, ed.), **Supp. VIII:** 272

Best American Essays 1989, The (Wolff, ed.), **Supp. XVII:** 208

Best American Essays 1993, The (J. Epstein, ed.), **Supp. XVI:** 275

Best American Essays 1997, The (Frazier, ed.), **Supp. VIII:** 272; **Supp. XVII:** 207

Best American Essays 1999, The (E. Hoagland and R. Atwan, eds.), **Supp. XVI:** 277

Best American Essays 2008, The, **Supp. XXIV:** 230

Best American Essays 2009, The, **Supp. XXIV:** 230

Best American Essays for College Students, The (R. Atwan, ed.), **Supp. XVI:** 273

Best American Fantasy, 2010 (Brockmeier, ed.), **Supp. XXII:** 49–50

Best American New Voices 2001 (C. Baxter, ed.), **Supp. XVII:** 22

Best American Poetry, The: 1988 (Ashbery, ed.), **Supp. III Part 1:** 26

Best American Poetry 2000, The (Dove and Lehman, eds.), **Supp. XXI:** 246

Best American Poetry 2006, The (Collins, ed.), **Supp. XXI:** 54

Best American Poetry 2016 (Hirsch, ed.), **Supp. XXVIII:** 22

Best American Short Stories, **I:**174; **II:** 587; **III:** 443; **Supp. IV Part 1:** 102, 315; **Supp. IX:** 114; **Supp. X:** 301

Best American Short Stories, 1915–1050, The, **Supp. IX:** 4

Best American Short Stories 1965, The (Foley, ed.), **Supp. XVI:** 225

Best American Short Stories 1979, The, **Supp. XXIII:** 290

Best American Short Stories 1982, The (Gardner, ed.), **Supp. XVII:** 16

Best American Short Stories 1983, The (A. Tyler, ed.), **Supp. XVI:** 37

Best American Short Stories 1986, The (Carver, ed.), **Supp. XVII:** 17

Best American Short Stories 1988, The (Helprin, ed.), **Supp. XVI:** 16

Best American Short Stories 1989, The (Atwood, ed.), **Supp. XVII:** 18; **Supp. XXI:** 39, 42

Best American Short Stories 1991, The (Adams and Kenison, eds.), **Supp. XVI:** 256

Best American Short Stories 1996, The, **Supp. XXIII:** 295

Best American Short Stories 1997, **Supp. XXII:** 75

Best American Short Stories 2001, The (Kenison and Kingsover, eds.), **Supp. XVI:** 24

Best American Short Stories 2007, The, **Supp. XXIII:** 290

Best American Short Stories 2010, The (Russo and Pitlor, eds.), **Supp. XXVII:** 228

Best American Short Stories of 1942, The, **Supp. V:** 316

Best American Short Stories of 1944, The, **Supp. IX:** 119

Best American Short Stories of the Century (Updike, ed.), **Supp. X:** 163

Best American Short Stories of the Eighties, The (Ravenal, ed.), **Supp. IV Part 1:** 93

Best American Sports Writing of the Century, The (Halberstam, ed.), **Supp. XVII:** 204

"Best China Saucer, The" (Jewett), **Retro. Supp. II:** 145–146

Best Creative Nonfiction, Vol. 1, The (Gutkind, ed.), **Supp. XXVI:** 53

Best Creative Nonfiction, Vol. 2, The (Gutkind, ed.), **Supp. XXIV:** 230

Bester, Alfred, **Supp. XVI:** 123

Best Hour of the Night, The (Simpson), **Supp. IX: 277–279**

Bestiaire, Le (Apollinaire), **IV:** 80

Bestiary, A (Wilbur), **Supp. III Part 2:** 552

"Bestiary for the Fingers of My Right Hand" (Simic), **Supp. VIII:** 274, 275

Best Man, The: A Play About Politics (Vidal), **Supp. IV Part 2:** 683

Best Mystery Stories (Wells, ed.), **Supp. XXVI:** 277

"Best of Everything, The" (Yates), **Supp. XI:** 341

Best of Pickering, The (Pickering), **Supp. XXI:** 192, 198

Best of Plimpton (Plimpton), **Supp. XVI:** 238, 239, 240

Beston, Henry, **Supp. XXVI: 31–44; Supp. XXVIII:** 251, 253, 254

Best Short Plays, The (Mayorga), **IV:** 381

Best Short Stories, The (O'Brien, ed.), **I:** 289

Best Short Stories by Negro Writers, The (Hughes, ed.), **Supp. I Part 1:** 345

Best Short Stories of 1926, The (O'Brien, ed.), **Supp. XVIII:** 279

Best Short Stories of 1934 (O'Brien, ed.), **Supp. XVIII:** 227

Best Short Stories of 1938 (O'Brien, ed.), **Supp. XIX:** 256; **Supp. XX: 34**

Best That Ever Did It, The (Lacy), **Supp. XV:** 201–202

Best Times, The: An Informal Memoir (Dos Passos), **I:** 475, 482

Best Women's Travel Writing 2010, The (Griest, ed.), **Supp. XXVIII:** 98

Best Words, Best Order: Essays on Poetry (Dobyns), **Supp. XIII:** 74, **76–78,** 87

Best Years of Our Lives, The (film; Wyler), **Supp. XV:** 195

"BETANCOURT" (Baraka), **Supp. II Part 1:** 33, 34

Bête humaine, La (Zola), **III:** 316, 318

"Beth Ann and Macrobioticism" (Christgau), **Supp. XXVII:** 37–39

"Bethe" (Hellman), **Supp. I Part 1:** 293

Bethea, David, **Supp. VIII:** 27

Bethel Merriday (Lewis), **II:** 455

Bethke, Bruce, **Supp. XVI:** 121

Bethlehem in Broad Daylight (Doty), **Supp. XI:** 121, **122–123**

Bethune, Jane, **Supp. XXVI:** 240, 245

Bethune, Mary McLeod, **Retro. Supp. I:** 197; **Supp. I Part 1:** 333

Bethurum, Dorothy, **IV:** 121

"Betrayal" (Lanier), **Supp. I Part 1:** 364

"Betrothed" (Bogan), **Supp. III Part 1:** 49–51

Bettelheim, Bruno, **Supp. I Part 2:** 622; **Supp. X:** 77, 84; **Supp. XIV:** 126; **Supp. XVI:** 33

Better Days (Price), **Supp. VI:** 264

Better Sort, The (James), **II:** 335

Better Than Sex (Thompson), **Supp. XXIV:** 283

"Better Things in Life, The" (Loos), **Supp. XVI:** 194

Betty Leicester (Jewett), **II:** 406

Betty Leicester's Christmas (Jewett), **II:** 406; **Retro. Supp. II:** 145

Betty's Summer Vacation (Durang), **Supp. XXIV:** 125–126

Between Angels (Dunn), **Supp. XI: 149–159**

"Between Angels" (Dunn), **Supp. XI:** 150

Between Fantoine and Agapa (Pinget), **Supp. V:** 39

Between Madison and Palmetto (Woodson), **Supp. XXVIII:** 287

"Between Memory and History: A Writer's Voice" (Kreisler), **Supp. XVI:** 155

"Between Queer Performances" (Hardin), **Supp. XXVI:** 242

Between Silences: A Voice from China (Jin), **Supp. XVIII:** 91, 92, 93

Between the Flowers (Arnow), **Supp. XXVIII:** 2, 3, 6, 11, 14–17, 18

"Between the Porch and the Altar" (R. Lowell), **II:** 540–541

"Between the World and Me" (Wright), **Supp. II Part 1:** 228

Between Time and Timbuktu (Vonnegut), **Supp. II Part 2:** 753, 759

Between Two Rivers (Kenny), **Supp. XXIII:** 143

Beuka, Robert A., **Supp. XIX:** 263; **Supp. XXI:** 47

"Be Very Afraid—Of Loss of Liberty at Home" (P. N. Warren), **Supp. XX: 272–273**

Bevis, Howard L., **Supp. I Part 2:** 611

Bevis, John, **Supp. I Part 2:** 503

Bewilderment: New Poems and Translations (Ferry), **Supp. XXIV: 160–161**

"Bewitched" (Wharton), **IV:** 316

Bewley, Marius, **I:** 336

Beyer, Werner, **Supp. XXIII:** 145

Beyle, Marie Henri. *See* Stendhal

Beyond (Goldbarth), **Supp. XII:** 192

Beyond a Boundary (C. L. R. James), **Supp. XXI:** 159, 170–171

Beyond Black Bear Lake (LaBastille), **Supp. X:** 95, **99–102,** 108

"Beyond Charles River to the Acheron" (R. Lowell), **II:** 541

Beyond Criticism (Shapiro), **Supp. II Part 2:** 703, 711

Beyond Culture (Trilling), **Supp. III Part 2:** 508–512

Beyond Desire (Anderson), **I:** 111

Beyond Document: The Art of Nonfiction Film (Warren, ed.), **Supp. IV Part 2:** 434

Beyond Forgetting (Hughes, ed.; foreword by Gallagher), **Supp. XXIV:** 167, 171

Beyond Good and Evil (Nietzsche), **Supp. IV Part 2:** 519

"Beyond Harm" (Olds), **Supp. X:** 210

Beyond Katrina: A Meditation on the Mississippi Gulf Coast (Trethewey), **Supp. XXI:** 248

"Beyond My Solitude" (Gibran), **Supp. XX: 119**

"Beyond the Alps" (R. Lowell), **II:** 547, 550

"Beyond the Bayou" (Chopin), **Supp. I Part 1:** 215

"Beyond the Black River" (Howard), **Supp. XXVII:** 126

Beyond the Boom: New Voices on American Life, Culture and Politics (Teachout), **Supp. XIX:** 137

Beyond the Horizon (O'Neill), **III:** 389; **Supp. XXI:** 13; **Supp. XXII:** 22

Beyond the Hundredth Meridian: John Wesley Powell and the Second Opening of the West (Stegner), **Supp. IV Part 2:** 599, 603–604, 611

"Beyond the Kittery Bridge" (Hatlen), **Supp. V:** 138

Beyond the Law (film) (Mailer), **Retro. Supp. II:** 205

Beyond Therapy (Durang), **Supp. XXIV: 119–120**

"Beyond the Sea (at the sanatorium)" (Salinas), **Supp. XIII:** 325

Beyond the Wall: Essays from the Outside (Abbey), **Supp. XIII:** 13

Beyond the Wall of Sleep (Lovecraft), **Supp. XXV:** 113

Beyond the Writers' Workshop: New Ways to Write Creative Nonfiction (C. Bly), **Supp. XVI:** 41

Beyond Tragedy (Niebuhr), **III:** 300–303

Bezner, Kevin, **Supp. XII:** 202

B. F.'s Daughter (Marquand), **III:** 59, 65, 68, 69

Bhagavad Gita, **III:** 566; **IV:** 183

"Biafra: A People Betrayed" (Vonnegut), **Supp. II Part 2:** 760

Bialosky, Jill, **Supp. XXVIII:** 85

Bianchi, Martha Dickinson, **I:** 470; **Retro. Supp. I:** 35, 37, 38

Bible, **I:** 191, 280, 414, 421, 490, 506; **II:** 6, 12, 15, 17, 108, 231, 237, 238, 252, 267, 302; **III:** 28, 199, 308–309, 341, 343, 350, 356, 402, 492, 519, 565, 577; **IV:** 11, 13, 42, 57, 60, 67, 152, 153, 154, 155, 164, 165, 296, 337, 341, 367, 369, 370, 371, 438; **Retro. Supp. I:** 91; **Supp. I Part 1:** 4, 6, 63, 101, 104, 105, 113, 193, 369; **Supp. I Part 2:** 388, 433, 494, 515, 516, 517, 583, 584, 587, 589, 653, 689, 690, 691; **Supp. IV Part 1:** 284; **Supp. IX:** 246; **Supp. VIII:** 20; **Supp. XIV:** 225. *See also* names of biblical books; New Testament; Old Testament

Biblia Americana (Mather), **Supp. II Part 2:** 442

Biblical Dialogues between a Father and His Family (Rowson), **Supp. XV:** 245–246

"Biblical Trees, Biblical Deliverance" (Weathers), **Retro. Supp. III:** 139–140

"Bibliography of the King's Book, A, or, Eikon Basilike" (Howe), **Supp. IV Part 2:** 435

Bibliography of the King's Book, A; or, Eikon Basilike (Almack), **Supp. IV Part 2:** 435

"Bicentennial" (Davison), **Supp. XXVI:** 73, 77

Bickel, Freddy. *See* March, Fredric

Bicycle Thieves (film, De Sica), **Supp. XXVI:** 134

Bidart, Frank, **Retro. Supp. II:** 48, 50, 52, 182, 183, 184; **Supp. XIX:** 82; **Supp. XV: 19–37; Supp. XVIII:** 91,92

Bid Me to Live (Doolittle), **Supp. I Part 1:** 258, 260, 268, 269, 270

"*Bien* Pretty" (Cisneros), **Supp. VII:** 70

"Bienvenidos" (Mora), **Supp. XIII:** 220

Bierce, Albert, **I:** 191, 209

Bierce, Ambrose, **I: 190–213,** 419; **II:** 74, 264, 271; **IV:** 350; **Retro. Supp. II:** 72; **Supp. XXV:** 26

Bierce, Mrs. Ambrose, **I:** 194–195, 199

Bierce, Day, **I:** 195, 199

Bierce, Helen, **I:** 210

Bierce, Leigh, **I:** 195, 198, 208

Bierce, General Lucius Verus, **I:** 191

Bierce, Marcus, **I:** 190, 191

Bierce, Mrs. Marcus, **I:** 190, 191

Bierds, Linda, **Supp. XVII: 25–37**

Biffle, Kent, **Supp. V:** 225

"Bi-Focal" (Stafford), **Supp. XI:** 318, 321

Bigamist's Daughter, A (McDermott), **Supp. XVIII:** 155, **156–158,** 160, 166

Big as Life (Doctorow), **Supp. IV Part 1:** 231, 234

Big Bad Love (film, Howard), **Supp. XXI:** 39

Big Bad Love (L. Brown), **Supp. XXI:** 40, 42, **44–45**

"Big Bite" (Mailer), **Retro. Supp. II:** 204

"Big Blonde" (Parker), **Supp. IX:** 189, 192, 193, 195, 196, 203

Big Box, The (Morrison and S. Morrison), **Retro. Supp. III:** 185

Big Bozo, The (Glaspell), **Supp. III Part 1:** 182

Bigelow, Gordon, **Supp. X:** 222, 227, 229

Bigelow, Jacob, **Supp. I Part 1:** 302

Bigelow Papers, Second Series, The (J. R. Lowell), **Supp. I Part 2:** 406, 415–416

Bigelow Papers, The (J. R. Lowell), **Supp. I Part 2:** 406, 407, 408, 410, 411–412, 415, 417, 424

"Big Fiddle" (Boyle), **Supp. XXIV:** 54

Big Fix, The (Lacy), **Supp. XV:** 204–205

Bigfoot Dreams (Prose), **Supp. XVI:** 253–254

Big Funk, The: A Casual Play (Shanley), **Supp. XIV:** 316, **327**

"Big Game" (Boyle), **Supp. XX: 20**

Big Game, The (film), **Supp. XIX:** 244

Big Gold Dream, The (C. Himes), **Supp. XVI:** 143, 144

"Bight, The" (Bishop), **Retro. Supp. II:** 38, 45

Big Hunger: Stories 1932–1959 (Fante), **Supp. XI:** 160

Big Knife, The (Odets), **Supp. II Part 2:** 546, 547, 548

Big Knockover, The (Hammett), **Supp. I Part 1:** 292; **Supp. IV Part 1:** 344, 345, 356

Big Laugh, The (O'Hara), **III:** 362, 373–375

Big Man (Neugeboren), **Supp. XVI:** 219, **220,** 221, 225

Big Money, The (Dos Passos), **I:** 482, 483, 486–487, 489; **Supp. I Part 2:** 646, 647

Big Picture (Everett), **Supp. XVIII:** 54, 66

"Big Picture" (Everett), **Supp. XVIII:** 66

"Big Picture" (Halliday), **Supp. XIX:** 93

"Big Rock Candy Figgy Pudding Pitfall, The" (Didion), **Supp. IV Part 1:** 195

Big Rock Candy Mountain, The (Stegner), **Supp. IV Part 2:** 596, 597, 598, 599, 600, 603, 604, 605, 606–607, 608, 610–611

Bigsby, C. W. E. (Christopher), **Supp. IX:** 137, 140; **Supp. XV:** 332

Big Sea, The (Hughes), **Retro. Supp. I:** 195, 197, 199, 201, 204; **Supp. I Part 1:** 322, 332, 333; **Supp. II Part 1:** 233–234; **Supp. XIX:** 77; **Supp. XXII:** 3

Big Sky, The (Mora), **Supp. XIII:** 221

Big Sleep, The (Chandler), **Supp. IV Part 1:** 122–125, 127, 128, 134

Big Sleep, The (film), **Retro. Supp. III:** 85; **Supp. IV Part 1:** 130; **Supp. XVIII:** 148

Big Strike, The (Ryan as Quin), **Supp. XVIII:** 226,**232–233**

Big Sur (Kerouac), **Supp. III Part 1:** 230

Big Sur and the Oranges of Hieronymous Bosch (H. Miller), **III:** 189–190

Big Time, The (Hayes), **Supp. XXVI:** 144

Big Town, The (Lardner), **II:** 426, 429

"Big Two-Hearted River" (Hemingway), **II:** 249; **Retro. Supp. I:** 170–171; **Supp. IX:** 106; **Supp. XIV:** 227, 235

"Big Wind" (Roethke), **III:** 531

"Big Winner Rises Late, The" (Dunn), **Supp. XI:** 146

"Bilingual/*Bilingüe*" (essay; Espaillat), *Supp. XXI:* 103

"Bilingual/*Bilingüe*" (poem; Espaillat), *Supp. XXI:* 104

"Bilingual Christmas" (Mora), **Supp. XIII:** 216–217

"Bilingual Sestina" (Alvarez), **Supp. VII:** 10

"Bill" (Winters), **Supp. II Part 2:** 792

"Bill, The" (Malamud), **Supp. I Part 2:** 427, 430, 434

"Bill Collector's Vacation, The" (Hampl), **Supp. XXII:** 83

"Billie Holiday" (Carruth), **Supp. XVI:** 50

Billings, Gladys. *See* Brooks, Mrs. Van Wyck

Billings, Josh, **Supp. XVIII:** 1, 4

Billips, Martha, **Supp. XXVIII:** 3, 4, 13, 14

Bill of Rites, a Bill of Wrongs, a Bill of Goods, A (Morris), **III:** 237

"Bill's Beans" (Nye), **Supp. XIII:** 283

"Billy" (Gordon), **Supp. IV Part 1:** 306

"Billy" (McCarriston), **Supp. XIV:** 265

Billy Bathgate (Doctorow), **Supp. IV Part 1:** 217, 219, 222, 224, 227, 229–231, 231, 232, 233, 238

Billy Bathgate (film), **Supp. IV Part 1:** 236

Billy Budd, Sailor (Melville), **III:** 40, 93–95; **IV:** 105; **Retro. Supp. I:** 249, **258–260; Retro. Supp. III:** 147, 149, 160, 161–162

Billy Collins Live: A Performance at the Peter Norton Symphony Space April 20, 2005 (CD, Collins), **Supp. XXI:** 51

"Billy Gardner's Ground Out" (Skloot), **Supp. XX: 205, 207**

Billy Phelan's Greatest Game (W. Kennedy), **Supp. VII:** 131, 132, 134, 135, 142–147, 149, 151, 153, 155

Billy Ray's Farm: Essays from a Place Called Tula (L. Brown), **Supp. XXI:** 48, 49

Billy's Boy (P. N. Warren), **Supp. XX: 261, 265–267**

Billy the Kid, **Supp. IV Part 2:** 489, 490, 492

Biloxi Blues (Simon), **Supp. IV Part 2:** 576, 577, 584, 586–587, 590

"Bimini" (Hemingway), **II:** 258

Bingham, Anne, **Supp. XV:** 239

Bingham, Millicent Todd, **I:** 470; **Retro. Supp. I:** 36

Bingham, Remica L., **Supp. XXI:** 256

Bingo Palace, The (Erdrich), **Supp. IV Part 1:** 259, 260, 261, 263–264, 265, 266–267, 268–269, 270, 271–273, 274, 275

"Binsey Poplars" (Hopkins), **Supp. I Part 1:** 94; **Supp. IV Part 2:** 639

Binswanger, Ludwig, **Supp. XV:** 26

Biographia Literaria (Coleridge), **II:** 10; **Retro. Supp. I:** 308

"Biography" (Francis), **Supp. IX:** 77

"Biography" (Pinsky), **Supp. VI:** 235, 236, 239, 241, **243,** 249, 250

Biography and Poetical Remains of the Late Margaret Miller Davidson (Irving), **II:** 314

"Biography in the First Person" (Dunn), **Supp. XI:** 144

"Biography of an Armenian Schoolgirl" (Nye), **Supp. XIII:** 275, 280

"Biography of a Story" (Jackson), **Supp. IX:** 113

Biondi, Joann, **Supp. XI:** 103

"Biopoetics Sketch for *Greenfield Review*" (Harjo), **Supp. XII:** 216

"Biotherm"(O'Hara), **Supp. XXIII:** 208, 218–219

"Birchbrook Mill" (Whittier), **Supp. I Part 2:** 699

"Birches" (Frost), **II:** 154; **Retro. Supp. I:** 132; **Retro. Supp. III:** 99–100; **Supp. XIII:** 147

Bird, Alan, **Supp. I Part 1:** 260

Bird, Gloria, **Supp. XII:** 216

Bird, Isabella, **Supp. X:** 103

Bird, Robert M., **III:** 423

"Bird, The" (Simpson), **Supp. IX:** 269–270

"Bird, the Bird, the Bird, The" (Creeley), **Supp. IV Part 1:** 149

"Bird, The"(Le Sueur), **Supp. XXIII:** 167

"Bird Banding with the Biologists" (Ray), **Supp. XVIII:** 194

Bird by Bird: Some Instructions on Writing and Life (Lamott), **Supp. XX: 132, 137–138**

"Bird came down the Walk, A" (Dickinson), **Retro. Supp. I:** 37

"Bird Frau, The" (Dove), **Supp. IV Part 1:** 245

"Bird in Hand" (screen story) (West and Ingster), **Retro. Supp. II:** 330

Bird Kingdom of the Mayas (LaBastille), **Supp. X:** 96

"Bird on a Wire" (Cohen), **Supp. XXVII:** 51

"Birds, Farrago"(Lea), **Supp. XXVIII:** 142

Birds and Beasts (W. J. Smith), **Supp. XIII:** 346

"Birds for Christmas, The" (Richard), **Supp. XIX:** 221

Bird's Nest, The (Jackson), **Supp. IX: 124–125**

Birds of America (McCarthy), **II:** 579–583; **Supp. X:** 177

Birds of America (Moore), **Supp. X:** 163, 165, 167, 168, 171, **177–179**

Birds of America, The (Audubon), **Supp. XVI:** 5–6, 7, 9, 10, 12, 13

"Birds of Killingsworth, The" (Longfellow), **Retro. Supp. II:** 164

Birds of North America (Audubon Society), **Supp. X:** 177

"Birds of Vietnam, The" (Carruth), **Supp. XVI:** 55

"Bird-Window-Flying" (Gallagher), **Supp. XXIV:** 169

"Bird-Witted" (Moore), **III:** 214

Birkelo, Cheryl, **Supp. XX: 220–221**

Birkerts, Sven, **Supp. IV Part 2:** 650; **Supp. V:** 212; **Supp. VIII:** 85; **Supp. X:** 311; **Supp. XX:** 92

Birkhead, L. M., **III:** 116

"Birmingham Sunday" (Hughes), **Supp. I Part 1:** 343

Birnbaum, Henry, **Supp. XII:** 128

Birnbaum, Michelle, **Supp. XXVIII:** 116, 122

Birnbaum, Robert, **Supp. X:** 13; **Supp. XVI:** 75; **Supp. XXIII:** 73, 75, 275

Birney, James G., **Supp. I Part 2:** 587, 588

Birstein, Ann, **Supp. VIII:** 100

"Birthday, A" (Untermeyer), **Supp. XV:** 296

Birthday Basket for Tía, A (Mora), **Supp. XIII:** 221

"Birthday Cake" (Carruth), **Supp. XVI:** 59

"Birthday Cake for Lionel, A" (Wylie), **Supp. I Part 2:** 721

"Birthday Girl: 1950" (McCarriston), **Supp. XIV:** 261

"Birthday of Mrs. Pineda, The" (Ríos), **Supp. IV Part 2:** 542, 546

"Birthday Poem, A" (Hecht), **Supp. X:** 64

"Birthday Present, A" (Plath), **Supp. I Part 2:** 531

"Birthmark" (July), **Supp. XXIV:** 206

"Birthmark, The" (Ellison), **Retro. Supp. II:** 116; **Supp. II Part 1:** 237–238

"Birth-mark, The" (Hawthorne), **Retro. Supp. I:** 152; **Retro. Supp. III:** 114

Birth-mark, The: Unsettling the Wilderness in American Literary History (Howe), **Supp. IV Part 2:** 422, 431, 434

Birth of a Nation, The (film), **Supp. I Part 1:** 66

Birth of a World: Bolívar in Terms of His Peoples (W. Frank), **Supp. XX: 80**

Birth of the Poet, The (Gordon), **Supp. XII:** 7

Birth of Tragedy, The (Nietzsche), **Supp. IV Part 1:** 105, 110; **Supp. IV Part 2:** 519; **Supp. VIII:** 182

"Birth of Venus, The" (Botticelli), **IV:** 410

"Birth of Venus, The" (Rukeyser), **Supp. VI:** 281

"Birth of Water Stories, The" (Vaz), **Supp. XXVI:** 260

"Birthplace: New Rochelle" (Oppen), **Supp. XXVI:** 231

"Birthplace Revisited" (Corso), **Supp. XII:** 123

"Birthright" (McKay), **Supp. X:** 136

Bisch, Louis E., **Supp. I Part 2:** 608

Bisco, John, **Supp. XVIII:** 11

"B is for Bachelors" (M. F. K. Fisher), **Supp. XVII:** 86

Bishop, Elizabeth, **Retro. Supp. I:** 140, 296, 303; **Retro. Supp. II: 37–56,** 175, 178, 189, 233, 234, 235; **Retro. Supp. III:** 251; **Supp. I Part 1: 72–97,** 239, 320, 326; **Supp. III Part 1:** 6, 7, 10, 18, 64, 239, 320, 326; **Supp. III Part 2:** 541, 561; **Supp. IV Part 1:** 249, 257; **Supp. IV Part 2:** 439, 626, 639, 641, 644, 647, 651, 653; **Supp. IX:** 40, 41, 45, 47, 48; **Supp. V:** 337; **Supp. X:** 58; **Supp. XI:** 123, 136; **Supp. XIII:** 115, 348; **Supp. XV:** 20–21, 100, 101, 112, 119, 249, 251; **Supp. XVII:** 36, 76; **Supp. XXI:** 58, 84, 131; **Supp. XXIII:** 117; **Supp. XXV:** 222; **Supp. XXVI:** 67, 78; **Supp. XXVII:** 228

Bishop, James, Jr., **Supp. XIII:** 1, 5, 6, 7, 9, 11, 15

Bishop, John Peale, **I:** 432, 440; **II:** 81, 85, 86–87, 91, 209; **IV:** 35, 140, 427; **Retro. Supp. I:** 109; **Supp. I Part 2:** 709

Bishop, John W., **Supp. I Part 1:** 83

Bishop, Judith, **Supp. XVI:** 295

Bishop, Morris, **Supp. I Part 2:** 676

Bishop, Rudine Sims, **Supp. XXVII:** 203

Bishop, William Thomas, **Supp. I Part 1:** 83

"Bishop Orders His Tomb at St. Praxed's Church, The" (R. Browning), **Supp. XV:** 127

"Bishop's Beggar, The" (Benét), **Supp. XI:** 56

"Bismarck" (Chapman), **Supp. XIV:** 52, 53

Bismark, Otto von, **Supp. I Part 2:** 643

Biss, Eula, **Supp. XXVI: 45–60**

"Bistro Styx, The" (Dove), **Supp. IV Part 1:** 250–251

Bitov, Andrei, **Retro. Supp. I:** 278

Bits of Gossip (R. H. Davis), **Supp. XVI:** 82–83, 84, 85, 89

"Bitte Nehmen Sie Die Blumen" (Boyle), **Supp. XXIV:** 57

"Bitter Drink, The" (Dos Passos), **Supp. I Part 2:** 647

"Bitter Farce, A" (Schwartz), **Supp. II Part 2:** 640, 657–658

Bitter Medicine (Paretsky), **Supp. XXV:** 174, 179, 183

"Bitter Pills for the Dark Ladies" (Jong), **Supp. V:** 118

Bitterroot (Burke), **Supp. XIV:** 34, 35

"Bittersweet Nightshade" (Skloot), **Supp. XX:** 202

Bitter Victory (Hardy; Kinnell, trans.), **Supp. III Part 1:** 235

Bittner, William, **Supp. XX:** 74,**Supp. XX:** 77, 76, 78, 80

Bitzer, G. W. "Billy", **Supp. XVI:** 183

Bixby, Horace, **IV:** 194

Bjerre, Thomas Aervold, **Supp. XXI:** 41, 47; **Supp. XXVII:** 218

Bjorkman, Frances Maule, **Supp. V:** 285

Bjorkman, Stig, **Supp. XV:** 6

Björnson, Björnstjerne, **II:** 275

Black, Cheryl, **Supp. XXI:** 6; **Supp. XXVIII:** 38

Black 100, The (Salley), **Supp. XIV:** 195

Blackamerican Literature, 1760-Present (R. Miller), **Supp. X:** 324

Black American Literature Forum, **Supp. XI:** 86, 92, 93

Black and Blue (Quindlen), **Supp. XVII:** 166, **176–178**

"Black and Tan" (Bell), **Supp. X:** 9

Black and White (Sorrentino), **Supp. XXI:** 228

Black Armour (Wylie), **Supp. I Part 2:** 708, 709, 712–714, 729

"Black Art" (Baraka), **Supp. II Part 1:** 49, 50–51, 59, 60

"Black Art, The" (Sexton), **Supp. II Part 2:** 682

"Black Aspen, The" (Davison), **Supp. XXVI:** 78

"Black Ball, The" (Ellison), **Retro. Supp. II:** 124

Black Bart and the Sacred Hills (Wilson), **Retro. Supp. III:** 318; **Supp. VIII:** 330, 331

Black Beetles in Amber (Bierce), **I:** 204, 209

"Blackberries" (Komunyakaa), **Supp. XIII:** 126

"Blackberry Eating" (Kinnell), **Supp. III Part 1:** 250

"Blackberrying" (D. West), **Supp. XVIII:** 283

Blackberry Winter (Warren), **IV:** 243, 251, 252

Black Betty (Mosley), **Supp. XIII:** 237, **Supp. XIII:** 240, 243

"Black Birch in Winter, A" (Wilbur), **Supp. III Part 2:** 561

Black Book, The (Morrison, ed.), **Retro. Supp. III:** 184, 191

"Black Boy" (Boyle), **Supp. XXIV:** 59

Black Boy (Wright), **IV:** 477, 478, 479, 480–482, 488, 489, 494; **Retro. Supp. II:** 117; **Supp. II Part 1:** 235–236; **Supp. IV Part 1:** 11; **Supp. XVIII:** 286

"Black Boys and Native Sons" (Howe), **Retro. Supp. II:** 112

Blackburn, Alex, **Supp. XIII:** 112

Blackburn, Paul, **Supp. XXII:** 164, 169; **Supp. XXIV:** 34, 37

Blackburn, William, **IV:** 100

"Black Buttercups" (Clampitt), **Supp. IX:** 42

Black Cargo, The (Marquand), **III:** 55, 60

Black Cargoes: A History of the Atlantic Slave Trade (Cowley), **Supp. II Part 1:** 140

"Black Cat, The" (Poe), **III:** 413, 414, 415; **Retro. Supp. II:** 264, 267, 269, 270; **Retro. Supp. III:** 227; **Supp. XXV:** 112

Black Cherry Blues (Burke), **Supp. XIV:** 30

"Black Christ, The" (Cullen), **Supp. IV Part 1:** 170, 171–172

Black Christ and Other Poems, The (Cullen), **Supp. IV Part 1:** 166, 170

"Black Clay Fish from Oaxaca, A" (Bronk), **Supp. XXI:** 31

"Black Colossus" (Howard), **Supp. XXVII:** 126

"Black Cottage, The" (Frost), **Retro. Supp. I:** 128

"BLACK DADA NIHILISMUS" (Baraka), **Supp. II Part 1:** 39, 41

"Black Death" (Hurston), **Supp. VI:** 153

Black Dog, Red Dog (Dobyns), **Supp. XIII:** 87, **88–89**

"Black Dog, Red Dog" (Dobyns), **Supp. XIII:** 89

Black Dog of Fate: A Memoir (Balakian), **Supp. XXIII:** 19, **20–24**, 24, 25

"Black Earth" (Moore), **III:** 197, 212

Black Echo, The (Connelly), **Supp. XXI:** 67, 68, 75, 80

Blacker the Berry, The (Thurman), **Retro. Supp. III:** 137

"Black Experience in Children's Books, The: One Step Forward, Two Steps Back" (Myers), **Supp. XXVII:** 200

Black Fire (Jones and Neal, eds.), **Supp. X:** 324, 328

Black Fire: An Anthology of Afro American Writing (Baraka, ed.), **Supp. II Part 1:** 53

Black Flame, The (Du Bois), **Supp. II Part 1:** 159, 185–186

Black Folk, Then and Now: An Essay in the History and Sociology of the Negro Race (Du Bois), **Supp. II Part 1:** 159, 178, 183, 185

Blackford, Holly, **Supp. XXII:** 300

"Black Fox, The" (Whittier), **Supp. I Part 2:** 692

Black Freckles (Levis), **Supp. XI:** 257, 271

"Black Gang", **IV:** 406, 407

Black Genius (Mosley, ed.), **Supp. XIII:** 246

Blackguard (Bodenheim), **Supp. XXV:** 17, 18, 22, 23–24

"Black Hood, The" (Francis), **Supp. IX:** 83, 91

Black House, The (Theroux), **Supp. VIII:** 319

Black Humor (C. Johnson), **Supp. VI:** 187, 199

Black Ice, The (Connelly), **Supp. XXI:** **70,** 75

Black Image in the White Mind, The (Fredrickson), **Supp. I Part 2:** 589

"Black Is My Favorite Color" (Malamud), **Supp. I Part 2:** 437

Black Jacobins, The (C. L. R. James), **Supp. XXI:** 159, 166–167

"Black Jewel, The" (Merwin), **Supp. III Part 1:** 355

Black Lamb and Grey Falcon (R. West), **Supp. XVI:** 152

"Black Laughter" (Taggard), **Supp. XXII:** 274

"Blacklegs" (B. Kelly), **Supp. XVII:** 131

Black Light (Kinnell), **Supp. III Part 1:** 235, 243

Black Like Me (Griffin), **Supp. XXV:** 51

Blacklist (Paretsky), **Supp. XXV:** 182, 184

"Blacklist and the Cold War, The" (Kramer), **Supp. I Part 1:** 295

Black Literature in America (Baker), **Supp. X:** 324

Black Magic, A Pictorial History of the Negro in American Entertainment (Hughes), **Supp. I Part 1:** 345

Black Magic: Collected Poetry 1961–1967 (Baraka), **Supp. II Part 1:** 45, 49–50

"Blackmailers Don't Shoot" (Chandler), **Supp. IV Part 1:** 121–122

Black Manhattan (J. W. Johnson), **Supp. IV Part 1:** 169

Black Mass, A (Baraka), **Supp. II Part 1:** 46, 48–49, 56, 57

"Black Mesa, The" (Merrill), **Supp. III Part 1:** 328

Black Metropolis (Cayton and Drake), **IV:** 475, 486, 488

Black Misery (Hughes), **Supp. I Part 1:** 336

Blackmur, Helen Dickson (Mrs. R. P. Blackmur), **Supp. II Part 1:** 90

Blackmur, Richard P., **I:** 50, 63, 67, 280, 282, 386, 455, 472; **II:** 320, 537; **III:** 194, 208, 462, 478, 497; **Supp. II Part 1: 87–112,** 136; **Supp. II Part 2:** 543, 643; **Supp. XII:** 45

Black Music (Baraka), **Supp. II Part 1:** 47, 51

Black Nativity (Hughes), **Retro. Supp. I:** 196

"Black News" (Biss), **Supp. XXVI:** 56

Black No More (Schuyler), **Supp. XIX:** 73; **Supp. XVI:** 142

Black on Black: "Baby Sister" and Selected Writings (C. Himes), **Supp. XVI:** 145

"Black or White" (Major), **Supp. XXII:** 185

"Blackout" (Hay), **Supp. XIV:** 121

Black Oxen (Atherton), **Supp. XXIV:** 25–26

Black Oxen (Atherton, Dawson, ed.), **Supp. XXIV:** 31

"Black Panther" (Hughes), **Retro. Supp. I:** 211

"Black Petal" (L.-Y. Lee), **Supp. XV:** 224–225

Black Power (Wright), **IV:** 478, 488, 494

"Black Rainbow, A: Modern Afro-American Poetry" (Dove and Waniek), **Supp. IV Part 1:** 244

Black Reconstruction (Du Bois), **Supp. II Part 1:** 159, 162, 171, 182

Black Riders and Other Lines, The (Crane), **I:** 406, 419

Black Riviera, The (Jarman), **Supp. XVII:** 109, 110, **115–116**

Blackrobe: Isaac Jogues (Kenny), **Supp. XXIII:** 143, 147, **151–152**, 153, 154

"Black Rook in Rainy Weather" (Plath), **Supp. I Part 2:** 543, 544; **Supp. XXIII:** 63

Blacks (Brooks), **Supp. III Part 1:** 69, 72, 86, 87

Blacks, The (Genet), **Supp. IV Part 1:** 8

"Black Ships Draw Up on a White Beach"(Wakoski), **Supp. XXVIII:** 271

Black Skin, White Masks (Fanon), **Retro. Supp. II:** 118

Black Sleuth, The (J. Bruce), **Supp. XVI:** 143

Blacksnake at the Family Reunion (Huddle), **Supp. XXVI:** 147, 151

Black Spear, The (Hayden), **Supp. II Part 1:** 375

Black Spring (H. Miller), **III:** 170, 175, 178, 180–182, 183, 184; **Supp. X:** 187

Blackstock, Carrie Galloway, **Retro. Supp. III:** 6

"Black Stone, The" (Howard), **Supp. XXVII:** 119

"Black Stone Lying on a White Stone" (Vallejo), **Supp. XIII:** 324

Black Sun (Abbey), **Supp. XIII:** 4, **8–9,** 17

"Black Swan" (B. Kelly), **Supp. XVII:** 130–131

"Black Swan, The" (Jarrell), **II:** 382

Black Swan, The (Merrill), **Supp. III Part 1:** 319, 320

"Black Tambourine" (Crane), **I:** 387–388; **II:** 371

Black Thunder (Bontemps), **Supp. XXII:** 4, 9

"Black Tuesday" (Swenson), **Supp. IV Part 2:** 646

Black Virgin Mountain (Heinemann), **Supp. XXII:** 103, **114–116**

Black Voices (Chapman), **IV:** 485

"Blackwater Mountain" (Wright), **Supp. V:** 335, 340

"Black Wedding, The" (Singer), **IV:** 12–13

Blackwell, Alice Stone, **Supp. XI:** 195, 197

Blackwell, Elizabeth, **Retro. Supp. II:** 146

Black Woman, The (Bambara, ed.), **Supp. XI:** 1

"Black Workers" (Hughes), **Retro. Supp. I:** 202

"Black Writer and the Southern Experience, The" (Walker), **Supp. III Part 2:** 521

Black Zodiac (Wright), **Supp. V:** 333, 344, 345

Blade Runner (film), **Supp. XI:** 84

Blades, John, **Supp. XX: 87**

"Blades of Steel" (R. Fisher), **Supp. XIX:** 72

Blaine, Anita McCormick, **Supp. I Part 1:** 5

Blaine, Nell, **Supp. XV:** 179; **Supp. XXIII:** 217

Blainville Testament, The (Lea), **Supp. XXVIII:** 136

"Blainville Testament, The"(Lea), **Supp. XXVIII:** 136, 140

Blair, Hugh, **II:** 8, 17; **Supp. I Part 2:** 422

Blair, Robert, **Supp. I Part 1:** 150

Blair, Walter, **II:** 20; **Retro. Supp. II:** 286

Blaisdell, Gus, **Supp. XIV:** 87

Blake, Casey Nelson, **Supp. XX: 69, 70, 78**

Blake, William, **I:** 381, 383, 389, 390, 398, 447, 476, 525, 526, 533; **II:** 321; **III:** 5, 19, 22, 195, 196, 197, 205, 485, 528, 540, 544–545, 567, 572; **IV:** 129; **Retro. Supp. II:** 76, 300; **Supp. I Part 1:** 80; **Supp. I Part 2:** 385, 514, 517, 539, 552, 708; **Supp. V:** 208, 257, 258; **Supp. VIII:** 26, 99, 103; **Supp. X:** 120; **Supp. XII:** 45; **Supp. XIV:** 344; **Supp. XVI:** 282; **Supp. XVII:** 119; **Supp. XX: 115, 116; Supp. XXII:** 225, 257; **Supp. XXIV:** 159; **Supp. XXV:** 248; **Supp. XXVI:** 235; **Supp. XXVII:** 292

Blakely, Barbara, **Supp. XIII:** 32

Blanc, Marie Thérèse, **Retro. Supp. II:** 135; **Supp. XXVIII:** 115

Blanc-Bentzon, Mme. Thérèse, **II:** 405

Blanchard, Paula, **Retro. Supp. II:** 131, 133–134, 135

Blanche, Jacques-Émile, **Supp. XX: 232**

Blanche of Brandywine (Lippard), **Supp. XXIII:** 178, 185

Blanchot, Maurice, **Supp. XVI:** 288; **Supp. XXIV:** 40

Blancs, Les (Hansberry), **Supp. IV Part 1:** 359, 364, 365, 369, 372–374

Blancs, Les: The Collected Last Plays of Lorraine Hansberry (Nemiroff, ed.), **Supp. IV Part 1:** 365, 368, 374

"'Blandula, Tenulla, Vagula'" (Pound), **III:** 463; **Supp. V:** 336, 337, 345

Blankenship, Tom, **IV:** 193

Blankfort, Michael, **Supp. XXVIII:** 72

"Blank Paper" (Peacock), **Supp. XIX:** 198–199

Blank Wall, The (Holding), **Supp. XXII:** 119, 120, 121, 130, **131–133,** 134

Blanshard, Rufus A., **I:** 67

Blassingame, John, **Supp. XX: 106**

Blauvelt, William Satake, **Supp. V:** 171, 173

Blavatsky, Elena Petrovna, **III:** 176

"Blazing in Gold and Quenching in Purple" (Dickinson), **Retro. Supp. I:** 30

Bleak House (Dickens), **II:** 291; **Supp. IV Part 1:** 293

Blechman, Burt, **Supp. I Part 1:** 290

"Bleeder" (Dobyns), **Supp. XIII:** 88

"Bleeding" (Swenson), **Supp. IV Part 2:** 646–647

Bleeding Kansas (Paretsky), **Supp. XXV:** 183

"Blessed Is the Man" (Moore), **III:** 215

"Blessed Man of Boston, My Grandmother's Thimble, and Fanning Island, The" (Updike), **IV:** 219

"Blessing, A" (Wright), **Supp. III Part 2:** 600, 606

Blessing on the Moon, A (Skibell), **Supp. XVII:** 48

Blessings (Quindlen), **Supp. XVII:** 167, **178–179**

"Blessing the Animals" (Komunyakaa), **Supp. XIII:** 129–130

"Blessing the Children" (Hogan), **Supp. IV Part 1:** 401

Bless Me, Ultima (Anya), **Supp. XIII:** 220

Blew, Mary Clearman, **Supp. XIV:** 227

Bligh, S. M., **I:** 226

"Blight"(Dybek), **Supp. XXIII:** 72

Blind Alleys (film), **Supp. XXI:** 146

Blind Assassin, The (Atwood), **Supp. XIII:** 20, **32**

Blind Bow-Boy, The (Van Vechten), **Supp. II Part 2:** 737, 740–742

"Blind Date" (Halliday), **Supp. XIX:** 85

Blind Date (Kosinski), **Supp. VII:** 215, 224–225

"Blinded by the Light" (Boyle), **Supp. XX: 20**

Blind Lion, The (Gunn Allen), **Supp. IV Part 1:** 324

"Blind Man's Holiday" (O. Henry), **Supp. II Part 1:** 401

Blind Man with a Pistol (C. Himes), **Supp. XVI:** 143, 144

Blindness and Insight (de Man), **Retro. Supp. I:** 67

"Blind Poet, The: Sidney Lanier" (Warren), **Supp. I Part 1:** 371, 373

"Blindsided" (E. P. Jones), **Supp. XXII:** 151–152

"Blind Tom" (R. H. Davis), **Supp. XVI:** 89, 90

"Blink"(Stuart), **Supp. XXVIII:** 233–234

Blithedale Romance, The (Hawthorne), **II:** 225, 231, 239, 241–242, 271, 282, 290; **IV:** 194; **Retro. Supp. I:** 63, 149, 152, 156–157, **162–163; Retro. Supp. III:** 119–121; **Supp. I Part 2:** 579; **Supp. II Part 1:** 280; **Supp. VIII:** 153, 201

Blitzstein, Marc, **Supp. I Part 1:** 277

Blix (Norris), **III:** 314, 322, 327, 328, 333

Blixen, Karen Denisen Baroness. *See* Dinesen, Isak

"Blizzard in Cambridge" (R. Lowell), **II:** 554

Blizzard Voices, The (Kooser), **Supp. XIX: 123**

Bloch, Ernest, **Supp. XX: 75**

Bloch, Robert, **Supp. XXV: 111, 145; Supp. XXVII: 119**

Block, Lawrence, **Supp. XXI: 67**

"Blocks"(O'Hara), **Supp. XXIII: 214**

Blok, Aleksandr Aleksandrovich, **IV: 443; Supp. XXVI: 144**

"Blond" (Trethewey), **Supp. XXI: 244**

Blonde Bait (Lacy), **Supp. XV: 204**

Blonde on Blonde (album, Dylan), **Supp. XVIII: 20, 27, 30**

Blondin, Antoine, **Supp. XVI: 230**

"Blood" (Hoffman), **Supp. XVIII: 86**

"Blood" (Singer), **IV: 15, 19**

"Blood, Bread, and Poetry" (Rich), **Retro. Supp. III: 251**

Blood, Bread, and Poetry: Selected Prose 1979–1985 (Rich), **Retro. Supp. III: 251**

Blood, Tin, Straw (Olds), **Supp. X: 212–215**

Blood and Guile (Hoffman), **Supp. XVIII: 83–84**

Blood and Guts in High School (Acker), **Supp. XII: 5, 6, 11–12**

Blood and Thunder (Finn), **Supp. XXVII: 128**

"Blood Bay, The" (Proulx), **Supp. VII: 262–263**

"Blood-Burning Moon" (Toomer), **Supp. III Part 2: 483; Supp. IX: 314–315**

"Bloodchild" (O. Butler), **Supp. XIII: 61, 69–70**

Bloodchild and Other Stories (O. Butler), **Supp. XIII: 69**

"Blood Donor" (Hay), **Supp. XIV: 121**

Blood for a Stranger (Jarrell), **II: 367, 368–369, 370–371, 375, 377**

"Blood from the Stone" (Oppen), **Supp. XXVI: 230–231**

Blood Issue (Crews), **Supp. XI: 103**

Bloodlines (Wright), **Supp. V: 332, 335, 340**

Blood Meridian (McCarthy), **Supp. XXIII: 42**

Blood Meridian; or, The Evening Redness in the West (McCarthy), **Supp. VIII: 175, 177, 180–182, 188, 190**

Blood of My Blood (Gambino), **Supp. XX: 35**

"Blood of the Conquistadores, The" (Alvarez), **Supp. VII: 7**

"Blood of the Lamb, The" (hymn), **Supp. I Part 2: 385**

Blood of the Martyr (Crane), **I: 422**

"Blood of the Martyrs, The" (Benét), **Supp. XI: 56, 58**

Blood of the Prophets, The (Masters), **Supp. I Part 2: 458, 459, 461**

Blood on the Forge (Attaway), **Supp. II Part 1: 234–235**

Blood on the Tracks (album, Dylan), **Supp. XVIII: 20, 27, 30**

"Blood Relatives" (Apple), **Supp. XVII: 6**

"Blood Returns, The" (Kingsolver), **Supp. VII: 209**

"Bloodroot" (Rash), **Supp. XXVII: 222**

"Bloodshed" (C. Ozick), **Supp. XVII: 43**

Bloodshed and Three Novellas (Ozick), **Supp. V: 259–260, 261, 266–268**

"Blood Soup"(Dybek), **Supp. XXIII: 71**

"Blood Stains" (Francis), **Supp. IX: 86**

Blood Work (Connelly), **Supp. XXI: 72**

Blood Work (film, Eastwood), **Supp. XXI: 74**

Bloody Crossroads, The: Where Literature and Politics Meet (Podhoretz), **Supp. VIII: 241–242**

"Bloody Massacre near Carson, A" (Twain), **Retro. Supp. III: 257**

Bloody News from My Friend (Samianto, trans. Balakian), **Supp. XXIII: 28**

Bloom, Alice, **Supp. IV Part 1: 308**

Bloom, Allan, **Retro. Supp. II: 19, 30, 31, 33–34**

Bloom, Claire, **Retro. Supp. II: 281; Supp. IX: 125**

Bloom, Harold, **Retro. Supp. I: 67, 193, 299; Retro. Supp. II: 81, 210, 262; Supp. IV Part 2: 620, 689; Supp. IX: 146, 259; Supp. V: 178, 272; Supp. VIII: 180; Supp. XII: 261; Supp. XIII: 46, 47; Supp. XIV: 14; Supp. XV: 134; Supp. XVII: 70, 141; Supp. XXIII: 42; Supp. XXV: 251**

Bloom, Larry, **Supp. XIII: 133**

Bloom, Leopold, **I: 27, 150; III: 10**

Bloom, Lynn Z., **Supp. IV Part 1: 6**

Bloomfield, Leonard, **I: 64**

Bloomingdale Papers, The (Carruth), **Supp. XVI: 48–50**

"Blossom and Fruit" (Benét), **Supp. XI: 52–53**

Blotner, Joseph, **Retro. Supp. I: 88; Retro. Supp. III: 75**

Blouin, Lenora, **Supp. VIII: 266**

"Blouse, The"(Rudman), **Supp. XXIII: 124**

"Blowing Soap Bubbles"(Crooker), **Supp. XXIII: 56**

"Blowin' in the Wind" (song, Dylan), **Supp. XVIII: 24, 25, 26, 29**

Bluckled Bag, The (Rinehart), **Supp. XXV: 197**

Blue Angel (Prose), **Supp. XVI: 249, 259–260**

Blue Angel, The (film), **Supp. XVIII: 243**

Blue Arabesque: A Search for the Sublime (Hampl), **Supp. XXII: 86, 98–99**

"Blue Battalions, The" (Crane), **I: 419–420**

"Blue Bead, The"(Hadas), **Supp. XXIII: 118, 119**

"Bluebeard" (Barthelme), **Supp. IV Part 1: 47**

"Bluebeard" (Millay), **III: 130**

"Blueberries" (Frost), **Retro. Supp. I: 121, 128**

"Blue Boy"(Dybek), **Supp. XXIII: 76**

Blue Calhoun (Price), **Supp. VI: 265–266**

Blue Caterpillar, The (Pickering), **Supp. XXI: 202–203**

Blue City (Macdonald, as Millar), **Supp. IV Part 2: 466–467**

Blue Devils of Nada, The: A Contemporary American Approach to Aesthetics (Murray), **Supp. XIX: 159–160**

Blue Estuaries, The: Poems, 1923–1968 (Bogan), **Supp. III Part 1: 48, 57, 66**

Blue Hammer, The (Macdonald), **Supp. IV Part 2: 462**

"Blue Hotel, The" (Crane), **I: 34, 415–416, 423**

"Blue Hour, The" (Komunyakaa), **Supp. XIII: 130**

"Blue Ice Wolf"(Wakoski), **Supp. XXVIII: 271–272**

Blue in the Face (Auster), **Supp. XII: 21**

Blue Jay's Dance, The: A Birth Year (Erdrich), **Supp. IV Part 1: 259–260, 265, 270, 272**

"Blue Juniata" (Cowley), **Supp. II Part 1: 144**

Blue Juniata: Collected Poems (Cowley), **Supp. II Part 1: 140**

"Blue Lick" (Offutt), **Supp. XIX: 164, 165**

Blue Light (Mosley), **Supp. XIII: 245–247, 248, 249**

"Blue Light Lounge Sutra for the Performance Poets at Harold Park Hotel" (Komunyakaa), **Supp. XIII: 125**

"Blue Meridian" (Toomer), **Supp. III Part 2: 476, 487; Supp. IX: 320**

"Blue Moles" (Plath), **Supp. I Part 2: 539**

"Blue Monday"(Wakoski), **Supp. XXVIII: 262, 263**

Blue Mountain Ballads (music) (Bowles), **Supp. IV Part 1: 84**

Blue Movie (Southern), **Supp. XI: 309**

"Blue Notes" (Matthews), **Supp. IX: 169**

Blue Pastoral (Sorrentino), **Supp. XXI: 226, 235–236**

Blue Pastures (Oliver), **Supp. VII: 229–230, 245**

"Blueprint for Negro Writing" (Wright), **Supp. XVIII: 282–283**

"Blueprints" (Kingsolver), **Supp. VII: 203**

Blue Religion, The (Connelly, ed.), **Supp. XXI: 74–75, 79**

Blue Rhine, Black Forest (Untermeyer), **Supp. XV: 310**

"Blue Ribbon at Amesbury, A" (Frost), **Retro. Supp. I: 138**

"Blues Ain't No Mockin Bird" (Bambara), **Supp. XI: 3**

"Blues and the Fable in the Flesh, The" (lecture, Murray), **Supp. XIX: 153**

Blues Baby: Early Poems (Mullen), **Supp. XXVII: 174**

"Blues Chant Hoodoo Rival" (Komunyakaa), **Supp. XIII: 117, 118**

Blue Screen (Parker), **Supp. XIX: 186**

"Blues for Another Time" (Dunn), **Supp. XI: 148**

"Blues for Jimmy" (McGrath), **Supp. X: 116**

"Blues for John Coltraine, Dead at 41" (Matthews), **Supp. IX: 157**

Blues for Mister Charlie (Baldwin), **Retro. Supp. II: 8; Supp. I Part 1: 48, 61–62, 63**

"Blues for Warren" (McGrath), **Supp. X: 116**

Blue Shoe (Lamott), **Supp. XX: 138–140**
Blues If You Want (Matthews), **Supp. IX: 155, 163–165**
"Blues I'm Playing, The" (Hughes), **Retro. Supp. I:** 204; **Supp. XIX:** 75
Blues Journey (Myers), **Supp. XXVII:** 211
"Blue Sky, The" (Snyder), **Supp. VIII:** 306
Blues Legacies and Black Feminism (A. Davis), **Supp. XXVI:** 50
Bluesman (Dubus III), **Supp. XXIV: 102–104**
"Blues on a Box" (Hughes), **Retro. Supp. I:** 208
"Blues People" (Ellison), **Retro. Supp. II:** 124
Blues People: Negro Music in White America (Baraka), **Retro. Supp. II:** 124; **Supp. II Part 1:** 30, 31, 33–35, 37, 41, 42, 53
"Blue Spruces in Pairs, a Bird Bath Between": (Bronk), **Supp. XXI:** 30
Bluest Eye, The (Morrison), **Retro. Supp. III:** 183, 184, 185–187, 199–200; **Supp. III Part 1:** 362, 363–367, 379; **Supp. IV Part 1:** 2, 253; **Supp. VIII:** 213, 214, 227; **Supp. XI:** 4, 91
Bluestone, George, **Supp. IX:** 7, 15
Blue Swallows, The (Nemerov), **III:** 269, 270, 271, 274–275, 278, 284, 286–288
"Blue Tattoo" (Nelson and Espeland), **Supp. XVIII:** 181
Blue Voyage (Aiken), **I:** 53, 56
Bluhm, Norman, **Supp. XXIII:** 217
Blum, Gustav, **Supp. XV:** 194
Blum, Morgan, **I:** 169
Blum, W. C (pseudonym). *See* Watson, James Sibley, Jr.
Blume, Judy, **Supp. XXVIII:** 279, 280
Blumenthal, Nathaniel. *See* Branden, Nathaniel
Blumenthal, Sidney, **Supp. VIII:** 241
Blunden, Edmund, **Supp. XIX:** 133
Blunt, Wilfrid Scawen, **III:** 459
Bly, Carol, **Supp. XVI: 31–43**
Bly, Robert, **I:** 291; **Supp. III Part 2:** 599; **Supp. IV Part 1: 59–77,** 177; **Supp. IV Part 2:** 623; **Supp. IX:** 152, 155, 265, 271, 290; **Supp. V:** 332; **Supp. VIII:** 279; **Supp. X:** 127; **Supp. XI:** 142; **Supp. XIII:** 284; **Supp. XV:** 74, 176; **Supp. XVI:** 32, 36, 39, 177, 212, 230; **Supp. XVII:** 243, 244; **Supp. XXI:** 83, 84–86, 87, 91, 93, 94, 95; **Supp. XXII:** 83; **Supp. XXIII:** 136; **Supp. XXIV:** 219
"B Negative" (X. J. Kennedy), **Supp. XV: 156–157**
"Boarder, The" (Simpson), **Supp. IX:** 269
Boarding House Blues (Farrell), **II:** 30, 43, 45
Boarding School, The (Foster), **Supp. XXV:** 35, 36, 37, 45–47
Boas, Franz, **I:** 214; **Retro. Supp. III:** 127, 130; **Supp. I Part 2:** 641; **Supp. IX:** 329; **Supp. VIII:** 295; **Supp. XIV:** 199, 209, 210
"Boat, The" (Oliver), **Supp. VII:** 247

"Boat, The" (Sexton), **Supp. II Part 2:** 692
Boating Party, The (Renoir), **Supp. XII:** 188
"Boat Is Tethered to the Floor,' The: After the Harlem Renaissance" (H. Johnson), **Supp. XXVI:** 175
Boat of Quiet Hours, The (Kenyon), **Supp. VII:** 167–169, 171
"Boat of Quiet Hours, The" (Kenyon), **Supp. VII:** 168
"Boat Ride" (Gallagher), **Supp. XXIV:** 169
"Bob and Spike" (Wolfe), **Supp. III Part 2:** 580
Bobbed Hair (Wells, et al), **Supp. XXVI:** 275
Bobbie, General Manager (Prouty), **Supp. XXVIII:** 177–178, 191
"Bobby Shafter's Gone to Sea" (Swados), **Supp. XIX:** 267
"Bob Dylan's 115th Dream" (song, Dylan), **Supp. XVIII:** 25
Bobrowski, Johannes, **Supp. XV:** 78
Bob the Gambler (F. Barthelme), **Supp. XI:** 30, 31, 32, 34–35, 36–37
Boccaccio, Giovanni, **III:** 283, 411; **IV:** 230
"Bocca della Verità, La" (Davison), **Supp. XXVI:** 74
Bocock, Maclin, **Supp. X:** 79
Boddy, Kasia, **Supp. XXII:** 261
Bodelson, Anders, **Supp. XVI:** 33
Bodenheim, Maxwell, **II:** 42, 530; **Retro. Supp. I:** 417; **Supp. I Part 1:** 257; **Supp. XXV:** 17–33; **Supp. XXVII:** 86, 87, 139
"Bodies" (Oates), **Supp. II Part 2:** 520
"Bodies and Souls: The Haitian Revolution and Madison Smartt Bell's *All Souls' Rising*" (Trouillot), **Supp. X:** 14
Bodies of Water (Cliff), **Supp. XXII:** 66–67, 74–75
Bodies of Work: Essays (Acker), **Supp. XII:** 7
Bodily Harm (Atwood), **Supp. XIII: 25–27**
Bodley Head Jack London (London), **II:** 483
Body (Crews), **Supp. XI: 108–109**
"Body, The" (Heldreth), **Supp. V:** 151
Body and Soul (Conroy), **Supp. XVI:** 63, **72–74,** 77
"Body and Soul: A Meditation" (Kumin), **Supp. IV Part 2:** 442, 452
Body and Soul: Essays on Poetry (Jarman), **Supp. XVII:** 110, **111–112**
"Body and Soul: Parts of a Life" (Jarman), **Supp. XVII:** 112, 113
Body and the Song, The (Bishop), **Retro. Supp. II:** 40
"Body Bright" (Sanders), **Supp. XVI:** 276
Body of Martin Aquilera, The (Everett), **Supp. XVIII:** 57
Body of Poetry, The: Essays on Women, Form, and the Poetic Self (A. Finch), **Supp. XVII:** 69–70, **77–78**

Body of This Death: Poems (Bogan), **Supp. III Part 1:** 47, 49–52, 58
Body of Waking (Rukeyser), **Supp. VI:** 274, 281
"Body of Waking" (Rukeyser), **Supp. VI:** 279
"Body on Fire, the Soul in Flight, The" (Jarman), **Supp. XVII:** 111, 112
Body Rags (Kinnell), **Supp. III Part 1:** 235, 236, 243–245, 250, 253, 254
"Body's Curse, The" (Dobyns), **Supp. XIII:** 87
"Body's Weight" (Espaillat), **Supp. XXI:** 111
"Body's Weight, The" (Dobyns), **Supp. XIII:** 89
Body Traffic (Dobyns), **Supp. XIII:** 87, 89
"'Body with the Lamp Lit Inside, The'" (Mills), **Supp. IV Part 1:** 64
Body Work (Paretsky), **Supp. XXV:** 177, 178, 179, 181, 184–185
Boehm, David, **Supp. XVII:** 58
Boehme, Jakob, **I:** 10
Bogan, Louise, **I:** 169, 185; **Retro. Supp. I:** 36; **Supp. I Part 2:** 707, 726; **Supp. III Part 1:** 47–68; **Supp. IX:** 229; **Supp. VIII:** 171, 265; **Supp. X:** 58, 102; **Supp. XIII:** 347; **Supp. XIV:** 129; **Supp. XVII:** 75; **Supp. XXIII:** 145; **Supp. XXVII:** 261
Bogan, Major Benjamin Lewis, **IV:** 120
Bogart, Humphrey, **Supp. I Part 2:** 623; **Supp. IV Part 1:** 130, 356
Bogdanovich, Peter, **Supp. V:** 226
Bogey Man, The (Plimpton), **Supp. XVI:** 241
Boggs, Francis W., **Supp. XVI:** 182
"Bogs" (Pickering), **Supp. XXI:** 198
"Bohemian, The" (Hapgood), **Supp. XVII:** 103
"Bohemian, The" (Harte), **Supp. II Part 1:** 339
"Bohemian Girl, The" (Cather), **Retro. Supp. I:** 7; **Retro. Supp. III:** 22, 26, 28
"Bohemian Hymn, The" (Emerson), **II:** 19
"Bohemians" (Saunders), **Supp. XIX:** 234
"Boids and Beasties" (Geisel), **Supp. XVI:** 100
Boissevain, Eugen, **III:** 124
Boissière, Ralph de, **Supp. XXI:** 160
Boit, Edward, **Retro. Supp. I:** 366
Bojorquez, Jennifer, **Supp. XII:** 318
"Boke, A" (Berrigan), **Supp. XXIV:** 42
Boker, George, **Supp. XV:** 269
Boland, Eavan, **Retro. Supp. III:** 14
Boland, Evan, **Supp. XXVIII:** 22
Bolaño, Roberto, **Supp. XXV:** 49
"Bold Words at the Bridge" (Jewett), **II:** 394
Boleslavsky, Richard, **Supp. XIV:** 240, 243
Boleyn, Anne, **Supp. I Part 2:** 461
Bolick, Katie, **Supp. XVI:** 167; **Supp. XXIII:** 135, 137, 138; **Supp. XXIV:** 167, 173, 177

Bolinas Journal (Brainard), **Supp. XXVII:** 20, 27

Bolivar, Simon, **Supp. I Part 1:** 283, 284, 285

Bolonik, Kera, **Supp. XVIII:** 60

"Bolshevik"(Lewisohn), **Supp. XXVIII:** 154

Bolton, Guy, **Supp. I Part 1:** 281

Bolts of Melody: New Poems of Emily Dickinson (Todd and Bingham, eds.), **I:** 470; **Retro. Supp. I:** 36

"Bomb" (Corso), **Supp. XII:** 117, 124, 125–126, 127

Bombeck, Erma, **Supp. XVII:** 168

Bombs Away (Steinbeck), **IV:** 51–52

"Bona and Paul" (Toomer), **Supp. IX:** 307, 318–319

Bonaparte, Darren, **Supp. XXVI:** 88

Bonaparte, Marie, **III:** 418; **Retro. Supp. II:** 264, 266

"Bon-Bon" (Poe), **III:** 425

Bond, The (Boyce), **Supp. XXI:** 5, 11–12

Bond, The (N. Boyce), **Supp. XVII:** 99, 100

Bondage (Hwang), **Supp. XXI:** 147

Bondsman, The (Massinger), **Supp. XV:** 238

Bondwoman's Narrative, by Hannah Crafts, a Fugitive Slave, Recently Escaped from North Carolina, The, **Supp. XX:** 105

Bone, Martyn, **Supp. XXII:** 247

Bone, Robert, **Supp. IX:** 318–319; **Supp. XI:** 283; **Supp. XVIII:** 285

Bone by Bone (Matthiessen), **Supp. V:** 199, 212, 213, 214

"Bone Deposit" (Ray), **Supp. XVIII:** 194

Boners (Abingdon). *See Schoolboy Howlers* (Abingdon)

"Bones" (Goldbarth), **Supp. XII: 173–174**

"Bones and Jewels" (Monette), **Supp. X:** 159

"Bones and Shells" (Sanders), **Supp. XVI:** 271–272

"Bones of a House" (Cowley). *See* "Blue Juniata"

Bones on Black Spruce Mountain, The (Budbill), **Supp. XIX:** 11–12

Bonetti, Kay, **Supp. VIII:** 47, 152, 159, 160, 165, 168, 170, 223; **Supp. XII:** 61; **Supp. XIV:** 232, 234; **Supp. XXI:** 36

"Bonfire" (Gallagher), **Supp. XXIV:** 170

"Bonfire, The" (Frost), **Retro. Supp. III:** 99

Bonfire of the Vanities, The (Wolfe), **Supp. III Part 2:** 584–586

Bonheur, Rosa, **Supp. XV:** 276

Bonhoeffer, Dietrich, **Supp. VIII:** 198

Boni, Charles, **Supp. XIV:** 288

Boni and Liveright, **Retro. Supp. I:** 59, 80, 178

Bonicelli, Vittorio, **Supp. XI:** 307

Bonifacius (Mather), **Supp. II Part 2:** 461, 464

Bonnefoy, Yves, **Supp. III Part 1:** 235, 243

"Bonne Maman"(King), **Supp. XXVIII:** 120

Bonner, Robert, **Retro. Supp. I:** 246

Bonneville, Mme. Marguerite, **Supp. I Part 2:** 520, 521

Bonneville, Nicolas de, **Supp. I Part 2:** 511, 518, 519

Bonney, William. *See* Billy the Kid

Bontemps, Arna, **Retro. Supp. I:** 194, 196, 203; **Supp. I Part 1:** 325; **Supp. IV Part 1:** 170; **Supp. IX:** 306, 309; **Supp. XVIII:** 282; **Supp. XXII:** 1–16

Book, A (Barnes), **Supp. III Part 1:** 36, 39, 44

Book about Myself, A (Dreiser), **I:** 515; **Retro. Supp. II:** 104

"Book as a Container of Consciousness, The" (Gass), **Supp. VI:** 92

Booker, Keith, **Supp. XV:** 197

"Bookies, Beware!" (Heller), **Supp. IV Part 1:** 383

"Book Notes and News" (column, Boyce), **Supp. XXI:** 2

Book of American Negro Poetry, The (J. W. Johnson, ed.), **Supp. IV Part 1:** 165, 166; **Supp. XXII:** 11; **Supp. XXVI:** 165

Book of Americans, A (Benét), **Supp. XI:** 46, 47, 51

Book of Beb, The (Buechner), **Supp. XII:** 53

Book of Breeething, The (Burroughs), **Supp. III Part 1:** 97, 103

Book of Burlesques, A (Mencken), **III:** 104

Book of Common Prayer, A (Didion), **Supp. IV Part 1:** 196, 198, 203–205, 207, 208

Book of Daniel, The (Doctorow), **Supp. IV Part 1:** 218, 219, 220–222, 227, 231, 237–238, 238; **Supp. V:** 45

Book of Dreams (Kerouac), **Supp. III Part 1:** 225

"Book of Ephraim, The" (Merrill), **Supp. III Part 1:** 330–334

Book of Folly, The (Sexton), **Supp. II Part 2:** 691, 692–694

Book of Gallant Vagabonds, The (Beston), **Supp. XXVI:** 33

Book of Gliders, The (Teale), **Supp. XXVIII:** 245–246

Book of Gods and Devils, The (Simic), **Supp. VIII: 281**

Book of Guys, The (Keillor), **Supp. XVI:** 177

"Book of Hours of Sister Clotilde, The" (A. Lowell), **II:** 522

"Book of Life" (Bidart), **Supp. XV:** 23

Book of Living Verse, The; English and American Poetry from the Thirteenth Century to the Present Day (Untermeyer, ed.), **Supp. XV:** 310

Book of Longing (Cohen), **Supp. XXVII:** 56

Book of Love, A (Vildrac; Bynner, trans.), **Supp. XV:** 50

Book of Lyrics (Bynner), **Supp. XV:** 51

Book of Martyrs (Fox). *See Acts and Monuments of These Latter and Perilous Days* (Fox)

Book of Medicines, The (Hogan), **Supp. IV Part 1:** 397, 410, 411–414

"Book of Medicines, The" (Hogan), **Supp. IV Part 1:** 412, 413

"Book of Memory, The" (Auster), **Supp. XII:** 21–22

Book of Mercy (Cohen), **Supp. XXVII:** 54

Book of My Nights (L.-Y. Lee), **Supp. XV:** 215, **223–226**

Book of Negro Folklore, The (Hughes, ed.), **Supp. I Part 1:** 345; **Supp. XXII:** 11–12

Book of Nightmares, The (Kinnell), **Supp. III Part 1:** 235, 236, 243, 244, 246–254

Book of One's Own, A: People and Their Diaries (Mallon), **Supp. XIX:** 134

Book of Prefaces, A (Mencken), **III:** 99–100, 105

Book of Repulsive Women, The (Barnes), **Supp. III Part 1:** 33

Book of Revelation, **Supp. XXIII:** 44

Book of Roses, The (Parkman), **Supp. II Part 2:** 597, 598

Book of the Body, The (Bidart), **Supp. XV:** 21, **25–27**

"Book of the Dead, The" (Rukeyser), **Supp. VI:** 272, 278, 279; **Supp. XV:** 349

"Book of the Grotesque, The" (Anderson), **I:** 106

Book of the Homeless, The (Wharton), **Retro. Supp. I:** 377

Book of the Hopi (Waters), **Supp. X:** 124

Book of Tobit (Bible), **Supp. XII:** 54

Book of Verses, A (Masters), **Supp. I Part 2:** 458

Book of Wonder (Dunsany), **Supp. XXV:** 113

Book of Yaak, The (Bass), **Supp. XVI: 18–19**

"Book of Yolek, The" (Hecht), **Supp. X:** 69, **70–71**

"Books" (Collins), **Supp. XXI:** 55

"Books Considered" (Bloom), **Supp. I Part 1:** 96

"Books I Left Behind, The" (Pickering), **Supp. XXI:** 196

Books in My Life, The (H. Miller), **II:** 176, 189

"Books/P,L,E, The" (Goldbarth), **Supp. XII:** 190

Bookviews, **Supp. XI:** 216

"Book World Live", **Supp. XVIII:** 143–144

"Boolean Algebra: X2=X" (Bronk), **Supp. XXI:** 30

"Boom" (Nemerov), **III:** 278

Boom! (T. Williams), **IV:** 383

Boomer Girls: Poems by Women of the Baby Boom Generation (Gemin and Sergi, eds.), **Supp. XXI:** 246

Boom Town (Wolfe), **IV:** 456

"Boom Town" (Wolfe), **IV:** 469

Boone, Daniel, **II:** 207; **III:** 444; **IV:** 192, 193

Boorstin, Daniel, **I:** 253

Booth, Charles, **Supp. I Part 1:** 13

Booth, John Wilkes, **III:** 588

Booth, Philip, **I:** 522; **Supp. IX:** 269; **Supp. XI:** 141; **Supp. XIII:** 277; **Supp. XV:** 92; **Supp. XXVI:** 68

Booth, General William, **Supp. I Part 2:** 384, 386

"Boot Theory"(Siken), **Supp. XXVIII:** 197, 199, 201

"Booze"(P. Benedict), **Supp. XXIII:** 36

Borah, William, **III:** 475

Borden, Lizzie, **II:** 5

Border and the Buffalo, The (J. Cook), **Supp. XXIV:** 248

"Border Crossings: An Interview with Eric Gansworth" (de la Paz and Purdy), **Supp. XXVI:** 101

Borderlands/La Frontera: The New Mestiza (Anzaldúa), **Supp. XIII:** 223

Border Matters (Saldívar), **Supp. XIX:** 112–113

Borders (Mora), **Supp. XIII:** 213, **215–217**

Border Trilogy (McCarthy), **Supp. VIII:** 175, 182

"Border View, Hot Springs, Texas" (W. V. Davis), **Supp. XXI:** 95

Bordo, Susan, **Supp. XXVIII:** 209

Borel, Pétrus, **III:** 320

Borges, Jorge Luis, **I:** 123, 135, 138, 140, 142; **Retro. Supp. III:** 235; **Supp. III Part 2:** 560; **Supp. IV Part 2:** 623, 626, 630; **Supp. V:** 238; **Supp. VIII:** 15, 348, 349; **Supp. XII:** 21, 147; **Supp. XIX:** 131; **Supp. XV:** 34; **Supp. XVI:** 201, 206; **Supp. XVII:** 47; **Supp. XXIII:** 68; **Supp. XXV:** 50, 69

"Borges and I" (Bidart), **Supp. XV:** 34, 35

"Borinken Blues" (Komunyakaa), **Supp. XIII:** 117

"Born, The" (Lamott), **Supp. XX: 143–144**

"Born a Square: The Westerner's Dilemma" (Stegner), **Supp. IV Part 2:** 595; **Supp. V:** 224

"Born Bad" (Cisneros), **Supp. VII:** 62

Born on the Fourth of July (Kovic), **Supp. XIX:** 17

"Borough of Cemeteries" (Shaw), **Supp. XIX:** 246

Borrowed Time: An AIDS Memoir (Monette), **Supp. X:** 145, 146, 147, 152, 154, 155

Boschman, Robert, **Retro. Supp. III:** 7

Bose, Sudip, **Supp. XXII:** 205, 206, 214

Bosmajian, Hamida, **Supp. XXII:** 290

"Bosque del Apache Wildlife Refuge" (Mora), **Supp. XIII:** 218

Boss Dog, The: A Story of Provence (M. F. K. Fisher), **Supp. XVII:** 91

Bossin, Gary, **Supp. XXVII:** 133, 143, 145

Bost, Suzanne, **Supp. XXII:** 66, 70, 75, 78

"Boston" (Hardwick), **Supp. III Part 1:** 201

Boston (Sinclair), **Supp. V:** 282, 288–289; **Supp. XXVIII:** 68

Boston, B. H., **Supp. XIII:** 312

Boston Adventure (Stafford), **Retro. Supp. II:** 177, 178

"Boston Common" (Berryman), **I:** 172

"Boston Evening Transcript, The" (T. S. Eliot), **Retro. Supp. III:** 60

"Boston Hymn" (Emerson), **II:** 13, 19

Bostonians, The (H. James), **I:** 9; **II:** 282; **IV:** 202; **Retro. Supp. I:** 216, 225

Boston Marriage (Mamet), **Supp. XIV:** 247

"Boston Nativity, The" (R. Lowell), **II:** 538

Boswell, James, **IV:** 431; **Supp. I Part 2:** 656

Boswell: A Modern Comedy (Elkin), **Supp. VI:** 42, **44–45,** 57

Bosworth, Patricia, **Supp. IV Part 2:** 573, 591

"Bothersome Sex and O'Brien, The" (Ryan as Quin), **Supp. XVIII:** 238

Botticelli (McNally), **Supp. XIII:** 197

Botticelli, Sandro, **IV:** 410; **Retro. Supp. I:** 422

"Botticellian Trees, The" (W. C. Williams), **Retro. Supp. I:** 422

"Bottled" (H. Johnson), **Supp. XXVI:** 164, 165

"Bottle of Milk for Mother, A" (Algren), **Supp. IX:** 3

"Bottle of Perrier, A" (Wharton), **IV:** 316

"Bottles" (Kenyon), **Supp. VII:** 171

"Bottom Line, The" (Elkin), **Supp. VI:** 52, **53**

Bottom: On Shakespeare (Zukofsky), **Supp. III Part 2:** 622, 624, 625, 626, 627, 629

Bottoms, David, **Supp. XXVIII: 21–36**

Boublil, Alain, **Supp. XXI:** 155

Boucher, Anthony, **Supp. IV Part 2:** 473; **Supp. XV:** 203, 205

Boucicault, Dion, **Supp. XXII:** 70

Boughton, Henrietta Breckenridge. *See* Young, Barbara

Boukreev, Anatoli, **Supp. XVIII:** 112

Boulanger, Nadia, **Supp. IV Part 1:** 81

"Boulot and Boulette" (Chopin), **Supp. I Part 1:** 211

Boulton, Agnes, **III:** 403; **Supp. XXII: 17–31**

Bound East for Cardiff (O'Neill), **III:** 388; **Supp. XXVIII:** 38

Bound for Glory (Guthrie), **Supp. XVIII:** 23

"Bounty" (Saunders), **Supp. XIX:** 226, 227

"Bounty"(P. Benedict), **Supp. XXIII:** 41

"Bouquet, The" (Stevens), **IV:** 90

"Bouquet of Dark Red Mums, The" (Notley), **Supp. XXII:** 230

"Bouquet of Roses in Sunlight" (Stevens), **IV:** 93

Bourdin, Henri L., **Supp. I Part 1:** 251

Bourgeois, Monique, **Supp. XXII:** 99–100

Bourgeois Poet, The (Shapiro), **Supp. II Part 2:** 701, 703, 704, 713, 714–716

Bourget, James, **IV:** 319

Bourget, Paul, **II:** 325, 338; **IV:** 311, 315; **Retro. Supp. I:** 224, 359, 373; **Retro. Supp. III:** 275; **Supp. XX: 232;**

Supp. XXIV: 23

Bourjaily, Vance, **III:** 43; **Supp. IX:** 260; **Supp. XXIV:** 225

Bourke-White, Margaret, **I:** 290, 293, 295, 297

Bourne, Charles Rogers, **I:** 215

Bourne, Mrs. Charles Rogers, **I:** 215

Bourne, Randolph, **I:** 214–238, 243, 245, 246–247, 251, 259; **Supp. I Part 2:** 524; **Supp. XV:** 141, 298, 301

Boursicot, Bernard, **Supp. XXI:** 152, 153, 154

Bouton, Jim "Bulldog", **Supp. XX: 274**

Bouton, John Bell, **Supp. XXIII:** 188, 189

Bowden, Charles, **Supp. XIII:** 17

Bowditch, Nathaniel, **Supp. I Part 2:** 482

Bowen, Barbara, **Supp. IX:** 311

Bowen, Elizabeth, **Retro. Supp. I:** 351; **Supp. IV Part 1:** 299; **Supp. IX:** 128; **Supp. VIII:** 65, 165, 251, 265

Bowen, Francis, **Supp. I Part 2:** 413

Bowen, Henry, **Supp. XVIII:** 4

Bowen, Louise de Koven, **Supp. I Part 1:** 5

Bowen, Michael, **Supp. VIII:** 73

Bowers, John, **Supp. XI:** 217–218

"Bowlers Anonymous" (Dobyns), **Supp. XIII:** 86

Bowles, Emily, **Supp. XVIII:** 200, 202

Bowles, Jane (Jane Auer), **II:** 586; **Supp. IV Part 1:** 89, 92

Bowles, Paul, **I:** 211; **II:** 586; **Supp. II Part 1:** 17; **Supp. IV Part 1: 79–99**

Bowles, Samuel, **I:** 454, 457; **Retro. Supp. I:** 30, 32, 33

"Bowl of Blood, The" (Jeffers), **Supp. II Part 2:** 434

"Bowl of Gardenias, The"(Wakoski), **Supp. XXVIII:** 272

"Bowls" (Moore), **III:** 196

Bowman, James, **III:** 193

"Bows to Drouth" (Snyder), **Supp. VIII:** 303

Box, Edgar (pseudonym). *See* Vidal, Gore

Box and Quotations from Chairman Mao Tse-tung (Albee), **I:** 89–91, 94

Boxer and the Spy, The (Parker), **Supp. XIX:** 190

Box Garden, The (Shields), **Supp. VII:** 314–315, 320

"Box of Pastels, A" (Kooser), **Supp. XIX:** 128

"Box of Rocks, A" (Gallagher), **Supp. XXIV:** 175

"Box Seat" (Toomer), **Supp. III Part 2:** 484; **Supp. IX:** 316, 318

Boy, A (Ashbery), **Supp. III Part 1:** 5

"Boy and Dog" (L. Brown), **Supp. XXI:** 38, 42, **43–44**

Boyce, Horace, **II:** 136

Boyce, Neith, **Supp. XVII:** 96, 97, 98–99, 100, 106; **Supp. XXI: 1–16**

Boyd, Brian, **Retro. Supp. I:** 270, 275

Boyd, Janet L., **Supp. X:** 229

Boyd, Kristen, **Supp. XXIII:** 246

Boyd, Nancy (pseudonym). *See* Millay, Edna St. Vincent

Boyd, Thomas, **I:** 99; **IV:** 427

Boyd, Valerie, **Retro. Supp. III:** 136

Boyelston, Matthew, **Supp. XXVII:** 216

Boyers, Robert, **Retro. Supp. III:** 245

Boyesen, H. H., **II:** 289

"Boy from Lam Kien, The" (July), **Supp. XXIV:** 200, 204

"Boyhood" (Collins), **Supp. XXI:** 64

"Boyhood" (Farrell), **II:** 28

"Boy in France, A" (Salinger), **III:** 552–553

"Boy in the Basement, The" (Inge), **Supp. XXV:** 105, 106

Boy in the Water (Dobyns), **Supp. XIII:** 75, **84**

Boyle, Kay, **IV:** 404; **Supp. XXIV: 49–66**

Boyle, T. Coraghessan, **Supp. VIII: 1–17; Supp. XX: 17–32; Supp. XXI:** 226; **Supp. XXII:** 262

Boyle, Thomas John. *See* Boyle, T. C.

Boynton, H. W., **Supp. IX:** 7

Boynton, Percy Holmes, **Supp. I Part 2:** 415

Boynton, Robert, **Supp. XVII:** 209; **Supp. XVIII:** 105, 107, 116

Boynton, Robert S., **Supp. XXV:** 158

"Boy on a Train" (Ellison), **Retro. Supp. II:** 124

"Boy Riding Forward Backward" (Francis), **Supp. IX:** 82

"Boys and Girls" (Cisneros), **Supp. VII:** 59–60

"Boys and Girls" (Munro), **Supp. XXVII:** 184

Boys' Book of Insects, The (Teale), **Supp. XXVIII:** 246

Boys' Book of Photography, The (Teale), **Supp. XXVIII:** 244

"Boy's Dream Ballad, The" (Very), **Supp. XXV:** 244

Boy's Froissart, The (Lanier), **Supp. I Part 1:** 361

"Boys"(Kenny), **Supp. XXIII:** 149

Boy's King Arthur, The (Lanier), **Supp. I Part 1:** 361

Boy's Mabinogion, The (Lanier), **Supp. I Part 1:** 361

"Boys of '29, The" (Holmes), **Supp. I Part 1:** 308

Boys of '76, The (Coffin), **III:** 577

Boy's Percy, The (Lanier), **Supp. I Part 1:** 361

"Boy Story" (Huddle), **Supp. XXVI:** 151

Boy's Town (Howells), **I:** 418

Boy's Will, A (Frost), **II:** 152, 153, 155–156, 159, 164, 166; **Retro. Supp. I:** 124, 127, 128, 131; **Retro. Supp. II:** 168; **Retro. Supp. III:** 95, 96

"Boy Up a Tree" (Hoffman), **Supp. XVIII:** 86

"Boy Who Wrestled with Angels, The" (Hoffman), **Supp. X:** 90

"Boy with One Shoe, The" (Jewett), **Retro. Supp. II:** 132

"Brace, The" (Bausch), **Supp. VII:** 48

Bracebridge Hall, or, The Humorists (Irving), **I:** 339, 341; **II:** 308–309, 313

Bracher, Frederick, **I:** 378, 380; **Supp. I Part 1:** 185

Brackenridge, Hugh Henry, **Supp. I Part 1:** 124, 127, 145; **Supp. II Part 1:** 65

Brackett, Leigh, **Supp. IV Part 1:** 130

Bradbury, John M., **I:** 288–289; **IV:** 130, 135

Bradbury, Malcolm, **Supp. VIII:** 124; **Supp. XVIII:** 140

Bradbury, Ray, **Supp. I Part 2:** 621–622; **Supp. IV Part 1: 101–118; Supp. XVI:** 122; **Supp. XVII:** 41; **Supp. XXIII:** 290; **Supp. XXV:** 141; **Supp. XXVII:** 295

"Brad Carrigan, American" (Saunders), **Supp. XIX:** 233

Braddon, Mary E., **Supp. I Part 1:** 35, 36

Bradfield, Scott, **Supp. VIII:** 88

Bradford, Gamaliel, **I:** 248, 250

Bradford, Roark, **Retro. Supp. I:** 80

Bradford, William, **Retro. Supp. II:** 161, 162; **Retro. Supp. III:** 9; **Supp. I Part 1:** 110, 112; **Supp. I Part 2:** 486, 494; **Supp. XXII: 33–47**

Bradlee, Ben, **Supp. V:** 201

Bradley, Bill, **Supp. VIII:** 47

Bradley, F. H., **Retro. Supp. I:** 57, 58

Bradley, Francis Herbert, **I:** 59, 567–568, 572, 573

Bradshaw, Barbara, **Supp. XIII:** 313

Bradstreet, Anne, **I:** 178–179, 180, 181, 182, 184; **III:** 505; **Retro. Supp. I:** 40; **Retro. Supp. III: 1–15; Supp. I Part 1: 98–123,** 300; **Supp. I Part 2:** 484, 485, 496, 546, 705; **Supp. V:** 113, 117–118; **Supp. XIII:** 152; **Supp. XIV:** 128; **Supp. XVIII:** 304; **Supp. XXII:** 46

Bradstreet, Elizabeth, **Supp. I Part 1:** 108, 122

Bradstreet, Simon, **I:** 178; **Supp. I Part 1:** 103, 110, 116

Bradstreet, Mrs. Simon. *See* Bradstreet, Anne

Brady, Alice, **III:** 399

Brady, Catherine, **Supp. XXIII:** 301

Brady, Matthew, **Supp. XVIII:** 4

Bragdon, Claude, **Supp. XX:** 117

"Bragdowdy and the Busybody, The" (Thurber), **Supp. I Part 2:** 617

Bragg, Rick, **Supp. XVIII:** 195

"Brahma" (Emerson), **II:** 19, 20

Brahms, Johannes, **III:** 118, 448

"Brahms in Delirium" (Skloot), **Supp. XX: 203**

Braided Creek (Kooser and Harrison), **Supp. XIX:** 126

"Braiding" (L.-Y. Lee), **Supp. XV:** 214

"Brain and the Mind, The" (James), **II:** 346

Brainard, Joe, **Supp. XV:** 33; **Supp. XXIII:** 217; **Supp. XXIV:** 33, 34, 35, 39, 41, 42, 43; **Supp. XXVII: 17–31**

"Brain Damage" (Barthelme), **Supp. IV Part 1:** 44

"Braindead Megaphone, The" (Saunders), **Supp. XIX:** 235

Braindead Megaphone, The: Essays (Saunders), **Supp. XIX: 234–236**

"Brain Scan" (Skloot), **Supp. XX: 200**

"Brain to the Heart, The" (Komunyakaa), **Supp. XIII:** 120

Braithwaite, Chris, **Supp. XXII:** 212

Braithwaite, Edward Kamau, **Supp. XXVII:** 160

Braithwaite, William Stanley, **Retro. Supp. I:** 131; **Supp. IX:** 309; **Supp. XV:** 296–297, 301–302, 305, 306

Brakhage, Stan, **Supp. XII:** 2

Braly, Malcolm, **Supp. XVIII:** 147

"Bramble, The" (Wrigley), **Supp. XVIII:** 301

Brame, Gloria, **Supp. XV:** 113; **Supp. XXIII:** 122

Bramen, Carrie Tirado, **Supp. XXIV:** 192

Bramer, Monte, **Supp. X:** 152

Branch Will Not Break, The (Wright), **Supp. III Part 2:** 596, 598–601; **Supp. IV Part 1:** 60; **Supp. IX:** 159

Brancusi, Constantin, **III:** 201; **Retro. Supp. I:** 292

Brancusi, Constantine, **Supp. XXVI:** 224

Brande, Dorothea, **Supp. I Part 2:** 608

Brandeis, Louis, **Supp. XXVIII:** 145

Brandel, Marc, **Supp. XXI:** 276

Branden, Nathaniel, **Supp. IV Part 2:** 526, 528

"Branding Cities" (Greenberg), **Supp. XXII:** 244

"Brand-Name Blues" (Kaufmann), **Supp. XI:** 39

Brand New Life, A (Farrell), **II:** 46, 48

Brando, Marlon, **II:** 588; **Supp. IV Part 2:** 560; **Supp. XVIII:** 251

Brandon, Henry, **Supp. I Part 2:** 604, 612, 618

Brandt, Alice, **Supp. I Part 1:** 92

Brandt, Carl, **Supp. XI:** 45

Branham, Kristi, **Supp. XXVIII:** 183

Brant, Sebastian, **III:** 447, 448

Brantley, Ben, **Supp. XXIV:** 268, 269–270, 271, 272, 274

Braque, Georges, **III:** 197; **Supp. IX:** 66; **Supp. XXVI:** 259

Brashford, Jake, **Supp. X:** 252

Brasil, Emanuel, **Supp. I Part 1:** 94

"Brasília" (Plath), **Supp. I Part 2:** 544, 545

"Brass Buttons" (McCoy), **Supp. XIII:** 161

"Brass Candlestick, The" (Francis), **Supp. IX:** 89

Brass Check, The (Sinclair), **Supp. V:** 276, 281, 282, 284–285

Brass Knuckles (Dybek), **Supp. XXIII: 68–69**

"Brass Ring, The" (Carver), **Supp. III Part 1:** 137

"Brass Spittoons" (Hughes), **Supp. I Part 1:** 326–327

Brass Verdict, The (Connelly), **Supp. XXI: 78–79**

Brats (X. J. Kennedy), **Supp. XV:** 163

Brautigan, Richard, **III:** 174; **Supp. VIII:** 42, 43; **Supp. XII:** 139; **Supp. XVI:** 172; **Supp. XXI:** 53

Brave Cowboy, The (Abbey), **Supp. XIII:** 4–5

Brave Men (Pyle), **Supp. XVII:** 61

Brave New World (Huxley), **II:** 454; **Supp. XIII:** 29; **Supp. XVIII:** 137

"Brave New World" (MacLeish), **III:** 18

Bravery of Earth, A (Eberhart), **I:** 522, 524, 525, 526, 530

"Brave Tailors of Maida, The" (Talese), **Supp. XVII:** 208

"Brave Words for a Startling Occasion" (Ellison), **Retro. Supp. II:** 118

Braving the Elements (Merrill), **Supp. III Part 1:** 320, 323, 325–327, 329

Bravo, The (Cooper), **I:** 345–346, 348

"Bravura" (Francis), **Supp. IX:** 90

Brawley, Benjamin, **Supp. I Part 1:** 327, 332

Brawl in a Tavern, A (Shaw), **Supp. XIX:** 241

Brawne, Fanny, **I:** 284; **II:** 531

Braxton, Joanne, **Supp. IV Part 1:** 12, 15

Brazil (Bishop), **Retro. Supp. II:** 45; **Supp. I Part 1:** 92

"Brazil" (Marshall), **Supp. XI:** 281

Brazil (Updike), **Retro. Supp. I:** 329, 330, 334

"Brazil, January 1, 1502" (Bishop), **Retro. Supp. II:** 47

Braziller, George, **Supp. X:** 24; **Supp. XXIII:** 214

Brazzi, Rossano, **Supp. IV Part 2:** 520

"Bread" (Dickey), **Supp. IV Part 1:** 182

"Bread" (Olds), **Supp. X:** 206

"Bread Alone" (Wylie), **Supp. I Part 2:** 727

Bread in the Wilderness (Merton), **Supp. VIII:** 197, 208

"Bread of Desire, The" (Nelson), **Supp. XVIII:** 177

Bread of Idleness, The (Masters), **Supp. I Part 2:** 460

"Bread of This World, The" (McGrath), **Supp. X:** 119, 127

Bread of Time, The (Levine), **Supp. V:** 180

Bread without Sugar (Stern), **Supp. IX:** 297–298

"Break, The" (Sexton), **Supp. II Part 2:** 689

"Breakaways, The" (Siddons), **Supp. XXII:** 244

Breakdown (Paretsky), **Supp. XXV:** 185

Breakfast at Tiffany's (Capote), **Supp. III Part 1:** 113, 117, 119–121, 124, 126

Breakfast of Champions (Vonnegut), **Supp. II Part 2:** 755, 759, 769, 770, 777–778

"Breakfast"(Wakoski), **Supp. XXVIII:** 267

Breaking and a Death, A (Kees), **Supp. XV:** 145

Breaking and Entering (X. J. Kennedy), **Supp. XV:** 153, **160–162**

Breaking Hard Ground (D. Hunter), **Supp. XVI:** 38

Breaking Ice (McMillan, ed.), **Supp. XIII:** 182–183

Breaking of the Day, The (Davison), **Supp. XXVI:** 65, 68–70

"Breaking of the Day, The" (Davison), **Supp. XXVI:** 68, 69

Breaking Open (Rukeyser), **Supp. VI:** 274, 281

"Breaking Open" (Rukeyser), **Supp. VI:** 286

Breaking Point, The (Rinehart), **Supp. XXV:** 196

Breaking Ranks: A Political Memoir (Podhoretz), **Supp. VIII:** 239–241, 245

"Breaking the Code of Silence: Ideology and Women's Confessional Poetry" (Harris), **Supp. XIV:** 269

"Breaking the Whistle" (Rash), **Supp. XXVII:** 218

"Breaking Up of the Winships, The" (Thurber), **Supp. I Part 2:** 616

Brearton, Fran, **Supp. XXIV:** 167

Breast, The (P. Roth), **Retro. Supp. II:** 287–288; **Supp. III Part 2:** 416, 418

"Breast, The" (Sexton), **Supp. II Part 2:** 687

"Breasts" (Gallagher), **Supp. XXIV:** 168, 174

"Breasts" (Simic), **Supp. VIII:** 275

"Breasts"(Dybek), **Supp. XXIII:** 77

"Breath" (Espaillat), **Supp. XXI:** 109

"Breath" (Levine), **Supp. V:** 185

Breathe No More, My Lady (Lacy), **Supp. XV:** 203

Breathing Lessons (Tyler), **Supp. IV Part 2:** 669–670

Breathing Room (Davison), **Supp. XXVI:** 66, 78–79

"Breathing Room" (Davison), **Supp. XXVI:** 79

Breathing the Monster Alive (Gansworth), **Supp. XXVI:** 112–113

Breathing the Water (Levertov), **Supp. III Part 1:** 274, 283, 284

"Breath of Life, The" (C. Baxter), **Supp. XVII:** 23

Breath's Burials (Sobin), **Supp. XVI:** 288–289

Breaux, Zelia, **Retro. Supp. II:** 114

Brecht, Bertolt, **I:** 60, 301; **III:** 161, 162; **IV:** 394; **Supp. I Part 1:** 292; **Supp. II Part 1:** 10, 26, 56; **Supp. IV Part 1:** 359; **Supp. IX:** 131, 133, 140; **Supp. X:** 112; **Supp. XIII:** 206, 286; **Supp. XIV:** 162; **Supp. XVIII:** 33; **Supp. XXIV:** 267

Breen, Jon L., **Supp. XXVI:** 277, 281

Breen, Joseph I., **IV:** 390

Breines, Ron, **Supp. XVIII:** 97

Breit, Harvey, **I:** 433; **III:** 575; **Retro. Supp. II:** 230; **Supp. XVIII:** 254; **Supp. XXI:** 277

Breman, Paul, **Supp. XXII:** 8

Bremer, Anne, **Supp. XXII:** 277

Bremer, Fredrika, **Supp. I Part 1:** 407

Bremer, Richard, **Supp. XXIII:** 236

Brendan: A Novel (Buechner), **Supp. XII:** 53

Brennan, Matthew C., **Supp. XIX:** 121; **Supp. XV:** 113, 125

Brent, David, **Supp. XXII:** 259

Brent, Linda, **Supp. IV Part 1:** 12, 13

Brentano, Franz, **II:** 350; **Supp. XIV:** 198, 199

Brer Rabbit (tales), **Supp. IV Part 1:** 11, 13; **Supp. XIV:** 88

Breslin, James E. B., **Retro. Supp. I:** 430

Breslin, John B., **Supp. IV Part 1:** 308

Breslin, Paul, **Supp. VIII:** 283

Bresson, Robert, **Supp. IV Part 1:** 156

"Bresson's Movies" (Creeley), **Supp. IV Part 1:** 156–157

"Bret Easton Ellis Podcast, The", **Supp. XXVII:** 79

Breton, André, **III:** 425; **Supp. XIII:** 114; **Supp. XVII:** 244

Brett, George, **II:** 466; **Supp. V:** 286

Brett, Reginald Baliol, **Supp. XX:** **230**

Brevoort, Henry, **II:** 298

Brew, Kwesi, **Supp. IV Part 1:** 10, 16

Brewer, Gaylord, **Supp. XV:** 330

"Brewing of Soma, The" (Whittier), **Supp. I Part 2:** 704

Brewsie and Willie (Stein), **IV:** 27

Brewster, Martha, **Supp. I Part 1:** 114

"Brewsterville Croesus, A" (Briggs), **Supp. XVIII:** 16

Brewsterville letters (Briggs), **Supp. XVIII:** 1, 5, **15–16**

"Brian Age 7" (Doty), **Supp. XI:** 136

Briand, Paul, **Supp. XVIII:** 155

"Briar Patch, The" (Warren), **IV:** 237

Briar Rose (Coover), **Supp. V:** 52

"Briar Rose (Sleeping Beauty)" (Sexton), **Supp. II Part 2:** 690

Brice, Fanny, **II:** 427

"Brick, The" (Nye), **Supp. XIII:** 276

"Bricklayer in the Snow" (Fante), **Supp. XI:** 164–165

"Brick Layer's Lunch Hour, The" (Ginsberg), **Supp. II Part 1:** 318

Brickman, Marshall, **Supp. XV:** 5

"Bricks, The" (Hogan), **Supp. IV Part 1:** 413

"Bridal Ballad, The" (Poe), **III:** 428

"Bridal Bed, The" (Gibran), **Supp. XX:** **124**

Bridal Dinner, The (Gurney), **Supp. V:** 109, 110

Bridal Hunt (Silver), **Supp. XXIV:** 264

"Bride Comes to Yellow Sky, The" (Crane), **I:** 34, 415, 416, 423

Bridegroom, The (Jin), **Supp. XVIII:** **97–98**

"Bridegroom, The" (Jin), **Supp. XVIII:** 98

Bridegroom Cometh, The (W. Frank), **Supp. XX:** **77**

"Bridegroom's Body, The" (Boyle), **Supp. XXIV:** 54, **55–56**

"Bride in the 30's, A" (Auden), **Supp. II Part 1:** 9

Bride of Lammermoor (Scott), **II:** 291

Bride of Samoa (film), **Supp. IV Part 1:** 82

"Bride of the Innisfallen, The" (Welty), **IV:** 278–279; **Retro. Supp. I:** 353

Bride of the Innisfallen, The, and Other Stories (Welty), **IV:** 261, 275–279; **Retro. Supp. I:** 352–353, 355

Brides of the South Wind: Poems 1917–1922 (Jeffers), **Supp. II Part 2:** 419

Bridge, Horatio, **II:** 226; **Retro. Supp. III:** 116

"BRIDGE, THE" (Baraka), **Supp. II Part 1:** 32, 36

Bridge, The (H. Crane), **I:** 62, 109, 266, 385, 386, 387, 395–399, 400, 402; **IV:** 123, 341, 418, 419, 420; **Retro. Supp. I:** 427; **Retro. Supp. II:** 76, 77, 81, 83, **84–87; Retro. Supp. III:** 42–43, 47, 48–49, 50–53, 54; **Supp. IX:** 306; **Supp. V:** 342; **Supp. XXIII:** 146; **Supp. XXVI:** 21, 25, 28

Bridge, The (Talese), **Supp. XVII:** 202, 203, 208

Bridge at Remagen, The (film), **Supp. XI:** 343

"Bridge Burners, The" (Van Vechten), **Supp. II Part 2:** 733

Bridgehead: The Drama of Israel (W. Frank), **Supp. XX:** 80

Bridge of San Luis Rey, The (Wilder), **I:** 360; **IV:** 356, 357, 360–363, 365, 366

"Bridge of Sighs"(P. Benedict), **Supp. XXIII:** 47–48

Bridge of Years, The (Sarton), **Supp. VIII:** 253

"Bridges" (Kingsolver), **Supp. VII:** 208

Bridges, Harry, **I:** 493; **Supp. XIX:** 264; **Supp. XVIII:** 238

Bridges, Lloyd, **Supp. XV:** 202

Bridges, Robert, **II:** 537; **III:** 527; **Supp. I Part 2:** 721; **Supp. II Part 1:** 21; **Supp. XIV:** 336, 341, 342, 343

"Bridging" (Apple), **Supp. XVII:** 5

Bridgman, P. W., **I:** 278

"Bridle, The" (Carver), **Supp. III Part 1:** 138

"Brief and Blameless Outline of the Ontogeny of Crow, A" (Wright), **Supp. XV:** 347

Brief and Frightening Reign of Phil, The (Saunders), **Supp. XIX:** 230–231, 233

"Brief Début of Tildy, The" (O. Henry), **Supp. II Part 1:** 408

"Brief Encounters on the Inland Waterway" (Vonnegut), **Supp. II Part 2:** 760

"Brief History of My Mother's Temper, A" (Huddle), **Supp. XXVI:** 150

Brief History of the Dead, The (Brockmeier), **Supp. XXII:** 57–59, 61

Briefings (Ammons), **Supp. VII:** 29

Brief Interviews with Hideous Men (Wallace), **Supp. X:** 308–310

"Brief Interviews with Hideous Men" (Wallace), **Supp. X:** 309

"Briefly It Enters, and Briefly Speaks" (Kenyon), **Supp. VII:** 174

"Brief Study of the British, A" (Saunders), **Supp. XIX:** 235

Brief Wondrous Life of Oscar Wao, The (Díaz), **Supp. XXIV:** 83, 84, 85, 87, **89–92,** 93

Brier, His Book (J. W. Miller), **Supp. XX:** **165, 168, 170**

"Brier Grows Wild, The" (J. W. Miller), **Supp. XX:** 170

"Brier Losing Touch with His Traditions, The" (J. W. Miller), **Supp. XX:** 165, 169

Brier Poems, The (J. W. Miller), **Supp. XX:** 168

"Brier Sermon, The—You Must Be Born Again" (J. W. Miller), **Supp. XX:** 165, **169–170**

Briffault, Robert, **Supp. I Part 2:** 560, 567

"Brigade de Cuisine" (McPhee), **Supp. III Part 1:** 307–308

Brigadier and the Golf Widow, The (Cheever), **Supp. I Part 1:** 184–185, 192

Briggs, Charles Frederick, **Supp. I Part 2:** 411; **Supp. XVIII:** 1–18

brigham, besmilr, **Supp. XV:** 349

"Bright and Morning Star" (Wright), **IV:** 488

Bright Book of Life: American Novelists and Storytellers from Hemingway to Mailer (Kazin), **Supp. VIII:** 102, 104

Bright Center of Heaven (Maxwell), **Supp. VIII:** 153–155, 164

"Brightness from the North" (B. Kelly), **Supp. XVII:** 131

Brighton Beach Memoirs (Simon), **Supp. IV Part 2:** 576, 577, 584, 586–587, 590

Bright Procession (Sedges), **Supp. II Part 1:** 125

Bright Room Called Day, A (Kushner), **Supp. IX:** 133, **138–141,** 142

Brillat-Savarin, Jean Anthelme, **Supp. XVII:** 82, 86, 87

"Brilliance" (Doty), **Supp. XI:** 124, 128

"Brilliant California Novelist, A" (Forman), **Supp. XXIV:** 30

"Brilliant Leaves" (Gordon), **II:** 199

"Brilliant Sad Sun" (W. C. Williams), **Retro. Supp. I:** 422

"Bring Brang Brung" (Muñoz), **Supp. XXV:** 135–136

"Bringing Back the Trumpeter Swan" (Kumin), **Supp. IV Part 2:** 454

Bringing It All Back Home (album, Dylan), **Supp. XVIII:** 20, 25, 26, 30

Bringing It All Back Home (McNally), **Supp. XIII:** 197–198

Bringing the Devil to His Knees (C. Baxter), **Supp. XVII:** 22

"Bringing the Strange Home" (Dunn), **Supp. XI:** 141

"Bring the Day!" (Roethke), **III:** 536

Brinkley, Douglas, **Supp. XIII:** 9; **Supp. XXIV:** 281, 293

Brinkmeyer, Robert H., Jr., **Supp. XI:** 38

Brinnin, John Malcolm, **IV:** 26, 27, 28, 42, 46; **Supp. XV:** 139

Brissot, Jacques Pierre, **Supp. I Part 2:** 511

"Britain's Negro Problem in Sierra Leone" (Du Bois), **Supp. I Part 1:** 176

"British Guiana" (Marshall), **Supp. XI:** 281–282

"British Poets, The" (Holmes), **Supp. I Part 1:** 306

"British Prison Ship, The" (Freneau), **Supp. II Part 1:** 261

Brittan, Gordon G., Jr., **Supp. XIV:** 234

Britten, Benjamin, **II:** 586; **Supp. II Part 1:** 17; **Supp. IV Part 1:** 84

Broadwater, Bowden, **II:** 562

Broadway, Broadway (McNally). *See It's Only a Play* (McNally)

Broadway, J. William, **Supp. V:** 316

Broadway Bound (Simon), **Supp. IV Part 2:** 576, 577, 584, 586–587, 590

Broadway Danny Rose (film; Allen), **Supp. XV:** 9

"Broadway Pageant, A" (Whitman), **Retro. Supp. III:** 305

"Broadway Sights" (Whitman), **IV:** 350

Broccoli, Albert R. "Cubby", **Supp. XI:** 307

Brock, H. I., **Retro. Supp. III:** 138

Bröck, Sabine, **Supp. XI:** 275, 277, 278

Brockmeier, Kevin, **Supp. XXII:** 49–63

Brodeur, Brian, **Supp. XXVI:** 150; **Supp. XXVIII:** 136

Brodhead, Richard, **Retro. Supp. II:** 139; **Supp. XIV:** 61

Brodkey, Harold, **Supp. VIII:** 151; **Supp. X:** 160

Brodkin, Joel, **Supp. XXV:** 261

Brodskii, Iosif Alexsandrovich. *See* Brodsky, Joseph

Brodsky, Joseph, **Supp. VIII:** 19–35; **Supp. X:** 65, 73; **Supp. XV:** 134, 135, 256; **Supp. XXIII:** 122

Brody, Alter, **Supp. XV:** 302, 307

Brodyar, Anatole, **Supp. XIV:** 106

Brokeback Mountain (film), **Supp. XX:** 273

"Brokeback Mountain" (Proulx), **Supp. VII:** 264–265

"Broken Balance, The" (Jeffers), **Supp. II Part 2:** 426

"Broken Field, The" (Teasdale), **Supp. XXVII:** 294

"Broken Field Running" (Bambara), **Supp. XI:** 10, 11

Broken Frieze, The (Everwine), **Supp. XV:** 74, 75, 89

Broken Glass (A. Miller), **Retro. Supp. III:** 176

Broken Ground, The (Berry), **Supp. X:** 30

"Broken Home, The" (Merrill), **Supp. III Part 1:** 319, 325

"Broken Oar, The" (Longfellow), **Retro. Supp. II:** 169

"Broken Promise" (MacLeish), **III:** 15

"Broken Ribs"(Prouty), **Supp. XXVIII:** 180

Broken Snare, The (Lewisohn), **Supp. XXVIII:** 148, 151

Broken Span, The (W. C. Williams), **IV:** 419; **Retro. Supp. I:** 424

"Broken Tower, The" (H. Crane), **I:** 385, 386, 400, 401–402; **Retro. Supp. II:** 89, 90; **Retro. Supp. III:** 53

Broken Vessels (Dubus), **Supp. VII:** 90–91; **Supp. XI:** 347

"Broken Vessels" (Dubus), **Supp. VII:** 90

Broken Wings, The (al-Ajni&hudot;a al-Mutakassirah) (Gibran), **Supp. XX:** 115, 124, 125

"Broker" (H. Roth), **Supp. IX:** 234

Bromfield, Louis, **IV:** 380

"Brompton Cocktail" (Mamet), **Supp. XIV:** 252

Bromwich, David, **Retro. Supp. I:** 305; **Supp. XII:** 162

"Broncho That Would Not Be Broken, The" (Lindsay), **Supp. I Part 2:** 383

Bronk, William, **Supp. XV:** 115; **Supp. XXI:** 17–34; **Supp. XXVI:** 237

Brontë, Anne, **Supp. IV Part 2:** 430

Brontë, Branwell, **I:** 462

Brontë, Charlotte, **I:** 458; **II:** 175; **Supp. IV Part 2:** 430; **Supp. IX:** 128; **Supp. XII:** 104, 303; **Supp. XV:** 338; **Supp. XVI:** 158; **Supp. XX:** 108

Brontë, Emily, **I:** 458; **Retro. Supp. I:** 43; **Supp. IV Part 2:** 430; **Supp. IX:** 128; **Supp. X:** 78, 89; **Supp. XV:** 338

"Bronze" (Francis), **Supp. IX:** 76

"Bronze" (Merrill), **Supp. III Part 1:** 336

Bronze Booklets on the History, Problems, and Cultural Contributions of the Negro series, **Supp. XIV:** 202

"Bronze Buckaroo, The" (Baraka), **Supp. II Part 1:** 49

"Bronze Horses, The" (A. Lowell), **II:** 524

"Bronze Tablets" (A. Lowell), **II:** 523

Bronzeville Boys and Girls (Brooks), **Supp. III Part 1:** 79

"Bronzeville Mother Loiters in Mississippi, A. Meanwhile, a Mississippi Mother Burns Bacon" (Brooks), **Supp. III Part 1:** 80

"Brooch, The" (Singer), **IV:** 20

Brook, Peter, **Retro. Supp. II:** 182

Brooke, Rupert, **II:** 82; **III:** 3

Brook Evans (Glaspell), **Supp. III Part 1:** 182–185

"Brooking Likeness" (Glück), **Supp. V:** 85

"Brooklyn" (Marshall), **Supp. XI:** 281, 282

"Brooklyn" (Shaw), **Supp. XIX:** 239, 240

Brooklyn Noir (McLoughlin, ed.), **Supp. XXIV:** 14

Brooks, Albert (Al Pew), **Supp. XXI:** 22

Brooks, Carrellin, **Supp. XXV:** 8

Brooks, Cleanth, **I:** 280, 282; **III:** 517; **IV:** 236, 279; **Retro. Supp. I:** 40, 41, 90; **Retro. Supp. II:** 235; **Retro. Supp. III:** 76; **Supp. I Part 2:** 423; **Supp. III Part 2:** 542; **Supp. IX:** 153, 155; **Supp. V:** 316; **Supp. X:** 115, 123; **Supp. XIV:** 1–20; **Supp. XIX:** 246; **Supp. XXVIII:** 2

Brooks, David, **Supp. IV Part 2:** 623, 626, 630; **Supp. VIII:** 232

Brooks, Gwendolyn, **Retro. Supp. I:** 208; **Supp. III Part 1:** 69–90; **Supp. IV Part 1:** 2, 15, 244, 251, 257; **Supp. XI:** 1, 278; **Supp. XIII:** 111, 112, 296; **Supp. XIV:** 73; **Supp. XVIII:** 175, 181, 185; **Supp. XXI:** 230

Brooks, Mel, **Supp. IV Part 1:** 390; **Supp. IV Part 2:** 591

Brooks, Paul, **Supp. IX:** 26, 31, 32

Brooks, Phillips, **II:** 542; **Retro. Supp. II:** 134; **Supp. XIII:** 142

Brooks, Van Wyck, **I:** 106, 117, 215, 222, 228, 230, 231, 233, 236, **239–263,** 266, 480; **II:** 30, 271, 285, 309, 337, 482; **III:** 394, 606; **IV:** 171, 312, 427, 433; **Retro. Supp. II:** 46, 137; **Supp. I Part 2:** 423, 424, 650; **Supp. II Part 1:** 137; **Supp. VIII:** 98, 101; **Supp. XIV:** 11; **Supp. XV:** 298, 301; **Supp. XX:** 68

Brooks, Mrs. Van Wyck (Eleanor Kenyon Stimson), **I:** 240, 245, 250, 252

Brooks, Mrs. Van Wyck (Gladys Billings), **I:** 258

Broom of the System, The (Wallace), **Supp. X:** 301, **302–305,** 310

"Brooms" (Simic), **Supp. VIII:** 275

Brosi, George, **Supp. XX: 166;** **Supp. XXIII:** 39

Brosnan, Jim, **II:** 424–425; **Supp. XX: 195**

Brossard, Chandler, **Supp. XXII:** 258

Brother Carl (Sontag), **Supp. III Part 2:** 452

"Brother Death" (Anderson), **I:** 114

Brother Fire (Di Piero), **Supp. XIX:** 35, 38, 45–47

Brotherhood of the Grape, The (Fante), **Supp. XI:** 160, **171–172**

"Brotherhood"(Stuart), **Supp. XXVIII:** 230

Brother in Elysium, The: Ideas of Friendship and Society in the United States (Bronk), **Supp. XXI:** 21, 22, 25, 31

"Brothers" (Anderson), **I:** 114

"Brothers" (Huddle), **Supp. XXVI:** 154

"Brothers" (Stone), **Supp. XXVII:** 254

"Brothers" (W. Stone), **Supp. XXVII:** 255

Brothers, The (F. Barthelme), **Supp. XI:** 25, 28, 29, 30, 32–33

Brothers and Keepers (Wideman), **Supp. X:** 320, 321–322, 323, **325–327,** 328, 329–330, 331, 332

Brothers Ashkenazi, The (Singer), **IV:** 2

Brothers Karamazov, The (Dostoevsky), **II:** 60; **III:** 146, 150, 283; **Supp. IX:** 102, 106; **Supp. XI:** 172; **Supp. XII:** 322

Brothers of No Kin (Richter), **Supp. XVIII:** 209

"Brothers of No Kin" (Richter), **Supp. XVIII:** 208

Brother to Dragons: A Tale in Verse and Voices (Warren), **IV:** 243–244, 245, 246, 251, 252, 254, 257

Broughton, James, **Supp. XV:** 146

Broughton, Rhoda, **II:** 174; **IV:** 309, 310; **Supp. XX: 232**

Broun, Heywood, **I:** 478; **II:** 417; **IV:** 432; **Supp. IX:** 190; **Supp. XXII:** 277

Broussais, François, **Supp. I Part 1:** 302

Brouwer, Joel, **Supp. XXII:** 223, 237

Browder, Earl, **I:** 515; **Supp. XX: 76, 77**

Brower, David, **Supp. X:** 29

Brower, Reuben, **Supp. XV:** 20

Brown, Alice, **II:** 523; **Retro. Supp. II:** 136

Brown, Andrew, **Supp. XVI:** 150

Brown, Ashley, **Retro. Supp. II:** 48; **Supp. I Part 1:** 79, 80, 82, 84, 92

Brown, Charles Brockden, **I:** 54, 211, 335; **II:** 74, 267, 298; **III:** 415; **Retro. Supp. III:** 226; **Supp. I Part 1:** 124–149; **Supp. II Part 1:** 65, 292; **Supp. XXIII:** 178

Brown, Mrs. Charles Brockden (Elizabeth Linn), **Supp. I Part 1:** 145, 146

Brown, Claude, Jr., **Retro. Supp. III:** 184

Brown, Clifford, **Supp. V:** 195

Brown, Clifford W., **Supp. XXVIII:** 164

Brown, Dan, **Supp. XXVII:** 5

Brown, Deborah, **Supp. XVII:** 75

Brown, Dee, **Supp. IV Part 2:** 504

Brown, Dorothy H., **Supp. XXVIII:** 233

Brown, Elijah, **Supp. I Part 1:** 125

Brown, Fleda, **Supp. XXIII:** 59

Brown, George Douglas, **III:** 473

Brown, Harry, **Supp. IV Part 2:** 560

Brown, Harvey, **Supp. XIV:** 148

Brown, Himan, **Supp. XIX:** 241, 242

Brown, H. Rap, **Supp. XXI:** 171

Brown, Jeffrey, **Supp. XXVII:** 205

Brown, Jennifer M., **Supp. XXVIII:** 277

Brown, John, **II:** 13; **IV:** 125, 126, 172, 237, 249, 254; **Supp. I Part 1:** 345; **Supp. VIII:** 204

Brown, Joseph Epes, **Supp. IV Part 2:** 487

Brown, Larry, **Supp. XVIII:** 195; **Supp. XXI:** 35–50

Brown, Leonard, **Supp. IX:** 117

Brown, Mary Armitt, **Supp. I Part 1:** 125

Brown, Mick, **Supp. XXVII:** 268, 270

Brown, Nell Porter, **Supp. XXV:** 130, 131, 138

Brown, Percy, **II:** 20

Brown, Robert (Anahalihs), **Supp. XXVI:** 89, 95

Brown, Robert E., **Supp. X:** 12

Brown, Scott, **Supp. XI:** 178

Brown, Slater, **IV:** 123; **Retro. Supp. II:** 79

Brown, Solyman, **Supp. I Part 1:** 156

Brown, Sterling, **Retro. Supp. I:** 198; **Supp. IV Part 1:** 169; **Supp. XIV:** 202; **Supp. XXII:** 1, 8, 12

Brown, Tina, **Supp. XVI:** 176–177

Brown, Wesley, **Supp. V:** 6

Brown, William Hill, **Supp. XXV:** 38

Brown, William Wells, **Supp. XXIII:** 184

Brown Angels (Myers), **Supp. XXVII:** 209

Brown Decades, The (Mumford), **Supp. II Part 2:** 475, 478, 491–492

Brown Dog (Harrison), **Supp. VIII:** 51

Brown Dog of the Yaak: Essays on Art and Activism (Bass), **Supp. XVI:** 22

"Brown Dwarf of Rügen, The" (Whittier), **Supp. I Part 2:** 696

Browne, Charles Farrar, **II:** 289; **IV:** 193, 196; **Supp. XVIII:** 1, 4

Browne, Roscoe Lee, **Supp. VIII:** 345

Browne, Thomas, **II:** 15–16, 304; **III:** 77, 78, 198, 487; **IV:** 147; **Supp. IX:** 136; **Supp. XII:** 45; **Supp. XVI:** 292

Browne, William, **Supp. I Part 1:** 98

Brownell, W. C., **II:** 14

Brownell, William Crary, **Retro. Supp. I:** 365, 366

Browner, Stephanie P., **Supp. XVIII:** 17

Brown Girl, Brownstones (Marshall), **Supp. XI:** 275, 276, **278–280,** 282

Brown Girl Dreaming (Woodson), **Supp. XXVIII:** 277, 279, 284

Brownies' Book, The (Hughes), **Supp. I Part 1:** 321

Browning, Dominique, **Supp. XXVI:** 131

Browning, Elizabeth Barrett, **I:** 458, 459; **Retro. Supp. I:** 33, 43; **Supp. XVIII:** 175–176; **Supp. XX:** 108; **Supp. XXVII:** 284

Browning, Oscar, **Supp. XX:** 231

Browning, Robert, **I:** 50, 66, 103, 458, 460, 468; **II:** 338, 478, 522; **III:** 5, 8, 467, 469, 484, 511, 521, 524, 606, 609; **IV:** 135, 245, 366, 416; **Retro. Supp. I:** 43, 55, 217; **Retro. Supp. II:** 188, 190; **Retro. Supp. III:** 60; **Supp. I Part 1:** 2, 6, 79, 311; **Supp. I Part 2:** 416, 468, 622; **Supp. III Part 1:** 5, 6; **Supp. IV Part 2:** 430; **Supp. X:** 65; **Supp. XV:** 92, 250, 275

Brownmiller, Susan, **Supp. X:** 252

Brownrigg, Sylvia, **Supp. XXV:** 59–60

"Brown River, Smile" (Toomer), **Supp. IV Part 1:** 16

Brownstone Eclogues and Other Poems (Aiken), **I:** 65, 67

Brown: The Last Discovery of America (Rodriguez), **Supp. XIV:** 297, 298, 300, **305–309,** 310, 311–312

"Browsing About the Ibsen Country"(Stuart), **Supp. XXVIII:** 230

Broyard, Anatole, **Supp. IV Part 1:** 39; **Supp. VIII:** 140; **Supp. X:** 186; **Supp. XI:** 348; **Supp. XVI:** 213

Broyles, Yolanda Julia, **Supp. XIX:** 112

Bruccoli, Matthew, **Retro. Supp. I:** 98, 102, 105, 114, 115, 359; **Supp. IV Part 2:** 468, 470

Bruce, John Edward, **Supp. XVI:** 143

Bruce, Lenny, **Supp. VIII:** 198

Bruce, Virginia, **Supp. XII:** 173

Bruce-Novoa, Juan, **Supp. VIII:** 73, 74

Bruchac, Joseph, **Supp. IV Part 1:** 261, 319, 320, 321, 322, 323, 325, 328, 398, 399, 403, 408, 414; **Supp. IV Part 2:** 502, 506

Brueghel, Pieter, **I:** 174; **Supp. I Part 2:** 475

Brueghel, Pieter, the Elder, **Retro. Supp. I:** 430

Bruell, Edwin, **Supp. VIII:** 126

Brugh, Spangler Arlington. *See* Taylor, Robert

"Bruja: Witch" (Mora), **Supp. XIII:** 214, 220, 221, **Supp. XIII:** 222

Brulé, Claude, **Supp. XI:** 307

Brumer, Andy, **Supp. XIII:** 88

Brummels, J. V., **Supp. XIX:** 119

Brunner, Emil, **III:** 291, 303

"Brush Fire" (J. Wright), **Supp. XVII:** 241

Brustein, Robert, **Retro. Supp. III:** 315, 319–320; **Supp. VIII:** 331; **Supp. XXIV:** 116

Brutus, **IV:** 373, 374; **Supp. I Part 2:** 471

"Brutus and Antony" (Masters), **Supp. I Part 2:** 472

"Bryan, Bryan, Bryan, Bryan" (Lindsay), **Supp. I Part 2:** 394, 395, 398

Bryan, George, **Retro. Supp. II:** 76

Bryan, Sharon, **Supp. IX:** 154

Bryan, William Jennings, **I:** 483; **IV:** 124; **Supp. I Part 2:** 385, 395–396, 455, 456

Bryant, Austin, **Supp. I Part 1:** 152, 153

Bryant, Frances, **Supp. I Part 1:** 153

Bryant, Louise, **Supp. X:** 136; **Supp. XXVIII:** 37–48

Bryant, Peter, **Supp. I Part 1:** 150, 151, 152, 153. *See also* George, Peter

Bryant, William Cullen, **I:** 335, 458; **II:** 311; **III:** 81; **IV:** 309; **Retro. Supp. I:** 217; **Retro. Supp. II:** 155; **Supp. I Part 1:** 150–173, 312, 362; **Supp. I Part 2:** 413, 416, 420; **Supp. IV Part 1:** 165; **Supp. XIII:** 145; **Supp. XIX:** 4; **Supp. XXV:** 250

Bryant, Mrs. William Cullen (Frances Fairchild), **Supp. I Part 1:** 153, 169

Bryer, Jackson R., **Supp. IV Part 2:** 575, 583, 585, 586, 589, 591; **Supp. XIII:** 200, **Supp. XIII:** 205

Bryher, Jackson R. (pseudonym). *See* Ellerman, Winifred

Brynner, Witter, **Supp. XXII:** 273

Bubber Goes to Heaven (Bontemps), **Supp. XXII:** 4

"Bubbs Creek Haircut" (Snyder), **Supp. VIII:** 306

Buber, Martin, **II:** 228; **III:** 45, 308, 528; **IV:** 11; **Supp. I Part 1:** 83, 88; **Supp. XVI:** 291; **Supp. XXVIII:** 151

Buccaneers, The (television miniseries), **Retro. Supp. III:** 290

Buccaneers, The (Wharton), **IV:** 327; **Retro. Supp. I:** 382; **Retro. Supp. III:** 289–290

Buchanan Dying (Updike), **Retro. Supp. I:** 331, 335

Buchbinder, David, **Supp. XIII:** 32

Buchwald, Art, **Supp. XII:** 124–125; **Supp. XVI:** 110–111

Buchwald, Emilie, **Supp. XVI:** 35, 36

Buck, Dudley, **Supp. I Part 1:** 362

Buck, Gene, **II:** 427

Buck, John, Sr., **Supp. XXVI:** 89

Buck, Pearl S., **Supp. II Part 1:** 113–134; **Supp. XIV:** 274

Buckdancer's Choice (Dickey), **Supp. IV Part 1:** 176, 177, 178, 180

"Buckdancer's Choice" (Dickey), **Supp. IV Part 1:** 191

Bucke, Richard Maurice, **Retro. Supp. I:** 407

"Buckeyes"(P. Benedict), **Supp. XXIII:** 46

"Buck Fever" (Humphrey), **Supp. IX:** 109

"Buck in the Snow, The" (Millay), **III:** 135

Buckley, Christopher, **Supp. IX:** 169; **Supp. XI:** 257, 329; **Supp. XV:** 76–77, 86

Buckley, James, Jr., **Supp. XVII:** 220

Buckminster, Joseph, **Supp. II Part 1:** 66–67, 69

Bucknell, Katherine, **Supp. XIV:** 170

Bucolics (Auden), **Supp. II Part 1:** 21, 24

Budbill, David, **Supp. XIX:** 1–16

Budd, Louis J., **IV:** 210

Buddha, **I:** 136; **II:** 1; **III:** 173, 179, 239, 567; **Supp. I Part 1:** 363; **Supp. I Part 2:** 397

Buddha, The: The Story of Siddhartha (film, Grubin), **Supp. XXIII:** 138, 140

"Buddha Boy" (Saunders), **Supp. XIX:** 235

"Buddha's Last Instruction, The" (Oliver), **Supp. VII:** 239

"Buddies"(Kenny), **Supp. XXIII:** 150

Budding Prospects (Boyle), **Supp. VIII:** 8–9; **Supp. XX:** 27–28

Buechner, Frederick, **III:** 310; **Supp. XII:** 41–59

Buell, Lawrence, **Supp. IX:** 29; **Supp. V:** 209; **Supp. XV:** 269, 282

"Buffalo" (Peacock), **Supp. XIX:** 198

"Buffalo, The" (Moore), **III:** 215

"Buffalo Bill". *See* Cody, William

Buffalo Girls (McMurtry), **Supp. V:** 229

Buffalo Girls (screenplay) (McMurtry), **Supp. V:** 232

Buffalo Hunters, The: The Story of the Hide Men (Sandoz), **Supp. XXIV:** 244, **247–249,** 256

Buffett, Jimmy, **Supp. VIII:** 42

Buffon, Comte de, **II:** 101

Buford, Fanny McConnell, **Retro. Supp. II:** 117

Bugeja, Michael, **Supp. X:** 201

Bugged for Murder (Lacy), **Supp. XV:** 205

"Buglesong" (Stegner), **Supp. IV Part 2:** 606

Buhle, Paul, **Supp. XXI:** 172

"Buick" (Shapiro), **Supp. II Part 2:** 705

"Builders" (Yates), **Supp. XI:** 342–343

Builders, The (Glasgow), **II:** 183–184, 193

"Builders, The" (Hay), **Supp. XIV:** 125

Builders in Sand (W. Frank), **Supp. XX:** 68

Builders of the Bay Colony (Morison), **Supp. I Part 2:** 484–485

"Builders of the Bridge, The" (Mumford), **Supp. II Part 2:** 475

"Building" (Snyder), **Supp. VIII:** 305

"Building, Dwelling, Thinking" (Heidegger), **Retro. Supp. II:** 87

Building a Character (Stanislavsky), **Supp. XIV:** 243

" 'Building' Larry Brown(s) at Algonquin Books of Chapel Hill" (Perry), **Supp. XXI:** 42

"Building of the Ship, The" (Longfellow), **II:** 498; **Retro. Supp. II:** 159, 167, 168

"Build Soil" (Frost), **Retro. Supp. I:** 138, 139; **Retro. Supp. III:** 103

"Build Soil" (Snyder), **Supp. VIII:** 304

Build-Up, The (W. C. Williams), **Retro. Supp. I:** 423

Bukiet, Melvin Jules, **Supp. XVII:** 39–51

Bukowski, Charles, **Supp. III Part 1:** 147; **Supp. XI:** 159, 161, 172, 173; **Supp. XVII:** 245

Bulgakov, Mikhail, **Supp. XIV:** 97

"Bulgarian Poetess, The" (Updike), **IV:** 215, 227; **Retro. Supp. I:** 329

Bull, Ole, **II:** 504

"Bulldozer, The" (Francis), **Supp. IX:** 87

"Bullet in the Brain" (Wolff), **Supp. VII:** 342–343

Bullet Park (Cheever), **Supp. I Part 1:** 185, 187–193, 194, 195

Bullets over Broadway (film; Allen), **Supp. XV:** 12, **12–13**

Bullfight, The (Mailer), **Retro. Supp. II:** 205

Bullfighter Checks Her Makeup, The: My Encounters with Extraordinary People (Orlean), **Supp. XXV:** 159, 163–164

Bullins, Ed, **Retro. Supp. III:** 316; **Supp. II Part 1:** 34, 42

Bullock, Sandra, **Supp. X:** 80

"Bull-Roarer, The" (Stern), **Supp. IX:** 297

"Bully, The" (Dubus), **Supp. VII:** 84

"Bulsh" (X. J. Kennedy), **Supp. XV:** 161

Bultmann, Rudolf, **III:** 309

Bulwark, The (Dreiser), **I:** 497, 506, 516–517; **Retro. Supp. II:** 95, 96, 105, 108

Bulwer-Lytton, Edward George, **IV:** 350

"Bums in the Attic" (Cisneros), **Supp. VII:** 62

Bunche, Ralph, **Supp. I Part 1:** 343; **Supp. XIV:** 202; **Supp. XXII:** 12

"Bunchgrass Edge of the World, The" (Proulx), **Supp. VII:** 263

Bunge, Nancy, **Supp. XVII:** 218; **Supp. XXII:** 175, 177, 178, 180, 183; **Supp. XXVI:** 257; **Supp. XXVIII:** 264

"Bunner Sisters, The" (Wharton), **IV:** 317

Bunting, Basil, **Retro. Supp. I:** 422; **Supp. III Part 2:** 616, 620, 624; **Supp. XIV:** 286

Buntline, Ned, **Supp. XXIII:** 182

Buñuel, Luis, **III:** 184; **Retro. Supp. II:** 337

Bunyan, John, **I:** 445; **II:** 15, 104, 228; **IV:** 80, 84, 156, 437; **Supp. I Part 1:** 32

Bunyan, Paul, **Supp. XXII:** 203

Burana, Lily, **Supp. XI:** 253

Burbank, Luther, **I:** 483

Burbank, Rex, **IV:** 363

Burch, Michael, **Supp. XXI:** 99

Burchfield, Alice, **Supp. I Part 2:** 652, 660

Burden of Proof, The (Turow), **Supp. XVII:** 216–217, 218

Burden of Southern History, The (Woodward), **Retro. Supp. I:** 75

Burdens of Formality, The (Lea, ed.), **Supp. X:** 58

Burger, Gottfried August, **II:** 306

Burgess, Anthony, **Supp. IV Part 1:** 227; **Supp. IV Part 2:** 685; **Supp. V:** 128; **Supp. XXIII:** 42

Burgh, James, **Supp. I Part 2:** 522

"Burglar of Babylon, The" (Bishop), **Retro. Supp. II:** 47; **Supp. I Part 1:** 93

Burgum, E. B., **IV:** 469, 470

Burham, Philip, **Supp. XX:** 44

"Burial of Jonathan Brown, The" (Hadas), **Supp. XXIII:** 115

Buried Child (Shepard), **Supp. III Part 2:** 433, 447, 448; **Supp. XIV:** 327

"Buried Lake, The" (Tate), **IV:** 136

Burkard, Michael, **Supp. XXIV:** 165

Burke, Carolyn, **Supp. XXII:** 156, 158, 162, 165, 167, 168

Burke, Edmund, **I:** 9; **III:** 310; **Supp. I Part 2:** 496, 511, 512, 513, 523; **Supp. II Part 1:** 80; **Supp. XVII:** 236

Burke, James Lee, **Supp. XIV:** 21–38; **Supp. XXI:** 67, 72, 80

Burke, Kenneth, **I:** 264–287, 291; **III:** 497, 499, 546; **IV:** 123, 408; **Retro. Supp. I:** 297; **Retro. Supp. II:** 117, 120; **Retro. Supp. III:** 48; **Supp. I Part 2:** 630; **Supp. II Part 1:** 136; **Supp. IX:** 229; **Supp. VIII:** 105; **Supp. XIV:** 3; **Supp. XXI:** 89

Burke, Rusty, **Supp. XXVII:** 128

Burke, William, **Supp. XXI:** 215

"Burl" (Mosher), **Supp. XXII:** 204, 211

Burley, Justin, **Supp. XVI:** 158

"Burly Fading One, The" (Hayden), **Supp. II Part 1:** 366

Burn, Stephen J., **Supp. XX:** 85; **Supp. XXII:** 266, 268

"Burned" (Levine), **Supp. V:** 186, 192

"Burned" (Stallings), **Supp. XXV:** 233

"Burned Diary, The" (Olds), **Supp. X:** 215

"Burned Man" (Huddle), **Supp. XXVI:** 148, 151

Burne-Jones, Edward, **Supp. XXII:** 156

Burnett, Allison, **Supp. XVII:** 22

Burnett, David, **Supp. XI:** 299

Burnett, Frances Hodgson, **Supp. I Part 1:** 44

Burnett, Whit, **III:** 551; **Supp. XI:** 294

Burnett, W. R., **Supp. XXVII:** 93

Burney, Fanny, **Supp. XV:** 232; **Supp. XX:** 108

Burnham, James, **Supp. I Part 2:** 648

Burnham, John Chynoweth, **I:** 59

"Burning, The" (Welty), **IV:** 277–278; **Retro. Supp. I:** 353

Burning Angel (Burke), **Supp. XIV:** 30, 32

Burning Bright (Rash), **Supp. XXVII:** 228–229

Burning Bright (Steinbeck), **IV:** 51, 61–62

Burning Bright: An Anthology of Sacred Poetry (Hampl, ed.), **Supp. XXII:** 87

"Burning Bush" (Cliff), **Supp. XXII:** 75

Burning Bush (Untermeyer), **Supp. XV:** 309

"Burning Bush" (Untermeyer), **Supp. XV:** 309

Burning Bush, The (Asch), **Supp. XXIII:** 7

Burning Bush, The (H. and G. Herczeg), **Supp. XVII:** 62

Burning Chrome (W. Gibson), **Supp. XVI:** 118, 122, **128**

"Burning Chrome" (W. Gibson), **Supp. XVI:** 117, 120, 123, 124, 128

Burning City (Benét), **Supp. XI:** 46, 58

Burning Daylight (London), **II:** 474, 481

Burning Down the House: Essays on Fiction (C. Baxter), **Supp. XVII:** 13, 20, 21

"Burning Down the Little House on the Prairie: Asian Pioneers in Contempo-

rary North America" (Martín-Lucas), **Supp. XXVI:** 218

Burning House, The (Beattie), **Supp. V:** 29

"Burning Ladder, The" (Gioia), **Supp. XV:** 118

Burning Mystery of Anna in 1951, The (Koch), **Supp. XV:** 182–183

"Burning of Paper Instead of Children, The" (Rich), **Retro. Supp. III:** 245; **Supp. I Part 2:** 558

"Burning Shit at An Khe" (Weigl), **Supp. XIX:** 279–280

Burning the Days (Salter), **Supp. XIX:** 252

Burning the Days: Recollections (Salter), **Supp. IX:** 245, 246, 248, 260, **261–262**

"Burning the Small Dead" (Snyder), **Supp. VIII:** 298

Burning Tigris, The: The Armenian Genocide and America's Response (Balakian), **Supp. XXIII:** 19, 21, 22, **25–28**, 30

"Burning Tobacco Beds" (J. W. Miller), **Supp. XX:** 167

Burn Marks (Paretsky), **Supp. XXV:** 174–175, 178, 180

Burns, Carol, **Supp. XVIII:** 162

Burns, David, **III:** 165–166

Burns, Ken, **Supp. XIV:** 14

Burns, Michael, **Supp. XV:** 339

Burns, Robert, **II:** 150, 306; **III:** 592; **IV:** 453; **Supp. I Part 1:** 158; **Supp. I Part 2:** 410, 455, 683, 685, 691, 692; **Supp. IX:** 173; **Supp. XII:** 171; **Supp. XIII:** 3; **Supp. XVIII:** 82

Burnshaw, Stanley, **Retro. Supp. I:** 298, 303; **Supp. III Part 2:** 615

"Burn the Cities" (West), **Retro. Supp. II:** 338

Burnt Mountain (Siddons), **Supp. XXII:** 253

"Burnt Norton" (T. S. Eliot), **I:** 575, 580–581, 582, 584, 585; **III:** 10; **Retro. Supp. I:** 66; **Retro. Supp. III:** 66–67, 68; **Supp. XV:** 216

Burnt-Out Case, A (Greene), **Supp. VIII:** 4

"Burnt-out Spa, The" (Plath), **Retro. Supp. II:** 246

Burn Witch Burn (A. Merritt), **Supp. XVII:** 58

Burr, Aaron, **I:** 7, 549, 550; **II:** 300; **IV:** 264; **Supp. I Part 2:** 461, 483

Burr: A Novel (Vidal), **Supp. IV Part 2:** 677, 682, 684, 685, 687, 688, 689, 691

Burr Oaks (Eberhart), **I:** 533, 535

Burroughs, Edgar Rice, **Supp. IV Part 1:** 101

Burroughs, John, **I:** 220, 236, 506; **IV:** 346; **Supp. IX:** 171; **Supp. XXVI:** 37; **Supp. XXVIII:** 228, 247, 253, 255

Burroughs, William S., **III:** 45, 174, 258; **Supp. II Part 1:** 320, 328; **Supp. III Part 1:** 91–110, 217, 226; **Supp. IV Part 1:** 79, 87, 90; **Supp. XI:** 297, 308; **Supp. XII:** 1, 3, 118, 121, 124, 129, 131, 136; **Supp. XIV:** 137, 140–141, 143–144, 150; **Supp. XVI:** 123,

135; **Supp. XVII:** 225; **Supp. XVIII:** 137; **Supp. XXIII:** 213; **Supp. XXIV:** 42

Burrow, Trigant, **Supp. II Part 1:** 6

Burrows, Ken, **Supp. V:** 115

Bursey, Jeff, **Supp. XXII:** 257

Burson, Claudia, **Supp. XV:** 343

Burstein, Janet, **Supp. XVII:** 41, 44, 48

"Bursts of Light" (Bronk), **Supp. XXI:** 33

Burt, Stephen, **Supp. XV:** 341, 342, 345, 347, 351; **Supp. XVII:** 18, 246

Burt, Steve, **Supp. V:** 83

Burtis, Thomson, **Supp. XIII:** 163

Burton, Robert, **II:** 535; **III:** 77, 78; **Supp. I Part 1:** 349

Burton, Sue D., **Supp. XIX:** 90

Burton, Susan, **Supp. XXVIII:** 206

Burton, William Evans, **III:** 412

"Burying Ground by the Ties" (MacLeish), **III:** 14

Bury My Heart at Wounded Knee (Brown), **Supp. IV Part 2:** 504

Bury the Dead (Shaw), **IV:** 381; **Supp. XIX:** 242–244, 249, 252

"Bus Along St. Clair: December, A" (Atwood), **Supp. XIII:** 33

Busch, Frederick, **Supp. X:** 78; **Supp. XII:** 343; **Supp. XVII:** 175; **Supp. XXVI:** 9

Bush, Barney, **Supp. XII:** 218, 222

Bush, Douglas, **Supp. I Part 1:** 268; **Supp. XIV:** 10

Bush, Harold K., **Retro. Supp. III:** 259

Bush, Robert, **Supp. XXVIII:** 112, 118, 125

"Busher Comes Back, The" (Lardner), **II:** 422

"Busher's Letters Home, A" (Lardner), **II:** 418–419, 421

Bushmiller, Ernie, **Supp. XXVII:** 21

Bushrui, Suheil, **Supp. XX:** 113, 117, 120, 122, 126–127

"Business and Poetry" (Gioia), **Supp. XV:** 113, 115

"Business Deal" (West), **IV:** 287

"Business Man, A" (Jewett), **Retro. Supp. II:** 132

Business of Memory, The: The Art of Remembering in an Age of Forgetting (C. Baxter, ed.), **Supp. XVII:** 21

"Business Trip" (Hoffman), **Supp. XVIII:** 86

"Bus Riley's Back in Town" (Inge), **Supp. XXV:** 95

Buss, Helen M., **Supp. IV Part 1:** 12

Bus Stop (Inge), **Supp. XXV:** 93, 99–100

Butcher, Fanny, **Supp. XXV:** 199

Butcher, Margaret Just, **Supp. XIV:** 203

"Butcher, The" (Southern), **Supp. XI:** 294

"Butcher, The"(Goodman), **Supp. XXVIII:** 92

"Butcher Cock, The"(P. Benedict), **Supp. XXIII:** 46–47

Butcher's Apron, The: New and Selected Poems (Wakoski), **Supp. XXVIII:** 271

"Butcher Shop" (Simic), **Supp. VIII:** 273

But Gentlemen Marry Brunettes (Loos), **Supp. XVI:** 190–191

"But He Says I Misunderstood" (Notley), **Supp. XXII:** 227

Butler, Benjamin, **I:** 457

Butler, Dorothy. *See* Farrell, Mrs. James T. (Dorothy Butler)

Butler, Elizabeth, **Supp. I Part 1:** 260

Butler, Ethel, **Supp. XIV:** 125

Butler, Hugo, **Supp. XVII:** 63

Butler, James D., **Supp. IX:** 175

Butler, Joseph, **II:** 8, 9

Butler, Judith, **Supp. XII:** 6

Butler, Maud. *See* Falkner, Mrs. Murray C. (Maud Butler)

Butler, Nicholas Murray, **I:** 223; **Supp. I Part 1:** 23; **Supp. III Part 2:** 499

Butler, Octavia, **Supp. XIII:** 59–72

Butler, Robert Olen, **Supp. XII:** 61–78, 319

Butler, Samuel, **II:** 82, 86; **IV:** 121, 440; **Supp. VIII:** 171

Butler-Evans, Elliot, **Retro. Supp. II:** 121

"But Only Mine" (Wright), **Supp. III Part 2:** 595

Butscher, Edward, **Supp. I Part 2:** 526

Butter Battle Book, The (Geisel), **Supp. XVI:** 110

"Buttercups" (R. Lowell), **Retro. Supp. II:** 187

Butterfield, R. W., **I:** 386

Butterfield, Stephen, **Supp. IV Part 1:** 3, 11

Butterfield 8 (O'Hara), **III:** 361

"Butterflies Under Persimmon" (Jarman), **Supp. XVII:** 120

Butterfly (Harvey), **Supp. XIII:** 184

"Butterfly, The" (Brodksy), **Supp. VIII:** 26

"Butterfly and the Traffic Light, The" (Ozick), **Supp. V:** 263, 265

Butterfly in the Typewriter (MacLaughlin), **Supp. XXVI:** 241, 243, 252

Butterfly Plague, The (Findley), **Supp. XX:** 50, 52, 53

Butterfly Stories (Vollmann), **Supp. XVII:** 226

"Butterfly-toed Shoes" (Komunyakaa), **Supp. XIII:** 126

Butter Hill and Other Poems (Francis), **Supp. IX:** 88, 89

"Button-Down Builders, The" (Siddons), **Supp. XXII:** 243–244

Buttons, Red, **Supp. IV Part 2:** 574

Buttrick, George, **III:** 301; **Supp. XII:** 47–48

"But What Is the Reader to Make of This?" (Ashbery), **Supp. III Part 1:** 25

Butz, Earl, **Supp. X:** 35

"Buz" (Alcott), **Supp. I Part 1:** 43

Buzinski, Jim, **Supp. XX:** 273

"By an *Objibwa Female* Pen: Invitation to sisters to a walk in the Garden, after a shower"(J. Schoolcraft), **Supp. XXIII:** 230

Byatt, A. S., **Supp. XXI:** 147

By Avon River (Doolittle), **Supp. I Part 1:** 272

"By Blue Ontario's Shore" (Whitman), **Retro. Supp. I:** 399, 400; **Retro.**

Supp. III: 305

"By Candlelight" (Major), **Supp. XXII:** 185

"By Disposition of Angels" (Moore), **III:** 214

"By Earth" (Olds), **Supp. X:** 214

"Bye for Now, Broadway, My New Friend" (Silver), **Supp. XXIV:** 276

"By Fire" (Olds), **Supp. X:** 214

Bygones (Untermeyer), **Supp. XV:** 304, 308–309, 312, 313

By Land, By Sea (Hoffman), **Supp. XVIII:** 86

By Land and by Sea (Morison), **Supp. I Part 2:** 492

Byles, Mather, **Supp. XX:** 279, 282

By-Line: Ernest Hemingway (Hemingway), **II:** 257–258

By Love Possessed (Cozens), **I:** 358, 365, 372–374, 375, 376, 377, 378, 379

"By Morning" (Swenson), **Supp. IV Part 2:** 642

"By Night" (Francis), **Supp. IX:** 76

Bynner, Witter, **II:** 513, 527; **Supp. XIII:** 347; **Supp. XV:** 39–54

Byrd, William, **Supp. IV Part 2:** 425; **Supp. XXI:** 35; **Supp. XXII:** 193

Byrne, Donn, **IV:** 67

Byrne, Edward, **Supp. XXV:** 226, 227

Byron, George Gordon, Lord, **I:** 343, 568, 577; **II:** 135, 193, 296, 301, 303, 310, 315, 331, 566; **III:** 82, 137, 170, 409, 410, 412, 469; **IV:** 245, 435; **Retro. Supp. III:** 44; **Supp. I Part 1:** 150, 312, 349; **Supp. I Part 2:** 580, 591, 683, 685, 719; **Supp. XIII:** 139; **Supp. XVI:** 188, 203, 206, 210

"Byron's Cain" (L. Michaels), **Supp. XVI:** 203

"Bystanders" (Matthews), **Supp. IX:** 160

By the Bias of Sound (Sobin), **Supp. XVI:** 281

By the North Gate (Oates), **Supp. II Part 2:** 504

"By the People" (Faulkner), **Retro. Supp. III:** 86

"By the People" (Stratton-Porter), **Supp. XX:** 221

"By the Sea" (Teasdale), **Supp. XXVII:** 294

By the Shores of Silver Lake (L. I. Wilder), **Supp. XXII:** 294, 295, 299

"By the Time You Get There, by the Time You Get Back" (Muñoz), **Supp. XXV:** 134

"By the Waters of Babylon" (Benét), **Supp. XI:** 56, 58

"By the Waters of Babylon"(Lewisohn), **Supp. XXVIII:** 154

By the Waters of Manhattan (Reznikoff), **Supp. XIV:** 288, 293, 294

By the Waters of Manhattan: An Annual (Reznikoff), **Supp. XIV:** 277, 280, 289

By the Waters of Manhattan: Selected Verse (Reznikoff), **Supp. XIV:** 281, 291

By the Well of Living and Seeing and the Fifth Book of the Maccabees (Reznikoff), **Supp. XIV:** 281

By the Well of Living and Seeing: New and Selected Poems 1918–1973 (Reznikoff), **Supp. XIV:** 281, 287–288, 295
By Way of Orbit (O'Neill), **III:** 405
Byways to Adventure: A Guide to Nature Hobbies (Teale), **Supp. XXVIII:** 247
Byzantine Parables (Notley), **Supp. XXII:** 235, 237

C

"C 33" (H. Crane), **I:** 384; **Retro. Supp. II:** 76; **Retro. Supp. III:** 44
Cabala, The (Wilder), **IV:** 356, 358–360, 369, 374
"Cabaret" (Boyle), **Supp. XXIV:** 61
Cabaret (film), **Supp. XIV:** 155, 162
Cabaret (play), **Supp. XIV:** 162; **Supp. XVII:** 45
Cabbages and Kings (O. Henry), **Supp. II Part 1:** 394, 409
Cabell, James Branch, **II:** 42; **III:** 394; **IV:** 67, 359, 360; **Retro. Supp. I:** 80; **Supp. I Part 2:** 613, 714, 718, 721; **Supp. X:** 223
"Cabin, The" (Carver), **Supp. III Part 1:** 137, 146
Cabin, The: Reminiscence and Diversions (Mamet), **Supp. XIV:** 240
Cabinet of Dr. Caligari, The (film), **Retro. Supp. I:** 268
Cable, George Washington, **II:** 289; **Retro. Supp. II:** 65; **Retro. Supp. III:** 265; **Supp. I Part 1:** 200; **Supp. II Part 1:** 198; **Supp. XIV:** 63; **Supp. XXVIII:** 113, 124, 226, 227, 228
Cables to the Ace; or, Familiar Liturgies of Misunderstanding (Merton), **Supp. VIII:** 208
Cabot, James, **II:** 14; **IV:** 173
Cabot, John, **Supp. I Part 2:** 496, 497
Cachoeira Tales and Other Poems, The (Nelson), **Supp. XVIII:** 178–179
"Cachoiera Tales, The" (Nelson), **Supp. XVIII:** 179
Cactus Flower (Barillet and Grédy), **Supp. XVI:** 194
"Caddy's Diary, A" (Lardner), **II:** 421–422
"Cadence" (Dubus), **Supp. VII:** 84–85
Cadieux, Isabelle, **Supp. XIII:** 127
"Cadillac Flambé" (Ellison), **Retro. Supp. II:** 119, 126; **Supp. II Part 1:** 248
Cadillac Jack (McMurtry), **Supp. V:** 225
Cadillac Jukebox (Burke), **Supp. XIV:** 32
Cadle, Dean, **Supp. I Part 2:** 429
Cady, Edwin H., **II:** 272
"Caedmon" (Garrett), **Supp. VII:** 96–97
Caesar, Julius, **II:** 12, 502, 561–562; **IV:** 372, 373
Caesar, Sid, **Supp. IV Part 2:** 574, 591
"Cafeteria, The" (Singer), **Retro. Supp. II:** 316
Cage, John, **Supp. IV Part 1:** 84; **Supp. V:** 337, 341; **Supp. XXIII:** 211
"Cage and the Prairie: Two Notes on Symbolism, The" (Bewley), **Supp. I**

Part 1: 251
Cage Keeper, The (Dubus III), **Supp. XXIV:** 99–102
"Cage Keeper, The" (Dubus III), **Supp. XXIV:** 101–102, 104
Cage of Age, The (Bronk), **Supp. XXI:** 32
Cage of Spines, A (Swenson), **Supp. IV Part 2:** 641–642, 647
"Cage of the Body, The"(Schott), **Supp. XXIII:** 243–244
Cagney, James, **Supp. IV Part 1:** 236; **Supp. XIII:** 174
Cagney, William, **Supp. XIII:** 174
Cahalan, James, **Supp. XIII:** 1, 2, 3, 4, 12
Cahan, Abraham, **Supp. IX:** 227; **Supp. XIII:** 106; **Supp. XXI:** 3, 14; **Supp. XXIII:** 1, 2, 9, 16; **Supp. XXVI:** 123; **Supp. XXVIII:** 78
Cahill, Tim, **Supp. XIII:** 13
Cahir, Linda Costanzo, **Retro. Supp. III:** 290
Cain, James M., **III:** 99; **Supp. IV Part 1:** 130; **Supp. XI:** 160; **Supp. XIII:** 159, 165
Cain, Kathleen Shine, **Supp. XX:** 247, 248
Caine Mutiny, The (film), **Supp. XXV:** 260, 261
Caine Mutiny, The (Wouk), **Supp. XXV:** 253, 255, 256, 259–261
Caine Mutiny Court-Martial, The (Wouk), **Supp. XXV:** 253, 256
Caird, G. B., **Supp. XXI:** 91–92
Cairns, Huntington, **III:** 103, 108, 114, 119
Cairo! Shanghai! Bombay! (Williams and Shapiro), **IV:** 380
C: A Journal of Poetry, **Supp. XXVII:** 18, 24
Cake (Bynner), **Supp. XV:** 50
Cakes and Ale (Maugham), **III:** 64
Calabria, Frank, **Supp. XIII:** 164
Calamity Jane (Martha Jane Canary), **Supp. V:** 229–230; **Supp. X:** 103
"Calamus" (Whitman), **IV:** 342–343; **Retro. Supp. I:** 52, 403, 404, 407; **Retro. Supp. III:** 302
Calasso, Roberto, **Supp. IV Part 1:** 301
Calavito, Jason, **Supp. XXV:** 123
Calder, William M., III, **Supp. XXIII:** 112
Calderón, Hector, **Supp. IV Part 2:** 544
Caldwell, Christopher, **Supp. IV Part 1:** 211
Caldwell, Erskine, **I:** 97, 211, **288–311;** **IV:** 286; **Supp. IV Part 2:** 601; **Supp. XXI:** 35; **Supp. XXII:** 196
Caldwell, Mrs. Erskine (Helen Lannegan), **I:** 289
Caldwell, Mrs. Erskine (Margaret Bourke-White), **I:** 290, 293–295, 297
Caldwell, Mrs. Erskine (Virginia Fletcher), **I:** 290
Caldwell, Gail, **Supp. XXVI:** 158
Caldwell, Reverend Ira Sylvester, **I:** 289, 305
Caldwell, Zoe, **Supp. XIII:** 207
Caleb Williams (Godwin), **III:** 415

"Calendar" (Creeley), **Supp. IV Part 1:** 158
Calendar of Saints for Unbelievers, A (Wescott), **Supp. XIV:** 342
Calendars (A. Finch), **Supp. XVII:** 76–77
Calhoun, John C., **I:** 8; **III:** 309
"Caliban in the Coal Mines" (Untermeyer), **Supp. XV:** 296
"California" (Carruth), **Supp. XVI:** 56
"California" (Didion), **Supp. IV Part 1:** 195
"California, This Is Minnesota Speaking" (Dunn), **Supp. XI:** 146
California and Oregon Trail, The (Parkman), **Supp. I Part 2:** 486
California: An Intimate History (Atherton), **Supp. XXIV:** 27
California Daughter (Leider), **Supp. XXIV:** 30
"California Hills in August" (Gioia), **Supp. XV:** 118–119
"California Indians of Today, The" (Zitkala-Ša), **Supp. XXV:** 284
"California Indian Trails and Prayer Trees" (Zitkala-Ša), **Supp. XXV:** 284
Californians (Jeffers), **Supp. II Part 2:** 415, 418, 420
Californians, The (Atherton), **Supp. XXIV:** 18, 21, 22
"California Oaks, The" (Winters), **Supp. II Part 2:** 798
"California Plush" (Bidart), **Supp. XV:** 23
"California Republic" (Didion), **Supp. IV Part 1:** 205
"California Requiem, A" (Gioia), **Supp. XV:** 126
California Suite (film), **Supp. IV Part 2:** 589
California Suite (Simon), **Supp. IV Part 2:** 581, 582
"Caligula" (R. Lowell), **II:** 554
Callahan, John F., **Retro. Supp. II:** 119, 126, 127
"Call at Corazón" (Bowles), **Supp. IV Part 1:** 82, 87
Calle, Sophia, **Supp. XII:** 22
"Called Back" (Kazin), **Supp. VIII:** 104
"Calle Visión" (Rich), **Retro. Supp. III:** 252
Calley, Captain William, **II:** 579
Calley, John, **Supp. XI:** 305
Callicott, J. Baird, **Supp. XIV:** 184
Calligrammes (Apollinaire), **I:** 432
"Calling Jesus" (Toomer), **Supp. III Part 2:** 484
Calling Myself Home (Hogan), **Supp. IV Part 1:** 397, 399, 400, 401, 413
Calling the Wind: Twentieth Century African-American Short Stories (Major, ed.), **Supp. XXII:** 172
Calling Western Union (Taggard), **Supp. XXII:** 271–272, **281–283**
Call It Experience (Caldwell), **I:** 290–291, 297
"Call It Fear" (Harjo), **Supp. XII:** 220
Call It Sleep (H. Roth), **Supp. IX:** 227, 228, **229–231;** **Supp. VIII:** 233; **Supp. XIII:** 106

"Call Letters: Mrs. V. B." (Angelou), **Supp. IV Part 1:** 15

Call Me Ishmael (Olson), **Supp. II Part 2:** 556; **Supp. XXI:** 21

Call Me Shakespeare (Endore), **Supp. XVII:** 65

"Call of Cthulhu, The" (Lovecraft), **Supp. XXV:** 109, 114, 116–117, 118; **Supp. XXVII:** 123

Call of the Gospel, The (Mather), **Supp. II Part 2:** 448

Call of the Wild, The (London), **II:** 466, 470–471, 472, 481

"Call of the Wild, The" (Snyder), **Supp. VIII:** 301

"Calloway's Code" (O. Henry), **Supp. II Part 1:** 404

"Call to Arms" (Mumford), **Supp. II Part 2:** 479

Call to Arms, The (film), **Retro. Supp. I:** 325

Calmer, Ned, **Supp. XI:** 219

Calvert, George H., **Supp. I Part 1:** 361

Calverton, V. F., **Supp. VIII:** 96; **Supp. XXVIII:** 73

Calvin, John, **II:** 342; **IV:** 160, 490

Calvino, Italo, **Supp. IV Part 2:** 623, 678; **Supp. XIX:** 34; **Supp. XXI:** 225; **Supp. XXII:** 263

Cambridge Companion to Native American Literature, The (Porter and Roemer, eds.), **Supp. XX:** 270

Cambridge Companion to Poe, The (Hayes, ed.), **Retro. Supp. III:** 237

Cambridge Edition of the Works of F. Scott Fitzgerald, The (Bruccoli, ed.), **Retro. Supp. I:** 115

Cambridge Film Handbook for *On the Waterfront* (Rapf), **Supp. XVIII:** 251

"Cambridge"(O'Hara), **Supp. XXIII:** 219

"Cambridge Thirty Years Ago" (J. R. Lowell), **Supp. I Part 2:** 419

Cambridge University Press, **Retro. Supp. I:** 115

"Camelia Riccardo"(Stuart), **Supp. XXVIII:** 227, 234

"Camellia Sabina" (Moore), **III:** 208, 215

"Cameo" (Trethewey), **Supp. XXI:** 250

"Cameo Appearance" (Simic), **Supp. VIII:** 283

"Camera Notes" (column, Stratton-Porter), **Supp. XX:** 217

Camera Obscura (Nabokov), **III:** 255

"Camera Obscura"(Wakoski), **Supp. XXVIII:** 262

Cameron, Angus, **Supp. XXI:** 268, 269, 275, 278

Cameron, Elizabeth, **I:** 10, 17

Cameron, Kenneth W., **II:** 16

Cameron, Peter, **Supp. XII: 79–95**

Cameron, Sharon, **Retro. Supp. I:** 43; **Retro. Supp. II:** 40

Camerson, Don, **I:** 10, 17

Camino, Léon Felipe, **Retro. Supp. II:** 89

Camino Real (T. Williams), **IV:** 382, 385, 386, 387, 388, 391, 392, 395, 398

Camões, Luiz Vaz de, **II:** 133; **Supp. I Part 1:** 94

"Camouflaging the Chimera" (Komunyakaa), **Supp. XIII: 122–123**

Camp, James, **Supp. XV:** 165

Camp, Walter, **II:** 423

Campana, Dino, **Supp. V:** 337

Campbell, Alan, **Supp. IV Part 1:** 353; **Supp. IX:** 196, 198, 201

Campbell, Alexander, **Supp. I Part 2:** 381, 395

Campbell, Donna, **Retro. Supp. II:** 139

Campbell, E. Simms, **Supp. XXII:** 12

Campbell, Helen, **Supp. XI:** 200, 206

Campbell, James, **Supp. XII:** 127

Campbell, James Edwin, **Supp. II Part 1:** 202

Campbell, Joanna (pseudonym). *See* Bly, Carol

Campbell, Joseph, **I:** 135; **IV:** 369, 370; **Supp. IX:** 245; **Supp. XXV:** 74

Campbell, Lewis, **III:** 476

Campbell, Thomas, **II:** 8, 303, 314; **III:** 410; **Supp. I Part 1:** 309, 310

Campbell, Virginia, **Supp. XIII:** 114

Campbell, Will D., **Supp. XXI:** 247

Campbell (Hale), Janet, **Supp. IV Part 2:** 503

"Campers Leaving: Summer 1981" (Kenyon), **Supp. VII:** 169

"Camp Evergreen" (Kenyon), **Supp. VII:** 168

"Campfire in a Light Rain"(Bottoms), **Supp. XXVIII:** 32

"Camping in Madera Canyon" (Swenson), **Supp. IV Part 2:** 649

Campion, Jane, **Supp. XXIV:** 172

Campion, Peter, **Supp. XXV:** 227, 233

Campion, Thomas, **I:** 439; **Supp. VIII:** 272

"Campo" (Muñoz), **Supp. XXV:** 130

Campo, Rafael, **Supp. XVII:** 112

Camus, Albert, **I:** 53, 61, 292, 294, 494; **II:** 57, 244; **III:** 292, 306, 453; **IV:** 6, 211, 236, 442, 487; **Retro. Supp. I:** 73; **Retro. Supp. II:** 20; **Supp. I Part 2:** 621; **Supp. VIII:** 11, 195, 241; **Supp. XI:** 96; **Supp. XIII:** 74, 165, 233, 247; **Supp. XVII:** 137

Camuto, Christopher, **Supp. V:** 212–213

"Canada" (Di Piero), **Supp. XIX:** 39

Canada Fragrant with Resin, **Supp. XVI:** 149

Canadé, Eugene, **Supp. XXI:** 22, 23

"Canadian Mosaic, The" (Beran), **Supp. XIII:** 25

Canadian Short Stories (radio show), **Supp. XXVII:** 181

"Can a Good Wife Be a Good Sport?" (T. Williams), **IV:** 380

"Canal, The: A Poem on the Application of Physical Science to Political Economy" (Barlow), **Supp. II Part 1:** 73

Canan, Peter, **Supp. XXV:** 123

Canary, Martha Jane. *See* Calamity Jane (Martha Jane Canary)

"Canary for One, A" (Hemingway), **Retro. Supp. I:** 170, 189

Canary in a Cat House (Vonnegut), **Supp. II Part 2:** 758

"Canary in Bloom" (Dove), **Supp. IV Part 1:** 248

Canby, Henry Seidel, **IV:** 65, 363

Canby, Vincent, **Retro. Supp. III:** 290

"Cancer" (McClatchy), **Supp. XII:** 266

"Cancer Match, The" (Dickey), **Supp. IV Part 1:** 182

"Canción y Glosa" (Merwin), **Supp. III Part 1:** 342

Candide (Hellman), **I:** 28; **Supp. I Part 1:** 288–289, 292

Candide (Voltaire), **Supp. I Part 1:** 288–289; **Supp. XI:** 297; **Supp. XVI:** 189

Candide (Voltaire; Wilbur, trans.), **Supp. III Part 2:** 560

"Candle Hat" (Collins), **Supp. XXI:** 60

Candle in the Cabin, The (Lindsay), **Supp. I Part 2:** 398, 400

"Candles" (Plath), **Retro. Supp. II:** 248, 257

Candles in Babylon (Levertov), **Supp. III Part 1:** 283

Candles in the Sun (T. Williams), **IV:** 381

Candles of Your Eyes, The (Purdy), **Supp. VII:** 278

Candy (Southern), **Supp. XI:** 297, **298–299,** 305

"Candy Land"(Goodman), **Supp. XXVIII:** 94

"Candy-Man Beechum" (Caldwell), **I:** 309

Cane (Toomer), **Supp. III Part 2:** 475, 481–486, 488; **Supp. IV Part 1:** 164, 168; **Supp. IX:** 305, 306, 307, **308–320; Supp. XIX:** 73; **Supp. XX:** 73

"Cane in the Corridor, The" (Thurber), **Supp. I Part 2:** 616

Canfield, Cass, **Supp. I Part 2:** 668

Canfield, Dorothy, **Retro. Supp. I:** 4, 11, 14, 18; **Retro. Supp. III:** 27; **Supp. XX:** 39. *See also* Fisher, Dorothy Canfield

Canfield, William W., **Supp. XXVI:** 86

Can Grande's Castle (A. Lowell), **II:** 518, 524

"Canicula di Anna" (Carson), **Supp. XII: 101–102**

"Can I Get You Anything?" (Carver and Gallagher), **Supp. XXIV:** 178

"Canis Major" (Frost), **Retro. Supp. I:** 137

"Canned Stuff" (Pickering), **Supp. XXI:** 198

Cannery Row (Steinbeck), **IV:** 50, 51, 64–65, 66, 68

Cannibal Galaxy, The (Ozick), **Supp. V:** 270

Cannibals and Christians (Mailer), **III:** 38–39, 40, 42; **Retro. Supp. II:** 203, 204, 205; **Supp. XXIV:** 281

Canning, George, **I:** 7, 8

Canning, Richard, **Supp. X:** 147

Cannon, Jimmy, **II:** 424

Cannon, Steve, **Retro. Supp. II:** 111

Cannon between My Knees, A (Gunn Allen), **Supp. IV Part 1:** 324

Canolle, Jean, **Supp. XVI:** 194

"Canonization, The" (Donne), **Supp. XIV:** 8

"Can Poetry Matter?" (Gioia), **Supp. XV:** 113, 114

Can Poetry Matter?: Essays on Poetry and American Culture (Gioia), **Supp. XV:** 112, **113–115**

"Canso" (Merwin), **Supp. III Part 1:** 344

Can Such Things Be? (Bierce), **I:** 203, 204, 205, 209

Canterbury Tales (Chaucer), **II:** 504; **III:** 411; **IV:** 65

Canterbury Tales, The (Chaucer), **Supp. XIX:** 4

"Canticle of Her Coming and Going" (Espaillat), **Supp. XXI:** 106

"Canto Amor" (Berryman), **I:** 173

Canto I (Pound), **III:** 469, 470; **Retro. Supp. I:** 286

Canto II (Pound), **III:** 470

Canto III (Pound), **III:** 470

Canto IV (Pound), **III:** 470

Canto VIII (Pound), **III:** 472

Canto IX (Pound), **III:** 472

Canto X (Pound), **III:** 472

Canto XIII (Pound), **III:** 472

Canto XXXIX (Pound), **III:** 468

Canto LXV (Pound), **Retro. Supp. I:** 292

Canto LXXXI (Pound), **III:** 459; **Retro. Supp. I:** 293

Cantor, Lois, **Supp. IV Part 1:** 285

Cantos (Pound), **I:** 482; **III:** 13–14, 17, 457, 462, 463, 466, 467, 469–470, 472–473, 474, 475, 476, 492; **Retro. Supp. I:** 284, 292, **292–293,** 293, 427; **Retro. Supp. III:** 50; **Supp. I Part 1:** 272; **Supp. II Part 1:** 5; **Supp. II Part 2:** 420, 557, 564, 644; **Supp. IV Part 1:** 153; **Supp. V:** 343, 345; **Supp. VIII:** 305; **Supp. XIV:** 55, 96; **Supp. XV:** 349

"Cantus Planis" (Pound), **III:** 466

Cantwell, Robert, **Retro. Supp. I:** 85; **Supp. VIII:** 96; **Supp. XIII:** 292

Can Women Be Gentlemen? (Atherton), **Supp. XXIV:** 20–21, 30

"Canyon de Chelly, Return, 1978"(Kenny), **Supp. XXIII:** 155

Canyons, The (film), **Supp. XXVII:** 79–80

"Can You Carry Me" (O'Hara), **III:** 369

Can You See Me Yet? (Findley), **Supp. XX:** 52–53

Canzoneri, Robert, **IV:** 114, 116

Canzoni (Pound), **Retro. Supp. I:** 286, 288, 413

"Cap" (Shaw), **Supp. IV Part 1:** 345

"Cape Breton" (Bishop), **Supp. I Part 1:** 92; **Supp. IX:** 45

Cape Cod (Thoreau), **II:** 540

"Cape Cod, Rome, and Jerusalem" (Chapman), **Supp. XIV:** 55

Capital City (Sandoz), **Supp. XXIV:** 244, **252–253,** 255

Capitalism: The Unknown Ideal (Rand), **Supp. IV Part 2:** 518, 527, 531, 532

Cap of Darkness (Wakoski), **Supp. XXVIII:** 266–267

Caponi, Gena Dagel, **Supp. IV Part 1:** 95

Capote, Truman, **Supp. I Part 1:** 291, 292; **Supp. III Part 1:** 111–133; **Supp. III Part 2:** 574; **Supp. IV Part 1:** 198, 220; **Supp. VIII:** 105; **Supp. XII:** 43, 249; **Supp. XV:** 146; **Supp. XVI:** 245–246; **Supp. XVII:** 236; **Supp. XXVIII:** 40

Capouya, Emile, **Supp. I Part 1:** 50

Cappetti, Carla, **Supp. IX:** 4, 8

Capra, Frank, **Supp. XVI:** 102

Capra, Fritjof, **Supp. X:** 261

"Capricious Gardens" (Eugenides), **Supp. XXIV:** 133–134

"Capricorn Rising" (Mackey), **Supp. XXVII:** 153

Capron, Marion, **Supp. IX:** 193

"Capsule History of Conservation, A" (Stegner), **Supp. IV Part 2:** 600

"Captain Carpenter" (Ransom), **III:** 491

Captain Craig (Robinson), **III:** 508, 523; **Supp. II Part 1:** 192

"Captain Jim's Friend" (Harte), **Supp. II Part 1:** 337

"Captain Jones's Invitation" (Freneau), **Supp. II Part 1:** 261

"Captain's Son, The" (Taylor), **Supp. V:** 314, 325, 327

"Captain's Wife, The" (Salter), **Supp. IX:** 261

"Capt Christopher Levett (of York)" (Olson), **Supp. II Part 2:** 576, 577

Captive Israel (Reznikoff), **Supp. XIV:** 283

"Captivity and Restoration of Mrs. Mary Rowlandson, The" (Howe), **Supp. IV Part 2:** 419, 431, 434

"Captivity of the Fly" (MacLeish), **III:** 19

"Captured Goddess, The" (A. Lowell), **II:** 520

Caputi, Jane, **Supp. IV Part 1:** 334, 335

Caputo, Philip, **Supp. XI:** 234; **Supp. XIX:** 17–31; **Supp. XXII:** 104; **Supp. XXV:** 153

Capuzzo, Michael, **Supp. XIII:** 254

Car (Crews), **Supp. XI:** 110–111

Carabi, Angels, **Supp. VIII:** 223; **Supp. XII:** 215

"Caramels" (Zinberg), **Supp. XV:** 195

"Caravaggio: Swirl & Vortex" (Levis), **Supp. XI:** 258, 269

Caravan (Bynner), **Supp. XV:** 50

Carby, Hazel B., **Supp. IV Part 1:** 13; **Supp. XXI:** 171

"Carcassonne" (Faulkner), **Retro. Supp. I:** 81

Card, Antha E., **Supp. I Part 2:** 496

Cárdenas, Lupe, **Supp. IV Part 2:** 538, 539, 540

Cardinale, Anthony, **Supp. XVII:** 239

Cardinale, Ernesto, **Supp. XII:** 225

"Cardinal Ideograms" (Swenson), **Supp. IV Part 2:** 645

"Cards" (Beattie), **Supp. V:** 31

"Career Woman" (Hay), **Supp. XIV:** 131

Carefree (film, Sandrich), **Supp. XVII:** 59

"Careful" (Carver), **Supp. III Part 1:** 138

Careful and Strict Enquiry into the Modern Prevailing Notions of That Freedom of Will, Which Is Supposed to be Essential to Moral Agency, Vertue and Vice, Reward and Punishment, Praise and Blame, A (Edwards), **I:** 549, 557, 558, 562

Carel: A Poem and Pilgrimage in the Holy Land (Melville), **III:** 92–93

Careless Love and Its Apostrophes (Bronk), **Supp. XXI:** 32

"Carentan O Carentan" (Simpson), **Supp. IX:** 267

Carew, Thomas, **IV:** 453

Carey, Gary, **Supp. XVI:** 186

Carey, Lynn, **Supp. XXIII:** 273

Carey, Mathew, **Supp. XV:** 238

"Car Games" (Conroy), **Supp. XVI:** 72

Cargill, Oscar, **Supp. II Part 1:** 117

Caribbean as Columbus Saw It (Morison and Obregon), **Supp. I Part 2:** 488

"Caribou Kitchen" (A. Finch), **Supp. XVII:** 76–77

Caribou Rising: Defending the Porcupine Herd, Gwich-'in Culture, and the Arctic National Wildlife Refuge (Bass), **Supp. XVI:** 27–28, 28

Carillo, Donna, **Supp. XXVII:** 204

"Caring for the World"(Schott), **Supp. XXIII:** 249–250

Carkeet, David, **Retro. Supp. III:** 265

Carl, K. A., **III:** 475

Carleton, George W., **Supp. XVIII:** 4

Carlin, George, **Supp. XXI:** 51

Carlin, Terry, **Supp. XXI:** 4, 5, 14

Carlisle, Harry, **Supp. XVIII:** 223, 233

Carl Krinken: His Christmas Stocking (S. and A. Warner), **Supp. XVIII:** 264

"Carlos Who Died, and Left Only This, The" (Ríos), **Supp. IV Part 2:** 547

Carlotta (empress of Mexico), **Supp. I Part 2:** 457

Carlotta's Intended and Other Tales (Stuart), **Supp. XXVIII:** 225, 228

"Carlotta's Intended"(Stuart), **Supp. XXVIII:** 225

Carl Sandburg (Golden), **III:** 579

Carlson, Susan L., **Supp. XV:** 323

Carlyle, Thomas, **I:** 103, 279; **II:** 5, 7, 11, 15–16, 17, 20, 145, 315; **III:** 82, 84, 85, 87; **IV:** 169, 182, 338, 350; **Retro. Supp. I:** 360, 408; **Retro. Supp. III:** 266; **Supp. I Part 1:** 2, 349; **Supp. I Part 2:** 410, 422, 482, 485, 552; **Supp. XXV:** 242

"Carma" (Toomer), **Supp. III Part 2:** 481–483; **Supp. IX:** 312–313

"Carmen de Boheme" (Crane), **I:** 384

Carmen Jones (film), **Supp. I Part 1:** 66

Carmina Burana, **Supp. X:** 63

Carmon, Walt, **Supp. XXII:** 277

Carnegie, Andrew, **I:** 483; **IV:** 192; **Supp. I Part 2:** 639, 644; **Supp. V:** 285

Carnegie, Dale, **Supp. I Part 2:** 608

"Carnegie Hall: Rescued" (Moore), **III:** 215

Carne-Ross, Donald S., **Supp. I Part 1:** 268, 269; **Supp. XXIV:** 153

Carnes, Mark C., **Supp. X:** 14

"Carnets" poems (Sobin), **Supp. XVI:** 286–287

Carnovsky, Morris, **III:** 154

"Carol for Carolyn, A" (A. Finch), **Supp. XVII:** 74, 75
"Carolina Parakeet" (Rash), **Supp. XXVII:** 220
Caroling Dusk: An Anthology of Verse by Negro Poets (Cullen, ed.), **Supp. IV Part 1:** 166, 169; **Supp. XXVI:** 165, 170
"Carol of Occupations" (Whitman), **I:** 486
"Carolyn Kizer and the Chain of Women" (A. Finch), **Supp. XVII:** 74–75
Carolyn Kizer: Perspectives on Her Life and Work (A. Finch), **Supp. XVII:** 74–75
"Carpe Diem" (Frost), **Supp. XII:** 303
"Carpe Noctem, if You Can" (Thurber), **Supp. I Part 2:** 620
Carpenter, Dan, **Supp. V:** 250
Carpenter, David, **Supp. VIII:** 297
Carpenter, Edward, **Supp. XX:** 230
Carpenter, Frederic I., **II:** 20
"Carpenter Bee" (Trethewey), **Supp. XXI:** 250
Carpentered Hen and Other Tame Creatures, The (Updike), **IV:** 214; **Retro. Supp. I:** 320
Carpenter's Gothic (Gaddis), **Supp. IV Part 1:** 288, 289–291, 293, 294
Carr, Dennis W., **Supp. IV Part 2:** 560
Carr, Elias, **Supp. XIV:** 57
Carr, Rosemary. *See* Benét, Rosemary
Carrall, Aaron, **Supp. IV Part 2:** 499
Carrel, Alexis, **IV:** 240
"Carrell/Klee/and Cosmos's Groom" (Goldbarth), **Supp. XII:** 183
"Carriage from Sweden, A" (Moore), **III:** 212
Carrie (King), **Supp. V:** 137
Carried Away (Harrison), **Supp. VIII:** 39
Carrier of Ladders (Merwin), **Supp. III Part 1:** 339, 346, 350–352, 356, 357
"Carriers of the Dream Wheel" (Momaday), **Supp. IV Part 2:** 481
Carriers of the Dream Wheel: Contemporary Native American Poetry (Niatum, ed.), **Supp. IV Part 2:** 484, 505
Carrington, Carroll, **I:** 199
"Carrion Spring" (Stegner), **Supp. IV Part 2:** 604
Carroll, Bart, **Supp. XXV:** 71
Carroll, Charles, **Supp. I Part 2:** 525
Carroll, Jonathan, **Supp. XXVIII:** 269, 270, 273
Carroll, Lewis, **I:** 432; **II:** 431; **III:** 181; **Supp. I Part 1:** 44; **Supp. I Part 2:** 622, 656; **Supp. XVI:** 103; **Supp. XXV:** 87; **Supp. XXVI:** 274
Carroll, Maureen P., **Supp. XXIV:** 177
"Carrots, Noses, Snow, Rose, Roses" (Gass), **Supp. VI:** 87
Carrouges, Michel, **Supp. IV Part 1:** 104
"Carrousel, The" (Rilke), **III:** 558
Carruth, Hayden, **Supp. IV Part 1:** 66; **Supp. IX:** 291; **Supp. VIII:** 39; **Supp. XIII:** 112; **Supp. XIV:** 273–274; **Supp. XIX:** 1; **Supp. XVI:** 45–61; **Supp. XXI:** 31; **Supp. XXIV:** 167
Carruth, Joe-Anne McLaughlin, **Supp. XVI:** 47

"Carry" (Hogan), **Supp. IV Part 1:** 412
Carrying Albert Home (Hickam), **Supp. XXVII:** 111
"Carrying On" (Dunn), **Supp. XI:** 145
Cars of Cuba (García), **Supp. XI:** 190
Carson, Anne, **Supp. XII:** 97–116; **Supp. XV:** 252; **Supp. XXV:** 222
Carson, Johnny, **Supp. IV Part 2:** 526
Carson, Rachel, **Supp. IX:** 19–36; **Supp. V:** 202; **Supp. X:** 99; **Supp. XVI:** 36; **Supp. XXVI:** 31; **Supp. XXVIII:** 243, 253, 256
Carson, Tom, **Supp. XI:** 227
Cart, Michael, **Supp. X:** 12; **Supp. XXVII:** 205; **Supp. XXVIII:** 288
"Car Tags" (Rash), **Supp. XXVII:** 222
Carter, Angela, **Supp. XXVII:** 190
Carter, Elliott, **Supp. III Part 1:** 21
Carter, Hodding, **Supp. XIV:** 2
Carter, Jared, **Supp. XVII:** 110
Carter, Jimmy, **Supp. I Part 2:** 638; **Supp. XIV:** 107
Carter, Lin, **Supp. XXVII:** 128
Carter, Marcia, **Supp. V:** 223
Carter, Mary, **Supp. IV Part 2:** 444
Carter, Paul, **Supp. XX:** 77, 78
Carter, Peter, **Supp. XVII:** 267
Carter, Stephen, **Supp. XI:** 220
Cartesian Sonata and Other Novellas (Gass), **Supp. VI:** 92–93
Cartier, Jacques, **Supp. I Part 2:** 496, 497
Cartier-Bresson, Henri, **Supp. VIII:** 98
"Cartographies of Silence" (Rich), **Supp. I Part 2:** 571–572
"Cartography" (Espaillat), **Supp. XXI:** 107
Cartwright, Louis, **Supp. XIV:** 147, 149, 151
Carver, Raymond, **Supp. III Part 1:** 135–151; **Supp. IV Part 1:** 342; **Supp. V:** 22, 23, 220, 326; **Supp. VIII:** 15; **Supp. X:** 85, 167; **Supp. XI:** 26, 65, 116, 153; **Supp. XII:** 79, 139, 289, 294; **Supp. XIX:** 209; **Supp. XXI:** 36, 115, 116, 118, 119; **Supp. XXIII:** 289, 296; **Supp. XXIV:** 97, 166, 167, 173, 177–178; **Supp. XXVI:** 147, 180; **Supp. XXVII:** 269
Carver: A Life in Poems (Nelson), **Supp. XVIII:** 171, 172, **181–182,** 183
Carville, James, **Supp. XXIV:** 282
Carving Hawk (Kenny), **Supp. XXIII:** 143, 150
Cary, Alice, **Retro. Supp. II:** 145; **Supp. XV:** 273; **Supp. XXII:** 206
Cary, Phoebe, **Supp. XV:** 273
Cary, Richard, **Retro. Supp. II:** 132, 137
"Casabianca" (Bishop), **Retro. Supp. II:** 42; **Supp. I Part 1:** 86
Casablanca (film), **Supp. VIII:** 61; **Supp. XV:** 14
Casanova: His Known and Unknown Life (Endore), **Supp. XVII:** 54
"Casa solariega, La" ("The Family Mansion") (Espaillat), **Supp. XXI:** 107
"Case Against Mist, The" (Halliday), **Supp. XIX:** 91

Casebook (Simpson), **Supp. XXVII:** 234, 244–246
Case for West-Indian Self-Government, The (C. L. R. James), **Supp. XXI:** 159, 161
Case in Diplomacy, A (Stuart), **Supp. XXVIII:** 235
Case of Jennie Brice, The (Rinehart), **Supp. XXV:** 193, 200
Case of Mr. Crump, The (Lewisohn), **Supp. XXVIII:** 145, 148, 149, 151, 159
Case of Rape, A (C. Himes), **Supp. XVI:** 143
Case of the Crushed Petunias, The (T. Williams), **IV:** 381
Case of the Officers of Excise (Paine), **Supp. I Part 2:** 503–504
Casey, Helen Marie, **Supp. XXIII:** 246
Casey, John, **Supp. X:** 164
Casey, Nell, **Supp. XXVIII:** 197
Cash, Arthur, **Supp. IV Part 1:** 299
Cashman, Nellie, **Supp. X:** 103
Casiero, Robert, **Supp. XIV:** 167
Casino Royale (film), **Supp. XI:** 306–307; **Supp. XXVII:** 96
Caskey, William, **Supp. XIV:** 166
"Cask of Amontillado, The" (Poe), **II:** 475; **III:** 413; **Retro. Supp. II:** 268, 269, 270, 273; **Retro. Supp. III:** 226, 229–230
Caso, Frank, **Supp. XVIII:** 95
Caspary, Vera, **Supp. XIX:** 78
Casper, Robert N., **Supp. XV:** 339, 347
Casper and His Friends (S. and A. Warner), **Supp. XVIII:** 264
Cassada (Salter), **Supp. IX:** 251–252
Cassada, Jackie, **Supp. XXIII:** 291
Cassady, Carolyn, **Supp. XIV:** 150
Cassady, Neal, **Supp. II Part 1:** 309, 311; **Supp. XIV:** 137, 144
"Cassandra" (Stallings), **Supp. XXV:** 233
"Cassandra Southwick" (Whittier), **Supp. I Part 2:** 693
Cassell, Verlin, **Supp. XI:** 315
Cassill, Ronald Verlin, **Supp. V:** 323; **Supp. XIX:** 266; **Supp. XVIII:** 72
Cassirer, Ernst, **I:** 265; **IV:** 87, 89
Cass Timberlane (Lewis), **II:** 455–456
Cast a Cold Eye (McCarthy), **II:** 566
Castaway (Cozzens), **I:** 363, 370, 374, 375, 379
"Caste in America" (Du Bois), **Supp. II Part 1:** 169
Castiglione, Baldassare, **I:** 279; **III:** 282
"Castilian" (Wylie), **Supp. I Part 2:** 714
Castillo, Ana, **Supp. XI:** 177; **Supp. XXIII:** 194
"Castle in Lynn, A" (McCarriston), **Supp. XIV:** 265, 268
"Castles and Distances" (Wilbur), **Supp. III Part 2:** 550
Castle Sinister (Marquand), **III:** 58
Cast of Thousands (Loos), **Supp. XVI:** 192, 193, 195
Castro, Fidel, **II:** 261, 434; **Supp. XX:** 80
Cast the First Stone (C. Himes), **Supp. XVI:** 135, 137–138

"Casual Incident, A" (Hemingway), **II:** 44

Casualties (Rash), **Supp. XXVII:** 227

"Casualty Report" (Halliday), **Supp. XIX:** 85

Caswell, Michelle, **Supp. XXII:** 262

"Cat, The" (Matthews), **Supp. IX: 157–158**

Cat, You Better Come Home (Keillor), **Supp. XVI:** 177

"Catalogues"(Prouty), **Supp. XXVIII:** 180

"Catbird Seat, The" (Thurber), **Supp. I Part 2:** 623

"Catch" (Francis), **Supp. IX:** 82

Catch-22 (Heller), **III:** 558; **Supp. IV Part 1:** 379, 380, 381–382, 383, 384–386, 387, 390, 391, 392, 393, 394; **Supp. V:** 244, 248; **Supp. XII:** 167–168; **Supp. XXIII:** 100; **Supp. XXVII:** 207

Catcher in the Rye, The (Salinger), **I:** 493; **III:** 551, 552, 553–558, 567, 571; **Retro. Supp. I:** 102; **Retro. Supp. II:** 222, 249; **Supp. I Part 2:** 535; **Supp. V:** 119; **Supp. VIII:** 242; **Supp. XI:** 65; **Supp. XVII:** 2; **Supp. XXIII:** 100; **Supp. XXIV:** 133

"Catching Frogs" (Kenyon), **Supp. VII:** 170

Catching the Mermother (A. Finch), **Supp. XVII:** 72

catechism of d neoamerican hoodoo church (Reed), **Supp. X:** 240, 241

Catered Affair, The (film), **Supp. IV Part 2:** 683

"Caterer, The"(Goodman), **Supp. XXVIII:** 91–92

"Catfish, The"(Bottoms), **Supp. XXVIII:** 25–26

"Cathay" (Goldbarth), **Supp. XII:** 185, 186

Cathay (Pound), **II:** 527; **Retro. Supp. I:** 289

Cathedral (Carver), **Supp. III Part 1:** 144–146; **Supp. XII:** 139

"Cathedral" (Carver), **Supp. III Part 1:** 144–145; **Supp. XXIV:** 177

Cathedral, The (J. R. Lowell), **Supp. I Part 2:** 407, 416–417

Cather, Willa, **I:** 312–334, 405; **II:** 96, 177, 404, 412; **III:** 453; **IV:** 190; **Retro. Supp. I: 1–23,** 355, 382; **Retro. Supp. II:** 71, 136; **Retro. Supp. III: 17–39; Supp. I Part 2:** 609, 719; **Supp. IV Part 1:** 31; **Supp. VIII:** 101, 102, 263; **Supp. X:** 103; **Supp. XIII:** 253; **Supp. XIV:** 112; **Supp. XIX:** 131; **Supp. XV:** 40, 51; **Supp. XVI:** 226; **Supp. XVIII:** 207; **Supp. XXIII:** 290; **Supp. XXIV:** 29, 30, 244; **Supp. XXV:** 201

Catherine, Saint, **II:** 211

Catherine II, **Supp. I Part 2:** 433

Catholic Art and Culture (Watkin), **Retro. Supp. II:** 187

"Catholic Novelist in the Protestant South, The" (O'Connor), **Retro. Supp. II:** 223, 224; **Retro. Supp. III:** 215

"Cathy Queen of Cats" (Cisneros), **Supp. VII:** 59

Cat Inside, The (Burroughs), **Supp. III Part 1:** 105

Cat in the Hat, The (Geisel), **Supp. XVI:** 106–107, 112

Cat in the Hat Come Back, The (Geisel), **Supp. XVI:** 107

"Cat in the Hat for President, The" (Coover), **Supp. V:** 44, 46–47

Cat in The Hat Songbook, The (Geisel), **Supp. XVI:** 104

Cato, **II:** 114, 117

Cat on a Hot Tin Roof (T. Williams), **II:** 190; **IV:** 380, 382, 383, 386, 387, 389, 390, 391, 394, 395, 397–398; **Supp. XXV:** 93

"Cat People: What Dr. Seuss Really Taught Us" (Menand), **Supp. XVI:** 106

Cats and Dogs (Silver), **Supp. XXIV:** 265, 274

Cat's Cradle (Vonnegut), **Supp. II Part 2:** 758, 759, 767–768, 770, 771, 772; **Supp. V:** 1

Cat's Eye (Atwood), **Supp. XIII: 29–30**

Catskill Eagle, A (Parker), **Supp. XIX:** 185

"Cat's Meow, A" (Brodsky), **Supp. VIII:** 31

"Cats of Ulthar, The" (Lovecraft), **Supp. XXV:** 114

Cat's Quizzer, The (Geisel), **Supp. XVI:** 111

"Catterskill Falls" (Bryant), **Supp. I Part 1:** 160

"Cattle Car Complex" (T. Rosenbaum), **Supp. XVII:** 48

Cattlemen from the Rio Grande Across the Far Marias (Sandoz), **Supp. XXIV:** 244, **249–251,** 256

Catullus, **Supp. XII:** 2, 13, **112; Supp. XV:** 23, 27, 35, 36

Catullus, Gaius Valerius, **I:** 381; **Supp. I Part 1:** 261; **Supp. I Part 2:** 728

Catullus (Gai Catulli Veronensis Liber) (Zukofsky), **Supp. III Part 2:** 625, 627, 628, 629

"Catullus: Carmina" (Carson), **Supp. XII:** 112

"Catullus: Excrucior" (Bidart), **Supp. XV:** 32, 35

"Cat Walked Through the Casserole, The" (Nelson and Espeland), **Supp. XVIII:** 181

Cat Walked Through the Casserole and Other Poems for Children (Nelson and Espeland), **Supp. XVIII:** 181

"Cat Who Aspired to Higher Things, The" (X. J. Kennedy), **Supp. XV:** 163

Cat Who Went to Heaven, The (Coatsworth), **Supp. XXVI:** 33

"Caucasian Storms Harlem, The" (R. Fisher), **Supp. XIX:** 78

Caudwell, Christopher, **Supp. X:** 112; **Supp. XXII:** 284

"Caul, The" (Banks), **Supp. V:** 10–11

Cause for Wonder (Morris), **III:** 232–233

"Causerie" (Tate), **IV:** 129

Causes and Consequences (Chapman), **Supp. XIV:** 41, 49, 51

"Causes of American Discontents before 1768, The" (Franklin), **II:** 120

Causley, Charles, **Supp. XV:** 117

Cavafy, Constantine P., **Supp. IX:** 275; **Supp. XI:** 119, 123; **Supp. XXI:** 131; **Supp. XXIII:** 150; **Supp. XXV:** 225, 233

Cavalcade of America, The (radio program), **III:** 146

Cavalcanti (Pound, opera), **Retro. Supp. I:** 287

Cavalcanti, Guido, **I:** 579; **III:** 467; **Supp. III Part 2:** 620, 621, 622, 623

Cavalieri, Grace, **Supp. IV Part 2:** 630, 631

"Cavalry Crossing the Ford" (Whitman), **IV:** 347

"Cave, The" (Bass), **Supp. XVI:** 23

Cave, The (Warren), **IV:** 255–256

Cavelieri, Grace, **Supp. XXIII:** 135

Cavell, Stanley, **Retro. Supp. I:** 306–307, 309

Cavender's House (Robinson), **III:** 510

Caver, Christine, **Supp. XXI:** 215

Caves of Death, The (Atherton; Joshi, ed.), **Supp. XXIV:** 23

"Caviar" (Boyle), **Supp. XX:** 19

Caviare at the Funeral (Simpson), **Supp. IX:** 266, **276–277**

"Cawdor" (Jeffers), **Supp. II Part 2:** 431

Caxton, William, **III:** 486

Cayton, Horace, **IV:** 475, 488

Cazamian, Louis, **II:** 529

C Comics, **Supp. XXVII:** 23

"Ceiling, The" (Brockmeier), **Supp. XXII:** 52–53

Celan, Paul, **Supp. X:** 149; **Supp. XII:** 21, 110–111; **Supp. XVI:** 284–285, 288; **Supp. XVII:** 241

"Celebrated Jumping Frog of Calaveras County, The" (Twain), **IV:** 196

Celebrated Jumping Frog of Calaveras County, The, and Other Sketches (Twain), **IV:** 197; **Retro. Supp. III:** 257, 260

Celebration (Crews), **Supp. XI:** 103, **108**

Celebration (Swados), **Supp. XIX: 269–270**

Celebration at Dark (W. J. Smith), **Supp. XIII:** 332

"Celebration for June 24th" (McGrath), **Supp. X:** 116

Celebration of the Sound Through (Sobin), **Supp. XVI:** 284–285

Celebrations after the Death of John Brennan (X. J. Kennedy), **Supp. XV:** 165

Celebrity (film; Allen), **Supp. XV:** 11

"Celebrity" (Pickering), **Supp. XXI:** 198

"Celery" (Stein), **IV:** 43

"Celestial Games" (Conroy), **Supp. XVI:** 72

"Celestial Globe" (Nemerov), **III:** 288

Celestial Navigation (Tyler), **Supp. IV Part 2:** 662–663, 671

"Celestial Railroad, The" (Hawthorne), **Retro. Supp. I:** 152; **Retro. Supp. III:** 115; **Supp. I Part 1:** 188

Celibate Season, A (Shields), **Supp. VII:**
323, 324
Cellini (Shanley), **Supp. XIV:** 316, **329–330**
"Cemetery at Academy, California"
(Levine), **Supp. V:** 182
Cemetery Nights (Dobyns), **Supp. XIII:**
85, 87, 89
"Cenotaph, The" (Stallings), **Supp. XXV:**
225, 234
"Censors As Critics: *To Kill a Mocking-
bird* As a Case Study" (May), **Supp.
VIII:** 126
"Census-Taker, The" (Frost), **Retro.
Supp. I:** 129
"Centaur, The" (Swenson), **Supp. IV
Part 2:** 641
Centaur, The (Updike), **IV:** 214, 216, 217,
218, 219–221, 222; **Retro. Supp. I:**
318, 322, 324, 331, 336
"Centennial Meditation of Columbia,
The" (Lanier), **Supp. I Part 1:** 362
Centeno, Agusto, **IV:** 375
"Centipede" (Dove), **Supp. IV Part 1:**
246
"Cento: A Note on Philosophy"
(Berrigan), **Supp. XXIV:** 42–43
"Central Man, The" (Bloom), **Supp. IV
Part 2:** 689
"Central Park" (R. Lowell), **II:** 552
Central Park (Wasserstein and Drattel),
Supp. XV: 333
"Central Park at Dusk" (Teasdale), **Supp.
XXVII:** 286, 289
Central Park West (Allen), **Supp. XV:** 13
Century Cycle (Wilson), **Retro. Supp.
III:** 313, 318, 321, 323, 325, 326
Century of Dishonor, A (Jackson), **Retro.
Supp. I:** 31
"Cerebral Snapshot, The" (Theroux),
Supp. VIII: 313
"Ceremonies" (Rukeyser), **Supp. VI:** 279
"Ceremony" (Monson), **Supp. XXIV:**
230
Ceremony (Silko), **Supp. IV Part 1:** 274,
333; **Supp. IV Part 2:** 557–558, 558–
559, 559, 561–566, 570; **Supp. XVIII:**
59
Ceremony (Wilbur), **Supp. III Part 2:**
550–551
"Ceremony, The" (Harjo), **Supp. XII:**
230
"Ceremony, The—Anatomy of a Mas-
sacre" (E. Hoffman, play), **Supp. XVI:**
160
Ceremony in Lone Tree (Morris), **III:**
229–230, 232, 238, 558
Ceremony of Brotherhood, A (Anaya and
Ortiz, eds.), **Supp. IV Part 2:** 502
Cerf, Bennett, **III:** 405; **IV:** 288; **Retro.
Supp. II:** 330; **Supp. XIII:** 172;
Supp. XIX: 244
"Certain Attention to the World, A"
(Haines), **Supp. XII:** 201
"Certain Beasts, Like Cats" (Bronk),
Supp. XXI: 30
Certain Distance, A (Francis), **Supp. IX:**
85
"Certain Music, A" (Rukeyser), **Supp.
VI:** 273

Certain Noble Plays of Japan (Pound),
III: 458
Certain People (Wharton), **Retro. Supp.
I:** 382
"Certain Poets" (MacLeish), **III:** 4
Certain Slant of Sunlight, A (Berrigan),
Supp. XXIV: 43
"Certain Testimony" (Bausch), **Supp.
VII:** 48
Certificate, The (Singer), **IV:** 1; **Retro.
Supp. II:** **314–315**
"Cerulean" (Everett), **Supp. XVIII:** 66
Cervantes, Lorna Dee, **Supp. IV Part 2:**
545
Cervantes, Miguel de, **I:** 130, 134; **II:** 8,
272, 273, 276, 289, 302, 310, 315; **III:**
113, 614; **IV:** 367; **Retro. Supp. I:**
91; **Supp. I Part 2:** 406; **Supp. V:**
277; **Supp. XIII:** 17; **Supp. XXIII:** 4
Cervantes. Lorna Dee, **Supp. XXVII:** 168
Césaire, Aimé, **Supp. X:** 132, 139; **Supp.
XIII:** 114
"Cesarean" (Kenyon), **Supp. VII:** 173
Cézanne, Paul, **II:** 576; **III:** 210; **IV:** 26,
31, 407; **Supp. V:** 333, 341–342;
Supp. XIX: 36
Chabon, Michael, **Supp. XI:** **63–81;**
Supp. XIX: 135, 138, 174, 223; **Supp.
XVI:** 259; **Supp. XX:** **177;** **Supp.
XXII:** 49; **Supp. XXIII:** 4
Chaboseau, Jean, **Supp. I Part 1:** 260
Chace, Bill, **Supp. XXI:** 256
Chagall, Marc, **Supp. XXIII:** 6
Chaikin, Joseph, **Supp. III Part 2:** 433,
436–437
"Chain, The" (Kumin), **Supp. IV Part 2:**
452
Chainbearer, The (Cooper), **I:** 351, 352–
353
"Chain of Love, A" (Price), **Supp. VI:**
258–259, 260
Chain Saw Dance, The (Budbill), **Supp.
XIX:** **5–6**
Chains of Dew (Glaspell), **Supp. III Part
1:** 181
Chalk Face (W. Frank), **Supp. XX:** **73–74**
Challacombe, Robert Hamilton, **III:** 176
Challenge (Untermeyer), **Supp. XV:** 296,
303
"Challenge" (Untermeyer), **Supp. XV:**
296
"Challenge from Beyond, The"
(Lovecraft, Howard, Long, Merritt,
and Moore), **Supp. XXV:** 122
Chalmers, George, **Supp. I Part 2:** 514,
521
"Chambered Nautilus, The" (Holmes),
Supp. I Part 1: 254, 307, 312–313,
314
Chamberlain, John, **Supp. I Part 2:** 647;
Supp. IV Part 2: 525
Chamberlain, Neville, **II:** 589; **Supp. I
Part 2:** 664
Chamber Music (Joyce), **III:** 16
Chambers, Richard, **Supp. III Part 2:**
610, 611, 612
Chambers, Whittaker, **Supp. III Part 2:**
610; **Supp. IV Part 2:** 526; **Supp. XV:**
143

Chameleon (C. Baxter), **Supp. XVII:**
14–15
"Champ, The" (Zinberg), **Supp. XV:** 193
"Champagne Regions" (Ríos), **Supp. IV
Part 2:** 553
"Champion" (Lardner), **II:** 420–421, 428,
430
Champion, Laurie, **Supp. VIII:** 128
"Champ of the Forecastle" (Howard),
Supp. XXVII: 124
Champollion-Figeac, Jean Jacques, **IV:**
426
"Chance" (Doolittle), **Supp. I Part 1:** 271
"Chance" (Munro), **Supp. XXVII:** 193
Chance, Frank, **II:** 418
Chance Acquaintance, A (Howells), **II:**
278
"Chance Encounter, A" (Swados), **Supp.
XIX:** 261, 262
"Chanclas" (Cisneros), **Supp. VII:** 61
Chandler, Raymond, **Supp. III Part 1:**
91; **Supp. IV Part 1:** **119–138,** 341,
344, 345; **Supp. IV Part 2:** 461, 464,
469, 470, 471, 472, 473; **Supp. XI:**
160, 228; **Supp. XII:** 307; **Supp.
XIII:** 159, 233; **Supp. XIV:** 21; **Supp.
XIX:** 178, 189; **Supp. XV:** 119; **Supp.
XVI:** 122; **Supp. XVII:** 137; **Supp.
XVIII:** 136,137, 137–138; **Supp.
XXI:** 67; **Supp. XXII:** 119; **Supp.
XXIV:** 284; **Supp. XXV:** 180
Chandler, Sherry, **Supp. XXIII:** 247
Chaney, "Professor" W. H., **II:** 463–464
Chang, Leslie C., **Supp. IV Part 1:** 72
"Change, The: Kyoto-Tokyo Express"
(Ginsberg), **Supp. II Part 1:** 313, 329
Changed Man, A (Prose), **Supp. XVI:**
261–262
"Changeling" (Espaillat), **Supp. XXI:**
100
Changeling (Middleton), **Retro. Supp. I:**
62
"Changeling, The" (J. R. Lowell), **Supp.
I Part 2:** 409
"Changeling, The" (Whittier), **Supp. I
Part 2:** 697
Change of World, A (Rich), **Retro. Supp.
III:** 241, 242; **Supp. I Part 2:** 551,
552
"Changes of Mind" (Baker), **Supp. XIII:**
52
"Changes of the Soul" (Taggard), **Supp.
XXII:** 280
"Change the Joke and Slip the Yoke"
(Ellison), **Retro. Supp. II:** 118
Change the World (Gold), **Supp.
XXVIII:** 78
"Change the World!"(column, Gold),
Supp. XXVIII: 78
Change Your Bedding! (O'Hara), **Supp.
XXIII:** 210
Changing Light at Sandover, The
(Merrill), **Supp. III Part 1:** 318, 319,
323, 327, 332, 335–336; **Supp. XII:**
269–270; **Supp. XV:** 264
"Changing Same, The" (Baraka), **Supp.
II Part 1:** 47, 51, 53
*Changing the Bully Who Rules the World:
Reading and Thinking about Ethics* (C.
Bly), **Supp. XVI:** 32, **39–40,** 41

Chanler, Mrs. Winthrop, **I:** 22; **IV:** 325

Channing, Carol, **IV:** 357

Channing, Edward, **Supp. I Part 2:** 479–480

Channing, Edward Tyrrel, **Supp. I Part 1:** 155; **Supp. I Part 2:** 422; **Supp. XXV:** 240

Channing, William Ellery, **I:** 336; **II:** 224, 495; **IV:** 172, 173, 176, 177; **Retro. Supp. I:** 54; **Supp. I Part 1:** 103; **Supp. I Part 2:** 589; **Supp. XXIV:** 67–81; **Supp. XXV:** 250

Channing, William Henry, **IV:** 178; **Supp. II Part 1:** 280, 285; **Supp. XXIV:** 68

Channing: The Reluctant Radical (Mendelsohn), **Supp. XXIV:** 72

Chanson de Roland, La, **I:** 13

"Chanson un Peu Naïve" (Bogan), **Supp. III Part 1:** 50–51

"Chanteuse" (Doty), **Supp. XI:** 119

"Chant for May Day" (Hughes), **Supp. I Part 1:** 331

Chants (Mora), **Supp. XIII: 214–215**

Chaos (Dove), **Supp. IV Part 1:** 243

Chapelle, Howard I., **Supp. XXV:** 217

"Chaperone, The" (Van Vechten), **Supp. II Part 2:** 728

Chaplin, Charles Spencer "Charlie," **I:** 27, 32, 43, 386, 447; **III:** 403; **Supp. I Part 2:** 607; **Supp. IV Part 1:** 146; **Supp. IV Part 2:** 574; **Supp. XX:** 75; **Supp. XXI:** 170; **Supp. XXII:** 25, 26

"Chaplinesque" (H. Crane), **Retro. Supp. II:** 79; **Retro. Supp. III:** 45, 49

"Chapman" (Rukeyser), **Supp. VI:** 273

Chapman, Abraham, **IV:** 485

Chapman, George, **Supp. I Part 2:** 422

Chapman, Ian, **Supp. XXVII:** 212

Chapman, John, **Supp. XXV:** 105

Chapman, John (Johnny Appleseed), **Supp. I Part 2:** 397

Chapman, John Jay, **IV:** 436; **Supp. XIV: 39–56**

Chapman, Stephen, **Supp. XIII:** 12

Chappell, Fred, **Supp. IV Part 1:** 69; **Supp. XI:** 317; **Supp. XVIII:** 87

Chapters in a Mythology: The Poetry of Sylvia Plath (Kroll), **Supp. I Part 2:** 541–543

Chapters on Erie (Adams and Adams), **Supp. I Part 2:** 644

Chapter Two (Simon), **Supp. IV Part 2:** 575, 586

"Chapter VI" (Hemingway), **II:** 252

Char, René, **Supp. XVI:** 282; **Supp. XVII:** 244

"Character" (Emerson), **II:** 6

"Characteristics of Negro Expression" (Hurston), **Retro. Supp. III:** 129, 137

"Character of Aboriginal Historical Tradition"(J. Schoolcraft), **Supp. XXIII:** 228–229

"Character of Presidents, The" (Doctorow), **Supp. IV Part 1:** 224

"Character of Socrates, The" (Emerson), **II:** 8–9

Character of the Poet, The (Simpson), **Supp. IX:** 273, 275, 278

"Characters in Fiction" (McCarthy), **II:** 562

"Charades" (Moore), **Supp. X:** 178

"Charge It" (Fante), **Supp. XI:** 164–165

"Charioteer, The" (Stallings), **Supp. XXV:** 233

Chariot in the Sky: A Story of the Jubilee Singers (Bontemps), **Supp. XXII:** 6, 13

"Charity" (Peacock), **Supp. XIX:** 221–222

Charity (Richard), **Supp. XIX: 220–222**

Charlatan, The (Singer), **IV:** 1

"Charles" (Jackson), **Supp. IX:** 125

Charles, Abram, **Supp. XXVI:** 87

Charles, Larry, **Supp. XVIII:** 21

Charles, Ron, **Supp. XXVIII:** 280, 283

"Charles Baxter, August Kleinzahler, Adrienne Rich: Contemporary Stevensians and the Problem of 'Other Lives' " (S. Burt), **Supp. XVII:** 18–19

Charles Goodnight: Cowman and Plainsman (Haley), **Supp. V:** 226

Charles Simic: Essays on the Poetry (Weigl), **Supp. VIII:** 269

Charles the Bold, Duke of Burgundy, **III:** 487

Charleville, Victoria Verdon, **Supp. I Part 1:** 200–201, 205, 206, 210

Charley's Aunt (B. Thomas), **II:** 138

Charlie Chan Is Dead: An Anthology of Contemporary Asian American Fiction (Hagedorn), **Supp. X:** 292

"Charlie Christian Story, The" (Ellison), **Retro. Supp. II:** 121

"Charlie Howard's Descent" (Doty), **Supp. XI:** 122

Charlie: The Improbable Life and Times of Charles MacArthur (Hecht), **Supp. XXVII:** 95

Charlotte: A Tale of Truth (Rowson), **Supp. I Part 1:** 128; **Supp. XV: 234–235,** 238. *See also Charlotte Temple* (Rowson)

Charlotte's Daughter; or, The Three Orphans (Rowson), **Supp. XV:** 246

Charlotte's Web (White), **Supp. I Part 2:** 655, 656, 658, 667, 670

Charlotte Temple (Rowson), **Supp. XV:** 229, **238–239; Supp. XXV:** 35, 36. *See also Charlotte: A Tale of Truth* (Rowson)

Charm, The (Creeley), **Supp. IV Part 1:** 139, 141, 144, 149–150

Charmed Life, A (McCarthy), **II:** 571–574

Charming Billy (McDermott), **Supp. XVIII:** 155, **162–164,** 166

Charms for the Easy Life (Gibbons), **Supp. X:** 45, **47–48**

Charnel Rose, The (Aiken), **I:** 50, 57, 62

Charney, Samuel, **Supp. XXIII:** 6

Charon's Cosmology (Simic), **Supp. VIII: 276–278**

Charterhouse, The (Percy), **Supp. III Part 1:** 388

Chart for Rough Water (W. Frank), **Supp. XX:** 78

Charvat, William, **II:** 244

Charyn, Jerome, **Supp. XVII:** 5

Chase, Mary Ellen, **Retro. Supp. II:** 243, 245; **Supp. XXIV:** 30

Chase, Richard, **IV:** 202, 443; **Retro. Supp. I:** 40, 395

Chase, Salmon P., **Supp. I Part 2:** 584

Chase, Stuart, **Supp. I Part 2:** 609

Chase, The (Foote), **Supp. I Part 1:** 281

Chasing the Dime (Connelly), **Supp. XXI: 74**

"Chaste Land, The" (Tate), **IV:** 122

Château, The (Maxwell), **Supp. VIII:** 152, 160, **165–167,** 168, 169

Chatham, Russell, **Supp. VIII:** 40

"Chattanooga Nights" (L. Brown), **Supp. XXI:** 39

Chatterdon, The Black Death, and Meriwether Lewis (Reznikoff), **Supp. XIV:** 288

Chatterton, Thomas, **Supp. I Part 1:** 349; **Supp. I Part 2:** 410, 716

Chatterton, Wayne, **Supp. IX:** 2, 4, 11–12

"Chatty Letters During a Journey from Aruba to Rio" (Thompson), **Supp. XXIV:** 282

Chatwin, Bruce, **Supp. VIII:** 322

Chaucer, Geoffrey, **I:** 131; **II:** 11, 504, 516, 542, 543; **III:** 283, 411, 473, 492, 521; **Retro. Supp. I:** 135, 426; **Supp. I Part 1:** 356, 363; **Supp. I Part 2:** 422, 617; **Supp. V:** 259; **Supp. XII:** 197; **Supp. XIX:** 4; **Supp. XVII:** 70

Chauncy, Charles, **I:** 546–547; **IV:** 147

Chavez, César, **Supp. V:** 199

Chávez, Denise, **Supp. IV Part 2:** 544; **Supp. XI:** 316

Chavez, Lydia, **Supp. VIII:** 75

Chavkin, Allan, **Supp. IV Part 1:** 259

Chavkin, Nancy Feyl, **Supp. IV Part 1:** 259

Chawla, Louise, **Supp. XXI:** 24

Chayefsky, Paddy, **Supp. XI:** 306

Cheang, Shu Lea, **Supp. XI:** 20

Cheap: New Poems and Ballads (Stone), **Supp. XXVII:** 249, 250, 257, 262

"Cheater's Guide To Love, The" (Díaz), **Supp. XXIV:** 84, 92, 93

"Cheat Takes Over" (Leopold), **Supp. XIV:** 189

"Cheers" (Carver), **Supp. III Part 1:** 138

Cheetham, James, **Supp. I Part 2:** 521

Cheever, Benjamin Hale, **Supp. I Part 1:** 175; **Supp. XXIV:** 97

Cheever, David W., **Supp. I Part 1:** 304

Cheever, Ezekiel, **Supp. I Part 1:** 174, 193

Cheever, Federico, **Supp. I Part 1:** 175

Cheever, Fred, **Supp. I Part 1:** 174

Cheever, Frederick L., **Supp. I Part 1:** 174

Cheever, John, **Retro. Supp. I:** 116, 333, 335; **Supp. I Part 1:** 174–199; **Supp. IX:** 114, 208; **Supp. V:** 23, 95; **Supp. VIII:** 151; **Supp. XI:** 65, 66, 99; **Supp. XII:** 140; **Supp. XIV:** 93; **Supp. XV:** 119, 142; **Supp. XXIII:** 104, 109, 275; **Supp. XXV:** 79, 142; **Supp. XXVI:** 147

Cheever, Mrs. John (Mary Winternitz), **Supp. I Part 1:** 175

Cheever, Mary Liley, **Supp. I Part 1:** 174

Cheever, Susan. *See* Cowley, Susan Cheever (Susan Cheever)

Cheever Evening, A (Gurney), **Supp. V:** 95

Chekhov, Anton, **I:** 52, 90; **II:** 27, 38, 44, 49, 198, 542; **III:** 362, 467; **IV:** 17, 53, 359, 446; **Retro. Supp. I:** 5, 355; **Retro. Supp. II:** 299; **Retro. Supp. III:** 25; **Supp. I Part 1:** 196; **Supp. II Part 1:** 6; **Supp. IV Part 2:** 585; **Supp. IX:** 260, 265, 274; **Supp. V:** 265; **Supp. VIII:** 153, 332; **Supp. XI:** 66; **Supp. XII:** 94, 307; **Supp. XIII:** 79; **Supp. XIV:** 87, 242; **Supp. XIX:** 172, 241; **Supp. XV:** 320, 329; **Supp. XVIII:** 102; **Supp. XXII:** 60; **Supp. XXIII:** 162, 290; **Supp. XXVII:** 218

"Chekhov's Sense of Writing as Seen Through His Letters" (Dobyns), **Supp. XIII:** 77–78

"Chemin de Fer" (Bishop), **Retro. Supp. II:** 41; **Supp. I Part 1:** 80, 85, 86

"Chemistry" (Rash), **Supp. XXVII:** 227

Chemistry and Other Stories (Rash), **Supp. XXVII:** 222, 225, 227–228

Cheney, Brainard, **Retro. Supp. II:** 229

Cheney, Matthew, **Supp. XXII:** 50

Chenzira, Ayoka, **Supp. XI:** 19

Chéri (Colette; stage adaptation, Loos), **Supp. XVI:** 194

Cherkovski, Neeli, **Supp. XII:** 118, 132, 134

Chernyshevski, Nikolai, **III:** 261, 262, 263; **Retro. Supp. I:** 269

Cherokee Lottery, The: A Sequence of Poems (W. J. Smith), **Supp. XIII:** **340–344**

"Cherríe Moraga's Radical Revision of *Death of a Salesman*"(Wiley), **Supp. XXIII:** 199

Cherry (Karr), **Supp. XI:** 239, **251–254**

"Cherrylog Road" (Dickey), **Supp. XVIII:** 191

Cherry Orchard, The (Chekhov), **IV:** 359, 426; **Supp. VIII:** 153

Cheslock, Louis, **III:** 99, 118, 119

Chesnutt, Charles Waddell, **Supp. II Part 1:** 174, 193, 211; **Supp. IV Part 1:** 257; **Supp. XIV:** **57–78**; **Supp. XXVIII:** 231, 234

"Chess House, The" (Dixon), **Supp. XII:** 139

Chessman, Caryl, **Supp. I Part 2:** 446

Chester, Alfred, **Retro. Supp. II:** 111, 112; **Supp. X:** 192

Chesterfield, Lord, **II:** 36

Chesterton, Gilbert Keith, **I:** 226; **IV:** 432

Cheuse, Alan, **Supp. IV Part 2:** 570

Chevigny, Bell Gale, **Supp. XI:** 283

Cheyenne Autumn (Sandoz), **Supp. XXIII:** 146; **Supp. XXIV:** 244, 248, 256, **258–260**

"Chicago" (Sandburg), **III:** 581, 592, 596; **Supp. III Part 1:** 71

Chicago (Shepard), **Supp. III Part 2:** 439

Chicago: City on the Make (Algren), **Supp. IX:** 1, 3

"*Chicago Defender* Sends a Man to Little Rock, The" (Brooks), **Supp. III Part 1:** 80–81

"Chicago Hamlet, A" (Anderson), **I:** 112

Chicago Loop (Theroux), **Supp. VIII:** 324

"Chicago Picasso, The" (Brooks), **Supp. III Part 1:** 70–71, 84

Chicago Poems (Sandburg), **III:** 579, 581–583, 586

"Chicano/Borderlands Literature and Poetry" (Ríos), **Supp. IV Part 2:** 537, 538, 542, 545

Chicano! The History of the Mexican American Civil Rights Movement (Rosales), **Supp. XXV:** 133

Chick, Nancy, **Supp. IV Part 1:** 1

"Chickamauga" (Bierce), **I:** 201

"Chickamauga" (Wolfe), **IV:** 460

Chickamauga (Wright), **Supp. V:** 333, 343–344

"Chickamauga" (Wright), **Supp. V:** 334

"Chicken Market" (Skloot), **Supp. XX:** **198, 200**

"Chiefly about War Matters" (Hawthorne), **II:** 227; **Retro. Supp. I:** 165

"Chiffon" (Hull), **Supp. XXI:** 138

"Child" (Plath), **Supp. I Part 2:** 544

Child, Greg, **Supp. XVIII:** 107

Child, Julia, **Supp. XVII:** 89, 90

Child, Lydia Maria, **Supp. XIII:** 141; **Supp. XVIII:** 11

"Child, The" (Ríos), **Supp. IV Part 2:** 543

"Child by Tiger, The" (Wolfe), **IV:** 451

"Childhood" (Wright), **Supp. V:** 341

Childhood, A: The Biography of a Place (Crews), **Supp. XI:** 102–103, 245

"Childhood, When You Are in It . . ." (Kenyon), **Supp. VII:** 160, 170

Childhood and Other Neighborhoods (Dybek), **Supp. XXIII:** 68, **69–70**

"Childhood Sketch" (Wright), **Supp. III Part 2:** 589

"Child Is Born, A" (Benét), **Supp. XI:** 46

"Child Is the Meaning of This Life, The" (Schwartz), **Supp. II Part 2:** 659–660

"Childlessness" (Merrill), **Supp. III Part 1:** 323

"Childless Woman" (Plath), **Supp. I Part 2:** 544

Child-Life (Whittier and Larcom, eds.), **Supp. XIII:** 142

Child-Life in Prose (Whittier and Larcom, eds.), **Supp. XIII:** 142

Childlike Life of the Black Tarantula, The (Acker), **Supp. XII:** 4, 6, **7–8**

"Child Margaret" (Sandburg), **III:** 584

"Child of Courts, The" (Jarrell), **II:** 378, 379, 381

Child of God (McCarthy), **Supp. VIII:** **177–178**

Child of My Heart (McDermott), **Supp. XVIII:** 155, **164–166**

Child of the Century, A (Hecht), **Supp. XXV:** 29; **Supp. XXVII:** 83, 84, 91, 95, 96

"CHILD OF THE THIRTIES" (Baraka), **Supp. II Part 1:** 60

"Child on Top of a Greenhouse" (Roethke), **III:** 531

Children (Gurney), **Supp. V:** 95, 96

"Children" (Stowe), **Supp. I Part 2:** 587

"Children, The" (Jarman), **Supp. XVII:** 116

Children, The (Wharton), **IV:** 321, 326; **Retro. Supp. I:** 381

"Children, the Sandbar, That Summer" (Rukeyser), **Supp. VI:** 274

Children and Others (Cozzens), **I:** 374

Children Is All (Purdy), **Supp. VII:** 277, 278, 282

"Children of Adam" (Whitman), **IV:** 342; **Retro. Supp. I:** 403, 405; **Retro. Supp. III:** 302, 308

Children of Job, The: American Second-Generation Witnesses to the Holocaust (A. Berger), **Supp. XVII:** 39

Children of Light (Stone), **Supp. V:** 304–306

Children of Light and the Children of Darkness, The (Niebuhr), **III:** 292, 306, 310

"Children of the Dirty War" (Goldman), **Supp. XXV:** 52

Children of the Frost (London), **II:** 469, 483

Children of the Holocaust (H. Epstein), **Supp. XVII:** 48; **Supp. XXII:** 95

"Children of the Lord's Supper, The" (Tegnér), **Retro. Supp. II:** 155, 157

Children of the Market Place (Masters), **Supp. I Part 2:** 471

"Children on Their Birthdays" (Capote), **Supp. III Part 1:** 114, 115

Children Playing Before a Statue of Hercules (Sedaris, ed.), **Supp. XXIII:** 289

"Children Selecting Books in a Library" (Jarrell), **II:** 371

Children's Hour, The (Hellman), **Supp. I Part 1:** 276–277, 281, 286, 297

"Children's Rhymes" (Hughes), **Supp. I Part 1:** 340

Childress, Mark, **Supp. X:** 89

Child's Garden of Verses, A (Stevenson), **Supp. IV Part 1:** 298, 314; **Supp. XIII:** 75

"Child's Nature, A" (Jin), **Supp. XVIII:** 93

"Child's Reminiscence, A" (Whitman), **IV:** 344

Childwold (Oates), **Supp. II Part 2:** 519–520

Chile Woman (G. Jones), **Supp. XXIV:** 185

Chill, The (Macdonald), **Supp. IV Part 2:** 473

Chills and Fever (Ransom), **III:** 490, 491–492, 493

Chilly Scenes of Winter (Beattie), **Supp. V:** 21, 22, 23, 24, 26, 27

Chime of Words, A: The Letters of Logan Pearsall Smith (Tribble, ed.), **Supp. XIV:** 348–349

Chimera (C. Frost), **Supp. XV:** 94, 95, 100

"Chimes for Yahya" (Merrill), **Supp. III Part 1:** 329

Chin, Frank, **Supp. V:** 164, 172

Chin, Mei, **Supp. XVIII:** 95

"China" (C. Johnson), **Supp. VI: 193–194**

Chinaberry Tree, The (Fauset), **Supp. XIX:** 73

"Chinaman's Hat" (Kingston), **Supp. V:** 169

China Men (Kingston), **Supp. V:** 157, 158, 159, 160, 161, 164–169; **Supp. X:** 292; **Supp. XV:** 220

"China Poet, The" (Sturgis), **Supp. XX: 233, 240**

China Trace (Wright), **Supp. V:** 332, 340, 341, 342

"Chinese Apples" (Di Piero), **Supp. XIX:** 40

Chinese Apples: New and Selected Poems (Di Piero), **Supp. XIX:** 33, 36, 37, 38, 39, 40, 44, 45, 46, 47–48

Chinese Classics (Legge), **III:** 472

Chinese Materia Medica (P. Smith), **III:** 572

"Chinese New Year" (Hull), **Supp. XXI:** 135

"Chinese Nightingale, The" (Lindsay), **Supp. I Part 2:** 392–393, 394

Chinese Nightingale and Other Poems, The (Lindsay), **Supp. I Part 2:** 392

Chinese Siamese Cat, The (Tan), **Supp. X:** 289

Chinese Translations, The (Bynner), **Supp. XV:** 47, 52

Chinitz, David, **Supp. XV:** 180, 185

"Chinoiseries" (A. Lowell), **II:** 524–525

Chip (Untermeyer), **Supp. XV:** 310

"Chipeta, Widow of Chief Ouray with a Word About a Deal in Blankets" (Zitkala-Ša), **Supp. XXV:** 281

"Chippings with a Chisel" (Hawthorne), **Retro. Supp. III:** 120

Chirico, Giorgio de, **Supp. III Part 1:** 14

Chirico, Miriam M., **Supp. XV:** 323

"Chiron" (Winters), **Supp. II Part 2:** 801

"Chitlins at the Waldorf" (Crouch), **Supp. XIX:** 158

"Chloroform Jags" (J. Scott), **Supp. XVII:** 189

"Chocklit Geography: Raymond Andrews's Mythical South" (Harris), **Supp. XXVI:** 14

Chodorov, Jerome, **IV:** 274

Choi, Susan, **Supp. XXVIII:** 214

"Choice, The" (Karr), **Supp. XI:** 251

"Choice of Accommodations, A" (Lahiri), **Supp. XXI:** 183

"Choice of Profession, A" (Malamud), **Supp. I Part 2:** 437

Choice of Wars, A (Shaw), **Supp. XIX:** 245

"Choices" (Gallagher), **Supp. XXIV:** 171

Chomei, Kamo No, **IV:** 171, 184

Chomsky, Noam, **Supp. IV Part 2:** 679

"Choose Something Like a Star" (Frost), **Retro. Supp. III:** 105

Choosing not Choosing (Cameron), **Retro. Supp. I:** 43

Chopin, Felix, **Supp. I Part 1:** 202

Chopin, Frédéric, **Supp. I Part 1:** 363

Chopin, Jean, **Supp. I Part 1:** 206

Chopin, Kate, **II:** 276; **Retro. Supp. I:** 10, 215; **Retro. Supp. II:** 57–74; **Supp. I Part 1:** 200–226; **Supp. V:** 304; **Supp. X:** 227; **Supp. XVIII:**

194; **Supp. XXVIII:** 225

"Chopin in Winter"(Dybek), **Supp. XXIII:** 72

"Choral: The Pink Church" (W. C. Williams), **Retro. Supp. I:** 428

"Chord" (Merwin), **Supp. III Part 1:** 356

"Chord"(Dybek), **Supp. XXIII:** 78

"Chords and Dischords" (column; Untermeyer), **Supp. XV:** 294

"Chorus, The"(Hadas), **Supp. XXIII:** 119–120

Choruses from Iphigenia in Aulis (Doolittle, trans.), **Supp. I Part 1:** 257, 268, 269

Chosen, The (Potok), **Supp. XXVI:** 125

"Chosen Blindness" (Karr), **Supp. XI:** 251

Chosen Country (Dos Passos), **I:** 475, 490–491

Chosen Place, The Timeless People, The (Marshall), **Supp. XI:** 275, 276, **282–284**

Chosŏn (P. Lowell), **II:** 513

Choukri, Mohamed, **Supp. IV Part 1:** 92

Chovteau, Mane Thérèse, **Supp. I Part 1:** 205

Chris Durang and Dawne (Durang), **Supp. XXIV:** 113, 124

"ChrisEaster" (Peacock), **Supp. XIX:** 198, 199

Chrisman, Robert, **Supp. IV Part 1:** 1

Christabel (Coleridge), **Supp. IV Part 2:** 465

"Christ for Sale" (R. Lowell), **II:** 538

Christgau, Robert, **Supp. XXVII:** 33–47

Christian, Graham, **Supp. XII:** 193

Christian Dictionary, A (Wilson), **IV:** 153

"Christian in World Crisis, The" (Merton), **Supp. VIII:** 203

Christianity and Power Politics (Niebuhr), **III:** 292, 303

"Christianity and the Survival of Creation" (Berry), **Supp. X:** 30

Christianity of Sholem Asch, The: An Appraisal from the Jewish Viewpoint (Lieberman), **Supp. XXIII:** 3, 7

"Christian Minister, The" (Emerson), **II:** 10

Christian Philosopher, The (Mather), **Supp. II Part 2:** 463–464

Christian Realism and Practical Problems (Niebuhr), **III:** 292, 308

"Christian Roommates, The" (Updike), **IV:** 226–227; **Retro. Supp. I:** 319, 323

Christian Science (Twain), **Retro. Supp. III:** 268

Christiansen, Carrie, **I:** 210

Christian's Secret of a Happy Life, The (H. W. Smith), **Supp. XIV:** 333–334

Christie, Agatha, **Supp. IV Part 1:** 341; **Supp. IV Part 2:** 469

Christ in Concrete (di Donato), **Supp. XX:** 33, 34–40, 42, 43, 46

"Christ in Concrete" (di Donato), **Supp. XX:** 34

Christine (King), **Supp. V:** 139, 148

"Christ Light, The" (Chopin), **Retro. Supp. II:** 61

"Christmas" (Saunders), **Supp. XIX:** 232

"Christmas, or the Good Fairy" (Stowe), **Supp. I Part 2:** 586

"Christmas 1944" (Levertov), **Supp. III Part 1:** 274

"Christmas Banquet, The" (Hawthorne), **II:** 227; **Retro. Supp. III:** 120

Christmas Card, A (Theroux), **Supp. VIII:** 322

Christmas Carol, A (Dickens), **Retro. Supp. I:** 196; **Supp. I Part 2:** 409–410; **Supp. X:** 252, 253; **Supp. XXV:** 149, 152

Christmas Carollin' (Wells), **Supp. XXVI:** 275

"Christmas Eve at Johnson's Drugs N Goods" (Bambara), **Supp. XI:** 11–12

"Christmas Eve in the Time of War: A Capitalist Meditates by a Civil War Monument" (R. Lowell), **II:** 538

"Christmas Eve under Hooker's Statue" (R. Lowell), **II:** 539–540

"Christmas Gift" (Warren), **IV:** 252–253

"Christmas Gifts"(Stuart), **Supp. XXVIII:** 232–233

"Christmas Greeting, A" (Wright), **Supp. III Part 2:** 601

"Christmas Hymn, A" (Wilbur), **Supp. III Part 2:** 557

Christmas Memory, A (Capote), **Supp. III Part 1:** 118, 119, 129

"Christmass Poem" (West), **Retro. Supp. II:** 338

Christmas Story (Mencken), **III:** 111

"Christmas to Me" (Lee), **Supp. VIII:** 113

Christographia (Taylor), **IV:** 164–165

Christ on a Clothesline (Loy), **Supp. XXII:** 168

"Christ on the Cross/Nuestro Señor Crucificado" (Mora), **Supp. XIII:** 229

Christopher, Mary (pseudonym). *See* West, Dorothy

Christopher and His Kind: 1929–1939 (Isherwood), **Supp. XIV:** 157, 163, 164, 171

"Christopher Cat" (Cullen), **Supp. IV Part 1:** 173

Christopher Columbus, Mariner (Morison), **Supp. I Part 2:** 488

Christopher Isherwood: A Critical Biography (Finney), **Supp. XIV:** 158

Christophersen, Bill, **Supp. IX:** 159, 167; **Supp. XI:** 155; **Supp. XIII:** 87; **Supp. XXI:** 103

"Christ's Passion" (Karr), **Supp. XI:** 251

Christus: A Mystery (Longfellow), **II:** 490, 493, 495, 505–507; **Retro. Supp. II:** 161, 165, 166

Chroma (F. Barthelme), **Supp. XI:** 30, 33, 34

"Chroma" (F. Barthelme), **Supp. XI:** 31

"Chronicle" (W. Stone), **Supp. XXVII:** 255

"Chronicle of Race Relations, A" (Du Bois), **Supp. II Part 1:** 182

Chronicle of the Conquest of Granada (Irving), **II:** 310

Chronicles: Volume One (Dylan), **Supp. XVIII:** 20, 21, 23, 24, 28, **32–33**

"Chronologues" (Goldbarth), **Supp. XII:** 183, 184

"Chrysanthemums, The" (Steinbeck), **IV:** 53

"Chrysaor" (Longfellow), **II:** 498

Chu, Louis, **Supp. X:** 291

Chuang, Hua, **Supp. X:** 291

Chuang-Tzu, **Supp. VIII:** 206

Chung, Haeja K., **Supp. XXVIII:** 3, 11

"Chunk of Amethyst, A" (R. Bly), **Supp. IV Part 1:** 72

Church, Margaret, **IV:** 466

"Church and the Fiction Writer, The" (O'Connor), **Retro. Supp. II:** 223, 233; **Supp. XVIII:** 161

"Church Going" (Larkin), **Supp. XXI:** 93

"Churchgoing" (Nelson), **Supp. XVIII:** 173

Churchill, Charles, **Supp. XV:** 232

Churchill, Winston, **I:** 9, 490; **Supp. I Part 2:** 491

Church of Dead Girls, The (Dobyns), **Supp. XIII:** 75, **83–84**

"Church of Omnivorous Light, The" (Wrigley), **Supp. XVIII:** 306–307

"Church of the Latter Day Saints, The" (Mosher), **Supp. XXII:** 208

"Church Porch, The" (Herbert), **IV:** 153

Church Psalmody, Selected from Dr. Watts and Other Authors (Mason and Greene, ed.), **I:** 458

Ciannic, Saint, **II:** 215

Ciano, Edda, **IV:** 249

Ciardi, John, **I:** 169, 179, 535; **III:** 268; **Supp. IV Part 1:** 243; **Supp. IV Part 2:** 639; **Supp. IX:** 269, 324; **Supp. XII:** 119

Cicada (Haines), **Supp. XII: 206–207**

"Cicadas" (Wilbur), **Supp. III Part 2:** 549

Cicero, **I:** 279; **II:** 8, 14–15; **III:** 23; **Supp. I Part 2:** 405

Cider House Rules, The (Irving), **Supp. VI:** 164, **173–175**

"Cigales" (Wilbur), **Supp. III Part 2:** 549

"Cigarette" (L. Michaels), **Supp. XVI:** 214

Cigarette Book, The (Brainard), **Supp. XXVII:** 20

Cimarron, Rose (Burke), **Supp. XIV:** 22, 35

"Cimetière Marin, Le" (Valéry), **IV:** 91–92

Cimino, Michael, **Supp. X:** 126

Cincinnati Kid, The (film), **Supp. XI: 306**

"Cinderella" (Jarrell), **II:** 386

"Cinderella" (Perrault), **IV:** 266, 267

"Cinderella" (Sexton), **Supp. II Part 2:** 691

"Cinema, The" (Salter), **Supp. IX:** 257

Cinema of Tony Richardson, The: Essays and Interviews (Phillips), **Supp. XI:** 306

Cinthio, **IV:** 370

Ciolkowski, Laura, **Supp. XVI:** 24

CIOPW (Cummings), **I:** 429

"Circe" (Welty), **Retro. Supp. I:** 353

Circle Game, The (Atwood), **Supp. XIII:** 20, 33

Circle in the Dirt (Moraga), **Supp. XXIII:** 195, 202

"Circle in the Fire, A" (O'Connor), **III:** 344–345, 349–350, 351, 353, 354; **Retro. Supp. II:** 229, 232

"Circle of Breath" (Stafford), **Supp. XI:** 318, 322

Circle of Hanh, The (Weigl), **Supp. XIX:** 273, 275, 282, **284–286**

Circle of the Seasons: The Journal of Naturalist's Year (Teale), **Supp. XXVIII:** 249–250, 251

"Circles" (Emerson), **I:** 455, 460

"Circles" (R. Lowell), **II:** 554

Circular Staircase, The (Rinehart), **Supp. XXV:** 189, 192, 200

Circumference: Varieties of Metaphysical Verse 1456–1928 (Taggard, ed.), **Supp. XXII:** 279

"Circus" (Huddle), **Supp. XXVI:** 150

"Circus, The" (Porter), **III:** 443, 445

"Circus Animals' Desertion" (Yeats), **I:** 389

Circus Fire, The (O'Nan), **Supp. XXV:** 153

"Circus in the Attic" (Warren), **IV:** 253

Circus in the Attic, The (Warren), **IV:** 243, 251–253

"Circus in Three Rings" (Plath), **Retro. Supp. II:** 243; **Supp. I Part 2:** 536

Circus of Needs, A (Dunn), **Supp. XI: 147–148**

"Cirque d'Hiver" (Bishop), **Supp. I Part 1:** 85

Cisneros, Sandra, **Supp. IV Part 2:** 544; **Supp. VII: 57–73; Supp. XI:** 177; **Supp. XVII:** 71; **Supp. XXII:** 177; **Supp. XXV:** 133

Cities and Men (Lewisohn), **Supp. XXVIII:** 158

Cities of the Interior (Nin), **Supp. X:** 182

Cities of the Plain (McCarthy), **Supp. VIII:** 175, **186–187**

Cities of the Red Night (Burroughs), **Supp. III Part 1:** 106

"Citizen Cain" (Baraka), **Supp. II Part 1:** 49

Citizen Kane (film), **Retro. Supp. I:** 115; **Supp. V:** 251; **Supp. XI:** 169

"Citizen of the World" (Goldsmith), **II:** 299

Citizens (Levin), **Supp. XXVII:** 133, 134, 139, 142, 143–144

Citro, Joseph, **Supp. XXII:** 208, 218

"City" (Francis), **Supp. IX:** 87

"City, The" (Stallings), **Supp. XXV:** 233

"City and Country" (Hadas), **Supp. XXIII:** 115, 116

City and the Island, The (Davison), **Supp. XXVI:** 65, 70–71

City and the Pillar, The (Vidal), **Supp. IV Part 2:** 677, 680–681; **Supp. XIV:** 170

"*City and the Pillar, The,* as Gay Fiction" (Summers), **Supp. IV Part 2:** 680–681

"City Articles" series (Briggs), **Supp. XVIII:** 12

City Block (W. Frank), **Supp. XX: 71, 72, 76**

City Boy (L. Michaels), **Supp. XVI:** 212

"City Boy" (L. Michaels), **Supp. XVI:** 203–204

City Boy (Thompson), **Supp. XXIII:** 294, **298–299**

City Boy, The (Wouk), **Supp. XXV:** 256, 259

City Dog (Di Piero), **Supp. XIX:** 33–34, 35, 38, 46, 48

"City Dog" (Di Piero), **Supp. XIX:** 47

City in History, The (Mumford), **Supp. II Part 2:** 495

"City in the Sea, The" (Poe), **III:** 411; **Retro. Supp. II:** 274

City in Which I Love You, The (L.-Y. Lee), **Supp. XV:** 212, **215–220**

"City in Which I Love You, The" (L.-Y. Lee), **Supp. XV:** 215, **217–218**

City in Winter, A (Helprin), **Supp. XXV:** 84, 87

City Life (Barthelme), **Supp. IV Part 1:** 44, 47

City of Bones (Connelly), **Supp. XXI: 74–75,** 77

"City of Change, A" (Bynner), **Supp. XV:** 45

City of Dreadful Night (Siegel), **Supp. XXII:** 258

City of Glass (Auster), **Supp. XII:** 22, **24–26**

City of God, The (St. Augustine), **IV:** 126

City of Names (Brockmeier), **Supp. XXII:** 55–56, 57

"City of Refuge, The" (R. Fisher), **Supp. XIX:** 65, 66, **67–68**

City of Refuge, The: The Collected Stories of Rudolph Fisher (McCluskey, ed.), **Supp. XIX:** 68–69

City of the Living and Other Stories, The (Stegner), **Supp. IV Part 2:** 599, 609, 613

City of Words: American Fiction 1950-1970 (T. Tanner), **Supp. XVI:** 69

City of Your Final Destination, The (Cameron), **Supp. XII:** 79, 82, **91–94**

"City on a Hill" (R. Lowell), **II: 552**

City on a Hill: Testing the American Dream at City College (Traub), **Supp. XXIV:** 221

"City Person Encountering Nature, A" (Kingston), **Supp. V:** 170

"City Planners, The" (Atwood), **Supp. XIII:** 33

"City Winter, A" (O'Hara), **Supp. XXIII:** 210

City Winter and Other Poems, A (O'Hara), **Supp. XXIII:** 210, 214

City Without Men (film), **Supp. XVIII:** 247

City Without Walls (Auden), **Supp. II Part 1:** 24

Civil Disobedience (Thoreau), **IV:** 185; **Supp. I Part 2:** 507

"Civil Disobedience" (Thoreau), **Supp. XXVIII:** 201

Civilization in the United States (Stearns), **I:** 245

"Civil Rights" (Lanier), **Supp. I Part 1:** 357

CivilWarLand in Bad Decline (Saunders), **Supp. XIX: 224–227**

"CivilWarLand in Bad Decline" (Saunders), **Supp. XIX:** 224–225, 227

Civitatis Anthology of African American Slave Narratives, The (H. L. Gates and Andrews, eds.), **Supp. XX: 105**

Cixous, Hélène, **Supp. X:** 102; **Supp. XIII:** 297; **Supp. XV:** 347

Clabough, Casey, **Supp. XXIV:** 194

Claiborne, Craig, **Supp. XVII:** 89

Claiborne, William, **I:** 132

"Claim, The" (Balakian), **Supp. XXIII:** 20

Claiming an Identity They Taught Me to Despise (Cliff), **Supp. XXII:** 66, 67–68, 70

Claiming of Sleeping Beauty, The (Rice), **Supp. VII:** 301

Claman, Emily Rosamund, **Supp. XXVI:** 175

Clampitt, Amy, **Supp. IX: 37–54; Supp. X:** 120; **Supp. XI:** 249; **Supp. XV:** 251, 256

Clancy's Wake, At (Crane), **I:** 422

"Clandeboye" (Leopold), **Supp. XIV:** 189

"Clara" (Hecht), **Supp. XXVII:** 95

Clara Howard; or, The Enthusiasm of Love (Brown), **Supp. I Part 1:** 145

Clara's Ole Man (Bullins), **Supp. II Part 1:** 42

Clara Wharton (Hayden), **Supp. XXV:** 38

Clare, John, **II:** 387; **III:** 528; **Supp. XVI:** 295

Clarel: A Poem and Pilgrimage in the Holy Land (Melville), **Retro. Supp. I:** 257; **Retro. Supp. III:** 149, 161

Clarence Major and His Art (Bell), **Supp. XXII:** 182

Clarissa (Richardson), **II:** 111; **Supp. I Part 2:** 714; **Supp. V:** 127; **Supp. XV:** 231; **Supp. XX: 236**

Clarissa Harlow (Richardson), **Supp. XXV:** 39

Clark, Alex, **Supp. XII:** 307

Clark, Charles, **I:** 470

Clark, Eleanor. *See* Warren, Mrs. Robert Penn (Eleanor Clark)

Clark, Francis Edward, **II:** 9

Clark, Geoffrey, **Supp. XI:** 342

Clark, Harry Hayden, **Supp. I Part 2:** 423

Clark, John Bates, **Supp. I Part 2:** 633

Clark, Kenneth, **Supp. XIV:** 342, 348; **Supp. XIX:** 151

Clark, Lewis Gaylord, **Supp. XVIII:** 4, 7, 8

Clark, Shirley, **Supp. XXI:** 22

Clark, Thomas, **Supp. III Part 2:** 629; **Supp. IV Part 1:** 140, 145, 147

Clark, Tom, **Supp. XXIV:** 36, 37, 41, 44

Clark, Walter, **Supp. XI:** 315

Clark, William, **III:** 14; **IV:** 179, 283

Clark, Willis Gaylord, **Supp. I Part 2:** 684

Clarke, Brock, **Supp. XXIII:** 109

Clarke, James Freeman, **Supp. II Part 1:** 280; **Supp. XXV:** 250

Clarke, John, **Supp. IV Part 1:** 8

Clarke, John J., **III:** 356

Clarke, Samuel, **II:** 108

Clark Lectures, **Retro. Supp. I:** 65

Claros varones de Belken (Hinojosa). *See Fair Gentlemen of Belken County* (Hinojosa)

Clash by Night (film), **Supp. XXVI:** 134

Clash by Night (Odets), **Supp. II Part 2:** 531, 538, 544–546, 550, 551

Classical Tradition, The (Highet), **Supp. I Part 1:** 268

Classic Ballroom Dances (Simic), **Supp. VIII:** 271, **276–278**, 283

Classics (Hadas), **Supp. XXIII: 124**

Classics and Commercials: A Literary Chronicle of the Forties (Wilson), **IV:** 433

"Classics" (Hadas), **Supp. XXIII:** 124

"CLASS STRUGGLE" (Baraka), **Supp. III Part 1:** 55

"Claude Glass, The: 1890" (Bierds), **Supp. XVII:** 27

Claudel, Paul, **I:** 60

Claudelle Inglish (Caldwell), **I:** 304

Clavel, Marcel, **I:** 343

"CLAY" (Baraka), **Supp. II Part 1:** 54

Clay, Henry, **I:** 8; **Supp. I Part 2:** 684, 686

Clay's Ark (O. Butler), **Supp. XIII:** 63

Clayton, John J., **Supp. IV Part 1:** 238

Clayton, Sarah Turner, **Supp. XXV:** 251

"Clean, Well Lighted Place, A" (Hemingway), **Retro. Supp. I:** 181

"Clear, with Light Variable Winds" (A. Lowell), **II:** 522

"Clear Days" (White), **Supp. I Part 2:** 664, 665

Clearing (Berry), **Supp. X:** 22

"Clearing, A" (Simpson), **Supp. IX:** 280

"Clearing, The" (Kenyon), **Supp. VII:** 174

"Clearing the Title" (Merrill), **Supp. III Part 1:** 336

"Clearing Up the Question of Stesichoros' Blinding by Helen" (Carson), **Supp. XII:** 107–108

"Clear Morning" (Glück), **Supp. V:** 88

"Clearness" (Wilbur), **Supp. III Part 2:** 544, 550

"Clear Night" (Wright), **Supp. V:** 341

Clear Pictures: First Loves, First Guides (Price), **Supp. VI:** 253, 254, 255, 256, 265

Clear Springs (Mason), **Supp. VIII:** 134–136, 137–138, 139, 147

Cleary, Rebecca Lauck, **Supp. XVIII:** 195

Cleaver, Eldridge, **Retro. Supp. II:** 12; **Supp. IV Part 1:** 206; **Supp. X:** 249

"Cleaving, The" (L.-Y. Lee), **Supp. XV:** 215, **218–220**

Cleland, John, **Supp. V:** 48, 127

Clemenceau, Georges, **I:** 490

"Clemency" (Wrigley), **Supp. XVIII:** 307–308

Clemens, Jane, **I:** 247

Clemens, Orion, **IV:** 193, 195

Clemens, Samuel Langhorne. *See* Twain, Mark

Clemens, Mrs. Samuel Langhorne (Olivia Langdon), **I:** 197, 208, 247; **Supp. I Part 2:** 457

Clemens, Susie, **IV:** 208

Clementine Recognitions (novel), **Supp. IV Part 1:** 280

Clements, Colin Campbell, **Supp. XVI:** 190

Clements, G. H., **Supp. XXVIII:** 237

Clemons, Walter, **Supp. IV Part 1:** 305, 307

Cleopatra, **III:** 44; **IV:** 373; **Supp. I Part 1:** 114

"Clepsydra" (Ashbery), **Supp. III Part 1: 10–15**

"Clerks, The" (Robinson), **III:** 517–518

"Cleveland" (Halliday), **Supp. XIX:** 90

Cleveland, Carol, **Supp. IX:** 120, 125

Cleveland, Ceil, **Supp. V:** 222

Cleveland, Grover, **II:** 126, 128, 129, 130, 137, 138; **Supp. I Part 2:** 486

"Clever Magician Carrying My Heart, A" (Salinas), **Supp. XIII:** 323

Cliff, Michelle, **Retro. Supp. III:** 242; **Supp. XXII: 65–80**

"Cliff, The" (C. Baxter), **Supp. XVII:** 16–17

Clifford, Craig, **Supp. IX:** 99

Clift, Montgomery, **III:** 161

Clifton, Lucille, **Supp. XVIII:** 177

Climate of Monastic Prayer, The (Merton), **Supp. VIII:** 205, 207

Climb, The (Boukreev), **Supp. XVIII:** 112

"Climber, The" (Mason), **Supp. VIII:** 140–141

Climbing High: A Woman's Account of Surviving the Everest Tragedy (Gammelgaard), **Supp. XVIII:** 112

"Climbing the Tower" (Crews), **Supp. XI:** 102

Clinton, De Witt, **I:** 338

"Clipped Wings" (H. Miller), **III:** 176–177

Clippinger, David, **Supp. XXI:** 24

Clive, Robert, **Supp. I Part 2:** 505

Clock Winder, The (Tyler), **Supp. IV Part 2:** 661–662, 670

Clock Without Hands (McCullers), **II:** 587–588, 604–606

Clockwork Orange, A (Burgess), **Supp. XIII:** 29

Clorindy (Cook), **Supp. II Part 1:** 199

"Close, The" (Jarman), **Supp. XVII:** 113

"Close Calls" (Wolff), **Supp. VII:** 332–333

"Closed Book, A" (Mosley), **Supp. XIII:** 237

"Closed for Good" (Frost), **Retro. Supp. III:** 105

Close Quarters (Heinemann), **Supp. XXII:** 103, **104–109**, 111, 115

Close Range: Wyoming Stories (Proulx), **Supp. VII:** 261–265

"Close Reading: Windows" (Hirshfield), **Supp. XXIII:** 131

Closers, The (Connelly), **Supp. XXI: 76–77**

Closest Possible Union, The (J. Scott), **Supp. XVII: 185–186,** 188, 191
"Closet, The" (Goodman), **Supp. XXVI:** 121
Close the Book (Glaspell), **Supp. III Part 1:** 179
"Close the Book" (R. Lowell), **II:** 554
Close to Me & Closer ... (The Language of Heaven) and Désamère (Notley), **Supp. XXII:** 234
Close to Shore: A True Story of Terror in an Age of Innocence (Capuzzo), **Supp. XIII:** 254
Closet Writing & Gay Reading: The Case of Melville's Pierre (Creech), **Retro. Supp. I:** 254
Closing Circle, The (Commoner), **Supp. XIII:** 264
Closing of the American Mind, The (Bloom), **Retro. Supp. II:** 19, 30, 31
"Closing of the Rodeo, The" (W. J. Smith), **Supp. XIII:** 332
Closing Time (Heller), **Supp. IV Part 1:** 382, 386, 391–394
Closset, Marie, **Supp. VIII:** 251, 265
Clotel (Brown), **Supp. XXIII:** 184
"Cloud, The" (Shelley), **Supp. I Part 2:** 720
"Cloud and Fame" (Berryman), **I:** 173
Cloud Atlas (D. Mitchell), **Supp. XXIV:** 86
Cloud Forest, The: A Chronicle of the South American Wilderness (Matthiessen), **Supp. V:** 202, 204
"Cloud on the Way, The" (Bryant), **Supp. I Part 1:** 171
"Cloud River" (Wright), **Supp. V:** 341
"Clouds" (Levine), **Supp. V:** 184
Cloudsplitter (Banks), **Supp. V:** 16
"Clover" (Lanier), **Supp. I Part 1:** 362–364
Clover and Other Poems (Lanier), **Supp. I Part 1:** 362
"Clown" (Corso), **Supp. XII:** 127
Clown in the Belfry, The: Writings on Faith and Fiction (Buechner), **Supp. XII:** 53
Cluck, Julia, **Supp. I Part 2:** 728
Clue, The (Wells), **Supp. XXVI:** 277
Clue of the Eyelash, The (Wells), **Supp. XXVI:** 280
Clum, John M., **Supp. XIII: 200,** 201, 209
Cluny, Hugo, **IV:** 290
Clurman, Harold, **I:** 93; **IV:** 381, 385
Clytus, Radiclani, **Supp. XIII:** 128, **Supp. XIII:** 129, 132
"C.O." (Wrigley), **Supp. XVIII:** 298
"Coal: Beginning and End" (Winters), **Supp. II Part 2:** 791
Coale, Howard, **Supp. XIII:** 15
Coale, Samuel, **Retro. Supp. III:** 111
"Coals" (Hoffman), **Supp. XVIII:** 86
Coalwood Way, The (Hickam), **Supp. XXVII:** 106, 107–108
"Coast, The" (column), **Supp. IV Part 1:** 198
"Coast Guard's Cottage, The" (Wylie), **Supp. I Part 2:** 723

Coast of Chicago, The (Dybek), **Supp. XXIII: 72–74,** 75
Coast of Trees, A (Ammons), **Supp. VII:** 24, 34
"Coast-Range Christ, The" (Jeffers), **Supp. II Part 2:** 414, 419
"Coast-Road, The" (Jeffers), **Supp. II Part 2:** 425
"Coat, The" (Everwine), **Supp. XV:** 80
Coates, Joseph, **Supp. VIII:** 80; **Supp. XXII:** 205
Coates, Robert, **I:** 54; **IV:** 298
"Coatlicue's Rules: Advice from an Aztec Goddess" (Mora), **Supp. XIII:** 223
"Coats" (Kenyon), **Supp. VII:** 172
Coats, Karen, **Supp. XXVIII:** 288
Coatsworth, Elizabeth Jane, **Supp. XXVI:** 33
Cobb, Lee J., **III:** 153
Cobb, Ty, **III:** 227, 229
Cobbett, William, **Supp. I Part 2:** 517; **Supp. XV:** 237
"Cobbler Keezar's Vision" (Whittier), **Supp. I Part 2:** 699
"Cobweb, The" (Carver), **Supp. III Part 1:** 148
Cobwebs From an Empty Skull (Bierce), **I:** 195
Coccimiglio, Vic, **Supp. XIII:** 114
"Cock-a-Doodle-Doo!" (Melville), **III:** 89
"Cockayne" (Emerson), **II:** 6
"Cock-Crow" (Gordon), **II:** 219
"Cockfight in a Loxahatchee Grove"(Bottoms), **Supp. XXVIII:** 24
Cock Pit (Cozzens), **I:** 359, 378, 379
Cockpit (Kosinski), **Supp. XII:** 21
Cockpit: A Novel (Kosinski), **Supp. VII:** 215, 223–224, 225
"Cock Robin Takes Refuge in the Storm House" (Snodgrass), **Supp. VI:** 319
Cocktail Hour, The (Gurney), **Supp. V:** 95, 96, 100, 101, 103, 105, 108
Cocktail Hour and Two Other Plays: Another Antigone and *The Perfect Party* (Gurney), **Supp. V:** 100
Cocktail Party, The (T. S. Eliot), **I:** 571, 582–583; **III:** 21; **Retro. Supp. I:** 65; **Retro. Supp. III:** 70; **Supp. V:** 101, 103
Cocoon, The: A Rest-Cure Comedy (Stuart), **Supp. XXVIII:** 225, 226, 230, 237–239
Cocteau, Jean, **III:** 471; **Retro. Supp. I:** 82, 378; **Supp. IV Part 1:** 82; **Supp. XVI:** 135; **Supp. XX: 236**
"Coda: Wilderness Letter" (Stegner), **Supp. IV Part 2:** 595
"Code, The" (Frost), **Retro. Supp. I:** 121, 128
Codex (Grossman), **Supp. XXV:** 64, 66–68
Codman, Florence, **Supp. II Part 1:** 92, 93
Codman, Ogden, Jr., **Retro. Supp. I:** 362, 363; **Retro. Supp. III:** 277, 280
Codrescu, Andrei, **Supp. XXII:** 155
Cody, William ("Buffalo Bill"), **I:** 440; **III:** 584; **Supp. V:** 230

"Coffee and Sweet Rolls" (Stone), **Supp. XXVII:** 253
"Coffee Lips" (Ferry), **Supp. XXIV:** 153, 162
Coffey, Michael, **Supp. V:** 243; **Supp. XV:** 65; **Supp. XX: 88**
Coffey, Warren, **III:** 358
Coffin, Charles, **III:** 577
Coffman, Frank, **Supp. XXVII:** 118
Cogan, David J., **Supp. IV Part 1:** 362
Cogan, Joshua, **Supp. XXI:** 247
Cogewea the Half-Blood: A Depiction of the Great Montana Cattle Range (Mourning Dove (Christal Quintasket)), **Supp. XXV:** 285
Coghill, Nevill, **Supp. II Part 1:** 4; **Supp. XIV:** 13
"Cognac in France"(Wakoski), **Supp. XXVIII:** 272
Cohan, George M., **II:** 427; **III:** 401
Cohen, Edward M., **Supp. XVI:** 212
Cohen, Esther, **Supp. XV:** 323
Cohen, Hettie, **Supp. II Part 1:** 30
Cohen, Joshua, **Supp. XXII:** 268
Cohen, Leonard, **Supp. XXVII: 49–65**
Cohen, Marty, **Supp. X:** 112
Cohen, Norman J., **Supp. IX:** 132, 143
Cohen, Rosetta, **Supp. XV:** 257
Cohen, Sarah Blacher, **Supp. V:** 273
Cohen, Victor, **Supp. XVIII:** 235, 236
"Coherent Decentering: Towards a New Model of the Poetic Self" (A. Finch), **Supp. XVII:** 76
Cohn, Jan, **Supp. XXV:** 192, 200
"Coin" (Goldbarth), **Supp. XII:** 187
Coindreau, Maurice, **III:** 339
Coiner, Constance, **Supp. XIII:** 297, 302
Coins and Coffins (Wakoski), **Supp. XXVIII:** 261, 262
Coit, Lille Hitchcock, **Supp. X:** 103
"Coitus" (Pound), **III:** 466
Coke, Desmond, **Supp. XX: 235**
Colburn, Nadia Herman, **Supp. XV:** 339, 341, 347
"Cold, The" (Kenyon), **Supp. VII:** 164
"Cold, The" (Winters), **Supp. II Part 2:** 790–791, 809, 811
"Cold-blooded Creatures" (Wylie), **Supp. I Part 2:** 729
Colden, Cadwallader, **Supp. I Part 1:** 250
"Colder the Air, The" (Bishop), **Supp. I Part 1:** 86
Cold Feet (Harrison), **Supp. VIII:** 39
Cold Frame (C. Frost), **Supp. XV:** 93, 96
Cold Ground Was My Bed Last Night (Garrett), **Supp. VII:** 98
"Cold Ground Was My Bed Last Night" (Garrett), **Supp. VII:** 100
"Cold Hill Side, The"(Hadas), **Supp. XXIII:** 121
"Cold Keener" (Hurston), **Retro. Supp. III:** 137
"Cold Night, The" (W. C. Williams), **Retro. Supp. I:** 418
"Cold Plunge into Skin Diving, A" (Knowles), **Supp. XII:** 241
Cold Spring, A (Bishop), **Retro. Supp. II:** 45

Cold Springs Harbor (Yates), **Supp. XI:** 348

Cold War American Poetry, **Supp. V:** 182

Cold War and the Income Tax, The (Wilson), **IV:** 430

Cole, Bruce, **Supp. XX: 106**

Cole, Goody, **Supp. I Part 2:** 696–697

Cole, Lester, **Retro. Supp. II:** 329

Cole, Nat King, **Retro. Supp. I:** 334; **Supp. X:** 255

Cole, Thomas, **Supp. I Part 1:** 156, 158, 171

Cole, William, **Supp. XIX:** 120

"Coleman" (Karr), **Supp. XI:** 244

Coleman, Wanda, **Supp. XI: 83–98**

Coleridge, Samuel Taylor, **I:** 283, 284, 447, 522; **II:** 7, 10, 11, 19, 71, 169, 273, 301, 502, 516, 549; **III:** 77, 83–84, 424, 461, 488, 523; **IV:** 74, 173, 250, 349, 453; **Retro. Supp. I:** 65, 308; **Retro. Supp. III:** 44, 109, 233; **Supp. I Part 1:** 31, 311, 349; **Supp. I Part 2:** 376, 393, 422; **Supp. IV Part 2:** 422, 465; **Supp. IX:** 38, 50; **Supp. V:** 258; **Supp. XIII:** 139; **Supp. XIV:** 21–22; **Supp. XV:** 250; **Supp. XXI:** 52, 55; **Supp. XXIII:** 231; **Supp. XXIV:** 74

Coles, Katharine, **Supp. IV Part 2:** 630

Coles, Robert, **Supp. XXIV:** 172, 265; **Supp. XXVI:** 250, 252

Colette, Sidonie-Gabrielle, **Supp. VIII:** 40, 171; **Supp. XVI:** 193–194

"Coliseum, The" (Poe), **III:** 411

Collage of Dreams (Spencer), **Supp. X:** 196

"Collapse of Tomorrow, The" (Mumford), **Supp. II Part 2:** 482

"Collected by a Valetudinarian" (E. Stoddard), **Supp. XV:** 286–287

Collected Earlier Poems (Hecht), **Supp. X:** 58, 59

Collected Earlier Poems (W. C. Williams), **Retro. Supp. I:** 414, 428

Collected Earlier Poems 1940–1960 (Levertov), **Supp. III Part 1:** 273, 275

Collected Essays (Tate), **IV:** 133–134

Collected Essays, Volume 2: Literary Criticism (Lovecraft), **Supp. XXV:** 121

Collected Essays of Ralph Ellison, The (Ellison), **Retro. Supp. II:** 119

Collected Essays of Robert Creeley, The (Creeley), **Supp. IV Part 1:** 153, 154

Collected Greed, Parts 1–13, The (Wakoski), **Supp. XXVIII:** 268–269

Collected Later Poems (W. C. Williams), **Retro. Supp. I:** 428

Collected Plays (A. Miller), **III:** 158; **Retro. Supp. III:** 165, 166–167

Collected Plays, 1974–1983 (Gurney), **Supp. V:** 99

Collected Poems (Aiken), **I:** 50

Collected Poems (Berrigan), **Supp. XXIV:** 39, 45, 46

Collected Poems (Burke), **I:** 269

Collected Poems (Cummings), **I:** 430, 439, 441

Collected Poems (Doolittle), **Supp. I Part 1:** 264–267, 269

Collected Poems (Frost), **Retro. Supp. I:** 136; **Retro. Supp. III:** 103

Collected Poems (H. Crane), **Retro. Supp. III:** 53

Collected Poems (Hull), **Supp. XXI:** 141

Collected Poems (Kees; Justice, ed.), **Supp. XV:** 134

Collected Poems (Lindsay), **Supp. I Part 2:** 380, 387, 392, 396–397, 400

Collected Poems (Markson), **Supp. XVII:** 143

Collected Poems (Moore), **III:** 194, 215

Collected Poems (O'Hara), **Supp. XXIII:** 207, 211, 220

Collected Poems (Price), **Supp. VI:** 267

Collected Poems (R. Lowell), **Supp. XV:** 20

Collected Poems (Simpson), **Supp. IX:** 279

Collected Poems (W. C. Williams), **IV:** 415; **Retro. Supp. I:** 430

Collected Poems (Winters), **Supp. II Part 2:** 791, 810

Collected Poems (Wright), **Supp. III Part 2:** 602

Collected Poems (Yeats), **Supp. XV:** 152

Collected Poems, 1909–1935 (T. S. Eliot), **I:** 580; **Retro. Supp. I:** 66

Collected Poems, 1909–1962 (T. S. Eliot), **I:** 583; **Retro. Supp. III:** 69

Collected Poems, 1918–1938 (Taggard), **Supp. XXII:** 283

Collected Poems, 1923–1953 (Bogan), **Supp. III Part 1:** 64

Collected Poems, 1936–1976 (Francis), **Supp. IX:** 77, 80, **87**

Collected Poems, The (Stevens), **III:** 273; **IV:** 75, 76, 87, 93; **Retro. Supp. I:** 296, 309

Collected Poems 1917–1952 (MacLeish), **III:** 3, 4, 19

Collected Poems 1921–1931 (W. C. Williams), **Retro. Supp. I:** 422; **Supp. XIV:** 285

Collected Poems 1930–1960 (Eberhart), **I:** 522, 525–526, 540, 541

Collected Poems: 1939–1989 (W. J. Smith), **Supp. XIII:** 332, 340, 343, 345

Collected Poems: 1940–1978 (Shapiro), **Supp. II Part 2:** 703, 717

Collected Poems: 1951–1971 (Ammons), **Supp. VII:** 24, 26–29, 32, 33

Collected Poems: 1956–1976 (Wagoner), **Supp. IX:** 323, **328–329**

Collected Poems of Amy Clampitt, The (Clampitt), **Supp. IX:** 37, 44, 53

Collected Poems of George Garrett (Garrett), **Supp. VII:** 109

Collected Poems of Hart Crane, The (Crane), **I:** 399–402

Collected Poems of James Agee, The (Fitzgerald, ed.), **I:** 27–28

Collected Poems of James T. Farrell, The (Farrell), **II:** 45

Collected Poems of Kay Boyle (Boyle), **Supp. XXIV:** 63

Collected Poems of Langston Hughes, The (Rampersad and Roessel, ed.), **Retro. Supp. I:** 194, 196, 212

Collected Poems of Muriel Rukeyser, The (Rukeyser), **Supp. VI:** 274

Collected Poems of Sara Teasdale, The (Teasdale), **Supp. XXVII:** 287, 294–295

Collected Poems of Thomas Merton, The, **Supp. VIII:** 207, 208

Collected Poetry (Auden), **Supp. II Part 1:** 18

Collected Prose (Wright), **Supp. III Part 2:** 596

Collected Prose, The (Bishop), **Retro. Supp. II:** 51

Collected Recordings (W. C. Williams), **Retro. Supp. I:** 431

Collected Shorter Poems, 1946-1991 (Carruth), **Supp. XVI:** 47

Collected Short Stories, The (Wharton), **Retro. Supp. I:** 362, 363, 366

Collected Short Stories of Harriette Simpson Arnow (Ballard and Chung, eds.), **Supp. XXVIII:** 3

Collected Sonnets (Millay), **III:** 136–137

Collected Stories (Carver), **Supp. XXIV:** 177

Collected Stories, 1939–1976 (Bowles), **Supp. IV Part 1:** 92

Collected Stories, The (Paley), **Supp. VI:** 218

Collected Stories, The (Price), **Supp. VI:** 266

Collected Stories, The (Theroux), **Supp. VIII:** 318

Collected Stories, The (Wharton), **Retro. Supp. I:** 361

Collected Stories of Amy Hempel, The (Hempel), **Supp. XXI:** 115, 117

Collected Stories of Eudora Welty, The (Welty), **Retro. Supp. I:** 355

Collected Stories of Isaac Bashevis Singer (Singer), **Retro. Supp. II: 307–308**

Collected Stories of Katherine Anne Porter (Porter), **III:** 454

Collected Stories of Peter Taylor (Taylor), **Supp. V:** 314, 320, 323–324, 325, 326

Collected Stories of Richard Yates, The, **Supp. XI:** 349

Collected Stories of Wallace Stegner (Stegner), **Supp. IV Part 2:** 599, 605

Collected Stories of William Faulkner (Faulkner), **II:** 72; **Retro. Supp. I:** 75; **Retro. Supp. III:** 86–87

Collected Stories of William Humphrey, The (Humphrey), **Supp. IX:** 106

Collected Works (Bierce), **I:** 204, 208–210

Collected Works of Buck Rogers in the 25th Century, The (Bradbury), **Supp. IV Part 1:** 101

Collected Works of Edgar Allan Poe (Mabbott, ed.), **Retro. Supp. III:** 237

Collected Writings (Brainard), **Supp. XXVII:** 17, 26–27, 29

Collected Writings, The (Z. Fitzgerald; Bruccoli, ed.), **Supp. IX:** 65, 68

Collecting the Animals (Everwine), **Supp. XV:** 73, 75, **78–81**, 85, 88

Collection of Epigrams, **II:** 111

Collection of Poems, on American Affairs, and a Variety of Other Subjects . . .

(Freneau), **Supp. II Part 1:** 274

Collection of Select Aphorisms and Maxims (Palmer), **II:** 111

"Collectors" (Carver), **Supp. III Part 1:** 141–142

Collette, **Supp. XVII:** 86

Collier, John, **Supp. XXI:** 8

Collier, Lucy Wood, **Supp. XXI:** 8

Collier, Michael, **Supp. XVII:** 23, 110

Collingwood, R. G., **I:** 278

Collins, Billy, **Supp. XI:** 143; **Supp. XIV:** 123; **Supp. XVII:** 245; **Supp. XXI:** 51–66; **Supp. XXIII:** 138

Collins, Brennan, **Supp. XXVI:** 12, 13

Collins, Doug, **Supp. V:** 5

Collins, Eddie, **II:** 416

Collins, John A., **Supp. XXVIII:** 173

Collins, L. M., **Supp. XXII:** 7

Collins, Richard, **Supp. XI:** 171

Collins, Ronald, **Supp. XXI:** 24

Collins, Wilkie, **Supp. I Part 1:** 35, 36; **Supp. IV Part 1:** 341; **Supp. XX:** 236

Collins, William, **Supp. I Part 2:** 714

Collinson, Peter , **II:** 114

Collinson, Peter (pseudonym). *See* Hammett, Dashiell

"Collision" (Huddle), **Supp. XXVI:** 155

Colloff, Pamela, **Supp. XIII:** 281

Colloque Sentimental (ballet), **Supp. IV Part 1:** 83

"Colloquy" (Kees), **Supp. XV:** 133

"Colloquy in Black Rock" (Lowell), **II:** 535

"Colloquy in Black Rock" (R. Lowell), **Retro. Supp. II:** 178

"Colloquy of Monos and Una, The" (Poe), **III:** 412

"Colloquy on a Bed" (Bronk), **Supp. XXI:** 31

Colonel's Dream, The (Chesnutt), **Supp. XIV:** 63, 75–76

Colônia, Regina, **Retro. Supp. II:** 53

Colony (Siddons), **Supp. XXII:** 239

Color (Cullen), **Supp. IV Part 1:** 164, 166, 167, 168

"Colorado" (Beattie), **Supp. V:** 27

Color and Democracy: Colonies and Peace (Du Bois), **Supp. II Part 1:** 184, 185

"Color-Blind Raspberry Picker, The"(Hadas), **Supp. XXIII:** 113

Color Curtain, The (Wright), **IV:** 478, 488

"Colored Americans" (Dunbar), **Supp. II Part 1:** 197

Colored People (H. L. Gates), **Supp. XX:** 101, 103, 104–105, 109, 111

"Color Line, The" (Douglass), **Supp. III Part 1:** 163–165

Color Line, The (W. B. Smith), **Supp. II Part 1:** 168

Color of Absence, The (Howe, ed.), **Supp. XXVIII:** 288

Color of a Great City, The (Dreiser), **Retro. Supp. II:** 104

Color of Darkness (Purdy), **Supp. VII:** 271

Color of Water, The (McBride), **Supp. XXVI:** 191

Color Purple, The (Walker), **Supp. III Part 2:** 517, 518, 520, 525–529, 532–537; **Supp. VIII:** 141; **Supp. X:** 252, 330; **Supp. XX: 107**

Color Schemes (Cheang; film), **Supp. XI:** 20

"Colors of Night, The" (Momaday), **Supp. IV Part 2:** 490

"Color Struck" (Hurston), **Retro. Supp. III:** 127, 137

"Colors without Objects" (Swenson), **Supp. IV Part 2:** 645

"Color: The Unfinished Business of Democracy" (Locke), **Supp. XIV:** 202, 207

Colossus, The (Plath), **Retro. Supp. II: 245–247; **Supp. I Part 2:** 529, 531, 536, 538, 540; **Supp. V:** 79; **Supp. XI:** 317

"Colossus, The" (Plath), **Retro. Supp. II:** 250; **Supp. XXIII:** 113

Colossus of Maroussi, The (H. Miller), **III:** 178, 185–186

"Colour out of Space, The" (Lovecraft), **Supp. XXV:** 109, 111, 114–116, 118, 121

"Colt, The" (Stegner), **Supp. IV Part 2:** 600

Coltelli, Laura, **Supp. IV Part 1:** 323, 330, 335, 409; **Supp. IV Part 2:** 493, 497, 559

Colter: The True Story of the Best Dog I Ever Had (Bass), **Supp. XVI:** 23

Coltrane, John, **Supp. VIII:** 197; **Supp. XXII:** 172

Coltrane, John (pseud.). *See* O'Nan, Stewart

Colum, Mary, **I:** 246, 252, 256; **Supp. I Part 2:** 708, 709

"Columba" (Cliff), **Supp. XXII:** 74, 76

Columbia Anthology of American Poetry (Parini, ed.), **Supp. XXV:** 251

Columbiad, The (Barlow), **Supp. II Part 1:** 67, 72, 73, 74, 75–77, 79

Columbia History of the American Novel, **Supp. XV:** 270

Columbia Literary History of the United States, **Supp. XV:** 270

"Columbian Ode" (Dunbar), **Supp. II Part 1:** 199

"Columbia U Poesy Reading—1975" (Corso), **Supp. XII:** 134

"Columbine, The" (Very), **Supp. XXV:** 242, 244

Columbus, Christopher, **I:** 253; **II:** 6, 310; **III:** 8; **Supp. I Part 2:** 397, 479, 480, 483, 486–488, 491, 495, 497, 498

"Columbus to Ferdinand" (Freneau), **Supp. II Part 1:** 255

Comanche Moon (McMurtry), **Supp. V:** 232

"Come, Break With Time" (Bogan), **Supp. III Part 1:** 52

Come, Thief (Hirshfield), **Supp. XXIII:** 134, 138

Come Along with Me (Jackson), **Supp. IX:** 117, 118, 122

Come Back, Charleston Blue (film), **Supp. XVI:** 144

Come Back, Little Sheba (film), **Supp. XXV:** 95

Come Back, Little Sheba (Inge), **Supp. XXV:** 94–95, 96–97

Comeback, The (Gurney), **Supp. V:** 97

"Come Back to the Raft Ag'in, Huck Honey!" (Fiedler), **Supp. XIII:** 93, 96–97, 101

Come Blow Your Horn (Simon), **Supp. IV Part 2:** 574, 575, 577, 578, 586, 587, 591

Come By Here (Major), **Supp. XXII:** 171, 182

"Come Dance with Me in Ireland" (Jackson), **Supp. IX:** 119

"Comedian as the Letter C, The" (Stevens), **IV:** 84–85, 88; **Retro. Supp. I:** 297, 301, 302

"Comedy Cop" (Farrell), **II:** 45

Comedy of a Country House (J. Sturgis), **Supp. XX: 238**

"Comedy's Greatest Era" (Agee), **I:** 31

"Come In" (Frost), **Retro. Supp. I:** 139

"Come On, Baby" (Zinberg), **Supp. XV:** 195

Come On All You Ghosts (Zapruder), **Supp. XXVI:** 54

"Come on Back" (Gardner), **Supp. VI:** 73

"Come Out into the Sun" (Francis), **Supp. IX:** 82

Come Out into the Sun: Poems New and Selected (Francis), **Supp. IX: 82–83**

"Come out the Wilderness" (Baldwin), **Supp. I Part 1:** 63

Comer, Anjanette, **Supp. XI:** 305

Comer, Cornelia, **I:** 214

"Come Rain or Come Shine" (song), **Supp. XXII:** 6

"Come Shining: The Spiritual South" (exhibition; Luster), **Supp. XV:** 350

Come with Me: Poems for a Journey (Nye), **Supp. XIII:** 279

"Comforts of Home, The" (O'Connor), **III:** 349, 351, 355; **Retro. Supp. II:** 237

Comic Artist, The (Glaspell and Matson), **Supp. III Part 1:** 182

"Comic Imagination of the Young Dickens, The" (Wright), **Supp. III Part 2:** 591

"Comic Textures and Female Communities 1937 and 1977: Clare Boothe and Wendy Wasserstein" (Carlson), **Supp. XV:** 323

Comic Tragedies (Alcott), **Supp. I Part 1:** 33

Coming After (Notley), **Supp. XXII:** 223, 227, 230, 232, 236

"Coming and Going" (Gallagher), **Supp. XXIV:** 175, 176–177

"Coming Close" (Levine), **Supp. V:** 192

Coming Forth by Day of Osiris Jones, The (Aiken), **I:** 59

"Coming Home" (Gordon), **Supp. IV Part 1:** 309

"Coming Home to Vermont" (McCarriston), **Supp. XIV:** 269

"Coming in From the Cold" (Walker), **Supp. III Part 2:** 526

Coming into Eighty (Sarton), **Supp. VIII:** 262

"Coming into Eighty" (Sarton), **Supp. VIII:** 262

Coming into the Country (McPhee), **Supp. III Part 1:** 298, 301–306, 309, 310

Coming Into Writing (Cixous), **Supp. X:** 102

Coming of Age in Mississippi (Moody), **Supp. IV Part 1:** 11

Coming on Home Soon (Woodson; Lewis, ill.), **Supp. XXVIII:** 279, 286

Comings Back (Goldbarth), **Supp. XII:** 180

"Coming to Canada--Age Twenty Two" (Shields), **Supp. VII:** 311

Coming to Canada: Poems (Shields), **Supp. VII:** 311–312

"Coming to Memoir as a Journalist" (Epstein), **Supp. XXII:** 95

"Coming to the Morning" (Merwin), **Supp. III Part 1:** 356

"Coming to This" (Strand), **Supp. IV Part 2:** 627

Comiskey, Charles, **II:** 422

Commager, Henry Steele, **I:** 253; **Supp. I Part 1:** 372; **Supp. I Part 2:** 484, 647, 650

Command the Morning (Buck), **Supp. II Part 1:** 125

"CommComm" (Saunders), **Supp. XIX:** 234

"Commencement Address, A" (Brodsky), **Supp. VIII:** 31

"Commencement Day Address, The" (Schwartz), **Supp. II Part 2:** 660

Commentaries (Caesar), **II:** 502, 561

"Commentary" (Auden), **Supp. II Part 1:** 13

"Comment on Curb" (Hughes), **Supp. I Part 1:** 340

"Comments/Questions" (Nelson), **Supp. XVIII:** 172

"Commerce" (Nye), **Supp. XIII:** 281

Commins, Saxe, **Retro. Supp. I:** 73; **Retro. Supp. II:** 337

Commodity of Dreams & Other Stories, A (Nemerov), **III:** 268–269, 285

Common Carnage (Dobyns), **Supp. XIII:** 87

"Common Ground, A" (Levertov), **Supp. III Part 1:** 277

"Common Life, The" (Auden), **Supp. IV Part 1:** 302, 313

"Common Meter" (R. Fisher), **Supp. XIX:** 71

Common Room, A: Essays 1954–1987 (Price), **Supp. VI:** 264–265, 267

Commons, John, **Supp. I Part 2:** 645

Common Sense (Paine), **II:** 117; **Supp. I Part 1:** 231; **Supp. I Part 2:** 505, 506–508, 509, 513, 516, 517, 521

Communal Cot (Loy), **Supp. XXII:** 168

"Communication" (Dobyns), **Supp. XIII:** 91

"Communion" (Dubus), **Supp. VII:** 91

Communion (Mora), **Supp. XIII:** 217–219

Communist Manifesto, The (Marx and Engels), **II:** 463; **Supp. XXI:** 162–163

"Community Life" (Moore), **Supp. X:** 178

"Community of Glaciers, The" (Bass), **Supp. XVI:** 23

Comnes, Gregory, **Supp. IV Part 1:** 283, 284, 291

"Companions, The" (Nemerov), **III:** 269, 278, 287

Company of Poets, A (Simpson), **Supp. IX:** 265, 275

Company of Women, The (Gordon), **Supp. IV Part 1:** 302–304, 304, 306, 313

Company She Keeps, The (McCarthy), **II:** 562, 563–566

"Comparisons of Wonder" (Jarman), **Supp. XVII:** 114

Compass Flower, The (Merwin), **Supp. III Part 1:** 353, 357

"Compassionate Friendship" (Doolittle), **Supp. I Part 1:** 257, 258, 259, 260, 271

"Compatibility" (C. Frost), **Supp. XV:** 103

"Compendium" (Dove), **Supp. IV Part 1:** 248

"Compensation" (Teasdale), **Supp. XXVII:** 293

"Complaint" (W. C. Williams), **Retro. Supp. I:** 418

"Complete Birth of the Cool, The" (Wright), **Supp. XV:** 343, 344

Complete Collected Poems of William Carlos Williams, 1906–1938, The (W. C. Williams), **Retro. Supp. I:** 424

"Complete Destruction" (W. C. Williams), **IV:** 413

"Complete Life of John Hopkins, The" (O. Henry), **Supp. II Part 1:** 405

Complete Poems (Frost), **II:** 155, 164

Complete Poems (Reznikoff), **Supp. XIV:** 281

Complete Poems (Sandburg), **III:** 590–592, 594, 596

Complete Poems, The (Bishop), **Retro. Supp. II:** 49; **Supp. I Part 1:** 72, 82, 94

Complete Poems, The (Bradbury), **Supp. IV Part 1:** 105

Complete Poems, The: 1927–1979 (Bishop), **Retro. Supp. II:** 51

Complete Poems of Emily Dickinson, The (Bianchi and Hampson, eds.), **Retro. Supp. I:** 35

Complete Poems of Emily Dickinson, The (T. H. Johnson, ed.), **I:** 470

Complete Poems of Frederick Goddard Tuckerman, The (Momaday), **Supp. IV Part 2:** 480

Complete Poems of Hart Crane, **Retro. Supp. II:** 81

Complete Poems of Robert Frost, The (Frost), **Retro. Supp. III:** 105

Complete Poems to Solve, The (Swenson), **Supp. IV Part 2:** 652

Complete Poetical Works (A. Lowell), **II:** 512, 516–517

Complete Poetical Works (Hulme), **III:** 464

Complete Poetical Works (Longfellow), **Retro. Supp. II:** 154

Complete Poetical Works of Amy Lowell, The (A. Lowell), **Supp. XV:** 295–296

Complete Prose of T. S. Eliot (T. S. Eliot), **Retro. Supp. III:** 58, 59

Complete Stories, The (O'Connor), **Retro. Supp. III:** 208; **Supp. X:** 1

Complete Tragedies, The: Euripedes II, **Supp. XV:** 50

"Complete with Starry Night and Bourbon Shots" (Goldbarth), **Supp. XII:** 192–193

Complete Works of Kate Chopin, The (Seyersted, ed.), **Supp. I Part 1:** 212, 225

Complete Works of the Gawain-Poet (Gardner), **Supp. VI:** 64, 65

"Complex Histories, Contested Memories: Some Reflections on Remembering Difficult Pasts" (E. Hoffman, lecture), **Supp. XVI:** 155

"Complicated Thoughts About a Small Son" (White), **Supp. I Part 2:** 678

"Compliments of the Season" (O. Henry), **Supp. II Part 1:** 392, 399

"Compline" (Auden), **Supp. II Part 1:** 23

"Composing a Life" (Pickering), **Supp. XXI:** 191, 196

Composition as Explanation (Stein), **IV:** 32, 33, 38

"Composition as Explanation" (Stein), **IV:** 27, 28

"Compound Eye, The" (Davison), **Supp. XXVI:** 74

"Compounding of Consciousness" (James), **II:** 358–359

Comprehensive Bibliography (Hanneman), **II:** 259

Compton-Burnett, Ivy, **I:** 93; **II:** 580; **Supp. XXIII:** 209

Compulsion (Levin), **Supp. XXVII:** 133, 139, 142, 144–145, 147

"Compulsory Heterosexuality and Lesbian Experience" (Rich), **Retro. Supp. III:** 251

"Comrade Laski, C.P.U.S.A. \[M.L.\]" (Didion), **Supp. IV Part 1:** 200

"Comrade Poets" (Hayes), **Supp. XXVI:** 144

Comstock, Anthony, **Retro. Supp. II:** 95

Comus (Milton), **II:** 12; **Supp. I Part 2:** 622

Conan Doyle, Arthur. *See* Doyle, Arthur Conan

Conan the Barbarian (comic), **Supp. XXVII:** 129

Conan the Barbarian (film), **Supp. XXVII:** 129

Conceptions of Reality in Modern American Poetry (Dembo), **Supp. I Part 1:** 272

"Concept of Character in Fiction, The" (Gass), **Supp. VI:** 85, **86**

Concept of Dread, The (Kierkegaard), **III:** 305

"Concerning a Woman of Sin" (Hecht), **Supp. XXVII:** 94

Concerning Children (Gilman), **Supp. XI:** 206

"Concerning Copyright" (Twain), **Retro. Supp. III:** 269

"Concerning Mold upon the Skin, Etc." (J. Scott), **Supp. XVII:** 188

"Concerning Necessity" (Carruth), **Supp. XVI:** 57

"Concerning Some Recent Criticism of His Work" (Doty), **Supp. XI:** 131

Concerning the End for Which God Created the World (Edwards), **I:** 549, 557, 559

"Concerning the Jews" (Twain), **Retro. Supp. III:** 268

Concerning the League (Woodbury, Henry, and Webster, trans.), **Supp. XXVI:** 81, 82, 87, 90

"Concerning Things That Can Be Doubled"(Crooker), **Supp. XXIII:** 64

Concerto for Two Pianos, Winds, and Percussion (Bowles), **Supp. IV Part 1:** 83

"Concert of Tenses, A" (Gallagher), **Supp. XXIV:** 172

Concert of Tenses, A: Essays on Poetry (Gallagher), **Supp. XXIV:** 166, 167, 171–172

Conchologist's First Book, The (Poe), **III:** 412; **Retro. Supp. III:** 234–235

Conclusive Evidence (Nabokov), **III:** 247–250, 252

"Concord Hymn" (Emerson), **II:** 19

Concrete Blonde, The (Connelly), **Supp. XXI:** 70–71, 78, 80

"Concrete Universal, The: Observations on the Understanding of Poetry" (Ransom), **III:** 480

Concurring Beasts (Dobyns), **Supp. XIII:** 76

Condé, Maryse, **Supp. XXIII:** 94

Condensed Novels and Other Papers (Harte), **Supp. II Part 1:** 342

"Condition, The" (Karmi; Everwine, trans.), **Supp. XV:** 78

Condition of Man, The (Mumford), **Supp. II Part 2:** 483, 484, 486, 495–496, 498

"Conditions for Work: The Common World of Women" (Rich), **Retro. Supp. III:** 248

"Condolence" (Parker), **Supp. IX:** 191

"Condominium, The" (Elkin), **Supp. VI:** 49, **50–51**, 55, 56

Condon, Charles R., **Supp. XIII:** 163

Condor and the Cows, The: A South American Travel Diary (Isherwood and Caskey), **Supp. XIV:** 166

"Condor and the Guests, The" (Connell), **Supp. XIV:** 86

Condorcet, Marquis de, **Supp. I Part 2:** 511

Conduct of Life, The (Emerson), **II:** 1–5, 8

Conduct of Life, The (Mumford), **Supp. II Part 2:** 485, 496–497

"Conductor of Nothing, The" (Levine), **Supp. V:** 189

"Coney Island" (Teasdale), **Supp. XXVII:** 289

Coney Island of the Mind, A (Ferlinghetti), **Supp. XIX:** 4; **Supp. XXI:** 53

Confederacy of Dunces, A (Toole), **Supp. XXVI:** 239, 240, 242, 243–244, 246, 250–253

"Conference Male, The" (Mora), **Supp. XIII:** 218

"Confession" (Peacock), **Supp. XIX:** 206

Confession, The (Rinehart), **Supp. XXV:** 200

"Confessional" (Bidart), **Supp. XV:** 29–30, 31

"Confessional Poem" (Nelson), **Supp. XVIII:** 174

Confession de Claude, La (Zola), **I:** 411

"Confession of a House-Breaker, The" (Jewett), **Retro. Supp. II:** 146–147

Confession of Jereboam O. Beauchamp, The (pamphlet), **IV:** 253

Confessions (Augustine), **I:** 279; **Retro. Supp. III:** 63; **Supp. XVI:** 288; **Supp. XXII:** 93

"Confessions" (Huddle), **Supp. XXVI:** 150

Confessions (Rousseau), **I:** 226

Confessions of a Barbarian: Selections from the Journals of Edward Abbey, 1951–1989 (Abbey; Petersen, ed.), **Supp. XIII:** 2, 4

"Confessions of a Latina Author" (Mora), **Supp. XIII:** 221

"Confessions of an Author Nomad"(Griest), **Supp. XXVIII:** 100

"Confessions of a Wannabe Negro" (McKnight), **Supp. XX: 152–153, 158**

Confessions of Nat Turner, The (Styron), **IV:** 98, 99, 105, 113–117; **Supp. X:** 16, 250

Confetti (Mora), **Supp. XIII:** 221

Confidence (James), **II:** 327, 328

Confidence-Man, The (Melville), **III:** 91; **Retro. Supp. I:** 255–256, 257; **Retro. Supp. II:** 121; **Supp. XIV:** 49

Confidence Man, The (Van Vechten), **Supp. II Part 2:** 737

Confidence-Man, The: His Masquerade (Melville), **Retro. Supp. III:** 147, 148, 160

Confidential Clerk, The (T. S. Eliot), **I:** 570, 571–572, 583, 584; **Retro. Supp. I:** 65; **Retro. Supp. III:** 70

Confident Years, 1885–1915, The (Brooks), **I:** 257, 259; **Supp. I Part 2:** 650

"Configurations" (Ammons), **Supp. VII:** 28

Configurations: New and Selected Poems, 1958–1998 (Major), **Supp. XXII: 182**

Conflict (Prouty), **Supp. XXVIII:** 177, 184, 185

Confronting the Horror: The Novels of Nelson Algren (Giles), **Supp. IX:** 11, 15

Confucius, **II:** 1; **III:** 456, 475; **Supp. IV Part 1:** 14

Confusion (Cozzens), **I:** 358, 359, 377, 378

"Confusion of Planes We Must Wander in Sleep, The" (Weigl), **Supp. XIX:** 283

Congdon, Don, **Supp. XXII:** 204

Congo (film), **Supp. IV Part 1:** 83

Congo (screenplay, Shanley), **Supp. XIV:** 316

"Congo, The" (Lindsay), **Supp. I Part 2:** 388–389, 392, 395

Congo and Other Poems, The (Lindsay), **Supp. I Part 2:** 379, 382, 389, 390, 391; **Supp. XXV:** 18

"Congregation" (Trethewey), **Supp. XXI:** 245, 247

"Congregation of Grackles, A"(Crooker), **Supp. XXIII:** 63

"Congress of the Insomniacs, The" (Simic), **Supp. VIII:** 281–282

Congreve, William, **III:** 195; **Supp. V:** 101; **Supp. XVIII:** 12

Coningsby (Disraeli), **II:** 127

"Conjectural Reading" (Bronk), **Supp. XXI:** 31

Conjectures of a Guilty Bystander (Merton), **Supp. VIII:** 197, 206, 207

Conjugal Bliss: A Comedy of Marital Arts (Nichols), **Supp. XIII:** 269

"Conjugation of the Paramecium, The" (Rukeyser), **Supp. VI:** 271

Conjugations and Reiterations (Murray), **Supp. XIX:** 161

"Conjuration" (Wilbur), **Supp. III Part 2:** 551

Conjure (recording), **Supp. X:** 241

Conjure (Reed), **Supp. X:** 240, 242

Conjure-Man Dies, The: A Mystery Tale of Dark Harlem (R. Fisher), **Supp. XIX:** 65, 71, **77–78; Supp. XVI:** 143

Conjure Woman, The (Chesnutt), **Supp. II Part 1:** 193; **Supp. XIV:** 57, **58–61,** 62, 63; **Supp. XXVIII:** 234

Conklin, Grof, **Supp. I Part 2:** 672

Conklin, Peggy, **Supp. XXII:** 27

Conkling, Hilda, **II:** 530

Conkling, Roscoe, **III:** 506

Conley, Robert J., **Supp. V:** 232

Conley, Susan, **Supp. XIII:** 111, 112

Connaroe, Joel, **Supp. IV Part 2:** 690

"Connecticut Lad, A" (White), **Supp. I Part 2:** 677

"Connecticut Valley" (Cowley), **Supp. II Part 1:** 141–142

Connecticut Yankee in King Arthur's Court, A (Twain), **I:** 209; **II:** 276; **IV:** 205; **Retro. Supp. III:** 255, 265–267

Connell, Evan S., **Supp. XIV: 79–100; Supp. XXIII:** 302

Connell, Norreys (pseudonym). *See* O'Riordan, Conal Holmes O'Connell

Connelly, Marc, **III:** 394; **Supp. I Part 2:** 679; **Supp. IX:** 190

Connelly, Michael, **Supp. XXI: 67–82**

Conner, Dan, **Supp. XXIII:** 125

Connery, Thomas B., **Supp. XVII:** 106

Connoisseur, The (Connell), **Supp. XIV:** 87

"Connoisseur of Chaos" (Stevens), **IV:** 89; **Retro. Supp. I:** 306

Connolly, Cyril, **Supp. XIV:** 158, 343, 348

Connors, Elizabeth. *See* Lindsay, Mrs. Vachel (Elizabeth Connors)
Connotations (Kenny), **Supp. XXIII:** 143, 144, 146, 150, 155
Conover, Roger, **Supp. I Part 1:** 95
Conover, Roger L., **Supp. XXII:** 155, 162
Conquering Horse (Manfred), **Supp. X:** 126
Conqueror, The (Atherton), **Supp. XXIV:** 23
"Conqueror Worm, The" (Poe), **Retro. Supp. II:** 261
Conquest of Canaan (Dwight), **Supp. I Part 1:** 124
Conquistador (MacLeish), **III:** 2, 3, 13–14, 15
Conrad, Alfred, **Retro. Supp. II:** 245
Conrad, Alfred H., **Supp. I Part 2:** 552
Conrad, C. A., **Supp. XXII:** 155
Conrad, David, **Supp. I Part 2:** 552
Conrad, Jacob, **Supp. I Part 2:** 552
Conrad, Joseph, **I:** 123, 343, 394, 405, 409, 415, 421, 485, 506, 575–576, 578; **II:** 58, 73, 74, 91, 92, 144, 263, 320, 338, 595; **III:** 28, 102, 106, 328, 464, 467, 491, 512; **IV:** 476; **Retro. Supp. I:** 80, 91, 106, 108, 231, 274, 377; **Retro. Supp. II:** 222; **Supp. I Part 1:** 292; **Supp. I Part 2:** 621, 622; **Supp. IV Part 1:** 197, 341; **Supp. IV Part 2:** 680; **Supp. V:** 249, 251, 262, 298, 307, 311; **Supp. VIII:** 4, 310; **Supp. XIV:** 112; **Supp. XIX:** 27; **Supp. XVI:** 158, 212; **Supp. XVIII:** 98, 102; **Supp. XX:** 195; **Supp. XXIV:** 286; **Supp. XXV:** 208
Conrad, Paul, **Supp. I Part 2:** 552
Conrad, Peter, **Supp. IV Part 2:** 688
"Conrad Aiken: From Savannah to Emerson" (Cowley), **Supp. I Part 1:** 43
Conrad Richter's Ohio Trilogy (Edwards), **Supp. XVIII:** 220
Conroy, Frank, **Supp. VIII:** 145; **Supp. XI:** 245; **Supp. XVI:** 63–78; **Supp. XXII:** 50
Conroy, Jack, **Supp. XXII:** 1, 5, 10
Conroy, Pat, **Supp. XVIII:** 193; **Supp. XXII:** 239
Cons, Scams, and Grifts (Gores), **Supp. XXI:** 70
"Conscience of the Court, The" (Hurston), **Retro. Supp. III:** 135–136
Conscience with the Power and Cases thereof (Ames), **IV:** 158
"Conscientious Objector, The" (Shapiro), **Supp. II Part 2:** 710
"Consciousness and Dining" (Harrison), **Supp. VIII:** 46
Conscious Stillness, A: Two Naturalists on Thoreau's Rivers (Teale and Zwinger), **Supp. XXVIII:** 251
"Conscript, The" (Lovecraft), **Supp. XXV:** 119
"Conscription Camp" (Shapiro), **Supp. II Part 2:** 705
"Consejos de Nuestra Señora de Guadalupe: Counsel from the Brown Virgin" (Mora), **Supp. XIII:** 224
"Conservation Esthetic" (Leopold), **Supp. XIV:** 179, 181, 186, 189–190

"Conserving Natural and Cultural Diversity: The Prose and Poetry of Pat Mora" (Murphy), **Supp. XIII:** 214
Considerable Town, A (M. F. K. Fisher), **Supp. XVII:** 90
"Considerations by the Way" (Emerson), **II:** 2, 5
Consider the Oyster (M. F. K. Fisher), **Supp. XVII:** 84, 87
Considine, Bob, **II:** 424
"Consolation" (Bausch), **Supp. VII:** 48
"Consolation for Tamar" (Stallings), **Supp. XXV:** 228
Consolation of Philosophy, The (Boethius), **Supp. XXVI:** 250
"Consolations" (Stafford), **Supp. XI:** 329
"Conspiracy of History, The: E. L. Doctorow's *The Book of Daniel*" (Levine), **Supp. IV Part 1:** 221
Conspiracy of Kings, The (Barlow), **Supp. II Part 1:** 80
Conspiracy of Pontiac, The (Parkman), **Supp. II Part 2:** 590, 595, 596, 599–600
Constab Ballads (McKay), **Supp. X:** 131, 133
Constance (Kenyon), **Supp. VII:** 170–172
Constancy (Boyce), **Supp. XVII:** 100; **Supp. XXI:** 6, 7, 12
"Constant Symbol, The" (Frost), **Retro. Supp. III:** 105
"Constellation Orion, The" (Kooser), **Supp. XIX:** 120
Constellations (Goodman), **Supp. XXVIII:** 88
Constitution of the Confederacy by Dekanawidah: Collected and Translated from \[the\] Mohawk Text by Chief Seth Newhouse, **Supp. XXVI:** 90
Constitution of the Five Nations, The (Parker), **Supp. XXVI:** 87
Construction of Boston, The (Koch), **Supp. XV:** 187
"Constructive Work" (Du Bois), **Supp. II Part 1:** 172
"Consumer's Report" (X. J. Kennedy), **Supp. XV:** 161–162
"Consumption" (Bryant), **Supp. I Part 1:** 169–170
Contact Collection of Contemporary Writers (McAlmon), **Supp. XXII:** 166
"Contagiousness of Puerperal Fever, The" (Holmes), **Supp. I Part 1:** 303–304
"Contemplation in a World of Action" (Merton), **Supp. VIII:** 204
"Contemplation of Poussin" (Sarton), **Supp. VIII:** 261
"Contemplations" (Bradstreet), **Retro. Supp. III:** 9–11, 12, 13; **Supp. I Part 1:** 112, 113, 119–122
Contemporaries (Kazin), **Supp. VIII:** 102, **103–104**
Contemporary American Playwrights (Bigsby), **Supp. XV:** 332
Contemporary American Poetry (Poulin, ed.), **Supp. IX:** 272; **Supp. XI:** 259
Contemporary Authors Autobiography, **Supp. XXII:** 225

Contending Forces (Hopkins), **Supp. XVIII:** 284
"Contentment" (Holmes), **Supp. I Part 1:** 307
"Contents" (Halliday), **Supp. XIX:** 92
"Contest, The" (Paley), **Supp. VI:** 223, 230, 231
"Contest for Aaron Gold, The" (P. Roth), **Supp. III Part 2:** 403
Continental Drift (Banks), **Supp. V:** 13–14, 16, 227
Continental Op, The (Hammett), **Supp. IV Part 1:** 344
Continent's End: An Anthology of Contemporary California Poets (Taggard, Sterling, and Rorty, eds.), **Supp. XXII:** 276
Continuing Education, A (Pickering), **Supp. XXI:** 194, 195–196
Continuity of American Poetry, The (Pearce), **Supp. I Part 1:** 111; **Supp. I Part 2:** 475
Continuous Harmony, A: Essays Cultural and Agricultural (Berry), **Supp. X:** 33
Continuous Life, The (Strand), **Supp. IV Part 2:** 630, 631–633
Contoski, Victor, **Supp. XII:** 181
"Contract" (Lardner), **II:** 432
"Contradictions: Tracking Poems" (Rich), **Retro. Supp. III:** 251
"Contraption, The" (Swenson), **Supp. IV Part 2:** 643
"Contrariness of the Mad Farmer, The" (Berry), **Supp. X:** 35
"Contrast, a Spenetic Effusion, The" (J. Schoolcraft), **Supp. XXIII:** 231–232
"Contrition" (Dubus), **Supp. VII:** 84
"Control Burn" (Snyder), **Supp. VIII:** 301
"Control Is the Mainspring" (Komunyakaa), **Supp. XIII:** 122, 124
"Controlling the 'Sloppiness of Things' in Frank Conroy's *Stop-Time*" (Strychacz), **Supp. XVI:** 69–70
Control of Nature, The (McPhee), **Supp. III Part 1:** 310–313
Controversial Sholem Asch, The (Siegel), **Supp. XXIII:** 3
"Conventional Wisdom, The" (Elkin), **Supp. VI:** 52–53
"Convergence" (Ammons), **Supp. VII:** 28
"Convergence of the Twain, The" (Hardy), **Supp. VIII:** 31, 32
Conversation (Aiken), **I:** 54
Conversation at Midnight (Millay), **III:** 138
"Conversation of Eiros and Charmion, The" (Poe), **III:** 412
"Conversation on Conversation" (Stowe), **Supp. I Part 2:** 587
"Conversations in Moscow" (Levertov), **Supp. III Part 1:** 282
Conversations on Some of the Old Poets (J. R. Lowell), **Supp. I Part 1:** 405
Conversations with Albert Murray (Maguire, ed.), **Supp. XIX:** 160–161
Conversations with Byron (Blessington), **Retro. Supp. II:** 58

Conversations with Eudora Welty (Prenshaw, ed.), **Retro. Supp. I:** 339, 340, 341, 342, 343, 352, 354
"Conversations with Helmholtz" (Allen), **Supp. XV:** 15
Conversations with Ishmael Reed (Dick and Singh, eds.), **Supp. X:** 244
Conversations with James Baldwin (Standley and Pratt, eds.), **Retro. Supp. II:** 6
Conversations with Richard Wilbur (Wilbur), **Supp. III Part 2:** 542–543
"Conversation with a Fireman from Brooklyn" (Gallagher), **Supp. XXIV:** 169–170
"Conversation with My Father, A" (Paley), **Supp. VI:** 220
"Conversion of the Jews, The" (P. Roth), **Retro. Supp. II:** 281; **Supp. III Part 2:** 404, 406; **Supp. XXVI:** 119
Convict, The: Stories (Burke), **Supp. XIV:** 25
"Convicta et Combusta" (J. Scott), **Supp. XVII:** 189
"Convolvulus" (Schott), **Supp. XXIII:** 248
"Convoy" (Weigl), **Supp. XIX:** 278
Conway, Jill, **Supp. I Part 1:** 19
Coode, John, **I:** 132
Cook, Bruce, **Supp. XII:** 130, 131, 133–134
Cook, Captain James, **I:** 2
Cook, Eleanor, **Retro. Supp. I:** 311
Cook, Elisha, **Supp. IV Part 1:** 356
Cook, Elizabeth Christine, **II:** 106
Cook, George Cram "Jig", **Supp. XXI:** 5, 6
Cook, Jessie W., **Supp. XXV:** 278
Cook, Johnny, **Supp. XXIV:** 248
Cook, Mercer, **Supp. IV Part 1:** 368
Cook, Richard, **Supp. XXII:** 158
"Cook, The"(Goodman), **Supp. XXVIII:** 93
Cook, Thomas R., **Supp. XXVIII:** 69
Cookbook Collector, The (Goodman), **Supp. XXVI:** 130–131
Cooke, Alistair, **III:** 113, 119, 120
Cooke, Delmar G., **II:** 271
Cooke, Grace MacGowan, **Supp. V:** 285
Cooke, Philip Pendleton, **III:** 420; **Retro. Supp. III:** 227
Cooke, Rose Terry, **II:** 401; **Retro. Supp. II:** 51, 136, 138; **Supp. XIII:** 152
"Cookie" (Taylor), **Supp. V:** 320
"Cookies, The" (Nye), **Supp. XIII:** 281
Cooking of Provincial France, The (M. F. K. Fisher), **Supp. XVII:** 89
Cook-Lynn, Elizabeth, **Supp. IV Part 1:** 325
"Cool Air" (Lovecraft), **Supp. XXV:** 110
Coolbrith, Ina, **I:** 193, 196
Cool Characters: Irony and American Fiction (Konstantinou), **Supp. XXVIII:** 222
"Coole Park" (Yeats), **Supp. VIII:** 155, 159
"Coole Park and Ballylee" (Yeats), **Supp. VIII:** 156
Cooler by the Lake (Heinemann), **Supp. XXII:** 103, **114**

Cooley, John, **Supp. V:** 214
Cooley, Peter, **Supp. XIII:** 76
Coolidge, Calvin, **I:** 498; **II:** 95; **Supp. I Part 2:** 647
Cooling Time: An American Poetry Vigil (Wright), **Supp. XV:** 353
Cool Million, A (West), **III:** 425; **IV:** 287, 288, 297–299, 300; **Retro. Supp. II:** 321, 322–323, 328, **335–337**
"Cool Million, A" (screen story) (West and Ingster), **Retro. Supp. II:** 330
"Cool Tombs" (Sandburg), **III:** 554
Coon, Ross, **IV:** 196
Cooney, Seamus, **Supp. XIV:** 289
"Coon Hunt" (White), **Supp. I Part 2:** 669
Co-op (Sinclair), **Supp. V:** 290
Cooper, Bernard, **Supp. XI:** 129
Cooper, Frederic Taber, **Supp. XX: 219–220; Supp. XXIV:** 28–29
Cooper, Gary, **Supp. IV Part 2:** 524
Cooper, James Fenimore, **I:** 211, 257, **335–357; II:** 74, 277, 295–296, 302, 306, 309, 313, 314; **III:** 51; **IV:** 205, 333; **Retro. Supp. I:** 246; **Retro. Supp. II:** 160; **Supp. I Part 1:** 141, 155, 156, 158, 171, 372; **Supp. I Part 2:** 413, 495, 579, 585, 652, 660; **Supp. IV Part 1:** 80; **Supp. IV Part 2:** 463, 469; **Supp. V:** 209–210; **Supp. VIII:** 189; **Supp. XIV:** 227; **Supp. XVIII:** 4; **Supp. XXIII:** 178
Cooper, Mrs. James Fenimore (Susan A. De Lancey), **I:** 338, 351, 354
Cooper, Jane, **Supp. XV:** 259
Cooper, Rand Richards, **Supp. XVI:** 74
Cooper, Susan Fenimore, **I:** 337, 354
Cooper, William, **I:** 337–338, 351
Cooper, Mrs. William, **I:** 337
Cooperman, Robert, **Supp. XXIII:** 247
Coover, Robert, **Supp. IV Part 1:** 388; **Supp. V: 39–55; Supp. XII:** 152; **Supp. XIV:** 96; **Supp. XVII:** 6; **Supp. XXI:** 236; **Supp. XXII:** 259
Copacetic (Komunyakaa), **Supp. XIII: 116–118,** 126
Cope, Wendy, **Supp. XV:** 117
Copelin, David, **Supp. XXIV:** 264
Copland, Aaron, **II:** 586; **Supp. I Part 1:** 281; **Supp. III Part 2:** 619; **Supp. IV Part 1:** 79, 80–81, 84; **Supp. XXII:** 283; **Supp. XXVI:** 134
Coplas de Don Jorge Manrique (Longfellow, trans.), **II:** 488, 492
Coppée, François Edouard Joachim, **II:** 325
Copperhead, The (Frederic), **II:** 134–135
"Copperhead, The"(Bottoms), **Supp. XXVIII:** 23
Copperhead Cane (J. W. Miller), **Supp. XX: 163, 164, 166–167**
Copper Sun (Cullen), **Supp. IV Part 1:** 167, 168
Coppola, Francis Ford, **Supp. XI:** 171, 172; **Supp. XII:** 75
"Coprinus Comatus: Evening Mushrooms, Morning Ink"(Wakoski), **Supp. XXVIII:** 267
Coprolites (Goldbarth), **Supp. XII: 177–178,** 180, 183

Coquette, The (Foster), **Supp. XXV:** 35, 36, 38–45
Coral and Captive Israel (Reznikoff), **Supp. XIV:** 288
"Coral Ring, The" (Stowe), **Supp. I Part 2:** 586
"Cora Unashamed" (Hughes), **Supp. I Part 1:** 329, 330
"Corazón del Corrido" (Mora), **Supp. XIII:** 225
Corban Ephphata (Li Lin Lee), **Supp. XV:** 225
Corbett, Gentlemen Jim, **II:** 416
Corbett, William, **Supp. XI:** 248; **Supp. XVI:** 286, 295; **Supp. XXIV:** 45
Corbière, Jean Antoine, **II:** 354–355, 528
Cordiall Water, A: A garland of Odd & Old Receipts to Assuage the Ills of Man and Beast (M. F. K. Fisher), **Supp. XVII:** 88, 90
Cording, Robert, **Supp. IX:** 328; **Supp. XII:** 184
Core, George, **Supp. XVIII:** 86; **Supp. XXI:** 193
Corelli, Marie, **III:** 579
Corey, Lewis, **Supp. I Part 2:** 645
"Corinna's Going a-Maying" (Herrick), **Supp. XIV:** 8, 9
"Coriolan" (Eliot), **I:** 580
"Coriolanus and His Mother" (Schwartz), **Supp. II Part 2:** 643, 644–645
"Corkscrew" (Hammett), **Supp. IV Part 1:** 345, 347
Corkum, Gerald, **I:** 37
Corky's Brother (Neugeboren), **Supp. XVI:** 225
"Corky's Brother" (Neugeboren), **Supp. XVI:** 225
Corliss, Richard, **Supp. VIII:** 73; **Supp. XXVII:** 96
Corman, Cid, **Supp. III Part 2:** 624, 625, 626, 627, 628; **Supp. IV Part 1:** 144; **Supp. VIII:** 292; **Supp. XV:** 74, 153; **Supp. XXI:** 23, 27
Corman, Roger, **Supp. XXV:** 154
"Corn" (Lanier), **Supp. I Part 1:** 352, 353, 354, 356–361, 364, 366
Corn, Alfred, **Supp. IX:** 156; **Supp. XV:** 250
Corneille, Pierre, **Supp. I Part 2:** 716; **Supp. IX:** 131
Cornelius, Randy, **Supp. XXVI:** 89
Cornell, Esther, **I:** 231
Cornell, Joseph, **Supp. XXI:** 131; **Supp. XXII:** 167, 168
Cornell, Katherine, **IV:** 356
Cornell, Valerie, **Supp. XX: 94–95**
"Corners" (Dunn), **Supp. XI:** 148
Cornhuskers (Sandburg), **III:** 583–585
"Corn-Planting, The" (Anderson), **I:** 114
"Corn-Pone Opinions" (Twain), **Retro. Supp. III:** 269
"Corn story (or the origin of corn)"(J. Schoolcraft), **Supp. XXIII:** 234–235
Cornucopia: New and Selected Poems, 1975–2002 (Peacock), **Supp. XIX: 203–204**
Corn Village (Le Sueur), **Supp. XXIII:** 167

Coronation Murder-Mystery, The (O'Hara, Ashbery, and Koch), **Supp. XXIII:** 217

"Coroner's Report" (Wrigley), **Supp. XVIII:** 295

"Corporal of Artillery" (Dubus), **Supp. VII:** 84, 85

"Corpse Bird, The" (Rash), **Supp. XXVII:** 219, 228

"Corpse Plant, The" (Rich), **Supp. I Part 2:** 555

Corpus Christi (McNally), **Supp. XIII:** 205–206, 209

Corradi, Juan, **Supp. IV Part 1:** 208

Corrections, The (Franzen), **Supp. XIX:** 54; **Supp. XX:** 83, 84, 85, 90, 91, 91–93, 95

Corregidora (G. Jones), **Supp. XXIV:** 183–184, **185–187,** 190, 193, 194, 195

"Correspondences" (Baudelaire), **I:** 63

"Corrido de Gregorio Cortez" (Mora), **Supp. XIII:** 225

"Corrigenda" (Komunyakaa), **Supp. XIII:** 115, 116

Corrosive Sublimate (Sorrentino), **Supp. XXI:** 226, 228

Corruption City (McCoy), **Supp. XIII:** 175

Corso, Gregory, **Supp. II Part 1:** 30; **Supp. IV Part 1:** 90; **Supp. XII:** 117–138; **Supp. XIV:** 150; **Supp. XVI:** 135; **Supp. XXI:** 53; **Supp. XXIII:** 215

Corsons Inlet (Ammons), **Supp. VII:** 25–26, 28–29, 36

"Corsons Inlet" (Ammons), **Supp. VII:** 25–26

Cortázar, Julio, **Retro. Supp. I:** 278; **Supp. XXII:** 265

"Cortège for Rosenbloom" (Stevens), **IV:** 81

Cortez, Hernando, **III:** 2

" 'Coruscating Glamour': Lynda Hull and the Movies" (Goldstein), **Supp. XXI:** 134

Cory, William Johnson, **Supp. XX:** 230, 231

Coser, Lewis, **Supp. I Part 2:** 650

Cosgrave, Patrick, **Retro. Supp. II:** 185

Cosmic Optimism: A Study of the Interpretation of Evolution by American Poets from Emerson to Robinson (Conner), **Supp. I Part 1:** 73

Cosmogony of the Iroquois Confederacy (Newhouse), **Supp. XXVI:** 87

Cosmological Eye, The (H. Miller), **III:** 174, 184

"Cosmological Eye, The" (H. Miller), **III:** 183

"Cosmos" (Beattie), **Supp. V:** 35

"Cost, The" (Hecht), **Supp. X:** 62–63

Costello, Bonnie, **Retro. Supp. II:** 40

Costello, Mark, **Supp. XXIII:** 290

Costner, Kevin, **Supp. VIII:** 45

"Cost of Living, The" (Malamud), **Supp. I Part 2:** 429, 437

"Costume as Metaphor" (Bronk), **Supp. XXI:** 26

Cott, Jonathan, **Supp. XVI:** 104, 106

"Cottagers' Corner" column (D. West), **Supp. XVIII:** 286

"Cottage Street, 1953" (Wilbur), **Supp. III Part 2:** 543, 561

"Cottagette, The" (Gilman), **Supp. XI:** 207

Cotten, Joseph, **Supp. IV Part 2:** 524

Cotter, Craig, **Supp. XXVIII:** 269, 270

Cotter, James Finn, **Supp. X:** 202

Cotton, John, **Supp. I Part 1:** 98, 101, 110, 111, 116

Cotton, Joseph, **Supp. XII:** 160

Cotton, Seaborn, **Supp. I Part 1:** 101

Cotton Club, The (Major), **Supp. XXII:** 174

"Cotton Club Classics" (Halliday), **Supp. XIX:** 92, 93

Cotton Comes to Harlem (C. Himes), **Supp. XVI:** 143, 144

Cotton Comes to Harlem (film, O. Davis), **Supp. XVI:** 144

"Cotton Song" (Toomer), **Supp. IX:** 312

Couch, W. T., **Supp. X:** 46

Coughlin, Ruth Pollack, **Supp. VIII:** 45

Coulette, Henri, **Supp. V:** 180; **Supp. XIII:** 312; **Supp. XV:** 74, 75

Coultrap-McQuin, Susan, **Supp. XVI:** 85, 92

"Council of State, A" (Dunbar), **Supp. II Part 1:** 211, 213

Count Bruga (Hecht), **Supp. XXV:** 27; **Supp. XXVII:** 89

"Count Dracula" (Allen), **Supp. XV:** 15

"Countee Cullen at 'The Heights' " (Tuttleton), **Supp. IV Part 1:** 166

Counterfeiters, The (Gide), **Supp. IV Part 1:** 80; **Supp. IV Part 2:** 681

"Countering" (Ammons), **Supp. VII:** 28

Counterlife, The (P. Roth), **Retro. Supp. II:** 279, 280, 291; **Supp. III Part 2:** 424–426

Counter-Statement (Burke), **I:** 270–272; **IV:** 431

"Countess, The" (Whittier), **Supp. I Part 2:** 691, 694

Count Frontenac and New France Under Louis XIV (Parkman), **Supp. II Part 2:** 607, 609–610

"Counting Small-Boned Bodies" (R. Bly), **Supp. IV Part 1:** 62

"Counting the Body" (Schott), **Supp. XXIII:** 251–252

"Counting the Children" (Gioia), **Supp. XV:** 122–123

"Counting the Mad" (Justice), **Supp. VII:** 117

"Count Lothar's Heart" (Boyle), **Supp. XXIV:** 58

Count of Monte Cristo, The (Dumas), **III:** 386, 396; **Supp. XVII:** 64, 216

"Countries We Live In, The" (Zach; Everwine, trans.), **Supp. XV:** 87

"Country Boy in Boston, The" (Howells), **II:** 255

Country By-Ways (Jewett), **II:** 402

Country Doctor, A (Jewett), **II:** 391, 392, 396, 404–405; **Retro. Supp. II:** 131, 141, 146

"Country Full of Swedes" (Caldwell), **I:** 297, 309

Country Girl, The (Odets), **Supp. II Part 2:** 546, 547, 548–549

"Country House" (Kumin), **Supp. IV Part 2:** 446

"Country Husband, The" (Cheever), **Supp. I Part 1:** 184, 189

"Country in the Woman, The" (Hurston), **Retro. Supp. III:** 127

"Country Life" (Pickering), **Supp. XXI:** 197

"Country Marriage" (C. Frost), **Supp. XV:** 99

Countrymen of Bones (R. O. Butler), **Supp. XII:** 62, **65–66**

"Country Mouse, The" (Bishop), **Retro. Supp. II:** 37, 38, 51

Country Music: Selected Early Poems (Wright), **Supp. V:** 332, 335, 338, 342

Country of a Thousand Years of Peace, The (Merrill), **Supp. III Part 1:** 321, 322, 331

"Country of Elusion, The" (O. Henry), **Supp. II Part 1:** 407

Country Of Language, The (Sanders), **Supp. XVI:** 277

Country of Marriage, The (Berry), **Supp. X:** 33

Country of Strangers, A (Richter), **Supp. XVIII:** 217

Country of Survivors (Di Piero), **Supp. XIX:** 36

Country of the Pointed Firs, The (Jewett), **II:** 392, 399, 405, 409–411; **Retro. Supp. I:** 6; **Retro. Supp. II:** 134, 136, 139, 140, 141, 145, 146, 147; **Retro. Supp. III:** 22; **Supp. VIII:** 126; **Supp. XIII:** 152; **Supp. XXIII:** 275, 278; **Supp. XXVIII:** 235

"Country Printer, The" (Freneau), **Supp. II Part 1:** 269

"Country Song" (Stallings), **Supp. XXV:** 222, 234

"Country Store and Moment of Grace" (Bottoms), **Supp. XXVIII:** 28

"Country Wife, The" (Gioia), **Supp. XV:** 120

Count Your Bullets (film), **Supp. XVII:** 141

Count Zero (W. Gibson), **Supp. XVI:** 19, **126–127,** 129

Coup, The (Updike), **Retro. Supp. I:** 331, 334, 335

"Coup de Grâce, The" (Bierce), **I:** 202

Couperin, François, **III:** 464

"Couple, The" (Olds), **Supp. X:** 206

"Couple of Hamburgers, A" (Thurber), **Supp. I Part 2:** 616

"Couple of Nuts, A" (Z. Fitzgerald), **Supp. IX:** 58, 71, 72

"Couple of Sad Experiences, A" (Twain), **Retro. Supp. III:** 265

"Couples" (Halliday), **Supp. XIX:** 89

Couples (Updike), **IV:** 214, 215, 216, 217, 227, 229–230; **Retro. Supp. I:** 320, 327, 330; **Supp. XII:** 296

Courlander, harold, **Retro. Supp. III:** 131

Cournos, John, **III:** 465; **Retro. Supp. III:** 85; **Supp. I Part 1:** 258

"Course in Creative Writing, A" (Stafford), **Supp. XI:** 327

"Course of a Particular, The" (Stevens), **Retro. Supp. I:** 312

"Coursier de Jeanne d'Arc, Le" (McCarriston), **Supp. XIV:** 267–268

Courtier, The (Castiglione), **III:** 282

" 'Courtin,' The" (J. R. Lowell), **Supp. I Part 2:** 415

"Courting" (Huddle), **Supp. XXVI:** 151

"Courting of Sister Wisby, The" (Jewett), **Retro. Supp. II:** 134, 135, 146

"Courting the Famous Figures at the Grotto of Improbable Thought" (B. Kelly), **Supp. XVII:** 127–128

Courtney, W. L., **Supp. XXIV:** 29

"Courtship" (Dove), **Supp. IV Part 1:** 248

"Courtship, A"(Thompson), **Supp. XXIII:** 293

"Courtship, Diligence" (Dove), **Supp. IV Part 1:** 248

Courtship of Miles Standish, The (Longfellow), **II:** 489, 502–503; **Retro. Supp. II:** 155, 161–162, 163, 166, 168

"Cousin Aubrey" (Taylor), **Supp. V:** 328

"Cousin Claire" (Andrews), **Supp. XXVI:** 11

Cousine Bette (Balzac), **Retro. Supp. II:** 98

Couturier, Maurice, **Supp. IV Part 1:** 44

Covarrubias, Miguel, **Supp. XVI:** 187

Cove, The (Rash), **Supp. XXVII:** 225–226

"Covered Bridges" (Kingsolver), **Supp. VII:** 203

"Cover Photograph" (Nelson), **Supp. XVIII:** 173

"Cover Stories" (Skloot), **Supp. XX: 195, 207**

"Cover Versions" (Halliday), **Supp. XIX:** 84

Cowan, Lester, **III:** 148

Cowan, Louise, **IV:** 120, 125

Coward, Noel, **Retro. Supp. I:** 65; **Retro. Supp. III:** 171; **Supp. I Part 1:** 332; **Supp. V:** 101; **Supp. XV:** 329; **Supp. XXIV:** 267

"Cowardice" (Theroux), **Supp. VIII:** 313

Cowboy Mouth (Shepard), **Supp. III Part 2:** 441–442

"Cowboys" (Salter). *See* "Dirt" (Salter)

Cowboys (Shepard), **Supp. III Part 2:** 432

Cowboys #2 (Shepard), **Supp. III Part 2:** 437, 438

Cowell, Henry, **Supp. IV Part 1:** 80, 82

Cowen, Philip, **Supp. XX: 2**

Cowen, Wilson Walker, **Supp. IV Part 2:** 435

Cowger, Ashley, **Supp. XXVIII:** 85

Cowie, Alexander, **IV:** 70

"Cow in Apple Time, The" (Frost), **II:** 154; **Retro. Supp. I:** 131

Cowl, Jane, **IV:** 357

Cowley, Abraham, **III:** 508; **IV:** 158; **Supp. I Part 1:** 357

Cowley, Malcolm, **I:** 246, 253, 254, 255, 256, 257, 283, 385; **II:** 26, 57, 94, 456; **III:** 606; **IV:** 123; **Retro. Supp. I:** 73, 91, 97; **Retro. Supp. II:** 77, 83, 89, 221, 330; **Retro. Supp. III:** 48, 75, 79; **Supp. I Part 1:** 174; **Supp. I Part 2:** 609, 610, 620, 647, 654, 678; **Supp. II Part 1:** 103, 135–156; **Supp. VIII:** 96; **Supp. XV:** 142; **Supp. XX: 76; Supp. XXVI:** 17

Cowley, Marguerite Frances Baird (Mrs. Malcolm Cowley), **Supp. I Part 2:** 615; **Supp. II Part 1:** 138, 139

Cowley, Muriel Maurer (Mrs. Malcolm Cowley), **Supp. II Part 1:** 139

Cowley, Susan Cheever (Susan Cheever), **Supp. I Part 1:** 175; **Supp. IX:** 133; **Supp. XXIV:** 97

Cowper, William, **II:** 17, 304; **III:** 508, 511; **Supp. I Part 1:** 150, 151, 152; **Supp. I Part 2:** 539; **Supp. XXVIII:** 169

"Cow Wandering in the Bare Field, The" (Jarrell), **II:** 371, 388

Cox, Martha Heasley, **Supp. IX:** 2, 4, 11–12

Cox, Sidney, **Retro. Supp. I:** 131; **Supp. XXI:** 19, 21

Cox, Stephen, **Supp. IV Part 2:** 523, 524

Cox, Steve, **Supp. XIX:** 116, 128

Coxey, Jacob, **II:** 464

"Coxon Fund, The" (James), **Retro. Supp. I:** 228

"Coy Mistress" (A. Finch), **Supp. XVII:** 72

Coyne, Patricia, **Supp. V:** 123

"Coyote Ortiz: *Canis latrans latrans* in the Poetry of Simon Ortiz" (P. C. Smith), **Supp. IV Part 2:** 509

Coyote's Daylight Trip (Gunn Allen), **Supp. IV Part 1:** 320, 324

Coyote Was Here (Ortiz), **Supp. IV Part 2:** 499

Cozzens, James Gould, **I:** 358–380; **II:** 459

Crabbe, George, **II:** 304; **III:** 469, 508, 511, 521; **Supp. XXIV:** 159

"Crab-Boil" (Dove), **Supp. IV Part 1:** 249

"Cracked Looking-Glass, The" (Porter), **III:** 434, 435, 446

"Cracker Chidlings" (Rawlings), **Supp. X:** 224, 228

Cracks (Purdy), **Supp. VII:** 277–278

Cracks Between What We Are and What We Are Supposed to Be, The (Mullen), **Supp. XXVII:** 175

"Cracks in the Universe" (Davison), **Supp. XXVI:** 78

Crack-Up, The (Fitzgerald), **II:** 80; **III:** 35, 45; **Retro. Supp. I:** 113, 115; **Supp. IX:** 61; **Supp. V:** 276

"Crack-Up, The" (Fitzgerald), **I:** 509; **Retro. Supp. I:** 113, 114

"Crack-up of American Optimism, The: Vachel Lindsay, the Dante of the Fundamentalists" (Viereck), **Supp. I Part 2:** 403

"Cradle and the Bookcase, The"(Hadas), **Supp. XXIII:** 122

"Cradle Me" (Biss), **Supp. XXVI:** 48

Cradle Will Rock, The (Blitzstein), **Supp. I Part 1:** 277, 278

Craft of Fiction, The (Lubbock), **I:** 504; **Supp. VIII:** 165

Craft of Peter Taylor, The (McAlexander, ed.), **Supp. V:** 314

Craig, David M., **Supp. XXII:** 187, 191, 192

Craig, Gordon, **III:** 394; **Supp. XXI:** 6

Craigie, William A., **Retro. Supp. III:** 265

Crain, Jane Larkin, **Supp. V:** 123; **Supp. XII:** 167, 168

Crais, Robert, **Supp. XXI:** 70

Cram, Ralph Adams, **I:** 19

Cramer, Steven, **Supp. XI:** 139; **Supp. XV:** 26

"Cramped Quarters" (Davison), **Supp. XXVI:** 77

"Cranbrook Schools: Adventures in Bourgeois Topologies" (Monson), **Supp. XXIV:** 235

Crandall, Reuben, **Supp. I Part 2:** 686

Crane, Agnes, **I:** 406

Crane, Edmund, **I:** 407

Crane, Frank, **Supp. XXVIII:** 245

Crane, Hart, **I:** 61, 62, 97, 109, 116, 266, **381–404; II:** 133, 215, 306, 368, 371, 536, 542; **III:** 260, 276, 453, 485, 521; **IV:** 122, 123–124, 127, 128, 129, 135, 139, 140, 141, 341, 380, 418, 419; **Retro. Supp. I:** 427; **Retro. Supp. II: 75–91; Retro. Supp. III: 41–55; Supp. I Part 1:** 86; **Supp. II Part 1:** 89, 152; **Supp. III Part 1:** 20, 63, 350; **Supp. IX:** 38, 229, 320; **Supp. V:** 342; **Supp. VIII:** 39; **Supp. X:** 115, 116, 120; **Supp. XI:** 123, 131; **Supp. XII:** 198; **Supp. XIX:** 35; **Supp. XV:** 138; **Supp. XX: 80; Supp. XXI:** 131, 132, 136, 230; **Supp. XXII:** 274; **Supp. XXIII:** 146, 174, 207; **Supp. XXV:** 19; **Supp. XXVI:** 21, 23–24, 25, 28, 143

Crane, Jonathan, Jr., **I:** 407

Crane, Jonathan Townley, **I:** 406

Crane, Mrs. Jonathan Townley, **I:** 406

Crane, Luther, **I:** 406

Crane, Milton, **Supp. XV:** 144

Crane, Nellie, **I:** 407

Crane, R. S., **Supp. I Part 2:** 423

Crane, Stephen, **I:** 34, 169–170, 201, 207, 211, **405–427,** 477, 506, 519; **II:** 58, 144, 198, 262, 263, 264, 276, 289, 290, 291; **III:** 314, 317, 334, 335, 454, 505, 585; **IV:** 207, 208, 256, 350, 475; **Retro. Supp. I:** 231, 325; **Retro. Supp. II:** 97, 123; **Supp. I Part 1:** 314; **Supp. III Part 2:** 412; **Supp. IV Part 1:** 350, 380; **Supp. IV Part 2:** 680, 689, 692; **Supp. IX:** 1, 14; **Supp. VIII:** 98, 105; **Supp. X:** 223; **Supp. XI:** 95; **Supp. XII:** 50; **Supp. XIV:** 21, 50, 51, 227; **Supp. XVII:** 71, 228; **Supp. XVIII:** 74, 75; **Supp. XXIII:** 26

Crane, William, **I:** 407

Cranford (Gaskell), **Supp. IX:** 79

Crash (film, Cronenberg), **Supp. XXVI:** 28

Crashaw, William, **IV:** 145, 150, 151, 165

"Crash Report" (McGrath), **Supp. X:** 116

Crater (Hickam), **Supp. XXVII:** 111
Crater, The (Cooper), **I:** 354, 355
Crater Trueblood and the Lunar Rescue Company (Hickam), **Supp. XXVII:** 111
Cratylus (Plato), **II:** 10
Cravan, Arthur, **Supp. XXII:** 164, 169
"Craven Street Gazette" (Franklin), **II:** 119
"Crawdad, The" (F. Wright), **Supp. XVII:** 244
Crawdad Creek (Sanders), **Supp. XVI:** 269
Crawford, Brad, **Supp. XI:** 133
Crawford, Eva, **I:** 199
Crawford, F. Marion, **III:** 320
Crawford, Joan, **Supp. I Part 1:** 67
Crawford, John E., **Supp. XXIII:** 165
Crawford, Kathleen, **I:** 289
Crawford, Neta C., **Supp. XXVI:** 85
Crawford, Robert, **Retro. Supp. III:** 57
"Crawling Out at Parties" (Bottoms), **Supp. XXVIII:** 25
"Crayon House" (Rukeyser), **Supp. VI:** 273
Crayon Miscellany, The (Irving), **II:** 312–313
Crazed, The (Jin), **Supp. XVIII: 99–100**
"Crazy about her Shrimp" (Simic), **Supp. VIII:** 282
"Crazy Cock" (H. Miller), **III:** 177
Crazy Gypsy (Salinas), **Supp. XIII:** 311, **313–315,** 316
"Crazy Gypsy" (Salinas), **Supp. XIII:** 313–314
Crazy Horse, **Supp. IV Part 2:** 488, 489
Crazy Horse (McMurtry), **Supp. V:** 233
Crazy Horse in Stillness (Heyen), **Supp. XIII:** 344
Crazy Horse: The Strange Man of the Oglaglas (Sandoz), **Supp. XXIV:** 244, 256, **257–258**
"Crazy Hunter, The" (Boyle), **Supp. XXIV: 54–55**
Crazy Hunter, The: Three Short Novels (Boyle), **Supp. XXIV: 54–56**
"Crazy in the Stir" (C. Himes), **Supp. XVI:** 137
Crazy Kill, The (C. Himes), **Supp. XVI:** 143
Crazy Man (Bodenheim), **Supp. XXV:** 22, 24
Creating a Personal Mythology (Wakoski), **Supp. XXVIII:** 261
Creating a Role (Stanislavsky), **Supp. XIV:** 243
"Creation, According to Coyote, The" (Ortiz), **Supp. IV Part 2:** 505
Creation: A Novel (Vidal), **Supp. IV Part 2:** 677, 685, 688
"Creation of Anguish" (Nemerov), **III:** 269
"Creation Story" (Gunn Allen), **Supp. IV Part 1:** 325
"Creative and Cultural Lag" (Ellison), **Retro. Supp. II:** 116; **Supp. II Part 1:** 229; **Supp. XVIII:** 283
Creative Criticism (Spingarn), **I:** 266
"Creative Democracy" (Locke), **Supp. XIV:** 208

Creative Present, The (Balkian and Simmons, eds.), **Supp. XI:** 230
"Creatures" (Gallagher), **Supp. XXIV:** 176, 177
Creatures in an Alphabet (illus. Barnes), **Supp. III Part 1:** 43
"Creatures of the Genitive" (Davison), **Supp. XXVI:** 74
"Credences of Summer" (Stevens), **IV:** 93–94
"Credentials" (Halliday), **Supp. XIX:** 90
"Credo" (Bynner), **Supp. XV:** 50
"Credo" (Du Bois), **Supp. II Part 1:** 169
"Credo" (Jeffers), **Supp. II Part 2:** 424
"Credos and Curios" (Thurber), **Supp. I Part 2:** 606, 613
Creech, James, **Retro. Supp. I:** 254
"Creed for Americans, A" (Benét), **Supp. XI:** 52
"Creed of a Beggar, The" (Lindsay), **Supp. I Part 2:** 379
Creegan, Andy, **Supp. XIX:** 205
Creekmore, Hubert, **II:** 586
Creeley, Robert, **Retro. Supp. I:** 411; **Supp. II Part 1:** 30; **Supp. III Part 1:** 2; **Supp. III Part 2:** 622, 626, 629; **Supp. IV Part 1: 139–161,** 322, 325; **Supp. XI:** 317; **Supp. XIII:** 104, 112; **Supp. XIV:** 150; **Supp. XVI:** 283; **Supp. XXII:** 227; **Supp. XXIV:** 35, 37; **Supp. XXVII:** 18, 22, 160
Creelman, James Ashmore, **Supp. XVI:** 186–187
"Cremona Violin, The" (A. Lowell), **II:** 523
Creole Families of New Orleans (King), **Supp. XXVIII:** 119
"Crêpe de Chine" (Doty), **Supp. XI:** 128
"Crêpes Flambeau" (Gallagher), **Supp. XXIV:** 170
Crescent (Hickam), **Supp. XXVII:** 111
"Cressy" (Harte), **Supp. II Part 1:** 354, 356
"Cretan Woman, The" (Jeffers), **Supp. II Part 2:** 435
Crèvecoeur, Michel-Guillaume Jean de, **I:** 229; **Supp. I Part 1: 227–252**
Crèvecoeur's Eighteenth-Century Travels in Pennsylvania and New York (Adams), **Supp. I Part 1:** 251
Crevel, René, **Supp. XIV:** 343
Crewe-Jones, Florence, **Supp. XVII:** 58
Crewe Train (Macaulay), **Supp. XII:** 88
Crews, Harry, **Supp. X:** 11, 12; **Supp. XI: 99–117,** 245; **Supp. XVIII:** 195; **Supp. XXI:** 35, 38, 40, 44
Crews, James, **Supp. XXIII:** 134–135
Crichton, Michael, **Supp. XIV:** 316
Crick, Philip, **Supp. XVI:** 289
Cricket (C. L. R. James; Grimshaw, ed.), **Supp. XXI:** 172
"Cricket" (C. Miller), **Supp. XXII:** 199
"Crickets" (R. O. Butler), **Supp. XII:** 71
Criers and Kibitzers, Kibitzers and Criers (Elkin), **Supp. VI: 45–46,** 57
Crime and Punishment (Dostoevsky), **II:** 60, 130; **IV:** 484; **Supp. IV Part 2:** 525; **Supp. VIII:** 282; **Supp. XII:** 281; **Supp. XIX:** 276; **Supp. XVII:**

155; **Supp. XVIII:** 278
Crime at Scottsboro, The (Endore), **Supp. XVII:** 59
Crime Beat (Connelly), **Supp. XXI:** 67, 79
Crimes and Misdemeanors (film; Allen), **Supp. XV:** 1, 2, **11,** 12
Crime Without Passion (film), **Supp. XXVII:** 90
"Criminal" (Strout), **Supp. XXIII:** 283, 285
"Crippled Hope, A" (King), **Supp. XXVIII:** 116
Crisis of the Negro Intellectual (Cruse), **Supp. XXVIII:** 71
Crisis papers (Paine), **Supp. I Part 2:** 508–509, 510
"Criteria of Negro Art" (Du Bois), **Supp. II Part 1:** 181; **Supp. XIX:** 66–67
"Critiad, The" (Winters), **Supp. II Part 2:** 794, 799
Critical Anthology A (Untermeyer), **Supp. XV:** 310
Critical Companion to Flannery O'Connor (Kirk), **Retro. Supp. III:** 210
Critical Essays on Charlotte Perkins Gilman (Karpinski, ed.), **Supp. XI:** 201
Critical Essays on Kay Boyle (Elkins, ed.), **Supp. XXIV:** 64
Critical Essays on Peter Taylor (McAlexander), **Supp. V:** 319, 320, 323–324
Critical Essays on Robert Bly (W. V. Davis), **Supp. IV Part 1:** 64, 69
Critical Essays on Wallace Stegner (Arthur), **Supp. IV Part 2:** 606
Critical Fable, A (A. Lowell), **II:** 511–512, 527, 529–530
Critical Guide to Leaves of Grass, A (J. Miller), **IV:** 352
Critical Mass (Paretsky), **Supp. XXV:** 185
Critical Response to Joan Didion, The (Felton), **Supp. IV Part 1:** 210
Critical Temper of Alain Locke, The: A Selection of His Essays on Art and Culture (Stewart, ed.), **Supp. XIV:** 196, **210–211,** 213
"Critic as Artist, The" (Wilde), **Supp. X:** 189
Criticism and Fiction (Howells), **II:** 288
Criticism and Ideology (Eagleton), **Retro. Supp. I:** 67
Criticism in the Borderlands (Calderón and Saldívar, eds.), **Supp. IV Part 2:** 544
"Critics, The" (Jong), **Supp. V:** 119
"Critics and Connoisseurs" (Moore), **III:** 209
Critic's Notebook, A (Howe), **Supp. VI:** 126–128
"Critic's Task, The" (Kazin), **Supp. VIII:** 103
"Critic Who Does Not Exist, The" (Wilson), **IV:** 431
"Critique de la Vie Quotidienne" (Barthelme), **Supp. IV Part 1:** 50
Critique of Pure Reason (Kant), **Supp. XVI:** 184

Croce, Benedetto, **I**: 58, 255, 265, 273, 281; **III**: 610

Crockett, Davy, **II**: 307; **III**: 227; **IV**: 266; **Supp. I Part 2**: 411

"Crocodilopolis" (Cliff), **Supp. XXII**: 76

Crofter and the Laird, The (McPhee), **Supp. III Part 1**: 301–302, 307

Croll, Nora Swan, **Supp. XXVII**: 262

Croly, Herbert, **I**: 229, 231, 235; **IV**: 436

Cromwell, Oliver, **IV**: 145, 146, 156; **Supp. I Part 1**: 111

Cronenberg, David, **Supp. XXI**: 152, 154

Cronin, A. J., **Supp. XVII**: 59

Cronin, Dr. Archibald, **III**: 578

Cronin, Gloria, **Supp. XXVI**: 123

Cronin, Justin, **Supp. X**: 10

Crooke, Dr. Helkiah, **Supp. I Part 1**: 98, 104

Crooked Little Heart (Lamott), **Supp. XX**: 138

Crooker, Barbara, **Supp. XXIII**: **51–66**, 245, 246, 251

Crooks, Alan, **Supp. V**: 226

Crooks, Robert, **Supp. XIII**: 237

"Crop, The" (O'Connor), **Retro. Supp. II**: 223–225

Crosby, Caresse, **I**: 385; **III**: 473; **Retro. Supp. II**: 85; **Supp. XII**: 198

Crosby, Harry, **I**: 385; **Retro. Supp. II**: 85

"Cross" (Hughes), **Supp. I Part 1**: 325; **Supp. XVIII**: 124

Cross, Charles, **Supp. XXIV**: 173

Crossan, John Dominic, **Supp. V**: 251

"Cross Country Snow" (Hemingway), **II**: 249

Cross Creek (Rawlings), **Supp. X**: 223, 226, 228, **231–232**, 233, 234, 235

Cross Creek Cookery (Rawlings), **Supp. X**: 233

"Cross Cut" (Davison), **Supp. XXVI**: 74

"Crossing, The" (Huddle), **Supp. XXVI**: 154

Crossing, The (McCarthy), **Supp. VIII**: 175, **184–186**

"Crossing, The" (Swenson), **Supp. IV Part 2**: 644

"Crossing Brooklyn Ferry" (Whitman), **IV**: 333, 340, 341; **Retro. Supp. I**: 389, 396, 397, 400–401; **Retro. Supp. III**: 304, 308–309; **Supp. XXIII**: 109

"Crossing into Poland" (Babel), **Supp. XIV**: 84

"Crossing New River" (Huddle), **Supp. XXVI**: 148, 150

Crossings (Chuang), **Supp. X**: 291

"Crossings" (Hogan), **Supp. IV Part 1**: 412

"Crossing the Void" (Davison), **Supp. XXVI**: 76

Crossing the Water (Plath), **Retro. Supp. II**: 248; **Supp. I Part 2**: 526, 538

Crossing to Safety (Stegner), **Supp. IV Part 2**: 599, 606, 612, 613–614

"Cross of Snow, The" (Longfellow), **II**: 490; **Retro. Supp. II**: 169–170

"Crossover" (O. Butler), **Supp. XIII**: 61

"Cross-PolliNation" (Gansworth), **Supp. XXVI**: 111

"Cross-Roads, The" (A. Lowell), **II**: 523

"Crossroads of the World Etc." (Merwin), **Supp. III Part 1**: 347, 348

Cross-Section (Seaver), **IV**: 485

Cross the Border, Close the Gap (Fiedler), **Supp. XIII**: 104

Cross Ties (X. J. Kennedy), **Supp. XV**: 165, **166–167**

"Cross Ties" (X. J. Kennedy), **Supp. XV**: 158

Crouch, Stanley, **Supp. XIX**: 158

"Croup" (Karr), **Supp. XI**: 243

Crouse, Russel, **III**: 284

"Crow" (Hogan), **Supp. IV Part 1**: 405

Crow (Hughes), **Supp. XV**: 347, 348

"Crow, The" (Creeley), **Supp. IV Part 1**: 148–149

Crow and the Heart, The (Carruth), **Supp. XVI**: 47–48

"Crowded Countries of the Bomb, The" (Oppen), **Supp. XXVI**: 232

"Crowded Street, The" (Bryant), **Supp. I Part 1**: 168

Crowder, A. B., **Supp. XI**: 107

"Crow Jane" (Baraka), **Supp. II Part 1**: 38

Crow Mercies (Schott), **Supp. XXIII**: **252–254**

"Crow Mercies" (Schott), **Supp. XXIII**: 253

Crowninshield, Frank, **III**: 123; **Supp. IX**: 201

Crown of Columbus (Erdrich and Dorris), **Supp. IV Part 1**: 260

"Crows, The" (Bogan), **Supp. III Part 1**: 50, 51

Crucial Instances (Wharton), **Retro. Supp. I**: 365, 367; **Retro. Supp. III**: 278

Crucible, The (A. Miller), **III**: 147, 148, 155, 156–158, 159, 166; **Retro. Supp. III**: 165, 166, 167, 169; **Supp. XIII**: 206; **Supp. XXV**: 93

"Crucified" (Gibran), **Supp. XX**: 119

"Crucifix in the Filing Cabinet" (Shapiro), **Supp. II Part 2**: 712

"Crude Foyer" (Stevens), **Retro. Supp. I**: 310

"Cruel and Barbarous Treatment" (McCarthy), **II**: 562, 563

"Cruel Mother, The" (B. Kelly), **Supp. XVII**: 126

Cruise of the Dazzler, The (London), **II**: 465

Cruise of the Snark, The (London), **II**: 476–477; **Supp. XXV**: 217

Cruisers, The (Myers), **Supp. XXVII**: 212

"Cruising with the Beach Boys" (Gioia), **Supp. XV**: 118

" 'Crumbling Idols' by Hamlin Garland" (Chopin), **Supp. I Part 1**: 217

"Crusade of the Excelsior, The" (Harte), **Supp. II Part 1**: 336, 354

Cruse, Harold, **Supp. XXVIII**: 71

Crush (Siken), **Supp. XXVIII**: 195, 196–200, 201

"Crusoe in England" (Bishop), **Retro. Supp. II**: 50; **Supp. I Part 1**: 93, 95, 96; **Supp. III Part 1**: 10, 18

Cruz, Angie, **Supp. XXVI**: 263–264

Cruz-Hacker, Alba, **Supp. XXI**: 107

Cry, the Beloved Country (Paton), **Supp. VIII**: 126

Cryer, Dan, **Supp. VIII**: 86, 88; **Supp. XII**: 164

Crying of Lot 49, The (Pynchon), **Supp. II Part 2**: 618, 619, 621, 630–633

"Crying Sisters, The" (Rand), **Supp. IV Part 2**: 524

"Crying Wolf" (C. Frost), **Supp. XV**: 101

"Cry of the Graves, The" (Gibran), **Supp. XX**: **124**

Cryptogram, The (Mamet), **Supp. XIV**: 240, 247, 255

"Crystal, The" (Aiken), **I**: 60

"Crystal, The" (Lanier), **Supp. I Part 1**: 364, 370

"Crystal Cage, The" (Kunitz), **Supp. III Part 1**: 258

Crystal Cup, The (Atherton), **Supp. XXIV**: 26

"Crystal Cup, The" (Teasdale), **Supp. XXVII**: 287

"Crystal Gazer, The" (Teasdale), **Supp. XXVII**: 287, 296

Crystal Vision (Sorrentino), **Supp. XXI**: 235, 236

"Crytal" (Sobin), **Supp. XVI**: 283

Cry to Heaven (Rice), **Supp. VII**: 300–301

"Cuba" (Hemingway), **II**: 258

"Cuba Libre" (Baraka), **Supp. II Part 1**: 33

Cuba: Prophetic Island (W. Frank), **Supp. XX**: **80, 81**

"Cubism, Barcelona" (Hull), **Supp. XXI**: 137

Cudjoe, Selwyn, **Supp. IV Part 1**: 6

"Cudjo's Own Story of the Last American Slaver" (Hurston), **Supp. VI**: 153

Cudlipp, Thelma, **I**: 501

Cudworth, Ralph, **II**: 9, 10

"Cuentista" (Mora), **Supp. XIII**: 224

"Cuento de agua santa, Un" (Mora), **Supp. XIII**: 224

"Cui Bono" (H. Johnson), **Supp. XXVI**: 167, 173

Cujo (King), **Supp. V**: 138–139, 143, 149, 152

Cukor, George, **Supp. XVI**: 192

Cullen, Countee, **Retro. Supp. I**: 207; **Retro. Supp. II**: 114; **Retro. Supp. III**: 127; **Supp. I Part 1**: 49, 325; **Supp. III Part 1**: 73, 75, 76; **Supp. IV Part 1**: **163–174**; **Supp. IX**: 306, 309; **Supp. X**: 136, 140; **Supp. XIII**: 186; **Supp. XIX**: 78; **Supp. XVIII**: 122,131, 185, 279, 280, 282, 284; **Supp. XXII**: 3, 6, 7, 8

"Cultivation of Christmas Trees, The" (Eliot), **I**: 579

Cult of Alien Gods, The: H. P. Lovecraft and Extraterrestrial Pop Culture (Calavito), **Supp. XXV**: 123

"Cult of Personality in American Letters, The" (Swados), **Supp. XIX**: 265

"Cult of the Best, The" (Arnold), **I**: 223

"Cultural Exchange" (Hughes), **Supp. I Part 1**: 341

"Cultural Pluralism: A New American-ism" (Locke), **Supp. XIV:** 195

"Cultural Relativism and Ideological Peace" (Locke), **Supp. XIV:** 202, 212

"Culture" (Emerson), **III:** 2, 4

"Culture, Self, and Style" (Gass), **Supp. VI:** 88

"Culture and Anarchy" (Rich), **Retro. Supp. III:** 249

"Culture and Religion" (Olds), **Supp. X:** 214

Culture of Cities, The (Mumford), **Supp. II Part 2:** 492, 494–495

Cummings, E. E., **I:** 44, 48, 64, 105, 176, **428–450,** 475, 477, 482, 526; **III:** 20, 196, 476; **IV:** 384, 402, 415, 427, 433; **Retro. Supp. II:** 178, 328; **Retro. Supp. III:** 48; **Supp. I Part 2:** 622, 678; **Supp. III Part 1:** 73; **Supp. IV Part 2:** 637, 641; **Supp. IX:** 20; **Supp. XV:** 312, 338; **Supp. XXVI:** 32; **Supp. XXVII:** 261

Cummings, Robert, **Supp. IV Part 2:** 524

Cummins, Ann, **Supp. XXIII:** 280

Cummins, James, **Supp. XVII:** 74

Cunard, Lady, **III:** 459

Cunard, Nancy, **Retro. Supp. III:** 129

Cunningham, Brent, **Supp. XXVII:** 153

Cunningham, J. V., **Supp. XV:** 169

Cunningham, Merce, **Supp. IV Part 1:** 83; **Supp. XV:** 187

Cunningham, Michael, **Supp. XII:** 80; **Supp. XV:** 55–71

Cunningham, Rodger, **Supp. XXIII:** 38–39

Cup of Gold (Steinbeck), **IV:** 51, 53, 61–64, 67

"Cupola, The" (Bogan), **Supp. III Part 1:** 53

"Curandera" (Mora), **Supp. XIII:** 214, 222

Curé de Tours, Le (Balzac), **I:** 509

Cure for Dreams, A: A Novel (Gibbons), **Supp. X:** 45–47, 48, 50

Curie, Marie, **IV:** 420, 421; **Supp. I Part 2:** 569

Curie, Pierre, **IV:** 420

Curiosa Americana (Mather), **Supp. II Part 2:** 463

Curiosities (Matthews), **Supp. IX:** 151, 152

"Curious Case of Sidd Finch, The" (Plimpton), **Supp. XVI:** 244

"Curious Shifts of the Poor" (Dreiser), **Retro. Supp. II:** 97

"Current" (Espaillat), **Supp. XXI:** 106

"Currents and Counter-Currents in Medical Science" (Holmes), **Supp. I Part 1:** 305

"Curried Cow" (Bierce), **I:** 200

Curry, Professor W. C., **IV:** 122

Curse of Downers Grove, The (film), **Supp. XXVII:** 80

Curse of the Jade Scorpion, The (film; Allen), **Supp. XV:** 11

Curse of the Starving Class (Shepard), **Supp. III Part 2:** 433, 447–448

Curse of the Werewolf, The (film), **Supp. XVII:** 56

"Curse of Yig, The" (Lovecraft and Bishop), **Supp. XXV:** 122

"Curse on a Thief, A" (X. J. Kennedy), **Supp. XV:** 171

"Curtain, The" (Chandler), **Supp. IV Part 1:** 122

Curtain Calls: British and American Women and the Theater, 1660–1820 (Saar), **Supp. XV:** 237

Curtain of Green, A (Welty), **IV:** 261–264, 268, 283

"Curtain of Green, A" (Welty), **IV:** 263–264

Curtain of Green and Other Stories, A (Welty), **Retro. Supp. I:** 343, 344, 345, 346, 347, 355

Curtain of Trees (opera), **Supp. IV Part 2:** 552

"Curtain Raiser, A" (Stein), **IV:** 43, 44

"Curtains" (Cisneros), **Supp. VII:** 66

Curtin, John, **Supp. IX:** 184

Curtis, George William, **Supp. I Part 1:** 307; **Supp. XVIII:** 3, 14

Curve (Goldbarth), **Supp. XII:** 181

Curve of Binding Energy, The (McPhee), **Supp. III Part 1:** 301

Curzon, Mary, **III:** 52

Cushing, Caleb, **Supp. I Part 2:** 684, 686

Cushman, Howard, **Supp. I Part 2:** 652

Cushman, Stephen, **Retro. Supp. I:** 430

Cusick, Albert, **Supp. XXVI:** 87

"Custard Heart, The" (Parker), **Supp. IX:** 201

Custer, General George, **I:** 489, 491

Custer Died for Your Sins (Deloria), **Supp. IV Part 1:** 323; **Supp. IV Part 2:** 504

"Custody"(Schott), **Supp. XXIII:** 241

"Customer, The"(Goodman), **Supp. XXVIII:** 92–93

"Custom House, The" (Hawthorne), **II:** 223; **Retro. Supp. I:** 147–148, 157; **Retro. Supp. III:** 116; **Supp. XXI:** 181

Custom of the Country, The (Wharton), **IV:** 318; **Retro. Supp. I:** 374, **375–376; Retro. Supp. III:** 284–285; **Supp. XXIV:** 23

"Cut" (Plath), **Retro. Supp. II:** 253

"Cut-Glass Bowl, The" (Fitzgerald), **II:** 88

Cutting, Bronson, **III:** 600

Cutting Lisa (Everett), **Supp. XVIII: 56**

"Cuttings, *later*" (Roethke), **III:** 532

"Cyberpunk" (Bethke), **Supp. XVI:** 121

Cyberspace trilogy (W. Gibson). *See* Sprawl trilogy (W. Gibson)

"Cyborg Manifesto"(Haraway), **Supp. XXVIII:** 220

"Cycles, The" (Pinsky), **Supp. VI:** 250–252

Cyclopedia of American Literature (Duyckinck and Duyckinck), **Supp. XXV:** 250

Cynic's Word Book, The (Bierce), **I:** 197, 205, 208, 209, 210

Cynthia Ozick (Lowin), **Supp. V:** 273

Cynthia Ozick's Comic Art (Cohen), **Supp. V:** 273

Cynthia Ozick's Fiction (Kauvar), **Supp. V:** 273

"Czar's Soliloquy, The" (Twain), **Retro. Supp. III:** 269

"Czeslaw Milosz and Memory" (Hampl), **Supp. XXII:** 92

D

Da Capo: Best Music Writing 2002 (Lethem, ed.), **Supp. XVIII:** 148

Dacey, Philip, **Supp. IV Part 1:** 70

Dacier, André, **II:** 10

"Dad" (Cullen), **Supp. IV Part 1:** 167

"Daddy" (Plath), **Retro. Supp. II:** 250–251; **Supp. I Part 2:** 529, 542, 545, 546; **Supp. II Part 2:** 688; **Supp. XXII:** 30; **Supp. XXIII:** 112, 113

Daddy Do-Funny's Wisdom Jingles (Stuart; Clements, ill.), **Supp. XXVIII:** 230, 237

"Daddy"(Hadas), **Supp. XXIII:** 112, 113

Daddy's Little Boy (Collins), **Supp. XXI:** 54

"Daemon, The" (Bogan), **Supp. III Part 1:** 58, 61

"Daemon Lover, The" (Jackson), **Supp. IX:** 116–117

"Daffodils" (Nelson and Espeland), **Supp. XVIII:** 181

"Daffodils" (Wordsworth), **Supp. XIII:** 284

"Daffy Duck in Hollywood" (Ashbery), **Supp. III Part 1:** 18

D'Agata, John, **Supp. XII:** 97, 98

"Dagon" (Lovecraft), **Supp. XXV:** 111, 121

Dago Red (Fante), **Supp. XI:** 160, 169

Dahl, Roald, **Supp. IX:** 114

Dahlberg, Edward, **I:** 231; **Retro. Supp. I:** 426; **Supp. III Part 2:** 624; **Supp. XIV:** 148; **Supp. XVIII:** 148; **Supp. XXII:** 257

Dahlberg, R'lene, **Supp. XIV:** 148

Daiches, David, **Retro. Supp. II:** 243; **Supp. I Part 2:** 536

Daily Horoscope (Gioia), **Supp. XV:** 112, **118–121,** 126

"Daily Horoscope" (Gioia), **Supp. XV:** 119

Daily Modernism (Podnieks), **Supp. X:** 189

Dain Curse, The (Hammett), **Supp. IV Part 1:** 348

"Daisies" (Glück), **Supp. V:** 88

"Daisy" (Oates), **Supp. II Part 2:** 523

Daisy (S. and A. Warner), **Supp. XVIII:** 268

Daisy-Head Mayzie (Geisel), **Supp. XVI:** 112

Daisy Miller (H. James), **Retro. Supp. I:** 216, 220, 222, 223, 228, 231; **Supp. XVIII:** 165; **Supp. XXIV:** 23

"Daisy Miller" (H. James), **II:** 325, 326, 327, 329; **IV:** 316

"Dakota (IV)" (Gansworth), **Supp. XXVI:** 111

Dale, Charlie, **Supp. IV Part 2:** 584

Daley, Yvonne, **Supp. XXII:** 216

Dali, Salvador, **II:** 586; **Supp. IV Part 1:** 83; **Supp. XIII:** 317
Dalibard, Thomas-François, **II:** 117
"Dallas-Fort Worth: Redband and Mistletoe" (Clampitt), **Supp. IX:** 45
"Dalliance of Eagles, The" (Whitman), **IV:** 348
Dalva (Harrison), **Supp. VIII:** 37, 45, 46, **48–49**
Daly, Carroll John, **Supp. IV Part 1:** 343, 345
Daly, John, **II:** 25, 26
Daly, Julia Brown, **II:** 25, 26
"Dalyrimple Goes Wrong" (Fitzgerald), **II:** 88
"Dam, The" (Rukeyser), **Supp. VI:** 283
Damas, Leon, **Supp. X:** 139
Damascus Gate (Stone), **Supp. V:** 308–311
Damballah (Wideman), **Supp. X:** 319, 320, 321, 322, 323, 326, 327, 331, 333–334
Dame de Saint Hermine, La (King), **Supp. XXVIII:** 119–120, 123
Dameshek, Brandon, **Supp. XIX:** 273, 277, 287
Damnation of Theron Ware, The (Frederic), **II:** 140–143, 144, 146, 147; **Retro. Supp. I:** 325
"Damned Agitator, The"(Gold), **Supp. XXVIII:** 72, 73
Damned Agitator and Other Stories, The (Gold), **Supp. XXVIII:** 72–73
Damned If I Do (Everett), **Supp. XVIII:** 66
"Damned Thing, The" (Bierce), **I:** 206
Damon, Matt, **Supp. VIII:** 175
Damon, S. Foster, **I:** 26; **II:** 512, 514, 515
"Damon and Vandalia" (Dove), **Supp. IV Part 1:** 252
Dana, H. W. L., **I:** 225
Dana, Richard Henry, Jr., **III:** 81; **Retro. Supp. III:** 150; **Supp. XX:** 227; **Supp. XXV:** 208
Dana, Richard Henry, Sr., **I:** 339, 351; **Supp. I Part 1:** 103, 154, 155; **Supp. I Part 2:** 414, 420; **Supp. XXV:** 250
Dana, Robert, **Supp. V:** 178, 180
"Dana Gioia and Fine Press Printing" (Peich), **Supp. XV:** 117
"Dance" (Kenny), **Supp. XXIII:** 148
"Dance, The" (Crane), **I:** 109
"Dance, The" (Roethke), **III:** 541
"Dance, The" (W. C. Williams), **Supp. XVII:** 113
"Dance, The"(Longstreet), **Supp. XXVIII:** 231
Dance and the Railroad, The (Hwang), **Supp. XXI:** 145, 146
"Dance in a Buffalo Skull" (Zitkala-Ša), **Supp. XXV:** 276
"Dance Me to the End of Love" (Cohen), **Supp. XXVII:** 61
Dance of Death, The (Auden), **Supp. II Part 1:** 10
Dance of Death, The (Bierce and Harcourt), **I:** 196
Dance of Life, The (Ellis), **Supp. XX:** 117

Dance of the Happy Shades (Munro), **Supp. XXVII:** 181, 182, 194
Dance of the Sleepwalkers (Calabria), **Supp. XIII:** 164
"Dance of the Solids, The" (Updike), **Retro. Supp. I:** 323
"Dancer" (Hoffman), **Supp. XVIII:** 86
Dancer (Myers), **Supp. XXVII:** 200
"Dancer, The" (Swados), **Supp. XIX:** 261, 263–264
Dancers, The (Myers), **Supp. XXVII:** 211
"Dancers Work by Forgetting" (Espaillat), **Supp. XXI:** 102
"Dances of Madness" (Schott), **Supp. XXIII:** 245
Dances with Wolves (film), **Supp. X:** 124
Dance to the Music of Time, A (Powell), **Supp. XVIII:** 146
Dancing After Hours (Dubus), **Supp. VII:** 91
Dancing Back Strong the Nation (Kenny), **Supp. XXIII:** 144, **148**
Dancing Bears, The (Merwin), **Supp. III Part 1:** 343–344
"Dancing"(Goodman), **Supp. XXVIII:** 94
"Dancing Mind, The" (speech, Morrison), **Retro. Supp. III:** 184
Dancing on the Grave of a Son of a Bitch (Wakoski), **Supp. XXVIII:** 265–266
Dancing on the Stones (Nichols), **Supp. XIII:** 256, 257, 259, 267, 269
"Dancing the Jig" (Sexton), **Supp. II Part 2:** 692
"Dancing with My Father"(Wakoski), **Supp. XXVIII:** 272
Dandelion Wine (Bradbury), **Supp. IV Part 1:** 101, 109–110
Dandurand, Karen, **Retro. Supp. I:** 30
"Dandy Frightening the Squatter, The" (Twain), **IV:** 193–194; **Retro. Supp. III:** 256, 259
Dangel, Mary Jo, **Supp. XVIII:** 156
Dangerous Crossroads (film), **Supp. XIII:** 163
Dangerous Day (Rinehart), **Supp. XXV:** 195
Dangerous Moonlight (Purdy), **Supp. VII:** 278
"Dangerous Road Before Martin Luther King" (Baldwin), **Supp. I Part 1:** 52
"Dangerous Summer, The" (Hemingway), **II:** 261
Dangerous Thoughts (Ryan as Quin), **Supp. XVIII:** 226
"Dangers of Authorship, The" (Blackmur), **Supp. II Part 1:** 147
Dangling Man (Bellow), **I:** 144, 145, 147, 148, 150–151, 153–154, 158, 160, 161, 162, 163; **Retro. Supp. II:** 19, 20–21, 22, 23; **Supp. VIII:** 234; **Supp. XIX:** 157
"Dang Little Squirt" (Bontemps), **Supp. XXII:** 4
Daniel (biblical book), **Supp. I Part 1:** 105
Daniel (film), **Supp. IV Part 1:** 236
Daniel, Arnaut, **III:** 467
Daniel, Robert W., **III:** 76

Daniel, Samuel, **Supp. I Part 1:** 369
Daniel Deronda (G. Eliot), **I:** 458
Daniels, Frank, **Supp. XXII:** 196
Daniels, Kate, **Supp. XVII:** 112
Danielson, Linda, **Supp. IV Part 2:** 569
"Dani"(Goodman), **Supp. XXVIII:** 89, 91
D'Annunzio, Gabriele, **II:** 515
Danny and the Deep Blue Sea: An Apache Dance (Shanley), **Supp. XIV:** 315, **318–319,** 320, 321, 323, 324
Danny O'Neill pentalogy (Farrell), **II:** 35–41
Danse Macabre (King), **Supp. IV Part 1:** 102; **Supp. V:** 144; **Supp. XXV:** 123
"Danse Russe" (W. C. Williams), **IV:** 412–413
"Dans le Restaurant" (Eliot), **I:** 554, 578
Dans l'ombre des cathédrales (Ambelain), **Supp. I Part 1:** 273
Dante Alighieri, **I:** 103, 136, 138, 250, 384, 433, 445; **II:** 8, 274, 278, 289, 490, 492, 493, 494, 495, 504, 508, 524, 552; **III:** 13, 77, 124, 182, 259, 278, 448, 453, 467, 533, 607, 609, 610–612, 613; **IV:** 50, 134, 137, 138, 139, 247, 437, 438; **Retro. Supp. I:** 62, 63, 64, 66, 360; **Retro. Supp. II:** 330; **Supp. I Part 1:** 256, 363; **Supp. I Part 2:** 422, 454; **Supp. III Part 2:** 611, 618, 621; **Supp. IV Part 2:** 634; **Supp. V:** 277, 283, 331, 338, 345; **Supp. VIII:** 27, 219–221; **Supp. X:** 120, 121, 125; **Supp. XII:** 98; **Supp. XV:** 254; **Supp. XVII:** 227, 241
Danvis Tales: Selected Stories (Robinson; Budbill, ed.), **Supp. XIX:** 6
Danziger, Adolphe, **I:** 199–200
Danziger, Jeff, **Supp. XXII:** 208
Dar (Nabokov), **III:** 246, 255
Darçan: Seeing the Divine Image in India (Eck), **Supp. XXVIII:** 52–53, 54, 58
D'Arcy, Randall, **Supp. XVII:** 76
Dardis, Tom, **Supp. XVIII:** 249
Dare, Philip, **Supp. XXVIII:** 62
"Dare's Gift" (Glasgow), **II:** 190
Darius & Twig (Myers), **Supp. XXVII:** 205
Dark and Feeling, The: Black American Writers and Their Work (Major), **Supp. XXII:** 180
Dark Angel, The (Bolton), **Supp. I Part 1:** 281
"Dark Angel Travels With Us to Canada and Blesses Our Vacation, The" (Dunn), **Supp. XI:** 146
Dark at the Top of the Stairs, The (film), **Supp. XXV:** 102
Dark at the Top of the Stairs, The (Inge), **Supp. XXV:** 93, 95, 100–102
Dark Barbarian, The (Howard, Herron ed.), **Supp. XXVII:** 118, 128
Dark Carnival (Bradbury), **Supp. IV Part 1:** 102
Darker (Strand), **Supp. IV Part 2:** 619, 626–628
Darker Face of the Earth, The (Dove), **Supp. IV Part 1:** 255–257

Dark Fields of the Republic: Poems 1991–1995 (Rich), **Retro. Supp. III:** 250, 252

"Dark Fire" (Hadas), **Supp. XXIII:** 126

Dark Green, Bright Red (Vidal), **Supp. IV Part 2:** 677

Dark Half, The (King), **Supp. V:** 141

Dark Harbor: A Poem (Strand), **Supp. IV Part 2:** 633–634

"Dark Hills, The" (Robinson), **III:** 523

Dark Horses (X. J. Kennedy), **Supp. XV: 167–170**

Dark Hours, The (W. V. Davis), **Supp. XXI: 91–92,** 93

"Dark Houses" (Davison), **Supp. XXVI:** 72

Dark Laughter (Anderson), **I:** 111, 116; **II:** 250–251

"Darkling Alphabet, A" (Snodgrass), **Supp. VI:** 323

Darkling Child (Merwin and Milroy), **Supp. III Part 1:** 346

"Darkling Summer, Ominous Dusk, Rumorous Rain" (Schwartz), **Supp. II Part 2:** 661

"Darkling Thrush" (Hardy), **Supp. IX:** 40

"Dark Man, The" (Howard), **Supp. XXVII:** 123

"Dark Men, The" (Dubus), **Supp. VII:** 86

Dark Mirrors (Sobin), **Supp. XVI:** 295

Dark Mother, The (W. Frank), **Supp. XX: 70–71**

Dark Mountains, The (Hoffman), **Supp. XVIII: 76–77**

Darkness and the Light, The (Hecht), **Supp. X:** 58

Darkness at Noon (Koestler), **Supp. XXIII:** 1

Darkness More Than Night, A (Connelly), **Supp. XXI: 73–74,** 80

"Darkness on the Edge of Town" (O'Brien), **Supp. V:** 246

Darkness Surrounding Us, The (Sorrentino), **Supp. XXI:** 227, 228

Darkness under the Trees/Walking behind the Spanish (Salinas), **Supp. XIII:** 311, **319–324**

"Dark Night" (St. John of the Cross), **Supp. XV:** 30

Dark Night of the Soul, The (St. John of the Cross), **I:** 1, 585

Dark of the Moon (Teasdale), **Supp. XXVII:** 284, 286, 295–296

"Dark Ones" (Dickey), **Supp. IV Part 1:** 182

Dark Power (Holding), **Supp. XXII: 122–123,** 124

Dark Princess: A Romance (Du Bois), **Supp. II Part 1:** 179, 181–182

Dark Room, The (T. Williams), **IV:** 381

Dark Sacred Night (CD), **Supp. XXI:** 75

Dark Shadows (television show), **Supp. XIX:** 57

"Dark Summer" (Bogan), **Supp. III Part 1:** 51, 53

Dark Summer: Poems (Bogan), **Supp. III Part 1:** 52–53, 57

"Dark Tower, The" (column), **Supp. IV Part 1:** 168, 170

Dark Tower, The: The Gunslinger (King), **Supp. V:** 152

Dark Tower IV, The: Wizard and Glass (King), **Supp. V:** 139

Dark Tunnel, The (Macdonald as Millar), **Supp. IV Part 2:** 465, 466

"Dark TV Screen" (Simic), **Supp. VIII:** 282

Dark Valley Destiny (Sprague de Camp), **Supp. XXVII:** 115, 128

"Dark Voyage, The" (McLay), **Supp. XIII:** 21

"Dark Walk, The" (Taylor), **Supp. V:** 320–321, 322, 326

Darkwater: Voices from Within the Veil (Du Bois), **Supp. II Part 1:** 178, 180, 183

Dark Waves and Light Matter (Goldbarth), **Supp. XII:** 176, 193

Dark World (Carruth), **Supp. XVI:** 55

"Darling" (Nye), **Supp. XIII:** 283–284

"Darling, The" (Chekhov), **Supp. IX:** 202

Darling-Darling (Barillet and Grédy; Loos, trans.), **Supp. XVI:** 194

Darnell, Linda, **Supp. XII:** 173

Darragh, Tina, **Supp. IV Part 2:** 427

Darreu, Robert Donaldson, **Supp. II Part 1:** 89, 98, 102

Darrow, Clarence, **Supp. I Part 1:** 5; **Supp. I Part 2:** 455; **Supp. XXVII:** 88

Dartmouth, Earl of, **Supp. XX: 284**

Darwin, Charles, **I:** 457; **II:** 323, 462, 481; **III:** 226, 231; **IV:** 69, 304; **Retro. Supp. I:** 254; **Retro. Supp. II:** 60, 65; **Supp. I Part 1:** 368; **Supp. IX:** 180; **Supp. XI:** 203; **Supp. XVI:** 13; **Supp. XX: 18; Supp. XXVII:** 34, 126

"Darwin in 1881" (Schnackenberg), **Supp. XV:** 253, 254, 258

Daryush, Elizabeth, **Supp. V:** 180

Dasburg, Andrew, **Supp. XXI:** 6

Dash, Julie, **Supp. XI:** 17, 18, 20

Dash, Robert, **Supp. XXVII:** 23

Dashell, Alfred, **Supp. X:** 224

"DAS KAPITAL" (Baraka), **Supp. II Part 1:** 55

"\[Date, 1601.\] Conversation, as it Was by the Social Fireside, in the Time of the Tudors" (Twain), **Retro. Supp. III:** 262

Datlow, Ellen, **Supp. XVI:** 123

"Datum Centurio" (Wallace), **Supp. X:** 309

Daudet, Alphonse, **II:** 325, 338

Daugher of Earth (Smedley), **Supp. XXVIII: 77–78**

"Daughter" (Caldwell), **I:** 309

"Daughter in the House" (X. J. Kennedy), **Supp. XV:** 160

Daughter of Earth (Smedly), **Supp. XIII:** 295

"Daughter of Erlik Khan, The" (Howard), **Supp. XXVII:** 121

Daughter of the Land, A (Stratton-Porter), **Supp. XX: 222**

Daughter of the Snows, A (London), **II:** 465, 469–470

Daughter of the Vine, A (Atherton), **Supp. XXIV:** 18, 22

"Daughters" (Anderson), **I:** 114

Daughters (Marshall), **Supp. XI:** 275, 276, 277, **286–288,** 289, 290

"Daughters, 1900" (Nelson), **Supp. XVIII:** 175

Daughters, I Love You (Hogan), **Supp. IV Part 1:** 397, 399, 401

"Daughter's Fever, A" (Bottoms), **Supp. XXVIII:** 28

"Daughters of Invention" (Alvarez), **Supp. VII:** 9

Daughters of the Dust (Dash; film), **Supp. XI:** 17, 18; **Supp. XX: 154**

Daughters of Valor: Contemporary Jewish American Women Writers (Halio and Siegel, eds.), **Supp. XXVI:** 123

Daumier, Honoré, **IV:** 412

Dave, R. A., **Supp. VIII:** 126

Davenport, Abraham, **Supp. I Part 2:** 699

Davenport, Basil, **Supp. XXV:** 27

Davenport, Gary, **Supp. IX:** 98

Davenport, Guy, **Supp. XIV:** 96; **Supp. XXI:** 235

Davenport, Herbert J., **Supp. I Part 2:** 642

Davenport, James, **I:** 546

Daves, E. G., **Supp. I Part 1:** 369

Davey, Frank, **Supp. XIII:** 33

"David" (Garrett), **Supp. VII:** 109–110

"David" (Gordon), **Supp. IV Part 1:** 298–299

David, Gray, **Supp. XX: 260**

"David and Agnes, a Romance" (Keillor), **Supp. XVI:** 175

David Blaize (Benson), **Supp. XX: 234**

David Copperfield (Dickens), **I:** 458; **II:** 290; **Retro. Supp. I:** 33; **Supp. XVI:** 65, 72; **Supp. XX: 234**

"David Crockett's Other Life" (Nye), **Supp. XIII:** 282

Davideis (Cowley), **IV:** 158

David Harum (Westcott), **I:** 216

David Huddle Reader, A: Selected Prose and Poetry (Huddle), **Supp. XXVI:** 160

"David Lynch Keeps His Head" (Wallace), **Supp. X:** 314

David Show, The (Gurney), **Supp. V:** 97

"David's Lamentation for Saul and Jonathan" (Bradstreet), **Retro. Supp. III:** 4

Davidson, Cathy, **Supp. XV:** 238

Davidson, Donald, **I:** 294; **III:** 495, 496; **IV:** 121, 122, 124, 125, 236; **Supp. II Part 1:** 139; **Supp. XIV:** 2; **Supp. XX: 164**

Davidson, James West, **Supp. XXII:** 218

Davidson, Jo, **Supp. XXI:** 7

Davidson, John, **Retro. Supp. I:** 55

Davidson, Michael, **Supp. VIII:** 290, 293, 294, 302–303; **Supp. XXVI:** 224

Davidson, Peter, **Supp. XXVIII:** 197

Davidson, Phebe, **Supp. XXIII:** 252

Davidson, Sara, **Supp. IV Part 1:** 196, 198, 203

Davidson, Sue, **Supp. XIX:** 260

Davidsz de Heem, Jan, **Supp. XI:** 133

Davie, Donald, **III:** 478; **Supp. IV Part 2:** 474; **Supp. V:** 331; **Supp. X:** 55, 59; **Supp. XVII:** 111, 112, 121

Davies, Arthur, **III:** 273

Davies, Sir John, **III:** 541

Davies, Marion, **Supp. XVI:** 186

Da Vinci, Leonardo, **I:** 274; **II:** 536; **III:** 210

Da Vinci Code, The (Brown), **Supp. XXVII:** 5

Davis, Allen F., **Supp. I Part 1:** 1, 7

Davis, Allison, **Supp. I Part 1:** 327

Davis, Angela, **Retro. Supp. III:** 184; **Supp. I Part 1:** 66; **Supp. X:** 249; **Supp. XXVI:** 50

Davis, Arthur B., **Supp. XVIII:** 119

Davis, Bette, **I:** 78; **Supp. I Part 1:** 67

Davis, Bill, **Supp. XIII:** 267

Davis, Christina, **Supp. XV:** 264

Davis, Cynthia, **Supp. XVIII:** 281, 286

Davis, Donald, **Supp. XIII:** 93

Davis, Elizabeth Gould, **Supp. I Part 2:** 567

Davis, George, **II:** 586

Davis, Glover, **Supp. V:** 180, 182, 186

Davis, Jefferson, **II:** 206; **IV:** 122, 125, 126

Davis, Jordan, **Supp. XV:** 178, 181, 186, 188

Davis, Katie, **Supp. VIII:** 83

Davis, L. J., **Supp. XI:** 234

Davis, Lydia, **Supp. XII:** 24; **Supp. XVII:** 21

Davis, Marcia, **Supp. XVIII:** 91, 100

Davis, Mary H., **Supp. XVIII:** 77

Davis, Miles, **Supp. XV:** 346; **Supp. XXII:** 172

Davis, Mollie Moore, **Supp. XXVIII:** 227

Davis, Ossie, Jr., **Supp. IV Part 1:** 362; **Supp. XVI:** 144

Davis, Rebecca Harding, **Supp. I Part 1:** 45; **Supp. XIII:** 292, 295, 305; **Supp. XVI:** **79–96**

Davis, Richard Harding, **III:** 328; **Supp. II Part 1:** 393; **Supp. XVI:** 85

Davis, Robert Gorham, **II:** 51; **IV:** 108

Davis, Stuart, **IV:** 409; **Supp. XV:** 295; **Supp. XXI:** 6

Davis, Thadious, **Supp. XVIII:** 120, 121, 123, 127, 129

Davis, Thulani, **Supp. XI:** 179; **Supp. XIII:** 233, 234, 239

Davis, William Virgil, **Supp. IV Part 1:** 63, 64, 68, 69, 70; **Supp. XXI:** **83–96**

Davison, Jane, **Supp. XXVI:** 64, 65

Davison, Peter, **Supp. XXI:** 91; **Supp. XXVI:** **61–80**

Davy's Lake (M. Finch), **Supp. XVII:** 69

Dawn (Dreiser), **I:** 498, 499, 503, 509, 515, 519

Dawn (O. Butler), **Supp. XIII:** 63, **64**

"Dawnbreaker" (Hayden), **Supp. II Part 1:** 370

Dawn in Russia (W. Frank), **Supp. XX:** 76

Dawn Patrol, The (film), **Supp. XIV:** 81

"Dawn Patrol: A Review of the Literature of the Negro for 1948" (Locke), **Supp. XIV:** 211

Dawson, Edward, **IV:** 151

Dawson, Emma, **I:** 199

Dawson, Melanie, **Supp. XXIV:** 25, 31

Dawson, Ruth, **Supp. XI:** 120

Day, Dorothy, **II:** 215; **Supp. I Part 2:** 524; **Supp. X:** 142; **Supp. XXV:** 19, 30; **Supp. XXVIII:** 79

Day, Douglas, **Retro. Supp. III:** 77

Day, Fred Holland, **Supp. XX:** **114, 115**

Day, Georgiana, **Supp. I Part 2:** 585

Day, Richard, **Supp. XVIII:** 251

"Day After Day of the Dead" (Mackey), **Supp. XXVII:** 156

Dayan, Joan, **Retro. Supp. II:** 270

"Day and Night" (Teasdale), **Supp. XXVII:** 293

"Day Book" (Notley), **Supp. XXII:** 230

Day Book, A (Creeley), **Supp. IV Part 1:** 155

"Daybreak" (Kinnell), **Supp. III Part 1:** 250

"Daybreak Blues" (Kees), **Supp. XV:** 133

"Day-Breakers, The" (Bontemps), **Supp. XXII:** 8

"Daybreak in Alabama" (Hughes), **Retro. Supp. I:** 211; **Supp. I Part 1:** 344

Day by Day (R. Lowell), **Retro. Supp. II:** 184, 186, 191

"Day-Care Field Trip: Aquarium" (Karr), **Supp. XI:** 243

"Day-Dream, A" (Bryant), **Supp. I Part 1:** 160

"Day-Dream of a Grocer, The" (Twain), **Supp. XVIII:** 9

"Day for Poetry and Song, A" (Douglass), **Supp. III Part 1:** 172

"Day in the Life of Half of Rumpelstiltskin, A" (Brockmeier), **Supp. XXII:** 50, 52, 53

"Day Lady Died, The" (O'Hara), **Supp. XIX:** 85; **Supp. XXIII:** 216, 219

Day Late and a Dollar Short, A (McMillan), **Supp. XIII:** 184, **Supp. XIII:** 185, **191–192**

"Day longs for the evening, The" (Levertov), **Supp. III Part 1:** 274

Daynard, Jodi, **Supp. XVIII:** 97

Day of a Stranger (Merton), **Supp. VIII:** 203

"Day of Days, A" (James), **II:** 322

Day of Doom (Wigglesworth), **IV:** 147, 155, 156

Day of the Body (C. Frost), **Supp. XV:** 93, **98–100**, 106

Day of the Locust, The (West), **I:** 298; **IV:** 288, 299–306; **Retro. Supp. II:** 321, 323, 324, 329, **337–338**; **Supp. II Part 2:** 626; **Supp. XI:** 296; **Supp. XII:** 173; **Supp. XIII:** 170; **Supp. XIV:** 328; **Supp. XVIII:** 246

"Day of Wrath" (Davison), **Supp. XXVI:** 74

"Day on the Big Branch, A" (Nemerov), **III:** 275–276

"Day on the Connecticut River, A" (Merrill), **Supp. III Part 1:** 336

Day Room, The (DeLillo), **Supp. VI:** 4

"Days" (Emerson), **II:** 19, 20

"Days and Nights" (Koch), **Supp. XV:** 179, 180

"Days and Nights: A Journal" (Price), **Supp. VI:** 265

Days Before, The (Porter), **III:** 433, 453

"Day's Ending (Tucson)" (Teasdale), **Supp. XXVII:** 288, 296

Days in the Yellow Leaf (Hoffman), **Supp. XVIII:** 75

"Days of 1935" (Merrill), **Supp. III Part 1:** 325, 328

"Days of 1941 and '44" (Merrill), **Supp. III Part 1:** 336

"Days of 1964" (Merrill), **Supp. III Part 1:** 328, 352

"Days of 1971" (Merrill), **Supp. III Part 1:** 328

"Days of 1981" (Doty), **Supp. XI:** 123

"Days of Awe: The Birth of Lucy Jane" (Wasserstein), **Supp. XV:** 332

"Days of Edward Hopper" (Haines), **Supp. XII:** 210

"Days of Heaven" (Bass), **Supp. XVI:** 20

Days of Obligation: An Argument with My Mexican Father (Rodriguez), **Supp. XIV:** 298, 300, **302–305**, 307, 310

Days of Our Lives (soap opera), **Supp. XI:** 83

Days of Our Lives Lie in Fragments: New and Old Poems (Garrett), **Supp. VII:** 109–110, 111

Days of the Phoenix (Brooks), **I:** 266

Days of Wine and Roses (J. P. Miller), **Supp. XIII:** 262

Days: Tangier Journal, 1987–1989 (Bowles), **Supp. IV Part 1:** 94

Days to Come (Hellman), **Supp. I Part 1:** 276, 277–278

Days without End (O'Neill), **III:** 385, 391, 397

Days Without Time (Teale), **Supp. XXVIII:** 247, 248

"Day's Work, A" (Capote), **Supp. III Part 1:** 120

"Day's Work, A" (Porter), **III:** 443, 446

"Day the Presidential Candidate Came to Ciudad Tamaulipas, The" (Caldwell), **I:** 309

"Day the Singer Fell, The" (Swados), **Supp. XIX:** 258

Day the World ended, The (Coover), **Supp. V:** 1

"Day with Conrad Green, A" (Lardner), **II:** 428–429, 430

"Deacon, The" (Huddle), **Supp. XXVI:** 151, 153–154, 158

"Deacon's Masterpiece, The" (Holmes), **Supp. I Part 1:** 302, 307

"Dead, The" (Collins), **Supp. XXI:** 64

"Dead, The" (Joyce), **I:** 285; **III:** 343; **Supp. XXIII:** 71

"Dead, The" (Very), **Supp. XXV:** 249

Dead and the Living, The (Olds), **Supp. X:** 201, **204–206**, 207

"Dead Body, The" (Olds), **Supp. X:** 210

"Dead by the Side of the Road, The" (Snyder), **Supp. VIII:** 301

"Dead Doe" (B. Kelly), **Supp. XVII:** 128–129

Dead End (Kingsley), **Supp. I Part 1:** 277, 281

Dead Father, The (Barthelme), **Supp. IV Part 1:** 43, 47, 50–51

"Dead Fiddler, The" (Singer), **IV:** 20

Dead Fingers Talk (Burroughs), **Supp. III Part 1:** 103

"Dead Hand" series (Sinclair), **Supp. V:** 276, 277, 281

"Dead Language Lessons" (Stallings), **Supp. XXV:** 233

"Dead Languages, The" (Humphrey), **Supp. IX:** 109

Dead Lecturer, The (Baraka), **Supp. II Part 1:** 31, 33, 35–37, 49

Dead Letters Sent (Kenny), **Supp. XXIII:** 143, 145

"Dead Letters Sent (By the Ontario Shores)"(Kenny), **Supp. XXIII:** 145

Deadline at Dawn (Odets), **Supp. II Part 2:** 546

Deadlock (Paretsky), **Supp. XXV:** 173, 176, 178–179

"Dead-Lock and Its Key, A" (E. Stoddard), **Supp. XV:** 286

"Dead Loon, The" (Bynner), **Supp. XV: 44–45**

Deadly Affair, A (Lacy), **Supp. XV:** 205–206

Deadly is the Female (film), **Supp. XVII:** 62

Dead Man's Walk (McMurtry), **Supp. V:** 231, 232

Dead Man's Walk (screenplay; McMurtry and Ossana), **Supp. V:** 231

Dead Man Walking (opera libretto, McNally), **Supp. XIII:** 207

Dead Poets Society (film), **Supp. XXI:** 192, 193, 194, 199

"Dead Reckoning" (Jarman), **Supp. XVII:** 113

"Dead Soldier's Talk, The" (Jin), **Supp. XVIII:** 92

Dead Souls (Gogol), **I:** 296

"Dead Souls on Campus" (Kosinski), **Supp. VII:** 222

"Dead Wingman, The" (Jarrell), **II:** 374

"Dead Wood, Green Wood" (Hadas), **Supp. XXIII:** 120

"Dead Yellow Women" (Hammett), **Supp. IV Part 1:** 345

Dead Zone, The (King), **Supp. V:** 139, 143, 144, 148, 152

Dean, James, **I:** 493

Dean, Man Mountain, **II:** 589

Deane, Silas, **Supp. I Part 2:** 509, 524

"Dean of Men" (Taylor), **Supp. V:** 314, 323

Dean's December, The (Bellow), **Retro. Supp. II:** 30–31

"Dear Adolph" (Benét), **Supp. XI:** 46

"Dear America" (Ortiz), **Supp. IV Part 2:** 503

Dearborn, Mary V., **Supp. XXVIII:** 39, 40, 41, 45

"Dear Dark Continent" (Notley), **Supp. XXII:** 223

"Dearest M—" (Carruth), **Supp. XVI:** 59

Dear Ghosts (Gallagher), **Supp. XXIV:** 166, 167, 170–171, 176

"Dear Judas" (Jeffers), **Supp. II Part 2:** 431–432, 433

Dear Juliette (Sarton), **Supp. VIII:** 265

Dear Life (Munro), **Supp. XXVII:** 195

Dear Lovely Death (Hughes), **Retro. Supp. I:** 203; **Supp. I Part 1:** 328

"Dear Mr. Walrus" (Boyle), **Supp. XXIV:** 58–59

Dear Rafe (Hinojosa), **Supp. XIX:** 98, **105–106**

"Dear Smoker" (Biss), **Supp. XXVI:** 51

"Dear Villon" (Corso), **Supp. XII:** 135

"Dear World" (Gunn Allen), **Supp. IV Part 1:** 321

Deasy, Philip, **Supp. XX: 42**

Death (Allen), **Supp. XV:** 3

"Death" (Corso), **Supp. XII:** 127

"Death" (Mailer), **III:** 38

"Death" (R. Lowell), **II:** 536

"Death" (W. C. Williams), **Retro. Supp. I:** 422

"Death" (West), **IV:** 286

"Death, Decay and Change" (Very), **Supp. XXV:** 243

"Death and Absence" (Glück), **Supp. V:** 82

Death and Birth of David Markand, The (W. Frank), **Supp. XX: 76–77**

Death and Taxes (Parker), **Supp. IX:** 192

"Death and the Child" (Crane), **I:** 414

"Death as a Society Lady" (Hecht), **Supp. X:** 71–72

Death before Bedtime (Vidal as Box), **Supp. IV Part 2:** 682

"Death Be Not Proud" (Donne), **Supp. XVI:** 158

"Death by Water" (Eliot), **I:** 395, 578

Death Comes for the Archbishop (Cather), **I:** 314, 327, 328–330; **Retro. Supp. I:** 16–18, 21; **Retro. Supp. III:** 24; **Supp. XIII:** 253; **Supp. XXIV:** 253; **Supp. XXVIII:** 119

"Death-Drag" (Faulkner), **Retro. Supp. III:** 84

Death in Paradise (Parker), **Supp. XIX:** 186

Death in the Afternoon (Hemingway), **II:** 253; **IV:** 35; **Retro. Supp. I:** 182; **Supp. VIII:** 182; **Supp. XIX:** 246; **Supp. XVI:** 205; **Supp. XX: 76**

"Death in the Country, A" (Benét), **Supp. XI:** 53–54

"Death in the Desert, A" (Cather), **Retro. Supp. III:** 21, 26

Death in the Family, A (Agee), **I:** 25, 29, 42, 45

Death in the Fifth Position (Vidal as Box), **Supp. IV Part 2:** 682

"Death in the Woods" (Anderson), **I:** 114, 115; **Supp. XXIV:** 136

Death in the Woods and Other Stories (Anderson), **I:** 112, 114, 115

Death in Venice (Mann), **III:** 231; **Supp. IV Part 1:** 392; **Supp. V:** 51

"Death in Viet Nam" (Salinas), **Supp. XIII:** 315

"Death in Winter" (C. Frost), **Supp. XV:** 98

Death Is a Lonely Business (Bradbury), **Supp. IV Part 1:** 102, 103, 111–112, 115

"Death Is Not the End" (Wallace), **Supp. X:** 309

Death Is the Place (Bronk), **Supp. XXI:** 32

Death Kit (Sontag), **Supp. III Part 2:** 451, 468–469

"Deathlight" (Huddle), **Supp. XXVI:** 150

Death Likes It Hot (Vidal as Box), **Supp. IV Part 2:** 682

"*Death*/Muerta" (Mora), **Supp. XIII:** 228

Death Notebooks, The (Sexton), **Supp. II Part 2:** 691, 694, 695

"Death of a Columnist" (Siddons), **Supp. XXII:** 241–242

Death of Adam, The: Essays on Modern Thought (Robinson), **Supp. XXI:** 212

"Death of a Hired Man" (Frost), **Retro. Supp. III:** 97, 98

"Death of a Jazz Musician" (W. J. Smith), **Supp. XIII:** 334

Death of a Kinsman, The (Taylor), **Supp. V:** 324, 326

"Death of a Lady's Man" (Cohen), **Supp. XXVII:** 58

Death of a Man (Boyle), **Supp. XXIV:** 60

"Death of an Old Seaman" (Hughes), **Retro. Supp. I:** 199

"Death of a Pig" (White), **Supp. I Part 2:** 665–668

Death of a Salesman (A. Miller), **I:** 81; **III:** 148, 149, 150, 153–154, 156, 157, 158, 159, 160, 163, 164, 166; **IV:** 389; **Retro. Supp. III:** 165, 167, 169–170, 171, 172–173; **Supp. IV Part 1:** 359; **Supp. XIV:** 102, 239, 254, 255; **Supp. XV:** 205; **Supp. XX: 27; Supp. XXIII:** 199

"Death of a Soldier, The" (Stevens), **Retro. Supp. I:** 299, 312. *see also* "Lettres d'un Soldat" (Stevens)

"Death of a Soldier, The" (Wilson), **IV:** 427, 445

"Death of a Toad" (Wilbur), **Supp. III Part 2:** 550

"Death of a Traveling Salesman" (Welty), **IV:** 261; **Retro. Supp. I:** 344

"Death of a Young Son by Drowning" (Atwood), **Supp. XIII:** 33

Death of Bessie Smith, The (Albee), **I:** 76–77, 92

Death of Billy the Kid, The (Vidal), **Supp. IV Part 2:** 683

Death of Cock Robin, The (Snodgrass), **Supp. VI:** 315, **317–319,** 324

Death of Dreams, A (Hoffman), **Supp. XVIII:** 79

"Death of General Wolfe, The" (Paine), **Supp. I Part 2:** 504

"Death of Halpin Frayser, The" (Bierce), **I:** 205

"Death of Justina, The" (Cheever), **Supp. I Part 1:** 184–185

Death of Life, The (Barnes), **Supp. III Part 1:** 34

Death of Malcolm X, The (Baraka), **Supp. II Part 1:** 47

"Death of Marilyn Monroe, The" (Olds), **Supp. X:** 205

"Death of Me, The" (Malamud), **Supp. I Part 2:** 437

"Death of Slavery, The" (Bryant), **Supp. I Part 1:** 168–169

"Death of St. Narcissus, The" (Eliot), **Retro. Supp. I:** 291

"Death of the Ball Turret Gunner, The" (Jarrell), **II:** 369–370, 372, 374, 375, 376, 378

"Death of the Fathers, The" (Sexton), **Supp. II Part 2:** 692

"Death of the Flowers, The" (Bryant), **Supp. I Part 1:** 170

Death of the Fox (Garrett), **Supp. VII:** 99, 101–104, 108

"Death of the Hat, The" (Collins), **Supp. XXI:** 59

"Death of the Hired Man, The" (Frost), **III:** 523; **Retro. Supp. I:** 121, 128; **Supp. IX:** 261

Death of the Kapowsin Tavern (Hugo), **Supp. VI:** 133–135

"Death of the Kapowsin Tavern" (Hugo), **Supp. VI:** 137, 141

"Death of the Lyric, The: The Achievement of Louis Simpson" (Jarman and McDowell), **Supp. IX:** 266, 270, 276

"Death of the Virgin, The (Rembrandt)" (Davison), **Supp. XXVI:** 70

"Death of Venus, The" (Creeley), **Supp. IV Part 1:** 143, 144–145

"Death on All Fronts" (Ginsberg), **Supp. II Part 1:** 326

"Deaths" (Dunn), **Supp. XI:** 147

"Death Sauntering About" (Hecht), **Supp. X:** 72

Deaths for the Ladies (and Other Disasters) (Mailer), **Retro. Supp. II:** 203

Death's Jest-Book (Beddoes), **Retro. Supp. I:** 285

Death Song (McGrath), **Supp. X:** 127

"Death the Carnival Barker" (Hecht), **Supp. X:** 72

"Death the Film Director" (Hecht), **Supp. X:** 72

"Death the Judge" (Hecht), **Supp. X:** 72

"Death the Mexican Revolutionary" (Hecht), **Supp. X:** 72

"Death the Oxford Don" (Hecht), **Supp. X:** 72

"Death the Painter" (Hecht), **Supp. X:** 72

Death the Proud Brother (Wolfe), **IV:** 456

"Death to Van Gogh's Ear!" (Ginsberg), **Supp. II Part 1:** 320, 322, 323

"Death Warmed Over!" (Bradbury), **Supp. IV Part 1:** 104–105, 112

Death Wish, The (Holding), **Supp. XXII:** 120, **123,** 134, 135

Deaver, Philip F., **Supp. XXVI:** 151, 160–161

Débâcle, La (Zola), **III:** 316

"Debate with the Rabbi" (Nemerov), **III:** 272

Debeljak, Ale&sacaron;, **Supp. VIII:** 272

De Bellis, Jack, **Supp. I Part 1:** 366, 368, 372

Debo, Annette, **Supp. XXI:** 254

DeBoer-Langworthy, Carol, **Supp. XVII:** 98, 99, 100

DeBold, Kathleen, **Supp. XXV:** 4

De Bosis, Lauro, **IV:** 372

"Debriefing" (Sontag), **Supp. III Part 2:** 468–470

Debs, Eugene, **I:** 483, 493; **III:** 580, 581; **Supp. I Part 2:** 524; **Supp. IX:** 1, 15; **Supp. XXIII:** 161, 162

"Debt" (Teasdale), **Supp. XXVII:** 290

Debt to Pleasure, The (Lanchester), **Retro. Supp. I:** 278

Debussy, Claude, **Retro. Supp. II:** 266; **Supp. XIII:** 44

"Decades" (Sorrentino), **Supp. XXI:** 229

Decameron (Boccaccio), **III:** 283, 411; **Supp. IX:** 215

de Camp, L. Sprague, **Supp. XXVII:** 115, 128

"Deceased" (Hughes), **Retro. Supp. I:** 208

"December" (Oliver), **Supp. VII:** 245

"December 1, 1994" (Stern), **Supp. IX:** 299

December 7 (film, Ford), **Supp. XVIII:** 247

"December 24" (Di Piero), **Supp. XIX:** 39

"December 28: Returning to Chicago" (Di Piero), **Supp. XIX:** 39

"December Dawn" (Skloot), **Supp. XX: 202**

"December Eclogue" (Winters), **Supp. II Part 2:** 794

"Decent Woman, A" (Boulton), **Supp. XXII:** 22–23

De Cenzo, Giorgia, **Supp. XXI:** 256

Deception (P. Roth), **Retro. Supp. II:** 291; **Supp. III Part 2:** 426–427

"Deceptions" (Dobyns), **Supp. XIII:** 77

De Chiara, Ann. *See* Malamud, Mrs. Bernard (Ann de Chiara)

De Chirico, Giorgio, **Supp. XIII:** 317

"Decided Loss, A" (Poe), **II:** 411

"Decision" (Boyle), **Supp. XXIV:** 54

"Decisions to Disappear" (Dunn), **Supp. XI:** 144

"Decisive Moment, The" (Auster), **Supp. XIV:** 292

Decker, James A., **Supp. III Part 2:** 621

Declaration of Gentlemen and Merchants and Inhabitants of Boston, and the Country Adjacent, A (Mather), **Supp. II Part 2:** 450

"Declaration of Paris, The" (Adams), **I:** 4

Declaration of the Rights of Man and the Citizen, **Supp. I Part 2:** 513, 519

Declaration of Universal Peace and Liberty (Paine), **Supp. I Part 2:** 512

Declension in the Village of Chung Luong (Weigl), **Supp. XIX:** 287, 288

Decline and Fall (Waugh), **Supp. I Part 2:** 607; **Supp. XV:** 142

Decline and Fall of the English System of Finance, The (Paine), **Supp. I Part 2:** 518

Decline and Fall of the Roman Empire, The (Gibbons), **Supp. III Part 2:** 629

"Decline of Book Reviewing, The" (Hardwick), **Supp. III Part 1:** 201–202

Decline of the West, The (Spengler), **I:** 270; **IV:** 125

"Decolonizing the Tongue: Reading Speech and Aphasia in the Work of Michelle Cliff" (Aguiar), **Supp. XXII:** 68

Deconstructing Harry (film; Allen), **Supp. XV:** 12, **13**

"Décor" (X. J. Kennedy), **Supp. XV:** 171

"Decoration Day" (Jewett), **II:** 412; **Retro. Supp. II:** 138

Decoration of Houses, The (Wharton and Codman), **IV:** 308; **Retro. Supp. I:** 362, 363–364, 366; **Retro. Supp. III:** 277, 280

"Decoy" (Ashbery), **Supp. III Part 1:** 13–14

Decter, Midge, **Supp. XX:** 248

Dedalus, Stephen, **Supp. XIX:** 47

"De Daumier-Smith's Blue Period" (Salinger), **III:** 560–561

"Dedication" (Nelson), **Supp. XVIII:** 173, 180

"Dedication and Household Map" (Erdrich), **Supp. IV Part 1:** 272

"Dedication Day" (Agee), **I:** 34

"Dedication for a Book" (Hay), **Supp. XIV:** 125

"Dedication for a Book of Criticism" (Winters), **Supp. II Part 2:** 801

"Dedication in Postscript, A" (Winters), **Supp. II Part 2:** 801

Dedications and Other Darkhorses (Komunyakaa), **Supp. XIII:** 112, **113–114**

"Dedication to Hunger" (Glück), **Supp. V:** 83

"Dedication to My Wife, A" (Eliot), **I:** 583

Dee, Jonathan, **Supp. XXIII:** 302; **Supp. XXVIII:** 208

Dee, Ruby, **Supp. IV Part 1:** 362

Deeck, William, **Supp. XXVI:** 278

Deeds of Utmost Kindness (Gander), **Supp. XV:** 340

Deegan, Thomas, **Supp. XXIII:** 100, 107–108

"Deep Breath at Dawn, A" (Hecht), **Supp. X:** 58

Deep End, The (film), **Supp. XXII:** 120, 131, 133

Deeper into Movies: The Essential Kael Collection from '69 to '72 (Kael), **Supp. IX:** 253

"Deeper Wisdom, The" (Hay), **Supp. XIV:** 129

Deep Green Sea (R. O. Butler), **Supp. XII:** 62, **74**

Deephaven (Jewett), **II:** 398–399, 400, 401, 410, 411; **Retro. Supp. II:** 133, 134, 135, 136, 137, 138, 140, 141, 143, 144

"Deep Sight and Rescue Missions" (Bambara), **Supp. XI:** 18–19

Deep Sightings and Rescue Missions: Fiction, Essays, and Conversations (Bambara), **Supp. XI:** 1, 3, **14–20**

Deep Sleep, The (Morris), **III:** 224–225

"Deep Song" (G. Jones), **Supp. XXIV:** 194

Deep South (Caldwell), **I:** 305, 309, 310

Deepstep Come Shining (Wright), **Supp. XV:** 337, 341, 344, **349–350,** 351, 353

"Deep Water" (Marquand), **III:** 56

"Deep Woods" (Nemerov), **III:** 272–273, 275

"Deer at Providencia, The" (Dillard), **Supp. VI:** 28, 32

Deer Camp: Last Light in the Northeast Kingdom (Ostrum, ed.), **Supp. XXII:** 218

"Deer Dancer" (Harjo), **Supp. XII:** 224–225

"Deer Ghost" (Harjo), **Supp. XII:** 225

Deer Park, The (Mailer), **I:** 292; **III:** 27, 31–33, 35–36, 37, 39, 40, 42, 43, 44; **Retro. Supp. II: 200–202,** 205, 207, 211

Deer Park, The: A Play (Mailer), **Retro. Supp. II:** 205

Deer Pasture, The (Bass), **Supp. XVI:** 15, 16, 23

Deerslayer, The (Cooper), **I:** 341, 349, 350, 355; **Supp. I Part 1:** 251

Deese, Helen, **Supp. XXV:** 251

"Defeat" (Boyle), **Supp. XXIV: 60–61**

Defeated, The (Lewisohn). *See Island Within, The* (Lewisohn)

Defence, The (Nabokov), **Supp. XXII:** 263

"Defence of General Funston, A" (Twain), **Retro. Supp. III:** 269

"Defence of Poesie, The" (Bronk), **Supp. XXI:** 32

"Defence of Poesy, The" (Sidney), **Supp. V:** 250

"Defence of Poetry" (Longfellow), **II:** 493–494

"Defence of Poetry, A" (Shelley), **Retro. Supp. III:** 41

"Defender of the Faith" (P. Roth), **Retro. Supp. II:** 281; **Supp. III Part 2:** 404, 407, 420

"Defending *The Searchers* (Scenes in the Life of an Obsession)" *(Lethem), Supp. XVIII:* 136,141

"Defenestration in Prague" (Matthews), **Supp. IX:** 168

Defenestration of Prague (Howe), **Supp. IV Part 2:** 419, 426, 429–430

Defense, The (Nabokov), **III:** 251–252; **Retro. Supp. I:** 266, 268, **270–272**

"Defense of Poetry" (Francis), **Supp. IX:** 83–84

DeFeo, Ronald, **Supp. XXIII:** 106

Defiant Ones, The (film), **Supp. I Part 1:** 67

"Defining the Age" (W. V. Davis), **Supp. IV Part 1:** 64

"Definition" (Ammons), **Supp. VII:** 28

Defoe, Daniel, **I:** 204; **II:** 104, 105, 159, 304–305; **III:** 113, 423; **IV:** 180; **Supp. I Part 2:** 523; **Supp. V:** 127

De Forest, John William, **II:** 275, 280, 288, 289; **IV:** 350

DeFrees, Madeline, **Supp. XVIII:** 293; **Supp. XXVI:** 180

Deganawida, the Peacemaker, **Supp. XXVI: 81–100**

"Deganawidah: The Peacemaker"(Kenny), **Supp. XXIII:** 151

Degas, Brian, **Supp. XI:** 307

Degler, Carl, **Supp. I Part 2:** 496

"Degrees of Fidelity" (Dunn), **Supp. XI:** 148, 156

Deguy, Michel, **Supp. XV:** 178

De Haven, Tom, **Supp. XI:** 39; **Supp. XII:** 338–339

Deitch, Joseph, **Supp. VIII:** 125

DeJean, Joan, **Supp. XXVIII:** 119

"Dejection" (Coleridge), **II:** 97

DeJong, Constance, **Supp. XII:** 4

DeJong, David Cornel, **I:** 35

Dekker,Thomas, **Supp. XVII:** 232

de Kooning, Elaine de, **Supp. XXIII:** 210, 217

de Kooning, Willem, **Supp. XII:** 198; **Supp. XV:** 177, 178

de Kooning, Willem de, **Supp. XXIII:** 208, 210, 211, 217, 220

Delacroix, Henri, **I:** 227

De La Mare, Walter, **III:** 429; **Supp. II Part 1:** 4; **Supp. XVII:** 69

Delamotte, Eugenia C., **Supp. XI:** 279

De Lancey, James, **I:** 338

De Lancey, Mrs. James (Anne Heathcote), **I:** 338

De Lancey, Susan A. *See* Cooper, Mrs. James Fenimore

De Lancey, William Heathcote, **I:** 338, 353

Delano, Amasa, **III:** 90

De la Paz, Oliver, **Supp. XXVI:** 101, 103, 111

Delattre, Roland A., **I:** 558

De Laurentiis, Dino, **Supp. XI:** 170, 307

De la Valdéne, Guy, **Supp. VIII:** 40, 42

Delbanco, Andrew, **Retro. Supp. III:** 152, 161, 162; **Supp. XXIV:** 69

Delbanco, Nicholas, **Supp. XXII:** 204

Del Cabral, Manuel, **Supp. XXI:** 104

DelCorso's Gallery (Caputo), **Supp. XIX:** 22–23

Delectorskaya, Lydia, **Supp. XXII:** 99

De l'éducation d'un homme sauvage (Itard), **Supp. I Part 2:** 564

Deleuze, Gilles, **Retro. Supp. III:** 159; **Supp. XXV:** 123

"Delft" (Goldbarth), **Supp. XII:** 189

Delft: An Essay-Poem (Goldbarth), **Supp. XII:** 187

"Delicate Affair, A"(King), **Supp. XXVIII:** 123

Delicate Balance, A (Albee), **I:** 86–89, 91, 93, 94

Delicate Balance, The (Hay), **Supp. XIV:** 121, 122, 124, 129, 133–134

"Delicate Balance, The" (Hay), **Supp. XIV:** 122

"Delicate Prey, The" (Bowles), **Supp. IV Part 1:** 86

Delicate Prey and Other Stories, The (Bowles), **Supp. IV Part 1:** 86–87

Délie (Scève), **Supp. III Part 1:** 11

Delights & Shadows (Kooser), **Supp. XIX:** 115, 116, 117, 121, **127–128**

DeLillo, Don, **Retro. Supp. I:** 278; **Retro. Supp. II:** 279; **Supp. IX:** 212; **Supp. VI: 1–18; Supp. XI:** 68; **Supp. XII:** 21, 152; **Supp. XIX:** 54; **Supp. XVII:** 183; **Supp. XVIII:** 136, 140; **Supp. XX: 83, 87, 91; Supp. XXIII:** 109; **Supp. XXVII:** 6; **Supp. XXVIII:** 206, 207

De Lint, Charles, **Supp. XXII:** 59

DeLisle, Anne, **Supp. VIII:** 175

Deliverance (Dickey), **Supp. IV Part 1:** 176, 186–188, 190; **Supp. X:** 30; **Supp. XX: 173–174; Supp. XXIII:** 43, 50

Deliverance, The (Glasgow), **II:** 175, 176, 177–178, 181

"Delivering" (Dubus), **Supp. VII:** 87

Dell, Floyd, **I:** 103, 105; **Supp. I Part 2:** 379; **Supp. XV:** 295; **Supp. XVII:** 96; **Supp. XXI:** 6; **Supp. XXII:** 275; **Supp. XXV:** 18; **Supp. XXVIII:** 38, 67, 69, 71, 75–76

Della Francesca, Piero, **Supp. XV:** 262

"Della Primavera Trasportata al Morale" (W. C. Williams), **Retro. Supp. I:** 419, 422

Del Negro, Janice, **Supp. XXVIII:** 286

DeLoria, Philip J., **Supp. XIV:** 306

Deloria, Vine, Jr., **Supp. IV Part 1:** 323; **Supp. IV Part 2:** 504; **Supp. XXVI:** 98

"Delta" (Rich), **Retro. Supp. III:** 250

"Delta Autumn" (Faulkner), **II:** 71

"Delta Factor, The" (Percy), **Supp. III Part 1:** 386

Delta of Venus: Erotica (Nin), **Supp. X:** 192, 195

Delta Wedding (Welty), **IV:** 261, 268–271, 273, 281; **Retro. Supp. I:** 349–350, 351

Delusions (Berryman), **I:** 170

De Man, Paul, **Retro. Supp. I:** 67; **Supp. XVII:** 70

DeMarinis, Rick, **Supp. XIV:** 22

DeMars, James, **Supp. IV Part 2:** 552

Dembo, L. S., **I:** 386, 391, 396, 397, 398, 402; **III:** 478; **Supp. I Part 1:** 272; **Supp. XIV:** 277, 282, 288, 290; **Supp. XXVI:** 226–227, 235

"Dementia Translucida" (Bierds), **Supp. XVII:** 33

"Demeter"(Crooker), **Supp. XXIII:** 61

"Demeters"(Hadas), **Supp. XXIII:** 113

Demetrakopoulous, Stephanie A., **Supp. IV Part 1:** 12

De Mille, Agnes, **Supp. XXVI:** 66

DeMille, Cecil B., **Supp. IV Part 2:** 520; **Supp. XV:** 42

Demme, Jonathan, **Retro. Supp. III:** 185; **Supp. V:** 14

Democracy (Adams), **I:** 9–10, 20; **Supp. IV Part 1:** 208; **Supp. XIX:** 139

Democracy (Didion), **Supp. IV Part 1:** 198, 208–210

"Democracy" (J. R. Lowell), **Supp. I Part 2:** 419

Democracy and Education (Dewey), **I:** 232

Democracy and Other Addresses (J. R. Lowell), **Supp. I Part 2:** 407

Democracy and Social Ethics (Addams), **Supp. I Part 1:** 8–11

Democracy in America (Tocqueville), **Retro. Supp. I:** 235; **Supp. XIV:** 306

Democratic Vistas (Whitman), **IV:** 333, 336, 348–349, 351, 469; **Retro. Supp. I:** 408; **Retro. Supp. III:** 302; **Supp. I Part 2:** 456

Democritus, **I:** 480–481; **II:** 157; **III:** 606; **Retro. Supp. I:** 247

"Demon Lover, The" (Rich), **Supp. I Part 2:** 556

"Demonstrators, The" (Welty), **IV:** 280; **Retro. Supp. I:** 355

DeMott, Benjamin, **Supp. IV Part 1:** 35; **Supp. V:** 123; **Supp. XIII:** 95; **Supp. XIV:** 106; **Supp. XXV:** 86

DeMott, Robert, **Supp. VIII:** 40, 41

Demuth, Charles, **IV:** 404; **Retro. Supp. I:** 412, 430; **Supp. XXI:** 6

"Demystified Zone" (Paley), **Supp. VI:** 227

Denby, Edwin, **Supp. XXIV:** 36, 45; **Supp. XXVII:** 23

Denmark Vesey (opera) (Bowles), **Supp. IV Part 1:** 83

Dennett, Daniel, **Supp. XXII:** 265

Denney, Joseph Villiers, **Supp. I Part 2:** 605

Denney, Reuel, **Supp. XII:** 121; **Supp. XXI:** 19

Dennie, Joseph, **II:** 298; **Supp. I Part 1:** 125

Denning, Michael, **Supp. XXVI:** 28

Denniston, Dorothy Hamer, **Supp. XI:** 276, 277

"Den of Lions" (Plath), **Retro. Supp. II:** 242

"Dental Assistant, The" (Simpson), **Supp. IX:** 280

Den Uyl, Douglas, **Supp. IV Part 2:** 528, 530

"Deodand, The" (Hecht), **Supp. X:** 65

"Departing" (Cameron), **Supp. XII:** 81

"Departmental" (Frost), **Retro. Supp. III:** 103

"Departure" (Glück), **Supp. V:** 89

"Departure" (Plath), **Supp. I Part 2:** 537

"Departure, The" (Freneau), **Supp. II Part 1:** 264

"Departure from Hydra, The" (Koch), **Supp. XV:** 180–181

Departures (Justice), **Supp. VII:** 124–127

Departures and Arrivals (Shields), **Supp. VII:** 320, 322

"Depressed by a Book of Bad Poetry, I Walk Toward an Unused Pasture and Invite the Insects to Join Me" (Wright), **Supp. III Part 2:** 600

"Depressed Person, The" (Wallace), **Supp. X:** 309

"Depression Days" (Mora), **Supp. XIII:** 224–225

"Deprived of Unhappiness" (Pickering), **Supp. XXI:** 203

De Puy, John, **Supp. XIII:** 12

De Quincey, Thomas, **Supp. XXVI:** 283

D'Erasmo, Stacey, **Supp. IX:** 121

Derby, J. C., **Supp. XVIII:** 4

De Reilhe, Catherine, **Supp. I Part 1:** 202

De Rerum Natura (Lucretius), **II:** 162

"De Rerum Virtute" (Jeffers), **Supp. II Part 2:** 424

De Rioja, Francisco, **Supp. I Part 1:** 166

"Derivative Sport in Tornado Alley" (Wallace), **Supp. X:** 314

Derleth, August, **Supp. I Part 2:** 465, 472; **Supp. XXV:** 111, 122; **Supp. XXVII:** 117, 119, 128

Deronda, Daniel, **II:** 179

Derricotte, Toi, **Supp. XVIII:** 177

Derrida, Jacques, **Retro. Supp. III:** 237; **Supp. IV Part 1:** 45; **Supp. XV:** 215, 224; **Supp. XVI:** 285, 288

Deruddere, Dominique, **Supp. XI:** 173

Der Wilde Jäger (Bürger), **II:** 306

Derzhavin, Gavrila Romanovich, **Supp. VIII:** 27

Desai, Anita, **Supp. XVI:** 156, 157, 158

Désamère (Notley), **Supp. XXII:** 226

De Santis, Christopher, **Retro. Supp. I:** 194

Descartes, René, **I:** 255; **III:** 618–619; **IV:** 133

"Descendant of Solomon and the Queen of Sheba" (Major), **Supp. XXII:** 182

Descendents, The (Glasgow), **II:** 173, 174–175, 176

Descending Figure (Glück), **Supp. V:** 83–84

"Descending Theology: Christ Human" (Karr), **Supp. XI:** 251

"Descending Theology: The Garden" (Karr), **Supp. XI:** 251

"Descent, The" (W. C. Williams), **Retro. Supp. I:** 428, 429

"Descent from the Cross" (Eliot), **Retro. Supp. I:** 57, 58

"Descent in the Maelström, A" (Poe), **Retro. Supp. II:** 274

"Descent into Proselito" (Knowles), **Supp. XII:** 237

"Descent into the Maelström, A" (Poe), **III:** 411, 414, 416, 424

Descent of Alette, The (Notley), **Supp. XXII:** 223, 224, 226, 227, 233–234

Descent of Man (Boyle), **Supp. VIII:** 1, 12–13; **Supp. XX:** 17, 18, 20

"Descent of Man" (Boyle), **Supp. VIII:** 14; **Supp. XX:** 18

Descent of Man, and Other Stories, The (Wharton), **Retro. Supp. III:** 278

Descent of Man, The (Darwin), **Supp. XIV:** 192

Descent of Man, The (Wharton), **IV:** 311; **Retro. Supp. I:** 367

Descent of Man and Other Stories, The (Wharton), **Retro. Supp. I:** 367

Descent of Winter, The (W. C. Williams), **Retro. Supp. I:** 419, 428

De Schloezer, Doris, **III:** 474

"Describers" (Halliday), **Supp. XIX:** 85

"Description" (Doty), **Supp. XI:** 126

"Description of the great Bones dug up at Clavarack on the Banks of Hudsons River A.D. 1705, The" (Taylor), **IV:** 163, 164

"Description without Place" (Stevens), **Retro. Supp. I:** 422

Desdemona (T. Morrison), **Retro. Supp. III:** 185

"Desert" (Hughes), **Retro. Supp. I:** 207

"Deserted Cabin" (Haines), **Supp. XII:** 203

Deserted Village, The (Goldsmith), **II:** 304

Desert Is My Mother, The/El desierto es mi madre (Mora), **Supp. XIII:** 214, 221

Desert Music, The (W. C. Williams), **IV:** 422; **Retro. Supp. I:** 428, 429

"Desert Music, The" (W. C. Williams), **Retro. Supp. I:** 428, 429

"Desert Places" (Frost), **II:** 159; **Retro. Supp. I:** 121, 123, 129, 138, 299; **Retro. Supp. III:** 103; **Supp. XIV:** 229

Desert Rose, The (McMurtry), **Supp. V:** 225, 231

Desert Solitaire (Abbey), **Supp. X:** 30; **Supp. XIII:** 7–8, 12; **Supp. XIV:** 177, 179; **Supp. XXV:** 208

"Design" (Frost), **II:** 158, 163; **Retro. Supp. I:** 121, 126, 138, 139; **Retro. Supp. III:** 103; **Supp. IX:** 81; **Supp. XVII:** 132; **Supp. XVIII:** 298

"Designated National Park, A" (Ortiz), **Supp. IV Part 2:** 509

"Designs on a Point of View" (Everwine), **Supp. XV:** 76

DeSilva, Bruce, **Supp. XXII:** 205, 206, 217

Des Imagistes (Pound), **II:** 513; **Supp. I Part 1:** 257, 261, 262

Desire (album, Dylan), **Supp. XVIII:** 28

"Desire" (Beattie), **Supp. V:** 29

Desire (Bidart), **Supp. XV:** 32–34, 35

"Desire" (Everwine), **Supp. XV:** 85

Desire, Desire, Desire (Durang), **Supp. XXIV:** 113

"Desire and Denial" (Bronk), **Supp. XXI:** 26

"Désirée's Baby" (Chopin), **Retro. Supp. II:** 64, 65; **Supp. I Part 1:** 213–215

"Desire"(Hadas), **Supp. XXIII:** 117

Desire under the Elms (O'Neill), **III:** 387, 390

"Desk, The"(Bottoms), **Supp. XXVIII:** 27

"Desolate Field, The" (W. C. Williams), **Retro. Supp. I:** 418

"Desolation, A" (Ginsberg), **Supp. II Part 1:** 313

Desolation Angels (Kerouac), **Supp. III Part 1:** 218, 225, 230

"Desolation Is a Delicate Thing" (Wylie), **Supp. I Part 2:** 729

"Desolation Row" (song, Dylan), **Supp. XVIII:** 30

De Soto and His Men in the Land of Florida (King), **Supp. XXVIII:** 116–117

Despair (Nabokov), **Retro. Supp. I:** 270, 274

Desperate Characters (Fox), **Supp. XX:** 91

"Despisals" (Rukeyser), **Supp. VI:** 282

Des Pres, Terrence, **Supp. X:** 113, 120, 124

"Destination Out" (Mackey), **Supp. XXVII:** 152

"Destiny and the Lieutenant" (McCoy), **Supp. XIII:** 171

"Destroyer, The" (Davison), **Supp. XXVI:** 71

"Destruction of Kreshev, The" (Singer), **IV:** 13; **Retro. Supp. II:** 307

Destruction of the European Jews, The (Hilberg), **Supp. V:** 267

"Destruction of the Goetheanum, The" (Salter), **Supp. IX:** 257

"Destruction of the Long Branch, The" (Pinsky), **Supp. VI:** 239, 240, 243–244, 245, 247, 250

Destructive Element, The (Spender), **Retro. Supp. I:** 216

"Detail of a Hayfield"(Siken), **Supp. XXVIII:** 202

"Detail & Parody for the poem 'Paterson' " (W. C. Williams), **Retro. Supp. I:** 424

Detmold, John, **Supp. I Part 2:** 670

De Tolnay, Charles, **Supp. XXII:** 255

Detour at Night (Endore), **Supp. XVII:** 64

Deuce, The (R. O. Butler), **Supp. XII:** 62, **69–70,** 72

Deus Lo Volt! (Connell), **Supp. XIV:** 80, 81, 95

Deuteronomy (biblical book), **II:** 166

Deutsch, Andre, **Supp. XI:** 297, 301

Deutsch, Babette, **Supp. I Part 1:** 328, 341; **Supp. XV:** 305; **Supp. XXV:** 21; **Supp. XXVII:** 293

Deutsch, Michel, **Supp. IV Part 1:** 104

"Devaluation Blues: Ruminations on Black Families in Crisis" (Coleman), **Supp. XI:** 87

Devane, William, **Supp. XI:** 234

Devasahayam, Madona, **Supp. XXII:** 260

"Development of My Mind and Character, The" (Notley), **Supp. XXII:** 227

Development of the American Short Story, The (Pattee), **Supp. XXVIII:** 124

"Development of the Literary West" (Chopin), **Retro. Supp. II:** 72

"Development of the Modern English Novel, The" (Lanier), **Supp. I Part 1:** 370–371

DeVeriante (Herbert of Cherbury), **II:** 108

"Devil and Daniel Webster, The" (Benét), **III:** 22; **Supp. XI:** 45–46, 47, 50–51, 52

Devil and Daniel Webster and Other Writings, The (Benét), **Supp. XI:** 48

"Devil and Tom Walker, The" (Irving), **II:** 309–310

Devil At Large, The: Erica Jong on Henry Miller (Jong), **Supp. V:** 115, 131

Devil-Doll, The (film, Browning), **Supp. XVII:** 58–59

Devil Finds Work, The (Baldwin), **Retro. Supp. II:** 14; **Supp. I Part 1:** 48, 52, 66–67

Devil in a Blue Dress (Mosley), **Supp. XIII:** 237, 239

"Devil in Manuscript, The" (Hawthorne), **II:** 226; **Retro. Supp. I:** 150–151

Devil in Paradise, A (H. Miller), **III:** 190

"Devil in the Belfry, The" (Poe), **III:** 425; **Retro. Supp. II:** 273

"Devil Is a Busy Man, The" (Wallace), **Supp. X:** 309

Devil's Dictionary, The (Bierce), **I:** 196, 197, 205, 208, 209, 210

Devil's Stocking, The (Algren), **Supp. IX:** 5, 16

"Devil's Thumb, The" (Krakauer), **Supp. XVIII:** 107

Devil's Tour, The (Karr), **Supp. XI:** 240, **242–244**

Devil Tree, The (Kosinski), **Supp. VII:** 215, 222, 223

"Devising" (Ammons), **Supp. VII:** 28

Devlin, Paul, **Supp. XIX:** 159

De Voe, Edward Thomas, **Supp. XXV:** 23, 29

De Voto, Bernard, **I:** 247, 248; **II:** 446; **Retro. Supp. III:** 84; **Supp. IV Part 2:** 599, 601

"Devout Meditation in Memory of Adolph Eichmann, A" (Merton), **Supp. VIII:** 198, 203

De Vries, Peter, **Supp. I Part 2:** 604

Dewberry, Elizabeth, **Supp. XII:** 62, 72

Dewey, John, **I:** 214, 224, 228, 232, 233, 266, 267; **II:** 20, 27, 34, 229, 361; **III:** 112, 294–295, 296, 303, 309–310, 599, 605; **IV:** 27, 429; **Supp. I Part 1:** 3, 5, 7, 10, 11, 12, 24; **Supp. I Part 2:** 493, 641, 647, 677; **Supp. IX:** 179; **Supp. V:** 290; **Supp. XIV:** 3; **Supp. XV:** 41

Dewey, Joseph, **Supp. IX:** 210

Dewey, Thomas, **IV:** 161

Dewey Defeats Truman (Mallon), **Supp. XIX:** 132, 137, **138**

Dexter, Peter, **Supp. XIV:** 221

De Young, Charles, **I:** 194

Dhairyam, Sagari, **Supp. IV Part 1:** 329, 330

Dharma Bums, The (Kerouac), **Supp. III Part 1:** 230, 231; **Supp. VIII:** 289, 305

"D. H. Lawrence" (Bynner), **Supp. XV:** 46

D. H. Lawrence: An Unprofessional Study (Nin), **Supp. X:** 182–183

D. H. Lawrence: The World of the Major Novels (Sanders), **Supp. XVI:** 267

D'Houdetot, Madame, **Supp. I Part 1:** 250

"Diabetes" (Dickey), **Supp. IV Part 1:** 182

Diaghilev, Sergei, **Supp. I Part 1:** 257

Dial (publication), **I:** 58, 109, 115, 116, 215, 231, 233, 245, 261, 384, 429; **II:** 8, 430; **III:** 194, 470, 471, 485; **IV:** 122, 171, 427; **Retro. Supp. I:** 58; **Retro. Supp. II:** 78; **Supp. I Part 2:** 642, 643, 647; **Supp. II Part 1:** 168, 279, 291; **Supp. II Part 2:** 474; **Supp. III Part 2:** 611

"Dialectical Materialism" (Weigl), **Supp. XIX:** 281

Dialectical Materialism and the Fate of Humanity (C. L. R. James), **Supp. XXI:** 169

"Dialectics of Love, The" (McGrath), **Supp. X:** 116

"Dialogue" (Rich), **Supp. I Part 2:** 560

Dialogue, A (Baldwin and Giovanni), **Supp. I Part 1:** 66

"Dialogue Between Franklin and the Gout" (Franklin), **II:** 121

"Dialogue Between General Wolfe and General Gage in a Wood near Boston, A" (Paine), **Supp. I Part 2:** 504

"Dialogue between Old England and New, A" (Bradstreet), **Retro. Supp. III:** 4, 7; **Supp. I Part 1:** 105–106, 110–111, 116

"Dialogue between the Writer and a Maypole Dresser, A" (Taylor), **IV:** 155

Dialogues (Bush, ed.), **III:** 4

Dialogues in Limbo (Santayana), **III:** 606

"Dialogue: William Harvey; Joan of Arc" (Goldbarth), **Supp. XII:** 178

Dialogue with a Dead Man (J. W. Miller), **Supp. XX:** 163, 164, 167

Diamond, Elin, **Retro. Supp. III:** 137

"Diamond as Big as the Ritz, The" (Fitzgerald), **II:** 88–89

"Diamond Cutters, The" (Rich), **Retro. Supp. III:** 243

Diamond Cutters and Other Poems, The (Rich), **Retro. Supp. III:** 241; **Supp. I Part 2:** 551, 552, 553

Diamond Dog, The (Wakoski), **Supp. XXVIII:** 271–272

"Diamond Guitar, A" (Capote), **Supp. III Part 1:** 124

Diamond Necklace, A (Notley), **Supp. XXII:** 228

"Diamonds in the Mine" (Cohen), **Supp. XXVII:** 51, 60

"Diana and Persis" (Alcott), **Supp. I Part 1:** 32, 41

"Diaper Brigade, The" (Ryan as Quin), **Supp. XVIII:** 230

Diaries (Coward), **Retro. Supp. III:** 171

Diaries of Charlotte Perkins Gilman (Knight, ed.), **Supp. XI:** 201

"Diary–1903" (Boyce), **Supp. XXI:** 8

"Diary Aug. 4–Aug. 5" (Brainard), **Supp. XXVII:** 18

Diary of a Chambermaid, The (film; Renoir), **Supp. XVI:** 193

Diary of Anaïs Nin, The (1931–1974), **Supp. X:** 181, 185–189, 191, 192, 193, 195

Diary of Anne Frank, The, **Supp. XXI:** 245

Diary of a Rapist, The: A Novel (Connell), **Supp. XIV:** 80, 82, 94

Diary of a Young Girl, The (Frank, tr. Mooyart-Doubleday), **Supp. XXVII:** 135, 137

Diary of a Yuppie (Auchincloss), **Supp. IV Part 1:** 31, 32–33

Diary of "Helena Morley", The (Bishop, trans.), **Retro. Supp. II:** 45, 51; **Supp. I Part 1:** 92

Dias, Robert Vas, **Supp. XXII:** 164, 169

Diay of Anne Frank, The (Goodrich and Hackett), **Supp. XXVII:** 136
Díaz, Junot, **Supp. XXIV: 83–95; Supp. XXV:** 49, 61
Díaz del Castillo, Bernál, **III:** 13, 14
Dick, Philip K., **Supp. XVI:** 123; **Supp. XVIII:** 136, 137, 138, 139, 142; **Supp. XXII:** 49
Dickens, Charles, **I:** 152, 198, 505; **II:** 98, 179, 186, 192, 271, 273–274, 288, 290, 297, 301, 307, 316, 322, 559, 561, 563, 577, 582; **III:** 146, 247, 325, 368, 411, 421, 426, 572, 577, 613–614, 616; **IV:** 21, 192, 194, 211, 429; **Retro. Supp. I:** 33, 91, 218; **Retro. Supp. II:** 204; **Retro. Supp. III:** 139; **Supp. I Part 1:** 13, 34, 35, 36, 41, 49; **Supp. I Part 2:** 409, 523, 579, 590, 622, 675; **Supp. IV Part 1:** 293, 300, 341; **Supp. IV Part 2:** 464; **Supp. IX:** 246; **Supp. VIII:** 180; **Supp. XI:** 277; **Supp. XII:** 335, 337; **Supp. XIII:** 233; **Supp. XV:** 62; **Supp. XVI:** 63, 65–66, 72–73, 202; **Supp. XVIII:** 7, 136, 146; **Supp. XX:** 21, 87, 195; **Supp. XXII:** 206; **Supp. XXIII:** 4, 85, 290; **Supp. XXIV:** 87; **Supp. XXV:** 258; **Supp. XXVII:** 269
Dickerson, Mary Jane, **Retro. Supp. III:** 81
Dickey, James, **I:** 29, 535; **III:** 268; **Retro. Supp. II:** 233; **Supp. III Part 1:** 354; **Supp. III Part 2:** 541, 597; **Supp. IV Part 1: 175–194; Supp. V:** 333; **Supp. X:** 30; **Supp. XI:** 312, 317; **Supp. XIX:** 282; **Supp. XV:** 115, 348; **Supp. XVIII:** 191, 299; **Supp. XXI:** 35; **Supp. XXIII:** 43, 50; **Supp. XXIV:** 42; **Supp. XXVI:** 67; **Supp. XXVIII:** 24, 26, 29
Dick Gibson Show, The (Elkin), **Supp. VI:** 42, **48–49**
Dickie, Margaret, **Retro. Supp. II:** 53, 84
Dickinson, Donald, **Retro. Supp. I:** 206, 212
Dickinson, Edward, **I:** 451–452, 453
Dickinson, Mrs. Edward, **I:** 451, 453
Dickinson, Emily, **I:** 384, 419, 433, **451–473; II:** 272, 276, 277, 530; **III:** 19, 194, 196, 214, 493, 505, 508, 556, 572, 576; **IV:** 134, 135, 331, 444; **Retro. Supp. I: 25–50; Retro. Supp. II:** 39, 40, 43, 45, 50, 76, 134, 155, 170; **Retro. Supp. III:** 248, 251; **Supp. I Part 1:** 29, 79, 188, 372; **Supp. I Part 2:** 375, 546, 609, 682, 691; **Supp. II Part 1:** 4; **Supp. III Part 1:** 63; **Supp. III Part 2:** 600, 622; **Supp. IV Part 1:** 31, 257; **Supp. IV Part 2:** 434, 637, 641, 643; **Supp. IX:** 37, 38, 53, 87, 90; **Supp. V:** 79, 140, 332, 335; **Supp. VIII:** 95, 104, 106, 108, 198, 205, 272; **Supp. XII:** 226; **Supp. XIII:** 153, 339; **Supp. XIV:** 45, 127–128, 133, 261, 284; **Supp. XIX:** 86; **Supp. XV:** 287, 303, 309; **Supp. XVI:** 288; **Supp. XVII:** 71, 73, 74, 75, 132; **Supp. XVIII:** 301; **Supp. XX: 106, 108; Supp. XXI:**
52, 61, 64, 132, 214; **Supp. XXII:** 81, 82, 225, 277–278; **Supp. XXIII:** 19, 165; **Supp. XXVII:** 261, 283, 292
Dickinson, Gilbert, **I:** 469
Dickinson, Goldsworthy Lowes, **Supp. XIV:** 336
Dickinson, Lavinia Norcross, **I:** 451, 453, 462, 470
Dickinson, Stephanie, **Supp. XXIII:** 250
Dickinson, Mrs. William A. (Susan Gilbert), **I:** 452, 453, 456, 469, 470
Dickinson, William Austin, **I:** 451, 453, 469
Dickinson and the Strategies of Reticence (Dobson), **Retro. Supp. I:** 29, 42
Dickson, Helen. *See* Blackmur, Helen Dickson
Dickstein, Morris, **Supp. XIII:** 106; **Supp. XXIV:** 222, 223
"Dick Whittington and His Cat", **Supp. I Part 2:** 656
"DICTATORSHIP OF THE PROLE-TARIAT, THE" (Baraka), **Supp. II Part 1:** 54
Dictionary of Afro-American Slang (Major), **Supp. XXII:** 172, 174, 180
Dictionary of American English (Craigie and Hulbert, eds.), **Retro. Supp. III:** 265
Dictionary of Literary Biography (Barron and Meyer, eds.), **Supp. XIX:** 195; **Supp. XVIII:** 173
Dictionary of Literary Biography (Gwynn, ed.), **Supp. XIX:** 121; **Supp. XVIII:** 173
Dictionary of Literary Biography (Kibler, ed.), **Supp. IX:** 94, 109; **Supp. XI:** 297
Dictionary of Literary Biography (Knight, ed.), **Supp. XIV:** 144
Dictionary of Literary Biography (Martine, ed.), **Supp. XXII:** 187
Dictionary of Literary Biography (Sicher, ed.), **Supp. XVII:** 41
Dictionary of Literary Biography (Twentieth-Century American Nature Poets, Bryson and Thompson, eds.), **Supp. XXIII:** 129
Dictionary of Modern English Usage, A (Fowler), **Supp. I Part 2:** 660
Dictionary of the Mohawk Language, A (Pyrlaeus), **Supp. XXVI:** 86
"Dictum: For a Masque of Deluge" (Merwin), **Supp. III Part 1:** 342–343
"Didactic Poem" (Levertov), **Supp. III Part 1:** 280
Diderot, Denis, **II:** 535; **IV:** 440; **Supp. XVI:** 293; **Supp. XVII:** 145
Did I Ever Tell You How Lucky You Are? (Geisel), **Supp. XVI:** 109
Di Dio, François, **Supp. XXVII:** 153
Didion, Joan, **Retro. Supp. I:** 116; **Retro. Supp. II:** 209; **Supp. I Part 1:** 196, 197; **Supp. III Part 1:** 302; **Supp. IV Part 1: 195–216; Supp. XI:** 221; **Supp. XII:** 307; **Supp. XXV:** 208; **Supp. XXVI:** 45, 49, 53; **Supp. XXVIII:** 40
Dido, **I:** 81
Dido, Queen of Hearts (Atherton), **Supp. XXIV:** 26
Di Donato, Peter, **Supp. XX: 34**
Di Donato, Pietro, **Supp. XX: 33–47**
"Did 'Paco's Story' Deserve Its Award" (Kakutani), **Supp. XXII:** 109
"Did You Ever Dream Lucky?" (Ellison), **Supp. II Part 1:** 246
Dieckmann, Katherine, **Supp. XXIII:** 295, 296
"Die-Hard, The" (Benét), **Supp. XI:** 54–55, 56
Diehl, Digby, **Supp. IV Part 1:** 204
Dien Cai Dau (Komunyakaa), **Supp. XIII:** 121, **122–124,** 125, 131, 132
Dies, Martin, **Supp. XVIII:** 229
"Dies Irae" (R. Lowell), **II:** 553
Die Zeit Ohne Beispiel, (Goebbels), **III:** 560
Difference Engine, The (W. Gibson and B. Sterling), **Supp. XVI:** 121, 124, **128–129**
Different Drummer, A (Larkin; film), **Supp. XI:** 20
Different Fleshes (Goldbarth), **Supp. XII:** 181–182, 188
Different Hours (Dunn), **Supp. XI:** 139, 142, 143, 155
"Different Road, A" (Strout), **Supp. XXIII:** 282–283
Different Seasons (King), **Supp. V:** 148, 152
Different Ways to Pray (Nye), **Supp. XIII:** 274, 275, 277, 285, 287
"Different Ways to Pray" (Nye), **Supp. XIII:** 275
"Difficulties of a Statesman" (Eliot), **I:** 580
"Difficulties of Modernism and the Modernism of Difficulty" (Poirier), **Supp. II Part 1:** 136
Diff'rent (O'Neill), **III:** 389; **Supp. XXII:** 22
Di Filippo, Paul, **Supp. XXII:** 260, 261
DiGaetani, John L., **Supp. XIII:** 200
Digges, Deborah, **Supp. XXIII:** 57
"Digging" (Sanders), **Supp. XVI:** 272
"Digging in the Garden of Age I Uncover a Live Root" (Swenson), **Supp. IV Part 2:** 649
Digging Up the Dirt (Moraga), **Supp. XXIII:** 197
Diggins, John P., **Supp. I Part 2:** 650
Digital Barbarism: A Writer's Manifesto (Helprin), **Supp. XXV:** 81, 84, 88–89
"Dignity of Life, The" (C. Bly), **Supp. XVI:** 34, 36–37
Digregorio, Charles, **Supp. XI:** 326
"Digression on *Number I,* 1948" (O'Hara), **Supp. XXIII:** 214
"Dilemma" (Budbill), **Supp. XIX:** 2
"Dilemma of Determinism, The" (James), **II:** 347–348, 352
"Dilemma of the Negro Writer, The" (speech, C. Himes), **Supp. XVI:** 140
"Dilettante, The" (Wharton), **IV:** 311, 313
"Dilettante, The: A Modern Type" (Dunbar), **Supp. II Part 1:** 199
Dillard, Annie, **Supp. VI: 19–39; Supp. VIII:** 272; **Supp. X:** 31; **Supp. XIII:**

154; **Supp. XXVI:** 31, 37; **Supp. XXVIII:** 247, 255–256

Dillard, R. H. W., **Supp. XII:** 16

Dillman, Bradford, **III:** 403; **Supp. XII:** 241

Dillon, Brian, **Supp. X:** 209

Dillon, George, **III:** 141; **Supp. III Part 2:** 621

Dillon, Millicent, **Supp. IV Part 1:** 95

Dilsaver, Paul, **Supp. XIII:** 112

Dilthey, Wilhelm, **I:** 58

Dime-Store Alchemy: The Art of Joseph Cornell, **Supp. VIII:** 272

"Diminuendo" (Dunn), **Supp. XI:** 152–153

"Dimout in Harlem" (Hughes), **Supp. I Part 1:** 333

"Dinah's Lament" (Nelson), **Supp. XVIII:** 183

Dinesen, Isak, **IV:** 279; **Supp. VIII:** 171; **Supp. XVI:** 250

Dining Room, The (Gurney), **Supp. V:** 105–106

"Dinner at ------, A" (O. Henry), **Supp. II Part 1:** 402

"Dinner at Sir Nigel's" (Bowles), **Supp. IV Part 1:** 94

Dinner at the Homesick Restaurant (Tyler), **Supp. IV Part 2:** 657, 667–668

"Dinner at Uncle Borris's" (Simic), **Supp. VIII:** 272

Dinner Bridge (Lardner), **II:** 435

Dinosaur Hunter, The (Hickam), **Supp. XXVII:** 111

Dinosaur Tales (Bradbury), **Supp. IV Part 1:** 103

"Diogenes Invents a Game" (Karr), **Supp. XI:** 240–241

"Diogenes Tries to Forget" (Karr), **Supp. XI:** 241

Diomede, Matthew, **Supp. XX: 46**

Dionysis in Doubt (Robinson), **III:** 510

Dionysus in 69 (Schechner), **Supp. XXIV:** 116

Diop, Birago, **Supp. IV Part 1:** 16

Diop, David, **Supp. IV Part 1:** 16

Di Piero, W. S., **Supp. XIX: 33–48; Supp. XVII:** 241

Di Prima, Diane, **Supp. III Part 1:** 30; **Supp. XIV:** 125, 144, 148, 150

Dirda, Michael, **Supp. XXI:** 233

Direction of Poetry, The: An Anthology of Rhymed and Metered Verse Written in the English Language since 1975 (Richman, ed.), **Supp. XV:** 250, 251

Direction of Poetry, The: Rhymed and Metered Verse Written in the English Language since 1975 (Richman), **Supp. XI:** 249

"Directive" (Bishop), **Retro. Supp. II:** 42

"Directive" (Frost), **III:** 287; **Retro. Supp. I:** 140; **Retro. Supp. III:** 105; **Supp. VIII:** 32, 33; **Supp. XXVI:** 77

"Dire Cure" (Matthews), **Supp. IX:** 168

"Dirge" (Dunbar), **Supp. II Part 1:** 199

"Dirge for My Brother: Dawn to Dawn"(Lea), **Supp. XXVIII:** 131

"Dirge Notes" (Huddle), **Supp. XXVI:** 148, 153

"Dirge without Music" (Millay), **III:** 126

"Dirt" (Salter), **Supp. IX:** 257, 260, 261

"Dirt and Desire: Essay on the Phenomenology of Female Pollution in Antiquity" (Carson), **Supp. XII:** 111

Dirty Bird Blues (Major), **Supp. XXII: 180–181**

Dirty Dingus Magee (film), **Supp. XVII:** 139

"Dirty English Potatoes" (X. J. Kennedy), **Supp. XV:** 165

"Dirty Memories" (Olds), **Supp. X:** 211

Dirty Story (Shanley), **Supp. XIV:** 316, 331

"Dirty Word, The" (Shapiro), **Supp. II Part 2:** 710

Dirty Work (L. Brown), **Supp. XXI:** 37, 39, 40, 42, **45**

"'Disabled Imagination' and the Masculine Metaphor in the Works of Leonard Kriegel, The" (Haugen), **Supp. XXIV:** 215

Disappearance of the Jews, The (Mamet), **Supp. XIV:** 249–250, 250–251, 252, 254

Disappearances (Auster), **Supp. XII:** 23

"Disappearances" (Hogan), **Supp. IV Part 1:** 401

Disappearances (Mosher), **Supp. XXII:** 204, 205, 206, 207, 208, 209, **210**

"Disappeared, The " (C. Baxter), **Supp. XVII:** 19

Disappearing Acts (McMillan), **Supp. XIII:** 182, 183, **188–189,** 192

Disappearing Ink: Poetry at the End of Print Culture (Gioia), **Supp. XV:** 112

"Disappointment, The" (Creeley), **Supp. IV Part 1:** 143

"Disappointment and Desire" (R. Bly), **Supp. IV Part 1:** 71

Disappointment Artist, The (Lethem), **Supp. XVIII:** 135, 141, **148**

"Disarmament"(Stuart), **Supp. XXVIII:** 230

"Discards" (Baker), **Supp. XIII:** 53, 55–56

Discerning the Signs of the Times (Niebuhr), **III:** 300–301, 307–308

Disch, Thomas M., **Supp. XIX:** 1

"Disciple of Bacon, The" (Epstein), **Supp. XII:** 163–164

"Discipline" (L. Brown), **Supp. XXI:** 44

Discomfort, Zone, The: A Personal History (Franzen), **Supp. XX: 83, 84, 95**

"Discordants" (Aiken), **I:** 65

Discourse on Method (Descartes), **I:** 255

"Discourtesies" (Kirsch), **Supp. XV:** 341

"Discovering Theme and Structure in the Novel" (Schuster), **Supp. VIII:** 126

"Discovery" (Freneau), **Supp. II Part 1:** 258

"Discovery of the Madeiras, The" (Frost), **Retro. Supp. I:** 139

"Discovery of What It Means to Be an American, The" (Baldwin), **Supp. I Part 1:** 54–55

Discovery! The Search for Arabian Oil (Stegner), **Supp. IV Part 2:** 599

Discrepancies and Apparitions (Wakoski), **Supp. XXVIII:** 261, 262

Discrepant Engagement (Mackey), **Supp. XXVII:** 159, 160, 161

Discrete Series (Oppen), **Supp. XXVI:** 224, 226–227, 230, 235

"Discrete Series" (Zukofsky), **Supp. III Part 2:** 616

"Discretions of Alcibiades" (Pinsky), **Supp. VI:** 241

"Disease, The" (Rukeyser), **Supp. VI:** 279

Disenchanted, The (play, Schulberg and Breit), **Supp. XVIII:** 254

Disenchanted, The (Schulberg), **II:** 98; **Retro. Supp. I:** 113; **Supp. XVIII: 247–250,** 253

Disenchantments: An Anthology of Modern Fairy Tale Poetry (Mieder), **Supp. XIV:** 126

"Dish of Green Pears, A" (Ríos), **Supp. IV Part 2:** 552

"Disillusion and Dogma" (Untermeyer), **Supp. XV:** 306

"Dislocated Room, The"(Siken), **Supp. XXVIII:** 199, 200, 201

"Disloyal to Civilization: Feminism, Racism, and Gynephobia" (Rich), **Retro. Supp. III:** 248

Dismantling the Silence (Simic), **Supp. VIII: 273–274,** 275, 276

Disney, Walt, **III:** 275, 426

"Disney of My Mind" (Chabon), **Supp. XI:** 63

Disobedience (Notley), **Supp. XXII:** 235, 236

Dispatches (Herr), **Supp. XI:** 245; **Supp. XIX:** 17

"Displaced Person, The" (O'Connor), **III:** 343–344, 350, 352, 356; **Retro. Supp. II:** 229, 232, 236

"Disposal" (Snodgrass), **Supp. VI:** 314

Dispossessed, The (Berryman), **I:** 170, 172, 173, 174, 175, 176, 178

"Disquieting Muses, The" (Plath), **Supp. I Part 2:** 538

Disraeli, Benjamin, **II:** 127

Dissent (Didion), **Supp. IV Part 1:** 208

"Dissent in Ashcroft's America" (P. N. Warren), **Supp. XX: 273**

"Dissenting Opinion on Kafka, A" (Wilson), **IV:** 437–438

Dissent in Three American Wars (Morison, Merk, and Freidel), **Supp. I Part 2:** 495

Dissertation on Liberty and Necessity, Pleasure and Pain, A (Franklin), **II:** 108

Dissertations on Government; the Affairs of the Bank: and Paper Money (Paine), **Supp. I Part 2:** 510

"Distance" (Carver), **Supp. III Part 1:** 146

"Distance" (Everwine), **Supp. XV:** 85

"Distance" (Paley), **Supp. VI:** 222

"Distance, The" (Karr), **Supp. XI:** 241

"Distance from the Sea, A" (Kees), **Supp. XV:** 147

"Distance Nowhere" (Hughes), **Retro. Supp. I:** 207

"Distance Up Close, The" (Peacock), **Supp. XIX:** 196–197, 198

"Distant Episode, A" (Bowles), **Supp. IV Part 1:** 84–85, 86, 90

Distant Episode, A: The Selected Stories (Bowles), **Supp. IV Part 1:** 79

Distant Rain: A Conversation Between Jakuch\[omacron\] Setouchi & Tess Gallagher (Setouchi and Gallagher), **Supp. XXIV:** 166, 178

Distinguished Guest, The (Miller), **Supp. XII: 299–301**

Distortions (Beattie), **Supp. V:** 21, 23, 24, 25, 27

"Distrest Shepherdess, The" (Freneau), **Supp. II Part 1:** 258

District of Columbia (Dos Passos), **I:** 478, 489–490, 492

Disturber of the Peace (Manchester), **III:** 103

Disturbing the Peace (Yates), **Supp. XI:** 345, 346

"Diver, The" (Hayden), **Supp. II Part 1:** 368, 372, 373

"Divided Life of Jean Toomer, The" (Toomer), **Supp. III Part 2:** 488

Divided Self, The (Laing), **Supp. XX: 95**

Divina Commedia (Longfellow, trans.), **II:** 490, 492, 493

"Divina Pastora, La" (C. L. R. James), **Supp. XXI:** 160

"Divine, The" (Di Piero), **Supp. XIX:** 41

"Divine Collaborator" (Simic), **Supp. VIII:** 282

Divine Comedies (Merrill), **Supp. III Part 1:** 324, 329–332

Divine Comedy (Dante), **I:** 137, 265, 400, 446; **II:** 215, 335, 490, 492, 493; **III:** 13, 448, 453; **Supp. V:** 283, 331, 338, 345; **Supp. X:** 253; **Supp. XIV:** 6; **Supp. XIX:** 36, 39

Divine Husband, The (Goldman), **Supp. XXV:** 49–50, 55–57

"Divine Image, The" (Blake), **Supp. V:** 257

Divine Pilgrim, The (Aiken), **I:** 50, 55

Divine Right's Trip (Norman), **Supp. XXIII:** 42

Divine Tragedy, The (Longfellow), **II:** 490, 500, 505, 506, 507; **Retro. Supp. II:** 165, 166

Divine Weekes and Workes (Sylvester, trans.), **Supp. I Part 1:** 104

Divine Weeks (Du Bartas), **IV:** 157–158

"Diving into the Wreck" (Rich), **Retro. Supp. III:** 246–247, 252

Diving into the Wreck: Poems 1971–1972 (Rich), **Retro. Supp. III:** 242, 246–247; **Supp. I Part 2:** 550, 559–565, 569; **Supp. XV:** 252

"Diving Past African Violets" (A. Finch), **Supp. XVII:** 72

Diving Rock on the Hudson, A (H. Roth), **Supp. IX:** 236, **237–238**

"Divinity in Its Fraying Fact, A" (Levis), **Supp. XI:** 271

"Divinity School Address" (Emerson), **II:** 12–13

"Divinity School or Trusting the Act of Writing" (Abraham), **Supp. XXIV:** 1, 3–4

"Divisions upon a Ground" (Hecht), **Supp. X:** 58

"Divorce" (Karr), **Supp. XI:** 244

"Divorced Fathers and Pizza Crusts" (Halliday), **Supp. XIX:** 93

Divorced in America: Marriage in an Age of Possibility (Epstein), **Supp. XIV:** 113

"Divorce Dream" (Halliday), **Supp. XIX:** 90

"Divorce in the United States" (Atherton), **Supp. XXIV:** 24

Dix, Douglas Shields, **Supp. XII:** 14

Dixie City Jam (Burke), **Supp. XIV:** 32

Dixon, Ivan, **Supp. IV Part 1:** 362

Dixon, Stephen, **Supp. XII: 139–158**

Dixon, Terrell F., **Supp. XVI:** 21

Dixon, Thomas, Jr., **Supp. II Part 1:** 169, 171, 177

Djbot Baghostus's Run (Mackey), **Supp. XXVII:** 158

Djinn (Robbe-Grillet), **Supp. V:** 48

D'Lugoff, Burt, **Supp. IV Part 1:** 362, 370

Dlugos, Tim, **Supp. XXVII:** 24

Dmytryk, Edward, **Supp. XX: 41**

Do, Lord, Remember Me (Garrett), **Supp. VII:** 98–100, 110

"Doaksology, The" (Wolfe), **IV:** 459

Do Androids Dream of Electric Sheep? (Dick), **Supp. XVIII:** 137

Dobard, Raymond G., **Supp. XXVI:** 200

Dobie, J. Frank, **Supp. V:** 225; **Supp. XIII:** 227

Döblin, Alfred, **Supp. XV:** 137

Dobriansky, Lev, **Supp. I Part 2:** 648, 650

Dobrin, Sidney I., **Supp. XVIII:** 192, 195

Dobson, Joanne, **Retro. Supp. I:** 29, 31, 42; **Supp. XVIII:** 259

Dobyns, Stephen, **Supp. XIII: 73–92**

"Docking at Palermo" (Hugo), **Supp. VI:** 137–138

"Dock Rats" (Moore), **III:** 213

"Dock-Witch, The" (Ozick), **Supp. V:** 262, 264

"Doc Mellhorn and the Pearly Gates" (Benét), **Supp. XI:** 55

"Doctor, The" (Dubus), **Supp. VII:** 80–81

"Doctor and the Doctor's Wife, The" (Hemingway), **II:** 248; **Retro. Supp. I:** 174, 175

Doctor Breen's Practice, a Novel (Howells), **I:** 282

Doctor Faustus (Mann), **III:** 283

Doctor Jazz (Carruth), **Supp. XVI:** 47, 59

"Doctor Jekyll" (Sontag), **Supp. III Part 2:** 469

"Doctor Leavis and the Moral Tradition" (Trilling), **Supp. III Part 2:** 512–513

"Doctor Marino" (Faulkner), **Retro. Supp. III:** 84

Doctor Martino and Other Stories (Faulkner), **II:** 72; **Retro. Supp. I:** 84; **Retro. Supp. III:** 84

"Doctor of the Heart, The" (Sexton), **Supp. II Part 2:** 692

Doctorow, E. L., **Retro. Supp. I:** 97; **Supp. III Part 2:** 590, 591; **Supp. IV Part 1: 217–240; Supp. V:** 45; **Supp. XVI:** 73; **Supp. XVII:** 183; **Supp. XX: 84, 90; Supp. XXI:** 18–19; **Supp. XXII:** 268

Doctor Sax (Kerouac), **Supp. III Part 1:** 220–222, 224–227

Doctor Sleep (Bell), **Supp. X: 9–11**

"Doctors' Row" (Aiken), **I:** 67

Doctor's Son and Other Stories, The (O'Hara), **III:** 361

Doctor Stories, The (W. C. Williams), **Retro. Supp. I:** 424

"Doctor's Wife, The" (Ozick), **Supp. V:** 262, 265

Doctor Zhivago (Pasternak), **IV:** 434, 438, 443

"Documentary" (Simic), **Supp. VIII:** 282

Dodd, Edward H., **Supp. XXVIII:** 252

Dodd, Elizabeth, **Supp. V:** 77

Dodd, Susan, **Supp. XXV:** 129

Dodd, Wayne, **Supp. IV Part 2:** 625

Dodge, Mabel, **Supp. XX: 69; Supp. XXI:** 5, 6, 8, 12; **Supp. XXII:** 158, 161. *See also* Luhan, Mabel Dodge

Dodge, Mary Mapes, **Supp. XXVIII:** 228

Dodson, Owen, **Supp. I Part 1:** 54

Dodsworth (Lewis), **II:** 442, 449–450, 453, 456

Doenitz, Karl, **Supp. I Part 2:** 491

Does Civilization Need Religion? (Niebuhr), **III:** 293–294

"Does 'Consciousness' Exist?" (James), **II:** 356

"Does Education Pay?" (Du Bois), **Supp. II Part 1:** 159

"Dog" (B. Kelly), **Supp. XVII:** 126

Dog (Shepard), **Supp. III Part 2:** 434

"Dog Act, The" (Komunyakaa), **Supp. XIII:** 114–115

"Dog and the Playlet, The" (O. Henry), **Supp. II Part 1:** 399

Dog Beneath the Skin, The (Auden), **Supp. II Part 1:** 10

"Dog Creek Mainline" (Wright), **Supp. V:** 340

"Dogdom of the Dead, The" (Stallings), **Supp. XXV:** 228

"Dogfight" (W. Gibson and Swanwick), **Supp. XVI:** 128

Dog in the Manger, The (Vega; Merwin, trans.), **Supp. III Part 1:** 341, 347

Dog of the Marriage, The (Hempel), **Supp. XXI:** 115, 116, 117, 118, **126–127**

"Dog"(P. Benedict), **Supp. XXIII:** 36–37, 39

Dogs Bark, but the Caravan Rolls On (Conroy), **Supp. XVI:** 63, 70, 74, **75–76**

Dogs Bark, The: Public People and Private Places (Capote), **Supp. III Part 1:** 120, 132

"Dog's Eye" (J. W. Miller), **Supp. XX: 167**

"Dogs of Bucharest, The" (Gallagher), **Supp. XXIV:** 171

Dogs of God (Benedict), **Supp. XXIII:** 35, **41–45,** 49–50

Dog Soldiers (Stone), **Supp. V:** 298, 299–301

"Dog's Tale, A" (Twain), **Retro. Supp. III:** 268

Dog Star, The (Di Piero), **Supp. XIX:** 38, **40–41,** 43

"Dog Stories" (Prose), **Supp. XVI:** 256

Dog & the Fever, The (Quevedo), **Retro. Supp. I:** 423

"Dogtown Letters, The" (Jarman and R. McDowell), **Supp. XVII:** 111

"Dogwood, The" (Levertov), **Supp. III Part 1:** 276

"Dogwood Tree, The: A Boyhood" (Updike), **IV:** 218; **Retro. Supp. I:** 318, 319

Doig, Ivan, **Supp. XIV:** 227

"Doing Battle with the Wolf" (Coleman), **Supp. XI:** 87–88

"Doing Jigsaw Puzzles" (Crooker), **Supp. XXIII:** 56

Doing Literary Business: American Women Writers in the Nineteenth Century (Coultrap-McQuin), **Supp. XVI:** 85

Doings and Undoings (Podhoretz), **Supp. VIII:** 236–237

"Do-It-Yourself" (C. Baxter), **Supp. XVII:** 14–15

Dolan, Jill, **Supp. XV:** 327

Dolben, Digby Mackworth, **Supp. XX:** 230

"Dolce Far' Niente" (Humphrey), **Supp. IX:** 106

Dolci, Carlo, **III:** 474–475

Dollars and Cents (A. Warner), **Supp. XVIII:** 264

"Dollhouse, The" (Haines), **Supp. XII:** 204

"Dollhouse, The" (Stallings), **Supp. XXV:** 231, 232

Dollmaker, The (Arnow), **Supp. XXVIII:** 1, 2–3, 8–11, 12, 13

Dollmaker's Ghost, The (Levis), **Supp. XI:** 259, 260, **264–268**

Doll's House, A (Ibsen), **III:** 523; **IV:** 357; **Supp. XVI:** 182; **Supp. XXVIII:** 230

Dolmetsch, Arnold, **III:** 464

Dolores Claiborne (King), **Supp. V:** 138, 141, 147, 148, 149–150, 152

"Dolph Heyliger" (Irving), **II:** 309

Dolphin, The (R. Lowell), **Retro. Supp. II:** 183, 186, 188, **190–191; Supp. XII:** 253–254

"Dolphins" (Francis), **Supp. IX:** 83

Dome of Many-Coloured Class, A (A. Lowell), **II:** 515, 516–517

Domesday Book (Masters), **Supp. I Part 2:** 465, 466–469, 471, 473, 476

"Domestic Economy" (Gilman), **Supp. XI:** 206

"Domestic Manners" (Hardwick), **Supp. III Part 1:** 211

Domestic Work (Trethewey), **Supp. XXI:** 243, 244, **248–251,** 254

"Domestic Work, 1937" (Trethewey), **Supp. XXI:** 248

"Dominant White, The" (McKay), **Supp. X:** 134

Dominguez, Robert, **Supp. VIII:** 83

Domini, John, **Supp. XIX:** 45; **Supp. XXI:** 235

Dominique, Jean. *See* Closset, Marie

Donahoe, Edward, **Supp. XVIII:** 132

Donahue, Deirdre, **Supp. XXV:** 9

Donahue, Phil, **Supp. IV Part 2:** 526; **Supp. X:** 311

Donaldson, Susan, **Supp. XXII:** 148

Doña Perfecta (Galdós), **II:** 290

Dong, Stella, **Supp. XVI:** 222

Don Juan (Byron), **Supp. XV:** 259

Don Juan (Lewisohn), **Supp. XXVIII:** 149, 151

"DON JUAN IN HELL" (Baraka), **Supp. II Part 1:** 33

Donkey of God, The (Untermeyer), **Supp. XV:** 310

"Donna mi Prega" (Cavalcanti), **Supp. III Part 2:** 620, 621, 622

Donn-Byrne, Brian Oswald. *See* Byrne, Donn

Donne, John, **I:** 358–359, 384, 389, 522, 586; **II:** 254; **III:** 493; **IV:** 83, 88, 135, 141, 144, 145, 151, 156, 165, 331, 333; **Retro. Supp. II:** 76; **Supp. I Part 1:** 80, 364, 367; **Supp. I Part 2:** 421, 424, 467, 725, 726; **Supp. III Part 2:** 614, 619; **Supp. IX:** 44; **Supp. VIII:** 26, 33, 164; **Supp. XII:** 45, 159; **Supp. XIII:** 94, 130; **Supp. XIV:** 122; **Supp. XV:** 92, 251; **Supp. XVI:** 158, 204; **Supp. XVIII:** 35, 39, 50–51, 307; **Supp. XXIV:** 167; **Supp. XXVII:** 220

Donne's Sermons: Selected Passages (L. P. Smith, ed.), **Supp. XIV:** 342

Donoghue, Denis, **I:** 537; **Supp. IV Part 1:** 39; **Supp. VIII:** 105, 189

Donohue, H. E. F., **Supp. IX:** 2, 3, 15, 16

Donoso, José, **Supp. XXIV:** 86

Do Not Deny Me (Thompson), **Supp. XXIII:** 300–301

"Do Not Weep Maiden, For War Is Kind" (Crane), **Supp. XVIII:** 75

Donovan, Josephine, **Retro. Supp. II:** 138, 139, 147

Don Quixote (Cervantes), **I:** 134; **II:** 291, 434; **III:** 113, 614; **Supp. I Part 2:** 422; **Supp. IX:** 94; **Supp. XXIV:** 87

Don Quixote: Which Was a Dream (Acker), **Supp. XII:** 5, **12–14**

Don't Ask (Levine), **Supp. V:** 178

Don't Ask Questions (Marquand), **III:** 58

Don't Bet on the Prince: Contemporary Feminist Fairy Tales in North America and England (Zipes), **Supp. XIV:** 126

Don't Drink the Water (Allen), **Supp. XV:** 3, **14**

Don't Look Back (film, Pennebaker), **Supp. XVIII:** 19

"Don't Miss It" (Stone), **Supp. XXVII:** 260

"Don't Neglect Your Wife" (script, Atherton), **Supp. XXIV:** 25

"Don't Shoot the Warthog" (Corso), **Supp. XII:** 123

Don't Stop the Carnival (Wouk), **Supp. XXV:** 257, 263–264

"Don't Tell Mother" (Wasserstein), **Supp. XV:** 319

"Don't Think Twice, It's All Right" (song, Dylan), **Supp. XVIII:** 24

Don't Worry About the Kids (Neugeboren), **Supp. XVI:** 226

"Don't Worry About the Kids" (Neugeboren), **Supp. XVI:** 226

Don't You Want to Be Free? (Hughes), **Retro. Supp. I:** 203; **Supp. I Part 1:** 339

"Doodler, The" (Merrill), **Supp. III Part 1:** 321

Doolan, Moira, **Retro. Supp. II:** 247

Doolittle, Hilda (H. D.), **II:** 517, 520–521; **III:** 194, 195–196, 457, 465; **IV:** 404, 406; **Retro. Supp. I:** 288, 412, 413, 414, 415, 417; **Supp. I Part 1:** **253–275; Supp. I Part 2:** 707; **Supp. III Part 1:** 48; **Supp. III Part 2:** 610; **Supp. IV Part 1:** 257; **Supp. V:** 79; **Supp. XV:** 43, 249, 301, 302; **Supp. XVII:** 77; **Supp. XXII:** 88; **Supp. XXIV:** 64; **Supp. XXVII:** 160, 261, 287

Doolittle, Thomas, **IV:** 150

"Doomed by Our Blood to Care" (Orfalea), **Supp. XIII:** 278

"Doomsday" (Plath), **Retro. Supp. II:** 242

Doomsters, The (Macdonald), **Supp. IV Part 2:** 462, 463, 472, 473

Doomswoman, The (Atherton), **Supp. XXIV:** 22

Doonesbury (Trudeau), **Supp. XXIV:** 283

"Door, The" (Creeley), **Supp. IV Part 1:** 145, 146, 156–157

Door, The (Rinehart), **Supp. XXV:** 197, 200

"Door, The" (White), **Supp. I Part 2:** 651, 675–676

"Door in the Dark, The" (Frost), **II:** 156

Door in the Hive, A (Levertov), **Supp. III Part 1:** 283, 284

"Door of the Trap, The" (Anderson), **I:** 112

"Doors" (Dybek), **Supp. XXIII:** 69

Doors (Hoffman), **Supp. XVIII:** 86–87

"Doors" (Hoffman), **Supp. XVIII:** 86–87

"Doors, Doors, Doors" (Sexton), **Supp. II Part 2:** 681

Doors, The, **Supp. X:** 186

"Doorways into the Depths" (Sanders), **Supp. XVI:** 272

Doreski, William, **Retro. Supp. II:** 185

Dorfman, Ariel, **Supp. IX:** 131, 138

Dorfman, Joseph, **Supp. I Part 2:** 631, 647, 650

Doris of Dobbs Ferry (Wells), **Supp. XXVI:** 277

Dorman, Jen, **Supp. XI:** 240

Dorn, Edward, **Supp. IV Part 1:** 154; **Supp. XXIV:** 33, 44; **Supp. XXVIII:** 268

Dorn, Sarah, **Supp. XXI:** 243

"Dorothea Dix, Samaritan" (J. Scott), **Supp. XVII:** 189

Dorr, Julia, **Supp. XV:** 286

Dorrance Doings (Wells), **Supp. XXVI:** 277

Dorrance Domain, The (Wells), **Supp. XXVI:** 277

Dorris, Michael, **Supp. IV Part 1:** 260, 272

Dos Passos, John, **I:** 99, 288, 374, 379, **474–496,** 517, 519; **II:** 74, 77, 89, 98; **III:** 2, 28, 29, 70, 172, 382–383; **IV:** 340, 427, 433; **Retro. Supp. I:** 105, 113, 187; **Retro. Supp. II:** 95, 196; **Supp. I Part 2:** 646; **Supp. III Part 1:** 104, 105; **Supp. V:** 277; **Supp. VIII:** 101, 105; **Supp. XIV:** 24; **Supp. XV:** 135, 137, 182; **Supp. XVII:** 105, 107; **Supp. XXI:** 8; **Supp. XXIII:** 68; **Supp. XXVI:** 17, 32, 133, 135; **Supp. XXVIII:** 68, 74

"Dos Passos: Poet Against the World" (Cowley), **Supp. II Part 1:** 143, 145

Dostoevsky: A Screenplay (Carver and Gallagher), **Supp. XXIV:** 178

Dostoevsky, Fyodor, **I:** 53, 103, 211, 468; **II:** 60, 130, 275, 320, 587; **III:** 37, 61, 155, 174, 176, 188, 189, 267, 272, 283, 286, 354, 357, 358, 359, 467, 571, 572; **IV:** 1, 7, 8, 17, 21, 50, 59, 106, 110, 128, 134, 285, 289, 476, 485, 491; **Retro. Supp. II:** 20, 204, 299; **Supp. I Part 1:** 49; **Supp. I Part 2:** 445, 466; **Supp. IV Part 2:** 519, 525; **Supp. VIII:** 175; **Supp. X:** 4–5; **Supp. XI:** 161; **Supp. XII:** 322; **Supp. XVI:** 63; **Supp. XVII:** 225; **Supp. XVIII:** 278, 280; **Supp. XX:** 45; **Supp. XXIII:** 4; **Supp. XXIV:** 132; **Supp. XXVIII:** 112

Doty, Mark, **Supp. IX:** 42, 300; **Supp. XI:** 119–138; **Supp. XXI:** 129, 130, 131, 139, 141; **Supp. XXIII:** 126, 221

Doty, M. R. *See* Dawson, Ruth; Doty, Mark

Double, The (Dostoevsky), **Supp. IX:** 105

"Double, The" (Levis), **Supp. XI:** 260, **261–263**

Double, The (Rank), **Supp. IX:** 105

Double Agent, The (Blackmur), **Supp. II Part 1:** 90, 108, 146

Double Axe, The (Jeffers), **Supp. II Part 2:** 416, 434

"Double Blind" (Skloot), **Supp. XX: 194, 208**

Doubleday, Frank, **I:** 500, 502, 515, 517; **III:** 327

Doubleday, Mrs. Frank, **I:** 500

Double Deuce (Parker), **Supp. XIX:** 183

Double Down (F. and S. Barthelme), **Supp. XI:** 27, 34, 35, 36–38

Double Dream of Spring, The (Ashbery), **Supp. III Part 1:** 11–13

Double Fold: Libraries and the Assault on Paper (Baker), **Supp. XIII:** 52, 56

Double Game (Calle), **Supp. XII:** 22

"Double Gap, The" (Auchincloss), **Supp. IV Part 1:** 33

"Double-Headed Snake of Newbury, The" (Whittier), **Supp. I Part 2:** 698

Double Honeymoon (Connell), **Supp. XIV:** 80, 87

Double Image, The (Levertov), **Supp. III Part 1:** 274, 276

"Double Image, The" (Sexton), **Supp. II Part 2:** 671, 677–678

Double Indemnity (film), **Supp. IV Part 1:** 130

Double Legacy: Reflections on a Pair of Deaths (Hadas), **Supp. XXIII:** 123, **126–127**

"Double Limbo" (Komunyakaa), **Supp. XIII:** 132

Double Man, The (Auden), **Supp. III Part 1:** 16; **Supp. X:** 118

"Double Ode" (Rukeyser), **Supp. VI:** 282–283, 286

Double Persephone (Atwood), **Supp. XIII:** 19

Double Play (Parker), **Supp. XIX: 189–190**

Doubles in Literary Psychology (Tymms), **Supp. IX:** 105

Double Vision: American Thoughts Abroad (Knowles), **Supp. XII:** 249

"Doubt" (Teasdale), **Supp. XXVII:** 291–292

"Doubt on the Great Divide" (Stafford), **Supp. XI:** 322

Dougherty, Robin, **Supp. XXII:** 205

Dougherty, Steve, **Supp. X:** 262

Douglas, Aaron, **Supp. I Part 1:** 326

Douglas, Alfred, **Supp. X:** 151

Douglas, Ann, **Supp. XII:** 136; **Supp. XVIII:** 258; **Supp. XX:** 69

Douglas, Claire, **III:** 552

Douglas, Ellen, **Supp. XXI:** 38

Douglas, George (pseudonym). *See* Brown, George Douglas

Douglas, Kirk, **Supp. XIII:** 5–6

Douglas, Lloyd, **IV:** 434

Douglas, Marjory Stoneman, **Supp. XVIII:** 195

Douglas, Melvyn, **Supp. V:** 223

Douglas, Michael, **Supp. XI:** 67

Douglas, Paul, **III:** 294

Douglas, Stephen A., **III:** 577, 588–589; **Supp. I Part 2:** 456, 471

Douglas, William O., **III:** 581

Douglass, Frederick, **Supp. I Part 1:** 51, 345; **Supp. I Part 2:** 591; **Supp. II Part 1:** 157, 195, 196, 292, 378; **Supp. III Part 1: 153–174; Supp. IV Part 1:** 1, 2, 13, 15, 256; **Supp. VIII:** 202; **Supp. XVIII:** 16; **Supp. XX: 109, 281; Supp. XXIII:** 167; **Supp. XXVIII:** 166, 173

Douglass, Thomas E., **Supp. XXIII:** 36

Douglass Pilot, The (Baldwin, ed.), **Supp. I Part 1:** 49

Dove, Belle, **I:** 451

Dove, Rita, **Supp. IV Part 1: 241–258; Supp. XVII:** 71, 110; **Supp. XVIII:** 172, 174; **Supp. XXI:** 243, 246, 247, 249, 251

Dove of the East and Other Stories, A (Helprin), **Supp. XXV:** 79, 83, 84–85

"Dover Beach" (Arnold), **Retro. Supp. I:** 325; **Supp. XIX:** 41

Dow, Lorenzo, **IV:** 265

Dowd, Douglas, **Supp. I Part 2:** 645, 650

"Do We Understand Each Other?" (Ginsberg), **Supp. II Part 1:** 311

Dowie, William, **Supp. V:** 199

Do with Me What You Will (Oates), **Supp. II Part 2:** 506, 515–517

Dowling, Eddie, **IV:** 394

Down and Out (Shanley), **Supp. XIV:** 317

"Down at City Hall" (Didion), **Supp. IV Part 1:** 211

"Down at the Cross" (Baldwin), **Retro. Supp. II:** 1, 2, 7, 12, 13, 15; **Supp. I Part 1:** 60, 61

"Down at the Dinghy" (Salinger), **III:** 559, 563

"Down by the Station, Early in the Morning" (Ashbery), **Supp. III Part 1:** 25

Downers Grove (Hornburg), **Supp. XXVII:** 80

Downey, Sharon D., **Supp. XX: 244**

Downhill Racer (film), **Supp. IX:** 253

"Down Home" (J. W. Miller), **Supp. XX: 169**

"Down in Alabam" (Bierce), **I:** 193

Downing, Ben, **Supp. XII:** 175, 189, 190–191

Downing, Major Jack (pseudonym). *See* Smith, Seba

Down in My Heart (Stafford), **Supp. XI:** 313, 315

Down Mailer's Way (Solotaroff), **Retro. Supp. II:** 203

Down the Airshaft (Gold), **Supp. XXVIII:** 69

"Down the Highway" (song, Dylan), **Supp. XVIII:** 24

Down the Rabbit Hole: Adventures and Misadventures in the Realm of Children's Literature (Lanes), **Supp. XVI:** 104

Down There on a Visit (Isherwood), **Supp. XIV:** 159, 161, 164, **168–169,** 170, 171

Down the River (Abbey), **Supp. XIII:** 12–13

"Down the River with Henry Thoreau" (Abbey), **Supp. XIII:** 12–13

Down These Mean Streets (P. Thomas), **Supp. XIII:** 264

Down the Starry River (Purdy), **Supp. VII:** 278

Down to the River: Portraits of Iowa Musicians (Dyas), **Supp. XIX:** 174

Downtown (Siddons), **Supp. XXII:** 239, 240, 242, **247–249, 251–252,** 253

"Downtrodden Mary's Failed Campaign of Terror" (Saunders), **Supp. XIX:** 226

"Downward Path to Wisdom, The" (Porter), **III:** 442, 443, 446

"Down Where I Am" (Hughes), **Supp. I Part 1:** 344

Down with Starvation Wages in Southeast Missouri (C. L. R. James), **Supp. XXI:** 169

"Dowsing for Joy" (Skloot), **Supp. XX: 203**

Dowson, Ernest C., **I:** 384

Doyle, Arthur Conan, **Retro. Supp. I:** 270; **Retro. Supp. III:** 226; **Supp. IV Part 1:** 128, 341; **Supp. IV Part 2:**

464, 469; **Supp. XI:** 63; **Supp. XXVI:** 282

Doyle, C. W., **I:** 199

Doyno, Victor, **Retro. Supp. III:** 265

"Draba" (Leopold), **Supp. XIV:** 186

Drabble, Margaret, **Supp. IV Part 1:** 297, 299, 305

Drabelle, Dennis, **Supp. XIII:** 13

Drach, Ivan, **Supp. III Part 1:** 268

Dracula (film), **Supp. IV Part 1:** 104; **Supp. XVII:** 57

Dracula (Stoker), **Supp. XXVI:** 58

"Draft Horse, The" (Frost), **Retro. Supp. I:** 141; **Retro. Supp. III:** 107

"Draft Lyrics for *Candide*" (Agee), **I:** 28

Draft of XVI Cantos, A (Pound), **III:** 472; **Retro. Supp. I:** 292

Draft of XXX Cantos, A (Pound), **III:** 196; **Retro. Supp. I:** 292

Drafts &Fragments (Pound), **Retro. Supp. I:** 293

"Dragon" (Lovecraft), **Supp. XXV:** 111

Dragon Country (T. Williams), **IV:** 383

Dragone, Nichole, **Supp. XXIII:** 157

Dragon Seed (Buck), **Supp. II Part 1:** 124

Dragons of Eden (Sagan), **Supp. XXVIII:** 23

Dragon's Teeth (Sinclair), **Supp. V:** 290

Dragon Takes a Wife, The (Myers), **Supp. XXVII:** 209

Drake, Benjamin, **Supp. I Part 2:** 584

Drake, Daniel, **Supp. I Part 2:** 584

Drake, Sir Francis, **Supp. I Part 2:** 497

Drake, Robert, **Supp. XX:** 274

Drake, St. Clair, **IV:** 475

Drake, Sylvia, **Supp. XXI:** 155

Drake, William, **Supp. XV:** 295; **Supp. XXVII:** 284, 285, 291, 293, 294, 297

Drama and the Stage, The (Lewisohn), **Supp. XXVIII:** 149

"Drama of an Evening, The"(King), **Supp. XXVIII:** 122

Dramatic Duologues (Masters), **Supp. I Part 2:** 461

"Drapery Factory, Gulfport. Mississippi, 1956" (Trethewey), **Supp. XXI:** 246

Drattel, Deborah, **Supp. XV:** 333

Drat These Brats (X. J. Kennedy), **Supp. XV:** 163

"Draught" (Cowley), **Supp. II Part 1:** 141, 142

Drayton, Michael, **IV:** 135; **Retro. Supp. II:** 76

"Dr. Bergen's Belief" (Schwartz), **Supp. II Part 2:** 650

Dr. Bloodmoney (Dick), **Supp. XVIII:** 138

"Dreadful Has Already Happened, The" (Strand), **Supp. IV Part 2:** 627

Dread Road, The (Le Sueur), **Supp. XXIII:** 168, 169, **169–170,** 173

"Dream, A" (Ginsberg), **Supp. II Part 1:** 312

"Dream, A" (Tate), **IV:** 129

"Dream, The" (Hayden), **Supp. II Part 1:** 368, 377

Dream at the End of the World, The: Paul Bowles and the Literary Renegades in Tangier (Green), **Supp. IV Part 1:** 95

"Dream Avenue" (Simic), **Supp. VIII:** 282

"Dream Boogie" (Hughes), **Retro. Supp. I:** 208; **Supp. I Part 1:** 339–340

"Dreambook Bestiary" (Komunyakaa), **Supp. XIII:** 120

Dreamer (C. Johnson), **Supp. VI:** 186, **196–199**

dreamer examines his pillow, the (Shanley), **Supp. XIV:** 315, **327**

"Dreamer in a Dead Language" (Paley), **Supp. VI:** 217

Dreaming Emmett (Morrison), **Retro. Supp. III:** 184

Dreaming in Cuban (García), **Supp. XI:** 178, **179–185,** 190

"Dreaming of Hair" (L.-Y. Lee), **Supp. XV:** 214

"Dreaming the Breasts" (Sexton), **Supp. II Part 2:** 692

"Dreaming Water" (Espaillat), **Supp. XXI:** 102

"Dream Interpretation" (Hadas), **Supp. XXIII:** 113, 121

"Dream Interpreted, The" (Paine), **Supp. I Part 2:** 505

Dream Jumbo (Longo), **Supp. XVI:** 124

Dream Keeper, The (Hughes), **Supp. I Part 1:** 328, 332, 333, 334

Dream Keeper and Other Poems, The (Hughes), **Retro. Supp. I:** 201, 202

Dreamland (Baker), **Supp. XIV:** 96

"Dream-Land" (Poe), **Retro. Supp. II:** 274

Dream Life of Balso Snell, The (West), **IV:** 286, 287, 288–290, 291, 297; **Retro. Supp. II:** 321, 322, 327, 328, **330–332**

"Dream Machine, The" (Hadas), **Supp. XXIII:** 122–123

Dream Me Home Safely: Writers on Growing up in America (Shreve, ed.), **Supp. XXIII:** 284

Dream of a Common Language, The: Poems, 1974–1977 (Rich), **Retro. Supp. III:** 242, 248–249, 253; **Supp. I Part 2:** 551, 554, 569–576

Dream of Arcadia: American Writers and Artists in Italy (Brooks), **I:** 254

Dream of Governors, A (Simpson), **Supp. IX:** 265, **269–270**

"Dream of Her Grandfather, A" (Zitkala-Ša), **Supp. XXV:** 282, 283

"Dream of Italy, A" (Masters), **Supp. I Part 2:** 458

"Dream of Mourning, The" (Glück), **Supp. V:** 84

"Dream of the Blacksmith's Room, A" (R. Bly), **Supp. IV Part 1:** 73

"Dream of the Cardboard Lover" (Haines), **Supp. XII:** 204

Dream of the Golden Mountains, The (Cowley), **Supp. II Part 1:** 139, 141, 142, 144

"Dream Pang, A" (Frost), **II:** 153

Dream-Quest of Unkown Kadath, The (Lovecraft), **Supp. XXV:** 113–114

"Dreams About Clothes" (Merrill), **Supp. III Part 1:** 328–329

"Dreams"(Dybek), **Supp. XXIII:** 73

Dreams from Bunker Hill (Fante), **Supp. XI:** 160, 166, **172–173**

"Dreams in the Witch House, The" (Lovecraft), **Supp. XXV:** 111, 123

"Dreams"(Kenny), **Supp. XXIII:** 153

"Dreams of Adulthood" (Ashbery), **Supp. III Part 1:** 26

"Dreams of Glory on the Mound" (Plimpton), **Supp. XVI:** 238–239

"Dreams of Math" (Kenyon), **Supp. VII:** 160–161

"Dreams of the Animals" (Atwood), **Supp. XIII:** 33

"Dream Variations" (Hughes), **Retro. Supp. I:** 198; **Supp. I Part 1:** 323

"Dream Vision" (Olsen), **Supp. XIII:** 295–296

"Dream Within a Dream" (Poe), **Retro. Supp. III:** 232

Dream with No Stump Roots in It, A (Huddle), **Supp. XXVI:** 152

"Dream with No Stumps in It, A" (Huddle), **Supp. XXVI:** 152

Dream Work (Oliver), **Supp. VII:** 234–235, 236–238, 240

Dred: A Tale of the Great Dismal Swamp (Stowe), **Supp. I Part 2:** 592

Dreiser, Theodore, **I:** 59, 97, 109, 116, 355, 374, 375, 475, 482, **497–520; II:** 26, 27, 29, 34, 38, 44, 74, 89, 93, 180, 276, 283, 428, 444, 451, 456–457, 467–468; **III:** 40, 103, 106, 251, 314, 319, 327, 335, 453, 576, 582; **IV:** 29, 35, 40, 135, 208, 237, 475, 482, 484; **Retro. Supp. I:** 325, 376; **Retro. Supp. II:** **93–110,** 114, 322; **Supp. I Part 1:** 320; **Supp. I Part 2:** 461, 468; **Supp. III Part 2:** 412; **Supp. IV Part 1:** 31, 236, 350; **Supp. IV Part 2:** 689; **Supp. IX:** 1, 14, 15, 308; **Supp. V:** 113, 120; **Supp. VIII:** 98, 101, 102; **Supp. XI:** 207; **Supp. XIV:** 111; **Supp. XVII:** 95, 96–97, 105, 155; **Supp. XVIII:** 1, 6, 76, 226; **Supp. XXI:** 275; **Supp. XXIII:** 161, 164; **Supp. XXV:** 18; **Supp. XXVI:** 133, 273; **Supp. XXVII:** 83, 88; **Supp. XXVIII:** 68, 145

"Drenched in Light" (Hurston), **Retro. Supp. III:** 129; **Supp. VI:** 150–151

Drennen, Eileen M., **Supp. XXII:** 241, 243

Dresner, Zita, **Supp. XXVIII:** 118

Dresser, Paul, **Retro. Supp. II:** 94, 103

Dress Gray (teleplay), **Supp. IV Part 2:** 683

Dress Gray (Truscott), **Supp. IV Part 2:** 683

"Dressing for Dinner" (Ríos), **Supp. IV Part 2:** 548

Dressing Up for the Carnival (Shields), **Supp. VII:** 328

"Dress of One Occasion" (Stallings), **Supp. XXV:** 233

"Dress Rehearsal" (Skloot), **Supp. XX:** 204

Drew, Bettina, **Supp. IX:** 2, 4

Drew, Elizabeth, **Retro. Supp. II:** 242, 243

Drexler, Eric, **Supp. XVI:** 121

Dreyfus, Alfred, **Supp. I Part 2:** 446

"Dr. Hanray's Second Chance" (Richter), **Supp. XVIII:** 218

"Dr. Heidegger's Experiment" (Hawthorne), **Retro. Supp. III:** 114

"Drift, The"(Lea), **Supp. XXVIII:** 137

Drift and Mastery (Lippmann), **I:** 222–223

"Driftwood" (C. Frost), **Supp. XV:** 106–107

"Drinker, The" (R. Lowell), **II:** 535, 550

"Drinking Cold Water" (Everwine), **Supp. XV:** 80–81

"Drinking from a Helmet" (Dickey), **Supp. IV Part 1:** 180

Drinking Gourd, The (Hansberry), **Supp. IV Part 1:** 359, 365–367, 374

Drinks before Dinner (Doctorow), **Supp. IV Part 1:** 231, 234–235

Drinkwater, John, **Retro. Supp. III:** 95

Driscoll, David, **Supp. XIX:** 241, 242

Driskill, Qwo-Li, **Supp. XXIII:** 147, 148, 149

Drive, He Said (Larner), **Supp. XVI:** 220

"Drive Home, The" (Banks), **Supp. V:** 7

"Driver" (Merrill), **Supp. III Part 1:** 331

"Driving Alone in Winter" (W. V. Davis), **Supp. XXI:** 89, 90, 94

"Driving Gloves"(Wakoski), **Supp. XXVIII:** 266

"Driving Through Minnesota During the Hanoi Bombings" (R. Bly), **Supp. IV Part 1:** 61; **Supp. XVII:** 243

"Driving through Oregon" (Haines), **Supp. XII:** 207

"Driving to Oregon"(Thompson), **Supp. XXIII:** 291

"Driving toward the Lac Qui Parle River" (R. Bly), **Supp. IV Part 1:** 61

"Dr. Jack-o'-Lantern" (Yates), **Supp. XI:** 340–341

Dr. Jekyll and Mr. Hyde (film), **Supp. XVII:** 57

"Drone" (Coleman), **Supp. XI:** 85–86

Drop City (Boyle), **Supp. XX: 30–31**

Drown (Díaz), **Supp. XXIV:** 83, 84, 85, 86, **88–89,** 90, 93

"Drowned Man, The: Death between Two Rivers" (McGrath), **Supp. X:** 116

"Drowning" (Boyle), **Supp. XX: 18**

"Drowning 1954" (Keillor), **Supp. XVI:** 172

Drowning Pool, The (film), **Supp. IV Part 2:** 474

Drowning Pool, The (Macdonald), **Supp. IV Part 2:** 470, 471

Drowning Season, The (Hoffman), **Supp. X: 82**

Drowning with Others (Dickey), **Supp. IV Part 1:** 176, 178, 179

"Drowsy Day, A" (Dunbar), **Supp. II Part 1:** 198

Dr. Seuss. *See* Geisel, Theodor Seuss (Dr. Seuss)

Dr. Seuss and Mr. Geisel (J. and N. Morgan), **Supp. XVI:** 103

Dr. Seuss Goes to War: The World War II Editorial Cartoons of Theodor Seuss Geisel (Minear), **Supp. XVI:** 101

Dr. Seuss's ABC (Geisel), **Supp. XVI:** 99

Dr. Strangelove; or, How I Learned to Stop Worrying and Love the Bomb (film), **Supp. XI:** 293, **301–305**

Drugiye Berega (Nabokov), **III:** 247–250, 252

"Drug Shop, The, or Endymion in Edmonstoun" (Benét), **Supp. XI:** 43

"Drug Store" (Shapiro), **Supp. II Part 2:** 705

"Drugstore in Winter, A" (Ozick), **Supp. V:** 272

Drukman, Steven, **Supp. XIII:** 195, 197, 202

"Drum" (Hogan), **Supp. IV Part 1:** 413

"Drum, The" (Alvarez), **Supp. VII:** 7

"Drumlin Woodchuck, A" (Frost), **II:** 159–160; **Retro. Supp. I:** 138

Drummond, William, **Supp. I Part 1:** 369

Drummond de Andrade, Carlos, **Supp. IV Part 2:** 626, 629, 630

Drums at Dusk (Bontemps), **Supp. XXII:** 5, 9–10

Drum-Taps (Whitman), **IV:** 346, 347, 444; **Retro. Supp. I:** 406; **Retro. Supp. III:** 301

"Drunken Fisherman, The" (R. Lowell), **II:** 534, 550

"Drunken Sisters, The" (Wilder), **IV:** 374

"Drunk Hunter, The"(Bottoms), **Supp. XXVIII:** 24

Drunk in the Furnace, The (Merwin), **Supp. III Part 1:** 345–346

"Drunk in the Furnace, The" (Merwin), **Supp. III Part 1:** 346

Druten, John van, **Supp. XIV:** 162

"Dr. Williams' Position" (Pound), **Supp. XVII:** 226–227

Dryden, John, **II:** 111, 542, 556; **III:** 15; **IV:** 145; **Retro. Supp. I:** 56; **Supp. I Part 1:** 150; **Supp. I Part 2:** 422; **Supp. IX:** 68; **Supp. XIV:** 5; **Supp. XV:** 258; **Supp. XX: 280**; **Supp. XXIV:** 158; **Supp. XXV:** 119

Drye, Captain Frank, **Retro. Supp. II:** 115

Dry Salvages, The (T. S. Eliot), **I:** 581

"Dry Salvages, The" (T. S. Eliot), **Retro. Supp. I:** 66; **Retro. Supp. III:** 66, 67–68

"Dry September" (Faulkner), **II:** 72, 73; **Retro. Supp. III:** 82

"Dry Spring"(Thompson), **Supp. XXIII:** 291

Dry Sun, Dry Wind (Wagoner), **Supp. IX:** 323, 324

D'Souza, Dinesh, **Supp. X:** 255

"Dual" (Goldbarth), **Supp. XII:** 188

"Dual Curriculum" (Ozick), **Supp. V:** 270

"Dualism" (Reed), **Supp. X:** 242

Duane's Depressed (McMurtry), **Supp. V:** 233

Du Bartas, Guillaume de Salluste, **Retro. Supp. III:** 3, 5, 8; **Supp. I Part 1:** 98, 104, 111, 118, 119

Dubek, Laura, **Retro. Supp. III:** 138

Duberman, Martin, **Supp. I Part 2:** 408, 409

Dubie, Norman, **Supp. XXIV:** 165

"Dubin's Lives" (Malamud), **Supp. I Part 2:** 451

Dubious Honors (M. F. K. Fisher), **Supp. XVII:** 91

"Dubliners" (J. Joyce), **Supp. XVI:** 41

Dubliners (Joyce), **I:** 130, 480; **III:** 471; **Supp. VIII:** 146; **Supp. XXVIII:** 207

Dublin's Lives (Malamud), **Supp. XIX:** 142

Du Bois, Nina Gomer (Mrs. W. E. B. Du Bois), **Supp. II P art 1:** 158; **Supp. XIV:** 200

Du Bois, Shirley Graham, **Supp. II Part 1:** 186; **Supp. XXI:** 171. *See also* Graham, Shirley

Du Bois, W. E. B., **I:** 260; **Supp. I Part 1:** 5, 345; **Supp. II Part 1:** 33, 56, 61, **157–189,** 195; **Supp. IV Part 1:** 9, 164, 170, 362; **Supp. X:** 133, 134, 137, 139, 242; **Supp. XIII:** 185, **Supp. XIII:** 186, 233, 238, 243, 244, 247; **Supp. XIV:** 54, 69, 72, 201, 202; **Supp. XIX:** 67, 69, 77; **Supp. XVI:** 135; **Supp. XVIII:** 119, 122, 126, 130; **Supp. XX: 102, 105, 106; Supp. XXI:** 166, 277; **Supp. XXII:** 3; **Supp. XXVI:** 88, 168; **Supp. XXVIII:** 65

DuBose, Martha Hailey, **Supp. XXV:** 192, 199, 200

Dubreuil, Jean, **Supp. IV Part 2:** 425

Dubus, Andre, **Supp. VII: 75–93; Supp. XI:** 347,**Supp. XI:** 349; **Supp. XIV:** 21; **Supp. XXIV:** 97

Dubus, Andre, III, **Supp. XXIV: 97–112**

Duchamp, Marcel, **IV:** 408; **Retro. Supp. I:** 416, 417, 418, 430; **Supp. IV Part 2:** 423, 424; **Supp. XII:** 124; **Supp. XV:** 157; **Supp. XXII:** 162, 163, 168

"Duchess at Prayer, The" (Wharton), **Retro. Supp. I:** 365

Duchess of Malfi, The (Webster), **IV:** 131

"Duckling Girl" (Dubus III), **Supp. XXIV:** 100–101, 105

Duck Soup (film), **Supp. IV Part 1:** 384

Duck Variations, The (Mamet), **Supp. XIV:** 239, 240, 249

Ducornet, Rikki, **Supp. XXII:** 261

Dudley, Anne. *See* Bradstreet, Anne

Dudley, Joseph, **III:** 52

Dudley, Thomas, **III:** 52; **Retro. Supp. III:** 3; **Supp. I Part 1:** 98, 99, 110, 116

"Duenna"(Schott), **Supp. XXIII:** 249

"Duet, With Muffled Brake Drums" (Updike), **Retro. Supp. I:** 319

Duet for Cannibals (Sontag), **Supp. III Part 2:** 452, 456

Duffey, Bernard, **Supp. I Part 2:** 458, 471

Duffield, Pitts, **Supp. XXI:** 3

Duffus, R. L., **Supp. I Part 2:** 650

Duffy, Martha, **Supp. IV Part 1:** 207; **Supp. XX: 244**

Duffy, William, **Supp. XVI:** 32

Du Fu (Tu Fu), **Supp. XV:** 217

Dufy, Raoul, **I:** 115; **IV:** 80

Dugan, Alan, **Supp. XIII:** 76

Dugan, James, **Supp. XV:** 197

"Dugout"(Kenny), **Supp. XXIII:** 155

Duhamel, Marcel, **Supp. XVI:** 135, 143

Dujardin, Edouard, **I:** 53

"Duke de l'Omelette, The" (Poe), **III:** 411, 425

Duke Herring (Bodenheim), **Supp. XXV:** 27

"Duke in His Domain, The" (Capote), **Supp. III Part 1:** 113, 126

Duke of Deception, The (G. Wolff), **Supp. II Part 1:** 97; **Supp. XI:** 246

"Duke's Child, The" (Maxwell), **Supp. VIII:** 172

"Dulce et Decorum Est" (Owen), **Supp. XVIII:** 92

"Dulham Ladies, The" (Jewett), **II:** 407, 408; **Retro. Supp. II:** 143

"Dulse" (Munro), **Supp. XXVII:** 188

Duluth (Vidal), **Supp. IV Part 2:** 677, 685, 689, 691–692

Dumas, Alexandre, **III:** 386; **Supp. XVII:** 64

Dumas, Henry, **Retro. Supp. III:** 184, 194

"Dumb Oax, The" (Lewis), **Retro. Supp. I:** 170

"Dummy, The" (Sontag), **Supp. III Part 2:** 469

"Dump Ground, The" (Stegner), **Supp. IV Part 2:** 601

Dunant, Sarah, **Supp. XIX:** 186

Dunayevskaya, Raya, **Supp. XXI:** 169

Dunbar, Alice Moore (Mrs. Paul Laurence Dunbar), **Supp. II Part 1:** 195, 200, 217

Dunbar, Paul Laurence, **Supp. I Part 1:** 320; **Supp. II Part 1:** 174, **191–219; Supp. III Part 1:** 73; **Supp. IV Part 1:** 15, 165, 170; **Supp. X:** 136; **Supp. XI:** 277; **Supp. XIII:** 111; **Supp. XXII:** 11; **Supp. XXVII:** 164

Duncan, Harry, **Supp. XV:** 75

Duncan, Isadora, **I:** 483; **Supp. XV:** 42, 50

Duncan, Isla, **Supp. XXVII:** 193

Duncan, Robert, **Retro. Supp. II:** 49; **Supp. III Part 2:** 625, 626, 630, 631; **Supp. VIII:** 304; **Supp. XVI:** 282–283; **Supp. XXIII:** 213; **Supp. XXVII:** 160

Dunciad, The (Pope), **I:** 204

Dune Boy: The Early Years of a Naturalist (Teale), **Supp. XXVIII:** 244, 247

Dunford, Judith, **Supp. VIII:** 107

Dunlap, William, **Supp. I Part 1:** 126, 130, 137, 141, 145

Dunn, Stephen, **Supp. XI: 139–158; Supp. XIX:** 85

Dunne, Finley Peter, **II:** 432

Dunne, John Gregory, **Supp. IV Part 1:** 197, 198, 201, 203, 207

"Dunnet Shepherdess, A" (Jewett), **II:** 392–393; **Retro. Supp. II:** 139

Dunning, Stephen, **Supp. XIV:** 126

Dunning, William Archibald, **Supp. II Part 1:** 170; **Supp. XIV:** 48

Dunnock, Mildred, **III:** 153

Dunster, Henry, **Supp. I Part 2:** 485

"Dunwich Horror, The" (Lovecraft), **Supp. XXV:** 111, 120

"Duo Tried Killing Man with Bacon" (Goldbarth), **Supp. XII:** 176

Dupee, F. W., **I:** 254; **II:** 548; **Supp. IX:** 93, 96; **Supp. VIII:** 231

DuPlessis, Rachel Blau, **Supp. IV Part 2:** 421, 426, 432; **Supp. XVI:** 284; **Supp. XXVI:** 228, 234, 237–238

Duplicate Keys (Smiley), **Supp. VI:** 292, **294–296**

Duplications, The (Koch), **Supp. XV:** 181, 183, 186

Durable Fire, A (Sarton), **Supp. VIII:** 260

Durand, Asher, B., **Supp. I Part 1:** 156, 157

Durand, Régis, **Supp. IV Part 1:** 44

Durang, Christopher, **Supp. XXIV: 113–130,** 263

"Durango Suite" (Gunn Allen), **Supp. IV Part 1:** 326

Durant, Kenneth, **Supp. XXII:** 278, 281

"Durations" (Matthews), **Supp. IX:** 152–153, 154

Dürer, Albrecht, **III:** 212; **Supp. XII:** 44

Durham, David Anthony, **Supp. XVIII:** 100

"During Fever" (R. Lowell), **II:** 547

Durkheim, Émile, **I:** 227; **Retro. Supp. I:** 55, 57; **Supp. I Part 2:** 637, 638

Durrell, Lawrence, **III:** 184, 190; **IV:** 430; **Supp. X:** 108, 187; **Supp. XVI:** 294

Dürrenmatt, Friedrich, **Supp. IV Part 2:** 683

Duse, Eleonora, **II:** 515, 528

Dusk and Other Stories (Salter), **Supp. IX: 260–261**

"Dusk in War Time" (Teasdale), **Supp. XXVII:** 294

Dusk of Dawn: An Essay Toward an Autobiography of a Race Concept (Du Bois), **Supp. II Part 1:** 159, 183, 186

Dusselier, Jane, **Supp. XXVI:** 210

"Dust" (R. Fisher), **Supp. XIX:** 71

"Dusting" (Alvarez), **Supp. VII:** 4

"Dusting" (Dove), **Supp. IV Part 1:** 247, 248

"Dusting" (Schnackenberg), **Supp. XV:** 256

"Dust of Snow" (Frost), **II:** 154; **Retro. Supp. III:** 101, 102

Dust Tracks on a Road (Hurston), **Retro. Supp. III:** 128, 131, 133–134; **Supp. IV Part 1:** 5, 11; **Supp. VI:** 149, 151, 158–159

"Dusty Braces" (Snyder), **Supp. VIII:** 302

Dutchman (Baraka), **Supp. II Part 1:** 38, 40, 42–44, 54, 55

"Dutch Nick Massacre, The" (Twain), **IV:** 195

"Dutch Picture, A" (Longfellow), **Retro. Supp. II:** 171

Dutton, Charles S., **Supp. VIII:** 332, 342

Dutton, Clarence Earl, **Supp. IV Part 2:** 598

Duvall, Robert, **Supp. V:** 227

"Duwamish" (Hugo), **Supp. VI:** 136

"Duwamish, Skagit, Hoh" (Hugo), **Supp. VI:** 136–137

"Duwamish No. 2" (Hugo), **Supp. VI:** 137

Duyckinck, Evert, **III:** 77, 81, 83, 85; **Retro. Supp. I:** 155, 247, 248; **Retro. Supp. III:** 154, 157, 158, 228; **Supp. I Part 1:** 122, 317; **Supp. XXV:** 250

Duyckinck, George, **Supp. I Part 1:** 122; **Supp. XXV:** 250

"Dvonya" (Simpson), **Supp. IX:** 274

Dwelling Places: Poems and Translations (Ferry), **Supp. XXIV: 152–153**

Dwellings: A Spiritual History of the Living World (Hogan), **Supp. IV Part 1:** 397, 410, 415–416, 417

Dwight, Sereno E., **I:** 547

Dwight, Timothy, **Supp. I Part 1:** 124; **Supp. I Part 2:** 516, 580; **Supp. II Part 1:** 65, 69

Dworkin, Andrea, **Supp. XII:** 6

Dwyer, Jim, **Supp. XVI:** 16, 19

Dyas, Sandra, **Supp. XIX:** 174

Dybbuk, A, or Between Two Worlds: Dramatic Legend in Four Acts (Kushner), **Supp. IX:** 138

Dybbuk, The (Ansky), **IV:** 6

Dybek, Stuart, **Supp. XXIII: 67–81**

Dybuk, The (Ansky), **Supp. XXIII:** 8

Dyer, Geoff, **Supp. X:** 169

Dyer, Joyce, **Supp. XX: 166**

Dyer, R. C., **Supp. XIII:** 162

Dyer, Richard, **Supp. XXII:** 261

Dyer's Thistle (Balakian), **Supp. XXIII:** 25

Dying Animal, The (P. Roth), **Retro. Supp. II:** 288

"Dying Elm, The" (Freneau), **Supp. II Part 1:** 258

"Dying Indian, The" (Freneau), **Supp. II Part 1:** 262

"Dying Man, The" (Roethke), **III:** 540, 542, 543–545

Dykeman, Wilma, **Supp. XX: 163**

Dykes to Watch Out For (Bechdel), **Supp. XXV:** 1, 3–4

Dylan, Bob, **Supp. VIII:** 202; **Supp. XIII:** 114, 119; **Supp. XV:** 349, 350; **Supp. XVIII: 19–34; Supp. XXII:** 83

Dylan's Visions of Sin (Ricks), **Supp. XVIII:** 20

"Dynamics of Heroic Action, The" (lecture, Murray), **Supp. XIX:** 153

Dynamo (O'Neill), **III:** 396

"Dynasties" (Gibran), **Supp. XX: 118**

"Dysfunctional Narratives: Or, 'Mistakes Were Made' " (C. Baxter), **Supp. XVII:** 20

"Dysfunctional Nation" (Karr), **Supp. XI:** 245

Dyson, A. E., **Retro. Supp. II:** 247

Dyson, Freeman, **Supp. XVII:** 42

E

"Each and All" (Emerson), **II:** 19

Each Happiness Ringer by Lions (Hirshfield), **Supp. XXIII:** 135

Each in His Season (Snodgrass), **Supp. VI:** 324, 327

Each Kindness (Woodson; Lewis, ill.), **Supp. XXVIII:** 287

"Each Like a Leaf" (Swenson), **Supp. IV Part 2:** 644

Eads, Martha Greene, **Supp. XVIII:** 49

Eady, Cornelius, **Supp. XXI:** 246

Eager, Allen, **Supp. XI:** 294

"Eagle, The" (Tate), **IV:** 128

"Eagle and the Mole, The" (Wylie), **Supp. I Part 2:** 710, 711, 713, 714, 729

"Eagle and the Skylark, The" (Gibran), **Supp. XX: 124**

Eagle as Wide as the World, The (X. J. Kennedy), **Supp. XV:** 162, 164

"Eagle Poem" (Harjo), **Supp. XII:** 224, 226

"Eagles" (Dickey), **Supp. IV Part 1:** 186

Eagle's Mile, The (Dickey), **Supp. IV Part 1:** 178, 185–186

"Eagle That Is Forgotten, The" (Lindsay), **Supp. I Part 2:** 382, 387

Eagleton, Terry, **Retro. Supp. I:** 67

Eakin, Paul John, **Supp. VIII:** 167, 168; **Supp. XIII:** 225; **Supp. XVI:** 70

Eakin, Sue, **Supp. XXVIII:** 166, 167

Eakins, Thomas, **Supp. XIV:** 338; **Supp. XXII:** 18–19

Eames, Emma, **Supp. XX: 232, 240**

Eames, Roscoe, **II:** 476

"Earl: My Life with a Louse" (Keillor), **Supp. XVI:** 176

"Earl Painter" (Banks), **Supp. V:** 14–15

"Early Adventures of Ralph Ringwood, The" (Irving), **II:** 314

Early Americana (Richter), **Supp. XVIII:** 208, 210, 211, 220

Early Autumn (Parker), **Supp. XIX:** 184–185

Early Ayn Rand, The: A Selection of Her Unpublished Fiction (Rand), **Supp. IV Part 2:** 520

Early Dark (Price), **Supp. VI:** 262

Early Diary of Anaïs Nin, The, **Supp. X:** 184, 192

Early Elkin (Elkin), **Supp. VI: 42–43,** 45

"Early Evenin' Blues" (Hughes), **Retro. Supp. I:** 205

"Early Evening, Frankfort, Kentucky" (Trethewey), **Supp. XXI:** 243, 250

"Early History of a Seamstress" (Reznikoff), **Supp. XIV:** 277, 289

Early History of a Sewing-Machine Operator (Reznikoff), **Supp. XIV:** 289

"Early History of a Sewing-Machine Operator" (Reznikoff), **Supp. XIV:** 277

"Early History of a Writer" (Reznikoff), **Supp. XIV:** 278, 290

"Early in the Morning" (L.-Y. Lee), **Supp. XV:** 214

Early Lectures of Ralph Waldo Emerson, The (Emerson), **II:** 11

Early Light (Di Piero), **Supp. XIX:** 38, **38–40**

Early Lives of Melville, The (Sealts), **Retro. Supp. I:** 257

"Early Marriage" (Richter), **Supp. XVIII:** 209

Early Martyr and Other Poems, An (W. C. Williams), **Retro. Supp. I:** 423

"Early Morning: Cape Cod" (Swenson), **Supp. IV Part 2:** 641

"Early Rooms" (Hirshfield), **Supp. XXIII:** 130

"Early Spring between Madison and Bellingham" (R. Bly), **Supp. IV Part 1:** 71

Early Writing (O'Hara), **Supp. XXIII:** 220

Earnhardt, Dale, **Supp. XII:** 310

Earnshaw, Doris, **Supp. IV Part 1:** 310

"Earth" (Bryant), **Supp. I Part 1:** 157, 164, 167

"Earth, The" (Sexton), **Supp. II Part 2:** 696

Earth Abides (Stewart), **Supp. XVIII:** 138

"Earth and Fire" (Berry), **Supp. X:** 27

Earth as Air, The: An Ars Poetica (Sobin), **Supp. XVI: 285–286**

"Earth Being" (Toomer), **Supp. IX:** 320

Earth Goat (online), **Supp. XXII:** 61

Earth Gods, The (Gibran), **Supp. XX: 116, 123**

"Earth is parched with heat, The" (Very), **Supp. XXV:** 239

"Earthlings" (King), **Supp. XXVIII:** 115

"Earthly Care a Heavenly Discipline" (Stowe), **Supp. I Part 2:** 586

"Earthly City of the Jews, The" (Kazin), **Retro. Supp. II:** 286

Earthly Meditations (Wrigley), **Supp. XVIII:** 304–305

"Earthly Meditations" (Wrigley), **Supp. XVIII:** 304–306

Earthly Possessions (Tyler), **Supp. IV Part 2:** 665–666, 671

Earth Power Coming (Ortiz, ed.), **Supp. IV Part 2:** 502

"Earth's Holocaust" (Hawthorne), **II:** 226, 231, 232, 242; **III:** 82; **Retro. Supp. I:** 152; **Retro. Supp. III:** 119

Earth Without You, The (F. Wright), **Supp. XVII:** 243

Eason, Laura, **Supp. XXIII:** 79

East Coker (T. S. Eliot), **I:** 580, 581, 582, 585, 587

"East Coker" (T. S. Eliot), **Retro. Supp. I:** 66; **Retro. Supp. III:** 66, 67; **Supp. VIII:** 195, 196

"Easter" (Toomer), **Supp. III Part 2:** 486

"Easter, an Ode" (R. Lowell), **II:** 536

"Easter 1916" (Yeats), **Supp. XXI:** 61

"Easter Island: The Statues Speak" (Davison), **Supp. XXVI:** 71

"Easter Morning" (Ammons), **Supp. VII:** 34

"Easter Morning" (Clampitt), **Supp. IX:** 45

"Eastern Standard" (Huddle), **Supp. XXVI:** 149

"Easter Ode, An" (Dunbar), **Supp. II Part 1:** 196

"Easter" (O'Hara), **Supp. XXIII:** 211

Easter Parade, The (Yates), **Supp. XI:** 346, 349

"Easter Sermon, 1866" (Nelson), **Supp. XVIII:** 177

"Easter Service" (Di Piero), **Supp. XIX:** 39–40

"Easter Shoes Epistle" (Bottoms), **Supp. XXVIII:** 30

"Easter Sunday: Recollection" (Gunn Allen), **Supp. IV Part 1:** 322

"Easter Wings" (Herbert), **Supp. IV Part 2:** 646

"Easter Wings" (Herbert), **Supp. XXVIII:** 198

"East European Cooking" (Simic), **Supp. VIII:** 277

East Is East (Boyle), **Supp. VIII:** 1–3; **Supp. XX: 23–24, 25,** 28

Eastlake, William, **Supp. XIII:** 12

East Lynne (Wood), **Supp. I Part 1:** 35, 36; **Supp. I Part 2:** 459, 462; **Supp. XVI:** 182

Eastman, Elaine Goodale, **Supp. X:** 103

Eastman, Max, **Supp. III Part 2:** 620; **Supp. X:** 131, 134, 135, 137; **Supp. XV:** 295; **Supp. XVI:** 185; **Supp. XVII:** 96; **Supp. XXI:** 6; **Supp. XXII:** 274, 275, 277; **Supp. XXVIII:** 67, 71

Eastman, P. D., **Supp. XXV:** 1

East of Eden (Steinbeck), **IV:** 51, 56–57, 59

"East of the Sun and West of the Moon" (Merwin), **Supp. III Part 1:** 344

Easton, Alison, **Retro. Supp. II:** 143, 144, 145

Easton, Bret Ellis, **Supp. XI:** 65

Easton, Nina J., **Supp. XIX:** 137

Easton, Robert, **Supp. IV Part 2:** 461, 474

East River (Asch), **Supp. XXIII:** 1, 3, 7, **14–15**

"East-Side: New York" (Bodenheim), **Supp. XXV:** 22

East Wind (A. Lowell), **II:** 527

East Wind: West Wind (Buck), **Supp. II Part 1:** 114–115

Easy Rawlins mysteries, **Supp. XIII:** 236, **237–241,** 242

Easy Rider (film), **Supp. XI:** 293, **308,** 309

Easy Rider (Hopper), **Supp. XXVI:** 26

"Easy to Love" (Lea), **Supp. XXVIII:** 142

Eat a Bowl of Tea (Chu), **Supp. X:** 291

"Eating " (Bass), **Supp. XVI:** 23–24

"Eating Alone" (L.-Y. Lee), **Supp. XV:** 214

"Eating Barley Sugar and Waiting to Be Ninety" (Hadas), **Supp. XXIII:** 120–121

Eating Naked (Dobyns), **Supp. XIII: 78–79**

"Eating Out" (L. Michaels), **Supp. XVI:** 209

"Eating Poetry" (Strand), **Supp. IV Part 2:** 626

"Eating the Whole" (C. Frost), **Supp. XV:** 101

"Eating Together" (L.-Y. Lee), **Supp. XV:** 214

"Eating with My Fingers" (C. Frost), **Supp. XV:** 97

Eaton, Edith, **Supp. X:** 291

Eaton, Mark A., **Supp. XXIII:** 129, 130, 136

Eaton, Peggy, **Supp. I Part 2:** 461

Eaton, Winnifred, **Supp. X:** 291

"Eatonville Anthology, The" (Hurston), **Supp. VI:** 152

Eat Pray Love (Gilbert), **Supp. XXII:** 83, 90

Eat the Document (film, Pennebaker), **Supp. XVIII:** 19, 26, 27, 28

Eat the Document (Spiotta), **Supp. XXVIII:** 207, 212–216

"Ebb and Flow, The" (Taylor), **IV:** 161

"Ebenezer Marsh, 1725" (Schnackenberg), **Supp. XV:** 256

Eben Holden (Bacheller), **I:** 216

Eberhardt, Isabelle, **Supp. IV Part 1:** 92

Eberhart, Mrs., **I:** 521–522, 530

Eberhart, Richard, **I:** 521–543; **II:** 535–536; **III:** 527; **IV:** 416; **Retro. Supp. II:** 176, 178; **Supp. I Part 1:** 83; **Supp. XII:** 119; **Supp. XXVI:** 68

Ebert, Roger, **Supp. XXVII:** 68

Eberwein, Jane Donahue, **Retro. Supp. III:** 5

Eble, Kenneth E., **Supp. I Part 1:** 201

Ebony and Topaz (C. S. Johnson, ed.), **Supp. XXVI:** 170

"Ecce Homo" (Cliff), **Supp. XXII:** 76

Eccentricities of a Nightingale (T. Williams), **IV:** 382, 385, 397, 398

Ecclesiastica Historia Integram Ecclesiae (Taylor), **IV:** 163

"Echart" (Sobin), **Supp. XVI:** 289

"Echo, The" (Bowles), **Supp. IV Part 1:** 84, 86, 87

Echo, Thomas William, **Supp. XXVI:** 87

"Echoes" (H. Crane), **Retro. Supp. III:** 45

Echoes inside the Labyrinth (McGrath), **Supp. X:** 127

Echo Park (Connelly), **Supp. XXI:** 77–78

Eck, Diana L., **Supp. XXVIII:** 49–63

Eckehart, Meister, **Supp. XV:** 225

Eckhart, Maria, **Supp. V:** 212

Eckley, William, **Supp. XXVIII:** 3–4

Eclipse (Hogan), **Supp. IV Part 1:** 397, 400, 402

Eclipse, a Nightmare (Montalembert), **Supp. XV:** 349

"Eclipse"(Schott), **Supp. XXIII:** 252

"Eclogue" (Oppen), **Supp. XXVI:** 232

Eclogues (Virgil), **Supp. VIII:** 31; **Supp. XXIV:** 156

Eclogues of Virgil, The (Ferry, trans.), **Supp. XXIV:** 156–157

"Ecologue" (Ginsberg), **Supp. II Part 1:** 326

"Ecologues of These States 1969–1971" (Ginsberg), **Supp. II Part 1:** 325

Ecology of a Cracker Childhood (Ray), **Supp. XVIII:** 189, 191, 192, 193, 195–199, 201, 202, 204

"Economics of Negro Emancipation in the United States, The" (Du Bois), **Supp. II Part 1:** 174

"Economics of the Cracker Landscape: Poverty as an Environmental Issue in Larry Brown's *Joe*" (Watson), **Supp. XXI:** 46

"Economic Theory of Women's Dress, The" (Veblen), **Supp. I Part 2:** 636

Economy of the Unlost: Reading Simonides of Keos with Paul Celan (Carson), **Supp. XII:** 110–111

Ecotactics: The Sierra Club Handbook for Environmental Activists (Mitchell and Stallings, eds.), **Supp. IV Part 2:** 488

"Ecstasy" (Bierds), **Supp. XVII:** 34

"Ecstasy" (Olds), **Supp. X:** 206

"Ecstasy of Influence, The" (Lethem), **Supp. XVIII:** 150

"Ecstatic" (Komunyakaa), **Supp. XIII:** 131

Edda, **Supp. X:** 114

Eddy, Mary Baker, **I:** 583; **III:** 506

Edel, Leon, **I:** 20; **II:** 338–339; **Retro. Supp. I:** 218, 224, 231

Edelberg, Cynthia, **Supp. IV Part 1:** 155

"Eden, Then and Now" (Stone), **Supp. XXVII:** 252

"Eden and My Generation" (Levis), **Supp. XI:** 270

Edenbaum, Robert, **Supp. IV Part 1:** 352

Eden Tree (Bynner), **Supp. XV:** 42, 51

Edenville Owls (Parker), **Supp. XIX:** 190

Eder, Richard, **Supp. XII:** 189; **Supp. XV:** 62, 187, 259, 261

Edgar Allan Poe: A Critical Biography (Quinn), **Retro. Supp. III:** 236–237

Edgar Allan Poe and the Masses (Whalen), **Retro. Supp. III:** 237

"Edgar Fane's Rosebud" (Hawthorne), **Retro. Supp. III:** 113

Edgar Huntly; or, Memoirs of a Sleep-Walker (Brown), **Supp. I Part 1:** 140–144, 145

"Edge" (Plath), **Retro. Supp. II:** 256; **Supp. I Part 2:** 527, 547

Edge, Mary E., **II:** 316

Edgell, David, **Supp. XXIV:** 71

Edgell, Zee, **Supp. XXIII:** 83–96

"Edge of Possibility, The: Susan Warner and the World of Sunday School Fiction" (S. Gates), **Supp. XVIII:** 267

"Edge of the Great Rift, The" (Theroux), **Supp. VIII:** 325

Edge of the Sea, The (Carson), **Supp. IX:** 19, 25–31, 32

Edge of the Woods, The: Iroquoia, 1534–1701 (Parmenter), **Supp. XXVI:** 85

Edgers, Geoff, **Supp. XV:** 113

Edgeworth, Maria, **II:** 8; **Supp. XV:** 231; **Supp. XX:** 108

Edible Woman, The (Atwood), **Supp. XIII:** 19, 20, 20–21

"Edict by the King of Prussia, An" (Franklin), **II:** 120

Edie: An American Biography (Stein), **Supp. XVI:** 245

Edinburgh Days: or, Doing What I Want to Do (Pickering), **Supp. XXI:** 200–201

Edison, Thomas A., **I:** 483; **Supp. I Part 2:** 392

Edith Wharton (Joslin), **Retro. Supp. I:** 376

Edith Wharton: A Biography (Lewis), **Retro. Supp. I:** 362

Edith Wharton: A Woman in Her Time (Auchincloss), **Retro. Supp. I:** 370

Edith Wharton: Matters of Mind and Spirit (Singley), **Retro. Supp. I:** 373

Edith Wharton's Argument with America (Ammons), **Retro. Supp. I:** 364

Edith Wharton's Brave New Politics (Bauer), **Retro. Supp. I:** 381

Edith Wharton's Letters from the Underworld (Waid), **Retro. Supp. I:** 360

Edith Wharton: Traveller in the Land of Letters (Goodwyn), **Retro. Supp. I:** 370

"Editing and Glosses" (Reznikoff), **Supp. XIV:** 283

Editing of Emily Dickinson, The (Franklin), **Retro. Supp. I:** 41

"Editor and the Schoolma'am, The" (Frederic), **II:** 130

"Editor's Easy Chair" (Howells), **II:** 276

"Editor's Study, The" (Howells), **II:** 275, 276, 285

"Editor Whedon" (Masters), **Supp. I Part 2:** 463

Edlin, Mari, **Supp. X:** 266

Edman, Irwin, **III:** 605; **Supp. XXV:** 255, 258

Edmond (Mamet), **Supp. XIV:** 241, 248, 249, 250

Edmonds, Dale, **Supp. XXIII:** 291

Edmondson, Belinda, **Supp. XXII:** 70

Edmundson, Mark, **Retro. Supp. II:** 262

Edmund Wilson (Kriegel), **Supp. XXIV:** 216–217

Edsel (Shapiro), **Supp. II Part 2:** 703, 704, 717–719

Edson, Margaret, **Supp. XVIII:** 35–52

Edson, Russell, **Supp. VIII:** 279

"Educated American Woman, An" (Cheever), **Supp. I Part 1:** 194

"Education, An" (Ozick), **Supp. V:** 267

Education and Living (Bourne), **I:** 252

"Education by Poetry" (Frost), **Retro. Supp. III:** 100; **Supp. XV:** 215

"Education of a Storyteller, The" (Bambara), **Supp. XI:** 20

Education of Black People, The (Du Bois), **Supp. II Part 1:** 186

Education of Harriet Hatfield, The (Sarton), **Supp. VIII:** 257–258

Education of Henry Adams, The (Adams), **I:** 1, 5, 6, 11, 14, 15–18, 19, 20–21, 111; **II:** 276; **III:** 504; **Retro. Supp. I:** 53, 59; **Supp. IX:** 19; **Supp. XIV:** 299

Education of H*y*m*a*n K*a*p*l*a*n, The (Rosten), **Supp. XVII:** 9

"Education of Mingo, The" (C. Johnson), **Supp. VI:** 193, 194

"Education of Norman Podhoretz, The" (Goldberg), **Supp. VIII:** 238

Education of Oscar Fairfax, The (Auchincloss), **Supp. IV Part 1:** 25, 36

"Education of the Poet" (Glück), **Supp. V:** 78, 80

Education sentimentale (Flaubert), **III:** 315

"Education the Imagination" (Koch), **Supp. XV:** 175–176, 177

Edwards, Clifford, **Supp. XVIII:** 220

Edwards, Eli. *See* McKay, Claude

Edwards, Esther, **I:** 545

Edwards, Harry Stillwell, **Supp. XXII:** 193

Edwards, John, **I:** 478

Edwards, Jonathan, **I: 544–566; II:** 432; **Retro. Supp. II:** 187; **Retro. Supp. III:** 9; **Supp. I Part 1:** 301, 302; **Supp. I Part 2:** 552, 594, 700; **Supp. IV Part 2:** 430; **Supp. VIII:** 205; **Supp. XXIV:** 72

Edwards, Sarah, **I:** 545

Edwards, Thomas, **Supp. XV:** 20

Edwards, Thomas R., **Supp. XVI:** 207

Edwards, Timothy, **I:** 545

Edwards-Yearwood, Grace, **Supp. VIII:** 81; **Supp. XXII:** 213

"Edwin Arlington Robinson" (Cowley), **Supp. II Part 1:** 144

Edwin Arlington Robinson (Winters), **Supp. II Part 2:** 812

Edwin Booth (play), **Supp. IV Part 1:** 89

E. E. Cummings (Marks), **I:** 438

E. E. Cummings: A Miscellany (Cummings), **I:** 429, 441

E. E. Cummings: A Miscellany, Revised (Cummings), **I:** 429

"Effects of Analogy" (Stevens), **Retro. Supp. I:** 297

"Effigy of a Nun" (Teasdale), **Supp. XXVII:** 296

Effluences from the Sacred Caves; More Selected Essays and Reviews (Carruth), **Supp. XVI:** 46

"Effort at Speech between Two People" (Rukeyser), **Supp. VI:** 276, 284

"Efforts of Affection" (Moore), **III:** 214

"Efforts of Affection: A Memoir of Marianne Moore" (Bishop), **Retro. Supp. II:** 52

Egan, Jennifer, **Supp. XIX: 49–63; Supp. XXIII:** 299, 300

Egan, Leona, **Supp. XXI:** 6

"Egg, The" (Anderson), **I:** 113, 114

"Egg, The" (Snyder), **Supp. VIII:** 302

Eggers, David, **Supp. XXIV:** 131, 200

Eggleston, George Cary, **Supp. XVIII:** 15

"Eggplant Epithalamion, The" (Jong), **Supp. V:** 119

"Eggs" (Olds), **Supp. X:** 206

"Eggshell" (Stern), **Supp. IX:** 299

Egoist, The (Meredith), **II:** 186

Egorova, Lubov, **Supp. IX:** 58

"Egotism, or the Bosom Serpent" (Hawthorne), **II:** 227, 239; **Retro. Supp. III:** 114, 116, 120

Egotist, The (Hecht), **Supp. XXVII:** 89

"Egyptian Pulled Glass Bottle in the Shape of a Fish, An" (Moore), **III:** 195, 213

Ehrenfels, Christian von, **Supp. XIV:** 198

Ehrenpreis, Irvin, **Supp. XII:** 128

Ehrenreich, Barbara, **Supp. XVII:** 210

Ehrhart, W. D., **Supp. XIX:** 281

Ehrlich, Gloria C., **Retro. Supp. III:** 278

Ehrlich, Gretel, **Supp. XIV:** 227; **Supp. XVIII:** 189; **Supp. XXVI:** 31, 187

"Ehue! fugaces, Posthume, Posthume, Labuntur anni" (Very), **Supp. XXV:** 243, 247

Eichmann, Adolf, **Supp. XII:** 166

Eichmann in Jerusalem (Arendt), **Retro. Supp. II:** 28; **Supp. VIII:** 243; **Supp. XII:** 166

"Eichmann in New York: The New York Intellectuals and the Hannah Arendt Controversy" (Rabinbach), **Supp. XII:** 166

"Eidolon" (Warren), **IV:** 239

"Eiger Dreams" (Krakauer), **Supp. XVIII:** 107

Eiger Dreams: Ventures Among Men and Mountains (Krakauer), **Supp. XVIII:** 105, 106, 107

Eight Cousins (Alcott), **Supp. I Part 1:** 29, 38, 42, 43

18 Pine Street series (Myers), **Supp. XXVII:** 211

18 Poems from the Quechua (Strand, trans.), **Supp. IV Part 2:** 630

"18 West 11th Street" (Merrill), **Supp. III Part 1:** 323, 328

1876: A Novel (Vidal), **Supp. IV Part 2:** 677, 684, 688, 689, 691, 692; **Supp. XIX:** 141

"18,000 CDs" (Halliday), **Supp. XIX:** 92

"Eighth Air Force" (Jarrell), **II:** 373–374, 377

Eight Harvard Poets, **I:** 429, 475

"Eighth Avenue Incident" (Halliday), **Supp. XIX:** 89–90

"Eighth Day, The" (Apple), **Supp. XVII:** 6, 50

"Eighth Ditch, The" (Baraka), **Supp. II Part 1:** 40

"'80s Pastoral: Frederick Barthelme's *Moon Deluxe* Ten Years On" (Peters), **Supp. XI:** 39

Eight Men (Wright), **IV:** 478, 488, 494

80 Flowers (Zukofsky), **Supp. III Part 2:** 631

Eikon Basilike, The, **Supp. IV Part 2:** 435

Eileen (Masters), **Supp. I Part 2:** 460

Eimi (Cummings), **I:** 429, 433, 434, 439–440

"Einstein" (MacLeish), **III:** 5, 8, 10–11, 18–19

Einstein, Albert, **I:** 493; **III:** 8, 10, 21, 161; **IV:** 69, 375, 410, 411, 421; **Retro. Supp. I:** 63; **Supp. I Part 2:** 609, 643; **Supp. III Part 2:** 621; **Supp. V:** 290; **Supp. XII:** 45

Eiseley, Loren, **III:** 227–228

Eisenberg, Deborah, **Supp. XXIII:** 290

Eisenhower, Dwight D., **I:** 136, 376; **II:** 548; **III:** 215; **IV:** 75; **Supp. I Part 1:** 291; **Supp. III Part 2:** 624; **Supp. V:** 45

Eisenstadt, Jill, **Supp. XVIII:** 135

Eisenstein, Sergei, **I:** 481; **Supp. XXI:** 170

Eisinger, Chester E., **I:** 302; **II:** 604; **Supp. IX:** 15

Eisner, Douglas, **Supp. X:** 155

Elam, Angela, **Supp. XI:** 290

Elam, Harry, **Retro. Supp. III:** 314

El Bernardo (Balbuena), **Supp. V:** 11

Elbert, Sarah, **Supp. I Part 1:** 34, 41

Elder, Donald, **II:** 417, 426, 435, 437; **Supp. XV:** 137

Elder, John, **Supp. IX:** 25; **Supp. XXVI:** 38

Elder, Lonne, III, **Supp. IV Part 1:** 362

Elder, Richard, **Supp. XII:** 172

"Elder Sister, The" (Olds), **Supp. X:** 205–206

Elder Statesman, The (T. S. Eliot), **I:** 572, 573, 583; **Retro. Supp. I:** 53, 65; **Retro. Supp. III:** 70

"Eldest Sister to Psyche, The" (Stallings), **Supp. XXV:** 234

E. L. Doctorow (Harter and Thompson), **Supp. IV Part 1:** 217

Eldredge, Kay, **Supp. IX:** 254, 259

Eldridge, Florence, **III:** 154, 403; **IV:** 357

Eleanor of Aquitaine, **III:** 470

Eleanor of Guienne, **I:** 14

Eleanor: or, Slave Catching in the Quaker City (Lippard), **Supp. XXIII:** 180, 185

"Elect, The" (Taylor), **Supp. V:** 323

"Elections, Nicaragua, 1984" (Kingsolver), **Supp. VII:** 208

Elective Affinities (Goethe; Bogan and Mayer, trans.), **Supp. III Part 1:** 63

Electra (Euripides), **III:** 398

Electra (Sophocles), **III:** 398; **IV:** 370; **Supp. IX:** 102

"Electra on Azalea Path" (Plath), **Supp. I Part 2:** 538

"Electrical Storm" (Bishop), **Supp. I Part 1:** 93

"Electrical Storm" (Hayden), **Supp. II Part 1:** 370

"Electric Arrows" (Proulx), **Supp. VII:** 256

"Electric Girl, The"(P. Benedict), **Supp. XXIII:** 40

"Electricity Saviour" (Olds), **Supp. X:** 215

Electric Kool-Aid Acid Test, The (Wolfe), **Supp. III Part 2:** 575–577, 582–584; **Supp. XI:** 239

Electric Lady, The (film), **Supp. XI:** 309

Electronic Book Review, **Supp. XXII:** 256, 257, 261

Elegant Extracts (Knox), **II:** 8

"Elegant Tom Dillar" (Briggs), **Supp. XVIII:** 17

"Elegiac" (Ferry), **Supp. XXIV:** 148–149

Elegiac Feelings American (Corso), **Supp. XII: 131–134**

"Elegiac Fragments" (Everwine), **Supp. XV:** 89

Elegies (Rukeyser), **Supp. VI:** 273

"Elegies" (Rukeyser), **Supp. VI:** 272

"Elegies for Paradise Valley" (Hayden), **Supp. II Part 1:** 363

"Elegy" (Bidart), **Supp. XV:** 25, 29

Elegy (Levis), **Supp. XI:** 257, 259, 261, **271–272**

"Elegy" (Merwin), **Supp. III Part 1:** 351

"Elegy" (Stafford), **Supp. XI:** 322

"Elegy" (Tate), **IV:** 128

"Elegy, for the U.S.N. Dirigible, Macon, An" (Winters), **Supp. II Part 2:** 810

"Elegy Ending in the Sound of a Skipping Rope" (Levis), **Supp. XI:** 271–272

"Elegy for 41 Whales Beached in Florence, Oregon, June 1979" (Bierds),

Supp. XVII: 27
"Elegy for D. H. Lawrence, An" (W. C. Williams), **Retro. Supp. I:** 421
"Elegy for My Father" (Strand), **Supp. IV Part 2:** 628
"Elegy for My Mother" (Wagoner), **Supp. IX:** 330
"Elegy for Redondo Beach" (Jarman), **Supp. XVII:** 112, 113
Elegy for September, An (Nichols), **Supp. XIII:** 268
"Elegy for Thelonious" (Komunyakaa), **Supp. XIII:** 118
"Elegy for the Lost Umbrella" (Stallings), **Supp. XXIII:** 124; **Supp. XXV:** 231, 232
"Elegy for the Native Guards" (Trethewey), **Supp. XXI:** 255
"Elegy for the U.S.N. Dirigible, Macon, A" (Winters), **Supp. II Part 2:** 810
"Elegy in Dialogue" (Taggard), **Supp. XXII:** 276
"Elegy"(J. Schoolcraft), **Supp. XXIII:** 231
"Elegy of Last Resort" (Nemerov), **III:** 271
"Elegy upon That Honorable and Renowned Knight Sir Philip Sidney, An" (Bradstreet), **Retro. Supp. III:** 7–8
"Elegy with a Thimbleful of Water in the Cage" (Levis), **Supp. XI:** 272
Elegy Written in a Country Churchyard (Gray), **I:** 68
"Elegy Written in a Country Churchyard" (Gray), **Supp. XIV:** 8
"Elementary Scene, The" (Jarrell), **II:** 387, 388, 389
"Elements" (M. Frank), **Supp. X:** 213
Elements of Style, The (Strunk), **Supp. I Part 2:** 670
"Elenita, Cards, Palm, Water" (Cisneros), **Supp. VII:** 64
"Eleonora" (Poe), **III:** 412
Eleothriambos (Lee), **IV:** 158
"Elephant & Ocean" (Notley), **Supp. XXII:** 230
"Elephants" (Moore), **III:** 203
"Elephant's Dance, The" (D. West), **Supp. XVIII:** 281
"Elevator, The" (Dixon), **Supp. XII:** 154
"Elevator Boy" (Hughes), **Retro. Supp. I:** 200; **Supp. I Part 1:** 326
"Eleven" (Cisneros), **Supp. VII:** 69
Eleven Essays in the European Novel (Blackmur), **Supp. II Part 1:** 91, 111
Eleven Heavy Things (installation, July), **Supp. XXIV:** 200
Eleven Kinds of Loneliness (Yates), **Supp. XI: 340–343,** 349
Eleven Poems on the Same Theme (Warren), **IV:** 239–241
"Eleven Times a Poem" (Corso), **Supp. XII:** 132, 133
Elfenbein, Anna Shannon, **Supp. XXVIII:** 121, 122, 123
El Greco (Doménikos Theotokópoulos), **I:** 387; **III:** 212
El-Hage, George N., **Supp. XX:** 116
"El-Hajj Malik El-Shabazz" (Hayden), **Supp. II Part 1:** 379

"Eli, the Fanatic" (P. Roth), **Supp. III Part 2:** 407–408
Elia, Nada, **Supp. XXII:** 73
Eliade, Mircea, **Supp. XVI:** 292
Elie, Paul, **Supp. XXII:** 91–92
Eliot, Charles William, **I:** 5; **II:** 345; **Retro. Supp. I:** 55; **Supp. I Part 2:** 479; **Supp. IX:** 94
Eliot, George, **I:** 375, 458, 459, 461, 467; **II:** 179, 181, 191–192, 275, 319, 324, 338, 577; **IV:** 311, 322; **Retro. Supp. I:** 218, 220, 225; **Supp. I Part 1:** 370; **Supp. I Part 2:** 559, 579; **Supp. IV Part 1:** 31, 297; **Supp. IV Part 2:** 677; **Supp. IX:** 38, 43, 51; **Supp. V:** 258; **Supp. XI:** 68; **Supp. XII:** 335; **Supp. XIV:** 344; **Supp. XX:** 108; **Supp. XXVIII:** 112
Eliot, T. S., **I:** 48, 49, 52, 59, 60, 64, 66, 68, 105, 107, 215–216, 236, 243, 256, 259, 261, 266, 384, 386, 395, 396, 399, 403, 430, 433, 441, 446, 475, 478, 479, 482, 521, 522, 527, **567–591;** **II:** 65, 96, 158, 168, 316, 371, 376, 386, 529, 530, 532, 537, 542, 545; **III:** 1, 4, 5, 6, 7–8, 9, 10, 11, 14, 17, 20, 21, 23, 26, 34, 174, 194, 195–196, 205–206, 220, 236, 239, 269, 270–271, 277–278, 301, 409, 428, 435, 436, 453, 456–457, 459–460, 461–462, 464, 466, 471, 476, 478, 485, 488, 492, 493, 498, 504, 509, 511, 517, 524, 527, 539, 572, 575, 586, 591, 594, 600, 613; **IV:** 27, 74, 82, 83, 95, 122, 123, 127, 129, 134, 138, 140, 141, 191, 201, 237, 331, 379, 402, 403, 418, 419, 420, 430, 431, 439, 442, 491; **Retro. Supp. I:** **51–71,** 74, 80, 89, 91, 171, 198, 210, 283, 289, 290, 292, 296, 298, 299, 311, 324, 359, 411, 413, 414, 416, 417, 420, 428; **Retro. Supp. II:** 79, 178, 189, 262, 326; **Retro. Supp. III:** 46, **57–72,** 74, 101, 103, 251, 255; **Supp. I Part 1:** 257, 264, 268, 270, 274, 299; **Supp. I Part 2:** 387, 423, 455, 536, 554, 624, 659, 721; **Supp. II Part 1:** 1, 4, 8, 20, 30, 91, 98, 103, 136, 314; **Supp. III Part 1:** 9, 10, 26, 31, 37, 41, 43, 44, 48, 62–64, 73, 91, 99–100, 105–106, 273; **Supp. III Part 2:** 541, 611, 612, 617, 624; **Supp. IV Part 1:** 40, 47, 284, 380, 404; **Supp. IV Part 2:** 436; **Supp. IX:** 158–159, 229; **Supp. V:** 79, 97, 101, 338, 343, 344; **Supp. VIII:** 19, 21, 93, 102, 105, 182, 195, 205, 290, 292; **Supp. X:** 59, 115, 119, 124, 187, 324; **Supp. XI:** 242; **Supp. XII:** 45, 159, 198, 308; **Supp. XIII:** 77, 104, 115, 332, 341–342, 344, 346; **Supp. XIV:** 5, 13, 107, 287, 290, 306, 347; **Supp. XIX:** 12; **Supp. XV:** 20, 51, 139, 177, 181, 186, 216, 218, 250, 251, 258, 298, 302, 303, 306, 307; **Supp. XVI:** 158–159, 204, 207, 282; **Supp. XVII:** 36, 71, 75, 111, 240; **Supp. XVIII:** 136; **Supp. XX: 86, 108, 199; Supp. XXIII:** 25, 60, 166; **Supp. XXVI:** 143; **Supp. XXVII:** 153, 284, 287

Eliot's Early Years (Gordon), **Retro. Supp. I:** 55
"Elizabeth" (Longfellow), **I:** 502
"Elizabeth, 1905" (Schnackenberg), **Supp. XV:** 253, 256
Elizabeth Appleton (O'Hara), **III:** 362, 364, 375–377
"Elizabeth Bishop (1911–1979)" (Merrill), **Retro. Supp. II:** 53
"Elizabeth Bishop in Brazil" (Brown), **Supp. I Part 1:** 96
"Elizabeth Bishop's *North & South*" (R. Lowell), **Retro. Supp. II:** 40–41
"Elizabeth Gone" (Sexton), **Supp. II Part 2:** 674, 681
Elizabeth Rex (Findley), **Supp. XX: 62–63**
Elizabeth Stoddard and the Boundaries of Bourgeois Culture (Mahoney), **Supp. XV:** 270
Elk Heads on the Wall (Ríos), **Supp. IV Part 2:** 540
Elkin, Stanley, **Supp. VI: 41–59**
Elkins, Andrew, **Supp. XXIII:** 131, 135
Elkins, Marilyn, **Supp. XXIV:** 64
"Elk Song" (Hogan), **Supp. IV Part 1:** 406
Ella in Bloom (Hearon), **Supp. VIII: 70–71**
Elledge, Jim, **Supp. XIII:** 88
Ellen Foster: A Novel (Gibbons), **Supp. X:** 41, **42–44,** 46, 47, 49, 50
Ellen Montgomery's Bookshelf (S. and A. Warner), **Supp. XVIII:** 264
Ellen Rogers (Farrell), **II:** 42–43
"Ellen's Dream" (Gioia), **Supp. XV:** 128
"Ellen West" (Bidart), **Supp. XV: 26–27**
Eller, Ernest, **Supp. I Part 2:** 497
Ellerman, Winifred, **Supp. I Part 1:** 258–259. *See also* McAlmon, Mrs. Robert (Winifred Ellerman)
"El libro de la sexualidad" (Simic), Supp. VIII: 283
Ellington, Duke, **Retro. Supp. II:** 115; **Supp. IV Part 1:** 360; **Supp. IX:** 164
Elliot, Charles, **Supp. V:** 161
Elliot, George P., **Supp. XV:** 92
Elliott, George B., **III:** 478
Elliott, J. W. M., **Supp. XXVI:** 87, 88
Elliott, Sarah Barnwell, **Supp. XXVIII:** 228
Ellipse, The: Selected Poems of Leonardo Sinisgalli (Di Piero, trans.), **Supp. XIX:** 34
"Ellipsis" (C. Frost), **Supp. XV:** 107
Ellis, Albert, **Supp. IV Part 2:** 527
Ellis, Anne, **Supp. XVI:** 38
Ellis, Bret Easton, **Supp. X:** 7; **Supp. XII:** 81; **Supp. XVIII:** 135; **Supp. XXVII: 67–81,** 269
Ellis, Charles, **Supp. I Part 1:** 99
Ellis, Havelock, **II:** 276; **Supp. XX: 117, 235; Supp. XXII:** 198
Ellis, John Harvard, **Supp. I Part 1:** 103
Ellis, Katherine, **IV:** 114
Ellis, Kelly, **Supp. XXI:** 249
Ellis, Ron, **Supp. XXII:** 209
Ellis, Thomas Sayers, **Supp. XXI:** 246
"Ellis Island" (Helprin), **Supp. XXV:** 85

Ellis Island and Other Stories (Helprin), **Supp. XXV:** 82, 83, 85

Ellison, Harlan, **Supp. XIII:** 61

Ellison, Ralph, **IV:** 250, 493; **Retro. Supp. II:** 3, **111–130; Retro. Supp. III:** 139; **Supp. II Part 1:** 33, **221–252; Supp. IV, Part 1:** 374; **Supp. IX:** 114, 316; **Supp. VIII:** 105, 245; **Supp. X:** 324; **Supp. XI:** 18, 92, 275; **Supp. XIII:** 186, 233, 305; **Supp. XIV:** 306; **Supp. XIX:** 148, 149, 155; **Supp. XV:** 194; **Supp. XVI:** 135, 139; **Supp. XVIII:** 59, 61, 62, 277, 283

Ellmann, Maud, **Supp. IV Part 1:** 302

Ellmann, Richard, **Supp. VIII:** 105; **Supp. XV:** 74

Ellroy, James, **Supp. XIV:** 26; **Supp. XXI:** 71

Elm, Damas, **Supp. XXVI:** 89

Elman, Richard, **Supp. V:** 40

"Elmer" (Faulkner), **Retro. Supp. I:** 79, 80

Elmer, Jonathan, **Retro. Supp. III:** 237

Elmer Gantry (Lewis), **I:** 26, 364; **II:** 447–449, 450, 455

Elmer the Great (Lardner), **II:** 427

"Elms" (Glück), **Supp. V:** 85

"Elms Dying, The—And My Friend, Lew Stillwell, Dead" (Bronk), **Supp. XXI:** 31

Elmslie, Kenward, **Supp. XXVII:** 19, 23, 26

Eloges (Perse), **Supp. XIII:** 344

"Eloquence of Grief, An" (Crane), **I:** 411

"El Paso Del Norte"(Kenny), **Supp. XXIII:** 150

"El Río Grande" (Mora), **Supp. XIII:** 224

El Round up" (Alvarez), **Supp. VII:** 11

"El Salvador: Requiem and Invocation" (Levertov), **Supp. III Part 1:** 284

Elsasser, Henry, **I:** 226

"Elsa Wertman" (Masters), **Supp. I Part 2:** 462–463

Elsie John and Joey Martinez: Two Stories (Huncke), **Supp. XIV:** 148

Elsie Venner (Holmes), **Supp. I Part 1:** 243, 315–316

Elton, Charles, **Supp. XIV:** 192

Éluard, Paul, **III:** 528; **Supp. IV Part 1:** 80; **Supp. XVII:** 244

Elvins, Kells, **Supp. III Part 1:** 93, 101

Ely, Richard T., **Supp. I Part 1:** 5; **Supp. I Part 2:** 640, 645

"Emancipation. A Life Fable" (Chopin), **Retro. Supp. II:** 59; **Supp. I Part 1:** 207–208

"Emancipation in the British West Indies" (Emerson), **II:** 13

"Emancipation Proclamation, The" (Emerson), **II:** 13

Emanuel, James, **Supp. I Part 1:** 346

Embargo, The (Bryant), **Supp. I Part 1:** 152–153

"Embarkation for Cythera, The" (Ferry), **Supp. XXIV:** 149

Embarrassments (James), **Retro. Supp. I:** 229

Embezzler, The (Auchincloss), **Supp. IV Part 1:** 24, 30–31

"Embraces" (Davison), **Supp. XXVI:** 72

"Embroidery, The" (C. Frost), **Supp. XV:** 97

"Emerald" (Doty), **Supp. XI:** 131

"Emerald, The" (Merrill), **Supp. III Part 1:** 328

Emerald City (Egan), **Supp. XIX:** 49, **52–53**

"Emerald City" (Egan), **Supp. XIX:** 52

Emerald City of Las Vegas, The (Wakoski), **Supp. XXVIII:** 269

Emerald Ice: Selected Poems, 1962–1987 (Wakoski), **Supp. XXVIII:** 268

"Emergence of Flight from Aristotle's Mud, The" (Goldbarth), **Supp. XII:** 190

Emergency Exit (Major), **Supp. XXII:** 174, **175,** 182

"Emergency Haying" (Carruth), **Supp. XVI:** 55

"Emergency Room" (Mora), **Supp. XIII:** 218

"Emerging Voices: The Teaching of Writing" (Mora), **Supp. XIII:** 220

Emerson, and Other Essays (Chapman), **Supp. XIV:** 41–44

Emerson, Ellen, **Supp. I Part 1:** 33

Emerson, John, **Supp. XVI:** 185, 186, 190, 192

Emerson, Ralph Waldo, **I:** 98, 217, 220, 222, 224, 228, 239, 246, 251, 252, 253, 257, 260, 261, 283, 386, 397, 402, 424, 433, 444, 447, 455, 458, 460–461, 463, 464, 485, 561; **II:** 1–24, 49, 92, 127–128, 169, 170, 226, 233, 237, 273–274, 275, 278, 289, 295, 301, 313, 315, 336, 338, 344, 402, 491, 503; **III:** 53, 82, 171, 174, 260, 277, 409, 424, 428, 453, 454, 507, 576–577, 606, 614; **IV:** 60, 167, 169, 170, 171, 172, 173–174, 176, 178, 183, 186, 187, 192, 201, 202, 211, 335, 338, 340, 342, 350; **Retro. Supp. I:** 34, 53, 54, 57, 62, 74–75, 76, 125, 148–149, 152–153, 159, 217, 250, 298, 392, 400, 403; **Retro. Supp. II:** 96, 113, 135, 142, 155, 207, 262; **Retro. Supp. III:** 223, 249, 255, 283; **Supp. I Part 1:** 2, 28–29, 31, 33, 188, 299, 308–309, 317, 358, 365, 366, 368; **Supp. I Part 2:** 374, 383, 393, 407, 413, 416, 420, 422, 474, 482, 580, 582, 602, 659, 679; **Supp. II Part 1:** 280, 288; **Supp. III Part 1:** 387; **Supp. IV Part 2:** 439, 597, 619; **Supp. IX:** 38, 90, 175, 176, 181; **Supp. V:** 118; **Supp. VIII:** 42, 105, 106, 108, 198, 201, 204, 205, 292; **Supp. X:** 42, 45, 121, 223; **Supp. XI:** 203; **Supp. XIII:** 141, 145, 233, 246, **Supp. XIII:** 247; **Supp. XIV:** 41–44, 46, 54, 104, 177; **Supp. XV:** 219, 224; **Supp. XVI:** 84; **Supp. XVII:** 42, 236; **Supp. XX: 115, 116; Supp. XXI:** 217; **Supp. XXIII:** 161, 190; **Supp. XXIV:** 4, 67, 74, 77; **Supp. XXV:** 241, 250; **Supp. XXVI:** 37; **Supp. XXVII:** 234; **Supp. XXVIII:** 158, 251

"Emerson and the Essay" (Gass), **Supp. VI:** 88

"Emerson the Lecturer" (J. R. Lowell), **Supp. I Part 2:** 420, 422

Emerson-Thoreau Award, **Retro. Supp. I:** 67

Emery, Amy Fass, **Retro. Supp. III:** 132

Emery, Clark, **III:** 478

Emery, Mary Lou, **Supp. XXII:** 73

E. M. Forster (Trilling), **Supp. III Part 2:** 496, 501, 504

"Emigre in Autumn, An" (Gioia), **Supp. XV:** 120

Emily, Alone (O'Nan), **Supp. XXV:** 145, 149, 150–151

"Emily Dickinson and Class" (Erkkila), **Retro. Supp. I:** 42–43

Emily Dickinson Editorial Collective, **Retro. Supp. I:** 47

Emily Dickinson in Southern California (X. J. Kennedy), **Supp. XV: 164–165**

"Emily Dickinson's Defunct" (Nelson), **Supp. XVIII:** 173

Emily Dickinson: Woman Poet (Bennett), **Retro. Supp. I:** 42

Eminent Victorians (Strachey), **Supp. I Part 2:** 485

Emma (Austen), **Supp. XVIII:** 149

"Emma and Eginhard" (Longfellow), **III:** 505

"Emma Enters a Sentence of Elizabeth Bishop's" (Gass), **Supp. VI:** 93

Emmanuel Appodocca: or, A Blighted Life (Philip), **Supp. XXI:** 160

"Emmaus" (Di Piero), **Supp. XIX:** 42, 43

Emma Who Saved My Life (Barnhardt), **Supp. XXVII:** 1, 3–5, 7

Emperor Jones, The (O'Neill), **II:** 278; **III:** 391, 392

Emperor of Haiti (Hughes), **Supp. I Part 1:** 339

"Emperor of Ice Cream, The" (Stevens), **IV:** 76, 80–81

"Emperors" (Dunn), **Supp. XI:** 155

"Emperor's New Clothes, The" (Anderson), **I:** 441

"Empire" (Ford), **Supp. V:** 69

Empire: A Novel (Vidal), **Supp. IV Part 2:** 677, 684, 686, 690; **Supp. XIX:** 132

"Empire Builders" (MacLeish), **III:** 14

Empire City, The: or, New York by Night and Day (Lippard), **Supp. XXIII:** 178, 180, 183, 184, 185

Empire Falls (Russo), **Supp. XII: 339–343**

Empire of Summer, The (Doty), **Supp. XI:** 120

Empire of the Senseless (Acker), **Supp. XII:** 5, **6, 14–16**

"Empires" (Simic), **Supp. VIII:** 282

"Emporium" (Shapiro), **Supp. II Part 2:** 705

Empress of the Splendid Season (Hijuelos), **Supp. VIII: 86–89**

Empson, William, **I:** 522, 533; **II:** 536; **III:** 286, 497, 498, 499; **IV:** 136, 431; **Retro. Supp. I:** 263; **Retro. Supp. II:** 253; **Supp. XVI:** 190

Empty Bed, The (Hadas), **Supp. XXIII: 117–118**

Empty Hands, The (Bronk), **Supp. XXI:** 31

"Empty Hills, The" (Winters), **Supp. II Part 2:** 792, 793, 796

"Empty Icon Frame" (Stallings), **Supp. XXV:** 233

Empty Mirror, Early Poems (Ginsberg), **Supp. II Part 1:** 308, 311, 313–314, 319, 329

"Empty Room" (Hughes), **Supp. I Part 1:** 337

"Empty Threat, An" (Frost), **II:** 159

Emshwiller, Ed, **Supp. XVIII:** 145

"Encantadas, The" (Melville), **III:** 89; **Retro. Supp. III:** 158; **Supp. XVIII:** 4

"Enchanted Bluff, The" (Cather), **Retro. Supp. III:** 28, 35

Enchanter, The (Nabokov), **Retro. Supp. I:** 266

"Enclosed Dreams, Highways and Labyrinths: Jonathan Lethem's *Amnesia Moon*" (Rossi), *Supp. XVIII:* 139

"Encomium Twenty Years Later" (Tate), **I:** 381

"Encounter" (Espaillat), **Supp. XXI:** 107

"Encounter, The" (Pound), **III:** 466

Encounter in April (Sarton), **Supp. VIII:** 259

"Encounter in April" (Sarton), **Supp. VIII:** 259

Encountering God: A Spiritual Journey from Bozeman to Banaras (Eck), **Supp. XXVIII:** 49–50, 52, 53, 54–56, 58, 60

"Encountering the Sublime" (McClatchy), **Supp. XII:** 261

"Encounter in Vindija Cave, Present-Day Croatia: Late October"(Schott), **Supp. XXIII:** 254

"Encounter on the Seine: Black Meets Brown" (Baldwin), **Retro. Supp. II:** 2

Encounters with Chinese Writers (Dillard), **Supp. VI:** 19, 23, 31

Encounters with the Archdruid (McPhee), **Supp. III Part 1:** 292–294, 301; **Supp. X:** 30

Encyclopedia of Arkansas History and Culture, The (online), **Supp. XXII:** 50

Encyclopedia of Scotland, The (A. Finch), **Supp. XVII:** 70–71

Encyclopedia of World Biography, The, **Supp. XXI:** 74

"End, The" (Olds), **Supp. X:** 205

"Endangered Species" (Mora), **Supp. XIII:** 219–220

Endecott and the Red Cross (R. Lowell), **II:** 545

Endgame (Beckett), **Supp. XIII:** 196; **Supp. XXII:** 263

"Endgame" (Tan), **Supp. X:** 290

"Endicott and the Red Cross" (Hawthorne), **Retro. Supp. II:** 181, 187–188

"End of Books, The" (Coover), **Supp. V:** 53

End of Books, The" (Coover), **Supp. XXII:** 259

End of Dreams, The (Skloot), **Supp. XX:** 196, 202–203

End of Education, The (Postman), **Supp. XI:** 275

"End of FIRPO in the World, The" (Saunders), **Supp. XIX:** 229

End of Me, The (Hayes), **Supp. XXVI:** 142–143

"End of Season" (Warren), **IV:** 239–240

"End of Something, The" (Hemingway), **II:** 248

End of the Affair, The (Greene), **Supp. XI:** 99

End of the Age of Innocence, The (Price), **Retro. Supp. I:** 377

End of the Candle, The (Bryant), **Supp. XXVIII:** 41

"End of the Line, The" (Helprin), **Supp. XXV:** 81

"End of the Line, The" (Jarrell), **III:** 527

"End of the Rainbow, The" (Jarrell), **II:** 386

End of the Road (film), **Supp. XI:** 309

End of the Road, The (Barth), **I:** 121, 122, 126–131; **Supp. XI:** 309; **Supp. XVIII:** 140, 141

"End of the World, The" (Gioia), **Supp. XV:** 126

"End of the World, The" (MacLeish), **III:** 8

Endor (Nemerov), **III:** 269, 270, 279

Endore, Guy, **Supp. XVII:** 53–67

"Endpapers" (Rich), **Retro. Supp. III:** 252

"Ends" (Dixon), **Supp. XII:** 153

End to Innocence, An: Essays on Culture and Politics (Fiedler), **Supp. XIII:** 98–99

Endure: The Diaries of Charles Walter Stetson (Stetson), **Supp. XI:** 196

"Enduring Chill, The" (O'Connor), **III:** 349, 351, 357; **Retro. Supp. II:** 236; **Retro. Supp. III:** 213

Enduring Vision of Norman Mailer, The (Leeds), **Retro. Supp. II:** 204

Endymion (Keats), **IV:** 405; **Retro. Supp. I:** 412

End Zone (DeLillo), **Supp. VI:** 2, 3, 4, 10, 11, 12

Enemies (Boyce and Hapgood), **Supp. XVII:** 100; **Supp. XXI:** 7, 13

Enemies: A Love Story (Singer), **IV:** 1; **Retro. Supp. II:** 310–311

Enemy, The: Time (T. Williams), **IV:** 391

Enemy of the People, An (adapt. Miller), **III:** 154–156

"Energy Vampire" (Ginsberg), **Supp. II Part 1:** 326

"Enforcement of the Slave Trade Laws, The" (Du Bois), **Supp. II Part 1:** 161

"Engaging the Past" (Bell), **Supp. X:** 17

Engel, Bernard F., **I:** 532

Engels, Friedrich, **IV:** 429, 443–444; **Supp. I Part 1:** 13; **Supp. XXI:** 162

Engels, John, **Supp. XXVI:** 152

Engineer of Beasts, The (Sanders), **Supp. XVI:** 270

Engineer of Moonlight (DeLillo), **Supp. VI:** 4

Engineers and the Price System, The (Veblen), **I:** 475–476; **Supp. I Part 2:** 638, 642, 648

Engines of Creation: the Coming Era of Nanotechnology (Drexler), **Supp. XVI:** 121

"England" (Moore), **III:** 203, 207, 214

Englander, Nathan, **Supp. XX: 177, 179; Supp. XXIV:** 131; **Supp. XXV:** 268

Engle, Paul, **III:** 542; **Retro. Supp. II:** 220, 221; **Supp. V:** 337; **Supp. XI:** 315; **Supp. XIII:** 76; **Supp. XVIII:** 72

English, Parker, **Retro. Supp. III:** 138

English, Zoë, **Supp. XVI:** 293

English Elegy, The: Studies in the Genre from Spenser to Yeats (Sacks), **Supp. IV Part 2:** 450

English Hours (James), **II:** 337; **Retro. Supp. I:** 235

English Language, The (L. P. Smith), **Supp. XIV:** 341

English-Latin Gradus or Verse Dictionary, An (Ainger), **Supp. XX: 230**

"English Lesson"(Strout), **Supp. XXIII:** 273–274, 284

Englishmen of Letters (James), **II:** 327

English Notebooks, The (Hawthorne), **II:** 226, 227–228

English Novel, The (Lanier), **Supp. I Part 1:** 371

English Poets, The: Lessing, Rousseau (J. R. Lowell), **Supp. I Part 2:** 407

English Prosody and Modern Poetry (Shapiro), **Supp. II Part 2:** 710

English Traits (Emerson), **II:** 1, 5, 6–7, 8

"English Writers on America" (Irving), **II:** 308

Engstrand, Stuart, **Supp. I Part 1:** 51

"Enigma Variations" (Nelson), **Supp. XVIII:** 177

"Enoch" (Very), **Supp. XXV:** 246, 247

"Enoch and the Gorilla" (O'Connor), **Retro. Supp. II:** 225

Enormous Changes at the Last Minute (Paley), **Supp. VI:** 218

"Enormous Changes at the Last Minute" (Paley), **Supp. VI:** 226, 232

"Enormous Radio, The" (Cheever), **Supp. I Part 1:** 175–177, 195

Enormous Radio and Other Stories, The (Cheever), **Supp. I Part 1:** 175–177

Enormous Room, The (Cummings), **I:** 429, 434, 440, 445, 477; **Supp. XXI:** 277

"Enough for a Lifetime" (Buck), **Supp. II Part 1:** 127

Enough Rope (Parker), **Supp. IX:** 189, 192

Enquiry Concerning Political Justice (Godwin), **Supp. I Part 1:** 126, 146

"En Route" (Boulton), **Supp. XXII:** 25

Entanglements of Nathaniel Hawthorne, The (Coale), **Retro. Supp. III:** 111

Entered From the Sun (Garrett), **Supp. VII:** 105–106, 107–109

"Entering the Building" (Notley), **Supp. XXII:** 237

"Entering the Kingdom" (Oliver), **Supp. VII:** 234

Entertaining Strangers (Gurney), **Supp. V:** 98, 99

Enter without Desire (Lacy), **Supp. XV:** 201

Entranced, The (Lippard), **Supp. XXIII:** 178, 180, 190

Entrance: Four Chicano Poets, **Supp. XIII:** 316

Entrance to Porlock, The (Buechner), **Supp. XII:** 52

Entries (Berry), **Supp. X:** 23

"Entropy" (Pynchon), **Supp. II Part 2:** 619, 621

"Entry" (Huddle), **Supp. XXVI:** 149

Entry in an Unknown Hand (F. Wright), **Supp. XVII:** 240, 244, 245

Environmental Imagination, The (Buell), **Supp. IX:** 29; **Supp. V:** 209

"Envoy" (Collins), **Supp. XXI:** 57

"Envoys, The" (Merrill), **Supp. III Part 1:** 326

"Envy; or, Yiddish in America" (Ozick), **Supp. V:** 263, 265–266

"Eolian Harp, The" (Coleridge), **I:** 284

"Eolian Harp, The"(Coleridge), **Supp. XXIII:** 231

"Eototo" (Sobin), **Supp. XVI:** 283–284

"Ephemera, The" (Franklin), **II:** 121

Ephesians (biblical book), **Supp. I Part 1:** 117

"Epic Poetry" (Very), **Supp. XXV:** 241

Epictetus, **III:** 566

"Epicurean, The" (Auchincloss), **Supp. IV Part 1:** 25

Epicurus, **I:** 59

Epidemic of Genius, An (Wolfert), **Supp. XXI:** 278

"Epigram" (R. Lowell), **II:** 550

"Epilogue" (R. Lowell), **Retro. Supp. II:** 191

"Epimanes" (Poe), **III:** 411

"Epimetheus" (Longfellow), **II:** 494

"Epiphany" (X. J. Kennedy), **Supp. XV:** 166, 167

"Epipsychidion" (Shelley), **Supp. I Part 2:** 718

"Episode, The" (Huddle), **Supp. XXVI:** 150

Episode in Palmetto (Caldwell), **I:** 297, 307

"Episode in the Life of an Ancestor" (Boyle), **Supp. XXIV:** 56

Episode of the Wandering Knife, The (Rinehart), **Supp. XXV:** 198, 200

"Epistle" (L.-Y. Lee), **Supp. XV:** 212

Epistles (Horace), **Supp. XXIV:** 156

Epistles of Horace, The (Ferry, trans.), **Supp. XXIV: 157–158**

Epistle to a Godson (Auden), **Supp. II Part 1:** 24

"Epistle to Be Left in the Earth" (MacLeish), **III:** 13

"Epistle to George William Curtis" (J. R. Lowell), **Supp. I Part 2:** 416

"Epistle to Léon-Paul Fargue" (MacLeish), **III:** 15

"Epitaph Ending in And, The" (Stafford), **Supp. XI:** 321–322

Epitaph for a Dead Beat (Markson), 139; **Supp. XVII: 136–138,** 141

Epitaph for a Desert Anarchist (Bishop), **Supp. XIII:** 1

Epitaph for a Tramp (Markson), **Supp. XVII:** 136, 137, 139 142

"Epitaph for Fire and Flower" (Plath), **Supp. I Part 2:** 537

"Epitaph for S.P." (Davison), **Supp. XXVI:** 71

"Epitaph for the Race of Man" (Millay), **III:** 127–128

"Epitaph on My Dear and Ever-Honoured Mother Mrs. Dorothy Dudley, An" (Bradstreet), **Retro. Supp. III:** 12

"Epithalamium" (Auden), **Supp. II Part 1:** 15

"Epstein" (P. Roth), **Retro. Supp. II:** 281; **Supp. III Part 2:** 404, 406–407, 412, 422

Epstein, Barbara, **Supp. XIX:** 268

Epstein, Helen, **Supp. XVII:** 47; **Supp. XXII:** 95

Epstein, Jacob, **Supp. XXIII:** 6

Epstein, Jason, **Supp. VIII:** 233

Epstein, Joseph, **Supp. IV Part 2:** 692; **Supp. VIII:** 236, 238; **Supp. XIV: 101–117; Supp. XVI:** 230, 275

Epstein, Leslie, **Supp. XII: 159–174; Supp. XVIII:** 92, 99

Epstein, Philip, **Supp. XII:** 159

"Equal in Paris" (Baldwin), **Retro. Supp. II:** 3; **Supp. I Part 1:** 52

"Equals" (Untermeyer), **Supp. XV:** 304

Equation for Evil (Caputo), **Supp. XIX:** 25–26

"Equations of the Light" (Gioia), **Supp. XV:** 125

"Equilibrists, The" (Ransom), **III:** 490, 494

"Equinox 1980" (Davison), **Supp. XXVI:** 77

"Equinox"(Crooker), **Supp. XXIII:** 55

"Equipment for Pennies" (H. Roth), **Supp. IX:** 233

Erasmus, Desiderius, **Supp. XV:** 258

Erasure (Everett), **Supp. XVIII:** 54, 60, **61–62**

"Erat Hora" (Pound), **III:** 463; **Retro. Supp. I:** 413

Erdrich, Louise, **Supp. IV Part 1: 259–278,** 333, 404; **Supp. X:** 290; **Supp. XVIII:** 189; **Supp. XXIV:** 245; **Supp. XXVI:** 102

"Erectus" (Karr), **Supp. XI:** 243

"Ere Sleep Comes Down to Soothe the Weary Eyes" (Dunbar), **Supp. II Part 1:** 199, 207–208

"Ergo Non Sum. Est." (Bronk), **Supp. XXI:** 31

"Ergotism"(Schott), **Supp. XXIII:** 245

"Eric Hermannson's Soul" (Cather), **Retro. Supp. III:** 25–26, 28

Erik Dorn (Hecht), **Supp. XXVII:** 83, 87–88, 89

Erikson, Erik, **I:** 58, 214, 218

Erisman, Fred, **Supp. VIII:** 126

Erkkila, Betsy, **Retro. Supp. I:** 42; **Supp. XX: 281, 287, 287–288**

Ernest, John, **Supp. XXI:** 24

"Ernest: or Parent for a Day" (Bourne), **I:** 232

Ernst, Max, **Retro. Supp. II:** 321

Eroding Witness (Mackey), **Supp. XXVII:** 152–153, 154, 157

"Eros" (Komunyakaa), **Supp. XIII:** 130

"Eros and Anteros" (E. Stoddard), **Supp. XV:** 283

Eros and Civilization (Marcuse), **Supp. XII:** 2

"Eros at Temple Stream" (Levertov), **Supp. III Part 1:** 278–279

Eros the Bittersweet (Carson), **Supp. XII:** 97, **98–99**

Eros Trilogy, The (Silver), **Supp. XXIV:** 264, 267

"Eros Turannos" (Robinson), **III:** 510, 512, 513–516, 517, 518

"Eroticism in Women" (Nin), **Supp. X:** 195

"Errand" (Carver), **Supp. III Part 1:** 149

Erskine, Albert, **IV:** 261; **Retro. Supp. II:** 117

Erskine, John, **I:** 223; **Supp. X:** 183; **Supp. XIV:** 120

Erstein, Hap, **Supp. IV Part 2:** 589, 590

"Escape" (MacLeish), **III:** 4

Escape Artist, The (Wagoner), **Supp. IX:** 324, **334–335**

"Escape"(Thompson), **Supp. XXIII:** 301

Escher, M. C., **Supp. XII:** 26; **Supp. XVI:** 102

"Escudilla" (Leopold), **Supp. XIV:** 188

Esenwein, J. Berg, **Supp. XXVI:** 281

Eshleman, Clayton, **Supp. XVI:** 284

"Eskimo Love" (Apple), **Supp. XVII:** 5

Espaillat, Rhina P., **Supp. XXI: 97–114**

Esparza, Laura, **Supp. XXIII:** 197

Especially Maine (Beston), **Supp. XXVI:** 32

Espeland, Pamela, **Supp. XVIII:** 180, 181

Espen, Hal, **Supp. X:** 15

Espey, John, **III:** 463, 468, 478

Esposito, Michael, **Supp. XX: 34, 40**

Esposito, Scott, **Supp. XVII:** 234

Esquibel, Catrióna Rueda, **Supp. XXIII:** 202

Essais (Renouvier), **II:** 344–345

Essay Concerning Human Understanding, An (Locke), **I:** 554; **II:** 8, 348–349

Essay on American Poetry (Brown), **Supp. I Part 1:** 156

"Essay on Aristocracy" (Paine), **Supp. I Part 2:** 515

Essay on Criticism, An (Pope), **Supp. XXVI:** 271, 284

"Essay on Friendship, An" (McClatchy), **Supp. XII:** 258–259

"Essay on Love" (Carruth), **Supp. XVI:** 56

Essay on Man (Pope), **II:** 111; **Supp. I Part 2:** 516

"Essay on Marriage" (Carruth), **Supp. XVI:** 48

Essay on Our Changing Order (Veblen), **Supp. I Part 2:** 629, 642

"Essay on Poetics" (Ammons), **Supp. VII:** 29–31

Essay on Projects (Defoe), **II:** 104

"Essay on Psychiatrists" (Pinsky), **Supp. VI:** 237, 238, 241, 242, 249, 250

Essay on Rime (Shapiro), **I:** 430; **Supp. II Part 2:** 702, 703, 708–711
"Essay on Sanity" (Dunn), **Supp. XI:** 147
"Essay on the Character of Robespierre" (Paine), **Supp. I Part 2:** 515
Essay on the Chinese Written Character (Fenollosa), **III:** 474
"Essay on What I Think About Most" (Carson), **Supp. XII:** 111–112
Essays (Emerson), **II:** 1, 7, 8, 12–13, 15, 21
Essays (Montaigne), **Supp. XXVI:** 39
Essays, Speeches, and Public Letters by William Faulkner (Meriweather, ed.), **Retro. Supp. I:** 77
Essays and Poems (Very), **Supp. XXV:** 247, 249–250
Essays in Anglo-Saxon Law (Adams), **I:** 5
Essays in London (James), **II:** 336
Essays in Radical Empiricism (James), **II:** 355, 356–357
Essays on Norman Mailer (Lucid), **Retro. Supp. II:** 195
Essays on the Nature and Principles of Taste (Alison), **Supp. I Part 1:** 151
Essays to Do Good (Mather), **II:** 104; **Supp. II Part 2:** 461, 467
"Essay: The Love of Old Houses" (Doty), **Supp. XI:** 136
"Essay Toward a Point of View, An" (Brooks), **I:** 244
"Essay Vanishes, The" (Monson), **Supp. XXIV:** 238
"Essence, Absence, and Sobin's *Venus Blue*" (English), **Supp. XVI:** 293
Essential Dykes to Watch Out For, The (Bechdel), **Supp. XXV:** 2
Essential Haiku, The (Hass), **Supp. VI:** 102
Essential Keats (Levine, ed.), **Supp. V:** 179
"Essential Oils—are wrung" (Dickinson), **I:** 471; **Retro. Supp. I:** 43, 46
"Essentials" (Toomer), **Supp. III Part 2:** 486
Essentials: A Philosophy of Life in Three Hundred Definitions and Aphorisms (Toomer), **Supp. III Part 2:** 486
Essentials: Definitions and Aphorisms (Toomer), **Supp. IX:** 320
"Essentials of Spontaneous Prose" (Kerouac), **Supp. III Part 1:** 227–228
Essential Works of the Founding Fathers, The (Kriegel, ed.), **Supp. XXIV:** 214
Estampas del valle y otras obras (Hinojosa). *See Valley, The* (Hinojosa)
Esta puente, mi espalda: Voces de mujeres tercermundistas en los Estados Unidos (Moraga, Castillo, and Alarcón, eds.), **Supp. XXIII:** 194
"Estate Sale" (Nye), **Supp. XIII:** 283
Estess, Sybil, **Supp. IV Part 2:** 449, 452
Esther (Adams), **I:** 9–10, 20
"Esther" (Toomer), **Supp. IX:** 313–314
"Esther Kahn" (Symons), **Supp. XX: 239**
"Esthétique du Mal" (Stevens), **IV:** 79; **Retro. Supp. I:** 300, 311, 312
"Estoy-eh-muut and the Kunideeyahs (Arrowboy and the Destroyers)" (film),

Supp. IV Part 2: 560
Estrada, Genaro, **Retro. Supp. II:** 89
Estray, The (Longfellow, ed.), **Retro. Supp. II:** 155
Esty, William, **III:** 358
"Eta Carinae" (Stone), **Supp. XXVII:** 260–261
"Etching, An" (Masters), **Supp. I Part 2:** 458
Eternal Feminine, The (Wells), **Supp. XXVI:** 275
"Eternal Goodness, The" (Whittier), **Supp. I Part 2:** 704
Eternal Quadrangle, The (Jack Reed), **Supp. XXVIII:** 38
Eternal Spring, The (Boyce), **Supp. XVII:** 100; **Supp. XXI:** 4, 5, 11
"Eternity, An" (W. C. Williams), **Retro. Supp. I:** 423
"Eternity Is Now" (Roethke), **III:** 544–545
"Ethan Brand" (Hawthorne), **II:** 227; **Retro. Supp. III:** 117
Ethan Frome (film, Madden), **Retro. Supp. III:** 290
Ethan Frome (Wharton), **IV:** 316–317, 327; **Retro. Supp. I:** 372–373; **Retro. Supp. III:** 283–284, 287; **Supp. IX:** 108; **Supp. XVIII:** 216; **Supp. XXIII:** 275, 281
"Ethical Turn in Postcolonial Theory and Narrative, The: Michelle Cliff's *No Telephone to Heaven*" (Moynagh), **Supp. XXII:** 73
Ethics (Spinoza), **IV:** 12; **Retro. Supp. II:** 300
"Ethics of Culture, The" (Locke), **Supp. XIV:** 211
"Ethnics of Frank Costello, The" (Talese), **Supp. XVII:** 202
Etiquette and Vitriol: The Food Chain and Other Plays (Silver), **Supp. XXIV:** 263, 264
"Étiquettes Jaunes, Les"(O'Hara), **Supp. XXIII:** 214
"Etude" (Kooser), **Supp. XIX:** 115
Etulain, Richard, **Supp. IV Part 2:** 597, 601, 604, 607, 608, 610, 611
"Etymology" (Nelson), **Supp. XVIII:** 185
Euclid, **III:** 6, 620
"Euclid Alone Has Looked on Beauty Bare" (Millay), **III:** 133
"Euclidean Spaces: Linear Time" (Bronk), **Supp. XXI:** 31
Eugene, Frank, **Supp. X:** 204
Eugene Onegin (Pushkin), **III:** 246, 263
Eugene Onegin (Pushkin; Nabokov, trans.), **Retro. Supp. I:** 266, 267, 272
Eugenides, Jeffrey, **Supp. XIX:** 138; **Supp. XXI:** 229; **Supp. XXIV:** 131–146
Eugénie, Empress, **IV:** 309
Eugénie Grandet (Balzac), **II:** 328
"Eugénie Grandet" (Barthelme), **Supp. IV Part 1:** 47
"Eulogy for Richard Hugo (1923–1982)" (Wagoner), **Supp. IX:** 330–331
"Eulogy on the Flapper" (Z. Fitzgerald), **Supp. IX:** 71

Eumenides (Aeschylus), **Retro. Supp. I:** 65
"E Unibus Pluram: Television and U.S. Fiction" (Wallace), **Supp. X:** 315–316
"Euphemisms" (Matthews), **Supp. IX:** 167–168
Eureka (Poe), **III:** 409, 424, 428–429; **Retro. Supp. III:** 225, 234
Eureka Mill (Rash), **Supp. XXVII:** 217–218
Eurekas (Goldbarth), **Supp. XII:** 181
Euripides, **I:** 325; **II:** 8, 282, 543; **III:** 22, 145, 398; **IV:** 370; **Supp. I Part 1:** 268, 269, 270; **Supp. I Part 2:** 482; **Supp. V:** 277
"Euripides and Professor Murray" (Eliot), **Supp. I Part 1:** 268
"Euripides—A Playwright" (West), **IV:** 286; **Retro. Supp. II:** 326
"Europe" (Ashbery), **Supp. III Part 1:** 7–10, 13, 18
European Discovery of America, The: The Northern Voyages (Morison), **Supp. I Part 2:** 496–497
Europeans, The (H. James), **I:** 452; **II:** 327, 328; **Retro. Supp. I:** 216, 220
Europe Central (Vollmann), **Supp. XVII:** 225, 226, 227, 229, 231, **233–235,** 236
"Europe! Europe!" (Ginsberg), **Supp. II Part 1:** 320, 322
Europe of Trusts, The: Selected Poems (Howe), **Supp. IV Part 2:** 420, 422, 426
Europe without Baedeker (Wilson), **IV:** 429
"Eurydice in Darkness" (Davison), **Supp. XXVI:** 71
Eurydice in the Underworld (Acker), **Supp. XII:** 7
"Eurydice Reveals Her Strength" (Stallings), **Supp. XXV:** 230
"Eurydice's Footnote" (Stallings), **Supp. XXV:** 230
Eustace, Saint, **II:** 215
Eustace Chisholm and the Works (Purdy), **Supp. VII:** 273–274, 279–280
"Euthanasia" (Tate), **IV:** 122
Eva (Levin), **Supp. XXVII:** 135, 143, 145
"Evaluation" (Bronk), **Supp. XXI:** 32
Eva-Mary (McCarriston), **Supp. XIV:** 259, 260, **263–268**
Evangeline (Dixon), **Supp. XII:** 153
Evangeline (Longfellow), **II:** 489, 501–502; **Retro. Supp. II:** 155, **156–159,** 162, 164; **Supp. I Part 2:** 586
Evanier, David, **Supp. XVI:** 212
Evans, Alice, **Supp. XVII:** 71, 72
Evans, Mary Ann. *See* Eliot, George
Evans, Oliver, **Supp. IV Part 1:** 85, 91
Evans, Sandy, **Supp. XIII:** 129
Evans, Walker, **I:** 36, 38, 293; **Retro. Supp. II:** 85
Eva's Man (G. Jones), **Supp. XXIV:** 183, 184, 185, **188–190,** 193
Eve (A. Finch), **Supp. XVII: 72–74**
"Eve" (W. C. Williams), **Retro. Supp. I:** 423
Even Cowgirls Get the Blues (Robbins), **Supp. X:** 259, 260, 261, 262–263,

264, 266, **269–271**, 272, 274, 277, 284; **Supp. XIII:** 11

"Evening" (Carver), **Supp. III Part 1:** 148

Evening (Minot), **Supp. VI:** 204–205, 208, **213–215**

"Evening at a Country Inn" (Kenyon), **Supp. VII:** 167

"Evening in Advent, An" (W. V. Davis), **Supp. XXI:** 92

"Evening in a Lumber Yard"(Le Sueur), **Supp. XXIII:** 165

"Evening in a Sugar Orchard" (Frost), **Retro. Supp. I:** 133

"Evening in Nuevo Leon, An" (Caldwell), **I:** 309

"Evening in the Sanitarium" (Bogan), **Supp. III Part 1:** 61

Evening Light, The (Skloot), **Supp. XX:** 196, 201–202

"Evening Love-of-Self" (Taggard), **Supp. XXII:** 280–281

"Evening of the 4th of July, The" (Kees), **Supp. XV:** 140, 142

"Evening on the Cote d'Azur" (Yates), **Supp. XI:** 349

Evening Performance, An: New and Selected Short Stories (Garrett), **Supp. VII:** 109

"Evenings at Home" (Hardwick), **Supp. III Part 1:** 195–196

"Evening's at Seven, The" (Thurber), **Supp. I Part 2:** 616

"Evening Star" (Bogan), **Supp. III Part 1:** 56

Evening Star, The (McMurtry), **Supp. V:** 230

Evening Star, The (screenplay, McMurtry), **Supp. V:** 232

"Evening Sun" (Kenyon), **Supp. VII:** 168

Evening Sun Turned Crimson, The (Huncke), **Supp. XIV:** 140, 149–150

"Evening Sun Turned Crimson, The" (Huncke), **Supp. XIV:** 137–138, 139

"Evening Wind, The" (Bryant), **Supp. I Part 1:** 164

"Evening without Angels" (Stevens), **Retro. Supp. I:** 302

Evening with Richard Nixon, An (Vidal), **Supp. IV Part 2:** 683

"Even Sea, The" (Swenson), **Supp. IV Part 2:** 641

Even Stephen (Perelman and West), **Retro. Supp. II:** 328

"Event, An" (Wilbur), **Supp. III Part 2:** 547, 554

"Event, The" (Dove), **Supp. IV Part 1:** 242, 247–248

"Even the Vanishing Housed"(Hirshfield), **Supp. XXIII:** 132

"Eventide" (Brooks), **Supp. III Part 1:** 73

"Eventide" (Purdy), **Supp. VII:** 270

"Event Itself, The" (Carruth), **Supp. XVI:** 47

Eve of Saint Agnes, The (Keats), **II:** 82, 531

"Eve of St. Agnes, The" (Clampitt), **Supp. IX:** 40

"Ever a Bridegroom: Reflections on the Failure of Texas Literature" (McMurtry), **Supp. V:** 225

Everett, Alexander Hill, **Supp. I Part 1:** 152

Everett, Percival, **Supp. XVIII:** 53–67

Everlasting Story of Nory, The (Baker), **Supp. XIII:** 52, **Supp. XIII:** 53–55

"Everly Brothers, The" (Skloot), **Supp. XX:** 199

Ever-Present Past, The (Hamilton), **Supp. XVI:** 196

Evers, Medgar, **IV:** 280; **Retro. Supp. II:** 13; **Supp. I Part 1:** 52, 65

Everson, William, **Supp. XXII:** 276

Everwine, Peter, **Supp. V:** 180; **Supp. XIII:** 312; **Supp. XV:** 73–90

"Everybody Knows" (Cohen), **Supp. XXVII:** 52, 62

"Everybody's Protest Novel" (Baldwin), **Retro. Supp. II:** 4; **Supp. I Part 1:** 50, 51

"Everybody's Reading Li Po' Silk-screened on a Purple T-Shirt" (Komunyakaa), **Supp. XIII:** 120

Everybody's Story: Writing by Older Minnesotans (C. Bly, ed.), **Supp. XVI:** 38

"Everybody Was Very Nice" (Benét), **Supp. XI:** 53

"Everyday Alchemy" (Taggard), **Supp. XXII:** 274–275, 276, 279

"Every-Day Girl, A" (Jewett), **Retro. Supp. II:** 132

Everyday People (O'Nan), **Supp. XXV:** 142, 146–147, 150

"Everyday Use" (Walker), **Supp. III Part 2:** 534

"Every-Day Work" (Jewett), **Retro. Supp. II:** 132

Everyman (Ashbery), **Supp. XXIII:** 210

Everyone Says I Love You (film; Allen), **Supp. XV:** 11

Every Pleasure (Goldbarth), **Supp. XII:** 181

Every Soul Is a Circus (Lindsay), **Supp. I Part 2:** 384, 394, 399

"Everything Is a Human Being" (Walker), **Supp. III Part 2:** 527

Everything Is Illuminated (Foer), **Supp. XII:** 169

Everything Is Now (Cliff), **Supp. XXII:** 67, 74, 76

"Everything Stuck to Him" (Carver), **Supp. III Part 1:** 143

Everything That Moves (Schulberg), **Supp. XVIII:** 254

Everything That Rises Must Converge (O'Connor), **III:** 339, 348–349, 350–351; **Retro. Supp. II:** 235, **236–237;** **Retro. Supp. III:** 208

"Everything That Rises Must Converge" (O'Connor), **III:** 349, 352, 357; **Retro. Supp. II:** 236; **Retro. Supp. III:** 213

Everything You Always Wanted to Know about Sex (film; Allen), **Supp. XV:** 4–5, 13

Eve's Diary (Twain), **IV:** 208–209

"Eve's Diary" (Twain), **Retro. Supp. III:** 269

"Eve Speaks" (Untermeyer), **Supp. XV:** 300

"Eve the Fox" (Gunn Allen), **Supp. IV Part 1:** 331

"Evidence" (Harjo), **Supp. XII:** 219

"Evidence-cum-Witness: Subaltern History, Violence, and the (De)formation of a Nation in Michelle Cliff's *No Telephone to Heaven*" (Sethuraman), **Supp. XXII:** 73

Evidence of the Senses, The (Kelley), **Supp. IV Part 2:** 529

Evidence of Things Not Seen, The (Baldwin), **Retro. Supp. II:** 15

"Evidences of Revealed Religion, The" (Channing), **Supp. XXIV:** 74

"Evil Seekers, The" (Sexton), **Supp. II Part 2:** 696

"Evolution" (Swenson), **Supp. IV Part 2:** 639

Evolving the Idol: The Poetry of Gustaf Sobin (Crick), **Supp. XVI:** 289

Ewing, Jon, **Supp. X:** 253

Ewings, The (O'Hara), **III:** 383

"Examination at the Womb Door" (Hughes), **Supp. XV:** 347

"Examination of the Hero in a Time of War" (Stevens), **Retro. Supp. I:** 305–306, 308

"Excavation of Troy" (MacLeish), **III:** 18

Excellent Becomes the Permanent, The (Addams), **Supp. I Part 1:** 25

"Excelsior" (Longfellow), **Retro. Supp. II:** 169

"Excerpts from Swan Lake" (Cameron), **Supp. XII:** 80, **84**

"Excerpts from the Epistemology Workshops" (Rand), **Supp. IV Part 2:** 529

"Excess of Charity" (Wylie), **Supp. I Part 2:** 720

"Exchange, The" (Swenson), **Supp. IV Part 2:** 644

"Excitement, The " (Jarman), **Supp. XVII:** 120–121

"Exclusive" (Olds), **Supp. X:** 206

"Excrement Poem, The" (Kumin), **Supp. IV Part 2:** 448

"Excursion" (Garrett), **Supp. VII:** 100

Excursions (Thoreau), **IV:** 188

"Excursion to Canada, An" (Thoreau), **Supp. XVIII:** 4

"Excursus of Reassurance in Begonia Time, An" (Carruth), **Supp. XVI:** 58

Executioner (Weigl), **Supp. XIX:** 277

Executioner's Song, The (Mailer), **Retro. Supp. II:** 108, 209

Exekiel, **Supp. XXI:** 91

Exemplar of Liberty: Native America and the Evolution of Democracy (Grinde and Johansen), **Supp. XXVI:** 98

"Exercise and Abstinence" (Swados), **Supp. XIX:** 265

Exercises in History, Chronology, and Biography, in Question and Answer (Rowson), **Supp. XV:** 245

Ex-Friends: Falling Out with Allen Ginsberg, Lionel and Diana Trilling, Lillian Hellman, Hannah Arendt, and Norman Mailer (Podhoretz), **Supp.**

VIII: 239, **242–244**
"Exhausted Bug, The" (R. Bly), **Supp. IV Part 1:** 73
"Exhortation" (Bogan), **Supp. III Part 1:** 58
"Exhortation" (McKay), **Supp. X:** 135
"Ex-husband"(Schott), **Supp. XXIII:** 249
"Exile" (Gass), **Supp. VI:** 92
"Exile" (Oates), **Supp. II Part 2:** 523
Exile, The (Buck), **Supp. II Part 1:** 119, 131
"Exiles, The" (Bradbury), **Supp. IV Part 1:** 113
"Exiles, The" (Whittier), **Supp. I Part 2:** 692–693
Exiles and Fabrications (Scott), **II:** 512
Exile's Daughter, The (Spencer), **Supp. II Part 1:** 121
"Exile's Departure, The" (Whittier), **Supp. I Part 2:** 683
Exiles from a Future Time (Wald), **Supp. XXVIII:** 66
Exiles from Paradise: Zelda and Scott Fitzgerald (Mayfield), **Supp. IX:** 65
"Exile's Letter" (Karr), **Supp. XI:** 241
Exile's Return (Cowley), **Supp. III Part 1:** 136, 138, 140, 141, 144, 147, 148
"Exile's Return, The" (R. Lowell), **II:** 539; **Retro. Supp. II:** 187
Exiles: Three Short Novels (Caputo), **Supp. XIX:** 25, **26–27**
"Existences" (Stafford), **Supp. XI:** 324
Existentialism from Dostoevsky to Sartre (W. Kaufmann), **Supp. XVII:** 137
Exit into History (Hoffman), **Supp. XVI:** 148, 150, **151–153**
Exit to Eden (Rampling), **Supp. VII:** 301–302
Exley (Clarke), **Supp. XXIII:** 109
Exley, Frederick, **Supp. XVI:** 69; **Supp. XVII:** 135; **Supp. XXIII:** 78, **97–110**
Exodus (biblical book), **IV:** 300
Exodus (film), **Supp. XX:** 246
Exodus (Uris), **Supp. IV Part 1:** 379; **Supp. XX: 243–244, 244, 245, 247, 248, 250–251, 257**
Exodus Revisited (Uris), **Supp. XX:** 247
"Exorcism" (Snodgrass), **Supp. VI:** 314
"Exorcism, An" (Malamud), **Supp. I Part 2:** 435
Exorcist, The (film), **Supp. I Part 1:** 66
"Expanded Composition, The" (Major), **Supp. XXII:** 174
"Expanding Rooms" (Notley), **Supp. XXII:** 229
"Expanding the Repertoire" (Mackey), **Supp. XXVII:** 161
"Expanses" (Dickey), **Supp. IV Part 1:** 186
"Ex Parte" (Lardner), **II:** 432
"Expatiation on the Combining of Weathers at Thirty-seventh and Indiana Where the Southern More or Less Crosses the Dog, The" (Carruth), **Supp. XVI:**51–52
"Expectant Father Compares His Wife to a Rabbit, An" (White), **Supp. I Part 2:** 678
"Expedition to the Pole, An" (Dillard), **Supp. VI:** 32, 34

"Expelled" (Cheever), **Supp. I Part 1:** 174, 186
Expense of Greatness, The (Blackmur), **Supp. II Part 1:** 90, 107
Expense of Vision, The (Holland), **Retro. Supp. I:** 216
"Expensive Gifts" (Miller), **Supp. XII:** 294
"Expensive Moment, The" (Paley), **Supp. VI:** 222, **227–228**, 230
Expensive People (Oates), **Supp. II Part 2:** 509, 510–511
"Experience" (Emerson), **Supp. XIV:** 42
"Experience" (Stone), **Supp. XXVII:** 251
"Experience and Fiction" (Jackson), **Supp. IX:** 121
"Experience and the Objects of Knowledge in the Philosophy of F. H. Bradley" (Eliot), **I:** 572; **Retro. Supp. I:** 59
Experience of Literature, The (Trilling), **Supp. III Part 2:** 493
"Experiences and Principles of an Historian" (Morison), **Supp. I Part 2:** 492
Experimental Death Unit # 1 (Baraka), **Supp. II Part 1:** 46
"Experimental Life, The" (Bourne), **I:** 217, 220
"Experiment in Misery, An" (S. Crane), **I:** 411; **Retro. Supp. II:** 97
Experiments and Observations on Electricity (Franklin), **II:** 102, 114–115
Experiments in Survival (Kriegel and Henrich, eds.), **Supp. XXIV:** 214
"Expiation" (Hoffman), **Supp. XVIII:** 86
"Expiation" (Wharton), **Retro. Supp. I:** 367
"Explaining an Affinity for Bats" (Stallings), **Supp. XXV:** 227, 233
"Explaining Evil" (Gordon), **Supp. IV Part 1:** 310
"Explaining Ted Kooser" (Gioia), **Supp. XIX:** 121
"Explanation" (Stevens), **IV:** 79
Explanation of America, An (Pinsky), **Supp. VI:** 237, **241–243**
Exploding Gravy (X. J. Kennedy), **Supp. XV:** 163
"Exploit" (Wharton), **IV:** 324
"Exploration in the Great Tuolumne Cañon" (Muir), **Supp. IX:** 181
"Explorer, The" (Brooks), **Supp. III Part 1:** 79–80
"Exploring the Magalloway" (Parkman), **Supp. II Part 2:** 591
"Exposed Nest, The" (Frost), **Supp. XXVI:** 74
Expositor's Bible, The (G. A. Smith), **III:** 199
Expression in America (Lewisohn), **Supp. XXVIII:** 145, 146, 158
Expressions of Sea Level (Ammons), **Supp. VII:** 24, 28, 36
"Exteriority" (Monson), **Supp. XXIV:** 230, 238
"Extinction of Silence, The" (Stallings), **Supp. XXV:** 234
Extract from Captain Stormfeld's Visit to Heaven (Twain), **IV:** 209–210

Extracts from Adam's Diary (Twain), **IV:** 208–209
Extra Indians (Gansworth), **Supp. XXVI:** 104, 107–108
"Extraño, Un" (Gallagher), **Supp. XXIV:** 170
"Exulting, The" (Roethke), **III:** 544
"Eye, The" (Bowles), **Supp. IV Part 1:** 93
Eye, The (Nabokov), **III:** 251
Eye-Beaters, Blood, Victory, Madness, Buckhead and Mercy, The (Dickey), **Supp. IV Part 1:** 178, 182–183
"Eye for an Eye, An" (Humphrey), **Supp. IX:** 108
"Eye in the Rock, The" (Haines), **Supp. XII:** 208, 209
Eye in the Sky (Dick), **Supp. XVIII:** 138
"Eye-Mote, The" (Plath), **Retro. Supp. II:** 246, 247
"Eye of Paris, The" (H. Miller), **III:** 183–184
"Eye of the Outside, The" (Rich), **Retro. Supp. III:** 251
Eye of the Poet, The: Six Views of the Art and Craft of Poetry (Citino, ed.), **Supp. XIII:** 115; **Supp. XXI:** 54
"Eye of the Rock, The" (Haines), **Supp. XII:** 208
"Eye of the Story, The" (Porter), **IV:** 279
Eye of the Story, The: Selected Essays and Reviews (Welty), **Retro. Supp. I:** 339, 342, 344, 345, 346, 351, 354, 355, 356
"Eyes, The" (Wharton), **IV:** 315
"Eyes like They Say the Devil Has" (Ríos), **Supp. IV Part 2:** 543, 544
Eyes of the Dragon, The (King), **Supp. V:** 139, 152
Eyes of the Heart: A Memoir of the Lost and Found (Buechner), **Supp. XII:** 53
"Eyes of Zapata" (Cisneros), **Supp. VII:** 70
"Eyes to See" (Cozzens), **I:** 374
Eye-to-Eye (Nye), **Supp. XIII:** 274
Eysturoy, Annie O., **Supp. IV Part 1:** 321, 322, 323, 328
Ezekiel (biblical book), **II:** 541
"Ezekiel" (R. Fisher), **Supp. XIX:** 71
Ezekiel, Mordecai, **Supp. I Part 2:** 645
"Ezekiel Learns" (R. Fisher), **Supp. XIX:** 71
"Ezra Pound" (Bynner), **Supp. XV:** 49
"Ezra Pound: His Cantos" (Zukofsky), **Supp. III Part 2:** 612, 619, 622
Ezra Pound's Mauberley (Espey), **III:** 463
"Ezra Pound's Very Useful Labors" (Schwartz), **Supp. II Part 2:** 644

F

Faas, Ekbert, **Supp. VIII:** 292
"Fabbri Tape, The" (Auchincloss), **Supp. IV Part 1:** 21–22
Fabens, Charles, **Supp. XXV:** 283
Faber, Geoffrey, **Retro. Supp. I:** 63
Faber Book of Movie Verse, The (French and Wlaschin, eds.), **Supp. XVI:** 294

Fabia (Prouty), **Supp. XXVIII:** 177, 189–191
"Fable" (Merwin), **Supp. III Part 1:** 343
"Fable" (Wylie), **Supp. I Part 2:** 714
Fable, A (Faulkner), **II:** 55, 73; **Retro. Supp. I:** 74; **Retro. Supp. III:** 87
"Fable, A" (Glück), **Supp. V:** 86
"Fable, The" (Winters), **Supp. II Part 2:** 792, 793, 796
"Fable Containing a Reflection the Size of a Match Head in Its Pupil, A" (Brockmeier), **Supp. XXII:** 59
"Fable Ending in the Sound of a Thousand Parakeets, A" (Brockmeier), **Supp. XXII:** 59
Fable for Critics, A (J. R. Lowell), **Supp. I Part 2:** 406, 407–408, 409, 412–413, 416, 420, 422
"Fable for Critics, A" (J. R. Lowell), **Supp. XVIII:** 3, 8
"Fable of the Fragile Butterfly, The"(Wakoski), **Supp. XXVIII:** 266
"Fable of the War, A" (Nemerov), **III:** 272
Fables (Gay), **II:** 111
Fables and Distances: New and Selected Essays (Haines), **Supp. XII:** 197, 199, 207–208, 211
Fables for Our Time (Thurber), **Supp. I Part 2:** 610
Fables of Identity: Studies in Poetic Mythology (Frye), **Supp. X:** 80
Fables of La Fontaine, The (Moore), **III:** 194, 215
"Fables of Representation: Poetry of the New York School" (Hoover), **Supp. XV:** 179
"Fables of the Fallen Guy" (Rosaldo), **Supp. IV Part 2:** 544
"Fables of the Moscow Subway" (Nemerov), **III:** 271
"Fable with a Photograph of a Glass Mobile on the Wall, A" (Brockmeier), **Supp. XXII:** 59
"Fable with Slips of White Paper Spilling from the Pockets, A" (Brockmeier), **Supp. XXII:** 59
Fabulators, The (Scholes), **Supp. V:** 40
Fabulous Small Jews (Epstein), **Supp. XIV:** 112
Face against the Glass, The (Francis), **Supp. IX:** 80–81
Face in the Crowd, A (film, Kazan), **Supp. XVIII:** 252–253
Face in the Crowd, A (O'Nan and King), **Supp. XXV:** 150, 152
Face of Time, The (Farrell), **II:** 28, 34, 35, 39
Faces of Jesus, The (Buechner), **Supp. XII:** 53
Face to the Wind (film), **Supp. XVII:** 141
Face Value (Hwang), **Supp. XXI:** 148, 154, 155
Fachinger, Petra, **Supp. XVI:** 153
"Facing It" (Komunyakaa), **Supp. XIII:** 117, 124, 125
Facing Shadows (Jin), **Supp. XVIII:** 92, 93
Facing the Music (L. Brown), **Supp. XXI:** 39, 42, **42–44**

"Facing the Music" (L. Brown), **Supp. XXI:** **38–39**, 41, **42**, 43
"Facing the Music: What's Wrong with All Those Happy Endings" (Neal), **Supp. XXI:** 41
"Facing West from California's Shores" (Jeffers), **Supp. II Part 2:** 437–438
Fact, Fiction, and Representation: Four Novels by Gilbert Sorrentino (Mackey), **Supp. XXI:** 236
"Fact and Fancy in *Mountain Path*"(Griffin), **Supp. XXVIII:** 4
"Fact in Fiction, The" (McCarthy), **II:** 562
Fact of a Doorframe, The (Rich), **Retro. Supp. III:** 243
"Fact of Blackness, The" (Fanon), **Supp. XX:** 152
"Facts" (Franzen), **Supp. XX:** **85**
"Facts" (Levine), **Supp. V:** 193
"Facts" (Oliver), **Supp. VII:** 231–232
"Facts" (Snyder), **Supp. VIII:** 301
"Facts, The" (Lardner), **II:** 431
Facts, The: A Novelist's Autobiography (P. Roth), **Retro. Supp. II:** 280, 291; **Supp. III Part 2:** 401, 405, 417, 426
"Facts and Traditions Respecting the Existence of Indigenous Intermittent Fever in New England" (Holmes), **Supp. I Part 1:** 303
"Facts Concerning the Recent Carnival of Crime in Connecticut" (Twain), **Retro. Supp. III:** 262
"Facts in the Case of M. Valdemar, The" (Poe), **III:** 416
Fader, Ellen, **Supp. XXVII:** 203–204
Faderman, Lillian, **Retro. Supp. II:** 135; **Supp. XIII:** 313
Fadiman, Clifton, **II:** 430, 431, 443, 591–592; **Supp. IX:** 8; **Supp. XVI:** 100, 106; **Supp. XVII:** 87, 90; **Supp. XXIII:** 2
Fading, My Parmacheene Belle (J. Scott), **Supp. XVII:** **184–185**, 188
Fading Smile, The (Davison), **Supp. XXVI:** 61, 66, 68
"Fado" (McClatchy), **Supp. XII:** 265–266
"Fado" (Vaz), **Supp. XXVI:** 261–262
Fado and Other Stories (Vaz), **Supp. XXVI:** 259–264, 268
Faerie Queene, The (Spenser), **III:** 487; **IV:** 253; **Supp. XIV:** 6; **Supp. XV:** 181
Faery, Rebecca Blevins, **Retro. Supp. I:** 374
Fagan, Kathy, **Supp. V:** 180; **Supp. XV:** 73
Fagan, Louise, **Supp. XIX:** 204, 205
Faggen, Robert, **Retro. Supp. III:** 105
Fahrenheit 451 (Bradbury), **Supp. IV Part 1:** 101, 102, 104, 107–109, 110, 113; **Supp. XIII:** 29
"Failure" (Gioia), **Supp. XV:** 125
"Failure" (Zach; Everwine, trans.), **Supp. XV:** 86
"Failure: A Meditation" (Monson), **Supp. XXIV:** 236
"Failure of David Barry, The" (Jewett), **Retro. Supp. II:** 132

Fainlight, Ruth, **Supp. XV:** 261, 264
Faint Perfume (Gale), **Supp. I Part 2:** 613
Fair, Bryan K., **Supp. VIII:** 128
Fairbanks, Douglas, **Supp. XVI:** 185, 186
Fairchild, Frances. *See* Bryant, Mrs. William Cullen (Frances Fairchild)
Fairchild, Hoxie, **Supp. XIV:** 120
Fairfield, Flora (pseudonym). *See* Alcott, Louisa May
Fair Gentlemen of Belken County (Hinojosa), **Supp. XIX:** 105
Fairly Conventional Woman, A (Shields), **Supp. VII:** 312, 316, 318
"Fairly Sad Tale, A" (Parker), **Supp. IX:** 192
Fair Warning (R. O. Butler), **Supp. XII:** 62, **75–76**
"Fairy-Tale Logic" (Stallings), **Supp. XXV:** 223, 234
Faith (Goldbarth), **Supp. XII:** 181, **182–183**
Faith and History (Niebuhr), **III:** 308
Faith and the Good Thing (C. Johnson), **Supp. VI:** 187, **188–190**, 191, 193, 194, 196
Faith for Living (Mumford), **Supp. II Part 2:** 479–480
Faithful Narrative of the Surprising Works of God in the Conversion of Many Hundred Souls in Northampton, and the Neighboring Towns and Villages of New-Hampshire in New-England, A (Edwards), **I:** 545, 562
Faithful: Two Diehard Boston Red Sox Fans Chronicle the Historic 2004 Season (O'Nan and King), **Supp. XXV:** 153
"Faith Healer" (Komunyakaa), **Supp. XIII:** 117
Faith Healer of Olive Avenue, The (Muñoz), **Supp. XXV:** 127, 131, 135–137
"Faith in a Tree" (Paley), **Supp. VI:** 217–218, 224, 230
"Faith in Search of Understanding" (Updike), **Retro. Supp. I:** 327
"Faith of an Historian" (Morison), **Supp. I Part 2:** 492
"Faith of Fishermen, The" (J. W. Miller), **Supp. XX: 170**
Faker's Dozen, A (Bukiet), **Supp. XVII:** 47
Falcoff, Mark, **Supp. VIII:** 88
Falcon (Hammett), **Supp. IV Part 1:** 351
Falconer (Cheever), **Supp. I Part 1:** 176, 193–195, 196
Falconer, A. F., **Supp. XIV:** 2
"Falcon of Ser Federigo, The" (Longfellow), **II:** 505
Falcon: Poems on Soviet Themes (Taggard), **Supp. XXII:** 284
Falk, Peter, **Supp. XI:** 174
Falkner, Dean, **II:** 55
Falkner, John, **II:** 55
Falkner, Murray, **II:** 55
Falkner, Murray C., **II:** 55
Falkner, Mrs. Murray C. (Maud Butler), **II:** 55
Falkner, William C., **II:** 55

"Fall" (Francis), **Supp. IX:** 76

"Fall, The" (Bass), **Supp. XVI:** 25

"Fall 1961" (R. Lowell), **II:** 550

Fallen Angels (Myers), **Supp. XXVII:** 204, 207

"Fallen Western Star: The Decline of San Francisco as a Literary Region" (Gioia), **Supp. XV:** 112, 115–116

"Fallen Western Star" Wars, The: A Debate about Literary California (Foley, ed.), **Supp. XV:** 112, 116

"Fall in Corrales" (Wilbur), **Supp. III Part 2:** 556

Falling (Dickey), **Supp. IV Part 1:** 178, 181–182

"Falling" (Dickey), **Supp. IV Part 1:** 182

"Falling Asleep over the Aeneid" (R. Lowell), **II:** 542; **Retro. Supp. II:** 188

Falling in Place (Beattie), **Supp. V:** 28–29

"Falling into Holes in Our Sentences" (R. Bly), **Supp. IV Part 1:** 71

Falling into Life (Kriegel), **Supp. XXIV:** 217–219

"Falling Water" (Davison), **Supp. XXVI:** 79

"Fall Journey" (Stafford), **Supp. XI:** 322

Fall of a Doll's House, The (J. Davison), **Supp. XXVI:** 65

Fall of America, The: 1965–1971 (Ginsberg), **Retro. Supp. III:** 247; **Supp. II Part 1:** 323, 325, 327; **Supp. XV:** 264

Fall of Eve, The (Loos), **Supp. XVI:** 187

Fall of the City, The: A Verse Play for Radio (MacLeish), **III:** 20

"Fall of the Dolls' House, The" (Davison), **Supp. XXVI:** 73–74

"Fall of the House of Usher, The" (Poe), **III:** 412, 414, 415, 419; **Retro. Supp. II:** 270; **Retro. Supp. III:** 224, 225, 226, 228; **Supp. XXV:** 112

Fall of the Magicians, The (Kees), **Supp. XV:** 144

Fall of the Year, The (Mosher), **Supp. XXII:** 205, 206, 208, 209, **214**

"Fall of Troy, Teh"(Hadas), **Supp. XXIII:** 113

Fallows, James, **Supp. VIII:** 241

Fall Quarter (Kees), **Supp. XV:** 141

Fall & Rise (Dixon), **Supp. XII:** 147–148, 148, 153, 157

Falls, Robert, **Supp. XXI:** 148; **Supp. XXIV:** 270

"Falls, The" (Olds), **Supp. X:** 215

"Falls, The" (Saunders), **Supp. XIX:** 229

"Falls Fight, The" (Howe), **Supp. IV Part 2:** 431–432

Falon, Janet Ruth, **Supp. IV Part 2:** 422

False Coin (Swados), **Supp. XIX:** 260–261, 263

"False Dawn" (Wharton), **Retro. Supp. I:** 381

"False Documents" (Doctorow), **Supp. IV Part 1:** 220, 236

"False Leads" (Komunyakaa), **Supp. XIII:** 116

Falwell, Jerry, **Supp. XX: 273**

Fame and Obscurity: Portraits by Gay Talese (Talese), **Supp. XVII:** 202, 203, 204

Fame & Folly: Essays (Ozick), **Supp. V:** 272

"Familiar Epistle to a Friend, A" (J. R. Lowell), **Supp. I Part 2:** 416

Familiar Territory: Observations on American Life (Epstein), **Supp. XIV:** 106

"Familiar Things" (Pickering), **Supp. XXI:** 204

"Family" (Sanders), **Supp. XVI:** 276

"Family" (Wilson), **IV:** 426

Family, Kinship, and Sympanthy in Nineteenth-Century America (Weinstein), **Supp. XVIII:** 261

"Family, The" (Taggard), **Supp. XXII:** 284

"Family Affair, A" (Chopin), **Retro. Supp. II:** 71

"Family and Socialism, The" (Ryan as Quin), **Supp. XVIII:** 238

Family Arsenal, The (Theroux), **Supp. VIII:** 322

"Family Barcus, The"(Thompson), **Supp. XXIII:** 299

Family Chronicle: An Odyssey from Russia to America (Reznikoff), **Supp. XIV:** 277, 288, 289

Family Devotions (Hwang), **Supp. XXI:** 145, 146

"Family History" (Mora), **Supp. XIII:** 217

"Family History, A" (R. H. Davis), **Supp. XVI:** 82

Family Honor (Parker), **Supp. XIX:** 186

Family Life (Banks), **Supp. V:** 7

Family Markowitz, The (Goodman), **Supp. XXVI:** 119, 121–123

"Family Matters" (Alvarez), **Supp. VII:** 10

Family Moskat, The (Singer), **IV:** 1, 17, 20, 46; **Retro. Supp. II:** 304

"Family of Little Feet, The" (Cisneros), **Supp. VII:** 61

"Family Parade, A"(Bottoms), **Supp. XXVIII:** 29

Family Party, A (O'Hara), **III:** 362

Family Pictures (Brooks), **Supp. III Part 1:** 69, 85, 86

Family Pictures (Miller), **Supp. XII:** 291, **295–297,** 299

"Family Portrait" (Trethewey), **Supp. XXI:** 250

"Family Reunion" (J. W. Miller), **Supp. XX: 167**

"Family Reunion" (X. J. Kennedy), **Supp. XV:** 169

Family Reunion, The (T. S. Eliot), **I:** 570–571, 572, 581, 584, 588; **Retro. Supp. I:** 62, 65; **Retro. Supp. III:** 70

"Family Secrets" (Kingsolver), **Supp. VII:** 208

"Family Sideshow, The" (Karr), **Supp. XI:** 245

"Family Story, The" (Skloot), **Supp. XX: 195**

"Family Ties" (Mora), **Supp. XIII:** 215

"Family Tree" (Komunyakaa), **Supp. XIII:** 117–118, 126

"Family Wasserstein, The" (Hoban), **Supp. XV:** 319, 325

Famous American Negroes (Hughes), **Supp. I Part 1:** 345

"Famous Gilson Bequest, The" (Bierce), **I:** 204

Famous Last Words (Findley), **Supp. XX: 49, 55–56**

Famous Negro Athletes (Bontemps), **Supp. XXII:** 6

Famous Negro Music Makers (Hughes), **Supp. I Part 1:** 345

"Famous New York Trials" (Ellison), **Supp. II Part 1:** 230

Fanatic, The (Levin), **Supp. XXVII:** 137, 141, 143, 145, 147

Fanatics, The (Dunbar), **Supp. II Part 1:** 213–214

Fancher, Edwin, **Retro. Supp. II:** 202

Fancher, Lou, **Supp. XVI:** 177

"Fancy and Imagination" (Poe), **III:** 421

Fancy Dancer, The (P. N. Warren), **Supp. XX: 267–268**

"Fancy Flights" (Beattie), **Supp. V:** 25

"Fancy's Show Box" (Hawthorne), **II:** 238

"Fancy Woman, The" (Taylor), **Supp. V:** 316–317, 319, 323

"Fang" (Goldbarth), **Supp. XII:** 190

Fanny: Being the True History of the Adventures of Fanny Hackabout-Jones (Jong), **Supp. V:** 115, 127

Fanny Hill (Cleland), **Supp. V:** 48, 127

Fan of Swords, The (al-Maghut), **Supp. XIII:** 278

Fanon, Frantz, **Retro. Supp. II:** 118; **Retro. Supp. III:** 194; **Supp. X:** 131, 141; **Supp. XX: 152**

"Fan's Further Notes, A"(Exley), **Supp. XXIII:** 108

Fanshawe (Hawthorne), **II:** 223–224; **Retro. Supp. I:** 149, 151; **Retro. Supp. III:** 110, 111

Fan's Notes, A: A Fictional Memoir (Exley), **Supp. XVI:** 69; **Supp. XXIII:** 78, 97, 98, **99–103,** 106, 109

"Fantasia on 'The Nut-Brown Maid' " (Ashbery), **Supp. III Part 1:** 19

"Fantasia on the Relations between Poetry and Photography" (Strand), **Supp. IV Part 2:** 631

"Fantastic Fables" (Bierce), **I:** 209

"Fantasy"(O'Hara), **Supp. XXIII:** 220

Fante, John, **Supp. XI:** 159–176

Fantzius Mallare: A Mysterious Oath (Hecht), **Supp. XXVII:** 88

Faraday, Michael, **I:** 480–481

Far and Away (Jarman), **Supp. XVII:** 110, 115

"Far and Away" (Jarman), **Supp. XVII:** 115

Farber, Jim, **Supp. XXVII:** 45

"Farewell" (Emerson), **II:** 13

"Farewell" (Ryan as Quin), **Supp. XVIII:** 229

Farewell, My Lovely (Chandler), **Supp. IV Part 1:** 122, 125–126, 127, 128, 130

"Farewell, My Lovely!" (White), **Supp. I Part 2:** 661–663, 665
Farewell, The (Gibran), **Supp. XX: 121**
"Farewell Performance" (Merrill), **Supp. III Part 1:** 336–337
Farewell-Sermon Preached at the First Precinct in Northampton, after the People's Publick Rejection of their Minister, A (Edwards), **I:** 548, 562
"Farewell Sweet Dust" (Wylie), **Supp. I Part 2:** 727–728
"Farewell to America, A" (Wheatley), **Supp. XX: 283**
Farewell to Arms, A (Hemingway), **I:** 212, 421, 476, 477; **II:** 68–69, 248–249, 252–253, 254, 255, 262, 265; **Retro. Supp. I:** 171, 178, **180–182**, 187, 189; **Retro. Supp. II:** 108; **Supp. IV Part 1:** 380–381, 381; **Supp. VIII:** 179; **Supp. XII:** 241–242; **Supp. XXI:** 277
"Farewell to Miles" (Berryman), **I:** 173
"Farewell to My Union Brothers" (Ryan as Quin), **Supp. XVIII:** 238
Farewell to Reform (Chamberlain), **Supp. I Part 2:** 647
Farewell to Sport (Gallico), **Supp. XVI:** 238
"Farewell to the Middle Class" (Updike), **Retro. Supp. I:** 321
Far Field, The (Roethke), **III:** 528, 529, 539, 545, 547–548
"Far Field, The" (Roethke), **III:** 537, 540
Far-Flung (Cameron), **Supp. XII:** 81
Far from the Madding Crowd (Hardy), **II:** 291
Fargason, William, **Supp. XXVIII:** 200
Fargnoli, Nicholas, **Retro. Supp. III:** 75
Faríd, 'Umar ibn al-, **Supp. XX: 117**
Faris, Athénaïse Charleville, **Supp. I Part 1:** 204
Farley, Abbie, **I:** 458
Farley, Harriet, **Supp. XIII:** 140
"Farm, The" (Creeley), **Supp. IV Part 1:** 155
Farmer (Harrison), **Supp. VIII:** 39, **44–45**
Farmer, Frances, **Supp. XV:** 196–197
Farmer, Richard, **Supp. XIV:** 2
"Farmer and the Fox, The" (Leopold), **Supp. XIV:** 188
Farmer Boy (L. I. Wilder), **Supp. XXII:** 294, 297, 299
"Farmers' Daughters, The" (W. C. Williams), **Retro. Supp. I:** 423
Farmers Hotel, The (O'Hara), **III:** 361
"Farmer's Sorrow, A" (Jewett), **Retro. Supp. II:** 132
"Farmer's Wife, The" (Sexton), **Supp. II Part 2:** 676
"Farmer & Wife" (Davison), **Supp. XXVI:** 79
"Farm Garden" (Nelson), **Supp. XVIII:** 186
"Farm Implements and Rutabagas in a Landscape" (Ashbery), **Supp. III Part 1:** 13
Farming: A Hand Book (Berry), **Supp. X:** 31, 35

"Farmlights in Iowa" (Kooser), **Supp. XIX:** 120
"Farm on the Great Plains, The" (Stafford), **Supp. XI:** 322
Farnol, Jeffrey, **Supp. I Part 2:** 653
Far North (Shepard), **Supp. III Part 2:** 433, 435
"Far Northern Birch, The" (Francis), **Supp. IX:** 90
Farnsworth, Elizabeth, **Supp. XI:** 139
"Farrago" (Kees), **Supp. XV:** 145
Farrand, Max, **II:** 122
Farrar, Geraldine, **Retro. Supp. I:** 10
Farrar, John, **II:** 191; **Supp. XI:** 47
Far Reaches, The (Hickam), **Supp. XXVII:** 111
Farrell, Barry, **Supp. XIV:** 142
Farrell, James Francis, **II:** 25, 26
Farrell, James T., **I:** 97, 288, 475, 508, 517, 519; **II: 25–53**, 416, 424; **III:** 28, 114, 116, 118, 119, 317, 382; **IV:** 211, 286; **Retro. Supp. II:** 196, 327; **Supp. I Part 2:** 679; **Supp. VIII:** 96, 97; **Supp. XIV:** 3; **Supp. XV:** 141; **Supp. XXVI:** 18; **Supp. XXVII:** 134
Farrell, Mrs. James T. (Dorothy Butler), **II:** 26
Farrell, Mrs. James T. (Hortense Alden), **II:** 26, 27, 45, 48
Farrell, John, **II:** 26
Farrell, John C., **Supp. I Part 1:** 24
Farrell, Kate, **Supp. XV:** 187–188, **Supp. XV:** 190
Farrell, Kevin, **II:** 26
Farrell, Mary, **II:** 25
Farrison, W. Edward, **Retro. Supp. III:** 133
"Far Rockaway" (Schwartz), **Supp. II Part 2:** 649
Farrow, Mia, **Supp. XV:** 8, 10
Far Side of the Dollar, The (Macdonald), **Supp. IV Part 2:** 473
Farther Off from Heaven (Humphrey), **Supp. IX:** 93, 96, 101, **103–104**, 105, 109
Farther Off from Heaven (Inge), **Supp. XXV:** 94, 100
Far Tortuga (Matthiessen), **Supp. V:** 201, 206–207
"Fascinating Fascism" (Sontag), **Supp. III Part 2:** 465
"Fascination of Cities, The" (Hughes), **Supp. I Part 1:** 325
Fashion, Power, Guilt and the Charity of Families (Shields), **Supp. VII:** 323
Fasman, Jonathan, **Supp. V:** 253
Fast, Howard, **Supp. I Part 1:** 295; **Supp. XXI:** 277; **Supp. XXIII:** 165
Fast, Jonathan, **Supp. V:** 115
Fast and Loose (Wharton), **Retro. Supp. I:** 361; **Retro. Supp. III:** 289
"Faster, America, Faster" (Gold), **Supp. XXVIII:** 73
"Faster than Light" (Nelson), **Supp. XVIII:** 178–179
"Fastest Runner on Sixty-first Street, The" (Farrell), **II:** 45
Fast Lane on a Dirt Road (Sherman), **Supp. XXII:** 205

Fast Sam, Cool Clyde, and Stuff (Myers), **Supp. XXVII:** 202, 210
Fast Sooner Hound, The (Bontemps and Conroy), **Supp. XXII:** 5, 10–11
"Fat" (Carver), **Supp. III Part 1:** 141
Fatal Interview (Millay), **III:** 128–129, 130
"Fatality" (Bausch), **Supp. VII:** 54
Fatal Lady (film), **Supp. XIII:** 166
"Fate" (Emerson), **II:** 2–3, 4, 16; **Supp. XIV:** 42
"Fate" (Koch), **Supp. XV:** 183
"Fate" (Mailer), **Retro. Supp. II:** 207
"Fate of Pleasure, The" (Trilling), **Supp. III Part 2:** 510
Fate of the Jury, The (Masters), **Supp. I Part 2:** 466, 468, 469
"Fat Girl, The" (Dubus), **Supp. VII:** 84, 85
"Father" (Kooser), **Supp. XIX:** 117, 127
"Father" (Levine), **Supp. V:** 188
"Father" (Sanders), **Supp. XVI:** 277
"Father" (Trethewey), **Supp. XXI:** 253
"Father" (Walker), **Supp. III Part 2:** 522
"Father, The" (Carver), **Supp. III Part 1:** 137, 140
Father, The (Olds), **Supp. X: 209–211**
"Father (Part I)" (Mullen), **Supp. XXVII:** 167
"Father Abraham" (Faulkner), **Retro. Supp. I:** 81, 82
Fatheralong: A Meditation on Fathers and Sons, Race and Society (Wideman), **Supp. X:** 320, 332–333, 334, 335
"Father and Daughter" (Eberhart), **I:** 539
Father and Glorious Descendant (Lowe), **Supp. X:** 291
"Father and Son" (Eberhart), **I:** 539
Father and Son (Farrell), **II:** 34, 35, 290, 291
Father and Son (Gosse), **Supp. VIII:** 157
"Father and Son" (Hughes), **Retro. Supp. I:** 204; **Supp. I Part 1:** 329, 339
"Father and Son" (Kunitz), **Supp. III Part 1:** 262
Father and Son (L. Brown), **Supp. XXI:** 36, 40, 41, **46–47**
"Father and Son" (Schwartz), **Supp. II Part 2:** 650
Father Bombo's Pilgrimage to Mecca (Freneau), **Supp. II Part 1:** 254
Father Fisheye (Balakian), **Supp. XXIII:** 19
"Father Fisheye" (Balakian), **Supp. XXIII:** 19
"Father Fitzgerald" (Nelson and Espeland), **Supp. XVIII:** 181
"Father Guzman" (Stern), **Supp. IX: 293,** 296
"Father John Melby and the Ghost of Amy Elizabeth" (Brockmeier), **Supp. XXII:** 60
"Father of My Country, The" (Wakoski), **Supp. XXVIII:** 262, 263, 271
Father of the Blues (Bontemps as Handy), **Supp. XXII:** 5
"Father out Walking on the Lawn, A" (Dove), **Supp. IV Part 1:** 246

"Fathers" (Creeley), **Supp. IV Part 1:** 157–158

Fathers, The (Tate), **IV:** 120, 127, 130, 131–133, 134, 141; **Supp. X:** 52

Fathers and Crows (Vollmann), **Supp. XVII:** 226, 231–232

"Fathers and Daughters, Mothers and Sons"(Hadas), **Supp. XXIII:** 119

"Fathers and Sons" (Hemingway), **II:** 249, 265–266; **Retro. Supp. I:** 175

"Father's Body, The" (Dickey), **Supp. IV Part 1:** 176

"Father's Day" (Connelly), **Supp. XXI:** 79–80

"Father's Game"(Lea), **Supp. XXVIII:** 130

"Father's Story, A" (Dubus), **Supp. VII:** 88

"Father's Voice" (Stafford), **Supp. XI:** 322

"Fathomless"(Lea), **Supp. XXVIII:** 136–137

"Fat Lady, The" (Carruth), **Supp. XVI:** 48

"Fat Man, Floating" (Dunn), **Supp. XI:** 144

Fat Men in Skirts (Silver), **Supp. XXIV:** 265–267, 275

Fatout, Paul, **Retro. Supp. III:** 268

"Fat Tuesday"(P. Benedict), **Supp. XXIII:** 38

Faulkes Chronicle, The (Huddle), **Supp. XXVI:** 148, 158, 159–160

Faulkner, Barry, **Supp. XV:** 41

Faulkner, William, **I:** 54, 97, 99, 105, 106, 115, 117, 118, 123, 190, 204–205, 211, 288, 289, 291, 292, 297, 305, 324, 374, 378, 423, 480, 517; **II:** 28, 51, **54–76,** 131, 174, 194, 217, 223, 228, 230, 259, 301, 306, 431, 458–459, 542, 594, 606; **III:** 45, 70, 108, 164, 218, 220, 222, 236–237, 244, 292, 334, 350, 382, 418, 453, 454, 482, 483; **IV:** 2, 4, 33, 49, 97, 98, 100, 101, 120, 131, 203, 207, 211, 217, 237, 257, 260, 261, 279, 280, 352, 461, 463; **Retro. Supp. I:** 73–95, 215, 339, 347, 356, 379, 382; **Retro. Supp. II:** 19, 221, 326; **Retro. Supp. III:** 73–90, 106, 194; **Supp. I Part 1:** 196, 197, 242, 372; **Supp. I Part 2:** 450, 621; **Supp. III Part 1:** 384–385, 396; **Supp. IV Part 1:** 47, 130, 257, 342; **Supp. IV Part 2:** 434, 463, 468, 502, 677, 682; **Supp. IX:** 20, 95; **Supp. V:** 58, 59, 138, 210, 226, 237, 261, 262, 334–336; **Supp. VIII:** 37, 39, 40, 104, 105, 108, 175, 176, 180, 181, 183, 184, 188, 189, 215; **Supp. X:** 44, 228; **Supp. XI:** 92, 247; **Supp. XII:** 16, 289, 310, 313; **Supp. XIII:** 100, 169; **Supp. XIV:** 1, 12–13, 21, 24, 93, 306; **Supp. XIX:** 97, 154, 166; **Supp. XV:** 92, 135, 338; **Supp. XVI:** 148, 189; **Supp. XVII:** 225; **Supp. XVIII:** 76, 84, 90, 148, 249; **Supp. XX: 137, 162, 185, 195; Supp. XXI:** 36, 38, 256; **Supp. XXII:** 193, 203, 205; **Supp. XXIII:** 166; **Supp. XXIV:** 54, 64, 132, 136, 215; **Supp. XXV:** 49; **Supp.**

XXVI: 1, 9, 45, 144, 147; **Supp. XXVII:** 11, 216, 218, 267, 276

Faulkner: A Collection of Critical Essays (Warren), **Retro. Supp. I:** 73

Faulkner at Nagano (Jelliffe, ed.), **I:** 289; **II:** 63, 65

Faulkner-Cowley File, The: Letters and Memories 1944–1962 (Cowley, ed.), **Retro. Supp. I:** 73, 92; **Supp. II Part 1:** 140, 141

"Faultlines"(Hadas), **Supp. XXIII:** 117–118

"Faun" (Plath), **Supp. I Part 2:** 537

"Fauna" (Jeffers), **Supp. II Part 2:** 415

Fauset, Arthur Huff, **Supp. XVIII:** 126

Fauset, Jessie Redmon, **Retro. Supp. III:** 127; **Supp. I Part 1:** 321, 325; **Supp. IV Part 1:** 164; **Supp. XIX:** 69, 78; **Supp. XVIII:** 122,127

Faust (Goethe), **I:** 396; **II:** 489; **III:** 395; **Supp. II Part 1:** 16; **Supp. IX:** 141

Faust, Beatrix Hapgood, **Supp. XXI:** 8

Faust, Clarence H., **II:** 20

Faute de l'Abbé Mouret, La (Zola), **III:** 322

"Favor, The" (Carver and Gallagher), **Supp. XXIV:** 178

Favor Island (Merwin), **Supp. III Part 1:** 346, 347

"Favor of Love, A" (Peacock), **Supp. XIX:** 203

Favourite Game, The (Cohen), **Supp. XXVII:** 51, 54, 56–57, 59

"Favrile" (Doty), **Supp. XI:** 131

"Fawn" (Davison), **Supp. XXVI:** 75

"Fawn, with a Bit of Green" (Swados), **Supp. XIX:** 258

Fay (L. Brown), **Supp. XXI:** 40, 41, 47

Fay, Bernard, **IV:** 41

"Fear, The" (Frost), **Retro. Supp. I:** 128

Fear and Loathing in Las Vegas (Thompson), **Supp. XXIV:** 280, 282, 283, 287, **288–292,** 293

Fear and Loathing on the Campaign Trail '72 (Thompson), **Supp. XXIV:** 279, 281, 282, 289, **292–293**

Fear and Trembling (Kierkegaard), **Supp. XX:** 132

"Fear & Fame" (Levine), **Supp. V:** 192

Fearful Child, The (C. Frost), **Supp. XV:** 96, 97, 106

"Fearful Child, The" (C. Frost), **Supp. XV:** 96

Fearing, Kenneth, **Supp. XV:** 138; **Supp. XXVI:** 134, 143

"Fearless" (Mosley), **Supp. XIII:** 241

Fearless Jones (Mosley), **Supp. XIII:** 241–242

"Fear of Concrete" (Halliday), **Supp. XIX:** 91

Fear of Fifty: A Midlife Memoir (Jong), **Supp. V:** 114, 115, 116, 131

Fear of Flying (Jong), **Supp. V:** 113, 115, 116, 119–123, 124, 129

"Feast, The" (Kinnell), **Supp. III Part 1:** 239, 250

Feast of All Saints, The (Rice), **Supp. VII:** 299–301

Feast of Love, The (C. Baxter), **Supp. XVII:** 13, 21–22

Feast of Love, The (film, R. Benton), **Supp. XVII:** 22

Feast of Snakes, A (Crews), **Supp. XI:** 102, **107–108; Supp. XXI:** 40

"Feast of Stephen, The" (Hecht), **Supp. X:** 63–64

Feast of the Goat, The (Llosa), **Supp. XXIV:** 89

"Featherbed for Critics, A" (Blackmur), **Supp. II Part 1:** 93, 151

Feather Crowns (Mason), **Supp. VIII: 146–147**

"Feathers" (Carver), **Supp. III Part 1:** 145

Feathers (Van Vechten), **Supp. II Part 2:** 736, 749

Feathers (Woodson), **Supp. XXVIII:** 287–288

"Feathers, The" (Hogan), **Supp. IV Part 1:** 416

Feathers Left Around (Wells), **Supp. XXVI:** 282

"February" (Ellison), **Supp. II Part 1:** 229

"February 14th" (Levine), **Supp. V:** 194

February in Sydney (Komunyakaa), **Supp. XIII: 124–125,** 129

"February in Sydney" (Komunyakaa), **Supp. XIII:** 125

"February: Thinking of Flowers" (Kenyon), **Supp. VII:** 171

"Feces" (McClatchy), **Supp. XII:** 266, 267–268

Fechner, Gustav, **II:** 344, 355, 358, 359, 363

Feder, Lillian, **IV:** 136; **Supp. XVI:** 49, 50

Federal Arts Project, **Supp. III Part 2:** 618

Federigo, or, The Power of Love (Nemerov), **III:** 268, 276, 282, 283–284, 285

"Fedge, The" (Halliday), **Supp. XIX:** 93

"Fedora" (Chopin), **Supp. I Part 1:** 220

Fedorko, Kathy A., **Retro. Supp. I:** 361, 374

"Feeling and Precision" (Moore), **III:** 206

Feeling Italian: The Art of Ethnicity in America (Ferraro), **Supp. XX:** 43

"Feeling of Effort, The" (James), **II:** 349

Feeling Very Strange: The Slipstream Anthology (Kelly and Kessel, eds.), **Supp. XIX:** 231

"Feel Like a Bird" (Swenson), **Supp. IV Part 2:** 639

"Feel Me" (Swenson), **Supp. IV Part 2:** 647

Feeney, Mary, **Supp. IX:** 152, 154

Feinsilver, Pamela, **Supp. XX: 135**

Feinstein, Herbert, **Supp. XIX:** 260

Feinstein, Sascha, **Supp. XIII:** 125

Feldman, Charles K., **Supp. XI:** 307

Feldman, Morton, **Supp. XXIII:** 211

Fellini, Federico, **Supp. XII:** 172; **Supp. XV:** 8

"Fellini the Cat" (Peacock), **Supp. XIX:** 206

"Fellow Citizens" (Sandburg), **III:** 553

Fellows, John, **Supp. I Part 2:** 520

Fellow Travelers (Mallon), **Supp. XIX:** 132, **143–144**

"Felo de Se" (Wylie), **Supp. I Part 2:** 727, 729

Felton, Sharon, **Supp. IV Part 1:** 210

"Female Author" (Plath), **Retro. Supp. II:** 243

"Female Frailty" (Freneau), **Supp. II Part 1:** 258

"Female Laughter and Comic Possibilities: *Uncommon Women and Others*" (Chirico), **Supp. XV:** 323

Female Patriot, The; or, Nature's Rights (Rowson), **Supp. XV:** 237–238

Female Prose Writers of America (Hart), **Supp. XVIII:** 257, 264

"Female Voice in *To Kill a Mockingbird*, The: Narrative Strategies in Film and Novel" (Shakelford), **Supp. VIII:** 129

" 'Feminine' Epic, The" (Notley), **Supp. XXII:** 232, 234, 236

"Feminine Landscape of Leslie Marmon Silko's *Ceremony*, The" (Gunn Allen), **Supp. IV Part 1:** 324

Feminine Mystique, The (Friedan), **Retro. Supp. III:** 241

Feminine Note in Fiction, The (Courtney), **Supp. XXIV:** 29

Feminism and the Politics of Literary Reputation: The Example of Erica Jong (Templin), **Supp. V:** 116

"Feminismo" (Robbins), **Supp. X:** 272

"Feminist Criticism in the Wilderness" (Showalter), **Supp. X:** 97

"Feminist Manifesto" (Loy), **Supp. XXII:** 160

Feminization of American Culture, The (Douglas), **Supp. XVIII:** 258

"Fence, The" (Oliver), **Supp. VII:** 232

"Fence Posts" (Snyder), **Supp. VIII:** 304

Fences (film, Washington), **Retro. Supp. III:** 321

Fences (Wilson), **Retro. Supp. III:** 318, 323–325, 325; **Supp. VIII:** 329, 330, 331, **334–337**, 350

Fenick, Elizabeth, **Retro. Supp. II:** 221

"Fenimore Cooper's Literary Offenses" (Twain), **IV:** 204–205; **Retro. Supp. III:** 265

Fennell, Frank L., **Supp. XVII:** 177–178

Fenollosa, Ernest, **III:** 458, 465, 466, 474, 475, 477; **Retro. Supp. I:** 289; **Supp. IV Part 1:** 154

Fenollosa, Mrs. Ernest, **III:** 458

"Fenstad's Mother" (C. Baxter), **Supp. XVII:** 18

Fenton, Charles, **Supp. XI:** 43

Fenton, James, **Supp. XV:** 117

Fenton, William, **Supp. XXVI:** 96

Ferber, Edna, **Retro. Supp. III:** 135; **Supp. XXVIII:** 69

Ferdinand: Including "It Was" (Zukofsky), **Supp. III Part 2:** 630

"Fergus" (Bourne), **I:** 229

Ferguson, James, **Supp. I Part 2:** 503

Ferguson, Otis, **Supp. IX:** 7

Ferguson, SallyAnn H., **Supp. XXVI:** 166

Ferguson, William, **Supp. XII:** 189

Ferguson Affair, The (Macdonald), **Supp. IV Part 2:** 473

Fergusson, Francis, **I:** 265, 440; **Supp. XV:** 20

Ferlinghetti, Lawrence, **Supp. IV Part 1:** 90; **Supp. VIII:** 290, 292; **Supp. XII:** 121, 125; **Supp. XIII:** 275; **Supp. XIX:** 4; **Supp. XXI:** 53; **Supp. XXIII:** 219

Fermata, The (Baker), **Supp. XIII:** 49–52, 54

"Fern" (Toomer), **Supp. III Part 2:** 481; **Supp. IX:** 313

Fern, Fanny, **Retro. Supp. I:** 246; **Supp. V:** 122

Fernández, Enrique, **Supp. VIII:** 73

Fernandez, Ramon, **Retro. Supp. I:** 302, 303; **Supp. XVI:** 214

"Fern-Beds in Hampshire Country" (Wilbur), **Supp. III Part 2:** 558

"Fern Hill" (D. Thomas), **IV:** 93; **Supp. XX:** **204**

"Fern-Life" (Larcom), **Supp. XIII:** 143

Ferragammo, Salvatore, **Supp. XVI:** 192

Ferraro, Thomas J., **Supp. XX:** 34, **43**

Ferreo, Guglielmo, **Supp. I Part 2:** 481

Ferris, Anthony, **Supp. XX:** 124

Ferris, Beth, **Supp. XXVI:** 183

Ferry, David, **Supp. XXIV:** **147–164**; **Supp. XXV:** 222

"Ferry, The" (Cliff), **Supp. XXII:** 74

Fessenden, Thomas Green, **II:** 300

Fessier, Michael, **Supp. XIII:** 164

"Festival Aspect, The" (Olson), **Supp. II Part 2:** 585

"Festival of Regrets, The" (Wasserstein), **Supp. XV:** 333

Festival of San Joaquin, The (Edgell), **Supp. XXIII:** 84, 85, **90–91**, 94

Fetching the Dead (Sanders), **Supp. XVI:** 269

Fêtes galantes (Verlaine), **IV:** 79

Fetherling, Doug, **Supp. XXVII:** 88, 90, 94

Fetid Itch (Silver), **Supp. XXIV:** 265

"Fetish" (McClatchy), **Supp. XII:** 256

Fetterley, Judith, **Retro. Supp. II:** 139; **Supp. XXIV:** 28

Fetterly, Judith, **Supp. XXV:** 285

"Feud" (Zinberg), **Supp. XV:** 195

"Feud, The"(Lea), **Supp. XXVIII:** 131–132, 136

"Fever" (Carver), **Supp. III Part 1:** 145

"Fever 103°'" (Plath), **Supp. I Part 2:** 541

Fever Pitch (Hornby), **Supp. XII:** 286; **Supp. XXIII:** 109

Fever: Twelve Stories (Wideman), **Supp. X:** 320

"Few Don'ts by an Imagiste, A" (Pound), **III:** 465; **Retro. Supp. I:** 288; **Supp. I Part 1:** 261–262

"Few Kind Words for Anger, A" (Kriegel), **Supp. XXIV:** 220

"Few Stray Comments on the Cultivation of the Lyric, A" (Sobin), **Supp. XVI:** 285

"Few Words of Introduction, A" (McNally), **Supp. XIII:** 198–199

Feydeau, Georges, **Supp. XXIV:** 271

Feynman, Richard, **Supp. XXV:** 267

Fiamengo, Janice, **Supp. XIII:** 35

"Fiat Lux" (H. Johnson), **Supp. XXVI:** 172

Fiber (Bass), **Supp. XVI:** 22

"*Fiber:* A Post-Pastoral Georgic" (Gifford), **Supp. XVI:** 22

Ficke, Arthur Davison, **Supp. XIII:** 347; **Supp. XV:** 40, 42, 43, 46, 48, 49

"Fiction" (Stafford), **Supp. XI:** 327

"Fiction: A Lens on Life" (Stegner), **Supp. IV Part 2:** 595, 596, 600

Fictional World of William Hoffman, The (Frank, ed.), **Supp. XVIII:** 74, 79, 80, 87

Fiction and the Figures of Life (Gass), **Supp. VI:** 85

Fiction of Joseph Heller, The (Seed), **Supp. IV Part 1:** 391

Fiction of Paule Marshall, The (Denniston), **Supp. XI:** 276

Fiction of the Forties (Eisinger), **I:** 302; **II:** 604

Fictions in Autobiography: Studies in the Art of Self-Invention (Eakin), **Supp. XVI:** 70

"Fiction Writer and His Country, The" (O'Connor), **III:** 342; **Retro. Supp. II:** 223, 225; **Supp. II Part 1:** 148

Fiddler's Trance, The (Skloot), **Supp. XX:** **196, 202**

Fidelity (Glaspell), **Supp. III Part 1:** 177

Fiedler, Leslie A., **II:** 27; **III:** 218; **Retro. Supp. II:** 280, 324; **Supp. II Part 1:** 87; **Supp. IV Part 1:** 42, 86; **Supp. IX:** 3, 227; **Supp. X:** 80; **Supp. XIII:** **93–110**; **Supp. XIV:** 11; **Supp. XIX:** 251; **Supp. XVIII:** 146; **Supp. XXIII:** 42; **Supp. XXV:** 268; **Supp. XXVII:** 133, 262

Fiedler on the Roof: Essays on Literature and Jewish Identity (Fiedler), **Supp. XIII:** 106–107

"Fie! Fie! Fi-Fi!" (Fitzgerald), **Retro. Supp. I:** 100

Field, Eugene, **Supp. II Part 1:** 197; **Supp. XXVIII:** 227

Field, John, **IV:** 179

"Field Events" (Bass), **Supp. XVI:** 19

"Field Full of Black Cats, A" (C. Frost), **Supp. XV:** 101

Field Guide (Hass), **Supp. VI:** 97–98, **99–101**, 102, 103, 106

Field Guide to Contemporary Poetry and Poetics (Friebert and Young, eds.), **Supp. XI:** 270

"Field Guide to the Western Birds" (Stegner), **Supp. IV Part 2:** 609

Fielding, Henry, **I:** 134; **II:** 302, 304–305; **III:** 61; **Supp. I Part 2:** 421, 422, 656; **Supp. IV Part 2:** 688; **Supp. IX:** 128; **Supp. V:** 127; **Supp. XI:** 277; **Supp. XVIII:** 2, 7; **Supp. XXV:** 258

Fielding, Richard, **Supp. XV:** 232

"Field-larks and Blackbirds" (Lanier), **Supp. I Part 1:** 355

Field of Honor (Hay), **Supp. XIV:** 120–121, 125, 130

"Field of Honor" (Hay), **Supp. XIV:** 120–121, 129–130

Field of Vision, The (Morris), **III:** 226–228, 229, 232, 233, 238
"Field Report" (Corso), **Supp. XII:** 124, **136**
"Fields" (Wright), **Supp. XV:** 342
Fields, Annie Adams, **II:** 401, 402, 403–404, 406, 412; **IV:** 177; **Retro. Supp. II:** 134, 135, 142; **Supp. I Part 1:** 317; **Supp. XVI:** 84, 88
Fields, James T., **II:** 274, 279, 402–403; **Retro. Supp. II:** 135; **Supp. I Part 1:** 317; **Supp. XIII:** 150; **Supp. XVI:** 84, 88
Fields, Mrs. James T., **Supp. XIV:** 44, 46. *See* Fields, Annie Adams
Fields, Jerry, **Supp. XXVI:** 86
Fields, Joseph, **IV:** 274
Fields, The (Richter), **Supp. XVIII: 213–214,** 220
Fields, W. C., **II:** 427; **IV:** 335
"Fields at Dusk, The" (Salter), **Supp. IX:** 260
Fields of Fire (Webb), **Supp. XXII:** 115
Fields of Praise, The (Nelson), **Supp. XVIII:** 171, 173, **177–178**
Fields of Wonder (Hughes), **Retro. Supp. I:** 206, 207; **Supp. I Part 1:** 333–334
Fierce Invalids Home from Hot Climates (Robbins), **Supp. X:** 267, 276–277, **282–285**
Fiery, Marion, **Supp. XXII:** 293
Fiery Chariot, The (Hurston), **Supp. VI:** 155–156
Fiesta (Gold), **Supp. XXVIII:** 70
"Fiesta, 1980" (Díaz), **Supp. XXIV:** 88
15 Poems (Banks), **Supp. V:** 5
"Fifteen Dollars' Worth" (Prouty), **Supp. XXVIII:** 180
"Fifteenth Farewell" (Bogan), **Supp. III Part 1:** 51, 58
"Fifth Avenue, Uptown" (Baldwin), **Supp. I Part 1:** 52
"Fifth Avenue—Spring Afternoon" (Untermeyer), **Supp. XV:** 296
Fifth Book of Peace, The (Kingston), **Supp. V:** 173
Fifth Chinese Daughter (Wong), **Supp. X:** 291
Fifth Column, The (Hemingway), **II:** 254, 258; **Retro. Supp. I:** 184
"Fifth Column of the Fencerow" (Leopold), **Supp. XIV:** 185
Fifth Decad of Cantos, The (Pound), **Retro. Supp. I:** 292
"Fifth Movement: *Autobiography*" (Zukofsky), **Supp. III Part 2:** 611
Fifth Sunday (Dove), **Supp. IV Part 1:** 251, 252–253
"Fifth Sunday" (Dove), **Supp. IV Part 1:** 252
Fifth Wheel, The (Prouty), **Supp. XXVIII:** 178–179, 186, 187, 191
50 Poems (Cummings), **I:** 430, 440, 442–443, 444–445, 446
Fifty Best American Short Stories (O'Brien), **III:** 56
"Fifty Dollars" (Elkin), **Supp. VI: 43–44**
"55 Miles to the Gas Pump" (Proulx), **Supp. VII:** 264

55 Poems (Zukofsky), **Supp. III Part 2:** 611, 621
"Fifty Grand" (Hemingway), **II:** 250, 424; **Retro. Supp. I:** 177
Fifty Shades of Grey (James), **Supp. XXVII:** 79
Fifty Stories (Boyle), **Supp. XXIV:** 58
"Fifty Suggestions" (Poe), **Retro. Supp. II:** 266
"52 Oswald Street" (Kinnell), **Supp. III Part 1:** 251
Fifty Years Among Authors, Editors, and Publishers (Derby), **Supp. XVIII:** 4
"Fifty Years Among the Black Folk" (Du Bois), **Supp. II Part 1:** 169
"Fifty Years of American Poetry" (Jarrell), **Retro. Supp. I:** 52
Fig Connection, The (Franzen and Siebert), **Supp. XX: 84**
Fight, The (Mailer), **Retro. Supp. II:** 207, 208
Fight Back: For the Sake of the People, For the Sake of the Land (Ortiz), **Supp. IV Part 2:** 497, 498, 499, 503, 510–512, 514
"Fighters, The" (Zinberg), **Supp. XV:** 193
Fight for Freedom (Hughes), **Supp. I Part 1:** 345
Fighting Angel (Buck), **Supp. II Part 1:** 119, 131
Fighting France; From Dunkerque to Belfort (Wharton), **Retro. Supp. I:** 377, 378; **Retro. Supp. III:** 285
Fightin': New and Collected Stories (Ortiz), **Supp. IV Part 2:** 513
"Figlia che Piange, La" (Eliot), **I:** 570, 584; **III:** 9
Figliola, Samantha, **Supp. V:** 143
"Figure a Poem Makes, The" (Frost), **Retro. Supp. I:** 139; **Retro. Supp. III:** 103–104, 105
"Figured Wheel, The" (Pinsky), **Supp. VI:** 243, 244, 245, 246
Figured Wheel, The: New and Collected Poems (Pinsky), **Supp. VI:** 247–248
"Figure in the Carpet, The" (James), **Retro. Supp. I:** 228, 229
"Figure in the Doorway, The" (Frost), **Retro. Supp. I:** 138
Figure of Fulfillment, The (Lerperger; Miller, trans.), **Supp. XX:** 165, 167–168
Figures from the Double World (McGrath), **Supp. X:** 118–119
Figures in Black: Words, Signs, and the "Racial" Self (H. L. Gates), **Supp. XX:** 99, 100, 106, 107
"Figures in the Clock, The" (McCarthy), **II:** 561–562
Figures Made Visible in the Sadness of Time (Everwine), **Supp. XV:** 75, 88
Figures of Time (Hayden), **Supp. II Part 1:** 367
Filbin, Thomas, **Supp. XXIII:** 299
"Filling Out a Blank" (Wagoner), **Supp. IX:** 324
Fillmore, Millard, **III:** 101
Film Flam: Essays on Hollywood (McMurtry), **Supp. V:** 228

Films of Ayn Rand, The (Cox), **Supp. IV Part 2:** 524
Filo, John, **Supp. XII:** 211
Filreis, Alan, **Supp. XXI:** 262, 267, 268, 269, 271, 273, 275, 277, 278
Filson, John, **Retro. Supp. I:** 421
Final Beast, The (Buechner), **Supp. XII: 49–51**
"Finale" (Longfellow), **II:** 505, 506–507
"Finale: Presto" (Davison), **Supp. XXVI:** 70
"Final Fear" (Hughes), **Supp. I Part 1:** 338
Final Harvest: Emily Dickinson's Poems (T. H. Johnson, ed.), **I:** 470, 471
"Finally Harriet" (Wolfert), **Supp. XXI: 265–267**
Final Payments (Gordon), **Supp. IV Part 1:** 297, 299, 300–302, 304, 306, 314
"Final Report, A" (Maxwell), **Supp. VIII:** 169
"Final Soliloquy of the Interior Paramour" (Stevens), **Retro. Supp. I:** 312
Final Solution, The (Reitlinger), **Supp. XII:** 161
Financier, The (Dreiser), **I:** 497, 501, 507, 509; **Retro. Supp. II:** 94, 101–102, 105; **Supp. XVIII:** 246
Finch, Annie, **Supp. XVII: 69–79**
Finch, Henry Leroy, **Supp. XVII:** 69
Finch, Margaret Rockwell, **Supp. XVII:** 69
Finch, Robert, **Supp. XIV:** 186–187; **Supp. XXVI:** 38
"Finches, Little Pats of Butter on the Wing" (Crooker), **Supp. XXIII:** 62
Find a Victim (Macdonald), **Supp. IV Part 2:** 467, 472, 473
Fin de Chéri, La (Colette; stage adaptation, Loos), **Supp. XVI:** 194
Finder, Henry, **Supp. XX: 90**
"Fin de Saison Palm Beach" (White), **Supp. I Part 2:** 673
"Fin de Siècle" (Lea), **Supp. XXVIII:** 137
"Finding a Bible in an Abandoned Cabin" (Wrigley), **Supp. XVIII: 293–294,** 296, 297, 300, 301, 303
Finding a Form (Gass), **Supp. VI:** 91–92, 93
Finding a Girl in America (Dubus), **Supp. VII:** 85–88
"Finding a Girl in America" (Dubus), **Supp. VII:** 87
"Finding Amy" (O'Nan), **Supp. XXV:** 143, 150
"Finding Beads" (Hogan), **Supp. IV Part 1:** 400
Finding Losses (Bronk), **Supp. XXI:** 31, 32
"Finding of Zach, The" (Dunbar), **Supp. II Part 1:** 212
Findings and Keepings: Analects for an Autobiography (Mumford), **Supp. II Part 2:** 483
Finding the Center: Narrative Poetry of the Zuni Indians (Tedlock), **Supp. IV Part 2:** 509
Finding the Islands (Merwin), **Supp. III Part 1:** 353, 357

"Finding the Place: A Migrant Child-hood" (Stegner), **Supp. IV Part 2:** 597

Findley, Timothy, **Supp. XX: 49–65**

"Find the Woman" (Macdonald, as Millar), **Supp. IV Part 2:** 466

Fine, David, **Supp. XI:** 160

Fine, Richard, **Supp. XVIII:** 248

Fine Clothes to the Jew (Hughes), **Retro. Supp. I:** 200, 201, 203, 205; **Supp. I Part 1:** 326–328

"Fine Old Firm, A" (Jackson), **Supp. IX:** 120

Fine Preserving (Plagemann), **Supp. XVII:** 91

Fine Preserving: M. F. K. Fisher's Annotated Edition of Catherine Plagemann's Cookbook (Plagemann; M. F. K. Fisher, ed.), **Supp. XVII:** 91

Finer Grain, The (James), **II:** 335

Fine Writing (L. P. Smith), **Supp. XIV:** 347

"Fingerprints" (Cohen), **Supp. XXVII:** 56

"Finis" (X. J. Kennedy), **Supp. XV:** 169

"Finished Basement" (Di Piero), **Supp. XIX:** 47

Finished Man, The (Garrett), **Supp. VII:** 96, 97–98

Finishing the Picture (A. Miller), **Retro. Supp. III:** 170, 172, 176

Fink, Jonathan, **Supp. XXI:** 244, 245, 248, 255, 256

Fink, Mike, **IV:** 266

Finkel, Donald, **Supp. XXVII:** 253

Finkelstein, Louis, **Supp. XXVIII:** 153

Finkelstein, Norman, **Supp. XXI:** 24, 33

Finkle, David, **Supp. XXI:** 47

Finley, John H., **II:** 418

Finn, David, **Supp. VIII:** 106–107

Finn, Mark, **Supp. XXVII:** 128

Finnegan, Robert (pseudonym). *See* Ryan, Paul William

Finnegans Wake (Joyce), **III:** 7, 12, 14, 261; **IV:** 182, 369–370, 418, 421; **Supp. I Part 2:** 620; **Supp. II Part 1:** 2; **Supp. XIII:** 191; **Supp. XVIII:** 32

Finney, Brian, **Supp. XIV:** 158, 160, 161, 165, 166, 167, 169

"Finnish Rhapsody" (Ashbery), **Supp. III Part 1:** 26

Finster, Howard, **Supp. XV:** 349

Firbank, Ronald, **IV:** 77, 436; **Supp. XXIII:** 209

"Fire" (Hughes), **Supp. I Part 1:** 327

"Fire and Cloud" (Wright), **IV:** 488

"Fire and Ice" (Frost), **II:** 154; **Retro. Supp. I:** 133; **Retro. Supp. III:** 101, 102; **Supp. XIX:** 122

Fire and Ice (Stegner), **Supp. IV Part 2:** 598, 607–608

"Fire and the Cloud, The" (Hurston), **Supp. VI:** 158

"Fire and the Hearth, The" (Faulkner), **II:** 71

Firebird (Doty), **Supp. XI:** 119–120, 121, **132–133,** 134

"Firebombing, The" (Dickey), **Supp. IV Part 1:** 180–181, 187, 189–190

"Fireborn Are at Home in Fire, The" (Sandburg), **III:** 591

"Fire by Night" (R. Fisher), **Supp. XIX:** 70–71

"Fire Chaconne" (Francis), **Supp. IX:** 87

Firecrackers (Van Vechten), **Supp. II Part 2:** 740, 742–744, 749

"Fire Dreams"(Thompson), **Supp. XXIII:** 296

Fire: From "A Journal of Love," the Unexpurgated Diary of Anaïs Nin, 1934–1937, **Supp. X:** 184, 185, 189, 194, 195

"Fire in the House, The" (Davison), **Supp. XXVI:** 71

Firelight Fairy Book, The (Beston), **Supp. XXVI:** 33

"Fireman, The " (Bass), **Supp. XVI:** 24

Fireman's Wife and Other Stories, The (Bausch), **Supp. VII:** 48, 54

Fire Next Time, The (Baldwin), **Retro. Supp. II:** 5, 8, 9; **Supp. I Part 1:** 48, 49, 52, 60–61

"Fire Next Time, The" (Baldwin). *See* "Down at the Cross" (Baldwin)

"Fire of Driftwood, The" (Longfellow), **II:** 499; **Retro. Supp. II:** 159, 168

"Fire of Life" (McCullers), **II:** 585

Fire on the Mountain (Abbey), **Supp. XIII:** 6

"Fire Poem" (Merrill), **Supp. III Part 1:** 321

"Fires" (Bass), **Supp. XVI:** 20

"Fires" (Carver), **Supp. III Part 1:** 136–139, 147

Fire Sale (Paretsky), **Supp. XXV:** 175–176, 178

Fire Screen, The (Merrill), **Supp. III Part 1:** 319, 325–329

"Fire Season" (Didion), **Supp. IV Part 1:** 199

"Fire Sequence" (Winters), **Supp. II Part 2:** 791, 796, 800

Fire Sermon (Morris), **III:** 238–239

"Fire Sermon, The" (T. S. Eliot), **Retro. Supp. I:** 60–61; **Retro. Supp. III:** 63

Fires: Essays, Poems, Stories (Carver), **Supp. III Part 1:** 136, 140, 142, 146–147

Fireside Travels (J. R. Lowell), **Supp. I Part 2:** 407, 419–420

Firestarter (King), **Supp. IX:** 114; **Supp. V:** 140, 141, 144

"fire the bastards" (Green), **Supp. IV Part 1:** 285

"Fire-Truck, A" (Wilbur), **Supp. III Part 2:** 556

"Fireweed" (Clampitt), **Supp. IX:** 44–45

"Firewood" (Banks), **Supp. V:** 15

"Fireworks" (Ford), **Supp. V:** 69

"Fireworks" (Shapiro), **Supp. II Part 2:** 707

Fireworks: A History and Celebration (Plimpton), **Supp. XVI:** 245

Fir-Flower Tablets (A. Lowell), **II:** 512, 526–527

Firger, Jessica, **Supp. XIX:** 51, 58, 59, 62

Firkins, Oscar W., **II:** 271; **Supp. XV:** 297, 309

"Firmament, The" (Bryant), **Supp. I Part 1:** 162

Firmat, Gustavo Pérez, **Supp. VIII:** 76, 77, 79; **Supp. XI:** 184

"First American, The" (Toomer), **Supp. III Part 2:** 480, 487

"First Birth" (Olds), **Supp. X:** 212

First Book of Africa, The (Hughes), **Supp. I Part 1:** 344–345

First Book of Jazz, The (Hughes), **Supp. I Part 1:** 345

First Book of Negroes, The (Hughes), **Supp. I Part 1:** 345

First Book of Rhythms, The (Hughes), **Supp. I Part 1:** 345

First Book of the West Indies, The (Hughes), **Supp. I Part 1:** 345

Firstborn (Glück), **Supp. V:** 80, 81, 82, 84

"Firstborn" (Wright), **Supp. V:** 340

"First Chaldaic Oracle" (Carson), **Supp. XII:** 111

"First Communion" (Fante), **Supp. XI:** 160

"First Confession" (X. J. Kennedy), **Supp. XV: 154–155**

"First Day of School, The" (Gibbons), **Supp. X:** 41, 42

"First Death in Nova Scotia" (Bishop), **Supp. I Part 1:** 73

"First Formal" (Olds), **Supp. X:** 212

First Four Books of Poems, The (Glück), **Supp. V:** 81, 83

First Four Years, The (L. I. Wilder), **Supp. XXII:** 296, 298, 299–300

"First Grade" (Stafford), **Supp. XI:** 328

First Hand (Bierds), **Supp. XVII:** 32, 34–36

"First Hawaiian Bank" (Nye), **Supp. XIII:** 278

"First Heat" (Taylor), **Supp. V:** 323

First Hour, The (Di Piero), **Supp. XIX:** 36–37, 40

"First Hour of the Night, The" (Bidart), **Supp. XV: 30–32**

"First Hunters and the Last, The" (Sobin), **Supp. XVI:** 292

First Indian on the Moon (Alexie), **Supp. XXVI:** 103

"First Job, The" (Cisneros), **Supp. VII:** 62

"1st Letter on Georges" (Olson), **Supp. II Part 2:** 578

First Light (C. Baxter), **Supp. XVII:** 15, **17–18,** 19, 22

First Light (Preston), **Supp. XVII:** 18

First Light (Wagoner), **Supp. IX:** 330

"Firstling, The" (Davison), **Supp. XXVI:** 69

"First Love" (Welty), **IV:** 264; **Retro. Supp. I:** 347

First Love: A Lyric Sequence (Untermeyer), **Supp. XV:** 295

"First Love: A Quiz" (Stallings), **Supp. XXV:** 221, 233

First Lover and Other Stories, The (Boyle), **Supp. XXIV: 57–58**

First Man, The (O'Neill), **III:** 390

First Manifesto (McGrath), **Supp. X:** 115

"First Meditation" (Roethke), **III:** 545–546

"First Noni Daylight, The" (Harjo), **Supp. XII:** 219
"First Passover" (Longfellow), **II:** 500–501
"First Person Female" (Harrison), **Supp. VIII:** 40, 41, 48
"First Place, The" (Wagoner), **Supp. IX:** 328
First Poems (Buechner), **Supp. XII:** 45
First Poems (Merrill), **Supp. III Part 1:** 318–321, 323
First Poems 1946–1954 (Kinnell), **Supp. III Part 1:** 235, 238–239
"First Praise" (W. C. Williams), **Retro. Supp. I:** 413
First Principles (Spencer), **Supp. I Part 1:** 368
"First Reader" (Collins), **Supp. XXI:** 55–56
"First Ride and First Walk" (Goldbarth), **Supp. XII:** 182–183
"First Seeing the St. Lawrence River"(Kenny), **Supp. XXIII:** 152
"First Seven Years, The" (Malamud), **Supp. I Part 2:** 431
"First Sex" (Olds), **Supp. X:** 208
"First Shift" (Rash), **Supp. XXVII:** 218, 220
"First Snow" (Mosher), **Supp. XXII:** 211
"First Snow in Alsace" (Wilbur), **Supp. III Part 2:** 545, 546, 559
"First Song" (Kinnell), **Supp. III Part 1:** 239
"First Spade in the West, The" (Fiedler), **Supp. XIII:** 103
"First Steps" (McClatchy), **Supp. XII:** 256
First There Is the Need (Reznikoff), **Supp. XIV:** 291
"First Things First" (Auden), **Supp. II Part 1:** 13
"First Thought, Best Thought" (Ginsberg), **Supp. II Part 1:** 327
"First Time I Saw Paris, The" (Fante), **Supp. XI:** 174
"First Travels of Max" (Ransom), **III:** 490–491
"First Tycoon of Teen, The" (Wolfe), **Supp. III Part 2:** 572
"First Views of the Enemy" (Oates), **Supp. II Part 2:** 508
"First Wife, The" (Buck), **Supp. II Part 1:** 127
"First Woods"(Bottoms), **Supp. XXVIII:** 31
First Words before Spring (Untermeyer), **Supp. XV:** 310
"First World War" (White), **Supp. I Part 2:** 665
"Fish" (F. Barthelme), **Supp. XI:** 26
"Fish" (Levis), **Supp. XI:** 259–260
Fish, Stanley, **Supp. IV Part 1:** 48; **Supp. XIV:** 14, 15
"Fish, The" (Bishop), **Supp. XV:** 100, 102; **Supp. XXVII:** 228
"Fish, The" (Moore), **III:** 195, 197, 209, 211, 213–214; **Supp. XXI:** 26
"Fish, The" (Oliver), **Supp. VII:** 236
"Fish, The/Lago Chapala" (Everwine), **Supp. XV:** 82–83

"Fish and Shadow" (Pound), **III:** 466
"Fishboy" (Richard), **Supp. XIX:** 212–213
Fishboy: A Ghost's Story (Richard), **Supp. XIX:** 209, **213–220,** 221
Fishburne, Laurence, **Supp. VIII:** 345
"Fish Cannery" (Fante), **Supp. XI:** 167
Fisher, Alexander Metcalf, **Supp. I Part 2:** 582
Fisher, Alfred, **Retro. Supp. II:** 243
Fisher, Barbara, **Supp. XXII:** 206
Fisher, Craig, **Supp. V:** 125
Fisher, Dorothy Canfield, **Retro. Supp. I:** 21, 133; **Supp. II Part 1:** 117. *See also* Canfield, Dorothy
Fisher, Mary, **Supp. I Part 2:** 455
Fisher, M. F. K., **Supp. XVII:** 81–93; **Supp. XXVIII:** 87
Fisher, Phillip, **Retro. Supp. I:** 39
Fisher, Rudolph, **Retro. Supp. I:** 200; **Supp. I Part 1:** 325; **Supp. X:** 139; **Supp. XIX:** 65–80; **Supp. XVI:** 143
Fisher, Vardis, **Supp. IV Part 2:** 598
Fisher King, The (Marshall), **Supp. XI:** 275–276, **288–290**
"Fisherman, The" (Merwin), **Supp. II Part 1:** 346
"Fisherman and His Wife, The" (Welty), **IV:** 266
"Fisherman from Chihuahua, The" (Connell), **Supp. XIV:** 86
"Fishing" (Harjo), **Supp. XII:** 227–228
"Fishing Idyll, A" (Mosher), **Supp. XXII:** 209
"Fish in the Stone, The" (Dove), **Supp. IV Part 1:** 245, 257
"Fish in the unruffled lakes" (Auden), **Supp. II Part 1:** 8–9
"Fish R Us" (Doty), **Supp. XI:** 135
Fisk, James, **I:** 4, 474
Fiske, David, **Supp. XXVIII:** 164, 166
Fiske, John, **Supp. I Part 1:** 314; **Supp. I Part 2:** 493
Fisketjon, Gary, **Supp. XXIV:** 178
"Fit Against the Country, A" (Wright), **Supp. III Part 2:** 591–592, 601
Fitch, Clyde, **Supp. IV Part 2:** 573
Fitch, Elizabeth. *See* Taylor, Mrs. Edward (Elizabeth Fitch)
Fitch, James, **IV:** 147
Fitch, Noël Riley, **Supp. X:** 186, 187
"Fits" (Munro), **Supp. XXVII:** 189, 196
"Fitting, The" (Hull), **Supp. XXI:** 134, 135
Fit to Be Tied (Silver), **Supp. XXIV: 271–272**
Fitts, Dudley, **I:** 169, 173; **Supp. I Part 1:** 342, 345; **Supp. XIII:** 346; **Supp. XXII:** 281; **Supp. XXVI:** 65
FitzGerald, Edward, **Supp. I Part 2:** 416; **Supp. III Part 2:** 610
Fitzgerald, Ella, **Supp. XIII:** 132
Fitzgerald, F. Scott, **I:** 107, 117, 118, 123, 188, 221, 288, 289, 358, 367, 374–375, 382, 423, 476, 482, 487, 495, 509, 511; **II: 77–100,** 257, 263, 272, 283, 415, 416, 417–418, 420, 425, 427, 430, 431, 432, 433, 434, 436, 437, 450, 458–459, 482, 560; **III:** 2, 26, 35, 36, 37, 40, 44, 45, 69, 106,

244, 284, 334, 350–351, 453, 454, 471, 551, 552, 572; **IV:** 27, 49, 97, 101, 126, 140, 191, 222, 223, 287, 297, 427, 471; **Retro. Supp. I:** 1, 74, **97–120,** 178, 180, 186, 215, 359, 381; **Retro. Supp. II:** 257, 321, 326, 328; **Supp. I Part 1:** 196, 197; **Supp. I Part 2:** 622; **Supp. III Part 2:** 409, 411, 585; **Supp. IV Part 1:** 123, 197, 200, 203, 341; **Supp. IV Part 2:** 463, 468, 607, 689; **Supp. IX:** 15, 20, 55, 57–63, 199; **Supp. V:** 23, 95, 226, 251, 262, 276, 313; **Supp. VIII:** 101, 103, 106, 137; **Supp. X:** 225; **Supp. XI:** 65, 221, 334; **Supp. XII:** 42, 173, 295; **Supp. XIII:** 170, 263; **Supp. XV:** 135; **Supp. XVI:** 64, 75, 191, 192, 294; **Supp. XVIII:** 148, 246, 248, 251, 254; **Supp. XX: 74; Supp. XXI:** 262; **Supp. XXII:** 82, 92; **Supp. XXIII:** 68, 101, 174
Fitzgerald, Robert, **I:** 27–28; **III:** 338, 348; **Retro. Supp. II:** 179, 221, 222, 223, 228, 229; **Supp. IV Part 2:** 631; **Supp. XV:** 112, 249; **Supp. XXII:** 281; **Supp. XXIII:** 112
Fitzgerald, Zelda (Zelda Sayre), **I:** 482; **II:** 77, 79, 82–85, 88, 90–91, 93, 95; **Supp. IV Part 1:** 310; **Supp. IX:** 55–73; **Supp. X:** 172. *See also* Sayre, Zelda
"Fitzgerald's Tragic Sense" (Schorer), **Retro. Supp. I:** 115
"Fitzgerald: The Romance of Money" (Cowley), **Supp. II Part 1:** 143
Fitzpatrick, Catherine, **Supp. XXVII:** 270
5 Detroits (Levine), **Supp. V:** 178
Five Came Back (West), **IV:** 287
Five Corners (screenplay, Shanley), **Supp. XIV:** 316
"Five-Dollar Bill, The" (D. West as Mary Christopher), **Supp. XVIII:** 282
"Five Dollar Guy, The" (W. C. Williams), **Retro. Supp. I:** 423
Five Easy Pieces (film), **Supp. V:** 26
"Five Elephants" (Dove), **Supp. IV Part 1:** 244–245
"Five Fucks" (Lethem), **Supp. XVIII:** 139
Five Groups of Verse (Reznikoff), **Supp. XIV:** 279, 282
Five Hundred Hats of Bartholomew Cubbins, The (Geisel), **Supp. XVI:** 100
Five Hundred Scorpions (Hearon), **Supp. VIII:** 57, 65, **66**
Five Indiscretions (Ríos), **Supp. IV Part 2:** 545–547
Five Men and Pompey (Benét), **Supp. XI:** 43, 44
Five Plays (Hughes), **Retro. Supp. I:** 197, 209
"Five Poems About Poetry" (Oppen), **Supp. XXVI:** 233
"Five Psalms" (Jarman), **Supp. XVII:** 120
Five Temperaments (Kalstone), **Retro. Supp. II:** 40
5,000 Fingers of Dr. T, The (film), **Supp. XVI:** 103

Five Young American Poets, **I:** 170; **II:** 367

Fixer, The (Malamud), **Supp. I Part 2:** 428, 435, 445, 446–448, 450, 451

"Fixin' Road" (Boulton), **Supp. XXII:** 23

"Fix It (Winter)"(Hadas), **Supp. XXIII:** 115

Fjellestad, Danuta Zadworna, **Supp. XVI:** 150

Flaccus, Kimball, **Retro. Supp. I:** 136

Flacius, Matthias, **IV:** 163

"Flagellant's Song" (X. J. Kennedy), **Supp. XV:** 165

Flag for Sunrise, A (Stone), **Supp. V:** 301–304

Flagg, Fannie, **Supp. XXII:** 213–214

Flag Is Born, A (Hecht), **Supp. XXVII:** 94–95

Flag of Childhood, The: Poems from the Middle East (Nye, ed.), **Supp. XIII:** 280

"Flag of Summer" (Swenson), **Supp. IV Part 2:** 645

Flagons and Apples (Jeffers), **Supp. II Part 2:** 413, 414, 417–418

Flags in the Dust (Faulkner), **Retro. Supp. I:** 81, 82, 83, 86, 88; **Retro. Supp. III:** 77

Flame and Shadow (Teasdale), **Supp. XXVII:** 284, 286, 292–295

Flamel, Nicolas, **Supp. XII:** 178

Flaming Corsage, The (W. Kennedy), **Supp. VII:** 133, 153–156

Flammarion, Camille, **Supp. I Part 1:** 260

Flanagan, John T., **Supp. I Part 2:** 464, 465, 468

Flanner, Janet, **Supp. XVI:** 195

"Flannery O'Connor: Poet to the Outcast" (Sister Rose Alice), **III:** 348

Flappers and Philosophers (Fitzgerald), **II:** 88; **Retro. Supp. I:** 103; **Supp. IX:** 56

"Flappers Were Her Daughters, The: The Liberated, Literary World of Gertrude Atherton" (Richey), **Supp. XXIV:** 30

Flash and Filigree (Southern), **Supp. XI:** 295, 296–297

"Flashcards" (Dove), **Supp. IV Part 1:** 250

Flash Fiction: Seventy-two Very Short Stories (J. Thomas, ed.), **Supp. XVI:** 268

"Flash in the Pan" (Shaw), **Supp. XIX:** 245

Flats (Wurlitzer), **Supp. XXVI:** 26

"Flat Sky of Summer"(Balakian), **Supp. XXIII:** 25

Flatt, Lester, **Supp. V:** 335

"Flatted Third, The" (Huddle), **Supp. XXVI:** 153

Flaubert, Gustave, **I:** 66, 123, 130, 272, 312, 314, 315, 477, 504, 506, 513, 514; **II:** 182, 185, 194, 198–199, 205, 209, 230, 289, 311, 316, 319, 325, 337, 392, 401, 577, 594; **III:** 196, 207, 251, 315, 461, 467, 511, 564; **IV:** 4, 29, 31, 37, 40, 134, 285, 428; **Retro. Supp. I:** 5, 215, 218, 222, 225, 235, 287; **Retro. Supp. III:** 25; **Supp. III Part 2:** 411, 412; **Supp. XI:** 334; **Supp. XIV:** 87, 336; **Supp. XXIII:** 254; **Supp. XXVII:** 2

"Flavia and Her Artists" (Cather), **Retro. Supp. I:** 5; **Retro. Supp. III:** 21, 26

Flavoring of New England, The (Brooks), **I:** 253, 256

Flavor of Man, The (Toomer), **Supp. III Part 2:** 487

"Flaw, The" (Peacock), **Supp. XIX:** 206

Flawed Texts and Verbal Icons: Literary Authority in American Fiction (Parker), **Retro. Supp. III:** 267

Flaxman, Josiah, **Supp. I Part 2:** 716

"Flea, The" (Donne), **Supp. XVIII:** 307

"Flèche d'Or" (Merrill), **Supp. III Part 1:** 328

Flecker, James Elroy, **Supp. I Part 1:** 257

"Flee on Your Donkey" (Sexton), **Supp. II Part 2:** 683, 685

Fleming, Ian, **Supp. XI:** 307; **Supp. XX:** 195; **Supp. XXVI:** 126

Fleming, Rene, **Supp. XII:** 321

Fleming, Robert E., **Supp. XVII:** 155; **Supp. XXII:** 184

Flesch, Rudolf, **Supp. XVI:** 105, 106

Flesh and Blood (Cunningham), **Supp. XV:** 63–65

Flesh and Blood (play; Cunnigham and Gaitens), **Supp. XV:** 65

"Flesh and the Spirit, The" (Bradstreet), **Retro. Supp. III:** 9, 11

"Fleshbody" (Ammons), **Supp. VII:** 27

Fletcher, H. D., **II:** 517, 529

Fletcher, John, **Supp. IV Part 2:** 621

Fletcher, John Gould, **I:** 243; **II:** 517, 529; **III:** 458; **Supp. I Part 1:** 263; **Supp. I Part 2:** 422; **Supp. XV:** 298, 302, 306, 307, 308

Fletcher, Marie, **Supp. XXVIII:** 123

Fletcher, Mary Frances, **Supp. XXVIII:** 231

Fletcher, Phineas, **Supp. I Part 1:** 369

Fletcher, Virginia. *See* Caldwell, Mrs. Erskine (Virginia Fletcher)

Fleurs du mal, Les (Beaudelaire; Millay and Dillon, trans.), **III:** 141–142

"Flight" (Bierds), **Supp. XVII:** 36

"Flight" (Updike), **IV:** 218, 222, 224; **Retro. Supp. I:** 318

Flight (White), **Supp. XVIII:** 127

"Flight, The" (Haines), **Supp. XII:** 204–205

"Flight, The" (Roethke), **III:** 537–538

Flight 115; or, Pas de Fumer sur la Piste (O'Hara and Berkson), **Supp. XXIII:** 217, 218

Flight among the Tombs (Hecht), **Supp. X:** 58, 71–74

"Flight for Freedom" (McCoy), **Supp. XIII:** 170

"Flight from Byzantium" (Brodsky), **Supp. VIII:** 30–31

"Flight of Besey Lane, The" (Jewett), **Retro. Supp. II:** 139

Flight of the Rocket, The (Fitzgerald), **II:** 89

Flights of the Harvest-Mare (Bierds), **Supp. XVII:** 26–27

Flight to Canada (Reed), **Supp. X:** 240, 249–252

Flinn, Mary, **Supp. XVII:** 110

Flint, F. S., **II:** 517; **III:** 459, 464, 465; **Retro. Supp. I:** 127; **Retro. Supp. III:** 95–96; **Supp. I Part 1:** 261, 262

Flint, Helen, **Supp. XXII:** 278

Flint, R. W., **Supp. XVI:** 47, 49, 57

"Flitting Flies" (X. J. Kennedy), **Supp. XV:** 166, 167

Flivver King, The (Sinclair), **Supp. V:** 290

Floating Candles, The (Lea), **Supp. XXVIII:** 131–132

Floating House, The (Sanders), **Supp. XVI:** 269

Floating Light Bulb, The (Allen), **Supp. XV:** 2, 3, 13

Floating Opera, The (Barth), **I:** 121, 122–126, 127, 129, 130, 131

"Floating Poem, Unnumbered, The" (Rich), **Supp. I Part 2:** 572–573

"Floating Trees" (Wright), **Supp. XV:** 348

Flood (Matthews), **Supp. IX:** 154, 160–161

Flood (Warren), **IV:** 252, 256–257

"Flood of Years, The" (Bryant), **Supp. I Part 1:** 159, 170, 171; **Supp. I Part 2:** 416

"Floor and the Ceiling, The" (W. J. Smith), **Supp. XIII:** 345, 346

"Floor Plans" (Komunyakaa), **Supp. XIII:** 114

"Floral Conversation" (Peacock), **Supp. XIX:** 200

"Floral Decorations for Bananas" (Stevens), **IV:** 8

Florentine Dagger, The: A Novel for Amateur Detectives (Hecht), **Supp. XXVII:** 89

Florida (Acker), **Supp. XII:** 5

"Florida" (Bishop), **Retro. Supp. II:** 43

"Florida Road Workers" (Hughes), **Retro. Supp. I:** 203

"Florida Sunday, A" (Lanier), **Supp. I Part 1:** 364, 366

Florist's Daughter, The (Hampl), **Supp. XXII:** 84, 85, 94, 95–98

"Flossie Cabanis" (Masters), **Supp. I Part 2:** 461–462

"Flossy Frills Helps Out" (Wells), **Supp. XXVI:** 276

"Flounder" (Trethewey), **Supp. XXI:** 244, 245, 246, 251

Flow Chart (Ashbery), **Supp. VIII:** 275

"Flowchart" (Ashbery), **Supp. III Part 1:** 26

Flower, Dean, **Supp. XXII:** 205, 212

Flower, Fruit, and Thorn Pieces (Richter), **Supp. XVI:** 182

Flower-de-Luce (Longfellow), **II:** 490

Flower Drum Song (Rodgers and Hammerstein), **Supp. XXI:** 148

Flower Drum Song, The (Lee), **Supp. XXI:** 148

Flower Fables (Alcott), **Supp. I Part 1:** 33

"Flower-Fed Buffaloes, The" (Lindsay), **Supp. I Part 2:** 398

"Flower Garden" (Jackson), **Supp. IX:** 119

"Flower-gathering" (Frost), **II:** 153

Flower Herding on Mount Monadnock (Kinnell), **Supp. III Part 1:** 235, 239, 241–244

"Flower Herding on Mount Monadnock" (Kinnell), **Supp. III Part 1:** 242

"Flowering Death" (Ashbery), **Supp. III Part 1:** 22

"Flowering Dream, The" (McCullers), **II:** 591

"Flowering Judas" (Porter), **III:** 434, 435–436, 438, 441, 445, 446, 450–451

Flowering Judas and Other Stories (Porter), **III:** 433, 434

Flowering of New England, The (Brooks), **IV:** 171–172; **Supp. VIII:** 101

Flowering of the Cumberland (Arnow), **Supp. XXVIII:** 3

Flowering of the Rod (Doolittle), **Supp. I Part 1:** 272

Flowering Peach, The (Odets), **Supp. II Part 2:** 533, 547, 549–550

"Flowering Plum" (Glück), **Supp. V:** 82

Flowers, The (Gilb), **Supp. XXV:** 138

Flowers for Hitler (Cohen), **Supp. XXVII:** 54

"Flowers for Marjorie" (Welty), **IV:** 262

"Flowers of the Fallow" (Larcom), **Supp. XIII:** 143, 145–146

"Flowers Well if anybody" (Dickinson), **Retro. Supp. I:** 30

"Fluff and Mr. Ripley" (D. West), **Supp. XVIII:** 284

"Fly, The" (Kinnell), **Supp. III Part 1:** 249

"Fly, The" (Shapiro), **Supp. II Part 2:** 705

"Fly, The" (Simic), **Supp. VIII:** 278

Flye, Father James Harold, **I:** 25, 26, 35–36, 37, 42, 46; **IV:** 215

"Fly in Buttermilk, A" (Baldwin), **Retro. Supp. II:** 8

Flying at Night: Poems 1965–1985 (Kooser), **Supp. XIX:** 128

"Flying High" (Levertov), **Supp. III Part 1:** 284

"Flying Home" (Ellison), **Retro. Supp. II:** 117, **125–126; Supp. II Part 1:** 235, 238–239

"Flying Home" (Kinnell), **Supp. III Part 1:** 250

"Flying Home" and Other Stories (Ellison), **Retro. Supp. II:** 119, 124

"Flying Home from Utah" (Swenson), **Supp. IV Part 2:** 645

"Flying over Clouds" (Gioia), **Supp. XV:** 118

Flying Solo (Kriegel), **Supp. XXIV: 219–221**

"Flying to Hanoi" (Rukeyser), **Supp. VI:** 279

Flynn, Elizabeth Gurley, **Supp. XVIII:** 225; **Supp. XXVIII:** 65, 67

Flynn, Richard, **Supp. XVII:** 115; **Supp. XVIII:** 183

Fly-Truffler, The (Sobin), **Supp. XVI: 294–295,** 296

Foata, Anne, **Supp. XI:** 104

FOB (Hwang), **Supp. XXI:** 143, 144, 145, 146, **148–150**

Focillon, Henri, **IV:** 90

Focus (A. Miller), **III:** 150–151, 156; **Retro. Supp. III:** 173, 174–175

Foer, Jonathan Safran, **Supp. XII:** 169; **Supp. XX: 177; Supp. XXIV:** 131; **Supp. XXV:** 268

Foerster, Norman, **I:** 222; **Supp. I Part 2:** 423, 424; **Supp. IV Part 2:** 598

"Fog" (Sandburg), **III:** 586

"Fog Galleon" (Komunyakaa), **Supp. XIII:** 127

"Foggy and dripping" (Kooser), **Supp. XIX:** 125

"Foggy Lane, The" (Simpson), **Supp. IX:** 274

"Fog Man, The" (Boyle), **Supp. XX: 20**

"Fog Patterns" (Hecht), **Supp. XXVII:** 85

Folded Leaf, The (Maxwell), **Supp. III Part 1:** 62; **Supp. VIII: 159–162**

Folding Star, The (Hollinghurst), **Supp. XIII:** 52

Foley, Barbara, **Supp. XXVI:** 28; **Supp. XXVIII:** 77–78

Foley, Jack, **Supp. X:** 125; **Supp. XV:** 112, 116; **Supp. XVII:** 77

Foley, Martha, **II:** 587; **Supp. XVI:** 225

Folk-Lore in the Old Testament (Frazer), **Supp. XX: 116–117**

Folks, Jeffrey, **Supp. XXVI:** 15

Folks from Dixie (Dunbar), **Supp. II Part 1:** 211–212

Folkways (Sumner), **III:** 102

Follain, Jean, **Supp. IX:** 152, 154

Follett, Wilson, **I:** 405; **Supp. XIII:** 173

Follower of Dusk (Salinas), **Supp. XIII:** 326

"Following the Bones" (W. V. Davis), **Supp. XXI:** 96

Following the Equator (Twain), **II:** 434; **IV:** 208; **Retro. Supp. III:** 255, 267

Follow Me Home (Hoffman), **Supp. XVIII:** 86

Folly (Minot), **Supp. VI:** 205, 208, **210–213**

Folly in the Forest (Wells), **Supp. XXVI:** 276

Folly of Others, The (Boyce), **Supp. XVII:** 100; **Supp. XXI:** 10

Folsom, Charles, **Supp. I Part 1:** 156

Folsom, Ed, **Retro. Supp. I:** 392

Folsom, Michael Brewster, **Supp. XXVIII:** 66, 67, 68, 71, 77, 78–79, 80

Folson, Marcia McClintock, **Retro. Supp. II:** 139

Fonda, Henry, **Supp. I Part 1:** 67; **Supp. IV Part 1:** 236

Fonda, Jane, **III:** 284; **Supp. XI:** 307; **Supp. XXVIII:** 3

Fonda, Peter, **Supp. VIII:** 42; **Supp. XI:** 293, 308

"Fondled Memories" (Molesworth), **Supp. XIX:** 121–122

"Fond Memories of a Black Childhood" (D. West), **Supp. XVIII:** 289

Foner, Eric, **Supp. I Part 2:** 523

Fong and the Indians (Theroux), **Supp. VIII:** 314, 315, **316–317**

Fontanne, Lynn, **III:** 397

Food and Drink (Untermeyer), **Supp. XV:** 310

Food Chain, The (Silver), **Supp. XXIV:** 265, **270–271,** 274

Fool for Love (Shepard), **Supp. III Part 2:** 433, 447, 448

Fooling with Words (PBS special, Moyers), **Supp. XXIII:** 139

"Foolishness" (Pickering), **Supp. XXI:** 197

Fools (Simon), **Supp. IV Part 2:** 584–585

Fools Crow (Welch), **Supp. XXIV:** 257

Fool's Progress, The: An Honest Novel (Abbey), **Supp. XIII:** 4, **13–15**

"Football Rebellion in Backwoods Georgia, A" (Andrews), **Supp. XXVI:** 3, 4

Foot Book, The (Geisel), **Supp. XVI:** 108

Foote, Bud, **Supp. XXVI:** 5

Foote, Horton, **Supp. I Part 1:** 281; **Supp. VIII:** 128, 129

Foote, Mary Hallock, **Retro. Supp. II:** 72; **Supp. IV Part 2:** 611

Foote, Roxanna. *See* Beecher, Mrs. Lyman (Roxanna Foote)

Foote, Samuel, **Supp. I Part 2:** 584

Foote, Stephanie, **Retro. Supp. II:** 139

"Foot Fault" (pseudonym). *See* Thurber, James

Footing on This Earth, A (Hay), **Supp. XIV:** 125, 126, 130

"Footing up a Total" (A. Lowell), **II:** 528

"Footnote to Howl" (Ginsberg), **Supp. II Part 1:** 316–317

"Footnote to Weather Forecasts, A" (Brodsky), **Supp. VIII:** 32

Footprints (Hearon), **Supp. VIII: 69–70**

Footprints (Levertov), **Supp. III Part 1:** 272, 281

"Footsteps of Angels" (Longfellow), **II:** 496

"For A, at Fourteen" (Weigl), **Supp. XIX:** 287

For a Bitter Season: New and Selected Poems (Garrett), **Supp. VII:** 99–100

"For a Dead Kitten" (Hay), **Supp. XIV:** 119–120

"For a Dead Lady" (Robinson), **III:** 508, 513, 517

"For a Ghost Who Once Placed Bets in the Park" (Levis), **Supp. XI:** 265

"Foraging" (H. Johnson), **Supp. XXVI:** 172

"For a Lamb" (Eberhart), **I:** 523, 530, 531

"For All" (Snyder), **Supp. VIII:** 304

"For All Tuesday Travelers" (Cisneros), **Supp. VII:** 67–68

"For a Lost Child" (Stafford), **Supp. XI:** 329

"For a Marriage" (Bogan), **Supp. III Part 1:** 52

"For an Emigrant" (Jarrell), **II:** 371

"For Anna Akmatova" (R. Lowell), **II:** 544

"For Anna Mae Pictou Aquash, Whose Spirit Is Present Here and in the Dappled Stars" (Harjo), **Supp. XII:** 225

"For Anne, at a Little Distance" (Haines), **Supp. XII:** 207

"For Annie" (Poe), **III:** 427; **Retro. Supp. II:** 263

"For an Old Friend Encountered Unexpectedly" (Espaillat), **Supp. XXI:** 111–112

"For a Southern Man" (Cisneros), **Supp. VII:** 67

"For Bailey" (Angelou), **Supp. IV Part 1:** 15

Forbes, Genevieve, **Supp. XXV:** 196

Forbes, Malcolm, **Supp. IV Part 1:** 94

"Forbidden, The" (Glück), **Supp. XIV:** 269

"Forbidden Magic" (Howard), **Supp. XXVII:** 118

"For Bill Nestrick (1940–96)" (Bidart), **Supp. XV:** 35

For Bread Alone (Choukri), **Supp. IV Part 1:** 92

"Force" (Di Piero), **Supp. XIX:** 35–36, 42, 44

Force of Desire, The (Bronk), **Supp. XXI:** 31, 32

Force of Evil (film, Polonsky), **Supp. XXI:** 261, 272, 275

Force of Spirit, The (Sanders), **Supp. XVI:** 277–278

Forché, Carolyn, **Supp. IV Part 1:** 208; **Supp. XIX:** 193

Ford, Arthur, **Supp. IV Part 1:** 140

Ford, Ford Madox, **I:** 288, 405, 409, 417, 421, 423; **II:** 58, 144, 198, 257, 263, 265, 517, 536; **III:** 458, 464–465, 470–471, 472, 476; **IV:** 27, 126, 261; **Retro. Supp. I:** 127, 177, 178, 186, 231, 286–287, 418; **Supp. I Part 1:** 107; **Supp. III Part 2:** 617; **Supp. VIII:** 107; **Supp. XIV:** 3

Ford, Harrison, **Supp. VIII:** 323

Ford, Harry, **Supp. V:** 179; **Supp. XIII:** 76

Ford, Henry, **I:** 295, 480–481; **III:** 292, 293; **Supp. I Part 1:** 21; **Supp. I Part 2:** 644; **Supp. III Part 2:** 612, 613; **Supp. IV Part 1:** 223; **Supp. V:** 290

Ford, John, **Supp. I Part 2:** 422; **Supp. III Part 2:** 619; **Supp. XVIII:** 247

Ford, Mark, **Supp. XXIII:** 220

Ford, Mary K., **Supp. XX:** **239**

Ford, Nick Aaron, **Retro. Supp. III:** 140

Ford, Richard, **Supp. IV Part 1:** 342; **Supp. V:** 22, **57–75**; **Supp. XXIV:** 97

Ford, Webster (pseudonym). *See* Masters, Edgar Lee

"Fording and Dread" (Harrison), **Supp. VIII:** 41

"Ford Madox Ford" (R. Lowell), **II:** 547; **Retro. Supp. II:** 188

"For Dudley" (Wilbur), **Supp. III Part 2:** 558

Fordyce, David, **II:** 113

For Eager Lovers (Taggard), **Supp. XXII:** 274–275

Foregone Conclusion, A (Howells), **II:** 278–279, 282

"Foreign Affairs" (Kunitz), **Supp. III Part 1:** 265

Foreign Correspondent (screenplay, Hecht), **Supp. XXVII:** 93

"Foreigner, A" (Bynner), **Supp. XV:** 46

"Foreigner, The" (Jewett), **II:** 409–410; **Retro. Supp. II:** 133, 142

"Foreigners" (Jarman), **Supp. XVII:** 113

"Foreign Language, The" (Franzen), **Supp. XX:** 84

"Foreign Shores" (Salter), **Supp. IX:** 260

Forensic and the Navigators (Shepard), **Supp. III Part 2:** 439

Forerunner, The (Boyce), **Supp. XXI:** 2, 4, **10–11**

Forerunner, The: His Parables and Poems (Gibran), **Supp. XX:** 115, **118–119**, 119

Foreseeable Future, The (Price), **Supp. VI:** 265

Foreseeable Futures (Matthews), **Supp. IX:** 155, **163**, 169

Foresman, Rebecca, **Supp. XXIV:** 171

"For Esmé with Love and Squalor" (Salinger), **III:** 560

"Forest" (Simic), **Supp. VIII:** 273

Forest, Jean-Claude, **Supp. XI:** 307

Forester's Letters (Paine), **Supp. I Part 2:** 508

"Forest Hymn, A" (Bryant), **Supp. I Part 1:** 156, 162, 163, 164, 165, 170

"Forest in the Seeds, The" (Kingsolver), **Supp. VII:** 203

Forest of the South, The (Gordon), **II:** 197

"Forest of the South, The" (Gordon), **II:** 199, 201

Forest without Leaves (Adams and Haines), **Supp. XII:** 209

"Forever, Said the Duck" (Lethem), **Supp. XVIII:** 139

"Forever and the Earth" (Bradbury), **Supp. IV Part 1:** 102

"Forever in That Year" (Carruth), **Supp. XVI:** 51

"Forever"(Thompson), **Supp. XXIII:** 296

For Ever Wilt Thou Love (Lewisohn), **Supp. XXVIII:** 152

"Forever Young" (Jarman and R. McDowell), **Supp. XVII:** 111

"For Fathers of Girls" (Dunn), **Supp. XI:** 146

For Frank O'Hara's Birthday (Notley), **Supp. XXII:** 224, 227

"For/From Lew" (Snyder), **Supp. VIII:** 303

"For Garrison Keillor, Fantasy Is a Lot More Fun then Reality" (Letofsky), **Supp. XVI:** 167

"For George Santayana" (R. Lowell), **II:** 547

"Forgetfulness" (Collins), **Supp. XXI:** 58

"Forgiveness" (Peacock), **Supp. XIX:** 200

Forgotten Helper, The: A Story for Children (Moore), **Supp. X:** 175

"Forgotten in an Old Notebook" (F. Wright), **Supp. XVII:** 244

Forgotten Village, The (Steinbeck), **IV:** 51

"For Grace, After a party"(O'Hara), **Supp. XXIII:** 214

"For Grizzel McNaught (1709–1792)" (A. Finch), **Supp. XVII:** 72

Forgue, Guy J., **III:** 118, 119

For Her Dark Skin (Everett), **Supp. XVIII:** 56, 60

"FOR HETTIE" (Baraka), **Supp. II Part 1:** 32

"FOR HETTIE IN HER FIFTH MONTH" (Baraka), **Supp. II Part 1:** 32, 38

"For Homer" (Corso), **Supp. XII:** 135

"For I'm the Boy" (Barthelme), **Supp. IV Part 1:** 47

"For James Dean"(O'Hara), **Supp. XXIII:** 214

"For Janice and Kenneth to Voyage"(O'Hara), **Supp. XXIII:** 214

"For Jeff" (Kooser), **Supp. XIX:** 125

"For Jessica, My Daughter" (Strand), **Supp. IV Part 2:** 629

"For John, Who Begs Me not to Enquire Further" (Sexton), **Supp. II Part 2:** 676

"For Johnny Pole on the Forgotten Beach" (Sexton), **Supp. II Part 2:** 675

"For Joy to Leave Upon" (Ortiz), **Supp. IV Part 2:** 508

"For Judy, Whose Husband Is Undergoing Surgery"(Crooker), **Supp. XXIII:** 61

"Fork" (Simic), **Supp. VIII:** 275

"For Karl Shapiro, Having Gone Back to the Sonnet" (Kooser), **Supp. XIX:** 118

"Forked Tongue" (Davison), **Supp. XXVI:** 71

"Forky" (Dubus III), **Supp. XXIV:** 99, 101

"For Lack of a Treaty" (Davison), **Supp. XXVI:** 79

For Lancelot Andrewes (T. S. Eliot), **Retro. Supp. I:** 64; **Retro. Supp. III:** 58

For Lizzie and Harriet (R. Lowell), **Retro. Supp. II:** 183, 186, 190

"Forlorn Hope of Sidney Lanier, The" (Leary), **Supp. I Part 1:** 373

For Love (Creeley), **Supp. IV Part 1:** 139, 140, 142–145, 147–149, 150, 154

"For Love" (Creeley), **Supp. IV Part 1:** 145

For Love (Miller), **Supp. XII:** 297–299, 299

For Love of Imabelle (C. Himes), **Supp. XVI:** 135, 143, 144

Form, Cycle, Infinity: Landscape Imagery in the Poetry of Robert Frost and George Seferis (Hadas), **Supp. XXIII:** 121–122

"Formal Elegy" (Berryman), **I:** 170

Formal Feeling Comes, A (A. Finch, ed.), **Supp. XVII:** 71–72

"Formalist Criticism: Its Principles and Limits" (Burke), **I:** 282

Forman, Henry James, **Supp. XXIV:** 29, 30

Forman, Milos, **Supp. IV Part 1:** 236

"Form and Function of the Novel, The" (Goldbarth), **Supp. XII:** 183

"For Marse Chouchoute" (Chopin), **Retro. Supp. II:** 60

"For Mary Ann Youngren" (Bidart), **Supp. XV:** 29

"Format and Form" (A. Rich), **Supp. XVII:** 74

"Formation of a Separatist, I" (Howe), **Supp. IV Part 2:** 427

"Form Is Emptiness" (Baraka), **Supp. II Part 1:** 51

"For Mr. Death Who Stands with His Door Open" (Sexton), **Supp. II Part 2:** 695

Forms of Discovery (Winters), **Supp. II Part 2:** 812, 813

Forms of Fiction, The (Gardner and Dunlap), **Supp. VI:** 64

"Forms of Love, The" (Oppen), **Supp. XXVI:** 225

"For My Children" (Karr), **Supp. XI:** 254

"For My Daughter" (Kees), **Supp. XV:** 141, 147

"For My Daughter" (Olds), **Supp. X:** 206

"For My Former Wife, Watching TV, in the Past" (Kooser), **Supp. XIX:** 120

"For My Lover, Returning to His Wife" (Sexton), **Supp. II Part 2:** 688

"For My Son Creston at the Solstice"(Lea), **Supp. XXVIII:** 131

Fornés, Maria Irene, **Supp. XXI:** 144; **Supp. XXIII:** 194, 200

"For Night to Come" (Stern), **Supp. IX:** 292

"For Once, Then, Something" (Frost), **II:** 156–157; **Retro. Supp. I:** 126, 133, 134; **Retro. Supp. III:** 101, 102

"For Peg: A Remnant of Song Still Distantly Sounding" (Carruth), **Supp. XVI:** 54

"For Pot-Boiling" (Hay), **Supp. XIV:** 128

"For Radicals" (Bourne), **I:** 221

"For Rainer Gerhardt" (Creeley), **Supp. IV Part 1:** 142–143, 147

Forrestal, James, **I:** 491; **Supp. I Part 2:** 489

Forrester, Fanny, **Supp. XVIII:** 13

Forrey, Carolyn, **Supp. XXIV:** 30

"For Richard After All" (Kingsolver), **Supp. VII:** 208

"For Sacco and Vanzetti" (Kingsolver), **Supp. VII:** 208

"Forsaken Brother, The"(J. Schoolcraft), **Supp. XXIII:** 235

"Forsaken Merman" (Arnold), **Supp. I Part 2:** 529

"Forsaking the Promised Land" (diss. Collins), **Supp. XXVI:** 12

"For S.F.S. 1875–1962" (J. W. Miller), **Supp. XX:** 166

For Spacious Skies (Buck), **Supp. II Part 1:** 131

Forster, E. M., **I:** 292; **IV:** 201; **Retro. Supp. I:** 59, 232; **Supp. III Part 2:** 503; **Supp. IX:** 128; **Supp. V:** 258; **Supp. VIII:** 155, 171; **Supp. XII:** 79,

81; **Supp. XIV:** 159, 160, 163; **Supp. XV:** 62; **Supp. XVI:** 236; **Supp. XVIII:** 143; **Supp. XX:** 229, 235, 239, 240; **Supp. XXI:** 233

Forster, John, **II:** 315

Forsythe, Robert, **Supp. XXVIII:** 77

Fort, Paul, **II:** 518, 528, 529; **Retro. Supp. I:** 55

"For the Ahkoond" (Bierce), **I:** 209

For the Body (Nelson), **Supp. XVIII:** 173

For the Century's End: Poems 1990–1999 (Haines), **Supp. XII:** 211–213

"For the Chinese New Year and Bill Berkson"(O'Hara), **Supp. XXIII:** 218

"For the Dedication of the New City Library, Boston" (Holmes), **Supp. I Part 1:** 308

"For the Fallen" (Levine), **Supp. V:** 188

For the Health of the Land: Previously Unpublished Essays and Other Writings (Leopold), **Supp. XIV:** 183

"For the Lady in the Black Raincoat Who Slept Through an Entire Poetry Reading" (Espaillat), **Supp. XXI:** 108

"For the Last Wolverine" (Dickey), **Supp. IV Part 1:** 182

"For the Losers of Things" (Stallings), **Supp. XXV:** 222

"For the Lovers of the Absolute" (Simic), **Supp. VIII:** 278–279

"For the Man Cutting the Grass" (Oliver), **Supp. VII:** 235

"For the Marriage of Faustus and Helen" (H. Crane), **I:** 395–396, 399, 402; **Retro. Supp. II:** 78–79, 82; **Retro. Supp. III:** 47–48

"For the Meeting of the National Sanitary Association, 1860" (Holmes), **Supp. I Part 1:** 307

For the New Intellectual (Rand), **Supp. IV Part 2:** 521, 526–527, 527, 532

"For the New Railway Station in Rome" (Wilbur), **Supp. III Part 2:** 554

"For the Night" (Kenyon), **Supp. VII:** 163

"For Theodore Roethke: 1908–1963" (R. Lowell), **II:** 554

"For the Poem *Patterson*" (W. C. Williams), **Retro. Supp. I:** 424

"For the Poets of Chile" (Levine), **Supp. V:** 188

"FOR THE REVOLUTIONARY OUTBURST BY BLACK PEOPLE" (Baraka), **Supp. II Part 1:** 55

"For the Sleepless" (Dunn), **Supp. XI:** 145

For the Time Being (Auden), **Supp. II Part 1:** 2, 17, 18

For the Time Being (Dillard), **Supp. VI:** 23, 27, 29, 32, 34–35

For the Time Being (Teale), **Supp. XXVIII:** 247

"For the Twentieth Century" (Bidart), **Supp. XV:** 35

For the Union Dead (R. Lowell), **II:** 543, 550–551, 554, 555; **Retro. Supp. II:** 181, 182, 186, 189; **Supp. X:** 53

"For the Union Dead" (R. Lowell), **II:** 551; **Retro. Supp. II:** 189

"For the Walking Dead" (Komunyakaa), **Supp. XIII:** 121

"For the West" (Snyder), **Supp. VIII:** 299

"For the Word Is Flesh" (Kunitz), **Supp. III Part 1:** 262–264

"Fortress, The" (Glück), **Supp. V:** 82

"Fortress, The" (Sexton), **Supp. II Part 2:** 682

Fortress of Solitude, The (Lethem), **Supp. XVIII:** 135, 136, **145–148,** 150

"Fort Robinson" (Kooser), **Supp. XIX:** 120

"Fortunate Traveler" (Hull), **Supp. XXI:** 140

Fortune, T. Thomas, **Supp. II Part 1:** 159

Fortune's Bones: The Manumission Requiem (Nelson), **Supp. XVIII:** 171, 172–173, 182–183

Fortune's Daughter (Hoffman), **Supp. X:** 77, 85

"Fortune Spill, The" (Nelson), **Supp. XVIII:** 175

45 Mercy Street (Sexton), **Supp. II Part 2:** 694, 695, 697

Forty Poems Touching on Recent American History (Bly, ed.), **Supp. IV Part 1:** 61

42nd Parallel, The (Dos Passos), **I:** 482, 484–485

Forty Stories (Barthelme), **Supp. IV Part 1:** 47, 49, 53, 54

For Whom the Bell Tolls (Hemingway), **II:** 249, 254–255, 261; **III:** 18, 363; **Retro. Supp. I:** 115, 176–177, 178, **184,** 187; **Supp. XVII:** 229; **Supp. XXV:** 146

For Whom the Southern Belle Tolls (Durang), **Supp. XXIV:** 113, 118, 125

Foscolo, Ugo, **II:** 543

Foss, Sam Walter, **Supp. II Part 1:** 197

"Fossils, The" (Kinnell), **Supp. III Part 1:** 244

Foster, Edward, **Supp. IV Part 2:** 431, 434; **Supp. XVI:** 281, 293; **Supp. XXI:** 33

Foster, Edward Halsey, **Supp. XII:** 120, 129, 130, 135; **Supp. XVIII:** 265, 268

Foster, Emily, **II:** 309

Foster, Frances Smith, **Supp. XX:** 287

Foster, Hannah Webster, **Supp. XV:** 234; **Supp. XXV:** 35–48

Foster, John Wilson, **Supp. XIII:** 32–33

Foster, Michael K., **Supp. XXVI:** 83

Foster, Phil, **Supp. IV Part 2:** 574

Foster, Richard, **Supp. XV:** 269

Foster, Stephen, **Supp. I Part 1:** 100–101; **Supp. I Part 2:** 699

Foucault, Michel, **Supp. VIII:** 5; **Supp. XII:** 98; **Supp. XV:** 344; **Supp. XVI:** 285

Foulke, Robert, **Supp. XXV:** 217

"Founder, The" (Stern), **Supp. IX:** 297

Founding of Harvard College, The (Morison), **Supp. I Part 2:** 485

"Foundry Workers" (Bodenheim), **Supp. XXV:** 22

"Fountain, The" (Bryant), **Supp. I Part 1:** 157, 165, 166, 168

Fountain, The (O'Neill), **III:** 391

Fountain and Other Poems, The (Bryant), **Supp. I Part 1:** 157

Fountainhead, The (film), **Supp. IV Part 2:** 524

Fountainhead, The (Rand), **Supp. IV Part 2:** 517, 521–523, 525, 531; **Supp. XXIV:** 281

Fountainhead, The: A Fiftieth Anniversary Celebration (Cox), **Supp. IV Part 2:** 523

"Fountain Piece" (Swenson), **Supp. IV Part 2:** 641

4-H Club (Shepard), **Supp. III Part 2:** 439

"Four Ages of Man, The" (Bradstreet), **Retro. Supp. III:** 1, 6; **Supp. I Part 1:** 111, 115

Four American Indian Literary Masters (Velie), **Supp. IV Part 2:** 486

"Four Angers"(Hadas), **Supp. XXIII:** 115

"Four Beasts in One; the Homo Cameleopard" (Poe), **III:** 425

Four Black Revolutionary Plays (Baraka), **Supp. II Part 1:** 45; **Supp. VIII:** 330

"Four Brothers" (Di Piero), **Supp. XIX:** 37

"Four Brothers, The" (Sandburg), **III:** 585

"Four Dancers at an Irish Wedding" (Gallagher), **Supp. XXIV:** 168, 170

Four Days (screenplay, P. Benedict), **Supp. XXIII:** 35

Four Dogs and a Bone and the Wild Goose (Shanley), **Supp. XIV:** 316, **328–329**

"Four Elements, The" (Bradstreet), **Retro. Supp. III:** 6

"Four Evangelists, The" (Komunyakaa), **Supp. XIII:** 131

"Four for Sir John Davies" (Roethke), **III:** 540, 541

Four for Trane (Mackey), **Supp. XXVII:** 153

"Four Girls, The" (Alvarez), **Supp. VII:** 7

"Four Horse Songs" (Harjo), **Supp. XII:** 220

"Four Humours, The" (Bradstreet), **Retro. Supp. III:** 5, 6

"400-Meter Free Style" (Kumin), **Supp. IV Part 2:** 442

"400-Pound CEO, The" (Saunders), **Supp. XIX:** 225

Fourier, Charles, **II:** 342

"Four in a Family" (Rukeyser), **Supp. VI:** 272

Four in Hand: A Quartet of Novels (Warner), **Supp. VIII:** 164

"Four Lakes' Days" (Eberhart), **I:** 525

"Four Mad Studies" (Di Piero), **Supp. XIX:** 37

"Four Meetings" (James), **II:** 327

Four Million, The (O. Henry), **Supp. II Part 1:** 394, 408

"Four Monarchies, The" (Bradstreet), **Retro. Supp. III:** 4, 6–7; **Supp. I Part 1:** 105, 106, 116

"Four Mountain Wolves" (Silko), **Supp. IV Part 2:** 561

Four of a Kind (Marquand), **III:** 54, 55

"Four of the Horsemen (Hypertense and Stroke, Coronary Occlusion and Cerebral Insult)" (Karr), **Supp. XI:** 250

"Four Poems" (Bishop), **Supp. I Part 1:** 92

"Four Poems at the End of Summer"(Hadas), **Supp. XXIII:** 117

"Four Preludes on Playthings of the Wind" (Sandburg), **III:** 586

Four Quartets (T. S. Eliot), **I:** 570, 576, 580–582, 585, 587; **II:** 537; **III:** 539; **Retro. Supp. I:** 66, 67; **Retro. Supp. III:** 58, 65–68, 69; **Supp. II Part 1:** 1; **Supp. IV Part 1:** 284; **Supp. V:** 343, 344; **Supp. VIII:** 182, 195; **Supp. XIII:** 344; **Supp. XIV:** 167; **Supp. XV:** 216, 260, 266

Four Saints in Three Acts (Stein), **IV:** 30, 31, 33, 43, 44–45

"Four Seasons, The" (Bradstreet), **Retro. Supp. III:** 6, 9, 10, 12; **Supp. I Part 1:** 112–113

Four Seasons of Success, The (Schulberg), **Supp. XVIII:** 254

"Four Sides of One Story" (Updike), **Retro. Supp. I:** 328

"Four Skinny Trees" (Cisneros), **Supp. VII:** 64

"14: In A Dark Wood: Wood Thrushes" (Oliver), **Supp. VII:** 244

"14 Men Stage Head Winter 1624/ 25" (Olson), **Supp. II Part 2:** 574

14 Stories (Dixon), **Supp. XII:** 141, **145–147**

Fourteen Hundred Thousand (Shepard), **Supp. III Part 2:** 439

Fourteen Sisters of Emilio Montez O'Brien, The (Hijuelos), **Supp. VIII: 82–85**

Fourteen Stories (Buck), **Supp. II Part 1:** 126

"Fourteenth Ward, The" (H. Miller), **III:** 175

Fourth Book of Peace, The (Kingston), **Supp. V:** 173

"Fourth Down" (Marquand), **III:** 56

Fourth Group of Verse, A (Reznikoff), **Supp. XIV:** 282, 284

"Fourth of July in Maine" (R. Lowell), **II:** 535, 552–553

Fourth Wall, The (Gurney), **Supp. V:** 109–110

Four Young Lady Poets (Baraka, ed.), **Supp. XXVIII:** 260

Fowler, Douglas, **Supp. IV Part 1:** 226, 227

Fowler, Gene, **Supp. VIII:** 290

Fowler, Henry Watson, **Supp. I Part 2:** 660

Fowler, Karen Joy, **Supp. XXII:** 49

Fowler, Singrid, **Supp. VIII:** 249, 258

Fowler, Virginia C., **Supp. VIII:** 224

Fox, Alan, **Supp. XIII:** 120

Fox, Dixon Ryan, **I:** 337

Fox, Joe, **Supp. IX:** 259, 261

Fox, John, **Supp. XIII:** 166; **Supp. XXII:** 36

Fox, Linda C., **Supp. XIII:** 217–218

Fox, Paula, **Supp. XX:** 91

Fox, Rose, **Supp. XXVIII:** 279, 284

Fox, Ruth, **Supp. I Part 2:** 619

"Fox, The" (Levine), **Supp. V:** 181, 189

Fox-Genovese, Elizabeth, **Supp. IV Part 1:** 286; **Supp. XXII:** 190, 192, 200

Fox in Socks (Geisel), **Supp. XVI:** 108, 112

"Fox Night" (Jarman), **Supp. XVII:** 120

Fox of Peapack, The (White), **Supp. I Part 2:** 676, 677–678

"Fox of Peapack, The" (White), **Supp. I Part 2:** 677

Fox: Poems 1998–2000 (Rich), **Retro. Supp. III:** 252

"Fox Point Health Clinic, 1974" (Halliday), **Supp. XIX:** 89, 93

Fox's Earth (Siddons), **Supp. XXII:** 239

Foye, Raymond, **Supp. XIV:** 150

Fradin, Judith and Dennis, **Supp. XXVIII:** 167

Fradkin, Lori, **Supp. XIX:** 52

Fraenkel, Michael, **III:** 178, 183

"Fragging" (Komunyakaa), **Supp. XIII:** 123

Fragile Beauty, A: John Nichols' Milagro Country: Text and Photographs from His Life and Work (Nichols), **Supp. XIII:** 268

"Fragility" (Shields), **Supp. VII:** 318

"Fragment" (A. Lowell), **II:** 516

"Fragment" (Ashbery), **Supp. III Part 1:** 11, 13, 14, 19, 20

"Fragment" (Ortiz), **Supp. IV Part 2:** 507

"Fragment of a Meditation" (Tate), **IV:** 129

"Fragment of an Agon" (Eliot), **I:** 579–580

"Fragment of a Prologue" (Eliot), **I:** 579–580

"Fragment of New York, 1929" (Eberhart), **I:** 536–537

"Fragments" (Emerson), **II:** 19

"Fragments for Fall" (Salinas), **Supp. XIII:** 320–321

"Fragments of a Hologram Rose" (W. Gibson), **Supp. XVI:** 122, 123, 128

"Fragments of a Liquidation" (Howe), **Supp. IV Part 2:** 426

"Fragments: On Dentistry" (Monson), **Supp. XXIV:** 236

Fragonard, Jean Honoré, **III:** 275; **IV:** 79

Fraiman, Susan, **Supp. IV Part 1:** 324

"Frame" (Rich), **Retro. Supp. III:** 249

"Frame for Poetry, A" (W. J. Smith), **Supp. XIII:** 333

France, Anatole, **IV:** 444; **Supp. I Part 2:** 631; **Supp. XIV:** 79

France and England in North America (Parkman), **Supp. II Part 2:** 596, 600–605, 607, 613–614

Franchere, Hoyt C., **II:** 131

Franchiser, The (Elkin), **Supp. VI: 51–52, 58**

Francini, Antonella, **Supp. XXVI:** 169

Franciosi, Robert, **Supp. XIV:** 283

Francis, Lee, **Supp. IV Part 2:** 499

Francis, Lesley Lee, **Retro. Supp. III:** 95, 107

Francis, Richard, **Supp. XV:** 121

Francis, Robert, **Supp. IX: 75–92**

Francis of Assisi, Saint, **III:** 543; **IV:** 69, 375, 410; **Supp. I Part 2:** 394, 397, 441, 442, 443
Franco, Francisco, **II:** 261
Franco, Harry (pseudonym). *See* Briggs, Charles Frederick
Franconia (Fraser), **Retro. Supp. I:** 136
"Franconia" tales (Abbott), **Supp. I Part 1:** 38
Frank, Anne, **Supp. X:** 149; **Supp. XVII:** 39
Frank, Frederick S., **Retro. Supp. II:** 273
Frank, Harriet, Jr., **Supp. XXV:** 102
Frank, James M., **Supp. XIV:** 1
Frank, Jerome, **Supp. I Part 2:** 645
Frank, Joseph, **II:** 587
Frank, Mary, **Supp. X:** 213
Frank, Robert, **Supp. XI:** 295; **Supp. XII:** 127; **Supp. XIV:** 150
Frank, Sheldon, **Supp. XXII:** 210
Frank, Waldo, **I:** 106, 109, 117, 229, 236, 245, 259, 400; **Retro. Supp. II:** 77, 79, 83; **Retro. Supp. III:** 47, 49, 50; **Supp. IX:** 308, 309, 311, 320; **Supp. XV:** 298; **Supp. XX:** 67–82
Frank, W. L., Jr., **Supp. XVIII:** 77
Frankel, Charles, **III:** 291
Frankel, Haskel, **Supp. I Part 2:** 448
Frankenberg, Lloyd, **I:** 436, 437, 445, 446; **III:** 194
Frankenheimer, John, **Supp. XI:** 343
Frankenstein (film), **Supp. IV Part 1:** 104; **Supp. XVII:** 57
Frankenstein (Gardner), **Supp. VI:** 72
Frankenstein (Shelley), **Supp. XII:** 79
Frankfurter, Felix, **I:** 489
"Frankie" (Keillor), **Supp. XVI:** 167
Frankie and Johnnie (Levin), **Supp. XXVII:** 134, 139
Frankie and Johnny (film), **Supp. XIII:** 206
Frankie and Johnny in the Clair de Lune (McNally), **Supp. XIII: 200,** 201
Franklin, Benjamin, **II:** 6, 8, 92, **101–125,** 127, 295, 296, 302, 306; **III:** 74, 90; **IV:** 73, 193; **Retro. Supp. III:** 112, 255; **Supp. I Part 1:** 306; **Supp. I Part 2:** 411, 503, 504, 506, 507, 510, 516, 518, 522, 524, 579, 639; **Supp. VIII:** 202, 205; **Supp. XIII:** 150; **Supp. XIV:** 306; **Supp. XVIII:** 12; **Supp. XX: 284; Supp. XXIV:** 224; **Supp. XXVI:** 83, 84
Franklin, Cynthia, **Supp. IV Part 1:** 332
Franklin, Ruth, **Supp. XVI:** 160
Franklin, R. W., **Retro. Supp. I:** 29, 41, 43, 47
Franklin, Sarah, **II:** 122
Franklin, Temple, **II:** 122
Franklin, Walt, **Supp. XXIII:** 54
Franklin, Wayne, **Supp. XXII:** 205
Franklin, William, **II:** 122; **Supp. I Part 2:** 504
Franklin Evans (Whitman), **Retro. Supp. I:** 393; **Retro. Supp. III:** 300
"Frank O'Connor and *The New Yorker*" (Maxwell), **Supp. VIII:** 172
Frank O'Hara: Poet Among Painters (Perloff), **Supp. XXIII:** 210
Franks, Lucinda, **Supp. XIII:** 12

"Frank Sinatra Has a Cold" (Talese), **Supp. XVII:** 203
"Frank Stanford of the Mulberry Family: An Arkansas Epilogue" (Wright), **Supp. XV:** 339–340
"Franny" (Salinger), **III:** 564, 565–566
Franny and Zooey (Salinger), **III:** 552, 564–567; **IV:** 216; **Supp. XIII:** 263
Franscell, Ron, **Supp. XXII:** 206, 216
Franzen, Jonathan, **Retro. Supp. II:** 279; **Supp. XIX:** 54; **Supp. XX: 83–97; Supp. XXII:** 255; **Supp. XXIV:** 131; **Supp. XXVIII:** 205–206
Fraser, G. S., **Supp. XII:** 128; **Supp. XIV:** 162
Fraser, Joe, **III:** 46
Fraser, Marjorie Frost, **Retro. Supp. I:** 136
Frayn, Michael, **Supp. IV Part 2:** 582
Frazee, E. S., **Supp. I Part 2:** 381
Frazee, Esther Catherine. *See* Lindsay, Mrs. Vachel Thomas (Esther Catherine Frazee)
Frazer, Sir James G., **I:** 135; **II:** 204; **III:** 6–7; **IV:** 70; **Retro. Supp. I:** 80; **Supp. I Part 1:** 18; **Supp. I Part 2:** 541; **Supp. XX:** 117
Frazier, Ian, **Supp. VIII:** 272
Frazier, Kathleen, **Supp. XXI:** 22
"Freak Power in the Rockies" (Thompson), **Supp. XXIV:** 286–287, 292, 293
"Freak Show, The" (Sexton), **Supp. II Part 2:** 695
Freaks: Myths and Images of the Secret Self (Fiedler), **Supp. XIII:** 106, 107
Freckles (film), **Supp. XX:** 223
Freckles (Stratton-Porter), **Supp. XX: 211, 218, 218–219, 222**
Fred Allen Show, **Supp. XXV:** 254
Freddy and Fredericka (Helprin), **Supp. XXV:** 81, 84, 87–88
Freddy's Book (Gardner), **Supp. VI: 72**
Frederic, Harold, **I:** 409; **II: 126–149,** 175, 276, 289; **Retro. Supp. I:** 325; **Supp. XXIV:** 30
"Frederick Douglass" (Dunbar), **Supp. II Part 1:** 197, 199
"Frederick Douglass" (Hayden), **Supp. II Part 1:** 363
Frederick Douglass: Slave, Fighter, Freeman (Bontemps), **Supp. XXII:** 13
Frederick the Great, **II:** 103; **Supp. I Part 2:** 433
Fredrickson, George M., **Supp. I Part 2:** 589
"Free" (O'Hara), **III:** 369
Free, and Other Stories (Dreiser), **Retro. Supp. II:** 104
Free Agents (Apple), **Supp. XVII:** 5–6
Free Air (Lewis), **II:** 441
Freeburg, Christopher, **Retro. Supp. III:** 158
Freedman, David, **Supp. XXV:** 255
Freedman, Monroe H., **Supp. VIII:** 127
Freedman, Richard, **Supp. V:** 244
Freedom (Franzen), **Supp. XXII:** 255
"Freedom" (Larsen), **Supp. XVIII:** 124
"Freedom" (White), **Supp. I Part 2:** 659

"Freedom, New Hampshire" (Kinnell), **Supp. III Part 1:** 238, 239, 251
"Freedom and Discipline" (Carruth), **Supp. XVI:** 50
Freedom Business, The (Nelson), **Supp. XVIII:** 186
Freedom Is the Right to Choose: An Inquiry into the Battle for the American Future (MacLeish), **III:** 3
"Freedom's a Hard-Bought Thing" (Benét), **Supp. XI:** 47, 48
"Freedom's Plow" (Hughes), **Supp. I Part 1:** 346
Free Enterprise (Cliff), **Supp. XXII:** 66–67, **77–78**
"Free Everything" (July), **Supp. XXIV:** 210
"Free Fantasia: Tiger Flowers" (Hayden), **Supp. II Part 1:** 363, 366
"Free Grace at Rose Hill"(Bottoms), **Supp. XXVIII:** 28
Freeing of the Dust, The (Levertov), **Supp. III Part 1:** 281–282
"Free Lance, The" (Mencken), **III:** 104, 105
Free-Lance Pallbearers, The (Reed), **Supp. X:** 240, **242–243,** 244
Freeland (Lane), **Supp. XXII:** 297
Free Life, A (Jin), **Supp. XVIII: 101– 102**
Freeloaders, The (Lacy), **Supp. XV:** 204
"Freely Espousing" (Schuyler), **Supp. XXVII:** 25
"Free Man" (Hughes), **Supp. I Part 1:** 333
Freeman, Chris, **Supp. XIV:** 157, 159
Freeman, Douglas Southall, **Supp. I Part 2:** 486, 493
Freeman, Jan, **Supp. XXVII:** 257, 262
Freeman, Jesse, **Supp. XXVI:** 11
Freeman, John, **Supp. XVIII:** 90
Freeman, Joseph, **II:** 26; **Supp. I Part 2:** 610; **Supp. XXII:** 274, 277; **Supp. XXVIII:** 75
Freeman, Mary E. Wilkins, **II:** 401; **Retro. Supp. II:** 51, 136, 138; **Supp. IX:** 79; **Supp. XXVIII:** 225, 229
Freeman, Morgan, **Supp. XII:** 317
Freeman, Suzanne, **Supp. X:** 83
Free Man, The (Richter), **Supp. XVIII:** 215
"Free Man's Worship, A" (Russell), **Supp. I Part 2:** 522
Freewheelin' Bob Dylan, The (album, Dylan), **Supp. XVIII:** 20, 24, 29
Free Will & Wanton Lust (Silver), **Supp. XXIV:** 265, **267–268,** 270
Freier, Mary, **Supp. XXV:** 197
Freilicher, Jane, **Supp. XV:** 178; **Supp. XXIII:** 209, 210, 212, 217
Freinman, Dorothy, **Supp. IX:** 94
Frémont, John Charles, **Supp. I Part 2:** 486
Fremont-Smith, Eliot, **Supp. XIII:** 263
Fremstad, Olive, **I:** 319; **Retro. Supp. I:** 10
French, Warren, **Supp. XII:** 118–119
French Chef, The (television program), **Supp. XVII:** 89

French Connection, The (film), **Supp. V:** 226

"French Informal Report, The"(Kenny), **Supp. XXIII:** 152

French Leave (X. J. Kennedy), **Supp. XV:** 165

Frenchman Must Die, A (Boyle), **Supp. XXIV:** 62

French Poets and Novelists (James), **II:** 336; **Retro. Supp. I:** 220

"French Scarecrow, The" (Maxwell), **Supp. VIII:** 169, 170

French Ways and Their Meaning (Wharton), **IV:** 319; **Retro. Supp. I:** 378

Freneau, Eleanor Forman (Mrs. Philip Freneau), **Supp. II Part 1:** 266

Freneau, Philip M., **I:** 335; **II:** 295; **Supp. I Part 1:** 124, 125, 127, 145; **Supp. II Part 1:** 65, 253–277

Frenzy (Everett), **Supp. XVIII: 59–60**

Frescoes for Mr. Rockefeller's City (MacLeish), **III:** 14–15

"Fresh Air" (Koch), **Supp. XV:** 181, 185

Fresh Air Fiend: Travel Writings, 1985–2000 (Theroux), **Supp. VIII:** 325

Fresh Brats (X. J. Kennedy), **Supp. XV:** 163

"Freshman" (Sanders), **Supp. XVI:** 277

"Freshman at Harvard, A"(column, Gold), **Supp. XXVIII:** 68

Freud, Sigmund, **I:** 55, 58, 59, 66, 67, 135, 241, 242, 244, 247, 248, 283; **II:** 27, 370, 546–547; **III:** 134, 390, 400, 418, 488; **IV:** 7, 70, 138, 295; **Retro. Supp. I:** 80, 176, 253; **Retro. Supp. II:** 104; **Supp. I Part 1:** 13, 43, 253, 254, 259, 260, 265, 270, 315; **Supp. I Part 2:** 493, 527, 616, 643, 647, 649; **Supp. IV Part 2:** 450; **Supp. IX:** 102, 155, 161, 308; **Supp. VIII:** 103, 196; **Supp. X:** 193, 194; **Supp. XII:** 14–15; **Supp. XIII:** 75; **Supp. XIV:** 83; **Supp. XV:** 219; **Supp. XVI:** 157–158, 161, 292; **Supp. XXII:** 165, 198; **Supp. XXVIII:** 145, 158

"Freud and Literature" (Trilling), **Supp. III Part 2:** 502–503

Freudenberger, Nell, **Supp. XXV:** 149

Freudian Psychology and Veblen's Social Theory, The (Schneider), **Supp. I Part 2:** 650

Freudian Wish and Its Place in Ethics, The (Holt), **I:** 59

"Freud in Turpentine" (Slaughter), **Retro. Supp. III:** 134

"Freud's Room" (Ozick), **Supp. V:** 268

Freud: The Mind of the Moralist (Sontag and Rieff), **Supp. III Part 2:** 455

"Freud: Within and Beyond Culture" (Trilling), **Supp. III Part 2:** 508

Frey, Charles, **Supp. XXII:** 301

Frey, Hillary, **Supp. XIX:** 55; **Supp. XXII:** 53

Frey, James, **Supp. XXII:** 95; **Supp. XXIII:** 109; **Supp. XXIV:** 230, 236

"Friday Morning Trial of Mrs. Solano, The" (Ríos), **Supp. IV Part 2:** 538, 548

Friebert, Stuart, **Supp. XIX:** 276

Frieburger, William, **Supp. XIII:** 239

Friede, Donald, **Supp. XVII:** 85, 86, 87, 90

Friedenberg, Edgar Z., **Supp. VIII:** 240

Friedman, Bruce Jay, **I:** 161; **Supp. IV Part 1:** 379

Friedman, Lawrence S., **Supp. V:** 273

Friedman, Milton, **Supp. I Part 2:** 648

Friedman, Norman, **I:** 431–432, 435, 439

Friedman, Stan, **Supp. XII:** 186

Friedmann, Georges, **Supp. I Part 2:** 645

"Fried Sausage" (Simic), **Supp. VIII:** 270

Friend, Julius, **Retro. Supp. I:** 80

Friend, The (Coleridge), **II:** 10

"Friend Husband's Latest" (Sayre), **Retro. Supp. I:** 104

"Friendly Debate between a Conformist and a Non-Conformist, A" (Wild), **IV:** 155

"Friendly Neighbor" (Keillor), **Supp. XVI:** 172

Friendly Way, The (Brainard), **Supp. XXVII:** 20

Friend of My Youth (Munro), **Supp. XXVII:** 190–191

"Friend of My Youth" (Munro), **Supp. XXVII:** 190

Friend of the Earth, A (Boyle), **Supp. VIII:** 12, 16; **Supp. XX: 29–30**

"Friend of the Fourth Decade, The" (Merrill), **Supp. III Part 1:** 327

"Friends" (Beattie), **Supp. V:** 23, 27

"Friends" (Paley), **Supp. VI:** 219, 226

"Friends" (Sexton), **Supp. II Part 2:** 693

Friend's Delight, The (Bierce), **I:** 195

"Friends from Philadelphia" (Updike), **Retro. Supp. I:** 319

"Friendship" (Emerson), **Supp. II Part 1:** 290; **Supp. XXV:** 250

Friends: More Will and Magna Stories (Dixon), **Supp. XII:** 148, 149

"Friends of Heraclitus, The" (Simic), **Supp. VIII:** 284

"Friends of Kafka, The" (Singer), **Retro. Supp. II:** 308

"Friends of the Family, The" (McCarthy), **II:** 566

"Friend to Alexander, A" (Thurber), **Supp. I Part 2:** 616

"Frigate Pelican, The" (Moore), **III:** 208, 210–211, 215

Frightened Wife, The (Rinehart), **Supp. XXV:** 198, 200

"Frill, The" (Buck), **Supp. XIV:** 274

"Fringe, The" (Bass), **Supp. XVI:** 19

Frings, Ketti, **Supp. XXV:** 95

Frobenius, Leo, **III:** 475; **Supp. III Part 2:** 620

Froebel, Friedrich, **Supp. XIV:** 52–53

Frog (Dixon), **Supp. XII:** 151

"Frog Dances" (Dixon), **Supp. XII:** 151

"Frog Pond, The" (Kinnell), **Supp. III Part 1:** 254

"Frogs" (Nelson), **Supp. XVIII:** 176

"Frog Takes a Swim" (Dixon), **Supp. XII:** 152

Frohock, W. M., **I:** 34, 42

Frolic of His Own, A (Gaddis), **Supp. IV Part 1:** 279, 291, 292–294; **Supp. XX: 91**

Frieburger, William, **Supp. XIII:** 239

From a Broken Bottle Traces of Perfume Still Emanate (Mackey), **Supp. XXVII:** 151, 157–159

"From a Mournful Village" (Jewett), **Retro. Supp. II:** 146

"From an Alabama Farm" (Nelson), **Supp. XVIII:** 182

"From an Old House in America" (Rich), **Supp. I Part 2:** 551, 565–567

From Another World (Untermeyer), **Supp. XV:** 293, 303, 310–311, 313

"From a Phrase of Simone Weil's and Some Words of Hegel's" (Oppen), **Supp. XXVI:** 236

"From a Roadside Motel" (F. Wright), **Supp. XVII:** 245

"From a Survivor" (Rich), **Supp. I Part 2:** 563

From A to Z (musical review; Allen), **Supp. XV:** 3, 13

From a Work in Progress (Notley), **Supp. XXII:** 232

"From a Work in Progress" (Notley), **Supp. XXII:** 232

From a Writer's Notebook (Brooks), **I:** 254

From Bauhaus to Our House (Wolfe), **Supp. III Part 2:** 580, 581, 584

From Bondage (H. Roth), **Supp. IX:** 236, **238–240**

"From *Chants* to *Borders* to *Communion*" (Fox), **Supp. XIII:** 217, 217–218

"From Chicago" (Anderson), **I:** 108–109

From Colony to Nation: Women Activists and the Gendering of Politics in Belize, 1912–1982 (Macpherson), **Supp. XXIII:** 84

From Death to Morning (Wolfe), **IV:** 450, 456, 458

"From Dick to Lethem: The Dickian Legacy, Postmodernism, and Avant-Pop in Jonathan Lethem's *Amnesia Moon*" (Rossi), **Supp. XVIII:** 137, 138–139

"From Discord, a Wife Makes a Nice New Life—Too Nice" (Linfield), **Supp. XVII:** 177

From Down to the Village (Budbill), **Supp. XIX: 6–7**

"From Feathers to Iron" (Kunitz), **Supp. III Part 1:** 261

"From Fifth Avenue Up" (Barnes), **Supp. III Part 1:** 33, 44

"From Gorbunov and Gorchakov" (Brodsky), **Supp. VIII:** 26

"From Grand Canyon to Burbank" (H. Miller), **III:** 186

"From Hell to Breakfast", **Supp. IX:** 326–327

From Here to Eternity (film), **Supp. XI:** 221

From Here to Eternity (J. Jones), **I:** 477; **Supp. XI:** 215, 216, 217, 218, **219–221**, 223, 224, 226, 229, 230, 231, 232, 234; **Supp. XIX:** 248; **Supp. XX: 248; Supp. XXII:** 140

From Here to Eternity (miniseries), **Supp. XI:** 234

From Jordan's Delight (Blackmur), **Supp. II Part 1:** 91

"From Lumaghi Mine" (Wrigley), **Supp. XVIII:** 295

Fromm, Erich, **I:** 58; **Supp. VIII:** 196

"From Mars"(Prouty), **Supp. XXVIII:** 180

From Morn to Midnight (Kaiser), **I:** 479

"From Native Son to Invisible Man" (Locke), **Supp. IX:** 306

"From Pico, the Women: A Life" (Creeley), **Supp. IV Part 1:** 149

"From Plane to Plane" (Frost), **Retro. Supp. III:** 105

From Plotzk to Boston (Antin), **Supp. XX:** 2

From Ritual to Romance (Weston), **II:** 540; **III:** 12; **Supp. I Part 2:** 439

From Room to Room (Kenyon), **Supp. VII:** 163–165, 166, 167

"From Room to Room" (Kenyon), **Supp. VII:** 159, 163–165

From Sand Creek: Rising in this Heart Which Is Our America (Ortiz), **Supp. IV Part 2:** 512–513

"From Sea Cliff, March" (Swenson), **Supp. IV Part 2:** 649

From Stone Orchard: A Collection of Memories (Findley), **Supp. XX: 57**

"From the Antigone" (Yeats), **III:** 459

From the Ashes: Voices of Watts (Schulberg, ed.), **Supp. XVIII:** 254

From the Barrio: A Chicano Anthology (Salinas and Faderman, eds.), **Supp. XIII:** 313

From the Beginning (Notley), **Supp. XXII:** 226, 235–236

From the Briarpatch File: On Context, Procedure, and American Identity (Murray), **Supp. XIX:** 161

"From the Childhood of Jesus" (Pinsky), **Supp. VI:** 244–245, 247

"From the Corpse Woodpiles, From the Ashes" (Hayden), **Supp. II Part 1:** 370

"From the Country to the City" (Bishop), **Supp. I Part 1:** 85, 86

"From the Cupola" (Merrill), **Supp. III Part 1:** 324–325, 331

"From the Dark Side of the Earth" (Oates), **Supp. II Part 2:** 510

"From the Diary of a New York Lady" (Parker), **Supp. IX:** 201

"From the Diary of One Not Born" (Singer), **IV:** 9

"From the Dreams" (Notley), **Supp. XXII:** 224

"From the East, Light" (Carver), **Supp. III Part 1:** 138

From the First Nine: Poems 1946–1976 (Merrill), **Supp. III Part 1:** 336

"From the Flats" (Lanier), **Supp. I Part 1:** 364

From the Flower Courtyard (Everwine), **Supp. XV:** 75

From the Heart of Europe (Matthiessen), **III:** 310

From the Meadow: Selected and New Poems (Everwine), **Supp. XV:** 75, **88–89**

"From the Memoirs of a Private Detective" (Hammett), **Supp. IV Part 1:** 343

From the Notebooks of Melanin Sun (Woodson), **Supp. XXVIII:** 280, 281

"From the Nursery" (Kenyon), **Supp. VII:** 171

"From the Poets in the Kitchen" (Marshall), **Supp. XI:** 277

"From the Reservation to *Dawn of the Dead* to James Dickey and Back Again" (Gansworth), **Supp. XXVI:** 113

From the Terrace (O'Hara), **III:** 362

"From the Thirties: Tillie Olsen and the Radical Tradition" (Rosenfelt), **Supp. XIII:** 296, 304

From the Western Door to the Lower West Side (Gansworth and Rogovin), **Supp. XXVI:** 112

"From Trollope's Journal" (Bishop), **Retro. Supp. II:** 47

"Front, A" (Jarrell), **II:** 374

Front, The (film), **Supp. I Part 1:** 295

Frontain, Raymond-Jean, **Supp. XXVI:** 242

"Front and the Back Parts of the House, The" (Maxwell), **Supp. VIII:** 169

Frontier Eden (Bigelow), **Supp. X:** 227

"Frontiers of Culture" (Locke), **Supp. XIV:** 213

"Front Lines" (Snyder), **Supp. VIII:** 301

Front Page, The (Hecht and MacArthur), **Supp. XXVII:** 83, 89–90, 96

Front Porch (Inge), **Supp. XXV:** 94

Front Runner, The (P. N. Warren), **Supp. XX:** 259, 262–264

Frost, A. B., **Retro. Supp. II:** 72

Frost, Carol, **Supp. XV: 91–109**

Frost, Elisabeth, **Supp. XXVII:** 171

Frost, Isabelle Moodie, **II:** 150, 151

Frost, Jeanie, **II:** 151

Frost, Richard, **Supp. XV:** 92

Frost, Robert, **I:** 26, 27, 60, 63, 64, 171, 229, 303, 326, 418; **II:** 55, 58, **150–172,** 276, 289, 388, 391, 471, 523, 527, 529, 535; **III:** 5, 23, 67, 269, 271, 272, 275, 287, 453, 510, 523, 536, 575, 581, 591; **IV:** 140, 190, 415; **Retro. Supp. I:** 67, **121–144,** 276, 287, 292, 298, 299, 311, 413; **Retro. Supp. II:** 40, 47, 50, 146, 178, 181; **Retro. Supp. III: 91–108,** 251; **Supp. I Part 1:** 80, 242, 263, 264; **Supp. I Part 2:** 387, 461, 699; **Supp. I Part 1:** 4, 19, 26, 103; **Supp. III Part 1:** 63, 74–75, 239, 253; **Supp. III Part 2:** 546, 592, 593; **Supp. IV Part 1:** 15; **Supp. IV Part 2:** 439, 445, 447, 448, 599, 601; **Supp. IX:** 41, 42, 75, 76, 80, 87, 90, 266, 308; **Supp. VIII:** 20, 30, 32, 98, 100, 104, 259, 292; **Supp. X:** 64, 65, 66, 74, 120, 172; **Supp. XI:** 43, 123, 150, 153, 312; **Supp. XII:** 130, 241, 303, 307; **Supp. XIII:** 143, 147, 334–335; **Supp. XIV:** 42, 122, 222, 229; **Supp. XIX:** 1, 123; **Supp. XV:** 21, 51, 65, 96, 212, 215, 250, 256, 293, 296, 299, 301, 302, 306, 348; **Supp. XVII:** 36, 110, 115–116; **Supp. XVIII:** 298, 300; **Supp. XX: 69, 199; Supp. XXI:** 19, 28, 51, 99, 104, 107, 205; **Supp. XXII:** 206; **Supp. XXIII:** 79, 145; **Supp. XXIV:** 159; **Supp. XXV:** 222; **Supp. XXVI:** 61, 62, 63, 65, 67, 164; **Supp. XXVII:** 217, 218, 219, 283, 290; **Supp. XXVIII:** 131

Frost, William Prescott, **II:** 150–151

"Frost: A Dissenting Opinion" (Cowley), **Supp. II Part 1:** 143

Frost: A Time to Talk (Francis), **Supp. IX:** 76, **85–86**

"Frost at Midnight" (Coleridge), **Supp. X:** 71

"Frost Flowers" (Kenyon), **Supp. VII:** 168

"Frost: He Is Sometimes a Poet and Sometimes a Stump-Speaker" (News-Week), **Retro. Supp. I:** 137

Frothingham, Nathaniel, **I:** 3

Frothingham, Octavius B., **IV:** 173

"Frozen City, The" (Nemerov), **III:** 270

"Frozen Fields, The" (Bowles), **Supp. IV Part 1:** 80

"Frozen Ship, The" (Very), **Supp. XXV:** 243

Frucht, Abby, **Supp. XXVI:** 156

"Fructifying a Cycle: Homage to Alan Ansen"(Hadas), **Supp. XXIII:** 123

"Fruit Garden Path, The" (A. Lowell), **II:** 516

"Fruit of the Flower" (Cullen), **Supp. IV Part 1:** 167

Fruit of the Tree, The (Wharton), **IV:** 314–315; **Retro. Supp. I:** 367, **370–371,** 373

"Fruit of Travel Long Ago" (Melville), **III:** 93

Fruits and Vegetables (Jong), **Supp. V:** 113, 115, 117, 118, 119

"Fruits of the Sea, The" (Di Piero), **Supp. XIX:** 47

Frumkes, Lewis Burke, **Supp. XII:** 335–336

Fry, Christopher, **Supp. I Part 1:** 270

Fry, Roger, **Supp. XIV:** 336

Fry, Stephen M., **Supp. XIX:** 159

Frye, Joanne, **Supp. XIII:** 292, 296, 298, 302

Frye, Northrop, **Supp. I Part 2:** 530; **Supp. II Part 1:** 101; **Supp. X:** 80; **Supp. XIII:** 19; **Supp. XIV:** 11, 15; **Supp. XVI:** 149, 156; **Supp. XX: 50; Supp. XXIII:** 42

Fryer, Judith, **Retro. Supp. I:** 379

F. Scott Fitzgerald: A Critical Portrait (Piper), **Supp. IX:** 65

"F. S. F., 1896–1996, R.I.P." (Doctorow), **Retro. Supp. I:** 97

Fuchs, Daniel, **Supp. XIII:** 106; **Supp. XXVII:** 134

Fuchs, Miriam, **Supp. IV Part 1:** 284

Fuehrer Bunker, The (Snodgrass), **Supp. VI:** 314, 315–317, 319–321

Fuel (Nye), **Supp. XIII:** 277, **282–284**

"Fuel" (Nye), **Supp. XIII:** 283

Fuertes, Gloria, **Supp. V:** 178

Fugard, Athol, **Retro. Supp. III:** 318; **Supp. VIII:** 330; **Supp. XIII:** 205

Fugitive Group, The (Cowan), **IV:** 120
Fugitive Kind, The (T. Williams), **IV:** 381, 383
Fugitives, The (group), **IV:** 122, 124, 125, 131, 237, 238
Fugitives, The: A Critical Account (Bradbury), **IV:** 130
"Fugitive Slave Law, The" (Emerson), **II:** 13
Fugitive's Return (Glaspell), **Supp. III Part 1:** 182–184
"Fulfillment" (H. Johnson), **Supp. XXVI:** 164, 173
Fuller, B. A. G., **III:** 605
Fuller, Edmund, **Supp. XXII:** 211, 212
Fuller, Hiram, **Supp. XVIII:** 12,14
Fuller, Jesse "Lonecat", **Supp. XV:** 147
Fuller, Margaret, **I:** 261; **II:** 7, 276; **IV:** 172; **Retro. Supp. I:** 155–156, 163; **Retro. Supp. II:** 46; **Retro. Supp. III:** 122; **Supp. I Part 2:** 524; **Supp. II Part 1:** 279–306; **Supp. IX:** 37; **Supp. XVIII:** 3, 11, 12, 16; **Supp. XXV:** 249
Fuller, Thomas, **II:** 111, 112
Fullerton, Morton, **Retro. Supp. III:** 280, 281–282, 284; **Supp. XX:** 231
Fullerton Street (Wilson), **Supp. VIII:** 331
"Full Fathom Five" (Plath), **Supp. I Part 2:** 538
Full Measure: Modern Short Stories on Aging (D. Sennett, ed.), **Supp. XVI:** 37
Full Monty, The (musical, McNally), **Supp. XIII:** 207
"Full Moon" (Hayden), **Supp. II Part 1:** 370
Full Moon and Other Plays (Price), **Supp. VI:** 266
"Full Moon and You're Not Here" (Cisneros), **Supp. VII:** 71–72
"Full Moon: New Guinea" (Shapiro), **Supp. II Part 2:** 707
"Fullness of Life, The" (Wharton), **Retro. Supp. I:** 363
Full of Life (Fante), **Supp. XI:** 160
Full of Life (film), **Supp. XI:** 170
Full of Lust and Good Usage (Dunn), **Supp. XI: 145–147**
Full Speed Ahead: Tales from the Log of a Correspondent with Our Navy (Beston), **Supp. XXVI:** 33
"Full Summer" (Olds), **Supp. X:** 212
Fulton, Ben, **Supp. XXII:** 207
Fulton, Joe B., **Retro. Supp. III:** 266
Fulton, Robert, **Supp. I Part 2:** 519; **Supp. II Part 1:** 73
Fun and Games (Major), **Supp. XXII:** 180
Funaroff, Sol, **Supp. XXVI:** 143
"Functional Poem" (Halliday), **Supp. XIX:** 85
Function of Criticism, The (Winters), **Supp. II Part 2:** 812, 813
"Fundamentalism" (Tate), **IV:** 125
"Fundamental Project of Technology, The" (Kinnell), **Supp. III Part 1:** 253
"Funeral of Bobò, The" (Brodsky), **Supp. VIII:** 27, 28

Fungi from Yuggoth (Lovecraft), **Supp. XXV:** 119–120
Fun Home: A Family Tragicomic (Bechdel), **Supp. XXV:** 1, 4–9
Funiculi-Funicula (Wellman), **Supp. XXV:** 20
Funkhouser, Christopher, **Supp. XXVII:** 151
"Funnel" (Sexton), **Supp. II Part 2:** 675
Fun to Be Free (Hecht and MacArthur), **Supp. XXVII:** 90
"Furious Seasons, The" (Carver), **Supp. III Part 1:** 137
Furious Seasons and Other Stories (Carver), **Supp. III Part 1:** 142, 143, 146
"Furious Versions" (L.-Y. Lee), **Supp. XV: 215–217**, 218, **220**
Furman, Jan, **Retro. Supp. III:** 187
"Furnished Room, The" (Hayden), **Supp. II Part 1:** 386–387, 394, 397, 399, 406, 408
"Furor Scribendi" (O. Butler), **Supp. XIII:** 70
Furors Die (Hoffman), **Supp. XVIII: 80–81**
Fur Person, The (Sarton), **Supp. VIII: 264–265**
Further Adventures with You (Wright), **Supp. XV:** 339, 342, **343–345**
Further Fables for Our Time (Thurber), **Supp. I Part 2:** 612
"Further in Summer than the Birds" (Dickinson), **I:** 471
Further Poems of Emily Dickinson (Bianchi and Hampson, ed.), **Retro. Supp. I:** 35
Further Range, A (Frost), **II:** 155; **Retro. Supp. I:** 132, 136, 137, 138, 139; **Retro. Supp. III:** 103, 104
Furthman, Charles, **Supp. XXVII:** 92
"Fury, The (Skloot), **Supp. XX: 197**
"Fury of Aerial Bombardment, The" (Eberhart), **I:** 535–536
"Fury of Flowers and Worms, The" (Sexton), **Supp. II Part 2:** 694
"Fury of Rain Storms, The" (Sexton), **Supp. II Part 2:** 695
Fury of the Jungle (film), **Supp. XIII:** 163
Fussell, Paul, **Supp. V:** 241
Fussell, Paul K., **Supp. XXV:** 253
"Futility" (H. Johnson), **Supp. XXVI:** 167, 172
"Future, if Any, of Comedy, The" (Thurber), **Supp. I Part 2:** 620
Future, The (album, Cohen), **Supp. XXVII:** 54
"Future, The" (Cohen), **Supp. XXVII:** 62
Future, The (film, July), **Supp. XXIV:** 199, 200, 202, **209**, 210
Future in the Present, The (C. L. R. James), **Supp. XXI:** 172
Future is Ours, Comrade, The: Conversations with the Russians (Kosinski), **Supp. VII:** 215
Futureland: Nine Stories of an Imminent World (Mosley), **Supp. XIII: 247–249**

"Future Life, The" (Bryant), **Supp. I Part 1:** 170
Future of Southern Letters, The (J. W. Miller), **Supp. XX:** 161
Future of the Race, The (H. L. Gates), **Supp. XX: 101, 104, 111**
Future Punishment of the Wicked, The (Edwards), **I:** 546

G

"Gabriel" (Rich), **Supp. I Part 2:** 557
Gabriel, Ralph H., **Supp. I Part 1:** 251
Gabriel, Trip, **Supp. V:** 212
Gabriel Conroy (Harte), **Supp. II Part 1:** 354
"Gabriel's Truth" (Kenyon), **Supp. VII:** 166
Gaddis, William, **Supp. IV Part 1: 279–296; Supp. IV Part 2:** 484; **Supp. IX:** 208; **Supp. V:** 52; **Supp. X:** 301, 302; **Supp. XX: 83, 91; Supp. XXI:** 226; **Supp. XXIII:** 107
Gadiot, Pud, **Supp. XI:** 295
Gaily, Gaily (film), **Supp. XXVII:** 95
Gaily, Gaily (Hecht), **Supp. XXVII:** 95
Gain (Powers), **Supp. IX:** 212, **220–221**
Gaines, Ernest J., **Supp. X:** 24, 250
Gaines, James R., **Supp. IX:** 190
Gainor, J. Ellen, **Supp. XXI:** 6
Gaitens, Peter, **Supp. XV:** 65
Gajarsa, Arthur, **Supp. XXVI:** 83
Galamain, Ivan, **Supp. III Part 2:** 624
Galassi, Jonathan, **Supp. XIX:** 34; **Supp. XVIII:** 92; **Supp. XXII:** 177
Galatea 2.2 (Powers), **Supp. IX:** 212, **219–220**
"Galatea Encore" (Brodsky), **Supp. VIII:** 31
Galbraith, John Kenneth, **Supp. I Part 2:** 645, 650
Galdós, Benito Pérez. *See* Pérez Galdós, Benito
Gale, Zona, **Supp. I Part 2:** 613; **Supp. VIII:** 155
Galehouse, Maggie, **Supp. XXI:** 215
"Gale in April" (Jeffers), **Supp. II Part 2:** 423
Galignani, Giovanni Antonio, **II:** 315
Galileo Galilei, **I:** 480–481; **Supp. XII:** 180; **Supp. XIII:** 75
Gallagher, Tess, **Supp. XVI:** 36; **Supp. XVII:** 110; **Supp. XXI:** 246; **Supp. XXIV: 165–181**
Gallant, Mavis, **Supp. VIII:** 151
"Gallant Fireman, A" (Twain), **Retro. Supp. III:** 256
Gallatin, Albert, **I:** 5
"Gallery" (Goldbarth), **Supp. XII:** 188
"Gallery of Real Creatures, A" (Thurber), **Supp. I Part 2:** 619
Gallico, Paul, **Supp. XVI:** 238
Gallows Songs (Snodgrass), **Supp. VI:** 317
Gallup, Dick, **Supp. XXIV:** 34, 35, 39, 44; **Supp. XXVII:** 18, 22, 23
Gallup, Donald, **III:** 404, 478
"Galop" (Davison), **Supp. XXVI:** 71
Galsworthy, John, **III:** 70, 153, 382

Galton Case, The (Macdonald), **Supp. IV Part 2:** 463, 473, 474

Galvin, Frances, **Supp. XXI:** 5

"Gal Young 'Un" (Rawlings), **Supp. X:** 228

Gambino, Richard, **Supp. XX: 35**

"Gambler, the Nun, and the Radio, The" (Hemingway), **II:** 250

"Gambler's Wife, The" (Dunbar), **Supp. II Part 1:** 196

Gambone, Philip, **Supp. XII:** 81

"Gambrel Roof, A" (Larcom), **Supp. XIII:** 144

Game, The (Bryant), **Supp. XXVIII:** 37, 38, 39

"Game at Salzburg, A" (Jarrell), **II:** 384, 389

Game Management (Leopold), **Supp. XIV:** 182

"Game of Catch, A" (Wilbur), **Supp. III Part 2:** 552

Game Players of Titan, The (Dick), **Supp. XVIII:** 138

"Games in Frank Conroy's *Stop-Time*" (T. Adams), **Supp. XVI:** 67

"Games Two" (Wilbur), **Supp. III Part 2:** 550

Gammelgaard, Lene, **Supp. XVIII:** 112

"Gamut, The" (Angelou), **Supp. IV Part 1:** 15

Gander, Forrest, **Supp. XV:** 339, 340, 342

Gandhi, Indira, **Supp. X:** 108

Gandhi, Mahatma, **III:** 179, 296–297; **IV:** 170, 185, 367; **Supp. VIII:** 203, 204; **Supp. X:** 27; **Supp. XXVIII:** 57

Gandhi on Non-Violence (Merton, ed.), **Supp. VIII:** 204–205

Gangemi, Merry, **Supp. XXV:** 6

Gang of Five: Leaders at the Center of the Conservative Crusade (Easton), **Supp. XIX:** 137

"Gang of Mirrors, The" (Simic), **Supp. VIII:** 283

Gannett, Ezra Stiles, **Supp. XXIV:** 74

Gansevoort, Guert, **III:** 94

Gansevoort, Peter, **III:** 92

Gansworth, Eric, **Supp. XXVI: 101–116**

"Gap" (Bierds), **Supp. XVII:** 35–36

Garabedian, Michael, **Supp. XIII:** 115

Garbage (Ammons), **Supp. VII:** 24, 35–36

Garbage (Dixon), **Supp. XII:** 147, 148

Garbage Man, The (Dos Passos), **I:** 478, 479, 481, 493

Garber, Frederick, **Supp. IX:** 294–295

Garbo, Greta, **Supp. I Part 2:** 616

García, Cristina, **Supp. VIII:** 74; **Supp. XI: 177–192**

García Lorca, Federico. *See* Lorca, Federico García

"García Lorca: A Photograph of the Granada Cemetery, 1966" (Levis), **Supp. XI:** 264

García Márquez, Gabriel, **Supp. V:** 244; **Supp. VIII:** 81, 82, 84, 85; **Supp. XII:** 147, 310, 316, 322; **Supp. XIII:** 226; **Supp. XVII:** 45; **Supp. XXIV:** 86, 89, 190; **Supp. XXV:** 49, 69

Gard, Claire, **Supp. XXIII:** 94

Gardaphe, Fred, **Supp. XX: 38, 41**

"Garden" (Marvell), **IV:** 161; **Supp. XVI:** 204

"Garden, The" (Glück), **Supp. V:** 83

"Garden, The" (Strand), **Supp. IV Part 2:** 629

"Garden, The" (Very), **Supp. XXV:** 248

"Garden Among Tombs" (B. Kelly), **Supp. XVII:** 126

"Garden by Moonlight, The" (A. Lowell), **II:** 524

"Gardener Delivers a Fawn, The" (C. Frost), **Supp. XV:** 99

Gardener's Son, The (McCarthy), **Supp. VIII:** 187

Garden God, The: A Tale of Two Boys (Reid), **Supp. XX:** 235

"Gardenias" (Doty), **Supp. XI:** 122

"Gardenias" (Monette), **Supp. X:** 159

"Garden Lodge, The" (Cather), **I:** 316, 317; **Retro. Supp. III:** 26

Garden of Adonis, The (Gordon), **II:** 196, 204–205, 209

Garden of Earthly Delights, A (Oates), **Supp. II Part 2:** 504, 507–509

Garden of Earthly Delights, The (Bosch), **Supp. XXII:** 255, 261

"Garden of Eden" (Hemingway), **II:** 259

Garden of Eden, The (Hemingway), **Retro. Supp. I:** 186, **187–188**

"Garden of Flesh, Garden of Stone" (B. Kelly), **Supp. XVII:** 128

Garden of Last Days, The (Dubus III), **Supp. XXIV:** 101, **107–108**

"Garden of the Moon, The" (Doty), **Supp. XI:** 122

Garden of the Prophet, The (Gibran), **Supp. XX: 119, 122**

"Garden of the Trumpet Tree, The" (B. Kelly), **Supp. XVII:** 131

"Gardens, The" (Oliver), **Supp. VII:** 236

"Gardens of Mont-Saint-Michel, The" (Maxwell), **Supp. VIII:** 169

"Gardens of the Villa D'Este, The" (Hecht), **Supp. X:** 59

"Gardens of Zuñi, The" (Merwin), **Supp. III Part 1:** 351

Garden Thieves, The: Twentieth Century African-American Poetry (Major, ed.), **Supp. XXII:** 172

Gardiner, Judith Kegan, **Supp. IV Part 1:** 205

Gardner, Erle Stanley, **Supp. IV Part 1:** 121, 345

Gardner, Isabella, **IV:** 127

Gardner, John, **Supp. I Part 1:** 193, 195, 196; **Supp. III Part 1:** 136, 142, 146; **Supp. VI: 61–76; Supp. XXV:** 152

Gardner, Thomas, **Supp. XXI:** 214

Gardner, Virginia, **Supp. XXVIII:** 43, 46

Gardons, S. S. *See* Snodgrass, W. D.

"Gare de Lyon" (M. F. K. Fisher), **Supp. XVII:** 91

Garfield, John, **Supp. XII:** 160

Gargoyles (Hecht), **Supp. XXVII:** 88

Garibaldi, Giuseppe, **I:** 4; **II:** 284

Garibay, Angel M., **Supp. XV:** 77

Garland, Hamlin, **I:** 407; **II:** 276, 289; **III:** 576; **Retro. Supp. I:** 133; **Retro. Supp. II:** 72; **Supp. I Part 1:** 217; **Supp. IV Part 2:** 502; **Supp. XVIII:** 6

Garland Companion, The (Zverev), **Retro. Supp. I:** 278

"Garments" (Gibran), **Supp. XX: 124**

Garments the Living Wear (Purdy), **Supp. VII:** 278–279, 280–281

Garner, Dwight, **Supp. X:** 202; **Supp. XVIII:** 89; **Supp. XXV:** 9

Garnett, Edward, **I:** 405, 409, 417; **III:** 27; **Retro. Supp. III:** 98; **Supp. XXVIII:** 119

Garrett, George P., **Supp. I Part 1:** 196; **Supp. VII: 95–113; Supp. X:** 3, 7; **Supp. XI:** 218; **Supp. XVIII:** 74, 75; **Supp. XXVI:** 153, 157

Garrigue, Jean, **Supp. XII:** 260

Garrison, Deborah, **Supp. IX:** 299

Garrison, Fielding, **III:** 105

Garrison, William Lloyd, **Supp. I Part 2:** 524, 588, 683, 685, 686, 687; **Supp. XIV:** 54; **Supp. XXIV:** 77; **Supp. XXVIII:** 173

"Garrison of Cape Ann, The" (Whittier), **Supp. I Part 2:** 691, 694

Garry Moore Show (television show), **Supp. IV Part 2:** 575

"Garter Motif" (White), **Supp. I Part 2:** 673

Gartner, Zsuzsi, **Supp. X:** 276

Garvey, Marcus, **Supp. III Part 1:** 175, 180; **Supp. IV Part 1:** 168; **Supp. X:** 135, 136; **Supp. XXI:** 166, 168; **Supp. XXII:** 7

Garvin, Viola, **Supp. XXVII:** 118

Gas (Kaiser), **I:** 479

Gas-House McGinty (Farrell), **II:** 41–42

Gaskell, Elizabeth, A., **Supp. I Part 2:** 580

Gasoline (Corso), **Supp. XII:** 118, **121–123**, 134

Gasoline Wars, The (Thompson), **Supp. XXIII:** 290

"Gasoline Wars, The" (Thompson), **Supp. XXIII:** 291

Gass, William H., **Supp. IX:** 208; **Supp. V:** 44, 52, 238; **Supp. VI: 77–96; Supp. XII:** 152; **Supp. XIV:** 305; **Supp. XVII:** 183

"Gassire's Lute: Robert Duncan's Vietnam War Poems" (Mackey), **Supp. XXVII:** 160

Gassner, John, **IV:** 381; **Supp. I Part 1:** 284, 292

"Gas Stations" (Apple), **Supp. XVII:** 4

Gastronomical Me, The (M. F. K. Fisher), **Supp. XVII:** 84, 85, 87, 91, 92

Gates, David, **Supp. V:** 24; **Supp. XIII:** 93; **Supp. XVI:** 73, 74; **Supp. XX: 92**

Gates, Elmer, **I:** 515–516

Gates, Henry Louis, Jr., **Retro. Supp. I:** 194, 195, 203; **Retro. Supp. III:** 130; **Supp. X:** 242, 243, 245, 247; **Supp. XIX:** 147, 149; **Supp. XVIII:** 287; **Supp. XX: 99–112, 279, 286; Supp. XXIV:** 192; **Supp. XXVI:** 13

Gates, Lewis E., **III:** 315, 330

Gates, Sondra Smith, **Supp. XVIII:** 267, 269

Gates, The (Rukeyser), **Supp. VI:** 271, 274, 281
"Gates, The" (Rukeyser), **Supp. VI:** 286
Gates, Tudor, **Supp. XI:** 307
Gates of Ivory, the Gates of Horn, The (McGrath), **Supp. X:** 118
Gates of Wrath, The; Rhymed Poems (Ginsberg), **Supp. II Part 1:** 311, 319
"Gathering" (Trethewey), **Supp. XXI:** 249
Gathering Forces, The (C. L. R. James), **Supp. XXI:** 171
"Gathering of Dissidents, A" (Applebaum), **Supp. XVI:** 153
Gathering of Fugitives, A (Trilling), **Supp. III Part 2:** 506, 512
Gathering of Zion, The: The Story of the Mormon Trail (Stegner), **Supp. IV Part 2:** 599, 602–603
Gather Together in My Name (Angelou), **Supp. IV Part 1:** 2, 3, 4–6, 11
Gathorne-Hardy, Robert, **Supp. XIV:** 344, 347, 348, 349
Gaudier-Brzeska, Henri, **III:** 459, 464, 465, 477
Gaughran, Richard, **Supp. XXI:** 47–48
Gauguin, Paul, **I:** 34; **IV:** 290; **Supp. IV Part 1:** 81; **Supp. XII:** 128
"Gauguin in Oregon" (Skloot), **Supp. XX: 203**
"Gauley Bridge" (Rukeyser), **Supp. VI:** 278
Gauss, Christian, **II:** 82; **IV:** 427, 439–440, 444
Gauthier, Jacquie, **Supp. XIX:** 204
Gautier, Théophile, **II:** 543; **III:** 466, 467; **Supp. I Part 1:** 277
Gay, John, **II:** 111; **Supp. I Part 2:** 523; **Supp. XIV:** 337
Gay, Peter, **I:** 560
Gay, Sydney Howard, **Supp. I Part 1:** 158; **Supp. XVIII:** 3
Gay, Walter, **IV:** 317
Gayarré, Charles, **Supp. XXVIII:** 112, 117, 124, 125
Gayatri Prayer, The, **III:** 572
Gay Canon, The (Drake), **Supp. XX: 274**
"Gay Chaps at the Bar" (Brooks), **Supp. III Part 1:** 74, 75
" 'Gay Culture': Still of the Wild Frontier" (P. N. Warren), **Supp. XX: 272**
Gaylord, Winfield R., **III:** 579–580
Gay Talese Reader, The: Portraits & Encounters (Talese), **Supp. XVII:** 202, 208
"Gaze, The"(Hadas), **Supp. XXIII:** 120
"Gazebo" (Carver), **Supp. III Part 1:** 138, 144, 145
Gazer's Spirit, The (Hollander), **Supp. XIX:** 121
Gazer Within, The, and Other Essays by Larry Levis, **Supp. XI:** 270
Gazzara, Ben, **Supp. VIII:** 319
Gazzo, Michael V., **III:** 155
"Geas" (Monson), **Supp. XXIV:** 238–239
Geddes, Virgil, **Supp. XXV:** 23
"Geese Flying over Hamilton, New York"(Balakian), **Supp. XXIII:** 24
"Geese Gone Beyond" (Snyder), **Supp. VIII:** 304

Geffen, David, **Supp. XXI:** 154
"Gegenwart" (Goethe), **Supp. II Part 1:** 26
Geisel, Theodor Seuss (Dr. Seuss), **Supp. X:** 56; **Supp. XVI: 97–115**
Geismar, Maxwell, **II:** 178, 431; **III:** 71; **Supp. IX:** 15; **Supp. XI:** 223
Geist, Bill, **Supp. XXIII:** 298
Gelb, Arthur, **IV:** 380; **Supp. XXI:** 12
Gelb, Barbara, **Supp. XXI:** 12; **Supp. XXVIII:** 40
Gelbart, Larry, **Supp. IV Part 2:** 591
Gelder, Robert Van, **Supp. XIII:** 166
Gelfant, Blanche H., **II:** 27, 41; **Supp. XVII:** 161
Gelfman, Jean, **Supp. X:** 3
Gellert, Hugo, **Supp. XXII:** 277
Gellhorn, Martha. *See* Hemingway, Mrs. Ernest (Martha Gellhorn)
Gelpi, Albert, **Retro. Supp. III:** 242, 250; **Supp. I Part 2:** 552, 554, 560
Gelpi, Barbara, **Supp. I Part 2:** 560
Gemin, Pamela, **Supp. XXI:** 246
Gemini (Innaurato), **Supp. XXIV:** 117
Gemini: an extended autobiographical statement on my first twenty-five years of being a black poet (Giovanni), **Supp. IV Part 1:** 11
Gem of the Ocean (Wilson), **Retro. Supp. III:** 321
"Gen" (Snyder), **Supp. VIII:** 302
"Gender Norms" (Radinovsky), **Supp. XV:** 285
"Gender of Sound, The" (Carson), **Supp. XII: 106**
"Genealogies"(Hadas), **Supp. XXIII:** 116
"Genealogy" (Komunyakaa), **Supp. XIII:** 129
"General Aims and Theories" (Crane), **I:** 389
General Died at Dawn, The (Odets), **Supp. II Part 2:** 546
"General Gage's Confession" (Freneau), **Supp. II Part 1:** 257
"General Gage's Soliloquy" (Freneau), **Supp. II Part 1:** 257
General History of the Robberies and Murders of the Most Notorious Pyrates from Their First Rise and Settlement in the Island of New Providence to the Present Year, A (C. Johnson), **Supp. V:** 128
General in His Labyrinth, The (García Márquez), **Supp. XXIV:** 89
"General Returns from One Place to Another, The"(O'Hara), **Supp. XXIII:** 216–217
"General William Booth Enters into Heaven" (Lindsay), **Supp. I Part 2:** 374, 382, 384, 385–388, 389, 392, 399
General William Booth Enters into Heaven and Other Poems (Lindsay), **Supp. I Part 2:** 379, 381, 382, 387–388, 391
"Generation of the Dispossessed" (P. N. Warren), **Supp. XX:** 272
"Generations"(Kenny), **Supp. XXIII:** 154
"Generations of Men, The" (Frost), **Retro. Supp. I:** 128; **Supp. XIII:** 147

Generation Without Farewell (Boyle), **Supp. XXIV:** 60, 62
"Generation Wuss" (Ellis), **Supp. XXVII:** 78, 79
Generous Man, A (Price), **Supp. VI:** 259, 260, 261
Genesis (biblical book), **I:** 279; **II:** 540; **Retro. Supp. I:** 250, 256; **Supp. XII:** 54
"Genesis" (Stegner), **Supp. IV Part 2:** 604
Genesis: Book One (Schwartz), **Supp. II Part 2:** 640, 651–655
Gene Stratton-Porter (Richards), **Supp. XX: 217–218**
Gene Stratton-Porter, Naturalist and Novelist (Long), **Supp. XX:** 212
"Gene Stratton-Porter: Women's Advocate" (Obuchowski), **Supp. XX:** 222
Genet, Jean, **I:** 71, 82, 83, 84; **Supp. IV Part 1:** 8; **Supp. XI:** 308; **Supp. XII:** 1; **Supp. XIII:** 74; **Supp. XVII:** 95; **Supp. XXIII:** 213; **Supp. XXIV:** 210
"Genetic Coding" (Sorrentino), **Supp. XXI:** 227
"Genetic Expedition" (Dove), **Supp. IV Part 1:** 249, 257
"Genetics of Justice" (Alvarez), **Supp. VII:** 19
"Genial Host, The" (McCarthy), **II:** 564
"Genie in the Bottle, The" (Davison), **Supp. XXVI:** 74
"Genie in the Bottle, The" (Wilbur), **Supp. III Part 2:** 542
"Genius, The" (MacLeish), **III:** 19
Genius and Lust: A Journey through the Major Writings of Henry Miller (Mailer), **Retro. Supp. II:** 208
"Genius Child" (Hughes), **Retro. Supp. I:** 203
"Genius of Bob Dylan, The" (Lethem), **Supp. XVIII:** 146
Genius of Hunger The (Goodman), **Supp. XXVIII:** 85, 86, 88–91
"Genius," The (Dreiser), **I:** 497, 501, 509–511, 519; **Retro. Supp. II:** 94–95, **102–103,** 104, 105
Genocide of the Mind: New Native America Writing (Moore, ed.), **Supp. XXVI:** 113
Genova, Lisa, **Supp. XXIII:** 127
"Genteel Tradition in American Philosophy, The" (Santayana), **I:** 222
Gent from Bear Creek, A (Howard), **Supp. XXVII:** 117, 126
"Gent from Bear Creek, A" (Howard), **Supp. XXVII:** 127
"Gentle Boys, The" (Hawthorne), **Retro. Supp. III:** 113
"Gentle Communion" (Mora), **Supp. XIII:** 218–219
Gentle Crafter, The (O. Henry), **Supp. II Part 1:** 410
Gentle Furniture-Shop, The (Bodenheim), **Supp. XXV:** 20
"Gentle Lena, The" (Stein), **IV:** 37, 40
Gentleman Caller, The (T. Williams), **IV:** 383
"Gentleman from Cracow, The" (Singer), **IV:** 9

"Gentleman of Bayou Têche, A" (Chopin), **Supp. I Part 1:** 211–212

"Gentleman of Shalott, The" (Bishop), **Supp. I Part 1:** 85, 86

Gentleman's Agreement (Hobson), **III:** 151

"Gentleman's Agreement" (Richard), **Supp. XIX:** 220–221

Gentlemen I Address You Privately (Boyle), **Supp. XXIV:** 53–54

Gentlemen Prefer Blondes (Loos; musical adaptation), **Supp. XVI:** 193

Gentlemen Prefer Blondes: The Illuminating Diary of a Professional Lady (Loos), **Supp. XVI:** 181, 183, 186, **188–189**

Gentlemen Prefer "Books" (J. Yeats), *Supp. XVI:* 190

Gentle People, The: A Brooklyn Fable (Shaw), **Supp. XIX:** 244–245, 249

Gentry, Marshall Bruce, **Supp. IV Part 1:** 236

"Genuine Man, The" (Emerson), **II:** 10

"Genus Narcissus" (Trethewey), **Supp. XXI:** 256

Geo-Bestiary (Harrison), **Supp. VIII:** 53

"Geode" (Frost), **II:** 161

Geographical History of America, The (Stein), **IV:** 31, 45; **Supp. XVIII:** 148

Geography and Plays (Stein), **IV:** 29–30, 32, 43, 44

Geography III (Bishop), **Retro. Supp. II:** 50; **Supp. I Part 1:** 72, 73, 76, 82, 93, 94, 95

Geography of a Horse Dreamer (Shepard), **Supp. III Part 2:** 432

Geography of Home, The: California's Poetry of Place (Bluckey and Young, eds.), **Supp. XIII:** 313

Geography of Lograire, The (Merton), **Supp. VIII:** 208

Geography of the Heart (F. Johnson), **Supp. XI:** 129

"Geometric Poem, The" (Corso), **Supp. XII:** 132, 133–134

George, Diana Hume, **Supp. IV Part 2:** 447, 449, 450

George, Henry, **II:** 276; **Supp. I Part 2:** 518

George, Jan, **Supp. IV Part 1:** 268

George, Lynell, **Supp. XIII:** 234–235, 237, 249

George, Peter, **Supp. XI:** 302, 303, 304

George and the Dragon (Shanley), **Supp. XIV:** 315

George Bernard Shaw: His Plays (Mencken), **III:** 102

George Mills (Elkin), **Supp. VI:** 53–54

George Oppen and the Fate of Modernism (Nicholls), **Supp. XXVI:** 228

George Palmer Putnam: Representative American Publisher (Greenspan), **Supp. XVIII:** 257

"George Robinson: Blues" (Rukeyser), **Supp. VI:** 279

George's Mother (Crane), **I:** 408

"George Thurston" (Bierce), **I:** 202

George Washington Crossing the Delaware (Koch), **Supp. XV:** 186

George Washington Jones: A Christmas Gift That Went A-Begging (Stuart), **Supp. XXVIII:** 235

"George Washington"(Kenny), **Supp. XXIII:** 154

George Washington Poems, The (Wakoski), **Supp. XXVIII:** 262, 271

Georgia Boy (Caldwell), **I:** 288, 305–306, 308, 309, 310

"Georgia Dusk" (Toomer), **Supp. IX:** 309

"Georgia: Invisible Empire State" (Du Bois), **Supp. II Part 1:** 179

"Georgia Night" (Toomer), **Supp. III Part 2:** 481

Georgia Scenes (Longstreet), **II:** 70, 313; **Supp. I Part 1:** 352; **Supp. XXVIII:** 231

Georgics (Virgil), **Retro. Supp. I:** 135; **Supp. XVI:** 22; **Supp. XXIV:** 153

Georgics of Virgil, The (Ferry. trans.), **Supp. XXIV:** 158–160

Georgie May (Bodenheim), **Supp. XXV:** 25

Georgoudaki, Ekaterini, **Supp. IV Part 1:** 12

Gerald McBoing-Boing (film), **Supp. XVI:** 102

"Geraldo No Last Name" (Cisneros), **Supp. VII:** 60–61

Gerald's Game (King), **Supp. V:** 141, 148–150, 151, 152

Gerald's Party (Coover), **Supp. V:** 49–50, 51, 52

Gérando, Joseph Marie de, **II:** 10

"Geranium, The" (O'Connor), **Retro. Supp. II:** 221, 236; **Retro. Supp. III:** 208

Gerard, Jeremy, **Supp. XXI:** 147

Gerber, Dan, **Supp. VIII:** 39

Gerber, Lisa, **Supp. XXVI:** 187

Gerhardt, Rainer, **Supp. IV Part 1:** 142

"German Girls! The German Girls!, The" (MacLeish), **III:** 16

"German Refugee, The" (Malamud), **Supp. I Part 2:** 436, 437

"Germany's Reichswehr" (Agee), **I:** 35

Germinal (Zola), **III:** 318, 322

Gernsback, Hugo, **Supp. IV Part 1:** 101

"Gernsback Continuum, The" (W. Gibson), **Supp. XVI:** 123, 128

"Gerontion" (Eliot), **I:** 569, 574, 577, 578, 585, 588; **III:** 9, 435, 436; **Retro. Supp. I:** 290; **Supp. XV:** 341; **Supp. XVI:** 158–159

Gerry, Elbridge, **Supp. I Part 2:** 486

"Gerry's Jazz" (Komunyakaa), **Supp. XIII:** 125

Gershwin, Ira, **Supp. I Part 1:** 281

"Gert" (Monette), **Supp. X:** 158

"Gertrude Atherton and the New Woman" (Forrey), **Supp. XXIV:** 30

Gertrude of Stony Island Avenue (Purdy), **Supp. VII:** 281–282

Gertrude Stein (Sprigge), **IV:** 31

Gertrude Stein: A Biography of Her Work (Sutherland), **IV:** 38

"Gertrude Stein and the Geography of the Sentence" (Gass), **Supp. VI:** 87

Gesell, Silvio, **III:** 473

"Gestalt at Sixty" (Sarton), **Supp. VIII:** 260

"Gesture of a Woman-in-Process" (Trethewey), **Supp. XXI:** 249–250

"Gesture toward an Unfound Renaissance, A" (Stafford), **Supp. XI:** 323

"Get It Again" (Halliday), **Supp. XIX:** 85

Getlin, Josh, **Supp. V:** 22; **Supp. VIII:** 75, 76, 78, 79

"Getting Along" (Larcom), **Supp. XIII:** 144

"Getting Along with Nature" (Berry), **Supp. X:** 31–32

"Getting Away from Already Pretty Much Being Away from It All" (Wallace), **Supp. X:** 314–315

"Getting Born" (Shields), **Supp. VII:** 311

Getting Even (Allen), **Supp. XV:** 3, 14, 15

"Getting Involved"(Lea), **Supp. XXVIII:** 138–139

"Getting Lucky" (L. Michaels), **Supp. XVI:** 205, 209

"Getting Out of Jail on Monday" (Wagoner), **Supp. IX:** 327

"Getting Over Arnette"(P. Benedict), **Supp. XXIII:** 39

"Getting over Robert Frost" (Davison), **Supp. XXVI:** 79

"Getting There" (Plath), **Supp. I Part 2:** 539, 542

"Getting to the Poem" (Corso), **Supp. XII:** 135

Getty, J. Paul, **Supp. X:** 108

Getty, Norris, **Supp. XV:** 136–137, 138, 139, 142, 143, 145, 146

Gettysburg, Manila, Acoma (Masters), **Supp. I Part 2:** 471

"Gettysburg: July 1, 1863" (Kenyon), **Supp. VII:** 172

Gevers, Nick, **Supp. XXII:** 59

Geyer, Bernadette, **Supp. XXIII:** 251

Ghachem, Malick, **Supp. X:** 17

Ghazálí, al-, **Supp. XX:** 117

"Ghazals: Homage to Ghalib" (Rich), **Supp. I Part 2:** 557

Ghost, The (Crane), **I:** 409, 421

"Ghost, The" (Peacock), **Supp. XIX:** 199

"Ghost Cat" (Peacock), **Supp. XIX:** 206

"Ghost Chant, et alii" (Komunyakaa), **Supp. XIII:** 114

Ghost Country (Paretsky), **Supp. XXV:** 183

Ghost in the Music, A (Nichols), **Supp. XIII:** 267

"Ghost Jam"(Hadas), **Supp. XXIII:** 119

"Ghostlier Demarcations, Keener Sounds" (Vendler), **Supp. I Part 2:** 565

"Ghostly Father, I Confess" (McCarthy), **II:** 565–566

Ghostly Lover, The (Hardwick), **Supp. III Part 1:** 194–196, 208, 209

Ghost Money (Hull), **Supp. XXI:** 129, **132–135,** 136

"Ghost of a Chance" (Rich), **Retro. Supp. III:** 244

Ghost of Meter, The (A. Finch), **Supp. XVII:** 71, 73

"Ghost of the Buffaloes, The" (Lindsay), **Supp. I Part 2:** 393

Ghost of Tradition, The (Walzer), **Supp. XVIII:** 174

Ghost Pain (Lea), **Supp. XXVIII:** 138–142

"Ghost Pain"(Lea), **Supp. XXVIII:** 141

Ghosts (Auster), **Supp. XII:** 22, **24, 26–27**

Ghosts (Ibsen), **III:** 152

Ghosts (Wharton), **IV:** 316, 327

Ghosts of Tsavo: Stalking the Mystery Lions of East Africa (Caputo), **Supp. XIX:** 28

Ghost Town (Coover), **Supp. V:** 52–53

Ghost Trio, The (Bierds), **Supp. XVII:** 29, **30**

Ghost Writer, The (P. Roth), **Retro. Supp. II:** 22, 290, 291; **Supp. III Part 2:** 420–421; **Supp. XVII:** 43

Giachetti, Fosco, **Supp. IV Part 2:** 520

"Giacometti" (Wilbur), **Supp. III Part 2:** 551

Giacometti, Alberto, **Supp. VIII:** 168, 169

Giacomo, Padre, **II:** 278–279

Giant's House, The: A Romance (McCracken), **Supp. X:** 86

"Giant Snail" (Bishop), **Retro. Supp. II:** 49

Giant Weapon, The (Winters), **Supp. II Part 2:** 810

"Giant Woman, The" (Oates), **Supp. II Part 2:** 523

Gibbon, Edward, **I:** 4, 378; **IV:** 126; **Supp. I Part 2:** 503; **Supp. III Part 2:** 629; **Supp. XIII:** 75; **Supp. XIV:** 97

Gibbons, James, **Supp. XVII:** 228

Gibbons, Kaye, **Supp. X:** 41–54; **Supp. XII:** 311

Gibbons, Reginald, **Supp. X:** 113, 124, 127; **Supp. XIX:** 40, 41–42, 281; **Supp. XV:** 105

Gibbons, Richard, **Supp. I Part 1:** 107

"Gibbs" (Rukeyser), **Supp. VI:** 273

Gibbs, Barbara, **Supp. IV Part 2:** 644

Gibbs, Wolcott, **Supp. I Part 2:** 604, 618; **Supp. VIII:** 151

Gibran, Kahlil, **Supp. XX: 69, 113–129**

"GIBSON" (Baraka), **Supp. II Part 1:** 54

Gibson, Charles Dana, **Supp. X:** 184

Gibson, Graeme, **Supp. XIII:** 20

Gibson, John Arthur, **Supp. XXVI:** 83, 84, 87, 89

Gibson, Simeon, **Supp. XXVI:** 96

Gibson, Wilfrid W., **Retro. Supp. I:** 128; **Retro. Supp. III:** 96

Gibson, William, **Supp. XVI: 117–133; Supp. XXII:** 49

Giddins, Gary, **Supp. XIII:** 245

Gide, André, **I:** 271, 290; **II:** 581; **III:** 210; **IV:** 53, 289; **Retro. Supp. III:** 275; **Supp. I Part 1:** 51; **Supp. IV Part 1:** 80, 284, 347; **Supp. IV Part 2:** 681, 682; **Supp. VIII:** 40; **Supp. X:** 187; **Supp. XIV:** 24, 348; **Supp. XVII:** 242

Gideon Planish (Lewis), **II:** 455

Gielgud, John, **I:** 82; **Supp. XI:** 305

Gierow, Dr. Karl Ragnar, **III:** 404

Gifford, Barry, **Supp. XXV:** 29

Gifford, Bill, **Supp. XI:** 38

Gifford, Terry, **Supp. XVI:** 22

"Gift, The" (Creeley), **Supp. IV Part 1:** 153

"Gift, The" (Doolittle), **Supp. I Part 1:** 267

Gift, The (Hyde), **Supp. XVIII:** 150

"Gift, The" (Jarman), **Supp. XVII:** 116

"Gift, The" (L.-Y. Lee), **Supp. XV:** 213, 214

Gift, The (Nabokov), **III:** 246, 255, 261–263; **Retro. Supp. I:** 264, 266, **268–270**, 273, 274–275, 278

"Gift from the City, A" (Updike), **Retro. Supp. I:** 320

"Gift of God, The" (Robinson), **III:** 512, 517, 518–521, 524

Gift of the Black Folk, The: The Negroes in the Making of America (Du Bois), **Supp. II Part 1:** 179

"Gift of the Magi, The" (O. Henry), **Supp. II Part 1:** 394, 406, 408

"Gift of the *Osuo,* The" (C. Johnson), **Supp. VI:** 194

"Gift of the Prodigal, The" (Taylor), **Supp. V:** 314, 326

"Gift Outright, The" (Frost), **II:** 152; **Retro. Supp. III:** 91, 106; **Supp. IV Part 1:** 15

"Gifts" (Davison), **Supp. XXVI:** 71

"Gifts of Our Fathers, The" (Gansworth), **Supp. XXVI:** 110

Gigi (Colette; stage adaptation, Loos), **Supp. XVI:** 193

"Gigolo" (Plath), **Retro. Supp. II:** 257

"G.I. Graves in Tuscany" (Hugo), **Supp. VI:** 138

"Gila Bend" (Dickey), **Supp. IV Part 1:** 185–186

Gilb, Dagoberto, **Supp. XXV:** 138

Gilbert, Elizabeth, **Supp. XXII:** 83, 90; **Supp. XXVII:** 258

Gilbert, Jack, **Supp. IX:** 287; **Supp. XXVIII:** 196

Gilbert, Peter, **Supp. IX:** 291, 300

Gilbert, Roger, **Supp. XI:** 124

Gilbert, Sandra M., **Retro. Supp. I:** 42; **Retro. Supp. II:** 324; **Supp. IX:** 66; **Supp. XV:** 270; **Supp. XXIV:** 28; **Supp. XXVII:** 261–262, 263

Gilbert, Susan. *See* Dickinson, Mrs. William A.

Gilbert and Sullivan, **Supp. IV Part 1:** 389

"Gilbert Stuart Portrait of Washington, The" (Kooser), **Supp. XIX:** 124

Gil Blas (Le Sage), **II:** 290

Gilded Age, The (Twain and Warner), **III:** 504; **IV:** 198; **Retro. Supp. III:** 262

Gilded Lapse of Time, A (Schnackenberg), **Supp. XV:** 258, **260–263**

"Gilded Lapse of Time, A" (Schnackenberg), **Supp. XV:** 257

"Gilded Six-Bits, The" (Hurston), **Retro. Supp. III:** 137, 139; **Supp. VI:** 154–155

Gilder, Richard Watson, **Retro. Supp. II:** 66; **Retro. Supp. III:** 279–280; **Supp. I Part 2:** 418; **Supp. XXVIII:** 113

Gildersleeve, Basil, **Supp. I Part 1:** 369

Gildner, Gary, **Supp. XXVI:** 4

Gilead (Robinson), **Supp. XXI:** 212, **216–220,** 223

Giles, H. A., **Retro. Supp. I:** 289

Giles, James R., **Supp. IX:** 11, 15; **Supp. XI:** 219, 223–224, 228, 234

"Giles Corey of the Salem Farms" (Longfellow), **II:** 505, 506; **Retro. Supp. II:** 166, 167

Giles Goat-Boy (Barth), **I:** 121, 122–123, 129, 130, 134, 135–138; **Supp. V:** 39

Gilgamesh: A New Rendering in English Verse (Ferry), **Supp. XXIV:** 147, **150–151**

Gill, Brendan, **Supp. I Part 2:** 659, 660

Gillespie, Nick, **Supp. XIV:** 298, 311

Gillette, Chester, **I:** 512

Gillian, Maria Mazziotti, **Supp. XXIII:** 248

Gilligan, Carol, **Supp. XIII:** 216; **Supp. XXII:** 18

Gillis, Jim, **IV:** 196

Gillis, Steve, **IV:** 195

Gilman, Charlotte Perkins, **Supp. I Part 2:** 637; **Supp. V:** 121, 284, 285; **Supp. XI: 193–211; Supp. XIII:** 295, 306; **Supp. XVI:** 84; **Supp. XXIII:** 26; **Supp. XXVIII:** 237

Gilman, Daniel Coit, **Supp. I Part 1:** 361, 368, 370

Gilman, Owen W., Jr., **Supp. XXVI:** 148

Gilman, Richard, **IV:** 115; **Supp. IV Part 2:** 577; **Supp. XIII:** 100; **Supp. XIX:** 251

Gilmore, Eddy, **Supp. I Part 2:** 618

Gilmore, Leigh, **Supp. XXVI:** 53

Gilmore, Lyman, **Supp. XXI:** 20, 22, 24

Gilmore, Mikal, **Supp. XVI:** 123, 124

Gilpin, Charles, **III:** 392

Gilpin, Dewitt, **Supp. XV:** 197

Gilpin, Laura, **Retro. Supp. I:** 7

Gilpin, Sam, **Supp. V:** 213

Gilpin, William, **Supp. IV Part 2:** 603

"Gil's Furniture Bought & Sold" (Cisneros), **Supp. VII:** 61–62, 64

Gilt Edged Guilt (Wells), **Supp. XXVI:** 281

Gilyard, Keith, **Supp. XXI:** 246

"Gimcrackery" articles (Briggs), **Supp. XVIII:** 8–9

"Gimpel the Fool" (Singer), **IV:** 14; **Retro. Supp. II:** 22, 307

Gimpel the Fool and Other Stories (Singer), **IV:** 1, 7–9, 10, 12

"Gin" (Levine), **Supp. V:** 193

"Gina"(Goodman), **Supp. XXVIII:** 90

"Gingerbread House, The" (Coover), **Supp. V:** 42–43

Gingerbread Lady, The (Simon), **Supp. IV Part 2:** 580, 583–584, 588

Gingerich, Willard, **Supp. IV Part 2:** 510

Gingertown (McKay), **Supp. X:** 132, 139

Gingold, Hermione, **Supp. XV:** 13

Gingrich, Arnold, **Retro. Supp. I:** 113; **Supp. XVII:** 88; **Supp. XX:** 34

Ginna, Robert, **Supp. IX:** 259

Ginsberg, Allen, **I:** 183; **Retro. Supp. I:** 411, 426, 427; **Retro. Supp. II:** 280; **Retro. Supp. III:** 54; **Supp. II Part 1:** 30, 32, 58, 307–333; **Supp. III Part 1:** 2, 91, 96, 98, 100, 222, 226; **Supp. III Part 2:** 541, 627; **Supp. IV Part 1:** 79, 90, 322; **Supp. IV Part 2:** 502; **Supp. IX:** 299; **Supp. V:** 168, 336; **Supp. VIII:** 239, 242–243, 289; **Supp. X:** 120, 204; **Supp. XI:** 135, 297; **Supp. XII:** 118–119, 121–122, 124, 126, 130–131, 136, 182; **Supp. XIV:** 15, 53, 54, 125, 137, 141, 142, 143–144, 148, 150, 269, 280, 283; **Supp. XV:** 134, 177, 263; **Supp. XVI:** 123, 135; **Supp. XVII:** 138, 243; **Supp. XVIII:** 20, 27, 29, 30; **Supp. XXI:** 53; **Supp. XXII:** 172, 225; **Supp. XXIII:** 211, 213, 215; **Supp. XXIV:** 34, 36, 37; **Supp. XXV:** 29; **Supp. XXVI:** 70; **Supp. XXVII:** 18

Gioia, Dana, **Supp. IX:** 279; **Supp. XII:** 209; **Supp. XIII:** 337; **Supp. XIX:** 117, 144; **Supp. XV:** 111–131, 251; **Supp. XVII:** 69, 72, 112; **Supp. XXI:** 99; **Supp. XXIII:** 112; **Supp. XXV:** 222

Giono, Jean, **Supp. XVI:** 135

Giordano, Tony J., **Supp. XXIII:** 125

Giotto di Bondone, **Supp. I Part 2:** 438; **Supp. XI:** 126

Giovani, Regula, **Supp. XV:** 270

Giovanni, Nikki, **Supp. I Part 1:** 66; **Supp. II Part 1:** 54; **Supp. IV Part 1:** 11; **Supp. VIII:** 214; **Supp. XXII:** 11; **Supp. XXVII:** 165, 200, 202; **Supp. XXVIII:** 279

Giovanni's Room (Baldwin), **Retro. Supp. II:** 5, 6, **6–7,** 8, 10; **Supp. I Part 1:** 51, 52, 55–56, 57, 60, 63, 67; **Supp. III Part 1:** 125

Giovannitti, Arturo, **I:** 476; **Supp. XV:** 299, 301, 302, 307

"Giraffe" (Swenson), **Supp. IV Part 2:** 651

Giraldi, Giovanni Battista. *See* Cinthio

"Girl" (Kincaid), **Supp. VII:** 182–183

Girl, The (Le Sueur), **Supp. XXIII:** 172–174

"Girl, The" (Olds), **Supp. X:** 207

"Girl Friend Poems" (Wright), **Supp. XV:** 349

"Girl from Lynn Bathes Horse!!" (McCarriston), **Supp. XIV:** 266

"Girl from Red Lion, P.A., A" (Mencken), **III:** 111

Girl in Glass, The: Love Poems (W. J. Smith), **Supp. XIII:** 335

Girl in Landscape (Lethem), **Supp. XVIII:** 136, **141–143**

"Girl in the Grave, The" (McCoy), **Supp. XIII:** 170

"Girl in the River, The" (Rash), **Supp. XXVII:** 224

"Girl in the River, The: The Wild and Scenic Chattooga, Ron Rash's *Saints at the River,* and the Drowning of Rachel Trois" (Lane), **Supp. XXVII:** 216

Girl Like I, A (Loos), **Supp. XVI:** 181, 183, 184, 187, 194, 196

"Girl of the Golden West" (Didion), **Supp. IV Part 1:** 195, 208, 211

Girl of the Golden West, The (Puccini), **III:** 139

Girl of the Limberlost (film), **Supp. XX:** 223

Girl of the Limberlost (Stratton-Porter), **Supp. XX: 211, 221–222**

"Girl on a Scaffold" (C. Frost), **Supp. XV:** 98

"Girl on the Baggage Truck, The" (O'Hara), **III:** 371–372

Girl on the Via Flaminia, The (Hayes), **Supp. XXVI:** 135, 136–137, 144

"Girls" (Gallagher), **Supp. XXIV:** 174–175, 177

Girls at Play (Theroux), **Supp. VIII:** 314, 315, 316, **317**

"Girls at the Sphinx, The" (Farrell), **II:** 45

"Girls in Their Summer Dresses, The" (Shaw), **Supp. XIX:** 246

"Girls in Their Upstairs Windows" (Lea), **Supp. XXVIII:** 137–138

Girl Sleuth, The: A Feminist Guide (Mason), **Supp. VIII:** 133, 135, **139,** 142

"Girl's Story, A" (Bambara), **Supp. XI:** 10–11

"Girl the Prince Liked, The" (Z. Fitzgerald), **Supp. IX:** 71

Girl Who Had to Die, The (Holding), **Supp. XXII: 126–127**

Girl Who Loved Tom Gordon, The (King), **Supp. V:** 138, 152

"Girl Who Raised Pigeons, The" (E. P. Jones), **Supp. XXII:** 143

Girl with Curious Hair (Wallace), **Supp. X:** 301, **305–308**

"Girl with Curious Hair" (Wallace), **Supp. X:** 306

"Girl with Silver Eyes, The" (Hammett), **Supp. IV Part 1:** 344, 345

"Girl with Talent, The" (Z. Fitzgerald), **Supp. IX:** 71

Girodias, Maurice, **III:** 171; **Supp. XI:** 297

Giroux, Robert, **Retro. Supp. II:** 177, 229, 235; **Supp. IV Part 1:** 280; **Supp. VIII:** 195; **Supp. XV:** 146

Gish, Dorothy, **Retro. Supp. I:** 103

Gish, Lillian, **Supp. XVI:** 184

Gissing, George, **II:** 138, 144

Gitagovinda, **Supp. XXII:** 258

Gita-govinda: Love Songs of Radha and Krishna (Jayadeva; Siegel, trans.), **Supp. XXII:** 258

Gittings, Robert, **II:** 531

Gittleman, Edwin, **Supp. XXV:** 237, 251

"Given" (C. Frost), **Supp. XV:** 96

Given Sugar, Given Salt (Hirshfield), **Supp. XXIII:** 133

"Give Us Back Our Country" (Masters), **Supp. I Part 2:** 472

Give Us This Day (film, Dmytryk), **Supp. XX: 40–41**

"Give Way, Ye Gates" (Roethke), **III:** 536

"Give Your Heart to the Hawks" (Jeffers), **Supp. II Part 2:** 433

"Giving Blood" (Updike), **IV:** 226; **Retro. Supp. I:** 332

Giving Good Weight (McPhee), **Supp. III Part 1:** 307

"Giving in to You" (X. J. Kennedy), **Supp. XV:** 160

"Giving Myself Up" (Strand), **Supp. IV Part 2:** 627

Giving Up America (Abraham), **Supp. XXIV:** 2, 3, **7–9**

Giving Up the Ghost (Moraga), **Supp. XXIII:** 197–199

G. K. the DJ (Keillor), **Supp. XVI:** 171

Glackens, William, **Retro. Supp. II:** 103

Gladden, Washington, **III:** 293; **Supp. I Part 1:** 5

Gladstone, William Ewart, **Supp. I Part 2:** 419

"Gladys Poem, The" (Alvarez), **Supp. VII:** 10

Glamorama (Ellis), **Supp. XXVII:** 68, 71, 75–76, 76, 78

"Glance at German 'Kultur,' A" (Bourne), **I:** 228

Glance Away, A (Wideman), **Supp. X:** 320

"Glance from the Bridge, A" (Wilbur), **Supp. III Part 2:** 551

"Glance in the Mirror, A" (Swados), **Supp. XIX:** 261–262

Glance toward Shakespeare, A (Chapman), **Supp. XIV:** 44

Glancy, Diane, **Supp. XXI:** 246

Glanville-Hicks, Peggy, **Supp. IV Part 1:** 84

Glare (Ammons), **Supp. VII:** 35–36

Glasgow, Cary, **II:** 173, 182

Glasgow, Ellen, **II: 173–195; IV:** 328; **Supp. X:** 228, 234; **Supp. XXIV:** 30; **Supp. XXV:** 201; **Supp. XXVI:** 276; **Supp. XXVIII:** 118, 123, 124

Glasmon, Kubec, **Supp. XIII:** 166

Glaspell, Susan, **Supp. III Part 1: 175–191; Supp. X:** 46; **Supp. XVII:** 99; **Supp. XXI:** 5; **Supp. XXVIII:** 68, 69

"Glass" (Francis), **Supp. IX:** 80

Glass, Irony, and God (Carson), **Supp. XII:** 97, **104–106**

Glass, Philip, **Supp. XXI:** 146, 147

"Glass Ark, The" (Komunyakaa), **Supp. XIII:** 129

Glass Bees, The (Jünger; Bogan and Mayer, trans.), **Supp. III Part 1:** 63

"Glass Blower of Venice" (Malamud), **Supp. I Part 2:** 450

"Glass Essay, The" (Carson), **Supp. XII:** 104–105

"Glass Face in the Rain, A: New Poems" (Stafford), **Supp. XI:** 327–328

Glass Key, The (Hammett), **Supp. IV Part 1:** 351–353

"Glass Meadows" (Bausch), **Supp. VII:** 53–54

Glass Menagerie, The (T. Williams), **I:** 81; **IV:** 378, 379, 380, 382, 383, 385, 386, 387, 388, 389, 390, 391, 392, 393–394, 395, 398; **Supp. IV Part 1:** 84; **Supp. XXV:** 101

"Glass Mountain, The" (Barthelme), **Supp. IV Part 1:** 47

"Glass Tent, The" (Everwine), **Supp. XV:** 76

Glatstein, Jacob, **Supp. X:** 70

Glazer, Nathan, **Supp. VIII:** 93, 243

"Gleaners, The" (Merwin), **Supp. III Part 1:** 346

Gleanings in Europe (Cooper), **I:** 346

Gleason, Ralph J., **Supp. IX:** 16

Gledhill, Christine, **Supp. XXVIII:** 183

Glenday, Michael, **Retro. Supp. II:** 210

Glengarry Glen Ross (film), **Supp. XIV:** 242

Glengarry Glen Ross (Mamet), **Supp. XIV:** 239, 240, 242, 245, 246, 250, 254, 255

Glimcher, Arne, **Supp. VIII:** 73

"Glimpses" (Jones), **Supp. XI:** 218

Glimpses of the Moon, The (Wharton), **II:** 189–190; **IV:** 322–323; **Retro. Supp. I:** 381; **Retro. Supp. III:** 288

"Glimpses of Vietnamese Life" (Levertov), **Supp. III Part 1:** 282

Glisson, J. T., **Supp. X:** 234

"Glittering Trout" (Davison), **Supp. XXVI:** 79

Gloria Mundi (Frederic), **II:** 144–145

Gloria Naylor (Fowler), **Supp. VIII:** 224

"Glorious Fourth, The" (Ryan as Quin), **Supp. XVIII:** 229

Glorious Ones, The (Prose), **Supp. XVI:** 251

Glory, The (Wouk), **Supp. XXV:** 254, 257, 265–266

Glory Field, The (Myers), **Supp. XXVII:** 208

Glory of Hera, The (Gordon), **II:** 196–197, 198, 199, 217–220

Glory of the Conquered, The (Glaspell), **Supp. III Part 1:** 176

Glory River (Huddle), **Supp. XXVI:** 151

Gloss, Molly, **Supp. XXIII:** 280

Glossary of Literary Terms (Abrams), **Supp. XVI:** 19

Glotfelty, Cheryll, **Supp. IX:** 25

Glover, Joyce Lee, **Supp. XIX:** 112

Glover, Michael, **Supp. XXIV:** 168

Glow, The (Wrigley), **Supp. XVIII:** 295

"Glow, The" (Wrigley), **Supp. XVIII:** 296–297, 307

Gluck, Christoph Willibald, **II:** 210, 211

Glück, Louise, **Supp. V: 77–94; Supp. VIII:** 272; **Supp. X:** 209; **Supp. XIV:** 269; **Supp. XV:** 19, 252; **Supp. XVII:** 241; **Supp. XXV:** 222; **Supp. XXVIII:** 197, 198

"Glue"(Siken), **Supp. XXVIII:** 201

"Glutton, The" (Shapiro), **Supp. II Part 2:** 705

"Glutton for Punishment, A" (Yates), **Supp. XI:** 341

Glyph (Everett), **Supp. XVIII: 60–61**

Gnädiges Fräulein, The (T. Williams), **IV:** 382, 395, 398

Gnomes and Occasions (Nemerov), **III:** 269

Gnomologia (Fuller), **II:** 111

"Gnothis Seauton" (Emerson), **II:** 11, 18–19

Go (Holmes), **Supp. XIV:** 144

"Go Ahead; Goodbye; Good Luck; and Watch Out" (Bronk), **Supp. XXI:** 31

"Goal of Intellectual Men, The" (Eberhart), **I:** 529–530

Go-Between, The (Hartley), **Supp. I Part 1:** 293

Gobineau, Joseph Arthur de, **Supp. XIV:** 209

Gobolinks; or, Shadow Pictures for Young and Old (Stuart and Paine), **Supp. XXVIII:** 229

God (Allen), **Supp. XV:** 3

God and the American Writer (Kazin), **Supp. VIII: 108–109**

Godard, Jean-Luc, **Supp. I Part 2:** 558

Godbey (Masters), **Supp. I Part 2:** 472

God Bless You, Mr. Rosewater (Vonnegut), **Supp. II Part 2:** 758, 767, 768–769, 771, 772

Goddess Abides, The (Buck), **Supp. II Part 1:** 129, 131–132

Gödel, Kurt, **Supp. IV Part 1:** 43

Godfather (Puzo), **Supp. IV Part 1:** 390

Godfires (Hoffman), **Supp. XVIII: 81–82**

God Help the Child (Morrison), **Retro. Supp. III:** 185, 199–200

God in Ruins, A (Uris), **Supp. XX: 247, 256**

"God in the Doorway" (Dillard), **Supp. VI:** 28

"God is a distant-stately Lover" (Dickinson), **I:** 471

Godkin, E. L., **II:** 274

God Knows (Heller), **Supp. IV Part 1:** 386, 388–389

God Made Alaska for the Indians (Reed), **Supp. X:** 241

God of His Fathers, The (London), **II:** 469

God of Vengeance, The (Asch), **IV:** 11; **Supp. XXIII: 5, 8–9**

Go Down, Moses (Faulkner), **Retro. Supp. I:** 75, 82, 85, 86, 88, 89, 90, 92; **Retro. Supp. III:** 86, 87; **Supp. XVIII:** 203

"Go Down, Moses" (Faulkner), **II:** 71–72

Go Down, Moses (Hayden), **Supp. II Part 1:** 365

Go Down, Moses and Other Stories (Faulkner), **II:** 71; **Supp. X:** 52

"Go Down Death A Funeral Sermon" (J. W. Johnson), **Supp. IV Part 1:** 7

"God Rest Ye Merry, Gentlemen" (Hemingway), **IV:** 122

Godric (Buechner), **Supp. XII:** 53

Gods, The (Goldbarth), **Supp. XII:** 189, 190

Gods Arrive, The (Wharton), **IV:** 326–327; **Retro. Supp. I:** 382

God Save the Child (Parker), **Supp. XIX:** 183–184

"God Save the Rights of Man" (Freneau), **Supp. II Part 1:** 268

"Gods|Children" (Swenson), **Supp. IV Part 2:** 645

"God's Christ Theory" (Carson), **Supp. XII: 106**

God's Country (Everett), **Supp. XVIII: 57–58, 64, 65**

God's Country and My People (Morris), **III:** 238

Gods Determinations touching his Elect: and the Elects Combat in their Conversion, and Coming up to God in Christ together with the Comfortable Effects thereof (Taylor), **IV:** 155–160, 165

God-Seeker, The (Lewis), **II:** 456

God Sends Sunday (Bontemps), **Supp. XXII:** 2, 3, 9

God's Favorite (Simon), **Supp. IV Part 2:** 575, 586, 588, 590

"God's Fool" (Gibran), **Supp. XX: 118**

God's Little Acre (Caldwell), **I:** 288, 289, 290, 297, 298–302, 305–306, 309, 310; **Supp. XXII:** 196

God's Man: A Novel in Wood Cuts (Ward), **I:** 31

Gods of Pegana, The (Dunsany), **Supp. XXV:** 113

Gods of Winter, The (Gioia), **Supp. XV:** 112, **121–125**

"Gods of Winter, The" (Gioia), **Supp. XV:** 117

"God's Peace in November" (Jeffers), **Supp. II Part 2:** 420

God's Silence (F. Wright), **Supp. XVII:** 240, 246–247

"God Stiff" (Carson), **Supp. XII: 106**

God's Trombones (J. W. Johnson), **Supp. II Part 1:** 201

"God's Youth" (Untermeyer), **Supp. XV:** 296

"God the Father and the Empty House" (McCarriston), **Supp. XIV:** 273

Godwin, William, **II:** 304; **III:** 415; **Supp. I Part 1:** 126, 146; **Supp. I Part 2:** 512, 513–514, 522, 709, 719

God without Thunder (Ransom), **III:** 495–496, 499

Godwulf Manuscript, The (Parker), **Supp. XIX: 178–182**

Goebbels, Josef, **III:** 560

Goebel, Irma, **Supp. X:** 95

Goen, C. C., **I:** 560

Goethe, Johann Wolfgang von, **I:** 181, 396, 587–588; **II:** 5, 6, 320, 344, 488, 489, 492, 502, 556; **III:** 395, 453, 607, 612, 616; **IV:** 50, 64, 173, 326; **Retro. Supp. I:** 360; **Retro. Supp. II:** 94; **Supp. I Part 2:** 423, 457; **Supp. II Part 1:** 26; **Supp. III Part 1:** 63; **Supp. IX:** 131, 308; **Supp. X:** 60; **Supp. XI:** 169; **Supp. XVIII:** 278; **Supp. XX: 84; Supp. XXIV:** 152

Go for the Body (Lacy), **Supp. XV:** 201, 204

Gogan, Robert, **Supp. XXI:** 24

Gogol, Nikolai, **I:** 296; **IV:** 1, 4; **Retro. Supp. I:** 266, 269; **Retro. Supp. III:** 139; **Supp. VIII:** 14; **Supp. XVII:** 45; **Supp. XVIII:** 102; **Supp. XXII:** 59

Goia, Dana, **Supp. XIX:** 121

Goines, Donald, **Supp. XXIII:** 174

"Going, Going, Gone" (Skloot), **Supp. XX: 207**

Going, William T., **Supp. VIII:** 126

"Going 1960–1970" (Huddle), **Supp. XXVI:** 148

Going After Cacciato (O'Brien), **Supp. V:** 237, 238, 239, 244–246, 248, 249

Going All the Way (Wakefield), **Supp. VIII:** 43

Going Away (Sigal), **Supp. XXVI:** 26

"Going Critical" (Bambara), **Supp. XI:** 14

Going Down (Markson), **Supp. XVII:** 136, 138, **139–140,** 141, 142–143, 144, 145

Going for the Rain (Ortiz), **Supp. IV Part 2:** 499, 505–508, 509, 514

"Going Home by Last Night" (Kinnell), **Supp. III Part 1:** 244

"Going Home in America" (Hardwick), **Supp. III Part 1:** 205

"Going Home"(Kenny), **Supp. XXIII:** 144, 148

Going into the City: Portrait of a Critic as a Young Man (Christgau), **Supp. XXVII:** 33, 39

"Going North" (Salinas), **Supp. XIII:** 316

Going Places (L. Michaels), **Supp. XVI:** 201, **203–206**

"Going Places" (L. Michaels), **Supp. XVI:** 203

"Going South" (J. W. Miller), **Supp. XX:** 169

Going South (Lardner and Buck), **II:** 427

Going To and Fro and Walking Up and Down (Reznikoff), **Supp. XIV:** 280, 282, 284, 285

Going to Meet the Man (Baldwin), **Supp. I Part 1:** 60, 62–63; **Supp. XX:** 147

"Going to Meet the Man" (Baldwin), **Retro. Supp. II:** 8, 9; **Supp. I Part 1:** 62–63

"Going to Naples" (Welty), **IV:** 278; **Retro. Supp. I:** 352, 353

"Going to Shrewsbury" (Jewett), **II:** 393

"Going to the Bakery" (Bishop), **Supp. I Part 1:** 93

Going-to-the-Stars (Lindsay), **Supp. I Part 2:** 398

Going-to-the-Sun (Lindsay), **Supp. I Part 2:** 397–398

Going to the Territory (Ellison), **Retro. Supp. II:** 119, 123–124

"Going towards Pojoaque, A December Full Moon/72" (Harjo), **Supp. XII:** 218

"Going Under" (Dubus), **Supp. VII:** 83

"Gold" (Francis), **Supp. IX:** 82

Gold (O'Neill), **III:** 391

Gold, Arthur, **Supp. XXIV:** 160, 161

Gold, Charles H., **Supp. XXVI:** 6

Gold, Don, **Supp. XXII:** 258

Gold, Michael, **II:** 26; **IV:** 363, 364, 365; **Retro. Supp. II:** 323; **Supp. I Part 1:** 331; **Supp. I Part 2:** 609; **Supp. XIV:** 288; **Supp. XXII:** 277; **Supp. XXVII:** 134; **Supp. XXVIII: 65–83**

Goldbarth, Albert, **Supp. XII: 175–195**

Goldbarth's Book of Occult Phenomena (Goldbarth), **Supp. XII:** 181

Goldberg, Carole, **Supp. XXII:** 207

Goldberg, Michael, **Supp. XXIII:** 210, 216, 217

Goldberg, S. L., **Supp. VIII:** 238

"Gold Bug, The" (Poe), **III:** 410, 413, 419, 420; **Retro. Supp. III:** 226, 230

Gold Bug Variations, The (Powers), **Supp. IX:** 210, 212, **216–217,** 219

Gold Cell, The (Olds), **Supp. X: 206–209**

Gold Diggers, The (Monette), **Supp. X:** 153

Golde, Miss (Mencken's Secretary), **III:** 104, 107

Golden, Harry, **III:** 579, 581; **Supp. VIII:** 244

Golden, Mike, **Supp. XI:** 294, 295, 297, 299, 303

Golden Age, The (Gurney), **Supp. V:** 101–103

Golden Apples (Rawlings), **Supp. X:** **228–229,** 230, 234

Golden Apples, The (Welty), **IV:** 261, 271–274, 281, 293; **Retro. Supp. I:** 341, 342, 343, **350–351,** 352, 355

Golden Apples of the Sun, The (Bradbury), **Supp. IV Part 1:** 102, 103

Golden Book of Springfield, The (Lindsay), **Supp. I Part 2:** 376, 379, 395, 396

Golden Bough, The (Frazer), **II:** 204, 549; **III:** 6–7; **Supp. I Part 1:** 18; **Supp. IX:** 123; **Supp. X:** 124

Golden Bowl, The (James), **II:** 320, 333, 335; **Retro. Supp. I:** 215, 216, 218–219, 232, **234–235,** 374

Golden Boy (Odets), **Supp. II Part 2:** 538, 539, 540–541, 546, 551

Golden Calves, The (Auchincloss), **Supp. IV Part 1:** 35

Golden Child (Hwang), **Supp. XXI:** 147–148

Golden Day, The (Mumford), **Supp. II Part 2:** 471, 475, 477, 483, 484, 488–489, 493

Golden Fleece, The (Gurney), **Supp. V:** 97

Golden Gate (film, Madden), **Supp. XXI:** 147

Golden Gate, The (Seth), **Supp. XVII:** 117

Golden Gate Country (Atherton), **Supp. XXIV:** 27

Golden Grove, The: Selected Passages from the Sermons and Writings of Jeremy Taylor (L. P. Smith), **Supp. XIV:** 345

"Golden Heifer, The" (Wylie), **Supp. I Part 2:** 707

"Golden Honeymoon, The" (Lardner), **II:** 429–430, 431

Golden Journey, The (W. J. Smith and Bogan, comps.), **Supp. XIII:** 347

Golden Ladder series (S. and A. Warner), **Supp. XVIII:** 267

"Golden Lads" (Marquand), **III:** 56

Golden Legend, The (Longfellow), **II:** 489, 490, 495, 505, 506, 507; **Retro. Supp. II:** 159, 165, 166

Golden Mean and Other Poems, The (Tate and Wills), **IV:** 122

Golden Mountain, The (Levin), **Supp. XXVII:** 134, 140

Golden Peacock (Atherton), **Supp. XXIV:** 26

"Golden Retrievals" (Doty), **Supp. XI:** 132

Golden Shakespeare, The: An Anthology (L. P. Smith), **Supp. XIV:** 349

Golden Slippers: An Anthology of Negro Poetry for Young Readers (Bontemps, ed.), **Supp. XXII:** 5, 11

Goldensohn, Lorrie, **Retro. Supp. II:** 51

Golden State (Bidart), **Supp. XV:** 21, **23–25**

"Golden State" (Bidart), **Supp. XV:** 23, 24, 25

Golden States (Cunningham), **Supp. XV:** 55, **56–59,** 63

Golden Throng, The: A Book About Bees (Teale), **Supp. XXVIII:** 246, 247

Golden Treasury of Best Songs and Lyrical Poems in the English Language (Palgrave), **Retro. Supp. I:** 124

Golden Treasury of the Best Songs and Lyrical Poems in the English Language (Palgrave), **Retro. Supp. III:** 91; **Supp. XIV:** 340

Golden Vase, The (Lewisohn), **Supp. XXVIII:** 152

"Golden Wedding, A"(Stuart), **Supp. XXVIII:** 231–232, 233

Golden Wedding and Other Tales, A (Stuart), **Supp. XXVIII:** 227, 231–235

Goldenweiser, Alexander Aleksandrovich, **Supp. XXVI:** 89

Golden Whales of California and Other Rhymes in the American Language, The (Lindsay), **Supp. I Part 2:** 394–395, 396

Golden Years, The (A. Miller), **Retro. Supp. III:** 166

Goldfinch, The (Tartt), **Supp. XXVII:** 268, 276–280

"Goldfish Bowl, The" (Francis), **Supp. IX:** 78

Gold Fools (Sorrentino), **Supp. XXI:** 237

Goldin Boys, The (Epstein), **Supp. XIV:** 112

Golding, Arthur, **III:** 467, 468

Golding, William, **Supp. IV Part 1:** 297

Goldini, Carlo, **II:** 274

Goldkorn Tales (Epstein), **Supp. XII:** **163–164**

Goldman, Albert, **Supp. XI:** 299

Goldman, Arnold, **Supp. XXI:** 13

Goldman, Emma, **III:** 176, 177; **Supp. I Part 2:** 524; **Supp. XVII:** 96, 103, 104; **Supp. XXIII:** 162; **Supp. XXVIII:** 43, 47, 67

Goldman, Francisco, **Supp. XXV: 49–62**

Goldman, William, **Supp. IV Part 2:** 474

Goldman-Price, Irene, **Retro. Supp. III:** 276, 277, 278

"Gold Mountain Stories" project (Kingston), **Supp. V:** 164

Gold of Chickaree, The (S. and A. Warner), **Supp. XVIII:** 267, 268, 269

Goldring, Douglas, **III:** 458

Goldsmith, Oliver, **II:** 273, 282, 299, 304, 308, 314, 315, 514; **Retro. Supp. I:** 335; **Supp. I Part 1:** 310; **Supp. I**

Part 2: 503, 714, 716; **Supp. XVIII:** 12

Gold Standard and the Logic of Naturalism, The (W. B. Michaels), **Retro. Supp. I:** 369

Goldstein, Laurence, **Supp. XXI:** 134

Goldstein, Rebecca, **Supp. XVII:** 44

Goldstein, Richard, **Supp. XXVII:** 43

Goldthwaite, Melissa, **Supp. XXVI:** 56

Goldwater, Barry, **I:** 376; **III:** 38

Goldwyn, Samuel, **Retro. Supp. II:** 199; **Supp. I Part 1:** 281; **Supp. XXIV:** 28; **Supp. XXV:** 195

Golem, The (Leivick), **IV:** 6; **Supp. XXIII:** 8

"Golgotha Is a Mountain" (Bontemps), **Supp. XXII:** 3, 8

"Goliardic Song" (Hecht), **Supp. X:** 63

"Go Like This" (Moore), **Supp. X:** 165

Goll, Ivan, **Supp. III Part 1:** 235, 243–244; **Supp. III Part 2:** 621

Gomes, Albert, **Supp. XXI:** 160

Goncharova, Natalya, **Supp. IX:** 66

Goncourt, Edmond de, **II:** 325, 328; **III:** 315, 317–318, 321; **Retro. Supp. I:** 226

Goncourt, Jules de, **II:** 328; **III:** 315, 317–318, 321

Gone Fishin' (Mosley), **Supp. XIII: 235–236,** 240

"Gone to Feed the Roses" (Vaz), **Supp. XXVI:** 268

"Gone to War" (E. Stoddard), **Supp. XV:** 282

"Gone West" (Rodriguez), **Supp. XIV:** 308

Gone with the Wind (film), **Retro. Supp. I:** 113; **Supp. XXVII:** 83

Gone with the Wind (Mitchell), **II:** 177; **Retro. Supp. I:** 340; **Supp. XX:** 243; **Supp. XXII:** 190, 195; **Supp. XXVIII:** 119

Gongora y Argote, Luis de, **II:** 552

Gonzalez, David, **Supp. VIII:** 85

González, Jovita, **Supp. XIX:** 99

Gonzo: The Life of Hunter S. Thompson (Wenner and Seymour), **Supp. XXIV:** 280, 281, 282, 288

Gooch, Brad, **Supp. XII:** 121; **Supp. XXIII:** 218, 220

Good, George, **Supp. XI:** 306

"Good, the Plaid, and the Ugly, The" (Wasserstein), **Supp. XV:** 327

"Good and Not So Good, The" (Dunn), **Supp. XI:** 141

"Good Anna, The" (Stein), **IV:** 37, 40, 43

Good As Gold (Heller), **Supp. IV Part 1:** 386, 388, 394

Good as I Been to You (album, Dylan), **Supp. XVIII:** 28

"Good As Yesterday" (Muñoz), **Supp. XXV:** 134, 135

Good Boys and Dead Girls and Other Essays (Gordon), **Supp. IV Part 1:** 309–310

"Good Brother" (Muñoz), **Supp. XXV:** 135

Good Brother, The (Offutt), **Supp. XIX:** 163, **168–169**

"Good-by and Keep Cold" (Frost), **Retro. Supp. I:** 135

"Goodbye" (Davison), **Supp. XXVI:** 69

"Good-bye" (Emerson), **II:** 19

"Goodbye, Christ" (Hughes), **Retro. Supp. I:** 202, 203

Goodbye, Columbus (P. Roth), **Retro. Supp. II:** 280, 281, 290; **Supp. III Part 2:** 403–406; **Supp. XIV:** 112; **Supp. XX: 177; Supp. XXVI:** 123

"Goodbye, Columbus" (P. Roth), **Supp. III Part 2:** 401, 404, 408–409, 411

Goodbye, Columbus and Five Short Stories (P. Roth), **Retro. Supp. II:** 279

"Goodbye, Goldeneye" (Swenson), **Supp. IV Part 2:** 651

"Goodbye, Mr. Chipstein" (Epstein), **Supp. XIV:** 103, 108

"Goodbye, My Brother" (Cheever), **Supp. I Part 1:** 175, 177, 193

"Goodbye and Good Luck" (Paley), **Supp. VI:** 219, 223

Goodbye Girl, The (film), **Supp. IV Part 2:** 589

Goodbye Girl, The (musical), **Supp. IV Part 2:** 576, 588

Goodbye Girl, The (Simon), **Supp. IV Part 2:** 575

Goodbye Look, The (Macdonald), **Supp. IV Part 2:** 473, 474

"Good-Bye My Fancy" (Whitman), **IV:** 348

"Good-Bye My Fancy"(Whitman), **Retro. Supp. III:** 303

"Goodbye to All That" (Biss), **Supp. XXVI:** 46, 47, 53

"Goodbye to All That" (Didion), **Supp. IV Part 1:** 197

Goodbye to All That (Graves), **I:** 477; **Supp. XXVI:** 53

Goodbye to Berlin (Isherwood), **Supp. XIV:** 159, 161, 162, 169

"Goodbye to My Twinkle Days" (Nguyen), **Supp. XXVI:** 209

"Good-Bye to the Mezzogiorno" (Auden), **Supp. II Part 1:** 19

"Goodbye to the Poetry of Calcium" (Wright), **Supp. III Part 2:** 599

"Good Company" (Matthews), **Supp. IX:** 160

"Good Country People" (O'Connor), **III:** 343, 350, 351, 352, 358; **Retro. Supp. II:** 229, 232; **Retro. Supp. III:** 213, 215, 217–218

Good Day to Die, A (Harrison), **Supp. VIII: 42–44,** 45, 47

Good Day to Die, A (O'Nan as James Coltrane), **Supp. XXV:** 146

Good Doctor, The (Simon), **Supp. IV Part 2:** 575, 585

Good Earth, The (Buck), **Supp. I Part 1:** 49; **Supp. II Part 1:** 115–175, 118, 125, 132

Good European, The (Blackmur), **Supp. II Part 1:** 91

Good Evening Mr. & Mrs. America, and All the Ships at Sea (Bausch), **Supp. VII:** 41, 47, 52

"Good Friday" (Jarman), **Supp. XVII:** 116

"Good Friday, 1613, Riding Westward" (Donne), **Supp. XXVII:** 220

"Good Friday, 1995, Driving Westward" (Rash), **Supp. XXVII:** 219–220

"Good Girl" (Peacock), **Supp. XIX:** 199

Good Gray Poet, The (O'Connor), **Retro. Supp. I:** 407

Good Health and How We Won It (Sinclair), **Supp. V:** 285–286

Good Hearts (Price), **Supp. VI:** 259, 265

"Good Job Gone, A" (Hughes), **Retro. Supp. I:** 204

Good Journey, A (Ortiz), **Supp. IV Part 2:** 497, 499, 503, 505, 509–510, 514

Good Life, The (Nearing and Nearing), **Supp. XXVI:** 35; **Supp. XXVIII:** 253

Good Lord Bird, The (McBride), **Supp. XXVI:** 191, 200, 202–204

Good Luck, Miss Wyckoff (Inge), **Supp. XXV:** 93, 95, 106–107

Good Luck in Cracked Italian (Hugo), **Supp. VI:** 133, 137–138

Goodman, Allegra, **Supp. XII:** 159; **Supp. XVI:** 205; **Supp. XX: 177; Supp. XXVI: 117–132**

Goodman, Diane, **Supp. XXVIII: 85–96**

Goodman, Ellen, **Supp. XVI:** 103

Goodman, Jack, **Supp. XXI:** 277

Goodman, Jenny, **Supp. XV:** 343, 344

Goodman, Kenneth Sawyer, **Supp. XXVII:** 89

Goodman, Paul, **I:** 218, 261; **III:** 39; **Supp. I Part 2:** 524; **Supp. VIII:** 239–240

Goodman, Philip, **III:** 105, 108

Goodman, Walter, **Supp. IV Part 2:** 532

Good Man Is Hard to Find, A (O'Connor), **III:** 339, 343–345; **Retro. Supp. III:** 208

"Good Man Is Hard to Find, A" (O'Connor), **III:** 339, 344, 353; **Retro. Supp. II:** 230–231; **Retro. Supp. III:** 212

Good Man Is Hard to Find and Other Stories, A (O'Connor), **Retro. Supp. II:** 229, **230–232**

Good Morning, America (Sandburg), **III:** 592–593

"Good Morning, Major" (Marquand), **III:** 56

Good Morning, Midnight (Rhys), **Supp. III Part 1:** 43

"Good Morning, Revolution" (Hughes), **Retro. Supp. I:** 201, 203

Good Morning Blues: The Autobiography of Count Basie (Murray), **Supp. XIX:** 159

Good Morning Revolution: Uncollected Writings of Social Protest (Hughes), **Retro. Supp. I:** 194, 201, 202, 209

Good Mother, The (Miller), **Supp. XII:** 289, **290–294,** 299, 301

Good News (Abbey), **Supp. XIII:** 11–12

"Good News from New-England" (E. Johnson), **Supp. I Part 1:** 115

Good News of Death and Other Poems (Simpson), **Supp. IX:** 265, **268–269**

"Goodnight, Saigon" (lecture, Caputo), **Supp. XIX:** 17, 30

Good Night, Willie Lee, I'll See You in the Morning (Walker), **Supp. III Part 2:** 520, 531
"Good Oak" (Leopold), **Supp. XIV:** 185, 187, 191
"Good Old Times, The: New York Fifty Years Ago" (Briggs), **Supp. XVIII:** 15
"Good Pine, A" (Offutt), **Supp. XIX:** 174
Goodrich, Chris, **Supp. XXII:** 206, 214
Goodrich, Frances, **Supp. XXVII:** 136
Goodrich, Samuel G., **Supp. I Part 1:** 38
Good Scent from a Strange Mountain, A (R. O. Butler), **Supp. XII:** 62, **70–72**
Good School, A (Yates), **Supp. XI:** 334, **346–347,** 348, 349
"*Good Shepherdess, The*/La Buena Pastora" (Mora), **Supp. XIII:** 228–229
Good Sports (Prouty), **Supp. XXVIII:** 180
Good Wife, The (O'Nan), **Supp. XXV:** 145, 149
Good Will (Smiley), **Supp. VI:** 292, **299–300**
Goodwin, K. L., **III:** 478
Goodwin, Stephen, **Supp. V:** 314, 316, 322, 323, 325
"Good Word for Winter, A" (J. R. Lowell), **Supp. I Part 2:** 420
Goodwyn, Janet, **Retro. Supp. I:** 370
Goody, Alex, **Supp. XXII:** 160
"Goophered Grapevine, The" (Chesnutt), **Supp. XIV:** 57, **58–61**
"Goose Fish, The" (Nemerov), **III:** 272, 284
"Goose Pond" (Kunitz), **Supp. III Part 1:** 262
Goose-Step, The (Sinclair), **Supp. V:** 276
Gordimer, Nadine, **Supp. XV:** 251
Gordon, Ambrose, **Supp. XV:** 144
Gordon, A. R., **III:** 199
Gordon, Caroline, **II: 196–222,** 536, 537; **III:** 454, 482; **IV:** 123, 126–127, 139, 282; **Retro. Supp. II:** 177, 222, 229, 233, 235; **Supp. II Part 1:** 139
Gordon, Charles G., **I:** 454
Gordon, Don, **Supp. X:** 119
Gordon, Eugene, **Supp. II Part 1:** 170; **Supp. XVIII:** 280
Gordon, Fran, **Supp. XIII:** 111
Gordon, James Morris, **II:** 197
Gordon, Lois, **Supp. IV Part 1:** 48; **Supp. V:** 46
Gordon, Lyndall, **Retro. Supp. I:** 55
Gordon, Mary, **Supp. IV Part 1: 297–317**
Gordon, Neil, **Supp. XVI:** 156
Gordon, Peter, **Supp. XII:** 3–4, 4–5, 8
Gordon, Ruth, **IV:** 357; **Supp. XX: 50**
Gore, Thomas Pryor, **Supp. IV Part 2:** 679
Gore and Igor (Levin), **Supp. XXVII:** 133
Gores, Joe, **Supp. XXI:** 70
Gorey, Edward, **IV:** 430, 436; **Supp. XXIII:** 209
"Gorge, The" (Huddle), **Supp. XXVI:** 154
Gorilla, My Love (Bambara), **Supp. XI:** 1, **2–7**

"Gorilla, My Love" (Bambara), **Supp. XI:** 2, 3–4
Gorki, Maxim, **I:** 478; **II:** 49; **III:** 402; **IV:** 299; **Supp. I Part 1:** 5, 51; **Supp. XIX:** 241
Gorky, Maxim, **Supp. XXIII:** 1, 4
Gorman, Herbert, **Supp. XXV:** 25
Gorney, Cynthia, **Supp. XVI:** 112
Gorra, Michael, **Supp. V:** 71
Goslings, The (Sinclair), **Supp. V:** 276, 281
Go South to Sorrow (Rowan), **Supp. XIV:** 306
Gospel (Barnhardt), **Supp. XXVII:** 1, 5–7, 8, 11, 13
Gospel According to Joe, The (Gurney), **Supp. V:** 99
"Gospel According to Saint Mark, The" (Gordon), **Supp. IV Part 1:** 310
Gospel according to the Son (Mailer), **Retro. Supp. II:** 213
"Gospel for the Twentieth Century, The" (Locke), **Supp. XIV:** 206
"Gospel of Beauty, The" (Lindsay), **Supp. I Part 2:** 380, 382, 384, 385, 391, 396
Gospels, The (di Donato), **Supp. XX: 45–46**
Gospel Singer, The (Crews), **Supp. XI:** 102, **109**
Gosse, Edmund, **II:** 538; **IV:** 350; **Supp. VIII:** 157
"Gossip" (Conroy), **Supp. XVI:** 71–72
Gossips, Gorgons, and Crones: The Fates of the Earth (Caputi), **Supp. IV Part 1:** 335
Go Tell It on the Mountain (Baldwin), **Retro. Supp. II:** 1, 2, 3, **4–5,** 7, 14; **Supp. I Part 1:** 48, 49, 50, 51, 52, 53–54, 55, 56, 57, 59, 61, 63, 64, 67; **Supp. II Part 1:** 170
Gotera, Vince, **Supp. XIII:** 115, 116, 119, 121, 127
Gothic Revival, The: An Essay on the History of Taste (Clark), **Supp. XIV:** 348
Gothic Writers (Thomson, Voller, and Frank, eds.), **Retro. Supp. II:** 273
"Go to the Devil and Shake Yourself" (song), **Supp. I Part 2:** 580
"Go to the Shine That's on a Tree" (Eberhart), **I:** 523
Go to the Widow-Maker (Jones), **Supp. XI:** 214, **225–226,** 227, 229, 233
"Gots Is What You Got" (Di Piero), **Supp. XIX:** 35, 36, 38, 41, 42, 45–46
Gottfried, Alex, **Supp. XIX:** 260
Gottfried, Martin, **Supp. IV Part 2:** 584
Gotthelf, Allan, **Supp. IV Part 2:** 528
Gottlieb, Adolph, **Supp. XV:** 144
Gottlieb, Edward, **Supp. XX: 250**
Gottlieb, Leopold, **Supp. XXIII:** 6
Gottlieb, Morton, **Supp. XVI:** 196
Gottlieb, Robert, **Supp. IV Part 2:** 474; **Supp. XXVI:** 244, 246, 250
Gottschalk and the Grande Tarantelle (Brooks), **Supp. III Part 1:** 86
"Gottschalk and the Grande Tarantelle" (Brooks), **Supp. III Part 1:** 86–87
Gould (Dixon), **Supp. XII:** 152, **153**
Gould, Edward Sherman, **I:** 346

Gould, Janice, **Supp. IV Part 1:** 322, 327; **Supp. XII:** 229
Gould, Jay, **I:** 4
Gould, Joe, **Supp. XV:** 143
Goulian, Jon-Jon, **Supp. XXVII:** 68
Gourd Dancer, The (Momaday), **Supp. IV Part 2:** 481, 487, 491, 493
Gourmont, Remy de, **I:** 270, 272; **II:** 528, 529; **III:** 457, 467–468, 477; **Retro. Supp. I:** 55
Gouverneurs de la Rosée (Roumain), **Supp. IV Part 1:** 360, 367
Government Girl (film, Nichols), **Supp. XVIII:** 247
"Governors of Wyoming, The" (Proulx), **Supp. VII:** 264
"Gowane"(Kenny), **Supp. XXIII:** 147–148
Goyen, William, **Supp. V:** 220
Grabhorn, Janet, **Supp. XV:** 142
"Grace" (Budbill), **Supp. XIX:** 2
"Grace" (Dubus), **Supp. VII:** 91
"Grace" (Harjo), **Supp. XII:** 224
Grace Notes (Dove), **Supp. IV Part 1:** 248–250, 252
Grace (Eventually): Thoughts on Faith (Lamott), **Supp. XX: 143–145**
Grade, Chaim, **Supp. XVII:** 41
"Grade School" (Stone), **Supp. XXVII:** 252
"Graduation" (Dubus), **Supp. VII:** 84
Grady, Henry W., **Supp. I Part 1:** 370; **Supp. XXVIII:** 123
Graeber, Laurel, **Supp. V:** 15
Graham, Billy, **I:** 308
Graham, David, **Supp. XIX:** 81; **Supp. XV:** 104
Graham, Don, **Supp. XI:** 252, 254
Graham, Jorie, **Supp. IX:** 38, 52; **Supp. X:** 73; **Supp. XII:** 209; **Supp. XIII:** 85; **Supp. XVII:** 110, 111, 133, 240, 241, 242
Graham, Martha, **Supp. XI:** 152
Graham, Maryemma, **Retro. Supp. I:** 201, 204
Graham, Nan, **Supp. XII:** 272
Graham, Sheilah, **II:** 94; **Retro. Supp. I:** 97, 113–114, 115; **Supp. IX:** 63
Graham, Shirley, **Supp. I Part 1:** 51; **Supp. XXI:** 277. *See also* Du Bois, Shirley Graham
Graham, Stephen, **Supp. I Part 2:** 397
Graham, Tom (pseudonym). *See* Lewis, Sinclair
"Graham House, April '76"(Balakian), **Supp. XXIII:** 24
Grahn, Judy, **Retro. Supp. III:** 248; **Supp. IV Part 1:** 325, 330; **Supp. XXIII:** 195
"Grain Field" (Crapsey), **Supp. XVII:** 77
Grainger, Percy, **Supp. I Part 2:** 386
Grain of Mustard Seed, A (Sarton), **Supp. VIII: 259–260,** 263
Gramar (Lowth), **II:** 8
"Gramercy Park" (Teasdale), **Supp. XXVII:** 289
Grammar of Motives, A (Burke), **I:** 272, 275, 276–278, 283, 284
Gramsci, Antonio, **Supp. XX: 35–36**
Granados, Gabriel Bernal, **Supp. XV:** 350

Granath, Jack, **Supp. XVIII:** 93

Granberry, Edwin, **I:** 288

Grand Canyon, Inc. (Everett), **Supp. XVIII:** 66

Grand Design, The (Dos Passos), **I:** 489–490

"Grande Malade, The" (Barnes), **Supp. III Part 1:** 36

"Grandfather" (Dunn), **Supp. XI:** 147

"Grandfather and Grandson" (Singer), **Retro. Supp. II:** 307

Grandfathers, The (Richter), **Supp. XVIII:** 219–220

"Grandfather's Blessing" (Alvarez), **Supp. VII:** 2

"Grand Forks" (Bierds), **Supp. XVII:** 34

"Grand Forks" (Simpson), **Supp. IX:** 280–281

"Grand Inquisitor" (Dostoevsky), **IV:** 106

Grandissimes (Cable), **II:** 291

"Grand-Master Nabokov" (Updike), **Retro. Supp. I:** 317

"Grand Miracle, The" (Karr), **Supp. XI:** 251

"Grandmother" (Gunn Allen), **Supp. IV Part 1:** 320, 325

"Grandmother in Heaven" (Levine), **Supp. V:** 186

"Grandmother of the Sun: Ritual Gynocracy in Native America" (Gunn Allen), **Supp. IV Part 1:** 328

Grandmothers of the Light: A Medicine Woman's Sourcebook (Gunn Allen, ed.), **Supp. IV Part 1:** 332, 333–334

"Grandmother Songs, The" (Hogan), **Supp. IV Part 1:** 413

"Grandpa and the Statue" (A. Miller), **III:** 147

"Grandparents" (R. Lowell), **II:** 550

"Grandsire Bells, The" (Bierds), **Supp. XVII:** 28–29

"Grandstand Complex, The" (McCoy), **Supp. XIII:** 166

Grange, Red, **II:** 416

Granger's Index to Poetry (anthology), **Retro. Supp. I:** 37, 39

Granite & Cedar (Miller), **Supp. XXII:** 214

Grant, Gavin, **Supp. XIX:** 175

Grant, Lee, **Supp. XIII:** 295

Grant, Madison, **Supp. II Part 1:** 170

Grant, Richard, **Supp. X:** 282

Grant, Ulysses S., **I:** 4, 15; **II:** 542; **III:** 506, 584; **IV:** 348, 446; **Supp. I Part 2:** 418; **Supp. XXIV:** 224

Grantwood, **Retro. Supp. I:** 416, 417

"Grapes, The" (Hecht), **Supp. X:** 65–66

"Grape Sherbet" (Dove), **Supp. IV Part 1:** 246

Grapes of Wrath, The (Steinbeck), **I:** 301; **III:** 589; **IV:** 51, 53–55, 59, 63, 65, 67, 68, 69; **Supp. V:** 290; **Supp. XI:** 169; **Supp. XIV:** 181; **Supp. XV:** 351; **Supp. XX:** 28

"Grapevine, The" (Ashbery), **Supp. III Part 1:** 4

"Grass" (Sandburg), **III:** 584

Grass, Günter, **Supp. VIII:** 40

Grass County (Kooser), **Supp. XIX:** 119

"Grasse: The Olive Trees" (Wilbur), **Supp. III Part 2:** 550

"Grass Figures" (Hecht), **Supp. XXVII:** 85

Grass Harp, The (Capote), **Supp. III Part 1:** 114–117, 123

Grassroot Jungles: A Book of Insects (Teale), **Supp. XXVIII:** 246, 255

Grass Still Grows, The (A. Miller), **III:** 146

"Gratified Desire" (Davison), **Supp. XXVI:** 74

"Grating Parmesan"(Crooker), **Supp. XXIII:** 56

Gratitude to Old Teachers (R. Bly), **Supp. IV Part 1:** 73

Grattan, Bill, **Supp. XXIII:** 273, 274, 275, 276, 279, 280

Graupner, Gottlieb, **Supp. XV:** 240, 244

"Grave, A" (Moore), **III:** 195, 202, 208, 213

Grave, The (Blair), **Supp. I Part 1:** 150

"Grave, The" (Porter), **III:** 433, 443, 445–446

"Grave, The" (Winters), **Supp. II Part 2:** 795, 796

"Graven Image" (O'Hara), **III:** 320

Grave of Light: New and Selected Poems, 1970–2005 (Notley), **Supp. XXII:** 226, 235, 236

Grave of the Right Hand, The (Wright), **Supp. V:** 332, 338, 339

"Grave Piece" (Eberhart), **I:** 533

Graver, Lawrence, **Supp. XXVII:** 136, 137, 140

Graves, Billy, **Supp. I Part 2:** 607

Graves, Jesse, **Supp. XXVII:** 216

Graves, John, **Supp. V:** 220

Graves, Morris, **Supp. X:** 264

Graves, Peter, **Supp. IV Part 2:** 474

Graves, Rean, **Supp. I Part 1:** 326

Graves, Robert, **I:** 437, 477, 523; **Supp. I Part 2:** 541; **Supp. IV Part 1:** 280, 348; **Supp. IV Part 2:** 685; **Supp. XXVI:** 53

"Graveyard, The" (Very), **Supp. XXV:** 249

"Graveyard Blues" (Trethewey), **Supp. XXI:** 245, 255, 256

Graveyard for Lunatics, A (Bradbury), **Supp. IV Part 1:** 102, 114–116

Gravity's Rainbow (Pynchon), **Supp. II Part 2:** 617, 618–619, 621–625, 627, 630, 633–636; **Supp. IV Part 1:** 279; **Supp. V:** 44; **Supp. XIV:** 49; **Supp. XVII:** 236; **Supp. XXII:** 255; **Supp. XXIV:** 140

Gray, Cecil, **Supp. I Part 1:** 258

Gray, Francine Du Plessix, **Supp. V:** 169

Gray, James, **III:** 207; **Supp. I Part 2:** 410

Gray, Jeffrey, **Supp. XV:** 27

Gray, Josie, **Supp. XXIV:** 166, 167, 172, 178

Gray, Paul, **Supp. IV Part 1:** 305; **Supp. IV Part 2:** 639; **Supp. XVI:** 74; **Supp. XVIII:** 94

Gray, Thomas, **I:** 68; **Supp. I Part 1:** 150; **Supp. I Part 2:** 422, 716

Gray, Thomas A., **Supp. I Part 2:** 710

"Gray Heron, The" (Kinnell), **Supp. III Part 1:** 250

"Gray Mills of Farley, The" (Jewett), **Retro. Supp. II:** 132, 144

"Gray Poem" (Everwine), **Supp. XV:** 81

Grayscale: Poems (Huddle), **Supp. XXVI:** 150

Grayson, Charles, **Supp. XIII:** 171

"Gray Squirrel" (Francis), **Supp. IX:** 90

"Gray Wolf's H 'ant, The" (Chesnutt), **Supp. XIV:** 60

Grayzel, Solomon, **Supp. XXVIII:** 150, 157

Grealy, Lucy, **Supp. XII:** 310

Greasy Lake (Boyle), **Supp. VIII:** 14–15

"Greasy Lake" (Boyle), **Supp. VIII:** 15; **Supp. XX:** 18–19

Greasy Lake & Other Stories (Boyle), **Supp. XX:** 17, 18–19

Great Action Stories (Kittredge and Krauzer), **Supp. XXVI:** 182

"Great Adventure of Max Breuck, The" (A. Lowell), **II:** 522

Great American Detective, The (Kittredge and Krauzer), **Supp. XXVI:** 182

Great American Novel, The (P. Roth), **Retro. Supp. II:** 283, 288–289; **Supp. III Part 2:** 414–416

Great American Poetry Bake-Off, The (Peters), **Retro. Supp. III:** 245

Great American Short Novels (Phillips, ed.), **Supp. VIII:** 156

Great Battles of the World (Crane), **I:** 415

"Great Carousel, The" (Untermeyer), **Supp. XV:** 296

Great Christian Doctrine of Original Sin Defended, The . . . (Edwards), **I:** 549, 557, 559

Great Circle (Aiken), **I:** 53, 55, 57

"Great Class-Reunion Bazaar, The" (Theroux), **Supp. VIII:** 312

Great Day, The (Hurston), **Retro. Supp. III:** 128, 129, 133, 137; **Supp. VI:** 154

Great Days (Barthelme), **Supp. IV Part 1:** 39

Great Days, The (Dos Passos), **I:** 491

Great Digest (Pound, trans.), **III:** 472

"Great Divider, The" (Saunders), **Supp. XIX:** 235

"Great Elegy for John Donne" (Brodsky), **Supp. VIII:** 21, 23

"Greater Good, A" (Di Piero), **Supp. XIX:** 39

Greater Inclination, The (Wharton), **Retro. Supp. I:** 363, 364–365, 366; **Retro. Supp. III:** 278, 279

Greater Sea, The (Gibran), **Supp. XX:** 118

"Greater Self, The" (Gibran), **Supp. XX:** 118

"Greater Torment, The" (Blackmur), **Supp. II Part 1:** 92

Greatest Hits 1969–1996 (Salinas), **Supp. XIII:** 311

"Greatest of These, The" (C. Miller), **Supp. XXII:** 188, 196

"Greatest Thing in the World, The" (Mailer), **Retro. Supp. II:** 196

Great Expectations (Acker), **Supp. XII:** 5, 9–11

Great Expectations (Dickens), **III:** 247; **Supp. I Part 1:** 35; **Supp. XVI:** 73; **Supp. XVIII:** 146; **Supp. XXVII:** 268

"Great Expectations, No Satisfaction" (D. Gates), **Supp. XVI:** 73

"Great Figure, The" (W. C. Williams), **IV:** 414

"Great Fillmore Street Buffalo Drive, The" (Momaday), **Supp. IV Part 2:** 493

Great Gatsby, The (Fitzgerald), **I:** 107, 375, 514; **II:** 77, 79, 83, 84, 85, 87, 91–93, 94, 96, 98; **III:** 244, 260, 372, 572; **IV:** 124, 297; **Retro. Supp. I:** 98, 105, **105–108**, 110, 114, 115, 335, 359; **Retro. Supp. II:** 107, 201; **Supp. II Part 2:** 626; **Supp. III Part 2:** 585; **Supp. IV Part 2:** 468, 475; **Supp. IX:** 57, 58; **Supp. X:** 175; **Supp. XI:** 65, 69, 334; **Supp. XVI:** 64, 75; **Supp. XVIII:** 76, 148, 165; **Supp. XX: 59, 60, 61, 72; Supp. XXII:** 81, 82, 88; **Supp. XXIII:** 101; **Supp. XXVII:** 9

Great Gatsby, The (Fitzgerald) (Modern Library), **Retro. Supp. I:** 113

Great God Brown, The (O'Neill), **III:** 165, 391, 394–395

Great Goodness of Life: A Coon Show (Baraka), **Supp. II Part 1:** 47

Great Heart: The History of a Labrador Adventure (Davidson and Rugge), **Supp. XXII:** 218

"Great Idea Lives Forever, A: Shouldn't Its Copyright?" (Helprin), **Supp. XXV:** 84, 88

Great Inclination, The (Wharton), **IV:** 310

"Great Infirmities" (Simic), **Supp. VIII:** 277

Great Jones Street (DeLillo), **Supp. VI:** 2, 3, 8–9, 11, 12

"Great Lawsuit, The: Man *versus* Men: Woman *versus* Women" (Fuller), **Retro. Supp. I:** 156; **Supp. II Part 1:** 292

Great Ledge, The (Davison), **Supp. XXVI:** 66, 77–78

"Great Ledge, The" (Davison), **Supp. XXVI:** 77, 78

"Great Men and Their Environment" (James), **II:** 347

"Great Mississippi Bubble, The" (Irving), **II:** 314

Great Mistake, The (Rinehart), **Supp. XXV:** 198, 200

"Great Prize Fight, The" (Twain), **Retro. Supp. III:** 259–260

Great Railway Bazaar, The: By Train through Asia (Theroux), **Supp. VIII:** 318, 319, **320–321,** 322

"Great Scott" (Conroy), **Supp. XVI:** 75, 77

Great Shark Hunt, The (Thompson), **Supp. XXIV:** 286

"Great Sleigh-Ride of Brewsterville, The" (Briggs), **Supp. XVIII:** 16

"Great Spirit, The" (Zitkala-Ša), **Supp. XXV:** 276, 282

"Great Stone Face, The" (Hawthorne), **Retro. Supp. III:** 117, 118

Great Stories of Suspense (Millar, ed.), **Supp. IV Part 2:** 474

Great Topics of the World (Goldbarth), **Supp. XII:** 187, 189, 191

Great Valley, The (Masters), **Supp. I Part 2:** 465

Great World and Timothy Colt, The (Auchincloss), **Supp. IV Part 1:** 25, 31, 32

Grédy, Jean-Pierre, **Supp. XVI:** 194

"Greed, Part 14"(Wakoski), **Supp. XXVIII:** 271

Greed, Parts 3 and 4 (Wakoski), **Supp. XXVIII:** 263

Greed, Parts 5–7 (Wakoski), **Supp. XXVIII:** 263–264

Greed, Parts 8–11 (Wakoski), **Supp. XXVIII:** 265

Greed, Parts One and Two (Wakoski), **Supp. XXVIII:** 263

"Greek Boy, The" (Bryant), **Supp. I Part 1:** 168

Greek Mind/Jewish Soul: The Conflicted Art of Cynthia Ozick (Strandberg), **Supp. V:** 273

"Greek Partisan, The" (Bryant), **Supp. I Part 1:** 168

"Greeks, The" (McCarriston), **Supp. XIV:** 271

"Greeks, the Chines, or Say the Mayans, The" (Bronk), **Supp. XXI:** 31

Greeley, Horace, **II:** 7; **IV:** 197, 286–287

Green, Anna Katharine, **Supp. XXV:** 199; **Supp. XXVI:** 277, 282

Green, Archie, **Supp. XXVI:** 134

Green, Ashbel, **Supp. IV Part 2:** 474

Green, David Gordon, **Supp. XXV:** 153

Green, Henry, **IV:** 279; **Retro. Supp. I:** 354; **Supp. III Part 1:** 3; **Supp. XI:** 294–295, 296, 297; **Supp. XII:** 315

Green, Jack, **Supp. IV Part 1:** 284–285

Green, Martin, **Supp. I Part 1:** 299

Green, Michelle, **Supp. IV Part 1:** 95

Green, Rose Basile, **Supp. XX: 33, 41**

"Green Automobile, The" (Ginsberg), **Supp. II Part 1:** 322

Greenberg, Clement, **Supp. XV:** 141, 143, 144, 145

Greenberg, Eliezer, **Supp. I Part 2:** 432; **Supp. XXIII:** 7

Greenberg, Hayim, **Supp. XXIII:** 3

Greenberg, Jonathan, **Supp. XII:** 285

Greenberg, Miriam, **Supp. XXII:** 244

Greenberg, Samuel, **I:** 393

Green Bough, A (Faulkner), **Retro. Supp. I:** 84; **Retro. Supp. III:** 84

"Green Canoe" (Halliday), **Supp. XIX:** 88

Green Centuries (Gordon), **II:** 196, 197–207, 209

"Green Crab's Shell, A" (Doty), **Supp. XI:** 126

"Green Door, The" (O. Henry), **Supp. II Part 1:** 395

Greene, A. C., **Supp. V:** 223, 225

Greene, Graham, **I:** 480; **II:** 62, 320; **III:** 57, 556; **Retro. Supp. I:** 215; **Supp. I Part 1:** 280; **Supp. IV Part 1:** 341; **Supp. IX:** 261; **Supp. V:** 298; **Supp. XI:** 99,**Supp. XI:** 104; **Supp. XIII:** 233; **Supp. XIX:** 29–30; **Supp. XVIII:** 79

Greene, Helga, **Supp. IV Part 1:** 134, 135

Greene, J. Lee, **Retro. Supp. II:** 121

Greene, Nathanael, **Supp. I Part 2:** 508

Greene, Richard Tobias, **III:** 76

Greene, Robert, **Supp. XVII:** 232

Green Eggs and Ham (Geisel), **Supp. XVI:** 108, 109

"Greene-ing of the Portables, The" (Cowley), **Supp. II Part 1:** 140

"Greenest Continent, The" (Stevens), **Retro. Supp. I:** 304

Greenfeld, Josh, **III:** 364

Greenfield, Josh, **Supp. XIX:** 269

"Green Hell" (Boyle), **Supp. XX:** 18

Green Hills of Africa (Hemingway), **II:** 253; **Retro. Supp. I:** 182, 186; **Retro. Supp. III:** 255, 264

Greening of America, The (C. Reich), **Supp. XVII:** 3

"Green Lagoons, The" (Leopold), **Supp. XIV:** 188

"Green Lampshade" (Simic), **Supp. VIII:** 283

Greenlanders, The (Smiley), **Supp. VI:** 292, **296–298,** 299, 305, 307

Greenlaw, Edwin A., **IV:** 453

"Greenleaf" (O'Connor), **III:** 350, 351; **Retro. Supp. II:** 233, 237; **Retro. Supp. III:** 208, 213

Greenman, Walter F., **I:** 217, 222

Green Memories (Mumford), **Supp. II Part 2:** 474, 475, 479, 480–481

Green Mountain Ghosts, Ghouls, and Unsolved Mysteries (Citro), **Supp. XXII:** 208, 218

"Green of Oxygen, The"(Wakoski), **Supp. XXVIII:** 272

"Green Pasture, The" (Leopold), **Supp. XIV:** 184

Green Pastures, The (Connelly), **Supp. II Part 1:** 223

"Green Red Brown and White" (Swenson), **Supp. IV Part 2:** 639

"Green River" (Bryant), **Supp. I Part 1:** 155, 164

Green Shadows, White Whale (Bradbury), **Supp. IV Part 1:** 102, 103, 116

"Green Shirt, The" (Olds), **Supp. X:** 209

"Greensleeves" (Jarman), **Supp. XVII:** 113

"Greensleeves" (Notley), **Supp. XXII:** 228

Greenslet, Ferris, **I:** 19; **Retro. Supp. I:** 9, 10, 11, 13; **Retro. Supp. II:** 41

Greenspan, Alan, **Supp. IV Part 2:** 526

Greenspan, Ezra, **Supp. XVIII:** 257

Greenstreet, Sydney, **Supp. IV Part 1:** 356

"Green Thought, A" (L. Michaels), **Supp. XVI:** 204

"Green-Thumb Boy" (Nelson), **Supp. XVIII:** 182

Green Treasury: A Journey Through the World's Great Nature Writing (Teale), **Supp. XXVIII:** 248

Greenwald, Ted, **Supp. IV Part 2:** 423

Green Wall, The (Wright), **Supp. III Part 2:** 591, 593, 595

Green Wave, The (Rukeyser), **Supp. VI:** 273, 280

"Green Ways" (Kunitz), **Supp. III Part 1:** 265

Green with Beasts (Merwin), **Supp. III Part 1:** 340, 344–346

Greenwood, Grace, **Supp. XIII:** 141

"Greeting Card Verse" (Peacock), **Supp. XIX:** 200

Greetings from Ice Country (Muñoz), **Supp. XXV:** 130

Gregerson, Linda, **Supp. IV Part 2:** 651; **Supp. X:** 204–205; **Supp. XI:** 142

"Gregorio Valdes" (Bishop), **Retro. Supp. II:** 51

Gregory, Alyse, **I:** 221, 226, 227, 231

Gregory, Horace, **II:** 512; **Supp. III Part 2:** 614, 615; **Supp. IX:** 229; **Supp. XV:** 143

Gregory, Lady Isabella Augusta, **III:** 458

Gregory, Sinda, **Supp. X:** 260, 268

Grendel (Gardner), **Supp. VI:** 63, **67,** 68, 74

Grenstone Poems (Bynner), **Supp. XV:** 44

"Gretel in Darkness" (Glück), **Supp. V:** 82

Gretta (Caldwell), **I:** 301, 302

Greuze, Jean Baptiste, **Supp. I Part 2:** 714

Grey, Zane, **Supp. XIII:** 5; **Supp. XXVI:** 186

Greyhounding This America (Kenny), **Supp. XXIII: 155**

Gridley Firing (Hayford), **Supp. XXII:** 204

"Grief Has Stamped" (Pedersen; Nelson, trans.), **Supp. XVIII:** 180

Grieg, Michael, **Supp. XV:** 133, 148

Griest, Stephanie Elizondo, **Supp. XXVIII: 97–110**

Griffin, Bartholomew, **Supp. I Part 1:** 369

Griffin, Joan R., **Supp. XXVIII:** 4

Griffin, John Howard, **Supp. VIII:** 208; **Supp. XXI:** 74; **Supp. XXV:** 51

Griffin, Merv, **Supp. IV Part 2:** 526

Griffith, Albert J., **Supp. V:** 325

Griffith, D. W., **I:** 31, 481–482; **Retro. Supp. I:** 103, 325; **Supp. XI:** 45; **Supp. XVI:** 183, 184; **Supp. XXI:** 170

Griffith, Paul, **Supp. XVIII:** 173, 175

Griffiths, Clyde, **I:** 511

Grile, Dod (pseudonym). *See* Bierce, Ambrose

Grimes, William, **Retro. Supp. III:** 320

Grimm, Herman, **II:** 17

Grimm brothers, **II:** 378; **III:** 101, 491, 492; **IV:** 266; **Supp. I Part 2:** 596, 622; **Supp. X:** 78, 84, 86

Grimshaw, Anna, **Supp. XXI:** 172

Grinde, Donald A., Jr, **Supp. XXVI:** 98

Grinnell, George Bird, **Supp. XVI:** 13

Gris, Juan, **I:** 442; **Retro. Supp. I:** 430

Griswold, Rufus Wilmot, **III:** 409, 429; **Retro. Supp. II:** 261, 262; **Retro. Supp. III:** 225, 236; **Supp. XV:** 277,

278; **Supp. XVI:** 8, 10–11; **Supp. XXV:** 250

"Grizzly" (Kittredge), **Supp. XXVI:** 187

Grogg, Sam, Jr., **Supp. IV Part 2:** 468, 471

Gromer, Crystal, **Supp. XII:** 297

Gronlund, Laurence, **II:** 276

Grooms, Red, **Supp. XV:** 178

Grooves: A Kind of Mystery (Brockmeier), **Supp. XXII:** 55, 56, 59

"Groping for Trouts" (Gass), **Supp. VI:** 87

Grosholz, Emily, **Supp. XII:** 185; **Supp. XIX:** 37–38, 278

Grosman un zun (Grosman and Son) (Asch), **Supp. XXIII:** 7

Gross, Robert A., **Supp. XIX:** 151

Gross, Terry, **Supp. XVI:** 167; **Supp. XXI:** 247, 255; **Supp. XXVIII:** 283

"Grosse Fuge" (Doty), *Supp. XI:* 126–127

Grossman, Allen, **Retro. Supp. II:** 83; **Supp. XIX:** 82, 86, 94; **Supp. XVIII:** 91

Grossman, Lev, **Supp. XXV:** 4, **63–78**

Grosz, George, **III:** 172; **IV:** 438; **Retro. Supp. II:** 321; **Supp. X:** 137; **Supp. XXVII:** 88

"Grotesque in Modern Fiction, The" (E. Hoffman, Ph.D. dissertation), **Supp. XVI:** 147

"Groundhog, The" (Eberhart), **I:** 523, 530–532, 533

"Ground on Which I Stand, The" (Wilson), **Retro. Supp. III:** 319; **Supp. VIII:** 331

"Ground Swell" (Jarman), **Supp. XVII:** 118

Group, The (McCarthy), **II:** 570, 574–578

"Group of Two, A" (Jarrell), **II:** 368

Group Therapy (Hearon), **Supp. VIII: 64–65**

"Grove" (Goldbarth), **Supp. XII:** 176

Groves of Academe, The (McCarthy), **II:** 568–571

Growing into Love (X. J. Kennedy), **Supp. XV:** 153, **158–160**

Growing Pains (J. S. Untermeyer), **Supp. XV:** 303

"Growing Season, The" (Caldwell), **I:** 309

Growing Up Gay: A Literary Anthology (Singer, ed.), **Supp. IV Part 1:** 330

"Growing Up Good in Maycomb" (Shaffer), **Supp. VIII:** 128

Growing Up Native American (Riley, ed.), **Supp. XXVI:** 104

"Grown-Up" (Jewett), **Retro. Supp. II:** 134

Grown Up All Wrong (Christgau), **Supp. XXVII:** 33, 35–36, 40–41

"Growth" (R. Lowell), **II:** 554

"Growth and Decay in Recent Verse" (Untermeyer), **Supp. XV:** 299

Growth of the American Republic, The (Morison and Commager), **Supp. I Part 2:** 484

"Growtown Buggle, The" (Jewett), **Retro. Supp. II:** 132

Grubin, David, **Supp. XXIII:** 138

Gruenberg, Louis, **III:** 392

Grumbach, Doris, **II:** 560

"Gryphon" (C. Baxter), **Supp. XVII:** 14, 17

"Guacamaja" (Leopold), **Supp. XIV:** 188–189

Guardian Angel (Paretsky), **Supp. XXV:** 178, 179

Guardian Angel, The (Holmes), **Supp. I Part 1:** 315–316

"Guardian of the Law" (R. Fisher), **Supp. XIX:** 71

Guard of Honor (Cozzens), **I:** 370–372, 375, 376–377, 378, 379

Guardsman, The (Molnar), **Supp. XVI:** 187

Guare, John, **Retro. Supp. III:** 318; **Supp. XIII:** 196, 207

Guattari, Félix, **Supp. XXV:** 123

Gubar, Susan, **Retro. Supp. I:** 42; **Retro. Supp. II:** 324; **Supp. IX:** 66; **Supp. XV:** 270; **Supp. XXIV:** 28

"Guenevere" (Teasdale), **Supp. XXVII:** 287

Guerard, Albert, Jr., **Supp. X:** 79; **Supp. XIII:** 172

Guérin, Maurice de, **I:** 241

"Guerrilla Handbook, A" (Baraka), **Supp. II Part 1:** 36

Guess and Spell Coloring Book, The (Swenson), **Supp. IV Part 2:** 648

Guess Who's Coming to Dinner (film), **Supp. I Part 1:** 67

Guest, Barbara, **Supp. XXIII:** 215; **Supp. XXVII:** 23

Guest, Judith, **Supp. XVI:** 36

Guest, Val, **Supp. XI:** 307

Guest Book (Bynner), **Supp. XV:** 51

"Guest Ellen at the Supper for Street People, The" (Ferry), **Supp. XXIV:** 152–153, 162

"Guests of Mrs. Timms, The" (Jewett), **II:** 408; **Retro. Supp. II:** 135

Guevara, Martha, **Supp. VIII:** 74

Guevara, Fray Miguel de, **Supp. XXI:** 104

"Guevara . . .Guevara" (Salinas), **Supp. XIII:** 312–313, 315

Guggenheim, Peggy, **Supp. XXII:** 165

Guided Tours of Hell (Prose), **Supp. XVI:** 257, 261

"Guided Tours of Hell" (Prose), **Supp. XVI:** 257

Guide for the Bedevilled, A (Hecht), **Supp. XXVII:** 94, 95

Guide for the Perplexed (Maimonides), **Supp. XVII:** 46

Guide in the Wilderness, A (Cooper), **I:** 337

"Guidelines" (Espaillat), **Supp. XXI:** 99

"Guide to Dungeness Spit, A" (Wagoner), **Supp. IX:** 325–326, 329

Guide to Ezra Pound's Selected Cantos' (Kearns), **Retro. Supp. I:** 292

Guide to Kulchur (Pound), **III:** 475

Guide to the Ruins (Nemerov), **III:** 269, 270–271, 272

Guillén, Jorge, **Supp. XXIV:** 152

Guillén, Nicolás, **Retro. Supp. I:** 202;
Supp. I Part 1: 345
Guillevic, Eugene, **Supp. III Part 1:** 283
"Guilt, The" (Peacock), **Supp. XIX:** 200
"Guilt and *Incident at Vichy*" (A. Miller),
Retro. Supp. III: 175
"Guilty Man, The" (Kunitz), **Supp. II
Part 1:** 263
*Guilty of Everything: The Autobiography
of Herbert Huncke* (Huncke), **Supp.
XIV:** 138, 140, 141, 150
Guilty Pleasures (Barthelme), **Supp. IV
Part 1:** 44, 45, 53
Guimond, James, **Supp. XXI:** 228
Guinness, Alec, **Retro. Supp. I:** 65;
Supp. XX: 50
Gulag Archipelago, The (Solzhenitsyn),
Supp. XVII: 229
"Gulf, The" (Dunn), **Supp. XI:** 149
Gulistan (Saadi), **II:** 19
Gullible's Travels (Lardner), **II:** 426, 427
Gulliver, Adelaide Cromwell, **Supp.
XVIII:** 286
"Gulliver Found" (Bronk), **Supp. XXI:**
33
Gulliver's Travels (Swift), **I:** 209, 348,
366; **II:** 301; **Retro. Supp. III:** 154;
Supp. I Part 2: 656; **Supp. XI:** 209;
Supp. XVI: 110
"Gulls" (Hayden), **Supp. II Part 1:** 367
"Gulls, The" (Nemerov), **III:** 272
"Gulls on Dumps" (Di Piero), **Supp.
XIX:** 41
"Gun, The" (Dobyns), **Supp. XIII:** 88
Gun, with Occasional Music (Lethem),
Supp. XVIII: 137–138
*Günderode: A Translation from the Ger-
man* (Fuller), **Supp. II Part 1:** 293
Gunderson, Gwen, **Supp. XXVI:** 134
Gundy, Jeff, **Supp. XI:** 315; **Supp. XVI:**
46, 265, 275
Gunfight at the O.K. Corral (film), **Supp.
XX: 246**
Gunga Din (screenplay, Hecht and
MacArthur), **Supp. XXVII:** 83, 90
"Gun Hand, The" (Davison), **Supp.
XXVI:** 71
Gun in Cheek (Pronzini), **Supp. XXVI:**
278
Gunman's Rhapsody (Parker), **Supp.
XIX:** 187
Gunn, Robin Wright, **Supp. XXI:** 243,
244
Gunn, Thom, **Supp. IX:** 269; **Supp.
XXVIII:** 260
Gunn, Thomas, **Supp. V:** 178
Gunn Allen, Paula, **Supp. IV Part 1:
319–340**, 404; **Supp. IV Part 2:** 499,
502, 557, 568; **Supp. XII:** 218
"Gunnar's Sword" (C. Bly), **Supp. XVI:**
34, 35, 37, 42
"Guns as Keys; and the Great Gate
Swings" (A. Lowell), **II:** 524
Gurdjieff, Georges, **Supp. IX:** 320; **Supp.
V:** 199
Gurganus, Allan, **Supp. XII:** 308–309,
310
Gurko, Leo, **III:** 62
Gurney, A. R., **Supp. IX:** 261; **Supp. V:
95–112**

Gurney, Mary (Molly) Goodyear, **Supp.
V:** 95
Gussow, Mel, **Supp. IX:** 93; **Supp. XII:**
325, 328, 341
Gustavus Vassa, the African (Vassa),
Supp. IV Part 1: 11
*Gusto, Thy Name Was Mrs. Hopkins: A
Prose Rhapsody* (Francis), **Supp. IX:**
89
Guston, Philip, **Supp. XXIII:** 210
Gute Mensch von Sezuan, Der (Brecht),
Supp. IX: 138
Gutenberg, Johann, **Supp. I Part 2:** 392
Guthrie, A. B., **Supp. X:** 103
Guthrie, Woody, **Supp. XVIII:** 23; **Supp.
XXVIII:** 255
Gutman, Herbert, **Supp. I Part 1:** 47
Guttenplan, D. D., **Supp. XI:** 38
"Gutting of Couffignal, The" (Hammett),
Supp. IV Part 1: 345
Guttmann, Allen, **Supp. XXVII:** 134;
Supp. XXVIII: 149
Guy, David, **Supp. XXVI:** 9
Guy Domville (James), **II:** 331; **Retro.
Supp. I:** 228
"Gwendolyn" (Bishop), **Retro. Supp. II:**
51
Gwynn, R. S., **Supp. XVIII:** 184
Gypsy Ballads (Hughes, trans.), **Supp. I
Part 1:** 345
Gypsy's Curse, The (Crews), **Supp. XI:
110**
"Gyroscope, The" (Rukeyser), **Supp. VI:**
271
Gysin, Brion, **Supp. XII:** 129

H

Ha, Quan Manh, **Supp. XXVI:** 213, 214,
215
Haardt, Sara. *See* Mencken, Mrs. H. L.
(Sara Haardt)
Haas, Robert, **Supp. XXII:** 177
Habakkuk (biblical book), **III:** 200, 347
Habibi (Nye), **Supp. XIII:** 273, **279**
"Habit" (James), **II:** 351
Habitations of the Word (Gass), **Supp.
VI:** 88
Habit of Being, The (O'Connor; Fitzger-
ald, ed.), **Retro. Supp. III:** 208
"Hack, The" (Swados), **Supp. XIX:** 267
"Hackberry"(P. Benedict), **Supp. XXIII:**
37–38, 39
Hacker, Marilyn, **Supp. XV:** 250; **Supp.
XVII:** 71, 76, 112; **Supp. XVIII:** 177,
178
Hacker, Randi, **Supp. XXVI:** 121
Hacket, Albert, **Supp. XXVII:** 136
Hackett, David, **Supp. XII:** 236
Hadas, Rachel, **Supp. XXIII:** 111–128;
Supp. XXIV: 157
Hadda, Janet, **Retro. Supp. II:** 317
Haddád, 'Abd al-Masíh, **Supp. XX: 116**
"Hades Welcomes His Bride" (Stallings),
Supp. XXV: 229–230
Haeckel, Ernst Heinrich, **II:** 480
Haegert, John, **Supp. XVI:** 69
Hafen, P. Jane, **Supp. XXV:** 280
Hafif, Marcia, **Supp. IV Part 2:** 423

Hagar's Daughter (P. Hopkins), **Supp.
XVI:** 143
Hagedorn, Jessica, **Supp. X:** 292
Hagen, Beulah, **Supp. I Part 2:** 679
Hager, Kelly, **Supp. XVIII:** 183
Hagestadt, Emma, **Supp. XXVI:** 212
Haggard, Rider, **III:** 189
Haggas, Carol, **Supp. XXVI:** 159, 160
Hagoromo (play), **III:** 466
Hagstrum, Jean, **Supp. XV:** 74
"Hail Mary" (Fante), **Supp. XI:** 160, 164
Haines, George, IV, **I:** 444
Haines, John, **Supp. XII: 197–214**
"Hair" (Corso), **Supp. XII:** 117, 126, 127
"Hair, The" (Carver), **Supp. III Part 1:**
137
"Haircut" (Lardner), **II:** 430, 436
"Hair Dressing" (Untermeyer), **Supp.
XV:** 304, 305
*Hairpiece: A Film for Nappy-Headed
People* (Chenzira; film), **Supp. XI:**
19–20
"Hairs" (Cisneros), **Supp. VII:** 59
Hairs/Pelitos (Cisneros), **Supp. VII:** 58
Hairy Ape, The (O'Neill), **III:** 391, 392,
393
"Haïta the Shepherd" (Bierce), **I:** 203
Haj, The (Uris), **Supp. XX: 244, 245,
247, 255–256**
Hajdu, David, **Supp. XXVII:** 153
Haldeman, Anna, **Supp. I Part 1:** 2
Hale, Edward Everett, **Supp. I Part 2:**
584; **Supp. XI:** 193, 200
Hale, John Parker, **Supp. I Part 2:** 685
Hale, Nancy, **Supp. VIII:** 151, 171
Hale, Sarah Josepha, **Retro. Supp. III:**
231
Haley, Alex, **Supp. I Part 1:** 47, 66
Haley, J. Evetts, **Supp. V:** 226
"Half a Century Gone" (R. Lowell), **II:**
554
"Half a Grapefruit" (Munro), **Supp.
XXVII:** 186–187
*Half-a-Hundred: Tales by Great American
Writers* (Grayson, ed.), **Supp. XIII:**
171
*Half and Half:Writers on Growing Up
Biracial and Bicultural* (Hearn, ed.),
Supp. XXV: 51
Half Asleep in Frog Pajamas (Robbins),
Supp. X: 259, **279–282**
Half Breed, The (film), **Supp. XVI:** 185
Half-Century of Conflict, A (Parkman),
Supp. II Part 2: 600, 607, 610
"Half Deity" (Moore), **III:** 210, 214, 215
"Half Hour of August" (Ríos), **Supp. IV
Part 2:** 552
"Half-Life of Cardio-Pulmonary Func-
tion, A" (Gansworth), **Supp. XXVI:**
111
*Half-Life of Cardio-Pulmonary Function,
A: Poems and Paintings* (Gansworth),
Supp. XXVI: 110–111
Half-Lives (Jong), **Supp. V:** 115, 119
Half Moon Street: Two Short Novels
(Theroux), **Supp. VIII:** 322, 323
Half of Paradise (Burke), **Supp. XIV:**
22, 24
Half-Past Nation Time (C. Johnson),
Supp. VI: 187

Half Remembered (Davison), **Supp. XXVI:** 61, 63, 65, 66–67, 70, 71

"Half-Skinned Steer, The" (Proulx), **Supp. VII:** 261–262

"Half Sonnets" (Jarman), **Supp. XVII:** 115

Half Sun Half Sleep (Swenson), **Supp. IV Part 2:** 645–646

Halfway (Kumin), **Supp. IV Part 2:** 441–442

"Halfway" (Rich), **Supp. I Part 2:** 553

Halfway Down the Hall: New and Selected Poems (Hadas), **Supp. XXIII:** 118–119

Halfway Home (Monette), **Supp. X:** 154

Halfway to Silence (Sarton), **Supp. VIII:** 261

Half You Don't Know, The: Selected Stories (Cameron), **Supp. XII:** 79, 80, 81

Haliburton, Thomas Chandler, **II:** 301; **IV:** 193; **Supp. I Part 2:** 411

Halifax, Lord, **II:** 111

Hall, Daniel, **Supp. XII:** 258

Hall, Donald, **I:** 567; **III:** 194; **Supp. IV Part 1:** 63, 72; **Supp. IV Part 2:** 621; **Supp. IX:** 269; **Supp. XIV:** 82, 126; **Supp. XV:** 21, 153, 176; **Supp. XVI:** 39, 230, 235; **Supp. XX:** 194; **Supp. XXI:** 86; **Supp. XXIII:** 209; **Supp. XXVI:** 68

Hall, Hazel, **Supp. XXII:** 275

Hall, James, **II:** 313; **Supp. I Part 2:** 584, 585

Hall, James Baker, **Supp. X:** 24

Hall, John, **Supp. XXVII:** 253

Hall, Louisa, **Retro. Supp. III:** 8

Hall, Rachel, **Supp. XXIII:** 301

Hall, Timothy L., **Supp. VIII:** 127, 128

Halleck, Fitz-Greene, **Supp. I Part 1:** 156, 158

"Hallelujah" (Cohen), **Supp. XXVII:** 52, 56, 61–62

"Hallelujah: A Sestina" (Francis), **Supp. IX:** 82

"Hallelujah on the Bum" (Abbey), **Supp. XIII:** 2

"Haller's Second Home" (Maxwell), **Supp. VIII:** 169

Halliday, Mark, **Supp. XIX: 81–95; Supp. XV:** 19, 20, 21, 23, 25, 27, 30

Hallock, Rev. Moses, **Supp. I Part 1:** 153

"Hall of Fantasy, The" (Hawthorne), **Retro. Supp. III:** 115

Hall of Mirrors, A (Stone), **Supp. V:** 295, 296–299, 300, 301

"Hallowe'en" (Huncke), **Supp. XIV:** 145

"Halloween Party, The" (Chabon), **Supp. XI:** 72

Halloween Tree, The (Bradbury), **Supp. IV Part 1:** 102, 112–113

"Halls, The" (Halliday), **Supp. XIX:** 90

Hallwas, John E., **Supp. I Part 2:** 454

Halpern, Daniel, **Supp. IV Part 1:** 94–95, 95

Halpern, Paul, **Supp. XXV:** 123

Halpern, Sue, **Supp. XXVI:** 128

Halsey, Theresa, **Supp. IV Part 1:** 330, 331

"Halt in the Desert, A" (Brodsky), **Supp. VIII:** 24

"Halves" (Dunn), **Supp. XI:** 149

Hamburg, Victoria, **Supp. XVI:** 126

Hamerik, Asger, **Supp. I Part 1:** 356

Hamill, Pete, **Supp. XX: 244, 255**

Hamill, Sam, **Supp. X:** 112, 125, 126, 127

Hamilton, Alexander, **I:** 485; **Supp. I Part 2:** 456, 483, 509

Hamilton, Alice, **Supp. I Part 1:** 5

Hamilton, David, **Supp. IX:** 296

Hamilton, Edith, **Supp. XVI:** 196

Hamilton, Lady Emma, **II:** 524

Hamilton, Hamish, **Supp. I Part 2:** 617

Hamilton, Virginia, **Supp. XXVIII:** 279

Hamilton, Walton, **Supp. I Part 2:** 632

Hamilton Stark (Banks), **Supp. V:** 8, 9–10, 11

"Hamlen Brook" (Wilbur), **Supp. III Part 2:** 564

"Hamlet" (Laforgue), **I:** 573; **III:** 11

Hamlet (Miller and Fraenkel), **III:** 178, 183

Hamlet (Shakespeare), **I:** 53, 183, 205, 377, 586–587; **II:** 158, 531; **III:** 7, 11, 12, 183; **IV:** 116, 131, 227; **Supp. I Part 1:** 369; **Supp. I Part 2:** 422, 457, 471; **Supp. IV Part 2:** 612; **Supp. IX:** 14

Hamlet, The (Faulkner), **II:** 69–71, 73, 74; **IV:** 131; **Retro. Supp. I:** 82, 91, 92; **Retro. Supp. III:** 85, 86; **Supp. IX:** 103; **Supp. VIII:** 178; **Supp. XI:** 247

"Hamlet and His Problems" (Eliot), **I:** 586–587

Hamlet of A. MacLeish, The (MacLeish), **III:** 11–12, 14, 15, 18

Hamlin, Eva, **Retro. Supp. II:** 115

"Hammer" (Bidart), **Supp. XV:** 35

Hammer, Adam, **Supp. XIII:** 112

Hammer, Langdon, **Retro. Supp. II:** 45, 53; **Supp. X:** 65

"Hammer Man, The" (Bambara), **Supp. XI:** 4–5

Hammett, Dashiell, **IV:** 286; **Retro. Supp. II:** 327; **Supp. I Part 1:** 286, 289, 291, 292, 293, 294, 295; **Supp. III Part 1:** 91; **Supp. IV Part 1:** 120, 121, **341–357; Supp. IV Part 2:** 461, 464, 468, 469, 472, 473; **Supp. IX:** 200; **Supp. XI:** 228; **Supp. XIII:** 159; **Supp. XIV:** 21; **Supp. XIX:** 178; **Supp. XVII:** 137; **Supp. XXI:** 68; **Supp. XXVI:** 277, 282

Hammon, Jupiter, **Supp. XXII:** 11

Hammond, John, **Supp. XVIII:** 24

Hammond, Karla, **Supp. IV Part 2:** 439, 442, 448, 637, 640, 644, 648

Hampl, Patricia, **Supp. IX:** 291; **Supp. XI:** 126; **Supp. XVII:** 21; **Supp. XXII: 81–101**

Hampson, Alfred Leete, **Retro. Supp. I:** 35–36, 38

"Hamrick's Polar Bear" (Caldwell), **I:** 309–310

Hamsun, Knut, **Supp. VIII:** 40; **Supp. XI:** 161, 167; **Supp. XII:** 21, 128

Hancock, John, **Supp. I Part 2:** 524; **Supp. XX:** 282

Hancock, Wade, **Supp. XVI:** 34

"Handbill Distributed in Buncombe County, North Carolina: 1915" (Rash), **Supp. XXVII:** 218

Handbook of North American Indians (Sando), **Supp. IV Part 2:** 510

Handcarved Coffins: A Nonfiction Account of an American Crime (Capote), **Supp. III Part 1:** 131

Handel, Georg Friedrich, **III:** 210; **IV:** 369

"Handfasting" (Wright), **Supp. XV:** 343

"Handfuls" (Sandburg), **III:** 584

"Handle with Care" (Fitzgerald), **Retro. Supp. I:** 114

Handley, William R., **Supp. XVIII:** 58

Handmaid's Tale, The (Atwood), **Supp. XIII:** 19, 20, **27–29**

"Hand of Casino, 1954, A" (Skloot), **Supp. XX: 194, 202**

"Hand of Emmagene, The" (Taylor), **Supp. V:** 314, 325–326

Hand of the Potter, The: A Tragedy in Four Acts (Dreiser), **Retro. Supp. II:** 104; **Supp. XVII:** 96

"Hands" (Anderson), **I:** 106, 107

"Hands" (Mora), **Supp. XIII:** 215

Hands of Orlac, The (M. Renard; Crewe-Jones, trans.), **Supp. XVII:** 58

Hand to Mouth (Auster), **Supp. XII:** 21

"Hand to Mouth" (Auster), **Supp. XII:** 31

Handy, Lowney, **Supp. XI:** 217, 220, 221, 225

Handy, W. C., **Supp. VIII:** 337

Handy Guide for Beggars, A (Lindsay), **Supp. I Part 2:** 376–378, 380, 382, 399

Haney, David, **Supp. XXI:** 253

"Hanged Man, A" (Cliff), **Supp. XXII:** 74

"Hanging Burley" (J. W. Miller), **Supp. XX: 167**

Hanging Garden, The (Wagoner), **Supp. IX:** 338–339

"Hanging Gardens of Tyburn, The" (Hecht), **Supp. X:** 58

"Hanging Man, The" (Davison), **Supp. XXVI:** 74

"Hanging of the Crane, The" (Longfellow), **Retro. Supp. II:** 169, 171

Hanging On (Conroy), **Supp. XVI:** 69

"Hanging Pictures in Nanny's Room" (Kenyon), **Supp. VII:** 164

"Hanging the Wash" (Alvarez), **Supp. VII:** 4

"Hangman, The" (Sexton), **Supp. II Part 2:** 680, 691

Hangover Mass (X. J. Kennedy), **Supp. XV:** 165

Hangsaman (Jackson), **Supp. IX:** 116, 123, **124**

Hanh, Thich Nhat, **Supp. V:** 199

Hanks, Lucy, **III:** 587

Hanks, Nancy. *See* Lincoln, Mrs. Thomas (Nancy Hanks)

Hanley, Lynne T., **Supp. IV Part 1:** 208

"Hanlon Mountain in Mist" (J. W. Miller), **Supp. XX: 164, 166–167**

Hanna, Mark, **Supp. I Part 2:** 395

Hannah, Barry, **Supp. X:** 285; **Supp. XIX:** 209; **Supp. XXI:** 38, 118; **Supp. XXVII:** 269

Hannah and Her Sisters (film; Allen), **Supp. XV:** 9, **10–11**

"Hannah Armstrong" (Masters), **Supp. I Part 2:** 461

"Hannah Binding Shoes" (Larcom), **Supp. XIII:** 141, 143

"Hannah Byde" (D. West), **Supp. XVIII:** 280

Hannah's House (Hearon), **Supp. VIII:** 58, **60–61**

Hanneman, Audre, **II:** 259

Hannibal Lecter, My Father (Acker), **Supp. XII:** 6

Hanoi (McCarthy), **II:** 579

"Hanoi Drifting, January 2003" (Weigl), **Supp. XIX:** 288

Hansberry, Lorraine, **Supp. IV Part 1: 359–377; Supp. VIII:** 329

Hanscom, Leslie, **Supp. XI:** 229

"Hansel and Gretel" (Prose), **Supp. XVI:** 256, 258

Hansen, Erik, **Supp. V:** 241

Hansen, Harry, **IV:** 366; **Supp. XXII:** 194, 277; **Supp. XXVII:** 85, 96

Han-shan, **Supp. VIII:** 292

Hanson, Curtis, **Supp. XI:** 67

Hanson, Elizabeth, **Supp. XXIV:** 220

Hanson, William F., **Supp. XXV:** 279, 280

Han Suyin, **Supp. X:** 291

Hanzlicek, C. G., **Supp. XV:** 73

Hapax (Stallings), **Supp. XXV:** 221, 222, 224, 231–233

Hapgood, Charles H., **II**, **Supp. XXI:** 6

Hapgood, Hutchins, **Supp. XVII: 95–108; Supp. XXI:** 1, 3, 9, 10

Hapgood, Norman, **Supp. XXI:** 2

Hapgoods, The: Three Earnest Brothers (Marcaccio), **Supp. XVII:** 106

"Happenings: An Art of Radical Juxtaposition" (Sontag), **Supp. III Part 2:** 456

"Happenstance" (Komunyakaa), **Supp. XIII:** 130

Happenstance (Shields), **Supp. VII:** 315–318, 320, 323, 324, 326

Happersberger, Lucien, **Supp. I Part 1:** 51

"Happiest Girl in the Whole U.S.A., The" (Muñoz), **Supp. XXV:** 131, 132

"Happiest I've Been, The" (Updike), **IV:** 219

Happily Ever After (Quindlen), **Supp. XVII:** 167

"Happiness" (Oliver), **Supp. VII:** 236

"Happiness" (Sandburg), **III:** 582–583

"Happiness" (Stone), **Supp. XXVII:** 254–255

"Happiness"(Hadas), **Supp. XXIII:** 117

Happiness of Getting It Down Right, The (Steinman, ed.), **Supp. VIII:** 172

"Happiness of the Garden Variety" (Richard), **Supp. XIX:** 212

"Happy Birthday" (Bambara), **Supp. XI:** 4

Happy Birthday (Loos), **Supp. XVI:** 193

Happy Birthday, Wanda June (Vonnegut), **Supp. II Part 2:** 759, 776–777

Happy Birthday of Death, The (Corso), **Supp. XII: 127–129**

Happy Childhood, A (Matthews), **Supp. IX:** 155, 160, **161–163**

Happy Days (Beckett), **Retro. Supp. I:** 206; **Supp. XXIV:** 123

Happy Days, 1880–1892 (Mencken), **III:** 100, 111, 120

"Happy End" (Simic), **Supp. VIII:** 276–277

"Happy Failure, The" (Melville), **III:** 90

Happy Families Are All Alike (Taylor), **Supp. V:** 322–323, 325

Happy Isles of Oceania, The: Paddling the Pacific (Theroux), **Supp. VIII:** 324

"Happy Journey to Trenton and Camden, The" (Wilder), **IV:** 366

"Happy Man, The" (Lethem), **Supp. XVIII:** 139

"Happy Marriage, The" (MacLeish), **III:** 15–16

Happy Marriage and Other Poems, The (MacLeish), **III:** 4

Happy to Be Here (Keillor), **Supp. XVI:** 165, 171

"Happy To Be Here" (Keillor), **Supp. XVI:** 168

"Hapworth 16, 1924" (Salinger), **III:** 552, 571–572

Haram, Karen, **Supp. XXIII:** 276

Haraway, Donna, **Supp. XXVIII:** 220

"Harbor Dawn, The" (H. Crane), **Supp. XXI:** 132, 136

"Harbor Lights" (Doty), **Supp. XI:** 122

Harcourt, Alfred, **II:** 191, 451–452; **III:** 587; **Retro. Supp. I:** 131; **Retro. Supp. III:** 101; **Supp. XV:** 308

Harcourt, Lewis, **Supp. XX: 232–233**

Harcourt, T. A., **I:** 196

Hardball (Paretsky), **Supp. XXV:** 177, 182, 184

Hard Candy, a Book of Stories (T. Williams), **IV:** 383

"Hardcastle Crags" (Plath), **Supp. I Part 2:** 537

"Hard Daddy" (Hughes), **Retro. Supp. I:** 200

"Hard Drive" (Huddle), **Supp. XXVI:** 151

"Hardened Criminals, The" (Lethem), **Supp. XVIII:** 139

Harder They Fall, The (Schulberg), **Supp. XV:** 194, 201

"Hardest Thing, The" (Huddle), **Supp. XXVI:** 151

Hard Facts (Baraka), **Supp. II Part 1:** 54, 55, 58

Hard Freight (Wright), **Supp. V:** 332, 339–340

Hard Hours, The (Hecht), **Supp. X:** 57, **59–62**, 63, 64

Hardie, Kier, **Supp. I Part 1:** 5

Hardin, Michael, **Supp. XXVI:** 242

Harding, Walter, **IV:** 177, 178

Harding, Warren G., **I:** 486; **II:** 253, 433; **Supp. I Part 1:** 24

"Hard Kind of Courage, The" (Baldwin), **Supp. I Part 1:** 52

Hard Laughter (Lamott), **Supp. XX: 132–133**

Hard Maple (S. and A. Warner), **Supp. XVIII:** 264

"Hard Rain's A-Gonna Fall, A" (song, Dylan), **Supp. XVIII:** 26, 29

Hard Time (Paretsky), **Supp. XXV:** 176, 177, 179, 182, 183

"Hard Time Keeping Up, A" (Ellison), **Retro. Supp. II:** 124

Hard Times (Dickens), **Supp. I Part 2:** 675

"Hard Times in Elfland, The" (Lanier), **Supp. I Part 1:** 365

"Hard Traveling: *Fay's* Deep South Landscape of Violence" (Beuka), **Supp. XXI:** 47

Hard Way Around, The: The Passages of Joshua Slocum (Wolff), **Supp. XXV:** 217

Hardwick, Elizabeth, **II:** 543, 554, 566; **Retro. Supp. II:** 179, 180, 183, 184, 190, 221, 228–229, 245; **Supp. I Part 1:** 196; **Supp. III Part 1: 193–215; Supp. IV Part 1:** 299; **Supp. V,** 319; **Supp. X,** 171; **Supp. XII:** 209; **Supp. XIV:** 89

"Hard Work 1956" (Dunn), **Supp. XI:** 147

Hardy, Barbara, **Supp. I Part 2:** 527

Hardy, Deborah, **Supp. XXVI:** 241, 242, 246

Hardy, Oliver, **Supp. I Part 2:** 607; **Supp. IV Part 2:** 574

Hardy, René, **Supp. III Part 1:** 235

Hardy, Thomas, **I:** 59, 103, 292, 317, 377; **II:** 181, 184–185, 186, 191–192, 271, 275, 372, 523, 542; **III:** 32, 453, 485, 508, 524; **IV:** 83, 135, 136; **Retro. Supp. I:** 141, 377–378; **Supp. I Part 1:** 217; **Supp. I Part 2:** 429, 512; **Supp. II Part 1:** 4, 26; **Supp. IX:** 40, 78, 85, 108, 211; **Supp. VIII:** 32; **Supp. X:** 228; **Supp. XI:** 311; **Supp. XIII:** 294, **Supp. XIII:** 130; **Supp. XIV:** 24; **Supp. XIX:** 86, 87; **Supp. XV:** 170; **Supp. XVIII:** 74; **Supp. XX:** 195; **Supp. XXI:** 109; **Supp. XXVI:** 67, 78; **Supp. XXVII:** 218

Hardy and the Poetry of Truth-Seeking (Halliday), **Supp. XIX:** 82

Harjo, Joy, **Supp. IV Part 1:** 325, 404; **Supp. IV Part 2:** 499, 507; **Supp. XII: 215–234; Supp. XVIII:** 189

Harlan's Race (P. N. Warren), **Supp. XX: 264–265**

"Harlem" (Hughes), **Retro. Supp. I:** 194, 204; **Supp. I Part 1:** 340; **Supp. VIII:** 213

Harlem (Myers), **Supp. XXVII:** 211

Harlem, Mecca of the New Negro (Locke), **Supp. XIV:** 201

"Harlem Dancer, The" (McKay), **Supp. X:** 134

Harlem Gallery (Tolson), **Retro. Supp. I:** 208, 209, 210

Harlem Glory: A Fragment of Aframerican Life (McKay), **Supp. X:** 132, **141–142**

Harlem Hellfighters, The: When Pride Met Courage (Myers), **Supp. XXVII:** 208

Harlem: Negro Metropolis (McKay), **Supp. X:** 132, 141, 142

Harlem Renaissance Remembered, The (Bontemps, ed.), **Supp. XXII:** 7

"Harlem Runs Wild" (McKay), **Supp. X:** 140

Harlem Shadows (McKay), **Supp. X:** 131–132, 136

Harlem Underground (Lacy), **Supp. XV:** 206

"Harlequin of Dreams, The" (Lanier), **Supp. I Part 1:** 365

Harlot's Ghost (Mailer), **Retro. Supp. II:** 211–212

Harlow, Jean, **IV:** 256; **Retro. Supp. I:** 110

"Harm" (C. Frost), **Supp. XV:** 101

Harmon, William, **Retro. Supp. I:** 37; **Supp. XI:** 248

"Harmonic" (F. Barthelme), **Supp. XI:** 26

Harmonium (Stevens), **III:** 196; **IV:** 76, 77, 78, 82, 87, 89, 92; **Retro. Supp. I:** 296, 297, 299, **300–302**, 301, 302

"Harmony of the Gospels" (Taylor), **IV:** 149

Harmony of the World (C. Baxter), **Supp. XVII:** 16–17

"Harmony of the World" (C. Baxter), **Supp. XVII:** 16

Harnett, Vincent, **Supp. XV:** 198

"Harp, The" (Weigl), **Supp. XIX:** 278

Harper (film), **Supp. IV Part 2:** 473

Harper, Donna, **Retro. Supp. I:** 194, 195, 209

Harper, Frances E. Watkins, **Supp. II Part 1:** 201–202; **Supp. XVIII:** 284; **Supp. XXII:** 11

Harper, Gordon Lloyd, **Retro. Supp. II:** 23

Harper, Michael S., **Retro. Supp. II:** 116, 123; **Supp. XV:** 74; **Supp. XXIV:** 184; **Supp. XXVII:** 152

Harper, William Rainey, **Supp. I Part 2:** 631

Harper's Anthology of 20th Century Native American Poetry (Niatum, ed.), **Supp. IV Part 1:** 331

"Harriet" (R. Lowell), **II:** 554

Harriette Arnow (Eckley), **Supp. XXVIII:** 3–4

Harrigan, Edward, **II:** 276; **III:** 14

Harriman, Margaret, **Supp. XXIV:** 19

Harrington, Michael, **I:** 306; **Supp. XXVIII:** 77

Harrington, Ollie, **Supp. XVI:** 142–143

Harris, Celia, **Retro. Supp. I:** 9

Harris, Corra, **Supp. XXII:** 190, 193, 196

Harris, George, **II:** 70

Harris, George Washington, **Supp. XXII:** 193

Harris, Joel Chandler, **III:** 338; **Supp. I Part 1:** 352; **Supp. II Part 1:** 192, 201; **Supp. XIV:** 61; **Supp. XX:** 103;

Supp. XXVIII: 226

Harris, John R., **Supp. XXVIII:** 256

Harris, Judith, **Supp. XIV:** 269

Harris, Julie, **II:** 587, 601; **Supp. IX:** 125

Harris, Leonard, **Supp. XIV:** 196, 211–212

Harris, MacDonald, **Supp. XI:** 65

Harris, Marie, **Supp. IX:** 153

Harris, Peter, **Supp. X:** 206, 207

Harris, Susan K., **Supp. XV:** 269

Harris, Thomas, **Supp. XIV:** 26; **Supp. XXI:** 67, 78

Harris, Trudier, **Supp. XXVI:** 13–14

Harris, Victoria Frenkel, **Supp. IV Part 1:** 68, 69

Harris, Violet J., **Supp. XXII:** 10, 13

Harris, William E., **Supp. XXIV:** 26

Harris, Wilson, **Supp. XXI:** 170; **Supp. XXVII:** 160, 161

Harrison, Colin, **Supp. XIV:** 26

Harrison, Hazel, **Retro. Supp. II:** 115

Harrison, Jim, **Supp. VIII: 37–56;** **Supp. XIX:** 125, 126

Harrison, Judy, **Supp. XXIII:** 278

Harrison, Kathryn, **Supp. X:** 191

Harrison, Ken, **Supp. IX:** 101

Harrison, Oliver (pseudonym). *See* Smith, Harrison

Harrod, Lois Marie, **Supp. XXIII:** 131–132

Harron, Mary, **Supp. XXVII:** 68

Harry: A Portrait (Boyce), **Supp. XVII:** 104; **Supp. XXI:** 7, **13–14**

Harryhausen, Ray, **Supp. IV Part 1:** 115

Harryman, Carla, **Supp. XV:** 344

"Harry of Nothingham" (Hugo), **Supp. VI:** 146–147

"Harry's Death" (Carver), **Supp. III Part 1:** 146

"Harsh Judgment, The" (Kunitz), **Supp. III Part 1:** 264

Hart, Albert Bushnell, **Supp. I Part 2:** 479, 480, 481

Hart, Bernard, **I:** 241, 242, 248–250, 256

Hart, Henry, **Retro. Supp. II:** 187; **Supp. XIV:** 97

Hart, James D., **Supp. XVIII:** 257

Hart, John Seely, **Supp. XVIII:** 257, 258, 264

Hart, Lorenz, **III:** 361

Hart, Moss, **Supp. IV Part 2:** 574; **Supp. XV:** 329

Hart, Pearl, **Supp. X:** 103

"Hart Crane" (Tate), **I:** 381

"Hart Crane and Poetry: A Consideration of Crane's Intense Poetics with Reference to 'The Return' " (Grossman), **Retro. Supp. II:** 83

Harte, Anna Griswold, **Supp. II Part 1:** 341

Harte, Bret, **I:** 193, 195, 203; **II:** 289; **IV:** 196; **Retro. Supp. II:** 72; **Supp. II Part 1: 335–359,** 399; **Supp. XV:** 115

Harte, Walter Blackburn, **I:** 199

Harter, Carol C., **Supp. IV Part 1:** 217

Hartigan, Grace, **Supp. XXIII:** 210, 212, 217

Hartley, David, **III:** 77

Hartley, Lois, **Supp. I Part 2:** 459, 464–465

Hartley, L. P., **Supp. I Part 1:** 293

Hartley, Marsden, **IV:** 409, 413; **Retro. Supp. I:** 430; **Supp. X:** 137; **Supp. XV:** 298

Hartman, Geoffrey, **Supp. IV Part 1:** 119; **Supp. XII:** 130, 253

Hartman, Saidiya, **Supp. XX:** 154

Harum, David, **II:** 102

"Harvard" (R. Lowell), **II:** 554

Harvard College in the Seventeenth Century (Morison), **Supp. I Part 2:** 485

"Harvest" (E. P. Jones), **Supp. XXII:** 141

"Harvest, The" (Hempel), **Supp. XXI:** 115, **122–123**

Harvest, The (Levin), **Supp. XXVII:** 143, 146

Harvester, The (Stratton-Porter), **Supp. XX: 211,** 212, 218, 221

"*Harvester, The:* The Natural Bounty of Gene Stratton-Porter" (Birkelo), **Supp. XX: 220–221**

"Harvesters of Night and Water" (Hogan), **Supp. IV Part 1:** 412

"Harvest Song" (Toomer), **Supp. III Part 2:** 483

Harvill Book of 20th Century Poetry in English, **Supp. X:** 55

Harvin, Emily, **Supp. XXIII:** 174

"Harv Is Plowing Now" (Updike), **Retro. Supp. I:** 318

Harwood, Lee, **Supp. XXVII:** 22

Haselden, Elizabeth Lee, **Supp. VIII:** 125

"Hasidic Noir" (Abraham), **Supp. XXIV: 14–15**

Haskell, Mary, **Supp. XX:** 115, 117

"Haskell's Mill" (Davison), **Supp. XXVI:** 73, 75, 76

Hass, Robert, **Supp. VI: 97–111; Supp. VIII:** 24, 28; **Supp. XI:** 142, 270; **Supp. XIV:** 83, 84; **Supp. XXI:** 60; **Supp. XXVI:** 61, 68; **Supp. XXVIII:** 196

Hassam, Childe, **Retro. Supp. II:** 136

Hassan, Ihab, **IV:** 99–100, 115; **Supp. XI:** 221

Hasse, Henry, **Supp. IV Part 1:** 102

Hasty-Pudding, The (Barlow), **Supp. II Part 1:** 74, 77–80

"Hater of Mediocrity, The" (Boulton), **Supp. XXII:** 23

Hateship, Friendship, Courtship, Loveship, Marriage (Munro), **Supp. XXVII:** 190, 192–193

Hate That Hate Produced, The (CBS documentary), **Supp. XX: 102**

Hatful of Rain, A (film), **Supp. XXVI:** 134

Hatful of Rain, A (Gazzo), **III:** 155

Hatlen, Burton, **Supp. V:** 138, 139–140; **Supp. XXI:** 24

"Hatred"(O'Hara), **Supp. XXIII:** 212

"Hattie Bloom" (Oliver), **Supp. VII:** 232

Haugen, Hayley Mitchell, **Supp. XXIV:** 215

Haunch, Paunch, and Jowl (Ornitz), **Supp. IX:** 227

Haunted Lady, The (Rinehart), **Supp. XXV:** 198, 200

"Haunted Landscape" (Ashbery), **Supp. III Part 1:** 22

Haunted Merchant, The (Briggs), **Supp. XVIII:** 2, 8

"Haunted Mind" (Simic), **Supp. VIII:** 282

"Haunted Mind, The" (Hawthorne), **II:** 230–231

"Haunted Oak, The" (Dunbar), **Supp. II Part 1:** 207, 208

"Haunted Palace, The" (Poe), **III:** 421

Haunted Photograph, The (Stuart), **Supp. XXVIII:** 235, 237

"Haunted Quack, The" (Hawthorne), **Retro. Supp. III:** 114

"Haunted Valley, The" (Bierce), **I:** 200

Haunting, The (film), **Supp. IX:** 125

Haunting of Hill House, The (Jackson), **Supp. IX:** 117, 121, 126

Hauptmann, Gerhart, **III:** 472

Haussmann, Sonja, **Supp. XIII:** 331, **Supp. XIII:** 347

"Havanna vanities come to dust in Miami" (Didion), **Supp. IV Part 1:** 210

Havel, Hippolyte, **Supp. XXI:** 4, 6

Haven (Lewisohn), **Supp. XXVIII:** 151, 156–157

Haven, Cynthia, **Supp. XV:** 252, 264; **Supp. XXIII:** 134, 138, 139

Haven's End (Marquand), **III:** 55, 56, 63, 68

"Have You Ever Faked an Orgasm" (Peacock), **Supp. XIX:** 199

"Have You Ever Tried to Enter the Long Black Branches" (Oliver), **Supp. VII:** 247

"Having a Coke with You"(O'Hara), **Supp. XXIII:** 219

"Having Been Interstellar" (Ammons), **Supp. VII:** 25

"Having It Out With Melancholy" (Kenyon), **Supp. VII:** 171

"Having Lost My Sons, I Confront the Wreckage of the Moon: Christmas, 1960" (Wright), **Supp. III Part 2:** 600

"Having Saints" (Davison), **Supp. XXVI:** 71

"Having Snow" (Schwartz), **Supp. II Part 2:** 652

"Having Words"(Thompson), **Supp. XXIII:** 293–294

"Hawaii, Washington, Vermont: A Frame for the Verse" (Taggard), **Supp. XXII:** 281–282

Hawaiian Hilltop (Taggard), **Supp. XXII:** 275

Hawai'i One Summer (Kingston), **Supp. V:** 157, 160, 166, 169–170

Haweis, Stephen, **Supp. XXII:** 157, 158, 159, 161, 163, 165

"Hawk, The" (Francis), **Supp. IX:** 81

Hawke, David Freeman, **Supp. I Part 2:** 511, 516

Hawkes, John, **I:** 113; **Retro. Supp. II:** 234; **Supp. III Part 1:** 2; **Supp. IX:** 212; **Supp. V:** 40; **Supp. XVII:** 183; **Supp. XXI:** 210

Hawkins, Gary, **Supp. XXI:** 35, 39

Hawkins, William, **II:** 587

Hawk in the Rain, The (Hughes), **Retro. Supp. II:** 244; **Supp. I Part 2:** 537, 540

Hawk Is Dying, The (Crews), **Supp. XI:** 111

Hawk Moon (Shepard), **Supp. III Part 2:** 445

Hawks, Howard, **Supp. IV Part 1:** 130; **Supp. XVIII:** 148

"Hawk's Cry in Autumn, The" (Brodsky), **Supp. VIII:** 29

"Hawks of Outremer" (Howard), **Supp. XXVII:** 120

"Hawk's Shadow" (Glück), **Supp. V:** 85

Hawk's Well, The (Yeats), **III:** 459–460

Hawley, Adelaide, **Supp. XIV:** 207

Hawley, Joseph, **I:** 546

Hawthorne (James), **II:** 372–378; **Retro. Supp. I:** 220, **223–224**

"Hawthorne" (Longfellow), **Retro. Supp. II:** 169

"Hawthorne" (R. Lowell), **II:** 550

Hawthorne, Julian, **II:** 225; **Supp. I Part 1:** 38; **Supp. XV:** 274

Hawthorne, Nathaniel, **I:** 106, 204, 211, 340, 355, 363, 384, 413, 458, 561–562; **II:** 7, 8, 40, 60, 63, 74, 89, 127–128, 138, 142, 198, **223–246,** 255, 259, 264, 267, 272, 274, 277, 281, 282, 295, 307, 309, 311, 313, 322, 324, 326, 402, 408, 446, 501, 545; **III:** 51, 81–82, 83, 84, 85, 87, 88, 91, 92, 113, 316, 359, 412, 415, 421, 438, 453, 454, 507, 565, 572; **IV:** 2, 4, 167, 172, 179, 194, 333, 345, 453; **Retro. Supp. I:** 1, 53, 59, 62, 63, 91, **145–167,** 215, 218, 220, 223, 248–249, 252, 257, 258, 330, 331, 365; **Retro. Supp. II:** 136, 142, 153, 156–157, 158, 159, 187, 221; **Retro. Supp. III:** 44, **109–124,** 155, 157, 194, 223, 225, 233; **Supp. I Part 1:** 38, 188, 197, 317, 372; **Supp. I Part 2:** 420, 421, 545, 579, 580, 582, 587, 595, 596; **Supp. III Part 2:** 501; **Supp. IV Part 1:** 80, 127, 297; **Supp. IV Part 2:** 463, 596; **Supp. IX:** 114; **Supp. V:** 152; **Supp. VIII:** 103, 105, 108, 153, 201; **Supp. X:** 78; **Supp. XI:** 51, 78; **Supp. XII:** 26; **Supp. XIII:** 102; **Supp. XIV:** 48; **Supp. XV:** 269, 272, 282; **Supp. XVI:** 83, 84, 157; **Supp. XVII:** 42; **Supp. XVIII:** 258, 260; **Supp. XXI:** 201; **Supp. XXIII:** 161, 190, 290; **Supp. XXV:** 242, 249

Hawthorne, Mrs. Nathaniel (Sophia Peabody), **II:** 224, 244; **III:** 75, 86

Hawthorne, Rose, **II:** 225

Hawthorne, Una, **II:** 225

"Hawthorne and His Mosses" (Melville), **Retro. Supp. I:** 254; **Supp. XIV:** 48

"Hawthorne Aspect \[of Henry James\], The" (Eliot), **Retro. Supp. I:** 63

"Hawthorne in Solitude" (Cowley), **Supp. II Part 1:** 143

Hay, John, **I:** 1, 10, 12, 14–15; **Supp. I Part 1:** 352

Hay, Mrs. John, **I:** 14

Hay, Sara Henderson, **Supp. XIV: 119–135**

Hayakawa, S. I., **I:** 448; **Supp. I Part 1:** 315; **Supp. XV:** 176

Haycroft, Howard, **Supp. XXV:** 199; **Supp. XXVI:** 277

Hayden, Robert, **Supp. II Part 1: 361–383; Supp. IV Part 1:** 169; **Supp. XIII:** 115, 127; **Supp. XIV:** 119, 123; **Supp. XXVIII:** 27

Hayden, Sterling, **Supp. XI:** 304

Hayden, William R., **Supp. XXV:** 38

Haydn, Hiram, **IV:** 100, 358

Hayduke Lives! (Abbey), **Supp. XIII:** 16

Hayek, Friedrich A. von, **Supp. IV Part 2:** 524

Hayes, Alfred, **Supp. XXVI: 133–146**

Hayes, Helen, **Supp. XVI:** 193, 195

Hayes, Ira, **Supp. IV Part 1:** 326

Hayes, Kevin, **Retro. Supp. III:** 237

Hayes, Richard, **Supp. V:** 320

Hayes, Rutherford B., **Supp. I Part 2:** 419

Hayford, James, **Supp. XXII:** 204, 218

Haygood, Wil, **Supp. VIII:** 79

"Haying While the Sun Shines" (L. I. Wilder), **Supp. XXII:** 290

Hayne, Paul Hamilton, **Supp. I Part 1:** 352, 354, 355, 360, 372

Haynes, Todd, **Supp. XVIII:** 23

Haynes-Smith, William, **Supp. XX: 231, 232, 233**

Hayward, Florence, **Retro. Supp. II:** 65

Hayward, John, **Retro. Supp. I:** 67

Hayward, Leland, **Supp. XIX:** 250

Haywood, "Big" Bill, **I:** 483; **Supp. V:** 286; **Supp. XXIII:** 162

Hazan, Joe, **Supp. XXIII:** 212

Hazard, Grace, **II:** 530

Hazard of Fortunes, A (Howells), **Retro. Supp. II:** 288

Hazard of New Fortunes, A (Howells), **II:** 275, 276, 286–297, 290

Hazel, Robert, **Supp. VIII:** 137, 138

Hazen, General W. B., **I:** 192, 193

Hazlitt, Henry, **Supp. IV Part 2:** 524

Hazlitt, William, **I:** 58, 378; **II:** 315; **Supp. XXI:** 205

Hazmat (McClatchy), **Supp. XII: 265–270**

Hazo, Samuel, **I:** 386; **Supp. XIV:** 123, 124

Hazzard, Shirley, **Supp. VIII:** 151

H.D. *See* Doolittle, Hilda

"He" (Porter), **III:** 434, 435

"Head and Shoulders" (Fitzgerald), **Retro. Supp. I:** 101

Headhunter (Findley), **Supp. XX: 57–59, 60, 61**

"Head-Hunter, The" (O. Henry), **Supp. II Part 1:** 403

"Headless Hawk, The" (Capote), **Supp. III Part 1:** 124

Headlines (T. Williams), **IV:** 381

Headlong Hall (Peacock), **Supp. I Part 1:** 307

Headmaster, The (McPhee), **Supp. III Part 1:** 291, 294, 298

"Head of Joaquín Murrieta, The" (Rodriguez), **Supp. XIV:** 303

Headsman, The (Cooper), **I:** 345–346

Heads of Grain (al-Sanábil) (Gibran), **Supp. XX: 124**

"Headwaters" (Momaday), **Supp. IV Part 2:** 486

"Head Wound" (Halliday), **Supp. XIX:** 92

Healey, Claire, **Supp. XXVIII:** 262

Healing, The (G. Jones), **Supp. XXIV:** 183, 185, **190–192,** 195

Healy, Eloise Klein, **Supp. XI:** 121, 124, 126, 127, 129, 137

Healy, Tim, **II:** 129, 137

Heaney, Sally, **Supp. XVII:** 241

Heaney, Seamus, **Retro. Supp. II:** 245; **Supp. IX:** 41, 42; **Supp. X:** 67, 122; **Supp. XI:** 249; **Supp. XV:** 256; **Supp. XXI:** 54, 243

"Heard through the Walls of the Race-track Glen Motel" (X. J. Kennedy), **Supp. XV:** 170

"Hearing, The" (Huddle), **Supp. XXVI:** 155

Hearn, Lafcadio, **I:** 211; **II:** 311

Hearon, Shelby, **Supp. VIII: 57–72**

Hearst, Patty, **Supp. IV Part 1:** 195

Hearst, William Randolph, **I:** 198, 207, 208; **IV:** 298

Heart and Perimeter (Bierds), **Supp. XVII: 28–29**

"Heart and the Lyre, The" (Bogan), **Supp. III Part 1:** 65

"Heart as Origami, The (Hirshfield), **Supp. XXIII:** 132

"Heartbeat" (Harjo), **Supp. XII:** 221–222

Heartbreak Hotel (Siddons), **Supp. XXII:** 239, 241, 242

Heartbreak Kid, The (film), **Supp. IV Part 2:** 575, 589

"Heart Failure"(Schott), **Supp. XXIII:** 252

"Heart Finds Its Own Conclusion, The" (Muñoz), **Supp. XXV:** 136

Heart for the Gods of Mexico, A (Aiken), **I:** 54

"Hearth" (Rash), **Supp. XXVII:** 222

"Hear the Nightingale Sing" (Gordon), **II:** 200

Hear the Wind Blow (Sanders), **Supp. XVI:** 268

Heart is a Lonely Hunter, The (McCullers), **II:** 586, 588–593, 604, 605

Heartland (film), **Supp. XXVI:** 183–184

Heart of a Woman, The (Angelou), **Supp. IV Part 1:** 2, 5, 7–9, 9, 14, 17

Heart of Darkness (Conrad), **Retro. Supp. II:** 292; **Supp. V:** 249, 311; **Supp. VIII:** 4, 316; **Supp. XIX:** 28; **Supp. XX: 18, 57–58; Supp. XXIV:** 286

"Heart of Darkness" (Conrad), **I:** 575, 578; **II:** 595; **Supp. XVI:** 212

Heart of Darkness (Didion), **Supp. IV Part 1:** 207

Heart of Dixie (film), **Supp. XXII:** 239, 241

Heart of Haiku, The (Hirshfield), **Supp. XXIII:** 137–138

Heart of Happy Hollow, The (Dunbar), **Supp. II Part 1:** 214

Heart of Knowledge, The: American Indians on the Bomb (Gunn Allen and Caputi, eds.), **Supp. IV Part 1:** 334–335

"Heart of Knowledge, The: Nuclear Themes in Native American Thought and Literature" (Caputi), **Supp. IV Part 1:** 335

Heart of the Earth (Moraga), **Supp. XXIII:** 196

"Heart of the Park, The " (O'Connor), **Retro. Supp. II:** 225

Heart of the West (O. Henry), **Supp. II Part 1:** 410

"Hearts, The" (Pinsky), **Supp. VI:** 245–247, 248

"'Hearts and Flowers' " (MacLeish), **III:** 8

"Hearts and Heads" (Ransom), **Supp. I Part 1:** 373

"Heart's Graveyard Shift, The" (Komunyakaa), **Supp. XIII:** 120

Heart-Shape in the Dust (Hayden), **Supp. II Part 1:** 365, 366

Heart's Needle (Snodgrass), **I:** 400; **Supp. XXVIII:** 86

"Heart's Needle" (Snodgrass), **Supp. VI: 311–313,** 320

"Hearts of Oak" (Rowson), **Supp. XV:** 243

"Heart Songs" (Proulx), **Supp. VII:** 254

Heart Songs and Other Stories (Proulx), **Supp. VII:** 252–256, 261

Heart to Artemis, The (Bryher), **Supp. I Part 1:** 259

"Heart to Heart" (Zitkala-Ša), **Supp. XXV:** 284

Heartwood (Burke), **Supp. XIV:** 35

Heath, Shirley, **Supp. XX:** 90

Heath Anthology of American Literature, The, **Supp. IX:** 4; **Supp. XV:** 270, 313

Heathcote, Anne. *See* De Lancey, Mrs. James

"Heathen Chinee, The" (Harte), **Supp. II Part 1:** 350–351, 352

Heathen Days, 1890–1936 (Mencken), **III:** 100, 111

Heath-Stubbs, John, **Supp. XV:** 153

Heaton, David, **Supp. XXVI:** 7

Heat's On, The (C. Himes), **Supp. XVI:** 143, 144

"Heaven" (Dunn), **Supp. XI:** 154

"Heaven" (Levine), **Supp. V:** 182

"Heaven" (Patchett), **Supp. XII:** 309

Heaven and Earth: A Cosmology (Goldbarth), **Supp. XII:** 187

"Heaven and Earth in Jest" (Dillard), **Supp. VI:** 24, 28

"Heaven as Anus" (Kumin), **Supp. IV Part 2:** 448

Heavenly Conversation, The (Mather), **Supp. II Part 2:** 460

"Heavenly Feast, The" (Schnackenberg), **Supp. XV:** 257, 259

Heavens (Untermeyer), **Supp. XV:** 306

Heavens and Earth (Benét), **Supp. XI:** 44

Heaven's Coast (Doty), **Supp. XI:** 119, 121, **129–130,** 134; **Supp. XXIII:** 126

Heaven's Prisoners (Burke), **Supp. XIV:** 23, 29

"Heavy Angel, The" (Everwine), **Supp. XV:** 80

"Heavy Bear Who Goes with Me, The" (Schwartz), **Supp. II Part 2:** 646

"Heavy Trash" (Halliday), **Supp. XIX:** 92, 93

Hebert, Ernest, **Supp. XXII:** 207

Heble, Ajay, **Supp. XXVII:** 183

"He Came Also Still" (Zukofsky), **Supp. III Part 2:** 612

Hecht, Anthony, **IV:** 138; **Supp. III Part 2:** 541, 561; **Supp. X: 55–75; Supp. XII:** 269–270; **Supp. XV:** 251, 256; **Supp. XXVII:** 218

Hecht, Ben, **I:** 103; **II:** 42; **Supp. I Part 2:** 646; **Supp. XI:** 307; **Supp. XIII:** 106; **Supp. XXV:** 18, 19, 22, 27, 29; **Supp. XXVII: 83–98,** 139

Hecht, S. Theodore, **Supp. III Part 2:** 614

Heckewelder, John, **II:** 503

"Hedge Island" (A. Lowell), **II:** 524

"Hedgerows in England, The" (Stone), **Supp. XXVII:** 258, 259–260

Hedges, William I., **II:** 311–312

"He 'Digesteth Harde Yron' " (Moore), **Supp. IV Part 2:** 454

Hedin, Robert, **Supp. XII:** 200, 202

Hedley, Jane, **Retro. Supp. III:** 249

Hedylus (Doolittle), **Supp. I Part 1:** 259, 270

"Heel & Toe To the End" (W. C. Williams), **Retro. Supp. I:** 430

Heffernan, Michael, **Supp. XII:** 177

"HEGEL" (Baraka), **Supp. II Part 1:** 53

Hegel, Georg Wilhelm Friedrich, **I:** 265; **II:** 358; **III:** 262, 308–309, 480, 481, 487, 607; **IV:** 86, 333, 453; **Supp. I Part 2:** 633, 635, 640, 645; **Supp. XVI:** 289; **Supp. XXVI:** 234

"Hegemony of Race, The" (Du Bois), **Supp. II Part 1:** 181

Hegger, Grace Livingston. *See* Lewis, Mrs. Sinclair (Grace Livingston Hegger)

"He Had Spent His Youth Dreaming" (Dobyns), **Supp. XIII:** 90

Heidegger, Martin, **II:** 362, 363; **III:** 292; **IV:** 491; **Retro. Supp. II:** 87; **Supp. V:** 267; **Supp. VIII:** 9; **Supp. XVI:** 283, 288; **Supp. XXVI:** 234

Heidenmauer, The (Cooper), **I:** 345–346

Heidi Chronicles, The (Wasserstein), **Supp. IV Part 1:** 309; **Supp. XV:** 319, **325–327**

"Height of the Ridiculous, The" (Holmes), **Supp. I Part 1:** 302

Heilbroner, Robert, **Supp. I Part 2:** 644, 648, 650

Heilbrun, Carolyn G., **Supp. IX:** 66; **Supp. XI:** 208; **Supp. XIV:** 161, 163; **Supp. XX: 108**

Heilman, Robert Bechtold, **Supp. XIV:** 11, 12

Heilpern, John, **Supp. XIV:** 242

Heim, Michael, **Supp. V:** 209

Heine, Heinrich, **II:** 272, 273, 277, 281, 282, 387, 544; **IV:** 5; **Supp. XV:** 293,

299; **Supp. XVI:** 188
Heineman, Frank, **Supp. III Part 2:** 619
Heinemann, Larry, **Supp. XXII: 103–117**
Heinlein, Robert, **Supp. IV Part 1:** 102; **Supp. XVI:** 122; **Supp. XVIII:** 149
Heinz, Helen. *See* Tate, Mrs. Allen (Helen Heinz)
Heiress, The (film), **Retro. Supp. I:** 222
"Heirs" (Nye), **Supp. XIII:** 284
"He Is Not Worth the Trouble" (Rowson), **Supp. XV:** 240
"He Knew" (C. Himes), **Supp. XVI:** 137
"Helas" (Creeley), **Supp. IV Part 1:** 150, 158
Helburn, Theresa, **IV:** 381
Heldreth, Leonard, **Supp. V:** 151
"Helen" (R. Lowell), **II:** 544
"Helen, Thy Beauty Is to Me" (Fante), **Supp. XI:** 169
"Helen: A Courtship" (Faulkner), **Retro. Supp. I:** 81
"Helen I Love You" (Farrell), **II:** 28, 45
Helen in Egypt (Doolittle), **Supp. I Part 1:** 260, 272, 273, 274; **Supp. XV:** 264
Helen in Egypt (H.D.), **Retro. Supp. III:** 51
Helen Keller: Sketch for a Portrait (Brooks), **I:** 254
Helen of Troy and Other Poems (Teasdale), **Supp. XXVII:** 283, 285–286, 288–289
"Helen of Tyre" (Longfellow), **II:** 496
Heliodora (Doolittle), **Supp. I Part 1:** 266
Helium-3 series (Hickam), **Supp. XXVII:** 111
"He Lives On the Landing" (Espaillat), **Supp. XXI:** 108
"Helix" (Sobin), **Supp. XVI:** 283
Hellbox (O'Hara), **III:** 361
Helle, Anita, **Supp. XXIII:** 117
Heller, Joseph, **III:** 2, 258; **IV:** 98; **Retro. Supp. II:** 324; **Supp. I Part 1:** 196; **Supp. IV Part 1: 379–396; Supp. V:** 244; **Supp. VIII:** 245; **Supp. XI:** 307; **Supp. XII:** 167–168; **Supp. XV:** 322; **Supp. XVII:** 139; **Supp. XXIII:** 100
"Hell-Heaven" (Lahiri), **Supp. XXI: 181–183,** 183, 184–186, 188
Hellman, Lillian, **I:** 28; **III:** 28; **Supp. I Part 1: 276–298; Supp. IV Part 1:** 1, 12, 83, 353, 355, 356; **Supp. IX:** 196, 198, 200–201, 204; **Supp. VIII:** 243; **Supp. XXVII:** 133, 136
Hellmann, Lillian, **Retro. Supp. II:** 327
Hello (Creeley), **Supp. IV Part 1:** 155, 157
"Hello, Hello Henry" (Kumin), **Supp. IV Part 2:** 446
"Hello, Stranger" (Capote), **Supp. III Part 1:** 120
Hello Dolly! (musical play), **IV:** 357
Hell's Angels: A Strange and Terrible Saga (Thompson), **Supp. XXIV:** 282, 283, 288, 290–291
Hellyer, John, **Supp. I Part 2:** 468
Helm, Bob, **Supp. XV:** 147
Helm, Levon, **Supp. XVIII:** 26
Helmets (Dickey), **Supp. IV Part 1:** 175, 178, 180

"Helmsman, The" (Doolittle), **Supp. I Part 1:** 266
"Help" (Barth), **I:** 139
"Help Her to Believe" (Olsen). *See* "I Stand There Ironing" (Olsen)
Helprin, Mark, **Supp. XIX:** 142; **Supp. XXV: 79–91**
Helsel, Philip Browning, **Supp. XXVI:** 53
"Helsinki Window" (Creeley), **Supp. IV Part 1:** 158
"Hema and Kaushik" (Lahiri), **Supp. XXI:** 183, 188
Hemenway, Robert E., **Retro. Supp. III:** 131, 137; **Supp. IV Part 1:** 6
Hemingway, Dr. Clarence Edwards, **II:** 248, 259
Hemingway, Ernest, **I:** 28, 64, 97, 99, 105, 107, 117, 150, 162, 190, 211, 221, 288, 289, 295, 367, 374, 378, 421, 423, 445, 476, 477, 478, 482, 484–485, 487, 488, 489, 491, 495, 504, 517; **II:** 27, 44, 51, 58, 68–69, 78, 90, 97, 127, 206, **247–270,** 289, 424, 431, 456, 457, 458–459, 482, 560, 600; **III:** 2, 18, 20, 35, 36, 37, 40, 61, 108, 220, 334, 363, 364, 382, 453, 454, 471–472, 476, 551, 575, 576, 584; **IV:** 27, 28, 33, 34, 35, 42, 49, 97, 108, 122, 126, 138, 190, 191, 201, 216, 217, 257, 297, 363, 404, 427, 433, 451; **Retro. Supp. I:** 74, 98, 108, 111, 112, 113, 115, **169–191,** 215, 292, 359, 418; **Retro. Supp. II:** 19, 24, 30, 68, 115, 123; **Retro. Supp. III:** 36, 194, 255, 264; **Supp. I Part 2:** 621, 658, 678; **Supp. II Part 1:** 221; **Supp. III Part 1:** 146; **Supp. III Part 2:** 617; **Supp. IV Part 1:** 48, 102, 123, 197, 236, 342, 343, 344, 348, 350, 352, 380–381, 383; **Supp. IV Part 2:** 463, 468, 502, 607, 679, 680, 681, 689, 692; **Supp. IX:** 16, 57, 58, 94, 106, 260, 262; **Supp. V:** 237, 240, 244, 250, 336; **Supp. VIII:** 40, 101, 105, 179, 182, 183, 188, 189, 196; **Supp. X:** 137, 167, 223, 225; **Supp. XI:** 214, 221; **Supp. XIII:** 96, 255, 270; **Supp. XIV:** 24, 83; **Supp. XIX:** 131, 154, 157, 246; **Supp. XV:** 69, 135; **Supp. XVI:** 203, 205–206, 208, 210, 233, 236–237, 281–282; **Supp. XVII:** 4, 105, 107, 137, 228, 229; **Supp. XVIII:** 74, 90, 102; **Supp. XX: 45, 74, 76; Supp. XXI:** 7, 8, 36, 262; **Supp. XXIII:** 4, 68, 166, 174, 275, 299; **Supp. XXIV:** 54, 64, 97, 284; **Supp. XXVI:** 17, 32, 135, 147, 180; **Supp. XXVII:** 134, 141
Hemingway, Mrs. Ernest (Hadley Richardson), **II:** 257, 260, 263
Hemingway, Mrs. Ernest (Martha Gellhorn), **II:** 260
Hemingway, Mrs. Ernest (Mary Welsh), **II:** 257, 260
Hemingway, Mrs. Ernest (Pauline Pfeiffer), **II:** 260
Hemingway, Mrs. Ernest (Martha Gellhorn), **Supp. XXVII:** 141

"Hemingway in Paris" (Cowley), **Supp. II Part 1:** 144
"Hemingway Story, A" (Dubus), **Supp. VII:** 91
"Hemingway: The Old Lion" (Cowley), **Supp. II Part 1:** 143
"Hemp, The" (Benét), **Supp. XI:** 44
Hempel, Amy, **Supp. XIX:** 209; **Supp. XXI: 115–128**
"Henchman, The" (Whittier), **Supp. I Part 2:** 696
Henderson, Alice Corbin, **Supp. I Part 2:** 387; **Supp. XV:** 302–303
Henderson, Darwin L., **Supp. XIII:** 213, 221–222
Henderson, Jane, **Supp. VIII:** 87; **Supp. XX:** 84
Henderson, Katherine, **Supp. IV Part 1:** 203, 207
Henderson, Linda. *See* Hogan, Linda
Henderson, Robert W., **Supp. VIII:** 124
Henderson, Stephen, **Supp. IV Part 1:** 365
Henderson, the Rain King (Bellow), **I:** 144, 147, 148, 152, 153, 154, 155, 158, 160, 161, 162–163; **Retro. Supp. II:** 19, **24–25,** 30
"Hen Flower, The" (Kinnell), **Supp. III Part 1:** 247–248
Henie, Sonja, **Supp. XII:** 165
Henkin, Joshua, **Supp. XXII:** 216
Henle, James, **II:** 26, 30, 38, 41; **Supp. IX:** 2
Henley, Beth, **Supp. XXI:** 145
Hennesy, Dale, **Supp. XV:** 5
Henning, Barbara, **Supp. XXVII:** 174
Henninger, Katherine, **Supp. XXI:** 253
Henri, Robert, **IV:** 411; **Supp. I Part 2:** 376
Henrich, Edith, **Supp. XXIV:** 214
Henry, Arthur, **I:** 515; **Retro. Supp. II:** 97
Henry, DeWitt, **Supp. XI:** 342
Henry, O., **I:** 201; **III:** 5; **Supp. I Part 2:** 390, 462; **Supp. II Part 1: 385–412; Supp. XV:** 40
Henry, Robert, **Retro. Supp. II:** 103
Henry, William A., III, **Supp. IV Part 2:** 574
Henry and Clara (Mallon), **Supp. XIX:** 132, **136–137,** 139, 141
Henry and June (film), **Supp. X:** 186
Henry and June: From the Unexpurgated Diary of Anaïs Nin, **Supp. X:** 184, 185, 187, 194
Henry Holt and Company, **Retro. Supp. I:** 121, 131, 133, 136
Henry IV (Shakespeare), **III:** 166; **Supp. VIII:** 164
"Henry James, Jr." (Howells), **II:** 289; **Retro. Supp. I:** 220
"Henry James and the Art of Teaching" (Rowe), **Retro. Supp. I:** 216
"Henry Lagoon" (Huddle), **Supp. XXVI:** 155
"Henry Manley, Living Alone, Keeps Time" (Kumin), **Supp. IV Part 2:** 451
"Henry Manley Looks Back" (Kumin), **Supp. IV Part 2:** 451

"Henry Manley" poems (Kumin), **Supp. IV Part 2:** 446

Henry Miller Reader, The (Durrell, ed.), **III:** 175, 190

"Henry's Confession" (Berryman), **I:** 186

Henry VIII (Shakespeare), **Supp. IX:** 235

Henslee, **Supp. IV Part 1:** 217

Henson, Josiah, **Supp. I Part 2:** 589

Hentoff, Margot, **Supp. IV Part 1:** 205

Henton, Alice, **Retro. Supp. III:** 8

Hentz, Caroline Lee, **Supp. I Part 2:** 584

Henze, Hans Werner, **Supp. II Part 1:** 24

"He of the Assembly" (Bowles), **Supp. IV Part 1:** 90

Hepburn, Katharine, **Supp. IX:** 189; **Supp. XI:** 17

Heraclitus, **II:** 1, 163; **IV:** 86

Herakles: A Play in Verse (MacLeish), **III:** 21, 22

Herald of the Autochthonic Spirit (Corso), **Supp. XII:** 134–136

He Ran All the Way (film), **Supp. XVII:** 63

Herberg, Will, **III:** 291

Herbert, Edward, **II:** 11

Herbert, Francis (pseudonym). *See* Bryant, William Cullen

Herbert, George, **II:** 12; **IV:** 141, 145, 146, 151, 153, 156, 165; **Retro. Supp. II:** 40; **Supp. I Part 1:** 80, 107, 108, 122; **Supp. IV Part 2:** 646; **Supp. XV:** 92, 212, 251; **Supp. XXI:** 109; **Supp. XXVIII:** 198

Herbert, Zbigniew, **Supp. VIII:** 20

Herbert Huncke Reader, The (Schafer, ed.), **Supp. XIV:** 137, 138, 139, 140, 145, 147, 150, 151–152

Herbert of Cherbury, Lord, **II:** 108

"Herbert West—Reanimator" (Lovecraft), **Supp. XXV:** 112

"Herbert White" (Bidart), **Supp. XV:** 24, 27

Herbs and the Earth (Beston), **Supp. XXVI:** 35–36

Herbst, Josephine, **Retro. Supp. II:** 325, 328; **Supp. XIII:** 295; **Supp. XXVI:** 18, 26, 28

"Her Choice" (Larcom), **Supp. XIII:** 144

"Her Dead Brother" (R. Lowell), **Retro. Supp. II:** 188

"Her Dream Is of the Sea" (Ríos), **Supp. IV Part 2:** 546

"Here" (Kenyon), **Supp. VII:** 164

Here and Beyond (Wharton), **Retro. Supp. I:** 382

Here and Now (Levertov), **Supp. III Part 1:** 275, 276

"Here and There" (Wallace), **Supp. X:** 305–306

Here Comes the Mystery Man (Sanders), **Supp. XVI:** 269

"Here Comes Winston, Full of the Holy Spirit" (Eugenides), **Supp. XXIV:** 133

Heredia, Juanita, **Supp. XI:** 185, 190

Heredity and Variation (Lock), **Retro. Supp. I:** 375

Heredity: A Psychological Study of Its Phenomena, Laws, Causes, and Consequences (Ribot), **Supp. XX: 238**

"Here Follows Some Verses upon the Burning of Our House, July 10th, 1666" (Bradstreet), **Retro. Supp. III:** 9, 11

Here in Harlem: Poems in Many Voices (Myers), **Supp. XXVII:** 211

"Here Inside My Forehead" (Rasmussen; Nelson and Espeland, trans.), **Supp. XVIII:** 180

Here is Your War (Pyle), **Supp. XVII:** 61

Here Let Us Feast (M. F. K. Fisher), **Supp. XVII:** 86, 87

Here Lies (Parker), **Supp. IX:** 192

Herendeen, Anne, **Supp. XXII:** 275

Here on Earth (Hoffman), **Supp. X:** 77, 89

Heresy and the Ideal: On Contemporary Poetry (Baker), **Supp. XI:** 142

"Here to Learn" (Bowles), **Supp. IV Part 1:** 93

"Here to Yonder" (Hughes), **Retro. Supp. I:** 205

"Her Father's Letters" (Milburn), **Supp. XI:** 242

"Her Favorite Story" (Richard), **Supp. XIX:** 211, 212

Herford, Beatrice, **Supp. XXVI:** 275

Herford, Oliver, **Supp. XXVI:** 275

Herford, Reverend Brooke, **I:** 471

Herford, Will, **Supp. XXII:** 275

"Her Game" (Skloot), **Supp. XX: 196, 202**

Hergesheimer, Joseph, **Supp. I Part 2:** 620; **Supp. XVI:** 187

"Heritage" (Cullen), **Supp. IV Part 1:** 164–165, 168, 170, 171

"Heritage" (Hogan), **Supp. IV Part 1:** 413

"Her Kind" (Sexton), **Supp. II Part 2:** 687

Herland (Gilman), **Supp. XI:** 208–209

Herman, Florence. *See* Williams, Mrs. William Carlos (Florence Herman)

Herman, Jan, **Supp. XIV:** 150–151

Herman, William (pseudonym). *See* Bierce, Ambrose

"Her Management" (Swenson), **Supp. IV Part 2:** 642

"Herman Melville" (Auden), **Supp. II Part 1:** 14

Herman Melville (Mumford), **Supp. II Part 2:** 471, 476, 489–491

"Hermes of the Ways" (Doolittle), **Supp. I Part 1:** 266

"Hermes: Port Authority: His Song" (Di Piero), **Supp. XIX:** 47

Hermetic Definition (Doolittle), **Supp. I Part 1:** 271, 272, 273, 274

Hermia Suydam (Atherton), **Supp. XXIV:** 21, 28

"Hermitage, The" (Haines), **Supp. XII:** 205–206

Hermit and the Wild Woman, The (Wharton), **IV:** 315; **Retro. Supp. I:** 371

"Hermit and the Wild Woman, The" (Wharton), **Retro. Supp. I:** 372

"Hermit Meets the Skunk, The" (Kumin), **Supp. IV Part 2:** 447

Hermit of 69th Street, The: The Working Papers or Norbert Kosky (Kosinski), **Supp. VII:** 215, 216, 223, 226–227

"Hermit of Saba, The" (Freneau), **Supp. II Part 1:** 259

"Hermit Picks Berries, The" (Kumin), **Supp. IV Part 2:** 447

Hermit's Story, The (Bass), **Supp. XVI:** 23–24

"Hermit Thrush, A" (Clampitt), **Supp. IX:** 40

Hermit-Woman, The (G. Jones), **Supp. XXIV:** 185, 194

Hernández, Miguel, **Supp. V:** 194; **Supp. XIII:** 315, 323; **Supp. XXI:** 104

Herne, James A., **II:** 276; **Supp. II Part 1:** 198

Hernton, Calvin, **Supp. X:** 240

"Hero, The" (Moore), **III:** 200, 211, 212

Hero, The: A Study in Tradition, Myth, and Drama (Raglan), **I:** 135; **Supp. XIX:** 147

Hero and the Blues, The (Murray), **Supp. XIX:** 153, 154

Hérodiade (Mallarmé), **I:** 66

Herodotus, **Supp. I Part 2:** 405

Heroes, The (Ashbery), **Supp. III Part 1:** 3

Heroes and Saints (Moraga), **Supp. XXIII:** 195, 196, 197, **203–204**

Heroes and Saints and Other Plays (Moraga), **Supp. XXIII:** 197

Hero in America, The (Van Doren), **II:** 103

"Heroines of Nature: Four Women Respond to the American Landscape" (Norwood), **Supp. IX:** 24

"Heroines of Novels" (King), **Supp. XXVIII:** 113

"Heron, The" (Roethke), **III:** 540–541

"Her One Bad Eye" (Karr), **Supp. XI:** 244

"Her Own People" (Warren), **IV:** 253

Her Place in These Designs (Espaillat), **Supp. XXI:** 99, 104

"Her Quaint Honour" (Gordon), **II:** 196, 199, 200

Herr, Michael, **Supp. XI:** 245; **Supp. XIX:** 17

Herreshoff, David, **Supp. XIX:** 265

Herrick, Robert, **II:** 11, 18, 444; **III:** 463, 592; **IV:** 453; **Retro. Supp. I:** 319; **Retro. Supp. II:** 101; **Supp. I Part 2:** 646; **Supp. XIII:** 334; **Supp. XIV:** 8, 9; **Supp. XV:** 155; **Supp. XXI:** 14

Herrmann, John, **Retro. Supp. II:** 328; **Supp. XXII:** 277

Herron, Don, **Supp. XXVII:** 128

Herron, George, **Supp. I Part 1:** 7

"Hers" (column, Prose), **Supp. XVI:** 254

Herschdorfer, Helen, **Supp. XXI:** 262

Herschel, Sir John, **Supp. I Part 1:** 314

"Her Sense of Timing" (Elkin), **Supp. VI:** 56, 58

Hersey, John, **IV:** 4; **Supp. I Part 1:** 196; **Supp. XVI:** 105–106; **Supp. XX:** 251

"Her Sweet turn to leave the Homestead" (Dickinson), **Retro. Supp. I:** 44

"Her Untold Story" (Thompson), **Supp. XXIII:** 301

Herzog (Bellow), **I:** 144, 147, 149, 150, 152, 153, 154, 155, 156, 157, 158, 159–160; **Retro. Supp. II:** 19, 26–27; **Supp. IV Part 1:** 30; **Supp. XIX:** 157

Herzog, Tobey C., **Supp. XXII:** 116

"He's About 22. I'm 63" (H. Johnson), **Supp. XXVI:** 174

Heschel, Abraham Joshua, **Supp. XXI:** 110, 112; **Supp. XXVIII:** 57

Hesford, Walter A., **Supp. XV:** 215, 217, 218

"He/She" (Dunn), **Supp. XI:** 149

"Hesitation Blues" (Hughes), **Retro. Supp. I:** 211

He Sleeps (McKnight), **Supp. XX:** 151, 152–155, 158

"He Sleeps" (McKnight), **Supp. XX:** 152, 155

Hesse, Hermann, **Supp. V:** 208

Hester, Carolyn, **Supp. XVIII:** 24

"Hetch Hetchy Valley" (Muir), **Supp. IX:** 185

He Who Gets Slapped (Andreyev), **II:** 425

"He Who Spits at the Sky" (Stegner), **Supp. IV Part 2:** 605

"He Will Not Leave a Note" (Ríos), **Supp. IV Part 2:** 548

Hewitt, James, **Supp. XV:** 240

Hewitt, J. N. B., **Supp. XXVI:** 81, 89, 90, 96, 97

Hewlett, Maurice, **I:** 359

Heyen, William, **Supp. XIII:** 285, 344; **Supp. XV:** 212

"Hey! Hey!" (Hughes), **Supp. I Part 1:** 327–328

Heyman, Stanley, **Supp. XXV:** 253

Hey Rub-a-Dub-Dub (Dreiser), **I:** 515; **II:** 26; **Retro. Supp. II:** 104, 105, 108

"Hey Sailor, What Ship?" (Olsen), **Supp. XIII:** 293, 294, 298, **299**

Heyward, DuBose, **Supp. XIX:** 78; **Supp. XVIII:** 281

Hiawatha, **Supp. XXVI:** 81, 82, 83, 86

Hiawatha (Longfellow), **Supp. I Part 1:** 79; **Supp. III Part 2:** 609, 610; **Supp. XXI:** 53

"Hibernaculum" (Ammons), **Supp. VII:** 26–27

Hichborn, Philip, **Supp. I Part 2:** 707, 708

Hichborn, Mrs. Philip. *See* Wylie, Elinor

"Hic Jacet" (W. C. Williams), **Retro. Supp. I:** 414

Hickam, Homer, **Supp. XXVII: 99–113**

Hickok, Guy, **Supp. XXI:** 7

Hickok, James Butler ("Wild Bill"), **Supp. V:** 229, 230

Hicks, Granville, **I:** 254, 259, 374; **II:** 26; **III:** 342, 355, 452; **Supp. I Part 1:** 361; **Supp. I Part 2:** 609; **Supp. IV Part 1:** 22; **Supp. IV Part 2:** 526; **Supp. VIII:** 96, 124; **Supp. XII:** 250; **Supp. XIII:** 263; **Supp. XXI:** 276; **Supp. XXII:** 279; **Supp. XXVI:** 144; **Supp. XXVII:** 134; **Supp. XXVIII:** 153

Hicks, Sally, **Supp. XXI:** 255

Hicok, Bethany, **Retro. Supp. II:** 39

"Hidden" (Nye), **Supp. XIII:** 283

"Hidden Gardens" (Capote), **Supp. III Part 1:** 125

Hidden in Plain View (Tobin and Dobard), **Supp. XXVI:** 200

Hidden Law, The (Hecht), **Supp. X:** 58

"Hidden Name and Complex Fate" (Ellison), **Supp. II Part 1:** 245

Hiddenness, Uncertainty, Surprise: Three Generative Energies of Poetry (Hirshfield), **Supp. XXIII:** 137

Hidden Wound, The (Berry), **Supp. X:** 23, 25, 26–27, 29, 34, 35

"Hide-and-Seek" (Francis), **Supp. IX:** 81

"Hiding" (Minot), **Supp. VI:** 203, 206

Hiding Place (Wideman), **Supp. X:** 320, 321, 327, 329, 331–332, 333

"Hidin' Out in Honky Heaven: On Race Relations in Vermont" (Budbill), **Supp. XIX:** 5

Hienger, Jorg, **Supp. IV Part 1:** 106

Hieronymus Bosch (De Tolnay), **Supp. XXII:** 255

Higgins, George, **Supp. IV Part 1:** 356

Higginson, Thomas Wentworth, **I:** 451–452, 453, 454, 456, 458, 459, 463, 464, 465, 470; **Retro. Supp. I:** 26, 31, 33, 35, 39, 40; **Supp. I Part 1:** 307, 371; **Supp. IV Part 2:** 430

Higgs, Robert, **Supp. XX:** 166

"High Bridge above the Tagus River at Toledo, The" (W. C. Williams), **Retro. Supp. I:** 429

"High Dive: A Variant" (Kumin), **Supp. IV Part 2:** 442

"High Diver" (Francis), **Supp. IX:** 82

"Higher Keys, The" (Merrill), **Supp. III Part 1:** 335–336

Higher Learning in America, The (Veblen), **Supp. I Part 2:** 630, 631, 641, 642

Highet, Gilbert, **Supp. I Part 1:** 268

"High Heav'd my breast"(J. Schoolcraft), **Supp. XXIII:** 235

High Noon (film), **Supp. V:** 46

"High on Sadness" (Komunyakaa), **Supp. XIII:** 114

"High School Senior" (Olds), **Supp. X:** 212

Highsmith, Patricia, **Supp. IV Part 1:** 79, 94, 132; **Supp. XXII:** 136

"High Spirits, The" (Huddle), **Supp. XXVI:** 154

High Spirits, The: Stories of Men and Women (Huddle), **Supp. XXVI:** 153–154

"High Tide" (Marquand), **III:** 56

High Tide in Tucson: Essays from Now or Never (Kingsolver), **Supp. VII:** 198, 201, 209

"High-Toned Old Christian Woman, A" (Stevens), **Retro. Supp. I:** 301

"High Water" (Mosher), **Supp. XXII:** 205, 211

"Highway, The" (Merwin), **Supp. III Part 1:** 346

Highway 61 Revisited (album, Dylan), **Supp. XVIII:** 20, 27, 30, 32

"Highway 61 Revisited" (song, Dylan), **Supp. XVIII:** 30

"Highway 99E from Chico" (Carver), **Supp. III Part 1:** 136

"Highway Apple Trees" (Espaillat), **Supp. XXI: 100–102**

High Window, The (Chandler), **Supp. IV Part 1:** 127–129, 130, 131

"High Yaller" (R. Fisher), **Supp. XIX:** 72

Hijuelos, Oscar, **Supp. IV Part 1:** 54; **Supp. VIII: 73–91**

Hike and the Aeroplane (Lewis), **II:** 440–441

Hilberg, Raul, **Supp. V:** 267

Hildebrand, Al, **III:** 118

Hiler, Hilaire, **Retro. Supp. II:** 327; **Supp. III Part 2:** 617

"Hill, A" (Hecht), **Supp. X:** 59–60, 63

Hill, Abram, **Supp. XV:** 194

Hill, Anita, **Supp. XX:** 110

Hill, Geoffrey, **Supp. XXVI:** 67

Hill, Hamlin, **Retro. Supp. II:** 286; **Retro. Supp. III:** 260

Hill, James J., **Supp. I Part 2:** 644

Hill, Joe, **I:** 493; **Supp. XVIII:** 224; **Supp. XXIII:** 162

Hill, Josiah, **Supp. XXVI:** 87, 88

Hill, Lee, **Supp. XI:** 293, 294, 297, 299, 301, 305, 307

Hill, Pamela Smith, **Supp. XXII:** 295

Hill, Patti, **I:** 289

Hill, Peggy, **Supp. XIII:** 163

"Hill, The" (Strand), **Supp. IV Part 2:** 627

"Hill, The" (Toomer), **Supp. III Part 2:** 486

Hill, Vernon, **Supp. I Part 2:** 397

"Hillcrest" (Robinson), **III:** 504

Hill-Lubin, Mildred A., **Supp. IV Part 1:** 13

Hillman, Sidney, **Supp. I Part 1:** 5

Hillringhouse, Mark, **Supp. IX:** 286, 288, 299

Hills Beyond, The (Wolfe), **IV:** 450, 451, 460, 461

"Hills Beyond, The" (Wolfe), **IV:** 460

Hillside and Seaside in Poetry (Larcom, ed.), **Supp. XIII:** 142

"Hillside Thaw, A" (Frost), **Retro. Supp. I:** 133

"Hills Like White Elephants" (Hemingway), **Retro. Supp. I:** 170

Hills of the Shatemuc, The (S. Warner), **Supp. XVIII:** 266

"Hill-Top View, A" (Jeffers), **Supp. II Part 2:** 417

Hill Towns (Siddons), **Supp. XXII:** 239, 253

"Hill Wife, The" (Frost), **II:** 154; **Retro. Supp. I:** 131; **Retro. Supp. III:** 99

Hillyer, Catherine, **Supp. XV:** 244

Hillyer, Robert, **I:** 475; **Supp. IX:** 75; **Supp. XIV:** 11

Hilton, James, **Supp. XIII:** 166

"Hiltons' Holiday, The" (Jewett), **II:** 391; **Retro. Supp. II:** 134

Him (Cummings), **I:** 429, 434–435

Himelstein, Morgan, **Supp. XXVIII:** 72

Himes, Chester Bomar, **Retro. Supp. II:** 117; **Supp. I Part 1:** 51, 325; **Supp. XIII:** 233; **Supp. XVI: 135–146**

Himes, Norman, **Supp. V:** 128
"Him on a Bicycle" (Weigl), **Supp. XIX:** 276
"Him with His Foot in His Mouth" (Bellow), **Retro. Supp. II:** 34
Him with His Foot in His Mouth and Other Stories (Bellow), **Retro. Supp. II:** 31
Hinchman, Sandra K., **Supp. IV Part 1:** 210
Hinckley, David, **Supp. XXII:** 215
Hindemith, Paul, **IV:** 357; **Supp. IV Part 1:** 81
Hindsell, Oliver, **Supp. XIII:** 162
Hindus, Milton, **Supp. XIV:** 288, 291, 292, 293; **Supp. XXIII:** 16
Hines, Suzanne, **Supp. XIV:** 151
Hinge Picture (Howe), **Supp. IV Part 2:** 423–424
Hinojosa, Rolando, **Supp. XIX:** 97–114
"Hinterlands" (W. Gibson), **Supp. XVI:** 123, 128
"Hippies: Slouching towards Bethlehem" (Didion), **Supp. IV Part 1:** 200
Hippolytus (Euripides), **II:** 543; **Supp. I Part 1:** 270
Hippolytus Temporizes (Doolittle), **Supp. I Part 1:** 270
"Hips" (Cisneros), **Supp. VII:** 61, 62
"Hipster's Hipster" (Ginsberg), **Supp. XIV:** 141
"Hired Girl" (Munro), **Supp. XXVII:** 194
Hirsch, Edward D., **Supp. IX:** 262; **Supp. V:** 177; **Supp. XIV:** 15; **Supp. XIX:** 202; **Supp. XV:** 78, 225; **Supp. XVII:** 23; **Supp. XXIII:** 124; **Supp. XXVIII:** 22, 23
Hirsch, Sidney, **Supp. XIV:** 1. *See* Mttron-Hirsch, Sidney
Hirschfeld, Jane, **Supp. XVII:** 241
Hirschorn, Clive, **Supp. IV Part 2:** 577, 579
Hirshfield, Jane, **Supp. XXIII:** 129–141
Hirson, Roger, **Supp. XI:** 343
"His Bride of the Tomb" (Dunbar), **Supp. II Part 1:** 196
"His Chest of Drawers" (Anderson), **I:** 113, 114
"His Daily Journal"(Kenny), **Supp. XXIII:** 153
"His Father's Whistle" (Wrigley), **Supp. XVIII:** 299
His First, Best Country (J. W. Miller), **Supp. XX:** 163, 166, 172–175
His Fortunate Grace (Atherton), **Supp. XXIV:** 22
His Girl Friday (film), **Supp. XXVII:** 83
His Human Majesty (Boyle), **Supp. XXIV:** 62
"His Last Day" (C. Himes), **Supp. XVI:** 137
"His Lover" (Dubus), **Supp. VII:** 86
"His Music" (Dunn), **Supp. XI:** 149
"His Own Key" (Ríos), **Supp. IV Part 2:** 543
His Picture in the Papers (film; Emerson), **Supp. XVI:** 185
His Religion and Hers (Gilman), **Supp. XI:** 209
Hiss, Alger, **Supp. XV:** 143

"Hiss, Chambers, and the Age of Innocence" (Fiedler), **Supp. XIII:** 99
"His Shield" (Moore), **III:** 211
"His Story" (Cisneros), **Supp. VII:** 67
His Thought Made Pockets & the Plane Buckt (Berryman), **I:** 170
"His Three Women" (Gioia), **Supp. XV:** 119–120
Histoire comparée des systèmes de philosophie (Gérando), **II:** 10
Histoire de la brume, L' (Dybek; trans. Beget), **Supp. XXIII:** 74
Historical and Moral View of the Origin and Progress of the French Revolution (Wollstonecraft), **Supp. I Part 1:** 126
"Historical Conceptualization" (Huizinga), **I:** 255
Historical Evidence and the Reading of Seventeenth-Century Poetry (Brooks), **Supp. XIV:** 11
"Historical Interpretation of Literature, The" (Wilson), **IV:** 431, 433, 445
Historical Jesus, The: The Life of a Mediterranean Jewish Peasant (Crossan), **Supp. V:** 251
Historical Life of Jesus, The (Pettis), **Supp. XXIII:** 189
"Historical Value of Crèvecoeur's *Voyage . . .,*" (Adams), *Supp. I Part 1:* 251
"History" (Emerson), **II:** 13, 15
"History" (Hughes), **Supp. I Part 1:** 344
History (R. Lowell), **Retro. Supp. II:** 183, 190
"History" (Simic), **Supp. VIII:** 279
"History, Myth, and the Western Writer" (Stegner), **Supp. IV Part 2:** 596, 601
"History among the Rocks" (Warren), **IV:** 252
History as a Literary Art (Morison), **Supp. I Part 2:** 493
"History as Fate in E. L. Doctorow's Tale of a Western Town" (Arnold), **Supp. IV Part 1:** 220
"History Is the Memory of Time" (Olson), **Supp. II Part 2:** 574
"History Lesson" (Trethewey), **Supp. XXI:** 248, 249
"History Lessons" (Komunyakaa), **Supp. XIII:** 126
History Man, The (Bradbury), **Supp. XVIII:** 140
"History of a Literary Movement" (Nemerov), **III:** 270
"History of a Literary Radical, The" (Bourne), **I:** 215, 235, 236
History of American Literature Since 1980, A (Pattee), **Supp. XXVIII:** 124
History of a Radical: Essays by Randolph Bourne (Brooks), **I:** 245
"History of Armenia, The"(Balakian), **Supp. XXIII:** 23, 24
"History of Buttons, The" (Goldbarth), **Supp. XII:** 187
History of English Literature (Taine), **III:** 323
History of English Prosody (Saintsbury), **Supp. XV:** 181
History of Fortus, The (Emerson), **II:** 8
History of Henry Esmond, The (Thackeray), **II:** 91, 130

History of Louisiana, A (King), **Supp. XXVIII:** 116
History of Modern Poetry, A (Perkins), **Supp. I Part 2:** 475; **Supp. XV:** 185
History of My Heart (Pinsky), **Supp. VI:** 243, 244, 245
History of New York, from the Beginning of the World to the End of the Dutch Dynasty, A (Irving), **II:** 300–303, 304, 310
History of Pendennis, The (Thackeray), **II:** 291
"History of Red, The" (Hogan), **Supp. IV Part 1:** 411
"History of Rodney, The" (Bass), **Supp. XVI:** 20
History of Roxbury Town (Ellis), **Supp. I Part 1:** 99
History of Southern Literature, The (Rubin), **Supp. XX:** 161
History of the African-American People (Proposed) by Strom Thurmond, The (Everett and Kincaid), **Supp. XVIII:** 62, **63–64**
History of the American Film, A (Durang), **Supp. XXIV:** 113, 117, **118–119**
"History of the Blues, A" (Biss), **Supp. XXVI:** 50
History of the Conquest of Mexico (Prescott), **Retro. Supp. I:** 123
History of the Conquest of Peru (Morison, ed.), **Supp. I Part 2:** 494
History of the Dividing Line betwixt Virginia and North Carolina (Byrd), **Supp. IV Part 2:** 425
History of the French Revolution (Carlyle), **Retro. Supp. III:** 266
History of the Life and Voyages of Christopher Columbus, A (Irving), **II:** 310, 314
History of the Navy of the United States of America (Cooper), **I:** 347
History of the Rise and Fall of the Slave-power in America (Wilson), **Supp. XIV:** 48, 49
History of the Russian Revolution, A (Trotsky), **Supp. XXI:** 161
History of the United States (Bancroft), **Supp. XXII:** 33
History of the United States of America during the Administrations of Thomas Jefferson and James Madison (Adams), **I:** 6–9, 10, 20, 21
History of the Work of Redemption, A (Edwards), **I:** 560
History of the World (Raleigh), **Retro. Supp. III:** 4, 6
History of United States Naval Operations in World War II (Morison), **Supp. I Part 2:** 490–492
History of Womankind in Western Europe, The, **Supp. XI:** 197
"History Teacher, The" (Collins), **Supp. XXI:** 57
"History Through a Beard" (Morison), **Supp. I Part 2:** 490
His Toy, His Dream, His Rest (Berryman), **I:** 169, 170, 183, 184–186
"His Words" (Roethke), **III:** 544

Hitchcock, Ada. *See* MacLeish, Mrs. Archibald (Ada Hitchcock)

Hitchcock, Alfred, **IV:** 357; **Supp. IV Part 1:** 132; **Supp. VIII:** 177; **Supp. XX:** 253; **Supp. XXII:** 119

Hitchcock, George, **Supp. X:** 127; **Supp. XVII:** 110

"Hitch Haiku" (Snyder), **Supp. VIII:** 297

"Hitch-Hikers, The" (Welty), **IV:** 262

"Hitchhikers"(Wakoski), **Supp. XXVIII:** 266

"Hitchhiking Is Illegal in Nevada" (Lethem), **Supp. XVIII:** 136

Hitchins, Christopher, **Supp. VIII:** 241

Hitler, Adolf, **I:** 261, 290, 492; **II:** 146, 454, 561, 565, 592; **III:** 2, 3, 110, 115, 140, 156, 246, 298, 446; **IV:** 5, 17, 18, 298, 372; **Supp. I Part 2:** 431, 436, 446, 664; **Supp. V:** 290

Hitler, Wendy, **III:** 404

Hitler Lives ? (film), **Supp. XVI:** 102

Hix, H. L., **Supp. XV:** 114

H. L. Mencken, a Portrait from Memory (Angoff), **III:** 107

"H. L. Mencken Meets a Poet in the West Side Y.M.C.A." (White), **Supp. I Part 2:** 677

H. L. Mencken: The American Scene (Cairns), **III:** 119

H. M. Pulham, Esquire (Marquand), **II:** 482–483; **III:** 58, 59, 65, 68–69

Hnizdovsky, Jacques, **Supp. XIII:** 346

"Hoadley's Test Case in Indiana" (Neugeboren), **Supp. XVI:** 219

Hoagland, Edward, **Supp. XIV:** 80; **Supp. XVI:** 277; **Supp. XXII:** 204, 206

Hoagland, Tony, **Supp. XIX:** 81, 89

"Hoarder, The" (Sexton), **Supp. II Part 2:** 692

"Hoarfrost" (C. Baxter), **Supp. XVII:** 15

Hoban, Phoebe, **Supp. XV:** 319, 325

Hoban, Russell, **Supp. XXIII:** 42

Hobb, Gormley, **I:** 203

Hobbes, Thomas, **I:** 277; **II:** 9, 10, 540; **III:** 306; **IV:** 88; **Supp. XII:** 33; **Supp. XIV:** 5, 7

Hobbit, The (Tolkien), **Supp. XXVII:** 124

Hobbs, Glenda, **Supp. XXVIII:** 4

Hoboken Blues (Gold), **Supp. XXVIII:** 74

Hobson, Geary, **Supp. IV Part 1:** 321; **Supp. IV Part 2:** 502

Hobson, J. A., **I:** 232

Hobson, John A., **Supp. I Part 2:** 650

Hobson, Laura Z., **III:** 151

Hocking, Agnes, **Supp. VIII:** 251

Hocking, William Ernest, **III:** 303

Hodge, Merle, **Supp. XXIII:** 94

Hodges, Campbell B., **Supp. XIV:** 8

Hodgson, Captain Joseph, **III:** 328

Hoffa, Jimmy, **I:** 493

Hoffenberg, Mason, **Supp. XI:** 294, 297, 299, 305

Hoffer, Eric, **Supp. VIII:** 188; **Supp. XIX:** 264

Hoffman, Abbie, **Supp. XIV:** 150

Hoffman, Alice, **Supp. X:** 77–94; **Supp. XIII:** 13

Hoffman, Allen, **Supp. XVII:** 42, 44

Hoffman, Daniel, **Retro. Supp. II:** 265

Hoffman, Daniel G., **I:** 405; **II:** 307; **Supp. XI:** 152

Hoffman, Dustin, **Supp. IV Part 1:** 236

Hoffman, E. T. A., **Supp. XVI:** 157

Hoffman, Eva, **Supp. XVI:** 147–164

Hoffman, Frederick J., **I:** 60, 67; **II:** 443; **IV:** 113

Hoffman, Josiah Ogden, **II:** 297, 300

Hoffman, Matilda, **II:** 300, 314

Hoffman, Paul, **Supp. XV:** 141–142

Hoffman, Roy, **Supp. XX:** 177

Hoffman, Todd, **Supp. XVIII:** 101

Hoffman, Tyler, **Retro. Supp. III:** 103

Hoffman, William, **Supp. XVIII:** 69–88

Hoffman, William M., **Supp. X:** 153

Hoffman-Jeep, Lynda, **Retro. Supp. III:** 127

Hoffmann, E. T. A., **III:** 415

Hofmann, Hans, **Supp. XV:** 144

Hofmeister, Tim, **Supp. XIX:** 115

Ho for a Hat (W. J. Smith), **Supp. XIII:** 346

Hofstadter, Richard, **Supp. VIII:** 98, 99, 108

Hogan, Linda, **Supp. IV Part 1:** 324, 325, 397–418; **Supp. XVIII:** 189

Hogan, Randolph, **Supp. XVI:** 252–253

Hogan, Ron, **Supp. XVIII:** 138, 139

Hogarth, William, **Supp. XII:** 44

Hogg, James, **I:** 53; **Supp. I Part 1:** 349; **Supp. IX:** 275

Hoggart, Richard, **Supp. XIV:** 299

"Hog-Nosed Snake, The" (Kooser), **Supp. XIX:** 128

Hogue, W. Lawrence, **Supp. XXII:** 175–176

Hohne, Karen, **Supp. V:** 147

Hojoki (Chomei), **IV:** 170

Holbrook, David, **Supp. I Part 2:** 526–527, 546

Holcroft, Thomas, **Supp. I Part 2:** 514

Holden, Jonathan, **Supp. XI:** 143

Holden, Raymond, **Supp. XIV:** 121–122

Holden, Stephen, **Retro. Supp. III:** 290

Holden, William, **Supp. XI:** 307

Hölderlin, Friedrich, **Supp. XVI:** 48; **Supp. XXIV:** 152

Holding, Elisabeth Sanxay, **Supp. XXII:** 119–137

"Holding On" (Levine), **Supp. V:** 184

Holding the Line: Women in the Great Arizona Mine Strike of 1983 (Kingsolver), **Supp. VII:** 197, 201–202, 204

"Holding the Mirror Up to Nature" (Nemerov), **III:** 275, 276

"Hold Me" (Levine), **Supp. V:** 186

Holdt, Jacob, **Supp. XXVI:** 26

Hold the Press (film), **Supp. XIII:** 163

Hold with the Hares (Zinberg), **Supp. XV:** 197–198, **Supp. XV:** 203

Hole in Texas, A (Wouk), **Supp. XXV:** 257, 266–267

"Hole in the Floor, A" (Wilbur), **Supp. III Part 2:** 556–557

Hole in the Sky: A Memoir (Kittredge), **Supp. XXVI:** 177, 179, 180–181, 182, 184–185

Holiday (Barry), **Retro. Supp. I:** 104

"Holiday" (Porter), **III:** 454

Holiday (W. Frank), **Supp. XX:** 72–73

Holiday, Billie, **Supp. I Part 1:** 80; **Supp. IV Part 1:** 2, 7; **Supp. XIX:** 147

Holiday Song for Four-Part Chorus of Mixed Voices with Piano Accompaniment (Taggard and Schuman), **Supp. XXII:** 283

Holinshed, Raphael, **IV:** 370

Holladay, Polly, **Supp. XXI:** 6

Holland, Josiah, **Supp. I Part 2:** 420

Holland, Laurence Bedwell, **Retro. Supp. I:** 216

Holland, Theodore, **I:** 453

Holland, Mrs. Theodore, **I:** 453, 455, 465

Holland, William, **IV:** 381

Hollander, John, **Supp. III Part 2:** 541; **Supp. IV Part 2:** 642; **Supp. IX:** 50, 153, 155; **Supp. XII:** 254, 255, 260; **Supp. XIX:** 121; **Supp. XV:** 256; **Supp. XVII:** 112; **Supp. XXIII:** 112; **Supp. XXVIII:** 202

Hollenberg, Donna, **Supp. XXIV:** 64

Holley, Marietta, **Supp. XIII:** 152

Holliday, Billie, **Supp. XXI:** 131

Hollinghurst, Alan, **Supp. XIII:** 52

Hollins Critic (Nelson), **Supp. XIX:** 3

Hollis, Thomas Brand, **Supp. I Part 2:** 514

Holloway, Karla F. C., **Retro. Supp. III:** 183

Hollow Men, The (Gold), **Supp. XXVIII:** 65

Hollow Men, The (T. S. Eliot), **I:** 574, 575, 578–579, 580, 585; **III:** 586; **Retro. Supp. I:** 63, 64

"Hollow Men, The" (T. S. Eliot), **Retro. Supp. III:** 65

"Hollow Tree, A" (R. Bly), **Supp. IV Part 1:** 64, 66

Holly and Pizen, and Other Stories (Stuart), **Supp. XXVIII:** 225, 229

Hollyberrys at the Shore, The, **Supp. X:** 42

"Hollywood!" (Vidal), **Supp. IV Part 2:** 688

Hollywood: American Movie-City (Rand, unauthorized), **Supp. IV Part 2:** 519

Hollywood: A Novel of America in the 1920s (Vidal), **Supp. IV Part 2:** 677, 684, 686, 688, 690, 691

Hollywood Ending (film; Allen), **Supp. XV:** 11

Hollywood on Trial (film), **Supp. I Part 1:** 295

Holmes, Abiel, **Supp. I Part 1:** 300, 301, 302, 310

Holmes, Mrs. Abiel (Sarah Wendell), **Supp. I Part 1:** 300

Holmes, John, **I:** 169; **Supp. II Part 1:** 87; **Supp. IV Part 2:** 440–441; **Supp. XIV:** 119; **Supp. XXVI:** 68

Holmes, John Clellon, **Supp. XII:** 118; **Supp. XIV:** 144, 150

Holmes, Martha Stoddard, **Supp. XX:** 205, 207

Holmes, Oliver Wendell, **I:** 487; **II:** 225, 273–274, 402, 403; **III:** 81–82, 590, 591–592; **IV:** 429, 436; **Retro. Supp. II:** 155; **Supp. I Part 1:** 103, 243,

254, **299–319; Supp. I Part 2:** 405, 414, 415, 420, 593, 704, 705; **Supp. XI:** 194; **Supp. XXIV:** 77

Holmes, Oliver Wendell, Jr., **I:** 3, 19; **Supp. IV Part 2:** 422

Holmes, Mrs. Oliver Wendell (Amelia Jackson), **Supp. I Part 1:** 303

Holmes, Steven J., **Supp. IX:** 172, 177

Holmes, Ted, **Supp. V:** 180

Holmes, William Henry, **Supp. IV Part 2:** 603–604

Holmquist, Kathryn, **Supp. XXVII:** 268

Holocaust (Reznikoff), **Supp. XIV:** 281, **291–293**

Holocaust in American Life, The (Novick), **Supp. XVI:** 154

Holt, Edwin E., **I:** 59

Holt, Felix, **II:** 179

Holt, Henry, **II:** 348; **III:** 587; **Retro. Supp. III:** 98

Holt, Patricia, **Supp. XIV:** 89

Holtby, Winifred, **Supp. I Part 2:** 720

Holtman, Janet, **Supp. XXVIII:** 7

Holy Ghostly, The (Shepard), **Supp. III Part 2:** 437–438, 447

"Holy Innocents, The" (R. Lowell), **II:** 539

Holy Sonnets (Donne), **IV:** 145; **Supp. I Part 1:** 367; **Supp. III Part 2:** 619; **Supp. XIII:** 130–131; **Supp. XVIII:** 50–51

"Holy Terror, A" (Bierce), **I:** 203

"Holy Terror, The" (Maxwell), **Supp. VIII:** 169

Holy the Firm (Dillard), **Supp. VI:** 23, **29**, 30, 31, 32

Holy War, The (Bunyan), **IV:** 156

"Holy Week"(Thompson), **Supp. XXIII:** 300

Holz, Patricia, **Supp. XXVII:** 267

"Homage to Arthur Rimbaud" (Wright), **Supp. V:** 339

Homage to Baudelaire (Duncan, ed.), **Supp. XV:** 75

Homage to Catalonia (Orwell), **Supp. XVII:** 229

"Homage to Che Guevara" (Banks), **Supp. V:** 5

Homage to Clio (Auden), **Supp. II Part 1:** 24

"Homage to Elizabeth Bishop" (Ivask, ed.), **Supp. I Part 1:** 96

"Homage to Ezra Pound" (Wright), **Supp. V:** 339

Homage to Frank O'Hara (Ashbery), **Supp. III Part 1:** 2–3

"Homage to Franz Joseph Haydn" (Hecht), **Supp. X:** 69

"Homage to Hemingway" (Bishop), **IV:** 35

Homage to Mistress Bradstreet (Berryman), **I:** 168, 169, 170–171, 172, 174, 175, 178–183, 184, 186

"Homage to Mistress Bradstreet" (Berryman), **Retro. Supp. III:** 14

"Homage to Paul Cézanne" (Wright), **Supp. V:** 341–342

Homage to Sextus Propertius (Pound), **Retro. Supp. I:** 290

"Homage to Sextus Propertius" (Pound), **III:** 462, 476; **Supp. III Part 2:** 622

"Homage to Shakespeare" (Cheever), **Supp. I Part 1:** 180

"Homage to the Empress of the Blues" (Hayden), **Supp. II Part 1:** 379

"Homage to the Memory of Wallace Stevens" (Justice), **Supp. VII:** 126

Homage to Theodore Dreiser (Warren), **I:** 517

Homans, Margaret, **Supp. X:** 229

"Home" (Hughes), **Supp. I Part 1:** 329, 330

"Home" (Mora), **Supp. XIII:** 217

Home (Morrison), **Retro. Supp. III:** 185, 198–199

Home (Robinson), **Supp. XXI:** 212, **220–223**

Home (Updike), **Retro. Supp. I:** 320

"Home" (Weigl), **Supp. XIX:** 287

"Home, Home on the Strange" (J. D. Reed), **Supp. XVI:** 174

"Home, Sweet Home" (Fante), **Supp. XI:** 164, 165

Home, The (Gilman), **Supp. XI: 206–207**

"Home, The" (Jarman), **Supp. XVII:** 116

"Home Address" (Bronk), **Supp. XXI:** 27

"Home after Three Months Away" (R. Lowell), **II:** 547

Home and Colonial Library (Murray), **Retro. Supp. I:** 246

"Home and the Open Road: The Nonfiction of Larry Brown" (Barrier), **Supp. XXI:** 48–49

Home as Found (Cooper), **I:** 348, 349, 350, 351

Home at the End of the World, A (Cunningham), **Supp. XV: 59–62**, 63

"Home Away from Home, A" (Humphrey), **Supp. IX:** 101

Home Book of Shakespeare Quotations (Stevenson), **Supp. XIV:** 120

"Home Burial" (Frost), **Retro. Supp. I:** 124, 125, 128, **129–130; Retro. Supp. III:** 97, 98; **Supp. VIII:** 31; **Supp. XIX:** 9; **Supp. XV:** 159

Homecoming (Alvarez), **Supp. VII:** 1, 3–5, 9

"Homecoming" (Carruth), **Supp. XVI:** 55

"Homecoming" (McGrath), **Supp. X:** 116

"Homecoming, The" (Gioia), **Supp. XV:** 123, 124

Homecoming, The (Wilson), **Supp. VIII:** 330

Homecoming Game, The (Nemerov), **III:** 268, 282, 284–285

"Home during a Tropical Snowstorm I Feed My Father Lunch" (Karr), **Supp. XI:** 241–242, 248

Home Economics (Berry), **Supp. X:** 28, 31–32, 35, 36, 37

"Home Economics for Halfbacks" (Skloot), **Supp. XX: 195, 207**

Home Fires and Reservation Roads (Gansworth), **Supp. XXVI:** 114

Home from the Hill (film), **Supp. IX:** 95

Home from the Hill (Humphrey), **Supp. IX:** 93, 95, **96–98**, 104, 106, 109

"Home Grown" (Vital), **Supp. XVI:** 160

"Homeland" (Merwin), **Supp. III Part 1:** 351

Homeland and Other Stories (Kingsolver), **Supp. VII:** 199, 202–204, 207

Homely Girl (A. Miller), **Retro. Supp. III:** 176

Home on the Range (Baraka), **Supp. II Part 1:** 47

Homeplace (Siddons), **Supp. XXII:** 253

Home Place, The (Morris), **III:** 221, 222, 232

Homeplace, The (Nelson), **Supp. XVIII: 174–175**

Home Port (Prouty), **Supp. XXVIII:** 180, 181, 188–189, 192

Homer, **I:** 312, 433; **II:** 6, 8, 133, 302, 543, 544, 552; **III:** 14, 21, 278, 453, 457, 473, 567; **IV:** 54, 371; **Retro. Supp. I:** 59; **Supp. I Part 1:** 158, 283; **Supp. I Part 2:** 494; **Supp. X:** 36, 120, 122; **Supp. XIV:** 21; **Supp. XVII:** 70, 227

Homer, Louise, **Retro. Supp. I:** 10

Homer, Winslow, **Supp. XXI:** 243

"Home Range" (Leopold), **Supp. XIV:** 184, 185

"Home Repairs" (Skloot), **Supp. XX: 204**

Homer's Art (Notley), **Supp. XXII:** 232

"Homer's Art" (Notley), **Supp. XXII:** 232–233

"Homesick Blues" (Hughes), **Supp. I Part 1:** 327

Home: Social Essays (Baraka), **Supp. II Part 1:** 45, 61

"Homesteading on the Extraterrestrial Frontier" (Abbott), **Supp. XVIII:** 142

Home to Harlem (McKay), **Supp. X:** 132, 137–138, **138–139; Supp. XVIII:** 127; **Supp. XXVIII:** 46

"Home Videos" (Brockmeier), **Supp. XXII:** 60

Homeward Bound (Cooper), **I:** 348

"Homeward Star, The" (Palmer), **Supp. XV:** 81–82

Homewood trilogy (Wideman), **Supp. X:** 319

"Homework" (Cameron), **Supp. XII:** 80, **83,** 84

"Homily" (Tate), **IV:** 121–122

Homing with the Birds (Stratton-Porter), **Supp. XX: 212, 216, 222**

"Homme Moyen Sensuel, L' " (Pound), **III:** 462

Homme révolté, L' (Camus), **III:** 306

"Homoeopathy and Its Kindred Delusions" (Holmes), **Supp. I Part 1:** 303–304, 305

Homo Ludens (Huizinga), **II:** 416–417, 425

"Homosexuality: Is It Disgusting, or Is It Delightful?" (Durang), **Supp. XXIV:** 114

"Homosexuality"(O'Hara), **Supp. XXIII:** 212

"Homosexual Villain, The" (Mailer), **III:** 36

"Homo Will Not Inherit" (Doty), **Supp. XI:** 128

"Homunculus, The: A Novel in One Chapter" (McKnight), **Supp. XX: 152**

Hone and Strong Diaries of Old Manhattan, The (Auchincloss, ed.), **Supp. IV Part 1:** 23

"Honey" (Beattie), **Supp. V:** 33

"Honey" (Wright), **Supp. III Part 2:** 589

Honey, Maureen, **Supp. XXVI:** 166

"Honey, We'll Be Brave" (Farrell), **II:** 45

Honey and Salt (Sandburg), **III:** 594–596

"Honey and Salt" (Sandburg), **III:** 594

"Honey Babe" (Hughes), **Supp. I Part 1:** 334

"Honey Tree, The" (Oliver), **Supp. VII:** 236

Hong, Maxine. *See* Kingston, Maxine Hong

Hong, Terry, **Supp. XXVI:** 216

Hongo, Garrett, **Supp. X:** 292; **Supp. XIII:** 114; **Supp. XVII:** 112

"Honkytonk" (Shapiro), **Supp. II Part 2:** 705

"Honky Tonk in Cleveland, Ohio" (Sandburg), **III:** 585

Honorable Men (Auchincloss), **Supp. IV Part 1:** 23

Honor Thy Father (Talese), **Supp. XVII:** 204–205, 210

Hood, Mary, **Supp. XXVI:** 15

Hood, Tom, **I:** 195

"Hoodoo in America" (Hurston), **Supp. VI:** 153–154

"Hook" (Wright), **Supp. III Part 2:** 604

Hook, Sidney, **I:** 265; **Supp. IV Part 2:** 527; **Supp. VIII:** 96, 100; **Supp. XIV:** 3

Hooker, Adelaide. *See* Marquand, Mrs. John P. (Adelaide Hooker)

Hooker, Isabella Beecher, **Supp. XI:** 193

Hooker, Samuel, **IV:** 162, 165

Hooker, Thomas, **II:** 15–16; **IV:** 162

Hooper, Marian. *See* Adams, Mrs. Henry (Marian Hooper)

Hoops (Myers), **Supp. XXVII:** 201, 204, 205–206

Hoosier Holiday, A (Dreiser), **Retro. Supp. II:** 104

Hoover, Herbert, **Supp. I Part 2:** 638

Hoover, J. Edgar, **Supp. XIII:** 170

Hoover, Paul, **Supp. XV:** 179

"Hope" (Bontemps), **Supp. XXII:** 2

"Hope" (Jarrell), **II:** 389

"Hope" (Matthews), **Supp. IX:** 163

Hope, A. D., **Supp. XIII:** 347

Hope, Lynn, **Supp. II Part 1:** 38

Hope, The (Wouk), **Supp. XXV:** 254, 257, 265–266

"Hope Atherton's Wanderings" (Howe), **Supp. IV Part 2:** 432

"Hopeless Kill, The" (Kenny), **Supp. XXIII:** 145

Hope of Heaven (O'Hara), **III:** 361

"Hopes Rise" (Boyle), **Supp. XX: 20**

"Hop-Frog; or, The Eight Chained Ourang-Outangs" (Poe), **Retro. Supp. II:** 264, 268, 269; **Retro. Supp. III:** 230

"Hop-Frog; or The Eight Chained Ourang-Outangs" (Poe), **Supp. XXV:** 112

Hopkin, Pauline, **Supp. XVI:** 143

Hopkins, Anne Yale, **Retro. Supp. III:** 3; **Supp. I Part 1:** 100, 102, 113

Hopkins, Gerard Manley, **I:** 171, 179, 397, 401, 522, 525, 533; **II:** 537; **III:** 197, 209, 523; **IV:** 129, 135, 141, 421; **Retro. Supp. II:** 40; **Supp. I Part 1:** 79, 81, 94; **Supp. III Part 2:** 551; **Supp. IV Part 1:** 178; **Supp. IV Part 2:** 637, 638, 639, 641, 643; **Supp. IX:** 39, 42; **Supp. V:** 337; **Supp. X:** 61, 115; **Supp. XIII:** 294; **Supp. XIV:** 83; **Supp. XV:** 250, 347; **Supp. XVI:** 282; **Supp. XVII:** 241; **Supp. XVIII:** 78, 79; **Supp. XX:** 230; **Supp. XXIII:** 121; **Supp. XXVII:** 222

Hopkins, Gerard Walter Sturgis, **Supp. XX: 229, 233, 240**

Hopkins, L. A., **I:** 502

Hopkins, Lemuel, **Supp. II Part 1:** 70

Hopkins, Miriam, **IV:** 381; **Supp. I Part 1:** 281

Hopkins, Pauline, **Supp. XVIII:** 284

Hopkins, Samuel, **I:** 547, 549; **Supp. XXIV:** 68

Hopkins, Vivian, **II:** 20

Hopkinson, Francis, **Supp. I Part 2:** 504

Hopler, Jay, **Supp. XXIII:** 132

Hopper (Strand), **Supp. IV Part 2:** 632

Hopper, Dennis, **Supp. XI:** 293, 308; **Supp. XXVI:** 26

Hopper, Edward, **IV:** 411, 413; **Supp. IV Part 2:** 619, 623, 631, 634; **Supp. XIX:** 117

Hopwood, Avery, **Supp. IV Part 2:** 573; **Supp. XXV:** 195

Horace, **II:** 8, 154, 169, 543, 552, 568; **III:** 15; **IV:** 89; **Retro. Supp. III:** 101; **Supp. I Part 2:** 423; **Supp. IX:** 152; **Supp. X:** 65; **Supp. XII:** 258, 260, 262

Horae Canonicae (Auden), **Supp. II Part 1:** 21

"Horatian Ode" (Marvell), **IV:** 135

"Horatian Ode upon Cromwell's Return from Ireland" (Marvell), **Supp. XIV:** 10

Horgan, Paul, **Supp. XV:** 46, 49, 52

Horkheimer, Max, **Supp. I Part 2:** 645; **Supp. IV Part 1:** 301

Horn, Dara, **Supp. XVII:** 50; **Supp. XX: 177**

Horn, Mother, **Supp. I Part 1:** 49, 54

Hornburg, Michael, **Supp. XXVII:** 80

Hornby, Nick, **Supp. XII:** 286; **Supp. XXIII:** 109

"Horn" (Lea), **Supp. XXVIII:** 132

Horn of Africa (Caputo), **Supp. XIX:** 21–23

Horn of Life, The (Atherton), **Supp. XXIV:** 26, 27

"Horn of Plenty" (Hughes), **Retro. Supp. I:** 210; **Supp. I Part 1:** 342

Horovitz, Israel, **Supp. XV:** 321

Horowitz, James. *See* Salter, James

Horowitz, Mark, **Supp. V:** 219, 231

"Horrible" (Halliday), **Supp. XIX:** 91

"Horror at Martin's Beach, The" (Lovecraft and Greene), **Supp. XXV:** 122

"Horror at Red Hook, The" (Lovecraft), **Supp. XXV:** 110

"Horse, The" (Levine), **Supp. V:** 182

"Horse, The" (Wright), **Supp. III Part 2:** 592, 601

"Horse, The" (Le Sueur), **Supp. XXIII:** 168

Horse Eats Hay (play), **Supp. IV Part 1:** 82

Horse Feathers (film), **Supp. IV Part 1:** 384

"Horseflies" (Wrigley), **Supp. XVIII:** 307

Horse Has Six Legs, The (Simic), **Supp. VIII:** 272

"Horselaugh on Dibber Lannon" (Fante), **Supp. XI:** 164

Horseman, Pass By (McMurtry), **Supp. V:** 220–221, 224

"Horses" (Doty), **Supp. XI:** 122

Horses and Men (Anderson), **I:** 112–113, 114

"Horses and Men in Rain" (Sandburg), **III:** 584

"Horse Show, The" (W. C. Williams), **Retro. Supp. I:** 423

Horses Make a Landscape More Beautiful (Walker), **Supp. III Part 2:** 521, 533

"Horse Thief" (Caldwell), **I:** 310

"Horseweed" (Offutt), **Supp. XIX:** 166, 167

Horse With a Green Vinyl Mane (P. N. Warren), **Supp. XX: 261**

"Horsie" (Parker), **Supp. IX:** 193

Horstmann, Steffen, **Supp. XXV:** 226

Horton, George Moses, **Supp. XXII:** 11

Horton, Philip, **I:** 383, 386, 387, 393, 441; **Supp. XV:** 138

Horton Hatches the Egg (Geisel), **Supp. XVI:** 100, 112

Horton Hears a Who! (Geisel), **Supp. XVI:** 102

"Horton's Ape" (P. Benedict), **Supp. XXIII:** 41

Horwitz, Tony, **Supp. XVIII:** 195–196

Hosea (biblical book), **II:** 166

Hospers, John, **Supp. IV Part 2:** 528

"Hospice" (Hull), **Supp. XXI:** 138

Hospital, Janette Turner, **Supp. IV Part 1:** 311–302

Hospital Sketches (Alcott), **Supp. I Part 1:** 34, 35

Hostages to Fortune (Humphrey), **Supp. IX:** 96, **104–106,** 109

Hostess to Murder (Holding), **Supp. XXII:** 126, **127**

Hostetler, Ann, **Retro. Supp. III:** 193

"Hot Combs" (Trethewey), **Supp. XXI:** 249

"Hot Cross Bum" (Loy), **Supp. XXII:** 168

"Hot Dog" (Stern), **Supp. IX: 298–299**

"Hotel, The" (Hadas), **Supp. XXIII:** 121

"Hotel Bar" (McClatchy), **Supp. XII:** 269

Hotel Dwellers, The (Lacy), **Supp. XV:** 205

Hotel Insomnia (Simic), **Supp. VIII:** 280, **281–282**

Hotel Lambosa and Other Stories (Koch), **Supp. XV:** 186

Hotel New Hampshire, The (Irving), **Supp. VI:** 163, 164, **172–173**, 177, 179; **Supp. XIX:** 164

"Hot-Foot Hannibal" (Chesnutt), **Supp. XIV:** 60

"Hot Ice"(Dybek), **Supp. XXIII:** 72–73

"Hot Night on Water Street" (Simpson), **Supp. IX:** 269, 270

"Hot Time, A" (Gunn Allen), **Supp. IV Part 1:** 333

Houdini, Harry, **IV:** 437; **Supp. XXV:** 121

"Hound of Heaven" (Thompson), **Retro. Supp. I:** 55

"Hourglass, The" (Kees), **Supp. XV:** 147

"Hour in Chartres, An" (Bourne), **I:** 228

"Hour of Peonies, The"(Crooker), **Supp. XXIII:** 58

Hour of the Dragon, The (Howard), **Supp. XXVII:** 126

Hours, The (Cunningham), **Supp. XII:** 80; **Supp. XV:** 65–68

"Hours before Eternity" (Caldwell), **I:** 291

House, Bridge, Fountain, Gate (Kumin), **Supp. IV Part 2:** 448, 449, 451, 454

House, Edward, **Supp. I Part 2:** 643

"House, The" (Merrill), **Supp. III Part 1:** 323

House at Pooh Corner, The (Milne), **Supp. IX:** 189

"House at the End of the World, The" (Brockmeier), **Supp. XXII:** 52, 53

House Behind the Cedars, The (Chesnutt), **Supp. XIV:** 69–71

Houseboat Days (Ashbery), **Supp. III Part 1:** 18–20

Housebreaker of Shady Hill and Other Stories, The (Cheever), **Supp. I Part 1:** 184

"House by the Sea, The" (E. Stoddard), **Supp. XV:** 277

House by the Sea, The (Sarton), **Supp. VIII:** 264

House Divided, A (Buck), **Supp. II Part 1:** 118

"House Divided, The/La Casa Divida" (Kingsolver), **Supp. VII:** 207

"House Guest" (Bishop), **Retro. Supp. II:** 49; **Supp. I Part 1:** 93

"House Holding" (Davison), **Supp. XXVI:** 73, 74

Household Saints (film), **Supp. XVI:** 256

Household Saints (Prose), **Supp. XVI:** 252–253, 254, 261

"House in Athens, The" (Merrill), **Supp. III Part 1:** 323

House in the Uplands, A (Caldwell), **I:** 297, 301, 306

"House in Turk Street, The" (Hammett), **Supp. IV Part 1:** 344

"House in Winter, The" (Sarton), **Supp. VIII:** 259

"House in Winter, The"(Hirshfield), **Supp. XXIII:** 132

House Is Made of Poetry, The (Baker and Gilbert, eds.), **Supp. XXVII:** 263

"Housekeeping" (Alvarez), **Supp. VII:** 3–5, 10

Housekeeping (Robinson), **Supp. XXI:** 210–211, **212–216**, 218, 223

"Housekeeping" (Trethewey), **Supp. XXI:** 249

"Housekeeping for Men" (Bourne), **I:** 231

House Made of Dawn (Momaday), **Supp. IV Part 1:** 274, 323, 326; **Supp. IV Part 2:** 479, 480, 481–484, 485, 486, 504, 562

Houseman, John, **Supp. IV Part 1:** 173

House Next Door, The (Siddons), **Supp. XXII:** 239

House Next Door, The (television movie), **Supp. XXII:** 239

"House of Caesar, The" (Garvin), **Supp. XXVII:** 118

House of Dust, The: A Symphony (Aiken), **I:** 50

House of Earth trilogy (Buck), **Supp. II Part 1:** 118, 123

House of Five Talents, The (Auchincloss), **Supp. IV Part 1:** 21, 25–27

"House of Flowers" (Capote), **Supp. III Part 1:** 123

House of Games (Mamet), **Supp. XIV:** 243

House of Houses (Mora), **Supp. XIII:** 213, 215, 218, 219, 223–224, **225–227**, 228, 229

House of Incest (Nin), **Supp. III Part 1:** 43; **Supp. X:** 187, 190, 193

House of Lee, The (Atherton), **Supp. XXIV:** 26–27

House of Life, The: Rachel Carson at Work (Brooks), **Supp. IX:** 26

House of Light (Oliver), **Supp. VII:** 238–240

House of Mirth, The (film, Davies), **Retro. Supp. III:** 290

House of Mirth, The (Wharton), **II:** 180, 193; **IV:** 311–313, 314, 316, 318, 323, 327; **Retro. Supp. I:** 360, 366, 367, **367–370**, 373, 380; **Retro. Supp. III:** 280–281, 288; **Supp. XX: 239, 240**

"House of Mist, The" (Rand), **Supp. IV Part 2:** 524

"House of My Own, A" (Cisneros), **Supp. VII:** 64

"House of Night, The" (Freneau), **Supp. II Part 1:** 259, 260

"House of Representatives and Me, The" (Conroy), **Supp. XVI:** 75

House of Sand and Fog (Dubus III), **Supp. XXIV:** 97, **104–107**

House of Sleeping Beauties, The (Hwang), **Supp. XXI:** 146

House of the Far and Lost, The (Wolfe), **IV:** 456

"House of the Injured, The" (Haines), **Supp. XII:** 203

"House of the One Father" (Antin), **Supp. XX: 3, 13**

House of the Prophet, The (Auchincloss), **Supp. IV Part 1:** 31

House of the Seven Gables (Hawthorne), **I:** 106; **II:** 60, 224, 225, 231, 237, 239, 240–241, 243, 244; **Retro. Supp. I:** 63, 149, **160–162**, 163, 164; **Retro.**

Supp. III: 118–119; **Supp. I Part 2:** 579

House of the Solitary Maggot, The (Purdy), **Supp. VII:** 274–275

"House of Women"(Lea), **Supp. XXVIII:** 142

"House on 15th S.W., The" (Hugo), **Supp. VI:** 140

"House on Main Street, The" (B. Kelly), **Supp. XVII:** 127

House on Mango Street, The (Cisneros), **Supp. VII:** 58, 59–64, 65, 66, 67, 68, 72; **Supp. XXV:** 133

"House on Mango Street, The" (Cisneros), **Supp. VII:** 59

House on Marshland, The (Glück), **Supp. V:** 81–83, 84

"House on Moscow Street, The" (Nelson), **Supp. XVIII:** 174

"House on the Heights, A" (Capote), **Supp. III Part 1:** 120

"House on the Hill, The" (Robinson), **III:** 505, 524

"House Raising" (Offutt), **Supp. XIX:** 166

"Houses" (Hogan), **Supp. IV Part 1:** 402

"Houses, The" (Merwin), **Supp. III Part 1:** 354

"Houses of Dreams" (Teasdale), **Supp. XXVII:** 292

"Houses of the Spirit" (Karr), **Supp. XI:** 250

"House Sparrows" (Hecht), **Supp. X: 68**

"House That Doesn't House, The" (Bronk), **Supp. XXI:** 34

House That Tai Maing Built, The (Lee), **Supp. X:** 291

"House Unroofed by the Gale" (Tu Fu), **II:** 526

"House Where Mark Twain Was Born, The" (Masters), **Supp. I Part 2:** 472

"Housewife" (Hempel), **Supp. XXI:** 124

"Housewife" (Sexton), **Supp. II Part 2:** 682

"Housewife's Paradise, The" (Davison), **Supp. XXVI:** 76

" 'Housing the Deliberations': New York, War, and Frank O'Hara"(Ward), **Supp. XXIII:** 218

Housman, A. E., **III:** 15, 136, 606; **Retro. Supp. III:** 27, 74; **Supp. II Part 1:** 4; **Supp. IV Part 1:** 165; **Supp. XV:** 40–41

Houston, Robert, **Supp. XXV:** 54

Houston Trilogy (McMurtry), **Supp. V:** 223–225

How" (Ginsberg), **Supp. XIV:** 142, 143

"How" (Moore), **Supp. X:** 167

"How About This?" (Carver), **Supp. III Part 1:** 141

"How America Came to the Mountains" (J. W. Miller), **Supp. XX: 169**

"How Annandale Went Out" (Robinson), **III:** 513

How a Poem Happens (blog, Brodeur), **Supp. XXVIII:** 136–137

Howard, Arliss, **Supp. XXI:** 39

Howard, Ben, **Supp. XVI:** 54

Howard, Gerald, **Supp. XII:** 21

Howard, Jane, **Retro. Supp. I:** 334

Howard, June, **Retro. Supp. II:** 139
Howard, Leon, **Supp. I Part 2:** 408, 422, 423
Howard, Maureen, **Supp. XII:** 285; **Supp. XVII:** 183
Howard, Richard, **Retro. Supp. II:** 43; **Supp. IV Part 2:** 624, 626, 640; **Supp. IX:** 324, 326; **Supp. VIII:** 273; **Supp. X:** 152; **Supp. XI:** 317; **Supp. XII:** 254; **Supp. XIII:** 76; **Supp. XV:** 23, 24; **Supp. XXIV:** 155
Howard, Robert E., **Supp. XXV:** 122; **Supp. XXVII: 115–131**
Howard, Vilma, **Retro. Supp. II:** 111, 112
Howards, J. Z., **Supp. VIII:** 178
Howards End (Forster), **Supp. XII:** 87
Howarth, Cora, **I:** 408, 409
Howbah Indians (Ortiz), **Supp. IV Part 2:** 513
How Beautiful the Ordinary: Twelve Stories of Identity (Cart, ed.), **Supp. XXVIII:** 288
"How Black Sees Green and Red" (McKay), **Supp. X:** 136
How Britain Rules Africa (Padmore), **Supp. XXI:** 166
"How David Did Not Care" (R. Bly), **Supp. IV Part 1:** 73
"How Did I Love Him?" (Nelson), **Supp. XVIII:** 176
"How Do I Love Thee?" (Browning), **Supp. XVIII:** 176
Howe, Daniel Walker, **Supp. XXIV:** 79
Howe, Darcus, **Supp. XXI:** 170
Howe, E.W., **I:** 106
Howe, Florence, **Supp. XIII:** 295, 306
Howe, Harriet, **Supp. XI:** 200, 201
Howe, Irving, **IV:** 10; **Retro. Supp. I:** 369; **Retro. Supp. II:** 112, 286; **Retro. Supp. III:** 85; **Supp. I Part 2:** 432; **Supp. II Part 1:** 99; **Supp. IX:** 227; **Supp. VI: 113–129; Supp. VIII:** 93, 232; **Supp. X:** 203, 245; **Supp. XII:** 160; **Supp. XIII:** 98; **Supp. XIV:** 103–104, 104; **Supp. XIX:** 257, 265; **Supp. XVII:** 50; **Supp. XXIII:** 3, 7; **Supp. XXIV:** 220–221, 222
Howe, James, **Supp. XXVIII:** 288
Howe, James Wong, **Supp. I Part 1:** 281; **Supp. V:** 223
Howe, Julia Ward, **III:** 505; **Retro. Supp. II:** 135; **Supp. XXVIII:** 113
Howe, LeAnne, **Supp. XXVI:** 84, 98
Howe, M. A. DeWolfe, **I:** 258; **II:** 406; **Supp. XIV:** 54
Howe, Mary Manning, **Supp. IV Part 2:** 422
Howe, Samuel, **Supp. I Part 1:** 153
Howe, Susan, **Retro. Supp. I:** 33, 43; **Supp. IV Part 2: 419–438; Supp. XVI:** 284
Howell, Chris, **Supp. XIII:** 112
Howell, James, **II:** 111
Howells, Margaret, **II:** 271
Howells, W. D., **Supp. XXVIII:** 117
Howells, William C., **II:** 273
Howells, William Dean, **I:** 109, 192, 204, 210, 211, 254, 355, 407, 411, 418, 459, 469; **II:** 127–128, 130, 131, 136, 137, 138, 140, **271–294,** 322, 331–332, 338, 397–398, 400, 415, 444, 451, 556; **III:** 51, 118, 314, 327–328, 461, 576, 607; **IV:** 192, 202, 342, 349; **Retro. Supp. I:** 220, 334, 362, 378; **Retro. Supp. II:** 93, 101, 135, 288; **Retro. Supp. III:** 258, 259, 262, 264, 268; **Supp. I Part 1:** 306, 318, 357, 360, 368; **Supp. I Part 2:** 414, 420, 645–646; **Supp. II Part 1:** 198, 352; **Supp. IV Part 2:** 678; **Supp. VIII:** 98, 101, 102; **Supp. XI:** 198, 200; **Supp. XIV:** 45–46; **Supp. XV:** 269, 274, 285, 287; **Supp. XVIII:** 6; **Supp. XXIV:** 24
Howells, Mrs. William Dean (Elinor Mead), **II:** 273
Howells, Winifred, **II:** 271
"Howells as Anti-Novelist" (Updike), **Retro. Supp. I:** 334
Howells: His Life and World (Brooks), **I:** 254
Hower, Edward, **Supp. XII:** 330, 343
Howes, Barbara, **Supp. XIII:** 331
How Good Is David Mamet, Anyway? (Heilpern), **Supp. XIV:** 242
"How Hard It Is to Keep from Being King When It's in You and in the Situation" (Frost), **Retro. Supp. III:** 107
"How I Became a Shadow" (Purdy), **Supp. VII:** 269
"How I Came to Vedanta" (Isherwood), **Supp. XIV:** 164
"How I Come to You" (Peacock), **Supp. XIX:** 198
"How I Learned to Sweep" (Alvarez), **Supp. VII:** 4
"How I Spent My Forties" (Wasserstein), **Supp. XV:** 325, 330, 332
"How It Began" (Stafford), **Supp. XI:** 327
"How It Feels to Be Colored Me" (Hurston), **Supp. VI:** 152
"How It Is" (Budbill), **Supp. XIX:** 10
"How It Is" (Everwine), **Supp. XV:** 79, 86
"How I Told My Child About Race" (Brooks), **Supp. III Part 1:** 78
"How I Went to the Mines" (Harte), **Supp. II Part 1:** 336
"How I Write" (Franzen), **Supp. XX: 84**
"How I Write" (Welty), **IV:** 279, 280
"How I Wrote *The Promised Land*" (Antin), **Supp. XX:** 3
"How Jonah Did Not Care" (R. Bly), **Supp. IV Part 1:** 73
Howl (Ginsberg), **Retro. Supp. I:** 426; **Supp. III Part 1:** 92; **Supp. IV Part 1:** 90; **Supp. V:** 336; **Supp. VIII:** 290; **Supp. XIV:** 15, 126, 157; **Supp. XVIII:** 20, 29
"How Laddie and the Princess Spelled Down at the Christmas Bee" (Stratton-Porter), **Supp. XX: 216**
Howl and Other Poems (Ginsberg), **Supp. II Part 1:** 308, 317–318, 319; **Supp. X:** 123
Howlett, William, **Retro. Supp. I:** 17
Howl: Original Draft Facsimile, Transcript and Variant Versions (Gimsberg), **Supp. XIV:** 142
"How Many Midnights" (Bowles), **Supp. IV Part 1:** 86–87
"How Many Nights" (Kinnell), **Supp. III Part 1:** 245–246
How Much? (Blechman), **Supp. I Part 1:** 290
"How Much Are You Worth" (Salinas), **Supp. XIII:** 325–326
"How Much Earth" (Levine), **Supp. V:** 184
How Much Earth: The Fresno Poets (Buckley, Oliveira, and Williams, eds.), **Supp. XIII:** 313
"How Not to Forget" (Bartov), **Supp. XVI:** 153–154
"How Poetry Comes to Me" (Corso), **Supp. XII:** 122
"How Poetry Comes to Me" (Snyder), **Supp. VIII:** 305
How Reading Changed My Life (Quindlen), **Supp. XVII:** 167, 179–180
"How She Came By Her Name: An Interview with Louis Massiah" (Bambara), **Supp. XI:** 20
"How Soon Hath Time" (Ransom), **IV:** 123
How Spring Comes (Notley), **Supp. XXII:** 226, 229
How Stella Got Her Groove Back (McMillan), **Supp. XIII:** 185, **190–191**
How the Alligator Missed Breakfast (Kinney), **Supp. III Part 1:** 235, 253
"How the Devil Came Down Division Street" (Algren), **Supp. IX:** 3
How the García Girls Lost Their Accents (Alvarez), **Supp. VII:** 3, 5–9, 11, 15, 17, 18
How the Grinch Stole Christmas! (Geisel), **Supp. XVI:** 102
How the Other Half Lives (Riis), **I:** 293
"How the Saint Did Not Care" (R. Bly), **Supp. IV Part 1:** 73
"How the Women Went from Dover" (Whittier), **Supp. I Part 2:** 694, 696, 697
"How They Got Her to Quiet Down" (Stone), **Supp. XXVII:** 263
"How This Magazine Wronged Herman Wouk" (Lewis), **Supp. XXV:** 253
"How To" (Carruth), **Supp. XVI:** 51
"How-To" (Monson), **Supp. XXIV:** 237
How To Be Alone: Essays (Franzen), **Supp. XX: 83, 90, 93–94**
"How to Be an Other Woman" (Moore), **Supp. X:** 165, 167, 168
"How to Become a Writer" (Moore), **Supp. X:** 167, 168
"How to Be Happy: Another Memo to Myself" (Dunn), **Supp. XI:** 145
"How to Catch Aunt Harriet" (Stone), **Supp. XXVII:** 251
How To Cook a Wolf (M. F. K. Fisher), **Supp. XVII:** 84–85, 87
"How to Date a Browngirl, Blackgirl, Whitegirl, or Halfie" (Díaz), **Supp. XXIV:** 88

How to Develop Your Personality (Shellow), **Supp. I Part 2:** 608

"How to Grow Orchids Without Grounds: A Manual" (Vaz), **Supp. XXVI:** 263

How to Know God: The Yoga Aphorisms of Patanjali (Isherwood and Prabhavananda)), **Supp. XIV:** 164

"How To Like It" (Dobyns), **Supp. XIII:** 85–86

"How to Live on $36,000 a Year" (Fitzgerald), **Retro. Supp. I:** 105

"How to Live. What to Do" (Stevens), **Retro. Supp. I:** 302

"How to Love a Bicycle" (Biss), **Supp. XXVI:** 48

"How Tom is Doin' " (Kees), **Supp. XV:** 143

How to Read (Pound), **Supp. VIII:** 291

How to Read a Novel (Gordon), **II:** 198

How to Read a Poem and Fall in Love with Poetry (Hirsch), **Supp. XIX:** 202

How to Read a Poem: And Fall in Love with Poetry (Hirsch), **Supp. XXIII:** 124

How to Read a Poem . . . and Start a Poetry Circle (Peacock), **Supp. XIX:** 194, 202–203, 205

How to Save Your Own Life (Jong), **Supp. V:** 115, 123–125, 130

"How to Study Poetry" (Pound), **III:** 474

"How to Talk to Your Mother" (Moore), **Supp. X:** 167, 172

"How to Tell a Story" (Twain), **Retro. Supp. III:** 262, 265

"How to Tell Stories to Children" (July), **Supp. XXIV:** 206–207

How to Win Friends and Influence People (Carnegie), **Supp. I Part 2:** 608

How to Worry Successfully (Seabury), **Supp. I Part 2:** 608

How to Write (Stein), **IV:** 32, 34, 35

"How to Write a Blackwood Article" (Poe), **III:** 425; **Retro. Supp. II:** 273

"How to Write a Memoir Like This" (Oates), **Supp. III Part 2:** 509

"How to Write Like Somebody Else" (Roethke), **III:** 540

How to Write Short Stories (Lardner), **II:** 430, 431

"How Vincentine Did Not Care" (R. Bly), **Supp. IV Part 1:** 73

How We Became Human: New and Selected Poems (Harjo), **Supp. XII:** 230–232

"How We Danced" (Sexton), **Supp. II Part 2:** 692

How We Got Insipid (Lethem), **Supp. XVIII:** 149

"How We Got in Town and Out Again" (Lethem), **Supp. XVIII:** 149

"How You Sound??" (Baraka), **Supp. II Part 1:** 30

Hoy, Philip, **Supp. X:** 56, 58

Hoyer, Linda Grace (pseudonym). *See* Updike, Mrs. Wesley

Hoyt, Constance, **Supp. I Part 2:** 707

Hoyt, Elinor Morton. *See* Wylie, Elinor

Hoyt, Helen, **Supp. XXII:** 275

Hoyt, Henry (father), **Supp. I Part 2:** 707

Hoyt, Henry (son), **Supp. I Part 2:** 708

Hoyt, Henry Martyn, **Supp. I Part 2:** 707

H. P. Lovecraft (Canan), **Supp. XXV:** 123

Hsu, Kai-yu, **Supp. X:** 292

Hsu, Ruth Y., **Supp. XV:** 212

Hubba City (Reed), **Supp. X:** 241

Hubbard, Elbert, **I:** 98, 383

Hubbell, Jay B., **Supp. I Part 1:** 372

"Hubbub, The" (Ammons), **Supp. VII:** 35

Huber, François, **II:** 6

Huckins, Olga, **Supp. IX:** 32

Huckleberry Finn (Twain). *See Adventures of Huckleberry Finn, The* (Twain)

Hucksters, The (Wakeman), **Supp. XXV:** 258

Hud (film), **Supp. V:** 223, 226

Huddle, David, **Supp. XXVI: 147–162**

Hudgins, Andrew, **Supp. X:** 206; **Supp. XVII:** 111, 112; **Supp. XVIII:** 176

Hudson, Henry, **I:** 230; **Supp. XXVI:** 86

Hudson, W. H., **Supp. XXVIII:** 255

"Hudsonian Curlew, The" (Snyder), **Supp. VIII:** 302

Hudson River Bracketed (Wharton), **IV:** 326–327; **Retro. Supp. I:** 382

Huebsch, B. W., **III:** 110

Hueffer, Ford Madox, **Supp. I Part 1:** 257, 262. *See also* Ford, Ford Madox

Huene-Greenberg, Dorothee von, **Supp. XX:** 46

Huff (television series), **Supp. XIX:** 222

"Hug, The" (Gallagher), **Supp. XXIV:** 168

Hug Dancing (Hearon), **Supp. VIII: 67–68**

Huge Season, The (Morris), **III:** 225–226, 227, 230, 232, 233, 238

Hugging the Jukebox (Nye), **Supp. XIII: 275–276,** 277

"Hugging the Jukebox" (Nye), **Supp. XIII:** 276

Hughes, Brigid, **Supp. XVI:** 247

Hughes, Carolyn, **Supp. XII:** 272, 285

Hughes, Frieda, **Supp. I Part 2:** 540, 541

Hughes, Glenn, **Supp. I Part 1:** 255

Hughes, H. Stuart, **Supp. VIII:** 240

Hughes, James Nathaniel, **Supp. I Part 1:** 321, 332

Hughes, John, **Supp. XXVII:** 5

Hughes, Ken, **Supp. XI:** 307

Hughes, Langston, **Retro. Supp. I: 193–214; Retro. Supp. II:** 114, 115, 117, 120; **Retro. Supp. III:** 125, 127, 128, 137; **Supp. I Part 1: 320–348; Supp. II Part 1:** 31, 33, 61, 170, 173, 181, 227, 228, 233, 361; **Supp. III Part 1:** 72–77; **Supp. IV Part 1:** 15, 16, 164, 168, 169, 173, 243, 368; **Supp. IX:** 306, 316; **Supp. VIII:** 213; **Supp. X:** 131, 136, 139, 324; **Supp. XI:** 1; **Supp. XIII:** 75, 111, 132, 233; **Supp. XIX:** 72, 75, 77; **Supp. XVI:** 135, 138; **Supp. XVIII:** 90, 277, 279, 280, 281, 282; **Supp. XXI:** 243; **Supp. XXII:** 3, 4, 5, 6, 8, 13–14; **Supp. XXIV:** 183; **Supp. XXVI:** 166; **Supp. XXVII:** 164; **Supp. XXVIII:** 279

Hughes, Nicholas, **Supp. I Part 2:** 541

Hughes, Robert, **Supp. X:** 73

Hughes, Ted, **IV:** 3; **Retro. Supp. II:** 244, 245, 247, 257; **Supp. I Part 2:** 536, 537, 538, 539, 540, 541; **Supp. XV:** 117, 347, 348; **Supp. XXII:** 30

Hughes, Thomas, **Supp. I Part 2:** 406

"Hugh Harper" (Bowles), **Supp. IV Part 1:** 94

Hughie (O'Neill), **III:** 385, 401, 405

Hugh Selwyn Mauberley (Pound), **I:** 66, 476; **III:** 9, 462–463, 465, 468; **Retro. Supp. I: 289–290,** 291, 299; **Supp. XIV:** 272

Hugo, Richard, **Supp. IX:** 296, 323, 324, 330; **Supp. VI: 131–148; Supp. XI:** 315, 317; **Supp. XII:** 178; **Supp. XIII:** 112, 113, 133; **Supp. XVIII:** 293, 299; **Supp. XXI:** 243; **Supp. XXVI:** 180, 187; **Supp. XXVIII:** 33

Hugo, Victor, **II:** 290, 490, 543; **Supp. IV Part 2:** 518; **Supp. IX:** 308

Hui-neng, **III:** 567

Huis Clos (Sartre), **Supp. IV Part 1:** 84

Huizinga, Johan, **I:** 225; **II:** 416–417, 418, 425

Hulbert, Ann, **Supp. XI:** 38–39

Hulbert, James R., **Retro. Supp. III:** 265

Hull, Lynda, **Supp. XI:** 131; **Supp. XXI: 129–142**

Hull, Thomas, **Supp. XXV:** 123

Hulme, Thomas E., **I:** 68, 69, 475; **III:** 196, 209, 463–464, 465; **IV:** 122; **Supp. I Part 1:** 261, 262; **Supp. XV:** 43

Human, All Too Human (Nietzsche), **Supp. X:** 48

"Human Culture" (Emerson), **II:** 11–12

Human Desire (film), **Supp. XXVI:** 134

Human Factor, The (Greene), **Supp. V:** 298

"Human Figures" (Doty), **Supp. XI:** 123–124

"Human Fly, The" (Boyle), **Supp. XX:** 19

"Human Geography" (Jarman), **Supp. XVII:** 116

"Human Immortality" (James), **II:** 353–354

"Human Life" (Emerson), **II:** 11–12

"Human Pig" (Jin), **Supp. XVIII:** 99

Human Rights, Human Wrongs: The Oxford Amnesty Lectures, 2001, **Supp. XVI:** 155

"Human Soul as a Rube Goldberg Device, The: A Choose-Your-Own-Adventure-Story" (Brockmeier), **Supp. XXII:** 60–61

Human Stain, The (P. Roth), **Retro. Supp. II:** 279, 289, 294–295

"Human Things" (Nemerov), **III:** 279

Human Universe (Olson), **Supp. II Part 2:** 571

"Human Universe" (Olson), **Supp. II Part 2:** 565, 567

Human Vibration (Richter), **Supp. XVIII:** 209

Human Wishes (Hass), **Supp. VI:** 105–106, 107

Human Work (Gilman), **Supp. XI:** 206

Humbert, Humbert, **Supp. X:** 283

Humble Inquiry into the Rules of the Word of God, An, Concerning the Qualifications Requisite to a Complete Standing and Full Communion in the Visible Christian Church (Edwards), **I:** 548

Humboldt, Alexander von, **III:** 428

Humboldt's Gift (Bellow), **Retro. Supp. II:** 19, 28–29, 34; **Supp. XIII:** 320

Hume, David, **I:** 125; **II:** 349, 357, 480; **III:** 618

Humes, Harold, **Supp. V:** 201; **Supp. XIV:** 82

Humes, Harry, **Supp. XIX:** 281; **Supp. XXIII:** 54

Humes, H. L. "Doc", **Supp. XI:** 294

"Humility" (Hoffman), **Supp. XVIII:** 86

Hummer, T. R., **Supp. XIX:** 278; **Supp. XXI:** 91

"Hummingbirds, The" (Welty), **IV:** 273

Humors and/or Not So Humorous (Kenny), **Supp. XXIII:** 155

Humphrey, William, **Supp. IX:** 93–112; **Supp. XV:** 353

Humphreys, Christmas, **Supp. V:** 267

Humphreys, David, **Supp. II Part 1:** 65, 69, 70, 268

Humphreys, Josephine, **Supp. XII:** 311

Humphries, Rolfe, **III:** 124; **Retro. Supp. I:** 137

Humpty Dumpty (Hecht), **Supp. XXVII:** 88

Hunchback of Notre Dame, The (film), **Supp. IV Part 1:** 101

Hunches in Bunches (Geisel), **Supp. XVI:** 111

Huncke, Herbert, **Supp. XII:** 118; **Supp. XIV:** 137–153

Huncke's Journal (Huncke), **Supp. XIV:** 139, 144, 145, 146

Hundred Camels in the Courtyard, A (Bowles), **Supp. IV Part 1:** 90

"Hundred Collars, A" (Frost), **Retro. Supp. I:** 128; **Supp. XIII:** 147

Hundred Secret Senses, The (Tan), **Supp. X:** 289, 293, 295, 297, 298, 299

Hundreds of Hens and Other Poems for Children by Halfdan Rasmussen (Nelson and Espeland, trans.), **Supp. XVIII:** 180

Hundred White Daffodils, A: Essays, Interviews, Newspaper Columns, and One Poem (Kenyon), **Supp. VII:** 160–162, 165, 166, 167, 174

Huneker, James, **III:** 102

"Hunger" (Davison), **Supp. XXVI:** 69

Hunger (Hamsun), **Supp. XI:** 167

"Hunger" (Hogan), **Supp. IV Part 1:** 411

"Hunger . . ." (Rich), **Supp. I Part 2:** 571

"Hunger" (Rich), **Retro. Supp. III:** 249

"Hungerfield" (Jeffers), **Supp. II Part 2:** 416–417, 436

Hungerfield and Other Poems (Jeffers), **Supp. II Part 2:** 422

Hunger of Memory: The Education of Richard Rodriguez (Rodriguez), **Supp. XIV:** 297, 298, **298–302,** 310

Hungry Ghosts, The (Oates), **Supp. II Part 2:** 504, 510

"Hungry Girl, The" (Goodman), **Supp. XXVIII:** 94

Hungry Hearts (Prose), **Supp. XVI:** 253

"Hungry Intellectual, A" (Le Sueur), **Supp. XXIII:** 164

Hungry Woman, The: A Mexican Medea (Moraga), **Supp. XXIII:** 196

Hunnewell, Susannah, **Supp. VIII:** 83

Hunt, Erica, **Supp. XXVII:** 163

Hunt, Harriot K., **Retro. Supp. II:** 146

Hunt, Leigh, **II:** 515–516; **Supp. XV:** 175

Hunt, Richard Morris, **IV:** 312

Hunt, Robert, **Supp. XV:** 42, 49, 52

Hunt, William, **II:** 343

"Hunter" (Bierds), **Supp. XVII:** 30

Hunter, Dianna, **Supp. XVI:** 38

Hunter, Dr. Joseph, **II:** 217

Hunter, J. Paul, **Supp. IV Part 1:** 332

Hunter, Kim, **Supp. I Part 1:** 286

"Hunter, The" (Arnow), **Supp. XXVIII:** 2, 6

"Hunter of Doves" (Herbst), **Retro. Supp. II:** 325

"Hunter of the West, The" (Bryant), **Supp. I Part 1:** 155

Hunters, The (film), **Supp. IX:** 250

Hunters, The (Salter), **Supp. IX:** 246, **249–250**

Hunters and Gatherers (Prose), **Supp. XVI:** 257

Hunter's Horn (Arnow), **Supp. XXVIII:** 1, 2, 3, 6–8, 11

"Hunters in the Snow" (Brueghel), **I:** 174; **Retro. Supp. I:** 430

"Hunters in the Snow" (Wolff), **Supp. VII:** 339–340

"Hunter's Moon—Eating the Bear" (Oliver), **Supp. VII:** 234

"Hunter's Vision, The" (Bryant), **Supp. I Part 1:** 160

Hunting for Hope: A Father's Journey (Sanders), **Supp. XVI:** 276–277, 278

"Hunting Is Not Those Heads on the Wall" (Baraka), **Supp. II Part 1:** 45

Huntington, Collis P., **I:** 198, 207

"Hunt in the Black Forest, The" (Jarrell), **II:** 379–380

Huntley, Jobe, **Supp. I Part 1:** 339

"Hurrah, Hurrah" (Nelson), **Supp. XVIII:** 175

Hurray Home (Wideman), **Supp. X:** 320

Hurricane (radio play, Boyce), **Supp. XXI:** 13

"Hurricane, The" (Crane), **I:** 401

"Hurricane, The" (Freneau), **Supp. II Part 1:** 262

"Hurricane Belle" (Notley), **Supp. XXII:** 228

"Hurry Kane" (Lardner), **II:** 425, 426, 427

"Hurry up Please It's Time" (Sexton), **Supp. II Part 2:** 694, 695

Hurst, Fannie, **Retro. Supp. III:** 127, 135, 137; **Supp. XVIII:** 278, 279

Hurston, Zora Neale, **Retro. Supp. I:** 194, 198, 200, 201, 203; **Retro. Supp. III:** **125–146; Supp. I Part 1:** 325, 326, 332; **Supp. II Part 1:** 33; **Supp. IV Part 1:** 5, 11, 12, 164, 257; **Supp. VI:** 149–161; **Supp. VIII:** 214; **Supp.** **X:** 131, 139, 232, 242; **Supp. XI:** 85; **Supp. XIII:** 185, 233, 236, 295, 306; **Supp. XIX:** 72, 75; **Supp. XVIII:** 122, 279, 280, 282; **Supp. XX: 107; Supp. XXII:** 12; **Supp. XXVI:** 1, 12, 164, 167

Hurt, John, **Supp. XIII:** 132

"Hurt Hawks" (Jeffers), **Supp. XXIII:** 145

Hurwitt, Robert, **Supp. XXIII:** 281

Husbands and Wives (film; Allen), **Supp. XV:** 12

"Husband's Song, The" (Di Piero), **Supp. XIX:** 39

Husband's Story, The (Shields), **Supp. VII:** 316. *See also* "Happenstance" (Shields)

"Husband's Tale, The" (Huddle), **Supp. XXVI:** 151

Hush (Woodson), **Supp. XXVIII:** 282

"Husks" (Bottoms), **Supp. XXVIII:** 32

Husserl, Edmund, **II:** 362, 363; **IV:** 491; **Supp. IV Part 1:** 42, 43

Hussey, Jo Ella, **Supp. XII:** 201

Hustler, The (film), **Supp. XI:** 306

Huston, John, **I:** 30, 31, 33, 35; **II:** 588; **III:** 161; **Retro. Supp. III:** 170; **Supp. IV Part 1:** 102, 116, 355; **Supp. XI:** 307; **Supp. XIII:** 174

Hustvedt, Siri, **Supp. XXVII:** 26; **Supp. XXVIII:** 206

"Huswifery" (Taylor), **IV:** 161; **Supp. I Part 2:** 386

"Hut, The" (Sobin), **Supp. XVI:** 284–285

Hutchens, John K., **Supp. IX:** 276

Hutcheon, Linda, **Supp. XXVIII:** 205

Hutcheson, Francis, **I:** 559

Hutchins, Patricia, **III:** 478

Hutchinson, Abigail, **I:** 562

Hutchinson, Anne, **Supp. I Part 1:** 100, 101, 113; **Supp. IV Part 2:** 434; **Supp. VIII:** 202, 205

Hutchinson, George, **Supp. XVIII:** 119–120, 121, 132

Hutchinson, Lucy, **Supp. XXV:** 224

Hutchinson, Paul E., **Supp. XXVI:** 156

Hutchinson, Percy, **Retro. Supp. III:** 133

Hutchinson, Thomas, **Supp. XX: 282**

Hutton, James, **Supp. IX:** 180

Hutton, Laurence, **Supp. XXVIII:** 228

Huwayyik, Yusuf, **Supp. XX: 115**

Huxley, Aldous, **II:** 454; **III:** 281, 428, 429–430; **IV:** 77, 435; **Supp. I Part 2:** 714; **Supp. XIV:** 3, 164; **Supp. XVI:** 189, 192; **Supp. XVIII:** 137; **Supp. XXIII:** 85–86; **Supp. XXIV:** 281

Huxley, Julian, **Supp. VIII:** 251; **Supp. X:** 108

Huxley, Juliette, **Supp. VIII:** 251, 265

Huxley, Thomas, **III:** 102, 108, 113, 281; **Retro. Supp. II:** 60, 65, 93; **Supp. XXVII:** 126

Huxley, Thomas Henry, **Supp. I Part 1:** 368

Huysmans, Joris Karl (Charles Marie Georges), **I:** 66; **III:** 315; **IV:** 286; **Retro. Supp. II:** 326; **Supp. XX: 239; Supp. XXVII:** 88

"Idea of Form at Spruce Creek, The" (Weigl), **Supp. XIX:** 283–284

"Idea of Ice, The" (C. Baxter), **Supp. XVII:** 15

"Idea of Order, An" (Wiman), **Supp. XVIII:** 173

"Idea of Order at Key West, The" (Stevens), **IV:** 89–90; **Retro. Supp. I:** 302, 303, 313

Ideas of Order (Stevens), **Retro. Supp. I:** 296, 298, **302–303,** 303, 305

Idema, James, **Supp. XXVII:** 7

"Identification Pleas" (Gansworth), **Supp. XXVI:** 114

"Identity Theft: True Memory, False Memory, and the Holocaust" (R. Franklin), **Supp. XVI:** 160

Ideograms in China (Michaux; Sobin, trans.), **Supp. XVI:** 288

"Ideographs" (Olds), **Supp. X:** 205

Ides of March, The (Wilder), **IV:** 357, 372

"I Did Not Learn Their Names" (Ellison), **Retro. Supp. II:** 124

"I Died with the First Blow & Was Reborn Wrong" (Coleman), **Supp. XI:** 91

"Idiom of a Self, The" (Pinsky), **Supp. VI:** 240

"Idiot, The" (Crane), **I:** 401

Idiot, The (Dostoevsky), **I:** 468

"Idiots First" (Malamud), **Supp. I Part 2:** 434–435, 437, 440–441

Idiots Karamazov, The (Durand and Innaurato), **Supp. XXIV:** 113, 116

"Idiot Wind" (song, Dylan), **Supp. XVIII:** 30

Idle Idylls (Wells), **Supp. XXVI:** 275

I Don't Need You Any More (A. Miller), **III:** 165

Idoru (W. Gibson), **Supp. XVI:** 119, 124, **129–130**

"I Dream I'm the Death of Orpheus" (Rich), **Supp. I Part 2:** 557–558

I Dreamt I Became a Nymphomaniac! Imagining (Acker), **Supp. XII:** 4, 6, 8, 11

"I Dreamt You Young" (Espaillat), **Supp. XXI:** 107

"Idyll" (Shaw), **Supp. XIX:** 241

Idylls of the King (Tennyson), **III:** 487; **Retro. Supp. III:** 266; **Supp. I Part 2:** 410; **Supp. XIII:** 146

Idyl of Work, An (Larcom), **Supp. XIII:** 139, 142, 146–147, 150

"If" (Creeley), **Supp. IV Part 1:** 158

If Beale Street Could Talk (Baldwin), **Retro. Supp. II:** 13–14; **Supp. I Part 1:** 48, 59–60, 67

"If Biblical Law Ruled Modern Society . . ." (P. N. Warren), **Supp. XX:** 272

If Blessing Comes (Bambara), **Supp. XI:** 1

"If Death Is Kind" (Teasdale), **Supp. XXVII:** 294

I Feel a Little Jumpy around You (Nye and Janeczko, eds.), **Supp. XIII:** 280

"I felt a Funeral, in my Brain" (Dickinson), **Retro. Supp. I:** 38

"If Grown-Ups Were Smart" (Nelson and Espeland), **Supp. XVIII:** 181

If He Hollers Let Him Go (C. Himes), **Supp. XVI:** 135, 138–139, 142

"If I Could Be Like Wallace Stevens" (Stafford), **Supp. XI:** 327

"If I Could Do Whatever I Wanted" (Nelson and Espeland), **Supp. XVIII:** 181

"If I Could Only Live at the Pitch That Is Near Madness" (Eberhart), **I:** 523, 526–527

If I Could Write This in Fire (Cliff), **Supp. XXII:** 67, 69

"If I Could Write This in Fire, I Would Write This in Fire" (Cliff), **Supp. XXII:** 65–66, 68–69

If I Die in a Combat Zone (O'Brien), **Supp. V:** 238, 239, 240, 245

If I Ever Get Out of Here (Gansworth), **Supp. XXVI:** 102, 108–109

If I Forget Thee, Jerusalem (Faulkner), **Retro. Supp. III:** 85

"If I Had My Way" (Creeley), **Supp. IV Part 1:** 157

"If I Might Be" (Chopin), *Retro. Supp. II:* 61

"I Find the Real American Tragedy" (Dreiser), **Retro. Supp. II:** 105

If I Ran the Circus (Geisel), **Supp. XVI:** 105

If I Ran the Zoo (Geisel), **Supp. XVI:** 104–105

If It Die (Gide), **I:** 290

"If It Were Not for You" (Carruth), **Supp. XVI:** 57

"If I Were a Man" (Gilman), **Supp. XI:** 207

"If I Were the Wind" (Leopold), **Supp. XIV:** 184

If Morning Ever Comes (Tyler), **Supp. IV Part 2:** 658–659

If Mountains Die: A New Mexico Memoir (Nichols), **Supp. XIII:** 255, 257, 267

"If Nancy Was a Boy" (Brainard), **Supp. XXVII:** 21

"If Nancy Was an Ashtray" (Brainard), **Supp. XXVII:** 21

I Forgot to Go to Spain (Harrison), **Supp. VIII:** 39, **52–53**

"If Poetry Were Not a Morality" (Gallagher), **Supp. XXIV:** 170

If the River Was Whiskey (Boyle), **Supp. VIII:** 15–16; **Supp. XX:** 17, 19

"If They Knew Yvonne" (Dubus), **Supp. VII:** 81

"If We Had Bacon" (H. Roth), **Supp. IX:** 232, 234

"If We Had Known" (Francis), **Supp. IX:** 78

"If We Must Die" (McKay), **Supp. IV Part 1:** 3; **Supp. X:** 132, 134

"If We Take All Gold" (Bogan), **Supp. III Part 1:** 52

If You Call This a Cry Song (Carruth), **Supp. XVI:** 56

If You Come Softly (Woodson), **Supp. XXVIII:** 280, 281, 282

If You Want to Write (Ueland), **Supp. XVII:** 13

I Gaspiri (Lardner), **II:** 435

"I Gather the Limbs of Osiris" (Pound), **Retro. Supp. I:** 287

I Get on the Bus (McKnight), **Supp. XX:** **148–150, 152**

"I Give You Back" (Harjo), **Supp. XII:** 223

Ignatius of Loyola, **IV:** 151; **Supp. XI:** 162

Ignatius Rising (Nevils and Hardy), **Supp. XXVI:** 241

Ignatow, David, **Supp. XIII:** 275

"Ignis Fatuus" (Tate), **IV:** 128

"Ignorant Lust after Knowledge, The" (Bronk), **Supp. XXI:** 31

"I Go Back to May 1937" (Olds), **Supp. X:** 207

I Go Dreaming Serenades (Salinas), **Supp. XIII:** 316

"I Got a Guy Once" (Gallagher), **Supp. XXIV:** 176

"I Got My Job on the *New York Times!*" (Schuyler and Brainard), **Supp. XXVII:** 23

I Got the Blues (Odets), **Supp. II Part 2:** 530

Iguana Killer, The (Ríos), **Supp. IV Part 2:** 542–544

"I Had Eight Birds Hatcht in One Nest" (Bradstreet), **Supp. I Part 1:** 102, 115, 117, 119

"I had no time to Hate" (Dickinson), **Retro. Supp. I:** 44–45, 46

I Hadn't Meant to Tell You This (Woodson), **Supp. XXVIII:** 280, 281

I Had Trouble in Getting to Solla Sollew (Geisel), **Supp. XVI:** 108, 109

I Hate Miranda July (blog), **Supp. XXIV:** 200

"I Have a Rendezvous with Life" (Cullen), **Supp. IV Part 1:** 168

"I Have Been Thinking About Snow" (Monson), **Supp. XXIV:** 235

"I Have Had to Learn to Live with My Face" (Wakoski), **Supp. XXVIII:** 264

"I Have Increased Power" (Ginsberg), **Supp. II Part 1:** 313

"I Have Moved West" (Taggard), **Supp. XXII:** 274

"I Have Seen Black Hands" (Wright), **Supp. II Part 1:** 228

"I Hear an Army" (Joyce), **Supp. I Part 1:** 262

"I heard a Fly buzz when I died" (Dickinson), **Retro. Supp. I:** 38

"I Heard Immanuel Singing" (Lindsay), **Supp. I Part 2:** 379

I Heard It Through the Grapevine (Turner), **Supp. XX:** 110

"I Hear It Was Charged against Me" (Whitman), **IV:** 343

I Hear Men Talking (Le Sueur), **Supp. XXIII:** 162, 167, **171–172**

"I Held a Shelley Manuscript" (Corso), **Supp. XII:** 128

"I Held His Name" (Ríos), **Supp. IV Part 2:** 547

"Ike and Nina" (Boyle), **Supp. XX:** 19

"I Kiss a Door" (July), **Supp. XXIV:** 204

I Knew a Phoenix (Sarton), **Supp. VIII:** 249, 251–252

"I Know a Man" (Creeley), **Supp. IV Part 1:** 147–148, 149

I Know Some Things: Stories about Childhood by Contemporary Writers (Moore, ed.), **Supp. X:** 175

"I Know the Stars" (Teasdale), **Supp. XXVII:** 293

"I Know Why the Caged Bird Cannot Read" (Prose), **Supp. XVI:** 259

I Know Why the Caged Bird Sings (Angelou), **Supp. IV Part 1:** 2–4, 5, 7, 11, 12, 13, 14, 15, 17; **Supp. XVI:** 259

"Ikon: The Harrowing of Hell" (Levertov), **Supp. III Part 1:** 284

"Iktomi and the Ducks" (Zitkala-Ša), **Supp. XXV:** 275–276

Ile (O'Neill), **III:** 388; **Supp. XXV:** 20

"I Led Three Lives" (television program), **Supp. XX:** 195

"I Let Him Take Me" (Cisneros), **Supp. VII:** 71

Iliad (Bryant, trans.), **Supp. I Part 1:** 158

Iliad (Chapman, trans.), **Supp. XXV:** 226

Iliad (Homer), **II:** 470; **Supp. IV Part 2:** 631; **Supp. IX:** 211; **Supp. X:** 114; **Supp. XVII:** 117; **Supp. XXI:** 36

Iliad (Pope, trans.), **Supp. I Part 1:** 152

"I Like" (Brainard), **Supp. XXVII:** 25

"I like to see it lap the Miles" (Dickinson), **Retro. Supp. I:** 37

"I Live Up Here" (Merwin), **Supp. III Part 1:** 349

"I'll Be Doing More of Same" (Franzen), **Supp. XX:** 89

"Illegal Alien" (Mora), **Supp. XIII:** 215

"Illegal Days, The" (Paley), **Supp. VI:** 222

Illegals, The (film), **Supp. XXVII:** 133, 140, 143

"Illegibility" (F. Wright), **Supp. XVII:** 244

Illig, Joyce, **Retro. Supp. II:** 20

"Illinois" (Masters), **Supp. I Part 2:** 458

"Illinois Bus Ride" (Leopold), **Supp. XIV:** 189

Illinois Poems (Masters), **Supp. I Part 2:** 472

"Illinois Village, The" (Lindsay), **Supp. I Part 2:** 381

"Ill-Lit" (F. Wright), **Supp. XVII:** 245

Ill-Lit: Selected & New Poems (F. Wright), **Supp. XVII:** 245

Illness as Metaphor (Sontag), **Supp. III Part 2:** 452, 461, 466

I'll Take My Stand ("Twelve Southerners"), **II:** 196; **III:** 496; **IV:** 125, 237; **Supp. X:** 25, 52–53; **Supp. XIV:** 3

"I'll Take You to Tennessee" (Connell), **Supp. XIV:** 82

Illumination (Frederic), **II:** 141

Illumination, The (Brockmeier), **Supp. XXII:** 61

Illumination Night (Hoffman), **Supp. X:** 85, **86,** 88, 89

Illuminations (Rimbaud), **Supp. XXI:** 233

"Illusion, An" (Wells), **Supp. XXVI:** 275

Illusion and Reality (Caudwell), **Supp. XXII:** 284

Illusion comique, L' (Corneille), **Supp. IX:** 138

"Illusion of Eternity, The" (Eberhart), **I:** 541

"Illusion of Fiction in Frank Conroy's *Stop-Time*, The" (R. Ramsey), **Supp. XVI:** 69

Illusions (Dash; film), **Supp. XI:** 20

"Illusions" (Emerson), **II:** 2, 5, 14, 16

Illustrated Man, The (Bradbury), **Supp. IV Part 1:** 102, 103, 113

Illustrations of China and Its People (Thompson), **Supp. XXI:** 151

Illustrations of Political Economy (Martineau), **Supp. II Part 1:** 288

"I Look at My Hand" (Swenson), **Supp. IV Part 2:** 638, 647

I Love Gootie: My Grandmother's Story (Apple), **Supp. XVII:** 9–10

I Love Myself When I Am Laughing . . . : A Zora Neale Hurston Reader (Walker), **Supp. III Part 2:** 531, 532

"I Love the Way It Goes" (O'Hara), **Supp. XXIII:** 220

"I'm a Fool" (Anderson), **I:** 113, 114, 116; **Supp. I Part 2:** 430

Image and Idea (Rahv), **Supp. II Part 1:** 146

Image and the Law, The (Nemerov), **III:** 268, 269–271, 272

"Image in the Mirror, The" (Swados), **Supp. XIX:** 265

"Images" (Hass), **Supp. VI:** 103

"Images and 'Images' " (Simic), **Supp. VIII:** 274

"Images for Godard" (Rich), **Supp. I Part 2:** 558

"Images of Walt Whitman" (Fiedler), **IV:** 352

"Imaginary Dialogue, An" (Espaillat), **Supp. XXI:** 103

"Imaginary Friendships of Tom McGrath, The" (Cohen), **Supp. X:** 112

"Imaginary Iceberg, The" (Bishop), **Retro. Supp. II:** 42; **Supp. I Part 1:** 86, 88

"Imaginary Jew, The" (Berryman), **I:** 174–175

Imaginary Letters (Pound), **III:** 473–474

Imaginary Paintings (C. Baxter), **Supp. XVII:** 18–19

"Imaginary Prisons" (Schnackenberg), **Supp. XV:** 257, 258

Imagination and Fancy; or, Selections from the English Poets, illustrative of those first requisites of their art; with markings of the best passages, critical notices of the writers, and an essay in answer to the question 'What is Poetry?' (Hunt), **II:** 515–516

"Imagination as Value" (Stevens), **Retro. Supp. I:** 298

"Imagination of Disaster, The" (Gordon), **Supp. IV Part 1:** 306

Imaginative Qualities of Actual Things (Sorrentino), **Supp. XXI:** 226, 230, 231–232, 234

"Imagine a Day at the End of Your Life" (Beattie), **Supp. V:** 33

Imagined London: A Tour of the World's Greatest Fictional City (Quindlen), **Supp. XVII:** 167, 180

Imagineering Atlanta (Rutheiser), **Supp. XXII:** 244

"Imagine Kissing Pete" (O'Hara), **III:** 372; **Supp. VIII:** 156

Imaging Robert: My Brother, Madness, and Survival (Neugeboren), **Supp. XVI:** 225, **226–229**

"Imagining How It Would Be to Be Dead" (Eberhart), **I:** 533

Imagining Los Angeles: A City in Fiction (Fine), **Supp. XI:** 160

"Imagining Their Own Hymns" (B. Kelly), **Supp. XVII:** 126–127

"Imagining the Midwest" (Sanders), **Supp. XVI:** 275–276

Imagining the Worst: Stephen King and the Representations of Women (Lant and Thompson), **Supp. V:** 141

"Imagisme" (Pound), **Retro. Supp. I:** 288

Imagistes, Des: An Anthology of the Imagists (Pound, ed.), **III:** 465, 471; **Retro. Supp. I:** 288

Imago (O. Butler), **Supp. XIII:** 63, **65–66**

"Imago" (Stevens), **IV:** 74, 89

Imagoes (Coleman), **Supp. XI:** 89–90

I Married a Communist (P. Roth), **Retro. Supp. II:** 289, 293–294

I Married an Angel (film), **Supp. XVI:** 193

"I May, I Might, I Must" (Moore), **III:** 215

Imbusch, Kevin, **Supp. XXIII:** 125

"I'm Crazy" (Salinger), **III:** 553

"I'm Here" (Roethke), **III:** 547

Imitations (R. Lowell), **II:** 550

Imitations (R. Lowell), **II:** 543, 544–545, 555; **Retro. Supp. II:** 181, 187

"Imitations of Drowning" (Sexton), **Supp. II Part 2:** 684, 686

"Immaculate Man" (Gordon), **Supp. IV Part 1:** 311

"Immanence of Dostoevsky, The" (Bourne), **I:** 235

"Immigrants" (Mora), **Supp. XIII:** 216

Immigrant Saint: The Life of Mother Cabrini (di Donato), **Supp. XX:** 44

"Immigrant Story, The" (Paley), **Supp. VI:** 230

Immobile Wind, The (Winters), **Supp. II Part 2:** 786

"Immobile Wind, The" (Winters), **Supp. II Part 2:** 788, 811

"Immolatus" (Komunyakaa), **Supp. XIII:** 126

"Immoral Proposition, The" (Creeley), **Supp. IV Part 1:** 144

"Immortal Autumn" (MacLeish), **III:** 13

"Immortality Ode" (Nemerov), **III:** 87

Immortality Ode (Wordsworth), **II:** 17; **Supp. I Part 2:** 673

Immortal Marriage, The (Atherton), **Supp. XXIV:** 26

"Immortal Woman, The" (Tate), **IV:** 130, 131, 137

"I'm Not Ready to Die Yet" (Harjo), **Supp. XII:** 231

I'm Not There (film, Haynes), **Supp. XVIII:** 23

"I'm on My Way" (Salinas), **Supp. XIII:** 320

"Impasse" (Hughes), **Supp. I Part 1:** 343

"Impatient Mary" (Taggard), **Supp. XXII:** 278

Imperative Duty, An, a Novel (Howells), **II:** 286

Imperial Bedrooms (Ellis), **Supp. XXVII:** 77–78

Imperial Eyes: Travel Writing and Transculturation (Pratt), **Retro. Supp. II:** 48

Imperial Germany and the Industrial Revolution (Veblen), **Supp. I Part 2:** 642, 643

Imperial Way, The: By Rail from Peshawar to Chittagong (Theroux), **Supp. VIII:** 323

"Implements from the 'Tomb of the Poet' " (Stallings), **Supp. XXV:** 232

"Implosions" (Rich), **Supp. I Part 2:** 556

"Imp of the Perverse, The" (Poe), **III:** 414–415; **Retro. Supp. II:** 267

Impolite Interviews, **Supp. XI:** 293

"Importance of Artists' Biographies, The" (Goldbarth), **Supp. XII:** 183, 184, 191

Importance of Being Earnest, The (Wilde), **Supp. XIV:** 324, 339

Importance of Gaining and Preserving the Friendship of the Indians to the British Interest Considered (Kennedy and Parker), **Supp. XXVI:** 84

"Important Houses, The" (Gordon), **Supp. IV Part 1:** 315

"Impossible Indispensability of the Ars Poetica, The" (Carruth), **Supp. XVI:** 57

"Impossible to Tell" (Pinsky), **Supp. VI:** 247, 248

"Imposter, The" (West), **Retro. Supp. II:** 322, 327

"Impressionism and Symbolism in *Heart of Darkness*" (Watt), **Supp. VIII:** 4

"Impressionism"(Crooker), **Supp. XXIII:** 57

"Impressions of a European Tour" (Bourne), **I:** 225

"Impressions of an Indian Childhood" (Zitkala-Ša), **Supp. XXV:** 272

"Impressions of a Plumber" (H. Roth), **Supp. IX:** 228, 234

"Impressions of Europe, 1913–1914" (Bourne), **I:** 225

"I Must Have Called and So He Comes" (Notley), **Supp. XXII:** 224

"I'm Walking behind the Spanish" (Salinas), **Supp. XIII:** 323–324

I'm Your Man (album, Cohen), **Supp. XXVII:** 54

"I'm Your Man" (Cohen), **Supp. XXVII:** 52, 61

"I/Myself" (Shields), **Supp. VII:** 311

"In a (Low) Bar" (Ferry), **Supp. XXIV:** 153

"In Absence" (Lanier), **Supp. I Part 1:** 364

"In Absentia" (Bowles), **Supp. IV Part 1:** 94

"In a Cab" (Untermeyer), **Supp. XV:** 296

"In a Coffee Pot" (Hayes), **Supp. XXVI:** 133–134, 144

"In a Country Cemetery" (Kooser), **Supp. XIX:** 120

Inada, Lawson Fusao, **Supp. V:** 180

"In a Dark Room, Furniture" (Nye), **Supp. XIII:** 274

"In a Dark Time" (Roethke), **III:** 539, 547, 548

In a Different Voice (Gilligan), **Supp. XXII:** 18

"In a Disused Graveyard" (Frost), **Retro. Supp. I:** 126, 133

In a Dusty Light (Haines), **Supp. XII:** 207

"In a Garden" (A. Lowell), **II:** 513

"In a Hard Intellectual Light" (Eberhart), **I:** 523

"In a Hollow of the Hills" (Harte), **Supp. II Part 1:** 354

In America (Sontag), **Supp. XIV:** 95–96

"In Amicitia" (Ransom), **IV:** 141

In a Narrow Grave: Essays on Texas (McMurtry), **Supp. V:** 220, 223

In an Iridescent Time, Poems, 1953–58 (Stone), **Supp. XXVII:** 250–251, 253, 262

"Inanna" (A. Finch), **Supp. XVII:** 72

"In Another Country" (Hemingway), **I:** 484–485; **II:** 249

In April Once (Percy), **Retro. Supp. I:** 341

"In a Prominent Bar in Secaucus One Day" (X. J. Kennedy), **Supp. XV:** 154, 155–156

"In Armenia, 1987"(Balakian), **Supp. XXIII:** 25

In A Shallow Grave (Purdy), **Supp. VII:** 272

In a shlekhter tsayt (In a bad time) (Asch), **Supp. XXIII:** 4

"In a Stadium" (A. Lowell), **Supp. XXVII:** 295

"In a Station of the Metro" (Pound), **Retro. Supp. I:** 288; **Supp. I Part 1:** 265; **Supp. XIV:** 284–285

"In a Strange Town" (Anderson), **I:** 114, 115

In a Summer Season (Lewisohn), **Supp. XXVIII:** 152

"In Athens Once" (Rodriguez), **Supp. XIV:** 303

"In a Tub" (Hempel), **Supp. XXI:** 119

In a U-Haul North of Damascus (Bottoms), **Supp. XXVIII:** 22, 26–27

In Battle for Peace: The Story of My 83rd Birthday (Du Bois), **Supp. II Part 1:** 185

In Bed One Night & Other Brief Encounters (Coover), **Supp. V:** 49, 50

"In Bertram's Garden" (Justice), **Supp. VII:** 117

"In Blackwater Woods" (Oliver), **Supp. VII:** 244, 246

In Black & Whitey (Lacy), **Supp. XV:** 206–207

"In Broad Daylight" (Jin), **Supp. XVIII:** 94

In Broken Country (Wagoner), **Supp. IX:** 330

"In California" (Simpson), **Supp. IX:** 271

"In Camp" (Stafford), **Supp. XI:** 329

"Incant against Suicide" (Karr), **Supp. XI:** 249

"In Celebration of My Uterus" (Sexton), **Supp. II Part 2:** 689

"Incendiary, The" (Rowson), **Supp. XV:** 234

"In Certain Places and Certain Times There Can Be More of You" (Dunn), **Supp. XI:** 144

Incest: From "A Journal of Love," the Unexpurgated Diary of Anaïs Nin, 1932–1934 (Nin), **Supp. X:** 182, 184, 185, 187, 191

"In Chandler Country" (Gioia), **Supp. XV:** 119

Inchbald, Elizabeth, **II:** 8

"In Cheever Country" (Gioia), **Supp. XV:** 119

Inchiquin, the Jesuit's Letters (Ingersoll), **I:** 344

"Incident" (Cullen), **Supp. IV Part 1:** 165, 166

Incidental Numbers (Wylie), **Supp. I Part 2:** 708

Incidentals (Sandburg), **III:** 579

Incidentals in the Day World (Notley), **Supp. XXII:** 223, 226, 227

Incident at Vichy (A. Miller), **III:** 165, 166; **Retro. Supp. III:** 173, 175–176

Incidents in the Life of a Slave Girl (Brent), **Supp. IV Part 1:** 13

Incidents in the Life of a Slavegirl (Jacobs), **Supp. XVI:** 85; **Supp. XXVIII:** 173

"Incipience" (Rich), **Supp. I Part 2:** 559

"In Clare" (McCarriston), **Supp. XIV:** 270–271

Including Horace (Untermeyer), **Supp. XV:** 301, 303–304

In Cold Blood: A True Account of a Multiple Murder and Its Consequences (Capote), **Retro. Supp. II:** 107–108; **Supp. I Part 1:** 292; **Supp. III Part 1:** 111, 117, 119, 122, 123, 125–131; **Supp. III Part 2:** 574; **Supp. IV Part 1:** 220; **Supp. XIV:** 162; **Supp. XXV:** 57

In Cold Hell, in Thicket (Olson), **Supp. II Part 2:** 571

"In Cold Hell, in Thicket" (Olson), **Supp. II Part 2:** 558, 563–564, 566, 572, 580

"Incoming Tide"(Strout), **Supp. XXIII:** 282, 285

"Incomparable Light, The" (Eberhart), **I:** 541

Incorporative Consciousness of Robert Bly, The (Harris), **Supp. IV Part 1:** 68

In Country (Mason), **Supp. VIII:** 133, **142–143,** 146

"In Country of Conscience" (J. W. Miller), **Supp. XX: 165**

" 'Incredible Eloquence': How Ron Rash's Novels Keep the Celtic Literary Tradition Alive" (K. Baldwin), **Supp. XXVII:** 216

"Incredible Survival of Coyote, The" (Snyder), **Supp. VIII:** 297

"Increment" (Ammons), **Supp. VII:** 28

In Defense of Ignorance (Shapiro), **Supp. II Part 2:** 703, 704, 713–714

In Defense of Reason (Winters), **Supp. I Part 1:** 268

In Defense of Women (Mencken), **III:** 109

Indelible (Hadas), **Supp. XXIII:** 119

Indelible Alison Bechdel, The (Bechdel), **Supp. XXV:** 4

Indemnity Only (Paretsky), **Supp. XXV:** 172–173, 176, 178

Independence Day (film), **Supp. X:** 80

Independence Day (Ford), **Supp. V:** 57, 62–63, 67–68

"Independent Candidate, The, a Story of Today" (Howells), **II:** 277

"Indestructible Mr. Gore, The" (Vidal), **Supp. IV Part 2:** 679

Index of American Design, **Supp. III Part 2:** 618

"India" (Rodriguez), **Supp. XIV:** 302

India: A Sacred Geography (Eck), **Supp. XXVIII:** 49, 60–62

"Indian at the Burial-Place of His Fathers, An" (Bryant), **Supp. I Part 1:** 155–156, 167–168

"Indian Burying Ground, The" (Freneau), **Supp. II Part 1:** 264, 266

"Indian Camp" (Hemingway), **II:** 247–248, 263; **Retro. Supp. I:** 174–175, 176, 177, 181; **Supp. XVI:** 208

Indian Country (Caputo), **Supp. XIX:** 22–25

Indian Country (Matthiessen), **Supp. V:** 211

"Indian Country" (McCarriston), **Supp. XIV:** 271

"Indian Country" (Simpson), **Supp. IX:** 274

Indian Earth (Bynner), **Supp. XV:** 46

"Indian Gifts to Civilized Man" (Zitkala-Ša), **Supp. XXV:** 281

"Indian Girls" (McCarriston), **Supp. XIV:** 272–273

"Indian Manifesto" (Deloria), **Supp. IV Part 1:** 323

"Indian Names" (Sigourney), **Retro. Supp. II:** 47

"Indian's Awakening, The" (Zitkala-Ša), **Supp. XXV:** 281

"Indian Student, The" (Freneau), **Supp. II Part 1:** 264

"Indian Student, The" (Simpson), **Supp. IX:** 280

Indian Summer (Howells), **II:** 275, 279–281, 282

Indian Summer (Knowles), **Supp. XII:** 249, 250

Indian Summer: Musings on the Gift of Life (Pickering), **Supp. XXI:** 204

Indian Summers (Gansworth), **Supp. XXVI:** 104

"Indian Teacher Among Indians, An" (Zitkala-Ša), **Supp. XXV:** 272

"Indian Uprising, The" (Barthelme), **Supp. IV Part 1:** 44

"Indian Wooing" (C. Miller), **Supp. XXII:** 197–198

Indifferent Children, The (Auchincloss), **Supp. IV Part 1:** 25

Indirections (Cox), **Supp. XXI:** 21

Indiscretions (Pound), **Retro. Supp. I:** 284

"Indispensability of the Eyes, The" (Olds), **Supp. X:** 202

"In Distrust of Merits" (Moore), **III:** 201, 214

"Individual and the State, The" (Emerson), **II:** 10

Individualism, Old and New (Dewey), **Supp. I Part 2:** 677

"Indolence" (Pickering), **Supp. XXI:** 203

In Dreams Begin Responsibilities (Schwartz), **Supp. II Part 2:** 642, 645–650

"In Dreams Begin Responsibilities" (Schwartz), **Supp. II Part 2:** 641, 649, 654

In Dubious Battle (Steinbeck), **IV:** 51, 55–56, 59, 63

"In Durance" (Pound), **Retro. Supp. I:** 285

"Industry of Hard Kissing, The" (Ríos), **Supp. IV Part 2:** 547

"In Duty Bound" (Gilman), **Supp. XI:** 196–197

"I Need, I Need" (Roethke), **III:** 535–536

"I Need Help" (Stern), **Supp. IX:** 290

"Ineffectual Marriage" (Loy), **Supp. XXII:** 165

"Inés in the Kitchen" (García), **Supp. XI:** 190

"I never saw a Moor" (Dickinson), **Retro. Supp. I:** 37

I Never Told Anybody: Teaching Poetry Writing in a Nursing Home (Koch), **Supp. XV:** 190

"I Never Will Be Married, I'd Rather Be Excus'd" (Rowson), **Supp. XV:** 240

Inevitable Exiles (Kielsky), **Supp. V:** 273

"Inevitable Trial, The" (Holmes), **Supp. I Part 1:** 318

"Inexhaustible Hat, The" (Wagoner), **Supp. IX:** 327

"In Extremis" (Berry), **Supp. X:** 23

Inez, Colette, **Supp. XXIII:** 54, 245

"Infancy" (Wilder), **IV:** 375

"Infant Boy at Midcentury" (Warren), **IV:** 244–245, 252

Infante, Guillermo Cabrera, **Retro. Supp. I:** 278

"Infant Sea Turtles" (F. Wright), **Supp. XVII:** 245

Infants of the Spring (Thurman), **Supp. XIX:** 73; **Supp. XVIII:** 281

Inferno (Dante), **IV:** 139; **Supp. V:** 338; **Supp. VIII:** 219–221

Inferno of Dante, The (Pinsky), **Supp. VI:** 235, 248

Infidel (Ali), **Supp. XXIV:** 15

"Infidelity" (Komunyakaa), **Supp. XIII:** 130

Infidels (album, Dylan), **Supp. XVIII:** 28

"Infiltration of the Universe" (MacLeish), **III:** 19

Infinite Jest: A Novel (Wallace), **Supp. X:** 301, **310–314; Supp. XX:** 91; **Supp. XXVII:** 6; **Supp. XXVIII:** 221

"Infinite Reason, The" (MacLeish), **III:** 19

"Infirmity" (R. Lowell), **II:** 554

"Infirmity" (Roethke), **III:** 548

In Five Years Time (Haines), **Supp. XII:** 206

"In Flower" (Snodgrass), **Supp. VI:** 325

"Influence of Landscape upon the Poet, The" (Eliot), **Retro. Supp. I:** 67

"In Football Season" (Updike), **IV:** 219

Informer, The (film), **Supp. III Part 2:** 619

Informers, The (Ellis), **Supp. XXVII:** 74–75

Informers, The (screenplay, Ellis and Jarecki), **Supp. XXVII:** 68, 79

Inge, William, **Supp. XXV: 93–108**

Ingersoll, Charles J., **I:** 344

Ingersoll, Robert Green, **Supp. II Part 1:** 198

Ingmundson, Kris, **Supp. XXIV:** 230, 234

Ingraham, Lloyd, **Supp. XVI:** 184

"Ingrained Reflexes" (Huddle), **Supp. XXVI:** 154

Ingster, Boris, **Retro. Supp. II:** 330

"In Guatemala, All Is Forgotten"(Goldman), **Supp. XXV:** 58

Inhabitants, The (Morris), **III:** 221–222

"Inheritance and Invention in Li-Young Lee's Poetry" (Xiaojing), **Supp. XV:** 214

"Inheritance"(Kenny), **Supp. XXIII:** 154

"Inheritance of Tools, The" (Sanders), **Supp. XVI:** 273

Inheritors (Glaspell), **Supp. III Part 1:** 175, 179–181, 186, 189

"In him we live, & move, & have our being" (Very), **Supp. XXV:** 246

"In Hollywood with the Zuni God of War" (Major), **Supp. XXII:** 180

"In Honor of David Anderson Brooks, My Father" (Brooks), **Supp. III Part 1:** 79

"In Honor of That High and Mighty Princess Queen Elizabeth of Happy Memory" (Bradstreet), **Retro. Supp. III:** 8–9

"Inhumanist, The" (Jeffers), **Supp. II Part 2:** 423, 426

"In Illo Tempore" (Karr), **Supp. XI:** 242

"In Interims: Outlyer" (Harrison), **Supp. VIII:** 38

"Initial" (F. Wright), **Supp. XVII:** 243

"In Jimmy's Grill"(Bottoms), **Supp. XXVIII:** 25

"Injudicious Gardening" (Moore), **III:** 198

"Injustice" (Paley), **Supp. VI:** 220

Injustice Collectors, The (Auchincloss), **Supp. IV Part 1:** 25

Ink, Blood, Semen (Goldbarth), **Supp. XII:** 181, 183

Ink Dark Moon, The: Love Poems by Ono no Komachi and Izumi Shikibu (Aratani and Hirshfield, trans.), **Supp.**

XXIII: 136

Ink Truck, The (W. Kennedy), **Supp. VII:** 132, 133–138, 140, 141, 149, 152

In Life Sentences: Literary Essays (Epstein), **Supp. XIV:** 112

"In Limbo" (Wilbur), **Supp. III Part 2:** 544, 561

In Limestone Country (Sanders), **Supp. XVI:** 272

"In Line" (Major), **Supp. XXII:** 185

In Love (Hayes), **Supp. XXVI:** 133, 139, 140–141

In Love and Trouble: Stories of Black Women (Walker), **Supp. III Part 2:** 520, 521, 530, 531, 532

In Mad Love and War (Harjo), **Supp. XII: 224–226**

"In Memoriam" (Emerson), **II:** 13

"In Memoriam" (Hay), **Supp. XIV:** 122, 127

"In Memoriam" (Tennyson), **Retro. Supp. I:** 325; **Supp. I Part 2:** 416

In Memoriam: 1933 (Reznikoff), **Supp. XIV:** 280, 285

In Memoriam to Identity (Acker), **Supp. XII:** 5, **16–18**

"In Memory of Arthur Winslow" (R. Lowell), **II:** 541, 547, 550; **Retro. Supp. II:** 187

"In Memory of Congresswoman Barbara Jordan" (Pinsky), **Supp. VI:** 250

"In Memory of Joe Brainard" (Bidart), **Supp. XV:** 33

"In Memory of My Dear Grandchild Elizabeth Bradstreet" (Bradstreet), **Retro. Supp. III:** 13

"In Memory of My Feelings" (O'Hara), **Supp. XV:** 215–216; **Supp. XXIII:** 208, 215–216

In Memory of My Feelings (O'Hara; Berkson, ed.), **Supp. XXIII:** 220

"In Memory of Vachel Lindsay" (Teasdale), **Supp. XXVII:** 297

"In Memory of W. B. Yeats" (Auden), **Supp. VIII:** 19, 30; **Supp. XI:** 243, 244; **Supp. XIX:** 85

"In Memory of W. H. Auden" (Stern), **Supp. IX:** 288

"In Memory"(Schott), **Supp. XXIII:** 254

"In Mercy on Broadway" (Doty), **Supp. XI:** 132

In Morocco (Wharton), **Retro. Supp. I:** 380; **Supp. IV Part 1:** 81

Inmost Leaf, The: A Selection of Essays (Kazin), **Supp. VIII:** 102, 103

In Motley (Bierce), **I:** 209

In My Father's Court (Singer), **IV:** 16–17; **Retro. Supp. II: 301–302**

"In My Life" (Dubus), **Supp. VII:** 81

"In My Other Life" (Huddle), **Supp. XXVI:** 151

Innaurato, Albert, **Supp. XXIV:** 113, 116, 117

"In Navaho Country" (Bronk), **Supp. XXI:** 30

Inner Circle, The (Boyle), **Supp. XX:** 24, **26**

Inner Landscape (Sarton), **Supp. VIII:** 259

Inner Room, The (Merrill), **Supp. III Part 1:** 336

"In Nine Sleep Valley" (Merrill), **Supp. III Part 1:** 328

Innocent Mrs. Duff, The (Holding), **Supp. XXII:** 119, 120, 123, **130–131**, 135, 136

Innocents, The: A Story for Lovers (Lewis), **II:** 441

Innocents Abroad, The (Twain), **Retro. Supp. III:** 257–258, 260–261, 267

Innocents Abroad, The; or, The New Pilgrim's Progress (Twain), **II:** 275, 434; **IV:** 191, 196, 197–198

Innocents and Others (Spiotta), **Supp. XXVIII:** 207, 216, 219–221

Innocents at Cedro, The: A Memoir of Thorstein Veblen and Some Others (Duffus), **Supp. I Part 2:** 650

"In Off the Cliffs of Moher" (McCarriston), **Supp. XIV:** 270

In Old Plantation Days (Dunbar), **Supp. II Part 1:** 214

In Ole Virginia (Page), **Supp. II Part 1:** 201

In Orbit (Morris), **III:** 236

In Other Words (Swenson), **Supp. IV Part 2:** 650–652

In Other Words: Literature by Latinas of the United States (Fernandez, ed.), **Supp. XXI:** 104

In Our Terribleness (Some elements and meaning in black style) (Baraka), **Supp. II Part 1:** 52, 53

In Our Time (Hemingway), **I:** 117; **II:** 68, 247, 252, 263; **IV:** 42; **Retro. Supp. I:** 170, 173, 174, 178, 180; **Supp. IX:** 106

"In Our Time" (Wolfe), **Supp. III Part 2:** 584

"Inpatient" (Kenyon), **Supp. VII:** 169

In Persuasion Nation (Saunders), **Supp. XIX: 231–234**

"In Persuasion Nation" (Saunders), **Supp. XIX:** 233–234

In Pharaoh's Army: Memories of the Lost War (Wolff), **Supp. VII:** 331–334, 335, 338

"In Plaster" (Plath), **Supp. I Part 2:** 540

"In Prague, in Montmartre" (Bierds), **Supp. XVII:** 27

"In Praise of Johnny Appleseed" (Lindsay), **Supp. I Part 2:** 397

"In Praise of Limestone" (Auden), **Supp. II Part 1:** 20–21; **Supp. VIII:** 23

In Pursuit of a Vanishing Star (Sobin), **Supp. XVI: 294**

"In Quercy, 1993" (Davison), **Supp. XXVI:** 78

In Quest of the Ordinary (Cavell), **Retro. Supp. I:** 307

Inquiry into the Moral and Religious Character of the American Government, An (H. Warner), **Supp. XVIII:** 259

Inquiry into the Nature of Peace, An (Veblen), **Supp. I Part 2:** 642

Inquisitor, The (Rowson), **Supp. XV: 232,** 238

In Radical Pursuit (Snodgrass), **Supp. VI:** 312, 316, 318

In Reckless Ecstasy (Sandburg), **III:** 579

In Recognition of William Gaddis (Kuehl and Moore), **Supp. IV Part 1:** 279

"In Reference to Her Children, 23 June 1659" (Bradstreet), **Retro. Supp. III:** 3, 13

"In Retirement" (Malamud), **Supp. I Part 2:** 437

"In Retrospect" (Angelou), **Supp. IV Part 1:** 15

"In Right" (Wolfert), **Supp. XXI:** 263, 264, 272

"Inroads of Time, The" (D. West), **Supp. XVIII:** 286–287

In Russia (A. Miller), **III:** 165

"In Sabine" (Chopin), **Supp. I Part 1:** 213

"In School-Days" (Whittier), **Supp. I Part 2:** 699–700

"Inscription for the Entrance to a Wood" (Bryant), **Supp. I Part 1:** 154, 155, 161–162

Inscriptions, 1944–1956 (Reznikoff), **Supp. XIV:** 281

In Search (Levin), **Supp. XXVII:** 133, 134, 138, 142, 143, 146–147

In Search of America: The Image of the United States in Travel Writing of the 1980s and 1990s (Rutkowska), **Supp. XXII:** 208

"In Search of a Motif for Expressive Female Figuration" (Major), **Supp. XXII:** 184

In Search of Bisco (Caldwell), **I:** 296

In Search of Lost Time (Proust), **Supp. XXV:** 71

In Search of Nella Larsen: A Biography of the Color Line (Hutchinson), **Supp. XVIII:** 120

"In Search of Our Mothers' Gardens" (Walker), **Supp. III Part 2:** 520–532, 524, 525, 527, 529, 532–533, 535, 536; **Supp. IX:** 306; **Supp. XVIII:** 200, 283

"In Search of Thomas Merton" (Griffin), **Supp. VIII:** 208

"In Search of Yage" (Burroughs), **Supp. III Part 1:** 98

Insect Friends (Teale), **Supp. XXVIII:** 247

"Insect Life in Florida" (Hull), **Supp. XXI:** 133

Insect World of J. Henri Fabre, The (Teale), **Supp. XXVIII:** 247

Insel (Loy), **Supp. XXII:** 167

"Insertion of Self into a Space of Borderless Possibilities, The" (Fjellestad), **Supp. XVI:** 150

"In Shadow" (Crane), **I:** 386

"In Shadow" (H. Crane), **Retro. Supp. III:** 45

"In Sickness and in Health" (Auden), **Supp. II Part 1:** 15

"In Sickness and in Health" (Humphrey), **Supp. IX:** 94

Inside, Outside (Wouk), **Supp. XXV:** 254, 255, 257, 265

Inside Diameter: The France Poems (Major), **Supp. XXII:** 182

Inside His Mind (A. Miller), **III:** 154

Inside Memory (Findley), **Supp. XX: 51, 63**

"Inside Norman Mailer" (Apple), **Supp. XVII:** 3, 4

"Insider Baseball" (Didion), **Supp. IV Part 1:** 211

Inside Sports magazine, **Supp. V:** 58, 61

Inside the Blood Factory (Wakoski), **Supp. XXVIII:** 262–263

In Simpkinsville: Character Tales (Stuart), **Supp. XXVIII:** 229, 236

"Insipid Profession of Jonathan Horneboom, The" (Lethem), **Supp. XVIII:** 149

"In So Many Dark Rooms" (Hogan), **Supp. IV Part 1:** 400

"Insomnia" (Bishop), **Supp. I Part 1:** 92

"Insomniac" (Plath), **Supp. I Part 2:** 539

"In Spain, Throwing Carnations" (P. N. Warren), **Supp. XX: 272**

"Inspiration for Greatness" (Caldwell), **I:** 291

"Instability of Race Types, The" (Boas), **Supp. XIV:** 209

"Installation #6" (Beattie), **Supp. V:** 33

"Instead of Dying" (Gallagher), **Supp. XXIV:** 171

"Intersities" (Berrigan), **Supp. XXIV:** 36

Instinct of Workmanship and the State of the Industrial Arts, The (Veblen), **Supp. I Part 2:** 642

Instincts of the Herd in Peace and War, The (Trotter), **I:** 249

Institute (Calvin), **IV:** 158, 160

"Instruction Manual, The" (Ashbery), **Supp. III Part 1:** 6–7, 10, 12

Instructions, The (Levin), **Supp. XXII:** 268

"Instructions for the Afternoon" (Gioia), **Supp. XV:** 120

Instructions to the Double (Gallagher), **Supp. XXIV:** 165, 167, 168, 169, 174

"Instructions to the Double" (Gallagher), **Supp. XXIV:** 168

"Instruction to Myself" (Brooks), **Supp. III Part 1:** 87

Instrument, The (O'Hara), **III:** 362, 364

"In Such Times, Ties Must Bind" (Nye), **Supp. XIII:** 286

In Sunlight and in Shadow (Helprin), **Supp. XXV:** 81, 88

"Insurance and Social Change" (Stevens), **Retro. Supp. I:** 297

Insurgent Mexico (Reed), **I:** 476

In Suspect Terrain (McPhee), **Supp. III Part 1:** 309, 310

"In Tall Grass" (Sandburg), **III:** 585

"Integer Vitae" (Horace), **Supp. XV:** 304

"Integrity" (Rich), **Retro. Supp. III:** 249

Intellectual History, An (Senghor), **Supp. X:** 139

"Intellectual Pre-Eminence of Jews in Modern Europe, The" (Veblen), **Supp. I Part 2:** 643–644

Intellectual Things (Kunitz), **Supp. III Part 1:** 260, 262–264

Intellectual versus the City, The (White), **I:** 258

"In Temporary Pain" (Bynner), **Supp. XV:** 41–42

Intensive Care (Myers), **Supp. XXVII:** 211

Intentions (Wilde), **Retro. Supp. I:** 56

"Interest in Life, An" (Paley), **Supp. VI:** 222, 224–225

Interest of Great Britain Considered, with Regard to Her Colonies and the Acquisition of Canada and Guadeloupe, The (Franklin), **II:** 119

"Interior" (H. Crane), **Retro. Supp. III:** 45

Interior Landscapes (Vizenor), **Supp. IV Part 1:** 262

Interiors (film; Allen), **Supp. IV Part 1:** 205; **Supp. XV:** 1, **7**, 10

Interlocking Lives (Koch), **Supp. XV:** 185

"Interlude" (A. Lowell), **Retro. Supp. II:** 46

"Interlude, An"(King), **Supp. XXVIII:** 122

Interlunar (Atwood), **Supp. XIII:** 35

"Intermezzo" (Schnackenberg), **Supp. XV:** 254

"In Terms of the Toenail: Fiction and the Figures of Life" (Gass), **Supp. VI:** 85

"International Episode, An" (James), **II:** 327

International Workers Order, **Retro. Supp. I:** 202

Interpretation of Christian Ethics, An (Niebuhr), **III:** 298–300, 301, 302

"Interpretation of Dreams, The" (Matthews), **Supp. IX:** 162–163

Interpretation of Music of the XVIIth and XVIIIth Centuries, The (Dolmetsch), **III:** 464

Interpretations and Forecasts: 1922–1972 (Mumford), **Supp. II Part 2:** 481

Interpretations of Poetry and Religion (Santayana), **III:** 611

Interpreter of Maladies (Lahiri), **Supp. XXI:** 175–176, **177–180**, 183

"Interpreter of Maladies" (Lahiri), **Supp. XXI:** 183, 184

Interpreters and Interpretations (Van Vechten), **Supp. II Part 2:** 729, 733–734

"Interrogate the Stones" (MacLeish), **III:** 9

"Interrogation of the Prisoner Bung By Mister Hawkins and Sergeant Tree, The" (Huddle), **Supp. XXVI:** 147, 149, 152

Interrogations at Noon (Gioia), **Supp. XV:** 112, **125–127**, 128, 129

"Interrupted Conversation, An" (Van Vechten), **Supp. II Part 2:** 735

"Interrupted Elegy" (Peacock), **Supp. XIX:** 200

Intersect: Poems (Shields), **Supp. VII:** 310–311

Intersexes, The (Prime-Stevenson as Mayne), **Supp. XX: 235**

Interstate (Dixon), **Supp. XII:** 140, 152–153, 153, 156

"Interview" (Hay), **Supp. XIV:** 132

"Interview, The" (Thurber), **Supp. I Part 2:** 616

"Interview With a Lemming" (Thurber), **Supp. I Part 2:** 603

"Interview with Larry Rivers, An"(O'Hara), **Supp. XXIII:** 214

"Interview with Peter Everwine, An" (Veinberg and Buckley), **Supp. XV:** 76–77

"Interview with the Crab" (Lethem), **Supp. XVIII:** 148

Interview with the Vampire (Rice), **Supp. VII:** 287, 288–291, 297–298, 303

"Interview with the Vampire" (Rice), **Supp. VII:** 288

Interzone (Burroughs), **Supp. IV Part 1:** 90

"In the Absence of Bliss" (Kumin), **Supp. IV Part 2:** 453

"In the Afternoon" (Dunn), **Supp. XI:** 146

"In the Alley" (Elkin), **Supp. VI: 46–47**

"In the Alley"(Lea), **Supp. XXVIII:** 136

In the American Grain (W. C. Williams), **Retro. Supp. I:** 420–421

In the American Jungle (W. Frank), **Supp. XX: 76**

In the American Tree (Silliman), **Supp. IV Part 2:** 426

"In the Arboretum" (Stone), **Supp. XXVII:** 260

In the Bank of Beautiful Sins (Wrigley), **Supp. XVIII: 300–302**

In the Bar of a Tokyo Hotel (T. Williams), **IV:** 382, 386, 387, 391, 393

In the Beauty of the Lilies (Updike), **Retro. Supp. I:** 322, 325, 326, 327, 333

"In the Beeyard" (Bierds), **Supp. XVII:** 29

"In the Beginning" (Quindlen), **Supp. XVII:** 166

"In the Beginning . . ." (Simic), **Supp. VIII:** 270, 271

In the Belly of the Beast: Letters from Prison (Abbott), **Retro. Supp. II:** 210

"In the Black Morning" (Wolfert), **Supp. XXI:** 265

"In the Black Museum" (Nemerov), **III:** 275

"In the Blink of God's Eye" (E. P. Jones), **Supp. XXII:** 150

"In the Bodies of Words" (Swenson), **Supp. IV Part 2:** 651

"In the Boston Children's Hospital" (Huddle), **Supp. XXVI:** 151

"In the Box"(Kenny), **Supp. XXIII:** 155

"In the Cage" (Gass), **Supp. VI:** 85

In the Cage (James), **Retro. Supp. I:** 229

"In the Cage" (James), **II:** 332; **Retro. Supp. I:** 231

"In the Cage" (R. Lowell), **Retro. Supp. II:** 187

"In the Cave at Lone Tree Meadow" (Haines), **Supp. XII:** 212

"In the Cemetery Where Al Jolson Is Buried" (Hempel), **Supp. XXI:** 115, **121–122**

"In the City Ringed with Giants" (Kingsolver), **Supp. VII:** 209

"In the Clearing" (Brodsky), **Supp. VIII:** 32

In the Clearing (Frost), **II:** 153, 155, 164; **Retro. Supp. I:** 121, 122, 141; **Retro. Supp. III:** 107

"In the Closet of the Soul" (Walker), **Supp. III Part 2:** 526

"In the Cold Air Register" (W. V. Davis), **Supp. XXI:** 94

"In the Confidence of a Story-Writer" (Chopin), **Retro. Supp. II:** 66–67; **Supp. I Part 1:** 217

In the Country of Last Things (Auster), **Supp. XII:** 23, **29–30,** 31, 32

"In the Courtyard of the Isleta Missions" (R. Bly), **Supp. IV Part 1:** 71

"In the Dark" (Levine), **Supp. V:** 194

In the Dark (Stone), **Supp. XXVII:** 257

"In the Dark New England Days" (Jewett), **Retro. Supp. II:** 139

"In the Days of Prismatic Colour" (Moore), **III:** 205, 213

In the Days of the Comet (Wells), **Supp. XX: 233, 240**

In the Electric Mist with Confederate Dead (Burke), **Supp. XIV:** 30, 31–32

"In the Field" (Wilbur), **Supp. III Part 2:** 558

"In the 51st State" (Berrigan), **Supp. XXIV:** 35

"In the First Stanza" (C. Kizer), **Supp. XVII:** 75

"In the Fleeting Hand of Time" (Corso), **Supp. XII:** 122–123

"In the Footsteps of Gutenberg" (Mencken), **III:** 101

"In the Forest" (Simpson), **Supp. IX:** 270

"In the Forest of the Laughing Elephant" (Caputo), **Supp. XIX:** 27

"In the Forties" (R. Lowell), **II:** 554

"In the Garden" (Ferry), **Supp. XXIV:** 153

In the Garden of the North American Martyrs (Wolff), **Supp. VII:** 341–342

In the Garret (Van Vechten), **Supp. II Part 2:** 735

"In the Grove: The Poet at Ten" (Kenyon), **Supp. VII:** 160

"In the Hall of Mirrors" (Merrill), **Supp. III Part 1:** 322

In the Harbor (Longfellow), **II:** 491

In the Heart of the Heart of the Country (Gass), **Supp. VI: 82–83,** 84, 85, 93

In the Heat of the Night (Ball), **Supp. XV:** 202

In the Heat of the Night (film), **Supp. I Part 1:** 67

In the Hollow of His Hand (Purdy), **Supp. VII:** 278–280

In the House of Light (Everwine, trans.), **Supp. XV:** 73, 75, **76–78,** 82

"In the Ice Pasture"(Bottoms), **Supp. XXVIII:** 27

"In the Laboratory of Kisses" (Gallagher), **Supp. XXIV:** 170

In the Lake of the Woods (O'Brien), **Supp. V:** 240, 243, 250–252

In the Land of the White Death: A Epic Story of Survival in the Siberian Arctic (Albanov), **Supp. XVIII:** 114

"In the Last Days" (Everwine), **Supp. XV:** 88, 89

"In the Late Summer Garden"(Crooker), **Supp. XXIII:** 55

In the Loyal Mountains (Bass), **Supp. XVI: 19–20**

"In the Loyal Mountains" (Bass), **Supp. XVI:** 20

"In the Mean Mud Season" (Huddle), **Supp. XXVI:** 154

In the Mecca (Brooks), **Supp. III Part 1:** 74

"In the Mecca" (Brooks), **Supp. III Part 1:** 70, 83–84

"In the Metropolitan Museum" (Teasdale), **Supp. XXVII:** 289

In the Midst of Life (Bierce), **I:** 200–203, 204, 206, 208, 212

"In the Miro District" (Taylor), **Supp. V:** 323

In the Miro District and Other Stories (Taylor), **Supp. V:** 325–326

In the Money (W. C. Williams), **Retro. Supp. I:** 423

"In the Motel" (X. J. Kennedy), **Supp. XV:** 163

"In the Naked Bed, in Plato's Cave" (Schwartz), **Supp. II Part 2:** 646–649

In the Name of the Neither (Sobin), **Supp. XVI:** 291

In the Next Galaxy (Stone), **Supp. XXVII:** 257, 262

"In the Next Galaxy" (Stone), **Supp. XXVII:** 253

"In the Night" (Kincaid), **Supp. VII:** 183

In the Night Season: A Novel (Bausch), **Supp. VII:** 52–53

"In the Old Neighborhood" (Dove), **Supp. IV Part 1:** 241, 257

"In the Old World" (Oates), **Supp. II Part 2:** 503, 504

"In the Park" (Biss), **Supp. XXVI:** 48

"In the Park" (Huncke), **Supp. XIV:** 139

In the Pines (Notley), **Supp. XXII:** 236–237

"In the Pit" (Proulx), **Supp. VII:** 255, 261

In the Pond (Jin), **Supp. XVIII: 95–96**

In the Presence of the Sun (Momaday), **Supp. IV Part 2:** 489, 490, 491–493, 493

"In the Quiet Night" (Li Po), **Supp. XV:** 47

"In the Realm of the Fisher King" (Didion), **Supp. IV Part 1:** 211

"In the Red Room" (Bowles), **Supp. IV Part 1:** 93

"In the Region of Ice" (Oates), **Supp. II Part 2:** 520

In the Room We Share (Simpson), **Supp. IX:** 279

"In These Dissenting Times" (Walker), **Supp. III Part 2:** 522

"In the Shadow of Gabriel, A.D.1550" (Frederic), **II:** 139

In the Shadow of Memory (Skloot), **Supp. XX:** 193, 196, 205, 205–206

"In the Shadow of Memory" (Skloot), **Supp. XX: 206**

In the Shadow of the Morning: Essays on Wild Lands, Wild Waters, and a Few Untamed People (Caputo), **Supp. XIX:** 28–29

In the Spirit of Crazy Horse (Matthiessen), **Supp. V:** 211

"In the Subway" (Untermeyer), **Supp. XV:** 296

In the Summer House (Jane Bowles), **Supp. IV Part 1:** 83, 89

"In the Syntax: Rewriting Joan Didion's 'Goodbye to All That' " (Biss), **Supp. XXVI:** 54

In the Tennessee Country (Taylor), **Supp. V:** 328

"In the Thick of Darkness" (Salinas), **Supp. XIII:** 325

In the Time of Butterflies (Alvarez), **Supp. XXIV:** 89

"In the Time of the Blossoms" (Mervin), **Supp. III Part 1:** 352

In the Time of the Butterflies (Alvarez), **Supp. VII:** 1, 12–15, 18

In the Time of the Present (Kenny), **Supp. XXIII:** 146, **156**

"In the Tube" (Jarman), **Supp. XVII:** 121

"In the Tunnel Bone of Cambridge" (Corso), **Supp. XII:** 120–121

"In the Upper Pastures" (Kumin), **Supp. IV Part 2:** 453

In the Valley (Frederic), **II:** 133–134, 136, 137

"In the Village" (Bishop), **Retro. Supp. II:** 38; **Supp. I Part 1:** 73, 74–75, 76, 77, 78, 88

"In the Waiting Room" (Bishop), **Retro. Supp. II:** 50; **Supp. I Part 1:** 81, 94, 95; **Supp. IV Part 1:** 249

In the Walled City (O'Nan), **Supp. XXV:** 142

"In the Ward: The Sacred Wood" (Jarrell), **II:** 376, 377

In the Western Night: Collected Poems 1965–90 (Bidart), **Supp. XV:** 19, **30–32**

"In the White Night" (Beattie), **Supp. V:** 30–31

"In the Wind My Rescue Is" (Ammons), **Supp. VII:** 25

"In the Winter Dark" (Peacock), **Supp. XIX:** 206

In the Winter of Cities (T. Williams), **IV:** 383

"In the X-Ray of the Sarcophagus of Tapero" (Goldbarth), **Supp. XII:** 191

"In the Yard" (Swenson), **Supp. IV Part 2:** 647

In the Zone (O'Neill), **III:** 388

In This, Our Life (film), **Supp. I Part 1:** 67

"In This Country, but in Another Language, My Aunt Refuses to Marry the Men Everyone Wants Her To" (Paley), **Supp. VI:** 225

"In This Dream" (J. W. Miller), **Supp. XX:** 170

In This Hung-up Age (Corso), **Supp. XII: 119–120,** 129

In This Our Life (Glasgow), **II:** 175, 178, 189

In This Our World (Gilman), **Supp. XI:** 196, 200, 202

"In Those Days" (Jarrell), **II:** 387–388

"Intimately Connected to the Zeitgeist" (Franzen), **Supp. XX:** 94

Intimates (Huddle), **Supp. XXVI:** 155–156

"In Time of War" (Auden), **Supp. II Part 1:** 8, 13

In Times Like These (Edgell), **Supp. XXIII:** 84, **89–90,** 94

"Into Egypt" (Benét), **Supp. XI:** 56, 57–58

Intolerance (film; Griffith), **Supp. XVI:** 184

"Into My Own" (Frost), **II:** 153; **Retro. Supp. I:** 127; **Retro. Supp. III:** 94–95

Into My Own: The English Years of Robert Frost (Walsh), **Retro. Supp. III:** 95

"Into Night" (McKnight), **Supp. XX:** **151–152**

"Into the Gorge" (Rash), **Supp. XXVII:** 228

Into the Interior (Cliff), **Supp. XXII:** 67, 78–79

"Into the Night Life . . ." (H. Miller), **III:** 180, 184

"Into the Nowhere" (Rawlings), **Supp. X:** 220

Into the Stone (Dickey), **Supp. IV Part 1:** 178

"Into the Stone" (Dickey), **Supp. IV Part 1:** 179

Into the Stone and Other Poems (Dickey), **Supp. IV Part 1:** 176

"Into the Streets May First" (Hayes), **Supp. XXVI:** 134, 144

Into the Wild (Krakauer), **Supp. XVIII:** 106, **107–108,** 116, 117

Into Thin Air: A Personal Account of the Mount Everest Disaster (Krakauer), **Supp. XVII:** 210; **Supp. XVIII:** 105, **109–113,** 117

In Touch: The Letters of Paul Bowles (J. Miller, ed.), **Supp. IV Part 1:** 95

"Intoxicated, The" (Jackson), **Supp. IX:** 116

"Intrigue" (Crane), **I:** 419

Introducing Irony: A Book of Poetic Short Stories and Poems (Bodenheim), **Supp. XXV:** 22–23

"Introducing the Fathers" (Kumin), **Supp. IV Part 2:** 452

Introductio ad Prudentiam (Fuller), **II:** 111

"Introduction"(Strout; *Ploughshares* spring 2010), **Supp. XXIII:** 284

"Introduction to a Haggadah" (Paley), **Supp. VI:** 219

Introduction to Objectivist Epistemology (Rand), **Supp. IV Part 2:** 527, 528–529

Introduction to Objectivist Epistemology 2nd ed. (Rand), **Supp. IV Part 2:** 529

"Introduction to Poetry" (Collins), **Supp. XXI:** 57

Introduction to Poetry, An (Gioia and X. J. Kennedy), **Supp. XV:** 113, 153

"Introduction to Some Poems, An" (Stafford), **Supp. XI:** 311, 324

Introduction to the Geography of Iowa, The (Doty), **Supp. XI:** 120

"Introduction to the Hoh" (Hugo), **Supp. VI:** 136–137

"Introduction to *The New Writing in the USA*" (Creeley), **Supp. IV Part 1:** 153–154

"Introduction to William Blake, An" (Kazin), **Supp. VIII:** 103

Introitus (Longfellow), **II:** 505, 506–507

"Intruder, The" (Dubus), **Supp. VII:** 76–78, 91

Intruder, The (Maeterlinck), **I:** 91

Intruder in the Dust (Faulkner), **II:** 71, 72; **Retro. Supp. III:** 86, 87; **Supp. XVI:** 148

Intuition (Goodman), **Supp. XXVI:** 128–130

"Invaders, The" (Haines), **Supp. XII:** 205

Invaders, The (W. Frank), **Supp. XX:** **79–80**

Invasion (Myers), **Supp. XXVII:** 207

Invasion of Privacy: The Cross Creek Trial of Marjorie Kinnan Rawlings (Acton), **Supp. X:** 233

Inventing Memory: A Novel of Mothers and Daughters (Jong), **Supp. V:** 115, 129

Inventing the Abbotts (Miller), **Supp. XII:** **294–295**

"Invention of Autobiography. The" (Hampl), **Supp. XXII:** 93–94

"Invention of God in a Mouthful of Milk, The" (Karr), **Supp. XI:** 250

Invention of Solitude, The (Auster), **Supp. XII:** 21–22

"Inventions of the March Hare" (Eliot), **Retro. Supp. I:** 55

Inventions of the March Hare (T. S. Eliot), **Retro. Supp. I:** 55–56, 58; **Retro. Supp. III:** 59

"Inventory" (Parker), **Supp. IX:** 192

Inverness, Amy Beth, **Supp. XXVII:** 103

"Inverted Forest, The" (Salinger), **III:** 552, 572

"Investigation" (Ryan as Quin), **Supp. XVIII:** 227–228

"Investigations of a Dog" (Kafka), **IV:** 438

"Investiture, The" (Banks), **Supp. V:** 7

"Investiture at Cecconi's" (Merrill), **Supp. III Part 1:** 336

"Invicibility"(O'Hara), **Supp. XXIII:** 214

"Invisible" (Pickering), **Supp. XXI:** 201

Invisible Circus, The (Egan), **Supp. XIX:** 49, **50–52**

Invisible Company, The (Sanders), **Supp. XVI:** 270–271

Invisible Man (Ellison), **IV:** 493; **Retro. Supp. II:** 3, 12, 111, 112, 113, 117, 119, **120–123,** 125; **Supp. II Part 1:** 40, 170, 221, 224, 226, 227, 230, 231–232, 235, 236, 241–245; **Supp. IX:** 306; **Supp. X:** 242; **Supp. XI:** 18, 92; **Supp. XIX:** 154, 155; **Supp. XVIII:** 59; **Supp. XXVI:** 215

Invisible: Poems (Nye), **Supp. XIII:** 277

Invisible Spectator, An (Sawyer-Lauçanno), **Supp. IV Part 1:** 95

Invisible Swords (Farrell), **II:** 27, 46, 48–49

Invisible Worm, The (Millar), **Supp. IV Part 2:** 465

Invitation to a Beheading (Nabokov), **III:** 252–253, 254, 257–258; **Retro. Supp. I:** 265, 270, 273

"Invitation to the Country, An" (Bryant), **Supp. I Part 1:** 160

"Invocation" (H. Johnson), **Supp. XXVI:** 166, 174

"Invocation" (McKay), **Supp. X:** 134

Invocation (Rash), **Supp. XXVII:** 217

"Invocation" (Untermeyer), **Supp. XV:** 296

"Invocation to Kali" (Sarton), **Supp. VIII:** 260

"Invocation: *To my Maternal Grand-father on hearing his descent from Chippewa ancestors misrepresented"(J. Schoolcraft),* Supp. XXIII: 232

"Invocation to the Social Muse" (MacLeish), **III:** 15

"In Weather" (Hass), **Supp. VI:** **102–103**

In Writing Huck Finn: Mark Twain's Creative Process (Doyno), **Retro. Supp. III:** 265

"In Your Fugitive Dream" (Hugo), **Supp. VI:** 143

"In Your Good Dream" (Hugo), **Supp. VI:** 143–144

"Iola, Kansas" (Clampitt), **Supp. IX:** **45–46**

Iola Leroy (Harper), **Supp. XVIII:** 284

Ion (Doolittle, trans.), **Supp. I Part 1:** 269, 274

Ion (Plato), **I:** 523

"Ione" (Dunbar), **Supp. II Part 1:** 199

Ionesco, Eugène, **I:** 71, 74, 75, 84, 295; **II:** 435; **Supp. VIII:** 201; **Supp. XIX:** 131; **Supp. XXIV:** 113

Ionica (Cory), **Supp. XX:** **230**

Ionica II (Cory), **Supp. XX:** **230**

"I Only Am Escaped Alone to Tell Thee" (Nemerov), **III:** 272, 273–274

"I Opened All the Portals Wide" (Chopin), **Retro. Supp. II:** 71

I Ought to Be in Pictures (Simon), **Supp. IV Part 2:** 584

Iphigenia (Notley), **Supp. XXII:** 226, 235

Iphigenia in Tauris (Euripedes), **Supp. XV:** 42, 50

I Promessi Sposi (Manzoni), **II:** 291

"I Put My Hand on My Son's Head" (Kooser), **Supp. XIX:** 120

Iram, Dhát al-'Imád (Gibran), **Supp. XX:** **116**

"Iraq Drifting, July 2003" (Weigl), **Supp. XIX:** 288

"Irascibles, The" (Kees), **Supp. XV:** 145–146

Ireland: A Terrible Beauty (Uris), **Supp. XX: 244, 245–246, 246, 254**

I Remember (Brainard), **Supp. XXVII:** 17, 18, 26, 29

I Remember (collected edition, Brainard), **Supp. XXVII:** 19

"I Remember" (Sexton), **Supp. II Part 2:** 680

I Remember Christmas (Brainard), **Supp. XXVII:** 19

I Remember More (Brainard), **Supp. XXVII:** 19

"Irene" (Poe), **Retro. Supp. III:** 231

"Irenicon" (Shapiro), **Supp. II Part 2:** 704

Irigaray, Luce, **Supp. XII:** 6

Iris (Jarman), **Supp. XVII:** 110, **116–117**

"Iris by Night" (Frost), **Retro. Supp. I:** 132

"Irises" (L.-Y. Lee), **Supp. XV:** 214–215

Irish in America, The (Coffey, ed.), **Supp. XIX:** 133

Irish Stories of Sarah Orne Jewett, The (Jewett), **Retro. Supp. II:** 142

Irish Triangle, An (Barnes), **Supp. III Part 1:** 34

"Iron Characters, The" (Nemerov), **III:** 279, 282

"Iron Hans" (Sexton), **Supp. II Part 2:** 691

Iron Heel, The (London), **II:** 466, 480

Iron John: A Book about Men (R. Bly), **Supp. IV Part 1:** 59, 67; **Supp. XVI:** 177

"Iron Table, The" (Jane Bowles), **Supp. IV Part 1:** 82–83

"Iron Throat, The" (Olsen), **Supp. XIII:** 292, 297, 299

Ironweed (W. Kennedy), **Supp. VII:** 132, 133, 134, 135, 142, 144, 145–147, 148, 150, 153

"Irony as Art: The Short Fiction of William Humphrey" (Tebeaux), **Supp. IX:** 109

"Irony Is Not Enough: Essay on My Life as Catherine Deneuve" (Carson), **Supp. XIII:** 112–113

Irony of American History, The (Niebuhr), **III:** 292, 306–307, 308

"Irrational Element in Poetry, The" (Stevens), **Retro. Supp. I:** 298, 301

"Irrevocable Diameter, An" (Paley), **Supp. VI:** 231–232

Irvine, Lorna, **Supp. XIII:** 26

Irving, Ebenezer, **II:** 296

Irving, Sir Henry, **IV:** 350

Irving, John, **Supp. VI:** 163–183; **Supp. X:** 77, 85

Irving, John Treat, **II:** 296

Irving, Peter, **II:** 296, 297, 298, 299, 300, 303

Irving, Washington, **I:** 211, 335, 336, 339, 343; **II: 295–318,** 488, 495; **III:** 113; **IV:** 309; **Retro. Supp. I:** 246; **Supp. I Part 1:** 155, 157, 158, 317; **Supp. I Part 2:** 377, 487, 585; **Supp. II Part 1:** 335; **Supp. IV Part 1:** 380; **Supp. XVIII:** 12; **Supp. XXIII:** 178

Irving, William, **II:** 296

Irving, William, Jr., **II:** 296, 297, 298, 299, 303

Irwin, Mark, **Supp. XII:** 21, 22, 24, 29

Irwin, Robert, **Supp. XX: 120**

Irwin, William Henry, **Supp. II Part 1:** 192

Is 5 (Cummings), **I:** 429, 430, 434, 435, 440, 445, 446, 447

"Isaac and Abraham" (Brodsky), **Supp. VIII:** 21

"Isaac and Archibald" (Robinson), **III:** 511, 521, 523

Isaacs, Neil D., **Supp. XIX:** 255

"Isabelle" (Saunders), **Supp. XIX:** 225

"Isabel Sparrow" (Oliver), **Supp. VII:** 232

Isaiah (biblical book), **Supp. I Part 1:** 236; **Supp. I Part 2:** 516; **Supp. XXI:** 107

"Isaiah Beethoven" (Masters), **Supp. I Part 2:** 461

I Sailed with Magellan (Dybek), **Supp. XXIII: 75–78,** 79

"I Saw in Louisiana a Live-Oak Growing" (Whitman), **I:** 220

"I Shall Be Released" (Dylan), **Supp. XV:** 349

"I Shall Live to Be Old" (Teasdale), **Supp. XXVII:** 296

I Shall Spit on Your Graves (film), **Supp. I Part 1:** 67

Isháq, Adib, **Supp. XX:** 117

Isherwood, Christopher, **II:** 586; **Supp. II Part 1:** 10, 11, 13; **Supp. IV Part 1:** 79, 82, 102; **Supp. XI:** 305; **Supp. XIV: 155–175; Supp. XVI:** 194

Isherwood Century, The (Berg and Freeman), **Supp. XIV:** 157, 159

Isherwood's Fiction (Schwerdt), **Supp. XIV:** 155

Ishiguro, Kazuo, **Supp. VIII:** 15

Ishi Means Man (Merton), **Supp. VIII:** 208

"Ishmael's Dream" (Stern), **Supp. IX:** 287

I Should Have Stayed Home (McCoy), **Supp. XIII:** 167, **168–170,** 171

"I Should Worry" (Kees), **Supp. XV:** 140

"I Sigh in the Afternoon" (Salinas), **Supp. XIII:** 318

"I Sing the Body Electric" (Whitman), **Retro. Supp. I:** 394, 395; **Retro. Supp. III:** 305

"Isis: Dorothy Eady, 1924" (Doty), **Supp. XI:** 122

"Is It O.K. to Be a Luddite?" (Pynchon), **Supp. XVI:** 128

"Is It True?" (Hughes), **Supp. I Part 1:** 342

I: Six Nonlectures (Cummings), **I:** 430, 433, 434

"Island" (Hughes), **Supp. I Part 1:** 340

"Island Fever" (Vaz), **Supp. XXVI:** 261

Island Garden, An (Thaxter), **Retro. Supp. II:** 136; **Supp. XIII:** 152

Island Holiday, An (Henry), **I:** 515

Island in the Atlantic (W. Frank), **Supp. XX:** 79

Island in the Sun (film), **Supp. XXVI:** 134

"Island of the Fay, The" (Poe), **III:** 412, 417

Islands (Siddons), **Supp. XXII:** 239

"Islands, The" (Hayden), **Supp. II Part 1:** 373

"Island Sheaf, An" (Doty), **Supp. XI:** 136

Islands in the Stream (Hemingway), **II:** 258; **Retro. Supp. I:** 186

Island Within, The (Lewisohn), **Supp. XXVIII:** 146, 149–150, 152–153, 156, 159

Isn't It Romantic (Wasserstein), **Supp. XV: 323–325,** 327

Is Objectivism a Religion? (Ellis), **Supp. IV Part 2:** 527

"Isolation of Modern Poetry, The" (Schwartz), **Supp. II Part 2:** 644

Israel (Lewisohn), **Supp. XXVIII:** 145, 146, 150, 157

"Israel" (Reznikoff), **Supp. XIV:** 283

Israel Potter: His Fifty Years of Exile (Melville), **III:** 90; **Retro. Supp. III:** 158–159; **Supp. XVIII:** 4

"Israfel" (Poe), **III:** 411

Is Sex Necessary? (Thurber and White), **Supp. I Part 2:** 607, 612, 614, 653

"Issues, The" (Olds), **Supp. X:** 205

"Istanbul" (Collins), **Supp. XXI:** 60

"I Stand Here Ironing" (Olsen), **Supp. XIII:** 292, 294, 296, 298, 300, 305

I Stole a Million (West), **IV:** 287

"Is Verse a Dying Technique?" (Wilson), **IV:** 431

It (Creeley), **Supp. IV Part 1:** 157, 158

IT (King), **Supp. V:** 139, 140, 141, 146–147, 151, 152

"It" (Olds), **Supp. X:** 208

It Ain't All for Nothin' (Myers), **Supp. XXVII:** 202–203

Italian American Reconciliation: A Folktale (Shanley), **Supp. XIV:** 315, **324–326,** 328, 330

Italian Backgrounds (Wharton), **Retro. Supp. I:** 370; **Retro. Supp. III:** 279

Italian Hours (James), **I:** 12; **II:** 337; **Retro. Supp. I:** 235

Italian Journeys (Howells), **II:** 274

"Italian Morning" (Bogan), **Supp. III Part 1:** 58

Italian Villas and Their Gardens (Wharton), **IV:** 308; **Retro. Supp. I:** 361, 367; **Retro. Supp. III:** 279–280

Italie, Hillel, **Supp. XV:** 128

It All Adds Up: From the Dim Past to the Uncertain Future (Bellow), **Retro. Supp. II:** 32

"It Always Breaks Out" (Ellison), **Retro. Supp. II:** 126; **Supp. II Part 1:** 248

Itard, Jean-Marc Gaspard, **Supp. I Part 2:** 564

"I taste a liquor never brewed" (Dickinson), **Retro. Supp. I:** 30, 37

It Came from Outer Space (film), **Supp. IV Part 1:** 102

It Can't Happen Here (Lewis), **II:** 454

It Chooses You (July), **Supp. XXIV:** 199, 209, 210

"It Don't Mean a Thing If It Ain't Got That Swing" (Matthews), **Supp. IX: 164–165**

I Tell You Now (Ortiz), **Supp. IV Part 2:** 500

"It Follows" (Stone), **Supp. XXVII:** 257

"It Goes Something Like This" (Gansworth), **Supp. XXVI:** 110

"Ithaca" (Glück), **Supp. V:** 89

It Happened One Night (Capra), **Supp. XV:** 197

It Has Come to Pass (Farrell), **II:** 26

"It Has Orange Teeth"(Lea), **Supp. XXVIII:** 137

"I think to live May be a Bliss" (Dickinson), **Retro. Supp. I:** 44

"I Thought It Was Harry" (Bronk), **Supp. XXI:** 31

I Thought of Daisy (Wilson), **IV:** 428, 434, 435

"It If Be Your Will" (Cohen), **Supp. XXVII:** 60

"Itinerary of an Obsession" (Kumin), **Supp. IV Part 2:** 450

"It Is a Strange Country" (Ellison), **Supp. II Part 1:** 238

"It Is Dangerous to Read Newspapers" (Atwood), **Supp. XIII:** 33

"It Is the Lesbian in Us ..." (Rich), **Retro. Supp. III:** 248

"It Must Be Abstract" (Stevens), **IV:** 95; **Retro. Supp. I:** 307

"It Must Change" (Stevens), **Retro. Supp. I:** 300, 307, 308

"It Must Give Pleasure" (Stevens), **Retro. Supp. I:** 307, 308, 309

"'It Out-Herods Herod. Pray You, Avoid It'" (Hecht), **Supp. X:** 62, 64

"It's All Over Now, Baby Blue" (song, Dylan), **Supp. XVIII:** 30

It's Loaded, Mr. Bauer (Marquand), **III:** 59

It's Nation Time (Baraka), **Supp. II Part 1:** 52, 53

"It's Nation Time" (Baraka), **Supp. II Part 1:** 53

It's Only a Play (McNally), **Supp. XIII:** 198

"It's Tartt—But Is It Art?" (*Vanity Fair*), **Supp. XXVII:** 277

It Was (Zukofsky), **Supp. III Part 2:** 630

"It Was Romance" (July), **Supp. XXIV:** 202–203

It Was the Nightingale (Ford), **III:** 470–471

"It Was When" (Snyder), **Supp. VIII:** 300

Ivanhoe (Scott), **I:** 216; **Supp. I Part 2:** 410

Ivan's Homecoming (Gold), **Supp. XXVIII:** 68, 69

Ivens, Bryna, **Supp. XV:** 311, 312

Ivens, Joris, **I:** 488; **Retro. Supp. I:** 184

"Iverson Boy, The" (Simpson), **Supp. IX:** 280

"Ives" (Rukeyser), **Supp. VI:** 273, 283

Ives, George H., **Supp. I Part 1:** 153

I've Seen the Promised Land (Myers), **Supp. XXVII:** 209

Ivory Grin, The (Macdonald), **Supp. IV Part 2:** 471, 472

"Ivory Novel, The" (Halliday), **Supp. XIX:** 90

Ivory Tower, The (James), **II:** 337–338

"Ivory Tower, The: Louis Untermeyer as Critic" (Aiken), **Supp. XV:** 298

Ivry, Sara, **Supp. XX:** 179

"Ivy Winding" (Ammons), **Supp. VII:** 33

Iwamatsu, Mako, **Supp. XXI:** 150

"I Wandered Lonely as a Cloud" (Wordsworth), **Retro. Supp. I:** 121–122; **Supp. X:** 73; **Supp. XIV:** 184

"I want, I want" (Plath), **Retro. Supp. II:** 246

"I Wanted to Be There When My Father Died" (Olds), **Supp. X:** 210

"I Want to Be a Father Like the Men" (Cisneros), **Supp. VII:** 71

"I Want to Be Miss America" (Alvarez), **Supp. VII:** 18

"I Want to Know Why" (Anderson), **I:** 114, 115, 116; **II:** 263

"I Want You Women Up North To Know" (Olsen), **Supp. XIII:** 292, 297

"I Was Born in Lucerne" (Levine), **Supp. V:** 181, 189

"'I Was Born': Slave Narratives, Their Status as Autobiography and as Literature"(Olney), **Supp. XXVIII:** 169

"I Was Marching"(Le Sueur), **Supp. XXIII:** 167

"I Was Really Very Hungry" (M. F. K. Fisher), **Supp. XVII:** 91

I Was Thinking of Beauty (Lea), **Supp. XXVIII:** 142

"I Went into the Maverick Bar" (Snyder), **Supp. VIII:** 301

"I Will Lie Down" (Swenson), **Supp. IV Part 2:** 640

I Will Say Beauty (C. Frost), **Supp. XV:** 96, **105–107**

I Wonder As I Wander (Hughes), **Retro. Supp. I:** 196, 203; **Supp. I Part 1:** 329, 332–333

I Would Have Saved Them If I Could (L. Michaels), **Supp. XVI:** 203, 205, **206–210**

"I Would Live in Your Love" (Teasdale), **Supp. XXVII:** 292

"Iya, the Camp-Eater" (Zitkala-Ša), **Supp. XXV:** 276

"Iyani: It goes this Way" (Gunn Allen), **Supp. IV Part 1:** 321

"I years had been from home" (Dickinson), **I:** 471

Iyer, Pico, **Supp. V:** 215

Izzo, David Garrett, **Supp. XIV:** 155, 156, 159, 160, 161, 163, 169, 171

J

Jab (Halliday), **Supp. XIX: 91–94**

"Jachid and Jechidah" (Singer), **IV:** 15

Jack and Jill (Alcott), **Supp. I Part 1:** 42

"Jack and the Beanstalk" (Hay), **Supp. XIV:** 124

"Jack in the Pot" (D. West), **Supp. XVIII:** 283

Jack Kelso (Masters), **Supp. I Part 2:** 456, 471–472

Jacklight (Erdrich), **Supp. IV Part 1:** 259, 270

Jack London, Hemingway, and the Constitution (Doctorow), **Supp. IV Part 1:** 220, 222, 224, 232, 235

Jackman, Harold, **Supp. XVIII:** 131

Jackpot (Caldwell), **I:** 304

"Jack Schmidt, Arts Administrator" (Keillor), **Supp. XVI:** 171

"Jack Schmidt on the Burning Sands" (Keillor), **Supp. XVI:** 171

Jackson, Amelia. *See* Holmes, Mrs. Oliver Wendell (Amelia Jackson)

Jackson, Andrew, **I:** 7, 20; **III:** 473; **IV:** 192, 248, 298, 334, 348; **Supp. I Part 2:** 456, 461, 473, 474, 493, 695

Jackson, Blyden, **Supp. I Part 1:** 337

Jackson, Charles, **Supp. I Part 1:** 303

Jackson, David Kelly, **Retro. Supp. III:** 237

Jackson, George, **Supp. I Part 1:** 66

Jackson, Helen Hunt, **I:** 459, 470; **Retro. Supp. I:** 26, 27, 30–31, 32, 33

Jackson, James, **Supp. I Part 1:** 302, 303

Jackson, J. O., **III:** 213

Jackson, Joe, **Supp. I Part 2:** 441

Jackson, Katherine Gauss, **Supp. VIII:** 124

Jackson, Lawrence, **Retro. Supp. II:** 113, 115

Jackson, Lawrence P., **Supp. XXII:** 140

Jackson, Melanie, **Supp. X:** 166

Jackson, Michael, **Supp. VIII:** 146

Jackson, Richard, **II:** 119; **Supp. IX:** 165

Jackson, Shelley, **Supp. XVIII:** 136

Jackson, Shirley, **Supp. IX: 113–130**

Jackson, Thomas J. ("Stonewall"), **IV:** 125, 126

"Jackson Hotel" (Hull), **Supp. XXI:** 134, 135

Jackson Pollock (O'Hara), **Supp. XXIII:** 214–215

"Jackson Square" (Levertov), **Supp. III Part 1:** 276

Jackstraws (Simic), **Supp. VIII:** 280, 282–283

"Jackstraws" (Simic), **Supp. VIII: 283**

Jack Tier (Cooper), **I:** 354, 355

"Jacob" (Garrett), **Supp. VII:** 109–110

"Jacob" (Schwartz), **Supp. II Part 2:** 663

Jacob, Max, **Supp. XV:** 178, 182

"Jacob and the Indians" (Benét), **Supp. XI:** 47–48

"Jacob Bayer and the Telephone" (Helprin), **Supp. XXV:** 81

Jacobs, Catherine Haydon, **Supp. XXI:** 98

Jacobs, Harriet, **Supp. XVI:** 85; **Supp. XXVIII:** 173

Jacobs, Jill Suzanne, **Supp. XX: 178, 186**

Jacobs, Rita D., **Supp. XII:** 339

Jacobsen, Jens Peter, **Retro. Supp. III:** 140

Jacobsen, Josephine, **Supp. XIII:** 346; **Supp. XIV:** 260

"Jacob's Ladder" (Rawlings), **Supp. X:** 224, 228

Jacob's Ladder, The (Levertov), **Supp. III Part 1:** 272, 276–278, 281

"Jacob's Ladder, The" (Levertov), **Supp. III Part 1:** 278

Jacobson, Dale, **Supp. X:** 112

Jacobson, Kristin, **Supp. XVIII:** 113

Jacobson, Leslie, **Supp. XV:** 323

Jacoby, Russell, **Supp. IV Part 2:** 692

"Jacquerie, The" (Lanier), **Supp. I Part 1:** 355, 356, 360, 364, 370

Jacques le fataliste (D. Diderot), **Supp. XVII:** 145

Jade Mountain, The: A Chinese Anthology, Being Three Hundred Poems of the T'ang Dynasty (Bynner, trans.), **II:** 527; **Supp. XV:** 46, 47, 48

Jafsie and John Henry: Essays on Hollywood, Bad Boys, and Six Hours of Perfect Poker (Mamet), **Supp. XIV:** 252

Jaggi, Maya, **Supp. XXV:** 50, 56, 57

Jaguar Totem (LaBastille), **Supp. X:** 99, 106, **107–109**

Jailbird (Vonnegut), **Supp. II Part 2:** 760, 779–780

Jailbirds (Sinclair), **Supp. XXVIII:** 74

Jaimes, M. Annette, **Supp. IV Part 1:** 330, 331

Jain, Devaki, **Supp. XXVIII:** 60

Jain, Manju, **Retro. Supp. I:** 53, 58

"Jake Flower, The" (Major), **Supp. XXII:** 182

Jake's Women (Simon), **Supp. IV Part 2:** 576, 588

"Jakie's Mother" (Fante), **Supp. XI:** 164

Jakobson, Roman, **Supp. IV Part 1:** 155

Jamaica 1968 (Brainard), **Supp. XXVII:** 27

"Jamaica Kincaid's New York" (Kincaid), **Supp. VII:** 181

James, Alice, **I:** 454; **Retro. Supp. I:** 228, 235

James, A. Lloyd, **Supp. XIV:** 343

James, Caryn, **Supp. X:** 302, 303

James, C. L. R., **Retro. Supp. III:** 162

James, C. L. R. (Cyril Lionel Robert), **Supp. XXI: 159–173**

James, Etta, **Supp. X:** 242

James, Henry, **I:** 4, 5, 9, 10, 12, 15, 16, 20, 52, 93, 109, 211, 226, 228, 244, 246, 251, 255, 258, 259, 336, 363, 374, 375, 379, 384, 409, 429, 436, 439, 452, 454, 459, 461–462, 463, 464, 485, 500, 504, 513, 514, 517–518, 571; **II:** 38, 58, 60, 73, 74, 95, 138, 140, 144, 147, 196, 198, 199, 228, 230, 234, 243, 259, 267, 271, 272, 275, 276, 278, 281, 282, 283, 284, 285, 286, 287, 288, 290, 306, 309, 316, **319–341,** 398, 404, 410, 415, 427, 444, 542, 544, 547–548, 556, 600; **III:** 44, 51, 136, 194–195, 199, 206, 208, 218, 228–229, 237, 281, 319, 325, 326, 334, 409, 453, 454, 457, 460, 461, 464, 511, 522, 576, 607; **IV:** 8, 27, 34, 37, 40, 53, 58, 73, 74, 134, 168, 172, 182, 198, 202, 285, 308, 309, 310, 311, 314, 316, 317, 318, 319, 321, 322, 323, 324, 328, 347, 352, 359, 433, 439, 476; **Retro. Supp. I:** 1, 8, 53, 56, 59, 108, 112, **215–242,** 272, 283, 284, 362, 366, 367, 368, 371, 373, 374, 375, 376, 377, 378, 379; **Retro. Supp. II:** 93, 135, 136, 203, 223; **Retro. Supp. III:** 20, 22, 26, 60, 275, 279, 281; **Supp. I Part 1:** 35, 38, 43; **Supp. I Part 2:** 414, 454, 608, 609, 612–613, 618, 620, 646; **Supp. II Part 1:** 94–95; **Supp. III Part 1:** 14, 200;

Supp. III Part 2: 410, 412; **Supp. IV Part 1:** 31, 35, 80, 127, 197, 349, 353; **Supp. IV Part 2:** 613, 677, 678, 682, 689, 693; **Supp. IX:** 121; **Supp. V:** 97, 101, 103, 258, 261, 263, 313; **Supp. VIII:** 98, 102, 156, 166, 168; **Supp. XI:** 153; **Supp. XIII:** 102; **Supp. XIV:** 40, 110, 112, 335, 336, 348, 349; **Supp. XV:** 41; **Supp. XVII:** 5, 47; **Supp. XVIII:** 160, 258; **Supp. XX: 227, 228, 232, 233, 238, 240; Supp. XXI:** 225; **Supp. XXII:** 89; **Supp. XXIV:** 132, 224; **Supp. XXVI:** 141, 145; **Supp. XXVII:** 268; **Supp. XXVIII:** 112, 237

James, Henry (father), **II:** 7, 275, 321, 337, 342–344, 364; **IV:** 174; **Supp. I Part 1:** 300

James, Henry (nephew), **II:** 360

James, Horace, **Supp. XIV:** 57

James, P. D., **Supp. XIX:** 131

James, William, **I:** 104, 220, 224, 227, 228, 255, 454; **II:** 20, 27, 165, 166, 276, 321, 337, **342–366,** 411; **III:** 303, 309, 509, 599, 600, 605, 606, 612; **IV:** 26, 27, 28–29, 31, 32, 34, 36, 37, 43, 46, 291, 486; **Retro. Supp. I:** 57, 216, 227, 228, 235, 295, 300, 306; **Retro. Supp. III:** 99; **Supp. I Part 1:** 3, 7, 11, 20; **Supp. XIV:** 40, 50, 197, 199, 212, 335; **Supp. XVII:** 97; **Supp. XXVII:** 33, 34

James, William (grandfather), **II:** 342

James Baldwin: The Legacy (Troupe, ed.), **Retro. Supp. II:** 15

James Baldwin—The Price of the Ticket (film), **Retro. Supp. II:** 2

James Dickey and the Politics of Canon (Suarez), **Supp. IV Part 1:** 175

"James Dickey on Yeats: An Interview" (Dickey), **Supp. IV Part 1:** 177

James Hogg: A Critical Study (Simpson), **Supp. IX:** 269, 276

"James Is a Girl" (Egan), **Supp. XIX:** 61

James Jones: A Friendship (Morris), **Supp. XI:** 234

James Jones: An American Literary Orientalist Master (Carter), **Supp. XI:** 220

"James Jones and Jack Kerouac: Novelists of Disjunction" (Stevenson), **Supp. XI:** 230

James Jones: Reveille to Taps (television documentary), **Supp. XI:** 234

Jameson, Anna Brownell, **Supp. XXIII:** 225, 226, 232, 235

Jameson, F. R., **Supp. IV Part 1:** 119

Jameson, Sir Leander Starr, **III:** 327

James Shore's Daughter (Benét), **Supp. XI:** 48

"James Thurber" (Pollard), **Supp. I Part 2:** 468

"James Whitcomb Riley (From a Westerner's Point of View)" (Dunbar), **Supp. II Part 1:** 198

Jammes, Francis, **II:** 528; **Retro. Supp. I:** 55

Jamming with the Band at the VFW (Bottoms), **Supp. XXVIII:** 23

"Jan, the Son of Thomas" (Sandburg), **III:** 593–594

Jan. 31 (Goldbarth), **Supp. XII:** 177, **178–179,** 180

"Jane Awake"(O'Hara), **Supp. XXIII:** 210

Janeczko, Paul, **Supp. XIII:** 280

Jane Eyre (Brontë), **Supp. XVI:** 158; **Supp. XXII:** 120

"Jane Lampton Clemens" (Twain), **Retro. Supp. III:** 256

Janet, Pierre, **I:** 248, 249, 252; **Retro. Supp. I:** 55, 57

Jane Talbot: A Novel (Brown), **Supp. I Part 1:** 145–146

"Janet Waking" (Ransom), **III:** 490, 491

"Janice" (Jackson), **Supp. IX:** 117

Janowitz, Tama, **Supp. X:** 7; **Supp. XXVII:** 68, 269

Jantz, Harold S., **Supp. I Part 1:** 112

"January" (Barthelme), **Supp. IV Part 1:** 54

"January" (W. V. Davis), **Supp. XXI:** 89, 90

January Man, The (screenplay, Shanley), **Supp. XIV:** 316

"January Thaw" (Leopold), **Supp. XIV:** 183–184

"Janus" (Beattie), **Supp. V:** 31

Janzen, Jean, **Supp. V:** 180

"Japan" (Collins), **Supp. XXI:** 56

Japanese Americans: The Formation and Transformations of an Ethnic Group (Spickard), **Supp. XXI:** 149

"Japanese Beetles" (X. J. Kennedy), **Supp. XV:** 161, 165

Japanese by Spring (Reed), **Supp. X:** 241, **253–255**

Japanese Cooking: A Simple Art (Tsuji), **Supp. XVII:** 90

"Japan's Young Dreams" (Geisel), **Supp. XVI:** 102

Jara, Victor, **Supp. IV Part 2:** 549

Jarecki, Dave, **Supp. XXIII:** 239

Jarecki, Nicholas, **Supp. XXVII:** 68

Jarman, Mark, **Supp. IV Part 1:** 68; **Supp. IX:** 266, 270, 276; **Supp. XII:** 209; **Supp. XV:** 251; **Supp. XVIII:** 178; **Supp. XXV:** 221–222

Jarmon, Mark, **Supp. XVII: 109–122**

Jarrell, Randall, **I:** 167, 169, 173, 180; **II: 367–390,** 539–540; **III:** 134, 194, 213, 268, 527; **IV:** 352, 411, 422; **Retro. Supp. I:** 52, 121, 135, 140; **Retro. Supp. II:** 44, 177, 178, 182; **Supp. I Part 1:** 89; **Supp. I Part 2:** 552; **Supp. II Part 1:** 109, 135; **Supp. III Part 1:** 64; **Supp. III Part 2:** 541, 550; **Supp. IV Part 2:** 440; **Supp. IX:** 94, 268; **Supp. V:** 315, 318, 323; **Supp. VIII:** 31, 100, 271; **Supp. XI:** 311, 315; **Supp. XII:** 121, 260, 297; **Supp. XV:** 93, 153; **Supp. XVII:** 111; **Supp. XXVI:** 67

Jarrell, Mrs. Randall (Mary von Schrader), **II:** 368, 385

Jarry, Alfred, **Retro. Supp. II:** 326; **Supp. XV:** 177–178, 182, 188

Jarvis, John Wesley, **Supp. I Part 2:** 501, 520

Jaskoski, Helen, **Supp. IV Part 1:** 325; **Supp. XXII:** 166

"Jasmine" (Komunyakaa), **Supp. XIII:** 132

"Jason" (Hecht), **Supp. X:** 62

"Jason" (MacLeish), **III:** 4

Jason and Medeia (Gardner), **Supp. VI:** 63, **68–69**

Jason the Sailor (Wakoski), **Supp. XXVIII:** 270

"Jasper Notes" (G. Jones), **Supp. XXIV:** 194

Jaspers, Karl, **III:** 292; **IV:** 491

Jauss, David, **Supp. XXI:** 129, 132, 133, 134, 139

Jay, William, **I:** 338

Jayber Crow (Berry), **Supp. X:** 28, 34

"Jaz Fantasia" (Sandburg), **III:** 585

Jazz (Morrison), **Retro. Supp. III:** 184, 193, 194, 195

Jazz (Myers), **Supp. XXVII:** 211

"Jazz Age Clerk, A" (Farrell), **II:** 45

Jazz Country: Ralph Ellison in America (Porter), **Retro. Supp. II:** 127

"Jazzonia" (Hughes), **Supp. I Part 1:** 324

Jazz Poetry Anthology, The (Komunyakaa and Feinstein, eds.), **Supp. XIII:** 125

"Jazztet Muted" (Hughes), **Supp. I Part 1:** 342

J. B.: A Play in Verse (MacLeish), **II:** 163, 228; **III:** 3, 21–22, 23; **Supp. IV Part 2:** 586

"Jealous" (Ford), **Supp. V:** 71

Jealous Gods, The (Atherton), **Supp. XXIV:** 26

Jealousies, The: A Faery Tale, by Lucy Vaughan Lloyd of China Walk, Lambeth (Keats), **Supp. XII:** 113

Jean Baptiste Le Moyne, Sieur de Bienville (King), **Supp. XXVIII:** 116

Jean-Christophe (Rolland), **Supp. XX:** 70

"Jean Harlow's Wedding Night" (Wasserstein), **Supp. XV:** 328

Jean Huguenot (Benét), **Supp. XI:** 44

"Jeff Briggs's Love Story" (Harte), **Supp. II Part 1:** 355

Jeffers, Robinson, **I:** 66; **III:** 134; **Retro. Supp. I:** 202; **Retro. Supp. III:** 250; **Supp. II Part 2: 413–440; Supp. IX:** 77; **Supp. VIII:** 33, 292; **Supp. X:** 112; **Supp. XI:** 312; **Supp. XV:** 113, 114, 115; **Supp. XVII:** 111, 112, 117; **Supp. XXI:** 87; **Supp. XXIII:** 145

Jeffers, Una Call Kuster (Mrs. Robinson Jeffers), **Supp. II Part 2:** 414

Jefferson, Blind Lemon, **Supp. VIII:** 349

Jefferson, Margo, **Supp. XX: 87; Supp. XXIV:** 271

Jefferson, Thomas, **I:** 1, 2, 5, 6–8, 14, 485; **II:** 5, 6, 34, 217, 300, 301, 437; **III:** 3, 17, 18, 294–295, 306, 310, 473, 608; **IV:** 133, 243, 249, 334, 348; **Retro. Supp. III:** 148; **Supp. I Part 1:** 146, 152, 153, 229, 230, 234, 235; **Supp. I Part 2:** 389, 399, 456, 474, 475, 482, 507, 509, 510, 511, 516, 518–519, 520, 522; **Supp. X:** 26; **Supp. XIV:** 191; **Supp. XX:** 285; **Supp. XXIV:** 85, 281

Jefferson and/or Mussolini (Pound), **Retro. Supp. I:** 292

"Jefferson Davis as a Representative American" (Du Bois), **Supp. II Part 1:** 161

J-E-L-L-O (Baraka), **Supp. II Part 1:** 47

"Jelly-Bean, The" (Fitzgerald), **II:** 88

"Jellyfish, A" (Moore), **III:** 215

Jemie, Onwuchekwa, **Supp. I Part 1:** 343

"Jemima of the Seventh Floor"(Stuart), **Supp. XXVIII:** 237

Jenkins, Jerry B., **Supp. XXVII:** 5

Jenkins, J. L., **I:** 456

Jenkins, Joe, **Supp. XX: 117, 120, 122**

Jenkins, Kathleen, **III:** 403

Jenkins, Susan, **IV:** 123

Jenks, Deneen, **Supp. IV Part 2:** 550, 554

Jenks, Tom, **Supp. XIX:** 51

Jenkyns, Richard, **Supp. XXV:** 223

Jennie Gerhardt (Dreiser), **I:** 497, 499, 500, 501, 504–505, 506, 507, 519; **Retro. Supp. II:** 94, **99–101**

"Jennie M'Grew" (Masters), **Supp. I Part 2:** 468

Jennifer Lorn (Wylie), **Supp. I Part 2:** 709, 714–717, 718, 721, 724

Jennison, Peter S., **Supp. XIX:** 268

"Jenny Garrow's Lover" (Jewett), **II:** 397

"Jerboa, The" (Moore), **III:** 203, 207, 209, 211–212

Jeremiah, **Supp. X:** 35

Jeremy's Version (Purdy), **Supp. VII:** 274

"Je Reviens"(Dybek), **Supp. XXIII:** 78

"Jericho" (R. Lowell), **II:** 536

Jerome, Judson, **Supp. XXIII:** 54

Jerry (Elliott), **Supp. XXVIII:** 228

"Jerry's Garage" (Budbill), **Supp. XIX:** 7

"Jersey City Gendarmerie, Je T'aime" (Lardner), **II:** 433

Jersey Rain (Pinsky), **Supp. VI:** 235, **247–250**

"Jerusalem" (Nye), **Supp. XIII:** 287

Jerusalem: Song of Songs (Uris), **Supp. XX: 244–245, 246, 255**

Jerusalem the Golden (Reznikoff), **Supp. XIV:** 280, 285, 286

"Jessekiah Brown's Courtship"(Stuart), **Supp. XXVIII:** 231

"Jessie and Jesus" (Andrews), **Supp. XXVI:** 11

Jessie and Jesus and Cousin Claire (Andrews), **Supp. XXVI:** 2, 10, 11–12

Jessup, Richard, **Supp. XI:** 306

"*Je Suis Perdu*" (Taylor), **Supp. V:** 314, 321–322

Jesuits in North America in the Seventeenth Century, The (Parkman), **Supp. II Part 2:** 597, 603–605

Jesus, **I:** 27, 34, 68, 89, 136, 552, 560; **II:** 1, 16, 197, 198, 214, 215, 216, 218, 219, 239, 373, 377, 379, 537, 538, 539, 549, 569, 585, 591, 592; **III:** 39, 173, 179, 270, 291, 296–297, 300, 303, 305, 307, 311, 339, 340, 341, 342, 344, 345, 346, 347, 348, 352, 353, 354, 355, 436, 451, 489, 534, 564, 566, 567, 582; **IV:** 51, 69, 86, 107, 109, 117, 137, 138, 141, 144, 147, 149, 150, 151, 152, 155, 156, 157, 158, 159, 163, 164, 232, 241, 289, 293, 294, 296, 331, 364, 392, 396, 418, 430; **Supp. I Part 1:** 2, 54, 104, 107, 108, 109, 121, 267, 371; **Supp. I Part 2:** 379, 386, 458, 515, 580, 582, 583, 587, 588, 683; **Supp. V:** 280

Jesus, the Son of Man (Gibran), **Supp. XX: 115–116, 117, 122–123**

"Jesus Asleep" (Sexton), **Supp. II Part 2:** 693

"Jesus of Nazareth, Then and Now" (Price), **Supp. VI:** 268

"Jesus Papers, The" (Sexton), **Supp. II Part 2:** 693

"Jesus Raises Up the Harlot" (Sexton), **Supp. II Part 2:** 693

"Jesus Shaves" (Davison), **Supp. XXVI:** 74

"Jesus Stories, The" (Brockmeier), **Supp. XXII:** 52

Jetée, La (film), **Supp. IV Part 2:** 436

"Jetty, The"(Lea), **Supp. XXVIII:** 139

"Jeune Parque, La" (Valéry), **IV:** 92

"Jew as Writer/The Writer as Jew, The: Reflections on Literature and Identity" (Apple), **Supp. XVII:** 1, 9

"Jewbird, The" (Malamud), **Supp. I Part 2:** 435

"Jewboy, The" (P. Roth), **Supp. III Part 2:** 412

"Jewels" (Teasdale), **Supp. XXVII:** 290, 291

Jewett, Caroline, **II:** 396

Jewett, Katharine, **Retro. Supp. II:** 46

Jewett, Mary, **II:** 396, 403

Jewett, Rutger, **Retro. Supp. I:** 381

Jewett, Sarah Orne, **I:** 313; **II: 391–414; Retro. Supp. I:** 6, 7, 19; **Retro. Supp. II:** 51, 52, **131–151**, 156; **Retro. Supp. III:** 22, 26, 37; **Supp. I Part 2:** 495; **Supp. IX:** 79; **Supp. VIII:** 126; **Supp. XIII:** 153; **Supp. XXIII:** 275, 278; **Supp. XXVIII:** 235

Jewett, Theodore Furber, **II:** 395

Jewett, Dr. Theodore Herman, **II:** 396–397, 402

"Jew for Export, The" (Mamet), **Supp. XIV:** 251–252

Jew in Love, A (Hecht), **Supp. XXVII:** 94

Jew in Our Day, The (W. Frank), **Supp. XX: 79**

Jew in the American Novel, The (Fiedler), **Supp. XIII:** 106

"Jewish Graveyards, Italy" (Levine), **Supp. V:** 190

"Jewish Hunter, The" (Moore), **Supp. X:** 163, 165, **174**

Jewison, Norman, **Supp. XI:** 306; **Supp. XIV:** 316

"Jew of Persia, A" (Helprin), **Supp. XXV:** 80, 85

Jews of Shklov (Schneour), **IV:** 11

Jews Without Money (Gold), **Supp. XIV:** 288–289; **Supp. XXVIII:** 65, 66, 67, 68, 69, 76–78, 79

JFK (film), **Supp. XIV:** 48

Jig Cook and the Provincetwon Players (Sarlós), **Supp. XXVIII:** 38–39

Jig of Forslin, The: A Symphony (Aiken), **I:** 50, 51, 57, 62, 66

Jigonsaseh, **Supp. XXVI:** 81, 82, 83, 86

"Jig Tune: Not for Love" (McGrath), **Supp. X:** 116

"Jihad" (McClatchy), **Supp. XII:** 266

"Jilting of Granny Weatherall, The" (Porter), **III:** 434, 435, 438

"Jim Baker's Blue-Jay Yarn" (Twain), **Retro. Supp. III:** 255, 268

Jim Crow's Last Stand (Hughes), **Retro. Supp. I:** 205

Jiménez, Juan Ramón, **Supp. XIII:** 315, 323

Jimmie Higgins (Sinclair), **Supp. V:** 288

"Jimmy Harlow" (X. J. Kennedy), **Supp. XV:** 170

Jimmy's Blues (Baldwin), **Retro. Supp. II:** 8, 9, 15

Jim's Book: A Collection of Poems and Short Stories (Merrill), **Supp. III Part 1:** 319

"Jim Smiley and His Jumping Frog" (Twain), **Retro. Supp. III:** 255, 257, 260

Jin, Ha, **Supp. XVIII: 89–104**

Jitney (Wilson), **Retro. Supp. III:** 318, 321; **Supp. VIII:** 330, 331, 351

Jitterbug Perfume (Robbins), **Supp. X:** 273, **274–276,** 279

Joachim, Harold, **Retro. Supp. I:** 58

Joan, Pope, **IV:** 165

"Joan"(Goodman), **Supp. XXVIII:** 88

Joanna and Ulysses (Sarton), **Supp. VIII: 254–255**

Joan of Arc, **IV:** 241; **Supp. I Part 1:** 286–288; **Supp. I Part 2:** 469

"Joan of Arc" (Cohen), **Supp. XXVII:** 59

Joans, Ted, **Supp. IV Part 1:** 169

Job (biblical book), **II:** 165, 166–167, 168; **III:** 21, 199, 512; **IV:** 13, 158; **Supp. I Part 1:** 125

Job, The (Burroughs and Odier), **Supp. III Part 1:** 97, 103

Job, The: An American Novel (Lewis), **II:** 441

"Job History" (Proulx), **Supp. VII:** 262

Jobim, Antonio Carlos, **Supp. IV Part 2:** 549

Jobim, Antônio Carlos, **Supp. XXI:** 100

"Job of the Plains, A" (Humphrey), **Supp. IX:** 101

Jocks, Christopher, **Supp. XXVI:** 97

"Jody Rolled the Bones" (Yates), **Supp. XI:** 335, 341

"Joe" (Alvarez), **Supp. VII:** 7–8

Joe (Brown), **Supp. XVIII:** 195

Joe (L. Brown), **Supp. XXI:** 41, **45–46,** 47

"Joe, the Vanishing American" (Swados), **Supp. XIX:** 258–259

Joe: A Memoir of Joe Brainard (Padgett), **Supp. XXVII:** 18

"Joe Hill" (Hayes), **Supp. XXVI:** 134

Joe Hill: A Biographical Novel (Stegner), **Supp. IV Part 2:** 599

Joe Jones (Lamott), **Supp. XX: 134–135**

"Joe"(King), **Supp. XXVIII:** 116

"Joe Louis: The King as a Middle-Aged Man" (Talese), **Supp. XVII:** 202

"Joe Messenger Is Dreaming"(P. Benedict), **Supp. XXIII:** 47

"Joe's Jitters" (Bronk), **Supp. XXI:** 27

Joe Turner's Come and Gone (Wilson), **Retro. Supp. III:** 318, 325–326; **Supp. VIII:** 334, **337–342,** 345

Joe versus the Volcano (screenplay, Shanley), **Supp. XIV:** 316

"Joey Martiney" (Huncke), **Supp. XIV:** 149

Johannes in Eremo (Mather), **Supp. II Part 2:** 453

Johansen, Bruce E., **Supp. XXVI:** 98

John XXIII, Pope, **Supp. I Part 2:** 492

John (biblical book), **I:** 68; **Supp. XV:** 222, 224

"John" (Shields), **Supp. VII:** 310–311

John, Augustus, **Supp. XXII:** 157

John, Elton, **Supp. XXI:** 148

"John, John Chinaman" (Buck), **Supp. II Part 1:** 128

John, Orrick, **Supp. XXVI:** 134

John Addington Symonds: A Biographical Study (Brooks), **I:** 240, 241

John-a Dreams: A Tale (J. Sturgis), **Supp. XX: 233**

"John Archer's Nose" (R. Fisher), **Supp. XIX:** 71–72, 78

John Barleycorn (London), **II:** 467, 481

John Brown (Du Bois), **Supp. II Part 1:** 171–172

"John Brown" (Emerson), **II:** 13

"John Brown" (Lindsay), **Supp. I Part 2:** 393

John Brown's Body (Benét), **II:** 177; **Supp. XI:** 45, 46, 47, **56–57**

John Brown: The Making of a Martyr (Warren), **IV:** 236

John Bull in America; or, The New Munchausen (Paulding), **I:** 344

"John Burke" (Olson), **Supp. II Part 2:** 579, 580

"John Burns of Gettysburg" (Harte), **Supp. II Part 1:** 343

"John Carter" (Agee), **I:** 27

John Chancellor Makes Me Cry (Siddons), **Supp. XXII:** 245

"John Coltrane: Where Does Art Come From?" (Baraka), **Supp. II Part 1:** 60

John Deth: A Metaphysical Legend and Other Poems (Aiken), **I:** 61

"John Endicott" (Longfellow), **II:** 505, 506; **Retro. Supp. II:** 165–166, 167

"John Evereldown" (Robinson), **III:** 524

John Fante Reader, The (Cooper, ed.), **Supp. XI:** 174

John Fante: Selected Letters, 1932–1981 (Cooney, ed.), **Supp. XI:** 170

"John Gardner: The Writer As Teacher" (Carver), **Supp. III Part 1:** 136, 146–147

John Gaunt (R. H. Davis), **Supp. XVI:** 89

John Jay Chapman and His Letters (Howe), **Supp. XIV:** 54

John Keats (A. Lowell), **II:** 530–531

John Kennedy Toole: The Omega Point (film, Sandord), **Supp. XXVI:** 240, 241, 243, 246, 253

"John Kinsella's Lament for Mrs. Mary Moore" (Yeats), **Supp. XVII:** 144

"John Lamar" (R. H. Davis), **Supp. XVI:** 89–90

John Lane, **Retro. Supp. I:** 59

"John L. Sullivan" (Lindsay), **Supp. I Part 2:** 394, 395

"John Marr" (Melville), **III:** 93

John Marr and Other Sailors (Melville), **III:** 93; **Retro. Supp. I:** 257; **Retro. Supp. III:** 161

John Muir: A Reading Bibliography (Kimes and Kimes), **Supp. IX:** 178

Johnny Appleseed and Other Poems (Lindsay), **Supp. I Part 2:** 397

"Johnny Bear" (Steinbeck), **IV:** 67

Johnny Got His Gun (Trumbo), **Supp. XXI:** 45

"Johnny Mnemonic" (W. Gibson), **Supp. XVI:** 122, 123–125, 128, 131

"Johnny Panic and the Bible of Dreams" (Plath), **Retro. Supp. II:** 245

"Johnny Ray" (Ríos), **Supp. IV Part 2:** 543

Johnny Tremain (Forbes), **Supp. XIX:** 235

John of the Cross (Saint), **I:** 585; **Supp. IV Part 1:** 284; **Supp. XV:** 223; **Supp. XVII:** 112

John Paul Jones: A Sailor's Biography (Morison), **Supp. I Part 2:** 494–495

"John Redding Goes to Sea" (Hurston), **Retro. Supp. III:** 127; **Supp. VI:** 150

"John Reed and the Real Thing"(Gold), **Supp. XXVIII:** 75

Johns, George Sibley, **Retro. Supp. II:** 65

Johns, Jasper, **Supp. XXIII:** 217

Johns, Orrick, **Retro. Supp. II:** 71; **Supp. XXVII:** 285

John Sloan: A Painter's Life (Brooks), **I:** 254

"John Smith Liberator" (Bierce), **I:** 209

Johnson, Alexandra, **Supp. X:** 86

Johnson, Alvin, **I:** 236; **Supp. XV:** 304

Johnson, Ben, **Retro. Supp. I:** 56

Johnson, Buffie, **Supp. IV Part 1:** 94

Johnson, Caitlin, **Supp. XXIII:** 281

Johnson, Carol Siri, **Supp. XXIII:** 257, 258, 264, 269

Johnson, Charles, **Supp. I Part 1:** 325; **Supp. V:** 128; **Supp. VI: 185–201;** **Supp. X:** 239; **Supp. XIII:** 182; **Supp. XIX:** 160

Johnson, Charles S., **Supp. IX:** 309; **Supp. XXII:** 6, 7

Johnson, Claudia Durst, **Supp. VIII:** 126–127

Johnson, Clifton, **Supp. XXI:** 248, 250

Johnson, Denis, **Supp. XIX:** 209; **Supp. XXI:** 118, 131

Johnson, Diane, **Retro. Supp. I:** 196; **Supp. XIII:** 127

Johnson, Eastman, **IV:** 321

Johnson, Edward, **IV:** 157; **Supp. I Part 1:** 110, 115

Johnson, Fenton, **Supp. XI:** 129

Johnson, Georgia Douglas, **Supp. IV Part 1:** 164

Johnson, Helene, **Supp. XVIII:** 282; **Supp. XXVI: 163–176**
Johnson, James Weldon, **Retro. Supp. II:** 114; **Retro. Supp. III:** 127; **Supp. I Part 1:** 324, 325; **Supp. II Part 1:** 33, 194, 200, 202–203, 206–207; **Supp. III Part 1:** 73; **Supp. IV Part 1:** 7, 11, 15, 16, 164, 165, 166, 169; **Supp. X:** 42, 136, **246; Supp. XIX:** 73; **Supp. XVIII:** 122, 127, 282
Johnson, Jeff, **Supp. XXV:** 98
Johnson, Joyce, **Supp. XIV:** 150
Johnson, Kent, **Supp. XV:** 347
Johnson, Lady Bird, **Supp. IV Part 1:** 22
Johnson, Laura K., **Retro. Supp. III:** 288
Johnson, Liza, **Supp. XXVIII:** 205, 206
Johnson, Lyndon B., **I:** 254; **II:** 553, 582; **Retro. Supp. II:** 27
Johnson, Marguerite. *See* Angelou, Maya
Johnson, Mat, **Retro. Supp. III:** 236
Johnson, Maurice, **Supp. XV:** 136, 137, 138
Johnson, Michael K., **Supp. XVIII:** 59, 64
Johnson, Mordecai, **Supp. XIV:** 202
Johnson, Nunnally, **Supp. IV Part 1:** 355
Johnson, Pamela Hansford, **IV:** 469
Johnson, Rafer, **Supp. I Part 1:** 271
Johnsrud, Reed, **Supp. IV Part 2:** 589
Johnson, Richard, **Supp. XIII:** 132
Johnson, Robert, **Supp. IV Part 1:** 146; **Supp. VIII:** 15, 134
Johnson, Robert K., **Supp. IV Part 2:** 573, 584
Johnson, Robert Underwood, **Supp. IX:** 182, 184, 185
Johnson, Samuel, **II:** 295; **III:** 491, 503; **IV:** 452; **Retro. Supp. I:** 56, 65; **Supp. I Part 1:** 33; **Supp. I Part 2:** 422, 498, 503, 523, 656; **Supp. IV Part 1:** 34, 124; **Supp. XI:** 209; **Supp. XII:** 159; **Supp. XIII:** 55, 347; **Supp. XVI:** 204; **Supp. XVII:** 1; **Supp. XXIV:** 152
Johnson, Samuel, Jr., **Supp. XXV:** 241, 250
Johnson, Sarah Anne, **Supp. XIX:** 49, 50, 52, 54, 55, 56, 58, 59, 60, 61; **Supp. XVIII:** 145
Johnson, Steve, **Supp. XVI:** 177
Johnson, Thomas H., **I:** 470–471; **IV:** 144, 158; **Retro. Supp. I:** 26, 28, 36, 39, 40, 41, 43
Johnson, Walter, **II:** 422
Johnson, Willard "Spud", **Supp. XV:** 42, 46
"Johnson Girls, The" (Bambara), **Supp. XI:** 7
Johnsrud, Harold, **II:** 562
Johnston, Basil, **Supp. IV Part 1:** 269
Johnston, Jill, **Supp. XXV:** 5
Johnston, Mary, **II:** 194
Johnston, Robert M., **Supp. I Part 1:** 369
"John Sutter" (Winters), **Supp. II Part 2:** 810
John's Wife (Coover), **Supp. V:** 51–52
John the Baptist, **I:** 389; **II:** 537, 591
John Wesley Harding (album, Dylan), **Supp. XVIII:** 27

Jolas, Eugène, **Retro. Supp. II:** 85, 328; **Supp. IV Part 1:** 80
Jolie Blon's Bounce (Burke), **Supp. XIV:** 26, 33–34
Jolly (Mamet), **Supp. XIV:** 240, 254
"Jolly Corner, The" (James), **I:** 571; **Retro. Supp. I:** 235
Jolly Plays for Holidays (Wells), **Supp. XXVI:** 275
"Jon" (Saunders), **Supp. XIX:** 232, 234
"Jonah" (R. Lowell), **II:** 536
Jonah's Gourd Vine (Hurston), **Retro. Supp. III:** 126, 128–129, 132, 139; **Supp. VI:** 149, 155
"Jonathan Edwards" (Holmes), **Supp. I Part 1:** 302, 315
"Jonathan Edwards in Western Massachusetts" (R. Lowell), **II:** 550
Jonathan Franzen at the End of Postmodernism (Burns), **Supp. XX: 85**
Jonathan Troy (Abbey), **Supp. XIII:** 4, 13
Jones, Anne, **Supp. X:** 8
Jones, Anne Goodwyn, **Supp. XXII:** 252; **Supp. XXVIII: 120–121, 123**
Jones, Carolyn M., **Supp. VIII:** 128; **Supp. XIX:** 160
Jones, Chuck, **Supp. XVI:** 102
Jones, David, **Supp. XVII:** 241
Jones, Dennis, **Supp. XXIII:** 228, 233
Jones, Derek Anson, **Supp. XVIII:** 38, 39
Jones, Edith Newbold. *See* Wharton, Edith
Jones, Edward P., **Supp. XXI:** 247; **Supp. XXII: 139–153**
Jones, E. Stanley, **III:** 297
Jones, Everett LeRoi. *See* Baraka, Imamu Amiri
Jones, Gayl, **Retro. Supp. III:** 184, 194; **Supp. XXIV: 183–197**
Jones, George Frederic, **IV:** 309
Jones, Grover, **Supp. XIII:** 166
Jones, Harry, **Supp. I Part 1:** 337
Jones, Harry L., **Supp. XXV:** 251
Jones, Howard Mumford, **I:** 353; **Supp. IV Part 2:** 606; **Supp. XIV:** 11; **Supp. XXVI:** 63
Jones, James, **III:** 40; **IV:** 98; **Supp. XI: 213–237; Supp. XIX:** 248, 252; **Supp. XX: 248; Supp. XXV:** 145
Jones, James Earl, **Supp. VIII:** 334; **Supp. XI:** 309
Jones, Jennifer, **Supp. IV Part 2:** 524
Jones, John Paul, **II:** 405–406; **Supp. I Part 2:** 479, 480, 494–495
Jones, Kirkland C., **Supp. XVIII:** 173, 174, 175; **Supp. XXII:** 9
Jones, LeRoi. *See* Baraka, Imamu Amiri
Jones, Louis B., **Supp. XVI:** 41
Jones, Loyal, **Supp. XX: 170**
Jones, Lucretia Stevens Rhinelander, **IV:** 309
Jones, Madison, **Retro. Supp. II:** 235; **Supp. X:** 1
Jones, Major (pseudonym). *See* Thompson, William T.
Jones, Malcolm, **Supp. V:** 219; **Supp. XX: 93, 138**
Jones, Mildred, **Supp. XVIII:** 281

Jones, Robert Edmond, **III:** 387, 391, 394, 399; **Supp. XXI:** 6, 12
Jones, Rodney, **Supp. XXVI:** 66
Jones, Sharon L., **Supp. XVIII:** 280, 285, 286
Jones, Tayari, **Supp. XXVIII:** 283
Jones, Tommy Lee, **Supp. V:** 227
Jones, Will Owen, **Retro. Supp. III:** 21
"Jones's Private Argyment" (Lanier), **Supp. I Part 1:** 352
"Jones's *The Thin Red Line:* The End of Innocence" (Michel-Michot), **Supp. XI:** 224–225
Jong, Allan, **Supp. V:** 115
Jong, Erica, **Supp. V: 113–135**
Jong-Fast, Molly Miranda, **Supp. V:** 115
Jonson, Ben, **I:** 58, 358; **II:** 11, 16, 17, 18, 436, 556; **III:** 3, 463, 575–576; **IV:** 395, 453; **Retro. Supp. II:** 76; **Supp. I Part 2:** 423; **Supp. IV Part 2:** 585; **Supp. XX: 197; Supp. XXIV:** 159
Jonsson, Thorsten, **Retro. Supp. I:** 73
Joplin, Janis, **Supp. IV Part 1:** 206; **Supp. XI:** 239
Joplin, Scott, **Supp. IV Part 1:** 223
Jordan, A. Van, **Supp. XVIII:** 172
Jordan, Barbara, **Supp. VIII:** 63; **Supp. XI:** 249
Jordan, David, **Supp. XIX:** 141
Jordan, Denise, **Supp. XXVII:** 209
Jordan, June, **Retro. Supp. III:** 184; **Supp. XII:** 217; **Supp. XXII:** 172; **Supp. XXIV:** 188
Jordan, Marie, **Supp. XV:** 224
Jo's Boys (Alcott), **Supp. I Part 1:** 32, 35, 40–41, 42
Joseph Heller (Ruderman), **Supp. IV Part 1:** 380
"Josephine Has Her Day" (Thurber), **Supp. I Part 2:** 606
Josephine Stories, The (Fitzgerald), **Retro. Supp. I:** 109
"Joseph Martinez" (Huncke), **Supp. XIV:** 149
"Joseph Pockets" (Stern), **Supp. IX:** 292
Josephson, Matthew, **I:** 259
"José's Country" (Winters), **Supp. II Part 2:** 789, 790
Joshi, S. T., **Supp. XXIV:** 23; **Supp. XXV:** 111, 118, 123; **Supp. XXVII:** 128
Josh Thurlow series (Hickam), **Supp. XXVII:** 111
Joshua (biblical book), **Supp. I Part 2:** 515
"Joshua Clark"(Kenny), **Supp. XXIII:** 154
Joslin, Katherine, **Retro. Supp. I:** 376
Journal (Emerson), **Supp. I Part 1:** 309
"Journal" (L. Michaels), **Supp. XVI:** 213
Journal (Thoreau), **IV:** 175
Journal (Woolman), **Supp. VIII:** 202
"Journal for My Daughter" (Kunitz), **Supp. III Part 1:** 268
"Journal of an Airman" (Auden), **Supp. XIX:** 151
Journal of Arthur Stirling, The (Sinclair), **Supp. V:** 280

"Journal of a Solitary Man, The" (Hawthorne), **II**: 226

Journal of a Solitude (Sarton), **Supp. VIII**: 256, 262–263

Journal of My Other Self (Rilke), **Retro. Supp. II**: 20

Journal of the Fictive Life (Nemerov), **III**: 267, 268, 269, 272, 273, 274, 280–281, 284–285, 286, 287

Journal of the Plague Year, A (Defoe), **III**: 423

"Journal of the Year of the Ox, A" (Wright), **Supp. V**: 343

Journals (Thoreau), **Supp. I Part 1**: 299

Journals and Other Documents on the Life and Voyages of Christopher Columbus (Morison, ed.), **Supp. I Part 2**: 494

Journals of Ralph Waldo Emerson, The (Emerson), **II**: 8, 17, 21

Journals of Susanna Moodie, The: Poems (Atwood), **Supp. XIII**: 33

"Journey, A" (Wharton), **Retro. Supp. I**: 364

"Journey, The" (Winters), **Supp. II Part 2**: 795

"Journey, The" (Wright), **Supp. III Part 2**: 605–606

"Journey, the Arrival and the Dream, The" (Gioia), **Supp. XV**: 120

"Journey, The: For Jane at Thirteen" (Kumin), **Supp. IV Part 2**: 442

Journey and Other Poems, The (Winters), **Supp. II Part 2**: 786, 794, 795, 796, 799, 800, 801

Journey Around My Room: The Autobiography of Louise Bogan—A Mosaic (Bogan), **Supp. III Part 1**: 47, 48, 52, 53

Journey Down, The (Bernstein), **IV**: 455

Journey Home, The (Abbey), **Supp. XIII**: 2, 12

"Journey into Speech, A" (Cliff), **Supp. XXII**: 69

Journey into Summer (Teale), **Supp. XXVIII**: 249

Journeyman (Caldwell), **I**: 297, 302–304, 307, 309; **Supp. XXVI**: 134

Journeyman: Travels of a Writer (Findley), **Supp. XX**: 50

"Journey of an Eyeball, The" (Vaz), **Supp. XXVI**: 261

Journey of Tai-me, The (Momaday), **Supp. IV Part 2**: 485

"Journey of the Magi" (Eliot), **Retro. Supp. I**: 64

Journey to a War (Auden and Isherwood), **Supp. II Part 1**: 13; **Supp. XIV**: 156, 158, 162

Journey to Love (W. C. Williams), **IV**: 422; **Retro. Supp. I**: 429

Journey to My Father; Isaac Bashevis Singer (Zamir), **Retro. Supp. II**: 317

"Journey to Nine Miles" (Walker), **Supp. III Part 2**: 527

"Journey to the Interior" (W. J. Smith), **Supp. XIII**: 339, 340

Journey with Genius: Recollections and Reflections Concerning the D. H. Lawrences (Bynner), **Supp. XV**: 46

Jowett, Benjamin, **Supp. XIV**: 335

"Joy" (Moore), **Supp. X**: 174

"Joy" (Singer), **IV**: 9; **Retro. Supp. II**: 307

Joyce, Cynthia, **Supp. X**: 194, 195, 196

Joyce, James, **I**: 53, 105, 108, 130, 174, 256, 285, 377, 395, 475–476, 478, 480, 483, 576; **II**: 27, 42, 58, 73, 74, 198, 209, 264, 320, 569; **III**: 7, 16, 26–27, 45, 174, 181, 184, 261, 273, 277, 343, 396, 398, 465, 471, 474; **IV**: 32, 73, 85, 95, 103, 171, 182, 211, 286, 370, 412, 418, 419, 428, 434, 456; **Retro. Supp. I**: 59, 63, 75, 80, 89, 91, 108, 109, 127, 287, 290, 292, 334, 335, 420; **Retro. Supp. II**: 221, 326; **Supp. I Part 2**: 257, 262, 270; **Supp. I Part 2**: 437, 546, 613, 620; **Supp. II Part 1**: 136; **Supp. III Part 1**: 35, 36, 65, 225, 229; **Supp. III Part 2**: 611, 617, 618; **Supp. IV Part 1**: 40, 47, 80, 227, 300, 310; **Supp. IV Part 2**: 424, 677; **Supp. IX**: 211, 229, 235, 308; **Supp. V**: 261, 331; **Supp. VIII**: 14, 40, 103; **Supp. X**: 115, 137, 194, 324; **Supp. XI**: 66; **Supp. XII**: 139, 151, 165, 191, 289; **Supp. XIV**: 83; **Supp. XIX**: 151, 172; **Supp. XVI**: 41, 189, 282; **Supp. XVII**: 44; **Supp. XXI**: 7; **Supp. XXII**: 141, 143–144; **Supp. XXIII**: 162; **Supp. XXVI**: 17, 135

"Joyce Carol Oates Plays the Saturn Piano"(Wakoski), **Supp. XXVIII**: 267–268

Joy Comes in the Morning (J. Rosen), **Supp. XVII**: 50

Joy in the Morning (B. Smith), **Supp. XXIII**: 257, 258, **269–270**

Joy Luck Club, The (Tan), **Supp. X**: 289, 291, 293, 294, 296, 297, 298, 299

"Joy of Sales Resistance, The" (Berry), **Supp. X**: 36

J R (Gaddis), **Supp. IV Part 1**: 279, 280, 285–289, 291, 294; **Supp. IV Part 2**: 484; **Supp. XXI**: 226

Juana Inés de la Cruz, Sor, **Supp. XXI**: 94, 104

Juan de la Cruz (John of the Cross), **Supp. XXI**: 99, 104

"Juan's Song" (Bogan), **Supp. III Part 1**: 50

Juba! (Myers), **Supp. XXVII**: 201, 202, 211

Juba to Jive: A Dictionary of African-American Slang (Major), **Supp. XXII**: 172, 180

Jubilate Agno (Smart), **Supp. IV Part 2**: 626

Judah, Hettie, **Supp. XIII**: 246

Judah the Pious (Prose), **Supp. XVI**: 249, 250, 262

"Judas Maccabaeus" (Longfellow), **II**: 506; **Retro. Supp. II**: 165, 167

Judd, Sylvester, **II**: 290; **Supp. I Part 2**: 420

Judd Rankin's Daughter (Glaspell), **Supp. III Part 1**: 186–188

Jude the Obscure (Hardy), **Supp. I Part 1**: 217

Judevine (Budbill), **Supp. XIX**: 4, **8–9**, 12

Judevine: A Play in Three Acts/Two Acts (Budbill), **Supp. XIX**: **12–13**

Judge, Jane, **Supp. XXII**: 191

"Judgement Day" (O'Connor), **III**: 349, 350; **Retro. Supp. II**: 236; **Retro. Supp. III**: 214

Judgment Day (Farrell), **II**: 29, 31, 32, 34, 39

"Judgment of Paris, The" (Merwin), **Supp. III Part 1**: 350

Judgment of Paris, The (Vidal), **Supp. IV Part 2**: 680, 682

"Judgment of the Sage, The" (Crane), **I**: 420

Judith (Farrell), **II**: 46, 48

"Judith" (Garrett), **Supp. VII**: 109–110

"Juggernaut" (Bass), **Supp. XVI**: 16–17

"Jug of Sirup, A" (Bierce), **I**: 206

"Jugurtha" (Longfellow), **II**: 499

"Juice or Gravy" (P. Roth), **Retro. Supp. II**: 279

"Juke Box Love Song" (Hughes), **Retro. Supp. I**: 209

"Julia" (Hellman), **Supp. I Part 1**: 280, 293

Julia France and Her Times (Atherton), **Supp. XXIV**: 24, 27

"Julia Miller" (Masters), **Supp. I Part 2**: 461

Julian (Vidal), **Supp. IV Part 2**: 677, 684–685, 685, 689

Julian, Norman, **Supp. XXVII**: 101

Julian the Apostate, **Retro. Supp. I**: 247

"Julian Vreden" (Bowles), **Supp. IV Part 1**: 94

Julie and Romeo (Ray), **Supp. XII**: 308, 310

Julien, Isaac, **Supp. XI**: 19

Julie; ou, La nouvelle Héloïse (Rousseau), **Supp. XVI**: 184

Julier, Laura, **Supp. IV Part 1**: 211

Julip (Harrison), **Supp. VIII**: 51

Julius Caesar (Shakespeare), **I**: 284; **Supp. XXVI**: 40

July, Miranda, **Supp. XXIV**: **199–211**

"July Midnight" (A. Lowell), **II**: 521

"July 1949" (Rash), **Supp. XXVII**: 218

"July Saturday"(Woodson), **Supp. XXVIII**: 280

Jumbo (Hecht and MacArthur), **Supp. XXVII**: 90

Jumel, Madame, **Supp. I Part 2**: 461

Jump at the Sun: Zora Neale Hurston's Cosmic Comedy (Lowe), **Retro. Supp. III**: 140

Jumping Out of Bed (R. Bly), **Supp. IV Part 1**: 71

"Jump-Up Day" (Kingsolver), **Supp. VII**: 203

Juncker, Clara, **Supp. XXVIII**: 122

"Junctions" (Lamott), **Supp. XX**: **143**

"June 1940" (Kees), **Supp. XV**: 141

"June Light" (Wilbur), **Supp. III Part 2**: 545

June Moon (Lardner and Kaufman), **II**: 427

"June Recital" (Welty), **IV**: 272–273

Juneteenth (Ellison), **Retro. Supp. II:** 119, 124, **126–128**

"Juneteenth" (Ellison), **Retro. Supp. II:** 119, 126; **Supp. II Part 1:** 248

"June the Third" (Gander), **Supp. XV:** 340

June-Tree: New and Selected Poems, 1974–2000 (Balakian), **Supp. XXIII:** 19, **24–25,** 32

Jung, Carl, **I:** 58, 135, 241, 248, 252, 402; **III:** 400, 534, 543; **Supp. I Part 2:** 439; **Supp. IV Part 1:** 68, 69; **Supp. VIII:** 45; **Supp. X:** 193; **Supp. XV:** 214; **Supp. XX:** 63, 117

Junger, Ernst, **Supp. III Part 1:** 63

Jungle, The (Sinclair), **III:** 580; **Supp. V:** 281–284, 285, 289; **Supp. XXVIII:** 77

Jungle Lovers (Theroux), **Supp. VIII:** 314, 315, 316, **317**

"Junior Addict" (Hughes), **Supp. I Part 1:** 343

"Juniper" (Francis), **Supp. IX:** 79

"Junk" (Wilbur), **Supp. III Part 2:** 556

Junker, Howard, **Supp. XV:** 116

Junkie: Confessions of an Unredeemed Drug Addict (Burroughs), **Supp. III Part 1:** 92, 94–96, 101

Junky (Burroughs), **Supp. XIV:** 143

Juno and the Paycock (O'Casey), **Supp. IV Part 1:** 361

"Jupiter Doke, Brigadier General" (Bierce), **I:** 204

Jupiter Laughs (A. Cronin), **Supp. XVII:** 59

Jurgen (Cabell), **III:** 394; **IV:** 286; **Retro. Supp. I:** 80; **Supp. I Part 2:** 718

Jury of Her Peers, A: American Women Writers from Anne Bradstreet to Annie Proulx (Showalter), **Supp. XX:** 274

Jusserand, Jules, **II:** 338

Just above My Head (Baldwin), **Retro. Supp. II:** 14–15

"Just a Little One" (Parker), **Supp. IX:** 191

Just and the Unjust, The (Cozzens), **I:** 367–370, 372, 375, 377, 378, 379

Just an Ordinary Day (Jackson), **Supp. IX:** 120

Just Before Dark: Collected Nonfiction (Harrison), **Supp. VIII:** 41, 45, 46, 53

Just Before the Divorce (Hayes), **Supp. XXVI:** 144

"Just Before the War with the Eskimos" (Salinger), **III:** 559

"Just Boys" (Farrell), **II:** 45

"Just for the Thrill: An Essay on the Difference Between Women and Men" (Carson), **Supp. XII:** 103–104

"Justice" (Hughes), **Supp. I Part 1:** 331

"Justice, A" (Faulkner), **Retro. Supp. I:** 83

Justice, Donald, **Retro. Supp. I:** 313; **Supp. III Part 2:** 541; **Supp. V:** 180, 337, 338, 341; **Supp. VII:** 115–130; **Supp. XI:** 141, 315; **Supp. XIII:** 76, 312; **Supp. XV:** 74, 93, 118, 119, 134; **Supp. XVII:** 110, 120, 246; **Supp. XX:** 199; **Supp. XXIV:** 165

Justice and Expediency (Whitter), **Supp. I Part 2:** 686

"Justice Denied in Massachusetts" (Millay), **III:** 140

Justice for Salcido (Endore), **Supp. XVII:** 63

"Justice Is Reason Enough"(Wakoski), **Supp. XXVIII:** 260, 261, 272

Justice of Gold in the Damnation of Sinners, The (Edwards), **I:** 559

"Justice to Feminism" (Ozick), **Supp. V:** 272

"Just Introduced" (Taggard), **Supp. XXII:** 274

Just Kids (Smith), **Supp. XXII:** 94

"Just Like a Woman" (Dylan), **Supp. XV:** 350

"Just Like Job" (Angelou), **Supp. IV Part 1:** 15

"Just One of the Boys" (Swados), **Supp. XIX:** 259

Just Whistle: A Valentine (Wright), **Supp. XV:** 346–348

Just Wild About Harry (H. Miller), **III:** 190

Just Write! Here's How (Myers), **Supp. XXVII:** 209–210

Juvenal, **II:** 8, 169, 552

K

K (Rinehart), **Supp. XXV:** 193–194, 200

"K, The" (Olson), **Supp. II Part 2:** 558, 563, 569

Kaaterskill Falls (Goodman), **Supp. XXVI:** 123–125

Kabir, **Supp. IV Part 1:** 74

"Kabnis" (Toomer), **Supp. III Part 2:** 481, 484; **Supp. IX:** 309, 310, **319–320**

Kachel, Elsie. *See* Stevens, Mrs. Wallace (Elsie Kachel)

"Kaddish" (Ginsberg), **Supp. II Part 1:** 319, 327

Kaddish and Other Poems, 1958–1960 (Ginsberg), **Supp. II Part 1:** 309, 319–320; **Supp. XIV:** 269

Kael, Pauline, **Supp. IX:** 253; **Supp. XV:** 147, 148

Kafka, Franz, **II:** 244, 565, 569; **III:** 51, 253, 418, 566, 572; **IV:** 2, 113, 218, 437–439, 442; **Retro. Supp. II:** 20, 221, 282; **Supp. I Part 1:** 197; **Supp. III Part 1:** 105; **Supp. III Part 2:** 413; **Supp. IV Part 1:** 379; **Supp. IV Part 2:** 623; **Supp. VIII:** 14, 15, 103; **Supp. XII:** 21, 37, 98, 168; **Supp. XIII:** 305; **Supp. XVI:** 17, 201, 206, 209; **Supp. XVII:** 244; **Supp. XX:** 18, 21, 85, 87; **Supp. XXII:** 89, 90, 94; **Supp. XXIII:** 68

Kafka Americana (Lethem and Scholtz), **Supp. XVIII:** 144–145

Kaganoff, Penny, **Supp. XI:** 122

Kagan's Superfecta (A. Hoffman), **Supp. XVII:** 42

Kahane, Jack, **III:** 171, 178

Kahn, Otto, **I:** 385; **IV:** 123; **Retro. Supp. II:** 81, 84, 85; **Supp. XX:** 75

Kahn, R. T., **Supp. XI:** 216

Kahn, Sholom Jacob, **Retro. Supp. III:** 107

"Kai, Today" (Snyder), **Supp. VIII:** 300

Kaiser, Georg, **I:** 479

Kaiser, Henry, **Supp. I Part 2:** 644

Kakutani, Michiko, **Supp. IV Part 1:** 196, 201, 205, 211, 212; **Supp. V:** 63; **Supp. VIII:** 81, 84, 86, 88, 141; **Supp. X:** 171, 301, 302, 310, 314; **Supp. XI:** 38, 179; **Supp. XII:** 165, 171, 172, 299; **Supp. XIX:** 142; **Supp. XVI:** 71; **Supp. XVII:** 6; **Supp. XX:** 92, 94; **Supp. XXII:** 109; **Supp. XXVI:** 246; **Supp. XXVII:** 274

Kalem, T. E., **Supp. IV Part 2:** 585

Kalevala (Finnish epic), **II:** 503, 504; **Retro. Supp. II:** 155

Kalevala (Lönnrot), **Retro. Supp. II:** 159, 160

Kalfus, Ken, **Supp. XVII:** 50

Kalki: A Novel (Vidal), **Supp. IV Part 2:** 677, 682, 685, 691, 692

Kallan, Richard A., **Supp. XX:** 244

Kallen, Horace, **I:** 229; **Supp. I Part 2:** 643; **Supp. XIV:** 195, 197, 198

Kallman, Chester, **II:** 586; **Supp. II Part 1:** 15, 17, 24, 26

"Kallundborg Church" (Whittier), **Supp. I Part 2:** 696

Kalstone, David, **Retro. Supp. II:** 40

Kamel, Rose, **Supp. XIII:** 306

Kamenev, Lev, **Supp. XXI:** 167

Kamera Obskura (Nabokov), **III:** 255

Kamhi, Michelle Moarder, **Supp. IV Part 2:** 529, 530

Kaminsky, Wally, **Supp. XVIII:** 72

Kamp, David, **Supp. XVIII:** 150

Kandy-Kolored Tangerine-Flake Streamline Baby, The (Wolfe), **Supp. III Part 2:** 569, 573–576, 580, 581

Kane, Daniel, **Supp. XXIV:** 37

Kane, Julie, **Supp. XVII:** 78

Kane, Lesley, **Supp. XIV:** 250

Kanellos, Nicolás, **Supp. VIII:** 82; **Supp. XIII:** 213

Kanin, Garson, **Supp. IV Part 2:** 574

"Kansas City Coyote" (Harjo), **Supp. XII:** 219, 222

"Kansas Emigrants, The" (Whittier), **Supp. I Part 2:** 687

Kant, Immanuel, **I:** 61, 277, 278; **II:** 10–11, 362, 480, 580–581, 582, 583; **III:** 300, 480, 481, 488, 612; **IV:** 90; **Supp. I Part 2:** 640; **Supp. IV Part 2:** 527; **Supp. XIV:** 198, 199; **Supp. XVI:** 184

Kanter, Hal, **IV:** 383

Kapital, Das (Marx), **III:** 580; **Supp. XXI:** 161, 162, 163

Kaplan, Abraham, **I:** 277

Kaplan, Carla, **Retro. Supp. III:** 138

Kaplan, E. Ann, **Supp. XXVIII:** 183

Kaplan, Justin, **I:** 247–248; **Retro. Supp. I:** 392; **Retro. Supp. III:** 261

Kaplan, Mary Jo, **Supp. XIX:** 266

Kaplan, Steven, **Supp. V:** 238, 241, 243, 248

Karate Is a Thing of the Spirit (Crews), **Supp. XI:** 112–113

Karbo, Karen, **Supp. X:** 259, 262

"Karintha" (Toomer), **Supp. IX:** 311

Karl, Frederick R., **Supp. IV Part 1:** 384; **Supp. XXI:** 234
Karloff, Boris, **Supp. XXVII:** 119
"Karloff and the Rock" (Di Piero), **Supp. XIX:** 44
Karl Shapiro's America (film), **Supp. II Part 2:** 703
Karmi, T., **Supp. XV:** 78, 88
Karr, Mary, **Supp. XI: 239–256; Supp. XIII:** 285; **Supp. XV:** 223; **Supp. XVI:** 63, 70, 77; **Supp. XVII:** 242
Karsner, David, **Supp. XXVII:** 83
Karyotakis, Konstantine, **Supp. XXIII:** 125
Kasabian, Linda, **Supp. IV Part 1:** 206
Kasper, Catherine, **Supp. XVI:** 294–295
Kate Chopin (Toth), **Retro. Supp. II:** 71
Kate Chopin: A Critical Biography (Seyersted), **Retro. Supp. II:** 65; **Supp. I Part 1:** 225
Kate Chopin and Edith Wharton: An Annotated Bibliographical Guide to Secondary Sources (Springer), **Supp. I Part 1:** 225
Kate Chopin and Her Creole Stories (Rankin), **Retro. Supp. II:** 57; **Supp. I Part 1:** 200, 225
"Kate Chopin's *The Awakening* in the Perspective of Her Literary Career" (Arms), **Supp. I Part 1:** 225
Kate Vaiden (Price), **Supp. VI:** 264, 265
"Käthe Kollwitz" (Rukeyser), **Supp. VI:** 283, 284
Katherine and Jean (Rice), **Supp. VII:** 288
"Kathleen" (Whittier), **Supp. I Part 2:** 693
Kathleen and Frank: The Autobiography of a Family (Isherwood), **Supp. XIV:** 158, 171
Kathy Goes to Haiti (Acker), **Supp. XII:** 5
Katz, Alan, **Supp. XXII:** 177
Katz, Alex, **Supp. XV:** 185; **Supp. XXVII:** 21, 22
Katz, Jonathan, **Supp. XII:** 179
Katz, Steve, **Supp. V:** 44
Katz, Steven T., **Supp. XVI:** 154
Katzenberg, Jffrey, **Supp. XXI:** 154
Kauffman, Carol, **Supp. XI:** 295
Kauffmann, Stanley, **III:** 452; **Supp. I Part 2:** 391; **Supp. XVI:** 74
Kaufman, Boris, **Supp. XVIII:** 251
Kaufman, Charlie, **Supp. XV:** 16
Kaufman, Ellen, **Supp. XXIII:** 132, 133
Kaufman, George S., **II:** 427, 435, 437; **III:** 62, 71–72, 394; **Retro. Supp. II:** 327; **Retro. Supp. III:** 177; **Supp. IV Part 2:** 574; **Supp. IX:** 190; **Supp. XV:** 329
Kaufmann, James, **Supp. XI:** 39
Kaufmann, Walter, **Supp. XVII:** 137
Kauvar, Elaine M., **Supp. V:** 273
Kavanaugh (Longfellow), **I:** 458; **II:** 489, 491; **Retro. Supp. II:** 156; **Supp. I Part 2:** 420
Kaveney, Roz, **Supp. XI:** 39
Kawabata, Yasunari, **Supp. XV:** 186; **Supp. XXI:** 146
Kawin, Bruce, **Retro. Supp. III:** 75

Kay, Terry, **Supp. XXVII:** 104
Kay Boyle: Artist and Activist (Spanier), **Supp. XXIV:** 64
Kay Boyle: Author of Herself (Mellen), **Supp. XXIV:** 64
Kay Boyle for the Twenty-First Century (Austenfeld, ed.), **Supp. XXIV:** 64
Kaye-Smith, Sheila, **Supp. XVIII:** 130–131
Kazan, Elia, **III:** 153, 163; **IV:** 383; **Retro. Supp. III:** 166, 171; **Supp. I Part 1:** 66, 295; **Supp. XVI:** 193; **Supp. XVIII:** 250–251, 252; **Supp. XXV:** 95, 102
Kazin, Alfred, **I:** 248, 417, 419, 517; **II:** 177, 459; **IV:** 236; **Retro. Supp. II:** 206, 243, 246, 286; **Supp. I Part 1:** 195, 196, 294, 295, 296; **Supp. I Part 2:** 536, 631, 647, 650, 678, 679, 719; **Supp. II Part 1:** 143; **Supp. IV Part 1:** 200, 382; **Supp. IX:** 3, 227; **Supp. V:** 122; **Supp. VIII: 93–111; Supp. XIII:** 98, 106; **Supp. XIV:** 11; **Supp. XV:** 142; **Supp. XXIII:** 2, 106; **Supp. XXIV:** 222; **Supp. XXVII:** 134; **Supp. XXVIII:** 66, 76, 157, 158
Keach, Stacey, **Supp. XI:** 309
Kean, Danuta, **Supp. XXI:** 80
Keane, Sarah, **Supp. I Part 1:** 100
Kearns, Cleo McNelly, **Retro. Supp. I:** 57
Kearns, George, **Retro. Supp. I:** 292
Keating, AnnLouise, **Supp. IV Part 1:** 330
Keaton, Buster, **I:** 31; **Supp. I Part 2:** 607; **Supp. IV Part 2:** 574
Keaton, Diane, **Supp. XV:** 5
Keats, John, **I:** 34, 103, 284, 314, 317–318, 385, 401, 448; **II:** 82, 88, 97, 214, 368, 512, 516, 530–531, 540, 593; **III:** 4, 10, 45, 122, 133–134, 179, 214, 237, 272, 275, 469, 485, 523; **IV:** 360, 405, 416; **Retro. Supp. I:** 91, 301, 313, 360, 395, 412; **Retro. Supp. III:** 74; **Supp. I Part 1:** 82, 183, 266, 267, 312, 349, 362, 363, 365; **Supp. I Part 2:** 410, 422, 424, 539, 552, 675, 719, 720; **Supp. III Part 1:** 73; **Supp. IV Part 1:** 123, 168, 325; **Supp. IV Part 2:** 455; **Supp. IX:** 38, 39, 45; **Supp. VIII:** 41, 273; **Supp. XI:** 43, 320; **Supp. XII:** 9, 113, 255; **Supp. XIII:** 131, 281; **Supp. XIV:** 274; **Supp. XIX:** 33, 276; **Supp. XV:** 92; **Supp. XVII:** 76, 112; **Supp. XX: 115,** 116; **Supp. XXI:** 131; **Supp. XXIV:** 159
Keats, John (other), **Supp. IX:** 190, 195, 200
Keegan, Abigail, **Supp. XXIII:** 129, 130, 136
"Keela, the Outcast Indian Maiden" (Welty), **IV:** 263
Keeley, Mary Paxton, **Supp. XV:** 136
"Keen Scalpel on Racial Ills" (Bruell), **Supp. VIII:** 126
Keep, The (Egan), **Supp. XIX:** 49, **56–61**
"*Keep A-Inchin' Along*" (Van Vechten), *Supp. III Part 2:* 744

Keeper's Son, The (Hickam), **Supp. XXVII:** 111–112
Keeping (Goldbarth), **Supp. XII:** 179–180, 180
"Keeping Accounts" (Davison), **Supp. XXVI:** 77
"Keeping Informed in D.C." (Nemerov), **III:** 287
Keeping Slug Woman Alive: A Holistic Approach to American Indian Texts (Sarris), **Supp. IV Part 1:** 329
"'Keeping Their World Large'" (Moore), **III:** 201–202
Keeping the Night (Everwine), **Supp. XV:** 75, **81–85,** 86
"Keeping Things Whole" (Strand), **Supp. IV Part 2:** 624
Keep It Simple: A Defense of the Earth (Nichols), **Supp. XIII:** 268
"Keep the Saving Habit" (L. I. Wilder), **Supp. XXII:** 290
"Keep Your Pity" (Boyle), **Supp. XXIV:** 58, 59
Kees, Weldon, **Supp. X:** 118; **Supp. XII:** 198; **Supp. XV:** 113, 114, 115, **133–149**
Kehe, Marjorie, **Supp. XXVI:** 209
Keillor, Garrison, **Supp. XII:** 343; **Supp. XIII:** 274; **Supp. XVI: 165–179; Supp. XXI:** 53, 62; **Supp. XXII:** 83; **Supp. XXIII:** 57, 58, 138
Keillor, Gary Edward. *See* Keiller, Garrison
Keith, Brian, **Supp. IV Part 2:** 474
Keith, Minor C., **I:** 483
Kelleghan, Fiona, **Supp. XVIII:** 136, 139, 140
Keller, A. G., **III:** 108
Keller, Christopher J., **Supp. XVIII:** 192, 195
Keller, Helen, **I:** 254, 258; **Supp. XXIII:** 161
Keller, Lynn, **Supp. IV Part 2:** 423; **Supp. V:** 78, 80
Kelley, David, **Supp. IV Part 2:** 528, 529
Kelley, Florence, **Supp. I Part 1:** 5, 7
Kelley, Mary, **Supp. XVIII:** 257, 260
Kelley, Robin, **Supp. XVIII:** 231
Kellogg, Reverend Edwin H., **III:** 200
Kellogg, Paul U., **Supp. I Part 1:** 5, 7, 12
Kelly, **II:** 464
Kelly, Adam, **Supp. XXVIII:** 205, 209, 213, 214, 222
Kelly, Brigit Pegeen, **Supp. XVII: 123–134; Supp. XXIII:** 54
Kelly, Emmett, **Supp. XI:** 99, 106
Kelly, Gene, **Supp. XXI:** 148
Kelly, James Patrick, **Supp. XIX:** 231; **Supp. XVIII:** 145
Kelly, Robert, **Supp. XXVIII:** 261
Kelly, Walt, **Supp. XI:** 105
Kelly, William, **Supp. XV:** 75, 88
Kelsey, Penelope Myrtle, **Supp. XXIII:** 143, 153–164
Kelsh, Nick, **Supp. XVII:** 167, 179
Kemble, E. W., **Supp. XXVIII:** 225, 237
Kemble, Fanny, **Retro. Supp. I:** 228
Kemble, Gouverneur, **II:** 298
Kemble, Peter, **II:** 298

Kempf, Andrea, **Supp. XXVI:** 212

Kempton, Murray, **Supp. VIII:** 104

Kempton-Wace Letters, The (London and Strunsky), **II:** 465

Kendall, Elaine, **Supp. XXVI:** 121

Kennan, George F., **Supp. VIII:** 241

Kennedy, Albert J., **Supp. I Part 1:** 19

Kennedy, Archibald, **Supp. XXVI:** 84

Kennedy, Arthur, **III:** 153

Kennedy, Burt, **Supp. IV Part 1:** 236

Kennedy, Jeffery, **Supp. XXI:** 6; **Supp. XXV:** 20

Kennedy, J. Gerald, **Retro. Supp. II:** 271; **Retro. Supp. III:** 237

Kennedy, John F., **I:** 136, 170; **II:** 49, 152–153; **III:** 38, 41, 42, 234, 411, 415, 581; **IV:** 229; **Supp. I Part 1:** 291; **Supp. I Part 2:** 496; **Supp. VIII:** 98, 104, 203; **Supp. XII:** 132; **Supp. XXVI:** 43

Kennedy, Mrs. John F., **I:** 136

Kennedy, John Pendleton, **II:** 313; **Retro. Supp. III:** 224; **Supp. XXII:** 193

Kennedy, Robert, **Supp. V:** 291

Kennedy, Robert F., **I:** 294; **Supp. I Part 1:** 52; **Supp. XI:** 343

Kennedy, Sarah, **Supp. XVIII:** 293, 299, 301

Kennedy, William, **Supp. VII: 131–157; Supp. XIX:** 141; **Supp. XVII:** 135; **Supp. XX: 90; Supp. XXIV:** 281, 282, 283

Kennedy, X. J., **Supp. V:** 178, 182; **Supp. XV:** 113, **151–173**

Kenner, Hugh, **III:** 475, 478; **IV:** 412; **Supp. I Part 1:** 255; **Supp. IV Part 2:** 474; **Supp. XV:** 147; **Supp. XXI:** 235; **Supp. XXVI:** 228

Kenneth Koch, a Tragedy (O'Hara and Rivers), **Supp. XXIII:** 217

"Kenneth Koch's 'Serious Moment' " (Spurr), **Supp. XV:** 183

Kenneth Millar/Ross Macdonald: A Checklist (Bruccoli), **Supp. IV Part 2:** 464, 469, 471

Kenney, Michael, **Supp. XIX:** 51, 52–53

Kenney, Susan, **Supp. XVIII:** 288, 289

Kenny, Maurice, **Supp. IV Part 2:** 502; **Supp. XXIII: 143–159**

Kent, George, **Supp. IV Part 1:** 11

Kent, Rockwell, **Supp. XV:** 41; **Supp. XXII:** 281

Kenton, Edna, **Supp. XXI:** 6; **Supp. XXV:** 21; **Supp. XXVIII:** 38

Kenton, Maxwell. *See* Burnett, David; Hoffenberg, Mason; Southern, Terry

"Kent State, May 1970" (Haines), **Supp. XII:** 211

"Kentucky Derby Is Decadent and Depraved, The" (Thompson), **Supp. XXIV:** 282, **287–288**

Kentucky Straight (Offutt), **Supp. XIX: 163–167,** 171, 172

Kentucky Trace, The: A Novel of the American Revolution (Arnow), **Supp. XXVIII:** 1, 3, 6, 11, 13–14

Kenya, the Land of Conflict (Kenyatta), **Supp. XXI:** 166

Kenyatta, Jomo, **Supp. X:** 135; **Supp. XXI:** 166

Kenyon, Jane, **Supp. VII: 159–177; Supp. VIII:** 272

Keogh, Tom, **Supp. XVI:** 230

Kepler, Johannes, **III:** 484; **IV:** 18

Keplinger, David, **Supp. XIX:** 273

Keppel, Frederick P., **I:** 214

"Kéramos" (Longfellow), **II:** 494; **Retro. Supp. II:** 167, 169

Kéramos and Other Poems (Longfellow), **II:** 490

Kerber, Linda K., **Supp. XXV:** 44

Kercheval, Jesse Lee, **Supp. XIX:** 51

Kerim, Ussin, **Supp. IX:** 152

Kermode, Frank, **IV:** 133; **Retro. Supp. I:** 301

Kern, Jerome, **II:** 427

Kerouac, Jack, **III:** 174; **Retro. Supp. I:** 102; **Supp. II Part 1:** 31, 307, 309, 318, 328; **Supp. III Part 1:** 91–94, 96, 100, 217–234; **Supp. IV Part 1:** 90, 146; **Supp. IX:** 246; **Supp. V:** 336; **Supp. VIII:** 42, 138, 289, 305; **Supp. XII:** 118, 121, 122, 123, 126, 131, 132; **Supp. XIII:** 275, 284; **Supp. XIV:** 137, 138, 141, 142, 143–144; **Supp. XV:** 134, 221; **Supp. XVI:** 123; **Supp. XVII:** 135, 138; **Supp. XX: 17; Supp. XXIII:** 100, 213; **Supp. XXIV:** 34, 44; **Supp. XXV:** 29; **Supp. XXVI:** 252; **Supp. XXVII:** 18; **Supp. XXVIII:** 254

Kerr, Deborah, **Supp. XI:** 307

Kerr, Orpheus C. (pseudonym). *See* Newell, Henry

Kerr, Walter, **Supp. IV Part 2:** 575, 579

Kerridge, Richard, **Supp. XVI:** 26

Kesey, Ken, **III:** 558; **Supp. III Part 1:** 217; **Supp. V:** 220, 295; **Supp. X:** 24, 265; **Supp. XI:** 104; **Supp. XXIII:** 100

Kessel, John, **Supp. XIX:** 231; **Supp. XVIII:** 145

Kessler, Milton, **Supp. XIX:** 195

Kessler, Rod, **Supp. XXVI:** 156

Kesten, Stephen, **Supp. XI:** 309

Ketchum, Liza, **Supp. XIX:** 266

Ketchup (Shanley), **Supp. XIV:** 315

Kevane, Bridget, **Supp. XI:** 185, 190

"Key, The" (Welty), **IV:** 262

"Keys" (Nye), **Supp. XIII:** 281

"Key to the Highway" (Halliday), **Supp. XIX:** 84

Key to Uncle Tom's Cabin, A (Stowe), **Supp. I Part 2:** 580; **Supp. XXVIII:** 167

Key West (H. Crane), **Retro. Supp. II:** 84

"Key West" (H. Crane), **I:** 400

Key West: An Island Sheaf (Crane), **I:** 385, 399–402

"Khalil the Heretic" (Gibran), **Supp. XX: 124**

Khrushchev, Nikita, **I:** 136

Kiang Kang-hu, **Supp. XV:** 45, 47

Kick (Myers and Workman), **Supp. XXVII:** 206

Kick for a Bite, A (Cobbett), **Supp. XV:** 237

"Kicking the Candles Out" (Jarman), **Supp. XVII:** 113

Kid, The (Aiken), **I:** 61

Kid, The (Chaplin), **I:** 386

Kidder, Tracy, **Supp. III Part 1:** 302; **Supp. XVIII:** 106, 114

Kiddush Ha-Shem: An Epic of 1648 (Asch), **Supp. XXIII:** 3, 6, **10,** 11, 12, 16

Kidesh ha-Shem (Sanctification of the name) (Asch), **Supp. XXIII:** 6

Kidman, Nicole, **Supp. X:** 80

"Kidnaper" (Gallagher), **Supp. XXIV:** 168, 174

"Kidnapping in the Family, A" (Fante), **Supp. XI:** 164

"Kid's Guide to Divorce, The" (Moore), **Supp. X:** 167, 172

Kidwell, Clara Sue, **Supp. IV Part 1:** 333

Kielsky, Vera Emuma, **Supp. V:** 273

Kiely, Brendan, **Supp. XVII:** 75

Kieran, John, **II:** 417

Kierkegaard, Søren Aabye, **II:** 229; **III:** 292, 305, 309, 572; **IV:** 438, 491; **Retro. Supp. I:** 326; **Retro. Supp. II:** 222; **Supp. V:** 9; **Supp. VIII:** 7–8; **Supp. XX: 132**

Kiernan, Robert F., **Supp. IV Part 2:** 684

Kieseritsky, L., **III:** 252

Kilcup, Karen, **Retro. Supp. III:** 101

Kilgo, Jim, **Supp. XVIII:** 192

"Kilim" (McClatchy), **Supp. XII:** 258

Kilina, Patricia (pseudonym). *See* Warren, Patricia Nell

"Killed at Resaca" (Bierce), **I:** 202

"Killed at the Ford" (Longfellow), **Retro. Supp. II:** 170–171

Killens, John Oliver, **Supp. IV Part 1:** 8, 369; **Supp. XXVII:** 202

"Killer in the Rain" (Chandler), **Supp. IV Part 1:** 122

"Killers, The" (Hemingway), **II:** 249; **Retro. Supp. I:** 188, 189

Killers, The: A Narrative of Real Life in Philadelphia (Lippard), **Supp. XXIII:** 178, 184

Killing Mister Watson (Matthiessen), **Supp. V:** 212, 214

"Killing of a State Cop, The" (Ortiz), **Supp. IV Part 2:** 499

Killing of Sister George, The (Marcus), **Supp. I Part 1:** 277

Killing Orders (Paretsky), **Supp. XXV:** 176, 177, 179, 182–813

"Killings" (Dubus), **Supp. VII:** 85–86

"Killing the Ghost of Ripton" (Carruth), **Supp. XIX:** 1

"Killing the Plants" (Kenyon), **Supp. VII:** 167, 168

Kilmer, Joyce, **Supp. I Part 2:** 387; **Supp. XV:** 294

Kilpatrick, James K., **Supp. X:** 145

Kilvert, Francis, **Supp. VIII:** 172

Kim (Kipling), **Supp. X:** 230

Kim, Alfred, **Supp. XI:** 140

Kim, Sharon, **Supp. XVIII:** 267

Kimball, Frederic, **Supp. XXI:** 146

Kimball, J. Golden, **Supp. IV Part 2:** 602

Kimbrough, Mary Craig. *See* Sinclair, Mary Craig (Mary Craig Kimbrough)

Kimes, Maymie B., **Supp. IX:** 178
Kimes, William F., **Supp. IX:** 178
Kimmelman, Bert, **Supp. XXI:** 24
Kimura, Takeshi, **Supp. XXVI:** 88
"Kin" (Welty), **IV:** 277; **Retro. Supp. I:** 353
Kinard, Agnes Dodds, **Supp. XIV:** 122, 123, 127
Kincaid, Jamaica, **Supp. VII: 179–196**
Kincaid, James, **Supp. XVIII:** 62, 63
"Kindness" (Dunn), **Supp. XI:** 149, 150
"Kindness" (Nye), **Supp. XIII:** 285
"Kindness" (Plath), **Retro. Supp. II:** 256
Kind of Light that Shines on Texas, The (McKnight), **Supp. XX: 151–152**
"Kind of Light that Shines on Texas, The" (McKnight), **Supp. XX: 151**
Kind of Order, A Kind of Folly, A: Essays and Conversations (Kunitz), **Supp. III Part 1:** 262, 268
Kindred (O. Butler), **Supp. XIII: 59–60,** 69
"Kind Sir: These Woods" (Sexton), **Supp. II Part 2:** 673
Kinds of Love (Sarton), **Supp. VIII: 253–254,** 256
Kinfolk (Buck), **Supp. II Part 1:** 126
King, Alexander, **IV:** 287
King, Carole, **Supp. XII:** 308
King, Clarence, **I:** 1
King, Ernest, **Supp. I Part 2:** 491
King, Fisher, **II:** 425
King, Francis, **Supp. XIV:** 155, 156, 166, 169
King, Grace, **Retro. Supp. II:** 136; **Supp. XXVIII: 111–127, 227,** 230
King, Martin Luther, Jr., **Retro. Supp. II:** 12, 13; **Supp. XVIII:** 24; **Supp. XX:** 281; **Supp. XXVIII:** 57
King, Michael, **Supp. XII:** 182
King, Queen, Knave (Nabokov), **III:** 251; **Retro. Supp. I:** 270
King, Starr, **Supp. II Part 1:** 341, 342
King, Stephen, **Supp. IV Part 1:** 102, 104; **Supp. IV Part 2:** 467; **Supp. IX:** 114; **Supp. V: 137–155;** **Supp. XIII:** 53; **Supp. XXIII:** 290; **Supp. XXV:** 123, 152, 153; **Supp. XXVII:** 276
King, Tabitha (Mrs. Stephen King), **Supp. V:** 137
King, The (Barthelme), **Supp. IV Part 1:** 47, 52
"King, The" (Gibran), **Supp. XX: 123–124**
King Arthur's Socks (Dell), **Supp. XXVIII:** 38
King Coffin (Aiken), **I:** 53–54, 57
"King David" (Benét), **Supp. XI:** 44
"King David" (Reznikoff), **Supp. XIV:** 283
Kingdom and the Power, The (Talese), **Supp. XVII:** 202, 203, 204, 210
Kingdom by the Sea, The: A Journey around Great Britain (Theroux), **Supp. VIII:** 323
"Kingdom County Come" (Mosher), **Supp. XXII:** 211–212
Kingdom Far and Clear, A: The Complete Swan Lake Trilogy (Helprin), **Supp. XXV:** 87

Kingdom of Earth (T. Williams), **IV:** 382, 386, 387, 388, 391, 393, 398
"Kingdom of Earth, The" (T. Williams), **IV:** 384
Kingdom of Fear (Thompson), **Supp. XXIV:** 283
"Kingdom of God Is Within You, The" (Very), **Supp. XXV:** 249
Kingfisher, The (Clampitt), **Supp. IX:** 38
"Kingfishers, The" (Olson), **Supp. II Part 2:** 557, 558–563, 582
King Jasper (Robinson), **III:** 523
King Kong (film), **Supp. IV Part 1:** 104; **Supp. XVII:** 58
King Lear (Shakespeare), **I:** 538; **II:** 540, 551; **Retro. Supp. I:** 248; **Supp. IV Part 1:** 31, 36; **Supp. IX:** 14; **Supp. XI:** 172; **Supp. XV:** 349
King Leopold's Soliloquy (Twain), **IV:** 208
"King Leopold's Soliloquy: A Defense of His Congo Rule" (Twain), **Retro. Supp. III:** 269
King My Father's Wreck, The (Simpson), **Supp. IX:** 266, 267, 270, 275, 276
King of Babylon Shall Not Come Against You, The (Garrett), **Supp. VII:** 110–111; **Supp. X:** 3
"King of Beasts" (P. N. Warren), **Supp. XX: 272**
"King of Folly Island, The" (Jewett), **II:** 394; **Retro. Supp. II:** 132, 133
King of Kings (film), **Supp. IV Part 2:** 520
King of Paris (Endore), **Supp. XVII:** 64
King of Spain, The (Bodenheim), **Supp. XXV:** 26
"King of the Bingo Game" (Ellison), **Retro. Supp. II:** 117, 125; **Supp. II Part 1:** 235, 238, 240–241
"King of the Cats, The" (Benét), **Supp. XI:** 49–50
"King of the Clock Tower" (Yeats), **III:** 473
"King of the Desert, The" (O'Hara), **III:** 369
King of the Fields, The (Singer), **Retro. Supp. II:** 317
King of the Jews (Epstein), **Supp. XII:** 161, **166–170,** 172
King of the Mountain (Garrett), **Supp. VII:** 96, 97
"King of the River" (Kunitz), **Supp. III Part 1:** 263, 267–268
"King of the Sea" (Marquand), **III:** 60
"King over the Water" (Blackmur), **Supp. II Part 1:** 107
"King Pandar" (Blackmur), **Supp. II Part 1:** 92, 102
"King Pest" (Poe), **Retro. Supp. II:** 273
Kingsblood Royal (Lewis), **II:** 456
Kingsbury, John, **Supp. I Part 1:** 8
"King's Daughters, Home for Unwed Mothers, 1948" (Stanford), **Supp. XV:** 345
King's Henchman, The (Millay), **III:** 138–139
Kingsley, Sidney, **Supp. I Part 1:** 277, 281

King's Mare, The (Canolle; Loos, trans.), **Supp. XVI:** 194
"King's Missive, The" (Whittier), **Supp. I Part 2:** 694
Kingsolver, Barbara, **Supp. VII: 197–214; Supp. XIII:** 16; **Supp. XVIII:** 189
King's Stilts, The (Geisel), **Supp. XVI:** 100, 104
Kingston, Earll, **Supp. V:** 160
Kingston, Maxine Hong, **Supp. IV Part 1:** 1, 12; **Supp. V: 157–175,** 250; **Supp. X:** 291–292; **Supp. XI:** 18, 245; **Supp. XV:** 220, 223
"King Volmer and Elsie" (Whittier), **Supp. I Part 2:** 696
Kinkaid, Jamaica, **Supp. XXII:** 65
Kinmont, Alexander, **Supp. I Part 2:** 588–589
Kinnaird, John, **Retro. Supp. I:** 399
Kinnell, Galway, **Supp. III Part 1: 235–256; Supp. III Part 2:** 541; **Supp. IV Part 2:** 623; **Supp. V:** 332; **Supp. VIII:** 39; **Supp. XI:** 139; **Supp. XII:** 241; **Supp. XV:** 212; **Supp. XVI:** 53; **Supp. XXII:** 83; **Supp. XXVI:** 67
Kinsella, Thomas, **Supp. XX: 195–196, 197, 207**
Kinsey, Alfred, **IV:** 230; **Supp. XIV:** 140
Kinzie, Mary, **Supp. XII:** 181; **Supp. XXIII:** 124
"Kipling" (Trilling), **Supp. III Part 2:** 495
Kipling, Rudyard, **I:** 421, 587–588; **II:** 271, 338, 404, 439; **III:** 55, 328, 508, 511, 521, 524, 579; **IV:** 429; **Supp. IV Part 2:** 603; **Supp. X:** 255; **Supp. XX: 23**
Kirby, David, **Supp. XIII:** 89; **Supp. XIX:** 81; **Supp. XXVIII:** 119, 122
Kirk, Connie, **Retro. Supp. III:** 210
Kirkland, Caroline, **Supp. XVIII:** 258
Kirkland, David, **Supp. XVI:** 186
Kirkland, Diane, **Supp. XXVIII:** 29–30
Kirkland, Jack, **I:** 297
Kirkland, John, **Supp. XXIV:** 70
Kirkpatrick, Jeane, **Supp. VIII:** 241
Kirkus, Virginia, **Supp. XV:** 198
Kirkwood, Cynthia A., **Supp. XI:** 177, 178, 179
Kirp, David L., **Supp. XI:** 129
Kirsch, Adam, **Supp. XV:** 251, 260, 264, 266, 341, 347, 350–351; **Supp. XXV:** 222, 233, 253, 262, 268; **Supp. XXVII:** 144
Kirsch, Robert, **Supp. XXVII:** 134
Kirstein, Lincoln, **Supp. II Part 1:** 90, 97; **Supp. IV Part 1:** 82, 83; **Supp. XXII:** 281
Kishef-makherin fun Kastilye, Di (The witch of Castle) (Asch), **Supp. XXIII:** 6
"Kiss, The" (Di Piero), **Supp. XIX:** 45, 47
Kiss, The (Harrison), **Supp. X:** 191
"Kiss, The" (Sexton), **Supp. II Part 2:** 687
"Kiss, The" (Teasdale), **Supp. XXVII:** 291

"Kiss Away" (C. Baxter), **Supp. XVII:** 20

Kissel, Howard, **Supp. IV Part 2:** 580

Kiss Hollywood Good-by (Loos), **Supp. XVI:** 190, 195

Kissinger, Henry, **Supp. IV Part 1:** 388; **Supp. XII:** 9, 14; **Supp. XXV:** 264

Kiss of the Spider Woman, the Musical (McNally), **Supp. XIII:** 207, **Supp. XIII:** 208

Kiss Tomorrow Good-bye (McCoy), **Supp. XIII:** 170, **172–173,** 174

"Kit and Caboodle" (Komunyakaa), **Supp. XIII:** 115

Kit Brandon: A Portrait (Anderson), **I:** 111

Kitchen, Judith, **Supp. IV Part 1:** 242, 245, 252; **Supp. IX:** 163; **Supp. XI:** 312, 313, 315, 317, 319, 320, 326, 329; **Supp. XV:** 215, 219; **Supp. XXVI:** 154–155

"Kitchenette" (Brooks), **Retro. Supp. I:** 208

Kitchen God's Wife, The (Tan), **Supp. X:** 289, 292, 293, 294–295, 296–297, 298–299

"Kitchen Terrarium: 1983" (McCarriston), **Supp. XIV:** 270

Kit O'Brien (Masters), **Supp. I Part 2:** 471

Kittel, Frederick August. *See* Wilson, August

Kittredge, Charmian. *See* London, Mrs. Jack (Charmian Kittredge)

Kittredge, William, **Supp. VIII:** 39; **Supp. XI:** 316; **Supp. XII:** 209; **Supp. XIII:** 16; **Supp. XXVI:** 177–190

"Kitty Hawk" (Frost), **II:** 164; **Retro. Supp. I:** 124, 141; **Retro. Supp. III:** 107

Kizer, Carolyn, **Supp. XVII:** 71, 72, 73, 74

Klaidman, Stephen, **Supp. XIX:** 269

Klail City (Hinojosa), **Supp. XIX:** 97, **101–103**

Klail City Death Trip (Hinojosa). *See Ask a Policeman* (Hinojosa); *Becky and Her Friends* (Hinojosa); *Dear Rafe* (Hinojosa); *Fair Gentlemen of Belken County* (Hinojosa); *Klail City* (Hinojosa); *Korean Love Songs from Klail City Death Trip* (Hinojosa); *Partners in Crime: A Rafe Buenrostro Mystery* (Hinojosa); *Rites and Witnesses: A Comedy* (Hinojosa); *Useless Servants, The* (Hinojosa); *Valley, The* (Hinojosa)

"Klassikal Lymnaeryx" (Stallings), **Supp. XXV:** 233

Klein, Joe, **Supp. XII:** 67–68

Klein, Marcus, **Supp. I Part 2:** 432; **Supp. XI:** 233

Kleist, Heinrich von, **Supp. IV Part 1:** 224

Kline, Franz, **Supp. XII:** 198; **Supp. XXIII:** 210, 211, 217

Kline, George, **Supp. VIII:** 22, 28

Klinghoffer, David, **Supp. XVI:** 74

Klinkowitz, Jerome, **Supp. IV Part 1:** 40; **Supp. X:** 263; **Supp. XI:** 347;

Supp. XXI: 233

Klise, James, **Supp. XXII:** 53

Kloefkorn, Bill, **Supp. XIX:** 119

Knapp, Adeline, **Supp. XI:** 200

Knapp, Friedrich, **III:** 100

Knapp, Samuel, **I:** 336

Knapp, Samuel Lorenzo, **Supp. XV:** 246

"Kneeling Down to Look into a Culvert" (R. Bly), **Supp. XXI:** 88

Kneel to the Rising Sun (Caldwell), **I:** 304, 309

"Knees/Dura-Europos" (Goldbarth), **Supp. XII:** 185

"Knife" (Simic), **Supp. VIII:** 275

"Knife Longs for the Ruby, The" (Vaz), **Supp. XXVI:** 266–267

Knight, Arthur, **Supp. XIV:** 144

Knight, Etheridge, **Supp. XI:** 239; **Supp. XXIII:** 174

Knight, Lania, **Supp. XXIII:** 273, 274, 275, 276, 279, 280

Knight, Michael, **Supp. XXVIII:** 167

"Knight, The" (Rich), **Retro. Supp. III:** 244

"Knight in Disguise, The" (Lindsay), **Supp. I Part 2:** 390

Knightly Quest, The (T. Williams), **IV:** 383

Knight's Gambit (Faulkner), **II:** 72

Knish, Anne. *See* Ficke, Arthur Davison

"Knit One, Purl Two" (K. Snodgrass), **Supp. XVI:** 42

"Knock" (Dickey), **Supp. IV Part 1:** 182

Knocked Out Loaded (album, Dylan), **Supp. XVIII:** 28

"Knocking Around" (Ashbery), **Supp. III Part 1:** 22

"Knocking on Heaven's Door" (Lamott), **Supp. XX: 140–141**

"Knocking on Three, Winston" (Epstein), **Supp. XIV:** 109

Knock on Any Door (film, Ray), **Supp. XVII:** 150

Knock on Any Door (W. Motley), 158; **Supp. XVII: 150–155,** 159, 160

Knockout Artist, The (Crews), **Supp. XI: 113–114**

Knoll, Robert E., **Supp. XV:** 118

Knopf, Alfred A., **III:** 99, 105, 106, 107; **Retro. Supp. I:** 13, 19, 317; **Supp. I Part 1:** 324, 325, 327; **Supp. IV Part 1:** 125, 354; **Supp. XIII:** 172

Knopf, Blanche, **Supp. I Part 1:** 324, 325, 327, 328, 332, 341; **Supp. IV Part 1:** 128, 346, 348; **Supp. XIII:** 169

"Knot, The" (Rich), **Supp. I Part 2:** 555

Knot-Holes (Bodenheim and Saphier), **Supp. XXV:** 20

Knotts, Kristina, **Supp. XIII:** 238

"Knowing, The" (Olds), **Supp. X:** 215

"Knowledge Forwards and Backwards" (Stern), **Supp. IX:** 296

"Knowledge of Plates" (Bronk), **Supp. XXI:** 33

Knowles, John, **Supp. IV Part 2:** 679; **Supp. XII: 235–250; Supp. XX:** 84

Known World, The (E. P. Jones), **Supp. XXII:** 139, 140, 142, **146–150,** 150

Knox, Bernard, **Supp. XXIV:** 153

Knox, Frank, **Supp. I Part 2:** 488, 489

Knox, Israel, **Supp. X:** 70

Knox, Vicesimus, **II:** 8

Knoxville: Summer of 1915 (Agee), **I:** 42–46

Knudson, R. Rozanne, **Supp. IV Part 2:** 648

Kober, Arthur, **Supp. I Part 1:** 292

Koch, Frederick, **IV:** 453

Koch, John, **Supp. VIII:** 88

Koch, Kenneth, **Supp. XIX:** 81; **Supp. XV: 175–192; Supp. XXIII:** 124, 207, 209, 210, 211, 215, 217, 220; **Supp. XXIV:** 33, 36, 42, 44; **Supp. XXVII:** 23, 26

Koch, Vivienne, **III:** 194; **IV:** 136, 140; **Retro. Supp. I:** 428, 430

"Kochinnenako in Academe: Three Approaches to Interpreting a Keres Indian Tale" (Gunn Allen), **Supp. IV Part 1:** 329

"Kodachromes of the Island" (Hayden), **Supp. II Part 1:** 367, 380

Koestler, Arthur, **I:** 258; **Supp. I Part 2:** 671; **Supp. XXIII:** 1

Kokkinen, Eila, **Supp. XIV:** 146, 148

"Kola Street"(Asch), **Supp. XXIII:** 7

Kolba, Ellen D., **Supp. XVIII:** 257

Kolbenheyer, Dr. Frederick, **Supp. I Part 1:** 207

Kolodny, Annette, **Supp. X:** 97, 103, 229

Komisarjevsky, W. P., **Supp. XXIII:** 5

"Komodo" (C. Frost), **Supp. XV:** 95

Komunyakaa, Yusef, **Supp. XIII: 111– 136; Supp. XXI:** 129, 139; **Supp. XXIII:** 254; **Supp. XXVII:** 166

Konigsberg, Allan Stewart. *See* Allen, Woody

Konstantinou, Lee, **Supp. XXVIII:** 222

Kon-Tiki (Heyerdahl), **II:** 477

Koopman, Harry Lyman, **Retro. Supp. I:** 40

Ko; or, A Season on Earth (Koch), **Supp. XV:** 175, 180, 181, 183, 186

Kooser, Ted, **Supp. XIX: 115–130; Supp. XV:** 113, 115; **Supp. XXI:** 243

Kootz, Samuel, **Supp. XV:** 144

Kora and Ka (Doolittle), **Supp. I Part 1:** 270

Kora in Hell (W. C. Williams), **Retro. Supp. I:** 416, **417–418,** 419, 430, 431; **Supp. XXI:** 232

Korb, Rena, **Supp. XI:** 2

Korczak, Janosz, **Supp. X:** 70

Korean Love Songs from Klail City Death Trip (Hinojosa), **Supp. XIX:** 98, **103– 104**

Kornblatt, Joyce Reiser, **Supp. XV:** 62

Kornfield, Jack, **Supp. XX:** 142; **Supp. XXIII:** 138

Korrektur (Bernhard), **Supp. XX:** 91

Kort, Amy, **Supp. XIII:** 148

Korwin, Yala, **Supp. XXI:** 99

Kosinski, Jerzy, **Supp. VII: 215–228; Supp. XII:** 21

"Kostas Tympakianakis" (Merrill), **Supp. III Part 1:** 326

Kostelanetz, Richard, **Supp. XXVII:** 166

Koteliansky, S. S., **Supp. VIII:** 251, 265

Kouidis, Virginia M., **Supp. XXII:** 161, 162, 166, 167, 169
Kovic, Ron, **Supp. XIX:** 17; **Supp. XXII:** 104
Kowloon Tong (Theroux), **Supp. VIII:** 325
Kozlenko, William, **IV:** 378, 381
Krabbenhoft, Ken, **Supp. XVII:** 112
Kraft, James, **Supp. XV:** 40, 41, 42, 43, 52
Krakauer, Jon, **Supp. XVII:** 210; **Supp. XVIII: 105–118**
Kramer, Dale, **Supp. I Part 2:** 669
Kramer, Glenn Philip, **Supp. XXIII:** 125
Kramer, Hilton, **III:** 537; **Supp. I Part 1:** 295, 296; **Supp. VIII:** 239; **Supp. XIX:** 269; **Supp. XV:** 113; **Supp. XXVII:** 23
Kramer, Lawrence, **Supp. IV Part 1:** 61, 65, 66; **Supp. IX:** 291
Kramer, Peter D., **Supp. XVI:** 229
Kramer, Robert, **Supp. XXVI:** 26
Kramer, Stanley, **II:** 421, 587
Krapp's Last Tape (Beckett), **I:** 71; **III:** 387; **Retro. Supp. I:** 206
Krassner, Paul, **Supp. IV Part 1:** 385; **Supp. XI:** 293
Kraus, Karl, **Supp. XX: 84**
Krauth, Leland, **Supp. XVIII:** 58
Krauzer, Steven M., **Supp. XXVI:** 181, 182, 188
Kreisler, Harry, **Supp. XVI:** 155
Kreitman, Esther, **IV:** 2
Krementz, Jill, **Supp. XXV:** 263
"Kremlin of Smoke" (Schnackenberg), **Supp. XV:** 257–258
Kreyling, Michael, **Supp. XXVI:** 14; **Supp. XXVIII:** 115
Kreymborg, Alfred, **II:** 530; **III:** 465; **IV:** 76; **Retro. Supp. I:** 417; **Supp. XV:** 301, 306; **Supp. XXII:** 161–162; **Supp. XXV:** 18, 19, 21
Kriegel, Leonard, **Supp. XXIV: 213–228**
Krim, Seymour, **Supp. XV:** 338; **Supp. XVI:** 217; **Supp. XVIII:** 285
Krisak, Len, **Supp. XXI:** 99, 104
Kristeva, Julia, **Supp. XII:** 6
Kristofferson, Kris, **Supp. XIII:** 119
Kristol, Irving, **Supp. VIII:** 93, 244; **Supp. XIII:** 98
Kristwald, Elfriede, **Supp. XXVI:** 4, 7
Krivak, Andrew, **Supp. XVII:** 242
Kroll, Jack, **Supp. IV Part 2:** 590; **Supp. XXIII:** 103
Kroll, Judith, **Supp. I Part 2:** 541–543, 544, 546
Kroll Ring, Frances. *See* Ring, Frances Kroll
Krondorfer, Björn, **Supp. XVI:** 160
Kronenberger, Louis, **Supp. XXII:** 191, 192
Krook, Dorothea, **Retro. Supp. II:** 243
Kropotkin, Peter, **I:** 493; **Supp. I Part 1:** 5; **Supp. IV Part 2:** 521
Krueger, Bill, **Supp. XXVII:** 13
Kruif, Paul de, **II:** 446
Krupat, Arnold, **Supp. IV Part 2:** 500
Krupnick, Mark, **Supp. XVI:** 153
Krutch, Joseph Wood, **II:** 459; **III:** 425; **IV:** 70, 175

Krutikov, Mikhail, **Supp. XXIII:** 11
Kubach, David, **Supp. XXVI:** 243, 245, 246, 248
Kublai Khan, **III:** 395
"Kubla Khan" (Coleridge), **Supp. XIII:** 131, 283
Kubrick, Stanley, **Supp. IV Part 1:** 392; **Supp. XI:** 293,**Supp. XI:** 301, 302–303
"Kubuku Rides (This Is It)" (L. Brown), **Supp. XXI:** 39, 42–43
Kuehl, John, **Supp. IV Part 1:** 279, 284, 285, 287
Kuehl, Linda, **Supp. IV Part 1:** 199
"Kugelmass Episode, The" (Allen), **Supp. XV:** 15, 16
Kukachin, Princess, **III:** 395
"Ku Klux" (Hughes), **Retro. Supp. I:** 205
Kulshrestha, Chirantan, **Retro. Supp. II:** 21
Kumin, Maxine, **Supp. IV Part 2: 439–457; Supp. XIII:** 294; **Supp. XVII:** 71, 75–76; **Supp. XX: 164; Supp. XXVI:** 68; **Supp. XXVII:** 256
Kundera, Milan, **Retro. Supp. III:** 320; **Supp. VIII:** 241
Kunerth, Jeff, **Supp. XXI:** 47
Kunitz, Stanley, **I:** 179, 180, 181, 182, 521; **II:** 545; **Supp. III Part 1: 257–270; Supp. V:** 79; **Supp. XI:** 259; **Supp. XIII:** 341; **Supp. XXVI:** 64, 67, 68
Kuo, Helena, **Supp. X:** 291
Kuropatkin, General Aleksei Nikolaevich, **III:** 247–248
Kurth, Peter, **Supp. XVIII:** 145
Kurzy of the Sea (Barnes), **Supp. III Part 1:** 34
Kushner, Rachel, **Supp. XXVIII:** 206
Kushner, Tony, **Retro. Supp. III:** 165; **Supp. IX: 131–149; Supp. XX: 177; Supp. XXI:** 145; **Supp. XXIV:** 263
Kussy, Bella, **IV:** 468
Kutnik, Jerzy, **Supp. XXII:** 177
Kuttner, Henry, **Supp. IV Part 1:** 102
Kuzma, Greg, **Supp. XV:** 118
Kyger, Joanne, **Supp. XXIV:** 37

L

LaBastille, Anne, **Supp. X: 95–110; Supp. XXVI:** 34
"Labor Day Dinner" (Munro), **Supp. XXVII:** 188
"Labor's Cultural Degradation" (Swados), **Supp. XIX:** 264–265
"Labours of Hercules, The" (Moore), **III:** 201
La Bruyère, Jean de, **I:** 58
La Bufera e Altro (Montale), **Supp. V:** 337
LaBute, Neil, **Supp. XXI:** 147
Labyrinth of Love (Untermeyer), **Supp. XV:** 312
Labyrinth of Solitude, The (Paz), **Supp. XIII:** 223
Lacan, Jacques, **Retro. Supp. III:** 237; **Supp. IV Part 1:** 45; **Supp. VIII:** 5; **Supp. XII:** 98

La Casa en Mango Street (Cisneros), **Supp. VII:** 58–59
Lacayo, Richard, **Supp. XXV:** 4
Lachaise, Gaston, **I:** 434
"Lackawanna" (Merwin), **Supp. III Part 1:** 350
Lackawanna Elegy (Goll; Kinnell, trans.), **Supp. III Part 1:** 235, 243–244
Laclède, Pierre, **Supp. I Part 1:** 205
"Lacquer Prints" (A. Lowell), **II:** 524–525
Lacy, Ed, **Supp. XV: 193–210**
Ladder, The (Rasmussen; Nelson, trans.), **Supp. XVIII:** 180–181
Ladder of Years (Tyler), **Supp. IV Part 2:** 657, 671–672
Ladders to Fire (Nin), **Supp. X:** 185
Laddie (Stratton-Porter), **Supp. XX: 211, 213**
"Laddie, the Princess and the Pie" (Stratton-Porter), **Supp. XX: 216**
"Ladies" (Coleman), **Supp. XI:** 93
Ladies Almanack (Barnes), **Supp. III Part 1:** 37–39, 42; **Supp. XXII:** 167
Ladies and Gentlemen (Hecht and MacArthur), **Supp. XXVII:** 90
Ladies Auxiliary, The (Mirvis), **Supp. XX: 177, 179–185**
"Ladies in Spring" (Welty), **IV:** 276–277; **Retro. Supp. I:** 353
Lady, The (Richter), **Supp. XVIII: 211–212,** 220
Lady Audley's Secret (Braddon), **Supp. I Part 1:** 35, 36
"Lady Barberina" (James), **Retro. Supp. I:** 227
"Lady Bates" (Jarrell), **II:** 380–381
Lady Chatterley's Lover (Lawrence), **III:** 170; **IV:** 434; **Retro. Supp. III:** 25; **Supp. XVI:** 267
Ladye Annabel (Lippard), **Supp. XXIII:** 178
Lady from Louisiana (film, Vorhaus), **Supp. XVII:** 59
"Lady from Redhorse, A" (Bierce), **I:** 203
Lady in Kicking Horse Reservoir, The (Hugo), **Supp. VI:** 134, **138–139**
Lady in the Lake, The (Chandler), **Supp. IV Part 1:** 127, 129–130
"Lady in the Lake, The" (Chandler), **Supp. IV Part 1:** 129
Lady in the Lake, The (film), **Supp. IV Part 1:** 130
"Lady in the Pink Mustang, The" (Erdrich), **Supp. IV Part 1:** 270
"Lady Is Civilized, The" (Taylor), **Supp. V:** 315
Lady Is Cold, The (White), **Supp. I Part 2:** 653
Lady Killer (Holding), **Supp. XXII:** 126, **127,** 130
"Lady Lazarus" (Plath), **Retro. Supp. II:** 250, 251, 255; **Supp. I Part 2:** 529, 535, 542, 545
Lady of Aroostook, The (Howells), **II:** 280
"Lady of Bayou St. John, A" (Chopin), **Retro. Supp. II:** 58
"Lady of the Lake, The" (Malamud), **Supp. I Part 2:** 437

Lady Oracle (Atwood), **Supp. XIII:** 21, **23–24**

"Lady or the Tiger, The?"(Stockton), **Supp. XXVIII:** 228

"Lady Poverty" (Notley), **Supp. XXII:** 234–235

Lady Sings the Blues (film), **Supp. I Part 1:** 67

"Lady's Maid's Bell, The" (Wharton), **IV:** 316

"Lady Wentworth" (Longfellow), **II:** 505

"Lady with a Lamp" (Parker), **Supp. IX:** 193

"Lady with the Heron, The" (Merwin), **Supp. III Part 1:** 343

"Lady with the Pet Dog, The" (Chekov), **Supp. XXII:** 60

"Lady with the Pet Tribble, The" (Brockmeier), **Supp. XXII:** 60

La Farge, John, **I:** 1, 2, 20; **II:** 322, 338; **Retro. Supp. I:** 217

La Farge, Oliver, **Supp. IV Part 2:** 503

Lafayette, Marquis de, **I:** 344, 345; **II:** 405–406; **Supp. I Part 2:** 510, 511, 683

"La Figlia Che Piange" (T. S. Eliot), **Retro. Supp. I:** 63; **Retro. Supp. III:** 60

La Follette, Robert, **I:** 483, 485, 492; **III:** 580

La Fontaine, Jean de, **II:** 154; **III:** 194; **IV:** 80

Laforgue, Jules, **I:** 386, 569, 570, 572–573, 575, 576; **II:** 528; **III:** 8, 11, 466; **IV:** 37, 79, 80, 122; **Retro. Supp. I:** 55, 56; **Retro. Supp. III:** 57, 59; **Supp. XIII:** 332, 335, 346; **Supp. XV:** 165

La Gallienne, Eva, **Supp. VIII:** 251

"Lager Beer" (Dunbar), **Supp. II Part 1:** 193

"La Gringuita: On Losing a Native Language" (Alvarez), **Supp. VII:** 18

Laguna Woman (Silko), **Supp. IV Part 2:** 557, 560–561

LaHaye, Tim, **Supp. XXVII:** 5

Lahiri, Jhumpa, **Supp. XXI: 175–189; Supp. XXIII:** 289

Lahr, John, **Supp. XXI:** 18

Laing, R. D., **Supp. I Part 2:** 527; **Supp. XX: 94**

Lainoff, Seymour, **Supp. XXVIII:** 146, 148, 151, 152, 153, 155, 156, 158

La kabbale pratique (Ambelain), **Supp. I Part 1:** 273

"Lake, The" (Bradbury), **Supp. IV Part 1:** 101

Lake, The (play), **Supp. IX:** 189

"Lake, The" (Poe), **Retro. Supp. III:** 231

Lakeboat (Mamet), **Supp. XIV:** 240–241

"Lake Chelan" (Stafford), **Supp. XI:** 321

Lake Effect Country (Ammons), **Supp. VII:** 34, 35

"Lake Isle of Innisfree, The" (Yeats), **Retro. Supp. I:** 413; **Supp. XIX:** 92

"Lake Return" (Wright), **Supp. XV:** 345

Lake Wobegon Days (Keillor), **Supp. XVI:** 165, 166, **173–174**

Lake Wobegon Summer 1956 (Keillor), **Supp. XVI:** 178

Lalic, Ivan V., **Supp. VIII:** 272

Lamantia, Philip, **Supp. VIII:** 289

Lamb, Brian, **Supp. XIX:** 156; **Supp. XX:** 101

Lamb, Charles, **III:** 111, 207; **Supp. VIII:** 125

Lamb, Wendy, **Supp. IV Part 2:** 658

Lambardi, Marilyn May, **Retro. Supp. II:** 45–46

Lamb in His Bosom (C. Miller), **Supp. XXII:** 187, **189–191**, 193–194, 195, 197, 198, 199, 200

"Lambkill" (Davison), **Supp. XXVI:** 75

"Lame Feet of Salvation, The" (W. V. Davis), **Supp. XXI:** 87–88

"Lament" (Wilbur), **Supp. III Part 2:** 550

Lament and Chastisement (O'Hara), **Supp. XXIII:** 209

"Lamentation in Winter"(Schott), **Supp. XXIII:** 243

"Lamentations" (Glück), **Supp. V:** 83, 84

"Lamentations of Jeremiah Johnson, The"(Stuart), **Supp. XXVIII:** 227

"Lament for Dark Peoples" (Hughes), **Retro. Supp. I:** 199

"Lament for Saul and Jonathan" (Bradstreet), **Supp. I Part 1:** 111

"Lament-Heaven" (Doty), **Supp. XI:** 125

"Lament of a New England Mother, The" (Eberhart), **I:** 539

Laments for the Living (Parker), **Supp. IX:** 192

"Lame Shall Enter First, The" (O'Connor), **III:** 348, 351, 352, 355, 356–357, 358; **Retro. Supp. II:** 237; **Retro. Supp. III:** 215

"Lamia" (Davison), **Supp. XXVI:** 74

Lamia (Keats), **II:** 512; **III:** 523

Lamming, George, **Supp. XXI:** 170

Lamott, Anne, **Supp. XX: 131–146**

La Motte-Fouqué, Friedrich Heinrich Karl, **III:** 77, 78

L'Amour, Louis, **Supp. XIII:** 5; **Supp. XXVI:** 186

Lamp for Nightfall, A (Caldwell), **I:** 297

Lamplit Answer, The (Schnackenberg), **Supp. XV:** 251, 254, **256–260**

"Lana Turner Has Collapsed!"(O'Hara), **Supp. XXIII:** 220

"Lance" (Nabokov), **Retro. Supp. I:** 266

Lancelot (Percy), **Supp. III Part 1:** 384, 395–396

Lancelot (Robinson), **III:** 513, 522

Lanchester, John, **Retro. Supp. I:** 278

"Land" (Emerson), **II:** 6

"Land Aesthetic, The" (Callicott), **Supp. XIV:** 184

Land and Freedom (film, Loach), **Supp. XXIII:** 163

"Land and Language" (J. W. Miller), **Supp. XX: 170**

Landau, Deborah, **Supp. XI:** 122, 123

"Land beyond the Blow" (Bierce), **I:** 209

"Land Ethic, The" (Leopold), **Supp. XIV:** 179, 180, 183, 191, 192

Landfall (Wagoner), **Supp. IX:** 330

"Landing in Luck" (Faulkner), **Retro. Supp. I:** 85

"Landing on the Moon" (Swenson), **Supp. IV Part 2:** 643

"Landings" (Hoffman), **Supp. XVIII:** 86

"Landing Under Water, I See Roots" (A. Finch), **Supp. XVII:** 76

"Land"(Kenny), **Supp. XXIII:** 147

Landlord at Lion's Head, The (Howells), **II:** 276, 287–288

Landmarks of Healing: A Study of House Made of Dawn (Scarberry-García), **Supp. IV Part 2:** 486

Land of Little Rain, The (Dillard), **Supp. VI: 27–28**

Land of Look Behind, The (Cliff), **Supp. XXII:** 65–66, 68–69

Land of the Free U.S.A. (MacLeish), **I:** 293; **III:** 16–17

Land of Unlikeness (R. Lowell), **II:** 537–538, 539, 547; **Retro. Supp. II:** 177, 178, **184–185**

Landor, Walter Savage, **III:** 15, 469; **Supp. I Part 2:** 422

"Landscape" (Sarton), **Supp. VIII:** 259

"Landscape #11" (Halliday), **Supp. XIX:** 93

Landscape and Journey (W. V. Davis), **Supp. XXI:** 83, 88, 90, **92–93**, 95

"Landscape as a Nude" (MacLeish), **III:** 14

Landscape at the End of the Century (Dunn), **Supp. XI:** 139, 143, **150–151**

"Landscape Chamber, The" (Jewett), **II:** 408–409

"Landscape for the Disappeared" (Komunyakaa), **Supp. XIII:** 120, 126

Landscape in American Poetry (Larcom), **Supp. XIII:** 142

"Landscape Painter, A" (James), **II:** 322; **Retro. Supp. I:** 219

"Landscape Symbolism in Kate Chopin's *At Fault*" (Arner), **Retro. Supp. II:** 62

"Landscape: The Eastern Shore" (Barth), **I:** 122

"Landscape with a Blur of Conquerors"(Siken), **Supp. XXVIII:** 202

"Landscape with Black Coats in Show"(Siken), **Supp. XXVIII:** 200

"Landscape with Boat" (Stevens), **Retro. Supp. I:** 306

"Landscape with Bottles"(Schott), **Supp. XXIII:** 242

"Landscape with the Fall of Icarus" (Brueghel), **Retro. Supp. I:** 430

Land's End: A Walk through Provincetown (Cunningham), **Supp. XV:** 69

Land That Drank the Rain, The (Hoffman), **Supp. XVIII:** 76, 80, 81, 82

"Land Where There Is No Death, The" (Benét), **Supp. XI:** 56

Lane, Ann, **Supp. XI:** 195, 208

Lane, Cornelia. See Anderson, Mrs. Sherwood

Lane, Homer, **Supp. II Part 1:** 6; **Supp. XIV:** 160

Lane, John, **Supp. XXIV:** 22; **Supp. XXVII:** 216

Lane, Nathan, **Supp. XIII:** 207

Lane, Rose Wilder, **Supp. IV Part 2:** 524; **Supp. XXII:** 293–294, 295, 296, 297, 301

Lanes, Selma G., **Supp. XVI:** 104, 107

Lang, Andrew, **Retro. Supp. I:** 127; **Supp. XXVI:** 33

Lang, John, **Supp. XXVII:** 215, 221, 227, 229

Lang, Violet, **Supp. XII:** 119

Lang, V. R. "Bunny", **Supp. XXIII:** 209

Langdon, Olivia. *See* Clemens, Mrs. Samuel Langhorne (Olivia Langdon)

Lange, Carl Georg, **II:** 350

Lange, Dorothea, **I:** 293; **Supp. XIV:** 181

Langland, Joseph, **III:** 542

Langston Hughes, American Poet (Walker), **Supp. III Part 2:** 530–531

Langston Hughes and the "Chicago Defender": Essays on Race, Politics, and Culture (De Santis, ed.), **Retro. Supp. I:** 194

Langston Hughes: Modern Critical Views (Bloom, ed.), **Retro. Supp. I:** 193

Langston Hughes Reader, The (Hughes), **Retro. Supp. I:** 202; **Supp. I Part 1:** 345

Langston Hughes: The Poet and His Critics (Barksdale), **Retro. Supp. I:** 202

"Language, Visualization and the Inner Library" (Shepard), **Supp. III Part 2:** 436, 438, 449

Language and Imagery of the Bible, The (Caird), **Supp. XXI:** 91–92

"Language and the Writer" (Bambara), **Supp. XI:** 18

Language As Gesture (Blackmur), **Supp. II Part 1:** 108

Language as Symbolic Action (Burke), **I:** 275, 282, 285

Language Book, The (Andrews and Bernstein), **Supp. IV Part 2:** 426

"Language Divine!" (J. Schoolcraft), **Supp. XXIII:** 225

Language God Talks, The: On Science and Religion (Wouk), **Supp. XXV:** 257, 267

Language in Thought and Action (Hayakawa), **I:** 448

"Language of Being and Dying, The" (Gass), **Supp. VI:** 91

"Language of Home, The" (Wideman), **Supp. X:** 320, 323–324

Language of Life, The (Moyers, television series), **Supp. XIII:** 274, 276

Language of the American South, The (Brooks), **Supp. XIV:** 14

"Language of the Brag, The" (Olds), **Supp. X:** 204

"Language We Know, The" (Ortiz), **Supp. IV Part 2:** 500

Lanier, Clifford, **Supp. I Part 1:** 349, 350, 353, 355, 356, 371

Lanier, James F. D., **Supp. I Part 1:** 350

Lanier, Lyle H., **Supp. X:** 25

Lanier, Robert Sampson, **Supp. I Part 1:** 349, 351, 355, 356, 361

Lanier, Mrs. Robert Sampson (Mary Jane Anderson), **Supp. I Part 1:** 349

Lanier, Sidney, **IV:** 444; **Supp. I Part 1:** **349–373; Supp. I Part 2:** 416; **Supp.**

IV Part 1: 165

Lanier, Mrs. Sidney (Mary Day), **Supp. I Part 1:** 351, 355, 357, 361, 362, 364, 370, 371

"Lanier as Poet" (Parks), **Supp. I Part 1:** 373

"Lanier's Reading" (P. Graham), **Supp. I Part 1:** 373

"Lanier's Use of Science for Poetic Imagery" (Beaver), **Supp. I Part 1:** 373

Lankes, J. J., **Supp. XXII:** 275

Lannegan, Helen. *See* Caldwell, Mrs. Erskine

Lannin, Paul, **II:** 427

Lanny Budd novels (Sinclair), **Supp. V:** 290

Lansdale, Joe R., **Supp. XXV:** 145

Lant, Kathleen Margaret, **Supp. V:** 141

Lanterns on the Levee (Percy), **Supp. XXII:** 193

Lanthenas, François, **Supp. I Part 2:** 515

"Lanyard, The" (Collins), **Supp. XXI:** 56, **62–64**

Laotzu, **III:** 173, 189, 567; **Supp. XV:** 39, 46, 48

Lapine, James, **Supp. XXI:** 147–148

"Lapis Lazuli" (Yeats), **I:** 532; **III:** 40

Laplace, Pierre Simon de, **III:** 428

Lapouge, M. G., **Supp. I Part 2:** 633

Lappa, Katherine, **Supp. XV:** 176

Lapsing to Grace (Espaillat), **Supp. XXI:** 99, 100

Lapsley, Gaillard, **Retro. Supp. III:** 289; **Supp. XX:** 231

Laqueur, Thomas, **Supp. XVI:** 154

Larbaud, Valery, **IV:** 404; **Supp. XIII:** 332; **Supp. XIV:** 338

Larcom, Lucy, **Retro. Supp. II:** 145; **Supp. XIII:** **137–157**

Larcom's Poetical Works (Larcom), **Supp. XIII:** 142

Lardner, James, **Supp. XXVII:** 141

Lardner, John, **II:** 437

Lardner, Ring, **I:** 487; **II:** 44, 91, 259, 263, **415–438; III:** 566, 572; **IV:** 433; **Retro. Supp. I:** 105; **Retro. Supp. II:** 222; **Supp. I Part 2:** 609; **Supp. IX:** 200; **Supp. XVI:** 189

Lardner, Ring, Jr., **Supp. XI:** 306

"Lardner, Shakespeare and Chekhov" (Matthews), **II:** 430

"Large Bad Picture" (Bishop), **Retro. Supp. II:** 43; **Supp. I Part 1:** 73, 80–82, 85, 86, 89, 90

"Large Coffee" (Lardner), **II:** 437

Large Glass, or The Bride Stripped Bare by Her Bachelors, Even (Duchamp), **Supp. IV Part 2:** 423, 424

Largo (Handel), **IV:** 369

"Lark" (Taggard), **Supp. XXII:** 280

Lark, The (Hellman), **Supp. I Part 1:** 286–288, 297

Lark: Four-Part Chorus for Mixed Voices (A Capella) with Baritone Solo (Taggard and Copland), **Supp. XXII:** 283

Larkin, Philip, **Supp. I Part 2:** 536; **Supp. XI:** 243, 249; **Supp. XIII:** 76, 85; **Supp. XV:** 117, 251; **Supp. XVII:**

110; **Supp. XVIII:** 173; **Supp. XX:** **199; Supp. XXI:** 84, 93; **Supp. XXVI:** 67

Larkin, Sharon Alile, **Supp. XI:** 20

Larmore, Phoebe, **Supp. X:** 266

Larner, Jeremy, **Supp. XVI:** 220

La Rochefoucauld, François de, **I:** 279; **II:** 111; **Supp. XIV:** 130

"La Rose des Vents" (Wilbur), **Supp. III Part 2:** 550

"Larry Brown's *Dirty Work*: A Study of Man's Responsibility for Suffering" (Prevost), **Supp. XXI:** 45

"Larry" (O'Hara), **Supp. XXIII:** 212

Larry's Party (Shields), **Supp. VII:** 324, 326–327

Larsen, Nella, **Retro. Supp. III:** 140; **Supp. I Part 1:** 325, 326; **Supp. IV Part 1:** 164; **Supp. XVIII:** 119–134

Larson, Charles, **Supp. IV Part 1:** 331

Larson, Clinton, **Supp. XI:** 328

Larson, Kelli, **Supp. XVIII:** 131

LaRue, Dorie, **Supp. XXI:** 43

"Larval Stage of a Bookworm" (Mencken), **III:** 101

La Salle and the Discovery of the Great West (Parkman), **Supp. II Part 2:** 595, 598, 605–607; **Supp. XVIII:** 114

Las Casas, Bartolomé de, **Supp. XXIV:** 87

Lasch, Christopher, **I:** 259

Lasdun, James, **Supp. XXIV:** 154

Lasher (Rice), **Supp. VII:** 299–300

Lask, Thomas, **III:** 576; **Supp. XVI:** 250

Laski, Harold, **Supp. I Part 2:** 632, 643

Lass, Abraham H., **Supp. XXIV:** 214

Lassalle, Ferdinand, **IV:** 429

Lasser, Louise, **Supp. XV:** 4

"Last Acts" (Olds), **Supp. X:** 210

Last Adam, The (Cozzens), **I:** 362–363, 364, 368, 375, 377, 378, 379

Last Analysis, The (Bellow), **I:** 152, 160, 161; **Retro. Supp. II:** 26

Last and Lost Poems of Delmore Schwartz (Phillips, ed.), **Supp. II Part 2:** 661, 665

Last Avant-Garde, The: The Making of the New York School of Poets (Lehman), **Supp. XV:** 178–179, 187

Last Beautiful Days of Autumn, The (Nichols), **Supp. XIII:** 254, 255, 267, 269

Last Best Place, The: A Montana Anthology (Kittredge and Smith, eds.), **Supp. XXVI:** 188

Last Blue (Stern), **Supp. IX:** 299–300

Last Book, The (Pickering), **Supp. XXI:** 203–204

Last Carousel, The (Algren), **Supp. IX:** 16

Last Centennial, The (P. N. Warren as Kilina), **Supp. XX:** 261–262

"Last Child" (X. J. Kennedy), **Supp. XV:** 162, 165

"Last Class with Roethke" (Gallagher), **Supp. XXIV:** 171

Last Clean Shirt, The (film, Leslie and O'Hara), **Supp. XXIII:** 217

Last Coyote, The (Connelly), **Supp. XXI:** **71**

"Last Dance" (Dubus III), **Supp. XXIV:** 100

"Last Day in the Field, The" (Gordon), **II:** 200

"Last Day of the Last Furlough" (Salinger), **III:** 552–553

"Last Days of Alice" (Tate), **IV:** 129

"Last Days of August, The" (Nye), **Supp. XIII:** 284

"Last Days of John Brown, The" (Thoreau), **IV:** 185

Last Days of Louisiana Red, The (Reed), **Supp. X:** 240, **248–249**

Last Days of Shylock, The (Lewisohn), **Supp. XXVIII:** 150, 152, 153

Last Decade, The (Trilling), **Supp. III Part 2:** 493, 499

"Last Demon, The" (Singer), **IV:** 15, 21

Last Detective, The (Crais), **Supp. XXI:** 70

Last Exit to Brooklyn (Selby), **Supp. III Part 1:** 125; **Supp. XXI:** 227, 231

Last Flower, The (Thurber), **Supp. I Part 2:** 610

"Last Frontier" (McCarriston), **Supp. XIV:** 272

Last Generation, The (Moraga), **Supp. XXIII:** 201

Last Gentleman, The (Percy), **Supp. III Part 1:** 383–388, 392–393

"Last Good Country, The" (Hemingway), **II:** 258–259

Last Good Time, The (Bausch), **Supp. VII:** 45–46

"Last Great Saloon, The"(Exley), **Supp. XXIII:** 103

"Last Hiding Places of Snow, The" (Kinnell), **Supp. III Part 1:** 252

"Last Hours, The" (Dunn), **Supp. XI:** 141

Last House: Reflections, Dreams, and Observations, 1943–1991 (M. F. K. Fisher), **Supp. XVII:** 92

Last Husband and Other Stories, The (Humphrey), **Supp. IX:** 94

"Last Interview" (Rash), **Supp. XXVII:** 218

Last Jew in America, The (Fiedler), **Supp. XIII:** 103

"Last Jew in America, The" (Fiedler), **Supp. XIII:** 103

Last Laugh, Mr. Moto (Marquand), **III:** 57

"Last Leaf, The" (Holmes), **Supp. I Part 1:** 302, 309

"Last Leaf, The" (Porter), **III:** 444

"Last Lie, The" (Weigl), **Supp. XIX:** 279

"Last Light" (Major), **Supp. XXII:** 185

"Last Look at the Lilacs" (Stevens), **IV:** 74

Last Man, The (Kees), **Supp. XV:** 142, 143, 145

"Last May" (Dixon), **Supp. XII: 143**

"Last Mermother, The" (A. Finch), **Supp. XVII:** 72

"Last Mohican, The" (Malamud), **Supp. I Part 2:** 437–438, 450, 451

"Lastness" (Kinnell), **Supp. III Part 1:** 248–249

"Last Night" (Olds), **Supp. X:** 212

Last Night at the Lobster (O'Nan), **Supp. XXV:** 149–150, 151

"Last Night at Tía's" (Alvarez), **Supp. VII:** 5

Last Night of Summer, The (Caldwell), **I:** 292–293

Last Notes from Home (Exley), **Supp. XXIII:** 97, 98, **106–108**

Last of Mr. Norris, The (Isherwood), **Supp. XIV:** 161

"Last of the Brooding Miserables, The" (Karr), **Supp. XI:** 250

"Last of the Caddoes, The" (Humphrey), **Supp. IX:** 101

Last of the Crazy People, The (Findley), **Supp. XX:** 51–52

"Last of the Gold Star Mothers, The" (C. Bly), **Supp. XVI:** 34, 35, 36

"Last of the Legions, The" (Benét), **Supp. XI:** 56, 57

Last of the Mohicans, The (Cooper), **I:** 341, 342, 349

Last of the Red Hot Lovers (Simon), **Supp. IV Part 2:** 575, 583, 589

"Last of the Valerii, The" (James), **II:** 327; **Retro. Supp. I:** 218

"Last One, The" (Merwin), **Supp. III Part 1:** 355

Last Picture Show, The (film), **Supp. V:** 223, 226

Last Picture Show, The (McMurtry), **Supp. V:** 220, 222–223, 233

Last Place on Earth, The: Scott and Amundsen's Race to the South Pole (Huntford), **Supp. XVIII:** 114

Last Puritan, The (Santayana), **III:** 64, 600, 604, 607, 612, 615–617

Last Radio Baby, The (Andrews), **Supp. XXVI:** 2–3, 7, 10

"Last Ride Together, The" (Browning), **I:** 468

"Last River, The" (Kinnell), **Supp. III Part 1:** 236

Last Song, The (Harjo), **Supp. XII:** 218

"Last Song for the Mend-It Shop" (Nye), **Supp. XIII:** 283

Last Summer with Maizon (Woodson), **Supp. XXVIII:** 279, 287

"Last Supper in Montana"(Bottoms), **Supp. XXVIII:** 28

"Last Tango in Fresno" (Salinas), **Supp. XIII:** 318

"Last Trip to Greece"(Hadas), **Supp. XXIII:** 118–119

Last Tycoon, The: An Unfinished Novel (Fitzgerald), **II:** 84, 98; **Retro. Supp. I:** 109, 114, **114–115; Retro. Supp. II:** 337; **Supp. IV Part 1:** 203; **Supp. IX:** 63; **Supp. XII:** 173; **Supp. XIII:** 170; **Supp. XVIII:** 248, 250

"Last WASP in the World, The" (Fiedler), **Supp. XIII:** 103

"Last Watch, The" (Gibran), **Supp. XX: 119**

Last Watch of the Night: Essays Too Personal and Otherwise (Monette), **Supp. X:** 147, 148, 153, **157–159**

"Last Will" (Stallings), **Supp. XXV:** 232

"Last Word, The" (column, Quindlen), **Supp. XVII:** 165, 167, 170

Last Word, The: Letters between Marcia Nardi and William Carlos Williams (O'Neil, ed.), **Retro. Supp. I:** 427

"Last Words" (Levine), **Supp. V:** 190

"Last Words" (Olds), **Supp. X:** 210

Last Worthless Evening, The (Dubus), **Supp. VII:** 87–88

Last Yankee, The (A. Miller), **Retro. Supp. III:** 170, 172

"Las Vegas (What?) Las Vegas (Can't Hear You! Too Noisy) Las Vegas! ! ! !" (Wolfe), **Supp. III Part 2:** 572

"Late" (Bogan), **Supp. III Part 1:** 53

"Late Air" (Bishop), **Supp. I Part 1:** 89

"Late Autumn" (Sarton), **Supp. VIII:** 261

"Late Bronze, Early Iron: A Journey Book" (Sobin), **Supp. XVI:** 290

Late Child, The (McMurtry), **Supp. V:** 231

"Late Conversation" (Doty), **Supp. XI:** 122

"Late Elegy for John Berryman, A" (W. V. Davis), **Supp. XXI:** 91

"Late Encounter with the Enemy, A" (O'Connor), **III:** 345; **Retro. Supp. II:** 232

Late Fire, Late Snow (Francis), **Supp. IX: 89–90**

"Late Fragment" (Gallagher), **Supp. XXIV:** 172

Late George Apley, The (Marquand), **II:** 482–483; **III:** 50, 51, 52, 56–57, 58, 62–64, 65, 66

Late George Apley, The (Marquand and Kaufman), **III:** 62

"Late Hour" (Everwine), **Supp. XV:** 85

Late Hour, The (Strand), **Supp. IV Part 2:** 620, 629–630

"Lately, at Night" (Kumin), **Supp. IV Part 2:** 442

"Late Moon" (Levine), **Supp. V:** 186

"Late Night Ode" (McClatchy), **Supp. XII:** 262–263

Later (Creeley), **Supp. IV Part 1:** 153, 156, 157

Later Life (Gurney), **Supp. V:** 103, 105

La Terre (Zola), **III:** 316, 322

Later the Same Day (Paley), **Supp. VI:** 218

"Late September in Nebraska" (Kooser), **Supp. XIX:** 120

Late Settings (Merrill), **Supp. III Part 1:** 336

"Late Sidney Lanier, The" (Stedman), **Supp. I Part 1:** 373

"Late Snow & Lumber Strike of the Summer of Fifty-Four, The" (Snyder), **Supp. VIII:** 294

"Late Start, A" (L. Brown), **Supp. XXI:** 40–41

"Latest Freed Man, The" (Stevens), **Retro. Supp. I:** 306

"Latest Injury, The" (Olds), **Supp. X:** 209

Latest Literary Essays and Addresses (J. R. Lowell), **Supp. I Part 2:** 407

"Late Subterfuge" (Warren), **IV:** 257

"Late Summer Lilies" (Weigl), **Supp. XIX:** 288

"Late Summer Love Song" (Davison), **Supp. XXVI:** 69

"Late Supper, A" (Jewett), **Retro. Supp. II:** 137

"Late Victorians" (Rodriguez), **Supp. XIV:** 303–304

"Late Walk, A" (Frost), **II:** 153; **Retro. Supp. I:** 127

Latham, Edyth, **I:** 289

Lathrop, George Parsons, **Supp. I Part 1:** 365

Lathrop, H. B., **Supp. III Part 2:** 612

Lathrop, Julia, **Supp. I Part 1:** 5

Latière de Trianon, La (Wekerlin), **II:** 515

"La Tigresse" (Van Vechten), **Supp. II Part 2:** 735, 738

Latimer, Hugh, **II:** 15

Latimer, Margery, **Supp. IX:** 320

La Tour Dreams of the Wolf Girl (Huddle), **Supp. XXVI:** 148, 151, 158, 159

La Traviata (Verdi), **III:** 139

"Latter-Day Warnings" (Holmes), **Supp. I Part 1:** 307

"Latter Rain, The" (Very), **Supp. XXV:** 249

"Lattice Work: Formal Tendencies in the Poetry of Robert Morgan and Ron Rash" (Graves), **Supp. XXVII:** 216

La Turista (Shepard), **Supp. III Part 2:** 440

Lauber, John, **Supp. XIII:** 21

Laud, Archbishop, **II:** 158

"Lauds" (Auden), **Supp. II Part 1:** 23

"Laughing Man, The" (Salinger), **III:** 559

Laughing Matters (Siegel), **Supp. XXII:** 260

Laughing to Keep From Crying (Hughes), **Supp. I Part 1:** 329–330

Laughing Wild (Durang), **Supp. XXIV:** 114, **124**

"Laughing with One Eye" (Schnackenberg), **Supp. XV:** 253

Laughlin, James, **III:** 171; **Retro. Supp. I:** 423, 424, 428, 430, 431; **Supp. VIII:** 195; **Supp. XV:** 140; **Supp. XVI:** 284; **Supp. XXI:** 29

Laughlin, Jay, **Supp. II Part 1:** 94

Laughlin, J. Laurence, **Supp. I Part 2:** 641

Laughter in the Dark (Nabokov), **III:** 255–258; **Retro. Supp. I:** 270

"Laughter of Women, The" (Davison), **Supp. XXVI:** 75

Laughter on the 23rd Floor (Simon), **Supp. IV Part 2:** 575, 576, 588, 591–592

"Launcelot" (Lewis), **II:** 439–440

"Laura Dailey's Story" (Bogan), **Supp. III Part 1:** 52

Laurel, Stan, **Supp. I Part 2:** 607; **Supp. IV Part 2:** 574

Laurel and Hardy Go to Heaven (Auster), **Supp. XII:** 21

Laurence, Alexander, **Supp. XVIII:** 138

Laurence, Dan H., **II:** 338–339

Laurens, John, **Supp. I Part 2:** 509

Lauter, Paul, **Supp. XV:** 313

Lautréamont, Comte de, **III:** 174

Lavender Locker Room, The (P. N. Warren), **Supp. XX:** 261, 273–274

Law, John, **Supp. XI:** 307

Law and Order (television), **Supp. XVII:** 153

Law and the Testimony, The (S. and A. Warner), **Supp. XVIII:** 264

Lawd Today (Wright), **IV:** 478, 492

Law for the Lion, A (Auchincloss), **Supp. IV Part 1:** 25

Lawgiver, The (Wouk), **Supp. XXV:** 253, 256, 257, 267–268

"Law Lane" (Jewett), **II:** 407

"Lawns of June, The" (Peacock), **Supp. XIX:** 196

"Law of Nature and the Dream of Man, The: Ruminations of the Art of Fiction" (Stegner), **Supp. IV Part 2:** 604

Lawrence, D. H., **I:** 291, 336, 377, 522, 523; **II:** 78, 84, 98, 102, 264, 517, 523, 532, 594, 595; **III:** 27, 33, 40, 44, 46, 172, 173, 174, 178, 184, 229, 261, 423, 429, 458, 546–547; **IV:** 138, 339, 342, 351, 380; **Retro. Supp. I:** 7, 18, 203, 204, 421; **Retro. Supp. II:** 68; **Retro. Supp. III:** 25, 147; **Supp. I Part 1:** 227, 230, 243, 255, 257, 258, 263, 329; **Supp. I Part 2:** 546, 613, 728; **Supp. II Part 1:** 1, 9, 20, 89; **Supp. IV Part 1:** 81; **Supp. VIII:** 237; **Supp. X:** 137, 193, 194; **Supp. XII:** 172; **Supp. XIV:** 310; **Supp. XV:** 45, 46, 158, 254; **Supp. XVI:** 267; **Supp. XX: 69; Supp. XXII:** 198; **Supp. XXIII:** 166, 275; **Supp. XXIV:** 51, 52, 57, 58, 64; **Supp. XXVI:** 144

Lawrence, Elizabeth, **Supp. XXIII:** 259, 264

Lawrence, Frieda, **Supp. XV:** 46

Lawrence, Rhoda, **Supp. I Part 1:** 45

Lawrence, Seymour, **Supp. IX:** 107; **Supp. XI:** 335, 346, 348

Lawrence, T. E., **Supp. XIV:** 159

Lawrence of Arabia (Aldington), **Supp. I Part 1:** 259

Lawrence of Arabia (film), **Supp. I Part 1:** 67

Laws (Hadas), **Supp. XXIII: 119–120,** 124

Laws (Plato), **Supp. IV Part 1:** 391

Laws of Ice, The (Price), **Supp. VI:** 264

Laws of Our Fathers, The (Turow), **Supp. XVII: 218–219**

Lawson, John Howard, **I:** 479, 482; **Supp. XXVIII:** 74, 79, 80

Lawton Girl, The (Frederic), **II:** 132–133, 144

Layachi, Larbi (Driss ben Hamed Charhadi), **Supp. IV Part 1:** 92, 93

Layard, John, **Supp. XIV:** 160

Lay Down My Sword and Shield (Burke), **Supp. XIV:** 22, 25, 34

"Layers, The" (Kunitz), **Supp. III Part 1:** 260, 266–267

"Layers, The: Some Notes on 'The Abduction' " (Kunitz), **Supp. III Part 1:** 266

"Lay-mans Lamentation, The" (Taylor), **IV:** 162–163

Lay of the Land, The: Metaphor as Experience and History in American

Life and Letters (Kolodny), **Supp. X:** 97

"Layover" (Hass), **Supp. VI:** 109

"Lay Preacher" (Dennie), **Supp. I Part 1:** 125

Layton, Irving, **Supp. XII:** 121

Lazar, Irving "Swifty", **Supp. XIX:** 250

Lazarillo de Tormes (Mendoza), **III:** 182

Lazar Malkin Enters Heaven (S. Stern), **Supp. XVII:** 42; **Supp. XX:** 178

Lazarus Laughed (O'Neill), **III:** 391, 395–396

Lazer, Hank, **Supp. IX:** 265

Lea, Luke, **IV:** 248

Lea, Sydney, **Supp. XXVIII: 129–143**

Leachman, Cloris, **Supp. XXI:** 146

Leacock, Stephen, **Supp. IV Part 2:** 464

"LEADBELLY GIVES AN AUTOGRAPH" (Baraka), **Supp. II Part 1:** 49

Leaflets: Poems, 1965–1968 (Rich), **Retro. Supp. III:** 242, 244; **Supp. I Part 2:** 551, 556–557

"League of American Writers, The: Communist Organizational Activity among American Writers 1929–1942" (Wolfe), **Supp. III Part 2:** 568

League of Brightened Philistines and Other Papers, The (Farrell), **II:** 49

Leahy, Anna, **Supp. XXI:** 246

"Leakage" (Skloot), **Supp. XX: 202**

Leal, Luis, **Supp. XIX:** 98, 112

"Leaning" (Webb), **Supp. XX: 56**

Leaning Forward (Paley), **Supp. VI:** 221

"Leaning Tower, The" (Porter), **III:** 442, 443, 446–447

Leaning Tower and Other Stories, The (Porter), **III:** 433, 442, 443–447

"Leap, The" (Dickey), **Supp. IV Part 1:** 182

"Leaping Up into Political Poetry" (R. Bly), **Supp. IV Part 1:** 61, 63

Leap Year (Cameron), **Supp. XII:** 79–80, 81, **85–86,** 88

Lear, Bernadette, **Retro. Supp. III:** 264

Lear, Edward, **III:** 428, 536; **Supp. XVI:** 103; **Supp. XXVI:** 274

Lear, Linda, **Supp. IX:** 19, 22, 25, 26

Learned Ladies, The (Molière; Wilbur, trans.), **Supp. III Part 2:** 560

"Learning a Dead Language" (Merwin), **Supp. III Part 1:** 345

Learning a Trade: A Craftsman's Notebooks, 1955–1997 (Price), **Supp. VI:** 254, 255, 267

"Learning Bones" (Espaillat), **Supp. XXI:** 107

Learning to Live in This World (Schott), **Supp. XXIII:** 248

Learning to Love: Exploring Solitude and Freedom (Merton), **Supp. VIII:** 200

Learning to Love You More (website), **Supp. XXIV:** 200

"Learning to Read" (Harper), **Supp. II Part 1:** 201–202

"Learning to Speak" (Everwine), **Supp. XV:** 79

"Learning to Speak" (Gansworth), **Supp. XXVI:** 111

"Learning to Think" (Kittredge), **Supp. XXVI:** 181

"Learning to Work Together" (L. I. Wilder), **Supp. XXII:** 290

Learning Tree, The (Park), **Supp. XIX:** 154

Leary, Lewis, **III:** 478

Leary, Paris, **Supp. IV Part 1:** 176

Leary, Timothy, **Supp. X:** 265; **Supp. XIV:** 150

Lease, Joseph, **Supp. XXI:** 246

Least Heat Moon, William, **Supp. V:** 169

Leather-Stocking Tales, The (Cooper), **I:** 335

Leatherwood God, The (Howells), **II:** 276, 277, 288

Leave It to Beaver (television show), **Supp. XX:** 103

"Leave Me Alone a Little" (Taggard), **Supp. XXII:** 274

"Leaves" (Updike), **Retro. Supp. I:** 323, 329, 335

Leaves and Ashes (Haines), **Supp. XII:** 206

Leaves from the Notebook of a Tamed Cynic (Niebuhr), **III:** 293

Leaves of Grass (Whitman), **II:** 8; **IV:** 331, 332, 333, 334, 335, 336, 340, 341–342, 348, 350, 405, 464; **Retro. Supp. I:** 387, 388, 389, 390, **392–395,** 406, 407, 408; **Retro. Supp. II:** 93; **Retro. Supp. III:** 298, 300, 302, 303–304, 310; **Supp. I Part 1:** 365; **Supp. I Part 2:** 416, 579; **Supp. III Part 1:** 156; **Supp. IX:** 265; **Supp. V:** 170; **Supp. VIII:** 275; **Supp. X:** 120; **Supp. XIV:** 334; **Supp. XIX:** 276; **Supp. XV:** 218; **Supp. XVIII:** 4; **Supp. XXI:** 205; **Supp. XXII:** 92; **Supp. XXIII:** 165; **Supp. XXIV:** 85

"Leaves of Grass" (Whitman), **IV:** 463

Leaves of Grass (1856) (Whitman), **Retro. Supp. I:** 399–402

Leaves of Grass (1860) (Whitman), **Retro. Supp. I:** 402–405

Leaves of the Tree, The (Masters), **Supp. I Part 2:** 460

"Leaving" (Hogan), **Supp. IV Part 1:** 400

"Leaving" (Wilbur), **Supp. III Part 2:** 563

"Leaving, The" (B. Kelly), **Supp. XVII:** 127, 132

Leaving a Doll's House: A Memoir (C. Bloom), **Retro. Supp. II:** 281

Leaving Another Kingdom: Selected Poems (Stern), **Supp. IX:** 296

"Leaving Bartram's Garden in Southwest Philadelphia" (Di Piero), **Supp. XIX:** 46

"Leaving Brooklyn" (Neugeboren), **Supp. XVI:** 226

Leaving Cheyenne (McMurtry), **Supp. V:** 220, 221–222, 224, 229

Leaving Home (Keillor), **Supp. XVI:** 175

"Leaving One, The" (Offutt), **Supp. XIX:** 165–166

"Leaving the Island" (Olds), **Supp. X:** 214

"Leaving the Yellow House" (Bellow), **Retro. Supp. II:** 27, 32

"Leaving Town" (Kenyon), **Supp. VII:** 163

Leavis, F. R., **I:** 522; **III:** 462–463, 475, 478; **Retro. Supp. I:** 67; **Retro. Supp. II:** 243; **Supp. I Part 2:** 536; **Supp. VIII:** 234, 236, 245

Leavis, Queenie, **Supp. XX: 232**

"Leavis-Snow Controversy, The" (Trilling), **Supp. III Part 2:** 512

Leavitt, Caroline, **Supp. XX: 186**

Leavitt, David, **Supp. VIII:** 88

Lebanon (C. Miller), **Supp. XXII:** 198–199

Le Braz, Anatole, **Supp. XIII:** 253

Le Carre, John, **Supp. XX: 195**

Lecker, Robert, **Supp. XIII:** 21

LeClair, Thomas (Tom), **Supp. IV Part 1:** 286; **Supp. V:** 53; **Supp. XII:** 152; **Supp. XX: 93; Supp. XXII:** 206, 210, 261, 264

Le Conte, Joseph, **II:** 479; **III:** 227–228

"Lecture, The" (Singer), **IV:** 21

"LECTURE PAST DEAD CATS" (Baraka), **Supp. II Part 1:** 52

Lectures in America (Stein), **IV:** 27, 32, 33, 35, 36, 41, 42

"Lectures on Poetry" (Bryant), **Supp. I Part 1:** 159, 161

Lectures on Rhetoric (Blair), **II:** 8

"Leda and the Swan" (Yeats), **III:** 347; **Supp. IX:** 52

Ledger (Fitzgerald), **Retro. Supp. I:** 109, 110

Lee (Masters), **Supp. I Part 2:** 471

Lee, Baayork, **Supp. XXI:** 148

Lee, C. Y., **Supp. XXI:** 148

Lee, Don, **Supp. XII:** 295; **Supp. XVII:** 13, 14, 15, 16

Lee, Don L. *See* Madhubuti, Haki R.

Lee, Gypsy Rose, **II:** 586; **III:** 161; **Supp. IV Part 1:** 84

Lee, Harper, **Supp. VIII: 113–131; Supp. XXVII:** 276

Lee, Harriett, **Supp. XV:** 230

Lee, Hermione, **Retro. Supp. III:** 277, 279, 283, 284, 287

Lee, James Kyun-Jin, **Supp. XV:** 213

Lee, James W., **Supp. IX:** 94, 97, 109

Lee, James Ward, **Supp. VIII:** 57

Lee, Lawrence, **Supp. XXV:** 29

Lee, Li Lin, **Supp. XV:** 211, 212

Lee, Li-Young, **Supp. XV: 211–228; Supp. XVII:** 241

Lee, Richard E., **Supp. XIX:** 226, 227

Lee, Robert E., **II:** 150, 206; **IV:** 126; **Supp. I Part 2:** 471, 486

Lee, Robert N., **Supp. XXVII:** 92

Lee, Samuel, **IV:** 158

Lee, Spike, **Retro. Supp. II:** 12; **Supp. XI:** 19; **Supp. XIII:** 179, 186; **Supp. XVI:** 144; **Supp. XX: 110; Supp. XXVI:** 199

Lee, Virginia Chin-lan, **Supp. X:** 291

Leeds, Barry, **Retro. Supp. II:** 204

Leeds, Daniel, **II:** 110

Leeds, Titan, **II:** 110, 111

Leeming, David, **Retro. Supp. II:** 4, 10

"Lees of Happiness, The" (Fitzgerald), **II:** 88

"Le Filme" (Weigl), **Supp. XIX:** 288

Left Behind series (LaHaye and Jenkins), **Supp. XXVII:** 5

Left Hand of God, The (film), **Supp. XXVI:** 134

Left Out in the Rain: New Poems 1947– 1985 (Snyder), **Supp. VIII:** 305

Leftovers, The (Perrota), **Supp. XXVII:** 6

"Legacy" (Dunn), **Supp. XI:** 148

"Legacy" (Komunyakaa), **Supp. XIII:** 132

"Legacy" (W. V. Davis), **Supp. XXI:** 93–94

"Legacy of Aldo Leopold, The" (Stegner), **Supp. XIV:** 193

"Legacy of Channing, The" (Robinson), **Supp. XXIV:** 79

Legacy of Fear, A (Farrell), **II:** 39

"Legacy of the Ancestral Arts, The" (Locke), **Supp. XIV:** 201

Legacy of the Civil War, The: Meditations on the Centennial (Warren), **IV:** 236

"Legal Alien" (Mora), **Supp. XIII:** 215

"Legal Tender Act, The" (Adams), **I:** 5

"Legend" (H. Crane), **Retro. Supp. III:** 45

Légende de la mort, La (Le Braz), **Supp. XIII:** 253

"Legend of Duluoz, The" (Kerouac), **Supp. III Part 1:** 218, 226, 227, 229

"Legend of Lillian Hellman, The" (Kazin), **Supp. I Part 1:** 297

"Legend of Monte del Diablo, The" (Harte), **Supp. II Part 1:** 339

"Legend of Paper Plates, The" (Haines), **Supp. XII:** 204

"Legend of Sammtstadt, A" (Harte), **Supp. II Part 1:** 355

"Legend of Sleepy Hollow, The" (Irving), **II:** 306–308

Legends (A. Lowell), **II:** 525–526

Legends and Dreams (P. N. Warren), **Supp. XX: 261**

Legends of Mexico (Lippard), **Supp. XXIII:** 178, 186

Legends of New England (Whittier), **Supp. I Part 2:** 684, 692

Legends of the Fall (Harrison), **Supp. VIII:** 38, 39, **45–46,** 48

"Legends of the Revolution"(series, Lippard), **Supp. XXIII:** 178

Legends of the West (Hall), **II:** 313

Léger, Fernand, **Retro. Supp. I:** 292

Legge, James, **III:** 472

Leggett, William, **Supp. I Part 1:** 157

"Legion, The" (Karr), **Supp. XI:** 243

"Legs" (Halliday), **Supp. XIX:** 90

Legs (W. Kennedy), **Supp. VII:** 133, 134, 138–142, 143, 151

Le Guin, Ursula K., **Supp. IV Part 1:** 333; **Supp. XXII:** 49

Lehan, Richard, **Retro. Supp. II:** 104

Lehman, David, **Supp. IX:** 161; **Supp. XIII:** 130; **Supp. XV:** 178–179, 180, 187, 190; **Supp. XXI:** 246; **Supp. XXVI:** 50

Lehmann, John, **Retro. Supp. II:** 243; **Supp. XIV:** 158, 159
Lehmann, Paul, **III:** 311
Lehmann-Haupt, Christopher, **Retro. Supp. II:** 291; **Supp. IV Part 1:** 205, 209, 306; **Supp. IX:** 95, 103; **Supp. XVI:** 73, 210, 294, 295; **Supp. XXII:** 205, 213; **Supp. XXIII:** 103
Lehrer, Jim, **Supp. XVIII:** 39
Leiber, Fritz, **Supp. XVI:** 123
Leibling, A. J., **Supp. XIV:** 112
Leibniz, Gottfried Wilhelm von, **II:** 103; **III:** 428
Leibowitz, Herbert A., **I:** 386; **Supp. XV:** 78
Leich, Roland, **Supp. XIV:** 123
Leichum, Laura, **Supp. XIX:** 197
Leider, Emily Wortis, **Supp. XXIV:** 19, 20, 22, 26, 27, 30
Leiding, Reba, **Supp. XXVI:** 159
Leighton, Betty, **Supp. XXI:** 42
Leimbach, Laura, **Supp. XXIII:** 54
Leithauser, Brad, **Retro. Supp. I:** 133; **Supp. XV:** 250; **Supp. XVII:** 112; **Supp. XXII:** 207
Leitz, Robert, **Supp. XIV:** 62
Leivick, H., **IV:** 6
Lekachman, Robert, **Supp. I Part 2:** 648
Leland, Charles, **Supp. II Part 1:** 193
Leland, Charles Godfrey, **I:** 257
Leland, John, **Supp. XIX:** 157; **Supp. XV:** 69
Lem, Stanislaw, **Supp. IV Part 1:** 103
"Le marais du cygne" (Whittier), **Supp. I Part 2:** 687
Lemay, Harding, **Supp. IX:** 98; **Supp. VIII:** 125
Lemercier, Eugène, **Retro. Supp. I:** 299
Lemkin, Raphael, **Supp. XXIII:** 31
"Lemorne *versus* Huell" (E. Stoddard), **Supp. XV:** 270, 273, 283
Le Morte D'Arthur Notes (Gardner), **Supp. VI:** 65, 66
Lena (Woodson), **Supp. XXVIII:** 280, 281
Lenhard, Elizabeth, **Supp. XXVII:** 267
Lenin, V. I., **I:** 366, 439, 440; **III:** 14–15, 262, 475; **IV:** 429, 436, 443–444; **Supp. I Part 2:** 647; **Supp. XXI:** 164
Lennertz, Carl, **Supp. XXVII:** 267
Lennon, J. Robert, **Supp. XXV:** 151
"Lenny Dying, Pacific Standard Time"(Thompson), **Supp. XXIII:** 294
"Lenore" (Poe), **III:** 411
"Lenox Avenue: Midnight" (Hughes), **Retro. Supp. I:** 198
"Lens of Poetry, The" (Bronk). *See Attendant, The* (Bronk)
Leonard, Elmore, **Supp. IV Part 1:** 356; **Supp. X:** 5; **Supp. XIV:** 26
Leonard, John, **Supp. IV Part 1:** 24; **Supp. IV Part 2:** 474; **Supp. V:** 164, 223–224; **Supp. XI:** 13; **Supp. XIX:** 269; **Supp. XVIII:** 147, 148; **Supp. XXI:** 233, 239
Leonardo da Vinci, **Supp. XII:** 44; **Supp. XXII:** 171
"Leonora's Kitchen"(Lea), **Supp. XXVIII:** 132
León-Portilla, Miguel, **Supp. XV:** 77

Leontiev, Constantine, **Supp. XIV:** 98
Leopard, The (Lampedusa), **Supp. XII:** 13–14
Leopardi, Giacomo, **II:** 543; **Supp. XIX:** 33, 43
"Leopard Man's Story, The" (London), **II:** 475
Leopard's Mouth Is Dry and Cold Inside, The (Levis), **Supp. XI:** 258
Leopold, Aldo, **Supp. V:** 202; **Supp. X:** 108; **Supp. XIV: 177–194; Supp. XXI:** 203; **Supp. XXVI:** 31; **Supp. XXVIII:** 243, 256
"Leper's Bell, the" (Komunyakaa), **Supp. XIII:** 118
Lerman, Leo, **Supp. X:** 188; **Supp. XVI:** 194
Lerner, Ben, **Supp. XXIV:** 45
Lerner, Max, **III:** 60; **Supp. I Part 2:** 629, 630, 631, 647, 650, 654; **Supp. XXVII:** 134
Lerperger, Emil, **Supp. XX: 165, 167**
Lesbian Nation: The Feminist Solution (Johnston), **Supp. XXV:** 5
"Lesbos" (Plath), **Retro. Supp. II:** 254
Lesesne, Teri, **Supp. XIII:** 277
LeSieg, Theo (pseudonym). *See* Geisel, Theodor Seuss (Dr. Seuss)
Leskov, Nikolai, **IV:** 299
Leslie, Alfred, **Supp. XII:** 127; **Supp. XXIII:** 217
"Less and Less Human, O Savage Spirit" (W. Stevens), **Supp. XVI:** 64
Lesser, Wendy, **Supp. IV Part 2:** 453; **Supp. XII:** 297; **Supp. XVI:** 201
Lessing, Gotthold, **Supp. I Part 2:** 422
"Lesson, The" (Bambara), **Supp. XI:** 5–6
"Lesson, The" (Dunbar), **Supp. II Part 1:** 199
"Lesson, The" (Olsen), **Supp. XIII:** 297
"Lesson, The"(Schott), **Supp. XXIII:** 254
"Lesson for the Ill Clothed and Ill Fed, A" (Ryan as Quin), **Supp. XVIII:** 230–231
Lesson of the Master, The (James), **Supp. XVIII:** 248
"Lesson of the Master, The" (James), **Retro. Supp. I:** 227
Lesson of the Masters: An Anthology of the Novel from Cervantes to Hemingway (Cowley-Hugo, ed.), **Supp. II Part 1:** 140
"Lesson on Concealment, A" (Brown), **Supp. I Part 1:** 133
"Lessons" (Epstein), **Supp. XII:** 163
"Lessons from an Older Man"(Thompson), **Supp. XXIII:** 293
"Lessons of the Body" (Simpson), **Supp. IX:** 267
Less than One (Brodsky), **Supp. VIII:** 22, 29–31
Less Than Zero (Ellis), **Supp. XXVII:** 67, 69–70, 71, 74, 75, 77, 78, 269
Less Than Zero (film), **Supp. XXVII:** 68, 77
Lester, Jerry, **Supp. IV Part 2:** 574
Lester, Ketty, **Supp. XV:** 133, 147
Le Style Apollinaire (Zukofsky), **Supp. III Part 2:** 616
Le Sueur, Arthur, **Supp. XXIII:** 161, 162

LeSueur, Joe, **Supp. XXIII:** 212, 216, 218, 220
Le Sueur, Meridel, **Supp. V:** 113, 130; **Supp. XII:** 217; **Supp. XXIII: 161–176; Supp. XXVI:** 28
Lesy, Michael, **Supp. XXV:** 146
"Let America Be America Again" (Hughes), **Retro. Supp. I:** 202; **Supp. I Part 1:** 331
Let Evening Come (Kenyon), **Supp. VII:** 160, 169–171
Lethem, Jonathan, **Supp. IX:** 122; **Supp. XVIII: 135–153; Supp. XXII:** 49; **Supp. XXVII:** 67
Let It Come Down (Bowles), **Supp. IV Part 1:** 87
Let It Ride (Pickering), **Supp. XXI:** 198–199
"Let Me Be" (Levine), **Supp. V:** 181, 189
"Let Me Begin Again" (Levine), **Supp. V:** 181, 189
"Let No Charitable Hope" (Wylie), **Supp. I Part 2:** 713–714, 729
Let No Man Write My Epitaph (film, Leacock), **Supp. XVII:** 150, 158
Let No Man Write My Epitaph (W. Motley), **Supp. XVII:** 150, **158–160**
Let Noon Be Fair (W. Motley), **Supp. XVII:** 161
Letofsky, Irv, **Supp. XVI:** 167
"Let one Eye his watches keep/While the Other Eye doth sleep" (Fletcher), **Supp. IV Part 2:** 621
Let's Balance the Books (radio show; Untermeyer), **Supp. XV:** 311
"Letter . . ." (Whittier), **Supp. I Part 2:** 687
"Letter, A" (Bogan), **Supp. III Part 1:** 54
"Letter, May 2, 1959" (Olson), **Supp. II Part 2:** 579, 580
"Letter, Much Too Late" (Stegner), **Supp. IV Part 2:** 613
"Letter, The" (Boulton), **Supp. XXII:** 22
"Letter, The" (Gioia), **Supp. XV:** 120
"Letter, The" (Malamud), **Supp. I Part 2:** 435–436
"Letter about Money, Love, or Other Comfort, If Any, The" (Warren), **IV:** 245
Letter Addressed to the People of Piedmont, on the Advantages of the French Revolution, and the Necessity of Adopting Its Principles in Italy, A (Barlow), **Supp. II Part 1:** 80, 81
"Letter for Marion, A" (McGrath), **Supp. X:** 116
"Letter from Aldermaston" (Merwin), **Supp. III Part 1:** 347
"Letter from a London Attic" (Pickering), **Supp. XXI:** 194
"Letter from a Region in My Mind" (Baldwin). *See* "Down at the Cross"
"Letter from Aunt Belle, A" (Kooser), **Supp. XIX:** 117
"Letter from Carson City" (Twain), **Retro. Supp. III:** 259
Letter from Li Po, A (Aiken), **I:** 68
"Letter from 'Manhattan' " (Didion), **Supp. IV Part 1:** 205

"Letter from the Country" (column, C. Bly), **Supp. XVI:** 33

Letter from the End of the Twentieth Century (Harjo), **Supp. XII:** 223

"Letter from the End of the Twentieth Century" (Harjo), **Supp. XII:** 227

"Letter Home" (Trethewey), **Supp. XXI:** 254

"Letter Number Three"(Wakoski), **Supp. XXVIII:** 264

"Letter on Céline" (Kerouac), **Supp. III Part 1:** 232

Letters (Cato), **II:** 114

Letters (Landor), **Supp. I Part 2:** 422

Letters (White), **Supp. I Part 2:** 651, 653, 675, 680

Letters (Wolfe), **IV:** 462

"Letters, The" (Swados), **Supp. XIX:** 261, 262

Letters and Leadership (Brooks), **I:** 228, 240, 245, 246

"Letters for the Dead" (Levine), **Supp. V:** 186

Letters from an American Farmer (Crèvecoeur), **Supp. I Part 1:** 227–251

Letters from Bohemia (Hecht), **Supp. XXVII:** 95

Letters from Maine (Sarton), **Supp. VIII:** 261

"Letters from Maine" (Sarton), **Supp. VIII:** 261

"Letters from My Father" (R. O. Butler), **Supp. XII:** 71

Letters from the Country (C. Bly), **Supp. XVI:** 33–34, 35, 37

Letters from the Earth (Twain), **IV:** 209

Letters from the East (Bryant), **Supp. I Part 1:** 158

"Letters from the Ming Dynasty" (Brodsky), **Supp. VIII:** 28

"Letters from the *Samantha*" (Helprin), **Supp. XXV:** 85

Letters of Angelicus and Fidelio Fobb (O'Hara and Berkson), **Supp. XXIII:** 218

Letters of a Traveller (Bryant), **Supp. I Part 1:** 158

Letters of a Traveller, Second Series (Bryant), **Supp. I Part 1:** 158

Letters of a Woman Homesteader (Stewart), **Supp. XXVI:** 183

Letters of Emily Dickinson, The (T. H. Johnson and Ward, eds.), **I:** 470; **Retro. Supp. I:** 28

Letters of William James (Henry James, ed.), **II:** 362

Letters on Various Interesting and Important Subjects . . . (Freneau), **Supp. II Part 1:** 272

Letters to a Niece (Adams), **I:** 22

Letters to a Teacher (Pickering), **Supp. XXI:** 195, 201–202

Letters to a Young Poet (Rilke), **Supp. XIII:** 74; **Supp. XV:** 93

"Letters to Dead Imagists" (Sandburg), **I:** 421

"Letters Written on a Ferry While Crossing Long Island Sound" (Sexton), **Supp. II Part 2:** 683

"Letter to Abbé Raynal" (Paine), **Supp. I Part 2:** 510

"Letter to a Kiss That Died for Us" (Gallagher), **Supp. XXIV:** 170

Letter to a Man in the Fire: Does God Exist or Does He Care? (Price), **Supp. VI:** 267–268

"Letter to American Teachers of History, A" (Adams), **I:** 19

Letter to an Imaginary Friend (McGrath), **Supp. X:** 111, 112–113, 116, **119–125**

"Letter to a Reader" (Sanders), **Supp. XVI:** 266, 267, 268, 269, 275

"Letter to a Young Author" (P. N. Warren), **Supp. XX:** 272

"Letter to a Young Contributor" (Higginson), **Retro. Supp. I:** 31

"Letter to a Young Writer" (Price), **Supp. VI:** 267

"Letter to Bell from Missoula" (Hugo), **Supp. VI:** 142–143

"Letter to E. Franklin Frazier" (Baraka), **Supp. II Part 1:** 49

"Letter to Elaine Feinstein" (Olson), **Supp. II Part 2:** 561

"Letter to Francis Picabia, A" (Boyle), **Supp. XXIV:** 63

"Letter to Freddy" (music) (Bowles), **Supp. IV Part 1:** 82

"Letter to Garber from Skye" (Hugo), **Supp. VI:** 146

"Letter to George Washington" (Paine), **Supp. I Part 2:** 517

"Letter to Her Husband, Absent upon Public Employment, A" (Bradstreet), **Retro. Supp. III:** 12

"Letter to His Brother" (Berryman), **I:** 172, 173

Letter to His Countrymen, A (Cooper), **I:** 346, 347, 349

"Letter to Kizer from Seattle" (Hugo), **Supp. VI:** 142

Letter to Lord Byron (Auden), **Supp. II Part 1:** 11

"Letter to Lord Byron" (Mumford), **Supp. II Part 2:** 494

"Letter to Matthews from Barton Street Flats" (Hugo), **Supp. VI:** 133

"Letter to Mexico" (Biss), **Supp. XXVI:** 48

"Letter to Minnesota" (Dunn), **Supp. XI:** 146

"Letter to Mr." (Poe), **III:** 411

"Letter Too Late to Vallejo" (Salinas), **Supp. XIII:** 313, 324

"Letter to Sister Madeline from Iowa City" (Hugo), **Supp. VI:** 142–143

"Letter to Soto" (Salinas), **Supp. XIII:** 325

"Letter to the Lady of the House" (Bausch), **Supp. VII:** 48

"Letter to the Rising Generation, A" (Comer), **I:** 214

"Letter to Walt Whitman" (Doty), **Supp. XI:** 135–136

"Letter to Wendell Berry, A" (Stegner), **Supp. IV Part 2:** 600

"Letter Writer, The" (Singer), **IV:** 20–21

"Let the Air Circulate" (Clampitt), **Supp. IX:** 45

Let the Hurricane Roar (Lane), **Supp. XXII:** 297

"Letting Down of the Hair, The" (Sexton), **Supp. II Part 2:** 692

Letting Go (P. Roth), **Retro. Supp. II:** 282, 283; **Supp. III Part 2:** 403, 404, 409–412

"Letting the Puma Go" (Dunn), **Supp. XI:** 149

"Lettres d'un Soldat" (Stevens), **Retro. Supp. I:** 299

Let Us Compare Mythologies (Cohen), **Supp. XXVII:** 53

Let Us Go into the Starry Night (Shanley), **Supp. XIV:** 317

Let Us Highly Resolve (Stratton-Porter), **Supp. XX:** 223

Let Us Now Praise Famous Men (Agee and Evans), **I:** 25, 27, 35, 36–39, 42, 45, 293

Let Your Mind Alone! (Thurber), **Supp. I Part 2:** 608

Leutze, Emanuel, **Supp. X:** 307

Levels of the Game (McPhee), **Supp. III Part 1:** 292, 294, 301

Levertov, Denise, **Retro. Supp. I:** 411; **Supp. III Part 1:** 271–287; **Supp. III Part 2:** 541; **Supp. IV Part 1:** 325; **Supp. VIII:** 38, 39; **Supp. XIX:** 282; **Supp. XVI:** 39, 40; **Supp. XXI:** 228; **Supp. XXII:** 83, 168, 177

Levi, Primo, **Supp. X:** 149; **Supp. XVII:** 48

Leviathan (Auster), **Supp. XII:** 27, **33–34**

"Leviathan" (Merwin), **Supp. III Part 1:** 345

"Leviathan" (R. Lowell), **II:** 537, 538

Levin, Adam, **Supp. XXII:** 268

Levin, Harry, **Supp. I Part 2:** 647

Levin, Jennifer, **Supp. X:** 305

Levin, Jonathan, **Retro. Supp. III:** 99

Levin, Meyer, **Supp. XX:** 34; **Supp. XXVII:** **133–149**

Lévinas, Emmanuel, **Supp. XVI:** 290, 291

Levine, Ellen, **Supp. V:** 4; **Supp. XI:** 178

Levine, Paul, **Supp. IV Part 1:** 221, 224

Levine, Philip, **Supp. III Part 2:** 541; **Supp. IX:** 293; **Supp. V:** **177–197**, 337; **Supp. XI:** 123, 257, 259, 267, 271, 315; **Supp. XIII:** 312; **Supp. XIX:** 45; **Supp. XV:** 73, 74, 212

Levine, Rosalind, **Supp. XII:** 123

Levine, Sherry, **Supp. XII:** 4

Levis, Larry, **Supp. IX:** 299; **Supp. V:** 180; **Supp. XI:** **257–274;** **Supp. XIII:** 312; **Supp. XV:** 73; **Supp. XVII:** 110

Lévi-Strauss, Claude, **Supp. I Part 2:** 636; **Supp. IV Part 1:** 45; **Supp. IV Part 2:** 490; **Supp. XVIII:** 190

Levitation: Five Fictions (Ozick), **Supp. V:** 268–270

"Levitation with Baby" (Nelson), **Supp. XVIII:** 173

Levitt, Saul, **Supp. XV:** 197

Levy, Alan, **Supp. IV Part 2:** 574, 589

Levy, D. A., **Supp. XXIII:** 174

Levy, G. Rachel, **Supp. I Part 2:** 567

Levy, Julien, **Supp. XXII:** 167, 168

Lévy-Bruhl, Lucien, **Retro. Supp. I:** 57

Levy Mayer and the New Industrial Era (Masters), **Supp. I Part 2:** 473

Lewallen, Constance M., **Supp. XXVII:** 20, 21

Lewes, George Henry, **II:** 569

Lewin, Albert, **Supp. XIV:** 279, 293

Lewis, C. Day, **III:** 527

Lewis, Dr. Claude, **II:** 442

Lewis, C. S., **Supp. XXV:** 73

Lewis, David Levering, **Supp. XIX:** 74, 75; **Supp. XVIII:** 127; **Supp. XXII:** 13

Lewis, E. B., **Supp. XXVIII:** 279, 285, 286, 287

Lewis, Edith, **I:** 313; **Retro. Supp. I:** 19, 21, 22; **Retro. Supp. III:** 24, 37

Lewis, Edwin, J., **II:** 439, 442

Lewis, Jerry, **Supp. IV Part 2:** 575; **Supp. X:** 172

Lewis, John L., **I:** 493

Lewis, Lilburn, **IV:** 243

Lewis, Lorene, **Supp. IV Part 2:** 596, 597

Lewis, Lucy, **IV:** 243

Lewis, Maggie, **Supp. V:** 23

Lewis, Meriwether, **II:** 217; **III:** 14; **IV:** 179, 243, 283

Lewis, Merrill, **Supp. IV Part 2:** 596, 597

Lewis, Michael, **II:** 451, 452; **Supp. XVII:** 210

Lewis, Michael J., **Supp. XXV:** 253

Lewis, Nancy, **Retro. Supp. III:** 282

Lewis, Robert Q., **Supp. IV Part 2:** 574

Lewis, R. W. B., **I:** 386, 561; **II:** 457–458; **Retro. Supp. I:** 362, 367; **Retro. Supp. III:** 282; **Supp. I Part 1:** 233; **Supp. XIII:** 93; **Supp. XXIII:** 42

Lewis, Sinclair, **I:** 116, 212, 348, 355, 362, 374, 378, 487, 495; **II:** 27, 34, 74, 79, 271, 277, 306, **439–461,** 474; **III:** 28, 40, 51, 60, 61, 63–64, 66, 70, 71, 106, 394, 462, 572, 606; **IV:** 53, 326, 366, 455, 468, 475, 482; **Retro. Supp. I:** 332; **Retro. Supp. II:** 95, 108, 197, 322; **Supp. I Part 2:** 613, 709; **Supp. IV Part 2:** 678; **Supp. IX:** 308; **Supp. V:** 278; **Supp. X:** 137; **Supp. XVII:** 41; **Supp. XVIII:** 278; **Supp. XXII:** 190; **Supp. XXIII:** 165, 166; **Supp. XXIV:** 29; **Supp. XXVIII:** 65

Lewis, Mrs. Sinclair (Dorothy Thompson), **II:** 449–450, 451, 453

Lewis, Mrs. Sinclair (Grace Livingston Hegger), **II:** 441

Lewis, Wyndham, **III:** 458, 462, 465, 470; **Retro. Supp. I:** 59, 170, 292; **Supp. III Part 2:** 617; **Supp. XXVI:** 144

Lewisohn, Ludwig, **Supp. XXIII:** 1; **Supp. XXVIII:** 145–161

Lexicon Tetraglotton (Howell), **II:** 111

"Lexington Avenue Musedog" (Peacock), **Supp. XIX:** 204

"Leyenda" (Mora), **Supp. XIII:** 214

Leyner, Mark, **Supp. XIX:** 223

Leyte (Morison), **Supp. I Part 2:** 491

"Liar, The" (Baraka), **Supp. II Part 1:** 36

"Liars, The" (Sandburg), **III:** 586

Liars' Club, The: A Memoir (Karr), **Supp. XI:** 239, 240, 241, 242, **244–248,** 252, 254; **Supp. XVI:** 70

Liar's Dice (C. Frost), **Supp. XV:** 93, 96

"Liar's Dice" (C. Frost), **Supp. XV:** 94, 107

Liars in Love (Yates), **Supp. XI:** 348, 349

Libation Bearers, The (Aeschylus), **III:** 398; **Supp. IX:** 103

Li Bay. *See* Li Po

Libby, Anthony, **Supp. XIII:** 87

Libera, Padre, **II:** 278

Liberal Imagination, The (Trilling), **III:** 308; **Retro. Supp. I:** 97, 216; **Supp. II Part 1:** 146; **Supp. III Part 2:** 495, 498, 501–504

Liberating Voices: Oral Tradition in African American Literature (G. Jones), **Supp. XXIV:** 185

Liberation (J. Scott), **Supp. XVII:** 192, **194–196**

"Liberation" (Winters), **Supp. II Part 2:** 791

Liber Brunenesis (yearbook), **IV:** 286

Liberties, The (Howe), **Supp. IV Part 2:** 426–428, 430, 432

Liberties of America, The (H. Warner), **Supp. XVIII:** 259

Liberty Jones (play), **Supp. IV Part 1:** 83

"Liberty Tree" (Paine), **Supp. I Part 2:** 505

Libra (DeLillo), **Supp. VI:** 2, **4, 5,** 6, **7,** 9, 10, 12, 13, 14, 16

Library for Juana, A (Mora), **Supp. XIII:** 218

Library of America, **Retro. Supp. I:** 2

"Library of Babel, The" (J. Borges), **Supp. XVII:** 47

"Library of Law, A" (MacLeish), **III:** 4

"Library of Moloch, The" (Bukiet), **Supp. XVII:** 47, 49

"Librettos for Eros" (Gander), **Supp. XV:** 340

Lice, The (Merwin), **Supp. III Part 1:** 339, 341–342, 346, 348, 349, 355

"License Plate, The" (Ferry), **Supp. XXIV:** 157

Lichtenberg, Georg Christoph, **Supp. XIV:** 339

Lichtenstein, Roy, **Supp. I Part 2:** 665; **Supp. XV:** 186; **Supp. XXVII:** 21

"Liddy's Orange" (Olds), **Supp. X:** 209

"Lie, The" (Antin), **Supp. XX:** 7, **9–10**

Lieberman, Herman (Chaim), **Supp. XXIII:** 3, 7

Lieberman, Laurence, **Supp. XI:** 323–324

Liebestod (Wagner), **I:** 284, 395

Liebling, A. J., **IV:** 290; **Supp. VIII:** 151; **Supp. XVI:** 167; **Supp. XXVII:** 46–47

Lie Down in Darkness (Styron), **IV:** 98, 99, 100–104, 105, 111; **Supp. XI:** 343

"Lie Down with the Lamb" (Gallagher), **Supp. XXIV:** 171

Lie of the Mind, A (Shepard), **Supp. III Part 2:** 433, 435, 441, 447–449

"Lies" (Haines), **Supp. XII:** 204

Lies (Hoffman), **Supp. XVIII:** **78–79**

"Lies and Consequences" (Pickering), **Supp. XXI:** 204

Lies Like Truth (Clurman), **IV:** 385

Lieutenant, The (Dubus), **Supp. VII:** 78

"Life" (Hecht), **Supp. XXVII:** 86

Life (Richards), **Supp. XXVII:** 40

"Life" (Wharton), **Retro. Supp. I:** 372

Life along the Passaic River (W. C. Williams), **Retro. Supp. I:** 423

Life Among the Savages (Jackson), **Supp. IX:** 115, **125**

Life and Adventures of Charles Anderson Chester, The (Lippard), **Supp. XXIII:** 184

"Life and Death Kisses, The" (Grossman), **Supp. XIX:** 87

Life and Death of the Salt Marsh (E. and N. Teale), **Supp. XXVIII:** 243

Life and Gabriella (Glasgow), **II:** 175, 176, 182–183, 184, 189

Life and I (Wharton), **Retro. Supp. I:** 360, 361, 362; **Retro. Supp. III:** 276

"Life and Letters" (Epstein), **Supp. XIV:** 104–105

"Life and Letters in New England" (Emerson), **Supp. XXIV:** 67

Life and Letters of Harrison Gray Otis, Federalist, 1765–1848, The (Morison), **Supp. I Part 2:** 480–481

Life and Letters of Sir Henry Wotton (L. P. Smith), **Supp. XIV:** 340–341

Life and Mind of Emily Dickinson, The (Taggard), **Supp. XXII:** 279

Life and Times of Frederick Douglass, Written by Himself, The (Douglass), **Supp. III Part 1:** 155, 159–163

Life and Writings of Horace McCoy, The (Wolfson), **Supp. XIII:** 172, 174

"Life Apart, The: L'Ame Close" (Wharton), **Retro. Supp. III:** 281–282

"Life as a Visionary Spirit" (Eberhart), **I:** 540, 541

"Life at Angelo's, A" (Benét), **Supp. XI:** 53

Life at Happy Knoll (Marquand), **III:** 50, 61

Life Before Man (Atwood), **Supp. XIII:** **24–25**

Lifeboat (screenplay, Hecht), **Supp. XXVII:** 93

"Life Cycle of Common Man" (Nemerov), **III:** 278

"Lifecycle Stairmaster" (Karr), **Supp. XI:** 250

Life Estates (Hearon), **Supp. VIII:** **68–69**

Life for Life's Sake (Aldington), **Supp. I Part 1:** 256

Life Full of Holes, A (Layachi), **Supp. IV Part 1:** 92

"Lifeguard" (Updike), **IV:** 226; **Retro. Supp. I:** 325

"Lifeguard, The" (Dickey), **Supp. IV Part 1:** 179–180

"Lifeguard, The"(Dickey), **Supp. XXVIII:** 26

"Life in the 30s" (column, Quindlen), **Supp. XVII:** 165, 167–169

Life in the Clearings (Shields), **Supp. VII:** 313

"Life in the Country: A City Friend Asks, 'Is It Boring?' " (Paley), **Supp. VI:** 231

Life in the Forest (Levertov), **Supp. III Part 1:** 282–283

Life in the Iron Mills (R. H. Davis), **Supp. XIII:** 292, 295, 299, 305; **Supp. XVI:** 79–82, **85–88,** 91

Life in the Iron Mills and Other Stories (T. Olson, ed.), **Supp. XVI:** 83

Life in the Theatre, A (Mamet), **Supp. XIV:** 241, 255

Life in the War Zone (Atherton), **Supp. XXIV:** 24

Life Is a Miracle: An Essay Against Modern Superstition (Berry), **Supp. X:** 35

"Life Is Fine" (Hughes), **Supp. I Part 1:** 334, 338

"Life Is Motion" (Stevens), **IV:** 74

Life & Letters of Gene Stratton-Porter (Meehan), **Supp. XX:** 213

Life of Albert Gallatin, The (Adams), **I:** 6, 14

"Life of a Man of the World, The"(Lippard), **Supp. XXIII:** 189

Life of an Ordinary Woman, The: Anne Ellis (A. Ellis), **Supp. XVI:** 38

Life of Captain Cipriani, The: An Account of British Government in the West Indies (C. L. R. James), **Supp. XXI:** 161

Life of Dryden (S. Johnson), **Retro. Supp. II:** 223

Life of Emily Dickinson, The (Sewall), **Retro. Supp. I:** 25

Life of Forms, The (Focillon), **IV:** 90

Life of Franklin Pierce (Hawthorne), **Retro. Supp. I:** 163

Life of George Cabot Lodge, The (Adams), **I:** 21

Life of George Washington (Irving), **II:** 314, 315–316

Life of Henry James (Edel), **Retro. Supp. I:** 224

"Life of Irony, The" (Bourne), **I:** 219

Life of Jesus (Renan), **Supp. XX: 122**

Life of John Brown, The (Gold), **Supp. XXVIII:** 72

"Life of Lincoln West, The" (Brooks), **Supp. III Part 1:** 86

Life of Mary, The (Rilke; F. Wright, trans.), **Supp. XVII:** 244

Life of Michelangelo (Grimm), **II:** 17

"Life of Nancy, The" (Jewett), **Retro. Supp. II:** 133, 144

Life of Oliver Goldsmith, The, with Selections from His Writings (Irving), **II:** 315

Life of Phips (Mather), **Supp. II Part 2:** 451, 452, 459

Life of Poetry, The (Rukeyser), **Supp. VI:** 271, 273, 275–276, 282, 283, 286

Life of Samuel Johnson (Boswell), **Supp. I Part 2:** 656

Life of Savage (S. Johnson), **Supp. I Part 2:** 523

Life of the Drama, The (Bentley), **IV:** 396

"Life of the Mind, The" (Kees), **Supp. XV:** 140

Life of the Right Reverend Joseph P. Machebeuf, The (Howlett), **Retro. Supp. I:** 17

Life of Thomas Paine, author of Rights of Men, With a Defence of his Writings (Chalmers), **Supp. I Part 2:** 514

Life of Thomas Paine, The (Cobbett), **Supp. I Part 2:** 517

"Life of Towne, The" (Carson), **Supp. XII:** 102

Life of William Ellery Channing (W. H. Channing), **Supp. XXIV:** 68

"Life on Beekman Place, A" (Naylor), **Supp. VIII:** 214

"Life on the Black List" (Endore), **Supp. XVII:** 63

Life on the Hyphen: The Cuban-American Way (Firmat), **Supp. VIII:** 76; **Supp. XI:** 184

Life on the Mississippi (Twain), **I:** 209; **IV:** 198, 199; **Retro. Supp. III:** 256, 264, 267; **Supp. I Part 2:** 440

"Life on the Rocks: The Galápagos" (Dillard), **Supp. VI:** 32

"Life Stories, East and West" (E. Hoffman), **Supp. XVI:** 157

Life Story (Baker), **II:** 259

Life Studies (R. Lowell), **I:** 400; **II:** 384, 386, 543, 546–550, 551, 555; **Retro. Supp. II:** 180, 185, 186, 188, 189, 191; **Retro. Supp. III:** 41; **Supp. I Part 2:** 543; **Supp. XI:** 240, 244, 250, 317; **Supp. XII:** 255; **Supp. XIV:** 15; **Supp. XV:** 252

"Life Studies" (R. Lowell), **Retro. Supp. II:** 188

"Life Styles in the Golden Land" (Didion), **Supp. IV Part 1:** 200

Life Supports: New and Collected Poems (Bronk), **Supp. XXI:** 19, 31, 32

"Life That Is, The" (Bryant), **Supp. I Part 1:** 169

"Life Work" (Stafford), **Supp. XI:** 329–330

"Life You Save May Be Your Own, The" (O'Connor), **III:** 344, 350, 354; **Retro. Supp. II:** 229, 230, 233; **Retro. Supp. III:** 208, 215, 219

Lifshin, Lyn, **Supp. XVI:** 37

"Lift Every Voice"(Woodson), **Supp. XXVIII:** 284

"Lifting, The" (Olds), **Supp. X:** 210

"Ligeia" (Poe), **III:** 412, 414; **Retro. Supp. II:** 261, 270, 271, 275; **Retro. Supp. III:** 228–229

Liggett, Walter W., **Supp. XIII:** 168

Light, James F., **IV:** 290; **Retro. Supp. II:** 325

Light, Kate, **Supp. XVII:** 109

Light and Dark (Bronk), **Supp. XXI:** 27–29, 31

"Light and the Sufferer" (Lethem), **Supp. XVIII:** 139–140

Light around the Body, The (R. Bly), **Supp. IV Part 1:** 61–62, 62; **Supp. XVII:** 243; **Supp. XXI:** 84–85

"Light Comes Brighter, The" (Roethke), **III:** 529–530

"Lighter than Air" (Stone), **Supp. XXVII:** 251

"Light from Above" (Eberhart), **I:** 541

Light in August (Faulkner), **II:** 63–64, 65, 74; **IV:** 207; **Retro. Supp. I:** 82, 84, 85, 86, 89, 92; **Retro. Supp. III:** 74, 80, 82–83; **Supp. XIV:** 12

Light in the Forest, The (Richter), **Supp. XVIII: 216–217**

Light in the Morning (Baker), **Supp. XVIII:** 263, 269

"Light in the Piazza, The" (Spencer), **Supp. XXVII:** 13

Light in the Window, A (Rinehart), **Supp. XXV:** 198–199, 202

"Light Man, A" (James), **II:** 322; **Retro. Supp. I:** 219

"Lightning" (Barthelme), **Supp. IV Part 1:** 53

"Lightning" (Bynner), **Supp. XV:** 44

"Lightning" (Oliver), **Supp. VII:** 235

"Lightning, The" (Swenson), **Supp. IV Part 2:** 645

Lightning Field (Spiotta), **Supp. XXVIII:** 207, 208–212, 213, 216, 219, 222

"Lightning Flash, The" (Gibran), **Supp. XX: 123**

"Lightning Rod Man, The" (Melville), **III:** 90; **Supp. XVIII:** 4

"Light of the Body, The" (Davison), **Supp. XXVI:** 71

"Light of the Sacred Harp"(Bottoms), **Supp. XXVIII:** 26

"Light of the World, The" (Hemingway), **II:** 249

"Lights"(Dybek), **Supp. XXIII:** 72

Lights in the Valley (Bodenheim), **Supp. XXV:** 29

"Lights in the Windows" (Nye), **Supp. XIII:** 280

"Lights Must Never Go Out, The"(Hadas), **Supp. XXIII:** 125

"Light Through the Window, The" (Brockmeier), **Supp. XXII:** 52, 59

Light Verse and Satires (Bynner), **Supp. XV:** 52

Light Years (Salter), **Supp. IX: 257–259**

"LIKE, THIS IS WHAT I MEANT!" (Baraka), **Supp. II Part 1:** 59

"Like All the Other Nations" (Paley), **Supp. VI:** 220

"Like a Rolling Stone" (song, Dylan), **Supp. XVIII:** 20, 30

"Like Decorations in a Nigger Cemetery" (Stevens), **IV:** 74, 79; **Retro. Supp. I:** 305

Like Ghosts of Eagles (Francis), **Supp. IX:** 86

"Like Life" (Moore), **Supp. X:** 163, 165, **172–173**

Like Life: Stories (Moore), **Supp. X:** 163, **171–175,** 177, 178

"Likeness to God" (Channing), **Supp. XXIV: 75–76,** 77, 78

"Like Talk" (Mills), **Supp. XI:** 311

"Like the New Moon I Will Live My Life" (R. Bly), **Supp. IV Part 1:** 71

Li'l Abner (Capp), **IV:** 198

"Lilacs" (A. Lowell), **II:** 527

"Lilacs, The" (Wilbur), **Supp. III Part 2:** 557–558

"Lilacs for Ginsberg" (Stern), **Supp. IX:** 299

Liliom (Molnar), **Supp. XVI:** 187

Lilith's Brood (O. Butler), **Supp. XIII:** 63

Lillabulero Press, **Supp. V:** 4, 5

Lillian Hellman (Adler), **Supp. I Part 1:** 297

Lillian Hellman (Falk), **Supp. I Part 1:** 297

Lillian Hellman: Playwright (Moody), **Supp. I Part 1:** 280

Lillo, George, **II:** 111, 112

"Lily Brown"(Goodman), **Supp. XXVIII:** 89, 92

"Lily Daw and the Three Ladies" (Welty), **IV:** 262

Lily for My Love, A (Berrigan), **Supp. XXIV:** 35

Lima, Agnes de, **I:** 231, 232

Lima, Frank, **Supp. XXIII:** 217, 221; **Supp. XXVII:** 23

Lima, Maria Helena, **Supp. XXII:** 73

Lima Beans (Kreymborg), **Supp. XXII:** 163

"Limbo: Altered States" (Karr), **Supp. XI:** 249–250

"Limen" (Trethewey), **Supp. XXI:** 250

Lime Orchard Woman, The (Ríos), **Supp. IV Part 2:** 538, 547–550, 553

"Lime Orchard Woman, The" (Ríos), **Supp. IV Part 2:** 548

Limitations (Turow), **Supp. XVII:** 222–223

"Limits" (Emerson), **II:** 19

Limits of Mortality, The: An Essay on Wordsworth's Major Poems (Ferry), **Supp. XXIV:** 147, 148

Lincoln, Abraham, **I:** 1, 4, 30; **II:** 8, 13, 135, 273, 555, 576; **III:** 576, 577, 580, 584, 587–590, 591; **IV:** 192, 195, 298, 347, 350, 444; **Supp. I Part 1:** 2, 8, 26, 309, 321; **Supp. I Part 2:** 379, 380, 382, 385, 390, 397, 399, 418, 424, 454, 456, 471, 472, 473, 474, 483, 579, 687; **Supp. IX:** 15; **Supp. VIII:** 108; **Supp. XIV:** 73

Lincoln, Kenneth, **Supp. IV Part 1:** 329; **Supp. IV Part 2:** 507

Lincoln, Thomas, **III:** 587

Lincoln, Mrs. Thomas (Nancy Hanks), **III:** 587

Lincoln: A Novel (Vidal), **Supp. IV Part 2:** 677, 684, 685, 688, 689–690, 691, 692

"Lincolnites" (Rash), **Supp. XXVII:** 229

Lincoln Lawyer, The (Connelly), **Supp. XXI:** 77, 78

Lincoln on Race and Slavery (H. L. Gates), **Supp. XX: 108–109**

"Lincoln Relics, The" (Kunitz), **Supp. III Part 1:** 269

Lincoln: The Man (Masters), **Supp. I Part 2:** 471, 473–474

Lindbergh, Charles A., **I:** 482

"Linden Branch, The" (MacLeish), **III:** 19, 20

Linden Hills (Naylor), **Supp. VIII:** 214, 218, **219–223**

Linderman, Lawrence, **Supp. IV Part 2:** 579, 583, 585, 589

Lindner, April, **Supp. XV:** 111, 119

"Lindo y Querido" (Muñoz), **Supp. XXV:** 135

Lindsay, Howard, **III:** 284

Lindsay, John, **Supp. I Part 2:** 374

Lindsay, Olive, **Supp. I Part 2:** 374, 375, 392

Lindsay, Vachel, **I:** 384; **II:** 263, 276, 530; **III:** 5, 505; **Retro. Supp. I:** 133; **Retro. Supp. III:** 101; **Supp. I Part 1:** 324; **Supp. I Part 2: 374–403**, 454, 473, 474; **Supp. III Part 1:** 63, 71; **Supp. XV:** 293, 297, 299, 301, 306; **Supp. XVI:** 184–185; **Supp. XXV:** 18; **Supp. XXVII:** 286, 294, 297

Lindsay, Mrs. Vachel (Elizabeth Connors), **Supp. I Part 2:** 398, 399, 473

Lindsay, Vachel Thomas, **Supp. I Part 2:** 374, 375

Lindsay, Mrs. Vachel Thomas (Esther Catherine Frazee), **Supp. I Part 2:** 374, 375, 384–385, 398

Lindsey, David, **Supp. XIV:** 26

"Line, The" (Olds), **Supp. X:** 206

Lineage of Ragpickers, Songpluckers, Elegiasts, and Jewelers, A (Goldbarth), **Supp. XII:** 191

"Line"(Crooker), **Supp. XXIII:** 58

Line Dance (Crooker), **Supp. XXIII:** 56, **58–60**

"Line Dance"(Crooker), **Supp. XXIII:** 59

"Line of Least Resistance, The" (Wharton), **Retro. Supp. I:** 366

Line Out for a Walk, A: Familiar Essays (Epstein), **Supp. XIV: 107**

"Liner Notes for the Poetically Unhep" (Hughes), **Retro. Supp. I:** 210

"Lines, Written on Reading Stuart's Account of the Treatment of Slaves in Charleston" (Very), **Supp. XXV:** 239

"Lines After Rereading T. S. Eliot" (Wright), **Supp. V:** 343

"Lines Composed a Few Miles Above Tintern Abbey" (Wordsworth), **Supp. III Part 1:** 12

"Lines Composed Over Three Thousand Miles from Tintern Abbey" (Collins), **Supp. XXI:** 57–58

"Lines for an Interment" (MacLeish), **III:** 15

"Lines for My Father" (Cullen), **Supp. IV Part 1:** 167

"Lines from Israel" (R. Lowell), **II:** 554

"Lines from Pietro Longhi" (Sobin), **Supp. XVI:** 289

"Lines on Revisiting the Country" (Bryant), **Supp. I Part 1:** 164

"Lines Suggested by a Tennessee Song" (Agee), **I:** 28

"Lines to a Friend Asleep"(J. Schoolcraft), **Supp. XXIII:** 228, 230

"Line-Storm Song, A" (Frost), **Retro. Supp. I:** 127

"Lines written at Castle Island, Lake Superior"(J. Schoolcraft), **Supp. XXIII:** 229, 232, 233

"Lines Written at Port Royal" (Freneau), **Supp. II Part 1:** 264

"Lines Written in an Asylum" (Carruth), **Supp. XVI:** 48

"Lines Written in Manassas", **Supp. XV:** 99–100

Lineup, The (Connelly), **Supp. XXI:** 67, 68–69

"Line Written in the Dark Illegible Next Day" (F. Wright), **Supp. XVII:** 242

Linfield, Susie, **Supp. XVII:** 169, 177

Lingeman, Richard, **Supp. X:** 82; **Supp. XXII:** 104

"Linguistics 101" (Huddle), **Supp. XXVI:** 152

Linn, Elizabeth. *See* Brown, Mrs. Charles Brockden (Elizabeth Linn)

Linn, John Blair, **Supp. I Part 1:** 145

Linnaeus, Carolus, **II:** 6; **Supp. I Part 1:** 245

"Linnets" (Levis), **Supp. XI:** 260, 261

"Linoleum" (Gallagher), **Supp. XXIV:** 170

"Linoleum Roses" (Cisneros), **Supp. VII:** 63, 66

Linotte: 1914–1920 (Nin), **Supp. X:** 193, 196, 197

Linschoten, Hans, **II:** 362, 363, 364

"Lion" (B. Kelly), **Supp. XVII:** 133

"Lion and Honeycomb" (Nemerov), **III:** 275, 278, 280

Lion and the Archer, The (Hayden), **Supp. II Part 1:** 366, 367

Lion and the Honeycomb, The (Blackmur), **Supp. II Part 1:** 91

Lion Country (Buechner), **Supp. XII:** 52, 53

Lionel Lincoln (Cooper), **I:** 339, 342

"Lion for Real, The" (Ginsberg), **Supp. II Part 1:** 320

Lionhearted, The: A Story about the Jews of Medieval England (Reznikoff), **Supp. XIV:** 280, 289

Lion in the Garden (Meriweather and Millgate), **Retro. Supp. I:** 91

"Lionizing" (Poe), **III:** 411, 425

"Lions, Harts, and Leaping Does" (Powers), **III:** 356

Lions and Shadows: An Education in the Twenties (Isherwood), **Supp. XIV:** 158, 159, 160, 162

"Lions in Sweden" (Stevens), **IV:** 79–80

Lipman, William R., **Supp. XIII:** 170

Li Po, **Supp. XI:** 241; **Supp. XII:** 218; **Supp. XV:** 47, 217

Lippard, George, **Supp. XXIII: 177–192**

Lippard, Lucy, **Supp. XXVII:** 39

Lippmann, Walter, **I:** 48, 222–223, 225; **III:** 291, 600; **IV:** 429; **Supp. I Part 2:** 609, 643; **Supp. VIII:** 104

Lipschitz, Moryce, **Supp. XXIII:** 6

Lips Together, Teeth Apart (McNally), **Supp. XIII: 201–202**, 208, 209

Lipsyte, Robert, **Supp. XVI:** 220

Lipton, James, **Supp. IV Part 2:** 576, 577, 579, 583, 586, 588

Lipton, Lawrence, **Supp. IX:** 3

Lisa Vale (Prouty), **Supp. XXVIII:** 186, 187, 189, 192
"Lisbon Story" (Vaz), **Supp. XXVI:** 267–268
Lisbon Traviata, The (McNally), **Supp. XIII:** 198, **199–200,** 201, 204, 208
Lish, Gordon, **Supp. XIX:** 209; **Supp. XXI:** 115, 121; **Supp. XXIII:** 274; **Supp. XXIV:** 166, 177; **Supp. XXVIII:** 207
Lisicky,Paul, **Supp. XI:** 120, 131, 135
Lisk, Thomas, **Supp. XXI:** 24
"Lisp, The" (Olds), **Supp. X:** 211
Listen, Ruben Fontanez (Neugeboren), **Supp. XVI: 220–221**
"Listeners, The" (de la Mare), **Supp. XVII:** 69
"Listeners and Readers: The Unforgetting of Vachel Lindsay" (Trombly), **Supp. I Part 2:** 403
"Listening" (J. W. Miller), **Supp. XX: 167**
"Listening" (Paley), **Supp. VI:** 218, 231, 232
"Listening" (Stafford), **Supp. XI:** 321, 322
Listening to Prozac (P. Kramer), **Supp. XVI:** 229
"Listening to the Desert" (Henderson), **Supp. XIII:** 221–222
"Listening to the Mockingbird" (Woodard), **Supp. VIII:** 128
Listening to Your Life: Daily Meditations with Frederick Buechner (Buechner), **Supp. XII:** 53
Listen to the Desert/Oye al desierto (Mora), **Supp. XIII:** 221
"Listen to the People" (Benét), **Supp. XI:** 51–52
Liston, Sonny, **III:** 38, 42
Li T'ai-po, **II:** 526
"Litany" (Ashbery), **Supp. III Part 1:** 21–22, 25, 26
"Litany" (Collins), **Supp. XXI:** 56–57
"Litany" (Sandburg), **III:** 593
"Litany, The" (Gioia), **Supp. XV:** 125, 126
"Litany for Dictatorships" (Benét), **Supp. XI:** 46, 58
"Litany for Survival, A" (Lorde), **Supp. XII:** 220
"Litany in Which Certain Things Are Crossed Out"(Siken), **Supp. XXVIII:** 199
"Litany of the Dark People, The" (Cullen), **Supp. IV Part 1:** 170, 171
"Litany of the Heroes" (Lindsay), **Supp. I Part 2:** 397
"Litany of Washington Street, The" (Lindsay), **Supp. I Part 2:** 376, 398–399
"Literary Achievement of Meyer Levin, The" (Bossin), **Supp. XXVII:** 133
Literary Anthropology (Trumpener and Nyce), **Retro. Supp. I:** 380
Literary Art and Activism of Rick Bass, The (Weltzien), **Supp. XVI:** 20–21
"Literary Blacks and Jews" (Ozick), **Supp. V:** 272

"Literary Career of Elizabeth Barstow Stoddard, The" (Matlack), **Supp. XV:** 269
Literary Criticism: A Short History (Brooks and Wimsatt), **Supp. XIV:** 12
"Literary Criticism of Georg Lukács, The" (Sontag), **Supp. III Part 2:** 453
"Literary Development or California, The" (Atherton), **Supp. XXIV:** 22
Literary Disruptions (Klinkowitz), **Supp. XXI:** 233
Literary Essays of Thomas Merton, The, **Supp. VIII:** 207
"Literary Folk As They Came and Went with Ourselves" (E. Stoddard), **Supp. XV:** 274
Literary Friends and Acquaintance (Howells), **Supp. I Part 1:** 318; **Supp. XV:** 287
"Literary Heritage of Tennyson, The" (Locke), **Supp. XIV:** 197
Literary History of the United States (Spiller et al., ed.), **Supp. I Part 1:** 104; **Supp. II Part 1:** 95
"Literary Importation" (Freneau), **Supp. II Part 1:** 264
"Literary Life of America, The" (Brooks), **I:** 245
"Literary London" (Atherton), **Supp. XXIV:** 24
Literary Outlaw: The Life and Times of William S. Burroughs (Morgan), **Supp. XIV:** 141
Literary Situation, The (Cowley), **Supp. II Part 1:** 135, 140, 144, 146, 147, 148
"Literary Worker's Polonius, The" (Wilson), **IV:** 431, 432
"Literature" (Emerson), **II:** 6
Literature (X. J. Kennedy), **Supp. XV:** 153
Literature and American Life (Boynton), **Supp. I Part 2:** 415
Literature and Insurgency: Ten Studies in Racial Evolution (Underwood), **Supp. XXIV:** 29
Literature and Life (Howells), **Supp. XIV:** 45–46
Literature and Morality (Farrell), **II:** 49
"Literature and Place: Varieties of Regional Experience" (Erisman), **Supp. VIII:** 126
"Literature and War" (Faulkner), **Retro. Supp. III:** 76
"Literature as a Symptom" (Warren), **IV:** 237
"Literature in Low Life" (Hapgood), **Supp. XVII:** 103
"Literature of Exhaustion, The" (Barth), **Supp. IV Part 1:** 48
"Lithuanian Nocturne" (Brodsky), **Supp. VIII:** 29
"Lit Instructor" (Stafford), **Supp. XI:** 321
Littauer, Kenneth, **Retro. Supp. I:** 114
Little Acts of Kindness (Budbill), **Supp. XIX:** 3, 14–15
"Little Annie's Ramble" (Hawthorne), **Retro. Supp. III:** 113
"Little Beast"(Siken), **Supp. XXVIII:** 198

"Little Bernhardt" (Shaw), **Supp. XIX:** 246
Little Big Man (Berger), **Supp. XII:** 171
Little Big Man (film), **Supp. X:** 124
Littlebird, Harold, **Supp. IV Part 2:** 499
Littlebird, Larry, **Supp. IV Part 2:** 499, 505
Little Birds: Erotica (Nin), **Supp. X:** 192, 195
"Little Brown Baby" (Dunbar), **Supp. II Part 1:** 206
"Little Brown Jug" (Baraka), **Supp. II Part 1:** 51
"Little Burst, A"(Strout), **Supp. XXIII:** 282
"Little by Little"(Hadas), **Supp. XXIII:** 115
Little Casino (Sorrentino), **Supp. XXI:** 237, 238
"Little Clown, My Heart" (Cisneros), **Supp. VII:** 71
"Little Convent Girl, The"(King), **Supp. XXVIII:** 120–121
"Little Cosmic Dust Poem" (Haines), **Supp. XII:** 209–210
"Little Country Girl, A" (Chopin), **Retro. Supp. II:** 71
"Little Curtis" (Parker), **Supp. IX:** 193
Little Disturbances of Man, The (Paley), **Supp. VI:** 218
"Little Dog" (Hughes), **Supp. I Part 1:** 329
Little Dorrit (Dickens), **Supp. I Part 1:** 35
"Little Edward" (Stowe), **Supp. I Part 2:** 587
"Little Elegy" (X. J. Kennedy), **Supp. XV:** 155
"Little Elegy for Antonio Machado"(O'Hara), **Supp. XXIII:** 220
Little Essays Drawn from the Writings of George Santayana (L. P. Smith), **Supp. XIV:** 342
"Little Expressionless Animals" (Wallace), **Supp. X:** 305
"Little Fable" (Hay), **Supp. XIV:** 131
Little Face and Other Stories (Thompson), **Supp. XXIII: 293–294**
"Little Face"(Thompson), **Supp. XXIII:** 293
Littlefield, Catherine, **Supp. IX:** 58
Little Fling, A (Pickering), **Supp. XXI:** 203
Little Foxes, The (Hellman), **Supp. I Part 1:** 276, 278–279, 281, 283, 297
"Little Fred, the Canal Boy" (Stowe), **Supp. I Part 2:** 587
"Little French Mary" (Jewett), **II:** 400
Little Friend, Little Friend (Jarrell), **II:** 367, 372, 375–376
Little Friend, The (Tartt), **Supp. XXVII:** 267, 269, 270, 274–276
"Little Gidding" (T. S. Eliot), **I:** 582, 588; **II:** 539; **Retro. Supp. I:** 66; **Retro. Supp. III:** 68
"Little Girl, My Stringbean, My Lovely Woman" (Sexton), **Supp. II Part 2:** 686
"Little Girl, The" (Paley), **Supp. VI:** 222, **228–229**

"Little Girl Tells a Story to a Lady, A" (Barnes), **Supp. III Part 1:** 36

"Little Goose Girl, The" (Grimm), **IV:** 266

Little Ham (Hughes), **Retro. Supp. I:** 203; **Supp. I Part 1:** 328, 339

Little House in the Big Woods (L. I. Wilder), **Supp. XXII:** 294, 295, 296, 297, 298–299, 300

Little House on the Prairie (L. I. Wilder), **Supp. XXII:** 294, 295–296, 297, 299, 301

Little House on the Prairie (television series), **Supp. XXII:** 289

"Little House" series (L. A. Wilder), **Supp. XXII:** 289

"Little House" series (L. I. Wilder), **Supp. XXVI:** 217–218

Little House Traveler, A (L. I. Wilder), **Supp. XXII:** 301

Little Ignorance, A (Schott), **Supp. XXIII:** 239, 241

Little King, The (Bynner), **Supp. XV:** 42, 50

Little Lady of the Big House, The (London), **II:** 481–482

Little Liar, The (film; Ingraham), **Supp. XVI:** 184–185

"Little Lion Face" (Swenson), **Supp. IV Part 2:** 651

"Little Lobelia's Song" (Bogan), **Supp. III Part 1:** 66

"Little Local Color, A" (Henry), **Supp. II Part 1:** 399

Little Lord Fauntleroy (Burnett), **Retro. Supp. I:** 188; **Supp. XVI:** 182

"Little Love, The" (H. Johnson), **Supp. XXVI:** 173

"Little Lyric" (Hughes), **Supp. I Part 1:** 334

Little Man, Little Man (Baldwin), **Supp. I Part 1:** 67

"Little Man at Chehaw Station, The" (Ellison), **Retro. Supp. II:** 123

"Little Match Girl, The"(Anderson), **Supp. XXVIII:** 279

Little Me (musical), **Supp. IV Part 2:** 575

Little Men (Alcott), **Supp. I Part 1:** 32, 39, 40

"Little Morning Music, A" (Schwartz), **Supp. II Part 2:** 662–663

Little Ocean (Shepard), **Supp. III Part 2:** 447

"Little Old Girl, A" (Larcom), **Supp. XIII:** 144

"Little Old Spy" (Hughes), **Supp. I Part 1:** 329

Little Orphan Annie (film), **Supp. XVIII:** 244

"Little Owl Who Lives in the Orchard" (Oliver), **Supp. VII:** 239

"Little Peasant, The" (Sexton), **Supp. II Part 2:** 690

"Little People"(Kenny), **Supp. XXIII:** 151

"Little Rapids, The" (Swenson), **Supp. IV Part 2:** 645

Little Red Song Book (Hill), **Supp. XVIII:** 224

Little Regiment and Other Episodes of the American Civil War, The (Crane), **I:** 408

Little River: New and Selected Poems (McCarriston), **Supp. XIV: 269–272**

"Little Road not made of Man , A" (Dickinson), **Retro. Supp. I:** 44

"Little Sawtooth" (Huddle), **Supp. XXVI:** 154, 155

Little Sister, The (Chandler), **Supp. IV Part 1:** 122, 130, 131–132

"Little Sleep's-Head Sprouting Hair in the Moonlight" (Kinnell), **Supp. III Part 1:** 247

"Little Snow White" (Grimm), **IV:** 266

"Little Spirit, or Boy-Man, The: An Odjibwa Tale"(J. Schoolcraft), **Supp. XXIII:** 234

Little Star (Halliday), **Supp. XIX:** 82, **84–85,** 87

"Little Star" (Halliday), **Supp. XIX:** 83, 84, 93

"Little Testament of Bernard Martin, Aet. 30" (Mumford), **Supp. II Part 2:** 472, 473, 474

"Little Things" (Olds), **Supp. X:** 208

Little Tour in France (James), **II:** 337

Little Town, The (Asch), **Supp. XXIII:** 4, 5, **7–8**

"Little Travel Diary, A"(O'Hara), **Supp. XXIII:** 220

Little Women (Alcott), **Supp. I Part 1:** 28, 29, 32, 35, 37, 38, 39–40, 41, 43, 44; **Supp. IX:** 128

Little Yellow Dog, A (Mosley), **Supp. XIII:** 237, 241

"Liturgy and Spiritual Personalism" (Merton), **Supp. VIII:** 199

Litz, A. Walton, **Retro. Supp. I:** 306

"Liu Ch'e" (Pound), **III:** 466

"Live" (Sexton), **Supp. II Part 2:** 684, 686

Live from Baghdad (screenplay, Shanley), **Supp. XIV:** 316

Live from Golgotha (Vidal), **Supp. IV Part 2:** 677, 682, 691, 692

Live Now and Pay Later (Garrett), **Supp. VII:** 111

"Live-Oak with Moss" (Whitman), **Retro. Supp. I:** 403

Live or Die (Sexton), **Supp. II Part 2:** 670, 683–687

Liveright, Horace, **Retro. Supp. I:** 80, 81, 83; **Supp. I Part 2:** 464; **Supp. XX:** 71, 75; **Supp. XXII:** 25; **Supp. XXIV:** 28; **Supp. XXV:** 24

Livermore, Elizabeth, **Supp. XXII:** 70

Lives (Plutarch), **II:** 5, 104

Lives of a Cell, The (L. Thomas), **Retro. Supp. I:** 322, 323

Lives of Distinguished American Naval Officers (Cooper), **I:** 347

Lives of Girls and Women (Munro), **Supp. XXVII:** 181, 182, 184

"Lives of Gulls and Children, The" (Nemerov), **III:** 271, 272

Lives of the Animals (Wrigley), **Supp. XVIII: 306–308**

Lives of the Artists (Vasari), **Supp. I Part 2:** 450

"Lives of the Bohemians" (Lethem), **Supp. XVIII:** 135

Lives of the Heart, The (Hirshfield), **Supp. XXIII:** 132–133, 135

Lives of the Muses, The: Nine Women and the Artists They Inspired (Prose), **Supp. XVI:** 250, 260

"Lives of the Philosophers, The" (Brockmeier), **Supp. XXII:** 59, 61

Lives of the Poets (Doctorow), **Supp. IV Part 1:** 234

"Lives of the Poets" (Doctorow), **Supp. IV Part 1:** 234

"Lives of the—Wha'?, The" (Goldbarth), **Supp. XII:** 191

"Living" (Wright), **Supp. XV:** 345

Living, The (Dillard), **Supp. VI:** 23

"Living at Home" (Gordon), **Supp. IV Part 1:** 311

Living by Fiction (Dillard), **Supp. VI:** 23, 31, **32,** 33

Living by the Word (Walker), **Supp. III Part 2:** 521, 522, 526, 527, 535

Living End, The (Elkin), **Supp. VI: 54,** 58

Living Instead (Bronk), **Supp. XXI:** 32

"Living in the Cult of Likability" (Ellis), **Supp. XXVII:** 79

"Living in the Flatlands" (Carruth), **Supp. XVI:** 54

Living in Time (Hadas), **Supp. XXIII:** 120, **122–123**

Living Is Easy, The (D. West), **Supp. XVIII:** 277, 280, **284–286,** 287

"Living Like Weasels" (Dillard), **Supp. VI:** 26, 33

Living My Life (Goldman), **Supp. XXVIII:** 47

Living Novel, The (Hicks), **III:** 342

Living of Charlotte Perkins Gilman, The (Gilman), **Supp. XI:** 193, 209

Living off the Country: Essays on Poetry and Place (Haines), **Supp. XII:** 199, 203, 207

"Living on a Giant" (X. J. Kennedy), **Supp. XV:** 163

Living Out Loud (Quindlen), **Supp. XVII:** 166, **167–169**

Living Present, The (Atherton), **Supp. XXIV:** 24

Living Reed, The (Buck), **Supp. II Part 1:** 129–130

Livingston, Myra Cohn, **Supp. XV:** 153, 162

Living Theater, **Retro. Supp. I:** 424

"Living There" (Dickey), **Supp. IV Part 1:** 182–183

Living the Spirit: A Gay American Indian Anthology (Roscoe, ed.), **Supp. IV Part 1:** 330

"Living Together: A Letter" (Biss), **Supp. XXVI:** 51

Living to Prowl (Pickering), **Supp. XXI:** 203

"Living with a Peacock" (O'Connor), **III:** 350

"Living Words and Cartoon Translations" (Jocks), **Supp. XXVI:** 97

"Livvie" (Welty), **IV:** 265; **Retro. Supp. I:** 348–349

"Livvie Is Back" (Welty), **Retro. Supp. I:** 351

Livy, **II:** 8

"Lizards in Jamshyd's Courtyard" (Faulkner), **Retro. Supp. III:** 85

Lizzie (film), **Supp. IX:** 125

"Llantos de La Llorona: Warnings from the Wailer" (Mora), **Supp. XIII:** 217, 224

"L'Lapse" (Barthelme), **Supp. IV Part 1:** 45–47, 48

Llosa, Mario Vargas, **Supp. XIX:** 131; **Supp. XXIV:** 89

Lloyd, Fabien. *See* Cravan, Arthur

Lloyd, Henry Demarest, **Supp. I Part 1:** 5

Lloyd George, Harold, **I:** 490

"LMFBR" (Snyder), **Supp. VIII:** 302

Loach, Ken, **Supp. XXIII:** 163

"Loaded Inflections" (Halliday), **Supp. XIX:** 90, 91

"Loam" (Sandburg), **III:** 584–585

"Loan, The" (Malamud), **Supp. I Part 2:** 427, 428, 431, 437

Loberer, Eric, **Supp. XV:** 339

"Local" (McCarriston), **Supp. XIV:** 270

Local Color (Capote), **Supp. III Part 1:** 120

"Local Color" (London), **II:** 475

"Local Family Keeps Son Happy" (Keillor), **Supp. XVI:** 168, 169

Local Girls (Hoffman), **Supp. X:** 77, **90–91,** 92

"Local Girls" (Hoffman), **Supp. X:** 90

Local Habitation & A Name, A (Kooser), **Supp. XIX:** 116, 118, **119–120**

Local Men (Whitehead), **Supp. XV:** 339

"Local Metaphysics" (Huddle), **Supp. XXVI:** 149

"Local Story: Reading the Signs"(Lea), **Supp. XXVIII:** 137

Local Time (Dunn), **Supp. XI:** 143, **148–149**

Local Wonders: Seasons in the Bohemian Alps (Kooser), **Supp. XIX:** 115, **126**

"Location" (Halliday), **Supp. XIX:** 87

Lock, Helen, **Supp. XIII:** 233, 237–238

Lock, Robert H., **IV:** 319; **Retro. Supp. I:** 375

Lockdown (Myers), **Supp. XXVII:** 204, 205

Locke, Alain, **Retro. Supp. II:** 115; **Retro. Supp. III:** 127, 128, 131, 140; **Supp. I Part 1:** 323, 325, 341; **Supp. II Part 1:** 53, 176, 182, 228, 247; **Supp. IV Part 1:** 170; **Supp. IX:** 306, 309; **Supp. X:** 134, 137, 139; **Supp. XIV: 195–219; Supp. XIX:** 69, 75; **Supp. XVIII:** 122; **Supp. XXII:** 7, 13

Locke, Duane, **Supp. IX:** 273

Locke, Jane Ermine, **Supp. XXV:** 38

Locke, John, **I:** 554–555, 557; **II:** 15–16, 113–114, 348–349, 480; **III:** 294–295; **IV:** 149; **Supp. I Part 1:** 130, 229, 230; **Supp. I Part 2:** 523

Locke, Sondra, **II:** 588

"Locked House, A" (Snodgrass), **Supp. VI:** 323

Locked Room, The (Auster), **Supp. XII:** 22, 24, **27–28**

Locket, The (Masters), **Supp. I Part 2:** 460

Lockridge, Ross, Jr., **Supp. XIX:** 263

"Locksley Hall" (Tennyson), **Supp. IX:** 19

Lockwood Concern, The (O'Hara), **III:** 362, 364, 377–382

Locomotion (Woodson), **Supp. XXVIII:** 284, 285

"Locus" (Ammons), **Supp. VII:** 28

"Locus" (Hayden), **Supp. II Part 1:** 361–362, 381

"Locusts, the Plaza, the Room, The" (Kees), **Supp. XV:** 141

Loden, Barbara, **III:** 163

Lodge, Henry Cabot, **I:** 11–12, 21

Lodge, Mrs. Henry Cabot, **I:** 11–12, 19

Lodge, Thomas, **IV:** 370

Loeb, Gerald, **Supp. IV Part 2:** 523

Loeb, Harold, **Supp. XXIV:** 49

Loeb, Jacques, **I:** 513; **Retro. Supp. II:** 104; **Supp. I Part 2:** 641

Loeffler, Jack, **Supp. XIII:** 1, 3, 12, 14, 16

Loft, William D., **Supp. XXVI:** 96

Loftus, Mary J., **Supp. XXI:** 245

Lofty Dogmas (A. Finch, M. Kumin and D. Brown, eds.), **Supp. XVII:** 75–76

"Log" (Merrlll), **Supp. III Part 1:** 328

Logan, Joshua, **Supp. XXV:** 95

Logan, Rayford W., **Supp. II Part 1:** 171, 194; **Supp. XIV:** 73

Logan, William, **Supp. X:** 201, 213; **Supp. XI:** 131, 132; **Supp. XII:** 98, 107, 113, 184; **Supp. XV:** 212, 226, 251, 257, 260–261, 262,**Supp. XV:** 263, 266

Log Book of "The Loved One," The, **Supp. XI:** 306

Logenbach, James, **Supp. XVII:** 183

"Logging and Pimping and 'Your Pal, Jim' " (Maclean), **Supp. XIV:** 229

"Logic"(Siken), **Supp. XXVIII:** 201, 202

"Logos" (W. Stone), **Supp. XXVII:** 255

Logsdon, Joseph, **Supp. XXVIII:** 166

Logue, Christopher, **Supp. XIV:** 82

Lohengrin (Wagner), **I:** 216

Lohrfinck, Rosalind, **III:** 107, 117

Lolita (Nabokov), **III:** 246, 247, 255, 258–261; **Retro. Supp. I:** 263, 264, 265, 266, 269, 270, **272–274,** 275; **Supp. V:** 127, 252; **Supp. VIII:** 133; **Supp. XVI:** 294; **Supp. XXII:** 260

"Lolita" (Parker), **Supp. IX:** 193

Lolly Dinks' Doings (E. Stoddard), **Supp. XV:** 273,**Supp. XV:** 286

Lombard, Kandace, **Supp. XXVII:** 262

Lombardi, Marilyn May, **Retro. Supp. II:** 40

Lomokome Papers, The (Wouk), **Supp. XXV:** 256, 262

London, Eliza, **II:** 465

London, Jack, **I:** 209; **II:** 264, 440, 444, 451, **462–485; III:** 314, 580; **Supp. IV Part 1:** 236; **Supp. IX:** 1, 14; **Supp. V:** 281; **Supp. XIII:** 312; **Supp. XIV:** 227; **Supp. XV:** 115; **Supp. XVI:** 181; **Supp. XVIII:** 90; **Supp.**

XXII: 203; **Supp. XXVII:** 126

London, Mrs. Jack (Bessie Maddern), **II:** 465, 466, 473, 478

London, Mrs. Jack (Charmian Kittredge), **II:** 466, 468, 473, 476, 478, 481

London, John, **II:** 464, 465

London, Scott, **Supp. XIV:** 301, 307, 311

"London 1972: Silent Zone" (Davison), **Supp. XXVI:** 72

London Embassy, The (Theroux), **Supp. VIII:** 323

London Fields (Amis), **Retro. Supp. I:** 278

"London Letter" (column; Eliot), **Supp. XV:** 306

London Magazine (Plath), **Supp. I Part 2:** 541

London Snow: A Christmas Story (Theroux), **Supp. VIII:** 322

London Suite (Simon), **Supp. IV Part 2:** 576, 581, 582, 588

London: The Biography (Ackroyd), **Supp. XVII:** 180

Loneliness of the Long Distance Runner, The (Sillitoe), **Supp. XX: 195**

Lonely Are the Brave (film), **Supp. XIII:** 6

"Lonely Coast, A" (Proulx), **Supp. VII:** 264

Lonely Crusade (C. Himes), **Supp. XVI:** 135, 139–140

Lonely for the Future (Farrell), **II:** 46, 47

"Lonely Gay Teen Seeking Same" (Egan), **Supp. XIX:** 61

Lonely Impulse of Delight, A (Shanley), **Supp. XIV:** 317–318

"Lonely Street, The" (W. C. Williams), **IV:** 413

"Lonely Worker, A" (Jewett), **Retro. Supp. II:** 132

Lonergan, Wayne, **Supp. I Part 1:** 51

Lonesome Boy (Bontemps), **Supp. XXII:** 6, 13–14

Lonesome Dove (McMurtry), **Supp. V:** 226–228, 231, 232, 233

Lonesome Traveler (Kerouac), **Supp. III Part 1:** 219, 225

"Lonesome Whistle Blowing" (Skow), **Supp. XVI:** 174

"Lone Striker, A" (Frost), **Retro. Supp. I:** 136, 137

Long, Ada, **Supp. V:** 178

Long, Frank Belknap, **Supp. XXV:** 111, 122; **Supp. XXVII:** 117

Long, Haniel, **Supp. XV:** 46, 49

Long, Huey, **I:** 489; **II:** 454; **IV:** 249; **Supp. IV Part 2:** 679; **Supp. XIV:** 14

Long, John Luther, **Supp. XXI:** 150

Long, Judith Reick, **Supp. XX: 212, 215, 217, 223**

Long, Ray, **II:** 430; **III:** 54

Long after Midnight (Bradbury), **Supp. IV Part 1:** 102

Long Ago in France: The Years in Dijon (M. F. K. Fisher), **Supp. XVII:** 91

Long and Happy Life, A (Price), **Supp. VI:** 258, **259–260,** 262, 264, 265

Long Approach, The (Kumin), **Supp. IV Part 2:** 452–453, 453

Longbottom, Robert, **Supp. XXI:** 148

Long Christmas Dinner, The (Wilder), **IV:** 357, 365; **Supp. V:** 105

Long Christmas Dinner and Other Plays (Wilder), **IV:** 365–366

Long Day's Dying, A (Buechner), **Supp. XII:** 45–47

Long Day's Journey into Night (O'Neill), **III:** 385, 401, 403–404; **Supp. IV Part 1:** 359; **Supp. XIV:** 327; **Supp. XXI:** 13; **Supp. XXII:** 27, 29, 30

Long Desire, A (Connell), **Supp. XIV:** 79, 80, 97

"Long Distance" (Stafford), **Supp. XI:** 329

"Long-Distance Runner, The" (Paley), **Supp. VI:** 221–222, 228, 230

Long Dream, The (Wright), **IV:** 478, 488, 494

"Long Embrace, The" (Levine), **Supp. V:** 187

"Long Enough" (Rukeyser), **Supp. VI:** 274

"Longest Night of My Life, The " (Nichols), **Supp. XIII:** 269

Longfellow, Henry Wadsworth, **I:** 458, 471; **II:** 274, 277, 295–296, 310, 313, 402, **486–510; III:** 269, 412, 421, 422, 577; **IV:** 309, 371; **Retro. Supp. I:** 54, 123, 150, 155, 362; **Retro. Supp. II: 153–174; Retro. Supp. III:** 106, 109, 113, 116, 225, 233, 255; **Supp. I Part 1:** 158, 299, 306, 317, 362, 368; **Supp. I Part 2:** 405, 406, 408, 409, 414, 416, 420, 586, 587, 602, 699, 704; **Supp. II Part 1:** 291, 353; **Supp. III Part 2:** 609; **Supp. IV Part 1:** 165; **Supp. IV Part 2:** 503; **Supp. XII:** 260; **Supp. XIII:** 141; **Supp. XIV:** 120; **Supp. XVIII:** 4; **Supp. XXI:** 51; **Supp. XXIII:** 223

"Long Feud" (Untermeyer), **Supp. XV:** 309

Long Feud: Selected Poems (Untermeyer), **Supp. XV:** 312

"Long Fourth, A" (Taylor), **Supp. V:** 313

Long Fourth and Other Stories, A (Taylor), **Supp. V:** 318–319

Long Gay Book, A (Stein), **IV:** 42

Long Goodbye, The (Chandler), **Supp. IV Part 1:** 120, 122, 132–134, 135

Long Goodbye, The (T. Williams), **IV:** 381

"Long Hair" (Snyder), **Supp. VIII:** 300

Longing for Home, The: Recollections and Reflections (Buechner), **Supp. XII:** 53

Longinus, Dionysius Cassius, **I:** 279

"Long-Legged House, The" (Berry), **Supp. X:** 21, 24–25, 27, 31

Long Live Man (Corso), **Supp. XII:** 129–130, 132

Long Love, The (Sedges), **Supp. II Part 1:** 125

Long Made Short (Dixon), **Supp. XII:** 152

Long March, The (Styron), **IV:** 97, 99, 104–107, 111, 113, 117

"Long Night, The" (Bambara), **Supp. XI:** 9

Long Night of White Chickens, The (Goldman), **Supp. XXV:** 49, 51–53

"Long Novel, A" (Ashbery), **Supp. III Part 1:** 6

Longo, Robert, **Supp. XVI:** 124

Long Patrol, The (Mailer), **III:** 46

"Long Peace Among Iroquois Nations, The" (Crawford), **Supp. XXVI:** 85

"Long Point Light" (Doty), **Supp. XI:** 127

Long Road of Woman's Memory, The (Addams), **Supp. I Part 1:** 17–18

"Long Run, The" (Wharton), **IV:** 314

Long Season, The (Brosnan), **II:** 424, 425; **Supp. XX: 195**

"Long Shadow of Lincoln, The: A Litany" (Sandburg), **III:** 591, 593

Longshot O'Leary (McGrath), **Supp. X:** 117

"Long Shower, The" (Francis), **Supp. IX:** 90

"Long Stemmed Roses" (Jarman), **Supp. XVII:** 115

Long Story Short (Gingher, ed.), **Supp. XXVII:** 12

Longstreet, Augustus B., **II:** 70, 313; **Supp. I Part 1:** 352; **Supp. V:** 44; **Supp. X:** 227

Longstreet, Augustus Baldwin, **Retro. Supp. III:** 259; **Supp. XXVIII:** 231

"Long Summer" (R. Lowell), **II:** 553–554

"Long Term" (Dunn), **Supp. XI:** 149

"Long Thoughts, The"(Dybek), **Supp. XXIII:** 71

Longtime Companion (film), **Supp. X:** 146, 152

Long Valley, The (Steinbeck), **IV:** 51

Long View (Taggard), **Supp. XXII: 283–284**

Long Voyage Home, The (O'Neill), **III:** 388

"Long Wail, A" (Crews), **Supp. XI:** 101

"Long Walk, The" (Bogan), **Supp. III Part 1:** 61

Long Walk Home, The (Kriegel), **Supp. XXIV:** 214–216

Long Walks and Intimate Talks (Paley), **Supp. VI:** 221

Long Way from Home, A (McKay), **Supp. X:** 132, 140

Long Winter, The (L. I. Wilder), **Supp. XXII:** 291, 294, 295

Lönnrot, Elias, **Retro. Supp. II:** 159

Looby, Christopher, **Supp. XIII:** 96

Look, Dan, **Supp. XXV:** 123

Look, Stranger! (Auden), **Supp. II Part 1:** 11

"Look, The" (Olds), **Supp. X:** 210

Look at Me (Egan), **Supp. XIX:** 49, 53–56, 60, 61

Look at the Harlequins (Nabokov), **Retro. Supp. I:** 266, 270

Lookaway, Lookaway (Barnhardt), **Supp. XXVII:** 1, 9–11, 13

"Look for My White Self" (Ammons), **Supp. VII:** 25

"Look Fred, You're a Doctor, My Problem Is Something Like This" (Berrigan), **Supp. XXIV:** 37

Look Homeward, Angel (Wolfe), **II:** 457; **IV:** 450, 452, 453, 454, 455–456, 461, 462, 463, 464, 468, 471; **Supp. XI:** 216

"Looking" (Sanders), **Supp. XVI:** 277

"Looking a Mad Dog Dead in the Eyes" (Komunyakaa), **Supp. XIII:** 114

"Looking at Each Other" (Rukeyser), **Supp. VI:** 280, 285–286

"Looking at Kafka" (P. Roth), **Supp. III Part 2:** 402

"Looking at Women" (Sanders), **Supp. XVI:** 274

"Looking Back" (Harjo), **Supp. XII:** 218

"Looking Back" (Merwin), **Supp. III Part 1:** 352

"Looking Back at Girlhood" (Jewett), **Retro. Supp. II:** 131, 133

Looking Backward (Bellamy), **II:** 276; **Supp. I Part 2:** 641; **Supp. XI:** 200

"Looking for a Ship" (McPhee), **Supp. III Part 1:** 312–313

"Looking for Dragon Smoke" (R. Bly), **Supp. IV Part 1:** 60

Looking for Holes in the Ceiling (Dunn), **Supp. XI:** 139, **143–145**

Looking for Langston (Julien; film), **Supp. XI:** 19, 20

Looking for Lincoln (television production), **Supp. XX:** 99

Looking for Luck (Kumin), **Supp. IV Part 2:** 453, 454–455

"Looking for Mr. Green" (Bellow), **Retro. Supp. II:** 27

"Looking for the Buckhead Boys" (Dickey), **Supp. IV Part 1:** 182, 183

"Looking Forward to Age" (Harrison), **Supp. VIII:** 49

"Looking from Inside My Body" (R. Bly), **Supp. IV Part 1:** 71

"Looking Glass, The" (Wharton), **Retro. Supp. I:** 382

"Lookout's Journal" (Snyder), **Supp. VIII:** 291

"Looks Like They'll Never Learn" (McCoy), **Supp. XIII:** 166

"Look to the Woods" (P. N. Warren), **Supp. XX: 272**

"Look to Thy Heart . . ." (Hay), **Supp. XIV:** 130

Loon, Hendrik Willem van, **Supp. XVI:** 185

Loon Lake (Doctorow), **Supp. IV Part 1:** 219, 222, 224–227, 230, 231, 232, 233

"Loon Point" (O'Brien), **Supp. V:** 237

Loos, Adolf, **Supp. XVI:** 187

Loos, Anita, **Supp. XVI: 181–199**

Loos, Mary Anita, **Supp. XVI:** 196

Loose Canons (H. L. Gates), **Supp. XX: 101, 108, 109–110, 111**

Loosestrife (Dunn), **Supp. XI: 152–154**

"Loosestrife" (Dunn), **Supp. XI:** 154

"Loose Woman" (X. J. Kennedy), **Supp. XV:** 159

Loose Woman: Poems (Cisneros), **Supp. VII:** 58, 71–72

Lopate, Edward, **Supp. XVI:** 266

Lopate, Philip, **Supp. XII:** 184; **Supp. XIII:** 280–281; **Supp. XVI:** 230

Lopatnikoff, Nikolai, **Supp. XIV:** 123

Lopez, Barry, **Supp. IV Part 1:** 416; **Supp. V:** 211; **Supp. X:** 29, 31; **Supp. XIII:** 16; **Supp. XIV:** 227

Lopez, Rafael, **Supp. IV Part 2:** 602

Lorax, The (Geisel), **Supp. XVI:** 109–110

Lorca, Federico García, **IV:** 380; **Supp. I Part 1:** 345; **Supp. IV Part 1:** 83; **Supp. VIII:** 38, 39; **Supp. XIII:** 315, 323, 324; **Supp. XV:** 186; **Supp. XXI:** 100; **Supp. XXVII:** 53, 151, 155, 160; **Supp. XXVIII:** 260

Lorch, Fred, **Retro. Supp. III:** 268

Lord, Audre, **Retro. Supp. III:** 247

Lord, Judge Otis P., **I:** 454, 457, 458, 470

Lorde, Audre, **Supp. I Part 2:** 550, 571; **Supp. IV Part 1:** 325; **Supp. XI:** 20; **Supp. XII:** 217, 220; **Supp. XIII:** 295; **Supp. XVII:** 71; **Supp. XXIII:** 194

Lord Jim (Conrad), **I:** 422; **II:** 26; **Retro. Supp. II:** 292; **Supp. I Part 2:** 623; **Supp. IV Part 2:** 680; **Supp. V:** 251

"Lord of Hosts" (Pinsky), **Supp. VI:** 244

Lord of the Flies (W. Golding), **Supp. XVI:** 65

Lord of the Rings (Tolkien), **Supp. V:** 140; **Supp. XXVII:** 128

Lords of Misrule, The (X. J. Kennedy), **Supp. XV:** 154, **170–171**

Lords of the Housetops (Van Vechten), **Supp. II Part 2:** 736

Lord's Prayer, **I:** 579

Lord Timothy Dexter of Newburyport, Mass. (Marquand), **III:** 55

Lord Weary's Castle (R. Lowell), **II:** 538, 542–551; **Retro. Supp. II:** 178, **186–187**, 188; **Supp. XV:** 252

"Lorelei" (Plath), **Retro. Supp. II:** 246; **Supp. I Part 2:** 538

Lorentzen, Christian, **Supp. XXVII:** 195–196

"Lorenzo" (Bynner), **Supp. XV:** 46, 50

Lorimer, George Horace, **II:** 430; **Retro. Supp. I:** 101, 113

Lori-Parks, Suzan, **Retro. Supp. III:** 319

Lorre, Peter, **Supp. IV Part 1:** 356

"Los Alamos" (Momaday), **Supp. IV Part 2:** 482

Los Amigos de Becky (Hinojosa). *See Becky and Her Friends* (Hinojosa)

"Los Angeles, 1980" (Gunn Allen), **Supp. IV Part 1:** 325

"Los Angeles Days" (Didion), **Supp. IV Part 1:** 211

Los Cerritos (Atherton), **Supp. XXIV:** 22

"Lo! School in Poetry, The" (Taggard), **Supp. XXII:** 276

"Loser, The" (Talese), **Supp. XVII:** 202, 208

Loser and Still Champion: Muhammad Ali (Schulberg), **Supp. XVIII:** 254

Losey, Joseph, **IV:** 383

Lose Your Mother: A Journey Along the Atlantic Slave Route (Hartman), **Supp. XX: 154**

"Losing a Language" (Merwin), **Supp. III Part 1:** 356

Losing Battles (Welty), **IV:** 261, 281–282; **Retro. Supp. I:** 341, 352, **353–354**

"Losing the Marbles" (Merrill), **Supp. III Part 1:** 337

"Losing Track of Language" (Clampitt), **Supp. IX:** 38, 40

Losses (Jarrell), **II:** 367, 372, 373–375, 376, 377, 380–381

"Losses" (Jarrell), **II:** 375–376

Lossky, N. O., **Supp. IV Part 2:** 519

"Loss of Breath" (Poe), **III:** 425–426

"Loss of My Arms and Legs, The" (Kingsolver), **Supp. VII:** 208

Loss of Roses, A (Inge), **Supp. XXV:** 95, 103–104, 106

"Loss of the Creature, The" (Percy), **Supp. III Part 1:** 387

"Lost" (Wagoner), **Supp. IX:** 328

"Lost, The" (Boyle), **Supp. XXIV:** 59

"Lost, The/Los Perdidos" (Kingsolver), **Supp. VII:** 208

"Lost and Found" (Levine), **Supp. V:** 188

"Lost and Found" (Nelson), **Supp. XVIII:** 176

"Lost Bodies" (Wright), **Supp. V:** 342

"Lost Boy, The" (Wolfe), **IV:** 451, 460, 466–467

"Lost Children, The" (Crooker), **Supp. XXIII:** 54

"Lost Decade, The" (Fitzgerald), **II:** 98

"Lost Dogs of Phnom Penh, The" (Boyle), **Supp. XXIV:** 64

Lost Ecstasy (Rinehart), **Supp. XXV:** 196

Lost Father, The (Simpson), **Supp. XXVII:** 237–239

"Lost Fugue for Chet" (Hull), **Supp. XXI:** 137–138, 141

Lost Galleon and Other Tales, The (Harte), **Supp. II Part 1:** 344

Lost Get-Back Boogie, The (Burke), **Supp. XIV:** 22, 25

"Lost Girls, The" (Hogan), **Supp. IV Part 1:** 406–407

Lost Grizzlies, The: A Search for Survivors in the Wilderness of Colorado (Bass), **Supp. XVI:** 25, 26

Lost Highway (film), **Supp. X:** 314

Lost Illusions (Balzac), **I:** 500

"Lost in Nostalgia: The Autobiographies of Eva Hoffman and Richard Rodriguez" (Fachinger), **Supp. XVI:** 153

Lost in the Bonewheel Factory (Komunyakaa), **Supp. XIII: 114–115,** 116

Lost in the City (E. P. Jones), **Supp. XXII:** 140, 142, **143–146,** 148, 149

Lost in the Cosmos: The Last Self-Help Book (Percy), **Supp. III Part 1:** 397

Lost in the Funhouse (Barth), **I:** 122, 135, 139; **Supp. X:** 307

"Lost in the Whichy Thicket" (Wolfe), **Supp. III Part 2:** 573, 574

Lost in Translation (E. Hoffman), **Supp. XVI:** 147, **148–151,** 153, 154, 159

"Lost in Translation" (Hass), **Supp. VIII:** 28

"Lost in Translation" (Merrill), **Supp. III Part 1:** 324, 329–330

Lost in Yonkers (film), **Supp. IV Part 2:** 588

Lost in Yonkers (Simon), **Supp. IV Part 2:** 576, 577, 584, 587–588, 590–591

"Lost Jerusalem" (Untermeyer), **Supp. XV:** 307

"Lost Keys of Glory, The" (Hurston), **Retro. Supp. III:** 139

Lost Lady, A (Cather), **I:** 323–325, 327; **Retro. Supp. I: 15–16,** 20, 21, 382; **Retro. Supp. III:** 24, 33–34, 36

Lost Light (Connelly), **Supp. XXI:** 72, **75–76**

"Lost Lives" (Sorrentino), **Supp. XXI:** 226

"Lost Lover, A" (Jewett), **II:** 400–401, 402; **Retro. Supp. II:** 137

"Lost Loves" (Kinnell), **Supp. III Part 1:** 237, 245

Lost Man's River (Matthiessen), **Supp. V:** 212, 213, 214, 215

"Lost on September Trail, 1967" (Ríos), **Supp. IV Part 2:** 540

Lost Puritan (Mariani), **Retro. Supp. II:** 189

Lost Roads Project, The: A Walk-In Book of Arkansas (exhibition; Wright and Luster), **Supp. XV:** 337, 348

"Lost Sailor, The" (Freneau), **Supp. II Part 1:** 264

Lost Son, The (Roethke), **III:** 529, 530–532, 533

"Lost Son, The" (Roethke), **III:** 536, 537–539, 542

"Lost Sons" (Salter), **Supp. IX:** 260

Lost Souls (Singer). *See* Meshugah (Singer)

"Lost"(Thompson), **Supp. XXIII:** 299, 300

"Lost Treaties of the California Indians" (Zitkala-Ša), **Supp. XXV:** 284

Lost Weekend, The (Jackson), **Supp. XIII:** 262

Lost Woods, The: Adventures of a Naturalist (Teale), **Supp. XXVIII:** 245, 247, 248

"Lost World, A" (Ashbery), **Supp. III Part 1:** 9

"Lost World, The" (Chabon), **Supp. XI:** 72–73

Lost World, The (Jarrell), **II:** 367, 368, 371, 379–380, 386, 387

"Lost World, The" cycle (Chabon), **Supp. XI: 71–73**

"Lost World of Richard Yates, The: How the Great Writer of the Age of Anxiety Disappeared from Print" (O'Nan), **Supp. XI:** 348

"Lost Young Intellectual, The" (Howe), **Supp. VI:** 113, **115–116**

Lost Zoo, The: (A Rhyme for the Young, But Not Too Young) (Cullen), **Supp. IV Part 1:** 173

Loti, Pierre, **II:** 311, 325; **Supp. IV Part 1:** 81

"Lot of People Bathing in a Stream, A" (Stevens), **IV:** 93

Lotringer, Sylvère, **Supp. XII:** 4

"Lot's Wife" (Nemerov), **III:** 270

"Lottery, The" (Jackson), **Supp. IX:** 113, 114, 118, 120, **122–123**

Lottery, The; or, The Adventures of James Harris (Jackson), **Supp. IX:** 113, 115, 116, 124, 125

Lotze, Hermann, **III:** 600

Loud and Clear (Quindlen), **Supp. XVII:** 167, **170–172**

"Loud Like Love" (video, Ellis), **Supp. XXVII:** 80

Loudspeaker (Lawson), **Supp. XXVIII:** 74

Louganis, Greg, **Supp. XX: 264**

"Louie, His Cousin & His Other Cousin" (Cisneros), **Supp. VII:** 60

Louinet, Patrice, **Supp. XXVII:** 128

Louis, Joe, **II:** 589; **Supp. IV Part 1:** 360

Louis, Pierre Charles Alexandre, **Supp. I Part 1:** 302, 303

"Louisa, Please Come Home" (Jackson), **Supp. IX:** 122

Louis Lambert (Balzac), **I:** 499

"Louis Simpson and Walt Whitman: Destroying the Teacher" (Lazer), **Supp. IX:** 265

"*Louis Zukofsky: All: The Collected Short Poems, 1923–1958*" (Creeley), **Supp. IV Part 1:** 154

"Lounge" (Francis), **Supp. IX:** 83

Lounsberry, Barbara, **Supp. XVII:** 208

Lounsbury, Floyd G., **Supp. XXVI:** 89

Lounsbury, Thomas R., **I:** 335

Louter, Jan, **Supp. XI:** 173

"Love" (Collins), **Supp. XXI:** 61

"Love," (Gibran), **Supp. XX: 119**

Love (Morrison), **Retro. Supp. III:** 185, 196–197

"Love" (Olson), **Supp. II Part 2:** 571

"Love" (Paley), **Supp. VI:** 219, 222, 230

Love, Deborah, **Supp. V:** 208, 210

Love Alone: 18 Elegies for Rog (Monette), **Supp. X:** 146, 154

Love Always (Beattie), **Supp. V:** 29, 30, 35

Love among the Cannibals (Morris), **III:** 228, 230–231

"Love Among the Ruins" (Mosley), **Supp. XIII:** 247

"Love and Art" (Huddle), **Supp. XXVI:** 150

Love and Death (film; Allen), **Supp. XV:** 2, **5–6,** 7, 11

Love and Death in the American Novel (Fiedler), **Supp. XIII:** 93, 96, **99–101,** 104

Love and Exile (Singer), **Retro. Supp. II: 302–304,** 315

Love and Fame (Berryman), **I:** 170

Love and Friendship (Bloom), **Retro. Supp. II:** 31, 33–34

Love and Glory (Parker), **Supp. XIX:** 189

"Love and How to Cure It" (Wilder), **IV:** 365

Love and Other Games of Chance (Siegel), **Supp. XXII:** 255, 256, **261–265,** 266, 267

Love and Scorn: New and Selected Poems (C. Frost), **Supp. XV:** 95, 96, 100, 103–105, 106

Love and Theft (album, Dylan), **Supp. XVIII:** 28, 31

"Love and the Hate, The" (Jeffers), **Supp. II Part 2:** 434–435

Love and the Incredibly Old Man (Siegel), **Supp. XXII: 267–268**

Love and Will (Dixon), **Supp. XII:** 148, 149

Love and Work (Price), **Supp. VI:** 261

"Love as a Great Power" (Bronk), **Supp. XXI:** 31

"Love Calls Us to the Things of This World" (Wilbur), **Supp. III Part 2:** 544, 552–553

Love Course, The (Gurney), **Supp. V:** 98

Lovecraft, H. P., **Retro. Supp. III:** 235; **Supp. XXII:** 49; **Supp. XXV: 109–126; Supp. XXVII:** 115, 117, 119, 128

Lovecraft and Influence (R. H. Waugh, ed.), **Supp. XXV:** 123

Loved One, The (film), **Supp. XI: 305–306,** 307

Loved One, The (Waugh), **Supp. XI:** 305

Love Expert, The (film; Kirkland), **Supp. XVI:** 186

Love Feast (Buechner), **Supp. XII:** 52

Love for Love (Congreve), **Supp. XVIII:** 12

"Love Fossil" (Olds), **Supp. X:** 203

"Love"(Hadas), **Supp. XXIII:** 117

Love in a Dead Language (Siegel), **Supp. XXII:** 255, **258–261,** 265–266, 267

Love in Buffalo (Gurney), **Supp. V:** 96

Love in Chartres (Asch), **Supp. XXVI:** 18, 19, 20–21, 25

"Love—In Other Words" (Lee), **Supp. VIII:** 113

"Love in the Air" (Jin), **Supp. XVIII:** 93–94

"Love in the Morning" (Dubus), **Supp. VII:** 91

Love in the Ruins: The Adventures of a Bad Catholic at a Time near the End of the World (Percy), **Supp. III Part 1:** 385, 387, 393–394, 397–398

Love in the Western World (de Rougemont), **Retro. Supp. I:** 328

"Love Is a Deep and a Dark and a Lonely" (Sandburg), **III:** 595

"Love Is a Fire" (Cohen), **Supp. XXVII:** 60

"Love Itself" (Cohen), **Supp. XXVII:** 61

Lovejoy, Elijah P., **Supp. I Part 2:** 588; **Supp. XXIV:** 78

Lovejoy, Owen R., **Supp. I Part 1:** 8

Lovejoy, Thomas, **Supp. X:** 108

"Lovejoy Street" (Stallings), **Supp. XXV:** 224

Lovelace, Richard, **II:** 590

"Love Letter (Schnackenberg), **Supp. XV:** 258–259

Love Letters (film), **Supp. IV Part 2:** 524

Love Letters (Gurney), **Supp. V:** 105, 108–109

Love Letters, The (Massie), **Supp. IV Part 2:** 524

Love Letters and Two Other Plays: The Golden Age and *What I Did Last Summer* (Gurney), **Supp. V:** 100

"Love Lies Sleeping" (Bishop), **Retro. Supp. II:** 42

Love Life (Mason), **Supp. VIII:** 145–146

"Love Life" (Mason), **Supp. VIII: 145–146**

Lovell, Julia, **Supp. XVIII:** 101

Lovely Bones, The (Sebold), **Supp. XXII:** 55

Lovely Lady, The (Lawrence), **Retro. Supp. I:** 203

"Lovely Lady, The" (Lawrence), **Supp. I Part 1:** 329

Love Me (Keillor), **Supp. XVI:** 178

Love Medicine (Erdrich), **Supp. IV Part 1:** 259, 260, 261, 263, 265, 266, 267–268, 270, 271, 274–275; **Supp. X:** 290

Love Medicine (expanded version) (Erdrich), **Supp. IV Part 1:** 263, 273, 274, 275

"Love Minus Zero/No Limit" (song, Dylan), **Supp. XVIII:** 31

"Love Nest, The" (Lardner), **II:** 427, 429

Love Nest, The, and Other Stories (Lardner), **II:** 430–431, 436

Lovenheim, Barbara, **Supp. X:** 169

Love of a Good Woman, The (Munro), **Supp. XXVII:** 190, 192

"Love of a Good Woman, The" (Munro), **Supp. XXVII:** 192

"Love of Annunziata, The" (di Donato), **Supp. XX: 40**

"Love of Elsie Barton: A Chronicle, The" (Warren), **IV:** 253

Love of Landry, The (Dunbar), **Supp. II Part 1:** 212

"Love of Morning, The" (Levertov), **Supp. III Part 1:** 284

Love of the Last Tycoon, The: A Western. See Last Tycoon, The

"Love on a Garbage Dump"(Gold), **Supp. XXVIII:** 68

"Love on the Bon Dieu" (Chopin), **Supp. I Part 1:** 213

Love on the Hoof (O'Hara and Lima), **Supp. XXIII:** 217

Love Poems (Sexton), **Supp. II Part 2:** 687–689

Love Poems (Tentative Title) (O'Hara), **Supp. XXIII:** 219

Love Poems of May Swenson, The (Swenson), **Supp. IV Part 2:** 652, 653

"Love Poet" (Agee), **I:** 28

"Lover" (Hoffman), **Supp. XVIII:** 87

"Love Ritual" (Mora), **Supp. XIII:** 215

Lover of Horses, The (Gallagher), **Supp. XXIV:** 166, 172, 173–174, 176

"Lover of Horses, The" (Gallagher), **Supp. XXIV:** 173–174, 176

Loveroot (Jong), **Supp. V:** 115, 130

"Lovers, The" (Berryman), **I:** 174

"Lovers, The" (Buck), **Supp. II Part 1:** 128

"Lover's Garden, A" (Ginsberg), **Supp. II Part 1:** 311

"Lovers of the Poor, The" (Brooks), **Supp. III Part 1:** 81, 85

Lovers Should Marry (Martin), **Supp. IV Part 1:** 351

"Lover's Song" (Yeats), **Supp. I Part 1:** 80

"Love Rushes By" (Salinas), **Supp. XIII:** 326–327

"Love's Ghost" (Nelson), **Supp. XVIII:** 176

Lovesick (Stern), **Supp. IX: 295–296**

Love's Labour's Lost (Shakespeare), **III:** 263

Love's Old Sweet Song (Saroyan), **Supp. IV Part 1:** 83

"Love Song During Riot with Many Voices" (Hull), **Supp. XXI:** 136

"Love Song of J. Alfred Prufrock, The" (T. S. Eliot), **I:** 52, 66, 569–570; **III:** 460; **Retro. Supp. I:** 55, 56, 57, 60; **Retro. Supp. III:** 61–62, 66; **Supp. II Part 1:** 5; **Supp. XIII:** 346; **Supp. XVI:** 150; **Supp. XXV:** 22; **Supp. XXVI:** 237

"Love Song of St. Sebastian" (Eliot), **Retro. Supp. I:** 57

"Lovesong of the Square Root of Negative One"(Siken), **Supp. XXVIII:** 201

"Love Songs" (Loy), **Supp. XXII:** 161

Love Songs (Teasdale), **Supp. XXVII:** 283, 289, 290–291

"Love Songs to Joannes" (Loy), **Supp. XXII:** 161, 163

Love's Pilgrimage (Sinclair), **Supp. V:** 286

"Love's Relative" (Stone), **Supp. XXVII:** 251

"Love the Wild Swan" (Jeffers), **Supp. VIII:** 33

Love to Mamá: A Tribute to Mothers (Mora, ed.), **Supp. XIII:** 221

Lovett, Robert Morss, **II:** 43

Lovett-Graff, Bennett, **Supp. XXV:** 123

"Love-Unknown" (Herbert), **Supp. I Part 1:** 80

Love! Valor! Compassion! (film), **Supp. XIII:** 206

Love! Valour! Compassion! (McNally), **Supp. XIII:** 199, **203–204**, 208, 209

"Love *versus* Law" (Stowe), **Supp. I Part 2:** 585–586

"Love Wall" (Peacock), **Supp. XIX:** 200

Love with a Few Hairs (Mrabet), **Supp. IV Part 1:** 92

Loving a Woman in Two Worlds (R. Bly), **Supp. IV Part 1:** 66, 67, 68–69, 71, 72

Loving in the War Years: Lo que nunca pasó por sus labios (Moraga), **Supp. XXIII:** 194, 195

"Loving on Borrowed Time" (J. W. Miller), **Supp. XX: 164**

"Loving Shepherdess, The" (Jeffers), **Supp. II Part 2:** 432

"Loving the Killer" (Sexton), **Supp. II Part 2:** 688

"Loving Wife" (C. Miller), **Supp. XXII:** 196–197, 199

Lovin' Molly (film), **Supp. V:** 223, 226

Low Country (Siddons), **Supp. XXII:** 239

Lowe, John, **Retro. Supp. III:** 133, 134, 138, 140; **Supp. XIII:** 238

Lowe, Pardee, **Supp. X:** 291

Lowell, Abbott Lawrence, **I:** 487; **II:** 513; **Supp. I Part 2:** 483

Lowell, Amy, **I:** 231, 384, 405, 475, 487; **II:** 174, **511–533**, 534; **III:** 465, 581, 586; **Retro. Supp. I:** 131, 133, 288;

Retro. **Supp. II:** 46, 175; **Retro. Supp. III:** 98, 101; **Supp. I Part 1:** 257–259, 261–263, 265, 266; **Supp. I Part 2:** 465, 466, 707, 714, 729; **Supp. XIV:** 128; **Supp. XV:** 43, 293, 295, 297, 298, 299, 300, 301, 303, 306; **Supp. XX: 69; Supp. XXII:** 161; **Supp. XXVII:** 288, 295

Lowell, Blanche, **Supp. I Part 2:** 409

Lowell, Harriet, **II:** 553, 554

Lowell, James Russell, **I:** 216, 458; **II:** 273, 274, 289, 302, 320, 402, 529, 530, 532, 534, 551; **III:** 409; **IV:** 129, 171, 175, 180, 182–183, 186; **Retro. Supp. I:** 228; **Retro. Supp. II:** 155, 175, 326; **Retro. Supp. III:** 106, 223, 232, 233, 236; **Supp. I Part 1:** 168, 299, 300, 303, 306, 311, 312, 317, 318, 362; **Supp. I Part 2: 404–426; Supp. II Part 1:** 197, 291, 352; **Supp. XV:** 278, 279; **Supp. XVI:** 84; **Supp. XVIII:** 2–3, 4, 8, 12

Lowell, Mrs. James Russell (Maria White), **Supp. I Part 2:** 405, 406, 414, 424

Lowell, Percival, **II:** 513, 525, 534

Lowell, Robert, **I:** 172, 381, 382, 400, 442, 521, 544–545, 550; **II:** 371, 376, 377, 384, 386–387, 532, **534–557; III:** 39, 44, 142, 508, 527, 528–529, 606; **IV:** 120, 138, 402, 430; **Retro. Supp. I:** 67, 140, 411; **Retro. Supp. II:** 27, 40, 44, 46, 48, 50, **175–193**, 221, 228–229, 235, 245; **Retro. Supp. III:** 41, 54, 243, 245; **Supp. I Part 1:** 89; **Supp. I Part 2:** 538, 543, 554; **Supp. III Part 1:** 6, 64, 84, 138, 147, 193, 194, 197–202, 205–208; **Supp. III Part 2:** 541, 543, 555, 561, 599; **Supp. IV Part 2:** 439, 620, 637; **Supp. IX:** 325; **Supp. V:** 81, 179, 180, 315–316, 337, 344; **Supp. VIII:** 27, 100, 271; **Supp. X:** 53, 58; **Supp. XI:** 146, 240, 244, 250, 317; **Supp. XII:** 253–254, 255; **Supp. XIII:** 76; **Supp. XIV:** 15, 126, 269; **Supp. XIX:** 197; **Supp. XV:** 20, 22, 93, 184, 249, 251, 253, 340; **Supp. XVII:** 239; **Supp. XX: 199, 203; Supp. XXI:** 131; **Supp. XXIII:** 211, 220; **Supp. XXIV:** 153; **Supp. XXVI:** 67, 68; **Supp. XXVIII:** 142

Lowell, Rose, **Supp. I Part 2:** 409

"Lowell in the Classrom" (Vendler), **Retro. Supp. II:** 191

Lowenthal, Michael, **Supp. XII:** 82

Lower Depths, The (Gorki), **III:** 402

"Lower the Standard" (Shapiro), **Supp. II Part 2:** 715

Lowes, John Livingston, **II:** 512, 516, 532; **IV:** 453, 455

Lowin, Joseph, **Supp. V:** 273

"Low Lands" (Davison), **Supp. XXVI:** 76

"Low-Lands" (Pynchon), **Supp. II Part 2:** 620, 624

Lowle, Percival, **Supp. I Part 2:** 404

Lownsbrough, John, **Supp. IV Part 1:** 209, 211

Lowry, Beverly, **Supp. XXI:** 48

Lowry, Malcolm, **Supp. XVII:** 135, 136; **Supp. XXVI:** 28

Lowth, Richard, **II:** 8

Loy, Mina, **III:** 194; **Supp. XXII: 155–170**

Loy, Myrna, **Supp. IV Part 1:** 355

"Loyal Woman's No, A" (Larcom), **Supp. XIII:** 142, 143–144

"Luani of the Jungle" (Hughes), **Supp. I Part 1:** 328

Lubbock, Percy, **I:** 504; **II:** 337; **IV:** 308, 314, 319, 322; **Retro. Supp. I:** 366, 367, 373; **Supp. VIII:** 165; **Supp. XX: 231**

Lubin, Isidor, **Supp. I Part 2:** 632

Lubow, Arthur, **Supp. VIII:** 310

Lucas, Craig, **Supp. XXIV:** 263

Lucas, Victoria (pseudonym). *See* Plath, Sylvia

Luce, Dianne C., **Supp. VIII:** 189

Lucid, Robert F., **Retro. Supp. II:** 195, 204

"Lucid Eye in Silver Town, The" (Updike), **IV:** 218

"Lucid Walking" (A. Finch), **Supp. XVII:** 72

"Lucinda Matlock" (Masters), **Supp. I Part 2:** 461, 465

"Luck" (Dunn), **Supp. XI:** 149

Luck, Jessica Lewis, **Supp. XXVII:** 173

Luck of Barry Lyndon, The (Thackeray), **II:** 290

"Luck of Roaring Camp, The" (Harte), **Supp. II Part 1:** 335, 344, 345–347

"Luck of the Bogans, The" (Jewett), **Retro. Supp. II:** 142

Lucky Life (Stern), **Supp. IX: 290–291**

"Lucky Lucy's Daily Dream Book" (Di Piero), **Supp. XIX:** 38–39

"Lucretia Smith's Soldier" (Twain), **Retro. Supp. III:** 260

Lucretius, **I:** 59; **II:** 162, 163; **III:** 600, 610–611, 612; **Supp. I Part 1:** 363

Lucy (Kincaid), **Supp. VII:** 180, 185, 186, 187–188, 194

Lucy, Saint, **II:** 211

Lucy Crown (Shaw), **Supp. XIX:** 251

Lucy Gayheart (Cather), **I:** 331; **Retro. Supp. I:** 19

"Lucy Tavish's Journey" (E. Stoddard), **Supp. XV:** 286

Lucy Temple (Rowson). *See Charlotte's Daughter; or, The Three Orphans*

Ludlow, Andrea, **Supp. XVIII:** 90

Ludvigson, Susan, **Supp. IV Part 2:** 442, 446, 447, 448, 451

Lueders, Edward, **Supp. XVI:** 265

"Luggage" (Bidart), **Supp. XV:** 35

Luhan, Mabel Dodge, **Retro. Supp. I:** 7; **Supp. XV:** 46, 50; **Supp. XXIV:** 30. *See also* Dodge, Mabel

Lu Ji, **Supp. VIII:** 303

Lukas, Michael, **Supp. XXVI:** 56

Luke (biblical book), **III:** 606

"Luke Havergal" (E. A. Robinson), **Supp. XVII:** 69

"Luke Havergal" (Robinson), **III:** 524

Lukeman, Gary, **Supp. XV:** 221

Luks, George, **IV:** 411; **Retro. Supp. II:** 103

"Lullaby" (Auden), **Supp. II Part 1:** 9
"Lullaby" (Bishop), **Supp. I Part 1:** 85
"Lullaby" (Everwine), **Supp. XV:** 89
"Lullaby" (Silko), **Supp. IV Part 2:** 560, 568–569
"Lullaby for Amy" (Jarman), **Supp. XVII:** 113, 121
"Lullaby of Cape Cod" (Brodsky), **Supp. VIII:** 27–28
Lullaby Raft (Nye), **Supp. XIII:** 278
Lullaby Raft (Nye, album), **Supp. XIII:** 274
Lullaby: The Comforting of Cock Robin (Snodgrass), **Supp. VI:** 324
"Lulls" (Walker), **Supp. III Part 2:** 525
"Lulu" (Wedekind), **Supp. XII:** 14
Lulu on the Bridge (film), **Supp. XII:** 21
Lulu's Library (Alcott), **Supp. I Part 1:** 43
"Lumber" (Baker), **Supp. XIII:** 55, 56
"Lumens, The" (Olds), **Supp. X:** 209
Lume Spento, A (Pound), **III:** 470
Lumet, Sidney, **Supp. IV Part 1:** 236; **Supp. IX:** 253
Luminous Debris: Reflecting on Vestige in Provence and Languedoc (Sobin), **Supp. XVI:** 291–293, 293–294
Luminous Face, The (Wells), **Supp. XXVI:** 280
"Lumumba's Grave" (Hughes), **Supp. I Part 1:** 344
"Luna, Luna" (Mora), **Supp. XIII:** 217
Lunar Baedecker (Loy), **Supp. XXII:** 165,**Supp. XXII:** 167, 166, 168
Lunar Baedecker and Time-Tables (Loy), **Supp. XXII:** 168
Lunar Follies (Sorrentino), **Supp. XXI:** 226, 237, 238–239
Lunar Park (Ellis), **Supp. XXVII:** 68, 71, 76–77
"Lunatic" (Hecht), **Supp. XXVII:** 95
Lunch Poems (O'Hara), **Supp. XXIII:** 219–220, 220
Lunsford, Bascom Lamar, **Supp. XX:** 163
Lupercal (Hughes), **Retro. Supp. II:** 245; **Supp. I Part 2:** 540
Lupton, Mary Jane, **Supp. IV Part 1:** 7
Lure of the Labrador Wild, The (Wallace), **Supp. XXII:** 218
Luria, Isaac, **IV:** 7
Lurie, Alison, **Supp. X:** 166; **Supp. XVI:** 103, 111–112
Lusitania Songspiel, Das (Durang), **Supp. XXIV:** 113, 116
Lust and Other Stories (Minot), **Supp. VI:** 205
Luster, Deborah, **Supp. XV:** 337,**Supp. XV:** 353, 348, 349, 350
Lustgarten, Edith, **III:** 107
Lustra (Pound), **Retro. Supp. I:** 289, 290
"Luther" (Huddle), **Supp. XXVI:** 152
Luther, Martin, **II:** 11–12, 506; **III:** 306, 607; **IV:** 490
"Luther on Sweet Auburn" (Bambara), **Supp. XI:** 16–17
Lux, Thomas, **Supp. XI:** 270; **Supp. XIX:** 276
Luxury Girl, The (McCoy), **Supp. XIII:** 163
Lyall, Sarah, **Supp. XIII:** 247

Lycidas (Milton), **II:** 540; **IV:** 347; **Retro. Supp. I:** 60; **Retro. Supp. II:** 186; **Supp. I Part 1:** 370; **Supp. IX:** 41
Lycographia (Paullini), **Supp. XVII:** 55
"Lydia and Marian" (Rowson), **Supp. XV:** 234
Lydon, Meghan, **Supp. XXVI:** 14–15
Lydon, Susan, **Supp. XII:** 170
Lyell, Charles, **Supp. IX:** 180
Lyell, Frank H., **Supp. VIII:** 125
Lyford, Harry, **Supp. I Part 2:** 679
"Lying" (Wilbur), **Supp. III Part 2:** 547, 562
"Lying and Looking" (Swenson), **Supp. IV Part 2:** 652
"Lying in a Hammock at William Duffy's Farm in Pine Island, Minnesota" (Wright), **Supp. III Part 2:** 589, 599, 600
"Lying in the Pollen and Water" (C. Frost), **Supp. XV:** 96
Lying Ladies, The (Ryan as Finnegan), **Supp. XVIII:** 233–235, 237
"Lying Next to the Knife" (McElwee), **Supp. XXIV:** 167, 173
Lyles, Lois F., **Supp. XI:** 7, 8
Lyly, John, **III:** 536; **Supp. I Part 1:** 369
Lynch, Anne, **Supp. XV:** 273
Lynch, Chris, **Supp. XXVIII:** 288
Lynch, Doris, **Supp. XVI:** 294
Lynchburg (Gander), **Supp. XV:** 340
"Lynched Man, The" (Karr), **Supp. XI:** 241
Lynchers, The (Wideman), **Supp. X:** 320
"Lynching, The" (McKay), **Supp. I Part 1:** 63
"Lynching of Jube Benson, The" (Dunbar), **Supp. II Part 1:** 214
"Lynching Song" (Hughes), **Supp. I Part 1:** 331
Lynd, Staughton, **Supp. VIII:** 240
Lynda Hull: Collected Poems (Hull), **Supp. XXI:** 129
Lynes, Katherine R., **Supp. XXVI:** 166, 170, 171, 175
Lynn, Kenneth S., **Retro. Supp. III:** 259; **Supp. XIII:** 96–97; **Supp. XIV:** 103
Lynn, Vera, **Supp. XI:** 304
Lyon, George Ella, **Supp. XX:** 161–162
Lyon, Kate, **I:** 409; **II:** 138, 143, 144
Lyon, Thomas, **Supp. IX:** 175
"Lyonnesse" (Plath), **Supp. I Part 2:** 541
Lyons, Bonnie, **Supp. V:** 58; **Supp. VIII:** 138
Lyons, Donald, **Supp. XXIV:** 274
Lyons, Nathan, **Supp. XXV:** 251
Lyons, The (Silver), **Supp. XXIV:** 263, **276**
Lyotard, Jean-François, **Supp. IV Part 1:** 54
Lyrical Ballads (Wordsworth), **III:** 583; **IV:** 120; **Supp. IX:** 274; **Supp. XI:** 243; **Supp. XIX:** 1; **Supp. XV:** 21
Lyrics of Love and Laughter (Dunbar), **Supp. II Part 1:** 207
Lyrics of Lowly Life (Dunbar), **Supp. II Part 1:** 197, 199, 200, 207
Lyrics of the Hearthside (Dunbar), **Supp. II Part 1:** 206
Lytal, Tammy, **Supp. XI:** 102

Lytle, Andrew, **IV:** 125; **Retro. Supp. II:** 220, 221, 235; **Supp. II Part 1:** 139; **Supp. X:** 1, 25; **Supp. XI:** 101
Lyttelton, Alfred, **Supp. XX:** 230
Lytton of Knebworth. *See* Bulwer-Lytton, Edward George

M

Mabbott, Thomas, **Retro. Supp. III:** 231, 232, 237
Mabie, Hamilton W., **Supp. XVIII:** 257
MCabe, Susan, **Supp. XXII:** 234
MacAdams, William, **Supp. XXVII:** 84, 91, 93, 96
McAlexander, Hubert H., **Supp. V:** 314, 319, 320, 323
McAlmon, Robert, **IV:** 404; **Retro. Supp. I:** 418, 419, 420; **Retro. Supp. II:** 328; **Supp. I Part 1:** 259; **Supp. III Part 2:** 614; **Supp. XXII:** 166, 215; **Supp. XXIV:** 62, 63
McAlmon, Mrs. Robert (Winifred Ellerman), **III:** 194. *See also* Ellerman, Winifred
McAlpine, Erica, **Supp. XXV:** 222, 233, 234
McAninch, Jerry, **Supp. XI:** 297, 298
MacArthur, Charles, **Supp. XXVII:** 83, 89
Macaulay, Catherine, **Supp. I Part 2:** 522
Macaulay, Rose, **Supp. XII:** 88; **Supp. XIV:** 348
Macaulay, Thomas, **II:** 15–16; **III:** 113, 591–592
Macauley, Robie, **Retro. Supp. II:** 228; **Supp. X:** 56
Macbeth (Shakespeare), **I:** 271; **IV:** 227; **Retro. Supp. I:** 131; **Supp. I Part 1:** 67; **Supp. I Part 2:** 457; **Supp. IV Part 1:** 87; **Supp. XIV:** 8; **Supp. XXVII:** 225
Macbeth (silent film), **Supp. XVI:** 184
MacBeth, George, **Retro. Supp. II:** 250
McBride, James, **Supp. XXVI:** 191–205
MacBride, Roger, **Supp. XXII:** 297, 301
McCabe, Tracy, **Supp. XXVI:** 166
McCafferty, Larry, **Supp. XVII:** 227
McCaffery, Larry, **Supp. IV Part 1:** 217, 227, 234; **Supp. V:** 53, 238; **Supp. VIII:** 13, 14; **Supp. X:** 260, 268, 301, 303, 307; **Supp. XVI:** 117; **Supp. XXII:** 177
McCann, Janet, **Supp. XXIII:** 51, 53, 54, 64
McCann, Jannet, **Supp. XXI:** 92
McCarriston, Linda, **Supp. X:** 204; **Supp. XIV:** 259–275
McCarthy, Charles Joseph, Jr. *See* McCarthy, Cormac
McCarthy, Cormac, **Supp. VIII:** 175–192; **Supp. XII:** 310; **Supp. XVII:** 185; **Supp. XXI:** 38, 40; **Supp. XXII:** 49; **Supp. XXIII:** 42, 44
McCarthy, Eugene, **Retro. Supp. II:** 182
McCarthy, Joseph, **I:** 31, 492; **II:** 562, 568; **Supp. I Part 1:** 294, 295; **Supp. I Part 2:** 444, 611, 612, 620; **Supp. XV:** 198, 311–312; **Supp. XXIII:** 7

McCarthy, Mary, **II: 558–584; Supp. I Part 1:** 84; **Supp. IV Part 1:** 209, 297, 310; **Supp. VIII:** 96, 99, 100; **Supp. X:** 177; **Supp. XI:** 246; **Supp. XIV:** 3; **Supp. XV:** 142; **Supp. XVI:** 64, 70; **Supp. XVII:** 43; **Supp. XXVII:** 89
McCay, Maura, **Supp. XII:** 271, 276
McClanahan, Ed, **Supp. X:** 24
McClanahan, Thomas, **Supp. XII:** 125–126
McClatchy, J. D., **Supp. XII: 253–270; Supp. XV:** 185, 257, 258
McClaurin, Irma, **Supp. XXIII:** 84, 86, 93, 94
McClellan, John L., **I:** 493
McClung, Isabelle, **Retro. Supp. I:** 5; **Retro. Supp. III:** 20, 22, 34, 37
McClure, Charlotte, **Supp. XXIV:** 29
McClure, H. H., **Retro. Supp. III:** 21
McClure, John, **Retro. Supp. I:** 80
McClure, Michael, **Supp. II Part 1:** 32; **Supp. VIII:** 289; **Supp. XVI:** 283
McClure, S. S., **I:** 313; **II:** 465; **III:** 327; **Retro. Supp. I:** 5, 6, 9; **Retro. Supp. III:** 21; **Supp. XV:** 40
McCluskey, John, Jr., **Supp. XIX:** 65, 68, 71, 72, 78
McCombs, Judith, **Supp. XIII:** 33
McConagha, Alan, **Supp. XVI:** 166
McConnell, Frank, **Supp. X:** 260, 274
McCorkle, Jill, **Supp. X:** 6; **Supp. XVIII:** 195; **Supp. XXV:** 129, 130
McCourt, Frank, **Supp. XII: 271–287**
McCoy, Horace, **Supp. XIII: 159–177; Supp. XXV:** 26
McCracken, Elizabeth, **Supp. X:** 86; **Supp. XII:** 310, 315–316, 321
McCrae, Fiona, **Supp. XVIII:** 60, 62
McCullers, Carson, **I:** 113, 190, 211; **II: 585–608; IV:** 282, 384, 385, 386; **Retro. Supp. II:** 324; **Supp. II Part 1:** 17; **Supp. IV Part 1:** 31, 84; **Supp. IV Part 2:** 502; **Supp. VIII:** 124; **Supp. XII:** 309; **Supp. XIV:** 120; **Supp. XV:** 338
McCullers, Reeves, **III:** 585, 586, 587
McCulloch, Jeanne, **Supp. XXVII:** 180
McDavid, Raven I., **III:** 120; **Supp. XIV:** 14
McDermott, Alice, **Supp. XII:** 311; **Supp. XVIII: 155–169**
McDermott, John J., **II:** 364
MacDiarmid, Hugh, **Supp. X:** 112
Macdonald, C. G., **Supp. XVII:** 73–74
MacDonald, Dwight, **Supp. XXV:** 268
Macdonald, Dwight, **I:** 233, 372, 379; **III:** 39; **Supp. V:** 265; **Supp. XIV:** 340; **Supp. XV:** 140
McDonald, E. J., **Supp. I Part 2:** 670
Macdonald, George, **Supp. XIII:** 75
MacDonald, Jeanette, **II:** 589
Macdonald, Ross, **Supp. IV Part 1:** 116, 136; **Supp. IV Part 2: 459–477; Supp. XIII:** 233; **Supp. XVIII:** 137,136; **Supp. XXI:** 67
MacDonald, Ruth K., **Supp. XVI:** 102
McDonnell, Thomas P., **Supp. XX: 45**
MacDougall, Ruth Doan, **Supp. XV:** 58; **Supp. XVI:** 174

MacDowell, Edward, **I:** 228; **III:** 504, 508, 524
McDowell, Frederick P. W., **II:** 194
McDowell, Mary, **Supp. I Part 1:** 5
MacDowell, Robert, **Supp. IX:** 266, 270, 276, 279
MacDowell, Robert, **Supp. XI:** 249
McDowell, Robert, **Supp. XVII:** 109, 110, 111
McDowell. Deborah, **Supp. XVIII:** 125, 129
McElderry, Margaret K., **Supp. XV:** 162
McElligot's Pool (Geisel), **Supp. XVI:** 104
McElrath, Joseph, **Supp. XIV:** 62
McElroy, Joseph, **Supp. IV Part 1:** 279, 285
McElwee, Caroline, **Supp. XXIV:** 167, 173
McEnery, Sarah, **Supp. XXVIII:** 230–231
McEuen, Kathryn, **II:** 20
McEwen, Arthur, **I:** 206
McFarland, Ron, **Supp. IX:** 323, 327, 328, 333
McGann, Jerome, **Retro. Supp. I:** 47
McGill, Meredith, **Supp. XVIII:** 17
McGillis, Ian, **Supp. XVIII:** 150
MacGillivray, William, **Supp. XVI:** 8
McGinity, Keren, **Supp. XX: 9**
McGovern, Edythe M., **Supp. IV Part 2:** 573, 582, 585
McGovern, George, **III:** 46
MacGowan, Christopher, **Retro. Supp. I:** 430
MacGowan, Kenneth, **III:** 387, 391
McGrath, Abigail, **Supp. XXVI:** 164, 165, 172
McGrath, Douglas, **Supp. XV:** 12
McGrath, Joseph, **Supp. XI:** 307, 309
McGrath, Patrick, **Supp. IX:** 113; **Supp. XXII:** 58
McGrath, Thomas, **Supp. X: 111–130**
"McGrath on McGrath" (McGrath), **Supp. X:** 119, 120
McGuane, Thomas, **Supp. V:** 53, 220; **Supp. VIII:** 39, 40, 42, 43
MacGuffin, The (Elkin), **Supp. VI: 55–56**
McGuiness, Daniel, **Supp. XV:** 261
McGuinniss, Joe, **Supp. XXVII:** 67
McGuirk, Kevin, **Retro. Supp. III:** 248
Machado y Ruiz, Antonio, **Supp. XIII:** 315, 323
Machan, Tibor, **Supp. IV Part 2:** 528
McHaney, Pearl, **Supp. XXI:** 244, 255, 256, 257
McHaney, Thomas, **Supp. XVIII:** 199,203
Machen, Arthur, **IV:** 286
McHenry, Tim, **Supp. XXV:** 161
Machiavelli, Niccolò, **I:** 485; **Supp. XIX:** 34
"Machiavellian Muzhiks of Moscow"(*The New York Times*), **Supp. XXVIII:** 45
"Machine-Gun, The" (Jarrell), **II:** 371
"Machines Mourn the Passing of People, The" (Stallings), **Supp. XXV:** 228
"Machine Song" (Anderson), **I:** 114
McHugh, Heather, **Supp. XIX:** 84; **Supp. XXIV:** 154

McHugh, Vincent, **Supp. XV:** 147
McInerney, Jay, **Supp. X:** 7, 166; **Supp. XI:** 65; **Supp. XII:** 81; **Supp. XVIII:** 148; **Supp. XXVII:** 68, 269
"Mac in Love" (Dixon), **Supp. XII: 142**
McIntire, Holly, **Supp. V:** 338
McIntosh, Maria, **Retro. Supp. I:** 246
Macintyre, Ben, **Supp. XXVII:** 270
Mack, Maynard, **Supp. XIV:** 12
Mackail, John William, **Supp. I Part 1:** 268; **Supp. I Part 2:** 461
McKay, Claude, **Supp. I Part 1:** 63; **Supp. III Part 1:** 75, 76; **Supp. IV Part 1:** 3, 79, 164; **Supp. IX:** 306; **Supp. X: 131–144; Supp. XI:** 91; **Supp. XIX:** 73; **Supp. XVII:** 74; **Supp. XVIII:** 122, 127, 280, 282; **Supp. XX: 69; Supp. XXII:** 275; **Supp. XXVIII:** 46, 71–72
McKay, Donald, **Supp. I Part 2:** 482
McKay, Nellie, **Retro. Supp. III:** 189
McKay, Nellie Y., **Supp. XX: 105**
McKee, Elizabeth, **Retro. Supp. II:** 221, 222
McKee, Ellen, **Retro. Supp. II:** 67
McKee, Kathryn B., **Supp. XXVIII:** 236
McKeen, William, **Supp. XXIV:** 279, 280, 281, 282, 288
McKeithan, Daniel Morley, **Retro. Supp. III:** 261
McKenney, Eileen, **IV:** 288; **Retro. Supp. II:** 321, 330
McKenney, Ruth, **IV:** 288; **Retro. Supp. II:** 321; **Supp. XVIII:** 238
MacKenzie, Agnes, **I:** 199
Mackenzie, Captain Alexander, **III:** 94
McKenzie, Cameron, **Retro. Supp. III:** 22
Mackenzie, Compton, **II:** 82; **Retro. Supp. I:** 100, 102
McKenzie, Geraldine, **Supp. XII:** 107
MacKenzie, Margaret, **I:** 199
Mackey, Louis, **Supp. XXI:** 236, 237
Mackey, Nathaniel, **Supp. XXVII: 151–162, 163, 168**
McKibben, Bill, **Supp. XVIII:** 192
McKinley, Gena, **Supp. XXVIII:** 228
McKinley, William, **I:** 474; **III:** 506; **Supp. I Part 2:** 395–396, 707
MacKinnon, Catharine, **Supp. XII:** 6
McKnight, Reginald, **Supp. XX: 147–159**
MacLachlan, Suzanne L., **Supp. XII:** 300,**Supp. XII:** 299
MacLauchlin, Cory, **Supp. XXVI:** 240, 241, 242, 243, 244, 246, 252
McLaverty, Michael, **Supp. X:** 67
McLay, Catherine, **Supp. XIII:** 21
Maclean, Alasdair, **Supp. V:** 244
McLean, Carolyn (pseudonym). See Bly, Carol
Maclean, Norman, **Supp. XIV: 221–237; Supp. XVI:** 98; **Supp. XXVI:** 184
MacLeish, Archibald, **I:** 283, 293, 429; **II:** 165, 228; **III: 1–25,** 427; **Supp. I Part 1:** 261; **Supp. I Part 2:** 654; **Supp. IV Part 1:** 359; **Supp. IV Part 2:** 586; **Supp. X:** 120; **Supp. XIV:** 11
MacLeish, Mrs. Archibald (Ada Hitchcock), **III:** 1

MacLeish, Kenneth, **III:** 1
McLellan, Dennis, **Supp. XXVII:** 5
McLellan, Joseph, **Supp. XXIV:** 226
McLennan, Gordon Lawson, **Supp. IX:** 89
McLeod, A. W., **Supp. I Part 1:** 257
MacLeod, Charlotte, **Supp. XXV:** 192
McLuhan, Marshall, **Supp. IV Part 2:** 474
McLure, Michael, **Supp. XIV:** 150
Macmahon, Arthur, **I:** 226
McMahon, Helen, **Supp. IV Part 2:** 579
McMichael, Barbara Lloyd, **Supp. XXII:** 206, 207, 215, 216
McMichael, George, **Supp. VIII:** 124
McMichael, Morton, **Supp. I Part 2:** 707
McMichaels, James, **Supp. XIII:** 114
McMillan, James B., **Supp. VIII:** 124
McMillan, Terry, **Supp. XIII: 179–193**
McMullan, Jim, **Supp. XIV:** 124
McMurtry, Josephine, **Supp. V:** 220
McMurtry, Larry, **Supp. V: 219–235; Supp. X:** 24; **Supp. XI:** 172
McNally, Terrence, **Supp. XIII: 195–211**
McNally, T. M., **Supp. XX: 92**
McNamee, Thomas, **Supp. XXII:** 218
McNamer, Deirdre, **Supp. XI:** 190
Macnaughton, William, **Retro. Supp. III:** 258
McNeese, Gretchen, **Supp. V:** 123
MacNeice, Louis, **II:** 586; **III:** 527; **Supp. II Part 1:** 17, 24; **Supp. IV Part 2:** 440; **Supp. X:** 116; **Supp. XIII:** 347
McNeil, Claudia, **Supp. IV Part 1:** 360, 362
M-a-c-n-o-l-i-a (Jordan), **Supp. XVIII:** 172
McPhee, John, **Supp. III Part 1: 289–316; Supp. X:** 29, 30; **Supp. XVIII:** 106–107, 114
MacPherson, Aimee Semple, **Supp. V:** 278
Macpherson, Anne, **Supp. XXIII:** 84
McPherson, Dolly, **Supp. IV Part 1:** 2, 3, 4, 6, 8, 11, 12
McPherson, James Alan, **Supp. XXII:** 141
McPherson, James Allen, **Retro. Supp. II:** 126
Macpherson, Jay, **Supp. XIII:** 19
MacPherson, Jennifer, **Supp. XXIII:** 248
MacPherson, Kenneth, **Supp. I Part 1:** 259
McPherson, Sandra, **Supp. XXIII:** 57
McPhillips, Robert, **Supp. XV:** 119, 250, 251, 252, 264, 266; **Supp. XXIII:** 111, 112, 114, 127
McQuade, Molly, **Supp. IX:** 151, 163; **Supp. VIII:** 277, 281; **Supp. XX:** 90
McQueen, Steve, **Supp. XI:** 306
Macrae, John, **I:** 252–253
McRobbie, Angela, **Supp. IV Part 2:** 691
MacShane, Frank, **Supp. IV Part 2:** 557; **Supp. XI:** 214, 216
"MacSwiggen" (Freneau), **Supp. II Part 1:** 259
McTaggart, John, **I:** 59
McTeague (Norris), **III:** 314, 315, 316–320, 322, 325, 327–328, 330, 331,

333, 335; **Retro. Supp. II:** 96; **Supp. IX:** 332
McWhorter, Dianne, **Supp. XXIII:** 38
McWilliams, Carey, **Supp. XI:** 169; **Supp. XXIV:** 282
Madama Butterfly (opera, Puccini), **III:** 139; **Supp. XXI:** 150, 155
"Madam and the Minister" (Hughes), **Supp. I Part 1:** 335
"Madam and the Wrong Visitor" (Hughes), **Supp. I Part 1:** 335
"Madame and Ahmad" (Bowles), **Supp. IV Part 1:** 93
"Madame Bai and the Taking of Stone Mountain" (Bambara), **Supp. XI:** 14–15
Madame Bovary (Flaubert), **II:** 185; **Retro. Supp. I:** 225; **Retro. Supp. II:** 70; **Supp. XI:** 334; **Supp. XX:** 58
"Madame Célestin's Divorce" (Chopin), **Supp. I Part 1:** 213
Madame Curie (film), **Retro. Supp. I:** 113
"Madame de Mauves" (James), **II:** 327; **Retro. Supp. I:** 218, 220
Madame de Treymes (Wharton), **IV:** 314, 323; **Retro. Supp. I:** 376; **Retro. Supp. III:** 281
"Madame Rose Hanie" (Gibran), **Supp. XX: 124**
"Madame Swann at Home"(Hadas), **Supp. XXIII:** 113
"Madam's Calling Cards" (Hughes), **Retro. Supp. I:** 206
Madden, David, **Supp. IV Part 1:** 285
Maddern, Bessie. *See* London, Mrs. Jack (Bessie Maddern)
Mad Dog Black Lady (Coleman), **Supp. XI:** 85–89, 90
Mad Dog Blues (Shepard), **Supp. III Part 2:** 437, 438, 441
Maddox, Lucy, **Supp. IV Part 1:** 323, 325
Mad Ducks and Bears: Football Revisited (Plimpton), **Supp. XVI:** 243
Mademoiselle Coeur-Brisé (Sibon, trans.), **IV:** 288
Mademoiselle de Maupin (Gautier), **Supp. I Part 1:** 277
"Mad Farmer, Flying the Flag of Rough Branch, Secedes from the Union, The" (Berry), **Supp. X:** 35
"Mad Farmer Manifesto, The: The First Amendment" (Berry), **Supp. X:** 35
"Mad Farmer's Love Song, The" (Berry), **Supp. X:** 35
Madheart (Baraka), **Supp. II Part 1:** 47
Madhouse, The (Farrell), **II:** 41
Madhubuti, Haki R. (Don L. Lee), **Supp. II Part 1:** 34, 247; **Supp. IV Part 1:** 244; **Supp. XXVII:** 165
Madison, Charles, **Supp. XXIII:** 6, 13
Madison, Dolley, **II:** 303
Madison, James, **I:** 1, 2, 6–9; **II:** 301; **Supp. I Part 2:** 509, 524
"Madison Smartt Bell: *The Year of Silence*" (Garrett), **Supp. X:** 7
Mad Love (film, Freund), **Supp. XVII:** 58

"Madman, A" (Updike), **Retro. Supp. I:** 320
Madman, The: His Parables and Poems (Gibran), **Supp. XX: 115, 118, 125**
"Madman's Song" (Wylie), **Supp. I Part 2: 711, 729**
Madonick, Michael, **Supp. XVII:** 123
"Madonna" (R. Lowell), **II:** 535–536
"Madonna of the Evening Flowers" (A. Lowell), **II:** 524
"Madonna of the Future, The" (James), **Retro. Supp. I:** 219
"Madrilène"(King), **Supp. XXVIII:** 120–121
"Mad Song" (Gioia), **Supp. XV:** 128
Madwoman in the Attic, The (Gilbert and Gubar), **Retro. Supp. I:** 42; **Supp. IX:** 66
"Maelzel's Chess-Player" (Poe), **III:** 419, 420
"Maestria" (Nemerov), **III:** 275, 278–279
Maeterlinck, Maurice, **I:** 91, 220; **Supp. XX: 115, 116**
"Magalu" (H. Johnson). *See* "Magula" (H. Johnson)
"Magazine-Writing Peter Snook" (Poe), **III:** 421
Magdeburg Centuries (Flacius), **IV:** 163
Magellan, Ferdinand, **Supp. I Part 2:** 497
Magellanic Clouds, The (Wakoski), **Supp. XXVIII:** 263
Maggie: A Girl of the Streets (S. Crane), **I:** 407, 408, 410–411, 416; **IV:** 208; **Retro. Supp. II:** 97, 107; **Supp. XVII:** 228; **Supp. XXIII:** 165
Maggie Cassidy (Kerouac), **Supp. III Part 1:** 220–221, 225, 227, 229, 232
Maggie-Now (B. Smith), **Supp. XXIII:** 258, **267–269**
"Maggie of the Green Bottles" (Bambara), **Supp. XI:** 2–3
"Maggie's Farm" (song, Dylan), **Supp. XVIII:** 25, 26
"Magi" (Plath), **Supp. I Part 2:** 544–545
"Magi, The" (Garrett), **Supp. VII:** 97
"Magic" (Pickering), **Supp. XXI:** 202
"Magic" (Porter), **III:** 434, 435
"Magical Thinking" (Hull), **Supp. XXI:** 137, 139
Magic Barrel, The (Malamud), **Supp. I Part 2:** 427, 428, 430–434
"Magic Barrel, The" (Malamud), **Supp. I Part 2:** 427, 428, 431, 432–433
Magic Christian, The (film), **Supp. XI:** 309
Magic Christian, The (Southern), **Supp. XI:** 297, **299–301**, 309
Magic City (Komunyakaa), **Supp. XIII: 125–127**, 128, 131
"Magic Flute, The" (Epstein), **Supp. XII:** 165
Magic Flute, The (Mozart), **III:** 164
Magician King, The (Grossman), **Supp. XXV:** 74–77
Magician of Lublin, The (Singer), **IV:** 6, 9–10; **Retro. Supp. II: 308–309**
Magicians, The (Grossman), **Supp. XXV:** 64, 68–74
Magician's Assistant, The (Patchett), **Supp. XII:** 307, 310, **317–320**, 322

Magician's Feastletters, The (Wakoski), **Supp. XXVIII:** 267

Magician's Land, The (Grossman), **Supp. XXV:** 77

"Magician's Wife, The" (Gordon), **Supp. IV Part 1:** 306

Magic Journey, The (Nichols), **Supp. XIII:** 266–267

Magic Keys, The (Murray), **Supp. XIX:** 157–158

Magic Kingdom, The (Elkin), **Supp. VI:** 42, **54–55,** 56, 58

"Magic Mirror, The: A Study of the Double in Two of Doestoevsky's Novels" (Plath), **Supp. I Part 2:** 536

Magic Mountain, The (Mann), **III:** 281–282; **Supp. IV Part 2:** 522; **Supp. XII:** 321; **Supp. XVII:** 137

Magic Tower, The (Willams), **IV:** 380

Magnaghi, Ambrogio, **Supp. XVI:** 286

Magnalia Christi Americana (Mather), **II:** 302; **Retro. Supp. III:** 4; **Supp. I Part 1:** 102; **Supp. I Part 2:** 584; **Supp. II Part 2:** 441, 442, 452–455, 460, 467, 468; **Supp. IV Part 2:** 434

Magnes, Judah, **Supp. XXIII:** 6

Magnificat (Nelson), **Supp. XVIII:** 176–177

"Magnificent Little Gift" (Salinas), **Supp. XIII:** 318

"Magnifying Mirror" (Karr), **Supp. XI:** 240

Magpie, The (Baldwin, ed.), **Supp. I Part 1:** 49

"Magpie Exhorts"(Schott), **Supp. XXIII:** 250

Magpie's Shadow, The (Winters), **Supp. II Part 2:** 786, 788

"Magpie's Song" (Snyder), **Supp. VIII:** 302

Magritte, René, **Supp. IV Part 2:** 623

Maguire, Roberta S., **Supp. XIX:** 160–161

"Magula" (H. Johnson), **Supp. XXVI:** 164, 166, 170–172, 174

Magus, The (Fowles), **Supp. XIX:** 58

Mahan, Albert Thayer, **Supp. I Part 2:** 491

Mahan, David C., **Supp. XXI:** 86

"Mahatma Joe" (Bass), **Supp. XVI:** 19

Mahin, John Lee, **Supp. XXVII:** 93

Mahlis, Kristen, **Supp. XXIII:** 90, 94

"Mahogany Tree, The" (M. F. K. Fisher), **Supp. XVII:** 88

Mahomet and His Successors (Irving), **II:** 314

Mahoney, Jeremiah, **IV:** 285

Mahoney, Lynn, **Supp. XV:** 270

"Maiden, Maiden" (Boyle), **Supp. XXIV:** 58

"Maiden in a Tower" (Stegner), **Supp. IV Part 2:** 613

Maiden's Prayer, The (Silver), **Supp. XXIV:** 275–276

"Maiden Without Hands" (Sexton), **Supp. II Part 2:** 691

"Maid of St. Philippe, The" (Chopin), **Retro. Supp. II:** 63

"Maid's Shoes, The" (Malamud), **Supp. I Part 2:** 437

Mailer, Fanny, **III:** 28

Mailer, Isaac, **III:** 28

Mailer, Norman, **I:** 261, 292, 477; **III:** **26–49,** 174; **IV:** 98, 216; **Retro. Supp. II:** 182, **195–217,** 279; **Supp. I Part 1:** 291, 294; **Supp. III Part 1:** 302; **Supp. IV Part 1:** 90, 198, 207, 236, 284, 381; **Supp. IV Part 2:** 689; **Supp. VIII:** 236; **Supp. XI:** 104, 218, 222, 229; **Supp. XIV:** 49, 53, 54, 111, 162; **Supp. XVII:** 225, 228, 236; **Supp. XVIII:** 19–20; **Supp. XX:** 90; **Supp. XXIII:** 105, 106; **Supp. XXIV:** 281; **Supp. XXV:** 145

"Maimed Man, The" (Tate), **IV:** 136

Maimonides, Moses, **Supp. XVII:** 46–47

Main Currents in American Thought: The Colonial Mind, 1625–1800 (Parrington), **I:** 517; **Supp. I Part 2:** 484

"Maine Roustabout, A" (Eberhart), **I:** 539

"Maine Speech" (White), **Supp. I Part 2:** 669–670

Maine Woods, The (Thoreau), **IV:** 188

Mains d'Orlac, Les (M. Renard), **Supp. XVII:** 58

Main Street (Lewis), **I:** 362; **II:** 271, 440, 441–442, 447, 449, 453; **III:** 394; **Supp. XIX:** 142; **Supp. XXII:** 282

"Maintenance" (Pickering), **Supp. XXI:** 204

Mainwaring, Marion, **Retro. Supp. III:** 289–290

Maitland, Margaret Todd, **Supp. XVI:** 292

Maizon at Blue Hill (Woodson), **Supp. XXVIII:** 287

Majdoubeh, Ahmad, **Supp. XX:** 116

"Majesty" (July), **Supp. XXIV:** 201–202, 203

Major, Clarence, **Supp. XXII:** 171–186

"Majorat, Das" (Hoffman), **III:** 415

Major Barbara (Shaw), **III:** 69

"Major Chord, The" (Bourne), **I:** 221

Majors and Minors (Dunbar), **Supp. II Part 1:** 197, 198

"Major's Tale, The" (Bierce), **I:** 205

Make Believe (J. Scott), **Supp. XVII:** **191–192,** 193, 194, 195

Make-Believe Town: Essays and Remembrances (Mamet), **Supp. XIV:** 240, 251

Make It New (Pound), **III:** 470

Makers and Finders (Brooks), **I:** 253, 254, 255, 257, 258

Makers of the Modern World (Untermeyer), **Supp. XV:** 312

"Making a Change" (Gilman), **Supp. XI:** 207

"Making a Living" (Sexton), **Supp. II Part 2:** 695

"Making a Sacher Torte"(Wakoski), **Supp. XXVIII:** 267

"Making Changes" (L. Michaels), **Supp. XVI:** 204

"Making Do" (Hogan), **Supp. IV Part 1:** 406

Making Face, Making Soul: Haciendo Caras, Creative and Critical Perspectives by Feminists of Color (Anzaldúa, ed.), **Supp. IV Part 1:** 330

Making It (Podhoretz), **Supp. VIII:** 231, 232, 233, **237–238,** 239, 244

"Making Light of Auntie" (X. J. Kennedy), **Supp. XV:** 163

"Making Love in 2003" (July), **Supp. XXIV:** 204–205, 210

"Making Marks" (Davison), **Supp. XXVI:** 72

"Making Much of Orioles" (Davison), **Supp. XXVI:** 74, 75

"Making of a Marginal Farm, The" (Berry), **Supp. X:** 22

Making of Americans, The (Stein), **IV:** 35, 37, 40–42, 45, 46; **Supp. III Part 1:** 37

"Making of Ashenden, The" (Elkin), **Supp. VI:** 49, 50

"Making of a Soldier USA, The" (Simpson), **Supp. IX:** 270

"Making of Garrison Keillor, The" (McConagha), **Supp. XVI:** 166"

Making of Modern Atlanta, The (documentary), **Supp. XXII:** 251

"Making of Paths, The" (Stegner), **Supp. IV Part 2:** 614

"Making of Poems, The" (W. J. Smith), **Supp. XIII:** 348

Making of the Modern Mind (Randall), **III:** 605

"Making Sense"(Lea), **Supp. XXVIII:** 132

Making the Light Come: The Poetry of Gerald Stern (Somerville), **Supp. IX:** 296–297

"Making Up Stories" (Didion), **Supp. IV Part 1:** 196, 203, 205

Making Your Own Days: The Pleasures of Reading and Writing Poetry (Koch), **Supp. XV:** 188; **Supp. XXIII:** 124

Maladies de la volonté, Les (Ribot), **Supp. XX:** **238**

Malady of the Ideal, The: Oberman, Maurice de Guérin, and Amiel (Brooks), **I:** 240, 241, 242

Malamud, Bernard, **I:** 144, 375; **II:** 424, 425; **III:** 40, 272; **IV:** 216; **Retro. Supp. II:** 22, 279, 281; **Supp. I Part 2:** **427–453;** **Supp. IV Part 1:** 297, 382; **Supp. IX:** 114, 227; **Supp. V:** 257, 266; **Supp. XIII:** 106, 264, 265, 294; **Supp. XVI:** 220; **Supp. XXVI:** 180

Malamud, Mrs. Bernard (Ann de Chiara), **Supp. I Part 2:** 451

Malandrinos, Cheryl C., **Supp. XXVI:** 219

Malanga, Gerard, **Supp. III Part 2:** 629; **Supp. XXIII:** 221

Malaquais, Jean, **Retro. Supp. II:** 199

Malatesta, Sigismondo de, **III:** 472, 473

Malcolm (Purdy), **Supp. VII:** 270–273, 277

"Malcolm Cowley and the American Writer" (Simpson), **Supp. II Part 1:** 147

Malcolm Lowry's "Volcano": Myth Symbol Meaning (Markson), **Supp. XVII:** 142, 144

"MALCOLM REMEMBERED (FEB. 77)" (Baraka), **Supp. II Part 1:** 60

Malcolm X, **Retro. Supp. II:** 12, 13; **Supp. I Part 1:** 52, 63, 65, 66; **Supp. IV Part 1:** 2, 10; **Supp. VIII:** 330, 345; **Supp. X:** 240; **Supp. XIV:** 306

Malcolm X (film), **Retro. Supp. II:** 12

Malcolm X: A Fire Burning Bright (Myers), **Supp. XXVII:** 209

Malcolm X: By Any Means Necessary (Myers), **Supp. XXVII:** 209

"Maldrove" (Jeffers), **Supp. II Part 2:** 418

Male, Roy, **II:** 239

Male Animal, The (Thurber), **Supp. I Part 2:** 605, 606, 610–611

"Malediction upon Myself" (Wylie), **Supp. I Part 2:** 722

Malefactors, The (Gordon), **II:** 186, 199, 213–216; **IV:** 139

"Malest Cornifici Tuo Catullo" (Ginsberg), **Supp. II Part 1:** 315

Malick, Terrence, **Supp. XI:** 234; **Supp. XV:** 351

Malin, Irving, **I:** 147; **Supp. XVI:** 71–72

"Malinche's Tips: Pique from Mexico's Mother" (Mora), **Supp. XIII:** 223

"Malinke's Atonement" (Antin), **Supp. XX:** 10

"Mallard" (C. Frost), **Supp. XV:** 98, 99

Mallarmé, Stéphane, **I:** 66, 569; **II:** 529, 543; **III:** 8, 409, 428; **IV:** 80, 86; **Retro. Supp. I:** 56; **Retro. Supp. III:** 57; **Supp. I Part 1:** 261; **Supp. II Part 1:** 1; **Supp. III Part 1:** 319–320; **Supp. III Part 2:** 630; **Supp. XIII:** 114; **Supp. XV:** 158; **Supp. XVI:** 282, 285

Malle, Louis, **Supp. XXIII:** 122

Mallia, Joseph, **Supp. XII:** 26, 29, 37

Mallon, Anne-Marie, **Supp. XXI:** 215

Mallon, Thomas, **Supp. IV Part 1:** 200, 209; **Supp. XIX:** 131–145

Maloff, Saul, **Supp. VIII:** 238

Malone, Tess, **Supp. XXVIII:** 283

Malory, Thomas, **II:** 302; **III:** 486; **IV:** 50, 61; **Supp. IV Part 1:** 47

"Mal Paso Bridge" (Jeffers), **Supp. II Part 2:** 415, 420

Malraux, André, **I:** 33–34, 127, 509; **II:** 57, 376; **III:** 35, 310; **IV:** 236, 247, 434; **Retro. Supp. I:** 73; **Retro. Supp. II:** 115–116, 119; **Supp. II Part 1:** 221, 232; **Supp. XIX:** 157

Maltese Falcon, The (film), **Supp. IV Part 1:** 342, 353, 355

Maltese Falcon, The (Hammett), **IV:** 286; **Supp. IV Part 1:** 345, 348–351

Mama (McMillan), **Supp. XIII:** 182, **187–188**

"Mama and Daughter" (Hughes), **Supp. I Part 1:** 334

Mama Day (Naylor), **Supp. VIII:** 223–**226**, 230

"Mama I Remember" (Nelson), **Supp. XVIII:** 173

Mama Poc: An Ecologist's Account of the Extinction of a Species (LaBastille), **Supp. X:** 99, **104–105**, 106

Mama Poems, The (Kenny), **Supp. XXIII:** 143, **154**

Mama's Bank Account (K. Forbes), **Supp. XVII:** 9

Mama's Promises (Nelson), **Supp. XVIII: 173–174**

"Mama Still Loves You" (Naylor), **Supp. VIII:** 214

Mambo Hips and Make Believe (Coleman), **Supp. XI: 94–96**

Mambo Kings, The (film), **Supp. VIII:** 73, 74

Mambo Kings Play Songs of Love, The (Hijuelos), **Supp. VIII:** 73–74, **79–82**

"Ma'me Pélagie" (Chopin), **Retro. Supp. II:** 64

Mamet, David, **Retro. Supp. III:** 165, 172; **Supp. XIV:** 239–258, 315

"Mamie" (Sandburg), **III:** 582

Mammedaty, Novarro Scott. *See* Momaday, N. Scott

"Mammon and the Archer" (O. Henry), **Supp. II Part 1:** 394, 408

Mammonart (Sinclair), **Supp. V:** 276–277

"Mammy" (D. West), **Supp. XVIII:** 283

"Mamouche" (Chopin), **Retro. Supp. II:** 66

Mamoulian, Rouben, **Supp. XVIII:** 281

"Man" (Corso), **Supp. XII:** 130

"Man" (Herbert), **II:** 12

"Man Against the Sky, The" (Robinson), **III:** 509, 523

"Manager, The"(Goodman), **Supp. XXVIII:** 91

"Man and a Woman Sit Near Each Other, A" (R. Bly), **Supp. IV Part 1:** 71

Man and Boy (Morris), **III:** 223, 224, 225

"Man and the Snake, The" (Bierce), **I:** 203

"Man and Woman" (Caldwell), **I:** 310

Manassas (Sinclair), **Supp. V:** 280, 281, 285

"Man Bring This Up Road" (T. Williams), **IV:** 383–384

"Man Carrying Thing" (Stevens), **IV:** 90

Manchester, William, **III:** 103

"Man Child, The" (Baldwin), **Supp. I Part 1:** 63

Man Could Stand Up, A (Ford), **I:** 423

"Mandarin's Jade" (Chandler), **Supp. IV Part 1:** 125

Mandel, Charlotte, **Supp. XVI:** 57

Mandelbaum, Maurice, **I:** 61

Mandelbaum, Michael, **Supp. XXV:** 264

Mandelstam, Osip, **Retro. Supp. I:** 278; **Supp. III Part 1:** 268; **Supp. VIII:** 21, 22, 23, 27; **Supp. XIII:** 77; **Supp. XV:** 254, 261, 263

"Mandelstam: The Poem as Event" (Dobyns), **Supp. XIII:** 78

"Mandolin" (Dove), **Supp. IV Part 1:** 247

"Mandoline" (Verlaine), **IV:** 79

"Mandrin Question, The" (Vaz), **Supp. XXVI:** 267

"Man Eating" (Kenyon), **Supp. VII:** 173

"Manet in Late Summer" (Skloot), **Supp. XX: 201**

"Man Feeding Pigeons" (Clampitt), **Supp. IX: 49–50**, 52

Manfred, Frederick, **Supp. X:** 126

Man from Kinvara, The (Gallagher), **Supp. XXIV:** 166, 172, 173

Man From Limbo, The (Endore), **Supp. XVII:** 55

Man fun natseres, Der (Asch), **Supp. XXIII:** 6

Mangione, Jerre, **Supp. XXV:** 28

"Mango Says Goodbye Sometimes" (Cisneros), **Supp. VII:** 64

Manhattan (film; Allen), **Supp. IV Part 1:** 205; **Supp. XV:** 5, **7–8**, 13

"Manhattan Dawn" (Justice), **Supp. VII:** 117

"Manhattan: Luminism" (Doty), **Supp. XI:** 135

Manhattan Murder Mystery (film; Allen), **Supp. XV:** 5, 11

Manhattan Transfer (Dos Passos), **I:** 26, 475, 478, 479, 480, 481, 482–484, 487; **II:** 286; **Supp. I Part 1:** 57; **Supp. XXVI:** 18

"Mania" (R. Lowell), **II:** 554

"Manic in the Moon, The" (Thurber), **Supp. I Part 2:** 620

Manifest; and Furthermore (Bronk), **Supp. XXI:** 32

"Manifest"(Lea), **Supp. XXVIII:** 135

"Manifesto: A Press Release from PRKA" (Saunders), **Supp. XIX:** 235

Manikin, The (J. Scott), **Supp. XVII: 189–191**, 192, 194

"Man in Black" (Plath), **Supp. I Part 2:** 538

Man in Lower Ten, The (Rinehart), **Supp. XXV:** 192, 200

Man in Prehistory (Chard), **Supp. XII:** 177–178

Man in the Black Coat Turns, The (R. Bly), **Supp. IV Part 1:** 66–68, 71, 73

"Man in the Brooks Brothers Shirt, The" (McCarthy), **II:** 563–564

"Man in the Drawer, The" (Malamud), **Supp. I Part 2:** 437

Man in the Flying Lawn Chair and Other Excursions and Observations, The (Plimpton), **Supp. XVI:** 234

Man in the Gray Flannel Suit, The (Wilson), **Supp. IV Part 1:** 387

Man in the High Castle, The (Dick), **Supp. XVIII:** 138

Man in the Middle, The (Wagoner), **Supp. IX:** 324, **332–333**

"Man in the Rain, The" (Ryan as Quin), **Supp. XVIII:** 226

"Man in the Toolhouse, The" (Swados), **Supp. XIX:** 263

Mankiewicz, Frank, **Supp. XXIV:** 279

Mankiewicz, Herman J., **Supp. XVI:** 189; **Supp. XXVII:** 91

Mankiewicz, Joseph, **Retro. Supp. I:** 113

Mankowitz, Wolf, **Supp. XI:** 307

"Man Made of Words, The" (Momaday), **Supp. IV Part 2:** 481, 484–485, 486, 487, 488

Man-Made World, The (Gilman), **Supp. XI:** 207

"Man-Moth, The" (Bishop), **Retro. Supp. II:** 42; **Supp. I Part 1:** 85–87, 88
Mann, Barbara Alice, **Supp. XXVI:** 81, 85, 86, 88, 90, 92, 95
Mann, Charles, **Retro. Supp. II:** 40
Mann, Erika, **Supp. II Part 1:** 11
Mann, Seymour (Samuel Weisman), **Supp. V:** 113
Mann, Thomas, **I:** 271, 490; **II:** 42, 539; **III:** 231, 281–282, 283; **IV:** 70, 73, 85; **Supp. IV Part 1:** 392; **Supp. IV Part 2:** 522; **Supp. IX:** 21; **Supp. V:** 51; **Supp. XI:** 275; **Supp. XII:** 173, 310, 321; **Supp. XIV:** 87; **Supp. XIX:** 147, 151, 157; **Supp. XVII:** 137; **Supp. XX:** 85; **Supp. XXIII:** 4; **Supp. XXVIII:** 145, 149
Mannequins' Demise: A Play in Eight Scenes (Budbill), **Supp. XIX:** 12
Mannerhouse (Wolfe), **IV:** 460
Manner Music, The (Reznikoff), **Supp. XIV: 293–295**
"Manners" (Bishop), **Supp. I Part 1:** 73
"Manners" (Emerson), **II:** 4, 6
"Manners, Morals, and the Novel" (Trilling), **Supp. III Part 2:** 502, 503
Mannheim, Karl, **I:** 279; **Supp. I Part 2:** 644
Manning, Ambrose, **Supp. XX: 166**
Manning, Frederic, **III:** 459
Manning, Robert, **Supp. IX:** 236
Mannix, Daniel P., **Supp. II Part 1:** 140
Man Nobody Knows, The (B. Barton), **Retro. Supp. I:** 179
Mano, D. Keith, **Supp. XVI:** 250
Mano, Guy Levis, **Supp. XVI:** 282
"Man of Indeterminate Age on a Subway Grate, A" (DI Piero), **Supp. XIX:** 47
"Man of Letters" (Pickering), **Supp. XXI:** 192, 195–196
"Man of Letters as a Man of Business, The" (Howells), **Supp. XIV:** 45–46
"Man of No Account, The" (Harte), **Supp. II Part 1:** 339
"Man of Property to His Muse, The" (W. Stone), **Supp. XXVII:** 255
"Man of the Crowd, The" (Poe), **III:** 412, 417; **Retro. Supp. I:** 154; **Retro. Supp. III:** 226
Man on Spikes (Asinof), **II:** 424
Man on Stage (Dixon), **Supp. XII:** 141, **154–155**
"Man on the Dump, The" (Stevens), **IV:** 74; **Retro. Supp. I:** 306
"Man on the Stairs, The" (July), **Supp. XXIV:** 202
"Man on the Train, The" (Percy), **Supp. III Part 1:** 387
Manor, The (Singer), **IV:** 6, 17–19
Manrique, Jorge, **Retro. Supp. II:** 154
Mansart Builds a School (Du Bois), **Supp. II Part 1:** 185–186
Man's Fate (Malraux), **I:** 127; **Retro. Supp. II:** 121
"Man's Fate A Film Treatment of the Malraux Novel" (Agee), **I:** 33–34
Mansfield, June, **Supp. X:** 183, 194
Mansfield, Katherine, **III:** 362, 453
Mansfield, Stephanie, **Supp. IV Part 1:** 227

Man's Hope (Malraux), **IV:** 247
Mansion, The (Faulkner), **II:** 73; **Retro. Supp. I:** 74, 82; **Retro. Supp. III:** 86
Man's Nature and His Communities (Niebuhr), **III:** 308
Manson, Charles, **Supp. IV Part 1:** 205
"Man Splitting Wood in the Daybreak, The" (Kinnell), **Supp. III Part 1:** 254
"Man's Pride" (Jeffers), **Supp. II Part 2:** 417
"Man's Story, The" (Anderson), **I:** 114
Man's Woman, A (Norris), **III:** 314, 322, 328, 329, 330, 332, 333
Man That Corrupted Hadleyburg, The (Twain), **I:** 204; **IV:** 208
"Man That Corrupted Hadleyburg, The" (Twain), **Retro. Supp. III:** 269
"Man That Was Used Up, The" (Poe), **III:** 412, 425
"Mantis" (Zukofsky), **Supp. III Part 2:** 617
"'Mantis': An Interpretation" (Zukofsky), **Supp. III Part 2:** 617–618
"Man to Know in the Restaurants, The" (Siddons), **Supp. XXII:** 244
Man to Send Rain Clouds, The (Rosen, ed.), **Supp. IV Part 2:** 499, 505, 513
"Man to Send Rain Clouds, The" (Silko), **Supp. IV Part 2:** 559
Mantrap (Lewis), **II:** 447
Manuductio Ad Ministerium (Mather), **Supp. II Part 2:** 465–467
"Manuelzinho" (Bishop), **Retro. Supp. II:** 47–48
Manuscript Books of Emily Dickinson, The (Franklin, ed.), **Retro. Supp. I:** 29, 41
"Manuscript Found in a Bottle, The" (Poe), **Retro. Supp. III:** 224
"Man Waiting for It to Stop, A" (Dunn), **Supp. XI:** 144
"Man Walked Out, A" (Lea), **Supp. XXVIII:** 140–141
"Man Who Became a Woman, The" (Anderson), **I:** 114
"Man Who Carries the Desert Around Inside Himself, The: For Wally" (Komunyakaa), **Supp. XIII:** 125
"Man Who Closed Shop, The" (Dunn), **Supp. XI:** 149
Man Who Gave Up His Name, The (Harrison), **Supp. VIII:** 45, 52
Man Who Had All the Luck, The (A. Miller), **III:** 148, 149, 164, 166; **Retro. Supp. III:** 166
"Man Who Knew Belle Star, The" (Bausch), **Supp. VII:** 46
"Man Who Knew Coolidge, The" (Lewis), **II:** 449
Man Who Knew Coolidge, The: Being the Soul of Lowell Schmaltz, Constructive and Nordic Citizen (Lewis), **II:** 450
Man Who Lived Underground, The (Wright), **Supp. II Part 1:** 40
"Man Who Lived Underground, The" (Wright), **IV:** 479, 485–487, 492; **Retro. Supp. II:** 121
"Man Who Made Me Love Him, The" (Weigl), **Supp. XIX:** 278

"Man Who Makes Brooms, The" (Nye), **Supp. XIII:** 276
Man Who Shook Hands, The (Wakoski), **Supp. XXVIII:** 266
"Man Who Studied Yoga, The" (Mailer), **III:** 35–36; **Retro. Supp. II:** 200
"Man Who Wanted to Win, The" (McCoy), **Supp. XIII:** 161
"Man Who Was Made of Netting, The" (Vaz), **Supp. XXVI:** 266
Man Who Was There, The (Morris), **III:** 220–221
"Man Who Was Used Up, The" (Poe), **Retro. Supp. III:** 225
"Man Who Writes Ants, The" (Merwin), **Supp. III Part 1:** 348
"Man with a Family" (Humphrey), **Supp. IX:** 94
Man without a Country, The (Hale), **I:** 488
"Man with the Blue Guitar, The" (Stevens), **I:** 266; **IV:** 85–87; **Retro. Supp. I: 303–305,** 306, 307, 309
Man with the Blue Guitar and Other Poems, The (Stevens), **IV:** 76; **Retro. Supp. I:** 303, 422
Man with the Golden Arm, The (Algren), **Supp. IX:** 1, 3, **9–11,** 14, 15; **Supp. V:** 4
Man with the Golden Arm, The (film), **Supp. IX:** 3
"Man with the Golden Beef, The" (Podhoretz), **Supp. IX:** 3
"Man with the Hoe, The" (Markham), **Supp. XV:** 115
Man with the Mask, The (Lippard), **Supp. XXIII:** 178, 183–184, 188
Many a Monster (Ryan as Finnegan), **Supp. XVIII:** 233, **236–238**
Manyan Letters (Olson), **Supp. II Part 2:** 571
Many Circles (Goldbarth), **Supp. XII:** 193
"Many Handles" (Sandburg), **III:** 594
"Many Happy Returns" (Auden), **Supp. II Part 1:** 15
Many Happy Returns (Berrigan), **Supp. XXII:** 224; **Supp. XXIV:** 37, 41
Many Loves (W. C. Williams), **Retro. Supp. I:** 424
"Many Mansions" (H. Roth), **Supp. IX:** 233, 234
Many Marriages (Anderson), **I:** 104, 111, 113
"Many of Our Waters: Variations on a Poem by a Black Child" (Wright), **Supp. III Part 2:** 602
"Many Swans" (A. Lowell), **II:** 526
"Many Thousands Gone" (Baldwin), **Retro. Supp. II:** 4; **Supp. I Part 1:** 51
"Many Wagons Ago" (Ashbery), **Supp. III Part 1:** 22
Many-Windowed House, A (Cowley), **Supp. II Part 1:** 141, 143
"Many-Windowed House, A" (Cowley), **Supp. II Part 1:** 137
Mao II (DeLillo), **Supp. VI:** 2, 4, **5,** 6, **7,** 8, 9, 14, 16

"Map, The" (Bishop), **Retro. Supp. II:** 41; **Supp. I Part 1:** 72, 82, 85–88, 93

"Map, The" (Strand), **Supp. IV Part 2:** 623–624

"Maple Leaf, The" (Joplin), **Supp. IV Part 1:** 223

"Maple Tree, The" (D. West), **Supp. XVIII:** 284

Map of Another Town: A Memoir of Provence (M. F. K. Fisher), **Supp. XVII:** 88, 89, 92

"Map of Montana in Italy, A" (Hugo), **Supp. VI:** 139

Mapp and Lucia (Benson), **Supp. XX: 229**

Mapping American Culture (Franklin and Steiner), **Supp. XXII:** 205

"Maps" (Hass), **Supp. VI:** 103–104

Mapson, Jo-Ann, **Supp. IV Part 2:** 440, 454

Map to the Next World, A: Poems and Tales (Harjo), **Supp. XII: 228–230**

"Maquillage" (Hull), **Supp. XXI:** 133

"Mara" (Jeffers), **Supp. II Part 2:** 434

Ma Rainey's Black Bottom (Wilson), **Retro. Supp. III:** 314–315, 318, 321–323, 325; **Supp. VIII:** 331, **332–334,** 346, 349, 350

Maranen (Asch), **Supp. XXIII:** 10

Marat, Jean Paul, **IV:** 117; **Supp. I Part 2:** 514, 515, 521

"Marathon" (Glück), **Supp. V:** 85

Marble Faun, The (Faulkner), **II:** 55, 56; **Retro. Supp. I:** 79; **Retro. Supp. III:** 74–75, 122–123

Marble Faun, The; or, The Romance of Monte Beni (Hawthorne), **II:** 225, 239, 242–243, 290, 324; **IV:** 167; **Retro. Supp. I:** 63, 149, 163, **164–165; Supp. I Part 1:** 38; **Supp. I Part 2:** 421, 596; **Supp. XIII:** 102

Marbles (Brodsky), **Supp. VIII:** 26–27

Marburg, Anita, **Supp. XXII:** 281

Marcaccio, Michael, **Supp. XVII:** 97, 106

Marcel, Kelly, **Supp. XXVII:** 79

"March" (W. C. Williams), **Retro. Supp. I:** 418

March, Alan, **Supp. XVI:** 242

March, Fredric, **III:** 154, 403; **IV:** 357; **Supp. X:** 220

"March, March on Down the Field" (Shaw), **Supp. XIX:** 246

Marchalonis, Shirley, **Supp. XIII:** 138, 140, 141, 143, 147–148

Marchand, Philip, **Supp. XXVII:** 196

"Marché aux Oiseaux" (Wilbur), **Supp. III Part 2:** 550

"Märchen, The" (Jarrell), **II:** 378–379

March Hares (Frederic), **II:** 143–144

Marching Men (Anderson), **I:** 99, 101, 103–105, 111

"Marching Music" (Simic), **Supp. VIII:** 281

"Marcia" (R. H. Davis), **Supp. XVI:** 91–92

Marcks, Greg, **Supp. XVIII:** 150

Marckwardt, Albert H., **Supp. XXIV:** 255

Marco Millions (O'Neill), **III:** 391, 395

Marcosson, Isaac, **III:** 322

Marcus, Greil, **Supp. XVIII:** 30, 53; **Supp. XXVI:** 142

Marcus, Steven, **Retro. Supp. II:** 196, 200

Marcus Aurelius, **II:** 1; **III:** 566; **Supp. XVIII:** 304

Marcuse, Herbert, **Supp. I Part 2:** 645; **Supp. VIII:** 196; **Supp. XII:** 2

Mardi and a Voyage Thither (Melville), **I:** 384; **II:** 281; **III:** 77–79, 84, 87, 89; **Retro. Supp. I:** 247, 254, 256; **Retro. Supp. III:** 147, 154, 157

Margaret (Judd), **II:** 290

Margaret & Dusty (Notley), **Supp. XXII:** 231

"Margaret Fuller, 1847" (Clampitt), **Supp. IX:** 43

"Marginalia" (Wilbur), **Supp. III Part 2:** 544

Margin of Hope, A: An Intellectual Autobiography (Howe), **Supp. VI:** 113–114, 117, 125, 128

"Margins of Maycomb, The: A Rereading of *To Kill a Mockingbird*" (Phelps), **Supp. VIII:** 128

Margoshes, Samuel, **Supp. X:** 70

"Margrave" (Jeffers), **Supp. II Part 2:** 426

Margret Howth (R. H. Davis), **Supp. XVI:** 81, 83, 84, **88–89**

Margret Howth: A Story of Today (J. Yellin, ed.), **Supp. XVI:** 88

Margulies, Donald, **Supp. XXI:** 145

"Maria Concepción" (Porter), **III:** 434–435, 451

Mariana (Vaz), **Supp. XXVI:** 258–259, 263

Mariani, Paul L., **Retro. Supp. I:** 412, 419; **Retro. Supp. II:** 189

Marianne Moore Reader, (Moore), **III:** 199

Marie Antoinette (film), **Retro. Supp. I:** 113

Marie Blythe (Mosher), **Supp. XXII:** 206, 209, **212**

Marie Grubbe (Jacobsen), **Retro. Supp. III:** 140

Marie Laveau (Prose), **Supp. XVI:** 251

Mariella Gable, Sister, **III:** 339, 355

"Marijuana and a Pistol" (C. Himes), **Supp. XVI:** 137

"Marijuana Notation" (Ginsberg), **Supp. II Part 1:** 313

Maril, Herman, **Supp. XXI:** 22, 23

Marilyn: A Biography (Mailer), **Retro. Supp. II:** 208

"Marilyn Gives Me a White Fleshed Peach"(Wakoski), **Supp. XXVIII:** 272

"Marin" (Cisneros), **Supp. VII:** 60, 61

Marin, Jay, **Retro. Supp. II:** 325

"Marina" (Eliot), **I:** 584, 585; **Retro. Supp. I:** 64

Mariners, Renegades, and Castaways (C. L. R. James), **Supp. XXI:** 159, 169–170

"Marine Surface, Low Overcast" (Clampitt), **Supp. IX: 47–48**

Marinetti, F. T., **Supp. XXII:** 159, 160, 161, 163

Marinetti, Tommaso, **Retro. Supp. I:** 59

Marion, Frances, **Supp. XXVIII:** 182

Marionettes, The (Faulkner), **Retro. Supp. I:** 79

"Mari Sandoz's *Slogum House*: Greed as a Woman" (Riley), **Supp. XXIV:** 252

Maritain, Jacques, **I:** 402; **Supp. XXVI:** 231, 232

Maritime Compact (Paine), **Supp. I Part 2:** 519

Maritime History of Massachusetts, 1783–1860, The (Morison), **Supp. I Part 2:** 481–483

Marjolin, Jean-Nicolas, **Supp. I Part 1:** 302

Marjorie Kinnan Rawlings: Sojourner at Cross Creek (Silverthorne), **Supp. X:** 220, 234

Marjorie Morningstar (film), **Supp. XXV:** 262

Marjorie Morningstar (Wouk), **Supp. XXV:** 253, 254, 256, 258, 261–262, 268

"Mark, The" (Bogan), **Supp. III Part 1:** 52

Marker, Chris, **Supp. IV Part 2:** 434, 436

"Market" (Hayden), **Supp. II Part 1:** 368, 369

Marketplace, The (Frederic), **II:** 145–146

Markham, Edwin, **I:** 199, 207; **Supp. XV:** 115

Markings (Hammarskjold), **Supp. II Part 1:** 26

Mark of the Vampire (film, Browning), **Supp. XVII:** 58

Markopoulos, Gregory, **Supp. XII:** 2

Markowick-Olczakova, Hanna, **Supp. X:** 70

Marks, Alison, **Supp. I Part 2:** 660

Marks, Barry A., **I:** 435, 438, 442, 446

Markson, David, **Supp. XVII: 135–147**

Mark Twain and Southwestern Humor (Lynn), **Retro. Supp. III:** 259

Mark Twain as a Literary Comedian (Sloane), **Retro. Supp. III:** 259

Mark Twain in Eruption (Twain), **IV:** 209

Mark Twain in the Margins (Fulton), **Retro. Supp. III:** 266

Mark Twain's America (De Voto), **I:** 248

Mark Twain's Autobiography (Twain), **IV:** 209

Mark Twain Speaking (Fatout), **Retro. Supp. III:** 268

Mark Twain: The Complete Interviews (Scharnhorst), **Retro. Supp. III:** 268

Marley, Bob, **Supp. IX:** 152

Marlowe, Christopher, **I:** 68, 368, 384; **II:** 590; **III:** 259, 491; **Retro. Supp. I:** 127; **Retro. Supp. II:** 76; **Supp. I Part 2:** 422; **Supp. XXI:** 227

Marlowe, Kimberly B., **Supp. XXII:** 214

"Marlowe Takes on the Syndicate" (Chandler), **Supp. IV Part 1:** 135

Marne, The (Wharton), **IV:** 319, 320; **Retro. Supp. I:** 378; **Retro. Supp. III:** 286

Marquand, John, **Supp. XI:** 301

Marquand, Mrs. John P. (Adelaide Hooker), **III:** 57, 61

Marquand, Mrs. John P. (Christina Sedgwick), **III:** 54, 57

Marquand, J. P., **I:** 362, 375; **II:** 459, 482–483; **III: 50–73,** 383; **Supp. I Part 1:** 196; **Supp. IV Part 1:** 31; **Supp. V:** 95

Marquand, Philip, **III:** 52

Marquis, Don, **Supp. I Part 2:** 668

Marra, Anthony, **Supp. XXVI:** 216

Marrásh, Francis al-, **Supp. XX: 117**

"Marriage" (Corso), **Supp. XII:** 117, 124, **127–128**

Marriage (Moore), **III:** 194

"Marriage" (Moore), **III:** 198–199, 213

"Marriage, A" (Untermeyer), **Supp. XV:** 305

Marriage A-la-Mode (Dryden), **Supp. IX:** 68

Marriage and Other Science Fiction (Goldbarth), **Supp. XII:** 189, 190

"Marriage in the Sixties, A" (Rich), **Retro. Supp. III:** 244; **Supp. I Part 2:** 554

Marriage of Bette and Boo, The (Durang), **Supp. XXIV:** 114, 121, **122–123**

Marriage of Heaven and Hell (Blake), **Supp. XXII:** 257

"Marriage of Heaven and Hell, The" (Blake), **III:** 544–545; **Supp. VIII:** 99

"Marriage of Phaedra, The" (Cather), **Retro. Supp. I:** 5; **Retro. Supp. III:** 26

Marriage Plot, The (Eugenides), **Supp. XXIV:** 135, **143–145**

"Marriage Rhapsody"(Hadas), **Supp. XXIII:** 114

Married (Strindberg), **Supp. XXII:** 23

"Married" (Taggard), **Supp. XXII:** 274

Married Men (Wolfert), **Supp. XXI:** 277

Married People (Rinehart), **Supp. XXV:** 201

Marrow of Tradition, The (Chesnutt), **Supp. XIV:** 63, **71–75,** 76

Marryat, Captain Frederick, **III:** 423

"Marrying Absurd" (Didion), **Supp. IV Part 1:** 200

"Marrying Iseult?' (Updike), **Retro. Supp. I:** 329

Marrying Man (Simon), **Supp. IV Part 2:** 588

"Marrying the Hangman" (Atwood), **Supp. XIII:** 34

Marry Me: A Romance (Updike), **Retro. Supp. I:** 329, 330, 332

"Mars and Hymen" (Freneau), **Supp. II Part 1:** 258

Marsden, Dora, **III:** 471; **Retro. Supp. I:** 416

Marsena (Frederic), **II:** 135, 136–137

Marsh, Edward, **Retro. Supp. III:** 96; **Supp. I Part 1:** 257, 263

Marsh, Frederick T., **Supp. XX: 39, 46**

Marsh, Fred T., **Supp. IX:** 232

Marsh, John R., **Supp. XIX:** 187

Marsh, Mae, **Supp. I Part 2:** 391

Marshall, George, **III:** 3

Marshall, John, **Supp. I Part 2:** 455; **Supp. XIX:** 62; **Supp. XVI:** 117; **Supp. XXIII:** 275, 276

Marshall, Paule, **Supp. IV Part 1:** 8, 14, 369; **Supp. XI:** 18, **275–292; Supp. XIII:** 295; **Supp. XX: 154**

Marshall, Tod, **Supp. XV:** 224; **Supp. XVII:** 25, 26, 29, 32

"Marshall Carpenter" (Masters), **Supp. I Part 2:** 463

"Marshes of Glynn, The" (Lanier), **Supp. I Part 1:** 364, 365–368, 370, 373

"'Marshes of Glynn, The': A Study in Symbolic Obscurity" (Ross), **Supp. I Part 1:** 373

Marsh Island, A (Jewett), **II:** 405; **Retro. Supp. II:** 134

"Marshland Elegy" (Leopold), **Supp. XIV:** 187, 189

"Mars Is Heaven!" (Bradbury), **Supp. IV Part 1:** 103, 106

Mars-Jones, Adam, **Supp. XXI:** 116

Marsman, Henrik, **Supp. IV Part 1:** 183

Marston, Ed, **Supp. IV Part 2:** 492

Marston, Elsa, **Supp. XXIII:** 241

Marta y Maria (Valdes), **II:** 290

"Martha's Lady" (Jewett), **Retro. Supp. II:** 140, 143

Marthe, Saint, **II:** 213

Martial, **II:** 1, 169; **Supp. IX:** 152

Martian Chronicles, The (Bradbury), **Supp. IV Part 1:** 102, 103, 106–107

Martian Time-Slip (Dick), **Supp. XVIII:** 142

Martien, Norman, **Supp. XXVIII:** 262

Martin, Benjamin, **Supp. I Part 2:** 503

Martin, Charles, **Supp. XVII:** 112

Martin, Dick, **Supp. XII:** 44

Martin, Jay, **I:** 55, 58, 60, 61, 67; **III:** 307; **Retro. Supp. II:** 326, 327, 329; **Supp. XI:** 162

Martin, John, **Supp. XI:** 172; **Supp. XXVIII:** 263

Martin, Judith, **Supp. V:** 128

Martin, Nell, **Supp. IV Part 1:** 351, 353

Martin, Reginald, **Supp. X:** 247, 249

Martin, Robert, **Retro. Supp. III:** 173; **Supp. XX: 165**

Martin, Robert E., **Supp. XXVIII:** 246

Martin, Stephen-Paul, **Supp. IV Part 2:** 430

Martin, Tom, **Supp. X:** 79

Martin du Gard, Roger, **Supp. I Part 1:** 51

Martineau, Harriet, **Supp. II Part 1:** 282, 288, 294; **Supp. XVIII:** 7; **Supp. XXIV:** 78

Martin Eden (London), **II:** 466, 477–481

Martinelli, Sheri, **Supp. IV Part 1:** 280

Martínez, Guillermo, **Supp. XIII:** 313

Martinez-Avila, Raul, **Supp. XXIII:** 125

Martini, Adrienne, **Supp. XVIII:** 35

Martín-Lucas, Belén, **Supp. XXVI:** 218

Mart'nez, Rafael, **Retro. Supp. I:** 423

Martone, John, **Supp. V:** 179

Marty (Chayefsky), **Supp. XV:** 205

"Martyr, The" (Porter), **III:** 454

Martz, Louis L., **IV:** 151, 156, 165; **Supp. I Part 1:** 107; **Supp. XIV:** 12; **Supp. XXI:** 85

Marvell, Andrew, **IV:** 135, 151, 156, 161, 253; **Retro. Supp. I:** 62, 127; **Retro. Supp. II:** 186, 189; **Supp. I Part 1:** 80; **Supp. XII:** 159; **Supp. XIV:** 10; **Supp. XVI:** 204; **Supp. XXI:** 227; **Supp. XXIII:** 62

"Marvella, for Borrowing" (Ríos), **Supp. IV Part 2:** 551

"Marvelous Sauce, The", **Supp. XVII:** 189

Marvels and Masterpieces (al-Badá'i' wa'l-Tará'if) (Gibran), **Supp. XX: 116, 124**

Marx, Eleanor, **Supp. XVI:** 85

Marx, Karl, **I:** 60, 267, 279, 283, 588; **II:** 376, 462, 463, 483, 577; **IV:** 429, 436, 443–444, 469; **Retro. Supp. I:** 254; **Supp. I Part 2:** 518, 628, 632, 633, 634, 635, 639, 643, 645, 646; **Supp. III Part 2:** 619; **Supp. IV Part 1:** 355; **Supp. IX:** 133; **Supp. VIII:** 196; **Supp. X:** 119, 134; **Supp. XIII:** 75; **Supp. XXI:** 162, 263

Marx, Leo, **Supp. I Part 1:** 233

"Marxism and Monastic Perpectives" (Merton), **Supp. VIII:** 196

Mary (Asch), **Supp. XXIII:** 2, 7, **14**

Mary (Nabokov), **Retro. Supp. I: 267–268,** 270, 277

"Mary" (Trethewey), **Supp. XXI:** 246

"Marygolds and Mules"(Arnow), **Supp. XXVIII:** 2

"Mary in Old Age" (Ferry), **Supp. XXIV:** 162

"Mary Karr, Mary Karr, Mary Karr, Mary Karr" (Harmon), **Supp. XI:** 248

Maryles, Daisy, **Supp. XII:** 271

Mary Magdalene, **I:** 303

"Mary Magdalene at Easter" (Davison), **Supp. XXVI:** 71

Mary; or, The Test of Honour (Rowson), **Supp. XV: 233,** 236

"Mary O'Reilly" (Anderson), **II:** 44

"Mary Osaka , I Love You" (Fante), **Supp. XI:** 169

Mary Roberts Rinehart Crime Book, The (Rinehart), **Supp. XXV:** 199

"Mary Snorak the Cook, Skermo the Gardener, and Jack the Parts Man Provide Dinner for a Wandering Stranger" (Grossman), **Supp. XIX:** 87

"Mary's Song" (Plath), **Supp. I Part 2:** 541

"Mary Winslow" (R. Lowell), **Retro. Supp. II:** 187

Marzynski, Marian, **Supp. XVI:** 153

"Masculinities and Murder: George Pemberton in Ron Rash's *Serena*" (Willis), **Supp. XXVII:** 216

Masefield, John, **II:** 552; **III:** 523

Masked and Anonymous (film, Dylan and Charles), **Supp. XVIII:** 21, 28

Mask for Janus, A (Merwin), **Supp. III Part 1:** 339, 341, 342

Maslin, Janet, **Supp. XVI:** 213; **Supp. XXI:** 79

Maslow, Abraham, **Supp. I Part 2:** 540

Maso, Carole, **Supp. XXII:** 261

Mason, Bobbie Ann, **Supp. VIII: 133–149; Supp. XI:** 26; **Supp. XII:** 294, 298, 311; **Supp. XX: 162; Supp. XXV:** 153

Mason, Charlotte Osgood, **Retro. Supp. III:** 127–128, 139; **Supp. XIV:** 201

Mason, David, **Supp. V:** 344; **Supp. XV:** 116, 251; **Supp. XVII:** 109, 110, 112,

121; **Supp. XVIII:** 182, 183

Mason, Jennifer, **Supp. XVIII:** 263

Mason, Lowell, **I:** 458

Mason, Margaret, **Supp. XXIII:** 209

Mason, Marsha, **Supp. IV Part 2:** 575, 586

Mason, Otis Tufton, **Supp. I Part 1:** 18

Mason, Walt, **Supp. XV:** 298

Mason & Dixon (Pynchon), **Supp. XVII:** 232

"Mason Jars by the Window" (Ríos), **Supp. IV Part 2:** 548

"Masque in Green and Black"(Hadas), **Supp. XXIII:** 121

Masque of Mercy, A (Frost), **II:** 155, 165, 167–168; **Retro. Supp. I:** 131, 140; **Retro. Supp. III:** 104, 105

"Masque of Mummers, The" (MacLeish), **III:** 18

"Masque of Pandora, The" (Longfellow), **Retro. Supp. II:** 167

Masque of Pandora, The, and Other Poems (Longfellow), **II:** 490, 494, 506; **Retro. Supp. II:** 169

Masque of Poets, A (Lathrop, ed.), **Retro. Supp. I:** 31; **Supp. I Part 1:** 365, 368

Masque of Reason, A (Frost), **II:** 155, 162, 165–167; **Retro. Supp. I:** 131, 140; **Retro. Supp. II:** 42; **Retro. Supp. III:** 104, 105

"Masque of the Red Death, The" (Poe), **III:** 412, 419, 424; **Retro. Supp. II:** 262, 268–269; **Retro. Supp. III:** 225

"Masquerade" (Banks), **Supp. V:** 7

Massachusetts, Its Historians and Its History (Adams), **Supp. I Part 2:** 484

"Massachusetts 1932" (Bowles), **Supp. IV Part 1:** 94

"Massachusetts to Virginia" (Whittier), **Supp. I Part 2:** 688–689

"Massacre and the Mastermind, The" (Bausch), **Supp. VII:** 49

"Massacre at Scio, The" (Bryant), **Supp. I Part 1:** 168

"Massacre of the Innocents, The" (Davison), **Supp. XXVI:** 70

"Massacre of the Innocents, The" (Simic), **Supp. VIII:** 282

Masses and Man (Toller), **I:** 479

"Masseur de Ma Soeur, Le" (Hecht), **Supp. X:** 58

Massey, Raymond, **Supp. IV Part 2:** 524

"Mass Eye and Ear: The Ward" (Karr), **Supp. XI:** 244

"Mass for the Day of St. Thomas Didymus" (Levertov), **Supp. III Part 1:** 283

Massie, Chris, **Supp. IV Part 2:** 524

Massing, Michael, **Supp. IV Part 1:** 208

Massinger, Philip, **Supp. I Part 2:** 422; **Supp. XV:** 238

Master Builder, The (Ibsen), **Supp. IV Part 2:** 522

Master Class (McNally), **Supp. XIII:** 204–205, 208

"Masterful" (Matthews), **Supp. IX:** 161–162

Mastering the Art of French Cooking (Child), **Supp. XVII:** 89

"Master Misery" (Capote), **Supp. III Part 1:** 117

Master of Dreams: A Memoir of Isaac Bashevis Singer (Telushkin), **Retro. Supp. II:** 317

"Master of Secret Revenges, The" (Gass), **Supp. VI:** 93

Master of the Crossroads (Bell), **Supp. X:** 16–17

"'Masterpiece of Filth, A': Portrait of Knoxville Forgets to Be Fair" (Howards), **Supp. VIII:** 178

Masterpieces of American Fiction, **Supp. XI:** 198

"Master Player, The" (Dunbar), **Supp. II Part 1:** 200

Masters, Edgar Lee, **I:** 106, 384, 475, 480, 518; **II:** 276, 529; **III:** 505, 576, 579; **IV:** 352; **Retro. Supp. I:** 131; **Supp. I Part 2:** 378, 386, 387, 454–478; **Supp. III Part 1:** 63, 71, 73, 75; **Supp. IV Part 2:** 502; **Supp. IX:** 308; **Supp. XIV:** 282–283; **Supp. XV:** 256, 293, 297, 301, 306; **Supp. XXV:** 18; **Supp. XXVII:** 283, 290

Masters, Hardin W., **Supp. I Part 2:** 468

Masters, Hilary, **Supp. IX:** 96

Masters of Sociological Thought (Coser), **Supp. I Part 2:** 650

Masters of the Dew (Roumain), **Supp. IV Part 1:** 367

Masters of the Short Story (Kriegel and Lass, eds.), **Supp. XXIV:** 214

"Masters of War" (song, Dylan), **Supp. XVIII:** 24

"Master's Pieces, The" (H. L. Gates), **Supp. XX: 109**

Matchmaker, The (Wilder), **IV:** 357, 369, 370, 374; **Supp. XX: 50**

Mate of the Daylight, The, and Friends Ashore (Jewett), **II:** 404; **Retro. Supp. II:** 146–147

Materassi, Mario, **Supp. IX:** 233

"Material" (Munro), **Supp. XXVII:** 185

Materials, The (Oppen), **Supp. XXVI:** 229–232

"Math Bending unto Angels" (Vaz), **Supp. XXVI:** 260

Mather, Cotton, **II:** 10, 104, 302, 506, 536; **III:** 442; **IV:** 144, 152–153, 157; **Retro. Supp. III:** 4; **Supp. I Part 1:** 102, 117, 174, 271; **Supp. I Part 2:** 584, 599, 698; **Supp. II Part 2: 441–470; Supp. IV Part 2:** 430, 434

Mather, Increase, **II:** 10; **IV:** 147, 157; **Supp. I Part 1:** 100

Mathews, Cornelius, **III:** 81; **Supp. I Part 1:** 317

Mathews, Shailer, **III:** 293

"Matinees" (Merrill), **Supp. III Part 1:** 319, 327

"Matins" (C. Frost), **Supp. XV:** 105

"Matins" (Glück), **Supp. V:** 88

"Matins" (Nelson), **Supp. XVIII:** 177

Matisse, Henri, **III:** 180; **IV:** 90, 407; **Supp. I Part 2:** 619; **Supp. IX:** 66; **Supp. VIII:** 168; **Supp. X:** 73, 74; **Supp. XXII:** 98, 99; **Supp. XXVI:** 259

"Matisse: Blue Interior with Two Girls–1947" (Hecht), **Supp. X: 73–74**

"Matisse: The Red Studio" (Snodgrass), **Supp. VI:** 316–317

Matlack, James, **Supp. XV:** 269, 271, 286

Matlock, Lucinda, **Supp. I Part 2:** 462

Matos, Juan, **Supp. XXI:** 104

Matrimaniac, The (film), **Supp. XVI:** 185, 186

Matrix Trilogy, The (film), **Supp. XVI:** 271

Matson, Harold, **Supp. XIII:** 164, 166, 167, 169, 172

Matson, Peter, **Supp. IV Part 1:** 299

Matson, Suzanne, **Supp. VIII:** 281

"Matter of Hannibal" (Twain), **Retro. Supp. III:** 258

"Matter of the River" (Twain), **Retro. Supp. III:** 258

Matters of Fact and Fiction: Essays 1973–1976 (Vidal), **Supp. IV Part 2:** 687

Matters of Life and Death: New American Stories (Wolff, ed.), **Supp. XXIII:** 289

Matthew (biblical book), **IV:** 164; **Supp. XV:** 222

Matthew Arnold (Trilling), **Supp. III Part 2:** 500–501

Matthews, Brander, **Retro. Supp. III:** 264

Matthews, Jackson, **Supp. XVI:** 282

Matthews, T. S., **II:** 430; **Supp. XV:** 142

Matthews, William, **Supp. IX: 151–170; Supp. V:** 4, 5; **Supp. XIII:** 112; **Supp. XXI:** 87; **Supp. XXVI:** 66

Matthiessen, F. O., **I:** 254, 259–260, 517; **II:** 41, 554; **III:** 310, 453; **IV:** 181; **Retro. Supp. I:** 40, 217; **Retro. Supp. II:** 137; **Supp. IV Part 2:** 422; **Supp. XIII:** 93; **Supp. XIV:** 3; **Supp. XXI:** 277; **Supp. XXV:** 251

Matthiessen, Peter, **Supp. V: 199–217,** 332; **Supp. XI:** 231, 294; **Supp. XIV:** 82; **Supp. XIX:** 268; **Supp. XVI:** 230; **Supp. XXVIII:** 253

Mattingly, Garrett, **Supp. IV Part 2:** 601

Mattos, Anita, **Supp. XXIII:** 197

Mattu, Ravi, **Supp. XVI:** 124

"Maud Island" (Caldwell), **I:** 310

Maud Martha (Brooks), **Supp. III Part 1:** 74, 78–79, 87; **Supp. XI:** 278

"Maud Muller" (Whittier), **Supp. I Part 2:** 698

Maugham, Somerset, **Supp. XXVIII:** 40

Maugham, W. Somerset, **III:** 57, 64; **Supp. IV Part 1:** 209; **Supp. X:** 58; **Supp. XIV:** 161

Maule's Curse: Seven Studies in the History of American Obscurantism (Winters), **Supp. II Part 2:** 807–808, 812

"Mau-mauing the Flak Catchers" (Wolfe), **Supp. III Part 2:** 577

Maupassant, Guy de, **I:** 309, 421; **II:** 191–192, 291, 325, 591; **IV:** 17; **Retro. Supp. II:** 65, 66, 67, 299; **Supp. I Part 1:** 207, 217, 223, 320; **Supp. XIV:** 336

"Maurice Barrès and the Youth of France" (Bourne), **I:** 228

Maurice Kenny: Celebrations of a Mo-hawk Writer (Kelsey, ed.), **Supp. XXIII:** 143
Maurier, George du, **II:** 338
Maurras, Charles, **Retro. Supp. I:** 55
Maus II: And Here My Troubles Began (A. Speigelman), **Supp. XVII:** 48
Mauve Gloves & Madmen, Clutter & Vine (Wolfe), **Supp. III Part 2:** 581
Maverick, Augustus, **Supp. XVIII:** 4
Maverick in Mauve (Auchincloss), **Supp. IV Part 1:** 26
"Mavericks, The" (play) (Auchincloss), **Supp. IV Part 1:** 34
"Mavericks, The" (story) (Auchincloss), **Supp. IV Part 1:** 32
"Max" (H. Miller), **III:** 183
Max, D. T., **Supp. XXI:** 117
Max and the White Phagocytes (H. Miller), **III:** 178, 183–184
Maximilian (emperor of Mexico), **Supp. I Part 2:** 457–458
Maximilian: A Play in Five Acts (Masters), **Supp. I Part 2:** 456, 457–458
"Maximus, to Gloucester" (Olson), **Supp. II Part 2:** 574
"Maximus, to himself" (Olson), **Supp. II Part 2:** 565, 566, 567, 569, 570, 572
Maximus Poems, The (Olson), **Retro. Supp. I:** 209; **Supp. II Part 2:** 555, 556, 563, 564–580, 584; **Supp. VIII:** 305; **Supp. XV:** 170, 264, 349; **Supp. XVI:** 287
Maximus Poems 1–10, The (Olson), **Supp. II Part 2:** 571
Maximus Poems IV, V, VI (Olson), **Supp. II Part 2:** 555, 580, 582–584
Maximus Poems Volume Three, The (Olson), **Supp. II Part 2:** 555, 582, 584–585
"Maximus to Gloucester, Letter 19 (A Pastoral Letter)" (Olson), **Supp. II Part 2:** 567
"Maximus to Gloucester, Sunday July 19" (Olson), **Supp. II Part 2:** 580
"Maximus to himself June 1964" (Olson), **Supp. II Part 2:** 584
Maxwell, Glyn, **Supp. XV:** 252, 253, 260, 261, 263, 264
Maxwell, William, **Supp. I Part 1:** 175; **Supp. III Part 1:** 62; **Supp. VIII:** 151–174; **Supp. XVII:** 23; **Supp. XXVIII:** 71, 74
May, Abigail (Abba). *See* Alcott, Mrs. Amos Bronson (Abigail May)
May, Charles, **Supp. XXVII:** 189, 196
May, Elaine Tyler, **Supp. XXII:** 81, 95
May, Jill, **Supp. VIII:** 126
"May 24, 1980" (Brodsky), **Supp. VIII:** 28
"May 1968" (Olds), **Supp. X:** 211–212
Mayakovsky, Vladimir, **Supp. XXIII:** 207; **Supp. XXVI:** 144
"Mayakovsky"(O'Hara), **Supp. XXIII:** 212, 214
"Mayan Glyphs Unread, The" (Bronk), **Supp. XXI:** 31
"Mayan Warning" (Mora), **Supp. XIII:** 214

Maybe (Hellman), **Supp. IV Part 1:** 12
"Maybe" (Oliver), **Supp. VII:** 239
"Maybe, Someday" (Ritsos), **Supp. XIII:** 78
May Blossom (Belasco), **Supp. XVI:** 182
"Mayday" (Faulkner), **Retro. Supp. I:** 80
"May Day" (Fitzgerald), **II:** 88–89; **Retro. Supp. I:** 103
"May Day Dancing, The" (Nemerov), **III:** 275
May Days (Pickering), **Supp. XXI:** 197–198
May Days: An Anthology of Verse from Masses-Liberator (Taggard, ed.), **Supp. XXII:** 275–276
"May Day Sermon to the Women of Gilmer County, Georgia, by a Woman Preacher Leaving the Baptist Church" (Dickey), **Supp. IV Part 1:** 182
Mayer, Bernadette, **Supp. XXIV:** 41
Mayer, Elizabeth, **Supp. II Part 1:** 16; **Supp. III Part 1:** 63
Mayer, John, **Retro. Supp. I:** 58
Mayer, Louis B., **Supp. XII:** 160; **Supp. XVIII:** 250
Mayes, Wendell, **Supp. IX:** 250
Mayfield, Sara, **Supp. IX:** 65
"May First" (Hayes), **Supp. XXVI:** 144
Mayflower, The (Stowe), **Supp. I Part 2:** 585, 586
Mayle, Peter, **Supp. XVI:** 295
Maynard, Joyce, **Supp. V:** 23
Maynard, Tony, **Supp. I Part 1:** 65
Mayne, Xavier. *See* Prime-Stevenson, Edward Irenaeus
Mayo, Robert, **III:** 478
Mayor (Allen), **Supp. XXII:** 245
Mayorga, Margaret, **IV:** 381
"Mayor of Glory River, The" (Huddle), **Supp. XXVI:** 151
"May-Pole of Merry Mount, The" (Hawthorne), **II:** 229; **Retro. Supp. III:** 113; **Supp. XXII:** 44
"May Queen" (Di Piero), **Supp. XIX:** 41
May Sarton: Selected Letters 1916–1954, **Supp. VIII:** 265
"May Sun Sheds an Amber Light, The" (Bryant), **Supp. I Part 1:** 170
"May Swenson: The Art of Perceiving" (Stanford), **Supp. IV Part 2:** 637
May the Generations Die in the Right Order (Schott), **Supp. XXIII:** 248–250
"Maze" (Eberhart), **I:** 523, 525–526, 527
Mazel (R. Goldstein), **Supp. XVII:** 44
Mazower, David, **Supp. XXIII:** 4, 5
Mazur, Gail, **Supp. XVIII:** 92
Mazurkiewicz, Margaret, **Supp. XI:** 2
Mazzeno, Laurence W., **Supp. XXV:** 253, 256, 258, 259, 263
Mazzini, Giuseppe, **Supp. I Part 1:** 2, 8; **Supp. II Part 1:** 299
M. Butterfly (Hwang), **Supp. X:** 292; **Supp. XXI:** 143, 147, **150–154**
Mc. Names starting with Mc are alphabetized as if spelled Mac.
McQueen, Steve, **Supp. XXVIII:** 167
"M. Degas Teaches Art & Science at Durfee Intermediate School, Detroit, 1942" (Levine), **Supp. V:** 181, 193

"Me, Boy Scout" (Lardner), **II:** 433
Me, Mop, and the Moondance Kid (Myers), **Supp. XXVII:** 206
Me, Vashya! (T. Williams), **IV:** 381
Mead, Elinor. *See* Howells, Mrs. William Dean (Elinor Mead)
Mead, George Herbert, **II:** 27, 34; **Supp. I Part 1:** 5; **Supp. I Part 2:** 641
Mead, Margaret, **Retro. Supp. III:** 133; **Supp. I Part 1:** 49, 52, 66; **Supp. IX:** 229
Mead, Taylor, **Supp. XV:** 187
Meade, Frank, **Retro. Supp. II:** 114
Meade, Marion, **Supp. IX:** 191, 193, 194, 195
Meadow, Lynne, **Supp. XIII:** 198
"Meadow House" (Carruth), **Supp. XVI:** 48
Meadowlands (Glück), **Supp. V:** 88–90
"Mean, Mrs." (Gass), **Supp. VI:** 83
"Me and the Mule" (Hughes), **Supp. I Part 1:** 334
Me and You and Everyone We Know (film, July), **Supp. XXIV:** 199, 200, 201, 203, 206, **207–209**
Mean Free Path (Lerner), **Supp. XXIV:** 45
Meaning a Life (M. Oppen), **Supp. XXVI:** 225, 228
"Meaningless Institution, A" (Ginsberg), **Supp. II Part 1:** 313
"Meaning of a Literary Idea, The" (Trilling), **Supp. III Part 2:** 498
"Meaning of Birds, The" (C. Smith), **Supp. X:** 177
"Meaning of Death, The, An After Dinner Speech" (Tate), **IV:** 128, 129
"Meaning of Life, The" (Tate), **IV:** 137
"Meaning of Simplicity, The" (Ritsos), **Supp. XIII:** 78
"Mean Mud Season, The" (Huddle), **Supp. XXVI:** 149
Means of Escape (Caputo), **Supp. XIX:** 18, 21, 25
Mean Spirit (Hogan), **Supp. IV Part 1:** 397, 404, 407–410, 415, 416–417
Means to Freedom, A: The Letters of H. P. Lovecraft and Robert Howard (Burke, Joshi, and Schultz eds.), **Supp. XXVII:** 128
Meantime, The (Bronk), **Supp. XXI:** 31
Mearns, Hughes, **III:** 220
"Measure" (Hass), **Supp. VI:** **99–100**, 101
Measure for Measure (Shakespeare), **Supp. XXVI:** 78
"Measuring My Blood" (Vizenor), **Supp. IV Part 1:** 262
Meatyard, Gene, **Supp. X:** 30
Me: By Jimmy (Big Boy) Valente (Keillor), **Supp. XVI:** 177
Mechan, Dennis B., **Supp. XVI:** 267–268
Mechanic, The (Bynner and DeMille), **Supp. XV:** 42, 50
"Mechanism" (Ammons), **Supp. VII:** 28
"Mechanism in Thought and Morals" (Holmes), **Supp. I Part 1:** 314
Mecom, Mrs. Jane, **II:** 122
"Meddlesome Jack" (Caldwell), **I:** 309

Medea (Jeffers), **Supp. II Part 2:** 435
Medea and Some Poems, The (Cullen), **Supp. IV Part 1:** 169, 173
Medea the Sorceress (Wakoski), **Supp. XXVIII:** 269–270
"Me Decade and the Third Great Awakening, The" (Wolfe), **Supp. III Part 2:** 581
"Médecin Malgré Lui, Le" (W. C. Williams), **IV:** 407–408
"Medfield" (Bryant), **Supp. I Part 1:** 157
Medical History of Contraception, A (Himes), **Supp. V:** 128
"Medicine Song" (Gunn Allen), **Supp. IV Part 1:** 326
Médicis, Marie de, **II:** 548
Medina (McCarthy), **II:** 579
"Meditation, A" (Eberhart), **I:** 533–535
"Meditation 1.6" (Taylor), **IV:** 165
"Meditation 1.20" (Taylor), **IV:** 165
"Meditation 2.68A" (Taylor), **IV:** 165
"Meditation 2.102" (Taylor), **IV:** 150
"Meditation 2.112" (Taylor), **IV:** 165
"Meditation 20" (Taylor), **IV:** 154–155
"Meditation 40" (Second Series) (Taylor), **IV:** 147
"Meditation at Lagunitas" (Hass), **Supp. VI:** 104–105; **Supp. XXI:** 60; **Supp. XXVI:** 61
"Meditation at Oyster River" (Roethke), **III:** 537, 549
Meditations (Descartes), **III:** 618
Meditations (Marcus Aurelius), **Supp. XVIII:** 304
"Meditations for a Savage Child" (Rich), **Supp. I Part 2:** 564–565
Meditations from a Movable Chair (Dubus), **Supp. VII:** 91
Meditations in an Emergency (O'Hara), **Supp. XXIII: 213–214,** 219, 220
"Meditations in an Emergency"(O'Hara), **Supp. XXIII:** 212, 214
"Meditations in a Swine Yard" (Komunyakaa), **Supp. XIII:** 131
"Meditations of an Old Woman" (Roethke), **III:** 529, 540, 542, 543, 545–547, 548
"Meditations on Grass"(Crooker), **Supp. XXIII:** 55
Meditations on the Insatiable Soul (R. Bly), **Supp. IV Part 1:** 72–73
Meditative Poems, The (Martz), **IV:** 151
"Mediterranean, The" (Tate), **IV:** 129
"Medium of Fiction, The" (Gass), **Supp. VI:** 85–86
"Medley" (Bambara), **Supp. XI:** 9
"Medusa" (Bogan), **Supp. III Part 1:** 50, 51
Meehan, Jeannette Porter, **Supp. XX: 213, 214, 217, 220, 224**
Meehan, Thomas, **Supp. IV Part 2:** 577–578, 586, 590
Meek, Martha, **Supp. IV Part 2:** 439, 440, 441, 442, 445, 447, 448
Meeker, Richard K., **II:** 190
Meese, Elizabeth, **Supp. XIII:** 297
"Meeting" (J. W. Miller), **Supp. XX: 167**
"Meeting, The" (F. Wright), **Supp. XVII:** 245

"Meeting and Greeting Area, The" (Cameron), **Supp. XII: 84–85**
Meeting by the River, A (Isherwood), **Supp. XIV:** 164, **170–171,** 172
"Meeting-House Hill" (A. Lowell), **II:** 522, 527
"Meeting in the Kitchen, The" (Schnackenberg), **Supp. XV:** 256
"Meeting of the Tisdale Fellows, The" (Huddle), **Supp. XXVI:** 155
"Meeting South, A" (Anderson), **I:** 115
"Meeting the Mountains" (Snyder), **Supp. VIII:** 300
Meeting Trees (Sanders), **Supp. XVI:** 269
Meet Me at the Morgue (Macdonald), **Supp. IV Part 2:** 472
Mehta, Sonny, **Supp. XI:** 178
Mehta, Ved, **Supp. XX: 87**
Meine, Curt, **Supp. XIV:** 179
Meiners, R. K., **IV:** 136, 137, 138, 140
Meinong, Alexius, **Supp. XIV:** 198, 199
Meisner, Sanford, **Supp. XIV:** 240, 242
Meister, Charles W., **II:** 112
Mejia, Jaime, **Supp. XIX:** 97
"Melancholia" (Dunbar), **Supp. II Part 1:** 194
Melancholy Baby (Parker), **Supp. XIX:** 186
"Melanctha" (Stein), **IV:** 30, 34, 35, 37, 38–40, 45
"Melancthon" (Moore), **III:** 212, 215
Melbourne House (S. and A. Warner), **Supp. XVIII:** 268
Meliboeus Hipponax (Lowell). *See Bigelow Papers, The* (Lowell)
Melinda and Melinda (Allen), **Supp. XV:** 16
Mellaart, James, **Supp. I Part 2:** 567
Mellard, James, **Supp. IV Part 1:** 387
Mellen, Joan, **Supp. XXIV:** 51, 52, 56, 64
Mellon, Andrew, **III:** 14
Mellor, W. M., **Supp. XX: 56**
Melnick, Jeffrey, **Supp. X:** 252
Melnick, Ralph, **Supp. XXVII:** 137–138; **Supp. XXVIII:** 147–148, 150–151, 158
Melnyczuk, Askold, **Supp. IV Part 1:** 70
Melodrama Play (Shepard), **Supp. III Part 2:** 440–441, 443, 445
Melodramatists, The (Nemerov), **III:** 268, 281–283, 284
Melopoeia (Espaillat and Tavano), **Supp. XXI:** 99–100
Melting-Pot, The (Zangwill), **I:** 229
"Melungeons" (Offutt), **Supp. XIX:** 171
Melville, Allan, **III:** 74, 77
Melville, Gansevoort, **III:** 76
Melville, Herman, **I:** 104, 106, 211, 288, 340, 343, 348, 354, 355, 561–562; **II:** 27, 74, 224–225, 228, 230, 232, 236, 255, 259, 271, 272, 277, 281, 295, 307, 311, 319, 320, 321, 418, 477, 497, 539–540, 545; **III:** 29, 45, 70, **74–98,** 359, 438, 453, 454, 507, 562–563, 572, 576; **IV:** 57, 105, 194, 199, 202, 250, 309, 333, 345, 350, 380, 444, 453; **Retro. Supp. I:** 54, 91, 160, 215, 220, **243–262; Retro. Supp. II:** 76; **Retro. Supp. III:** 147–164, 194,

223; **Supp. I Part 1:** 147, 238, 242, 249, 309, 317, 372; **Supp. I Part 2:** 383, 495, 579, 580, 582, 602; **Supp. IV Part 2:** 463, 613; **Supp. V:** 279, 281, 298, 308; **Supp. VIII:** 48, 103, 104, 105, 106, 108, 156, 175, 181, 188; **Supp. XI:** 83; **Supp. XII:** 282; **Supp. XIII:** 294, 305; **Supp. XIV:** 48, 227; **Supp. XV:** 287; **Supp. XVII:** 42, 185; **Supp. XVIII:** 1, 4, 6, 7, 9; **Supp. XXI:** 169; **Supp. XXII:** 174, 262; **Supp. XXIII:** 164, 165, 174, 190; **Supp. XXIV:** 88
Melville, Mrs. Herman (Elizabeth Shaw), **III:** 77, 91, 92
Melville, Maria Gansevoort, **III:** 74, 77, 85
Melville, Thomas, **III:** 77, 79, 92; **Supp. I Part 1:** 309
Melville, Whyte, **IV:** 309
Melville Goodwin, USA (Marquand), **III:** 60, 65–66
Melville's Marginalia (Cowen), **Supp. IV Part 2:** 435
"Melville's Marginalia" (Howe), **Supp. IV Part 2:** 435
Member of the Wedding, The (McCullers), **II:** 587, 592, 600–604, 605, 606; **Supp. VIII:** 124
"Meme Ortiz" (Cisneros), **Supp. VII:** 60
Memnon (song cycle) (Bowles), **Supp. IV Part 1:** 82
Memmott, Carol, **Supp. XXVI:** 209
Memnoch the Devil (Rice), **Supp. VII:** 289, 290, 294, 296–299
"Memoir" (Hempel), **Supp. XXI:** 118
"Memoir" (Untermeyer), **II:** 516–517
"Memoir, A" (Koch), **Supp. XV:** 184
Memoir from Antproof Case (Helprin), **Supp. XXV:** 84, 87
"Memoirist's Apology, A" (Karr), **Supp. XI:** 245, 246
Memoir of Mary Ann, A (O'Connor), **III:** 357
Memoir of Thomas McGrath, A (Beeching), **Supp. X:** 114, 118
Memoirs (W. Frank), **Supp. XX: 67, 69, 70, 81**
Memoirs of a Preacher, a Revelation of the Church and the Home, The (Lippard), **Supp. XXIII:** 178, 183–184, 188, 190
Memoirs of Arii Taimai (Adams), **I:** 2–3
"Memoirs of Carwin, the Biloquist" (Brown), **Supp. I Part 1:** 132
Memoirs of Hecate County (Wilson), **IV:** 429
Memoirs of Margaret Fuller Ossoli (Fuller), **Supp. II Part 1:** 280, 283, 285
"Memoirs of Stephen Calvert" (Brown), **Supp. I Part 1:** 133, 144
Memorabilia (Xenophon), **II:** 105
Memorable Providences (Mather), **Supp. II Part 2:** 458
Memorial, The: Portrait of a Family (Isherwood), **Supp. XIV:** 156, 159, 160–161
"Memorial Day" (Cameron), **Supp. XII:** 80, **82–83**

"Memorial for the City" (Auden), **Supp. II Part 1:** 20

"Memorial Rain" (MacLeish), **III:** 15

"Memorial to Ed Bland" (Brooks), **Supp. III Part 1:** 77

"Memorial Tribute" (Wilbur), **Supp. IV Part 2:** 642

"Memories" (Whittier), **Supp. I Part 2:** 699

Memories of a Catholic Girlhood (McCarthy), **II:** 560–561, 566; **Supp. XI:** 246; **Supp. XVI:** 64, 70

Memories of a Southern Woman of Letters (King), **Supp. XXVIII:** 111, 124–125

"Memories of East Texas" (Karr), **Supp. XI:** 239

"Memories of Uncle Neddy" (Bishop), **Retro. Supp. II:** 38; **Supp. I Part 1:** 73, 93

"Memories of West Street and Lepke" (R. Lowell), **II:** 550

"Memory" (Epstein), **Supp. XII:** 163

"Memory" (Everwine), **Supp. XV:** 82

"Memory, A" (Welty), **IV:** 261–262; **Retro. Supp. I:** 344–345

"Memory, Narrative, and the Discourses of Identity in *Abeng* and *No Telephone to Heaven*" (Smith), **Supp. XXII:** 70

"Memory, The" (Gioia), **Supp. XV:** 119

Memory and Enthusiasm: Essays, 1975–1985 (Di Piero), **Supp. XIX:** 34, 41, 42

"Memory and Imagination" (Hampl), **Supp. XXII:** 94

Memory Gardens (Creeley), **Supp. IV Part 1:** 141, 157

"Memory Harbor" (Skloot), **Supp. XX:** 201

Memory of Murder, A (Bradbury), **Supp. IV Part 1:** 103

Memory of Old Jack, The (Berry), **Supp. X:** 34

Memory of Two Mondays, A (A. Miller), **III:** 153, 156, 158–159, 160, 166

"Memory's Power" (Huddle), **Supp. XXVI:** 160

"Memo to Non-White Peoples" (Hughes), **Retro. Supp. I:** 209

"Men" (Boyle), **Supp. XXIV:** 61

Men, Women and Ghosts (A. Lowell), **II:** 523–524

"Menace of the Peyote, The" (Zitkala-Ša), **Supp. XXV:** 281

Menaker, Charlotte, **Supp. XIX:** 266

Menaker, Daniel, **Supp. VIII:** 151; **Supp. XXIII:** 276

Menand, Louis, **Supp. XIV:** 40, 197; **Supp. XVI:** 106, 107; **Supp. XXIII:** 104–105

Men and Angels (Gordon), **Supp. IV Part 1:** 304–305, 306, 308

Men and Brethen (Cozzens), **I:** 363–365, 368, 375, 378, 379

Men and Cartoons (Lethem), **Supp. XVIII:** 145, **148**

"Men and Women" (R. Bly), **Supp. IV Part 1:** 72

"Men at Forty" (Justice), **Supp. VII:** 126–127

Mencius (Meng-tzu), **IV:** 183

Mencken, August, **III:** 100, 108

Mencken, August, Jr., **III:** 99, 109, 118–119

Mencken, Mrs. August (Anna Abhau), **III:** 100, 109

Mencken, Burkhardt, **III:** 100, 108

Mencken, Charles, **III:** 99

Mencken, Gertrude, **III:** 99

Mencken, H. L., **I:** 199, 210, 212, 235, 245, 261, 405, 514, 515, 517; **II:** 25, 27, 42, 89, 90, 91, 271, 289, 430, 443, 449; **III:** **99–121**, 394, 482; **IV:** 76, 432, 440, 475, 482; **Retro. Supp. I:** 1, 101; **Retro. Supp. II:** 97, 98, 102, 265; **Supp. I Part 2:** 484, 629–630, 631, 647, 651, 653, 659, 673; **Supp. II Part 1:** 136; **Supp. IV Part 1:** 201, 314, 343; **Supp. IV Part 2:** 521, 692, 693; **Supp. XI:** 163–164, 166; **Supp. XIII:** 161; **Supp. XIV:** 111; **Supp. XV:** 297, 301, 303; **Supp. XVI:** 187–188, 189; **Supp. XVII:** 106; **Supp. XXII:** 23, 187, 277; **Supp. XXIV:** 26, 281; **Supp. XXVII:** 86

Mencken, Mrs. H. L. (Sara Haardt), **III:** 109, 111

"Men Deified Because of Their Cruelty" (Simic), **Supp. VIII:** 282

Mendelbaum, Paul, **Supp. V:** 159

Mendele, **IV:** 3, 10

Mendelief, Dmitri Ivanovich, **IV:** 421

Mendelsohn, Daniel, **Supp. X:** 153, 154; **Supp. XV:** 257, 258, 261, 266

Mendelsohn, Jack, **Supp. XXIV:** 72, 77

Mendelsohn, Jane, **Supp. XXVI:** 158

Mendelssohn, Moses, **Supp. XXIII:** 4; **Supp. XXVIII:** 155

Mendes, Alfred, **Supp. XXI:** 160

Mending Skins (Gansworth), **Supp. XXVI:** 103, 104, 106

"Mending Wall" (Frost), **II:** 153–154; **Retro. Supp. I:** 128, 130; **Retro. Supp. III:** 97, 98; **Supp. X:** 64

"Meneseteung" (Munro), **Supp. XXVII:** 190–191

Men from the Boys, The (Lacy), **Supp. XV:** 202, 205

"Menielle" (Stallings), **Supp. XXV:** 223

Men in the Off Hours (Carson), **Supp. XII:** **111–113**

"Men in the Storm, The" (Crane), **I:** 411

"Men Loved Wholly Beyond Wisdom" (Bogan), **Supp. III Part 1:** 50

"Men Made Out of Words" (Stevens), **IV:** 88

Men Must Act (Mumford), **Supp. II Part 2:** 479

Mennes, John, **II:** 111

Mennoti, Gian Carlo, **Supp. IV Part 1:** 84

Men of Brewster Place, The (Naylor), **Supp. VIII:** 213, **228–230**

"Men of Color, to Arms!" (Douglass), **Supp. III Part 1:** 171

Men of Good Hope: A Story of American Progressives (Aaron), **Supp. I Part 2:** 650

Mens' Club, The (film), **Supp. XVI:** 212–213

Men's Club, The (L. Michaels), **Supp. XVI:** 206, **210–212**

"Men's Sauna" (Huddle), **Supp. XXVI:** 150

"Menstruation at Forty" (Sexton), **Supp. II Part 2:** 686

"Mental Hospital Garden, The" (W. C. Williams), **Retro. Supp. I:** 428

Mental Radio (Sinclair), **Supp. V:** 289

Mentoria; or, The Young Lady's Friend (Rowson), **Supp. XV:** **233–234**, 238

"Men We Carry in Our Minds, The" (Sanders), **Supp. XVI:** 273

Men Who Made the Nation, The (Dos Passos), **I:** 485

"*Men Who Raised the Dead, The*" (Rash), **Supp. XXVII:** 220

Men Without Women (Hemingway), **II:** 249; **Retro. Supp. I:** 170, 176; **Supp. IX:** 202

"Merced" (Rich), **Supp. I Part 2:** 563

"Mercedes" (E. Stoddard), **Supp. XV:** 278

"Mercedes Hospital" (Bishop), **Retro. Supp. II:** 51

"Mercenary, A" (Ozick), **Supp. V:** 267

Mercer, Johnny, **Supp. XXII:** 6

Merchandising (Hwang), **Supp. XXI:** 147

Merchant of Venice, The (Shakespeare), **IV:** 227; **Supp. XIV:** 325

Merchants of Venice (Shakespeare), **Supp. XXVIII:** 153

Mercury Theatre, **Retro. Supp. I:** 65

Mercy, A (Morrison), **Retro. Supp. III:** 185, 197–198

Mercy, Pity, Peace, and Love (Ozick), **Supp. V:** 257, 258

Mercy, The (Levine), **Supp. V:** 194–195

Mercy of a Rude Stream (H. Roth), **Supp. IX:** 231, 234, **235–242**

"Mercy"(P. Benedict), **Supp. XXIII:** 49

Mercy Philbrick's Choice (Jackson), **Retro. Supp. I:** 26, 27, 33

Mercy Street (Sexton), **Supp. II Part 2:** 683, 689

"Mercy"(Thompson), **Supp. XXIII:** 295, 296

Meredith, George, **II:** 175, 186; **Supp. IV Part 1:** 300

Meredith, Mary. *See* Webb, Mary

Meredith, William, **II:** 545; **Retro. Supp. II:** 181

"Merely by Wilderness" (Peacock), **Supp. XIX:** 199

"Merely to Know" (Rich), **Supp. I Part 2:** 554

"Mère Pochette" (Jewett), **II:** 400

"Merger II, The" (Auchincloss), **Supp. IV Part 1:** 34

Meri (Asch), **Supp. XXIII:** 5, 11

"Mericans" (Cisneros), **Supp. VII:** 69

"Merida, 1969" (Matthews), **Supp. IX:** 151

"Meridian" (Clampitt), **Supp. IX:** **48–49**

Meridian (Walker), **Supp. III Part 2:** 520, 524, 527, 528, 531–537

Mérimée, Prosper, **II:** 322

Merington, Marguerite, **Supp. XXVIII:** 228

Meriwether, James B., **Retro Supp. I:** 77, 91

"Meriwether Connection, The" (Cowley), **Supp. II Part 1:** 142

Merker, Kim K., **Supp. XI:** 261; **Supp. XV:** 75, 77

"Merlin" (Emerson), **II:** 19, 20

Merlin (Robinson), **III:** 522

"Merlin Enthralled" (Wilbur), **Supp. III Part 2:** 544, 554

"Mermother" (A. Finch), **Supp. XVII:** 72

Merril, Judith, **Supp. XVI:** 123

Merrill, Cavafy, Poems, and Dreams (Hadas), **Supp. XXIII: 123–124**

Merrill, Christopher, **Supp. XI:** 329

Merrill, Flora, **Retro. Supp. III:** 33

Merrill, James, **Retro. Supp. I:** 296; **Retro. Supp. II:** 53; **Supp. III Part 1: 317–338; Supp. III Part 2:** 541, 561; **Supp. IX:** 40, 42, 48, 52; **Supp. X:** 73; **Supp. XI:** 123, 131, 249; **Supp. XII:** 44, 254, 255, 256, 261–262, 269–270; **Supp. XIII:** 76, 85; **Supp. XV:** 249, 250, 253; **Supp. XVII:** 123; **Supp. XXIII:** 112, 122, 123; **Supp. XXV:** 222, 227–228; **Supp. XXVI:** 67

Merrill, Mark (pseudonym). *See* Markson, David

Merrill, Robert, **Retro. Supp. II:** 201

Merrill, Ronald, **Supp. IV Part 2:** 521

Merritt, A., **Supp. XXV:** 122

Merritt, Abraham, **Supp. XVII:** 58

Merritt, Theresa, **Supp. VIII:** 332

Merritt, Vernon, **Supp. XXII:** 245

"Merry-Go-Round" (Hughes), **Retro. Supp. I:** 194, 205; **Supp. I Part 1:** 333

Merry-Go-Round, The (Van Vechten), **Supp. II Part 2:** 734, 735

Merry Month of May, The (Jones), **Supp. XI: 227–228**

Merry Widow, The (Lehar), **III:** 183

Merton, Thomas, **III:** 357; **Supp. VIII: 193–212; Supp. XXII:** 83, 90; **Supp. XXIV:** 133

Merwin, W. S., **Supp. III Part 1: 339–360; Supp. III Part 2:** 541; **Supp. IV Part 2:** 620, 623, 626; **Supp. IX:** 152, 155, 290; **Supp. V:** 332; **Supp. XIII:** 274, 277; **Supp. XIX:** 82; **Supp. XV:** 222, 342; **Supp. XXI:** 95; **Supp. XXVI:** 67, 68; **Supp. XXVIII:** 196

Meryman, Richard, **Supp. IV Part 2:** 579, 583

Meshiekhs tsaytn (Times of the Messiah) (Asch), **Supp. XXIII:** 5

Meshugah (Singer), **Retro. Supp. II: 315–316**

Mesic, Michael, **Supp. IV Part 1:** 175

Mesic, Penelope, **Supp. X:** 15

Message in the Bottle, The (Percy), **Supp. III Part 1:** 387–388, 393, 397

"Message in the Bottle, The" (Percy), **Supp. III Part 1:** 388

"Message of Flowers and Fire and Flowers, The" (Brooks), **Supp. III Part 1:** 69

Messengers Will Come No More, The (Fiedler), **Supp. XIII:** 103

Messerli, Douglas, **Supp. XVI:** 293

Messiah (Vidal), **Supp. IV Part 2:** 677, 680, 681–682, 685, 691, 692

"Messiah, The" (Wasserstein), **Supp. XV:** 328

Messiah of Stockholm, The (Ozick), **Supp. V:** 270–271; **Supp. XVII:** 42

"Mess of Pork, A"(Arnow), **Supp. XXVIII:** 2

Messud, Claire, **Supp. XVIII:** 98

Metamorphic Tradition in Modern Poetry (Quinn), **IV:** 421

Metamorphoses (Golding, trans.), **Supp. XXV:** 226

Metamorphoses (Ovid), **II:** 542–543; **III:** 467, 468; **Supp. XV:** 33; **Supp. XVI:** 20; **Supp. XX:** 280; **Supp. XXIV:** 132

Metamorphoses (Pound, trans.), **III:** 468–469

"Metamorphosis" (Huddle), **Supp. XXVI:** 151

Metamorphosis, The (Kafka), **IV:** 438; **Retro. Supp. II:** 287–288; **Supp. VIII:** 3; **Supp. XXI:** 89

"Metamorphosis and Survival" (Woodcock), **Supp. XIII:** 33

"Metaphor as Mistake" (Percy), **Supp. III Part 1:** 387–388

"Metaphor for Guatemala, A: The Long Night of White Chickens"(Perera), **Supp. XXV:** 50

Metaphor & Memory: Essays (Ozick), **Supp. V:** 272

Metaphor of Trees and Last Poems (Bronk), **Supp. XXI:** 32

"Metaphors of a Magnifico" (Stevens), **IV:** 92

Metaphysical Club, The (Menand), **Supp. XIV:** 40, 197

"Metaphysical Poets, The" (Eliot), **I:** 527, 586

"Metaphysics" (Ginsberg), **Supp. II Part 1:** 313

Metcalf, Paul, **Supp. XIV:** 96; **Supp. XXIII:** 163, 174

"Meteor, The" (Bradbury), **Supp. IV Part 1:** 102

Methinks the Lady...(Endore), **Supp. XVII:** 61–62

"Metonymy as an Approach to the Real World" (Bronk), **Supp. XXI:** 30

Metress, Christopher P., **Supp. V:** 314

Metrical History of Christianity, The (Taylor), **IV:** 163

"Metrical Regularity" (Lovecraft), **Supp. XXV:** 120

Metropolis, The (Sinclair), **Supp. V:** 285

"Metropolitan Tower, The" (Teasdale), **Supp. XXVII:** 286, 289

"Metterling Lists, The" (Allen), **Supp. XV:** 15

"Metzengerstein" (Poe), **III:** 411, 417

Mew, Charlotte, **Retro. Supp. II:** 247

Mewshaw, Michael, **Supp. V:** 57; **Supp. X:** 82

Mexican Enough: My Life Between the Borderlines (Griest), **Supp. XXVIII:** 97, 100, 106–110

"Mexican Hands" (Ryan as Quin), **Supp. XVIII:** 227

"Mexico" (R. Lowell), **II:** 553, 554

"Mexico, Age Four" (Salinas), **Supp. XIII:** 315

Mexico City Blues (Kerouac), **Supp. III Part 1:** 225, 229

"Mexico Is a Foreign Country: Five Studies in Naturalism" (Warren), **IV:** 241, 252

"Mexico's Children" (Rodriguez), **Supp. XIV:** 302

Meyer, Carolyn, **Supp. XIX:** 194–195, 197

Meyer, Donald B., **III:** 298

Meyer, Ellen Hope, **Supp. V:** 123

Meyer, Robert, **Supp. XXI:** 23

Meyers, Jeffrey, **Retro. Supp. I:** 124, 138; **Retro. Supp. II:** 191

Meynell, Alice, **Supp. I Part 1:** 220

Mezey, Robert, **Supp. IV Part 1:** 60; **Supp. V:** 180; **Supp. XIII:** 312; **Supp. XV:** 74

Mezzanine, The (Baker), **Supp. XIII: 41–43,** 44, 45, 48, 55

"Mezzo Cammin" (Longfellow), **II:** 490

"Mi Abuelo" (Ríos), **Supp. IV Part 2:** 541

Miami (Didion), **Supp. IV Part 1:** 199, 210

Miami and the Siege of Chicago (Mailer), **Retro. Supp. II:** 206

Miasma (Holding), **Supp. XXII: 121–122**

"Michael" (Wordsworth), **III:** 523

Michael, Magali Cornier, **Supp. XIII:** 32

"Michael Angelo: A Fragment" (Longfellow), **II:** 490, 494, 495, 506; **Retro. Supp. II:** 167

"Michael Egerton" (Price), **Supp. VI:** 257–258, 260

Michael Kohlhaas (Kleist), **Supp. IV Part 1:** 224

Michael O'Halloran (Stratton-Porter), **Supp. XX: 222**

Michaels, Leonard, **Supp. XVI: 201–215**

Michaels, Walter Benn, **Retro. Supp. I:** 115, 369, 379

Michael Scarlett (Cozens), **I:** 358–359, 378

"Michael's Veterans Remember" (Espaillat), **Supp. XXI:** 110

Michaux, Henri, **Supp. XVI:** 288; **Supp. XXVIII:** 138–139

Michelangelo, **I:** 18; **II:** 11–12; **III:** 124; **Supp. I Part 1:** 363; **Supp. XVII:** 112

Michel-Michot, Paulette, **Supp. XI:** 224–225

Michelson, Albert, **IV:** 27

"Michigan Avenue" (Hecht), **Supp. XXVII:** 85

Mickelsson's Ghosts (Gardner), **Supp. VI:** 63, **73–74**

Mickiewicz, Adam, **Supp. II Part 1:** 299

"Microscope" (Trethewey), **Supp. XXI:** 251

Midair (Conroy), **Supp. XVI:** 63, **71–72**

"Mid-Air" (Conroy), **Supp. XVI:** 69, 71

Mid-American Chants (Anderson), **I:** 109, 114

"Midas" (Winters), **Supp. II Part 2:** 801

"Mid-August at Sourdough Mountain Lookout" (Snyder), **Supp. VIII:** 292–293

Midcentury (Dos Passos), **I:** 474, 475, 478, 490, 492–494; **Supp. I Part 2:** 646

Mid-Century American Poets, **III:** 532

Mid-Channel (Lewisohn), **Supp. XXVIII:** 151, 152, 156

"Mid-Day" (Doolittle), **Supp. I Part 1:** 266–267

"Middle Age" (R. Lowell), **II:** 550

"Middle-Aged, Middle-Class Woman at Midnight, A" (Taggard), **Supp. XXII:** 282–283

"Middleaged Man, The" (Simpson), **Supp. IX:** 274–275

Middle Ages, The (Gurney), **Supp. V:** 96, 105, 108

Middlebrook, Diane Wood, **Supp. IV Part 2:** 444, 451; **Supp. XXVI:** 66

"Middle Daughter, The" (Kingsolver), **Supp. VII:** 209

Middlemarch (G. Eliot), **I:** 457, 459; **II:** 290, 291; **Retro. Supp. I:** 225; **Supp. I Part 1:** 174; **Supp. IX:** 43; **Supp. XI:** 68; **Supp. XII:** 335

Middle of My Tether, The: Familiar Essays (Epstein), **Supp. XIV: 106–107**

"Middle of Nowhere, The" (Wagoner), **Supp. IX:** 327–328

Middle of the Journey, The (Trilling), **Supp. III Part 2:** 495, 504–506

"Middle of the Way" (Kinnell), **Supp. III Part 1:** 242

Middle Passage (C. Johnson), **Supp. VI: 194–196,** 198, 199; **Supp. XIII:** 182

"Middle Passage" (Hayden), **Supp. II Part 1:** 363, 375–376

Middlesex (Eugenides), **Supp. XXIV:** 131, 134–135, **138–142**

"Middle Toe of the Right Foot, The" (Bierce), **I:** 203

Middleton, Thomas, **Retro. Supp. I:** 62

"Middle Way, The"(Hadas), **Supp. XXIII:** 121

Middle Years, The (James), **II:** 337–338; **Retro. Supp. I:** 235

"Middle Years, The" (James), **Retro. Supp. I:** 228, 272

"Midnight" (Dunn), **Supp. XI:** 147

"Midnight Consultations, The" (Freneau), **Supp. II Part 1:** 257

Midnight Cry, A (Mather), **Supp. II Part 2:** 460

"Midnight Gladness" (Levertov), **Supp. III Part 1:** 284–285

Midnight Lantern (Gallagher), **Supp. XXIV:** 167, 171

"Midnight Lantern" (Gallagher), **Supp. XXIV:** 171

"Midnight Magic" (Mason), **Supp. VIII:** 146

Midnight Magic: Selected Stories of Bobbie Ann Mason (Mason), **Supp. VIII:** 148

Midnight Mass (Bowles), **Supp. IV Part 1:** 93

"Midnight Postscript" (F. Wright), **Supp. XVII:** 245, 246

Midnight Queen, The (Lippard), **Supp. XXIII:** 180

"Midnight Salvage" (Rich), **Retro. Supp. III:** 252

Midnight Salvage: Poems 1995–1998 (Rich), **Retro. Supp. III:** 252

"Midnight Show" (Shapiro), **Supp. II Part 2:** 705

"Midpoint" (Updike), **Retro. Supp. I:** 321, 323, 327, 330, 335

Midpoint and Other Poems (Updike), **IV:** 214

"Midrash on Happiness" (Paley), **Supp. VI:** 217

"Midsummer" (Bronk), **Supp. XXI:** 30

"Midsummer in the Blueberry Barrens" (Clampitt), **Supp. IX:** 40–41

"Midsummer Letter" (Carruth), **Supp. XVI:** 47

Midsummer Night's Dream, A (Shakespeare), **Supp. I Part 1:** 369–370; **Supp. X:** 69

Midsummer Night's Sex Comedy, A (film; Allen), **Supp. XV:** 8

"Midwest" (Stafford), **Supp. XI:** 317

"Midwest Poetics" (C. Baxter), **Supp. XVII:** 18

Mieder, Wolfgang, **Supp. XIV:** 126

Mies van der Rohe, Ludwig, **Supp. IV Part 1:** 40

Mighty Aphrodite (film; Allen), **Supp. XV:** 11

"Mighty Fortress, A" (Leopold), **Supp. XIV:** 185

"Mighty Lord, The (Rowson), **Supp. XV:** 243

"Migration, The" (Tate), **IV:** 130

Mihailovitch, Bata, **Supp. VIII:** 272

Mikado, The (Gilbert and Sullivan), **Supp. XXI:** 151

Miklitsch, Robert, **Supp. IV Part 2:** 628, 629

Mikolowski, Ken and Ann, **Supp. XXIV:** 43

Mila 18 (Uris), **Supp. IV Part 1:** 379; **Supp. XX: 244, 247, 248, 251–252, 253**

Milagro Beanfield War, The (film), **Supp. XIII:** 267

Milagro Beanfield War, The (Nichols), **Supp. XIII:** 253, **265–266**

Milburn, Michael, **Supp. XI:** 239, 242

Milch, David, **Supp. XI:** 348

Mild Day, The (Bronk), **Supp. XXI:** 32

Miles, Barry, **Supp. XII:** 123

Miles, Diana, **Retro. Supp. III:** 139

Miles, Jack, **Supp. VIII:** 86

Miles, Josephine, **Supp. XIII:** 275; **Supp. XXVIII:** 259–260

Miles, Julie, **I:** 199

Miles, Kitty, **I:** 199

"Miles of Night, The" (Halliday), **Supp. XIX:** 91

Milestone, Lewis, **Supp. I Part 1:** 281

Milestones (Kramer), **Supp. XXVI:** 26

Miles Wallingford (Cooper). *See Afloat and Ashore* (Cooper)

Milford, Kate, **Supp. XVIII:** 150

Milford, Nancy, **II:** 83; **Supp. IX:** 60

Milhaud, Darius, **Supp. IV Part 1:** 81

Miligate, Michael, **IV:** 123, 130, 132

"Militant Nudes" (Hardwick), **Supp. III Part 1:** 210–211

"Military Parachuting Exercise" (Huddle), **Supp. XXVI:** 150, 153

Milk (film), **Supp. XX: 269**

"Milk Bottles" (Anderson), **I:** 114

"Milk Prose" (Weigl), **Supp. XIX:** 278

Milk Train Doesn't Stop Here Anymore, The (T. Williams), **IV:** 382, 383, 384, 386, 390, 391, 392, 393, 394, 395, 398

Mill, James, **II:** 357

Mill, John Stuart, **III:** 294–295; **Supp. XI:** 196; **Supp. XIV:** 22

Millar, Kenneth. *See* Macdonald, Ross

Millar, Margaret (Margaret Sturm), **Supp. IV Part 2:** 464, 465

Millay, Cora, **III:** 123, 133–134, 135–136

Millay, Edna St. Vincent, **I:** 482; **II:** 530; **III: 122–144; IV:** 433, 436; **Retro. Supp. II:** 48; **Supp. I Part 2:** 707, 714, 726; **Supp. IV Part 1:** 168; **Supp. IV Part 2:** 607; **Supp. IX:** 20; **Supp. V:** 113; **Supp. XIV:** 120, 121, 122, 127; **Supp. XV:** 42, 46, 51, 250, 293, 307; **Supp. XVII:** 69, 75, 96; **Supp. XXII:** 273; **Supp. XXIII:** 164; **Supp. XXVI:** 170, 171; **Supp. XXVII:** 261, 283, 284

Millennium Approaches (Kushner), **Supp. IX:** 141, 142, 145

Miller, Arthur, **I:** 81, 94; **III: 145–169; Retro. Supp. III: 165–181,** 313; **Supp. IV Part 1:** 359; **Supp. IV Part 2:** 574; **Supp. VIII:** 334; **Supp. XIII:** 127; **Supp. XIV:** 102, 239; **Supp. XVI:** 194

Miller, Mrs. Arthur (Ingeborg Morath), **III:** 162–163

Miller, Mrs. Arthur (Marilyn Monroe), **III:** 161, 162–163

Miller, Mrs. Arthur (Mary Grace Slattery), **III:** 146, 161

Miller, Brown, **Supp. IV Part 1:** 67

Miller, Carol, **Supp. IV Part 1:** 400, 405, 409, 410, 411

Miller, Caroline, **Supp. XXII: 187–201**

Miller, Danny L., **Supp. XXVIII:** 2

Miller, Henry, **I:** 97, 157; **III:** 40, **170–192; IV:** 138; **Retro. Supp. II:** 327; **Supp. I Part 2:** 546; **Supp. V:** 119, 131; **Supp. X:** 183, 185, 187, 194, 195; **Supp. XIII:** 1, 17; **Supp. XXII:** 88, 256, 257, 258; **Supp. XXIII:** 100; **Supp. XXIV:** 52, 281

Miller, Henry (actor), **Supp. XVI:** 182

Miller, Herman, **Supp. I Part 2:** 614, 617

Miller, James E., Jr., **IV:** 352

Miller, Jean Baker, **Supp. XXII:** 18

Miller, Jeffrey, **Supp. IV Part 1:** 95

Miller, J. Hillis, **Supp. IV Part 1:** 387

Miller, Jim Wayne, **Supp. XX: 161–176; Supp. XXIII:** 39

Miller, Joaquin, **I:** 193, 195, 459; **Supp. II Part 1:** 351

Miller, John Duncan, **Supp. I Part 2:** 604

Miller, John E., **Supp. XXII:** 295

Miller, John M., **Supp. XXII:** 214, 218

Miller, Jonathan, **Retro. Supp. II:** 181

Miller, Laura, **Supp. XIII:** 48; **Supp. XIX:** 53, 54, 56; **Supp. XXII:** 239; **Supp. XXV:** 12, 13
Miller, Marilyn, **Supp. XVI:** 187
Miller, Matt, **Supp. XV:** 211
Miller, Matthew, **Supp. XVI:** 47, 51
Miller, Orilla, **Supp. I Part 1:** 48
Miller, Perry, **I:** 546, 547, 549, 550, 560; **IV:** 186; **Supp. I Part 1:** 31, 104; **Supp. I Part 2:** 484; **Supp. IV Part 2:** 422; **Supp. VIII:** 101; **Supp. XXV:** 251
Miller, R. Baxter, **Retro. Supp. I:** 195, 207
Miller, Rebecca, **Retro. Supp. III:** 177
Miller, Robert Ellis, **II:** 588
Miller, Ruth, **Supp. X:** 324
Miller, Stuart, **Supp. XVI:** 242
Miller, Sue, **Supp. X:** 77, 85; **Supp. XI:** 190; **Supp. XII: 289–305**
Miller of Old Church, The (Glasgow), **II:** 175, 181
"Miller's Tale" (Chaucer), **III:** 283
Miller Williams and the Poetry of the Particular (Burns), **Supp. XV:** 339
Millet, Lydia, **Supp. XXVIII:** 221
Millett, Kate, **Supp. X:** 193, 196
Millgate, Michael, **Retro. Supp. I:** 91
Mill Hand's Lunch Bucket (Bearden), **Supp. VIII:** 337
Millhauser, Steven, **Supp. XXII:** 49
Millier, Brett C., **Retro. Supp. II:** 39
Milligan, Bryce, **Supp. XIII:** 274, 275, 277
Million Little Pieces, A (Frey), **Supp. XXII:** 95; **Supp. XXIII:** 109; **Supp. XXIV:** 230, 236
Millions of Strange Shadows (Hecht), **Supp. X:** 57, **62–65**
"Million Young Workmen, 1915, A" (Sandburg), **III:** 585
Millroy the Magician (Theroux), **Supp. VIII:** 325
Mills, Alice, **Supp. XIII:** 233
Mills, Benjamin Fay, **III:** 176
Mills, C. Wright, **Supp. I Part 2:** 648, 650
Mills, Florence, **Supp. I Part 1:** 322
Mills, Ralph J., Jr., **III:** 530; **Supp. IV Part 1:** 64; **Supp. XI:** 311
Mills, Tedi López, **Supp. XVI:** 281
Mills of the Kavanaughs, The (R. Lowell), **II:** 542–543, 546, 550; **III:** 508; **Retro. Supp. II:** 178, 179, 188; **Supp. XXIII:** 211
"Mills of the Kavanaughs, The" (R. Lowell), **II:** 542–543
Milne, A. A., **Supp. IX:** 189; **Supp. XXIV:** 132, 133
Milne, A. J. M., **I:** 278
Milosz, Czeslaw, **Supp. III Part 2:** 630; **Supp. VIII:** 20, 22; **Supp. XI:** 267, 312; **Supp. XVII:** 241; **Supp. XX: 165; Supp. XXI:** 132; **Supp. XXII:** 92; **Supp. XXIII:** 134, 140
Miltner, Robert, **Supp. XI:** 142
Milton, Edith, **Supp. VIII:** 79; **Supp. X:** 82
Milton, John, **I:** 6, 138, 273, 587–588; **II:** 11, 15, 113, 130, 411, 540, 542;

III: 40, 124, 201, 225, 274, 468, 471, 486, 487, 503, 511; **IV:** 50, 82, 126, 137, 155, 157, 241, 279, 347, 422, 461, 494; **Retro. Supp. I:** 60, 67, 127, 360; **Retro. Supp. II:** 161, 295; **Retro. Supp. III:** 104; **Supp. I Part 1:** 124, 150, 370; **Supp. I Part 2:** 412, 422, 491, 501, 522, 622, 722, 724; **Supp. IV Part 2:** 430, 634; **Supp. VIII:** 294; **Supp. X:** 22, 23, 36; **Supp. XII:** 180; **Supp. XIV:** 5, 7; **Supp. XX: 108; Supp. XXIII:** 122; **Supp. XXIV:** 159
Milton, John R., **Supp. IV Part 2:** 503
Milton and His Modern Critics (L. P. Smith), **Supp. XIV:** 347
"Milton by Firelight" (Snyder), **Supp. II Part 1:** 314; **Supp. VIII:** 294
"Miltonic Sonnet, A" (Wilbur), **Supp. III Part 2:** 558
Mimesis (Auerbach), **III:** 453
"Mimnermos and the Motions of Hedonism" (Carson), **Supp. XII: 99–100**
"Mimnermos Interviews, The" (Carson), **Supp. XII: 100–101**
Mims, Edwin, **Supp. I Part 1:** 362, 364, 365, 371
"Mind" (Wilbur), **Supp. III Part 2:** 554
"Mind, The" (Kinnell), **Supp. III Part 1:** 245
Mind Breaths: Poems 1972–1977 (Ginsberg), **Supp. II Part 1:** 326
Mindfield: New and Selected Poems (Corso), **Supp. XII: 136**
"Mind in the Modern World" (Trilling), **Supp. III Part 2:** 512
"Mind Is Shapely, Art Is Shapely" (Ginsberg), **Supp. II Part 1:** 327
Mindlin, Henrique, **Supp. I Part 1:** 92
Mind of My Mind (O. Butler), **Supp. XIII:** 62, 63
Mind of Primitive Man, The (Boas), **Supp. XIV:** 209
Mind-Reader, The (Wilbur), **Supp. III Part 2:** 560–562
"Mind-Reader, The" (Wilbur), **Supp. III Part 2:** 561–562
"Mind's Landscape on an Early Winter Day, The" (Bronk), **Supp. XXI:** 28
"Mind's Own Place, The" (Oppen), **Supp. XXVI:** 227
Mindwheel (Pinsky), **Supp. VI:** 235
Minear, Richard H., **Supp. XVI:** 101, 102
"Mined Country" (Wilbur), **Supp. III Part 2:** 546–548
"Minefields" (Espaillat), **Supp. XXI:** 106
"Mine Own John Berryman" (Levine), **Supp. V:** 179–180
Miner, Bob, **Supp. V:** 23
Miner, Earl, **III:** 466, 479
Miner, Madonne, **Supp. XIII:** 29
Miner, Valerie, **Supp. XXIII:** 295, 296
"Minerva Writes Poems" (Cisneros), **Supp. VII:** 63–64, 66
Mingus, Charles, **Supp. IX:** 152
"Mingus in Diaspora" (Matthews), **Supp. IX:** 166
"Mingus in Shadow" (Matthews), **Supp. IX:** 168–169
Ming Yellow (Marquand), **III:** 56
"Minimal, The" (Roethke), **III:** 531–532

Minimus Poems, The (X. J. Kennedy), **Supp. XV:** 169–170
"Mini-novela: *Rosa y sus espinas"* (Mora), *Supp. XIII:* 218
"Minions of Midas, The" (London), **II:** 474–475
Minister's Charge, The, or The Apprenticeship of Lemuel Barber (Howells), **II:** 285–286, 287
Minister's Wooing, The (Stowe), **II:** 541
"Minister's Wooing, The" (Stowe), **Supp. I Part 2:** 592–595
"Ministration of Our Departed Friends, The" (Stowe), **Supp. I Part 2:** 586–587
Minna and Myself (Bodenheim), **Supp. XXV:** 21
"Minneapolis Poem, The" (Wright), **Supp. III Part 2:** 601–602
Minnesota Grain Show, The (radio, Keillor), **Supp. XVI:** 170
"Minnesota Transcendentalist" (Peseroff), **Supp. IV Part 1:** 71
Minnie, Temple, **II:** 344
Minock, Daniel, **Supp. XXVI:** 187
Minority Report: H. L. Mencken's Notebooks (Mencken), **III:** 112
Minor Pleasures of Life, The (Macaulay), **Supp. XIV:** 348
"Minor Poems" (Eliot), **I:** 579
"Minor Poet" (Hay), **Supp. XIV:** 127
"Minor Topics" (Howells), **II:** 274
Minot, Stephen, **Supp. XXIII:** 290
Minot, Susan, **Supp. VI: 203–215**
"Minotaur Loves His Labyrinth, The" (Simic), **Supp. VIII:** 270, 279, 281
"Minstrel Man" (Hughes), **Supp. I Part 1:** 325
Mint (Nye), **Supp. XIII:** 277
"Minting Time" (Sarton), **Supp. VIII:** 259
Mint Snowball (Nye), **Supp. XIII:** 277–278, **284–285**
"Mint Snowball" (Nye), **Supp. XIII:** 278, 284
"Mint Snowball II" (Nye), **Supp. XIII:** 284, 285
Minty Alley (C. L. R. James), **Supp. XXI:** 159, 161
Mintz, Susannah B., **Supp. XXVI:** 52
Mintzlaff, Dorothy, **Supp. XV:** 153
Minus, Marian, **Supp. XVIII:** 282
Minutes to Go (Corso, Gysin, Beiles and Burroughs), **Supp. XII:** 129
Mi querido Rafa (Hinojosa). See *Dear Rafe* (Hinojosa)
Mirabai: Ecstatic Poems (Hirshfield and Bly, trans.), **Supp. XXIII:** 136
Mirabell: Books of Number (Merrill), **Supp. III Part 1:** 332–334
"Miracle" (Carver), **Supp. III Part 1:** 139–140
Miracle at St. Anna (film, Lee), **Supp. XXVI:** 199
Miracle at St. Anna (McBride), **Supp. XXVI:** 194–199
Miracle at Verdun (Chlumberg), **Supp. XIX:** 242
Miracle Boy and Other Stories (P. Benedict), **Supp. XXIII:** 35, **45–50**

"Miracle Boy"(P. Benedict), **Supp. XXIII:** 45–46, 50

"Miracle for Breakfast, A" (Bishop), **Retro. Supp. II:** 43

Miracle of Catfish, A (L. Brown), **Supp. XXI:** 39–40, 47, **48**

"Miracle of Lava Canyon, The" (Henry), **Supp. II Part 1:** 389, 390

Miracle of Mindfulness, The: A Manual on Meditation (Thich Nhat Hanh), **Supp. V:** 199–200

Miracle's Boys (miniseries), **Supp. XXVIII:** 282

Miracle's Boys (Woodson), **Supp. XXVIII:** 280, 282

Mirage (Masters), **Supp. I Part 2:** 459, 470, 471

"Mirages, The" (Hayden), **Supp. II Part 1:** 373

"Miranda" (Buck), **Supp. II Part 1:** 128

Miranda, Carmen, **Supp. XII:** 165

Miranda, Francisco de, **Supp. I Part 2:** 522

"Miranda Over the Valley" (Dubus), **Supp. VII:** 81–83

"Miriam" (Capote), **Supp. III Part 1:** 117, 120, 122

"Miriam" (Whittier), **Supp. I Part 2:** 691, 703

"Miriam Tazewell" (Ransom), **Supp. X:** 58

"Mirror" (Merrill), **Supp. III Part 1:** 322

"Mirror" (Plath), **Retro. Supp. II:** 248–249, 257

"Mirror" (Rash), **Supp. XXVII:** 222

"Mirror, The" (Glück), **Supp. V:** 83

"Mirror, The"(Hadas), **Supp. XXIII:** 116

"Mirroring Evil: Nazi Images/Recent Art" (Epstein), **Supp. XII:** 166

"Mirror of Leopold Leopoldovitch Siegelevsky, The" (Siegel), **Supp. XXII:** 257–258

Mirrors (Creeley), **Supp. IV Part 1:** 156

Mirrors and Windows (Nemerov), **III:** 269, 275–277

Mirrors of Astonishment (Hadas), **Supp. XXIII:** 115–116

"Mirrors of Chartres Street" (Faulkner), **II:** 56

Mirrors of Moscow (Bryant), **Supp. XXVIII:** 37, 40, 41, 42, 44, 45

"Mirrors of Tuzun Thune, The" (Howard), **Supp. XXVII:** 123

Mirsky, Norman, **Supp. XX:** 244

Mirvis, Tova, **Supp. XX:** 177–191

Misanthrope, The (Molière; Wilbur, trans.), **Supp. III Part 2:** 552, 560

Miscellaneous Poems (Rowson), **Supp. XV:** 243

Miscellaneous Works of Mr. Philip Freneau, Containing His Essays and Additional Poems (Freneau), **Supp. II Part 1:** 263, 264, 266

Miscellany of American Poetry, A (Untermeyer, ed.), **Supp. XV:** 305, 310

Misérables, Les (Hugo), **II:** 179; **Supp. I Part 1:** 280

Misery (King), **Supp. V:** 140, 141, 142, 147–148, 151, 152

Mises, Ludwig von, **Supp. IV Part 2:** 524

Misfits, The (A. Miller), **III:** 147, 149, 156, 161–162, 163; **Retro. Supp. III:** 170, 172

Misfit: The Strange Life of Frederick Exley (Yardley), **Supp. XXIII:** 97

Mish, Jeanetta Calhoun, **Supp. XXVI:** 112

Mishler, Peter, **Supp. XXVIII:** 195, 197, 202

"Mishōsha, or the Magician and his daughters: A Chippewa Tale"(J. Schoolcraft), **Supp. XXIII:** 234, 235

"Misogamist, The" (Dubus), **Supp. VII:** 86–87

Misread City, The: New Literary Los Angeles (Gioia and Timberg, eds.), **Supp. XV:** 116

Misrepresentations Corrected, and Truth Vindicated, in a Reply to the Rev. Mr. Solomon Williams's Book (Edwards), **I:** 549

Miss Crandall's School for Young Ladies & Little Misses of Color (Nelson and Alexander), **Supp. XVIII:** 171, 175, 181, **185–186**

"Miss Cynthie" (R. Fisher), **Supp. XIX:** 65, 69

Miss Doll, Go Home (Markson), **Supp. XVII:** 138

"Miss Ella" (Z. Fitzgerald), **Supp. IX:** 57, 59, **71–72**

"Miss Emily and the Bibliographer" (Tate), **Supp. II Part 1:** 103

"Miss Furr and Miss Skeene" (Stein), **IV:** 29–30

"Missing Child" (Simic), **Supp. VIII:** 282

"Missing in Action" (Komunyakaa), **Supp. XIII:** 123, 124

Missing/Kissing: Missing Marisa, Kissing Christine (Shanley), **Supp. XIV:** 316

Missing Link (X. J. Kennedy), **Supp. XV:** 165

Missing Link, The (Wells), **Supp. XXVI:** 281

"Missing Poem, The" (Halliday), **Supp. XIX:** 93–94

"Missionary Brings a Young Native to America, A" (H. Johnson), **Supp. XXVI:** 167, 173, 174

"Mission of Jane, The" (Wharton), **Retro. Supp. I:** 367

"Missions, The" (Rodriguez), **Supp. XIV:** 303

Mission to Moscow (film), **Supp. I Part 1:** 281

"Mississippi" (Bass), **Supp. XVI:** 17

"Mississippi" (Faulkner), **Retro. Supp. I:** 77

"Mississippi" (Simpson), **Supp. IX:** 271

"Missive Missile, A" (Frost), **Retro. Supp. III:** 104

"Miss Kate in H-1" (Twain), **IV:** 193

Miss Kelly (Holding), **Supp. XXII:** 133–134

Miss Leonora When Last Seen (Taylor), **Supp. V:** 323

Miss Lonelyhearts (West), **I:** 107; **II:** 436; **III:** 357; **IV:** 287, 288, 290–297, 300, 301, 305, 306; **Retro. Supp. II:** 321, 322, 325, 328, **332–335**

"Miss Lora" (Díaz), **Supp. XXIV:** 86

Miss Mamma Aimee (Caldwell), **I:** 308, 309, 310

"Miss Mary Pask" (Wharton), **IV:** 316; **Retro. Supp. I:** 382

"Miss McEnders" (Chopin), **Retro. Supp. II:** 67

Miss Morissa: Doctor of the Gold Trail (Sandoz), **Supp. XXIV:** 244, **255–256**

"Missoula Softball Tournament" (Hugo), **Supp. VI:** 132

Miss Pinkerton (Rinehart), **Supp. XXV:** 197

Miss Ravenel's Conversion from Secession to Loyalty (De Forest), **IV:** 350

Miss Saigon (musical), **Supp. XXI:** 155

"Miss Tempy's Watchers" (Jewett), **II:** 401; **Retro. Supp. II:** 139

"Miss Terriberry to Wed in Suburbs" (Updike), **Retro. Supp. I:** 335

"Miss Urquhart's Tiara" (Jarman), **Supp. XVII:** 116

Miss Witherspoon (Durang), **Supp. XXIV:** 113, **126**

"Mist, The" (King), **Supp. V:** 144

"Mistaken Charity, A" (Freeman), **Retro. Supp. II:** 138

"Mister Brother" (Cunningham), **Supp. XV:** 68

Misterioso (Sorrentino), **Supp. XXI:** 236, 237

"Mister Toussan" (Ellison), **Retro. Supp. II:** 124–125; **Supp. II Part 1:** 238

"Mistress of Sydenham Plantation, The" (Jewett), **Retro. Supp. II:** 141

Mitcham, Matthew, **Supp. XX: 264**

Mitchell, Burroughs, **Supp. XI:** 218, 222, 227

Mitchell, David, **Supp. XXIV:** 86

Mitchell, Don, **Supp. XXII:** 207, 211, 212

Mitchell, Joan, **Supp. XXIII:** 210

Mitchell, Margaret, **II:** 177; **Supp. XX: 243; Supp. XXII:** 195; **Supp. XXVIII:** 119

Mitchell, Pat, **Supp. XXIV:** 35, 42; **Supp. XXVII:** 18, 24

Mitchell, Roger, **Supp. IV Part 1:** 70; **Supp. XV:** 213, 215

Mitchell, Dr. S. Weir, **IV:** 310

Mitchell, Tennessee. *See* Anderson, Mrs. Sherwood (Tennessee Mitchell)

Mitchell, Verner, **Supp. XVIII:** 281, 286

Mitchell, Werner, **Supp. XXVI:** 165, 170, 171–172, 174

Mitchell, Wesley C., **Supp. I Part 2:** 632, 643

"Mitchie-Gawa" (Taggard), **Supp. XXII:** 272

Mitch Miller (Masters), **Supp. I Part 2:** 456, 466, 469–471, 474, 475, 476

Mitchum, Robert, **Supp. IX:** 95, 250

Mitgang, Herbert, **Supp. IV Part 1:** 220, 226, 307; **Supp. VIII:** 124; **Supp. XIX:** 251; **Supp. XX: 243**

Mitla Pass (Uris), **Supp. XX: 244, 247, 248, 256**

Mixed Company: Collected Short Stories (Shaw), **Supp. XIX:** 251

"Mixed Sequence" (Roethke), **III:** 547

Miyazawa Kenji, **Supp. VIII:** 292

Mizener, Arthur, **II:** 77, 81, 84, 94; **IV:** 132; **Supp. XVIII:** 249

Mizner, Addison, **Supp. XVI:** 191

Mizner, Wilson, **Supp. XVI:** 191, 195

Mladenoff, Nancy, **Supp. X:** 176

"M'liss: An Idyl of Red Mountain" (Harte), **Supp. II Part 1:** 339

"Mnemonic Devices" (Goldbarth), **Supp. XII:** 183

"Mnemosyne" (Hölderlin), **Supp. XXIV:** 152

"Mobile in Back of the Smithsonian, The" (Swenson), **Supp. IV Part 2:** 646

Mobilio, Albert, **Supp. VIII:** 3; **Supp. XIX:** 45; **Supp. XVIII:** 144

Moby Dick (film), **Supp. IV Part 1:** 102, 116

Moby Dick; or, The Whale (Melville), **I:** 106, 354; **II:** 33, 224–225, 236, 539–540; **III:** 28–29, 74, 75, 77, 81, 82, 83–86, 87, 89, 90, 91, 93, 94, 95, 359, 453, 556; **IV:** 57, 199, 201, 202; **Retro. Supp. I:** 160, 220, 243, 244, 248, **249–253**, 254, 256, 257, 335; **Retro. Supp. II:** 121, 186, 275; **Retro. Supp. III:** 147, 148–149, 150, 151, 155, 156–157, 160, 161; **Supp. I Part 1:** 249; **Supp. I Part 2:** 579; **Supp. IV Part 2:** 613; **Supp. V:** 281; **Supp. VIII:** 106, 188, 198; **Supp. XXI:** 159; **Supp. XXII:** 81, 268; **Supp. XXIV:** 88

Mock, John, **Supp. XIII:** 174

"Mocking-Bird, The" (Bierce), **I:** 202

"Mock Orange" (Glück), **Supp. V:** 84–85

Modarressi, Mitra, **Supp. IV Part 2:** 657

"Model Father" (Huddle), **Supp. XXVI:** 150

"Model of Christian Charity, A" (Winthrop), **Retro. Supp. III:** 2

Models of Misrepresentation: On the Fiction of E. L. Doctorow (Morris), **Supp. IV Part 1:** 231

Model World and Other Stories, A (Chabon), **Supp. XI:** 66

Modern American and British Poetry (Untermeyer, ed.), **Supp. XV:** 306

Modern American Poetry (Untermeyer, ed.), **Retro. Supp. III:** 100; **Supp. XV:** 293, 303, 306, 312

Modern American Poets (Aiken, ed.), **Supp. XXVI:** 225

Modern American Verse (Untermeyer, ed.), **Supp. XV:** 301

Modern Brazilian Architecture (Bishop, trans.), **Supp. I Part 1:** 92

Modern British Poetry (Untermeyer, ed.), **Supp. XV:** 305, 308, 312

Modern Fiction Studies, **Supp. V:** 238

Modern Fiction Studies (Haegert), **Supp. XVI:** 69

"Modern Greek for 'Nightmare' Is *Ephialtes*, The" (Stallings), **Supp. XXV:** 233

Modern Instance a Novel, A (Howells), **II:** 275, 279, 282–283, 285

Modern Library, The, **Retro. Supp. I:** 112, 113

Modern Mephistopheles, A (Alcott), **Supp. I Part 1:** 37–38

Modern Poetic Sequence, The (Rosenthal), **Supp. V:** 333

"Modern Poetry" (Crane), **I:** 390

Modern Poetry and the Tradition (Brooks), **Supp. XIV:** 5–7

"Modern Primer: Helpful Hints to Tell Appearances from Truth" (Taubman), **Supp. XXV:** 106

"Modern Race Creeds and Their Fallacies" (Locke), **Supp. XIV:** 210

Modern Rhetoric, with Readings (Brooks and Warren), **Supp. XIV:** 11

"Modern Sorcery" (Simic), **Supp. VIII:** 283

Modern Times (album, Dylan), **Supp. XVIII:** 28, 31, 33

"Modern Times" (Zukofsky), **Supp. III Part 2:** 624

Modern Writer, The (Anderson), **I:** 117

Modersohn, Otto, **Supp. I Part 2:** 573

Modersohn, Mrs. Otto (Paula Becker), **Supp. I Part 2:** 573–574

"Modes of Being" (Levertov), **Supp. III Part 1:** 282

Modest Enquiry into the Nature and Necessity of a Paper-Currency, A (Franklin), **II:** 108–109

"Modest Proposal, A" (Swift), **I:** 295; **Retro. Supp. II:** 287

"Modest Proposal with Feline Feeling, A" (Neugeboren), **Supp. XVI:** 219

"Modest Self-Tribute, A" (Wilson), **IV:** 431, 432

Modigliani, Amedeo, **Supp. XXVI:** 259

Moeller, Philip, **III:** 398, 399

"Moench von Berchtesgaden, Der" (Voss), **I:** 199–200

Moers, Ellen, **Retro. Supp. II:** 99

Moe's Villa and Other Stories (Purdy), **Supp. VII:** 270, 280

Moffat, Juan, **Supp. XX: 52**

Moffet, Penelope, **Supp. XXIV:** 165, 167

Mogen, David, **Supp. IV Part 1:** 106

Mohammed, **I:** 480; **II:** 1

Mohawk (Russo), **Supp. XII: 326–328**

Moir, William Wilmerding, **Supp. V:** 279

Mojo Hand (Phillips), **Supp. XXIII:** 174

Moldaw, Carol, **Supp. XV:** 264; **Supp. XVII:** 127, 130

"Moles" (Oliver), **Supp. VII:** 235

Molesworth, Charles, **Supp. IV Part 1:** 39; **Supp. VIII:** 292, 306; **Supp. XIX:** 121–122

Molière (Jean-Baptiste Poquelin), **III:** 113; **Supp. I Part 2:** 406; **Supp. III Part 2:** 552, 560; **Supp. IV Part 2:** 585; **Supp. V:** 101

"Molino Rojo, El" (Ríos), **Supp. IV Part 2:** 544

Moll Flanders (Defoe), **Supp. V:** 127; **Supp. XIII:** 43

"Molloch in State Street" (Whittier), **Supp. I Part 2:** 687

"Moll Pitcher" (Whittier), **Supp. I Part 2:** 684

"Molly Brant, Iroquois Matron" (Gunn Allen), **Supp. IV Part 1:** 331

"Molly Brant to Willie"(Kenny), **Supp. XXIII:** 153

Molnar, Ferenc, **Supp. XVI:** 187

"Moloch" (H. Miller), **III:** 177

Momaday, N. Scott, **Supp. IV Part 1:** 274, 323, 324, 404; **Supp. IV Part 2: 479–496,** 504, 557, 562; **Supp. XII:** 209; **Supp. XVIII:** 58

" 'Momentary Stay against Confusion,' A: Frank Conroy's *Stop-Time*" (T. Adams), **Supp. XVI:** 69

Moment of Untruth (Lacy), **Supp. XV:** 206, 207

Moments of the Italian Summer (Wright), **Supp. III Part 2:** 602

Moment to Moment: Poems of a Mountain Recluse (Budbill), **Supp. XIX: 2, 7, 9–10**

"Momus" (Robinson), **III:** 508

Monaghan, Charles, **Supp. XIX:** 155

Monaghan, Pat, **Supp. XI:** 121

Monaghan, Patricia, **Supp. XVII:** 76, 123, 127, 129

Mona Lisa Overdrive (W. Gibson), **Supp. XVI:** 119, 120, **127–128**

"Mon Ami" (Bourne), **I:** 227

Monday Night (Boyle), **Supp. XXIV:** 54

Monet, Claude, **Retro. Supp. I:** 378

"Monet's 'Waterlilies' " (Hayden), **Supp. II Part 1:** 361–362

Monette, Paul, **Supp. X: 145–161**

Money (Amis), **Retro. Supp. I:** 278

Money (Gold), **Supp. XXVIII:** 69

"Money" (Matthews), **Supp. IX:** 166

"Money" (Nemerov), **III:** 287

Money, Money, Money (Wagoner), **Supp. IX:** 324, **333–334**

Moneyball: The Art of Winning an Unfair Game (M. Lewis), **Supp. XVII:** 210

Moneychangers, The (Sinclair), **Supp. V:** 285

Money Writes! (Sinclair), **Supp. V:** 277

Monica, Saint, **IV:** 140

Monikins, The (Cooper), **I:** 348, 354

Monk, Craig, **Supp. XXIV:** 64

Monk, Thelonious, **Supp. XVIII:** 62

Monk and the Hangman's Daughter, The (Bierce), **I:** 199–200, 209

"Monkey" (Weigl), **Supp. XIX:** 278

Monkey Business (screenplay, Hecht), **Supp. XXVII:** 91, 94

"Monkey Garden, The" (Cisneros), **Supp. VII:** 63

"Monkey Junk: A Satire on Modern Divorce" (Hurston), **Retro. Supp. III:** 127

"Monkey Puzzle, The" (Moore), **III:** 194, 207, 211

Monkeys (Minot), **Supp. VI:** 203–205, **206–210**

"Monkeys, The" (Moore), **III:** 201, 202

Monkey Wars, The (Weigl), **Supp. XIX:** 276, 278–280

Monkey Wrench Gang, The (Abbey), **Supp. VIII:** 42; **Supp. XIII: 9–11,** 16

"Monk of Casal-Maggiore, The" (Longfellow), **II:** 505

"Monocle de Mon Oncle, Le" (Stevens), **IV:** 78, 84; **Retro. Supp. I:** 301; **Supp. III Part 1:** 20; **Supp. X:** 58

"Monody to the Sound of Zithers" (Boyle), **Supp. XXIV:** 63

"Monolog from a Mattress" (Untermeyer), **Supp. XV:** 307

"Monologue for Mothers" (Taggard), **Supp. XXII:** 279

"Mon Plaisir" (July), **Supp. XXIV:** 205–206

Monro, Harold, **III:** 465; **Retro. Supp. I:** 127; **Supp. XV:** 296

Monroe, Harriet, **I:** 235, 384, 390, 393; **III:** 458, 581, 586; **IV:** 74; **Retro. Supp. I:** 58, 131; **Retro. Supp. II:** 82, 83; **Supp. I Part 1:** 256, 257, 258, 262, 263, 267; **Supp. I Part 2:** 374, 387, 388, 464, 610, 611, 613, 614, 615, 616; **Supp. XIV:** 286; **Supp. XV:** 43, 299, 302; **Supp. XXV:** 18; **Supp. XXVII:** 283, 286, 289–290, 297

Monroe, James, **Supp. I Part 2:** 515, 517

Monroe, Lucy, **Retro. Supp. II:** 70

Monroe, Marilyn, **III:** 161, 162–163; **Supp. XXVII:** 95

Monroe's Embassy; or, the Conduct of the Government in Relation to Our Claims to the Navigation of the Mississippi (Brown), **Supp. I Part 1:** 146

Monsieur Motte (King), **Supp. XXVIII:** 114

"Monsieur Motte" (King), **Supp. XXVIII:** 113–114, 116, 118, 122

Monson, Ander, **Supp. XXIV: 229–242**

"Monsoon Season" (Komunyakaa), **Supp. XIII:** 122

Monsour, Leslie, **Supp. XV:** 125

Monster (graphic novel, Myers), **Supp. XXVII:** 199, 202, 203, 204, 205

"Monster, The" (Crane), **I:** 418

Monster, The, and Other Stories (Crane), **I:** 409

"Monstro" (Díaz), **Supp. XXIV:** 86

Montage of a Dream Deferred (Hughes), **Retro. Supp. I:** 194, **208–209; Supp. I Part 1:** 333, 339–341

Montagu, Ashley, **Supp. I Part 1:** 314

"Montaigne" (Emerson), **II:** 6

Montaigne, Michel de, **II:** 1, 5, 6, 8, 14–15, 16, 535; **III:** 600; **Retro. Supp. I:** 247; **Supp. XIV:** 105; **Supp. XXI:** 111, 205; **Supp. XXVI:** 39

Montale, Eugenio, **Supp. III Part 1:** 320; **Supp. V:** 337–338; **Supp. VIII:** 30; **Supp. XV:** 112

Montalembert, Hughes de, **Supp. XV:** 349

"Montana Memory" (Maclean), **Supp. XIV:** 221

"Montana; or the End of Jean-Jacques Rousseau" (Fiedler), **Supp. XIII: 97–98**

"Montana Ranch Abandoned" (Hugo), **Supp. VI:** 139

"Montana Wedding Day" (Bottoms), **Supp. XXVIII:** 32

"Mont Blanc" (Shelley), **Supp. IX:** 52

Montcalm, Louis Joseph de, **Supp. I Part 2:** 498

Montcalm and Wolfe (Parkman), **Supp. II Part 2:** 596, 609, 610, 611–613

Montemarano, Nicholas, **Supp. XVI:** 227

Montgomery, Benilde, **Supp. XIII:** 202

Montgomery, George, **Supp. XXIII:** 209

Montgomery, Robert, **Supp. I Part 2:** 611; **Supp. IV Part 1:** 130

Month of Sundays, A (Updike), **Retro. Supp. I:** 325, 327, 329, 330, 331, 333, 335

Monti, Luigi, **II:** 504

Montoya, José, **Supp. IV Part 2:** 545

"Montrachet-le-Jardin" (Stevens), **IV:** 82

Mont-Saint-Michel and Chartres (Adams), **I:** 1, 9, 12–14, 18, 19, 21; **Supp. I Part 2:** 417

Montserrat (Hellman), **Supp. I Part 1:** 283–285

Montserrat (Robles), **Supp. I Part 1:** 283–285

"Monument, The" (Bishop), **Supp. I Part 1:** 89

Monument, The (Strand), **Supp. IV Part 2:** 629, 630

"Monument in Utopia, A" (Schnackenberg), **Supp. XV:** 261, 263

"Monument Mountain" (Bryant), **Supp. I Part 1:** 156, 162

"Monument to After-Thought Unveiled, A" (Frost), **Retro. Supp. I:** 124

Moo (Smiley), **Supp. VI:** 292, **303–305**

Moods (Alcott), **Supp. I Part 1:** 33, 34–35, 43

Moody, Anne, **Supp. IV Part 1:** 11

Moody, Richard, **Supp. I Part 1:** 280

Moody, Rick, **Supp. XXI:** 117; **Supp. XXIV:** 131

Moody, Ron, **Supp. XXII:** 49

Moody, William Vaughn, **III:** 507; **IV:** 26

Moody, Mrs. William Vaughn, **I:** 384; **Supp. I Part 2:** 394

Moody-Freeman, Julie, **Supp. XXIII:** 91, 94, 95

"Moon" (A. Finch), **Supp. XVII:** 77

Moon, Henry Lee, **Supp. XVIII:** 281, 285

"Moon and the Night and the Men, The" (Berryman), **I:** 172

"Moon and the Yew Tree, The" (Plath), **Supp. XXVII:** 296

Moon Crossing Bridge (Gallagher), **Supp. XXIV:** 166, 170

"Moon Deluxe" (F. Barthelme), **Supp. XI:** 26, 27, 33, 36

Mooney, Tom, **I:** 505

"Moon-Face" (London), **II:** 475

Moon-Face and Other Stories (London), **II:** 483

"Moon Flock" (Dickey), **Supp. IV Part 1:** 186

Moon for the Misbegotten, A (O'Neill), **III:** 385, 401, 403, 404

Moon in a Mason Jar (Wrigley), **Supp. XVIII: 295–298**

Moon in Its Flight, The (Sorrentino), **Supp. XXI:** 226

"Moon in Its Flight, The" (Sorrentino), **Supp. XXI:** 229

Moon Is a Gong, The (Dos Passos). *See Garbage Man, The* (Dos Passos)

Moon Is Down, The (Steinbeck), **IV:** 51

Moon Lady, The (Tan), **Supp. X:** 289

"Moonlight Alert" (Winters), **Supp. II Part 2:** 801, 811, 815

"Moonlight: Chickens on a Road" (Wrigley), **Supp. XVIII:** 295–296, 297

"Moonlit Night" (Reznikoff), **Supp. XIV:** 285–286

Moon of the Caribbees, The (O'Neill), **III:** 388

Moon Palace (Auster), **Supp. XII:** 22, 27, **30–32**

"Moonshine" (Komunyakaa), **Supp. XIII:** 127, 128

Moons of Jupiter, The (Munro), **Supp. XXVII:** 182, 187–189

"Moons of Jupiter, The" (Munro), **Supp. XXVII:** 188–189

"Moon Solo" (Laforgue), **Supp. XIII:** 346

Moonstone, The (Collins), **Supp. XX: 236**

Moonstruck (screenplay, Shanley), **Supp. XIV:** 315, 316, **321–324**

"Moon upon her fluent Route, The" (Dickinson), **I:** 471

Moony's Kid Don't Cry (T. Williams), **IV:** 381

Moore, Arthur, **Supp. I Part 1:** 49

Moore, C. L., **Supp. XXV:** 122

Moore, Deborah Dash, **Supp. XX: 246**

Moore, Dennis, **Supp. XXVII:** 275

Moore, George, **I:** 103

Moore, Hannah, **Supp. XV:** 231

Moore, Jack B., **Supp. XXV:** 24, 26, 27

Moore, John Milton, **III:** 193

Moore, Julie L., **Supp. XXIII:** 252

Moore, Lorrie, **Supp. VIII:** 145; **Supp. X: 163–180; Supp. XXV:** 142

Moore, Marianne, **I:** 58, 285, 401, 428; **III: 193–217,** 514, 592–593; **IV:** 74, 75, 76, 91, 402; **Retro. Supp. I:** 416, 417; **Retro. Supp. II:** 39, 44, 48, 50, 82, 178, 179, 243, 244; **Supp. I Part 1:** 84, 89, 255, 257; **Supp. I Part 2:** 707; **Supp. II Part 1:** 21; **Supp. III Part 1:** 58, 60, 63; **Supp. III Part 2:** 612, 626, 627; **Supp. IV Part 1:** 242, 246, 257; **Supp. IV Part 2:** 454, 640, 641; **Supp. XIV:** 124, 130; **Supp. XV:** 306, 307; **Supp. XVII:** 131; **Supp. XXI:** 98; **Supp. XXII:** 273–274

Moore, Marie Lorena. *See* Moore, Lorrie

Moore, MariJo, **Supp. XXVI:** 113

Moore, Mary Tyler, **Supp. V:** 107

Moore, Mary Warner, **III:** 193

Moore, Dr. Merrill, **III:** 506

Moore, Steven, **Supp. IV Part 1:** 279, 283, 284, 285, 287; **Supp. XII:** 151; **Supp. XVII:** 230, 231, 232; **Supp. XXII:** 261, 265

Moore, Sturge, **III:** 459

Moore, Thomas, **II**: 296, 299, 303; **Supp. IX**: 104; **Supp. X**: 114; **Supp. XXIII**: 138

Moore, Virginia, **Supp. XV**: 308

Moorehead, Caroline, **Supp. XIV**: 337

Moorepack, Howard, **Supp. XV**: 199

"Moorings" (Hoffman), **Supp. XVIII**: 87

Moos, Malcolm, **III**: 116, 119

"Moose, The" (Bishop), **Retro. Supp. II**: 50; **Supp. I Part 1**: 73, 93, 94, 95; **Supp. IX**: 45, 46

"Moose Wallow, The" (Hayden), **Supp. II Part 1**: 367

"Moowis, The Indian Coquette"(J. Schoolcraft), **Supp. XXIII**: 234

Mooyart-Doubleday, B. M., **Supp. XXVII**: 135

Mop, Moondance, and the Nagasaki Knights (Myers), **Supp. XXVII**: 206

"Moquihuitzin's Answer" (Everwine), **Supp. XV**: 78

Mora, Pat, **Supp. XIII**: **213–232**

Moraga, Cherríe, **Supp. XXIII**: **193–206**

"Moral Argument Against Calvinism, The" (Channing), **Supp. XXIV**: **73–74**, 75

"Moral Bully, The" (Holmes), **Supp. I Part 1**: 302

"Moral Character, the Practice of Law, and Legal Education" (Hall), **Supp. VIII**: 127

"Moral Equivalent for Military Service, A" (Bourne), **I**: 230

"Moral Equivalent of War, The" (James), **II**: 361; **Supp. I Part 1**: 20

"Moral Imperatives for World Order" (Locke), **Supp. XIV**: 207, 213

Moralités Légendaires (Laforgue), **I**: 573

"Morality and Mercy in Vienna" (Pynchon), **Supp. II Part 2**: 620, 624

"Morality of Indian Hating, The" (Momaday), **Supp. IV Part 2**: 484

"Morality of Poetry, The" (Wright), **Supp. III Part 2**: 596–597, 599

Moral Man and Immoral Society (Niebuhr), **III**: 292, 295–297

"Morals Is Her Middle Name" (Hughes), **Supp. I Part 1**: 338

"Morals of Chess, The" (Franklin), **II**: 121

"Moral Substitute for War, A" (Addams), **Supp. I Part 1**: 20

"Moral Theology of Atticus Finch, The" (Shaffer), **Supp. VIII**: 127

"Moral Thought, A" (Freneau), **Supp. II Part 1**: 262

Moran, Thomas, **Supp. IV Part 2**: 603–604

Moran, William L., **Supp. XXIV**: 150–151, 152

Moran of the Lady Letty (Norris), **II**: 264; **III**: 314, 322, 327, 328, 329, 330, 331, 332, 333

Morath, Ingeborg. *See* Miller, Mrs. Arthur (Ingeborg Morath)

Moravec, Paul, **Supp. XIX**: 123

Moravia, Alberto, **I**: 301

More (Crooker), **Supp. XXIII**: **60–62**

Moré, Gonzalo, **Supp. X**: 185

More, Henry, **I**: 132

More, Paul Elmer, **I**: 223–224, 247; **Supp. I Part 2**: 423

Moreau, Gustave, **I**: 66

"More Blues and the Abstract Truth" (Wright), **Supp. XV**: 345

More Boners (Abingdon), **Supp. XVI**: 99

More Conversations with Eudora Welty (Prenshaw, ed.), **Retro. Supp. I**: 340, 341, 342, 343, 344, 352, 353, 354

More Dangerous Thoughts (Ryan as Quin), **Supp. XVIII**: 226, **229–230**, 231, 238

More Die of Heartbreak (Bellow), **Retro. Supp. II**: 31, 33, 34

"More Girl Than Boy" (Komunyakaa), **Supp. XIII**: 117

More I Remember More (Brainard), **Supp. XXVII**: 19

"More Light! More Light! (Hecht), **Supp. X**: 60

"More Like an Extension of the Spirit: Clothing in Lyric Poems"(Hadas), **Supp. XXIII**: 124

"Morella" (Poe), **III**: 412; **Retro. Supp. II**: 270

"More Love in the Western World" (Updike), **Retro. Supp. I**: 327–328, 329

"Morels" (W. J. Smith), **Supp. XIII**: **336–339**

Moreno, Gary, **Supp. XV**: 5

"More Observations Now" (Conroy), **Supp. XVI**: 75

"More of a Corpse Than a Woman" (Rukeyser), **Supp. VI**: 280

"More Pleasant Adventures" (Ashbery), **Supp. III Part 1**: 1

More Poems to Solve (Swenson), **Supp. IV Part 2**: 640, 642, 648

More Stately Mansions (O'Neill), **III**: 385, 401, 404–405

"More Than Human" (Chabon), **Supp. XI**: 71–72

More Things Change The More They Stay the Same, The (J. W. Miller), **Supp. XX**: **164**

More Tish (Rinehart), **Supp. XXV**: 194

More Triva (L. P. Smith), **Supp. XIV**: 339

Morgan, Edmund S., **IV**: 149; **Supp. I Part 1**: 101, 102; **Supp. I Part 2**: 484

Morgan, Edwin, **Supp. IV Part 2**: 688

Morgan, Emanuel. *See* Bynner, Witter

Morgan, Henry, **II**: 432; **IV**: 63; **Supp. XXV**: 255

Morgan, Jack, **Retro. Supp. II**: 142

Morgan, J. P., **I**: 494; **III**: 14, 15

Morgan, Judith, **Supp. XVI**: 103

Morgan, Neil, **Supp. XVI**: 103

Morgan, Robert, **Supp. V**: 5; **Supp. XX**: **161**, **162**

Morgan, Robin, **Supp. I Part 2**: 569

Morgan, Ted, **Supp. XIV**: 141

Morgan's Passing (Tyler), **Supp. IV Part 2**: 666–667, 668, 669

Morgenstern, Dan, **Supp. XIX**: 159

Morgenthau, Hans, **III**: 291, 309

Morgenthau, Henry, Sr., **Supp. XXIII**: 21, 22, 26, 30

Morgesons, The (E. Stoddard), **Supp. XV**: 270, 273, 274, 278, **279–282**, 283

Morgesons and Other Writings, Published and Unpublished, The (Buell and Zagarell), **Supp. XV**: 269

Moriah's Mourning and Other Half-Hour Sketches (Stuart), **Supp. XXVIII**: 229, 235

Moricand, Conrad, **III**: 190

Morison, Samuel Eliot, **Supp. I Part 2**: **479–500**; **Supp. XXII**: 35

Morison, Mrs. Samuel Eliot (Elizabeth Shaw Greene), **Supp. I Part 2**: 483

Morison, Mrs. Samuel Eliot (Priscilla Barton), **Supp. I Part 2**: 493, 496, 497

Morita, Pat, **Supp. XXI**: 146

"Morituri Salutamus" (Longfellow), **II**: 499, 500; **Retro. Supp. II**: 169; **Supp. I Part 2**: 416

"Moriturus" (Millay), **III**: 126, 131–132

Morley, Christopher, **III**: 481, 483, 484; **Supp. I Part 2**: 653; **Supp. IX**: 124

Morley, Edward, **IV**: 27

Morley, Lord John, **I**: 7

Mormon Country (Stegner), **Supp. IV Part 2**: 598, 601–602

"Morning, The" (Updike), **Retro. Supp. I**: 329

"Morning after My Death, The" (Levis), **Supp. XI**: 260, 263–264

"Morning Arrives" (F. Wright), **Supp. XVII**: 244

Morning Face (Stratton-Porter), **Supp. XX**: 223

Morning for Flamingos, A (Burke), **Supp. XIV**: 30, 31, 32

"Morning from the Gospel of John, A"(Bottoms), **Supp. XXVIII**: 28, 29

"Morning Glory" (Merrill), **Supp. III Part 1**: 337

Morning Glory, The (R. Bly), **Supp. IV Part 1**: 63–65, 66, 71

"Morning Imagination of Russia, A" (W. C. Williams), **Retro. Supp. I**: 428

Morning in Antibes (Knowles), **Supp. XII**: 249

Morning in the Burned House (Atwood), **Supp. XIII**: 20, 35

Morning Is Near Us, The (Glaspell), **Supp. III Part 1**: 184–185

Morning Noon and Night (Cozzens), **I**: 374, 375, 376, 377, 379, 380

"Morning of the Day They Did It, The" (White), **Supp. I Part 2**: 663

"Morning Prayers" (Harjo), **Supp. XII**: 231

"Morning Roll Call" (Anderson), **I**: 116

"Morning Roudup" (Sorrentino), **Supp. XXI**: 228

"Mornings, I Walk Past the First Cemetery of Athens" (Stallings), **Supp. XXV**: 225

"Morning Shadows" (Skloot), **Supp. XX**: **199**

"Mornings in a New House" (Merrill), **Supp. III Part 1**: 327

"Mornings in Ormos"(Hadas), **Supp. XXIII**: 112, 113, 123

Mornings Like This (Dillard), **Supp. VI**: 23, 34

"Morning Song" (Plath), **Retro. Supp. II:** 252; **Supp. XXIII:** 115

"Morning Star"(Wakoski), **Supp. XXVIII:** 270

Morning Watch, The (Agee), **I:** 25, 39–42

"Morning with Broken Window" (Hogan), **Supp. IV Part 1:** 405

"Moro Like Me"(Goldman), **Supp. XXV:** 51

Morrell, Ottoline, **Retro. Supp. I:** 60

Morris, Bernard E., **Supp. XV:** 154, 169

Morris, Christopher D., **Supp. IV Part 1:** 231, 236

Morris, Gary, **Supp. XXII:** 262

Morris, George Sylvester, **Supp. I Part 2:** 640

Morris, Gouverneur, **Supp. I Part 2:** 512, 517, 518

Morris, Lloyd, **III:** 458

Morris, Robert, **Supp. I Part 2:** 510

Morris, Timothy, **Retro. Supp. I:** 40

Morris, William, **II:** 323, 338, 523; **IV:** 349; **Supp. I Part 1:** 260, 356; **Supp. XI:** 202

Morris, Willie, **Supp. XI:** 216, 231, 234; **Supp. XIX:** 151, 252; **Supp. XXVII:** 269

Morris, Wright, **I:** 305; **III: 218–243,** 558, 572; **IV:** 211

Morrison, Charles Clayton, **III:** 297

Morrison, Jim, **Supp. IV Part 1:** 206

Morrison, Kay, **Retro. Supp. III:** 104

Morrison, Toni, **Retro. Supp. II:** 15, 118; **Retro. Supp. III: 183–205; Supp. III Part 1: 361–381; Supp. IV Part 1:** 2, 13, 14, 250, 253, 257; **Supp. V:** 169, 259; **Supp. VIII:** 213, 214; **Supp. X:** 85, 239, 250, 325; **Supp. XI:** 4, 14, 20, 91; **Supp. XII:** 289, 310; **Supp. XIII:** 60, 185; **Supp. XVI:** 143; **Supp. XVII:** 183; **Supp. XX: 108; Supp. XXI:** 172, 243; **Supp. XXII:** 65, 78; **Supp. XXIV:** 183, 184, 185; **Supp. XXV:** 142; **Supp. XXVI:** 14

"Morro Bay" (Jeffers), **Supp. II Part 2:** 422

Morrow, Christopher, **Supp. XXVII:** 216, 225

Morrow, W. C., **I:** 199

Morse, Jedidiah, **Supp. XV:** 243

Morse, Robert, **Supp. XI:** 305

Morse, Samuel F. B., **Supp. I Part 1:** 156

Morse, Samuel French, **Supp. XXI:** 17, 19, 23, 27

Mortal Acts, Mortal Words (Kinnell), **Supp. III Part 1:** 235, 236, 237, 249–254

Mortal Antipathy, A (Holmes), **Supp. I Part 1:** 315–316

"Mortal Enemies" (Humphrey), **Supp. IX:** 109

"Mortal Eternal" (Olds), **Supp. X:** 214

Mortal No, The (Hoffman), **IV:** 113

Mortal Stakes (Parker), **Supp. XIX:** 183–184

Morte D'Arthur, Le (Malory), **Supp. IV Part 1:** 47

Mortmere Stories, The (Isherwood and Upward), **Supp. XIV:** 159

Morton, David, **Supp. IX:** 76

Morton, Jelly Roll, **Supp. X:** 242

Morton, Thomas, **Supp. XXII:** 44, 45, 46

"Mosaic of the Nativity: Serbia, Winter 1993" (Kenyon), **Supp. VII:** 173

Mosby's Memoirs and Other Stories (Bellow), **Retro. Supp. II:** 27

"Moscow, Idaho" (Offutt), **Supp. XIX:** 170

Moscow under Fire (Caldwell), **I:** 296

Moser, Barry, **Supp. XIV:** 223

Moses (Asch), **Supp. XXIII:** 7

Moses (Untermeyer), **Retro. Supp. III:** 133; **Supp. XV: 309**

Moses, Man of the Mountain (Hurston), **Retro. Supp. III:** 130, 132–133, 139; **Supp. VI:** 149, 158, 160

"Moses on Sinai" (Untermeyer), **Supp. XV:** 300

Mosher, Howard Frank, **Supp. XXII: 203–221**

Moskowitz, Alfred, **Supp. XXI:** 98, 106

Mosle, Sara, **Supp. XI:** 254

Mosley, Walter, **Supp. XIII: 233–252; Supp. XVI:** 143

Mosquito (G. Jones), **Supp. XXIV:** 183, 184, 185, 190, **192–194,** 195

Mosquito Coast, The (film), **Supp. VIII:** 323

Mosquito Coast, The (Theroux), **Supp. VIII:** 321, **322–323**

Mosquitoes (Faulkner), **II:** 56; **Retro. Supp. I:** 79, 81; **Retro. Supp. III:** 77

Moss, Howard, **III:** 452; **Supp. IV Part 2:** 642; **Supp. IX:** 39; **Supp. XIII:** 114; **Supp. XV:** 143, 152

Moss, Stanley, **Supp. XI:** 321

Moss, Thylias, **Supp. XI:** 248

Mosses from an Old Manse (Hawthorne), **I:** 562; **II:** 224; **III:** 82, 83; **Retro. Supp. I:** 157, 248; **Retro. Supp. III:** 114–116, 122, 156

Moss Mystery, The (Wells), **Supp. XXVI:** 278

"Moss of His Skin" (Sexton), **Supp. II Part 2:** 676

Most, Doug, **Supp. XVIII:** 101

"Most Extraordinary Case, A" (James), **II:** 322; **Retro. Supp. I:** 218

"Most Girl Part of You, The" (Hempel), **Supp. XXI:** 116

Most Likely to Succeed (Dos Passos), **I:** 491

"Most of It, The" (Frost), **Retro. Supp. I:** 121, 125, 129, 139; **Retro. Supp. III:** 104; **Supp. XVIII:** 300

"Most Popular Novels in America, The" (Mabie), **Supp. XVIII:** 257

Motel Chronicles (Shepard), **Supp. III Part 2:** 445

"Mother" (Kooser), **Supp. XIX:** 117, 126, 127

"Mother" (Paley), **Supp. VI: 222–223**

Mother (Schjeldahl), **Supp. XXIV:** 44

"Mother" (Snyder), **Supp. VIII:** 298

Mother (Whistler), **IV:** 369

Mother, The (Buck), **Supp. II Part 1:** 118–119

"Mother and Child #3" (Davison), **Supp. XXVI:** 77

"Mother and Jack and the Rain" (Sexton), **Supp. II Part 2:** 686

"Mother and Son" (Tate), **IV:** 128, 137–138

Mother Country: Britain, the Welfare State and Nuclear Pollution (Robinson), **Supp. XXI:** 211

Mother Courage and Her Children (Brecht), **III:** 160; **Supp. IX:** 140; **Supp. XII:** 249

"Mother Earth: Her Whales" (Snyder), **Supp. VIII:** 302

"Motherhood" (Swenson), **Supp. IV Part 2:** 645

Mother Hubbard (Reed), **Supp. X:** 241

Motherless Brooklyn (Lethem), **Supp. XXII:** 49

Motherless in Brooklyn (Lethem), **Supp. XVIII:** 135, **143–144**

Mother Love (Dove), **Supp. IV Part 1:** 250–251, 254

"Mother Marie Therese" (R. Lowell), **Retro. Supp. II:** 188

Mother Night (Vonnegut), **Supp. II Part 2:** 757, 758, 767, 770, 771

"Mother-Right" (Rich), **Retro. Supp. III:** 249

"Mother Rosarine" (Kumin), **Supp. IV Part 2:** 442

"Mothers and Daughters in the Fiction of the New Republic" (Davidson), **Supp. XV:** 238

"Mother's lament for the absence of a child, A"(J. Schoolcraft), **Supp. XXIII:** 236

"Mother Song" (Huddle), **Supp. XXVI:** 151

Mother's Recompense, The (Wharton), **IV:** 321, 324; **Retro. Supp. I:** 382; **Retro. Supp. III:** 288–289

"Mother's Tale, A" (Agee), **I:** 29–30

"Mother's Things" (Creeley), **Supp. IV Part 1:** 141

"Mother Suite, The"(Crooker), **Supp. XXIII:** 61

"Mother's Voice" (Creeley), **Supp. IV Part 1:** 156

Mother to Daughter, Daughter to Mother (Olsen, ed.), **Supp. XIII:** 295

"Mother Tongue" (Simic), **Supp. VIII:** 283

"Mother to Son" (Hughes), **Retro. Supp. I:** 199, 203; **Supp. I Part 1:** 321–322, 323

Motherwell, Robert, **Supp. XV:** 145; **Supp. XXI:** 125

"Mother Writes to the Murderer, The: A Letter" (Nye), **Supp. XIII:** 276

Moths of the Limberlost (Stratton-Porter), **Supp. XX: 218**

"Motion, The" (Olson), **Supp. II Part 2:** 571

Motion of History, The (Baraka), **Supp. II Part 1:** 55, 56

"Motive for Metaphor, The" (Stevens), **IV:** 89; **Retro. Supp. I:** 310

Motiveless Malignity (Auchincloss), **Supp. IV Part 1:** 31

Motke ganef (Asch), **Supp. XXIII:** 5
Motley, John Lothrop, **Supp. I Part 1:** 299; **Supp. I Part 2:** 479; **Supp. XX:** 228, 231
Motley, Willard, **Supp. XVII:** 149–163; **Supp. XXIII:** 145
"Motor Car, The" (White), **Supp. I Part 2:** 661
Motorcycle Betrayal Poesm, The (Wakoski), **Supp. XXVIII:** 264–265
Motor-Flight Through France (Wharton), **I:** 12; **Retro. Supp. I:** 372
Motown and Didi (Myers), **Supp. XXVII:** 204, 211
Mott, Michael, **Supp. VIII:** 204, 208
Motta, Gustavo, **Supp. XXIII:** 125
Mottetti: Poems of Love: The Motets of Eugenio Montale (Montale; Gioia, trans.), **Supp. XV:** 112, **127–128**
Mottke, the Thief (Asch), **Supp. XXIII:** 9, 12
Mottke, the Thief (Asch; tr. Willa and Edwin Muir), **Supp. XXIII:** 5
Mouawad, Nelly, **Supp. XX:** 126
"Mound, The" (Lovecraft and Bishop), **Supp. XXV:** 122
"Mountain, The" (Frost), **Retro. Supp. I:** 121
"Mountain Hermitage, The: Pages from a Japanese Notebook" (Passin), **Supp. XIII:** 337
Mountain Interval (Frost), **II:** 154; **Retro. Supp. I:** 131, 132, 133; **Retro. Supp. III:** 99–100
"Mountain Lion" (Hogan), **Supp. IV Part 1:** 412
"Mountain Music" essays (Sanders), **Supp. XVI:** 276–277
Mountain on the Desert, The (Richter), **Supp. XVIII:** 216, 219
Mountainous Journey, A (Tuqan), **Supp. XIII:** 278
Mountain Path (Arnow), **Supp. XXVIII:** 1, 2, 3–6, 11, 14, 16
"Mountains" (Dubus III), **Supp. XXIV:** 101
Mountains, The (Wolfe), **IV:** 461
Mountains and Rivers without End (Snyder), **Supp. VIII:** 295, **305–306**
"Mountains grow unnoticed, The" (Dickinson), **Retro. Supp. I:** 46
Mountains Have Come Closer, The (J. W. Miller), **Supp. XX:** 165, 168, 169–170
Mountains Look Down, The: A History of Chichester, a Company Town in the Catskills (Bennett), **Supp. XXII:** 218
Mountains of California, The (Muir), **Supp. IX:** 183
"Mountain Whippoorwill, The" (Benét), **Supp. XI:** 44–45, 46, 47
"Mount-Joy: or Some Passages Out of the Life of a Castle-Builder" (Irving), **II:** 314
"Mount Venus" (Wright), **Supp. XV:** 346
Mount Vernon on the Potomac: History of the Mount Vernon Ladies' Association of the Union (King), **Supp. XXVIII:** 120
"Mourners" (Kooser), **Supp. XIX:** 127

"Mourners, The" (Malamud), **Supp. I Part 2:** 431, 435, 436–437
Mourners Below (Purdy), **Supp. VII:** 274, 280
"Mourning and Melancholia" (Freud), **Supp. IV Part 2:** 450; **Supp. XVI:** 161
Mourning Becomes Electra (O'Neill), **III:** 391, 394, 398–400
"Mourning Doves" (Pedersen; Nelson, trans.), **Supp. XVIII:** 180
"Mourning Poem for the Queen of Sunday" (Hayden), **Supp. II Part 1:** 379–380
"Mouse Elegy" (Olds), **Supp. X:** 209
Mouse Is Born, A (Loos), **Supp. XVI:** 193
"Mouse Roulette Wheel, The" (C. Bly), **Supp. XVI:** 34
Moustapha's Eclipse (McKnight), **Supp. XX:** 147, 150
"Mouth of Brass" (Humphrey), **Supp. IX:** 101
Moveable Feast, A (Hemingway), **II:** 257; **Retro. Supp. I:** 108, 171, **186–187**
Movement, The: Documentary of a Struggle for Equality (Student Nonviolent Coordinating Committee), **Supp. IV Part 1:** 369
"Move over Macho, Here Comes Feminismo" (Robbins), **Supp. X:** 272
Movers and Shakers (Sochen), **Supp. XXI:** 1
"Moves, The" (July), **Supp. XXIV:** 205
"Move to California, The" (Stafford), **Supp. XI:** 318, 321
"Movie" (Shapiro), **Supp. II Part 2:** 707
Movie at the End of the World, The (McGrath), **Supp. X:** 127
Moviegoer, The (Percy), **Supp. III Part 1:** 383–385, 387, 389–392, 394, 397
"Movie Magazine, The: A Low 'Slick' " (Percy), **Supp. III Part 1:** 385
Movies (Dixon), **Supp. XII:** 147
Movies About the Movies (Ames), **Supp. XVIII:** 242–243
"Movie Star Peter at the Supper for Street People" (Ferry), **Supp. XXIV:** 153
"Moving Around" (Matthews), **Supp. IX:** 155
"Moving Finger, The" (Wharton), **Retro. Supp. I:** 365
"Moving Inward at Last" (Bly), **Supp. XXI:** 84–85
Moving On (McMurtry), **Supp. V:** 223–224
"Moving On" (Pickering), **Supp. XXI:** 197
Moving Pictures: Memoirs of a Hollywood Prince (Schulberg), **Supp. XVIII:** 242, 243, 254
"Moving Sale" (Stallings), **Supp. XXV:** 228
Moving Target, The (Macdonald), **Supp. IV Part 2:** 462, 463, 467, 470, 471, 473, 474
Moving Target, The (Merwin), **Supp. III Part 1:** 346, 347–348, 352, 357
Mowat, Farley, **Supp. XXVI:** 61

"Mowbray Family, The" (Farrell and Alden), **II:** 45
"Mowing" (Frost), **II:** 169–170; **Retro. Supp. I:** 127, 128; **Retro. Supp. III:** 96
"Moxan's Master" (Bierce), **I:** 206
Moxley, Jennifer, **Supp. XVII:** 70
Moyers, Bill, **Supp. IV Part 1:** 267; **Supp. VIII:** 331; **Supp. XI:** 126, 132; **Supp. XII:** 217; **Supp. XIII:** 274, 276; **Supp. XV:** 212; **Supp. XXIII:** 129, 130, 131, 139
Moylan, Virginia Lynn, **Retro. Supp. III:** 136
Moynagh, Maureen, **Supp. XXII:** 73
Moynihan, Daniel Patrick, **Retro. Supp. II:** 123; **Supp. VIII:** 241; **Supp. XIX:** 150–151
"Moyshele"(Asch), **Supp. XXIII:** 4
"Mozart" (C. Frost), **Supp. XV:** 94
Mozart, Wolfgang Amadeus, **I:** 479, 588; **IV:** 74, 358; **Supp. IV Part 1:** 284
"Mozart and the Gray Steward" (Wilder), **IV:** 358
Mrabet, Mohammed, **Supp. IV Part 1:** 92, 93
Mr. and Mrs. Baby and Other Stories (Strand), **Supp. IV Part 2:** 631
"Mr. and Mrs. Fix-It" (Lardner), **II:** 431
Mr. Arcularis (Aiken), **I:** 54, 56
"Mr. Big" (Allen), **Supp. XV:** 15
Mr. Bridge (Connell), **Supp. XIV:** 80, 82, 93; **Supp. XXIII:** 302
Mr. Brown Can Moo! Can You? (Geisel), **Supp. XVI:** 104
"Mr. Bruce" (Jewett), **II:** 397; **Retro. Supp. II:** 134, 143
"Mr. Burnshaw and the Statue" (Stevens), **Retro. Supp. I:** 298, 303
"Mr. Carson Death on His Nights Out" (McGrath), **Supp. X:** 118
Mr. Clemens and Mark Twain (Kaplan), **I:** 247–248
"Mr. Coffee and Mr. Fixit" (Carver), **Supp. III Part 1:** 145
"Mr. Cornelius Johnson, Office-Seeker" (Dunbar), **Supp. II Part 1:** 211, 213
"Mr. Costyve Duditch" (Toomer), **Supp. III Part 2:** 486
"Mr. Dajani, Calling from Jericho" (Nye), **Supp. XIII:** 286–287
"Mr. Edwards and the Spider" (R. Lowell), **I:** 544; **II:** 550; **Retro. Supp. II:** 187
Mr. Field's Daughter (Bausch), **Supp. VII:** 47–48, 51–52
"Mr. Flood's Party" (Robinson), **III:** 512
"Mr. Forster's Pageant" (Maxwell), **Supp. VIII:** 172
"Mr. Frost's Chickens" (Oliver), **Supp. VII:** 232–233
"Mr. Higginbotham's Catastrophe" (Hawthorne), **Retro. Supp. III:** 113
Mr. Hodge and Mr. Hazard (Wylie), **Supp. I Part 2:** 708, 709, 714, 721–724
"Mr. Hueffer and the Prose Tradition" (Pound), **III:** 465
Mr. Ives' Christmas (Hijuelos), **Supp. VIII:** 85–86

Mr. Kelso's Lion (Bontemps), **Supp. XXII:** 7
"Mr. Longfellow and His Boy" (Sandburg), **III:** 591
"Mr. Luna and History" (Ríos), **Supp. IV Part 2:** 551
"Mr. Mitochondria" (Stollman), **Supp. XVII:** 50
Mr. Moto Is So Sorry (Marquand), **III:** 57, 58
Mr. Norris Changes Trains (Isherwood), **Supp. XIV:** 161
Mr Peters' Connections (A. Miller), **Retro. Supp. III:** 170, 172, 176
"Mr. Preble Gets Rid of His Wife" (Thurber), **Supp. I Part 2:** 615
"Mr. Rat"(Thompson), **Supp. XXIII:** 301–302
"Mr. Rolfe" (Wilson), **IV:** 436
Mr. Rutherford's Children (S. and A. Warner), **Supp. XVIII:** 264
"Mrs. Adis" (Kaye-Smith), **Supp. XVIII:** 130–131
Mrs. Albert Grundy: Observations in Philistia (Frederic), **II:** 138–139
Mr. Sammler's Planet (Bellow), **I:** 144, 147, 150, 151, 152, 158; **Retro. Supp. II:** 19, 28, 30
Mrs. Balfame (Atherton), **Supp. XXIV:** 20
"Mrs. Bilingsby's Wine" (Taylor), **Supp. V:** 323
Mrs. Bob Cratchit's Wild Christmas Binge (Durang), **Supp. XXIV:** 113, 125
Mrs. Bridge: A Novel (Connell), **Supp. XIV:** 79, 80, 81, 82, **89–94,** 95; **Supp. XXIII:** 302
"Mrs. Cassidy's Last Year" (Gordon), **Supp. IV Part 1:** 306
"Mrs. Cross and Mrs. Kidd" (Munro), **Supp. XXVII:** 188
Mrs. Dalloway (Woolf), **Supp. IV Part 1:** 299; **Supp. VIII:** 5; **Supp. XV:** 55, 65–66
"Mrs. Dimbleby" (Barnhardt), **Supp. XXVII:** 12
"Mrs. Green" (Huddle), **Supp. XXVI:** 148
"Mr. Shelley Speaking" (Wylie), **Supp. I Part 2:** 719
"Mrs. Jellison" (Hay), **Supp. XIV:** 123
"Mrs. Krikorian" (Olds), **Supp. X:** 211
"Mrs. Maecenas" (Burke), **I:** 271
"Mrs. Mandrill" (Nemerov), **III:** 278
"Mrs. Manstey's View" (Wharton), **Retro. Supp. I:** 362, 363
"Mrs. Mobry's Reason" (Chopin), **Retro. Supp. II:** 61
Mr. Spaceman (R. O. Butler), **Supp. XII:** 62, **74–75**
Mrs. Reynolds (Stein), **IV:** 43
"Mrs. Sen's" (Lahiri), **Supp. XXI:** 177–178, 180–181
Mrs. Stevens Hears the Mermaids Singing (Sarton), **Supp. VIII:** 252–253, **256–257**
Mrs. Ted Bliss (Elkin), **Supp. VI: 56,** 58
"Mrs. Turner Cutting the Grass" (Shields), **Supp. VII:** 319–320

"Mrs. Walpurga" (Rukeyser), **Supp. VI:** 273
"Mr. Thompson's Prodigal" (Harte), **Supp. II Part 1:** 354
"Mr. Trumm's Eyes"(Schott), **Supp. XXIII:** 243
Mr. Vertigo (Auster), **Supp. XII: 34–35,** 36
"Mr. Vonnegut in Sumatra" (Saunders), **Supp. XIX:** 235
"Mr. Whittier" (Scott), **Supp. I Part 2:** 705
Mr. Wilson's War (Dos Passos), **I:** 485
"Mr. Woodriff's Neckties" (Gallagher), **Supp. XXIV:** 175–176
"MS. Found in a Bottle" (Poe), **III:** 411, 416; **Retro. Supp. II:** 274
"Ms. Lot" (Rukeyser), **Supp. VI:** 281
Ms. Magazine, **Supp. V:** 259
Mttron-Hirsch, Sidney, **III:** 484–485
Mu (album, Do Cherry), **Supp. XXVII:** 154
"mu" (Mackey), **Supp. XXVII:** 155, 156
"Muchas Gracias Por Todo" (Nye), **Supp. XIII:** 282–283
"Much Madness is divinest Sense" (Dickinson), **Retro. Supp. I:** 37–38
"Muck-A-Muck" (Harte), **Supp. II Part 1:** 342
"Mud Below, The" (Proulx), **Supp. VII:** 262
Mudge, Alden, **Supp. XIV:** 35
"Mudman"(P. Benedict), **Supp. XXIII:** 47
Mudrick, Marvin, **Retro. Supp. II:** 289
"Mud Season" (Kenyon), **Supp. VII:** 167–168
Mueller, Lisel, **Supp. I Part 1:** 83, 88; **Supp. XIV:** 268
Muggli, Mark, **Supp. IV Part 1:** 207
Muhammad, Elijah, **Supp. I Part 1:** 60
Muir, Edwin, **I:** 527; **II:** 368; **III:** 20; **Supp. XXII:** 166; **Supp. XXIII:** 1; **Supp. XXVI:** 67
Muir, John, **Supp. IX:** 33, **171–188; Supp. VIII:** 296; **Supp. X:** 29; **Supp. XIV:** 177, 178, 181; **Supp. XXVI:** 34, 37, 43; **Supp. XXVIII:** 249, 251, 253, 255
Muir, Willa, **Supp. XXIII:** 1
Muirhead, Deborah, **Supp. XVIII:** 186
Mujica, Barbara, **Supp. VIII:** 89
Mulas, Franco, **Supp. XX:** 38
Mulatto (Hughes), **Retro. Supp. I:** 197, 203; **Supp. I Part 1:** 328, 339
Mulching of America, The (Crews), **Supp. XI:** 107
Muldoon, William, **I:** 500–501
Mule Bone (Hughes and Hurston), **Retro. Supp. I:** 194, 203; **Supp. VI:** 154
Mule Bone (Hurston), **Retro. Supp. III:** 128
Mules and Men (Hurston), **Retro. Supp. III:** 128, 130, 132, 137, 138; **Supp. VI:** 149, 153, 154, 160
Mulford, Prentice, **I:** 193
Mullen, Harryette, **Supp. XXVII: 163–177**
Mullennix, Joel, **Supp. XXIII:** 281
Muller, Kathryn, **Supp. XXVI:** 95

Mulligan, Robert, **Supp. VIII:** 128, 129
Mulligan Stew (Sorrentino), **Supp. XII:** 139; **Supp. XXI:** 233
Mullins, Eustace, **III:** 479
Mullins, Priscilla, **II:** 502–503
"Multiplication of Wool, The" (Sanders), **Supp. XVI:** 268
"Multitraditional Faith: A Personal View of Christians in Dialogue with People of Other Religious Traditions"(Eck), **Supp. XXVIII:** 53
Multitudes, Multitudes (Clampitt), **Supp. IX:** 39
Mumbo Jumbo (Reed), **Supp. X:** 240, 242, **245–248,** 251
Mumford, Lewis, **I:** 245, 250, 251, 252, 259, 261; **II:** 271, 473–474; **Supp. I Part 2:** 632, 638; **Supp. II Part 2: 471–501**
Mumford, Sophia Wittenberg (Mrs. Lewis Mumford), **Supp. II Part 2:** 474, 475
"Mummers, The" (Di Piero), **Supp. XIX:** 44
Mummy, The (film), **Supp. IV Part 1:** 104; **Supp. XVII:** 57
Mundo y Palabra (Espaillat), **Supp. XXI:** 104
"Mundus et Infans" (Auden), **Supp. II Part 1:** 15
Mundy, Talbot, **Supp. XXVII:** 121
"Munich, 1938" (R. Lowell), **II:** 554
"Munich Mannequins, The" (Plath), **Retro. Supp. II:** 256
"Municipal Report, A" (Henry), **Supp. II Part 1:** 406–407
Muñoz, Manuel, **Supp. XXV: 127–139**
Munro, Alice, **Supp. IX:** 212; **Supp. X:** 290; **Supp. XII:** 289–290, 310; **Supp. XXIII:** 289, 296; **Supp. XXVII: 179–198**
Munsey, Frank, **I:** 501; **Supp. XXVII:** 120
Munson, Gorham, **I:** 252, 388, 432; **Retro. Supp. II:** 77, 78, 79, 82, 83; **Retro. Supp. III:** 45, 48; **Supp. I Part 2:** 454; **Supp. XX: 70, 74**
Münsterberg, Hugo, **Supp. XIV:** 197
Murakami, Haruki, **Supp. XVI:** 124
"Muralist, The" (Rich), **Retro. Supp. III:** 241
"Murano" (Doty), **Supp. XI:** 131
Murasaki, Lady, **II:** 577
Muratori, Fred, **Supp. XVI:** 281
Muray, Nicholas, **Supp. I Part 2:** 708
Murchison, Ginger, **Supp. XXV:** 222, 223, 226
Murder, My Sweet (film), **Supp. IV Part 1:** 130
"Murder Comes for the Bishop"(Goldman), **Supp. XXV:** 57
"Murderer Guest, The" (Gordon), **Supp. IV Part 1:** 306
"Murderers" (L. Michaels), **Supp. XVI:** 207–208
"Murderer's Grog" (Howard), **Supp. XXVII:** 121
Murder in Mount Holly (Theroux), **Supp. VIII:** 315–316
Murder in the Cathedral (T. S. Eliot), **I:** 571, 573, 580, 581; **II:** 20; **Retro.**

Supp. I: 65; **Retro. Supp. II:** 222; **Retro. Supp. III:** 66, 69–70

Murder of Lidice, The (Millay), **III:** 140

"Murders in the Rue Morgue, The" (Poe), **III:** 412, 416, 419–420; **Retro. Supp. II:** 271, 272; **Retro. Supp. III:** 225–226, 226–227; **Supp. XIX:** 77

Murdoch, Iris, **Supp. VIII:** 167; **Supp. XVIII:** 136,149

Murfree, Mary Noailles (ps. Charles Egbert Craddock), **Supp. XXVIII:** 113, 239

Murnau, F. W., **Supp. XV:** 128

Murphy, Brenda, **Supp. XXI:** 6

Murphy, Cullen, **Supp. XXVI:** 61

Murphy, Jacqueline Shea, **Retro. Supp. II:** 143

Murphy, Patrick, **Supp. XIII:** 214

Murphy, Richard, **Retro. Supp. II:** 250; **Supp. XXIII:** 75

Murray, Albert, **Retro. Supp. II:** 119, 120; **Supp. XIX:** 147–162

Murray, Bill, **Supp. XXI:** 51

Murray, Edward, **I:** 229

Murray, G. E., **Supp. X:** 201; **Supp. XI:** 143, 155

Murray, Gilbert, **III:** 468–469

Murray, Jan, **Supp. IV Part 2:** 574

Murray, John, **II:** 304; **III:** 76, 79; **Retro. Supp. I:** 246

Murray, Judith Sargent, **Supp. XV:** 236–237

Murray, Les, **Supp. XIX:** 131

Murray, Margaret A., **Supp. V:** 128

Murrell, John A., **IV:** 265

Mursell, James L., **Supp. I Part 2:** 608

"Muse" (Ammons), **Supp. VII:** 29

"Muse, Postmodern and Homeless, The" (Ozick), **Supp. V:** 272

Muse & Drudge (Mullen), **Supp. XXVII:** 171–172, 176

"Musée des Beaux Arts" (Auden), **Retro. Supp. I:** 430; **Supp. II Part 1:** 14

"Musée des Beaux Arts Revisited" (Collins), **Supp. XXI:** 60

"Muse of Aboutness, The" (Baker), **Supp. XVI:** 288

Muses Are Heard, The (Capote), **Supp. III Part 1:** 126

"Muses of Terrence McNally, The" (Zinman), **Supp. XIII:** 207–208

"Muse's Tragedy, The" (Wharton), **Retro. Supp. I:** 364; **Retro. Supp. III:** 279

Museum (Dove), **Supp. IV Part 1:** 245–247, 248

"Museum" (Hass), **Supp. VI:** 107

Museums and Women (Updike), **Retro. Supp. I:** 321

"Museum Vase" (Francis), **Supp. IX:** 83

"Mushrooms" (Plath), **Retro. Supp. II:** 246; **Supp. I Part 2:** 539

"Music" (Huddle), **Supp. XXVI:** 150

"Music" (Oliver), **Supp. VII:** 236

Music (al-Músíqá) (Gibran), **Supp. XX:** 115, 124

Music After the Great War (Van Vechten), **Supp. II Part 2:** 732

Music and Bad Manners (Van Vechten), **Supp. II Part 2:** 733

Music Appreciation (Skloot), **Supp. XX:** 196, 197–201

"Music for a Farce" (Bowles), **Supp. IV Part 1:** 83

Music for Chameleons (Capote), **Supp. III Part 1:** 120, 125–127, 131, 132

"Music for Museums?" (Van Vechten), **Supp. II Part 2:** 732

"Music for the Movies" (Van Vechten), **Supp. II Part 2:** 733

"Music from Spain" (Welty), **IV:** 272

Music Like Dirt (Bidart), **Supp. XV:** 35

"Music Like Dirt" (Bidart), **Supp. XV:** 35

Music of Chance, The (Auster), **Supp. XII:** 21, 23, 32–33

"Music of My Own Kind Too, The" (Budbill), **Supp. XIX:** 10

"Music of Prose, The" (Gass), **Supp. VI:** 92

Music of Spain, The (Van Vechten), **Supp. II Part 2:** 734, 735

"Music of the Spheres" (Epstein), **Supp. XII:** 165

"Music School" (B. Kelly), **Supp. XVII:** 124

Music School, The (Updike), **IV:** 214, 215, 219, 226, 227; **Retro. Supp. I:** 320, 328, 329, 330

"Music School, The" (Updike), **Retro. Supp. I:** 326, 329, 335

"Music Swims Back to Me" (Sexton), **Supp. II Part 2:** 673

Muske, Carol, **Supp. IV Part 2:** 453–454

"Mussel Hunter at Rock Harbor" (Plath), **Supp. I Part 2:** 529, 537

Musset, Alfred de, **I:** 474; **II:** 543

Mussolini, Benito, **III:** 115, 473, 608; **IV:** 372, 373; **Supp. I Part 1:** 281, 282; **Supp. I Part 2:** 618; **Supp. V:** 290; **Supp. XVI:** 191

"Mustafa Ferrari" (X. J. Kennedy), **Supp. XV:** 170–171

Mustich, James, **Supp. XXI:** 52

"Must the Novelist Crusade?" (Welty), **IV:** 280

"Mutability of Literature, The" (Irving), **II:** 308

"Mutation of the Spirit" (Corso), **Supp. XII:** 132, 133

Mute, The (McCullers), **II:** 586

Mutilated, The (T. Williams), **IV:** 382, 386, 393

Mutiny of the Elsinore, The (London), **II:** 467

"Muttsy" (Hurston), **Supp. XVIII:** 279; **Supp. XXVI:** 164

Muyumba, Walton, **Supp. XIX:** 158

"My Adventures as a Social Poet" (Hughes), **Retro. Supp. I:** 194, 207

"My Alba" (Ginsberg), **Supp. II Part 1:** 320, 321

My Alexandria (Doty), **Supp. XI:** 119, 120, 121, **123–125,** 130

"My Amendment" (Saunders), **Supp. XIX:** 232

My Amputations (Major), **Supp. XXII:** 174, **175–176**

My Ántonia (Cather), **I:** 321–322; **Retro. Supp. I:** 1, 3, 4, **11–13,** 14, 17, 18, 22; **Retro. Supp. III:** 18, 20, 23, 30–32, 36; **Supp. IV Part 2:** 608; **Supp. XVI:** 226

"My Appearance" (Wallace), **Supp. X:** 306–307

My Argument with the Gestapo: A Macaronic Journal (Merton), **Supp. VIII:** 207; **Supp. XV:** 344

"My Arkansas" (Angelou), **Supp. IV Part 1:** 15

"My Aunt" (Holmes), **Supp. I Part 1:** 302, 310

"My Beginnings" (Simpson), **Supp. IX:** 273

"My Bird Problem" (Franzen), **Supp. XX:** 94

My Black Horse (Gallagher), **Supp. XXIV:** 170

"My Bodyguard" (Notley), **Supp. XXII:** 230

My Bondage and My Freedom (Douglass), **Supp. III Part 1:** 155, 173

"My Bones Here Are Waiting for Yours" (Vaz), **Supp. XXVI:** 265–266

My Brother (Kincaid), **Supp. VII:** 191–193

"My Brother Paul" (Dreiser), **Retro. Supp. II:** 94

"My Brothers the Silent" (Merwin), **Supp. III Part 1:** 349–350

"My Brother's Work" (Dunn), **Supp. XI:** 147

"My Brother Takes a Hammer to the Mirror" (F. Wright), **Supp. XVII:** 244

"My Butterfly" (Frost), **II:** 151; **Retro. Supp. I:** 124; **Retro. Supp. III:** 91–92, 94

"My Children, and a Prayer for Us" (Ortiz), **Supp. IV Part 2:** 507

My Children! My Africa! (Fugard), **Supp. XXIV:** 267

"My College Sex Group" (Peacock), **Supp. XIX:** 199

"My Coney Island Uncle" (Swados), **Supp. XIX:** 267–268

"My Confession" (McCarthy), **II:** 562

"My Confessional Sestina" (Gioia), **Supp. XV:** 123

"My Corner" (Major), **Supp. XXII:** 184

My Country and My People (Yutang), **Supp. X:** 291

"My Country Tish of Thee" (Rinehart), **Supp. XXV:** 194

"My Country 'Tis of Thee" (Reznikoff), **Supp. III Part 2:** 616

"My Daughter at the Gymnastics Party"(Bottoms), **Supp. XXVIII:** 29

"My Daughter Considers Her Body" (Skloot), **Supp. XX: 197–198,** 200

"My Daughter Works the Heavy Bag"(Bottoms), **Supp. XXVIII:** 32

My Days of Anger (Farrell), **II:** 34, 35–36, 43

"My Dear Niece" (Boyce), **Supp. XXI:** 10

"My Dear Republican Mother" (C. Bly), **Supp. XVI:** 31–32

My Death My Life by Pier Paolo Pasolini (Acker), **Supp. XII:** 7
My Dog Stupid (Fante), **Supp. XI:** 160, **170–171**
My Dog Tulip (Ackerley), **Supp. XX: 237**
"My Ear-Rings"(J. Schoolcraft), **Supp. XXIII:** 226
My Emily Dickinson (Howe), **Retro. Supp. I:** 33, 43; **Supp. IV Part 2:** 430–431
"My English" (Alvarez), **Supp. VII:** 2
Myers, Christopher, **Supp. XXVII:** 211
Myers, John Bernard, **Supp. XXIII:** 210, 219
Myers, Linda A., **Supp. IV Part 1:** 10
Myers, Walter Dean, **Supp. XXVII: 199– 214**
Myerson, Julie, **Supp. XXVII:** 278
"My Extended Family" (Theroux), **Supp. VIII:** 311
My Face for the World to See (Hayes), **Supp. XXVI:** 139, 141–142
"My Father" (Biss), **Supp. XXVI:** 47
"My Father" (Budbill), **Supp. XIX:** 5
"My Father" (L. Michaels), **Supp. XVI:** 214
"My Father" (Sterne), **IV:** 466
"My Father at Eighty-Five" (R. Bly), **Supp. IV Part 1:** 73
"My Father Is a Simple Man" (Salinas), **Supp. XIII:** 324
"My Father Is with Me" (Budbill), **Supp. XIX:** 15
"My Father: October 1942" (Stafford), **Supp. XI:** 323
My Father Photographed with Friends (Bronk), **Supp. XXI:** 26–27,**Supp. XXI:** 31
"My Father Photographed with Friends" (Bronk), **Supp. XXI:** 23, 27
"My Fathers Came From Kentucky" (Lindsay), **Supp. I Part 2:** 395
"My Father's Employment"(Schott), **Supp. XXIII:** 247
"My Father's Friends" (Maxwell), **Supp. VIII:** 171
"My Father's Ghost" (Wagoner), **Supp. IX:** 330
"My Father's God" (Fante), **Supp. XI:** 160, 174
My Father's House (film), **Supp. XXVII:** 141
"My Father's House" (L.-Y. Lee), **Supp. XV:** 225
"My Father's Love Letters" (Gallagher), **Supp. XXIV:** 171–172
"My Father's Love Letters" (Komunyakaa), **Supp. XIII:** 127
"My Father Speaks to me from the Dead" (Olds), **Supp. X:** 210
"My Father's Telescope" (Dove), **Supp. IV Part 1:** 246, 248
"My Father with Cigarette Twelve Years Before the Nazis Could Break His Heart" (Levine), **Supp. V:** 194
"My Favorite Murder" (Bierce), **I:** 205
My Favorite Plant: Writers and Gardeners on the Plants They Love (Kincaid), **Supp. VII:** 193–194

My Favorites in Suspense (Hitchcock, ed.), **Supp. XXII:** 119
"My Fifty-Plus Years Celebrate Spring" (Salinas), **Supp. XIII:** 327
"My First Book" (Harte), **Supp. II Part 1:** 343
My First Summer in the Sierra (Muir), **Supp. IX:** 172, 173, **178–181**, 183, 185; **Supp. XIV:** 177
"My Flamboyant Grandson" (Saunders), **Supp. XIX:** 231–232
"My Fountain Pen" (McClatchy), **Supp. XII:** 254, 260
My Friend, Henry Miller (Perlès), **III:** 189
My Friend, Julia Lathrop (Addams), **Supp. I Part 1:** 25
"My Friend, Walt Whitman" (Oliver), **Supp. VII:** 245
"My Garden Acquaintance" (J. R. Lowell), **Supp. I Part 2:** 420
My Garden \[Book\]: (Kincaid), **Supp. VII:** 193–194
"My Good-bye" (Weigl), **Supp. XIX:** 288
"My Good Man" (Gansworth), **Supp. XXVI:** 114
"My Grandfather" (R. Lowell), **II:** 554
"My Grandmother's Love Letters" (H. Crane), **Retro. Supp. II:** 78; **Retro. Supp. III:** 46
"My Grandpa Builds an Airplane"(Bottoms), **Supp. XXVIII:** 32
My Grandparents Were Married for Sixty-five Years (Schott), **Supp. XXIII:** 240–241
"My Grandson, Home at Last" (Angelou), **Supp. IV Part 1:** 13
My Green Hills of Jamaica (McKay), **Supp. X:** 132, 142
"My Gun" (Gallagher), **Supp. XXIV:** 175
My Guru and His Disciple (Isherwood), **Supp. XIV:** 157, 164, 172
"My Heart" (Collins), **Supp. XXI:** 58
My Heart's in the Highlands (Saroyan), **Supp. IV Part 1:** 83
"My Hell's Angel"(Wakoski), **Supp. XXVIII:** 264
"My High School Reunion" (Kingston), **Supp. V:** 169
My Hollywood (Simpson), **Supp. XXVII:** 242–244
"My House New-Painted" (Bronk), **Supp. XXI:** 30
"My Hunt for King Sebastião" (Vaz), **Supp. XXVI:** 260
"My Ideal Home" (Stratton-Porter), **Supp. XX: 222**
"My Indigo" (L.-Y. Lee), **Supp. XV:** 214
My Kind of Place: Travel Stories from a Woman Who's Been Everywhere (Orlean), **Supp. XXV:** 160, 164–165
"My Kinsman, Major Molineux" (Hawthorne), **II:** 228, 229, 237–239, 243; **Retro. Supp. I:** 153–154, 158, 160, 161; **Retro. Supp. II:** 181, 187; **Retro. Supp. III:** 110, 112; **Supp. XVI:** 157
My Kinsman, Major Molineux (R. Lowell), **II:** 545–546

"My Last Afternoon with Uncle Devereux Winslow" (R. Lowell), **II:** 547–548; **Retro. Supp. II:** 189
"My Last Drive" (Hardy), **Supp. VIII:** 32
"My Last Duchess" (R. Browning), **Supp. XV:** 121; **Supp. XXV:** 229; **Supp. XXVII:** 218
Myles, Eileen, **Supp. XXIV:** 45
"My Life" (Strand), **Supp. IV Part 2:** 627
My Life, Starring Dara Falcon (Beattie), **Supp. V:** 31, 34–35
My Life a Loaded Gun: Dickinson, Plath, Rich, and Female Creativity (Bennett), **Retro. Supp. I:** 29
My Life and Hard Times (Thurber), **Supp. I Part 2:** 607, 609
My Life and Loves in Greenwich Village (attr. Bodenheim), **Supp. XXV:** 30
My Life as a Man (P. Roth), **Retro. Supp. II:** 281, 286, 289; **Supp. III Part 2:** 401, 404, 405, 417–418
"My Life as a P.I.G., or the True Adventures of Smokey the Cop" (Abbey), **Supp. XIII:** 3
"My life closed twice before its close" (Dickinson), **Retro. Supp. I:** 38
"My Life had stood a Loaded Gun" (Dickinson), **Retro. Supp. I:** 42, 43, 45, 46; **Supp. IV Part 2:** 430
My Life of Absurdity (C. Himes), **Supp. XVI:** 145
"My Life with Medicine" (Nye), **Supp. XIII:** 282
"My Life with *Playboy*" (Plimpton), **Supp. XVI:** 246
"My Life with R. H. Macy" (Jackson), **Supp. IX:** 118
"My Little Utopia" (Simic), **Supp. VIII:** 283
My Lives and How I Lost Them (Cullen), **Supp. IV Part 1:** 173
"My Lord Bag of Rice" (C. Bly), **Supp. XVI:** 40
My Lord Bag of Rice: New and Selected Stories (C. Bly), **Supp. XVI:** 41
"My Lost City" (Fitzgerald), **Retro. Supp. I:** 102
"My Lost Youth" (Longfellow), **II:** 487, 499; **Retro. Supp. II:** 168
My Love Affair with America: The Cautionary Tale of a Cheerful Conservative (Podhoretz), **Supp. VIII:** 232, 233, 237, **244–246**
"My Lover Has Dirty Fingernails" (Updike), **Retro. Supp. I:** 332, 333
"My lover is tall and handsome"(J. Schoolcraft), **Supp. XXIII:** 235
"My Lucy Friend Who Smells Like Corn" (Cisneros), **Supp. VII:** 68–69
"My Mammogram" (McClatchy), **Supp. XII:** 263–264
"My Man Bovanne" (Bambara), **Supp. XI:** 2
"My Mariner" (Larcom), **Supp. XIII:** 147
My Mark Twain (Howells), **II:** 276; **Retro. Supp. III:** 262
"My Metamorphosis" (Harte), **Supp. II Part 1:** 339

My Mistress's Sparrow Is Dead (Eugenides, ed.), **Supp. XXIV:** 135

"My Moby Dick" (Humphrey), **Supp. IX:** 95

"My Monkey" (Nelson), **Supp. XVIII:** 178

"My Moral Life" (Halliday), **Supp. XIX:** 89

My Mortal Enemy (Cather), **I:** 327–328; **Retro. Supp. I:** 16–17; **Supp. I Part 2:** 719

"My Mother" (Biss), **Supp. XXVI:** 47

My Mother, My Father and Me (Hellman), **Supp. I Part 1:** 290–291

"My Mother and My Sisters" (Ortiz), **Supp. IV Part 2:** 499

My Mother: Demonology (Acker), **Supp. XII:** 6

"My Mother Is Speaking from the Desert" (Gordon), **Supp. IV Part 1:** 309, 314

"My Mother Milkman"(Wakoski), **Supp. XXVIII:** 267

"My Mother Remembers That She Was Beautiful" (Gallagher), **Supp. XXIV:** 169

"My Mother's Goofy Song" (Fante), **Supp. XI:** 164

"My Mother's Memoirs, My Father's Lie, and Other True Stories" (Banks), **Supp. V:** 15

"My Mother's Nipples" (Hass), **Supp. VI:** 109

"My Mother's Story" (Kunitz), **Supp. III Part 1:** 259

"My Mother's Voice" (Very), **Supp. XXV:** 244

"My Mother"(Taylor), **Supp. XXIII:** 231

"My Mother Then and Now" (Wasserstein), **Supp. XV:** 327

"My Mother with Purse the Summer They Murdered the Spanish Poet" (Levine), **Supp. V:** 194

My Movie Business: A Memoir (Irving), **Supp. VI:** 164

"My Name" (Cisneros), **Supp. VII:** 60

"My Negro Problem—And Ours" (Podhoretz), **Supp. VIII: 234–236**

"My Neighborhood"(Dybek), **Supp. XXIII:** 69

"My New Diet" (Karr), **Supp. XI:** 241

My Next Bride (Boyle), **Supp. XXIV: 53,** 59

"My November Guest" (Frost), **Retro. Supp. III:** 96

"My Number" (Collins), **Supp. XXI:** 64

"My Old Man" (Hemingway), **II:** 263

My Other Life (Theroux), **Supp. VIII:** 310, 324

"My Own Story" (E. Stoddard), **Supp. XV:** 273, 279, 283

My Own True Name: New and Selected Poems for Young Adults, 1984–1999 (Mora), **Supp. XIII:** 222

"My Papa's Waltz" (Roehke), **Supp. XXVII:** 250

"My Parents Have Come Home Laughing" (Jarman), **Supp. XVII:** 113

"My Passion for Ferries" (Whitman), **IV:** 350

"My People" (Hughes), **Retro. Supp. I:** 197; **Supp. I Part 1:** 321–322, 323

"My Philosophy" (Allen), **Supp. XV:** 15

"My Playmate" (Whittier), **Supp. I Part 2:** 699–700

"My Priests" (Monette), **Supp. X:** 159

"My Public" (Rinehart), **Supp. XXV:** 201

Myra Breckinridge (Vidal), **Supp. IV Part 2:** 677, 685–686, 689, 691

"My Race" (H. Johnson), **Supp. XXVI:** 163

"My Raptor" (A. Finch), **Supp. XVII:** 72

"My Recollections of S. B. Fairchild" (Jackson), **Supp. IX:** 118–119

"My Religion" (Carson), **Supp. XII:** 105–106

Myrer, Anton, **Supp. XXV:** 145

"My Road to Hell Was Paved" (Patchett), **Supp. XII:** 310–311

Myron (Vidal), **Supp. IV Part 2:** 677, 685, 686, 691

"My Roomy" (Lardner), **II:** 420, 421, 428, 430

"My Sad Self" (Ginsberg), **Supp. II Part 1:** 320

My San Francisco (Atherton), **Supp. XXIV:** 27

My Secret History (Theroux), **Supp. VIII:** 310, 324

"Myself" (Audubon), **Supp. XVI:** 1–2, 5, 12

Myself Painting (Major), **Supp. XXII: 184–185**

"My Shoes" (Simic), **Supp. VIII:** 275

"My Side of the Matter" (Capote), **Supp. III Part 1:** 114, 115

My Silk Purse and Yours: The Publishing Scene and American Literary Art (Garrett), **Supp. VII:** 111; **Supp. X:** 7

My Sister Eileen (McKenney), **IV:** 288; **Retro. Supp. II:** 321

My Sister's Hand in Mine: The Collected Works of Jane Bowles, **Supp. IV Part 1:** 82–83

"My Son" (Strand), **Supp. IV Part 2:** 629

My Son, John (film), **Supp. I Part 1:** 67

"My Son, the Murderer" (Malamud), **Supp. I Part 2:** 437

My Son Is a Splendid Driver (Inge), **Supp. XXV:** 93, 95, 107

"My Son the Man" (Olds), **Supp. X:** 212

"My Speech to the Graduates" (Allen), **Supp. XV:** 16

"Mysteries of Caesar, The" (Hecht), **Supp. X:** 73

"Mysteries of Eleusis, The" (Hardwick), **Supp. III Part 1:** 195

Mysteries of Paris, The (Sue), **Supp. XXIII:** 182

Mysteries of Pittsburgh, The (Chabon), **Supp. XI:** 65, 68, **69–71; Supp. XIX:** 135

Mysteries of Small Houses (Notley), **Supp. XXII:** 223, 224, 226, 234–235

"Mysterious Case of R, The" (Conroy), **Supp. XVI:** 72

Mysterious Stranger, The (Twain), **IV:** 190–191, 210; **Retro. Supp. III:** 269

Mystery, A (Shields). *See Swann* (Shields)

"Mystery, The" (Dunbar), **Supp. II Part 1:** 199, 210

"Mystery, The" (Glück), **Supp. V:** 91

"Mystery, The" (Teasdale), **Supp. XXVII:** 293

Mystery and Manners (O'Connor), **Retro. Supp. II:** 230; **Retro. Supp. III:** 208

"'Mystery Boy' Looks for Kin in Nashville" (Hayden), **Supp. II Part 1:** 366, 372

"Mystery of Coincidence, The" (Conroy), **Supp. XVI:** 74

"Mystery of Heroism, A" (Crane), **I:** 414

"Mystery of Marie Rogêt, The" (Poe), **III:** 413, 419; **Retro. Supp. II:** 271

"Mystic" (Plath), **Retro. Supp. II:** 257; **Supp. I Part 2:** 539, 541

"Mystical Poet, A" (Bogan), **Retro. Supp. I:** 36

"Mystic of Sex, The—A First Look at D. H. Lawrence" (Nin), **Supp. X:** 188

"Mystic Vision in 'The Marshes of Glynn'" (Warfel), **Supp. I Part 1:** 366, 373

"Mystification" (Poe), **III:** 425

"My Story" (Monroe), **Supp. XXVII:** 95

"My Strange New Poetry" (Halliday), **Supp. XIX:** 88, 94

My Study Windows (J. R. Lowell), **Supp. I Part 2:** 407

"My Teacher" (Conroy), **Supp. XVI:** 75

"Myth" (Rukeyser), **Supp. VI:** 281–282

"Myth" (Trethewey), **Supp. XXI:** 245, 255, 256

"Myth"(Hadas), **Supp. XXIII:** 119

"Mythmaker" (Trethewey), **Supp. XXI:** 243

Myth of American Manhood, The (Kriegel, ed.), **Supp. XXIV:** 214

Myth of Sisyphus, The (Camus), **I:** 294; **Supp. XIII:** 165

"Myth of the Happy Worker, The" (Swados), **Supp. XIX:** 265

"Myth of the Isolated Artist, The" (Oates), **Supp. II Part 2:** 520

Myth of the Machine, The (Mumford), **Supp. II Part 2:** 476, 478, 482, 483, 493, 497

"Myth of the Powerful Worker, The" (Swados), **Supp. XIX:** 265

Mythology and the Romantic Tradition in English Poetry (Bush), **Supp. I Part 1:** 268

Myths and Texts (Snyder), **Supp. VIII: 295–296**

"Myths of Bears, The" (Bass), **Supp. XVI:** 19, 20

"My Tocaya" (Cisneros), **Supp. VII:** 69

My Uncle Dudley (Morris), **I:** 305; **III:** 219–220

"My Uncle's Favorite Coffee Shop" (Nye), **Supp. XIII:** 283

"My Uncle Sowing Beatitudes"(Bottoms), **Supp. XXVIII:** 28

"My Unopened Life" (Gallagher), **Supp. XXIV:** 171

"My Weariness of Epic Proportions" (Simic), **Supp. VIII:** 276

My Wicked Wicked Ways (Cisneros), **Supp. VII:** 58, 64–68, 71

"My Wicked Wicked Ways" (Cisneros), **Supp. VII:** 58, 64–66
My Wisdom (Thompson), **Supp. XXIII: 291–293**
"My Word-house" (Mora), **Supp. XIII:** 219, 225
My Works and Days (Mumford), **Supp. II Part 2:** 475, 477, 481
"My World and My Critics" (Stratton-Porter), **Supp. XX: 220**
My World and Welcome to It (Thurber), **Supp. I Part 2:** 610

N

Nabokov, Peter, **Supp. IV Part 2:** 490
Nabokov, Véra, **Retro. Supp. I:** 266, 270
Nabokov, Vladimir, **I:** 135; **III: 244–266,** 283, 286; **Retro. Supp. I: 263–281,** 317, 335; **Supp. I Part 1:** 196; **Supp. II Part 1:** 2; **Supp. IV Part 1:** 135; **Supp. IX:** 152, 212, 261; **Supp. V:** 127, 237, 251, 252, 253; **Supp. VIII:** 105, 133, 138; **Supp. X:** 283; **Supp. XI:** 66; **Supp. XII:** 310; **Supp. XIII:** 46, 52; **Supp. XVI:** 148, 294; **Supp. XVIII:** 98, 102; **Supp. XXII:** 263; **Supp. XXIV:** 133
Nabokov's Dozen (Nabokov), **Retro. Supp. I:** 266
Nabokov's Garden: A Guide to Ada (Mason), **Supp. VIII:** 138
Naca, Kristin, **Supp. XIII:** 133
Nadeau, Robert, **Supp. X:** 261, 270
Nadel, Alan, **Supp. IV Part 1:** 209
Nafisi, Azar, **Supp. XXVIII:** 80–81
Naimy, Mikhail, **Supp. XX: 116, 119, 120**
Naipaul, V. S., **Supp. IV Part 1:** 297; **Supp. VIII:** 314; **Supp. X:** 131; **Supp. XIV:** 111; **Supp. XX: 87; Supp. XXI:** 170; **Supp. XXII:** 240, 241, 242, 246, 253
Naison, Mark, **Supp. XVIII:** 231
Naked and the Dead, The (Mailer), **I:** 477; **III:** 26, 27, 28–30, 31, 33, 35, 36, 44; **Retro. Supp. II: 197–199; Supp. IV Part 1:** 381; **Supp. XI:** 218; **Supp. XIX:** 248; **Supp. XX:** 248; **Supp. XXI:** 277
Naked Author (di Donato), **Supp. XX: 45**
Naked Babies (Quindlen and Kelsh), **Supp. XVII:** 167, 179
Naked in Garden Hills (Crews), **Supp. XI:** 102, **110**
Naked Lunch (Burroughs), **Supp. III Part 1:** 92–95, 97–105; **Supp. IV Part 1:** 90
"Naked Nude" (Malamud), **Supp. I Part 2:** 450
Naked on Roller Skates (Bodenheim), **Supp. XXV:** 27
Naked Poetry (Berg and Mezey, eds.), **Supp. IV Part 1:** 60
Naked Poetry (Levine), **Supp. V:** 180
Naked Revenge (film), **Supp. XVII:** 141
Nall, Gus, **Supp. XXII:** 172, 184
Namedropping: Mostly Literary Memoirs (Coover), **Supp. V:** 40
"Name in the Papers" (Hughes), **Supp. I Part 1:** 330

Name Is Archer, The (Macdonald, under Millar), **Supp. IV Part 2:** 466
"Name Is Burroughs, The" (Burroughs), **Supp. III Part 1:** 93
Name Is Fogarty, The: Private Papers on Public Matters (Farrell), **II:** 49
"Names" (Carruth), **Supp. XVI:** 54, 56
"Names, The" (Collins), **Supp. XXI:** 54, 61–62
Names, The (DeLillo), **Supp. VI:** 3, 10, 13, 14
Names, The (Momaday), **Supp. IV Part 2:** 479, 480, 483, 486, 487, 488, 489
Namesake, The (Lahiri), **Supp. XXI:** 176, 184, **186–188**
Names and Faces of Heroes, The (Price), **Supp. VI:** 258, 260
Names of the Dead, The (O'Nan), **Supp. XXV:** 142, 143–144, 149, 151
Names of the Lost, The (Levine), **Supp. V:** 177–178, 179, 187–188
"Naming for Love" (Carruth), **Supp. XVI:** 48
"Naming Myself" (Kingsolver), **Supp. VII:** 208
"Naming of Names, The" (Sanders), **Supp. XVI:** 268
Naming of the Beasts, The (Stern). *See Rejoicings: Selected Poems, 1966–1972* (Stern)
Naming the Unseen (Ray), **Supp. XVIII:** 192, **193–195**
"Naming the Unseen" (Ray), **Supp. XVIII:** 203
Nana (Zola), **III:** 321
Nance, Kevin, **Supp. XXVI:** 58; **Supp. XXVII:** 268
"Nancy Culpepper" (Mason), **Supp. VIII:** 141
Nancy Drew stories, **Supp. VIII:** 133, 135, 137, 142
"Nancy Knapp" (Masters), **Supp. I Part 2:** 461
"Naola Beauty Academy, New Orleans, 1943" (Trethewey), **Supp. XXI:** 246
"Naomi Counting Time"(Thompson), **Supp. XXIII:** 293
"Naomi Shihab Nye: U.S. Mideast-History a Harbinger of 9-11?" (Nye), **Supp. XIII:** 286
"Naomi Trimmer" (X. J. Kennedy), **Supp. XV:** 170
"Nap, The" (Banks), **Supp. V:** 7
"Napoleon" (Emerson), **II:** 6
Napoleon I, **I:** 6, 7, 8, 474; **II:** 5, 309, 315, 321, 523; **Supp. I Part 1:** 153; **Supp. I Part 2:** 518, 519
Napoleon Jackson: The Gentleman of the Plush Rocker (Stuart), **Supp. XXVIII:** 233, 235
Napoli, Mary, **Supp. XXVIII:** 285
Napolitano, Louise, **Supp. XX: 35, 45, 46–47**
Narcissa and Other Fables (Auchincloss), **Supp. IV Part 1:** 21, 34
"Narcissus as Narcissus" (Tate), **IV:** 124
"Narcissus Leaves the Pool" (Epstein), **Supp. XIV:** 110
Narcissus Leaves the Pool: Familiar Essays (Epstein), **Supp. XIV:** 110

Nardal, Paulette, **Supp. X:** 139
Nardi, Marcia, **Retro. Supp. I:** 426, 427
"Narragansett Boulevard" (Halliday), **Supp. XIX:** 91
Narration (Stein), **IV:** 27, 30, 32, 33, 36
Narrative of a Four Months' Residence among the Natives of a Valley of the Marquesas Islands (Melville), **III:** 76
Narrative of Arthur Gordon Pym, The (Poe), **III:** 412, 416; **Retro. Supp. II:** 265, **273–275; Retro. Supp. III:** 224, 234, 235–236; **Supp. XI:** 293; **Supp. XXII:** 58
Narrative of the Life of Frederick Douglass, an American Slave, Written by Himself (Douglass), **Supp. III Part 1:** 154–159, 162, 165; **Supp. IV Part 1:** 13; **Supp. VIII:** 202
"Narrativity Scenes" (Wright), **Supp. XV:** 345
Narrenschiff, Das (Brant), **III:** 447
"Narrow Fellow in the Grass, A" (Dickinson), **Retro. Supp. I:** 30, 37
Narrow Heart, A: Portrait of a Woman (Gordon), **II:** 197, 217
Narrow Rooms (Purdy), **Supp. VII:** 274
Narrows, The (Connelly), **Supp. XXI:** 71, **76**
Nasby, Petroleum, **Supp. XVIII:** 1
Nash, Noreen, **Supp. XXII:** 256
Nash, Ogden, **Supp. XXI:** 51; **Supp. XXIV:** 45
Nash, Roderick, **Supp. IX:** 185; **Supp. XIV:** 191–192
Nash, Susan Smith, **Supp. XVI:** 274
Nash, Thomas, **Supp. III Part 1:** 387–388
Nashe, Thomas, **I:** 358; **Supp. XVII:** 232
Nashville (film), **Supp. IX:** 143
"Nashville Gone to Ashes" (Hempel), **Supp. XXI:** 115, 118, **120–121**
Nashville Skyline (album, Dylan), **Supp. XVIII:** 27
Nason, Elias, **Supp. XV:** 242
Nasser, Gamal Abdel, **IV:** 490
Nasty Bits (Silver), **Supp. XXIV:** 265
Natalie Mann (Toomer), **Supp. III Part 2:** 484–486
Nathan, Amy, **Supp. XXVII:** 200
Nathan, George Jean, **II:** 91; **III:** 103, 104, 106, 107; **IV:** 432; **Supp. IV Part 1:** 343; **Supp. IX:** 56–57; **Supp. XIII:** 161; **Supp. XXII:** 23; **Supp. XXVII:** 86
"Nathanael West" (Herbst), **Retro. Supp. II:** 325
Nathanael West: The Art of His Life (Martin), **Retro. Supp. II:** 325
Nathan Coulter (Berry), **Supp. X:** 24, 33
National Dream, The: Building the Impossible Railway (Findley and Whitehead), **Supp. XX: 51**
"Nationalist, The" (Anderson), **I:** 115
"Nation Is Like Ourselves, The" (Baraka), **Supp. II Part 1:** 53
"Native, The" (Olds), **Supp. X:** 215
"Native American Attitudes to the Environment" (Momaday), **Supp. IV Part 2:** 481, 491

Native American Renaissance (Lincoln), **Supp. IV Part 2:** 507
Native American Testimony (Nabokov, ed.), **Supp. IV Part 2:** 490
"Native Blessing" (Ray), **Supp. XVIII:** 202
Native Guard (Trethewey), **Supp. XXI:** 243, 244, 247, **254–257**
"Native Guard" (Trethewey), **Supp. XXI:** 256
"Native Hill, A" (Berry), **Supp. X:** 21
Native in a Strange Land: Trials & Tremors (Coleman), **Supp. XI:** 84–85, 87
Native of Winby and Other Tales, A (Jewett), **II:** 396; **Retro. Supp. II:** 138
"Natives Don't Cry" (Boyle), **Supp. XXIV:** 57–58
Native Son (Wright), **IV:** 476, 477, 478, 479, 481, 482–484, 485, 487, 488, 491, 495; **Retro. Supp. II:** 107, 116; **Supp. I Part 1:** 51, 64, 67, 337; **Supp. II Part 1:** 170, 235–236; **Supp. IX:** 306; **Supp. XIV:** 73; **Supp. XVII:** 155; **Supp. XVIII:** 283, 286; **Supp. XXI:** 169
"Native Trees" (Merwin), **Supp. III Part 1:** 355
Natorp, Paul, **Supp. XIV:** 198
Natural, The (Malamud), **II:** 424, 425; **Retro. Supp. II:** 288; **Supp. I Part 2:** 438–441, 443; **Supp. XXVI:** 180
"*Natural, The:* Malamud's World Ceres" (Wasserman), **Supp. I Part 2:** 439
Natural Affection (Inge), **Supp. XXV:** 95, 103, 104–105, 106
"Natural History" (Olds), **Supp. X:** 210
Natural History and Antiquities of Selborne, The (White), **Supp. XXVIII:** 247
"Natural History Note" (Hay), **Supp. XIV:** 124, 130
"Natural History of Some Poems, A" (Harrison), **Supp. VIII:** 53
"Natural History of the Dead" (Hemingway), **II:** 206; **Retro. Supp. I:** 176
Naturalist Buys an Old Farm, A (Teale), **Supp. XXVIII:** 251, 255
Natural Laws of Good Luck, The (Graf), **Supp. XXVI:** 46
"Naturally Superior School, A" (Knowles), **Supp. XII:** 235, 240–241
"Natural Method of Mental Philosophy" (Emerson), **II:** 14
"Natural Resources" (Rich), **Retro. Supp. III:** 249; **Supp. I Part 2:** 575
Natural Selection (F. Barthelme), **Supp. XI:** 2, 28, 32, 33
Nature (Emerson), **I:** 463; **II:** 1, 8, 12, 16; **IV:** 171, 172–173; **Supp. XXIV:** 75, 79; **Supp. XXV:** 241
"Nature" (Emerson), **Retro. Supp. I:** 250; **Supp. I Part 2:** 383; **Supp. III Part 1:** 387; **Supp. IX:** 178
"Nature" (Very), **Supp. XXV:** 242
"Nature, Inc." (Lewis), **II:** 441
Nature and Destiny of Man, The (Niebuhr), **III:** 292, 303–306, 310
"Nature and Life" (Emerson), **II:** 19

"Nature and New America Painting"(O'Hara), **Supp. XXIII:** 212
"Nature and Nurture: When It Comes to Twins, Sometimes It's Hard to Tell the Two Apart" (Bausch), **Supp. VII:** 40
Nature and Purpose of the Universe, The (Durang), **Supp. XXIV:** 115–116
"Nature-Metaphors" (Lanier), **Supp. I Part 1:** 352
Nature Morte (Brodsky), **Supp. VIII:** 25
Nature of Evil, The (James), **II:** 343
Nature of Generosity, The (Kittredge), **Supp. XXVI:** 186, 187–188, 189
Nature of Peace, The (Veblen), **Supp. I Part 2:** 642
Nature of Things, The (Lucretius; Stallings, trans.), **Supp. XXV:** 221, 226–227
Nature of Things, The (television show), **Supp. XX: 51**
Nature of True Virtue, The (Edwards), **I:** 549, 557–558, 559
Nature of Yearning, The (Huddle), **Supp. XXVI:** 149–150
Nature: Poems Old and New (Swenson), **Supp. IV Part 2:** 652
Nature's Economy: A History of Ecological Ideas (Worster), **Supp. IX:** 19
Nature's Way (Wouk), **Supp. XXV:** 253
Naumburg, Margaret, **Supp. XX: 68, 74–75**
Nausea (Sartre), **Supp. VIII:** 7
"Navajo Blanket, A" (Swenson), **Supp. IV Part 2:** 649
Navarette, Don Martín de, **II:** 310
Navarro, Ramon, **Supp. IV Part 1:** 206
Navigator, The (film), **I:** 31
Navratilova, Martina, **Supp. XX: 264**
Naylor, Gloria, **Supp. VIII: 213–230; Supp. XX: 108**
Naylor, Paul Kenneth, **Supp. IV Part 2:** 420
Nazarene, The (Asch), **Supp. XXIII:** 2, 3, 4, 6, 9, **12–13**, 14, 15, 16
Nazarene, The: or, The Last of the Washingtons (Lippard), **Supp. XXIII:** 183, 184, 187, 190
Nazimova, **III:** 399
Neal, Darlin', **Supp. XXI:** 41
Neal, Larry, **Retro. Supp. II:** 112, 128; **Retro. Supp. III:** 316; **Supp. X:** 324, 328
Neal, Lawrence P., **Supp. II Part 1:** 53
Neal, Patricia, **Supp. I Part 1:** 286; **Supp. IV Part 2:** 524; **Supp. V:** 223
Neale, Walter, **I:** 192, 208
"Near Damascus" (Di Piero), **Supp. XIX:** 43
Nearer the Moon: From "A Journal of Love," the Unexpurgated Diary of Anaïs Nin, 1937–1939, **Supp. X:** 184, 185
Near Horizons: The Story of an Insect Garden (Teale), **Supp. XXVIII:** 247
Nearing, Helen and Scott, **Supp. XXVI:** 35
Near-Johannesburg Boy and Other Poems, The (Brooks), **Supp. III Part 1:** 86

Near Klamath (Carver), **Supp. III Part 1:** 137
"Near Perigord" (Pound), **Retro. Supp. I:** 289, 290
"Near Spring" (Pickering), **Supp. XXI:** 198
Near the Ocean (R. Lowell), **II:** 543, 550, 551–553, 554, 555; **Retro. Supp. II:** 182, 186, 189–190
"Near View of the High Sierra, A" (Muir), **Supp. IX:** 183
Nebeker, Helen, **Supp. IX:** 122
"Nebraska Blizzard" (F. Wright), **Supp. XVII:** 247
Necessary Angel, The (Stevens), **IV:** 76, 79, 89, 90
"Necessities of Life" (Rich), **Retro. Supp. III:** 244
Necessities of Life: Poems, 1962–1965 (Rich), **Retro. Supp. III:** 242, 244; **Supp. I Part 2:** 553, 555
"Necessity of Blacks' Writing Fiction About the South, The" (Andrews), **Supp. XXVI:** 1, 13
"Necessity of Lemons, The"(Schott), **Supp. XXIII:** 247, 248
Nechayev, Sergey, **Supp. XXI:** 164
Neck Deep and Other Predicaments (Monson), **Supp. XXIV:** 230, **234–236**, 241
"Necrological" (Ransom), **III:** 486–489, 490, 492
Ned Christie's War (Conley), **Supp. V:** 232
"Need for a Cultural Base to Civil Rites & Bpower Mooments, The" (Baraka), **Supp. II Part 1:** 48
"Need for Christian Preaching, The" (Buechner), **Supp. XII:** 49
Needful Things (King), **Supp. V:** 139, 146
"Needle" (Simic), **Supp. VIII:** 275
"Needle Trade" (Reznikoff), **Supp. XIV:** 277, 289
"Need of Being Versed in Country Things, The" (Frost), **II:** 154; **Retro. Supp. I:** 133, 135
"Need to Say It, The" (Hampl), **Supp. XXII:** 94
Neel, Philippe, **Supp. XIV:** 338
Neelakantappa, Tara, **Supp. XV:** 104–105
Neeley, Barbara, **Supp. XVI:** 143
"Negative Capability" (Komunyakaa), **Supp. XIII:** 131
Negligible Tales (Bierce), **I:** 209
"Negotiating the Darkness, Fortified by Poets' Strength" (Karr), **Supp. XI:** 254; **Supp. XIII:** 285
Negotiating with the Dead (Atwood), **Supp. XIII:** 20, 35
Negritude movement, **Supp. X:** 131, 139
"Negro" (Hughes), **Supp. I Part 1:** 321–322
Negro, The (Du Bois), **Supp. II Part 1:** 178, 179, 185
Negro, The: The Southerner's Problem (Page), **Supp. II Part 1:** 168
Negro: An Anthology (Cunard, ed.), **Retro. Supp. III:** 129
Negro and His Music, The (Locke), **Supp. XIV:** 202

"Negro-Art Hokum, The" (Schuyler), **Supp. XXVI:** 167

"Negro Artisan, The" (Du Bois), **Supp. II Part 1:** 166

"Negro Artist and the Racial Mountain, The" (Hughes), **Retro. Supp. I:** 200, 207; **Supp. I Part 1:** 323, 325; **Supp. IV Part 1:** 169

Negro Art: Past and Present (Locke), **Supp. XIV:** 202

"Negro Assays the Negro Mood, A" (Baldwin), **Supp. I Part 1:** 52

"Negro Citizen, The" (Du Bois), **Supp. II Part 1:** 179

"Negro Dancers" (Hughes), **Retro. Supp. I:** 199; **Supp. I Part 1:** 324

"Negroes" (Bodenheim), **Supp. XXV:** 22

Negroes in America, The (McKay), **Supp. X:** 132, 136

"Negroes of Farmville, Virginia, The: A Social Study" (Du Bois), **Supp. II Part 1:** 166

Negro Family, The: The Case for National Action (Moynihan), **Retro. Supp. II:** 123

"Negro Farmer, The" (Du Bois), **Supp. II Part 1:** 167

"Negro Fight, The" (column, C. L. R. James), **Supp. XXI:** 169

"Negro Ghetto" (Hughes), **Supp. I Part 1:** 331

Negro in America, The (Locke), **Supp. XIV:** 208

Negro in American Civilization, The (Du Bois), **Supp. II Part 1:** 179

Negro in American Culture, The (Locke and Butcher), **Supp. XIV:** 202–203

Negro in Art, The: A Pictorial Record of the Negro Artist and of the Negro Theme in Art (Locke), **Supp. XIV:** 202

"Negro in Large Cities, The" (Du Bois), **Supp. II Part 1:** 169

"Negro in Literature and Art, The" (Du Bois), **Supp. II Part 1:** 174

Negro in New York, The (Ellison), **Supp. II Part 1:** 230

"Negro in the Black Belt, The: Some Social Sketches" (Du Bois), **Supp. II Part 1:** 166

Negro in the Caribbean, The (Williams), **Supp. XXI:** 166

"Negro in the Three Americas, The" (Locke), **Supp. XIV:** 211

"Negro in the Well, The" (Caldwell), **I:** 309

"Negro Love Song, A" (Dunbar), **Supp. II Part 1:** 204

"Negro Martyrs Are Needed" (C. Himes), **Supp. XVI:** 138

Negro Mother, The (Hughes), **Supp. I Part 1:** 328

Negro Mother and Other Dramatic Recitations, The (Hughes), **Retro. Supp. I:** 203

Negro Novel in America, The (Bone), **Supp. IX:** 318–319; **Supp. XVIII:** 285

Negro Publication Society of America, **Retro. Supp. I:** 205

"Negro Renaissance, The: Jean Toomer and the Harlem of the 1920s" (Bontemps), **Supp. IX:** 306

"Negro Schoolmaster in the New South, A" (Du Bois), **Supp. II Part 1:** 168

"Negro's Contribution to American Culture, The" (Locke), **Supp. XIV:** 210, 211

"Negro Sermon, A: Simon Legree" (Lindsay), **Supp. I Part 2:** 393

"Negro Sings of Rivers, The" (Hughes), **Supp. IV Part 1:** 16

"Negro Speaks of Rivers, The" (Hughes), **Retro. Supp. I:** 199; **Supp. I Part 1:** 321

"Negro Spirituals, The (Locke), **Supp. XIV:** 201

"Negro Takes Stock, The" (Du Bois), **Supp. II Part 1:** 180

"Negro Theatre, The" (Van Vechten), **Supp. II Part 2:** 735

"Negro Voter Sizes Up Taft, A" (Hurston), **Supp. VI:** 160

"Negro Writer and His Roots, The: Toward a New Romanticism" (Hansberry), **Supp. IV Part 1:** 364

"Negro Youth Speaks" (Locke), **Supp. XIV:** 201

"Nehemias Americanus" (Mather), **Supp. II Part 2:** 453

Nehru, Jawaharlal, **IV:** 490

"Neighbor" (Hugo), **Supp. VI:** 135–136

"Neighborhood Drunk"(Dybek), **Supp. XXIII:** 71

"Neighbors" (Carver), **Supp. III Part 1:** 135, 139, 141; **Supp. XI:** 153

"Neighbors" (Hogan), **Supp. IV Part 1:** 405

"Neighbors, The" (Hay), **Supp. XIV:** 126

"Neighbour Rosicky" (Cather), **I:** 331–332

Neil Simon (R. K. Johnson), **Supp. IV Part 2:** 573

"Neil Simon's Jewish-Style Comedies" (Walden), **Supp. IV Part 2:** 584, 591

"Neil Simon: Toward Act III?" (Walden), **Supp. IV Part 2:** 591

Neilson, Heather, **Supp. IV Part 2:** 681

Neiman, Gilbert, **Supp. XV:** 140

"Neither Out Far nor In Deep" (Frost), **I:** 303; **Retro. Supp. I:** 121, 138; **Retro. Supp. III:** 103

"Nellie Clark" (Masters), **Supp. I Part 2:** 461

Nelson, Alice Dunbar, **Supp. XVII:** 75

Nelson, Cary, **Supp. XVIII:** 226, 227, 230, 231; **Supp. XXII:** 271

Nelson, Ernest, **I:** 388

Nelson, Howard, **Supp. IV Part 1:** 66, 68; **Supp. XIX:** 3; **Supp. XXI:** 95

Nelson, Lord Horatio, **II:** 524

Nelson, Lynn (pseudonym). *See* Nelson, Marilyn

Nelson, Marilyn, **Supp. XVII:** 74, 112; **Supp. XVIII:** 171–188

Nelson, Shirley, **Supp. XII:** 293

Nelson, Steve, **Supp. XVIII:** 226

Nelson Algren (Cox and Chatterton), **Supp. IX:** 11–12

Nelson Algren: A Life on the Wild Side (Drew), **Supp. IX:** 2

Nemerov, David, **II:** 268

Nemerov, Howard, **III:** 267–289; **IV:** 137, 140; **Supp. III Part 2:** 541; **Supp. IV Part 2:** 455, 650; **Supp. IX:** 114

"Nemesis" (Lovecraft), **Supp. XXV:** 119

Nemesis (P. Roth), **Supp. XXIV:** 214

Nemiroff, Robert Barron, **Supp. IV Part 1:** 360, 361, 365, 369, 370, 374

Neoconservative Criticism: Norman Podhoretz, Kenneth S. Lynn, and Joseph Epstein (Winchell), **Supp. VIII:** 241; **Supp. XIV:** 103

"Neo-Formalism: A Dangerous Nostalgia" (Sadoff), **Supp. XXI:** 100

"Neo-Hoodoo Manifesto, The" (Reed), **Supp. X:** 242

Neon Bible, The (Toole), **Supp. XXVI:** 239, 241, 242, 246–250, 253

Neon Rain, The (Burke), **Supp. XIV:** 22, 24, 26–27, 28–29, 30

Neon Vernacular (Komunyakaa), **Supp. XIII:** 121, 127–128, 131

Neon Wilderness, The (Algren), **Supp. IX:** 3, 4

Neo-Slave Narratives (Rushdy), **Supp. X:** 250

Nepantla: Essays from the Land in the Middle (Mora), **Supp. XIII:** 213, 219–221, 227

Nephew, The (Purdy), **Supp. VII:** 271, 273, 282

"Nereids of Seriphos, The" (Clampitt), **Supp. IX:** 41

Nericcio, William, **Supp. XIV:** 304–305

Neruda, Pablo, **Supp. I Part 1:** 89; **Supp. IV Part 2:** 537; **Supp. IX:** 157, 271; **Supp. V:** 332; **Supp. VIII:** 272, 274; **Supp. X:** 112; **Supp. XI:** 191; **Supp. XII:** 217; **Supp. XIII:** 114, 315, 323; **Supp. XXI:** 61, 100; **Supp. XXIV:** 170

"Nerves" (Huddle), **Supp. XXVI:** 149

Nesbit, Edith, **Supp. VIII:** 171

Nesbit, Lynn, **Supp. XXIII:** 100

Nesbitt, Robin, **Supp. VIII:** 89

Nessmuk (George Washington Sears), **Supp. XIX:** 10

Nesting Ground, The (Wagoner), **Supp. IX:** 324, 325–326

Nest of Ninnies, A (Ashbery and Schuyler), **Supp. III Part 1:** 3; **Supp. XV:** 178

"Nests"(Le Sueur), **Supp. XXIII:** 165

Net of Cobwebs (Holding), **Supp. XXII:** 126, 129–130, 134

Net of Magic: Wonders and Deceptions in India (Siegel), **Supp. XXII:** 262

Nets to Catch the Wind (Wylie), **Supp. I Part 2:** 709, 710–712, 714

Nettleton, Asahel, **I:** 458

"Net to Snare the Moonlight, A" (Lindsay), **Supp. I Part 2:** 387

Neubauer, Carol E., **Supp. IV Part 1:** 9

Neugeboren, Jacob Mordecai. *See* Neugeboren, Jay

Neugeboren, Jay, **Supp. XVI: 217–231**

Neugroschel, Joachim, **Supp. IX:** 138

Neuhaus, Richard John, **Supp. VIII:** 245; **Supp. XIX:** 144

Neumann, Erich, **Supp. I Part 2:** 567; **Supp. IV Part 1:** 68, 69

Neuromancer (W. Gibson), **Supp. XII:** 15; **Supp. XVI:** 117, 119–120, 122, 124, **125–126,** 127, 129, 131

Neurotica: Jewish Writers on Sex (Bukiet, ed.), **Supp. XVII:** 48

"Neurotic America and the Sex Impulse" (Dreiser), **Retro. Supp. II:** 105

Neutra, Richard, **Supp. XVI:** 192

"Never Again Would Birds' Song Be the Same" (Frost), **Retro. Supp. III:** 104

"Never Been" (Huddle), **Supp. XXVI:** 150

"Never Bet the Devil Your Head" (Poe), **III:** 425; **Retro. Supp. II:** 273

Never Come Morning (Algren), **Supp. IX:** 3, **7–9**

Never in a Hurry: Essays on People and Places (Nye), **Supp. XIII:** 273, **280–282,** 286

"Never Marry a Mexican" (Cisneros), **Supp. VII:** 70

"Never Room with a Couple" (Hughes), **Supp. I Part 1:** 330

"Nevertheless" (Moore), **III:** 214

Nevils, René Pol, **Supp. XXVI:** 241, 242, 246

Nevins, Allan, **I:** 253; **Supp. I Part 2:** 486, 493

"Nevsky Prospekt" (Olds), **Supp. X:** 205

New Adam, The (Untermeyer), **Supp. XV:** 304, 305

New Addresses (Koch), **Supp. XV:** 177, 184

"New Age of the Rhetoricians, The" (Cowley), **Supp. II Part 1:** 135

New American Cyclopedia, **Supp. XVIII:** 4

New American Literature, The (Pattee), **II:** 456

New American Novel of Manners, The (Klinkowitz), **Supp. XI:** 347

"New American Ode, The" (Wright), **Supp. XV:** 346

New American Poetry (Allen, ed.), **Supp. XXVI:** 223

New American Poetry, 1945–1960, The (Allen, ed.), **Supp. VIII:** 291, 292; **Supp. XIII:** 112; **Supp. XXIII:** 215–216

New American Poetry, The (Allen, ed.), **Supp. XXVII:** 25

"New American Writer, A" (W. C. Williams), **Retro. Supp. II:** 335

New and Collected Poems (Reed), **Supp. X:** 241

New and Collected Poems (Wilbur), **Supp. III Part 2:** 562–564

New and Selected Poems (Nemerov), **III:** 269, 275, 277–279

New and Selected Poems (Oliver), **Supp. VII:** 240–241, 245

New and Selected Poems (W. J. Smith), **Supp. XIII:** 332

New and Selected Poems (Wagoner), **Supp. IX: 326–327**

New and Selected Poems, 1958–1998 (Sorrentino), **Supp. XXI:** 229

New and Selected Poems: 1974–1994 (Dunn), **Supp. XI: 151–152**

New and Selected Things Taking Place (Swenson), **Supp. IV Part 2:** 648–650, 651

"New Aristocracy, The" (Atherton), **Supp. XXIV:** 24

"New Art Gallery Society, The" (Wolfe), **Supp. III Part 2:** 580

Newberger, Julee, **Supp. XVIII:** 168

"New Birth, The" (Very), **Supp. XXV:** 246, 247, 248

New Black Poetry, The (Major, ed.), **Supp. XXII:** 172, 174, 176, 180

New Bridge, The (Levin), **Supp. XXVII:** 133

"New Capitalist Tool, The" (Wasserstein), **Supp. XV:** 328

New Collected Poems (Oppen), **Supp. XXVI:** 224

Newcomb, Ralph, **Supp. XIII:** 12

Newcomb, Robert, **II:** 111

New Conscience and an Ancient Evil, A (Addams), **Supp. I Part 1:** 14–15, 16

"New Conservatism in American Poetry, The" (Wakoski), **Supp. XVII:** 112

"New Conservatives, The: Intellectuals in Retreat" (Epstein), **Supp. XIV:** 103

New Critical Essays on H. P. Lovecraft (Simmons, ed.), **Supp. XXV:** 123

New Criticism, The (Ransom), **III:** 497–498, 499, 501

"New Day, A" (Levine), **Supp. V:** 182

Newdick, Robert Spangler, **Retro. Supp. I:** 138

Newdick's Season of Frost (Newdick), **Retro. Supp. I:** 138

New Dictionary of Quotations, A (Mencken), **III:** 111

New Directions Anthology in Prose and Poetry (Laughlin, ed.), **Supp. XVI:** 284

"New Directions in Poetry" (D. Locke), **Supp. IX:** 273

"New Dog, The: Variations on a Text by Jules Laforgue" (C. Frost), **Supp. XV:** 98

Newell, Henry, **IV:** 193

"New England" (R. Lowell), **II:** 536

"New England" (Robinson), **III:** 510, 524

"New England Bachelor, A" (Eberhart), **I:** 539

"New Englander, The" (Anderson), **I:** 114

New England Girlhood, A (Larcom), **Supp. XIII:** 137, 142, 143, 144, **147–154**

New England Gothic Literature (Ringel), **Supp. XXII:** 205

New England: Indian Summer (Brooks), **I:** 253, 256

New England Local Color Literature (Donovan), **Retro. Supp. II:** 138

"New England Nun, A"(Freeman), **Supp. XXVIII:** 225

"New England Sabbath-Day Chace, The" (Freneau), **Supp. II Part 1:** 273

New-England Tale, A (Sedgwick), **I:** 341

New England Tragedies, The (Longfellow), **II:** 490, 505, 506; **Retro. Supp. II:** 165, 167

New English Canaan (Morton), **Supp. XXII:** 45

New Era in American Poetry, The (Untermeyer, ed.), **Supp. XV:** 301, 303, 306

Newer Ideals of Peace (Addams), **Supp. I Part 1:** 11–12, 15, 16–17, 19, 20–21

"New Experience in Millinery, A" (Stratton-Porter), **Supp. XX: 216**

New Feminist Criticism, The: Essays on Women, Literature, and Theory (Showalter), **Supp. X:** 97

New Fire: To Put Things Right Again (Moraga), **Supp. XXIII:** 197

"New Folsom Prison" (Matthews), **Supp. IX:** 165

New Formalism, The: A Critical Introduction (McPhillips), **Supp. XV:** 250, 251, 252, 264

Newfound (J. W. Miller), **Supp. XX: 163, 166, 170–172**

New Found Land: Fourteen Poems (MacLeish), **III:** 12–13

New Hampshire (Frost), **II:** 154–155; **Retro. Supp. I:** 132, 133, 135; **Retro. Supp. III:** 101–102, 105

"New Hampshire" (Frost), **Retro. Supp. III:** 101, 102; **Retro. Supp. XXVI:** 78

"New Hampshire, February" (Eberhart), **I:** 536

New Hard-Boiled Writers (Panek), **Supp. XIV:** 27

"New Home" (Richter), **Supp. XVIII:** 209

Newhouse, Seth, **Supp. XXVI:** 87, 89, 90

New Industrial State, The (Galbraith), **Supp. I Part 2:** 648

"New Journalism, The" (Wolfe), **Supp. III Part 2:** 571

New Journalism, The (Wolfe and E. W. Johnson, eds.), **Supp. III Part 2:** 570, 579–581, 583, 586; **Supp. XXIV:** 282; **Supp. XXVII:** 38

New Left, The: The Anti-Industrial Revolution (Rand), **Supp. IV Part 2:** 527

"New Letters from Thomas Jefferson" (Stafford), **Supp. XI:** 324

New Letters on the Air: Contemporary Writers on Radio, **Supp. X:** 165, 169, 173

"New Life" (Glück), **Supp. V:** 90

New Life, A (Malamud), **Supp. I Part 2:** 429–466

"New Life, The" (Bynner), **Supp. XV:** 44

"New Life, The"(Schott), **Supp. XXIII:** 242

"New Life at Kyerefaso" (Sutherland), **Supp. IV Part 1:** 9

"New Light on Veblen" (Dorfman), **Supp. I Part 2:** 650

"New Man, A" (E. P. Jones), **Supp. XXII:** 144

Newman, Charles, **Supp. I Part 2:** 527, 546–548

Newman, Edwin, **Supp. IV Part 2:** 526

Newman, Frances, **Supp. XXII:** 198
Newman, Judie, **Supp. IV Part 1:** 304, 305
Newman, Paul, **Supp. IV Part 2:** 473, 474
New Man, The (Merton), **Supp. VIII:** 208
"New Mecca, The" (Saunders), **Supp. XIX:** 235, 236
"New Medea, The" (Howells), **II:** 282
New Mexico trilogy (Nichols), **Supp. XIII:** 269
New Morning (album, Dylan), **Supp. XVIII:** 27, 33
"New Mother" (Olds), **Supp. X:** 206
"New Mothers, The" (Shields), **Supp. VII:** 310
New Music (Price), **Supp. VI:** 264, 265
"New Mutants, The" (Fiedler), **Supp. XIII:** 104
"New Name for Some Old Ways of Thinking, A" (James), **II:** 353
New Native American Novel, The: Works in Progress (Bartlett), **Supp. IV Part 1:** 335
"New Natural History, A" (Thurber), **Supp. I Part 2:** 619
New Negro, The (Locke), **Supp. XIX:** 69
"New Negro, The" (Locke), **Supp. XIV:** 201
New Negro, The (Locke, ed.), **Supp. II Part 1:** 176; **Supp. IX:** 309; **Supp. X:** 137; **Supp. XXII:** 8
New Negro, The: An Interpretation (Locke, ed.), **Retro. Supp. I:** 199; **Supp. IV Part 1:** 170; **Supp. XIV:** 195, 201–202
New Negro for a New Century, A (Washington, Wood, and Williams), **Supp. XIV:** 201
New New Journalism, The (R. Boynton), **Supp. XVII:** 209
"New Nomads, The" (E. Hoffman), **Supp. XVI:** 161
"New Orleans" (Carruth), **Supp. XVI:** 50
New Orleans Sketches (Faulkner), **Retro. Supp. I:** 80
New Orleans: The Place and the People (King), **Supp. XXVIII:** 116, 121
New Path to the Waterfall, A (Carver), **Supp. III Part 1:** 138–140, 147, 149; **Supp. XXIV:** 172
"New Patricians, The" (Untermeyer), **Retro. Supp. III:** 47
New Perspectives on Women and Comedy (Dresner), **Supp. XXVIII:** 188
"New Poem, The" (Wright), **Supp. V:** 339, 340
"New Poems" (MacLeish), **III:** 19
"New Poems" (Oliver), **Supp. VII:** 240
New Poems 1960 (Bynner), **Supp. XV:** 51
New Poems: 1980–88 (Haines), **Supp. XII: 209–210**
New Poetry, The (Monroe and Henderson, eds.), **Supp. I Part 2:** 387
"New Poetry Handbook, The" (Strand), **Supp. IV Part 2:** 626
New Poetry of Mexico (Strand, trans.), **Supp. IV Part 2:** 630

New Poets of England and America (Hall, Pack, and Simpson, eds.), **Supp. IV Part 2:** 621
"Newport of Anchuria" (Henry), **Supp. II Part 1:** 409
New Princeton Encyclopedia of Poetry and Poetics (Preminger and Brogan, eds.), **Supp. XV:** 250
New Religious America, A: How a "Christian Country" Has Become the World's Most Religiously Diverse Nation (Eck), **Supp. XXVIII:** 49, 57–59
"*New Republic* Moves Uptown, The" (Cowley), **Supp. II Part 1:** 142
"New Rose Hotel" (W. Gibson), **Supp. XVI:** 120, 122, 124
"News, The" (McClatchy), **Supp. XII:** 269
News Crew (Cruisers) series (Myers), **Supp. XXVII:** 212
"New Season" (Levine), **Supp. V:** 188
New Seeds of Contemplation (Merton), **Supp. VIII:** 200, 208
News from the Glacier: Selected Poems 1960–1980 (Haines), **Supp. XII:** 207, 208–209
"News Item" (Parker), **Supp. IX:** 190
News of a Kidnapping (García Márquez), **Supp. XXV:** 57
New Song, A (Hughes), **Retro. Supp. I:** 202; **Supp. I Part 1:** 328, 331–332
"New Song"(Kenny), **Supp. XXIII:** 156
Newson-Horst, Adele, **Supp. XXIII:** 95
"New South, The" (Lanier), **Supp. I Part 1:** 352, 354, 370
"New South, The"(speech, Grady), **Supp. XXVIII:** 123
New Southern Girl, The: Female Adolescence in the Works of 12 Women Authors (Town), **Supp. XVIII:** 195
Newspaper Days, 1899–1906 (Mencken), **III:** 100, 102, 120
"New Spirit, The" (Ashbery), **Supp. III Part 1:** 14, 15
New Spoon River, The (Masters), **Supp. I Part 2:** 461–465, 473
New Star Chamber and Other Essays, The (Masters), **Supp. I Part 2:** 455–456, 459
New Tales of the Vampires (Rice), **Supp. VII:** 290
New Tenant, The (Ionesco), **Supp. XXIV:** 113
New Testament, **I:** 303, 457, 458; **II:** 167; **III:** 305; **IV:** 114, 134, 152; **Retro. Supp. I:** 58, 140, 360; **Supp. I Part 1:** 104, 106; **Supp. I Part 2:** 516; **Supp. XVII:** 155; **Supp. XXIII:** 13. *See also* names of New Testament books
New Testament, A (Anderson), **I:** 101, 114
"New Theory of Thorstein Veblen, A" (Galbraith), **Supp. I Part 2:** 650
Newton, Benjamin Franklin, **I:** 454
Newton, Huey P., **Supp. I Part 1:** 66; **Supp. IV Part 1:** 206; **Supp. XXVII:** 168
Newton, Isaac, **I:** 132, 557; **II:** 6, 103, 348–349; **III:** 428; **IV:** 18, 149
Newton, Maud, **Supp. XXIII:** 290

Newton, Sarah Emily, **Supp. XV:** 234
"New-Wave Format, A" (Mason), **Supp. VIII:** 141, 143, 147
New West of Edward Abbey, The (Ronald), **Supp. XIII:** 4
"New Wife" (Halliday), **Supp. XIX:** 89
New Wolves, The: The Return of the Mexican Wolf to the American Southwest (Bass), **Supp. XVI:** 26–27
New Woman's Survival Sourcebook, The (Rennie and Grimstead, eds.), **Supp. I Part 2:** 569
New World, The (Bronk), **Supp. XXI:** 25–26, 31
New World, The (Bynner), **Supp. XV:** 41, 42
"New World, The" (Very), **Supp. XXV:** 248
New World, The: Tales (Banks), **Supp. V:** 8, 9, 10
New World Naked, A (Mariani), **Retro. Supp. I:** 419
New Worlds of Literature (Beaty and Hunter, eds.), **Supp. IV Part 1:** 331
New World Writing (Updike), **IV:** 217
"New Year, The" (Very), **Supp. XXV:** 240, 244
New Year Letter (Auden), **Supp. II Part 1:** 14, 16
"New Year's Day" (Wharton), **Retro. Supp. I:** 381
"New Year's Eve" (Schwartz), **Supp. II Part 2:** 640, 656–657
New Year's Eve/1929 (Farrell), **II:** 43
"New Year's Eve 1968" (R. Lowell), **II:** 554
New Year's Eve: A Play (W. Frank), **Supp. XX: 75**
"New Year's Gift, The" (Stowe), **Supp. I Part 2:** 587
"New Year Two Thousand, The" (Weigl), **Supp. XIX:** 287–288
"New York" (Capote), **Supp. III Part 1:** 122
"New York" (Moore), **III:** 196, 198, 202, 206
"New York 1965" (Bowles), **Supp. IV Part 1:** 94
New York: A Serendipiter's Journey (Talese), **Supp. XVII:** 202, 203
"New York Breeze" (Halliday), **Supp. XIX:** 85
New York City Arts Project, **Supp. III Part 2:** 618
"New York City in 1979"(Acker), **Supp. XII:** 5
New York Edition, **Retro. Supp. I:** 235
"New York Edition" (James), **II:** 336, 337
"New York Gold Conspiracy, The" (Adams), **I:** 4
New York Hat, The (film; Griffith), **Supp. XVI:** 183
New York Intellectuals, **Supp. VIII:** 93
"New York Intellectuals, The" (Howe), **Supp. VI:** 120
"New York Is a City of Things Unnoticed" (Talese), **Supp. XVII:** 202, 209

New York: Its Upper Ten and Lower Million (Lippard), **Supp. XXIII:** 180, 183, 184

New York Jew (Kazin), **Supp. VIII:** 95, **97–100**

New York Madness (Bodenheim), **Supp. XXV:** 28

"New York Theater: Isn't It Romantic" (Wasserstein), **Supp. XV:** 320

New York Trilogy, The (Auster), **Supp. XII:** 21, **24–28**

Next (McNally), **Supp. XIII:** 197

"Next in Line, The" (Bradbury), **Supp. IV Part 1:** 102

"Next Rodeo, The" (Kittredge), **Supp. XXVI:** 185–186

Next Rodeo, The: New and Selected Essays (Kittredge), **Supp. XXVI:** 185–186

Next Room of the Dream, The (Nemerov), **III:** 269, 275, 278, 279–280, 284

"Next Time I Crossed the Line into Oklahoma, The" (Wright), **Supp. XV:** 345

Next-to-Last Things: New Poems and Essays (Kunitz), **Supp. III Part 1:** 257–259, 261, 262, 265, 266, 268

"'Next to Reading Matter' " (Henry), **Supp. II Part 1:** 399

Nexus (H. Miller), **III:** 170, 187, 188, 189

Ngai, Sianne, **Supp. XXVIII:** 222

Nguyen, Bich Minh, **Supp. XXVI: 207–222**

Niatum, Duane, **Supp. IV Part 1:** 331; **Supp. IV Part 2:** 505

Nice and Noir (Schwartz), **Supp. XIV:** 23

"Nice Girl" (Nelson), **Supp. XVIII:** 178

Nice Jewish Boy, The (P. Roth), **Supp. III Part 2:** 412

"Nice Part f Town, A" (Hayes), **Supp. XXVI:** 144

Nicholas II, Tsar, **Supp. I Part 2:** 447

"Nicholas in the Park" (Halliday), **Supp. XIX:** 88

Nicholls, Peter, **Supp. XIX:** 232; **Supp. XXVI:** 228, 232

Nichols, Charles, **Retro. Supp. I:** 194

Nichols, Dudley, **Supp. XVIII:** 247

Nichols, John Treadwell, **Supp. XIII: 253–272**

Nichols, Luther, **Supp. X:** 265

Nichols, Mike, **Supp. IV Part 1:** 234; **Supp. IV Part 2:** 577

Nicholson, Colin, **Supp. VIII:** 129

Nicholson, Harold, **Supp. XIV:** 163

Nicholson, Jack, **Supp. V:** 26; **Supp. VIII:** 45; **Supp. XI:** 308

Nicholson, John, **Supp. XVI:** 293

Nick Adams Stories, The (Hemingway), **II:** 258; **Retro. Supp. I:** 174

"Nick and the Candlestick" (Plath), **Supp. I Part 2:** 544

Nickel and Dimed: On (Not) Getting By in America (Ehrenreich), **Supp. XVII:** 210

Nickel Eclipse: Iroquois Moon (Gansworth), **Supp. XXVI:** 110

Nickel Mountain: A Pastoral Novel (Gardner), **Supp. VI:** 63, 64, 68, **69**

Nickerson, Catherine Ross, **Supp. XXV:** 192, 200, 202

"Nicodemus" (Keillor), **Supp. XVI:** 167

Nicoll, Allardyce, **III:** 400

Nicoloff, Philip, **II:** 7

Niebuhr, Gustav, **III:** 292

Niebuhr, H. Richard, **I:** 494

Niebuhr, Lydia, **III:** 292

Niebuhr, Reinhold, **III: 290–313; Supp. I Part 2:** 654; **Supp. XX:** 79

Niedecker, Lorine, **Supp. III Part 2:** 616, 623; **Supp. XIV:** 287; **Supp. XXIII:** 174

Nielsen, Ed, **Supp. IX:** 254

Nielson, Dorothy, **Supp. I Part 2:** 659

Nietzsche, Friedrich Wilhelm, **I:** 227, 283, 383, 389, 396, 397, 402, 509; **II:** 7, 20, 27, 42, 90, 145, 262, 462, 463, 577, 583, 585; **III:** 102–103, 113, 156, 176; **IV:** 286, 491; **Supp. I Part 1:** 254, 299, 320; **Supp. I Part 2:** 646; **Supp. IV Part 1:** 104, 105–106, 107, 110, 284; **Supp. IV Part 2:** 519; **Supp. V:** 277, 280; **Supp. VIII:** 11, 181, 189; **Supp. X:** 48; **Supp. XII:** 98; **Supp. XIV:** 339; **Supp. XX:** 117; **Supp. XXVII:** 34

Nieves, Felipe, **Supp. XVIII:** 90

Niflis, N. Michael, **Supp. IV Part 1:** 175

Niger, S. *See* Charney, Samuel

Nigger Heaven (Van Vechten), **Supp. II Part 2:** 739, 744–746; **Supp. XIX:** 76; **Supp. XVIII:** 123, 127

"Nigger Jeff" (Dreiser), **Retro. Supp. II:** 97

Nigger of the "Narcissus," The (Conrad), **II:** 91; **Retro. Supp. I:** 106; **Supp. XVIII:** 224; **Supp. XXIV:** 286

"NIGGY THE HO" (Baraka), **Supp. II Part 1:** 54

"Night" (H. Johnson), **Supp. XXVI:** 173

"Night" (Huddle), **Supp. XXVI:** 155

"Night, Death, Mississippi" (Hayden), **Supp. II Part 1:** 369

'Night, Mother (Norman), **Supp. VIII:** 141

"Night above the Avenue" (Merwin), **Supp. III Part 1:** 355

"Night among the Horses, A" (Barnes), **Supp. III Part 1:** 33–34, 39, 44

"Night and the Madman" (Gibran), **Supp. XX:** 118

Night at the Movies, A, or, You Must Remember This: Fictions (Coover), **Supp. V:** 50–51

"Night at the Opera, A" (Matthews), **Supp. IX:** 167

"Night before the Sentence Is Carried Out, The" (Wright), **Supp. XV:** 341

"Nightbird" (Komunyakaa), **Supp. XIII:** 132

Night-Blooming Cereus, The (Hayden), **Supp. II Part 1:** 367, 373

"Night-Blooming Cereus, The" (Hayden), **Supp. II Part 1:** 367

Night-Born, The (London), **II:** 467

"Nightbreak" (Rich), **Retro. Supp. III:** 244; **Supp. I Part 2:** 556

"Nightclub" (Collins), **Supp. XXI:** 60

Night Country, The (O'Nan), **Supp. XXV:** 141, 148–149, 150

Night Dance (Price), **Supp. VI:** 264

"Night Dances, The" (Plath), **Supp. I Part 2:** 544

"Night Dream, The" (MacLeish), **III:** 15

"Nightfall" (Teasdale), **Supp. XXVII:** 293

"Night Ferry" (Doty), **Supp. XI:** 124

"Nightfishing" (Schnackenberg), **Supp. XV:** 254

"Nighthawks"(Dybek), **Supp. XXIII:** 73, 74

"Night I Met Little Floyd, The" (Wright), **Supp. XV:** 345–346

Night in Acadie, A (Chopin), **Retro. Supp. II: 66–67,** 73; **Supp. I Part 1:** 200, 219, 220, 224

"Night in Acadie, A" (Chopin), **Retro. Supp. II:** 66

"Night in June, A" (W. C. Williams), **Retro. Supp. I:** 424

"Night in New Arabia, A" (Henry), **Supp. II Part 1:** 402

Night in Question, The: Stories (Wolff), **Supp. VII:** 342–344

"Night Journey" (Roethke), **Supp. III Part 1:** 260

"Night Letter to the Reader" (Collins), **Supp. XXI:** 55

Night Light (Justice), **Supp. VII:** 126–127

"Nightmare" (Kumin), **Supp. IV Part 2:** 442

Nightmare Factory, The (Kumin), **Supp. IV Part 2:** 444–447, 451

"Nightmare Factory, The" (Kumin), **Supp. IV Part 2:** 445, 453

Nightmare on Main Street (Poe), **Retro. Supp. II:** 262

"Nightmare" poems (Benét), **Supp. XI:** 46, 58

"Night Mirror" (L.-Y. Lee), **Supp. XV:** 225

Night Music (Odets), **Supp. II Part 2:** 541, 543, 544

"Night of First Snow" (R. Bly), **Supp. IV Part 1:** 71

Night of January 16th (Rand), **Supp. IV Part 2:** 527

Night of the Iguana, The (T. Williams), **IV:** 382, 383, 384, 385, 386, 387, 388, 391, 392, 393, 394, 395, 397, 398

"Night of the Iguana, The" (T. Williams), **IV:** 384

"Night of the Living Beanfield: How an Unsuccessful Cult Novel Became an Unsuccessful Cult Film in Only Fourteen Years, Eleven Nervous Breakdowns, and $20 Million" (Nichols), **Supp. XIII:** 267

Night Passage (Parker), **Supp. XIX:** 185–186

Night Rider (Warren), **IV:** 243, 246–247

Nights (Doolittle), **Supp. I Part 1:** 270, 271

Nights and Days (Merrill), **Supp. III Part 1:** 319, 320, 322–325

"Nights and Days" (Rich), **Supp. I Part 2:** 574

"Night's for Cryin,' The" (C. Himes), **Supp. XVI:** 137

"Night Shift" (Plath), **Supp. I Part 2:** 538

"Nightshine Beyond Memory, A: Ten More Years with Ray" (Gallagher), **Supp. XXIV:** 167, 172

Night-Side (Oates), **Supp. II Part 2:** 522

"Night-Side" (Oates), **Supp. II Part 2:** 523

Night-Side, The (Skloot), **Supp. XX:** 193, **196, 205, 208**

Nights in the Gardens of Brooklyn (Swados), **Supp. XIX:** 261–264

"Nights in the Gardens of Brooklyn" (Swados), **Supp. XIX:** 261

"Night Sketches: Beneath an Umbrella" (Hawthorne), **II:** 235–237, 238, 239, 242; **Supp. XXI:** 201

"Night Sport" (Hoffman), **Supp. XVIII:** 86, 87

"Night Strategies"(Bottoms), **Supp. XXVIII:** 29

"Night-Sweat" (R. Lowell), **II:** 554

"Night-Talk" (Ellison), **Retro. Supp. II:** 126; **Supp. II Part 1:** 248

Night the New Jesus Fell to Earth, The (Rash), **Supp. XXVII:** 216–217, 227

Night Thoughts (Young), **III:** 415

"Night-Time River Road, A" (Ferry), **Supp. XXIV:** 150

Night Traveler, The (Oliver), **Supp. VII:** 233

"Night Watch" (Gioia), **Supp. XV:** 117

"Night Watch, The" (Wright), **Supp. V:** 339

"Night We All Had Grippe, The" (Jackson), **Supp. IX:** 118

Nightwood (Barnes), **Supp. III Part 1:** 31, 32, 35–37, 39–43

Night World and the Word Night, The (F. Wright), **Supp. XVII:** 240, 244–245

"Nihilist as Hero, The" (R. Lowell), **II:** 554; **Retro. Supp. II:** 190

Nijinsky, Vaslav, **Supp. XV:** 28–29

Nikolai Gogol (Nabokov), **Retro. Supp. I:** 266

"Nilda" (Díaz), **Supp. XXIV:** 92

Niles, Thomas, **Retro. Supp. I:** 35

Niles, Thomas, Jr., **Supp. I Part 1:** 39

Nilsson, Christine, **Supp. I Part 1:** 355

Nilsson, Harry, **Supp. XI:** 309

Nilsson, Jenny Lind, **Supp. XVI:** 177

Nimitz, Chester, **Supp. I Part 2:** 491

"Nimram" (Gardner), **Supp. VI:** 73

Nims, John Frederick, **III:** 527; **Supp. XVII:** 112

Nin, Anaïs, **III:** 182, 184, 190; **Supp. III Part 1:** 43; **Supp. IV Part 2:** 680; **Supp. X:** 181–200; **Supp. XIX:** 134

"9" (Oliver), **Supp. VII:** 244

"9 Failures of the Imagination" (Lethem), **Supp. XVIII:** 148

"Nine-Ball" (Offutt), **Supp. XIX:** 166, 167

Nine Dragons (Connelly), **Supp. XXI:** 74, **79–80**

"Nine from Eight" (Lanier), **Supp. I Part 1:** 352–354

Nine Gates: Entering the Mind of Poetry (Hirshfield), **Supp. XXIII:** 136, 137

Nine Headed Dragon River: Zen Journals 1969–1982 (Matthiessen), **Supp. V:** 199

Nine Horses (Collins), **Supp. XXI:** 55, 60, 61, 62, 65

"Nine Horses" (Collins), **Supp. XXI:** 61

Ninemile Wolves,The (Bass), **Supp. XVI:** 24–25, 26

"Nine Nectarines" (Moore), **III:** 203, 209, 215

Nine Plays (Reznikoff), **Supp. XIV:** 288

"Nine Poems for the Unborn Child" (Rukeyser), **Supp. VI:** 280–281, 284

Nine Stories (Nabokov), **Retro. Supp. I:** 266

Nine Stories (Salinger), **III:** 552, 558–564

"19 Hadley Street" (Schnackenberg), **Supp. XV:** 253

19 Necromancers from Now (Reed), **Supp. X:** 240

19 Varieties of Gazelle (Nye), **Supp. XIII:** 275, **286–288**

"19 Varieties of Gazelle" (Nye), **Supp. XIII:** 286

1984 (Orwell), **Supp. XIII:** 29; **Supp. XVIII:** 137, 138

"1959"(Lea), **Supp. XXVIII:** 138

"1953 Dodge Coronet" (Huddle), **Supp. XXVI:** 151

"1940" (Stafford), **Supp. XI:** 328–329

"1945–1985: Poem for the Anniversary" (Oliver), **Supp. VII:** 237

"1941" (Stone), **Supp. XXVII:** 253

1919 (Dos Passos), **I:** 482, 485–486, 487, 489, 490, 492

"1975" (Wright), **Supp. V:** 341

"1973"(Hirshfield), **Supp. XXIII:** 130

"1910" (Mora), **Supp. XIII:** 215

Nineteenth-Century Minor Poets (Auden), **Supp. XXV:** 237

"1938" (Komunyakaa), **Supp. XIII:** 114

1939 (Boyle), **Supp. XXIV:** 62

"1939" (Taylor), **Supp. V:** 316

1933 (Levine), **Supp. V:** 185–187

"1933" (Levine), **Supp. V:** 188

"Nineteenth New York, The" (Doctorow), **Supp. IV Part 1:** 232

"1929" (Auden), **Supp. II Part 1:** 6

"1926" (Kees), **Supp. XV:** 135

"93990" (Saunders), **Supp. XIX:** 233

"90 North" (Jarrell), **II:** 370, 371

90 Trees (Zukofsky), **Supp. III Part 2:** 631

95 Poems (Cummings), **I:** 430, 433, 435, 439, 446, 447

"91 Revere Street" (R. Lowell), **II:** 547; **Retro. Supp. II:** 188; **Supp. XI:** 240

Ninety Percent of Everything (Lethem, Kelly and Kessel), **Supp. XVIII:** 145

"92 Days" (L. Brown), **Supp. XXI:** 44–45

"Nine Years Later" (Brodsky), **Supp. VIII:** 32

Ninth Avenue (Bodenheim), **Supp. XXV:** 24–25

"Nirvana" (Lanier), **Supp. I Part 1:** 352

Nirvana Blues, The (Nichols), **Supp. XIII:** 266, 267

Nishikigi (play), **III:** 466

Niven, David, **Supp. XI:** 307

Nixon (film), **Supp. XIV:** 48

Nixon, Richard M., **I:** 376; **III:** 38, 46; **Supp. I Part 1:** 294, 295; **Supp. V:** 45, 46, 51; **Supp. XII:** 14; **Supp. XIV:** 306

"NJ Transit" (Komunyakaa), **Supp. XIII:** 132

Nketia, J. H., **Supp. IV Part 1:** 10

Nketsia, Nana, **Supp. IV Part 1:** 2, 10

Nkize, Julius, **Supp. IV Part 1:** 361

Nkrumah, Kwame, **I:** 490, 494; **Supp. IV Part 1:** 361; **Supp. X:** 135

Nkrumah and the Ghana Revolution (C. L. R. James), **Supp. XXI:** 159, 171–172

NO (Major), **Supp. XXII:** 174

"Noah" (Biss), **Supp. XXVI:** 48

Noailles, Anna de, **IV:** 328

Noa Noa (Gauguin), **I:** 34

Nobel Lecture (Singer), **Retro. Supp. II:** 300

"No Better Than a 'Withered Daffodil' " (Moore), **III:** 216

Noble, David W., **Supp. I Part 2:** 650

Noble, Marianne, **Supp. XVIII:** 267

"Noble Rider and the Sound of Words, The" (Stevens), **Retro. Supp. I:** 299

Noble Savage, The (Coover), **Supp. V:** 40

"No Bobolink reverse His Singing" (Dickinson), **Retro. Supp. I:** 45

Nobodaddy (MacLeish), **III:** 5–6, 8, 10, 11, 18, 19, 20

"Nobodaddy" (W. Blake), **Supp. XVII:** 245

"Nobody in Hollywood" (Bausch), **Supp. VII:** 54

Nobody Knows My Name (Baldwin), **Supp. XIII:** 111

"Nobody Knows My Name" (Baldwin), **Retro. Supp. II:** 8; **Supp. I Part 1:** 52

Nobody Knows My Name: More Notes of a Native Son (Baldwin), **Retro. Supp. II:** 6, 8; **Supp. I Part 1:** 47, 52, 55

"Nobody knows this little Rose" (Dickinson), **Retro. Supp. I:** 30

"Nobody Said Anything" (Carver), **Supp. III Part 1:** 141

"Nobody's Business" (Lahiri), **Supp. XXI:** 183

Nobody's Fool (Russo), **Supp. XII:** 326, **331–335,** 340

"No Change of Place" (Auden), **Supp. II Part 1:** 5

"Noche Triste, La" (Frost), **Retro. Supp. I:** 123

Nock, Albert Jay, **I:** 245; **Supp. IV Part 2:** 521, 524

"No Coward Soul Is Mine" (Brontë), **I:** 458

"No Crime in the Mountains" (Chandler), **Supp. IV Part 1:** 129

"Nocturne" (Komunyakaa), **Supp. XIII:** 126

"Nocturne" (MacLeish), **III:** 8

"Nocturne at Bethesda" (Bontemps), **Supp. XXII:** 3, 8

"Nocturne in a Deserted Brickyard" (Sandburg), **III:** 586

Nocturne of Remembered Spring (Aiken), **I:** 50

Nod House (Mackey), **Supp. XXVII:** 156

No Direction Home (documentary film, Scorsese), **Supp. XVIII:** 22, 23, 29

No Direction Home (Shelton), **Supp. XVIII:** 21

No Door (Wolfe), **IV:** 451–452, 456

"No Door" (Wolfe), **IV:** 456

No Doubt the Nameless (Lea), **Supp. XXVIII:** 142

"No End" (Huddle), **Supp. XXVI:** 151

"No Epitaph" (Carson), **Supp. XII:** 111

No Exit (Sartre), **I:** 82, 130; **Supp. XIV:** 320

No Exit (Sartre; Bowles, trans.), **Supp. IV Part 1:** 84

No Gifts from Chance (Benstock), **Retro. Supp. I:** 361

"No-Good Blues" (Komunyakaa), **Supp. XIII:** 130

No Hero (Marquand), **III:** 57

No Heroes: A Memoir of Coming Home (Offutt), **Supp. XIX:** 163, **172–174,** 175

No! In Thunder (Fiedler), **Supp. XIII:** 101

"Noir" (Stallings), **Supp. XXV:** 232

"Noiseless Patient Spider" (Whitman), **III:** 555; **IV:** 348; **Supp. IV Part 1:** 325

Noises Off (Frayn), **Supp. IV Part 2:** 582

Noi vivi. See We the Living (film)

"No Jury Would Convict" (Shaw), **Supp. XIX:** 245

"No Lamp Has Ever Shown Us Where to Look" (MacLeish), **III:** 9

Nolan, Sidney, **Retro. Supp. II:** 189

No Laughing Matter (Heller and Vogel), **Supp. IV Part 1:** 384, 389

No Love Lost, a Romance of Travel (Howells), **II:** 277

Nomad (Ali), **Supp. XXIV:** 15

Nomad's Land (Rinehart), **Supp. XXV:** 195

No Man Is an Island (Merton), **Supp. VIII:** 207

"No Man's Land" (Biss), **Supp. XXVI:** 47, 56

"No More This Home" (Taggard), **Supp. XXII:** 277, 280

No Mother to Guide Her (Loos), **Supp. XVI:** 194

No Name in the Street (Baldwin), **Retro. Supp. II:** 13, 14; **Supp. I Part 1:** 47, 48, 52, 65–66, 67

No Nature: New and Selected Poems (Snyder), **Supp. VIII:** 305

Nonconformist's Memorial, The (Howe), **Supp. IV Part 2:** 434, 435–436

Nonconformity (Algren), **Supp. IX:** 15

None but the Lonely Heart (film), **Supp. II Part 2:** 546

Nones (Auden), **Supp. II Part 1:** 21

"Nones" (Auden), **Supp. II Part 1:** 22–23

None Shall Look Back (Gordon), **II:** 205–207, 208

"No No, Bad Daddy" (Nelson), **Supp. XVIII:** 177, 178

"Non-Tenured" (Halliday), **Supp. XIX:** 90, 91

Nonverbal Communication: Notes on the Visual Perception of Human Relations (Kees and Ruesch), **Supp. XV:** 147

"Noon" (Bryant), **Supp. I Part 1:** 157

No One Belongs Here More Than You (July), **Supp. XXIV:** 199, **200–207**

"No One Remembers" (Levine), **Supp. V:** 187

"Noon Walk on the Asylum Lawn" (Sexton), **Supp. II Part 2:** 673

"Noon Wine" (Porter), **III:** 436, 437–438, 442, 446

"No Pain Whatsoever" (Yates), **Supp. XI:** 341

"No Place for You, My Love" (Welty), **IV:** 278, 279; **Retro. Supp. I:** 353

No Plays of Japan, The (Waley), **III:** 466

No Pockets in a Shroud (McCoy), **Supp. XIII:** 166–168, 171, 172, 173, 174

"No Poem So Fine" (Francis), **Supp. IX:** 83

Norcross, Frances, **I:** 456, 462

Norcross, Louise, **I:** 456, 462

Nordfeldt, B. J. O., **Supp. XXI:** 6

Nordfeldt, Margaret, **Supp. XXI:** 6

Nordyke, Lewis, **Supp. XIII:** 5

No Relief (Dixon), **Supp. XII:** 139, **142–143**

No Resting Place (Humphrey), **Supp. IX:** 94, **106–108**

Norfolk Poems, The (Carruth), **Supp. XVI:** 47, 48

Norma (Bellini), **IV:** 309

Norma Ashe (Glaspell), **Supp. III Part 1:** 175, 186–187

"Normal Life, A"(Thompson), **Supp. XXIII:** 300

"Normal Motor Adjustments" (Stein and Solomons), **IV:** 26

Norman, Charles, **III:** 479

Norman, Gurney, **Supp. X:** 24; **Supp. XXIII:** 42

Norman, Jessye, **Supp. XX: 110**

Norman, Marsha, **Supp. VIII:** 141; **Supp. XXI:** 145; **Supp. XXIV:** 124

Norman Mailer (Poirier), **Retro. Supp. II:** 207–208

Norman Mailer: Modern Critical Views (Bloom), **Retro. Supp. II:** 205

Norman Mailer Revisited (Merrill), **Retro. Supp. II:** 201

Norna; or, The Witch's Curse (Alcott), **Supp. I Part 1:** 33

Norris, Charles, **III:** 320; **Retro. Supp. I:** 100; **Supp. XVIII:** 226

Norris, Frank, **I:** 211, 355, 500, 506, 517, 518, 519; **II:** 89, 264, 276, 289, 307; **III:** 227, **314–336,** 596; **IV:** 29; **Retro. Supp. I:** 100, 325; **Retro. Supp. II:** 96, 101; **Supp. III Part 2:** 412; **Supp. IX:** 14, 15; **Supp. VIII:** 101, 102; **Supp. XV:** 115

"North" (Budbill), **Supp. XIX:** 7–8

"North" (Hugo), **Supp. VI:** 135

North, Milou (pseudonym), **Supp. IV Part 1:** 260. *See also* Dorris, Michael; Erdrich, Louise

North, Sir Thomas, **IV:** 370

"North American Sequence" (Roethke), **I:** 171–172, 183; **III:** 529, 545, 547, 548

"North American Time" (Rich), **Retro. Supp. III:** 250

"North Beach" (Snyder), **Supp. VIII:** 289

North Country: A Personal Journey Through the Borderland (Mosher), **Supp. XXII: 203–204,** 206, 212, **217–218**

"North Country Sketches" (McClatchy), **Supp. XII:** 256

"Northeast Playground" (Paley), **Supp. VI:** 226–227, 229

Northern Borders (Mosher), **Supp. XXII:** 203, 204, 206, 207, 208, 209, **213–214**

Northern Lights (O'Brien), **Supp. V:** 237, 239, 241–244, 250

"Northern Motive" (Levine), **Supp. V:** 195

Northfield Poems (Ammons), **Supp. VII:** 29

"Northhanger Ridge" (Wright), **Supp. V:** 335, 340

"North Haven" (Bishop), **Retro. Supp. II:** 50

"North Labrador" (H. Crane), **I:** 386; **Retro. Supp. III:** 45

North of Boston (Frost), **II:** 152, 153–154, 527; **Retro. Supp. I:** 121, 125, 127, **128–130,** 131; **Retro. Supp. III:** 97–98; **Supp. I Part 1:** 263; **Supp. XIII:** 146

North of Jamaica (Simpson), **Supp. IV Part 2:** 448; **Supp. IX:** 275, 276

North of the Danube (Caldwell), **I:** 288, 290, 293, 294, 309, 310

North: Poems of Home (Kenny), **Supp. XXIII: 147–148**

Northrup, Cyrus, **Supp. I Part 1:** 350

North Sea (Jarman), **Supp. XVII:** 110, 113

"North Sea Undertaker's Complaint, The" (R. Lowell), **II:** 550

North & South (Bishop), **Retro. Supp. II: 41–43;** **Supp. I Part 1:** 72, 84, 85, 89

North Star, The (Hellman), **Supp. I Part 1:** 281

Northup, Solomon, **Supp. XIV:** 32; **Supp. XXVIII: 163–176**

"Northwest Writers at Work" (Baker), **Supp. XXIV:** 178

"North Winter" (Carruth), **Supp. XVI:** 53

North with the Spring (Teale), **Supp. XXVIII:** 243, 249, 254

Norton, Charles Eliot, **I:** 223, 568; **II:** 279, 322–323, 338; **Retro. Supp. II:** 371; **Retro. Supp. II:** 135; **Supp. I Part 1:** 103; **Supp. I Part 2:** 406, 479

Norton, Jody, **Supp. VIII:** 297

Norton, John, **Supp. I Part 1:** 99, 110, 112, 114

Norton Anthology of African American Literature, The (H. L. Gates and McKay, eds.), **Supp. X:** 325; **Supp. XX: 105**

Norton Anthology of American Literature, **Supp. X:** 325; **Supp. XV:** 270

Norton Anthology of Literature by Women (Gilbert and Gubar, eds.), **Supp. XV:** 270

Norton Anthology of Modern Poetry, The, **Supp. XI:** 259; **Supp. XV:** 258; **Supp. XXIV:** 35, 39

Norton Anthology of Poetry, The, **Supp. XVIII:** 20

Norton Anthology of Short Fiction, The, **Supp. IX:** 4

Norton Book of Personal Essays, The, **Supp. XIV:** 105

Norton Lectures, **Retro. Supp. I:** 65

Norwood, Vera, **Supp. IX:** 24

No Safe Harbour (Porter), **III:** 447

Nosferatu: An Opera Libretto (Gioia), **Supp. XV:** 112, **128**

"Nosferatu's Serenade" (Gioia), **Supp. XV:** 128

No Siege Is Absolute (Char; version of F. Wright), **Supp. XVII:** 244

No Sign (Lea), **Supp. XXVIII:** 132–133

"No Snake" (A. Finch), **Supp. XVII:** 72

"No Speak English" (Cisneros), **Supp. VII:** 63

"Nostalgia" (Collins), **Supp. XXI:** 57

"Nostalgia" (Saunders), **Supp. XIX:** 235

Nostalgia for 70 (J. W. Miller), **Supp. XX: 165**

"Nostalgia of the Lakefronts" (Justice), **Supp. VII:** 118, 119, 120

"Nostalgic Mood" (Farrell), **II:** 45

No Star Is Lost (Farrell), **II:** 34, 35, 44

Nostrandt, Jeanne, **Supp. XVIII:** 80–81

Nostromo (Conrad), **II:** 600; **IV:** 245

"Nosty Fright, A" (Swenson), **Supp. IV Part 2:** 651

"Not" (Huddle), **Supp. XXVI:** 157

Not about Nightingales (T. Williams), **IV:** 381

"Not a Sparrow" (Gallagher), **Supp. XXIV:** 171

Not: A Trio (Huddle), **Supp. XXVI:** 150, 156–157

"Not a Womb in the House" (Quindlen), **Supp. XVII:** 166, 171

"(Not) Born in he U.S.A." (Gansworth), **Supp. XXVI:** 111

Not Coming to Be Barked At (Kooser), **Supp. XIX:** 116, **120**

Not Dancing (Dunn), **Supp. XI:** 143, **148**

"Note about *Iconographs,* A" (Swenson), **Supp. IV Part 2:** 646

Notebook (R. Lowell), **Retro. Supp. II:** 186, 190; **Supp. V:** 343

Notebook 1967–68 (R. Lowell), **II:** 553–555; **Retro. Supp. II:** 182, 186, 190

Notebook of Malte Laurids Brigge, The (Rilke), **III:** 571

Notebooks (Fitzgerald), **Retro. Supp. I:** 110

Notebooks of Captain George, The (Renoir), **Supp. XXII:** 257

"Notebooks on Poetry and Politics" (Rich), **Retro. Supp. III:** 251

No Telephone to Heaven (Cliff), **Supp. XXII:** 66, 69, 71–72

"Note on Abraham Lincoln" (Vidal), **Supp. IV Part 2:** 688

"Note on Commercial Theatre" (Hughes), **Retro. Supp. I:** 207

"Note on Ezra Pound, A" (Eliot), **Retro. Supp. I:** 290

"Note on Lanier's Music, A" (P. Graham), **Supp. I Part 1:** 373

Note on Literary Criticism, A (Farrell), **II:** 26, 49

"Note on Poetry, A" (Doolittle), **Supp. I Part 1:** 254, 267–268

"Note on Realism, A" (Anderson), **I:** 110

"Note on the Limits of 'History' and the Limits of 'Criticism,' A" (Brooks), **Supp. XIV:** 11

"Note on the Poetry of Love, A" (Untermeyer), **Supp. XV:** 304

"Note on the Truth of the Tales, A" (Vollmann), **Supp. XVII:** 230

"Notes" (Dove), **Supp. IV Part 1:** 246

"Notes for a Moving Picture: The House" (Agee), **I:** 33, 34

"Notes for an Autobiography" (Van Vechten), **Supp. II Part 2:** 749

"Notes for a Novel About the End of the World" (Percy), **Supp. III Part 1:** 393

"Notes for a Preface" (Sandburg), **III:** 591, 596–597

"NOTES FOR A SPEECH" (Baraka), **Supp. II Part 1:** 33

Notes for the Green Box (Duchamp), **Supp. IV Part 2:** 423

Notes for the Two-Dollar Window: Portraits from an American Neighborhood (Kriegel), **Supp. XXIV: 223–224**

Notes from a Bottle Found on the Beach at Carmel (Connell), **Supp. XIV:** 80, 87, 96, 97

Notes from a Sea Diary: Hemingway All the Way (Algren), **Supp. IX:** 16

Notes from No Man's Land (Biss), **Supp. XXVI:** 45, 46, 47, 48, 50, 53, 55–57

"Notes from the Childhood and Girlhood" (Brooks), **Supp. III Part 1:** 77

"Notes from the River" (Stern), **Supp. IX:** 285, 287, 294, 295

Notes from Underground (Dostoevsky), **III:** 571; **IV:** 485; **Retro. Supp. II:** 121

Notes Left Behind: Last and Selected Poems (Hayford), **Supp. XXII:** 218

"Notes of a Faculty Wife" (Jackson), **Supp. IX:** 126

"Notes of a Native Daughter" (Didion), **Supp. IV Part 1:** 196, 197, 200, 201

Notes of a Native Son (Baldwin), **Retro. Supp. II:** 1, 2, 3, 5, 6; **Supp. I Part 1:** 50, 52, 54; **Supp. IV Part 1:** 163

"Notes of a Native Son" (Baldwin), **Supp. I Part 1:** 50, 54

Notes of a Son and Brother (James), **II:** 337; **Retro. Supp. I:** 235

"Notes on a Departure" (Trilling), **Supp. III Part 2:** 498

"Notes on Babbitt and More" (Wilson), **IV:** 435

"Notes on 'Camp' " (Sontag), **Supp. III Part 2:** 455–456; **Supp. XIV:** 167

Notes on Democracy (Mencken), **III:** 104, 107–108, 109, 116, 119

Notes on Dialectics (C. L. R. James), **Supp. XXI:** 169

"Notes on Free Verse" (Dobyns), **Supp. XIII:** 77

"Notes on 'Layover' " (Hass), **Supp. VI:** 109

"Notes on Memory and Enthusiasm" (Di Piero), **Supp. XIX:** 42

Notes on Novelists (James), **II:** 336, 337; **Retro. Supp. I:** 235

"Notes on Nukes, Nookie, and Neo-Romanticism" (Robbins), **Supp. X:** 272

"Notes on Poetry" (Eberhart), **I:** 524, 527–528, 529

"Notes on Teaching"(Hadas), **Supp. XXIII:** 122

"Notes on the Craft of Poetry" (Strand), **Supp. IV Part 2:** 626

"Notes on the Decline of Outrage" (Dickey), **Supp. IV Part 1:** 181

"Notes on the New Formalism" (Gioia), **Supp. XV:** 113, 114–115

"Notes on the Novel-as-Autobiography" (P. Bailey), **Supp. XVI:** 69

"Notes on 'The Poetry of Everday Life' " (Notley), **Supp. XXII:** 232

Notes on the State of Virginia (1781–1782) (Jefferson), **Supp. XIV:** 191

"Notes on Writing Weird Fiction" (Lovecraft), **Supp. XXV:** 120–121

"Notes to Be Left in a Cornerstone" (Benét), **Supp. XI:** 46, 58

"Notes Toward a Politics of Location" (Rich), **Retro. Supp. III:** 251

"Notes toward a Supreme Fiction" (Stevens), **IV:** 87–89; **Retro. Supp. I:** 300, 306, **306–309,** 311; **Retro. Supp. III:** 51; **Supp. I Part 1:** 80

"Notes towards a Poem That Can Never Be Written" (Atwood), **Supp. XIII:** 34–35

"Not Exactly for Talia" (Halliday), **Supp. XIX:** 94

"Not Forgotten" (Davison), **Supp. XXVI:** 70

No Thanks (Cummings), **I:** 430, 431, 432, 436, 437, 441, 443, 446

Not Heaven: A Novel in the Form of Prelude, Variations, and Theme (W. Frank), **Supp. XX: 80**

"Nothing" (C. Frost), **Supp. XV:** 94

"Nothing Big" (Komunyakaa), **Supp. XIII:** 121

Nothing Can Make Me Do This (Huddle), **Supp. XXVI:** 147, 151–152, 158–159

Nothing Ever Breaks Except the Heart (Boyle), **Supp. XXIV:** 59

Nothing for Tigers (Carruth), **Supp. XVI:** 47, 48, 50

"Nothing Gold Can Stay" (Frost), **Retro. Supp. I:** 133; **Retro. Supp. III:** 102

Nothing Gold Can Stay (Rash), **Supp. XXVII:** 215, 224, 229–230

"Nothing in Heaven Functions as It Ought" (X. J. Kennedy), **Supp. XV:** 158–159

Nothing Makes You Free: Writings by Descendants of Jewish Holocaust Survivors (Bukiet, ed.), **Supp. XVII:** 39–40, 48–49

"Nothing Missing" (O'Hara), **III:** 369

Nothing Personal (Baldwin), **Supp. I Part 1:** 58, 60

Nothing Sacred (film), **Supp. XVIII:** 243

Nothing Sacred (screenplay, Hecht), **Supp. XXVII:** 83, 91, 93

"Nothing Song, The" (Snodgrass), **Supp. VI:** 326

"Nothing Stays Put" (Clampitt), **Supp. IX:** 42

"Nothing Sudden" (Davison), **Supp. XXVI:** 76

Nothing to Write Home About (Brainard), **Supp. XXVII:** 20, 28

"Nothing Will Yield" (Nemerov), **III:** 279

No Third Path (Kosinski), **Supp. VII:** 215

"Not Ideas About the Thing but the Thing Itself" (Stevens), **IV:** 87

"No Time" (Collins), **Supp. XXI:** 61

Notions of the Americans: Picked up by a Travelling Bachelor (Cooper), **I:** 343–345, 346

"Not-Knowing" (Barthelme), **Supp. IV Part 1:** 48

"Not Leaving the House" (Snyder), **Supp. VIII:** 300

Notley, Alice, **Supp. XXII:** 223–238; **Supp. XXIII:** 221; **Supp. XXIV:** 35, 37, 39, 41, 43, 45

"'Not Marble nor the Gilded Monument'" (MacLeish), **III:** 12

Not Mine to Finish: Poems, 1928–1934 (Taggard), **Supp. XXII:** 280

"Not My Bones" (Nelson), **Supp. XVIII:** 183

Not Now But Now (M. F. K. Fisher), **Supp. XVII:** 86, 90

Notorious (screenplay, Hecht), **Supp. XXVII:** 83, 91, 93

"Not Quite Social" (Frost), **II:** 156

"Not Sappho, Sacco" (Rukeyser), **Supp. VI:** 277

"Not Sixteen" (Anderson), **I:** 114

"Not Slightly" (Stein), **IV:** 44

Not Smart (Steele), **Supp. XXVIII:** 38

Not So Deep as a Well (Parker), **Supp. IX:** 192

"Not Somewhere Else, but Here" (Rich), **Supp. I Part 2:** 552, 573

Not-So-Simple Neil Simon (McGovern), **Supp. IV Part 2:** 573

Not So Simple: The "Simple" Stories by Langston Hughes (Harper), **Retro. Supp. I:** 194, 209

"Not the Point" (Cameron), **Supp. XII:** 83

"Not They Who Soar" (Dunbar), **Supp. II Part 1:** 199

Not This Pig (Levine), **Supp. V:** 178, 181, 182–183

"Not to Be Satan nor to Deal with Him" (Bronk), **Supp. XXI:** 32

Not to Eat; Not for Love (Weller), **III:** 322

Not Under Forty (Cather), **Retro. Supp. III:** 17, 24, 36

Not Wanted on the Voyage (Findley), **Supp. XX:** 50, 56–57, 59

Not Without Laughter (Hughes), **Retro. Supp. I:** 197, 198, 201; **Supp. I Part 1:** 328, 332; **Supp. XIX:** 73, 154

Nouvelle Héloïse, La (Rousseau), **Supp. XV:** 232

Nova Express (Burroughs), **Supp. III Part 1:** 93, 103, 104; **Supp. XVIII:** 137

Novel, The (Bulwer), **Retro. Supp. II:** 58

Novel, The: An Alternative History (Moore), **Supp. XXII:** 261

"Novel as a Function of American Democracy, The" (Ellison), **Retro. Supp. II:** 124

"Novel Démeublé, The" (Cather), **Retro. Supp. I:** 15; **Retro. Supp. III:** 17, 24

Novel History: Historians and Novelists Confront America's Past (and Each Other) (Carnes), **Supp. X:** 14

"Novelist and Believer" (O'Connor), **Retro. Supp. III:** 209

"Novelists of 2007" (Halliday), **Supp. XIX:** 90

Novella (Goethe; Bogan and Mayer, trans.), **Supp. III Part 1:** 63

Novellas and Other Writings (Wharton), **Retro. Supp. I:** 360

"Novel of the Thirties, A" (Trilling), **Supp. III Part 2:** 499

Novels and Other Writings (Bercovitch), **Retro. Supp. II:** 325

Novels and Tales of Henry James, The (James), **Retro. Supp. I:** 232

"Novel-Writing and Novel-Reading" (Howells), **II:** 276, 290

"November" (Larcom), **Supp. XIII:** 143

"November Cotton Flower" (Toomer), **Supp. IX:** 312

"November"(Lea), **Supp. XXVIII:** 137

November Twenty Six Nineteen Sixty Three (Berry), **Supp. X:** 24

"Novices" (Moore), **III:** 200–201, 202, 213

Novick, Peter, **Supp. XVI:** 154–155

"Novogodnee" ("New Year's Greetings") (Tsvetaeva), **Supp. VIII:** 30

"Novotny's Pain" (P. Roth), **Supp. III Part 2:** 403

"No Voyage" (Oliver), **Supp. VII:** 231

No Voyage and Other Poems (Oliver), **Supp. VII:** 230–231, 232

Now, Voyager (film), **Supp. XXVIII:** 177, 184, 188

Now, Voyager (Prouty), **Supp. XXVIII:** 177, 179, 180, 186–188, 189, 191

Now and Another Time (Hearon), **Supp. VIII:** 58, 61–62

Now and Then (Buechner), **Supp. XII:** 49, 53

"Now and Then, America" (Mora), **Supp. XIII:** 217

"Nowhere" (J. Scott), **Supp. XVII:** 189

Nowhere Is a Place: Travels in Patagonia (Theroux and Chatwin), **Supp.**

VIII: 322

"Now I Am Married" (Gordon), **Supp. IV Part 1:** 299

"Now I Lay Me" (Hemingway), **II:** 249; **Retro. Supp. I:** 175

"Now I Lay Me" (Olds), **Supp. X:** 208

"Now Is the Air Made of Chiming Balls" (Eberhart), **I:** 523

Now Is Your Time! The African American Struggle for Freedom (Myers), **Supp. XXVII:** 209

"No Word" (Kunitz), **Supp. III Part 1:** 263

"No Worst" (Nelson), **Supp. XVIII:** 177, 178

Now Sheba Sings the Song (Angelou), **Supp. IV Part 1:** 16

"Now That We Live" (Kenyon), **Supp. VII:** 165

"Now the Servant's Name Was Malchus" (Wilder), **IV:** 358

"Now We Know" (O'Hara), **III:** 368–369

NOW with Bill Moyers (television), **Supp. XIII:** 286

Noyes, Alfred, **IV:** 434

Nuamah, Grace, **Supp. IV Part 1:** 10

"Nuances of a Theme by Williams" (Stevens), **Retro. Supp. I:** 422

Nuclear Age, The (O'Brien), **Supp. V:** 238, 243, 244, 246–248, 249, 251

"Nuclear Arms and Morality" (Sanders), **Supp. XVI:** 266

"Nude at a Dressing Table" (Peacock), **Supp. XIX:** 204

Nude Croquet (Fiedler), **Supp. XIII:** 103

"Nude Descendig a Staircase" (X. J. Kennedy), **Supp. XV:** 168

Nude Descending a Staircase (Duchamp), **IV:** 408; **Retro. Supp. I:** 416; **Supp. XXII:** 162

Nude Descending a Staircase (X. J. Kennedy), **Supp. XV:** 153, **154–157**

Nugent, Bruce, **Retro. Supp. I:** 200

Nugent, Elliot, **Supp. I Part 2:** 606, 611, 613

Nuggets and Dust (Bierce), **I:** 195

"Nullipara" (Olds), **Supp. X:** 209

Number One (Dos Passos), **I:** 489

"Numbers" (Skloot), **Supp. XX: 196, 207**

"Numbers, Letters" (Baraka), **Supp. II Part 1:** 50

"Numbers Trouble" (Stallings), **Supp. XXV:** 224

Nunc Dimittis (Brodsky), **Supp. VIII:** 25–26, 28

"Nun No More, A" (Fante), **Supp. XI:** 160

"Nun's Priest's Tale" (Chaucer), **III:** 492

Nunzio, Nanzia, **IV:** 89

Nuptial Flight, The (Masters), **Supp. I Part 2:** 460, 471

"Nuptials" (Tate), **IV:** 122

Nursery Rhymes from Mother Stone (Stone), **Supp. XXVII:** 257

"Nurse Whitman" (Olds), **Supp. X:** 203

Nurture (Kumin), **Supp. IV Part 2:** 453–454, 455

Nussbaum, Emily, **Supp. XI:** 143

Nussbaum, Felicity A., **Supp. X:** 189

Nutcracker, The (Tchaikovsky), **Retro. Supp. I:** 196

"Nux Postcoenatica" (Holmes), **Supp. I Part 1:** 303

Nyberg, Björn, **Supp. XXVII:** 128

Nyce, James M., **Retro. Supp. I:** 380

Nye, Naomi Shihab, **Supp. XI:** 316; **Supp. XIII: 273–290; Supp. XXIII:** 253; **Supp. XXVII:** 166

Nyerere, Julius, **Supp. X:** 135

"Nympholepsy" (Faulkner), **Retro. Supp. I:** 81

Nymphs of the Valley ('Ará'is al-Murúj) (Gibran), **Supp. XX: 115, 124, 125**

O

"Ö" (Dove), **Supp. IV Part 1:** 245

Oak and Ivy (Dunbar), **Supp. II Part 1:** 98

"Oak Bluffs" column (D. West), **Supp. XVIII:** 286

Oak Openings, The (Cooper), **I:** 354, 355

Oandasan, Bill, **Supp. IV Part 2:** 499

Oasis, The (McCarthy), **II:** 566–568

Oates, Joyce Carol, **Supp. II Part 2: 503–527; Supp. IV Part 1:** 205; **Supp. IV Part 2:** 447, 689; **Supp. V:** 323; **Supp. XI:** 239; **Supp. XII:** 343; **Supp. XIII:** 306; **Supp. XIV:** 26, 109; **Supp. XXIII:** 35; **Supp. XXV:** 86, 123; **Supp. XXVI:** 126

Oates, Stephen B., **Retro. Supp. III:** 75, 77

"Oath, The" (Tate), **IV:** 127

Obbligati (Hecht), **Supp. X:** 57

Ober, Harold, **Retro. Supp. I:** 101, 103, 105, 110, 113

Oberndorf, Clarence P., **Supp. I Part 1:** 315

Obey, André, **IV:** 356, 375

"Obit" (R. Lowell), **II:** 554

"Obituaries" (Collins), **Supp. XXI:** 65

"Obituary Writer, The" (Davison), **Supp. XXVI:** 72

"Objective Value of a Social Settlement, The" (Addams), **Supp. I Part 1:** 4

"Objective Woman, The" (Jong), **Supp. V:** 119

Objectivist Anthology, An, **Supp. XIV:** 287

"Objectivist Ethics, The" (Rand), **Supp. IV Part 2:** 530–532

"Objectivists" Anthology, An (Zukofsky), **Supp. III Part 2:** 613, 615

Objectivist's Anthology, An (Zukofsky, ed.), **Supp. XXVI:** 226

Object Lessons (Quindlen), **Supp. XVII: 173–174**

"Objects" (Wilbur), **Supp. III Part 2:** 545–547

Oblique Prayers (Levertov), **Supp. III Part 1:** 283

"Oblivion" (Justice), **Supp. VII:** 121

Oblivion Seekers, The (Eberhardt), **Supp. IV Part 1:** 92

"Oblong Box, The" (Poe), **III:** 416

"Obnoxious Truth, The" (Notley), **Supp. XXII:** 234

Obregon, Maurice, **Supp. I Part 2:** 488

O'Briant, Don, **Supp. X:** 8

O'Brien, Edward, **Supp. XV:** 140

O'Brien, Edward J., **I:** 289; **III:** 56; **Supp. XIX:** 256; **Supp. XVIII:** 227; **Supp. XX: 34**

O'Brien, Edwin, **Supp. XVIII:** 208

O'Brien, Fitzjames, **I:** 211

O'Brien, Geoffrey, **Supp. IV Part 2:** 471, 473

O'Brien, Joe, **Supp. XXI:** 5, 6

O'Brien, John, **Supp. V:** 48, 49; **Supp. X:** 239, 244; **Supp. XXI:** 228, 229, 233

O'Brien, Sharon, **Retro. Supp. III:** 19, 25, 37

O'Brien, Tim, **Retro. Supp. III:** 104; **Supp. V: 237–255; Supp. XI:** 234; **Supp. XVII:** 14; **Supp. XXI:** 122; **Supp. XXV:** 142, 143, 153

"Obscene Poem, An" (Creeley), **Supp. IV Part 1:** 150

Obscure Destinies (Cather), **I:** 331–332; **Retro. Supp. I:** 19

"Observation Relative to the Intentions of the Original Founders of the Academy in Philadelphia" (Franklin), **II:** 114

"Observations" (Dillard), **Supp. VI:** 34

Observations (Moore), **III:** 194, 195–196, 197, 199, 203, 205, 215

"Observations Now" (Conroy), **Supp. XVI:** 75

Observations: Photographs by Richard Avedon: Comments by Truman Capote, **Supp. III Part 1:** 125–126

Obsession, The (Levin), **Supp. XXVII:** 133, 136, 138, 143, 147

Obsession with Anne Frank, An: Meyer Levin and the Diary (Graver), **Supp. XXVII:** 136, 137

Obuchowski, Mary DeJong, **Supp. XX: 222**

O Canada: An American's Notes on Canadian Culture (Wilson), **IV:** 429–430

"O Captain! My Captain" (Whitman), **Retro. Supp. III:** 297

"O Carib Isle!" (H. Crane), **I:** 400–401; **Retro. Supp. III:** 43–44

O'Casey, Sean, **III:** 145; **Supp. IV Part 1:** 359, 361, 364

"Occidentals" (Ford), **Supp. V:** 71–72

Occom, Samuel, **Supp. XX: 288**

"Occultation of Orion, The" (Longfellow), **Retro. Supp. II:** 168

"Occurrence at Owl Creek Bridge, An" (Bierce), **I:** 200–201; **II:** 264; **Supp. XXV:** 26

"Ocean 1212-W" (Plath), **Supp. I Part 2:** 528

"Ocean of Words" (Jin), **Supp. XVIII:** 94

Ocean of Words: Army Stories (Jin), **Supp. XVIII:** 89, 92, **93–94**

O'Connell, Nicholas, **Supp. IX:** 323, 325, 334

O'Connell, Shaun, **Supp. XXI:** 231

O'Connor, Edward F., Jr., **III:** 337

O'Connor, Flannery, **I:** 113, 190, 211, 298; **II:** 606; **III: 337–360; IV:** 4, 217, 282; **Retro. Supp. II:** 179, **219–239,** 272, 324; **Retro. Supp. III: 207–221; Supp. I Part 1:** 290; **Supp. III Part 1:** 146; **Supp. V:** 59, 337; **Supp. VIII:** 13, 14, 158; **Supp. X:** 1, 26, 69, 228, 290; **Supp. XI:** 104; **Supp. XIII:** 294; **Supp. XIV:** 93; **Supp. XIX:** 166, 209, 223; **Supp. XV:** 338; **Supp. XVI:** 219; **Supp. XVII:** 43, 114; **Supp. XVIII:** 156, 161, 194; **Supp. XXI:** 197; **Supp. XXIII:** 289; **Supp. XXV:** 142; **Supp. XXVI:** 152, 252; **Supp. XXVII:** 11, 216, 218, 230, 267, 276; **Supp. XXVIII:** 30

O'Connor, Frank, **III:** 158; **Retro. Supp. II:** 242; **Supp. I Part 2:** 531; **Supp. VIII:** 151, 157, 165, 167, 171; **Supp. XV:** 74

O'Connor, Philip F., **Supp. XXIII:** 290

O'Connor, Richard, **II:** 467

O'Connor, T. P., **II:** 129

O'Connor, William, **IV:** 346; **Retro. Supp. I:** 392, 407

O'Connor, William Van, **III:** 479; **Supp. I Part 1:** 195

O'Crowley, Peggy, **Supp. XXVII:** 201

"Octascope" (Beattie), **Supp. V:** 27, 28

"Octaves" (Robinson), **Supp. III Part 2:** 593

"Octet" (Wallace), **Supp. X:** 309

"October" (Frost), **Retro. Supp. III:** 96

October (Isherwood), **Supp. XIV:** 157, 164

"October" (Oliver), **Supp. VII:** 241

"October" (Swenson), **Supp. IV Part 2:** 649

"October, 1866" (Bryant), **Supp. I Part 1:** 169

"October 1913" (McCarriston), **Supp. XIV:** 266

"October and November" (R. Lowell), **II:** 554

"October in the Railroad Earth" (Kerouac), **Supp. III Part 1:** 225, 227, 229

October Light (Gardner), **Supp. VI:** 63, **69–71,** 72

"October Maples, Portland" (Wilbur), **Supp. III Part 2:** 556

October Palace, The (Hirshfield), **Supp. XXIII:** 131

October Sky (film), **Supp. XXVII:** 101, 103, 106

"October: With Rain" (W. V. Davis), **Supp. XXI:** 94

"Octopus, An" (Moore), **III:** 202, 207–208, 214

"Octopus, The" (Merrill), **Supp. III Part 1:** 321

Octopus, The (Norris), **I:** 518; **III:** 314, 316, 322–326, 327, 331–333, 334, 335

"O Daedalus, Fly Away Home" (Hayden), **Supp. II Part 1:** 377–378

"OD and Hepatitis Railroad or Bust, The" (Boyle), **Supp. VIII:** 1

Odd Couple, The (1985 version, Simon), **Supp. IV Part 2:** 580

Odd Couple, The (film), **Supp. IV Part 2:** 589

Odd Couple, The (Simon), **Supp. IV Part 2:** 575, 579–580, 585, 586; **Supp. XVII:** 8

Odd Jobs (Updike), **Retro. Supp. I:** 334

Odd Mercy (Stern), **Supp. IX:** 298–299

Odd Number (Sorrentino), **Supp. XXI:** 236

"Odds, The" (Hecht), **Supp. X:** 64–65

Odds, The (O'Nan), **Supp. XXV:** 150, 151–152

"Odds, The" (Salinas), **Supp. XIII:** 321

"Ode" (Emerson), **II:** 13

"Ode" (Sobin), **Supp. XVI:** 284–285

"Ode" (X. J. Kennedy), **Supp. XV:** 160

"Ode (Intimations of Immortality)" (Matthews), **Supp. IX:** 162

"Ode for Memorial Day" (Dunbar), **Supp. II Part 1:** 199

"Ode for the American Dead in Asia" (McGrath), **Supp. X:** 119

"Ode: For the Budding of Islands" (Sobin), **Supp. XVI:** 287

"Ode Inscribed to W. H. Channing" (Emerson), **Supp. XIV:** 46

"Ode: Intimations of Immortality" (Wordsworth), **Supp. I Part 2:** 729; **Supp. III Part 1:** 12; **Supp. XIV:** 8

"Ode in Time of Crisis" (Taggard), **Supp. XXII:** 271

Odell, Margaretta Matilda, **Supp. XX:** **278, 284, 288**

"Ode: My 24th Year" (Ginsberg), **Supp. II Part 1:** 312

"Ode on a Grecian Urn" (Keats), **I:** 284; **III:** 472; **Supp. XII:** 113; **Supp. XIV:** 8, 9–10; **Supp. XV:** 100; **Supp. XXI:** 64

"Ode on Human Destinies" (Jeffers), **Supp. II Part 2:** 419

"Ode on Indolence" (Keats), **Supp. XII:** 113

"Ode on Melancholy" (Keats), **Retro. Supp. I:** 301

Ode Recited at the Harvard Commemoration (J. R. Lowell), **Supp. I Part 2:** 416–418, 424

"Ode Recited at the Harvard Commemoration" (R. Lowell), **II:** 551

Odes (Horace), **Supp. XXIV:** 153

Odes (O'Hara), **Supp. XXIII:** 216

"Ode: Salute to the French Negro Poets"(O'Hara), **Supp. XXIII:** 216

"Ode Secrète" (Valéry), **III:** 609

"Odes of Estrangement" (Sobin), **Supp. XVI:** 289

Odes of Horace, The (Ferry, trans.), **Supp. XXIV:** **153–156**

"Odes to Natural Processes" (Updike), **Retro. Supp. I:** 323

"Ode: The Capris" (Halliday), **Supp. XIX:** 88

"Ode to a Lebanese Crock of Olives"(Wakoski), **Supp. XXVIII:** 266

"Ode to a Nightingale" (Keats), **II:** 368; **Retro. Supp. II:** 261; **Supp. IX:** 52

"Ode to Autumn" (Masters), **Supp. I Part 2:** 458

"Ode to Cervantes" (Salinas), **Supp. XIII:** 324

"Ode to Coit Tower" (Corso), **Supp. XII:** 122

"Ode to Ethiopia" (Dunbar), **Supp. II Part 1:** 199, 207, 208, 209

"Ode to Fear" (Tate), **IV:** 128

Ode to Harvard and Other Poems, An (Bynner), **Supp. XV:** 41, 44

"Ode to Joy"(O'Hara), **Supp. XXIII:** 208, 216

"Ode to Meaning" (Pinsky), **Supp. VI:** **249–250,** 251

"Ode to Michael Goldberg ('s Birth and Other Births)"(O'Hara), **Supp. XXIII:** 209, 216, 218

"Ode to Night" (Masters), **Supp. I Part 2:** 458

"Ode to Our Young Pro-Consuls of the Air" (Tate), **IV:** 135

"Ode to the Austrian Socialists" (Benét), **Supp. XI:** 46, 58

"Ode to the Confederate Dead" (Tate), **II:** 551; **IV:** 124, 133, 137; **Supp. X:** 52

"Ode to the Johns Hopkins University" (Lanier), **Supp. I Part 1:** 370

"Ode to the Maggot" (Komunyakaa), **Supp. XIII:** 130

"Ode to the Mexican Experience" (Salinas), **Supp. XIII:** 316–317

"Ode to the Virginian Voyage" (Drayton), **IV:** 135

"Ode to the West Wind" (Shelley), **Retro. Supp. I:** 308; **Supp. I Part 2:** 728; **Supp. IX:** 52; **Supp. XII:** 117; **Supp. XIV:** 271–272; **Supp. XV:** 221

"Ode to Walt Whitman" (Benét), **Supp. XI:** 52

"Ode to Willem de Kooning"(O'Hara), **Supp. XXIII:** 208, 216

Odets, Clifford, **Supp. I Part 1:** 277, 295; **Supp. I Part 2:** 679; **Supp. II Part 2:** **529–554;** **Supp. IV Part 2:** 587; **Supp. V:** 109; **Supp. VIII:** 96; **Supp. XVIII:** 238; **Supp. XX:** **34;** **Supp. XXVII:** 134

Odier, Daniel, **Supp. III Part 1:** 97

"Odi et Amo" (Catullus), **Supp. XV:** 27, 32, 35

"Odom"(P. Benedict), **Supp. XXIII:** 41

O'Donnell, George Marion, **II:** 67

O'Donnell, Mary King, **Supp. XVIII:** 232

O'Donnell, Thomas F., **II:** 131

"Odor of Verbena, An" (Faulkner), **II:** 66; **Retro. Supp. III:** 85

O'Doul, Lefty, **II:** 425

Odysseus (Homer), **Supp. XXVI:** 79

"Odysseus to Telemachus" (Brodsky), **Supp. VIII:** 25

Odyssey (Bryant, trans.), **Supp. I Part 1:** 158

Odyssey (Homer), **III:** 14, 470; **Retro. Supp. I:** 286, 290; **Retro. Supp. II:** 121; **Supp. I Part 1:** 185; **Supp. IV Part 2:** 631; **Supp. IX:** 211; **Supp. X:** 114; **Supp. XIV:** 191; **Supp. XVII:** 117; **Supp. XXI:** 36

"Odyssey of a Wop, The" (Fante), **Supp. XI:** 164, 165

Oedipus at Colonus (Sophocles), **Retro. Supp. III:** 70

Oedipus Rex (Sophocles), **I:** 137; **III:** 145, 151, 152, 332; **Supp. I Part 2:** 428

Oedipus Tyrannus (Sophocles), **II:** 203; **Supp. XV:** 265

Oehlschlaeger, Fritz, **Supp. IX:** 123

Oelze, Richard, **Supp. XXII:** 167

"Of Alexander Crummell" (Du Bois), **Supp. II Part 1:** 170

O'Faoláin, Seán, **Supp. II Part 1:** 101

Of a World That Is No More (Singer), **IV:** 16

Of Being Numerous (Oppen), **Supp. XXVI:** 223, 230, 233–234, 237

"Of Being Numerous" (Oppen), **Supp. XXVI:** 232, 233–234, 236

"Of Booker T. Washington and Others" (Du Bois), **Supp. II Part 1:** 168

"Of Bright & Blue Birds & the Gala Sun" (Stevens), **IV:** 93

"Of Christian Heroism" (Ozick), **Supp. V:** 272

"Of Dying Beauty" (Zukofsky), **Supp. III Part 2:** 610

"Of Epiphanies and Poets" (Phillips), **Supp. XX:** 221

"Of 'Father and Son' " (Kunitz), **Supp. III Part 1:** 262

Offenbach, Jacques, **II:** 427

"Offering for Mr. Bluehart, An" (Wright), **Supp. III Part 2:** 596, 601

"Offerings" (Mason), **Supp. VIII:** 141

"Offertory" (Hempel), **Supp. XXI:** **126–127**

Office, The (Asch), **Supp. XXVI:** 18–20, 21, 25

"Office, The" (Munro), **Supp. XXVII:** 183–184

Official Entry Blank (Kooser), **Supp. XIX:** 116, **117–118**

"Official Entry Form" (Kooser), **Supp. XIX:** 117

"Official Piety" (Whittier), **Supp. I Part 2:** 687

Off Keck Road (Simpson), **Supp. XXVII:** 240–242

"Offloading for Mrs. Schwartz" (Saunders), **Supp. XIX:** 225–226

"Of Freemasons, Kings, and Constitutions" (P. N. Warren), **Supp. XX:** **273**

"Off-Shore Pirates, The" (Fitzgerald), **II:** 88

Off the Beaten Path (Proulx), **Supp. VII:** 261

Off the Beaten Path: Stories of Place, **Supp. XVI:** 22

"Off the Cuff" (Simpson), **Supp. IX:** 278

"Off the Highway" (Wolfert), **Supp. XXI:** 265

Off the Map (Levine), **Supp. V:** 178

Offut, Chris, **Supp. XIX:** **163–176**

Offutt, Chris, **Supp. XXVII:** 217

Of Gravity and Angels (Hirshfield), **Supp. XXIII:** 131

O'Flaherty, George, **Supp. I Part 1:** 202, 205–206

O'Flaherty, Kate. *See* Chopin, Kate

O'Flaherty, Thomas, **Supp. I Part 1:** 202, 203–204, 205
O'Flaherty, Thomas, Jr., **Supp. I Part 1:** 202
"Of Maids and Other Muses" (Alvarez), **Supp. VII:** 11
"Of Margaret" (Ransom), **III:** 491
Of Mice and Men (Steinbeck), **IV:** 51, 57–58
"Of Modern Poetry" (Stevens), **IV:** 92
Of Nature, Time and Teale: A Biographical Sketch of Edwin Way Teale (Dodd), **Supp. XXVIII:** 252
Of No Country I Know: New and Selected Poems and Translations (Ferry), **Supp. XXIV: 157**
Of Plymouth Plantation (Bradford), **Retro. Supp. II:** 161, 162; **Retro. Supp. III:** 9; **Supp. XXII:** 33, **35–47**
Of Plymouth Plantation (Morison, ed.), **Supp. I Part 2:** 494
"Ofrenda for Lobo" (Mora), **Supp. XIII:** 224
"Often" (Kenyon), **Supp. VII:** 171
"Often, in Dreams, He Moved through a City" (Dobyns), **Supp. XIII:** 90
"Of the Coming of John" (Du Bois), **Supp. II Part 1:** 170
"Of the Culture of White Folk" (Du Bois), **Supp. II Part 1:** 175
Of the Farm (Updike), **IV:** 214, 217, 223–225, 233; **Retro. Supp. I:** 318, 329, 332
"Of the Four-Winged Cherubim as Signature" (Sobin), **Supp. XVI:** 287
"Of 'The Frill' " (McCarriston), **Supp. XIV:** 274
"Of the Passing of the First-Born" (Du Bois), **Supp. II Part 1:** 170
"Of the Sorrow Songs" (Du Bois), **Supp. II Part 1:** 170
"Of the Vanity of All Worldly Creature" (Bradstreet), **Retro. Supp. III:** 4
"Of the Wings of Atlanta" (Du Bois), **Supp. II Part 1:** 170
Of This Time, Of This Place (Trilling), **Supp. III Part 2:** 498, 504
Of Time and the River (Wolfe), **IV:** 450, 451, 452, 455, 456, 457, 458, 459, 462, 464–465, 467, 468, 469
Of Woman Born: Motherhood as Experience and Institution (Rich), **Retro. Supp. III:** 242, 246; **Supp. I Part 2:** 554, 567–569
Of Women and Their Elegance (Mailer), **Retro. Supp. II:** 209
Ogden, Archie, **Supp. XIII:** 174
Ogden, Henry, **II:** 298
Ogden, Uzal, **Supp. I Part 2:** 516
Ogle, Connie, **Supp. XXIII:** 300, 301
Oglethorpe's Dream: A Picture of Georgia (Bottoms and Kirkland), **Supp. XXVIII:** 29–30
"Oh, Atonement" (Weigl), **Supp. XIX:** 287
"Oh, Fairest of the Rural Maids" (Bryant), **Supp. I Part 1:** 169
"Oh, Immobility, Death's Vast Associate" (Dobyns), **Supp. XIII:** 89

"Oh, Joseph, I'm So Tired" (Yates), **Supp. XI:** 348
Oh, the Places You'll Go! (Geisel), **Supp. XVI:** 111
Oh, the Thinks You can Think! (Geisel), **Supp. XVI:** 111
"O'Halloran's Luck" (Benét), **Supp. XI:** 47
O'Hara, Frank, **Supp. XII:** 121; **Supp. XIX:** 81, 85; **Supp. XV:** 93, 176, 177, 178, 179–180, 182, 186, 187, 215–216; **Supp. XXII:** 226, 236; **Supp. XXIII: 207–222; Supp. XXIV:** 33, 34, 36, 42, 43, 44; **Supp. XXVII:** 19, 22, 23
O'Hara, J. D., **Supp. IV Part 1:** 43; **Supp. V:** 22; **Supp. XVI:** 221; **Supp. XXI:** 228
O'Hara, John, **I:** 375, 495; **II:** 444, 459; **III:** 66, **361–384; IV:** 59; **Retro. Supp. I:** 99, 112; **Supp. I Part 1:** 196; **Supp. II Part 1:** 109; **Supp. IV Part 1:** 31, 383; **Supp. IV Part 2:** 678; **Supp. IX:** 208; **Supp. V:** 95; **Supp. VIII:** 151, 156; **Supp. XIX:** 209
O'Hara, John Myers, **Supp. XXVII:** 285, 289
O'Hara's Choice (Uris), **Supp. XX:** 247, **256–257**
"O Heaven born muse! inspire my humble lay" (Very), **Supp. XXV:** 239
O'Hehir, Andrew, **Supp. XII:** 280
O. Henry Biography (C. A. Smith), **Supp. II Part 1:** 395
"Ohio Pagan, An" (Anderson), **I:** 112, 113
Ohio trilogy (Richter), **Supp. XVIII:** 212–215
Oh Mercy (album, Dylan), **Supp. XVIII:** 28, 33
Oh Say Can You Say? (Geisel), **Supp. XVI:** 111
Oil! (Sinclair), **Supp. V:** 276, 277–279, 282, 288, 289
Oil Notes (Bass), **Supp. XVI:** 17
"Oil Painting of the Artist as the Artist" (MacLeish), **III:** 14
"O-jib-way Maid, The"(J. Schoolcraft), **Supp. XXIII:** 235
O'Keeffe, Georgia, **Supp. IX:** 62, 66; **Supp. XX: 75**
"Oklahoma" (Levis), **Supp. XI:** 267
Oklahoma's Poor Rich Indians: An Orgy of Graft and Exploitation of the Five Civilized Tribes—Legalized Robbery (Zitkala-Ša, Sniffen, and Fabens), **Supp. XXV:** 283
Oktenberg, Adrian, **Supp. XVII:** 76; **Supp. XXI:** 253; **Supp. XXIII:** 133
"Old, Old, Old, Old Andrew Jackson" (Lindsay), **Supp. I Part 2:** 398
"Old Amusement Park, An" (Moore), **III:** 216
"Old Angel Midnight" (Kerouac), **Supp. III Part 1:** 229–230
"Old Apple Dealer, The" (Hawthorne), **II:** 227, 233–235, 237, 238
"Old Apple-Tree, The" (Dunbar), **Supp. II Part 1:** 198

"Old Army Game, The" (Garrett), **Supp. VII:** 100–101
"Old Aunt Peggy" (Chopin), **Retro. Supp. II:** 64
"Old Barn at the Bottom of the Fogs, The" (Frost), **Retro. Supp. I:** 138
Old Battle-Ax, The (Holding), **Supp. XXII: 128–129**
Old Beauty and Others, The (Cather), **I:** 331
"Old Boys, Old Girls" (E. P. Jones), **Supp. XXII:** 151
Old Bruin: Commodore Matthew C. Perry, 1794–1858 (Morison), **Supp. I Part 2:** 494–495
Old Bunch, The (Levin), **Supp. XXVII:** 134, 139, 143
Old Burnside: A Memoir of a Southern Girlhood (Arnow), **Supp. XXVIII:** 1, 3, 13, 17–18
"Old Cracked Tune, An" (Kunitz), **Supp. III Part 1:** 264
Old Creole Days (Cable), **Supp. XXVIII:** 116
Old Curiosity Shop, The (Dickens), **I:** 458; **Supp. I Part 2:** 409
"Old Enemy, The" (Teasdale), **Supp. XXVII:** 296
Oldest Killed Lake in North America, The (Carruth), **Supp. XVI:** 51
"Oldest Man, The" (M. F. K. Fisher), **Supp. XVII:** 91
"Old Farmer, The" (Jeffers), **Supp. II Part 2:** 418
Old-Fashioned Girl, An (Alcott), **Supp. I Part 1:** 29, 41, 42
"Old Father Morris" (Stowe), **Supp. I Part 2:** 586
Old Favorites and New Fancies for 1909 (Wells), **Supp. XXVI:** 275
"Old Flame, The" (R. Lowell), **II:** 550
"Old Florist" (Roethke), **III:** 531
"Old Folsom Prison" (Matthews), **Supp. IX:** 165
Old Forest, The (Taylor), **Supp. V:** 320, 321, 326, 327
"Old Forest, The" (Taylor), **Supp. V:** 313, 321, 323, 326
Old Forest and Other Stories (Taylor), **Supp. V:** 326
Old Friends and New (Jewett), **II:** 402; **Retro. Supp. II:** 137, 140
Old Glory, The (R. Lowell), **II:** 543, 545–546, 555; **Retro. Supp. II:** 188
Old Helmet, The (S. and A. Warner), **Supp. XVIII:** 267
"Old Homestead, The" (Dunbar), **Supp. II Part 1:** 198
"Old House" (Espaillat), **Supp. XXI:** 112, 113
Old Indian Legends (Zitkala-Ša), **Supp. XXV:** 275, 278, 285
"Old Iron" (Nye), **Supp. XIII:** 276
"Old Ironsides" (Holmes), **Supp. I Part 1:** 302
Old Jules (Sandoz), **Supp. XXIV:** 243, 244, **245–246,** 249, 251, 255, 257
"Old Lady's Restoration, The"(King), **Supp. XXVIII:** 124

"Old Lady We Saw, An" (Shields), **Supp. VII:** 310–311

"Old Love" (Singer), **Retro. Supp. II:** 307

"Old McGrath Place, The" (McGrath), **Supp. X:** 114

"Old Maid, The" (Wharton), **Retro. Supp. I:** 381, 382

"Old Man, The" (Faulkner), **II:** 68, 69; **Retro. Supp. III:** 85

Old Man and the Sea, The (Hemingway), **II:** 250, 256–257, 258, 265; **III:** 40; **Retro. Supp. I:** 180, **185,** 186

"Old Man Drunk" (Wright), **Supp. III Part 2:** 595

"Old Man Feeding Hens" (Francis), **Supp. IX:** 78

"Old Man on the Hospital Porch" (Ríos), **Supp. IV Part 2:** 546–547

Old Man Rubbing His Eyes (R. Bly), **Supp. IV Part 1:** 65

"Old Manse, The" (Hawthorne), **II:** 224

"Old Man's Winter Night, An" (Frost), **Retro. Supp. I:** 126, 131

Old Man Who Love Cheese, The (Keillor), **Supp. XVI:** 177

"Old Man with a Dog" (Wright), **Supp. XV:** 346

Old Marriage and New (Kooser), **Supp. XIX:** 120–121

"Old Meeting House, The" (Stowe), **Supp. I Part 2:** 586

"Old Memory, An" (Dunbar), **Supp. II Part 1:** 198

"Old Men, Old Horses" (P. N. Warren as Kilina), **Supp. XX:** 262

"Old Men, The" (McCarthy), **II:** 566

"Old Men Pitching Horseshoes" (X. J. Kennedy), **Supp. XV:** 166

Old Money (Wasserstein), **Supp. XV:** **333–334**

"Old Morgue, The" (Prose), **Supp. XVI:** 250

Old Morning Program, The (radio show, Keillor). *See Prairie Home Companion, A* (radio show, Keillor)

"Old Mortality" (Porter), **III:** 436, 438– 441, 442, 445, 446

"Old Mrs. Harris" (Cather), **I:** 332; **Retro. Supp. I:** 19

Old Neighborhood, The (Mamet), **Supp. XIV:** 240, 241, 242, 249–250, 251, 252, 254

"Old News" (Hawthorne), **Retro. Supp. III:** 111

Old New York (Wharton), **IV:** 322; **Retro. Supp. I:** 381; **Retro. Supp. III:** 288

"Ol' Doc Hyar" (Campbell), **Supp. II Part 1:** 202

"Old of the Moon" (Offutt), **Supp. XIX:** 165, 166

Old One-Two, The (Gurney), **Supp. V:** 98

"Old Order, The" (Porter), **III:** 443, 444– 445, 451

"Old Osawatomie" (Sandburg), **III:** 584

Old Patagonia Express, The: By Train through the Americas (Theroux), **Supp. VIII:** 322

"Old People" (Ferry), **Supp. XXIV:** 162

"Old People, The" (Faulkner), **II:** 71–72

"Old Photograph" (Davison), **Supp. XXVI:** 72

"Old Photograph, An" (Kooser), **Supp. XIX:** 121

"Old Poet Moves to a New Apartment 14 Times, The" (Zukofsky), **Supp. III Part 2:** 628

Old Possum's Book of Practical Cats (T. S. Eliot), **Supp. XIII:** 228, 344

"Old Red" (Gordon), **II:** 199, 200, 203

Old Red and Other Stories (Gordon), **II:** 157

Old Régime in Canada, The (Parkman), **Supp. II Part 2:** 600, 607, 608–609, 612

Old Religion, The (Mamet), **Supp. XIV:** 253

Olds, Sharon, **Supp. X:** 201–217; **Supp. XI:** 139, 142, 244; **Supp. XII:** 229; **Supp. XIV:** 265; **Supp. XVII:** 114, 240; **Supp. XXI:** 249

"Old Saws" (Garrett), **Supp. VII:** 96–97

Old South, The: "A Summer Tragedy" and Other Stories (Bontemps), **Supp. XXII:** 7

"Old Stories" (Skloot), **Supp. XX:** 200

Old Testament, **I:** 109, 181, 300, 328, 401, 410, 419, 431, 457, 458; **II:** 166, 167, 219; **III:** 270, 272, 348, 390, 396; **IV:** 41, 114, 152, 309; **Retro. Supp. I:** 122, 140, 249, 311, 360; **Retro. Supp. II:** 299; **Supp. I Part 1:** 60, 104, 106, 151; **Supp. I Part 2:** 427, 515, 516; **Supp. IX:** 14. *See also* names of Old Testament books

"Old Things, The" (James), **Retro. Supp. I:** 229

"Old Times on the Mississippi" (Twain), **IV:** 199; **Retro. Supp. III:** 256, 264

Oldtown Folks (Stowe), **Supp. I Part 2:** 587, 596–598

"Old Town of Berwick, The" (Jewett), **Retro. Supp. II:** 132

"Old Trails" (Robinson), **III:** 513, 517

"Old Tyrannies" (Bourne), **I:** 233

"Old West" (Bausch), **Supp. VII:** 48

"Old Whorehouse, An" (Oliver), **Supp. VII:** 235

"Old Woman" (Pinsky), **Supp. VI:** 238

"Old Woman of Beare, The" (X. J. Kennedy), **Supp. XV:** 156

"Old Woman's Tale, An" (Hawthorne), **Retro. Supp. III:** 111

"Old Word, The" (Simic), **Supp. VIII:** 282

"Old-World Landowners" (Gogol), **Supp. XV:** 262

Oldys, Francis. *See* Chalmers, George

Oleanna (Mamet), **Supp. XIV:** 239, 241, 245, 248, 250

Olendorf, Donna, **Supp. IV Part 1:** 196

"Olga Poems, The" (Levertov), **Supp. III Part 1:** 279–281

"Olive Groves of Thasos, The" (Clampitt), **Supp. IX:** **51–52**

Olive Kitteridge (Strout), **Supp. XXIII:** 273, 275, **280–284,** 285

Oliver, Bill, **Supp. VIII:** 138

Oliver, Douglas, **Supp. XXII:** 225, 226, 233, 235

Oliver, Mary, **Supp. VII: 229–248; Supp. X:** 31; **Supp. XVI:** 39; **Supp. XVII:** 111, 240; **Supp. XXIII:** 51

Oliver, Sydney, **I:** 409

Oliver Goldsmith: A Biography (Irving), **II:** 315

Oliver Twist (Dickens), **I:** 354; **Supp. IV Part 2:** 464

Olives (Stallings), **Supp. XXV:** 221, 223, 224, 233–234

"Olivia" (Salinas), **Supp. XIII:** 316

"Olivier Bergmann" (Halliday), **Supp. XIX:** 93–94

Olivieri, David (pseudonym), **Retro. Supp. I:** 361. *See also* Wharton, Edith

Ollive, Samuel, **Supp. I Part 2:** 503

Olmsted, Frederick Law, **Supp. I Part 1:** 355

Olney, James, **Supp. XXVIII:** 169

Olor de la memoria, El/The Scent of Memory (Espaillat), **Supp. XXI:** 104

Olsen, Lance, **Supp. IV Part 1:** 54; **Supp. IV Part 2:** 623

Olsen, Tillie, **Supp. V:** 114, 220; **Supp. XIII: 291–309; Supp. XVI:** 83, 90

Olshan, Joseph, **Supp. XIX:** 52

Olson, Charles, **Retro. Supp. I:** 209; **Retro. Supp. III:** 245; **Supp. II Part 1:** 30, 328; **Supp. II Part 2: 555–587; Supp. III Part 1:** 9, 271; **Supp. III Part 2:** 542, 624; **Supp. IV Part 1:** 139, 144, 146, 153, 154, 322; **Supp. IV Part 2:** 420, 421, 423, 426; **Supp. VIII:** 290, 291; **Supp. XII:** 2, 198; **Supp. XIII:** 104; **Supp. XIV:** 96; **Supp. XV:** 177; **Supp. XXI:** 19, 21, 23; **Supp. XXIV:** 42; **Supp. XXVII:** 160

Olson, Clarence, **Supp. XX:** 84, 85, 86

Olson, Ray, **Supp. XVII:** 111, 112, 119

Olson, Sigurd F., **Supp. XXVIII:** 255

Olson, Tillie, **Supp. XXVII:** 256

"Ol' Tunes, The" (Dunbar), **Supp. II Part 1:** 197

"O Lull Me, Lull Me" (Roethke), **III:** 536–537

O'Malley, Anne, **Supp. XXII:** 56

Omar Khayyam, **Supp. I Part 1:** 363

O'Meally, Robert, **Retro. Supp. II:** 112

Omega the Unknown (comic book series), **Supp. XVIII:** 149

"Omen" (Komunyakaa), **Supp. XIII:** 126, 127

Omensetter's Luck (Gass), **Supp. VI: 80– 82,** 87

Omeros (Walcott), **Supp. XV:** 264

"Ominous Baby, An" (Crane), **I:** 411

Ommateum, with Doxology (Ammons), **Supp. VII:** 24–26, 27, 28, 36

Omni-Americans, The: New Perspectives on Black Experience and American Culture (Murray), **Supp. XIX:** 147, **149–151,** 154

"Omnibus Jaunts and Drivers" (Whitman), **IV:** 350

Omoo (Melville), **III:** 76–77, 79, 84; **Retro. Supp. I:** 247; **Retro. Supp. III:** 147, 152, 153, 154, 155

O My Land, My Friends (H. Crane), **Retro. Supp. II:** 76

"On Abrigador Hill" (Nelson), **Supp. XVIII:** 183

"On a Certain Condescension in Foreigners" (J. R. Lowell), **Supp. I Part 2:** 419

"On a Certain Engagement South of Seoul" (Carruth), **Supp. XVI:** 47

"On a Child Who Lived One Minute" (X. J. Kennedy), **Supp. XV:** 152, 155

"On Acquiring Riches" (Banks), **Supp. V:** 5

On a Darkling Plain (Stegner), **Supp. IV Part 2:** 598, 607

On a Fire on the Moon (Mailer), **Retro. Supp. II:** 206

"On a Hill Far Away" (Dillard), **Supp. VI:** 28

"On a Honey Bee, Drinking from a Glass and Drowned Therein" (Freneau), **Supp. II Part 1:** 273

"On a Monument to a Pigeon" (Leopold), **Supp. XIV:** 187–188

"On a Mountainside" (Wagoner), **Supp. IX:** 332

O'Nan, Stewart, **Supp. XI:** 348; **Supp. XXV: 141–155**

"On a New Novel" (Ellis), **Supp. XXVII:** 78

"On an Old Photograph of My Son" (Carver), **Supp. III Part 1:** 140

"Onan's Soliloquy" (X. J. Kennedy), **Supp. XV:** 165

"On Antiphon Island" (Mackey), **Supp. XXVII:** 156

"On a Proposed Trip South" (W. C. Williams), **Retro. Supp. I:** 413

"On a Scale of 1 to 10: Life Writing and Lyrical Pain" (Mintz), **Supp. XXVI:** 52–53

Onassis, Jacqueline Kennedy, **Supp. XVIII:** 287

"On a Tree Fallen across the Road" (Frost), **Retro. Supp. I:** 134

"On a View of Pasadena from the Hills" (Winters), **Supp. II Part 2:** 795, 796–799, 814

"On a Visit to a Halfway House after a Long Absence" (Salinas), **Supp. XIII:** 325

"On a Windy Night" (Dixon), **Supp. XII:** 155

On Becoming a Novelist (Gardner), **Supp. VI:** 64

"On Being an American" (Toomer), **Supp. III Part 2:** 479

"On Being Asked to Write a Poem against the War in Vietnam" (Carruth), **Supp. XVI:** 55–56

"On Being a Woman" (Parker), **Supp. IX:** 201

On Being Blue (Gass), **Supp. VI:** 77, 78, 86, 94; **Supp. XIV:** 305

"On Being Brought from Africa to America" (Wheatley), **Supp. XX:** 280–281, 286–287

"On Being Too Inhibited" (Hay), **Supp. XIV:** 130

"On Being Unable to Read" (Cornell), **Supp. XX: 94–95**

On Beyond Zebra! (Geisel), **Supp. XVI:** 105

"On Burroughs' Work" (Ginsberg), **Supp. II Part 1:** 320

Once (Walker), **Supp. III Part 2:** 519, 522, 530

Once at Antietam (Gaddis), **Supp. IV Part 1:** 285

"Once by the Pacific" (Frost), **II:** 155; **Retro. Supp. I:** 122, 137; **Retro. Supp. III:** 102

Once in a Blue Moon (film), **Supp. XXVII:** 90

"Once More, the Round" (Roethke), **III:** 529

Once More around the Block: Familiar Essays (Epstein), **Supp. XIV:** 107

"Once More to the Lake" (White), **Supp. I Part 2:** 658, 668, 673–675

"On Certain Political Measures Proposed to Their Consideration" (Barlow), **Supp. II Part 1:** 82

"Once There Was Light" (Kenyon), **Supp. VII:** 171–172

Once Upon a Time in Atlanta (Andrews), **Supp. XXVI:** 3, 11

"On *Credo Ut Intelligam*" (Bronk), **Supp. XXI:** 31

Ondaatje, Michael, **Supp. IV Part 1:** 252

"On Dining Alone" (M. F. K. Fisher), **Supp. XVII:** 83

On Distant Ground (R. O. Butler), **Supp. XII:** 62, **66–68,** 69, 74

"On Divers Geometries" (Bronk), **Supp. XXI:** 31

"On Dreams"(Hadas), **Supp. XXIII:** 117

"One, The" (Weigl), **Supp. XIX:** 282–283

"1 January 1965" (Brodsky), **Supp. VIII:** 23–24

One-Act Plays (Clark and Cook, eds.), **Supp. XXVIII:** 69

O'Neale, Sondra, **Supp. IV Part 1:** 2

"One A.M. with Voices" (X. J. Kennedy), **Supp. XV:** 157

"One Arm" (T. Williams), **IV:** 383

One Arm, and Other Stories (T. Williams), **IV:** 383

"One Art" (Bell), **Supp. X:** 2

One Art (Bishop), **Retro. Supp. II:** 51

"One Art" (Bishop), **Retro. Supp. II:** 50; **Supp. I Part 1:** 72, 73, 82, 93, 94–95, 96; **Supp. XV:** 126; **Supp. XXI:** 58; **Supp. XXIII:** 117; **Supp. XXV:** 222

"One Art: The Poetry of Elizabeth Bishop, 1971–1976" (Schwartz), **Supp. I Part 1:** 81

One Big Self: Prisoners of Louisiana (Wright and Luster), **Supp. XV:** 337, 344, 350, **351–353**

"One Blessing had I than the rest" (Dickinson), **Retro. Supp. I:** 45

"One Body" (Hass), **Supp. VI:** 106

One Boy's Boston, 1887–1901 (Morison), **Supp. I Part 2:** 494

"One Coat of Paint" (Ashbery), **Supp. III Part 1:** 26

"One Dash-Horses" (Crane), **I:** 416

One Day (Morris), **III:** 233–236

One Day, When I Was Lost (Baldwin), **Retro. Supp. II:** 13; **Supp. I Part 1:** 48, 66, 67

"One Dead Friend" (Kumin), **Supp. IV Part 2:** 441

One Destiny: An Epistle to the Christians (Asch), **Supp. XXIII:** 2, 7

"One Down" (Goodman), **Supp. XXVI:** 122–123

One Fish Two Fish Red Fish Blue Fish (Geisel), **Supp. XVI:** 108

One Flesh (Major), **Supp. XXII: 183–184**

One Flew Over the Cuckoo's Nest (Kesey), **III:** 558

One Flew Over the Cuckoo's Nest (Kesey), **Supp. XXIII:** 100

One Foot in Eden (Rash), **Supp. XXVII:** 222–223, 226

"One for the Road" (Swados), **Supp. XIX:** 259

One for the Rose (Levine), **Supp. V:** 178, 179, 181, 187, 189–191

"One for the Rose" (Levine), **Supp. V:** 181, 190

"One Friday Morning" (Hughes), **Supp. I Part 1:** 330

"One Holy Night" (Cisneros), **Supp. VII:** 69–70

"One Home" (Stafford), **Supp. XI:** 321

100 Faces of Death, The, Part IV (Boyle), **Supp. VIII:** 16

100 Great Poets of the English Language (Gioia, ed.), **Supp. XXI:** 99

100 Places Every Woman Should Go (Griest), **Supp. XXVIII:** 97, 100, 105–106

100 Years of Negro Freedom (Bontemps), **Supp. XXII:** 6

145 Street: Short Stories (Myers), **Supp. XXVII:** 210, 211

$106,000 Blood Money (Hammett), **Supp. IV Part 1:** 345

"$106,000 Blood Money" (Hammett), **Supp. IV Part 1:** 345, 346

One Hundred Days in Europe (Holmes), **Supp. I Part 1:** 317

180 More: Extraordinary Poems for Every Day (Collins, ed.), **Supp. XXI:** 54

120 Million (Gold), **Supp. XXVIII:** 73

158-Pound Marriage, The (Irving), **Supp. VI:** 163, 164, **167–170**

O'Neil, Elizabeth Murrie, **Retro. Supp. I:** 427

O'Neill, Brendan, **Supp. XII:** 286

O'Neill, Eugene, **I:** 66, 71, 81, 94, 393, 445; **II:** 278, 391, 427, 585; **III:** 151, 165, **385–408; IV:** 61, 383; **Retro. Supp. II:** 82, 104; **Retro. Supp. III:** 48, 165, 174, 177, 313; **Supp. III Part 1:** 177–180, 189; **Supp. IV Part 1:** 359; **Supp. IV Part 2:** 587, 607; **Supp. V:** 277; **Supp. VIII:** 332, 334; **Supp. XIV:** 239, 320, 328; **Supp. XVI:** 193; **Supp. XVII:** 96, 99–100, 103, 105, 107; **Supp. XX: 69; Supp. XXI:** 6, 13; **Supp. XXII:** 17, 18, 22, 28; **Supp. XXV:** 19; **Supp. XXVIII:**

38, 39, 68, 69–70, 74

O'Neill, Oona, **Supp. XXII:** 25, 26

"One Is a Wanderer" (Thurber), **Supp. I Part 2:** 616

One Is the Sun (P. N. Warren), **Supp. XX: 269–270**

One L (Turow), **Supp. XVII: 214,** 215, 217

"One Last Look at the Adige: Verona in the Rain" (Wright), **Supp. III Part 2:** 603

One Life (Rukeyser), **Supp. VI:** 273, 281, 283

One Life at a Time, Please (Abbey), **Supp. XIII:** 13

One Man in His Time (Glasgow), **II:** 178, 184

"One Man's Fortunes" (Dunbar), **Supp. II Part 1:** 211, 212–213

One Man's Initiation (Dos Passos), **I:** 476–477, 479, 488

One Man's Meat (White), **Supp. I Part 2:** 654, 669, 676

"One Man's Meat" (White), **Supp. I Part 2:** 655

One Matchless Time: A Life of William Faulkner (Parini), **Retro. Supp. III:** 73; **Supp. XXII:** 205

"One Moment on Top of the Earth" (Nye), **Supp. XIII:** 282

One More July: A Football Dialogue with Bill Curry (Plimpton), **Supp. XVI:** 243

"One More"(Kenny), **Supp. XXIII:** 156

"One More Song" (Lindsay), **Supp. I Part 2:** 400–401

"One More Thing" (Carver), **Supp. III Part 1:** 138, 144

"One More Time" (Gordon), **II:** 200

One Nation (Stegner), **Supp. IV Part 2:** 599, 608

"One-Night Homecoming" (X. J. Kennedy), **Supp. XV:** 167

"ONE NIGHT STAND" (Baraka), **Supp. II Part 1:** 32

"One of Our Conquerors" (Bourne), **I:** 223

One of Ours (Cather), **I:** 322–323; **Retro. Supp. I:** 1, 3, **13–15,** 20; **Retro. Supp. III:** 23, 36

One of the Dangerous Trades (Davison), **Supp. XXVI:** 61, 67–68

"One of the Missing" (Bierce), **I:** 201–202

"One of the Rooming Houses of Heaven" (Doty), **Supp. XI:** 131

"One of the Smallest" (Stern), **Supp. IX:** 299–300

"One of Us" (Fante), **Supp. XI:** 165

Oneóta: or, The Red Race of America (H. Schoolcraft), **Supp. XXIII:** 232

"One Out of Twelve: Writers Who Are Women in Our Century" (Olsen), **Supp. XIII:** 294

"One Part Humor, 2 Parts Whining" (Kakutani), **Supp. XI:** 38

"One Person" (Wylie), **Supp. I Part 2:** 709, 724–727

"One Reel Tragedy" (Stone), **Supp. XXVII:** 254

"One Sister have I in our house" (Dickinson), **Retro. Supp. I:** 34

165 Meeting House Lane (Notley), **Supp. XXII:** 224, 225, 226

"One Song, The" (Strand), **Supp. IV Part 2:** 619

"One Summer in Spain" (Coover), **Supp. V:** 40

One That Got Away, The (Everett), **Supp. XVIII:** 54

1000 Airplanes on the Roof (Glass, Hwang, and Sirlin), **Supp. XXI:** 147

1001 Afternoons in Chicago (Hecht), **Supp. XXVII:** 83, 85, 88

One Thousand Avant-Garde Plays (Koch), **Supp. XV:** 187

"One Thousandth, The" (Weigl), **Supp. XIX:** 288

One Time, One Place: Mississippi in the Depression, a Snapshot Album (Welty), **Retro. Supp. I:** 339, 343, 344

1 x 1 (One Times One) (Cummings), **I:** 430, 436, 438–439, 441, 446, 447, 448

"One Touch of Nature" (McCarthy), **II:** 580

One Train (Koch), **Supp. XV:** 177, 184

"One Trip Abroad" (Fitzgerald), **II:** 95

One True Thing (film), **Supp. XVII:** 176

One True Thing (Quindlen), **Supp. XVII:** 166, **174–176**

"One Way" (Creeley), **Supp. IV Part 1:** 150–151

One Way or Another (Cameron), **Supp. XII:** 81

One-Way Ticket (Hughes), **Retro. Supp. I:** 206, 207, 208; **Supp. I Part 1:** 333–334

One Way to Heaven (Cullen), **Supp. IV Part 1:** 170, 172

One Way to Reconstruct the Scene (W. V. Davis), **Supp. XXI:** 83, **88–91**

"One Way to Reconstruct the Scene" (W. V. Davis), **Supp. XXI:** **88–89,** 90, 91, 92, **93**

One Way to Spell Man (Stegner), **Supp. IV Part 2:** 595, 598, 601, 609

"One Way to Spell Man" (Stegner), **Supp. IV Part 2:** 601

One Whose Eyes Open When You Close Your Eyes, The (F. Wright), **Supp. XVII:** 240, 243

"One Who Skins Cats, The" (Gunn Allen), **Supp. IV Part 1:** 331

One Who Walked Alone (Price), **Supp. XXVII:** 117

"One Who Went Forth to Feel Fear" (Grimms), **Supp. X:** 86

"One Winter I Devise a Plan of My Own" (Ríos), **Supp. IV Part 2:** 549

One Winter Night in August (X. J. Kennedy), **Supp. XV:** 154, 162

One World at a Time (Kooser), **Supp. XIX:** 116, **122–123**

One Writer's Beginnings (Welty), **Retro. Supp. I:** 339, 340, 341, 343, 344, 355–356

"One Year" (Olds), **Supp. X:** 210

On Fire (L. Brown), **Supp. XXI:** 41, **48–49**

On Fire (Silver), **Supp. XXIV:** 264

"On First Looking Into Chapman's Homer" (Keats), **Supp. XXI:** 64; **Supp. XXV:** 226

"On First Looking Out through Juan de la Cosa's Eyes" (Olson), **Supp. II Part 2:** 565, 566, 570, 579

"On First Opening *The Lyric Year*" (W. C. Williams), **Retro. Supp. I:** 414

"On Freedom's Ground" (Wilbur), **Supp. III Part 2:** 562

On Glory's Course (Purdy), **Supp. VII:** 275–276, 279, 280

On Grief and Reason (Brodsky), **Supp. VIII:** 31–32

"On Hearing a Symphony of Beethoven" (Millay), **III:** 132–133

"On Hearing the Airlines Will Use a Psychological Profile to Catch Potential Skyjackers" (Dunn), **Supp. XI:** 144–145

On Human Finery (Bell), **Supp. I Part 2:** 636

"On *Imagerie*: Esther Williams, 1944" (Sobin), **Supp. XVI:** 294

"On Imagination" (Wheatley), **Supp. XX: 281**

"On Imminence: An Essay" (Sobin), **Supp. XVI:** 291

On Immunity: An Inoculation (Biss), **Supp. XXVI:** 45, 57–58, 59

Onion's Dark Core, The: A Little Book of Poetry Talk (Bottoms), **Supp. XXVIII:** 22, 23, 26–27, 33

"Onionskin" (Goodman), **Supp. XXVI:** 121, 125

"On Ithaka" (Davison), **Supp. XXVI:** 79

On Kingdom Mountain (Mosher), **Supp. XXII:** 203, 205, 206, 207, 208, 209, 212, 214, **216**

Onkl Mozes (Uncle Moses) (Asch), **Supp. XXIII:** 5

"On leaving my children John and Jane at School, in the Atlantic states, and preparing to return to the interior"(J. Schoolcraft), **Supp. XXIII:** 227, 228, 232, 233, 235, 236

On Liberty (Mill), **Supp. XI:** 196

On Lies, Secrets, and Silence: Selected Prose 1966–1978 (Rich), **Retro. Supp. III:** 242, 246, 247–248

"On Looking Alone at a Place" (M. F. K. Fisher), **Supp. XVII:** 91

"On Looking at a Copy of Alice Meynell's Poems, Given Me, Years Ago, by a Friend" (A. Lowell), **II:** 527–528

"On Lookout Mountain" (Hayden), **Supp. II Part 1:** 380

Only a Few of Us Left (Marquand), **III:** 55

"Only Animal, The" (F. Wright), **Supp. XVII:** 245

"Only a Pawn in Their Game" (song, Dylan), **Supp. XVIII:** 24

Only as Far as Brooklyn (Kenny), **Supp. XXIII: 148–151,** 152

"Only Bar in Dixon, The" (Hugo), **Supp. VI:** 140, 141

Only Dangerous Thing, The (Di Piero), **Supp. XIX: 37–38**

Only Dark Spot in the Sky, The (Dove), **Supp. IV Part 1:** 244

"Only Good Indian, The" (Humphrey), **Supp. IX:** 101

Only in America (Golden), **Supp. VIII:** 244

"Only in the Dream" (Eberhart), **I:** 523

"Only Path to Tomorrow, The" (Rand), **Supp. IV Part 2:** 524

"Only Professional Player of the Toy Piano, Margaret Leng Tan, The" (Biss), **Supp. XXVI:** 51

"Only Rose, The" (Jewett), **II:** 408

"Only Son of the Doctor, The" (Gordon), **Supp. IV Part 1:** 305, 306

"Only the Cat Escapes", **Supp. XII:** 150–151

"Only the Dead Know Brooklyn" (Wolfe), **IV:** 451

Only the Little Bone (Huddle), **Supp. XXVI:** 152–153

"Only the Little Bone" (Huddle), **Supp. XXVI:** 151, 153

"Only When I Am Quiet and Do Not Speak"(Hirshfield), **Supp. XXIII:** 133

Only When I Laugh (Simon), **Supp. IV Part 2:** 575

Only World, The (Hull), **Supp. XXI:** 129, **138–141**

On Man and Manhood (Kriegel), **Supp. XXIV: 224–225**

"On Manhood, Disease, and the Authentic Self" (Kriegel), **Supp. XXIV:** 215

"On Meditation"(J. Schoolcraft), **Supp. XXIII:** 229

"On Meeting My Father in a Bar for the First Time" (Gansworth), **Supp. XXVI:** 110

"On Messrs. Hussey and Coffin" (Wheatley), **Supp. XX: 280**

On Moral Fiction (Gardner), **Supp. VI:** 61, **71,** 72, 73

"On Morality" (Didion), **Supp. IV Part 1:** 196

"On Mt. Philo in November" (Di Piero), **Supp. XIX:** 37, 39

"On Murder Considered as One of the Fine Arts" (De Quincey), **Supp. XXVI:** 283

"On My Own" (Levine), **Supp. V:** 181, 189–190

"On My Own Work" (Wilbur), **Supp. III Part 2:** 541–542

On Native Grounds: An Interpretation of Modern American Prose Literature (Kazin), **I:** 517; **Supp. I Part 2:** 650; **Supp. VIII:** 93, 96–97, 98, **100–102; Supp. XXVIII:** 157

"On Not Being a Dove" (Updike), **Retro. Supp. I:** 323

"On Open Form" (Merwin), **Supp. III Part 1:** 347–348, 353

On Photography (Sontag), **Supp. III Part 2:** 451, 458, 462–465

"On Poetry"(Hadas), **Supp. XXIII:** 115, 116

"On Political Poetry" (R. Bly), **Supp. IV Part 1:** 61

On Politics: A Carnival of Buncombe (Moos, ed.), **III:** 116

"On Pretentiousness" (Kushner), **Supp. IX:** 131–132

"On Quitting a Little College" (Stafford), **Supp. XI:** 321

"On Reading Eckerman's Conversations with Goethe" (Masters), **Supp. I Part 2:** 458

On Reading Shakespeare (L. P. Smith), **Supp. XIV:** 345–346

"On Reading to Oneself" (Gass), **Supp. VI:** 88, 89

"On Recollection" (Wheatley), **Supp. XX:** 287

On Revolution (Arendt), **Retro. Supp. I:** 87

On Second Thought (Kenny), **Supp. XXIII:** 144

"On Seeing Larry Rivers's *Washington Crossing the Delaware* at the Museum of Modern Art" (O'Hara), **Supp. XV:** 186; **Supp. XXIII:** 208, 214

"On Seeing Red" (Walker), **Supp. III Part 2:** 527

"On Seeing Two Goldfinches Fly Out of an Alder Tree, the Way You Are Swiftly Flying out of My Life"(Wakoski), **Supp. XXVIII:** 266

"On Social Plays" (A. Miller), **III:** 147, 148, 159

Onstad, Katrina, **Supp. XXIV:** 209

"On Steinbeck's Story 'Flight' " (Stegner), **Supp. IV Part 2:** 596

"On Style" (Sontag), **Supp. III Part 2:** 456–459, 465–466

"On Suicide" (Hay), **Supp. XIV:** 130, 132

"On Teaching the Young Laurel to Shoot" (Bynner), **Supp. XV:** 50

"On the Antler" (Proulx), **Supp. VII:** 252–253

"On the Avenue" (Espaillat), **Supp. XXI:** 112

On the Banks of Plum Creek (L. I. Wilder), **Supp. XXII:** 294, 299

"On the Banks of the Wabash" (Paul Dresser), **Retro. Supp. II:** 94

"On the Beach, at Night" (Whitman), **IV:** 348

"On the Bosom of This Grave and Wasted Land I Will Lay My Head" (Ray), **Supp. XVIII:** 189

On the Boundary (Tillich), **Retro. Supp. I:** 326

"On the Building of Springfield" (Lindsay), **Supp. I Part 2:** 381

"On the Coast of Maine" (Hayden), **Supp. II Part 1:** 381

On the Contrary: Articles of Belief (McCarthy), **II:** 559, 562

"On the Death of a Friend's Child" (J. R. Lowell), **Supp. I Part 2:** 409

"On the Death of Cardinal Tisserant" (Bronk), **Supp. XXI:** 32

"On the Death of General Wooster" (Wheatley), **Supp. XX:** 287

"On the Death of Rev. Mr. George White-field—1770" (Wheatley), **Supp. XX: 280,Supp. XX: 282–283**

"On the Death of Senator Thomas J. Walsh" (Winters), **Supp. II Part 2:** 802, 806

"On the Death of Yeats" (Bogan), **Supp. III Part 1:** 59

"On the Death of Zhukov" (Brodsky), **Supp. VIII:** 27

"On the Disadvantages of Central Heating" (Clampitt), **Supp. IX:** 41, 47, 52

"On the Doric Rock, Lake Superior"(J. Schoolcraft), **Supp. XXIII:** 232

On the Drumhead: A Selection from the Writing of Mike Quin (Carlisle, ed.), **Supp. XVIII:** 223, 226

"On the Edge" (Levine), **Supp. V:** 181–182

On the Edge and Over (Levine), **Supp. V:** 178, 180–182, 186

On the Edge of the Great Rift: Three Novels of Africa (Theroux), **Supp. VIII:** 316

"On the Edge of Visible Light"(Schott), **Supp. XXIII:** 242

"On the Eve of the Feast of the Immaculate Conception, 1942" (R. Lowell), **II:** 538; **Retro. Supp. II:** 185

"On the Eyes of an SS Officer" (Wilbur), **Supp. III Part 2:** 548

"On the Failure of Meaning in the Absence of Objective Analogs" (Bronk), **Supp. XXI:** 31

"On the Fall of General Earl Cornwallis" (Freneau), **Supp. II Part 1:** 261

"On the Folly of Writing Poetry" (Freneau), **Supp. II Part 1:** 263

"On the Four Parts of the World" (Dudley), **Retro. Supp. III:** 3

On the Frontier (Auden and Isherwood), **Supp. II Part 1:** 13; **Supp. XIV:** 163

On the Great Atlantic Rainway: Selected Poems, 1950–1988 (Koch), **Supp. XV:** 177

"On the History of Poetry" (Halliday), **Supp. XIX:** 88, 89

"On the Hysterical Playground" (Watman), **Supp. XX: 93**

"On the Island" (Stern), **Supp. IX:** 290

"On the Late Eclipse" (Bryant), **Supp. I Part 1:** 152

On the Laws of the Poetic Art (Hecht), **Supp. X:** 58

On the Line (Swados), **Supp. XIX: 258–260**

"On the Line" (Swados), **Supp. XIX:** 259

"On the Marginal Way" (Wilbur), **Supp. III Part 2:** 558, 559

On the Mesa (Nichols), **Supp. XIII:** 268

"On the Moon and Matriarchal Consciousness" (Neumann), **Supp. IV Part 1:** 68

"On the Morning after the Sixties" (Didion), **Supp. IV Part 1:** 205, 206

On the Motion and Immobility of Douve (Bonnefoy; Kinnell, trans.), **Supp. III Part 1:** 235

"On the Mullica"(Schott), **Supp. XXIII:** 253

"On the Murder of Lieutenant José del Castillo by the Falangist Bravo Marti-

nez, July 12, 1936" (Levine), **Supp. V:** 187

"On the Night of a Friend's Wedding" (Robinson), **III:** 524

"On the Occasion of a Poem: Richard Hugo" (Wright), **Supp. III Part 2:** 596

On the Occasion of My Last Afternoon (Gibbons), **Supp. X:** 46, **50–53**

On the Origin of Species (Darwin), **Supp. XIV:** 192

"On the Parapet" (Tanner), **Retro. Supp. II:** 205

"On the Platform" (Nemerov), **III:** 287

On the Poetry of Philip Levine: Stranger to Nothing (Levis), **Supp. XI:** 257

"On the Pottlecombe Cornice" (Sturgis), **Supp. XX: 233, 240**

"On the Powers of the Human Under-standing" (Freneau), **Supp. II Part 1:** 274

On the Prejudices, Predilections, and Firm Beliefs of William Faulkner (Brooks), **Supp. XIV:** 13

"On the Pulse of Morning" (Angelou), **Supp. IV Part 1:** 15–17

"On the Railway Platform" (Jarrell), **II:** 370

"On the Rainy River" (O'Brien), **Supp. V:** 250

On the Rebound: A Story and Nine Poems (Purdy), **Supp. VII:** 276–277

"On the Religion of Nature" (Freneau), **Supp. II Part 1:** 275

"On the River" (Dunbar), **Supp. II Part 1:** 193

"On the River" (Levine), **Supp. V:** 193

On the River Styx and Other Stories (Matthiessen), **Supp. V:** 212

On the Road (Kerouac), **Retro. Supp. I:** 102; **Supp. III Part 1:** 92, 218, 222–224, 226, 230–231; **Supp. V:** 336; **Supp. X:** 269; **Supp. XIII:** 275; **Supp. XIV:** 138, 150; **Supp. XV:** 221; **Supp. XVIII:** 20, 138; **Supp. XXI:** 53; **Supp. XXIV:** 281; **Supp. XXVI:** 26, 252; **Supp. XXVIII:** 254

"On the Road Home" (Stevens), **Retro. Supp. I:** 306

On the Road with the Archangel (Buechner), **Supp. XII:** 54

"On the Rope" (Richard), **Supp. XIX:** 211–212

"On the Run" (Boyle), **Supp. XXIV:** 52

On These I Stand: An Anthology of the Best Poems of Countee Cullen (Cullen), **Supp. IV Part 1:** 173

"On the Skeleton of a Hound" (Wright), **Supp. III Part 2:** 593

"On the Staten Island Ferry"(Kenny), **Supp. XXIII:** 154

"On the Street" (Peacock), **Supp. XIX:** 199

"On the Street: Monument" (Gunn Allen), **Supp. IV Part 1:** 326

"On the Subway" (Olds), **Supp. X:** 207

"On the System of Policy Hitherto Pursued by Their Government" (Barlow), **Supp. II Part 1:** 82

"On the Teaching of Modern Literature" (Trilling), **Supp. III Part 2:** 509–510

"On the Uniformity and Perfection of Nature" (Freneau), **Supp. II Part 1:** 275

"On the Universality and Other Attributes of the God of Nature" (Freneau), **Supp. II Part 1:** 275

"On the Use of Trisyllabic Feet in Iambic Verse" (Bryant), **Supp. I Part 1:** 156

On the Verge: Emerging Poets (Ellis and Lease, eds.), **Supp. XXI:** 246

On the Waterfront (film, Kazan), **Supp. XVIII: 250–251,** 252, 253

"On the Way" (Stone), **Supp. XXVII:** 251, 253

"On the Way Home" (L. I. Wilder), **Supp. XXII:** 292

On the Way to the Island (Ferry), **Supp. XXIV:** 147, **148–149,** 150

"On the Way to the San Remo"(O'Hara), **Supp. XXIII:** 212, 219

On the Way toward a Phenomenological Psychology: The Psychology of William James (Linschoten), **II:** 362

"On the Way to Work" (Dunn), **Supp. XI:** 149–150

"On the Wide Heath" (Millay), **III:** 130

"On the Writing of Novels" (Buck), **Supp. II Part 1:** 121

On the Yard (Braly), **Supp. XVIII:** 147

On This Island (Auden), **Supp. II Part 1:** 11

On This Side of the River (Ferry), **Supp. XXIV: 161–162**

"On Time" (O'Hara), **III:** 369–370

"Ontological Episode of the Asylum" (Carruth), **Supp. XVI:** 48, 50

"Ontology of the Sentence, The" (Gass), **Supp. VI:** 77

"On Top" (Leopold), **Supp. XIV:** 188

"On Top" (Snyder), **Supp. VIII:** 304

"On Translating Akhmatova" (Kunitz), **Supp. III Part 1:** 268

"On Turning Ten" (Collins), **Supp. XXI:** 64

"On Visiting a Borrowed Country House in Arcadia" (Stallings), **Supp. XXV:** 233–234

"On Waking to Old Debts" (Keillor), **Supp. XVI:** 167

On William Stafford: The Worth of Local Things (Andrews, ed.), **Supp. XI:** 311, 312, 317, 321, 324, 326

On Writers and Writing (O'Nan, ed.), **Supp. XXV:** 152–153

"On Writing" (Carver), **Supp. III Part 1:** 142–143

"On Writing" (Nin), **Supp. X:** 182

On Your Own (Gallagher), **Supp. XXIV:** 166

Opatoshu, Joseph, **IV:** 9

"Open Boat, The" (Crane), **I:** 408, 415, 416–417, 423; **Retro. Supp. I:** 325; **Supp. XIV:** 51

Open Boat and Other Stories (Crane), **I:** 408

Open Door, The (Skloot), **Supp. XX: 194, 196, 208**

Open Heart: A Patient's Story of Life-Saving Medicine and Life-Giving Friendship (Neugeboren), **Supp. XVI:** 217, **229–230**

Open House (Roethke), **III:** 529–530, 540

"Open House" (Roethke), **III:** 529

"Opening, An" (Swenson), **Supp. IV Part 2:** 639

Opening of the Field, The (Duncan), **Supp. III Part 2:** 625

Opening the Hand (Merwin), **Supp. III Part 1:** 341, 353, 355

"Open Letter" (Roethke), **III:** 532, 534

"Open Letter to Surrealists Everywhere, An" (H. Miller), **III:** 184

Open Meeting, The (Gurney), **Supp. V:** 98

Open Net (Plimpton), **Supp. XVI:** 241

"Open Road, The" (Dreiser), **II:** 44

Open Sea, The (Masters), **Supp. I Part 2:** 471

Open Season: Sporting Adventures (Humphrey), **Supp. IX:** 95

"Open Secret" (Nelson), **Supp. XVIII:** 185

Open Secrets (Munro), **Supp. XXVII:** 190, 191–192

"Open Secrets" (Munro), **Supp. XXVII:** 191–192

"Open the Gates" (Kunitz), **Supp. III Part 1:** 264–265, 267

"Opera, The" (Whitman), **Retro. Supp. III:** 309–310

"Opera Company, The" (Merrill), **Supp. III Part 1:** 326

Operating Instructions: A Journal of My Son's First Year (Lamott), **Supp. XX: 136–137, 142**

"Operation, The" (Sanders), **Supp. XVI:** 266

"Operation, The" (Sexton), **Supp. II Part 2:** 675, 679

Operation Shylock: A Confession (P. Roth), **Retro. Supp. II:** 279, 280, 291

Operation Sidewinder (Shepard), **Supp. III Part 2:** 434–435, 439, 446–447

Operations in North African Waters (Morison), **Supp. I Part 2:** 490

Operation Wandering Soul (Powers), **Supp. IX:** 212, **217–219**

Opffer, Emil, **Retro. Supp. II:** 80; **Retro. Supp. III:** 46, 48

"Opinion" (Du Bois), **Supp. II Part 1:** 173

Opinionator, The (Bierce), **I:** 209

Opinions of Oliver Allston (Brooks), **I:** 254, 255, 256

O Pioneers! (Cather), **I:** 314, 317–319, 320; **Retro. Supp. I:** 1, 5, 6, **7–9,** 10, 13, 20; **Retro. Supp. II:** 136; **Retro. Supp. III:** 18, 20, 22, 23, 28–30, 36

Oppen, George, **IV:** 415; **Supp. III Part 2:** 614, 615, 616, 626, 628; **Supp. XIV:** 285, 286, 287; **Supp. XVI:** 282, 283; **Supp. XVII:** 243; **Supp. XXI:** 19,**Supp. XXI:** 29, 23; **Supp. XXIII:** 165–166, 168; **Supp. XXVI: 223–238**

Oppen, Mary, **Supp. XXVI:** 225

Oppenheim, James, **I:** 106, 109, 239, 245; **Supp. XV:** 294, 296, 298, 299, 301, 302, 307, 313; **Supp. XX: 68**

Oppenheimer, J. Robert, **I:** 137, 492

Oppenheimer, Judy, **Supp. IX:** 115, 116, 118, 120, 126

"Opportunity for American Fiction, An" (Howells), **Supp. I Part 2:** 645–646

Opposing Self, The (Trilling), **Supp. III Part 2:** 506–507

"Opposition" (Lanier), **Supp. I Part 1:** 368, 373

Oprah's Roots: An African American Lives Special (television production), **Supp. XX:** 99

Opticks: A Poem in Seven Sections (Goldbarth), **Supp. XII:** 177, **178**

Optimist's Daughter, The (Welty), **IV:** 261, 280; **Retro. Supp. I:** 339, 355

"Optimist's Daughter, The" (Welty), **IV:** 280–281

Options (O. Henry), **Supp. II Part 1:** 410

Opus Posthumous (Stevens), **IV:** 76, 78

Opus Posthumous (W. Stevens), **Supp. XVII:** 241

Oracle at Stoneleigh Court, The (Taylor), **Supp. V:** 328

Orage, Alfred, **III:** 473

"O/Rain-in-the-Face"(Kenny), **Supp. XXIII:** 156

"Oral History" (Goodman), **Supp. XXVI:** 118, 119

Orange, Max (pseudonym). *See* Heller, Joseph

"Orange, The"(Wakoski), **Supp. XXVIII:** 269

Orange Fish, The (Shields), **Supp. VII:** 318, 320, 323, 328

Orangery, The (Sorrentino), **Supp. XXI:** 228

Oranges (exhibition, Hartigan), **Supp. XXIII:** 210

Oranges (McPhee), **Supp. III Part 1:** 298–299, 301, 309

Oranges: 12 Pastorals (O'Hara), **Supp. XXIII:** 210

"Oranging of America, The" (Apple), **Supp. XVII:** 3–4, 6

Oranging of America and Other Short Stories, The (Apple), **Supp. XVII:** 1–2, **3–4**, 7, 8

Oration Delivered at Washington, July Fourth, 1809 (Barlow), **Supp. II Part 1:** 80, 83

Orations and Addresses (Bryant), **Supp. I Part 1:** 158

Orators, The (Auden), **Supp. II Part 1:** 6, 7, 11, 18–19

Orazem, Kate, **Supp. XXVIII:** 196

Orbach, Jerry, **Supp. XXIII:** 103

Orb Weaver, The (Francis), **Supp. IX:** **81–82**

"Orchard" (Doolittle), **Supp. I Part 1:** 263–264, 265, 266

"Orchard" (Eberhart), **I:** 539

Orchard, The (B. Kelly), **Supp. XVII:** 123, 127, **130–133**

"Orchard, The" (B. Kelly), **Supp. XVII:** 133

Orchard Keeper, The (McCarthy), **Supp. VIII:** **175–176**

Orchestra (Davies), **III:** 541

"Orchid Fever" (Orlean), **Supp. XXV:** 160

"Orchids" (Roethke), **III:** 530–531

Orchid Thief, The: A True Story of Beauty and Obsession (Orlean), **Supp. XXV:** 160, 161–162

"Or Consider Prometheus" (Clampitt), **Supp. IX:** 44

Ordeal of Mansart, The (Du Bois), **Supp. II Part 1:** 185–186

Ordeal of Mark Twain, The (Brooks), **I:** 240, 247, 248; **II:** 482

Ordering the Façade: Photography and Contemporary Southern Women's Writing (Henninger), **Supp. XXI:** 253

"Order of Insects" (Gass), **Supp. VI:** 83

Order Out of Chaos (McPherson), **Supp. IV Part 1:** 2, 12

"Orders" (Duncan), **Supp. XXVII:** 160

"Ordinary Afternoon in Charlottesville, An" (Wright), **Supp. V:** 344

"Ordinary Days" (Dunn), **Supp. XI:** 151

"Ordinary Evening in New Haven, An" (Stevens), **IV:** 91–92; **Retro. Supp. I:** 297, 300, 311, 312

Ordinary Heroes (Turow), **Supp. XVII:** **221–222**, 223

Ordinary Life (Crooker), **Supp. XXIII:** **56**

Ordinary Love (Smiley), **Supp. VI:** 292, **299–300**

Ordinary Love; and Good Will: Two Novellas (Smiley), **Supp. VI:** 292, **299–300**

Ordinary Miracles (Jong), **Supp. V:** 115, 130–131

Ordinary Seaman, The (Goldman), **Supp. XXV:** 49, 50, 53–54

"Ordinary Time: Virginia Woolf and Thucydides on War" (Carson), **Supp. XII:** 111

"Ordinary Women, The" (Stevens), **IV:** 81

Ordinary Words (Stone), **Supp. XXVII:** 257, 262

Ordways, The (Humphrey), **Supp. IX:** 95, **98–100**, 109; **Supp. XV:** 353

"Oread" (Doolittle), **II:** 520–521; **Supp. I Part 1:** 265–266

Oregon Message, An (Stafford), **Supp. XI:** **328–329**

Oregon Trail, The (Parkman), **II:** 312; **Supp. II Part 2:** 592, 595–596, 598, 606

Oresteia (Aeschylus), **Supp. IX:** 103

"Orestes at Tauris" (Jarrell), **II:** 376, 377

Orfalea, Gregory, **Supp. XIII:** 278

Orfeo ed Euridice (Gluck), **II:** 210, 211

Orff, Carl, **Supp. X:** 63

"Organizer's Wife, The" (Bambara), **Supp. XI:** 8–9

"Organmeister: Hasse After Marienkirche" (Bierds), **Supp. XVII:** 34

"Orgy" (Rukeyser), **Supp. VI:** 280

Orgy, The (Rukeyser), **Supp. VI:** 274, 283

"Orgy of Southerness, An" (Pickering), **Supp. XXI:** 203

"Oriental Rug"(Balakian), **Supp. XXIII:** 23, 24–25

"Orientation of Hope, The" (Locke), **Supp. XIV:** 212–213

Orient Express (Dos Passos), **I:** 480

"Orient Express, The" (Jarrell), **II:** 382, 383–384

Origen, Adamantius, **IV:** 153

"Origin" (Harjo), **Supp. XII:** 219

Original Child Bomb: Points for Meditation to Be Scratched on the Walls of a Cave (Merton), **Supp. VIII:** 203

Original Essays on the Poetry of Anne Sexton (George), **Supp. IV Part 2:** 450

"Original Follies Girl, The" (Z. Fitzgerald), **Supp. IX:** 71

Original Light (Goldbarth), **Supp. XII:** 181, **183–184**, 188

Original Love (Peacock), **Supp. XIX:** **199–201,** 206

Original of Laura, The (Nabokov), **Retro. Supp. I:** 266

"Original Sin" (Jeffers), **Supp. II Part 2:** 426

"Original Sin" (Vaz), **Supp. XXVI:** 259–260

"Original Sin" (Warren), **IV:** 245

"Original Story" (Gansworth), **Supp. XXVI:** 114

Origin: Hawaii (Taggard), **Supp. XXII:** 272, 284

"Origin of Extermination in the Imagination, The" (Gass), **Supp. VI:** 89

Origin of Species (Darwin), **Supp. XXVII:** 34

Origin of Species, The (Darwin), **II:** 173, 462; **Supp. XVI:** 13

Origin of the Brunists, The (Coover), **Supp. V:** 39, 41, 52

"Origin of the Miscodeed, or the Maid of Taquimenon"(J. Schoolcraft), **Supp. XXIII:** 235

"Origin of the Robin, The"(J. Schoolcraft), **Supp. XXIII:** 234, 235

"Origins and History of Consciousness" (Rich), **Retro. Supp. III:** 249; **Supp. I Part 2:** 570

"Origins of a Nonfiction Writer" (Talese), **Supp. XVII:** 208

"Origins of a Poem" (Levertov), **Supp. III Part 1:** 273

"Origins of the Beat Generation, The" (Kerouac), **Supp. III Part 1:** 231

Origo, Iris, **IV:** 328

"O'Riley's Late-Bloomed Little Son" (X. J. Kennedy), **Supp. XV:** 159

"Orion" (Rich), **Retro. Supp. III:** 244, 245; **Supp. I Part 2:** 557

O'Riordan, Conal Holmes O'Connell, **III:** 465

Orlacs Hände (film, Weine), **Supp. XVII:** 58

Orlando (V. Woolf), **Supp. XVII:** 86

Orlando (Woolf), **Supp. I Part 2:** 718; **Supp. VIII:** 263; **Supp. XII:** 9

Orlando Furioso (Ariosto), **Supp. XV:** 175

Orlean, Susan, **Supp. XXV: 157–167**

Orlik, Emil, **Supp. XXIII:** 6

Orloff, Chana, **Supp. XXIII:** 6

Orlovsky, Peter, **Supp. XII:** 121, 126; **Supp. XIV:** 150; **Supp. XVIII:** 27

Ormonde, Czenzi, **Supp. IV Part 1:** 132

Ormond; or, The Secret Witness (Brown), **Supp. I Part 1:** 133–137
Ornament and Crime (Loos), **Supp. XVI:** 187
Orne, Sarah. *See* Jewett, Sarah Orne
Ornithological Biography; or, An Account of the Habits of the Birds of the United States of America, and Interspersed with Delineations of American Scenery and Manners (Audubon), 7–10; **Supp. XVI:** 13
"Ornithology" (Hull), **Supp. XXI:** 138–139
Ornitz, Samuel, **Supp. IX:** 227; **Supp. XIII:** 166
Ornstein, Leo, **Supp. XX:** 75
O'Rourke, Meghan, **Supp. XXV:** 10; **Supp. XXVIII:** 197
O'Rourke, William, **Supp. XXII:** 213
Orphan Angel, The (Wylie), **Supp. I Part 2:** 707, 709, 714, 717, 719–721, 722, 724
Orphan's Tale, An (Neugeboren), **Supp. XVI:** 222, 223
Orpheus (film), **Supp. XXVII:** 80
Orpheus (Rukeyser), **Supp. VI:** 273
"Orpheus" (Winters), **Supp. II Part 2:** 801
"Orpheus, Eurydice, Hermes" (Rilke), **Supp. VIII:** 31, 32
"Orpheus (1)" (Atwood), **Supp. XIII:** 35
"Orpheus (2)" (Atwood), **Supp. XIII:** 35
"Orpheus Alone" (Strand), **Supp. IV Part 2:** 632
Orpheus Descending (T. Williams), **IV:** 380, 381, 382, 385, 386, 387, 389, 391–392, 395, 396, 398
Orr, David, **Retro. Supp. III:** 99; **Supp. XXI:** 62
Orr, Peter, **Supp. I Part 2:** 538, 540, 543
Orse, Brian, **Supp. XX:** 264
Ortega y Gasset, José, **I:** 218, 222; **Supp. IV Part 2:** 521; **Supp. XXIII:** 165
Ortiz, Simon J., **Supp. IV Part 1:** 319, 404; **Supp. IV Part 2:** 497–515, 557; **Supp. XII:** 217, 218
"Ortlieb's Uptown Taproom" (Di Piero), **Supp. XIX:** 46, 47
Orton, Joe, **Supp. XXIV:** 113, 126, 263
O'Ruddy, The (Crane), **I:** 409, 424
Orwell, George, **I:** 489; **II:** 454, 580; **Supp. I Part 2:** 523, 620; **Supp. II Part 1:** 143; **Supp. IV Part 1:** 236; **Supp. V:** 250; **Supp. VIII:** 241; **Supp. XIV:** 112, 158; **Supp. XVII:** 228, 229; **Supp. XVIII:** 137, 138; **Supp. XX:** 86
Osborn, Dwight, **III:** 218–219, 223
"Osborn Look, The" (Morris), **III:** 221
Osgood, Frances, **Supp. XVII:** 75
Osgood, J. R., **II:** 283
O'Shea, Kitty, **II:** 137
O'Shea, Milo, **Supp. XI:** 308
"Oshkikwe's Baby" (traditional Chippewa story), **Supp. IV Part 1:** 333
Oshogay, Delia, **Supp. IV Part 1:** 333
Osofsky, Gilbert, **Supp. XXVIII:** 167
Ossana, Diana, **Supp. V:** 230–231, 232
Ossian, **Supp. I Part 2:** 491
Ossip, Kathleen, **Supp. X:** 201

"Osso Bucco" (Collins), **Supp. XXI:** 60
Ostanovka v Pustyne (A halt in the wilderness) (Brodsky), **Supp. VIII:** 21
Oster, Judith, **Supp. XVI:** 151
Ostriker, Alicia, **Supp. I Part 2:** 540; **Supp. IV Part 2:** 439, 447, 449; **Supp. X:** 207, 208; **Supp. XI:** 143; **Supp. XV:** 251; **Supp. XXVII:** 261
Ostrom, Hans, **Retro. Supp. I:** 195
Oswald, Lee Harvey, **III:** 234, 235
Oswald II (DeLillo), **Supp. VI:** 16
Oswald's Tale (Mailer), **Retro. Supp. II:** 212–213
"Otagamiad, The"(J. Schoolcraft), **Supp. XXIII:** 223
O Taste and See (Levertov), **Supp. III Part 1:** 278–279, 281
Othello (Shakespeare), **I:** 284–285
"Other, The" (Sexton), **Supp. II Part 2:** 692
Other America, The (Harrington), **I:** 306
"Other American Renaissance, The" (Tompkins), **Supp. XVIII:** 258
Other Destinies: Understanding the American Indian Novel (Owens), **Supp. IV Part 1:** 404
otherelectricities.com, **Supp. XXIV:** 240–241
Other Electricities: Stories (Monson), **Supp. XXIV:** 230, 231–234, 235–236, 238, 241
"Other Frost, The" (Jarrell), **Retro. Supp. I:** 121
"Other Gods, The" (Lovecraft), **Supp. XXV:** 114
Other Gods: An American Legend (Buck), **Supp. II Part 1:** 123, 130–131
Other House, The (James), **Retro. Supp. I:** 229
"Other League of Nations, The" (Ríos), **Supp. IV Part 2:** 552
"Other Margaret, The" (Trilling), **Supp. III Part 2:** 504–505
"Other Miller, The" (Wolff), **Supp. VII:** 343–344
"Other Mothers" (Paley), **Supp. VI:** 225
"Other Mothers, The"(Goodman), **Supp. XXVIII:** 95–96
"Other Night at Columbia, The" (Trilling), **Supp. XII:** 126
"Other People's Secrets" (Hampl), **Supp. XXII:** 94
"Other Robert Frost, The" (Jarrell), **Retro. Supp. I:** 135
Others (Shields), **Supp. VII:** 310
Other Side, The (Gordon), **Supp. IV Part 1:** 299, 306, 307–309, 310–311
Other Side, The (Woodson and Lewis), **Supp. XXVIII:** 285–286
Other Side, The/El Otro Lado (Alvarez), **Supp. VII:** 9–12
"Other Side, The"(Hadas), **Supp. XXIII:** 120
Other Side of the River, The (Wright), **Supp. V:** 332–333, 342
"Other Side of the River, The" (Wright), **Supp. V:** 335
"Other Tradition, The" (Ashbery), **Supp. III Part 1:** 15, 18

"Other Two, The" (Wharton), **Retro. Supp. I:** 367
Other Voices, Other Rooms (Capote), **Supp. III Part 1:** 113–118, 121, 123–124
"Other Wanderer, The" (Gibran), **Supp. XX:** 124
"Other War, The" (Cowley), **Supp. II Part 1:** 144
"Otherwise" (Kenyon), **Supp. VII:** 172, 174
Otherwise: New and Selected Poems (Kenyon), **Supp. VII:** 167, 172–174
Otherwise Than Being; or, Beyond Essence (Lévinas), **Supp. XVI:** 290, 291
"Other Woman, The" (Anderson), **I:** 114
"Other World, The" (Wrigley), **Supp. XVIII:** 307
"Otherworld, Underworld, Prayer Porch"(Bottoms), **Supp. XXVIII:** 33–34
Other Worlds Than This (Hadas), **Supp. XXIII:** 118, **124–125**
Otho the Great: A Tragedy in Five Acts (Keats), **Supp. XII:** 113
Otis, Harrison Gray, **Supp. I Part 2:** 479–481, 483, 486, 488
Otis, James, **III:** 577; **Supp. I Part 2:** 486; **Supp. XV:** 229
O to Be a Dragon (Moore), **III:** 215
"Otravida, Otravez" (Díaz), **Supp. XXIV:** 93
Ott, Bill, **Supp. XXVI:** 187
"Ottawa Valley, The" (Munro), **Supp. XXVII:** 185–186
Otter, Samuel, **Retro. Supp. III:** 157
Otto, Rudolf, **Supp. XVII:** 243
"Ouija" (McClatchy), **Supp. XII:** 269–270
Oupensky, Peter, **Supp. XIV:** 188
Our America (Michaels), **Retro. Supp. I:** 379
Our America (W. Frank), **I:** 229; **Supp. IX:** 308; **Supp. XX:** **69–70, 75**
Our American Humorists (Masson), **Supp. XXVI:** 275
Our Aperture (Monson), **Supp. XXIV:** 230, 239
"Our Assistant's Column" (Twain), **IV:** 193
"Our Bourgeois Literature" (Sinclair), **Supp. V:** 281
Our Brains and What Ails Them (Gilman), **Supp. XI:** 207
Our Century (Wilder), **IV:** 374
"Our Christmas Party" (E. Stoddard), **Supp. XV:** 273, 278
Our Country (Strong), **Supp. XIV:** 64
"Our Countrymen in Chains!" (Whittier), **Supp. I Part 2:** 688
"Our Cultural Humility" (Bourne), **I:** 223, 228
Our Depleted Society (Seymour), **Supp. XIII:** 264
"Our Dust" (Wright), **Supp. XV:** 345, 346
"Our Eyes" (Davison), **Supp. XXVI:** 78
"Our Father Who Drowns the Birds" (Kingsolver), **Supp. VII:** 208–209

"Our Fellow Savages of the Sandwich Islands" (Twain), **Retro. Supp. III:** 268

"Our First House" (Kingston), **Supp. V:** 169

Our Gang (P. Roth), **Retro. Supp. II:** 287; **Supp. III Part 2:** 414; **Supp. IV Part 1:** 388

"Our Good Day" (Cisneros), **Supp. VII:** 60

Our Ground Time Here Will Be Brief (Kumin), **Supp. IV Part 2:** 450–452

Our House in the Last World (Hijuelos), **Supp. VIII:** 73, **76–79,** 87, 88

"Our Lady" (A. Finch), **Supp. XVII:** 77

"*Our Lady of the Annunciation*/Nuestra Señora de Anunciación" (Mora), **Supp. XIII:** 217, 224, 228

"Our Lady of the Artichokes" (Vaz), **Supp. XXVI:** 265

Our Lady of the Artichokes and Other Portuguese-American Stories (Vaz), **Supp. XXVI:** 264–268

"Our Lady of Troy" (MacLeish), **III:** 3, 20

"Our Limitations" (Holmes), **Supp. I Part 1:** 314

"Our Martyred Soldiers" (Dunbar), **Supp. II Part 1:** 193

"Our Master" (Whittier), **Supp. I Part 2:** 704

"Our Mother Pocahontas" (Lindsay), **Supp. I Part 2:** 393

Our Mr. Wrenn: The Romantic Adventures of a Gentle Man (Lewis), **II:** 441

Our National Parks (Muir), **Supp. IX:** 181, 184

Our New York: A Personal Vision in Words and Photographs (Kazin), **Supp. VIII: 106–107**

Our Nig (Wilson), **Supp. XX: 105**

"Our Old Aunt Who Is Now in a Retirement Home" (Shields), **Supp. VII:** 310

Our Old Home (Hawthorne), **II:** 225; **Retro. Supp. I:** 163; **Retro. Supp. III:** 122

"Our Own Movie Queen" (Z. Fitzgerald), **Supp. IX:** 71

"Our Presbyterian Christmas"(Bottoms), **Supp. XXVIII:** 29

"Our River Now" (L.-Y. Lee), **Supp. XV:** 224, 225

Our Selves (Bronk), **Supp. XXI:** 32

Ourselves to Know (O'Hara), **III:** 362, 365

Our Sister Killjoy: or, Reflections from a Black-Eyed Squint (Aidoo), **Supp. XXII:** 68

"Our Story Begins" (Wolff), **Supp. VII:** 345

"Our Sweating Selves" (Di Piero), **Supp. XIX:** 36

Our Town (Wilder), **IV:** 357, 364, 365, 366, 368–369

"Our Unplanned Cities" (Bourne), **I:** 229, 230

Our Wonder World, **Retro. Supp. I:** 341

Ouspensky, P. D., **I:** 383; **Supp. XX: 116**

"Out" (Harjo), **Supp. XII:** 219

" 'Out, Out—' " (Frost), **Retro. Supp. I:** 131; **Retro. Supp. III:** 99

"Outcast" (McKay), **Supp. X:** 135

"Outcasts of Poker Flats, The" (Harte), **Supp. II Part 1:** 345, 347–348

Outcroppings (Harte), **Supp. II Part 1:** 343

Out Cry (T. Williams), **IV:** 383, 393

Outcry, The (James), **Retro. Supp. I:** 235

"Outdoor Shower" (Olds), **Supp. X:** 214

Outer Banks (Siddons), **Supp. XXII:** 239

Outerbridge Reach (Stone), **Supp. V:** 306–308

Outer Dark (McCarthy), **Supp. VIII: 176–177**

Outermost Dream, The: Essays and Reviews (Maxwell), **Supp. VIII: 171–172**

Outermost House, The (Beston), **Supp. XXVI:** 31, 34, 37–43; **Supp. XXVIII:** 254

"Outing, The" (Baldwin), **Supp. I Part 1:** 63

"Outlantish" (Mackey), **Supp. XXVII:** 154–155

Outlaw Journalist (McKeen), **Supp. XXIV:** 279, 288

"Out Like a Lamb" (Dubus), **Supp. VII:** 91

"Outline of an Autobiography" (Toomer), **Supp. III Part 2:** 478

"Outline Toward a Theory of the Mine Versus the Mind and the Harvard Outline" (Monson), **Supp. XXIV:** 235

Outlyer and Ghazals (Harrison), **Supp. VIII:** 41

"Out of Business" (Mora), **Supp. XIII:** 217

Out of Eden: Essays on Modern Art (Di Piero), **Supp. XIX:** 41, 42

"Out of My Deeper Heart" (Gibran), **Supp. XX:** 118

Out of My League (Plimpton), **Supp. XVI:** 233, 239

"Out of Nowhere into Nothing" (Anderson), **I:** 113

"Out of Season" (Hemingway), **II:** 263

"Out of the Cradle Endlessly Rocking" (Whitman), **IV:** 342, 343–345, 346, 351; **Retro. Supp. I:** 404, 406; **Retro. Supp. III:** 304, 306–308

"Out of the Deeps" (E. Stoddard), **Supp. XV:** 286

"Out of the Hospital and Under the Bar" (Ellison), **Retro. Supp. II:** 118–119; **Supp. I Part 1:** 246

"Out of the Rainbow End" (Sandburg), **III:** 594–595

"Out of the Sea, Early" (Swenson), **Supp. IV Part 2:** 645

"Out of the Snow" (Dubus), **Supp. VII:** 91

Out of the Stars (Purdy), **Supp. VII:** 281–282

"Out of the Woods" (Offutt), **Supp. XIX:** 169–170

Out of the Woods: Stories (Offutt), **Supp. XIX:** 163, 167, **169–172,** 175

"Out of Your Nakedness, Out of My Nakedness"(Hadas), **Supp. XXIII:** 125

"Outrageous" (Pickering), **Supp. XXI:** 202

Outre-Mer: A Pilgrimage beyond the Sea (Longfellow), **II:** 313, 491; **Retro. Supp. II:** 155, 165

"Outside" (Stafford), **Supp. XI:** 318

Outside, The (Glaspell), **Supp. III Part 1:** 179, 187

"Outside In" (Pickering), **Supp. XXI:** 197

Outsider, The (Wright), **IV:** 478, 481, 488, 491–494, 495

Outside Shot, The (Myers), **Supp. XXVII:** 205, 206

Outside World, The (Mirvis), **Supp. XX: 177, 178, 185–190**

Out Went the Candle (Swados), **Supp. XIX: 257**

Out West (Shanley), **Supp. XIV:** 317

"Out with the Old" (Yates), **Supp. XI:** 342

"Ouzo for Robin" (Merrill), **Supp. III Part 1:** 326

"Oval Portrait, The" (Poe), **III:** 412, 415; **Retro. Supp. II:** 270

"Oven Bird, The" (Frost), **Retro. Supp. I:** 131; **Retro. Supp. XI:** 99; **Supp. XI:** 153; **Supp. XIX:** 15

"Over 2,000 Illustrations and a Complete Concordance" (Bishop), **Retro. Supp. II:** 45; **Supp. I Part 1:** 90–91

"Over Brogno"(Lea), **Supp. XXVIII:** 135–136

"Over by the River" (Maxwell), **Supp. VIII:** 169, 170

"Overcoat, The" (Gogol), **Supp. XXII:** 59

"Overgrown Pasture, The" (A. Lowell), **II:** 523

"Overheard through the Walls of the Invisible City" (Bidart), **Supp. XV:** 32

"Over Kansas" (Ginsberg), **Supp. II Part 1:** 320

Overland to the Islands (Levertov), **Supp. III Part 1:** 275, 276

Overlook, The (Connelly), **Supp. XXI: 78**

"Overlooking Lake Champlain" (Di Piero), **Supp. XIX:** 47

"Overnight Pass" (X. J. Kennedy), **Supp. XV:** 168

Overreachers, The (Talese), **Supp. XVII:** 202

"Over-Soul, The" (Emerson), **II:** 7

Over the Blue Mountain (Richter), **Supp. XVIII:** 220

"Over the Edge"(Hadas), **Supp. XXIII:** 115

"Over the Hill" (Dubus), **Supp. VII:** 76, 79–80

Overtime (Gurney), **Supp. V:** 104

Overton, Grant, **Supp. XXV:** 200

"Overwhelming Question, An" (Taylor), **Supp. V:** 323

Ovid, **I:** 62; **II:** 542–543; **III:** 457, 467, 468, 470; **Retro. Supp. I:** 63; **Supp. IV Part 2:** 634; **Supp. XII:** 264

"Ovid in Exile" (Di Piero), **Supp. XIX:** 44

"Ovid's Farewell" (McClatchy), **Supp. XII:** 257–258

Owen, David, **II:** 34

Owen, Maureen, **Supp. IV Part 2:** 423

Owen, Wilfred, **II:** 367, 372; **III:** 524; **Supp. X:** 146; **Supp. XIX:** 17; **Supp. XVII:** 245; **Supp. XVIII:** 92; **Supp. XXVII:** 295

Owens, Hamilton, **III:** 99, 109

Owens, Louis, **Supp. IV Part 1:** 404

"O Where Are You Going?" (Auden), **Supp. X:** 116

"Owl, The" (Wrigley), **Supp. XVIII:** 297–298, 301

Owl in the Attic, The (Thurber), **Supp. I Part 2:** 614

Owl in the Mask of the Dreamer, The: Collected Poems (Haines), **Supp. XII:** 211

"Owl in the Sarcophagus, The" (Stevens), **Retro. Supp. I:** 300

Owl's Clover (Stevens), **Retro. Supp. I:** 298, **303–304**

"Owl's Clover" (Stevens), **IV:** 75

Owl's Insomnia, Poems by Rafael Alberti, The (Strand, trans.), **Supp. IV Part 2:** 630

Owl Spirit Dwelling (Gallagher), **Supp. XXIV:** 170

Owlstone Crown, The (X. J. Kennedy), **Supp. XV:** 162, **164**

"Owl Who Was God, The" (Thurber), **Supp. I Part 2:** 610

Owning It All (Kittredge), **Supp. XXVI:** 184, 187

Owning Jolene (Hearon), **Supp. VIII:** **66–67**

"Owning the Masters" (Nelson), **Supp. XVIII:** 171

Oxford Anthology of American Literature, The, **III:** 197; **Supp. I Part 1:** 254

Oxford Book of American Verse (Matthiessen, ed.), **Retro. Supp. I:** 40

Oxford Book of Children's Verse in America, The (Hall, ed.), **Supp. XIV:** 126

Oxford Companion to African American Literature, The (Andrews et al., eds), **Supp. XXVI:** 166

Oxford Companion to Twentieth-Century Poetry (Hamilton, ed.), **Supp. XVII:** 243

Oxford History of the American People, The (Morison), **Supp. I Part 2:** 495–496

Oxford History of the United States, 1783–1917, The (Morison), **Supp. I Part 2:** 483–484

"Oxford Town" (song, Dylan), **Supp. XVIII:** 24

Oxherding Tale (C. Johnson), **Supp. VI:** **190–192,** 193, 194, 196

Oxley, William, **Supp. XV:** 125

"O Yes" (Olsen), **Supp. XIII:** 294, 298, **299–300,** 301

"O Youth and Beauty!" (Cheever), **Retro. Supp. I:** 335

"Oysters" (Sexton), **Supp. II Part 2:** 692

"Ozark Odes" (Wright), **Supp. XV:** 346

Ozick, Cynthia, **Supp. V:** **257–274;** **Supp. VIII:** 141; **Supp. X:** 192; **Supp. XVII:** 42, 43, 49, 50

O-Zone (Theroux), **Supp. VIII:** 323–324

P

Pace, Patricia, **Supp. XI:** 245

Pacernik, Gary, **Supp. IX:** 287, 291

Pacific and Other Stories, The (Helprin), **Supp. XXV:** 84, 85

"Pacific Distances" (Didion), **Supp. IV Part 1:** 211

"Pacific Village" (M. F. K. Fisher), **Supp. XVII:** 83

"Pacifist War Song" (Lovecraft), **Supp. XXV:** 119

Pack, Robert, **Supp. IV Part 2:** 621

"Packed Dirt, Churchgoing, a Dying Cat, a Traded Car" (Updike), **IV:** 219

Packer, Nancy Huddleston, **Supp. XXIII:** 290

"Packing Mother's Things" (C. Frost), **Supp. XV:** 97

Pack of Lies (Sorrentino), **Supp. XXI:** 236, 237

Paco's Story (Heinemann), **Supp. XXII:** 103, **109–114,** 115

Paddock, Joe, **Supp. XVI:** 36

Paddock, Nancy, **Supp. XVI:** 36

Padel, Ruth, **Supp. XII:** 107

Padgett, Ron, **Supp. XV:** 190; **Supp. XXIII:** 218, 221; **Supp. XXIV:** 33, 34, 35, 37, 38, 39, 41, 42, 43, 44; **Supp. XXVII:** 18, 19, 20, 22, 24, 26, 28, 29

Padmore, Dorothy, **Supp. XXI:** 166

Padmore, George, **Supp. XXI:** 166

"Paesano with a Trowel" *(Time),* **Supp. XX:** 46

Pafko at the Wall (DeLillo), **Supp. VI:** 4

"Paganini and the Powers of Darkness" (Skloot), **Supp. XX:** 201

"Pagan Prayer" (Cullen), **Supp. IV Part 1:** 170

"Pagan Rabbi, The" (Ozick), **Supp. V:** 262, 264, 265; **Supp. XVII:** 43

Pagan Rabbi and Other Stories, The (Ozick), **Supp. V:** 260, 261, 263–265

Pagan Spain (Wright), **IV:** 478, 488, 495

Page, Geraldine, **Supp. XV:** 7

Page, Kirby, **III:** 297

Page, Myra, **Supp. XXIII:** 166

"Page, The" (Huddle), **Supp. XXVI:** 155

Page, Thomas Nelson, **II:** 174, 176, 194; **Supp. XIV:** 61; **Supp. XXII:** 193

Page, Walter Hines, **II:** 174, 175; **Supp. I Part 1:** 370

Page, William, **Supp. XVIII:** 2, 11

Pages from a Cold Island (Exley), **Supp. XXIII:** 97, **103–106,** 108

"Pages from Cold Point" (Bowles), **Supp. IV Part 1:** 85, 86, 87

Paid on Both Sides: A Charade (Auden), **Supp. II Part 1:** 6, 18–19

Paige, Satchel, **Supp. I Part 1:** 234

Paige, T. D. D., **III:** 475

"Pail, The" (R. Bly), **Supp. XXI:** 85

Pain, Joseph, **Supp. I Part 2:** 502

Paine, Albert Bigelow, **I:** 249; **Retro. Supp. III:** 269; **Supp. XXVIII:** 229

Paine, Thomas, **I:** 490; **II:** 117, 302; **III:** 17, 148, 219; **Retro. Supp. I:** 390; **Supp. I Part 1:** 231; **Supp. I Part 2:** **501–525; Supp. XI:** 55

"Pain has an Element of Blank" (Dickinson), **Retro. Supp. I:** 44

"Pain Scale, The" (Biss), **Supp. XXVI:** 51–53

"Painstaking Historian, The" (Skloot), **Supp. XX:** **205–206**

"Paint and Powder" (Z. Fitzgerald), **Supp. IX:** 71

Painted Bird, The (Kosinski), **Supp. VII:** 215–217, 219–221, 222, 227

Painted Desert (F. Barthelme), **Supp. XI:** 28–29, 32

Painted Dresses (Hearon), **Supp. VIII:** 63

"Painted Head" (Ransom), **III:** 491, 494; **Supp. II Part 1:** 103, 314

Painted Turtle: Woman with Guitar (Major), **Supp. XXII: 178–180,** 182

Painted Word, The (Wolfe), **Supp. III Part 2:** 580–581, 584; **Supp. XV:** 143

Painter, Pamela, **Supp. XXIII:** 295

"Painter, The" (Ashbery), **Supp. III Part 1:** 5–6, 13

Painter Dreaming in the Scholar's House, The (Nemerov), **III:** 269

"Painters" (Rukeyser), **Supp. VI:** 281

"Painting a Mountain Stream" (Nemerov), **III:** 275

"Pair a Spurs" (Proulx), **Supp. VII:** 263–264

"Pair of Bright Blue Eyes, A" (Taylor), **Supp. V:** 321

"Pair of Glasses, A" (Gallagher), **Supp. XXIV:** 174, 176

Paisan (film, Rossellini), **Supp. XXVI:** 134

"Pajamas" (Olds), **Supp. X:** 206

Pakula, Alan, **Supp. XIII:** 264

Palace at 4 A.M. (Giacometti), **Supp. VIII:** 169

Palahniuk, Chuck, **Supp. XXI:** 116

"Palantine, The" (Whittier), **Supp. I Part 2:** 694, 696

Palatella, John, **Retro. Supp. II:** 48; **Supp. XXIV:** 39

"Palatski Man, The" (Dybek), **Supp. XXIII:** 70

Pale Fire (Nabokov), **III:** 244, 246, 252, 263–265; **Retro. Supp. I:** 264, 265, 266, 270, 271, 272, 276, 278, 335; **Supp. V:** 251, 253; **Supp. XXII:** 260

"Pale Horse, Pale Rider" (Porter), **III:** 436, 437, 441–442, 445, 446, 449

Pale Horse, Pale Rider: Three Short Novels (Porter), **III:** 433, 436–442; **Supp. VIII:** 157

"Pale Pink Roast, The" (Paley), **Supp. VI:** 217

"Pale Rider" (B. Kelly), **Supp. XVII:** 132–133

Paley, Grace, **Supp. IX:** 212; **Supp. VI:** **217–233; Supp. X:** 79, 164; **Supp. XII:** 309; **Supp. XXI:** 118; **Supp. XXII:** 172

Paley, William, **II:** 9
Palgrave, Francis Turner, **Retro. Supp. I:** 124; **Retro. Supp. III:** 91; **Supp. XIV:** 340
Palgrave's Golden Treasury (Palgrave), **IV:** 405
Palimpsest (Doolittle), **Supp. I Part 1:** 259, 268, 269, 270–271
Palimpsest (Vidal), **Supp. X:** 186
"Palingenesis" (Longfellow), **II:** 498
Pal Joey (O'Hara), **III:** 361, 367–368
"Pal Joey" stories (O'Hara), **III:** 361
Pallbearers Envying the One Who Rides (Dobyns), **Supp. XIII:** 89
Palm, Edward Frederick, **Supp. XXII:** 103
"Palm, The" (Merwin), **Supp. III Part 1:** 355
Palmer, Charles, **II:** 111
Palmer, Elihu, **Supp. I Part 2:** 520
Palmer, George Herbert, **Supp. XIV:** 197
Palmer, Michael, **Supp. IV Part 2:** 421; **Supp. XVI:** 284; **Supp. XVII:** 240
Palmer, Samuel, **Supp. XV:** 81
Palmerston, Lord, **I:** 15
Palm-of-the-Hand-Stories (Kawabata), **Supp. XV:** 186
"Palm Wine" (McKnight), **Supp. XX:** 155
"Palo Alto: The Marshes" (Hass), **Supp. VI:** 100
Palpable God, A: Thirty Stories Translated from the Bible with an Essay on the Origins and Life of Narrative (Price), **Supp. VI:** 262, 267
Palubinskas, Helen, **Supp. X:** 292
Palumbo, Carmine, **Supp. XXVI:** 241
Pamela (Richardson), **Supp. V:** 127; **Supp. XX: 236; Supp. XXII:** 120
Pamela's First Musical (Wasserstein), **Supp. XV:** 333
Panache de bouquets (Komunyakaa; Cadieux, trans.), **Supp. XIII:** 127
Pan-African movement, **Supp. II Part 1:** 172, 175
Pancake, Breece D'J, **Supp. XXIII:** 35
Pandaemonium (Epstein), **Supp. XII:** 161, **172–173**
"Pandora" (Adams), **I:** 5
Pandora: New Tales of Vampires (Rice), **Supp. VII:** 295
Panek, LeRoy, **Supp. XIV:** 27
"Pangolin, The" (Moore), **III:** 210
Panic: A Play in Verse (MacLeish), **III:** 2, 20
Panic in Needle Park (film), **Supp. IV Part 1:** 198
Pankey, Eric, **Supp. XIX:** 44
Pantagruel (Rabelais), **II:** 112
"Pantaloon in Black" (Faulkner), **II:** 71
"Panther, The: A Bedtime Story"(P. Benedict), **Supp. XXIII:** 40
Panther and the Lash, The (Hughes), **Retro. Supp. I:** 204, 211; **Supp. I Part 1:** 342–344, 345–346
"Panthers, The" (Southern), **Supp. XI:** 295
"Panties and the Buddha" (Peacock), **Supp. XIX:** 199

"Pan *versus* Moses" (Ozick), **Supp. V:** 262
"Paolo Castelnuovo" (Everwine), **Supp. XV:** 83–84
"Papa and Mama Dance, The" (Sexton), **Supp. II Part 2:** 688
"Papago II"(Kenny), **Supp. XXIII:** 149–150
"Papago I"(Kenny), **Supp. XXIII:** 149–150
"Papa Who Wakes Up Tired in the Dark" (Cisneros), **Supp. VII:** 62
Pape, Greg, **Supp. V:** 180; **Supp. XIII:** 312; **Supp. XV:** 73
Paper Boy (Huddle), **Supp. XXVI:** 148, 150, 151
"Paper Covers Rock"(Thompson), **Supp. XXIII:** 291
Paper Doll (Parker), **Supp. XIX:** 184
"Paper Dolls Cut Out of a Newspaper" (Simic), **Supp. VIII:** 282
"Paper House, The" (Mailer), **III:** 42–43
Paper Lion (film, March), **Supp. XVI:** 242
Paper Lion: Confessions of a Last-String Quarterback (Plimpton), **Supp. XVI: 242–243**
Papernick, Jon, **Supp. XVII:** 50
Papers on Literature and Art (Fuller), **Supp. II Part 1:** 292, 299
Papini, Giovanni, **Supp. XVI:** 195; **Supp. XXII:** 159, 161, 163
Papp, Joseph, **Supp. IV Part 1:** 234; **Supp. XXI:** 145
"Paprika Johnson" (Barnes), **Supp. III Part 1:** 33
"Par" (Bausch), **Supp. VII:** 54
"Parable from a Christian" (Notley), **Supp. XXII:** 235
"Parable in the Later Novels of Henry James" (Ozick), **Supp. V:** 257
"Parable of the Gift" (Glück), **Supp. V:** 89
"Parable of the Hostages" (Glück), **Supp. V:** 89
"Parable of the King" (Glück), **Supp. V:** 89
Parable of the Sower (O. Butler), **Supp. XIII: 66–67,** 69
Parable of the Talents (O. Butler), **Supp. XIII:** 61,**Supp. XIII:** 66, **67–69**
"Parable of the Trellis" (Glück), **Supp. V:** 89
Parachutes & Kisses (Jong), **Supp. V:** 115, 123, 125–126, 129
Paracritical Hinge: Essays, Talks, Notes, Interviews (Mackey), **Supp. XXVII:** 159, 160–161
"Paradelle for Susan" (Collins), **Supp. XXI:** 58
"Parade of Painters" (Swenson), **Supp. IV Part 2:** 645
"Paradigm, The" (Tate), **IV:** 128
Paradine Case, The (screenplay, Hecht), **Supp. XXVII:** 93
Paradise (Barthelme), **Supp. IV Part 1:** 52
"Paradise" (Caputo), **Supp. XIX:** 26–27
"Paradise" (Doty), **Supp. XI:** 123

Paradise (Morrison), **Retro. Supp. III:** 184, 194–195
Paradise, Piece by Piece (Peacock), **Supp. XIX:** 193, 194–195, 195–196, **201–202**
Paradise Lost (Milton), **I:** 137; **II:** 168, 549; **IV:** 126; **Retro. Supp. III:** 139; **Supp. XII:** 173, 297; **Supp. XV:** 181; **Supp. XX: 280**
Paradise Lost (Odets), **Supp. II Part 2:** 530, 531, 538–539, 550
Paradise Now (Living Theater), **Supp. XXIV:** 116
"Paradise of Bachelors and the Tartarus of Maids, The" (Melville), **III:** 91; **Retro. Supp. III:** 159
Paradise of Bombs, The (Sanders), **Supp. XVI:** 265, 272–273
Paradise Park (Goodman), **Supp. XXVI:** 126–128
Paradise Poems (Stern), **Supp. IX: 293–294,** 295
Paradiso (Dante), **Supp. IX:** 50
"Paradoxes and Oxymorons" (Ashbery), **Supp. III Part 1:** 23–24
Paradox of Progressive Thought, The (Noble), **Supp. I Part 2:** 650
Paragon, The (Knowles), **Supp. XII:** 249
"Paragraphs" (Carruth), **Supp. XVI:** 52–53
"Parameters" (Dunn), **Supp. XI:** 154
"Para Mi Tataranieto El Astropionero" (Espaillat), **Supp. XXI:** 104
"Paraphrase" (Crane), **I:** 391–392, 393
"Pardon, The" (Wilbur), **Supp. III Part 2:** 544, 550
Paredes, Américo, **Supp. XIII:** 225; **Supp. XIX:** 97, 98, 100
Paredes, Raymund A., **Supp. XIII:** 320, 321
"Parentage" (Stafford), **Supp. XI:** 321, 322
Parentheses: An Autobiographical Journey (Neugeboren), **Supp. XVI:** 217, 218, 219, 221, 226
"Parents" (F. Barthelme), **Supp. XI:** 34
"Parents Taking Shape" (Karr), **Supp. XI:** 243
"Parents' Weekend: Camp Kenwood" (Kenyon), **Supp. VII:** 169
Pareto, Vilfredo, **II:** 577
Paretsky, Sara, **Supp. IV Part 2:** 462; **Supp. XIV:** 26; **Supp. XXV: 169–187**
Parini, Jay, **Retro. Supp. III:** 73, 75, 88, 91, 105; **Supp. X:** 17; **Supp. XIX:** 120, 129; **Supp. XX: 243; Supp. XXI:** 192; **Supp. XXII:** 205; **Supp. XXV:** 251; **Supp. XXVIII:** 130
"Paris" (Collins), **Supp. XXI:** 60
"Paris" (Stern), **Supp. IX:** 300
"Paris, 7 A.M." (Bishop), **Retro. Supp. II:** 41, 42; **Supp. I Part 1:** 85, 89
Paris, Bob, **Supp. XX: 264**
Paris, Paris (Shaw), **Supp. XIX:** 240
Paris France (Stein), **IV:** 45
Park, Ed, **Supp. XXII:** 255
Park, Robert, **IV:** 475
"Park Bench" (Hughes), **Supp. I Part 1:** 331–332
Park City (Beattie), **Supp. V:** 24, 35–36

"Park City" (Beattie), **Supp. V:** 35
Parker, Arthur C., **Supp. XXVI:** 87, 88
Parker, Charlie, **Supp. I Part 1:** 59; **Supp. X:** 240, 242, 246; **Supp. XIII:** 129
Parker, Dorothy, **Retro. Supp. II:** 327; **Supp. IV Part 1:** 353; **Supp. IX:** 62, 114, **189–206; Supp. X:** 164; **Supp. XI:** 28; **Supp. XVIII:** 242, 246, 252; **Supp. XXVI:** 275; **Supp. XXVII:** 283, 284
Parker, Emily, **Supp. XVIII:** 102
Parker, Hershel, **Retro. Supp. III:** 152, 267
Parker, Idella, **Supp. X:** 232, 234–235
Parker, James, **Supp. XXVI:** 84
Parker, Joan, **Supp. XIX:** 187
Parker, Lonnae O'Neal, **Supp. XXIII:** 276
Parker, Muriel, **Supp. IX:** 232
Parker, Patricia, **Supp. XV:** 242
Parker, Robert B., **Supp. IV Part 1:** 135, 136; **Supp. XIX: 177–192**
Parker, Robert Dale, **Supp. XXIII:** 223, 228, 229
Parker, Theodore, **Supp. I Part 1:** 38; **Supp. I Part 2:** 518; **Supp. XXIV:** 70
Parker, Thomas, **Supp. I Part 1:** 102
"Parker's Back" (O'Connor), **III:** 348, 352, 358; **Retro. Supp. III:** 213, 216–217
"Parkersburg" (Halliday), **Supp. XIX:** 92
Parkes, Henry Bamford, **Supp. I Part 2:** 617
Park-Fuller, Linda, **Supp. XIII:** 297
Parkinson, Tom, **Supp. XXVIII:** 260
Parkman, Francis, **II:** 278, 310, 312; **IV:** 179, 309; **Supp. I Part 2:** 420, 479, 481–482, 486, 487, 493, 498; **Supp. II Part 2: 589–616**
Parkman Reader, The (Morison, ed.), **Supp. I Part 2:** 494
Parks, Gordon, Sr., **Supp. XI:** 17
Parks, Larry, **Supp. I Part 1:** 295
Parks, Rosa, **Supp. I Part 1:** 342
"Park Street Cemetery, The" (R. Lowell), **II:** 537, 538
Par le Détroit (cantata) (Bowles), **Supp. IV Part 1:** 82
Parliament of Fowls, The (Chaucer), **III:** 492
Parmenides (Plato), **II:** 10
Parmenter, Jon, **Supp. XXVI:** 85
Parnassus (Emerson), **II:** 8, 18
Parnell, Charles Stewart, **II:** 129, 137
Parole (film), **Supp. XIII:** 166
Parole Fixer (film), **Supp. XIII:** 170
Parrington, Vernon Louis, **I:** 254, 517, 561; **III:** 335, 606; **IV:** 173; **Supp. I Part 2:** 484, 640
Parrish, Dillwyn, **Supp. XVII:** 83–84, 90
Parrish, Robert, **Supp. XI:** 307
"Parrot, The" (Merrill), **Supp. III Part 1:** 320
"Parsley" (Dove), **Supp. IV Part 1:** 245, 246
Parson, Annie, **Supp. I Part 2:** 655
Parsons, Elsie Clews, **I:** 231, 235
Parsons, Ian, **Supp. IX:** 95
Parsons, Louella, **Supp. XII:** 173

Parsons, Talcott, **Supp. I Part 2:** 648
Parsons, Theophilus, **II:** 396, 504; **Retro. Supp. II:** 134; **Supp. I Part 1:** 155
"Parthian Shot, The" (Hammett), **Supp. IV Part 1:** 343
Partial Glossary, A (Bronk), **Supp. XXI:** 26
Partial Payments: Essays on Writers and Their Lives (Epstein), **Supp. XIV:** 111
Partial Portraits (James), **II:** 336
"Partial Relief" (Halliday), **Supp. XIX:** 91
Partial Truth (Nelson), **Supp. XVIII: 175–176,** 178
"Particulars" (Pickering), **Supp. XXI:** 197
Parties (Van Vechten), **Supp. II Part 2:** 739, 747–749
"Parting" (Kunitz), **Supp. III Part 1:** 263
"Parting Gift" (Wylie), **Supp. I Part 2:** 714
"Parting Glass, The" (Freneau), **Supp. II Part 1:** 273
"Partings" (Hogan), **Supp. IV Part 1:** 413
Partington, Blanche, **I:** 199
Partisans (Matthiessen), **Supp. V:** 201
"Partner, The" (Roethke), **III:** 541–542
Partners, The (Auchincloss), **Supp. IV Part 1:** 31, 34
Partners in Crime: A Rafe Buenrostro Mystery (Hinojosa), **Supp. XIX: 107–108**
"Part of a Letter" (Wilbur), **Supp. III Part 2:** 551
Part of a Long Story: Eugene O'Neill as a Young Man in Love (Boulton), **Supp. XXII:** 18, 21, 27–30
Part of Speech, A (Brodsky), **Supp. VIII:** 22
"Part of the Bee's Body Embedded in the Flesh, The" (C. Frost), **Supp. XV:** 105, 107
"Part of the Story" (Dobyns), **Supp. XIII:** 79
Part of Vermont, A (Taggard), **Supp. XXII:** 284
Parton, Sara, **Retro. Supp. I:** 246
Partridge, Jeffrey F., **Supp. XV:** 219
Partridge, John, **II:** 110, 111
"Parts of a Journal" (Gordon), **Supp. IV Part 1:** 310
Parts of a World (Stevens), **Retro. Supp. I: 305–306,** 307, 309, 313
"Parturition" (Loy), **Supp. XXII:** 159, 160–161
"Party, The" (Dunbar), **Supp. II Part 1:** 198, 205–206
"Party, The" (Taylor), **Supp. V:** 315
Party at Jack's, The (Wolfe), **IV:** 451–452, 469
"Party Down at the Square, A" (Ellison), **Retro. Supp. II:** 124
Party Girls (Goodman), **Supp. XXVIII:** 88, 93–96
Party of Five (television series), **Supp. XIX:** 222
"Party Poem" (Huddle), **Supp. XXVI:** 149

Pascal, Blaise, **II:** 8, 159; **III:** 292, 301, 304, 428; **Retro. Supp. I:** 326, 330
"Paskudnyak" (Pilcer), **Supp. XVII:** 50
"Pass, The" (Neugeboren), **Supp. XVI:** 225
"Passage" (Crane), **I:** 391
"Passage in the Life of Mr. John Oakhurst, A" (Harte), **Supp. II Part 1:** 353–354
Passage in the Night, A (Asch), **Supp. XXIII:** 7
"Passages" (Duncan), **Supp. XVI:** 287
"Passages for Puritans" (Davison), **Supp. XXVI:** 62
"Passages from a Relinquished Work" (Hawthorne), **Retro. Supp. I:** 150
Passages toward the Dark (McGrath), **Supp. X:** 126, 127
"Passage to India" (Whitman), **IV:** 348; **Retro. Supp. III:** 308
Passage to India, A (Forster), **II:** 600; **Supp. XVIII:** 143
Passaro, Vince, **Supp. X:** 167, 302, 309, 310
"Passenger, The" (Brockmeier), **Supp. XXII:** 52
"Passenger Pigeons" (Jeffers), **Supp. II Part 2:** 437
Passin, Herbert, **Supp. XIII:** 337
Passing (Larsen), **Supp. XVIII:** 119, 123, **127–130**
"Passing Beauty" (C. Frost), **Supp. XV:** 97
"Passing of Grandison, The" (Chesnutt), **Supp. XIV:** 62, **66–69**
"Passing of Sister Barsett, The" (Jewett), **Retro. Supp. II:** 138–139, 143
"Passing Ports and Crossing Walks" (Gansworth), **Supp. XXVI:** 114
"Passing Show, The" (Bierce), **I:** 208
"Passing Through" (Kunitz), **Supp. III Part 1:** 265
"Passion, The" (Barnes), **Supp. III Part 1:** 36
"Passion, The" (Merwin), **Supp. III Part 1:** 343
Passionate, Accurate Story, The: Making Your Heart's Truth into Literature (C. Bly), **Supp. XVI: 41–42**
Passionate Pilgrim, A (James), **II:** 324; **Retro. Supp. I:** 219
"Passionate Pilgrim, A" (James), **II:** 322, 323–324; **Retro. Supp. I:** 218
Passion Play (Kosinski), **Supp. VII:** 215, 225–226
Passions of Uxport, The (Kumin), **Supp. IV Part 2:** 444
Pass It On (Hadas), **Supp. XXIII:** 115, 123
"Pass It On, I"(Hadas), **Supp. XXIII:** 115
"Pass It On, II"(Hadas), **Supp. XXIII:** 115
"Passive Resistance" (McKay), **Supp. X:** 133
Passport to the War (Kunitz), **Supp. III Part 1:** 261–264
Passwords (Stafford), **Supp. XI: 329–330**
"Past, The" (Bryant), **Supp. I Part 1:** 157, 170

Past, The (Kinnell), **Supp. III Part 1:** 235, 253–254
"Past, The" (Kinnell), **Supp. III Part 1:** 254
Past and Present (Carlyle), **Supp. I Part 2:** 410
Pasternak, Boris, **II:** 544; **Supp. XXIII:** 209
"Pastiches et Pistaches" (Van Vechten), **Supp. II Part 2:** 732
"Past Is the Present, The" (Moore), **III:** 199–200
"Pastoral" (Carver), **Supp. III Part 1:** 137, 146
"Pastoral" (Dove), **Supp. IV Part 1:** 249
"Pastoral" (Trethewey), **Supp. XXI:** 257
"Pastoral Hat, A" (Stevens), **IV:** 91
Pastoralia (Saunders), **Supp. XIX: 227–229**
"Pastoralia" (Saunders), **Supp. XIX:** 227, 229
"Pastor Dowe at Tacaté" (Bowles), **Supp. IV Part 1:** 87
Pastorela (ballet) (Kirstein), **Supp. IV Part 1:** 83
Pastorius, Francis Daniel, **Supp. I Part 2:** 700
"Pasture, The" (Frost), **Retro. Supp. III:** 97
"Pasture Poems" (Kumin), **Supp. IV Part 2:** 446
Pastures of Heaven, The (Steinbeck), **IV:** 51
Patch, Jerry, **Supp. XVIII:** 38
Patchen, Kenneth, **Supp. III Part 2:** 625
Patchett, Ann, **Supp. XII: 307–324; Supp. XXVIII:** 85
Patchwork Planet (Lethem), **Supp. XVIII:** 150
Pater, Walter, **I:** 51, 272, 476; **II:** 27, 338; **III:** 604; **IV:** 74; **Retro. Supp. I:** 56, 79; **Retro. Supp. II:** 326; **Supp. I Part 2:** 552; **Supp. IX:** 66
Paterna (Mather), **Supp. II Part 2:** 451
Paternostro, Silvana, **Supp. XXV:** 55, 58
"Paterson" (Ginsberg), **Supp. II Part 1:** 314–315, 321, 329
Paterson (W. C. Williams), **I:** 62, 446; **IV:** 418–423; **Retro. Supp. I:** 209, 284, 413, 419, 421, **424–428,** 428, 429, 430; **Retro. Supp. II:** 321, 328; **Retro. Supp. III:** 50; **Supp. II Part 2:** 557, 564, 625; **Supp. VIII:** 275, 305; **Supp. XIV:** 96; **Supp. XV:** 264, 349
Paterson, Book Five (W. C. Williams), **IV:** 422–423
Paterson, Book One (W. C. Williams), **IV:** 421–422
Paterson, Isabel, **Supp. IV Part 2:** 524
Paterson, Part Three (W. C. Williams), **IV:** 420–421
Pat Garrett and Billy the Kid (film, Peckinpah), **Supp. XVIII:** 27
"Path, The" (Bryant), **Supp. I Part 1:** 169
Pathfinder, The (Cooper), **I:** 349, 350, 355
Pat Hobby Stories, The (Fitzgerald), **Retro. Supp. I:** 114

"Pathos of Low Life, The" (Hapgood), **Supp. XVII:** 103
"Patience of a Saint, The" (Humphrey), **Supp. IX:** 106
Patience Sparhawk and Her Times (Atherton), **Supp. XXIV:** 18, 20, 22, 27
Patient 002 (Skloot), **Supp. XX: 194, 208**
Patinkin, Mandy, **Supp. IV Part 1:** 236
Paton, Alan, **Supp. VIII:** 126
Paton, Priscilla, **Retro. Supp. III:** 95
Patria Mia (Pound), **III:** 460–461; **Retro. Supp. I:** 284
"Patria Mia" (Pound), **Retro. Supp. I:** 284
"Patriarch, The" (Alvares), **Supp. V:** 11
"Patrick Kavanagh at First Light" (Skloot), **Supp. XX: 204**
Patrimony: A True Story (P. Roth), **Retro. Supp. II:** 279, 280, 291; **Supp. III Part 2:** 427
Patriot, The (Buck), **Supp. II Part 1:** 122–123
Patriot, The (Connell), **Supp. XIV:** 94–95
Patriot Act (Gansworth), **Supp. XXVI:** 114
Patriotic Gore: Studies in the Literature of the American Civil War (Wilson), **III:** 588; **IV:** 430, 438, 443, 445–445, 446; **Supp. VIII:** 100
"Patriotic Thing, The" (Ryan as Quin), **Supp. XVIII:** 229
"Patriots, The/Los Patriotas" (Kingsolver), **Supp. VII:** 209
Patrol (Myers), **Supp. XXVII:** 208
Patron Saint of Liars, The (Patchett), **Supp. XII:** 307, 310, **311–314,** 317
Pattee, Fred L., **II:** 456; **Supp. XXVIII:** 124
Patten, Gilbert, **II:** 423
Patten, Simon, **Supp. I Part 2:** 640
Patternmaster (O. Butler), **Supp. XIII:** 61, 62, 63
Patternmaster Series (O. Butler), **Supp. XIII: 62–63**
Pattern Recognition (W. Gibson), **Supp. XVI:** 124, **130–131**
"Patterns" (A. Lowell), **II:** 524
Patterson (Williams), **Supp. XXVIII:** 265
Patterson, Floyd, **III:** 38
Patterson, Margot, **Supp. XXII:** 85
Patterson, William M., **Supp. I Part 1:** 265
Patton, General George, **III:** 575; **Supp. I Part 2:** 664
Patton, Jessica Ray, **Supp. XXVIII:** 281
Patton, Venetra K., **Supp. XXVI:** 166
"Patty-Cake, Patty-Cake...A Memoir" (Apple), **Supp. XVII:** 7
Patty Fairfield series (Wells), **Supp. XXVI:** 276
Paul, Saint, **I:** 365; **II:** 15, 494; **IV:** 122, 154, 164, 335; **Retro. Supp. I:** 247; **Supp. I Part 1:** 188
Paul, Sherman, **I:** 244; **IV:** 179
"Paula Becker to Clara Westhoff" (Rich), **Retro. Supp. III:** 249; **Supp. I Part 2:** 573–574

"Paula Gunn Allen" (Ruppert), **Supp. IV Part 1:** 321
Paul Ardenheim, the Monk of Wissahikon (Lippard), **Supp. XXIII:** 178, 186, 187, 189, 190
Paul Bowles: Romantic Savage (Caponi), **Supp. IV Part 1:** 95
Paulding, James Kirke, **I:** 344; **II:** 298, 299, 303; **Supp. I Part 1:** 157
Pauley, Jane, **Supp. XXI:** 39
Paul Jones (Hapgood), **Supp. XVII:** 100–101
Paul Marchand, F.M.C. (Chesnutt), **Supp. XIV:** 76
"Paul Monette: The Brink of Summer's End" (film), **Supp. X:** 152
"Paul Revere" (Longfellow), **II:** 489, 501
"Paul Revere's Ride" (Longfellow), **Retro. Supp. II:** 163
"Paul's Case" (Cather), **I:** 314–315; **Retro. Supp. I:** 3, 5; **Retro. Supp. III:** 20, 27
Paulsen, Friedrich, **III:** 600
"Pauper Witch of Grafton, The" (Frost), **Retro. Supp. II:** 42
"Pause by the Water, A" (Merwin), **Supp. III Part 1:** 354
"Pavane for the Nursery, A" (W. J. Smith), **Supp. XIII:** 335
"Pavement, The" (Olson), **Supp. II Part 2:** 571
Pavese, Cesare, **Supp. XXI:** 132
Pavic, Milorad, **Supp. XXII:** 265
Pavilion of Women (Buck), **Supp. II Part 1:** 125–126
"Pawnbroker, The" (Kumin), **Supp. IV Part 2:** 442, 443–444, 451
Pawnbroker, The (Wallant), **Supp. XVI:** 220
Pay Day (Asch), **Supp. XXVI:** 19, 21–23
"Paying Dues" (Bass), **Supp. XVI:** 16
Paylor, Diane R., **Supp. XXVIII:** 283, 288
Payne, Daniel, **Supp. V:** 202; **Supp. XXVI:** 33, 35, 37, 40
Payne, John Howard, **II:** 309
Payne Tom, **Supp. XXII:** 266
Paz, Octavio, **Supp. III Part 2:** 630; **Supp. VIII:** 272; **Supp. XI:** 191; **Supp. XIII:** 223
P. D. Kimerakov (Epstein), **Supp. XII:** 160, **162**
Peabody, Elizabeth Palmer, **Retro. Supp. I:** 155–156, 225; **Supp. XXIV:** 75; **Supp. XXV:** 242, 246, 250
Peabody, Francis G., **III:** 293; **Supp. I Part 1:** 5
Peabody, Josephine Preston, **III:** 507; **Supp. XX: 115**
Peace (Woodson), **Supp. XXVIII:** 285
Peaceable Kingdom, The (Prose), **Supp. XVI:** 256–257
Peace and Bread in Time of War (Addams), **Supp. I Part 1:** 21, 22–23
"Peace Between Black and White in the United States" (Locke), **Supp. XIV:** 205
Peace Breaks Out (Knowles), **Supp. XII:** 249
"Peacemaker"(Kenny), **Supp. XXIII:** 151

"Peace March, The" (Simpson), **Supp. IX:** 279

"Peace of Cities, The" (Wilbur), **Supp. III Part 2:** 545

"Peace of Mind" (Boyle), **Supp. XX:** 19

"Peaches" (Davison), **Supp. XXVI:** 77

"Peaches—Six in a Tin Box, Sarajevo" (Cisneros), **Supp. VII:** 67

Peachtree Road (Siddons), **Supp. XXII:** 239, 240, 242, **246–247, 248–251,** 252

Peaco, Ed, **Supp. XXIV:** 221

Peacock, Doug, **Supp. VIII:** 38; **Supp. XIII:** 12

Peacock, Gibson, **Supp. I Part 1:** 360

Peacock, Molly, **Supp. XIX:** 193–207; **Supp. XVII:** 74

"Peacock, The" (Merrill), **Supp. III Part 1:** 320

"Peacock, The" (Mosher), **Supp. XXII:** 211

Peacock, Thomas Love, **Supp. I Part 1:** 307; **Supp. VIII:** 125

"Peacock Room, The" (Hayden), **Supp. II Part 1:** 374–375

"Peacocks of Avignon, The" (Swados), **Supp. XIX:** 263

Pearce, Richard, **Supp. IX:** 254

Pearce, Roy Harvey, **II:** 244; **Supp. I Part 1:** 111, 114; **Supp. I Part 2:** 475

"Pearl" (Kooser), **Supp. XIX:** 127–128

Pearl, The (Steinbeck), **IV:** 51, 62–63

Pearlman, Daniel, **III:** 479

Pearlman, Mickey, **Supp. XIII:** 293, 306

Pearl of Orr's Island, The (Stowe), **Supp. I Part 2:** 592–593, 595

"Pearls" (A. Finch), **Supp. XVII:** 72

Pears, Peter, **II:** 586; **Supp. IV Part 1:** 84

Pearson, Drew, **Supp. XIV:** 126

Pearson, Norman Holmes, **Supp. I Part 1:** 259, 260, 273

Pearson, Tom, **Supp. XXVI:** 113

"Pear Tree" (C. Frost), **Supp. XV:** 105

"Peasants' Way O' Thinkin' " (McKay), **Supp. X:** 133

Pease, Donald E., **Supp. IV Part 2:** 687

"Peboan and Seegwun (Winter and Spring): A Chippewa Allegory"(J. Schoolcraft), **Supp. XXIII:** 235

Peck, Gregory, **Supp. VIII:** 128, 129; **Supp. XII:** 160, 173

Peckinpah, Sam, **Supp. XI:** 306; **Supp. XVIII:** 27

"Peck of Gold, A" (Frost), **II:** 155

Peculiar Treasures: A Biblical Who's Who (Buechner), **Supp. XII:** 53

Pedagogy of the Oppressed (Freire), **Supp. XXV:** 133

"Pedal Point" (Francis), **Supp. IX:** 87

Pedersen, Inge, **Supp. XVIII:** 179

"Pedersen Kid, The" (Gass), **Supp. VI:** 83

"Pedigree, The" (Creeley), **Supp. IV Part 1:** 150

Peebles, Melvin Van, **Supp. XI:** 17; **Supp. XVI:** 144

"Peed Onk" (Moore). *See* "People Like That Are the Only People Here: Canonical Babbling in Peed Onk" (Moore)

"Peeler, The" (O'Connor), **Retro. Supp. II:** 225

"Peeper, The" (Davison), **Supp. XXVI:** 69

Peich, Michael, **Supp. XV:** 113, 117; **Supp. XXV:** 222

Peikoff, Leonard, **Supp. IV Part 2:** 520, 526, 529

Peirce, Charles Sanders, **II:** 20, 352–353; **III:** 599; **Supp. I Part 2:** 640; **Supp. III Part 2:** 626

Pelagius, **III:** 295

"Pelican, The" (Merrill), **Supp. III Part 1:** 320

"Pelican, The" (Wharton), **IV:** 310; **Retro. Supp. I:** 364

Pellacchia, Michael, **Supp. XIII:** 16

Pelley, Denise, **Supp. XIX:** 205

Pelonero, Michael, **Supp. XXIII:** 125

Peltier, Leonard, **Supp. V:** 212

"Pemberton's Bride" (Rash), **Supp. XXVII:** 225

"Penance"(Dybek), **Supp. XXIII:** 69

"Pen and Paper and a Breath of Air" (Oliver), **Supp. VII:** 245

Pence, Amy, **Supp. XV:** 211, 223

"Pencil, The" (Chandler), **Supp. IV Part 1:** 135

Pencillings by the Way (Willis), **II:** 313; **Supp. XVIII:** 12

"Pencils" (Sandburg), **III:** 592

Pencil Shavings (Prouty), **Supp. XXVIII:** 177, 191

Pendleton, Devon, **Supp. XVIII:** 151

"Pendulum" (Bradbury and Hasse), **Supp. IV Part 1:** 102

"Penelope's Song" (Glück), **Supp. V:** 89

Penelope: The Story of the Half-Scalped Woman (Schott), **Supp. XXIII:** 240, **244–245**

Penhally (Gordon), **II:** 197, 199, 201–203, 204

"Penis" (McClatchy), **Supp. XII:** 266–267

Penitent, The (di Donato), **Supp. XX:** 44, 45

Penitent, The (Singer), **Retro. Supp. II:** 309–310, 313

Penland, Nell Bates, **Supp. XXII:** 188

Penn, Robert, **I:** 489

Penn, Sean, **Supp. XI:** 107

Penn, Thomas, **II:** 118

Penn, William, **Supp. I Part 2:** 683

Penna, Sandro, **Supp. XIX:** 34

Pennebaker, D. A., **Supp. XVIII:** 19, 26

Penney, Rob, **Retro. Supp. III:** 317

"Pennsylvania Pilgrim, The" (Whittier), **Supp. I Part 2:** 700

"Pennsylvania Planter, The" (Freneau), **Supp. II Part 1:** 268

"Pennsylvania Station" (Faulkner), **Retro. Supp. III:** 84

Penny, Rob, **Supp. VIII:** 330

"Penny, The" (D. West), **Supp. XVIII:** 283–284

Penrod (Tarkington), **III:** 223

"Penseroso, Il" (Milton), **Supp. XIV:** 8

Pensieri (Leopardi; Di Piero, trans.), **Supp. XIX:** 34

"Pensive Hours"(J. Schoolcraft), **Supp. XXIII:** 230–231

Pentagon of Power, The (Mumford), **Supp. II Part 2:** 498

"Pentecostal, The"(Bottoms), **Supp. XXVIII:** 28

Pentimento (Hellman), **Supp. I Part 1:** 280, 292–294, 296; **Supp. IV Part 1:** 12; **Supp. VIII:** 243; **Supp. XXVII:** 137

"Peonies at Dusk" (Kenyon), **Supp. VII:** 171

People, The (Glaspell), **Supp. III Part 1:** 179

People, Yes, The (Sandburg), **III:** 575, 589, 590, 591

"PEOPLE BURNING, THE" (Baraka), **Supp. II Part 1:** 49

"People in Hell Just Want a Drink of Water" (Proulx), **Supp. VII:** 263

"People Like That Are the Only People Here: Canonical Babbling in Peed Onk" (Moore), **Supp. X:** 168, **178–179**

People Live Here: Selected Poems 1949–1983 (Simpson), **Supp. IX:** 269, 277

"People Next Door, The" (Simpson), **Supp. IX:** 279

People of the Abyss, The (London), **II:** 465–466

"People on the Roller Coaster, The" (Hardwick), **Supp. III Part 1:** 196

People Shall Continue, The (Ortiz), **Supp. IV Part 2:** 510

People's History of the United States, A (Zinn), **Supp. XXIV:** 87; **Supp. XXVIII:** 100

"People's Surroundings" (Moore), **III:** 201, 202, 203

"People v. Abe Lathan, Colored, The" (Caldwell), **I:** 309

"Peppermint Lounge Revisited, The" (Wolfe), **Supp. III Part 2:** 571

Peppis, Paul, **Supp. XXII:** 160

Pepys, Samuel, **Supp. I Part 2:** 653

"Perchance to Dream" (Franzen), **Supp. XX:** 90, 93

Perchance to Dream: Robert B. Parker's Sequel to Raymond Chandler's "Big Sleep" (Parker), **Supp. XIX:** 189

"Perch'io non spero di tornar giammai" (Cavalcanti), **Supp. III Part 2:** 623

Perch of the Devil (Atherton), **Supp. XXIV:** 24, 29

Percy, Thomas, **Supp. XIV:** 2

Percy, Walker, **Supp. III Part 1:** 383–400; **Supp. IV Part 1:** 297; **Supp. V:** 334; **Supp. X:** 42; **Supp. XIV:** 21; **Supp. XIX:** 209; **Supp. XXVI:** 253

Percy, William, **Supp. V:** 334

Percy, William Alexander, **Retro. Supp. I:** 341; **Supp. XXII:** 193

Peregrin, Tony, **Supp. XV:** 69

"Peregrine" (Wylie), **Supp. I Part 2:** 712–713, 714

Perelman, Bob, **Supp. XII:** 23

Perelman, S. J., **IV:** 286; **Retro. Supp. I:** 342; **Retro. Supp. II:** 321, 322, 325, 326, 327, 336; **Supp. IV Part 1:** 353; **Supp. XI:** 66

Perera, Victor, **Supp. XXV:** 50, 52

Perestroika (Kushner), **Supp. IX:** 141, 142, 145

Péret, Benjamin, **Supp. VIII:** 272

Peretz, Isaac Leib, **IV:** 1, 3; **Retro. Supp. II:** 299; **Supp. XXIII:** 4, 7, 8–9

Pérez Galdós, Benito, **II:** 275

Perfect Analysis Given by a Parrot, A (T. Williams), **IV:** 395

"Perfect Couple, The" (Nelson), **Supp. XVIII:** 173

"Perfect Day for Bananafish, A" (Salinger), **III:** 563–564, 571

Perfect Fiction, The (Sorrentino), **Supp. XXI:** 228

Perfect Ganesh, A (McNally), **Supp. XIII: 202–203,** 208, 209

"Perfect Gerbil, The: Reading Barthelme's 'The School' " (Saunders), **Supp. XIX:** 235

"Perfection" (Helprin), **Supp. XXV:** 80

"Perfect Knight, The" (Chandler), **Supp. IV Part 1:** 120

Perfect Mother, The (Schott), **Supp. XXIII: 241–242**

Perfect Party, The (Gurney), **Supp. V:** 100, 105, 106–107

"Perfect Things" (F. Barthelme), **Supp. XI:** 30, 33–34

Perfidy (Hecht), **Supp. XXVII:** 95

"Performance, The" (Dickey), **Supp. IV Part 1:** 178–179, 181

"Perfume" (Mora), **Supp. XIII:** 218

"Perhaps the World Ends Here" (Harjo), **Supp. XII:** 228, 231

Perhaps Women (Anderson), **I:** 114

Pericles (Shakespeare), **I:** 585; **Supp. III Part 2:** 624, 627, 629

Perillo, Lucia, **Supp. XXVI:** 68

"Period Metaphor" (Bronk), **Supp. XXI:** 33

Period of Adjustment (T. Williams), **IV:** 382, 386, 387, 388, 389, 390, 392, 393, 394, 397

"Period Pieces from the Mid-Thirties" (Agee), **I:** 28

"Peripheral Vision" (Davison), **Supp. XXVI:** 69–70

"Periphery" (Ammons), **Supp. VII:** 28

Perkins, David, **Supp. I Part 2:** 459, 475; **Supp. XV:** 185

Perkins, Maxwell, **I:** 252, 289, 290; **II:** 87, 93, 95, 252; **IV:** 452, 455, 457, 458, 461, 462, 463, 469; **Retro. Supp. I:** 101, 105, 108, 109, 110, 113, 114, 178; **Supp. IX:** 57, 58, 60, 232; **Supp. X:** 219, 224, 225, 229, 230, 233; **Supp. XI:** 218, 227

Perlès, Alfred, **III:** 177, 183, 187, 189

Perloff, Marjorie, **Supp. I Part 2:** 539, 542; **Supp. IV Part 1:** 68; **Supp. IV Part 2:** 420, 424, 432; **Supp. XXII:** 161, 271; **Supp. XXIII:** 210, 220

Permanence and Change (Burke), **I:** 274

Permanent Errors (Price), **Supp. VI:** 261

Permanent Horizon, The: A New Search for Old Truths (Lewisohn), **Supp. XXVIII:** 157

"Permanent Traits of the English National Genius" (Emerson), **II:** 18

Permit Me Voyage (Agee), **I:** 25, 27

"Perosa Canavese" (Everwine), **Supp. XV:** 84

Perrault, Charles, **IV:** 266; **Supp. I Part 2:** 622

Perrin, Noel, **Supp. XVI:** 34; **Supp. XXII:** 205, 207, 211, 218

Perrins, Carol. *See* Frost, Carol

Perrota, Tom, **Supp. XXVII:** 5

Perry, Anne, **Supp. V:** 335

Perry, Bliss, **I:** 243

Perry, Donna, **Supp. IV Part 1:** 322, 327, 335

Perry, Edgar A., **III:** 410

Perry, Keith Ronald, **Supp. XXI:** 42

Perry, Lincoln, **Supp. V:** 24, 33

Perry, Matthew C., **Supp. I Part 2:** 494–495

Perry, Pam, **Supp. XXVI:** 12

Perry, Patsy Brewington, **Supp. I Part 1:** 66

Perry, Phyllis Alesia, **Supp. XVIII:** 96

Perry, Ralph Barton, **I:** 224; **II:** 356, 362, 364; **Supp. XIV:** 197

Perry, Dr. William, **II:** 395, 396

Perse, St.-John, **III:** 12, 13, 14, 17; **Supp. III Part 1:** 14; **Supp. IV Part 1:** 82; **Supp. XIII:** 344; **Supp. XV:** 178

"Persephone in Hell" (Dove), **Supp. IV Part 1:** 250, 251

"Persephone"(Le Sueur), **Supp. XXIII:** 162, 165, **170–171**

"Persephone to Psyche" (Stallings), **Supp. XXV:** 234

"Persephone Writes a Letter to Her Mother" (Stallings), **Supp. XXV:** 228

"Persimmons" (L.-Y. Lee), **Supp. XV:** 211, 213

"Persistence of Desire, The" (Updike), **IV:** 222–223, 228

"Persistence of Poetry, The" (Bynner), **Supp. XV:** 49

"Persistences" (Hecht), **Supp. X: 68–69**

Person, Place, and Thing (Shapiro), **Supp. II Part 2:** 702, 705

Personae of Ezra Pound (Pound), **III:** 458

Personae: The Collected Poems (Pound), **Retro. Supp. I:** 285, 286; **Supp. I Part 1:** 255; **Supp. XVII:** 32

"Personal" (Stern), **Supp. IX:** 299

"Personal and Occasional Pieces" (Welty), **Retro. Supp. I:** 355

"Personal and the Individual, The" (L. Michaels), **Supp. XVI:** 201

Personal Injuries (Turow), **Supp. XVII: 219–220,** 221, 223

"Personalities" (column, Briggs), **Supp. XVIII:** 15

"Personal Narrative" (Edward), **Retro. Supp. III:** 9

Personal Narrative (Edwards), **I:** 545, 552, 553, 561, 562; **Supp. I Part 2:** 700

"Personal Poem #9" (Berrigan), **Supp. XXIV:** 34, 35

"Personal Poem"(O'Hara), **Supp. XXIII:** 219

Personal Recollection of Joan of Arc (Twain), **IV:** 208

Personals (Bontemps), **Supp. XXII:** 7, 8

"Personals" (Didion), **Supp. IV Part 1:** 200

"Personism" (O'Hara), **Supp. XV:** 181

"Personism: A Manifesto" (O'Hara), **Supp. XXIII:** 212, 215; **Supp. XXIV:** 43

Persons and Places (Santayana), **III:** 615

Persons in Hiding (film), **Supp. XIII:** 170

Persons in Hiding (Hoover), **Supp. XIII:** 170

Person Sitting in Darkness, A (Twain), **IV:** 208

"Persons Who Interest Us" (*Harper's Bazaar*), **Supp. XXV:** 277–278

"Perspective" (Francis), **Supp. IX:** 78

"Perspective: Anniversary D-Day" (Karr), **Supp. XI:** 241

Perspectives by Incongruity (Burke), **I:** 284–285

"Perspectives: Is It Out of Control?" (Gleason), **Supp. IX:** 16

Perspectives on Cormac McCarthy (Arnold and Luce, eds.), **Supp. VIII:** 189

Persse, Dudley Jocelyn, **Supp. XX: 232**

Pertes et Fracas (McCoy), **Supp. XIII:** 175

"Peruvian Child" (Mora), **Supp. XIII:** 218

Peseroff, Joyce, **Supp. IV Part 1:** 71

Pesetsky, Bette, **Supp. XXIV:** 173

"Pestilence" (Nelson), **Supp. XVIII:** 186

Pest Maiden, The (Schott), **Supp. XXIII: 245–246**

"Peter" (Cather), **Retro. Supp. I:** 4

"Peter" (Moore), **III:** 210, 212

Peter, Saint, **III:** 341, 346; **IV:** 86, 294

"Peter Goldthwaite's Treasure" (Hawthorne), **Retro. Supp. III:** 113

Peterkin, Julia, **Supp. I Part 1:** 328; **Supp. XXII:** 12, 189

"Peter Klaus" (German tale), **II:** 306

Peter Pan (Barrie), **Supp. XV:** 319

"Peter Parley" works (Goodrich), **Supp. I Part 1:** 38

"Peter Pendulum" (Poe), **III:** 425

"Peter Quince at the Clavier" (Stevens), **IV:** 81, 82

Peter Rabbit tales, **Retro. Supp. I:** 335

Peters, Cora, **Supp. I Part 2:** 468

Peters, Jacqueline, **Supp. XII:** 225

Peters, Margot, **Supp. VIII:** 252

Peters, Robert, **Retro. Supp. III:** 245; **Supp. XIII:** 114

Peters, S. H. (pseudonym). *See* Henry, O.

Peters, Timothy, **Supp. XI:** 39

"Peter's Avocado" (Rodriguez), **Supp. XIV:** 308–309

Petersen, David, **Supp. XIII:** 2

Petersen, Donald, **Supp. V:** 180; **Supp. XV:** 74, 92

Peterson, Dorothy, **Supp. XVIII:** 131, 132

Peterson, George, **Supp. XXII:** 250

Peterson, Houston, **I:** 60

Peterson, Roger Tory, **Supp. V:** 202; **Supp. XXVIII:** 243, 249, 255

Peterson, Virgilia, **Supp. IV Part 1:** 30

Peter Whiffle: His Life and Works (Van Vechten), **Supp. II Part 2:** 728–729, 731, 735, 738–741, 749

"Petey and Yotsee and Mario" (H. Roth), **Supp. IX:** 234

"Petition, A" (Winters), **Supp. II Part 2:** 785

"Pet Milk"(Dybek), **Supp. XXIII:** 74

"'Pet Negro' System, The" (Hurston), **Supp. VI:** 159

"Petra and Its Surroundings" (Frost), **Retro. Supp. I:** 124

Petrarch, **I:** 176; **II:** 590; **III:** 4

"Petrarch, Shakespeare, and the Blues" (C. Frost), **Supp. XV:** 92, 104, 105

"Petrified Man" (Welty), **IV:** 262; **Retro. Supp. I:** 345, 351

"Petrified Man, The" (Twain), **IV:** 195; **Retro. Supp. III:** 257

"Petrified Woman, The" (Gordon), **II:** 199

Petronius, **III:** 174, 179

Petry, Ann, **Supp. VIII:** 214; **Supp. XI:** 6, 85; **Supp. XVIII:** 286

Pet Sematary (King), **Supp. V:** 138, 143, 152

Pettengill, Claire C., **Supp. XXV:** 40

Pettengill, Richard, **Supp. VIII:** 341, 345, 348

Pettingell, Phoebe, **Supp. XV:** 251, 256–257, 262

Pettis, Joyce, **Supp. XI:** 276, 277, 278, 281

Pettis, Olive G., **Supp. XXIII:** 189

Petty, Jill, **Supp. XXI:** 244, 248, 249, 250

Pfaelzer, Jean, **Supp. XVI:** 88, 90

Pfaff, Timothy, **Supp. V:** 166

Pfeil, Fred, **Supp. XIV:** 36

Pfister, Karin, **IV:** 467, 475

Phaedo (Plato), **II:** 10

Phaedra (Lowell and Barzun, trans.), **II:** 543–544

"Phantasia for Elvira Shatayev, The" (Rich), **Retro. Supp. III:** 249; **Supp. I Part 2:** 570

Phantasms of War (A. Lowell), **II:** 512

"Phantom of the Movie Palace, The" (Coover), **Supp. V:** 50–51

Phantom Ship, The (Marryat), **Supp. XVII:** 55

"Pharaoh, The" (Kenyon), **Supp. VII:** 172

"Pharmacy"(Strout), **Supp. XXIII:** 281

Pharr, Mary, **Supp. V:** 147

"Phases" (E. Stoddard), **Supp. XV:** 273

"Phases" (Stevens), **Retro. Supp. I:** 299

"Phases—in praise of Zoloft"(Lea), **Supp. XXVIII:** 138

Phases of an Inferior Planet (Glasgow), **II:** 174–175

"Pheasant, The" (Carver), **Supp. III Part 1:** 146

Phelan, Alice, **Supp. XXII:** 193

Pheloung, Grant, **Supp. XI:** 39

Phelps, Donald, **Supp. XXIII:** 174

Phelps, Elizabeth Stuart, **Retro. Supp. II:** 146; **Supp. XIII:** 141; **Supp. XVI:** 80

Phelps, Teresa Godwin, **Supp. VIII:** 128

Phelps, William Lyon "Billy", **Supp. XX:** 68, 75, 220

"Phenomena and Laws of Race Contacts, The" (Locke), **Supp. XIV:** 210

Phenomenal Fauna, A (Wells), **Supp. XXVI:** 275

"Phenomenology of Anger, The" (Rich), **Retro. Supp. III:** 247; **Supp. I Part 2:** 562–563, 571

Phenomenology of Moral Experience, The (Mandelbaum), **I:** 61

"Phenomenology of *On Moral Fiction*" (C. Johnson), **Supp. VI:** 188

Phidias, **Supp. I Part 2:** 482

Philadelphia Fire (Wideman), **Supp. X:** 320, 334

Philadelphia Negro, The (Du Bois), **Supp. II Part 1:** 158, 163–164, 166

Philbrick, Thomas, **I:** 343

"Philemon and Baucis"(Hadas), **Supp. XXIII:** 114

"Phil in the Marketplace" (Lethem), **Supp. XVIII:** 148

Philip, Jim, **Supp. XII:** 136

Philip, Maxwell, **Supp. XXI:** 160

Philip, Prince, **Supp. X:** 108

"Philip of Pokanoket" (Irving), **II:** 303

Philippians (biblical book), **IV:** 154

"Philippine Conquest, The" (Masters), **Supp. I Part 2:** 456

"Philip Roth Reconsidered" (Howe), **Retro. Supp. II:** 286

"Philistinism and the Negro Writer" (Baraka), **Supp. II Part 1:** 39, 44

Phillips, Adam, **Supp. XII:** 97–98

Phillips, Anne K., **Supp. XX:** 221

Phillips, Carl, **Supp. XXI:** 246

Phillips, David Graham, **II:** 444; **Retro. Supp. II:** 101

Phillips, Gene D., **Supp. XI:** 306

Phillips, Jayne Anne, **Supp. XIV:** 21

Phillips, J. J., **Supp. XXIII:** 174

Phillips, J. O. C., **Supp. I Part 1:** 19

Phillips, Robert, **Supp. XIII:** 335, 344

Phillips, Wendell, **Supp. I Part 1:** 103; **Supp. I Part 2:** 524

Phillips, Willard, **Supp. I Part 1:** 154, 155

Phillips, William, **Supp. VIII:** 156

Phillips, William L., **I:** 106

"Philly Babylon" (Di Piero), **Supp. XIX:** 46

"Philoctetes"(Hadas), **Supp. XXIII:** 115

"Philoctetes: The Wound and the Bow" (Wilson), **Supp. XXIV:** 217

"Philosopher, The" (Farrell), **II:** 45

Philosopher of the Forest (pseudonym). *See* Freneau, Philip

Philosophes classiques, Les (Taine), **III:** 323

"Philosophical Cobbler, The" (Sanders), **Supp. XVI:** 268

"Philosophical Concepts and Practical Results" (James), **II:** 352

"Philosophical Investigation of Metaphor, A" (Gass), **Supp. VI:** 79

Philosophical Transactions (Watson), **II:** 114

"Philosophy, Or Something Like That" (P. Roth), **Supp. III Part 2:** 403

"Philosophy and Its Critics" (James), **II:** 360

"Philosophy and the Form of Fiction" (Gass), **Supp. VI:** 85

"Philosophy for People" (Emerson), **II:** 14

"Philosophy in Warm Weather" (Kenyon), **Supp. VII:** 168

"Philosophy Lesson" (Levine), **Supp. V:** 195

Philosophy of Alain Locke, The: Harlem Renaissance and Beyond (Harris, ed.), **Supp. XIV:** 196, 211–212

"Philosophy of Composition, The" (Poe), **III:** 416, 421; **Retro. Supp. II:** 266, 267, 271; **Retro. Supp. III:** 233–234; **Supp. XXV:** 120, 121

Philosophy of Friedrich Nietzsche, The (Mencken), **III:** 102–103

"Philosophy of Handicap, A" (Bourne), **I:** 216, 218

"Philosophy of History" (Emerson), **II:** 11–12

Philosophy of Literary Form, The (Burke), **I:** 275, 281, 283, 291

Philosophy of the Human Mind, The (Stewart), **II:** 8

Philosophy: Who Needs It (Rand), **Supp. IV Part 2:** 517, 518, 527, 533

Philoxenes, **Supp. VIII:** 201

"Phineas" (Knowles), **Supp. XII:** 238–240

Phineas: Six Stories (Knowles), **Supp. XII:** 249

"Phocion" (R. Lowell), **II:** 536

Phoebe Light (Notley), **Supp. XXII:** 227

Phoenix and the Turtle, The (Shakespeare), **I:** 284

"Phoenix Lyrics" (Schwartz), **Supp. II Part 2:** 665

"Phoenix on the Sword, The" (Howard), **Supp. XXVII:** 117, 124–125

"Phone Booths, The" (Jarman), **Supp. XVII:** 112–113

"Phony War Films" (Jones), **Supp. XI:** 217, 232

"Photo, The"(Wakoski), **Supp. XXVIII:** 266

"Photograph: Carlisle Indian School (1879–1918)"(Kenny), **Supp. XXIII:** 156

"Photograph: Migrant Worker, Parlier, California, 1967" (Levis), **Supp. XI:** 272

"Photograph of a Bawd Drinking Raleigh Rye" (Trethewey), **Supp. XXI:** 254

"Photograph of a Child on a Vermont Hillside" (Kenyon), **Supp. VII:** 168

"Photograph of My Mother as a Young Girl" (Gioia), **Supp. XV:** 119

"Photograph of the Girl" (Olds), **Supp. X:** 205

"Photograph of the Unmade Bed" (Rich), **Supp. I Part 2:** 558

Photographs (Welty), **Retro. Supp. I:** 343

"Photographs, The" (Barthelme), **Supp. IV Part 1:** 53

"Photography" (Levine), **Supp. V:** 194

"Phyllis"(Goodman), **Supp. XXVIII:** 87, 89

Phyrrho, **Retro. Supp. I:** 247

"Physical Universe" (Simpson), **Supp. IX:** 278

"Physicist We Know, A" (Shields), **Supp. VII:** 310

"Physics and Cosmology in the Fiction of Tom Robbins" (Nadeau), **Supp. X:** 270

Physiologie du goût (Brillat-Savarin), **Supp. XVII:** 82, 86

Physiology of Taste, The; or, Meditations on Transcendent Gastronomy (Brillat-Savarin; M. F. K. Fisher, trans.), **Supp. XVII:** 86, 87, 91

"Physiology of Versification, The: Harmonies of Organic and Animal Life" (Holmes), **Supp. I Part 1:** 311

Physique de l'Amour (Gourmont), **III:** 467–468

Piaf, Edith, **Supp. IV Part 2:** 549

Piaget, Jean, **Supp. XIII:** 75

"Piano" (Lawrence), **Supp. XV:** 254

"Piano Fingers" (Mason), **Supp. VIII:** 146

Piano Lesson, The (Bearden), **Supp. VIII:** 342

Piano Lesson, The (television film), **Retro. Supp. III:** 326

Piano Lesson, The (Wilson), **Retro. Supp. III:** 318, 325, 326–328; **Supp. VIII: 342–345**

Piano Man's Daughter, The (Findley), **Supp. XX: 59–61**

"Piano Player, The"(Strout), **Supp. XXIII:** 283, 285

Piatt, James, **Supp. I Part 2:** 420

Piatt, John J., **II:** 273

Piazza, Ben, **Supp. XIII:** 163

Piazza, Paul, **Supp. XIV:** 157, 160, 171

"Piazza de Spagna, Early Morning" (Wilbur), **Supp. III Part 2:** 553

Piazza Tales, The (Melville), **III:** 91; **Retro. Supp. III:** 158

Picabia, Francis, **Retro. Supp. I:** 416; **Retro. Supp. II:** 331; **Supp. XXII:** 162

Picasso (Stein), **IV:** 28, 32, 45

Picasso, Pablo, **I:** 429, 432, 440, 442, 445; **II:** 602; **III:** 197, 201, 470; **IV:** 26, 31, 32, 46, 87, 407, 436; **Retro. Supp. I:** 55, 63; **Supp. IV Part 1:** 81; **Supp. IX:** 66

"Picayune: A Child's Story"(Stuart), **Supp. XXVIII:** 225

Piccione, Anthony, **Supp. XV:** 212

"Piccola Comedia" (Wilbur), **Supp. III Part 2:** 561

Pickard, Samuel T., **Supp. I Part 2:** 682

Picked-Up Pieces (Updike), **Retro. Supp. I:** 320, 322, 323, 335

Picker, Lauren, **Supp. VIII:** 78, 83

Picker, Tobias, **Supp. XII:** 253

Pickering, Sam, **Supp. XXI: 191–207**

Pickford, Mary, **Retro. Supp. I:** 325; **Supp. I Part 2:** 391

"Picking and Choosing" (Moore), **III:** 205

"Pickman's Model" (Lovecraft), **Supp. XXV:** 113, 114

Picnic (film), **Supp. XXV:** 95

Picnic (Inge), **Supp. XXV:** 93, 95, 97–99

"Picnic" (Peacock), **Supp. XIX:** 206

Picnic, Lightning (Collins), **Supp. XXI:** 54, 60

"Picnic, Lightning" (Collins), **Supp. XXI:** 64–65

Picnic Cantata (music) (Bowles), **Supp. IV Part 1:** 89

"Picnic Remembered" (Warren), **IV:** 240

Pictorial History of the Negro in America, A (Hughes), **Supp. I Part 1:** 345

"Picture" (Huddle), **Supp. XXVI:** 150

"Picture, The" (Olson), **Supp. II Part 2:** 574

Picture Bride (Son), **Supp. X:** 292

"Picture I Want, The" (Olds), **Supp. X:** 209

Picture of Dorian Gray, The (Wilde), **Supp. IX:** 105

"Picture of Little J. A. in a Prospect of Flowers, A" (Ashbery), **Supp. III Part 1:** 3

Picture Palace (Theroux), **Supp. VIII:** 322

"Pictures" (Pickering), **Supp. XXI:** 197

"Pictures at an Extermination" (Epstein), **Supp. XII:** 161

"Pictures from an Expedition" (Duffy), **Supp. IV Part 1:** 207

Pictures from an Institution (Jarrell), **II:** 367, 385

Pictures from Brueghel (W. C. Williams), **Retro. Supp. I:** 429–431

"Pictures from Brueghel" (W. C. Williams), **Retro. Supp. I:** 419

"Pictures of Columbus, the Genoese, The" (Freneau), **Supp. II Part 1:** 258

Pictures of Fidelman: An Exhibition (Malamud), **Supp. I Part 2:** 450–451

"Pictures of the Artist" (Malamud), **Supp. I Part 2:** 450

Pictures of the Floating World (A. Lowell), **II:** 521, 524–525; **Supp. XXVII:** 295

Pictures of Travel (Heine), **II:** 281

Picturesque America; or, the Land We Live In (Bryant, ed.), **Supp. I Part 1:** 158

"Picturesque Ghetto, The" (Hapgood), **Supp. XVII:** 101

"Picturesque: San Cristóbal de las Casas" (Mora), **Supp. XIII:** 218

Picture This (Heller), **Supp. IV Part 1:** 386, 388, 390–391

Picturing Will (Beattie), **Supp. V:** 29, 31–32, 34

"Pie" (X. J. Kennedy), **Supp. XV:** 170

"Piece, A" (Creeley), **Supp. IV Part 1:** 155, 156

"Piece of Moon, A" (Hogan), **Supp. IV Part 1:** 407

Piece of My Heart, A (Ford), **Supp. V:** 57, 58–61, 62

Piece of My Mind, A: Reflections at Sixty (Wilson), **IV:** 426, 430, 438, 441

"Piece of News, A" (Welty), **IV:** 263; **Retro. Supp. I:** 345, 346

Pieces (Creeley), **Supp. IV Part 1:** 155

Pieces and Pontifications (Mailer), **Retro. Supp. II:** 209–210

Pieces of the Frame (McPhee), **Supp. III Part 1:** 293

"Pie of the Month"(Thompson), **Supp. XXIII:** 300

Pierce, Franklin, **II:** 225, 226, 227; **III:** 88; **Retro. Supp. I:** 150, 163, 164, 165

Pierce, Frederick, **Retro. Supp. I:** 136

Piercy, Josephine, **Retro. Supp. III:** 9

Piercy, Josephine K., **Supp. I Part 1:** 103

"Pierian Handsprings" (column, Untermeyer), **Supp. XV:** 294

Pierpont, Claudia Roth, **Supp. X:** 192, 193, 196

Pierre et Jean (Maupassant), **I:** 421

Pierre: or The Ambiguities (Melville), **III:** 86–88, 89; **IV:** 194; **Retro. Supp. I:** 249, 253–254, 256; **Retro. Supp. III:** 147, 149, 150, 157–158; **Supp. I Part 2:** 579

Pierrepont, Sarah. *See* Edwards, Sarah

Pierrot qui pleure et Pierrot qui rit (Rostand), **II:** 515

Pierson, George W, **Supp. XXII:** 289

Pig Cookies (Ríos), **Supp. IV Part 2:** 537, 550, 552–554

Pigeon Feathers (Updike), **IV:** 214, 218, 219, 221–223, 226

"Pigeon Feathers" (Updike), **Retro. Supp. I:** 318, 322, 323

"Pigeons" (Rilke), **II:** 544

"Pigeons, The" (Espaillat), **Supp. XXI:** 98

"Pigeons from Hell" (Howard), **Supp. XXVII:** 116, 119–120

"Pigeon Woman" (Swenson), **Supp. IV Part 2:** 644

"Pig Helmet and the Wall of Life"(P. Benedict), **Supp. XXIII:** 48–49

Pigs in Heaven (Kingsolver), **Supp. VII:** 197, 199, 209–210

Pike County Ballads, The (Hay), **Supp. I Part 1:** 352

Piket, Vincent, **Supp. IV Part 1:** 24

Pilar San-Mallafre, Maria del, **Supp. V:** 40

Pilcer, Sonya, **Supp. XVII:** 50

Pilgrim (Findley), **Supp. XX: 61–62**

"Pilgrim" (Freneau), **Supp. I Part 1:** 125

"Pilgrimage" (Ray), **Supp. XVIII:** 193

"Pilgrimage" (Sontag), **Supp. III Part 2:** 454–455

"Pilgrimage" (Trethewey), **Supp. XXI:** 255

"Pilgrimage, The" (Maxwell), **Supp. VIII:** 169, 171

Pilgrimage of Festus, The (Aiken), **I:** 50, 55, 57

Pilgrimage of Henry James, The (Brooks), **I:** 240, 248, 250; **IV:** 433

Pilgrim at Tinker Creek (Dillard), **Supp. VI:** 22, **23–26**, 28, 29, **30–31**, 34; **Supp. XVIII:** 189; **Supp. XXVIII:** 255

"Pilgrim Makers" (R. Lowell), **II:** 541

Pilgrim's Harbor (Skloot), **Supp. XX: 196, 207**

Pilgrim's Progress (Bunyan), **I:** 92; **II:** 15, 168, 572; **Supp. I Part 1:** 32, 38; **Supp. I Part 2:** 599

Pili's Wall (Levine), **Supp. V:** 178, 183–184

"Pillar of Fire" (Bradbury), **Supp. IV Part 1:** 113–114

Pillars of Hercules, The: A Grand Tour of the Mediterranean (Theroux), **Supp. VIII:** 325

"Pillow" (L.-Y. Lee), **Supp. XV:** 224

Pilot, The (Cooper), **I:** 335, 337, 339, 342–343, 350

"Pilot from the Carrier, A" (Jarrell), **II:** 374

"Pilots, Man Your Planes" (Jarrell), **II:** 374–375

"Pilots, The" (Levertov), **Supp. III Part 1:** 282

Pilsudski, Joseph, **Supp. XXIII:** 6

"Pimp's Revenge, A" (Malamud), **Supp. I Part 2:** 435, 450, 451

Pinball (Kosinski), **Supp. VII:** 215, 226

Pinchot, Gifford, **Supp. IX:** 184; **Supp. XIV:** 178

Pindar, **I:** 381; **II:** 543; **III:** 610

"Pine" (Dickey), **Supp. IV Part 1:** 183

Pine Barrens, The (McPhee), **Supp. III Part 1:** 298–301, 309

"Pineys, The" (Stern), **Supp. IX:** 288, 296

Pinget, Robert, **Supp. V:** 39

Pinhook: Finding Wholeness in a Fragmented Land (Ray), **Supp. XVIII:** 189, 192, 202–204

"Pink Dog" (Bishop), **Retro. Supp. II:** 48

"Pink Dress, The" (Boulton), **Supp. XXII:** 19

"Pink Dress, The" (Wakoski), **Supp. XXVIII:** 264

Pinker, James B., **I:** 409; **Retro. Supp. I:** 231

Pinkerton, Jan, **Supp. V:** 323–324

"Pink Moon—The Pond" (Oliver), **Supp. VII:** 234

Pinktoes (C. Himes), **Supp. XVI: 142**

Pinocchio in Venice (Coover), **Supp. V:** 40, 51

Pinsker, Sanford, **Retro. Supp. II:** 23; **Supp. IX:** 293, 327; **Supp. V:** 272; **Supp. XI:** 251, 254, 317

Pinsky, Robert, **Retro. Supp. II:** 50; **Supp. IX:** 155, 158; **Supp. VI: 235–251; Supp. XIII:** 277, 285; **Supp. XXI:** 243; **Supp. XXIII:** 111, 124

Pinter, Harold, **I:** 71; **Supp. XIII:** 20, 196; **Supp. XIV:** 239; **Supp. XVI:** 207

Pinto, Ferdinand Mendes (pseudonym). *See* Briggs, Charles Frederick

Pinto and Sons (Epstein), **Supp. XII:** 170, **171–172**

Pinto letters (Briggs), **Supp. XVIII:** 3, **12–13**

"Pinup" (Collins), **Supp. XXI:** 59

"Pioneer Girl" (L. I. Wilder), **Supp. XXII:** 290, 293, 294, 295

Pioneer Girl (Nguyen), **Supp. XXVI:** 216–220

Pioneers, The (Cooper), **I:** 336, 337, 339, 340–341, 342, 348; **II:** 313

Pioneers of France in the New World (Parkman), **Supp. III Part 2:** 599, 602

"Pioneers! O Pioneers!" (Whitman), **Retro. Supp. I:** 8

"Pioneer's Vision, The" (Larcom), **Supp. XIII:** 140

Pious and Secular America (Niebuhr), **III:** 308

Pipe Night (O'Hara), **III:** 361, 368

Piper, Dan, **Supp. IX:** 65

Pipers at the Gates of Dawn: The Wisdom of Children's Literature (Cott), **Supp. XVI:** 104

"Piper's Rocks" (Olson), **Supp. IV Part 1:** 153

"Pipistrelles" (B. Kelly), **Supp. XVII:** 129–130

Pipkin, Charles W., **Supp. XIV:** 3

Pippa Passes (Browning), **IV:** 128

Piquion, René, **Supp. I Part 1:** 346

Pirandello, Luigi, **Supp. IV Part 2:** 576, 588

Piranesi, Giovanni Battista, **Supp. XV:** 258

Pirate, The (Robbins), **Supp. XII:** 6

Pirate, The (Scott), **I:** 339

Pirates of Penzance, The (Gilbert and Sullivan), **IV:** 386

Pisan Cantos, The (Pound), **III:** 476; **Retro. Supp. I:** 140, 283, 285, 293; **Supp. III Part 1:** 63; **Supp. V:** 331, 337; **Supp. XIV:** 11; **Supp. XV:** 351

Pisarev, Dimitri, **Supp. XXI:** 164

Piscator, Erwin, **IV:** 394

"Pissaro: Tropical Impressions" (Kenny), **Supp. XXIII:** 146

Pissarro, Camille, **I:** 478

"Pissing off the Back of the Boat into the Nevernais Canal" (Matthews), **Supp. IX:** 160–161

Pistol, The (Jones), **Supp. XI:** 219, **223–224,** 227, 234

"Pistol Politics" (Howard), **Supp. XXVII:** 128

Pit, The (Norris), **III:** 314, 322, 326–327, 333, 334

"Pit, The" (Roethke), **III:** 538

"Pit and the Pendulum, The" (Poe), **III:** 413, 416; **Retro. Supp. II:** 264, 269–270, 273

"Pitcher" (Francis), **Supp. IX:** 82

"Pitcher, The" (Dubus), **Supp. VII:** 87

Pitchford, Nicola, **Supp. XII:** 13

"Pits, The" (D. Graham), **Supp. XI:** 252, 254

Pitt, William, **Supp. I Part 2:** 510, 518

Pitts, Rebecca, **Supp. XXII:** 280, 281

"Pittsburgh" (Carruth), **Supp. XVI:** 58

Pittsburgh Cycle (Wilson). *See Century Cycle* (Wilson)

"Pity" (Huddle), **Supp. XXVI:** 151

"Pity Me" (Wylie), **Supp. I Part 2:** 729

Pity the Monsters (Williamson), **Retro. Supp. II:** 185

Pius II, Pope, **III:** 472

Pius IX, Pope, **II:** 79

"Piute Creek" (Snyder), **Supp. VIII:** 293

Pixley, Frank, **I:** 196

Pizer, Donald, **III:** 321; **Retro. Supp. II:** 100, 199

"Place" (Hoffman), **Supp. XVIII:** 86

"Place at the Outskirts" (Simic), **Supp. VIII:** 282

Place Called Estherville, A (Caldwell), **I:** 297, 307

Place Called Freedom, A (Sanders), **Supp. XVI:** 269

Place for My Head, A (Hoffman), **Supp. XVIII:** 76

"Place in Fiction" (Welty), **IV:** 260, 279

Place in Mind, A (Lea), **Supp. XXVIII:** 133–134

Place of Dead Roads, The (Burroughs), **Supp. III Part 1:** 196

Place of Love, The (Shapiro), **Supp. II Part 2:** 702, 706

"Place of Poetry, The" (Stevens), **Retro. Supp. I:** 304

Place of Science in Modern Civilization and Other Essays, The (Veblen), **Supp. I Part 2:** 629, 642

"Place of Trumpets, The" (B. Kelly), **Supp. XVII:** 127

Place on Earth, A (Berry), **Supp. X:** 33–34, 36

Places I Never Meant to Be (Blume, ed.), **Supp. XXVIII:** 280

Places Left Unfinished at the Time of Creation (Santos), **Supp. XIII:** 274

"Places to Look for Your Mind" (Moore), **Supp. X:** 174–175

"Place They'd Never Seen, A: The Theater" (Wasserstein), **Supp. XV:** 332

"Place to Live, A" (Levertov), **Supp. III Part 1:** 281

"Place to Stand, A" (Price), **Supp. VI:** 258

Place to Stand, A (Wagoner), **Supp. IX:** 324

"Place (Any Place) to Transcend All Places, A" (W. C. Williams), **Retro. Supp. I:** 422

"Place Where My Poems Are Coming From, The" (Crooker), **Supp. XXIII:** 64

Placi, Carlo, **IV:** 328

Plagemann, Catherine, **Supp. XVII:** 91

"Plagiarist, The" (Singer), **IV:** 19

Plagued by the Nightingale (Boyle), **Supp. XXIV: 51–52,** 53, 56

Plague of Dreamers, A (Stern), **Supp. XX: 178**

Plainest Narrative, The (Bronk), **Supp. XXI:** 31

"Plain Language from Truthful James" (Harte). *See* "Heathen Chinee, The"

"Plain Sense of Things, The" (Stevens), **Retro. Supp. I:** 298, 299, 307, 312

"Plain Song" (Carruth), **Supp. XVI:** 54

Plain Song (Harrison), **Supp. VIII: 38–39**

"Plain Song" (Kooser), **Supp. XIX:** 120

"Plain Song for Comadre, A" (Wilbur), **Supp. III Part 2:** 554

"Plain Talk". *See Common Sense* (Paine)

Plaint of a Rose, The (Sandburg), **III:** 579

Plain Truth: Or, Serious Considerations on the Present State of the City of Philadelphia, and Province of Pennsylvania (Franklin), **II:** 117–119
Plainwater: Essays and Poetry (Carson), **Supp. XII:** 97, **99–104**
Plan B (C. Himes), **Supp. XVI:** 143, 144
Plan B: Further Thoughts on Faith (Lamott), **Supp. XX:** **142–143**
"Planchette" (London), **II:** 475–476
"Planetarium" (Rich), **Retro. Supp. III:** 245; **Supp. I Part 2:** 557
Planet News: 1961–1967 (Ginsberg), **Supp. II Part 1:** 321
"Planet of Love"(Siken), **Supp. XXVIII:** 199, 200
Planet Waves (album, Dylan), **Supp. XVIII:** 27
"Plantation a beginning, a" (Olson), **Supp. II Part 2:** 573
Plantation Songs and Other Verse (Stuart), **Supp. XXVIII:** 225, 230, 237, 239
Plant Dreaming Deep (Sarton), **Supp. VIII:** 250, 263
Plante, David, **Supp. IV Part 1:** 310
Planting a Sequoia (Gioia), **Supp. XV:** 117
"Planting a Sequoia" (Gioia), **Supp. XV:** 111, 112, 117, **121–122**
"Plants Fed On By Fawns" (B. Kelly), **Supp. XVII:** 133
Plarr, Victor, **III:** 459, 477
Plated Heart, The (Goodman), **Supp. XXVIII:** 85, 88, 91–93
Plath, James, **Retro. Supp. I:** 334; **Supp. XXIII:** 73, 74, 80
Plath, Sylvia, **Retro. Supp. II:** 181, **241–260; Retro. Supp. III:** 243; **Supp. I Part 2: 526–549,** 554, 571; **Supp. III Part 2:** 543, 561; **Supp. IV Part 2:** 439; **Supp. V:** 79, 81, 113, 117, 118, 119, 344; **Supp. X:** 201, 202, **203,** 215; **Supp. XI:** 146, 240, 241, 317; **Supp. XII:** 217, 308; **Supp. XIII:** 35, 76, 312; **Supp. XIV:** 269; **Supp. XV:** 123, 148, 184, 252, 253, 340; **Supp. XVII:** 239; **Supp. XXI:** 58; **Supp. XXII:** 30, 92, 93; **Supp. XXIII:** 63, 64, 112, 113, 254; **Supp. XXV:** 222; **Supp. XXVI:** 45, 64, 67, 68, 77; **Supp. XXVII:** 261, 296; **Supp. XXVIII:** 177, 192, 265
Plath, Warren, **Supp. I Part 2:** 528
Plato, **I:** 224, 279, 383, 389, 485, 523; **II:** 5, 8, 10, 15, 233, 346, 391–392, 591; **III:** 115, 480, 600, 606, 609, 619–620; **IV:** 74, 140, 333, 363, 364; **Retro. Supp. I:** 247; **Retro. Supp. II:** 31; **Supp. I Part 2:** 595, 631; **Supp. IV Part 1:** 391; **Supp. IV Part 2:** 526; **Supp. X:** 78
"Plato" (Emerson), **II:** 6
"Platonic Relationship, A" (Beattie), **Supp. V:** 22
Platonic Scripts (Justice), **Supp. VII:** 115
Platonov, Dmitri, **Supp. VIII:** 30
Platt, Anthony M., **Supp. I Part 1:** 13–14
Platt, Edward, **Supp. XXIII:** 97
Platte River (Bass), **Supp. XVI:** 19

"Platte River" (Bass), **Supp. XVI:** 20
"Plausible Man" (Davison), **Supp. XXVI:** 71
Plausible Prejudices: Essays on American Writing (Epstein), **Supp. XIV:** 111
Plautus, Titus Maccius, **IV:** 155; **Supp. III Part 2:** 630
"Play, A" (Brainard), **Supp. XXVII:** 18
Play and Other Stories, The (Dixon), **Supp. XII:** 148, 149
Playback (Chandler), **Supp. IV Part 1:** 134–135; **Supp. XVIII:** 138
Playback (script) (Chandler), **Supp. IV Part 1:** 131
"Play Ball!" (Francis), **Supp. IX:** 89
Playboy of the Western World, The (Synge), **Supp. III Part 1:** 34
Play Days (Jewett), **Retro. Supp. II:** 135
Play Days: A Book of Stories for Children (Jewett), **II:** 401–402
Player Piano (Vonnegut), **Supp. II Part 2:** 756, 757, 760–765
Players (DeLillo), **Supp. VI:** 3, 6, 8, 14
"Players, The" (W. J. Smith), **Supp. XIII:** 340, 343
"Playground, The" (Bradbury), **Supp. IV Part 1:** 104
"Playing" (Huddle), **Supp. XXVI:** 151, 154
Playing at Stillness (Espaillat), **Supp. XXI:** 112
Playing for Time (A. Miller), **Retro. Supp. III:** 174
Playing in the Dark (Morrison), **Retro. Supp. II:** 118; **Retro. Supp. III:** 184, 194; **Supp. XIII:** 185–186
"Playing the Bawd at Twenty" (Skloot), **Supp. XX:** **204–205**
Play in Poetry (Untermeyer), **Supp. XV:** 310
"Playin with Punjab" (Bambara), **Supp. XI:** 6
Play It Again Sam (Allen), **Supp. XV:** 2, 3, 14
Play It as It Lays (Didion), **Supp. IV Part 1:** 198, 201–203, 203, 211
Play It as It Lays (film), **Supp. IV Part 1:** 198
"Plays and Operas Too" (Whitman), **IV:** 350
Plays of Negro Life: A Source-Book of Native American Drama (Locke and Gregory), **Supp. XIV:** 202
Plays: Six (A. Miller), **Retro. Supp. III:** 176
Plays: Winesburg and Others (Anderson), **I:** 113
"Playthings" (Komunyakaa), **Supp. XIII:** 126
"Playtime: Danish Fun" (Larsen), **Supp. XVIII:** 120, 122–123
"Playtime: Three Scandinavian Stories" (Larsen), **Supp. XVIII:** 122–123
Playwright's Voice, The (Savran), **Supp. XIII:** 209; **Supp. XV:** 321; **Supp. XXIV:** 263
Plaza Suite (Simon), **Supp. IV Part 2:** 575, 581–582, 583, 589
"Pleaders, The" (Davison), **Supp. XXVI:** 71

Pleading Guilty (Turow), **Supp. XVII:** **218,** 219
"Plea for Captain Brown, A" (Thoreau), **IV:** 185
"Plea of a Plebeian" (H. Johnson), **Supp. XXVI:** 173
Pleasant Ways of St. Médard, The (King), **Supp. XXVIII:** 117–119, 120, 121, 122, 123
"Please" (Komunyakaa), **Supp. XIII:** 122
"Please Don't Kill Anything" (A. Miller), **III:** 161
"Please Don't Take My Sunshine Away" (Conroy), **Supp. XVI:** 69
Please Louise (Morrison and S. Morrison), **Retro. Supp. III:** 185
"Pleasure" (Very), **Supp. XXV:** 242, 244
Pleasure Dome (Frankenberg), **I:** 436
Pleasure Dome (Komunyakaa), **Supp. XIII:** 113, 121, **131–133**
Pleasure of Hope, The (Emerson), **II:** 8
"Pleasure of Ruins, The" (McClatchy), **Supp. XII:** 256
"Pleasures of Formal Poetry, The" (Bogan), **Supp. III Part 1:** 51
"Pleasures of Peace, The" (Koch), **Supp. XV:** 180
"Plea to the Protestant Churches, A" (Brooks), **Supp. XIV:** 4
Plimpton, George, **Retro. Supp. III:** 88; **Supp. IV Part 1:** 386; **Supp. IX:** 256; **Supp. V:** 201; **Supp. VIII:** 82, 157; **Supp. XI:** 294; **Supp. XIV:** 82; **Supp. XVI:** **233–248**
Pliny the Elder, **Supp. XVI:** 292
Pliny the Younger, **II:** 113
"Ploesti Isn't Long Island" (Zinberg), **Supp. XV:** 195
"Plot against the Giant, The" (Stevens), **IV:** 81
Plotinus, **Supp. XV:** 33; **Supp. XVI:** 291
Plough and the Stars, The (O'Casey), **III:** 159
"Ploughing on Sunday" (Stevens), **IV:** 74
Plowing the Dark (Powers), **Supp. IX:** 212–213, **221–224**
"Pluck"(Prouty), **Supp. XXVIII:** 180
Plum Bun (Fauset), **Supp. XIX:** 73; **Supp. XVIII:** 127
Plumed Serpent, The (Lawrence), **Supp. XV:** 46
"Plumet Basilisk, The" (Moore), **III:** 203, 208, 215
Plumly, Stanley, **Supp. IV Part 2:** 625
Plummer, Amanda, **Supp. IV Part 1:** 236
Plunder (serial movie), **Supp. IV Part 2:** 464
Plunket, Robert, **Supp. XV:** 68
Plunkett, Edward (Lord Dunsany), **Supp. XXV:** 113
"Plunkville Patriot" (O'Henry), **Supp. II Part 1:** 389
"Pluralism and Ideological Peace" (Locke), **Supp. XIV:** 202, 212
"Pluralism and Intellectual Democracy" (Locke), **Supp. XIV:** 202, 208, 212
Pluralistic Universe, A (James), **II:** 342, 348, 357–358
Plutarch, **II:** 5, 8, 16, 555; **Retro. Supp. I:** 360; **Supp. XVI:** 292

Plymell, Charles, **Supp. XIV:** 149

Plymell, Pam, **Supp. XIV:** 149

Pnin (Nabokov), **III:** 246; **Retro. Supp. I:** 263, 265, 266, 275, 335

"Po' Boy Blues" (Hughes), **Supp. I Part 1:** 327

Pocahontas, **I:** 4; **II:** 296; **III:** 584

"Pocahontas to Her English Husband, John Rolfe" (Gunn Allen), **Supp. IV Part 1:** 331

"Pocketbook and Sauerkraut" (Di Piero), **Supp. XIX:** 35, 36, 41, 42, 45

"Pocketknives" (Rash), **Supp. XXVII:** 222

"Pocket Poem" (Kooser), **Supp. XIX:** 128

Podhoretz, Norman, **IV:** 441; **Retro. Supp. II:** 323; **Supp. IV Part 1:** 382; **Supp. IX:** 3; **Supp. VIII:** 93, **231–247**; **Supp. XIV:** 103; **Supp. XXV:** 253, 268

Podnieks, Elizabeth, **Supp. X:** 189, 190, 191, 192

"Pod of the Milkweed" (Frost), **Retro. Supp. I:** 141

Podulka, Fran, **Supp. XXVI:** 6

Poe (screenplay, O'Nan), **Supp. XXV:** 154

Poe, Edgar Allan, **I:** 48, 53, 103, 190, 194, 200, 210, 211, 261, 340, 459; **II:** 74, 77, 194, 255, 273, 295, 308, 311, 313, 421, 475, 482, 530, 595; **III:** 259, **409–432**, 485, 507, 593; **IV:** 123, 129, 133, 141, 187, 261, 345, 350, 432, 438, 439, 453; **Retro. Supp. I:** 41, 273, 365, 421; **Retro. Supp. II:** 102, 104, 160, 164, 220, **261–277**, 322; **Retro. Supp. III:** 44, 194, **223–239**; **Supp. I Part 1:** 36, 309; **Supp. I Part 2:** 376, 384, 385, 388, 393, 405, 413, 421, 474, 682; **Supp. II Part 1:** 385, 410; **Supp. III Part 2:** 544, 549–550; **Supp. IV Part 1:** 80, 81, 101, 128, 341, 349; **Supp. IV Part 2:** 464, 469; **Supp. IX:** 115; **Supp. VIII:** 105; **Supp. X:** 42, 78; **Supp. XI:** 85, 293; **Supp. XIII:** 100, 111; **Supp. XV:** 275; **Supp. XVI:** 294; **Supp. XVIII:** 3, 11; **Supp. XX: 74; Supp. XXI:** 51; **Supp. XXIII:** 161, 164, 169, 177, 178; **Supp. XXIV:** 54; **Supp. XXV:** 111, 119; **Supp. XXVI:** 282; **Supp. XXVII:** 84

Poe Abroad: Influence, Reputation, Affinities (Vines), **Retro. Supp. II:** 261

"Poe-et's Nightmare, The" (Lovecraft), **Supp. XXV:** 119

Poe Log, The: A Documentary Life, 1809–1849 (Thomas and Jackson), **Retro. Supp. III:** 237

"Poem" (Bishop), **Retro. Supp. II:** 40; **Supp. I Part 1:** 73, 76–79, 82, 95

"Poem" (Harrison), **Supp. VIII:** 38

"Poem" (Justice), **Supp. VII:** 125

"Poem" (Kunitz), **Supp. III Part 1:** 263

"Poem" (Notley), **Supp. XXII:** 228–229

"Poem" (O'Hara), **Supp. XIX:** 85

"Poem" (Wright), **Supp. III Part 2:** 590

"Poem, the Snow, Jane Goodall, the Vase of Daffodils, The" (Huddle), **Supp. XXVI:** 150

"Poem, The"(Wakoski), **Supp. XXVIII:** 265

"Poem About Black Power, A" (Boyle), **Supp. XXIV:** 64

"Poem About George Doty in the Death House, A" (Wright), **Supp. III Part 2:** 594–595, 597–598

"Poem about People" (Pinsky), **Supp. VI:** 240–241, 244, 248

"Poem as Mask, The" (Rukeyser), **Supp. VI:** 281, 285

"Poem as Time Machine, The" (Gallagher), **Supp. XXIV:** 172

"Poem Beginning 'The' " (Zukofsky), **Supp. III Part 2:** 610, 611, 614

"Poem Catching Up with an Idea" (Carruth), **Supp. XVI:** 56

"Poem for a Birthday" (Plath), **Supp. I Part 2:** 539

"POEM FOR ANNA RUSS AND FANNY JONES, A" (Baraka), **Supp. II Part 1:** 58

"Poem for Black Hearts, A" (Baraka), **Supp. II Part 1:** 50

"POEM FOR DEEP THINKERS, A" (Baraka), **Supp. II Part 1:** 55

"Poem for D. H. Lawrence" (Creeley), **Supp. IV Part 1:** 141

"Poem for Don Cherry" (Mackey), **Supp. XXVII:** 154

"Poem for Dorothy, A" (Merwin), **Supp. III Part 1:** 342

"Poem for Hemingway and W. C. Williams" (Carver), **Supp. III Part 1:** 147

"Poem for my Son" (Kumin), **Supp. IV Part 2:** 442

"Poem for People Who Are Understandably Too Busy to Read Poetry" (Dunn), **Supp. XI:** 147

"Poem for Someone Killed in Spain, A" (Jarrell), **II:** 371

"Poem for the Blue Heron, A" (Oliver), **Supp. VII:** 235–236

"Poem for Two Voices" (Everwine), **Supp. XV:** 89

"Poem For Willie Best, A" (Baraka), **Supp. II Part 1:** 36

"Poem in Prose" (Bogan), **Supp. III Part 1:** 58

"Poem in the Park, The" (Davison), **Supp. XXVI:** 74

"Poem in Which I Refuse Contemplation" (Dove), **Supp. IV Part 1:** 249

"Poem Is a Walk, A" (Ammons), **Supp. VII:** 36

"Poem Like a Grenade, A" (Haines), **Supp. XII:** 204

"Poem of Flight, The" (Levine), **Supp. V:** 189

"Poem of Liberation, The" (Stern), **Supp. IX:** 292

Poem of the Cid (Merwin, trans.), **Supp. III Part 1:** 347

"Poem of the Forgotten" (Haines), **Supp. XII:** 202–203

"Poem (V (F) W)"(O'Hara), **Supp. XXIII:** 219

"Poem on a Line by Anne Sexton, 'We Are All Writing God's Poem' "(Crooker), **Supp. XXIII:** 59

"Poem on the Memorable Victory Obtained by the Gallant Captain Paul Jones" (Freneau), **Supp. II Part 1:** 261

"Poem out of Childhood" (Rukeyser), **Supp. VI:** 272, 277

Poem-Paintings (O'Hara and Bluhm), **Supp. XXIII:** 217

"Poem Read at the Dinner Given to the Author by the Medical Profession" (Holmes), **Supp. I Part 1:** 310–311

Poems (Auden), **Supp. II Part 1:** 6

Poems (Berryman), **I:** 170

Poems (Bryant), **II:** 311; **Supp. I Part 1:** 155, 157

Poems (Cummings), **I:** 430, 447

Poems (E. Stoddard), **Supp. XV:** 274

Poems (Eliot), **I:** 580, 588; **IV:** 122; **Retro. Supp. I:** 59, 291

Poems (Emerson), **II:** 7, 8, 12–13, 17

Poems (Holmes), **Supp. I Part 1:** 303

Poems (J. R. Lowell), **Supp. I Part 2:** 405

Poems (Koch), **Supp. XV:** 179

Poems (Moore), **III:** 194, 205, 215

Poems (Poe), **III:** 411; **Retro. Supp. III:** 224, 231

Poems (Reznikoff), **Supp. XIV:** 282, 283, 284, 285

Poems (Tate), **IV:** 121

Poems (W. C. Williams), **Retro. Supp. I:** 412–413, 416, 424

Poems (W. J. Smith), **Supp. XIII:** 332

Poems (Williams), **Supp. XXIV:** 35

Poems (Winters), **Supp. II Part 2:** 809, 810

Poems (Wordsworth), **I:** 468

Poems, 1909–1925 (Eliot), **Retro. Supp. I:** 64

Poems, 1924–1933 (MacLeish), **III:** 7, 15

Poems, 1943–1956 (Wilbur), **Supp. III Part 2:** 554

Poems, 1953–58 (W. Stone), **Supp. XXVII:** 254

Poems, The (Freneau), **Supp. II Part 1:** 263

Poems 1918–1975 : The Complete Poems of Charles Reznikoff (Cooney, ed.), **Supp. XIV:** 289

Poems 1940–1953 (Shapiro), **Supp. II Part 2:** 703, 711

Poems 1947–1954 (Kees), **Supp. XV:** 147

Poems: 1947–1957 (W. J. Smith), **Supp. XIII:** 333

Poems 1957–1967 (Dickey), **Supp. IV Part 1:** 178, 181

Poems about God (Ransom), **III:** 484, 486, 491; **IV:** 121

"Poems about Painting" (Snodgrass), **Supp. VI:** 316

Poems and Essays (Ransom), **III:** 486, 490, 492

Poems and New Poems (Bogan), **Supp. III Part 1:** 60–62

"Poems and Places" (Haines), **Supp. XII:** 203

Poems and Poetry of Europe, The (Longfellow, ed.), **Retro. Supp. II:** 155

Poems by Emily Dickinson (Todd and Higginson, eds.), **I:** 469, 470; **Retro. Supp. I:** 35, 39

Poems by Emily Dickinson, Second Series (Todd and Higginson, eds.), **I:** 454; **Retro. Supp. I:** 35

Poems by Emily Dickinson, The (Bianchi and Hampson, eds.), **Retro. Supp. I:** 35

Poems by Emily Dickinson, Third Series (Todd, ed.), **Retro. Supp. I:** 35

Poems by James Russell Lowell, Second Series (J. R. Lowell), **Supp. I Part 2:** 406, 409

Poems by Sidney Lanier, (Lanier), **Supp. I Part 1:** 364

Poems from Black Africa (Hughes, ed.), **Supp. I Part 1:** 344

"Poems I Have Lost, The" (Ortiz), **Supp. IV Part 2:** 507

Poems: North & South–A Cold Spring, (Bishop), **Supp. I Part 1:** 83, 89

Poems of a Jew (Shapiro), **Supp. II Part 2:** 703, 712–713

"Poems of a Mountain Recluse" (Budbill), **Supp. XIX:** 9, 10

Poems of Anna Akhmatova, The (Kunitz and Hayward, trans.), **Supp. III Part 1:** 269

Poems of Emily Dickinson, The (Bianchi and Hampson, eds.), **Retro. Supp. I:** 35

Poems of Emily Dickinson, The (T. H. Johnson, ed.), **I:** 470

Poems of François Villon (Kinnell, trans.), **Supp. III Part 1:** 235, 243, 249

"Poems of Our Climate, The" (Stevens), **Retro. Supp. I:** 313

Poems of Peter Davison, The (Davison), **Supp. XXVI:** 66, 78

Poems of Philip Freneau, Written Chiefly during the Late War (Freneau), **Supp. II Part 1:** 261

Poems of Places (Longfellow, ed.), **II:** 490; **Retro. Supp. II:** 155; **Supp. I Part 1:** 368

Poems of Stanley Kunitz, The (Kunitz), **Supp. III Part 1:** 258, 263, 264, 266, 268

"Poems of These States" (Ginsberg), **Supp. II Part 1:** 323, 325

Poems of Two Friends (Howells and Piatt), **II:** 273, 277

"POEM SOME PEOPLE WILL HAVE TO UNDERSTAND, A" (Baraka), **Supp. II Part 1:** 49

Poems on Slavery (Longfellow), **II:** 489; **Retro. Supp. II:** 157, 168; **Supp. I Part 2:** 406

Poems on Various Subjects (Rowson), **Supp. XV:** 232

Poems on Various Subjects, Religious and Moral (Wheatley), **Supp. XX: 277, 282, 284, 285, 289**

Poem Spoken at the Public Commencement at Yale College, in New Haven; September 1, 1781, A (Barlow), **Supp. II Part 1:** 67–68, 74, 75

Poems Retrieved (O'Hara), **Supp. XXIII:** 220

Poems: Selected and New, 1950–1974 (Rich), **Retro. Supp. III:** 247

Poems to Solve (Swenson), **Supp. IV Part 2:** 642

Poems Written and Published during the American Revolutionary War (Freneau), **Supp. II Part 1:** 273, 274

Poems Written between the Years 1768 and 1794 (Freneau), **Supp. II Part 1:** 269

"Poem That Took the Place of a Mountain" (Olson), **Supp. II Part 2:** 582

"Poem to My First Lover" (Olds), **Supp. X:** 206

"Poem to the Reader" (Olds), **Supp. X:** 213

"Poem with No Ending, A" (Levine), **Supp. V:** 186, 190

"Poem You Asked For, The" (Levis), **Supp. XI:** 259–260

Poe Poe Poe Poe Poe Poe Poe (Hoffman), **Retro. Supp. II:** 265

Poesía Náhuatl, **Supp. XV:** 77

Poésies 1917–1920 (Cocteau), **Retro. Supp. I:** 82

"Poesis: A Conceit" (Sobin), **Supp. XVI:** 288

"Poet" (Taggard), **Supp. XXII:** 284

Poet, The (Connelly), **Supp. XXI: 71,** 78

"Poet, The" (Dunbar), **Supp. II Part 1:** 207, 209–210

"Poet, The" (Emerson), **II:** 13, 19, 20, 170; **Retro. Supp. III:** 301

"Poet, The" (Ortiz), **Supp. IV Part 2:** 505

"Poet and His Book, The" (Millay), **III:** 126, 138

"Poet and His Public, The" (Jarrell), **Supp. I Part 1:** 96

"Poet and His Song, The" (Dunbar), **Supp. II Part 1:** 199

"Poet and the Person, The" (Kinard), **Supp. XIV:** 127

"Poet and the Queen, The" (Shaw), **Supp. XIX:** 241

"Poet and the World, The" (Cowley), **Supp. II Part 1:** 145

"Poet as Anti-Specialist, The" (Swenson), **Supp. IV Part 2:** 638, 643

"Poet as *Curandera*" (Mora), **Supp. XIII:** 214, 220

"Poet as Hero, The: Keats in His Letters" (Trilling), **Supp. III Part 2:** 506–507

"Poet as Religious Moralist, The" (Larson), **Supp. XI:** 328

"Poet at Seven, The" (Rimbaud), **II:** 545

Poet at the Breakfast-Table, The (Holmes), **Supp. I Part 1:** 313–314

"Poète contumace, Le" (Corbiere), **II:** 384–385

"Poet for President, A" (Mora), **Supp. XIII:** 220–221

Poetic Achievement of Ezra Pound, The (Alexander), **Retro. Supp. I:** 293

Poetic Diction: A Study in Meaning (Barfield), **III:** 274, 279

"Poetic Principle, The" (Poe), **III:** 421, 426; **Retro. Supp. II:** 266; **Retro.**

Supp. III: 225, 234

"Poetics" (Ammons), **Supp. VII:** 29–30

Poetics (Aristotle), **III:** 422; **Supp. XI:** 249; **Supp. XIII:** 75; **Supp. XIV:** 243; **Supp. XV:** 265

Poetics of Space, The (Bachelard), **Supp. XIII:** 225; **Supp. XVI:** 292

"Poetics of the Periphery: Literary Experimentalism in Kathy Acker's *In Memoriam to Identity*" (Acker), **Supp. XII:** 17

"Poetics of the Physical World, The" (Kinnell), **Supp. III Part 1:** 239

"Poetics of Tourette Syndrome, The: Language, Neurobiology, and Poetry" (Schleifer), **Supp. XVIII:** 144

Poet in the World, The (Levertov), **Supp. III Part 1:** 271, 273, 278, 282

"Poet or the Growth of a Lit'ry Figure" (White), **Supp. I Part 2:** 676

Poetry (Barber), **Supp. IV Part 2:** 550

"Poetry" (Moore), **III:** 204–205, 215

"Poetry" (Nye), **Supp. XIII:** 282

"Poetry" (Wrigley), **Supp. XVIII:** 301–302

"Poetry, Community and Climax" (Snyder), **Supp. VIII:** 290

"Poetry, Pleasure, and the Hedonist Reader" (Collins), **Supp. XXI:** 54

"Poetry: A Metrical Essay" (Holmes), **Supp. I Part 1:** 310

"Poetry and Belief in Thomas Hardy" (Schwartz), **Supp. II Part 2:** 666

Poetry and Criticism (Nemerov, ed.), **III:** 269

"Poetry and Drama" (Eliot), **I:** 588

Poetry and Fiction: Essays (Nemerov), **III:** 269, 281

"Poetry and Place" (Berry), **Supp. X:** 22, 28, 31, 32

Poetry and Poets (A. Lowell), **II:** 512

"Poetry and Religion" (Jarman), **Supp. XVII:** 111

Poetry and the Age (Jarrell), **IV:** 352; **Retro. Supp. I:** 121; **Supp. II Part 1:** 135

"Poetry and the Primitive: Notes on Poetry as an Ecological Survival Technique" (Snyder), **Supp. VIII:** 291, 292, 299, 300

"Poetry and the Public World" (MacLeish), **III:** 11

Poetry and the World (Pinsky), **Supp. VI:** 236, 239, 244, 247

Poetry and Truth (Olson), **Supp. II Part 2:** 583

"Poetry and Uncertainty"(Hirshfield), **Supp. XXIII:** 137

"Poetry As a Way of Life" (Bishop interview), **Retro. Supp. II:** 53

"Poetry as Survival" (Harrison), **Supp. VIII:** 45

"Poetry Baron, The" (Gallagher), **Supp. XXIV:** 166, 177

"Poetry Failure" (Halliday), **Supp. XIX:** 92

Poetry for Students (Taibl), **Supp. XV:** 255

"Poetry for the Advanced" (Baraka), **Supp. II Part 1:** 58

"Poetry Friendship on Earth" (Halliday), **Supp. XIX:** 90, 91

Poetry Handbook, A (Oliver), **Supp. VII:** 229, 245

Poetry Home Repair Manual, The (Kooser), **Supp. XIX:** 116, 128

Poetry in Motion (film), **Supp. XXIV:** 33

Poetry in Motion: 100 Poems from the Subways and Buses (Peacock, ed.), **Supp. XIX:** 195

"Poetry in Translation: Literary Imperialism or, Defending the Musk Ox" (Gallagher), **Supp. XXIV:** 172

"Poetry of Barbarism, The" (Santayana), **IV:** 353

Poetry of Chaucer, The (Gardner), **Supp. VI:** 63

Poetry of Meditation, The (Martz), **IV:** 151; **Supp. I Part 1:** 107

Poetry of Mourning: The Modern Elegy from Hardy to Heaney (Ramazani), **Supp. IV Part 2:** 450

Poetry of Stephen Crane, The (Hoffman), **I:** 405

Poetry of the Negro, 1746–1949, The (Hughes and Bontemps), **Supp. I Part 1:** 345; **Supp. XXII:** 11

Poetry 180: A Turning Back to Poetry (Collins, ed.), **Supp. XXI:** 54

Poetry Reading against the Vietnam War, A (Bly and Ray, eds.), **Supp. IV Part 1:** 61, 63

"Poetry Workshop, The" (column, Kumin), **Supp. XX: 164**

"Poetry Wreck, The" (Shapiro), **Supp. II Part 2:** 717

Poetry Wreck, The: Selected Essays (Shapiro), **Supp. II Part 2:** 703, 704, 717

"Poets" (X. J. Kennedy), **Supp. XV:** 158

Poet's Alphabet, A: Reflections on the Literary Art and Vocation (Bogan), **Supp. III Part 1:** 55, 64

Poets and Poetry of America (Griswold), **Supp. XV:** 277; **Supp. XXV:** 250

Poets and Poetry of America, The (Griswold), **Retro. Supp. III:** 236

Poet's Choice (Engle and Langland, eds.), **III:** 277, 542

Poet's Guide to Poetry, A (Kinzie), **Supp. XXIII:** 124

"Poet's Husband Engages in Gourmet Cooking, The" (Espaillat), **Supp. XXI:** 99

Poets of the Old Testament, The (Gordon), **III:** 199

Poets of Today (Hall, ed.), **Supp. XXVII:** 253, 256

Poets of Today (Wheelock, ed.), **Supp. IV Part 2:** 639

Poets on Poetry (Nemerov, ed.), **III:** 269

"Poet's Tact, and a Necessary Tactlessness, The" (C. Frost), **Supp. XV:** 94–95

"Poet's View, A" (Levertov), **Supp. III Part 1:** 284

"Poet's Voice, The" (Oliver), **Supp. VII:** 245

"Poets with History and Poets Without History"(Tsvetaeva), **Supp. XXIII:** 168

"Poet Turns on Himself, The" (Dickey), **Supp. IV Part 1:** 177, 181, 185

Poganuc People (Stowe), **Supp. I Part 2:** 581, 596, 599–600

Pogo (comic strip), **Supp. XI:** 105

Pohl, R. D., **Supp. XXVI:** 102

Pohrt, Tom, **Supp. XIX:** 123

Poincaré, Raymond, **IV:** 320

"Point, The" (Hayden), **Supp. II Part 1:** 373

"Point at Issue!, A" (Chopin), **Retro. Supp. II:** 61; **Supp. I Part 1:** 208

"Point of Age, A" (Berryman), **I:** 173

Point of No Return (Marquand), **III:** 56, 59–60, 65, 67, 69

Point Reyes Poems (R. Bly), **Supp. IV Part 1:** 71

"Points" (Hoffman), **Supp. XVIII:** 86

Points for a Compass Rose (Connell), **Supp. XIV:** 79, 80, 96

"Point Shirley" (Plath), **Supp. I Part 2:** 529, 538

Points in Time (Bowles), **Supp. IV Part 1:** 93

"Points West" (column), **Supp. IV Part 1:** 198

Poirier, Richard, **I:** 136, 239; **III:** 34; **Retro. Supp. I:** 134; **Retro. Supp. II:** 207–208; **Retro. Supp. III:** 102; **Supp. I Part 2:** 660, 665; **Supp. IV Part 2:** 690

"Poison Oak" (Huddle), **Supp. XXVI:** 148, 152

Poison Pen (Garrett), **Supp. VII:** 111

Poisonwood Bible, The (Kingsolver), **Supp. VII:** 197–198, 202, 210–213

Poitier, Sidney, **Supp. IV Part 1:** 360, 362

Pokerface (Collins), **Supp. XXI:** 53

"Polack Reverie" (Halliday), **Supp. XIX:** 88

Polanco, Richard, **Supp. XX: 260**

"Polar Bear" (Heller), **Supp. IV Part 1:** 383

"Polar Bears and Others" (Boyle), **Supp. XXIV:** 57

"Polar Seas and Sir John Franklin, The" (Briggs), **Supp. XVIII:** 14

Pole, Rupert, **Supp. X:** 185

"Pole Star" (MacLeish), **III:** 16

Po Li, **Supp. I Part 1:** 262

Police (Baraka), **Supp. II Part 1:** 47

"Police" (Corso), **Supp. XII:** 117, 127

"Police Court Saturday Morning" (X. J. Kennedy), **Supp. XV:** 170

"Police Dreams" (Bausch), **Supp. VII:** 47

Politian (Poe), **III:** 412; **Retro. Supp. III:** 234

"Political and Practical Conceptions of Race, The" (Locke), **Supp. XIV:** 209–210

Political Essays (J. R. Lowell), **Supp. I Part 2:** 407

Political Fable, A (Coover), **Supp. V:** 44, 46, 47, 49, 51

"Political Fables" (Mather), **Supp. II Part 2:** 450

"Political Interests" (Stevens), **Retro. Supp. I:** 295

"Political Litany, A" (Freneau), **Supp. II Part 1:** 257

"Political Migrations: A Family Story" (Mallon), **Supp. XIX:** 141–142

"Political Pastoral" (Frost), **Retro. Supp. I:** 139

"Political Poem" (Baraka), **Supp. II Part 1:** 36

Politics (Acker), **Supp. XII:** 3, 4

Politics (Macdonald), **I:** 233–234

"Politics" (Paley), **Supp. VI:** 217

"Politics, Structure, and Poetic Development" (McCombs), **Supp. XIII:** 33

"Politics and the English Language" (Orwell), **Retro. Supp. II:** 287; **Supp. I Part 2:** 620

Politics and the Novel (Howe), **Supp. VI:** 113

"Politics and the Personal Lyric in the Poetry of Joy Harjo and C. D. Wright" (Goodman), **Supp. XV:** 344

"Politics of Ethnic Authorship, The: Li-Young Lee, Emerson, and Whitman at the Banquet Table" (Partridge), **Supp. XV:** 219

"Politics of Silence, The" (Monette), **Supp. X:** 148

Polito, Robert, **Supp. XVIII:** 33; **Supp. XXIV:** 234; **Supp. XXVI:** 55; **Supp. XXVIII:** 284

Politt, Katha, **Supp. XII:** 159

Poliziano (Angelo Ambrogini), **Supp. XXIV:** 152

Polk, James, **Supp. XIII:** 20

Polk, James K., **I:** 17; **II:** 433–434

Pollack, Sydney, **Supp. XIII:** 159

"Pollen" (Nye), **Supp. XIII:** 284

Pollitt, Katha, **Supp. X:** 186, 191, 193; **Supp. XVI:** 39

Pollock, Jackson, **IV:** 411, 420; **Supp. XIX:** 33; **Supp. XV:** 145, 177, 178; **Supp. XXIII:** 208, 210, 211

"Polly" (Chopin), **Retro. Supp. II:** 72

Polo, Marco, **III:** 395

Polonsky, Abraham, **Supp. XXI:** 261, 275

Polybius, **Supp. I Part 2:** 491

"Polydore" (Chopin), **Retro. Supp. II:** 66

"Pomegranate" (Glück), **Supp. V:** 82

"Pomegranate Seed" (Wharton), **IV:** 316; **Retro. Supp. I:** 382

Ponce de Leon, Luis, **III:** 391

"Pond, The" (Nemerov), **III:** 272

"Pond at Dusk, The" (Kenyon), **Supp. VII:** 168

Ponder Heart, The (Welty), **IV:** 261, 274–275, 281; **Retro. Supp. I:** 351–352

"Ponderosa Pine" (Huncke), **Supp. XIV:** 146

Ponsot, Margaret, **Supp. XVII:** 241

"Pony" (Sanders), **Supp. XVI:** 277

"Pony Car"(P. Benedict), **Supp. XXIII:** 47

Poodle Springs (Parker and Chandler), **Supp. IV Part 1:** 135; **Supp. XIX:** 189

Poodle Springs Story, The (Chandler), **Supp. IV Part 1:** 135

"Pool, The" (Doolittle), **Supp. I Part 1:** 264–265

Poole, Ernest, **II:** 444

"Pool Lights" (F. Barthelme), **Supp. XI:** 25, 26–27, 36

"Pool Room in the Lions Club" (Merwin), **Supp. III Part 1:** 346

"Poolside" (Skloot), **Supp. XX: 202–203**

"Poor Black Fellow" (Hughes), **Retro. Supp. I:** 204

"Poor Bustard, The" (Corso), **Supp. XII:** 134

"Poor but Happy" (Mamet), **Supp. XIV:** 252, 253

"Poor Dead Feet of My First Husband, The"(Schott), **Supp. XXIII:** 241

Poore, Charles, **III:** 364; **Supp. XIX:** 257, 264; **Supp. XX:** 38

Poor Fool (Caldwell), **I:** 291, 292, 308

"Poor Fool Blues"(Lea), **Supp. XXVIII:** 137

Poorhouse Fair, The (Updike), **IV:** 214, 228–229, 232; **Retro. Supp. I:** 317, 320

"Poor Joanna" (Jewett), **II:** 394

"Poor Man's Pudding and Rich Man's Crumbs" (Melville), **III:** 89–90

"Poor Richard" (James), **II:** 322

Poor Richard's Almanac for 1733 (Franklin), **II:** 108, 110

Poor Richard's Almanac for 1739 (Franklin), **II:** 112

Poor Richard's Almanac for 1758 (Franklin), **II:** 101

Poor Richard's Almanac (undated) (Franklin), **II:** 112

Poor White (Anderson), **I:** 110–111

"Poor Working Girl" (Z. Fitzgerald), **Supp. IX:** 71

Popa, Vasko, **Supp. VIII:** 272

Pope, Alexander, **I:** 198, 204; **II:** 17, 114; **III:** 263, 267, 288, 517; **IV:** 145; **Retro. Supp. I:** 335; **Supp. I Part 1:** 150, 152, 310; **Supp. I Part 2:** 407, 422, 516, 714; **Supp. II Part 1:** 70, 71; **Supp. X:** 32, 36; **Supp. XII:** 260; **Supp. XV:** 258; **Supp. XX: 280;** **Supp. XXV:** 119; **Supp. XXVI:** 284

Pope, James, **Supp. XXII:** 196

Pope-Hennessy, James, **Supp. XIV:** 348

"Pope's Penis, The" (Olds), **Supp. X:** 207

"Poplar, Sycamore" (Wilbur), **Supp. III Part 2:** 549

Popo and Fifina: Children of Haiti (Hughes and Bontemps), **Retro. Supp. I:** 203; **Supp. XXII:** 4, 10, 12

"Poppies" (Oliver), **Supp. VII:** 240

"Poppies in July" (Plath), **Supp. I Part 2:** 544

"Poppies in July"(Crooker), **Supp. XXIII:** 61

"Poppies in October" (Plath), **Supp. I Part 2:** 544

"Poppycock" (Francis), **Supp. IX:** 87

"Poppy Juice" (Taggard), **Supp. XXII:** 276

"Poppy Seed" (A. Lowell), **II:** 523

"Popular Art and the Cultural Tradition" (C. L. R. James), **Supp. XXI:** 170

Popular Book, The: A History of America's Literary Taste (Hart), **Supp. XVIII:** 257, 258

Popular Culture (Goldbarth), **Supp. XII: 186**

Popular History of the United States (Gay), **Supp. I Part 1:** 158

Popular Problems (album, Cohen), **Supp. XXVII:** 63

"Popular Songs" (Ashbery), **Supp. III Part 1:** 6

"Populist Manifesto" (Ferlinghetti), **Supp. VIII:** 290

"Porcelain Bowl" (Glück), **Supp. V:** 83

Porcher, Frances, **Retro. Supp. II:** 71

Porco, Mike, **Supp. XVIII:** 24

"Porcupine, The" (Kinnell), **Supp. III Part 1:** 244

Porcupine's Kiss, The (Dobyns), **Supp. XIII: 89–90**

"Por esas coases que pasan" (Hinojosa), **Supp. XIX:** 101

Porgy and Bess (film), **Supp. I Part 1:** 66

Porgy and Bess (play), **Supp. IV Part 1:** 6

"Porn Bought my Football" (Offutt), **Supp. XIX:** 163

"Porphyria's Lover" (Browning), **II:** 522

Portable Beat Reader, The (Charters, ed.), **Supp. XIV:** 152

Portable Blake, The (Kazin, ed.), **Supp. VIII:** 103

Portable Faulkner, The (Cowley, ed.), **II:** 57, 59; **Retro. Supp. I:** 73

Portable Kisses: Love Poems (Gallagher), **Supp. XXIV:** 170

Portable Paul and Jane Bowles, The (Dillon), **Supp. IV Part 1:** 95

Portable Veblen, The (Veblen), **Supp. I Part 2:** 630, 650

"Porte-Cochere" (Taylor), **Supp. V:** 320

"Porter" (Hughes), **Supp. I Part 1:** 327

"Porter" (Nelson), **Supp. XVIII:** 175

Porter, Bern, **III:** 171

Porter, Cole, **Supp. IX:** 189

Porter, Eliot, **Supp. IV Part 2:** 599

Porter, Fairfield, **Supp. XV:** 178; **Supp. XXIII:** 209, 211, 212; **Supp. XXIV:** 41; **Supp. XXVII:** 21

Porter, Herman W., **Supp. I Part 1:** 49

Porter, Horace, **Retro. Supp. II:** 4, 127

Porter, Jacob, **Supp. I Part 1:** 153

Porter, Katherine Anne, **I:** 97, 385; **II:** 194, 606; **III: 433–455,** 482; **IV:** 26, 138, 246, 261, 279, 280, 282; **Retro. Supp. I:** 354; **Retro. Supp. II:** 233, 235; **Retro. Supp. III:** 36, 37, 53; **Supp. IV Part 1:** 31, 310; **Supp. IX:** 93, 94, 95, 98, 128; **Supp. V:** 225; **Supp. VIII:** 156, 157; **Supp. X:** 50; **Supp. XIII:** 294; **Supp. XIV:** 3; **Supp. XV:** 338; **Supp. XXIV:** 52; **Supp. XXVI:** 23; **Supp. XXVIII:** 68

Porter, Nicodemus, **Supp. XXVI:** 87

Porter, Noah, **Supp. I Part 2:** 640

Porter, William Sydney. *See* Henry, O.

"Porter Paints a Picture"(O'Hara), **Supp. XXIII:** 212

Porteus, Beilby, **Supp. I Part 1:** 150

Portis, Rowe, **Supp. XXVI:** 147

"Portland Going Out, The" (Merwin), **Supp. III Part 1:** 345

Portnoy's Complaint (P. Roth), **Retro. Supp. II: 282–286,** 291; **Supp. III Part 2:** 401, 404, 405, 407, 412–414, 426; **Supp. V:** 119, 122; **Supp. XI:** 140; **Supp. XVII:** 8, 43; **Supp. XX:** 177; **Supp. XXVII:** 142

Port of Saints (Burroughs), **Supp. III Part 1:** 106

"Portrait" (Dixon), **Supp. XII:** 154

"Portrait, A" (Parker), **Supp. IX:** 192–193

"Portrait, The" (Kunitz), **Supp. III Part 1:** 263

"Portrait, The" (Wharton), **Retro. Supp. I:** 364

"Portrait d'une Femme" (Pound), **Retro. Supp. I:** 288

Portrait in Brownstone (Auchincloss), **Supp. IV Part 1:** 21, 23, 27, 31

"Portrait in Georgia" (Toomer), **Supp. IX:** 314

"Portrait in Greys, A" (W. C. Williams), **Retro. Supp. I:** 416

"Portrait of a Girl in Glass" (T. Williams), **IV:** 383

"Portrait of a Jewelry Drummer" (Untermeyer), **Supp. XV:** 299–300

"Portrait of a Lady" (T. S. Eliot), **I:** 569, 570, 571, 584; **III:** 4; **Retro. Supp. I:** 55, 56, 62; **Retro. Supp. III:** 60–61

Portrait of a Lady, The (James), **I:** 10, 258, 461–462, 464; **II:** 323, 325, 327, 328–329, 334; **Retro. Supp. I:** 215, 216, 217, 219, 220, 223, **224–225,** 232, 233, 381

"Portrait of an Artist" (P. Roth), **Supp. III Part 2:** 412

Portrait of an Eye: Three Novels (Acker), **Supp. XII:** 6, **7–9**

"Portrait of an Invisible Man" (Auster), **Supp. XII:** 21

"Portrait of a Supreme Court Judge" (Untermeyer), **Supp. XV:** 299

Portrait of Bascom Hawkes, A (Wolfe), **IV:** 451–452, 456

Portrait of Edith Wharton (Lubbock), **Retro. Supp. I:** 366

Portrait of Logan Pearsall Smith, Drawn from His Letters and Diaries, A (Russell, ed.), **Supp. XIV:** 349

Portrait of Picasso as a Young Man (Mailer), **Retro. Supp. II:** 213

"Portrait of the Artist as an Old Man, A" (Humphrey), **Supp. IX:** 109

Portrait of the Artist as a Young Man, A (Joyce), **I:** 475–476; **III:** 471, 561; **Retro. Supp. I:** 127; **Retro. Supp. II:** 4, 331; **Supp. IX:** 236; **Supp. XIII:** 53, 95

"Portrait of the Artist with Hart Crane" (Wright), **Supp. V:** 342

"Portrait of the Great White Hunter Fox-hunting in the Absence of Big Game" (Major), **Supp. XXII:** 183

"Portrait of the Intellectual as a Yale Man" (McCarthy), **II:** 563, 564–565

"Portrait of the Reader with a Bowl of Cereal, A" (Collins), **Supp. XXI:** 55

"Portrait of the Self . . . , A" (Sobin), **Supp. XVI:** 288

Portraits and Elegies (Schnackenberg), **Supp. XV:** 249, **253–256**

"Portraits of Grief" *(New York Times),* **Supp. XIX:** 142

"Port Town" (Hughes), **Retro. Supp. I:** 199

Portuguese Voyages to America in the Fifteenth Century (Morison), **Supp. I Part 2:** 488

"Po' Sandy" (Chesnutt), **Supp. XIV:** 60

Poseidon Adventure, The (film), **Supp. XII:** 321

Poseidon Adventure, The (Gallico), **Supp. XVI:** 238

"Poseidon and Company" (Carver), **Supp. III Part 1:** 137

"Positive Obsession" (O. Butler), **Supp. XIII:** 70

Poss, Stanley, **Supp. XIV:** 166

Possession (Byatt), **Supp. XXI:** 147

"Possessions" (H. Crane), **I:** 392–393; **Retro. Supp. II:** 78

Possible World, A (Koch), **Supp. XV:** 184

Postal Inspector (film), **Supp. XIII:** 166

"Postcard from Greece" (Stallings), **Supp. XXV:** 229, 231

Postcards (Proulx), **Supp. VII:** 249, 256–258, 262

"Postcard to Send to Sumer, A" (Bronk), **Supp. XXI:** 31

"Postcolonialism and Autobiography" (Skinner and Waller), **Supp. XXII:** 78

"Postcolonial Tale, A" (Harjo), **Supp. XII:** 227

"Posthumous Letter to Gilbert White" (Auden), **Supp. II Part 1:** 26

"Post-Larkin Triste" (Karr), **Supp. XI:** 242–243

Postlethwaite, Diana, **Supp. XII:** 317–318; **Supp. XVI:** 176

"Postlude" (W. C. Williams), **Retro. Supp. I:** 415

Post-Luria, Sheila, **Retro. Supp. III:** 158, 160

Postman, Neil, **Supp. XI:** 275

Postman Always Rings Twice, The (Cain), **Supp. XIII:** 165–166

Postman Always Rings Twice, The (film), **Supp. XIV:** 241

"Postmaster and the Clerk, The" (Budbill), **Supp. XIX:** 9

"Postmortem Guide, A" (Dunn), **Supp. XI:** 155

Post Oaks and Sand Roughs (Howard), **Supp. XXVII:** 116

Postrel, Virginia, **Supp. XIV:** 298, 311

"Postscript" (Du Bois), **Supp. II Part 1:** 173

"Postscript" (Nye), **Supp. XIII:** 287

Postsouthern Sense of Place, The (Bone), **Supp. XXII:** 247

"Potato" (Wilbur), **Supp. III Part 2:** 545

"Potatoes' Dance, The" (Lindsay), **Supp. I Part 2:** 394

Pot of Earth, The (MacLeish), **III:** 5, 6–8, 10, 12, 18

Potok, Chaim, **Supp. XXVI:** 124

"Pot Roast" (Strand), **Supp. IV Part 2:** 629

Potshot (Parker), **Supp. XIX:** 185

Pot Shots at Poetry (Francis), **Supp. IX: 83–84**

Potter, Beatrix, **Supp. I Part 2:** 656; **Supp. XVI:** 100

Potter, Stephen, **IV:** 430

Potter's House, The (Stegner), **Supp. IV Part 2:** 598, 606

Poulenc, Francis, **Supp. IV Part 1:** 81

Poulin, Al, Jr., **Supp. IX:** 272; **Supp. XI:** 259

Pound, Ezra, **I:** 49, 58, 60, 66, 68, 69, 105, 236, 243, 256, 384, 403, 428, 429, 475, 476, 482, 487, 521, 578; **II:** 26, 55, 168, 263, 316, 371, 376, 513, 517, 520, 526, 528, 529, 530; **III:** 2, 5, 8, 9, 13–14, 17, 174, 194, 196, 278, 430, 453, **456–479**, 492, 504, 511, 523, 524, 527, 575–576, 586, 590; **IV:** 27, 28, 407, 415, 416, 433, 446; **Retro. Supp. I:** 51, 52, 55, 58, 59, 63, 82, 89, 127, 140, 171, 177, 178, 198, 216, **283–294**, 298, 299, 359, 411, 412, 413, 414, 417, 418, 419, 420, 423, 426, 427, 430, 431; **Retro. Supp. II:** 178, 183, 189, 326; **Retro. Supp. III:** 58, 59, 74, 96; **Supp. I Part 1:** 253, 255–258, 261–268, 272, 274; **Supp. I Part 2:** 387, 721; **Supp. II Part 1:** 1, 8, 20, 30, 91, 136; **Supp. III Part 1:** 48, 63, 64, 73, 105, 146, 225, 271; **Supp. III Part 2:** 542, **609–617**, 619, 620, 622, 625, 626, 628, 631; **Supp. IV Part 1:** 153, 314; **Supp. IX:** 291; **Supp. V:** 331, 338, 340, 343, 345; **Supp. VIII:** 39, 105, 195, 205, 271, 290, 291, 292, 303; **Supp. X:** 24, 36, 112, 120, 122; **Supp. XII:** 97; **Supp. XIV:** 11, 55, 83, 272, 284, 286, 287, 347; **Supp. XIX:** 42; **Supp. XV:** 20, 42, 43, 51, 93, 161, 181, 297, 298, 299, 301, 302, 306; **Supp. XVI:** 47, 282; **Supp. XVII:** 111, 226–227; **Supp. XXI:** 33; **Supp. XXII:** 165; **Supp. XXIII:** 26, 166, 174; **Supp. XXIV:** 37; **Supp. XXVI:** 143, 144, 224, 226; **Supp. XXVII:** 261, 284, 287, 288

Pound, Louise, **Retro. Supp. I:** 4; **Supp. XV:** 137

Pound, T. S., **I:** 428

"Pound Reweighed" (Cowley), **Supp. II Part 1:** 143

Powell, Anthony, **Supp. XIX:** 131; **Supp. XVIII:** 136, 146

Powell, Betty, **Retro. Supp. II:** 140

Powell, D. A., **Supp. XXIII:** 221

Powell, Dawn, **Supp. IV Part 2:** 678, 682; **Supp. XIX:** 143

Powell, Dick, **Supp. IX:** 250

Powell, John Wesley, **Supp. IV Part 2:** 598, 604, 611

Powell, Lawrence Clark, **III:** 189

Powell, Margaret K., **Supp. XXIV:** 170

Powell, William, **Supp. IV Part 1:** 355

"Power" (Corso), **Supp. XII:** 117, 126, 127, **128**

"Power" (Emerson), **II:** 2, 3

"Power" (Rich), **Retro. Supp. III:** 249; **Supp. I Part 2:** 569

Power, Samantha, **Supp. XXIII:** 25, 26, 27

"Power and Danger: Works of a Common Woman" (Rich), **Retro. Supp. III:** 248

"Power and Light" (Dickey), **Supp. IV Part 1:** 182

Power and the Glory, The (Greene), **III:** 556

"Powerhouse" (Welty), **Retro. Supp. I:** 343, 346

"Power Never Dominion" (Rukeyser), **Supp. VI:** 281

"Power of Fancy, The" (Freneau), **Supp. II Part 1:** 255

Power of Myth, The (Campbell), **Supp. IX:** 245

"Power of Prayer, The" (Lanier), **Supp. I Part 1:** 357

"Power of Stories, The" (Sanders), **Supp. XVI:** 278

"Power of Suggestion" (Auchincloss), **Supp. IV Part 1:** 33

Power of Sympathy, The (W. H. Brown), **Supp. II Part 1:** 74; **Supp. XXV:** 38

Power Politics (Atwood), **Supp. XIII:** 20, 33–34, 35

Powers, Catherine A., **Supp. XXII:** 217

Powers, J. F., **Supp. V:** 319; **Supp. XVII:** 43

Powers, Kim, **Supp. VIII:** 329, 340

Powers, Richard, **Supp. IX: 207–225; Supp. XVII:** 183; **Supp. XX: 93; Supp. XXII:** 49; **Supp. XXIV:** 131

Powers of Attorney (Auchincloss), **Supp. IV Part 1:** 31, 32, 33

"Powers of Darkness" (Wharton), **Retro. Supp. I:** 379

"Powers of Recuperation" (Rich), **Retro. Supp. III:** 252

Powless, Peter, **Supp. XXVI:** 87

Powys, John Cowper, **Supp. I Part 2:** 454, 476; **Supp. IX:** 135

Poynton, Jerome, **Supp. XIV:** 147, 150

Pozorski, Aimee L., **Supp. XXII:** 160, 166

Practical Agitation (Chapman), **Supp. XIV:** 41

"Practical Application in This Life, by Men as Social and Intellectual Beings, of the Certainty of a Future State, The" (Very), **Supp. XXV:** 240

Practical Criticism: A Study of Literary Judgment (Richards), **Supp. XIV:** 3, 16

Practical Magic (film), **Supp. X:** 80

Practical Magic (Hoffman), **Supp. X:** 78, 82, **88–89**

"Practical Methods of Meditation, The" (Dawson), **IV:** 151

Practical Navigator, The (Bowditch), **Supp. I Part 2:** 482

Practice of Perspective, The (Dubreuil), **Supp. IV Part 2:** 425

Practice of Reading, The (Donoghue), **Supp. VIII:** 189

Pragmatism (W. James), **Supp. XXVII:** 33

Pragmatism: A New Name for Some Old Ways of Thinking (James), **II:** 352

"Pragmatism's Conception of Truth" (James), **Supp. XIV:** 40

Prague Orgy, The (P. Roth), **Retro. Supp. II:** 280

"Praire, The" (Clampitt), **Supp. IX:** 42

"Prairie" (Sandburg), **III:** 583, 584

Prairie, The (Cooper), **I:** 339, 342

"Prairie Birthday" (Leopold), **Supp. XIV:** 185

Prairie Home Companion, A (Keillor, radio program), **Supp. XIII:** 274; **Supp. XVI:** 169–171, 173–178

Prairie Home Morning Show, A (Keillor, radio program), **Supp. XVI:** 171

"Prairie Life, A Citizen Speaks" (Dunn), **Supp. XI:** 145

"Prairies, The" (Bryant), **Supp. I Part 1:** 157, 162, 163, 166

"Prairie Spring" (Cather), **Retro. Supp. III:** 23

Praise (Hass), **Supp. VI:** 104–105, 106

"Praise for an Urn" (Crane), **I:** 388

"Praise for Sick Women" (Snyder), **Supp. VIII:** 294

"Praise in Summer" (Wilbur), **Supp. III Part 2:** 546–548, 560, 562

"Praise of a Palmtree" (Levertov), **Supp. III Part 1:** 284

"Praise of the Committee" (Rukeyser), **Supp. VI:** 278

"Praises, The" (Goldbarth), **Supp. XII:** 185

"Praises, The" (Olson), **Supp. II Part 2:** 558, 560, 563, 564

Praises and Dispraises (Des Pres), **Supp. X:** 120

Praisesong for the Widow (Marshall), **Supp. IV Part 1:** 14; **Supp. XI:** 18, 276, 278, **284–286**, 287; **Supp. XX:** 154

"Praise to the End!" (Roethke), **III:** 529, 532, 539

Prajadhipok, King of Siam, **I:** 522

Prater Violet (Isherwood), **Supp. XIV:** **164–166**, 169–170, 171

Pratt, Anna (Anna Alcott), **Supp. I Part 1:** 33

Pratt, Louis H., **Retro. Supp. II:** 6

Pratt, Mary Louise, **Retro. Supp. II:** 48

Pratt, Parley, **Supp. IV Part 2:** 603

"Prattler" (newspaper column), **I:** 207

"Prattler, The" (Bierce), **I:** 196

"Prayer" (Gioia), **Supp. XV:** 117

"Prayer" (Olds), **Supp. X:** 204

"Prayer" (Peacock), **Supp. XIX:** 198, 199, 200

"Prayer" (Toomer), **Supp. IX:** 318

"Prayer, A" (Kushner), **Supp. IX:** **134**

"Prayer for Columbus" (Whitman), **IV:** 348

"Prayer for My Daughter" (Yeats), **II:** 598

"Prayer for My Grandfather to Our Lady, A" (R. Lowell), **II:** 541–542

"Prayer for my Son" (C. Frost), **Supp. XV:** 98–99

"Prayer for Our Daughters" (Jarman), **Supp. XVII:** 120

Prayer for Owen Meany, A (Irving), **Supp. VI:** 164, 165, 166, **175–176**

"PRAYER FOR SAVING" (Baraka), **Supp. II Part 1:** 52–53

Prayer for the Dying, A (O'Nan), **Supp. XXV:** 141, 142, 144, 145–146, 148

Prayer for the Little City (Lea), **Supp. XXVIII:** 134–136

"Prayer in Spring, A" (Frost), **II:** 153, 164

"Prayer Meeting" (Di Piero), **Supp. XIX:** 46, 47

"Prayer on All Saint's Day" (Cowley), **Supp. II Part 1:** 138, 153

Prayers for Dark People (Du Bois), **Supp. II Part 1:** 186

"Prayer to Hermes" (Creeley), **Supp. IV Part 1:** 156, 157

"Prayer to Masks" (Senghor), **Supp. IV Part 1:** 16

"Prayer to the Child of Prague" (Salinas), **Supp. XIII:** 327

"Prayer to the Good Poet" (Wright), **Supp. III Part 2:** 603

"Prayer to the Pacific" (Silko), **Supp. IV Part 2:** 560

"Prayer to the Verb" (Davison), **Supp. XXVI:** 79

Praying Wrong (Davison), **Supp. XXVI:** 66, 76–77

"Pray without Ceasing" (Emerson), **II:** 9–10

Praz, Mario, **IV:** 430

"Preacher, The" (Whittier), **Supp. I Part 2:** 698–699

Preacher and the Slave, The (Stegner), **Supp. IV Part 2:** 599, 608, 609

"Preacher Is Called to Testify for the Accused, The" (Rash), **Supp. XXVII:** 219

"Preacher Who Takes Up Serpents Laments the Presence of Skeptics in His Church, A" (Rash), **Supp. XXVII:** 219

Precaution (Cooper), **I:** 337, 339

"Precautions"(Karyotakis, trans. Hadas), **Supp. XXIII:** 125

"Preconceptions of Economic Science, The" (Veblen), **Supp. I Part 2:** 634

Predecessors, Et Cetera (Clampitt), **Supp. IX:** 37

"Predicament, A" (Poe), **Retro. Supp. II:** 273

Predilections (Moore), **III:** 194

Prefaces and Prejudices (Mencken), **III:** 99, 104, 106, 119

Preface to a Twenty Volume Suicide Note. . . . (Baraka), **Supp. II Part 1:** 31, 33–34, 51, 61

"Preference" (Wylie), **Supp. I Part 2:** 713

"Prejudice against the Past, The" (Moore), **IV:** 91

Prejudices (Mencken), **Supp. I Part 2:** 630

Prejudices: A Selection (Farrell, ed.), **III:** 116

Prejudices: First Series (Mencken), **III:** 105

"Preliminary Remarks on the Poetry in the First Person" (Wright), **Supp. XV:** 339

Prell (exhibition, Brainard), **Supp. XXVII:** 21

Prelude, A: Landscapes, Characters and Conversations from the Earlier Years of My Life (Wilson), **IV:** 426, 427, 430, 434, 445

Prelude, The (Wordsworth), **III:** 528; **IV:** 331, 343; **Supp. I Part 2:** 416, 676; **Supp. XI:** 248

Prelude and Liebestod (McNally), **Supp. XIII:** 201

"Preludes" (T. S. Eliot), **I:** 573, 576, 577; **Retro. Supp. I:** 55; **Retro. Supp. III:** 60; **Supp. IV Part 2:** 436

Preludes for Memnon (Aiken), **I:** 59, 65

Preludes from Memnon (Aiken), **Supp. X:** 50

"Prelude to an Evening" (Ransom), **III:** 491, 492–493

Prelude to Darkness (Salinas), **Supp. XIII:** 311, **318–319**, 320

"Prelude to the Present" (Mumford), **Supp. II Part 2:** 471

"Premature Burial, The" (Poe), **III:** 415, 416, 418; **Retro. Supp. II:** 270

"Premeditations"(Schott), **Supp. XXIII:** 247

Preminger, Otto, **Supp. IX:** 3, 9; **Supp. XX:** **246–247**

"Premonition" (Hay), **Supp. XIV:** 122

"Premonitions of the Bread Line" (Komunyakaa), **Supp. XIII:** 114, 115

Prenshaw, Peggy Whitman, **Supp. X:** 229

"Preparations" (Silko), **Supp. IV Part 2:** 560

Preparatory Meditations (Taylor), **IV:** 145, 148, 149, 150, 152, 153, 154–155, 164, 165

"Prepare" (Carruth), **Supp. XVI:** 59

Prepositions: The Collected Critical Essays of Louis Zukofsky (Zukofsky), **Supp. III Part 2:** 630

Prescott, Anne, **Supp. IV Part 1:** 299

Prescott, Orville, **Supp. IV Part 2:** 680; **Supp. XI:** 340; **Supp. XXIII:** 13

Prescott, Peter, **Supp. X:** 83

Prescott, Peter S., **Supp. XVI:** 212

Prescott, William, **Retro. Supp. I:** 123

Prescott, William Hickling, **II:** 9, 310, 313–314; **IV:** 309; **Supp. I Part 2:** 414, 479, 493, 494

"Prescription of Painful Ends" (Jeffers), **Supp. II Part 2:** 424

"Presence, The" (Gordon), **II:** 199, 200

"Presence, The" (Kumin), **Supp. IV Part 2:** 445, 455

Presence and Desire: Essays on Gender, Sexuality, Performance (Dolan), **Supp. XV:** 327

"Presence of Others, The" (Kenyon), **Supp. VII:** 164

Presences (Taylor), **Supp. V:** 325

"Present Age, The" (Emerson), **II:** 11–12

Present Danger, The: Do We Have the Will to Reverse the Decline of American Power? (Podhoretz), **Supp. VIII:** 241

"Present for the Boy, A" (Swados), **Supp. XIX:** 259

Present for Young Ladies, A (Rowson), **Supp. XV:** 245

"Present Hour" (Sandburg), **III:** 593–594

Presenting Walter Dean Myers (Bishop), **Supp. XXVII:** 203

Present Philosophical Tendencies (Perry), **I:** 224

"Present State of Ethical Philosophy, The" (Emerson), **II:** 9

"Present State of Poetry, The" (Schwartz), **Supp. II Part 2:** 666

"Preservation of Innocence" (Baldwin), **Supp. I Part 1:** 51

"Preserving Wildness" (Berry), **Supp. X:** 28, 29, 32

"President and Other Intellectuals, The" (Kazin), **Supp. VIII:** 104

Presidential Papers, The (Mailer), **III:** 35, 37–38, 42, 45; **Retro. Supp. II:** 203, 204, 206

"Presidents" (Merwin), **Supp. III Part 1:** 351

Presnell, Robert, Sr., **Supp. XIII:** 166

Pressley, Nelson, **Supp. XVIII:** 37–38

"PRES SPOKE IN A LANGUAGE" (Baraka), **Supp. II Part 1:** 60

"Presto Manifesto" (Stallings), **Supp. XXV:** 227

Presumed Innocent (Turow), 217; **Supp. XVII:** 214–216, 223

Pretending to Be Asleep (Davison), **Supp. XXVI:** 65, 71–72

"Pretext, The" (Wharton), **Retro. Supp. I:** 371

Pretty Baby (film), **Supp. XXI:** 252

Pretty Boy Floyd (McMurtry), **Supp. V:** 231

"Pretty Girl, The" (Dubus), **Supp. VII:** 87–88

"Pretty Mouth and Green My Eyes" (Salinger), **III:** 560

"Previous Condition" (Baldwin), **Supp. I Part 1:** 51, 55, 63

"Previous Tenant, The" (Simpson), **Supp. IX:** 278–279

Prevost, Verbie Lovorn, **Supp. XXI:** 45

Priaulx, Allan, **Supp. XI:** 228

Price, Alan, **Retro. Supp. I:** 377

Price, E. Hoffman, **Supp. XXV:** 114

Price, Novalyne, **Supp. XXVII:** 117

Price, Reynolds, **Supp. IX:** 256, 257; **Supp. VI: 253–270**

Price, Richard, **II:** 9; **Supp. I Part 2:** 522; **Supp. XX: 85**

Price, The (A. Miller), **III:** 165–166; **Retro. Supp. III:** 172, 173–174

"*Price, The:* The Power of the Past" (A. Miller), **Retro. Supp. III:** 174

"Price Is Right, The" (Skloot), **Supp. XX: 198–199**

"Price of Poetry, The" (Biss), **Supp. XXVI:** 48

"Price of the Harness, The" (Crane), **I:** 414

Pricksongs & Descants; Fictions (Coover), **Supp. V:** 39, 42, 43, 49, 50

"Pride" (Hughes), **Supp. I Part 1:** 331

Pride and Prejudice (Austen), **II:** 290; **Supp. XXVI:** 117–118

Prideaux, Tom, **Supp. IV Part 2:** 574, 590

"Priesthood, The" (Winters), **Supp. II Part 2:** 786

Priestly, Joseph, **Supp. I Part 2:** 522

Prima, Diane di, **Supp. XXVIII:** 260

Primary Colors, The (A. Theroux), **Supp. VIII:** 312

"Primary Ground, A" (Rich), **Supp. I Part 2:** 563

"Prime" (Auden), **Supp. II Part 1:** 22

"Primer Class" (Bishop), **Retro. Supp. II:** 38, 51

Primer for Blacks (Brooks), **Supp. III Part 1:** 85

Primer for Combat (Boyle), **Supp. XXIV:** 62

"Primer for the Nuclear Age" (Dove), **Supp. IV Part 1:** 246

"Primer for the Small Weird Loves, A"(Siken), **Supp. XXVIII:** 199

Primer mensaje a la América Hispana (W. Frank), **Supp. XX:** 76

Primer of Ignorance, A (Blackmur), **Supp. II Part 1:** 91

Prime-Stevenson, Edward Irenaeus, **Supp. XX: 235**

Primitive (Oppen), **Supp. XXVI:** 237

Primitive, The (C. Himes), **Supp. XVI:** 139, **141–142**

"Primitive Black Man, The" (Du Bois), **Supp. II Part 1:** 176

"Primitive Like an Orb, A" (Stevens), **IV:** 89; **Retro. Supp. I:** 309

Primitive People (Prose), **Supp. XVI:** 255, 256, 257

"Primitive Singing" (Lindsay), **Supp. I Part 2:** 389–390

Primitivism and Decadence (Winters), **Supp. II Part 2:** 786, 803–807, 812

Primrose, Archibald Philip, **Supp. XX: 230**

Prince, F. T., **Supp. XXIV:** 45

Prince, Richard, **Supp. XII:** 4

"Prince, The" (Jarrell), **II:** 379

"Prince, The" (Winters), **Supp. II Part 2:** 802

Prince and the Pauper, The (Twain), **IV:** 200–201, 206; **Retro. Supp. III:** 255, 262, 264

Prince Hagen (Sinclair), **Supp. V:** 280

Prince of a Fellow, A (Hearon), **Supp. VIII:** 58, **62–63**

Princess, The (Tennyson), **Supp. I Part 2:** 410

Princess and the Goblins, The (Macdonald), **Supp. XIII:** 75

Princess Casamassima, The (James), **II:** 276, 291; **IV:** 202; **Retro. Supp. I:** 216, 221, 222, 225, **226–227**

"Princess Casamassima, The" (Trilling), **Supp. III Part 2:** 502, 503

Princess of Arcady, A (Henry), **Retro. Supp. II:** 97

"Principles" (Du Bois), **Supp. II Part 1:** 172

Principles of Literary Criticism (Richards), **I:** 274; **Supp. I Part 1:** 264; **Supp. XIV:** 3

Principles of Psychology, The (James), **II:** 321, 350–352, 353, 354, 357, 362, 363–364; **IV:** 28, 29, 32, 37

Principles of Psychology, The (W. James), **Supp. XVII:** 97

Principles of Zoölogy (Agassiz), **Supp. I Part 1:** 312

Prior, Sir James, **II:** 315

Prior, Matthew, **II:** 111; **III:** 521

"Prison, The" (Malamud), **Supp. I Part 2:** 431, 437

"Prisoned Love" (Boyce), **Supp. XXI:** 9

"Prisoner of Ours, The" (Weigl), **Supp. XIX:** 288

Prisoner of Second Avenue, The (Simon), **Supp. IV Part 2:** 583, 584

Prisoner of Sex, The (Mailer), **III:** 46; **Retro. Supp. II:** 206

Prisoner of Zenda, The (film), **Supp. I Part 2:** 615

Prisoner's Dilemma (Powers), **Supp. IX:** 212, **214–216**, 221

Prison Memoirs of an Anarchist (A. Berkman), **Supp. XVII:** 103–104

Pritchard, William H., **Retro. Supp. I:** 131, 141; **Retro. Supp. III:** 104, 105; **Supp. IV Part 1:** 285; **Supp. IV Part 2:** 642; **Supp. XI:** 326; **Supp. XVI:** 71

Pritchett, V. S., **II:** 587; **Supp. II Part 1:** 143; **Supp. VIII:** 171; **Supp. XIII:** 168

Pritikin, Renny, **Supp. XXIV:** 40

"Privatation and Publication" (Cowley), **Supp. II Part 1:** 149

Private Contentment (Price), **Supp. VI:** 263

"Private History of a Campaign That Failed, The" (Twain), **IV:** 195; **Retro. Supp. III:** 256

Private I, The: Privacy in a Public World (Peacock, ed.), **Supp. XIX:** 193, 203

Private Life of Axie Reed, The (Knowles), **Supp. XII:** 249

Private Line (Major), **Supp. XXII:** 174

"Private Man Confronts His Vulgarities at Dawn, A" (Dunn), **Supp. XI:** 146

Private Memoirs and Confessions of a Justified Sinner, The (Hogg), **Supp. IX:** 276

"Private Property and the Common Wealth" (Berry), **Supp. X:** 25

Private Snafu series (Geisel), **Supp. XVI:** 102

"Private Theatricals" (Howells), **II:** 280

Private Women, Public Stage: Literary Domesticity in Nineteenth-Century America (Kelley), **Supp. XVIII:** 257

"Privilege" (Munro), **Supp. XXVII:** 186, 187

Privilege, The (Kumin), **Supp. IV Part 2:** 442–444, 451

Prize Stories 1918 : The O. Henry Awards, **Supp. XVI:** 16

"Probe" (Ryan as Quin), **Supp. XVIII:** 229

"Probing the Dark" (Komunyakaa), **Supp. XIII:** 131

"Problem from Hell, A": America and the Age of Genocide (Power), **Supp. XXIII:** 25, 27–28

"Problem from Milton, A" (Wilbur), **Supp. III Part 2:** 550

"Problem of Anxiety, The" (Koch), **Supp. XV:** 183

"Problem of Being, The" (James), **II:** 360

Problem of Classification in the Theory of Value, The (Locke), **Supp. XIV:** 199

"Problem of Evil into Cocoon" (Taggard), **Supp. XXII:** 284

"Problem of Housing the Negro, The" (Du Bois), **Supp. II Part 1:** 168

"Problem of the Religious Novel, The" (Isherwood), **Supp. XIV:** 172

Problems and Other Stories (Updike), **Retro. Supp. I:** 322, 329

Problems of Dostoevsky's Poetics (Bakhtin), **Supp. XXII:** 259

"Problem Solving" (Goldbarth), **Supp. XII:** 185

Procedures for Underground (Atwood), **Supp. XIII:** 33

"Procedures for Underground" (Atwood), **Supp. XIII:** 33

Process (Boyle), **Supp. XXIV:** 51

Procession, The (al-Mawákib) (Gibran), **Supp. XX:** 116, **124**

Processional (Lawson), **I:** 479

"Procession at Candlemas, A" (Clampitt), **Supp. IX:** 41

"Proclamation" (Saunders), **Supp. XIX:** 235

Proclus, **Retro. Supp. I:** 247

"Prodigal" (Ammons), **Supp. VII:** 29

"Prodigal" (Hoffman), **Supp. XVIII:** 86

"Prodigal, The" (Bishop), **Supp. I Part 1:** 90, 92

Prodigal Parents, The (Lewis), **II:** 454–455

"Prodigy" (Simic), **Supp. VIII:** 278

Producers, The (film, M. Brooks), **Supp. XVII:** 45

"Proem" (Crane), **I:** 397

"Proem, The: By the Carpenter" (O. Henry), **Supp. II Part 1:** 409

"Professions for Women" (Woolf), **Supp. XIII:** 305

"Professor" (Hughes), **Supp. I Part 1:** 330

"Professor, The" (Bourne), **I:** 223

Professor at the Breakfast Table, The (Holmes), **Supp. I Part 1:** 313, 316

"Professor Clark's Economics" (Veblen), **Supp. I Part 2:** 634

Professor of Desire, The (P. Roth), **Retro. Supp. II:** 288; **Supp. III Part 2:** 403, 418–420

Professor's House, The (Cather), **I:** 325–336; **Retro. Supp. I:** 16; **Retro. Supp. III:** 24, 32–33, 34–35

"Professor Veblen" (Mencken), **Supp. I Part 2:** 630

Proffer, Carl R., **Supp. VIII:** 22

Profile Makers, The (Bierds), **Supp. XVII:** 29, **30–32,** 33

"Profile of the Tenderloin Street Prostitute, A" (Vollmann), **Supp. XVII:** 230

Profits of Religion, The (Sinclair), **Supp. V:** 276

"Prognosis" (Warren), **IV:** 245

"Progress" (F. Wright), **Supp. XVII:** 247

Progress of Love, The (Munro), **Supp. XXVII:** 189

"Progress of Love, The" (Munro), **Supp. XXVII:** 189

"Progress Report" (Simic), **Supp. VIII:** 278

"Project for a Trip to China" (Sontag), **Supp. II Part 2:** 454, 469

"Project for *The Ambassadors*" (James), **Retro. Supp. I:** 229

"Projection" (Nemerov), **III:** 275

"Projective Verse" (Olson), **Supp. III Part 1:** 30; **Supp. III Part 2:** 555, 556, 557, 624; **Supp. IV Part 1:** 139, 153; **Supp. VIII:** 290

"Projector, The" (Baker), **Supp. XIII:** 53, 55

Prokofiev, Sergey Sergeyevich, **Supp. IV Part 1:** 81

"Prolegomena, Section 1" (Pound), **Supp. III Part 2:** 615–616

"Prolegomena, Section 2" (Pound), **Supp. III Part 2:** 616

"Prolegomenon to a Biography of Mailer" (Lucid), **Retro. Supp. II:** 195

"Proletarian as New Negro, The: Mike Gold's Harlem Renaissance"(Maxwell), **Supp. XXVIII:** 71

Proletarian Literature in the United States (Hicks), **Supp. I Part 2: 609–610; Supp. XXVI:** 134

"Proletarian Realism"(Gold), **Supp. XXVIII:** 76

"Prologue" (MacLeish), **III:** 8, 14

Prologue, for Full Chorus of Mixed Voices and Orchestra (Taggard and Schuman), **Supp. XXII:** 283

"Prologue, The" (Bradstreet), **Retro. Supp. III:** 1, 4, 5, 7, 8, 10

"Prologue to a Life" (D. West), **Supp. XVIII:** 280

"Prologue to Our Time" (Mumford), **Supp. III Part 2:** 473

"Prometheus" (Longfellow), **II:** 494

Prometheus Bound (R. Lowell), **II:** 543, 544, 545, 555

Promise, The (Buck), **Supp. II Part 1:** 124

"Promise, The" (Olds), **Supp. X:** 213

"Promise and Fulfillment" (D. West), **Supp. XVIII:** 278

Promised Land (Parker), **Supp. XIX:** 183, 184, 190

Promised Land, The (M. Antin), **Supp. IX:** 227; **Supp. XVI:** 148, 149; **Supp. XX:** 1, 2, 3, **4–9,** 11; **Supp. XXVIII:** 159

Promised Land, The (Porter), **III:** 447

"Promised Land, The" (R. Fisher), **Supp. XIX:** 72

Promised Lands (Sontag), **Supp. III Part 2:** 452

Promise of American Life, The (Croly), **I:** 229

"Promise of Blue Horses, The" (Harjo), **Supp. XII:** 228

Promise of Rest, The (Price), **Supp. VI:** 262, 266

Promises (Warren), **Supp. XIV:** 15

Promises, Promises (musical), **Supp. IV Part 2:** 575

Promises: Poems 1954–1956 (Warren), **IV:** 244–245, 249, 252

"Promise This When You Be Dying" (Dickinson), **Retro. Supp. I:** 44, 46

"Pronoun Variations"(Hadas), **Supp. XXIII:** 120

Pronzini, Bill, **Supp. XXVI:** 277, 278, 282

Proof, The (Winters), **Supp. II Part 2:** 786, 791, 792–794

"Proofreader, The" (Huddle), **Supp. XXVI:** 151, 152

Proofs and Theories: Essays on Poetry (Glück), **Supp. V:** 77, 79, 92; **Supp. XIV:** 269

"Propaganda of History, The" (Du Bois), **Supp. II Part 1:** 182

Propertius, Sextus, **III:** 467; **Retro. Supp. II:** 187; **Supp. XII:** 2

Property Of: A Novel (Hoffman), **Supp. X:** 77, 79, **80–82**

"Property of Loss" (W. V. Davis), **Supp. XXI:** 95

"Prophecy of Samuel Sewall, The" (Whittier), **Supp. I Part 2:** 699

Prophet, The (Asch), **Supp. XXIII:** 7

Prophet, The (Gibran), **Supp. XX: 113, 115, 119–121, 126**

"Prophet, The" (Notley), **Supp. XXII:** 229

"Prophet, The" (Very), **Supp. XXV:** 248–249

"Prophet and the Child, The" (Gibran), **Supp. XX: 123**

Propheteers, The (Apple), **Supp. XVII: 6–7**

"Prophetic Pictures, The" (Hawthorne), **II:** 227

"Proportion" (A. Lowell), **Retro, Supp. II:** 525

"Proposal" (Carver), **Supp. III Part 1:** 149

Proposals Relating to the Education of Youth in Pensilvania (Franklin), **II:** 113

"Proposed New Version of the Bible" (Franklin), **II:** 110

Prose, Francine, **Supp. XII:** 333; **Supp. XIX:** 209; **Supp. XVI: 249–264; Supp. XXIII:** 300; **Supp. XXVI:** 121, 130

"Prose for Departure" (Merrill), **Supp. III Part 1:** 336

Prose Pieces (Bynner), **Supp. XV:** 52

"Prose Poem as an Evolving Form, The" (R. Bly), **Supp. IV Part 1:** 64

"Proserpina and the Devil" (Wilder), **IV:** 358

"Prosody" (Espaillat), **Supp. XXI:** 102

"Prosody" (Shapiro), **Supp. II Part 2:** 710

Prospect before Us, The (Dos Passos), **I:** 491

"Prospective Immigrants Please Note" (Rich), **Supp. I Part 2:** 555

Prospect of Peace, The (Barlow), **Supp. II Part 1:** 67, 68, 75

Prospects of Literature, The (L. P. Smith), **Supp. XIV:** 343

Prospects on the Rubicon (Paine), **Supp. I Part 2:** 510–511

Prospectus of a National Institution, to Be Established in the United States (Barlow), **Supp. II Part 1:** 80, 82

Prospice (Browning), **IV:** 366

"Protestant Easter" (Sexton), **Supp. II Part 2:** 684

"Prothalamion" (Schwartz), **Supp. II Part 2:** 649, 652

"Prothalamion" (Spenser), **Retro. Supp. I:** 62

Proud, Robert, **Supp. I Part 1:** 125

"Proud Farmer, The" (Lindsay), **Supp. I Part 2:** 381

Proud Flesh (Humphrey), **Supp. IX:** 94, 95, 96, **102–103,** 104, 105, 109

"Proud Flesh" (Warren), **IV:** 243

Proud Highway, The (Thompson), **Supp. XXIV:** 283

Proud Lady (Boyce), **Supp. XXI:** 7, 12

"Proud Lady" (Wylie), **Supp. I Part 2:** 711–712

"Proud Music of the Storms" (Whitman), **Retro. Supp. III:** 305

Proulx, Annie, **Supp. VII: 249–267; Supp. XXIV:** 245, 251; **Supp. XXVI:** 186

Proust, Marcel, **I:** 89, 319, 327, 377, 461; **II:** 377, 514, 606; **III:** 174, 181, 184, 244–245, 259, 471; **IV:** 32, 201, 237, 301, 312, 328, 359, 428, 431, 434, 439, 443, 466, 467; **Retro. Supp. I:** 75, 89, 169, 335; **Supp. III Part 1:** 10, 12, 14, 15; **Supp. IV Part 2:** 600; **Supp. IX:** 211; **Supp. VIII:** 103; **Supp. X:** 193, 194; **Supp. XII:** 289; **Supp. XIV:** 24, 83, 95; **Supp. XVI:** 295; **Supp. XXI:** 231; **Supp. XXIII:** 122

Prouty, Olive Higgins, **Supp. XXVIII: 177–194**

Proverbs, **Supp. X:** 45

"Proverbs" (Jarman), **Supp. XVII:** 118

"Providence" (Komunyakaa), **Supp. XIII:** 132

"Provident Woman, A" (Boyce), **Supp. XXI:** 10

Provincetown Players and the Playwrights' Theatre, 1915–1922, The (Kenton), **Supp. XXVIII:** 38

"Provincetown Postcards" (F. Wright), **Supp. XVII:** 244

"Provincia deserta" (Pound), **Retro. Supp. I:** 289

"Provisional Remarks on Being / A Poet / of Arkansas" (Wright), **Supp. XV:** 337

"Prue" (Munro), **Supp. XXVII:** 188

Pruette, Lorine, **Supp. IV Part 2:** 522

Prufrock and Other Observations (T. S. Eliot), **I:** 569–570, 571, 573, 574, 576–577, 583, 584, 585; **Retro. Supp. I:** 59, 62; **Retro. Supp. III:** 58, 59–60

"Prufrock's Perivigilium" (T. S. Eliot), **Retro. Supp. I:** 57

Pryor, Richard, **Supp. XIII:** 343

Pryse, Marjorie, **Retro. Supp. II:** 139, 146; **Supp. XXV:** 285

"Psalm" (Ginsberg), **Supp. II Part 1:** 312

"Psalm" (Oppen), **Supp. XXVI:** 232–233, 235

"Psalm" (Simic), **Supp. VIII:** 282

"Psalm, A, or Supplication for mercy, and confession of Sin, addressed to the Author of Life, in the Odjibway-Alqonquin tongue"(J. Schoolcraft), **Supp. XXIII:** 232

"Psalm and Lament" (Justice), **Supp. VII:** 116, 117–118, 120–122, 124

"Psalm for Pinhook" (Ray), **Supp. XVIII:** 202

"Psalm Jew, The"(Asch). *See Salvation* (Asch)

"Psalm of Life, A" (Longfellow), **II:** 489, 496; **Retro. Supp. II:** 164, 168, 169; **Supp. I Part 2:** 409

"Psalm of the West" (Lanier), **Supp. I Part 1:** 362, 364

"Psalm: Our Fathers" (Merwin), **Supp. III Part 1:** 350

Psalms (biblical book), **I:** 83; **II:** 168, 232; **Retro. Supp. I:** 62; **Supp. I Part 1:** 125

Psalms, Hymns, and Spiritual Songs of the Rev. Isaac Watts, The (Worcester, ed.), **I:** 458

Psychiatric Novels of Oliver Wendell Holmes, The (Oberndorf), **Supp. I Part 1:** 315

"Psychology and Form" (Burke), **I:** 270

Psychology: Briefer Course (James), **II:** 351–352

Psychology of Art (Malraux), **IV:** 434

Psychology of Insanity, The (Hart), **I:** 241–242, 248–250

Psychopathia Sexualis (Shanley), **Supp. XIV:** 316, **329**

Psychophysiks (Fechner), **II:** 358

Pterodactyls (Silver), **Supp. XXIV: 268–270**

Ptomaine Street (Wells), **Supp. XXVI:** 275

"Pu-239" (Kalfus), **Supp. XVII:** 50

"Publication is the Auction" (Dickinson), **Retro. Supp. I:** 31

"Public Bath, The" (Snyder), **Supp. VIII:** 298

Public Burning, The (Coover), **Supp. IV Part 1:** 388; **Supp. V:** 44, 45, 46–47, 48, 51, 52; **Supp. XVII:** 6

"Public Burning of Julius and Ethel Rosenberg, The: An Historical Romance" (Coover), **Supp. V:** 44

"Public Figure" (Hay), **Supp. XIV:** 124

"Public Garden, The" (R. Lowell), **II:** 550

Public Good (Paine), **Supp. I Part 2:** 509–510

Public Poetry of Robert Lowell, The (Cosgrave), **Retro. Supp. II:** 185

"Public & Private" (column, Quindlen), **Supp. XVII:** 165, 167, 169–170

Public Speech: Poems (MacLeish), **III:** 15–16

Public Spirit (Savage), **II:** 111

"Public Woman, A" (Cliff), **Supp. XXII:** 76

Puccini, Giacomo, **Supp. XXI:** 150, 151

"Puck" (Monette), **Supp. X:** 157–158

Pudd'nhead Wilson (Twain), **I:** 197; **Retro. Supp. III:** 267

"Pudd'nhead Wilson's Calendar" (Twain), **I:** 197

"Pueblo Revolt, The" (Sando), **Supp. IV Part 2:** 510

Puella (Dickey), **Supp. IV Part 1:** 178, 185

Pulitzer, Alfred, **Retro. Supp. I:** 257

Pull Down Vanity (Fiedler), **Supp. XIII:** 103

Pullman, George, **Supp. I Part 1:** 9

"Pullman Car Hiawatha" (Wilder), **IV:** 365–366

Pull My Daisy (film), **Supp. XII:** 126–127

"Pulp Cutters' Nativity, A" (Budbill), **Supp. XIX:** 9

"Pulpit and the Pew, The" (Holmes), **Supp. I Part 1:** 302

"Pulse-Beats and Pen-Strokes" (Sandburg), **III:** 579

"Pump, The" (Humphrey), **Supp. IX:** 101

Pump House Gang, The (Wolfe), **Supp. III Part 2:** 575, 578, 580, 581

Punch, Brothers, Punch and Other Sketches (Twain), **IV:** 200

Punch: The Immortal Liar, Documents in His History (Aiken), **I:** 57, 61

Punishment Without Vengeance (Vega; Merwin, trans.), **Supp. III Part 1:** 341, 347

"Pupil" (F. Barthelme), **Supp. XI:** 26

"Pupil, The" (H. James), **Supp. XX: 233**

"Pupil, The" (James), **II:** 331; **Retro. Supp. I:** 217, 219, 228

"Purchase" (Banks), **Supp. V:** 6

"Purchase of Some Golf Clubs, A" (O'Hara), **III:** 369

"Purdah" (Plath), **Supp. I Part 2:** 602

Purdy, Charles, **Supp. VIII:** 330

Purdy, James, **Supp. VII: 269–285**

Purdy, John Lloyd, **Supp. XXVI:** 101, 103, 105, 111

Purdy, Theodore, **Supp. VIII:** 153

Pure (C. Frost), **Supp. XV:** 93, **101–102,** 104, 106

"Pure" (C. Frost), **Supp. XV:** 101–102

"Pure and the Good, The: On Baseball and Backpaking" (Maclean), **Supp. XIV:** 222

"Pure Good of Theory, The" (Stevens), **Retro. Supp. I:** 310

Purgatorio (Dante), **III:** 182; **Retro. Supp. III:** 65

"Purim Parade" (Espaillat), **Supp. XXI:** 108

Puritan Family (Morgan), **Supp. I Part 1:** 101

"Puritanical Pleasures" (Hardwick), **Supp. III Part 1:** 213–214
Puritan Origins of the American Self, The (Bercovitch), **Supp. I Part 1:** 99
Puritan Pronaos, The: Studies in the Intellectual Life of New England in the Seventeenth Century (Morison), **Supp. I Part 2:** 485
"Puritan Realism: *The Wide, Wide World* and *Robinson Crusoe*" (Kim), **Supp. XVIII:** 267
Puritans, The (P. Miller), **Supp. VIII:** 101
"Puritan's Ballad, The" (Wylie), **Supp. I Part 2:** 723
"Purloined Letter, The" (Poe), **Retro. Supp. II:** 271, 272; **Retro. Supp. III:** 225, 227
Purple Cane Road (Burke), **Supp. XIV:** 32, 33
Purple Decades, The (Wolfe), **Supp. III Part 2:** 584
"Purple Hat, The" (Welty), **IV:** 264
Purple Rose of Cairo, The (film; Allen), **Supp. XV:** 1, 9–10, 12, 14
Purser, John T., **Supp. XIV:** 4
Pursuit of a Wound (Lea), **Supp. XXVIII:** 137–138
"Pursuit of Happiness" (Simpson), **Supp. IX:** 279
"Pursuit of Happiness, The" (Ashbery), **Supp. III Part 1:** 23
Pursuit of the Prodigal, The (Auchincloss), **Supp. IV Part 1:** 25
Pushcart at the Curb, A (Dos Passos), **I:** 478, 479
"Pushcart Man" (Hughes), **Supp. I Part 1:** 330
Pushcart Prize, XIII, The (Ford), **Supp. V:** 58
Pushcart Prize VII, The (Hendeson, ed.), **Supp. XVII:** 16
Pushcart Prize XIV, The (Henderson, ed.), **Supp. XVII:** 18
Pushcart Prize XX, The (Henderson, ed.), **Supp. XVII:** 20
"Pushing 100" (Mora), **Supp. XIII:** 215
Pushkin, Aleksander, **III:** 246, 261, 262; **Retro. Supp. I:** 266, 269; **Supp. XVI:** 188
Pussy, King of the Pirates (Acker), **Supp. XII:** 6–7
"Pussycat and the Expert Plumber Who Was a Man, The" (A. Miller), **III:** 146–147
Pussycat Fever (Acker), **Supp. XII:** 6
Putnam, George Haven, **Supp. XVIII:** 257, 260
Putnam, George P., **II:** 314; **Supp. XVIII:** 3–4, 14, 260
Putnam, Phelps, **I:** 288
Putnam, Samuel, **II:** 26; **III:** 479; **Supp. III Part 2:** 615
"Put Off the Wedding Five Times and Nobody Comes to It" (Sandburg), **III:** 586–587
Puttenham, George, **Supp. I Part 1:** 113
Puttermesser Papers, The (Ozick), **Supp. V:** 269

"Putting a Burden Down" (Peacock), **Supp. XIX:** 199
Putting It Together (Sondheim), **Supp. XXIV:** 124
"Putting on *Visit to a Small Planet*" (Vidal), **Supp. IV Part 2:** 683
Puttin' on Ole Massa: The Slave Narratives of Henry Bibb, William Wells Brown, and Solomon Northup (Osofsky), **Supp. XXVIII:** 167
Put Yourself in My Shoes (Carver), **Supp. III Part 1:** 139
"Put Yourself in My Shoes" (Carver), **Supp. III Part 1:** 139, 141
Putzi, Jennifer, **Supp. XV:** 284
Puzo, Mario, **Supp. IV Part 1:** 390
"Puzzle of Modern Society, The" (Kazin), **Supp. VIII:** 103
Pygmalion (Shaw), **Supp. XII:** 14
Pyle, Ernie, **III:** 148; **Supp. V:** 240; **Supp. XVII:** 61
Pylon (Faulkner), **II:** 64–65, 73; **Retro. Supp. I:** 84, 85; **Retro. Supp. III:** 77, 83
Pym (M. Johnson), **Retro. Supp. III:** 236
Pynchon, Thomas, **III:** 258; **Retro. Supp. I:** 278; **Retro. Supp. II:** 279, 324; **Supp. II Part 2:** 557, **617–638**; **Supp. III Part 1:** 217; **Supp. IV Part 1:** 53, 279; **Supp. IV Part 2:** 570; **Supp. IX:** 207, 208, 212; **Supp. V:** 40, 44, 52; **Supp. VIII:** 14; **Supp. X:** 260, 301, 302; **Supp. XI:** 103; **Supp. XII:** 289; **Supp. XIV:** 49, 53, 54, 96; **Supp. XIX:** 223; **Supp. XVI:** 123, 128; **Supp. XVII:** 183, 225, 232, 236; **Supp. XX: 21, 83, 87; Supp. XXIII:** 42, 101; **Supp. XXVII:** 183
Pyne, John, **Supp. XXI:** 7
Pyne, Mary, **Supp. XXI:** 7
Pyrah, Gill, **Supp. V:** 126
"Pyramid Club, The" (Doctorow), **Supp. IV Part 1:** 234
Pyrlaeus, Johann Christopher, **Supp. XXVI:** 86
"Pyrography" (Ashbery), **Supp. III Part 1:** 18
Pyros, John, **Supp. XXVIII:** 66
Pythagoras, **I:** 332
Pythagorean Silence (Howe), **Supp. IV Part 2:** 426, 428–429

Q

QBVII (television movie), **Supp. XX:** 247
QBVII (Uris), **Supp. XX: 244, 247, 248, 251, 253–254**
"Qebehseneuf" (Goldbarth), **Supp. XII:** 186
"Quadroons, The" (Child), **Supp. XVIII:** 124
"Quai d'Orléans" (Bishop), **Supp. I Part 1:** 89
"Quail for Mr. Forester" (Humphrey), **Supp. IX:** 94
"Quail in Autumn" (W. J. Smith), **Supp. XIII:** 334–335, 339
Quaker City, The: or, The Monks of Monk Hall (Lippard), **Supp. XXIII:** 177,

178–179, **180–183,** 184, 187, 188–189, 190
"Quaker Graveyard in Nantucket, The" (R. Lowell), **II:** 54, 550; **Retro. Supp. II:** 178, 186–187
"Quake Theory" (Olds), **Supp. X:** 203
Qualey, Carlton C., **Supp. I Part 2:** 650
Quality of Hurt, The (C. Himes), **Supp. XVI:** 137, 145
"Quality of Wine" (Carruth), **Supp. XVI:** 59
"Quality Time" (Kingsolver), **Supp. VII:** 203
"Quandary" (F. Wright), **Supp. XVII:** 244
Quang-Ngau-chè, **III:** 473
Quarles, Francis, **I:** 178, 179
"Quarrel" (Taggard), **Supp. XXII:** 276
Quarry, The (Chesnutt), **Supp. XIV:** 76
"Quarry, The" (Nemerov), **III:** 272
Quarry, The: New Poems (Eberhart), **I:** 532, 539
Quartermain, Peter, **Supp. IV Part 2:** 423, 434
Quatermain, Peter, **Supp. XXII:** 163
"Quaternions, The" (Bradstreet), **Supp. I Part 1:** 104–106, 114, 122
"Quatrains for Ishi" (Komunyakaa), **Supp. XIII:** 129
Quatuor pour la fin du temps (Messiaen), **Supp. XXVII:** 152
Queechy (S. Warner as Wetherell), **Supp. XVIII:** 257, **264–266**
Queen Christmas (Wells), **Supp. XXVI:** 275
"Queen Elizabeth and the Blind Girl or Music for the Dead Children" (B. Kelly), **Supp. XVII:** 124, 125
Queen of Outer Space (film), **Supp. XXVII:** 94
"Queen of the Black Coast" (Howard), **Supp. XXVII:** 125
"Queen of the Blues" (Brooks), **Supp. III Part 1:** 75
Queen of the Damned, The (Rice), **Supp. VII:** 290, 292–293, 297, 299
Queen of the Mob (film), **Supp. XIII:** 170
"Queens of France" (Wilder), **IV:** 365
"Queen's Twin, The" (Jewett), **Retro. Supp. II:** 138
Queen's Twin, The, and Other Stories (Jewett), **Retro. Supp. II:** 140
Queen Victoria (Strachey), **Supp. I Part 2:** 485, 494; **Supp. XIV:** 342
Queer (Burroughs), **Supp. III Part 1:** 93–102
"Queer Aztlán"(Moraga), **Supp. XXIII:** 201
"Queer Beer" (Hansberry), **Supp. IV Part 1:** 374
"Quelques considérations sur la méthode subjective" (James), **II:** 345–346
"Quest, The" (Gibran), **Supp. XX: 124**
"Question" (Swenson), **Supp. IV Part 2:** 640
"Question and Answer" (Hughes), **Retro. Supp. I:** 211
"Questioning Faces" (Frost), **Retro. Supp. I:** 141

"Question Mark in the Circle, The" (Stegner), **Supp. IV Part 2:** 597

"Questionnaire, The" (Snodgrass), **Supp. VI:** 318

"Question of Fidelity, A" (Beauvoir), **Supp. IX:** 4

"Question of Loneliness, A" (Swados), **Supp. XIX:** 262

"Question of Our Speech, The" (Ozick), **Supp. V:** 272

"Question of Simone de Beauvoir, The" (Algren), **Supp. IX:** 4

Questions About Angels (Collins), **Supp. XXI:** 54, 58, 59, 60, 64

Questions for Ecclesiastes (Jarman), **Supp. XVII:** 109, 110, **118–119**

"Questions of Geography" (Hollander), **Supp. I Part 1:** 96

"Questions of Swimming, 1935" (Davison), **Supp. XXVI:** 76

Questions of Travel (Bishop), **Retro. Supp. II: 46–48; Supp. I Part 1:** 72, 83, 92, 94

"Questions of Travel" (Bishop), **Retro. Supp. II:** 47

"Questions to Tourists Stopped by a Pineapple Field" (Merwin), **Supp. III Part 1:** 355

"Questions without Answers" (T. Williams), **IV:** 384

"Quest of the Purple-Fringed, The" (Frost), **Retro. Supp. I:** 139; **Retro. Supp. III:** 104

Quest of the Silver Fleece, The (Du Bois), **Supp. II Part 1:** 176–178

Quevedo y Villegas, Francisco Gómez, **Retro. Supp. I:** 423

Quickly: A Column for Slow Readers (Mailer), **Retro. Supp. II:** 202

Quicksand (Larsen), **Supp. XVIII:** 119, 121, 122, **124–127**

Quicksand and Passing (Larsen; McDowell, ed.), **Supp. XVIII:** 125

"Quies," (Pound), **Retro. Supp. I:** 413

Quiet American, The (Greene), **Supp. XIX:** 29

"Quiet and clear" (Kooser), **Supp. XIX:** 125

Quiet City (Shaw), **Supp. XIX:** 244

Quiet Days in Clichy (H. Miller), **III:** 170, 178, 183–184, 187

"Quiet Desperation" (Simpson), **Supp. IX:** 277–278

"Quiet Hour" (Huddle), **Supp. XXVI:** 149–150

"Quiet Light, A" (Skloot), **Supp. XX:** 203

"Quiet of the Mind" (Nye), **Supp. XIII:** 284

"Quiet Woman, The" (Taggard), **Supp. XXII:** 274

"QUILLA" (Trethewey), **Supp. XXI:** 246

"Quilting" (D. West), **Supp. XVIII:** 283

Quin, Mike (pseudonym). *See* Ryan, Paul William

Quincy, Edmund, **Supp. XVIII:** 4

Quindlen, Anna, **Supp. XVI:** 108; **Supp. XVII: 165–181**

Quinlan, Kathleen, **Supp. X:** 80

Quinn, Anthony, **Supp. XXI:** 46

Quinn, Arthur Hobson, **Retro. Supp. III:** 236

Quinn, John, **III:** 471

Quinn, Paul, **Supp. V:** 71

Quinn, Sister M. Bernetta, **III:** 479; **IV:** 421

Quinn, Vincent, **I:** 386, 401, 402; **Supp. I Part 1:** 270

"Quinnapoxet" (Kunitz), **Supp. III Part 1:** 263

Quinn's Book (W. Kennedy), **Supp. VII:** 133, 148–150, 153

Quintero, José, **III:** 403

Quintilian, **IV:** 123

Quinzaine for This Yule, A (Pound), **Retro. Supp. I:** 285

Quite Contrary: The Mary and Newt Story (Dixon), **Supp. XII: 144,** 153

Quitting Time (Kriegel), **Supp. XXIV: 225–227**

Quod Erat Demonstrandum (Stein), **IV:** 34

Quo Vadis? (Sienkiewicz), **Supp. IV Part 2:** 518; **Supp. XVI:** 182

R

Raab, Max, **Supp. XI:** 309

Raban, Jonathan, **Supp. XXV:** 208, 217

"Rabbi, The" (Hayden), **Supp. II Part 1:** 363, 369

Rabbit, Run (Updike), **IV:** 214, 223, 230–234; **Retro. Supp. I:** 320, 325, 326, 327, 331, 333, 335; **Supp. XI:** 140; **Supp. XII:** 298; **Supp. XVI:** 220

"Rabbit, The" (Barnes), **Supp. III Part 1:** 34

Rabbit at Rest (Updike), **Retro. Supp. I:** 334

Rabbit Dance (Gansworth), **Supp. XXVI:** 114

Rabbit Factory, The (L. Brown), **Supp. XXI:** 40, **47–48**

"*Rabbit Factory, The:* Escaping the Isolation of the Cage" (Gaughran), **Supp. XXI:** 47–48

Rabbit Is Rich (Updike), **Retro. Supp. I:** 334; **Supp. XXVI:** 142

Rabbit novels (Updike), **Supp. V:** 269

Rabbit Redux (Updike), **IV:** 214; **Retro. Supp. I:** 332, 333

Rabbit's Umbrella, The (Plimpton), **Supp. XVI:** 244

"Rabbits Who Caused All the Trouble, The" (Thurber), **Supp. I Part 2:** 610

Rabe, David, **Supp. XXIV:** 117; **Supp. XXV:** 153

Rabelais, and His World (Bakhtin), **Retro. Supp. II:** 273

Rabelais, François, **I:** 130; **II:** 111, 112, 302, 535; **III:** 77, 78, 174, 182; **IV:** 68; **Supp. I Part 2:** 461

Rabelais and His World (Bakhtin), **Supp. X:** 120

Rabinbach, Anson, **Supp. XII:** 166

Rabinowitz, Dorothy, **Supp. XXVII:** 134

Rabinowitz, Paula, **Supp. V:** 161

"Race" (Emerson), **II:** 6

"Race, Privilege, and the Politics of (Re)Writing History: An Analysis of the Novels of Michelle Cliff" (Edmondson), **Supp. XXII:** 70

"Race Cannot Become Great Until It Recognizes Its Talent" (Hurston), **Retro. Supp. III:** 129

Race Contacts and Interracial Relations: Lectures on the Theory and Practice of Race (Locke), **Supp. XIV:** 196, 199, 209, **209–210,** 211

"'RACE LINE' IS A PRODUCT OF CAPITALISM, THE" (Baraka), **Supp. II Part 1:** 61

"Race of Life, The" (Thurber), **Supp. I Part 2:** 614

"Race Problems and Modern Society" (Toomer), **Supp. III Part 2:** 486

Race Questions, Provincialism, and Other American Problems (Royce), **Supp. XIV:** 199

"Race Riot, Tulsa, 1921" (Olds), **Supp. X:** 205

Race Rock (Matthiessen), **Supp. V:** 201

"Races, The" (R. Lowell), **II:** 554

"Rachel" (D. West), **Supp. XVIII:** 289

Rachel Carson: Witness for Nature (Lear), **Supp. IX:** 19

Rachel River (film, Smolan), **Supp. XVI:** 36

"Racial Progress and Race Adjustment" (Locke), **Supp. XIV:** 210

Racine, Jean Baptiste, **II:** 543, 573; **III:** 145, 151, 152, 160; **IV:** 317, 368, 370; **Supp. I Part 2:** 716

Radcliffe, Ann, **Supp. XX: 108**

Radiance (Crooker), **Supp. XXIII: 57–58**

"Radical" (Moore), **III:** 211

"Radical Chic" (Wolfe), **Supp. III Part 2:** 577–578, 584, 585

Radical Chic & Mau-mauing the Flak Catchers (Wolfe), **Supp. III Part 2:** 577–578

Radical Empiricism of William James, The (Wild), **II:** 362, 363–364

Radicalism in America, The (Lasch), **I:** 259

"Radical Jewish Humanism: The Vision of E. L. Doctorow" (Clayton), **Supp. IV Part 1:** 238

"Radically Condensed History of Postindustrial Life, A" (Wallace), **Supp. X:** 309

Radical's America, A (Swados), **Supp. XIX: 264–265**

Radinovsky, Lisa, **Supp. XV:** 284, 285

"Radio" (O'Hara), **III:** 369

Radio Days (film; Allen), **Supp. XV:** 9

Radio Golf (Wilson), **Retro. Supp. III:** 321

"Radio Pope" (Goldbarth), **Supp. XII:** 188, 192

Raditzer (Matthiessen), **Supp. V:** 201

Radkin, Paul, **Supp. I Part 2:** 539

"Rafaela Who Drinks Coconut & Papaya Juice on Tuesdays" (Cisneros), **Supp. VII:** 63

Rafelson, Bob, **Supp. XIV:** 241

Raffalovich, Marc-André, **Supp. XIV:** 335

Rafferty, Terence, **Supp. XX: 87, 92**

"Raft, The" (Lindsay), **Supp. I Part 2:** 393

Rag and Bone Shop of the Heart, The: Poems for Men (Bly, Hillman, and Meade, eds.), **Supp. IV Part 1:** 67

Rage in Harlem (C. Himes). *See For Love of Imabelle* (C. Himes)

Rage to Live, A (O'Hara), **III:** 361

Raglan, Lord, **I:** 135

Rago, Henry, **Supp. III Part 2:** 624, 628, 629

"Rag Rug"(Hadas), **Supp. XXIII:** 118

Ragtime (Doctorow), **Retro. Supp. II:** 108; **Supp. IV Part 1:** 217, 222–224, 231, 232, 233, 234, 237, 238; **Supp. V:** 45; **Supp. XXIV:** 227

"Ragtime" (Doctorow), **Supp. IV Part 1:** 234

Ragtime (film), **Supp. IV Part 1:** 236

Ragtime (musical, McNally), **Supp. XIII:** 207

Rahab (W. Frank), **Supp. XX: 71–72,** 76

Rahaim, Liz, **Supp. XVII:** 2

Rahv, Philip, **Retro. Supp. I:** 112; **Supp. II Part 1:** 136; **Supp. IX:** 8; **Supp. VIII:** 96; **Supp. XIV:** 3; **Supp. XV:** 140; **Supp. XXVII:** 134

"Raid" (Hughes), **Retro. Supp. I:** 208

Raids on the Unspeakable (Merton), **Supp. VIII:** 201, 208

Raikin, Judith, **Supp. XXII:** 66

Rail, DeWayne, **Supp. XIII:** 312

"Rain, the Rez, and Other Things, The" (Gansworth), **Supp. XXVI:** 111

Rain and Other Fictions (Kenny), **Supp. XXIII:** 157

"Rain and the Rhinoceros" (Merton), **Supp. VIII:** 201

Rainbow, The (Lawrence), **III:** 27

"Rainbows" (Marquand), **III:** 56

Rainbow Stories, The (Vollmann), **Supp. XVII:** 226, 227, 230, 231, 233

Rainbow Tulip, The (Mora), **Supp. XIII:** 221

"Rain Country" (Haines), **Supp. XII:** 210

"Rain-Dream, A" (Bryant), **Supp. I Part 1:** 164

Raine, Kathleen, **I:** 522, 527

"Rain Falling Now, The" (Dunn), **Supp. XI:** 147

"Rain Flooding Your Campfire" (Gallagher), **Supp. XXIV:** 177

"Rain in the Heart" (Taylor), **Supp. V:** 317, 319

Rain in the Trees, The (Merwin), **Supp. III Part 1:** 340, 342, 345, 349, 354–356

"Rainmaker, The" (Humphrey), **Supp. IX:** 101

Raintree County (Lockridge), **Supp. XIX:** 263

Rainwater, Catherine, **Supp. V:** 272

"Rainy Day" (Longfellow), **II:** 498

"Rainy Day, The" (Buck), **Supp. II Part 1:** 127

"Rainy Mountain Cemetery" (Momaday), **Supp. IV Part 2:** 486

Rainy Mountain Christmas Doll (painting) (Momaday), **Supp. IV Part 2:** 493

"Rainy Season: Sub-Tropics" (Bishop), **Supp. I Part 1:** 93

"Rainy Sunday" (Espaillat), **Supp. XXI:** 106

Raised in Captivity (Silver), **Supp. XXIV: 271**

"Raise High the Roof Beam, Carpenters" (Salinger), **III:** 567–569, 571

Raise High the Roof Beam, Carpenters; and Seymour: An Introduction (Salinger), **III:** 552, 567–571, 572

Raise Race Rays Raze: Essays Since 1965 (Baraka), **Supp. II Part 1:** 47, 52, 55

Raisin (musical), **Supp. IV Part 1:** 374

Raising Demons (Jackson), **Supp. IX: 125–126**

Raising the Dead (Rash), **Supp. XXVII:** 220–221, 222

Raisin in the Sun, A (film: Columbia Pictures), **Supp. IV Part 1:** 360, 367

Raisin in the Sun, A (Hansberry), **Supp. IV Part 1:** 359, 360, 361, 362–364; **Supp. VIII:** 343

Raisin in the Sun, A (television film: American Playhouse), **Supp. IV Part 1:** 367, 374

Raisin in the Sun, A (unproduced screenplay) (Hansberry), **Supp. IV Part 1:** 360

Rajan, R., **I:** 390

"Rake, The" (Mamet), **Supp. XIV:** 240

Rake's Progress, The (opera), **Supp. II Part 1:** 24

Rakosi, Carl, **Supp. III Part 2:** 614, 615, 616, 617, 618, 621, 629; **Supp. XIV:** 286, 287

Ralegh, Sir Walter, **Supp. I Part 1:** 98

Raleigh, John Henry, **IV:** 366

Raleigh, Walter, **Retro. Supp. III:** 4, 6

Ralph, Brett, **Supp. XVII:** 245

Ramakrishna, Sri, **III:** 567

Ramakrishna and His Disciples (Isherwood), **Supp. XIV:** 164

Ramazani, Jahan, **Supp. IV Part 2:** 450

"Ramble of Aphasia, A" (O. Henry), **Supp. II Part 1:** 410

Ramey, Phillip, **Supp. IV Part 1:** 94

Ramírez, Juan, **Supp. XXIII:** 203

Ramona (Jackson), **Supp. XXIV:** 27

Rampersad, Arnold, **Retro. Supp. I:** 196, 200, 201, 204; **Supp. IV Part 1:** 244, 250

Rampling, Anne, **Supp. VII:** 201. *See also* Rice, Anne

Rampling, Charlotte, **Supp. IX:** 253

Ramsey, Priscilla R., **Supp. IV Part 1:** 15

Ramsey, Roger, **Supp. XVI:** 69

Ramsey, William, **Supp. XVIII:** 66

Ramus, Petrus, **Supp. I Part 1:** 104

Rancière, Jacques, **Supp. XXVI:** 18, 135, 136, 141

Rand, Ayn, **Supp. I Part 1:** 294; **Supp. IV Part 2:** 517–535

Randall, Jarrell, 1914–1965 (Lowell, Taylor, and Warren, eds.), **II:** 368, 385

Randall, John H., **III:** 605

Randolph, John, **I:** 5–6

Randolph, Ladette, **Supp. XXIII:** 274

"Randolphs of the Redwoods, The" (Atherton), **Supp. XXIV:** 18

"Range-Finding" (Frost), **Retro. Supp. I:** 131

Range of the Possible (T. Marshall), **Supp. XVII:** 36

Rangoon (F. Barthelme), **Supp. XI:** 25

Rangus, Eric, **Supp. XXI:** 244, 254

Rank, Otto, **I:** 135; **Supp. IX:** 105; **Supp. X:** 183, 185, 193

Ranke, Leopold von, **Supp. I Part 2:** 492

Rankin, Daniel, **Retro. Supp. II:** 57, 72; **Supp. I Part 1:** 200, 203, 225

Rankin, Tom, **Supp. XXI:** 36

Rankine, Annette, **Supp. XX: 69**

Ranlett, William H., **Supp. XVIII:** 3

Ransohoff, Martin, **Supp. XI:** 305, 306

Ransom, John Crowe, **I:** 265, 301; **II:** 34, 367, 385, 389, 536–537, 542; **III:** 454, **480–502,** 549; **IV:** 121, 122, 123, 124, 125, 127, 134, 140, 141, 236, 237, 433; **Retro. Supp. I:** 90; **Retro. Supp. II:** 176, 177, 178, 183, 220, 228, 246; **Supp. I Part 1:** 80, 361; **Supp. I Part 2:** 423; **Supp. II Part 1:** 90, 91, 136, 137, 139, 318; **Supp. II Part 2:** 639; **Supp. III Part 1:** 318; **Supp. III Part 2:** 542, 591; **Supp. IV Part 1:** 217; **Supp. V:** 315, 331, 337; **Supp. X:** 25, 56, 58; **Supp. XIV:** 1; **Supp. XIX:** 123; **Supp. XXIII:** 145

Ransome, Arthur, **Supp. XXV:** 205

Ransome, James, **Supp. XXVIII:** 285

"Rape" (Coleman), **Supp. XI:** 89–90

"Rape" (Rich), **Retro. Supp. III:** 247

"Rape, The" (Baraka), **Supp. II Part 1:** 40

Rape of Bunny Stuntz, The (Gurney), **Supp. V:** 109

"Rape of Philomel, The" (Shapiro), **Supp. II Part 2:** 720

"Rape of the Lock, The" (Pope), **Supp. XIV:** 8

Rapf, Joanna, **Supp. XVIII:** 251

Raphael, **I:** 15; **III:** 505, 521, 524; **Supp. I Part 1:** 363

"Rapist" (Dunn), **Supp. XI:** 144

Rap on Race, A (Baldwin and Mead), **Supp. I Part 1:** 66

Rapoport, Nessa, **Supp. XXVI:** 124

"Rappaccini's Daughter" (Hawthorne), **II:** 229; **Retro. Supp. III:** 115, 117

"Rapture of the Deep" (Hempel), **Supp. XXI: 123**

"Rapunzel" (Sexton), **Supp. II Part 2:** 691

Rare & Endangered Species: A Novella & Short Stories (Bausch), **Supp. VII:** 51, 54

"Raree Show" (MacLeish), **III:** 9

Rascoe, Burton, **III:** 106, 115

Rash, Ron, **Supp. XXVII: 215–231**

Raskin, Jonah, **Supp. XV:** 116

Raskin, Saul, **Supp. XXIII:** 6

"Raskolnikov" (Simic), **Supp. VIII:** 282

Rasmussen, Douglas, **Supp. IV Part 2:** 528, 530

Rasmussen, Halfdan, **Supp. XVIII:** 180

"Raspberries" (Rash), **Supp. XXVII:** 222

Rasporich, Beverly, **Supp. XXVII:** 180, 182
Rasselas (S. Johnson), **Supp. XI:** 209
Rathmann, Andrew, **Supp. XV:** 34
Ratiner, Steven, **Supp. XXIII:** 134
"Rat in the Engine" (Espaillat), **Supp. XXI:** 106
"Ration" (Baraka), **Supp. II Part 1:** 50
"Rationale of Verse, The" (Poe), **III:** 427–428; **Retro. Supp. II:** 266
Ratner, Rochelle, **Supp. XV:** 105; **Supp. XXIV:** 168; **Supp. XXVI:** 160
Ratner's Star (DeLillo), **Supp. VI:** 1, 2, 3, 4, 10, 12, 14; **Supp. XVIII:** 140
"Rat of Faith, The" (Levine), **Supp. V:** 192
"Rats in the Walls, The" (Lovecraft), **Supp. XXV:** 109, 112
Rattigan, Terence, **III:** 152
Raugh, Joseph, **Supp. I Part 1:** 286
Rauh, Ida, **Supp. XXI:** 6
Rauschenberg, Robert, **Supp. XV:** 187
Rauschenbusch, Walter, **III:** 293; **Supp. I Part 1:** 7
Ravelstein (Bellow), **Retro. Supp. II:** 19, 33–34
Raven, Simon, **Supp. XII:** 241
Raven, The (film, Friedlander), **Supp. XVII:** 58
"Raven, The" (Poe), **III:** 413, 421–422, 426; **Retro. Supp. II:** 265, 266–267; **Retro. Supp. III:** 225, 232, 234, 237; **Supp. XVII:** 58
Raven, The, and Other Poems (Poe), **III:** 413
Ravenal, Shannon, **Supp. IV Part 1:** 93
"Raven Days, The" (Lanier), **Supp. I Part 1:** 351
Ravenel, Shannon, **Supp. XXI:** 39
Ravenna, Michael. *See* Welty, Eudora
"Ravens at Deer Creek" (Wrigley), **Supp. XVIII:** 299–300, 306
Raven's Road (Gunn Allen), **Supp. IV Part 1:** 330, 335
Raver, Anne, **Supp. XVIII:** 191
Ravetch, Irving, **Supp. XXV:** 102
"Ravine, The" (Carruth), **Supp. XVI:** 53
Ravits, Martha, **Supp. XXI:** 215
Raw Heaven (Peacock), **Supp. XIX: 196–197**
Rawlings, Marjorie Kinnan, **Retro. Supp. III:** 134, 135; **Supp. X: 219–237; Supp. XVIII:** 194–195
Rawlins, C. L., **Supp. XVII:** 72, 73
Ray, David, **Supp. IV Part 1:** 61
Ray, Janisse, **Supp. XVIII: 189–206**
Ray, Jeanne Wilkinson, **Supp. XII:** 308, 310
Ray, John, **II:** 111, 112
Ray, Man, **IV:** 404; **Retro. Supp. I:** 416; **Supp. XII:** 124; **Supp. XXIII:** 6
Ray, Nicholas, **Supp. XVIII:** 253
Ray Bradbury Theatre, The (television show), **Supp. IV Part 1:** 103
Raymond, Henry J., **Supp. XVIII:** 4
"Raymond and Ann" (Budbill), **Supp. XIX:** 9
"Raymond Andrews as Griot" (Collins), **Supp. XXVI:** 13

Raymond Carver: A Writer's Life (Sklenicka), **Supp. XXIV:** 166
"Raymond Carver: The Kindest Cut" (Wood), **Supp. XXIV:** 166
"Razor's Edge, The" (Wasserstein), **Supp. XV:** 328
Reactionary Essays on Poetry and Ideas (Tate), **Supp. II Part 1:** 106, 146
Read, Deborah, **II:** 122
Read, Forrest, **III:** 478
Read, Herbert, **I:** 523; **II:** 372–373, 377–378; **Retro. Supp. I:** 54; **Supp. III Part 1:** 273; **Supp. III Part 2:** 624, 626
Read, William A., **Supp. XIV:** 4
Reade, Charles, **Supp. I Part 2:** 580
Reader, Constant. *See* Parker, Dorothy
Reader, Dennis J., **Supp. I Part 2:** 454
"Reader, The" (F. Wright), **Supp. XVII:** 246
Reader's Block (Markson), **Supp. XVII: 143–145,** 146
Reader's Encyclopedia, The: An Encyclopedia of World Literature and the Arts (W. Benét), **Supp. XI:** 44
Reader's Guide to William Gaddis's The Recognitions, A (Moore), **Supp. IV Part 1:** 283
Reader's Map of Arkansas (Wright), **Supp. XV:** 348
"Reader's Tale, A" (Doty), **Supp. XI:** 119, 120, 128, 129
"Reading" (Auden), **Supp. VIII:** 155
"Reading, The" (Di Piero), **Supp. XIX:** 41
"Reading, Writing, Region" (J. W. Miller), **Supp. XX: 165**
"Reading an Anthology of Chinese Poems of the Sung Dynasty, I Pause to Admire the Length and Clarity of Their Titles" (Collins), **Supp. XXI:** 56
"Reading at Forty" (Pickering), **Supp. XXI:** 196
Reading at the Social Limit (Elmer), **Retro. Supp. III:** 237
"Reading Group Guide", **Supp. XI:** 244–245
"Reading Lao Tzu Again in the New Year" (Wright), **Supp. V:** 343
"Reading Late of the Death of Keats" (Kenyon), **Supp. VII:** 169
Reading Lolita in Tehran (Nafisi), **Supp. XXVIII:** 80, 81
"Reading Myself" (R. Lowell), **II:** 555
Reading Myself and Others (P. Roth), **Retro. Supp. II:** 282; **Supp. V:** 45
"Reading *Ode to the West Wind* 25 Years Later" (McCarriston), **Supp. XIV:** 271–272
"Reading of the Psalm, The" (Francis), **Supp. IX:** 79
"Reading Ovid" (Di Piero), **Supp. XIX:** 44
"Reading Philosophy at Night" (Simic), **Supp. VIII:** 272
Reading Rilke: Reflections on the Problems of Translation (Gass), **Supp. VI:** 92, **93–94**
"Reading Rorty and Paul Celan One Morning in Early June" (Wright),

Supp. V: 343
"Reading Sarcophagi: An Essay" (Sobin), **Supp. XVI:** 290
"Readings of History" (Rich), **Supp. I Part 2:** 554
"Reading the Russians" (Stone), **Supp. XXVII:** 251–252
"Reading the Signs, Empowering the Eye" (Bambara), **Supp. XI:** 17–18
"Reading the Slender Body"(Bordo), **Supp. XXVIII:** 209
Reading the Spirit (Eberhart), **I:** 525, 527, 530
Ready, Richard M., **Supp. XIX:** 154
"Ready Or Not" (Baraka), **Supp. II Part 1:** 50
Reagan, Ronald, **Supp. IV Part 1:** 224–225
"Real Bowery, The" (Hapgood), **Supp. XVII:** 103
"Real Class" (Vidal), **Supp. IV Part 1:** 35
Real Cool Killers, The (C. Himes), **Supp. XVI:** 143
Real Dope, The (Lardner), **II:** 422–423
"Real Estate" (Moore), **Supp. X:** 178
"Real Gone Guy, A" (McGrath), **Supp. X:** 117
"Real Horatio Alger Story, The" (Cowley), **Supp. II Part 1:** 143
"Realities" (MacLeish), **III:** 4
"Reality in America" (Trilling), **Supp. III Part 2:** 495, 502
"Reality! Reality! What Is It?" (Eberhart), **I:** 536
Reality Sandwiches, 1953–60 (Ginsberg), **Supp. II Part 1:** 315, 320
"Reality U.S.A." (Halliday), **Supp. XIX:** 89
Real Life of Sebastian Knight, The (Nabokov), **III:** 246; **Retro. Supp. I:** 266, 269, 270, 274
"Really Good Jazz Piano, A" (Yates), **Supp. XI:** 342
"Real Movie, with Stars, The" (Hull), **Supp. XXI:** 136
Real Presence: A Novel (Bausch), **Supp. VII:** 42–43, 50
"Real Revolution Is Love, The" (Harjo), **Supp. XII:** 224, 225–226
"Real Surrounding, The: On Canaletto's Venice" (Bronk), **Supp. XXI:** 32
"Real Thing, The" (H. James), **Retro. Supp. I:** 228; **Retro. Supp. II:** 223
"Real Two-Party System" (Vidal), **Supp. IV Part 2:** 679
Real West Marginal Way, The (Hugo), **Supp. VI:** 132, 134; **Supp. XVIII:** 299
"Real World around Us, The" (Carson), **Supp. IX:** 21
Reaper Essays, The (Jarman and McDowell), **Supp. IX:** 270; **Supp. XVII:** 110–111
"*Reaper* Interviews Jean Doh and Sean Dough, The" (Jarman and McDowell), **Supp. XVII:** 110
"Reapers" (Toomer), **Supp. III Part 2:** 481; **Supp. IX:** 312

Reason and Other Women (Notley), **Supp. XXII:** 224, 227, 235, 236, 237
"Reason and Race: A Review of the Literature of the Negro for 1946" (Locke), **Supp. XIV:** 206
"Reason for Moving, A" (Strand), **Supp. IV Part 2:** 624
"Reason for Stories, The: Toward a Moral Fiction" (Stone), **Supp. V:** 298, 300
Reasons for Moving (Strand), **Supp. IV Part 2:** 624–626, 626
"Reasons for Music" (MacLeish), **III:** 19
"Reasons of the Body" (Sanders), **Supp. XVI:** 274
"Reasons to Hate Poetry"(Lea), **Supp. XXVIII:** 137
Reasons to Live (Hempel), **Supp. XXI:** 115, 117, 118, **119–122**
Rebecca (du Maurier), **Supp. XIX:** 57–58; **Supp. XXII:** 120
Rebecca, or, The Fille de Chambre (Rowson), **Supp. XV:** 229, **235–236,** 238
Rebecca Harding Davis Reader, A (Pfaelzer, ed.), **Supp. XVI:** 88, 90
Rebel Angels: Twenty-five Poets of the New Formalism (Jarman and Mason, eds.), **Supp. XV:** 251; **Supp. XVII:** 109, 110, 112, 121
"Rebellion" (R. Lowell), **Retro. Supp. II:** 187
Rebel Powers (Bausch), **Supp. VII:** 41, 45–46, 49–51
Rebel without a Cause (film), **Supp. XII:** 9
"Rebirth" (McKnight), **Supp. XX: 147, 157**
"Rebirth of God and the Death of Man, The " (Fiedler), **Supp. XIII:** 108
Rebolledo, Tey Diana, **Supp. XIII:** 214
Reb Shloyme nogid: A poeme fun yidishn leben (Shloyme the wealthy: A poem of Jewish life)(Asch), **Supp. XXIII:** 4, 5
Recapitulation (Stegner), **Supp. IV Part 2:** 598, 600, 612–613
"Recapitulation, The" (Eberhart), **I:** 522
"Recapitulations" (Shapiro), **Supp. II Part 2:** 701, 702, 708, 710–711
"Receding Horizons" (Lethem and Scholtz), **Supp. XVIII:** 145
"Recencies in Poetry" (Zukofsky), **Supp. III Part 2:** 615
Recent Killing, A (Baraka), **Supp. II Part 1:** 55
"Recent Negro Fiction" (Ellison), **Supp. II Part 1:** 233, 235
"Recessional" (A. Finch), **Supp. XVII:** 70–71
"Recital, The" (Ashbery), **Supp. III Part 1:** 14
"Recitative" (H. Crane), **I:** 390; **Retro. Supp. II:** 78
Reckless Eyeballing (Reed), **Supp. X:** 241
Reckless Moment, The (film), **Supp. XXII:** 120, 131, 132
Recognition of Robert Frost: Twenty-Fifth Anniversary (Thornton, ed.), **Retro. Supp. III:** 103

Recognitions, The (Gaddis), **Supp. IV Part 1:** 279, 280–285, 286, 287, 288, 289, 291, 292, 294; **Supp. XX: 91; Supp. XXIV:** 140
"Recollection and Perhaps a Tribute, A" (Espaillat), **Supp. XXI:** 103–104
Recollections (R. H. Stoddard), **Supp. XV:** 271
Recollections of Logan Pearsall Smith: The Story of a Friendship (Gathorne-Hardy), **Supp. XIV:** 344
"Reconciliation" (Whitman), **IV:** 347
"Reconstructed but Unregenerate" (Ransom), **III:** 496
"Reconstruction and Its Benefits" (Du Bois), **Supp. II Part 1:** 171
"Recording the Spirit Voices"(Bottoms), **Supp. XXVIII:** 26
Recovering (Sarton), **Supp. VIII:** 264
Recovering the U.S. Hispanic Literary Heritage (Paredes), **Supp. XIII:** 320
"Recovery" (Dove), **Supp. IV Part 1:** 248
Re-Creation Story (Gansworth), **Supp. XXVI:** 113–114
Rector of Justin, The (Auchincloss), **Supp. IV Part 1:** 21, 23, 27–30, 36
"Recurrent Dream" (Nelson), **Supp. XVIII:** 176
Recyclopedia: Trimmings, S*PeRM**K*T, and Muse & Drudge (Mullen), **Supp. XXVII:** 171, 174–175
"RED AUTUMN" (Baraka), **Supp. II Part 1:** 55
Red Badge of Courage, The (S. Crane), **I:** 201, 207, 212, 405, 406, 407, 408, 412–416, 419, 421, 422, 423, 477, 506; **II:** 264; **III:** 317; **IV:** 350; **Retro. Supp. II:** 108; **Supp. IV Part 1:** 380; **Supp. XIV:** 51; **Supp. XVII:** 228; **Supp. XVIII:** 75; **Supp. XXI:** 277; **Supp. XXVII:** 207
"Redbirds" (C. Frost), **Supp. XV:** 99
"Red Bow, The" (Saunders), **Supp. XIX:** 232–233, 234
"Redbreast in Tampa" (Lanier), **Supp. I Part 1:** 364
"Red Brocade" (Nye), **Supp. XIII:** 288
Redburn: His First Voyage (Melville), **III:** 79–80, 84; **Retro. Supp. I:** 245, 247–248, 249; **Retro. Supp. III:** 147, 148, 150–151, 152, 154–155; **Supp. XVIII:** 6
Red Calico (Miller and Bowden), **Supp. XXII:** 188
"Red Carpet for Shelley, A" (Wylie), **Supp. I Part 2:** 724
Red Channels (Harnett), **Supp. XV:** 198
"Red Clowns" (Cisneros), **Supp. VII:** 63
Red Coal, The (Stern), **Supp. IX: 291–292**
Red Coat, The (Shanley), **Supp. XIV:** 316–317
"Red Cords" (Lamott), **Supp. XX: 142**
"Red"(Crooker), **Supp. XXIII:** 63
"Red Cross" (Hughes), **Retro. Supp. I:** 205
Red Cross (Shepard), **Supp. III Part 2:** 440, 446

Red Death, A (Mosley), **Supp. XIII:** 237, 239, 240
"Red Deer" (C. Frost), **Supp. XV:** 101
Redding, Josephine, **Supp. XXI:** 2
Redding, Saunders, **Supp. I Part 1:** 332, 333
Reddings, J. Saunders, **Supp. IV Part 1:** 164
Red Dust (Levine), **Supp. V:** 178, 183–184, 188
"Red Dust" (Levine), **Supp. V:** 184
"Redemption" (Gardner), **Supp. VI:** 72
Redemption (Uris), **Supp. XX: 244, 246, 247, 248, 254, 255**
"Red Ensign, The" (Gallagher), **Supp. XXIV:** 175, 176
"Redeployment" (Nemerov), **III:** 267, 272
Redfield, Robert, **IV:** 475
Redford, Robert, **Supp. IX:** 253, 259; **Supp. XIII:** 267; **Supp. XIV:** 223
Redgrave, Lynn, **Supp. V:** 107
Red Harvest (Hammett), **Supp. IV Part 1:** 346–348, 348; **Supp. IV Part 2:** 468; **Supp. XXI:** 272
"Red Hat, The"(Hadas), **Supp. XXIII:** 111, 113, 118, 119, 124, 128
Red-Headed Woman (film), **Retro. Supp. I:** 110; **Supp. XVI:** 191
Red Helmet (Hickam), **Supp. XXVII:** 110–111
"Red Horse Wind over Albuquerque" (Harjo), **Supp. XII:** 219
Red Hot Vacuum, The (Solotaroff), **Retro. Supp. II:** 281
Rediscovery of America, The (W. Frank), **Supp. XX: 75**
Rediscovery of Man, The (W. Frank), **Supp. XX: 67–68, 80**
"Red Leaves" (Faulkner), **II:** 72
"Red Meat: What Difference Did Stesichoros Make?" (Carson), **Supp. XII:** 107
"Red Nails" (Howard), **Supp. XXVII:** 126
"Red Pawn" (Rand), **Supp. IV Part 2:** 520
Red Pony, The (Steinbeck), **IV:** 50, 51, 58, 70
Redrawing the Boundaries (Fisher), **Retro. Supp. I:** 39
Red Robins, The (Koch), **Supp. XV:** 185–186, 187
Red Roses for Bronze (Doolittle), **Supp. I Part 1:** 253, 268, 271
Red Rover, The (Cooper), **I:** 342–343, 355
Red Ryder (comic books), **Supp. XXVII:** 23
"Red Rydler and His Dog" (O'Hara and Brainard), **Supp. XXVII:** 23
Reds (Beatty), **Supp. XXIV:** 227
Reds (film), **Supp. XXVIII:** 40, 46
"Red Shadows" (Howard), **Supp. XXVII:** 122
"Red Shift" (Berrigan), **Supp. XXIV:** 46
"Red Silk Stockings" (Hughes), **Retro. Supp. I:** 200
Redskins, The (Cooper), **I:** 351, 353
Red Sox and Bluefish: And Other Things That Make New England New England

(Orlean), **Supp. XXV:** 159

"Red Sox Nation, North" (Mosher), **Supp. XXII:** 209

"Red Star, Winter Orbit" (W. Gibson and B. Sterling), **Supp. XVI:** 123

Red Suitcase (Nye), **Supp. XIII:** 277, 278, 287

Red the Fiend (Sorrentino), **Supp. XXI:** 227, 231, 237

Red Wallflower, A (S. Warner), **Supp. XVIII:** 260

"Red Wheelbarrow, The" (W. C. Williams), **IV:** 411–412; **Retro. Supp. I:** 419, 430

"Red Wind" (Chandler), **Supp. IV Part 1:** 122

"Red Wing Church, The" (Kooser), **Supp. XIX:** 119

"Redwings" (Wright), **Supp. III Part 2:** 603

Reed, Edward Bliss, **Supp. XV:** 297, 298, 300

Reed, Ishmael, **Retro. Supp. II:** 111, 324–325; **Supp. II Part 1:** 34; **Supp. X: 239–257,** 331; **Supp. XIII:** 181, 182; **Supp. XVI:** 143; **Supp. XX:** 107; **Supp. XXII:** 172; **Supp. XXVII:** 167

Reed, J. D., **Supp. XVI:** 174

Reed, John, **I:** 48, 476, 483; **Supp. X:** 136; **Supp. XV:** 295, 299; **Supp. XVII:** 96, 99, 100; **Supp. XVIII:** 225; **Supp. XXI:** 6, 12; **Supp. XXII:** 274, 275; **Supp. XXIII:** 161, 162; **Supp. XXVIII:** 37, 38, 39, 40, 47

Reed, Lou, **Retro. Supp. II:** 266

"Reedbeds of the Hackensack, The" (Clampitt), **Supp. IX:** 41

"Reed of Pan, A" (McCullers), **II:** 585

Reedy, Billy, **Retro. Supp. II:** 65, 67, 71, 73

Reedy, William Marion, **Supp. I Part 2:** 456, 461, 465; **Supp. XXVII:** 287

Reef, The (Wharton), **IV:** 317–318, 322; **Retro. Supp. I:** 372, **373–374; Retro. Supp. III:** 284, 285

Reena and Other Stories (Marshall), **Supp. XI:** 275, 277, 278

Reese, Debbie, **Supp. XXVI:** 108–109

"Reese in Evening Shadow" (Skloot), **Supp. XX: 204**

Reeve, F. D., **Retro. Supp. III:** 107; **Supp. XV:** 344, 349

Reeve's Tale (Chaucer), **I:** 131

"Refiguring the Postcolonial Imagination: Tropes of Visuality in Writing by Rhys, Kincaid, and Cliff" (Emery), **Supp. XXII:** 73

Refiner's Fire: The Life and Adventures of Marshall Pearl, a Foundling (Helprin), **Supp. XXV:** 83, 85–86

"Reflection from Anita Loos" (Empson), **Supp. XVI:** 190

"Reflections" (Carruth), **Supp. XVI:** 54

"Reflections" (Komunyakaa), **Supp. XIII:** 117

Reflections at Fifty and Other Essays (Farrell), **II:** 49

"Reflections by a Fire" (Sarton), **Supp. VIII:** 259

Reflections in a Golden Eye (McCullers), **II:** 586, 588, 593–596, 604; **IV:** 384, 396

Reflections of a Jacobite (Auchincloss), **Supp. IV Part 1:** 31

Reflections on a Gift of Watermelon Pickle (Dunning), **Supp. XIV:** 126

Reflections on Poetry and Poetics (Nemerov), **III:** 269

"Reflections on the Constitution of Nature" (Freneau), **Supp. II Part 1:** 274

"Reflections on the Death of the Reader" (Morris), **III:** 237

Reflections on the End of an Era (Niebuhr), **III:** 297–298

"Reflections on the Life and Death of Lord Clive" (Paine), **Supp. I Part 2:** 505

Reflections on the Revolution in France (Burke), **Supp. I Part 2:** 511, 512

Reflections: Thinking Part I (Arendt), **Supp. I Part 2:** 570

"Reflex Action and Theism" (James), **II:** 345, 363

Reflex and Bone Structure (Major), **Supp. XXII: 174–175**

"Refrains/Remains/Reminders" (Goldbarth), **Supp. XII:** 180–181, 181

"Refuge" (Kingsolver), **Supp. VII:** 208

"Refuge" (Teasdale), **Supp. XXVII:** 291

"Refuge, A" (Goldbarth), **Supp. XII:** 190

Refugee Children: Theory, Research, and Services (Ahearn and Athey, eds.), **Supp. XI:** 184

"Refugees, The" (Jarrell), **II:** 371

"Refusal" (C. Frost), **Supp. XV:** 102

"Refusal to Publish Fifth Book" (Halliday), **Supp. XIX:** 94

"Regalia" (H. Johnson), **Supp. XXVI:** 172

Regarding Wave (Snyder), **Supp. VIII: 299–300**

Regina (Epstein), **Supp. XII: 170–171**

"Regional Literature of the South" (Rawlings), **Supp. X:** 228

"Regional Writer, The" (O'Connor), **Retro. Supp. II:** 223, 225

Régnier, Henri de, **II:** 528–529

Regular Guy, A (Simpson), **Supp. XXVII:** 239–240

Regulators, The (King), **Supp. V:** 141

Rehder, Robert, **Supp. IV Part 1:** 69

Rehearsing Absence (Espaillat), **Supp. XXI:** 99

Reich, Tova, **Supp. XVI:** 158

Reichel, Hans, **III:** 183

Reichl, Ruth, **Supp. X:** 79, 85

Reid, B. L., **II:** 41, 47

Reid, Forrest, **Supp. XX: 235**

Reid, Thomas, **II:** 9; **Supp. I Part 1:** 151

Reign of Snakes (Wrigley), **Supp. XVIII:** 293, **302–306**

"Reign of Snakes" (Wrigley), **Supp. XVIII:** 302–304

Reign of Wonder, The (Tanner), **I:** 260

Rein, Yevgeny, **Supp. VIII:** 22

Reinagle, Alexander, **Supp. XV:** 238, 240

"Reincarnation" (Dickey), **Supp. IV Part 1:** 181–182

Reine des pommes, La (C. Himes). *See For Love of Imabelle* (C. Himes)

Reiner, Carl, **Supp. IV Part 2:** 591

Reinfeld, Linda, **Supp. IV Part 2:** 421

Reinhardt, Max, **Supp. XV:** 307

Reinventing the Enemy's Language: Contemporary Native Women's Writing of North America (Bird and Harjo, eds.), **Supp. XII:** 216, 217

Reisman, Jerry, **Supp. III Part 2:** 618

Reiter, Amy, **Supp. XIX:** 54, 56

Reitlinger, Gerald, **Supp. XII:** 161

Reivers, The: A Reminiscence (Faulkner), **I:** 305; **II:** 57, 73; **Retro. Supp. I:** 74, 82, 91; **Retro. Supp. III:** 87–88

"Rejoicings" (Stern), **Supp. IX:** 289–290

Rejoicings: Selected Poems, 1966–1972 (Stern), **Supp. IX: 289–290**

Relation of My Imprisonment, The (Banks), **Supp. V:** 8, 12–13

"Relations" (Biss), **Supp. XXVI:** 56

"Relations between Poetry and Painting, The" (Stevens), **Retro. Supp. I:** 312

Relations of the Alabama-Georgia Dialect to the Provincial Dialects of Great Britain, The (Brooks), **Supp. XIV:** 3

Relative Stranger, A (C. Baxter), **Supp. XVII:** 19, 22

"Relativity of Beauty, The" (Rawlings), **Supp. X:** 226

Relearning the Alphabet (Levertov), **Supp. III Part 1:** 280, 281

"Release" (C. Baxter), **Supp. XVII:** 15

"Release, The" (MacLeish), **III:** 16

Reles, Abe ("Kid Twist"), **Supp. IV Part 1:** 382

"Relevance of an Impossible Ethical Ideal, The" (Niebuhr), **III:** 298

"Religion" (Dunbar), **Supp. II Part 1:** 199

"Religion" (Emerson), **II:** 6

Religion of Nature Delineated, The (Wollaston), **II:** 108

"Religious Instruction" (Peacock), **Supp. XIX:** 200, 201

Religious Rebel, A: The Letters of "H. W. S." (Mrs. Pearsall Smith) (L. P. Smith), **Supp. XIV:** 349

"Reluctance" (Frost), **II:** 153; **Retro. Supp. III:** 96

Reluctantly: Autobiographical Essays (Carruth), **Supp. XVI:** 45–46, 50

Remains (Snodgrass), **Supp. VI:** 311, **313–314**

"Remains, The" (Strand), **Supp. IV Part 2:** 627

"Remains of Princess Kaiulani's Garden, The" (Vaz), **Supp. XXVI:** 262–263

"Remarks on Color" (Wright), **Supp. XV:** 346

"Remarks on National Literature" (Channing), **Supp. XXIV: 76–77**

"Remarks on Spencer's *Definition of Mind as Correspondence*" (James), **II:** 345

Remarque, Erich Maria, **Retro. Supp. I:** 113; **Supp. IV Part 1:** 380

Rembrandt, **II:** 536; **IV:** 310; **Supp. IV Part 1:** 390, 391

"Rembrandt, The" (Wharton), **IV:** 310

"Rembrandt's Hat" (Malamud), **Supp. I Part 2:** 435, 437

Rembrandt Takes a Walk (Strand), **Supp. IV Part 2:** 631

"Rembrandt to Rembrandt" (Robinson), **III:** 521–522

Remembered Earth, The: An Anthology of Contemporary Native American Literature (Hobson, ed.), **Supp. IV Part 1:** 321

Remembered Yesterdays (R. U. Johnson), **Supp. IX:** 184

"Remembering" (Angelou), **Supp. IV Part 1:** 15

"Remembering Allen Tate" (Cowley), **Supp. II Part 1:** 153

"Remembering Barthes" (Sontag), **Supp. III Part 2:** 451, 471

"Remembering Guston" (Kunitz), **Supp. III Part 1:** 257

"Remembering James Laughlin" (Karr), **Supp. XI:** 242

Remembering Laughter (Stegner), **Supp. IV Part 2:** 598, 606, 607, 608, 611, 614

"Remembering Lobo" (Mora), **Supp. XIII:** 220, 227

"Remembering My Father" (Berry), **Supp. X:** 23

"Remembering My Parents Remembering the Books They Read" (Espaillat), **Supp. XXI:** 107

"Remembering that Island" (McGrath), **Supp. X:** 116

"Remembering the Children of Auschwitz" (McGrath), **Supp. X:** 127

"Remembering the Lost World" (Jarrell), **II:** 388

"Remembering the Sixties" (Simpson), **Supp. IX:** 279

Remember Me to Tom (T. Williams), **IV:** 379–380

"Remember Not" (H. Johnson), **Supp. XXVI:** 166

"Remember the Moon Survives" (Kingsolver), **Supp. VII:** 209

Remember to Remember (H. Miller), **III:** 186

"Remembrance, A" (Gioia), **Supp. XV:** 112

Remembrance of Things Past (Proust), **Supp. IV Part 2:** 600; **Supp. XII:** 9; **Supp. XIII:** 44

Remembrance Rock (Sandburg), **III:** 590

Reminiscence, A (Ashbery), **Supp. III Part 1:** 2

Remnick, David, **Supp. XVI:** 246

"Remora" (Merrill), **Supp. III Part 1:** 326

"Removal" (White), **Supp. I Part 2:** 664–665

"Removal, The" (Merwin), **Supp. III Part 1:** 350, 351

"Removal Service Request" (Halliday), **Supp. XIX:** 90

Removed from Time (Matthews and Feeney), **Supp. IX:** 154

Remsen, Ira, **Supp. I Part 1:** 369

"Rémy de Gourmont, A Distinction" (Pound), **III:** 467

"Renaissance" (Carruth), **Supp. XVI:** 56

Renaissance in the South (Bradbury), **I:** 288–289

Renaldo and Clara (film, Dylan and Shepard), **Supp. XVIII:** 21, 28, 31

"Renaming the Kings" (Levine), **Supp. V:** 184

Renan, Ernest, **Supp. XX:** 122

Renan, Joseph Ernest, **II:** 86; **IV:** 440, 444

Renard, Jules, **IV:** 79

"Renascence" (Millay), **III:** 123, 125–126, 128; **Supp. XV:** 42

Renault, Mary, **Supp. IV Part 2:** 685

"Rendezvous, The" (Kumin), **Supp. IV Part 2:** 455

René, Norman, **Supp. X:** 146, 152

Renée (anonymous author), **Supp. XVI:** 64, 66

Renegade (Lewisohn), **Supp. XXVIII:** 150, 152, 155

"Renegade, The" (Jackson), **Supp. IX:** 120

Renewal of Life series (Mumford), **Supp. II Part 2:** 476, 479, 481, 482, 485, 495, 497

"Reno Hill ... Little Bighorn"(Kenny), **Supp. XXIII:** 155

Renoir, Jean, **Supp. XII:** 259; **Supp. XXII:** 256

Renouvrier, Charles, **II:** 344–345, 346

"Renunciation" (Banks), **Supp. V:** 10

Renza, Louis A., **Retro. Supp. II:** 142

"Repair" (Peacock), **Supp. XIX:** 204

"Repeating Dream" (Gander), **Supp. XV:** 340

Repent in Haste (Marquand), **III:** 59

Reperusals and Re-Collections (L. P. Smith), **Supp. XIV:** 346–347

"Repetitive Heart, The: Eleven Poems in Imitation of the Fugue Form" (Schwartz), **Supp. II Part 2:** 645–646

"Replacing Regionalism" (Murphy), **Retro. Supp. II:** 143

Replansky, Naomi, **Supp. X:** 119

Replenishing Jessica (Bodenheim), **Supp. XXV:** 24, 25

"Reply to Mr. Wordsworth" (MacLeish), **III:** 19

"Reply to the Editor of 'The Art of Authorship' " (Twain), **Retro. Supp. III:** 265

"Report, A" (Jin), **Supp. XVIII:** 93

Reporter, The (Levin), **Supp. XXVII:** 139

"Report from a Forest Logged by the Weyhaeuser Company" (Wagoner), **Supp. IX:** 328

"Report from North Vietnam" (Paley), **Supp. VI:** 227

Report from Part One (Brooks), **Supp. III Part 1:** 70, 72, 80, 82–85

Report from Part Two (Brooks), **Supp. III Part 1:** 87

Report on a Game Survey of the North Central States (Leopold), **Supp. XIV:** 182

"Report on the Barnhouse Effect" (Vonnegut), **Supp. II Part 2:** 756

"Report to an Academy, A" (Kafka), **Supp. XX:** 18

"Report to Crazy Horse" (Stafford), **Supp. XI: 324–325**

"Repose of Rivers" (H. Crane), **I:** 393; **Retro. Supp. II:** 78, 81

"Repossession of a Heritage, The" (Zagarell), **Supp. XV:** 270, 281

Repp, John, **Supp. XXIII:** 302

"Representation and the War for Reality" (Gass), **Supp. VI:** 88

"Representative Indian, The" (*Outlook*), **Supp. XXV:** 277, 278

Representative Men (Emerson), **II:** 1, 5–6, 8

"Representing Far Places" (Stafford), **Supp. XI:** 321

Repression and Recovery (Nelson), **Supp. XVIII:** 226

"REPRISE OF ONE OF A. G.'S BEST POEMS" (Baraka), **Supp. II Part 1:** 59

"RepRoach" (Stallings), **Supp. XXV:** 230–231

"Reproducing Ourselves Is All Very Well" (E. Hoffman), **Supp. XVI:** 155

Republic (Plato), **I:** 485; **Retro. Supp. III:** 94

"Republican Manifesto, A" (Paine), **Supp. I Part 2:** 511

"Republican Mother, The: Woman and the Enlightenment—An American Perspective" (Kerber), **Supp. XXV:** 44

Republic of Love, The (Shields), **Supp. VII:** 323–324, 326, 327

"Requa" (Olsen), **Supp. XIII:** 294, **302–303,** 304

Requa, Kenneth A., **Supp. I Part 1:** 107

"Requa I" (Olsen). See "Requa" (Olsen)

"Request for Offering" (Eberhart), **I:** 526

"Requiem" (Akhmatova), **Supp. VIII:** 20

"Requiem" (LaBastille), **Supp. X:** 105

Requiem for a Nun (Faulkner), **II:** 57, 72–73; **Retro. Supp. III:** 73, 86, 87

Requiem for Harlem (H. Roth), **Supp. IX:** 235, 236, **240–242**

"Rescue, The" (Updike), **IV:** 214

Rescued Year, The (Stafford), **Supp. XI: 321–322**

"Rescued Year, The" (Stafford), **Supp. XI:** 322, 323

"Rescue with Yul Brynner" (Moore), **III:** 215

"Rescuing Moon"(P. Benedict), **Supp. XXIII:** 40

"Resemblance" (Bishop), **Supp. I Part 1:** 86

"Resemblance" (Ferry), **Supp. XXIV:** 161

"Resemblance between a Violin Case and a Coffin, A" (T. Williams), **IV:** 378–379

"Reservations" (Taylor), **Supp. V:** 323

"Reserved Memorials" (Mather), **Supp. II Part 2:** 446, 449

"Resignación" (Espaillat), **Supp. XXI:** 104

"Resignation"(J. Schoolcraft), **Supp. XXIII:** 228, 229–230

"Resistance to Civil Government" (Thoreau), **Supp. X:** 27, 28

Resist Much, Obey Little (Berry), **Supp. XIII:** 2

Resolution (Parker), **Supp. XIX:** 187

"Resolution" (Rash), Supp. XXVII: 221

"Resolution and Independence" (Wordsworth), **Supp. XV:** 346

"Resonance" (Stone), **Supp. XXVII:** 253

"Resort" (Hampl), **Supp. XXII:** 86–87

Resort and Other Poems (Hampl), **Supp. XXII:** 83, 86–87

Resources of Hope (R. Williams), **Supp. IX:** 146

"Respectable Place, A" (O'Hara), **III:** 369

"Respectable Woman, A" (Chopin), **Retro. Supp. II:** 66

"Respite" (Pedersen; Nelson, trans.), **Supp. XVIII:** 180

Responses (Wilbur), **Supp. III Part 2:** 541

"Response to a Rumor that the Oldest Whorehouse in Wheeling, West Virginia, Has Been Condemned" (Wright), **Supp. III Part 2:** 602

"Rest Cure" (Boyle), **Supp. XXIV:** 57

Restif de La Bretonne, Nicolas, **III:** 175

"Rest of Life, The" (Gordon), **Supp. IV Part 1:** 311

Rest of Life, The: Three Novellas (Gordon), **Supp. IV Part 1:** 310–312

Rest of My Life, The (Wells), **Supp. XXVI:** 271, 283

Rest of the Way, The (McClatchy), **Supp. XII:** 255, **258–259**

Restoration comedy, **Supp. I Part 2:** 617

Restorers, The (Di Piero), **Supp. XIX:** 42–43, 44

"Restorers, The" (Di Piero), **Supp. XIX:** 43

"Restraint" (F. Barthelme), **Supp. XI:** 26

"Result" (Emerson), **II:** 6

"Résumé" (Parker), **Supp. IX:** 189

"Resurrecting Methuselah" (E. P. Jones), **Supp. XXII:** 151

Resurrection (Della Francesca), **Supp. XV:** 262

"Resurrection" (Harjo), **Supp. XII:** 224

"Resurrection" (Jin), **Supp. XVIII:** 94–95

Resurrection, The (Gardner), **Supp. VI:** 61, 63, **64–65,** 68, 69, 73, 74

"Resurrection, The" (Very), **Supp. XXV:** 247–248

Resurrection Blues (A. Miller), **Retro. Supp. III:** 176–177

"Retort" (Hay), **Supp. XIV:** 133

Retour amont (Char; Sobin, trans.), **Supp. XVI:** 282

Retrieval System, The (Kumin), **Supp. IV Part 2:** 449, 451, 452

"Retrievers in Translation" (Doty), **Supp. XI:** 132

"Retroduction to American History" (Tate), **IV:** 129

"Retrospects and Prospects" (Lanier), **Supp. I Part 1:** 352

"Return" (Corso), **Supp. XII:** 135

"Return" (Creeley), **Supp. IV Part 1:** 141, 145

"Return" (MacLeish), **III:** 12

"Return" (Oppen), **Supp. XXVI:** 231

"Return, The" (Bidart), **Supp. XV:** 32–33

"Return, The" (Bontemps), **Supp. XXII:** 3, 8

"Return, The" (Pound), **Retro. Supp. I:** 288

"Return, The" (Ray), **Supp. XVIII:** 194

"Return, The" (Roethke), **III:** 533

"Return, The: Orihuela, 1965" (Levine), **Supp. V:** 194

"Return: An Elegy, The" (Warren), **IV:** 239

"Return: Buffalo" (Hogan), **Supp. IV Part 1:** 411

"Returning" (Komunyakaa), **Supp. XIII:** 122

"Returning a Lost Child" (Glück), **Supp. V:** 81

"Returning from the Enemy" (Harjo), **Supp. XII:** 229–230

Returning North with the Spring (Harris), **Supp. XXVIII:** 256

"Returning the Borrowed Road" (Komunyakaa), **Supp. XIII:** 113, 133

"Return of Alcibiade, The" (Chopin), **Retro. Supp. II:** 58, 64

Return of Ansel Gibbs, The (Buechner), **III:** 310; **Supp. XII: 48**

"Return of Eros to Academe, The" (Bukiet), **Supp. XVII:** 47

"Return of Spring" (Winters), **Supp. II Part 2:** 791

Return of the Native, The (Hardy), **II:** 184–185, 186

Return of the Vanishing American, The (Fiedler), **Supp. XIII:** 103

Return to a Place Lit by a Glass of Milk (Simic), **Supp. VIII:** 274, 276, 283

"Return to Lavinia" (Caldwell), **I:** 310

"Return to Thin Air: The Everest Disaster Ten Years Later" *(Outside),* **Supp. XVIII:** 113

Return to Zion, The (Asch), **Supp. XXIII:** 5

Reuben (Wideman), **Supp. X:** 320

Reuben and Rachel; or, Tales of Old Times (Rowson), **Supp. XV: 240–241**

Reunion (Mamet), **Supp. XIV:** 240, 247, 254

"Reunion in Brooklyn" (H. Miller), **III:** 175, 184

"Reunion Joke, The" (Huddle), **Supp. XXVI:** 156

Reuther brothers, **I:** 493

"Reveille" (Kingsolver), **Supp. VII:** 208

"Reveille" (Untermeyer), **Supp. XV:** 300

"Reveille, The" (Harte), **Supp. II Part 1:** 342–343

Revelation (biblical book), **II:** 541; **IV:** 104, 153, 154; **Supp. I Part 1:** 105, 273

"Revelation" (O'Connor), **III:** 349, 353–354; **Retro. Supp. II:** 237; **Retro. Supp. III:** 208, 212–213

"Revelation" (Warren), **III:** 490

Revelations of Divine Love (Julian of Norwich), **Retro. Supp. III:** 68

Revenge (Harrison), **Supp. VIII:** 39, 45

"Revenge of Hamish, The" (Lanier), **Supp. I Part 1:** 365

"Revenge of Hannah Kemhuff, The" (Walker), **Supp. III Part 2:** 521

"Revenge of Rain-in-the-Face, The" (Longfellow), **Retro. Supp. II:** 170

"Reverberation"(Kenny), **Supp. XXIII:** 155

Reverberator, The (James), **Retro. Supp. I:** 227

"Reverdure" (Berry), **Supp. X:** 22

Reverdy, Pierre, **Supp. XV:** 178, 182; **Supp. XXIII:** 208

"Reverend Father Gilhooley" (Farrell), **II:** 45

Reverse Transcription (Kushner), **Supp. IX:** 138

Reversible Errors (Turow), **Supp. XVII: 220–221**

"Rev. Freemont Deadman" (Masters), **Supp. I Part 2:** 463

Reviewer's ABC, A (Aiken), **I:** 58

Review of Contemporary Fiction, 1990 (Tabbi, ed.), **Supp. XVII:** 143

"Revolt, against the Crepuscular Spirit in Modern Poetry" (Pound), **Retro. Supp. I:** 286

"Revolution" (C. L. R. James), **Supp. XXI:** 160

"Revolution" (Taggard), **Supp. XXII:** 275

"Revolutionary Answer to the Negro Problem in the USA, The" (statement, C. L. R. James), **Supp. XXI:** 169

Revolutionary Petunias (Walker), **Supp. III Part 2:** 520, 522, 530

Revolutionary Road (Yates), **Supp. XI:** 334, **335–340**

"Revolutionary Symbolism in America" (Burke), **I:** 272

"Revolutionary Theatre, The" (Baraka), **Supp. II Part 1:** 42

Revolution in Taste, A: Studies of Dylan Thomas, Allen Ginsberg, Sylvia Plath, and Robert Lowell (Simpson), **Supp. IX:** 276

"Revolution in the Revolution in the Revolution" (Snyder), **Supp. VIII:** 300

Revon, Marcel, **II:** 525

"Rewaking, The" (W. C. Williams), **Retro. Supp. I:** 430

"Rewrite" (Dunn), **Supp. XI:** 147

"Rewriting Tradition in the Digital Era: The Vision of Eric Gansworth" (Purdy), **Supp. XXVI:** 105

Rexroth, Kenneth, **II:** 526; **Supp. II Part 1:** 307; **Supp. II Part 2:** 436; **Supp. III Part 2:** 625, 626; **Supp. IV Part 1:** 145–146; **Supp. VIII:** 289; **Supp. XIII:** 75; **Supp. XIV:** 287; **Supp. XV:** 140, 141, 146; **Supp. XXII:** 168

Reynolds, Ann (pseudonym). See Bly, Carol

Reynolds, Clay, **Supp. XI:** 254

Reynolds, David, **Supp. XV:** 269; **Supp. XXIII:** 187

Reynolds, Sir Joshua, **Supp. I Part 2:** 716

Reynolds, Quentin, **IV:** 286

Reza, Yasmina, **Supp. XXI:** 148

Rezanov (Atherton), **Supp. XXIV:** 23

Reznikoff, Charles, **IV:** 415; **Retro. Supp. I:** 422; **Supp. III Part 2:** 615,

616, 617, 628; **Supp. XIV: 277–296;**
Supp. XXIII: 174; **Supp. XXIV:** 36,
45; **Supp. XXVI:** 226
"Rhapsodist, The" (Brown), **Supp. I Part**
1: 125–126
"Rhapsody on a Windy Night" (T. S.
Eliot), **Retro. Supp. I:** 55; **Retro.**
Supp. III: 60
Rhetoric of Motives, A (Burke), **I:** 272,
275, 278, 279
Rhetoric of Religion, The (Burke), **I:** 275,
279
"Rhobert" (Toomer), **Supp. IX:** 316–317
"Rhode Show" (Mallon), **Supp. XIX:**
137–138
"Rhododendrons" (Levis), **Supp. XI:**
260, 263
Rhubarb Show, The (radio, Keillor),
Supp. XVI: 178
"Rhyme of Sir Christopher, The"
(Longfellow), **II:** 501
Rhymes to Be Traded for Bread (Lindsay),
Supp. I Part 2: 380, 381–382
Rhys, Ernest, **III:** 458
Rhys, Jean, **Supp. III Part 1:** 42, 43;
Supp. XVIII: 131
"Rhythm" (Stone), **Supp. XXVII:** 249–
250
"Rhythm & Blues" (Baraka), **Supp. II**
Part 1: 37–38
Rhythms (Reznikoff), **Supp. XIV:** 279,
282, 283
Rhythms II (Reznikoff), **Supp. XIV:** 282,
283, 284
"Rialto, The"(Woodson and Lynch),
Supp. XXVIII: 288
Ribalow, Harold, **Supp. IX:** 236; **Supp.**
XXVII: 133
Ribbentrop, Joachim von, **IV:** 249
Ribicoff, Abraham, **Supp. IX:** 33
Ribot, Théodule Armand, **Supp. XX: 238**
Ricardo, David, **Supp. I Part 2:** 628, 634
Rice, Allen Thorndike, **Retro. Supp. I:**
362
Rice, Anne, **Supp. VII: 287–306**
Rice, Elmer, **I:** 479; **III:** 145, 160–161
Rice, Mrs. Grantland, **II:** 435
Rice, Philip Blair, **IV:** 141
Rice, Stan, **Supp. XII:** 2
Rice, Tim, **Supp. XXI:** 148
Rice, Tom, **Supp. XIV:** 125
Rich, Adrienne, **Retro. Supp. I:** 8, 36,
42, 47, 404; **Retro. Supp. II:** 43, 191,
245; **Retro. Supp. III:** 1, 12, 14, **241–**
254; Supp. I Part 2: 546–547, **550–**
578; Supp. III Part 1: 84, 354; **Supp.**
III Part 2: 541, 599; **Supp. IV Part**
1: 257, 325; **Supp. V:** 82; **Supp. VIII:**
272; **Supp. XII:** 217, 229, 255; **Supp.**
XIII: 294; **Supp. XIV:** 126, 129;
Supp. XIX: 83, 193; **Supp. XV:** 176,
252; **Supp. XVII:** 32, 74; **Supp.**
XXII: 65, 66; **Supp. XXV:** 3; **Supp.**
XXVI: 45, 68; **Supp. XXVII:** 165;
Supp. XXVIII: 196
Rich, Arnold, **Supp. I Part 2:** 552
Rich, Frank, **Supp. IV Part 2:** 585, 586;
Supp. V: 106; **Supp. XXI:** 146; **Supp.**
XXIV: 121, 124
Richard, Mark, **Supp. XIX: 209–222**

Richard Cory (Gurney), **Supp. V:** 99–
100, 105
"Richard Hunt's 'Arachne' " (Hayden),
Supp. II Part 1: 374
Richard II (Shakespeare), **Supp. XVII:**
244
Richard III (Shakespeare), **Supp. I Part**
2: 422
Richards, Bertrand F., **Supp. XX: 217–**
218
Richards, Constance S., **Supp. XXII:** 73
Richards, David, **Supp. IV Part 2:** 576;
Supp. XXIV: 266, 269
Richards, Grant, **I:** 515
Richards, I. A., **I:** 26, 273–274, 279, 522;
III: 498; **IV:** 92; **Supp. I Part 1:** 264,
265; **Supp. I Part 2:** 647; **Supp.**
XXVI: 63
Richards, Ivor Armonstrong, **Supp. XIV:**
2–3, 16
Richards, Keith, **Supp. XXVII:** 40, 41,
45
Richards, Laura E., **II:** 396; **III:** 505–
506, 507
Richards, Leonard, **Supp. XIV:** 48
Richards, Lloyd, **Retro. Supp. III:** 315,
318, 323; **Supp. IV Part 1:** 362;
Supp. VIII: 331
Richards, Rosalind, **III:** 506
Richards, Tad, **Supp. XVII:** 77
Richardson, Alan, **III:** 295
Richardson, Charles F., **Retro. Supp. III:**
261; **Supp. XVIII:** 14, 15
Richardson, Dorothy, **I:** 53; **II:** 320;
Supp. III Part 1: 65
Richardson, Helen Patges, **Retro. Supp.**
II: 95
Richardson, Henry Hobson, **I:** 3, 10
Richardson, Maurice, **Supp. XII:** 241
Richardson, Samuel, **I:** 134; **II:** 104, 111,
322; **Supp. IX:** 128; **Supp. V:** 127;
Supp. XV: 232; **Supp. XX: 236**
Richardson, Tony, **Supp. XI:** 305, 306
"Richard Wright and Recent Negro Fic-
tion" (Ellison), **Retro. Supp. II:** 116
"Richard Wright's Blues" (Ellison),
Retro. Supp. II: 117, 124
"Richard Yates: A Requiem" (Lawrence),
Supp. XI: 335
"Rich Boy, The" (Fitzgerald), **II:** 94;
Retro. Supp. I: 98, 108
Richer, the Poorer, The: Sketches and
Reminiscences (D. West), **Supp.**
XVIII: 277, 289
"Riches" (Bausch), **Supp. VII:** 54
"Riches" (Teasdale), **Supp. XXVII:** 290
Richey, Elinor, **Supp. XXIV:** 30
Richler, Mordecai, **Supp. XI:** 294, 297
Rich Man, Poor Man (miniseries), **Supp.**
XIX: 252
Rich Man, Poor Man (Shaw), **Supp.**
XIX: 251–252
Richman, Robert, **Supp. XI:** 249; **Supp.**
XV: 120–121, 251
Richman, Shira, **Supp. XXIV:** 167
Richmond (Masters), **Supp. I Part 2:** 471
Richmond, M. A., **Supp. XX: 277, 279,**
282, 286, 289, 290
Rich Relations (Hwang), **Supp. XXI:**
146–147

Richter, Conrad, **Supp. X:** 103; **Supp.**
XVIII: 207–222
Richter, Jean Paul, **II:** 489, 492; **Supp.**
XVI: 182
Rick Bass (Weltzien), **Supp. XVI:** 20
Rickman, Clio, **Supp. I Part 2:** 519
Ricks, Christopher, **Retro. Supp. I:** 56;
Supp. XVIII: 20, 30, 32
Riddel, Joseph N., **IV:** 95
"Riddle, The" (Hay), **Supp. XIV:** 130
Ride down Mt Morgan, The (A. Miller),
Retro. Supp. III: 173
"Ride in an Omnibus, A" (Briggs), **Supp.**
XVIII: 9, 16
Rideout, Walter B., **Supp. XXVI:** 28
"Riders to the Blood-Red Wrath"
(Brooks), **Supp. III Part 1:** 82–83
Riders to the Sea (Synge), **III:** 157
Ridge, Lola, **Supp. IX:** 308; **Supp. XV:**
307; **Supp. XXIV:** 49, 52; **Supp.**
XXVI: 23
Riding, Alan, **Supp. XVI:** 294
Riding, Laura, **I:** 437
"Riding Out at Evening" (McCarriston),
Supp. XIV: 262–263
Riding the Iron Rooster: By Train through
China (Theroux), **Supp. VIII:** 324
Ridley, Clifford, **Supp. XXIV:** 282
Riesenberg, Felix, **I:** 360, 361
Riesman, David, **Supp. I Part 2:** 649,
650
"Rif, to Music, The" (Bowles), **Supp. IV**
Part 1: 89
"Riff"(Lea), **Supp. XXVIII:** 137
Riffs & Reciprocities (Dunn), **Supp. XI:**
154–155
Rifkin, Libby, **Supp. XXIV:** 39, 44
Rifles, The (Vollmann), **Supp. XVII:** 226,
233
Riggs, Kate Douglas Wiggin, **Supp.**
XXVIII: 229
Riggs, Marlon, **Supp. XI:** 19
Right Distance, The (Pickering), **Supp.**
XXI: 196–197
Right Madness on Skye, The (Hugo),
Supp. VI: 145–147
Rights of Man (Paine), **Supp. I Part 2:**
508, 511, 512–514, 516, 519, 523
"Rights of Woman" (Rowson), **Supp. XV:**
243
"Rights of Women, The" (Brown). *See*
Alcuin: A Dialogue (Brown)
Right Stuff, The (Wolfe), **Supp. III Part**
2: 581–584
Right Thoughts in Sad Hours (Mather),
IV: 144
Rigney, Barbara Hill, **Supp. VIII:** 215
"Rigorists" (Moore), **III:** 198
Rihani, Ameen, **Supp. XX: 115**
Rihoku, **Supp. XXII:** 228
Riis, Jacob A., **I:** 293; **Supp. I Part 1:**
13; **Supp. XVII:** 101, 106
Riley, Glenda, **Supp. XXIV:** 252
Riley, James Whitcomb, **I:** 205; **Supp. II**
Part 1: 192, 193, 196, 197
Rilke, Rainer Maria, **I:** 445, 523; **II:** 367,
381, 382–383, 389, 543, 544; **III:** 552,
558, 563, 571, 572; **IV:** 380, 443;
Retro. Supp. II: 20, 187; **Supp. I**
Part 1: 264; **Supp. I Part 2:** 573;

Supp. III Part 1: 239, 242, 246, 283, 319–320; **Supp. IV Part 1:** 284; **Supp. V:** 208, 343; **Supp. VIII:** 30, 40; **Supp. X:** 164; **Supp. XI:** 126; **Supp. XIII:** 74, 88; **Supp. XV:** 93, 212, 222,**Supp. XV:** 223, 225; **Supp. XVI:** 292; **Supp. XVII:** 244; **Supp. XXII:** 89, 90, 94; **Supp. XXIII:** 207; **Supp. XXIV:** 37, 38, 152, 162; **Supp. XXVI:** 259

Rilke on Love and Other Difficulties (Rilke), **Supp. X:** 164

"Rilke's Growth as a Poet" (Dobyns), **Supp. XIII:** 77

"Rimbaud" (Kerouac), **Supp. III Part 1:** 232

Rimbaud, Arthur, **I:** 381, 383, 389, 391, 526; **II:** 528, 543, 545; **III:** 23, 174, 189; **IV:** 286, 380, 443; **Retro. Supp. I:** 56; **Retro. Supp. II:** 187, 326; **Supp. III Part 1:** 14, 195; **Supp. IV Part 2:** 624; **Supp. VIII:** 39, 40; **Supp. XII:** 1, 16, 128, 255; **Supp. XIII:** 284; **Supp. XIV:** 338; **Supp. XVIII:** 23, 33; **Supp. XXI:** 225, 233; **Supp. XXIII:** 207; **Supp. XXIV:** 39, 40

Rindge, Debora, **Supp. XXI:** 246

Rinehart, Mary Roberts, **Supp. XXV:** 189–203; **Supp. XXVI:** 276, 281, 282

Rinehart, Stanley, **III:** 36

Ring, Frances Kroll, **Supp. IX:** 63, 64

Ring and the Book, The (Browning), **Supp. I Part 2:** 416, 468

Ring cycle (Wagner), **Supp. IV Part 1:** 392

Ringe, Donald, **I:** 339, 343; **Retro. Supp. II:** 270

Ringel, Faye, **Supp. XXII:** 205, 207

"Ringing" (Bierds), **Supp. XVII:** 28

"Ringing the Bells" (Sexton), **Supp. II Part 2:** 672, 687

Ringle, Ken, **Supp. X:** 15

"Ringless"(Wakoski), **Supp. XXVIII:** 263

Ring of Heaven: Poems (Hongo), **Supp. X:** 292

Rings of Saturn, The (Wakoski), **Supp. XXVIII:** 267

Rink, The (musical, McNally), **Supp. XIII:** 207

Rin Tin Tin: The Life and the Legend (Orlean), **Supp. XXV:** 160, 165–166

Rio Lobo (film), **Supp. XVI:** 246

Ríos, Alberto Alvaro, **Supp. IV Part 2:** 537–556

"Riot" (Brooks), **Supp. III Part 1:** 71, 84–85

Riot (Myers), **Supp. XXVII:** 208

Ripening (Le Sueur), **Supp. XXIII:** 165

Ripley, Ezra, **II:** 8; **IV:** 172

Rip-off Red, Girl Detective (Acker), **Supp. XII:** 3–4

Ripostes (Pound), **Retro. Supp. I:** 287–288, 413

Ripostes of Ezra Pound, The, Whereunto Are Appended the Complete Poetical Works of T. E. Hulme, with Prefatory Note (Pound), **III:** 458, 464, 465

Riprap (Snyder), **Supp. VIII:** 292–294, 295

"Riprap" (Snyder), **Supp. VIII:** 293–294

"Rip Van Winkle" (Irving), **II:** 304–306; **Supp. I Part 1:** 185

Rischin, Moses, **Supp. XVII:** 101, 103, 106

Risco-Lozado, Eliezar, **Supp. XIII:** 313

Rise and Shine (Quindlen), **Supp. XVII:** 179

Rise of David Levinsky, The (Cahan), **Supp. IX:** 227; **Supp. XIII:** 106; **Supp. XXVI:** 123; **Supp. XXVIII:** 78

Rise of Silas Lapham, The (Howells), **II:** 275, 279, 283–285; **IV:** 202; **Retro. Supp. II:** 93, 101

"Rise of the Middle Class" (Banks), **Supp. V:** 10

Rising and Falling (Matthews), **Supp. IX:** 154, **160**

"Rising Daughter, The" (Olds), **Supp. X:** 204

Rising from the Plains (McPhee), **Supp. III Part 1:** 309–310

Rising Glory of America, The (Brackenridge and Freneau), **Supp. I Part 1:** 124; **Supp. II Part 1:** 67, 253, 256, 263

"Rising of the Storm, The" (Dunbar), **Supp. II Part 1:** 199

Rising Sun in the Pacific, The (Morison), **Supp. I Part 2:** 490

Rising Up and Rising Down (Vollmann), **Supp. XVII:** 225, 226, **229–230**, 232, 233, 235–236

Risk Pool, The (Russo), **Supp. XII:** 328–331

Ristovic, Aleksandar, **Supp. VIII:** 272

"Rita Dove: Identity Markers" (Vendler), **Supp. IV Part 1:** 247, 257

Ritchey, John, **Supp. XIV:** 122

Ritchie, Anne Thackeray, **Supp. XX:** 231, 233

"Rite of Passage" (Olds), **Supp. X:** 206

"Rites and Ceremonies" (Hecht), **Supp. X:** 61

Rites and Witnesses: A Comedy (Hinojosa), **Supp. XIX:** 106–107

"Rites of Spring, The" (Morris), **III:** 223

Ritholtz, Emily Rose, **Supp. XXVIII:** 285

Ritivoi, Andreea Deciu, **Supp. XVI:** 148

Ritschl, Albrecht, **III:** 309, 604

Ritsos, Yannis, **Supp. X:** 112

"Ritsos and the Metaphysical Moment" (Dobyns), **Supp. XIII:** 78

Rittenhouse, David, **Supp. I Part 2:** 507

Rittenhouse, Jessie, **Supp. XV:** 295; **Supp. XXVII:** 286, 288, 289, 297

"Ritual, The" (Jarman), **Supp. XVII:** 114

"Ritual and Renewal: Keres Traditions in the Short Fiction of Leslie Silko" (Ruoff), **Supp. IV Part 2:** 559

Ritz, The (film), **Supp. XIII:** 206

Ritz, The (McNally), **Supp. XIII:** 198

"Rival, The" (Plath), **Retro. Supp. II:** 254

Riven Rock (Boyle), **Supp. VIII:** 5–6; **Supp. XX:** 25–26

"River" (Ammons), **Supp. VII:** 28

"River, The" (O'Connor), **III:** 344, 352, 353, 354, 356; **Retro. Supp. II:** 229, 231–232; **Retro. Supp. III:** 213

Rivera, Tomás, **Supp. XIII:** 216, 221; **Supp. XIX:** 97, 102

Riverbed (Wagoner), **Supp. IX:** 327–328

"River Driftwood" (Jewett), **Retro. Supp. II:** 132, 133, 147

"River Jordan, The" (DeLillo), **Supp. VI:** 3, 4

River King, The (Hoffman), **Supp. X:** 78, 85, 90, **91–92**

"River Merchant's Wife: A Letter, The" (Pound), **III:** 463

"River Now, The" (Hugo), **Supp. VI:** 144

River of Forgetfulness, The (Hadas), **Supp. XXIII:** **120**

"River of Rivers in Connecticut, The" (Stevens), **Retro. Supp. I:** 313

River of the Mother of God and Other Essays by Aldo Leopold, The (Leopold), **Supp. XIV:** 180

"River"(O'Hara), **Supp. XXIII:** 212

"River Profile" (Auden), **Supp. II Part 1:** 26

"River Road" (Kunitz), **Supp. III Part 1:** 260

River Runs Through It, A (film), **Supp. XXVI:** 184

"River Runs Through It, A" (Maclean), **Supp. XIV:** 222–223, **223–229**, 233, 234, 235; **Supp. XVI:** 98

River Runs Through It and Other Stories, A (Maclean), **Supp. XIV:** 221, 223

Rivers, Allison, **Supp. XXIII:** 51

Rivers, Larry, **Supp. III Part 1:** 3; **Supp. XV:** 177, 178, 186; **Supp. XXIII:** 209, 210, 211, 212, 215, 216, 217, 220

Rivers and Mountains (Ashbery), **Supp. III Part 1:** 10, 26

River's Children, The: An Idyl of the Mississippi (Stuart), **Supp. XXVIII:** 233, 235

Riverside Drive (Simpson), **Supp. IX:** 275–276

Riverside Poetry (Auden, Moore, and Shapiro, eds.), **Supp. XXI:** 98

Rivers to the Sea (Teasdale), **Supp. XV:** 295; **Supp. XXVII:** 283, 286, 289, 290, 294

"River"(Strout), **Supp. XXIII:** 283

River Styx, Ohio, and Other Poems, The (Oliver), **Supp. VII:** 231, 232

"River That Is East, The" (Kinnell), **Supp. III Part 1:** 241–242

"River"(theater performance, Strout), **Supp. XXIII:** 281

"River Towns" (Masters), **Supp. I Part 2:** 473

Rives, Amélie, **II:** 194

Rivière, Jacques, **Retro. Supp. I:** 63

"Rivington's Last Will and Testament" (Freneau), **Supp. II Part 1:** 261

"Rivulet, The" (Bryant), **Supp. I Part 1:** 155, 162

Rix, Alice, **I:** 199

RL's Dream (Mosley), **Supp. XIII:** 234, **244–245**, 249

Roach, Max, **Supp. X:** 239

"Road, Roadsides, and the Disparate Frames of a Sequence" (Sobin), **Supp. XVI:** 288

"Road, The" (H. Johnson), **Supp. XXVI:** 164

Road, The (McCarthy), **Supp. XXII:** 49

Road, The: In Search of America (Asch), **Supp. XXVI:** 17, 21, 23, 25, 26–28

"Road Agent"(Lea), **Supp. XXVIII:** 136

Road Between, The (Farrell), **II:** 29, 38, 39–40

"Road Between Here and There, The" (Kinnell), **Supp. III Part 1:** 254

"Road Home, The" (Hammett), **Supp. IV Part 1:** 343

Road Home, The (Harrison), **Supp. VIII:** 37, 45, 48, **49–50,** 53

Road Is Before Us, The (Boulton), **Supp. XXII:** 17, 25–26

Roadless Yaak, The: Reflections and Observations about One of Our Last Great Wild Places (Bass, ed.), **Supp. XVI:** 23

"Road Not Taken, The" (Frost), **II:** 154; **Retro. Supp. I:** 131; **Retro. Supp. III:** 99; **Supp. XI:** 150; **Supp. XV:** 127

Road Not Taken, The: Finding America in the Poem Everyone Loves and Almost Everyone Gets Wrong (Orr), **Retro. Supp. III:** 99

"Roadside Flowers" (Collins), **Supp. XXI:** 61

Roadside Poems for Summer Travellers (Larcom, ed.), **Supp. XIII:** 142

"Roadside Resurrection, A" (L. Brown), **Supp. XXI:** 40, 42

Roads of Destiny (O. Henry), **Supp. II Part 1:** 410

Road through the Wall, The (Jackson), **Supp. IX:** 115, 118, 120, 123–124

"Road to Avignon, The" (A. Lowell), **II:** 516

"Road to Hell, The" (Fante), **Supp. XI:** 160

Road to Los Angeles, The (Fante), **Supp. XI:** 160, 166, 167, **168,** 172

Road to Many a Wonder, The (Wagoner), **Supp. IX:** 327, **336**

Road to the Temple, The (Glaspell), **Supp. III Part 1:** 175, 182, 186; **Supp. XXI:** 6

Road to Wellville, The (Boyle), **Supp. VIII:** 6–8; **Supp. XX:** 24–25, 26, 28

Road to Xanadu, The (Lowes), **IV:** 453

"Road Warrior" (Pickering), **Supp. XXI:** 204

"Roan Stallion" (Jeffers), **Supp. II Part 2:** 428–429

"Roast-beef" (Stein), **IV:** 43

Roast Leviatham (Untermeyer), **Supp. XV:** 307

"Roast Possum" (Dove), **Supp. IV Part 1:** 247, 248

Robards, Jason, Jr., **III:** 163, 403

Robb, Christina, **Supp. XV:** 251

Robbe-Grillet, Alain, **I:** 123; **IV:** 95; **Supp. IV Part 1:** 42; **Supp. V:** 47, 48; **Supp. XXIII:** 213

Robber Bride, The (Atwood), **Supp. XIII:** 30–31

Robber Bridegroom, The (Welty), **IV:** 261, 266–268, 271, 274; **Retro. Supp. I:** 347

Robbins, Amy Moorman, **Supp. XXVII:** 170

Robbins, Harold, **Supp. XII:** 6

Robbins, Henry, **Supp. IV Part 1:** 198, 201, 210, 211

Robbins, Katherine Robinson, **Supp. X:** 264

Robbins, Thomas, **Supp. XV:** 271

Robbins, Tom, **Supp. IV Part 1:** 227; **Supp. VIII:** 14; **Supp. X:** 259–288; **Supp. XIII:** 11

"Robe, The" (Douglas), **IV:** 434

Robert Bly (Sugg), **Supp. IV Part 1:** 68

"Robert Bly" (W. V. Davis), **Supp. IV Part 1:** 70

"Robert Bly and the Trouble with America" (Mitchell), **Supp. IV Part 1:** 70

Robert Bly: An Introduction to the Poetry (Nelson), **Supp. IV Part 1:** 66

Robert Bly: The Poet and His Critics (W. V. Davis), **Supp. IV Part 1:** 63; **Supp. XXI:** 84, **85–86,** 87, 95

Robert Coover: The Universal Fiction-making Process (Gordon), **Supp. V:** 46

Robert Creeley (Ford), **Supp. IV Part 1:** 140

Robert Creeley and the Genius of the American Common Place (Clark), **Supp. IV Part 1:** 140

Robert Creeley's Poetry: A Critical Introduction (Edelberg), **Supp. IV Part 1:** 155

Robert E. Howard: Selected Poems (Coffman, ed.), **Supp. XXVII:** 118

Robert Frost (Meyers), **Retro. Supp. I:** 138

Robert Lowell (Meyers), **Retro. Supp. II:** 191

Robert Lowell and the Sublime (Hart), **Retro. Supp. II:** 187

Robert Lowell's Shifting Colors (Doreski), **Retro. Supp. II:** 185

Robert Lowell: The First Twenty years (Staples), **Retro. Supp. II:** 187

Roberts, Carol, **Supp. XX: 53**

Roberts, David, **Supp. XVIII:** 106

Roberts, Diane, **Supp. X:** 15; **Supp. XXVII:** 2

Roberts, J. M., **IV:** 454

Roberts, Leo, **II:** 449

Roberts, Margaret, **II:** 449; **IV:** 453, 454

Roberts, Matthew, **Retro. Supp. II:** 324

Roberts, Meade, **IV:** 383

Roberts, Michael, **I:** 527, 536

Roberts, Richard, **III:** 297

Roberts, Victoria, **Supp. XIX:** 205

Roberts, Wally, **Supp. XI:** 119, 120, 126

Roberts, William, **Supp. XI:** 343

Roberts Brothers, **Retro. Supp. I:** 31, 35

Robertson, David, **Supp. VIII:** 305

Robertson, D. B., **III:** 311

Robertson, Lisa, **Supp. XXII:** 155

Robertson, Nan, **Supp. IV Part 1:** 300

Robertson, William, **II:** 8

Robert the Devil (Merwin, trans.), **Supp. III Part 1:** 341, 346

Robeson, Paul, **III:** 392; **Supp. IV Part 1:** 360, 361; **Supp. X:** 137; **Supp. XIX:** 66; **Supp. XXI:** 167

Robeson, Susan L., **Supp. XVIII:** 268

Robespierre, Maximilien, **Supp. I Part 2:** 514, 515, 517

"Robinson" (Kees), **Supp. XV:** 143–144

Robinson, Christopher L., **Supp. XII:** 13, 14

Robinson, David, **Supp. XXIV:** 70, 71, 78–79

Robinson, Dean, **III:** 506

Robinson, Edward, **III:** 505

Robinson, Edward G., **Supp. XI:** 306

Robinson, Edwin Arlington, **I:** 480; **II:** 388, 391, 529, 542; **III:** 5, **503–526,** 576; **Retro. Supp. III:** 104; **Supp. I Part 2:** 699; **Supp. II Part 1:** 191; **Supp. III Part 1:** 63, 75; **Supp. III Part 2:** 592, 593; **Supp. IX:** 77, 266, 276, 308; **Supp. XIX:** 123; **Supp. XV:** 256, 299, 300, 301, 306; **Supp. XVII:** 69; **Supp. XXVII:** 283

Robinson, Forrest G., **Supp. IV Part 2:** 597, 601, 604

Robinson, Herman, **III:** 506–507

Robinson, H. M., **IV:** 369, 370

Robinson, Jackie, **Supp. I Part 1:** 338

Robinson, James Harvey, **I:** 214; **Supp. I Part 2:** 492

Robinson, James K., **Supp. IX:** 328

Robinson, Margaret G., **Supp. IV Part 2:** 597, 601, 604

Robinson, Marilynne, **Supp. XXI: 209–224; Supp. XXII:** 50; **Supp. XXVI:** 45, 187

Robinson, Mary, **Supp. XI:** 26

Robinson, Rowland E., **Supp. XIX:** 6

Robinson, Roxana, **Supp. XXV:** 60

Robinson, Sugar Ray, **Supp. IV Part 1:** 167

Robinson, Ted, **Supp. XIII:** 166

Robinson Crusoe (Defoe), **II:** 159; **III:** 113, 423; **IV:** 369; **Retro. Supp. II:** 274; **Supp. I Part 2:** 714; **Supp. IV Part 2:** 502

Robison, Lori, **Supp. XXVIII:** 115

Robison, Mary, **Supp. V:** 22; **Supp. XXI:** 115, 116, 118

Roblès, Emmanuel, **Supp. I Part 1:** 283

"Robstown" (Salinas), **Supp. XIII:** 315

Rochefort, Christina, **Supp. XVI:** 143

Rochefoucauld, Louis Alexandre, **Supp. I Part 2:** 510

Rochman, Hazel, **Supp. XXVII:** 204; **Supp. XXVIII:** 285–286, 287

"Rock" (Nye), **Supp. XIII:** 287

Rock (Wagoner), **Supp. IX:** 324, **334,** 335

Rock, Catherine, **Supp. XII:** 17

Rock, The (Stevens), **Retro. Supp. I:** 309, 312

"Rock, The" (Stevens), **Retro. Supp. I:** 312

Rock, The (T. S. Eliot), **Retro. Supp. I:** 65; **Retro. Supp. III:** 69, 70

Rockaway (Shanley), **Supp. XIV:** 315

"Rock Climbers, The" (Francis), **Supp. IX:** 82

Rock-Drill (Pound), **Retro. Supp. I:** 293

Rockefeller, John D., **I:** 273; **III:** 580; **Supp. I Part 2:** 486; **Supp. V:** 286; **Supp. XXIII:** 26

Rockefeller, Nelson, **III:** 14, 15

Rocket Boys (Hickam), **Supp. XXVII:** 101, 103–106

Rocket Boys (musical), **Supp. XXVII:** 103

Rockets and Rodeos and Other American Spectacles (Mallon), **Supp. XIX:** 137

Rocket to the Moon (Odets), **Supp. II Part 2:** 541–543, 544

Rock Garden, The (Shepard), **Supp. III Part 2:** 432, 447

"Rocking Horse Winner, The" (Lawrence), **Supp. I Part 1:** 329

Rocking the Boat (Vidal), **Supp. IV Part 2:** 683

"Rockpile, The" (Baldwin), **Supp. I Part 1:** 63

Rock Springs (Ford), **Supp. V:** 57, 58–59, 68–69

Rockwell, John, **Supp. XXVII:** 45, 46

Rocky Mountains, The: or, Scenes, Incidents, and Adventures in the Far West; Digested from the Journal of Captain E. L. E Bonneville, of the Army of the United States, and Illustrated from Various Other Sources (Irving), **II:** 312

Rodden, John, **Supp. XVI:** 63, 69, 72

Roddenberry, Gene, **Supp. XXII:** 60

Rodefer, Stephen, **Supp. XXIV:** 38

Roderick, David, **Supp. XV:** 223

Roderick Hudson (James), **II:** 284, 290, 324, 326, 328; **Retro. Supp. I:** 219, **220–221,** 221, 226; **Supp. IX:** 142

Rodgers, Richard, **III:** 361

Rodgers, Ronald, **Supp. IV Part 2:** 503

Rodker, John, **III:** 470

Rodman, Selden, **Supp. I Part 1:** 83; **Supp. X:** 115

Rodney, Walter, **Supp. XXI:** 171

"Rodrigo Returns to the Land and Linen Celebrates" (Cisneros), **Supp. VII:** 68

Rodríguez, Diane, **Supp. XXIII:** 203

Rodriguez, Randy A., **Supp. XIV:** 312

Rodriguez, Richard, **Supp. XIV: 297–313**

Roessel, David, **Supp. XXVIII:** 69

Roethke, Charles, **III:** 531

Roethke, Theodore, **I:** 167, 171–172, 183, 254, 285, 521; **III:** 273, **527–550; IV:** 138, 402; **Retro. Supp. II:** 178, 181, 246; **Supp. I Part 2:** 539; **Supp. III Part 1:** 47, 54, 56, 239, 253, 260–261, 350; **Supp. IV Part 2:** 626; **Supp. IX:** 323; **Supp. XV:** 140, 145, 212; **Supp. XVIII:** 90; **Supp. XX: 199; Supp. XXIII:** 19; **Supp. XXIV:** 165, 171; **Supp. XXVII:** 250

"Roger Malvin's Burial" (Hawthorne), **II:** 243; **Retro. Supp. I:** 153

Rogers, Michael, **Supp. X:** 265, 266

Rogers, Pattiann, **Supp. XVIII:** 189

Rogers, Samuel, **II:** 303; **Supp. I Part 1:** 157

Rogers, Will, **I:** 261; **IV:** 388

Roger's Version (Updike), **Retro. Supp. I:** 325, 327, 330

Roget, Peter Mark, **Supp. I Part 1:** 312

Rogin, Michael Paul, **Retro. Supp. III:** 150

"Rogue River Jet-Board Trip, Gold Beach, Oregon, July 4, 1977" (Carver), **Supp. III Part 1:** 140

"Rogue's Gallery" (McCarthy), **II:** 563

Rohr, Richard, **Supp. XX: 143**

Roiphe, Katie, **Supp. XXV:** 10

Roland de La Platière, Jean Marie, **II:** 554

Rolando Hinojosa and the American Dream (Glover), **Supp. XIX:** 112

Rolando Hinojosa: A Reader's Guide (Zilles), **Supp. XIX:** 112

Rolando Hinojosa Reader, The (Saldívar, ed.), **Supp. XIX:** 112

Rôle du Nègre dans la culture des Amériques, La (Locke), **Supp. XIV:** 202

"Role of a Lifetime, The" (Skloot), **Supp. XX: 203**

"Role of Society in the Artist, The" (Ammons), **Supp. VII:** 34

Rolfe, Alfred, **IV:** 427

Rolfe, Frederick, **Supp. XX: 235**

"Roll, Jordan, Roll" (spiritual), **Supp. IV Part 1:** 16

Rolland, Romain, **Supp. XX: 70**

"Roll Call" (Hoffman), **Supp. XVIII:** 86

"Roll Call" (Komunyakaa), **Supp. XIII:** 123

Rolle, Esther, **Supp. IV Part 1:** 367

Rollin, Charles, **II:** 113

Rolling Stones (O. Henry), **Supp. II Part 1:** 410

Rolling Thunder Logbook (Shepard), **Supp. III Part 2:** 433

Rolling Thunder Logbook, The (Shepard), **Supp. XVIII:** 31

"Rolling Up" (Simpson), **Supp. IX:** 265, 274, 280

Rollins, Howard E., Jr., **Supp. IV Part 1:** 236

Rollins, Hyder E., **Supp. IV Part 1:** 168

Rollins, Sonny, **Supp. V:** 195

"Rollo" tales (Abbott), **Supp. I Part 1:** 38

"Roma I" (Wright), **Supp. V:** 338

"Roma II" (Wright), **Supp. V:** 338

Romains, Jules, **I:** 227

Román, David, **Supp. XIII:** 208

Romance, A (Weigl), **Supp. XIX:** 277–278

"Romance, A" (Weigl), **Supp. XIX:** 278

"Romance and a Reading List" (Fitzgerald), **Retro. Supp. I:** 101

Romance of a Plain Man, The (Glasgow), **II:** 175, 180–181

"Romance of Certain Old Clothes, The" (James), **II:** 322; **Retro. Supp. I:** 218

Romance Reader, The (Abraham), **Supp. XXIV:** 1–2, 3, **4–7**

Romancing the Shadow: Poe and Race (Kennedy and Weissberg, eds.), **Retro. Supp. III:** 237

"Roman Elegies" (Brodsky), **Supp. VIII:** 29

"Roman Fever" (Wharton), **Retro. Supp. I:** 382

"Roman Fountain" (Bogan), **Supp. III Part 1:** 56

"Romanitas of Gore Vidal, The" (Tatum), **Supp. IV Part 2:** 684

Romaniuk, Zbigniew, **Supp. XVI:** 154

Romano, John, **Supp. XV:** 253

"Roman Sarcophagus, A" (R. Lowell), **II:** 544

Roman Spring of Mrs. Stone, The (T. Williams), **IV:** 383, 385

Roman Summer (Lewisohn), **Supp. XXVIII:** 149, 151–152

"Romantic, The" (Bogan), **Supp. III Part 1:** 50

"Romantic, The" (Lewisohn), **Supp. XXVIII:** 154

Romantic Comedians, The (Glasgow), **II:** 175, 186, 190, 194

Romantic Education, A (Hampl), **Supp. XXII:** 82, 83, **87–90,** 91

Romantic Egoists, The (Auchincloss), **Supp. IV Part 1:** 25

Romantic Egotist, The (Fitzgerald), **II:** 82

"Romantic Egotist, The" (Fitzgerald), **Retro. Supp. I:** 100

"Romanticism and Classicism" (Hulme), **III:** 196

"Romanticism Comes Home" (Shapiro), **Supp. II Part 2:** 713

Romantic Manifesto, The: A Philosophy of Literature (Rand), **Supp. IV Part 2:** 521, 523, 527, 529–530

"Romantic Regionalism of Harper Lee, The" (Erisman), **Supp. VIII:** 126

Romantics, The (Rinehart), **Supp. XXV:** 196

"Rome" (W. C. Williams), **Retro. Supp. I:** 420

Rome Brothers, **Retro. Supp. I:** 393

Romeo and Juliet (Shakespeare), **Supp. V:** 252; **Supp. VIII:** 223

Romola (G. Eliot), **II:** 291; **IV:** 311

Romulus: A New Comedy (Vidal), **Supp. IV Part 2:** 683

Romulus der Grosse (Dürrenmatt), **Supp. IV Part 2:** 683

Ronald, Ann, **Supp. XIII:** 4, 5, 6, 7, 9, 11

"Rondel for a September Day" (White), **Supp. I Part 2:** 676

"Ron Narrative Reconstructions, The" (Coleman), **Supp. XI:** 83

"Ron Padgett's Visual Imagination" (Notley), **Supp. XXII:** 224

Ron Rash Reader, The (Rash; Wilhelm, ed.), **Supp. XXVII:** 215

Ronsard, Pierre de, **Supp. X:** 65; **Supp. XV:** 165

Rood, John, **IV:** 261

"Roof, the Steeple, and the People, The" (Ellison), **Retro. Supp. II:** 118, 126; **Supp. II Part 1:** 248

"Room" (Levertov), **Supp. III Part 1:** 282

Roomates (film, P. Yates), **Supp. XVII:** 8, 9

Roomates: My Grandfather's Story (Apple), **Supp. XVII:** 2, **7–9**

"Room at the Heart of Things, A" (Merrill), **Supp. III Part 1:** 337

Room Called Remember, A: Uncollected Pieces (Buechner), **Supp. XII:** 53

"Roomful of Hovings, A" (McPhee), **Supp. III Part 1:** 291, 294

Room of One's Own, A (Woolf), **Supp. IX:** 19; **Supp. V:** 127; **Supp. XIII:** 305

Room Rented by a Single Woman (Wright), **Supp. XV:** 340–341

"Rooms" (Collins), **Supp. XXI:** 61

Room Temperature (Baker), **Supp. XIII:** 41, **43–45,** 48, 50

Room to Swing (Lacy), **Supp. XV:** 202, 203, 205, 207

"Room Upstairs, The" (Gioia), **Supp. XV:** 120–121, 124

Roosevelt, Eleanor, **IV:** 371; **Supp. IV Part 2:** 679; **Supp. XXVII:** 137

Roosevelt, Franklin, **Supp. V:** 290

Roosevelt, Franklin Delano, **I:** 482, 485, 490; **II:** 553, 575; **III:** 2, 18, 69, 110, 297, 321, 376, 476, 580, 581; **Supp. I Part 2:** 488, 489, 490, 491, 645, 654, 655

Roosevelt, Kermit, **III:** 508

Roosevelt, Theodore, **I:** 14, 62; **II:** 130; **III:** 508; **IV:** 321; **Retro. Supp. I:** 377; **Supp. I Part 1:** 1, 21; **Supp. I Part 2:** 455, 456, 502, 707; **Supp. IX:** 184; **Supp. V:** 280, 282; **Supp. XIX:** 29; **Supp. XX:** 221; **Supp. XXIII:** 26

Roosevelt After Inauguration And Other Atrocities (Burroughs), **Supp. III Part 1:** 98

"Roosevelt Chair, The" (Skloot), **Supp. XX:** 205

"Roosters" (Bishop), **Retro. Supp. II:** 39, 43, 250; **Supp. I Part 1:** 89

Root, Abiah, **I:** 456

Root, Elihu, **Supp. IV Part 1:** 33

Root, Simeon, **I:** 548

Root, Timothy, **I:** 548

Rootabaga Stories (Sandburg), **III:** 583, 587

"Rootedness: The Ancestor as Foundation" (Morrison), **Supp. III Part 1:** 361

"Roots" (Halliday), **Supp. XIX:** 88

Roots in the Soil (film), **Supp. IV Part 1:** 83

"Rope" (Porter), **III:** 451

Rope (screenplay, Hecht), **Supp. XXVII:** 93

Rope, The (O'Neill), **III:** 388

Ropemakers of Plymouth, The (Morison), **Supp. I Part 2:** 494

"Ropes" (Nye), **Supp. XIII:** 276

"Rope's End, The" (Nemerov), **III:** 282

Roquelaure, A. N., **Supp. VII:** 301. *See also* Rice, Anne

Rorem, Ned, **Supp. IV Part 1:** 79, 84; **Supp. XXIII:** 217

Rorschach Test (F. Wright), **Supp. XVII:** 240, 245

Rorty, James, **Supp. XXII:** 276, 277

"Rosa" (Ozick), **Supp. V:** 271

Rosa, Rodrigo Rey, **Supp. IV Part 1:** 92

Rosaldo, Renato, **Supp. IV Part 2:** 544

"Rosalia" (Simic), **Supp. VIII:** 278

Roscoe, Will, **Supp. IV Part 1:** 330

"Roscoe in Hell" (McKnight), **Supp. XX:** 151

"Rose" (Dubus), **Supp. VII:** 88

Rose (L.-Y. Lee), **Supp. XV:** 211, **212–215,** 218

Rose, Alice, Sister, **III:** 348

Rose, Charlie, **Supp. XIX:** 26, 30; **Supp. XXVII:** 270

Rose, Lloyd, **Supp. XXIV:** 267

Rose, Mickey, **Supp. XV:** 3

Rose, Philip, **Supp. IV Part 1:** 362

"Rose, The" (Roethke), **III:** 537

"Rose, The" (W. C. Williams), **Retro. Supp. I:** 419

Rose, Where Did You Get That Red?: Teaching Great Poetry to Children (Koch), **Supp. XV:** 189

"Rose for Emily, A" (Faulkner), **II:** 72; **Retro. Supp. III:** 82, 84; **Supp. IX:** 96; **Supp. XX:** 179; **Supp. XXIV:** 136

Rose-Hued Cities (P. N. Warren), **Supp. XX:** 261

Rose in Bloom (Alcott), **Supp. I Part 1:** 42

"Rose-Johnny" (Kingsolver), **Supp. VII:** 203

Rose Madder (King), **Supp. V:** 141, 148, 150, 152

"Rose-Morals" (Lanier), **Supp. I Part 1:** 364

Rosen, Jody, **Supp. XXVII:** 46

Rosen, Jonathan, **Supp. XVII:** 50; **Supp. XX:** 179

Rosen, Kenneth, **Supp. IV Part 2:** 499, 505, 513

Rosen, Norma, **Supp. XVII:** 49, 50

Rosenbaum, Alissa Zinovievna. *See* Rand, Ayn

Rosenbaum, Thane, **Supp. XVII:** 48

Rosenberg, Bernard, **Supp. I Part 2:** 650

Rosenberg, Harold, **Supp. XIX:** 159; **Supp. XV:** 143; **Supp. XXIII:** 211

Rosenberg, Isaac, **Supp. XXVII:** 295

Rosenberg, Julia, **Supp. XVIII:** 136

Rosenberg, Julius and Ethel, **Supp. I Part 1:** 295; **Supp. I Part 2:** 532; **Supp. V:** 45

Rosenberg, Liz, **Supp. XV:** 251

Rosenberg, Shlomo, **Supp. XXIII:** 6

Rosenbloom, Joel, **Supp. IV Part 2:** 527

Rosenblum, Martin, **Supp. XXVI:** 236

Rosenfeld, Alvin H., **Supp. I Part 1:** 120

Rosenfeld, Isaac, **Supp. XII:** 160

Rosenfeld, Paul, **I:** 116, 117, 231, 245

Rosenfelt, Deborah, **Supp. XIII:** 296, 304

Rosenfield, Isaac, **IV:** 3

Rosengarten, Theodore, **Supp. XVIII:** 183

Rosenthal, Ira, **Supp. XIV:** 146–147

Rosenthal, Lois, **Supp. VIII:** 258

Rosenthal, M. L., **II:** 550; **III:** 276, 479; **Supp. V:** 333

Rosenthal, Peggy, **Supp. XVII:** 119

Rose of Wissahikon, The (Lippard), **Supp. XXIII:** 178

"Rose Pogonias" (Frost), **Retro. Supp. I:** 127

"Rose Red and Snow White" (Grimms), **Supp. X:** 82

"Rose Room" (Sorrentino), **Supp. XXI:** 228

"Roses" (Conroy), **Supp. XVI:** 72

"Roses" (Dove), **Supp. IV Part 1:** 246

"Roses and Skulls" (Goldbarth), **Supp. XII:** 192

"Roses for Lubbock" (Nye), **Supp. XIII:** 281

"Roses Only" (Moore), **III:** 195, 198, 200, 202, 215

Rose Tattoo, The (T. Williams), **IV:** 382, 383, 387, 388, 389, 392–393, 394, 397, 398

Rose Theatre (Sorrentino), **Supp. XXI:** 236

"Rosewood, Ohio" (Matthews), **Supp. IX:** 160

Rosie (Lamott), **Supp. XX:** 133–134

"Rosie Baby" (Huddle), **Supp. XXVI:** 147, 152

Rosiebelle Lee Wildcat Tennessee (Andrews), **Supp. XXVI:** 6–7

"Rosie"(Goodman), **Supp. XXVIII:** 89–90, 95

Rosinante to the Road Again (Dos Passos), **I:** 478

Roskies, David, **Supp. XVII:** 39, 44, 49–50

Roskolenko, Harry, **Supp. XV:** 179

Rosmersholm (Ibsen), **III:** 152

Rosmond, Babette, **II:** 432

Ross, Eleanor. *See* Taylor, Eleanor Ross

Ross, Harold, **Supp. I Part 1:** 174; **Supp. I Part 2:** 607, 617, 653, 654, 655, 660; **Supp. IX:** 190; **Supp. VIII:** 151, 170

Ross, Herbert, **Supp. XV:** 2

Ross, Jean, **Supp. XXI:** 144, 146

Ross, John F., **II:** 110

Ross, Lillian, **Retro. Supp. II:** 198

Ross, Mary, **Supp. XXII:** 195

Ross, Mitchell S., **Supp. IV Part 2:** 692; **Supp. X:** 260

Ross, Robert, **Supp. XXIV:** 167

Rossen, Robert, **Supp. XI:** 306

Rosset, Barney, **III:** 171

Rossetti, Christina, **Supp. XIV:** 128; **Supp. XXVII:** 284

Rossetti, Dante Gabriel, **I:** 433; **II:** 323; **Retro. Supp. I:** 128, 286; **Supp. I Part 2:** 552; **Supp. XXII:** 156

Rossetti, William Michael, **Retro. Supp. I:** 407

Rossi, Umberto, **Supp. XVIII:** 137, 138–139

Rossini, Clare, **Supp. XVII:** 111

Rosskam, Edwin, **IV:** 477

Ross Macdonald (Bruccoli), **Supp. IV Part 2:** 468, 470

Rostand, Edmond, **II:** 515; **Supp. IV Part 2:** 518

Rosten, Leo, **Supp. XVII:** 9

Rosy Crucifixion, The (H. Miller), **III:** 170, 187, 188–189, 190

Rotella, Mark, **Supp. XXVIII:** 279, 284

Rote Walker, The (Jarman), **Supp. XVII:** 110, **113–115**

Roth, Henry, **Supp. IV Part 1:** 314; **Supp. IX: 227–243; Supp. VIII:** 233; **Supp. XIII:** 106; **Supp. XXVII:** 134

Roth, Philip, **I:** 144, 161; **II:** 591; **Retro. Supp. II:** 22, **279–297; Supp. I Part 1:** 186, 192; **Supp. I Part 2:** 431, 441, 443; **Supp. II Part 1:** 99; **Supp. III Part 2: 401–429; Supp. IV Part 1:** 236, 379, 388; **Supp. IX:** 227; **Supp. V:** 45, 119, 122, 257, 258; **Supp. VIII:** 88, 236, 245; **Supp. XI:** 64, 68, 99, 140; **Supp. XII:** 190, 310; **Supp. XIV:** 79, 93, 111, 112; **Supp. XVI:** 206; **Supp. XVII:** 43, 48, 183; **Supp. XVIII:** 89; **Supp. XXI:** 234; **Supp. XXII:** 268; **Supp. XXVI:** 119, 123; **Supp. XXVII:** 142

Roth, Rita, **Supp. XVI:** 112

Roth, William, **Supp. XV:** 142

Rothenberg, Jerome, **Supp. VIII:** 292; **Supp. XII:** 3; **Supp. XXIV:** 37; **Supp. XXVIII:** 260–261, 266

Rothermere, Lady Mary, **Retro. Supp. I:** 63

Rothko, Mark, **Supp. XV:** 144

Rothstein, Mervyn, **Supp. VIII:** 142

"Rouen, France"(Kenny), **Supp. XXIII:** 152

"Rouge High" (Hughes), **Supp. I Part 1:** 330

Rougemont, Denis de, **II:** 586; **IV:** 216; **Retro. Supp. I:** 328, 329, 330, 331

Rough Edges (Skloot), **Supp. XX: 196**

Roughing It (Twain), **II:** 312; **IV:** 195, 197, 198; **Retro. Supp. III:** 258, 261, 267

Roughing It in the Bush (Shields), **Supp. VII:** 313

"Rough Outline" (Simic), **Supp. VIII:** 276

"Rough-Skinned Newt, The"(Schott), **Supp. XXIII:** 253–254

Rough South of Larry Brown, The (film, Hawkins), **Supp. XXI:** 39

Rougon-Macquart, Les (Zola), **II:** 175–176

Roumain, Jacques, **Retro. Supp. I:** 202; **Supp. IV Part 1:** 360, 367

"Round, The" (Kunitz), **Supp. III Part 1:** 268

"Roundelay Between Two Shepherdesses, A" (Notley), **Supp. XXII:** 229

"Round Trip" (Dunn), **Supp. XI:** 148–149

Round Up (Lardner), **II:** 426, 430, 431

Rountree, Owen (pseud.). *See* Kittredge, William; Krauzer, Steven M.

Rourke, Constance, **I:** 258; **IV:** 339, 352

Rourke, Milton, **Retro. Supp. II:** 89

Rousseau, Jean-Jacques, **I:** 226; **II:** 8, 343; **III:** 170, 178, 259; **IV:** 80, 173, 440; **Retro. Supp. III:** 109; **Supp. I Part 1:** 126; **Supp. I Part 2:** 637, 659; **Supp. IV Part 1:** 171; **Supp. XI:** 245; **Supp. XVI:** 292; **Supp. XXI:** 83; **Supp. XXVI:** 38–39

Roussel, Raymond, **Supp. III Part 1:** 6, 7, 10, 15, 16, 21; **Supp. XV:** 182

"Route 302" (Halliday), **Supp. XIX:** 93

"Routes" (Everwine), **Supp. XV:** 82

"Route Six" (Kunitz), **Supp. III Part 1:** 258

Route Two (Erdrich and Dorris), **Supp. IV Part 1:** 260

"Routine Things Around the House, The" (Dunn), **Supp. XI:** 148

Rover Boys (Winfield), **III:** 146

Rovit, Earl, **IV:** 102

Rowan, Carl T., **Supp. XIV:** 306

Rowe, Anne E., **Supp. X:** 223

Rowe, John Carlos, **Retro. Supp. I:** 216

Rowe, Kenneth Thorpe, **Supp. XXIII:** 258

Rowell, Charles, **Supp. XXI:** 250, 254, 255; **Supp. XXIV:** 184

"Rowing" (Sexton), **Supp. II Part 2:** 696

"Rowing Endeth, The" (Sexton), **Supp. II Part 2:** 696

Rowlandson, Mary, **Supp. IV Part 2:** 430, 431; **Supp. XXVIII:** 170

Rowling, J. K., **Supp. XXV:** 70

"Rows of Cold Trees, The" (Winters), **Supp. II Part 2:** 790–791, 800

Rowson, Susanna, **Supp. I Part 1:** 128; **Supp. XV: 229–248**

Roxanna Slade (Price), **Supp. VI:** 267

Roxie Hart (Watkins), **Supp. XVI:** 188

Royal Family, The (Vollmann), **Supp. XVII:** 226, 230, 233

"Royal Palm" (Crane), **I:** 401

Royce, Josiah, **I:** 443; **III:** 303, 600; **IV:** 26; **Retro. Supp. I:** 57; **Supp. XIV:** 197, 199; **Supp. XVII:** 97

"Roy McInnes" (Budbill), **Supp. XIX:** 6–7

"Roy Spivey" (July), **Supp. XXIV:** 210

Royster, Sarah Elmira, **III:** 410, 429

Royte, Elizabeth, **Supp. XV:** 59

Rózewicz, Tadeusz, **Supp. X:** 60

R. S. Thomas: Poetry and Theology (W. V. Davis), **Supp. XXI: 86–87**

Ruas, Charles, **Supp. IV Part 1:** 383

Ruback, Max, **Supp. XXIII:** 290

Rubáiyát (Khayyám), **I:** 568

Rubáiyát of Omar Khayyam (Fitzgerald), **Supp. I Part 2:** 416; **Supp. III Part 2:** 610; **Supp. XV:** 156; **Supp. XXVII:** 262

"Rubber Life" (Prose), **Supp. XVI:** 256

"Rubbing the Faces of Angels"(Bottoms), **Supp. XXVIII:** 26

Rubel, Nora L., **Supp. XXIV:** 7

Rub from Snub, A (Swanwick), **Supp. XV:** 237

"Rubicon" (Cliff), **Supp. XXII:** 76

Rubin, Louis, **Supp. I Part 2:** 672, 673, 679; **Supp. X:** 42

Rubin, Louis D., Jr., **IV:** 116, 462–463

Rubin, Stan, **Supp. XIV:** 307, 310

Rubin, Stan Sanvel, **Supp. IV Part 1:** 242, 245, 252

Rubins, Josh, **Supp. XX: 89**

"Ruby Brown" (Hughes), **Supp. I Part 1:** 327

"Ruby Daggett" (Eberhart), **I:** 539

Rucker, Rudy, **Supp. X:** 302

Rudd, Hughes, **Supp. XII:** 141

"Rude Awakening, A" (Chopin), **Retro. Supp. II:** 64

Rudens (Plautus), **Supp. III Part 2:** 630

Ruderman, Judith, **Supp. IV Part 1:** 380

Rudge, Olga, **Supp. V:** 338

Rudikoff, Sonya, **Supp. XIV:** 113

Rudman, Mark, **Supp. XXIII:** 124; **Supp. XXIV:** 153

Rueckert, William, **I:** 264

Ruesch, Jurgen, **Supp. XV:** 147

Rugby Chapel (Arnold), **Supp. I Part 2:** 416

"Rugby Road" (Garrett), **Supp. VII:** 100

Rugge, John, **Supp. XXII:** 218

Ruhl, Arthur, **Supp. XXVIII:** 45

Ruining the New Road (Matthews), **Supp. IX:** 154, **155–157**

"Ruins of Italica, The" (Bryant, trans.), **Supp. I Part 1:** 166

Rukeyser, Muriel, **Retro. Supp. II:** 48; **Retro. Supp. III:** 251; **Supp. VI: 271–289; Supp. XV:** 349; **Supp. XVII:** 74; **Supp. XXVIII:** 196

"Rule of Phase Applied to History, The" (Adams), **I:** 19

Rule of the Bone (Banks), **Supp. V:** 16

Rulers of Kings (Atherton), **Supp. XXIV:** 23

"Rules by Which a Great Empire May Be Reduced to a Small One" (Franklin), **II:** 120

Rules For the Dance: A Handbook for Reading and Writing Metrical Verse (Oliver), **Supp. VII:** 229, 247

Rules of Attraction, The (Ellis), **Supp. XXVII:** 68, 70–71, 74, 76

Rules of the Game, The (film), **Supp. XII:** 259

Rulfo, Juan, **Supp. IV Part 2:** 549

Rumba (film, Gering), **Supp. XVII:** 57

Rumbaut, Rubén, **Supp. XI:** 184

Rum Diary, The (Thompson), **Supp. XXIV:** 281, **283–286,** 293

Rümelin-Oesterlen, Natalie, **Supp. XX: 235**

Rumens, Carol, **Supp. XI:** 14; **Supp. XVI:** 212

Rumi, **Supp. XX: 117**

"Rumination of Rivers, The" (Bronk), **Supp. XXI:** 32

Rumkowski, Chaim, **Supp. XII:** 168

Rummel, Mary Kay, **Supp. XIII:** 280

"Rumor and a Ladder" (Bowles), **Supp. IV Part 1:** 93

Rumor of War, A (Caputo), **Supp. XIX:** 17–21, 25, 30

Rumors (Simon), **Supp. IV Part 2:** 582–583, 591

Rumpelstiltskin (Gardner), **Supp. VI:** 72

"Rumpelstiltskin" (Grimm), **IV:** 266

"Rumpelstiltskin" (Sexton), **Supp. II Part 2:** 690

Run, Sheep, Run (Bodenheim), **Supp. XXV:** 27

"Runagate Runagate" (Hayden), **Supp. II Part 1:** 377

Runaway (Munro), **Supp. XXVII:** 190, 193–194

"Runes" (Nemerov), **III:** 267, 277–278

Run Man Run (C. Himes), **Supp. XVI:** 142, 143

"Runner, The" (Grossman), **Supp. XIX:** 83

"Running" (Wilbur), **Supp. III Part 2:** 558–559

"RUNNING-AWAY"(Strout), **Supp. XXIII:** 274

Running Dog (DeLillo), **Supp. VI:** 3, 6, 8, 14

"Running in Church" (A. Finch), **Supp. XVII:** 72

"Running the Table" Conroy), **Supp. XVI:** 75

"Run of Bad Luck, A" (Proulx), **Supp. VII:** 253–254

Run of Jacks, A (Hugo), **Supp. VI:** 131, 133, 134, 135, 136

Run River (Didion), **Supp. IV Part 1:** 197, 199–200, 201

Ruoff, A. LaVonne Brown, **Supp. IV Part 1:** 324, 327; **Supp. IV Part 2:** 559

Rupert, Jim, **Supp. XII:** 215

Ruppert, James, **Supp. IV Part 1:** 321

Rural Hours (Cooper), **Supp. XIII:** 152

"Rural Route" (Wright), **Supp. V:** 340

"Rural South, The" (Du Bois), **Supp. II Part 1:** 174

Rush, Benjamin, **Supp. I Part 2:** 505, 507

Rushdie, Salman, **Supp. IV Part 1:** 234, 297

Rushdy, Ashraf, **Supp. X:** 250

Rushing, Jimmy, **Retro. Supp. II:** 113

Rusk, Dean, **II:** 579

Ruskin, John, **II:** 323, 338; **IV:** 349; **Retro. Supp. I:** 56, 360; **Supp. I Part 1:** 2, 10, 87, 349; **Supp. I Part 2:** 410

Rusnak, Karl, **Supp. XVIII:** 149

Russ, Joanna, **Retro. Supp. III:** 36, 37

Russell, Ada Dwyer, **II:** 513, 527

Russell, Bertrand, **II:** 27; **III:** 605, 606; **Retro. Supp. I:** 57, 58, 59, 60; **Supp. I Part 2:** 522; **Supp. V:** 290; **Supp. XII:** 45; **Supp. XIV:** 337

Russell, Diarmuid, **Retro. Supp. I:** 342, 345, 346–347, 349–350

Russell, George, **Retro. Supp. I:** 342

Russell, Herb, **Supp. I Part 2:** 465–466

Russell, John, **Supp. XIV:** 344, 347, 348; **Supp. XXVII:** 22

Russell, Legacy, **Supp. XXVIII:** 195

Russell, Peter, **III:** 479

Russell, Richard, **Supp. XI:** 102

Russell, Robert, **Supp. XX: 195**

Russell, Sue, **Supp. IV Part 2:** 653

Russello, Gerald, **Supp. XXIV:** 159

Russert, Margaret, **Supp. XVIII:** 62

Russert, Tim, **Supp. XII:** 272

Russia at War (Caldwell), **I:** 296

"Russia Between Myth and Reality: From *Meri* to *Three Cities*"(Krutikov), *Supp. XXIII:* 11

"Russia Europe's Only Solvent Nation, Says Lenin, Soviet Chief"(Bryant), **Supp. XXVIII:** 43

"Russian Gay-Girl and the War, The"(Bryant), **Supp. XXVIII:** 41

Russian Journal, A (Steinbeck), **IV:** 52, 63

Russo, Richard, **Supp. XI:** 349; **Supp. XII: 325–344; Supp. XXIII:** 302

"Rusty Autumn" (Swenson), **Supp. IV Part 2:** 640

Rutabaga-Roo: I've Got a Song and It's for You (Nye, album), **Supp. XIII:** 274

Ruth (biblical book), **Supp. I Part 2:** 516

Ruth, George Herman ("Babe"), **II:** 423; **Supp. I Part 2:** 438, 440

Rutheiser, Charles, **Supp. XXII:** 244

Ruth Hall (Fern), **Supp. V:** 122

Ruthven, K. K., **Supp. XXII:** 261

Rutkowska, Malgorzata, **Supp. XXII:** 208

Rutledge, Ann, **III:** 588; **Supp. I Part 2:** 471

Ruwe, Donelle R., **Supp. XII:** 215

Ryan, Alan, **Supp. XXVI:** 5

Ryan, Katy, **Supp. XXI:** 215

Ryan, Kay, **Supp. XXI:** 20; **Supp. XXV:** 222

Ryan, Maureen, **Supp. XXI:** 215

Ryan, Paul William, **Supp. XVIII: 223–239; Supp. XXI:** 264–265

Ryder (Barnes), **Supp. III Part 1:** 31, 36–38, 42, 43

"Ryder" (Rukeyser), **Supp. VI:** 273, 283

"Ry¿kan Says" (Budbill), **Supp. XIX:** 11

Ryle, Herbert Edward, **Supp. XX: 230**

Rymer, Thomas, **IV:** 122

S

S. (Updike), **Retro. Supp. I:** 330, 331, 332, 333

S-1 (Baraka), **Supp. II Part 1:** 55, 57

Saadi, **II:** 19

Saar, Doreen Alvarez, **Supp. XV:** 237

Sabbatai Zevi (Asch), **Supp. XXIII:** 12

"Sabbath, The" (Stowe), **Supp. I Part 2:** 587

"Sabbath Mom" (White), **Supp. I Part 2:** 671–672

Sabbaths (Berry), **Supp. X:** 31

Sabbath's Theater (P. Roth), **Retro. Supp. II:** 279, 288

"Sabbatical, The" (Stallings), **Supp. XXV:** 234

"Sabbioneta to Parma" (Di Piero), **Supp. XIX:** 36–37

Sabines, Jaime, **Supp. V:** 178

Sabol, Cathy, **Supp. XXVI:** 160

"Sabotage" (Baraka), **Supp. II Part 1:** 49, 53

"Saboteur" (Jin), **Supp. XVIII:** 97

Sacco, Nicola, **I:** 482, 486, 490, 494; **II:** 38–39, 426; **III:** 139–140; **Supp. I Part 2:** 446; **Supp. IX:** 199; **Supp. V:** 288–289; **Supp. XXII:** 277

Sachs, Hanns, **Supp. I Part 1:** 259; **Supp. X:** 186

Sack Full of Old Quarrels, A (Weigl), **Supp. XIX:** 277

"Sacks" (Carver), **Supp. III Part 1:** 143–144

Sacks, Oliver, **Supp. XVIII:** 143

Sacks, Peter, **Supp. IV Part 2:** 450

Sackville-West, Vita, **Supp. VIII:** 263

"Sacrament of Divorce, The" (Patchett), **Supp. XII:** 309

"Sacrament of Self: Catholic Roots of Contemporary Memoir" (lecture,

Hampl), **Supp. XXII:** 81

"Sacraments" (Dubus), **Supp. VII:** 91

Sacred and Profane Memories (Van Vechten), **Supp. II Part 2:** 735, 749

"Sacred Chant for the Return of Black Spirit and Power" (Baraka), **Supp. II Part 1:** 51

"Sacred Factory, The" (Toomer), **Supp. IX:** 320

Sacred Fount, The (James), **II:** 332–333; **Retro. Supp. I:** 219, 228, 232

"Sacred Heart" (Egan), **Supp. XIX:** 52

"Sacred Hoop, The: A Contemporary Perspective" (Gunn Allen), **Supp. IV Part 1:** 324

Sacred Hoop, The: Recovering the Feminine in American Indian Traditions (Gunn Allen), **Supp. IV Part 1:** 319, 320, 322, 324, 325, 328–330, 331, 333, 334

Sacred Journey, The (Buechner), **Supp. XII:** 42, 53

"Sacred Thing, The" (Ryan as Quin), **Supp. XVIII:** 227

Sacred Wood, The (T. S. Eliot), **IV:** 431; **Retro. Supp. I:** 59, 60; **Retro. Supp. III:** 66; **Supp. I Part 1:** 268; **Supp. II Part 1:** 136, 146

Sacrifice, The (Bidart), **Supp. XV:** 22, 27–30, 35

"Sacrifice, The" (Bidart), **Supp. XV:** 29

"Sacrifice, The" (Oates), **Supp. II Part 2:** 523

Sacrilege of Alan Kent, The (Caldwell), **I:** 291–292

"Sad Brazil" (Hardwick), **Supp. III Part 1:** 210

Sad Days of Light (Balakian), **Supp. XXIII:** 20

"Sad Dust Glories" (Ginsberg), **Supp. II Part 1:** 376

Sad Dust Glories: Poems Written Work Summer in Sierra Woods (Ginsberg), **Supp. II Part 1:** 326

Sade, Marquis de, **III:** 259; **IV:** 437, 442; **Supp. XII:** 1, 14–15

Sad-Faced Boy (Bontemps), **Supp. XXII:** 5, 12

Sad Flower in the Sand, A (film), **Supp. XI:** 173

Sad Heart at the Supermarket, A (Jarrell), **II:** 386

"Sadie" (Matthiessen), **Supp. V:** 201

"Sadie and Maud" (Brooks), **Supp. XVIII:** 175

Sadness and Happiness (Pinsky), **Supp. VI:** 235, 237–241

"Sadness of Brothers, The" (Kinnell), **Supp. III Part 1:** 237, 251

"Sadness of Days, The" (Salinas), **Supp. XIII:** 325

Sadness of Days, The: Selected and New Poems (Salinas), **Supp. XIII:** 311, 324–326

"Sadness of Lemons, The" (Levine), **Supp. V:** 184

Sadoff, Ira, **Supp. XVII:** 241; **Supp. XXI:** 100

"Sad Rite" (Karr), **Supp. XI:** 243

"Sad Strains of a Gay Waltz" (Stevens), **Retro. Supp. I:** 302

"Safe" (Gordon), **Supp. IV Part 1:** 299, 306

"Safe in their Alabaster Chambers" (Dickinson), **Retro. Supp. I:** 30

Safer, Morley, **Supp. XIX:** 25

"Safe Subjects" (Komunyakaa), **Supp. XIII:** 118

Safety Features (Monson), **Supp. XXIV:** 230

"Safeway" (F. Barthelme), **Supp. XI:** 26, 27, 36

Saffin, John, **Supp. I Part 1:** 115

Saffy, Edna, **Supp. X:** 227

Sagan, Carl, **Supp. XXVIII:** 23

Sagan, Miriam, **Supp. XXIII:** 133

"Saga of an American Ranch" (P. N. Warren), **Supp. XX: 261**

"Saga of Arturo Bandini" (Fante), **Supp. XI:** 159, **166–169**

"Saga of King Olaf, The" (Longfellow), **II:** 489, 505; **Retro. Supp. II:** 154, 155, 164

"Sage of Stupidity and Wonder, The" (Goldbarth), **Supp. XII:** 191

Sahl, Mort, **II:** 435–436

"Sah Sin" (Gallagher), *Supp. XXIV:* 171

"Said" (Dixon), **Supp. XII:** 149–150

Said, Edward, **Retro. Supp. III:** 194; **Supp. XXI:** 153

"Sailing after Lunch" (Stevens), **IV:** 73

Sailing Alone Around the Room: New and Selected Poems (Collins), **Supp. XXI:** 54, 56, 62

Sailing Alone Around the World (Slocum), **Supp. XXV:** 205, 206, 208, 213–216, 218

"Sailing Home from Rapallo" (R. Lowell), **Retro. Supp. II:** 189

Sailing through China (Theroux), **Supp. VIII:** 323

"Sailing to Byzantium" (Yeats), **III:** 263; **Supp. VIII:** 30; **Supp. X:** 74; **Supp. XI:** 281

"Sail Made of Rags, The" (Nye), **Supp. XIII:** 277

"Sailor off the Bremen" (Shaw), **Supp. XIX:** 247

"Sailor's Grudge" (Howard), **Supp. XXVII:** 124

"Sailors Lost at Sea" (Shields), **Supp. VII:** 318

"Saint, The"(Lewisohn), **Supp. XXVIII:** 154

"St Anne/Santa Ana" (Mora), **Supp. XIII:** 229

"Saint Anthony of Padua/San Antonio de Padua" (Mora), **Supp. XIII:** 228

"St. Augustine and the Bullfights" (Porter), **III:** 454

Sainte-Beuve, Charles Augustin, **IV:** 432

St. Elmo (Wilson), **Retro. Supp. I:** 351–352

"Saint Emmanuel the Good, Martyr" (Unamuno; Everwine, trans.), **Supp. XV:** 79

Sainte Vierge, La (Picabia), **Retro. Supp. II:** 331

Saint-Exupéry, Antoine de, **Supp. IX:** 247

"St. Francis Einstein of the Daffodils" (W. C. Williams), **IV:** 409–411

Saint-Gaudens, Augustus, **I:** 18, 228; **II:** 551

Saint-Gaudens, Homer, **Supp. XV:** 41

"St. George, the Dragon, and the Virgin" (R. Bly), **Supp. IV Part 1:** 73

St. George and the Godfather (Mailer), **III:** 46; **Retro. Supp. II:** 206, 208

Saint Jack (Theroux), **Supp. VIII:** 319

St. John, David, **Supp. V:** 180; **Supp. XI:** 270, 272; **Supp. XIII:** 312

St. John, Edward B., **Supp. IV Part 2:** 490

St. John, James Hector. *See* Crèvecoeur, Michel-Guillaume Jean de

"Saint John and the Back-Ache" (Stevens), **Retro. Supp. I:** 310

Saint Judas (Wright), **Supp. III Part 2: 595–599**

"Saint Judas" (Wright), **Supp. III Part 2:** 598–599

St. Louis Woman (Bontemps and Cullen), **Supp. IV Part 1:** 170

St. Mawr (Lawrence), **II:** 595

Saint Maybe (Tyler), **Supp. IV Part 2:** 670–671

"Saint Nicholas" (Moore), **III:** 215

"Saint"(O'Hara), **Supp. XXIII:** 219

St. Petersburg (Biely), **Supp. XII:** 13

Saint-Phalle, Niki de, **Supp. XV:** 187

"St. Roach" (Rukeyser), **Supp. VI:** 286

"Saint Robert" (Dacey), **Supp. IV Part 1:** 70

Saints at the River (Rash), **Supp. XXVII:** 222, 223–224, 226

Saintsbury, George, **IV:** 440; **Supp. XV:** 181

Saints' Everlasting Rest, The (Baxter), **III:** 199; **IV:** 151, 153

Saint-Simon, Claude Henri, **Supp. I Part 2:** 648

"St. Thomas Aquinas" (Simic), **Supp. VIII:** 281

Saks, Gene, **Supp. IV Part 2:** 577, 588

Salamun, Tomaz, **Supp. VIII:** 272

Salazar, Dixie, **Supp. V:** 180; **Supp. XV:** 73

Saldívar, José David, **Supp. IV Part 2:** 544, 545; **Supp. XIX:** 110, 112–113

Sale, Richard, **Supp. IV Part 1:** 379

Sale, Roger, **Supp. V:** 244

Saleh, Dennis, **Supp. V:** 182, 186

"Salem" (R. Lowell), **II:** 550

Salemi, Joseph, **Supp. IV Part 1:** 284

Salem's Lot (King), **Supp. V:** 139, 144, 146, 151

"Sale of the Hessians, The" (Franklin), **II: 120**

"Salesman at Fifty" (A. Miller), **Retro. Supp. III:** 173

Salick, Roydan, **Supp. XXIII:** 93, 94

Salinas, Luis Omar, **Supp. IV Part 2:** 545; **Supp. V:** 180; **Supp. XIII: 311–330; Supp. XV:** 73

"Salinas Is on His Way" (Salinas), **Supp. XIII:** 317

"Salinas Sends Messengers to the Stars" (Salinas), **Supp. XIII:** 317

"Salinas Summering at the Caspian and Thinking of Hamlet" (Salinas), **Supp. XIII:** 320

"Salinas Wakes Early and Goes to the Park to Lecture Sparrows" (Salinas), **Supp. XIII:** 320

Salinger, Doris, **III:** 551

Salinger, J. D., **II:** 255; **III: 551–574; IV:** 190, 216, 217; **Retro. Supp. I:** 102, 116, 335; **Supp. IV Part 2:** 502; **Supp. V:** 23, 119; **Supp. VIII:** 151; **Supp. XI:** 2, 66; **Supp. XIV:** 93; **Supp. XXIII:** 100; **Supp. XXVI:** 119

Salisbury, Harrison, **Supp. I Part 2:** 664

Salle, David, **Supp. XII:** 4

Salley, Columbus, **Supp. XIV:** 195

"Sally" (Cisneros), **Supp. VII:** 63

"Sally's Choice" (E. Stoddard), **Supp. XV:** 282

Salmagundi; or, The Whim-Whams and Opinions of Launcelot Langstaff Esq., and Others (Irving), **II:** 299, 300, 304

Salmon, Edward G., **Supp. XVIII:** 258

Salome (Strauss), **IV:** 316

Salon (online magazine), **Supp. VIII:** 310; **Supp. X:** 202

"Salt"(Crooker), **Supp. XXIII:** 62

Salt Eaters, The (Bambara), **Supp. XI:** 1, **12–14**

Salt Ecstasies, The (White), **Supp. XI:** 123

Salter, James, **Supp. IX: 245–263; Supp. XIX:** 252; **Supp. XVI:** 237, 247

Salter, Mary Jo, **Supp. IV Part 2:** 653; **Supp. IX:** 37, 292; **Supp. XV:** 251, 253; **Supp. XVII:** 112; **Supp. XXIII:** 112

Salter, Sarah, **Supp. XXVI:** 57

Salt Garden, The (Nemerov), **III:** 269, 272–275, 277

"Salt Garden, The" (Nemerov), **III:** 267–268

Salting the Ocean (Nye, ed.), **Supp. XIII:** 280

Salt Lesson, The (C. Frost), **Supp. XV:** 92, 96

"Salt Lesson, The" (C. Frost), **Supp. XV:** 99

"Salts and Oils" (Levine), **Supp. V:** 190

Salt to the Devil (film, Dmytryk), **Supp. XX:** 41

Saltzman, Arthur, **Supp. XIII:** 48

Saltzman, Harry, **Supp. XI:** 307

"Salut au Monde!" (Whitman), **Retro. Supp. I:** 387, 396, 400

"Salute" (MacLeish), **III:** 13

Salute (Shaw), **Supp. XIX:** 244

"Salute to Mister Yates, A" (Dubus), **Supp. XI:** 347, 349

Salute to Spring (Le Sueur), **Supp. XXIII:** 164, 165, 166, 172

Salvador (Didion), **Supp. IV Part 1:** 198, 207–208, 210

"Salvage" (Clampitt), **Supp. IX:** 41

"Salvage" (Rinehart), **Supp. XXV:** 194

Salvation (Asch), **Supp. XXIII:** 3, **4, 12,** 13, 15

Salvos: An Informal Book About Books and Plays (W. Frank), **Supp. XX:** 75

Samain, Albert, **II:** 528

Same Door, The (Updike), **IV:** 214, 219, 226; **Retro. Supp. I:** 320

"Same in Blues" (Hughes), **Retro. Supp. I:** 208

"Same Kiss After Many Years, The" (Gallagher), **Supp. XXIV:** 169

Same River Twice, The (Offutt), **Supp. XIX:** 163, 164, **167–168,** 175

"Samhain" (A. Finch), **Supp. XVII:** 72

Sam Lawson's Oldtown Fireside Stories (Stowe), **Supp. I Part 2:** 587, 596, 598–599

Sam Patch, the High, Wide & Handsome Jumper (Bontemps and Conroy), **Supp. XXII:** 5, 11

"Sa'm Pèdi" (Bell), **Supp. X:** 17

"Sampler, A" (MacLeish), **III:** 4

Sampoli, Maria, **Supp. V:** 338

Sampson, Edward, **Supp. I Part 2:** 664, 673

Sampson, Martin, **Supp. I Part 2:** 652

Sams, Stanhope, **Supp. XXVIII:** 229

"Sam's Dad" (Lamott), **Supp. XX:** 142–143

Sam's Legacy (Neugeboren), **Supp. XVI:** 221, 222

Samson, John, **Retro. Supp. III:** 152

Samson Agonistes (Milton), **III:** 274

"Samson and Delilah" (Masters), **Supp. I Part 2:** 459

Samuel, Maurice, **Supp. XXIII:** 1, 7

Samuel de Champlain: Father of New France (Morison), **Supp. I Part 2:** 496–497

Samuels, Charles Thomas, **Retro. Supp. I:** 334

"Samuel Sewall" (Hecht), **Supp. X:** 58

"Samwheel" (Lamott), **Supp. XX:** 144–145

Sanborn, Franklin B., **IV:** 171, 172, 178

Sanborn, Geoffrey, **Retro. Supp. III:** 152

Sanborn, Kate, **Supp. XIII:** 152

Sanborn, Sara, **Supp. XIV:** 113

Sanburg, Carl, **Supp. XXVIII:** 79

Sanchez, Carol Anne, **Supp. IV Part 1:** 335

Sanchez, Carol Lee, **Supp. IV Part 2:** 499, 557

Sanchez, Sonia, **Retro. Supp. III:** 316; **Supp. II Part 1:** 34; **Supp. XXVII:** 167

Sánchez Beras, César, **Supp. XXI:** 100, 104

Sanctified Church, The (Hurston), **Supp. VI:** 150

"Sanctified Church, The" (Hurston), **Retro. Supp. III:** 133

"Sanction of the Victims, The" (Rand), **Supp. IV Part 2:** 528

Sanctuary (Faulkner), **II:** 57, 61–63, 72, 73, 74, 174; **Retro. Supp. I:** 73, 84, 86–87, 87; **Retro. Supp. III:** 81–82, 87; **Supp. I Part 2:** 614; **Supp. XII:** 16

"Sanctuary" (Larsen), **Supp. XVIII:** 119, 130–131

Sanctuary (Wharton), **IV:** 311; **Retro. Supp. III:** 278

"Sanctuary" (Wylie), **Supp. I Part 2:** 711

"Sanctuary, The" (Nemerov), **III:** 272, 274

"Sanctuary, The" (Teasdale), **Supp. XXVII:** 294

Sanctuary V (Schulberg), **Supp. XVIII:** 254

"Sanctus" (Nelson), **Supp. XVIII:** 183

Sand, George, **II:** 322; **Retro. Supp. I:** 235, 372; **Supp. XV:** 275; **Supp. XXVIII:** 115

"Sandalphon" (Longfellow), **II:** 498

Sand and Foam: A Book of Aphorisms (Gibran), **Supp. XX:** 115, 121–122

Sandbox, The (Albee), **I:** 74–75, 89

Sandburg, Carl, **I:** 103, 109, 384, 421; **II:** 529; **III:** 3, 20, **575–598; Retro. Supp. I:** 133, 194; **Supp. I Part 1:** 257, 320; **Supp. I Part 2:** 387, 389, 454, 461, 653; **Supp. III Part 1:** 63, 71, 73, 75; **Supp. IV Part 1:** 169; **Supp. IV Part 2:** 502; **Supp. IX:** 1, 15, 308; **Supp. XIII:** 274, 277; **Supp. XV:** 293, 299, 300, 301, 302, 306; **Supp. XXII:** 275; **Supp. XXIII:** 161, 165; **Supp. XXV:** 18; **Supp. XXVII:** 83

Sandburg, Mrs. Carl (Lillian Steichen), **III:** 580

Sandburg, Helga, **III:** 583

Sandburg, Janet, **III:** 583, 584

Sandburg, Margaret, **III:** 583, 584

Sand County Almanac and Sketches Here and There, A (Leopold), **Supp. XIV:** 177, 178, **182–192**

"Sand Creek, Colorado" (Kenny), **Supp. XXIII:** 155

"Sand Dabs" (Oliver), **Supp. VII:** 245

"Sand Dunes" (Frost), **Retro. Supp. I:** 137; **Retro. Supp. II:** 41

Sander, August, **Supp. IX:** 211

Sanders, Mark, **Supp. XIX:** 119, 121

Sanders, Scott Russell, **Supp. XVI: 265–280**

Sandlin, Tim, **Supp. XXII:** 114

"Sandman, The" (Barthelme), **Supp. IV Part 1:** 47

Sandman's Dust (Bukiet), **Supp. XVII:** 40, 41

Sando, Joe S., **Supp. IV Part 2:** 510

Sandoe, James, **Supp. IV Part 1:** 131; **Supp. IV Part 2:** 470

Sandoval, Chela, **Supp. XXIII:** 204

Sandoz, Mari, **Supp. XV:** 141; **Supp. XXIII:** 146; **Supp. XXIV:** **243–261**

Sandperl, Ira, **Supp. VIII:** 200

"Sand-Quarry and Moving Figures" (Rukeyser), **Supp. VI:** 271, 278

Sand Rivers (Matthiessen), **Supp. V:** 203

"Sand Roses, The" (Hogan), **Supp. IV Part 1:** 401

Sandrow, Nahma, **Supp. XXVIII:** 70

Sands, Diana, **Supp. IV Part 1:** 362

Sands, Robert, **Supp. I Part 1:** 156, 157

"Sands at Seventy" (Whitman), **IV:** 348

"Sandstone Farmhouse, A" (Updike), **Retro. Supp. I:** 318

Sandy Bottom Orchestra, The (Keillor and Nilsson), **Supp. XVI:** 177

Sanford, John, **IV:** 286, 287

San Francisco (film), **Supp. XVI:** 181, 192

"San Francisco" (Hempel), **Supp. XXI:** 118

"San Francisco Blues" (Kerouac), **Supp. III Part 1:** 225

Sangamon County Peace Advocate, The (Lindsay), **Supp. I Part 2:** 379

Sanger, Margaret, **Supp. I Part 1:** 19; **Supp. XXI:** 6; **Supp. XXIII:** 161

Sankofa (film), **Supp. XX: 154**

Sansom, William, **IV:** 279

Sans Soleil (film), **Supp. IV Part 2:** 436

"Santa" (Sexton), **Supp. II Part 2:** 693

Santa Claus: A Morality (Cummings), **I:** 430, 441

"Santa Fe, New Mexico" (Kenny), **Supp. XXIII:** 150

"Santa Fé Trail, The" (Lindsay), **Supp. I Part 2:** 389

"Santa Lucia" (Hass), **Supp. VI:** 105–106

"Santa Lucia II" (Hass), **Supp. VI:** 105–106

Santayana, George, **I:** 222, 224, 236, 243, 253, 460; **II:** 20, 542; **III:** 64, **599–622; IV:** 26, 339, 351, 353, 441; **Retro. Supp. I:** 55, 57, 67, 295; **Retro. Supp. II:** 179; **Supp. I Part 2:** 428; **Supp. II Part 1:** 107; **Supp. X:** 58; **Supp. XIV:** 199, 335, 340, 342; **Supp. XVI:** 189; **Supp. XVII:** 97, 106; **Supp. XX: 228, 229, 231**

Santiago, Esmeralda, **Supp. XI:** 177

"Santorini: Stopping the Leak" (Merrill), **Supp. III Part 1:** 336

Santos, John Phillip, **Supp. XIII:** 274

Santos, Sherod, **Supp. VIII:** 270

Saphier, William, **Supp. XXV:** 19, 20

Sapir, Edward, **Supp. VIII:** 295; **Supp. XVI:** 283

"Sapphics for Patience" (A. Finch), **Supp. XVII:** 72

Sapphira and the Slave Girl (Cather), **I:** 331; **Retro. Supp. I:** 2, **19–20; Retro. Supp. III:** 18. **Retro. Supp. III:** 33, 24

Sappho, **II:** 544; **III:** 142; **Retro. Supp. III:** 19; **Supp. I Part 1:** 261, 269; **Supp. I Part 2:** 458; **Supp. XII:** 98, 99; **Supp. XVII:** 74; **Supp. XXV:** 222; **Supp. XXVII:** 171, 283, 288

"Sappho" (Wright), **Supp. III Part 2:** 595, 604

"Sappho, Keats" (Hadas), **Supp. XXIII:** 113

"Sara" (song, Dylan), **Supp. XVIII:** 28

"Sarah" (Schwartz), **Supp. II Part 2:** 663

Sarah; or, The Exemplary Wife (Rowson), **Supp. XV:** 242

"Saratoga" mysteries (Dobyns), **Supp. XIII:** 79–80

Sardonic Arm, The (Bodenheim), **Supp. XXV:** 22, 23

Sargent, John Singer, **II:** 337, 338; **Supp. XX: 231**

Sarlós, Robert K., **Supp. XXI:** 7, 12, 13; **Supp. XXVIII:** 38

Saroyan, Aram, **Supp. XV:** 182

Saroyan, William, **III:** 146–147; **IV:** 393; **Supp. I Part 2:** 679; **Supp. IV Part 1:** 83; **Supp. IV Part 2:** 502; **Supp. XIII:** 280; **Supp. XXIII:** 20; **Supp. XXV:** 29

Sarris, Greg, **Supp. IV Part 1:** 329, 330

Sarton, George, **Supp. VIII:** 249

Sarton, May, **Supp. III Part 1:** 62, 63; **Supp. VIII: 249–268; Supp. XIII:** 296; **Supp. XVII:** 71

Sartoris (Faulkner), **II:** 55, 56–57, 58, 62; **Retro. Supp. I:** 77, 81, 82, 83, 88; **Retro. Supp. III:** 74, 77–78

Sartor Resartus (Carlyle), **II:** 26; **III:** 82

Sartre, Jean-Paul, **I:** 82, 494; **II:** 57, 244; **III:** 51, 204, 292, 453, 619; **IV:** 6, 223, 236, 477, 487, 493; **Retro. Supp. I:** 73; **Supp. I Part 1:** 51; **Supp. IV Part 1:** 42, 84; **Supp. IX:** 4; **Supp. VIII:** 11; **Supp. XIII:** 74, 171; **Supp. XIV:** 24; **Supp. XVII:** 137; **Supp. XXIV:** 281

Sassone, Ralph, **Supp. X:** 171

Sassoon, Siegfried, **II:** 367; **Supp. XIX:** 18; **Supp. XV:** 308; **Supp. XXVII:** 295

Satan in Goray (Singer), **IV:** 1, 6–7, 12; **Retro. Supp. II:** 303, **304–305**

Satan Says (Olds), **Supp. X:** 201, 202, **202–204,** 215

"Satan Says" (Olds), **Supp. X:** 202; **Supp. XVII:** 114

Satanstoe (Cooper), **I:** 351–352, 355

"Sather Gate Illumination" (Ginsberg), **Supp. II Part 1:** 329

"Satire as a Way of Seeing" (Dos Passos), **III:** 172

Satires of Persius, The (Merwin, trans.), **Supp. III Part 1:** 347

Satirical Rogue on Poetry, The (Francis). *See Pot Shots at Poetry* (Francis)

Satori in Paris (Kerouac), **Supp. III Part 1:** 231

"Saturday" (Salinas), **Supp. XIII:** 315

"Saturday Matinee" (Trethewey), **Supp. XXI:** 251

Saturday Night (Orlean), **Supp. XXV:** 159, 161

Saturday Night at the War (Shanley), **Supp. XIV:** 315

"Saturday Rain" (Kees), **Supp. XV:** 136

"Saturday Route, The" (Wolfe), **Supp. III Part 2:** 580

Satyagraha (Gandhi), **IV:** 185

"Satyr's Heart, The" (B. Kelly), **Supp. XVII:** 132

Saucedo, José Guadalupe, **Supp. XXIII:** 197

Saudade (Vaz), **Supp. XXVI:** 256–258, 263

Saul and Patsy (C. Baxter), **Supp. XVII:** 22–23

"Saul and Patsy" (C. Baxter), **Supp. XVII:** 17

"Saul and Patsy Are Getting Comfortable in Michigan" (C. Baxter), **Supp. XVII:** 22

"Saul and Patsy Are in Labor" (C. Baxter), **Supp. XVII:** 20, 22

"Saul and Patsy Are Pregnant" (C. Baxter), **Supp. XVII:** 22

Saunders, George, **Supp. XIX: 223–237; Supp. XXII:** 49; **Supp. XXIV:** 199

Saunders, Richard, **II:** 110

Savage, Augusta, **Retro. Supp. II:** 115

Savage, James, **II:** 111

Savage, Tom, **Supp. XXIV:** 45

Savage Holiday (Wright), **IV:** 478, 488

Savage in Limbo: A Concert Play (Shanley), **Supp. XIV:** 315, **319–321,** 323, 324

Savage Love (Shepard and Chaikin), **Supp. III Part 2:** 433

Savage Place, A (Parker), **Supp. XIX:** 185

Savage Sword of Conan, The (comic), **Supp. XXVII:** 129

Savage Wilds (Reed), **Supp. X:** 241

Save Me, Joe Louis (Bell), **Supp. X:** 7, 10, **11–12**

Save Me the Waltz (Z. Fitzgerald), **II:** 95; **Retro. Supp. I:** 110; **Supp. IX:** 58, 59, 65, **66–68**

"Save One for Mainz" (Huddle), **Supp. XXVI:** 150, 153

Savers, Michael, **Supp. XI:** 307

"Saving Herself"(Goodman), **Supp. XXVIII:** 95

"Saving Julie"(Goodman), **Supp. XXVIII:** 95

Saving Lives (Goldbarth), **Supp. XII:** 192

Saving Private Ryan (film), **Supp. V:** 249; **Supp. XI:** 234

Savings (Hogan), **Supp. IV Part 1:** 397, 404, 405, 406, 410

Saving Sebastian (Taylor), **Supp. XXIII:** 57

Savo, Jimmy, **I:** 440

Savran, David, **Supp. IX:** 145; **Supp. XIII:** 209; **Supp. XV:** 321; **Supp. XXIV:** 263, 264

"Sawdust" (Offutt), **Supp. XIX:** 164

Sawyer-Lauçanno, Christopher, **Supp. IV Part 1:** 95

Saxon, Lyle, **Retro. Supp. I:** 80

"Saxophone" (Di Piero), **Supp. XIX:** 38

"Sax's and Selves" (Halliday), **Supp. XIX:** 88

"Say All" (Ray), **Supp. XVIII:** 193

Say and Seal (S. and A. Warner), **Supp. XVIII:** 258, 266

Saye and Sele, Lord, **Supp. I Part 1:** 98

Sayer, Mandy, **Supp. XIII:** 118

Sayers, Dorothy, **Supp. IV Part 1:** 341; **Supp. IV Part 2:** 464

Sayers, Valerie, **Supp. XI:** 253; **Supp. XVIII:** 99

"Say Good-bye" (Weigl), **Supp. XIX:** 288

Say Her Name (Goldman), **Supp. XXV:** 50, 59–62

"Sayings/For Luck" (Goldbarth), **Supp. XII:** 176

"Saying What Needs To Be Said" (Skloot), **Supp. XX: 201**

"Saying Your Names"(Siken), **Supp. XXVIII:** 197

Say! Is This the U.S.A.? (Caldwell), **I:** 293, 294–295, 304, 309, 310

Saylor, Bruce, **Supp. XII:** 253

Sayre, Joel, **Supp. XIII:** 166

Sayre, Nora, **Supp. XII:** 119

Sayre, Zelda, **Retro. Supp. I:** 101, 102–103, 104, 105, 108, 109, 110, 113, 114. *See also* Fitzgerald, Zelda (Zelda Sayre)

"Say Yes" (Wolff), **Supp. VII:** 344

"Say You Love Me" (Peacock), **Supp. XIX:** 198

Scafe, Suzanne, **Supp. XXIII:** 94, 95

"Scale" (Halliday), **Supp. XIX:** 92

"Scales of the Eyes, The" (Nemerov), **III:** 272, 273, 277

Scalpel (McCoy), **Supp. XIII: 174–175**

Scalpel (screen treatment, McCoy), **Supp. XIII:** 174

Scandalabra (Zelda Fitzgerald), **Supp. IX:** 60, 61, 65, 67, **68–70**

"Scandal Detectives, The" (Fitzgerald), **II:** 80–81; **Retro. Supp. I:** 99

Scarberry-García, Susan, **Supp. IV Part 2:** 486

Scarborough, Dorothy, **Supp. XVIII:** 279–280

Scarecrow, The (Connelly), **Supp. XXI:** 71, 74, 78, **79**

"Scarecrow, The" (Farrell), **II:** 45

"Scarf, A" (Shields), **Supp. VII:** 328

Scarface (screenplay, Hecht), **Supp. XXVII:** 83, 91, 92–93

Scarlet Cabinet, The (Notley), **Supp. XXII:** 233

"Scarlet Citadel, The" (Howard), **Supp. XXVII:** 125, 126

Scarlet Letter, The (Hawthorne), **II:** 63, 223, 224, 231, 233, 239–240, 241, 243, 244, 255, 264, 286, 290, 291, 550; **Retro. Supp. I:** 63, 145, 147, 152, **157–159,** 160, 163, 165, 220, 248, 330, 335; **Retro. Supp. II:** 100; **Retro. Supp. III:** 116–117; **Supp. I Part 1:** 38; **Supp. II Part 1:** 386; **Supp. VIII:** 108, 198; **Supp. XII:** 11; **Supp. XVII:** 143; **Supp. XX: 178, 183; Supp. XXII:** 147

"Scarlet Letter Aleph, The" (Mirvis), **Supp. XX: 183**

Scarlet Plague, The (London), **II:** 467

Scarlet Sister Mary (Peterkin), **Supp. XXII:** 189

Scar Lover (Crews), **Supp. XI:** 103, 107, **114–115**

"Scarred Girl, The" (Dickey), **Supp. IV Part 1:** 180

Scates, Maxine, **Supp. XIV:** 264, 265, 274

"Scenario" (H. Miller), **III:** 184

"Scene" (Howells), **II:** 274

"Scene in Jerusalem, A" (Stowe), **Supp. I Part 2:** 587

"Scenes" (Shields), **Supp. VII:** 318

Scènes d'Anabase (chamber music) (Bowles), **Supp. IV Part 1:** 82

"Scenes from a Documentary History of Mississippi" (Trethewey), **Supp. XXI:** 255–256

Scenes from American Life (Gurney), **Supp. V:** 95, 96, 105, 108

Scenes from Another Life (McClatchy), **Supp. XII:** 255–256

"Scenes from Childhood" (W. V. Davis), **Supp. XXI:** 95

"Scenes of Childhood" (Merrill), **Supp. III Part 1:** 322, 323, 327

"Scented Herbage of My Breast" (Whitman), **IV:** 342–343

"Scent of a Woman's Ink" (Prose), **Supp. XVI:** 259

"Scent of Unbought Flowers, The" (Ríos), **Supp. IV Part 2:** 547

Scepticisms (Aiken), **I:** 58

Scève, Maurice, **Supp. III Part 1:** 11

Schad, Christian, **Supp. IV Part 1:** 247

Schafer, Benjamin G., **Supp. XIV:** 144

Schafer, William, **Supp. XIX:** 164, 172

Schaller, George, **Supp. V:** 208, 210–211

Schapiro, Meyer, **II:** 30

Scharmann, Hermann Balthazar, **Supp. XII:** 41

Scharnhort, Gary, **Retro. Supp. III:** 268

Scharper, Alice, **Supp. XXII:** 175

Scharper, Diane, **Supp. XXIII:** 134

Schary, Dore, **Supp. IV Part 1:** 365; **Supp. XIII:** 163

Schatz, Tom, **Supp. XVIII:** 242

Schaum, Melita, **Supp. XXII:** 166

Schaumbergh, Count de, **II:** 120

Schechner, Richard, **Supp. XXIV:** 116

Scheele, Roy, **Supp. XVI:** 54; **Supp. XXI:** 103

Scheeman, George, **Supp. XXII:** 230

Scheffauer, G. H., **I:** 199

"Scheherazade" (Ashbery), **Supp. III Part 1:** 18

"Scheherazade Is Nailed and Mailed in Five Days" (Stone), **Supp. XXVII:** 257

"Scheherazade"(Siken), **Supp. XXVIII:** 199

Scheick, William, **Supp. V:** 272

Schelberg, Budd, **Supp. XVIII:** 241–256

Scheler, Max, **I:** 58

Schelling, Friedrich, **Supp. I Part 2:** 422

Schenck, Joseph, **Supp. XVI:** 186

Schenk, Margaret, **I:** 199

Scheponik, Peter, **Supp. X:** 210

Scherer, Loline, **Supp. XIII:** 161

"Scherzo"(Hadas), **Supp. XXIII:** 113

Schevill, James, **I:** 116

Schickel, Richard, **Supp. XV:** 1

Schifano, Mario, **Supp. XXIII:** 217

Schifino, Martin, **Supp. XXVI:** 145

Schilder, Paul, **Supp. I Part 2:** 622

Schildkraut, Rudolph, **Supp. XXIII:** 8

Schiller, Andrew, **II:** 20

Schiller, Frederick, **Supp. V:** 290

Schiller, Johann Christoph Friedrich von, **I:** 224; **Supp. IV Part 2:** 519; **Supp. XVI:** 292

Schiller, Lawrence, **Retro. Supp. II:** 208, 212, 214

Schimmel, Harold, **Supp. V:** 336

"Schizoid Nature of the Implied Author in Twentieth-Century American Ethnic Novels, The" (Nelson), **Supp. XVIII:** 172

Schjeldahl, Peter, **Supp. XXIV:** 44; **Supp. XXVII:** 23

Schlegel, Augustus Wilhelm, **III:** 422, 424

Schlegell, David von, **Supp. IV Part 2:** 423

Schleiermacher, Friedrich, **III:** 290–291, 309

Schleifer, Ronald, **Supp. XVIII:** 144

Schlepping Through the Alps (S. Apple), **Supp. XVII:** 8

Schlesinger, Arthur, Jr., **III:** 291, 297–298, 309

Schleuning, Neala, **Supp. XXIII:** 165

Schmidt, Jon Zlotnik, **Supp. IV Part 1:** 2

Schmidt, Kaspar. *See* Stirner, Max

Schmidt, Michael, **Supp. X:** 55

Schmidt, Peter, **Supp. XXVIII:** 234

Schmitt, Carl, **I:** 386–387

Schmitz, Neil, **Supp. X:** 243

Schnackenberg, Gjertrud, **Supp. XV:** 249–268

Schneeman, George, **Supp. XXIV:** 41

Schneider, Alan, **I:** 87

Schneider, Dean, **Supp. XXVII:** 208; **Supp. XXVIII:** 286

Schneider, Louis, **Supp. I Part 2:** 650

Schneider, Romy, **Supp. IV Part 2:** 549

Schneider, Steven, **Supp. IX:** 271, 274

Schneiderman, Jason, **Supp. XXVIII:** 196

Schnellock, Emil, **III:** 177

Schneour, Zalman, **IV:** 11

"Schnetzer Day" (Halliday), **Supp. XIX:** 93

Schnitzler, Arthur, **Supp. XV:** 307; **Supp. XVI:** 187

Schoen, Carol, **Supp. XXVII:** 297

Schoerke, Meg, **Supp. XVII:** 110

"Scholar Gypsy, The" (Arnold), **II:** 541

"Scholastic and Bedside Teaching" (Holmes), **Supp. I Part 1:** 305

Schöler, Bo, **Supp. IV Part 1:** 399, 400, 403, 407, 409; **Supp. IV Part 2:** 499

Scholes, Robert, **Supp. V:** 40, 42

Scholtz, Carter, **Supp. XVIII:** 144

Schomburg, Arthur, **Supp. X:** 134; **Supp. XXII:** 6

Schomburg Library of Nineteenth-Century Black Women Writers (H. L. Gates, ed.), **Supp. XX:** 105

Schönberg, Claude-Michel, **Supp. XXI:** 155

"School Among the Ruins, The" (Rich), **Retro. Supp. III:** 252

School Among the Ruins, The: Poems 2000–2004 (Rich), **Retro. Supp. III:** 252

Schoolboy Howlers (Abingdon), **Supp. XVI:** 99

Schoolcraft, Henry Rowe, **II:** 503; **Retro. Supp. II:** 160; **Supp. XXIII:** 223, 227, 228, 232, 233–234

Schoolcraft, Jane Johnston (Bamewawagezhikaquay), **Supp. XXIII:** 223–238

"School Days of an Indian Girl, The" (Zitkala-Ša), **Supp. XXV:** 272

"School Daze" (Bambara), **Supp. XI:** 19

School Daze (film), **Supp. XI:** 19, 20

"Schoolhouse" (Levis), **Supp. XI:** 258

"School of Giorgione, The" (Pater), **I:** 51

School of Udhra (Mackey), **Supp. XXVII:** 154–155

"School Play, The" (Merrill), **Supp. III Part 1:** 336

"Schooner Fairchild's Class" (Benét), **Supp. XI:** 55

Schopenhauer, Arthur, **III:** 600, 604; **IV:** 7; **Retro. Supp. I:** 256; **Retro. Supp. II:** 94; **Supp. I Part 1:** 320; **Supp. I Part 2:** 457; **Supp. X:** 187; **Supp. XVI:** 184

Schorer, Mark, **II:** 28; **III:** 71; **Retro. Supp. I:** 115; **Supp. IV Part 1:** 197, 203, 211; **Supp. XVI:** 206

Schott, Penelope Scambly, **Supp. XXIII:** 239–256

Schott, Webster, **Supp. IX:** 257

Schøtt-Khristensen, Lene, **Supp. XXVI:** 124, 125

Schotts, Jeffrey, **Supp. XII:** 193

Schrader, Mary von. *See* Jarrell, Mrs. Randall (Mary von Schrader)

Schreiber, Jan, **Supp. XXI:** 105, 111

Schreiner, Olive, **I:** 419; **Supp. XI:** 203

"Schreuderspitze, The" (Helprin), **Supp. XXV:** 85

Schroeder, Eric James, **Supp. V:** 238, 244

Schubert, Bernard L., **Supp. XVII:** 58

Schubert, David, **Supp. XXIV:** 45

Schubert, Franz Peter, **Supp. I Part 1:** 363

Schubnell, Matthias, **Supp. IV Part 2:** 486

Schudel, Matt, **Supp. XXII:** 205, 214

Schuessler, Jennifer, **Supp. XXVI:** 126

Schulberg, Budd, **II:** 98; **Retro. Supp. I:** 113; **Supp. XIII:** 170; **Supp. XV:** 194; **Supp. XXVII:** 142

Schulberg, Stuart, **Supp. XVIII:** 254

Schulman, Grace, **Supp. XXIII:** 58

Schulman, Tom, **Supp. XXI:** 193, 194

Schultz, David E., **Supp. XXVII:** 128

Schulz, Bruno, **Supp. IV Part 2:** 623; **Supp. XVII:** 41

Schuman, William, **Supp. XII:** 253; **Supp. XXII:** 283

Schumann, Dr. Alanson Tucker, **III:** 505

Schuster, Edgar H., **Supp. VIII:** 126

Schuyler, George S., **III:** 110; **Supp. XIX:** 78; **Supp. XVI:** 142; **Supp. XXVI:** 167

Schuyler, James, **Supp. XV:** 177, 178; **Supp. XXIII:** 207, 212, 215, 217; **Supp. XXIV:** 33; **Supp. XXVII:** 21, 23, 24, 26, 28

Schuyler, William, **Supp. I Part 1:** 211

"Schuylkill, The" (Halliday), **Supp. XIX:** 92

Schwartz, Delmore, **I:** 67, 168, 188, 288; **IV:** 128, 129, 437; **Retro. Supp. II:** 29, 178; **Supp. II Part 1:** 102, 109; **Supp. II Part 2:** 639–668; **Supp. IX:** 299; **Supp. VIII:** 98; **Supp. XIII:** 320; **Supp. XIV:** 3; **Supp. XIX:** 257; **Supp. XV:** 184

Schwartz, Leonard, **Supp. XVI:** 289

Schwartz, Lloyd, **Supp. I Part 1:** 81; **Supp. XXIV:** 160

Schwartz, Marilyn, **Supp. XII:** 126, 128, 130, 132

Schwartz, Meryl F., **Supp. XXII:** 65, 66

Schwartz, Richard B., **Supp. XIV:** 23, 27

Schwarz, A. B. Christa, **Supp. XIX:** 77, 79

Schwed, Peter, **Supp. XXII:** 119

Schweitzer, Albert, **Supp. IV Part 1:** 373

Schweitzer, Harold, **Supp. X:** 210

Schwerdt, Lisa M., **Supp. XIV:** 155, 171

Schwind, Jean, **Retro. Supp. III:** 36

Schwitters, Kurt, **III:** 197; **Retro. Supp. II:** 322, 331, 336; **Supp. IV Part 1:** 79

"Science" (Jeffers), **Supp. II Part 2:** 426

Science and Health with Key to the Scriptures (Eddy), **I:** 383

"Science Favorable to Virtue" (Freneau), **Supp. II Part 1:** 274

Science of English Verse, The (Lanier), **Supp. I Part 1:** 368, 369

"Science of the Night, The" (Kunitz), **Supp. III Part 1:** 258, 265

"Sci-Fi Floater Genius" (Halliday), **Supp. XIX:** 91

Sciolino, Martina, **Supp. XII:** 9

"Scissors" (C. Baxter), **Supp. XVII:** 19

Scofield, Sandra, **Supp. XXI:** 119

Scooter tetralogy (Murray). *See Magic Keys, The* (Murray); *Seven League Boots, The* (Murray); *Spyglass Tree, The* (Murray); *Train Whistle Guitar* (Murray)

Scopes, John T., **III:** 105, 495

"Scorched Face, The" (Hammett), **Supp. IV Part 1:** 344

"Scorn" (C. Frost), **Supp. XV:** 105

"Scorpion, The" (Bowles), **Supp. IV Part 1:** 84, 86

Scorpions (Myers), **Supp. XXVII:** 203, 204, 205

Scorsese, Martin, **Supp. IV Part 1:** 356; **Supp. XVIII:** 22

"Scotland" (Huddle), **Supp. XXVI:** 155

Scott, Anne Firor, **Supp. I Part 1:** 19

Scott, A. O., **Supp. X:** 301, 302; **Supp. XII:** 343

Scott, Duncan C., **Supp. XXVI:** 87

Scott, Evelyn, **Retro. Supp. I:** 73; **Supp. XXII:** 198

Scott, Gavin, **Supp. XXII:** 218

Scott, George C., **III:** 165–166; **Supp. XI:** 304

Scott, George Lewis, **Supp. I Part 2:** 503, 504

Scott, Hazel, **Supp. XXII:** 12

Scott, Herbert, **Supp. V:** 180

Scott, Howard, **Supp. I Part 2:** 645

Scott, Joanna, **Supp. XVII: 183–197**

Scott, Lizabeth, **Supp. IV Part 2:** 524

Scott, Lynn Orilla, **Retro. Supp. II:** 12

Scott, Mark, **Retro. Supp. I:** 127

Scott, Mary Ellen, **Supp. XXVI:** 235

Scott, Nathan A., Jr., **II:** 27

Scott, Paul, **Supp. IV Part 2:** 690

Scott, Ridley, **Supp. XIII:** 268

Scott, Walter, **Supp. XVI:** 7, 13

Scott, Sir Walter, **I:** 204, 339, 341, 343, 354; **II:** 8, 17, 18, 217, 296, 301, 303, 304, 308; **III:** 415, 482; **IV:** 204, 453;

Retro. Supp. I: 99; Supp. I Part 2: 579, 580, 685, 692; **Supp. IV Part 2:** 690; **Supp. IX:** 175; **Supp. X:** 51, 114

Scott, Whitney, **Supp. XXVI:** 49; **Supp. XXVIII:** 284

Scott, Winfield Townley, **II:** 512; **Supp. I Part 2:** 705; **Supp. XV:** 51

Scottsboro boys, **I:** 505; **Supp. I Part 1:** 330

Scottsboro Limited (Hughes), **Retro. Supp. I:** 203; **Supp. I Part 1:** 328, 330–331, 332

Scoundrel, The (film), **Supp. XXVII:** 90

Scoundrel Time (Hellman), **Supp. I Part 1:** 294–297; **Supp. IV Part 1:** 12; **Supp. VIII:** 243

Scrambled Eggs Super! (Geisel), **Supp. XVI:** 105

Scrambled Eggs & Whiskey: Poems, 1991–1995 (Carruth), **Supp. XVI:** 47

Scratch (MacLeish), **III:** 22–23

"Scratch Music" (Wright), **Supp. XV:** 343

"Scream, The" (R . Lowell), **II:** 550

"Screamer, The" (Coleman), **Supp. XI: 92–93**

"Screamers, The" (Baraka), **Supp. II Part 1:** 38

"Screech Owl" (Huddle), **Supp. XXVI:** 151

"Screen Guide for Americans" (Rand), **Supp. IV Part 2:** 524

"Screen Memory" (Cliff), **Supp. XXII:** 75

"Screeno" (Schwartz), **Supp. II Part 2:** 660

Screens, The (Genet), **Supp. XII:** 12

Screen Sirens Scream! (Parla and Mitchell), **Supp. XXII:** 256

Scribblers on the Roof: Contemporary American Jewish Fiction (Bukiet and Roskies, eds.), **Supp. XVII:** 39, 49–50

Scripts for the Pageant (Merrill), **Supp. III Part 1:** 332, 333, 335

Scrolls from the Dead Sea, The (Wilson), **IV:** 429

Scruggs, Earl, **Supp. V:** 335

Scudder, Horace Elisha, **II:** 400, 401; **Retro. Supp. II:** 67; **Supp. I Part 1:** 220; **Supp. I Part 2:** 410, 414

Scully, James, **Supp. XII:** 131

"Sculpting the Whistle" (Ríos), **Supp. IV Part 2:** 549

"Sculptor" (Plath), **Supp. I Part 2:** 538

"Sculptor's Funeral, The" (Cather), **I:** 315–316; **Retro. Supp. I:** 5, 6; **Retro. Supp. III:** 20, 26; **Supp. XV:** 40

Scum (Singer), **Retro. Supp. II:** 316–317

Scupoli, Lorenzo, **IV:** 156

"Scythe Song" (Lang), **Retro. Supp. I:** 128

Sea and the Mirror, The: A Commentary on Shakespeare's "The Tempest" (Auden), *Supp. II Part 1:* 2, 18

Sea around Us, The (Carson), **Supp. IX:** 19, **23–25**

Sea around Us, The (film), **Supp. IX:** 25

Sea Birds Are Still Alive, The (Bambara), **Supp. XI:** 1, 4, **7–12**

"Sea Birds Are Still Alive, The" (Bambara), **Supp. XI:** 8

"Sea-Blue and Blood-Red" (A. Lowell), **II:** 524

Seabrook, John, **Supp. VIII:** 157

"Sea Burial from the Cruiser Reve" (Eberhart), **I:** 532–533

Seabury, David, **Supp. I Part 2:** 608

"Sea Calm" (Hughes), **Retro. Supp. I:** 199

"Sea Chanty" (Corso), **Supp. XII:** 118

"Sea Dream, A" (Whitter), **Supp. I Part 2:** 699

"Seafarer, The" (Pound, trans.), **Retro. Supp. I:** 287

Seagall, Harry, **Supp. XIII:** 166

Sea Garden (Doolittle), **Supp. I Part 1:** 257, 259, 266, 269, 272; **Supp. XXVII:** 288

Seager, Allan, **IV:** 305

Seagull on the Step, The (Boyle), **Supp. XXIV:** 60, 62

"Seagulls and Children" (C. Frost), **Supp. XV:** 95

Sea Lady, The (Boyce), **Supp. XXI:** 8, 13

"Sea Lily" (Doolittle), **Supp. I Part 1:** 266

Sea Lions, The (Cooper), **I:** 354, 355

Sealts, Merton M., Jr., **Retro. Supp. I:** 257

Seaman, Benjamin, **Supp. XXIII:** 69–70, 72

Seaman, Donna, **Supp. VIII:** 86; **Supp. X:** 1, 4, 12, 16, 213; **Supp. XIX:** 53, 55, 57, 58, 59, 60, 61; **Supp. XV:** 65; **Supp. XVIII:** 102; **Supp. XXI:** 236; **Supp. XXII:** 266; **Supp. XXIII:** 71, 74, 134, 135, 298; **Supp. XXIV:** 167, 171; **Supp. XXVI:** 150–151, 158

"Seamy Side, The"(Hadas), **Supp. XXIII:** 119

"Séance, The" (Singer), **IV:** 20

Séance and Other Stories, The (Singer), **IV:** 19–21

"Sea Oak" (Saunders), **Supp. XIX:** 228, 229, 231

Sea of Cortez (Steinbeck), **IV:** 52, 54, 62, 69

Sea of Grass, The (film), **Supp. XVIII:** 211

Sea of Grass, The (Richter), **Supp. XVIII: 210–211**, 215–216, 217, 220

"Sea Pieces" (Melville), **III:** 93

Searchers, The (film, Ford), **Supp. XVIII:** 57, 58, 135–136, 141

Searches and Seizures (Elkin), **Supp. VI:** 49

"Search for Southern Identity, The" (Woodward), **Retro. Supp. I:** 75; **Supp. XXII:** 194

Search for the King, A: A Twelfth-Century Legend (Vidal), **Supp. IV Part 2:** 681

Searching for Caleb (Tyler), **Supp. IV Part 2:** 663–665, 671

"Searching for Poetry: Real *vs.* Fake" (B. Miller), **Supp. IV Part 1:** 67

Searching for Survivors (Banks), **Supp. V:** 7

"Searching for Survivors (I)" (Banks), **Supp. V:** 8

"Searching for Survivors (II)" (Banks), **Supp. V:** 7, 8

Searching for the Ox (Simpson), **Supp. IX:** 266, **274–275**

"Searching for the Ox" (Simpson), **Supp. IX:** 275, 280

"Searching in the Britannia Tavern" (Wagoner), **Supp. IX:** 327

Searching the Drowned Man (Lea), **Supp. XXVIII:** 130–131

"Searching the Drowned Man: The Third Day"(Lea), **Supp. XXVIII:** 131

Searching Wing, The, (Hellman), **Supp. I Part 1:** 277, 278, 281–282, 283, 292, 297

Search-Light. *See* Frank, Waldo

"Search Party, The" (Matthews), **Supp. IX:** 156

Searle, Ronald, **Supp. I Part 2:** 604, 605

Sea Road to the Indies (Hart), **Supp. XIV:** 97

"Seascape" (Bishop), **Retro. Supp. II:** 42–43

Seascape: Needle's Eye (Oppen), **Supp. XXVI:** 236–237

"Sea's Green Sameness, The" (Updike), **IV:** 217

Seaside and the Fireside, The (Longfellow), **II:** 489; **Retro. Supp. II:** 159, 168

"Season, The" (Stone), **Supp. XXVII:** 250–251

Season in Hell, A (Rimbaud), **III:** 189

Seasons, The (Thomson), **II:** 304; **Supp. I Part 1:** 151

Seasons' Difference, The (Buechner), **Supp. XII:** 47

Seasons of Celebration (Merton), **Supp. VIII:** 199, 208

Seasons of the Heart: In Quest of Faith (Kinard, comp.), **Supp. XIV:** 127

"Seasons of the Soul" (Tate), **IV:** 136–140

Seasons on Earth (Koch), **Supp. XV:** **183–184**

"Sea Surface Full of Clouds" (Stevens), **IV:** 82

"Sea Tides" (Hoffman), **Supp. XVIII:** 87

"Sea Treader" (Hoffman), **Supp. XVIII:** 87

"Sea Unicorns and Land Unicorns" (Moore), **III:** 202–203

Seaver, Edwin, **Supp. XXV:** 28

Seaver, Richard, **Supp. XI:** 301

"Seaweed" (Longfellow), **II:** 498

Sea-Wolf, The (London), **II:** 264, 466, 472–473

Sebald, W. G., **Supp. XIV:** 96; **Supp. XXI:** 92

Sebold, Alice, **Supp. XXII:** 55

Seckler, David, **Supp. I Part 2:** 650

"2nd Air Force" (Jarrell), **II:** 375

Second American Revolution and Other Essays (1976–1982), The (Vidal), **Supp. IV Part 2:** 679, 687, 688

Secondary Colors, The (A. Theroux), **Supp. VIII:** 312

Second Avenue (O'Hara), **Supp. XXIII:** 216

"Second Avenue"(O'Hara), **Supp. XXIII:** 208, 211, 218

Second Blush, The (Peacock), **Supp. XIX:** 197, **205–206**

Second Chance (Auchincloss), **Supp. IV Part 1:** 33

"Second Chances" (Hugo), **Supp. VI:** 144, 145

Second Coming, The (Percy), **Supp. III Part 1:** 383, 384, 387, 388, 396–397

"Second Coming, The" (Yeats), **III:** 294; **Retro. Supp. I:** 290, 311; **Supp. VIII:** 24; **Supp. XIX:** 85; **Supp. XVI:** 159

Second Decade, The. See Stephen King, The Second Decade: "Danse Macabre" to "The Dark Half" (Magistrale)

Second Dune, The (Hearon), **Supp. VIII:** 58, **59–60**

Second Flowering, A: Works and Days of the Lost Generation (Cowley), **Retro. Supp. II:** 77; **Supp. II Part 1:** 135, 141, 143, 144, 147, 149

Second Growth (Stegner), **Supp. IV Part 2:** 599, 608

Second-Hand Coat: Poems New and Selected (Stone), **Supp. XXVII:** 250, 257, 262

"Second Hour of the Night, The" (Bidart), **Supp. XV:** 32, **33–34**

Second Marriage (F. Barthelme), **Supp. XI:** 32, 33

"Second Marriage" (McCarriston), **Supp. XIV:** 262

"Second Mortgage" (Shaw), **Supp. XIX:** 245–246

Second Nature (Hoffman), **Supp. X:** 88, 89

"Second Nesting" (Davison), **Supp. XXVI:** 77

Seconds, The (Bierds), **Supp. XVII:** **33–34**

Second Set, The (Komunyakaa and Feinstein, eds.), **Supp. XIII:** 125

Second Sex, The (Beauvoir), **Retro. Supp. III:** 243; **Supp. IV Part 1:** 360

"Second Sight" (Mosher), **Supp. XXII:** 214

Second Stone, The (Fiedler), **Supp. XIII:** 102

"Second Swimming, The" (Boyle), **Supp. VIII:** 13, 14

Second Tree from the Corner (White), **Supp. I Part 2:** 654

"Second Tree from the Corner" (White), **Supp. I Part 2:** 651

Second Twenty Years at Hull-House, The: September 1909 to September 1929, with a Record of a Growing World Consciousness (Addams), **Supp. I Part 1:** 24–25

Second Voyage of Columbus, The (Morison), **Supp. I Part 2:** 488

Second Wooing of Salina Sue and Other Stories, The (Stuart), **Supp. XXVIII:** 235

Second Words, (Atwood), **Supp. XIII:** 35

Second World, The (Blackmur), **Supp. II Part 1:** 91

Secret, The (E. Hoffman), **Supp. XVI:** 151, **155–158,** 161

"Secret, The" (Levine), **Supp. V:** 195

Secret Agent, The (Conrad), **Supp. IV Part 1:** 341

Secret Agent X-9 (Hammett), **Supp. IV Part 1:** 355

"Secret Courts of Men's Hearts, The: Code and Law in Harper Lee's *To Kill a Mockingbird*" (C. D. Johnson), **Supp. VIII:** 126

"Secret Dog, The" (Cameron), **Supp. XII: 83–84**

Secret Garden, The (Burnett), **Supp. I Part 1:** 44

"Secret Garden, The" (Hoffman), **Supp. XVIII:** 86

"Secret Gladness, A" (C. Frost), **Supp. XV:** 91

Secret Historie (J. Smith), **I:** 131

Secret History, The (Tartt), **Supp. XXVII:** 267, 268, 269, 270–273

Secret History of the Dividing Line (Howe), **Supp. IV Part 2:** 424, 425–426

"Secret Integration, The" (Pynchon), **Supp. II Part 2:** 624

"Secret Life of Musical Instruments, The" (Wright), **Supp. XV:** 343

"Secret Life of Walter Mitty, The" (Thurber), **Supp. I Part 2:** 623; **Supp. XVI:** 233

"Secret Lion, The" (Ríos), **Supp. IV Part 2:** 543, 544

"Secret Nature of the Mechanical Rabbit, The"(P. Benedict), **Supp. XXIII:** 49

"Secret Ocean, The" (Jarman), **Supp. XVII:** 120

Secret of Poetry, The: Essays (Jarman), **Supp. XVII:** 110, 111, 120

"Secret of the Russian Ballet, The" (Van Vechten), **Supp. II Part 2:** 732

"Secret Profession, The" (Stone), **Supp. XXVII:** 258–259

"Secret Prune" (Ríos), **Supp. IV Part 2:** 549

Secret River, The (Rawlings), **Supp. X:** 233

Secrets and Surprises (Beattie), **Supp. V:** 23, 27, 29

Secrets from the Center of the World (Harjo), **Supp. XII: 223–224**

"Secret Sharer, The" (J. Conrad), **Supp. IX:** 105; **Supp. XVI:** 158; **Supp. XXV:** 217

"Secret Society, A" (Nemerov), **III:** 282

Secrets of the Heart (Gibran), **Supp. XX:** 116

"Secrets of the Summer, The" (Ellis), **Supp. XXVII:** 75

Secrets of the Universe: Scenes from the Journey Home (Sanders), **Supp. XVI:** 273–274

"Secret World of Women, The"(Goodman), **Supp. XXVIII:** 95

"Secular" (Trethewey), **Supp. XXI:** 249

Secular Journal of Thomas Merton, The, **Supp. VIII:** 206

"Security" (Boyle), **Supp. XXIV:** 58

"Security" (Stafford), **Supp. XI:** 329

"Security"(Strout), **Supp. XXIII:** 283

Sedaris, David, **Supp. XXIII:** 289

Sedges, John (pseudonym). *See* Buck, Pearl S.
Sedgwick, Catherine Maria, **I:** 341; **Supp. I Part 1:** 155, 157
Sedgwick, Christina. *See* Marquand, Mrs. John P. (Christina Sedgwick)
Sedgwick, Ellery, **I:** 217, 229, 231; **III:** 54–55
Sedgwick, Eve, **Supp. XX:** 267
Sedgwick, Henry, **Supp. I Part 1:** 156
Sedgwick, Robert, **Supp. I Part 1:** 156
Sedore, Timothy, **Supp. XIV:** 312
"Seduction and Betrayal" (Hardwick), **Supp. III Part 1:** 207
Seduction and Betrayal: Women and Literature (Hardwick), **Supp. III Part 1:** 194, 204, 206–208, 212, 213; **Supp. XIV:** 89
See, Carolyn, **Supp. XXII:** 206, 217
Seed, David, **Supp. IV Part 1:** 391
"Seed Eaters, The" (Francis), **Supp. IX:** 82
"Seed Leaves" (Wilbur), **Supp. III Part 2:** 558
"Seeds" (Anderson), **I:** 106, 114
Seeds of Contemplation (Merton), **Supp. VIII:** 199, 200, 207, 208
Seeds of Destruction (Merton), **Supp. VIII:** 202, 203, 204, 208
Seedtime on the Cumberland (Arnow), **Supp. XXVIII:** 3
Seeger, Pete, **Supp. XXVIII:** 65, 79
"Seeing Red" (column, Ryan as Quin), **Supp. XVIII:** 226
Seeing through the Sun (Hogan), **Supp. IV Part 1:** 397, 400, 401–402, 402, 413
"See in the Midst of Fair Leaves" (Moore), **III:** 215
"Seekers, The" (McGrath), **Supp. X:** 117
"Seeking a Vision of Truth, Guided by a Higher Power" (Burke), **Supp. XIV:** 21, 23
"See(k)ing the Self: Mirrors and Mirroring in Bicultural Texts" (Oster), **Supp. XVI:** 151
"Seele im Raum" (Jarrell), **II:** 382–383
"Seele im Raum" (Rilke), **II:** 382–383
"See Naples and Die" (Hecht), **Supp. X:** 69, 70
"Seen from the 'L'" (Barnes), **Supp. III Part 1:** 33
"See the Moon?" (Barthelme), **Supp. IV Part 1:** 42, 49–50, 50
Sefarim, Mendele Mokher, **Supp. XXIII:** 4
Seferis, George, **Supp. XXV:** 225
Segal, D. (pseudonym). *See* Singer, Isaac Bashevis
Segal, George, **Supp. XI:** 343
Segal, Lore, **Supp. XVI:** 203
Segregation: The Inner Conflict in the South (Warren), **IV:** 237, 238, 246, 252
"*Se*: Hegel's Absolute and Heidegger's *Ereignis*" (Agamben), **Supp. XVI:** 289
Seidel, Frederick, **I:** 185
Seidman, Hugh, **Supp. XXI:** 228
Seize the Day (Bellow), **I:** 144, 147, 148, 150, 151, 152, 153, 155, 158, 162; **Retro. Supp. II:** 19, **23–24**, 27, 32, 34; **Supp. I Part 2:** 428
Selby, Hubert, **Supp. III Part 1:** 125
Selby, Hubert, Jr., **Supp. XXI:** 227
Selby, John, **Retro. Supp. II:** 221, 222
Selden, John, **Supp. XIV:** 344
Seldes, Gilbert, **II:** 437, 445; **Retro. Supp. I:** 108
Selected Criticism: Prose, Poetry (Bogan), **Supp. III Part 1:** 64
Selected Essays (Eliot), **I:** 572
Selected Essays and Reviews (Carruth), **Supp. XVI:** 46
Selected Journals and Other Writings (Audubon), **Supp. XVI:** 10, 12, 13
Selected Letters (Bynner), **Supp. XV:** 52
Selected Letters (Oppen), **Supp. XXVI:** 228
Selected Letters (W. C. Williams), **Retro. Supp. I:** 430
Selected Letters, 1940–1956 (Kerouac), **Supp. XIV:** 137, 144
Selected Letters of Robert Frost (Thompson, ed.), **Retro. Supp. I:** 125
Selected Letters of Willa Cather, The, **Retro. Supp. III:** 37
Selected Levis, The (Levis), **Supp. XI:** 257, 272
Selected Plays (O'Hara), **Supp. XXIII:** 216
Selected Poems (A. Lowell), **II:** 512, 516
Selected Poems (Aiken), **I:** 69
Selected Poems (Ashbery), **Supp. III Part 1:** 25–26
Selected Poems (Berrigan), **Supp. XXIV:** 37
Selected Poems (Bodenheim), **Supp. XXV:** 29
Selected Poems (Brodsky), **Supp. VIII:** 22
Selected Poems (Brooks), **Supp. III Part 1:** 82–83
Selected Poems (Bynner), **Supp. XV:** 51, 52
Selected Poems (Corso), **Supp. XII:** 129
Selected Poems (Dove), **Supp. IV Part 1:** 241, 243, 250
Selected Poems (Frost), **Retro. Supp. I:** 133, 136; **Retro. Supp. III:** 102, 103
Selected Poems (Guillevic; Levertov, trans.), **Supp. III Part 1:** 283
Selected Poems (Hayden), **Supp. II Part 1:** 363, 364, 367
Selected Poems (Hughes), **Retro. Supp. I:** 202; **Supp. I Part 1:** 341, 345, 346
Selected Poems (Hugo), **Supp. VI:** 143
Selected Poems (Jarrell), **II:** 367, 370, 371, 374, 377, 379, 380, 381, 382, 384
Selected Poems (Justice), **Supp. VII:** 115
Selected Poems (Kinnell), **Supp. III Part 1:** 235, 253
Selected Poems (Levine, 1984), **Supp. V:** 178, 179
Selected Poems (Merton), **Supp. VIII:** 207, 208
Selected Poems (Moore), **III:** 193, 194, 205–206, 208, 215
Selected Poems (Notley), **Supp. XXII:** 234
Selected Poems (O'Hara; Allen, ed.), **Supp. XXIII:** 220
Selected Poems (O'Hara; Ford, ed.), **Supp. XXIII:** 220
Selected Poems (Pound), **Retro. Supp. I:** 289, 291
Selected Poems (R. Bly), **Supp. IV Part 1:** 60, 62, 65, 66, 68, 69–71
Selected Poems (R. Lowell), **Retro. Supp. II:** 184, 186, 188, 190
Selected Poems (Ransom), **III:** 490, 492
Selected Poems (Reznikoff), **Supp. XIV:** 288
Selected Poems (Rukeyser), **Supp. VI:** 274
Selected Poems (Sexton), **Supp. IV Part 2:** 449
Selected Poems (Sorrentino), **Supp. XXI:** 226
Selected Poems (Strand), **Supp. IV Part 2:** 630
Selected Poems, 1923–1943 (Warren), **IV:** 241–242, 243
Selected Poems, 1928–1958 (Kunitz), **Supp. III Part 1:** 261, 263–265
Selected Poems, 1938–1988 (McGrath), **Supp. X:** 127
Selected Poems, 1958–1980 (Sorrentino), **Supp. XXI:** 228
Selected Poems, 1963–1983 (Simic), **Supp. VIII:** 275
Selected Poems 1936–1965 (Eberhart), **I:** 541
Selected Poems: 1957–1987 (Snodgrass), **Supp. VI:** 314–315, 323, 324
Selected Poems 1965–1975 (Atwood), **Supp. XIII:** 32–34
Selected Poems: 1975–2005 (Skloot), **Supp. XX:** 196
Selected Poems II: Poems Selected and New, 1976–1986 (Atwood), **Supp. XIII:** 20, 34–35
Selected Poems of Ezra Pound (Pound), **Supp. V:** 336
Selected Poems of Gabriela Mistral (Hughes, trans.), **Supp. I Part 1:** 345
Selected Poems of Stanley Kunitz, The, **Supp. XXVI:** 64
Selected Poetry of Amiri Baraka/LeRoi Jones (Baraka), **Supp. II Part 1:** 58
Selected Poetry of Hayden Carruth, The (Carruth), **Supp. XVI:** 53
Selected Stories (Dubus), **Supp. VII:** 88–89
Selected Stories of Richard Bausch, The (Bausch), **Supp. VII:** 42
Selected Translations (Snodgrass), **Supp. VI:** 318, 324, **325–326**
Selected Verse of Margaret Haskins Durber, The (Keillor), **Supp. XVI:** 171
Selected Witter Bynner, The, **Supp. XV:** 52
Selected Works of Djuna Barnes, The (Barnes), **Supp. III Part 1:** 44
Selected Writings (Brainard), **Supp. XXVII:** 20
Selected Writings 1950–1990 (Howe), **Supp. VI:** 116–117, 118, 120
Selected Writings of Edgar Allan Poe: Authoritative Texts, Backgrounds and Contexts, Criticism (Thompson, ed.), **Retro. Supp. III:** 237

Selected Writings of John Jay Chapman, The (Barzun), **Supp. XIV:** 54

Select Epigrams from the Greek Anthology (Mackail), **Supp. I Part 2:** 461

"Selecting a Reader" (Kooser), **Supp. XIX:** 119–120

"Selene Afterwards" (MacLeish), **III:** 8

"Self" (James), **II:** 351

Self, William, **Supp. XXII:** 172

Self and the Dramas of History, The (Niebuhr), **III:** 308

"Self-Appraisal" (Davison), **Supp. XXVI:** 68

Self-Consciousness (Updike), **Retro. Supp. I:** 318, 319, 320, 322, 323, 324

"Self-Culture" (Channing), **Supp. XXIV: 78–79**

"Self-Exposed, The" (X. J. Kennedy), **Supp. XV:** 159

Self-Help: Stories (Moore), **Supp. X:** 163, 166, **167–169**, 174, 175

"Self-Importance" (Halliday), **Supp. XIX:** 90

Self-Interviews (Dickey), **Supp. IV Part 1:** 179

"Selfish Giant, The"(Wilde), **Supp. XXVIII:** 279

"Selfish Giant, The"(Woodson), **Supp. XXVIII:** 277

"Self-Made Man, A" (Crane), **I:** 420

"Self Pity" (C. Frost), **Supp. XV:** 93, 94, 101, 102, 104

Self Portrait (album, Dylan), **Supp. XVIII:** 27

Self-Portrait (Brainard and Waldman), **Supp. XXVII:** 23–24

"Self-Portrait" (Creeley), **Supp. IV Part 1:** 156

"Self-Portrait" (Davison), **Supp. XXVI:** 68

"Self-Portrait" (Mumford), **Supp. II Part 2:** 471

"(Self) Portrait" (Trethewey), **Supp. XXI:** 253

"Self-Portrait" (Wylie), **Supp. I Part 2:** 729

"Self-Portrait Against Red Wallpaper"(Siken), **Supp. XXVIII:** 202

"Self Portrait at Fifty-three" (Weigl), **Supp. XIX:** 288

Self-Portrait: Ceaselessly into the Past (Millar, ed. Sipper), **Supp. IV Part 2:** 464, 469, 472, 475

"Self-Portrait in a Convex Mirror" (Ashbery), **Supp. III Part 1:** 5, 7, 9, 16–19, 22, 24, 26

"Self-Portrait on a Christmas Night" (Brainard), **Supp. XXVII:** 24–25

"Self-Portrait with 1911 NY Yankees Cap" (Skloot), **Supp. XX: 202**

"Self-Reliance" (Emerson), **II:** 7, 15, 17; **Retro. Supp. I:** 159; **Retro. Supp. II:** 155; **Supp. X:** 42, 45

Selfwolf (Halliday), **Supp. XIX:** 81, **89–91,** 93

Seligman, Rachel, **Supp. XXVIII:** 164

Sélincourt, Ernest de, **Supp. I Part 2:** 676

Selinger, Eric, **Supp. XVI:** 47

Selinger, Eric Murphy, **Supp. XI:** 248

Sell, Henry, **Supp. XVI:** 188

Sellers, Isaiah, **IV:** 194–195

Sellers, Peter, **Supp. XI:** 301, 304, 306, 307, 309

Sellers, William, **IV:** 208

Seltzer, Mark, **Retro. Supp. I:** 227

Selznick, David O., **Retro. Supp. I:** 105, 113; **Supp. IV Part 1:** 353; **Supp. XVIII:** 242; **Supp. XXII:** 195

Semi, Allen (pseudonym). *See* Larsen, Nella

"Semi-Lunatics of Kilmuir, The" (Hugo), **Supp. VI:** 145

"Semiotics/The Doctor's Doll" (Goldbarth), **Supp. XII:** 183–184

Semmelweiss, Ignaz, **Supp. I Part 1:** 304

Senancour, Étienne Divert de, **I:** 241

Senator North (Atherton), **Supp. XXIV:** 22

Sendak, Maurice, **Supp. IX:** 207, 208, 213, 214; **Supp. XVI:** 110

Seneca, **II:** 14–15; **III:** 77

Senghor, Leopold Sédar, **Supp. IV Part 1:** 16; **Supp. X:** 132, 139

Senier, Siobhan, **Supp. IV Part 1:** 330

"Senility" (Anderson), **I:** 114

Senior, Olive, **Supp. XXIII:** 94

"Senior Partner's Ethics, The" (Auchincloss), **Supp. IV Part 1:** 33

Senlin: A Biography (Aiken), **I:** 48, 49, 50, 52, 56, 57, 64

Sennett, Dorothy, **Supp. XVI:** 43

Sennett, Mack, **III:** 442

"Señora X No More" (Mora), **Supp. XIII:** 218

"Señor Ong and Señor Ha" (Bowles), **Supp. IV Part 1:** 87

Señor Presidente, El (Asturias), **Supp. XXIV:** 89

"Señor X" (Muñoz), **Supp. XXV:** 135

Sensational Designs: The Cultural Work of American Fiction, 1790–1860 (Tompkins), **Supp. XVIII:** 258–259

Sense and Sensibility (Austen), **Supp. XXVI:** 130, 212

Sense of Beauty, The (Santayana), **III:** 600

Sense of Life in the Modern Novel, The (Mizener), **IV:** 132

"Sense of Shelter, A" (Updike), **Retro. Supp. I:** 318

"Sense of the Meeting, The" (Conroy), **Supp. XVI:** 72

Sense of the Past, The (James), **II:** 337–338

"Sense of the Past, The" (Trilling), **Supp. III Part 2:** 503

"Sense of the Present, The" (Hardwick), **Supp. III Part 1:** 210

"Sense of the Sleight-of-Hand Man, The" (Stevens), **IV:** 93

"Sense of Where You Are, A" (McPhee), **Supp. III Part 1:** 291, 296–298

"Sensibility! O La!" (Roethke), **III:** 536

"Sensible Emptiness, A" (Kramer), **Supp. IV Part 1:** 61, 66

Sensualists, The (Hecht), **Supp. XXVII:** 96

"Sensuality Plunging Barefoot Into Thorns" (Cisneros), **Supp. VII:** 68

"Sentence" (Barthelme), **Supp. IV Part 1:** 47

Sent for You Yesterday (Wideman), **Supp. X:** 320, 321

Sentimental Education (Flaubert), **Supp. XXVII:** 2

"Sentimental Education, A" (Banks), **Supp. V:** 10

"Sentimental Journey" (Oates), **Supp. II Part 2:** 522, 523

"Sentimental Journey, A" (Anderson), **I:** 114

Sentimental Journey, A (Sterne), **Supp. I Part 2:** 714

"Sentimental Journeys" (Didion), **Supp. IV Part 1:** 211

Sentimental Journey through France and Italy, A (Sterne), **Supp. XV:** 232

"Sentiment of Rationality, The" (James), **II:** 346–347

"Separated Father" (Halliday), **Supp. XIX:** 92, 93

Separate Flights (Dubus), **Supp. VII:** 78–83

"Separate Flights" (Dubus), **Supp. VII:** 83

Separate Peace, A (Knowles), **Supp. IV Part 2:** 679; **Supp. XII: 241–249**

Separate Way (Reznikoff), **Supp. XIV:** 280

"Separating" (Updike), **Retro. Supp. I:** 321

"Separation, The" (Kunitz), **Supp. III Part 1:** 263

"Sepia High Stepper" (Hayden), **Supp. II Part 1:** 379

Septagon (Levin), **Supp. XXVII:** 139

September (film; Allen), **Supp. XV:** 11

"September" (Komunyakaa), **Supp. XIII:** 130

"September" (Pickering), **Supp. XXI:** 198

"September 1, 1939" (Auden), **Supp. II Part 1:** 13; **Supp. IV Part 1:** 225; **Supp. VIII:** 30, 32; **Supp. XV:** 117–118

September 11, 2001: American Writers Respond (Heyen), **Supp. XIII:** 285

"September's Book" (Notley), **Supp. XXII:** 229

September Song (Humphrey), **Supp. IX:** 101, 102, **108–109**

"September Twelfth, 2001" (X. J. Kennedy), **Supp. XV:** 171

Septet for the End of Time (Mackey), **Supp. XXVII:** 152

"Sept Vieillards, Les" (Millay, trans.), **III:** 142

Sequel to Drum-Taps (Whitman), **Retro. Supp. I:** 406

"Sequence, Sometimes Metaphysical" (Roethke), **III:** 547, 548

Sequence of Seven Plays with a Drawing by Ron Slaughter, A (Nemerov), **III:** 269

Sequoya, Jana, **Supp. IV Part 1:** 334

Seraglio, The (Merrill), **Supp. III Part 1:** 331

Seraphita (Balzac), **I:** 499
Seraph on the Suwanee (Hurston), **Retro. Supp. III:** 134–135; **Supp. VI:** 149, 159–160
Serena (film), **Supp. XXVII:** 222
Serena (Rash), **Supp. XXVII:** 222, 224–225, 226
Serenissima: A Novel of Venice (Jong). *See Shylock's Daughter: A Novel of Love in Venice (Serenissima)* (Jong)
Sergeant, Elizabeth Shepley, **I:** 231, 236, 312, 319, 323, 328; **Retro. Supp. III:** 18, 21, 22, 23, 24, 29, 30, 36
Sergeant Bilko (television show), **Supp. IV Part 2:** 575
Sergi, Paula, **Supp. XXI:** 246
"Serious Talk, A" (Carver), **Supp. III Part 1:** 138, 144
Serly, Tibor, **Supp. III Part 2:** 617, 619
"Sermon, Now Encrypted" (Monson), **Supp. XXIV:** 239–240
"Sermon by Doctor Pep" (Bellow), **I:** 151
Sermones (Horace), **II:** 154
"Sermon for Our Maturity" (Baraka), **Supp. II Part 1:** 53
"Sermon in the Cotton Field" (Nelson), **Supp. XVIII:** 177
"Sermon in the Depths, The" (Hecht), **Supp. XXVII:** 86
"Sermon of the Fallen"(Bottoms), **Supp. XXVIII:** 26
Sermons and Soda Water (O'Hara), **III:** 362, 364, 371–373, 382
"Sermons on the Warpland" (Brooks), **Supp. III Part 1:** 84
"Serpent in the Wilderness, The" (Masters), **Supp. I Part 2:** 458
"Servant of History, A" (Rash), **Supp. XXVII:** 229
Servant of the Bones (Rice), **Supp. VII:** 298, 302
"Servant to Servants, A" (Frost), **Retro. Supp. I:** 125, 128; **Supp. X:** 66
Serve It Forth (M. F. K. Fisher), **Supp. XVII:** 83, 86, 87, 89, 92
Service, Robert W., **Supp. XXI:** 51; **Supp. XXII:** 203
Seshachari, Neila, **Supp. V:** 22
"Session, The" (Adams), **I:** 5
"Sestina" (Bishop), **Supp. I Part 1:** 73, 88
"Sestina from the Home Gardener, A"(Wakoski), **Supp. XXVIII:** 263
Set-angya, **Supp. IV Part 2:** 493
Seth, Vikram, **Supp. XVII:** 117
Seth's Brother's Wife (Frederic), **II:** 131–132, 137, 144
Sethuraman, Ramchandran, **Supp. XXII:** 73
Setouchi, Jakuch\[omacron\], **Supp. XXIV:** 166
Set This House on Fire (Styron), **IV:** 98, 99, 105, 107–113, 114, 115, 117
Setting Free the Bears (Irving), **Supp. VI:** 163, **166–167,** 169–170
Setting the Tone (Rorem), **Supp. IV Part 1:** 79
Settle, Mary Lee, **Supp. IX:** 96
Settlement Horizon, The: A National Estimate (Woods and Kennedy), **Supp. I Part 1:** 19
Settlers, The (Levin), **Supp. XXVII:** 134, 143, 146
"Settling the Colonel's Hash" (McCarthy), **II:** 559, 562
Setzer, Helen, **Supp. IV Part 1:** 217
"Seurat's Sunday Afternoon along the Seine" (Schwartz), **Supp. II Part 2:** 663–665
Sevag, Aris, **Supp. XXIII:** 28, 29
7 Years from Somehwere (Levine), **Supp. V:** 178, 181, 188–189
Seven against Thebes (Aeschylus; Bacon and Hecht, trans.), **Supp. X:** 57
Seven Ages of Man, The (Wilder), **IV:** 357, 374–375
Seven Deadly Sins, The (Wilder), **IV:** 357, 374–375
Seven Descents of Myrtle, The (T. Williams), **IV:** 382
"Seven Fat Brides, The" (P. Abraham), **Supp. XVII:** 50
Seven Guitars (Wilson), **Retro. Supp. III:** 318; **Supp. VIII:** 331, **348–351**
Seven Lady Godivas, The (Geisel), **Supp. XVI:** 100, 103
Seven League Boots, The (Murray), **Supp. XIX: 156–157**
Seven-League Crutches, The (Jarrell), **II:** 367, 372, 381, 382, 383–384, 389
Seven Mountains of Thomas Merton, The (Mott), **Supp. VIII:** 208
Seven-Ounce Man, The (Harrison), **Supp. VIII:** 51
"Seven Places of the Mind" (Didion), **Supp. IV Part 1:** 200, 210
Seven Plays (Shepard), **Supp. III Part 2:** 434
"Seven Selves, The" (Gibran), **Supp. XX: 118**
"Seven Sentences"(Dybek), **Supp. XXIII:** 74
"Seven Stanzas at Easter" (Updike), **IV:** 215
Seven Storey Mountain, The (Merton), **Supp. VIII:** 193, 195, 198, 200, 207, 208
Seventeen (Berrigan and Padgett), **Supp. XXIV:** 41
Seventh Beggar, The (Abraham), **Supp. XXIV:** 2, 3, **9–12,** 13, 14
Seventh Heaven (Hoffman), **Supp. X:** 87, 89
"Seventh of March" (Webster), **Supp. I Part 2:** 687
"7000 Romaine, Los Angeles 38" (Didion), **Supp. IV Part 1:** 200
"Seventh Street" (Toomer), **Supp. IX:** 316
Seven Types of Ambiguity (Empson), **II:** 536; **IV:** 431
77 Dream Songs (Berryman), **I:** 168, 169, 170, 171, 174, 175, 183–188
73 Poems (Cummings), **I:** 430, 431, 446, 447, 448
Seven Valleys and the Four Valleys, The (Bahá'u'lláh), **Supp. XX: 121**
"Several Short Questions About Crumbs"(Schott), **Supp. XXIII:** 249
Sevier, Jack, **IV:** 378
Sévigné, Madame de, **IV:** 361
Sewall, Richard, **Retro. Supp. I:** 25
Sewall, Samuel, **IV:** 145, 146, 147, 149, 154, 164; **Supp. I Part 1:** 100, 110
Sewell, Elizabeth, **Supp. XIII:** 344
"Sex" (Carruth), **Supp. XVI:** 58
Sex, Economy, Freedom and Community (Berry), **Supp. X:** 30, 36
"Sex Camp" (Mamet), **Supp. XIV:** 240
Sex Castle, The (Lacy), **Supp. XV:** 206
Sex & Character (Weininger), **Retro. Supp. I:** 416
"Sext" (Auden), **Supp. II Part 1:** 22
Sexton, Anne, **Retro. Supp. II:** 245; **Supp. I Part 2:** 538, 543, 546; **Supp. II Part 2: 669–700;** **Supp. III Part 2:** 599; **Supp. IV Part 1:** 245; **Supp. IV Part 2:** 439, 440–441, 442, 444, 447, 449, 451, 620; **Supp. V:** 113, 118, 124; **Supp. X:** 201, 202, 213; **Supp. XI:** 146, 240, 317; **Supp. XII:** 217, 253, 254, 256, 260, 261; **Supp. XIII:** 35, 76, 294, 312; **Supp. XIV:** 125, 126, 132, 269; **Supp. XIX:** 82, 203; **Supp. XV:** 123, 252, 340; **Supp. XVII:** 239; **Supp. XX: 199;** **Supp. XXVI:** 68; **Supp. XXVII:** 261
Sexual Behavior in the American Male (Kinsey), **Supp. XIII:** 96–97
Sexual Perversity in Chicago (Mamet), **Supp. XIV:** 239, 240, 246–247, 249
"Sexual Revolution, The" (Dunn), **Supp. XI:** 142
Sexus (H. Miller), **III:** 170, 171, 184, 187, 188
"Sex Without Love" (Olds), **Supp. X:** 206
"Sexy" (Lahiri), **Supp. XXI:** 183–184
Seyersted, Per E., **Retro. Supp. II:** 65; **Supp. I Part 1:** 201, 204, 211, 216, 225; **Supp. IV Part 2:** 558
Seyfried, Robin, **Supp. IX:** 324
Seymour, Corey, **Supp. XXIV:** 280
Seymour, Miranda, **Supp. VIII:** 167
"Seymour: An Introduction" (Salinger), **III:** 569–571, 572
Sgt. Pepper column (Christgau), **Supp. XXVII:** 42–44
"Shack" (L. Brown), **Supp. XXI:** 49
Shacochis, Bob, **Supp. VIII:** 80
"Shadow" (Creeley), **Supp. IV Part 1:** 158
"Shadow, The" (A. Lowell), **II:** 522
Shadow and Act (Ellison), **Retro. Supp. II:** 119; **Supp. II Part 1:** 245–246
"Shadow and Shade" (Tate), **IV:** 128
"Shadow and the Flesh, The" (London), **II:** 475
"Shadow A Parable" (Poe), **III:** 417–418
Shadow Country (Gunn Allen), **Supp. IV Part 1:** 322, 324, 325–326
"Shadow Kingdom, The" (Howard), **Supp. XXVII:** 122–123, 127
Shadow-Line, The (Conrad), **Supp. XXV:** 217
Shadow Man, The (Gordon), **Supp. IV Part 1:** 297, 298, 299, 312–314, 315
Shadow of a Dream, The, a Story (Howells), **II:** 285, 286, 290
Shadow of a Man (Moraga), **Supp. XXIII:** 195, 197, **199–203**

Shadow of Heaven (Hayes), **Supp. XXVI:** 137–139

"Shadow of the Crime, The: A Word from the Author" (Mailer), **Retro. Supp. II:** 214

"Shadow of the Vulture, The" (Howard), **Supp. XXVII:** 120–121

Shadow on the Dial, The (Bierce), **I:** 208, 209

"Shadow out of Time, The" (Lovecraft), **Supp. XXV:** 111

Shadow over Innsmouth, The (Lovecraft), **Supp. XXV:** 111, 117–118, 120, 121

"Shadow Passing" (Merwin), **Supp. III Part 1:** 355

Shadowplay (C. Baxter), **Supp. XVII:** 15, 19–20

Shadows (Gardner), **Supp. VI:** 74

Shadows and Fog (film; Allen), **Supp. XV:** 11

Shadows Burning (Di Piero), **Supp. XIX:** 42, 43–44

Shadows by the Hudson (Singer), **IV:** 1

Shadows of Africa (Matthiessen), **Supp. V:** 203

"Shadows of Zamboula" (Howard), **Supp. XXVII:** 125–126

Shadows on the Hudson (Singer), **Retro. Supp. II:** 311–313

Shadows on the Rock (Cather), **I:** 314, 330–331, 332; **Retro. Supp. I:** 18; **Retro. Supp. III:** 24

"Shadows over Lovecraft: Reactionary Fantasy and Immigrant Eugenics" (Lovett-Graff), **Supp. XXV:** 123

Shadow Train (Ashbery), **Supp. III Part 1:** 23–24, 26

"Shad-Time" (Wilbur), **Supp. III Part 2:** 563

Shaffer, Thomas L., **Supp. VIII:** 127, 128

Shaft (Parks; film), **Supp. XI:** 17

Shaftesbury, Earl of, **I:** 559

Shahid, Irfan, **Supp. XX:** 113, 127

Shahn, Ben, **Supp. X:** 24

Shakedown for Murder (Lacy), **Supp. XV:** 203

Shakelford, Dean, **Supp. VIII:** 129

Shaker, Why Don't You Sing? (Angelou), **Supp. IV Part 1:** 16

Shakespear, Mrs. Olivia, **III:** 457; **Supp. I Part 1:** 257

"Shakespeare" (Emerson), **II:** 6

"Shakespeare" (Very), **Supp. XXV:** 244

Shakespeare, William, **I:** 103, 271, 272, 284–285, 358, 378, 433, 441, 458, 461, 573, 585, 586; **II:** 5, 8, 11, 18, 72, 273, 297, 302, 309, 320, 411, 494, 577, 590; **III:** 3, 11, 12, 82, 83, 91, 124, 130, 134, 145, 153, 159, 183, 210, 263, 286, 468, 473, 492, 503, 511, 567, 575–576, 577, 610, 612, 613, 615; **IV:** 11, 50, 66, 127, 132, 156, 309, 313, 362, 368, 370, 373, 453; **Retro. Supp. I:** 43, 64, 91, 248; **Retro. Supp. II:** 114, 299; **Retro. Supp. III:** 156; **Supp. I Part 1:** 79, 150, 262, 310, 356, 363, 365, 368, 369, 370; **Supp. I Part 2:** 397, 421, 422, 470, 494, 622, 716, 720; **Supp. II Part 2:** 624, 626; **Supp. IV Part 1:**

31, 83, 87, 243; **Supp. IV Part 2:** 430, 463, 519, 688; **Supp. IX:** 14, 133; **Supp. V:** 252, 280, 303; **Supp. VIII:** 160, 164; **Supp. X:** 42, 62, 65, 78; **Supp. XII:** 54–57, 277, 281; **Supp. XIII:** 111, 115, 233; **Supp. XIV:** 97, 120, 225, 245, 306; **Supp. XV:** 92; **Supp. XVIII:** 278; **Supp. XXII:** 206; **Supp. XXIV:** 33, 34, 40, 87, 159

Shakespeare and His Forerunners (Lanier), **Supp. I Part 1:** 369

Shakespeare in Harlem (Hughes), **Retro. Supp. I:** 194, 202, 205, 206, 207, 208; **Supp. I Part 1:** 333, 334, 345

Shalit, Gene, **Supp. VIII:** 73

Shalit, Wendy, **Supp. XX:** 179, 182, 186

Shall We Gather at the River (Wright), **Supp. III Part 2:** 601–602; **Supp. XVII:** 241

"Shame" (Oates), **Supp. II Part 2:** 520

"Shame" (Wilbur), **Supp. III Part 2:** 556

"Shame and Forgetting in the Information Age" (C. Baxter), **Supp. XVII:** 21

"Shameful Affair, A" (Chopin), **Retro. Supp. II:** 61

Shamela (Fielding), **Supp. V:** 127

"Shampoo, The" (Bishop), **Retro. Supp. II:** 46; **Supp. I Part 1:** 92

Shange, Ntozake, **Supp. VIII:** 214; **Supp. XVII:** 70; **Supp. XVIII:** 172; **Supp. XXI:** 172

Shank, Randy, **Supp. X:** 252

Shankaracharya, **III:** 567

Shanley, John Patrick, **Retro. Supp. III:** 318; **Supp. XIV:** 315–332

Shannon, Sandra, **Supp. VIII:** 333, 348

"Shape of Flesh and Bone, The" (MacLeish), **III:** 18–19

Shape of Me and Other Stuff, The (Geisel), **Supp. XVI:** 111

Shape of the Journey, The (Harrison), **Supp. VIII:** 53

Shapes of Clay (Bierce), **I:** 208, 209

Shaping Joy, A: Studies in the Writer's Craft (Brooks), **Supp. XIV:** 13

Shapiro, Alan, **Supp. XXIV:** 157

Shapiro, Charles, **Supp. XIX:** 257, 259–260

Shapiro, David, **Supp. XII:** 175, 185; **Supp. XXIV:** 34

Shapiro, Dorothy, **IV:** 380

Shapiro, Edward S., **Supp. XXV:** 253

Shapiro, Karl, **I:** 430, 521; **II:** 350; **III:** 527; **Supp. II Part 2:** 701–724; **Supp. III Part 2:** 623; **Supp. IV Part 2:** 645; **Supp. X:** 116; **Supp. XI:** 315; **Supp. XIX:** 117, 118, 119; **Supp. XXI:** 98; **Supp. XXV:** 30

Shapiro, Laura, **Supp. IX:** 120; **Supp. XX:** 87, 89

Share, Don, **Supp. XXVII:** 152

"Sharecropping in the Golden Ladn" (Kawin), **Retro. Supp. III:** 75

"Shared Patio, The" (July), **Supp. XXIV:** 201, 202

Sharif, Omar, **Supp. IX:** 253

"Sharing" (Huddle), **Supp. XXVI:** 153

"Shark Meat" (Snyder), **Supp. VIII:** 300

Shatayev, Elvira, **Supp. I Part 2:** 570

Shaviro, Steven, **Supp. VIII:** 189

Shaw, Bernard, **Retro. Supp. III:** 165

Shaw, Chris, **Supp. XXIII:** 155–156

Shaw, Colonel Robert Gould, **II:** 551

Shaw, Elizabeth. *See* Melville, Mrs. Herman (Elizabeth Shaw)

Shaw, George Bernard, **I:** 226; **II:** 82, 271, 276, 581; **III:** 69, 102, 113, 145, 155, 161, 162, 163, 373, 409; **IV:** 27, 64, 397, 432, 440; **Retro. Supp. I:** 100, 228; **Supp. IV Part 1:** 36; **Supp. IV Part 2:** 585, 683; **Supp. IX:** 68, 308; **Supp. V:** 243–244, 290; **Supp. XI:** 202; **Supp. XII:** 94; **Supp. XIV:** 343; **Supp. XVII:** 100; **Supp. XXIV:** 33, 34

Shaw, Irwin, **IV:** 381; **Supp. IV Part 1:** 383; **Supp. IX:** 251; **Supp. XI:** 221, 229, 231; **Supp. XIX:** 239–254

Shaw, Joseph Thompson ("Cap"), **Supp. IV Part 1:** 121, 345, 351; **Supp. XIII:** 161

Shaw, Judge Lemuel, **III:** 77, 88, 91

Shaw, Lytle, **Supp. XXIII:** 208; **Supp. XXIV:** 44

Shaw, Peter, **Supp. XVI:** 70

Shaw, Robert B., **Supp. XXIII:** 112

Shaw, Sarah Bryant, **Supp. I Part 1:** 169

Shaw, Wilbur, Jr., **Supp. XIII:** 162

Shawl, The (Mamet), **Supp. XIV:** 245

Shawl, The (Ozick), **Supp. V:** 257, 260, 271

"Shawl, The" (Ozick), **Supp. V:** 271–272

Shawl and Prarie du Chien, The: Two Plays (Mamet), **Supp. XIV:** 243–244

Shawn, William, **Supp. VIII:** 151, 170

"Shawshank Redemption, The" (King), **Supp. V:** 148

She (Haggard), **III:** 189

Shea, Renee, **Supp. XXIII:** 85, 86, 90, 95

Sheaffer, Louis, **Supp. XXI:** 6

Shearer, Flora, **I:** 199

"Sheaves, The" (Robinson), **III:** 510, 524

"She Came and Went" (J. R. Lowell), **Supp. I Part 2:** 409

"She Devil" (Howard), **Supp. XXVII:** 121

"She-Devil" (Nelson), **Supp. XVIII:** 178

She-Devil Circus (Nelson), **Supp. XVIII:** 176, 178

Sheed, Wilfrid, **IV:** 230; **Supp. XI:** 233; **Supp. XXI:** 233

Sheeler, Charles, **IV:** 409; **Retro. Supp. I:** 430

"Sheep Child" (B. Kelly), **Supp. XVII:** 131–132

"Sheep Child, The" (Dickey), **Supp. XVII:** 131–132

Sheeper (Rosenthal), **Supp. XIV:** 147

"Shee-Show" (Rash), **Supp. XXVII:** 220

Sheffer, Jonathan, **Supp. IV Part 1:** 95

She Had Some Horses (Harjo), **Supp. XII:** 220–223, 231

"She Had Some Horses" (Harjo), **Supp. XII:** 215, 222

"Shell, The" (Humphrey), **Supp. IX:** 94

Shelley, Mary, **Supp. XX:** 108

Shelley, Percy Bysshe, **I:** 18, 68, 381, 476, 522, 577; **II:** 331, 516, 535, 540;

III: 412, 426, 469; IV: 139; **Retro. Supp. I:** 308, 360; **Retro. Supp. III:** 44; **Supp. I Part 1:** 79, 311, 349; **Supp. I Part 2:** 709, 718, 719, 720, 721, 722, 724, 728; **Supp. IV Part 1:** 235; **Supp. IX:** 51; **Supp. V:** 258, 280; **Supp. XII:** 117, 132, 136–137, 263; **Supp. XIV:** 271–272; **Supp. XV:** 92, 175, 182; **Supp. XX:** 115; **Supp. XXI:** 131

Shellow, Sadie Myers, **Supp. I Part 2:** 608

Shelnut, Blevin, **Supp. XXV:** 36

"Shelter" (C. Baxter), **Supp. XVII:** 19

"Shelter" (Doty), **Supp. XI:** 132

Sheltered Life, The (Glasgow), II: 174, 175, 179, 186, 187–188

Sheltering Sky, The (Bowles), **Supp. IV Part 1:** 82, 84, 85–86, 87

Sheltering Sky, The (film), **Supp. IV Part 1:** 94, 95

Shelton, Frank, **Supp. IV Part 2:** 658

Shelton, Richard, **Supp. XI:** 133; **Supp. XIII:** 7

Shelton, Robert, **Supp. XVIII:** 20, 21, 22, 23, 24, 25, 26

Shelton, Mrs. Sarah. *See* Royster, Sarah Elmira

"Shelton Laurel" (Rash), **Supp. XXVII:** 221

Shenandoah (Schwartz), **Supp. II Part 2:** 640, 651–652

"Shenandoah" (Shapiro), **Supp. II Part 2:** 704

Shepard, Alice, IV: 287

Shepard, Gregory, **Supp. XXII:** 119

Shepard, Harvey, **Supp. XVII:** 240

Shepard, Jim, **Supp. XXI:** 115

Shepard, Odell, II: 508; **Supp. I Part 2:** 418

Shepard, Richard F., **Supp. XXIV:** 216

Shepard, Sam, **Supp. III Part 2: 431–450; Supp. XVIII:** 21, 28, 31; **Supp. XXI:** 144, 145

Shepard, Thomas, I: 554; IV: 158

"Shepherd of Resumed Desire, The" (Wright), **Supp. XV:** 349

Sheppard Lee (Bird), III: 423

"She Remembers the Future" (Harjo), **Supp. XII:** 222

Sheridan, Richard Brinsley, **Retro. Supp. I:** 127

Sherlock, William, IV: 152

Sherman, Joe, **Supp. XXII:** 205

Sherman, Sarah Way, **Retro. Supp. II:** 145

Sherman, Stuart Pratt, I: 222, 246–247; **Supp. I Part 2:** 423

Sherman, Susan, **Supp. VIII:** 265

Sherman, Tom, IV: 446

Sherman, William T., IV: 445, 446

"She Rock" (Hurston), **Retro. Supp. III:** 127

Sherry, Denver William, **Supp. XXII:** 190

Sherwood, Robert, II: 435; **Supp. IX:** 190

Sherwood Anderson & Other Famous Creoles (Faulkner), I: 117; II: 56

Sherwood Anderson Reader, The (Anderson), I: 114, 116

Sherwood Anderson's Memoirs (Anderson), I: 98, 101, 102, 103, 108, 112, 116

Sherwood Anderson's Notebook (Anderson), I: 108, 115, 117

She's Having a Baby (film, Hughes), **Supp. XXVII:** 5

"She Sings" (Taggard), **Supp. XXII:** 272

She Stoops to Conquer (Goldsmith), II: 514

Shestov, Lev, **Supp. VIII:** 20, 24

Shetley, Vernon, **Supp. IX:** 292; **Supp. XI:** 123

"She Wept, She Railed" (Kunitz), **Supp. III Part 1:** 265

"Shiddah and Kuziba" (Singer), IV: 13, 15

Shidyak, Paris al-, **Supp. XX:** 117

Shield of Achilles, The (Auden), **Supp. II Part 1:** 21

"Shield of Achilles, The" (Auden), **Supp. II Part 1:** 21, 25

Shields, Art, **Supp. XXVIII:** 74

Shields, Carol, **Supp. VII: 307–330**

Shields, John C., **Supp. XX: 279, 280, 281, 286**

Shifting Landscape: A Composite, 1925–1987 (H. Roth), **Supp. IX: 233–235**

Shifts of Being (Eberhart), I: 525

Shigematsu, Soiko, **Supp. III Part 1:** 353

Shihab, Aziz, **Supp. XIII:** 273

Shih-hsiang Chen, **Supp. VIII:** 303

Shiksa Goddess; or, How I Spent My Forties (Wasserstein), **Supp. XV:** 319, 320, 325, 332, 333

Shilling, Jane, **Supp. XXVII:** 276

"Shiloh" (Mason), **Supp. VIII:** 140

Shiloh and Other Stories (Mason), **Supp. VIII:** 133, **139–141,** 143, 145

Shilts, Randy, **Supp. X:** 145

Shimmering Verge, The (one-woman show, Peacock), **Supp. XIX:** 194, **204–205**

Shining, The (King), **Supp. V:** 139, 140, 141, 143–144, 146, 149, 151, 152

"Shining Ones, The" (P. N. Warren), **Supp. XX: 272**

Shining Victory (film, Rapper), **Supp. XVII:** 60

Shinn, Everett, **Retro. Supp. II:** 103

Shi Pei Pu, **Supp. XXI:** 152, 153, 154

"Ship in a Bottle" (Strout), **Supp. XXIII:** 283

"Ship of Death" (Lawrence), **Supp. I Part 2:** 728

Ship of Fools (Porter), III: 433, 447, 453, 454; IV: 138

Shipping News, The (Proulx), **Supp. VII:** 249, 258–259

"Ships" (O. Henry), **Supp. II Part 1:** 409

Ships Going into the Blue: Essays and Notes on Poetry (Simpson), **Supp. IX:** 275

Ship to America, A (Singer), IV: 1

"Shipwreck, The" (Merwin), **Supp. III Part 1:** 346

Shirley, John, **Supp. XVI:** 123, 128

"Shirt" (Pinsky), **Supp. VI: 236–237,** 239, 240, 241, 245, 247

"Shirt Poem, The" (Stern), **Supp. IX:** 292

"Shirts, The" (Gallagher), **Supp. XXIV:** 169

"Shirts of a Single Color" (Ryan), **Supp. XVIII:** 227

"Shiva and Parvati Hiding in the Rain" (Pinsky), **Supp. VI:** 244

"Shiva" (Goodman), **Supp. XXVIII:** 89

Shively, Charley, **Retro. Supp. I:** 391; **Supp. XII:** 181, 182

Shnayerson, Michael, **Supp. XIX:** 248

Shneidman, Edwin, **Supp. XXVI:** 246

"Shock of Good Poetry, The" (Hirshfield), **Supp. XXIII:** 136

Shock of Recognition, The (Wilson), II: 530

Shock of the New, The (Hughes), **Supp. X:** 73

Shoe Bird, The (Welty), IV: 261; **Retro. Supp. I:** 353

Shoemaker of Dreams (Ferragammo), **Supp. XVI:** 192

"Shoes" (O. Henry), **Supp. II Part 1:** 409

"Shoes of Wandering, The" (Kinnell), **Supp. III Part 1:** 248

Sholem Asch: Zayn levn un zayne verk (Sholem Asch: His life and his work), **Supp. XXIII:** 6

Sholl, Betsy, **Supp. XXI:** 129, 131

Shooter (Myers), **Supp. XXVII:** 203, 204

"Shooters, Inc." (Didion), **Supp. IV Part 1:** 207, 211

"Shooting, The" (Dubus), **Supp. VII:** 84, 85

"Shooting Niagara; and After?" (Carlyle), **Retro. Supp. I:** 408

"Shooting of the Red Eagle" (Zitkala-Ša), **Supp. XXV:** 275

Shooting Rats at the Bibb County Dump (Bottoms), **Supp. XXVIII:** 22, 23–26

"Shooting Rats at the Bibb County Dump" (Bottoms), **Supp. XXVIII:** 24

"Shooting Rats in the Afterlife" (Bottoms), **Supp. XXVIII:** 30

"Shooting Script" (Rich), **Retro. Supp. III:** 245; **Supp. I Part 2:** 558; **Supp. IV Part 1:** 257

Shooting Star, A (Stegner), **Supp. IV Part 2:** 599, 608–609

"Shooting the Works" (Di Piero), **Supp. XIX:** 41–42

Shooting the Works: On Poetry and Pictures (Di Piero), **Supp. XIX: 41–42**

"Shooting Whales" (Strand), **Supp. IV Part 2:** 630

"Shopgirls" (F. Barthelme), **Supp. XI:** 26, 27, 33, 36

Shopping for Joe (O'Hara and Steven Rivers), **Supp. XXIII:** 217

"Shopping with Bob Berwick" (Halliday), **Supp. XIX:** 88

Shop Talk (P. Roth), **Retro. Supp. II:** 282

Shoptaw, John, **Supp. IV Part 1:** 247

Shore Acres (Herne), **Supp. II Part 1:** 198

Shorebirds of North America, The (Matthiessen), **Supp. V:** 204

"Shore House, The" (Jewett), **II:** 397

Shore Leave (Wakeman), **Supp. IX:** 247

"Shoreline Horses" (Ríos), **Supp. IV Part 2:** 553

"Shoreline Life" (Skloot), **Supp. XX:** 201

Shores of Light, The: A Literary Chronicle of the Twenties and Thirties (Wilson), **IV:** 432, 433

Shorey, Paul, **III:** 606

Short Account of the Destruction of the Indies, A (Las Casas), **Supp. XXIV:** 87

Short and the Long of It, The (Kenny), **Supp. XXIII:** 155–156

Short Cuts (film, Altman), **Supp. IX:** 143; **Supp. XXIV:** 166, 172, 178

"Short End, The" (Hecht), **Supp. X:** 65

"Shorter View, The" (X. J. Kennedy), **Supp. XV:** 160, 168

Short Fiction of Norman Mailer, The (Mailer), **Retro. Supp. II:** 205

"Short Flight, The" (Huddle), **Supp. XXVI:** 156

Short Friday and Other Stories (Singer), **IV:** 14–16

Short Girls (Nguyen), **Supp. XXVI:** 212–216

Short Guide to a Happy Life, A (Quindlen), **Supp. XVII:** 167, 179

"Short Happy Life of Francis Macomber, The" (Hemingway), **II:** 250, 263–264; **Retro. Supp. I:** 182; **Supp. IV Part 1:** 48; **Supp. IX:** 106

Short Night, The (Turner), **Supp. XV:** 201

Short Novels of Thomas Wolfe, The (Wolfe), **IV:** 456

Short Poems (Berryman), **I:** 170

"SHORT SPEECH TO MY FRIENDS" (Baraka), **Supp. II Part 1:** 35

Short Stories (Rawlings), **Supp. X:** 224

Short Stories: Five Decades (Shaw), **Supp. XIX:** 252–253

"Short Story, The" (Welty), **IV:** 279

Short Story Masterpieces, **Supp. IX:** 4

Short Studies of American Authors (Higginson), **I:** 455

"Short-timer's Calendar" (Komunyakaa), **Supp. XIII:** 125

"Short Weight" (Davison), **Supp. XXVI:** 75

Shosha (Singer), **Retro. Supp. II:** 313–314

Shostak, Debra, **Supp. XXIV:** 136

Shostakovich, Dimitri, **IV:** 75; **Supp. VIII:** 21

"Shotgun Wedding" (Stone), **Supp. XXVII:** 253

Shot of Love (album, Dylan), **Supp. XVIII:** 28

"Shots" (Ozick), **Supp. V:** 268

Shotts, Jeffrey, **Supp. XV:** 103, 104

"Should Wizard Hit Mommy?" (Updike), **IV:** 221, 222, 224; **Retro. Supp. I:** 335

Shoup, Barbara, **Supp. XV:** 55, 59, 62, 69

"Shoveling Snow with Buddha" (Collins), **Supp. XXI:** 60

"Shovel Man, The" (Sandburg), **III:** 553

Showalter, Elaine, **Retro. Supp. I:** 368; **Supp. IV Part 2:** 440, 441, 444; **Supp. X:** 97; **Supp. XVI:** 80, 92; **Supp. XX:** 274; **Supp. XXIV:** 28

"Shower of Gold" (Welty), **IV:** 271–272

Show Way (Woodson; Talbott, ill.), **Supp. XXVIII:** 286–287

Show World (Barnhardt), **Supp. XXVII:** 1, 7–9

Shreve, Porter, **Supp. XXVI:** 209

Shribman, David M., **Supp. XXII:** 205, 218

"Shrike and the Chipmunks, The" (Thurber), **Supp. I Part 2:** 617

Shrimp Girl (Hogarth), **Supp. XII:** 44

"Shrine and the Burning Wheel, The" (Jarman), **Supp. XVII:** 116

"Shrine with Flowers" (Di Piero), **Supp. XIX:** 43, 44

"Shriveled Meditation" (X. J. Kennedy), **Supp. XV:** 170

Shropshire Lad, A (Housman), **Supp. XV:** 41

"Shrouded Stranger, The" (Ginsberg), **Supp. II Part 1:** 312

"Shroud of Color, The" (Cullen), **Supp. IV Part 1:** 166, 168, 170, 171

Shrunken Head of Pancho Villa, The (Valdez), **Supp. XXIII:** 203

Shtetl (film; Marzynski), **Supp. XVI:** 153

Shtetl: The Life and Death of a Small Town and the World of Polish Jews (E. Hoffman), **Supp. XVI:** 152, **153–155**

Shue, Elizabeth, **Supp. XXIII:** 276

Shuffle (L. Michaels), **Supp. XVI:** 202, 203, 213

Shuffle Along (musical), **Supp. I Part 1:** 322; **Supp. X:** 136

Shulman, Polly, **Supp. XXVI:** 158

Shultz, George, **Supp. IV Part 1:** 234

Shuman, R. Baird, **Supp. XXV:** 96

Shurr, William, **Retro. Supp. I:** 43

Shuster, Joel, **Supp. XI:** 67

Shusterman, Richard, **Retro. Supp. I:** 53

"Shut a Final Door" (Capote), **Supp. III Part 1:** 117, 120, 124

Shut Up, He Explained (Lardner), **II:** 432

Shylock's Daughter: A Novel of Love in Venice (Serenissima) (Jong), **Supp. V:** 115, 127, 128–129

Siamanto (Atom Yarjanian), **Supp. XXIII:** 28

"Siasconset: How It Arose and What It Is" (Briggs), **Supp. XVIII:** 9

Siberian Village, The (Dove), **Supp. IV Part 1:** 255, 256

Sibley, Celestine, **Supp. XXII:** 194, 199

Sibley, Mulford Q., **Supp. I Part 2:** 524

"Sibling Mysteries" (Rich), **Supp. I Part 2:** 574

Siblings (Quindlen and Kelsh), **Supp. XVII:** 167, 179

Siblings in Paradise (or Moscow when It Sizzles) (Silver), **Supp. XXIV:** 265

Sibon, Marcelle, **IV:** 288

"Sicilian Emigrant's Song" (W. C. Williams), **Retro. Supp. I:** 413

Sicilian Miniatures (Sobin), **Supp. XVI:** 288

"Sick Wife, The" (Kenyon), **Supp. VII:** 173, 174

"'Sic transit gloria mundi'" (Dickinson), **Retro. Supp. I:** 30

Sid Caesar Show (television show), **Supp. IV Part 2:** 575

Siddons, Anne Rivers, **Supp. XXII: 239–254**

Siddons, Sarah, **II:** 298

Side Effects (Allen), **Supp. XV:** 3, 14, **15–16**

"Side Effects of Lucille, The" (Huddle), **Supp. XXVI:** 155–156

Side of Paradise, This (Fitgerald), **Supp. IX:** 56

"Sidewalk, The" (Biss), **Supp. XXVI:** 48

Sidnee Poet Heroical, The (Baraka), **Supp. II Part 1:** 55

Sidney, Algernon, **II:** 114

Sidney, Mary, **Supp. I Part 1:** 98

Sidney, Philip, **II:** 470; **Retro. Supp. III:** 3, 7; **Supp. I Part 1:** 98, 111, 117–118, 122; **Supp. I Part 2:** 658; **Supp. II Part 1:** 104–105; **Supp. V:** 250; **Supp. XII:** 264; **Supp. XIV:** 128

Sidney, Sylvia, **Supp. I Part 1:** 67

Sidney Lanier: A Bibliographical and Critical Study (Starke), **Supp. I Part 1:** 371

Sidney Lanier: A Biographical and Critical Study (Starke), **Supp. I Part 1:** 371

Siebert, Kathy, **Supp. XX: 84**

Siege (Shaw), **Supp. XIX:** 244

Siegel, Barry, **Supp. XIV:** 82

Siegel, Ben, **Supp. XXIII:** 3, 4, 10, 11, 12, 14, 16

Siegel, Catherine, **Supp. XII:** 126

Siegel, Jerry, **Supp. XI:** 67

Siegel, Lee, **Supp. XXII: 255–269; Supp. XXV:** 56

"Siege of London, The" (James), **Retro. Supp. I:** 227

Siegle, Robert, **Supp. XII:** 8

Sienkiewicz, Henryk, **Supp. IV Part 2:** 518; **Supp. XVI:** 182

"Sierra Kid" (Levine), **Supp. V:** 180–181

Sigal, Clancy, **Supp. XXI:** 44; **Supp. XXIII:** 166; **Supp. XXVI:** 26

Sigg, Eric, **Retro. Supp. I:** 53

"Sight" (Merwin), **Supp. III Part 1:** 356

Sighted Singer, The (Halliday), **Supp. XIX:** 82, **86–87**

"Sight in Camp in the Daybreak Gray and Dim, A" (Whitman), **II:** 373

Sights and Spectacles (McCarthy), **II:** 562

"Sights from a Steeple" (Hawthorne), **Retro. Supp. I:** 62; **Retro. Supp. III:** 113, 120; **Supp. XXI:** 201

Sights Unseen (Gibbons), **Supp. X: 49–50**

Sight Unseen and the Confession (Rinehart), **Supp. XXV:** 195, 200

"Signals" (Carver), **Supp. III Part 1:** 143

"Signature for Tempo" (MacLeish), **III:** 8–9

"Signed Confession of Crimes against the State" (Merton), **Supp. VIII:** 201

"Sign for My Father, Who Stressed the Bunt"(Bottoms), **Supp. XXVIII:** 26–27

Signifying Monkey, The (Hughes), **Retro. Supp. I:** 195

Signifying Monkey, The: A Theory of Afro-American Literary Criticism (H. L. Gates), **Supp. X:** 243; **Supp. XX: 99, 106–107**

"Signing, The (Dixon), **Supp. XII: 146**

Sign in Sidney Brustein's Window, The (Hansberry), **Supp. IV Part 1:** 359, 365, 369, 370–372

"Sign in the Sky, A: Dating the League of the Haudenosaunee" (Mann and Fields), **Supp. XXVI:** 86

Sign of Jonas, The (Merton), **Supp. VIII:** 194–195, 195, 197, 200, 206, 207

"Sign of Saturn, The" (Olds), **Supp. X:** 206

"Signs" (Rash), **Supp. XXVII:** 219

"Signs, Oakvale, Mississippi, 1941" (Trethewey), **Supp. XXI:** 248–249

Signs and Wonders (Bukiet), **Supp. XVII: 45–46**

Sigourney, Lydia, **Supp. I Part 2:** 684

Siken, Richard, **Supp. XXVIII: 195–203**

Sikora, Malgorzata, **Retro. Supp. II:** 324

Silas Marner (G. Eliot), **II:** 26

Silberg, Richard, **Supp. XV:** 116

Silberman, James, **Supp. XXIV:** 288

"Silence" (Moore), **III:** 212

"Silence" (Munro), **Supp. XXVII:** 193–194

"Silence" (Poe), **III:** 416

"Silence" (Sanders), **Supp. XVI:** 278

"Silence, A" (Clampitt), **Supp. IX:** 53

"Silence—A Fable" (Poe), **III:** 416

Silence and Metaphor (Bronk), **Supp. XXI:** 31, 32

"Silence Before Harvest, The" (Merwin), **Supp. III Part 1:** 352

Silence Dogood Papers, The (Franklin), **II:** 106–107

Silence in the Snowy Fields (R. Bly), **Supp. IV Part 1:** 60–61, 62, 63, 65, 66, 72; **Supp. XXI:** 84, 85

Silence of History, The (Farrell), **II:** 46–47

Silence of the Lambs, The (T. Harris), **Supp. XXI:** 78

Silence Opens, A (Clampitt), **Supp. IX: 53**

Silences (Olsen), **Supp. XIII:** 293, 294, 295, 296, **304–306**

"Silences: When Writers Don't Write" (Olsen), **Supp. XIII:** 294

Silencing the Past: Power and the Production of History (Trouillot), **Supp. X:** 14

"Silent in America" (Levine), **Supp. V:** 183

Silent Life, The (Merton), **Supp. VIII:** 208

Silent Partner, The (Odets), **Supp. II Part 2:** 539

"Silent Piano, The" (Davison), **Supp. XXVI:** 78

"Silent Poem" (Francis), **Supp. IX:** 86

"Silent Season of a Hero, The" (Talese), **Supp. XVII:** 203–204

"Silent Slain, The" (MacLeish), **III:** 9

"Silent Snow, Secret Snow" (Aiken), **I:** 52

Silent Spring (Carson), **Supp. IX:** 19, 24, **31–34; Supp. V:** 202; **Supp. XIV:** 177; **Supp. XVI:** 36; **Supp. XVIII:** 189

Silhouettes of American Life (R. H. Davis), **Supp. XVI:** 85

"Silken Tent, The" (Frost), **Retro. Supp. I:** 138–139; **Retro. Supp. III:** 104; **Supp. IV Part 2:** 448

Silko, Leslie Marmon, **Supp. IV Part 1:** 274, 319, 325, 333–334, 335, 404; **Supp. IV Part 2:** 499, 505, **557–572; Supp. V:** 169; **Supp. XI:** 18; **Supp. XII:** 217; **Supp. XVIII:** 58; **Supp. XXVI:** 102

Silliman, Ron, **Supp. IV Part 2:** 426; **Supp. XV:** 344; **Supp. XVII:** 70, 77

Silliman's Blog (R. Silliman), **Supp. XVII:** 70

Silman, Roberta, **Supp. X:** 6

Silver, Nicky, **Supp. XXIV:** 128, **263–277**

Silver, Sam, **Supp. XXVII:** 36

"Silver, The"(Wakoski), **Supp. XXVIII:** 271

Silverblatt, Michael, **Supp. XV:** 224

"Silver Crown, The" (Malamud), **Supp. I Part 2:** 434–435, 437; **Supp. V:** 266

"Silver Dish, The" (Bellow), **Retro. Supp. II:** 30

"Silver Filigree" (Wylie), **Supp. I Part 2:** 707

"Silver Key, The" (Lovecraft), **Supp. XXV:** 114

"Silver Lake" (B. Kelly), **Supp. XVII:** 130

Silverman, Joseph, **Supp. XXIII:** 8

Silvers, Phil, **Supp. IV Part 2:** 574

Silverthorne, Elizabeth, **Supp. X:** 220, 221, 222, 226, 234

"Silver To Have and to Hurl" (Didion), **Supp. IV Part 1:** 197

Simic, Charles, **Supp. V:** 5, 332; **Supp. VIII:** 39, **269–287; Supp. XI:** 317; **Supp. XIX:** 277, 282; **Supp. XV:** 179, 185

"Similar Cases" (Gilman), **Supp. XI:** 200, 202

Similitudes, from the Ocean and Prairie (Larcom), **Supp. XIII:** 141

Simmel, Georg, **Supp. I Part 2:** 644; **Supp. XVII:** 98

Simmons, Charles, **Supp. XI:** 230

Simmons, David, **Supp. XXV:** 123

Simmons, Maggie, **Retro. Supp. II:** 21

Simms, Michael, **Supp. XII:** 184

Simms, William Gilmore, **I:** 211

Simon, Greg, **Supp. XXIV:** 166

Simon, John, **Supp. IV Part 2:** 691

Simon, Neil, **Supp. IV Part 2: 573–594; Supp. XVII:** 8

Simone, Nina, **Supp. XXI:** 243

"Simone Weil's Passion Mysticism: The Paradox of Chronic Pain and the Transformation of the Cross" (Helsel),

Supp. XXVI: 53

"Simon Gerty" (Wylie), **Supp. I Part 2:** 713

Simonides, **Supp. XII:** 110–111

"Simon Ortiz" (Gingerich), **Supp. IV Part 2:** 510

Simon Ortiz (Wiget), **Supp. IV Part 2:** 509

Simonson, Lee, **III:** 396; **Supp. XXI:** 6

"Simple" (Peacock), **Supp. XIX:** 200

"Simple Art of Murder, The" (Chandler), **Supp. IV Part 1:** 121, 341

"Simple Autumnal" (Bogan), **Supp. III Part 1:** 52–53

Simple Heart (Flaubert), **I:** 504

Simple Honorable Man, A (Richter), **Supp. XVIII:** 208, 218, **219,** 220

"Simple Purchase, A" (Peacock), **Supp. XIX:** 199

Simple Speaks his Mind (Hughes), **Retro. Supp. I:** 209; **Supp. I Part 1:** 337

Simple Stakes a Claim (Hughes), **Retro. Supp. I:** 209; **Supp. I Part 1:** 337

Simple's Uncle Sam (Hughes), **Retro. Supp. I:** 209; **Supp. I Part 1:** 337

Simple Takes a Wife (Hughes), **Retro. Supp. I:** 209; **Supp. I Part 1:** 337

Simple Truth, The (Hardwick), **Supp. III Part 1:** 199, 200, 208

Simple Truth, The (Levine), **Supp. V:** 178, 179, 193–194

"Simple Widsom, The" (Skloot), **Supp. XX:** 207

"Simplicity" (Sanders), **Supp. XVI:** 276

Simplicity (Stone), **Supp. XXVII:** 257, 262

Simply, Trixi, **Supp. XXV:** 2

Simply Heavenly (Hughes), **Retro. Supp. I:** 209; **Supp. I Part 1:** 338, 339

Simpson, Ethel C., **Supp. XXVIII:** 227

Simpson, Louis, **Supp. III Part 2:** 541; **Supp. IV Part 2:** 448, 621; **Supp. IX: 265–283,** 290; **Supp. VIII:** 39, 279; **Supp. XI:** 317; **Supp. XII:** 130; **Supp. XIII:** 337

Simpson, Mona, **Supp. XVI:** 206; **Supp. XXVII:** 180, **233–237**

"Sin" (C. Frost), **Supp. XV:** 96

Sinatra, Frank, **Supp. IX:** 3; **Supp. X:** 119; **Supp. XI:** 213

"Since Death Brushed Past Me" (Teasdale), **Supp. XXVII:** 297

Sincere Convert, The (Shepard), **IV:** 158

Sincerely, Willis Wayde (Marquand), **III:** 61, 63, 66, 67–68, 69

Sincerity (Rowson), **Supp. XV:** 242

Sincerity and Authenticity (Trilling), **Supp. III Part 2:** 510–512

"Sincerity and Objectification: With Special Reference to the Work of Charles Reznikoff" (Zukofsky), **Supp. XIV:** 286

Sinclair, Mary Craig (Mary Craig Kimbrough), **Supp. V:** 275, 286, 287

Sinclair, Upton, **II:** 34, 440, 444, 451; **III:** 580; **Retro. Supp. II:** 95; **Supp. V: 275–293; Supp. VIII:** 11; **Supp. XXVIII:** 43, 68

Sinclair Lewis: An American Life (Schorer), **II:** 459

"Sine Qua Non" (Stallings), **Supp. XXV:** 232

"Singapore" (Oliver), **Supp. VII:** 239, 240

Singer, Bennett L., **Supp. IV Part 1:** 330

Singer, Beth, **Supp. XIV:** 203

Singer, Isaac Bashevis, **I:** 144; **IV: 1–24; Retro. Supp. II:** 22, **299–320; Supp. IX:** 114; **Supp. XVIII:** 215, 220; **Supp. XXI:** 106; **Supp. XXII:** 258

Singer, Israel Joshua, **IV:** 2, 16, 17; **Retro. Supp. II:** 302; **Supp. XVII:** 41

Singer, Joshua, **IV:** 4

Singer, Rabbi Pinchos Menachem, **IV:** 16

Singin' and Swingin' and Gettin' Merry Like Christmas (Angelou), **Supp. IV Part 1:** 2, 5, 6–7, 9, 13, 14

"Singing & Doubling Together" (Ammons), **Supp. VII:** 34–35

Singing Jailbirds (Sinclair), **Supp. V:** 277

"Singing the Black Mother" (Lupton), **Supp. IV Part 1:** 7

Single Hound, The (Sarton), **Supp. VIII:** 251, 265

Single Hound, The: Poems of a Lifetime (Dickinson; Bianchi, ed.), **Retro. Supp. I:** 35

Single Man, A (Isherwood), **Supp. XIV:** 157, 164, **169–170,** 171

"Single Sonnet" (Bogan), **Supp. III Part 1:** 56–58

Singley, Carol, **Retro. Supp. I:** 373

Singular Family, A: Rosacoke and Her Kin (Price), **Supp. VI: 258–259,** 260

"Singular First Person, The" (Sanders), **Supp. XVI:** 274

Singularities (Howe), **Supp. IV Part 2:** 431

Sin in Their Blood (Lacy), **Supp. XV:** 200

"Sinister Adolescents, The" (Dos Passos), **I:** 493

Sinister Street (Mackenzie), **II:** 82

Sinking of Clay City, The (Wrigley), **Supp. XVIII: 294–295**

Sinners in the Hands of an Angry God (Edwards), **I:** 546, 552–553, 559, 562; **Supp. XXIV:** 72

Sinning with Annie, and Other Stories (Theroux), **Supp. VIII:** 318

"Sins of Kalamazoo, The" (Sandburg), **III:** 586

Sintram and His Companions (La Motte-Fouqué), **III:** 78

"Siope" (Poe), **III:** 411

"Sioux Woman's Love for Her Grandchild, A" (Zitkala-Ša), **Supp. XXV:** 281

"Sipapu: A Cultural Perspective" (Gunn Allen), **Supp. IV Part 1:** 323

Sipchen, Bob, **Supp. X:** 145

Sipper, Ralph B., **Supp. IV Part 2:** 475

"Sire" (Cisneros), **Supp. VII:** 62–63, 64

"Siren and Signal" (Zukofsky), **Supp. III Part 2:** 611, 612

Sirens of Titan, The (Vonnegut), **Supp. II Part 2:** 757, 758, 760, 765–767

"Sir Galahad" (Tennyson), **Supp. I Part 2:** 410

Sirin, V. (pseudonym), **Retro. Supp. I:** 266. *See also* Nabokov, Vladimir

Sirlin, Jerome, **Supp. XXI:** 147

Sir Vadia's Shadow: A Friendship across Five Continents (Theroux), **Supp. VIII:** 309, 314, 321, 325

"Sir William's Reply to Molly"(Kenny), **Supp. XXIII:** 153

"Sis" (F. Barthelme), **Supp. XI:** 26

"S is for Sad" (M. F. K. Fisher), **Supp. XVII:** 86

Sisley, Alfred, **I:** 478

Sissman, L. E., **Supp. X:** 69; **Supp. XXVI:** 68, 74

"Sister" (Hughes), **Retro. Supp. I:** 208

"Sister" (Lamott), **Supp. XX:** 142

"Sister, The" (July), **Supp. XXIV:** 202

Sister Age (M. F. K. Fisher), **Supp. XVII:** 88, 91

Sister Carrie (Dreiser), **I:** 482, 497, 499, 500, 501–502, 503–504, 505, 506, 515, 519; **III:** 327; **IV:** 208; **Retro. Supp. I:** 376; **Retro. Supp. II:** 93, **96–99; Supp. XVIII:** 76, 243; **Supp. XXIII:** 165; **Supp. XXV:** 129; **Supp. XXVIII:** 145

Sister Mary Ignatius Explains It All for You (Durang), **Supp. XXIV:** 114, **119–120**

"Sister of the Minotaur" (Stevens), **IV:** 89; **Supp. IX:** 332

"Sisters" (Boulton), **Supp. XXII:** 20

"Sisters" (Nelson), **Supp. XVIII:** 176

"Sisters, The" (Whittier), **Supp. I Part 2:** 696

Sister's Choice (Showalter), **Retro. Supp. I:** 368

Sisters-in-Law, The (Atherton), **Supp. XXIV:** 25

Sisters of the Earth: Women's Prose and Poetry About Nature (Anderson, ed.), **Supp. XVIII:** 189

Sisters Rosensweig, The (Wasserstein), **Supp. XV:** 320, **328–330**

"Sisyphus" (Kumin), **Supp. IV Part 2:** 443, 444, 451

"Sitalkas" (Doolittle), **Supp. I Part 1:** 266

"Site of Memory, The" (Morrison), **Retro. Supp. III:** 191, 194

"Sites of Memory" (Cliff), **Supp. XXII:** 69, 74

Sitney, P. Adams, **Supp. XII:** 2

"Sitting Blind by the Sea"(Stuart), **Supp. XXVIII:** 239

Sitting Bull, **Supp. IV Part 2:** 492

"Sitting in a Rocking Chair Going Blind" (Komunyakaa), **Supp. XIII:** 114

Sitting In: Selected Writings on Jazz, Blues, and Related Topics (Carruth), **Supp. XVI:** 46

"Sitting Up Late with My Father, 1977" (F. Wright), **Supp. XVII:** 247

Sitti's Secrets (Nye), **Supp. XIII:** 278

Situation Normal (A. Miller), **III:** 148, 149, 156, 164

Situation of Poetry, The: Contemporary Poetry and Its Traditions (Pinsky), **Supp. VI: 237–238,** 239, 241, 242

Sitwell, Edith, **IV:** 77; **Supp. I Part 1:** 271

6 A.M. (Bodenheim), **Supp. XXV:** 27

"Six Brothers" (Cisneros), **Supp. VII:** 67

Six Characters in Search of an Author (Pirandello), **Supp. IV Part 2:** 576

"Six Days: Some Rememberings" (Paley), **Supp. VI:** 226

"65290" (Leopold), **Supp. XIV:** 184–185

Six French Poets (A. Lowell), **II:** 528–529

"Six in All" (Bierds), **Supp. XVII:** 31

Six Lips (Schott), **Supp. XXIII:** 251–252

"Six Persons" (Baraka), **Supp. II Part 1:** 53

Six Red Months in Russia (Bryant), **Supp. XXVIII:** 37, 40, 41–43, 44, 45

Six Sections from Mountains and Rivers without End (Snyder), **Supp. VIII:** 305

"Six Sundays Toward a Seventh"(Lea), **Supp. XXVIII:** 134

"Sixteen Months" (Sandburg), **III:** 584

1601, or Conversation as It Was by the Fireside in the Time of the Tudors (Twain), **IV:** 201

"Sixth-Month Song in the Foothills" (Snyder), **Supp. VIII:** 297

Sixties, The (magazine) (R. Bly), **Supp. IV Part 1:** 60; **Supp. IX:** 271

"Sixty" (Dunn), **Supp. XI:** 155

"Sixty Acres" (Carver), **Supp. III Part 1:** 141

"64 Elmgrove" (Halliday), **Supp. XIX:** 88

"69 Hidebound Opinions, Propositions, and Several Asides from a Manila Folder concerning the Stuff of Poetry" (Wright), **Supp. XV:** 344–345

Sixty Seconds (Bodenheim), **Supp. XXV:** 26

Sixty Stories (Barthelme), **Supp. IV Part 1:** 41, 42, 44, 47, 49, 50

63: Dream Palace (Purdy), **Supp. VII:** 270–271

"Six Variations" (Levertov), **Supp. III Part 1:** 277–278

"Six-Year-Old Boy" (Olds), **Supp. X:** 206

"Six Years Later" (Brodsky), **Supp. VIII:** 26, 28

"Size and Sheer Will" (Olds), **Supp. X:** 206

Size of Thoughts, The: Essays and Other Lumber (Baker), **Supp. XIII: 52–53,** 55, 56

Sizwe Bansi Is Dead (Fugard), **Supp. VIII:** 330

Sjöwall, Maj, **Supp. XX: 87**

"Skagway" (Haines), **Supp. XII:** 206

"Skaters, The" (Ashbery), **Supp. III Part 1:** 10, 12, 13, 18, 25

"Skaters, The" (Jarrell), **II:** 368–369

Skau, Michael, **Supp. XII:** 129, 130, 132, 134

Skeeters Kirby (Masters), **Supp. I Part 2:** 459, 470, 471

Skeleton at the Feast, The (Wells), **Supp. XXVI:** 278, 282

Skeleton Crew (King), **Supp. V:** 144

"Skeleton in Armor, The" (Longfellow), **Retro. Supp. II**: 168

"Skeleton's Cave, The" (Bryant), **Supp. I Part 1**: 157

Skelton, John, **III**: 521

Skepticisms (Aiken), **Supp. XV**: 298, 302

Sketch Book of Geoffrey Crayon, Gent., The (Irving), **II**: 295, 303, 304–308, 309, 311, 491; **Supp. I Part 1**: 155

Sketches of Art (Jameson), **Retro. Supp. II**: 58

Sketches of Eighteenth Century America (Crèvecoeur), **Supp. I Part 1**: 233, 240–241, 250, 251

"Sketches of Female Biography" (Rowson), **Supp. XV**: 245

Sketches of Switzerland (Cooper), **I**: 346

Sketches Old and New (Twain), **IV**: 198

"Sketch for a Job-Application Blank" (Harrison), **Supp. VIII**: 38

"Sketch"(Kenny), **Supp. XXIII**: 155

Sketch of Old England, by a New England Man (Paulding), **I**: 344

Skibell, Joseph, **Supp. XVII**: 48

"Skier and the Mountain, The" (Eberhart), **I**: 528–529

"Skiing by Moonlight" (Davison), **Supp. XXVI**: 74

"Skin-Boats: 1830, The" (Bierds), **Supp. XVII**: 28

Skinker, Mary Scott, **Supp. IX**: 20

Skinner, Ewart, **Supp. XXII**: 78

Skinny Island (Auchincloss), **Supp. IV Part 1**: 33

Skinny Legs and All (Robbins), **Supp. X**: 267, 273, **276–279**

Skin of Our Teeth, The (Wilder), **IV**: 357, 358, 369–372; **Supp. IV Part 2**: 586; **Supp. XX**: 50

"Skins" (Wright), **Supp. V**: 340

Skins and Bones: Poems 1979–1987 (Gunn Allen), **Supp. IV Part 1**: 321, 331

"Skipper Ireson's Ride" (Whittier), **Supp. I Part 2**: 691, 693–694

"Skirmish at Sartoris" (Faulkner), **II**: 67

"Skirt" (Halliday), **Supp. XIX**: 90

Skirts and Slacks (Di Piero), **Supp. XIX**: 35, 36, 38, 45–47

Sklenicka, Carol, **Supp. XXIV**: 166

Skloot, Floyd, **Supp. XX**: **193–209**

Skotheim, Robert Allen, **Supp. XVII**: 104

Skow, John, **Supp. V**: 213; **Supp. XVI**: 174

Skube, Michael, **Supp. XVIII**: 96

"Skunk Cabbage" (Bronk), **Supp. XXI**: 31

"Skunk Cabbage" (Oliver), **Supp. VII**: 235, 236

"Skunk Hour" (R. Lowell), **II**: 548–550; **Retro. Supp. II**: 188, 189; **Supp. XIV**: 269; **Supp. XX**: 203

Skurnick, Lizzie, **Supp. XXVI**: 49

Sky, The Stars, The Wilderness, The (Bass), **Supp. XVI**: 19, 20

Sky Changes, The (Sorrentino), **Supp. XXI**: 228, 230, 231; **Supp. XXVI**: 26

"Sky Dance" (Leopold), **Supp. XIV**: 186

"Sky Line" (Taylor), **Supp. V**: 316

"Sky Line, The" (Mumford), **Supp. II Part 2**: 475

Sky of Stone (Hickam), **Supp. XXVII**: 101, 106, 108–110

"Skyscraper" (Sandburg), **III**: 581–582

Sky's the Limit, The: A Defense of the Earth (Nichols), **Supp. XIII**: 268

"Sky Valley Rider" (Wright), **Supp. V**: 335, 340

Sky-Walk; or the Man Unknown to Himself (Brown), **Supp. I Part 1**: 127–128

Slam! (Myers), **Supp. XXVII**: 201, 202, 206

"Slang in America" (Whitman), **IV**: 348

Slappy Hooper, the Wonderful Sign Painter (Bontemps and Conroy), **Supp. XXII**: 5, 11

Slapstick (Vonnegut), **Supp. II Part 2**: 753, 754, 778

Slapstick Tragedy (T. Williams), **IV**: 382, 393

Slate, Lane, **Supp. IX**: 251, 253

Slater Brown, William, **Retro. Supp. III**: 48

Slattery, Mary Grace. *See* Miller, Mrs. Arthur (Mary Grace Slattery)

Slattery's Hurricane (Wouk), **Supp. XXV**: 257, 262–263

Slaughter, Frank G., **Retro. Supp. III**: 134

"Slaughterer, The" (Singer), **IV**: 19

Slaughterhouse-Five (Vonnegut), **Supp. II Part 2**: 755, 758–759, 760, 770, 772–776; **Supp. V**: 41, 244; **Supp. XIX**: 235

Slaughter Rule, The (film; Alex and Andrew Smith), **Supp. XIX**: 174

Slave, The (Baraka), **Supp. II Part 1**: 42, 44, 56

Slave, The: A Novel (Singer), **IV**: 13; **Retro. Supp. II**: **305–307**

"Slave Canal" (Ray), **Supp. XVIII**: 193

"Slave Coffle" (Angelou), **Supp. IV Part 1**: 16

"Slave of the Sky" (P. N. Warren), **Supp. XX**: 261

"Slave on the Block" (Hughes), **Supp. I Part 1**: 329

Slave Power, The: The Free North and Southern Domination, 1780–1860 (Richards), **Supp. XIV**: 48

"Slave Quarters" (Dickey), **Supp. IV Part 1**: 181

Slavery (Channing), **Supp. XXIV**: 77–78

"Slave's Dream, The" (Longfellow), **Supp. I Part 2**: 409

Slave Ship: A Historical Pageant (Baraka), **Supp. II Part 1**: 47–49, 53, 56–57

"Slave-Ships, The" (Whittier), **Supp. I Part 2**: 687–688

Slaves in Algiers; or, A Struggle for Freedom (Rowson), **Supp. XV**: **236–237**

"Slave Trade, The: View from the Middle Passage" (Major), **Supp. XXII**: 182

Slavs! Thinking about the Longstanding Problems of Virtue and Happiness (Kushner), **Supp. IX**: **146**

Sledge, Eugene, **Supp. V**: 250

Sleek for the Long Flight (Matthews), **Supp. IX**: 154, 155, **157–158**

Sleep (Dixon), **Supp. XII**: 154

"Sleep, The" (Strand), **Supp. IV Part 2**: 627

Sleeper (film; Allen), **Supp. XV**: 5

"Sleeper, The" (Poe), **III**: 411; **Retro. Supp. III**: 231–232

"Sleeper 1, The" (Hay), **Supp. XIV**: 132–133

"Sleeper 2, The" (Hay), **Supp. XIV**: 132–133

"Sleepers, The" (Whitman), **IV**: 336; **Retro. Supp. III**: 308

"Sleepers in Jaipur" (Kenyon), **Supp. VII**: 172

Sleepers in Moon-Crowned Valleys (Purdy), **Supp. VII**: 274, 275

Sleepers Joining Hands (R. Bly), **Supp. XXI**: 85

"Sleepers Joining Hands" (R. Bly), **Supp. IV Part 1**: 63, 73

Sleeping Beauty (Macdonald), **Supp. IV Part 2**: 474, 475

Sleeping Beauty, The (Carruth), **Supp. XVI**: 53, 57–58

"Sleeping Beauty IV" (Stone), **Supp. XXVII**: 263

"Sleeping Beauty Syndrome, The: The New Agony of Single Men" (Wasserstein), **Supp. XV**: 328

Sleeping Dogs (Wells), **Supp. XXVI**: 280–281

Sleeping Fires (Atherton), **Supp. XXIV**: 25

"Sleeping Fury, The" (Bogan), **Supp. III Part 1**: 58

Sleeping Fury, The: Poems (Bogan), **Supp. III Part 1**: 55–58

Sleeping Gypsy and Other Poems, The (Garrett), **Supp. VII**: 96–98

Sleeping in the Forest (Oliver), **Supp. VII**: 233

"Sleeping in the Forest" (Oliver), **Supp. VII**: 233–234

Sleeping in the Woods (Wagoner), **Supp. IX**: **328**

Sleeping on Fists (Ríos), **Supp. IV Part 2**: 540

Sleeping on the Wing: An Anthology of Modern Poetry (Koch and Farrell, eds.), **Supp. XV**: 187–188

"Sleeping on the Wing"(O'Hara), **Supp. XXIII**: 214

"Sleeping Standing Up" (Bishop), **Supp. I Part 1**: 85, 89, 93

"Sleeping with Animals" (Kumin), **Supp. IV Part 2**: 454

Sleeping with One Eye Open (Strand), **Supp. IV Part 2**: 621–624, 623, 628

Sleeping with the Dictionary (Mullen), **Supp. XXVII**: 173–174, 176

Sleep in Thunder (Lacy), **Supp. XV**: 206

"Sleepless, The" (L.-Y. Lee), **Supp. XV**: 224

"Sleepless at Crown Point" (Wilbur), **Supp. III Part 2**: 561

Sleepless Nights (Hardwick), **Supp. III Part 1**: 193, 208–211

"Sleepless Nights" (Nelson), **Supp. XVIII:** 174

"Sleep-Walkers, The" (Gibran), **Supp. XX: 118**

Sleepy Lagoon Mystery, The (Endore), **Supp. XVII:** 60

"Sleepy People" (Lethem), **Supp. XVIII:** 140

Sleigh, Tom, **Supp. XIX:** 38, 40

Sleight, Ken, **Supp. XIII:** 12

"Slicing Oranges for Jeremiah"(Wakoski), **Supp. XXVIII:** 262, 263

Slick, Sam (pseudonym). *See* Haliburton, Thomas Chandler

"Slick Gonna Learn" (Ellison), **Retro. Supp. II:** 116; **Supp. II Part 1:** 237–238

"Slight Rebellion off Madison" (Salinger), **III:** 553

"Slight Sound at Evening, A" (White), **Supp. I Part 2:** 672

"Slim Graves Show, The" (Keillor), **Supp. XVI:** 172

"Slim Greer" series (Hayden), **Supp. II Part 1:** 369

"Slim in Hell" (Hayden), **Supp. II Part 1:** 369

"Slim Man Canyon" (Silko), **Supp. IV Part 2:** 560

"Slip, Shift, and Speed Up: The Influence of Robinson Jeffers's Narrative Syntax" (Jarman), **Supp. XVII:** 111, 112

"Slippery Fingers" (Hammett), **Supp. IV Part 1:** 343

Slipping-Down Life, A (Tyler), **Supp. IV Part 2:** 660–661

Sloan, Jacob, **IV:** 3, 6

Sloan, John, **I:** 254; **IV:** 411; **Retro. Supp. II:** 103; **Supp. XXII:** 277

Sloane, David E. E., **Retro. Supp. III:** 259

Sloane, John, **Supp. XV:** 295

"Slob" (Farrell), **II:** 25, 28, 31

Slocum, Joshua, **Supp. I Part 2:** 497; **Supp. XXV: 205–219**

Slogum House (Sandoz), **Supp. XXIV:** 244, **251–252,** 255

Slomovitz, Philip, **Retro. Supp. III:** 133

Slonim, Véra. *See* Nabokov, Véra

Slopen, Beverly, **Supp. XX:** 59

Slouching towards Bethlehem (Didion), **Supp. IV Part 1:** 196, 197, 200–201, 202, 206, 210

Slovic, Scott, **Supp. XVI:** 277

"Slow Child with a Book of Birds" (Levis), **Supp. XI:** 268

"Slow Dance with Icarus" (Monson), **Supp. XXIV:** 240

Slow Dancing Through Ether: A Fine Binding Project (Monson and Ingmundson), **Supp. XXIV:** 230, 234

"Slow Down for Poetry" (Strand), **Supp. IV Part 2:** 620

Slow Music (Taggard), **Supp. XXII:** 284

"Slow Pacific Swell, The" (Winters), **Supp. II Part 2:** 790, 793, 795, 796, 799

Slow Parade (Kees), **Supp. XV:** 137

Slow Train Coming (album, Dylan), **Supp. XVIII:** 28

Slow Transparency (Hadas), **Supp. XXIII: 113–114**

Slow Vision (Bodenheim), **Supp. XXV:** 28

"Slum Church" (Espaillat), **Supp. XXI:** 110–111

"Slumgullions" (Olsen), **Supp. IV Part 1:** 54

Slumgullion Stew: An Edward Abbey Reader (Abbey), **Supp. XIII:** 4

Slung, Michelle, **Supp. XX: 87**

"S & M" (Komunyakaa), **Supp. XIII:** 114

"Small" (C. Frost), **Supp. XV:** 102

Small, Albion, **Supp. I Part 1:** 5

"Small, Good Thing, A" (Carver), **Supp. III Part 1:** 145, 147

Small, Miriam Rossiter, **Supp. I Part 1:** 319

Small Boy and Others, A (James), **II:** 337, 547; **Retro. Supp. I:** 235

"Small but Urgent Request to the Unknowable" (Karr), **Supp. XI:** 243

Small Ceremonies (Shields), **Supp. VII:** 312–315, 320

Small Craft Warnings (T. Williams), **IV:** 382, 383, 384, 385, 386, 387, 392, 393, 396, 398

"Small Degrees" (Brockmeier), **Supp. XXII:** 52, 59

"Small Fry" (Peacock), **Supp. XIX:** 206

Small Place, A (Kincaid), **Supp. VII:** 186–187, 188, 191

"Small Rain, The" (Pynchon), **Supp. II Part 2:** 620

Small Room, The (Sarton), **Supp. VIII:** 252, **255–256**

Smalls, Bob, **II:** 128

"Small Song for Andrew" (Weigl), **Supp. XIX:** 280

Small Time Crooks (film; Allen), **Supp. XV:** 11

Small Town, A (Hearon), **Supp. VIII: 65–66**

"Small Vases from Hebron, The" (Nye), **Supp. XIII:** 283

"Small Vision, The" (Goldbarth), **Supp. XII:** 180

"Small Voice from the Wings" (Everwine), **Supp. XV:** 76

"Small Wire" (Sexton), **Supp. II Part 2:** 696

Small Worlds (A. Hoffman), **Supp. XVII:** 44

Smardz, Zofia, **Supp. XVI:** 155

Smart, Christopher, **III:** 534; **Supp. I Part 2:** 539; **Supp. IV Part 2:** 626

Smart, Joyce H., **Supp. XI:** 169

"Smart Cookie, A" (Cisneros), **Supp. VII:** 64

"Smash"(Thompson), **Supp. XXIII:** 301, 302

"Smashup" (Thurber), **Supp. I Part 2:** 616

Smedley, Agens, **Supp. XXVIII:** 77

Smedly, Agnes, **Supp. XIII:** 295

"Smell of a God, The" (Peacock), **Supp. XIX:** 199

"Smelt Fishing" (Hayden), **Supp. II Part 1:** 367

"Smile of the Bathers, The" (Kees), **Supp. XV:** 145

"Smile on the Face of a Kouros, The" (Bronk), **Supp. XXI:** 31

"Smiles" (Dunn), **Supp. XI:** 151

Smiles, Samuel, **Supp. X:** 167

Smiley, Jane, **Supp. VI: 291–309; Supp. XII:** 73, 297; **Supp. XIII:** 127; **Supp. XIX:** 54

Smith, Aaron, **Supp. XXVIII:** 196

Smith, Adam, **II:** 9; **Supp. I Part 2:** 633, 634, 639; **Supp. XVII:** 235

Smith, Amanda, **Supp. XXVII:** 211

Smith, Annick, **Supp. XIV:** 223; **Supp. XXVI:** 183, 186, 188

Smith, Barbara, **Supp. XXIII:** 194

Smith, Bardwell, **Supp. XXVIII:** 62

Smith, Benjamin, **IV:** 148

Smith, Bernard, **I:** 260

Smith, Bessie, **Retro. Supp. I:** 343; **Retro. Supp. III:** 314; **Supp. VIII:** 330; **Supp. XIX:** 147

Smith, Betty, **Supp. XXIII: 257–271**

Smith, Charlie, **Supp. X:** 177

Smith, Clark Ashton, **Supp. XXV:** 111; **Supp. XXVII:** 117

Smith, Dale, **Supp. XV:** 136, 138, 139

Smith, Dave, **Supp. V:** 333; **Supp. XI:** 152; **Supp. XII:** 178, 198; **Supp. XIX:** 277, 282

Smith, David, **Supp. XIII:** 246, 247

Smith, David Nichol, **Supp. XIV:** 2

Smith, Dinitia, **Supp. VIII:** 74, 82, 83; **Supp. XVIII:** 162; **Supp. XXIV:** 2–3; **Supp. XXVIII:** 207

Smith, Elihu Hubbard, **Supp. I Part 1:** 126, 127, 130

Smith, Ernest J., **Supp. XXIII:** 111, 113, 117

Smith, George Adam, **III:** 199

Smith, Hannah Whitall, **Supp. XIV:** 333, 334, 338

Smith, Harriet, **Retro. Supp. III:** 261

Smith, Harrison, **II:** 61

Smith, Henry Justin, **Supp. XXVII:** 85

Smith, Henry Nash, **IV:** 210; **Retro. Supp. III:** 78, 266; **Supp. I Part 1:** 233

Smith, Herbert F., **Supp. I Part 2:** 423

Smith, Iain Crichton, **Supp. XVIII:** 196

Smith, James, **II:** 111

Smith, Jedediah Strong, **Supp. IV Part 2:** 602

Smith, Jerome, **Supp. IV Part 1:** 369

Smith, Joe, **Supp. IV Part 2:** 584

Smith, John, **I:** 4, 131; **II:** 296

Smith, John Allyn, **I:** 168

Smith, Johnston (pseudonym). *See* Crane, Stephen

Smith, Katherine Capshaw, **Supp. XXII:** 10, 13–14; **Supp. XXVIII:** 124

Smith, Kellogg, **Supp. I Part 2:** 660

Smith, Lamar, **II:** 585

Smith, Mrs. Lamar (Marguerite Walters), **II:** 585, 587

Smith, Lane, **Supp. XIX:** 231

Smith, Larry David, **Supp. XVIII:** 22

Smith, Lee, **Supp. XII:** 311; **Supp. XVIII:** 195; **Supp. XXII:** 206, 213

Smith, Lillian, **Supp. XXII:** 67

Smith, Logan Pearsall, **Supp. XIV: 333–351**

Smith, Lula Carson. *See* McCullers, Carson

Smith, Mark, **Supp. XVIII:** 155

Smith, Martha Nell, **Retro. Supp. I:** 33, 43, 46, 47

Smith, Mary Rozet, **Supp. I Part 1:** 5, 22

Smith, Oliver, **II:** 586

Smith, Patricia Clark, **Supp. IV Part 1:** 397, 398, 402, 406, 408, 410; **Supp. IV Part 2:** 509; **Supp. XII:** 218

Smith, Patrick, **Supp. VIII:** 40, 41

Smith, Patti, **Supp. XII:** 136; **Supp. XIV:** 151

Smith, Porter, **III:** 572

Smith, Red, **II:** 417, 424

Smith, Robert McClure, **Supp. XV:** 270

Smith, Robert Pearsall, **Supp. XIV:** 333

Smith, Sarah A., **Supp. XVIII:** 99

Smith, Seba, **Supp. I Part 2:** 411

Smith, Sidonie, **Supp. IV Part 1:** 11; **Supp. XXII:** 70

Smith, Stevie, **Supp. V:** 84

Smith, Sydney, **II:** 295; **Supp. XIV:** 112

Smith, Thorne, **Supp. IX:** 194

Smith, Valerie, **Supp. XXII:** 146

Smith, Wallace, **Supp. XXVII:** 88

Smith, Wendy, **Supp. XII:** 330, 335; **Supp. XVIII:** 89, 92

Smith, Wilford Bascom "Pitchfork", **Supp. XIII:** 168

Smith, William, **II:** 114

Smith, William Gardner, **Supp. XVI:** 142–143

Smith, William Jay, **Supp. XIII: 331–350**

Smitherman, Geneva, **Supp. XXVI:** 13

"Smoke" (Di Piero), **Supp. XIX:** 38

Smoke (film), **Supp. XII:** 21

"Smoke" (Huddle), **Supp. XXVI:** 149

Smoke and Steel (Sandburg), **III:** 585–587, 592

Smoke Dancing (Gansworth), **Supp. XXVI:** 104–105

"Smokehouse" (Offutt), **Supp. XIX:** 166, 167

"Smokers" (Wolff), **Supp. VII:** 340–341

Smokey Bites the Dust (film, C. Griffith), **Supp. XVII:** 9

"Smoking in an Open Grave"(Bottoms), **Supp. XXVIII:** 24

Smoking Mountain, The: Stories of Postwar Germany (Boyle), **Supp. XXIV:** 61

"Smoking My Prayers" (Ortiz), **Supp. IV Part 2:** 503

"Smoking Room, The" (Jackson), **Supp. IX:** 116

"Smoky Gold" (Leopold), **Supp. XIV:** 186

Smolan, Sandy, **Supp. XVI:** 36

Smollett, Tobias G., **I:** 134, 339, 343; **II:** 304–305; **III:** 61; **Supp. XVIII:** 7; **Supp. XXV:** 258

Smooding, Robert, **Supp. XXIII:** 294

Smudging (Wakoski), **Supp. XXVIII:** 265

Smuggler's Bible, A (McElroy), **Supp. IV Part 1:** 285

Smuggler's Handbook, The (Goldbarth), **Supp. XII:** 181, 183

Smugglers of Lost Soul's Rock, The (Gardner), **Supp. VI:** 70

Smyth, Albert Henry, **II:** 123

Smyth, Jacqui, **Supp. XXI:** 215

"Snack Firm Maps New Chip Push" (Keillor), **Supp. XVI:** 168, 169

"Snail, The" (Hay), **Supp. XIV:** 124

"Snake, The" (Berry), **Supp. X:** 31

"Snake, The" (Crane), **I:** 420

"Snakecharmer" (Plath), **Supp. I Part 2:** 538

"Snakes, Mongooses" (Moore), **III:** 207

"Snakeskin" (Kooser), **Supp. XIX:** 123

"Snakes of September, The" (Kunitz), **Supp. III Part 1:** 258

"Snapshot of 15th S.W., A" (Hugo), **Supp. VI:** 141

"Snapshot Rediscovered, A" (X. J. Kennedy), **Supp. XV:** 170

"Snapshots in an Album" (Espaillat), **Supp. XXI:** 111

"Snapshots of a Daughter-in-Law" (Rich), **Retro. Supp. III:** 243; **Supp. I Part 2:** 553–554

Snapshots of a Daughter-in-Law: Poems, 1954–1962 (Rich), **Retro. Supp. III:** 241, 243–244; **Supp. I Part 2:** 550–551, 553–554; **Supp. XII:** 255

Snaring the Flightless Birds (Bierds), **Supp. XVII:** 26

Sneetches and Other Stories, The (Geisel), **Supp. XVI:** 109

"Sneeze, The" (Chekhov), **Supp. IV Part 2:** 585

Snell, Ebenezer, **Supp. I Part 1:** 151

Snell, Thomas, **Supp. I Part 1:** 153

Sniffen, Matthew, **Supp. XXV:** 283

Sniper, The (O'Neill), **Supp. XXVIII:** 68–69

"Snob, The" (Boulton), **Supp. XXII:** 23

"Snob, The" (Shapiro), **Supp. II Part 2:** 705

Snobbery: The America Version (Epstein), **Supp. XIV:** 102, 114–115

Snodgrass, Kathleen, **Supp. XVI:** 42

Snodgrass, W. D., **I:** 400; **Retro. Supp. II:** 179; **Supp. III Part 2:** 541; **Supp. V:** 337; **Supp. VI: 311–328;** **Supp. XI:** 141, 315; **Supp. XIII:** 312; **Supp. XV:** 92, 153; **Supp. XVII:** 239

Snodgrass, W. F., **Supp. XXVIII:** 86

"Snow" (C. Baxter), **Supp. XVII:** 19

"Snow" (Frost), **Retro. Supp. I:** 133

"Snow" (Haines), **Supp. XII:** 212

"Snow" (Sexton), **Supp. II Part 2:** 696

"Snow" (W. V. Davis), **Supp. XXI:** 89, 90, 93

Snow, C. P., **Supp. I Part 2:** 536

Snow, Dean, **Supp. XXVI:** 86

Snow, Hank, **Supp. V:** 335

"Snow and Dirty Rain"(Siken), **Supp. XXVIII:** 199

Snow Angels (film), **Supp. XXV:** 153–154

Snow Angels (O'Nan), **Supp. XXV:** 142, 143, 150

Snow Ball, The (Gurney), **Supp. V:** 99

"Snow-Bound" (Whittier), **Supp. I Part 2:** 700–703

"Snow Bound at Eagle's" (Harte), **Supp. II Part 1:** 356

Snow-Cap Sister, The: A Farce (Stuart), **Supp. XXVIII:** 229

"Snowflakes" (Longfellow), **II:** 498

"Snow Goose, The" (Gallico), **Supp. XVI:** 238

Snow-Image, The (Hawthorne), **Retro. Supp. III:** 110, 117–118

"Snow-Image, The" (Hawthorne), **Retro. Supp. III:** 117–118

Snow-Image and Other Twice Told Tales, The (Hawthorne), **II:** 237; **Retro. Supp. I:** 160

"Snowing in Greenwich Village" (Updike), **IV:** 226; **Retro. Supp. I:** 321

"Snow in New York" (Swenson), **Supp. IV Part 2:** 644

Snow Leopard, The (Matthiessen), **Supp. V:** 199, 207–211

"Snow Man, The" (Stevens), **IV:** 82–83; **Retro. Supp. I:** 299, 300, 302, 306, 307, 312; **Supp. XXI:** 60

"Snowmass Cycle, The" (Dunn), **Supp. XI:** 152

Snow: Meditations of a Cautious Man in Winter (Banks), **Supp. V:** 6

Snow Poems, The (Ammons), **Supp. VII:** 32–34

Snowshoe Trek to Otter River (Budbill), **Supp. XIX:** 11

Snow's Music, The (Skloot), **Supp. XX: 196, 204–205**

"Snows of Kilimanjaro, The" (Hemingway), **II:** 78, 257, 263, 264; **Retro. Supp. I:** 98, 182; **Supp. XII:** 249

"Snows of Studiofiftyfour, The" (Plimpton), **Supp. XVI:** 245

"Snow Songs" (Snodgrass), **Supp. VI:** 324

"Snowstorm, The" (Oates), **Supp. II Part 2:** 523

"Snowstorm as It Affects the American Farmer, A" (Crèvecoeur), **Supp. I Part 1:** 251

Snow White (Barthelme), **Supp. IV Part 1:** 40, 47, 48–49, 50, 52; **Supp. V:** 39

"Snowy Egret" (Weigl), **Supp. XIX:** 280–281

"Snowy Mountain Song, A" (Ortiz), **Supp. IV Part 2:** 506

Snyder, Gary, **Supp. III Part 1:** 350; **Supp. IV Part 2:** 502; **Supp. V:** 168–169; **Supp. VIII:** 39, **289–307;** **Supp. XVI:** 283; **Supp. XXII:** 276

Snyder, Mike, **Supp. XIV:** 36

Snyder, Phillip A., **Retro. Supp. III:** 134

Soak the Rich (film), **Supp. XXVII:** 90

"So-and-So Reclining on Her Couch" (Stevens), **IV:** 90

"Soapland" (Thurber), **Supp. I Part 2:** 619

Soares, Lota de Macedo, **Retro. Supp. II:** 44; **Supp. I Part 1:** 89, 94

"Sobbin' Women, The" (Benét), **Supp. XI:** 47

Sobin, Gustaf, **Supp. XVI: 281–298**

Sochen, June, **Supp. XXI:** 1

Social Ethics (Gilman), **Supp. XI:** 207

"Social Function of the Story Teller, The" (lecture, Murray), **Supp. XIX:** 153

"Socialism and the Negro" (McKay), **Supp. X:** 135

"Socialism of the Skin, A (Liberation, Honey!)" (Kushner), **Supp. IX:** 135

Social Thought in America: The Revolt against Formalism (White), **Supp. I Part 2:** 648, 650

"Society, Morality, and the Novel" (Ellison), **Retro. Supp. II:** 118, 123–124

"Society of Eros" (Kittredge), **Supp. XXVI:** 178, 184

"Sociological Habit Patterns in Linguistic Transmogrification" (Cowley), **Supp. II Part 1:** 143

"Sociological Poet, A" (Bourne), **I:** 228

Socrates, **I:** 136, 265; **II:** 8–9, 105, 106; **III:** 281, 419, 606; **Supp. I Part 2:** 458; **Supp. XII:** 98

Socrates Fortlow stories (Mosley), **Supp. XIII: 242–243**

So Forth (Brodsky), **Supp. VIII:** 32–33

"So Forth" (Brodsky), **Supp. VIII:** 33

"Soft Flame" (Skloot), **Supp. XX: 203**

"Soft-Hearted Sioux, The" (Zitkala-Ša), **Supp. XXV:** 274, 282

Soft Machine, The (Burroughs), **Supp. III Part 1:** 93, 103, 104

"Soft Mask" (Karr), **Supp. XI:** 243

Soft Side, The (James), **II:** 335; **Retro. Supp. I:** 229

"Soft Spring Night in Shillington, A" (Updike), **Retro. Supp. I:** 318, 319

"Soft Wood" (R. Lowell), **II:** 550–551

"So Help Me" (Algren), **Supp. IX:** 2

Soil and Survival: Land Stewardship and the Future of American Agriculture (C. Bly, J. Paddock and N. Paddock), **Supp. XVI:** 36–37

"Soirée in Hollywood" (H. Miller), **III:** 186

Sojourner, The (Rawlings), **Supp. X:** 233–234

"Sojourn in a Whale" (Moore), **III:** 211, 213

"Sojourns" (Didion), **Supp. IV Part 1:** 205

Sokolow, Jayme, **Supp. XIX:** 134

Solanus, Jane, **Supp. XVI:** 293

Solar Lottery (Dick), **Supp. XVIII:** 138

Solar Storms (Hogan), **Supp. IV Part 1:** 397, 410, 414–415

"Soldier, The" (Frost), **II:** 155

"Soldier Asleep at the Tomb" (Schnackenberg), **Supp. XV:** 262–263

Soldier Blue (film), **Supp. X:** 124

"Soldier of Fortune" (Wright), **Supp. XV:** 341

Soldier of the Great War, A (Helprin), **Supp. XXV:** 83–84, 86–87

"Soldier's Home" (Hemingway), **Retro. Supp. I:** 189

Soldier's Joy (Bell), **Supp. X:** 7, **7–8,** 10, 11; **Supp. XXIII:** 43

Soldiers of the Storm (film), **Supp. XIII:** 163

Soldiers' Pay (Faulkner), **I:** 117; **II:** 56, 68; **Retro. Supp. I:** 80, 81; **Retro. Supp. III:** 76–77

"Soldier's Testament, The" (Mumford), **Supp. II Part 2:** 473

"Soliloquy: Man Talking to a Mirror" (Komunyakaa), **Supp. XIII:** 116–117

"Solipsism" (Monson), **Supp. XXIV:** 230

"Solitary, The" (Teasdale), **Supp. XXVII:** 296

"Solitary Confinement" (X. J. Kennedy), **Supp. XV:** 157

"Solitary Pond, The" (Updike), **Retro. Supp. I:** 323

So Little Time (Marquand), **III:** 55, 59, 65, 67, 69

"Solitude" (Maupassant), **Supp. I Part 1:** 223

Solnit, Rebecca, **Supp. XXVI:** 45

Solo Faces (Salter), **Supp. IX: 259–260**

Solomon, Andy, **Supp. X:** 11

Solomon, Carl, **Supp. XIV:** 143, 150

Solomon, Charles, **Supp. VIII:** 82

Solomon, Deborah, **Supp. XXI:** 245

Solomon, Henry, Jr., **Supp. I Part 2:** 490

Solomon Crow's Christmas Pockets and Other Tales (Stuart), **Supp. XXVIII:** 229

Solomon Northup's Odyssey (television movie), **Supp. XXVIII:** 167

Solomons, Leon, **IV:** 26

"So Long, Marianne" (Cohen), **Supp. XXVII:** 51, 60

So Long, See You Tomorrow (Maxwell), **Supp. VIII:** 156, 160, 162, **167–169;** **Supp. XVII:** 23

"So Long Ago" (Bausch), **Supp. VII:** 41–42

Solotaroff, Robert, **Retro. Supp. II:** 203

Solotaroff, Theodore, **III:** 452–453; **Retro. Supp. II:** 281; **Supp. I Part 2:** 440, 445; **Supp. X:** 79; **Supp. XI:** 340; **Supp. XII:** 291; **Supp. XIX:** 268; **Supp. XXVI:** 118

Solstice (Di Piero), **Supp. XIX:** 36

"Solstice" (Jeffers), **Supp. II Part 2:** 433, 435

"Solstice, The" (Merwin), **Supp. III Part 1:** 356

"Solus Rex" (Nabokov), **Retro. Supp. I:** 274

Solution, The (Stone), **Supp. XXVII:** 257

"Solutions" (McCarthy), **II:** 578

"Solving the Puzzle" (Dunn), **Supp. XI:** 152

Solzhenitsyn, Alexandr, **Retro. Supp. I:** 278; **Supp. VIII:** 241

"Some Afternoon" (Creeley), **Supp. IV Part 1:** 150–151

Some American People (Caldwell), **I:** 292, 294, 295, 296, 304, 309

"Some Ashes Drifting above Piedra, California" (Levis), **Supp. XI:** 264–265

"Some Aspects of the Grotesque in Southern Fiction" (O'Connor), **Retro. Supp.**

II: 223, 224

"Some Birds on a Dun Field" (Bronk), **Supp. XXI:** 27

"Somebody Always Grabs the Purple" (H. Roth), **Supp. IX:** 234

Somebody Else, Somewhere Else: The Raymond Andrews Story (film, Freeman), **Supp. XXVI:** 11

Somebody in Boots (Algren), **Supp. IX:** 3, **5–7,** 12

Somebody's Darling (McMurtry), **Supp. V:** 225

Some Came Running (film), **Supp. XI:** 213

Some Came Running (Jones), **Supp. XI:** 214, 215, 220, **222–223,** 226, 227, 232

Some Can Whistle (McMurtry), **Supp. V:** 229

"Some Children of the Goddess" (Mailer), **Retro. Supp. II:** 204

Someday, Maybe (Stafford), **Supp. XI: 323–325; Supp. XIII:** 281

Some Drawings and Some Notes to Myself (Brainard), **Supp. XXVII:** 20

"Some Dreamers of the Golden Dream" (Didion), **Supp. IV Part 1:** 200

"Some Esoteric Aspects of the League of the Iroquois" (Hewitt), **Supp. XXVI:** 96

Some Faces in the Crowd (Schulberg), **Supp. II:** 252

"Some Foreign Letters" (Sexton), **Supp. II Part 2:** 674

"Some General Instructions" (Koch), **Supp. XV:** 182

"Some Good News" (Olson), **Supp. II Part 2:** 575, 576, 577

"Some Grass along a Ditch Bank" (Levis), **Supp. XI:** 266

"Some Greek Writings" (Corso), **Supp. XII:** 130

Some Honorable Men: Political Conventions, 1960–1972 (Mailer), **Retro. Supp. II:** 208

Some Imagist Poets (A. Lowell), **III:** 511, 518, 520; **Supp. I Part 1:** 257, 261

"Some keep the Sabbath going to Church" (Dickinson), **Retro. Supp. I:** 30; **Supp. XVIII:** 301

"Some Laughed" (L. Michaels), **Supp. XVI:** 207

"Some Like Indians Endure" (Gunn Allen), **Supp. IV Part 1:** 330

"Some Like Them Cold" (Lardner), **II:** 427–428, 430, 431; **Supp. IX:** 202

"Some Lines from Whitman" (Jarrell), **IV:** 352

"Some Matters Concerning the Occupant" (Keillor), **Supp. XVI:** 167

"Some Musicians Play Chamber Music for Us" (Bronk), **Supp. XXI:** 27–28

"Some Negatives: X. at the Chateau" (Merrill), **Supp. III Part 1:** 322

"Some Neglected Points in the Theory of Socialism" (Veblen), **Supp. I Part 2:** 635

"Some Notes for an Autobiographical Lecture" (Trilling), **Supp. III Part 2:** 493, 497, 500

"Some Notes on French Poetry" (R. Bly), **Supp. IV Part 1:** 61

"Some Notes on Miss L." (West), **IV:** 290–291, 295; **Retro. Supp. II:** 322

"Some Notes on Organic Form" (Levertov), **Supp. III Part 1:** 272, 279

"Some Notes on Teaching: Probably Spoken" (Paley), **Supp. VI:** 225

"Some Notes on the Gazer Within" (Levis), **Supp. XI:** 270

"Some Notes on Violence" (West), **IV:** 304; **Retro. Supp. II:** 322, 323

"Some Observations Now" (Conroy), **Supp. XVI:** 75

Some Observations of a Stranger at Zuni in the Later Part of the Century (Major), **Supp. XXII:** 179–180

"Some Observations of a Stranger at Zuni in the Later Part of the Century" (Major), **Supp. XXII:** 179

Some of the Dharma (Kerouac), **Supp. III Part 1:** 225

"Some of Us Have Fewer" (Monson), **Supp. XXIV:** 240

"Someone Is Buried" (Salinas), **Supp. XIII:** 324

"Someone Is Writing a Poem" (Rich), **Retro. Supp. III:** 251

"Someone Puts a Pineapple Together" (Stevens), **IV:** 90–91

"Someone's Blood" (Dove), **Supp. IV Part 1:** 245

"Someone Talking" (Harjo), **Supp. XII:** 219–220

"Someone Talking to Himself" (Wilbur), **Supp. III Part 2:** 557

"Someone to Watch Over Me" (Stern), **Supp. IX:** 300

Someone to Watch Over Me: Stories (Bausch), **Supp. VII:** 53

Some People, Places, & Things That Will Not Appear in My Next Novel (Cheever), **Supp. I Part 1:** 184–185

"Some Poets' Criticism and the Age" (Yenser), **Supp. XV:** 113–114

Some Problems of Philosophy: A Beginning of an Introduction to Philosophy (James), **II:** 360–361

"Some Questions You Might Ask" (Oliver), **Supp. VII:** 238–239

"Some Remarks on Humor" (White), **Supp. I Part 2:** 672

"Some Remarks on Rhythm" (Roethke), **III:** 548–549

Somers, Fred, **I:** 196

Somerville, Jane, **Supp. IX:** 289, 296–297

"Some Secrets" (Stern), **Supp. IX:** 286, 287, 288, 289, 295

Some Sort of Epic Grandeur (Bruccoli), **Retro. Supp. I:** 115, 359

"Something" (Oliver), **Supp. VII:** 236

"Something Broken" (Rich), **Retro. Supp. III:** 244

Something Happened (Heller), **Supp. IV Part 1:** 383, 386–388, 389, 392

"*Something Happened*: The Imaginary, the Symbolic, and the Discourse of the Family" (Mellard), **Supp. IV Part 1:** 387

Something in Common (Hughes), **Supp. I Part 1:** 329–330

Something Inside: Conversations with Gay Fiction Writers (Gambone), **Supp. XII:** 81

Something I've Been Meaning to Tell You (Munro), **Supp. XXVII:** 182, 184–185

"Something Matters but We Don't " (Bronk), **Supp. XXI:** 32

"Something Might Be Gaining" (Mosher), **Supp. XXII:** 209

"Something New" (Stern), **Supp. IX:** 290

"Something Rich and Strange" (Rash), **Supp. XXVII:** 223–224

Some Things (Berrigan, Padgett, and Brainard), **Supp. XXIV:** 41

Something Said (Sorrentino), **Supp. XXI:** 226, 227, 229, 235

"Something's Going to Happen" (Zinberg), **Supp. XV:** 196

"Something Spurious from the Mindinao Deep" (Stegner), **Supp. IV Part 2:** 605

"Something That Needs Nothing" (July), **Supp. XXIV:** 203

"Something to Believe In" (Pitts), **Supp. XXII:** 280

Something to Declare (Alvarez), **Supp. VII:** 1, 2, 11, 17–19

Something to Remember Me By (Bellow), **Retro. Supp. II:** 32

"Something to Remember Me By" (Bellow), **Retro. Supp. II:** 32

"Something Wicked" (O'Nan), **Supp. XXV:** 148

Something Wicked This Way Comes (Bradbury), **Supp. IV Part 1:** 101, 110–111; **Supp. XXV:** 148

"Something Wild . . ." (T. Williams), **IV:** 381

"Some Thoughts" (McNally), **Supp. XIII:** 207

"Some Thoughts on the Line" (Oliver), **Supp. VII:** 238

"Some Thoughts on the Science of Onanism" (Twain), **Retro. Supp. III:** 262

"Sometimes, Reading" (Stafford), **Supp. XI:** 314

"Sometimes It Just Happens That Way, That's All" (Hinojosa), **Supp. XIX:** 101

"Sometimes I Wonder" (Hughes), **Supp. I Part 1:** 337

Sometimes Mysteriously (Salinas), **Supp. XIII:** 311, **326–328**

"Sometimes Mysteriously" (Salinas), **Supp. XIII:** 328

Some Trees (Ashbery), **Supp. III Part 1:** 3–7, 12

"Some Trees" (Ashbery), **Supp. III Part 1:** 2

"Some Truths About American Readers" (Atherton), **Supp. XXIV:** 24, 27

"Some Views on the Reading and Writing of Short Stories" (Welty), **Retro. Supp. I:** 351

"Somewhere" (Nemerov), **III:** 279–280

"Somewhere Else" (Paley), **Supp. VI:** 227

"Somewhere in Africa" (Sexton), **Supp. II Part 2:** 684–685

Somewhere in the Darkness (Myers), **Supp. XXVII:** 203–204

"Somewhere Is Such a Kingdom" (Ransom), **III:** 492

"Somewhere near Phu Bai" (Komunyakaa), **Supp. XIII:** 123–124

Some Words (Bronk), **Supp. XXI:** 32

"Some Words with a Mummy" (Poe), **III:** 425

"Some Yips and Barks in the Dark" (Snyder), **Supp. VIII:** 291

Sommers, Michael, **Supp. IV Part 2:** 581

Sommers, William, **I:** 387, 388

"Somnambulism" (Brown), **Retro. Supp. III:** 226

"Somnambulisma" (Stevens), **Retro. Supp. I:** 310

"So Much Summer" (Dickinson), **Retro. Supp. I:** 26, 44, 45

"So Much the Worse for Boston" (Lindsay), **Supp. I Part 2:** 398

"So Much Water So Close to Home" (Carver), **Supp. III Part 1:** 143, 146

Son, Cathy, **Supp. X:** 292

"Son, The" (Dove), **Supp. IV Part 1:** 245

"Son and Father" (Pickering), **Supp. XXI:** 197

"Sonata" (Schnackenberg), **Supp. XV:** 259

"Sonata for the Invisible" (Harjo), **Supp. XII:** 228

Sonata for Two Pianos (Bowles), **Supp. IV Part 1:** 83

Son at the Front, A (Wharton), **II:** 183; **IV:** 320; **Retro. Supp. I:** 378; **Retro. Supp. III:** 286

Sondheim, Stephen, **Supp. XII:** 260; **Supp. XVI:** 194

Son Excellence Eugène Rougon (Zola), **III:** 322

Son from Sleep, A (Hadas), **Supp. XXIII:** 114–115

Song (B. Kelly), **Supp. XVII:** 123, **127–130**

"Song" (B. Kelly), **Supp. XVII:** 127

"Song" (Bogan), **Supp. III Part 1:** 57

"Song" (Bryant). *See* "Hunter of the West, The"

"Song" (Dunbar), **Supp. II Part 1:** 199

"Song" (Espaillat), **Supp. XXI:** 106–107

"Song" (Ginsberg), **Supp. II Part 1:** 317

"Song" (Kenyon), **Supp. VII:** 169

"Song" (Rich), **Supp. I Part 2:** 560

"Song" (Wylie), **Supp. I Part 2:** 729

"Song, A" (Creeley), **Supp. IV Part 1:** 145

"Song, The" (Gioia), **Supp. XV:** 117

"Song, The" (Very), **Supp. XXV:** 242

Song and Idea (Eberhart), **I:** 526, 529, 533, 539

"Song: Enlightenment" (X. J. Kennedy), **Supp. XV:** 169

"Song for a Lover Killed in Battle" (J. Schoolcraft), **Supp. XXIII:** 235

Song for Anninho (G. Jones), **Supp. XXIV:** 185, 195

Song for My Father, A: A Play in Two Acts (Budbill), **Supp. XIX:** 3, **15–16**

"Song for Myself and the Deer to Return On" (Harjo), **Supp. XII:** 225

"Song for My Sixtieth Year" (Carruth), **Supp. XVI:** 54

"Song for Occupations, A" (Whitman), **Retro. Supp. I:** 394; **Retro. Supp. III:** 305

"Song for Simeon, A" (Eliot), **Retro. Supp. I:** 64

"Song for the Coming of Smallpox" (Wagoner), **Supp. IX:** 329, 330

"Song for the End of Time" (Gioia), **Supp. XV:** 126–127

"Song for the First People" (Wagoner), **Supp. IX:** 328

"Song for the Last Act" (Bogan), **Supp. III Part 1:** 64

"Song for the Middle of the Night, A" (Wright), **Supp. III Part 2:** 594

"Song for the Rainy Season" (Bishop), **Supp. I Part 1:** 93–94, 96

"Song for the Romeos, A" (Stern), **Supp. IX:** 296

"Song for Woody" (song, Dylan), **Supp. XVIII:** 24

"Song from a Courtyard Window" (Gioia), **Supp. XV:** 119

"Song III" (Taggard), **Supp. XXII:** 284

"Song in the Front Yard, A" (Brooks), **Supp. XVIII:** 181

"Songline of Dawn" (Harjo), **Supp. XII:** 229

"Song: Love in Whose Rich Honor" (Rukeyser), **Supp. VI:** 285

"Song: Now That She Is Here" (Carruth), **Supp. XVI:** 59

"Song of Absinthe Granny, The" (Stone), **Supp. XXVII:** 263

"Song of Advent, A" (Winters), **Supp. II Part 2:** 789

"Song of a Man Who Rushed at the Enemy" (Wagoner), **Supp. IX:** 329, 330

"Song of Courage, A" (Masters), **Supp. I Part 2:** 458

Song of God, The: Bhagavad-Gita (Isherwood and Prabhavananda, trans.), **Supp. XIV:** 156, 157, 164

Song of Hiawatha, The (Longfellow), **II:** 501, 503–504; **Retro. Supp. II:** 155, **159–161,** 162, 163; **Supp. XXIII:** 223, 234–235

"Song of Innocence, A" (Ellison), **Retro. Supp. II:** 126; **Supp. II Part 1:** 248

"Song of My Fiftieth Birthday, The" (Lindsay), **Supp. I Part 2:** 399

"Song of Myself" (Whitman), **II:** 544; **III:** 572, 584, 595; **IV:** 333, 334, 337–339, 340, 341, 342, 344, 348, 349, 351, 405; **Retro. Supp. I:** 388, 389, 395–399, 400; **Retro. Supp. III:** 299, 305, 308; **Supp. IX:** 131, 136, 143, 328, 331; **Supp. V:** 122; **Supp. XIV:** 139; **Supp. XVIII:** 194, 304; **Supp. XXII:** 81

Song of Napalm (Weigl), **Supp. XIX:** 278–282

"Song of Napalm" (Weigl), **Supp. XIX:** 276–277

Song of Russia (film), **Supp. I Part 1:** 281, 294; **Supp. XVII:** 60–61

"Song of Self" (Huncke), **Supp. XIV:** 138–139, 145

Song of Solomon (biblical book), **III:** 118; **IV:** 150

Song of Solomon (Morrison), **Retro. Supp. III:** 184, 189–190; **Supp. III Part 1:** 364, 368, 369, 372, 379; **Supp. XVIII:** 55

Song of Songs (biblical book), **II:** 538; **IV:** 153–154; **Supp. XV:** 221

"Song of the Adoumboulou: 3" (Mackey), **Supp. XXVII:** 157

"Song of the Adoumboulou: 6" (Mackey), **Supp. XXVII:** 157

"Song of the Adoumboulou: 7" (Mackey), **Supp. XXVII:** 157

"Song of the Andoumboulou" (Mackey), **Supp. XXVII:** 153–154, 155, 156

"Song of the Andoumboulou: 1" (Mackey), **Supp. XXVII:** 153–154

"Song of the Andoumboulou: 8" (Mackey), **Supp. XXVII:** 154

"Song of the Andoumboulou: 16" (Mackey), **Supp. XXVII:** 155

"Song of the Andoumboulou: 26" (Mackey), **Supp. XXVII:** 155

"Song of the Answerer" (Whitman), **Retro. Supp. I:** 393, 399

Song of the Cardinal, The (Stratton-Porter), **Supp. XX: 217, 218, 219**

"Song of the Chattahoochee, The" (Lanier), **Supp. I Part 1:** 365, 368

"Song of the Degrees, A" (Pound), **III:** 466

"Song of the Drunkard" (Ferry), **Supp. XXIV:** 153, 162

"Song of the Dryads" (Taggard), **Supp. XXII:** 272

"Song of the Exposition" (Whitman), **IV:** 332

"Song of the Gavilan" (Leopold), **Supp. XIV:** 189

"Song of the Gourd" (Wright), **Supp. XV:** 348–349

"Song of the Greek Amazon" (Bryant), **Supp. I Part 1:** 168

Song of the Lark, The (Cather), **I:** 312, 319–321, 323; **Retro. Supp. I:** 1, 3, 7, **9–11,** 13, 19, 20; **Retro. Supp. III:** 18, 23, 30

"Song of the Okogis, or Frog in Spring"(J. Schoolcraft), **Supp. XXIII:** 232, 233, 235

"Song of the Open Road" (McGrath), **Supp. X:** 127

"Song of the Open Road" (Whitman), **IV:** 340–341, 414; **Retro. Supp. I:** 400; **Retro. Supp. III:** 305; **Supp. III:** 265

"Song of the Redwood Tree" (Whitman), **IV:** 348

"Song of the Scullery" (McCarriston), **Supp. XIV:** 272

"Song of the Sky Loom" (traditional Tewa poem), **Supp. IV Part 1:** 325

"Song of the Son" (Toomer), **Supp. III Part 2:** 482–483; **Supp. IX:** 313

"Song of the Sower, The" (Bryant), **Supp. I Part 1:** 169

"Song of the Stars" (Bryant), **Supp. I Part 1:** 163

"Song of the Swamp-Robin, The" (Frederic), **II:** 138

"Song of the Vermonters, The" (Whittier), **Supp. I Part 2:** 692

"Song of Three Smiles" (Merwin), **Supp. III Part 1:** 344

"Song of Wandering Aengus, The" (Yeats), **IV:** 271; **Retro. Supp. I:** 342, 350

"Song of Welcome" (Brodsky), **Supp. VIII:** 32

"Song on Captain Barney's Victory" (Freneau), **Supp. II Part 1:** 261

"Song/Poetry and Language-Expression and Perception" (Ortiz), **Supp. IV Part 2:** 500, 508

"Song Rehearsal, The" (Stallings), **Supp. XXV:** 233

"Song: 'Rough Winds Do Shake the Darling Buds of May' " (Simpson), **Supp. IX:** 268

Songs (Boyce), **Supp. XXI:** 9

Songs and Satires (Masters), **Supp. I Part 2:** 465–466

Songs and Sonnets (L. P. Smith), **Supp. XIV:** 341

Songs and Sonnets (Masters), **Supp. I Part 2:** 455, 459, 461, 466

"Songs for a Colored Singer" (Bishop), **Supp. I Part 1:** 80, 85

Songs for a Summer's Day (A Sonnet Cycle) (MacLeish), **III:** 3

Songs for Eve (MacLeish), **III:** 3, 19

"Songs for Eve" (MacLeish), **III:** 19

"Songs for My Father" (Komunyakaa), **Supp. XIII:** 128

Songs for the Missing (O'Nan), **Supp. XXV:** 143, 148, 150

Songs for the Unborn Second Baby (Notley), **Supp. XXII:** 228

"Songs for Two Seasons" (C. Frost), **Supp. XV:** 95–96

Songs from a Room (album, Cohen), **Supp. XXVII:** 54

Songs from This Earth on Turtle's Back: Contemporary American Indian Poetry (Bruchac, ed.), **Supp. IV Part 1:** 320, 328

"Songs of a Housewife" (Rawlings), **Supp. X:** 221–222

"Songs of Billy Bathgate, The" (Doctorow), **Supp. IV Part 1:** 230

Songs of Innocence (Blake), **Supp. I Part 2:** 708

Songs of Jamaica (McKay), **Supp. X:** 131, 133

Songs of Leonard Cohen (album, Cohen), **Supp. XXVII:** 54, 59

Songs of Love and Hate (album, Cohen), **Supp. XXVII:** 54

"Songs of Maximus, The" (Olson), **Supp. II Part 2:** 567

"Songs of Parting" (Whitman), **IV:** 348

Songs of the Doomed (Thompson), **Supp. XXIV:** 283

Songs of the North: A Sigurd Olson Reader (Mosher, ed.), **Supp. XXII:** 218

Songs of the Sierras (J. Miller), **I:** 459
Songs of Three Centuries (Whittier and Larcom, eds.), **Supp. XIII:** 142
"Song to David" (Smart), **III:** 534
"Song to No Music, A" (Brodsky), **Supp. VIII:** 26
"Song V" (Taggard), **Supp. XXII:** 284
Song Yet Sung (McBride), **Supp. XXVI:** 194, 199–201, 204
Soniat, Katherine, **Supp. XXI:** 245
Sonneschein, Rosa, **Retro. Supp. II:** 65
"Sonnet" (Rukeyser), **Supp. VI:** 284
"Sonnet, A" (Very), **Supp. XXV:** 242
"Sonnet Crown for Two Voices" (Bierds), **Supp. XVII:** 35
"Sonnet"(J. Schoolcraft), **Supp. XXIII:** 229
"Sonnet of Good Cheer, A" (Howard), **Supp. XXVII:** 118–119
"Sonnets" (Carruth), **Supp. XVI:** 56
Sonnets, The (Berrigan), **Supp. XXII:** 224; **Supp. XXIV:** 33, 34, 35, 37, 38–41, 45
"Sonnets at Christmas" (Tate), **IV:** 135
Sonnets to Duse and Other Poems (Teasdale), **Supp. XXVII:** 287
Sonnets to Orpheus (Rilke), **Supp. XV:** 222; **Supp. XXIV:** 38
"Sonnet to a Negro in Harlem" (H. Johnson), **Supp. XXVI:** 166, 167–170
"Sonnet—To Science" (Poe), **Retro. Supp. III:** 231
"Sonnet-To Zante" (Poe), **III:** 421
"Sonnet XV" (Berrigan), **Supp. XXIV:** 38–39, 44
Sonny: A Christmas Gift (Stuart), **Supp. XXVIII:** 226, 229, 235–236
"Sonny's Blues" (Baldwin), **Retro. Supp. II:** 7, 8, 10, 14; **Supp. I Part 1:** 58–59, 63, 67; **Supp. XI:** 288; **Supp. XXVII:** 201
Sonny's Father (Stuart), **Supp. XXVIII:** 226, 236, 237
Son of Laughter, The: A Novel (Buechner), **Supp. XII:** 54
Son of Perdition, The (Cozzens), **I:** 359–360, 377, 378, 379
Son of the Circus, A (Irving), **Supp. VI:** 165, 166, **176–179**
Son of the Gamblin' Man: The Youth of an Artist (Sandoz), **Supp. XXIV:** 244, **256–257**
"Son of the Gods, A" (Bierce), **I:** 202
Son of the Morning (Oates), **Supp. II Part 2:** 518, 519, 520–522
Son of the Morning Star: Custer and the Little Bighorn (Connell), **Supp. XIV:** 80, 82, 97
"Son of the Romanovs, A" (Simpson), **Supp. IX:** 273–274
"Son of the White Wolf" (Howard), **Supp. XXVII:** 121
Son of the Wolf, The (London), **II:** 465, 469
"Son of the Wolfman" (Chabon), **Supp. XI:** 76
"Sonrisas" (Mora), **Supp. XIII:** 216, 219
Sons (Buck), **Supp. II Part 1:** 117–118
"Sons" (Teasdale), **Supp. XXVII:** 295
Sons and Lovers (Lawrence), **III:** 27

Sons of Kai, The: The Story the Indian Told (Beston), **Supp. XXVI:** 33
Sontag, Kate, **Supp. XV:** 104
Sontag, Susan, **IV:** 13, 14; **Retro. Supp. II:** 279; **Supp. I Part 2:** 423; **Supp. III Part 2: 451–473; Supp. XIV:** 14, 15, 95–96, 167; **Supp. XVI:** 201, 204, 206; **Supp. XX: 205; Supp. XXI:** 243; **Supp. XXVI:** 45
"Soon" (Munro), **Supp. XXVII:** 193, 194
"Soonest Mended" (Ashbery), **Supp. III Part 1:** 1, 13
"Sootfall and Fallout" (White), **Supp. I Part 2:** 671
Sophisticates, The (Atherton), **Supp. XXIV:** 20, 25
Sophocles, **I:** 274; **II:** 291, 385, 577; **III:** 145, 151, 152, 153, 159, 398, 476, 478, 609, 613; **IV:** 291, 363, 368, 370; **Supp. I Part 1:** 153, 284; **Supp. I Part 2:** 491; **Supp. V:** 97; **Supp. VIII:** 332; **Supp. XV:** 265, 266
"Sophronsiba" (Bourne), **I:** 221
Sorayam, Aram, **Supp. XXII:** 25
Sorby, Angela, **Supp. XXIII:** 132
Sorcerer's Apprentice, The: Tales and Conjurations (C. Johnson), **Supp. VI: 192–193,** 194
"Sorcerer's Eye, The" (Nemerov), **III:** 283
Sordello (Browning), **III:** 467, 469, 470
"Sordid? Good God!" (Williams), **Retro. Supp. II:** 334
So Red the Rose (Young), **Supp. XXII:** 190, 193
"Sorghum" (Mason), **Supp. VIII:** 146
Sorkin, Adam, **Supp. XXIV:** 178
Sorokin, Pitirim, **Supp. I Part 2:** 679
Sorrentino, Christopher, **Supp. XVIII:** 148
Sorrentino, Gilbert, **Retro. Supp. I:** 426; **Supp. IV Part 1:** 286; **Supp. XII:** 139; **Supp. XXI: 225–241; Supp. XXII:** 261; **Supp. XXVI:** 26; **Supp. XXVII:** 18
Sorrento (Notley), **Supp. XXII:** 231
"Sorrow" (Komunyakaa), **Supp. XIII:** 119
Sorrow Dance, The (Levertov), **Supp. III Part 1:** 279–280, 283
"Sorrowful Guest, A" (Jewett), **Retro. Supp. II:** 137
Sorrows of Fat City, The: A Selection of Literary Essays and Reviews (Garrett), **Supp. VII:** 111
Sorrows of Young Werther, The (Goethe), **Supp. XI:** 169; **Supp. XX: 234, 236**
Sorrows of Young Werther, The (Goethe; Bogan and Mayer, trans.), **Supp. III Part 1:** 63
"Sorry Fugu" (Boyle), **Supp. XX:** 19
"Sorting Facts; or, Nineteen Ways of Looking at Marker" (Howe), **Supp. IV Part 2:** 434, 436
"Sort of Song, A" (W. C. Williams), **Supp. XVII:** 243
"S O S" (Baraka), **Supp. II Part 1:** 50
"So Sassafras" (Olson), **Supp. II Part 2:** 574

So Short a Time (Gelb), **Supp. XXVIII:** 40
"So There" (Creeley), **Supp. IV Part 1:** 157
"So This Is Nebraska" (Kooser), **Supp. XIX:** 120
Sotirov, Vasil, **Supp. IX:** 152
Soto, Gary, **Supp. IV Part 2:** 545; **Supp. V:** 180; **Supp. XI:** 270; **Supp. XIII:** 313, 315, 316, 320, 323; **Supp. XV:** 73; **Supp. XXV:** 130
"Soto Thinking of the Ocean" (Salinas), **Supp. XIII:** 321
"Sotto Voce" (Kunitz), **Supp. III Part 1:** 265
Sot-Weed Factor, The (Barth), **I:** 122, 123, 125, 129, 130, 131–134, 135; **Supp. XXII:** 259
"Soul" (Ferry), **Supp. XXIV:** 162
Soul, The (Brooks), **I:** 244
Soul and Body of John Brown, The (Rukeyser), **Supp. VI:** 273
Soul Barnacles: Ten More Years with Ray (Gallagher; Simon, ed.), **Supp. XXIV:** 166, 167, 171, 172
Soul Clap Hands and Sing (Marshall), **Supp. XI:** 276, 278, **280–282**
Soul Expeditions (Singer). *See Shosha* (Singer)
Soul Gone Home (Hughes), **Retro. Supp. I:** 203; **Supp. I Part 1:** 328
"Soul inside the Sentence, The" (Gass), **Supp. VI:** 88
Soul Is Here for Its Own Joy, The (Bly, ed.), **Supp. IV Part 1:** 74
Soul of Man under Socialism, The (Wilde), **Supp. IX:** 134–135
"Soul of Spain, The \[In the manner of Gertrude Stein\]" (Hemingway), **Supp. XX: 74**
Soul of the Far East, The (P. Lowell), **II:** 513
"Soul on Bench" (Halliday), **Supp. XIX:** 91
Soul on Ice (Cleaver), **Retro. Supp. II:** 12, 13
"Souls Belated" (Wharton), **Retro. Supp. I:** 364; **Retro. Supp. III:** 278–279, 287
"Soul selects her own Society, The" (Dickinson), **Retro. Supp. I:** 37
Souls of Black Folk, The (Du Bois), **Supp. II Part 1:** 33, 40, 160, 168–170, 176, 183; **Supp. IV Part 1:** 164; **Supp. IX:** 305, 306; **Supp. X:** 133; **Supp. XIII:** 185, 238, 243
Souls of Black Folk. The (Du Bois), **Supp. XX: 102**
"Sound, The" (Olds), **Supp. X:** 214
Sound and Beauty (Hwang), **Supp. XXI:** 146
"Sound and Fury" (O. Henry), **Supp. II Part 1:** 402
Sound and the Fury, The (Faulkner), **I:** 480; **II:** 55, 57, 58–60, 73; **III:** 237; **IV:** 100, 101, 104; **Retro. Supp. I:** 73, 75, 77, 82, **83–84**, 86, 88, 89, 90, 91, 92; **Retro. Supp. III:** 74, 78–80, 82, 84; **Supp. IX:** 103; **Supp. VIII:** 215; **Supp. X:** 44; **Supp. XII:** 33;

Supp. XIV: 12; Supp. XVII: 138; Supp. XVIII: 84; Supp. XXVII: 11

"Sound Bites" (Alvarez), Supp. VII: 11

Sound I Listened For, The (Francis), Supp. IX: 78–79, 87

"Soundless Trumpet, The" (Antin), Supp. XX: 12

"Sound Mind, Sound Body" (R. Lowell), II: 554

Sound of a Voice, The (Hwang), Supp. XXI: 146

"Sound of Distant Thunder, A" (Elkin), Supp. VI: 42–43, 44

"Sound of Light, The" (Merwin), Supp. III Part 1: 356

Sound of Mountain Water, The (Stegner), Supp. IV Part 2: 595, 596, 598, 600, 608

"Sound of Talking" (Purdy), Supp. VII: 270

Sounds of Poetry (television special, Moyers), Supp. XXIII: 139

Sounds of Poetry, The (Pinsky), Supp. VI: 236, 247, 248; Supp. XXIII: 124

Sound the Stars Make Rushing Through the Sky, The: The Writings of Jane Johnston Schoolcraft (Parker, ed.), Supp. XXIII: 223–224, 227, 228

Soupault, Philippe, IV: 288, 404; Retro. Supp. II: 85, 321, 324

Source (Doty), Supp. XI: 121, **134–137**

"Source" (Doty), Supp. XI: 136

"Source, The" (Olds), Supp. X: 211

"Source, The" (Porter), III: 443

Source of Light, The (Price), Supp. VI: **262,** 266

"Sources" (Rich), Retro. Supp. III: 250

"Sources of Soviet Conduct, The" (Kennan), Supp. VIII: 241

Sour Grapes (W. C. Williams), Retro. Supp. I: 418

"Sour Grapes"(Moraga), Supp. XXIII: 202

"Sourwood Nocturne" (Skloot), Supp. XX: **202**

"South" (Levis), Supp. XI: 266

"South" (Trethewey), Supp. XXI: 247, 256

"South, The" (Hughes), Supp. I Part 1: 321

South American Journey (W. Frank), Supp. XX: **79**

"Southampton Variations"(O'Hara), Supp. XXIII: 212

"Southbound on the Freeway" (Swenson), Supp. IV Part 2: 643

South Dakota Guidebook, The (C. Baxter), Supp. XVII: 15

Southern, Terry, Supp. IV Part 1: 379; Supp. V: 40, 201; Supp. XI: 293–310; Supp. XVI: 230

Southern Cross, The (Wright), Supp. V: 332, 342

"Southern Cross, The" (Wright), Supp. V: 338

"Southerner's Problem, The" (Du Bois), Supp. II Part 1: 168

"Southern Girl" (Zelda Fitzgerald), Supp. IX: 71

"Southern Gothic" (Trethewey), Supp. XXI: 256

"Southern History" (Trethewey), Supp. XXI: 256, 257

"Southern Mode of the Imagination, A" (Tate), IV: 120

"Southern Road, A" (H. Johnson), Supp. XXVI: 165, 167, 172, 174

"Southern Romantic, A" (Tate), Supp. I Part 1: 373

"Southern Sojourn, A" (Hoffman), Supp. XVIII: 87

Southern Terry, Supp. XIV: 82

Southern Writers: A New Biographical Dictionary (Flora, Vogel, and Giemza, eds.), Supp. XXVI: 148

Southey, Robert, II: 304, 502; Supp. I Part 1: 154; Supp. XXIV: 74

"South Lingers On, The" (R. Fisher), Supp. XIX: 69–70

South Moon Under (Rawlings), Supp. X: **225–226,** 229, 233

South Pacific Affair (Lacy), Supp. XV: 206

Southpaw, The (Harris), II: 424–425

"South Sangamon" (Cisneros), Supp. VII: 66

"South State Street: Chicago" (Bodenheim), Supp. XXV: 22

South to a Very Old Place (Murray), Supp. XIX: **151–153**

Southwell, Robert, IV: 151

Southwestern Homelands (Kittredge), Supp. XXVI: 188

Southwick, Marcia, Supp. XI: 259

Southworth, E. D. E. N, Retro. Supp. I: 246

Souvenir of the Ancient World, Selected Poems of Carlos Drummond de Andrade (Strand, trans.), Supp. IV Part 2: 630

Sovereign Bones: New Native American Writing (Gansworth, ed.), Supp. XXVI: 113

Sovereignty and Goodness of God, The (Rowlandson), Supp. XXVIII: 170

"Sow" (Plath), Supp. I Part 2: 537

"Sowing and Reaping in *Furors Die*" (Nostrandt), Supp. XVIII: 80–81

Soyinka, Wole, Supp. XX: **100**

"Space" (Brockmeier), Supp. XXII: 51

Space between Our Footsteps, The: Poems and Paintings from the Middle East (Nye, ed.), Supp. XIII: 280

"Space Quale, The" (James), II: 349

"Spaces Between, The" (Kingsolver), Supp. VII: 209

"Spaceships Have Landed" (Munro), Supp. XXVII: 191

"Space Where Sex Should Be, The: Toward a Definition of the Black Literary Tradition" (Nelson), Supp. XVIII: 172

Spack, Ruth, Supp. XXV: 278

Spackman, Peter, Supp. XVI: 221

Spacks, Patricia, Supp. XVI: 251

"Spain" (Auden), Supp. II Part 1: 12–13, 14

"Spain in Fifty-Ninth Street" (White), Supp. I Part 2: 677

Spanier, Sandra, Supp. XXIV: 51, 64

"Spanish-American War Play" (Crane), I: 422

Spanish Ballads (Merwin, trans.), Supp. III Part 1: 347

Spanish Bayonet (Benét), Supp. XI: 45, 47

Spanish Earth, The (film), Retro. Supp. I: 184

Spanish Love (Rinehart), Supp. XXV: 195

Spanish Papers and Other Miscellanies (Irving), II: 314

"Spanish Revolution, The" (Bryant), Supp. I Part 1: 153, 168

Spanish Student, The (Longfellow), II: 489, 506; Retro. Supp. II: 165

"Spanish Winter" (Egan), Supp. XIX: 52

Spanking the Maid (Coover), Supp. V: 47, 48, 49, 52

Spare Change (Parker), Supp. XIX: 186–187

Spargo, John, Supp. I Part 1: 13

"Spark, The" (Wharton), Retro. Supp. I: 381

"Sparkles from the Wheel" (Whitman), IV: 348

Sparks, Debra, Supp. X: 177

Sparks, Jared, Supp. I Part 1: 156; Supp. XXIV: 71

"Sparrow" (Berry), Supp. X: 31

Sparrow, Henry, III: 587

Sparrow, Mrs. Henry, III: 587

"Sparrow's Gate, The" (B. Kelly), Supp. XVII: 133

Spaulding, William, Supp. XVI: 106

"Spawning Run, The" (Humphrey), Supp. IX: 95

"Speak, Gay Memory" (Kirp), Supp. XI: 129

"Speak, Hoyt-Schermerhorn" (Lethem), Supp. XVIII: 148

Speak, Memory (Nabokov), III: 247–250, 252; Retro. Supp. I: 264, 265, 266, 267, 268, 277; Supp. XVI: 148

Speak, Memory (V. Nabakov), Supp. XVII: 47

Speaking and Language (Shapiro), Supp. II Part 2: 721

Speaking for Nature: How Literary Naturalists from Henry Thoreau to Rachel Carson Have Shaped America (Brooks), Supp. IX: 31

Speaking for Ourselves: American Ethnic Writing (Faderman and Bradshaw, eds.), Supp. XIII: 313

Speaking of Accidents (Everwine), Supp. XV: 75, 88

"Speaking of Accidents" (Everwine), Supp. XV: 88–89

"Speaking of Counterweights" (White), Supp. I Part 2: 669

Speaking of Faith: Global Perspectives on Women, Religion, and Social Change (Eck and Jain, eds.), Supp. XXVIII: 60

Speaking of Literature and Society (Trilling), Supp. III Part 2: 494, 496, 499

"Speaking of Love" (Gioia), **Supp. XV:** 124–125

Speaking of Race, Speaking of Sex: Hate Speech, Civil Rights, and Civil Liberties (H. L. Gates, Griffin, Lively, and Strossen), **Supp. XX:** 111

Speaking on Stage (Kolin and Kullman, eds.), **Supp. IX:** 145

Speaking on Stage: Interviews with Contemporary American Playwrights (Balakian), **Supp. XV:** 327

"Speaking Passions" (Kitchen), **Supp. XV:** 215

Speak of the Devil (Holding), **Supp. XXII:** 127

Speak What We Feel (Not What We Ought to Say): Reflections on Literature and Faith (Buechner), **Supp. XII:** 57

Spear, Roberta, **Supp. V:** 180; **Supp. XV:** 73

"Spear and Fang" (Howard), **Supp. XXVII:** 116

"Special Kind of Fantasy, A: James Dickey on the Razor's Edge" (Niflis), **Supp. IV Part 1:** 175

"Special Pleading" (Lanier), **Supp. I Part 1:** 364

"Special Problems in Teaching Leslie Marmon Silko's *Ceremony*" (Gunn Allen), **Supp. IV Part 1:** 333

Special Providence, A (Yates), **Supp. XI:** 342, **344–345**

"Special Time, a Special School, A" (Knowles), **Supp. XII:** 236

Special View of History, The (Olson), **Supp. II Part 2:** 566, 569, 572

Specimen Days (Whitman), **IV:** 338, 347, 348, 350; **Retro. Supp. I:** 408

Specimens of the American Poets, **Supp. I Part 1:** 155

"Speckled Trout" (Rash), **Supp. XXVII:** 222

"Spectacles, The" (Poe), **III:** 425

Spectator Bird, The (Stegner), **Supp. IV Part 2:** 599, 604, 606, 611–612

Spector, Herman, **Supp. XXV:** 26; **Supp. XXVI:** 143

Spector, Robert, **Supp. XIII:** 87

Spectra: A Book of Poetic Experiments (Bynner and Ficke), **Supp. XV:** 43

"Spectre Bridegroom, The" (Irving), **II:** 304

"Spectre Pig, The" (Holmes), **Supp. I Part 1:** 302

"Speculating Woman" (X. J. Kennedy), **Supp. XV:** 168

"Speech Sounds" (O. Butler), **Supp. XIII:** 61, **70**

"Speech to a Crowd" (MacLeish), **III:** 16

"Speech to the Detractors" (MacLeish), **III:** 16

"Speech to the Young" (Brooks), **Supp. III Part 1:** 79, 86

"Speech to Those Who Say Comrade" (MacLeish), **III:** 16

Speedboat (Adler), **Supp. X:** 171

Speed of Darkness, The (Rukeyser), **Supp. VI:** 274, 281

Speed Queen, The (O'Nan), **Supp. XXV:** 142, 144

Speed-the-Plow (Mamet), **Supp. XIV:** 241, 246, 249, 250, 251

"Speedy Gonzales Was the Fastest Mouse in Mexico" (P. N. Warren as Kilina), **Supp. XX: 262**

Speilberg, Steven, **Supp. XI:** 234

Speirs, Logan, **Supp. XIX:** 282

"Spell" (Francis), **Supp. IX:** 87

"Spell, The" (Peacock), **Supp. XIX:** 198, 200

Spellbound (screenplay, Hecht), **Supp. XXVII:** 93

"Spell for the Manufacture & Use of a Magic Carpet" (Hull), **Supp. XXI:** 132–133, 139, 141

Spelling Dictionary, A (Rowson), **Supp. XV:** 244

Spence, Thomas, **Supp. I Part 2:** 518

Spence + Lila (Mason), **Supp. VIII:** 133, **143–145**

Spencer, Edward, **Supp. I Part 1:** 357, 360

Spencer, Elizabeth, **Supp. XXVII:** 13

Spencer, Herbert, **I:** 515; **II:** 345, 462–463, 480, 483, 536; **III:** 102, 315; **IV:** 135; **Retro. Supp. II:** 60, 65, 93, 98; **Supp. I Part 1:** 368; **Supp. I Part 2:** 635; **Supp. XXVII:** 126; **Supp. XXVIII:** 112

Spencer, Sharon, **Supp. X:** 185, 186, 195, 196

Spencer, Theodore, **I:** 433; **Supp. III Part 1:** 2

Spender, Natasha, **Supp. IV Part 1:** 119, 127, 134

Spender, Stephen, **II:** 371; **III:** 504, 527; **Retro. Supp. I:** 216; **Retro. Supp. II:** 243, 244; **Supp. I Part 2:** 536; **Supp. II Part 1:** 11; **Supp. IV Part 1:** 82, 134; **Supp. IV Part 2:** 440; **Supp. X:** 116

"Spending the New Year with the Man from Receiving at Sears"(Wakoski), **Supp. XXVIII:** 267

Spengler, Oswald, **I:** 255, 270; **II:** 7, 577; **III:** 172, 176; **Retro. Supp. II:** 324; **Supp. I Part 2:** 647

Spens, Sir Patrick, **Supp. I Part 2:** 404

Spenser, Edmund, **I:** 62; **III:** 77, 78, 89; **IV:** 155, 453; **Retro. Supp. I:** 62; **Supp. I Part 1:** 98, 152, 369; **Supp. I Part 2:** 422, 719; **Supp. XXIV:** 159

"Spenser's Ireland" (Moore), **III:** 211, 212

"Spermaceti Papers"(Lippard), **Supp. XXIII:** 178

S*PeRM**K*T (Mullen), **Supp. XXVII:** 169, 170–171

Sperry, Margaret, **Supp. IV Part 1:** 169

Spheres of Existence (C. L. R. James), **Supp. XXI:** 172

Sphere: The Form of a Motion (Ammons), **Supp. VII:** 24, 32, 33, 35, 36

"Sphinx" (Hayden), **Supp. II Part 1:** 373

Spice-Box of Earth, The (Cohen), **Supp. XXVII:** 54

"Spiced Plums" (Ríos), **Supp. IV Part 2:** 553

Spickard, Paul, **Supp. XXI:** 149

"Spider and the Ghost of the Fly, The" (Lindsay), **Supp. I Part 2:** 375

Spider Bay (Van Vechten), **Supp. II Part 2:** 746

"Spider Heart, The" (Peacock), **Supp. XIX:** 200

"Spiders" (Schwartz), **Supp. II Part 2:** 665

Spider's House, The (Bowles), **Supp. IV Part 1:** 87–89, 90, 91

Spider Woman's Granddaughters: Traditional Tales and Contemporary Writing by Native American Women (Gunn Allen, ed.), **Supp. IV Part 1:** 320, 326, 332–333; **Supp. IV Part 2:** 567

Spiegel, Sam, **Supp. XVIII:** 251, 252

Spiegelman, Art, **Supp. XVII:** 48

Spiegelman, Willard, **Supp. XI:** 126

Spielberg, Steven, **Supp. XXI:** 154

Spillane, Mickey, **Supp. IV Part 2:** 469, 472; **Supp. XV:** 200; **Supp. XVIII:** 236, 237

"Spillcorn" (Rash), **Supp. XXVII:** 222

Spiller, Robert E., **I:** 241; **Supp. I Part 1:** 104

Spillers, Hortense, **Supp. XX: 109**

"Spillikins: Gregor Mendel at the Table" (Bierds), **Supp. XVII:** 34–35

Spillville (Hampl), **Supp. XXII:** 98

Spillway (Barnes), **Supp. III Part 1:** 44

Spingarn, Amy, **Supp. I Part 1:** 325, 326

Spingarn, Joel, **I:** 266; **Supp. I Part 1:** 325

Spinoza, Baruch, **I:** 493; **II:** 590, 593; **III:** 600; **IV:** 5, 7, 11, 12, 17; **Retro. Supp. II:** 300; **Supp. I Part 1:** 274; **Supp. I Part 2:** 643; **Supp. XVI:** 184

"Spinoza of Market Street, The" (Singer), **IV:** 12–13; **Retro. Supp. II:** 307

"Spinster" (Plath), **Supp. I Part 2:** 536

"Spinster's Tale, A" (Taylor), **Supp. V:** 314–315, 316–317, 319, 323

Spiotta, Dana, **Supp. XXVIII: 205–223**

Spiral of Memory, The: Interviews (Coltelli, ed.), **Supp. XII:** 215

"'Spiral Staircase, The': Apples vs. Oragnes"(Wakoski), **Supp. XXVIII:** 272

Spires, Elizabeth, **Supp. X:** 8

"Spire Song" (Bowles), **Supp. IV Part 1:** 80

Spirit and Flame: An Anthology of African American Poetry (Gilyard, ed.), **Supp. XXI:** 246

Spirit and the Flesh, The: Sexual Diversity in American Indian Culture (W. L. Williams), **Supp. IV Part 1:** 330

"Spirit Birth" (Cullen), **Supp. IV Part 1:** 168

Spirit Brides (Gibran). See *Nymphs in the Valley*

"Spirit"(Goodman), **Supp. XXVIII:** 86–87, 91

Spirit in Man, The (Jung), **Supp. IV Part 1:** 68

"Spirit in Me, The" (Hoffman), **Supp. XVIII:** 87

"Spirit Made Visible" (art exhibit), **Supp. XXII:** 180

Spirit of Culver (West), **IV:** 287

Spirit of Labor, The (Hapgood), **Supp. XVII:** 96, 99, 101–102; **Supp. XXI:** 4

Spirit of Romance, The (Pound), **III:** 470; **Retro. Supp. I:** 286

Spirit of the Ghetto, The: Studies of the Jewish Quarter of New York (Hapgood), **Supp. XVII:** 96, 101, 103, 106

Spirit of Youth and the City Streets, The (Addams), **Supp. I Part 1:** 6–7, 12–13, 16, 17, 19

"Spirits" (Bausch), **Supp. VII:** 46–47

Spirits, and Other Stories (Bausch), **Supp. VII:** 46–47, 54

"Spirit Says, You Are Nothing, The" (Levis), **Supp. XI:** 265–266

Spirits Rebellious (al-Arwá&hudot; al-Mutamarrida) (Gibran), **Supp. XX:** 115, 124, 125

Spiritual Adventures (Symons), **Supp. XX:** 239

Spiritual Conflict, The (Scupoli), **IV:** 156

Spiritual Exercises, The (Loyola), **IV:** 151; **Supp. XI:** 162

"Spiritual Manifestation, A" (Whittier), **Supp. I Part 2:** 699

"Spirituals and Neo-Spirituals" (Hurston), **Supp. VI:** 152–153

"Spirituals and Non-Spirituals" (Hurston), **Retro. Supp. III:** 129

Spits, Ellen Handler, **Supp. XII:** 166

"Spitzbergen Tales" (Crane), **I:** 409, 415, 423

Spitzer, Philip, **Supp. XIV:** 21

Splay Anthem (Mackey), **Supp. XXVII:** 152, 155–156, 159

"Spleen" (Eliot), **I:** 569, 573–574

Spleen de Paris, Le (Baudelaire), **Supp. XIV:** 337

Splendid Drunken Twenties, The (Van Vechten), **Supp. II Part 2:** 739–744

Splendide-Hôtel (Sorrentino), **Supp. XXI:** 233

Splendid Offer, A (King), **Supp. XXVIII:** 120

Splendid Table, The (radio show), **Supp. XXIII:** 138

Splendor in the Grass (screenplay, Inge), **Supp. XXV:** 93, 95, 102–103, 104

"Splinters" (Bukiet), **Supp. XVII:** 47

"Split at the Root: An Essay on Jewish Identity" (Rich), **Retro. Supp. III:** 241, 251

"Split Infinitive" (Pickering), **Supp. XXI:** 204

"Splitting an Order" (Kooser), **Supp. XIX:** 128–129

"Splittings" (Rich), **Retro. Supp. III:** 249; **Supp. I Part 2:** 570–571

"Splitting Wood at Six Above" (Kumin), **Supp. IV Part 2:** 449

Spofford, Harriet Prescott, **Supp. XIII:** 143

Spoils of Poynton, The (James), **I:** 463; **Retro. Supp. I:** 229–230

Spoken Page, The (Nye), **Supp. XIII:** 274

"Spokes" (Auster), **Supp. XII:** 23

Spokesmen (Whipple), **II:** 456

Spook Sonata, The (Strindberg), **III:** 387, 392

Spooky Art, The: A Book about Writing (Mailer), **Retro. Supp. II:** 214

"Spoon, The" (Simic), **Supp. VIII:** 275

Spoon River Anthology (Masters), **I:** 106; **III:** 579; **Supp. I Part 2:** 454, 455, 456, 460–465, 466, 467, 471, 472, 473, 476; **Supp. IX:** 306; **Supp. XIV:** 282–283; **Supp. XIX:** 121; **Supp. XXII:** 282; **Supp. XXVII:** 211, 290

Sport and a Pastime, A (Salter), **Supp. IX:** 254–257; **Supp. XVI:** 237

Sporting Club, The (McGuane), **Supp. VIII:** 43

Sport of the Gods, The (Dunbar), **Supp. II Part 1:** 193, 200, 207, 214–217

Sports Illustrated Training with Weights (Parker and Marsh), **Supp. XIX:** 187

"Sportsman Born and Bred, A" (Plimpton), **Supp. XVI:** 241

Sportsman's Sketches, A (Turgenev), **I:** 106; **IV:** 277

Sportswriter, The (Ford), **Supp. V:** 57, 58, 62–67

"Spotted Horses" (Faulkner), **IV:** 260; **Retro. Supp. III:** 85

Sprague, Morteza, **Retro. Supp. II:** 115

Spratling, William, **II:** 56; **Retro. Supp. I:** 80

Sprawl trilogy (W. Gibson), **Supp. XVI:** 117, 122, 124

"Spray, The" (Lethem), **Supp. XVIII:** 148

"Spray Paint King, The" (Dove), **Supp. IV Part 1:** 252–253

Spreading Fires (Knowles), **Supp. XII:** 249

Sprigge, Elizabeth, **IV:** 31

"Spring" (Kooser), **Supp. XIX:** 126

"Spring" (Millay), **III:** 126

"Spring" (Mora), **Supp. XIII:** 217

"Spring 1967" (Carruth), **Supp. XVI:** 55

Spring and All (W. C. Williams), **Retro. Supp. I:** 412, 418, 418–420, 427, 430, 431

"Spring and All" (W. C. Williams), **Retro. Supp. I:** 419

Spring Awakening (Wedeking, trans. Franzen), **Supp. XX: 85**

"Spring Break-Up" (Carruth), **Supp. XVI:** 56

"Spring Bulletin" (Allen), **Supp. XV:** 15

Springer's Progress (Markson), **Supp. XVII: 141–142,** 143, 146

"Spring Evening" (Farrell), **II:** 45

"Spring Evening" (Kenyon), **Supp. VII:** 173

"Springfield Magical" (Lindsay), **Supp. I Part 2:** 379

Spring in New Hampshire and Other Poems (McKay), **Supp. X:** 131, 135

"Spring in the Naugatuck Valley" (Teasdale), **Supp. XXVII:** 294

"Spring Lizards" (Rash), **Supp. XXVII:** 219

"Spring Notes from Robin Hill" (Carruth), **Supp. XVI:** 48

"Spring Pastoral" (Wylie), **Supp. I Part 2:** 707

"Spring Pools" (Frost), **II:** 155; **Retro. Supp. I:** 137

"Spring Snow" (Matthews), **Supp. IX:** 160

"SPRING SONG" (Baraka), **Supp. II Part 1:** 60

Springsteen, Bruce, **Supp. VIII:** 143

"Spring Strains" (W. C. Williams), **Retro. Supp. I:** 416

Spring Tides (Morison), **Supp. I Part 2:** 494

Springtime and Harvest (Sinclair), **Supp. V:** 280

"Springtime for You" (Halliday), **Supp. XIX:** 87

Springtime in Britain (Teale), **Supp. XXVIII:** 251

"Spring Torrents" (Teasdale), **Supp. XXVII:** 293

Spruance, Raymond, **Supp. I Part 2:** 479, 491

"Spruce Has No Taproot, The" (Clampitt), **Supp. IX:** 41–42

Spruijt-Metz, Donna, **Supp. XXVIII:** 200

"Spunk" (Hurston), **Retro. Supp. III:** 127, 139; **Supp. VI:** 150, 151–152

Spunk: The Selected Stories (Hurston), **Supp. VI:** 150

Spurr, David, **Supp. XV:** 183

Spy, The (Cooper), **I:** 335, 336, 337, 339, 340; **Supp. I Part 1:** 155

"Spy, The" (Francis), **Supp. IX:** 81

Spy, The (Freneau), **Supp. II Part 1:** 260

Spyglass Tree, The (Murray), **Supp. XIX: 155–156**

Spy in the House of Love, A (Nin), **Supp. X:** 186

Squanto, **Supp. I Part 2:** 486

"Square Business" (Baraka), **Supp. II Part 1:** 49

Square Root of Wonderful, The (McCullers), **II:** 587–588

"Squash in Blossom" (Francis), **Supp. IX:** 81

"Squatter on Company Land, The" (Hugo), **Supp. VI:** 133

"Squatter's Children" (Bishop), **Retro. Supp. II:** 47

"Squeak, Memory" (Bukiet), **Supp. XVII:** 47

Squeeze Play (Auster), **Supp. XII:** 21

Squires, Radcliffe, **IV:** 127; **Supp. XV:** 118

Squirrels (Mamet), **Supp. XIV:** 240

S.S. Gliencairn (O'Neill), **III:** 387, 388, 405

S.S. San Pedro (Cozzens), **I:** 360–362, 370, 378, 379

Ssshh (Olds), **Supp. X:** 215

"Stacking the Straw" (Clampitt), **Supp. IX:** 41

Stade, George, **Supp. IV Part 1:** 286

Staël, Madame de, **II:** 298

"Staff of Life, The" (H. Miller), **III:** 187

Stafford, Jean, **II:** 537; **Retro. Supp. II:** 177; **Supp. V:** 316

Stafford, William, **Supp. IV Part 1:** 72; **Supp. IV Part 2:** 642; **Supp. IX:** 273; **Supp. XI: 311–332; Supp. XIII:** 76, 274, 276, 277, 281, 283; **Supp. XIV:**

119, 123; **Supp. XX: 161; Supp. XXI:** 246

"Stag and the Quiver, The"(Siken), **Supp. XXVIII:** 201

"Stage All Blood, The" (MacLeish), **III:** 18

"Staggerlee Wonders" (Baldwin), **Retro. Supp. II:** 15

Stained White Radiance, A (Burke), **Supp. XIV:** 28, 31

Stalin, Joseph, **I:** 261, 490; **II:** 39, 40, 49, 564; **III:** 30, 298; **IV:** 372; **Supp. V:** 290; **Supp. XXI:** 164, 165, 167

"Stalking" (J. W. Miller), **Supp. XX: 167**

"Stalking the Billion-Footed Beast: A Literary Manifesto for the New Social Novel" (Wolfe), **Supp. III Part 2:** 586

Stallings, A. E., **Supp. XXIII:** 111, 124; **Supp. XXV: 221–236**

Stallings, H. A., **Supp. XXII:** 194

Stallman, R. W., **I:** 405

Stamberg, Susan, **Supp. IV Part 1:** 201; **Supp. XII:** 193

Stamford, Anne Marie, **Supp. XII:** 162

Stanard, Mrs. Jane, **III:** 410, 413

Stand, The (King), **Supp. V:** 139, 140–141, 144–146, 148, 152

"Standard of Liberty, The" (Rowson), **Supp. XV:** 243

"Standard of Living, The" (Parker), **Supp. IX: 198–199**

Stander, Lionel, **Supp. I Part 1:** 289

"Standing and the Waiting, The" (M. F. K. Fisher), **Supp. XVII:** 83

Standing by Words (Berry), **Supp. X:** 22, 27, 28, 31, 32, 33, 35

Standing Fast (Swados), **Supp. XIX: 268–269**

"Standing Fast: Fox into Hedgehog" (Davison), **Supp. XXVI:** 72

"Standing Halfway Home" (Wagoner), **Supp. IX:** 324

"Standing Humbly Before Nature" (Gerber), **Supp. XXVI:** 187

"Standing In" (Caputo), **Supp. XIX:** 26

Standing Still and Walking in New York (O'Hara), **Supp. XXIII:** 220

Stand in the Mountains, A (Taylor), **Supp. V:** 324

Standish, Burt L. (pseudonym). *See* Patten, Gilbert

Standish, Miles, **I:** 471; **II:** 502–503

Standley, Fred L., **Retro. Supp. II:** 6

Stand Still Like the Hummingbird (H. Miller), **III:** 184

"Stand Up" (Salinas), **Supp. XIII:** 315

Stand with Me Here (Francis), **Supp. IX:** 76

Stanford, Ann, **Retro. Supp. I:** 41; **Retro. Supp. III:** 1, 9; **Supp. I Part 1:** 99, 100, 102, 103, 106, 108, 109, 113, 117; **Supp. IV Part 2:** 637

Stanford, Charles Villiers, **Supp. XX: 228**

Stanford, Donald E., **II:** 217

Stanford, Frank, **Supp. XV:** 338, 339, 341, 342–343, 343, 345, 348, 350

Stanford, Ginny (Crouch), **Supp. XV:** 339

Stanford, Leland, **I:** 196, 198

Stanislavsky, Konstantin, **Supp. XIV:** 240, 243

Stanley, Jodee, **Supp. XIX:** 52

Stanley, Marion Cummings, **Supp. XXVII:** 288

"Stanley Kunitz" (Oliver), **Supp. VII:** 237

Stansell, Christine, **Supp. XVII:** 106; **Supp. XXI:** 4

Stanton, Frank L., **Supp. II Part 1:** 192

Stanton, Robert J., **Supp. IV Part 2:** 681

"Stanzas, Written in 1815 before going to hear my Father read religious services"(J. Schoolcraft), **Supp. XXIII:** 229

"Stanzas from the Grande Chartreuse" (Arnold), **Supp. I Part 2:** 417

Stanzas in Meditation (Stein), **Supp. III Part 1:** 13

Staples, Hugh, **Retro. Supp. II:** 187

Star, Alexander, **Supp. X:** 310

Starbuck, George, **Retro. Supp. II:** 53, 245; **Supp. I Part 2:** 538; **Supp. IV Part 2:** 440; **Supp. XIII:** 76; **Supp. XXVI:** 68

Star Child (Gunn Allen), **Supp. IV Part 1:** 324

"Star Dust" (Wrigley), **Supp. XVIII:** 296

Stardust Lounge, The (Digges), **Supp. XXIII:** 57

Stardust Memories (film; Allen), **Supp. XV:** 1, 4, **8,** 9, 13

"Stare, The" (Updike), **Retro. Supp. I:** 329

"Starfish, The" (R. Bly), **Supp. IV Part 1:** 72

"Star in a Stoneboat" (Frost), **Retro. Supp. III:** 101

"Staring at the Sea on the Day of the Death of Another" (Swenson), **Supp. IV Part 2:** 652

Star in the Window, The (Prouty), **Supp. XXVIII:** 179, 184, 187

Star Is Born, A (film), **Supp. IV Part 1:** 198; **Supp. IX:** 198; **Supp. XVIII:** 242, 243

Stark, David, **Supp. XII:** 202

Stark, Heidi, **Supp. XXIII:** 228, 233

"Stark Boughs on the Family Tree" (Oliver), **Supp. VII:** 232

Starke, Aubrey Harrison, **Supp. I Part 1:** 350, 352, 356, 360, 362, 365, 370, 371

Starkey, David, **Supp. XII:** 180, 181

Star Ledger (Hull), **Supp. XXI:** 129, **136–138**

"Star Ledger" (Hull), **Supp. XXI:** 136

"Starlight" (Levine), **Supp. V:** 188

"Starlight Scope Myopia" (Komunyakaa), **Supp. XIII:** 123, 124

Starlight Wonder Book, The (Beston), **Supp. XXVI:** 33

Starna, William A., **Supp. XXVI:** 85, 86

Starnino, Carmine, **Supp. XVII:** 74

"Star of the Nativity" (Brodsky), **Supp. VIII:** 33

Starr, Ellen Gates, **Supp. I Part 1:** 4, 5, 11

Starr, Jean. *See* Untermeyer, Jean Starr

Starr, Kevin, **Supp. XXIV:** 17, 22

Starr, Ringo, **Supp. XI:** 309

Star Rover, The (London), **II:** 467

"Starry Night, The" (Sexton), **Supp. II Part 2:** 681

"Stars" (Frost), **II:** 153

Stars, the Snow, the Fire, The: Twenty-five Years in the Northern Wilderness (Haines), **Supp. XII: 199–201,** 206, 209

Star Shines over Mt. Morris Park, A (H. Roth), **Supp. IX:** 227, 236, **236–237**

"Stars of the Summer Night" (Longfellow), **II:** 493

"Stars over Harlem" (Hughes), **Retro. Supp. I:** 207

"Star-Spangled" (García), **Supp. XI:** 177, 178

Star-Spangled Girl, The (Simon), **Supp. IV Part 2:** 579

"Star-Splitter, The" (Frost), **Retro. Supp. I:** 123, 133

Stars Principal (McClatchy), **Supp. XII: 256–258**

"Start Again Somewhere" (Gallagher), **Supp. XXIV:** 169

"Star That Would Not Shine, The" (C. L. R. James), **Supp. XXI:** 160

"Starting from Paumanok" (Whitman), **IV:** 333; **Retro. Supp. III:** 305

Starting from Troy (Hadas), **Supp. XXIII:** 113

Starting Out in the Thirties (Kazin), **Supp. VIII: 95–97; Supp. XXIV:** 223

Starting Over (Spencer), **Supp. XXVII:** 13

Star Trek television series, **Supp. XXII:** 60

"Starved Lovers" (MacLeish), **III:** 19

Starved Rock (Masters), **Supp. I Part 2:** 465

"Starving Again" (Moore), **Supp. X:** 163, 172, 175

"Starving"(Strout), **Supp. XXIII:** 283, 285

"Star Watcher, The" (Davison), **Supp. XXVI:** 69

"State, The" (Bourne), **I:** 233

State and Main (Mamet), **Supp. XIV:** 241

"Statement of Principles" (Ransom), **III:** 496

"Statement of Randolph Carter, The" (Lovecraft), **Supp. XXV:** 114, 123

"Statement: Phillipa Allen" (Rukeyser), **Supp. VI:** 283–284

"Statements on Poetics" (Snyder), **Supp. VIII:** 291, 292

"Statement with Rhymes" (Kees), **Supp. XV:** 139

"State of the Art, The" (Elkin), **Supp. VI:** 52

"State of the Arts, The" (Wasserstein), **Supp. XV:** 332

State of the Nation (Dos Passos), **I:** 489

"State of the Union" (Vidal), **Supp. IV Part 2:** 678

State of the Union: 50 Political Poems (Beckman and Zapruder, eds.), **Supp. XXVIII:** 202

State Versus Elinor Norton, The (Rinehart), **Supp. XXV:** 197, 200

Static Element, The: Selected Poems of Natan Zach (Everwine, trans.), **Supp.**

XV: 73, 75, **85–88**
"Statue, The" (Berryman), **I:** 173
"Statue and Birds" (Bogan), **Supp. III Part 1:** 50
"Statue of an Unkown Soldier, The" (Kooser), **Supp. XIX:** 124
"Statues, The" (Schwartz), **Supp. II Part 2:** 654, 659
"Stature of Michael Gold, The"(Lawson), **Supp. XXVIII:** 79
"Status Rerum" (Pound), **Supp. I Part 1:** 257
Stavans, Ilan, **Supp. XI:** 190
"Stave Church" (W. V. Davis), **Supp. XXI:** 93, 94
"Staying Afloat"(Strout), **Supp. XXIII:** 274
"Staying Alive" (Levertov), **Supp. III Part 1:** 281
Staying Alive (Wagoner), **Supp. IX:** 324, **326**
"Staying at Ed's Place" (Swenson), **Supp. IV Part 2:** 648
Staying Put : Making a Home in a Restless World (Sanders), **Supp. XVI:** 274–275
Stay Me, Oh Comfort Me: Journals and Stories, 1933–1941 (M. F. K. Fisher), **Supp. XVII:** 92
Stayton, Richard, **Supp. IX:** 133
Steadman, Goodman, **IV:** 147
Steadman, Ralph, **Supp. XXIV:** 288
"Steak" (Snyder), **Supp. VIII:** 301
Steal Away: Selected and New Poems (Wright), **Supp. XV:** 337, 340, 348, 350–351
Stealing Beauty (Minot), **Supp. VI:** 205
Stealing Buddha's Dinner (Nguyen), **Supp. XXVI:** 208, 209–212, 217, 218, 219–220
Stealing Glimpses (McQuade), **Supp. IX:** 151
Stealing the Language: The Emergence of Women's Poetry in America (Ostriker), **Supp. XV:** 251
"Stealing the Thunder: Future Visions for American Indian Women, Tribes, and Literary Studies" (Gunn Allen), **Supp. IV Part 1:** 331
"Steam Shovel Cut" (Masters), **Supp. I Part 2:** 468
Stearns, Harold, **I:** 245; **Supp. XVII:** 106
Stedman, Edmund Clarence, **Supp. I Part 1:** 372; **Supp. II Part 1:** 192; **Supp. XV:** 115, 269, 273, 274, 282, 286; **Supp. XXVIII:** 228
Steel, Sharon, **Supp. XIX:** 61
Steele, Lloyd, **Supp. XXV:** 96
Steele, Margaret, **Supp. XXI:** 5
Steele, Max, **Supp. XIV:** 82
Steele, Sir Richard, **I:** 378; **II:** 105, 107, 300; **III:** 430
Steele, Timothy, **Supp. XV:** 251; **Supp. XVII:** 112; **Supp. XXIII:** 111
Steele, Wilbur Daniel, **Supp. XXI:** 5; **Supp. XXVIII:** 38
"Steel Mills: South Chicago" (Bodenheim), **Supp. XXV:** 22
Steelwork (Sorrentino), **Supp. XXI:** 227, 230, 231, 232

Steenburgen, Mary, **Supp. IV Part 1:** 236
Steeple Bush (Frost), **II:** 155; **Retro. Supp. I:** 140; **Retro. Supp. II:** 42; **Retro. Supp. III:** 105
"Steeple-Jack, The" (Moore), **III:** 212, 213, 215
"Steerage" (Goldbarth), **Supp. XII:** 187
Steers, Nina, **Retro. Supp. II:** 25
Stefans, Brian Kim, **Supp. XXII:** 226
Steffens, Lincoln, **II:** 577; **III:** 580; **Retro. Supp. I:** 202; **Retro. Supp. II:** 101; **Supp. I Part 1:** 7; **Supp. XVII:** 98, 101, 106–107; **Supp. XXI:** 2, 3, 5, 7, 10; **Supp. XXIII:** 162
Stegner, Page, **IV:** 114, 116; **Supp. IV Part 2:** 599
Stegner, Wallace, **Retro. Supp. III:** 83; **Supp. IV Part 2:** 595–618; **Supp. V:** 220, 224, 296; **Supp. X:** 23, 24; **Supp. XIV:** 82, 193, 230, 233; **Supp. XVIII:** 192; **Supp. XXII:** 204, 205, 208; **Supp. XXVIII:** 253
"Stegner's Short Fiction" (Ahearn), **Supp. IV Part 2:** 604
Steichen, Edward, **III:** 580, 594–595
Steichen, Lillian. *See* Sandburg, Mrs. Carl (Lillian Steichen)
Steiger, Rod, **Supp. VIII:** 269; **Supp. XI:** 305
Stein, Edith, **Supp. XXII:** 92–93, 167
Stein, Gertrude, **I:** 103, 105, 476; **II:** 56, 251, 252, 257, 260, 262–263, 264, 289; **III:** 71, 454, 471–472, 600; **IV:** **24–48,** 368, 375, 404, 415, 443, 477; **Retro. Supp. I:** 108, 170, 176, 177, 186, 418, 422; **Retro. Supp. II:** 85, 207, 326, 331; **Retro. Supp. III:** 194; **Supp. I Part 1:** 292; **Supp. III Part 1:** 13, 37, 225, 226; **Supp. III Part 2:** 626; **Supp. IV Part 1:** 11, 79, 80, 81, 322; **Supp. IV Part 2:** 468; **Supp. IX:** 55, 57, 62, 66; **Supp. V:** 53; **Supp. XII:** 1, 139; **Supp. XIV:** 336; **Supp. XVI:** 187; **Supp. XVII:** 98, 105, 107; **Supp. XVIII:** 148; **Supp. XXI:** 7, 33; **Supp. XXII:** 158, 159; **Supp. XXIII:** 166, 207; **Supp. XXVII:** 26; **Supp. XXVIII:** 260
Stein, Howard, **Supp. XXIV:** 116
Stein, Jean, **Retro. Supp. III:** 77; **Supp. XVI:** 245
Stein, Karen F., **Supp. XIII:** 29, 30
Stein, Leo, **IV:** 26; **Supp. XIV:** 336; **Supp. XV:** 298
Stein, Lorin, **Supp. XII:** 254; **Supp. XVIII:** 137, 139
Stein, Rachel, **Retro. Supp. III:** 245
Steinbeck, John, **I:** 107, 288, 301, 378, 495, 519; **II:** 272; **III:** 382, 453, 454, 589; **IV:** **49–72;** **Retro. Supp. II:** 19, 196; **Supp. IV Part 1:** 102, 225; **Supp. IV Part 2:** 502; **Supp. IX:** 33, 171; **Supp. V:** 290, 291; **Supp. VIII:** 10; **Supp. XI:** 169; **Supp. XIII:** 1, 17; **Supp. XIV:** 21, 181; **Supp. XIX:** 3; **Supp. XVII:** 228; **Supp. XVIII:** 90, 102, 254
Steinbeck, Olive Hamilton, **IV:** 51
Steinberg, Saul, **Supp. VIII:** 272

Steinberg, Sybil, **Supp. XVII:** 165, 166; **Supp. XXIII:** 241; **Supp. XXVI:** 258
Steinem, Gloria, **Supp. IV Part 1:** 203; **Supp. XXIII:** 104, 105, 106
Steiner, George, **Retro. Supp. I:** 327; **Supp. IV Part 1:** 286; **Supp. XVI:** 230
Steiner, Michael, **Supp. XXII:** 205
Steiner, Nancy, **Supp. I Part 2:** 529
Steiner, Stan, **Supp. IV Part 2:** 505
Steinfels, Margaret, **Supp. XVII:** 170
Steinhoff, Eirik, **Supp. XVI:** 290
Steinman, Michael, **Supp. VIII:** 172
Steinmetz, Charles P., **Supp. XXIII:** 161
Steinmetz, Charles Proteus, **I:** 483
Steinway Quintet Plus Four, The (Epstein), **Supp. XII:** 159, **162–166**
Stekel, Wilhelm, **III:** 554
Stella (film, 1990), **Supp. XXVIII:** 183–184, 193
Stella (Goethe), **Supp. IX:** 133, 138
Stella (Kushner), **Supp. IX:** 133
Stella, Joseph, **I:** 387
Stella Dallas (film, 1925), **Supp. XXVIII:** 177, 182, 183, 193
Stella Dallas (film, 1937), **Supp. XXVIII:** 177, 182–183, 188, 193
Stella Dallas (Prouty), **Supp. XXVIII:** 177, 180–182, 185
"Stellaria" (Francis), **Supp. IX:** 83
Stelligery and Other Essays (Wendell), **Supp. I Part 2:** 414
St. Elmo (Evans), **Supp. XXII:** 120
Sten, Christopher, **Retro. Supp. III:** 153
Stendhal, **I:** 316; **III:** 465, 467; **Supp. I Part 1:** 293; **Supp. I Part 2:** 445
Stepanchev, Stephen, **Supp. XI:** 312
Stephen, Leslie, **IV:** 440
Stephen, Sir Leslie, **IV:** 440; **Supp. I Part 1:** 306
Stephen, Saint, **II:** 539; **IV:** 228
Stephen Crane (Berryman), **I:** 169–170, 405
Stephen Escott (Lewisohn), **Supp. XXVIII:** 151–152
Stephen King, The Second Decade: "Danse Macabre" to "The Dark Half" (Magistrale), **Supp. V:** 138, 146, 151
Stephen King: The Art of Darkness (Winter), **Supp. V:** 144
Stephens, Alexander, **Supp. XXVIII:** 231
Stephens, Jack, **Supp. X:** 11, 14, 15, 17
Stephens, James, **Supp. XIX:** 204
Stephens, Uriah, **Supp. XXIII:** 187
Stephenson, Gregory, **Supp. XII:** 120, 123
Stephenson, Neal, **Supp. XXII:** 49
"Stepping Out" (Dunn), **Supp. XI:** 140, 141
Stepping Outside (Gallagher), **Supp. XXIV:** 165, 167
Steps (Kosinski), **Supp. VII:** 215, 221–222, 225
"Steps" (Nye), **Supp. XIII:** 288
Steps to the Temple (Crashaw), **IV:** 145
"Steps Toward Poverty and Death" (R. Bly), **Supp. IV Part 1:** 60
Stepto, Robert B., **Retro. Supp. II:** 116, 120, 123

Sterile Cuckoo, The (Nichols), **Supp. XIII:** 258, **259–263,** 264

Sterling, Bruce, **Supp. XVI:** 118, 121, 123, 124, 128–129

Sterling, George, **I:** 199, 207, 208, 209; **II:** 440; **Supp. V:** 286; **Supp. XXII:** 276, 277

Sterling, Phillip, **Supp. XXIII:** 102

Stern, Bernhard J., **Supp. XIV:** 202, 213

Stern, Daniel, **Supp. VIII:** 238

Stern, Frederick C., **Supp. X:** 114, 115, 117

Stern, Gerald, **Supp. IX: 285–303; Supp. XI:** 139, 267; **Supp. XV:** 211, 212

Stern, Madeleine B., **Supp. I Part 1:** 35

Stern, Maurice, **IV:** 285

Stern, Philip Van Doren, **Supp. XIII:** 164

Stern, Richard, **Retro. Supp. II:** 291

Stern, Richard G., **Retro. Supp. II:** 204

Stern, Steven, **Supp. XVII:** 42, 48, 49; **Supp. XX: 178**

"Sterne" (Schwartz), **Supp. II Part 2:** 663

Sterne, Laurence, **II:** 302, 304–305, 308; **III:** 454; **IV:** 68, 211, 465; **Supp. I Part 2:** 714; **Supp. IV Part 1:** 299; **Supp. V:** 127; **Supp. X:** 324; **Supp. XV:** 232

Sterritt, David, **Supp. IV Part 2:** 574

Stetson, Caleb, **IV:** 178

Stetson, Charles Walter, **Supp. XI:** 195, 196, 197, 202, 204, 209

Steve Nelson, American Radical (Nelson), **Supp. XVIII:** 226

Stevens, Frances Simpson, **Supp. XXII:** 159, 162

Stevens, Hampton, **Supp. XXVII:** 45

Stevens, James, **Supp. XXIII:** 152

Stevens, Wallace, **I:** 60, 61, 266, 273, 462, 521, 528, 540–541; **II:** 56, 57, 530, 552, 556; **III:** 19, 23, 194, 216, 270–271, 272, 278, 279, 281, 453, 463, 493, 509, 521, 523, 600, 605, 613, 614; **IV: 73–96,** 140, 141, 332, 402, 415; **Retro. Supp. I:** 67, 89, 193, 284, 288, **295–315,** 335, 403, 411, 416, 417, 422; **Retro. Supp. II:** 40, 44, 326; **Retro. Supp. III:** 251; **Supp. I Part 1:** 80, 82, 257; **Supp. II Part 1:** 9, 18; **Supp. III Part 1:** 2, 3, 12, 20, 48, 239, 318, 319, 344; **Supp. III Part 2:** 611; **Supp. IV Part 1:** 72, 393; **Supp. IV Part 2:** 619, 620, 621, 634; **Supp. IX:** 41; **Supp. V:** 337; **Supp. VIII:** 21, 102, 195, 271, 292; **Supp. X:** 58; **Supp. XI:** 123, 191, 312; **Supp. XIII:** 44, 45; **Supp. XIX:** 7, 40, 86, 87; **Supp. XV:** 39, 41, 92, 115, 250, 261, 298, 302, 306, 307; **Supp. XVI:** 64, 158, 202, 210, 288; **Supp. XVII:** 36, 42, 110, 129, 130, 240, 241; **Supp. XXI:** 19, 28, 60, 133; **Supp. XXII:** 162; **Supp. XXIII:** 53, 57, 65; **Supp. XXIV:** 41, 45; **Supp. XXVI:** 67; **Supp. XXVII:** 261; **Supp. XXVIII:** 131, 260, 268

Stevens, Mrs. Wallace (Elsie Kachel), **IV:** 75

"Stevens and the Idea of the Hero" (Bromwich), **Retro. Supp. I:** 305

Stevens and the Interpersonal (Halliday), **Supp. XIX: 85–86**

Stevenson, Adlai, **II:** 49; **III:** 581

Stevenson, Anne, **Supp. XV:** 121; **Supp. XVII:** 74; **Supp. XXVI:** 66

Stevenson, Burton E., **Supp. XIV:** 120

Stevenson, David, **Supp. XI:** 230

Stevenson, David L., **Retro. Supp. III:** 86

Stevenson, Ellen Borden, **Supp. XXV:** 30

Stevenson, Robert Louis, **I:** 2, 53; **II:** 283, 290, 311, 338; **III:** 328; **IV:** 183–184, 186, 187; **Retro. Supp. I:** 224, 228; **Supp. I Part 1:** 49; **Supp. II Part 1:** 404–405; **Supp. IV Part 1:** 298, 314; **Supp. VIII:** 125; **Supp. XIII:** 75; **Supp. XIV:** 40; **Supp. XVII:** 69; **Supp. XXI:** 204; **Supp. XXVIII:** 227

Stevick, Robert D., **III:** 509

Stewart, Dugald, **II:** 8, 9; **Supp. I Part 1:** 151, 159; **Supp. I Part 2:** 422

Stewart, Elinore Pruitt, **Supp. XXVI:** 183

Stewart, George, **Supp. XVIII:** 138

Stewart, Jeffrey C., **Supp. XIV:** 196, 209, 210

Stewart, Randall, **II:** 244; **Supp. XX: 164**

Stewart, Robert E., **Supp. XI:** 216

"St. Francis of Assisi" (Di Piero), **Supp. XIX:** 43

Stickeen (Muir), **Supp. IX:** 182

Sticks and Bones (Rabe), **Supp. XXIV:** 117

"Sticks and Stones" (L. Michaels), **Supp. XVI:** 205

Sticks and Stones (Mumford), **Supp. II Part 2:** 475, 483, 487–488

Sticks & Stones (Matthews), **Supp. IX:** 154, 155, 157, 158

"St. Idyl's Light"(Stuart), **Supp. XXVIII:** 226

Stieglitz, Alfred, **Retro. Supp. I:** 416; **Retro. Supp. II:** 103; **Supp. VIII:** 98; **Supp. XVII:** 96; **Supp. XX: 74, 75**

"Stigmata" (Oates), **Supp. II Part 2:** 520

Stiles, Ezra, **I:** 108, 122; **IV:** 144, 146, 148; **Supp. XXIV:** 68

Still, James, **Supp. XX: 163; Supp. XXVII:** 217

Still, William Grant, **Retro. Supp. I:** 203

Still Alice (Genova), **Supp. XXIII:** 127

"Stillborn" (Plath), **Supp. I Part 2:** 544

"Still Here" (Hughes), **Retro. Supp. I:** 211

"Still Just Writing" (Tyler), **Supp. IV Part 2:** 658

"Still Life" (Hecht), **Supp. X:** 68

"Still Life" (Malamud), **Supp. I Part 2:** 450

Still Life (Pickering), **Supp. XXI:** 198

"Still Life" (Pickering), **Supp. XXI:** 198

"Still Life" (Sandburg), **III:** 584

"Still Life" (Vaz), **Supp. XXVI:** 261

"Still Life: Moonlight Striking up on a Chess-Board" (A. Lowell), **II:** 528

"Still Life Or" (Creeley), **Supp. IV Part 1:** 141, 150, 158

Still Life with Oysters and Lemon (Doty), **Supp. XI:** 119, 121, **133–134**

Still Life with Woodpecker (Robbins), **Supp. X:** 260, **271–274,** 282

"Still Moment, A" (Welty), **IV:** 265; **Retro. Supp. I:** 347

Stillness (Gardner), **Supp. VI:** 74

"Stillness in the Air" (Dickinson), **Supp. XV:** 261

Stillness of Dancing, The (Bierds), **Supp. XVII: 27–28**

"Still Small Voices, The" (Fante), **Supp. XI:** 164

Still Such (Salter), **Supp. IX:** 246

"Still the Place Where Creation Does Some Work on Itself" (W. V. Davis), **Supp. IV Part 1:** 68

Stimpson, Catharine R., **Supp. IV Part 2:** 686

Stimson, Eleanor Kenyon. *See* Brooks, Mrs. Van Wyck

"Stimulants, Poultices, Goads" (Wright), **Supp. XV:** 349

"Stings" (Plath), **Retro. Supp. II:** 255; **Supp. I Part 2:** 541

"Stirling Street September" (Baraka), **Supp. II Part 1:** 51

Stirner, Max, **II:** 27

"Stirrup-Cup, The" (Lanier), **Supp. I Part 1:** 364

Stitt, Peter, **Supp. IV Part 1:** 68; **Supp. IV Part 2:** 628; **Supp. IX:** 152, 163, 291, 299; **Supp. XI:** 311, 317; **Supp. XIII:** 87; **Supp. XIX:** 121; **Supp. XV:** 98, 99

Stivers, Valerie, **Supp. X:** 311

St. John, David, **Supp. XV:** 73, 253

St. Louis Woman (Bontemps and Cullen), **Supp. XXII:** 6

St. Mark, Tyler, **Supp. XX: 260**

Stock, Noel, **III:** 479

Stockbroker, the Bitter Young Man, and the Beautiful Girl, The (Hayes), **Supp. XXVI:** 143

Stockton, Frank R., **I:** 201; **Supp. XXVIII:** 228

Stoddard, Charles Warren, **I:** 193, 195, 196; **Supp. II Part 1:** 192, 341, 351

Stoddard, Elizabeth, **II:** 275; **Supp. XV: 269–291**

Stoddard, Richard, **Supp. I Part 1:** 372

Stoddard, Richard Henry, **Supp. XV:** 269, 271, 272, 273, 274, 278, 279, 286

Stoddard, Solomon, **I:** 545, 548; **IV:** 145, 148

Stoffman, Judy, **Supp. XVIII:** 97

Stoic, The (Dreiser), **I:** 497, 502, 508, 516; **Retro. Supp. II:** 95, 96, 101, 108

Stoker, Bram, **Supp. XXVI:** 58

Stokes, Geoffrey, **Supp. XV:** 256

Stokes, Olivia Egleston Phelps, **Supp. XVIII:** 261

"Stolen Calf, The" (Dunbar), **Supp. II Part 1:** 196

Stolen Jew, The (Neugeboren), **Supp. XVI: 222–224,** 225

Stolen Legacy of Anne Frank, The: Meyer Levin, Lillian Hellman, and the Staging of the Diary (Melnick), **Supp. XXVII:** 137–138

Stolen Past, A (Knowles), **Supp. XII:** 249

Stolen Words: Forays into the Origins and Ravages of Plagiarism (Mallon), **Supp. XIX: 134–135**

Stollman, Aryeh Lev, **Supp. XVII:** 49; **Supp. XXIV:** 2, 8, 10–11

Stolmar, Thomas, **Supp. XVIII:** 138

"Stoma" (Barnhardt), **Supp. XXVII:** 12

Stomping the Blues (Murray), **Supp. XIX: 158–159**

"Stone" (Ozick), **Supp. XVII:** 50

Stone, Edward, **III:** 479

Stone, Herbert S., **Supp. XXI:** 2

Stone, I. F., **Supp. XIV:** 3

Stone, Irving, **II:** 463, 466, 467

Stone, Oliver, **Supp. XIV:** 48, 316

Stone, Phil, **II:** 55; **Retro. Supp. III:** 74

Stone, Richard, **Supp. XIV:** 54

Stone, Robert, **Supp. V: 295–312; Supp. X:** 1; **Supp. XIX:** 54

Stone, Rosetta (pseudonym). *See* Geisel, Theodor Seuss (Dr. Seuss)

Stone, Ruth, **Supp. XXVII: 249–265**

Stone, Wilmer, **Supp. I Part 1:** 49

Stone and the Shell, The (Hay), **Supp. XIV:** 122, 123, 127, 130

Stone Arabia (Spiotta), **Supp. XXVIII:** 207, 209, 216–219

"Stone Bear, The" (Haines), **Supp. XII:** 206–207, 212

"Stone City" (Proulx), **Supp. VII:** 251–253

Stone Country (Sanders), **Supp. XVI:** 271–272

Stone Diaries, The (Shields), **Supp. VII:** 307, 315, 324–326, 327

"Stone Dreams" (Kingsolver), **Supp. VII:** 203

Stone Harp, The (Haines), **Supp. XII: 204,** 205, 206, 207

Stonemason, The (McCarthy), **Supp. VIII:** 175, 187

"Stones" (Hoffman), **Supp. XVIII:** 86

"Stones" (Kumin), **Supp. IV Part 2:** 447

Stones (lithograph series, O'Hara and Rivers), **Supp. XXIII:** 217

"Stones, The" (Plath), **Supp. I Part 2:** 535, 539

"Stones in My Passway, Hellhounds on My Trail" (Boyle), **Supp. VIII:** 15

Stones of Florence, The (McCarthy), **II:** 562

"Stonewall Jackson" (Melville), **Retro. Supp. III:** 161

"Stone Walls" (Sarton), **Supp. VIII:** 259

"Stop" (Wilbur), **Supp. III Part 2:** 556

Stop-Loss (screenplay, Richard), **Supp. XIX:** 222

"Stop Me If You've Heard This One" (Lardner), **II:** 433

Stopover: Tokyo (Marquand), **III:** 53, 57, 61, 70

Stoppard, Tom, **Retro. Supp. I:** 189

Stopping by Home (Huddle), **Supp. XXVI:** 149

"Stopping by Woods on a Snowy Evening" (Frost), **II:** 154; **Retro. Supp. I:** 129, 133, 134, 135, 139; **Retro. Supp. III:** 95, 102

"Stopping the Bullies" (Myers and Carillo), **Supp. XXVII:** 204

Stopping Westward (Richards), **II:** 396

"Stop Player. Joke No. 4" (Gaddis), **Supp. IV Part 1:** 280

Stop-Time (Conroy), **Supp. XVI: 63–71,** 72, 75, 76–77

"Store, The" (E. P. Jones), **Supp. XXII:** 144–145

Store, The (Stribling), **Supp. VIII:** 126; **Supp. XXII:** 195

"*Store* and *Mockingbird:* Two Pulitzer Novels about Alabama" (Going), **Supp. VIII:** 126

Store of a Million Items, The (Cliff), **Supp. XXII:** 67, 74, 75

"Store of a Million Items, The" (Cliff), **Supp. XXII:** 75

Storer, Edward, **Supp. I Part 1:** 261, 262

Stories, Fables and Other Diversions (Nemerov), **III:** 268–269, 285

Stories: Elizabeth Stoddard, **Supp. XV:** 270

"Stories for Sale" (Kolba), **Supp. XVIII:** 257

Stories for the Sixties (Yates, ed.), **Supp. XI:** 343

Stories from Our Living Past (Prose), **Supp. XVI:** 251

Stories from the Italian Poets (Hunt), **Supp. XV:** 175

Stories from the Old Testament Retold (L. P. Smith), **Supp. XIV:** 342

Stories from World Literature, **Supp. IX:** 4

"Stories in the Snow" (Leopold), **Supp. XIV:** 183

Stories into Film (Kittredge and Krauzer), **Supp. XXVI:** 182

Stories of an Imaginary Childhood (Bukiet), **Supp. XVII: 41–44,** 45

Stories of F. Scott Fitzgerald, The (Cowley, ed.), **Retro. Supp. I:** 115

Stories of F. Scott Fitzgerald, The (Fitzgerald), **II:** 94

Stories of Modern America, **Supp. IX:** 4

Stories of Stephen Dixon, The (Dixon), **Supp. XII:** 152

Stories of the American Experience (Kriegel and Lass, eds.), **Supp. XXIV:** 214

Stories of the Spanish Civil War (Hemingway), **II:** 258

Stories Revived (James), **II:** 322

Stories that Could Be True (Stafford), **Supp. XI: 325–327**

Stories Toto Told Me (Rolfe), **Supp. XX:** 235

Storm, The (Buechner), **Supp. XII: 54–57**

"Storm, The" (Chopin), **Retro. Supp. II:** 60, 68; **Supp. I Part 1:** 218, 224

Storm, The (al-'Awásif) (Gibran), **Supp. XX: 116, 124, 125**

"Storm Fear" (Frost), **II:** 153; **Retro. Supp. I:** 127

"Storm Ship, The" (Irving), **II:** 309

"Storm Warning" (Rich), **Retro. Supp. III:** 242

"Storm Warnings" (Kingsolver), **Supp. VII:** 207–208

"Stormy Weather" (Ellison), **Supp. II Part 1:** 233

"Story" (Everwine), **Supp. XV:** 89

"Story, A" (Jarrell), **II:** 371

Story, Julian, **Supp. XX:** 232

Story, Richard David, **Supp. IV Part 2:** 575, 588

Story, William Wetmore, **Supp. XX:** 228

"Story about Chicken Soup, A" (Simpson), **Supp. IX:** 272–273

"Story about the Anteater, The" (Benét), **Supp. XI:** 53

"Story About the Body, A" (Hass), **Supp. VI:** 107–108

Story Behind the Story, The (Turchi and Barrett, eds.), **Supp. XXVII:** 1, 12

"Story for Teddy, A" (Swados), **Supp. XIX:** 266–267

Story for Teddy, A—and Others (Swados), **Supp. XIX: 266–268**

"Story Hearer, The" (Paley), **Supp. VI:** 230, 231

"Story Hour" (Hay), **Supp. XIV:** 124

"Story Hour" (Jarman), **Supp. XVII:** 116

Story Hour: A Second Look at Cinderella, Bluebeard, and Company (Hay), **Supp. XIV:** 119, 124, 125, 132, 133

Story of a Country Town, The (Howe), **I:** 106

Story of a Lover, The (Hapgood), **Supp. XVII:** 99, 100, 104; **Supp. XXI:** 3, 5, 7

"Story of America, The: A Tribalography" (Howe), **Supp. XXVI:** 84

Story of a Million Years, The (Huddle), **Supp. XXVI:** 147, 152, 157–158

Story of an American Family, The: Letters of the Hapgood Family, 1648–1917 (Boyce), **Supp. XVII:** 97; **Supp. XXI:** 9, 14

"Story of an Hour, The" (Chopin), **Retro. Supp. II:** 72; **Supp. I Part 1:** 212–213, 216

Story of a Novel, The (Wolfe), **IV:** 456, 458

"Story of a Proverb, The" (Lanier), **Supp. I Part 1:** 365

"Story of a Proverb, The: A Fairy Tale for Grown People" (Lanier), **Supp. I Part 1:** 365

Story of a Story and Other Stories, The: A Novel (Dixon), **Supp. XII:** 155

Story of a Wonder Man, The (Lardner), **II:** 433–434

"Story of a Year, The" (James), **Retro. Supp. I:** 218

Story of Babette, The: A Little Creole Girl (Stuart), **Supp. XXVIII:** 228, 233

Story of George Washington Carver, The (Bontemps), **Supp. XXII:** 13

Story of G.I. Joe, The (film, Wellman), **Supp. XVII:** 61, 62

"Story of Gus, The" (A. Miller), **III:** 147–148

"Story of How a Wall Stands, A" (Ortiz), **Supp. IV Part 2:** 499, 507

Story of Mist, The (Dybek), **Supp. XXIII: 74–75,** 78

"Story of Mist, The" (Dybek), **Supp. XXIII:** 74–75

Story of Mount Desert Island, Maine, The (Morison), **Supp. I Part 2:** 494

Story of My Boyhood and Youth, The (Muir), **Supp. IX: 172–174,** 176

Story of My Father, The: A Memoir (Miller), **Supp. XII:** 301

Story of O, The (Réage), **Supp. XII:** 9, 10

Story of Our Lives, The (Strand), **Supp. IV Part 2:** 620, 628–629, 629

"Story of Poppy Van Buster, The" (Briggs), **Supp. XVIII:** 8

"Story of the Bad Little Boy That Bore a Charmed Life, The" (Twain), **Retro. Supp. III:** 263

"Story of the Good Little Boy Who Did Not Prosper, The" (Twain), **Retro. Supp. III:** 263

Story of the Negro (Bontemps), **Supp. XXII:** 6, 12–13

Story of the Normans, The, Told Chiefly in Relation to Their Conquest of England (Jewett), **II:** 406

Story of the Telegraph, The (Briggs, and Maverick), **Supp. XVIII:** 4

"Story of Toby, The" (Melville), **III:** 76

"Story of To-day, A" (Davis). *See also Margret Howth*

"Story of To-day, A" (R. H. Davis), **Supp. XVI:** 88, 89

Story of Utopias, The (Mumford), **Supp. II Part 2:** 475, 483–486, 495

Story of Wine in California, The (M. F. K. Fisher), **Supp. XVII:** 88

Story on Page One, The (Odets), **Supp. II Part 2:** 546

Storyteller (Silko), **Supp. IV Part 2:** 558, 559, 560, 561, **566–570**

"Storyteller" (Silko), **Supp. IV Part 2:** 569

"*Storyteller:* Grandmother Spider's Web" (Danielson), **Supp. IV Part 2:** 569

"Storyteller's Notebook, A" (Carver), **Supp. III Part 1:** 142–143

Story Teller's Story, A: The Tale of an American Writer's Journey through His Own Imaginative World and through the World of Facts . . . (Anderson), **I:** 98, 101, 114, 117

"Story That Could Be True, A" (Stafford), **Supp. XI:** 326

Stothard, Peter, **Supp. XXV:** 221

"Stout Gentleman, The" (Irving), **II:** 309

Stover at Yale (Johnson), **III:** 321

Stowe, Calvin, **IV:** 445; **Supp. I Part 2:** 587, 588, 590, 596, 597

Stowe, Charles, **Supp. I Part 2:** 581, 582

Stowe, Eliza, **Supp. I Part 2:** 587

Stowe, Harriet Beecher, **II:** 274, 399, 403, 541; **Retro. Supp. I:** 34, 246; **Retro. Supp. II:** 4, 138, 156; **Supp. I Part 1:** 30, 206, 301; **Supp. I Part 2:** **579–601; Supp. III Part 1:** 154, 168, 171; **Supp. IX:** 33; **Supp. X:** 223, 246, 249, 250; **Supp. XI:** 193; **Supp. XIII:** 141, 295; **Supp. XV:** 278; **Supp. XVI:** 82, 85; **Supp. XXVIII:** 114, 167–168

Stowe, Samuel Charles, **Supp. I Part 2:** 587

Stowe, William, **Supp. IV Part 1:** 129

Strachey, Lytton, **I:** 5; **IV:** 436; **Retro. Supp. I:** 59; **Supp. I Part 2:** 485, 494; **Supp. XIV:** 342; **Supp. XVI:** 191

"Stradivari" (Bierds), **Supp. XVII:** 28

Straight Cut (Bell), **Supp. X:** 5, **6–7,** 10

Straight Man (Russo), **Supp. XII: 335–339,** 340

Straits: Poems (Koch), **Supp. XV:** 184

Strand, Mark, **Supp. IV Part 2: 619–636; Supp. IX:** 155; **Supp. V:** 92, 332, 337, 338, 343; **Supp. XI:** 139, 145; **Supp. XII:** 254; **Supp. XIII:** 76; **Supp. XV:** 74; **Supp. XXIV:** 165

Strand, Paul, **Supp. VIII:** 272

Strandberg, Victor, **Supp. V:** 273

Strange, Sharan, **Supp. XXI:** 246

"Strange Beautiful Woman, A" (Nelson), **Supp. XVIII:** 173

Strange Bedfellows (Woods), **Supp. XXI:** 70

Strange Case of Dr. Jekyll and Mr. Hyde, The (Stevenson), **II:** 290

Strange Children, The (Gordon), **II:** 196, 197, 199, 211–213

Strange Commonplace, A (Sorrentino), **Supp. XXI:** 232, 237, 238

Strange Crime in Bermuda, The (Holding), **Supp. XXII: 124–125,** 127, 129

Strange Fire (Bukiet), **Supp. XVII:** 46

"Strange Fruit" (Harjo), **Supp. XII:** 224, 225

"Strange Fruit" (song), **Supp. I Part 1:** 80; **Supp. XVIII:** 228

"Strange Funeral at Braddock, The"(Gold), **Supp. XXVIII:** 73–74

Strange Interlude (O'Neill), **III:** 391, 397–398; **IV:** 61; **Supp. XXII:** 24; **Supp. XXVIII:** 39

Strange Lives of Familiar Insects, The (Teale), **Supp. XXVIII:** 297

Stranger, The (Camus), **I:** 53, 292; **Supp. VIII:** 11; **Supp. XV:** 352

"Stranger, The" (Rich), **Supp. I Part 2:** 555, 560

"Stranger, The" (Salinger), **III:** 552–553

Strange Relation (Hadas), **Supp. XXIII:** 111, 113, 120, **127**

"Stranger in My Own Life, A: Alienation in American Indian Poetry and Prose" (Gunn Allen), **Supp. IV Part 1:** 322

Stranger in the Kingdom, A (Mosher), **Supp. XXII:** 204, 205, 206, 207, 208, 209, **212–213**

"Stranger in the Village" (Baldwin), **Retro. Supp. II:** 3; **Supp. I Part 1:** 54; **Supp. IV Part 1:** 10

"Stranger in Town" (Hughes), **Supp. I Part 1:** 334

Stranger Music (Cohen), **Supp. XXVII:** 54

"Strangers" (Howe), **Supp. VI:** 120

Strangers: A Book of Poems (Ferry), **Supp. XXIV: 149–150**

Strangers and Wayfarers (Jewett), **Retro. Supp. II:** 138

"Strangers from the Horizon" (Merwin), **Supp. III Part 1:** 356

"Stranger's Gift, The" (Very), **Supp. XXV:** 242

Strangers on a Train (Highsmith), **Supp. IV Part 1:** 132

Strangers on a Train (screenplay, Hecht), **Supp. XXVII:** 93

"Strange Story, A" (Taylor), **Supp. V:** 323

"Strange Story, A" (Wylie), **Supp. I Part 2:** 723

Strange Things (Atwood), **Supp. XIII:** 35

Strange Victory (Teasdale), **Supp. XXVII:** 284, 296–297

"Strategy"(Prouty), **Supp. XXVIII:** 180

"Strato in Plaster" (Merrill), **Supp. III Part 1:** 328

Stratton-Porter, Gene, **Supp. XX: 211–225**

Straub, Peter, **Supp. XXV:** 145

Straus, Ralph, **Supp. XIII:** 168

Straus, Roger, **Supp. VIII:** 82; **Supp. XV:** 59

Strauss, Harold, **Supp. XV:** 137

Strauss, Helen, **Supp. XXIII:** 258

Strauss, Johann, **I:** 66

Strauss, Richard, **IV:** 316

Strauss, Robert, **Supp. XI:** 141, 142

Stravinsky (De Schloezer), **III:** 474

Stravinsky, Igor, **Retro. Supp. I:** 378; **Supp. IV Part 1:** 81; **Supp. XI:** 133; **Supp. XV:** 265

"Stravinsky's Three Pieces 'Grotesques,' for String Quartet" (A. Lowell), **II:** 523

Straw, The (O'Neill), **III:** 390

"Strawberry Milkshake" (Halliday), **Supp. XIX:** 92, 94

"Straw House, Straw Dog"(Siken), **Supp. XXVIII:** 197

"Stray Document, A" (Pound), **II:** 517

"Strays" (Richard), **Supp. XIX:** 210–211, 220

Streaks of the Tulip, The: Selected Criticism (W. J. Smith), **Supp. XIII:** 333, 334, 344, **347–348**

Streamline Your Mind (Mursell), **Supp. I Part 2:** 608

Strecker, Trey, **Supp. XXI:** 238

"Street, Cloud" (Ríos), **Supp. IV Part 2:** 549

Street, The (Petry), **Supp. XVIII:** 286

Streetcar Named Desire, A (T. Williams), **IV:** 382, 383, 385, 386, 387, 389–390, 395, 398; **Supp. IV Part 1:** 359

Street in Bronzeville, A (Brooks), **Retro. Supp. I:** 208; **Supp. III Part 1:** 74–78

"Street Moths" (X. J. Kennedy), **Supp. XV:** 170

"Street Musicians" (Ashbery), **Supp. III Part 1:** 18

"Street of Crocodiles" (Hull), **Supp. XXI:** 130

"Street off Sunset, A" (Jarrell), **II:** 387

Street of Seven Stars, The (Rinehart), **Supp. XXV:** 193

"Streets" (Dixon), **Supp. XII: 145–146**

Streets in Their Own Ink (Dybek), **Supp. XXIII:** 78

Streets in the Moon (MacLeish), **III:** 5, 8–11, 15, 19

Streets of Laredo (McMurtry), **Supp. V:** 230

"Streets of Laredo" (screenplay) (McMurtry and Ossana), **Supp. V:** 226, 230

Streets of Night (Dos Passos), **I:** 478, 479–480, 481, 488

Streitfield, David, **Supp. XIII:** 234; **Supp. XVI:** 63

Strength of Fields, The (Dickey), **Supp. IV Part 1:** 178

"Strength of Fields, The" (Dickey), **Supp. IV Part 1:** 176, 184–185

"Strength of Gideon, The" (Dunbar), **Supp. II Part 1:** 212

Strength of Gideon and Other Stories, The (Dunbar), **Supp. II Part 1:** 211, 212

"Strenuous Artistry" (Zagarell), **Supp. XV:** 281

Strether, Lambert, **II:** 313

"Stretto" (Davison), **Supp. XXVI:** 77

Stribling, T. S., **Supp. VIII:** 126

Strickland, Barbara, **Supp. XIX:** 102

Strickland, Joe (pseudonym). *See* Arnold, George W.

"Strictly Bucolic" (Simic), **Supp. VIII:** 278

Strictly Business (O. Henry), **Supp. II Part 1:** 410

"Strike, The" (Olsen), **Supp. XIII:** 292, 297

Strike at Shane's, The (Skloot), **Supp. XX:** 216

"Strikers" (Untermeyer), **Supp. XV:** 296

Strindberg, August, **I:** 78; **III:** 145, 165, 387, 390, 391, 392, 393; **IV:** 17; **Supp. XVII:** 100; **Supp. XXII:** 23

"String, The" (Dickey), **Supp. IV Part 1:** 179

String Light (Wright), **Supp. XV:** 345–346

"String Quartet, The" (Weigl), **Supp. XIX:** 278

"Strivings of the Negro People" (Du Bois), **Supp. II Part 1:** 167

Stroby, W. C., **Supp. XIV:** 26

Strohbach, Hermann, **Supp. XI:** 242

"Stroke of Good Fortune, A" (O'Connor), **III:** 344; **Retro. Supp. II:** 229, 232

Strom, Stephen, **Supp. XII:** 223

Strong, Anna Louise, **Supp. XVIII:** 238; **Supp. XXIII:** 166

Strong, George Templeton, **IV:** 321

Strong, Josiah, **Supp. XIV:** 64

"Strong Draughts of Their Refreshing Minds" (Dickinson), **Retro. Supp. I:** 46

Stronghold, The (Levin), **Supp. XXVII:** 143, 145–146

Strong Motion (Franzen), **Supp. XX:** 85, 88–89, 92, 95

Strong Opinions (Nabokov), **Retro. Supp. I:** 263, 266, 270, 276

"Strong Room of the House, The" (Bronk), **Supp. XXI:** 32

"Strong Women" (Dorman), **Supp. XI:** 240

Strout, Elizabeth, **Supp. X:** 86; **Supp. XXIII: 273–287**

Structure of Nations and Empires, The (Niebuhr), **III:** 292, 308

"Structure of Rime, The" (Duncan), **Supp. XVI:** 287

Structuring the Void (Klinkowitz), **Supp. XXI:** 233

Struggle, The (film; Griffith), **Supp. XVI:** 191

"Strumpet Song" (Plath), **Retro. Supp. II:** 246; **Supp. I Part 2:** 536

Strunk, William, **Supp. I Part 2:** 652, 662, 670, 671, 672

Strunsky, Anna, **II:** 465

"Strut for Roethke, A" (Berryman), **I:** 188

Strychacz, Thomas F., **Supp. XVI:** 69–70

Stuart, Dabney, **Supp. XVIII:** 79

Stuart, Gilbert, **I:** 16

Stuart, J. E. B., **III:** 56

Stuart, Jesse, **Supp. XX: 162–163, 165**

Stuart, Michael, **Supp. XV:** 140

Stuart, Ruth McEnery, **Supp. XXVIII: 225–241**

Stuart Little (White), **Supp. I Part 2:** 655–658

"Stubborn Kisses" (Gallagher), **Supp. XXIV:** 170

Stuckey, W. J., **Supp. XXII:** 191–192

"Student, The" (Moore), **III:** 212, 215

"Student of Clouds" (Collins), **Supp. XXI:** 60

"Student of Salmanaca, The" (Irving), **II:** 309

"Student's Wife, The" (Carver), **Supp. III Part 1:** 141

Studies in American Indian Literature: Critical Essays and Course Designs (Gunn Allen), **Supp. IV Part 1:** 324, 333

Studies in Classic American Literature (Lawrence), **II:** 102; **III:** 33; **IV:** 333; **Retro. Supp. I:** 421

Studies in Short Fiction (Edmonds), **Supp. XXIII:** 291

Studies in Short Fiction (Malin), **Supp. XVI:** 71

Studies in the Psychology of Sex (Ellis), **Supp. XX: 235**

"Studs" (Farrell), **II:** 25, 28, 31

Studs Lonigan: A Trilogy (Farrell), **II:** 25, 26, 27, 31–34, 37, 38, 41–42

"Study in Orange and White" (Collins), **Supp. XXI:** 60

"Study of Images" (Stevens), **IV:** 79

"Study of Lanier's Poems, A" (Kent), **Supp. I Part 1:** 373

Study of Milton's Prosody (Bridges), **II:** 537

"Study of the Negro Problems, The" (Du Bois), **Supp. II Part 1:** 165

Stuewe, Paul, **Supp. IV Part 1:** 68

Stuhlmann, Gunther, **Supp. X:** 182, 184, 185, 187

Stull, William L., **Supp. XXIV:** 177

Stultifera Navis (Brant), **III:** 447

"Stumps" (Davison), **Supp. XXVI:** 72

"Stumptown Attends the Picture Show"(Bottoms), **Supp. XXVIII:** 24–25, 33

Sturak, John Thomas, **Supp. XIII:** 162, 163, 165, 168

Sturgeon, Theodore, **Supp. XVIII:** 145

Sturgis, George, **III:** 600

Sturgis, Howard, **IV:** 319; **Retro. Supp. I:** 367, 373

Sturgis, Howard Overing, **Supp. XX: 227–242**

Sturgis, Julian Russell, **Supp. XX: 228, 233, 238**

Sturgis, Susan, **III:** 600

Sturm, Margaret. *See* Millar, Margaret

Stuttaford, Genevieve, **Supp. IX:** 279

Stuyvesant, Peter, **II:** 301

"Style" (Nemerov), **III:** 275

Styles of Radical Will (Sontag), **Supp. III Part 2:** 451, 459, 460–463

"Stylist, The" (Egan), **Supp. XIX:** 51, 52

Styne, Jule, **Supp. XVI:** 193

Styron, William, **III:** 40; **IV:** 4, **97–119,** 216; **Supp. IX:** 208; **Supp. V:** 201; **Supp. X:** 15–16, 250; **Supp. XI:** 229, 231, 343; **Supp. XIV:** 82; **Supp. XVI:** 235–236; **Supp. XXIII:** 107, 109

Suares, J. C., **Supp. IV Part 1:** 234

Suarez, Ernest, **Supp. IV Part 1:** 175; **Supp. V:** 180

Suarez, Ray, **Supp. XXI:** 243

"Sub, The" (Dixon), **Supp. XII:** 146

Subjection of Women, The (Mill), **Supp. XI:** 196, 203

"Subjective Necessity for Social Settlements" (Addams), **Supp. I Part 1:** 4

"Subject of Childhood, A" (Paley), **Supp. VI:** 221; **Supp. XXI:** 118

"Submarginalia" (Howe), **Supp. IV Part 2:** 422

Substance and Shadow (James), **II:** 344

"Subterranean Homesick Blues" (song, Dylan), **Supp. XVIII:** 25

Subterraneans, The (Kerouac), **Supp. III Part 1:** 225, 227–231

"Subtitle" (Kees), **Supp. XV:** 139

Subtreasury of American Humor, A (White and White), **Supp. I Part 2:** 668

"Suburban Culture, Imaginative Wonder: The Fiction of Frederick Barthelme" (Brinkmeyer), **Supp. XI:** 38

Suburban Sketches (Howells), **II:** 274, 277

"Subversive Element, The" (Ryan as Quin), **Supp. XVIII:** 230

"Subverted Flower, The" (Frost), **Retro. Supp. I:** 139

"Subway, The" (Tate), **IV:** 128

"Subway Singer, The" (Clampitt), **Supp. IX:** 45

"Success" (Mora), **Supp. XIII:** 217

Successful Love and Other Stories (Schwartz), **Supp. II Part 2:** 661, 665

Successful Women (Taves), **Supp. XXV:** 198

Succession, The: A Novel of Elizabeth and James (Garrett), **Supp. VII:** 104–107, 108

"Success is counted sweetest" (Dickinson), **Retro. Supp. I:** 30, 31–32, 38; **Supp. XV:** 126

Success Stories (Banks), **Supp. V:** 14–15

"Success Story" (Banks), **Supp. V:** 15

"Such Counsels You Gave to Me" (Jeffers), **Supp. II Part 2:** 433

Such Silence (Milburn), **Supp. XI:** 242

"Such Things Happen Only in Books" (Wilder), **IV:** 365

Such Was the Season (Major), **Supp. XXII: 177–178,** 179, 182

"Sudden Journey" (Gallagher), **Supp. XXIV:** 169

Suddenly, Last Summer (film) (Vidal), **Supp. IV Part 2:** 683

Suddenly Last Summer (T. Williams), **I:** 73; **IV:** 382, 383, 385, 386, 387, 389, 390, 391, 392, 395–396, 397, 398

Suder (Everett), **Supp. XVIII: 54–55**

Sudermann, Hermann, **I:** 66

Sue, Eugène, **Supp. XXIII:** 182

Sugg, Richard P., **Supp. IV Part 1:** 68

"Suggestion from a Friend" (Kenyon), **Supp. VII:** 171

"Suicide" (Barnes), **Supp. III Part 1:** 33

"Suicide off Egg Rock" (Plath), **Supp. I Part 2:** 529, 538

Suicides and Jazzers (Carruth), **Supp. XVI:** 46

"Suicide's Note" (Hughes), **Retro. Supp. I:** 199

"Suitable Surroundings, The" (Bierce), **I:** 203

"Suitcase, The" (Ozick), **Supp. V:** 262, 264

"Suite for Augustus, A" (Dove), **Supp. IV Part 1:** 245

"Suite for Emily" (Hull), **Supp. XXI:** 139–140

"Suite for Lord Timothy Dexter" (Rukeyser), **Supp. VI:** 283, 285

"Suite from the Firebird" (Stravinsky), **Supp. XI:** 133

"Suitor, The" (Kenyon), **Supp. VII:** 164–165

Sukarno, **IV:** 490

Sukenick, Ronald, **Supp. V:** 39, 44, 46; **Supp. XII:** 139

Sula (Morrison), **Retro. Supp. III:** 184, 187–189; **Supp. III Part 1:** 362, 364, 367, 368, 379; **Supp. VIII:** 219

Sullivan, Andrew, **Supp. IX:** 135

Sullivan, Arthur, **Supp. XX: 228**

Sullivan, Frank, **Supp. IX:** 201

Sullivan, Harry Stack, **I:** 59

Sullivan, Jack, **Supp. X:** 86; **Supp. XII:** 331

Sullivan, Noel, **Retro. Supp. I:** 202; **Supp. I Part 1:** 329, 333

Sullivan, Patrick, **Supp. XXVI:** 158

Sullivan, Richard, **Supp. VIII:** 124

Sullivan, Walter, **Supp. VIII:** 168

"Sullivan County Sketches" (Crane), **I:** 407, 421

"Sumach and Goldenrod: An American Idyll" (Mumford), **Supp. II Part 2:** 475

Suma Genji (Play), **III:** 466

Sumerian Vistas (Ammons), **Supp. VII:** 34, 35

"Summa Lyrica" (Grossman), **Supp. XIX:** 86

"Summer" (Emerson), **II:** 10

Summer (Gioia), **Supp. XV:** 117

"Summer" (R. Lowell), **II:** 554

Summer (Wharton), **IV:** 317; **Retro. Supp. I:** 360, 367, 374, **378–379,** 382;

Retro. **Supp. III:** 286–287; **Supp. XXIII:** 275, 281

Summer, Bob, **Supp. X:** 1, 5, 6, 42

Summer and Smoke (T. Williams), **IV:** 382, 384, 385, 386, 387, 395, 397, 398; **Supp. IV Part 1:** 84

Summer Anniversaries, The (Justice), **Supp. VII:** 115, 117

Summer Blue (Skloot), **Supp. XX: 196, 207–208**

Summer Brave (Inge), **Supp. XXV:** 99

"Summer Commentary, A" (Winters), **Supp. II Part 2:** 808

"Summer Day" (O'Hara), **III:** 369

"Summer Days, The" (Oliver), **Supp. VII:** 239

"Summer Evening" (Boyle), **Supp. XXIV:** 61

"Summer Lake" (Huddle), **Supp. XXVI:** 150

Summer Lake: New and Selected Poems (Huddle), **Supp. XXVI:** 150

"Summer Love Overheated" (Díaz), **Supp. XXIV:** 89

"Summer Matures" (H. Johnson), **Supp. XXVI:** 174

Summer Never Ends (W. Frank), **Supp. XX:** 78

"Summer Night" (Hughes), **Supp. I Part 1:** 325

"Summer Night, A" (Auden), **Supp. II Part 1:** 8

"Summer Night—Broadway" (Untermeyer), **Supp. XV:** 296

"Summer Noon: 1941" (Winters), **Supp. II Part 2:** 811

"Summer of '82" (Merwin), **Supp. III Part 1:** 355–356

Summer on the Lakes in 1843 (Fuller), **Supp. II Part 1:** 279, 295–296

"Summer People" (Hemingway), **II:** 258–259

"Summer People, The" (Jackson), **Supp. IX:** 120

"Summer People, The" (Merrill), **Supp. III Part 1:** 325–326

"Summer Perdu" (Halliday), **Supp. XIX:** 89

"Summer Planning" (Halliday), **Supp. XIX:** 92

"Summer Ramble, A" (Bryant), **Supp. I Part 1:** 162, 164

Summers, Claude J., **Supp. IV Part 2:** 680–681; **Supp. XIV:** 161, 169

Summers, Robert, **Supp. IX:** 289

"Summer School" (Davison), **Supp. XXVI:** 69

"Summer Solstice, New York City" (Olds), **Supp. X:** 207

"Summer's Reading, A" (Malamud), **Supp. I Part 2:** 430–431, 442

"Summer Storm" (Gioia), **Supp. XV:** 127

"Summer Storm" (Simpson), **Supp. IX:** 268

"'Summertime and the Living . . .'" (Hayden), **Supp. II Part 1:** 363, 366

Summertime Island (Caldwell), **I:** 307–308

"Summer Tragedy" (Bontemps), **Supp. XXII:** 9

"Summer: West Side" (Updike), **Retro. Supp. I:** 320

"Summer with Tu Fu, A" (Carruth), **Supp. XVI:** 55, 58

Summit Beach, 1921 (Dove), **Supp. IV Part 1:** 249

Summoning of Stones, A (Hecht), **Supp. X:** 57, 58, **58–59**

"Summons" (Gansworth), **Supp. XXVI:** 114

"Summons" (Untermeyer), **Supp. XV:** 296

Summons to Memphis, A (Taylor), **Supp. V:** 313, 314, 327

Summons to the Free, A (Benét), **Supp. XI:** 47

Sumner, Charles, **I:** 3, 15; **Supp. I Part 2:** 685, 687

Sumner, John, **Retro. Supp. II:** 95

Sumner, John B., **I:** 511

Sumner, William Graham, **III:** 102, 108; **Supp. I Part 2:** 640

"Sumptuous Destination" (Wilbur), **Supp. III Part 2:** 553

"Sun" (Moore), **III:** 215

"Sun" (Swenson), **Supp. IV Part 2:** 640

"Sun, Rising"(Lea), **Supp. XXVIII:** 135

"Sun, Sea, and Sand" (Marquand), **III:** 60

Sun Also Rises, The (Hemingway), **I:** 107; **II:** 68, 90, 249, 251–252, 260, 600; **III:** 36; **IV:** 35, 297; **Retro. Supp. I:** 171, **177–180,** 181, 189; **Supp. I Part 2:** 614; **Supp. XIII:** 263; **Supp. XVIII:** 74; **Supp. XXVII:** 87

"Sun and Moon" (Kenyon), **Supp. VII:** 168

"Sun and the Still-born Stars, The" (Southern), **Supp. XI:** 295

Sun at Midnight (Soseki; Merwin and Shigematsu, trans.), **Supp. III Part 1:** 353

"Sun Crosses Heaven from West to East Bringing Samson Back to the Womb, The" (R. Bly), **Supp. IV Part 1:** 73

Sun Dance Land (Hanson), **Supp. XXV:** 280

Sun Dance Opera, The (Zitkala-Ša and Hanson), **Supp. XXV:** 279–280

"Sun Dance Shield" (Momaday), **Supp. IV Part 2:** 491

Sunday, Billy, **II:** 449

"Sunday Afternoon" (Munro), **Supp. XXVII:** 194

"Sunday Afternoons" (Komunyakaa), **Supp. XIII:** 127

Sunday after the War (H. Miller), **III:** 184

"Sunday at Home" (Hawthorne), **II:** 231–232; **Retro. Supp. III:** 113

"Sunday Evening at Middlefork Creek Pentecostal Church" (Rash), **Supp. XXVII:** 219

"Sunday Following Mother's Day, The" (E. P. Jones), **Supp. XXII:** 145

"Sunday Morning" (Stevens), **II:** 552; **III:** 278, 463, 509; **IV:** 92–93; **Retro. Supp. I:** 296, 300, 301, 304, 307, 313; **Supp. XIX:** 40; **Supp. XV:** 120; **Supp. XVI:** 210; **Supp. XVII:** 42;

Supp. XXI: 28, 133; Supp. XXIII: 57

"Sunday Morning Apples" (Crane), I: 387

"Sunday Morning Prophecy" (Hughes), Supp. I Part 1: 334

"Sunday Morning with the Sensational Nightingales" (Collins), Supp. XXI: 60

"Sundays" (B. Kelly), Supp. XVII: 124–125

"Sundays" (Salter), Supp. IX: 257

"Sundays, They Sleep Late" (Rukeyser), Supp. VI: 278

"Sundays of Satin-Legs Smith, The" (Brooks), Supp. III Part 1: 74, 75

"Sundays Visiting" (Ríos), Supp. IV Part 2: 541

Sundial, The (Jackson), Supp. IX: 126–127

Sundog (Harrison), Supp. VIII: 46–48

Sun Dogs (R. O. Butler), Supp. XII: 64–65

Sun Do Move, The (Hughes), Supp. I Part 1: 339

Sundquist, Eric, Supp. XIV: 66, 71

"Sunfish" (C. Frost), Supp. XV: 100–101, 102

"Sunflower Sutra" (Ginsberg), Supp. II Part 1: 317, 321; Supp. XV: 215

Sung Sex (Elmslie), Supp. XXVII: 20

Sunlight Dialogues, The (Gardner), Supp. VI: 63, 68, 69, 70

"Sunlight Is Imagination" (Wilbur), Supp. III Part 2: 549

"Sunny Ridge, The" (Halliday), Supp. XIX: 92

Sun Out: Selected Poems, 1952–1954 (Koch), Supp. XV: 179

"Sunrise" (Lanier), Supp. I Part 1: 370

"Sunrise and the Bomb" (Halliday), Supp. XIX: 84, 85, 92

Sunrise over Fallujah (Myers), Supp. XXVII: 207

"Sunrise runs for Both, The" (Dickinson), Retro. Supp. I: 45

Sunrise with Seamonsters: Travels and Discoveries, 1964–1984 (Theroux), Supp. VIII: 311, 313, 323, 325

"Sun Rising" (Donne), Supp. VIII: 164

"Sunset" (Ransom), III: 484

"Sunset from Omaha Hotel Window" (Sandburg), III: 584

Sunset Gun (Parker), Supp. IX: 192

Sunset Limited (Burke), Supp. XIV: 32, 33

Sunset Limited (Harrison), Supp. VIII: 51

"Sunset Maker, The" (Justice), Supp. VII: 123

Sunset Maker, The: Poems, Stories, a Memoir (Justice), Supp. VII: 116, 118, 119, 123–124

Sunshine Boys, The (film), Supp. IV Part 2: 589

Sunshine Boys, The (Simon), Supp. IV Part 2: 575, 584–585

"Sunthin' in the Pastoral Line" (J. R. Lowell), Supp. I Part 2: 415–416

Sun to Sun (Hurston), Supp. VI: 154

Sun Tracks (Ortiz), Supp. IV Part 2: 499, 500

Sun Under Wood (Hass), Supp. VI: 103, 108–109

"Superb Lily, The" (Pinsky), Supp. VI: 250

"Super Goat Man" (Lethem), Supp. XVIII: 148

"Superman Comes to the Supermarket" (Mailer), Retro. Supp. II: 204

"Supermarket in California, A" (Ginsberg), Retro. Supp. III: 54; Supp. XI: 135

"Supernatural Horror in Literature" (Lovecraft), Supp. XXV: 120

"Supernatural Love" (Schnackenberg), Supp. XV: 257, 259–260

Supernatural Love: Poems 1976–1992 (Schnackenberg), Supp. XV: 253, 256, 260, 263

Suplee, Curt, Supp. XVI: 202

"Supper After the Last, The" (Kinnell), Supp. III Part 1: 239

"Supposedly Fun Thing I'll Never Do Again, A" (Wallace), Supp. X: 315

Supposedly Fun Thing I'll Never Do Again, A: Essays and Arguments (Wallace), Supp. X: 314–316

Suppressed Desires (Glaspell and Cook), Supp. III Part 1: 178; Supp. XXI: 6

Suppression of the African Slave Trade to the United States of America, 1638–1870 (Du Bois), Supp. II Part 1: 157, 162

Supreme Fiction, The (Stevens), Supp. XVI: 158

"Supremes, The" (Jarman), Supp. XVII: 115

Sure Hand of God, The (Caldwell), I: 297, 302

Sure Signs: New and Selected Poems (Kooser), Supp. XIX: 116, 117, 121–122

"Surety and Fidelity Claims" (Stevens), Retro. Supp. I: 296, 309

Surface of Earth, The (Price), Supp. VI: 261–262

"Surfaces" (Ammons), Supp. VII: 36

Surfaces and Masks (Major), Supp. XXII: 180

Surfacing (Atwood), Supp. XIII: 20, 21, 22–23, 24, 33, 35

"Surgeon at 2 A.M." (Plath), Supp. I Part 2: 545

Surmmer Knowledge (Schwartz), Supp. II Part 2: 662, 665

"Surprise" (Kenyon), Supp. VII: 173

Surprised by Sin: The Reader in Paradise Lost (Fish), Supp. XIV: 15

Surreal South (eds. P. Benedict and L. Benedict), Supp. XXIII: 35

"Surround, The Imagining Herself as the Environment,/She Speaks to James Wright at Sundow" (Dickey), Supp. IV Part 1: 185

"Surrounded by Weasels" (Gray and Gallagher), Supp. XXIV: 178

"Survey of Literature" (Ransom), III: 480

"Survey of the Literature, A" (Saunders), Supp. XIX: 235

"Surveyor, The" (H. Roth), Supp. IX: 233, 234

Survival (Atwood), Supp. XIII: 20, 22, 35

"Survival, Infantry" (Oppen), Supp. XXVI: 232

"Survival as Tao, Beginning at 5:00 A.M." (Carruth), Supp. XVI: 56

Survival of the Bark Canoe, The (McPhee), Supp. III Part 1: 301, 302, 308, 313

Survival This Way: Interviews with American Indian Poets (Bruchac), Supp. IV Part 2: 506

"Surviving Love" (Berryman), I: 173

Survivor (O. Butler), Supp. XIII: 62, 63

Susan and Anna Warner (Foster), Supp. XVIII: 265

Susan and God (film; Cukor), Supp. XVI: 192

Susanna Moodie: Voice and Vision (Shields), Supp. VII: 313

Susan Warner ("Elizabeth Wetherell") (A. Warner), Supp. XVIII: 259, 260

Suspect in Poetry, The (Dickey), Supp. IV Part 1: 177

"Sustained by Fiction" (Hoffman), Supp. X: 90, 92

"Susto" (Ríos), Supp. IV Part 2: 553

Sutherland, Donald, IV: 38, 44; Supp. IX: 254

Sutherland, Efua, Supp. IV Part 1: 9, 16

Sutherland, Zena, Supp. XXVII: 202

Sutherland-Smith, James, Supp. X: 211, 212

Sut Lovingood (Harris), II: 70; Supp. XXII: 193

Sutton, Roger, Supp. X: 266; Supp. XXVII: 212; Supp. XXVIII: 281

Sutton, Walter, III: 479

"Sutton Pie Safe, The"(P. Benedict), Supp. XXIII: 36

Suttree (McCarthy), Supp. VIII: 178–180, 189

Suvero, Mark di, Supp. IX: 251

"Suzanne" (Cohen), Supp. XXVII: 51, 54, 59

Svevo, Italo, Supp. XIV: 112

Swados, Harvey, Supp. XI: 222; Supp. XIX: 255–271

Swales, Martin, Supp. XIX: 183

Swallow, Alan, Supp. X: 112, 115, 116, 120, 123

Swallow Barn (J. P. Kennedy), II: 313

Swallow Barn (Kennedy), Supp. XXII: 193

Swallow the Lake (Major), Supp. XXII: 174

"Swamp Boy" (Bass), Supp. XVI: 20

Swan, Barbara, Supp. IV Part 2: 447

Swan, Jon, Supp. IV Part 1: 176

Swan Lake (Helprin), Supp. XXV: 83, 87

Swan Lake (Tchaikovsky), Supp. IX: 51

Swan Lake Trilogy (Helprin), Supp. XXV: 81, 84, 87

"Swan Legs" (Stern), Supp. IX: 299

Swann (Shields), Supp. VII: 315, 318–323, 326

Swann, Brian, Supp. IV Part 2: 500

Swanson, Gloria, **II:** 429

Swanson, Stevenson, **Supp. XIV:** 111

Swan Song (Hecht and MacArthur), **Supp. XXVII:** 90

Swanton, John Reed, **Supp. VIII:** 295

Swan Watch (Schulberg), **Supp. XVIII:** 254

Swanwick, John, **Supp. XV:** 237

Swanwick, Michael, **Supp. XVI:** 128

"Swarm, The" (Plath), **Retro. Supp. II:** 255

"Sway" (Simpson), **Supp. IX:** 276

Sweat (Hurston), **Supp. VI:** 152

"Sweat" (Hurston), **Retro. Supp. III:** 139

Swedenborg, Emanuel, **II:** 5, 10, 321, 342, 343–344, 396

Sweeney Agonistes (T. S. Eliot), **I:** 580; **Retro. Supp. I:** 64, 65; **Retro. Supp. II:** 247; **Retro. Supp. III:** 58, 69

"Sweeney Among the Nightingales" (Eliot), **III:** 4

"Sweeper, The" (Kooser), **Supp. XIX:** 125

Sweet, Blanche, **Supp. I Part 2:** 391

Sweet, Timothy, **Supp. IV Part 1:** 330

Sweet and Lowdown (film; Allen), **Supp. XV:** 11

Sweet and Sour (O'Hara), **III:** 361

"Sweet Armageddon" (Hoffman), **Supp. XVIII:** 85, 86

Sweet Bird of Youth (T. Williams), **IV:** 382, 383, 385, 386, 387, 388, 389, 390, 391, 392, 395, 396, 398; **Supp. IV Part 1:** 84, 89

Sweet Charity (musical), **Supp. IV Part 2:** 575

Sweet Flypaper of Life, The (Hughes), **Supp. I Part 1:** 335–336

"Sweetgrass"(Kenny), **Supp. XXIII:** 148

"Sweetheart" (Notley), **Supp. XXII:** 231

"Sweetheart of the Song Tra Bong, The" (O'Brien), **Supp. V:** 243, 249

"Sweethearts" (Ford), **Supp. V:** 69

Sweet Hereafter, The (Banks), **Supp. V:** 15–16

Sweet Illusions (Myers), **Supp. XXVII:** 208–209

Sweet Lorain (Weigl), **Supp. XIX:** 282

Sweet Machine (Doty), **Supp. XI:** 121, **131–132,** 135

Sweet Science, The (Liebling), **Supp. XXVII:** 46–47

Sweet Sue (Gurney), **Supp. V:** 105, 107–108

Sweet Sweetback's Baadasss Song (Peebles; film), **Supp. XI:** 17

Sweet Thursday (Steinbeck), **IV:** 50, 52, 64–65

Sweet Will (Levine), **Supp. V:** 178, 187, 189, 190

"Sweet Will" (Levine), **Supp. V:** 190

"Sweet Willy"(J. Schoolcraft), **Supp. XXIII:** 226, 231

"Sweet Words on Race" (Hughes), **Retro. Supp. I:** 211

Sweezy, Paul, **Supp. I Part 2:** 645

"Swell-Looking Girl, A" (Caldwell), **I:** 310

Swenson, May, **Retro. Supp. II:** 44; **Supp. IV Part 2: 637–655; Supp.**

XIX: 123; **Supp. XXVI:** 66, 67

Swetman, Glenn R., **Supp. XXI:** 91

"Swift" (Schwartz), **Supp. II Part 2:** 663

Swift, Jonathan, **I:** 125, 194, 209, 441; **II:** 110, 302, 304–305, 577; **III:** 113; **IV:** 68; **Retro. Supp. I:** 66; **Retro. Supp. III:** 109, 139; **Supp. I Part 2:** 406, 523, 603, 656, 665, 708, 714; **Supp. IV Part 1:** 51; **Supp. IV Part 2:** 692; **Supp. XI:** 105, 209; **Supp. XII:** 276; **Supp. XV:** 258; **Supp. XVI:** 110; **Supp. XVIII:** 2, 12; **Supp. XXV:** 87

"Swimmer" (Francis), **Supp. IX:** 82

"Swimmer" (Skloot), **Supp. XX: 199, 200**

"Swimmer, The" (Cheever), **Supp. I Part 1:** 185, 187

"Swimmer, The" (Glück), **Supp. V:** 82

"Swimmers" (Untermeyer), **Supp. XV:** 300

"Swimmers, The" (Fitzgerald), **Retro. Supp. I:** 110, 111

"Swimmers, The" (Tate), **IV:** 136

"Swimming" (Harjo), **Supp. XII:** 218

Swimming Pool, The (Rinehart), **Supp. XXV:** 189, 198, 200, 202

"Swimming Pool, The"(Strout), **Supp. XXIII:** 284

"Swim Team, The" (July), **Supp. XXIV:** 201

Swinburne, Algernon C., **I:** 50, 384, 568; **II:** 3, 4, 129, 400, 524; **IV:** 135; **Retro. Supp. I:** 100; **Retro. Supp. III:** 44, 60, 74; **Supp. I Part 1:** 79; **Supp. I Part 2:** 422, 552; **Supp. XIV:** 120, 344

"Swinburne as Poet" (Eliot), **I:** 576

Swinger of Birches, A: A Portrait of Robert Frost (Cox), **Retro. Supp. I:** 132

"Swinging an Arc Before Him As He Goes" (Espaillat), **Supp. XXI:** 108

"Swinging on a Birch-Tree" (Larcom), **Supp. XIII:** 147

Swiss, Tom, **Supp. XIX:** 40

Switch, The (Dixon), **Supp. XII:** 141

Swope, D. B., **Supp. IX:** 95

Sword Blades and Poppy Seed (A. Lowell), **II:** 518, 520, 522, 532

Sword of God, The: Jeanne D'Arc (Endore), **Supp. XVII:** 55

Sybil (Auchincloss), **Supp. IV Part 1:** 25

Sybil and Chryssa (S. and A. Warner), **Supp. XVIII:** 264

"Sycamore" (Frost), **Retro. Supp. III:** 104

"Sycamore" (Stern), **Supp. IX:** 294

"Sycamore, The" (Moore), **III:** 216

"Sycamores, The" (Whittier), **Supp. I Part 2:** 699

Sylvester, Johnny, **Supp. I Part 2:** 438

Sylvester, Joshua, **I:** 178, 179; **II:** 18; **III:** 157; **Supp. I Part 1:** 98, 104, 114, 116

Sylvia (Gurney), **Supp. V:** 105

"Sylvia" (L. Michaels), **Supp. XVI:** 202, 213

"Sylvia" (Larcom), **Supp. XIII:** 144

"Sylvia" (Stern), **Supp. IX:** 297

Sylvia: A Fictional Memoir (L. Michaels), **Supp. XVI:** 202, 213

Sylvia Plath: Method and Madness (Butscher), **Supp. I Part 2:** 526

Sylvia Plath: Poetry and Existence (Holbrook), **Supp. I Part 2:** 526–527

"Sylvia's Death" (Sexton), **Supp. II Part 2:** 671, 684, 685

"Symbol and Image in the Shorter Poems of Herman Melville" (Dickey), **Supp. IV Part 1:** 176

Symbolist Movement in Literature, The (Symons), **I:** 50, 569; **Retro. Supp. I:** 55; **Retro. Supp. III:** 57

Symonds, John Addington, **I:** 241, 242, 251, 259; **IV:** 334; **Supp. XIV:** 329, 335; **Supp. XX: 230**

Symons, Arthur, **I:** 50, 569; **Retro. Supp. I:** 55; **Retro. Supp. III:** 57; **Supp. XX: 239; Supp. XXVII:** 287

Symons, Julian, **Supp. IV Part 1:** 343, 351

"Sympathy" (Dunbar), **Supp. IV Part 1:** 15

Sympathy of Souls, A (Goldbarth), **Supp. XII:** 175, 176, **186–187**

"Symphony, The" (Lanier), **Supp. I Part 1:** 352, 360–361, 364; **Supp. I Part 2:** 416

Symposium (Plato), **Retro. Supp. II:** 31; **Supp. IV Part 1:** 391

Symposium: To Kill a Mockingbird (Alabama Law Review), **Supp. VIII:** 127, 128

Symptoms and Madness (Major), **Supp. XXII:** 174

Symptoms of Being 35 (Lardner), **II:** 434

Synanon (Endore), **Supp. XVII:** 65

Synanon (film, Quine), **Supp. XVII:** 65

Synanon City (Endore), **Supp. XVII:** 65

Syncopated Cakewalk, The (Major), **Supp. XXII:** 174

Synge, John Millington, **I:** 434; **III:** 591–592; **Supp. III Part 1:** 34; **Supp. VIII:** 155

Synthetic Philosophy (Spencer), **II:** 462–463

"Syringa" (Ashbery), **Supp. III Part 1:** 19–21, 25

"Syrinx" (Clampitt), **Supp. IX:** 53

"Syrinx" (Merrill), **Supp. III Part 1:** 328

Syrkin, Marie, **Supp. XIV:** 279, 288, 291; **Supp. XXVII:** 133–134

"System, The" (Ashbery), **Supp. III Part 1:** 14, 15, 18, 21–22

System of Dante's Hell, The (Baraka), **Supp. II Part 1:** 39–41, 55

"System of Dante's Inferno, The" (Baraka), **Supp. II Part 1:** 40

"System of Doctor Tarr and Professor Fether, The" (Poe), **III:** 419, 425

System of General Geography, A (Brown), **Supp. I Part 1:** 146

Szaylay, Michael, **Supp. XXI:** 267; **Supp. XXVIII:** 206, 218, 222

Sze, Mai-mai, **Supp. X:** 291

Szentgyorgyi, Tom, **Supp. IX:** 135, 136, 140, 141–142

Szilagyi, Anca, **Supp. XXVI:** 218

Szukalski, Stanislaus, **Supp. XXV:** 19, 23

Szulc, Tad, **Supp. XVI:** 154

Szumskyj, Benjamin, **Supp. XXVII:** 128

Szwarc, Marek, **Supp. XXVII:** 140

Szymborka, Wislawa, **Supp. XI:** 267

Szymborska, Wislawa, **Supp. XVIII:** 29

T

"T-2 Tanker Blues" (Snyder), **Supp. VIII:** 294

Tabios, Eileen, **Supp. XV:** 214, 225, 226

"Table of Delectable Contents, The" (Simic), **Supp. VIII:** 276

Tabloid Dreams (R. O. Butler), **Supp. XII:** 70–72, 74

Tacey Cromwell (Richter), **Supp. XVIII:** 211, 215, 217

Tacitus, Cornelius, **I:** 485; **II:** 113

Tadic, Novica, **Supp. VIII:** 272

Taft (Patchett), **Supp. XII:** 307, 312, **314–317**

"Tag" (Hughes), **Supp. I Part 1:** 341

Taggard, Genevieve, **IV:** 436; **Supp. XXII:** 271–287; **Supp. XXVI:** 144

Taggart, John, **Supp. IV Part 2:** 421

Tagore, Rabindranath, **I:** 383; **Supp. XX:** 117

"Taibele and Her Demon" (Singer), **Retro. Supp. II:** 307

Taibl, Erika, **Supp. XV:** 255

"Tailor Shop, The" (H. Miller), **III:** 175

"Tails" (Dixon), **Supp. XII:** 154

Taine, Hippolyte, **I:** 503; **II:** 271; **III:** 323; **IV:** 440, 444

"Tain't So" (Hughes), **Supp. I Part 1:** 330

"Taipei Tangle" (Halliday), **Supp. XIX:** 91

Takasago (play), **III:** 466

Takazauckas, Albert, **Supp. XXIII:** 203

Take Away the Darkness (Bynner), **Supp. XV:** 51

Take Heart (Peacock), **Supp. XIX: 197–199**, 206

Take Me Back: A Novel (Bausch), **Supp. VII:** 41, 43–45, 46, 49

"Take My Saddle from the Wall: A Valediction" (McMurtry), **Supp. V:** 219

"'Take No for an Answer' " (Didion), **Supp. IV Part 1:** 203

"Take Pity" (Malamud), **Supp. I Part 2:** 427, 428, 435, 436, 437

"Takers, The" (Olds), **Supp. X:** 205

"Take the I Out" (Olds), **Supp. X:** 213

Take the Money and Run (film; Allen), **Supp. XV:** 3–4, 6

"Taking a Stitch in a Dead Man's Arm" (Vaz), **Supp. XXVI:** 264

"Taking Away the Name of a Nephew" (Ríos), **Supp. IV Part 2:** 545–546

Taking Care of Mrs. Carroll (Monette), **Supp. X:** 153

Taking Care: Thoughts on Storytelling and Belief (Kittredge), **Supp. XXVI:** 181, 182, 183, 185

"Taking of Captain Ball, The" (Jewett), **Retro. Supp. II:** 134

"Taking Off Emily Dickinson's Clothes" (Collins), **Supp. XXI:** 59, 60

"Taking Out the Lawn Chairs" (Karr), **Supp. XI:** 241

"Taking the Bypass" (J. Epstein), **Supp. XIV:** 110; **Supp. XVI:** 230

"Taking the Forest" (Howe), **Supp. IV Part 2:** 433

"Taking the Lambs to Market" (Kumin), **Supp. IV Part 2:** 455

Talbot, Daniel, **Supp. XIX:** 264

Talbott, Hudson, **Supp. XXVIII:** 286

"Tale, A" (Bogan), **Supp. III Part 1:** 50, 51

Taleb-Khyar, Mohamed, **Supp. IV Part 1:** 242, 243, 244, 247, 257

Talented Mr. Ripley, The (Highsmith), **Supp. XXII:** 119

"Tale of Jerusalem, A" (Poe), **III:** 411

Tale of Possessors Self-Dispossessed, A (O'Neill), **III:** 404

Tale of the Body Thief, The (Rice), **Supp. VII:** 290, 293–294, 297

"Tale of the White Pyramid, The" (Cather), **Retro. Supp. III:** 25

Tale of Two Cities, A (film), **Supp. I Part 1:** 67

"Tale of Two Liars, A" (Singer), **IV:** 12

Tales (Baraka), **Supp. II Part 1:** 39, 55

Tales (Poe), **III:** 413; **Retro. Supp. III:** 225

Tales and Stories for Black Folks (Bambara, ed.), **Supp. XI:** 1

Tales before Midnight (Benét), **Supp. XI:** 46, 53, 57

Talese, Gay, **Supp. XVI:** 273; **Supp. XVII:** 199–211; **Supp. XXIV:** 282

Tales of a Traveller (Irving), **II:** 309–310

Tales of a Wayside Inn (Longfellow), **II:** 489, 490, 501, 502, 504–505; **Retro. Supp. II:** 154, **162–165**

Tales of Glauber-Spa (Bryant, ed.), **Supp. I Part 1:** 157

Tales of H. P. Lovecraft (Oates, ed.), **Supp. XXV:** 123

"Tales of Lone Oak"(Teale), **Supp. XXVIII:** 244

Tales of Manhattan (Auchincloss), **Supp. IV Part 1:** 23

Tales of Men and Ghosts (Wharton), **IV:** 315; **Retro. Supp. I:** 372

Tales of My People (Asch), **Supp. XXIII:** 7

Tales of Rhoda, The (Rice), **Supp. VII:** 288

Tales of Soldiers and Civilians (Bierce), **I:** 200–203, 204, 206, 208, 212

Tales of the Argonauts (Harte), **Supp. II Part 1:** 337, 348, 351

Tales of the Fish Patrol (London), **II:** 465

Tales of the Grotesque and Arabesque (Poe), **II:** 273; **III:** 412, 415; **Retro. Supp. II:** 270; **Retro. Supp. III:** 225, 228

Tales of the Jazz Age (Fitzgerald), **II:** 88; **Retro. Supp. I:** 105; **Supp. IX:** 57

Tales You Won't Believe (Stratton-Porter), **Supp. XX: 217**

Taliaferro, Frances, **Supp. XXII:** 210

"Talisman, A" (Moore), **III:** 195–196

Talisman, The (King), **Supp. V:** 140, 144, 152

"Talkin Bout Sonny" (Bambara), **Supp. XI:** 6–7

"Talking" (Merwin), **Supp. III Part 1:** 354

Talking All Morning (R. Bly), **Supp. IV Part 1:** 59, 60, 61, 62, 64, 65

Talking Dirty to the Gods (Komunyakaa), **Supp. XIII: 130–131**

Talking History (television program), **Supp. XXI:** 172

"Talking Horse" (Malamud), **Supp. I Part 2:** 435

Talking Soft Dutch (McCarriston), **Supp. XIV: 260–263**, 266, 270, 271

"Talking to Barr Creek" (Wagoner), **Supp. IX:** 328

"Talking to Sheep" (Sexton), **Supp. II Part 2:** 695

Talking to the Sun: An Illustrated Anthology of Poems for Young People (Koch and Farrell, eds.), **Supp. XV:** 188

"Talking Water" (Taggard), **Supp. XXII:** 276

"Talk of Heroes" (C. Bly), **Supp. XVI:** 34

"Talk of the Town" (*The New Yorker* column), **IV:** 215; **Supp. IV Part 1:** 53, 54

"Talk on Guadalcanal" (Wolfert), **Supp. XXI:** 264

Talk Talk (Boyle), **Supp. XX:** 24

"Talk with the Yellow Kid, A" (Bellow), **I:** 151

Tallent, Elizabeth, **Supp. IV Part 2:** 570

Tallman, Warren, **Supp. IV Part 1:** 154

TallMountain, Mary, **Supp. IV Part 1:** 324–325

Talma, Louise, **IV:** 357

Talmadge, Constance, **Supp. XVI:** 186, 187, 196

Talmadge, Norma, **Supp. XVI:** 186, 187, 196

Talmadge Girls, The (Loos), **Supp. XVI:** 186, 196

Talmey, Allene, **Supp. IV Part 1:** 197; **Supp. XIII:** 172

Talmud, **IV:** 8, 17

Taltos: Lives of the Mayfair Witches (Rice), **Supp. VII:** 299–300

"Tamar" (Jeffers), **Supp. II Part 2:** 427–428, 436

Tamar and Other Poems (Jeffers), **Supp. II Part 2:** 416, 419

"Tambourine Life" (Berrigan), **Supp. XXIV:** 42

Tambourines to Glory (Hughes), **Supp. I Part 1:** 338–339

"Tame Indians" (Jewett), **Retro. Supp. II:** 141

"Tamerlane" (Poe), **III:** 426

Tamerlane and Other Poems (Poe), **III:** 410; **Retro. Supp. III:** 224, 231

"Tammany Man, The" (Hapgood), **Supp. XVII:** 103

"Tam O'Shanter" (Burns), **II:** 306

Tamsen Donner: A Woman's Journey (Whitman), **Supp. XXI:** 246

Tan, Amy, **Supp. X:** 289–300

Tangential Views (Bierce), **I:** 209
"Tangier 1975" (Bowles), **Supp. IV Part 1:** 94
Tanguay, Pablo, **Supp. XXIII:** 299
"Tankas" (McClatchy), **Supp. XII:** 266
Tanner, Laura E., **Supp. X:** 209; **Supp. XXI:** 217
Tanner, Obour, **Supp. XX: 281, 288**
Tanner, Tony, **I:** 260, 261; **Retro. Supp. II:** 205; **Supp. IV Part 1:** 285; **Supp. XVI:** 65, 69
Tannhäuser (Wagner), **I:** 315
"Tan Ta Ra, Cries Mars...," (Wagoner), **Supp. IX:** 325
Tao of Physics, The (Capra), **Supp. X:** 261
Tao Teh Ching (Bynner, trans.), **Supp. XV:** 46, 47
Tapahonso, Luci, **Supp. IV Part 1:** 404; **Supp. IV Part 2:** 499, 508
Tape for the Turn of the Year (Ammons), **Supp. VII:** 31–33, 35
"Tapestry" (Ashbery), **Supp. III Part 1:** 22–23
"Tapestry" (E. P. Jones), **Supp. XXII:** 152
Tapestry Room Murder, The (Wells), **Supp. XXVI:** 282
"Tapiama" (Bowles), **Supp. IV Part 1:** 89–90
"Tapiola" (W. C. Williams), **Retro. Supp. I:** 429
Tappan, Arthur, **Supp. I Part 2:** 588
Tapping the White Cane of Solitude (F. Wright), **Supp. XVII:** 243
Taps at Reveille (Fitzgerald), **II:** 94, 96; **Retro. Supp. I:** 113
Taradash, Daniel, **Supp. XXV:** 95
Tar: A Midwest Childhood (Anderson), **I:** 98, 115; **II:** 27
Tarantino, Quentin, **Supp. IV Part 1:** 356
Tarantula (Dylan), **Supp. XVIII:** 21, 29, **31–32**
Tar Baby (Morrison), **Retro. Supp. III:** 190–191; **Supp. III Part 1:** 364, 369–372, 379; **Supp. IV Part 1:** 13
Tarbell, Ida, **III:** 322, 580; **Retro. Supp. II:** 101
"Target Practice" (Offutt), **Supp. XIX:** 171
"Target Study" (Baraka), **Supp. II Part 1:** 49–50, 54
Tarkington, Booth, **II:** 444; **III:** 70; **Retro. Supp. I:** 100; **Supp. XV:** 41
Tarnawsky, Yuriy (George) Orest, **Supp. XX:** 259
Tarpon (film), **Supp. VIII:** 42
Tarr, Rodger L., **Supp. X:** 222, 224, 226
Tárrega, Francisco, **Supp. XXI:** 100
Tartt, Donna, **Supp. XVIII:** 135; **Supp. XXVII:** 67, **267–281**
Tartuffe (Molière; Wilbur, trans.), **Supp. III Part 2:** 560
Tarumba, Selected Poems of Jaime Sabines (Levine and Trejo, trans.), **Supp. V:** 178
Tarzan Finds a Son (film, Weismuller), **Supp. XX: 18**
"Tarzan Is an Expatriate" (Theroux), **Supp. VIII:** 313

Tasis, Juan de, **Supp. XXI:** 104
Task, The (Cowper), **II:** 304
Tasker Street (Halliday), **Supp. XIX:** 82, **87–89**
Tasso, Torquato, **I:** 276
Taste of Palestine, A: Menus and Memories (Shihab), **Supp. XIII:** 273
Tate, Alan, **Supp. XV:** 141
Tate, Allen, **I:** 48, 49, 50, 67, 69, 381, 382, 386, 390, 396, 397, 399, 402, 441, 468; **II:** 197–198, 367, 536, 537, 542, 551, 554; **III:** 424, 428, 454, 482, 483, 485, 493, 495, 496, 497, 499, 500, 517; **IV:** 120–143, 236, 237, 433; **Retro. Supp. I:** 37, 41, 90; **Retro. Supp. II:** 77, 79, 82, 83, 89, 176, 178, 179; **Retro. Supp. III:** 48, 49, 50; **Supp. I Part 1:** 364, 371; **Supp. I Part 2:** 423; **Supp. II Part 1:** 90–91, 96, 98, 103–104, 136, 139, 144, 150, 151, 318; **Supp. II Part 2:** 643; **Supp. III Part 2:** 542; **Supp. V:** 315, 331; **Supp. X:** 1, 52; **Supp. XIV:** 2; **Supp. XXI:** 256; **Supp. XXII:** 277
Tate, Mrs. Allen (Caroline Gordon). See Gordon, Caroline
Tate, Mrs. Allen (Helen Heinz), **IV:** 127
Tate, Mrs. Allen (Isabella Gardner), **IV:** 127
Tate, Benjamin Lewis Bogan, **IV:** 127
Tate, Greg, **Supp. XIII:** 233, 237
Tate, James, **Supp. V:** 92, 338; **Supp. VIII:** 39, 279; **Supp. XV:** 250; **Supp. XVII:** 242; **Supp. XXVIII:** 196
Tate, John Allen, **IV:** 127
Tate, Michael Paul, **IV:** 127
Tate, Nancy, **II:** 197
Tatonetti, Lisa, **Supp. XXIII:** 149–150
Tattooed Countess, The (Van Vechten), **I:** 295; **Supp. II Part 2:** 726–728, 738, 742
Tattooed Feet (Nye), **Supp. XIII:** 274
"Tattoos" (McClatchy), **Supp. XII:** 266–267, 268
"Tattoos" (Wright), **Supp. V:** 335, 340
Tatum, Anna, **I:** 516
Tatum, James, **Supp. IV Part 2:** 684
Taubman, Howard, **Supp. XXV:** 106
Taupin, René, **II:** 528, 529; **Supp. III Part 2:** 614, 615, 617, 621
Tavano, John, **Supp. XXI:** 99
"Tavern, The"(Goodman), **Supp. XXVIII:** 92
Taves, Isabella, **Supp. XXV:** 198
Tawney, Richard Henry, **Supp. I Part 2:** 481
Taylor, Ann, **Supp. XXIII:** 231
Taylor, Bayard, **II:** 275; **Supp. I Part 1:** 350, 361, 362, 365, 366, 372; **Supp. XV:** 269
Taylor, Chuck, **Supp. XXIII:** 57
Taylor, Cora. See Howarth, Cora
Taylor, Deems, **III:** 138
Taylor, Edward, **III:** 493; **IV:** 144–166; **Retro. Supp. III:** 3; **Supp. I Part 1:** 98; **Supp. I Part 1:** 375, 386, 546
Taylor, Mrs. Edward (Elizabeth Fitch), **IV:** 147, 165
Taylor, Mrs. Edward (Ruth Wyllys), **IV:** 148

Taylor, Eleanor Ross, **Supp. V:** 317, 318
Taylor, Elizabeth, **II:** 588
Taylor, Frank, **III:** 81
Taylor, Frederick Winslow, **Supp. I Part 2:** 644
Taylor, Graham, **Supp. I Part 1:** 5
Taylor, Helen, **Supp. XXVIII:** 121, 122, 234, 237–238
Taylor, Henry, **Retro. Supp. I:** 212; **Supp. XI:** 317; **Supp. XIII:** 333
Taylor, Henry W., **IV:** 144
Taylor, Jeremy, **II:** 11; **III:** 487; **Supp. I Part 1:** 349; **Supp. XII:** 45; **Supp. XIV:** 344, 345
Taylor, John, **IV:** 149
Taylor, Katherine, **Supp. VIII:** 251
Taylor, Kezia, **IV:** 148
Taylor, Nathaniel W., **Supp. I Part 2:** 580
Taylor, Paul, **I:** 293
Taylor, Peter, **Retro. Supp. II:** 179; **Supp. V: 313–329; Supp. XIV:** 3
Taylor, Raynor, **Supp. XV:** 238
Taylor, Richard, **IV:** 146
Taylor, Robert, **Supp. I Part 1:** 294; **Supp. XV:** 135, 138; **Supp. XVI:** 277
Taylor, Samuel A., **Supp. XX: 253**
Taylor, Stephan, **Supp. XVI:** 203
Taylor, Thomas, **II:** 10
Taylor, William, **IV:** 145–146
Taylor, Zachary, **I:** 3; **II:** 433–434
Tchelitchew, Peter, **II:** 586
Tea and Sympathy (Anderson), **Supp. I Part 1:** 277; **Supp. V:** 108
"Tea at the Palaz of Hoon" (Stevens), **Retro. Supp. I:** 300, 302, 306
"Teacher's Pet" (Thurber), **Supp. I Part 2:** 605–606
"Teaching and Story Telling" (Maclean), **Supp. XIV:** 234
Teaching a Stone to Talk: Expeditions and Encounters (Dillard), **Supp. VI:** 23, 26, 28, 32, 33, 34–35
"Teaching Emily Dickenson"(Hadas), **Supp. XXIII:** 115
"Teaching Hanh the Blues" (Weigl), **Supp. XIX:** 287
Teachings of Don B., The (Barthelme), **Supp. IV Part 1:** 53
Teachout, Terry, **Supp. XIX:** 137
Teale, Edwin Way, **Supp. XIII:** 7; **Supp. XXVIII: 243–258**
Teall, Dorothy, **I:** 221
"Team Blue/Team Square: Revisiting the Lyric and the Narrative" (Biss and Zapruder), **Supp. XXVI:** 54–55
"Team Players" (Biss), **Supp. XXVI:** 46
Team Team Team (film), **Supp. IX:** 251
"Tea on the Mountain" (Bowles), **Supp. IV Part 1:** 90
"Tea Party, The" (MacLeish), **III:** 11
Tear and a Smile, A (Dam'a wa Ibtisáma) (Gibran), **Supp. XX: 116, 118, 124**
Teare, Brian, **Supp. XXII:** 236
"Tears, Idle Tears" (Lord Tennyson), **Supp. XIV:** 8
"Tears of the Pilgrims, The" (McClatchy), **Supp. XII:** 256
Teasdale, Sara, **Retro. Supp. I:** 133; **Supp. I Part 2:** 393, 707; **Supp. XIV:**

127; **Supp. XV:** 295, 297, 301, 305, 307, 308; **Supp. XVII:** 69, 75; **Supp. XXVII:** 283–298

"Tease" (Swados), **Supp. XIX:** 267

Tebeaux, Elizabeth, **Supp. IX:** 109

"Technical Manifesto of Futurist Literature" (Marinetti), **Supp. XXII:** 161

Technics and Civilization (Mumford), **Supp. I Part 2:** 638; **Supp. II Part 2:** 479, 493, 497

Technics and Human Development (Mumford), **Supp. I Part 2:** 638; **Supp. II Part 2:** 497

Technique of the Mystery Story, The (Wells), **Supp. XXVI:** 277, 280, 281–282

"Technology, The" (Egan), **Supp. XIX:** 61

"Teddy" (Salinger), **III:** 561–563, 571

"Te Deum" (Reznikoff), **Supp. XIV:** 281

Tedlock, Dennis, **Supp. IV Part 2:** 509

"Teeth Mother Naked at Last, The" (R. Bly), **Supp. IV Part 1:** 63, 68, 73

Teggart, Richard, **Supp. I Part 2:** 650

Tegnér, Esaias, **Retro. Supp. II:** 155

Teilhard de Chardin, Pierre, **Supp. I Part 1:** 314

Tekonwatonti/Molly Brant (Kenny), **Supp. XXIII:** 143, 147, 151, **152–153,** 154

"Telegraphs from a Distracted Sibyl" (Mullen), **Supp. XXVII:** 166, 176

Telephone, The (film), **Supp. XI:** 309

"Telephone Call, A" (Parker), **Supp. IX:** **202–203**

"Telephone Number of the Muse, The" (Justice), **Supp. VII:** 124–125

Telephone Poles and Other Poems (Updike), **IV:** 214, 215

"Television" (Beattie), **Supp. V:** 33

Teller, Edward, **I:** 137

"Tell Him About Brother John" (Muñoz), **Supp. XXV:** 136

"Telling" (Ortiz), **Supp. IV Part 2:** 509

"Telling It in Black and White: The Importance of the Africanist Presence in *To Kill a Mockingbird*" (Baecker), **Supp. VIII:** 128

Telling Secrets (Buechner), **Supp. XII:** 53–54

Telling Stories (Didion), **Supp. IV Part 1:** 197

"Telling Stories" (Didion), **Supp. IV Part 1:** 197

"Telling the Bees" (Whittier), **Supp. I Part 2:** 694–695

Telling the Little Secrets (J. Burstein), **Supp. XVII:** 44

Telling the Truth: The Gospel as Tragedy, Comedy, and Fairy Tale (Buechner), **Supp. XII:** 53

"Tell Me" (Hughes), **Supp. VIII:** 213

"Tell Me, Sir, ... What Is 'Black' Literature?" (H. L. Gates), **Supp. XX: 108**

Tell Me, Tell Me (Moore), **III:** 215

Tell Me Again (Notley), **Supp. XXII:** 224, 230–231

Tell Me Again How the White Heron Rises and Flies across the Nacreous River at Twilight toward the Distant

Islands (Carruth), **Supp. XVI:**56

Tell Me a Riddle (film), **Supp. XIII:** 295

Tell Me a Riddle (Olsen), **Supp. XIII:** 294, 296, **298–302,** 303, 305

"Tell Me a Riddle" (Olsen), **Supp. XIII:** 294, 297, 298, **300–302,** 305

"Tell Me a Story" (McDermott), **Supp. XVIII:** 177

Tell Me How Long the Train's Been Gone (Baldwin), **Retro. Supp. II:** 9, **11–12,** 14; **Supp. I Part 1:** 48, 52, 63–65, 67

"Tell Me My Fortune" (Epstein), **Supp. XII:** 163

Tell Me True: Memoir, History, and Writing a Life (Hampl and May, eds.), **Supp. XXII:** 81–82, 84, **94–95**

Tell Me Your Answer True (Sexton), **Supp. II Part 2:** 683

Tell My Horse (Hurston), **Retro. Supp. III:** 130, 131–132; **Supp. VI:** 149, 156, 158

"Tell-Tale Heart, The" (Poe), **III:** 413, 414–415, 416; **Retro. Supp. II:** 267, 269, 270; **Retro. Supp. III:** 227; **Supp. XXV:** 112

"Tell the Women We're Going" (Carver), **Supp. III Part 1:** 138, 144

"Telluride Blues—A Hatchet Job" (Abbey), **Supp. XIII:** 10

Telushkin, Dvorah, **Retro. Supp. II:** 317

Temblor (Howe), **Supp. IV Part 2:** 431

Temperamental People (Rinehart), **Supp. XXV:** 196

Tempering of Eugene O'Neill, The (D. Alexander), **Supp. XVII:** 99

"Temper of Steel, The" (Jones), **Supp. XI:** 218

Tempers, The (W. C. Williams), **Retro. Supp. I: 413–414,** 415, 416, 424

Tempest, The (Shakespeare), **I:** 394; **II:** 12; **III:** 40, 61, 263; **Retro. Supp. I:** 61; **Retro. Supp. III:** 190–191; **Supp. IV Part 2:** 463; **Supp. V:** 302–303; **Supp. XII:** 54–57; **Supp. XV:** 255, 256

Temple, Minnie, **II:** 323

Temple, The (Herbert), **IV:** 145, 153

Temple, William, **III:** 303

Temple House (E. Stoddard), **Supp. XV:** 273, **284–286**

Temple of My Familiar, The (Walker), **Supp. III Part 2:** 521, 527, 529, 535, 537; **Supp. IV Part 1:** 14

"Temple of the Holy Ghost, A" (O'Connor), **III:** 344, 352; **Retro. Supp. II:** 232; **Retro. Supp. III:** 215–216

Templin, Charlotte, **Supp. V:** 116

Temporary Shelter (Gordon), **Supp. IV Part 1:** 299, 305–307

"Temporary Shelter" (Gordon), **Supp. IV Part 1:** 306

Temptation Game, The (Gardner), **Supp. VI:** 72

Temptation of Don Volpi, The (Hayes), **Supp. XXVI:** 135, 137

"Temptation of St. Anthony, The" (Barthelme), **Supp. IV Part 1:** 47

Temptations, The, **Supp. X:** 242

"10 Best Weathers of 1983, The" (Notley), **Supp. XXII:** 224

"10 Things I Do Every Day" (Berrigan), **Supp. XXII:** 224; **Supp. XXIV:** 41

"Tenancy, A" (Merrill), **Supp. III Part 1:** 322, 323

"Tenant" (Hoffman), **Supp. XVIII:** 86

Tenants, The (Malamud), **Supp. I Part 2:** 448–450

"Ten Best Issues of Comic Books, The" (Notley), **Supp. XXII:** 224

Ten Commandments (McClatchy), **Supp. XII:** 262–265

Ten Days That Shook the World (Reed), **II:** 577; **Supp. X:** 136; **Supp. XVIII:** 225; **Supp. XXVIII:** 40, 43

Tendencies in Modern American Poetry (A. Lowell), **II:** 529; **Retro. Supp. III:** 100

"Tender, Hilarious Reminiscences of Life in Mythical Lake Wobegon" (MacDougall), **Supp. XVI:** 174

Tender Buttons (G. Stein), **I:** 103, 105; **IV:** 27, 42–43; **Retro. Supp. II:** 331; **Supp. XV:** 347; **Supp. XXVII:** 169

"Tenderfoot" (Haines), **Supp. XII:** 209

Tender Is the Night (Fitzgerald), **I:** 375; **II:** 79, 84, 91, 95–96, 97, 98, 420; **Retro. Supp. I:** 105, 108, 109, **110–112,** 114; **Supp. IX:** 59, 60, 61; **Supp. XV:** 197; **Supp. XXI:** 11

"Tenderloin" (Crane), **I:** 408

"Tenderly" (Dobyns), **Supp. XIII:** 86–87

'Tender Man, A" (Bambara), **Supp. XI:** 9–10

"Tenderness" (Dunn), **Supp. XI:** 149, 150

"Tender Offer, The" (Auchincloss), **Supp. IV Part 1:** 34

"Tender Organizations, The" (C. Bly), **Supp. XVI:** 40, 42

"Tenebrae" (Komunyakaa), **Supp. XIII:** 132

Tenenbaum, Joseph, **Supp. XX: 253**

"Ten Forty-Four" (Kingsolver), **Supp. VII:** 208

Ten Indians (Bell), **Supp. X:** 7, **12**

Ten Introductions: A Collection of Modern Verse (Taggard and Fitts, ed.), **Supp. XXII:** 281

Tennant, Agnieszka, **Supp. XX: 140**

"Ten Neglected American Writers Who Deserve to Be Better Known" (Cantor), **Supp. IV Part 1:** 285

Tennent, Gilbert, **I:** 546

Tennessee Day in St. Louis (Taylor), **Supp. V:** 324

"Tennessee's Partner" (Harte), **Supp. II Part 1:** 345, 348–350

"Tennis" (Pinsky), **Supp. VI:** 241, 242

Tennis Court Oath, The (Ashbery), **Supp. III Part 1:** 7, 9, 12, 14, 26

Ten North Frederick (O'Hara), **III:** 361

Tennyson, Alfred, Lord, **I:** 587–588; **II:** 18, 82, 273, 338, 404, 439, 604; **III:** 5, 409, 469, 485, 511, 521, 523; **Retro. Supp. I:** 100, 325; **Retro. Supp. II:** 135; **Retro. Supp. III:** 60, 266; **Supp. I Part 1:** 349, 356; **Supp. I Part 2:** 410, 416, 552; **Supp. IX:** 19; **Supp. X:** 157; **Supp. XIII:** 111; **Supp. XIV:**

40, 120; **Supp. XV:** 275; **Supp. XVIII:** 78; **Supp. XXVII:** 261

"Tenochtitlan" (Bronk), **Supp. XXI:** 31

"Ten O'Clock News" (Ortiz), **Supp. IV Part 2:** 503–504

"Te-Non-An-At-Che"(Kenny), **Supp. XXIII:** 151

Tenorman (Huddle), **Supp. XXVI:** 150, 151, 153, 156, 159

Ten Poems (Dove), **Supp. IV Part 1:** 244

Ten Poems of Francis Ponge Translated by Robert Bly and Ten Poems of Robert Bly Inspired by the Poems by Francis Ponge (R. Bly), **Supp. IV Part 1:** 71

"Tension in Poetry" (Tate), **IV:** 128, 129, 135

Tenth Muse, The (Bradstreet), **Retro. Supp. III:** 1, 4–14; **Supp. I Part 1:** 102, 103, 114

10,000 Days of Thunder: A History of the Vietnam War (Caputo), **Supp. XIX:** 29

Tenting Tonight (Rinehart), **Supp. XXV:** 195

"Tent on the Beach, The" (Whittier), **Supp. I Part 2:** 703

"Ten True Things" (July), **Supp. XXIV:** 205

"Teodoro Luna Confesses after Years to His Brother, Anselmo the Priest, Who Is Required to Understand, But Who Understands Anyway, More Than People Think" (Ríos), **Supp. IV Part 2:** 552

Teodoro Luna's Two Kisses (Ríos), **Supp. IV Part 2:** 550–552, 553

"Tepeyac" (Cisneros), **Supp. VII:** 69

"Terce" (Auden), **Supp. II Part 1:** 22

Terence, **IV:** 155, 363; **Supp. I Part 2:** 405

Terkel, Studs, **Supp. IV Part 1:** 364

"Term" (Merwin), **Supp. III Part 1:** 356–357

"Terminal Days at Beverly Farms" (R. Lowell), **Retro. Supp. II:** 189

Terminating, or Sonnet LXXV, or "Lass Meine Schmerzen nicht verloren sein, or Ambivalence" (Kushner), **Supp. IX:** 132

Terminations (James), **Retro. Supp. I:** 229

"Terminus" (Emerson), **II:** 13, 19

"Terminus" (Wharton), **Retro. Supp. I:** 371; **Retro. Supp. III:** 283

"Terms in Which I Think of Reality, The" (Ginsberg), **Supp. II Part 1:** 311

Terms of Endearment (film), **Supp. V:** 226

Terms of Endearment (McMurtry), **Supp. V:** 224–225

"Terrace, The" (Wilbur), **Supp. III Part 2:** 550

Terrarium (Sanders), **Supp. XVI:** 270

"Terrence McNally" (Bryer), **Supp. XIII:** 200

"Terrence McNally" (Di Gaetani), **Supp. XIII:** 200

Terrence McNally: A Casebook (Zinman), **Supp. XIII:** 209

"Terrestrial Cuckoo"(O'Hara), **Supp. XXIII:** 210

"Terrible Peacock, The" (Barnes), **Supp. III Part 1:** 33

Terrible Threes, The (Reed), **Supp. X:** 241, 253

Terrible Twos, The (Reed), **Supp. X:** 241, **252–253**

"Terrific Mother" (Moore), **Supp. X:** 178

Territory Ahead, The (Morris), **III:** 228–229, 236

Terrorism (Wright), **Supp. XV:** 341, 342

"Terrorism" (Wright), **Supp. XV:** 341

"Terrors of the Amazon"(Grossman), **Supp. XXV:** 66

Terry, Edward A., **II:** 128, 129

Terry, Rose, **Supp. I Part 2:** 420

Tertium Organum (Ouspensky), **I:** 383; **Supp. XX:** **116**

"Terza Rima" (Rich), **Retro. Supp. III:** 252

Terzian, Peter, **Supp. XXV:** 12, 13

Tess of the d'Ubervilles (Hardy), **II:** 181; **Retro. Supp. II:** 100

"Testament" (Berry), **Supp. X:** 36

"Testament" (Carruth), **Supp. XVI:** 59

"Testament (Or, Homage to Walt Whitman)" (Jong), **Supp. V:** 130

"Testament of Flood" (Warren), **IV:** 253

Testament of François Villon, The (Pound, opera), **Retro. Supp. I:** 287

"Testament: Vermeer in December" (Bierds), **Supp. XVII:** 33

"Testimonia on the Question of Stesichoros' Blinding by Helen" (Carson), **Supp. XII:** 107

"Testimonies of a Roasted Chicken" (Jarman), **Supp. XVII:** 120

"Testimony" (Komunyakaa), **Supp. XIII:** 129

"Testimony of James Apthorp, The" (Kees), **Supp. XV:** 146

Testimony: The United States (1885–1890): Recitative (Reznikoff), **Supp. XIV:** 279, 280, 281, 285, **289–291**

Testimony: The United States (1891–1900): Recitative (Reznikoff), **Supp. XIV:** 291

Testing-Tree, The (Kunitz), **Supp. III Part 1:** 260, 263, 264, 267, 268

"Testing-Tree, The" (Kunitz), **Supp. III Part 1:** 269

Test of Poetry, A (Zukofsky), **Supp. III Part 2:** 618, 622

Teuton, Christopher, **Supp. XXVI:** 102, 110, 111

"Teutonic Scholar" (X. J. Kennedy), **Supp. XV:** 161

"Texas Moon, and Elsewhere, The" (McMurtry), **Supp. V:** 225

Texas Poets in Concert: A Quartet (Gwynn, ed.), **Supp. XIII:** 277

Texas Summer (Southern), **Supp. XI:** 309

Texasville (McMurtry), **Supp. V:** 228, 233

Thacher, Molly Day, **IV:** 381

Thacker, Robert, **Supp. XXVII:** 180, 182

Thackeray, William Makepeace, **I:** 194, 354; **II:** 182, 271, 282, 288, 316, 321, 322; **III:** 64, 70; **IV:** 326; **Retro. Supp. I:** 218; **Supp. I Part 1:** 307; **Supp. I Part 2:** 421, 495, 579; **Supp. IV Part 1:** 297; **Supp. IX:** 200; **Supp. XI:** 277; **Supp. XIV:** 306; **Supp. XX:** **228**

Thaddeus, Janice Farrar, **Supp. IV Part 1:** 299

"Thailand" (Barthelme), **Supp. IV Part 1:** 41

Thalberg, Irving, **Retro. Supp. I:** 109, 110, 114; **Supp. XVI:** 191, 192

Thales, **I:** 480–481

Thalia Trilogy (McMurtry), **Supp. V:** 220–223, 234

Tham, Claire, **Supp. VIII:** 79

"Thanatopsis" (Bryant), **Supp. I Part 1:** 150, 154, 155, 170

Thanatos Syndrome, The (Percy), **Supp. III Part 1:** 385, 397–399

"Thanking My Mother for Piano Lessons"(Wakoski), **Supp. XXVIII:** 264

"Thanks Can Be Named to Death" (Peacock), **Supp. XIX:** 199

"Thanksgiving" (Davison), **Supp. XXVI:** 74

"Thanksgiving" (Glück), **Supp. V:** 83

"Thanksgiving, A" (Auden), **Supp. II Part 1:** 26

"Thanksgiving for a Habitat" (Auden), **Supp. II Part 1:** 24

Thanksgivings (Traherne), **Supp. XVI:** 288

"Thanksgiving Spirit" (Farrell), **II:** 45

Thanksgiving Visitor, The (Capote), **Supp. III Part 1:** 116, 118, 119

"Thank You, Esther Forbes" (Saunders), **Supp. XIX:** 235

Thank You, Fog (Auden), **Supp. II Part 1:** 24

"Thank You, Lord" (Angelou), **Supp. IV Part 1:** 15

Thank You, Mr. Moto (Marquand), **III:** 57, 58

Thank You and Other Poems (Koch), **Supp. XV:** 180–181

"Thank You in Arabic" (Nye), **Supp. XIII:** 273, 281

"Thar's More in the Man Than Thar Is in the Land" (Lanier), **Supp. I Part 1:** 352–353, 359–360

That Affair Next Door (Green), **Supp. XXVI:** 277

"That Evening Sun" (Faulkner), **II:** 72; **Retro. Supp. I:** 75, 83; **Retro. Supp. III:** 82

That Horse (Hogan), **Supp. IV Part 1:** 397, 404, 405

"That House, This Room" (W. V. Davis), **Supp. XXI:** 90

"That I Had the Wings" (Ellison), **Supp. II Part 1:** 238

That Night (McDermott), **Supp. XVIII:** 155, **158–160,** 162, 163, 166

"That's the Place Indians Talk About" (Ortiz), **Supp. IV Part 2:** 511

That Tantalus (Bronk), **Supp. XXI:** 31

"That the Soul May Wax Plump" (Swenson), **Supp. IV Part 2:** 650

"That the Universe Is Chrysalid" (Sobin), **Supp. XVI:** 284

"That Tree" (Porter), **III:** 434–435, 446, 451

That Was the Week That Was (television program), **Supp. XIV:** 125

"That Winter" (Stone), **Supp. XXVII:** 253

"That Year" (Olds), **Supp. X:** 203

"Thaw" (C. Frost), **Supp. XV:** 93, 104, 105

Thaxter, Celia, **Retro. Supp. II:** 136, 147; **Supp. XIII:** 143, 153

Thayer, Abbott, **I:** 231

Thayer, Scofield, **I:** 231; **Retro. Supp. I:** 58

Thayer and Eldridge, **Retro. Supp. I:** 403

"Theater" (Toomer), **Supp. IX:** 309, 317–318

"Theater Chronicle" (McCarthy), **II:** 562

"Theater Problems? Call Dr. Chekhov" (Wasserstein), **Supp. XV:** 320

Theatricals (James), **Retro. Supp. I:** 228

The Blacker the Berry: A Novel of Negro Life (Thurman), **Supp. XIX:** 73; **Supp. XVIII:** 281

"Theft" (Porter), **III:** 434, 435

Theft, A (Bellow), **Retro. Supp. II:** 31–32, 34

The Harder They Fall (Schulberg), **Supp. XVIII:** 247, 253

The Harder They Fall: Celebrities Tell Their Real-Life Stories of Addiction and Recovery (F. Wright), **Supp. XVII:** 240

"Their Ancient, Glittering Eyes" (Rash), **Supp. XXVII:** 227–228

Their Dogs Came with Them (Viramontes), **Supp. XXV:** 130, 138

Their Eyes Were Watching God (Hurston), **Retro. Supp. III:** 130–131, 132, 135, 137, 138, 139, 140; **Supp. VI:** 149, 152, 156–157; **Supp. XX: 107**

Their Heads Are Green and Their Hands Are Blue: Scenes from the Non-Christian World (Bowles), **Supp. IV Part 1:** 89

"Their Losses" (Taylor), **Supp. V:** 320

"Their Name is Macaroni" (Boyle), **Supp. XXIV:** 61

"Their Sleep" (W. V. Davis), **Supp. XXI:** 93

Their Wedding Journey (Howells), **II:** 277–278; **Retro. Supp. I:** 334

them (Oates), **Supp. II Part 2:** 503, 511–514

Theme Is Freedom, The (Dos Passos), **I:** 488–489, 492, 494

Theme Time Radio Hour (radio show, Dylan), **Supp. XVIII:** 28

"Theme with Variations" (Agee), **I:** 27

"Then" (Barthelme), **Supp. IV Part 1:** 48

"Then as Now" (Cliff), **Supp. XXII:** 76

"The Night Rhonda Ferguson Was Killed" (E. P. Jones), **Supp. XXII:** 144

"The 1950s"(Lea), **Supp. XXVIII:** 142

"Then It All Came Down" (Capote), **Supp. III Part 1:** 125, 131

Theocritus, **II:** 169; **Retro. Supp. I:** 286; **Supp. XXIV:** 156

Theodore Roethke's Far Fields: The Evolution of His Poetry (Balakian), **Supp. XXIII:** 19

"Theodore the Poet" (Masters), **Supp. I Part 2:** 461

Theological Position, A (Coover), **Supp. V:** 44

Theophrastus, **I:** 58

"Theoretical and Scientific Conceptions of Race, The" (Locke), **Supp. XIV:** 209

"Theoretical Subject(s) of *This Bridge Called My Back,* The"(Alarcón), **Supp. XXIII:** 204–205

"Theories of Time and Space" (Trethewey), **Supp. XXI:** 255

"Theory" (Huddle), **Supp. XXVI:** 149

Theory and Practice of Rivers and Other Poems, The (Harrison), **Supp. VIII:** 47, 49

Theory of Business Enterprise, The (Veblen), **Supp. I Part 2:** 638, 641, 644

Theory of Flight (Rukeyser), **Supp. VI:** 272, 275, **277–278,** 284

"Theory of Flight" (Rukeyser), **Supp. VI:** 277–278

Theory of Moral Sentiments, The (A. Smith), **Supp. I Part 2:** 634

Theory of the Leisure Class, The (Veblen), **I:** 475–476; **Supp. I Part 2:** 629, 633, 641, 645; **Supp. IV Part 1:** 22

"There" (Taylor), **Supp. V:** 323

"There Are No Such Trees in Alpine California" (Haines), **Supp. XII:** 207

"There Goes (Varoom! Varoom!) That Kandy-Kolored Tangerine-Flake Streamline Baby" (Wolfe), **Supp. III Part 2:** 569–571

"There Have Been Changes" (Pickering), **Supp. XXI:** 202–203

"There Is a Lesson" (Olsen), **Supp. XIII:** 292, 297

"There is a Man" (Espaillat), **Supp. XXI:** 108–109

"There Is Only One of Everything" (Atwood), **Supp. XIII:** 34

There Is Something Out There (McNally). *See And Things That Go Bump in the Night* (McNally)

"There Must Be" (Peacock), **Supp. XIX:** 199

"There's a certain Slant of light" (Dickinson), **Retro. Supp. I:** 38

There's a Wocket in My Pocket! (Geisel), **Supp. XVI:** 111

Thérèse de Lisieux, Saint, **Supp. VIII:** 195

"There She Is She Is Taking Her Bath" (Anderson), **I:** 113, 114

"There Was a Child Went Forth" (Whitman), **IV:** 348; **Retro. Supp. III:** 304–306; **Supp. XXVI:** 230

"There Was a Man, There Was a Woman" (Cisneros), **Supp. VII:** 70

"There Was an Old Woman She Had So Many Children She Didn't Know What to Do" (Cisneros), **Supp. VII:** 60

"There Was a Youth Whose Name Was Thomas Granger" (Olson), **Supp. II Part 2:** 558, 560, 563

There Were Giants in the Land (Benét), **Supp. XI:** 50

"There Will Come Soft Rains" (Teasdale), **Supp. XXVII:** 295

There You Are (Simpson), **Supp. IX:** 279–280

"There You Are" (Simpson), **Supp. IX:** 279

"Thermopylae" (Clampitt), **Supp. IX:** 43

Theroux, Alexander, **Supp. VIII:** 312

Theroux, Marcel, **Supp. VIII:** 325

Theroux, Paul, **Supp. V:** 122; **Supp. VIII: 309–327**

"These Are My People" (Hayden), **Supp. II Part 1:** 365

These Are My Same Hands (Schott), **Supp. XXIII:** 241, 242

"These are the days when Birds come back" (Dickinson), **Retro. Supp. I:** 30

"These Days" (Davison), **Supp. XXVI:** 79

"These Days" (Olds), **Supp. X:** 215

"These Flames and Generosities of the Heart: Emily Dickinson and the Illogic of Sumptuary Values" (Howe), **Supp. IV Part 2:** 431

"These Hands" (Brockmeier), **Supp. XXII:** 51, 52, 53

These Happy Golden Years (L. I. Wilder), **Supp. XXII:** 294, 297, 299

These Low Grounds (Turpin), **Supp. XVIII:** 283

"These Nerves" (Biss), **Supp. XXVI:** 50–51

"These saw Visions" (Dickinson), **Retro. Supp. I:** 46

These 13 (Faulkner), **II:** 72; **Retro. Supp. III:** 82

These Three (film), **Supp. I Part 1:** 281

These Times (Untermeyer), **Supp. XV: 299–300,** 303

"These Times" (Untermeyer), **Supp. XV:** 300

"Thessalonica: A Roman Story" (Brown), **Supp. I Part 1:** 133

Thévenaz, Paul, **Supp. XV:** 42

Thew, Harvey, **Supp. XIII:** 166

"They Ain't the Men They Used To Be" (Farrell), **II:** 45

"They Burned the Books" (Benét), **Supp. XI:** 46

They Came Like Swallows (Maxwell), **Supp. VIII: 155–159,** 168, 169

"They Can't Turn Back" (Baldwin), **Supp. I Part 1:** 52

They Do Not: The Letters of a Non-Professional Lady Arranged for Public Consumption (Clements), **Supp. XVI:** 190

They Feed They Lion (Levine), **Supp. V:** 178, 179, 181, 184–185, 186

"They Feed They Lion" (Levine), **Supp. V:** 188

"They Lion Grow" (Levine), **Supp. V:** 184–185

"They're Not Your Husband" (Carver), **Supp. III Part 1:** 141, 143

They're Playing Our Song (musical), **Supp. IV Part 2:** 589

They Seek a City (Bontemps and Conroy), **Supp. XXII:** 5, 11

They Shall Inherit the Laughter (Jones), **Supp. XI:** 217, 218, 232

"They Shall Not Die" (Ryan as Quin), **Supp. XVIII:** 228–229

They Shoot Horses (film), **Supp. XIII:** 159

They Shoot Horses, Don't They? (McCoy), **Supp. XIII:** 159, **164–166,** 168, 171, 172, 174; **Supp. XXV:** 26

"They Sing, They Sing" (Roethke), **III:** 544

They Stooped to Folly (Glasgow), **II:** 175, 186–187

They Were Expendable (film), **Supp. XVIII:** 247

"They Weren't Going to Die" (Boyle), **Supp. XXIV:** 61

They Whisper (R. O. Butler), **Supp. XII:** **72–73**

They Who Knock at Our Gates: A Complete Gospel of Immigration (Antin), **Supp. XX:** 2–3, 10–11, 12

"Thick and Thin"(Hadas), **Supp. XXIII:** 119

Thidwick the Big-Hearted Moose (Geisel), **Supp. XVI:** 104

Thief's Journal, The (Genet), **Supp. XXIV:** 210

"Thief's Philosophy of Life, The" (Hapgood), **Supp. XVII:** 103

"Thief's Wife, The" (B. Kelly), **Supp. XVII:** 125–126

"Thieves" (Yates), **Supp. XI:** 349

Thieves of Paradise (Komunyakaa), **Supp. XIII:** 113, **128–130,** 132

"Thimble, The" (Kenyon), **Supp. VII:** 164

"Thing and Its Relations, The" (James), **II:** 357

" 'Thing Not Named, The': Willa Cather as a Lesbian Writer" (O'Brien), **Retro. Supp. III:** 37

"Things" (Haines), **Supp. XII:** 207

"Things" (Kenyon), **Supp. VII:** 169

"Things, The" (Kinnell), **Supp. III Part 1:** 246

Things As They Are (Stein), **IV:** 34, 37, 40

"Things Can Be Named to Death" (Peacock), **Supp. XIX:** 199

"Things Don't Stop" (Nye), **Supp. XIII:** 287

Things Gone and Things Still Here (Bowles), **Supp. IV Part 1:** 91

"Things of August" (Stevens), **Retro. Supp. I:** 309

Things of This World (Wilbur), **Supp. III Part 2:** 552–555

Things That Fall from the Sky (Brockmeier), **Supp. XXII: 50–53**

"Things That Fall from the Sky" (Brockmeier), **Supp. XXII:** 51, 53

Things Themselves: Essays and Scenes (Price), **Supp. VI:** 261

Things They Carried, The (T. O'Brien), **Supp. V:** 238, 239, 240, 243, 248–

250; **Supp. XVII:** 14; **Supp. XXI:** 122

"Things to Do in New York City" (Berrigan), **Supp. XXII:** 224

Things We Don't Understand and Definitely Are Not Going to Talk About (performance piece, July), **Supp. XXIV:** 200

"Thing That Killed My Father Off, The" (Carver), **Supp. III Part 1:** 143

Thingy World!: or, How We Got to Where We Are: A Satire in One Act (Budbill), **Supp. XIX: 13–14**

"Think about It" (Conroy), **Supp. XVI:** 75

Think Back on Us . . . (Cowley), **Supp. II Part 1:** 139, 140, 142

Think Fast, Mr. Moto (Marquand), **III:** 57, 58

"Thinking about Barbara Deming" (Paley), **Supp. VI:** 227

"Thinking about Being Called Simple by a Critic" (Stafford), **Supp. XI:** 328

Thinking about the Longstanding Problems of Virtue and Happiness: Essays, a Play, Two Poems, and a Prayer (Kushner), **Supp. IX:** 131, 134, 135

"Thinking about the Past" (Justice), **Supp. VII:** 123–124

"Thinking about Western Thinking" (Didion), **Supp. IV Part 1:** 204, 206

"'Thinking against Oneself': Reflections on Cioran" (Sontag), **Supp. III Part 2:** 459–460

"Thinking Back Through Our Mothers: Traditions in Canadian Women's Writing" (Shields), **Supp. VII:** 307–308

"Thinking for Berky" (Stafford), **Supp. XI:** 320

"Thinking in Subversion" (Gansworth), **Supp. XXVI:** 114

"Thinking like a Mountain" (Leopold), **Supp. XIV:** 188, 189

"Thinking of the Lost World" (Jarrell), **II:** 338–389

Thinking Out Loud (Quindlen), **Supp. XVII:** 167, **169–170**

Thin Man, The (film), **Supp. IV Part 1:** 342, 355

Thin Man, The (Hammett), **Supp. IV Part 1:** 354–355

"Thinnest Shadow, The" (Ashbery), **Supp. III Part 1:** 5

"Thin People, The" (Plath), **Supp. I Part 2:** 538, 547

Thin Red Line, The (film; Malick), **Supp. V:** 249; **Supp. XV:** 351

Thin Red Line, The (Jones), **Supp. XI:** 219, **224–225,** 229, 231, 232, 233, 234

"Thin Strips" (Sandburg), **III:** 587

"Third and Final Continent, The" (Lahiri), **Supp. XXI: 178–180**

"Third Avenue in Sunlight" (Hecht), **Supp. X:** 61

"Third Body, A" (R. Bly), **Supp. IV Part 1:** 71

Third Circle, The (Norris), **III:** 327

"Third Expedition, The" (Bradbury), **Supp. IV Part 1:** 103, 106

Third Generation, The (C. Himes), **Supp. XVI:** 135, **140–141**

Third Life of Grange Copeland, The (Walker), **Supp. III Part 2:** 520, 527–536

Third Mind, The (Burroughs), **Supp. XII:** 3

"Third Myth, The" (Muñoz), **Supp. XXV:** 134

Third Rose, The (Brinnin), **IV:** 26

"Third Sermon on the Warpland, The" (Brooks), **Supp. III Part 1:** 85

"Third Thing That Killed My Father Off, The" (Carver), **Supp. III Part 1:** 144

Third Violet, The (Crane), **I:** 408, 417–418

Thirlwall, John C., **Retro. Supp. I:** 430

Thirst (O'Neill), **Supp. XXVIII:** 38

"Thirst: Introduction to Kinds of Water" (Carson), **Supp. XII: 103**

"13, 1977, 21" (Lethem), **Supp. XVIII:** 148

13 by Shanley (Shanley), **Supp. XIV:** 316

13 Seconds: A Look Back at the Kent State Shootings (Caputo), **Supp. XIX:** 29

Thirteen Hands: A Play in Two Acts (Shields), **Supp. VII:** 322–323

Thirteen O'Clock (Benét), **Supp. XI:** 46

Thirteen Other Stories (Purdy), **Supp. VII:** 278

Thirteen Stories and Thirteen Epitaphs (Vollmann), **Supp. XVII:** 226

"Thirteenth and Pennsylvania" (Stafford), **Supp. XI:** 324

Thirteenth Month, The (Pedersen; Nelson, trans.), **Supp. XVIII:** 179–180

"Thirteen Ways of Looking at a Blackbird" (Stevens), **IV:** 94; **Supp. IX:** 47; **Supp. XVII:** 130; **Supp. XXIII:** 253

"Thirteen Ways of Looking at a Blackbird" (W. Stevens), **Supp. XX: 110**

Thirteen Ways of Looking at a Black Man (H. L. Gates), **Supp. XX: 102, 110**

30/6 (poetry chapbook), **Supp. V:** 5, 6

"30. Meditation. 2. Cor. 5.17. He Is a New Creature" (Taylor), **IV:** 144

30: Pieces of a Novel (Dixon), **Supp. XII:** 152, **153–154**

"Thirty Bob a Week" (Davidson), **Retro. Supp. I:** 55

"Thirty Delft Tiles" (Doty), **Supp. XI:** 131

"35/10" (Olds), **Supp. X:** 206

"35,000 Feet—The Lanterns" (Goldbarth), **Supp. XII:** 182

31 Letters and 13 Dreams (Hugo), **Supp. VI:** 141–144

Thirty Poems (Bryant), **Supp. I Part 1:** 157, 158

Thirty-Six Poems (Warren), **IV:** 236, 239, 240

"33" (Alvarez), **Supp. VII:** 4

"3275" (Monette), **Supp. X:** 148, 159

Thirty Years (Marquand), **III:** 56, 60–61

Thirty Years of Treason (Bentley), **Supp. I Part 1:** 297

This, My Letter (Hay), **Supp. XIV:** 121, 122, 129, 131

"This, That & the Other" (Nemerov), **III:** 269

This Body Is Made of Camphor and Go-pherwood (R. Bly), **Supp. IV Part 1:** 63–65, 66, 71; **Supp. XXI:** 85

This Boy's Life: A Memoir (T. Wolff), **Supp. VII:** 334–339, 340, 343; **Supp. XI:** 246, 247; **Supp. XXV:** 208

This Bridge Called My Back: Writings by Radical Women of Color (Moraga and Anzaldúa, eds.), **Supp. XXIII:** 193, 194, 196, **204–205**

"This Bright Dream" (Benét), **Supp. XI:** 55

This Coffin Has No Handles (McGrath), **Supp. X:** 117

"This Configuration" (Ashbery), **Supp. III Part 1:** 22

"This Corruptible" (Wylie), **Supp. I Part 2:** 727, 729

"This Crazy Wickedness, Little Nests of Light" (Notley), **Supp. XXII:** 228

"This Crutch That I Love" (Nye), **Supp. XIII:** 288

"This Gentile World" (H. Miller), **III:** 177

"This Hand" (Wylie), **Supp. I Part 2:** 713

"This Hour" (Olds), **Supp. X:** 212

"This House I Cannot Leave" (Kingsolver), **Supp. VII:** 208

This Hunger (Nin), **Supp. X:** 185

This in Which (Oppen), **Supp. XXVI:** 225, 230, 232–233, 234

"This Is a Photograph of Me" (Atwood), **Supp. XIII:** 33

"This Is a Poem, Good Afternoon" (Keillor), **Supp. XVI:** 167

"This Is a Young World" (Howard), **Supp. XXVII:** 118

"This Is for You" (Cohen), **Supp. XXVII:** 60

This Is How You Lose Her (Díaz), **Supp. XXIV:** 83, 84, 86, 88, **92–93**

"This Is It" (Stern), **Supp. IX:** 290

"This Is Just to Say" (W. C. Williams), **Supp. XI:** 328

This Is My God: The Jewish Way of Life (Wouk), **Supp. XXV:** 253, 255–256, 263, 268

"This Is My Heart" (Harjo), **Supp. XII:** 230

This Is Not a Novel (Markson), **Supp. XVII:** 145–146

"This Is Not Who We Are" (Nye), **Supp. XIII:** 285, 286

This Is Our Time: Secular Cantata No. 1, Mixed Voice Chorus and Orchestra (Taggard, Schuman and Weissleder), **Supp. XXII:** 283

"This Is Us, Excellent" (Richard), **Supp. XIX:** 212

"This Is What I Said" (Salinas), **Supp. XIII:** 322

This Journey (Wright), **Supp. III Part 2:** 605–606

"This Land Is Your Land"(Guthrie), **Supp. XXVIII:** 255

"This Lime-Tree Bower My Prison" (Coleridge), **Supp. XXI:** 52, 55

This Man and This Woman (Farrell), **II:** 42

"This Monkey, My Back" (Boyle), **Supp. XX:** 17

"This Morning" (Huddle), **Supp. XXVI:** 151

"This Morning" (Kenyon), **Supp. VII:** 164

"This Morning, This Evening, So Soon" (Baldwin), **Supp. I Part 1:** 63

"This Morning Again It Was in the Dusty Pines" (Oliver), **Supp. VII:** 240

This Music Crept by Me upon the Waters (MacLeish), **III:** 21

"This New England: Newport, Vermont" (Mosher), **Supp. XXII:** 209

This Old House (J. Davison), **Supp. XXVI:** 65

This People (Lewisohn), **Supp. XXVIII:** 150, 152, 153–154

This People Israel: The Meaning of Jewish Existence (Baeck), **Supp. V:** 260

"This Person" (July), **Supp. XXIV:** 202

"This Personal Maze Is Not the Prize" (Selinger), **Supp. XI:** 248

"This Place in the Ways" (Rukeyser), **Supp. VI:** 273–274

This Property Is Condemned (T. Williams), **IV:** 378

This Proud Heart (Buck), **Supp. II Part 1:** 119–120

This Same Sky: A Collection of Poems from around the World (Nye, ed.), **Supp. XIII:** 280

"This Sandwich Has No Mayonnaise" (Salinger), **III:** 552–553

This Shape We're In (Lethem), **Supp. XVIII:** 145

"This Shape We're In" (Lethem), **Supp. XVIII:** 148

This Side of Paradise (Fitzgerald), **I:** 358; **II:** 77, 80, 81, 82–83, 84, 85–87, 88; **Retro. Supp. I:** 99–100, **101–102,** 103, 105, 106, 110, 111; **Supp. XVIII:** 248

This Singing World: An Anthology of Modern Poetry for Young People (Untermeyer, ed.), **Supp. XV:** 306

This Strange Joy: Selected Poems of Sandro Penna (Di Perio, trans.), **Supp. XIX:** 34

This Stubborn Self: Texas Autobiographies (Almon), **Supp. XIII:** 288

"This They Took with Them" (Boyle), **Supp. XXIV:** 61

This Thing Don't Lead to Heaven (Crews), **Supp. XI:** 112

This Time: New and Selected Poems (Stern), **Supp. IX:** 290–291, **299**

"Thistle Seed in the Wind" (Francis), **Supp. IX:** 81

"Thistles in Sweden, The" (Maxwell), **Supp. VIII:** 169

"This Tokyo" (Snyder), **Supp. VIII:** 298

This Tree Will Be Here for a Thousand Years (R. Bly), **Supp. IV Part 1:** 65–66, 71, 72

This Tree Will Be Here for a Thousand Years (revised edition) (R. Bly), **Supp. IV Part 1:** 66

This Very Earth (Caldwell), **I:** 297, 302

This Waiting for Love (Mitchell, ed.), **Supp. XXVI:** 165, 173

This Wheel's on Fire: Levon Helm and the Story of the Band (Helm), **Supp. XVIII:** 26

This Woman (di Donato), **Supp. XX:** 33, **41–42, 46**

Thoens, Karen, **Supp. V:** 147

Thomas, Brandon, **II:** 138

Thomas, Dave, **Supp. XXVI:** 18

Thomas, Debra, **Supp. XIII:** 114

Thomas, D. M., **Supp. VIII:** 5

Thomas, Dwight, **Retro. Supp. III:** 237

Thomas, Dylan, **I:** 49, 64, 382, 432, 526, 533; **III:** 21, 521, 528, 532, 534; **IV:** 89, 93, 136; **Supp. I Part 1:** 263; **Supp. III Part 1:** 42, 47; **Supp. IX:** 114; **Supp. V:** 344; **Supp. VIII:** 21; **Supp. X:** 115; **Supp. XV:** 74; **Supp. XVII:** 135; **Supp. XX:** 199, 204; **Supp. XXIV:** 54; **Supp. XXVII:** 222

Thomas, Edna Lewis, **Supp. XVIII:** 281

Thomas, Edward, **II:** 154; **Retro. Supp. I:** 127, 131, 132; **Retro. Supp. III:** 98; **Supp. I Part 1:** 263; **Supp. II Part 1:** 4

Thomas, Jacob ("Jake"), **Supp. XXVI:** 83

Thomas, James, **Supp. XVI:** 268

Thomas, Joseph, **Supp. XVIII:** 183

Thomas, J. Parnell, **Supp. I Part 1:** 286; **Supp. XV:** 198

Thomas, June, **Supp. XXV:** 2, 3

Thomas, Lewis, **Retro. Supp. I:** 323

Thomas, Lorenzo, **Supp. XXIV:** 37; **Supp. XXVII:** 166, 167

Thomas, Louisa, **Supp. XXIII:** 280, 283

Thomas, Rob, **Supp. XVIII:** 100, 101

Thomas, R. S., **Supp. XXI:** 83, 86–87, 93, 95, 96

Thomas, William I., **Supp. I Part 2:** 641

Thomas-a-Kempis, **Retro. Supp. I:** 247

Thomas and Beulah (Dove), **Supp. IV Part 1:** 242, 247–248, 249; **Supp. XVIII:** 174; **Supp. XXI:** 249

Thomas Aquinas (Saint), **I:** 13, 14, 265, 267; **III:** 270; **Retro. Supp. II:** 222; **Supp. IV Part 2:** 526

"Thomas at the Wheel" (Dove), **Supp. IV Part 1:** 248

"Thomas Eakins and the Photograph of a Man in Motion" (Major), **Supp. XXII:** 183

"Thomas Eakins' Delaware River Paintings" (Major), **Supp. XXII:** 183

"Thomas McGrath: Words for a Vanished Age" (Vinz), **Supp. X:** 117

Thomas Merton on Peace, **Supp. VIII:** 208

Thomas Merton Studies Center, The, **Supp. VIII:** 208

Thompson, Barbara, **Supp. V:** 322

Thompson, Caroline, **Supp. XXIII:** 291

Thompson, Cy, **I:** 538

Thompson, Daniel, **Supp. XXIII:** 174

Thompson, Dorothy, **II:** 449–450, 451, 453; **Supp. XV:** 307; **Supp. XXVIII:** 156

Thompson, Edward, **Supp. XXI:** 172

Thompson, E. P., **Supp. X:** 112, 117

Thompson, Francis, **Retro. Supp. I:** 55

Thompson, Frank, **II:** 20

Thompson, George, **Supp. I Part 2:** 686; **Supp. XXIII:** 182

Thompson, Hunter S., **Supp. VIII:** 42; **Supp. XI:** 105; **Supp. XIII:** 1, 17; **Supp. XVII:** 95, 102, 228; **Supp. XXIV:** 279–294; **Supp. XXVIII:** 40

Thompson, James R., **Supp. IV Part 1:** 217

Thompson, Jean, **Supp. XXIII: 289–305**

Thompson, John, **Supp. V:** 323; **Supp. XXI:** 151

Thompson, Juliet, **Supp. XX: 117**

Thompson, Lawrance Roger, **II:** 508; **Retro. Supp. I:** 138, 141; **Retro. Supp. III:** 102

Thompson, Lisa B., **Supp. XXIII:** 202

Thompson, Morton, **Supp. XIII:** 170

Thompson, Theresa, **Supp. V:** 141

Thompson, William T., **Supp. I Part 2:** 411

Thomson, James, **II:** 304; **Supp. I Part 1:** 150, 151; **Supp. XXIV:** 159

Thomson, Virgil, **IV:** 45; **Supp. IV Part 1:** 81, 83, 84, 173; **Supp. XVI:** 195

"Thoreau" (J. R. Lowell), **Supp. I Part 2:** 420, 422

Thoreau, Henry David, **I:** 98, 104, 228, 236, 257, 258, 261, 305, 433; **II:** 7, 8, 13, 17, 101, 159, 224, 273–274, 295, 312–313, 321, 457–458, 540, 546–547; **III:** 171, 174, 186–187, 189, 208, 214–215, 453, 454, 507, 577; **IV: 167–189,** 191, 341; **Retro. Supp. I:** 51, 62, 122; **Retro. Supp. II:** 13, 96, 142, 158; **Retro. Supp. III:** 249; **Supp. I Part 1:** 29, 34, 116, 188, 299, 358; **Supp. I Part 2:** 383, 400, 420, 421, 507, 540, 579, 580, 655, 659, 660, 664, 678; **Supp. III Part 1:** 340, 353; **Supp. IV Part 1:** 236, 392, 416; **Supp. IV Part 2:** 420, 430, 433, 439, 447; **Supp. IX:** 25, 90, 171; **Supp. V:** 200, 208; **Supp. VIII:** 40, 42, 103, 105, 198, 201, 204, 205, 292, 303; **Supp. X:** 21, 27, 28–29, 101, 102; **Supp. XI:** 155; **Supp. XIII:** 1, 17; **Supp. XIV:** 40, 54, 106, 177, 181; **Supp. XVIII:** 4; **Supp. XX: 116, 221; Supp. XXI:** 203, 217; **Supp. XXII:** 206; **Supp. XXIII:** 174; **Supp. XXVI:** 31, 34, 37; **Supp. XXVIII:** 158, 201, 243, 249, 251, 253

Thoreau, John, **IV:** 171, 182

Thoreau, Mrs. John, **IV:** 172

"Thoreau's Hound: On Hiddenness"(Hirshfield), **Supp. XXIII:** 137

"Thorn, The" (Gordon), **Supp. IV Part 1:** 314

Thorne, Francis, **Supp. XII:** 253

"Thorn Merchant, The" (Komunyakaa), **Supp. XIII:** 119–120

Thornton, Billy Bob, **Supp. VIII:** 175

Thornton, Lionel, **III:** 291

Thornton, Richard, **Retro. Supp. III:** 103

"Thorofare" (Minot), **Supp. VI: 209–210**

"Thorow" (Howe), **Supp. IV Part 2:** 419, 420, 421, 431, 433–434

Thorp, Willard, **Supp. XIII:** 101

Thorpe, Thomas Bangs, **Retro. Supp. III:** 259

Thorslev, Peter L., Jr., **I:** 524

Thorstein Veblen (Dowd), **Supp. I Part 2:** 650

Thorstein Veblen (Qualey, ed.), **Supp. I Part 2:** 650

Thorstein Veblen: A Chapter in American Economic Thought (Teggart), **Supp. I Part 2:** 650

Thorstein Veblen: A Critical Interpretation (Riesman), **Supp. I Part 2:** 649, 650

Thorstein Veblen: A Critical Reappraisal (Dowd, ed.), **Supp. I Part 2:** 650

Thorstein Veblen and His America (Dorfman), **Supp. I Part 2:** 650

Thorstein Veblen and the Institutionalists: A Study in the Social Philosophy of Economics (Seckler), **Supp. I Part 2:** 650

"Those before Us" (R . Lowell), **II:** 550

"Those Being Eaten by America" (R. Bly), **Supp. IV Part 1:** 62

Those Bones Are Not My Child (Bambara), **Supp. XI:** 1, 14, **20–22**

Those Extraordinary Twins (Twain), **IV:** 205–206; **Retro. Supp. III:** 267

"Those Graves in Rome" (Levis), **Supp. XI:** 266

"Those of Us Who Think We Know" (Dunn), **Supp. XI:** 146

Those That Be in Bondage (Webber), **Supp. XXI:** 160

"Those Times . . ." (Sexton), **Supp. II Part 2:** 670, 684

"Those Various Scalpels" (Moore), **III:** 202

"Those Were the Days" (Levine), **Supp. V:** 190

"Those Who Don't" (Cisneros), **Supp. VII:** 60

"Those Who Love" (Teasdale), **Supp. XXVII:** 296

"Those Who Thunder" (Hogan), **Supp. IV Part 1:** 406

"Those Winter Sundays"(Hayden), **Supp. XXVIII:** 27

"Thought, A" (Sarton), **Supp. VIII:** 262

Thought and Character of William James (Perry), **II:** 362

Thoughtbook of Francis Scott Key Fitzgerald (Fitzgerald), **Retro. Supp. I:** 99

"Thought Experiment" (Saunders), **Supp. XIX:** 235

"Thoughtful Roisterer Declines the Gambit, The" (Hecht), **Supp. X:** 63

"Thought of Heaven, The" (Stern), **Supp. IX:** 297

"Thoughts after Lambeth" (Eliot), **I:** 587; **Retro. Supp. I:** 324

Thoughts and Reflections (Lord Halifax), **II:** 111

Thoughts in Solitude (Merton), **Supp. VIII:** 207

Thoughts of Thoreau, The (Teale), **Supp. XXVIII:** 248

"Thoughts on Being Bibliographed" (Wilson), **IV:** 435

"Thoughts on the Establishment of a Mint in the United States" (Paine), **Supp. I Part 2:** 512

"Thoughts on the Gifts of Art" (Kenyon), **Supp. VII:** 167

Thousand Acres, A (Smiley), **Supp. VI:** 292, **301–303**

"Thousand and Second Night, The" (Merrill), **Supp. III Part 1:** 324

"Thousand Dollar Vagrant, The" (Olsen), **Supp. XIII:** 292, 297

"Thousand Faces of Danny Torrance, The" (Figliola), **Supp. V:** 143

"Thousand Genuflections, A" (McCarriston), **Supp. XIV:** 266

Thousand-Mile Walk to the Gulf, A (Muir), **Supp. IX:** 177–178

Thousand Plateaus, A (Deleuze and Guattari), **Supp. XXV:** 123

"Thou Shalt Not Steal" (McClatchy), **Supp. XII:** 264

"Thread, The" (Merwin), **Supp. III Part 1:** 351

Three (film), **Supp. IX:** 253

3-3-8 (Marquand), **III:** 58

"3 A.M. Kitchen: My Father Talking" (Gallagher), **Supp. XXIV:** 169

"Three Academic Pieces" (Stevens), **IV:** 90

"Three Agee Wards, The" (Morris), **III:** 220–221

"Three American Singers" (Cather), **Retro. Supp. I:** 10

"Three Around the Old Gentleman" (Berryman), **I:** 188

"Three Avilas, The" (Jeffers), **Supp. II Part 2:** 418

"Three Black Women Writers" (C. L. R. James), **Supp. XXI:** 172

Three Books of Song (Longfellow), **II:** 490

"Three Bushes" (Yeats), **Supp. I Part 1:** 80

Three Cantos (Pound), **Retro. Supp. I:** 290

Three Centuries of Harvard (Morison), **Supp. I Part 2:** 485

Three Changes (Silver), **Supp. XXIV:** 275

Three Circles of Light (di Donato), **Supp. XX: 33, 42–43, 44, 46**

Three Cities: A Trilogy (Asch), **Supp. XXIII:** 1, 5, **10–12**

Three Comrades (Remarque), **Retro. Supp. I:** 113

"Three Corollaries of Cultural Relativism" (Locke), **Supp. XIV:** 202

"Three-Day Blow, The" (Hemingway), **II:** 248

Three Essays on America (Brooks), **I:** 246

Three Farmers on Their Way to a Dance (Powers), **Supp. IX:** 211–212, **213–214,** 222

"Three Fates, The" (Benét), **Supp. XI:** 48–49, 50

"Three Generations of Secrets" (A. Finch), **Supp. XVII:** 73

"Three Gifts, The" (Gibran), **Supp. XX:** **124**

Three Gospels (Price), **Supp. VI:** 267

365 Days (Boyle), **Supp. XXIV:** 50, 60

"Three Kings, The: Hemingway, Faulkner, and Fitzgerald" (Ford), **Supp. V:** 59

Three Lives (Auchincloss), **Supp. IV Part 1:** 25

Three Lives (Stein), **I:** 103; **IV:** 26, 27, 31, 35, 37–41, 42, 45, 46; **Supp. IX:** 306; **Supp. XXIII:** 166

"THREE MOVEMENTS AND A CODA" (Baraka), **Supp. II Part 1:** 50

Three One Act Plays (*Riverside Drive, Old Saybrook,* and *Central Park West*) (Allen), **Supp. XV:** 3

Three on the Tower: The Lives and Works of Ezra Pound, T. S. Eliot, and William Carlos Williams (Simpson), **Supp. IX:** 276

Three Papers on Fiction (Welty), **IV:** 261

Three-Penny Opera (Brecht), **I:** 301; **Supp. XIV:** 162

"Three Percent Own All the Wealth" (Ryan as Quin), **Supp. XVIII:** 231–232

Three Philosophical Poets (Santayana), **III:** 610–612

"Three Pigs in Five Days" (Prose), **Supp. XVI:** 257, 258

"Three Players of a Summer Game" (T. Williams), **IV:** 383

Three Poems (Ashbery), **Supp. III Part 1:** 2, 3, 14, 15, 18, 24–26

"Three Poems for my Daughter" (Di Piero), **Supp. XIX:** 40

"Three Pokes of a Thistle" (Nye), **Supp. XIII:** 281

"Three Proofs"(Siken), **Supp. XXVIII:** 201

Three Prophets of Religious Liberalism (Wright), **Supp. XXIV:** 71

Three Roads, The (Macdonald, under Millar), **Supp. IV Part 2:** 466, 467

Three Short Plays with Long Titles (Silver and Ann), **Supp. XXIV:** 264

"Three Silences of Molinos, The" (Longfellow), **Retro. Supp. II:** 169

Three Sisters, The (Chekhov), **Supp. XV:** 323

"Three Sisters, The" (Cisneros), **Supp. VII:** 64

Three Soldiers (Dos Passos), **I:** 477–478, 480, 482, 488, 493–494; **Supp. XXI:** 277

"Three Songs at the End of Summer" (Kenyon), **Supp. VII:** 169–170

"Three Steps to the Graveyard" (Wright), **Supp. III Part 2:** 593, 596

Three Stories and Ten Poems (Hemingway), **II:** 68, 263; **Supp. XVII:** 105

Three Tall Women (Albee), **Supp. XXIV:** 270

Three Taverns, The (Robinson), **III:** 510

"Three Taverns, The" (Robinson), **III:** 521, 522

Three Tenant Families (Agee), **I:** 37–38

Three Tenors, One Vehicle: A Book of Songs (X. J. Kennedy, Camp, and Waldrop), **Supp. XV:** 165

"Three Types of Poetry" (Tate), **IV:** 131

"Three Vagabonds of Trinidad" (Harte), **Supp. II Part 1:** 338

"Three Waterfalls, The" (Lanier), **Supp. I Part 1:** 350

"Three-Way Mirror" (Brooks), **Supp. III Part 1:** 69–70

Three Weeks in Spring (Parker and Parker), **Supp. XIX:** 187

"Three Whose Hatred Killed Them"(Gold), **Supp. XXVIII:** 67

"Three Women" (Plath), **Supp. I Part 2:** 539, 541, 544, 545, 546

Three Young Poets (Swallow, ed.), **Supp. X:** 116

Threnody (Emerson), **Supp. I Part 2:** 416

"Threnody" (Emerson), **II:** 7

"Threnody for a Brown Girl" (Cullen), **Supp. IV Part 1:** 166

"Threshing-Floor, The" (Baldwin), **Supp. I Part 1:** 50

"Threshing Wheat" (Huddle), **Supp. XXVI:** 148

Threshold (film), **Supp. IX:** 254

"Threshold" (Goldbarth), **Supp. XII:** 175

Threshold (Jackson), **Supp. IX:** 117

Thriller (television show), **Supp. XXVII:** 119

"Throat" (Goldbarth), **Supp. XII:** 177–178

Throne of Labdacus, The (Schnackenberg), **Supp. XV:** 260, **263–266**

Thrones (Pound), **Retro. Supp. I:** 293

Through Dooms of Love (Kumin), **Supp. IV Part 2:** 444

Through Glacier Park in 1915 (Rinehart), **Supp. XXV:** 195

"Through the Black Curtain" (Kingston), **Supp. V:** 169

Through the Forest: New and Selected Poems, 1977–1987 (Wagoner), **Supp. IX:** **330–331**

"Through the Gates of the Silver Key" (Lovecraft and Price), **Supp. XXV:** 114, 123

"Through the Hills of Spain" (Salinas), **Supp. XIII:** 315

"Through the Hole in the Mundane Millstone" (West), **Retro. Supp. II:** 321, 322

Through the Ivory Gate (Dove), **Supp. IV Part 1:** 242, 243, 251, 252, 253–254, 254

"Through the Kitchen Window, Chiapas" (Nye), **Supp. XIII:** 277

Through the Safety Net (C. Baxter), **Supp. XVII:** 17, 22

"Through the Smoke Hole" (Snyder), **Supp. VIII:** 299

Throw Like a Girl (Thompson), **Supp. XXIII:** **299–300**

"Throw Like a Girl"(Thompson), **Supp. XXIII:** 299, 300

"Thrush Relinquished, The" (Grossman), **Supp. XIX:** 83

Thucydides, **II:** 418; **IV:** 50; **Supp. I Part 2:** 488, 489, 492; **Supp. IV Part 1:** 391; **Supp. XIII:** 233

Thunderbolt and Lightfoot (film), **Supp. X:** 126

"Thunder from a Cloudless Sky" (Mosher), **Supp. XXII:** 209

"Thunderhead" (MacLeish), **III:** 19

Thurber, James, **I:** 487; **II:** 432; **IV:** 396; **Supp. I Part 2: 602–627,** 653, 654, 668, 672, 673, 679; **Supp. II Part 1:** 143; **Supp. IV Part 1:** 349; **Supp. IX:** 118; **Supp. XIV:** 104; **Supp. XVI:** 167; **Supp. XVII:** 4

Thurber, Mrs. James (Althea Adams), **Supp. I Part 2:** 613, 615, 617

Thurber, Mrs. James (Helen Muriel Wismer), **Supp. I Part 2:** 613, 617, 618

Thurber, Robert, **Supp. I Part 2:** 613, 617

Thurber, Rosemary, **Supp. I Part 2:** 616

Thurber, William, **Supp. I Part 2:** 602

Thurber Album, The (Thurber), **Supp. I Part 2:** 611, 619

Thurber Carnival, The (Thurber), **Supp. I Part 2:** 620; **Supp. XIV:** 104

Thurman, Judith, **Supp. IV Part 1:** 309; **Supp. XXV:** 2

Thurman, Wallace, **Retro. Supp. I:** 200; **Retro. Supp. III:** 127, 137; **Supp. I Part 1:** 325, 326, 328, 332; **Supp. IV Part 1:** 164; **Supp. X:** 136, 139; **Supp. XIX:** 78; **Supp. XVI:** 135; **Supp. XVIII:** 279, 281; **Supp. XXII:** 2

"Thursday" (Millay), **III:** 129

"Thurso's Landing" (Jeffers), **Supp. II Part 2:** 433

"Thus Do I Refute Gioia" (Junker), **Supp. XV:** 116

"Thus Far by Faith" (Nelson), **Supp. XVIII:** 177

Thus Spake Zarathustra (Nietzsche), **II:** 463; **Supp. IV Part 1:** 110; **Supp. IV Part 2:** 519

Thwaite, Lady Alicia. *See* Rawlings, Marjorie Kinnan

"Thyme" (Stallings), **Supp. XXV:** 232–233

Thy Neighbor's Wife (Talese), **Supp. XVII:** 204, 205–206, 207, 208, 210

"Tiara" (Doty), **Supp. XI:** 122

"Tibetan Time" (Prose), **Supp. XVI:** 255

Ticket for a Seamstitch, A (Harris), **II:** 424–425

Tickets for a Prayer Wheel (Dillard), **Supp. VI:** 22, 34

Ticket That Exploded, The (Burroughs), **Supp. III Part 1:** 93, 103, 104

Tickless Time (Glaspell), **Supp. III Part 1:** 179

Ticknor, George, **II:** 488; **Supp. I Part 1:** 313

Ticknor, William, **Supp. XVIII:** 258

"Ti Démon" (Chopin), **Supp. I Part 1:** 225

Tide of Time, The (Masters), **Supp. I Part 2:** 471

"Tide of Voices" (Hull), **Supp. XXI:** 132, 133–134, 136

"Tide Rises, the Tide Falls, The" (Longfellow), **I:** 498

"Tides" (Hoffman), **Supp. XVIII:** 86

Tidewater Blood (Hoffman), **Supp. XVIII: 82–83**

Tidyman, Ernest, **Supp. V:** 226

Tietjens, Eunice, **Supp. XV:** 47, 297; **Supp. XXVII:** 286

"Tiger" (Blake), **Supp. I Part 1:** 80; **Supp. VIII:** 26

Tiger (Bynner), **Supp. XV:** 42, 50

"Tiger, The" (Buechner), **Supp. XII:** 48

Tiger in the House, The (Van Vechten), **Supp. II Part 2:** 736

Tiger Joy (Benét), **Supp. XI:** 45

Tiger-Lilies (Lanier), **Supp. I Part 1:** 350–351, 357, 360, 371

Tiger Who Wore White Gloves, The: or, What You Are, You Are (Brooks), **Supp. III Part 1:** 86

"Tignon, The"(King), **Supp. XXVIII:** 122

Till, Emmett, **Supp. I Part 1:** 61

Till, Eric, **Supp. XXIII:** 103

Tillich, Paul, **II:** 244; **III:** 291, 292, 303, 309; **IV:** 226; **Retro. Supp. I:** 325, 326, 327; **Supp. V:** 267; **Supp. XIII:** 74, 91

Tillie Olsen: A Study of the Short Fiction (Frye), **Supp. XIII:** 292, 296, 298, 299, 302

Tillman, Lynne, **Supp. XII:** 4

Tillotson, John, **II:** 114

Tillotson, Kristen, **Supp. XVII:** 23

Tillstrom, Burr, **Supp. XIV:** 125

Till the Day I Die (Odets), **Supp. II Part 2:** 530, 533–536, 552

Tilton, Eleanor, **Supp. I Part 1:** 317

Tilton, Theodore, **Supp. XVIII:** 4

Timaeus (Plato), **II:** 10; **III:** 609

Tim: A Story of School Life (Sturgis), **Supp. XX: 227, 230, 232, 233–235**

Timber (Jonson), **II:** 16

Timberg, Scott, **Supp. XV:** 116

"Timberwolf' (Halliday), **Supp. XIX:** 91

Timbuktu (Auster), **Supp. XII:** 34, **35–36**

"Time" (Matthews), **Supp. IX: 165–166**

"Time" (Merrill), **Supp. III Part 1:** 325

"Time" (Very), **Supp. XXV:** 249

"Time and Again" (Sanders), **Supp. XVI:** 269

Time and a Place, A (Humphrey), **Supp. IX:** 95, 98, **100–102**

"Time and Distance Overcome" (Biss), **Supp. XXVI:** 55–56

"Time and the Garden" (Winters), **Supp. II Part 2:** 801, 809

"Time and the Liturgy" (Merton), **Supp. VIII:** 199

Time and the River (Edgell), **Supp. XXIII:** 84, 85, **91–93**

Time and Tide: A Walk through Nantucket (Conroy), **Supp. XVI:** 63, 71, **76–77**

Timebends (A. Miller), **Retro. Supp. III:** 172

"Time Exposure" (C. Baxter), **Supp. XVII:** 20–21

Time Exposures, by Search-Light (W. Frank), **Supp. XX:** 75

Time in the Rock (Aiken), **I:** 65

Time Is Noon, The (Buck), **Supp. II Part 1:** 129, 130–131

Time & Money (Matthews), **Supp. IX:** 155, **165–167**

"Time of Death, A" (Munro), **Supp. XXVII:** 180

"Time of Friendship, The" (Bowles), **Supp. IV Part 1:** 90–91

"Time of Her Time, The" (Mailer), **III:** 37, 45; **Retro. Supp. II:** 200

Time of Our Time, The (Mailer), **Retro. Supp. II:** 213–214

Time of the Assassins, The: A Study of Rimbaud (H. Miller), **III:** 189

"Time of the Missile" (Oppen), **Supp. XXVI:** 232

Time Out of Mind (album, Dylan), **Supp. XVIII:** 28

"Time Past" (Morris), **III:** 232

"Time Present" (Morris), **III:** 232

"Times" (Beattie), **Supp. V:** 31

"Times, The" (Emerson), **II:** 11–12

Times Are Never So Bad, The (Dubus), **Supp. VII:** 87–88

Time's Arrow (Amis), **Retro. Supp. I:** 278

"Time Shall Not Die" (Chandler), **Supp. IV Part 1:** 120

Times of Melville and Whitman, The (Brooks), **I:** 257

Time's Power: Poems 1985–1988 (Rich), **Retro. Supp. III:** 250

Times They Are A-Changin', The (album, Dylan), **Supp. XVIII:** 20, 25

"Times They Are A-Changin,' The" (song, Dylan), **Supp. XVIII:** 30

"Timesweep" (Sandburg), **III:** 595–596

Time to Act, A (MacLeish), **III:** 3

Time to Be Born, A (Powell), **Supp. XIX:** 143

Time to Go (Dixon), **Supp. XII:** 147

Time to Kill (film), **Supp. IV Part 1:** 130

Time to Speak, A (MacLeish), **III:** 3

Time Will Darken It (Maxwell), **Supp. VIII:** 159, **162–164,** 169

"Timing of Sin, The" (Dubus), **Supp. VII:** 91

Tim O'Brien (Herzog), **Supp. V:** 239

Timoleon (Melville), **III:** 93; **Retro. Supp. I:** 257; **Retro. Supp. III:** 161

Timothy Dexter Revisited (Marquand), **III:** 55, 62, 63

Timothy Findley: Stories from a Life (Roberts), **Supp. XX: 53**

Timrod, Henry, **Supp. XVIII:** 31, 33

Tin Can, The (W. J. Smith), **Supp. XIII:** 334, **Supp. XIII:** 336, 337

"Tin Can, The" (W. J. Smith), **Supp. XIII: 337–339**

Tin Can Tree, The (Tyler), **Supp. IV Part 2:** 659–660

Tinguely, Jean, **Supp. XV:** 187

Tinker, Chauncey Brewster, **Supp. XIV:** 12

"Tinseled Bucks: A Historical Study of Indian Homosexuality"(Kenny), **Supp. XXIII:** 149

Tintern Abbey (Wordsworth), **Supp. I Part 2:** 673, 675

Tiny Alice (Albee), **I:** 81–86, 87, 88, 94

"Tiny Closet, The" (Inge), **Supp. XXV:** 105–106

"Tiny Mummies! The True Story of the Ruler of 43rd Street's Land of the Walking Dead" (Wolfe), **Supp. III Part 2:** 573, 574

Tip on a Dead Jockey and Other Stories (Shaw), **Supp. XIX:** 251

"Tip-Top Club, The" (Keillor), **Supp. XVI:** 172

"Tired" (Hughes), **Supp. I Part 1:** 331

"Tired and Unhappy, You Think of Houses" (Schwartz), **Supp. II Part 2:** 649

"Tiresias" (Garrett), **Supp. VII:** 96–97

'Tis (McCourt), **Supp. XII:** 271, **279–286**

Tisch (Dixon), **Supp. XII:** 141, **155–156**

" 'Tis Finished" (Very), **Supp. XXV:** 249

Tish (Rinehart), **Supp. XXV:** 194

Tish Marches On (Rinehart), **Supp. XXV:** 194

Tish Plays the Game (Rinehart), **Supp. XXV:** 194

Titan, The (Dreiser), **I:** 497, 501, 507–508, 509, 510; **Retro. Supp. II:** 94, 101, 102

Titanic Operas (Dickinson Electronic Archives), **Supp. XXVII:** 261

Titian, **Supp. I Part 2:** 397, 714

"Tito's Goodbye" (García), **Supp. XI:** 190

"To a Bird, Seen Under My Window in the Garden"(J. Schoolcraft), **Supp. XXIII:** 230

To a Blossoming Pear Tree (Wright), **Supp. III Part 2:** 602–605

"To a Blossoming Pear Tree" (Wright), **Supp. III Part 2:** 604

"To Abolish Children" (Shapiro), **Supp. II Part 2:** 717

To Abolish Children and Other Essays (Shapiro), **Supp. II Part 2:** 703

"To a Calvinist in Bali" (Millay), **Supp. XXVI:** 170

"To a Caty-Did, the Precursor of Winter" (Freneau), **Supp. II Part 1:** 274–275

"To a Chameleon" (Moore), **III:** 195, 196, 215

"To a Conscript of 1940" (Read), **II:** 372–373, 377–378

"To a Contemporary Bunk Shooter" (Sandburg), **III:** 582

"To a Cough in the Street at Midnight" (Wylie), **Supp. I Part 2:** 727, 729–730

"To a Defeated Savior" (Wright), **Supp. III Part 2:** 593–594, 596

"To a Face in the Crowd" (Warren), **IV:** 239

"To a Fish Head Found on the Beach near Malaga" (Levine), **Supp. V:** 185

"To a Friend" (Nemerov), **III:** 272

"To a Friend"(O'Hara), **Supp. XXIII:** 212

"To a Friend Whose Work Has Come to Triumph" (Sexton), **Supp. II Part 2:** 683

To a God Unknown (Steinbeck), **I:** 107; **IV:** 51, 59–60, 67

"To a Greek Marble" (Aldington), **Supp. I Part 1:** 257

"To a Locomotive in Winter" (Whitman), **IV:** 348

"To a Mad Friend" (Davison), **Supp. XXVI:** 69

"To a Military Rifle" (Winters), **Supp. II Part 2:** 810, 811, 815

"To a Mouse" (Burns), **Supp. IX:** 173

"To an American Workman Dying of Starvation" (Taggard), **Supp. XXII:** 282

"To an Athlete Dying Young" (Houseman), **Supp. XVII:** 121

"To a Negro Jazz Band in a Parisian Cabaret" (Hughes), **Supp. I Part 1:** 325

"To an Old Philosopher in Rome" (Stevens), **III:** 605; **Retro. Supp. I:** 312

"To an Old Poet in Peru" (Ginsberg), **Supp. II Part 1:** 322

"To a Now-Type Poet" (X. J. Kennedy), **Supp. XV:** 161

"To Answer Your Question" (Jarman), **Supp. XVII:** 114–115

"To Any Would-Be Terrorists" (Nye), **Supp. XIII:** 285, 286

"To a Picture of Eleonora Duse" (Teasdale), **Supp. XXVII:** 287

"To a Poet" (Rich), **Supp. I Part 2:** 571; **Supp. XIX:** 83

"To a Prize Bird" (Moore), **III:** 215

"To a Republican, with Mr. Paine's Rights of Man" (Freneau), **Supp. II Part 1:** 267

"To a Revolutionary Girl" (Bodenheim), **Supp. XXV:** 28

"To a Shade" (Yeats), **III:** 18

"To a Skylark" (Shelley), **Supp. I Part 2:** 720; **Supp. X:** 31

"Toast to Harlem, A" (Hughes), **Supp. I Part 1:** 338

"To Aunt Rose" (Ginsberg), **Supp. II Part 1:** 320

"To Autumn" (Keats), **Supp. IX:** 50

"To a Waterfowl" (Bryant), **Supp. I Part 1:** 154, 155, 162, 171

"To a Young Poet" (X. J. Kennedy), **Supp. XV:** 161

"To a Young Writer" (Stegner), **Supp. X:** 24

"Tobacco" (Rash), **Supp. XXVII:** 218

Tobacco Road (Caldwell), **I:** 288, 289, 290, 295–296, 297, 298, 302, 307, 309, 310; **IV:** 198; **Supp. XXII:** 196

"To Be a Monstrous Clever Fellow" (Fante), **Supp. XI:** 167

"To Become Music or Break" (Jauss), **Supp. XXI:** 133

To Bedlam and Part Way Back (Sexton), **Retro. Supp. II:** 245; **Supp. II Part 2:** 672–678; **Supp. IV Part 2:** 441; **Supp. XI:** 317

"To Beethoven" (Lanier), **Supp. I Part 1:** 364

To Begin Again: Stories and Memoirs, 1908–1929 (M. F. K. Fisher), **Supp. XVII:** 92

Tobey, Mark, **Supp. X:** 264

To Be Young, Gifted, and Black: Lorraine Hansberry in Her Own Words (Nemiroff), **Supp. IV Part 1:** 372, 374

"To Big Mary from an Ex-Catholic" (Mora), **Supp. XIII:** 217, 224, 228

Tobin, Jacqueline L., **Supp. XXVI:** 200

"Tobin's Palm" (O. Henry), **Supp. II Part 1:** 408; **Supp. XV:** 40

Tobit (apocryphal book), **I:** 89

"To Brooklyn Bridge" (H. Crane), **Retro. Supp. III:** 51

"To Build a Fire" (London), **II:** 468

Toby Tyler: or, Ten Weeks with a Circus (Otis), **III:** 577

"To Change in a Good Way" (Ortiz), **Supp. IV Part 2:** 511

"To Charlotte Cushman" (Lanier), **Supp. I Part 1:** 364

"To Cole, the Painter, Departing for Europe" (Bryant), **Supp. I Part 1:** 157, 161

Tocqueville, Alexis de, **III:** 261; **IV:** 349; **Retro. Supp. I:** 235; **Supp. I Part 1:** 137; **Supp. I Part 2:** 659, 660; **Supp. II Part 1:** 281, 282, 284; **Supp. XIV:** 306, 312

"To Crispin O'Conner" (Freneau), **Supp. II Part 1:** 268

"To Da-Duh, In Memoriam" (Marshall), **Supp. XI:** 276

"TODAY" (Baraka), **Supp. II Part 1:** 55

"Today" (Ginsberg), **Supp. II Part 1:** 328

"Today Is a Good Day To Die" (Bell), **Supp. X:** 7

"Today"(O'Hara), **Supp. XXIII:** 210–211

Today We Live (film), **Retro. Supp. III:** 84

Today Will Be a Quiet Day" (Hempel), **Supp. XXI:** 117,**Supp. XXI:** 118

Todd, Mabel Loomis, **I:** 454, 470; **Retro. Supp. I:** 33, 34, 35, 39, 47

"To Death" (Levertov), **Supp. III Part 1:** 274

"To Delmore Schwartz" (R. Lowell), **II:** 547; **Retro. Supp. II:** 188

"to disembark" (Brooks), **Supp. III Part 1:** 86

"To Dorothy on Her Exclusion from The Guinness Book of Records" (X. J. Kennedy), **Supp. XV:** 166

"To Dream of Bears" (Gallagher), **Supp. XXIV:** 176

"To Dr. Thomas Shearer" (Lanier), **Supp. I Part 1:** 370

"To Earthward" (Frost), **II:** 154

"To Edward John Moreton Drax Plunkett, Eighteenth Baron Dunsany" (Lovecraft), **Supp. XXV:** 113

"To Edwin V. McKenzie" (Winters), **Supp. II Part 2:** 801

"To Eleonora Duse" (A. Lowell), **II:** 528

"To Elizabeth Ward Perkins" (A. Lowell), **II:** 516

"To Elsie" (W. C. Williams), **Retro. Supp. I:** 419

"To Emily Dickinson" (H. Crane), **Retro. Supp. II:** 76

"To E. T." (Frost), **Retro. Supp. I:** 132

To Feel These Things (L. Michaels), **Supp. XVI:** 205, **213–214**

"To Feel These Things" (L. Michaels), **Supp. XVI:** 214

Toffler, Alvin, **Supp. IV Part 2:** 517

"To Fill" (Moore), **Supp. X:** 168, 169

"To Gabriela, a Young Writer" (Mora), **Supp. XIII:** 220

"To George May" (Bodenheim), **Supp. XXV:** 25

To Have and Have Not (film), **Retro. Supp. III:** 85; **Supp. XV:** 347

To Have and Have Not (Hemingway), **I:** 31; **II:** 253–254, 264; **Retro. Supp. I:** 182, **183,** 187

"To Helen" (Poe), **III:** 410, 411, 427; **Retro. Supp. II:** 102; **Retro. Supp. III:** 224, 232

"To Hell With Dying" (Walker), **Supp. III Part 2:** 523

"To Her Father with Some Verses" (Bradstreet), **Retro. Supp. III:** 2, 12

"To His Coy Mistress"(Marvell), **Supp. XXIII:** 62

"To His Excellency General Washington" (Wheatley), **Supp. XX: 289**

"To His Father" (Jeffers), **Supp. II Part 2:** 415

Toilet, The (Baraka), **Supp. II Part 1:** 37, 40–42

"To James Russell Lowell" (Holmes), **Supp. I Part 1:** 311

To Jerusalem and Back (Bellow), **Retro. Supp. II:** 29

"To Jesus on His Birthday" (Millay), **III:** 136–137

"To John Keats" (A. Lowell), **II:** 516

"To Judge Faolain, Dead Long Enough: A Summons" (McCarriston), **Supp. XIV:** 264–265

"To Justify My Singing" (Wright), **Supp. III Part 2:** 590

"To Kill a Deer" (C. Frost), **Supp. XV:** 102

To Kill a Mockingbird (film), **Supp. VIII:** 128–129

To Kill a Mockingbird (Lee), **Supp. VIII: 113–129; Supp. XIX:** 142; **Supp. XVI:** 259; **Supp. XXVII:** 13

"To Kill a Mockingbird: Harper Lee's Tragic Vision" (Dave), **Supp. VIII:** 126

To Kill a Mockingbird: Threatening Boundaries (C. D. Johnson), **Supp. VIII:** 126

Toklas, Alice B., **IV:** 27; **Supp. IV Part 1:** 81, 91; **Supp. XVI:** 187

"Tokyo Story" (Wasserstein), **Supp. XV:** 328

"To Larry Rivers"(O'Hara), **Supp. XXIII:** 212

"To Light" (Hogan), **Supp. IV Part 1:** 402

"To Ligurinus" (Horace; Ferry, trans.), **Supp. XXIV:** 155

"To Ligurinus" (Horace; Howard, trans.), **Supp. XXIV:** 155
"To Live and Diet" (Wasserstein), **Supp. XV:** 328
Tolkien, J. R. R., **Supp. V:** 140
Tolkin, Michael, **Supp. XI:** 160
Toller, Ernst, **I:** 479
"To Lose the Earth" (Sexton), **Supp. II Part 2:** 684, 685
Tolson, Melvin, **Retro. Supp. I:** 208, 209, 210
Tolstoy, Leo, **I:** 6, 7, 58, 103, 312, 376; **II:** 191–192, 205, 271, 272, 275, 276, 281, 285, 286, 320, 407, 542, 559, 570, 579, 606; **III:** 37, 45, 61, 323, 467, 572; **IV:** 17, 21, 170, 285; **Retro. Supp. I:** 91, 225; **Retro. Supp. II:** 299; **Supp. I Part 1:** 2, 3, 6, 20; **Supp. IV Part 1:** 392; **Supp. IX:** 246; **Supp. V:** 277, 323; **Supp. XI:** 68; **Supp. XII:** 310, 322; **Supp. XIV:** 87, 97, 98; **Supp. XIX:** 241; **Supp. XXIII:** 4, 11, 275; **Supp. XXIV:** 132; **Supp. XXV:** 142; **Supp. XXVIII:** 112
"To Lu Chi" (Nemerov), **III:** 275
"To Lydia" (Horace; Ferry, trans.), **Supp. XXIV:** 154
"To Lydia" (Horace; McHugh, trans.), **Supp. XXIV:** 154
Tom (Cummings), **I:** 430
"Tom" (Oliver), **Supp. VII:** 232
"To M." (Teasdale), **Supp. XXVII:** 297
"Tom, Tom, the Piper's Son" (Ransom), **Supp. X:** 58
"To M, with a Rose" (Lanier), **Supp. I Part 1:** 364
To Make a Prairie (Kumin), **Supp. IV Part 2:** 440, 441
"To Make Words Disappear" (Simpson), **Supp. IX:** 265–266
Tomás and the Library Lady (Mora), **Supp. XIII:** 216, 221
"Tomatoes" (Francis), **Supp. IX:** 82
"Tom Ball's Barn" (Kooser), **Supp. XIX:** 119
"Tom Brown at Fisk" (Du Bois), **Supp. II Part 1:** 160
Tom Brown's School Days (Hughes), **Supp. I Part 2:** 406
"Tomb Stone" (Dickey), **Supp. IV Part 1:** 185
"Tombstone Blues" (song, Dylan), **Supp. XVIII:** 30
Tomcat in Love (O'Brien), **Supp. V:** 238, 240, 243, 252–254
"Tomcat's Wife, The" (C. Bly), **Supp. XVI:** 40
Tomcat's Wife and Other Stories, The (C. Bly), **Supp. XVI:** 40–41
"Tom Fool at Jamaica" (Moore), **III:** 215
To Mix with Time (Swenson), **Supp. IV Part 2:** 637, 643–645, 645
Tom Jones (Fielding), **I:** 131; **Supp. V:** 127
Tomlinson, Charles, **Supp. XVI:** 284
Tommy Gallagher's Crusade (Farrell), **II:** 44
Tommyknockers, The (King), **Supp. V:** 139, 144

"Tommy's Burglar" (Henry), **Supp. II Part 1:** 399, 401
"Tommy Stames" (Budbill), **Supp. XIX:** 8
Tomo Cheeki (pseudonym). *See* Freneau, Philip
Tomorrow Is Another Day (E. P. Jones), **Supp. XXII:** 252
Tomorrow is Another Day (film, Feist), **Supp. XVII:** 62
"Tomorrow the Moon" (Dos Passos), **I:** 493
Tomorrow Will Be Better (B. Smith), **Supp. XXIII:** 258, **264–267**
"Tom Outland's Story" (Cather), **I:** 325–326
Tompkins, Jane, **Supp. XVI:** 89; **Supp. XVIII:** 258, 259, 263
Tompson, Benjamin, **Supp. I Part 1:** 110, 111
"Tom-Rock Through Eels" (Hempel), **Supp. XXI:** 116, 118, **123–124**
Tom Sawyer (Twain). *See Adventures of Tom Sawyer, The* (Twain)
Tom Sawyer Abroad (Twain), **II:** 482; **IV:** 19, 204
Tom Sawyer Detective (Twain), **IV:** 204
Tom Sawyer (musical) (Gurney), **Supp. V:** 96
"Tom's Husband" (Jewett), **Retro. Supp. II:** 132, 141
Tom Swift (Stratemeyer), **III:** 146
Tom-Walker, The (Sandoz), **Supp. XXIV:** 244, **253–255**
"Tom Wolfe's Guide to Etiquette" (Wolfe), **Supp. III Part 2:** 578
"To My Brother Killed: Haumont Wood: October, 1918" (Bogan), **Supp. III Part 1:** 58
"To My Class, on Certain Fruits and Flowers Sent Me in Sickness" (Lanier), **Supp. I Part 1:** 370
"To My Dear and Loving Husband" (Bradstreet), **Retro. Supp. III:** 12
"To My Dear Children" (Bradstreet), **Retro. Supp. III:** 13
"To my ever beloved & lamented son William Henry"(J. Schoolcraft), **Supp. XXIII:** 226, 231
"To My Father's Ghost" (Everwine), **Supp. XV:** 76
"To My Ghost Reflected in the Auxvasse River" (Levis), **Supp. XI:** 265
"To My Greek" (Merrill), **Supp. III Part 1:** 326
"To My Missionary Critics" (Twain), **Retro. Supp. III:** 268–269
"To My Mother" (Berry), **Supp. X:** 23
"To My Sister—Ernestine Kealoha Taggard, 1900–1943" (Taggard), **Supp. XXII:** 284
"To My Small Son, at the Photographer's" (Hay), **Supp. XIV:** 121
"To My Small Son, on Certain Occasions" (Hay), **Supp. XIV:** 121
"To My Students" (Taggard), **Supp. XXII:** 280
"To Name is to Possess" (Kincaid), **Supp. VII:** 194
Tone, Aileen, **I:** 21–22

"Tongue Is, The" (Komunyakaa), **Supp. XIII:** 113
"Tongue of the Jews" (Bukiet), **Supp. XVII:** 47
Tongues (Shepard and Chaikin), **Supp. III Part 2:** 433
Tongues of Angels, The (Price), **Supp. VI:** 265
Tongues Untied (Riggs; film), **Supp. XI:** 19, 20
"Tonight" (R. Lowell), **II:** 538
"Tonight Is Part of the Struggle"(Le Sueur), **Supp. XXIII:** 172
Tonight Is the Night of the Prom (Jarman), **Supp. XVII:** 110, **112–113**
"Tonight Is the Night of the Prom" (Jarman), **Supp. XVII:** 113
Tonight No Poetry Will Serve: Poems 2007–2010 (Rich), **Retro. Supp. III:** 252
Tonkin, Boyd, **Supp. XXVII:** 270
Tony Kushner in Conversation (Vorlicky, ed.), **Supp. IX:** 132
"Too Anxious for Rivers" (Frost), **II:** 162
"Too Blue" (Hughes), **Retro. Supp. I:** 207
"Too Damn Close: Thresholds and Their Maintenance in Rick Bass's Work" (Kerridge), **Supp. XVI:** 26
"Too Early" (Leopold), **Supp. XIV:** 186
"Too Early Spring" (Benét), **Supp. XI:** 53
"Too Far from Home" (Bowles), **Supp. IV Part 1:** 94–95
Too Far from Home: Selected Writings of Paul Bowles (Halpern, ed.), **Supp. IV Part 1:** 94, 95
Too Far to Go: The Maples Stories (Updike), **Retro. Supp. I:** 321
"Too Good To Be True": The Life and Art of Leslie Fiedler (Winchell), **Supp. XIII:** 94, 98, 99, 101
Toohey, John Peter, **Supp. IX:** 190
Toolan, David, **Supp. IV Part 1:** 308
Too Late (Dixon), **Supp. XII:** 143–144
"Too Late" (Pickering), **Supp. XXI:** 197
"Too-Late Born, The" (Hemingway), **III:** 9
Toole, John Kennedy, **Supp. XIV:** 21; **Supp. XXVI:** 239–254
"Toolless" (Pickering), **Supp. XXI:** 204
Too Many Bottles (Holding), **Supp. XXII:** 126, **134–135**
"Too Many Friends" (video, Ellis), **Supp. XXVII:** 80
Toomer, Jean, **Retro. Supp. II:** 79; **Retro. Supp. III:** 48; **Supp. I Part 1:** 325, 332; **Supp. III Part 2: 475–491;** **Supp. IV Part 1:** 16, 164, 168; **Supp. IX: 305–322; Supp. XIII:** 305; **Supp. XVIII:** 122; **Supp. XX:** 73; **Supp. XXII:** 6
Toomer, Nathan Eugene Pinchback. *See* Toomer, Jean
Too Much Happiness (Munro), **Supp. XXVII:** 195
"Too Much Happiness" (Munro), **Supp. XXVII:** 195
Too Much Johnson (film), **Supp. IV Part 1:** 83

"To One Who Said Me Nay" (Cullen), **Supp. IV Part 1:** 166

"Tooth, The" (Jackson), **Supp. IX:** 122

Tooth and Claw (Boyle), **Supp. XX: 20**

Tooth of Crime, The (Shepard), **Supp. III Part 2:** 432, 441–445, 447

"To Our Son"(Lea), **Supp. XXVIII:** 130–131

"Too Young" (O'Hara), **III:** 369

Topaz (film), **Supp. XX: 253**

Topaz (Uris), **Supp. XX: 247, 248, 253**

"Top Israeli Official Hints at 'Shared' Jerusalem" (Nye), **Supp. XIII:** 287

"To P. L., 1916–1937" (Levine), **Supp. V:** 185

"To Please a Shadow" (Brodsky), **Supp. VIII:** 30

"Top of the Food Chain" (Boyle), **Supp. XX:** 20

"Top of the Hill" (Jewett), **II:** 406

"Topography" (Olds), **Supp. X:** 208

Topography and Other Poems (Stone), **Supp. XXVII:** 256, 262

Topper (T. Smith), **Supp. IX:** 194

To Praise the Music (Bronk), **Supp. XXI:** 31, 32

To Quito and Back (Hecht), **Supp. XXVII:** 89

Torah, **IV:** 19

"Torch Songs" (Wrigley), **Supp. XVIII:** 296

Torday, Daniel, **Supp. XXII:** 151

"To Reach Japan" (Munro), **Supp. XXVII:** 195

"Torn-up Road, The"(Siken), **Supp. XXVIII:** 198

"Toronto, More or Less, in Fifteen Years" (Gansworth), **Supp. XXVI:** 110

Torpedo 8: The Story of Swede Larsen's Bomber Squadron (Wolfert), **Supp. XXI:** 267

Torpedo Junction (Hickam), **Supp. XXVII:** 103, 111

"Torquemada" (Bukiet), **Supp. XVII:** 44

"Torquemada" (Longfellow), **II:** 505; **Retro. Supp. II:** 164

Torrence, Ridgely, **III:** 507

Torrent and the Night Before, The (Robinson), **III:** 504

Torrents of Spring, The (Hemingway), **I:** 117; **II:** 250–251

Torres, Ben Fong, **Supp. XXVI:** 209

Torres, Héctor A., **Supp. XIII:** 225

Torres, Louis, **Supp. IV Part 2:** 529, 530

Torres-Saillant, Silvio, **Supp. XXI:** 104, 105, 108, 109

Torsney, Cheryl, **Retro. Supp. I:** 224

Tortilla Curtain, The (Boyle), **Supp. VIII: 9–10; Supp. XX: 28–29**

Tortilla Flat (Steinbeck), **IV:** 50, 51, 61, 64

Tortilla Flats (Steinbeck), **Supp. XX: 28**

Tortured Skins, and Other Fictions (Kenny), **Supp. XXIII:** 150, 156, 157

Tory Lover, The (Jewett), **II:** 406; **Retro. Supp. II:** 144–145

"Toscana" (Dixon), **Supp. XII:** 154

"To Sestius" (Horace; Ferry, trans.), **Supp. XXIV:** 155

"To Sestius" (Horace; Lasdun, trans.), **Supp. XXIV:** 154

"To Sir Toby" (Freneau), **Supp. II Part 1:** 269

"To Sophy, Expectant" (Mumford), **Supp. II Part 2:** 475

"To Speak of Woe That Is in Marriage" (R. Lowell), **II:** 550

"To Statecraft Embalmed" (Moore), **III:** 197

To Stay Alive (Levertov), **Supp. III Part 1:** 280–282

"Total Eclipse" (Dillard), **Supp. VI:** 28

"Total Eclipse of the Moon"(Crooker), **Supp. XXIII:** 55

Total Immersion (Goodman), **Supp. XXVI:** 118–121, 125

"Total Immersion" (Goodman), **Supp. XXVI:** 120

Total Recall (Paretsky), **Supp. XXV:** 172, 180, 181, 183–184

Toth, Emily, **Retro. Supp. II:** 71

Toth, Susan Allan, **Retro. Supp. II:** 138

"To the Americans of the United States" (Freneau), **Supp. II Part 1:** 271

"To the Apennines" (Bryant), **Supp. I Part 1:** 157, 164

"To the Bleeding Hearts Association of American Novelists" (Nemerov), **III:** 281

"To the Bone"(Lea), **Supp. XXVIII:** 137, 138

To the Bone: New and Selected Poems (Lea), **Supp. XXVIII:** 130, 137

"To the Botequim & Back" (Bishop), **Retro. Supp. II:** 51

To the Bright and Shining Sun (Burke), **Supp. XIV:** 22, 25

"To the Citizens of the United States" (Paine), **Supp. I Part 2:** 519–520

"To the Dandelion" (J. R. Lowell), **Supp. I Part 2:** 424

"To the End" (Haines), **Supp. XII:** 212–213

To the Ends of the Earth: The Selected Travels of Paul Theroux, **Supp. VIII:** 324

"To the Fabulous Constellation" (Ferry), **Supp. XXIV:** 148–149

"To the Film Industry in Crisis"(O'Hara), **Supp. XXIII:** 213–214

To the Finland Station: A Study in the Writing and Acting of History (Wilson), **IV:** 429, 436, 443–444, 446

"To the Governor & Legislature of Massachusetts" (Nemerov), **III:** 287

To the Green Man (Jarman), **Supp. XVII:** 110, 120–121

"To the Harbormaster" (O'Hara), **Supp. XXIII:** 208, 212, 214; **Supp. XXIV:** 42

To the Holy Spirit (Winters), **Supp. II Part 2:** 810

"To the Keeper of the King's Water Works" (Freneau), **Supp. II Part 1:** 269

"To the Lacedemonians" (Tate), **IV:** 134

"To the Laodiceans" (Jarrell), **Retro. Supp. I:** 121, 140

To the Lighthouse (Woolf), **I:** 309; **II:** 600; **Retro. Supp. II:** 337; **Retro. Supp. III:** 128; **Supp. VIII:** 155

"To the Man on Trail" (London), **II:** 466

"To the Memory of My Dear and Ever Honoured Father Thomas Dudley" (Bradstreet), **Retro. Supp. III:** 12

"To the Memory of the Brave Americans Under General Greene" (Freneau), **Supp. II Part 1:** 262, 274

"To the Miscodeed"(J. Schoolcraft), **Supp. XXIII:** 230

"To the Muse" (Wright), **Supp. III Part 2:** 601

"To the Natural World: at 37" (Taggard), **Supp. XXII:** 279–280

"To the Nazi Leaders" (Hay), **Supp. XIV:** 121

"To the New World" (Jarrell), **II:** 371

"To the One of Fictive Music" (Stevens), **IV:** 89; **Retro. Supp. I:** 297, 300

"To the One Upstairs" (Simic), **Supp. VIII:** 283

"To the Peoples of the World" (Du Bois), **Supp. II Part 1:** 172

"To the Person Sitting in Darkness" (Twain), **Retro. Supp. III:** 268

"To the Pine Tree on first seeing it on returning from Europe"(J. Schoolcraft), **Supp. XXIII:** 225, 228, 232–233

To the Place of Trumpets (B. Kelly), 132; **Supp. XVII: 123–127**

"To the Pliocene Skull" (Harte), **Supp. II Part 1:** 343–344

"To the Powers of Darkness" (Taggard), **Supp. XXII:** 279, 280

"To the Powers of Desolation" (Taggard), **Supp. XXII:** 280

"To the pure all things are pure" (Very), **Supp. XXV:** 242, 248

"To the Queen of Heaven" (Taggard), **Supp. XXII:** 280

"To the Reader" (Baudelaire), **II:** 544–545

"To The Reader" (Jarman), **Supp. XVII:** 115

"To the Reader" (Levertov), **Supp. III Part 1:** 277

"To the Republic" (Horace; Ferry, trans.), **Supp. XXIV:** 154

"To the Right Honourable William, Earl of Dartmouth" (Wheatley), **Supp. XX: 278, 284, 287–288**

"To the River Arve" (Bryant), **Supp. I Part 1:** 163

"To the Snake" (Levertov), **Supp. III Part 1:** 277

"To the Stone-Cutters" (Jeffers), **Supp. II Part 2:** 420

"To the Unseeable Animal" (Berry), **Supp. X:** 31

"To the Western World" (Simpson), **Supp. IX:** 269, 270

To the White Sea (Dickey), **Supp. IV Part 1:** 186, 190–191

"To the Young Who Want to Die" (Brooks), **Supp. III Part 1:** 85–86

"To Tlaoc of the Rain" (Everwine), **Supp. XV:** 77

"To Train a Writer" (Bierce), **I:** 199

"Touch, The" (Sexton), **Supp. II Part 2:** 687

Touch and Go (M. F. K. Fisher and D. Parrish), **Supp. XVII:** 84

"Touching the Tree" (Merwin), **Supp. III Part 1:** 355

Touching the World (Eakin), **Supp. VIII:** 167

Touch of Danger, A (Jones), **Supp. XI:** 226, **228–229**

Touch of the Poet, A (O'Neill), **III:** 385, 401, 404

Touchstone, The (Wharton), **Retro. Supp. I:** 365; **Retro. Supp. III:** 278, 279

Touchstone Anthology of Contemporary Nonfiction, The: Work from 1970 to the Present (Williford and Martone, eds.), **Supp. XXVI:** 53

"Touch-up Man" (Komunyakaa), **Supp. XIII:** 119

Tough Guys Don't Dance (Mailer), **Retro. Supp. II:** 211

"Tough People" (Offutt), **Supp. XIX:** 170–171

Toulet, Paul Jean, **IV:** 79

Tour (McNally), **Supp. XIII:** 197

"Tour 5" (Hayden), **Supp. II Part 1:** 381

To Urania (Brodsky), **Supp. VIII:** 22, 28–29

Tourgée, Albion W., **Supp. XIV:** 63

"Tour Guide" (Komunyakaa), **Supp. XIII:** 114

"Tourist Death" (MacLeish), **III:** 12

Tourmaline (J. Scott), **Supp. XVII:** 192–**194,** 195

Tour of Duty (Dos Passos), **I:** 489

"Tour of the Labyrinth" (Stallings), **Supp. XXV:** 229

Touron the Prairies, A (Irving), **II:** 312–313

Toussaint L'Ouverture, **Supp. XXI:** 166

Toussaint L'Ouverture (C. L. R. James), **Supp. XXI:** 167

Tovey, Donald Francis, **Supp. XIV:** 336

"To Virgil" (Horace; Ferry, trans.), **Supp. XXIV:** 155

"To Virgil" (Horace; Wright, trans.), **Supp. XXIV:** 155

To Walk a Crooked Mile (McGrath), **Supp. X:** 117

Toward a New Poetry (Wakoski), **Supp. XXVIII:** 262

Toward a New Synthesis (Begiebing), **Retro. Supp. II:** 210

"Toward an Understanding of the Public Life" (Davison), **Supp. XXVI:** 73

"Toward a Woman-Centered University" (Rich), **Retro. Supp. III:** 248

"Toward Nightfall" (Simic), **Supp. VIII:** 277

Towards a Better Life (Burke), **I:** 270

"Towards a Chicano Poetics: The Making of the Chicano Subject, 1969–1982" (Saldívar), **Supp. IV Part 2:** 544

Towards an Enduring Peace (Bourne), **I:** 232

"Towards Morning" (Pedersen; Nelson, trans.), **Supp. XVIII:** 180

"Towards Proletarian Art"(Gold), **Supp. XXVIII:** 71, 80

Toward the Blanched Alphabets (Sobin), **Supp. XVI:** 290

Toward the Gulf (Masters), **Supp. I Part 2:** 465–466

"Toward the Solstice" (Rich), **Supp. I Part 2:** 575–576

Toward Wholeness in Paule Marshall's Fiction (Pettis), **Supp. XI:** 276

"Tower" (Merwin), **Supp. III Part 1:** 343

"Tower Beyond Tragedy, The" (Jeffers), **Supp. II Part 2:** 429–430

Tower of Ivory (Atherton), **Supp. XXIV:** 21, 23

Tower of Ivory (MacLeish), **III:** 3–4

"Tower of Song" (Cohen), **Supp. XXVII:** 52

"Tower of the Elephant, The" (Howard), **Supp. XXVII:** 117, 125

Towers, Robert, **Supp. IX:** 259; **Supp. XVI:** 211; **Supp. XXV:** 86

"To What Red Hell" (C. Himes), **Supp. XVI:** 137

"To Whistler, American" (Pound), **III:** 465–466

"To Wine" (Bogan), **Supp. III Part 1:** 57, 58

Towle, Tony, **Supp. XXIII:** 221; **Supp. XXVII:** 23

Town, Caren J., **Supp. XVIII:** 195, 199

Town, The (Faulkner), **II:** 57, 73; **Retro. Supp. I:** 74, 82; **Retro. Supp. III:** 86

Town, The (Richter), **Supp. XVIII:** 207, **214–215,** 217

Town and the City, The (Kerouac), **Supp. III Part 1:** 222–224; **Supp. XIV:** 143

"Town Crier" (Bierce), **I:** 193, 194, 195, 196

"*Town Crier* Exclusive, Confessions of a Princess Manqué: 'How Royals Found Me "Unsuitable" to Marry Their Larry' " (Elkin), **Supp. VI:** 56

Town Down the River, The (Robinson), **III:** 508

"Town Dump, The" (Nemerov), **III:** 272, 275, 281

Towne, Robert, **Supp. XI:** 159, 172, 174

"Townhouse Interior with Cat" (Clampitt), **Supp. IX:** 40

Townie (Dubus III), **Supp. XXIV:** 98, **108–111**

"Townies" (Dubus), **Supp. VII:** 86

Town in the Forest, The: Life Story of Richmond, New Hampshire (Boyce; Faust, ed.), **Supp. XXI:** 8

"Town of the Sound of a Twig Breaking" (Carson), **Supp. XII:** **102**

"Town Poor, The" (Jewett), **Retro. Supp. II:** 138, 139, 143

Townsend, Alison, **Supp. XIII:** 222; **Supp. XXIII:** 132, 139

Townsend, Ann, **Supp. V:** 77

Townsend, Jim, **Supp. XXII:** 243

"Towns in Colour" (A. Lowell), **II:** 523–524

Townsman, The (Sedges), **Supp. II Part 1:** 124–125

Town Smokes (P. Benedict), **Supp. XXIII:** **35–39**

"Town Smokes"(P. Benedict), **Supp. XXIII:** 37

"To World War Two" (Koch), **Supp. XV:** 184

Toys in a Field (Komunyakaa), **Supp. XIII:** **121–122**

"Toys in a Field" (Komunyakaa), **Supp. XIII:** 122

Toys in the Attic (Hellman), **Supp. I Part 1:** 289–290

Toyter mentsh, Der (The dead man) (Asch), **Supp. XXIII:** 9

Tracer (F. Barthelme), **Supp. XI:** 31–32, 33

Traces of Thomas Hariot, The (Rukeyser), **Supp. VI:** 273, 274, 283

"Tracing Life with a Finger" (Caldwell), **I:** 291

Tracker (Wagoner), **Supp. IX:** 329, **336–337**

"Tracking" (Wagoner), **Supp. IX:** 329

"Track Meet, The" (Schwartz), **Supp. II Part 2:** 665

Tracks (Erdrich), **Supp. IV Part 1:** 259, 262–263, 269, 272, 273–274, 274, 275

"Track-Workers" (Bodenheim), **Supp. XXV:** 22

"Tract" (W. C. Williams), **Retro. Supp. I:** 414

"Tract against Communism, A" (Twelve Southerners), **IV:** 125, 237

Tractatus (Wittgenstein), **Supp. XVII:** 143

Tracy, Benjamin, **Supp. XVIII:** 4

Tracy, D. H., **Supp. XVIII:** 178

Tracy, Lee, **IV:** 287, 288

Tracy, Steven, **Retro. Supp. I:** 195

"Trade, The" (Levine), **Supp. V:** 193

Trading Twelves (Callahan and Murray, eds.), **Retro. Supp. II:** 119

Trading Twelves: The Selected Letters of Ralph Ellison and Albert Murray (Murray and Callahan, eds.), **Supp. XIX:** 148, 158

Traditional History of the Confederacy of the Six Nations (Scott), **Supp. XXVI:** 87

" 'Traditional' Marriage: A Secular Affair" (P. N. Warren), **Supp. XX:** 273

"Tradition and Industrialization" (Wright), **IV:** 489–490

"Tradition and Mythology: Signatures of Landscape in Chicana Poetry" (Rebolledo), **Supp. XIII:** 214

"Tradition and the Individual Talent" (Eliot), **I:** 441, 574, 585; **Retro. Supp. I:** 59, 286

"Tradition and the Individual Talent" (T. S. Eliot), **Retro. Supp. III:** 66

Tragedies, Life and Letters of James Gates Percival (Swinburne), **Supp. I Part 2:** 422

Tragedy of Bees, A (P. N. Warren), **Supp. XX:** **261**

"Tragedy of Bees, A" (P. N. Warren), **Supp. XX:** **272**

Tragedy of Don Ippolito, The (Howells), **II:** 279

"Tragedy of Error, A" (James), **II:** 322; **Retro. Supp. I:** 218

Tragedy of Pudd'nhead Wilson, The (Twain), **IV:** 206–207

Tragic America (Dreiser), **Retro. Supp. II:** 95

"Tragic Dialogue" (Wylie), **Supp. I Part 2:** 724

Tragic Ground (Caldwell), **I:** 297, 306

Tragic Muse, The (James), **Retro. Supp. I:** 227

Traherne, Thomas, **IV:** 151; **Supp. III Part 1:** 14; **Supp. V:** 208; **Supp. XV:** 212; **Supp. XVI:** 282, 288, 295

"Trail, The" (W. J. Smith), **Supp. XIII:** 342

Trailerpark (Banks), **Supp. V:** 12

"Trailing Arbutus, The" (Whittier), **Supp. I Part 2:** 691

Trail of the Lonesome Pine, The (Fox), **Supp. XIII:** 166

"Train, The" (O'Connor), **Retro. Supp. II:** 225

"Train Dreams" (Berrigan), **Supp. XXIV:** 45

"Train Ride" (Berrigan), **Supp. XXIV:** 42, 43–44

"Train Rising Out of the Sea" (Ashbery), **Supp. III Part 1:** 22

"Trains" (Banks), **Supp. V:** 8

"Train Tune" (Bogan), **Supp. III Part 1:** 64

Train Whistle Guitar (Murray), **Supp. XIX: 153–155,** 157

Traitor, The (Wouk), **Supp. XXV:** 256, 259

"Traits of Indian Character" (Irving), **II:** 303

Trakl, Georg, **Supp. XVII:** 241

Tramp Abroad, A (Twain), **IV:** 200; **Retro. Supp. III:** 267, 268

Tramping With a Poet in the Rockies (S. Graham), **Supp. I Part 2:** 397

Tramp's Excuse, The (Lindsay), **Supp. I Part 2:** 379, 380, 382

Tran, Sharon, **Supp. XXVI:** 216, 218

"Trance, The" (Taggard), **Supp. XXII:** 280

"Transaction" (Cliff), **Supp. XXII:** 75

"Transatlantic" (Toomer), **Supp. III Part 2:** 486

Transatlantic Sketches (James), **II:** 324; **Retro. Supp. I:** 219

"Transcendental Etude" (Rich), **Retro. Supp. III:** 249; **Supp. I Part 2:** 576

"Transcontinental Highway" (Cowley), **Supp. II Part 1:** 141

"Transducer" (Ammons), **Supp. VII:** 28

"Transfiguration" (Jarman), **Supp. XVII:** 118, 119

"Transfigured Bird" (Merrill), **Supp. III Part 1:** 320–321

"Transformations" (Harjo), **Supp. XII:** 226

Transformations (Sexton), **Supp. II Part 2:** 689–691; **Supp. IV Part 2:** 447; **Supp. XIV:** 125

Transforming Madness: New Lives for People Living with Mental Illness (Neugeboren), **Supp. XVI:** 229

"Transit" (Conroy), **Supp. XVI:** 72

Transit to Narcissus, A (Mailer), **Retro. Supp. II:** 196

"Translation" (Espaillat), **Supp. XXI:** 107

"Translation and Transposition" (Carne-Ross), **Supp. I Part 1:** 268–269

"Translation of a Fragment of Simonides" (Bryant), **Supp. I Part 1:** 153, 155

"Translations" (Rich), **Supp. I Part 2:** 563

Translations of Ezra Pound, The (Kenner, ed.), **III:** 463

Translations of the Gospel Back into Tongues (Wright), **Supp. XV: 342–343,** 346

"Translator's Task, The"(Benjamin), **Supp. XXIII:** 28

"Trans-National America" (Bourne), **I:** 229, 230

"Transparency" (X. J. Kennedy), **Supp. XV:** 159–160

"Transparent Itineraries: 1983" (Sobin), **Supp. XVI:** 287

"Transparent Itineraries: 1984" (Sobin), **Supp. XVI:** 287

"Transparent Itineraries: 1992" (Sobin), **Supp. XVI:** 289

"Transparent Itineraries" poems (Sobin), **Supp. XVI:** 290

Transparent Man, The (Hecht), **Supp. X: 57, 69–71**

"Transparent Man, The" (Hecht), **Supp. X: 69–70**

Transparent Things (Nabokov), **Retro. Supp. I:** 266, 270, 277

"Transport" (Simic), **Supp. VIII:** 282

Transport to Summer (Stevens), **IV:** 76, 93; **Retro. Supp. I:** 309–312

Tranströmer, Thomas, **Supp. IV Part 2:** 648

"Traps for the Unwary" (Bourne), **I:** 235

Trash Trilogy (McMurtry), **Supp. V:** 225–226, 231

Traub, James, **Supp. XXIV:** 221, 222

Traubel, Horace, **IV:** 350

"Travel: After a Death" (Kenyon), **Supp. VII:** 169

Travel Alarm (Nye), **Supp. XIII:** 277

"Traveled World, The" (Pickering), **Supp. XXI:** 203

"Traveler, The" (Haines), **Supp. XII:** 203–204, 210

"Traveler, The" (Stegner), **Supp. IV Part 2:** 605

Traveler at Forty, A (Dreiser), **I:** 515

Traveler from Altruria, a Romance A, (Howells), **II:** 285, 287

Traveler's Tree, The: New and Selected Poems (W. J. Smith), **Supp. XIII:** 332, 347

"Traveling" (Paley), **Supp. VI:** 230

"Traveling Light" (Wagoner), **Supp. IX:** 329

Traveling Mercies: Some Thoughts on Faith (Lamott), **Supp. XX: 132, 140–142**

"Traveling Onion, The" (Nye), **Supp. XIII:** 276

Traveling through the Dark (Stafford), **Supp. XI:** 311, 316, **318–321**

"Traveling through the Dark" (Stafford), **Supp. XI:** 318–320, 321, 323, 329

Traveling with the Innocents Abroad (McKeithan), **Retro. Supp. III:** 261

Travelling in Amherst: A Poet's Journal, 1931–1954, **Supp. IX: 88–89**

Travelling Standing Still: Poems, 1918–1928 (Taggard), **Supp. XXII:** 278

Travelling Thirds, The (Atherton), **Supp. XXIV:** 23

Travels in Alaska (Muir), **Supp. IX:** 182, 185–186

"Travels in Georgia" (McPhee), **Supp. III Part 1:** 293–294

"Travels in North America" (Kees), **Supp. XV:** 133–134

Travels in the Congo (Gide), **III:** 210

"Travels in the South" (Ortiz), **Supp. IV Part 2:** 506

Travels with Charley (Steinbeck), **IV:** 52

"Travel Writing: Why I Bother" (Theroux), **Supp. VIII:** 310

Travis, Merle, **Supp. V:** 335

Travisano, Thomas, **Retro. Supp. II:** 40

Treadway, Jessica, **Supp. XXIII:** 280

Treasure Hunt (Buechner), **Supp. XII:** 52

Treasure Island (Stevenson), **Retro. Supp. III:** 88; **Supp. X:** 230

Treasure of the Humble, The (Maeterlinck), **Supp. XX:** 116

"Treasure of the Redwoods, A" (Harte), **Supp. II Part 1:** 337

Treasury of Art Masterpieces, A: From the Renaissance to the Present Day (Craven), **Supp. XII:** 44

Treasury of English Aphorisms, A (L. P. Smith), **Supp. XIV:** 344

Treasury of English Prose, A (L. P. Smith, ed.), **Supp. XIV:** 341

Treasury of the Theatre, A (Gassner), **Supp. I Part 1:** 292

Treasury of Yiddish Stories, A (Howe and Greenberg, eds.), **Supp. I Part 2:** 432; **Supp. XXIII:** 7

Treat 'Em Rough (Lardner), **II:** 422–423

Treatise Concerning Religious Affections (Edwards), **I:** 547, 552, 554, 555, 557, 558, 560, 562

Treatise Concerning the Lord's Supper (Doolittle), **IV:** 150

"Treatise on Poetry" (Milosz), **Supp. VIII:** 20

Treatise on Right and Wrong, A (Mencken), **III:** 110, 119

"Treatise on Tales of Horror, A" (Wilson), **IV:** 438

Treatise on the Gods, A (Mencken), **III:** 108–110, 119

"Treatment" (Wright), **Supp. XV:** 343

Trece poetas del mundo azteca (León-Portilla), **Supp. XV:** 77

Tre Croce (Tozzi), **Supp. III Part 2:** 616

"Tree, a Rock, a Cloud, A" (McCullers), **II:** 587

"Tree, The" (Pound), **Retro. Supp. I:** 286; **Supp. I Part 1:** 255

"Tree, The" (Stone), **Supp. XXVII:** 250

"Tree, the Bird, The" (Roethke), **III:** 548

"Tree at My Window" (Frost), **II:** 155

Tree Grows in Brooklyn, A (B. Smith), **Supp. XVII:** 9; **Supp. XXIII:** 257, 259–264, 265, 271

Tree Grows in Brooklyn, A (film; Kazan), **Supp. XVI:** 193

"Tree House at Night, The" (Dickey), **Supp. IV Part 1:** 179

"Tree House"(Thompson), **Supp. XXIII:** 301

Tree Is Older Than You Are, The (Nye, ed.), **Supp. XIII:** 280

"Tree of Laughing Bells, The" (Lindsay), **Supp. I Part 2:** 376

"Tree of Life, The" (Swados), **Supp. XIX:** 268

"Tree of Night, A" (Capote), **Supp. III Part 1:** 114, 120

Tree of Night and Other Stories, A (Capote), **Supp. III Part 1:** 114

"Trees, The" (Rich), **Supp. I Part 2:** 555

Trees, The (Richter), **Supp. XVIII: 212–213,** 220

"Trees at Night" (H. Johnson), **Supp. XXVI:** 174

"Trees Listening to Bach" (Merrill), **Supp. III Part 1:** 336

Tree Tall Woman (Mullen), **Supp. XXVII:** 166–167, 169, 170, 172, 174, 176

Tree That Came to Stay, The (Quindlen), **Supp. XVII:** 167

Tree Where Man Was Born, The (Matthiessen), **Supp. V:** 199, 203, 204

Trejo, Ernesto, **Supp. V:** 178, 180; **Supp. XIII:** 313, 316; **Supp. XV:** 73

Trelawny, Edward John, **Supp. I Part 2:** 721

"Trellis for R., A" (Swenson), **Supp. IV Part 2:** 647

Tremblay, Bill, **Supp. XIII:** 112

Tremble (Wright), **Supp. XV: 348–349**

"Trespass" (Frost), **Retro. Supp. I:** 139

Trespassing (Pickering), **Supp. XXI:** 202

"Trespassing" (Pickering), **Supp. XXI:** 202

Trethewey, Eric, **Supp. XXI:** 243, 244

Trethewey, Natasha, **Supp. XXI: 243–259**

"Tretitoli, Where the Bomb Group Was" (Hugo), **Supp. VI:** 138

Trevelyan, Robert C., **Supp. XIV:** 334

Trevor-Roper, Hugh, **Supp. XIV:** 348

Trial, The (Kafka), **IV:** 113; **Retro. Supp. II:** 20

"Trial, The" (Rukeyser), **Supp. VI:** 278

"Trial by Existence, The" (Frost), **II:** 166; **Retro. Supp. III:** 94

"Trial for Arson, The"(Hadas), **Supp. XXIII:** 114

Trial of a Poet, The (Shapiro), **Supp. II Part 2:** 710

Trial of the Hawk, The: A Comedy of the Seriousness of Life (Lewis), **II:** 441

"Trial path, The" (Zitkala-Ša), **Supp. XXV:** 274–275, 282

Trials of the Human Heart (Rowson), **Supp. XV:** 237, 239

Tribal Secrets: Recovering American Indian Intellectual Traditions (Warrior), **Supp. IV Part 1:** 329

"Tribute" (A. Finch), **Supp. XVII:** 72, 73–74

"Tribute, A" (Easton), **Supp. IV Part 2:** 461

"Tribute, The" (Doolittle), **Supp. I Part 1:** 267

"Tribute (To My Mother)" (Cullen), **Supp. IV Part 1:** 166

Tribute to Freud (Doolittle), **Supp. I Part 1:** 253, 254, 258, 259, 260, 268

Tribute to the Angels (Doolittle), **Supp. I Part 1:** 272

"Trick on the World, A" (Ríos), **Supp. IV Part 2:** 553

"Tricks" (Olds), **Supp. X:** 203–204

"Trick Scenery" (F. Barthelme), **Supp. XI:** 26

Trifler, The (Masters), **Supp. I Part 2:** 459–460

Trifles (Glaspell), **Supp. III Part 1:** 175, 178, 179, 182, 186, 187; **Supp. X:** 46; **Supp. XXI:** 12

Trifonov, Iurii V., **Retro. Supp. I:** 278

Triggering Town, The: Lectures and Essays on Poetry and Writing (Hugo), **Supp. VI:** 133, 140

Trilling, Diana, **II:** 587, 600; **Supp. I Part 1:** 297; **Supp. XII:** 126; **Supp. XXI:** 271, 275

Trilling, Lionel, **I:** 48; **II:** 579; **III:** 308, 310, 319, 327; **IV:** 201, 211; **Retro. Supp. I:** 19, 97, 121, 216, 227; **Retro. Supp. III:** 78, 106; **Supp. III Part 2: 493–515; Supp. IX:** 266, 287; **Supp. V:** 259; **Supp. VIII:** 93, 98, 190, 231, 236, 243; **Supp. XIII:** 100–101; **Supp. XIV:** 280, 288–289; **Supp. XV:** 20, 140, 152

Trilogy (Doolittle), **Supp. I Part 1:** 271, 272

Trilogy (Wakoski), **Supp. XXVIII:** 261

Trilogy of Desire (Dreiser), **I:** 497, 508; **Retro. Supp. II:** 94, 96, **101–102**

Trimberger, Ellen Kay, **Supp. XVII:** 96, 106; **Supp. XXI:** 12

Trimmed Lamp, The (O. Henry), **Supp. II Part 1:** 410

Trimmings (Mullen), **Supp. XXVII:** 169–170, 171

"Trinc" (McGrath), **Supp. X:** 127

Trinity (Uris), **Supp. XX: 243, 244, 245, 246, 247, 248, 253, 254–255**

Trio (Baker), **Supp. I Part 1:** 277

Trio (Saroyan), **Supp. XXII:** 25

"Triolets for Triolet" (Nelson), **Supp. XVIII:** 179

"Trip" (F. Barthelme), *Supp. XI:* 26

Triple Thinkers, The: Ten Essays on Literature (Wilson), **IV:** 428, 431; **Supp. II Part 1:** 146

"Triplex" (Doolittle), **Supp. I Part 1:** 271

Tripmaster Monkey: His Fake Book (Kingston), **Supp. V:** 157, 158, 169, 170–173

Trippings in Authorland (Forrester), **Supp. XVIII:** 13

Trippings of Tom Pepper, The (Briggs), **Supp. XVIII:** 3, 13–14

"Trip to Hanoi" (Sontag), **Supp. III Part 2:** 460–462

Trip to Parnassus, A; or, The Judgement of Apollo on Dramatic Authors and Performers (Rowson), **Supp. XV: 232–233**

"Triptych" (Eberhart), **I:** 522, 539

Tristam Shandy (Sterne), **Supp. XXII:** 267

Tristan and Iseult, **Retro. Supp. I:** 328, 329, 330, 331

Tristessa (Kerouac), **Supp. III Part 1:** 225, 227, 229

Tristram (Robinson), **III:** 521, 522, 523

Tristram Shandy (Sterne), **I:** 299; **IV:** 465–466; **Supp. V:** 127; **Supp. XVIII:** 60

"Triumph" (C. L. R. James), **Supp. XXI:** 160

"Triumphal March" (Eliot), **I:** 580; **III:** 17; **Retro. Supp. I:** 64

Triumph of Achilles, The (Glück), **Supp. V:** 79, 84–86, 92

"Triumph of a Modern, The, or, Send for the Lawyer" (Anderson), **I:** 113, 114

"Triumph of the Egg, The" (Anderson), **I:** 113

Triumph of the Egg, The: A Book of Impressions from American Life in Tales and Poems (Anderson), **I:** 112, 114

Triumph of the Spider Monkey, The (Oates), **Supp. II Part 2:** 522

Triumphs of the Reformed Religion in America (Mather), **Supp. II Part 2:** 453

Trivial Breath (Wylie), **Supp. I Part 2:** 709, 722–724

Trivia; or, the Art of Walking the Streets of London (Gay), **Supp. XIV:** 337

Trivia: Printed from the Papers of Anthony Woodhouse, Esq. (L. P. Smith), **Supp. XIV:** 336, **337–340**

"Trivia Tea" (Skloot), **Supp. XX: 205**

Trocchi, Alexander, **Supp. XI:** 294, 295, 301

Troilus and Criseyde (Chaucer), **Retro. Supp. I:** 426

Trois contes (Flaubert), **IV:** 31, 37

Trojan Horse, The: A Play (MacLeish), **III:** 21

"Trojan Women, The" (Maxwell), **Supp. VIII:** 169

Troll Garden, The (Cather), **I:** 313, 314–316, 322; **Retro. Supp. I:** 5, 6, 8, 14; **Retro. Supp. III:** 20, 21, 22, 26–28, 36

"Trolling for Blues" (Wilbur), **Supp. III Part 2:** 563–564

Trollope, Anthony, **I:** 10, 375; **II:** 192, 237; **III:** 51, 70, 281, 382; **Retro. Supp. I:** 361

Trombly, Albert Edmund, **Supp. I Part 2:** 403

Trombold, John, **Supp. XVIII:** 111

"Trompe L'Oeil" (Collins), **Supp. XXI:** 60

"Troop Train" (Shapiro), **Supp. II Part 2:** 707

"Tropes of the Text" (Gass), **Supp. VI:** 88

Tropic of Cancer (H. Miller), **III:** 170, 171, 174, 177, 178–180, 181, 182, 183, 187, 190; **Supp. V:** 119; **Supp. X:** 187; **Supp. XXII:** 230, 257

Tropic of Capricorn (H. Miller), **III:** 170, 176–177, 178, 182, 183, 184, 187, 188–189, 190

"Tropic of Cuba" (di Donato), **Supp. XX: 45**

Trotsky, Leon, **I:** 366; **II:** 562, 564; **IV:** 429; **Supp. XXI:** 161, 164, 165, 167, 168

Trotter, W., **I:** 249

"Trouble at the Home Office" (Huddle), **Supp. XXVI:** 156

Troubled Air, The (Shaw), **Supp. XIX: 249–250**

Troubled Island (opera; Hughes and Still), **Retro. Supp. I:** 203

Troubled Lovers in History (Goldbarth), **Supp. XII:** 176, **192–193**

Trouble Follows Me (Macdonald, under Millar), **Supp. IV Part 2:** 466

Trouble in July (Caldwell), **I:** 297, 304–305, 306, 309

Trouble Island (Hughes), **Supp. I Part 1:** 328

"Trouble of Marcie Flint, The" (Cheever), **Supp. I Part 1:** 186

Trouble with Francis, The: An Autobiography (Francis), **Supp. IX:** 76, 77, 82, **84–85**

Trouble with God, The (Francis), **Supp. IX:** 88

"Trouble with Poetry, The" (Collins), **Supp. XXI:** 57

Trouble with Poetry and Other Poems, The (Collins), **Supp. XXI:** 55, 57, 62

"Trouble with the Stars and Stripes" (Nye), **Supp. XIII:** 277

Trouillot, Michel-Rolphe, **Supp. X:** 14–15

Troupe, Quincy, **Retro. Supp. II:** 15, 111; **Supp. X:** 242

"Trout" (Hugo), **Supp. VI:** 135

Trout Fishing in America (Brautigan), **Supp. VIII:** 43

"Trouvée" (Bishop), **Retro. Supp. II:** 49

Trowbridge, John Townsend, **Retro. Supp. III:** 303

Troy (film), **Supp. XX: 273**

"Truce" (Taggard), **Supp. XXII:** 276–277

"Truce of the Bishop, The" (Frederic), **II:** 139–140

"Truck Stop: Minnesota" (Dunn), **Supp. XI:** 145–146

Trudeau, Garry, **Supp. XXIV:** 283

True Account, The: A Novel of the Lewis & Clark & Kinneson Expeditions (Mosher), **Supp. XXII:** 206, 207, 208, **214–215**

True and False: Heresy and Common Sense for the Actor (Mamet), **Supp. XIV:** 241, 243

True Blood (television series), **Supp. XIX:** 174

Trueblood, Valerie, **Supp. XIII:** 306

True Confessions (Dunne), **Supp. IV Part 1:** 198

True Confessions (film), **Supp. IV Part 1:** 198

"True Crime" (Gansworth), **Supp. XXVI:** 114

"True Feeling Leaves No Memory" (Davison), **Supp. XXVI:** 69

Trueheart, Charles, **Supp. XXI:** 238

True History of the Conquest of New Spain, The (Castillo), **III:** 13

True Intellectual System of the Universe, The (Cuddleworth), **II:** 10

"True Love" (Olds), **Supp. X:** 212

Trueman, Matthew (pseudonym). *See* Lowell, James Russell

"True Morality" (Bell), **Supp. X:** 13

"True Romance" (Everett), **Supp. XVIII:** 65

Truesdale, C. W., **Supp. XXI:** 246

True Stories (Atwood), **Supp. XIII:** 34–35

"True Stories" (Atwood), **Supp. XIII:** 34

"True Stories of Bitches" (Mamet), **Supp. XIV:** 246, 252

True Stories of History and Biography (Hawthorne), **Retro. Supp. III:** 121

"True Story, A" (Twain), **Retro. Supp. III:** 262

"Truest Sport, The: Jousting with Sam and Charlie" (Wolfe), **Supp. III Part 2:** 581–582

"True Vine" (Wylie), **Supp. I Part 2:** 723

True West (Shepard), **Supp. III Part 2:** 433, 441, 445, 447, 448

Truman, Harry, **III:** 3

Truman Capote: In Which Various Friends, Enemies, Acquaintances, and Detractors Recall His Turbulent Career (Plimpton), **Supp. XVI:**245

Truman Show, The (film), **Supp. XVI:** 271

Trumbo, Dalton, **Supp. I Part 1:** 295; **Supp. XIII:** 6; **Supp. XVII:** 63; **Supp. XX:** 246; **Supp. XXI:** 45

Trumbull, John, **Supp. II Part 1:** 65, 69, 70, 268

Trump, Donald, **Supp. IV Part 1:** 393

Trumpener, Katie, **Retro. Supp. I:** 380

Trumpet of Jubilee (Lewisohn), **Supp. XXVIII:** 150, 152, 154–155, 156

"Trumpet Player" (Hughes), **Supp. I Part 1:** 333

"Trumpet Player, 1963" (Halliday), **Supp. XIX:** 92

Trumpet Shall Sound, The (Wilder), **IV:** 356

Trumpet Unblown, The (Hoffman), **Supp. XVIII:** 71, **74–75**

Trunk Music (Connelly), **Supp. XXI:** 72, 75

"Truro Bear, The" (Oliver), **Supp. VII:** 234

Truscott, Lucian K., **Supp. IV Part 2:** 683

Trust (Ozick), **Supp. V:** 257–258, 259, 260–263, 270, 272

Trust Me (Updike), **Retro. Supp. I:** 322

"Trusty, The" (Rash), **Supp. XXVII:** 229–230

"Trust Yourself" (Emerson), **II:** 10

"Truth" (Emerson), **II:** 6

"Truth, The" (Halliday), **Supp. XIX:** 87, 88, 94

"Truth, The" (Jarrell), **II:** 381–382

Truth About Celia, The (Brockmeier), **Supp. XXII: 53–55**

"Truth about God, The" (Carson), **Supp. XII: 105–106**

"Truth be told" (Trethewey), **Supp. XXI:** 255, 256

"Truthful James" (Harte), **IV:** 196

"Truth Is, The" (Hogan), **Supp. IV Part 1:** 401–402

"Truth Is Forced, The" (Swenson), **Supp. IV Part 2:** 652

"Truth of the Matter, The" (Nemerov), **III:** 270

Truth Serum (Cooper), **Supp. XI:** 129

"Truth the Dead Know, The" (Sexton), **Supp. II Part 2:** 681

"Trying to Evangelize a Cut Flower" (Peacock), **Supp. XIX:** 199

Trying to Find Chinatown (Hwang), **Supp. XXI:** 147

Trying to Save Piggy Sneed (Irving), **Supp. VI:** 19–165

"Trying to Talk with a Man" (Rich), **Retro. Supp. III:** 247; **Supp. I Part 2:** 559

"Tryptich I" (Bell), **Supp. X:** 7

"Tryst, The" (Wharton), **Retro. Supp. I:** 378

"Try the Girl" (Chandler), **Supp. IV Part 1:** 125

Try! Try! (O'Hara), **Supp. XXIII:** 209, 210, 216

"Ts'ai Chih" (Pound), **III:** 466

T. S. Eliot and American Philosophy (Jain), **Retro. Supp. I:** 58

T. S. Eliot's Silent Voices (Mayer), **Retro. Supp. I:** 58

Tsuji, Shizuo, **Supp. XVII:** 90

Tsurikgekumen (The return) (Asch), **Supp. XXIII:** 5

Tsvetaeva, Marina, **Supp. VIII:** 30; **Supp. XXIII:** 168

"Tuberoses" (E. Stoddard), **Supp. XV:** 282

Tubert, Susana, **Supp. XXIII:** 203

Tuck, James A., **Supp. XXVI:** 83

Tucker, Benjamin R., **Supp. XXI:** 9

Tuckerman, Frederick Goddard, **IV:** 144; **Supp. XXV:** 241

Tucker's People (Wolfert), **Supp. XXI:** 261, 262, 263, 267, **267–275,** 278

Tuerk, Richard, **Supp. XXVIII:** 78

"Tuesday, November 5th, 1940" (Benét), **Supp. XI:** 46, 52

"Tuesday April 25th 1966" (Olson), **Supp. II Part 2:** 585

"Tuesday Night at the Savoy Ballroom" (Komunyakaa), **Supp. XIII:** 132

Tuffield, Aviva, **Supp. XVI:** 147, 148

"Tuft of Flowers, The" (Frost), **II:** 153; **Retro. Supp. I:** 126, 127; **Retro. Supp. III:** 94, 95, 99

Tufts, James Hayden, **Supp. I Part 2:** 632

Tu Fu, **II:** 526; **Supp. XV:** 47

Tu Fu (Ayscough), **II:** 527

Tugwell, Rexford Guy, **Supp. I Part 2:** 645

"Tulip" (Hammett), **Supp. IV Part 1:** 356

"Tulip Man, The" (McCarriston), **Supp. XIV:** 261

"Tulips" (Nye), **Supp. XIII:** 281

"Tulips" (Plath), **Retro. Supp. II:** 252–253; **Supp. I Part 2:** 540, 542, 544

"Tulips" (Snodgrass), **Supp. VI:** 325

Tulips and Chimneys (Cummings), **I:** 436, 437, 440, 445, 447

"Tulips"(Strout), **Supp. XXIII:** 283, 285

"Tulips"(theater performance, Strout), **Supp. XXIII:** 281

Tully, Jim, **III:** 103, 109

Tumble Home (Hempel), **Supp. XXI:** 115, **124–125**

"Tumble Home" (Hempel), **Supp. XXI:** 115, 116, **124–125,** 126

Tumble Tower (Modarressi and Tyler), **Supp. IV Part 2:** 657

"Tuned in Late One Night" (Stafford), **Supp. XI:** 327–328

Tunnel, The (Gass), **Supp. V:** 44; **Supp. VI: 89–91,** 94

"Tunnel, The" (Strand), **Supp. IV Part 2:** 622

"Tunnels" (Komunyakaa), **Supp. XIII:** 123

Tunnel Vision (Paretsky), **Supp. XXV:** 173–174, 177, 178, 181

Tuon, Bunkong, **Supp. XXVI:** 211, 220

Tuqan, Fadwa, **Supp. XIII:** 278

Tura, Cosimo, **III:** 474–475

Turandot and Other Poems (Ashbery), **Supp. III Part 1:** 3

Turco, Lewis, **Supp. XV:** 118

Turgenev, Ivan Sergeevich, **I:** 106; **II:** 263, 271, 275, 280, 281, 288, 319, 320, 324–325, 338, 407; **III:** 461; **IV:** 17, 277; **Retro. Supp. I:** 215, 222; **Supp. VIII:** 167

Turgot, Anne Robert Jacques, **II:** 103; **Supp. I Part 1:** 250

"Turkey and Bones and Eating and We Liked It" (Stein), **IV:** 44

"Turkey Season, The" (Munro), **Supp. XXVII:** 188

Turman, Glynn, **Supp. IV Part 1:** 362

"Turnabout" (Faulkner), **Retro. Supp. III:** 84

Turnbull, Dr. George, **II:** 113

Turnbull, Lawrence, **Supp. I Part 1:** 352

"Turned" (Gilman), **Supp. XI:** 207

Turner, Addie, **IV:** 123

Turner, Darwin, **Supp. I Part 1:** 339; **Supp. IV Part 1:** 165

Turner, Frederick Jackson, **Supp. I Part 2:** 480, 481, 632, 640; **Supp. IV Part 2:** 596

Turner, Guinevere, **Supp. XXVII:** 68

Turner, Jenny, **Supp. XXVIII:** 214

Turner, Nat, **IV:** 113–114, 115, 116, 117

Turner, Patricia A., **Supp. XIII:** 237; **Supp. XX:** 110

Turner, Russell. *See* Lacy, Ed

Turner, Victor, **Supp. IV Part 1:** 304

"Turning Away Variations on Estrangement" (Dickey), **Supp. IV Part 1:** 183

Turning Point, The (McCoy), **Supp. XIII:** 175

"Turning Thirty, I Contemplate Students Bicycling Home" (Dove), **Supp. IV Part 1:** 250

Turning Wind, A (Rukeyser), **Supp. VI:** 272–273, 279–280

Turn in the South, A (Naipaul), **Supp. XXII:** 240

Turn of the Screw, The (H. James), **Retro. Supp. I:** 219, 231; **Supp. IV Part 2:** 682

"Turn of the Screw, The" (H. James), **II:** 331–332; **Retro. Supp. I:** 228, 229, 231, 232; **Supp. XVII:** 143

Turns and Movies and Other Tales in Verse (Aiken), **I:** 65

"Turn with the Sun, A" (Knowles), **Supp. XII:** 237–238

"Turn Your Radio On" (J. W. Miller), **Supp. XX: 169**

Turow, Scott, **Supp. V:** 220; **Supp. XVII: 213–224**

"Turpentine" (Gallagher), **Supp. XXIV:** 174, 175, 176

Turpin, E. Walters, **Supp. XVIII:** 283

Turrinus, Lucius Mamilius, **IV:** 373

"Turtle" (Hogan), **Supp. IV Part 1:** 401

Turtle, Swan (Doty), **Supp. XI: 121–122**

"Turtle, Swan" (Doty), **Supp. XI:** 121–122

Turtle Island (Snyder), **Supp. VIII: 300–303**

Turtle Moon (Hoffman), **Supp. X:** 77, **87–88,** 89

"Turtle Shrine near Chittagong, The" (Nye), **Supp. XIII:** 277

Turtotte, James, **Supp. XXIII:** 125

Turturro, John, **Supp. XI:** 174

Tuscan Cities (Howells), **II:** 280

Tuskegee movement, **Supp. II Part 1:** 169, 172

Tuten, Frederic, **Supp. VIII:** 75, 76; **Supp. XIII:** 237, 249

Tuten, James, **Supp. XVIII:** 195

Tuthill, Louisa Cavolne, **Supp. I Part 2:** 684

"Tutored Child, The" (Kunitz), **Supp. III Part 1:** 264

Tuttleton, James W., **Supp. IV Part 1:** 166, 168

"T.V.A." (Agee), **I:** 35

Tvedten, Brother Benet, **Supp. IV Part 2:** 505

"TV Men" (Carson), **Supp. XII: 105, 112**

Twain, Mark, **I:** 57, 103, 107, 109, 190, 192, 193, 195, 197, 203, 209, 245, 246, 247–250, 255, 256, 257, 260, 261, 292, 342, 418, 469, 485; **II:** 70, 140, 259, 262, 266–268, 271, 272, 274–275, 276, 277, 280, 285–286, 287, 288, 289, 301, 304, 306, 307, 312, 415, 432, 434, 436, 446, 457, 467, 475, 476, 482; **III:** 65, 101, 102, 112–113, 114, 220, 347, 357, 409, 453, 454, 504, 507, 554, 558, 572, 575, 576; **IV: 190–213,** 333, 349, 451; **Retro. Supp. I:** 169, 194, 195; **Retro. Supp. II:** 123; **Retro. Supp. III: 255–273; Supp. I Part 1:** 37, 39, 44, 247, 251, 313, 317; **Supp. I Part 2:** 377, 385, 393, 410, 455, 456, 457, 473, 475, 579, 602, 604, 618, 629, 651, 660; **Supp. II Part 1:** 193, 344, 354, 385; **Supp. IV Part 1:** 386, 388; **Supp. IV Part 2:** 463, 468, 603, 607, 693; **Supp. IX:** 14, 171; **Supp. V:** 44, 113, 131; **Supp. VIII:** 40, 189; **Supp. X:** 51, 227; **Supp. XII:** 343; **Supp. XIII:** 1, 17; **Supp. XV:** 41; **Supp. XVI:** 66, 208; **Supp. XVIII:** 1, 9, 13; **Supp. XXI:** 205; **Supp. XXII:** 89, 203, 205, 206; **Supp. XXIII:** 85; **Supp. XXVII:** 84, 218; **Supp. XXVIII:** 114, 115, 118, 119, 228, 229

"Twa Sisters, The" (ballad), **Supp. I Part 2:** 696

Twelfth Night (Shakespeare), **Supp. IV Part 1:** 83; **Supp. IX:** 14; **Supp. XXII:** 229

Twelve (Blok), **Supp. XXVI:** 144

"12 O'Clock News" (Bishop), **Retro. Supp. II:** 48

12 Years a Slave (film), **Supp. XXVIII:** 167

Twelve Men (Dreiser), **Retro. Supp. II:** 94, 104

Twelve Moons (Oliver), **Supp. VII:** 231, 233–236, 238, 240

Twelve Southerners, **IV:** 125; **Supp. X:** 25

Twelve Years a Slave (Northup), **Supp. XIV:** 32; **Supp. XXVIII:** 163, 166–167, 169–176

Twentieth Century (Hecht and MacArthur), **Supp. XXVII:** 90

Twentieth Century Authors, **I:** 376, 527

"Twentieth Century Fiction and the Black Mask of Humanity" (Ellison), **Retro. Supp. II:** 118

Twentieth Century Pleasures (Hass), **Supp. VI:** 103, 106, 109

Twenty Drawings (Gibran), **Supp. XX: 116**

"28" (Levine), **Supp. V:** 187, 191

"Twenty-Four Poems" (Schwartz), **Supp. II Part 2:** 646, 649

"2433 Agnes, First Home, Last House in Missoula" (Hugo), **Supp. VI:** 139–140

"Twenty Hill Hollow" (Muir), **Supp. IX:** 178

Twenty Love Poems and a Song of Despair (Neruda), **Supp. XXIV:** 170

"Twenty Minutes" (Salter), **Supp. IX:** 260

29 Mini-Essays (Brainard), **Supp. XXVII:** 28

Twenty-One Love Poems (Rich), **Retro. Supp. II:** 242, 248; **Supp. I Part 2:** 572–573

"Twenty-One Poems" (MacLeish), **III:** 19

Twenty Poems (Haines), **Supp. XII:** 204, **205–206**

Twenty Poems of Anna Akhmatova (Kenyon), **Supp. VII:** 165–166

Twenty Questions: (Posed by Poems) (McClatchy), **Supp. XII:** 254, **259–262**

27 Views of Raleigh (Barnhardt, ed.), **Supp. XXVII:** 12

27 Wagons Full of Cotton and Other One-Act Plays (T. Williams), **IV:** 381, 383

Twenty-seventh City, The (Franzen), **Supp. XX:** 83–84, 84, 85, 86–88, 88, 89, 91, 92, 95

Twentysomething Essays by Twentysomething Writers (Kellogg and Quint, eds.), **Supp. XXVI:** 53

Twenty Thousand Leagues under the Sea (Verne), **I:** 480; **Supp. XI:** 63

"Twenty Years Ago" (Lindsay), **Supp. I Part 2:** 384, 399

Twenty Years at Hull-House (Addams), **Supp. I Part 1:** 3, 4, 11, 16

Twersky, David, **Supp. XX:** 244

Twice over Lightly: New York Ten and Now (Hayes and Loos), **Supp. XVI:** 195

Twice-Told Tales (Hawthorne), **I:** 354; **II:** 224; **III:** 412, 421; **Retro. Supp. I:** 154–155, 160; **Retro. Supp. III:** 109, 110, 113–114, 225, 233, 234

Twichell, Chase, **Supp. V:** 16; **Supp. XVII:** 110, 112

Twilight (Frost), **II:** 151

"Twilight's Last Gleaming" (Burroughs and Elvins), **Supp. III Part 1:** 93, 94, 101

Twilight Sleep (Wharton), **IV:** 320–322, 324–325, 327, 328; **Retro. Supp. I:** 381

"Twin, The" (Olds), **Supp. X:** 207

"Twin Beds in Rome" (Updike), **Retro. Supp. I:** 332

"Twins of Table Mountain, The" (Harte), **Supp. II Part 1:** 355

"Twist, The" (Olson), **Supp. II Part 2:** 570

Twitch and Shout (film), **Supp. XVIII:** 143

Twitchell-Waas, Jeffrey, **Supp. XVIII:** 99; **Supp. XXII:** 163

"Two" (Huddle), **Supp. XXVI:** 150

Two Admirals, The (Cooper), **I:** 350

Two against One (F. Barthelme), **Supp. XI:** 32, 33, 36

"Two and One"(Hadas), **Supp. XXIII:** 114–115

"Two Boys" (Moore), **Supp. X:** 173

"Two Brothers, The" (Jewett), **Retro. Supp. II:** 132

Two-Character Play, The (T. Williams), **IV:** 382, 386, 393, 398

"Two Chets"(Lea), **Supp. XXVIII:** 134–135

Two Citizens (Wright), **Supp. III Part 2:** 602–604

"Two Deer" (Bass), **Supp. XVI:** 24

"Two Domains, The" (Goldbarth), **Supp. XII:** 192

"Two-Eleven All Around" (Offutt), **Supp. XIX:** 170

"Two Environments, The" (Trilling), **Supp. III Part 2:** 510

"Two-Fisted Self Pity" (Broyard), **Supp. XI:** 348

Two for Texas (Burke), **Supp. XIV:** 25, 34

"Two Friends" (Cather), **I:** 332

"Two Gardens in Linndale" (Robinson), **III:** 508

Two Gentlemen in Bonds (Ransom), **III:** 491–492

Two: Gertrude Stein and Her Brother (Stein), **IV:** 43

"Two Ghosts" (Francis), **Supp. IX:** 87

Two-Gun Bob (Szumskyj), **Supp. XXVII:** 128

"Two Hangovers" (Wright), **Supp. III Part 2:** 596

Two-Headed Poems (Atwood), **Supp. XIII:** 34

Two Hot to Handle (Lacy), **Supp. XV:** 206

Two Hours to Doom (Bryant), **Supp. XI:** 302

"Two Hundred Years in an Hour" (Boyce), **Supp. XXI:** 8

"Two Hunters, The"(Arnow), **Supp. XXVIII:** 2

"Two Kitchens in Provence" (M. F. K. Fisher), **Supp. XVII:** 88, 91

"Two Ladies in Retirement" (Taylor), **Supp. V:** 320

Two Letters to the Citizens of the United States, and One to General Washington (Barlow), **Supp. II Part 1:** 80

Two Little Women on a Holiday (Wells), **Supp. XXVI:** 277

"Two Lives, The" (Hogan), **Supp. IV Part 1:** 400, 402, 403, 406, 411

Two Long Poems (Stern), **Supp. IX:** 296

"Two Look at Two" (Frost), **Supp. XXI:** 26

"Two Lovers and a Beachcomber by the Real Sea" (Plath), **Supp. I Part 2:** 536

"Two Men" (McClatchy)", **Supp. XII:** 269

Two Men (E. Stoddard), **Supp. XV:** 272, 273, **283–284**

Two Men of Sandy Bar (Harte), **Supp. II Part 1:** 354

"Two Mexicos"(Gold), **Supp. XXVIII:** 70, 73

Twomey, Jay, **Supp. XVII:** 111

"Two Moods of Love" (Cullen), **Supp. IV Part 1:** 166

Two Moons (Mallon), **Supp. XIX:** 132, **138–141**

"Two Morning Monologues" (Bellow), **I:** 150; **Retro. Supp. II:** 20

"'Two Mothers United': Interclass Femal Friendship in *Stella Dallas*"(Branham), **Supp. XXVIII:** 183

"Two Nations of Black America, The" *(Frontline)*, **Supp. XX:** 99

Two-Ocean War, The (Morison), **Supp. I Part 2:** 491

"Two of Hearts" (Hogan), **Supp. IV Part 1:** 410

"Two on a Party" (T. Williams), **IV:** 388

"Two or Three Things I Dunno About John Cassavetes" (Lethem), **Supp. XVIII:** 148

"Two Pendants: For the Ears" (W. C. Williams), **Retro. Supp. I:** 423

"Two Poems of Going Home" (Dickey), **Supp. IV Part 1:** 182–183

"Two Portraits" (Chopin), **Supp. I Part 1:** 218

"Two Presences, The" (R. Bly), **Supp. IV Part 1:** 65

"Two Rivers" (Stegner), **Supp. IV Part 2:** 605

Tworkov, Jack, **Supp. XII:** 198

"Two Scenes" (Ashbery), **Supp. III Part 1:** 4

Two Serious Ladies (Jane Bowles), **Supp. IV Part 1:** 82

"Two Silences" (Carruth), **Supp. XVI:** 55

"Two Sisters" (Farrell), **II:** 45

Two Sisters: A Memoir in the Form of a Novel (Vidal), **Supp. IV Part 2:** 679

"Two Sisters of Persephone" (Plath), **Retro. Supp. II:** 246

"Two Songs on the Economy of Abundance" (Agee), **I:** 28

Two Sons, The (Boyce), **Supp. XXI:** 7, 13

"Two Tales of Clumsy" (Schnackenberg), **Supp. XV:** 258

"Two Temples, The" (Melville), **III:** 89–90

Two Thousand Seasons (Armah), **Supp. IV Part 1:** 373

Two Towns in Provence (M. F. K. Fisher), **Supp. XVII:** 91

Two Trains Running (Wilson), **Supp. VIII:** 345–348

"Two Tramps in Mudtime" (Frost), **II:** 164; **Retro. Supp. I:** 137; **Supp. IX:** 261

"Two Trams in Mudtime" (Frost), **Retro. Supp. III:** 103

"Two Twilights for William Carlos Williams" (Boyle), **Supp. XXIV:** 63

"Two Views of a Cadaver Room" (Plath), **Supp. I Part 2:** 538

"Two Villages" (Paley), **Supp. VI:** 227

"Two Voices in a Meadow" (Wilbur), **Supp. III Part 2:** 555

Two Weeks in Another Town (Shaw), **Supp. XIX:** 251

"Two Witches" (Frost), **Retro. Supp. I:** 135

"Two Words" (Francis), **Supp. IX:** 81

Two Worlds Walking: A Mixed-Blood Anthology (Glancy and Truesdale, eds.), **Supp. XXI:** 246

Two Years Before the Mast (Dana), **I:** 351; **Retro. Supp. III:** 150; **Supp. XXV:** 208

"Tyger, The" (Blake), **Supp. XVII:** 128

Tyler, Anne, **Supp. IV Part 2: 657–675;** **Supp. V:** 227, 326; **Supp. VIII:** 141; **Supp. X:** 1, 77, 83, 85; **Supp. XII:** 307; **Supp. XVI:** 37; **Supp. XVIII:** 157, 195; **Supp. XXIII:** 298

Tyler, Royall, **I:** 344; **Retro. Supp. I:** 377

Tymms, Ralph, **Supp. IX:** 105

Tyndale, William, **II:** 15

Tyndall, John, **Retro. Supp. II:** 93

Typee: A Peep at Polynesian Life (Melville), **III:** 75–77, 79, 84; **Retro.**

Supp. I: 245–246, 249, 252, 256; **Retro. Supp. III:** 147, 149, 151, 152–153

Types From City Streets (Hapgood), **Supp. XVII:** 103

"Typewriter, The" (D. West), **Supp. XVIII:** 279; **Supp. XXVI:** 164

Typewriter Town (W. J. Smith), **Supp. XIII:** 332

"Typhus" (Simpson), **Supp. IX:** 277

Tyranny of the Normal (Fiedler), **Supp. XIII: 107–108**

"Tyranny of the Normal" (Fiedler), **Supp. XIII:** 107–108

"Tyrant of Syracuse" (MacLeish), **III:** 20

"Tyrian Businesses" (Olson), **Supp. II Part 2:** 567, 568, 569

Tytell, John, **Supp. XIV:** 140

Tzara, Tristan, **Supp. III Part 1:** 104, 105

U

U and I (Baker), **Supp. XIII: 45–47,** 48, 52, 55

Überdie Seelenfrage (Fechner), **II:** 358

Ubik (Dick), **Supp. XVIII:** 136

"*Ubi Sunt* Lament for the Eccentric Museums of My Childhood" (Stallings), **Supp. XXV:** 232

Ubu Roi (Jarry), **Supp. XV:** 178, 186

Ueland, Brenda, **Supp. XVII:** 13

Ugly Feelings (Ngai), **Supp. XXVIII:** 222

Uhry, Alfred, **Supp. XX:** 177

ukanhavyrfuckinciti back (Phillips), **Supp. XXIII:** 174

Ukrainian Dumy (P. N. Warren as Kilina and Tarnawsky, trans.), **Supp. XX: 261**

"Ulalume" (Poe), **III:** 427; **Retro. Supp. II:** 264, 266

Ulin, David, **Supp. XIII:** 244; **Supp. XVI:** 74

Ullman, Leslie, **Supp. IV Part 2:** 550; **Supp. XVIII:** 175

Ultimate Good Luck, The (Ford), **Supp. V:** 57, 61–62

Ultimate Punishment: A Lawyer's Reflections on Dealing with the Death Penalty (Turow), **Supp. XVII:** 220–221

Ultima Thule (Longfellow), **II:** 490; **Retro. Supp. II:** 169

"Ultima Thule" (Nabokov), **Retro. Supp. I:** 274

Ultramarine (Carver), **Supp. III Part 1:** 137, 138, 147, 148

"Ultrasound" (Stallings), **Supp. XXV:** 225, 233, 234

Ulysses (Joyce), **I:** 395, 475–476, 478, 479, 481; **II:** 42, 264, 542; **III:** 170, 398; **IV:** 103, 418, 428, 455; **Retro. Supp. I:** 59, 63, 290, 291; **Retro. Supp. II:** 121; **Supp. I Part 1:** 57; **Supp. III Part 2:** 618, 619; **Supp. IV Part 1:** 285; **Supp. IV Part 2:** 424; **Supp. IX:** 102; **Supp. V:** 261; **Supp. X:** 114; **Supp. XIII:** 43, 191; **Supp. XV:** 305; **Supp. XVII:** 140, 227; **Supp. XXV:** 65; **Supp. XXVII:** 6, 70;

Supp. XXVIII: 207

"*Ulysses,* Order and Myth" (Eliot), **Retro. Supp. I:** 63

"Ulysses, Order and Myth" (T. S. Eliot), **Retro. Supp. III:** 63

"Umbrella, The" (Peacock), **Supp. XIX:** 203–204

Unaccountable Worth of the World, The (Price), **Supp. VI:** 267

Unaccustomed Earth (Lahiri), **Supp. XXI:** 176, **181–183,** 183, 188

"Unaccustomed Earth" (Lahiri), **Supp. XXI:** 186

Unamuno y Jugo, Miguel de, **III:** 310; **Supp. XV:** 79

"Unattached Smile, The" (Crews), **Supp. XI:** 101

"Unbelievable Thing Usually Goes to the Heart of the Story, The: Magic Realism in the Fiction of Rick Bass" (Dwyer), **Supp. XVI:** 16

"Unbeliever, The" (Bishop), **Retro. Supp. II:** 43

"Unborn Song" (Rukeyser), **Supp. VI:** 274

Unbought Spirit: A John Jay Chapman Reader (Stone, ed.), **Supp. XIV:** 54

Uncalled, The (Dunbar), **Supp. II Part 1:** 200, 211, 212

Uncentering the Earth: Copernicus and The Revolutions of the Heavenly Spheres (Vollmann), **Supp. XVII:** 226

Uncertain Certainty, The: Interviews, Essays, and Notes on Poetry (Simic), **Supp. VIII:** 270, 273, 274

Uncertainty and Plenitude: Five Contemporary Poets (Stitt), **Supp. IX:** 299

"Uncle" (Levine), **Supp. V:** 186

"Uncle Adler" (Kooser), **Supp. XIX:** 120

"Uncle Christmas" (Ríos), **Supp. IV Part 2:** 552

"Uncle Jim's Baptist Revival Hymn" (Lanier and Lanier), **Supp. I Part 1:** 353

"Uncle Lot" (Stowe), **Supp. I Part 2:** 585–586

"Uncle Mingo's Speculatioms"\[sic\] (Stuart), **Supp. XXVIII:** 225, 226, 227

Uncle Moses (Asch), **Supp. XXIII:** 14

"Uncle Moustapha's Eclipse" (McKnight), **Supp. XX:** 148

Uncle Remus Tales (Harris), **Supp. II Part 1:** 201

"Uncle Tomitudes" (Briggs), **Supp. XVIII:** 14

Uncle Tom's Cabin (Stowe), **II:** 291; **Supp. I Part 1:** 49; **Supp. I Part 2:** 410, 579, 582, 589–592; **Supp. II Part 1:** 170; **Supp. III Part 1:** 154, 171; **Supp. IX:** 19; **Supp. X:** 246, 249, 250; **Supp. XIII:** 95; **Supp. XVI:** 82, 85, 88; **Supp. XVIII:** 14; **Supp. XXVIII:** 114, 167

Uncle Tom's Children (Wright), **IV:** 476, 478, 488; **Retro. Supp. III:** 131; **Supp. II Part 1:** 228, 235; **Supp. XVIII:** 283

"Uncle Wiggily in Connecticut" (Salinger), **III:** 559–560, 563

"Unclouded Day, The" (Proulx), **Supp. VII:** 254–255

"Uncommon Visage" (Brodsky), **Supp. VIII:** 31

"Uncommon Woman: An Interview with Wendy Wasserstein" (Cohen), **Supp. XV:** 323

Uncommon Women and Others (Wasserstein), **Supp. XV:** 320–321, **322–323;** **Supp. XXIV:** 117

Uncompromising Fictions of Cynthia Ozick (Pinsker), **Supp. V:** 272

"Unconscious Came a Beauty" (Swenson), **Supp. IV Part 2:** 646

"Uncreation, The" (Pinsky), **Supp. VI:** 245

"Undead, The" (Wilbur), **Supp. III Part 2:** 556

"Undefeated, The" (Hemingway), **II:** 250; **Retro. Supp. I:** 180

Under a Glass Bell (Nin), **Supp. X:** 186

"Under Ben Bulben" (Yeats), **Supp. V:** 220

Undercliff: Poems 1946–1953 (Eberhart), **I:** 528, 536–537

Under Cover (Goldbarth), **Supp. XII:** 177, 180, 193

Undercover Doctor (film), **Supp. XIII:** 170

"Under Cygnus" (Wilbur), **Supp. III Part 2:** 558

"Under Forty" (Trilling), **Supp. III Part 2:** 494

"Underground" (Hayes), **Supp. XXVI:** 144

Underground, The Story of a People (Tenenbaum), **Supp. XX:** 253

Underground Man, The (film), **Supp. IV Part 2:** 474

Underground Man, The (Macdonald), **Supp. IV Part 2:** 474, 475

Underground Woman, The (Boyle), **Supp. XXIV:** 62

"Under Libra: Weights and Measures" (Merrill), **Supp. III Part 1:** 328

Under Milk Wood (D. Thomas), **III:** 21

"Undersea" (Carson), **Supp. IX:** 21

Understanding Cynthia Ozick (Friedman), **Supp. V:** 273

Understanding Drama (Brooks and Heilman), **Supp. XIV:** 12

Understanding E. L. Doctorow (Fowler), **Supp. IV Part 1:** 226

Understanding Fiction (Brooks and Warren), **IV:** 279; **Supp. XIV:** 11

Understanding Fiction (Brooks and Warren, eds.), **Supp. XIX:** 246

Understanding Flannery O'Connor (Whitt), **Retro. Supp. II:** 226

Understanding Nicholson Baker (Saltzman), **Supp. XIII:** 48

Understanding Poetry: An Anthology for College Students (Brooks and Warren), **IV:** 236; **Retro. Supp. I:** 40, 41; **Supp. XIV:** 4–5

Understanding Robert Bly (W. V. Davis), **Supp. XXI:** 84–85, 88

Understanding Ron Rash (Lang), **Supp. XXVII:** 215–216

"Understandings of Food as Culture" (Dusselier), **Supp. XXVI:** 210

Understanding Tim O'Brien (Kaplan), **Supp. V:** 241

Understanding To Kill a Mockingbird: A Student Casebook to Issues, Sources, and Documents (C. D. Johnson), **Supp. VIII:** 127

Under Stars (Gallagher), **Supp. XXIV:** 166, 167, 168–169, 170

Undertaker's Garland, The (Wilson and Bishop), **IV:** 427

Under Taos Mountain: The Terrible Quarrel of Magpie and Tía (Schott), **Supp. XXIII: 250–251**

Under the Banner of Heaven: A Story of Violent Faith (Krakauer), **Supp. XVIII:** 105, **114–116,** 117

"Under the Boathouse"(Bottoms), **Supp. XXVIII:** 26

"Under the Cedarcroft Chestnut" (Lanier), **Supp. I Part 1:** 364

Under the Feet of Jesus (Viramontes), **Supp. XXV:** 130

"Under the Harbour Bridge" (Komunyakaa), **Supp. XIII:** 125

"Under the Influence" (Sanders), **Supp. XVI:** 274, 277

"Under the Language Sea" (Davison), **Supp. XXVI:** 79

Under the Lilacs (Alcott), **Supp. I Part 1:** 42–43, 44

"Under the Maud Moon" (Kinnell), **Supp. III Part 1:** 246–247

Under the Mountain Wall: A Chronicle of Two Seasons in the Stone Age (Matthiessen), **Supp. V:** 202

Under the Red Flag (Jin), **Supp. XVIII:** 89, **94–95**

"Under the Roof of Memory" (Davison), **Supp. XXVI:** 78

"Under the Rose" (Pynchon), **Supp. II Part 2:** 620

"Under the Seal of My Widowhood" (Lombard), **Supp. XXVII:** 262

Under the Sea-Wind: A Naturalist's Picture of Ocean Life (Carson), **Supp. IX:** 19, **22–23**

Under the Shadow (Sorrentino), **Supp. XXI:** 236–237

Under the Sign of Saturn (Sontag), **Supp. III Part 2:** 451, 452, 458, 470–471

"Under the Sign of Saturn" (Sontag), **Supp. III Part 2:** 470

"Under the Sky" (Bowles), **Supp. IV Part 1:** 87

"Under the Sun"(Schott), **Supp. XXIII:** 247, 248

" 'Under the Umbrella of Black Civilization': A Conversation with Reginald McKnight" (Ashe), **Supp. XX: 154**

Under the Volcano (M. Lowry), **Supp. XVII:** 135, 139, 140; **Supp. XXVI:** 28

Under the Vulture-Tree (Bottoms), **Supp. XXVIII:** 22, 27–28

"Under the Vulture-Tree"(Bottoms), **Supp. XXVIII:** 27–28

"Under the Willows" (J. R. Lowell), **Supp. I Part 2:** 416

Under the Willows and Other Poems (J. R. Lowell), **Supp. I Part 2:** 424

"Undertow" (Boyce), **Supp. XXI:** 10

"Underwater Spring" (Huddle), **Supp. XXVI:** 153

Underwood, John Curtis, **Supp. XXIV:** 29

Underwood, Wilbur, **Retro. Supp. II:** 79; **Retro. Supp. III:** 46

Underworld (DeLillo), **Supp. VI:** 2, 4–5, 6–7, 8, 9, 10, 11, **13–15; Supp. XI:** 68; **Supp. XX:** 91; **Supp. XXVII:** 6

Underworld (screenplay, Hecht), **Supp. XXVII:** 83, 90, 91

Underworld, The (Wolfert). *See Tucker's World* (Wolfert)

"Undesirable, The" (Huddle), **Supp. XXVI:** 148, 153

Undine (La Motte-Fouqué), **II:** 212; **III:** 78

Undiscovered Country, The (Howells), **II:** 282

"Undressing, The" (C. Frost), **Supp. XV:** 98

"Undressing the Vanity Dolls" (Vaz), **Supp. XXVI:** 260–261

Undset, Sigrid, **Retro. Supp. III:** 24

Uneasy Chair, The (Stegner), **Supp. IV Part 2:** 599

"Unemployed, Disabled, and Insane, The" (Haines), **Supp. XII:** 211–212

Unending Blues (Simic), **Supp. VIII: 278–279**

Unending Dialogue: Voices from an AIDS Poetry Workshop (Hadas, Barber, et al), **Supp. XXIII:** 118, **125–126**

"Unexpected Freedom" (Peacock), **Supp. XIX:** 199

"Unexpressed" (Dunbar), **Supp. II Part 1:** 199

"Unfinished Bronx, The" (Paley), **Supp. VI:** 228

Unfinished Crime, The (Holding), **Supp. XXII:** 120, **123–124,** 135, 136

"Unfinished Duet"(Siken), **Supp. XXVIII:** 198, 200

"Unfinished Poems" (Eliot), **I:** 579

"Unfinished Song" (C. Frost), **Supp. XV:** 97

Unfinished Woman, An (Hellman), **Supp. I Part 1:** 292, 293, 294; **Supp. IV Part 1:** 12, 353–354; **Supp. IX:** 196, 200–201

Unforeseen Wilderness, The: An Essay on Kentucky's Red River Gorge (Berry), **Supp. X:** 28, 29, 30, 36

Unforgotten Years (L. P. Smith), **Supp. XIV:** 333, 334, 335, 336, 347

"Unfortunate Coincidence" (Parker), **Supp. IX:** 190

Unframed Originals (Merwin), **Supp. III Part 1:** 341

Ungar, Sanford, **Supp. XI:** 228

Ungaretti, Giuseppe, **Supp. V:** 337

Unguided Tour (Sontag), **Supp. III Part 2:** 452

"Unheimliche, Das" (The Uncanny) (Freud), **Supp. XVI:** 157–158

Unholy Garden (screenplay, Hech and MacArthur), **Supp. XXVII:** 90

Unholy Sonnets (Jarman), **Supp. XVII:** 109, 110, **119–120; Supp. XVIII:** 178

"Unholy Sonnets" (Jarman), **Supp. XVII:** 118, 119–120

"Unidentified Flying Object" (Hayden), **Supp. II Part 1:** 368

"Unifying Principle, The" (Ammons), **Supp. VII:** 28

"Unimportant Man, An" (D. West), **Supp. XVIII:** 280

"Union" (Hughes), **Supp. I Part 1:** 331

"Union" (Stone), **Supp. XXVII:** 254

"Union Square" (Teasdale), **Supp. XXVII:** 286, 289

"Union Street: San Francisco, Summer 1975" (Carver), **Supp. III Part 1:** 138

"Unitarian Christianity" (Channing), **Supp. XXIV: 71–73,** 77

Unitarians and the Universalists, The (Robinson), **Supp. XXIV:** 70

"United"(Kenny), **Supp. XXIII:** 149

United States Army in World War II (Morison), **Supp. I Part 2:** 490

United States Constitution, **I:** 6, 283

United States Essays, 1951–1991 (Vidal), **Supp. IV Part 2:** 678, 687

"United States of Huck, The: Introduction to *Adventures of Huckleberry Finn*" (Saunders), *Supp. XIX:* 235

"United States of Lyncherdom, The" (Twain), **Retro. Supp. III:** 268

United States of Poetry, The (television series), **Supp. XIII:** 274

"Unity through Diversity" (Locke), **Supp. XIV:** 212, 213

Universal Baseball Asociation, Inc., J. Henry Waugh, Prop., The (Coover), **Supp. V:** 39, 41–42, 44, 46

Universal Passion (Young), **III:** 111

"Universe of Death, The" (H. Miller), **III:** 184

Universe of Time, A (Anderson), **II:** 27, 28, 45, 46, 48, 49

"Universities" (Emerson), **II:** 6

"Universities: A Mirage? " (Mora), **Supp. XIII:** 219

"University" (Shapiro), **Supp. II Part 2:** 704–705, 717

"University Avenue" (Mora), **Supp. XIII:** 216

"University Days" (Thurber), **Supp. I Part 2:** 605

"University Hospital, Boston" (Oliver), **Supp. VII:** 235

"University's Peril, The" (Taggard), **Supp. XXII:** 273

"Unknowable, The" (Levine), **Supp. V:** 195

"Unknown Girl in the Maternity Ward" (Sexton), **Supp. II Part 2:** 676

"Unknown Love, The" (Chandler), **Supp. IV Part 1:** 120

Unknown Messages (Stone), **Supp. XXVII:** 257

Unknown Rilke, The (Rilke; F. Wright, trans.), **Supp. XVII:** 244

"Unknown War, The" (Sandburg), **III:** 594

Unkown Constellations, The (Swados), **Supp. XIX:** 256

Unleashed (anthology), **Supp. XI:** 132

Unleashed: Poems by Writers' Dogs (Hempel and Shepard, eds.), **Supp. XXI:** 115

"Unlighted Lamps" (Anderson), **I:** 112

Unlit Lamp, The (Holding), **Supp. XXII: 121,** 130

Unlived Life of Little Mary Ellen, The (Stuart), **Supp. XXVIII:** 230

"Unlived Life of Little Mary Ellen, The"(Stuart), **Supp. XXVIII:** 236

Unloved Wife, The (Alcott), **Supp. I Part 1:** 33

Unmarried Woman, An (film), **Supp. IV Part 1:** 303

"Unnatural Mother, The" (Gilman), **Supp. XI:** 207

"Unnatural State of the Unicorn" (Komunyakaa), **Supp. XIII:** 119

"Unparalleled Adventure of One Hans Pfaall, The" (Poe), **III:** 424

"Unpleasant Profession of Jonathan Hoag, The" (Heinlein), **Supp. XVIII:** 149

Unprecedented Era, The (Goebbels), **III:** 560

"Unprofitable Servant, The" (O. Henry), **Supp. II Part 1:** 403

Unpublished Poems of Emily Dickinson (Bianchi and Hampson, ed.), **Retro. Supp. I:** 35

Unpunished (Gilman), **Supp. XI:** 208

Unraveling Strangeness, The (Weigl), **Supp. XIX: 287–288**

"Unreal City" (Eliot), **Supp. XV:** 218

"Unreality of Modern Realism, The" (Rinehart), **Supp. XXV:** 201

"Unreasoning Heart" (Untermeyer), **Supp. XV:** 309

Unsaid (Gioia), **Supp. XV:** 129

"Unseen, The" (Pinsky), **Supp. VI:** 243–244

"Unseen, The" (Singer), **Retro. Supp. II:** 307

Unseen Hand, The (Shepard), **Supp. III Part 2:** 439, 445–446

Unselected Poems (Levine), **Supp. V:** 179

Unsettling of America, The: Culture and Agriculture (Berry), **Supp. X:** 22, 26, 29, 32, 33, 35; **Supp. XIV:** 177, 179

Unspeakable Gentleman, The (Marquand), **III:** 53–54, 60, 63

Unspeakable Practices, Unnatural Acts (Barthelme), **Supp. IV Part 1:** 39

"Unspeakable Things Unspoken: The Afro-American Presence in American Literature" (Morrison), **Retro. Supp. III:** 194; **Supp. III Part 1:** 375, 377–379

Unspoken and Other Poems, The (Bremer), **Supp. XXII:** 277

"Untelling, The" (Strand), **Supp. IV Part 2:** 629

Unterecker, John, **I:** 386

Untermeyer, Jean Starr, **II:** 530; **Supp. XV:** 294, 295, 303, 307, 308, 310; **Supp. XXVII:** 286

Untermeyer, Louis, **II:** 516–517, 530, 532; **III:** 268; **Retro. Supp. I:** 124, 133, 136; **Retro. Supp. III:** 47, 100, 133; **Supp. III Part 1:** 2; **Supp. IX:** 76; **Supp. XIV:** 119, 123; **Supp. XV: 293–318; Supp. XXI:** 277; **Supp. XXV:** 21, 23; **Supp. XXVII:** 252, 286, 289

Untimely Papers (Bourne), **I:** 218, 233

"Untitled" (C. Frost), **Supp. XV:** 103

"Untitled Blues" (Komunyakaa), **Supp. XIII:** 117

Unto the Sons (Talese), **Supp. XVII:** 199–200, **206–207,** 208, 209, 210

"Untrustworthy Speaker, The" (Glück), **Supp. V:** 86

"Unused" (Anderson), **I:** 112, 113

Unvanquished, The (Faulkner), **II:** 55, 67–68, 71; **Retro. Supp. I:** 84; **Retro. Supp. III:** 85; **Supp. I Part 2:** 450

"Unvexed Isles, The" (Warren), **IV:** 253

"Unwanted Lucretia"(Prouty), **Supp. XXVIII:** 180

"Unwedded" (Larcom), **Supp. XIII:** 144

"Unweepables, The" (Karr), **Supp. XI:** 243

"Unwelcome Guest, An" (Papernick), **Supp. XVII:** 50

Unwelcome Man, The (W. Frank), **Supp. XX: 70, 76**

Unwelcome Words (Bowles), **Supp. IV Part 1:** 93, 94

"Unwelcome Words" (Bowles), **Supp. IV Part 1:** 94, 95

Unwin, T. Fisher, **Supp. XI:** 202

"Unwithered Garland, The" (Kunitz), **Supp. III Part 1:** 265

Unwobbling Pivot, The (Pound, trans.), **III:** 472

"Unwritten, The" (Merwin), **Supp. III Part 1:** 352

"Unwritten Law" (Glück), **Supp. V:** 91

Up (Sukenick), **Supp. V:** 39

Up Above the World (Bowles), **Supp. IV Part 1:** 82, 91, 92

"Up and Down" (Merrill), **Supp. III Part 1:** 328

Upanishads, **IV:** 183

Up Country: Poems of New England (Kumin), **Supp. IV Part 2:** 446, 447–448, 453

"Update" (Dunn), **Supp. XI:** 150–151

Updike, John, **I:** 54; **III:** 572; **IV:** 214–235; **Retro. Supp. I:** 116, **317–338; Retro. Supp. II:** 213, 279, 280; **Supp. I Part 1:** 186, 196; **Supp. IV Part 2:** 657; **Supp. IX:** 208; **Supp. V:** 23, 43, 95, 119; **Supp. VIII:** 151, 167, 236; **Supp. XI:** 65, 66, 99, 140; **Supp. XII:** 140, 296, 298, 310; **Supp. XIII:** 45–46, 47, 52; **Supp. XIV:** 79, 93, 111; **Supp. XVI:** 205, 207, 220; **Supp. XX:** 17; **Supp. XXI:** 116, 226; **Supp. XXIII:** 109

Updike, Mrs. Wesley, **IV:** 218, 220

Up from Slavery (Washington), **Supp. II Part 1:** 169; **Supp. IX:** 19

Upham, Thomas Goggswell, **II:** 487

"Upholsterers, The" (Lardner), **II:** 435

"Up in Michigan" (Hemingway), **II:** 263; **Supp. XIX:** 241

Upjohn, Richard, **IV:** 312

"Upon a Fit of Sickness, Anno 1632" (Bradstreet), **Retro. Supp. III:** 13

"Upon a Spider Catching a Fly" (Taylor), **IV:** 161

"Upon a Wasp Child with Cold" (Taylor), **IV:** 161

"Upon Meeting Don L. Lee, in a Dream" (Dove), **Supp. IV Part 1:** 244

"Upon My Dear and Loving Husband His Going into England, Jan. 16, 1661" (Bradstreet), **Supp. I Part 1:** 110

"Upon My Mother's Death"(Hadas), **Supp. XXIII:** 118

"Upon Returning to the Country Road" (Lindsay), **Supp. I Part 2:** 382

"Upon Some Distemper of Body" (Bradstreet), **Retro. Supp. III:** 2

"Upon the Burning of Our House, July 10th, 1666" (Bradstreet), **Supp. I Part 1:** 107–108, 122

"Upon the Sweeping Flood" (Taylor), **IV:** 161

"Upon Wedlock, and Death of Children" (Taylor), **IV:** 144, 147, 161

"Upon Westminster Bridge" (Wordsworth), **Supp. XXIV:** 148

"Upset, An" (Merrill), **Supp. III Part 1:** 336

Upstairs and Downstairs (Vonnegut), **Supp. II Part 2:** 757

Upstate (Wilson), **IV:** 447

Up Stream (Lewisohn), **Supp. XXVIII:** 146–147, 148–149, 155–156, 157, 159

Upton, Lee, **Supp. X:** 209

"Upturned Face" (Crane), **I:** 423

Upward, Allen, **Supp. I Part 1:** 262

Upward, Edward, **Supp. XIV:** 159, 160

"Upward Moon and the Downward Moon, The" (R. Bly), **Supp. IV Part 1:** 71

Urama, Kelechi, **Supp. XXVII:** 202

Urania: A Rhymed Lesson (Holmes), **Supp. I Part 1:** 300

"Urban Convalescence, An" (Merrill), **Supp. III Part 1:** 322–324

"Urban Renewal" (Komunyakaa), **Supp. XIII:** 113

Urban Tumbleweed: Notes from a Tanka Diary (Mullen), **Supp. XXVII:** 175–176

Urdang, Constance, **Supp. XV:** 74

"Uganda and Fatima" (Rowson), **Supp. XV:** 234

Urial Accosta: A Play (Reznikoff), **Supp. XIV:** 282, 288

Urich, Robert, **Supp. V:** 228

"Uriel" (Emerson), **II:** 19

Uris, Leon, **Supp. IV Part 1:** 285, 379; **Supp. XX: 243–258; Supp. XXVII:** 147

Uroff, Margaret D., **Supp. I Part 2:** 542

Ursu, Liliana, **Supp. XXIV:** 178

"Us" (Sexton), **Supp. II Part 2:** 687

U.S. 1 (Rukeyser), **Supp. VI:** 272, 278, 283, 285

U.S.A. (Dos Passos), **I:** 379, 475, 478, 482–488, 489, 490, 491, 492, 493,

494, 495; **Retro. Supp. II:** 197; **Supp. I Part 2:** 646; **Supp. III Part 1:** 104, 105; **Supp. XIV:** 24; **Supp. XXVI:** 23

"U.S.A. School of Writing, The" (Bishop), **Retro. Supp. II:** 43

USA the Movie (film), **Supp. XXVII:** 263

"U.S. Commercial Orchid, The" (Agee), **I:** 35

"Used-Boy Raisers, The" (Paley), **Supp. VI:** 218, 228

"Used Cars on Oahu" (Nye), **Supp. XIII:** 282

"Used Side of the Sofa, The" (Ríos), **Supp. IV Part 2:** 551

Useless Servants, The (Hinojosa), **Supp. XIX:** 98, 103, 104, **109–110**

Use of Fire, The (Price), **Supp. VI:** 265

"Use of Force, The" (W. C. Williams), **Retro. Supp. I:** 424

Use of Poetry and the Use of Criticism, The (Eliot), **Retro. Supp. I:** 65

Uses of Enchantment, The: The Meaning and Importance of Fairy Tales (Bettelheim), **Supp. X:** 77; **Supp. XIV:** 126

"Uses of Hell, The" (E. Hoffman), **Supp. XVI:** 154

"Uses of Hell, The: An Exchange"(Novick, Katz, and Szulc), **Supp. XVI:** 154

Uses of Literacy, The (Hoggart), **Supp. XIV:** 299

Uses of Literature, The (Calvino), **Supp. XXII:** 263

"Uses of Poetry, The" (W. C. Williams), **Retro. Supp. I:** 412

"Uses of the Blues, The" (Baldwin), **Retro. Supp. II:** 8

"Use-Unuse of Us, The" (Bronk), **Supp. XXI:** 32

"USFS 1919: The Ranger, the Cook, and a Hole in the Sky" (Maclean), **Supp. XIV:** 230, 234

Ushant: An Essay (Aiken), **I:** 49, 54, 55, 56, 57

"Usher 11" (Bradbury), **Supp. I Part 2:** 622

U.S.I. (Kramer), **Supp. XXVI:** 26

"Using Jacqueline Woodson's *Locomotion* with Middle School Students"(Napoli and Ritholz), **Supp. XXVIII:** 285

"Using Parrots to Kill Mockingbirds: Yet Another Racial Prosecution and Wrongful Conviction in Maycomb" (Fair), **Supp. VIII:** 128

USS Constellation: Pride of the American Navy (Myers), **Supp. XXVII:** 208

Ustedes y Nosotros: Nuevo Mensaje a Ibero-América (W. Frank), **Supp. XX:** **79**

"Usual Objects"(Schott), **Supp. XXIII:** 248

Usual Star, The (Doolittle), **Supp. I Part 1:** 270

"Usurpation (Other People's Stories)" (Ozick), **Supp. V:** 268, 271

Utopia 14 (Vonnegut), **Supp. II Part 2:** 757

V

V. (Pynchon), **Supp. II Part 2:** 618, 620–622, 627–630; **Supp. IV Part 1:** 279

"Vacation" (Stafford), **Supp. XI:** 321, 322

Vacationland (Monson), **Supp. XXIV:** 230, 231, 234

"Vacation Trip" (Stafford), **Supp. XI:** 322

Vachel Lindsay: A Poet in America (Masters), **Supp. I Part 2:** 473, 474

"Vachel Lindsay: The Midwest as Utopia" (Whitney), **Supp. I Part 2:** 403

"Vachel Lindsay Writes to Floyd Dell" (Tanselle), **Supp. I Part 2:** 403

"Vacillation" (Yeats), **Supp. XV:** 253

Vadim, Roger, **Supp. XI:** 293, 307

"Vag" (Dos Passos), **I:** 487–488

Vagina Monologues, The (Ensler), **Supp. XIX:** 204–205

Vagrant Grace (Bottoms), **Supp. XXVIII:** 22, 28–29

Vail, Laurence, **Supp. XXIV:** 50

Valdez, Luis, **Supp. XXIII:** 203

"Vale" (Stallings), **Supp. XXV:** 230, 231

Valediction (Parker), **Supp. XIX:** 185

"Valediction Forbidding Mourning, A" (Rich), **Retro. Supp. III:** 245–246

"Valene"(Goodman), **Supp. XXVIII:** 89, 90, 95

Valentine, Jean, **Supp. V:** 92

Valentine, Saint, **IV:** 396

Valentines (Kooser), **Supp. XIX:** 116, 123, **128–129**

Valentino, Rudolph, **I:** 483

Valéry, Paul, **II:** 543, 544; **III:** 279, 409, 428, 609; **IV:** 79, 91, 92, 428, 443; **Retro. Supp. II:** 187

"Valhalla" (Francis), **Supp. IX:** 77

Valhalla and Other Poems (Francis), **Supp. IX:** 76

Valiant Runaways, The (Atherton), **Supp. XXIV:** 22

Validity in Interpretation (Hirsch), **Supp. XIV:** 15

Valitsky, Ken, **Supp. XII:** 7

Vallejo, César, **Supp. IX:** 271; **Supp. V:** 332; **Supp. XIII:** 114, 315, 323; **Supp. XXI:** 132

Valley, The (Asch), **Supp. XXVI:** 17, 21, 23–26

"Valley, The" (Bass), **Supp. XVI:** 20, 22

Valley, The (Hinojosa), **Supp. XIX:** 97, 99, **100–101**

"Valley Between, The" (Marshall), **Supp. XI:** 278

Valley of Decision, The (Wharton), **IV:** 311, 315; **Retro. Supp. I:** 365–367; **Retro. Supp. III:** 279

"Valley of the Monsters, The" (Peacock), **Supp. XIX:** 198

Valley of the Moon, The (London), **II:** 467, 481

"Valley of Unrest, The" (Poe), **III:** 411

Valli, Alida, **Supp. IV Part 2:** 520

"Valor" (Bausch), **Supp. VII:** 54

Valparaiso (DeLillo), **Supp. VI:** 4, 12

"Value of a Place, The" (Bass), **Supp. XVI:** 18

"Value of Folklore in Literature"(Stuart), **Supp. XXVIII:** 230

"Values and Fictions" (Toomer), **Supp. III Part 2:** 485–486

"Values and Imperatives" (Locke), **Supp. XIV:** 199, 202, 212

Values of Veblen, The: A Critical Appraisal (Rosenberg), **Supp. I Part 2:** 650

"Vampire" (Karr), **Supp. XI:** 241

Vampire Armand, The (Rice), **Supp. VII:** 290, 294–295

Vampire Chronicles, The (Rice), **Supp. VII:** 290

Vampire Lestat, The (Rice), **Supp. VII:** 290–292, 298, 299

Van Aalst, Mariska, **Supp. XIX:** 50, 51

Van Arsdale, Sarah, **Supp. XXV:** 4

Van Buren, Floyd, **Retro. Supp. III:** 82

Van Buren, Martin, **II:** 134, 312; **III:** 473

"Vandals" (Munro), **Supp. XXVII:** 192

Vande Kieft, Ruth M., **IV:** 260

Vanderbilt, Cornelius, **III:** 14

VanDerWerff, Todd, **Supp. XXV:** 75

Van Dine, S. S., **Supp. IV Part 1:** 341; **Supp. XXVI:** 283

Van Doren, Carl, **I:** 252–253, 423; **II:** 103, 111, 112; **Supp. I Part 2:** 474, 486, 707, 709, 717, 718, 727; **Supp. II Part 1:** 395; **Supp. VIII:** 96–97

Van Doren, Mark, **I:** 168; **III:** 4, 23, 589; **Supp. I Part 2:** 604; **Supp. III Part 2:** 626; **Supp. IX:** 266, 268; **Supp. VIII:** 231; **Supp. XV:** 152, 305, 307; **Supp. XXII:** 275

Vandover and the Brute (Norris), **III:** 314, 315, 316, 320–322, 328, 333, 334

Van Duyn, Mona, **Supp. IX:** 269

Van Dyke, Annette, **Supp. IV Part 1:** 327

Van Dyke, Henry, **I:** 223; **II:** 456

Van Engen, Abram, **Retro. Supp. III:** 12

Van Gogh, Vincent, **I:** 27; **IV:** 290; **Supp. I Part 2:** 451; **Supp. IV Part 1:** 284; **Supp. XXII:** 171–172

Van Gogh Field and Other Stories, The (Kittredge), **Supp. XXVI:** 181, 182, 184

Van Gogh's Room at Arles (Elkin), **Supp. VI:** 56

"Vanilla Dunk" (Lethem), **Supp. XVIII:** 139

"Vanisher, The" (Whittier), **Supp. I Part 2:** 691

Vanishing of Betty Varian, The (Wells), **Supp. XXVI:** 278

Vanishing Point (Markson), **Supp. XVII:** 135, 137, 138, 145–146

"Vanishing Point, The" (Davison), **Supp. XXVI:** 76

"Vanishing Point: Former City" (Monson), **Supp. XXIV:** 238

"Vanishing Point for Solo Voice" (Monson), **Supp. XXIV:** 239

Vanishing Point: Not a Memoir (Monson), **Supp. XXIV:** 230, **236–239**, 241–242

"Vanishing Point: Panera" (Monson), **Supp. XXIV:** 238

"Vanishing Red, The" (Frost), **Retro. Supp. II:** 47; **Retro. Supp. III:** 99

"Vanity" (B. Diop), **Supp. IV Part 1:** 16

Vanity Fair (Thackeray), **I:** 354; **II:** 91; **III:** 70; **Supp. IX:** 200

"Vanity of All Worldly Things, The" (Bradstreet), **Retro. Supp. III:** 11; **Supp. I Part 1:** 102, 119

Vanity of Duluoz (Kerouac), **Supp. III Part 1:** 221, 222

"Vanity of Existence, The" (Freneau), **Supp. II Part 1:** 262

Van Matre, Lynn, **Supp. V:** 126

Vann, Barbara, **Supp. XV:** 187

Vanquished, The (Faulkner), **I:** 205

"Vanquished, The" (Rash), **Supp. XXVII:** 220

Van Rensselaer, Stephen, **I:** 351

Van Vechten, Carl, **I:** 295; **IV:** 76; **Retro. Supp. I:** 199; **Retro. Supp. III:** 127, 134, 137; **Supp. I Part 1:** 324, 327, 332; **Supp. I Part 2:** 715; **Supp. II Part 2:** 725–751; **Supp. X:** 247; **Supp. XIX:** 76; **Supp. XVI:** 135; **Supp. XVII:** 96, 97, 101, 104; **Supp. XVIII:** 123, 131, 132, 279, 280; **Supp. XX:** 69; **Supp. XXI:** 5, 8; **Supp. XXII:** 5, 158, 160

Van Vliet, Don, **Supp. XXIII:** 174

Vanya and Sonia and Masha and Spike (Durang), **Supp. XXIV: 127–128**

Vanzetti, Bartolomeo, **I:** 482, 486, 490, 494; **II:** 38–39, 426; **III:** 139–140; **Supp. I Part 2:** 446, 610, 611; **Supp. IX:** 199; **Supp. V:** 288–289; **Supp. XXII:** 277

"Vapor Trail Reflected in the Frog Pond" (Kinnell), **Supp. III Part 1:** 242–243

"Vapor Trails" (Snyder), **Supp. VIII:** 298

"Variant Text" (Goodman), **Supp. XXVI:** 118

"Variation: Ode to Fear" (Warren), **IV:** 241

"Variation on a Sentence" (Bogan), **Supp. III Part 1:** 60

"Variation on Gaining a Son" (Dove), **Supp. IV Part 1:** 248

"Variation on Pain" (Dove), **Supp. IV Part 1:** 248

"Variations: The air is sweetest that a thistle guards" (Merrill), **Supp. III Part 1:** 321

"Variations: White Stag, Black Bear" (Merrill), **Supp. III Part 1:** 321

"Varick Street" (Bishop), **Supp. I Part 1:** 90, 92

Varieties of Metaphysical Poetry, The (Eliot), **Retro. Supp. I:** 65

Varieties of Religious Experience, The (William James), **II:** 344, 353, 354, 359–360, 362; **IV:** 28, 291; **Supp. IX:** 19

Variety (film), **Supp. XII:** 7

Variorum (Whitman), **Retro. Supp. I:** 406

Various Antidotes (J. Scott), **Supp. XVII: 188–189**

Various Miracles (Shields), **Supp. VII:** 318–320, 323, 324

"Various Miracles" (Shields), **Supp. VII:** 318–319, 324

Various Poems (Zach), **Supp. XV:** 86

Various Positions (album, Coen), **Supp. XXVII:** 54

"Various Tourists" (Connell), **Supp. XIV:** 79

"Varmint Question, The" (Leopold), **Supp. XIV:** 180–181

Varno, David, **Supp. XIX:** 205

Varvogli, Aliki, **Supp. XXVIII:** 214

Vasari, Giorgio, **Supp. I Part 2:** 450; **Supp. III Part 1:** 5

Vasquez, Robert, **Supp. V:** 180

Vassall Morton (Parkman), **Supp. II Part 2:** 595, 597–598

Vasse, W. W., **III:** 478

Vaudeville for a Princess (Schwartz), **Supp. II Part 2:** 661–662

"Vaudeville Moment" (Bodenheim), **Supp. XXV:** 22

Vaughan, Henry, **IV:** 151; **Supp. XV:** 251

Vaughn, Robert, **Supp. XI:** 343

Vaughn, Stephanie, **Supp. XXV:** 142

"Vaunting Oak" (Ransom), **III:** 490

Vaz, Katherine, **Supp. XXVI: 255–269**

Vazirani, Reetika, **Supp. XIII:** 133

Veblen (Hobson), **Supp. I Part 2:** 650

Veblen, Andrew, **Supp. I Part 2:** 640

Veblen, Oswald, **Supp. I Part 2:** 640

Veblen, Thorstein, **I:** 104, 283, 475–476, 483, 498, 511; **II:** 27, 272, 276, 287; **Supp. I Part 2:** 628–650; **Supp. IV Part 1:** 22

Veblen, Mrs. Thorstein (Ellen Rolfe), **Supp. I Part 2:** 641

Veblenism: A New Critique (Dobriansky), **Supp. I Part 2:** 648, 650

"Veblen's Attack on Culture" (Adorno), **Supp. I Part 2:** 650

Vecsey, Christopher, **Supp. XXVI:** 90

Vectors and Smoothable Curves (Bronk), **Supp. XXI: 24–26,** 32

Vedanta for Modern Man (Isherwood, ed.), **Supp. XIV:** 164

Vedanta for the Western World (Isherwood, ed.), **Supp. XIV:** 164

Vedas, **IV:** 183

Vega, Janine Pommy, **Supp. XIV:** 148

Vega, Lope de, **Retro. Supp. I:** 285; **Supp. III Part 1:** 341, 347

Vegetable, The (Fitzgerald), **Retro. Supp. I:** 105; **Supp. IX:** 57

Vegetable, The, or From President to Postman (Fitzgerald), **II:** 91

"Vegetable Love" (Apple), **Supp. XVII:** 4

"Vegetable Love"(Crooker), **Supp. XXIII:** 62

"Vegetable Wisdom" (Halliday), **Supp. XIX:** 88

Veg tsu zikh, Der (The road to one's self) (Asch), **Supp. XXIII:** 5, 11

Veil of Snows, A (Helprin), **Supp. XXV:** 84, 87

Veinberg, Jon, **Supp. V:** 180; **Supp. XIII:** 313; **Supp. XV:** 76–77, 86

Vein of Iron (Glasgow), **II:** 175, 186, 188–189, 191, 192, 194

Vein of Riches, A (Knowles), **Supp. XII:** 249

Vein of Words (J. W. Miller), **Supp. XX: 165**

Velie, Alan R., **Supp. IV Part 2:** 486

Velocities: New and Selected Poems, 1966–1992 (Dobyns), **Supp. XIII:** 86–87, 87, 88

"Velocity" (Collins), **Supp. XXI:** 61

"Velorio" (Cisneros), **Supp. VII:** 66

"Velvet Gentleman, The" (Skloot), **Supp. XX: 201**

"Velvet Shoes" (Wylie), **Supp. I Part 2:** 711, 714

Venant, Elizabeth, **Supp. XI:** 343

Vencloca, Thomas, **Supp. VIII:** 29

Vendler, Helen H., **Retro. Supp. I:** 297; **Retro. Supp. II:** 184, 191; **Supp. I Part 1:** 77, 78, 92, 95; **Supp. I Part 2:** 565; **Supp. IV Part 1:** 245, 247, 249, 254, 257; **Supp. IV Part 2:** 448; **Supp. V:** 78, 82, 189, 343; **Supp. XII:** 187, 189; **Supp. XV:** 20, 184

"Vendor, The"(Goodman), **Supp. XXVIII:** 92

"Venetian Blind, The" (Jarrell), **II:** 382–383

Venetian Glass Nephew, The (Wylie), **Supp. I Part 2:** 707, 709, 714, 717–719, 721, 724

Venetian Life (Howells), **II:** 274, 277, 279

Venetian Vespers, The (Hecht), **Supp. X:** 57, **65–69**

"Venetian Vespers, The" (Hecht), **Supp. X:** 65, **66–67**

Venice Observed (McCarthy), **II:** 562

Ventadorn, Bernard de, **Supp. IV Part 1:** 146

"Ventriloquists' Conversations" (Gentry), **Supp. IV Part 1:** 236

Venturesome Voyages of Captain Voss, The (Voss), **Supp. XXV:** 217

"Venus, Cupid, Folly and Time" (Taylor), **Supp. V:** 322–323

Venus and Adonis (film), **Supp. IV Part 1:** 82

Venus and Don Juan (C. Frost), **Supp. XV:** 93, **102–103,** 104, 107

"Venus and Don Juan" (C. Frost), **Supp. XV:** 103

Venus Blue (Sobin), **Supp. XVI: 293–294,** 294

Venus in Sparta (Auchincloss), **Supp. IV Part 1:** 25

"Venus Pandemos" (Halliday), **Supp. XIX:** 85, 89, 90, 93

"Venus's-flytraps" (Komunyakaa), **Supp. XIII:** 126, 127

"Veracruz" (Hayden), **Supp. II Part 1:** 371, 373

Verducci, Tom, **Supp. XXII:** 209

"Verdun" (Beston), **Supp. XXVI:** 32

Verga, Giovanni, **II:** 271, 275

Verghese, Abraham, **Supp. X:** 160

Verhaeren, Emile, **I:** 476; **II:** 528, 529

Verlaine, Paul, **II:** 529, 543; **III:** 466; **IV:** 79, 80, 86, 286; **Retro. Supp. I:** 56, 62; **Retro. Supp. II:** 326

"Vermeer" (Nemerov), **III:** 275, 278, 280

Vermeer, Jan, **Retro. Supp. I:** 335

"Vermont" (Carruth), **Supp. XVI:** 54

"Vermont" (Huddle), **Supp. XXVI:** 161

Vermont Journal: 1971 (Brainard), **Supp. XXVII:** 27

Vermont Notebook, The (Ashbery), **Supp. III Part 1:** 1

"Vermont Tale, A" (Helprin), **Supp. XXV:** 85

Vermont Writers: A State of Mind (Daley), **Supp. XXII:** 216

"Vernal Ague, The" (Freneau), **Supp. II Part 1:** 258

Verne, Jules, **I:** 480; **Retro. Supp. I:** 270; **Retro. Supp. III:** 235; **Supp. XI:** 63

Vernon, John, **Supp. X:** 15

Verplanck, Gulian C., **Supp. I Part 1:** 155, 156, 157, 158

Verrazano, Giovanni da, **Supp. I Part 2:** 496, 497

Verse (Zawacki), **Supp. VIII:** 272

"Verse for Urania" (Merrill), **Supp. III Part 1:** 329, 330

Verses (Wharton), **Retro. Supp. I:** 362; **Retro. Supp. III:** 276

Verses, Printed for Her Friends (Jewett), **II:** 406

"Verses for Children" (A. Lowell), **II:** 516

"Verses Made at Sea in a Heavy Gale" (Freneau), **Supp. II Part 1:** 262

"Verses on the Death of T. S. Eliot" (Brodsky), **Supp. VIII:** 19

"Version of a Fragment of Simonides" (Bryant), **Supp. I Part 1:** 153, 155

"Vers Libre Epidemic, The" (Lovecraft), **Supp. XXV:** 120

Verulam, Baron. *See* Bacon, Francis

Very, Jones, **III:** 507; **Supp. XXV: 237–252**

"Very Hot Sun in Bermuda, The" (Jackson), **Supp. IX:** 126

Very Old Bones (W. Kennedy), **Supp. VII:** 133, 148, 150–153

"Very Old Man with Enormous Wings, A" (García Márquez), **Supp. XXIV:** 190

Very Persistent Gappers of Frip, The (Saunders), **Supp. XIX: 229–230**

"Very Proper Gander, The" (Thurber), **Supp. I Part 2:** 610

"Very Short Story, A" (Hemingway), **II:** 252; **Retro. Supp. I:** 173

"Vesalius in Zante" (Wharton), **Retro. Supp. I:** 372

Vesey, Denmark, **Supp. I Part 2:** 592

Vesey, Desmond, **Supp. XIV:** 162

"Vespers" (Auden), **Supp. II Part 1:** 23

"Vespers" (Glück), **Supp. V:** 88

"Vespers"(Dybek), **Supp. XXIII:** 78

Vestal Lady on Brattle, The (Corso), **Supp. XII:** 119, **120–121,** 134

Vested Interests and the Common Man, The (Veblen), **Supp. I Part 2:** 642

"Vesuvius at Home" (Rich), **Retro. Supp. I:** 42; **Retro. Supp. III:** 248

"Veteran, The" (Crane), **I:** 413

"Veterans' Cemetery" (Gioia), **Supp. XV:** 117

"Veteran Sirens" (Robinson), **III:** 512, 524

"Veterinarian" (X. J. Kennedy), **Supp. XV:** 168

"Vetiver" (Ashbery), **Supp. III Part 1:** 26

Vetter, Lara, **Supp. XXII:** 166

"Via Dieppe-Newhaven" (H. Miller), **III:** 183

"Via Negativa" (Salter), **Supp. IX:** 257

Vicar of Wakefield, The (Goldsmith), **I:** 216

Vicious Circle, The (film, Wilder), **Supp. XVII:** 62

"Vicissitudes of the Avant-Garde, The" (Gass), **Supp. VI:** 91

Vicky Van (Wells), **Supp. XXVI:** 280

Vico, Giambattista, **Supp. XX:** 38

Victim, The (Bellow), **I:** 144, 145, 147, 149, 150, 151, 152, 153, 155, 156, 158, 159, 164; **IV:** 19; **Retro. Supp. II:** 21, 22, 34

"Victor" (Mumford), **Supp. II Part 2:** 476

Victoria (Rowson), **Supp. XV:** 231

Victorian in the Modern World, A (Hapgood), **Supp. XVII:** 95, 97, 100, 101, 103, 105, 106; **Supp. XXI:** 8

"Victoria's Secret" (Collins), **Supp. XXI:** 58–59

"Victories" (Untermeyer), **Supp. XV:** 300

"Victory at Sea" (television series), **Supp. I Part 2:** 490

"Victory comes late" (Dickinson), **Retro. Supp. I:** 45

"Victory of the Moon, The" (Crane), **I:** 420

Vida, Vendela, **Supp. XIX:** 49, 50, 53, 57, 58, 59, 61, 62

Vidal, Gore, **II:** 587; **IV:** 383; **Supp. IV Part 1:** 22, 35, 92, 95, 198; **Supp. IV Part 2: 677–696; Supp. IX:** 96; **Supp. X:** 186, 195; **Supp. XIV:** 156, 170, 338; **Supp. XIX:** 131, 132

Video Poems (Collins), **Supp. XXI:** 53

Viebahn, Fred, **Supp. IV Part 1:** 248

Viera, Joseph M., **Supp. XI:** 178, 186

Viereck, Peter, **Supp. I Part 2:** 403

Viertel, Berthold, **Supp. XIV:** 165

Viertel, Salka, **Supp. XVI:** 192

Viet Journal (Jones), **Supp. XI: 230–231**

Vietnam (McCarthy), **II:** 578–579

"Vietnam in Me, The" (O'Brien), **Supp. V:** 241, 252

Vietnamization of New Jersey, The (Durang), **Supp. XXIV:** 113, **117–118**

Vietnam Reader, The: The Definitive Collection of Fiction and Nonfiction on the War (O'Nan, ed.), **Supp. XXV:** 153

Vie unanime, La (Romains), **I:** 227

"View, The" (Roussel), **Supp. III Part 1:** 15, 16, 21

View from 80, The (Cowley), **Supp. II Part 1:** 141, 144, 153

"View from an Institution" (F. Wright), **Supp. XVII:** 244

View from Castle Rock, The (Munro), **Supp. XXVII:** 194–195

"View from the Backyard" (W. V. Davis), **Supp. XXI:** 96

View from the Bridge, A (A. Miller), **III:** 147, 148, 156, 158, 159–160; **Retro. Supp. III:** 165, 167, 168–169, 173; **Supp. XXV:** 93

View from the Seventh Layer, The (Brockmeier), **Supp. XXII: 59–61**

"View from the Seventh Layer, The" (Brockmeier), **Supp. XXII:** 61

View of My Own, A: Essays in Literature and Society (Hardwick), **Supp. III Part 1:** 194, 200

"View of the Capital from the Library of Congress" (Bishop), **Retro. Supp. II:** 45

View of the Soil and Climate of the United States, A (Brown, trans.), **Supp. I Part 1:** 146

"View of the Woods, A" (O'Connor), **III:** 349, 351, 358; **Retro. Supp. II:** 237

"Viewpoint" (column, Siddons), **Supp. XXII:** 240, 245

"Views of the Mysterious Hill: The Appearance of Parnassus in American Poetry" (Strand), **Supp. IV Part 2:** 631

"Vigil" (Karr), **Supp. XI:** 241

"Vigil, The" (Dante), **III:** 542

"Vigil at Heiligenkreuz" (W. V. Davis), **Supp. XXI:** 93

"Vigil"(Dybek), **Supp. XXIII:** 78

"Vignette" (Trethewey), **Supp. XXI:** 253, 254

Vigny, Alfred Victor de, **II:** 543

Vildrac, Charles, **Supp. XV:** 50

Vile Bodies (Waugh), **Supp. I Part 2:** 607

Villa, Pancho, **I:** 210; **III:** 584

"Villa dei Pini" (Davison), **Supp. XXVI:** 79

"Village, The" (Huddle), **Supp. XXVI:** 156

"Village Blacksmith, The" (Longfellow), **Retro. Supp. II:** 167, 168; **Supp. I Part 2:** 409

Village Hymns, a Supplement to Dr. Watts's Psalms and Hymns (Nettleton), **I:** 458

"Village Improvement Parade, The" (Lindsay), **Supp. I Part 2:** 388, 389

Village Magazine, The (Lindsay), **Supp. I Part 2:** 379–380, 382

Village Virus, The (Lewis), **II:** 440

"Villanelle at Sundown" (Justice), **Supp. VII:** 119, 122–123

"Villanelle of Change" (Robinson), **III:** 524

Villard, Oswald, **Supp. I Part 1:** 332

"Villa Selene" (Simpson), **Supp. IX:** 279

Villon, François, **II:** 544; **III:** 9, 174, 592; **Retro. Supp. I:** 286; **Supp. I Part 1:** 261; **Supp. III Part 1:** 235, 243, 249, 253; **Supp. III Part 2:** 560; **Supp. IX:** 116

"Villonaud for This Yule" (Pound), **Retro. Supp. I:** 286

Vincent, Steven, **Supp. XXV:** 201

"Vincenzo Tailor" (Di Piero), **Supp. XIX:** 38

Vindication of the Rights of Woman (Wollstonecraft), **Supp. I Part 1:** 126; **Supp. XI:** 203

Viner, Katherine, **Supp. XXVII:** 276

Vines, Lois Davis, **Retro. Supp. II:** 261

"Vineyard of Red Wine, The" (Beston), **Supp. XXVI:** 32

Vintage Book of Amnesia, The (Lethem, ed.), **Supp. XVIII:** 138
"Vintage Thunderbird, A" (Beattie), **Supp. V:** 27
Vinz, Mark, **Supp. X:** 117
Viol de Lucrèce, Le (Obey), **IV:** 356
Violence (Bausch), **Supp. VII:** 48–49, 54
Violent Bear It Away, The (O'Connor), **III:** 339, 345–348, 350, 351, 354, 355, 356, 357; **Retro. Supp. II:** 233, **234–236; Retro. Supp. III:** 208, 210–211, 213, 215
Violent Hero, Wilderness Heritage and Urban Reality, The: A Study of the Private Eye in the Novels of Dashiell Hammett, Raymond Chandler and Ross Macdonald (Parker), **Supp. XIX:** 177
"Violent Vet, The" (O'Brien), **Supp. V:** 238
"Violets"(Bottoms), **Supp. XXVIII:** 31–32
Violin (Rice), **Supp. VII:** 302
Viorst, Judith, **Supp. X:** 153
Viper Run (Karr), **Supp. XI: 248–251**
Viramontes, Helene María, **Supp. XXV:** 130, 133, 138
Virgil, **I:** 312, 322, 587; **II:** 133, 542; **IV:** 137, 359; **Retro. Supp. I:** 135; **Supp. I Part 1:** 153; **Supp. I Part 2:** 494; **Supp. IV Part 2:** 631
"Virgin and Child with Music and Numbers" (Bronk), **Supp. XXI:** 30
"Virgin and the Dynamo" (Adams), **III:** 396
"Virgin Carrying a Lantern, The" (Stevens), **IV:** 80
Virgin Huntress, The (Holding), **Supp. XXII:** 119, 124, **135–136**
Virginia (Glasgow), **II:** 175, 178, 181–182, 193, 194
"Virginia" (Lindsay), **Supp. I Part 2:** 398
"Virginia Britannia" (Moore), **III:** 198, 208–209
"Virginians Are Coming Again, The" (Lindsay), **Supp. I Part 2:** 399
Virginia Reels (Hoffman), **Supp. XVIII:** 79, 86
Virgin Spain (W. Frank), **Supp. XX: 76**
"Virgins Plus Curtains Minus Dots" (Loy), **Supp. XXII:** 161
Virgin Suicides, The (Eugenides), **Supp. XXIV:** 134, **136–138**, 141, 142
Virgin Time: In Search of the Contemplative Life (Hampl), **Supp. XXII:** 82, 83–84, **90–92**
"Virgin Violeta" (Porter), **III:** 454
"Virility" (Ozick), **Supp. V:** 262, 265
Virtual Light (W. Gibson), **Supp. XVI:** 124, **129,** 130
Virtue of Selfishness, The: A New Concept of Egoism (Rand), **Supp. IV Part 2:** 527, 530–532
"Virtuoso" (Francis), **Supp. IX:** 82
Virtuoso Literature for Two and Four Hands (Wakoski), **Supp. XXVIII:** 266
Virtuous Girl, A (Bodenheim), **Supp. XXV:** 27
Virtuous Woman, A (Gibbons), **Supp. X:** **44–45,** 46, 50

Visconti, Luchino, **Supp. V:** 51
Viscusi, Robert, **Supp. XX: 46**
Visible Saints: The History of a Puritan Idea (Morgan), **IV:** 149
"Vision, A" (Olds), **Supp. X:** 214
"Vision, A" (Winters), **Supp. II Part 2:** 785, 795
"Vision and Prayer" (D. Thomas), **I:** 432
"Visionary, The" (Poe), **III:** 411
Visionary Farms, The (Eberhart), **I:** 537–539
Visioning, The (Glaspell), **Supp. III Part 1:** 175–177, 180, 187, 188
Vision in Spring (Faulkner), **Retro. Supp. I:** 79
Vision of Columbus (Barlow), **Supp. I Part 1:** 124; **Supp. II Part 1:** 67, 68, 70–75, 77, 79
Vision of Sir Launfal, The (J. R. Lowell), **Supp. I Part 1:** 311; **Supp. I Part 2:** 406, 409, 410
"Vision of the World, A" (Cheever), **Supp. I Part 1:** 182, 192
"Visions and Voices" (Davison), **Supp. XXVI:** 71
"Visions of Budhardin"(Dybek), **Supp. XXIII:** 70–71
Visions of Cody (Kerouac), **Supp. III Part 1:** 225–227
Visions of Gerard (Kerouac), **Supp. III Part 1:** 219–222, 225, 227, 229
"Visions of the Daughters of Albion" (Blake), **III:** 540
"Visit" (Ammons), **Supp. VII:** 28–29
"Visit, The" (Kenyon), **Supp. VII:** 169
"Visitant, The" (Dunn), **Supp. XI:** 147
"*Visitation, The*/La Visitación" (Mora), **Supp. XIII:** 217, 224, 228
"Visitation"(Kenny), **Supp. XXIII:** 157
"Visit Home, A" (Stafford), **Supp. XI:** 318
Visit in 2001, The (musical, McNally), **Supp. XIII:** 207
Visiting Day (Woodson; Ransome, ill.), **Supp. XXVIII:** 278, 285
"Visiting My Own House in Iowa City" (Stern), **Supp. IX:** 300
Visiting Villain, The (Wells), **Supp. XXVI:** 278, 280
"Visit of Charity, A" (Welty), **IV:** 262
"Visit of the Hawk" (Huddle), **Supp. XXVI:** 149
"Visitors" (J. W. Miller), **Supp. XX: 167**
"Visitors" (Salinas), **Supp. XIII:** 318
"Visitors, The/Los Visitantes" (Kingsolver), **Supp. VII:** 208
"Visits to St. Elizabeths" (Bishop), **Retro. Supp. II:** 47
Visit to a Small Planet: A Comedy Akin to Vaudeville (Vidal), **Supp. IV Part 2:** 682–683
"Visit to a Small Planet" (teleplay) (Vidal), **Supp. IV Part 2:** 682
"Visit to Avoyelles, A" (Chopin), **Supp. I Part 1:** 213
"Visit to Manafon, A" (W. V. Davis), **Supp. XXI:** 96
"Vissi d'Arte" (Moore), **Supp. X: 173–174**

Vistas of History (Morison), **Supp. I Part 2:** 492
"Vita" (Stafford), **Supp. XI:** 330
"Vita Brevis" (Hull), **Supp. XXI:** 138
Vital, David, **Supp. XVI:** 160
Vital Provisions (Price), **Supp. VI:** 262–263
"Vitamins" (Carver), **Supp. III Part 1:** 138
Vita Nova (Glück), **Supp. V:** 90–92
Vita Nuova, La (Dante), **Retro. Supp. III:** 65
Vitruvius, **Supp. XVI:** 292
Vittorio, the Vampire (Rice), **Supp. VII:** 295–296
Viudas (Dorfman), **Supp. IX:** 138
"Vivaldi"(Dybek), **Supp. XXIII:** 68
"Viva Vargas!" (Allen), **Supp. XV:** 15
Viva Villa! (screenplay, Hecht), **Supp. XXVII:** 93
Viviparous Quadrupeds of North America, The (Audubon and Bachman), **Supp. XVI:** 10
Vivisections (Siegel), **Supp. XXII:** 257
Vizenor, Gerald, **Supp. IV Part 1:** 260, 262, 329, 404; **Supp. IV Part 2:** 502
Vladimir Nabokov: The American Years (Nabokov), **Retro. Supp. I:** 275
Vlag, Piet, **Supp. XV:** 295
"Vlemk, the Box Painter" (Gardner), **Supp. VI:** 73
"V-Letter" (Shapiro), **Supp. II Part 2:** 707
V-Letter and Other Poems (Shapiro), **Supp. II Part 2:** 702, 706
"Vocabulary of Dearness" (Nye), **Supp. XIII:** 284
"Vocation" (Stafford), **Supp. XI:** 312, 321
Vocation and a Voice, A (Chopin), **Retro. Supp. II:** 67, 72
"Vocation and a Voice, A" (Chopin), **Retro. Supp. II:** 72; **Supp. I Part 1:** 200, 220, 224, 225
Vogel, David, **Supp. XV:** 88
Vogel, Speed, **Supp. IV Part 1:** 390
"Vogue Vista" (Peacock), **Supp. XIX:** 200
"Voice" (F. Wright), **Supp. XVII:** 245
"Voice" (Notley), **Supp. XXII:** 230
"Voice, The" (Dunn), **Supp. XI:** 152
Voice at the Back Door, The (Spencer), **Supp. XXVII:** 13
Voiced Connections of James Dickey, The (Dickey), **Supp. IV Part 1:** 177
"Voice from the Wilderness" (Ray), **Supp. XVIII:** 202
"Voice from the Woods, A" (Humphrey), **Supp. IX:** 101
"Voice from Under the Table, A" (Wilbur), **Supp. III Part 2:** 553, 554
Voice in the Mountain, A (Davison), **Supp. XXVI:** 65, 73–75, 77
"Voice of God, The" (Very), **Supp. XXV:** 243
Voice of Reason, The: Essays in Objectivist Thought (Rand), **Supp. IV Part 2:** 527, 528, 532

"Voice of Rock, The" (Ginsberg), **Supp. II Part 1:** 313

Voice of the Butterfly, The (Nichols), **Supp. XIII:** 270

Voice of the City, The (O. Henry), **Supp. II Part 1:** 410

"Voice of the Mountain, The" (Crane), **I:** 420

Voice of the Negro (Barber), **Supp. II Part 1:** 168

"Voice of the Past, The" (Skloot), **Supp. XX:** 207

Voice of the People, The (Glasgow), **II:** 175, 176

Voice of the Turtle: American Indian Literature 1900–1970 (Gunn Allen, ed.), **Supp. IV Part 1:** 332, 334

Voices from the Moon (Dubus), **Supp. VII:** 88–89

"Voices from the Other World" (Merrill), **Supp. III Part 1:** 331

Voices in the House (Sedges), **Supp. II Part 1:** 125

Voices of a Summer Day (Shaw), **Supp. XIX:** 251

Voices of the Night (Longfellow), **II:** 489, 493; **Retro. Supp. II:** 154, 157, 168

"Voices of Village Square, The" (Wolfe), **Supp. III Part 2:** 571–572

Voice That Is Great within Us, The (Caruth, ed.), **Supp. XIII:** 112

Void Moon (Connelly), **Supp. XXI:** 73, 74

Voigt, Ellen Bryan, **Supp. XIII:** 76

"Voir Dire" (Monson), **Supp. XXIV:** 237

Voix humaine, La (Cocteau), **Supp. XX:** 236

Volkening, Henry, **Retro. Supp. II:** 117; **Supp. XV:** 142

Vollmann, William T., **Supp. XIV:** 96; **Supp. XVII: 225–237; Supp. XX:** 93

Volney, Constantin François de Chasseboeuf, **Supp. I Part 1:** 146

Voltaire, **I:** 194; **II:** 86, 103, 449; **III:** 420; **IV:** 18; **Retro. Supp. II:** 94; **Retro. Supp. III:** 109; **Supp. I Part 1:** 288–289; **Supp. I Part 2:** 669, 717; **Supp. XV:** 258; **Supp. XX:** 285

Voltaire! Voltaire! (Endore), **Supp. XVII:** 65

Volunteer Poilu, A (Beston), **Supp. XXVI:** 32

Volunteers, The (Rowson and Reinagle), **Supp. XV:** 238

Volynsky, Akim (Chaim Flekser), **Supp. XXIII:** 11

Vonnegut, Kurt, **Retro. Supp. I:** 170; **Supp. II Part 2:** 557, 689, **753–784; Supp. IV Part 1:** 227, 392; **Supp. V:** 40, 42, 237, 244, 296; **Supp. X:** 260; **Supp. XI:** 104; **Supp. XII:** 139, 141; **Supp. XVIII:** 242, 252; **Supp. XXI:** 226; **Supp. XXIII:** 42, 101, 109

Vonnegut, Kurt, Jr., **Supp. XIX:** 223; **Supp. XVII:** 41, 135

"Voracities and Verities" (Moore), **III:** 214

Vore, Nellie, **I:** 199

Vorlicky, Robert, **Supp. IX:** 132, 135, 136, 141, 144, 147

Vorse, Mary Heaton, **Supp. XVII:** 99; **Supp. XX: 76; Supp. XXI:** 5, 6, 9, 13

Vortex, The (Coward), **Supp. XXIV:** 267

"Vorticism" (Pound), **Retro. Supp. I:** 288

Vosjoli, Philippe de, **Supp. XX:** 253

Voss, J. C., **Supp. XXV:** 217

Voss, Ralph E., **Supp. XXV:** 93

Voss, Richard, **I:** 199–200

"Vow, The" (Hecht), **Supp. X:** 64

"Vowels 2" (Baraka), **Supp. II Part 1:** 51

Vow of Conversation, A: Journal, 1964–1965 (Merton), **Supp. VIII:** 206

Vox (Baker), **Supp. XIII: 47–49,** 50, 52, 53

"Voyage" (MacLeish), **III:** 15

Voyage, The (Caputo), **Supp. XIX:** 25, 27–28

"Voyage, The" (Irving), **II:** 304

Voyage, The, and Other Versions of Poems by Baudelaire (R. Lowell), **Retro. Supp. II:** 187

Voyage dans la Haute Pennsylvanie et dans l'état de New-York (Crèvecoeur), **Supp. I Part 1:** 250–251

Voyage of the Beagle (Darwin), **Supp. IX:** 211

Voyage of the Dawn Treader (C. S. Lewis), **Supp. XXV:** 74

Voyage of the Destroyer *from New York to Brazil, The* (Slocum), **Supp. XXV:** 208, 212–213

Voyage of the Liberdade, The (Slocum), **Supp. XXV:** 208, 210–212

Voyage Out, The (Woolf), **Supp. XV:** 65

"Voyager, The" (Everwine), **Supp. XV:** 75

"Voyages" (H. Crane), **I:** 393–395; **Retro. Supp. II:** 78, 80, 81; **Retro. Supp. III:** 46, 49

"Voyages" (Levine), **Supp. V:** 190

Voyages and Discoveries of the Companions of Columbus (Irving), **II:** 310

Voyage to Pagany, A (W. C. Williams), **IV:** 404; **Retro. Supp. I:** 418–419, **420–421,** 423

Voyaging Portraits (Sobin), **Supp. XVI:** 282, 287

"Voyeur, The" (Gioia), **Supp. XV:** 125

"Voz de America" (column, W. Frank), **Supp. XX:** 80

Voznesensky, Andrei, **II:** 553; **Supp. III Part 1:** 268; **Supp. III Part 2:** 560

Vrbovska, Anca, **Supp. IV Part 2:** 639

V. S. Naipaul: An Introduction to His Work (Theroux), **Supp. VIII:** 314, 318

"V. S. Pritchett's Apprenticeship" (Maxwell), **Supp. VIII:** 172

Vukelich, James, **Supp. XXIII:** 228, 233

"Vulgarity in Literature" (Huxley), **III:** 429–430

"Vultures" (Oliver), **Supp. VII:** 235

"Vultures of Wahpeton" (Howard), **Supp. XXVII:** 126–127

"V. V." (Alcott), **Supp. I Part 1:** 37

W

W (Viva) (Cummings), **I:** 429, 433, 434, 436, 443, 444, 447

Wabash (R. O. Butler), **Supp. XII:** 61, **68–69**

Wade, Grace, **I:** 216

"Wading at Wellfleet" (Bishop), **Retro. Supp. II:** 42, 43; **Supp. I Part 1:** 80, 85, 86

Wadsworth, Charles, **I:** 454, 470; **Retro. Supp. I:** 32, 33

Wage, William, **Supp. XXVI:** 87

Wagenknecht, Edward, **II:** 508; **Supp. I Part 2:** 408, 584; **Supp. IV Part 2:** 681

"Wages of Poetry, The" (Wright), **Supp. XV:** 337

Wagner, Erica, **Supp. XXI:** 117

Wagner, Jean, **Supp. I Part 1:** 341, 346; **Supp. IV Part 1:** 165, 167, 171

Wagner, Karl, **Supp. XXVII:** 128

Wagner, Richard, **I:** 284, 395; **II:** 425; **III:** 396, 507; **Supp. IV Part 1:** 392

Wagner, Robert, **Supp. IX:** 250

"Wagnerians, The" (Auchincloss), **Supp. IV Part 1:** 23

"Wagner Matinée, A" (Cather), **I:** 315–316; **Retro. Supp. I:** 5, 8; **Retro. Supp. III:** 21, 25, 27–28

Wagoner, David, **Supp. IX: 323–340; Supp. XII:** 178; **Supp. XX: 200**

Wahlöö, Per, **Supp. XX:** 87

Waid, Candace, **Retro. Supp. I:** 360, 372, 373

Waif, The (Longfellow, ed.), **Retro. Supp. II:** 155

"Waif of the Plains, A" (Harte), **Supp. II Part 1:** 354

Wain, John, **Supp. XIV:** 166

"Wait" (Kinnell), **Supp. III Part 1:** 250

"Waiter in a California Vietnamese Restaurant" (Major), **Supp. XXII:** 182

"Waiting" (Dubus), **Supp. VII:** 87

Waiting (Jin), **Supp. XVIII:** 89, **96–97,** 99

"Waiting" (W. C. Williams), **Retro. Supp. I:** 418

"Waiting, The" (L.-Y. Lee), **Supp. XV:** 218

"Waiting, The" (Olds), **Supp. X:** 209

"Waiting between the Trees" (Tan), **Supp. X:** 290

"Waiting by the Gate" (Bryant), **Supp. I Part 1:** 171

Waiting for God (Weil), **I:** 298

Waiting for Godot (Beckett), **I:** 78, 91, 298; **Supp. IV Part 1:** 368–369; **Supp. XXIII:** 213

Waiting for Lefty (Odets), **Supp. I Part 1:** 277; **Supp. II Part 2:** 529, 530–533, 540; **Supp. V:** 109; **Supp. XIX:** 242

Waiting for Sweet Betty (Major), **Supp. XXII: 183**

Waiting for Teddy Williams (Mosher), **Supp. XXII:** 205, 206, 207, 208, 209, **215–216**

"Waiting for the Armistice" (Lea), **Supp. XXVIII:** 132

Waiting for the End of the World (Bell), **Supp. X: 4–5,** 11
Waiting for the King of Spain (Wakoski), **Supp. XXVIII:** 266
"Waiting for the Ladies" (L. Brown), **Supp. XXI:** 44
Waiting for the Verdict (R. H. Davis), **Supp. XVI:** 85, 89, 90
"Waiting in a Rain Forest" (Wagoner), **Supp. IX:** 329
Waiting in the Wings (Loraga), **Supp. XXIII:** 195
Waiting Room, The (Kees), **Supp. XV:** 133, 148
Waiting to Exhale (McMillan), **Supp. XIII:** 184, 185, **189–190,** 191
"Waiting to Freeze" (Banks), **Supp. V:** 5, 6
Waiting to Freeze: Poems (Banks), **Supp. V:** 6, 8
Waits, Tom, **Supp. VIII:** 12
Wait until Spring, Bandini (Fante), **Supp. XI:** 160, 161, 164, 165, **166–167**
Wait until Spring, Bandini (film), **Supp. XI:** 173
"Wake, The" (Dove), **Supp. IV Part 1:** 250
"Wakefield" (Hawthorne), **Retro. Supp. I:** 154, 159; **Retro. Supp. III:** 118, 120
Wakefield, Dan, **Supp. VIII:** 43; **Supp. XIX:** 257, 258; **Supp. XVI:** 220
Wakefield, Richard, **Supp. IX:** 323
"Wake Island" (Rukeyser), **Supp. VI:** 273
"Wake"(Kenny), **Supp. XXIII:** 155
Wakeman, Frederic, **Supp. IX:** 247
Wake Up and Live! (Brande), **Supp. I Part 2:** 608
"Waking" (C. Frost), **Supp. XV:** 93
Waking (Rash), **Supp. XXVII:** 220, 221–222, 224
Waking, The (Roethke), **III:** 541
"Waking Early Sunday Morning" (R. Lowell), **II:** 552
"Waking Early Sunday Morning" (R. Lowell), **Retro. Supp. II:** 190
"Waking in the Blue" (R. Lowell), **II:** 547; **Retro. Supp. II:** 180
"Waking in the Dark" (Rich), **Supp. I Part 2:** 559
"Waking Up the Rake" (Hogan), **Supp. IV Part 1:** 415–416, 416
Wakoski, Diane, **Supp. V:** 79; **Supp. XII:** 184; **Supp. XV:** 252; **Supp. XVII:** 112; **Supp. XXIII:** 52; **Supp. XXIV:** 37; **Supp. XXVIII:** **259–275**
"Wakulla: Chasing the Gator's Eye"(Bottoms), **Supp. XXVIII:** 26
Walbridge, John, **Supp. XX: 125**
Walcott, Charles C., **II:** 49
Walcott, Derek, **Supp. VIII:** 28; **Supp. X:** 122, 131; **Supp. XV:** 256; **Supp. XXIV:** 86
Walcott, Jersey Joe, **Supp. V:** 182
Wald, Alan, **Supp. XV:** 202; **Supp. XVIII:** 223; **Supp. XXI:** 261, 262, 271, 275–276, 277, 278; **Supp. XXVIII:** 66, 67, 70, 74, 77
Wald, Lillian, **Supp. I Part 1:** 12

Walden (Thoreau), **Supp. XIV:** 177, 227; **Supp. XV:** 275; **Supp. XVIII:** 14, 80, 189; **Supp. XXIV:** 73; **Supp. XXVI:** 34, 41, 43
Walden, Daniel, **Supp. IV Part 2:** 584, 591; **Supp. V:** 272
Walden; or, Life in the Woods (Thoreau), **I:** 219, 305; **II:** 8, 142, 159, 312–313, 458; **IV:** 168, 169, 170, 176, 177–178, 179–182, 183, 187; **Retro. Supp. I:** 62; **Supp. I Part 2:** 579, 655, 664, 672; **Supp. VIII:** 296; **Supp. X:** 27, 101; **Supp. XIII:** 152; **Supp. XXVIII:** 248
Waldman, Anne, **Supp. XIV:** 150; **Supp. XXIII:** 221; **Supp. XXIV:** 33, 41, 45; **Supp. XXVII:** 22, 23, 26
Waldmeir, Joseph, **III:** 45
Waldmeir, Joseph J., **Supp. I Part 2:** 476
Waldo (Theroux), **Supp. VIII:** 313, 314, **314–315**
Waldo Frank: A Study (Munson), **Supp. XX:** 74
Waldron, Jeremy, **Supp. XVII:** 235
Waldron, Nan Turner, **Supp. XXVI:** 37
Waldrop, Keith, **Supp. XV:** 153, 165
Waley, Arthur, **II:** 526; **III:** 466; **Supp. V:** 340
"Walk, A" (Snyder), **Supp. VIII:** 297
Walkabout Year: Twelve Months in Australia (Pickering), **Supp. XXI:** 199, 200
"Walk at Sunset, A" (Bryant), **Supp. I Part 1:** 155
"Walk before Mass, A" (Agee), **I:** 28–29
Walker, Alice, **Retro. Supp. I:** 215; **Retro. Supp. III:** 136, 137, 184, 247; **Supp. I Part 2:** 550; **Supp. III Part 2:** 488, **517–540; Supp. IV Part 1:** 14; **Supp. IX:** 306, 311; **Supp. VIII:** 141, 214; **Supp. X:** 85, 228, 252, 325, 330; **Supp. XIII:** 179, 185, 291, 295; **Supp. XVI:** 39; **Supp. XVIII:** 200, 283; **Supp. XX: 84, 107, 108; Supp. XXI:** 172; **Supp. XXII:** 172
Walker, Cheryl, **Supp. XI:** 145; **Supp. XXVII:** 284, 296
Walker, David, **Supp. V:** 189; **Supp. XVII:** 246
Walker, Franklin D., **III:** 321
Walker, Gue, **Supp. XII:** 207
Walker, Margaret, **Supp. XVIII:** 282; **Supp. XX: 106**
Walker, Marianne, **Supp. VIII:** 139
Walker, Obadiah, **II:** 113
Walker, Scott, **Supp. XV:** 92
Walker in the City, A (Kazin), **Supp. VIII: 93–95,** 99
Walk Hard (Blum and Hill), **Supp. XV:** 194
Walk Hard-Talk Loud (Zinberg), **Supp. XV:** 194, 202
"Walking" (Hogan), **Supp. IV Part 1:** 416
"Walking" (Thoreau), **Supp. IV Part 1:** 416; **Supp. IX:** 178
"Walking a Battlefield: A Love Story"(Bottoms), **Supp. XXVIII:** 32–33

"Walking Along in Winter" (Kenyon), **Supp. VII:** 167
"Walking around the Block with a Three-Year-Old" (Wagoner), **Supp. IX:** 331–332
"Walking at Noon Near the Burlington Depot in Lincoln, Nebraska" (Kooser), **Supp. XIX:** 122
"Walking Backwards into the Future" (R. Williams), **Supp. IX:** 146
Walking Down the Stairs: Selections from Interviews (Kinnell), **Supp. III Part 1:** 235, 249
"Walking Home" (Schnackenberg). *See* "Laughing with One Eye" (Schnackenberg)
"Walking Home at Night" (Ginsberg), **Supp. II Part 1:** 313
"Walking Is Almost Falling" (Peacock), **Supp. XIX:** 196, 197
Walking Light (Dunn), **Supp. XI:** 140, 141, 153
"Walking Man of Rodin, The" (Sandburg), **III:** 583
"Walking Sticks and Paperweights and Water Marks" (Moore), **III:** 215
Walking Tall (Dunn), **Supp. XI:** 140
Walking the Black Cat (Simic), **Supp. VIII:** 280, **282–284**
Walking the Boundaries (Davison), **Supp. XXVI:** 65, 72–73, 74
"Walking the Boundaries" (Davison), **Supp. XXVI:** 73
Walking to Gatlinburg (Mosher), **Supp. XXII:** 204, 205, 206, 207, 208, 209, 215, **216–217**
Walking to Martha's Vineyard (F. Wright), **Supp. XVII:** 240, 241, 245, 246
Walking to Sleep (Wilbur), **Supp. III Part 2:** 557–560
"Walking to Sleep" (Wilbur), **Supp. III Part 2:** 544, 557, 559, 561, 562
"Walking Wounded" (Shaw), **Supp. XIX:** 248
Walkin' the Dog (Mosley), **Supp. XIII:** 242
"Walk in the Moonlight, A" (Anderson), **I:** 114
Walk Me to the Distance (Everett), **Supp. XVIII: 55–56,** 57
Walk on the Wild Side, A (Algren), **Supp. IX:** 3, **12–13,** 14; **Supp. V:** 4
"Walks in Rome" (Merrill), **Supp. III Part 1:** 337
Walk Through the Year, A (Teale), **Supp. XXVIII:** 251
Walk to the River, A (Hoffman), **Supp. XVIII: 77–78**
Walk with Tom Jefferson, A (Levine), **Supp. V:** 179, 187, 190–191
Wall, Cheryl, **Supp. XXVI:** 165, 166
"Wall, The" (Bronk), **Supp. XXI:** 31
"Wall, The" (Brooks), **Supp. III Part 1:** 70, 71, 84
Wall, The (Hersey), **IV:** 4; **Supp. XX: 251**
Wall, The (Rinehart), **Supp. XXV:** 197–198, 200
"Wall, The" (Roethke), **III:** 544

"Wall, The" (Sexton), **Supp. II Part 2:** 696

Wallace, Daniel, **Supp. XXII:** 49

Wallace, David, **Supp. XXI:** 277

Wallace, David Foster, **Retro. Supp. II:** 279; **Supp. X: 301–318; Supp. XIX:** 223; **Supp. XVII:** 226; **Supp. XX: 91, 93; Supp. XXII:** 260, 261; **Supp. XXVII:** 6, 79; **Supp. XXVIII:** 209, 221

Wallace, Henry, **I:** 489; **III:** 111, 475; **Supp. I Part 1:** 286; **Supp. I Part 2:** 645

Wallace, Jim, **Supp. XX: 143**

Wallace, Mike, **Supp. IV Part 1:** 364; **Supp. IV Part 2:** 526; **Supp. XX: 102**

Wallace, Paul, **Supp. XXVI:** 90, 96–97

Wallace, Richard, **Supp. XVIII:** 101–102

Wallace Stevens (Kermode), **Retro. Supp. I:** 301

Wallace Stevens: The Poems of our Climate (Bloom), **Retro. Supp. I:** 299

Wallace Stevens: Words Chosen out of Desire (Stevens), **Retro. Supp. I:** 297

Wallach, Eli, **III:** 161

Wallant, Edward Lewis, **Supp. XVI:** 220

Wallas, Graham, **Supp. I Part 2:** 643

"Walled City" (Oates), **Supp. II Part 2:** 524

Wallenstein, Anna. *See* Weinstein, Mrs. Max (Anna Wallenstein)

Waller, Edmund, **III:** 463

Waller, Fats, **IV:** 263

Waller, Nicole, **Supp. XXII:** 78

"Wallet, The" (Rash), **Supp. XXVII:** 222

Walling, William English, **Supp. I Part 2:** 645; **Supp. XV:** 295

"Wall of Paintings, The" (Notley), **Supp. XXII:** 230

Wall of the Sky, the Wall of the Eye, The (Lethem), **Supp. XVIII:** 139

Walls Do Not Fall, The (Doolittle), **Supp. I Part 1:** 271, 272

Walls of Jericho, The (R. Fisher), **Supp. XIX:** 65, 67, 70, **72–77**, 78

"Wall Songs" (Hogan), **Supp. IV Part 1:** 413

Wall Writing (Auster), **Supp. XII:** 23–24

Walpole, Horace, **I:** 203; **Supp. I Part 2:** 410, 714

Walpole, Hugh, **Retro. Supp. I:** 231; **Supp. XX: 232**

Walpole, Robert, **IV:** 145

Walsh, David M., **Supp. XV:** 5

Walsh, Ed, **II:** 424

Walsh, Ernest, **Supp. XXIV:** 50

Walsh, George, **Supp. IV Part 2:** 528

Walsh, John Evangelist, **Retro. Supp. III:** 95, 98

Walsh, Keenan, **Supp. XXVI:** 152

Walsh, Raoul, **Supp. XIII:** 174

Walsh, Richard J., **Supp. II Part 1:** 119, 130

Walsh, William, **Supp. IV Part 1:** 242, 243, 246, 248, 252, 254, 257; **Supp. XXVI:** 4, 9; **Supp. XXVIII:** 34

"Walt, the Wounded" (Di Piero), **Supp. XIX:** 37

"Walt and Will" (Apple), **Supp. XVII:** 6

Walter, Eugene, **Supp. XVI:** 230

Walter, Joyce, **Supp. XV:** 121

Walter, Natasha, **Supp. XXVII:** 275

Walter Benjamin at the Dairy Queen: Reflections at Sixty and Beyond (McMurtry), **Supp. V:** 232

Walters, Barbara, **Supp. XIV:** 125

Walters, Marguerite. *See* Smith, Mrs. Lamar (Marguerite Walters)

"Walter T. Carriman" (O'Hara), **III:** 368

Walton, Izaak, **Supp. I Part 2:** 422

"Walt Whitman" (Kooser), **Supp. XIX:** 118

"Walt Whitman" (Masters), **Supp. I Part 2:** 458

"Walt Whitman at Bear Mountain" (Simpson), **Supp. IX:** 265

Walt Whitman Bathing (Wagoner), **Supp. IX: 331–332**

Walt Whitman Handbook (Allen), **IV:** 352

Walt Whitman Reconsidered (Chase), **IV:** 352

"Waltz, The" (Parker), **Supp. IX:** 204

"Waltzer in the House, The" (Kunitz), **Supp. III Part 1:** 258

Waltzing Matilda (Notley), **Supp. XXII:** 229–230

"Waltzing Matilda" (Notley), **Supp. XXII:** 230

Waltzing the Magpies: A Year in Australia (Pickering), **Supp. XXI:** 199, 200

Waltzing Through the Endtime (Bottoms), **Supp. XXVIII:** 29, 30–31

Walzer, Kevin, **Supp. XII:** 202; **Supp. XV:** 118; **Supp. XVIII:** 174

Wambaugh, Joseph, **Supp. X:** 5; **Supp. XXI:** 67

Wampeters, Foma, & Granfalloons (Vonnegut), **Supp. II Part 2:** 758, 759–760, 776, 779

Wand, David Hsin-fu, **Supp. X:** 292

"Wanderer, The" (W. C. Williams), **Retro. Supp. I:** 414, 421

Wanderer, The: His Parables and His Sayings (Gibran), **Supp. XX: 116, 123–124**

"Wanderers, The" (Welty), **IV:** 273–274

"Wandering Jew, The" (Robinson), **III:** 505, 516–517

Wanderings of Oisin (Yeats), **Supp. I Part 1:** 79

Wandering Through Winter (Teale), **Supp. XXVIII:** 243, 249, 254

Wang, Dorothy, **Supp. X:** 289

Wang Wei, **Supp. XV:** 47

Waniek, Marilyn Nelson, **Supp. IV Part 1:** 244. *See also* Nelson, Marilyn

Wanking 'Tards (Silver), **Supp. XXIV:** 265

"Wan Lee, the Pagan" (Harte), **Supp. II Part 1:** 351

"Want, The" (Olds), **Supp. X:** 210

Want Bone, The (Pinsky), **Supp. VI:** 236–237, 244–245, 247

"Wanted: An Ontological Critic" (Ransom), **III:** 498

"Wanting to Die" (Sexton), **Supp. II Part 2:** 684, 686; **Supp. XIV:** 132

"Wants" (Paley), **Supp. VI:** 219

Waples, Dorothy, **I:** 348

Wapshot Chronicle, The (Cheever), **Supp. I Part 1:** 174, 177–180, 181, 196

Wapshot Scandal, The (Cheever), **Supp. I Part 1:** 180–184, 187, 191, 196

"War" (Findley), **Supp. XX: 49**

"War" (H. Johnson), **Supp. XXVI:** 173

"War" (Jin), **Supp. XVIII:** 93

"War" (Kingston), **Supp. V:** 169

"War" (Simic), **Supp. VIII:** 282

"War, Response, and Contradiction" (Burke), **I:** 283

"War and Peace" (Sanders), **Supp. XVI:** 277

War and Peace (Tolstoy), **I:** 6, 7; **II:** 191, 205, 291; **IV:** 446; **Supp. V:** 277; **Supp. XI:** 68; **Supp. XIV:** 97; **Supp. XXIII:** 11

War and Remembrance (miniseries), **Supp. XXV:** 265

War and Remembrance (Wouk), **Supp. XX: 243; Supp. XXV:** 253, 254, 257, 258, 264–265

"War and the Small Nations" (Gibran), **Supp. XX: 127**

War and War (F. Barthelme), **Supp. XI:** 25

"War Between Men and Women, The" (Thurber), **Supp. I Part 2:** 615

"War Bride"(Prouty), **Supp. XXVIII:** 180

War Bulletins (Lindsay), **Supp. I Part 2:** 378–379

Ward, Aileen, **II:** 531

Ward, Artemus (pseudonym). *See* Browne, Charles Farrar

Ward, Cynthia, **Retro. Supp. III:** 138

Ward, Douglas Turner, **Supp. IV Part 1:** 362

Ward, Geoff, **Supp. XXIII:** 218

Ward, Henry, **Supp. I Part 2:** 588

Ward, Mrs. Humphry, **II:** 338

Ward, Leo R., **Supp. VIII:** 124

Ward, Lester F., **Supp. I Part 2:** 640; **Supp. XI:** 202, 203

Ward, Lynn, **I:** 31

Ward, Nathaniel, **Retro. Supp. III:** 4; **Supp. I Part 1:** 99, 102, 111, 116

Ward, Susan, **Supp. XXIII:** 146

Ward, Theodora, **I:** 470; **Retro. Supp. I:** 28

Ward, William Hayes, **Supp. I Part 1:** 371

"War Debt, A" (Jewett), **Retro. Supp. II:** 138, 141

"War Diary" (Boyce), **Supp. XVII:** 104; **Supp. XXI:** 6

"War Diary, A" (Bourne), **I:** 229

War Dispatches of Stephen Crane, The (Crane), **I:** 422

"Ward Line, The" (Morris), **III:** 220

Ware, Amy, **Supp. XXVI:** 113

Warfel, Harry R., **Supp. I Part 1:** 366

War Games (Morris), **III:** 238

War Goes On, The (Asch), **Supp. XXIII:** 6

"Warhol / Blue Jackie"(Balakian), **Supp. XXIII:** 32

War in Heaven, The (Shepard and Chaikin), **Supp. III Part 2:** 433

War Is Kind (S. Crane), **I:** 409; **III:** 585

"War Is Kind" (S. Crane), **I:** 419; **Supp. XXVI:** 173

Warlock (Harrison), **Supp. VIII:** 45, **46**

Warm as Wool (Sanders), **Supp. XVI:** 269

"Warming" (Trethewey), **Supp. XXI:** 245

Warner, Anna, **Supp. XVIII:** 258–275

Warner, Charles Dudley, **II:** 405; **IV:** 198; **Retro. Supp. III:** 262; **Supp. XXVIII:** 113, 227

Warner, Jack, **Supp. XII:** 160–161; **Supp. XVIII:** 249; **Supp. XXVII:** 92

Warner, John R., **III:** 193

Warner, Oliver, **I:** 548

Warner, Susan, **Retro. Supp. I:** 246; **Supp. XV:** 275; **Supp. XVIII:** 257–275

Warner, Sylvia Townsend, **Supp. VIII:** 151, 155, 164, 171

Warner, W. Lloyd, **III:** 60

Warner Family and the Warner Books, The (Baker), **Supp. XVIII:** 259, 267

"Warning" (Hughes), **Supp. I Part 1:** 343

"Warning" (Pound), **III:** 474

"Warning, A" (Howard), **Supp. XXVII:** 118

"Warning, The" (Creeley), **Supp. IV Part 1:** 150

"Warning, The" (Longfellow), **II:** 498

Warning Hill (Marquand), **III:** 55–56, 60, 68

"War of Eyes, A" (Coleman), **Supp. XI:** 93–94

War of Eyes and Other Stories, A (Coleman), **Supp. XI:** 91–92

War of the Classes (London), **II:** 466

War of the Foxes (Siken), **Supp. XXVIII:** 195, 196, 199, 200–202

"War of the Foxes"(Siken), **Supp. XXVIII:** 201, 202

"War of the Wall, The" (Bambara), **Supp. XI:** 15–16

"War of Vaslav Nijinsky, The" (Bidart), **Supp. XV:** 21–22, **27–29**

Warp (Grossman), **Supp. XXV:** 64, 65–66

"War Poems" (Sandburg), **III:** 581

Warren, Austin, **I:** 265, 268, 271; **Supp. I Part 2:** 423

Warren, David, **Supp. XXIV:** 269

Warren, Earl, **III:** 581

Warren, Gabriel, **IV:** 244

Warren, Mercy Otis, **Supp. XV:** 230

Warren, Patricia Nell, **Supp. XX:** 259–276

Warren, Robert Penn, **I:** 190, 211, 517; **II:** 57, 217, 228, 253; **III:** 134, 310, 382–383, 454, 482, 485, 490, 496, 497; **IV:** 121, 122, 123, 125, 126, **236–259**, 261, 262, 279, 340–341, 458; **Retro. Supp. I:** 40, 41, 73, 90; **Retro. Supp. II:** 220, 235; **Supp. I Part 1:** 359, 371; **Supp. I Part 2:** 386, 423; **Supp. II Part 1:** 139; **Supp. III Part 2:** 542; **Supp. IX:** 257; **Supp. V:** 261, 316, 318, 319, 333; **Supp. VIII:** 126, 176; **Supp. X:** 1, 25, 26; **Supp. XI:** 315; **Supp. XII:** 254, 255; **Supp. XIV:** 1, 2, 3, 4, 11, 14, 15; **Supp. XIX:** 246; **Supp. XVIII:** 77, 78–79; **Supp. XXI:** 256; **Supp. XXVI:** 63, 67, 78; **Supp. XXVIII:** 2, 22

Warren, Mrs. Robert Penn (Eleanor Clark), **IV:** 244

Warren, Rosanna, **IV:** 244; **Supp. XIX:** 34; **Supp. XV:** 251, 261, 262, 263

Warren, Vincent, **Supp. XXIII:** 218, 219

Warrington Poems, The (Ríos), **Supp. IV Part 2:** 540

Warrior, Robert Allen, **Supp. IV Part 1:** 329

"Warrior, The" (Gunn Allen), **Supp. IV Part 1:** 326

"Warrior: 5th Grade" (Olds), **Supp. X:** 214

"Warrior Road" (Harjo), **Supp. XII:** 217

"Warrior's Daughter, A" (Zitkala-Ša), **Supp. XXV:** 274, 275, 282

Wars, The (Findley), **Supp. XX:** 53–54

Warsh, Lewis, **Supp. XXIV:** 41

Warshavsky, Isaac (pseudonym). *See* Singer, Isaac Bashevis

Warshow, Robert, **Supp. I Part 1:** 51

Wars I Have Seen (Stein), **IV:** 27, 36, 477

Wartime (Fussell), **Supp. V:** 241

War Trash (Jin), **Supp. XVIII:** 89, **100–101**

"War Widow, The" (Frederic), **II:** 135–136

"Was" (Creeley), **Supp. IV Part 1:** 155

"Was" (Faulkner), **II:** 71

"Was Blind but Now"(Lea), **Supp. XXVIII:** 139–140

"Wash" (Faulkner), **II:** 72; **Retro. Supp. III:** 84

Wash, Richard, **Supp. XII:** 14

"Washboard Wizard" (Nelson), **Supp. XVIII:** 182

Washburn, Keith, **Supp. XXVI:** 148–149

"Washed in the Rain" (Fante), **Supp. XI:** 165

"Washerwoman's Day, The"(Arnow), **Supp. XXVIII:** 2

"Washing of Hands, A" (Kooser), **Supp. XIX:** 115

Washington, Booker T., **Supp. I Part 2:** 393; **Supp. II Part 1:** 157, 160, 167, 168, 171, 225; **Supp. XIV:** 198, 199, 201; **Supp. XVIII:** 121–122

Washington, D.C. (Vidal), **Supp. IV Part 2:** 677, 684, 686–687, 690

"Washington, D.C. Journal" (Brainard), **Supp. XXVII:** 27

Washington, George, **I:** 453; **II:** 313–314; **Supp. I Part 2:** 399, 485, 508, 509, 511, 513, 517, 518, 520, 599

Washington, Mary Helen, **Supp. XVIII:** 119, 284

Washington, Teresa, **Retro. Supp. III:** 130

Washington and His Generals (Lippard), **Supp. XXIII:** 178, **185–186,** 187

Washington Crossing the Delaware (Rivers), **Supp. XV:** 186

Washington Post Book World (Lesser), **Supp. IV Part 2:** 453; **Supp. VIII:** 80, 84, 241; **Supp. X:** 282

Washington Square (James), **II:** 327, 328; **Retro. Supp. I:** 215, 220, **222–223**

"Washington Square, 1946" (Ozick), **Supp. V:** 272

Washington Square Ensemble, The (Bell), **Supp. X:** 1, **3–4**

"Washman"(P. Benedict), **Supp. XXIII:** 40

"Was Lowell an Historical Critic?" (Altick), **Supp. I Part 2:** 423

Wasserman, Earl R., **Supp. I Part 2:** 439, 440

Wasserman, Jakob, **Supp. I Part 2:** 669

Wasserstein, Wendy, **Retro. Supp. III:** 318; **Supp. IV Part 1:** 309; **Supp. XV: 319–336; Supp. XXIV:** 116, 117, 119, 128

Wasson, Ben, **Retro. Supp. I:** 79, 83

"Waste Carpet, The" (Matthews), **Supp. IX: 158–159**

Waste Land, The (T. S. Eliot), **I:** 107, 266, 298, 395, 396, 482, 570–571, 572, 574–575, 577–578, 580, 581, 584, 585, 586, 587; **III:** 6–8, 12, 196, 277–278, 453, 471, 492, 586; **IV:** 122, 123, 124, 140, 418, 419, 420; **Retro. Supp. I:** 51, 60, **60–62,** 63, 64, 66, 210, 290, 291, 299, 311, 420, 427; **Retro. Supp. II:** 85, 121, 190; **Retro. Supp. III:** 47, 50–51, 58, 59, 62–65, 66, 67, 101; **Supp. I Part 1:** 272; **Supp. I Part 2:** 439, 455, 614; **Supp. II Part 1:** 4, 5, 11, 96; **Supp. III Part 1:** 9, 10, 41, 63, 105; **Supp. IV Part 1:** 47, 284; **Supp. IX:** 158, 305; **Supp. V:** 338; **Supp. X:** 125; **Supp. XIII:** 341–342, 344, 346; **Supp. XIV:** 6, 284; **Supp. XIX:** 288; **Supp. XV:** 21, 181, 261, 306; **Supp. XVI:** 204; **Supp. XVII:** 140–141, 144, 227; **Supp. XVIII:** 78, 79–80; **Supp. XXIII:** 23, 25, 79, 165; **Supp. XXIV:** 140; **Supp. XXVII:** 287

"Waste Land, The": A Facsimile and Transcript of the Original Drafts Including the Annotations of Ezra Pound (Eliot, ed.), **Retro. Supp. I:** 58

Waste Land and Other Poems, The (T. S. Eliot), **Supp. XV:** 305

Wat, Alexander, **Supp. XVI:** 155, 161

Watch, The (Bass), **Supp. XVI: 16–17**

"Watch, The, —" (Bass), **Supp. XVI:** 17

Watch and Ward (James), **II:** 323; **Retro. Supp. I:** 218, **219,** 220

"Watcher" (Trethewey), **Supp. XXI:** 247

"Watcher, The" (R. Bly), **Supp. IV Part 1:** 71

"Watcher by the Dead, A" (Bierce), **I:** 203

Watchfires (Auchincloss), **Supp. IV Part 1:** 23

"Watching Crow, Looking toward the Manzano Mountains" (Harjo), **Supp. XII:** 219

"Watching Gators at Ray Boone's Reptile Farm"(Bottoms), **Supp. XXVIII:** 24

"Watching the Oregon Whale" (A. Finch), **Supp. XVII:** 77

"Watching the Sunset" (Coleman), **Supp. XI:** 92

"Watching the Vulture at the Road Kill" (Stallings), **Supp. XXV:** 230

Watch on the Rhine (Hellman), **Supp. I Part 1:** 276, 278, 279–281, 283–284; **Supp. IV Part 1:** 83

"Watch Out for Landmines" (Biss), **Supp. XXVI:** 47, 51, 56
"Water" (Emerson), **II:** 19
"Water" (Komunyakaa), **Supp. XIII:** 132
"Water" (R. Lowell), **II:** 550
"Waterbird" (Swenson), **Supp. IV Part 2:** 651
"Water Borders" (Dillard), **Supp. VI:** 27
"Water Buffalo" (Komunyakaa), **Supp. XIII:** 122
"Watercolor of Grantchester Meadows" (Plath), **Supp. I Part 2:** 537
Water Cure, The (Everett), **Supp. XVIII: 64–66**
"Water Drum"(Kenny), **Supp. XXIII:** 144
"Waterfall, The" (Clampitt), **Supp. IX:** 44
Waterfront (Schulberg), **Supp. XVIII: 251–252**
"Water Hose Is on Fire, The" (Simic), **Supp. XV:** 185
Waterhouse, Keith, **Supp. VIII:** 124
"Waterlily Fire" (Rukeyser), **Supp. VI:** 285, 286
Waterlily Fire: Poems 1935–1962 (Rukeyser), **Supp. VI:** 274, 283, 285
Watermark (Brodsky), **Supp. VIII:** 29
Water-Method Man, The (Irving), **Supp. VI:** 163, **167–179,** 180
Water Music (Boyle), **Supp. VIII:** 1, 3–5, 8, 14; **Supp. XX: 20–22**
"Water Music for the Progress of Love in a Life-Raft Down the Sammamish Slough" (Wagoner), **Supp. IX:** 326
"Water People" (Burke), **Supp. XIV:** 21
"Water Picture" (Swenson), **Supp. IV Part 2:** 641
"Water Quilt" (Rash), **Supp. XXVII:** 222
"Water Rising" (Hogan), **Supp. IV Part 1:** 400
Waters, Ethel, **II:** 587
Waters, Frank, **Supp. X:** 124
Waters, Muddy, **Supp. VIII:** 345
Watershed (Everett), **Supp. XVIII: 58–59,** 64
"Watershed" (Kingsolver), **Supp. VII:** 208
"Watershed" (Warren), **IV:** 239
"Watershed, The" (Auden), **Supp. II Part 1:** 5
Waters of Kronos, The (Richter), **Supp. XVIII:** 207, 208, **218–219,** 220
Waters of Siloe, The (Merton), **Supp. VIII:** 196, 208
Waterston, Sam, **Supp. IX:** 253
Water Street (Merrill), **Supp. III Part 1:** 321–323
"Water Walker" (Wilbur), **Supp. III Part 2:** 548, 560
Water-Witch, The (Cooper), **I:** 342–343
"Water Witch"(P. Benedict), **Supp. XXIII:** 38
Waterworks, The (Doctorow), **Supp. IV Part 1:** 218, 222, 223, 231–233, 234
"Water Works, The" (Doctorow), **Supp. IV Part 1:** 234
Watkin, E. I., **Retro. Supp. II:** 187
Watkins, Floyd C., **IV:** 452
Watkins, James T., **I:** 193, 194

Watkins, Maureen, **Supp. XVI:** 188
Watkins, Mel, **Supp. X:** 330; **Supp. XIII:** 246
Watman, Max, **Supp. XX:** 92
Watrous, Peter, **Supp. VIII:** 79
Watson, Brook, **Supp. XX:** 284
Watson, Burton, **Supp. XV:** 47
Watson, James Sibley, Jr., **I:** 261
Watson, Jay, **Supp. XVIII:** 195; **Supp. XXI:** 46
Watson, J. B., **II:** 361
Watson, Julia, **Supp. XXV:** 8
Watson, Richard, **Supp. I Part 2:** 516, 517
Watson, William, **II:** 114
Watsonville: Some Place Not Here (Moraga), **Supp. XXIII:** 195, 196, 202, 203
Watt, Ian, **Supp. VIII:** 4
Watteau, Jean Antoine, **III:** 275; **IV:** 79
Watts, Emily Stipes, **Supp. I Part 1:** 115
Waugh, Arthur, **Supp. XXIV:** 30
Waugh, Evelyn, **I:** 480; **III:** 281; **Supp. I Part 2:** 607; **Supp. IV Part 2:** 688; **Supp. XI:** 305, 306; **Supp. XIX:** 131; **Supp. XXV:** 70
Waugh, Robert H., **Supp. XXV:** 123
"Wave" (Snyder), **Supp. VIII:** 299
Wave, A (Ashbery), **Supp. III Part 1:** 1, 4, 24–26
"Wave, A" (Ashbery), **Supp. III Part 1:** 9, 19, 24–25
"Wave, The" (MacLeish), **III:** 19
"Wave, The" (Untermeyer), **Supp. XV:** 300
Wave Amplitude in the Mona Passage (Schott), **Supp. XXIII: 242–243**
"Wavemaker Falters, The" (Saunders), **Supp. XIX:** 225
"Waxwings" (Francis), **Supp. IX:** 82
Way, The (Steiner and Witt, eds.), **Supp. IV Part 2:** 505
"Way Down, The" (Kunitz), **Supp. III Part 1:** 263
"Way It Is, The" (Ellison), **Supp. II Part 1:** 245
"Way It Is, The" (Jones), **Supp. XI:** 229
Way It Is, The (Stafford), **Supp. XIII:** 274
"Way It Is, The" (Strand), **Supp. IV Part 2:** 627
"Wayland" (Sanders), **Supp. XVI:** 275
Wayne, John, **Supp. IV Part 1:** 200
Way of Chuang-Tzu, The (Merton), **Supp. VIII:** 208
"Way of Exchange in James Dickey's Poetry, The" (Weatherby), **Supp. IV Part 1:** 175
Way of Life According to Laotzu, The (Bynner), **Supp. XV:** 46, 48
Way Out, A (Frost), **Retro. Supp. I:** 133; **Retro. Supp. III:** 100
Wayside Motor Inn, The (Gurney), **Supp. V:** 96, 105, 109
"Ways of Breaking: Lynda Hull's 'Ornithology' " (Jauss), **Supp. XXI:** 139
"Ways of Talking" (Jin), **Supp. XVIII:** 93
Ways of the Hour, The (Cooper), **I:** 354

Ways of White Folks, The (Hughes), **Retro. Supp. I:** 203, 204; **Supp. I Part 1:** 329, 330, 332
Way Some People Die, The (Macdonald), **Supp. IV Part 2:** 470, 471, 472, 474
Way Some People Live, The (Cheever), **Supp. I Part 1:** 175
"Way the Cards Fall, The" (Komunyakaa), **Supp. XIII:** 117
"Way the Luck Runs, The" (Wolfert), **Supp. XXI:** 265
"Way Things Are, The" (Turow, unpub.), **Supp. XVII:** 215, 218
Way to Rainy Mountain, The (Momaday), **Supp. IV Part 2:** 485–486, 487–489, 491, 493
Way to Wealth, The (Franklin), **II:** 101–102, 110; **Supp. XX: 27**
Wayward and the Seeking, The: A Collection of Writings by Jean Toomer (Toomer), **Supp. III Part 2:** 478–481, 484, 487
Wayward Bus, The (Steinbeck), **IV:** 51, 64–65
"Way We Live Now, The" (Sontag), **Supp. III Part 2:** 467–468
"Way You'll Never Be, A" (Hemingway), **II:** 249
"W. D. Sees Himself Animated" (Snodgrass), **Supp. VI:** 327
"W. D. Sits in Kafka's Chair and Is Interrogated Concerning the Assumed Death of Cock Robin" (Snodgrass), **Supp. VI:** 319
"W. D. Tries to Warn Cock Robin" (Snodgrass), **Supp. VI:** 319
"We" (Alexander), **Supp. XVIII:** 185
Weaks, Mary Louise, **Supp. X:** 5
Weales, Gerald, **II:** 602
We Almost Disappear (Bottoms), **Supp. XXVIII:** 31–33
"Wealth," from *Conduct of Life, The* (Emerson), **II:** 2, 3–4
"Wealth," from *English Traits* (Emerson), **II:** 6
Wealth of Nations, The (A. Smith), **II:** 109
"We Are Looking at You, Agnes" (Caldwell), **I:** 309
We Are Not Afraid (Hickam), **Supp. XXVII:** 99, 100
We Are Not in This Together (Kittredge), **Supp. XXVI:** 182, 183, 184
We Are Still Married: Stories and Letters (Keillor), **Supp. XVI:** 176, 177
"We Are the Crazy Lady and Other Feisty Feminist Fables" (Ozick), **Supp. V:** 259
Weary Blues, The (Hughes), **Retro. Supp. I:** 195, 197, 198, 199, 200, 203, 205; **Supp. I Part 1:** 325
"Weary Blues, The" (Hughes), **Retro. Supp. I:** 198, 199; **Supp. I Part 1:** 324, 325
"Weary Kingdom" (Irving), **Supp. VI:** 163
Weasels and Wisemen: Ethics and Ethnicity in the Work of David Mamet (Kane), **Supp. XIV:** 250

Weather and the Women Treat Me Fair, The (Everett), **Supp. XVIII:** 66

Weatherby, H. L., **Supp. IV Part 1:** 175

Weather Central (Kooser), **Supp. XIX:** 116, **123–125**

Weatherford, Carole Boston, **Supp. XXVIII:** 280, 286, 287

"Weathering Out" (Dove), **Supp. IV Part 1:** 248

"Weather Report" (Huddle), **Supp. XXVI:** 152

Weathers. Glenda, **Retro. Supp. III:** 139–140

"Weather Within, The" (M. F. K. Fisher), **Supp. XVII:** 88, 91

Weaver, Harriet, **III:** 471

Weaver, James, **Supp. XVIII:** 72

Weaver, Michael, **Supp. XVIII:** 176, 177

Weaver, Mike, **Retro. Supp. I:** 430

Weaver, Raymond, **Retro. Supp. III:** 162

Weaver, Robert, **Supp. XXVII:** 181

Weaver, Will, **Supp. XVI:** 39

"Weaving" (Larcom), **Supp. XIII:** 142, **Supp. XIII:** 144–145, 150, 151

"Web" (Oliver), **Supp. VII:** 236

Web and the Rock, The (Wolfe), **IV:** 451, 455, 457, 459–460, 462, 464, 467, 468

Webb, Beatrice, **Supp. I Part 1:** 5

Webb, Mary, **I:** 226

Webb, Phyllis, **Supp. XX:** 56

Webb, Sidney, **Supp. I Part 1:** 5

Webb, W. P., **Supp. V:** 225

Webber, A. R. F., **Supp. XXI:** 160

Weber, Brom, **I:** 383, 386

Weber, Carl, **Supp. IX:** 133, 138, 141

Weber, Max, **I:** 498; **Supp. I Part 2:** 637, 648

Weber, Sarah, **Supp. I Part 1:** 2

Weberman, A. J., **Supp. XVIII:** 27

Web of Earth, The (Wolfe), **IV:** 451–452, 456, 458, 464, 465

Web of Iniquity, The (Nickerson), **Supp. XXV:** 200

"Web of Life, The" (Nemerov), **III:** 282

Webster, Brenda, **Supp. XVI:** 157, 161

Webster, Daniel, **II:** 5, 9; **Supp. I Part 2:** 659, 687, 689, 690

Webster, John, **I:** 384; **Supp. I Part 2:** 422

Webster, Noah, **Supp. I Part 2:** 660; **Supp. II Part 1:** 77

Wector, Dixon, **II:** 103

Wedding, The (D. West), **Supp. XVIII:** 277, **287–289; Supp. XXVI:** 174

"Wedding, The" (Everwine), **Supp. XV:** 83

"Wedding, The" (Major), **Supp. XXII:** 185

Wedding, The (television miniseries), **Supp. XVIII:** 277, 289

"Wedding Cake" (Nye), **Supp. XIII:** 283

"Wedding Dance, The" (Di Piero), **Supp. XIX:** 47

"Wedding Day" (Boyle), **Supp. XXIV:** 56–57

Wedding Day and Other Stories (Boyle), **Supp. XXIV: 56–57**

"Wedding in Brownsville, A" (Singer), **IV:** 15

Wedding in Hell, A (Simic), **Supp. VIII:** 280, **282**

"Wedding of Henry Markowitz, The" (Goodman), **Supp. XXVI:** 121–122

"Wedding of the Rose and Lotus, The" (Lindsay), **Supp. I Part 2:** 387

"Wedding Supper, The" (Rowson), **Supp. XV:** 243

"Wedding Toast, A" (Wilbur), **Supp. III Part 2:** 561

Wedekind, Frank, **III:** 398; **Supp. XX:** 85; **Supp. XXII:** 23

Wedge, The (W. C. Williams), **Retro. Supp. I:** 424

"We Didn't"(Dybek), **Supp. XXIII:** 77–78

"Wednesday at the Waldorf" (Swenson), **Supp. IV Part 2:** 647

We Don't Live Here Anymore (Dubus), **Supp. XXIV:** 97

"We Don't Live Here Anymore" (Dubus), **Supp. VII:** 78–79, 85

"Weed" (McCarriston), **Supp. XIV:** 259, 273

"Weed, The" (Bishop), **Supp. I Part 1:** 80, 88–89

"Weed, The" (Taggard), **Supp. XXII:** 284

Weedkiller's Daughter, The (Arnow), **Supp. XXVIII:** 3, 11–13, 14

"Weeds, The" (McCarthy), **II:** 566

"Weekend" (Beattie), **Supp. V:** 27

"Weekend" (Hempel), **Supp. XXI:** 124

Weekend, The (Cameron), **Supp. XII:** 80, 81, **86–88**

"Weekend at Ellerslie, A" (Wilson), **IV:** 431

Weekend Edition (National Public Radio), **Supp. IX:** 299; **Supp. XVII:** 240, 242

Weekend in Dinlock (Sigal), **Supp. XXIII:** 166

"Week in the Word, A" (Hampl), **Supp. XXII:** 85

Week on the Concord and Merrimack Rivers, A (Thoreau), **IV:** 168, 169, 177, 182–183; **Supp. I Part 2:** 420; **Supp. XIV:** 227; **Supp. XXVIII:** 251

Weeks, Edward, **III:** 64

Weeks, Jerome, **Supp. VIII:** 76

"Weeping Burgher" (Stevens), **IV:** 77

"Weeping Women" (Levertov), **Supp. III Part 1:** 282

We Fished All Night (W. Motley), **Supp. XVII:** 155–158, 159, 160

We Fly Away (Francis), **Supp. IX:** 79–80, 84

" ' We Had Some Good Times Anyway' " (Gansworth), **Supp. XXVI:** 114

We Happy Few (Hinojosa), **Supp. XIX:** 99, 111–112

We Have Always Lived in the Castle (Jackson), **Supp. IX:** 121, 126, **127–128**

"We Have Our Arts So We Won't Die of Truth" (Bradbury), **Supp. IV Part 1:** 105

We Have Tomorrow (Bontemps), **Supp. XXII:** 6, 12

Weich, Dave, **Supp. XII:** 321; **Supp. XVIII:** 91

Weidman, Jerome, **Supp. XXVII:** 142

"Weighing In" (Espaillat), **Supp. XXI:** 111

"Weight" (Wideman), **Supp. X:** 321

"Weights" (C. Baxter), **Supp. XVII:** 16

Weigl, Bruce, **Supp. VIII:** 269, 274; **Supp. XIX: 273–290; Supp. XV:** 342

Weik, Alexa, **Supp. XXIV:** 64

Weil, Dorothy, **Supp. XV:** 231

Weil, James L., **Supp. XXI:** 23, 31

Weil, Robert, **Supp. IX:** 236

Weil, Simone, **I:** 298; **Supp. XV:** 259; **Supp. XXII:** 93; **Supp. XXVI:** 234

Weiland (C. B. Brown), **Supp. XIII:** 100

Weinauer, Ellen, **Supp. XV:** 270, 284

Weinberger, Eliot, **Supp. IV Part 1:** 66; **Supp. VIII:** 290, 292; **Supp. XVI:** 284

Weinberger, Eric, **Supp. XXII:** 264

Weinfield, Henry, **Supp. XXI:** 24, 28, 33

Weininger, Otto, **Retro. Supp. I:** 416

Weinraub, Judith, **Supp. XXI:** 39

Weinreb, Mindy, **Supp. X:** 24

Weinreich, Regina, **Supp. XIV:** 22

Weinstein, Cindy, **Supp. XVIII:** 261

Weinstein, Hinda, **IV:** 285

Weinstein, Max, **IV:** 285

Weinstein, Mrs. Max (Anna Wallenstein), **IV:** 285, 287

Weinstein, Nathan. *See* West, Nathanael

Weinstein, Selma, **Supp. XXI:** 170

Weir, Sybil, **Supp. XXIV:** 20

Weisheit, Rabbi, **IV:** 76

Weismuller, Johnny, **Supp. X:** 264; **Supp. XX: 18**

Weiss, David, **Supp. XVI:** 55

Weiss, Jane, **Supp. XVIII:** 267, 269

Weiss, Peter, **IV:** 117

Weiss, Theodore, **Supp. IV Part 2:** 440; **Supp. IX:** 96

Weissberg, Liliane, **Retro. Supp. III:** 237

Weissleder, Paul, **Supp. XXII:** 283

Weist, Dianne, **Supp. X:** 80

Weithas, Art, **Supp. XI:** 231

Welch, Dave, **Supp. XXI:** 118

Welch, Don, **Supp. XIX:** 119

Welch, James, **Supp. IV Part 1:** 404; **Supp. IV Part 2:** 503, 513, 557, 562; **Supp. XXIV:** 257; **Supp. XXVI:** 186, 188

Welch, Lew, **Supp. V:** 170; **Supp. VIII:** 303; **Supp. XXII:** 276

"Welcome from War" (Rukeyser), **Supp. VI:** 286

"Welcome Morning" (Sexton), **Supp. II Part 2:** 696

"Welcome the Wrath" (Kunitz), **Supp. III Part 1:** 261

Welcome to Hard Times (Doctorow), **Supp. IV Part 1:** 218, 219–220, 222, 224, 230, 238

Welcome to Hard Times (film), **Supp. IV Part 1:** 236

"Welcome to New Dork" (Leonard), **Supp. XVIII:** 148

Welcome to Our City (Wolfe), **IV:** 461

Welcome to the Castle (Hayes), **Supp. XXVI:** 144

Welcome to the Monkey House (Vonnegut), **Supp. II Part 2:** 758

Welcome to the Moon (Shanley), **Supp. XIV:** 318

Welcome to the Moon and Other Plays (Shanley), **Supp. XIV:** 315, **316–319**

Weld, Theodore, **Supp. I Part 2:** 587, 588

Weld, Tuesday, **Supp. XI:** 306

Welded (O'Neill), **III:** 390; **Supp. XXII:** 24

"Welfare Worker, Disenchanted, Contemplates Friday Afternoon, The" (Trethewey), **Supp. XXI:** 246

"Well, Everything"(Lea), **Supp. XXVIII:** 137

"Well, The" (Momaday), **Supp. IV Part 2:** 483

"Well Dressed Man with a Beard, The" (Stevens), **Retro. Supp. I:** 297

Wellek, René, **I:** 253, 261, 282; **II:** 320; **Supp. XIV:** 12, 14

Weller, George, **III:** 322

Welles, Gideon, **Supp. I Part 2:** 484

Welles, Orson, **IV:** 476; **Supp. I Part 1:** 67; **Supp. IV Part 1:** 82, 83; **Supp. V:** 251; **Supp. VIII:** 46; **Supp. XI:** 169, 307

"Wellfleet Whale, The" (Kunitz), **Supp. III Part 1:** 263, 269

Wellfleet Whale and Companion Poems, The (Kunitz), **Supp. III Part 1:** 263

Wellink, Yvonne, **Supp. XVIII:** 257

Wellman, Flora, **II:** 463–464, 465

Wellman, Rita, **Supp. XXV:** 20

"Well Rising, The" (Stafford), **Supp. XI:** 318

Wells, Carolyn, **Supp. XXVI: 271–287**

Wells, H. G., **I:** 103, 226, 241, 243, 253, 405, 409, 415; **II:** 82, 144, 276, 337, 338, 458; **III:** 456; **IV:** 340, 455; **Retro. Supp. I:** 100, 228, 231; **Supp. XVI:** 190; **Supp. XXI:** 8

Wellspring, The (Olds), **Supp. X: 211–212**

Well Wrought Urn, The: Studies in the Structure of Poetry (Brooks), **Supp. XIV:** 1, **8–9,** 14, 15, 16

Welsh, Mary, **Supp. XIX:** 248. *See also* Hemingway, Mrs. Ernest (Mary Welsh)

Welty, Eudora, **II:** 194, 217, 606; **IV: 260–284; Retro. Supp. I:** 339–358; **Retro. Supp. II:** 235; **Retro. Supp. III:** 36; **Supp. IV Part 2:** 474; **Supp. V:** 59, 315, 336; **Supp. VIII:** 94, 151, 171; **Supp. X:** 42, 290; **Supp. XII:** 310, 322; **Supp. XIV:** 3; **Supp. XV:** 338; **Supp. XXIV:** 223; **Supp. XXVI:** 152; **Supp. XXVII:** 216, 218, 267

Welty, Eurora, **Supp. XIX:** 151

Weltzien, O. Alan, **Supp. XVI:** 20–21, 28

"We miss Her, not because We see—" (Dickinson), **Retro. Supp. I:** 46

We Must Dance My Darlings (Trilling), **Supp. I Part 1:** 297

Wendell, Barrett, **III:** 507; **Supp. I Part 2:** 414; **Supp. XIV:** 197

Wendell, Sarah. *See* Holmes, Mrs. Abiel (Sarah Wendell)

Wendy Wasserstein: A Casebook (Barnett), **Supp. XV:** 323, 330

"Wendy Wasserstein's Three Sisters: Squandered Privilege" (Brewer), **Supp. XV:** 330

Wenner, Jann S., **Supp. XXIV:** 280, 283

Wept of Wish-ton-Wish, The (Cooper), **I:** 339, 342, 350

Werbe, Peter, **Supp. XIII:** 236

"We Real Cool" (Brooks), **Supp. III Part 1:** 80

"We're All Pharaohs When We Die" (Gallagher), **Supp. XXIV:** 170

We're Back! A Dinosaur's Story (screenplay, Shanley), **Supp. XIV:** 316

"We're Friends Again" (O'Hara), **III:** 372–373

"Were the Whole Realm of Nature Mine" (Watts), **I:** 458

Werewolf (M. Sommers), **Supp. XVII:** 55

Were-Wolf, The (C. Housman), **Supp. XVII:** 55

Werewolf of Paris, The (Endore), **Supp. XVII:** 55–56

Werewolves in Their Youth (Chabon), **Supp. XI:** 66, **76–77**

Werlock, Abby, **Supp. XIII:** 293

Werthman, Michael, **Supp. V:** 115

"Wer-Trout, The" (Proulx), **Supp. VII:** 255–256

Wescott, Glenway, **I:** 288; **II:** 85; **III:** 448, 454; **Supp. VIII:** 156; **Supp. XIV:** 342; **Supp. XVI:** 195

"We Shall All Be Born Again But We Shall Not All Be Saved" (Matthews), **Supp. IX:** 162

West, Anthony, **Supp. IV Part 1:** 284

West, Benjamin, **Supp. I Part 2:** 511

West, Dorothy, **Retro. Supp. III:** 127; **Supp. XIII:** 295; **Supp. XIX:** 72; **Supp. XVIII: 277–291; Supp. XXVI:** 164, 173, 174

West, James, **II:** 562

West, M. Genevieve, **Retro. Supp. III:** 127

West, Nathanael, **I:** 97, 107, 190, 211, 298; **II:** 436; **III:** 357, 425; **IV: 285–307; Retro. Supp. II: 321–341; Supp. IV Part 1:** 203; **Supp. VIII:** 97; **Supp. XI:** 85, 105, 159, 296; **Supp. XII:** 173, 310; **Supp. XIII:** 106, 170; **Supp. XIX:** 223; **Supp. XVIII:** 251, 253, 254

West, Ray, **Supp. XV:** 142

West, Rebecca, **II:** 412, 445; **Supp. XVI:** 152, 153

Westall, Julia Elizabeth. *See* Wolfe, Mrs. William Oliver (Julia Elizabeth Westall)

"We Stand United" (Benét), **Supp. XI:** 46

"West Authentic, The: Willa Cather" (Stegner), **Supp. IV Part 2:** 608

"West Coast, The: Region with a View" (Stegner), **Supp. IV Part 2:** 608–609

"West Coast Waterfront: End of an Era" (Swados), **Supp. XIX:** 264

Westcott, Edward N., **II:** 102

"Western Association of Writers" (Chopin), **Supp. I Part 1:** 217

"Western Ballad, A" (Ginsberg), **Supp. II Part 1:** 311

Western Borders, The (Howe), **Supp. IV Part 2:** 424–425

Western Canon (Bloom), **Supp. XXV:** 251

Western Canon: The Books and Schools of the Ages (Bloom), **Supp. IX:** 146

Western Lands, The (Burroughs), **Supp. III Part 1:** 106

"Western North Carolina" (Halliday), **Supp. XIX:** 85

Western Star (Benét), **Supp. XI:** 46, 47, 57

"Westland" (C. Baxter), **Supp. XVII:** 18, 19

"West Marginal Way" (Hugo), **Supp. VI:** 131, 135

West of Eden: Writers in Hollywood, 1928–1940 (Fine), **Supp. XVIII:** 248

West of Yesterday, East of Summer: New and Selected Poems, 1973–1993 (Monette), **Supp. X:** 159

West of Your City (Stafford), **Supp. XI:** 316, **317–318,** 321, 322

Weston, Jessie L., **II:** 540; **III:** 12; **Supp. I Part 2:** 438

"West Real" (Ríos), **Supp. IV Part 2:** 539, 540

West-running Brook (Frost), **II:** 155; **Retro. Supp. I:** 136, 137; **Retro. Supp. III:** 102

"West-running Brook" (Frost), **II:** 150, 162–164; **Retro. Supp. III:** 102

"West Wall" (Merwin), **Supp. III Part 1:** 355

"Westward Beach, A" (Jeffers), **Supp. II Part 2:** 418

Westward Ho (Harrison), **Supp. VIII:** 51, **52**

Westward the Course of Empire (Leutze), **Supp. X:** 307

"Westward the Course of Empire Takes Its Way" (Wallace), **Supp. X: 307–308; Supp. XXII:** 260

"West Wind" (Oliver), **Supp. VII:** 246

"West Wind, The" (Bryant), **Supp. I Part 1:** 155

West Wind: Poems and Prose Poems (Oliver), **Supp. VII:** 243, 246–248

"We Take My Grandpa Fishing"(Bottoms), **Supp. XXVIII:** 32

"Wet Casements" (Ashbery), **Supp. III Part 1:** 18–20

We the Living (film), **Supp. IV Part 2:** 520

We the Living (Rand), **Supp. IV Part 2:** 520–521

Wetherell, Elizabeth (pseudonym). *See* Warner, Susan

Wet Parade (Sinclair), **Supp. V:** 289

Wetzsteon, Ross, **Supp. XXI:** 12

"We've Adjusted Too Well" (O'Brien), **Supp. V:** 247

Wevill, David, **Retro. Supp. II:** 247, 249

"We Wear the Mask" (Dunbar), **Supp. II Part 1:** 199, 207, 209–210

We Were Heroes: The Journal of Scott Pendleton Collins, a World War II Soldier, Normandy, France, 1944 (Myers), **Supp. XXVII:** 208

We Will Be Citizens: New Essays on Gay and Lesbian Theatre (Fischer, ed.), **Supp. XXIV:** 263

We Will Never Die (Hecht), **Supp. XXVII:** 94

Weybright, Victor, **Supp. XIII:** 172

Weyden, Rogier van der, **Supp. IV Part 1:** 284

Whalen, Marcella, **Supp. I Part 1:** 49

Whalen, Philip, **Supp. VIII:** 289; **Supp. XXII:** 226

Whalen, Terence, **Retro. Supp. III:** 237

Whalen-Bridge, John, **Retro. Supp. II:** 211–212

"Whales off Wales, The" (X. J. Kennedy), **Supp. XV:** 163

"Whales Weep" (Boyle), **Supp. XX:** 19

"Whales Weep Not!" (D. H. Lawrence), **Supp. XVII:** 77

Wharton, Edith, **I:** 12, 375; **II:** 96, 180, 183, 186, 189–190, 193, 283, 338, 444, 451; **III:** 69, 175, 576; **IV:** 8, 53, 58, **308–330; Retro. Supp. I:** 108, 232, **359–385; Retro. Supp. III: 275–293; Supp. IV Part 1:** 23, 31, 35, 36, 80, 81, 310; **Supp. IX:** 57; **Supp. XII:** 308; **Supp. XIV:** 337, 347; **Supp. XVI:** 189; **Supp. XVIII:** 278; **Supp. XX: 227, 229, 232, 239, 240; Supp. XXIII:** 275; **Supp. XXIV:** 29, 64; **Supp. XXV:** 201; **Supp. XXVI:** 145, 276; **Supp. XXVII:** 4; **Supp. XXVIII:** 112, 125

Wharton, Edward Robbins, **IV:** 310, 313–314, 319

"What" (Dunn), **Supp. XI:** 144

What a Kingdom It Was (Kinnell), **Supp. III Part 1:** 235, 238, 239

"What America Would Be Like without Blacks" (Ellison), **Retro. Supp. II:** 123

What Are Masterpieces (Stein), **IV:** 30–31

What Are Years (Moore), **III:** 208–209, 210, 215

"What Are Years?" (Moore), **III:** 211, 213

What a Way to Go (Morris), **III:** 230–232

"What a Wonder among the Instruments Is the Walloping Trombone!" (Carruth), **Supp. XVI:** 51

"What Became of the Flappers?" (Zelda Fitzgerald), **Supp. IX:** 71

"What Can I Tell My Bones?" (Roethke), **III:** 546, 549

What Century? (O'Hara), **Supp. XXIII:** 216

"What Child Is This?" (Jarman), **Supp. XVII:** 113–114, 115

"What Do I Care?" (Teasdale), **Supp. XXVII:** 284

"What Do I Care for Morning" (H. Johnson), **Supp. XXVI:** 173

"What Do We Have Here" (Carson), **Supp. XII: 101**

"What Do We See" (Rukeyser), **Supp. VI:** 282

What Do Women Want? Bread Roses Sex Power (Jong), **Supp. V:** 115, 117, 129, 130

"What Do You Do in San Francisco?" (Carver), **Supp. III Part 1:** 143

What Dreams My Come (Atherton as Frank Lin), **Supp. XXIV:** 28

What D'Ya Know for Sure (Zinberg), **Supp. XV:** 196

Whatever Happened to Gloomy Gus of the Chicago Bears? (Coover), **Supp. V:** 51, 52

Whatever Happened to Jacy Farrow? (Cleveland), **Supp. V:** 222

"What Every Boy Should Know" (Maxwell), **Supp. VIII:** 169

"What Feels Like the World" (Bausch), **Supp. VII:** 46

"What Fort Sumter Did for Me" (E. Stoddard), **Supp. XV:** 282

"What Girls Read" (Salmon), **Supp. XVIII:** 258

"What God Is Like to Him I Serve" (Bradstreet), **Supp. I Part 1:** 106–107

"What Happened Here Before" (Snyder), **Supp. VIII:** 302

"What Happened to Georgia" (Ray), **Supp. XVIII:** 194

"What Happened?" (Wakoski), **Supp. XXVIII:** 268

What Happens (Herrmann), **Supp. XXII:** 277

What Have I Ever Lost by Dying? (R. Bly), **Supp. IV Part 1:** 71–72

What Have You Lost? (Nye, ed.), **Supp. XIII:** 280

What I Believe (Asch), **Supp. XXIII:** 2

"What I Believe" (Mumford), **Supp. II Part 2:** 479

"What I Call What They Call Onanism" (Goldbarth), **Supp. XII:** 175

What I Did Last Summer (Gurney), **Supp. V:** 96, 100, 107, 108

"What if God" (Olds), **Supp. X:** 208

What I Have Done with Birds: Character Studies of Native American Birds (Stratton-Porter), **Supp. XX:** 218

"What I Have to Defend, What I Can't Bear Losing" (Stern), **Supp. IX:** 286, 287, 288, 298

"What I Knew" (Nelson), **Supp. XVIII:** 178

"What I Know about Being a Playwright" (McNally), **Supp. XIII:** 195, 207

"What I Mean" (Ortiz), **Supp. IV Part 2:** 497

"What Is an Emotion" (James), **II:** 350

What Is Art? (Tolstoy), **I:** 58

"What Is Civilization? Africa's Answer" (Du Bois), **Supp. II Part 1:** 176

"What Is College For?" (Bourne), **I:** 216

"What Is Exploitation?" (Bourne), **I:** 216

What Is Found There: Notebooks on Poetry and Politics (Rich), **Retro. Supp. III:** 241, 251; **Supp. XVII:** 74

"What Is It?" (Carver), **Supp. III Part 1:** 139

What Is Man? (Twain), **II:** 434; **IV:** 209

"What Is Man" (Twain), **Retro. Supp. III:** 269

"What Is Poetry" (Ashbery), **Supp. III Part 1:** 19

"What Is Seized" (Moore), **Supp. X:** 164, 168, 169, 172, 175

"What Is the Earth?" (Olds), **Supp. X:** 213

What Is This Jewish Heritage? (Lewisohn), **Supp. XXVIII:** 145, 150, 157, 158–159

"What Is This Poet" (Stern), **Supp. IX:** 295

What Is To Be Done? (Lenin), **Supp. XXI:** 164

"What I Think" (Hogan), **Supp. IV Part 1:** 406

What Love Comes To: New & Selected Poems (Stone), **Supp. XXVII:** 249, 257, 262

What Maisie Knew (H. James), **II:** 332; **Retro. Supp. I:** 229, **230; Supp. XVIII:** 160

What Makes Sammy Run? (NBC broadcast, Schulberg and Schulberg), **Supp. XVIII:** 254

What Makes Sammy Run (Schulberg), **Supp. XXVII:** 142

What Makes Sammy Run? (Schulberg), **Supp. XIII:** 170; **Supp. XVIII:** 241, **244–247,** 248, 249, 253

"What Makes Sammy Run?" (Schulberg), **Supp. XVIII:** 241

What Moon Drove Me to This? (Harjo), **Supp. XII: 218–220**

"What Must" (MacLeish), **III:** 18

What My Father Believed (Wrigley), **Supp. XVIII:** 298–300

"What My Father Believed" (Wrigley), **Supp. XVIII: 298–299**

What Price Hollywood? (film), **Supp. XVIII:** 243

Whatsaid Serif (Mackey), **Supp. XXVII:** 155, 156

"What Sally Said" (Cisneros), **Supp. VII:** 63

What Saves Us (Weigl), **Supp. XIX:** 282

"What's Happening in America" (Sontag), **Supp. III Part 2:** 460–461

"What She Couldn't Tell" (Hampl), **Supp. XXII:** 92

"What's in Alaska?" (Carver), **Supp. III Part 1:** 141, 143

"What's in a Name" (H. L. Gates), **Supp. XX:** 101

What's New, Pussycat? (film; Allen), **Supp. XI:** 307; **Supp. XV:** 1, 2, 14

"What's New in American and Canadian Poetry" (R. Bly), **Supp. IV Part 1:** 67

What's O'Clock (A. Lowell), **II:** 511, 527, 528

What's the Story: Reflections on a Life Grown Long (Lea), **Supp. XXVIII:** 142–143

What's Up, Tiger Lily? (film; Allen), **Supp. XV:** 2, **3**

"What the Arts Need Now" (Baraka), **Supp. II Part 1:** 47

"What the Bed Knows" (Schott), **Supp. XXIII:** 249

"What the Body Can Say" (Trethewey), **Supp. XXI:** 255

"What the Brand New Freeway Won't Go By" (Hugo), **Supp. VI:** 132–133

"What the Gypsies Told My Grandmother While She Was Still a Young Girl" (Simic), **Supp. VIII:** 283

"What the Prose Poem Carries with It" (R. Bly), **Supp. IV Part 1:** 64

"What the Stone Says" (Huddle), **Supp. XXVI:** 151

What They Found: Love on 145th Street (Myers), **Supp. XXVII:** 210–211

"What They Wanted" (Dunn), **Supp. XI:** 151

What Thou Lovest Well (Hugo), **Supp. VI:** 140, 141

"What Thou Lovest Well Remains American" (Hugo), **Supp. VI:** 140, 141

What Time Collects (Farrell), **II:** 46, 47–48

What to Do? (Chernyshevsky), **Retro. Supp. I:** 269

"What to Keep, What to Discard" (Taggard), **Supp. XXII:** 280

"What to the Slave is Your Fourth of July?"(Douglass), **Supp. XXIII:** 167

What Use Are Flowers? (Hansberry), **Supp. IV Part 1:** 359, 368–369, 374

What Was Literature? (Fiedler), **Supp. XIII:** 96–97, **105–106**

What Was Mine (Beattie), **Supp. V:** 33, 35

What Was the Relationship of the Lone Ranger to the Means of Production? (Baraka), **Supp. II Part 1:** 58

"What We Came Through" (Goldbarth), **Supp. XII:** 179–180

"What Were the White Things?" (Hempel), **Supp. XXI:** 126

What We Talk About When We Talk About Love (Carver), **Supp. III Part 1:** 142–146; **Supp. XII:** 139; **Supp. XXIV:** 177

"What Why When How Who" (Pinsky), **Supp. VI:** 244

What Will Suffice: Contemporary American Poets on the Art of Poetry (Buckley and Young, eds.), **Supp. XIII:** 313

What Work Is (Levine), **Supp. V:** 181, 187, 192–193

"What You Hear from Em" (Taylor), **Supp. V:** 314, 320, 324

"What You Live For" (Huddle), **Supp. XXVI:** 150

What You See in the Dark (Muñoz), **Supp. XXV:** 127, 137–139

"What You Want" (O. Henry), **Supp. II Part 1:** 402

"What You Would Do" (Weigl), **Supp. XIX:** 288

Wheatley, Phillis, **Supp. XIII:** 111; **Supp. XVII:** 74–75; **Supp. XX:** 106, **277–291**

Whedon, Tony, **Supp. XXI:** 131, 132

"Wheelchairs" (Kriegel), **Supp. XXIV:** 220

Wheeler, Candace, **Supp. XXVIII:** 228, 230

Wheeler, David, **Supp. XVI:** 277

Wheeler, John, **II:** 433

Wheeler, Monroe, **Supp. XV:** 295

Wheelock, John Hall, **IV:** 461; **Supp. IX:** 268; **Supp. XIV:** 120; **Supp. XV:** 301; **Supp. XXVII:** 286, 291, 293, 294, 297

Wheel of Life, The (Glasgow), **II:** 176, 178, 179, 183

Wheelwright, Philip, **Supp. XV:** 20

"When" (Olds), **Supp. X:** 207

When Boyhood Dreams Come True (Farrell), **II:** 45

Whence and Whither (Stuart), **Supp. XXVIII:** 235

"When Death Came April Twelve 1945" (Sandburg), **III:** 591, 593

"When Death Comes" (Oliver), **Supp. VII:** 241

"When De Co'n Pone's Hot" (Dunbar), **Supp. II Part 1:** 202–203

"When God First Said" (Zach; Everwine trans.), **Supp. XV:** 87

"When Grandma Died—1942" (Shields), **Supp. VII:** 311

"When Howitzers Began" (Carruth), **Supp. XVI:** 55

"When I Buy Pictures" (Moore), **III:** 205

"When I Came from Colchis" (Merwin), **Supp. III Part 1:** 343

"When I Have Fears I May Cease to Be" (Keats), **Supp. XIX:** 92

"When I Left Business for Literature" (Anderson), **I:** 101

"When I Love You" (Peacock), **Supp. XIX:** 199

"When in Rome—Apologia" (Komunyakaa), **Supp. XIII:** 120

"When It Comes" (Olds), **Supp. X:** 213

"When It's Clear and Hot" (Trethewey), **Supp. XXI:** 246

When I Was Alive (Notley), **Supp. XXII:** 228

"When I Was Alive" (Notley), **Supp. XXII:** 229

"When I Was Seventeen" (Kincaid), **Supp. VII:** 181

"When I Was Thirty-Five, You Took My Photograph" (Stone), **Supp. XXVII:** 254

"When I Was Twenty-five" (Talese), **Supp. XVII:** 202

When Knighthood Was in Flower (Major), **III:** 320

"\[When\] Let by rain" (Taylor), **IV:** 160–161

"When Lilacs Last in the Dooryard Bloom'd" (Whitman), **IV:** 347–348, 351; **Retro. Supp. I:** 406; **Supp. IV Part 1:** 16; **Supp. XV:** 215

"When Malindy Sings" (Dunbar), **Supp. II Part 1:** 200, 204–205

When Peoples Meet: A Study of Race and Culture (Locke and Stern), **Supp. XIV:** 202, 213

When She Was Good (P. Roth), **Retro. Supp. II:** 282, 283, 284; **Supp. III Part 2:** 403, 405, 410–413

"When Sue Wears Red" (Hughes), **Retro. Supp. I:** 195, 204

"When the Acacia Blooms"(Crooker), **Supp. XXIII:** 60

"When the Dead Ask My Father about Me" (Olds), **Supp. X:** 210

"When the Frost Is on the Punkin" (Riley), **Supp. II Part 1:** 202

When the Jack Hollers (Hughes), **Retro. Supp. I:** 203; **Supp. I Part 1:** 328

"When the Last Riders" (Zach; Everwine, trans.), **Supp. XV:** 75, 86

"When the Light Gets Green" (Warren), **IV:** 252

"When the Model Does Not Show" (Major), **Supp. XXII:** 184

"When the Peace Corps Was Young" (Theroux), **Supp. VIII:** 314

When the Sun Tries to Go On (Koch), **Supp. XV:** 185

"When the Sun Tries to Go On" (Koch), **Supp. XV:** 179, 180

"When the World Ended as We Knew It" (Harjo), **Supp. XII:** 231

When Time Was Born (Farrell), **II:** 46, 47

"When We Dead Awaken" (Rich), **Retro. Supp. III:** 246

"When We Dead Awaken: Writing as Revision" (Rich), **Retro. Supp. III:** 246; **Supp. I Part 2:** 552–553, 560

"When We Gonna Rise" (Baraka), **Supp. II Part 1:** 48

"When We Have To" (Salinas), **Supp. XIII:** 322–323

"WHEN WE'LL WORSHIP JESUS" (Baraka), **Supp. II Part 1:** 54

"When We Sold the Tent" (Espaillat), **Supp. XXI:** 102

"When we speak of God, is it God we speak of?" (J. Logan), **Supp. XVII:** 113

"When Women Throw Down Bundles: Strong Women Make Strong Nations" (Gunn Allen), **Supp. IV Part 1:** 328

"When You Come into Your Kingdom" (Muñoz), **Supp. XXV:** 136

"'When You Finally See Them': The Unconquered Eye in *To Kill a Mockingbird*" (Champion), **Supp. VIII:** 128

"When You Lie Down, the Sea Stands Up" (Swenson), **Supp. IV Part 2:** 643

"Where Are the People of Color?" (Myers), **Supp. XXVII:** 199

"Where Blue Is Blue" (Richard), **Supp. XIX:** 221

Where Does One Go When There's No Place Left to Go? (Crews), **Supp. XI:** 103

Where Does the Day Go? (Myers), **Supp. XXVII:** 199, 200, 202

"Where Go the Boats" (R. Stevenson), **Supp. XVII:** 69

Where Horizons Go (Espaillat), **Supp. XXI:** 99, 103, 104

"Where I Come from Is Like This" (Gunn Allen), **Supp. IV Part 1:** 319

"Where I'm Calling From" (Carver), **Supp. III Part 1:** 145

Where I'm Calling From: New and Selected Stories (Carver), **Supp. III Part 1:** 138, 148; **Supp. XXIV:** 178

"Where I Ought to Be" (Erdrich), **Supp. IV Part 1:** 265

Where Is My Wandering Boy Tonight? (Wagoner), **Supp. IX: 335–336**
"Where Is the Island?" (Francis), **Supp. IX:** 78
"Where Is the Voice Coming From?" (Welty), **IV:** 280; **Retro. Supp. I:** 355
Where Joy Resides (Isherwood), **Supp. XIV:** 156
"Where Knock Is Open Wide" (Roethke), **III:** 533–535
"Where My Sympathy Lies" (H. Roth), **Supp. IX:** 234
Where's Daddy? (Inge), **Supp. XXV:** 95, 105, 106
Where's My Money? (Shanley), **Supp. XIV:** 316, 328, **330–331**
Where the Bluebird Sings to the Lemonade Springs (Stegner), **Supp. IV Part 2:** 596, 597, 598, 600, 604, 606, 613; **Supp. XXII:** 205
"Where the Bones Move" (W. V. Davis), **Supp. XXI:** 92
Where the Cross Is Made (O'Neill), **III:** 388, 391
Where There's a Will (Rinehart), **Supp. XXV:** 193
Where the Rivers Flow North (Mosher), **Supp. XXII:** 205, 207, 208, **210–212**
"Where the Rivers Flow North" (Mosher), **Supp. XXII:** 204, 206, 207, 208, 209, **210–211**
Where the Sea Used to Be (Bass), **Supp. XVI:** 21
"Where the Sea Used to Be" (Bass), **Supp. XVI:** 20, 21
"*Where the Sea Used to Be:* Rick Bass and the Novel of Ecological Education" (Dixon), **Supp. XVI:** 21
"Where the Soft Air Lives" (Nye), **Supp. XIII:** 275
Where the Twilight Never Ends (Haines), **Supp. XII:** 211
Where the Wild Grape Grows: Selected Writings, 1930–1950 (D. West; Mitchell and Davis, eds.), **Supp. XVIII:** 283, 286
Where the Wild Things Are (Sendak), **Supp. IX:** 207
"Wherever Home Is" (Wright), **Supp. III Part 2:** 605, 606
"Wherever I Am Not" (Huddle), **Supp. XXVI:** 156–157
Where Water Comes Together With Other Water (Carver), **Supp. III Part 1:** 147, 148
"Where We Crashed" (Hugo), **Supp. VI:** 138
"Where We Must Look for Help" (R. Bly), **Supp. XXI:** 84
"Where You Are" (Doty), **Supp. XI:** 131
Where You'll Find Me, and Other Stories (Beattie), **Supp. V:** 30–31
Whicher, Stephen, **II:** 20
"Which Is More Than I Can Say for Some People" (Moore), **Supp. X:** 177, 178
Which Ones Are the Enemy? (Garrett), **Supp. VII:** 98
"Which Theatre Is the Absurd One?" (Albee), **I:** 71

"Which Way to the Future?" (Rehder), **Supp. IV Part 1:** 69
"While Hendrix Played a Solo: 'Burning of the Midnight Lamp' " (Gansworth), **Supp. XXVI:** 112
While I Was Gone (Miller), **Supp. XII:** 290, **301–303**
"While Seated in a Plane" (Swenson), **Supp. IV Part 2:** 645
While the Messiah Tarries (Bukiet), **Supp. XVII:** 43, **46–47**
While We've Still Got Feet (Budbill), **Supp. XIX:** 5, 7, **10–11**, 15
Whilomville Stories (Crane), **I:** 414
"Whip, The" (Robinson), **III:** 513
Whipple, Thomas K., **II:** 456, 458; **IV:** 427
"Whippoorwill, The" (Francis), **Supp. IX:** 90
"Whip-poor-will, The" (Thurber), **Supp. I Part 2:** 616
Whirl Asunder, A (Atherton), **Supp. XXIV:** 22
Whirlpool (film, Preminger), **Supp. XVII:** 62
"Whisperer in Darkness, The" (Lovecraft), **Supp. XXV:** 114
"Whispering Gallery, The" (Komunyakaa), **Supp. XIII:** 132
"Whispering Leaves" (Glasgow), **II:** 190
Whispering to Fool the Wind (Ríos), **Supp. IV Part 2:** 540–541, 544, 545
"Whispers in the Next Room" (Simic), **Supp. VIII:** 278
"Whispers of Heavenly Death" (Whitman), **IV:** 348
"Whispers of Immortality" (Eliot), **Supp. XI:** 242
Whistle (Jones), **Supp. XI:** 219, 224, **231–234**
"Whistle, The" (Franklin), **II:** 121
"Whistle, The" (Komunyakaa), **Supp. XIII:** 111, 126
"Whistle, The" (Welty), **IV:** 262
Whistler, James, **I:** 484; **III:** 461, 465, 466; **IV:** 77, 369
Whistler, James Abbott McNeill, **Supp. XIV:** 335–336
"Whistling Dick's Christmas Stocking" (O. Henry), **Supp. II Part 1:** 390, 392
Whistling in the Dark (Garrett), **Supp. VII:** 111
Whistling in the Dark: True Stories and Other Fables (Garrett), **Supp. VII:** 95
Whitcher, Frances Miriam Berry, **Supp. XIII:** 152
"White" (Simic), **Supp. VIII: 275–276**
White, Barbara, **Retro. Supp. I:** 379
White, Dana, **Supp. XXII:** 251
White, E. B., **Retro. Supp. I:** 335; **Supp. I Part 2:** 602, 607, 608, 612, 619, 620, **651–681**; **Supp. II Part 1:** 143; **Supp. IX:** 20, 32; **Supp. VIII:** 171; **Supp. XVI:** 167
White, Elizabeth Wade, **Retro. Supp. III:** 3; **Supp. I Part 1:** 100, 103, 111
White, Gilbert, **Supp. XXVIII:** 247, 255
White, Henry Kirke, **Supp. I Part 1:** 150
White, James L., **Supp. XI:** 123
White, Joel, **Supp. I Part 2:** 654, 678

White, Katharine (Katharine Sergeant Angell), **Supp. I Part 2:** 610, 653, 655, 656, 669; **Supp. VIII:** 151, 171; **Supp. XXVIII:** 45
White, Lillian, **Supp. I Part 2:** 651
White, Lucia, **I:** 258
White, Maria. *See* Lowell, Mrs. James Russell (Maria White)
White, Morton, **I:** 258; **Supp. I Part 2:** 647, 648, 650
White, Roberta, **Supp. XII:** 293
White, Stanford, **Supp. IV Part 1:** 223
White, Stanley, **Supp. I Part 2:** 651, 655
White, T. H., **III:** 522
White, T. W., **III:** 411, 415
White, Walter, **Supp. I Part 1:** 345; **Supp. XIX:** 73; **Supp. XVIII:** 123, 127
White, William, **Retro. Supp. II:** 326
White, William A., **I:** 252
White Album, The (Didion), **Supp. IV Part 1:** 198, 202, 205–207, 210
"White Album, The" (Didion), **Supp. IV Part 1:** 205, 206
"White Angel" (Cunningham), **Supp. XV:** 59
"White Apache" (Markson), **Supp. XVII:** 136
"White as Snow" (Boyle), **Supp. XXIV:** 58, 59
White Boys (McKnight), **Supp. XX: 155–157**
"White Boys, The" (McKnight), **Supp. XX: 155–157**
White Buildings (H. Crane), **I:** 385, 386, 390–395, 400; **Retro. Supp. II:** 77–78, **80–81**, 82, 83, 85; **Retro. Supp. III:** 49, 50
White Butterfly (Mosley), **Supp. XIII:** 237, 238, 240
White Center (Hugo), **Supp. VI:** 144–145
"White Center" (Hugo), **Supp. VI:** 144, 146
Whited, Stephen, **Supp. XI:** 135
White Deer, The (Thurber), **Supp. I Part 2:** 606
White Doves at Morning (Burke), **Supp. XIV:** 22–23, 32, 35–36
"White Eagle, The" (Chopin), **Retro. Supp. II:** 72
White Fang (London), **II:** 471–472, 481
White Fawn (Prouty), **Supp. XXVIII:** 184–185, 187, 189
Whitefield, George, **I:** 546; **Supp. XX: 280**
White-Footed Deer and Other Poems (Bryant), **Supp. I Part 1:** 157
White Goddess, The (Graves), **Supp. IV Part 1:** 280
White-Haired Lover (Shapiro), **Supp. II Part 2:** 703, 717
Whitehead, Alfred North, **III:** 605, 619, 620; **IV:** 88; **Supp. I Part 2:** 554, 647
Whitehead, Mrs. Catherine, **IV:** 116
Whitehead, Colson, **Supp. XIII:** 233, 241
Whitehead, James, **Supp. XV:** 339
Whitehead, Margaret, **IV:** 114, 115, 116
Whitehead, William, **Supp. XX: 50–51**, 53

White Heat (Walsh), **Supp. XIII:** 174
"White Heron, A" (Jewett), **II:** 409;
Retro. Supp. II: 17
White Heron and Other Stories, A
(Jewett), **II:** 396
White Horses (Hoffman), **Supp. X: 83–85,** 90, 92
"White Horses of Vienna, The" (Boyle),
Supp. XXIV: 59–60
*White Horses of Vienna, The, and Other
Stories* (Boyle), **Supp. XXIV: 57,
58–59**
White House Diary, A (Lady Bird
Johnson), **Supp. IV Part 1:** 22
White-Jacket (Melville), **III:** 80, 81, 84,
94; **Retro Supp. I:** 248, 249, 254;
Retro. Supp. III: 147, 152, 154, 155,
156; **Supp. XVIII:** 7, 9
White Lantern, The (Connell), **Supp.
XIV:** 97
"White Lies" (Trethewey), **Supp. XXI:**
244, 246, 251
"White Lights, The" (Robinson), **III:** 524
"White Lilies, The" (Glück), **Supp. V:** 88
White Man, Listen! (Wright), **IV:** 478,
488, 489, 494
White Morning, The (Atherton), **Supp.
XXIV:** 24, 29
"White Mulberry Tree, The" (Cather), **I:**
319; **Retro. Supp. I:** 7, 9, 17
White Mule (W. C. Williams), **Retro.
Supp. I:** 423
"White Negro, The" (Mailer), **III:** 36–37;
Retro. Supp. II: 202
"Whiteness of the Whale, The"
(Melville), **III:** 84, 86
"White Night" (Oliver), **Supp. VII:** 236
"White Nights" (Auster), **Supp. XII:**
23–24
White Noise (DeLillo), **Supp. VI:** 1, 3–4,
5–7, 10, 11–12, 16; **Supp. XVIII:**
140; **Supp. XX:** 91
White Oxen and Other Stories, The
(Burke), **I:** 269, 271
*White Paper on Contemporary American
Poetry* (McClatchy), **Supp. XII:** 253,
259–260
"White Phosphorous" (Notley), **Supp.
XXII:** 232, 233
"White Pine" (Oliver), **Supp. VII:** 244
White Pine: Poems and Prose Poems
(Oliver), **Supp. VII:** 243–246
White Poems, The (Crooker), **Supp.
XXIII: 54–55**
White Rat (G. Jones), **Supp. XXIV:** 185
White Roots of Peace (Wallace), **Supp.
XXVI:** 90, 96–97
White Sail (Sorrentino), **Supp. XXI:** 228
"White Ship, The" (Lovecraft), **Supp.
XXV:** 113
"White Silence, The" (London), **II:** 468
"White Silk" (Nye), **Supp. XIII:** 275
"White Snake, The" (Sexton), **Supp. II
Part 2:** 691
"White Spot" (Anderson), **I:** 116
"White-Tailed Hornet, The" (Frost),
Retro. Supp. I: 138
"White Trash Cowboys of *Father and
Son,* The" (Bjerre), **Supp. XXI:** 41

"White Trees, Hammer Moon" (Dubus
III), **Supp. XXIV:** 101, 104
Whitfield, Raoul, **Supp. IV Part 1:** 345
Whitfield, Stephen J., **Supp. XX: 243,
244**
Whitlock, Brand, **II:** 276
Whitman (Masters), **Supp. I Part 2:** 473,
475, 476
Whitman, George, **IV:** 346, 350
Whitman, Ruth, **Supp. XXI:** 246
Whitman, Sarah Helen, **Retro. Supp. III:**
225, 236
Whitman, Sarah Wyman, **Retro. Supp.
II:** 136
Whitman, Walt, **I:** 61, 68, 98, 103, 104,
109, 219, 220, 227, 228, 242, 246,
250, 251, 260, 261, 285, 381, 384,
386, 396, 397, 398, 402, 419, 430,
459, 460, 483, 485, 486, 577; **II:** 7, 8,
18, 127, 140, 273–274, 275, 289, 295,
301, 320, 321, 373, 445, 446, 451,
457, 494, 529, 530, 552; **III:** 171, 175,
177, 181–182, 189, 203, 234, 260,
426, 430, 453, 454, 461, 505, 507–508, 511, 528, 548, 552, 555, 559,
567, 572, 576, 577, 579, 584, 585,
595, 606, 609; **IV:** 74, 169, 191, 192,
202, **331–354,** 405, 409, 416, 444,
450–451, 457, 463, 464, 469, 470,
471; **Retro. Supp. I:** 8, 52, 194, 254,
283, 284, 333, **387–410,** 412, 417,
427; **Retro. Supp. II:** 40, 76, 93, 99,
155, 156, 158, 170, 262; **Retro. Supp.
III:** 41, 44, 49, 244, 245, 251, 283,
295–311; Supp. I Part 1: 6, 79, 167,
311, 314, 325, 365, 368, 372; **Supp. I
Part 2:** 374, 384, 385, 387, 389, 391,
393, 399, 416, 436, 455, 456, 458,
473, 474, 475, 525, 540, 579, 580,
582, 682, 691; **Supp. III Part 1:** 6,
20, 156, 239–241, 253, 340; **Supp. III
Part 2:** 596; **Supp. IV Part 1:** 16,
169, 325; **Supp. IV Part 2:** 597, 625;
Supp. IX: 8, 9, 15, 38, 41, 44, 48, 53,
131, 292, 298, 299, 308, 320; **Supp.
V:** 113, 118, 122, 130, 170, 178, 183,
277, 279, 332; **Supp. VIII:** 42, 95,
105, 126, 198, 202, 269; **Supp. X:** 36,
112, 203, 204; **Supp. XI:** 83, 123,
132, 135, 203, 321; **Supp. XII:** 132,
185, 190, 256; **Supp. XIII:** 1, 77, 115,
153, 221, 304, 335; **Supp. XIV:** 89,
312, 334, 335, 338; **Supp. XIX:** 118,
276; **Supp. XV:** 41, 93, 181, 183, 212,
213, 218, 250, 275, 301, 302, 303,
309, 352; **Supp. XVI:** 209; **Supp.
XVII:** 42, 71, 112, 133; **Supp. XVIII:**
4, 194, 196, 304; **Supp. XX: 69, 115,
116, 221; Supp. XXI:** 169, 217, 227,
256; **Supp. XXII:** 81, 82, 86, 92;
Supp. XXIII: 19, 109, 166, 207;
Supp. XXVI: 227, 230, 233, 234;
Supp. XXVII: 160; **Supp. XXVIII:**
71, 74, 268
"Whitman Pinch Hits, 1861" (Skloot),
Supp. XX: 203
"Whitman: The Poet and the Mask"
(Cowley), **Supp. II Part 1:** 143
Whitmarsh, Jason, **Supp. VIII:** 283
Whitmer, Peter, **Supp. X:** 264, 265

Whitney, Blair, **Supp. I Part 2:** 403
Whitney, Josiah, **Supp. IX:** 180, 181
Whitt, Margaret Earley, **Retro. Supp. II:**
226
Whittemore, Reed, **III:** 268; **Supp. XI:**
315
Whittier, Elizabeth, **Supp. I Part 2:** 700,
701, 703; **Supp. XIII:** 141, 142
Whittier, John Greenleaf, **I:** 216; **II:** 275;
III: 52; **Retro. Supp. I:** 54; **Retro.
Supp. II:** 155, 163, 169; **Supp. I Part
1:** 168, 299, 313, 317, 372; **Supp. I
Part 2:** 420, 602, **682–707; Supp.
VIII:** 202, 204; **Supp. XI:** 50; **Supp.
XIII:** 140, 145; **Supp. XV:** 246; **Supp.
XXIII:** 156
Whittier, Mary, **Supp. I Part 2:** 683
"Whittier Birthday Speech" (Twain),
Retro. Supp. III: 262, 268; **Supp. I
Part 1:** 313
"Who" (Kenyon), **Supp. VII:** 174
"Who" (Sobin), **Supp. XVI:** 284–285
"Who Am I—Who I Am" (Corso), **Supp.
XII:** 134
"Who Be Kind To" (Ginsberg), **Supp. II
Part 1:** 323
Who Do You Love (Thompson), **Supp.
XXIII: 289, 295–296**
Who Do You Think You Are? (Munro),
Supp. XXVII: 181, 182, 184, 186–187, 194
"Whoever Was Using This Bed" (Carver),
Supp. III Part 1: 148
"Whoever You Are Holding Me Now in
Hand" (Whitman), **IV:** 342; **Retro.
Supp. I:** 52
Who Gathered and Whispered behind Me
(Goldbarth), **Supp. XII:** 181, 182
"Who in One Lifetime" (Rukeyser),
Supp. VI: 276, 279
Who Is the Widow's Muse? (Stone), **Supp.
XXVII:** 257, 262
Who Is Witter Bynner? (Kraft), **Supp.
XV:** 40, 52
"Who Is Your Mother? Red Roots of
White Feminism" (Gunn Allen), **Supp.
IV Part 1:** 329
Whole Hog (Wagoner), **Supp. IX: 337–338**
"Whole Mess...Almost, The" (Corso),
Supp. XII: 135
"Whole Moisty Night, The" (R. Bly),
Supp. IV Part 1: 69
Whole New Life, A (Price), **Supp. VI:**
265, **266,** 267
"Whole Self, The" (Nye), **Supp. XIII:**
275
"Whole Soul, The" (Levine), **Supp. V:**
192
"Whole Story, The" (Strand), **Supp. IV
Part 2:** 622
Whole Town's Talking, The (Loos), **Supp.
XVI:** 187
Whole Wide World, The (film), **Supp.
XXVII:** 117
"Whole World Knows, The" (Welty), **IV:**
272; **Retro. Supp. I:** 343
Who'll Stop the Rain (film), **Supp. V:** 301
Who Lost an American? (Algren), **Supp.
IX: 15–16**

Who Owns America? (symposium), **Supp. XIV:** 4

Who Owns the West? (Kittredge), **Supp. XXVI:** 185

"Who Puts Together" (Hogan), **Supp. IV Part 1:** 403, 405, 412–413

"Whore of Mensa, The" (Allen), **Supp. XV:** 15

Whores for Gloria (Vollmann), **Supp. XVII:** 226, 230

Whorf, Benjamin Lee, **Supp. XVI:** 283

Who's Afraid? (Holding), **Supp. XXII:** 120, **125–126**

Who's Afraid of Virginia Woolf? (Albee), **I:** 71, 77–81, 83, 85, 86, 87, 94; **IV:** 230

Who Shall Be the Sun? Poems Based on the Lore, Legends, and Myths of the Northwest Coast and Plateau Indians (Wagoner), **Supp. IX:** 328, **329–330,** 337

"Whosis Kid, The" (Hammett), **Supp. IV Part 1:** 344

"Who Sit Watch in Daylight" (Wright), **Supp. XV:** 342

"Who's Passing for Who?" (Hughes), **Supp. I Part 1:** 330

"Who Speak on the Page?" (Sanders), **Supp. XVI:** 278

Who We Are: On Being (and Not Being) a Jewish American Writer (Rubin, ed.), **Supp. XXIV:** 3

Who Will Run the Frog Hospital?: A Novel (Moore), **Supp. X:** 163, 165, 169, **175–177**

Who Wrote the Book of Love? (Siegel), **Supp. XXII: 265–267,** 267

Why Are We in Vietnam? (Mailer), **III:** 27, 29, 30, 33, 34–35, 39, 42, 44; **Retro. Supp. II:** 205–206

"Why Bother?" (Franzen). *See* "Perchance to Dream" (Franzen)

"Why China?" (Egan), **Supp. XIX:** 51, 52

"Why Did the Balinese Chicken Cross the Road?" (Walker), **Supp. III Part 2:** 527

"Why Do the Heathens Rage?" (O'Connor), **III:** 351

"Why Do They Prate?" (H. Johnson), **Supp. XXVI:** 174

"Why Do You Write About Russia?" (Simpson), **Supp. IX:** 277

"Why Have We Not More Great Novelists?" (Atherton), **Supp. XXIV:** 24

"Why I Am a Danger to the Public" (Kingsolver), **Supp. VII:** 204

"Why I Am a Pagan" (Zitkala-Ša), **Supp. XXV:** 276–277

Why I Am Not a Christian (Russell), **Supp. I Part 2:** 522

"Why I Am Not a Painter"(O'Hara), **Supp. XXIII:** 208

Why I Came to Judevine (Budbill), **Supp. XIX:** 2, **7–8,** 15

"Why I Do Not Wish to Float in Space"(Schott), **Supp. XXIII:** 251

"Why I Entered the Gurdjieff Work" (Toomer), **Supp. III Part 2:** 481

"Why I Like Laurel" (Patchett), **Supp. XII:** 309

"Why I Live at the P.O." (Welty), **IV:** 262; **Retro. Supp. I:** 345

"Why I Make Sam Go to Church" (Lamott), **Supp. XX:** 141

"Why Is American Literature Bourgeois?" (Atherton), **Supp. XXIV:** 24, 28

"Why Is Economics Not an Evolutionary Science?" (Veblen), **Supp. I Part 2:** 634

"Why I Write" (Didion), **Supp. IV Part 1:** 201, 203

"Why I Wrote *Phil:* An Exclusive Essay for Amazon.com" (Saunders), **Supp. XIX:** 230–231

Why Johnny Can't Read: And What You Can Do About It (Flesch), **Supp. XVI:** 105

"Why Negro Women Leave Home" (Brooks), **Supp. III Part 1:** 75

Why Poetry Matters (Parini), **Supp. XIX:** 120, 129

"Why"(Prouty), **Supp. XXVIII:** 180

"Why Resign from the Human Race?" (Swados), **Supp. XIX:** 265

"Why the Little Frenchman Wears His Hand in a Sling" (Poe), **III:** 425

Why Torture Is Wrong, and the People Who Love Them (Durang), **Supp. XXIV: 126–127**

"Why We Are Forgiven" (Weigl), **Supp. XIX:** 282–283

Why We Behave Like Microbe Hunters (Thurber), **Supp. I Part 2:** 606

Why We Were in Vietnam (Podhoretz), **Supp. VIII:** 241

"Why Write?" (Updike), **Retro. Supp. I:** 317

"Wichita Vortex Sutra" (Ginsberg), **Supp. II Part 1:** 319, 321, 323–325, 327

Wickenden, Dorothy, **Supp. XXIII:** 291

Wickes, George, **Supp. XIV:** 165

Wickford Point (Marquand), **III:** 50, 58, 64–65, 69

Wicks, Robert Russell, **Supp. XII:** 49

Wide, Wide World, The (S. Warner as Wetherell), **Supp. XV:** 275; **Supp. XVIII:** 257, 260, **262–264,** 265

Wide Blue Yonder (Thompson), **Supp. XXIII:** 289, **296–298**

"Wide Empty Landscape with a Death in the Foreground" (Momaday), **Supp. IV Part 2:** 492

Wideman, Edgar, **Supp. XXV:** 146, 147

Wideman, John Edgar, **Retro. Supp. II:** 123; **Supp. X:** 239, 250, **319–336;** **Supp. XI:** 245; **Supp. XIII:** 247; **Supp. XVIII:** 89; **Supp. XXI:** 246; **Supp. XXIV:** 183

Widener, Jeff, **Supp. XVIII:** 91

"Wideness" (Pickering), **Supp. XXI:** 203

"Wide Net, The" (Welty), **IV:** 266

Wide Net and Other Stories, The (Welty), **IV:** 261, 264–266, 271; **Retro. Supp. I:** 347–349, 352, 355

Widening Spell of the Leaves, The (Levis), **Supp. XI:** 258, 259, 261, **268–269,** 271

"Wide Prospect, The" (Jarrell), **II:** 376–377

Wide Sargasso Sea (Rhys), **Supp. XVIII:** 131

"Widespread Enigma Concerning Blue-Star Woman" (Zitkala-Ša), **Supp. XXV:** 282–283

"Widow" (Peacock), **Supp. XIX:** 206

"Widower" (Robison), **Supp. XXI:** 118

Widow for One Year, A (Irving), **Supp. VI:** 165, **179–181**

Widow's Mite (Holding), **Supp. XXII:** 136

Widows of Thornton, The (Taylor), **Supp. V:** 320, 321

Widow's Story, A (Oates), **Supp. XXV:** 60

"Widow's Wish, The" (Briggs), **Supp. XVIII:** 15

Wieland; or, The Transformation (Brown), **Retro. Supp. III:** 226; **Supp. I Part 1:** 128–132, 133, 137, 140

Wiene, Robert, **Retro. Supp. I:** 268

Wiener, John, **Supp. IV Part 1:** 153

Wieners, John, **Supp. II Part 1:** 32; **Supp. XXIII:** 215

Wiesel, Elie, **Supp. XVII:** 47, 48, 49

Wiest, Dianne, **Supp. XV:** 12

"Wife, Forty-five, Remembers Love, A" (Shields), **Supp. VII:** 310

"Wifebeater, The" (Sexton), **Supp. II Part 2:** 693

"Wife for Dino Rossi, A" (Fante), **Supp. XI:** 165

"Wife of His Youth, The" (Chesnutt), **Supp. XIV: 63–66; Supp. XXVIII:** 231

Wife of His Youth and Other Stories of the Color Line, The (Chesnutt), **Supp. XIV:** 62, 63

"Wife of Jesus Speaks, The" (Karr), **Supp. XI:** 250–251

"Wife of Nashville, A" (Taylor), **Supp. V:** 320

"Wife's Story, The" (R. H. Davis), **Supp. XVI:** 85, 91, 92–93

Wife's Story, The (Shields), **Supp. VII:** 316. *See also* Happenstance

"Wife-Wooing" (Updike), **IV:** 226

Wigan, Gareth, **Supp. XI:** 306

Wiget, Andrew, **Supp. IV Part 2:** 509

Wigglesworth, Michael, **IV:** 147, 156; **Supp. I Part 1:** 110, 111

Wilbur, Richard, **III:** 527; **Retro. Supp. II:** 50; **Supp. III Part 1:** 64; **Retro. Supp. III Part 2: 541–565; Supp. IV Part 2:** 626, 634, 642; **Supp. V:** 337; **Supp. VIII:** 28; **Supp. X:** 58, 120; **Supp. XII:** 258; **Supp. XIII:** 76, 336; **Supp. XV:** 51, 251, 256; **Supp. XVII:** 26; **Supp. XVIII:** 178; **Supp. XX: 199; Supp. XXI:** 247; **Supp. XXIV:** 36, 45; **Supp. XXVI:** 64, 68

Wilcocks, Alexander, **Supp. I Part 1:** 125

Wilcox, Ella Wheeler, **Supp. II Part 1:** 197

Wilcox, Kirstin, **Supp. XX: 283, 284, 285**

Wild, John, **II:** 362, 363–364

Wild, Peter, **Supp. V:** 5

Wild, Robert, **IV:** 155

"Wild, The" (Berry), **Supp. X:** 30

Wild 90 (film) (Mailer), **Retro. Supp. II:** 205

Wild and Woolly (film), **Supp. XVI:** 185

"Wild Boar in These Woods: The Influence of Seamus Heaney on the Poetry of Ron Rash" (Boyelston), **Supp. XXVII:** 216

Wild Boy of Aveyron, The (Itard). *See* De l'éducation d'un homme sauvage

Wild Boys, The: A Book of the Dead (Burroughs), **Supp. III Part 1:** 106–107

Wild Card Quilt: Taking A chance on Home (Ray), **Supp. XVIII:** 189, 192, 193, 196, 198, **200–202,** 204

Wilde, Oscar, **I:** 50, 66, 381, 384; **II:** 515; **IV:** 77, 350; **Retro. Supp. I:** 56, 102, 227; **Retro. Supp. II:** 76, 326; **Retro. Supp. III:** 44; **Supp. IV Part 2:** 578, 679, 683; **Supp. IX:** 65, 66, 68, 189, 192; **Supp. V:** 106, 283; **Supp. X:** 148, 151, 188–189; **Supp. XIV:** 324, 334; **Supp. XV:** 350; **Supp. XXIV:** 263

Wilder, Alec, **Supp. XXVII:** 42

Wilder, Amos Parker, **IV:** 356

Wilder, Mrs. Amos Parker (Isabella Thornton Niven), **IV:** 356

Wilder, Billy, **Supp. IV Part 1:** 130; **Supp. XI:** 307

Wilder, Isabel, **IV:** 357, 366, 375

Wilder, Laura Ingalls, **Supp. XXI:** 2; **Supp. XXII: 289–303; Supp. XXVI:** 217

Wilder, Thornton, **I:** 360, 482; **IV: 355–377,** 431; **Retro. Supp. I:** 109, 359; **Supp. I Part 2:** 609; **Supp. IV Part 2:** 586; **Supp. IX:** 140; **Supp. V:** 105; **Supp. XII:** 236–237; **Supp. XX: 50; Supp. XXVIII:** 76

"Wilderness" (Leopold), **Supp. XIV:** 190

Wilderness (Parker), **Supp. XIX:** 177, **188–189**

"Wilderness" (Sandburg), **III:** 584, 595

Wilderness (Warren), **IV:** 256

"Wilderness, The" (Merwin), **Supp. III Part 1:** 340, 345

"Wilderness, The" (Robinson), **III:** 524

Wilderness of Vision, The: On the Poetry of John Haines (Bezner and Walzer, eds.), **Supp. XII:** 202

Wilderness Plots: Tales about the Settlement of the American Land (Sanders), **Supp. XVI:** 267–268, 269

"Wilderness Station, A" (Munro), **Supp. XXVII:** 191

"Wilderness"(Thompson), **Supp. XXIII:** 301

Wilderness World of Anne LaBastille, The (LaBastille), **Supp. X: 105,** 106

Wilderness World of John Muir, The (Teale), **Supp. XXVIII:** 248

"Wilder: Prophet of the Genteel Christ"(Gold), **Supp. XXVIII:** 76

Wild Flag, The (White), **Supp. I Part 2:** 654

"Wildflower, The" (W. C. Williams), **Retro. Supp. I:** 420

"Wild Flowers" (Caldwell), **I:** 310

"Wildflowers" (Minot), **Supp. VI:** 208

"Wild Geese" (Oliver), **Supp. VII:** 237

"Wild Honey Suckle, The" (Freneau), **Supp. II Part 1:** 253, 264, 266

Wild in the Country (Odets), **Supp. II Part 2:** 546

"Wild in the Woods" (Skloot), **Supp. XX:** 206

Wild Iris, The (Glück), **Supp. V:** 79, 87–89, 91

Wildlife (Ford), **Supp. V:** 57, 69–71

Wildlife in America (Matthiessen), **Supp. V:** 199, 201, 204

"Wildlife in American Culture" (Leopold), **Supp. XIV:** 190, 191

"Wild Light" (Skloot), **Supp. XX: 200**

Wild Man, The (P. N. Warren), **Supp. XX: 260, 270–272**

"Wildness" (Sanders), **Supp. XVI:** 276

Wild Old Wicked Man, The (MacLeish), **III:** 3, 20

Wild Palms, The (Faulkner), **II:** 68–69; **Retro. Supp. I:** 85. *See also If I Forget Thee, Jerusalem* (Faulkner)

"Wild Palms, The" (Faulkner), **II:** 68; **Retro. Supp. III:** 85

Wild Patience Has Taken Me This Far, A: Poems 1978–1981 (Rich), **Retro. Supp. III:** 249

"Wild Peaches" (Wylie), **Supp. I Part 2:** 707, 712

Wild Roses of Cape Ann and Other Poems (Larcom), **Supp. XIII:** 142, 147

Wild Seed (O. Butler), **Supp. XIII:** 62, 63

"Wild Swans at Coole, The " (W. B. Yeats), **Supp. XVI:** 48

"Wild Swans at Norfolk, The" (Carruth), **Supp. XVI:** 48

"Wild Thing" (L. Brown), **Supp. XXI:** 44

Wild Thorn (Hoffman), **Supp. XVIII: 84–85**

Wild to the Heart (Bass), **Supp. XVI:** 16

"Wild Turkeys: Dignity of the Damned" (B. Kelly), **Supp. XVII:** 129

"Wildwest" (MacLeish), **III:** 14

Wiley, Catherine, **Supp. XXIII:** 199

Wiley, Craig, **Supp. VIII:** 313

Wilhelm, Randall, **Supp. XXVII:** 215, 224

Wilhelm Meister (Goethe), **II:** 291

Wilkes, John, **Supp. I Part 2:** 503, 519, 522

Wilkie, Curtis, **Supp. V:** 11

Wilkins, Roy, **Supp. I Part 1:** 345

Wilkinson, Alec, **Supp. VIII:** 164, 168, 171

Wilkinson, Marguerite, **Supp. XXVII:** 292–293

Wilkinson, Max, **Supp. IX:** 251

Will, The (Swados), **Supp. XIX: 265–266**

Willa Cather: The Emerging Voice (O'Brien), **Retro. Supp. III:** 19, 37

Willard, Nancy, **Supp. XIX:** 138

Willard, Samuel, **IV:** 150

Willard Gibbs (Rukeyser), **Supp. VI:** 273, 283, 284

Willcutts, Tim, **Supp. XVII:** 239, 241, 246

Willett, Ralph, **Supp. XIV:** 27

Willey, Basil, **Retro. Supp. II:** 243

"William Butler Yeats Among the Ghosts" (Skloot), **Supp. XX: 204–205**

William Carlos Williams (Koch), **Retro. Supp. I:** 428

William Carlos Williams: An American Artist (Breslin), **Retro. Supp. I:** 430

William Carlos Williams and Alterity (Ahearn), **Retro. Supp. I:** 415

William Carlos Williams and the Meanings of Measure (Cushman), **Retro. Supp. I:** 430

William Carlos Williams: The American Background (Weaver), **Retro. Supp. I:** 430

William Ellery Channing: An Intellectual Portrait (Edgell), **Supp. XXIV:** 71

William Ellery Channing: Selected Writings (Robinson, ed.), **Supp. XXIV:** 71

William Faulkner: A Critical Study (Howe), **Supp. VI:** 119–120, 125

William Faulkner: A Literary Companion (Fargnoli), **Retro. Supp. III:** 75

William Faulkner: Early Prose and Poetry (Faulkner), **Retro. Supp. I:** 80

William Faulkner: First Encounters (Brooks), **Supp. XIV:** 13

"William Faulkner's Legend of the South" (Cowley), **Supp. II Part 1:** 143

"William Faulkner: The Stillness of *Light in August*" (Kazin), *Supp. VIII:* 104

William Faulkner: The Yoknapatawpha Country (Brooks), **Supp. XIV: 12–13,** 16

William Faulkner: Toward Yoknapatawpha and Beyond (Brooks), **Supp. XIV:** 13

"William Humphrey, 73, Writer of Novels about Rural Texas" (Gussow), **Supp. IX:** 93

William Humphrey, Destroyer of Myths (Almon), **Supp. IX:** 93

William Humphrey. Boise State University Western Writers Series (Winchell), **Supp. IX:** 109

"William Humphrey Remembered" (Masters), **Supp. IX:** 96

William Humphrey. Southwestern Series (Lee), **Supp. IX:** 109

William Inge and the Subversion of Gender (J. Johnson), **Supp. XXV:** 98

"William Ireland's Confession" (A. Miller), **III:** 147–148

William James and Phenomenology: A Study of the "Principles of Psychology" (Wilshire), **II:** 362

William Lloyd Garrison (Chapman), **Supp. XIV:** 46–51, 52, 53, 55

William Maxwell Portrait, A: Memories and Appreciations (C. Baxter, Collier, and Hirsch, eds.), **Supp. XVII:** 23

Williams, Annie Laurie, **Supp. IX:** 93

Williams, Blanch Colton, **Supp. XVIII:** 279

Williams, Cecil, **II:** 508

Williams, Charles, **Supp. II Part 1:** 15, 16

Williams, C. K., **Supp. XIII:** 114; **Supp. XVII:** 112

Williams, Cratis, **Supp. XX: 163**

Williams, Dakin, **IV:** 379

Williams, David Reichard, **Supp. XIII:** 162

Williams, Edward, **IV:** 404

Williams, Edwina Dakin, **IV:** 379

Williams, Eric, **Supp. XXI:** 166, 170, 171

Williams, Esther, **Supp. XII:** 165

Williams, Fannie Barrier, **Supp. XIV:** 201

Williams, Garth, **Supp. XXII:** 301

Williams, George, **Supp. V:** 220

Williams, Henry Sylvester, **Supp. XXI:** 166

Williams, Horace, **IV:** 453

Williams, Joan, **Supp. IX:** 95

Williams, John A., **Supp. XVI:** 143

Williams, John Alexander, **Supp. XXIII:** 39

Williams, John Sharp, **IV:** 378

Williams, Jonathan, **Supp. XXII:** 168

Williams, Kenny J., **Supp. XX: 281, 286**

Williams, Linda, **Supp. XXVIII:** 183

Williams, Lyle, **Supp. XIV:** 22

Williams, Michael, **Supp. V:** 286

Williams, Miller, **Supp. XIV:** 126; **Supp. XV:** 339; **Supp. XVIII:** 177

Williams, Paul, **IV:** 404

Williams, Raymond, **Supp. IX:** 146

Williams, Roger, **Supp. I Part 2:** 699; **Supp. XXIII:** 15

Williams, Rose, **IV:** 379

Williams, Sherley Anne, **Supp. V:** 180

Williams, Solomon, **I:** 549

Williams, Stanley T., **II:** 301, 316; **Supp. I Part 1:** 251

Williams, Stephen, **IV:** 148

Williams, Ted, **IV:** 216; **Supp. IX:** 162

Williams, Ted. C., **Supp. XXVI:** 102

Williams, Tennessee, **I:** 73, 81, 113, 211; **II:** 190, 194; **III:** 145, 147; **IV:** 4, 378–401; **Retro. Supp. III:** 165, 177, 313; **Supp. I Part 1:** 290, 291; **Supp. IV Part 1:** 79, 83, 84, 359; **Supp. IV Part 2:** 574, 682; **Supp. IX:** 133; **Supp. XI:** 103; **Supp. XIII:** 331; **Supp. XIV:** 250, 315; **Supp. XVI:** 194; **Supp. XXIV:** 113; **Supp. XXV:** 94, 96, 97

Williams, Terry Tempest, **Supp. XIII:** 16; **Supp. XVIII:** 189

Williams, Walter L., **Supp. IV Part 1:** 330, 331

Williams, William, **IV:** 404, 405

Williams, William Carlos, **I:** 61, 62, 229, 255, 256, 261, 285, 428, 438, 446, 539; **II:** 133, 536, 542, 543, 544, 545; **III:** 194, 196, 198, 214, 269, 409, 453, 457, 458, 464, 465, 591; **IV:** 30, 74, 75, 76, 94, 95, 286, 287, **402–425**; **Retro. Supp. I:** 51, 52, 62, 209, 284, 285, 288, 296, 298, **411–433**; **Retro. Supp. II:** 178, 181, 189, 250, 321, 322, 326, 327, 328, 334, 335; **Retro. Supp. III:** 47, 52, 245, 251; **Supp. I Part 1:** 254, 255, 259, 266; **Supp. II Part 1:** 9, 30, 308, 318; **Supp. II Part**

2: 421, 443; **Supp. III Part 1:** 9, 147, 239, 271, 275, 276, 278, 350; **Supp. III Part 2:** 542, 610, 613, 614, 615, 616, 617, 621, 622, 626, 628; **Supp. IV Part 1:** 151, 153, 246, 325; **Supp. IX:** 38, 268, 291; **Supp. V:** 180, 337; **Supp. VIII:** 195, 269, 272, 277, 292; **Supp. X:** 112, 120, 204; **Supp. XI:** 311, 328; **Supp. XII:** 198; **Supp. XIII:** 77, 90, 335; **Supp. XIV:** 280, 284, 285, 293; **Supp. XIX:** 1, 42, 117, 119, 121; **Supp. XV:** 42, 51, 182, 250, 306, 307; **Supp. XVI:** 48, 282; **Supp. XVII:** 36, 113, 227, 243; **Supp. XXI:** 226, 227, 230, 233; **Supp. XXII:** 162, 165, 168, 226, 227, 228; **Supp. XXIII:** 164, 207, 211; **Supp. XXIV:** 39, 41, 52, 63; **Supp. XXV:** 19; **Supp. XXVI:** 78, 143, 224, 226; **Supp. XXVII:** 284; **Supp. XXVIII:** 265

Williams, Mrs. William Carlos (Florence Herman), **IV:** 404

Williams, Wirt, **Supp. XIV:** 24

Williamson, Alan, **Retro. Supp. II:** 185; **Supp. XIX:** 91

Williamson, J. W., **Supp. XX: 164**

William Styron's Nat Turner: Ten Black Writers Respond (Clarke, ed.), **IV:** 115

Williams-Walsh, Mary Ellen, **Supp. IV Part 2:** 611

William the Conqueror, **Supp. I Part 2:** 507

William Wetmore Story and His Friends (James), **Retro. Supp. I:** 235; **Supp. XX: 228**

William Wilson (Gardner), **Supp. VI:** 72

"William Wilson" (Poe), **II:** 475; **III:** 410, 412; **Retro. Supp. II:** 269; **Retro. Supp. III:** 224, 225; **Supp. IX:** 105

"Willie" (Angelou), **Supp. IV Part 1:** 15

Willie Masters' Lonesome Wife (Gass), **Supp. VI:** 77, **84–85, 86–87**

"Willing" (Moore), **Supp. X:** 178

Willingly (Gallagher), **Supp. XXIV:** 166, 168, 169, 170, 176

Willis, Bruce, **Supp. IV Part 1:** 236

Willis, Dail, **Supp. XXIII:** 298

Willis, Gordon, **Supp. XV:** 7

Willis, Mary Hard, **Supp. V:** 290–291

Willis, Meredith, **Supp. XXVI:** 153

Willis, Nathaniel Parker, **II:** 313; **Retro. Supp. III:** 232, 236; **Supp. I Part 2:** 405; **Supp. XVIII:** 12

Willis, Rachel, **Supp. XXVII:** 216

Williwaw (Vidal), **Supp. IV Part 2:** 677, 680, 681

Willow Field, The (Kittredge), **Supp. XXVI:** 184

"Willow Woman" (Francis), **Supp. IX:** 78

Wills, Garry, **Supp. I Part 1:** 294; **Supp. IV Part 1:** 355

Wills, Ridley, **IV:** 122

Wills, Ross B., **Supp. XI:** 169

"Will to Believe, The" (James), **II:** 352; **Supp. XIV:** 50

Will to Believe, The, and Other Essays in Popular Philosophy (James), **II:** 356; **IV:** 28

Will to Change, The: Poems, 1968–1970 (Rich), **Retro. Supp. III:** 242, 244, 245; **Supp. I Part 2:** 551, 557–559

Will to Live On, The: This Is Our Heritage (Wouk), **Supp. XXV:** 257, 266

"Will We Plug Chips into Our Brains?" (W. Gibson), **Supp. XVI:** 117–118

Will You Please Be Quiet, Please? (Carver), **Supp. III Part 1:** 138, 140, 144

"Will You Please Be Quiet, Please?" (Carver), **Supp. III Part 1:** 137, 141

"Will You Tell Me?" (Barthelme), **Supp. IV Part 1:** 42, 47

Wilsdorf, Anne, **Supp. XVI:** 177

Wilsey, Sean, **Supp. XXV:** 1, 8

Wilshire, Bruce, **II:** 362, 364

Wilshire, Gaylord, **Supp. V:** 280

Wilson, Adrian, **Supp. XV:** 147

Wilson, Alexander, **Supp. XVI:** 4, 6

Wilson, Angust, **IV:** 430, 435

Wilson, August, **Retro. Supp. III: 313–329; Supp. VIII: 329–353; Supp. XIX:** 132

Wilson, Augusta Jane Evans, **Retro. Supp. I:** 351

Wilson, David, **Supp. XXVIII:** 166, 169, 174

Wilson, Earl, **Supp. X:** 264

Wilson, Edmund, **I:** 67, 185, 236, 247, 260, 434, 482; **II:** 79, 80, 81, 86, 87, 91, 97, 98, 146, 276, 430, 530, 562, 587; **III:** 588; **IV:** 308, 310, **426–449**; **Retro. Supp. I:** 1, 97, 100, 101, 103, 104, 105, 115, 274; **Retro. Supp. II:** 321, 327, 329; **Supp. I Part 1:** 372; **Supp. I Part 2:** 407, 646, 678, 709; **Supp. II Part 1:** 19, 90, 106, 136, 137, 143; **Supp. III Part 2:** 612; **Supp. IV Part 2:** 693; **Supp. IX:** 55, 65, 190; **Supp. VIII:** 93, 95, 96, 97, 98–99, 100, 101, 103, 105, 162; **Supp. X:** 186; **Supp. XI:** 160; **Supp. XIII:** 170; **Supp. XIV:** 338; **Supp. XV:** 142, 308; **Supp. XVI:** 194; **Supp. XX: 76, 81; Supp. XXII:** 278; **Supp. XXIII:** 104–105, 106; **Supp. XXIV:** 62, 217, 222, 281; **Supp. XXVIII:** 76

Wilson, Edmund (father), **IV:** 441

Wilson, E. O., **Supp. X:** 35

Wilson, Harriet, **Supp. XX: 105**

Wilson, Henry, **Supp. XIV:** 48

Wilson, Mary Ann, **Supp. XXVIII:** 115

Wilson, Reuel, **II:** 562

Wilson, Robert, **Supp. XI:** 144

Wilson, Robley, **Supp. XXIII:** 290

Wilson, Sloan, **Supp. IV Part 1:** 387

Wilson, Thomas, **IV:** 153

Wilson, Tracy, **Supp. XVIII:** 101

Wilson, Victoria, **Supp. X:** 166

Wilson, Woodrow, **I:** 245, 246, 490; **II:** 183, 253; **III:** 105, 581; **Supp. I Part 1:** 21; **Supp. I Part 2:** 474, 643; **Supp. V:** 288

Wilton, David, **IV:** 147

Wiman, Christian, **Supp. XV:** 251, 253, 264; **Supp. XVII:** 74; **Supp. XVIII:** 173, 174

Wimberly, Lowry, **Supp. XV:** 136, 137

"Wimp, The" (Gallagher), **Supp. XXIV:** 174

Wimsatt, William K., **Supp. XIV:** 12

Winch, Terence, **Supp. XXIII:** 291

Winchell, Mark, **Supp. VIII:** 176, 189

Winchell, Mark Royden, **Supp. IX:** 97, 98, 109; **Supp. VIII:** 241; **Supp. XIII:** 94, 98, 99, 101; **Supp. XIV:** 103, 106, 111

Winchell, Walter, **Supp. XXV:** 29

Winckelmann, Johann Joachim, **Supp. XII:** 178

Wind, Lee, **Supp. XXVIII:** 285

Wind, Sand, and Stars (Saint-Exupéry), **Supp. IX:** 247

Wind Across the Everglades (film, Ray), **Supp. XVIII:** 253

Wind Chrysalid's Rattle (Sobin), **Supp. XVI:** 283

"Windfall" (B. Kelly), **Supp. XVII:** 132

Windflower Home Almanac of Poetry, The (Kooser, ed.), **Supp. XIX:** 119

Windham, Donald, **IV:** 382

"Windhover" (Hopkins), **I:** 397; **II:** 539; **Supp. IX:** 43

Winding Stair and Other Poems, The (Yeats), **Supp. XV:** 253

"Winding Street, The" (Petry), **Supp. XI:** 6

"Window" (Pinsky), **Supp. VI:** 237, 247

"Window, The" (Hull), **Supp. XXI:** 140–141

Window at the White Cat, The (Rinehart), **Supp. XXV:** 192

Windows (Creeley), **Supp. IV Part 1:** 157, 158

"Windows" (Jarrell), **II:** 388, 389

"Window Seat, A" (Goldbarth), **Supp. XII:** 185

Wind Remains, The (opera) (Bowles), **Supp. IV Part 1:** 83

"Winds, The" (Welty), **IV:** 265; **Retro. Supp. I:** 348, 350

"Winds and Clouds over a Funeral" (Jin), **Supp. XVIII:** 94

Winds of War, The (miniseries), **Supp. XXV:** 265

Winds of War, The (Wouk), **Supp. XX:** 243; **Supp. XXV:** 254, 257, 258

"Wind up Sushi" (Goldbarth), **Supp. XII:** 186–187

Windy City Blues (Paretsky), **Supp. XXV:** 171

"Windy Day at the Reservoir, A" (Beattie), **Supp. V:** 33

Windy McPherson's Son (Anderson), **I:** 101, 102–103, 105, 111

"Wine" (Carver), **Supp. III Part 1:** 138

"Wine Menagerie, The" (H. Crane), **I:** 389, 391; **Retro. Supp. II:** 82

Wine of the Puritans, The: A Study of Present-Day America (Brooks), **I:** 240

"Wine of Wizardry, A" (Sterling), **I:** 208

Winer, Linda, **Supp. IV Part 2:** 580; **Supp. XV:** 332

Winesburg, Ohio (Anderson), **I:** 97, 102, 103, 104, 105–108; **III:** 112, 113, 114, 116, 224, 579; **Retro. Supp. III:** 76; **Supp. IX:** 306, 308; **Supp. V:** 12; **Supp. XI:** 164; **Supp. XVI:** 17; **Supp.**

XXII: 282; **Supp. XXIV:** 281

Winet, Kristin, **Supp. XXVIII:** 99

Winfrey, Oprah, **Retro. Supp. III:** 183; **Supp. XIX:** 194, 204; **Supp. XX:** 83, 93

Wing-and-Wing, The (Cooper), **I:** 350, 355

Winged Seed, The: A Remembrance (L.-Y. Lee), **Supp. XV:** 211, **220–223**

Winged Words: American Indian Writers Speak (Coltelli), **Supp. IV Part 2:** 493, 497

"Wingfield" (Wolff), **Supp. VII:** 341–342

"Wings, The" (Doty), **Supp. XI:** 124

"Wings in the Night" (Howard), **Supp. XXVII:** 122

Wings of the Dove, The (James), **I:** 436; **II:** 320, 323, 333, 334–335; **Retro. Supp. I:** 215, 216, 217, 232, **233–234;** **Supp. II Part 1:** 94–95; **Supp. IV Part 1:** 349

Winik, Marion, **Supp. XXVI:** 212

Winkelberg (Hecht), **Supp. XXVII:** 95

"Wink of the Zenith, The" (Skloot), **Supp. XX: 207**

Wink of the Zenith, The: The Shaping of a Writer's Life (Skloot), **Supp. XX: 195, 196, 207**

"Winkte"(Kenny), **Supp. XXIII:** 148–149

"Winky" (Saunders), **Supp. XIX:** 228–229, 229

"Winner, The" (Davison), **Supp. XXVI:** 64

Winner Names the Age, The: A Collection of Works by Lillian Smith (Cliff, ed.), **Supp. XXII:** 67

Winners, Viola Hopkins, **Retro. Supp. III:** 289

Winner Take Nothing (Hemingway), **II:** 249; **Retro. Supp. I:** 170, 175, 176, 181

"Winnie" (Brooks), **Supp. III Part 1:** 86

Winokur, Maxine. *See* Kumin, Maxine

Winslow, Art, **Supp. XVIII:** 102

Winslow, Devereux, **II:** 547

Winslow, Harriet, **II:** 552–553

Winslow, Ola Elizabeth, **I:** 547

Winslow, Warren, **II:** 540

Winston, Andrew, **Supp. XII:** 189

Winston, Michael R., **Supp. XIV:** 197

Winter, Douglas, **Supp. V:** 144

Winter, Johnny and Edgar, **Supp. V:** 334

Winter, Kate, **Supp. X:** 104

"Winter Branch, A" (Irving), **Supp. VI:** 163

"Winter Burial, A" (Clampitt), **Supp. IX:** 48

Winter Carnival (film), **Retro. Supp. I:** 113

"Winter Concert"(Strout), **Supp. XXIII:** 283

"Winter Daybreak at Vence, A" (Wright), **Supp. III Part 1:** 249–250

Winter Diary, A (Van Doren), **I:** 168

"Winter Dreams" (Fitzgerald), **II:** 80, 94; **Retro. Supp. I:** 108

"Winter Drive, A" (Jewett), **Retro. Supp. II:** 147

"Winter Eden, A" (Frost), **Retro. Supp. I:** 137

"Winter Father, The" (Dubus), **Supp. VII:** 83, 87

Winter Hours: Prose, Prose Poems, and Poems (Oliver), **Supp. VII:** 230, 247

"Winter in Dunbarton" (R. Lowell), **II:** 547; **Retro. Supp. II:** 187

"Wintering" (Plath), **Retro. Supp. II:** 255

"Wintering Over" (Davison), **Supp. XXVI:** 76

Winter Insomnia (Carver), **Supp. III Part 1:** 138

Winter in the Blood (Welch), **Supp. IV Part 2:** 562

"Winter Landscape" (Berryman), **I:** 174; **Retro. Supp. I:** 430

Winter Light (W. V. Davis), **Supp. XXI: 92,** 93

"Winter Light" (W. V. Davis), **Supp. XXI:** 90, 92

Winter Lightning (Nemerov), **III:** 269

Winter Morning Walks: One Hundred Postcards to Jim Harrison (Kooser), **Supp. XIX:** 116, **125–126**

Winter News (Haines), **Supp. XII:** 199, **201–204,** 207–208, 208

"Winter Night, A" (Teasdale), **Supp. XXVII:** 289

Winternitz, Mary. *See* Cheever, Mrs. John (Mary Winternitz)

Winter: Notes from Montana (Bass), **Supp. XVI:** 17–18

Winter of Our Discontent, The (Steinbeck), **IV:** 52, 65–66, 68

"Winter on Earth" (Toomer), **Supp. III Part 2:** 486

"Winter Piece, A" (Bryant), **Supp. I Part 1:** 150, 155

"Winter Rains, Cataluña" (Levine), **Supp. V:** 182

"Winter Remembered" (Ransom), **III:** 492–493

"Winter Roses" (W. V. Davis), **Supp. XXI:** 94

Winterrowd, Prudence, **I:** 217, 224

Winters, Ivor, **Retro. Supp. III:** 50

Winters, Jonathan, **Supp. XI:** 305

Winters, Yvor, **I:** 59, 63, 386, 393, 397, 398, 402, 471; **III:** 194, 498; **IV:** 153; **Retro. Supp. II:** 76, 77, 78, 82, 83, 85, 89; **Supp. I Part 1:** 268; **Supp. II Part 2:** 416, 666, **785–816; Supp. IV Part 2:** 480; **Supp. V:** 180, 191–192; **Supp. XIV:** 287; **Supp. XV:** 74, 341; **Supp. XXV:** 250

"Winter Sacrament" (Bronk), **Supp. XXI:** 33

"Winter Scenes" (Bryant). *See* "Winter Piece, A"

Winterset (Anderson), **III:** 159

"Winter Shrub, A" (Bronk), **Supp. XXI:** 28

"Winter Skyline Late" (F. Wright), **Supp. XVII:** 245

"Winter Sleep" (Wylie), **Supp. I Part 2:** 711, 729

Winter's Night (Boyce), **Supp. XXI:** 7, **12–13**

Winter's Tale (film, Goldsman), **Supp. XXV:** 86

Winter's Tale (Helprin), **Supp. XXV:** 79–80, 81, 82, 83, 86

Winter's Tale, The (Shakespeare), **Supp. XIII:** 219

Winter Stars (Levis), **Supp. XI:** 259, **266–268**

"Winter Stars" (Levis), **Supp. XI:** 267–268

"Winter Stars" (Teasdale), **Supp. XXVII:** 295

Winter Stop-Over (Everwine), **Supp. XV:** 74, 76

"Winter Stop-Over" (Everwine), **Supp. XV:** 76

Winter Studies and Summer Rambles in Canada (Jameson), **Supp. XXIII:** 225, 226

"Winter Sunrise" (Davison), **Supp. XXVI:** 69

"Winter Swan" (Bogan), **Supp. III Part 1:** 52

"Winter Thunder" (Sandoz), **Supp. XXIV:** 255

Winter Thunder (X. J. Kennedy), **Supp. XV:** 167

"Winter Thunder" (X. J. Kennedy), **Supp. XV:** 169

"Winter Trees" (Pedersen; Nelson, trans.), **Supp. XVIII:** 180

Winter Trees (Plath), **Retro. Supp. II:** 257; **Supp. I Part 2:** 526, 539, 541; **Supp. XXVII:** 296

"Winter Walk" (W. V. Davis), **Supp. XXI:** 92

"Winter Weather Advisory" (Ashbery), **Supp. III Part 1:** 26

"Winter Wheat" (Hoffman), **Supp. XVIII:** 86, 87

"Winter Wind" (Munro), **Supp. XXVII:** 185

"Winter without Snow, The" (C. Frost), **Supp. XV:** 96, 105–106

"Winter Words" (Levine), **Supp. V:** 192

Winthrop, John, **Retro. Supp. III:** 3; **Supp. I Part 1:** 99, 100, 101, 102, 105; **Supp. I Part 2:** 484, 485

Winthrop Covenant, The (Auchincloss), **Supp. IV Part 1:** 23

"Wires of the Night, The" (Collins), **Supp. XXI:** 64

Wirt, William, **I:** 232

Wirth, Louis, **IV:** 475

Wisconsin Death Trip (Lesy), **Supp. XXV:** 146

Wisconsin Death Trip (Levy), **Supp. XIX:** 102

"Wisdom" (Teasdale), **Supp. XXVII:** 291

"Wisdom Cometh with the Years" (Cullen), **Supp. IV Part 1:** 166

Wisdom of the African World (McKnight, ed.), **Supp. XX: 157–158**

Wisdom of the Desert, The: Sayings from the Desert Fathers of the Fourth Century (Merton), **Supp. VIII:** 201

Wisdom of the Heart, The (H. Miller), **III:** 178, 184

Wise, Stephen S., **Supp. XXVIII:** 153

Wise Blood (O'Connor), **III:** 337, 338, 339–343, 344, 345, 346, 350, 354, 356, 357; **Retro. Supp. II:** 219, 221, 222, 223, **225–228; Retro. Supp. III:** 208, 209–210, 213, 215

Wise Men, The (Price), **Supp. VI:** 254

"Wiser Than a God" (Chopin), **Retro. Supp. II:** 61; **Supp. I Part 1:** 208

"Wishbone"(Siken), **Supp. XXVIII:** 200

Wishes, Lies, and Dreams: Teaching Children to Write Poetry (Koch), **Supp. XV:** 176, 189; **Supp. XXVII:** 26

"Wish for a Young Wife" (Roethke), **III:** 548

Wishful Thinking: A Theological ABC (Buechner), **Supp. XII:** 53

Wishing Tree, The: Christopher Isherwood on Mystical Religion (Adjemian, ed.), **Supp. XIV:** 164, 173

"Wish List" (Goodman), **Supp. XXVI:** 119–120

Wish You Were Here (O'Nan), **Supp. XXV:** 142, 147–148, 150, 152

Wismer, Helen Muriel. *See* Thurber, Mrs. James (Helen Muriel Wismer)

Wisse, Ruth, **Supp. XII:** 167, 168

Wister, Owen, **I:** 62; **Retro. Supp. II:** 72; **Supp. XIV:** 39

Wit (Edson), **Supp. XVIII:** 35–36, 37, **38–51**

"Witchbird" (Bambara), **Supp. XI:** 11

"Witch Burning" (Plath), **Supp. I Part 2:** 539

Witchcraft of Salem Village, The (Jackson), **Supp. IX:** 121

"Witch Doctor" (Hayden), **Supp. II Part 1:** 368, 380

Witches of Eastwick, The (Updike), **Retro. Supp. I:** 330, 331

Witch from Castile, The (Asch), **Supp. XXIII:** 6, 10

Witching Hour, The (Rice), **Supp. VII:** 299–300

"Witch of Coös, The" (Frost), **II:** 154–155; **Retro. Supp. I:** 135; **Retro. Supp. II:** 42

"Witch of Owl Mountain Springs, The: An Account of Her Remarkable Powers" (Taylor), **Supp. V:** 328

"Witch of Wenham, The" (Whittier), **Supp. I Part 2:** 694, 696

Witek, Terri, **Supp. XVII:** 117

"With a Little Help from My Friends" (Kushner), **Supp. IX:** 131

With Bold Knife and Fork (M. F. K. Fisher), **Supp. XVII:** 89, 91

"With Che at Kitty Hawk" (Banks), **Supp. V:** 6

"With Che at the Plaza" (Banks), **Supp. V:** 7

"With Che in New Hampshire" (Banks), **Supp. V:** 6

"With Child" (Taggard), **Supp. XXII:** 276, 278

"Withdrawal Symptoms" (Mora), **Supp. XIII:** 216

"Withered Leaf, A—Seen on a Poet's Table" (Very), **Supp. XXV:** 243

"Withered Skins of Berries" (Toomer), **Supp. III Part 2:** 485; **Supp. IX:** 320

Withers, Harry Clay, **Supp. XIII:** 161

Witherspoon, John, **Supp. I Part 2:** 504

With Eyes at the Back of Our Heads (Levertov), **Supp. III Part 1:** 276–277

With Her in Ourland (Gilman), **Supp. XI:** 208–209

With His Pistol in His Hand (Paredes), **Supp. XIII:** 225; **Supp. XIX:** 98

"Within the Words: An Apprenticeship" (Haines), **Supp. XII:** 197

"With Kit, Age 7, at the Beach" (Stafford), **Supp. XI:** 323

With Love to Lesbia (Kenny), **Supp. XXIII:** 145

"With Mercy for the Greedy" (Sexton), **Supp. II Part 2:** 680

With My Trousers Rolled (Epstein), **Supp. XIV:** 101, 105

Without a Hero (Boyle), **Supp. VIII:** 16; **Supp. XX: 20**

Without Feathers (Allen), **Supp. XV:** 3, 14, 15

Without Stopping (Bowles), **Supp. IV Part 1:** 79, 81, 85, 90, 91, 92

"Without Tradition and within Reason: Judge Horton and Atticus Finch in Court" (C. D. Johnson), **Supp. VIII:** 127

With Shuddering Fall (Oates), **Supp. II Part 2:** 504–506

"With the Dog at Sunrise" (Kenyon), **Supp. VII:** 170

With the Empress Dowager of China (Carl), **III:** 475

"With the Horse in the Winter Pasture" (McCarriston), **Supp. XIV:** 262

With the Old Breed: At Peleliu and Okinawa (Sledge), **Supp. V:** 249–250

"With the Violin" (Chopin), **Retro. Supp. II:** 61

"Witness" (Clampitt), **Supp. IX:** 42–43, 45, 46

"Witness" (Dubus), **Supp. VII:** 89

"Witness" (Harjo), **Supp. XII:** 227–228

Witness (McNally), **Supp. XIII:** 197

"Witness" (Nelson), **Supp. XVIII:** 186

"Witness, The" (Porter), **III:** 443–444

"Witness for Poetry, A" (Stafford), **Supp. XI:** 324

"Witness for the Defense" (Hay), **Supp. XIV:** 124

"Witnessing My Father's Will" (Karr), **Supp. XI:** 241

"Witnessing to a Shared World" (Sanders), **Supp. XVI:** 278

Witness to the Times! (McGrath), **Supp. X:** 118

Witness Tree, A (Frost), **II:** 155; **Retro. Supp. I:** 122, 137, 139; **Retro. Supp. III:** 104

Wit's End: Days and Nights of the Algonquin Round Table (Gaines), **Supp. IX:** 190

Wits Recreations (Mennes and Smith), **II:** 111

Witt, Shirley Hill, **Supp. IV Part 2:** 505

Witte, John, **Supp. XX: 200**

Wittels, Anne F., **Supp. XV:** 59
Wittenberg, Judith Bryant, **Retro. Supp. II:** 146
Wittgenstein, Ludwig, **Retro. Supp. I:** 53; **Supp. III Part 2:** 626–627; **Supp. X:** 304; **Supp. XII:** 21; **Supp. XV:** 344, 346
Wittgensteins' Mistress (Markson), **Supp. XVII:** 135, 142, 143, 145
Wittliff, William, **Supp. V:** 227
"Witty War, A" (Simpson), **Supp. IX:** 268
Witz (Cohen), **Supp. XXII:** 268
"Wives and Mistresses" (Hardwick), **Supp. III Part 1:** 211–212
"Wives of the Dead, The" (Hawthorne), **Retro. Supp. III:** 110–111
Wizard of Loneliness, The (Nichols), **Supp. XIII:** 259, 263, 264
Wizard of Oz, The (Baum), **Supp. IV Part 1:** 113
Wizard of Oz, The (film), **Supp. X:** 172, 214
Wizard's Tide, The: A Story (Buechner), **Supp. XII:** 54
"WLT (The Edgar Era)" (Keillor), **Supp. XVI:** 172
WLT: A Radio Romance (Keillor), **Supp. XVI:** 176
Wobegon Boy (Keillor), **Supp. XVI:** 177
Wodehouse, P. G., **Supp. IX:** 195; **Supp. XXI:** 204–205
Woiwode, Larry, **Supp. VIII:** 151; **Supp. XVI:** 206
Wojahn, David, **Supp. IX:** 161, 292, 293; **Supp. XXI:** 130, 131, 132, 138, 139, 141
Wolcott, Derek, **Retro. Supp. III:** 318
Wolcott, James, **Supp. IX:** 259
Wolf, Christa, **Supp. IV Part 1:** 310, 314
Wolf, Daniel, **Retro. Supp. II:** 202
Wolf, Robert L., **Supp. XXII:** 274, 277, 279, 280
Wolf: A False Memoir (Harrison), **Supp. VIII:** 40, **41–42,** 45
Wolfe, Ben, **IV:** 454
Wolfe, Gregory, **Supp. XIV:** 307
Wolfe, James, **Supp. I Part 2:** 498
Wolfe, Linnie, **Supp. IX:** 176
Wolfe, Mabel, **IV:** 454
Wolfe, Thomas, **I:** 288, 289, 374, 478, 495; **II:** 457; **III:** 40, 108, 278, 334, 482; **IV:** 52, 97, 357, **450–473; Retro. Supp. I:** 382; **Supp. I Part 1:** 29; **Supp. IV Part 1:** 101; **Supp. IX:** 229; **Supp. X:** 225; **Supp. XI:** 213, 216, 217, 218; **Supp. XIII:** 17; **Supp. XIV:** 122; **Supp. XVIII:** 78; **Supp. XX: 163; Supp. XXVII:** 38
Wolfe, Tom, **Supp. III Part 2:** 567–588; **Supp. IV Part 1:** 35, 198; **Supp. V:** 296; **Supp. X:** 264; **Supp. XI:** 239; **Supp. XV:** 143; **Supp. XVII:** 202; **Supp. XVIII:** 72, 117; **Supp. XXIV:** 282, 283
Wolfe, William Oliver, **IV:** 454
Wolfe, Mrs. William Oliver (Julia Elizabeth Westall), **IV:** 454
"Wolfe Homo Scribens" (Cowley), **Supp. II Part 1:** 144
Wolfert, Ira, **Supp. XXI: 261–279**

Wolfert's Roost (Irving), **II:** 314
Wolff, Cynthia Griffin, **Retro. Supp. I:** 379; **Supp. IV Part 1:** 203
Wolff, Donald, **Supp. XIII:** 316, 317, 326
Wolff, Geoffrey, **Supp. II Part 1:** 97; **Supp. XI:** 239, 245, 246; **Supp. XXII:** 206, 211; **Supp. XXV:** 217
Wolff, Tobias, **Retro. Supp. I:** 190; **Supp. V:** 22; **Supp. VII: 331–346; Supp. X:** 1; **Supp. XI:** 26, 239, 245, 246, 247; **Supp. XV:** 223; **Supp. XVI:** 39, 41, 63, 70, 77; **Supp. XXIII:** 289; **Supp. XXV:** 142, 208
"Wolf in the Bed, The"(Hadas), **Supp. XXIII:** 118
Wolfreys, Julian, **Supp. XVIII:** 61
"Wolfshead" (Howard), **Supp. XXVII:** 116, 119
Wolfson, P. J., **Supp. XIII:** 172
"Wolf Town" (Carson), **Supp. XII: 102**
Wolf Willow: A History, a Story, and a Memory of the Last Plains Frontier (Stegner), **Supp. IV Part 2:** 595, 596, 597, 598, 599, 600, 601, 604, 606, 611, 613, 614
Wolitzer, Hilma, **Supp. XV:** 55; **Supp. XXIII:** 108
Wolitzer, Meg, **Supp. XV:** 65
Wolkomir, Richard, **Supp. XXII:** 218
Wollaston, William, **II:** 108
Wollstonecraft, Mary, **Supp. I Part 1:** 126; **Supp. I Part 2:** 512, 554
"Wolves in the Asheville Zoo, The" (Rash), **Supp. XXVII:** 220
"Wolves in the Marsh" (Dubus III), **Supp. XXIV:** 99–100
Womack, Craig, **Supp. XXIII:** 147, 153, 154–155
"Woman" (Bogan), **Supp. X:** 102
"Woman, I Got the Blues" (Komunyakaa), **Supp. XIII:** 117
"Woman, Why Are You Weeping?" (Kenyon), **Supp. VII:** 174–175
"Woman, Young and Old, A" (Paley), **Supp. VI:** 222, 225
Woman Aroused, The (Lacy), **Supp. XV:** 199–200
"Woman at the Pond, The" (Rash), **Supp. XXVII:** 215, 230
Woman at the Washington Zoo, The (Jarrell), **II:** 367, 386, 387, 389
Woman Before an Aquarium (Hampl), **Supp. XXII:** 83, 86, 98
"Woman Before an Aquarium" (Hampl), **Supp. XXII:** 85, 98
"Womand and the Woman's Movement" (Briggs), **Supp. XVIII:** 14
"Woman Dead in Her Forties, A" (Rich), **Retro. Supp. III:** 249; **Supp. I Part 2:** 574–575
Woman Driver, The (Thompson), **Supp. XXIII:** 291, **294–295**
"Woman Enough" (Gallagher), **Supp. XXIV:** 169
"Woman Hanging from the Thirteenth Floor Window, The" (Harjo), **Supp. XII:** 216, 221
"Woman Hollering Creek" (Cisneros), **Supp. VII:** 70

Woman Hollering Creek and Other Stories (Cisneros), **Supp. VII:** 58, 68–70
"Womanhood" (Brooks), **Supp. III Part 1:** 77
"Woman in Rain" (X. J. Kennedy), **Supp. XV:** 168
Woman in the Dark (Hammett), **Supp. IV Part 1:** 343
"Woman in the House, A" (Caldwell), **I:** 310
Woman in the Nineteenth Century (Fuller), **Retro. Supp. I:** 156; **Supp. II Part 1:** 279, 292, 294–296; **Supp. XI:** 197, 203; **Supp. XVIII:** 3, 11
"Woman in the Shoe, The" (Ryan as Quin), **Supp. XVIII:** 231
Woman in White, The (Collins), **Supp. I Part 1:** 35, 36
"Woman Is Talking to Death, A"(Grahn), **Supp. XXIII:** 195
"Womanizer, The" (Ford), **Supp. V:** 71, 72
"Woman Like Yourself, A" (C. Frost), **Supp. XV:** 107
Woman Lit by Fireflies, The (Harrison), **Supp. VIII: 50–51**
"Woman Loses Cookie Bake-Off, Sets Self on Fire" (R. O. Butler), **Supp. XII:** 72
Woman of Andros, The (Wilder), **IV:** 356, 363–364, 367, 368, 374
Woman of Means, A (Taylor), **Supp. V:** 319–320
"Woman of Tomorrow, The" (Atherton), **Supp. XXIV:** 29
Woman on the Edge of Time (Piercy), **Supp. XIII:** 29
Woman on the Porch, The (Gordon), **II:** 199, 209–211
"Woman on the Stair, The" (MacLeish), **III:** 15–16
"Woman's Dream, A" (E. Stoddard), **Supp. XV:** 278
"Woman's Exchange in Simpkinsville, The"(Stuart), **Supp. XXVIII:** 227, 234–235
Woman's Fiction: A Guide to Novels By and About Women in America, 1820–1870 (Baym), **Supp. XVIII:** 258
"Woman's Heartlessness" (Thaxter), **Retro. Supp. II:** 147
Woman's Honor (Glaspell), **Supp. III Part 1:** 179
"Woman Singing" (Ortiz), **Supp. IV Part 2:** 513
Woman's Place, A (C. L. R. James and Weinstein), **Supp. XXI:** 170
Woman's Share in Primitive Culture (Mason), **Supp. I Part 1:** 18
"Woman Struck by Car Turns into Nymphomaniac" (R. O. Butler), **Supp. XII:** 72
"Woman's Work" (Alvarez), **Supp. VII:** 4
"Woman Taken in Adultery, A"(Thompson), **Supp. XXIII:** 300
"Woman Uses Glass Eye to Spy on Philandering Husband" (R. O. Butler), **Supp. XII:** 70, 72

Woman Warrior (Kingston), **Supp. IV Part 1:** 12; **Supp. V:** 157, 158, 159, 160–164, 166, 169; **Supp. X:** 291–292; **Supp. XIV:** 162

Woman Warrior, The (Kingston), **Supp. XV:** 220

"Woman Who Believed in Jaguars, The" (Rash), **Supp. XXVII:** 228

Woman Who Fell from the Sky, The (Harjo), **Supp. XII: 226–228**

"Woman Who Fell From the Sky, The" (Iroquois creation story), **Supp. IV Part 1:** 327

Woman Who Owned the Shadows, The (Gunn Allen), **Supp. IV Part 1:** 320, 322, 326, 327–328

"Woman Who Plays Trumpet Is Deported, A" (Cliff), **Supp. XXII:** 74

"Woman Who Prayed, The" (Gallagher), **Supp. XXIV:** 175

"Woman Who Raised Goats, The" (Gallagher), **Supp. XXIV:** 168

"Woman Who Went Backwards, The" (Schott), **Supp. XXIII:** 241

Woman Within, The (Glasgow), **II:** 183, 190–191; **Supp. XXVIII:** 124

"Womanwork" (Gunn Allen), **Supp. IV Part 1:** 326

Women (Bukowski), **Supp. XI:** 172

"Women" (Didion), **Supp. IV Part 1:** 205

"Women" (Swenson), **Supp. IV Part 2:** 647

Women, The (Boyle), **Supp. XX: 24, 26–27**

Women, The (film), **Retro. Supp. I:** 113

Women, The (film; Cukor), **Supp. XVI:** 181, 192

"Women, The" (Stuart), **Supp. XXVIII:** 236

Women, Violence, and Testimony in the Works of Zora Neale Hurston (Miles), **Retro. Supp. III:** 139

"Women and Children First" (Prose), **Supp. XVI:** 254

Women and Children First: Stories (Prose), **Supp. XVI:** 254

Women and Economics (Gilman), **Supp. I Part 2:** 637; **Supp. V:** 284; **Supp. XI:** 200, **203–204,** 206

"Women and Honor: Some Notes on Lying" (Rich), **Retro. Supp. III:** 247–248

"Women and Poetry" (Notley), **Supp. XXII:** 236

Women and Thomas Harrow (Marquand), **III:** 50, 61, 62, 66, 68, 69–70, 71

Women and Vodka (Markson as Merrill, ed.), **Supp. XVII:** 136

Women and Wilderness (LaBastille), **Supp. X:** 97, **102–104**

"Women as They Are" (Rowson), **Supp. XV:** 243

Women at Point Sur, The (Jeffers), **Supp. II Part 2:** 430–431

Women Authors of Our Day in Their Homes (Halsey), **Supp. XXIV:** 20

Women in Love (Lawrence), **III:** 27, 34; **Supp. XXIV:** 58

Women in Praise of the Sacred: 43 Centuries of Spiritual Poetry by Women (Hirshfield, ed.), **Supp. XXIII:** 136, 137

"Women of Auschwitz, The" (Gallagher), **Supp. XXIV:** 171

Women of Belize: Gender and Change in Central America (McClaurin), **Supp. XXIII:** 84

Women of Brewster Place, The: A Novel in Seven Stories (Naylor), **Supp. VIII:** 213, **214–218**

Women of Manhattan: An Upper West Side Story (Shanley), **Supp. XIV:** 315, **326–327**

"Women of My Color" (Coleman), **Supp. XI:** 88–89

Women of Mystery: The Lives and Works of Notable Women Crime Novelists (DuBose), **Supp. XXV:** 199

Women of Provincetown, The (Black), **Supp. XXVIII:** 38

Women of Trachis (Pound, trans.), **III:** 476

"Women on the Breadlines" (Le Sueur), **Supp. XXIII:** 166, 167

Women on the Wall, The (Stegner), **Supp. IV Part 2:** 599, 605, 606

Women Poets in English (Stanford, ed.), **Retro. Supp. I:** 41

"Women Reformers and American Culture, 1870–1930" (Conway), **Supp. I Part 1:** 19

Women's Barracks (T. Levin), **Supp. XXVII:** 140

"Women's Movement, The" (Didion), **Supp. IV Part 1:** 206

"Women Waiting" (Shields), **Supp. VII:** 320

"Women We Love Whom We Never See Again" (R. Bly), **Supp. IV Part 1:** 66

"Women We Never See Again" (R. Bly), **Supp. IV Part 1:** 66

Women Who Make Our Novels, The (Overton), **Supp. XXV:** 200

Women with Men (Ford), **Supp. V:** 57, 71–72

"Wonder" (Olds), **Supp. X:** 210

Wonder-Book for Girls and Boys, A (Hawthorne), **Retro. Supp. III:** 121

Wonder Boys (Chabon), **Supp. XI:** 67, **73–75,** **Supp. XI:** 78; **Supp. XVI:** 259

Wonder Boys (film), **Supp. XI:** 67

Wonderful O, The (Thurber), **Supp. I Part 2:** 612

"Wonderful Old Gentleman, The" (Parker), **Supp. IX:** 197

"Wonderful Pen, The" (Swenson), **Supp. IV Part 2:** 650

Wonderful Wizard of Oz, The (Baum), **Supp. XXV:** 129

Wonderful Words, Silent Truth: Essays on Poetry and a Memoir (Simic), **Supp. VIII:** 270

Wonder Hat and Other One-Act Plays, The (Hecht and Goodman), **Supp. XXVII:** 89

Wonderland (Oates), **Supp. II Part 2:** 511, 512, 514–515

"Wonder: Red Beans and Ricely" (Lea), **Supp. XXVIII:** 141–142

Wonders Hidden (Sanders), **Supp. XVI:** 269

Wonders of the African World (television series), **Supp. XX:** 99

Wonders of the Invisible World, The (Mather), **Supp. II Part 2:** 456–459, 460, 467

Wonder-Working Providence (E. Johnson), **IV:** 157

Wong, Hertha, **Supp. IV Part 1:** 275

Wong, Jade Snow, **Supp. X:** 291

Wong, Nellie, **Supp. XVII:** 72

Wong, Shawn, **Supp. XV:** 221

Wong, Timothy, **Supp. XVIII:** 94

"Wood" (Nye), **Supp. XIII:** 276

Wood, Audrey, **IV:** 381

Wood, Charles Erskine Scott, **Supp. XV:** 301

Wood, Clement, **Supp. XV:** 298

Wood, Clement Biddle, **Supp. XI:** 307

Wood, Gaby, **Supp. XXIV:** 166

Wood, Harrison, **Supp. XXII:** 283

Wood, Mrs. Henry, **Supp. I Part 1:** 35

Wood, James, **Supp. XIV:** 95–96; **Supp. XIX:** 138

Wood, Mabel, **I:** 199

Wood, Michael, **Supp. IV Part 2:** 691

Wood, Norman Barton, **Supp. XIV:** 201

Wood, Susan, **Supp. XVI:** 123

Woodard, Calvin, **Supp. VIII:** 128

Woodard, Charles L., **Supp. IV Part 2:** 484, 493

Woodard, Deborah, **Supp. XIII:** 114

Woodberry, George Edward, **III:** 508

Woodbridge, Frederick, **I:** 217, 224

Woodbridge, John, **Retro. Supp. III:** 3, 4; **Supp. I Part 1:** 101, 102, 114

Woodbury, Hanni, **Supp. XXVI:** 8, 82, 87, 90, 95

"Wood-Choppers, The" (Chopin), **Retro. Supp. II:** 72

Woodcock, George, **Supp. XIII:** 33

Woodcome, Beth, **Supp. XVII:** 240

"Wood Dove at Sandy Spring, The" (MacLeish), **III:** 19

"Wooden Spring" (Rukeyser), **Supp. VI:** 285

"Wooden Umbrella, The" (Porter), **IV:** 26

Woodhull, Victoria, **Supp. XVIII:** 4

"Woodnotes" (Emerson), **II:** 7, 19

"Wood-Pile, The" (Frost), **Retro. Supp. I:** 128; **Retro. Supp. III:** 97; **Supp. IV Part 2:** 445

Woodress, James, **Retro. Supp. III:** 21

Woodrow, James, **Supp. I Part 1:** 349, 366

"Woods, Books, and Truant Officers, The" (Maclean), **Supp. XIV:** 221, 225

Woods, James, **Supp. XXVII:** 277

"Woods, New York, The" (Bronk), **Supp. XXI:** 27

Woods, Paula L., **Supp. XXI:** 70

Woods, Robert A., **Supp. I Part 1:** 19

Woods, The (Mamet), **Supp. XIV:** 241, 254–255

Woodson, Jacqueline, **Supp. XXVIII: 277–290**

Woodson, Jon, **Retro. Supp. III:** 140

Woodswoman (LaBastille), **Supp. X:** 95, **96–99,** 108

Woodswoman III: Book Three of the Woodswoman's Adventures (LaBastille), **Supp. X:** 95, **106–107**

"Wood Thrush" (Kenyon), **Supp. VII:** 172

Woodward, C. Vann, **IV:** 114, 470–471; **Retro. Supp. I:** 75, 76; **Supp. XIX:** 152; **Supp. XXII:** 194

"Woof: A Plea of Sorts" (Saunders), **Supp. XIX:** 235

"Woofing" (Hurston), **Retro. Supp. III:** 137

"Wooing the Inanimate" (Brodsky), **Supp. VIII:** 32

Woolcott, Alexander, **Supp. IX:** 197

Wooley, Bryan, **Supp. V:** 225

Woolf, Douglas, **Supp. XXIII:** 174

Woolf, Leonard, **Supp. IX:** 95

Woolf, Virginia, **I:** 53, 79, 112, 309; **II:** 320, 415; **IV:** 59; **Retro. Supp. I:** 59, 75, 170, 215, 291, 359; **Supp. I Part 2:** 553, 714, 718; **Supp. IV Part 1:** 299; **Supp. IX:** 66, 109; **Supp. V:** 127; **Supp. VIII:** 5, 155, 251, 252, 263, 265; **Supp. XI:** 134, 193; **Supp. XII:** 81, 98, 289; **Supp. XIII:** 305; **Supp. XIV:** 341–342, 342, 343, 346, 348; **Supp. XIX:** 134; **Supp. XV:** 55, 65; **Supp. XXIII:** 275; **Supp. XXVII:** 183

Woollcott, Alexander, **IV:** 432; **Retro. Supp. II:** 327; **Supp. I Part 2:** 664; **Supp. IX:** 190, 194

Woolley, Leonard, **Supp. XXIII:** 33

Woollstonecraft, Mary, **Supp. XVI:** 184

"Woolly Mammoth" (X. J. Kennedy), **Supp. XV:** 163–164

Woolman, John, **Supp. VIII:** 202, 204, 205

Woolsey, Sarah Chauncey, **Supp. XXVIII:** 228

Woolson, Constance Fenimore, **Retro. Supp. I:** 224, 228

Woolverton, Linda, **Supp. XXI:** 148

Wooster, David, **Supp. XX:** 288

Worcester, Samuel, **I:** 458

Word and Idioms: Studies in the English Language (L. P. Smith), **Supp. XIV:** 343

"Word by Word" (column, Lamott), **Supp. XX:** 140

"Word from the Outer Dark, A" (Howard), **Supp. XXVII:** 118

"Wordless Winter" (Davison), **Supp. XXVI:** 75–76

Word of God and the Word of Man, The (Barth), **Retro. Supp. I:** 327

"Word out of the Sea, A" (Whitman), **IV:** 344

Words (Creeley), **Supp. IV Part 1:** 139, 150–153, 154, 155, 158

"Words" (Creeley), **Supp. IV Part 1:** 152

"Words" (Gioia), **Supp. XV:** 125

"Words" (Merwin), **Supp. III Part 1:** 352

"Words" (Plath), **Supp. I Part 2:** 547

"Words" (Shields), **Supp. VII:** 323

"Words, The" (Wagoner), **Supp. IX:** 326

"Words above a Narrow Entrance" (Wagoner), **Supp. IX:** 325

"Words for a Bike-Racing, Osprey-Chasing Wine-Drunk Squaw Man" (Gunn Allen), **Supp. IV Part 1:** 325

Words for Dr. Y (Sexton), **Supp. II Part 2:** 698

"Words for Hart Crane" (R. Lowell), **I:** 381; **II:** 547; **Retro. Supp. II:** 188; **Retro. Supp. III:** 41, 54

"Words for Love" (Berrigan), **Supp. XXIV:** 35

"Words for Maria" (Merrill), **Supp. III Part 1:** 327

"Words for My Father" (Davison), **Supp. XXVI:** 72

"Words for My Grandmother" (Balakian), **Supp. XXIII:** 19, 20

Words for the Chisel (Taggard), **Supp. XXII:** **276–277**

"Words for the Unknown Makers" (Kunitz), **Supp. III Part 1:** 264

Words for the Wind (Roethke), **III:** 529, 533, 541, 543, 545

"Words for the Wind" (Roethke), **III:** 542–543

Words in the Mourning Time (Hayden), **Supp. II Part 1:** 361, 366, 367

"Words in the Mourning Time" (Hayden), **Supp. II Part 1:** 370–371

"Words into Fiction" (Welty), **IV:** 279

"Words into Worlds Won't Go" (Major), **Supp. XXII:** 174

"Words Like Freedom" (Hughes), **Retro. Supp. I:** 207

"Words of a Young Girl" (R. Lowell), **II:** 554

"Words of Prey" (Stallings), **Supp. XXV:** 230

Words under the Words: Selected Poems (Nye), **Supp. XIII:** 277

Wordsworth, Dorothy, **Supp. IX:** 38

Wordsworth, William, **I:** 283, 522, 524, 525, 588; **II:** 7, 11, 17, 18, 97, 169, 273, 303, 304, 532, 549, 552; **III:** 219, 263, 277, 278, 511, 521, 523, 528, 583; **IV:** 120, 331, 343, 453, 465; **Retro. Supp. I:** 121, 196; **Supp. I Part 1:** 150, 151, 154, 161, 163, 312, 313, 349, 365; **Supp. I Part 2:** 375, 409, 416, 422, 607, 621, 622, 673, 674, 675, 676, 677, 710–711, 729; **Supp. II Part 1:** 4; **Supp. III Part 1:** 12, 15, 73, 279; **Supp. IV Part 2:** 597, 601; **Supp. IX:** 38, 41, 265, 274; **Supp. V:** 258; **Supp. VIII:** 273; **Supp. X:** 22, 23, 65, 120; **Supp. XI:** 248, 251, 312; **Supp. XIII:** 214; **Supp. XIV:** 184; **Supp. XIX:** 1; **Supp. XV:** 93, 250; **Supp. XX:** 108, 116; **Supp. XXI:** 131; **Supp. XXIV:** 74, 159

" 'Word Which Made All Clear, The': The Silent Close of *The House of Mirth*" (Benstock), **Supp. XX:** 240

Work (Alcott), **Supp. I Part 1:** 32–33, 42

Work (Dixon), **Supp. XII:** 141, **143**

"Work" (Halliday), **Supp. XIX:** 85

"Work" (Huddle), **Supp. XXVI:** 149

"Work" (Oliver), **Supp. VII:** 243

Work and Love (Dunn), **Supp. XI:** 147–**148**

"Worker" (Coleman), **Supp. XI:** 89

Worker Writers (Le Sueur), **Supp. XXIII:** 165

Working a Passage; or, Life on a Liner (Briggs), **Supp. XVIII:** 2, **9–10**

Working Class Movement in America, The (E. Marx and E. Aveling), **Supp. XVI:** 85

Working Papers: Selected Essays and Reviews (Carruth), **Supp. XVI:** 46

"Working Roots: A Collection of Poetry and Prose" (Trethewey), **Supp. XXI:** 245

"Working the Landscape" (Dunn), **Supp. XI:** 151

Working Through: A Teacher's Journey in the Urban University (Kriegel), **Supp. XXIV:** **222–223**

Workin' on the Chain Gang: Shaking Off the Dead Hand of History (Mosley), **Supp. XIII:** 247, 248

Workman, Ross, **Supp. XXVII:** 206, 209–210

"Work Notes '66" (Baraka), **Supp. II Part 1:** 47

Work of Art (Lewis), **II:** 453–454

"Work of Shading, The" (Simic), **Supp. VIII:** 277–278

Work of Stephen Crane, The (Follett, ed.), **I:** 405

"Work on Red Mountain, The" (Harte), **Supp. II Part 1:** 339

Works and Days (Erga Kai H¿merai) (Hesiod; Stallings, trans.), **Supp. XXV:** 221

"Workshop" (Espaillat), **Supp. XXI:** 105

Works of Love, The (Morris), **III:** 223–224, 225, 233

Works of the Late Edgar Allan Poe: With Notices of His Life and Genius (Griswold, Parker, and Lowell, eds.), **Retro. Supp. III:** 236

Works of Witter Bynner, The (Kraft, ed.), **Supp. XV:** 52

"World, The" (Bronk), **Supp. XXI:** 32

"World, The" (Simic), **Supp. VIII:** 282

"World, the Flesh, and the Devil, The" (P. Benedict), **Supp. XXIII:** 48

World, the Worldless, The (Bronk), **Supp. XXI:** **29–31**

"World, World—" (Oppen), **Supp. XXVI:** 233

World According to Garp, The (Irving), **Supp. VI:** 163, 164, **170–173,** 181

World and Africa, The: An Inquiry into the Part Which Africa Has Played in World History (Du Bois), **Supp. II Part 1:** 184–185

"World and All Its Teeth, The" (Nye), **Supp. XIII:** 282

"World and the Door, The" (O. Henry), **Supp. II Part 1:** 402

"World and the Jug, The" (Ellison), **Retro. Supp. II:** 112, 119, 123

"World as We Know It, The" (Barresi), **Supp. XV:** 100

World Authors 1950–1970, **Supp. XIII:** 102

World Away, A (O'Nan), **Supp. XXV:** 141, 144–145, 149

World Below, The (Miller), **Supp. XII: 303–304**

World Below the Window, The: Poems 1937–1997 (W. J. Smith), **Supp. XIII:** 332, 340, 345

World Doesn't End, The (Simic), **Supp. VIII:** 272, **279–280**

World Elsewhere, A: The Place of Style in American Literature (Poirier), **I:** 239

"World Ends Here, The" (Harjo), **Supp. XII:** 227–228

World Enough and Time (Warren), **IV:** 243, 253–254

World Gone Wrong (album, Dylan), **Supp. XVIII:** 28

"World I Live In, The" (T. Williams), **IV:** 388

World I Never Made, A (Farrell), **II:** 34, 35, 424

World in the Attic, The (Morris), **III:** 222–223, 224

World in the Evening, The (Isherwood), **Supp. XIV:** 157, 164, 165, **166–167,** 170

World Is a Wedding, The (Schwartz), **Supp. II Part 2:** 643, 654–660

"World Is a Wedding, The" (Schwartz), **Supp. II Part 2:** 655–656, 657

"World Is Too Much with Us, The" (Wordsworth), **Supp. I Part 1:** 312

Worldly Hopes (Ammons), **Supp. VII:** 34

Worldly Philosophers, The (Heilbroner), **Supp. I Part 2:** 644, 650

World Made Straight, The (film), **Supp. XXVII:** 222

World Made Straight, The (Rash), **Supp. XXVII:** 222, 224, 228, 229

World of Apples, The (Cheever), **Supp. I Part 1:** 191, 193

World of David Wagoner, The (McFarland), **Supp. IX:** 323

"World of Easy Rawlins, The" (Mosley), **Supp. XIII:** 234, 236

World of Gwendolyn Brooks, The (Brooks), **Supp. III Part 1:** 83, 84

World of H. G. Wells, The (Brooks), **I:** 240, 241, 242

World of Light, A (Skloot), **Supp. XX: 196, 205, 206–207**

"World of Light, A" (Skloot), **Supp. XX: 194, 207**

World of Light, A: Portraits and Celebrations (Sarton), **Supp. III Part 1:** 62; **Supp. VIII:** 249, 253, 262

World of Our Fathers: The Journey of the Eastern European Jews to America and the Life They Found and Made (Howe), **Supp. VI:** 113, 114, 116, 118, 119, **120–125; Supp. XIV:**104; **Supp. XXIII:** 3; **Supp. XXIV:** 220–221

"World of Pure Experience, A" (James), **II:** 356–357

World of Raymond Chandler, The (Spender), **Supp. IV Part 1:** 119

World of Sex, The (H. Miller), **III:** 170, 178, 187

"World of the Perfect Tear, The" (McGrath), **Supp. X:** 116, 118

World of the Ten Thousand Things, The: Selected Poems (Wright), **Supp. V:** 333

"World of Tomorrow, The" (White), **Supp. I Part 2:** 663

World of Washington Irving, The (Brooks), **I:** 256–257

World of Willa Cather, The (Bannet), **Retro. Supp. III:** 18

World Over, The (Wharton), **Retro. Supp. I:** 382

World Revolution (C. L. R. James), **Supp. XXI:** 167

"Worlds" (Goldbarth), **Supp. XII:** 183, 189

World's Body, The (Ransom), **III:** 497, 499; **Supp. II Part 1:** 146

World's End (Boyle), **Supp. VIII:** 11–12; **Supp. XX:** 22–23

World's End and Other Stories (Theroux), **Supp. VIII:** 322

"World's Fair" (Berryman), **I:** 173

World's Fair (Doctorow), **Supp. IV Part 1:** 217, 224, 227–229, 234, 236–237

World's Fair, The (Fitzgerald), **II:** 93

Worlds of Color (Du Bois), **Supp. II Part 1:** 185–186

"Worlds of Color" (Du Bois), **Supp. II Part 1:** 175

World So Wide (Lewis), **II:** 456

"World's Worst Boyfriends, The" (Wasserstein), **Supp. XV:** 328

"World-Telegram" (Berryman), **I:** 173

World to Come, The (D. Horn), **Supp. XVII:** 50

"World Trade Center / Mail runner / '73"(Balakian), **Supp. XXIII:** 32–33

World View on Race and Democracy: A Study Guide in Human Group Relations (Locke), **Supp. XIV:** 205, 206

World within the Word, The (Gass), **Supp. VI:** 77

"World Without Objects Is a Sensible Place, A" (Wilbur), **Supp. III Part 2:** 550

"World Without Rodrigo, The" (Cisneros), **Supp. VII:** 68

"Worm King's Lullaby, The"(Siken), **Supp. XXVIII:** 201

"Worm Moon" (Oliver), **Supp. VII:** 234

Wormser, Baron, **Supp. XXIII:** 57

"Worms of the Earth" (Howard), **Supp. XXVII:** 123–124

"Worn Path, A" (Welty), **IV:** 262; **Retro. Supp. I:** 345–346

"Worsening Situation" (Ashbery), **Supp. III Part 1:** 17–18

"Worship" (Emerson), **II:** 2, 4–5

"Worship" (H. Johnson), **Supp. XXVI:** 172

"Worship and Church Bells" (Paine), **Supp. I Part 2:** 521

Worster, Donald, **Supp. IX:** 19

Worthington, Marjorie, **Supp. XII:** 13

Wouk, Herman, **Supp. XX: 243; Supp. XXV:** 253–270; **Supp. XXVII:** 134, 147

Wouldn't Take Nothing for My Journey Now (Angelou), **Supp. IV Part 1:** 10, 12, 14, 15, 16

"Wound" (Pedersen; Nelson, trans.), **Supp. XVIII:** 180

Wound and the Bow, The: Seven Studies in Literature (Wilson), **IV:** 429; **Supp. XXIV:** 217

Wounded (Everett), **Supp. XVIII:** 54, **64,** 65

Wounds in the Rain (Crane), **I:** 409, 414, 423

Woven Stone (Ortiz), **Supp. IV Part 2:** 501, 514

Woven Stories (Ortiz), **Supp. IV Part 2:** 503

"Wraith, The" (Roethke), **III:** 542

"Wrath of God, The" (Fante), **Supp. XI:** 160, 164

"Wreath for a Bridal" (Plath), **Supp. I Part 2:** 537

"Wreath for Emmet Till, A" (Nelson), **Supp. XVIII:** 177

Wreath for Emmett Till, A (Nelson), **Supp. XVIII:** 171, 173, 175, 181, **183–185**

Wreath for Garibaldi and Other Stories, A (Garrett), **Supp. VII:** 99–101

"Wreath of Women" (Rukeyser), **Supp. VI:** 280

Wreckage (Jin), **Supp. XVIII: 98–99**

Wreckage of Agathon, The (Gardner), **Supp. VI:** 63, **65–66**

Wrecking Crew (Levis), **Supp. XI: 259–260**

Wrecking Yard, The (Benedict), **Supp. XXIII: 35, 39–41**

"Wrecking Yard, The" (P. Benedict), **Supp. XXIII:** 39–40

"Wreck of Rivermouth, The" (Whittier), **Supp. I Part 2:** 694, 696–697

"Wreck of the Deutschland" (Hopkins), **Supp. X:** 61

"Wreck of the Hesperus, The" (Longfellow), **Retro. Supp. II:** 168, 169

Wrestler's Cruel Study, The (Dobyns), **Supp. XIII: 82–83**

"Wrestler with Sharks, A" (Yates), **Supp. XI:** 341

"Wrestling Angels"(Bottoms), **Supp. XXVIII:** 24

"Wrestling with Augie March" (Kriegel), **Supp. XXIV:** 220

Wright, Bernie, **I:** 191, 193

Wright, C. D. (Carolyn Doris), **Supp. XV: 337–355**

Wright, Charles, **Supp. V:** 92, **331–346; Supp. VIII:** 272; **Supp. XIII:** 114; **Supp. XVII:** 71; **Supp. XXI:** 95, 255; **Supp. XXIV:** 155

Wright, Chauncey, **II:** 344

Wright, Conrad, **Supp. XXIV:** 71, 72

Wright, Farnworth, **Supp. XXVII:** 120, 125

Wright, Frank Lloyd, **I:** 104, 483

Wright, Franz, **Supp. XVII: 239–249**

Wright, George, **III:** 479

Wright, Harold Bell, **II:** 467–468

Wright, Holly, **Supp. VIII:** 272

Wright, James, **I:** 291; **Supp. III Part 1:** 249; **Supp. III Part 2:** 541, **589–607; Supp. IV Part 1:** 60, 72; **Supp. IV Part 2:** 557, 558, 561, 566, 571, 623;

Supp. IX: 152, 155, 159, 265, 271, 290, 293, 296; **Supp. V:** 332; **Supp. X:** 69, 127; **Supp. XI:** 150; **Supp. XII:** 217; **Supp. XIII:** 76; **Supp. XIX:** 122, 273; **Supp. XV:** 79, 93, 212; **Supp. XVII:** 239, 241, 243, 244; **Supp. XXVI:** 68

Wright, Nathalia, **IV:** 155

Wright, Philip Green, **III:** 578, 579, 580

Wright, Richard, **II:** 586; **IV:** 40, **474–497**; **Retro. Supp. II:** 4, 111, 116, 120; **Retro. Supp. III:** 131, 140; **Supp. I Part 1:** 51, 52, 64, 332, 337; **Supp. II Part 1:** 17, 40, 221, 228, 235, 250; **Supp. IV Part 1:** 1, 11, 84, 374; **Supp. IX:** 316; **Supp. VIII:** 88; **Supp. X:** 131, 245, 254; **Supp. XI:** 85; **Supp. XII:** 316; **Supp. XIII:** 46, 233; **Supp. XIV:** 73; **Supp. XVI:** 135, 139, 141, 143; **Supp. XVIII:** 277, 282, 286; **Supp. XXI:** 169; **Supp. XXIII:** 166

Wright, Mrs. Richard (Ellen Poplar), **IV:** 476

Wright, Sarah, **Supp. IV Part 1:** 8; **Supp. XIII:** 295

Wright, William, **Retro. Supp. II:** 76, 77; **Retro. Supp. III:** 45

Wrigley, Robert, **Supp. XVIII: 293–308**

"Writer" (Sanders), **Supp. XVI:** 277

"Writer, The" (Wilbur), **Supp. III Part 2:** 561, 562

"Writer and the Jewish Community, The" (Levin), **Supp. XXVII:** 134

"Writer and the Land, The"(Billips), **Supp. XXVIII:** 14

"Writer as Alaskan, The" (Haines), **Supp. XII:** 199

Writer in America, The (Brooks), **I:** 253, 254, 257

Writer in America, The (Stegner), **Supp. IV Part 2:** 597, 599, 607

"Writers" (R. Lowell), **II:** 554

Writer's Almanac, The (Keillor, radio program), **Supp. XIII:** 274; **Supp. XVI:** 178; **Supp. XXIII:** 138

Writer's America, A: Landscape in Literature (Kazin), **Supp. VIII:** 106

Writers and Their Craft (Delbanco, ed.), **Supp. XXII:** 204

"Writer's Bed, A" (Mirvis), **Supp. XX: 179**

Writer's Capital, A (Auchincloss), **Supp. IV Part 1:** 21, 23, 24, 31

"Writer's Credo, A" (Abbey), **Supp. XIII:** 1, 17

Writer's Eye, A: Collected Book Reviews (Welty), **Retro. Supp. I:** 339, 354, 356

Writers in America (Schulberg), **Supp. XVIII:** 242, 243, 250, 254

Writers in Revolt (Southern, Seaver, and Trocchi, eds.), **Supp. XI:** 301

Writer's Life, A (Talese), **Supp. XVII:** 208–209, 210

Writer's Notebook, A (Maugham), **Supp. X:** 58

Writers on America (U.S. Department of State, ed.), **Supp. XIII:** 288

Writers on the Left (Aaron), **IV:** 429; **Supp. II Part 1:** 137

Writers on Writing (Prose), **Supp. XVI:** 259

"Writer's Prologue to a Play in Verse" (W. C. Williams), **Retro. Supp. I:** 424

"Writer's Quest for a Parnassus, A" (T. Williams), **IV:** 392

Writers' Workshop (University of Iowa), **Supp. V:** 42

"Writers Workshop, The" (Conroy), **Supp. XVI:** 76

"Writing" (Nemerov), **III:** 275

"Writing About the Universe" (Mosley), **Supp. XIII:** 247

"Writing American Fiction" (P. Roth), **Retro. Supp. II:** 279; **Supp. I Part 1:** 192; **Supp. I Part 2:** 431; **Supp. III Part 2:** 414, 420, 421; **Supp. V:** 45

"Writing and a Life Lived Well" (Patchett), **Supp. XII:** 308

"Writing and Writers: *Disjecta Membra*" (Sorrentino), *Supp. XXI:* 235

Writing a Woman's Life (Heilbrun), **Supp. IX:** 66

"Writing Between Worlds" (Mirvis), **Supp. XX: 177, 178, 179**

Writing Brave and Free: Encouraging Words for People Who Want to Start Writing (Kooser and Cox), **Supp. XIX:** 116, 128

Writing Chicago: Modernism, Ethnography, and the Novel (Cappetti), **Supp. IX:** 4, 8

Writing Creative Nonfiction: The Literature of Reality (Talese and Lounsberry, eds.), **Supp. XVII:** 208

Writing Dylan: The Songs of a Lonesome Traveler (Smith), **Supp. XVIII:** 22

Writing from the Center (Sanders), **Supp. XVI:** 266, 275–276

"Writing from the Inside Out: Style Is Not the Frosting; It's the Cake" (Robbins), **Supp. X:** 266

Writing Habit, The (Huddle), **Supp. XXVI:** 152, 160

"Writing Habit, The" (Huddle), **Supp. XXVI:** 160

"Writing here last autumn of my hopes of seeing a hoopoe" (Updike), **Retro. Supp. I:** 335

Writing Home (Crooker), **Supp. XXIII:** 54

Writing in an Age of Silence (Paretsky), **Supp. XXV:** 169, 181

Writing in Restaurants (Mamet), **Supp. XIV:** 246

"Writing Is Work" (Rinehart), **Supp. XXV:** 198

"Writing Lesson, The" (Gordon), **Supp. IV Part 1:** 306

Writing Life, The (Dillard), **Supp. VI:** 23, 31

"Writing of Apollinaire, The" (Zukofsky), **Supp. III Part 2:** 616, 617

"Writing of *Fearless Jones*, The" (Mosley), **Supp. XIII:** 242

"Writing on Napkins at the Sunshine Club"(Bottoms), **Supp. XXVIII:** 23

Writing on the Wall, The, and Literary Essays (McCarthy), **II:** 579

Writings to an Unfinished Accompaniment (Merwin), **Supp. III Part 1:** 352

"Writing the Rez: Popular Obsessions in the Works of Eric Gansworth" (de la Paz and Purdy), **Supp. XXVI:** 102, 111

"Writing the Universe-Mind" (Tabios), **Supp. XV:** 225

Writing the World (Stafford), **Supp. XI:** 314

"Writing to Save Our Lives" (Milligan), **Supp. XIII:** 274

Writing Vietnam, Writing Life: Caputo, Heinemann, O'Brien, Butler (Herzog), **Supp. XXII:** 116

Writin' Is Fightin' (Reed), *Supp. X:* 241

"Writ of Divorcement"(Lewisohn), **Supp. XXVIII:** 154

"Writ on the Eve of My 32nd Birthday" (Corso), **Supp. XII:** 129–130

"Written History as an Act of Faith" (Beard), **Supp. I Part 2:** 492

"Written on the Land" (J. W. Miller), **Supp. XX: 170**

"Wrong Man, The" (Larsen), **Supp. XVIII:** 124

"Wrong Notes" (S. Kauffmann), **Supp. XVI:** 74

"Wrought Figure" (McCarriston), **Supp. XIV:** 272

Wrozynski, Henryk, **Supp. XXIII:** 64

"Wunderkind" (McCullers), **II:** 585

Wunderlich, Mark, **Supp. XI:** 119, 132

Wundt, Wilhelm, **II:** 345

Wurlitzer, Rudolph, **Supp. XXVI:** 26

Wurster, William Wilson, **Supp. IV Part 1:** 197

WUSA (film), **Supp. V:** 301

Wuthering Heights (E. Brontë), **Supp. V:** 305; **Supp. X:** 89

Wuthering Heights (screenplay, Hecht and MacArthur), **Supp. XXVII:** 90

WWII (Jones), **Supp. XI:** 219, 231

Wyandotté (Cooper), **I:** 350, 355

Wyatt, Robert B., **Supp. V:** 14

Wyatt, Thomas, **Supp. I Part 1:** 369

Wyce, Marion, **Supp. XXVI:** 57

Wycherly Woman, The (Macdonald), **Supp. IV Part 2:** 473

Wych Hazel (S. and A. Warner), **Supp. XVIII:** 267, **268–269**

Wydra, Ewa. See Hoffman, Eva

Wyeth, Andrew, **Supp. XIX:** 117

Wyler, William, **Supp. XV:** 195

Wylie, Elinor, **IV:** 436; **Supp. I Part 2: 707–730**; **Supp. III Part 1:** 2, 63, 318–319; **Supp. XI:** 44; **Supp. XIV:** 127; **Supp. XV:** 307; **Supp. XXVII:** 283, 284

Wylie, Horace, **Supp. I Part 2:** 708, 709

Wylie, Philip, **III:** 223

Wyllys, Ruth. See Taylor, Mrs. Edward (Ruth Wyllys)

"Wyoming Valley Tales" (Crane), **I:** 409

Wyzewa, Théodore de, **Supp. XIV:** 336

X

Xaipe (Cummings), **I:** 430, 432–433, 447
Xarque and Other Poems (G. Jones), **Supp. XXIV:** 194
Xenogenesis trilogy (O. Butler), **Supp. XIII: 63–66,** 69
Xenophon, **II:** 105
X Factor, The: A Quest for Excellence" (Plimpton), **Supp. XVI:** 241
X Files (television series), **Supp. XVI:** 125
Xiaojing, Zhou, **Supp. XV:** 214
Xicana Codex of Changing Consciousness, A: Writings, 2000–2010 (Moraga), **Supp. XXIII:** 197
Xingu and Other Stories (Wharton), **IV:** 314, 320; **Retro. Supp. I:** 378
Xionia (Wright), **Supp. V:** 333
XLI Poems (Cummings), **I:** 429, 432, 440, 443
Xu, Wenying, **Supp. XXVI:** 212
"Xuthal of the Dusk" (Howard), **Supp. XXVII:** 126

Y

Yabroff, Jennie, **Supp. XIX:** 50, 58, 61
Yacoubi, Ahmed, **Supp. IV Part 1:** 88, 92, 93
Yage Letters, The (Burroughs), **Supp. III Part 1:** 94, 98, 100
Yagoda, Ben, **Supp. VIII:** 151
Yamamoto, Isoroku, **Supp. I Part 2:** 491
Yancey's War (Hoffman), **Supp. XVIII:** 71, **75–76**
Yankee City (Warner), **III:** 60
Yankee Clipper (ballet) (Kirstein), **Supp. IV Part 1:** 82
Yankee in Canada, A (Thoreau), **IV:** 188
Yankey in London (Tyler), **I:** 344
"Yánnina" (Merrill), **Supp. III Part 1:** 329
"Yanosz Korczak's Last Walk" (Markowick-Olczakova), **Supp. X:** 70
Yarboro, Chelsea Quinn, **Supp. V:** 147
Yarbro-Bejarano, Yvonne, **Supp. XXIII:** 196, 201
Yardley, Jonathan, **Supp. V:** 326; **Supp. XI:** 67; **Supp. XXIII:** 97, 99, 103, 104, 107, 108, 109
"Yard Sale" (Kenyon), **Supp. VII:** 169
Yates, Richard, **Supp. XI: 333–350; Supp. XXIII:** 289; **Supp. XXIV:** 97; **Supp. XXV:** 154
"Year, The" (Sandburg), **III:** 584
Year at the Races, A (Parker and Parker), **Supp. XIX:** 187
Year Before Last (Boyle), **Supp. XXIV: 52–53**
"Year Between, The" (Neugeboren), **Supp. XVI:** 226
Year in Provence, A (Mayle), **Supp. XVI:** 295
Yearling, The (Rawlings), **Supp. X:** 219, **230–231,** 233, 234; **Supp. XXII:** 195
"Year of Grace" (Swados), **Supp. XIX:** 262–263
Year of Happy, A (Goldbarth), **Supp. XII:** 180
Year of Magical Thinking, The (Didion), **Supp. XXV:** 60, 208

"Year of Mourning, The" (Jeffers), **Supp. II Part 2:** 415
Year of Silence, The (Bell), **Supp. X:** 1, **5–6,** 7
"Year of Silence, The" (Brockmeier), **Supp. XXII:** 59
"Year of the Double Spring, The" (Swenson), **Supp. IV Part 2:** 647
Year's Best Fantasy and Horror, 2004, **Supp. XXII:** 55
Year's Best Science Fiction, The (Merril, ed.), **Supp. XVI:** 123
Year's Life, A (J. R. Lowell), **Supp. I Part 2:** 405
"Years of Birth" (Cowley), **Supp. II Part 1:** 149
Years of Conscience: The Muckrakers: An Anthology of Reform Journalism (Swados, ed.), **Supp. XIX:** 264
Years of My Youth (Howells), **II:** 276
"Years of Wonder" (White), **Supp. I Part 2:** 652, 653
"Years Without Understanding, The" (Weigl), **Supp. XIX:** 282–283
Years With Ross, The (Thurber), **Supp. I Part 2:** 619
Year the Lights Came On, The (Kay), **Supp. XXVII:** 104
Year We Left Home, The (Thompson), **Supp. XXIII:** 301, **302–303**
Yeats, Jack, **Supp. XVI:** 190
Yeats, Jack B., **Supp. XX: 201**
Yeats, John Butler, **III:** 458; **Supp. XX:** 69
Yeats, William Butler, **I:** 69, 172, 384, 389, 403, 434, 478, 494, 532; **II:** 168–169, 566, 598; **III:** 4, 5, 8, 18, 19, 20, 23, 29, 40, 205, 249, 269, 270–271, 272, 278, 279, 294, 347, 409, 457, 458–460, 472, 473, 476–477, 521, 523, 524, 527, 528, 533, 540, 541, 542, 543–544, 591–592; **IV:** 89, 93, 121, 126, 136, 140, 271, 394, 404; **Retro. Supp. I:** 59, 66, 127, 141, 270, 283, 285, 286, 288, 290, 311, 342, 350, 378, 413; **Retro. Supp. II:** 185, 331; **Retro. Supp. III:** 74; **Supp. I Part 1:** 79, 80, 254, 257, 262; **Supp. I Part 2:** 388, 389; **Supp. II Part 1:** 1, 4, 9, 20, 26, 361; **Supp. III Part 1:** 59, 63, 236, 238, 253; **Supp. IV Part 1:** 81; **Supp. IV Part 2:** 634; **Supp. IX:** 43, 119; **Supp. V:** 220; **Supp. VIII:** 19, 21, 30, 155, 156, 190, 239, 262, 292; **Supp. X:** 35, 58, 119, 120; **Supp. XI:** 140; **Supp. XII:** 132, 198, 217, 266; **Supp. XIII:** 77, **Supp. XIII:** 87; **Supp. XIV:** 7; **Supp. XV:** 36, 41, 181, 186; **Supp. XVI:** 47–48, 159; **Supp. XVII:** 36; **Supp. XXI:** 61; **Supp. XXVII:** 227, 228; **Supp. XXVIII:** 260
Yee, Amy, **Supp. XVIII:** 93, 94
"Ye Have Your Closes" (Davison), **Supp. XXVI:** 78
Yehuda (Levin), **Supp. XXVII:** 139, 146
Yellin, Jean Fagan, **Supp. XVI:** 88, 89
Yellow Back Radio Broke-Down (Reed), **Supp. X:** 240, 242, **243–245**
"Yellow Dog Café" (Komunyakaa), **Supp. XIII:** 126

Yellow Face (Hwang), **Supp. XXI:** 143, 148, **154–156**
"Yellow Girl" (Caldwell), **I:** 310
Yellow Glove (Nye), **Supp. XIII:** 275, **276–277**
"Yellow Glove" (Nye), **Supp. XIII:** 276
"Yellow Gown, The" (Anderson), **I:** 114
Yellow House on the Corner, The (Dove), **Supp. IV Part 1:** 244, 245, 246, 254
"Yellow Raft, The" (Connell), **Supp. XIV: 85–86**
"Yellow River" (Tate), **IV:** 141
Yellow Room, The (Rinehart), **Supp. XXV:** 198, 200
"Yellowstone, The"(Kenny), **Supp. XXIII:** 155
"Yellow Violet, The" (Bryant), **Supp. I Part 1:** 154, 155
"Yellow Wallpaper, The" (Gilman), **Supp. XI: 198–199,** 207; **Supp. XVI:** 84; **Supp. XXVIII:** 237
"Yellow Woman" (Keres stories), **Supp. IV Part 1:** 327
"Yellow Woman" (Silko), **Supp. IV Part 2:** 567–568
Yelverton, Theresa, **Supp. IX:** 181
"Ye Merry Peacemakers"(Stuart), **Supp. XXVIII:** 230
Yenser, Stephen, **Supp. X:** 207, 208; **Supp. XV:** 113–114
"Yentl the Yeshiva Boy" (Singer), **IV:** 15, 20
Yerkes, Charles E., **I:** 507, 512
Yerma (opera) (Bowles), **Supp. IV Part 1:** 89
Yertle the Turtle and Other Stories (Geisel), **Supp. XVI:** 109
"Yes" (Stafford), **Supp. XI:** 329
Yes, Mrs. Williams (W. C. Williams), **Retro. Supp. I:** 423
Yes, Yes, No, No (Kushner), **Supp. IX:** 133
"Yes and It's Hopeless" (Ginsberg), **Supp. II Part 1:** 326
"Yes"(Crooker), **Supp. XXIII:** 62
Yesenin, Sergey, **Supp. VIII:** 40
"Yes: I Mean So OK–Love" (Bronk), **Supp. XXI:** 31
"Yes! No!" (Oliver), **Supp. VII:** 243–244
Yesterday and Today: A Comparative Anthology of Poetry (Untermeyer, ed.), **Supp. XV:** 309
Yesterdays (Wheeler), **Supp. XXVIII:** 228
Yesterday's Self: Nostalgia and the Immigrant Identity (Ritivoi), **Supp. XVI:** 148
Yesterday Will Make You Cry (C. Himes), **Supp. XVI:** 137
"Yet Another Example of the Porousness of Certain Borders" (Wallace), **Supp. X:** 309
"Yet Do I Marvel" (Cullen), **Supp. IV Part 1:** 165, 169
Yet Other Waters (Farrell), **II:** 29, 38, 39, 40
"Yevtushenko" (Kooser), **Supp. XIX:** 124
Yevtushenko, Yevgeny, **Supp. III Part 1:** 268
Yezzi, David, **Supp. XII:** 193

Yiddish Policemen's Union, The (Chabon), **Supp. XXII:** 49

Yizkor Book, **Supp. XVI:** 154

...y no se lo tragó la tierra (Rivera), **Supp. XIX:** 99, 101

Y no se lo trago la tierra (And the Earth Did Not Cover Him) (Rivera), **Supp. XIII:** 216

¡Yo! (Alvarez), **Supp. VII:** 1, 15–17

"Yogurt of Vasirin Kefirovsky, The" (Apple), **Supp. XVII:** 3, 4

Yohannan, J. D., **II:** 20

"Yoke, The" (Bidart), **Supp. XV:** 33

"Yoked Together"(Lea), **Supp. XXVIII:** 137

"Yom Kippur 1984" (Rich), **Retro. Supp. III:** 250–251

Yonge, Charlotte, **II:** 174

"Yonnondio" (Whitman), **Supp. XIII:** 304

Yonnondio: From the Thirties (Olsen), **Supp. XIII:** 295, 295, **Supp. XIII:** 292, 296, **303–304,** 305

"Yore" (Nemerov), **III:** 283

York, Jake Adam, **Supp. XXI:** 257

York, Lorraine, **Supp. XX:** 51

"York Beach" (Toomer), **Supp. III Part 2:** 486

Yorke, Dorothy, **Supp. I Part 1:** 258

Yorke, Henry Vincent. *See* Green, Henry

"York Garrison, 1640" (Jewett), **Retro. Supp. II:** 141

Yosemite, The (Muir), **Supp. IX:** 185

"Yosemite Glaciers: Ice Streams of the Great Valley" (Muir), **Supp. IX:** 181

Yoshe Kalb (Singer), **IV:** 2

"You, Andrew Marvell" (MacLeish), **III:** 12–13

"You, Dr. Martin" (Sexton), **Supp. II Part 2:** 673

You, Emperors, and Others: Poems 1957–1960 (Warren), **IV:** 245

"You, Genoese Mariner" (Merwin), **Supp. III Part 1:** 343

"You, Reader" (Collins), **Supp. XXI:** 55

"You, Too, Will Have This Printed Word (World) of Your Own" (Gansworth), **Supp. XXVI:** 114

"You All Know the Story of the Other Woman" (Sexton), **Supp. II Part 2:** 688

"You Are Gorgeous and I'm Coming"(O'Hara), **Supp. XXIII:** 219

You Are Happy (Atwood), **Supp. XIII:** 34

"You Are Happy" (Atwood), **Supp. XIII:** 34

"You Are in Bear Country" (Kumin), **Supp. IV Part 2:** 453, 455

"You Are Jeff"(Siken), **Supp. XXVIII:** 198, 199

"You Are Not I" (Bowles), **Supp. IV Part 1:** 87

"You Begin" (Atwood), **Supp. XIII:** 34

You Bright and Risen Angels (Vollmann), **Supp. XVII:** 225, 226

"You Bring Out the Mexican in Me" (Cisneros), **Supp. VII:** 71

You Came Along (film), **Supp. IV Part 2:** 524

"You Can Go Home Again" (TallMountain), **Supp. IV Part 1:** 324–325

"You Can Have It" (Levine), **Supp. V:** 188–189

You Can't Go Home Again (Wolfe), **IV:** 450, 451, 454, 456, 460, 462, 468, 469, 470

You Can't Keep a Good Woman Down (Walker), **Supp. III Part 2:** 520, 525, 531

You Can't Pet a Possom (Bontemps), **Supp. XXII:** 4, 12

You Can't Take It with You (Kaufman and Hart), **Supp. XIV:** 327

"You Can't Tell a Man by the Song He Sings" (P. Roth), **Supp. III Part 2:** 406

"You Don't Know Us Negroes" (Hurston), **Retro. Supp. III:** 129

"You Don't Know What Love Is" (Carver), **Supp. III Part 1:** 147

You Don't Love Me Yet (Lethem), **Supp. XVIII:** 149–150

"You Have Left Your Lotus Pods on the Bus" (Bowles), **Supp. IV Part 1:** 91

You Have Seen Their Faces (Caldwell), **I:** 290, 293–294, 295, 304, 309

You Know Me, Al: A Busher's Letters (Lardner), **Supp. XVI:** 189

You Know Me Al (comic strip), **II:** 423

You Know Me Al (Lardner), **II:** 26, 415, 419, 422, 431

"You Know More Than You Think You Do"(Hadas), **Supp. XXIII:** 124

"You Know What" (Beattie), **Supp. V:** 33

"You Know Who You Are" (Nye), **Supp. XIII:** 275

"You Live Like a God" (Cohen), **Supp. XXVII:** 60

You Might As Well Live: The Life and Times of Dorothy Parker (Keats), **Supp. IX:** 190

"You Must Relax!" (J. Scott), **Supp. XVII:** 189

You Must Revise Your Life (Stafford), **Supp. XI:** 312–313, 313–314, 315

"Young" (Sexton), **Supp. II Part 2:** 680

Young, Al, **Supp. X:** 240; **Supp. XXVI:** 12

Young, Art, **IV:** 436

Young, Barbara, **Supp. XX: 119, 123**

Young, Brigham, **Supp. IV Part 2:** 603

Young, Courtland, **Supp. XXII:** 21

Young, David, **Supp. XIX:** 276

Young, Dianne, **Supp. XXII:** 252

Young, Edward, **II:** 111; **III:** 415, 503

Young, Gary, **Supp. XV:** 88

Young, Hershini Bhana, **Supp. XXIV:** 189

Young, Mary, **Supp. XIII:** 236, 238, 239, 240

Young, Philip, **II:** 306; **Retro. Supp. I:** 172

Young, Stark, **Retro. Supp. III:** 74; **Supp. XXII:** 193; **Supp. XXVIII:** 70

Young Adventure (Benét), **Supp. XI:** 44

"Young America" (Brooks), **Supp. XV:** 298

Youngblood Hawke (film), **Supp. XXV:** 263

Youngblood Hawke (Wouk), **Supp. XXV:** 256, 257, 258, 259, 263

"Young Child and His Pregnant Mother, A" (Schwartz), **Supp. II Part 2:** 650

Young Christian, The (Abbott), **Supp. I Part 1:** 38

"Young Dr. Gosse" (Chopin), **Supp. I Part 1:** 211, 216

Younger, Paul, **Supp. XXVIII:** 62

Younger Choir, The (anthology), **Supp. XV:** 294

Younger Quire, The (Untermeyer), **Supp. XV:** 294, 297

"Young Folks, The" (Salinger), **III:** 551

Young Folk's Cyclopaedia of Persons and Places (Champlin), **III:** 577

"Young Girl's Lament, A" (Jin), **Supp. XVIII:** 99

"Young Goodman Brown" (Hawthorne), **II:** 229; **Retro. Supp. I:** 151–152, 153, 154; **Retro. Supp. III:** 110, 111–112; **Supp. XI:** 51; **Supp. XIV:** 48, 50

Young Harvard: First Poems of Witter Bynner (Bynner), **Supp. XV:** 41

Young Hearts Crying (Yates), **Supp. XI:** 348

"Young Housewife, The" (W. C. Williams), **Retro. Supp. I:** 415

Young Immigrants, The (Lardner), **II:** 426

"Young Lady's Friend, The: Verses, Addressed to a Young Lady, on Her Leaving School" (Rowson), **Supp. XV:** 234

Young Landlords (Myers), **Supp. XXVII:** 204

"Young Lions" (E. P. Jones), **Supp. XXII:** 145

Young Lions, The (Shaw), **Supp. XIX: 248–249**

Young Lonigan: A Boyhood in Chicago Streets (Farrell), **II:** 31, 41

Young Manhood of Studs Lonigan, The (Farrell), **II:** 31, 34

"Young Man Leaving Home"(Lea), **Supp. XXVIII:** 130

"Young Man on the Go" (column, Siddons), **Supp. XXII:** 244

Young Martin's Promise (Myers), **Supp. XXVII:** 209

Young Men and Fire (Maclean), **Supp. XIV:** 221, **231–233**

Young of the Year (Lea), **Supp. XXVIII:** 142

Young People's Pride (Benét), **Supp. XI:** 44

Young Poet's Primer (Brooks), **Supp. III Part 1:** 86

Youngren, J. Alan, **Supp. XVI:** 174

"Young Sammy's First Wild Oats" (Santayana), **III:** 607, 615

"Young Sor Juana, The" (Mora), **Supp. XIII:** 218

"Your Arkansas Traveler" (Schulberg), **Supp. XVIII:** 252

"Your Dailiness" (Notley), **Supp. XXII:** 227

"Your Death" (Dove), **Supp. IV Part 1:** 250

"You're History" (Hampl), **Supp. XXII:** 84, 95

You're Only Old Once! (Geisel), **Supp. XVI:** 111

"You're Ugly, Too" (Moore), **Supp. X:** 171

"Your Face on the Dog's Neck" (Sexton), **Supp. II Part 2:** 686

"Your Hand, Your Hand" (Hoffman), **Supp. XVIII:** 79

Your Job in Germany (film, Capra), **Supp. XVI:** 102

Your Job in Japan (film, Capra), **Supp. XVI:** 102

"Your Life" (Stafford), **Supp. XI:** 329

"Your Mother's Eyes" (Kingsolver), **Supp. VII:** 209

Your Native Land, Your Life: Poems (Rich), **Retro. Supp. III:** 250–251

"You Take a Train through a Foreign Country" (Dobyns), **Supp. XIII:** 90

"Youth" (Hughes), **Supp. I Part 1:** 321; **Supp. XXII:** 12

"Youth" (Huncke), **Supp. XIV:** 145

Youth and Life (Bourne), **I:** 217–222, 232

Youth and the Bright Medusa (Cather), **I:** 322; **Retro. Supp. I:** 14

"Youthful Religious Experiences" (Corso), **Supp. XII:** 117

Youth of Parnassus, and Other Stories, The (L. P. Smith), **Supp. XIV:** 336

Youth's First Steps in Geography (Rowson), **Supp. XV:** 243

You Touched Me! (Williams and Windham), **IV:** 382, 385, 387, 390, 392–393

"You Touch Me" (X. J. Kennedy), **Supp. XV:** 166

You Went Away (Findley), **Supp. XX: 49**

"You Who Sleep Soundly Through Our Bleakest Hour" (Espaillat), **Supp. XXI:** 110

Yurchenco, Henrietta, **Supp. XVIII:** 20

Yurka, Blanche, **Supp. I Part 1:** 67

Yutang, Adet, **Supp. X:** 291

Yutang, Anor, **Supp. X:** 291

Yutang, Lin, **Supp. X:** 291; **Supp. XVI:** 190

Yutang, Mei-mei, **Supp. X:** 291

Yvernelle: A Legend of Feudal France (Norris), **III:** 314

Y & X (Olson), **Supp. II Part 2:** 556

Z

Zabel, Morton Dauwen, **II:** 431; **III:** 194, 215; **Supp. I Part 2:** 721

Zach, Natan, **Supp. XV:** 75, 82, 85

Zaehner, R. C., **Supp. XXII:** 258

Zagajewski, Adam, **Supp. XVII:** 241

Zagarell, Sandra, **Supp. XV:** 269, 270, 278, 281, 282

Zagarell, Sandra A., **Retro. Supp. II:** 140, 143

"Zagrowsky Tells" (Paley), **Supp. VI:** 229

Zaino, Nick, **Supp. XXII:** 207

Zakrzewska, Marie, **Retro. Supp. II:** 146

Zaleski, Jeff, **Supp. XI:** 143; **Supp. XIX:** 54; **Supp. XXVI:** 158

Zall, Paul, **Supp. XIV:** 156

Zaltzberg, Charlotte, **Supp. IV Part 1:** 374

"Zambesi and Ranee" (Swenson), **Supp. IV Part 2:** 647

Zamir, Israel, **Retro. Supp. II:** 303, 317

Zamora, Bernice, **Supp. IV Part 2:** 545

Zamoyski, Adam, **Supp. XV:** 257

Zangwill, Israel, **I:** 229; **Supp. XX: 2**; **Supp. XXVIII:** 147

Zanita: A Tale of the Yosemite (Yelverton), **Supp. IX:** 181

Zanuck, Darryl F., **Supp. XI:** 170; **Supp. XII:** 165

Zapata, Emiliano, **Supp. XIII:** 324

"Zapatos" (Boyle), **Supp. VIII:** 15

Zapruder, Matthew, **Supp. XVI:** 55; **Supp. XXVI:** 54; **Supp. XXVIII:** 202

Zarathustra, **III:** 602

Zawacki, Andrew, **Supp. VIII:** 272

"Zaydee" (Levine), **Supp. V:** 186

Zebra-Striped Hearse, The (Macdonald), **Supp. IV Part 2:** 473

Zechariah (biblical book), **IV:** 152

Zeidner, Lisa, **Supp. IV Part 2:** 453; **Supp. XXIII:** 297

"Zeitl and Rickel" (Singer), **IV:** 20

Zeke and Ned (McMurtry and Ossana), **Supp. V:** 232

Zeke Proctor, Cherokee Outlaw (Conley), **Supp. V:** 232

Zelazny, Roger, **Supp. XXV:** 73

Zelazo, Suzanne, **Supp. XXII:** 158, 167

Zelda: A Biography (Milford), **Supp. IX:** 60

"Zelda and Scott: The Beautiful and Damned" (National Portrait Gallery exhibit), **Supp. IX:** 65

Zelig (film; Allen), **Supp. XV:** 4, 6, **8–9**

Zeller, Maya Jewell, **Supp. XXIV:** 167

Zen and the Birds of Appetite (Merton), **Supp. VIII:** 205–206, 208

Zend-Avesta (Fechner), **II:** 358

"Zenith: Walker Creek" (Davison), **Supp. XXVI:** 74

Zeno, **Retro. Supp. I:** 247

Zero db and Other Stories (Bell), **Supp. X:** 1, 5, 6

"Zeus over Redeye" (Hayden), **Supp. II Part 1:** 380

Zevi, Sabbatai, **IV:** 6

Ziegfeld, Florenz, **II:** 427–428

Ziegler, Cyd, **Supp. XX: 273**

Ziegler, Heidi, **Supp. XXII:** 260

Ziggurat (Balakian), **Supp. XXIII:** 19, **32–33**

Zigrosser, Carl, **I:** 226, 228, 231

Zigzagger (Muñoz), **Supp. XXV:** 127, 132, 133, 134

"Zigzagger" (Muñoz), **Supp. XXV:** 134

Zilles, Klaus, **Supp. XIX:** 112

Zimmerman, Paul D., **Supp. IV Part 2:** 583, 589, 590

Zimmerman, Robert. *See* Dylan, Bob

Zimmerman, Robert Allen. *See* Dylan, Bob

Zinberg, Leonard S. *See* Lacy, Ed

Zinman, Toby Silverman, **Supp. XIII:** 207–208, 209

Zinn, Howard, **Supp. V:** 289; **Supp. XXIV:** 87; **Supp. XXVIII:** 100

Zinovyev, Grigory, **Supp. XXI:** 167

Zinsser, Hans, **I:** 251, 385

"Zion Hill"(Bottoms), **Supp. XXVIII:** 28

Zip: A Novel of the Left and Right (Apple), **Supp. XVII:** 4–5

Zipes, Jack, **Supp. XIV:** 126

"Zipper, The" (L. Michaels), **Supp. XVI:** 214

Zitkala-Ša (Gertrude Simmons Bonnin), **Supp. XXV: 271–287**

"Zizi's Lament" (Corso), **Supp. XII:** 123

Zodiac, The (Dickey), **Supp. IV Part 1:** 178, 183–184, 185

"Zog-19: A Scientific Romance"(P. Benedict), **Supp. XXIII:** 49

Zola, Émile, **I:** 211, 411, 474, 500, 502, 518; **II:** 174, 175–176, 182, 194, 275, 276, 281, 282, 319, 325, 337, 338; **III:** 315, 316, 317–318, 319–320, 321, 322, 323, 393, 511, 583; **IV:** 326; **Retro. Supp. I:** 226, 235; **Retro. Supp. II:** 93; **Supp. I Part 1:** 207; **Supp. II Part 1:** 117

Zolotow, Maurice, **III:** 161

"Zone" (Bogan), **Supp. III Part 1:** 60–61

Zone Journals (Wright), **Supp. V:** 332–333, 342–343

"Zooey" (Salinger), **III:** 564–565, 566, 567, 569, 572

"Zoo Revisited" (White), **Supp. I Part 2:** 654

Zoo Story, The (Albee), **I:** 71, 72–74, 75, 77, 84, 93, 94; **III:** 281

Zorach, William, **I:** 260; **Supp. XXVIII:** 38, 39

"Zora Neale Hurston's *Dust Tracks:* Autobiography and Artist Novel" (Snyder), **Retro. Supp. III:** 134

Zu-Bolton, Ahmos, **Supp. XXVII:** 166, 168

Zuccotti, Susan, **Supp. XVI:** 154

Zuckerman Bound: A Trilogy and Epilogue (P. Roth), **Supp. III Part 2:** 423

Zuckerman Unbound (P. Roth), **Retro. Supp. II:** 283; **Supp. III Part 2:** 421–422

Zueblin, Charles, **Supp. I Part 1:** 5

Zuger, Abigail, **Supp. X:** 160

Zukofsky, Celia (Mrs. Louis), **Supp. III Part 2:** 619–621, 623, 625, 626–629, 631

Zukofsky, Louis, **IV:** 415; **Retro. Supp. I:** 422; **Supp. III Part 2: 619–636**; **Supp. IV Part 1:** 154; **Supp. XIV:** 279, 282, 285, 286–287; **Supp. XXVI:** 224, 226, 227, 229

Zukofsky, Paul, **Supp. III Part 2:** 622, 623–626, 627, 628

Zuleika Dobson (Beerbohm), **Supp. I Part 2:** 714

Zulus (Everett), **Supp. XVIII:** 54, **56–57**

"Zuni Potter: Drawing the Heartline" (Bierds), **Supp. XVII:** 26

Zverev, Aleksei, **Retro. Supp. I:** 278

Zwinger, Ann, **Supp. X:** 29; **Supp. XXVIII:** 251, 253

Zyda, Joan, **Retro. Supp. II:** 52